D1267039

PROF
011.62
BES

Madison County - Canton
Public Library
Madison County Library System

# Best Books for Children

# Best Books for Children™
## Preschool through Grade 6

SIXTH EDITION

John T. Gillespie

EDITOR

R. R. BOWKER®

A Unit of Cahners Business Information

New Providence, New Jersey

Published by R. R. Bowker, a unit of Cahners Business Information
Copyright © 1998 by Reed Elsevier Inc.
*All rights reserved*
Printed and bound in the United States of America

Bowker® is a registered trademark of Reed Elsevier Inc.
No part of this publication may be reproduced of transmitted in any
form or by any means, or stored in any information storage and
retrieval system, without prior written permission of R. R. Bowker,
121 Chanlon Road, New Providence, New Jersey 07974.

**Library of Congress Cataloging-in-Publication Data**

Best books for children : preschool through grade 6 /
John T. Gillespie, editor. — 6th ed.
Includes bibliographical references (p.     ) and index.
ISBN 0-8352-4099-1
1. Children's literature—Bibliography
2. Children—United States—Books and reading.
3. Best books—United States.     I. Gillespie, John
Thomas, 1928–
Z1037.B5476    1998

011.62—dc21                                                    98-35713
                                                                    CIP

ISBN 0 - 8352 - 4099 - 1

9  780835  240994

# Contents

# Biography

# Social Institutions and Issues

# CONTENTS

# Recreation

# Major Subjects Arranged Alphabetically

# Preface

This is the sixth edition of *Best Books for Children*. As with the earlier editions, the primary aim of this work is to provide a list of books that are recommended to satisfy both a child's recreational reading needs and the demands of a typical school curriculum. These recommendations are gathered from a number of sources, which are discussed on the following page. For greatest depth, coverage has been limited to the age group including preschool children through readers in the sixth grade. Books that could be used with advanced sixth-graders but are best suited to readers in grades seven through nine are listed in the companion volumes, *Best Books for Junior High Readers* (Bowker, 1991) and *Best Books for Young Adult Readers* (Bowker, 1997). It is suggested that these titles be used to enrich collections for gifted fifth- and sixth-grade readers.

Of the 18,707 titles in this sixth edition of *Best Books for Children*, 17,684 are individually numbered entries. The remaining 1,023 titles—those cited in the annotations—are additional recommended titles by the main entry author. These related titles are listed with publication date and—if the publisher differs from that cited for the main entry title—with the publisher's name. In some cases where there are a large number of titles in a series, additional entries have been used. Also, some series are so extensive that, due to space limitations, only representative titles are included. More than half of the 17,684 numbered entries are new to this edition.

For most titles, at least two recommendations were required from the sources consulted for a title to be considered for listing. However, in some cases, a single recommendation could also make a title a candidate for inclusion. This was particularly true of nonfiction books in a series. The reviewing policies of many journals do not allow the inclusion of all titles in a series. Some give little or no coverage for series books while others review only representative titles or list titles without reviews. Where only a single recommendation was available, the reviewing history of the series was taken into consideration and, in many cases, the books were examined and evaluated by the editor from copies supplied by the publisher. In these cases such criteria as availability, up-to-dateness, accuracy, usefulness, and relevance were applied.

Several sources were used to compile this annotated bibliography. At the outset there was a thorough perusal and evaluation of the entries in the fifth (1994) edition of *Best Books for Children*. All out-of-print titles were dropped as well as those that were considered no longer timely or suitable. The other sources consulted were numerous and varied. A review was made of such retrospective sources as *Children's Catalog* (H.W. Wilson) and *The Elementary School Library Collection* (Brodart), but the major tools were current periodicals and annual bibliographies such as *Children's Books* (New York Public Library) as well as annual roundups in such periodicals as *School Library Journal* and *Social Education*. Many special subject bibliographies were also used. Current book reviewing periodicals were consulted, especially those issues from July 1993 (where coverage of the fifth edition ceased) through March 1998. The four main periodicals consulted were *Booklist; Bulletin of the Center for Children's Books; Horn Book;* and *School Library Journal*.

It is hoped that this bibliography will be used in four different ways: (1) as a tool to evaluate the adequacy of existing collections; (2) as a book-selection instrument for beginning and expanding collections; (3) as an aid for giving reading guidance to children; and (4) as a base for the preparation of bibliographies and reading lists. To increase the book's usefulness, particularly in the two latter areas, the chosen titles are arranged under broad interest areas or, as in the case on nonfiction works, by curriculum-oriented subjects rather than by using the Dewey Decimal Classification System. In this way, analogous titles that otherwise would have been separated are brought together and can be seen in relation to other books on the same broad topic. For this sixth edition, a thorough review of each broad subject area and its subdivisions was made—new ones added, others dropped, and many rearranged, often to provide easier alphabetical access. It is hoped that these changes will reflect current reading needs and will aid the usability of this bibliography. In this regard, some arbitrary decisions had to be made; for example, books of mathematical puzzles are placed in the Mathematics section. In general, the titles that appear in the section Books for Younger Readers are those usually read to children or used in assisted reading situations. Basic readers are found in Books for Beginning Readers. Simple chapter books and similar nonfiction that bridge the reading abilities and interests of children in the upper primary grades and early middle grades are found in the sections for older readers.

Some types of books have been omitted from this bibliography. These include reference books such as dictionaries and encyclopedias, professional books (for example, other bibliographies), and such mass-market series as Nancy Drew and Hardy Boys books, though individual libraries might wish to purchase them.

Special features that have been retained in this edition include a listing of "Major Subjects Arranged Alphabetically." This special list provides both entry numbers as well as page numbers for the largest subject areas covered in the volume. Other features also continued are the International Standard Book Number (ISBN) for both hardcover and paperback editions, information on pagination, nonfiction series titles, and Dewey Decimal numbers for nonfiction titles. Also included are review citations for all books published and reviewed from 1985 through March 1998. These review citations will give librarians sources from which to find out more detailed information about each of the books listed. The four sources are:

*Booklist* (BL)
*Bulletin of the Center for Children's Books* (BCCB)
*Horn Book* (HB)
*School Library Journal* (SLJ)

The citing of only one review does not necessarily mean that the book received only a single recommendation. It might easily also have been listed in one or more of the other bibliographies consulted. Books without review citations are pre-1985 imprints and reprints of older recommended books recently brought back into print (the original publication date is indicated within the annotation if it was readily available). An asterisk following a review citation denotes an outstanding recommendation from that source.

If a book has won the prestigious Caldecott or Newbery medals, this information is given at the end of the annotation.

## Entry Information

As in previous editions, titles in the main section of the book are assigned an entry number. The entry contains the following information where applicable: (1) author or editor; (2) title; (3) suitable grade levels; (4) adapter or translator; (5) indication of illustrations or illustrator's name (usually only for picture books); (6) series title for nonfiction books; (7) date of publication; (8) publisher and price of hardbound edition (LB=library binding); (9) ISBN of hardbound edition; (10) paperback (paper) publisher and price (if no publisher is listed, it is the same as the hardbound edition); (11) ISBN of paperback edition; (12) annotation; (13) review citations; (14) Dewey Decimal number. Bibliographic information and prices were verified in *Books in Print 1997–1998*, as well as many publishers' catalogs.

## Indexes

*Best Books for Children* includes four indexes: author, illustrator, book title, and subject/grade level. In both the Author Index and the Illustrator

Index, joint authors and joint illustrators are listed separately, and book titles and entry numbers are given; fiction titles are indicated by (F). In the Title Index, both main entry titles and internal titles cited within the annotation are included, all with entry numbers and (F) notations.

The Subject/Grade Level Index includes several thousand subject headings. Within each subject, entries are listed according to grade-level suitabilities. For example, under the subject Humorous Stories there may be numerous entry numbers given first for Primary (P) readers; then for the Primary-Intermediate (PI) group; for the Intermediate (I) group; for the Intermediate-Junior High (IJ) readers; and finally for all readers, covering grades from preschool through grade 8 (All). This will enable the professional to select the most appropriate titles for use. Biographical entries are listed in this index by the last name of the subject of the biography. The following codes are used to give approximate grade level:

P (Primary) preschool through grade 3
PI (Primary-Intermediate) grades 2 through 4
I (Intermediate) grades 4 through 6
IJ (Intermediate-Junior High) grades 5 through 8
All (All readers) preschool through grade 8

Specific, more exact grade-level suitabilities are given (parenthetically) for each book in its main text entry.

To facilitate quick reference, all listings in all indexes refer the user to entry number, not page number.


Many people were involved in the preparation of this bibliography. I am especially grateful to Nancy Bucenec, Managing Editor, whose painstaking care and infinite patience have resulted in the fine editorial work on these pages. Thanks are also due to the staff at Rock Hill Press for their work on the database, editing, and typesetting of this large book: Catherine Barr, Chris McNaull, and Julie Miller.

# Best Books for Children

# Literature

# Books for Younger Readers

## Alphabet, Concept, and Counting Books

### Alphabet Books

**1** Alda, Arlene. *Arlene Alda's ABC* (PS–K). Illus. 1993, Tricycle Pr. $12.95 (1-883672-01-5). 32pp. Objects turn into letters in this unusual alphabet book. (Rev: BL 1/1/94)

**2** Anglund, Joan Walsh. *In a Pumpkin Shell* (PS–2). Illus. by author. 1977, Harcourt paper $6.00 (0-15-644425-9). 32pp. A Mother Goose ABC book.

**3** Anno, Mitsumasa. *Anno's Alphabet: An Adventure in Imagination* (PS–2). Illus. by author. 1992, HarperCollins paper $19.95 (0-06-443315-3). 64pp. A most unusual and distinctive alphabet book that shows the letters as pieces of rough-grained wood and, on the opposite pages, objects beginning with that letter. An excellent introduction to art as well.

**4** Aylesworth, Jim. *The Folks in the Valley: A Pennsylvania Dutch ABC* (PS–2). Illus. by Stefano Vitale. 1994, HarperCollins paper $5.95 (0-064-43363-3). 32pp. Celebrating the way of life for a Pennsylvania Dutch family, from the alarm clock to the Z sound of sleep. (Rev: BL 5/1/92*; HB 1–2/92; SLJ 5/92)

**5** Aylesworth, Jim. *Old Black Fly* (PS–2). Illus. by Stephen Gammell. 1992, Holt $15.95 (0-8050-1401-2). 32pp. A fun alphabet book that describes the 26 awful things Old Black Fly did one day. (Rev: BCCB 7–8/92; BL 2/15/92*; HB 5–6/92; SLJ 4/92*)

**6** Baker, Alan. *Black and White Rabbit's ABC* (PS–K). Illus. 1994, Kingfisher $7.95 (1-85697-951-2). 24pp. A simple ABC book about a rabbit and his antics. (Rev: BL 7/94)

**7** Balian, Lorna. *Humbug Potion: An A-B-Cipher* (1–2). Illus. 1993, Humbug $12.95 (0-687-37102-3).

32pp. Each letter is given a number (1 to 26) in this unusual alphabet book.

**8** Bayer, Jane. *A, My Name Is Alice* (K–3). Illus. by Steven Kellogg. 1984, Dial paper $4.95 (0-8037-0130-6). 32pp. Through the alphabet with jump rope rhymes.

**9** Berg, Cami. *D Is for Dolphin* (PS–3). Illus. by Janet Biondi. 1991, Windom $18.95 (1-879244-01-2). 56pp. In this alphabet book, every letter stands for a word associated with dolphins. (Rev: BCCB 6/91; BL 9/15/91; SLJ 7/91)

**10** Blackwell, Deborah. *An ABC Bestiary* (PS–2). Illus. 1989, Farrar $15.00 (0-374-30005-4). 28pp. This story is geared to the visually sophisticated child who can appreciate the humor of "chicken cooking croissants." (Rev: BL 1/15/90; SLJ 1/90)

**11** Bond, Michael. *Paddington's ABC* (PS–2). Illus. by John Lobban. Series: Paddington. 1991, Viking paper $11.99 (0-670-84104-8). 32pp. In an imaginative way, the bear Paddington introduces the alphabet. (Rev: BCCB 1/92; BL 12/15/91; SLJ 2/92)

**12** Bourke, Linda. *Eye Spy: A Mysterious Alphabet* (2–5). Illus. 1991, Chronicle $15.95 (0-87701-805-7). 64pp. A wordless alphabet book offering a guessing game with one puzzle for each alphabet letter. (Rev: BL 11/15/91; HB 1–2/92; SLJ 12/91)

**13** Boynton, Sandra. *A Is for Angry: An Animal and Adjective Alphabet* (PS–K). Illus. 1987, Workman paper $6.95 (0-89480-507-X). 48pp. Adjectives are used in this alphabet book.

**14** Bragg, Ruth G. *Alphabet Out Loud* (1–2). Illus. 1992, Picture Book paper $14.95 (0-88708-172-X). An unusual book in which the letters of the alphabet are used to introduce various activities. (Rev: SLJ 4/92)

**15** Brown, Ruth. *Alphabet Times Four: An International ABC* (PS–4). Illus. by author. 1991, Dutton paper $13.95 (0-525-44831-4). An alphabet book in which the key words are given in English, Spanish, French, and German. (Rev: BCCB 11/91*; SLJ 10/91)

**16** Browne, Philippa-Alys. *African Animals ABC* (PS–3). Illus. 1995, Sierra Club $15.95 (0-87156-372-X). 32pp. This picture book uses African animals in an ABC format and gives facts about each one's habitats and physical features. (Rev: BL 11/15/95)

**17** Bruce, Lisa. *Oliver's Alphabets* (1–2). Illus. by Debi Gliori. 1993, Bradbury $13.95 (0-02-735996-4). The alphabet is introduced using everyday people and events in young Oliver's life, like his family, friends, and home. (Rev: SLJ 12/93)

**18** Bunting, Jane. *My First ABC* (PS–1). Illus. 1993, DK Publg. $12.95 (1-56458-403-8). 32pp. In this alphabet book, children play with objects starting with each letter of the alphabet. (Rev: BL 12/15/93; SLJ 5/94)

**19** Carlson, Nancy. *ABC I Like Me!* (PS–1). Illus. 1997, Viking $14.99 (0-670-87458-2). 32pp. A little pig and his friends take a trip through the alphabet. (Rev: BL 4/1/97; SLJ 6/97)

**20** Chaplin, Susan Gibbons. *I Can Sign My ABCs* (K–3). Illus. by Laura McCaul. 1986, Gallaudet Univ. $9.95 (0-930323-19-X). 56pp. The ABCs of sign language, with color illustrations. (Rev: BL 2/15/87)

**21** Chin-Lee, Cynthia. *A Is for Asia* (K–4). Illus. by Yumi Heo. 1997, Orchard LB $16.99 (0-531-33011-7). 32pp. A variety of topics, from geography to holidays, are covered in this unique alphabet book. (Rev: BCCB 5/97; BL 3/1/97; SLJ 4/97)

**22** Chwast, Seymour. *The Alphabet Parade* (K–3). Illus. by author. 1991, Smithmark $3.98 (0-831-70005-X). In this wordless book, the letters of the alphabet join a parade filled with other fascinating paraders. (Rev: SLJ 10/91)

**23** Crowther, Robert. *My Pop-up Surprise ABC* (PS–K). Illus. by author. 1997, Orchard $16.95 (0-531-30038-2). A simple alphabet book that uses large, easily manipulated flaps and pull tabs. (Rev: SLJ 8/97)

**24** Darling, Kathy. *Amazon ABC* (PS–1). Illus. by Tara Darling. 1996, Lothrop LB $15.93 (0-688-13779-2). 32pp. In a series of striking photographs, the alphabet is introduced through animals of the rain forest surrounding the Amazon River. (Rev: BL 3/1/96; SLJ 5/96)

**25** Dragonwagon, Crescent. *Alligator Arrived with Apples: A Potluck Alphabet Feast* (PS–2). Illus. by Jose Aruego and Ariane Dewey. 1987, Macmillan $15.95 (0-02-733090-7); paper $5.99 (0-689-71613-3). 40pp. An alliterative alphabet story about the menu and guests of an unusual Thanksgiving feast. (Rev: BL 9/15/87; SLJ 11/87)

**26** Drucker, Malka. *A Jewish Holiday ABC* (PS–2). Illus. by Rita Pocock. 1992, Harcourt $13.95 (0-15-200482-3). 40pp. Using a picture-book approach, Jewish holidays and religious concepts are introduced. (Rev: BCCB 5/92; BL 2/15/92; HB 5–6/92; SLJ 7/92)

**27** Edens, Cooper, et al. *An ABC of Fashionable Animals* (PS–K). Illus. 1989, Simon & Schuster $12.95 (0-88138-122-5). 56pp. Costumed animals team up with the alphabet to amuse young readers. (Rev: BL 7/89)

**28** Ehlert, Lois. *Eating the Alphabet: Fruits and Vegetables from A to Z* (PS–1). Illus. by author. 1989, Harcourt $15.00 (0-15-224435-2); paper $5.95 (0-15-201036-X). 32pp. An eye-catching alphabet book. (Rev: BL 3/15/89; HB 5–6/89; SLJ 6/89)

**29** Eichenberg, Fritz. *Ape in a Cape: An Alphabet of Odd Animals* (PS–1). Illus. by author. 1952, Harcourt $17.00 (0-15-203722-5); paper $7.00 (0-15-607830-9). 32pp. Each letter of the alphabet is represented by a full-page color picture of an animal with a brief nonsense rhyme explaining it.

**30** Ernst, Lisa Campbell. *The Letters Are Lost!* (PS–1). Illus. 1996, Viking paper $14.99 (0-670-86336-X). 32pp. Alphabet blocks find homes that match their letters (e.g., *A* is an airplane) in this imaginative alphabet book. (Rev: BL 1/1–15/96; HB 3–4/96)

**31** Feelings, Muriel. *Jambo Means Hello: Swahili Alphabet Book* (K–3). Illus. by Tom Feelings. 1974, Dial LB $13.89 (0-8037-4350-5); Puffin paper $4.99 (0-8037-4428-5). 60pp. An alphabet book that concentrates on the positive, beautiful aspects of African-Swahili life.

**32** Fisher, Leonard Everett. *The ABC Exhibit* (PS–1). Illus. 1991, Macmillan $15.95 (0-02-735251-X). 32pp. An unusual picture book that teaches the alphabet through full-color paintings. (Rev: BCCB 7–8/91; BL 3/15/91; SLJ 5/91)

**33** Gag, Wanda. *The ABC Bunny* (PS–1). Illus. by author. 1997, Putnam paper $5.95 (0-698-11438-8). 32pp. Bunny scampers through the alphabet in this classic ABC book.

**34** Geisert, Arthur. *Pigs from A to Z* (1–4). Illus. by author. 1986, Houghton $17.95 (0-395-38509-1). 64pp. Complicated etchings hide letters throughout and it will take somewhat older than usual alphabet book readers to figure them out. (Rev: BL 11/15/86; HB 1–2/87; SLJ 12/86)

**35** Grimes, Nikki. *C Is for City* (PS–2). Illus. by Pat Cummings. 1995, Lothrop LB $15.93 (0-688-11809-

7). 40pp. Signs, objects, and inhabitants associated with a city are used in this clever alphabet book. (Rev: BCCB 12/95; BL 10/1/95; SLJ 11/95)

**36** Hague, Kathleen. *Alphabears: An ABC Book* (PS–K). Illus. by Michael Hague. 1984, Holt $12.95 (0-8050-0841-1); paper $4.95 (0-8050-1637-6). 32pp. Twenty-six different lovable bears are introduced, one for each letter.

**37** Hansen, Biruta A. *Parading with Piglets: A Playful ABC Pop-up* (PS–1). Illus. 1996, National Geographic $16.95 (0-7922-2711-5). 14pp. Animals move when tabs are pulled in this alphabet book. (Rev: BL 12/15/96)

**38** Harrison, Ted. *A Northern Alphabet: A Is for Arctic* (K–2). Illus. by author. 1989, Tundra paper $7.95 (0-88776-233-6). 32pp. Scenes, people, and objects associated with the Far North are used in this alphabet book. A reissue.

**39** Heidelbach, Nikolaus. *Where the Girls Are* (2–4). Trans. from German by A. W. Millyard. Illus. by author. 1994, Annick paper $8.95 (1-55037-974-7). In this imaginative alphabet book, 26 different girls engage in some unusual activities. (Rev: SLJ 12/94)

**40** Heller, Nicholas. *Goblins in Green* (PS–1). Illus. by Joseph A. Smith. 1995, Greenwillow LB $15.93 (0-688-12803-3). 32pp. Goblins and their articles of clothing are used to introduce the alphabet. (Rev: BL 9/1/95; SLJ 9/95)

**41** Helman, Andrea. *O Is for Orca: A Pacific Northwest Alphabet Book* (K–2). Photos by Art Wolfe. 1995, Sasquatch $14.95 (1-57061-038-X). Stunning color photos are used in this alphabet book presenting some of the animals, people, plants, and geographical features of the Pacific Northwest. (Rev: SLJ 2/96)

**42** Hepworth, Cathi. *ANTics! An Alphabetical Anthology* (K–2). Illus. by author. 1992, Putnam LB $15.95 (0-399-21862-9). 32pp. This inventive picture book for older children features the names of people and concepts that contain the word "ant." (Rev: BL 5/15/92*; SLJ 7/92*)

**43** Hoban, Tana. *26 Letters and 99 Cents* (PS–1). Illus. by author. 1987, Greenwillow LB $15.93 (0-688-06362-4). 32pp. An ABC and counting book combined by turning the book upside down. (Rev: BCCB 4/87; BL 3/1/87; SLJ 4/87)

**44** Howland, Naomi. *ABCDrive! A Car Trip Alphabet* (PS–1). Illus. 1994, Clarion $15.00 (0-395-66414-4). 32pp. An alphabet book that uses names of vehicles and terms connected with traveling. (Rev: BCCB 6/94; BL 4/15/94; SLJ 6/94)

**45** Hubbard, Woodleigh. *C Is for Curious: An ABC of Feelings* (PS–3). Illus. 1990, Chronicle $13.95 (0-87701-679-8). 32pp. One word for each alphabet let-

ter — such as A is for angry, B is for bored — with colorful graphics. (Rev: BL 3/1/91)

**46** Hughes, Langston. *The Sweet and Sour Animal Book* (PS–1). Illus. 1994, Oxford $17.95 (0-19-509185-X). 48pp. An alphabet book by the distinguished poet that uses illustrations by children from the Harlem School of the Arts. (Rev: BCCB 1/95; BL 10/15/94; SLJ 2/95)

**47** Isadora, Rachel. *City Seen from A to Z* (PS–2). Illus. by author. 1983, Greenwillow LB $15.93 (0-688-01803-3). 32pp. Everyday objects in the city are used in this alphabet book.

**48** Jahn-Clough, Lisa. *ABC Yummy* (PS–2). Illus. 1997, Houghton $5.95 (0-395-84542-4). 32pp. A tiny picture book that uses fruits and vegetables on a trip through the alphabet. (Rev: BL 4/1/97; SLJ 6/97)

**49** Jernigan, Gisela. *Agave Blooms Just Once* (2–4). Illus. by E. Wesley Jernigan. 1989, Harbinger paper $10.95 (0-943173-44-2). An introduction to flora and fauna in the Sonoran Desert and an alphabet book, in rhyming verse. (Rev: BL 3/1/90)

**50** Johnson, Jean. *Firefighters A to Z* (PS–1). Illus. 1985, Walker LB $11.85 (0-8027-6590-4). 39pp. An alphabet book organized around the workings of a fire-fighting unit. Others in this series are: *Librarians A to Z* (1989); *Police Officers A to Z* (1986); *Postal Workers A to Z* (1987); *Teachers A to Z* (1987). (Rev: BL 3/1/86)

**51** Johnson, Odette, and Bruce Johnson. *Apples, Alligators and Also Alphabets* (PS–K). Illus. 1992, Stoddart paper $3.95 (0-19-540906-X). 32pp. An inventive alphabet book with whimsical words and actions. (Rev: BL 4/15/91; SLJ 6/91)

**52** Jordan, Martin, and Tanis Jordan. *Amazon Alphabet* (PS–2). Illus. 1996, Kingfisher $17.95 (1-85697-666-1). 40pp. The wildlife of the Amazon rain forest provides the subjects for this oversize alphabet book. (Rev: BL 4/15/96; SLJ 5/96)

**53** Kaye, Buddy, et al. *A You're Adorable* (PS–1). Illus. by Martha Alexander. 1994, Candlewick $9.95 (1-56402-237-4). 32pp. A charming alphabet book that uses the words of a song that was popular more than 40 years ago. (Rev: BL 7/94)

**54** Kellogg, Steven. *Aster Aardvark's Alphabet Adventures* (PS–3). Illus. 1987, Morrow paper $3.95 (0-688-11571-3). 40pp. The alphabet is interpreted through 26 vignettes, 1 to 3 pages long. (Rev: BL 9/1/87; HB 11–12/87; SLJ 12/87)

**55** King-Smith, Dick. *Dick King-Smith's Alphabeasts* (PS–K). Illus. by Quentin Blake. 1992, Macmillan $14.95 (0-02-750720-3). 64pp. Mirth-provoking verses celebrate the animal kingdom. (Rev: BCCB 12/92; BL 9/15/92; SLJ 12/92)

**56** Kitamura, Satoshi. *From Acorn to Zoo and Everything in Between in Alphabetical Order* (PS–1). Illus. 1992, Farrar $15.00 (0-374-32470-0). 32pp. A number of objects starting with the same letter are pictured on each page of this attractive British alphabet book. (Rev: BL 7/92; HB 5–6/92*; SLJ 7/92)

**57** Kitamura, Satoshi. *What's Inside? The Alphabet Book* (PS–1). Illus. by author. 1985, Farrar $12.95 (0-374-38306-5). 32pp. An offbeat alphabet book for young readers who know their letters and enjoy some visual fun. (Rev: BL 9/1/85; SLJ 9/86)

**58** Kitchen, Bert. *Animal Alphabet* (PS–2). Illus. by author. 1984, Puffin paper $4.95 (0-8037-0431-3). 32pp. A stylistic ABC book using both familiar and unfamiliar animals.

**59** Lester, Alison. *Alice and Aldo* (K–3). Illus. 1998, Houghton $15.00 (0-395-87092-5). 32pp. Young Alice and her stuffed toy, Aldo, present the alphabet through a series of everyday activities. (Rev: BL 3/1/98)

**60** Lindbergh, Reeve. *The Awful Aardvarks Go to School* (PS–2). Illus. by Tracey Campbell Pearson. 1997, Viking paper $15.99 (0-670-85920-6). 32pp. In this hilarious alphabet book, 3 aardvarks create chaos when they invade a classroom. (Rev: BL 10/15/97*; SLJ 12/97)

**61** Linscott, Jody. *Once upon A to Z: An Alphabet Odyssey* (K–4). Illus. by Claudia Porges Holland. 1991, Doubleday $15.00 (0-385-41893-0). A story that introduces the alphabet through the journey of Andy and Daisy. (Rev: SLJ 1/92)

**62** Livingston, Myra Cohn. *B Is for Baby: An Alphabet of Verses* (PS–K). Photos by Steel Stillman. 1996, Simon & Schuster $15.00 (0-689-80950-6). This alphabet book celebrates babyhood in a series of simple, catchy rhymes. (Rev: SLJ 9/96)

**63** Lobel, Anita. *Alison's Zinnia* (PS–2). Illus. 1990, Greenwillow LB $15.93 (0-688-08866-X). 32pp. In this alphabet book, flowers are used to guide youngsters through their ABCs. (Rev: BCCB 10/90; BL 9/1/90*; HB 11–12/90; SLJ 10/90)

**64** Lobel, Anita. *Away from Home* (PS–3). Illus. 1994, Greenwillow LB $15.93 (0-688-10355-3). 32pp. Each letter of the alphabet depicts a boy in a different place, e.g., Adam arrives in Amsterdam. (Rev: BCCB 9/94; BL 8/94; SLJ 10/94)

**65** Lobel, Anita. *Pierrot's ABC Garden* (PS–1). Illus. 1993, Western $12.95 (0-307-17551-0). 24pp. In this alphabet book, Pierrot gathers a variety of vegetables to take to his Pierrette. (Rev: BL 11/15/93)

**66** Lobel, Arnold. *On Market Street* (PS–1). Illus. by Anita Lobel. 1981, Greenwillow LB $16.93 (0-688-84309-3); Morrow paper $5.95 (0-688-08745-0). 40pp. A merry alphabet book with objects from apples to zippers.

**67** Lyne, Alice. *A My Name Is . . .* (PS–2). Illus. by Lynne W. Cravath. 1997, Whispering Coyote $14.95 (1-879085-40-2); paper $5.95 (1-879085-41-0). Introduces the alphabet through pictures of animals and humans. (Rev: SLJ 5/97)

**68** MacDonald, Suse. *Alphabatics* (PS–1). Illus. by author. 1986, Macmillan $16.95 (0-02-761520-0). 64pp. An alphabet book that forms a letter into part of the picture illustrating the sound of the letter, such as "m" as part of the mustache on a face. (Rev: BL 12/15/86; SLJ 12/86)

**69** McDonnell, Flora. *Flora McDonnell's ABC* (PS–K). Illus. 1997, Candlewick $16.99 (0-7636-0118-7). 32pp. A witty, delightful introduction to the alphabet using animals and fish engaging in zany activities. (Rev: BCCB 7–8/97; BL 4/15/97)

**70** McKenzie, Ellen Kindt. *The Perfectly Orderly House* (K–2). Illus. by Megan Lloyd. 1994, Holt $14.95 (0-8050-1946-4). 32pp. In this picture book, an old woman decides to put some order in her house and sorts out objects for storage alphabetically. (Rev: BCCB 12/94; BL 12/1/94; SLJ 1/95)

**71** MacKinnon, Debbie. *My First ABC* (PS). Illus. by Anthea Sieveking. 1993, Barron's $11.95 (0-8120-6331-7). Children interact with various common objects in this charming alphabet book. (Rev: SLJ 7/93)

**72** Magee, Doug, and Robert Newman. *All Aboard ABC* (PS–2). Illus. 1990, Dutton paper $15.99 (0-525-65036-9). 48pp. Vivid photos enhance this ABC book that captures trains from many angles. (Rev: BCCB 9/90; BL 10/1/90; SLJ 11/90)

**73** Mahurin, Tim. *Jeremy Kooloo* (PS–K). Illus. 1995, Dutton paper $13.99 (0-525-45203-6). 32pp. Jeremy Kooloo, a frisky cat, acts up in this humorous alphabet book. (Rev: BCCB 2/95; BL 12/15/94; HB 5–6/95; SLJ 3/95)

**74** Marshall, Janet. *Look Once, Look Twice* (K–2). Illus. 1995, Ticknor $13.95 (0-395-71644-6). 64pp. A clever alphabet book that uses interesting patterns to introduce letters and words that begin with each letter. (Rev: BCCB 4/95; BL 2/1/95; HB 5–6/95; SLJ 4/95)

**75** Martin, Bill, Jr., and John Archambault. *Chicka Chicka Boom Boom* (PS–2). Illus. by Lois Ehlert. 1989, Simon & Schuster paper $15.00 (0-671-67949-X). 32pp. The letters of the alphabet enjoy a series of adventures. (Rev: BL 10/15/89*; HB 1–2/90*; SLJ 11/89)

**76** Martin, Mary Jane. *From Anne to Zach* (PS–K). Illus. by Michael Grejniec. 1996, Boyds Mills $14.95 (1-56397-573-4). This ABC book introduces the alphabet by using a lot of first names, both common and obscure. (Rev: SLJ 12/96)

**77** Maurer, Donna. *Annie, Bea, and Chi Chi Dolores: A School Day Alphabet* (PS–4). Illus. by Denys Cazet. 1993, Orchard LB $16.99 (0-531-08617-8). A day in a kindergarten supplies the letters to introduce an alphabet. (Rev: BL 2/13/93; HB 7–8/93; SLJ 5/93)

**78** Mayer, Marianna. *The Unicorn Alphabet* (3–5). Illus. by Michael Hague. 1989, Dial LB $14.89 (0-8037-0373-2). 32pp. Using unicorn tapestries, this alphabet book presents many objects familiar to Middle Ages mythology. (Rev: BCCB 11/89; BL 9/1/89; SLJ 12/89)

**79** Mayers, Florence Cassen. *ABC: The Alef-Bet Book* (K–4). Illus. 1989, Abrams $12.95 (0-8109-1885-4). Each letter of the Hebrew alphabet is illustrated by an object from the Israel Museum. (Rev: SLJ 11/89)

**80** Mayers, Florence Cassen. *ABC: The Museum of Modern Art, New York* (PS–4). Illus. 1986, Abrams $12.95 (0-8109-1849-8). 32pp. Introducing children to the alphabet and fine art. (Rev: BL 2/15/87)

**81** Mayers, Florence Cassen. *Baseball ABC* (1–3). Illus. 1994, Abrams $12.95 (0-8109-1938-9). An unusual alphabet book that uses baseball terminology, equipment, teams, and players to introduce the ABCs. (Rev: SLJ 12/94)

**82** Mayers, Florence Cassen. *A Russian ABC: Featuring Masterpieces from the Hermitage* (K–4). Illus. 1992, Abrams $12.95 (0-8109-1919-2). 36pp. An ABC series featuring art reproductions from the museum's collection. (Rev: BL 11/1/92; SLJ 2/93)

**83** Merriam, Eve. *Goodnight to Annie: An Alphabet Lullaby* (PS–K). Illus. by Carol Schwartz. 1992, Hyperion LB $15.49 (1-56282-206-3). 32pp. While waiting for sleep, a young girl plays with her alphabet blocks. (Rev: BL 10/15/92; SLJ 1/93)

**84** Merriam, Eve. *Where Is Everybody? An Animal Alphabet* (PS–3). Illus. by Diane De Groat. 1992, Simon & Schuster paper $14.95 (0-671-64964-7). 40pp. An alphabet book with many, many details in each picture. (Rev: BL 6/15/89; HB 7–8/89)

**85** Metaxas, Eric. *The Birthday ABC* (K–3). Illus. by Tim Raglin. 1995, Simon & Schuster paper $15.00 (0-671-88306-2). 32pp. Animals in proper 18th century attire illustrate the letters of the alphabet. (Rev: BL 8/95; SLJ 6/95)

**86** Micklethwait, Lucy, ed. *I Spy: An Alphabet in Art* (K–2). Illus. 1992, Greenwillow $19.00 (0-688-11679-5). 64pp. Young readers are asked to find objects in full-page reproductions of paintings. (Rev: BCCB 2/93; BL 11/1/92; HB 1–2/93; SLJ 10/92)

**87** Miller, Jane. *Farm Alphabet Book* (PS–K). Illus. 1987, Scholastic paper $2.99 (0-590-31991-4). 32pp. Photographs of farm life make an unusual ABC book.

**88** Miranda, Anne. *Pignic: An Alphabet Book in Rhyme* (PS–2). Illus. by Rosekrans Hoffman. 1996, Boyds Mills $14.95 (1-56397-558-0). 32pp. A pig picnic is used as a locale for introducing the 26 letters through objects and activities. (Rev: BL 3/1/96; SLJ 5/96)

**89** Modesitt, Jeanne. *The Story of Z* (K–2). Illus. by Lonni S. Johnson. 1990, Picture Book paper $14.95 (0-88708-105-3). 28pp. Z becomes tired of being last and decides to leave the alphabet. (Rev: BL 6/1/90; SLJ 1/91)

**90** Onyefulu, Ifeoma. *A Is for Africa* (K–3). Illus. 1993, Dutton paper $15.99 (0-525-65147-0). 32pp. A series of photos of people, places, and things taken in Nigeria introduce the alphabet. (Rev: BL 8/93)

**91** Owens, Mary Beth. *A Caribou Alphabet* (PS–1). Illus. by author. 1988, Farrar paper $4.95 (0-374-41043-7). 40pp. An alphabet book featuring caribous. (Rev: BL 9/1/88; HB 11–12/88; SLJ 10/88)

**92** Oxenbury, Helen. *Helen Oxenbury's ABC of Things* (PS–K). Illus. by author. 1993, Simon & Schuster paper $3.95 (0-689-71761-X). 56pp. Groups of unlikely animals and objects are pictured together in this imaginative and humorous alphabet book.

**93** Pallotta, Jerry. *The Frog Alphabet Book . . . and Other Awesome Amphibians* (PS–1). Illus. by Ralph Masiello. 1990, Charlesbridge $15.95 (0-88106-463-7); paper $6.95 (0-88106-462-9). 32pp. This alphabet book introduces amphibians and gives salient facts about different varieties. (Rev: BL 9/1/90)

**94** Pandell, Karen. *Animal Action ABC* (PS–1). Illus. by Art Wolfe and Nancy Sheehan. 1996, Dutton paper $15.99 (0-525-45486-1). 40pp. The alphabet is introduced by 26 action words that are skillfully illustrated to show motion. (Rev: BL 11/15/96)

**95** Paul, Ann W. *Eight Hands Round: A Patchwork Alphabet* (1–4). Illus. by Jeanette Winter. 1991, HarperCollins LB $14.89 (0-06-024704-5). 32pp. An alphabet book that shows how the art of patchwork grew and why. (Rev: BCCB 7–8/91; BL 6/1/91; SLJ 7/91)

**96** Pelham, David. *A Is for Animals: An Animal ABC* (PS–1). 1991, Simon & Schuster $16.95 (0-671-72495-9). Animals pop out of squares in this alphabet book. (Rev: BL 9/15/91)

**97** Pelletier, David. *The Graphic Alphabet* (4–8). Illus. 1996, Orchard $17.95 (0-531-36001-6). 32pp. Letters of the alphabet are pictured in various imaginative positions. (Rev: BCCB 12/96; BL 11/1/96; HB 11–12/96; SLJ 11/96)

**98** Pomeroy, Diana. *Wildflower ABC: An Alphabet of Potato Prints* (PS–2). Illus. 1997, Harcourt $15.00 (0-15-201041-6). 40pp. Different wildflowers like the columbine and dandelion are pictured in potato prints in this alphabet book. (Rev: BL 2/15/97; SLJ 11/97)

**99** Pratt, Kristin J. *A Swim Through the Sea* (PS–3). Illus. by author. 1994, Dawn $16.95 (1-883220-03-3); paper $7.95 (1-883220-04-1). An alphabet book in which Seamore the seahorse introduces a number of creatures from the deep. (Rev: SLJ 8/94)

**100** Pratt, Kristin J. *A Walk in the Rainforest* (2–4). Illus. by author. 1992, Dawn $16.95 (1-878265-99-7); paper $7.95 (1-878265-53-9). 33pp. In this book written and illustrated by a high school student, plants and animals found in the rain forest are used to introduce the alphabet. (Rev: SLJ 7/92)

**101** Press, Judy. *Alphabet Art: With A to Z Animal Art and Fingerplays* (PS–K). Illus. by Sue Dennen. Series: Little Hands Book. 1998, Williamson paper $12.95 (1-885593-14-7). 134pp. For teachers and parents, this book explains how to teach the alphabet using crafts, games, poems, and fingerplays. (Rev: SLJ 3/98)

**102** Provensen, Alice, and Martin Provensen. *A Peaceable Kingdom: The Shaker Abecedarius* (PS–K). Illus. by authors. 1981, Puffin paper $5.99 (0-14-050370-6). 40pp. A newly illustrated version of the Shaker's *Animal Rhymes*, first published in 1882.

**103** Reed, Lynn R. *Pedro, His Perro, and the Alphabet Sombrero* (PS–3). Illus. 1995, Hyperion LB $15.49 (0-7868-2058-6). 32pp. Pedro and his dog decorate a large sombrero using items that start with letters of the Spanish alphabet. (Rev: BL 4/15/95; SLJ 4/95)

**104** Rey, H. A. *Curious George Learns the Alphabet* (K–2). Illus. by author. 1963, Houghton $14.95 (0-395-16031-6); paper $5.95 (0-395-13718-7). 72pp. George makes learning the alphabet a wonderful and amusing game.

**105** Rosen, Michael. *Michael Rosen's ABC* (PS–1). Illus. by Bee Willey. 1997, Millbrook LB $24.90 (1-56294-138-0). 64pp. Strange characters and happenings in the woods are used in this whimsical ABC book. (Rev: BL 6/1–15/97; SLJ 3/97)

**106** Rosenberg, Liz. *A Big and a Little Alphabet* (PS–1). Illus. by Vera Rosenberry. 1997, Orchard LB $16.99 (0-531-33050-8). 32pp. An ABC book that uses big and small animals to show the differences between upper and lowercase. (Rev: BL 11/1/97; SLJ 10/97)

**107** Rotner, Shelley. *Action Alphabet* (PS–2). Illus. 1996, Simon & Schuster $16.00 (0-689-80086-X). 32pp. An alphabet book that uses as its focus a variety of outdoor activities. (Rev: BCCB 6/96; BL 8/96; SLJ 1/97)

**108** Ryden, Hope. *ABC of Crawlers and Flyers* (2–4). Illus. 1996, Clarion $14.95 (0-395-72808-8).

32pp. Each letter of the alphabet introduces a different insect. (Rev: BL 9/15/96; SLJ 10/96)

**109** Sanders, Eve. *What's Your Name? From Ariel to Zoe* (PS–1). Illus. by Marilyn Sanders. 1995, Holiday LB $15.95 (0-8234-1209-1). 36pp. Using photographs of children, this ABC book devotes a separate page to each name and its derivation. (Rev: BL 10/15/95; SLJ 3/96)

**110** Sandved, Kjell B. *The Butterfly Alphabet* (K–3). Illus. 1996, Scholastic $15.95 (0-590-48003-0). 72pp. In double-page spreads, the alphabet is introduced with breathtaking close-ups of wing patterns of butterflies and moths. (Rev: BL 3/15/96; SLJ 5/96)

**111** Seeley, Laura L. *The Book of Shadowboxes: A Story of the ABC's* (PS–3). Illus. 1990, Peachtree $16.95 (0-934601-65-8). Using objects in shadowboxes as illustrations, the letters of the alphabet are introduced. (Rev: SLJ 4/91)

**112** Seuss, Dr. *Dr. Seuss' ABC* (K–2). Illus. by author. 1963, Random LB $11.99 (0-394-90030-8). 72pp. A master author creates a strikingly popular alphabet book.

**113** Shannon, George. *Tomorrow's Alphabet* (1–3). Illus. by Donald Crews. 1996, Greenwillow LB $15.93 (0-688-13505-6). 56pp. A sophisticated alphabet book using letters to represent future developments, e.g., A is for seed — tomorrow's apple. (Rev: BCCB 4/96; BL 3/1/96*; SLJ 4/96*)

**114** Shaw, Eve. *Grandmother's Alphabet* (PS–K). Illus. by author. 1996, Pfeifer-Hamilton paper $14.95 (1-57025-127-4). An alphabet book that describes a number of activities and professions that grandmothers can be involved in. (Rev: SLJ 5/97)

**115** Shepard, Ernest H. *Winnie-the-Pooh's ABC: Inspired by A. A. Milne* (PS–K). Illus. 1995, Dutton paper $9.99 (0-525-45365-2). 32pp. An alphabet book that uses illustrations that first appeared in the Pooh books. (Rev: BL 1/15/95)

**116** Slate, Joseph. *Miss Bindergarten Gets Ready for Kindergarten* (PS–1). Illus. by Ashley Wolff. 1996, Dutton paper $15.99 (0-525-45446-2). 32pp. Each of Miss Bindergarten's class represents a letter of the alphabet, like Adam Krupp — an alligator. (Rev: BL 8/96; SLJ 8/96*)

**117** Snow, Alan. *The Monster Book of ABC Sounds* (PS–K). Illus. 1991, Dial paper $12.95 (0-8037-0935-8). 32pp. Starting with hide-and-seek between monsters and rats, this is a fun tour of the alphabet. (Rev: BL 7/91; SLJ 9/91)

**118** Staake, Bob. *My Little ABC Book* (PS–K). Illus. by author. 1998, Simon & Schuster paper $6.99 (0-689-81659-6). The letters of the alphabet are presented in this board book that uses bright colors and pleasant graphics. (Rev: SLJ 3/98)

**119** Stutson, Caroline. *Prairie Primer: A to Z* (PS–2). Illus. by Susan C. Lamb. 1996, Dutton paper $15.99 (0-525-45163-3). 32pp. The alphabet is introduced by objects and activities associated with farm life 100 years ago. (Rev: BL 10/15/96; SLJ 10/96)

**120** Tapahonso, Luci, and Eleanor Schick. *Navajo ABC: A Dine Alphabet Book* (PS–3). Illus. by Eleanor Schick. 1995, Simon & Schuster $16.00 (0-689-80316-8). 24pp. Various objects and words associated with the Navajo people are used to introduce their alphabet and the English alphabet. (Rev: BL 12/15/95; SLJ 12/95)

**121** Testa, Fulvio. *A Long Trip to Z* (PS–1). Illus. 1997, Harcourt $15.00 (0-15-201610-4). 32pp. The alphabet is explored during a magical flight on a red airplane where different objects are seen and heard. (Rev: BL 10/1/97; SLJ 10/97)

**122** *The Timbertoes ABC Alphabet Book* (PS–1). Illus. 1997, Boyds Mills $7.95 (1-56397-604-8). 32pp. The Timbertoes, a family of wooden figures, introduce the letters of the alphabet. (Rev: BL 3/1/97; SLJ 7/97)

**123** Tryon, Leslie. *Albert's Alphabet* (PS–1). Illus. by author. 1991, Macmillan $16.00 (0-689-31642-9). 40pp. Out of a variety of materials, a school carpenter creates an alphabet for the playground. (Rev: BL 4/15/91; SLJ 7/91)

**124** Turner, Priscilla. *The War Between the Vowels and the Consonants* (K–3). Illus. by Whitney Turner. 1996, Farrar $15.00 (0-374-38236-0). 30pp. Rivalry between vowels and consonants is used as a lively introduction to letters. (Rev: BL 12/1/96; SLJ 10/96)

**125** Viorst, Judith. *The Alphabet from Z to A: With Much Confusion on the Way* (1–3). Illus. by Richard Hull. 1994, Atheneum $15.00 (0-689-31768-9). 32pp. The alphabet is presented backward in amusing verses. (Rev: BL 3/1/94; SLJ 4/94)

**126** Walker, John. *Ridiculous Rhymes from A to Z* (1–3). Illus. by David Catrow. 1995, Holt $16.95 (0-8050-1581-7). 56pp. A charming alphabet book for older kids who like to play with words, sounds, and unusual meanings. (Rev: BL 1/1–15/96; SLJ 2/96)

**127** Watson, Clyde. *Applebet: An ABC* (PS–2). Illus. by Wendy Watson. 1982, Farrar paper $3.95 (0-374-40427-5). 32pp. An alphabet book in which apples and a country fair provide the links from letter to letter.

**128** Wells, Ruth. *A to Zen: A Book of Japanese Culture* (2–4). Illus. by Yoshi. 1992, Picture Book $16.00 (0-88708-175-4). 32pp. An alphabet-book format introduces young readers to Japanese culture and life. (Rev: BCCB 12/92; BL 1/15/93; SLJ 4/93)

**129** Willard, Nancy. *An Alphabet of Angels* (PS–3). Illus. 1994, Scholastic $16.95 (0-590-48480-X). 64pp. Using the alphabet as a framework, the artist

has created and photographed pieces of sculpture that depict various angels. (Rev: BCCB 10/94; BL 9/15/94; SLJ 10/94)

**130** Wilner, Isabel. *B Is for Bethlehem: A Christmas Alphabet* (K–3). Illus. by Elisa Kleven. 1990, Dutton paper $14.99 (0-525-44622-2). 32pp. A Christmas story alphabet book. (Rev: BL 9/15/90*)

**131** Wood, Jakki. *Animal Parade* (PS–1). Illus. 1993, Macmillan $14.95 (0-02-793394-6). 32pp. Each page of this alphabet book contains several animals whose names start with the same letter. (Rev: BL 3/1/93; SLJ 7/93)

## Concept Books

### GENERAL

**132** Aliki. *Feelings* (K–2). Illus. 1984, Greenwillow LB $15.93 (0-688-03832-8); Morrow paper $4.95 (0-688-06518-X). 32pp. An introduction to various emotions.

**133** Anholt, Catherine, and Laurence Anholt. *One, Two, Three, Count with Me* (PS–1). Illus. 1996, Puffin paper $4.99 (0-14-055596-X). 32pp. This counting book also introduces the concepts of size, color, and the days of the week. (Rev: BL 6/1–15/94; SLJ 8/94)

**134** Ayres, Pam. *Guess What?* (PS–K). Illus. by Julie Lacome. 1994, Candlewick $3.99 (1-56402-346-X). 32pp. Readers guess objects in answer to rhymed questions. (Rev: BL 6/1/88; SLJ 7/88)

**135** *Baby's First Words* (PS). Illus. by Lars Wik. 1985, Random $3.99 (0-394-86945-1). 28pp. Photos of everyday objects known by toddlers and babies. (Rev: BL 6/15/85)

**136** Baker, Alan. *Brown Rabbit's Day* (PS–K). Illus. by author. Series: Little Rabbit Books. 1995, Kingfisher $7.95 (1-85697-584-3). In this concept book, Brown Rabbit invites friends over for a party where they have an opportunity to identify colors, count, and tell time. (Rev: SLJ 3/96)

**137** Baker, Alan. *Gray Rabbit's Odd One Out* (PS–K). Illus. by author. Series: Little Rabbit Books. 1995, Kingfisher $7.95 (1-85697-585-1). Object identification and the use of various colors to build objects are covered in this concept book. (Rev: SLJ 3/96)

**138** Bartlett, Alison. *Cat Among the Cabbages* (PS–K). Illus. 1997, Dutton paper $9.99 (0-525-45755-0). 24pp. Colors, sizes, and opposites are demonstrated in this story of a cat's walk in a garden. (Rev: BL 2/1/97; SLJ 1/97)

**139** Bauman, A. F. *Guess Where You're Going, Guess What You'll Do* (PS–3). Illus. by True Kelley. 1995, Houghton paper $4.95 (0-395-74512-8). 32pp.

This concept book explores the relationship between cause and effect. (Rev: BL 11/1/89; SLJ 12/89)

**140** Berenstain, Stan, and Jan Berenstain. *Inside, Outside, Upside Down* (PS–1). Illus. by authors. 1968, Random LB $11.99 (0-394-91142-3). A bear has a brief trip that explains various concepts.

**141** Bond, Michael. *Paddington's Opposites* (PS–2). Illus. by John Lobban. Series: Paddington. 1991, Viking paper $11.99 (0-670-84105-6). 32pp. The concept of opposites is introduced by Paddington by using common experiences and objects. (Rev: BL 12/15/91)

**142** Bown, Deni. *Happy Times* (PS). Illus. Series: Snapshot. 1995, DK Publg. $3.95 (0-7894-0229-7). 10pp. Children learn about the concept of time through a series of colorful illustrations. Also use *Color Fun* (1995). (Rev: BL 1/1–15/96; SLJ 7/96)

**143** Carle, Eric. *From Head to Toe* (PS). Illus. 1997, HarperCollins LB $16.89 (0-06-023516-0). 32pp. Children make the same movements as animals in this concept book illustrated with lively collages. (Rev: BCCB 6/97; BL 4/15/97; SLJ 4/97) [613.7]

**144** Carrier, Lark. *Do Not Touch* (1–3). Illus. by author. 1991, Picture Book paper $15.95 (0-88708-061-8). 28pp. A picture book with the concept of words within words. (Rev: BL 4/1/89)

**145** Carter, David A. *More Bugs in Boxes* (PS–3). Illus. 1990, Simon & Schuster $13.95 (0-671-69577-0). A board book that explores the world of shapes and colors. (Rev: SLJ 8/90)

**146** Cendrars, Blaise. *Shadow* (K–3). Trans. and illus. by Marcia Brown. 1982, Macmillan $17.00 (0-684-17226-7). 40pp. The Caldecott Medal winner (1983) that explores the mysterious world of shadows.

**147** Charles, N. N. *What Am I? Looking Through Shapes at Apples and Grapes* (PS–K). Illus. by Leo Dillon and Diane Dillon. 1994, Scholastic $13.95 (0-590-47891-5). 36pp. Geometric shapes are used creatively to illustrate a number of clever riddles in this interactive book. (Rev: BL 11/15/94; SLJ 1/95)

**148** Chesanow, Neil. *Where Do I Live?* (K–3). Illus. by Ann Iosa. 1995, Barron's paper $5.95 (0-8120-9241-4). 48pp. The concept of belonging is explored, from a room of one's own to being a part of the solar system. (Rev: BL 2/1/95) [910]

**149** Ford, Miela. *What Color Was the Sky Today?* (PS–1). Illus. by Sally Noll. 1997, Greenwillow LB $14.93 (0-688-14559-0). 24pp. Using fewer than 100 words, this book introduces the concepts of colors, counting, time, and the weather. (Rev: BL 5/1/97; SLJ 3/97)

**150** Fowler, Allan. *North, South, East, and West* (1–2). Illus. Series: Rookie Read-About Science.

1993, Children's Book Pr. $18.50 (0-516-06011-2); Children's paper $4.95 (0-516-46011-0). 32pp. This is an introduction to the concept of directions for beginning readers in an attractive small format using many color photographs. (Rev: BL 9/1/93) [526]

**151** Gibbons, Gail. *Playgrounds* (PS–1). Illus. by author. 1985, Holiday LB $15.95 (0-8234-0553-2). 32pp. A concept book that shows young readers playground scenes that are familiar. (Rev: BCCB 6/85; BL 5/15/85; SLJ 5/85)

**152** Goley, Elaine P. *Learn the Value of Trust* (PS–2). Illus. by Debbie Crocker. 1987, Rourke LB $15.94 (0-86592-378-7). 32pp. A simple text with examples drawn from a child's experiences. Others in this series are: *Learn the Value of Understanding Others; Learn the Value of Patience* (all 1988). (Rev: BL 6/15/88)

**153** Goor, Ron, and Nancy Goor. *Shadows: Here, There, and Everywhere* (PS–3). Illus. by authors. 1981, HarperCollins LB $14.89 (0-690-04133-0). 48pp. A simple book that explains what shadows are and how to make them.

**154** Grejniec, Michael. *Good Morning, Good Night* (PS). Illus. 1997, North-South paper $6.95 (1-55858-704-7). 28pp. A concept book with basic vocabulary that demonstrates opposites. (Rev: BL 3/15/93; SLJ 8/93)

**155** Grunwald, Lisa. *Now Soon Later* (PS). Illus. by Jane Johnson. 1996, Greenwillow $15.00 (0-688-13946-9). 24pp. Concepts involving time — like "now," "soon," and "later" — are explained through a girl's day-long activities. (Rev: BCCB 10/96; BL 7/96; SLJ 9/96)

**156** Harris, Pamela. *Hot, Cold, Shy, Bold* (PS–K). Illus. 1998, Kids Can $10.95 (1-55074-153-5). 32pp. A successful book of opposites that uses a rhyming text and color photos. (Rev: BL 3/15/98) [428.1]

**157** Hartman, Gail. *As the Crow Flies: A First Book of Maps* (PS–1). Illus. by Harvey Stevenson. 1993, Aladdin paper $5.95 (0-689-71762-8). 32pp. The concept of maps is introduced by using the environments of different animals. (Rev: BL 3/1/91; HB 5–6/91; SLJ 3/91)

**158** Hewitt, Sally. *Puzzles* (PS–3). Illus. Series: Take Off With. 1996, Raintree Steck-Vaughn LB $21.40 (0-8172-4115-9). 32pp. A concept book that involves counting as well as identifying patterns and shapes. (Rev: BL 5/15/96; SLJ 6/96)

**159** Hewitt, Sally. *Sorting and Sets* (PS–3). Illus. Series: Take Off With. 1996, Raintree Steck-Vaughn LB $21.40 (0-8172-4112-4). 32pp. Relationships between objects are explored in this general-concept book. (Rev: BL 5/15/96; SLJ 6/96)

**160** Hill, Eric. *Spot's Big Book of Colors, Shapes and Numbers* (PS–K). Illus. 1994, Putnam $10.95

(0-399-22679-6). 26pp. The dog Spot guides youngsters in this introduction to colors, shapes, and numbers. (Rev: BL 6/1–15/94)

**161** Hoban, Tana. *Animal, Vegetable, or Mineral?* (K–2). Illus. 1995, Greenwillow $15.00 (0-688-12746-0). 32pp. Pictures illustrate each of these categories and the often subtle differences between them. (Rev: BL 8/95; SLJ 9/95) [508]

**162** Hoban, Tana. *Black on White* (PS). Illus. 1993, Greenwillow paper $4.95 (0-688-11918-2). The photographs show black objects on a white background. A companion book is: *White on Black* (1993). (Rev: HB 7–8/93; SLJ 8/93)

**163** Hoban, Tana. *Dots, Spots, Speckles, and Stripes* (PS–K). Illus. 1987, Greenwillow LB $15.93 (0-688-06863-4). 32pp. Viewers pick out patterns in photographs, like speckles in strawberries. (Rev: BL 9/1/87; HB 11–12/87; SLJ 9/87)

**164** Hoban, Tana. *Exactly the Opposite* (PS–1). Illus. 1990, Greenwillow LB $15.93 (0-688-08862-7). 32pp. A concept book that challenges children to think on more than one level. (Rev: BCCB 10/90; BL 9/1/90; HB 11–12/90*; SLJ 10/90)

**165** Hoban, Tana. *Look Book* (PS–3). Illus. 1997, Greenwillow LB $15.93 (0-688-14972-3). 40pp. Everyday objects are featured in this concept book that changes one's perceptions by peeking through a series of holes. (Rev: BL 7/97; HB 9–10/97; SLJ 8/97) [779]

**166** Hoban, Tana. *Shadows and Reflections* (PS–1). Illus. 1990, Greenwillow LB $12.88 (0-688-07090-6). 32pp. This captures visual concepts for young children with water and shadows. (Rev: BL 2/15/90; HB 5–6/90; SLJ 5/90)

**167** Hoban, Tana. *What Is It?* (PS). Illus. by author. 1985, Greenwillow paper $4.95 (0-688-02577-3). 12pp. An array of toddler objects — a blue tennis shoe, a red sock, keys — in attractive board-book format. (Rev: BL 3/15/85; HB 9–10/85; SLJ 9/85)

**168** Hoban, Tana. *What Is That?* (PS). Illus. 1994, Greenwillow paper $4.95 (0-688-12920-X). 12pp. Using black silhouettes, a number of common animals are pictured in this board book. Also use *Who Are They?* (1994). (Rev: BL 12/1/94; HB 11–12/94; SLJ 11/94)

**169** Hoberman, Mary Ann. *A House Is a House for Me* (K–2). Illus. by Betty Fraser. 1978, Puffin paper $4.99 (0-14-050394-3). 48pp. This picture book explores the idea that various objects can serve as houses.

**170** Hughes, Shirley. *The Nursery Collection* (PS–K). Illus. 1994, Lothrop $17.00 (0-688-13583-8). 64pp. Explores and explains the concepts of shapes, numbers, sizes, sounds, and experiences. (Rev: BL 9/1/94)

**171** Inkpen, Mick. *Kipper's Book of Opposites* (PS–K). Illus. by author. 1995, Harcourt paper $6.00 (0-15-200668-0). Kipper, a friendly dog, introduces a number of simple opposites in text and brightly colored pictures. (Rev: SLJ 8/95)

**172** Jenkins, Sandra. *Flip-Flap* (PS). Illus. 1995, DK Publg. $14.95 (0-7894-0121-5). 24pp. By lifting flaps and turning wheels, one explores concepts like colors, numbers, and shapes. (Rev: BL 2/1/96) [910]

**173** Koch, Michelle. *By the Sea* (PS). Illus. n.d., Smithmark paper $3.98 (0-8317-1125-6). 24pp. Opposites are introduced in a seaside setting. (Rev: BL 2/15/91; SLJ 7/91) [428.1]

**174** Krauss, Ruth. *A Hole Is to Dig* (PS). Illus. by Maurice Sendak. 1952, HarperCollins $14.95 (0-06-023405-9); paper $4.95 (0-06-443205-X). 48pp. Child-perceived definitions, such as "the world is so you have something to stand on," complemented by whimsical drawings.

**175** Lillie, Patricia. *When This Box Is Full* (PS–2). Illus. by Donald Crews. 1993, Greenwillow LB $13.93 (0-688-12017-2); paper $4.99 (0-14-055831-4). 24pp. A youngster stores objects throughout the year in a wooden box in this concept book about "full" and "empty." (Rev: BCCB 12/93; BL 12/1/93; HB 11–12/93; SLJ 1/94)

**176** Llewellyn, Claire. *My First Book of Time* (PS–2). Illus. 1992, DK Publg. $14.95 (1-879431-78-5). 32pp. An oversize book with enticing photos and drawings provides an excellent introduction to the concept of time. (Rev: BCCB 7–8/92; BL 5/1/92; HB 7–8/92; SLJ 8/92) [529.7]

**177** Lynn, Sara. *Clothes* (PS). Illus. by author. 1986, Macmillan paper $2.95 (0-689-71095-X). 14pp. A baby's board book that focuses on familiar clothes. (Rev: BL 1/1/87; SLJ 3/87)

**178** Maccarone, Grace. *Monster Math School Time* (K–2). Illus. by Margaret A. Hartelius. Series: Hello Math Reader, Level 1. 1997, Scholastic $3.50 (0-590-30859-9). A beginning reader that teaches how to tell time through the antics of 12 monsters and their daily activities. (Rev: SLJ 1/98)

**179** McGuire, Richard. *What's Wrong with This Book?* (K–3). Illus. 1997, Viking paper $14.99 (0-670-86852-3). 32pp. Witty pictures and cutouts fool the eye in this book filled with unexpected pleasures. (Rev: BCCB 4/97; BL 2/1/97; HB 3–4/97; SLJ 3/97)

**180** MacKinnon, Debbie. *What Am I?* (PS). Illus. by Anthea Sieveking. 1996, Dial paper $10.99 (0-8037-1826-8). 24pp. Children with their toys act out adult occupations, such as firefighter, musician, doctor, or clown. (Rev: BCCB 10/94; BL 1/1–15/96; SLJ 3/96)

**181** McMillan, Bruce. *Eating Fractions* (PS–2). Illus. 1991, Scholastic $15.95 (0-590-43770-4).

32pp. Challenging fractions at the beginning level. (Rev: BCCB 9/91; BL 8/91; SLJ 9/91*) [513.2]

**182** Maestro, Betsy, and Giulio Maestro. *Traffic: A Book of Opposites* (PS–2). Illus. by Giulio Maestro. 1991, Crown $16.00 (0-517-54427-X). 32pp. Various forms of opposites are explored in this concept book.

**183** Manning, Linda. *Dinosaur Days* (PS–1). Illus. by Vlasta Van Kampen. 1994, Troll paper $12.95 (0-8167-3315-5). 32pp. Days of the week are introduced by 7 dinosaurs, each of which causes a household emergency. (Rev: BL 7/94; SLJ 8/94)

**184** Marzollo, Jean. *I Spy School Days: A Book of Picture Riddles* (PS–2). Illus. by Walter Wick. Series: I Spy. 1995, Scholastic $12.95 (0-590-48135-5). 38pp. Riddles and puzzles using photographs are featured, each related to school activities. (Rev: BL 12/1/95; SLJ 10/95)

**185** Matthias, Catherine. *Over-Under* (PS–1). Illus. by Gene Sharp. 1984, Children's LB $17.00 (0-516-02048-X); paper $4.95 (0-516-42048-8). 32pp. Spatial concepts are explained in an easy-to-read format.

**186** Miller, Margaret. *Can You Guess?* (PS–K). Illus. 1993, Greenwillow LB $14.93 (0-688-11181-5). 40pp. Concepts about everyday objects are explored in this book of questions and answers. (Rev: BCCB 10/93; BL 12/1/93; HB 11–12/93; SLJ 1/94)

**187** Modesitt, Jeanne. *Sometimes I Feel Like a Mouse: A Book About Feelings* (PS–1). Illus. by Robin Spowart. 1996, Scholastic paper $3.95 (0-590-44836-6). 32pp. Various emotions, like happy and proud, are pictured through poses of familar animals. (Rev: BL 10/1/92; SLJ 5/93)

**188** Murphy, Stuart J. *The Best Vacation Ever* (PS–3). Illus. by Nadine Bernard Westcott. 1997, HarperCollins LB $14.89 (0-06-026767-4); paper $4.95 (0-06-446706-6). 40pp. The concepts of collecting and analyzing data and making charts are introduced as a girl helps her family decide on a vacation spot. (Rev: BL 2/1/97; SLJ 3/97)

**189** Murphy, Stuart J. *Give Me Half!* (PS–3). Illus. by G. Brian Karas. 1996, HarperCollins LB $14.89 (0-06-025874-8). 40pp. A boy and his sister learn how to share when they find they have only one pizza and a single can of juice. (Rev: BCCB 5/96; BL 5/1/96; SLJ 6/96)

**190** *My First Look at Noises* (PS). Illus. Series: My First Look at. 1991, Random $6.95 (0-679-81161-3). 20pp. Crisp color photos are used to explore the world of sound in this beginner's book. (Rev: BL 6/1/91) [534]

**191** *My First Look at Opposites* (PS). Illus. Series: My First Look at. 1990, Random $7.00 (0-679-80620-2). 20pp. In bright, attractive photos, the idea

of opposites is introduced. (Rev: BL 10/15/90) [428.1]

**192** Paul, Ann W. *Hello Toes! Hello Feet!* (PS). Illus. by Nadine Bernard Westcott. 1998, DK Publg. $15.95 (0-7894-2481-9). An interactive picture book in which a girl introduces her hands and feet and describes all of the things they do. (Rev: BL 3/1/98; SLJ 3/98)

**193** Pluckrose, Henry. *Beginnings and Endings* (PS–K). Illus. by Stephen Shott. Series: New Look. 1996, Children's LB $15.60 (0-516-08236-1). 32pp. A concept book that explores items that have beginnings and ends (e.g., a rope) and those that do not (e.g., a necklace). (Rev: BL 6/1–15/96) [428]

**194** Priddy, Roger. *Baby's Book of Nature* (PS). Illus. 1995, DK Publg. $9.95 (0-7894-0003-0). 21pp. Photographs are used to introduce various concepts in nature, such as color, shapes, and patterns. (Rev: BL 6/1–15/95) [508]

**195** Rose, Emma. *Pumpkin Faces: A Glowing Book You Can Read in the Dark!* (PS–K). Illus. by Judith Moffatt. 1997, Scholastic $6.95 (0-590-13454-X). A simple concept book that uses the faces of Halloween jack-o'-lanterns to express a variety of emotions. (Rev: SLJ 11/97)

**196** Salt, Jane. *First Words for Babies and Toddlers* (PS). Illus. by Gerald Hawksley. 1991, Random $9.95 (0-679-80831-0). 192pp. A chunky picture book of objects familiar to young children. (Rev: BL 4/15/91) [428.1]

**197** Scarry, Richard. *Richard Scarry's Lowly Worm Word Book* (PS). Illus. by author. 1981, Random $3.99 (0-394-84728-8). 28pp. A tiny book showing familiar objects belonging to Lowly Worm.

**198** Sendak, Maurice. *The Nutshell Library* (PS–3). Illus. by author. 1962, HarperCollins $15.95 (0-06-025500-5). Miniature volumes include an alphabet book, *Alligators All Around,* and a counting book, *One Was Johnny* (both 1962).

**199** Serfozo, Mary. *What's What? A Guessing Game* (PS–K). Illus. by Keiko Narahashi. 1996, Simon & Schuster paper $15.00 (0-689-80653-1). 32pp. A concept book that explores various physical properties and their opposites, like soft and hard. (Rev: BCCB 10/96; BL 10/1/96I; SLJ 10/96*)

**200** Szekeres, Cyndy. *I Love My Busy Book* (PS–1). Illus. 1997, Scholastic $12.95 (0-590-69195-3). 48pp. Concepts like colors, manners, and parts of the body are introduced in double-page spreads. (Rev: BCCB 3/97; BL 2/1/97; SLJ 4/97)

**201** Tafuri, Nancy. *My Friends* (PS). Illus. by author. 1987, Greenwillow paper $3.95 (0-688-07187-2). 12pp. Small animals are displayed as the friends of a toddler in this board book. (Rev: BL 10/1/87; SLJ 11/87)

**202** Tomczyk, Mary. *Shapes, Sizes and More Surprises!* (PS–1). Illus. by Loretta Braren. Series: Little Hands Early Learning Books. 1996, Williamson paper $12.95 (0-913589-95-0). 141pp. An activity book for youngsters filled with stories, puzzles, counting exercises, and games. (Rev: SLJ 10/96)

**203** *Understanding Opposites: Tab Board Book* (PS). Illus. Series: Ages and Stages. 1997, Dutton $5.99 (0-525-45785-2). 14pp. Seven pairs of common opposites — e.g., clean and dirty — are introduced with pictures of children and objects to illustrate the meanings. (Rev: BL 4/15/97)

**204** Van Fleet, Matthew. *One Yellow Lion* (PS). Illus. by author. 1992, Dial paper $8.95 (0-8037-1099-2). This book, with foldout pages and plenty of drawings of animals, presents the concepts of color and counting. (Rev: SLJ 9/92)

**205** Walton, Rick. *So Many Bunnies: A Bedtime ABC and Counting Book* (PS). Illus. by Paige Miglio. 1998, Lothrop LB $15.93 (0-688-13657-5). A combination ABC and counting book that is also a bedtime book because it tells how Mother Rabbit tucked her 26 babies in for the night. (Rev: SLJ 3/98)

**206** Wilbur, Richard. *Opposites* (5–7). Illus. by author. 1991, Harcourt $11.95 (0-15-258720-9). 39pp. Through verses and cartoonlike illustrations, a series of antonyms are given for words.

**207** Wildsmith, Brian. *What the Moon Saw* (PS–1). Illus. by author. 1978, Oxford paper $11.95 (0-19-272157-7). 32pp. The Sun shows the Moon many things that involve such basic concepts as numbers and weight.

**208** Ziefert, Harriet. *A Dozen Dozens* (PS–3). Illus. by Chris L. Demarest. Series: Math Easy-to-Read, Level 2. 1998, Viking paper $3.99 (0-14-038819-2). The concept of dozens and half-dozens is explored in this happy picture book easy reader. (Rev: SLJ 2/98)

### COLORS

**209** Baker, Alan. *White Rabbit's Color Book* (PS–K). Illus. 1994, Kingfisher $7.95 (1-85697-953-9). 24pp. A rabbit falls into different pots of paint in this book that identifies many colors. (Rev: BL 7/94)

**210** Bond, Michael. *Paddington's Colors* (PS–2). Illus. by John Lobban. Series: Paddington. 1991, Viking paper $11.99 (0-670-84102-1). 32pp. While Paddington does his spring cleaning, various colors are introduced. (Rev: BL 12/15/91)

**211** Bown, Deni. *Color Fun* (PS). Illus. Series: Snapshot. 1995, DK Publg. $3.95 (0-7894-0230-0). 12pp. Colors are revealed by pulling tabs that open double-page spreads filled with objects of a particular color. (Rev: BL 1/1–15/96; SLJ 7/96) [701.85]

**212** Bryant-Mole, Karen. *Blue* (PS–1). Illus. Series: Images Series. 1996, Silver Pr. LB $10.95 (0-382-39590-5); paper $4.95 (0-382-39626-X). 24pp. A concept book that focuses on a single color, blue, and a variety of objects. Also use *Texture* (1996). (Rev: SLJ 1/97)

**213** Cabrera, Jane. *Cat's Colors* (PS). Illus. 1997, Dial paper $13.99 (0-8037-2090-4). 32pp. A concept book in which a black-and-orange cat is asked to choose its favorite color. (Rev: BL 4/15/97; SLJ 5/97)

**214** *Colors* (PS). Illus. Series: World Wildlife Fund. 1997, Cedco $5.95 (0-7683-2008-9). 14pp. Sharp color photos of animals are used effectively in this board book that teaches basic colors. Other books in this series are: *Spots* and *Stripes* (both 1997). (Rev: BL 10/15/97)

**215** De Brunhoff, Laurent. *Babar's Book of Color* (PS–1). Illus. by author. 1984, Random $13.00 (0-394-86896-X). 36pp. When Babar's children and Cousin Arthur visit his studio, they learn about color. (Rev: BL 3/1/85; SLJ 2/85)

**216** Dodds, Dayle Ann. *The Color Box* (PS–1). Illus. by Giles Laroche. 1992, Little, Brown $14.95 (0-316-18820-4). 32pp. Alexander, a young monkey, opens doors and discovers a variety of colors. (Rev: BCCB 3/92; BL 5/1/92; SLJ 6/92)

**217** Ehlert, Lois. *Color Farm* (PS–K). Illus. 1990, HarperCollins LB $14.89 (0-397-32441-3). 40pp. Various animals are pictured by using a number of different shapes and colors. (Rev: BL 11/15/90; HB 1–2/91; SLJ 11/90)

**218** Ehlert, Lois. *Color Zoo* (PS–2). Illus. by author. 1989, HarperCollins LB $15.89 (0-397-32260-7). 32pp. How basic shapes can be combined to make familiar objects. (Rev: BL 5/15/89; SLJ 4/89)

**219** Faulkner, Keith. *My Colors: Let's Learn About Colors* (PS). Illus. by Jonathan Lambert. 1995, Simon & Schuster $7.95 (0-671-89829-9). 22pp. In a series of double-page spreads, white pages are filled with colored objects when tabs are pulled in this book that introduces 10 colors. (Rev: BL 6/1–15/95)

**220** Goldsen, Louise. *Colors* (K–2). Illus. by P. M. Valet and Sylvaine Perols. 1991, Scholastic paper $11.95 (0-590-45236-3). Through the use of clear acetate sheets, various colors are introduced and identified. (Rev: SLJ 5/92) [535.5]

**221** Hill, Eric. *Spot Looks at Colors* (PS). Illus. by author. 1986, Putnam $3.95 (0-399-21349-X). 14pp. A board book with Spot, the puppy, as he lures young readers into this basic concept book. (Rev: BL 10/15/86; SLJ 10/86)

**222** Hoban, Tana. *Colors Everywhere* (PS–K). Illus. 1995, Greenwillow LB $15.93 (0-688-12763-0).

32pp. A wordless picture book that identifies the colors found in each of the photographs used. (Rev: BCCB 3/95; BL 5/1/95; HB 7–8/95; SLJ 7/95)

**223**   Hoban, Tana. *Is It Red? Is It Yellow? Is It Blue?* (PS). Illus. 1978, Greenwillow LB $15.93 (0-688-84171-6); Morrow paper $4.95 (0-688-07034-5). 32pp. Without words, this picture book explains the concept of color.

**224**   Hoban, Tana. *Of Colors and Things* (PS–1). Illus. by author. 1989, Greenwillow LB $15.93 (0-688-07535-5). 24pp. Colors explained in picture-book style. (Rev: BCCB 3/89; BL 4/1/89; SLJ 4/89)

**225**   Hoban, Tana. *Red, Blue, Yellow Shoe* (PS). Illus. by author. 1986, Greenwillow paper $4.95 (0-688-06563-5). 12pp. A very simple introduction to color in a board book. (Rev: BCCB 1/87; BL 10/15/86; HB 11–12/86)

**226**   Hughes, Shirley. *Colors* (PS). Illus. by author. 1986, Lothrop paper $4.95 (0-688-04206-6). 24pp. Rhymes help to explain the concept of color. (Rev: BL 12/15/86; HB 1–2/87; SLJ 12/86)

**227**   Inkpen, Mick. *Kipper's Book of Colors* (PS–K). Illus. by author. 1995, Harcourt paper $6.00 (0-15-200647-8). Kipper, a brown-and-white dog, takes the reader on a tour that introduces colors. (Rev: SLJ 8/95)

**228**   Jonas, Ann. *Color Dance* (PS–K). Illus. 1989, Greenwillow LB $15.93 (0-688-05991-0). 32pp. Dancers wave colored scarves and introduce various colors. (Rev: BL 8/89; SLJ 12/89)

**229**   Lionni, Leo. *Little Blue and Little Yellow* (PS–1). Illus. by author. 1959, Astor-Honor $14.95 (0-8392-3018-4). All the characters are blobs of color; an ingenious story intended to give the young child an awareness of color.

**230**   McMillan, Bruce. *Growing Colors* (PS–2). Illus. 1988, Lothrop LB $15.93 (0-688-07845-1). 40pp. An effective use of the camera for probing color in nature. (Rev: BL 9/1/88)

**231**   McMillan, Naomi. *Baby's Colors* (PS). Illus. by Keaf Holliday. 1996, Golden Bks. $3.99 (0-307-12873-3). 16pp. A board book that introduces basic colors to an African American girl. (Rev: BL 6/1–15/96)

**232**   Martin, Bill, Jr. *Brown Bear, Brown Bear, What Do You See?* (PS–1). Illus. by Eric Carle. 1992, Holt $15.95 (0-8050-1744-5). 32pp. This brightly illustrated easy-reader book first appeared in 1967 and is a fine introduction to colors. (Rev: BL 3/1/92; SLJ 5/92)

**233**   Murphy, Chuck. *Color Surprises* (PS–1). Illus. 1997, Simon & Schuster paper $12.95 (0-689-81504-2). Introduces colors using flaps of the same color as the animal underneath. (Rev: BL 12/15/97)

**234**   *My First Look at Colors* (PS). Illus. Series: My First Look at. 1990, Random $9.00 (0-679-80535-4). A basic color identification book that uses many well-labeled objects as examples. (Rev: SLJ 12/90) [535.6]

**235**   Pienkowski, Jan. *Colors* (K–1). Illus. by author. 1989, Simon & Schuster $3.50 (0-671-68134-6). 14pp. Ten objects are used as examples of colors.

**236**   Rockwell, Anne. *Mr. Panda's Painting* (PS–K). Illus. 1993, Macmillan LB $14.95 (0-02-777451-1). 32pp. Mr. Panda, a painter, brings a variety of colors back with him when he goes shopping in a paint store. (Rev: BL 11/1/93)

**237**   Serfozo, Mary. *Who Said Red?* (PS–K). Illus. by Narahashi Keiko. 1988, Macmillan paper $4.95 (0-689-71592-7). 32pp. A little boy is looking for his lost kite in this picture book about colors. (Rev: BL 9/1/88; SLJ 1/89)

**238**   Seuss, Dr. *My Many Colored Days* (PS). Illus. by Steve Johnson and Lou Fancher. 1996, Knopf LB $17.99 (0-679-97597-7). 32pp. Various moods are linked with colors in this rhyming picture book. (Rev: BL 11/1/96; SLJ 12/96)

**239**   Sharratt, Nick. *The Green Queen* (PS). Illus. by author. 1992, Candlewick $5.95 (1-56402-093-2). A green queen introduces the readers to colors in objects around her. (Rev: SLJ 11/92)

**240**   Spinelli, Eileen. *If You Want to Find Golden* (PS–2). Illus. by Stacey Schuett. 1993, Albert Whitman LB $15.95 (0-8075-3585-0). 32pp. An unusual book on colors in which they are introduced through objects found in a big city. (Rev: BL 12/1/93; SLJ 1/94)

**241**   Westray, Kathleen. *A Color Sampler* (2–5). Illus. 1993, Ticknor $14.95 (0-395-65940-X). 32pp. This book uses objects found in classic quilts to illustrate and introduce various colors. (Rev: BL 7/93) [535.6]

**242**   Winograd, Deborah. *My Color Is Panda* (PS). Illus. by author. 1993, Simon & Schuster $13.00 (0-671-79152-4). 20pp. A panda introduces his world and a number of colors. (Rev: BL 8/93)

**243**   Yamaka, Sara. *The Gift of Driscoll Lipscomb* (1–3). Illus. by Joung Un Kim. 1995, Simon & Schuster paper $15.00 (0-02-793599-X). 32pp. Through gifts from an artist neighbor, a young girl learns the nature and value of colors. (Rev: BL 6/1–15/95; SLJ 8/95)

**244**   Yee, Patrick. *Rosie Rabbit's Colors* (PS). Illus. 1998, Simon & Schuster $3.99 (0-689-81842-4). 16pp. This is one of 4 small, square, very simple board books that introduce concepts. The others are *Rosie Rabbit's Shapes, Rosie Rabbit's Numbers* and *Rosie Rabbit's Opposites* (all 1998). (Rev: BL 2/1/98; SLJ 2/98)

## PERCEPTION

**245**  Ahlberg, Janet, and Allan Ahlberg. *Peek-a-Boo!* (PS). Illus. 1981, Puffin paper $4.99 (0-14-050107-X). 32pp. Scenes are visible through a peephole in each page.

**246**  Aruego, Jose, and Ariane Dewey. *We Hide, You Seek* (PS). Illus. by authors. 1979, Greenwillow LB $15.93 (0-688-84201-1); Morrow paper $4.95 (0-688-07815-X). 32pp. An almost wordless picture book in which a rhinoceros sets out to find his friends who are playing hide-and-seek with him.

**247**  Baylor, Byrd. *The Other Way to Listen* (K–3). Illus. by Peter Parnall. 1978, Macmillan $15.00 (0-684-16017-X). 32pp. An old man teaches a young boy how to listen.

**248**  Carrier, Lark. *There Was a Hill . . .* (PS–1). Illus. by author. 1991, Picture Book paper $15.95 (0-907234-70-4). 40pp. An attractive picture book with a guessing game woven into the irresistible pages. (Rev: BL 9/15/85; SLJ 10/85)

**249**  Hoban, Tana. *I Read Signs* (PS–2). Illus. by author. 1983, Greenwillow LB $17.93 (0-688-02318-5); Morrow paper $4.95 (0-688-07331-X). 32pp. An introduction to some common signs and their meaning. Also use: *I Read Symbols* (1983).

**250**  Hoban, Tana. *Is It Rough? Is It Smooth? Is It Shiny?* (PS). Illus. by author. 1984, Greenwillow $18.00 (0-688-03823-9). 32pp. Textures are explored in a series of photographs.

**251**  Hoban, Tana. *Just Look* (PS–3). Illus. 1996, Greenwillow LB $15.93 (0-688-14041-6). 40pp. Using paper peepholes and later revealing the entire subject, the author introduces a variety of objects and teaches observation skills. (Rev: BCCB 6/96; BL 4/15/96; HB 5–6/96; SLJ 4/96)

**252**  Hoban, Tana. *Look Again!* (PS–2). Illus. by author. 1971, Macmillan $15.00 (0-02-744050-8). 40pp. A concept book in which photographs of objects appear in part, as a whole, and then as a part within a composition.

**253**  Hoban, Tana. *Look Up, Look Down* (PS–K). Illus. 1992, Greenwillow LB $13.93 (0-688-10578-5). The camera catches such perspectives as a pavement oil slick, birds perched on wires, and the peace of a snow-filled park. (Rev: BL 4/15/92; SLJ 4/92)

**254**  McMillan, Bruce. *Mouse View: What the Class Pet Saw* (PS–3). Illus. 1993, Holiday LB $16.95 (0-8234-1008-0). 32pp. Familiar classroom sights are shown from a mouse's point of view. (Rev: BL 3/15/93*; SLJ 4/93)

**255**  Magnus, Erica. *Around Me* (PS–2). Illus. n.d., Smithmark $3.98 (0-8317-3213-X). This concept book shows a variety of scenes and situations that change depending on who is viewing them. (Rev: SLJ 8/92)

**256**  Rey, H. A. *See the Circus* (K–3). Illus. 1956, Houghton paper $3.50 (0-395-07068-6). Under the flap on each page is a secret.

**257**  Shaw, Charles. *It Looked Like Spilt Milk* (K–2). Illus. by author. 1947, HarperCollins LB $13.89 (0-06-025565-X); paper $4.95 (0-06-443159-2). 30pp. White material appears on each page, but its identity is not revealed until the end. Originally published in 1947.

**258**  West, Colin. *One Day in the Jungle* (PS–K). Illus. 1995, Candlewick $9.95 (1-56402-646-9). 24pp. The sounds made by various jungle animals get louder and louder as a sneezing fit progresses from a tiny butterfly to a huge elephant. (Rev: BL 1/1–15/96; SLJ 2/96)

**259**  Wood, A. J. *Hidden Pictures* (2–4). Illus. 1996, Millbrook LB $22.90 (1-56294-369-3). 40pp. A number of animals are hidden in a series of pictures that depict various habitats. (Rev: BL 4/15/96; SLJ 5/96) [591]

## SIZE AND SHAPE

**260**  Baker, Alan. *Brown Rabbit's Shape Book* (PS–K). Illus. 1994, Kingfisher $7.95 (1-85697-950-4). 24pp. A rabbit explores different shapes when he finds an assortment of balloons that he blows up. (Rev: BL 7/94)

**261**  Cohen, Caron L. *Where's the Fly?* (PS–3). Illus. by Nancy Barnet. 1996, Greenwillow $15.00 (0-688-14044-0). 32pp. Color pictures are used to explore the concepts of relative size and distance using, for example, closeups. (Rev: BCCB 4/96; BL 3/1/96; HB 7–8/96; SLJ 5/96)

**262**  Falwell, Cathryn. *Shape Space* (PS–2). Illus. 1992, Houghton $14.95 (0-395-61305-1). 32pp. A cut-paper girl plays and builds with colorful cut-paper shapes. (Rev: BL 10/15/92; HB 1–2/93; SLJ 10/92)

**263**  Fosberg, John. *Cookie Shapes* (PS). Illus. by author. 1997, Simon & Schuster $4.99 (0-689-81288-4). A board book that uses cookies to introduce 10 different shapes. Also use *Ice Cream Colors* (1997). (Rev: SLJ 12/97)

**264**  Greene, Rhonda Gowler. *When a Line Bends . . . A Shape Begins* (PS–2). Illus. by James Kaczman. 1997, Houghton $16.00 (0-395-78606-1). In this concept book, 10 different shapes — including a circle, square, triangle, diamond, and heart — are introduced. (Rev: SLJ 10/97)

**265**  Henkes, Kevin. *The Biggest Boy* (PS). Illus. by Nancy Tafuri. 1995, Greenwillow LB $14.93 (0-688-12830-0). 32pp. The concept of size is explored in this story of a youngster who dreams of being the biggest boy in the world. (Rev: BL 3/1/95; HB 5–6/95; SLJ 4/95)

**266** Hoban, Tana. *Circles, Triangles, and Squares* (PS–2). Illus. by author. 1974, Macmillan LB $15.00 (0-02-744830-4). 32pp. A series of 5 photographs show the 3 most familiar geometric forms.

**267** Hoban, Tana. *Is It Larger? Is It Smaller?* (PS–1). Illus. by author. 1997, Morrow paper $4.95 (0-688-15287-2). 32pp. Effective photographs and design illustrate the concepts of large and small, without words. (Rev: BCCB 4/85; BL 3/15/85; SLJ 4/85)

**268** Hoban, Tana. *Look! Look! Look!* (PS–1). Illus. 1988, Greenwillow LB $16.93 (0-688-07240-2). 24pp. Photos entice the reader into this wordless picture book. (Rev: BCCB 10/88; BL 9/1/88; HB 11–12/89)

**269** Hoban, Tana. *Over, Under and Through and Other Spacial Concepts* (K–2). Illus. by author. 1973, Macmillan LB $16.00 (0-02-744820-7). 32pp. Spacial concepts are conveyed through brief text and photographs.

**270** Hoban, Tana. *Shapes, Shapes, Shapes* (PS–1). Illus. by author. 1986, Greenwillow LB $15.93 (0-688-05833-7). 32pp. Eleven shapes are sought in the color photos. (Rev: BCCB 4/86; BL 3/1/86; HB 5–6/86)

**271** Hoban, Tana. *So Many Circles, So Many Squares* (PS–1). Illus. 1998, Greenwillow $15.00 (0-688-15165-5). 32pp. In this wordless concept book, the author explores different things that are round or square. (Rev: BL 3/1/98; SLJ 3/98) [516]

**272** Hoban, Tana. *Spirals, Curves, Fanshapes, and Lines* (PS–2). Illus. 1992, Greenwillow LB $13.93 (0-688-11229-3). 32pp. Form and grace are explored in everyday objects. (Rev: BL 11/15/92; HB 11–12/92; SLJ 12/92) [516.15]

**273** Hutchins, Pat. *Shrinking Mouse* (PS–K). Illus. 1997, Greenwillow LB $14.93 (0-688-13962-0). 32pp. A clever exploration of space and perspective using woodland animals and birds. (Rev: BL 2/15/97; SLJ 4/97*)

**274** Jenkins, Steve. *Big and Little* (PS–2). Illus. 1996, Houghton $14.95 (0-395-72664-6). 32pp. The concept of size is explored in this book that contrasts various animals. (Rev: BL 10/1/96; SLJ 10/96*)

**275** Jonas, Ann. *Holes and Peeks* (PS–K). Illus. by author. 1984, Greenwillow LB $15.93 (0-688-02538-2). 24pp. A young black child explains the difference between scary holes and pleasant objects to peek through.

**276** Kalan, Robert. *Blue Sea* (K–3). Illus. by Donald Crews. 1979, Greenwillow LB $15.93 (0-688-

84184-8); Morrow paper $4.95 (0-688-11509-8). 24pp. Big fish and little fish in the sea convey the idea of size.

**277** MacDonald, Suse. *Sea Shapes* (PS–K). Illus. 1994, Harcourt $13.95 (0-15-200027-5); paper $6.00 (0-15-201700-3). 32pp. Sea creatures and attractive collages are used to introduce a number of shapes. (Rev: BL 9/1/94; HB 11–12/94; SLJ 11/94)

**278** Murphy, Stuart J. *The Best Bug Parade* (PS–1). Illus. by Holly Keller. Series: MathStart. 1996, HarperCollins LB $14.89 (0-06-025872-1); paper $4.95 (0-06-446700-7). 33pp. A parade of bugs is used to introduce the concept of size. (Rev: BCCB 5/96; SLJ 6/96)

**279** Murphy, Stuart J. *Circus Shapes* (PS). Illus. by Edward Miller. Series: Mathstart. 1998, Harper-Collins LB $15.89 (0-06-027437-9). 40pp. Objects associated with the circus are pictured in this concept book that introduces various shapes. (Rev: BL 3/1/98; SLJ 4/98)

**280** *My First Look at Shapes* (PS). Illus. Series: My First Look at. 1990, Random $8.00 (0-679-80534-6). Basic shapes are illustrated. Also use: *My First Look at Sizes* (1990). (Rev: SLJ 12/90) [516.2]

**281** Myller, Rolf. *How Big Is a Foot?* (K–2). Illus. by author. 1991, Dell paper $3.50 (0-440-40495-9). The problem of relative sizes, humorously and imaginatively described.

**282** Rotner, Shelley, and Richard Olivo. *Close, Closer, Closest* (PS–1). Illus. 1997, Simon & Schuster $13.00 (0-689-80762-7). 40pp. This concept book explores perspective and scale in a series of pictures that show objects at different distances. (Rev: BCCB 4/97; BL 4/1/97; HB 5–6/97; SLJ 7/97) [152.14]

**283** *Shapes Galore* (PS). Illus. Series: Snapshot. 1995, DK Publg. $3.95 (0-7894-0231-9). 12pp. Preschoolers learn about shapes like triangles and circles through everyday objects, such as sailboats and a sandwich. (Rev: BL 1/1–15/96; SLJ 7/96) [561.15]

**284** Wegman, William. *Triangle, Square, Circle* (PS–K). Illus. 1995, Hyperion $6.95 (0-7868-0104-2). 16pp. Shapes are introduced in a series of photographs involving dogs. (Rev: BCCB 7–8/95; BL 5/15/95; SLJ 8/95)

**285** Wells, Robert E. *Is a Blue Whale the Biggest Thing There Is?* (PS–3). Illus. 1993, Albert Whitman LB $13.95 (0-8075-3655-5); paper $6.95 (0-8075-3656-3). 32pp. The concept of size is explored, first by comparing an elephant to the huge blue whale and ending with our galaxy being compared to the universe. (Rev: BCCB 11/93; BL 12/15/93; SLJ 1/94)

**286** Wells, Robert E. *What's Smaller Than a Pygmy Shrew?* (1–4). Illus. 1995, Albert Whitman $13.95 (0-8075-8837-7); paper $6.95 (0-8075-8838-5). 32pp.

The concept of smallness is explored using examples from nature. (Rev: BL 8/95; SLJ 5/95)

**287** Wexler, Jerome. *Everyday Mysteries* (K–4). Illus. 1995, Dutton paper $15.99 (0-525-45363-6). 40pp. Close-ups of parts of familiar objects become exercises in identification puzzles. (Rev: BCCB 9/95; BL 10/15/95; HB 11–12/95; SLJ 9/95) [683]

## Counting and Number Books

**288** Anno, Mitsumasa. *Anno's Counting Book: An Adventure in Imagination* (PS–K). Illus. by author. 1977, HarperCollins LB $15.89 (0-690-01288-8); paper $6.95 (0-06-443123-1). 32pp. An appealing book on numbers in which the same landscapes are used throughout; houses, birds, trees, and people are added as the seasons progress.

**289** Anno, Mitsumasa. *Anno's Magic Seeds* (K–3). Illus. 1995, Putnam $15.99 (0-399-22538-2). 42pp. An arithmetic allegory about the beginnings of agriculture that involves magic seeds given to Jack by a wizard. (Rev: BCCB 4/95; BL 4/1/95*; HB 9–10/95; SLJ 9/95)

**290** Appelt, Kathi. *Bat Jamboree* (PS–2). Illus. by Melissa Sweet. 1996, Morrow LB $15.93 (0-688-13883-7). A delightful counting book that focuses on the annual Bat Jamboree staged by some enterprising bats. (Rev: SLJ 9/96)

**291** Ashton, Elizabeth A. *An Old-Fashioned 1 2 3 Book* (PS–K). Illus. by Jessie Willcox Smith. 1991, Viking paper $14.95 (0-670-83499-8). A quaintly illustrated book of verses, celebrating numbers. (Rev: SLJ 6/91)

**292** Aylesworth, Jim. *One Crow: A Counting Rhyme* (PS–K). Illus. by Ruth Young. 1990, HarperCollins paper $5.95 (0-06-443242-4). 32pp. Farm life introduces numbers. (Rev: BL 6/15/88; SLJ 12/88)

**293** Baker, Keith. *Big Fat Hen* (PS–1). Illus. 1994, Harcourt $13.95 (0-15-292869-3). 32pp. A counting book that uses the rhyme "One, two, buckle my shoe" as a basis. (Rev: BL 4/1/94; SLJ 4/94)

**294** Bang, Molly. *Ten, Nine, Eight* (PS–1). Illus. by author. 1983, Greenwillow LB $15.93 (0-688-00907-7); Morrow paper $4.95 (0-688-10480-0). 24pp. A counting-down book (from 10 to 1) involving a black child going to bed.

**295** Bassede, Francine. *George's Store at the Shore* (PS). Illus. 1998, Orchard paper $14.95 (0-531-30083-8). 32pp. In this delightful counting book, George the duck and Mary the cat go to the beach. (Rev: BL 2/15/98; SLJ 4/98)

**296** Bender, Robert. *The A to Z Beastly Jamboree* (PS–2). Illus. by author. 1996, Lodestar paper $14.99 (0-525-67520-5). An animal ABC that can also serve as a counting book because the number of animals changes with each letter. (Rev: SLJ 7/96)

**297** Bennett, David. *One Cow Moo Moo!* (PS–2). Illus. by Andy Cooke. 1990, Holt $15.95 (0-8050-1416-0). In this cumulative story about farm animals and their sounds, counting skills are presented. (Rev: SLJ 12/90)

**298** Bertrand, Lynne. *Dragon Naps* (K–3). Illus. by Janet Street. 1996, Viking paper $14.99 (0-670-85403-4). 32pp. A counting book that also tells the story of 2 nappers who do everything but sleep. (Rev: BL 1/1–15/96; SLJ 4/96)

**299** Blackstone, Stella. *Grandma Went to Market: A Round-the-World Counting Rhyme* (PS–2). Illus. by Bernard Lodge. 1996, Houghton $13.95 (0-395-74045-2). 32pp. In this counting rhyme, Grandma goes on a global shopping spree. (Rev: BL 2/1/96; SLJ 4/96)

**300** Bloom, Valerie. *Fruits: A Caribbean Counting Poem* (PS–2). Illus. by David Axtell. 1997, Holt $15.95 (0-8050-5171-6). 32pp. Using unusual fruits found on the Caribbean islands — like pawpaws, guavas, and sweetsop — plus a humorous story, numbers are introduced. (Rev: BCCB 4/97; BL 3/15/97; SLJ 7/97)

**301** Bohdal, Susi. *1, 2, 3 What Do You See?* (PS–1). Illus. 1997, North-South LB $15.88 (1-55858-647-4). 32pp. In this charming counting book, a little girl brings presents to various numbers of animals. (Rev: BL 8/97)

**302** Bond, Michael. *Paddington's 1, 2, 3* (PS–2). Illus. by John Lobban. Series: Paddington. 1991, Viking paper $11.99 (0-670-84103-X). 32pp. The beloved bear introduces very young children to the world of counting. (Rev: BL 12/15/91; SLJ 2/92)

**303** Bown, Deni. *Let's Count* (PS). Illus. Series: Snapshot. 1995, DK Publg. $3.95 (0-7894-0232-7). 12pp. Using photos of favorite animals, food, and toys, children learn to count from 1 to 10. Also use *Shapes Galore* (1995). (Rev: BL 1/1–15/96; SLJ 7/96) [513.2]

**304** Brooks, Alan. *Frogs Jump: A Counting Book* (PS–1). Illus. by Steven Kellogg. 1996, Scholastic $15.95 (0-590-45528-1). 48pp. Madcap animals introduce basic numbers through unusual activities. (Rev: BL 10/15/96; SLJ 10/96)

**305** Brooks, Bruce. *NBA by the Numbers* (K–3). Illus. 1997, Scholastic $10.95 (0-590-97578-1). 32pp. This book uses basketball terms to introduce the numbers 1–10, 20, 30, 40, and 50. (Rev: BL 3/1/97)

**306** Brown, Paula. *Moon Jump: A Cowntdown* (PS–1). Illus. 1996, Puffin paper $4.99 (0-140-54454-2). 32pp. A group of cows enter a contest to see which one can jump over the moon; also can be used as a counting book. (Rev: BCCB 3/93; BL 1/1/93)

**307** Brusca, Maria C., and Tona Wilson. *Three Friends: A Counting Book/Tres Amigos: Un Cuento para Contar* (PS–2). Illus. by Maria C. Brusca. 1995, Holt $14.95 (0-8050-3707-1). 32pp. Learning to count from 1 to 10 in Spanish and English through watching the actions of a cowboy, a cowgirl, and a horse. (Rev: BL 11/15/95; SLJ 12/95)

**308** Burns, Marilyn. *How Many Feet? How Many Tails? A Book of Math Riddles* (1–2). Illus. by Lynn Adams. 1996, Scholastic paper $3.50 (0-590-67360-2). 32pp. During a walk with Grandpa, a child learns about numbers in this easy-to-read book. (Rev: BL 2/1/97)

**309** Burton, Katherine. *One Gray Mouse* (PS). Illus. by Kim Fernandes. 1997, Kids Can $9.95 (1-55074-225-6). 24pp. Different numbers of animals are presented in this pleasant picture book that teaches the concepts of counting and colors. (Rev: BL 11/15/97; SLJ 12/97) [513.2]

**310** Carle, Eric. *1, 2, 3 to the Zoo* (PS–K). Illus. by author. 1968, Putnam $15.95 (0-399-61172-X); paper $7.95 (0-399-21970-6). 34pp. A counting book illustrated with pictures of animals in a zoo train. Originally published in 1968.

**311** Carle, Eric. *Roosters Off to See the World* (PS–K). Illus. by author. 1991, Picture Book $16.00 (0-88708-042-1). 28pp. In this counting book originally published in 1972, a rooster gathers together a group of animals to explore the world. Addition and subtraction are also introduced.

**312** Carlstrom, Nancy White. *Let's Count It Out, Jesse Bear* (PS–1). Illus. by Bruce Degen. 1996, Simon & Schuster paper $15.00 (0-689-80478-4). 28pp. In rhyming couplets, the numbers 1 to 20 are introduced. (Rev: BCCB 9/96; BL 9/15/96; SLJ 9/96)

**313** Chandra, Deborah. *Miss Mabel's Table* (PS–2). Illus. by Max Grover. 1994, Harcourt $14.95 (0-15-276712-6). 32pp. A counting book about Miss Mabel, her restaurant, and the food she serves. (Rev: BCCB 4/94; BL 3/15/94; SLJ 6/94)

**314** Charles, Faustin. *A Caribbean Counting Book* (K–3). Illus. by Roberta Arenson. 1996, Houghton $13.95 (0-395-77944-8). 32pp. Using Caribbean settings, this colorful counting book uses 12 rhymes from 9 islands. (Rev: BCCB 5/96; BL 4/15/96; SLJ 6/96)

**315** Chorao, Kay. *Number One Number Fun* (PS–1). Illus. 1995, Holiday LB $15.95 (0-8234-1142-7). 32pp. Simple arithmetic is highlighted through a series of clever rhymes involving addition and subtraction. (Rev: BCCB 2/95; BL 2/15/95; SLJ 3/95)

**316** Christelow, Eileen, reteller. *Five Little Monkeys Jumping on the Bed* (PS–K). Illus. by Eileen Christelow. 1989, Ticknor $15.00 (0-89919-769-8); paper $5.95 (0-395-55701-1). An exuberant rendition of the favorite nursery rhyme. (Rev: BL 6/1/89)

**317** Christelow, Eileen. *Five Little Monkeys Sitting in a Tree* (PS–K). Illus. 1991, Houghton $15.00 (0-395-54434-3). 32pp. The numbers 1 through 5 are taught through the antics of 5 little monkeys. A sequel is: *Don't Wake Up Mama!* (1992). (Rev: BL 5/15/91; SLJ 8/91)

**318** Chwast, Seymour. *The Twelve Circus Rings* (K–3). Illus. 1993, Harcourt $14.95 (0-15-200627-3). 32pp. A math concept book with a circus theme and bright poster art. (Rev: BL 3/15/93; SLJ 4/93) [945]

**319** Clark, Emma C. *Little Miss Muffet's Count-Along Surprise* (K–2). Illus. 1997, Doubleday $15.95 (0-385-32517-7). 32pp. Miss Muffet is joined by a spider and numbers of other animals, ending with 19 crocodiles, in this humorous counting book. (Rev: BL 12/15/97; SLJ 10/97)

**320** Cleveland, David. *The April Rabbits* (PS–1). Illus. by Nurit Karlin. 1986, Scholastic paper $2.95 (0-590-42369-X). 32pp. The days of the month and a group of rabbits are used in this counting book. Reissue of a 1978 edition.

**321** Coats, Laura J. *Ten Little Animals* (PS–1). Illus. 1990, Macmillan LB $14.00 (0-02-719054-4). 32pp. A young boy's bedtime is disturbed by his 10 rollicking stuffed animals. (Rev: BL 4/15/90; HB 3–4/90; SLJ 9/90)

**322** Crews, Donald. *Ten Black Dots* (PS–K). Illus. by author. 1986, Greenwillow LB $15.93 (0-688-06068-4). 32pp. Dots form an integral part of this counting book, originally published in 1968, such as "5 dots make buttons on a coat." (Rev: BL 3/1/86; SLJ 5/86)

**323** Crowther, Robert. *My Pop-up Surprise 123* (PS–K). Illus. by author. 1997, Orchard $16.95 (0-531-30039-0). A simple counting book using easily manipulated flaps and pull tabs. (Rev: SLJ 8/97)

**324** De Regniers, Beatrice S. *So Many Cats!* (PS–1). Illus. by Ellen Weiss. 1985, Houghton paper $6.95 (0-89919-700-0). 32pp. One by one, new cats arrive at the narrator's house, until there are 12. (Rev: BL 1/1/86; HB 11–12/85; SLJ 1/86)

**325** Duke, Kate. *One Guinea Pig Is Not Enough* (PS–1). Illus. 1998, Dutton $15.99 (0-525-45918-9). 48pp. A group of guinea pigs enjoy different zany activities in this counting book, which also introduces addition. (Rev: BL 2/1/98; SLJ 3/98)

**326** Dunbar, Joyce. *Ten Little Mice* (PS–1). Illus. by Maria Majewska. 1990, Harcourt $13.95 (0-15-

200601-X). 24pp. Ten frolicking mice depart, one by one, to their cozy nest. (Rev: BL 4/15/90)

**327** Edens, Cooper. *How Many Bears?* (1–3). Illus. by Marjett Schille. 1994, Atheneum $14.95 (0-689-31923-1). A clever math problem is solved by studying the answer to the question "How many bears does it take to run the bakery in Little Animal Town?" (Rev: SLJ 12/94)

**328** Ehlert, Lois. *Fish Eyes: A Book You Can Count On* (PS–K). Illus. 1990, Harcourt $14.95 (0-15-228050-2). 32pp. Compelling color and design introduce this counting book. (Rev: BL 3/1/90*; SLJ 5/90)

**329** Enderle, Judith R., and Stephanie G. Tessler. *Six Snowy Sheep* (PS–2). Illus. by John O'Brien. 1994, Boyds Mills $14.95 (1-56397-138-0). A humorous counting book involving sheep and a story that counts down from 6 to 1. (Rev: SLJ 12/94)

**330** Enderle, Judith R., and Stephanie G. Tessler. *Where Are You, Little Zack?* (PS–1). Illus. by Brian Floca. 1997, Houghton $14.95 (0-395-73092-9). A counting book that involves 4 duck brothers and their adventures in New York City. (Rev: SLJ 4/97)

**331** Ernst, Lisa Campbell. *Up to Ten and Down Again* (PS–K). Illus. by author. 1995, Morrow paper $4.95 (0-688-14391-1). 32pp. Beginning with "1 duck is swimming," this simple counting book teaches numbers and tells a story. (Rev: BCCB 3/86; BL 3/1/86; SLJ 8/86)

**332** Falwell, Cathryn. *Feast for 10* (PS–K). Illus. 1993, Houghton $14.95 (0-395-62037-6). 32pp. Using the common experience of shopping and preparing dinner, this book, which features an African-American family, teaches youngsters the numbers from 1 to 10. (Rev: BCCB 6/93; BL 6/1–15/93; SLJ 6/93)

**333** Feelings, Muriel. *Moja Means One: Swahili Counting Book* (K–3). Illus. by Tom Feelings. 1971, Peter Smith $18.50 (0-844-66900-8); Dial paper $4.95 (0-8037-5711-5). 32pp. The sights and sounds of East Africa come alive in this charming counting book.

**334** Fleming, Denise. *Count!* (PS–K). Illus. by author. 1992, Holt $14.95 (0-8050-1595-7). Brightly colored animals and birds are used to introduce basic numbers. (Rev: SLJ 3/92)

**335** French, Vivian. *One Ballerina Two* (3–5). Illus. by Jan Ormerod. 1991, Lothrop $13.95 (0-688-10333-2). 32pp. The focus is on ballet in this simple counting book. (Rev: BCCB 12/91; BL 12/1/91; SLJ 12/91)

**336** Friedman, Aileen. *The King's Commissioners* (K–2). Illus. by Susan Guevara. 1995, Scholastic $15.95 (0-590-48989-5). 40pp. In this sophisticated counting book, a king decides to take an inventory of his employees. (Rev: BCCB 2/95; BL 2/15/95; SLJ 3/95)

**337** Galdone, Paul. *Over in the Meadow: An Old Nursery Counting Rhyme* (PS–K). Illus. by author. 1989, Simon & Schuster paper $5.95 (0-671-67837-X). The old nursery rhyme in a full-color picture book featuring 10 animal families. (Rev: BL 12/15/86; SLJ 2/87)

**338** Garne, S. T. *One White Sail: A Caribbean Counting Book* (PS–1). Illus. by Lisa Etre. 1992, Simon & Schuster $14.00 (0-671-75579-X). 32pp. A counting book that uses the colors and objects of the Caribbean to illustrate numbers. (Rev: BL 5/15/92; HB 9–10/92; SLJ 5/92)

**339** Geisert, Arthur. *Pigs from 1 to 10* (PS–2). Illus. by author. 1991, Houghton $16.00 (0-395-58519-8). 32pp. In a series of hidden-picture illustrations, pigs search for a lost place and uncover the numbers 0 to 10. (Rev: BL 11/1/92; HB 9–10/92*)

**340** Gerstein, Mordicai. *Roll Over!* (PS–K). Illus. 1988, Crown $12.00 (0-517-55209-4). 32pp. A counting rhyme that starts with 10 in a bed until someone says "Roll over."

**341** Giganti, Paul. *Each Orange Had Eight Slices* (PS–3). Illus. by Donald Crews. 1992, Greenwillow LB $15.93 (0-688-10429-0). This well-designed book challenges young readers to think analytically about what it portrays. (Rev: BCCB 4/92; BL 3/15/92; SLJ 3/92) [513.5]

**342** Giganti, Paul. *How Many Snails?* (PS–K). Illus. by Donald Crews. 1988, Greenwillow LB $16.00 (0-688-06370-5). 24pp. A counting book that focuses on visual discrimination as well as numbers. (Rev: BL 8/88; SLJ 3/89)

**343** Green, Kate. *A Number of Animals* (PS–K). Illus. by Christopher Wormell. 1995, Harcourt $19.95 (0-15-200926-4). 32pp. A counting book involving a little chick who has lost his mother and asks for help from various numbers of animals. (Rev: SLJ 4/94)

**344** Grossman, Bill. *My Little Sister Ate One Hare* (K–3). Illus. by Kevin Hawkes. 1996, Crown LB $18.99 (0-517-59601-6). A counting book with outrageous illustrations about swallowing a variety of slimy creatures. (Rev: BCCB 1/97; SLJ 12/96*)

**345** Grossman, Virginia. *Ten Little Rabbits* (PS–1). Illus. by Sylvia Long. 1991, Chronicle $13.95 (0-87701-552-X). 32pp. This counting book of rabbits dressed as Indians introduces the cultures of various American tribes. (Rev: BL 4/1/91; SLJ 6/91)

**346** Grover, Max. *Amazing and Incredible Counting Stories: A Number of Tall Tales* (K–3). Illus. 1995, Harcourt $14.00 (0-15-200090-9). 32pp. These 27 delightful stories feature numbers and the counting concept. (Rev: BL 2/15/96; SLJ 12/95)

**347** Gunson, Christopher. *Over on the Farm* (PS). Illus. 1997, Scholastic $15.95 (0-590-13445-0). 32pp. This counting book uses a farm setting and the folk rhyme "Over in the Meadow" to introduce numbers. (Rev: BL 2/1/97; SLJ 3/97)

**348** Gustafson, Scott. *Scott Gustafson's Animal Orchestra: A Counting Book* (K–3). Illus. 1995, Greenwich Workshop paper $14.95 (0-86713-030-X). 32pp. An assembly of animals in tuxedo splendor. (Rev: BL 1/15/89; SLJ 2/89)

**349** Guy, Ginger F. *¡Fiesta!* (PS–2). Illus. by René K. Moreno. 1996, Greenwillow $15.00 (0-688-14331-8). Numbers are introduced in both English and Spanish in this book about collecting articles to celebrate a Mexican fiesta. (Rev: SLJ 9/96)

**350** Halsey, Megan. *3 Pandas Planting* (PS–2). Illus. 1994, Macmillan paper $14.95 (0-02-742035-3). 32pp. A reverse counting book that shows all sorts of endangered species helping to save the earth — for example, condors collecting litter. (Rev: BL 5/15/94; SLJ 6/94)

**351** Hamm, Diane J. *How Many Feet in the Bed?* (PS–2). Illus. by Kate S. Palmer. 1991, Simon & Schuster paper $14.00 (0-671-72638-2). 32pp. As more people hop into the family bed, there are more feet to count. (Rev: BL 7/91; SLJ 10/91)

**352** Harshman, Marc. *Only One* (PS–3). Illus. by Barbara Garrison. 1993, Dutton paper $14.99 (0-525-65116-0). 32pp. This counting book shows that a collective noun consists of several parts, for example, 9 players make a baseball team. (Rev: BL 5/15/93)

**353** Hartmann, Wendy. *One Sun Rises: An African Wildlife Counting Book* (PS–3). Illus. by Nicolaas Maritz. 1994, Dutton paper $13.99 (0-525-45225-7). 32pp. Using paintings of African daytime and nocturnal animals, this counting book goes from 1 to 10 and back. (Rev: BL 12/1/94; SLJ 11/94) [513.2]

**354** Heinst, Marie. *My First Number Book* (PS–3). Illus. 1992, DK Publg. $14.95 (1-879431-73-4). 48pp. A bright, absorbing introduction to mathematics. (Rev: BL 6/15/92; SLJ 6/92) [513.2]

**355** Helman, Andrea. *1, 2, 3 Moose: A Pacific Northwest Counting Book* (PS–2). Illus. by Art Wolfe. 1996, Sasquatch $15.95 (1-57061-078-9). 32pp. A 1-to-20 counting book that employs the flora and fauna of the Pacific Northwest. (Rev: BL 11/1/96; SLJ 1/97) [428.1]

**356** Hill, Eric. *Spot Counts from 1 to 10* (PS–1). Illus. by author. Series: Little Spot Board Books. 1989, Putnam $3.95 (0-399-21672-3). In this simple counting board book, Spot the dog counts many different barnyard animals. (Rev: SLJ 8/89)

**357** Hoban, Tana. *Count and See* (PS–K). Illus. 1972, Macmillan LB $15.00 (0-02-744800-2). 40pp.

Beginning with numbers 1 to 15, then going to 100; clear photographs of familiar objects are easily recognized and fun to count.

**358** Hoban, Tana. *1, 2, 3* (PS). Illus. by author. 1985, Greenwillow paper $4.95 (0-688-02579-X). 12pp. Starting with 1 birthday cake, photos present objects in a baby's world. (Rev: BCCB 3/85; BL 3/15/85; SLJ 9/85)

**359** Holder, Heidi. *Crows: An Old Rhyme* (K–2). Illus. 1987, Farrar $14.95 (0-374-31660-0). 32pp. The promises of 12 crows are woven into the wordless tale of a mink and a weasel in this lovely reinterpretation of an old English counting rhyme. (Rev: BL 1/15/88)

**360** Hulme, Joy N. *Sea Squares* (K–3). Illus. by Carol Schwartz. 1993, Hyperion paper $5.95 (1-56282-520-8). 32pp. Children can visualize multiplication in this picture book with an underwater theme. (Rev: BL 12/1/91; SLJ 1/92) [513.5]

**361** Hutchins, Pat. *One Hunter* (PS–2). Illus. by author. 1982, Greenwillow LB $16.93 (0-688-00615-9); Morrow paper $4.95 (0-688-06522-8). 24pp. A counting book with a hunter and hidden African animals.

**362** Inkpen, Mick. *Kipper's Book of Numbers* (PS–K). Illus. by author. 1995, Harcourt paper $6.00 (0-15-200646-X). Using other animal friends, Kipper, a brown-and-white dog, introduces the basic numbers. (Rev: SLJ 8/95)

**363** Inkpen, Mick. *Kipper's Toybox* (PS–K). Illus. 1992, Harcourt $13.95 (0-15-200501-3). 32pp. A young dog counts his toys and finds that his toy box has 2 visitors — a pair of mice. (Rev: BL 10/15/92; SLJ 1/93)

**364** Jahn-Clough, Lisa. *1 2 3 Yippie* (PS). Illus. 1998, Houghton $5.95 (0-395-87003-8). 32pp. A small, square counting book that deals with 2 children who have a party for different numbers of animals. (Rev: BL 3/15/98)

**365** Jonas, Ann. *Splash!* (PS–1). Illus. 1995, Greenwillow LB $14.93 (0-688-11052-5). 24pp. Principles of addition and subtraction are shown by counting the animal life in and around a backyard pond. (Rev: BCCB 6/95; BL 6/1–15/95; HB 9–10/95; SLJ 6/95)

**366** Kharms, Daniil. *First, Second* (PS–3). Trans. by Richard Pevear. Illus. by Marc Rosenthal. 1996, Farrar $16.00 (0-374-32339-9). 32pp. The concepts of "first" through "tenth" are introduced in this rollicking cumulative story. (Rev: BCCB 2/96; BL 4/15/96; HB 9–10/96; SLJ 4/96)

**367** Kitamura, Satoshi. *When Sheep Cannot Sleep: The Counting Book* (PS–1). Illus. by author. 1986, Farrar $14.00 (0-374-38311-1); paper $4.95 (0-374-48359-0). 32pp. Woolly the sheep can't sleep so he takes a walk — chasing 1 butterfly, watching 2 ladybugs, and so on. (Rev: BL 10/1/86; HB 11–12/86; SLJ 12/86)

**368**   Kitchen, Bert. *Animal Numbers* (PS–1). Illus. by author. 1987, Puffin paper $4.95 (0-8037-0910-2). 24pp. Readers count the babies in each brood in this simple counting book. (Rev: BCCB 10/87; BL 10/1/87; SLJ 10/87)

**369**   Kneen, Maggie. *When You're Not Looking: A Storytime Counting Book* (PS–2). Illus. by author. 1996, Simon & Schuster paper $15.00 (0-689-80026-6). Ten double-page spreads invite children to make up their own stories and find a number of objects hidden in the pictures in this unusual counting book. (Rev: SLJ 12/96)

**370**   Kuskin, Karla. *James and the Rain* (PS–1). Illus. by Reg Cartwright. 1995, Simon & Schuster paper $15.00 (0-671-88808-0). 32pp. During his outing on a rainy day, James meets a variety of animals in this amusing counting book. (Rev: BL 6/1–15/95; SLJ 7/95)

**371**   Kusugak, Michael A. *My Arctic 1, 2, 3* (K–3). Illus. by Vladyana Krykorka. 1996, Annick $16.95 (1-55037-505-9); paper $6.95 (1-55037-504-0). Using Arctic animals as a focus, this counting book presents the numbers 1 through 10, 20, 100, and a million in both English and the Inuit language. (Rev: SLJ 5/97)

**372**   Lavis, Steve. *Cock-a-Doodle-Doo: A Farmyard Counting Book* (PS–K). Illus. 1997, Dutton paper $13.99 (0-525-67542-6). 32pp. Farmyard animals and their sounds are used to introduce basic numbers. (Rev: BL 11/15/96; SLJ 1/97)

**373**   Leedy, Loreen. *Fraction Action* (K–2). Illus. 1994, Holiday LB $16.95 (0-8234-1109-5). 32pp. How to divide various objects and the meaning of fractions are explored in this simple, colorful arithmetic book. (Rev: BCCB 3/94; BL 3/15/94) [513.2]

**374**   Le Sieg, Theo. *Wacky Wednesday* (PS–1). Illus. by George Booth. 1974, Random LB $11.99 (0-394-92912-8). 48pp. In this counting book, every page has a number of things out of place.

**375**   Leuck, Laura. *My Baby Brother Has Ten Tiny Toes* (PS–K). Illus. by Clara Vulliamy. 1997, Albert Whitman LB $14.95 (0-8075-5310-7). 24pp. A charming counting book that uses characteristics of a baby as its focus. (Rev: BL 4/15/97; SLJ 3/97)

**376**   Loomis, Christine. *One Cow Coughs: A Counting Book for the Sick and Miserable* (PS–K). Illus. by Pat Dypold. 1994, Ticknor $14.95 (0-395-67899-4). 32pp. A counting book that uses sick animals and the treatments they receive as its subjects. (Rev: BL 10/15/94; SLJ 10/94)

**377**   Lyon, George E. *Counting on the Woods* (PS–4). Illus. by Ann W. Olson. 1998, DK Publg. $15.95 (0-7894-2480-0). This gem of a counting book can also be used as a science book because of its brilliant color photos of animals. (Rev: BL 3/1/98*; SLJ 4/98) [513.2]

**378**   McCourt, Lisa. *The Rain Forest Counts!* (PS–1). Illus. by Cheryl Nathan. 1997, Troll $15.95 (0-8167-4388-6). 32pp. This rhyming counting book features the animals and plants of the rain forest. (Rev: BL 12/15/97; SLJ 11/97)

**379**   MacDonald, Elizabeth. *Mike's Kite* (3–5). Illus. by Robert Kendall. 1993, Harcourt paper $9.75 (0-15-300320-0). 32pp. In this counting book, Mike and a number of bystanders get carried away on the tail of a kite. (Rev: BL 7/90; SLJ 9/90)

**380**   MacDonald, Suse. *Puzzlers* (2–5). Illus. by Bill Oakes. 1989, Dial $13.89 (0-8037-0690-1). 32pp. In double-page spreads, numbers that change into animal puzzles are cleverly presented. For sophisticated readers. (Rev: BCCB 10/89; BL 9/15/89*; HB 1–2/90; SLJ 10/89)

**381**   Mack, Stan. *Ten Bears in My Bed: A Goodnight Countdown* (PS–K). Illus. by author. 1974, Pantheon LB $13.99 (0-394-92902-0). 32pp. In this children's favorite, based on a counting song, when the "little one" says "Roll over, Roll over," one by one the bears leave the bed.

**382**   McMillan, Bruce. *Counting Wildflowers* (PS–1). Illus. 1986, Lothrop LB $15.93 (0-688-02860-8). 32pp. A counting book that features American wildflowers in color photos. (Rev: BCCB 4/86; BL 6/15/86; SLJ 8/86)

**383**   McMillan, Bruce. *Jelly Beans for Sale* (PS–2). Illus. 1996, Scholastic $15.95 (0-590-86584-6). 32pp. Counting and basic math concepts are illustrated in this book about selling candies. (Rev: BCCB 10/96; BL 9/1/96; SLJ 10/96) [332.4]

**384**   McMillan, Bruce. *One, Two, One Pair!* (PS). Illus. 1996, Scholastic paper $4.99 (0-590-46082-X). 32pp. The concept of pairs is explored with sharp color images. (Rev: BCCB 2/91; BL 1/15/91; SLJ 2/91) [515.5]

**385**   Marzollo, Jean. *Ten Cats Have Hats: A Counting Book* (PS–K). Illus. by David McPhail. 1994, Scholastic $6.95 (0-590-20656-7). A counting book that uses intriguing pictures containing unusual details to present numbers 1 to 10. (Rev: SLJ 11/94)

**386**   Masurel, Claire. *Ten Dogs in the Window* (PS–K). Illus. by Pamela Paparone. 1997, North-South LB $15.88 (1-55858-755-1). 32pp. This amusing counting book starts with 10 and goes to 1 by using the sale of dogs in a pet store as a framework. (Rev: BL 11/15/97; SLJ 12/97)

**387**   Miller, Jane. *Farm Counting Book* (PS–1). Illus. by author. 1992, Simon & Schuster LB $5.95 (0-671-66552-9). 24pp. A counting book using photographs of farm animals.

**388** Min, Laura. *Mrs. Sato's Hens* (1–2). Illus. by Benrei Huang. 1994, Scott Foresman/GoodYear $2.95 (0-673-36193-4). 8pp. In an easy-to-read counting book, every morning Mrs. Sato counts the eggs that her hens are laying. (Rev: BL 1/1/95)

**389** Moore, Elaine. *Roly-Poly Puppies: A Counting Book* (PS–K). Illus. by Jacqueline Rogers. 1996, Scholastic $6.95 (0-590-46665-8). 32pp. The numbers 1 to 10 are introduced through the antics of 10 roly-poly puppies. (Rev: BL 9/15/96; SLJ 12/96)

**390** Mora, Pat. *Uno, Dos, Tres: One, Two, Three* (PS–2). Illus. by Barbara Lavallee. 1996, Clarion $14.95 (0-395-67294-5). 43pp. The numbers 1 to 10 are introduced in both English and Spanish. (Rev: BL 6/1–15/96; HB 5–6/96; SLJ 4/96)

**391** Morozumi, Atsuko. *One Gorilla: A Counting Book* (PS–K). Illus. 1990, Farrar $15.00 (0-374-35644-0). 26pp. This counting book contains different animals, always accompanied by one gorilla. (Rev: BL 11/1/90; SLJ 1/91)

**392** Mullins, Patricia. *One Horse Waiting for Me* (PS–1). Illus. 1998, Simon & Schuster $16.00 (0-689-81381-3). 32pp. All kinds of horses, even those from fantasies, appear in this handsome counting book. (Rev: BL 3/1/98*)

**393** Murphy, Stuart J. *Divide and Ride* (PS–3). Illus. by George Ulrich. Series: MathStart. 1997, HarperCollins LB $14.89 (0-06-026777-1). 40pp. Concepts of division are illustrated by problems posed when 11 friends visit various carnival attractions. (Rev: BL 2/1/97; SLJ 3/97) [513.2]

**394** Murphy, Stuart J. *Every Buddy Counts* (PS–3). Illus. by Fiona Dunbar. Series: MathStart. 1997, HarperCollins LB $14.89 (0-06-026773-9). 40pp. A simple counting book in which a girl counts up the number of friends she has. (Rev: BL 2/1/97; SLJ 3/97)

**395** Murphy, Stuart J. *A Fair Bear Share* (1–2). Illus. by John Speirs. Series: MathStart. 1998, HarperCollins LB $14.89 (0-06-027439-5). Bear cubs count out the food they have gathered into groups of 10 in this simple math book. (Rev: BL 3/1/98)

**396** *My First Look at Counting* (PS). Illus. Series: My First Look at. 1991, Random $7.00 (0-679-81163-X). 20pp. With bright, attractive photos, this book introduces the concepts of numbers and counting. (Rev: BL 6/1/91) [513.5]

**397** *My First Look at Numbers* (PS). Illus. Series: My First Look at. 1990, Random $9.00 (0-679-80533-8). This basic numbers book uses familiar objects to illustrate numbers from 1 to 10, 20, and 100. (Rev: SLJ 12/90) [513.2]

**398** Nagel, Karen. *The Lunch Line* (2–4). Illus. by Jerry Zimmerman. 1996, Scholastic $3.50 (0-590-60246-2). 32pp. Kim has lost her lunch and must buy it in this simple book on calculation. (Rev: BL 2/1/97)

**399** Naylor, Phyllis Reynolds. *Ducks Disappearing* (PS–K). Illus. by Tony Maddox. 1997, Simon & Schuster $13.00 (0-689-31902-9). 30pp. A young child solves the mystery of missing ducklings in this counting book. (Rev: BCCB 2/97; BL 2/1/97; SLJ 3/97)

**400** Nikola-Lisa, W. *One Hole in the Road* (PS–2). Illus. by Dan Yaccarino. 1996, Holt $15.95 (0-8050-4285-7). 24pp. Events caused by a pothole are used to introduce numbers in this clever counting book. (Rev: BL 10/1/96; SLJ 10/96)

**401** Nikola-Lisa, W. *1, 2, 3 Thanksgiving!* (PS–1). Illus. by Robin Kramer. 1991, Whitman LB $14.95 (0-8075-6109-6). 32pp. Each page adds something new to the traditional feast. (Rev: BL 9/1/91)

**402** Noll, Sally. *Surprise!* (PS–K). Illus. 1997, Greenwillow LB $14.93 (0-688-15171-X). 24pp. A subtle counting book in which a young girl is surprised by the gift of a kitten. (Rev: BL 10/1/97; SLJ 10/97)

**403** Ochs, Carol P. *When I'm Alone* (PS–3). Illus. by Vicki Jo Redenbaugh. 1993, Carolrhoda LB $14.95 (0-87614-752-X). 32pp. In this counting book, various animals upset a girl's attempts to keep her part of the house tidy. (Rev: BL 2/1/93; SLJ 6/93)

**404** O'Donnell, Elizabeth Lee. *I Can't Get My Turtle to Move* (K–2). Illus. by Maxie Chambliss. 1989, Morrow LB $11.88 (0-688-07324-7). In this counting book with rhyming text, a little girl tries to get her turtle to move. (Rev: SLJ 7/89)

**405** O'Donnell, Elizabeth Lee. *Winter Visitors* (PS–K). Illus. by Carol Schwartz. 1997, Morrow LB $15.93 (0-688-13064-X). 40pp. A counting book in which a number of unwanted animals visit a girl and her cat. (Rev: BL 9/15/97; SLJ 10/97)

**406** O'Keefe, Susan Heyboer. *One Hungry Monster: A Counting Book in Rhyme* (PS–1). Illus. by Lynn Munsinger. 1989, Little, Brown $12.95 (0-316-63385-2); paper $5.95 (0-316-63388-7). 32pp. A little boy tries to keep 10 hungry monsters out of trouble. (Rev: BL 6/1/89; HB 7–8/89)

**407** Olyff, Clotilde. *1 2 3 . . .* (3–5). Illus. by author. 1994, Ticknor $13.95 (0-395-70736-6). A pop-up book that introduces numbers from 1 to the 0 in 10, each in a different, attractive typeface. (Rev: SLJ 11/94)

**408** Onyefulu, Ifeoma. *Emeka's Gift: An African Counting Story* (K–2). Illus. 1995, Dutton paper $14.99 (0-525-65205-1). 32pp. Using photographs shot in Nigeria, this counting book from 2 to 10 involves objects encountered by a boy going on a visit to his grandmother's house. (Rev: BCCB 5/95; BL 6/1–15/95; SLJ 7/95) [960]

**409**  Orgel, Doris. *Two Crows Counting* (PS–1). Illus. by Judith Moffatt. 1995, Byron Preiss paper $4.50 (0-553-37573-3). 32pp. Two crows fly over a landscape and count from 1 to 10 and back again in this easily read book. (Rev: BL 10/1/95; SLJ 2/96)

**410**  Ormerod, Jan. *Joe Can Count* (PS–3). Illus. 1993, Mulberry paper $3.95 (0-688-04588-X). 24pp. An African-American toddler uses animals to count to 10. A reissue.

**411**  Parker, Vic. *Bearobics: A Hip-Hop Counting Story* (PS–3). Illus. by Emily Bolam. 1997, Viking paper $14.99 (0-670-87034-X). 32pp. A bear turns on his boom box in the forest and brings out a variety of dancing animals in this counting book. (Rev: BL 2/15/97; SLJ 2/97*)

**412**  Peek, Merle. *Roll Over! A Counting Song* (PS). Illus. by author. 1991, Houghton paper $5.95 (0-395-58105-2). 32pp. A counting book from 10 to 1 about animals in a bed.

**413**  Piers, Helen. *Is There Room on the Bus?* (PS–1). Illus. by Hannah Giffard. 1996, Simon & Schuster $14.00 (0-689-80610-8). 32pp. In this cumulative counting story, Sam picks up various numbers of animals as he travels around the world in his bus. (Rev: BL 5/1/96; SLJ 7/96)

**414**  Pinczes, Elinor J. *Arctic Fives Arrive* (K–2). Illus. by Holly Berry. 1996, Houghton $14.95 (0-395-73577-7). 32pp. Counting by 5s is introduced in this book about animals on an ice floe. (Rev: BL 9/15/96; SLJ 11/96)

**415**  Pinczes, Elinor J. *One Hundred Hungry Ants* (K–3). Illus. by Bonnie Mackain. 1993, Houghton $15.95 (0-395-63116-5). 32pp. Ants group and regroup on their march to a picnic site. (Rev: BL 3/1/93; SLJ 8/93)

**416**  Pinczes, Elinor J. *A Remainder of One* (PS–2). Illus. by Bonnie Mackain. 1995, Houghton $14.95 (0-395-69455-8). 32pp. An arithmetic book that uses a parade of beetles before the queen as a focal point. (Rev: BL 3/1/95*; SLJ 5/95)

**417**  Pomerantz, Charlotte. *One Duck, Another Duck* (PS). Illus. by Jose Aruego and Ariane Dewey. 1984, Greenwillow LB $15.93 (0-688-03745-3). 24pp. Danny tries to count ducks but has problems.

**418**  Pomeroy, Diana. *One Potato: A Counting Book of Potato Prints* (PS–2). Illus. 1996, Harcourt $16.00 (0-15-200300-2). 32pp. A counting book from 1 to 100 using imaginative potato prints, with additional information on how to create your own prints. (Rev: BL 4/1/96; HB 7–8/96; SLJ 6/96) [513.2]

**419**  Raffi. *Five Little Ducks* (PS–1). Illus. by Jose Aruego and Ariane Dewey. 1988, Crown $15.00 (0-517-56945-0); paper $5.99 (0-517-58360-7). 32pp. Mother Duck and her ducklings waddle "over the

hills and far away" in this addition to the Songs to Read series. (Rev: BL 6/1/89; HB 5–6/89)

**420**  Roche, Denis. *Only One Ollie* (PS). Illus. 1997, Houghton $4.95 (0-395-81123-6). 14pp. Ollie, a little dog, counts objects in his house from 1 to 10 in this charming board book. (Rev: BCCB 6/97; BL 4/15/97; SLJ 8/97)

**421**  Rocklin, Joanne. *One Hungry Cat* (1–2). Illus. by Rowan Barnes-Murphy. Series: Hello Math Reader. 1997, Scholastic paper $3.99 (0-590-93972-6). A slapstick easy reader that introduces simple arithmetic by using cookies that a hungry cat enjoys eating. (Rev: BL 5/1/97; SLJ 7/97)

**422**  Roth, Susan L. *My Love for You* (PS–K). Illus. 1997, Dial paper $12.89 (0-8037-2032-7). 26pp. A mouse expresses his love for a friend using numbers in this charming counting book. (Rev: BL 2/1/97; SLJ 2/97)

**423**  Ryan, Pam M. *One Hundred Is a Family* (PS–3). Illus. by Benrei Huang. 1994, Hyperion LB $14.49 (1-56282-673-5). 32pp. Different kinds of families are highlighted in this counting book that goes from 1 to 10 and then by tens to 100. (Rev: BL 11/1/94; SLJ 10/94)

**424**  Samton, Sheila W. *Moon to Sun: An Adding Book* (PS–1). Illus. 1991, Boyds Mills $9.95 (1-878093-13-4). Moon and clouds and other sky objects introduce adding. Also use: *On the River: An Adding Book* (1991). (Rev: SLJ 1/92)

**425**  Samton, Sheila W. *Ten Tiny Monsters* (PS–1). Illus. by author. 1997, Crown LB $18.99 (0-517-70942-2). A countdown book in which 10 apprentice monsters try unsuccessfully to frighten people. (Rev: SLJ 12/97)

**426**  Schlein, Miriam. *More Than One* (PS–3). Illus. by Donald Crews. 1996, Greenwillow LB $14.93 (0-688-14103-X). 24pp. Using the concept of "one" as a framework, other numbers and groups of numbers are introduced. (Rev: BCCB 1/97; BL 11/1/96; SLJ 12/96) [513]

**427**  Scott, Ann H. *One Good Horse: A Cowpuncher's Counting Book* (PS–1). Illus. by Lynn Sweat. 1990, Greenwillow LB $14.93 (0-688-09147-4). As a father and his son ride through their ranch, they count the various animals and objects they see. (Rev: HB 7–8/90; SLJ 4/90)

**428**  Sendak, Maurice. *Seven Little Monsters* (K–2). Illus. by author. 1977, HarperCollins LB $14.89 (0-06-025478-5). 16pp. A counting book involving monsters that townspeople try to eliminate.

**429**  Serfozo, Mary. *Who Wants One?* (PS–1). Illus. by Keiko Narahashi. 1989, Macmillan paper $15.00 (0-689-50474-8). 32pp. A young girl dressed as a magician brings forth many objects that introduce the numbers from 1 to 10. (Rev: BL 11/1/89; SLJ 12/89)

**430**  Simon, Charnan. *One Happy Classroom* (1–2). Illus. by Rebecca M. Thornburgh. 1997, Children's LB $17.00 (0-516-20318-5). 32pp. An easy-to-read counting book that takes place in a classroom and involves counting from 1 to 10 and back. (Rev: BL 5/1/97)

**431**  Sis, Peter. *Waving: A Counting Book* (PS–1). Illus. 1988, Greenwillow LB $12.88 (0-688-07160-0). 24pp. A story chain of people waving provides the fun in this counting book. (Rev: BL 3/15/88; HB 5–6/88)

**432**  Slater, Teddy. *Stay in Line* (1–2). Illus. 1996, Scholastic paper $3.50 (0-590-22713-0). 32pp. Children on a field trip learn various numerical ways of lining up. (Rev: BL 8/96)

**433**  Sloat, Teri. *From One to One Hundred* (PS–2). Illus. 1991, Dutton paper $14.99 (0-525-44764-4). 32pp. Each page offers the young reader opportunities to count to a certain number. (Rev: BCCB 9/91; BL 10/1/91; SLJ 12/91)

**434**  Smith, Maggie. *Counting Our Way to Maine* (PS–2). Illus. 1995, Orchard LB $16.99 (0-531-08734-4). 32pp. In this counting book, numbers from 1 to 20 are introduced by using a family's summer trip to Maine. (Rev: BCCB 3/95; BL 4/1/95; SLJ 5/95*)

**435**  Staake, Bob. *My Little 123 Book* (PS–K). Illus. by author. 1998, Simon & Schuster paper $6.99 (0-689-81660-X). A board book that uses bright colors and pleasant graphics to present numbers from 1 to 20. (Rev: SLJ 3/98)

**436**  Stickland, Paul. *Ten Terrible Dinosaurs* (PS–1). Illus. by author. 1997, Dutton $14.99 (0-525-45905-7). Using a countdown from 10 to 1, misbehaving dinosaurs engage in some antisocial behavior. (Rev: SLJ 10/97)

**437**  Sturges, Philemon. *Ten Flashing Fireflies* (PS–1). Illus. by Anna Vojtech. 1995, North-South LB $15.88 (1-55858-421-8). 32pp. Ten fireflies are captured by 2 youngsters in this counting book that also introduces subtraction. (Rev: BCCB 7–8/95; BL 6/1–15/95; SLJ 8/95*)

**438**  Tafuri, Nancy. *Who's Counting?* (PS). Illus. by author. 1986, Greenwillow LB $15.93 (0-688-06131-1). 24pp. Each double-page spread is devoted to one number from 1 to 10. (Rev: BL 3/1/86; HB 5–6/86; SLJ 4/86)

**439**  Testa, Fulvio. *If You Take a Pencil* (PS–1). Illus. by author. 1985, Dial paper $4.95 (0-8037-0165-9). 32pp. A handsome collection of pictures is used in this counting book.

**440**  Thompson, Susan L. *One More Thing, Dad* (PS–2). Illus. by Dora Leder. 1980, Whitman LB $10.75 (0-8075-6095-2). A simple counting book involving a boy going out of the house.

**441**  Tildes, Phyllis L. *Counting on Calico* (PS–K). Illus. 1995, Charlesbridge LB $15.88 (0-88106-864-0); paper $6.95 (0-88106-862-4). 32pp. The features of a calico cat are used to introduce basic numbers, ending with 20 wet paw prints. (Rev: BL 6/1–15/95)

**442**  *The Timbertoes 123 Counting Book* (PS–1). Illus. 1997, Boyds Mills $7.95 (1-56397-627-7). 32pp. Basic numbers are introduced by the Timbertoes, a family of wooden figures, when they visit an apple orchard. (Rev: BL 3/1/97; SLJ 7/97)

**443**  Trinca, Rod, and Kerry Argent. *One Woolly Wombat* (PS–2). Illus. by Kerry Argent. 1985, Kane/Miller $12.95 (0-916291-00-6); paper $6.95 (0-916291-10-3). 32pp. A charming 1-14 counting book featuring Australian animals. (Rev: BL 7/85; HB 7–8/85; SLJ 9/85)

**444**  Walsh, Ellen S. *Mouse Count* (PS–K). Illus. 1991, Harcourt $12.00 (0-15-256023-8). 32pp. In this counting book, 10 little mice fall asleep unaware that a hungry snake is nearby. (Rev: BL 2/15/91; HB 5–6/91; SLJ 5/91*)

**445**  Walton, Rick. *How Many How Many How Many* (PS–1). Illus. by Cynthia Jabar. 1993, Candlewick $14.95 (1-56402-062-2). A variety of items are used in this effective counting book that covers the numbers 1 through 12. (Rev: SLJ 2/94)

**446**  Watson, Amy, et al. *The Folk Art Counting Book* (PS–2). Illus. 1992, Abrams $12.95 (0-8109-3306-3). 40pp. Collections from the Rockefeller Folk Art Center in Williamsburg, Virginia, invite the younger reader to count to 20. (Rev: BL 6/15/92; SLJ 8/92) [745]

**447**  Wing, Natasha L. *Hippity Hop, Frog on Top* (PS–K). Illus. by DeLoss McGraw. 1994, Simon & Schuster paper $15.00 (0-671-87045-9). 32pp. In this counting book, 10 frogs hop on each other to get over a wall. (Rev: BL 7/94; SLJ 7/94)

**448**  Winter, Jeanette. *Josefina* (PS–3). Illus. 1996, Harcourt $15.00 (0-15-201091-2). 36pp. An original counting book that features the Mexican woman Josefina and her amazing collection of clay figures. (Rev: BCCB 10/96; BL 10/15/96*; SLJ 10/96)

**449**  Wise, William. *Ten Sly Piranhas: A Counting Story in Reverse (A Tale of Wickedness — and Worse!)* (PS–3). Illus. by Victoria Chess. 1993, Dial LB $13.89 (0-8037-1201-4). 32pp. A counting book featuring the murderous antics of 10 sly piranhas. (Rev: BL 5/1/93; HB 7–8/93)

**450**  Wood, Jakki. *Moo Moo, Brown Cow* (PS–1). Illus. by Rog Bonner. 1992, Harcourt $14.00 (0-15-200533-1). 28pp. In this large-sized counting book, a kitten asks farm animals about their young. (Rev: BL 6/15/92; SLJ 8/92)

**451**   Yektai, Niki. *Bears at the Beach: Counting 10 to 20* (PS–1). Illus. 1996, Millbrook LB $21.90 (0-7613-0047-3). 32pp. A wordless counting book that covers numbers from 10 to 20. (Rev: BL 7/96; SLJ 6/96)

**452**   Zabar, Abbie. *55 Friends* (PS–3). Illus. by author. 1994, Hyperion $13.95 (0-7868-0021-6). In a fanciful text, animals from 1 to 10 are introduced and then combined in various ways to reach 55. (Rev: SLJ 11/94)

# Bedtime Books and Nursery Rhymes

## Bedtime Books

**453**   Alda, Arlene. *Sheep, Sheep, Sheep, Help Me Fall Asleep* (PS–1). Illus. 1995, Dell paper $4.99 (0-440-40957-8). 32pp. This bedtime book gives a new twist to counting sheep to help someone fall asleep. (Rev: BL 11/1/92; SLJ 1/93)

**454**   Alexander, Martha. *You're a Genius, Blackboard Bear* (PS–K). Illus. 1995, Candlewick $12.95 (1-56402-238-2). 32pp. Anthony and Blackboard Bear build a rocket ship but decide it is better to remain at home. (Rev: BCCB 6/96; BL 5/1/95; SLJ 6/95)

**455**   Anholt, Catherine, and Laurence Anholt. *The Twins, Two by Two* (PS–K). Illus. 1992, Candlewick $13.95 (1-56402-041-X). 32pp. Twins Minnie and Max learn how to go to bed, from the story of Noah's ark. (Rev: BL 2/1/92)

**456**   Appelt, Kathi. *Bayou Lullaby* (PS–1). Illus. by Neil Waldman. 1995, Morrow LB $15.93 (0-688-12857-2). 40pp. A Cajun bedtime tale of a land ruled over by the king of the bullfrogs. (Rev: BL 3/15/95; SLJ 4/95*)

**457**   Appelt, Kathi. *I See the Moon* (PS–K). Illus. by Debra R. Jenkins. 1997, Eerdmans $15.00 (0-8028-5118-5). 24pp. A bedtime book about a little girl all alone on the sea in a tiny boat. (Rev: BCCB 5/97; BL 3/15/97)

**458**   Arnold, Tedd. *Five Ugly Monsters* (PS–K). Illus. 1995, Scholastic $6.95 (0-590-22226-0). 24pp. Several groups of monsters interrupt a little boy's plans to go to sleep. (Rev: BCCB 10/95; BL 11/15/95; SLJ 12/95)

**459**   Asch, Frank. *Barnyard Lullaby* (PS–2). Illus. 1998, Simon & Schuster $15.00 (0-689-81363-5). 40pp. At first, it is only a mother hen who is singing a lullaby, but soon all the other animals and the farmer's wife join in. (Rev: BL 1/1–15/98*; SLJ 2/98)

**460**   Aylesworth, Jim. *The Good-Night Kiss* (PS–1). Illus. by Walter L. Krudop. 1993, Atheneum $14.95 (0-689-31515-5). 32pp. Various animals view one another, but the last to be seen is a child getting a good-night kiss. (Rev: BL 9/1/93; SLJ 12/93)

**461**   Aylesworth, Jim. *Teddy Bear Tears* (PS–1). Illus. by Jo Ellen McAllister-Stammen. 1997, Simon & Schuster $16.00 (0-689-31776-X). 32pp. When the lights go out at bedtime, a young boy tells his 4 teddy bears that they must not be scared. (Rev: BL 4/1/97; SLJ 6/97)

**462**   Balan, Bruce. *The Moose in the Dress* (PS–K). Illus. by Denise Teasdale. 1993, Random paper $4.99 (0-517-10895-X). Is a young boy visited by a moose every night or is it a shadow from the curtains? (Rev: SLJ 3/92)

**463**   Banks, Kate. *And If the Moon Could Talk* (PS–2). Illus. by Georg Hallensleben. 1998, Farrar $15.00 (0-374-30299-5). 32pp. At bedtime, a little girl's actions are duplicated in the outside world with a number of different animals. (Rev: BL 2/15/98; SLJ 2/98*)

**464**   Bartalos, Michael. *Shadowville* (K–3). Illus. 1995, Viking paper $13.99 (0-670-86161-8). 40pp. Explains what shadows do at night when there isn't any light. (Rev: BL 5/1/95; SLJ 8/95)

**465**   Brown, Margaret Wise. *A Child's Good Night Book* (PS–K). Illus. by Jean Charlot. 1986, Harper-Collins $10.95 (0-060-21028-1); paper $4.95 (0-06-443114-2). 32pp. Animals and children prepare for bed in this rhythmically told story.

**466**   Brown, Margaret Wise. *Goodnight Moon* (PS). Illus. by Clement Hurd. 1947, HarperCollins LB $14.89 (0-06-020706-X); paper $5.95 (0-06-443017-0). 32pp. A soothing go-to-sleep story. A pop-up book version is: *The Goodnight Moon Room: A Pop-Up Book* (1985).

**467**   Brown, Margaret Wise. *Little Donkey Close Your Eyes* (PS–K). Illus. by Ashley Wolff. 1995, HarperCollins LB $13.89 (0-06-024483-6). 32pp. As night falls, different animals are told to close their eyes in this bedtime book. (Rev: BL 11/15/95; HB 11–12/95; SLJ 9/95*)

**468**   Brown, Margaret Wise. *The Sleepy Men* (PS–K). Illus. by Robert Rayevsky. 1996, Hyperion LB $15.49 (0-7868-2126-4). 32pp. A bedtime story about a big sleepy man who tells a little sleepy man a bedtime story. (Rev: BCCB 1/97; BL 10/1/96; SLJ 12/96)

**469**   Buchholz, Quint. *Sleep Well, Little Bear* (K–3). Trans. by Peter F. Neumeyer. Illus. 1994, Farrar $14.00 (0-374-37026-5). 33pp. At night, a stuffed toy bear thinks about the day just past and about the mysterious night outside. (Rev: BL 12/1/94; SLJ 12/94)

**470** Bunting, Eve. *No Nap* (PS–1). Illus. by Susan Meddaugh. 1989, Houghton $15.95 (0-89919-813-9). 28pp. Whenever bedtime is suggested, Susie says, "No nap." (Rev: BCCB 10/89; BL 9/15/89; HB 1–2/90; SLJ 10/89)

**471** *The Candlewick Book of Bedtime Stories* (PS–2). Illus. 1995, Candlewick $19.99 (1-56402-652-3). 96pp. Nineteen well-known picture books suitable for bedtime reading are reprinted, often with abridged illustrations. (Rev: BL 11/15/95; SLJ 12/95)

**472** Carlstrom, Nancy White. *Swim the Silver Sea, Joshie Otter* (PS–K). Illus. by Ken Kuroi. 1997, Putnam paper $5.95 (0-698-11447-7). 40pp. At bedtime, a baby otter swims back to his mother and the love she gives him. (Rev: BL 4/1/93; SLJ 5/93)

**473** Carlstrom, Nancy White. *Where Does the Night Hide?* (PS–1). Illus. by Thomas B. Allen and Laura Allen. 1990, Macmillan LB $13.95 (0-02-717390-9). 32pp. A mother and daughter search in many places to find where the night hides during the day. (Rev: BL 10/15/90; SLJ 2/91)

**474** Cazet, Denys. *Night Lights: 24 Poems to Sleep On* (PS–2). Illus. by author. 1997, Orchard LB $16.99 (0-531-33010-9). There are 24 bedtime rhymes in this nighttime collection; some are lullabies, others are amusing poems about animals at night. (Rev: SLJ 5/97)

**475** Chislett, Gail. *Whump* (PS–1). Illus. by Vladyana Krykorka. 1992, Firefly $.99 (1-55037-253-X). A little boy has trouble adjusting to his big new bed. (Rev: SLJ 3/90)

**476** Chorao, Kay. *The Baby's Bedtime Book* (PS–K). Illus. by author. 1984, Dutton paper $15.99 (0-525-44149-2). 64pp. Twenty-seven verses suitable for bedtime reading.

**477** Christiana, David. *Drawer in a Drawer* (K–3). Illus. 1990, Farrar $13.95 (0-374-31874-3). 32pp. A first picture book of a surreal world with quick-changing patterns. (Rev: BL 7/90; SLJ 10/90)

**478** Cleary, Beverly. *Petey's Bedtime Story* (K–3). Illus. by David Small. 1993, Morrow LB $14.93 (0-688-10661-7). 32pp. Petey prolongs his bedtime rituals until his parents fall asleep from exhaustion. (Rev: BL 9/1/93; SLJ 2/94)

**479** Conrad, Pam. *Animal Lullabies* (K–3). Illus. by Richard Cowdrey. 1997, HarperCollins LB $14.89 (0-06-024719-3). 32pp. Each of the different animals sings a lullaby that brings out one of their characteristics. (Rev: BL 9/1/97; SLJ 1/98)

**480** Cooper, Helen. *The Boy Who Wouldn't Go to Bed* (PS–1). Illus. 1997, Dial paper $14.99 (0-8037-2253-2). 32pp. A boy who is tired but doesn't want

to go to bed finally succumbs to his mother's wishes. (Rev: BL 8/97*; SLJ 7/97)

**481** Cooper, Susan. *Matthew's Dragon* (K–2). Illus. by Joseph A. Smith. 1991, Macmillan $14.95 (0-689-50512-4). After a bedtime story involving dragons, Matthew is visited by a friendly one. (Rev: SLJ 10/91)

**482** Corentin, Philippe. *Papa!* (PS–1). Illus. by author. 1997, Chronicle $13.95 (0-8118-1640-0). At night, a little boy and a monster child frighten each other and are comforted by their respective parents. (Rev: SLJ 9/97)

**483** Daly, Niki. *Mary Malloy and the Baby Who Wouldn't Sleep* (PS–K). Illus. 1993, Golden Bks. $14.95 (0-307-17501-4). 32pp. In this bedtime story, Mr. Fez, a crocodile, tricks Moon into giving up the baby he has taken. (Rev: BL 9/15/93; SLJ 12/93)

**484** Davis, Karen. *Star Light, Star Bright* (PS–1). Illus. 1993, Simon & Schuster $15.00 (0-671-79455-8). 24pp. Louisa searches throughout her house and in the sky for a special star on which she can wish. (Rev: BL 6/1–15/93)

**485** Dotlich, Rebecca. *Sweet Dreams of the Wild: Poems for Bedtime* (PS–K). Illus. by Katharine Dodge. 1996, Boyds Mills $15.95 (1-56397-180-1). 32pp. A delightful picture book that explores in poetry and illustrations the many places animals sleep. (Rev: BL 1/1–15/96; SLJ 3/96) [811.54]

**486** Dragonwagon, Crescent. *Half a Moon and One Whole Star* (PS–1). Illus. by Jerry Pinkney. 1990, Simon & Schuster paper $5.99 (0-689-71415-7). 32pp. Susan is falling asleep as the sights and sounds of the night surround her. (Rev: BCCB 5/86; BL 3/15/86; SLJ 4/86)

**487** Dyer, Jane. *Animal Crackers: A Delectable Collection of Pictures, Poems, and Lullabies for the Very Young* (PS). Illus. 1996, Little, Brown $17.95 (0-316-19766-1). 64pp. An immensely appealing collection of lullabies, poems, and nursery rhymes accompanied by muted illustrations. (Rev: BCCB 3/96; BL 4/15/96; SLJ 5/96)

**488** Emberley, Ed. *Go Away, Big Green Monster!* (PS–1). Illus. 1993, Little, Brown $14.95 (0-316-23653-5). 32pp. This toy book deals with a child's nighttime fears in a lighthearted way that will be both a joy and a comfort to young people. (Rev: BCCB 3/93; BL 4/15/93*; HB 7–8/93)

**489** Erskine, Jim. *Bedtime Story* (PS). Illus. by Ann Schweninger. 1981, Crown LB $8.95 (0-517-54540-3). 32pp. A little boy goes to sleep, as do many animal friends.

**490** Feldman, Eve B. *Animals Don't Wear Pajamas: A Book About Sleeping* (PS–1). Illus. by Mary Beth Owens. 1992, Holt $14.95 (0-8050-1710-0). 32pp. In watercolors and simple text, the sleeping habits of different animals are described. (Rev: BL 3/1/92; HB 5–6/92; SLJ 6/92) [591.51]

**491** Field, Eugene. *Wynken, Blynken, and Nod: A Poem* (PS–K). Illus. by Johanna Westerman. 1995, North-South LB $15.88 (1-55858-423-4). 24pp. New illustrations enhance this edition of the classic bedtime poem. (Rev: BL 11/1/95; SLJ 11/95) [811]

**492** Foreman, Michael. *Dad! I Can't Sleep* (PS–K). Illus. 1995, Harcourt $13.95 (0-15-200307-X). 32pp. A young panda tries to go to sleep by counting a number of different animals. (Rev: BL 3/1/95; SLJ 7/95)

**493** Foreman, Michael. *Surprise! Surprise!* (PS–1). Illus. 1995, Harcourt $14.00 (0-15-200038-0). 32pp. Little Panda is afraid of the dark and has become used to relying on Moonlight for help. (Rev: BL 12/15/95; SLJ 3/96)

**494** Fox, Mem. *A Bedtime Story* (PS–2). Illus. by Elivia Savadier. 1996, Mondo $13.95 (1-57255-136-4). Polly and Bed Rabbit look forward to a bedtime story from their parents. (Rev: SLJ 12/96)

**495** Fox, Mem. *Time for Bed* (PS). Illus. by Jane Dyer. 1993, Harcourt $15.00 (0-15-288183-2). 32pp. Various animals put their babies to sleep in this quiet bedtime book. (Rev: BCCB 10/93; BL 10/1/93; SLJ 10/93)

**496** French, Vivian. *A Song for Little Toad* (PS–1). Illus. by Barbara Firth. 1995, Candlewick $14.99 (1-56402-614-0). Every animal thinks that Mother Toad's croaking lullaby is ugly except Little Toad. (Rev: HB 11–12/95; SLJ 9/95)

**497** Garelick, May. *Look at the Moon* (K–3). Illus. by Barbara Garrison. 1996, Mondo $14.95 (1-57255-142-9). 30pp. A young girl wonders if animals experience the same thrill of seeing moonlight as she does. (Rev: BL 11/15/96; SLJ 1/97)

**498** Gerber, Carole. *Hush! A Gaelic Lullaby* (PS–2). Illus. by Marty Husted. 1997, Whispering Coyote $15.95 (1-879085-57-7). In this lullaby, an Irish family puts baby to bed while taking precautions against a storm that is approaching their farm. (Rev: HB 1–2, 3–4, 5-6/97; SLJ 1/98)

**499** Gerstein, Mordicai. *Bedtime, Everybody!* (PS–2). Illus. 1996, Hyperion LB $13.49 (0-7868-2138-8). 32pp. Daisy has difficulty getting her many stuffed animals to go to bed. (Rev: BL 6/1–15/96; SLJ 6/96)

**500** Ginsburg, Mirra. *Asleep, Asleep* (PS–K). Illus. by Nancy Tafuri. 1992, Greenwillow LB $13.93 (0-688-09154-7). 24pp. A bedtime book that shows a variety of animals asleep. (Rev: BL 5/1/92; HB 5–6/92*; SLJ 4/92*)

**501** Ginsburg, Mirra, adapt. *The Sun's Asleep Behind the Hill* (PS–1). Illus. by Paul O. Zelinsky. 1982,

Greenwillow LB $15.93 (0-688-00825-9). 32pp. At the end of the day all life prepares for rest.

**502** Goode, Diane. *I Hear a Noise* (PS–1). Illus. by author. 1988, Puffin paper $3.99 (0-525-44884-5). 32pp. A monster steals a boy and his mother and then gets yelled at by his mother. (Rev: BL 12/1/88; HB 9–10/88; SLJ 2/89)

**503** Graff, Nancy P. *In the Hush of the Evening* (PS–2). Illus. by G. Brian Karas. 1998, Harper-Collins $14.95 (0-06-022099-6). 32pp. In this bedtime book, a mother tells her child about all the sounds of the evening. (Rev: BL 3/15/98)

**504** Griffin, Sandra U. *Earth Circles* (PS–3). Illus. by author. 1989, Walker LB $13.85 (0-8027-6845-8). The circle of life from birth to death, including the need to sleep at the end of each day, is introduced as it appears in nature. (Rev: SLJ 11/89)

**505** Grimes, Nikki. *Baby's Bedtime* (PS). Illus. by Sylvia Walker. 1996, Golden Bks. $3.95 (0-307-12872-5). 16pp. A board book in which a baby gets a bath and is tucked into bed. (Rev: BL 5/15/96)

**506** Hagen, Jeff. *Hiawatha Passing* (K–3). Illus. by Kenneth Shue. 1995, Holt $15.95 (0-8050-1832-8). 32pp. A boy listens to the sounds of a train in the night before he falls asleep. (Rev: BL 11/15/95; SLJ 1/96)

**507** Hague, Michael. *Sleep, Baby, Sleep: Lullabies and Night Poems* (PS–K). Illus. 1994, Morrow $18.00 (0-688-10877-6). 80pp. This collection of 26 lullabies includes the standard favorites and some new ones. (Rev: BL 8/94; SLJ 10/94)

**508** Hamm, Diane J. *Rockabye Farm* (PS). Illus. by Rick Brown. 1992, Simon & Schuster paper $15.00 (0-671-74773-8). One by one, a farmer rocks the farm animals to sleep, including his own baby. (Rev: SLJ 7/92)

**509** Harley, Bill. *Nothing Happened* (K–2). Illus. by Ann Miya. 1995, Tricycle Pr. $14.95 (1-883672-09-0). 32pp. Jack is determined to stay awake so he can share in all the exciting things he believes happen to his family when he is asleep. (Rev: BL 4/15/95; SLJ 6/95)

**510** Hazelaar, Cor. *Zoo Dreams* (PS–1). Illus. by author. 1997, Farrar $14.00 (0-374-39730-9). A bedtime book that shows how zoo animals sleep in a simple text and muted watercolors. (Rev: HB 3–4/97; SLJ 3/97)

**511** Hillert, Margaret. *The Sky Is Not So Far Away: Night Poems for Children* (PS–1). Illus. by Thomas Werner. 1996, Boyds Mills $15.95 (1-56397-223-9). 32pp. A simple poetry book that contains poems on night themes, such as dreams and bedtime rituals. (Rev: BCCB 11/96; SLJ 9/96) [811]

**512** Ho, Minfong. *Hush! A Thai Lullaby* (PS–3). Illus. by Holly Meade. 1996, Orchard LB $16.99 (0-531-08850-2). 32pp. In this Thai lullaby, a mother silences some animals, one by one, so that her baby can sleep. (Rev: BCCB 4/96; BL 4/15/96; HB 11–12/96; SLJ 3/96)

**513** Hoellwarth, Cathryn C. *The Underbed* (PS–K). Illus. by Sibyl G. Grieg. 1990, Good Books $12.95 (0-934672-79-2). 24pp. Mother helps Tucker get rid of the monster he believes is under the bed. (Rev: BL 3/1/91; SLJ 7/91)

**514** Hort, Lenny. *How Many Stars in the Sky?* (PS–1). Illus. by James E. Ransome. 1991, Morrow LB $15.93 (0-688-10104-6). 32pp. A boy and his father go out into the night to count the stars in the sky. (Rev: BCCB 6/91; BL 5/1/91; SLJ 5/91)

**515** Howe, James. *There's a Monster Under My Bed* (PS–1). Illus. by David S. Rose. 1986, Macmillan $15.00 (0-689-31178-8); paper $4.95 (0-689-71409-2). 32pp. A child is sure there are monsters under his bed, only to find that the noises come from little brother Alex, who sees monsters of his own. (Rev: BL 5/1/86; HB 7–8/86; SLJ 5/86)

**516** *Hush, Little Baby: A Traditional Lullaby* (PS). Illus. by Shari Halpern. 1997, North-South LB $15.88 (1-55858-808-6). 22pp. This traditional lullaby is illustrated with fresh pictures that resemble parts of a quilt. (Rev: BL 10/15/97; SLJ 1/98)

**517** James, Betsy. *The Dream Stair* (K–3). Illus. by Richard J. Watson. 1990, HarperCollins $13.95 (0-06-022787-7). 32pp. After Grandmother tucks her in bed, a little girl dreams of wandering "past clouds, past angels." (Rev: BL 3/1/90; SLJ 7/90)

**518** Janovitz, Marilyn. *Is It Time?* (PS–K). Illus. 1994, North-South LB $12.88 (1-55858-332-7). 24pp. Ted, a wolf cub, prepares for bed with his father's help. (Rev: BCCB 11/94; BL 1/1/95; SLJ 1/95)

**519** Jordan, Sandra. *Down on Casey's Farm* (PS–K). Illus. by author. 1996, Orchard LB $16.99 (0-531-08853-7). A bedtime book that introduces a number of farm animals through the fantasies of a young boy. (Rev: SLJ 10/96)

**520** Kalman, Maira. *Hey Willy, See the Pyramids* (K–2). Illus. by author. 1988, Viking $16.99 (0-670-82163-2). 40pp. Sister Lulu tells a young boy an off-beat story about a woman and 3 cross-eyed dogs. (Rev: BL 2/1/89; SLJ 9/88)

**521** Khalsa, Dayal Kaur. *Sleepers* (PS–K). Illus. by author. 1988, Crown LB $7.95 (0-517-56917-5). 24pp. A little girl discusses all the sleepers she knows — such as her grandfather who sleeps after every meal. (Rev: BL 4/1/88; HB 9–10/88; SLJ 2/88)

**522** Kherdian, David. *Lullaby for Emily* (PS). Illus. by Nonny Hogrogian. 1995, Holt $15.95 (0-8050-

2957-5). 28pp. This book pictures the scenes described in a lullaby that a mother sings to her sleepy child. (Rev: BL 5/1/95; SLJ 7/95)

**523** Knutson, Kimberley. *Bed Bouncers* (PS–K). Illus. 1995, Simon & Schuster paper $14.00 (0-02-750871-4). 32pp. A brother and sister bounce from their beds into space in this bedtime story. (Rev: BL 5/15/95; SLJ 8/95)

**524** Koller, Jackie F. *No Such Thing* (K–3). Illus. by Betsy Lewin. 1997, Boyds Mills $14.95 (1-56397-490-8). 32pp. A monster and her son under the bed are undergoing the same comforting bedtime rituals as a real mother and son. (Rev: BCCB 3/97; BL 4/1/97; SLJ 6/97)

**525** Kramsky, Jerry. *The Cranky Sun* (K–2). Illus. by Lorenzo Mattotti. 1996, Little, Brown $16.95 (0-316-50361-4). A bedtime story about a cranky sun that refuses to set. (Rev: SLJ 7/96)

**526** Laimgruber, Monika. *Susannah and the Sandman* (PS–2). Trans. by Marianne Martens. Illus. by author. 1996, North-South LB $15.88 (1-55858-602-4). The Sandman has to wait until Susannah has a pillow fight with her toys and pets before he can sprinkle his magic dust on her. (Rev: SLJ 2/97)

**527** Lansky, Bruce. *Sweet Dreams: Bedtime Poems, Songs and Lullabies* (PS). Illus. by Vicki Wehrman. 1996, Meadowbrook Pr. $15.00 (0-671-57046-3). 32pp. A collection of original poems and traditional songs and rhymes about going to bed and to sleep. (Rev: SLJ 10/96)

**528** Lesser, Carolyn. *The Goodnight Circle* (PS–2). Illus. by Lorinda Bryan Cauley. 1984, Harcourt $14.95 (0-15-232158-6); paper $7.00 (0-15-232159-4). 30pp. What animals do between night and morning. 

**529** Leuck, Laura. *Sun Is Falling, Night Is Calling* (PS). Illus. by Ora Eitan. 1994, Simon & Schuster paper $15.00 (0-671-86940-X). 32pp. A loving bunny, Mama, soothes her child to sleep in this quiet bedtime book. (Rev: BCCB 6/94; BL 6/1–15/94)

**530** Lewison, Wendy C. *Going to Sleep on the Farm* (PS–1). Illus. by Juan Wijngaard. 1992, Dial LB $13.89 (0-8037-1097-6). 32pp. Father explains to his dozing son how farm animals go to sleep. (Rev: BCCB 7–8/92; BL 4/15/92*; HB 5–6/92; SLJ 6/92)

**531** Lindgren, Astrid. *I Don't Want to Go to Bed* (PS–1). Trans. by Barbara Lucas. Illus. by Ilon Wikland. 1988, Farrar $12.95 (91-29-59066-3). 32pp. Five-year-old Larry won't go to bed until Aunt Lottie gives him a pair of magic glasses. (Rev: BL 12/1/88; SLJ 4/89)

**532** Lipniacka, Ewa. *To Bed . . . or Else!* (PS–2). Illus. by Basia Bogdanowicz. 1991, Crocodile $13.95 (0-940793-85-7). Two girls find it difficult to go to sleep until one of their mothers finds a solution. (Rev: SLJ 3/92)

**533** Loh, Morag. *Tucking Mommy In* (PS–1). Illus. by Donna Rawlins. 1988, Orchard paper $5.95 (0-531-07025-5). 40pp. Mommy falls asleep and the children tuck her in. (Rev: BCCB 9/88; BL 10/1/88; SLJ 10/88)

**534** London, Jonathan. *Fireflies, Fireflies, Light My Way* (PS–1). Illus. by Linda Messier. 1996, Viking paper $14.99 (0-670-85442-5). 32pp. One by one, animals lead each other, ending with a child being taken to a place where they are all present. (Rev: BL 7/96; SLJ 6/96)

**535** London, Jonathan. *Into This Night We Are Rising* (K–3). Illus. by G. Brian Karas. 1996, Puffin paper $4.99 (0-14-055773-3). 32pp. Children fly through the night sky but later return to their beds. (Rev: BL 8/93; HB 7–8/93)

**536** Long, Sylvia. *Hush Little Baby* (PS–1). Illus. 1997, Chronicle $12.95 (0-8118-1416-5). 32pp. This song, a tender lullaby, focuses on the tender relationship between a mother and her baby bunny. (Rev: BL 6/1–15/97)

**537** *Lullabies: An Illustrated Songbook* (PS–1). Illus. 1997, Harcourt $23.00 (0-15-201728-3). 96pp. Thirty-seven lullabies with simple piano accompaniment and guitar chords, as well as background information on each song. (Rev: BL 12/15/97; SLJ 1/98) [782]

**538** McBratney, Sam. *Guess How Much I Love You* (PS–K). Illus. by Anita Jeram. 1995, Candlewick $15.99 (1-56402-473-3). 32pp. In this bedtime book, a young rabbit tries to tell his father how much he loves him. (Rev: BL 3/15/95*; HB 7–8/95; SLJ 5/95)

**539** McCourt, Lisa. *I Love You, Stinky Face* (PS–K). Illus. by Cyd Moore. 1997, Troll $15.95 (0-8167-4392-4). 32pp. In this tender bedtime story, a young girl tests the limits of her mother's love with a series of questions like "Would you love me if I were a big scary ape?" (Rev: BL 10/15/97*; SLJ 10/97)

**540** MacDonald, Margaret Read. *Tuck-Me-In Tales: Bedtime Stories from Around the World* (PS–1). Illus. by Yvonne Davis. 1996, August House $19.95 (0-87483-461-9). 64pp. Five traditional bedtime stories from around the world are lavishly illustrated. (Rev: BL 10/1/96; SLJ 11/96) [398.2]

**541** McDonald, Megan. *My House Has Stars* (PS–3). Illus. by Peter Catalanotto. 1996, Orchard LB $16.99 (0-531-08879-0). 32pp. Eight children from around the world tell about their homes in the evening and at night. (Rev: BCCB 11/96; BL 11/1/96; SLJ 10/96)

**542** McGilvray, Richard. *Don't Climb Out of the Window Tonight* (K–2). Illus. by Alan Snow. n.d., Smithmark $3.98 (0-8317-5003-0). 32pp. A young girl imagines all the terrible things that might happen if her teddy bear climbed out of the window at night. (Rev: BL 6/1–15/93)

**543** McKellar, Shona, ed. *A Child's Book of Lullabies* (1–4). Illus. by Mary Cassatt. 1997, DK Publg. $12.95 (0-7894-1507-0). 32pp. Using 13 reproductions of Mary Cassatt's paintings, several traditional lullabies are introduced. (Rev: BL 6/1–15/97)

**544** McMullan, Kate. *If You Were My Bunny* (PS–K). Illus. by David McPhail. 1996, Scholastic $6.95 (0-590-52749-5). 32pp. A bedtime book with lullabies sung by different loving animal mothers to their attentive offspring. (Rev: BL 5/1/96; HB 7–8/96)

**545** McPhail, David. *The Dream Child* (PS–K). Illus. by author. 1988, Puffin paper $4.95 (0-525-44366-5). 32pp. Dream Child and Tame Bear come down from the sky for nighttime adventures in this soothing lullaby. (Rev: BL 4/1/85; SLJ 3/85)

**546** Maris, Ron. *My Book* (PS–K). Illus. by author. 1986, Puffin paper $4.99 (0-14-050523-7). 32pp. A peek-a-boo book that leads a cat to bed.

**547** Marshall, James. *What's the Matter with Carruthers? A Bedtime Story* (K–3). Illus. by author. 1972, Houghton $18.00 (0-395-13895-7). 32pp. Carruthers, a very large bear, gets grumpy because it's time for his sleep.

**548** Mayer, Mercer. *There's a Nightmare in My Closet* (K–3). Illus. by author. 1968, Dial LB $14.89 (0-8037-8683-2); paper $4.95 (0-8037-8574-7). 32pp. A boy brings a creature out of the closet into a more friendly atmosphere.

**549** Mayer, Mercer. *There's an Alligator Under My Bed* (PS–1). Illus. by author. 1987, Dial LB $14.89 (0-8037-0375-9). 32pp. No matter what anyone says, there is an alligator under the young hero's bed. (Rev: BL 4/1/87; SLJ 6–7/87)

**550** Melmed, Laura K. *I Love You As Much . . .* (PS–K). Illus. by Henri Sorensen. 1993, Lothrop LB $15.93 (0-688-11719-8). 24pp. In a series of double-page spreads, various animal mothers tell their offspring how much they love them in this attractive bedtime book. (Rev: BL 9/1/93; SLJ 3/94)

**551** Miranda, Anne. *Night Songs* (PS–K). Illus. 1993, Macmillan LB $13.95 (0-02-767250-6). 32pp. This lullaby describes the rising of the moon in words and pictures. (Rev: BL 4/1/93; SLJ 6/93)

**552** Moore, Julia. *While You Sleep* (PS). Illus. by Lyn Gilbert. 1996, Dutton paper $11.99 (0-525-45462-4). In this bedtime book, rhyming couplets are used to describe what animals are doing around the world while a child sleeps. (Rev: SLJ 8/96)

**553** Morris, Winifred. *What If the Shark Wears Tennis Shoes?* (PS). Illus. by Betsy Lewin. 1990, Macmillan $13.95 (0-689-31587-2). 32pp. A mother patiently answers her son's farfetched questions about being left alone at night. (Rev: BL 12/15/90; SLJ 10/90)

**554** Morrissey, Dean. *Ship of Dreams* (K–3). Illus. by author. 1994, Millpond: Abrams $17.95 (0-8109-3848-0). In this bedtime book, Joey takes off in his red wagon on a flight to see if the sandman really exists. (Rev: SLJ 12/94)

**555** Narahashi, Keiko. *Is That Josie?* (PS–1). Illus. 1994, Macmillan paper $14.95 (0-689-50606-6). 32pp. A young girl pretends to be a number of different animals before allowing her mother to hug her at bedtime. (Rev: BCCB 10/94; BL 11/1/94; SLJ 11/94*)

**556** Newfield, Marcia. *Where Did You Put Your Sleep?* (PS–1). Illus. by Andrea Da Rif. 1983, Macmillan LB $13.95 (0-689-50286-9). 32pp. A little girl who can't go to sleep plays a game with her father.

**557** Nye, Naomi S. *Benito's Dream Bottle* (PS–3). Illus. by Yu Cha Pak. 1995, Simon & Schuster $15.00 (0-02-768467-9). 32pp. A young boy tries to find out what dreams are and where they come from. (Rev: BL 5/1/95; SLJ 6/95)

**558** Nye, Naomi S. *Lullaby Raft* (PS–1). Illus. by Vivienne Flesher. 1997, Simon & Schuster $16.00 (0-689-80521-7). 32pp. A fantasy world is introduced to a youngster by his mother through the words of her lullaby. (Rev: BL 11/1/97; SLJ 9/97)

**559** Oppenheim, Joanne. *The Story Book Prince* (PS–3). Illus. by Rosanne Litzinger. 1987, Harcourt $12.95 (0-15-200590-0). 32pp. The young prince can't sleep, and so members of the kingdom try to wear him out. (Rev: BL 3/1/87; SLJ 4/87)

**560** Ormerod, Jan. *Midnight Pillow Fight* (PS–1). Illus. 1993, Candlewick $14.95 (1-56402-169-6). 32pp. At bedtime, Polly and her pillow engage in a fight with other cushions. (Rev: BL 1/15/93; SLJ 5/93)

**561** Osofsky, Audrey. *Dreamcatcher* (PS–3). Illus. by Ed Young. 1992, Orchard LB $16.99 (0-531-08588-0). 32pp. An Ojibway baby watches everyday events in his family's life and later sleeps peacefully. (Rev: BCCB 7–8/92; BL 2/15/92; SLJ 4/92)

**562** Pank, Rachel. *Sonia and Barnie and the Noise in the Night* (PS–K). Illus. 1991, Scholastic paper $13.95 (0-590-44657-6). 32pp. Her cowardly cat may hide up in a tree, but brave and bossy Sonia takes on the "monster" who frightened them. (Rev: BL 6/1/91; SLJ 12/91)

**563** Prelutsky, Jack. *My Parents Think I'm Sleeping* (K–3). Illus. by Yossi Abolafia. 1985, Greenwillow LB $15.93 (0-688-04019-5). 48pp. These poems take place at the midnight hour when a young boy thinks about what goes on when the lights are off. (Rev: BCCB 1/86; BL 11/15/85; HB 1–2/86)

**564** Raschka, Chris. *Can't Sleep* (PS–1). Illus. 1995, Orchard LB $15.99 (0-531-08779-4). 32pp. A young dog with insomnia takes comfort in having the moon watch over him until he goes to sleep. (Rev: BCCB 10/95; BL 9/15/95; SLJ 9/95*)

**565** Ray, Karen. *Sleep Song* (PS). Illus. by Rhonda Mitchell. 1995, Orchard LB $16.99 (0-531-08728-X). 32pp. Nightly rituals like taking a bath are highlighted in this charming bedtime book. (Rev: BCCB 3/95; BL 2/15/95; SLJ 4/95)

**566** Roberts, Bethany. *A Mouse Told His Mother* (PS–K). Illus. by Maryjane Begin. 1997, Little, Brown $14.95 (0-316-74982-6). 32pp. Though a little mouse claims he is about to embark on different wild adventures, he is really getting ready for bed. (Rev: BL 4/1/97; SLJ 5/97)

**567** Rosenberg, Liz. *Adelaide and the Night Train* (PS–K). Illus. by Lisa Desimini. 1989, Harper-Collins LB $13.89 (0-06-025103-4). 32pp. A young girl takes a long train ride through country and city and then back to her own bed. (Rev: BCCB 9/89; BL 10/1/89; SLJ 1/90)

**568** Rydell, Katy. *Wind Says Good Night* (PS–1). Illus. by David Jorgensen. 1994, Houghton $14.95 (0-395-60474-5). 42pp. This cumulative bedtime story tells how all the animals and birds cooperate so a little girl can go to sleep. (Rev: BCCB 5/94; BL 4/1/94; SLJ 4/94*)

**569** Rylant, Cynthia. *Night in the Country* (PS–1). Illus. by Mary Szilagyi. 1986, Macmillan LB $14.95 (0-02-777210-1); paper $4.95 (0-689-71473-4). 32pp. A description of the sounds of night in the country that makes the dark seem not at all frightening. (Rev: BCCB 9/86; BL 3/15/86; SLJ 5/86)

**570** Rymill, Linda R. *Good Knight* (PS–2). Illus. by G. Brian Karas. 1998, Holt $15.95 (0-8050-4129-X). The bedtime rituals of a young boy, ending with a story from his mother. (Rev: SLJ 3/98)

**571** Scarry, Patsy. *Patsy Scarry's Big Bedtime Storybook* (PS–1). Illus. by Cyndy Szekeres. 1990, Random $9.95 (0-679-80756-X). 72pp. Sixteen stories featuring Little Richard, a rabbit, and his friends.

**572** Schlein, Miriam. *Sleep Safe, Little Whale: A Lullaby* (PS–K). Illus. by Peter Sís. 1997, Greenwillow $14.95 (0-688-14757-7). 24pp. This soothing lullaby describes a number of baby animals that are in safe places when they go to sleep. (Rev: BL 11/15/97)

**573** Schotter, Roni. *Bunny's Night Out* (PS–1). Illus. by Margot Apple. 1989, Little, Brown $13.95 (0-316-77465-0). A bunny sneaks out at night and experiences adventures before coming home to his welcome bed. (Rev: SLJ 7/89)

**574** Shepperson, Rob. *The Sandman* (PS–1). Illus. 1989, Farrar $13.95 (0-374-36405-2). 32pp. Jay decides to stay up to see if the sandman really exists. (Rev: BL 12/1/89; SLJ 4/90)

**575** Spinelli, Eileen. *Naptime, Laptime* (PS). Illus. by Melissa Sweet. 1995, Scholastic $6.95 (0-590-48510-5). 24pp. A child wonders where various animals sleep and then decides it's best on grandmother's lap. (Rev: BCCB 2/96; BL 12/1/95; SLJ 2/96)

**576** Spooner, Michael. *A Moon in Your Lunch Box* (K–3). Illus. by Ib Ohlsson. 1995, Holt paper $4.95 (0-8050-3545-1). 67pp. This is a collection of original poems about the moon, night, and changes they produce. (Rev: BCCB 7–8/93; BL 6/1–15/93; SLJ 6/93) [811]

**577** Stafford, Kim R. *We Got Here Together* (PS–K). Illus. by Debra Frasier. 1994, Harcourt $13.95 (0-15-294891-0). 32pp. A short bedtime story that uses geometric patterns in cut-paper compositions. (Rev: BCCB 7–8/94; BL 5/1/94; SLJ 5/94)

**578** Stevenson, Harvey. *Big, Scary Wolf* (PS–1). Illus. 1997, Clarion $14.00 (0-395-74213-7). 32pp. At bedtime, a father reassures his daughter that there isn't a wolf hiding in her room. (Rev: BL 9/1/97; SLJ 8/97)

**579** Stevenson, James. *What's Under My Bed?* (1–3). Illus. by author. 1983, Greenwillow LB $15.93 (0-688-02327-4); Morrow paper $4.95 (0-688-09350-7). 32pp. A grandfather helps reduce his grandchildren's fears. A sequel is: *Worse Than Willy!* (1984).

**580** Stoddard, Sandol. *Turtle Time: A Bedtime Story* (PS–3). Illus. by Lynn Munsinger. 1995, Houghton $13.95 (0-395-56754-8). 32pp. A bedtime story about a little girl and her pet turtle. (Rev: BL 4/1/95; SLJ 4/95)

**581** Storm, Theodor. *Little Hobbin* (PS–1). Trans. by Anthea Bell. Illus. by Lisbeth Zwerger. 1995, North-South LB $15.88 (1-55858-461-7). 18pp. In this soothing bedtime lullaby, Little Hobbin takes a journey in his bed at night. (Rev: BL 2/1/96; SLJ 1/96)

**582** Szekeres, Cyndy. *The Deep Blue Sky Twinkles with Stars* (PS–K). Illus. 1998, Scholastic $12.95 (0-590-69198-8). 40pp. This bedtime book shows 5 young rabbits getting ready for bed and a story from dad. (Rev: BL 2/15/98; SLJ 3/98)

**583** Szekeres, Cyndy. *Good Night, Sammy* (PS). Illus. by author. 1985, Western $3.50 (0-307-12238-7). A little fox gets ready for a good night's sleep. (Rev: BL 12/1/85; SLJ 3/86)

**584** Tafuri, Nancy. *I Love You, Little One* (PS–1). Illus. 1998, Scholastic $15.95 (0-590-92159-2). 32pp. In this bedtime story, different animal mothers try to tell their children how much they love them. (Rev: BL 2/1/98; SLJ 3/98)

**585** Thomas, Shelley M. *Putting the World to Sleep* (PS–1). Illus. by Bonnie Christensen. 1995, Houghton $13.95 (0-395-71283-1). 32pp. Universal bedtime customs and nocturnal conditions around the world are celebrated in this nighttime book. (Rev: BL 11/15/95; SLJ 10/95*)

**586** Titherington, Jeanne. *Baby's Boat* (PS). Illus. 1992, Greenwillow LB $15.93 (0-688-08556-3). 24pp. A gentle, loving rhyme in a well-designed and well-illustrated picture book. (Rev: BL 5/15/92*; SLJ 4/92*)

**587** Tyers, Jenny. *When It Is Night, When It Is Day* (PS–2). Illus. 1996, Houghton $14.95 (0-395-71546-6). 32pp. The behavior of various animals at night is explored in this charming bedtime book. (Rev: BL 3/1/96; SLJ 4/96)

**588** Vulliamy, Clara. *Good Night, Baby* (PS). Illus. by author. 1996, Candlewick $4.99 (1-56402-817-8). A board book featuring a blond, blue-eyed baby being put to bed. Also use *Wide Awake!* (1996). (Rev: SLJ 6/96)

**589** Waddell, Martin. *Can't You Sleep, Little Bear?* (PS). Illus. by Barbara Firth. 1992, Candlewick $15.99 (1-56402-007-X). 32pp. Even lanterns don't comfort Little Bear, who is scared of the dark, until Father Bear offers the comfort of his arms. (Rev: BCCB 4/92; BL 3/1/92*; SLJ 1/92*)

**590** Wahl, Jan. *Humphrey's Bear* (PS–1). Illus. by William Joyce. 1987, Holt $15.95 (0-8050-0332-0); paper $5.95 (0-8050-1169-2). 32pp. Father thinks Humphrey is too old to sleep with a toy bear, but he doesn't know of their great adventures. (Rev: BCCB 6/87; BL 5/15/87; SLJ 8/87)

**591** Walter, Mildred P. *Darkness* (PS–2). Illus. by Marcia Jameson. 1995, Simon & Schuster $15.00 (0-689-80305-2). 32pp. The comforting aspects of darkness are sure to reassure people who are afraid of the dark. (Rev: BL 11/15/95; SLJ 11/95)

**592** Weiss, Nicki. *Where Does the Brown Bear Go?* (PS–K). Illus. by author. 1989, Puffin paper $5.99 (0-14-054181-0). 24pp. A bedtime story that asks where different animals go when night comes. (Rev: BCCB 3/89; BL 4/15/89; SLJ 3/89)

**593** Whitman, Candace. *The Night Is Like an Animal* (PS–1). Illus. 1995, Farrar $13.00 (0-374-35521-5). 32pp. Night, a little furry animal, goes to sleep close to a little child's dreams. (Rev: BCCB 10/95; BL 11/15/95; SLJ 11/95)

**594** Winthrop, Elizabeth. *Asleep in a Heap* (PS–1). Illus. by Mary Morgan. 1993, Holiday LB $15.95 (0-8234-0992-9). 32pp. Julia is much too busy to go to bed, but her antics send the rest of the family to sleep. (Rev: BL 11/15/93; SLJ 1/94)

**595** Winthrop, Elizabeth. *Maggie and the Monster* (PS–K). Illus. by Tomie dePaola. 1987, Holiday LB

$15.95 (0-8234-0639-3); paper $5.95 (0-8234-0698-9). 32pp. Every single night a small girl monster comes into Maggie's room. (Rev: BL 4/1/87; SLJ 5/87)

**596** Wood, Douglas. *Northwoods Cradle Song: From a Menominee Lullaby* (PS–K). Illus. by Lisa Desimini. 1996, Simon & Schuster paper $15.00 (0-689-80503-9). An American Indian song in which animals, including a mother and child, fall asleep at night, while around them the nocturnal world awakens. (Rev: HB 5–6/96; SLJ 5/96)

**597** Yaccarino, Dan. *Good Night, Mr. Night* (PS–3). Illus. 1997, Harcourt $15.00 (0-15-201319-9). 40pp. A gentle bedtime story in which Mr. Night enters a boy's bedroom to close his eyes. (Rev: BL 11/1/97; SLJ 10/97)

**598** Yolen, Jane. *Baby Bear's Bedtime Book* (PS–2). Illus. by Jane Dyer. 1990, Harcourt $14.95 (0-15-205120-1). 32pp. A baby bear asks his sitter to tell him a story at bedtime. (Rev: BL 3/15/90; SLJ 5/90)

**599** Yolen, Jane, ed. *Sleep Rhymes Around the World* (PS–4). Illus. 1994, Boyds Mills $16.95 (1-56397-243-3). 40pp. Twenty-one lullabies from as far away as Iran and Uganda are included in this handsome anthology that includes the text in English and the original language. (Rev: BL 2/1/94; SLJ 3/94) [808.81]

**600** Zerner, Amy, and Jessie S. Zerner. *The Dream Quilt* (K–4). Illus. 1995, Tuttle $19.95 (0-8048-1999-8). 96pp. Alex has dreams of adventure when he wraps himself up in his great-great-grandfather's quilt at bedtime. (Rev: BL 8/95; SLJ 6/95)

**601** Zolotow, Charlotte. *Sleepy Book* (PS–1). Illus. by Ilse Plume. 1988, HarperCollins LB $14.89 (0-06-026968-1). 32pp. Spare text tells how various birds, insects, and animals sleep. (Rev: BL 5/15/88; SLJ 12/88)

## Nursery Rhymes

**602** Ahlberg, Janet, and Allan Ahlberg. *Jeremiah in the Dark Woods* (1–3). Illus. by authors. 1990, Puffin paper $4.99 (0-14-032811-4). 48pp. Well-known nursery rhyme characters in different roles. (Rev: BL 5/1/87) [398.8]

**603** Anholt, Catherine, et al. *The Candlewick Book of First Rhymes* (PS–K). Illus. 1996, Candlewick $17.99 (0-7636-0015-6). 64pp. A selection of well-known rhymes taken from prestigious, previously published collections. (Rev: BL 11/15/96; SLJ 1/97) [811]

**604** Arnold, Tedd. *Mother Goose's Words of Wit and Wisdom: A Book of Months* (PS–2). Illus. 1990, Dial paper $14.95 (0-8037-0825-4). 64pp. Using cross-stitched samplers as illustrations, some 80 nursery rhymes are grouped, using months as topics. (Rev: BL 8/90*; SLJ 11/90) [398.8]

**605** Aylesworth, Jim. *The Completed Hickory Dickory Dock* (PS–K). Illus. by Eileen Christelow. 1994, Aladdin paper $5.99 (0-689-71862-4). 32pp. The "whole" story of what happened when the clock struck 12. (Rev: BL 10/1/90; SLJ 2/91) [811]

**606** Benjamin, Floella. *Skip Across the Ocean: Nursery Rhymes from Around the World* (PS–K). Illus. by Sheila Moxley. 1995, Orchard $15.95 (0-531-09455-3). 48pp. Thirty-two nursery rhymes from around the world, including several lullabies. (Rev: BL 10/1/95; SLJ 11/95)

**607** Bornstein, Harry, and Karen L. Saulnier. *Nursery Rhymes from Mother Goose Told in Signed English* (K–2). Illus. by Patricia Peters and Linda C. Tom. 1993, Gallaudet Univ. $14.95 (0-930323-99-8). 41pp. Fourteen rhymes with signing symbols for the deaf. (Rev: SLJ 6/93) [398.8]

**608** Brown, Marc. *Play Rhymes* (PS–1). Illus. 1993, Puffin paper $5.99 (0-140-54936-6). 32pp. There is humor, warmth, and coziness in these play rhymes. Also use: *Hand Rhymes* (1985). (Rev: BL 12/1/87; HB 11–12/87; SLJ 10/87) [398.8]

**609** Brown, Ruth. *Ladybug, Ladybug* (PS–1). Illus. by author. 1992, Puffin paper $4.99 (0-14-054543-3). 32pp. An extended version of the Mother Goose rhyme. (Rev: BL 11/1/88) [398.8]

**610** Chorao, Kay. *The Baby's Good Morning Book* (PS–K). Illus. by author. 1986, Dutton paper $13.95 (0-525-44257-X). 64pp. Familiar verses, such as Stevenson's "Time to Rise," that evoke the feeling of morning are included in this book for young children. (Rev: BCCB 10/86; BL 9/1/86; HB 11–12/86) [398.8]

**611** Cole, Joanna, and Stephanie Calmenson, eds. *Pat-a-Cake and Other Play Rhymes* (PS). Illus. by Alan Tiegreen. 1992, Morrow LB $13.93 (0-688-11039-8). 48pp. Lots of fun for the young reader in this charming collection. (Rev: BL 12/15/92; SLJ 12/92) [398.8]

**612** Conover, Chris. *Froggie Went a-Courting* (PS–1). Illus. by author. 1986, Farrar $15.00 (0-374-32466-2); paper $4.95 (0-374-42474-8). 32pp. A world in full-color miniature as the debonair Froggie woos Miss Mouse. (Rev: BL 10/1/86; SLJ 9/86) [398.8]

**613** Cook, Scott. *Mother Goose* (PS–K). Illus. 1994, Knopf LB $16.99 (0-679-90949-4). 44pp. Using soft, impressionistic paintings as illustrations, 51 rhymes are presented. (Rev: BL 11/15/94; SLJ 1/95)

**614** Cousins, Lucy. *Humpty Dumpty and Other Nursery Rhymes* (PS). Illus. 1996, Dutton paper $6.99 (0-525-45675-9). 14pp. This board book contains 11 well-known nursery rhymes. (Rev: BL 9/15/96; SLJ 1/97)

**615** Cousins, Lucy. *Jack and Jill and Other Nursery Rhymes* (PS). Illus. 1996, Dutton paper $5.99 (0-525-45676-7). 14pp. Eleven popular nursery rhymes are contained in this attractive board book. (Rev: BL 9/15/96; SLJ 1/97)

**616** Dabcovich, Lydia. *The Keys to My Kingdom: A Poem in Three Languages* (PS–2). Illus. 1992, Smithmark $3.98 (0-831-73052-8). 32pp. A girl and her dog travel to Grandma's from city to country in this trilingual — English, French, Spanish — retelling of the nursery rhyme. (Rev: BL 4/1/92; SLJ 4/92) [398.8]

**617** dePaola, Tomie. *The Comic Adventures of Old Mother Hubbard and Her Dog* (PS–3). Illus. by author. 1981, Harcourt $13.95 (0-15-219541-6); paper $4.95 (0-15-219542-4). 32pp. A handsome version of the classic nursery rhyme. [398.8]

**618** Downes, Belinda. *A Stitch in Rhyme: A Nursery Rhyme Sampler with Embroidered Illustrations* (PS–K). Illus. 1996, Knopf LB $19.99 (0-679-97679-5). 44pp. Many favorite nursery rhmes are pictured as embroidery samplers. (Rev: BL 11/1/96; SLJ 12/96) [398.8]

**619** Emerson, Sally, comp. *Nursery Rhyme Songbook with Easy Music to Play for Piano and Guitar* (PS–K). Illus. by Colin Maclean and Moira Maclean. 1995, Kingfisher paper $9.95 (1-85697-635-1). 72pp. A collection of nursery rhymes accompanied by easy-to-play scoring for piano and guitar. (Rev: SLJ 3/93) [784]

**620** Emerson, Sally, ed. *The Nursery Treasury: A Collection of Baby Games, Rhymes, and Lullabies* (PS). Illus. by Moira Maclean and Colin Maclean. 1988, Doubleday $22.50 (0-385-24650-1). 128pp. All sorts of songs and rhymes for young children. (Rev: BL 11/1/88; SLJ 1/89) [398.8]

**621** *Five Little Ducks: An Old Rhyme* (PS–K). Illus. by Pamela Paparone. 1995, North-South LB $15.88 (1-55858-474-9). 30pp. Though they wander into the woods during the day, the 5 little ducks always return home to their mother at night. (Rev: BL 12/15/95)

**622** Foreman, Michael. *Michael Foreman's Mother Goose* (PS–K). Illus. by author. 1991, Harcourt $20.00 (0-15-255820-9). 160pp. A rewarding visual tour of nursery rhymes. (Rev: BL 9/15/91; SLJ 10/91*) [398.8]

**623** Galdone, Paul. *Three Little Kittens* (2–4). Illus. by author. 1986, Houghton $15.00 (0-89919-426-5); paper $5.95 (0-89919-796-5). 32pp. A lively reworking of the old nursery rhyme. (Rev: BL 10/1/86; SLJ 12/86) [398.8]

**624** Hale, Sarah Josepha. *Mary Had a Little Lamb* (PS–1). Illus. by Tomie dePaola. 1984, Holiday LB $15.95 (0-8234-0509-5). 32pp. A nicely illustrated version of this nursery rhyme. Another recommend-

ed edition is illustrated by Bruce McMillan (Scholastic, 1990). [398.8]

**625** Hale, Sarah Josepha. *Mary Had a Little Lamb* (PS–1). Illus. by Salley Mavor. 1995, Orchard LB $16.99 (0-531-08725-5). 32pp. An effective version of the famous rhyme using collages for illustrations. (Rev: BCCB 5/95; BL 5/15/95; HB 3–4/95, 7–8/95, 11–12/95; SLJ 6/95*) [811]

**626** Hallworth, Grace, ed. *Down by the River: Afro-Caribbean Rhymes, Games, and Songs for Children* (PS–1). Illus. by Caroline Binch. 1996, Scholastic $16.95 (0-590-69320-4). 40pp. More than 20 playground rhymes from the Caribbean are included in this joyful book illustrated with watercolors. (Rev: BCCB 1/97; BL 10/15/96; SLJ 12/96) [811]

**627** Harbour, Elizabeth. *A First Picture Book of Nursery Rhymes* (PS–2). Illus. 1996, Viking paper $12.99 (0-670-85030-6). 32pp. With soft, delicate illustrations, this book is a fine collection of the most popular nursery rhymes. (Rev: BL 4/15/96; SLJ 8/96) [398.8]

**628** Hawkins, Colin, and Jacqui Hawkins. *Hey Diddle Diddle* (PS). Illus. by authors. 1992, Candlewick $6.95 (1-56402-014-2). This board book contains 5 attractively illustrated rhymes. Five more are found in: *Humpty Dumpty* (1992). (Rev: SLJ 5/92) [398.8]

**629** Hayes, Sarah. *This Is the Bear* (PS). Illus. by Helen Craig. 1993, HarperCollins LB $11.89 (0-397-32171-6); Candlewick paper $2.50 (0-06-443103-7). 32pp. Written in "House That Jack Built" style, the story of the bear named Fred who is taken to the local dump and awaits rescue. A reissue. A sequel is: *This Is the Bear and the Picnic Lunch* (1989). (Rev: BL 4/1/86; SLJ 9/86) [398.8]

**630** Heller, Nicholas. *This Little Piggy* (PS–K). Illus. by Sonja Lamut. 1997, Greenwillow LB $14.93 (0-688-15175-2). 24pp. This reworking of the "This Little Piggy" rhyme adds humorous modern touches. (Rev: BL 2/15/97; SLJ 5/97)

**631** Hennessy, B. G. *The Missing Tarts* (PS–K). Illus. by Tracey Campbell Pearson. 1989, Viking $12.95 (0-670-82039-3). 32pp. Clever version of the familiar rhyme. (Rev: BL 2/1/89; HB 3–4/89; SLJ 4/89) [398.8]

**632** *Hey Diddle Diddle* (PS–K). Illus. by Marilyn Janovitz. 1992, Hyperion LB $6.89 (1-56282-169-5). This book is illustrated with watercolors that humorously reproduce the old nursery rhyme. (Rev: SLJ 8/92) [398.8]

**633** *Hickory Dickory Dock and Other Nursery Rhymes* (PS–1). Illus. by Carol Jones. 1992, Houghton $10.95 (0-395-60834-1). 48pp. Eleven familiar nursery rhymes are illustrated, with 4 pages devoted to a single rhyme, each ending with a circular hole that leads to the next rhyme. (Rev: BL 3/1/92; SLJ 6/92) [398.8]

**634** Hopkins, Lee Bennett. *Animals from Mother Goose* (PS–2). Illus. by Kathryn Hewitt. 1989, Harcourt $6.95 (0-15-200406-8). 28pp. In this puzzle book, questions about animals in Mother Goose rhymes are answered by lifting page flaps. A companion volume is: *People from Mother Goose: A Question Book* (1989). (Rev: BL 11/1/89; SLJ 1/90) [398.8]

**635** *If All the Seas Were One Sea* (PS–1). Illus. by Janina Domanska. 1987, Macmillan LB $15.00 (0-02-732540-7). 32pp. First published in 1971, this nursery rhyme is given new dimensions by swirling illustrations. A 1972 Caldecott Honor Book. [398.8]

**636** Ivimey, John W. *The Complete Story of the Three Blind Mice* (PS–K). Illus. by Paul Galdone. 1987, Houghton $13.95 (0-89919-481-8). 32pp. A collection of antique British stories in this illustrator's last book. (Rev: BL 11/1/87)

**637** *Little Robin Redbreast: A Mother Goose Rhyme* (PS–1). Illus. by Shari Halpern. 1994, North-South LB $14.88 (1-55858-248-7). 32pp. The old nursery rhyme is given new life in this large-print edition with illustrations of collages with acrylics. (Rev: BL 3/15/94; SLJ 7/94)

**638** Lobel, Arnold. *Whiskers and Rhymes* (PS–3). Illus. by author. 1985, Morrow paper $4.95 (0-688-08291-2). 48pp. Original nursery rhymes featuring cats in old-fashioned costumes. (Rev: BCCB 10/85; BL 9/15/85; SLJ 10/85) [398.8]

**639** Lodge, Bernard. *There Was an Old Woman Who Lived in a Glove* (PS–K). Illus. 1992, Whispering Coyote LB $14.95 (1-879085-55-0). 25pp. A round, white-haired lady and her dove set out to see the world in this takeoff on the classic rhyme. (Rev: BL 10/15/92; SLJ 2/92) [398.8]

**640** Manson, Christopher. *The Tree in the Wood* (K–4). Illus. 1993, North-South LB $14.88 (1-55858-193-6). 28pp. This book illustrated by woodcuts is an adaptation of the nursery song "The Green Grass Grew All Around." (Rev: BL 3/1/93; SLJ 5/93) [398.8]

**641** Marks, Alan, ed. *Over the Hills and Far Away: A Book of Nursery Rhymes* (PS–1). Illus. 1994, North-South $19.95 (1-55858-285-1). 97pp. Sixty of the most popular Mother Goose rhymes are contained in this well-designed volume. (Rev: BL 9/1/94*; SLJ 10/94) [398.8]

**642** Marks, Alan. *Ring-a-Ring O'Roses and Ding, Dong Bell* (PS–K). Illus. by author. 1991, Picture Book $19.95 (0-88708-187-8). 96pp. A delightful collection of 76 familiar nursery rhymes with watercolor and ink illustrations. (Rev: BL 3/1/92; HB 5–6/92; SLJ 3/92) [398.8]

**643** Marshall, James. *James Marshall's Mother Goose* (PS–1). Illus. by author. 1979, Farrar $15.00 (0-374-33653-9); paper $6.95 (0-374-43723-8). 40pp. An ebullient, breezy treatment of traditional material. [398.8]

**644** Martin, Bill, Jr. *"Fire! Fire!" Said Mrs. McGuire* (PS–K). Illus. by Richard Egielski. 1996, Harcourt $15.00 (0-15-227562-2). 32pp. With humorous illustrations, the traditional nursery rhyme is given a modern touch. (Rev: BCCB 4/96; BL 3/15/96; SLJ 6/96) [398.8]

**645** Mother Goose. *The Baby's Lap Book* (PS–K). Illus. by Kay Chorao. 1990, Dutton $12.95 (0-525-26100-1). 64pp. Soft pencil drawings illustrate such familiar Mother Goose rhymes as "Jack Be Nimble" and "Old King Cole." [398.8]

**646** Mother Goose. *Gregory Griggs and Other Nursery Rhyme People* (PS–1). Illus. by Arnold Lobel. 1987, Macmillan paper $3.95 (0-688-07042-6). Out-of-the-ordinary nursery rhymes are included in this refreshingly different collection. Reissue of 1978 edition. [398.8]

**647** Mother Goose. *The House That Jack Built* (PS–1). Illus. by Elizabeth Falconer. 1990, Ideals $13.95 (0-8249-8459-5). A rebus format illustrates this familiar rhyme. (Rev: BL 12/1/90; SLJ 1/91) [398.8]

**648** Mother Goose. *If Wishes Were Horses: Mother Goose Rhymes* (K–1). Illus. by Susan Jeffers. 1987, Dutton paper $3.95 (0-525-44325-8). 32pp. Eight Mother Goose rhymes involving horses. [398.8]

**649** Mother Goose. *Mother Goose* (PS–2). Illus. by Brian Wildsmith. 1982, Oxford $22.95 (0-19-279611-9); paper $11.95 (0-19-272180-1). 80pp. Original artistic conceptions of the old rhymes with wonderful action in brilliantly colored animal and human figures. [398.8]

**650** Mother Goose. *Mother Goose: A Collection of Classic Nursery Rhymes* (PS–K). Illus. by Michael Hague. 1984, Holt $15.95 (0-8050-0214-6). 80pp. Forty-five nursery rhymes delicately illustrated. [398.8]

**651** Mother Goose. *The Random House Book of Mother Goose* (PS). Illus. by Arnold Lobel. 1986, Random LB $16.99 (0-394-96799-2). 176pp. Many moods and styles are reflected in the text and illustrations. (Rev: BCCB 1/87; BL 11/15/86; SLJ 12/86) [398.8]

**652** Mother Goose. *Real Mother Goose* (PS–3). Illus. by Blanche Fisher Wright. 1991, Checkerboard $12.95 (1-56288-041-1). 128pp. A reprint of the golden anniversary edition with introduction by May Hill Arbuthnot. [398.8]

**653** Mother Goose. *The Real Mother Goose Clock Book* (PS–1). Illus. by Blanche Fisher Wright. n.d.,

Checkerboard $6.95 (1-56288-095-0). 22pp. Time-related rhymes and a clock with movable hands help children associate the clock with daily routines. [398.8]

**654** Mother Goose. *Tomie dePaola's Mother Goose* (PS–1). Illus. by Tomie dePaola. 1985, Putnam $24.95 (0-399-21258-2). 127pp. Large format and lavish illustrations accompany these old favorites. (Rev: BCCB 11/85; BL 9/1/85; HB 1–2/86) [398.8]

**655** *Mother Goose: A Canadian Sampler* (PS–1). 1996, Groundwood $18.95 (0-88899-213-0). 63pp. Using illustrations from 29 of Canada's prominent picture book illustrators, this is a fine edition of Mother Goose rhymes. (Rev: SLJ 5/96)

**656** *Mother Goose: A Sampler* (PS–K). Illus. 1996, Douglas & McIntyre $18.95 (0-88899-260-2). 64pp. Twenty-eight modern Canadian artists illustrate favorite rhymes from Mother Goose. (Rev: BL 6/1–15/96)

**657** *Old Mother Hubbard and Her Wonderful Dog* (PS–K). Illus. by James Marshall. 1991, Farrar $13.95 (0-374-35621-1). 32pp. While Mother Hubbard tries to get some food for her dog, he is busy dancing a jig or playing a flute. (Rev: BL 6/15/91; HB 7–8/91; SLJ 8/91*) [398.8]

**658** Opie, Iona. *Humpty Dumpty and Other Rhymes* (PS–K). Illus. by Rosemary Wells. 1997, Candlewick $6.99 (0-7636-0353-8). 16pp. A board book version of popular Mother Goose rhymes featuring all sorts of animals. Also use *Little Boy Blue and Other Rhymes; Pussycat, Pussycat and Other Rhymes;* and *Wee Willie Winkie and Other Rhymes* (all 1997). (Rev: BL 3/1/98; SLJ 12/97)

**659** Opie, Iona, ed. *My Very First Mother Goose* (PS). Illus. by Rosemary Wells. 1996, Candlewick $19.99 (1-56402-620-5). 108pp. A basic collection of 60 standard rhymes illustrated with imagination and charm. (Rev: BCCB 12/96; BL 9/1/96; HB 11–12/96; SLJ 10/96*) [398.8]

**660** Opie, Peter, and Iona Opie. *Tail Feathers from Mother Goose: The Opie Rhyme Book* (2–5). Illus. 1988, Random $7.99 (0-517-05555-4). 124pp. A collection of more than 60 rhymes. (Rev: BCCB 10/88; SLJ 10/88) [398.8]

**661** Ormerod, Jan. *Jan Ormerod's To Baby with Love* (PS). Illus. 1994, Lothrop $16.00 (0-688-12558-1). 40pp. Five catchy nursery rhymes that are attractively illustrated. (Rev: BL 8/94; SLJ 10/94)

**662** Patz, Nancy, reteller. *Moses Supposes His Toeses Are Roses: And Seven Other Silly Old Rhymes* (K–3). Illus. by Nancy Patz. 1983, Harcourt $13.95 (0-15-255690-7); paper $6.00 (0-15-255691-5). 32pp. Eight wonderful nonsense rhymes are well illustrated. [398.8]

**663** Penney, Ian. *Ian Penney's Book of Nursery Rhymes* (PS–K). Illus. 1994, Abrams $14.95 (0-8109-3733-6). 40pp. Using pictures based on scenes from English formal gardens, this book presents 14 Mother Goose rhymes in lavish settings. (Rev: BL 11/15/94; SLJ 3/95)

**664** Petersham, Maud, and Miska Petersham. *The Rooster Crows: A Book of American Rhymes and Jingles* (K–2). Illus. by authors. 1969, Macmillan LB $14.95 (0-02-773100-6). 64pp. Rope skipping, counting, and other game rhymes form the bulk of this jaunty collection. A reissue of the 1946 Caldecott Medal winner. [398.8]

**665** *A Pocket Full of Posies* (PS–2). Illus. by Roy Gerrard. 1991, Farrar $9.95 (0-374-36032-4). This beautifully designed little book contains 10 favorite Mother Goose rhymes. (Rev: SLJ 12/91) [398.8]

**666** Prelutsky, Jack. *Beneath a Blue Umbrella* (PS–2). Illus. by Garth Williams. 1990, Greenwillow $15.95 (0-688-06429-9). 64pp. A miscellany of 28 gaily illustrated rhymes by Mother Goose; good read-aloud material. (Rev: BCCB 3/90; HB 3–4/90; SLJ 6/90) [398.8]

**667** Roffey, Maureen, and Bernard Lodge. *The Grand Old Duke of York* (PS–2). Illus. 1993, Whispering Coyote $13.95 (1-879085-79-8). 32pp. A book of familiar rhymes with added verses. (Rev: BL 3/15/93) [398.8]

**668** Scieszka, Jon. *The Book That Jack Wrote* (2–4). Illus. by Daniel Adel. 1994, Viking paper $14.99 (0-670-84330-X). 32pp. A zany cumulative story that is a takeoff on "The House that Jack Built." (Rev: BCCB 9/94; BL 11/1/94; SLJ 9/94)

**669** Sendak, Maurice. *Hector Protector, and As I Went over the Water* (K–1). Illus. by author. 1965, HarperCollins paper $7.95 (0-06-443237-8). 64pp. Two brief Mother Goose rhymes expanded with many drawings that make them both humorous and appealing. [398.8]

**670** Sewall, Marcia. *Animal Song* (PS–K). Illus. by author. 1988, Little, Brown $14.95 (0-316-78191-6). 128pp. An old chanting rhyme using animal names. (Rev: BL 3/15/88; SLJ 6–7/88) [398.8]

**671** Sharon, Lois, and Bram Staff. *Sharon, Lois and Bram's Mother Goose: Songs, Finger Rhymes, Tickling Verses, Games, and More* (PS–1). Illus. by Maryann Kovalski. 1986, Little, Brown $16.95 (0-316-78281-5); paper $9.95 (0-316-78282-3). 92pp. A lively collection, including modern poems and songs and well-known selections. (Rev: BL 4/1/86; SLJ 8/86) [398.8]

**672** Sutherland, Zena, ed. *The Orchard Book of Nursery Rhymes* (PS–1). Illus. by Faith Jaques. 1990, Orchard $22.95 (0-531-05903-0). 88pp. A collection of 72 familiar and lesser-known rhymes.

(Rev: BCCB 10/90; BL 9/1/90; HB 1–2/91; SLJ 9/90*) [398.8]

**673** *Teddy Bear, Teddy Bear: A Classic Action Rhyme* (PS). Illus. by Michael Hague. 1993, Morrow LB $13.93 (0-688-12085-7). 32pp. A sweet version of the traditional rhyme. (Rev: BL 3/15/93; SLJ 5/93) [398.8]

**674** *The Three Little Pigs* (PS). Illus. by Terri Super. 1984, Putnam $3.95 (0-448-10214-5). 18pp. A favorite nursery rhyme retold in traditional fashion with color illustrations and sturdy binding. [398.8]

**675** *Twinkle, Twinkle: An Animal Lover's Mother Goose* (PS–1). Illus. by Bobbi Fabian. 1997, Dutton paper $14.99 (0-525-45906-5). 40pp. Photos of animals are used to illustrate this unusual Mother Goose album. (Rev: BL 12/1/97; SLJ 10/97)

**676** Willebeck le Mair, Henriette. *Granny's Little Rhyme Book: A Collection of Favorite Nursery Rhymes* (PS–K). Illus. by author. 1990, Putnam $6.95 (0-399-22174-3). 24pp. This small book contains 10 rhymes illustrated by the famous Dutch artist. (Rev: BL 6/1/90) [398.8]

**677** Wood, Jakki. *Fiddle-i-fee* (PS–1). Illus. 1994, Bradbury paper $14.95 (0-02-793396-2). 32pp. A lively version of the nursery rhyme that begins "I had a cat; and the cat pleased me." (Rev: BL 6/1–15/94)

**678** Yolen, Jane, ed. *The Lap-Time Song and Play Book* (PS). Illus. by Margot Tomes. 1989, Harcourt $15.95 (0-15-243588-3). 32pp. A collection of 16 nursery games and songs with a history for each and simple piano arrangements. (Rev: BL 10/1/89; HB 11–12/89; SLJ 10/89) [782.42]

**679** Yolen, Jane, and Adam Stemple. *Jane Yolen's Mother Goose Songbook* (PS–2). Illus. by Rosekrans Hoffman. 1992, Boyds Mills LB $16.95 (1-878093-52-5). 96pp. This Mother Goose collection, with brief folklore and history notes for each rhyme, is attractive to older children. (Rev: BL 12/15/92; HB 3–4/93) [398.8]

**680** Ziefert, Harriet, ed. *Mother Goose Math* (PS–1). Illus. by Emily Bolam. 1997, Viking paper $14.99 (0-670-87569-4). 32pp. This charming picture book contains nursery rhymes that deal with numbers, like "One, two, buckle my shoe." (Rev: BCCB 7–8/97; BL 6/1–15/97; SLJ 2/98)

## Stories without Words

**681** Aliki. *Tabby* (PS–1). Illus. 1995, HarperCollins LB $13.89 (0-06-024916-1). 32pp. A wordless story about the first year in a kitten's life. (Rev: BL 7/95; HB 7–8/95; SLJ 8/95)

**682** Anderson, Lena. *Bunny Bath* (PS–K). Illus. 1990, R&S $3.95 (91-29-59652-1). In this wordless book, a boy and his bunny prepare to take a bath. Also use: *Bunny Surprise* (1990). (Rev: SLJ 11/90)

**683** Anderson, Lena. *Bunny Box* (PS). Illus. 1991, Farrar $3.95 (91-29-59858-3). Like its companion *Bunny Fun* (1991), this wordless book tells about a preschooler and his friends, a mother rabbit and her bunny. (Rev: SLJ 9/91)

**684** Anderson, Lena. *Bunny Party* (PS). Illus. by author. 1989, Farrar $3.95 (91-29-59134-1). A child and his bunny play together in this wordless story from Sweden. Also use: *Bunny Story* (1989). (Rev: HB 7–8/89; SLJ 6/89)

**685** Aruego, Jose. *Look What I Can Do!* (K–2). Illus. by author. 1971, Macmillan paper $4.95 (0-689-71205-7). 32pp. Almost wordless picture book about the antics that result when one caribou challenges another.

**686** Baker, Jeannie. *Window* (3–5). Illus. 1991, Greenwillow LB $15.93 (0-688-08918-6). 24pp. The changes from a rural to an urban setting are traced in the changes seen through a window. (Rev: BCCB 3/91; BL 4/15/91; HB 5–6/91; SLJ 3/91*)

**687** Bang, Molly. *The Grey Lady and the Strawberry Snatcher* (PS–1). Illus. by author. 1984, Macmillan $16.00 (0-02-708140-0). 48pp. The snatcher tries to get the strawberries from the Grey Lady.

**688** Banyai, Istvan. *Zoom* (1–3). Illus. 1995, Viking paper $13.99 (0-670-85804-8). 64pp. A clever picture book that begins with small objects and zooms to larger perspectives. (Rev: BCCB 2/95; BL 2/1/95; SLJ 3/95)

**689** Blake, Quentin. *Clown* (PS–1). Illus. 1996, Holt $15.95 (0-8050-4399-3). 32pp. A wordless book in which a discarded toy clown has amazing adventures alone in a big city. (Rev: BL 4/15/96; HB 7–8/96; SLJ 5/96)

**690** Blue, Rose. *Good Yontif: A Picture Book of the Jewish Year* (K–2). Illus. by Lynne Feldman. 1997, Millbrook $16.95 (0-7613-0142-9). A wordless book that shows how a family celebrates such Jewish holy days as Rosh Hashanah, Yom Kippur, Purim, Passover, and Shabbat. (Rev: SLJ 3/97)

**691** Briggs, Raymond. *The Snowman* (K–3). Illus. by author. 1978, Random $17.00 (0-394-83973-0); paper $7.99 (0-394-88466-3). 32pp. A small boy has adventures with the snowman he has made.

**692** Carle, Eric. *Do You Want to Be My Friend?* (PS–K). Illus. by author. 1971, HarperCollins LB $14.89 (0-690-01137-7); paper $5.95 (0-06-443127-4). 32pp. The end of an animal's tail appears on each page, and the child must guess the animal before turning the page to see the front end.

**693** Collington, Peter. *The Tooth Fairy* (K–3). Illus. 1995, Knopf $17.00 (0-679-87168-3). 32pp. A wordless picture book about a tooth fairy's busy night. (Rev: BCCB 11/95; BL 10/1/95; SLJ 11/95)

**694** Crews, Donald. *Truck* (1–3). Illus. by author. 1980, Greenwillow LB $15.93 (0-688-84244-5); Morrow paper $4.95 (0-688-10481-9). 32pp. The picture book that traces a truck trip from loading dock to its San Francisco destination.

**695** Cristini, Ermanno, and Luigi Puricelli. *In My Garden* (PS–2). Illus. by authors. 1991, Picture Book paper $12.95 (0-907234-05-4). 28pp. A journey across a garden where a variety of plants, animals, and insects live.

**696** Day, Alexandra. *Carl's Masquerade* (PS–1). Illus. 1992, Farrar $12.95 (0-374-31094-7). 32pp. Carl, the rottweiler baby-sitter, takes his young charge and follows its parents to a masquerade ball. (Rev: BCCB 12/92; BL 2/1/93; SLJ 11/92)

**697** dePaola, Tomie. *The Hunter and the Animals: A Wordless Picture Book* (K–3). Illus. by author. 1981, Holiday LB $16.95 (0-8234-0397-1); paper $6.95 (0-8234-0428-5). 32pp. A hunter lost in the forest is helped by the animals.

**698** Geisert, Arthur. *Oink Oink* (PS–2). Illus. 1993, Houghton $13.95 (0-395-64048-2). 32pp. This saga of 8 piglets on an adventure uses only the word oink. (Rev: BL 3/1/93; HB 5–6/93; SLJ 6/93)

**699** Goodall, John S. *Creepy Castle* (PS–K). Illus. by author. 1992, Smithmark $4.98 (0-831-74679-3). 60pp. Depicted in a medieval setting, this concerns the adventures of 2 mice who get locked in a castle, are rescued, and foil the villain.

**700** Goodall, John S. *Paddy Under Water* (PS–1). Illus. by author. 1991, Harcourt $12.95 (0-689-50297-4). 32pp. A cleverly designed book without words that tells of the aquatic adventures of a young pig. A reissue.

**701** Hutchins, Pat. *Changes, Changes* (PS–1). Illus. by author. 1971, Macmillan LB $13.95 (0-02-745870-9). 32pp. A wooden doll couple rearrange a set of building blocks to suit different situations.

**702** Jenkins, Steve. *Looking Down* (PS–2). Illus. 1995, Houghton $14.95 (0-395-72665-4). 32pp. A wordless picture book that starts with a view of earth from space and ends with a close-up of a ladybug. (Rev: BL 8/95; HB 11–12/95; SLJ 9/95)

**703** Lionel. *Peekaboo Babies* (PS–K). Illus. 1997, Orchard $12.95 (0-531-30016-1). 12pp. A counting book that uses tabs and flaps to find baby animals. (Rev: BL 12/15/97)

**704** McCully, Emily Arnold. *Picnic* (PS–2). Illus. by author. 1984, HarperCollins LB $15.89 (0-06-024100-4). 32pp. An eventful picnic for the mouse family.

**705** McCully, Emily Arnold. *School* (PS–1). Illus. by author. 1987, HarperCollins LB $14.89 (0-06-024133-0); paper $4.95 (0-06-443233-5). 32pp. The littlest mouse decides to follow her siblings to school to see what it's like. (Rev: BL 9/1/87; SLJ 10/87)

**706** Mariotti, Mario. *Hands Off!* (PS–3). Illus. 1990, Kane/Miller $10.95 (0-916291-29-4). This wordless picture book depicts photos of a soccer game in action. (Rev: SLJ 1/91)

**707** Mariotti, Mario. *Hanimations* (PS–3). Illus. 1989, Kane/Miller $10.95 (0-916291-22-7). In this wordless book, hands are transformed into all kinds of familiar animals and birds. (Rev: SLJ 1/90)

**708** Martin, Rafe. *Will's Mammoth* (K–2). Illus. by Stephen Gammell. 1989, Putnam $15.95 (0-399-21627-8). 32pp. A boy named Will travels back in time to when mammoths and saber-toothed tigers roamed the earth. (Rev: BCCB 11/89; BL 9/15/89; HB 3–4/90*; SLJ 10/89*)

**709** Mayer, Mercer. *A Boy, a Dog and a Frog* (PS–1). Illus. by author. 1967, Dial LB $9.89 (0-8037-0767-3); paper $3.50 (0-8037-0769-X). 32pp. Engaging pen-and-ink drawings will delight youngsters into supplying the story line for the boy and his dog on their frog hunt. Sequel: *Frog, Where Are You?* (1969). Also from the same author and publisher: *A Boy, a Dog, a Frog and a Friend* (1971); *Frog on His Own* (1973); *Frog Goes to Dinner* (1974); *One Frog Too Many* by Mercer Mayer and Marianna Mayer (1975).

**710** Mayer, Mercer. *Hiccup* (PS–1). Illus. by author. 1976, Dial paper $3.95 (0-8037-3590-1). 32pp. A female hippo with a severe case of hiccups is helped by her male companion in this wordless tale.

**711** Muller, Gerda. *Circle of Seasons* (PS–1). Illus. 1995, Dutton paper $13.99 (0-525-45394-6). 48pp. In this wordless picture book, the joys and characteristics of the 4 seasons are celebrated. (Rev: BL 11/15/95; SLJ 3/96)

**712** Oxenbury, Helen. *Dressing* (PS). Illus. by author. 1981, Simon & Schuster $4.95 (0-671-42113-1). 14pp. For 1- and 2-year olds, a wordless book that shows common objects. Also part of this series is: *Working* (1981).

**713** Popov, Nikolai. *Why?* (1–4). Illus. by author. 1996, North-South LB $15.88 (1-55858-535-4). A wordless antiwar fable about a frog that is annoyed by a troublesome mouse. (Rev: BCCB 6/96; SLJ 4/96)

**714** Rohmann, Eric. *Time Flies* (PS–3). Illus. 1994, Crown $17.00 (0-517-59598-2). 32pp. A wordless fantasy about a bird's adventures in a natural-history museum. (Rev: BL 3/1/94; SLJ 5/94)

**715** Schories, Pat. *Mouse Around* (PS–1). Illus. 1991, Farrar $13.00 (0-374-35080-9). 40pp. A young mouse finds he is transported in surprising ways when he sets out to see the town. (Rev: BCCB 7–8/91; BL 6/15/91; SLJ 8/91)

**716** Tafuri, Nancy. *Early Morning in the Barn* (PS). Illus. by author. 1983, Greenwillow LB $16.93 (0-688-02329-0). 24pp. Only the sounds of farm animals are heard in the pages of this book.

**717** Tafuri, Nancy. *Follow Me!* (PS–1). Illus. 1990, Greenwillow LB $15.93 (0-688-08774-4). 24pp. A young sea lion, under the watchful eyes of his mother, has an adventure following a crab on the beach. (Rev: BCCB 4/90; BL 6/1/90; HB 9–10/90; SLJ 4/90*)

**718** Tafuri, Nancy. *Junglewalk* (PS–K). Illus. by author. 1988, Greenwillow LB $15.93 (0-688-07183-X). 32pp. A bedtime story sends a young boy off to dreamland and adventures with a majestic tiger. (Rev: BL 3/1/88; HB 3–4/88)

**719** Turkle, Brinton. *Deep in the Forest* (PS–1). Illus. by author. 1976, Dutton paper $3.95 (0-525-44322-3). 32pp. In a reversal of the Goldilocks story, a mischievous bear tries the porridge, chairs, and beds.

**720** Van Allsburg, Chris. *The Mysteries of Harris Burdick* (1–8). Illus. by author. 1984, Houghton $17.95 (0-395-35393-9). 32pp. A group of pictures are presented and youngsters are asked to supply the stories.

**721** Ward, Lynd. *The Silver Pony: A Story in Pictures* (2–4). Illus. by author. 1973, Houghton $17.95 (0-395-14753-0); paper $6.95 (0-395-64377-5). Handsome pictures grace this story about a farm boy's imaginative adventures on a magnificent winged horse.

**722** Wiesner, David. *Free Fall* (PS–K). Illus. by author. 1988, Lothrop LB $16.93 (0-688-05584-2); paper $4.95 (0-688-10990-X). 32pp. An atlas falls from a boy's lap as he sleeps and opens his imagination to exotic places. (Rev: BCCB 5/88; BL 6/1/88; SLJ 6–7/88)

**723** Winter, Paula. *The Bear and the Fly: A Story* (PS). Illus. by author. 1981, Crown LB $12.95 (0-517-52605-0). The havoc caused when a fly interrupts the Bear family's dinner.

# Picture Books

## Imaginative Stories

### FANTASIES

**724** Ada, Alma F. *Dear Peter Rabbit* (PS–1). Illus. by Leslie Tryon. 1994, Atheneum $16.00 (0-689-31850-2). 48pp. A number of fairy tale characters like Goldilocks and Peter Rabbit write letters to each other in this clever picture book. (Rev: BCCB 4/94; BL 5/1/94; SLJ 7/94*)

**725** Ada, Alma F. *Jordi's Star* (PS–3). Illus. by Susan Gaber. 1996, Putnam $15.95 (0-399-22832-2). 32pp. A shepherd befriends a star whose reflection he sees every night in a pool. (Rev: BCCB 12/96; BL 12/1/96*; SLJ 12/96)

**726** Adinolfi, JoAnn. *The Egyptian Polar Bear* (PS–1). Illus. 1994, Houghton $14.95 (0-395-68074-3). 32pp. A lost polar bear finds himself in Egypt and a friend of the young pharaoh. (Rev: BL 11/1/94; SLJ 1/95)

**727** Adoff, Arnold. *Flamboyan* (PS–3). Illus. by Karen Barbour. 1988, Harcourt $14.95 (0-15-228404-4). 32pp. Named for the tree outside her window, red-haired Flamboyan yearns to fly. (Rev: BCCB 10/88; BL 10/15/88; SLJ 10/88)

**728** Agee, Jon. *The Incredible Painting of Felix Clousseau* (PS–3). Illus. by author. 1988, Farrar $15.00 (0-374-33633-4); paper $4.95 (0-374-43582-0). 32pp. A very laid-back artist is oblivious to the havoc his paintings cause. (Rev: BCCB 11/88; BL 11/1/88; HB 1–2/89)

**729** Ahlberg, Janet, and Allan Ahlberg. *Each Peach Pear Plum* (PS). Illus. by authors. 1985, Puffin paper $4.99 (0-14-050639-X). 32pp. A pictorial guessing game revealed in pictures and rhymes.

**730** Ahlberg, Janet, and Allan Ahlberg. *Funnybones* (PS–2). Illus. by authors. 1981, Greenwillow LB $14.93 (0-688-84238-0); Morrow paper $4.95 (0-688-09927-0). 32pp. Three skeletons set out one dark night to frighten somebody in town.

**731** Alborough, Jez. *Watch Out! Big Bro's Coming!* (PS–K). Illus. 1997, Candlewick $16.99 (0-7636-0130-6). 24pp. A little mouse warns the other animals that Big Bro is coming and all of them wonder what the fuss is about. (Rev: BL 9/1/97; SLJ 8/97)

**732** Alexander, Lloyd. *The House Gobbaleen* (K–3). Illus. by Diane Goode. 1995, Dutton paper $15.99 (0-525-45289-3). 40pp. Tooly believes that the little monster he invites into his house will bring him good luck. (Rev: BCCB 12/95; BL 7/95; SLJ 9/95*)

**733** Allen, Judy. *Whale* (K–3). Illus. by Tudor Humphries. 1993, Candlewick $15.95 (1-56402-160-2). 32pp. As Anya and her parents are in a boat, they witness a whale and her calf being saved by the ghosts of dead whales. (Rev: BCCB 5/93; BL 7/93)

**734** Amoss, Berthe. *Old Hannibal and the Hurricane* (K–2). Illus. by author. 1991, Smithmark $3.98 (0-8317-6949-1). To escape a terrible hurricane, Old Hannibal attaches wings to his rowboat. (Rev: SLJ 2/92)

**735** Anderson, Janet S. *The Key into Winter* (PS–3). Illus. by David Soman. 1994, Albert Whitman LB $15.95 (0-8075-4170-2). 32pp. In this fantasy, the keys that unlock the seasons are used to explain the coming of death to old people. (Rev: BCCB 4/94; BL 2/15/94; SLJ 4/94)

**736** Anderson, Joan. *Richie's Rocket* (1–3). Photos by George Ancona. 1993, Morrow LB $14.93 (0-688-11305-2). 32pp. Richie discovers that he really has blasted off into space in his cardboard spaceship. (Rev: BL 9/15/93; SLJ 10/93)

**737** Anholt, Catherine, and Laurence Anholt. *Come Back, Jack!* (PS–3). Illus. 1994, Candlewick $12.95 (1-56402-313-3). 32pp. A little girl follows her brother into a book, where they meet characters from 4 nursery rhymes. (Rev: BCCB 3/94; BL 6/1–15/94; SLJ 7/94)

**738** Appelt, Kathi. *Elephants Aloft* (1–3). Illus. by Keith Baker. 1993, Harcourt $13.95 (0-15-225384-X). 40pp. In this language book, various prepositions are introduced during a flight to Africa by 2 elephants in a hot-air balloon. (Rev: BL 12/15/93; SLJ 1/94)

**739** Appelt, Kathi. *A Red Wagon Year* (PS–1). Illus. by Laura M. Kvasnosky. 1996, Harcourt $11.00 (0-15-277991-4). 28pp. A journey through the 12 months on a red wagon that changes its role with the seasons. (Rev: BL 10/1/96; SLJ 12/96)

**740** Argueta, Manlio. *Magic Dogs of the Volcanoes: Los Perros Mágicos de los Volcanoes* (K–3). Illus. by Elly Simmons. 1990, Children's Book Pr. $15.50 (0-89239-064-6). 30pp. From El Salvador, this dual-language book tells the story of the magical dogs that live at the foot of volcanoes. (Rev: SLJ 2/91)

**741** Armour, Peter. *Stop That Pickle!* (K–3). Illus. by Andrew Shachat. 1993, Houghton $14.95 (0-395-66375-X). 32pp. The last pickle in the jar flees the deli and is pursued by a number of food items in this comic gem. (Rev: BL 1/1/94; SLJ 2/94)

**742** Armstrong, Jennifer. *King Crow* (K–4). Illus. by Eric Rohmann. 1995, Crown LB $16.99 (0-517-59635-0). 32pp. Cormac's kindness toward an injured crow is rewarded by a return of his kingdom. (Rev: BCCB 5/95; BL 7/95; SLJ 5/95)

**743** Armstrong, Jennifer. *The Snowball* (K–1). Illus. by Jean Pidgeon. 1996, Random paper $3.99 (0-679-86444-X). 32pp. A snowball gathers up children as it rolls down a hill. (Rev: BL 2/1/97)

**744** Armstrong, Jennifer. *Wan Hu Is in the Stars* (K–2). Illus. by Barry Root. 1995, Morrow LB $14.93 (0-688-12458-5). 32pp. Poet Wan Hu tries various schemes to fly to the stars and finally succeeds. (Rev: BCCB 7–8/95; BL 6/1–15/95; SLJ 7/95)

**745** Arnold, Tedd. *Green Wilma* (PS–3). Illus. by author. 1993, Dial LB $13.89 (0-8037-1314-2). 32pp. Wilma wakes up one morning to discover she is a green frog. (Rev: BCCB 2/93; BL 3/1/93; SLJ 5/93)

**746** Arnold, Tedd. *No Jumping on the Bed!* (PS–3). Illus. by author. 1987, Dial LB $13.89 (0-8037-0039-3). 32pp. Walter jumps so high and hard on his bed that he goes right through to the apartment below, and so on down . . . Also use: *Ollie Forgot* (1988). (Rev: BL 10/15/87; SLJ 10/87)

**747** Arnold, Tedd. *No More Water in the Tub!* (PS). Illus. 1995, Dial paper $14.89 (0-8037-1583-8). 32pp. When his bathtub comes away from the wall, William becomes the captain of a floating tub that explores different floors of his apartment building. (Rev: BCCB 9/95; BL 12/15/95; SLJ 10/95)

**748** Arnold, Tim. *The Winter Mittens* (2–4). Illus. 1988, Macmillan LB $13.95 (0-689-50449-7). 32pp. Addie uses the magic mittens she finds to make it snow. (Rev: BCCB 12/88; BL 12/15/88; HB 11–12/88)

**749** Auch, Mary Jane. *The Easter Egg Farm* (PS–2). Illus. 1992, Holiday LB $16.95 (0-8234-0917-1). 32pp. Humor and chaos infect a chicken ranch where the owner wears dangling earrings and trendy clothes and Pauline the hen lays "ugly" eggs. (Rev: BL 3/1/92*; SLJ 4/92)

**750** Auch, Mary Jane. *Monster Brother* (PS–2). Illus. 1994, Holiday LB $15.95 (0-8234-1095-1). 32pp. Rodney is visited by a monster every night, but his brother, Sidney, has a unique solution. (Rev: BCCB 11/94; BL 11/15/94; SLJ 11/94)

**751** Aylesworth, Jim. *My Sister's Rusty Bike* (K–3). Illus. by Richard Hull. 1996, Simon & Schuster $16.00 (0-689-31798-0). 32pp. A fantasy in which a boy meets unusual creatures as he travels American byways. (Rev: BL 11/15/96; SLJ 10/96)

**752** Babbitt, Natalie. *Bub; or, The Very Best Thing* (PS–1). Illus. 1994, HarperCollins $15.95 (0-06-205044-3). 32pp. A king and queen discover that the best way to raise their young prince is with plenty of love. (Rev: BCCB 6/94; BL 2/15/94; HB 5–6/94; SLJ 4/94)

**753** *Baby Bear's Treasury: 25 Stories for the Very, Very Young* (PS). Illus. 1995, Candlewick $19.99 (1-56402-655-8). 64pp. A fine collection of previously published stories and rhymes by famous authors and artists. (Rev: BL 12/15/95)

**754** Baker, Keith. *The Dove's Letter* (1–4). Illus. by author. 1993, Harcourt paper $6.00 (0-15-224134-5). 32pp. A dove finds an obviously lost letter and attempts to deliver it to the proper person. (Rev: BL 5/1/88; SLJ 7/88)

**755** Baker, Keith. *The Magic Fan* (PS–2). Illus. 1989, Harcourt $14.95 (0-15-250750-7). 32pp. Village people don't like Yoshi's magic bridge until it saves them from a tidal wave. (Rev: BCCB 2/90; BL 11/1/89; HB 1–2/90; SLJ 10/89*)

**756** Balian, Lorna. *Humbug Witch* (1–3). Illus. by author. 1992, Humbug LB $14.95 (1-881772-24-1). 32pp. A little witch doesn't seem to get the hang of witchcraft.

**757** Balian, Lorna. *Leprechauns Never Lie* (K–3). Illus. by author. 1994, Humbug LB $14.95 (1-881-77207-1). 32pp. Lazy Ninny Nanny is outwitted by a clever leprechaun.

**758** Balian, Lorna. *Wilbur's Space Machine* (PS–1). Illus. 1990, Holiday LB $19.95 (0-8234-0836-1). 32pp. Violet and Wilbur build a space machine to escape the world's pollution and an unwelcome guest, Googie. (Rev: BL 10/15/90; SLJ 2/91)

**759** Bang, Molly. *Delphine* (PS–1). Illus. by author. 1988, Morrow $12.95 (0-688-05636-9). 32pp. Delphine takes a wild ride down the mountain to the post office where Gram's gift awaits her. (Rev: BCCB 10/88; HB 9–10/88; SLJ 9/88)

**760** Bang, Molly. *One Fall Day* (PS–1). Illus. 1994, Greenwillow LB $14.93 (0-688-07016-7). 24pp. A group of toys act out the activities that a normal child would engage in during a day. (Rev: BCCB 10/94; BL 9/1/94; SLJ 10/94)

**761** Bang, Molly. *The Paper Crane* (PS–1). 1985, Greenwillow paper $4.95 (0-688-07333-6). 32pp. A paper crane left by a thankful stranger leads to good fortune for a restaurant owner down on his luck. (Rev: BCCB 3/86; BL 1/15/86; HB 1–2/86)

**762** Banks, Kate. *Alphabet Soup* (K–2). Illus. by Peter Sis. 1994, Knopf paper $4.99 (0-679-86723-6). 32pp. Instead of eating his alphabet soup, a little boy daydreams. (Rev: BL 11/1/88; SLJ 1/89)

**763** Banks, Kate. *Spider Spider* (K–1). Illus. by Georg Hallensleben. 1996, Farrar $14.00 (0-374-37151-2). A disturbing story about a boy who dreams of being a spider and is transformed into one. (Rev: SLJ 11/96)

**764** Bannerman, Helen. *The Story of Little Babaji* (PS–1). Illus. by Fred Marcellino. 1996, Harper-Collins LB $14.89 (0-06-205065-6). 72pp. An excellent new version of *Little Black Sambo,* now set in India and without racial slurs. (Rev: BL 9/1/96*; HB 9–10/96; SLJ 10/96)

**765** Banyai, Istvan. *REM: Rapid Eye Movement* (PS–4). Illus. 1997, Viking paper $14.99 (0-670-87492-2). 32pp. A series of engrossing pictures that are actually part of a boy's dream. (Rev: BCCB 4/97; BL 7/97; HB 5–6/97; SLJ 6/97)

**766** Barber, Antonia. *The Enchanter's Daughter* (K–3). Illus. by Errol LeCain. 1994, Farrar paper $5.95 (0-374-42143-9). 32pp. As the enchanter

grows older, he longs to find the secret of youth and his daughter yearns for a past she doesn't remember. (Rev: BCCB 11/88; BL 11/1/88; SLJ 12/88)

**767** Barrett, Judith. *Cloudy with a Chance of Meatballs* (K–3). Illus. by Ron Barrett. 1978, Macmillan $16.00 (0-689-30647-4); paper $4.99 (0-689-70749-5). 32pp. In the land of Chewandswallow, food falls from the skies.

**768** Barrett, Judith. *Pickles to Pittsburgh: The Sequel to Cloudy with a Chance of Meatballs* (K–2). Illus. by Ron Barrett. 1997, Simon & Schuster $16.00 (0-689-80104-1). The people of the town of Chewandswallow take all their excess food and distribute it around the world — for example, eggplants to Ecuador and pickles to Pittsburgh. (Rev: SLJ 11/97)

**769** Bartlett, T. C. *Tuba Lessons* (PS–3). Illus. by Monique Felix. 1997, Harcourt $18.00 (0-15-201643-0). 32pp. On his way to a music lesson, a boy travels through the woods on a path that looks like a music staff and, from a perch in a tree, sees animals that resemble notes. (Rev: BL 11/1/97; SLJ 11/97)

**770** Base, Graeme. *The Sign of the Seahorse: A Tale of Greed and High Adventure in Two Acts* (1–3). Illus. 1992, Abrams $19.95 (0-8109-3825-1). 48pp. A fable about undersea life that brings a lesson about the dangers of pollution. (Rev: BL 11/15/92; SLJ 11/92)

**771** Bateson-Hill, Margaret. *Lao Lao of Dragon Mountain* (K–3). Illus. by Francesca Pelizzoli. 1998, Larousse $14.95 (1-84089-035-5). 32pp. The story of Lao Lao and her beautiful cutouts is told in both English and Chinese. (Rev: BCCB 1/97; BL 12/15/96; SLJ 1/97)

**772** Baum, L. Frank. *The Wizard of Oz* (K–3). Illus. by Lisbeth Zwerger. 1996, North-South $19.95 (1-55858-638-5). 103pp. A Viennese artist reworks this classic tale with unusual, refreshing illustrations and an abridged text. (Rev: BL 10/15/96; SLJ 11/96*)

**773** Beck, Ian. *Emily and the Golden Acorn* (K–2). Illus. 1992, Simon & Schuster paper $14.00 (0-671-75979-5). Emily's favorite oak tree is transformed into a sailing ship. (Rev: SLJ 11/92)

**774** *Benjamin's First Book* (PS). Illus. 1997, Sterling $5.95 (0-8069-0389-9). 26pp. A board book that features photos of a delightful teddy bear named Benjamin. Also use *Benjamin's Toys* and *Shopping with Benjamin* (both 1997). (Rev: BL 2/1/98)

**775** Berger, Barbara Helen. *The Jewel Heart* (PS–3). Illus. 1994, Putnam $15.95 (0-399-22681-8). 28pp. The clown doll Gemino loses his jewel heart in the woods, and the ballerina Pavelle tries to help him. (Rev: BL 9/1/94; SLJ 10/94)

**776** Berger, Barbara Helen. *A Lot of Otters* (PS). Illus. by author. 1997, Philomel $16.99 (0-399-

22910-8). At night, a toddler climbs into a cardboard box with his book and sails off into waters filled with fun-loving otters. (Rev: SLJ 9/97*)

**777** *Big Bear's Treasury: A Children's Anthology* (K–3). Illus. 1992, Candlewick $19.95 (1-56402-113-0). 93pp. This is volume 2 of an oversized book that contains picture-book stories, excerpts from longer works, and verse by well-known British writers. Also use volume 1, with the same title (1992). (Rev: BCCB 4/92; BL 2/1/93; SLJ 9/92)

**778** Birchmore, Daniel A. *The White Curtain* (PS–2). Illus. by Gail Lucas. 1997, Cucumber Island Storytellers $15.95 (1-887813-09-8). Gusts of wind blow a white curtain outdoors, where it can enjoy exploring the world. (Rev: SLJ 2/98)

**779** Blake, Robert J. *Spray* (1–4). Illus. 1996, Putnam $15.95 (0-399-22770-9). 32pp. When Justin gets lost in his boat, the ghost of the mariner Joshua Slocum brings him to safety. (Rev: BL 6/1–15/96; SLJ 6/96)

**780** Blos, Joan W. *Martin's Hats* (K–2). Illus. by Marc Simont. 1987, Morrow paper $4.95 (0-688-07039-6). 32pp. Each of Martin's hats brings him a new adventure.

**781** Blos, Joan W. *Nellie Bly's Monkey* (K–2). Illus. by Catherine Stock. 1996, Morrow LB $14.93 (0-688-12678-2). 40pp. Nellie Bly's exciting trip around the world in 1890 is recalled by the monkey McGinty, who accompanied her. (Rev: BCCB 5/96; BL 2/15/96; SLJ 4/96)

**782** Boesky, Amy. *Planet Was* (K–3). Illus. by Nadine Bernard Westcott. 1990, Little, Brown $14.95 (0-316-10084-6). 32pp. Young Prince Hierre introduces change into the life of Planet Was. (Rev: BL 12/1/90; SLJ 1/91)

**783** Bontemps, Arna, and Langston Hughes. *The Pasteboard Bandit* (K–3). Illus. by Peggy Turley. 1997, Oxford $16.95 (0-19-511476-0). 96pp. A fantasy written in the 1930s about the friendship between a Mexican boy and an American boy and of their pasteboard carnival toy. (Rev: BL 1/1–15/98; HB 11–12/97; SLJ 1/98)

**784** Boo, Marcial. *The Butterfly Kiss* (PS–1). Illus. by Tim Vyner. 1995, Harcourt $14.00 (0-15-200841-1). 32pp. A kiss in the shape of a butterfly finally finds a home with a child and his grandfather at bedtime. (Rev: BL 12/15/95; SLJ 2/96)

**785** Bowden, Joan. *Why the Tides Ebb and Flow* (1–3). Illus. by Marc Brown. 1979, Houghton $16.00 (0-395-28378-7); paper $5.95 (0-395-54952-3). 48pp. In her search for a hut, Old Woman causes the tides.

**786** Boyd, Lizi. *Willy and the Cardboard Boxes* (PS). Illus. 1999, NAL paper $3.95 (0-140-54342-2). 32pp. In his father's office, a small boy imagines all

sorts of adventures when he plays with large cardboard boxes. (Rev: BL 6/15/91; SLJ 8/91)

**787** Brett, Jan. *Trouble with Trolls* (PS–3). Illus. 1992, Putnam $15.95 (0-399-22336-3). 32pp. In this Scandinavian-type tale, Treva has trouble with trolls when they try to steal her dog Tuffi. (Rev: BCCB 12/92; BL 9/1/92*; SLJ 9/92)

**788** Briggs, Raymond. *The Bear* (PS–3). Illus. 1994, Random LB $20.99 (0-679-96944-6). 36pp. Tilly is befriended by a white bear that crawls into her bedroom when she is asleep. (Rev: BCCB 3/95; BL 2/1/95; SLJ 2/95)

**789** Briggs, Raymond. *Jim and the Beanstalk* (PS–2). Illus. by author. 1997, Putnam paper $5.95 (0-698-11577-5). 40pp. A humorous, fast-moving sequel to the well-known tale.

**790** Bright, Robert. *Georgie and the Robbers* (K–2). Illus. by author. 1963, Scholastic paper $1.50 (0-590-08725-8). 28pp. Adventures of Georgie, the friendly little ghost who haunted the Whittaker's attic. Another title by the same author and publisher: *Georgie* (1944).

**791** Brown, Jeff. *Flat Stanley* (1–3). Illus. by Tomi Ungerer. 1964, HarperCollins LB $15.89 (0-06-020681-0). 64pp. A falling bulletin board flattens Stanley so he is only one-half-inch thick.

**792** Brown, Jeff. *Invisible Stanley* (2–3). Illus. by Steve Bjorkman. 1996, HarperTrophy paper $3.95 (0-06-442029-9). 81pp. When Stanley suddenly becomes invisible, he performs many humanitarian acts, including foiling a bank robbery. (Rev: SLJ 12/96)

**793** Brown, M. K. *Let's Go Swimming with Mr. Sillypants* (PS–1). Illus. by author. 1992, Crown paper $5.99 (0-517-59030-1). 32pp. Mr. Sillypants is so anxious about his first swimming lesson that he dreams he turns into a fish and then into a fierce sea creature. (Rev: BL 8/86; SLJ 2/87)

**794** Brown, Marc. *Witches Four* (PS–1). Illus. by author. 1980, Parents LB $5.95 (0-8193-1014-X). 48pp. Four witches lose their magic hats and they are found by 4 homeless cats.

**795** Brown, Margaret Wise. *David's Little Indian* (K–2). Illus. by Remy Charlip. 1989, Hopscotch $10.95 (0-929077-02-4). 48pp. David finds a little Indian who comes to live with him and together they share a friendship. A reissue.

**796** Buehner, Caralyn. *A Job for Wittilda* (K–3). Illus. by Mark Buehner. 1993, Dial LB $13.89 (0-8037-1150-6). 32pp. A witch with 47 cats decides she must find a job to feed them. (Rev: BL 7/93)

**797** Buffett, Jimmy, and Savannah Buffett. *The Jolly Mon* (2–5). Illus. by Lambert Davis. 1988, Harcourt $16.00 (0-15-240530-5). 32pp. The story of Jolly

Mon in the Caribbean whose musical voice gains him a magical guitar. (Rev: BCCB 6/88; BL 4/1/88; SLJ 7/88)

**798** Buffett, Jimmy, and Savannah Buffett. *Trouble Dolls* (K–3). Illus. by Lambert Davis. 1991, Harcourt $16.00 (0-15-290790-4). 32pp. Four tiny dolls come alive to help a young girl search for her missing father. (Rev: BL 3/15/91; SLJ 6/91)

**799** Bunting, Eve. *Ducky* (PS–2). Illus. by David Wisniewski. 1997, Clarion $15.00 (0-395-75185-3). 32pp. A yellow plastic duck has many adventures when he is washed overboard from an ocean liner. (Rev: BL 8/97; HB 11–12/97; SLJ 9/97)

**800** Bunting, Eve. *The Man Who Could Call Down Owls* (K–3). Illus. by Charles Mikolaycak. 1984, Macmillan LB $16.00 (0-02-715380-0). 32pp. A fantasy about a man who could communicate with owls.

**801** Bunting, Eve. *Night of the Gargoyles* (PS–3). Illus. by David Wiesner. 1994, Clarion $14.95 (0-395-66553-1). 28pp. A horror story in which gargoyles come alive at night. (Rev: BCCB 11/94; BL 10/1/94; SLJ 10/94*)

**802** Burningham, John. *Cloudland* (PS–1). Illus. 1996, Crown LB $20.99 (0-517-70929-5). 48pp. When Albert falls off a cliff, he is rescued by cloud children. (Rev: BL 12/15/96; SLJ 10/96)

**803** Burningham, John. *Come Away from the Water, Shirley* (K–2). Illus. by author. 1977, HarperCollins LB $14.89 (0-690-01361-2). 32pp. While her parents nap on the beach, Shirley goes adventuring at sea — in her imagination.

**804** Burningham, John. *John Patrick Norman McHennessy — The Boy Who Was Always Late* (PS–2). Illus. 1988, Crown $14.95 (0-517-56805-5). 32pp. Young McHennessy's farfetched excuses for always being late for school are not believed until . . . (Rev: BL 2/1/88; HB 3–4/88; SLJ 4/88)

**805** Burns, Marilyn. *The Greedy Triangle* (K–3). Illus. by Gordon Silveria. 1995, Scholastic $15.95 (0-590-48991-7). 40pp. A little triangle is tired of his shape and becomes a quadrilateral. (Rev: BCCB 3/95; BL 2/1/95; SLJ 3/95)

**806** Bursik, Rose. *Amelia's Fantastic Flight* (PS–3). Illus. 1994, Holt paper $5.95 (0-8050-3386-6). 32pp. Amelia flies from country to country in the plane she has built, returning home in time for dinner. (Rev: BL 3/1/92)

**807** Butterworth, Nick. *The Rescue Party* (PS–1). Illus. by author. 1993, Little, Brown $14.95 (0-316-11923-7). A park keeper enjoys playing with his animal buddies until a young rabbit falls down a well. (Rev: SLJ 2/94)

**808** Calhoun, Mary. *Wobble the Witch Cat* (PS–1). Illus. by Roger Duvoisin. 1958, Morrow LB $14.93 (0-688-31621-2). 32pp. A cat hides a witch's broomstick because he can't ride it.

**809** Carle, Eric. *Draw Me a Star* (4–7). Illus. 1992, Putnam $16.95 (0-399-21877-7). 36pp. The story of creation is told through the artist's drawings of various objects. (Rev: BCCB 12/92; BL 9/15/92; SLJ 10/92)

**810** Carle, Eric. *Little Cloud* (PS–K). Illus. 1996, Putnam $15.95 (0-399-23034-3). 32pp. A little cloud transforms itself into a variety of shapes and finally produces rain. (Rev: BL 4/1/96; HB 5–6/96; SLJ 5/96)

**811** Carle, Eric. *Papa, Please Get the Moon for Me* (PS–K). Illus. by author. 1986, Picture Book $19.00 (0-88708-026-X). 32pp. A little girl's father gets a high ladder to climb to the moon, but has to admit it's too large to bring home. (Rev: BL 6/1/86; SLJ 8/86)

**812** Carlstrom, Nancy White. *Who Gets the Sun out of Bed?* (PS–K). Illus. by David McPhail. 1996, Little, Brown paper $4.95 (0-316-12829-5). 32pp. The moon, a rabbit, and a young boy all help to get the sun up in the morning. (Rev: BL 9/1/92; SLJ 9/92)

**813** Carr, Jan. *The Nature of the Beast* (K–3). Illus. by G. Brian Karas. 1996, Morrow LB $15.93 (0-688-13597-8). 32pp. Isabelle acquires an unusual pet whose behavior mystifies her family. (Rev: BCCB 4/96; BL 4/15/96; HB 7–8/96; SLJ 7/96)

**814** Carrick, Carol. *Melanie* (K–3). Illus. by Alisher Dianov. 1996, Clarion $14.95 (0-395-66555-8). 32pp. Blind Melanie sets out to find her grandfather, who has disappeared in the Dark Forest. (Rev: BCCB 11/96; BL 9/15/96; SLJ 11/96)

**815** Cecil, Laura, ed. *A Thousand Yards of Sea: A Collection of Sea Stories and Poems* (PS–3). Illus. by Emma C. Clark. 1993, Greenwillow $18.00 (0-688-11437-7). 80pp. A delightful collection of poems and stories that explore various aspects of the sea and its inhabitants. (Rev: BL 4/15/93)

**816** Chapman, Carol. *Barney Bipple's Magic Dandelions* (K–3). Illus. by Steven Kellogg. 1992, Puffin paper $5.99 (0-14-054540-9). 32pp. A reissue of a 1977 title in which Barney gets 3 magic dandelions and 3 wishes.

**817** Charlton, Nancy Lee. *Derek's Dog Days* (PS–1). Illus. by Chris L. Demarest. 1996, Harcourt $14.00 (0-15-223219-2). Derek wants to be a dog and acts like one until he goes to school and finds out it's better to be a boy. (Rev: SLJ 7/96)

**818** Chesworth, Michael. *Rainy Day Dream* (PS–1). Illus. 1992, Farrar $14.00 (0-374-36177-0). 32pp. On a windy day, a young boy is swept aloft with his umbrella and has an adventure flying over the countryside. (Rev: BL 11/15/92; SLJ 11/92)

**819** Christiana, David. *The First Snow* (PS–3). Illus. 1996, Scholastic $15.95 (0-590-22855-2). 32pp. Aunt Arctica persuades Mother Nature to let Winter come into her kingdom. (Rev: BL 2/1/97; SLJ 2/97)

**820** Christiana, David. *A Tooth Fairy's Tale* (K–2). Illus. 1994, Farrar $16.00 (0-374-37677-8). 32pp. The tooth fairy wants to get possession of a beautiful blue stone owned by a giant. (Rev: BL 5/1/94; SLJ 7/94)

**821** Christiana, David. *White Nineteens* (K–2). Illus. 1992, Farrar $15.00 (0-374-38390-1). 32pp. A tree sprite goes out in search of a pair of wings. (Rev: SLJ 8/92)

**822** Chwast, Seymour. *Mr. Merlin and the Turtle* (PS). Illus. by author. 1996, Greenwillow $11.95 (0-688-14632-5). Merlin is bored with his pet turtle and transforms him into a variety of other animals until he decides that having a turtle isn't so bad. (Rev: SLJ 10/96)

**823** Clark, Emma C. *Catch That Hat!* (K–2). Illus. 1990, Little, Brown $12.95 (0-316-14496-7). 28pp. A rhymed story about the adventures of a runaway hat. (Rev: BL 5/15/90*; SLJ 8/90)

**824** Clement, Rod. *Just Another Ordinary Day* (K–3). Illus. by author. 1997, HarperCollins LB $14.89 (0-06-027667-3). A clever picture book from Australia in which ordinary daily occurrences are pictured in very extraordinary ways with outlandish characters. (Rev: BCCB 9–8/97; SLJ 6/97*)

**825** Coffelt, Nancy. *Dogs in Space* (PS–2). Illus. 1993, Harcourt $14.95 (0-15-200440-8). 32pp. High-flying dogs visit one planet after another. (Rev: BL 2/15/93; SLJ 4/93)

**826** Coffelt, Nancy. *Tom's Fish* (PS–2). Illus. 1994, Harcourt $13.95 (0-15-200587-0). 32pp. Tom can't understand why his pet goldfish, Jessie, swims upside down. (Rev: BL 3/15/94; HB 9–10/94; SLJ 5/94)

**827** Cohen, Caron L. *Crookjaw* (1–3). Illus. by Linda Bronson. 1997, Holt $15.95 (0-8050-5300-X). When her husband is swallowed by a giant whale named Crookjaw, Smilinda decides to save him by using a silver harpoon in this comic fantasy. (Rev: SLJ 9/97)

**828** Cole, Babette. *The Trouble with Mom* (K–2). Illus. by author. 1997, Putnam paper $5.95 (0-698-11593-7). 32pp. In this humorous fantasy, a boy has a witch for a mother. Originally published in 1984.

**829** Cole, Brock. *Alpha and the Dirty Baby* (K–2). Illus. 1995, Farrar $5.95 (0-374-40357-0). 32pp. When Mama and Papa have a spat, the imp behind

the couch changes the entire family. (Rev: BCCB 12/91; BL 10/1/91*; SLJ 11/91*)

**830** Cole, Brock. *The Winter Wren* (K–2). Illus. by author. 1984, Farrar $15.00 (0-374-38454-1); paper $4.95 (0-374-48408-2). 32pp. Simon and Meg go out looking for spring.

**831** Cole, Joanna. *Golly Gump Swallowed a Fly* (PS–3). Illus. by Bari Weissman. 1982, Parents $5.95 (0-8193-1069-7). 48pp. A new version of "The Old Woman Who Swallowed a Fly" story.

**832** Cole, Joanna, and Stephanie Calmenson, eds. *The Scary Book* (1–4). Illus. by Chris L. Demarest, et al. 1991, Morrow $12.95 (0-688-10654-4). 128pp. Lots of ghosts, goblins, and ghoulies will delight picture-book enthusiasts and older readers too. (Rev: BCCB 12/91; BL 8/91; SLJ 9/91)

**833** Compton, Kenn, and Joanne Compton. *Granny Greenteeth and the Noise in the Night* (PS–2). Illus. by Kenn Compton. 1993, Holiday LB $14.95 (0-8234-1051-X). In this humorous cumulative tale, Granny Greenteeth tries to get help to discover what is making the noise that comes from under her bed. (Rev: SLJ 3/94)

**834** Conover, Chris. *Sam Panda and Thunder Dragon* (K–3). Illus. 1992, Farrar $16.00 (0-374-36393-5). 32pp. Thunder Dragon comes to earth seeking help to repair his broken rain machine. (Rev: BCCB 2/93; BL 1/1/93; SLJ 3/93)

**835** Conrad, Pam. *The Tub Grandfather* (PS–1). Illus. by Richard Egielski. 1993, HarperCollins LB $14.89 (0-06-022896-2). 32pp. Little wooden figures find a missing grandfather when their ball rolls under a radiator. (Rev: BL 10/15/93; SLJ 3/94*)

**836** Conrad, Pam. *The Tub People* (PS–2). Illus. by Richard Egielski. 1989, HarperCollins $15.00 (0-060-21340-X); paper $4.95 (0-06-443306-4). 32pp. In this fantasy, wooden figures who enjoy playing in the tub are swept down the drain. (Rev: BCCB 11/89; BL 8/89; HB 11–12/89*; SLJ 12/89)

**837** Cooke, Trish. *Mr. Pam Pam and the Hullabazoo* (PS–2). Illus. by Patrice Aggs. 1994, Candlewick $14.95 (1-56402-411-3). Mr. Pam Pam amuses a young boy and his mother in this fantastic story about seeing the Hullabazoo, a creature with yellow hands, a green mustache, and red-and-black dots on his face. (Rev: BCCB 11/94; SLJ 11/94)

**838** Coombs, Patricia. *Dorrie and the Haunted Schoolhouse* (PS–1). Illus. 1992, Houghton $13.95 (0-395-60116-9). 32pp. When their teacher is missing, the little witch, Dorrie, and her friends try to teach themselves. (Rev: BL 9/1/92; SLJ 2/93)

**839** Cottringer, Anne. *Ella and the Naughty Lion* (PS–1). Illus. by Russell Ayto. 1996, Houghton $14.95 (0-395-79753-5). 32pp. Ella saves her baby brother when their pet lion becomes too playful. (Rev: BCCB 10/96; BL 9/1/96; SLJ 12/96)

**840** Cousins, Lucy. *Katy Cat and Beaky Boo* (PS). Illus. by author. 1996, Candlewick $14.99 (1-56402-884-4). 24pp. A flap book in which Katy Cat and puffin friend Beaky Boo discuss different characteristics of animals. (Rev: SLJ 1/97)

**841** Coville, Bruce. *William Shakespeare's A Midsummer Night's Dream* (1–4). Illus. by Dennis Nolan. 1996, Dial paper $16.89 (0-8037-1785-7). 48pp. A delightful retelling of Shakespeare's comedy. (Rev: BL 9/1/96; SLJ 10/96)

**842** Coville, Bruce, and Katherine Coville. *The Foolish Giant* (1–3). Illus. by authors. 1978, HarperCollins LB $13.89 (0-397-31800-6); paper $3.95 (0-06-443229-7). 48pp. In spite of not being too bright, a giant named Harry saves a town from a wicked wizard.

**843** Cowan, Catherine, trans. and adapt. *My Life with the Wave: Based on the Story by Octavio Paz* (K–3). Illus. by Mark Buehner. 1997, Lothrop LB $15.93 (0-688-12661-8). At the seashore, a boy captures a wave and takes it home, with unfortunate results. (Rev: HB 9–10/97; SLJ 8/97*)

**844** Cowen-Fletcher, Jane. *Baby Angels* (PS). Illus. 1996, Candlewick $15.99 (1-56402-666-3). 24pp. Baby angels protect a toddler when the baby begins exploring its immediate surroundings. (Rev: BL 3/1/96; SLJ 5/96)

**845** Cowley, Joy. *Singing Down the Rain* (K–2). Illus. by Jan S. Gilchrist. 1997, HarperCollins LB $14.89 (0-06-027603-7). 32pp. Fantasy and reality blend in this story about a young girl, a drought, and a tiny woman who is a rain singer. (Rev: BL 11/15/97; SLJ 10/97)

**846** Cretan, Gladys. *Joey's Head* (2–4). Illus. by Blanche Sims. 1991, Simon & Schuster paper $13.95 (0-671-73201-3). 48pp. A boy tries to make his younger brother disappear but only his head vanishes. (Rev: BL 8/91; SLJ 12/91)

**847** Crews, Nina. *I'll Catch the Moon* (PS–K). Illus. by author. 1996, Greenwillow LB $14.93 (0-688-14135-8). A mood piece in which a young boy fantasizes about climbing to the moon and circling the earth. (Rev: BCCB 5/96; HB 5–6/96; SLJ 5/96)

**848** Cummings, Pat. *Carousel* (K–2). Illus. 1994, Bradbury $14.95 (0-02-725512-3). 32pp. When Alex breaks the carousel given to her on her birthday, she dreams that the animals on the carousel come to life and take her on a ride in the night sky. (Rev: BL 7/94; SLJ 8/94)

**849** Czernecki, Stefan. *Zorah's Magic Carpet* (K–3). Illus. by author. 1996, Hyperion LB $15.49 (0-7868-2066-7). In this tale set in Morocco, a young woman weaves a magic carpet that takes her to exotic places

she later weaves into other carpets. (Rev: HB 7–8/96; SLJ 4/96)

**850** Dahl, Roald. *The Minpins* (PS–3). Illus. by Patrick Benson. 1991, Viking paper $17.00 (0-670-84168-4). 48pp. Little Billy encounters a monster when he disobeys orders and goes into the Forest of Sin. (Rev: BCCB 11/91; BL 10/15/91; HB 1–2/92; SLJ 11/91)

**851** Dale, Penny. *Wake Up, Mr. B.!* (PS–1). Illus. by author. 1992, Candlewick $14.95 (1-56402-104-1). Annie goes on a fantasy trip with the family dog, Mr. B. (Rev: SLJ 10/92)

**852** Daly, Niki. *Mama, Papa, and Baby Joe* (PS–K). Illus. 1999, Puffin paper $4.99 (0-140-54969-2). 32pp. A most unusual family goes out on a weird shopping trip. (Rev: BL 9/15/91; SLJ 10/91)

**853** Darling, Christina. *Mirror* (PS–2). Illus. by Alexandra Day. 1997, Farrar $16.00 (0-374-34720-4). 32pp. A fifth-grader tells about the magical mirror that hung in her bedroom when she was only 7. (Rev: BL 3/1/97; SLJ 3/97)

**854** Davol, Marguerite W. *How Snake Got His Hiss* (PS–3). Illus. by Mercedes McDonald. 1996, Orchard LB $15.99 (0-531-08768-9). 32pp. Not only does this tale tell how a snake got its hiss but also how the hyena got its spots and the lion its mane. (Rev: BCCB 4/96; BL 4/15/96; SLJ 3/96)

**855** Davol, Marguerite W. *The Paper Dragon* (PS–3). Illus. by Robert Sabuda. 1997, Simon & Schuster $17.00 (0-689-31992-4). 60pp. This story set in China tells how Mi Fei accomplishes his task of putting a destructive dragon to sleep. (Rev: BL 10/15/97*; SLJ 11/97)

**856** Day, Alexandra. *Carl Makes a Scrapbook* (PS–4). Illus. 1994, Farrar $12.95 (0-374-31129-3). 32pp. Madeleine, with the help of her dog, Carl, combine pages of her mother's photo album with those from Carl's scrapbook about dogs. (Rev: BCCB 11/94; BL 11/15/94; SLJ 11/94)

**857** Deedy, Carmen A. *The Library Dragon* (K–2). Illus. by Michael P. White. 1994, Peachtree $16.95 (1-56145-091-X). The new librarian is a real fire-breathing dragon who in time learns to trust children with her books. (Rev: BCCB 2/95; SLJ 12/94)

**858** Dematons, Charlotte. *Looking for Cinderella* (PS–3). Illus. 1996, Front Street $15.95 (1-886910-13-8). 32pp. In an old windmill, Hilda encounters many fairy tale characters, including Hansel and Gretel and Tom Thumb. (Rev: BCCB 10/96; BL 9/15/96; SLJ 1/97)

**859** Demi. *Liang and the Magic Paintbrush* (2–4). Illus. by author. 1980, Holt paper $5.95 (0-8050-0801-2). 32pp. A boy in Old China finds everything he dreams comes to life.

**860** Denton, Kady M. *Would They Love a Lion?* (PS–K). Illus. 1995, Kingfisher $14.95 (1-85697-546-0). 32pp. A young child who is anxious to be noticed imagines herself as various animals. (Rev: BCCB 7–8/95; BL 8/95; SLJ 7/95)

**861** dePaola, Tomie. *Bill and Pete* (K–2). Illus. by author. 1996, Putnam paper $5.95 (0-698-11400-0). 32pp. Pete is a toothbrush (alias a bird) who helps young Bill in a series of world misadventures.

**862** dePaola, Tomie. *Sing, Pierrot, Sing: A Picture Book in Mime* (PS–2). Illus. by author. 1983, Harcourt paper $3.95 (0-15-274989-6). 32pp. A group of children comfort Pierrot at his loss of Columbine.

**863** dePaola, Tomie. *Strega Nona Meets Her Match* (K–2). Illus. 1993, Putnam $15.95 (0-399-22421-1). 34pp. Strega Amelia comes to town and takes away business from the other witch in town, Strega Nona. (Rev: BCCB 12/93; BL 11/1/93; HB 11–12/93)

**864** dePaola, Tomie. *The Unicorn and the Moon* (PS–3). Illus. 1994, Silver Burdett LB $14.95 (0-382-24658-6). 32pp. A unicorn tries to save the moon that is trapped between 2 mountains. (Rev: BL 1/1/95)

**865** DeSaix, Deborah Durland. *In the Back Seat* (PS–3). Illus. 1993, Farrar $14.00 (0-374-33639-3). 30pp. To pass the time during a car trip, Ariel tells younger brother Jeffrey a fantastic story that incorporates the scenery they are viewing. (Rev: BL 9/1/93; SLJ 8/93)

**866** DeSaix, Deborah Durland. *Returning Nicholas* (PS–3). Illus. by author. 1995, Farrar $16.00 (0-374-36251-3). A carousel horse comes to life and takes Antonia for a ride into the past. (Rev: SLJ 1/96)

**867** Desimini, Lisa. *Moon Soup* (PS–3). Illus. 1993, Hyperion LB $15.49 (1-56282-464-3). 32pp. An unusual man concocts a brew he calls moon soup and flies to the moon to eat it. (Rev: BL 11/1/93; SLJ 1/94)

**868** Devlin, Wende, and Harry Devlin. *Old Black Witch!* (K–3). Illus. by Harry Devlin. 1992, Macmillan $13.95 (0-02-729185-5). 32pp. When Nicky and his mother buy an old house, they find a witch living in the chimney. (Rev: BL 11/15/92)

**869** Dewan, Ted. *The Sorcerer's Apprentice* (K–2). Illus. 1998, Doubleday $15.95 (0-385-32537-1). 32pp. A variation on "The Sorcerer's Apprentice" in which an inventor creates a robot to clean up his workshop. (Rev: BL 2/1/98; HB 3–4/97; SLJ 2/98)

**870** Dewan, Ted. *Top Secret* (K–2). Illus. 1997, Doubleday $15.95 (0-385-32324-7). 32pp. A humorous story that debunks the tooth fairy myth and explains how a band of tiny fellows manage to complete missions of exchanging teeth for money every night. (Rev: BL 4/1/97; SLJ 3/97)

**871** Diller, Harriet. *Grandaddy's Highway* (PS–3). Illus. by Henri Sorensen. 1993, Boyds Mills $14.95 (1-878093-63-0). 32pp. Maggie and her grandfather imagine driving a truck together across the United States to the Pacific. (Rev: BL 5/1/93; SLJ 5/93)

**872** Dillon, Jana. *Jeb Scarecrow's Pumpkin Patch* (PS–2). Illus. 1992, Houghton $16.00 (0-395-57578-8). 32pp. Tension builds between Jeb Scarecrow and the crows as he guards the family's pumpkin patch. (Rev: BL 10/1/92*; SLJ 9/92)

**873** Donnelly, Liza. *Dinosaur Beach* (PS–2). Illus. by author. 1991, Scholastic paper $2.50 (0-685-43744-2). A boy and his dog spend a lovely day playing with the dinosaurs at a beach. (Rev: SLJ 7/89)

**874** Donnelly, Liza. *Dinosaur Garden* (PS–3). Illus. 1991, Scholastic paper $2.99 (0-590-43172-2). 32pp. Rex's seedlings sprout into a tropical jungle that is soon home to plant-eating dinosaurs. (Rev: BL 4/15/90; SLJ 3/90)

**875** Dorros, Arthur. *Abuela* (K–2). Illus. by Elisa Kleven. 1991, Dutton paper $15.99 (0-525-44750-4). 40pp. Rosalba and her grandmother fly over New York City in her imagination. (Rev: BCCB 9/92; BL 10/15/91*; HB 11–12/91*; SLJ 10/91)

**876** Dorros, Arthur. *Isla* (PS–3). Illus. by Elisa Kleven. 1995, Dutton paper $15.99 (0-525-45149-8). 40pp. A little girl and her grandmother fly through the air to the Caribbean island where her grandmother grew up. A sequel to *Abuela* (1991). (Rev: BL 11/1/95; SLJ 9/95)

**877** Downes, Belinda. *Every Little Angel's Handbook* (PS–3). Illus. 1997, Dial $14.99 (0-8037-2264-8). 32pp. A fantasy about all the different angels that surround us, even those that make angel food cake. (Rev: BL 12/1/97; SLJ 12/97)

**878** Dragonwagon, Crescent. *Brass Button* (K–3). Illus. by Susan Paradise. 1997, Simon & Schuster $16.00 (0-689-80582-9). 40pp. Mrs. Morrison loses a button from her new red coat, and it falls into several different hands before she gets it back. (Rev: BL 6/1–15/97; SLJ 6/97)

**879** Drawson, Blair. *Flying Dimitri* (K–3). Illus. 1997, Orchard $14.95 (0-531-30037-4). 40pp. A fantasy in which a young boy flies to Mars to save a princess but is happy to get home, where his father tucks him into bed. (Rev: BL 12/15/97; SLJ 4/98)

**880** Drawson, Blair. *Mary Margaret's Tree* (K–3). Illus. 1996, Orchard LB $16.99 (0-531-08871-5). 32pp. In this fantasy, Mary Margaret views the change of seasons from atop a tree that she has planted. (Rev: BL 10/1/96; SLJ 10/96)

**881** Drescher, Henrik. *The Boy Who Ate Around* (K–3). Illus. 1994, Hyperion LB $15.49 (0-7868-2011-X). 40pp. When young Mo objects to the family dinner fare, he turns into a ravenous warthog that eats everything in sight. (Rev: BL 11/1/94; SLJ 10/94)

**882** Drescher, Henrik. *Simon's Book* (PS–1). Illus. by author. 1983, Lothrop LB $15.93 (0-688-02086-0); paper $3.95 (0-688-10484-3). 32pp. A frightening monster chases Simon through the pages of his drawing pad.

**883** Drummond, Allan. *The Willow Pattern Story* (2–4). Illus. 1992, North-South $14.95 (1-558-58171-5); paper $5.95 (1-558-58413-7). 28pp. The author spins a tale from the story depicted on willow pattern china. (Rev: BL 10/15/92; SLJ 12/92)

**884** Dunrea, Olivier. *The Tale of Hilda Louise* (PS–2). Illus. by author. 1996, Farrar $16.00 (0-374-37380-9). A fantasy involving a lonely child in an orphanage who gains the power to float but loses it when she finds a relative who loves her. (Rev: SLJ 9/96)

**885** Duquennoy, Jacques. *The Ghosts' Trip to Loch Ness* (PS–2). Illus. by author. 1996, Harcourt $11.00 (0-15-201440-3). A quartet of ghosts travels to Scotland for a glimpse of the Loch Ness monster in this amusing fantasy. (Rev: BCCB 10/96; SLJ 10/96)

**886** Dwyer, Mindy. *Aurora: A Tale of the Northern Lights* (K–2). Illus. by author. 1997, Alaska Northwest $15.95 (0-88240-494-6). A fantasy that traces the origins of the aurora borealis through the story of a young girl's search for a place filled with darkness. (Rev: SLJ 2/98)

**887** Eaton, Deborah, and Susan Halter. *No One Told the Aardvark* (PS–2). Illus. by Jim Spence. 1997, Charlesbridge $15.95 (0-88106-872-1); paper $6.95 (0-88106-871-3). In this humorous story, a young boy thinks of all the advantages there would be if he were different animals. (Rev: SLJ 6/97)

**888** Egan, Tim. *Distant Feathers* (K–3). Illus. 1998, Houghton $15.00 (0-395-85808-9). 32pp. A giant bird taps on Sedrick Van Pelt's window and asks for bread in this humorous picture book. (Rev: BL 3/15/98)

**889** Egielski, Richard. *Buz* (PS–2). Illus. 1995, HarperCollins LB $14.89 (0-06-023567-5). 32pp. A bug that is eaten accidently by a boy finally finds an escape route via the boy's ear. (Rev: BCCB 10/95; BL 8/95; SLJ 9/95)

**890** Emerson, Scott, and Howard Post. *The Magic Boots* (PS–1). Illus. by Howard Post. 1994, Gibbs Smith $15.95 (0-87905-603-7). 32pp. When William travels anywhere he wants, he thinks it is because he owns magic boots. (Rev: BL 12/15/94; SLJ 1/95)

**891** Enright, Elizabeth. *Tatsinda* (K–4). Illus. by Katie T. Treherne. 1991, Harcourt $16.95 (0-15-284280-2). 64pp. A golden-haired girl is carried off by an ogre. (Rev: SLJ 7/91)

**892** Erlbruch, Wolf. *Leonard: A Fable* (K–3). Illus. by author. 1995, Orchard LB $16.99 (0-531-08782-4). Leonard is so intrigued with dogs that when a fairy grants him a wish he decides that he wants to be turned into a dog. (Rev: SLJ 1/96)

**893** Esterl, Arnica. *Okino and the Whales* (K–3). Illus. by Marek Zawadzki. 1995, Harcourt $16.00 (0-15-200377-0). 32pp. A mother tells her son the story of how his great-great-grandmother rescued her daughter from the underwater kingdom of Iwa. (Rev: BL 10/15/95; SLJ 1/96)

**894** Eversole, Robyn. *The Flute Player/La Flautista* (PS–2). Illus. by G. Brian Karas. 1995, Orchard LB $15.99 (0-531-08769-7). 32pp. A bilingual book (English and Spanish) about a young girl who is able to extract a number of presents from a broken flute. (Rev: BL 10/1/95; SLJ 11/95)

**895** Eyles, Heather. *Well, I Never!* (K–2). Illus. by Terry Ross. 1990, Overlook $11.95 (0-87951-383-7). Polly complains to her mother that there are monsters in her room — and she's right. (Rev: BCCB 3/90; SLJ 3/90)

**896** Farber, Norma. *The Boy Who Longed for a Lift* (PS–1). Illus. by Brian Selznick. 1997, Harper-Collins LB $15.89 (0-06-027109-4). 32pp. A tired boy gets offers of a lift from different animals, but he prefers to go home and get the perfect lift from his father. (Rev: BL 5/15/97; HB 5–6/97; SLJ 6/97)

**897** Farber, Norma. *Return of the Shadows* (K–3). Illus. by Andrea Baruffi. 1992, HarperCollins LB $14.89 (0-06-020519-9). 32pp. In this picture book, a group of shadows decides to run free and roam the world on its own. (Rev: BL 7/92; SLJ 10/92*)

**898** Farmer, Nancy. *Runnery Granary* (K–2). Illus. by Joseph A. Smith. 1996, Greenwillow LB $14.93 (0-688-14188-9). 32pp. Mrs. Runnery discovers that gnomes are eating her grain. (Rev: BL 6/1–15/96; HB 9–10/96; SLJ 8/96)

**899** Fisher, Leonard Everett. *Sailboat Lost* (PS–2). Illus. 1991, Macmillan $15.95 (0-02-735351-6). 32pp. A toy sailboat has adventures during the time it is adrift at sea. (Rev: BL 9/1/91)

**900** Florian, Douglas. *Monster Motel* (PS–1). Illus. 1993, Harcourt $13.95 (0-15-255320-7). Many of the 13 poems that are presented deal with monsters who live in a motel. (Rev: SLJ 6/93)

**901** Flournoy, Vanessa, and Valerie Flournoy. *Celie and the Harvest Fiddler* (K–4). Illus. by James E. Ransome. 1995, Morrow LB $14.93 (0-688-11458-X). 32pp. In a story set in the 1870s, an African American girl receives from a mysterious fiddler a mask that grants wishes. (Rev: BL 9/15/95; SLJ 11/95)

**902** Foreman, Michael. *Jack's Fantastic Voyage* (K–3). Illus. 1992, Harcourt $14.95 (0-15-239496-

6). 32pp. Jack doubts that his grandfather really had the adventures he claims until one night the 2 experience together an equally amazing voyage. (Rev: BL 11/15/92; SLJ 11/92)

**903** Fox, Mem. *Feathers and Fools* (1–4). Illus. by Nicholas Wilton. 1996, Harcourt $16.00 (0-15-200473-4). An antiwar allegory about the rivalry between peacocks and swans. (Rev: SLJ 7/96)

**904** Fox, Mem. *The Straight Line Wonder* (K–4). Illus. by Marc Rosenthal. 1997, Mondo $14.95 (1-57255-206-9). 24pp. Three straight lines are dear friends until one of them wants to change its shape. (Rev: BL 10/15/97; SLJ 1/98)

**905** Franklin, Jonathan. *Don't Wake the Baby* (K–3). Illus. by author. 1991, Farrar $13.95 (0-374-31826-3). In this fantasy, when his young brother's crib suddenly becomes a ship and takes off, Marvin has a hard time preventing his brother from waking up. (Rev: SLJ 8/91)

**906** Frascino, Edward. *Nanny Noony and the Magic Spell* (PS–3). Illus. by author. 1988, Pippin $15.95 (0-945912-00-5). 32pp. How the spell on the farm is undone. (Rev: BL 11/15/88; SLJ 1/89)

**907** Freeman, Don. *A Rainbow of My Own* (K–3). Illus. by author. 1966, Puffin paper $4.99 (0-14-050328-5). 32pp. A boy's search for a rainbow ends in his own home.

**908** Freeman, Don. *Tilly Witch* (1–3). Illus. by author. 1978, Viking $13.95 (0-670-71303-1); Puffin paper $4.99 (0-14-050262-9). 32pp. Tilly attends Miss Fitch's Finishing School for Witches.

**909** French, Vivian. *Once upon a Time* (PS–K). Illus. by John Prater. 1993, Candlewick $14.99 (1-56402-177-7). 32pp. In this story in verse, a family moves into a country house in a neighborhood where all sorts of nursery rhyme characters live. (Rev: BCCB 4/93; BL 5/1/93)

**910** Frieden, Sarajo. *The Care and Feeding of Fish* (K–3). Illus. 1996, Houghton $15.95 (0-395-71251-3). 32pp. Loulou's pet fish grows to the size of a human and shares many adventures with her. (Rev: BCCB 10/96; BL 11/15/96; SLJ 10/96)

**911** Friend, Catherine. *My Head Is Full of Colors* (PS–3). Illus. by Kiki. 1994, Hyperion $14.95 (1-56282-360-4). 32pp. Maria finds she has amazing hair that each day contains a different set of objects. (Rev: BL 3/15/94; SLJ 6/94)

**912** Frissen. *Yann and the Whale* (K–3). Illus. by Hanze. Series: A Cranky Nell Book. 1997, Kane/Miller $13.95 (0-916291-71-5). When Yann is saved from drowning by a whale, he vows never to hunt these creatures again. (Rev: SLJ 6/97)

**913** Gackenbach, Dick. *Barker's Crime* (PS–2). Illus. 1996, Harcourt $15.00 (0-15-200628-1). 32pp. Greedy Mr. Gobble takes Barker the dog to court for inhaling the aroma of the miser's meals. (Rev: BL 3/1/96; SLJ 7/96)

**914** Gackenbach, Dick. *Harry and the Terrible Whatzit* (PS–2). Illus. by author. 1979, Houghton $15.00 (0-395-28795-2); paper $6.95 (0-89919-223-8). 32pp. Harry follows his mother into the dark cellar to confront the terrible 2-headed Whatzit.

**915** Gaffney, Timothy R. *Grandpa Takes Me to the Moon* (K–2). Illus. by Barry Root. 1996, Morrow LB $15.93 (0-688-13938-8). At bedtime, Grandpa, a former astronaut, takes his grandson on an imaginary walk on the moon. (Rev: BCCB 10/96; SLJ 9/96*)

**916** Galchutt, David. *There Was Magic Inside* (1–3). Illus. 1993, Simon & Schuster paper $14.00 (0-671-75978-7). In this tale set in an Asian land, Toshi accidentally awakens a dangerous sea monster. (Rev: SLJ 8/93)

**917** Galdone, Paul. *The Magic Porridge Pot* (K–3). Illus. by author. 1976, Houghton $15.95 (0-395-28805-3). 32pp. The familiar tale of the magic pot that produces porridge but runs amuck when the words that stop it are forgotten.

**918** Gammell, Stephen. *Is That You, Winter?* (PS–2). Illus. 1997, Harcourt $16.00 (0-15-201415-2). 32pp. Old Man Winter discovers for whom he is busy making snow. (Rev: BL 9/1/97; SLJ 10/97)

**919** Geeslin, Campbell. *In Rosa's Mexico* (PS–1). Illus. by Andrea Arroyo. 1996, Knopf LB $18.99 (0-679-96721-4). 32pp. Three short stories about an angelic Mexican girl and her good works. (Rev: BCCB 1/97; BL 11/15/96; SLJ 12/96)

**920** Geisert, Arthur. *The Etcher's Studio* (PS–2). Illus. 1997, Houghton $15.95 (0-395-79754-3). 32pp. After describing the etching process, a young boy imagines that he is in his grandfather's pictures. (Rev: BCCB 6/97; BL 4/1/97; HB 5–6/97; SLJ 4/97)

**921** Geraghty, Paul. *The Hunter* (K–3). Illus. 1994, Crown LB $15.99 (0-517-59693-8). 32pp. Jamina discovers an orphaned baby elephant in the bush and tries to get herself and the elephant home. (Rev: BL 9/1/94; SLJ 8/94*)

**922** Geras, Adele. *From Lullaby to Lullaby* (PS–1). Illus. by Kathryn Brown. 1997, Simon & Schuster $16.00 (0-689-80568-3). 40pp. Each of the objects that are depicted in a blanket that a mother is knitting for her daughter comes to life and expresses its wishes. (Rev: BL 4/15/97; SLJ 7/97)

**923** Gershator, David, and Phillis Gershator. *Palampam Day* (PS–2). Illus. by Enrique O. Sanchez. 1997, Marshall Cavendish LB $15.95 (0-7614-5002-5). 32pp. Set in the West Indies, this story tells about a boy who is suddenly having conversations with all sorts of objects, like a coconut, a dog, and a bowl of bananas. (Rev: BL 8/97; SLJ 9/97)

**924** Gershator, Phillis. *Sambalena Show-Off* (PS–1). Illus. by Leonard Jenkins. 1995, Simon & Schuster $15.00 (0-689-80314-1). Sambalena gets so swell-headed that when he puts a clay pot on his head at a party he can't get it off. (Rev: SLJ 2/96)

**925** Gerstein, Mordicai. *Behind the Couch* (2–3). Illus. by author. 1996, Hyperion paper $3.95 (0-7868-1139-0). 57pp. In this fantasy, a young boy discovers a whole new world after his stuffed toy falls behind the couch. (Rev: BCCB 9/96; SLJ 7/96)

**926** Getz, David. *Floating Home* (1–3). Illus. by Michael Rex. 1997, Holt $15.95 (0-8050-4497-3). 32pp. When teacher wants Maxine to see her home in a new way, she becomes an astronaut to see it from space. (Rev: BCCB 5/97; BL 5/1/97; SLJ 5/97)

**927** Giblin, James Cross. *The Dwarf, the Giant, and the Unicorn: A Tale of King Arthur* (2–4). Illus. by Claire Ewart. 1996, Clarion $15.95 (0-395-60520-2). 44pp. When King Arthur's ship is stranded on an island, he encounters 3 unusual creatures. (Rev: BL 12/1/96; SLJ 10/96)

**928** Gillerlain, Gayle, reteller. *The Reverend Thomas's False Teeth* (K–3). Illus. by Dena Schutzer. 1995, BridgeWater paper $14.95 (0-8167-3303-1). When the Reverend Thomas's false teeth fall into deep water, Gracie thinks of an ingenious way to retrieve them. (Rev: SLJ 12/95)

**929** Gilliland, Judith Heide. *Not in the House, Newton!* (PS–3). Illus. by Elizabeth Sayles. 1995, Clarion $15.00 (0-395-61195-4). 32pp. When Newton draws objects using his magical red crayon, they jump off the pages. (Rev: BL 12/15/95; SLJ 1/96)

**930** Gilman, Phoebe. *The Gypsy Princess* (PS–3). Illus. 1997, Scholastic $15.95 (0-590-86543-9). 32pp. Cinnamon tires of being a princess and longs for the gypsy life. (Rev: BCCB 3/97; BL 2/1/97; SLJ 3/97)

**931** Ginsburg, Mirra. *Where Does the Sun Go at Night?* (PS–1). Illus. by Jose Aruego and Ariane Dewey. 1980, Morrow paper $4.95 (0-688-07041-8). 32pp. A question-and-answer format is used in this adaptation of an Armenian song.

**932** Givens, Terryl. *Dragon Scales and Willow Leaves* (PS–1). Illus. by Andrew Portwood. 1997, Putnam $12.95 (0-399-22619-2). 32pp. In this fantasy, 2 children on a walk in the woods imagine different experiences. The boy sees adventure and the girl finds beauty. (Rev: BL 10/15/97; SLJ 12/97)

**933** Glassman, Peter. *My Working Mom* (K–3). Illus. by Tedd Arnold. 1994, Morrow LB $15.93 (0-688-12260-4). This working mom is different from others because she is a practicing witch. (Rev: BCCB 5/94; SLJ 8/94)

**934** Goble, Paul. *Dream Wolf* (K–2). Illus. by author. 1990, Macmillan LB $14.95 (0-02-736585-9). 32pp. A friendly wolf leads 2 lost Plains Indian children home. (Rev: BL 2/15/90)

**935** Goennel, Heidi. *I Pretend* (PS). Illus. 1995, Morrow LB $15.93 (0-688-13593-5). 32pp. A child imagines wonderful adventures out of commonplace events. (Rev: BL 4/1/95; SLJ 6/95)

**936** Gogol, Nikolai. *Sorotchintzy Fair* (1–4). Trans. by Daniel Reynolds. Illus. by Gennady Spirin. 1991, Godine $16.95 (0-87923-879-8). 24pp. Based on a Gogol story, this is a tale about a young girl who falls in love with a stranger she meets at a county fair. (Rev: BCCB 6/92; BL 5/15/91; HB 9–10/91; SLJ 8/91)

**937** Gordon, Amy. *Midnight Magic* (2–4). Illus. by Judy Clifford. 1995, BridgeWater paper $12.95 (0-8167-3660-X). 63pp. When colorful Uncle Harry comes to baby-sit for his 2 young nephews, so many strange things happen that the boys think he uses magic. (Rev: SLJ 12/95)

**938** Gray, Libba M. *Is There Room on the Feather Bed?* (PS–1). Illus. by Nadine Bernard Westcott. 1997, Orchard $16.95 (0-531-30013-7). 32pp. On a rainy night, animals ask to be allowed to share the comfortable feather bed of a farm couple. (Rev: BL 3/1/97; SLJ 4/97)

**939** Greaves, Margaret. *The Naming* (PS–3). Illus. by Pauline Baynes. 1993, Harcourt $14.95 (0-15-200534-X). 32pp. In Eden, Adam meets all the animals and gives them names, including the magical unicorn. (Rev: BL 3/15/93; SLJ 5/93)

**940** Greenfield, Eloise. *Daydreamers* (1–4). Illus. by Tom Feelings. 1985, Dial paper $4.95 (0-8037-0167-5). 32pp. A celebration of daydreaming and the pleasures it can bring.

**941** Greenstein, Elaine. *Mattie's Hats Won't Wear That!* (K–2). Illus. 1997, Knopf LB $18.99 (0-679-98349-X). 32pp. A group of hats rebel at all the decorations that Mattie piles on them in her hat shop. (Rev: BL 12/15/97)

**942** Greenstein, Elaine. *Mrs. Rose's Garden* (PS–2). Illus. 1996, Simon & Schuster paper $15.00 (0-689-80215-3). 32pp. When Mr. and Mrs. Rose produce enormous vegetables from a super fertilizer, complications arise. (Rev: BCCB 6/96; BL 6/1–15/96; SLJ 6/96)

**943** Gruelle, Johnny. *Raggedy Ann Stories* (PS–3). Illus. 1993, Macmillan LB $16.00 (0-02-737585-4). 96pp. This story features the lovable rag doll. A reissue. Also use: *Raggedy Andy Stories* (1993).

**944** Guthrie, Donna. *The Witch Who Lives Down the Hall* (PS–2). Illus. by Amy Schwartz. 1985, Harcourt $12.95 (0-15-298610-3). 32pp. A young boy thinks his new high-rise neighbor is a witch, and proves it when the 2 of them fly above the city on her magic carpet. (Rev: BCCB 1/86; BL 9/15/85; SLJ 10/85)

**945** Guy, Ginger F. *Black Crow, Black Crow* (PS–2). Illus. by Nancy Winslow Parker. 1991, Greenwillow $13.95 (0-688-08956-9). 24pp. A little girl imagines that crows lead the same kind of life that she does. (Rev: BL 4/15/91; HB 3–4/91; SLJ 6/91)

**946** Haas, Irene. *The Maggie B* (K–2). Illus. by author. 1975, Macmillan $16.00 (0-689-50021-1); Simon & Schuster paper $5.99 (0-689-81507-7). 32pp. Beautiful watercolors enhance this story of a little girl and her adventures on an imaginary ship named for her — The Maggie B.

**947** Haas, Irene. *A Summertime Song* (PS–3). Illus. 1997, Simon & Schuster paper $16.00 (0-689-50549-3). 32pp. A frog presents a little girl with a magic paper hat that shrinks her so she is able to attend a birthday party with little animals like a mouse and an inchworm. (Rev: BL 5/15/97; HB 5–6/97; SLJ 6/97)

**948** Haley, Gail E. *Jack and the Bean Tree* (K–2). Illus. by author. 1986, Crown $13.95 (0-517-55717-7). 48pp. The old tale is retold in the traditional version with an Appalachian background. (Rev: BCCB 7–8/86; BL 8/86; SLJ 9/86)

**949** Haley, Gail E. *Jack and the Fire Dragon* (PS–3). Illus. by author. 1988, Crown LB $14.95 (0-517-56814-4). 40pp. The Appalachians are the backdrop for this retelling of how Jack, of beanstalk fame, battles the dragon. (Rev: BL 7/88; SLJ 9/88)

**950** Hancock, Sibyl. *Esteban and the Ghost* (1–3). Illus. by Dirk Zimmer. 1983, Dial LB $10.89 (0-8037-2411-X). 32pp. Esteban sets out to find a ghost and collect a reward.

**951** Hanel, Wolfram. *The Gold at the End of the Rainbow* (K–3). Illus. by Loek Koopmans. 1997, North-South LB $15.88 (1-55858-693-8). 32pp. Because Brendon and his grandfather refuse to steal a leprechaun's treasure, they are rewarded. (Rev: BCCB 9/96; BL 4/1/97; SLJ 7/97)

**952** Harley, Bill. *Sarah's Story* (K–2). Illus. by Eve Aldridge. 1996, Tricycle Pr. $15.95 (1-883672-20-1). Sarah has some amazing adventures when she visits an ant colony. (Rev: BCCB 3/97; SLJ 1/97)

**953** Harrison, David L. *The Animals' Song* (PS–K). Illus. by Chris L. Demarest. 1997, Boyds Mills $14.95 (1-56397-144-5). 32pp. When a little girl and boy play their flute and drum, all the animals join in. (Rev: BCCB 6/97; BL 4/1/97; SLJ 3/97)

**954** Harrison, Joanna. *When Mom Turned into a Monster* (PS–3). Illus. 1996, Carolrhoda $14.95 (1-57505-013-7). 32pp. Her pesky and interfering children cause Mom to gradually turn into a monster. (Rev: BL 11/15/96)

**955** Harrison, Troon. *Don't Dig So Deep, Nicholas!* (PS–1). Illus. by Gary Clement. 1997, Firefly $17.95 (1-895688-51-5); paper $6.95 (1-895688-60-4). 32pp.

Nicholas digs such a big hole in the sand that he reaches Australia, and soon the beach is covered with kangaroos, dingos, wombats, koalas, and other creatures from Down Under. (Rev: SLJ 10/97)

**956** Harter, Debbie. *Walking Through the Jungle* (PS–1). Illus. by author. 1997, Orchard $14.95 (0-531-30035-8). A humorous fantasy in which a young girl encounters a number of fierce creatures on her walk through the jungle. (Rev: SLJ 10/97)

**957** Hartman, Gail. *As the Roadrunner Runs: A First Book of Maps* (PS–1). Illus. by Cathy Bobak. 1994, Bradbury paper $14.95 (0-02-743092-8). 32pp. The separate worlds of different animals of the U.S. Southwest are described and then brought together into one large map that shows the combined region. A companion to *As the Crow Flies* (1991). (Rev: BCCB 1/95; BL 11/15/94; SLJ 1/95)

**958** Hautzig, Deborah, adapt. *The Pied Piper of Hamelin* (K–2). Illus. by S. D. Schindler. 1989, Random LB $9.99 (0-394-96579-5); paper $3.99 (0-394-86579-0). 47pp. A simple adaptation of the story about a piper who inflicts a terrible payment on the town of Hamelin. (Rev: SLJ 3/90)

**959** Hawkes, Kevin. *His Royal Buckliness* (PS–2). Illus. 1992, Smithmark $3.98 (0-8317-3051-X). 32pp. A nonsense tale about the kidnapping of Lord Buckley by the giants. (Rev: BL 12/1/92; SLJ 12/92)

**960** Hawkins, Colin, and Jacqui Hawkins. *Come for a Ride on the Ghost Train* (PS–1). Illus. by authors. 1993, Candlewick $12.95 (1-56402-236-6). Ugly monsters take the reader on trips to such scary places as a graveyard, a dark crypt, and a haunted chapel. (Rev: SLJ 2/94)

**961** Haywood, Carolyn. *How the Reindeer Saved Santa* (PS–1). Illus. by Victor G. Ambrus. 1986, Morrow LB $12.88 (0-688-05904-X). 64pp. Santa trades in his reindeer for a helicopter, and then ends up in a snowbank. (Rev: BL 9/1/86; SLJ 12/86)

**962** Heckman, Philip. *Waking Upside Down* (1–4). Illus. by Dwight Been. 1996, Simon & Schuster $16.00 (0-689-31930-4). 32pp. A boy discovers that he can walk on the ceiling. (Rev: BCCB 5/96; BL 7/96; SLJ 7/96)

**963** Heller, Nicholas. *Peas* (PS–1). Illus. 1993, Greenwillow LB $13.93 (0-688-12407-0). 24pp. Lewis dreams about the peas that he has refused to eat at dinner and how they get their revenge. (Rev: BL 9/15/93)

**964** Hendrick, Mary J. *If Anything Ever Goes Wrong at the Zoo* (PS–2). Illus. by Jane Dyer. 1993, Harcourt $14.00 (0-15-238007-8). 32pp. When the zoo floods, Leslie and her mother make room in their home and yard for the animals. (Rev: BL 6/1–15/93; SLJ 7/93*)

**965** Henwood, Simon. *A Piece of Luck* (2–3). Illus. 1990, Farrar $13.95 (0-374-35925-3). 26pp. A tale about the value of sharing. (Rev: BL 6/1/90; SLJ 8/90)

**966** Henwood, Simon. *The Troubled Village* (K–2). Illus. by author. 1991, Farrar $13.95 (0-374-37780-4). The residents of Troubled Village get particularly upset when the sky caves in and a little boy falls into the void left behind. (Rev: SLJ 12/91)

**967** Hiatt, Fred. *If I Were Queen of the World* (PS–2). Illus. by Mark Graham. 1997, Simon & Schuster paper $16.00 (0-689-80700-7). 32pp. A little girl thinks of all the benefits she could enjoy if she were queen of the whole wide world. (Rev: BCCB 6/97; BL 5/1/97; SLJ 5/97)

**968** Hickox, Rebecca. *Per and the Dala Horse* (PS–3). Illus. by Yvonne Gilbert. 1995, Doubleday $15.95 (0-385-32075-2). 32pp. With the help of his magic wooden horse, Per, the youngest in his family, is able to retrieve the Communion cup from the trolls. (Rev: BL 11/15/95; SLJ 1/96)

**969** Hill, Susan. *Beware Beware* (K–2). Illus. by Angela Barrett. 1993, Candlewick $14.95 (1-56402-245-5). 32pp. A girl thinks she sees all sorts of scary beasts when she explores the woods in the evening in this picture book set in Victorian England. (Rev: BCCB 12/93; BL 11/15/93; SLJ 2/94)

**970** Hillman, Elizabeth. *Min-Yo and the Moon Dragon* (PS–3). Illus. by John Wallner. 1992, Harcourt $14.95 (0-15-254230-2). 32pp. Little Min-Yo volunteers to go to the moon by climbing a cobweb staircase to find the moon dragon. (Rev: BL 3/15/92; SLJ 6/92)

**971** Hissey, Jane. *Hoot* (PS–1). Illus. 1997, Random $18.00 (0-679-88387-8). 32pp. Five friends, who are really stuffed toys, make a new pal when they find a nocturnal roommate, Hoot the owl. (Rev: BL 6/1–15/97; SLJ 7/97)

**972** Hobbs, Will. *Beardream* (1–4). Illus. by Jill Kastner. 1997, Simon & Schuster $16.00 (0-689-31973-8). 32pp. When a great bear fails to reappear in the spring, a boy climbs into the mountains to look for it. (Rev: BL 4/15/97; SLJ 4/97)

**973** Hodges, Margaret. *Molly Limbo* (PS–2). Illus. by Elizabeth Miles. 1996, Simon & Schuster $16.00 (0-689-80581-0). 32pp. Mr. Means saves money for rent by living in a haunted house. (Rev: BCCB 10/96; BL 9/15/96; HB 11–12/96; SLJ 9/96)

**974** Holabird, Katharine. *Alexander and the Magic Boat* (PS–K). Illus. by Helen Craig. 1991, Crown $11.95 (0-517-58142-6). Using his imagination, Alexander takes his mother on a sea cruise to the other side of the world. (Rev: SLJ 3/91)

**975** Hooker, Ruth. *Matthew the Cowboy* (PS–1). Illus. by Cat B. Smith. 1990, Whitman LB $14.95 (0-8075-4999-1). When Matthew gets a cowboy suit for his birthday, he sets out for an adventure in the Wild West. (Rev: BCCB 12/90; SLJ 2/91)

**976** Hough, Libby. *If Somebody Lived Next Door* (PS). Illus. by Laura M. Kvasnosky. 1997, Dutton paper $10.99 (0-525-45497-7). 32pp. Olivia imagines what would happen if the house next door were inhabited by a family and a number of different animals. (Rev: BL 6/1–15/97; SLJ 7/97)

**977** Howe, James. *There's a Dragon in My Sleeping Bag* (PS–2). Illus. by David S. Rose. 1994, Atheneum $15.00 (0-689-31873-1). 40pp. Alex invents imaginary playmates but decides that being with his brother is best. (Rev: BL 12/15/94; SLJ 3/95)

**978** Hubbard, Patricia. *My Crayons Talk* (PS–1). Illus. by G. Brian Karas. 1996, Holt $15.95 (0-8050-3529-X). 32pp. Crayons in a box unite to produce a series of colorful pictures. (Rev: BCCB 5/96; BL 4/1/96; SLJ 5/96)

**979** Hughes, Shirley. *Stories by Firelight* (K–3). Illus. 1993, Lothrop $16.00 (0-688-04568-5). 64pp. This collection of stories, many of which are fantasies, explore wintry themes and are linked by poems. (Rev: BL 12/1/93; SLJ 1/94)

**980** Hutchins, Pat. *Silly Billy!* (K–3). Illus. 1992, Greenwillow LB $13.93 (0-688-10818-0). 32pp. Hazel, a monster child, has trouble with her pesty young brother, Billy. (Rev: BL 1/1/93; SLJ 9/92)

**981** Hutchins, Pat. *The Very Worst Monster* (K–2). Illus. by author. 1985, Greenwillow LB $16.88 (0-688-04011-X); paper $3.95 (0-688-07816-8). 32pp. A monster family has a new addition, and Hazel is not happy with her baby brother. (Rev: BCCB 4/85; HB 5–6/87; SLJ 5/85)

**982** Hutchins, Pat. *Where's the Baby?* (PS–K). Illus. by author. 1988, Greenwillow LB $12.88 (0-688-05934-1). 32pp. Hazel despairs of the mess her baby brother makes in the house wherever he goes in this story of a monster family. (Rev: BL 3/1/88; HB 5–6/88; SLJ 3/88)

**983** Huth, Holly Young. *Darkfright* (K–3). Illus. by Jenny Stow. 1996, Simon & Schuster $16.00 (0-689-80188-2). 32pp. A wounded star helps a Caribbean woman conquer her fear of the dark. (Rev: BCCB 1/97; BL 11/1/96; SLJ 1/97)

**984** Ichikawa, Satomi. *Isabela's Ribbons* (PS–1). Illus. 1995, Putnam $15.95 (0-399-22772-5). 32pp. In this fantasy set in Puerto Rico, Isabela makes friends when her collection of ribbons lead her to children. (Rev: BL 12/1/95; SLJ 11/95)

**985** Ichikawa, Satomi. *Nora's Castle* (PS–1). Illus. by author. 1997, Putnam $5.95 (0-698-11587-2). 32pp. As a little girl explores a deserted castle with her stuffed animals, they come alive and explore with her. (Rev: BCCB 6/86; BL 4/1/86; SLJ 5/86)

**986** Inkpen, Mick. *Nothing* (PS–K). Illus. 1998, Orchard $14.95 (0-531-30076-5). 32pp. A stuffed toy that is left behind when a family moves finds a new home with the help of a cat. (Rev: BL 3/15/98)

**987** Ishinabe, Fusako. *Spring Snowman* (PS–1). Illus. 1991, Garrett LB $14.60 (0-944483-83-6). 32pp. Animals in the forest find that when spring comes their snowman disappears. (Rev: BL 5/1/91)

**988** Jackson, Shelley. *The Old Woman and the Wave* (1–3). Illus. by author. Series: Richard Jackson Book. 1998, DK Publg. $15.95 (0-7894-2484-3). An old woman has lived her life under a wave that hovers over her house. (Rev: SLJ 3/98*)

**989** James, J. Alison. *Eucalyptus Wings* (PS–3). Illus. by Demi. 1995, Simon & Schuster $16.00 (0-689-31886-3). 40pp. Through the use of magical powers, Kiria and her friend Mica are able to fly like the eucalyptus leaves that float from the trees. (Rev: BL 1/1–15/96; SLJ 3/96)

**990** James, Simon. *Sally and the Limpet* (PS–1). Illus. 1991, Macmillan $13.95 (0-689-50528-0). At the beach, Sally finds a shell that attaches itself to her. (Rev: HB 3–4/91; SLJ 6/91)

**991** Jarrett, Clare. *Catherine and the Lion* (PS–K). Illus. 1997, Carolrhoda $19.93 (1-57505-035-8). 24pp. One day in her bedroom, Catherine finds a new friend, a lion. (Rev: BL 12/15/96; SLJ 2/97)

**992** Jessup, Harley. *What's Alice Up To?* (PS–1). Illus. 1997, Viking paper $14.99 (0-670-87396-9). 32pp. A puzzled dog looks on as his owner, Alice, prepares a birthday party for him. (Rev: BL 9/15/97)

**993** Johnson, Paul B. *The Cow Who Wouldn't Come Down* (K–2). Illus. 1993, Orchard LB $15.99 (0-531-08631-3). 32pp. Miss Rosemary has problems getting her cow back to earth once it learns how to fly. (Rev: BCCB 7–8/93; BL 2/1/93; HB 5–6/93; SLJ 5/93*)

**994** Johnson, Paul B. *A Perfect Pork Stew* (K–2). Illus. 1998, Orchard $15.95 (0-531-30070-6). 32pp. In this original Baba Yaga tale, a witch mistakes some dirt for a pig and makes a stew of it that gives her a tummy ache. (Rev: BL 3/15/98; SLJ 4/98)

**995** Johnston, Tony. *Alice Nizzy Nazzy: The Witch of Santa Fe* (PS–1). Illus. by Tomie dePaola. 1995, Putnam $15.95 (0-399-22788-1). 32pp. In a variation on the Baba Yaga stories, Manuela almost becomes the dinner of a witch named Alice Nizzy Nazzy. (Rev: BCCB 5/95; BL 3/15/95; SLJ 4/95)

**996** Jonas, Ann. *The Quilt* (PS–1). Illus. by author. 1984, Greenwillow LB $15.93 (0-688-03826-3). 32pp. A girl has a nightmare involving the designs on a quilt.

**997** Jonas, Ann. *The Trek* (PS–1). Illus. by author. 1985, Greenwillow LB $15.93 (0-688-04800-5); Morrow paper $3.95 (0-688-08742-6). 32pp. A young girl imagines she is trekking through a dangerous jungle on her way to school. (Rev: BCCB 3/86; BL 11/15/85; SLJ 10/85)

**998** Jonell, Lynne. *Mommy Go Away!* (PS). Illus. by Petra Mathers. 1997, Putnam $12.95 (0-399-23001-7). 25pp. In this role-reversal fantasy, Christopher makes his bossy mother so tiny that he can lecture her as she does him. (Rev: BL 10/15/97; HB 9–10/97; SLJ 12/97)

**999** Jordan, Jennifer. *Albert Goes to Town* (PS–3). Illus. by Shannon McNeill. 1997, Chronicle $13.95 (0-8118-0860-2). 32pp. In this fantasy, a neighbor creates a car for Albert big enough that he can take a ride around the town. (Rev: BL 2/1/98; SLJ 1/98)

**1000** Karim, Roberta. *This Is a Hospital, Not a Zoo!* (K–3). Illus. by Sue Truesdell. 1998, Clarion $15.00 (0-395-72070-2). 48pp. When nurses and doctors want to poke or prod young Filbert MacFee, he simply turns himself into a wild animal like a penguin or giraffe. (Rev: BL 3/1/98)

**1001** Karlin, Nurit. *The Tooth Witch* (PS–K). Illus. by author. 1985, HarperCollins LB $13.89 (0-397-32120-1). 32pp. The story of Abra Cadabra and how she becomes the first Tooth Fairy. (Rev: BCCB 10/85; BL 6/15/85; SLJ 9/86)

**1002** Karlins, Mark. *Salmon Moon* (K–3). Illus. by Hans Poppel. 1993, Simon & Schuster paper $14.00 (0-671-73624-8). 32pp. In this fantasy, Mr. Lutz finds a salmon in a fish store and plots with his friends to return it to the ocean. (Rev: BL 11/1/93)

**1003** Keats, Ezra Jack. *Regards to the Man in the Moon* (PS–1). Illus. by author. 1987, Macmillan paper $4.99 (0-689-71160-3). 32pp. Lewis and his friend visit outer space via their imaginations. Originally published in 1981.

**1004** Keller, Debra. *The Trouble with Mister* (PS–2). Illus. by Shannon McNeill. 1995, Chronicle $13.95 (0-8118-0358-9). 32pp. Alex draws a picture of a dog he wants as a pet and names him Mister. Suddenly, to Alex's astonishment, Mister appears. (Rev: BL 1/1–15/96; SLJ 2/96)

**1005** Kellogg, Steven. *Ralph's Secret Weapon* (PS–3). Illus. by author. 1983, Dial paper $3.95 (0-8037-0307-4). 32pp. Ralph's bassoon playing is so bad, his aunt thinks it will charm a bothersome sea monster.

**1006** Kerins, Tony. *The Brave Ones* (PS). Illus. 1996, Candlewick $9.99 (1-56402-812-7). 24pp. Five courageous toy animals are frightened by Little Clancy, a tiny turtle. (Rev: BL 7/96; SLJ 7/96)

**1007** Ketteman, Helen. *Bubba, The Cowboy Prince: A Fractured Texas Tale* (K–3). Illus. by James Warhola. 1997, Scholastic $15.95 (0-590-25506-1). 32pp. A Western version of the Cinderella story in which a cow is the fairy godmother. (Rev: BL 12/1/97)

**1008** Ketteman, Helen. *Heat Wave* (K–3). Illus. by Scott Goto. 1998, Walker LB $16.85 (0-8027-8645-6). 32pp. In this hilarious fantasy, a heat wave gets stuck on a rural weather vane causing a great upheaval for plants and animals. (Rev: BL 2/1/98; SLJ 3/98)

**1009** Ketteman, Helen. *Luck with Potatoes* (1–3). Illus. by Brian Floca. 1995, Orchard LB $15.99 (0-531-08773-5). 32pp. A tall tale about a farmer who finds his lost cows in the giant potatoes he has been growing. (Rev: BL 10/1/95; SLJ 10/95)

**1010** Khalsa, Dayal Kaur. *The Snow Cat* (PS–3). Illus. 1992, Crown $14.00 (0-517-59183-9). 32pp. God sends a huge Snow Cat down to Elsie, but it melts in her house and turns into a frozen pond. (Rev: BL 12/1/92*)

**1011** Kilborne, Sarah S. *Peach and Blue* (K–3). Illus. by Lou Fancher and Steve Johnson. 1994, Knopf $18.00 (0-679-83929-1). 32pp. A tender story about the friendship between Blue, a toad, and a peach and how Blue helps the peach see the world. (Rev: BCCB 11/94; BL 12/15/94; SLJ 10/94)

**1012** Killion, Bette. *Think of It* (PS–1). Illus. by Denise Saldutti. 1993, HarperCollins LB $11.89 (0-06-023258-7). A little girl imagines what various animals would do if given the admonishments she gets. (Rev: SLJ 8/93)

**1013** Kimmel, Eric A. *The Tale of Ali Baba and the Forty Thieves: A Story from the Arabian Nights* (1–3). Illus. by Will Hillenbrand. 1996, Holiday LB $15.95 (0-8234-1258-X). 30pp. Ali Baba and the story of his amazing treasure trove are covered in colorful prose. (Rev: BCCB 2/97; BL 12/1/96; SLJ 12/96)

**1014** Kimmel, Margaret Mary. *Magic in the Mist* (1–3). Illus. by Trina S. Hyman. 1975, Macmillan $15.00 (0-689-50026-2). 32pp. A young Welsh boy and his toad Jeremy find a dragon.

**1015** Kinsey-Warnock, Natalie. *The Fiddler of the Northern Lights* (K–3). Illus. by Leslie Bowman. 1996, Dutton paper $14.99 (0-525-65215-9). 32pp. A fantasy set in the Far North about a fiddler whose music makes the northern lights dance. (Rev: BL 11/15/96; SLJ 11/96)

**1016** Kinsey-Warnock, Natalie. *On a Starry Night* (PS–1). Illus. by David McPhail. 1994, Orchard LB $16.99 (0-531-08670-4). 32pp. When her father throws her into the air, a young girl visits the stars before returning to his arms. (Rev: BL 2/1/94; HB 7–8/94; SLJ 5/94)

**1017** Kinsey-Warnock, Natalie, and Helen Kinsey. *The Bear That Heard Crying* (K–3). Illus. by Ted Rand. 1993, Dutton paper $14.99 (0-525-65103-9).

32pp. When Sarah wanders off into the woods, she is cared for by a black bear. (Rev: BL 8/93)

**1018** Kipling, Rudyard. *How the Camel Got His Hump* (K–4). Illus. by Tim Raglin. Series: Rabbit Ears Storybook Classics. 1989, Picture Book $19.95 (0-88708-097-9). An effective presentation of the Kipling story that is also available with a cassette read by Jack Nicholson. (Rev: SLJ 2/90)

**1019** Kipling, Rudyard. *Just So Stories* (PS–K). Illus. by Isabelle Brent. 1993, Viking paper $19.99 (0-670-85196-5). 160pp. A beautifully illustrated edition of this classic. (Rev: BL 12/15/93; SLJ 12/93)

**1020** Kipling, Rudyard. *Rikki-Tikki-Tavi* (1–3). Illus. by Lambert Davis. 1992, Harcourt $18.00 (0-15-267015-7). 44pp. A mongoose overcomes snakes that live in the garden of an English family in India. (Rev: BL 9/15/92)

**1021** Kirk, Daniel. *Trash Trucks!* (PS–1). Illus. 1997, Putnam $15.95 (0-399-22927-2). 32pp. Kirk imagines the great trucks with jagged teeth that eat up the mountains of trash collected every day. (Rev: BL 5/15/97)

**1022** Kirkpatrick, Karey. *Disney's James and the Giant Peach* (K–3). Illus. by Lane Smith. 1996, Disney LB $17.49 (0-7868-5039-6). 48pp. A simplified retelling of Roald Dahl's work, aimed at the primary grades. (Rev: BCCB 6/96; BL 5/1/96)

**1023** Kitamura, Satoshi. *UFO Diary* (PS–3). Illus. 1989, Farrar $14.00 (0-374-38026-0). 32pp. A visitor takes a wrong turn at the Milky Way and lands on Earth. (Rev: BL 12/1/89; HB 3–4/90*; SLJ 1/90)

**1024** Kleven, Elisa. *The Paper Princess* (K–2). Illus. 1994, Dutton paper $15.99 (0-525-45231-1). 32pp. A paper princess created by a little girl flies over the city and learns about life. (Rev: BL 7/94; SLJ 6/94*)

**1025** Knox, Bob. *Dave and Jane in Outer Space* (1–4). Illus. by author. 1995, Rizzoli $15.95 (0-8478-1916-7). With their robot and dog, 10-year-olds Dave and Jane tour the solar system. (Rev: SLJ 4/96)

**1026** Komaiko, Leah. *My Perfect Neighborhood* (K–2). Illus. by Barbara Westman. 1990, HarperCollins $13.95 (0-06-023287-0). 32pp. In jiving rhymes, a young girl surveys her most unusual neighborhood. (Rev: BL 3/1/90; SLJ 8/90)

**1027** Krauss, Ruth. *The Carrot Seed* (K–1). Illus. by Crockett Johnson. 1945, HarperCollins LB $13.89 (0-06-023351-6); paper $4.95 (0-06-443210-6). 24pp. A young boy is convinced that the seeds he plants will grow, in spite of his family's doubts.

**1028** Kroll, Steven. *The Candy Witch* (PS–1). Illus. by Marylin Hafner. 1979, Scholastic paper $2.50 (0-590-44509-X). 32pp. A family of witches perform good work except for the youngest, who undoes their work.

**1029** Kroll, Steven. *The Tyrannosaurus Game* (PS–3). Illus. by Tomie dePaola. 1976, Holiday paper $5.95 (0-8234-0620-2). 40pp. A group of first-graders plays a game involving an imaginary purple tyrannosaurus.

**1030** Kroll, Virginia. *Faraway Drums* (K–3). Illus. by Floyd Cooper. 1998, Little, Brown $14.95 (0-316-50449-1). 32pp. Growing up in a noisy, violent, inner-city neighborhood, a young African American girl gets comfort from remembering stories about her family's African past. (Rev: BL 2/15/98)

**1031** Kroll, Virginia. *Wood-Hoopoe Willie* (K–3). Illus. by Katherine Roundtree. 1993, Charlesbridge LB $15.88 (0-88106-410-6). 32pp. Grandpa is convinced that a wood-hoopoe, a colorful African bird, is living inside his grandson. (Rev: BL 3/1/93)

**1032** Kroninger, Stephen. *If I Crossed the Road* (PS–1). Illus. 1997, Simon & Schuster $16.00 (0-689-81190-X). 32pp. In this fantasy, a young boy realizes he is too young to engage in many kinds of activities, but he can certainly dream about them. (Rev: BL 12/15/97; SLJ 12/97)

**1033** Krudop, Walter L. *Something Is Growing* (K–3). Illus. 1995, Simon & Schuster $15.00 (0-689-31940-1). 32pp. When Peter plants a tiny seed, he does not realize that the plant will grow out of control. (Rev: BL 6/1–15/95; SLJ 6/95*)

**1034** Kurt, Kemal. *The Five Fingers and the Moon* (1–3). Trans. by Anthea Bell. Illus. by Aljoscha Blau. 1997, North-South LB $15.88 (1-55858-802-7). 32pp. The fairy people enlist the help of the Five Fingers of the Hand when the Moon fails to function properly. (Rev: BL 10/15/97)

**1035** Kuskin, Karla. *The Upstairs Cat* (K–3). Illus. by Howard Fine. 1997, Clarion $15.00 (0-395-70146-5). 32pp. The story of 2 vicious cats who are obsessed with harming each other becomes a parable about the foolishness and waste of wars. (Rev: BL 11/15/97; SLJ 12/97)

**1036** Kvasnosky, Laura McGee. *What Shall I Dream?* (K–2). Illus. by Judith Byron Schachner. 1996, Dutton paper $14.99 (0-525-45207-9). A young prince gets advice from others about what he should dream, but his nursemaid tells him that dreams come from within. (Rev: BCCB 1/97; SLJ 9/96)

**1037** Lachner, Dorothea. *Andrew's Angry Words* (K–2). Illus. by The Tjong-Khing. 1995, North-South LB $15.88 (1-55858-436-6). 24pp. Andrew's angry words have a surprising effect on a number of people until a lady offers him some kind words to reverse the situation. (Rev: BL 4/15/95; SLJ 6/95)

**1038** Lachner, Dorothea. *Meredith: The Witch Who Wasn't* (K–4). Trans. by J. Alison James. Illus. by

Christa Unzner. 1997, North-South LB $15.88 (1-55858-782-9). 32pp. Meredith, a novice who has a mind of her own, is afraid she will not be certified as a witch. (Rev: BL 9/1/97; SLJ 11/97)

**1039** Lacome, Julie. *I'm a Jolly Farmer* (PS–K). Illus. 1994, Candlewick $13.95 (1-56402-318-4). 32pp. A little girl and her dog fantasize about all the things they could be and places that they could go. (Rev: BL 6/1–15/94; SLJ 8/94)

**1040** Larrick, Nancy, and Wendy Lamb, eds. *To Ride a Butterfly: Original Pictures, Stories, Poems and Songs for Children* (PS–4). Illus. 1991, Dell $17.00 (0-440-50402-3). 96pp. Well-known writers and artists contribute original material to this attractive book. (Rev: BL 10/15/91; HB 1–2/92; SLJ 11/91) [810]

**1041** Lasky, Kathryn. *The Gates of the Wind* (PS–3). Illus. by Janet Stevens. 1995, Harcourt $15.00 (0-15-204264-4). Even though she is living a comfortable life, Gamma Lee decides one day to set out with her donkey to explore the Gates of the Wind. (Rev: SLJ 10/95)

**1042** Laslett, Stephanie. *The Monster Party: A Spooky Story* (K–2). Illus. by Nigel McMullen. 1996, Dutton paper $10.99 (0-525-45691-0). A witch is so anxious to attend a Monster Party, where witches are not allowed, that she lets herself be turned into an ugly troll. (Rev: SLJ 12/96)

**1043** Latimer, Jim. *James Bear and the Goose Gathering* (K–3). Illus. by Betsy Franco-Feeney. 1994, Scribners paper $14.95 (0-684-19526-7). 32pp. A flock of geese are tricked by James Bear into performing in a muddy hollow as, they think, their ancestors once did. A sequel to *James Bear's Pie* (1992). (Rev: BL 3/1/94; SLJ 4/94)

**1044** Lavis, Steve. *Jump!* (PS). Illus. 1998, Dutton $14.99 (0-525-67578-7). 32pp. An interactive book in which a boy marches, roars, and dances with a variety of toys and animals. (Rev: BL 1/1–15/98; HB 5–6/97)

**1045** Leedy, Loreen. *How Humans Make Friends* (1–4). Illus. 1996, Holiday LB $15.95 (0-8234-1223-7). 32pp. Zork, an extraterrestrial, learns about human behavior, the nature of friendship, and the importance of sharing. (Rev: BL 4/1/96; SLJ 7/96)

**1046** Leedy, Loreen. *The Potato Party and Other Troll Tales* (PS–2). Illus. by author. 1989, Holiday LB $14.95 (0-8234-0761-6). 32pp. A delightful collection of 7 original stories about trolls. (Rev: SLJ 12/89)

**1047** Le Guin, Ursula K. *A Ride on the Red Mare's Back* (PS–2). Illus. by Julie Downing. 1992, Orchard LB $17.99 (0-531-08591-0). 48pp. This original fairy tale tells how a girl rescues her brother from the trolls. (Rev: BCCB 10/92; BL 6/15/92; HB 3–4/93; SLJ 9/92*)

**1048** Lehrer, Jamie. *The Magic Costumes: A Story with Pop-ups, Foil, and More* (PS–K). Illus. by Tracey Morgan. 1996, Dial paper $14.99 (0-8037-1967-1). 24pp. Pop-ups and other interactive devices are used to illustrate 2 children and their trip to Fairyland. (Rev: BL 12/15/96)

**1049** Lent, Blair. *Molasses Flood* (K–3). Illus. 1992, Houghton $14.95 (0-395-45314-3). 32pp. When an old molasses tank explodes, Charlie takes an unexpected tour of Boston on a sea of molasses. (Rev: BCCB 1/93; BL 9/1/92; HB 11–12/92; SLJ 10/92)

**1050** Lester, Alison. *Isabella's Bed* (PS–1). Illus. 1993, Houghton $14.95 (0-395-65565-X). 32pp. Grandmother tells her 2 grandchildren a story that results in their being taken on a fantastic ride in a magical bed. (Rev: BL 6/1–15/93; SLJ 6/93)

**1051** Lester, Alison. *The Journey Home* (PS–1). Illus. 1991, Houghton $14.95 (0-395-53355-4). 32pp. Two children fall through a hole in their sandbox and experience a series of amazing adventures. (Rev: BL 7/91; HB 7–8/91)

**1052** Lester, Helen. *Pookins Gets Her Way* (PS–1). Illus. by Lynn Munsinger. 1990, Houghton paper $6.95 (0-395-53965-X). 32pp. Pookins gets nasty if she doesn't get her own way, but she learns a lesson in self-indulgence from a gnome. (Rev: BL 4/15/87; SLJ 8/87)

**1053** Lester, Helen. *Princess Penelope's Parrot* (PS–1). Illus. by Lynn Munsinger. 1996, Houghton $14.95 (0-395-78320-8). 32pp. A browbeaten parrot gets revenge on a bossy princess. (Rev: BCCB 1/97; BL 9/1/96; HB 1–12/96; SLJ 10/96)

**1054** Lester, Helen. *The Wizard, the Fairy and the Magic Chicken* (K–2). Illus. by Lynn Munsinger. 1983, Houghton $14.95 (0-395-33885-9); paper $5.95 (0-395-47945-2). 32pp. Three friends are in competition with their magic tricks.

**1055** Lester, Julius. *Sam and the Tigers: A New Telling of Little Black Sambo* (PS–3). Illus. by Jerry Pinkney. 1996, Dial paper $15.89 (0-8037-2029-7). 40pp. A charming retelling of *Little Black Sambo* without any hint of racism. (Rev: BCCB 7–8/96; BL 6/1–15/96*; HB 9–10/96; SLJ 8/96*)

**1056** Leverich, Kathleen. *Hilary and the Troublemakers* (PS–K). Illus. by Walter Lorraine. 1992, Greenwillow $13.00 (0-688-10857-1). 144pp. In a story that illustrates how real a child's imaginary life can seem, Hilary is beset by such troublemakers as an enormous owl and a piggy bank that will not let her take out money. (Rev: BL 4/1/92*; SLJ 7/92)

**1057** Lindbergh, Reeve. *There's a Cow in the Road!* (K–1). Illus. by Tracey Campbell Pearson. 1993, Dial $13.99 (0-8037-1335-5). 32pp. A small girl getting ready for school is amazed to find farmyard animals outside her house. (Rev: BL 7/93)

**1058** Lipson, Michael. *How the Wind Plays* (PS–1). Illus. by Daniel Kirk. 1994, Hyperion LB $15.49 (1-56282-326-4). 32pp. The wind, in the shape of a little boy, travels around the world creating fun and excitement. (Rev: BL 5/1/94; SLJ 5/94)

**1059** London, Jonathan. *If I Had a Horse* (PS–1). Illus. by Brooke Scudder. 1997, Chronicle $13.95 (0-8118-1112-3). 32pp. A young girl dreams of riding a horse through all sorts of exotic places. (Rev: BL 9/15/97; SLJ 9/97)

**1060** London, Jonathan. *Let the Lynx Come In* (PS–2). Illus. by Patrick Benson. 1996, Candlewick $15.99 (1-56402-531-4). 32pp. A young boy is taken on a ride to the moon on the back of a lynx. (Rev: BL 9/15/96; SLJ 10/96)

**1061** London, Jonathan. *The Owl Who Became the Moon* (PS–2). Illus. by Ted Rand. 1993, Dutton paper $15.99 (0-525-45054-8). 32pp. A young boy imagines a train rattling through the night that frightens all the animals but the owl. (Rev: BCCB 2/93; BL 1/15/93)

**1062** Loredo, Elizabeth. *Boogie Bones* (K–3). Illus. by Kevin Hawkes. 1997, Putnam $15.95 (0-399-22763-6). 32pp. Boogie Bones, a skeleton, disguises himself as a human to enter a dance contest. (Rev: BL 9/1/97; SLJ 9/97)

**1063** Low, Alice. *Stories to Tell a Five-Year-Old* (PS–1). Illus. by Heather H. Maione. 1996, Little, Brown paper $8.95 (0-316-53416-1). 150pp. Twenty-one short stories to delight the kindergarten set. (Rev: BL 6/1–15/96)

**1064** Lowell, Susan. *The Bootmaker and the Elves* (K–4). Illus. by Tom Curry. 1997, Orchard LB $16.99 (0-531-33044-3). 32pp. The old folktale is given a new setting, the Old West, and a new subject, cowboy boots. (Rev: BL 9/15/97; HB 11–12/97; SLJ 11/97)

**1065** Luenn, Nancy. *Songs for the Ancient Forest* (K–3). Illus. by Jill Kastner. 1993, Macmillan $14.95 (0-689-31719-0). 32pp. Raven has a dream about the fate of the lovely forests of the Pacific Northwest. (Rev: BL 3/1/93; SLJ 3/93)

**1066** Luenn, Nancy. *Unicorn Crossing* (2–3). Illus. by Peter E. Hanson. 1987, Troll paper $2.50 (0-8167-1321-9). 64pp. Jenny and Mrs. Donovan look for unicorns during a summer on an island. (Rev: BCCB 9/87; BL 9/1/87; SLJ 10/87)

**1067** Lyon, George E. *The Outside Inn* (K–3). Illus. by Vera Rosenberry. 1991, Orchard $15.95 (0-531-05936-7); paper $6.95 (0-531-07086-7). 32pp. All kinds of creatures seek their food, while in the foreground, youngsters prepare a "pretend" meal. (Rev: BL 7/91; SLJ 9/91)

**1068** McAllister, Angela. *The Enchanted Flute* (K–4). Illus. by Margaret Chamberlain. 1991, Delacorte $14.95 (0-385-30326-2). A goldsmith creates for Queen Pernickety a flute that only plays what the listener wants to hear. (Rev: BCCB 1/92; SLJ 12/91)

**1069** McCloskey, Kevin. *Mrs. Fitz's Flamingos* (PS–2). Illus. 1992, Lothrop LB $13.93 (0-688-10475-4). 32pp. To brighten the view from her windows, Mrs. Fitz places plastic flamingos on her neighbor's roof. (Rev: BL 4/15/92; SLJ 6/92)

**1070** McCully, Emily Arnold. *Starring Mirette and Bellini* (K–4). Illus. 1997, Putnam $15.99 (0-399-22636-2). 32pp. In this sequel to *Mirette on the High Wire*, high-wire artist Bellini is saved from a czarist prison by his protégé, Mirette. (Rev: BCCB 7–8/97; BL 4/15/97*; SLJ 5/97)

**1071** MacDonald, Betty. *The Won't-Take-a-Bath Cure* (PS–2). Illus. by Bruce Whatley. 1997, Harper-Collins $12.95 (0-06-027630-4). A picture version of a story featuring Mrs. Piggle-Wiggle, who lives in an upside-down house. (Rev: SLJ 10/97)

**1072** MacDonald, Elizabeth. *John's Picture* (PS–2). Illus. by David McTaggart. 1999, Dutton paper $3.95 (0-14-054344-9). 32pp. After John draws a picture of a man, it becomes alive and begins drawing other objects. (Rev: BL 3/15/91; SLJ 10/91)

**1073** McGee, Marni. *Forest Child* (K–3). Illus. by A. Scott Banfill. 1994, Simon & Schuster $15.00 (0-671-86608-7). A feral girl, who has been raised by animal friends, is rescued by them when she is captured by a hunter. (Rev: SLJ 3/95)

**1074** McGeorge, Constance W. *Snow Riders* (PS–3). Illus. by Mary Whyte. 1995, Chronicle $13.95 (0-8118-0873-4). 32pp. Snow horses created by a brother and sister come to life and take the children on a magic ride. (Rev: BL 1/1–15/96)

**1075** Machado, Ana María. *Niña Bonita* (PS–3). Trans. from Spanish by Elena Iribarren. Illus. by Rosana Faría. Series: Cranky Nell Books. 1996, Kane/Miller $9.95 (0-916291-63-4). A rabbit envies the dark skin of a little girl he meets in this story set in a South American coastal town. (Rev: SLJ 12/96)

**1076** McKissack, Patricia. *Mirandy and Brother Wind* (2–3). Illus. by Jerry Pinkney. 1988, Knopf LB $18.99 (0-394-98765-9). 32pp. Mirandy wants Brother Wind to be her partner at the junior cakewalk contest. (Rev: BCCB 12/88; BL 1/1/89; HB 3–4/89)

**1077** McMillan, Bruce. *Ghost Doll* (K–1). Illus. by author. 1997, Apple Island paper $10.00 (0-934313-01-6). 32pp. Chrissy changes a ghost doll into the real thing.

**1078** McMillan, Bruce. *The Remarkable Riderless Runaway Tricycle* (K–3). Illus. by author. 1985, Apple Island paper $10.00 (0-934313-00-8). 48pp. A tricycle, unwilling to be consigned to the dump, sets out on its own trip. This reissued picture book was first published in 1978 and contains black-and-white photographs.

**1079** McMullan, Kate. *Hey, Pipsqueak!* (PS–2). Illus. by Jim McMullan. 1995, HarperCollins $14.95 (0-06-205100-8). In his miniature car, a little boy tries to deliver a present but is stopped by a troll. (Rev: SLJ 11/95)

**1080** McNaughton, Colin. *Captain Abdul's Pirate School* (1–4). Illus. 1994, Candlewick $16.95 (1-56402-429-6). 40pp. A pirate crew operates a school in which rewards are given for bad deeds and deplorable manners. (Rev: BCCB 12/94; BL 10/15/94; SLJ 1/95)

**1081** McNaughton, Colin. *Who's That Banging on the Ceiling?* (PS–3). Illus. 1994, Candlewick paper $5.99 (1-56402-384-2). 32pp. Tenants in a high rise are disturbed by a noisemaker in the building. (Rev: BL 1/15/93; SLJ 3/93)

**1082** McPhail, David. *Edward and the Pirates* (PS–3). Illus. 1997, Little, Brown $15.95 (0-316-56344-7). 32pp. The pirates that Edward is reading about come alive and kidnap him. (Rev: BCCB 7–8/97; BL 4/15/97; SLJ 5/97)

**1083** McPhail, David. *Moony B. Finch, the Fastest Draw in the West* (PS–2). Illus. by author. 1994, Artists & Writers Guild $12.95 (0-307-17554-5). When his picture of a train comes to life, a young boy hops on board for an adventure out west. (Rev: SLJ 7/94)

**1084** McPhail, David. *The Party* (PS–1). Illus. 1990, Little, Brown $14.95 (0-316-56330-7). 32pp. A little boy and his stuffed toys have a party even after Dad falls asleep. (Rev: BL 10/1/90; SLJ 11/90)

**1085** McPhail, David. *The Puddle* (PS–2). Illus. 1998, Farrar $15.00 (0-374-36148-7). 32pp. A fantasy about a boy who goes out in the rain to sail his boat and encounters various animals that play with him. (Rev: BL 2/1/98; SLJ 3/98)

**1086** McPhail, David. *The Train* (PS). Illus. 1977, Little, Brown $15.95 (0-316-56316-1); paper $5.95 (0-316-56331-5). 32pp. Matthew's toy train comes to life in this fantasy. A reissue.

**1087** Madden, Don. *The Wartville Wizard* (K–3). Illus. by author. 1986, Macmillan paper $5.99 (0-689-71667-2). 32pp. An old man who picks up litter is given the "power over trash" by Mother Nature in this tale about littering. (Rev: BL 11/1/86; SLJ 1/87)

**1088** Madinaveitia, Horacio. *Sir Robert's Little Outing* (K–3). Illus. 1992, Wonder Well LB $13.95 (1-879567-01-6); paper $7.95 (1-879567-00-8). 30pp. An oafish knight, Sir Robert, sets out on a quest to win the fair Princess Dorothea. (Rev: BL 1/1/93)

**1089** Mahy, Margaret. *Boom, Baby, Boom, Boom!* (PS–K). Illus. by Patricia MacCarthy. 1997, Viking paper $15.99 (0-670-87314-4). 32pp. When Mama quietly plays her drum, animals enter the house and share a baby's dinner. (Rev: BL 3/1/97; SLJ 5/97)

**1090** Mahy, Margaret. *The Great White Man-Eating Shark: A Cautionary Tale* (1–4). Illus. by Jonathan Allen. 1990, Dial paper $13.99 (0-8037-0749-5). 32pp. A boy who looks and swims like a shark misuses his unusual appearance and talents. (Rev: BL 2/15/90; HB 3–4/90*; SLJ 1/90*)

**1091** Mahy, Margaret. *The Queen's Goat* (PS–3). Illus. by Emma C. Clark. 1995, Smithmark $3.98 (0-8317-2210-X). 32pp. The queen chooses the gardener's goat, Carmen, as her pet and finds that goats have minds of their own. (Rev: BL 8/91; SLJ 11/91)

**1092** Mahy, Margaret. *Tick Tock Tales: Twelve Stories to Read Around the Clock* (K–3). Illus. by Wendy Smith. 1994, Simon & Schuster paper $16.95 (0-689-50604-X). 92pp. Twelve unusual, imaginative tales from a master storyteller. (Rev: SLJ 4/94*)

**1093** Maizlish, Lisa. *The Ring* (PS–1). Illus. 1996, Greenwillow $15.00 (0-688-14217-6). 24pp. A magic ring turns winter to summer and allows a boy to fly over New York City. (Rev: BL 6/1–15/96; HB 7–8/96; SLJ 5/96)

**1094** Manning, Mick. *Honk! Honk! A Story of Migration* (K–2). Illus. by Brita Granström. 1997, Kingfisher $14.95 (0-7534-5103-4). In this fantasy, a child hitches a ride on a Canada goose and migrates to the North and back. (Rev: SLJ 11/97)

**1095** Mariconda, Barbara. *Witch Way to the Beach* (1–3). Illus. by Jon McIntosh. Series: First Choice Chapter Book. 1997, Bantam $13.95 (0-385-32265-8); paper $3.99 (0-440-41268-4). 48pp. Constance, a witch, does not expect all the adventures she has when she goes to the beach. (Rev: SLJ 11/97)

**1096** Mark, Jan. *Fun with Mrs. Thumb* (PS–2). Illus. by Nicola Bayley. 1993, Candlewick $9.95 (1-56402-247-1). 32pp. Simple rhymes describe how a ginger cat attacks the wooden dollhouse in which Mrs. Thumb, a doll, lives. (Rev: BL 1/1/94; SLJ 3/94)

**1097** Martin, Jacqueline B. *Higgins Bend Song and Dance* (1–4). Illus. by Brad Sneed. 1997, Houghton $16.00 (0-395-67583-9). Simon Henry vows to use any method possible to catch Oscar, a wily catfish. (Rev: SLJ 9/97)

**1098** Marzollo, Jean. *Snow Angel* (PS–2). Illus. by Jacqueline Rogers. 1995, Scholastic $14.95 (0-590-48748-5). In this fantasy, a little girl is taken on a flight by a snow angel on a wintry day. (Rev: SLJ 12/95)

**1099** Maynard, Bill. *Incredible Ned* (K–2). Illus. by Frank Remkiewicz. 1997, Putnam $15.95 (0-399-23023-8). Ned has a strange problem: every time he mentions an object or animal, it appears. (Rev: SLJ 11/97)

**1100** Meddaugh, Susan. *Beast* (K–2). Illus. by author. 1985, Houghton paper $3.95 (0-317-18511-X). 32pp. Anna frightens a timid monster.

**1101** Meddaugh, Susan. *Cinderella's Rat* (K–2). Illus. 1997, Houghton $15.00 (0-395-86833-5). 32pp. An amusing picture book that tells what happened to the rat that was turned into Cinderella's coachman. (Rev: BL 10/1/97; HB 9–10/97; SLJ 10/97*)

**1102** Meddaugh, Susan. *Martha Blah Blah* (PS–2). Illus. 1996, Houghton $14.95 (0-395-79755-1). 32pp. Martha, who talks after eating alphabet soup, finds her vocabulary constricted when the soup company reduces the letters in each can. (Rev: BCCB 12/96; BL 9/15/96; HB 11–12/96; SLJ 11/96*)

**1103** Medearis, Angela Shelf. *The Ghost of Sifty Sifty Sam* (K–3). Illus. by Jacqueline Rogers. 1997, Scholastic $15.95 (0-590-48290-4). 32pp. A chef named Dan uses his cooking to tame a ghost whose wailings have made a house unfit for living. (Rev: BL 12/1/97; SLJ 11/97)

**1104** Melmed, Laura K. *The First Song Ever Sung* (PS–3). Illus. by Ed Young. 1993, Lothrop LB $15.93 (0-688-08231-9). 32pp. A young boy in ancient Japan asks different people and animals what was the first song ever sung and gets, in each case, a different answer. (Rev: BCCB 7–8/93; BL 9/1/93; SLJ 6/93*)

**1105** Metaxas, Eric, adapt. *Pinocchio: The Classic Italian Tale* (K–3). Illus. by Brian Ajhar. 1996, Simon & Schuster paper $19.95 (0-689-80230-7). A simple retelling of some of the key episodes from the original story, with handsome illustrations. (Rev: SLJ 8/96)

**1106** Michelson, Richard. *Did You Say Ghosts?* (K–2). Illus. by Leonard Baskin. 1993, Macmillan LB $14.95 (0-02-766915-7). 32pp. Ghosts, monsters, and various supernatural beings scare each other in this cumulaive tale. (Rev: BL 9/1/93)

**1107** Milgrim, David. *Dog Brain* (PS–2). Illus. 1996, Viking paper $13.99 (0-670-86935-X). 32pp. In simple text and childlike pictures, a dog tells about a typical day's activities. (Rev: BL 9/1/96; SLJ 9/96)

**1108** Milich, Melissa. *Miz Fannie Mae's Fine New Easter Hat* (K–3). Illus. by Yong Chen. 1997, Little, Brown $14.95 (0-316-57159-8). 32pp. Tandy and her father buy a magical hat for Mama's Easter. (Rev: BL 5/15/97; SLJ 6/97)

**1109** Miller, William. *The Conjure Woman* (PS–3). Illus. by Terea D. Shaffer. 1996, Simon & Schuster $15.00 (0-689-31962-2). 32pp. A "conjure woman" magically transports a sick Toby to the family's African homeland, Ghana, where he is made well. (Rev: BL 2/15/96; SLJ 3/96)

**1110** Mills, Lauren. *Fairy Wings* (PS–3). Illus. by Dennis Nolan. 1995, Little, Brown $15.95 (0-316-57397-3). 32pp. Fia is the only fairy in the land of fairies without gossamer wings. (Rev: BL 11/1/95; SLJ 1/96)

**1111** Moers, Hermann. *Katie and the Big, Brave Bear* (PS–3). Illus. by Jozef Wilkon. 1995, North-South LB $14.88 (1-55858-398-X). 32pp. Big, Brave Bear comes to life out of a storybook to protect Katie when her mother goes to the supermarket and leaves her alone. (Rev: BL 6/1–15/95; SLJ 8/95)

**1112** Mohr, Nicholasa. *Old Letivia and the Mountain of Sorrows* (PS–3). Illus. by Rudy Gutierrez. 1996, Viking paper $15.99 (0-670-84419-5). 32pp. A witch and 2 friends set out to conquer the Wild Wind in this tale set in ancient Puerto Rico. (Rev: BL 5/15/96; SLJ 8/96)

**1113** Morozumi, Atsuko. *My Friend Gorilla* (PS–K). Illus. 1998, Farrar $15.00 (0-374-35458-8). 32pp. When a zoo closes down, a boy adopts a gorilla; but in time, his friend must go back to his home in Africa. (Rev: BL 2/1/98; SLJ 3/98)

**1114** Moss, Miriam. *Jigsaw* (K–3). Illus. by Tony Smith. 1997, Millbrook LB $22.40 (0-7613-0044-9). 32pp. An unusual picture book in which items on a journey become parts of a jigsaw puzzle. (Rev: BL 9/15/97; SLJ 12/97)

**1115** Munsch, Robert. *Mud Puddle* (PS–2). Illus. by Sami Suomalainen. 1996, Annick LB $16.95 (1-55037-469-9); paper $5.95 (1-55037-468-0). 32pp. Jule Ann is attacked by a mud puddle every time she leaves her house. (Rev: BL 4/1/96)

**1116** Murdocca, Salvatore. *Baby Wants the Moon* (PS–2). Illus. 1995, Lothrop LB $14.93 (0-688-13665-6). 32pp. Sunny fantasizes that his new baby sister is eating so much she will become a giant. (Rev: BL 6/1–15/95; SLJ 6/95*)

**1117** Murphy, Stuart J. *A Pair of Socks* (PS–1). Illus. by Lois Ehlert. 1996, HarperCollins LB $14.89 (0-06-025880-2). 40pp. A sock sets out to find its lost mate. (Rev: BL 10/1/96; SLJ 12/96)

**1118** Mutchnick, Brenda, and Ron Casden. *A Noteworthy Tale* (1–4). Illus. by Ian Penney. 1997, Abrams $17.95 (0-8109-1386-0). A fantasy about 2 lands, one in which music is created and cherished and the other where it is banned. (Rev: SLJ 1/98)

**1119** Myers, Walter Dean. *The Story of the Three Kingdoms* (5–8). Illus. by Ashley Bryan. 1995, HarperCollins LB $14.89 (0-06-024287-6). 32pp. In this fable, humans gradually take over mastery of the land, sea, and sky. (Rev: BCCB 7–8/95; BL 6/1–15/95; SLJ 7/95*)

**1120** Nash, Ogden. *The Tale of Custard the Dragon* (PS–3). Illus. by Lynn Munsinger. 1995, Little, Brown $14.95 (0-316-59880-1). 32pp. Custard, a cowardly dragon, saves the day when a pirate king terrorizes everyone. (Rev: BL 3/1/95; HB 7–8/95; SLJ 7/95)

**1121** Naylor, Phyllis Reynolds. *The Boy with the Helium Head* (K–3). Illus. by Kay Chorao. 1992, Dell $3.50 (0-440-40644-7). By mistake, Jonathan receives a helium shot and becomes famous.

**1122** Newman, Nanette. *There's a Bear in the Bath!* (PS–3). Illus. by Michael Foreman. 1994, Harcourt $13.95 (0-15-285512-2). 32pp. Liza finds a bear in her yard that likes coffee and crosswords. (Rev: BL 3/15/94; SLJ 7/94)

**1123** Nichol, Barbara. *Dippers* (3–5). Illus. by Barry Moser. 1997, Tundra $17.95 (0-88776-396-0). A fantasy about a sick child in Toronto in 1912 and about her sister, who sees dippers, creatures that look like prairie dogs with wings. (Rev: SLJ 9/97)

**1124** Nightingale, Sandy. *Cider Apples* (K–3). Illus. 1996, Harcourt $15.00 (0-15-201244-3). 32pp. Fairies help a young girl and her grandmother save an ailing apple tree. (Rev: BL 9/1/96; SLJ 11/96)

**1125** Nightingale, Sandy. *A Giraffe on the Moon* (PS). Illus. 1992, Harcourt $13.95 (0-15-230950-0). 32pp. A fine visual feast in a picture book that begins "I didn't expect to see . . ." (Rev: BL 2/15/92*; SLJ 3/92)

**1126** Nolen, Jerdine. *Harvey Potter's Balloon Farm* (K–3). Illus. by Mark Buehner. 1994, Morrow $16.00 (0-688-07887-7). 32pp. In this tall tale, a little girl learns all the secrets of trade when she visits Harvey's balloon farm and discovers how they are grown. (Rev: BL 4/15/94; HB 7–8/94; SLJ 5/94)

**1127** Nones, Eric Jon. *Angela's Wings* (PS–3). Illus. 1995, Farrar $16.00 (0-374-30331-2). 32pp. Angela tries to hide the fact that she has grown wings until she learns to fly. (Rev: BL 9/15/95; SLJ 10/95)

**1128** Oliviero, Jamie. *Som See and the Magic Elephant* (1–3). Illus. by Jo'Anne Kelly. 1995, Hyperion $14.95 (0-7868-0025-9). 32pp. Before Som See's great aunt dies, she wants to touch a white elephant; and with the help of magical powers, Som See is eventually able to grant her wish. (Rev: BL 5/1/95; SLJ 5/95)

**1129** Olofsdotter, Marie. *Sofia and the Heartmender* (K–3). Illus. 1993, Free Spirit $14.95 (0-915793-50-4). 32pp. Sofia is taken to a magical world where she is able to confront and conquer her fears. (Rev: BL 11/1/93)

**1130** O'Malley, Kevin. *Carl Caught a Flying Fish* (K–1). Illus. by author. 1996, Simon & Schuster $13.00 (0-689-80098-3). When Carl takes his new friend, a goldfish with wings, to school, the fish wreaks havoc. (Rev: SLJ 7/96)

**1131** Oram, Hiawyn. *A Boy Wants a Dinosaur* (PS–2). Illus. by Satoshi Kitamura. 1991, Farrar $13.95 (0-374-30939-6). 28pp. Alex and his dad go to the Dino Store to pick out a pet dinosaur. (Rev: BL 4/15/91; SLJ 7/91)

**1132** Oram, Hiawyn. *In the Attic* (PS–K). Illus. by Satoshi Kitamura. 1985, Holt $13.95 (0-8050-0779-2); paper $4.95 (0-8050-0780-6). 32pp. A little boy climbs his fire engine ladder into his attic, where he has exciting adventures, even though, as his mother tells him, "we don't have an attic." (Rev: BCCB 3/85; BL 6/15/85; SLJ 10/85)

**1133** Orgel, Doris. *Button Soup* (K–3). Illus. by Pau Estrada. Series: Bank Street Easy-to-Read. 1994, Bantam paper $3.99 (0-553-37341-2). 32pp. A variation on the "Stone Soup" story in which an old woman makes soup using a button and water as the only 2 ingredients. (Rev: SLJ 2/95)

**1134** Ottley, Matt. *What Faust Saw* (K–2). Illus. 1996, Dutton paper $13.99 (0-525-45650-3). 32pp. A dog isn't believed when he tries to warn a family about aliens landing in the front yard. (Rev: BL 6/1–15/96; SLJ 6/96)

**1135** Palatini, Margie. *Piggie Pie!* (K–3). Illus. by Howard Fine. 1995, Clarion $14.00 (0-395-71691-8). 32pp. Gritch the Witch is off to Old MacDonald's farm in search of 8 plump pigs for her favorite pie. (Rev: BL 9/1/95*; SLJ 11/95*)

**1136** Palazzo, Tony. *Magic Crayon* (PS–2). Illus. by author. 1967, Lion LB $12.95 (0-87460-089-8). Imaginative fun for very young readers.

**1137** Paraskevas, Betty. *The Tangerine Bear* (PS–2). Illus. by Michael Paraskevas. 1997, HarperCollins LB $14.89 (0-06-205147-4). 32pp. Toy Tangerine Bear wants to become part of a family, but nobody wants him because his smile was sewn on upside down. (Rev: BL 11/1/97)

**1138** Parnall, Peter. *Spaces* (1–3). Illus. 1993, Millbrook LB $21.90 (1-56294-336-7). 32pp. A fantastic view of what unusual creatures and thoughts can fill all sorts of spaces. (Rev: BL 12/1/93; SLJ 12/93)

**1139** Pastuchiv, Olga. *Minas and the Fish* (PS–2). Illus. by author. 1997, Houghton $14.95 (0-395-79756-X). 32pp. Minas is granted a single wish if he frees a strange sea creature that has been caught by his father and brothers. (Rev: BCCB 5/97; SLJ 5/97)

**1140** Paterson, Katherine. *The King's Equal* (2–5). Illus. by Vladimir Vagin. 1992, HarperCollins LB $16.89 (0-06-022497-5). 64pp. An arrogant king learns humility when the bride he wants does not want him. (Rev: BCCB 1/93; BL 7/92; SLJ 9/92*)

**1141** Paton, Priscilla. *Howard and the Sitter Surprise* (PS–2). Illus. by Paul Meisel. 1996, Houghton $15.95 (0-395-71814-7). Howard is a terror to all the baby-sitters until he meets his match in Sarah the bear. (Rev: SLJ 10/96)

**1142** Paxton, Tom. *The Story of the Tooth Fairy* (K–3). Illus. by Robert Sauber. 1996, Morrow LB $15.93 (0-688-12988-9). 32pp. Emily realizes that the girl in her garden is really a fairy. (Rev: BCCB 3/96; BL 8/96; SLJ 9/96)

**1143** Pearson, Susan. *Well, I Never!* (PS–1). Illus. by James Warhola. 1990, Simon & Schuster paper $15.00 (0-671-69199-6). 24pp. Strange things are happening on the farm, such as pigs learning to fly. (Rev: BL 11/15/90; SLJ 2/91)

**1144** Peet, Bill. *Big Bad Bruce* (K–3). Illus. by author. 1982, Houghton $16.00 (0-395-25150-8); paper $6.95 (0-395-32922-1). Bruce encounters a witch and is shrunk to the size of a chipmunk.

**1145** Peet, Bill. *The Caboose Who Got Loose* (K–3). Illus. by author. 1980, Houghton $16.00 (0-395-14805-7); paper $6.95 (0-395-28715-4). 48pp. When Katy Caboose is jarred loose from the rest of the train, she gets her wish to be a "cabin in the trees," free from noise and smoke.

**1146** Peet, Bill. *Jennifer and Josephine* (1–3). Illus. by author. 1980, Houghton paper $6.95 (0-395-29608-0). Jennifer, an old touring car, is driven through several adventures by a reckless driver and is accompanied by a friendly cat named Josephine.

**1147** Peppe, Rodney. *The Magic Toy Box* (PS). Illus. 1996, Candlewick $15.99 (0-7636-0010-5). 32pp. Toys leave their magical toy box to play with Pongo, a stuffed animal. (Rev: BL 9/15/96; SLJ 11/96)

**1148** Perry, Sarah. *If . . .* (K–4). Illus. 1995, J. Paul Getty Museum $16.95 (0-89236-321-5). 46pp. Using a number of unconventional statements beginning with "if," this imaginative book presents a series of eyecatching, ingenious pictures to illustrate each phrase. (Rev: BCCB 1/96; BL 10/15/95*; SLJ 2/96)

**1149** Peters, Lisa Westberg. *When the Fly Flew In . . .* (PS–2). Illus. by Brad Sneed. 1994, Dial paper $14.89 (0-8037-1432-7). 32pp. A pesky fly is the inadvertent cause of a group of animals cleaning up their room. (Rev: BCCB 9/95; BL 7/94*; SLJ 9/94)

**1150** Peterson, Beth. *Myrna Never Sleeps* (1–3). Illus. by John O'Brien. 1995, Atheneum $13.00 (0-689-31893-6). 51pp. When Myrna can't get to sleep, she imagines herself as a superwoman in all sorts of adventures. (Rev: SLJ 7/95)

**1151** Pflieger, Pat. *The Fog's Net* (PS–3). Illus. by Ruth Gamper. 1994, Houghton $14.95 (0-395-68194-4). 32pp. A fantasy about a girl who weaves a deadly net at the insistence of the devil. (Rev: BL 9/15/94; SLJ 1/95)

**1152** Pienkowski, Jan. *Haunted House* (K–2). Illus. by Jane Walmsley. 1979, Dutton paper $16.99 (0-525-31520-9). 12pp. All kinds of ghosts emerge from various places in this unusual house.

**1153** Pilkey, Dav. *God Bless the Gargoyles* (K–3). Illus. 1996, Harcourt $15.00 (0-15-200248-0). 40pp. To comfort the despised gargoyles, angels take them on flights. (Rev: BL 10/1/96; SLJ 11/96)

**1154** Pilkey, Dav. *When Cats Dream* (PS–3). Illus. 1992, Orchard LB $16.99 (0-531-08597-X). 32pp. Cats' dreams are more fun and more colorful than their reality. (Rev: BCCB 9/92; BL 8/92; HB 3–4/93; SLJ 9/92*)

**1155** Pinkney, Brian. *The Adventures of Sparrowboy* (PS–3). Illus. 1997, Simon & Schuster $16.00 (0-689-81071-7). 40pp. A paperboy named Henry discovers that, like the sparrows, he can fly. (Rev: BCCB 6/97; BL 4/1/97; HB 7–8/97, 9–10/97; SLJ 4/97)

**1156** Pinkwater, Daniel. *The Phantom of the Lunch Wagon* (K–3). Illus. 1992, Macmillan LB $13.95 (0-02-774641-0). 32pp. The lunch wagon that Chris has repaired is haunted by its old ghost, who does not want to leave. (Rev: BCCB 11/92; BL 9/1/92; SLJ 12/92)

**1157** Pinkwater, Daniel. *Wempires* (PS–3). Illus. 1991, Macmillan paper $13.95 (0-02-774411-6). 32pp. A boy is obsessed by vampires until he has a visit from 3 of them. (Rev: BCCB 10/91; BL 8/91; SLJ 11/91)

**1158** Pinkwater, Daniel. *Young Larry* (K–3). Illus. by Jill Pinkwater. 1997, Marshall Cavendish LB $14.95 (0-7614-5004-1). 32pp. Larry, a polar bear, gets his first job being a lifeguard. Also use *At the Hotel Larry* (1997). (Rev: BL 9/1/97; SLJ 10/97*)

**1159** Polacco, Patricia. *Appelemando's Dreams* (PS–2). Illus. 1991, Putnam $15.95 (0-399-21800-9). 32pp. Appelemando teaches the townspeople that they should never question the importance of dreams. (Rev: BL 10/15/91; SLJ 9/91)

**1160** Polacco, Patricia. *Babushka's Doll* (PS–2). Illus. 1990, Simon & Schuster paper $16.00 (0-671-68343-8). 32pp. Natasha, a pest, learns her lesson when a doll comes alive and begins nagging. (Rev: BCCB 11/90; BL 9/15/90*; HB 1–2/91; SLJ 11/90)

**1161** Polacco, Patricia. *Rechenka's Eggs* (K–2). Illus. by author. 1988, Putnam $15.95 (0-399-21501-8). 32pp. Old Babushka saves a wild goose, and when her decorated eggs are broken, the goose repays her kindness by laying her own decorated eggs. (Rev: BCCB 6/88; BL 4/1/88; SLJ 5/88)

**1162** Pomerantz, Charlotte. *Mangaboom* (K–4). Illus. by Anita Lobel. 1997, Greenwillow LB $15.93 (0-688-12957-9). 40pp. When Daniel climbs to the top of a huge mango tree, he meets a gorgeous lady giant named Mangaboom. (Rev: BCCB 5/97; BL 4/1/97; SLJ 4/97)

**1163** Powers, Daniel. *Jiro's Pearl* (PS–3). Illus. 1997, Candlewick $15.99 (1-56402-631-0). 32pp. A Japanese tale about a foolish young boy who is sent by his ailing grandmother to buy medicine. (Rev: BL 10/1/97; SLJ 7/97)

**1164** Poydar, Nancy. *Cool Ali* (PS–1). Illus. 1996, Simon & Schuster paper $13.00 (0-689-80755-4). 26pp. Ali cools her neighborhood by drawing items that suggest moderate temperatures. (Rev: BCCB 10/96; BL 8/96; HB 9–10/96; SLJ 9/96)

**1165** Prater, John. *Once upon a Picnic* (PS–2). Illus. 1996, Candlewick $14.99 (1-56402-810-0). 32pp. All kinds of fantastic creatures are having picnics at the same time as a very ordinary family is having its picnic. (Rev: BCCB 4/96; BL 8/96; SLJ 8/96)

**1166** Preiss, Byron, ed. *The Best Children's Books in the World: A Treasury of Illustrated Stories* (K–3). Illus. 1996, Abrams $29.95 (0-8109-1246-5). 319pp. A fascinating collection of 15 distinguished picture books published in countries around the world as they originally appeared, with translations when necessary. (Rev: SLJ 12/96)

**1167** Price, Mathew. *Have You Seen My Sister?* (3–5). Illus. by Errol LeCain. 1991, Harcourt $12.95 (0-15-200467-X). 28pp. While looking for his baby sister, Ben gets help from a goose, a doll, and a stuffed rabbit. (Rev: BL 12/1/91)

**1168** Prior, R. W. N. *The Great Monarch Butterfly Chase* (PS–2). Illus. by Beth Glick. 1993, Bradbury $14.95 (0-02-775145-7). In this fantasy based on fact, 2 boys follow a monarch butterfly on its migration to Mexico. (Rev: SLJ 2/94)

**1169** Pyle, Howard. *Bearskin* (1–4). Illus. by Trina S. Hyman. 1997, Morrow LB $15.93 (0-688-09838-X). 48pp. An abandoned youngster is cared for by a bear and grows up to be a dragon-slaying hero. (Rev: BL 11/1/97*; HB 9–10/97; SLJ 8/97*)

**1170** Rascal. *Oregon's Journey* (K–3). Illus. by Louis Joos. 1994, Troll paper $15.95 (0-8167-3305-8). 40pp. A dwarf and a performing bear leave the circus and head west to Oregon and freedom. (Rev: BCCB 6/94; BL 4/15/94*; SLJ 8/94)

**1171** Ray, Mary L. *Pumpkins: A Story for a Field* (K–4). Illus. by Barry Root. 1992, Harcourt $13.95 (0-15-252252-2). 32pp. A farmer reaches an agreement with a vacant field and together they grow a bumper crop of pumpkins. (Rev: BL 10/15/92; HB 11–12/92; SLJ 3/93)

**1172** Reasoner, Charles. *Who Drives This?* (PS). Illus. by author. Series: Sliding Surprise Books. 1996, Price Stern Sloan $9.95 (0-8431-3939-0). A board book that uses sliding panels to reveal animals driving various vehicles. Also use *Who Pretends?* (1996). (Rev: SLJ 8/96)

**1173** Reiner, Annie. *A Visit to the Art Galaxy* (1–3). Illus. 1990, Simon & Schuster $15.95 (0-671-74957-9). 56pp. Two children and their mother enter the Land of Modern Art and discover new ways of looking at paintings. (Rev: BL 5/15/91)

**1174** Richardson, Jean. *The Bear Who Went to the Ballet* (PS–1). Illus. by Susan Winter. 1995, DK Publg. $14.95 (0-7894-0318-8). 32pp. A teddy bear discovers she is not suited to becoming a ballerina, so she decides to be a teller of ballet stories instead. (Rev: BL 2/15/96; SLJ 3/96)

**1175** Richardson, Judith B. *Old Winter* (PS–1). Illus. by R. W. Alley. 1996, Orchard LB $15.99 (0-531-08883-9). 32pp. Old Winter is so angry at people criticizing his season that he decides to remain in the North although spring is scheduled to arrive. (Rev: BCCB 12/96; BL 10/1/96; SLJ 12/96)

**1176** Ringgold, Faith. *Aunt Harriet's Underground Railroad in the Sky* (1–4). Illus. 1992, Crown $16.00 (0-517-58767-X). 32pp. Cassie and brother Be Be soar among the stars and meet Harriet Tubman. (Rev: BCCB 12/92; BL 11/1/92; SLJ 12/92*)

**1177** Ringgold, Faith. *Bonjour, Lonnie* (1–4). Illus. 1996, Hyperion LB $16.49 (0-7868-2062-4). 32pp. Love Bird takes Lonnie to Paris to explore his family tree. (Rev: BL 10/1/96; SLJ 1/97)

**1178** Ringgold, Faith. *Tar Beach* (PS–2). Illus. 1991, Crown LB $18.99 (0-517-58031-4). 32pp. A little girl on the rooftop of her apartment building dreams of soaring over New York City. (Rev: BCCB 3/91; BL 1/1/91; HB 5–6/91*; SLJ 2/91*)

**1179** Robinson, Fay. *Where Did All the Dragons Go?* (PS–3). Illus. by Victor Lee. 1996, Troll paper $15.95 (0-8167-3808-4). 32pp. All kinds of dragons swirl about in the pages of this unusual picture book. (Rev: BL 12/15/96)

**1180** Rodriguez, Anita. *Jamal and the Angel* (PS–2). Illus. 1992, Crown LB $15.99 (0-517-59115-4). 32pp. Through the help of his guardian angel, Jamal is able to get the guitar he has wanted. (Rev: BL 12/1/92)

**1181** Rohmann, Eric. *The Cinder-Eyed Cats* (K–4). Illus. 1997, Crown LB $18.99 (0-517-70897-3). 40pp. A memorable picture book about a trip that a boy takes to a lush tropical island and the fantastic animals and fish that keep him company there. (Rev: BL 11/15/97; SLJ 11/97)

**1182** Root, Phyllis. *Aunt Nancy and Old Man Trouble* (K–2). Illus. by David Parkins. 1996, Candlewick $16.99 (1-56402-374-8). 32pp. Aunt Nancy outwits Old Man Trouble by posing a question he can't answer. (Rev: BCCB 3/96; BL 5/1/96; HB 9–10/96; SLJ 5/96)

**1183** Root, Phyllis. *One Windy Wednesday* (PS–K). Illus. by Helen Craig. 1996, Candlewick $9.99 (0-7636-0054-7). 24pp. A strong wind causes the barnyard animals to change the sounds they make so that the cow begins to oink. (Rev: BL 10/15/96; SLJ 11/96)

**1184** Root, Phyllis. *Rosie's Fiddle* (K–3). Illus. by Kevin O'Malley. 1997, Lothrop LB $15.93 (0-688-12853-X). 32pp. Rosie O'Grady is challenged by the devil to engage in a fiddling contest in this somewhat scary picture book. (Rev: BCCB 4/97; BL 4/15/97; SLJ 4/97)

**1185** Rosenberg, Liz. *The Carousel* (K–3). Illus. by Jim LaMarche. 1995, Harcourt $16.00 (0-15-200853-5). 32pp. Two girls discover that the horses of the carousel in the park have come alive. (Rev: BCCB 12/95; BL 11/15/95; SLJ 1/96*)

**1186** Rosenberg, Liz. *Eli and Uncle Dawn* (PS–3). Illus. by Susan Gaber. 1997, Harcourt $15.00 (0-15-200947-7). 32pp. Eli's Uncle Dawn is a real magician who takes the boy on a magical nighttime flight. (Rev: BL 5/15/97; SLJ 6/97)

**1187** Rosenberg, Liz. *Monster Mama* (PS–3). Illus. by Stephen Gammell. 1993, Putnam $15.95 (0-399-21989-7). 32pp. Patrick turns into a monster to protect his mother when local bullies insult her. (Rev: BCCB 7–8/93; BL 1/15/93*; HB 3–4/93; SLJ 6/93)

**1188** Ross, Michael E. *Become a Bird and Fly!* (PS–3). Illus. by Peter Parnall. 1992, Millbrook LB $21.40 (1-56294-074-0). 32pp. A boy wants so much to fly that he imagines he has become a bird. (Rev: BL 1/15/93; SLJ 2/93)

**1189** Ross, Tom. *Eggbert: The Slightly Cracked Egg* (PS–3). Illus. by Rex Barron. 1994, Putnam $15.95 (0-399-22416-5). 32pp. When Eggbert the egg gets cracked, he notices that the whole world and the objects in it contain many cracks. (Rev: BL 2/1/94; SLJ 5/94)

**1190** Rubel, Nicole. *The Ghost Family Meets Its Match* (K–3). Illus. 1992, Dial paper $13.89 (0-8037-1094-1). 32pp. A group of ghosts tries to drive out humans who have just moved into the house the ghosts love. (Rev: BL 6/15/92; HB 1–2/93; SLJ 11/82)

**1191** Ryder, Joanne. *Bears Out There* (K–2). Illus. by Jo Ellen McAllister-Stammen. 1995, Macmillan $15.00 (0-689-31780-8). 32pp. A boy imagines that bears do the same things that he does during a typical summer day. (Rev: BL 4/15/95; SLJ 5/95)

**1192** Ryder, Joanne. *The Snail's Spell* (K–2). Illus. by Lynne Cherry. 1992, Puffin paper $5.99 (0-14-050891-0). 32pp. A little boy knows how a snail feels when he shrinks to that size. Originally published in 1982.

**1193** Ryder, Joanne. *Winter Whale* (K–3). Illus. by Michael Rothman. 1991, Morrow LB $13.88 (0-688-07177-5). 32pp. When he is turned into a whale, a young boy experiences all the joys of living in the sea. (Rev: BL 10/15/91; SLJ 10/91)

**1194** Rylant, Cynthia. *Cat Heaven* (PS–3). Illus. 1997, Scholastic $15.95 (0-590-10054-8). 40pp. A picture book about the activities in cat heaven. (Rev: BL 9/1/97; SLJ 10/97)

**1195** Rylant, Cynthia. *The Dreamer* (PS–3). Illus. by Barry Moser. 1993, Scholastic $15.95 (0-590-47341-7). 32pp. A fantasy about an artist who creates a new world of joy through the drawings he sees in his imagination. (Rev: BCCB 12/93; BL 11/1/93; SLJ 2/94)

**1196** Sabraw, John. *I Wouldn't Be Scared* (K–3). Illus. 1989, Orchard LB $13.99 (0-531-08418-3). 32pp. When a young boy sets out alone to find his lost dog, he imagines all sorts of terrible monsters are after him. (Rev: BL 11/1/89; HB 1–2/90; SLJ 9/89)

**1197** Sadler, Marilyn. *Alistair and the Alien Invasion* (PS–3). Illus. by Roger Bollen. 1994, Simon & Schuster paper $15.00 (0-671-75957-4). 42pp. Alistair makes contact with some space aliens who help him with his science project. (Rev: BL 6/1–15/94; SLJ 7/94)

**1198** Sadler, Marilyn. *Alistair in Outer Space* (PS–2). Illus. by Roger Bollen. 1989, Simon & Schuster paper $15.00 (0-671-66678-9). Nerdy Alistair is carried off by a space ship on his way to the library. (Rev: BL 2/1/85; SLJ 11/89)

**1199** Sadler, Marilyn. *Alistair Underwater* (PS–3). Illus. by Roger Bollen. 1990, Simon & Schuster paper $5.95 (0-671-79246-6). 44pp. Alistair, in his own submarine, saves a colony of friendly frogs. (Rev: BL 7/90; SLJ 6/90)

**1200** Samton, Sheila W. *Jenny's Journey* (PS–2). Illus. 1991, Viking paper $4.99 (0-14-054308-2). 32pp. Jenny imagines an eventful voyage to visit her friend who has moved away. (Rev: BCCB 6/91; BL 4/15/91; HB 9–10/91; SLJ 8/91)

**1201** Sandburg, Carl. *The Wedding Procession of the Rag Doll and the Broom Handle and Who Was in It* (1–3). Illus. by Harriet Pincus. 1978, Harcourt paper $3.95 (0-15-695487-7). 32pp. Illustrated edition of one of the Rootabaga Stories.

**1202** Sanfield, Steve. *The Girl Who Wanted a Song* (K–3). Illus. by Stephen T. Johnson. 1996, Harcourt $16.00 (0-15-200969-8). Through contact with a lost Canada goose, orphaned Marici finds that she has a distinctive song to sing, like the birds and animals around her. (Rev: SLJ 7/97)

**1203** San Souci, Robert D. *The Boy and the Ghost* (K–3). Illus. by Brian Pinkney. 1989, Simon & Schuster paper $16.00 (0-671-67176-6). 32pp. While spending a night in a haunted house, a black boy encounters a ghost. (Rev: BCCB 12/89; BL 10/1/89)

**1204** San Souci, Robert D. *Pedro and the Monkey* (K–3). Illus. by Michael Hays. 1996, Morrow LB $15.93 (0-688-13744-X). 32pp. A Filipino version of the beloved Puss-in-Boots story. (Rev: BCCB 11/96; BL 9/1/96; SLJ 10/96) [398.2]

**1205** Say, Allen. *River Dream* (1–3). Illus. by author. 1988, Houghton $14.95 (0-395-48294-1); paper $5.95 (0-395-65749-0). 32pp. In a dream sequence Mark learns you don't need to kill fish to enjoy fishing. (Rev: HB 11–12/88)

**1206** Schaefer, Carole L. *The Squiggle* (PS–1). Illus. by Pierr Morgan. 1996, Crown LB $18.99 (0-517-70048-4). 30pp. In a young Chinese girl's imagination, a piece of red string becomes all sorts of wonderful things. (Rev: BCCB 2/97; BL 12/1/96*; SLJ 12/96*)

**1207** Schubert, Ingrid, and Dieter Schubert. *Abracadabra* (PS–1). Illus. 1997, Front Street $15.95 (1-886910-17-0). 32pp. Macrobius the Magician delights in causing confusion by having animals exchange body parts. (Rev: BL 7/97)

**1208** Scieszka, Jon. *The Good, the Bad and the Goofy* (2–5). Illus. by Lane Smith. 1992, Viking paper $12.99 (0-670-84380-6). 70pp. There are many near escapes when Joe, Fred, and Sam are taken back in time to 1868 and the days of the Chisholm Trail. (Rev: SLJ 7/92)

**1209** Seabrook, Elizabeth. *Cabbages and Kings* (PS–3). Illus. by Jamie Wyeth. 1997, Viking paper $15.99 (0-670-87462-0). 32pp. The story of an asparagus stalk that becomes friendly with a young cabbage. (Rev: BL 8/97; SLJ 11/97)

**1210** Seabrooke, Brenda. *The Swan's Gift* (PS–3). Illus. by Wenhai Ma. 1995, Candlewick $15.95 (1-56402-360-5). 32pp. A starving farmer is rewarded when he refuses to shoot a beautiful swan for food. (Rev: BL 12/15/95)

**1211** Selden, George. *Harry Kitten and Tucker Mouse* (3–5). Illus. by Garth Williams. 1986, Farrar $16.00 (0-374-32860-9); Dell paper $3.99 (0-440-40124-0). 64pp. Harry and Tucker meet and set up housekeeping in the Times Square subway station in New York City. (Rev: BL 2/15/87; SLJ 2/87)

**1212** Sendak, Maurice. *Kenny's Window* (K–3). Illus. by author. 1956, HarperCollins $13.95 (0-06-025494-7); paper $4.95 (0-06-443209-2). 64pp. Kenny remembers a garden he has been dreaming about.

**1213** Sendak, Maurice. *Maurice Sendak's Really Rosie* (1–4). Illus. by author. 1975, HarperCollins paper $10.95 (0-06-443138-X). 48pp. A book based on the TV presentation, including 7 songs used in the program.

**1214** Sendak, Maurice. *Outside Over There* (PS–3). Illus. by author. 1981, HarperCollins paper $8.95 (0-06-443185-1). 40pp. Goblins steal Ira's baby sister and leave another made of ice.

**1215** Sendak, Maurice. *Very Far Away* (PS–2). Illus. by author. 1957, HarperCollins LB $16.89 (0-06-025515-3). 56pp. Martin decides to go away after his mother doesn't have time to answer his questions.

**1216** Sendak, Maurice. *Where the Wild Things Are* (K–3). Illus. by author. 1988, HarperCollins LB $15.89 (0-06-025493-9); paper $5.95 (0-06-443178-9). 48pp. The few moments' wild reverie of a small unruly boy who has been sent supperless to his room. Caldecott Medal winner, 1964.

**1217** Seuss, Dr. *And to Think That I Saw It on Mulberry Street* (K–3). Illus. by author. 1989, Random LB $15.99 (0-394-94494-1). 32pp. A rhyme about what Marco saw on Mulberry Street.

**1218** Seuss, Dr. *Bartholomew and the Oobleck* (K–2). Illus. by author. 1949, Random LB $15.99 (0-394-90075-8). What happens when sticky green stuff begins falling instead of snow? Also use: *McElligot's Pool* (1947).

**1219** Seuss, Dr. *The Butter Battle Book* (K–2). Illus. by author. 1984, Random LB $15.99 (0-394-96580-9). 48pp. A warning about the nuclear arms race in words and pictures.

**1220** Seuss, Dr. *The 500 Hats of Bartholomew Cubbins* (K–2). Illus. by author. 1989, Random LB $15.99 (0-394-94484-4). 48pp. What happened when Bartholomew couldn't take his hat off before the king.

**1221** Seuss, Dr. *On Beyond Zebra!* (K–2). Illus. by author. 1955, Random LB $15.99 (0-394-90084-7). A nonsense alphabet that begins after Z.

**1222** Shannon, Margaret. *Elvira* (PS–2). Illus. 1993, Ticknor $13.95 (0-395-66597-3). 32pp. A peace-loving dragon leaves home to live with princesses who will appreciate her kindly ways. (Rev: BL 8/93)

**1223** Shaw-MacKinnon, Margaret. *Tiktala* (1–3). Illus. by Laszlo Gal. 1996, Holiday $15.95 (0-8234-1221-0). 32pp. In this fantasy, an Inuit girl gains sufficient knowledge and wisdom to become a soapstone carver. (Rev: BL 7/96; HB 7–8/96; SLJ 5/96)

**1224** Sheldon, Dyan. *Under the Moon* (K–3). Illus. by Gary Blythe. 1994, Dial paper $15.99 (0-8037-1670-2). 32pp. Jenny sleeps outdoors and dreams of living long ago, when the land was inhabited by Indians. (Rev: BCCB 5/94; BL 6/1–15/94; SLJ 6/94*)

**1225** Sheldon, Dyan. *Unicorn Dreams* (PS–2). Illus. by Neil Reed. 1997, Dial $14.99 (0-8037-2284-2). 32pp. Danny befriends a unicorn who later takes the

boy and his classmates to an enchanted land. (Rev: BL 2/1/98; SLJ 1/98)

**1226** Sheldon, Dyan. *The Whales' Song* (K–3). Illus. by Gary Blythe. 1991, Dial paper $16.99 (0-8037-0972-2). 32pp. Grandma tells Lilly of a time when whales practically danced on the water. (Rev: BCCB 5/91; BL 6/1/91*; SLJ 7/91)

**1227** Shepard, Aaron. *The Legend of Lightning Larry* (K–3). Illus. by Toni Goffe. 1993, Macmillan $14.95 (0-684-19433-3). 32pp. Evil-Eye McNeevil controls the town until Lightning Larry challenges him. (Rev: BL 3/1/93)

**1228** Shields, Carol D. *I Wish My Brother Was a Dog* (PS–3). Illus. by Paul Meisel. 1997, Dutton paper $14.99 (0-525-45464-0). 32pp. In this fantasy, a boy imagines that his baby brother is a dog that he can control and train. (Rev: BL 6/1–15/97; SLJ 7/97)

**1229** Showers, Paul. *Somebody and the Three Blairs* (PS–K). Illus. by Simone Abel. 1991, Orchard LB $16.99 (0-531-08478-7). 32pp. In this variation on Goldilocks, a bear cub comes into the Blairs' house. (Rev: BL 5/1/91)

**1230** Silver, Norman. *Cloud Nine* (PS–2). Illus. by Jan Ormerod. 1995, Clarion $15.95 (0-395-73545-9). A boy, tired of all the noise his family makes, builds a ladder to the clouds, where he hopes to have peace and quiet. (Rev: SLJ 9/95)

**1231** Silverman, Erica. *Big Pumpkin* (PS–1). Illus. by S. D. Schindler. 1992, Macmillan $16.00 (0-02-782683-X). 32pp. A witch gets help from several friends, including a ghost, a vampire, and a bat, to pick a huge pumpkin in her garden. (Rev: BL 9/1/92; HB 3–4/93; SLJ 9/92)

**1232** Silverman, Erica. *Gittel's Hands* (K–3). Illus. by Deborah N. Lattimore. 1996, Troll paper $14.95 (0-8167-3798-3). 32pp. A beggar, who is the prophet Elijah in disguise, helps a young girl fashion objects from a silver coin. (Rev: BL 5/15/96; HB 7–8/96; SLJ 6/96)

**1233** Simon, Carly. *Midnight Farm* (PS–2). Illus. by David Delamare. 1997, Simon & Schuster paper $16.00 (0-689-81237-X). A nighttime fantasy in which twin brothers play with plants and animals that behave like humans — dancing, playing musical instruments, and having fun. (Rev: SLJ 9/97)

**1234** Simon, Francesca. *Spider School* (K–2). Illus. by Peta Coplans. 1996, Dial paper $14.99 (0-8037-1975-2). A young girl has a nightmare about a horrible day in which her school teacher is a gorilla who calls her a knucklehead. (Rev: SLJ 9/96)

**1235** Sis, Peter. *The Three Golden Keys* (1–4). Illus. 1994, Doubleday $22.50 (0-385-47292-7). 64pp. In this fantasy, the author returns to Prague, the city of his childhood, where he receives, from mysterious figures, keys that unlock his past. (Rev: BCCB 1/95; BL 12/1/94; SLJ 12/94)

**1236** Small, David. *Imogene's Antlers* (K–2). Illus. by author. 1985, Crown $16.00 (0-517-55564-6); paper $5.99 (0-517-56242-1). 32pp. Imogene wakes up one morning to find she has antlers, which she takes in stride, although her mother doesn't. (Rev: BCCB 5/85; BL 6/1/85; SLJ 4/85)

**1237** Small, David. *Paper John* (PS–2). Illus. by author. 1987, Farrar $15.00 (0-374-35738-2); paper $5.95 (0-374-45725-5). 32pp. Gentle John is kind to an evil man who steals money and escapes in John's magnificent kite. (Rev: BCCB 6/87; BL 6/15/87; SLJ 6–7/87)

**1238** Smax, Willy. *Jack Tractor: Five Stories from Smallbill's Garage* (PS–2). Illus. by Keren Ludlow. 1996, Crown $18.00 (0-517-70911-2). 60pp. This picture book features many vehicles, including Alfie Romeo, Jack Tractor, and Benny the Breakdown Truck, who is the hero of these 5 adventures. (Rev: BL 1/1–15/96; SLJ 2/96)

**1239** Smee, Nicola. *The Tusk Fairy* (PS–K). Illus. by author. 1994, BridgeWater paper $3.95 (0-8167-3312-0). When Lizzie's toy elephant begins to unravel, she places it under her pillow, hoping for a visit from the tusk fairy. (Rev: SLJ 8/94)

**1240** Smith, Lane. *The Big Pets* (PS–1). Illus. 1991, Viking paper $14.95 (0-670-83378-9). 32pp. On the back of her pet cat, a little girl has many adventures. (Rev: BCCB 3/91; BL 2/1/91; SLJ 6/91)

**1241** Smith, Lane. *The Happy Hocky Family* (K–4). Illus. by author. 1993, Viking paper $13.99 (0-670-85206-6). 60pp. A parody on basal readers that features the Hocky family and the flat repetitive writing style that satirizes the dull Dick and Jane readers. (Rev: SLJ 9/93*)

**1242** Speed, Toby. *Whoosh! Went the Wish* (K–3). Illus. by Barry Root. 1997, Putnam $15.95 (0-399-23000-9). On 4 different tries, the wish fairy mixes up Henry's wish for a cat, with hilarious results. (Rev: SLJ 9/97)

**1243** Steig, William. *Caleb and Kate* (PS–3). Illus. by author. 1977, Farrar $16.00 (0-374-31016-5); paper $5.95 (0-374-41038-0). 32pp. Because he constantly quarrels with his wife, Caleb is transformed into a dog by a witch.

**1244** Steig, William. *Shrek!* (1–4). 1990, Farrar $10.95 (0-374-36877-5). 32pp. A warty creature sets out to find the ugly princess he is supposed to marry. (Rev: BCCB 12/90; BL 11/15/90; HB 1–2/91; SLJ 12/90*)

**1245** Steig, William. *The Toy Brother* (K–4). Illus. 1996, HarperCollins LB $14.89 (0-06-205079-6). 32pp. In this tale set in the Middle Ages, Yorick accidentally shrinks himself until he becomes his younger brother's favorite toy. (Rev: BCCB 2/96; BL 2/15/96; HB 5–6/96; SLJ 2/96*)

**1246** Stevenson, James. *Rolling Rose* (PS). Illus. 1992, Greenwillow LB $15.93 (0-688-10675-7). 24pp. No one pays attention to baby Rose in her rolling walker, so she just rolls out the door for adventure. (Rev: BL 3/1/92*; SLJ 6/92)

**1247** Stewart, Sarah. *The Money Tree* (PS). Illus. by David Small. 1991, Farrar $14.95 (0-374-35014-0). 32pp. Miss McGillicuddy's pleasant life is interrupted when a strange tree begins blooming with paper money. (Rev: BCCB 12/91*; BL 10/15/91; HB 1–2/92; SLJ 1/92)

**1248** Stewig, John W. *The Moon's Choice* (K–3). Illus. by Jan Palmer. 1993, Simon & Schuster paper $15.00 (0-671-76962-6). A silly girl is rescued from her mean-spirited sisters by the moon in this fantasy. (Rev: SLJ 9/93)

**1249** Stone, Phoebe. *When the Wind Bears Go Dancing* (PS–1). Illus. 1997, Little, Brown $15.95 (0-316-81701-5). 32pp. While the wind makes noises outside, a little girl dreams of dancing with 5 white bears in the midnight sky. (Rev: BL 1/1–15/98; SLJ 1/98)

**1250** Strete, Craig Kee, and Michelle Netten Chacon. *How the Indians Bought the Farm* (PS–3). Illus. by Francisco Mora. 1996, Greenwillow $15.00 (0-688-14130-7). 32pp. A group of wild animals help some North American Indians outwit white government officials. (Rev: BCCB 7–8/96; BL 5/15/96; HB 7–8/96)

**1251** Sun, Chyng Feng. *Cat and Cat-face* (K–3). Illus. by Lesley Liu. 1996, Houghton $14.95 (0-395-72038-9). 32pp. A pansy (known as "Cat-face" in Chinese) and a real cat become friends in spite of their differences. (Rev: BL 3/15/96; SLJ 4/96)

**1252** Sweeten, Sami. *Wolf* (K–2). Illus. by author. 1994, Albert Whitman LB $14.95 (0-8075-9160-2). One day, Leon meets a wolf who conveniently eats everything that the boy dislikes. (Rev: SLJ 7/94)

**1253** Swope, Sam. *The Krazees* (PS–K). Illus. by Eric Brace. 1997, Farrar $16.00 (0-374-34281-4). 32pp. In this wild romp, Iggie gets the Krazees on wet gray days, and soon the Krazees take over the house. (Rev: BL 11/15/97; SLJ 12/97)

**1254** Székessy, Tanja. *A Princess in Boxland* (PS–1). Trans. from German by J. Alison James. Illus. by author. 1996, North-South LB $15.88 (1-55858-540-0). In this fantasy, a girl climbs inside a cardboard carton and is transported to a magic land. (Rev: SLJ 7/96)

**1255** Taber, Anthony. *The Boy Who Stopped Time* (K–3). Illus. by author. 1993, Macmillan $13.95 (0-689-50460-8). 32pp. Annoyed that he has to go to bed so early, Julian stops the family clock — and time. (Rev: BL 3/1/93)

**1256** Tafuri, Nancy. *What the Sun Sees/What the Moon Sees* (PS–K). Illus. 1997, Greenwillow LB $15.93 (0-688-14494-2). 32pp. Two contrasting stories — one from the sun's point of view and the other from the moon's — are told, beginning from opposite covers of this book. (Rev: BL 11/15/97; SLJ 10/97)

**1257** Tate, Lindsey. *Claire and the Friendly Snakes* (PS–2). Illus. by Jonathan Franklin. 1993, Farrar $15.00 (0-374-31337-7). Claire imagines that many common household items are really friendly snakes. (Rev: SLJ 8/93)

**1258** Tazewell, Charles. *The Littlest Angel* (PS–3). Illus. by Paul Micich. 1991, Ideals $16.95 (0-8249-8516-8). 32pp. A young angel in heaven keeps getting into trouble because there is nothing to do. (Rev: BL 9/15/91)

**1259** Teague, Mark. *The Field Beyond the Outfield* (PS–2). Illus. 1992, Scholastic $14.95 (0-590-45173-1). 32pp. Ludlow Grebe sees monsters everywhere, even on the baseball field. (Rev: BL 5/1/92; SLJ 6/92)

**1260** Teague, Mark. *The Secret Shortcut* (PS–3). Illus. 1996, Scholastic $14.95 (0-590-67714-4). 32pp. Pirates, space aliens, and a plague of frogs are only 3 of the obstacles that prevent Wendell and Floyd from getting to school on time. (Rev: BL 9/15/96; SLJ 11/96)

**1261** Thayer, Jane. *Gus Loves His Happy Home* (PS–2). Illus. by Seymour Fleishman. 1989, Shoe String LB $16.50 (0-208-02249-X). With time on his hands, Gus the Friendly Ghost goes for a ride on the tail of a kite. (Rev: BL 2/15/90; SLJ 2/90)

**1262** Thiel, Elizabeth. *The Polka Dot Horse* (PS). Illus. by Terry Milne. 1993, Simon & Schuster paper $14.00 (0-671-79419-1). 28pp. A discarded toy sets out to find a new home. (Rev: BL 1/15/93; SLJ 4/93)

**1263** Thomas, Frances. *The Bear and Mr. Bear* (PS–1). Illus. by Ruth Brown. 1995, Dutton paper $14.99 (0-525-45362-8). 32pp. A grumpy old man nicknamed Mr. Bear frees a misused carnival bear who becomes his friend. (Rev: BL 1/15/95; SLJ 3/95)

**1264** Tibo, Gilles. *Simon and the Snowflakes* (PS–1). Illus. 1991, Tundra paper $4.95 (0-88776-274-3). 24pp. Young Simon likes to count snowflakes as they come down. (Rev: BL 12/15/88; SLJ 4/89)

**1265** Tompert, Ann. *Grandfather Tang's Story* (K–3). Illus. by Robert Andrew Parker. 1990, Crown LB $17.99 (0-517-57272-9). 32pp. As a Chinese grandfather tells his granddaughter a tale about 2 foxes, he arranges Chinese puzzles to form the animals' shapes. (Rev: BCCB 4/90; BL 4/15/90; SLJ 5/90)

**1266** Turkle, Brinton. *Do Not Open* (1–3). Illus. by author. 1981, Dutton paper $3.95 (0-525-44224-3). 32pp. Miss Moody finds a bottle on the shore labeled "Do Not Open."

**1267** Turnbull, Ann. *The Sand Horse* (PS–3). Illus. by Michael Foreman. 1989, Macmillan LB $13.95 (0-689-31581-3). At night, a horse sculpted out of sand at a beach comes alive and joins the "white horses" in the waves. (Rev: SLJ 1/90)

**1268** Tusa, Tricia. *Camilla's New Hairdo* (PS–3). Illus. 1991, Farrar $14.95 (0-374-31021-1). 32pp. In her isolated tower, Camilla fashions her long hair into the shape of the animals she sees from afar. (Rev: BL 9/1/91; SLJ 12/91)

**1269** Tusa, Tricia. *Maebelle's Suitcase* (PS–1). Illus. by author. 1987, Macmillan paper $5.99 (0-689-71444-0). 32pp. An offbeat picture book concerning a 108-year-old woman who lives in a treehouse. (Rev: BCCB 7–8/87; BL 4/1/87; SLJ 6–7/87)

**1270** Tzannes, Robin. *Professor Puffendorf's Secret Potions* (K–4). Illus. by Korky Paul. 1992, Checkerboard $16.95 (1-56288-267-8). 36pp. A scientist's secret potions are used in her absence by her lazy assistant, Slag. (Rev: BL 2/1/93)

**1271** Udry, Janice May. *The Moon Jumpers* (K–2). Illus. by Maurice Sendak. 1959, HarperCollins $15.00 (0-06-026145-5). 32pp. The pleasure and enjoyment of 4 children as they dance in the moonlight.

**1272** Ulmer, Wendy K. *A Campfire for Cowboy Billy* (1–3). Illus. by Kenneth J. Spengler. 1997, Northland LB $15.95 (0-87358-681-6). 32pp. Growing up in a big city, little Billy imagines all the sights around him are really part of the Old West, like making a "curbside food stand," a chuck wagon. (Rev: BL 12/1/97; SLJ 1/98)

**1273** Utton, Peter. *Jennifer's Room* (PS–3). Illus. 1995, Orchard $15.95 (0-531-06842-0). 32pp. Jennifer's imagination is so great that she can transform the objects in her room into living things. (Rev: BL 4/1/95; SLJ 3/95)

**1274** Utton, Peter. *The Witch's Hand* (1–3). Illus. 1989, Farrar $13.95 (0-374-38463-0). 32pp. Dad tells his son how he and the boy's mother fought off a witch who wanted to steal the youngster. (Rev: BL 1/15/90; SLJ 4/90)

**1275** Vainio, Pirkko. *The Dream House* (K–3). Trans. by J. Alison James. Illus. by author. 1997, North-South LB $15.88 (1-55858-750-0). The land on which Lucas is building his dream house is so small that he must stack the rooms. (Rev: SLJ 1/98)

**1276** Van Allsburg, Chris. *Bad Day at Riverbend* (K–3). Illus. 1995, Houghton $17.95 (0-395-67347-X). 32pp. This book, set in the Old West, is about a strange light that freezes everything that it touches. (Rev: BCCB 9/95; BL 10/15/95; SLJ 10/95)

**1277** Van Allsburg, Chris. *Ben's Dream* (2–4). Illus. by author. 1982, Houghton $16.95 (0-395-32084-4). 32pp. Ben dreams that he is in a flood and passing the great landmarks of the world.

**1278** Van Allsburg, Chris. *Jumanji* (1–4). Illus. by author. 1981, Houghton $17.95 (0-395-30448-2). A board game that 2 children play brings out a jungle world. Caldecott Medal winner, 1982.

**1279** Van Allsburg, Chris. *Just a Dream* (K–3). Illus. 1990, Houghton $17.95 (0-395-53308-2). 48pp. Walter, who doesn't recycle his trash, takes a trip into the future and finds the situation bleak. (Rev: BCCB 11/90; BL 10/15/90; HB 1–2/91; SLJ 12/90)

**1280** Van Allsburg, Chris. *The Stranger* (K–2). Illus. by author. 1986, Houghton $17.95 (0-395-42331-7). 32pp. Farmer Bailey hits a man with his car and brings him home. Autumn is unaccountably delayed until the strange man departs. (Rev: BL 10/1/86; HB 11–12/86; SLJ 11/86)

**1281** Van Allsburg, Chris. *The Widow's Broom* (K–2). Illus. 1992, Houghton $17.95 (0-395-64051-2). 32pp. In this tale of good and evil, a witch's broom falls from the sky with the witch still on it. (Rev: BCCB 10/92*; BL 9/15/92*; HB 1–2/93; SLJ 11/92*)

**1282** Van Allsburg, Chris. *The Wretched Stone* (K–3). Illus. 1991, Houghton $17.95 (0-395-53307-4). 32pp. A magical stone that some sailors find turns them into monkeys. (Rev: BCCB 11/91; BL 10/1/91; HB 1–2/92*; SLJ 11/91)

**1283** Van Camp, Richard. *A Man Called Raven* (K–3). Illus. by George Littlechild. 1997, Children's Book Pr. $15.95 (0-89239-144-8). A man appears to 2 boys who have injured a raven and tells them the story of the terrible consequences that befell a man who did the same thing. (Rev: SLJ 6/97)

**1284** Van Laan, Nancy. *A Mouse in My House* (PS–K). Illus. by Marjorie Priceman. 1990, Knopf LB $10.99 (0-679-90043-8). 32pp. A boy identifies with many wild animals in his activities. (Rev: BL 10/1/90; HB 11–12/90; SLJ 12/90*)

**1285** Varvasovszky, Laszlo. *Henry in Shadowland* (1–4). Illus. 1990, Godine $17.95 (0-87923-785-6). Henry enters his shadow-box theater world to find the king of Shadowland. (Rev: SLJ 2/91)

**1286** Vaughan, Marcia. *Dorobo the Dangerous* (K–2). Illus. by Kazuko Stone. Series: Animal Fair. 1994, Silver Burdett LB $14.95 (0-382-24070-7); paper $4.95 (0-382-24453-2). This fantasy with a Japanese setting tells how a young girl sets out to find the culprit that is stealing her fish. (Rev: SLJ 1/95)

**1287** Vesey, Amanda. *The Princess and the Frog* (K–3). Illus. by author. 1985, Little, Brown $14.95 (0-316-90036-2). 32pp. Unlike the Grimm Brothers' tale, this frog remains a frog even after the princess's kiss. (Rev: BCCB 5/85; HB 3–4/86; SLJ 1/86)

**1288** Vigna, Judith. *Boot Weather* (PS–K). Illus. by author. 1989, Whitman LB $14.95 (0-8075-0837-3). 32pp. Kim puts on her boots to play in the snow and imagines all sorts of exciting adventures. (Rev: BCCB 2/89; BL 3/1/89; SLJ 5/89)

**1289** Vigna, Judith. *Uncle Alfredo's Zoo* (K–3). Illus. 1994, Albert Whitman $14.95 (0-8075-8292-1). 32pp. A miracle restores the collection of stone animals to the front of the house formerly owned by Anna's deceased uncle. (Rev: BL 5/1/94; SLJ 6/94)

**1290** Waber, Bernard. *You're a Little Kid with a Big Heart* (PS–2). Illus. by author. 1980, Houghton $14.95 (0-395-29163-1). A little girl is granted her wish — to be an adult.

**1291** Wagerin, Walter. *Probity Jones and the Fear Not Angel* (PS–2). Illus. by Tim Ladwig. 1996, Augsburg $15.99 (0-8066-2992-4). 32pp. When Probity is too sick to appear in a Christmas pageant, an angel takes her to witness what she is missing. (Rev: BL 12/15/96)

**1292** Wahl, Jan. *I Met a Dinosaur* (K–3). Illus. by Chris Sheban. 1997, Harcourt $18.00 (0-15-201644-9). 32pp. After a visit to a natural history museum, a little girl sees dinosaurs every place she goes. (Rev: BL 11/1/97; SLJ 11/97)

**1293** Wahl, Jan. *Once When the World Was Green* (1–4). Illus. by Fabricio Vandenbroeck. 1996, Tricycle Pr. $14.95 (1-883672-12-0). 32pp. When a Mayan farmer begins killing the animals around him to clothe himself, eagles respond by stealing his son. (Rev: BL 5/1/96; SLJ 7/96)

**1294** Wakefield, Ali. *Those Calculating Crows!* (K–2). Illus. by Christy Hale. 1996, Simon & Schuster paper $16.00 (0-689-80483-0). 28pp. A farmer and his wife are outwitted by crows intent on eating small corn plants. (Rev: BL 11/15/96; SLJ 12/96)

**1295** Walter, Mildred P. *Brother to the Wind* (K–2). Illus. by Leo Dillon and Diane Dillon. 1985, Lothrop LB $15.93 (0-688-03812-3). 32pp. A folklike tale set in Africa about a boy who wants to fly. (Rev: BCCB 3/85; HB 7–8/85; SLJ 5/85)

**1296** Walton, Rick. *Noah's Square Dance* (PS–3). Illus. by Thor Wickstrom. 1995, Lothrop $16.00 (0-688-11186-6). 32pp. Noah acts as caller during a square dance involving the animals on his ark. (Rev: BL 9/1/95; SLJ 10/95)

**1297** Walton, Rick. *You Don't Always Get What You Hope For* (PS). Illus. by Heidi S. Mario. 1996, Gibbs Smith $14.95 (0-87905-739-4). Instead of an ordinary Monday, as expected, a young boy has a series of fantastic adventures. (Rev: SLJ 11/96)

**1298** Watts, Irene N. *The Fish Princess* (1–3). Illus. by Steve Mennie. 1996, Tundra $17.95 (0-88776-366-9). A young girl, rescued from the sea by a fisherman, is accused of bringing bad luck to the villagers. (Rev: SLJ 3/97)

**1299** Wayland, April Halprin. *To Rabbittown* (PS–1). Illus. by Robin Spowart. 1989, Scholastic paper $3.95 (0-590-44777-7). 32pp. A poem about a girl and her pet rabbit and their journey. (Rev: BL 2/1/89; SLJ 4/89)

**1300** Weatherby, Mark A. *My Dinosaur* (PS–1). Illus. 1997, Scholastic paper $15.95 (0-590-97203-0). 32pp. A little girl travels through the night sky with her dinosaur before returning to bed. (Rev: BCCB 5/97; BL 3/1/97; SLJ 3/97)

**1301** Weilerstein, Sadie R. *K'tonton's Sukkot Adventure* (PS–3). Illus. by Joe Boddy. 1993, Jewish Publication Soc. $12.95 (0-8276-0502-1). A tiny boy disobeys his father and attends Sukkot services in the synagogue by hiding in a small box. (Rev: SLJ 3/94)

**1302** Wellington, Monica. *Night House, Bright House* (PS–1). Illus. 1997, Dutton paper $11.99 (0-525-45491-8). 24pp. When a cat and mice play at night, household objects come alive and talk to them. (Rev: BL 2/1/97; SLJ 4/97)

**1303** Weninger, Brigitte. *Lumina* (PS–2). Illus. by Julie Wintz-Litty. 1997, North-South LB $15.88 (1-55858-791-8). 32pp. A little orphan girl named Lumina is helped by an owl and later meets a young boy who takes her to his house, where she shares Christmas with his family. (Rev: BL 10/15/97; SLJ 11/97)

**1304** Westcott, Nadine Bernard. *The Giant Vegetable Garden* (PS–K). Illus. by author. 1981, Little, Brown $14.95 (0-316-93129-2); paper $4.95 (0-316-93130-6). 32pp. A mayor gets his town's residents to grow large vegetables.

**1305** Whelan, Gloria. *The Miracle of Saint Nicholas* (PS–3). Illus. by Judith G. Brown. 1997, Ignatius $12.95 (1-883937-18-3). 32pp. After the end of Communism, a young Russian boy who vows to clean up his local church is helped by a miracle. (Rev: BL 11/1/97)

**1306** Whitcher, Susan. *The Key to the Cupboard* (K–4). Illus. by Andrew Glass. 1997, Farrar $16.00 (0-374-34127-3). 32pp. A girl and the witch in the attic join forces to fly into the night to make mischief. (Rev: BL 9/1/97; SLJ 9/97)

**1307** Whitcher, Susan. *Moonfall* (K–3). Illus. by Barbara Lehman. 1993, Farrar $14.00 (0-374-35056-6). 25pp. Sylvie tries to save the moon that has fallen from the sky. (Rev: BL 7/93)

**1308** Whitcher, Susan. *Something for Everyone* (1–3). Illus. by Barbara Lehman. 1995, Farrar $15.00 (0-374-37138-5). When Great Aunt Elsie moves away, she leaves behind possessions that are a great help to a neighbor when she, in turn, travels. (Rev: SLJ 11/95)

**1309** Wiesner, David. *June 29, 1999* (PS–3). Illus. 1992, Houghton $15.95 (0-395-59762-5). 32pp. Holly sends small growing vegetables into space in balloons and reaps a fantastic harvest. (Rev: BCCB 11/92; BL 10/15/92; HB 1–2/93*; SLJ 11/92*)

**1310** Wild, Margaret. *Going Home* (PS–1). Illus. by Wayne Harris. 1994, Scholastic $14.95 (0-590-47958-X). 32pp. A variety of animals from the zoo take Hugo from his hospital bed to exotic places like an Amazon jungle. (Rev: BL 4/1/94; SLJ 4/94)

**1311** Wildsmith, Brian. *Professor Noah's Spaceship* (K–3). Illus. by author. 1980, Oxford paper $11.95 (0-19-272149-6). 32pp. A modern Noah takes off to escape the world's pollution.

**1312** Wildsmith, Brian, and Rebecca Wildsmith. *Jack and the Meanstalk* (K–2). Illus. by authors. 1994, Knopf LB $15.99 (0-679-95810-X). Professor Jack produces a plant in his lab that grows so large that it threatens the life of animals and other plants. (Rev: BCCB 5/94; SLJ 9/94)

**1313** Willard, Nancy. *The Nightgown of the Sullen Moon* (PS–3). Illus. by David McPhail. 1983, Harcourt $14.95 (0-15-257429-8). 32pp. The story of the moon, her nightgown, and why on some nights she doesn't shine.

**1314** Willard, Nancy. *Pish, Posh, Said Hieronymus Bosch* (K–3). Illus. by Leo Dillon and Diane Dillon. 1991, Harcourt $22.00 (0-15-262210-1). 32pp. Willard's fanciful poem introduces readers to the strange world of grotesque creatures created by Hieronymus Bosch. (Rev: BCCB 12/91; BL 11/15/91; SLJ 12/91*) [811]

**1315** Willard, Nancy. *The Sorcerer's Apprentice* (1–4). Illus. by Leo Dillon and Diane Dillon. 1993, Scholastic $15.95 (0-590-47329-8). 32pp. Sylvia, the sorcerer's apprentice, is overcome when she is directed to make clothes for the many creatures found in the magician's house. (Rev: BCCB 1/94; BL 11/1/93; SLJ 1/94)

**1316** Williams, Arlene. *Dragon Soup* (K–3). Illus. by Sally J. Smith. 1996, H. J. Kramer $15.95 (0-915811-63-4). 32pp. Tonlu visits the Cloud Dragons to get help in avoiding an arranged marriage. (Rev: BL 7/96; SLJ 6/96)

**1317** Williams, Laura E. *The Long Silk Strand* (PS–3). Illus. by Grayce Bochak. 1995, Boyds Mills $15.95 (1-56397-236-0). 32pp. Using a Japanese setting, this is the story of the bond between a girl and her grandmother that is so strong it conquers death. (Rev: BL 2/1/96)

**1318** Williams, Linda. *The Little Old Lady Who Was Not Afraid of Anything* (PS–1). Illus. by Megan Lloyd. 1986, HarperCollins LB $14.89 (0-690-04586-7); paper $5.95 (0-06-443183-5). 32pp. The scary tale of a little old woman who comes upon 2 big shoes in the forest going CLOMP CLOMP all by themselves. (Rev: BCCB 10/86; BL 10/1/86; SLJ 1/87)

**1319** Willis, Jeanne. *Earthlets: As Explained by Professor Xargle* (1–3). 1989, Dutton paper $14.99 (0-525-44465-3). 32pp. An amusing lesson as a green alien monster explains Earthlets to his students. (Rev: BCCB 4/89; BL 5/1/89; SLJ 5/89)

**1320** Willis, Val. *The Mystery in the Bottle* (K–3). 1991, Farrar $14.95 (0-374-35194-5). 32pp. The adventures of mischievous Bobby Bell and the mermaid he finds on a beach. (Rev: BL 1/15/92; SLJ 1/92)

**1321** Willis, Val. *The Secret in the Matchbox* (K–3). Illus. by John Shelley. 1990, Farrar paper $4.95 (0-374-46593-2). The dragon in Bobby's matchbox grows larger and larger, and nearly destroys the school. (Rev: BCCB 7–8/88; BL 7/88; SLJ 6–7/88)

**1322** Willis, Val. *The Surprise in the Wardrobe* (K–4). Illus. by John Shelley. 1990, Farrar $15.00 (0-374-37309-4). Bobby Bell brings a special surprise to school — a witch. (Rev: SLJ 1/91)

**1323** Winch, John. *The Old Man Who Loved to Sing* (PS–3). Illus. 1996, Scholastic $14.95 (0-590-22640-1). 40pp. The animals in the valley are unhappy when their neighbor, an old man, stops serenading them. (Rev: BL 4/15/96; HB 7–8/96; SLJ 4/96)

**1324** Winch, John. *The Old Woman Who Loved to Read* (PS–1). Illus. 1997, Holiday $15.95 (0-8234-1281-4); paper $6.95 (0-8234-1348-9). 32pp. An old woman buys a farmhouse in which to retire and read, but she finds unexpected chores awaiting her. (Rev: BL 3/1/97; SLJ 5/97)

**1325** Winthrop, Elizabeth. *A Very Noisy Girl* (PS–K). Illus. by Ellen Weiss. 1991, Holiday LB $14.95 (0-8234-0858-2). When Elizabeth's mother asks her to be quiet, Elizabeth responds by turning herself into a dog. (Rev: SLJ 5/91)

**1326** Wise, William. *Perfect Pancakes If You Please* (PS–3). Illus. by Richard Egielski. 1997, Dial paper $14.89 (0-8037-1447-5). 32pp. An evil chef hopes to marry the king's daughter by making perfect pancakes. (Rev: BL 12/1/96; SLJ 2/97)

**1327** Wolf, Jake. *And Then What?* (PS–1). Illus. by Marylin Hafner. 1993, Greenwillow LB $13.93 (0-688-10286-7). 32pp. After each of Mother's explanations of the day's activities, Willy exclaims "And

then what?" until she runs out of activities. (Rev: BL 12/1/93; SLJ 12/93)

**1328** Wolff, Ferida. *Seven Loaves of Bread* (K–4). Illus. by Katie Keller. 1993, Morrow LB $15.93 (0-688-11112-2). 32pp. Rose does a poor job when she takes over the bread-baking chores that Milly has to abandon because of illness. (Rev: BL 9/15/93; SLJ 11/93*)

**1329** Wolff, Patricia R. *The Toll-Bridge Troll* (PS–2). Illus. by Kimberly B. Root. 1995, Harcourt $14.00 (0-15-277665-6). 24pp. Trigg outwits a troll who demands a toll for crossing the bridge that leads to Trigg's school. (Rev: BL 4/15/95; HB 9–10/95; SLJ 6/95)

**1330** Wood, Audrey. *The Bunyans* (K–3). Illus. by David Shannon. 1996, Scholastic $15.95 (0-590-48089-8). 32pp. Meet the rest of the Bunyan family, including 2 gigantic children. (Rev: BCCB 1/97; BL 9/15/96; SLJ 12/96*)

**1331** Wood, Audrey. *Elbert's Bad Word* (PS–1). Illus. by author. 1988, Harcourt $15.00 (0-15-225320-3). 32pp. A bad word flies into Elbert's mouth, which gets him in trouble, so he goes to the local wizard for help. (Rev: BL 10/1/88; HB 1–2/89; SLJ 10/88)

**1332** Wood, Audrey. *The Rude Giants* (PS–3). Illus. 1993, Harcourt $13.95 (0-15-269412-9). 32pp. Clever Gerda convinces 2 dirty, ugly, rude giants to clean up the castle before they eat everybody. (Rev: BCCB 6/93; BL 3/1/93*; SLJ 5/93)

**1333** Wood, Audrey. *Sweet Dream Pie* (PS–2). Illus. by Mark Teague. 1998, Scholastic $15.95 (0-590-96204-3). 32pp. Eating too much of Ma Brindle's delicious pie will give one nightmares, and unfortunately everyone but Ma Brindle overindulges. (Rev: BL 2/15/98; SLJ 3/98)

**1334** Wood, Audrey. *Tickleoctopus* (PS–1). Illus. by Don Wood. 1994, Harcourt $16.00 (0-15-287000-8). 46pp. A young cave boy discovers a friendly monster who tickles him; and for the first time in human history, a smile is born. (Rev: BCCB 7–8/94; BL 3/1/94; SLJ 5/94)

**1335** Wood, Audrey, and Mark Teague. *The Flying Dragon Room* (PS–3). Illus. 1996, Scholastic $14.95 (0-590-48193-2). 32pp. With a set of tools he has been given, young Patrick creates a fantastic home, complete with a friendly dinosaur. (Rev: BL 4/1/96*; SLJ 3/96)

**1336** Wood, Audrey, and Don Wood. *Piggies* (PS–K). Illus. by Don Wood. 1991, Harcourt $13.95 (0-15-256341-5). 32pp. Fingers can become piggies in this imaginative book with elaborate artwork. (Rev: BCCB 4/91*; BL 3/1/91*; SLJ 5/91*)

**1337** Woodruff, Elvira. *The Wing Shop* (PS–2). Illus. by Stephen Gammell. 1991, Holiday LB $16.95 (0-

8234-0825-6). 32pp. In an effort to get back to the street where he once lived, Matthew tries to fly with a variety of wings. (Rev: BCCB 6/91; BL 3/15/91; HB 5–6/91; SLJ 11/91)

**1338** Yaccarino, Dan. *If I Had a Robot* (PS–1). Illus. 1996, Viking paper $14.99 (0-670-86936-8). 32pp. Phil dreams of owning a robot that will perform all the unpleasant tasks, like eating vegetables. (Rev: BCCB 9/96; BL 7/96; SLJ 9/96)

**1339** Yaccarino, Dan. *Zoom! Zoom! Zoom! I'm Off to the Moon* (PS–K). Illus. 1997, Scholastic $15.95 (0-590-95610-8). 32pp. A little boy boards his red rocket for a trip to the moon and back. (Rev: BL 11/15/97; HB 9–10/97; SLJ 12/97)

**1340** Yardley, Joanna. *The Red Ball* (K–2). Illus. by author. 1991, Harcourt $14.95 (0-15-200894-2). In this fantasy, Joanie chases her red ball as it bounces in and out of a series of photographs. (Rev: SLJ 10/91)

**1341** Yen, Clara. *Why Rat Comes First: A Story of the Chinese Zodiac* (PS–1). Illus. by Hideo C. Yoshida. 1991, Children's Book Pr. LB $14.95 (0-89239-072-7). 32pp. The story of how the 12 years in the Chinese calendar were named after particular animals. (Rev: BL 9/15/91; SLJ 10/91)

**1342** Yep, Laurence. *The Butterfly Boy* (PS–2). Illus. by Jeanne M. Lee. 1993, Farrar $16.00 (0-374-31003-3). 32pp. A young boy incurs the derision of others when he dreams of experiencing life from a butterfly's point of view. (Rev: BL 10/15/93; SLJ 2/94)

**1343** Yep, Laurence. *The City of Dragons* (K–3). Illus. by Jean Tseng and Mou-Sien Tseng. 1995, Scholastic $14.95 (0-590-47865-6). 32pp. A boy's very sad face moves dragons to shed tears of pearls. (Rev: BL 11/15/95; SLJ 11/95)

**1344** Yep, Laurence. *The Curse of the Squirrel* (2–4). Illus. by Dirk Zimmer. 1987, Random LB $6.99 (0-394-98200-2); paper $3.99 (0-394-88200-8). 64pp. Shag, a giant monster squirrel, puts a curse on Howie the dog who becomes a squirrel himself at night. (Rev: BCCB 11/87; BL 10/1/87; SLJ 12/87)

**1345** Yolen, Jane. *The Girl in the Golden Bower* (K–3). Illus. by Jane Dyer. 1994, Little, Brown $15.95 (0-316-96894-3). 32pp. Aurea guards the magic comb her dying mother gave her from the clutches of an evil sorceress. (Rev: BCCB 10/94; BL 10/15/94; SLJ 10/94)

**1346** Yorinks, Arthur. *It Happened in Pinsk* (1–3). Illus. by Richard Egielski. 1983, Farrar $14.00 (0-374-33651-2); paper $3.95 (0-374-43649-5). 32pp. A self-satisfied man wakes up one morning to find his head is missing.

**1347** Yorinks, Arthur. *Louis the Fish* (PS–2). Illus. by Richard Egielski. 1980, Farrar $13.95 (0-374-34658-5); paper $5.95 (0-374-44598-2). 32pp. The story of an unhappy man who is turned into a fish.

**1348** Yorinks, Richard. *Ugh* (PS–3). Illus. by Richard Egielski. 1990, Farrar $13.95 (0-374-38028-7). 32pp. During prehistoric times, a young boy named Ugh invents the first bicycle. (Rev: BCCB 11/90*; BL 10/15/90; SLJ 12/90)

**1349** York, Sarah Mountbatten-Windsor, Duchess of. *Budgie at Bendick's Point* (PS–1). Illus. by John Richardson. 1989, Simon & Schuster paper $14.00 (0-671-67684-9). 36pp. The story of Budgie, a helicopter, and how he saved 2 boys caught in a gale. Also use: *Budgie the Little Helicopter* (1989). (Rev: BL 12/1/89)

**1350** Zadrzynska, Ewa. *The Girl with a Watering Can* (K–3). Illus. by Arnold Skolnick. 1990, Chameleon $15.95 (0-915829-64-9). 32pp. Characters from several famous paintings in our National Gallery of Art come alive. (Rev: BL 12/1/90; SLJ 12/90)

**1351** Zelinsky, Paul O. *The Maid and the Mouse and the Odd-Shaped House* (PS–3). Illus. 1993, Dutton paper $14.99 (0-525-45095-5). 32pp. The improvements that a maid and a mouse make on a house result in cleverly disguised objects found in the illustrations. A reissue.

**1352** Zemach, Harve, and Kaethe Zemach. *The Princess and Froggie* (PS–2). Illus. by Margot Zemach. 1992, Farrar paper $4.95 (0-374-46011-6). These brief tales are charmingly presented by the Zemachs and their teenage daughter.

**1353** Zemach, Kaethe. *The Character in the Book* (PS–2). Illus. 1998, HarperCollins $14.95 (0-06-205060-5). 32pp. Character, who lives in a book, discovers how he can leave his book and visit a different one. (Rev: BL 2/15/98; SLJ 4/98)

**1354** Zemach, Margot. *Jake and Honeybunch Go to Heaven* (1–3). Illus. by author. 1982, Farrar $16.00 (0-374-33652-0); paper $4.95 (0-374-43714-9). 40pp. A controversial (because of charges of stereotyping) picture book about a black workingman and his pet mule.

**1355** Zeman, Ludmila. *The First Red Maple Leaf* (PS–2). Illus. by author. 1997, Tundra $15.95 (0-88776-372-3). An American Indian boy saves his people from the cruel Iceheart with the help of the magical goose, Branta. (Rev: SLJ 9/97)

### IMAGINARY ANIMALS

**1356** Agee, Jon. *Ellsworth* (K–2). Illus. by author. 1989, Farrar paper $3.95 (0-374-42082-3). Ellsworth, a dog who is also an economics professor, faces unemployment.

**1357** Alborough, Jez. *Where's My Teddy?* (PS–1). Illus. 1992, Candlewick $15.95 (1-56402-048-7).

32pp. Eddie loses his teddy bear and retraces his steps in the forest trying to find him. (Rev: BCCB 9/92*; BL 10/1/92; SLJ 8/92)

**1358** Alexander, Martha. *Blackboard Bear* (PS–1). Illus. by author. 1988, Dial paper $3.50 (0-8037-0629-4). Spurred on by the older children, a small boy draws a picture of a big bear on his blackboard. The bear steps right down and becomes his playmate. Two sequels are: *I Sure Am Glad to See You, Blackboard Bear* (Puffin 1976); *And My Mean Old Mother Will Be Sorry, Blackboard Bear* (1977).

**1359** Alexander, Martha. *Even That Moose Won't Listen to Me* (PS–1). Illus. by author. 1988, Dial LB $11.89 (0-8037-0188-8). 32pp. Rebecca finds a moose in the garden, but no one believes her. (Rev: BCCB 4/88; BL 4/1/88; SLJ 5/88)

**1360** Alexander, Sue. *There's More . . . Much More* (PS–1). Illus. by Patience Brewster. 1987, Harcourt $12.95 (0-15-200605-2). 32pp. A squirrel helps a little girl to fill a flower basket and understand the beauties of the forest. (Rev: BL 11/15/87; SLJ 12/87)

**1361** Allard, Harry. *Bumps in the Night* (K–3). Illus. by James Marshall. 1994, Bantam paper $2.25 (0-553-15284-X). 48pp. Dudley the Stork thinks his house is haunted.

**1362** Allard, Harry. *The Cactus Flower Bakery* (PS–1). Illus. by Ned Delaney. 1993, HarperCollins paper $4.95 (0-0644-3297-1). 32pp. A nearsighted armadillo becomes friendly with an unpopular snake. (Rev: BL 5/1/91; SLJ 8/91)

**1363** Allen, Jonathan. *Mucky Moose* (PS–2). Illus. 1996, Simon & Schuster paper $5.95 (0-689-80651-5). 32pp. Mucky Moose smells so bad that even a wolf won't hunt him. (Rev: BL 3/1/91; HB 9–10/91; SLJ 8/91)

**1364** Allen, Pamela. *Who Sank the Boat?* (PS–2). Illus. 1996, Putnam paper $4.95 (0-698-11373-X). 32pp. One of 5 animal friends is guilty of sinking the boat.

**1365** Arnold, Katya. *Duck, Duck, Goose?* (PS–1). Illus. 1997, Holiday $15.95 (0-8234-1296-2). 32pp. Goose tries in vain to improve her appearance by swapping body parts with other animals. (Rev: BL 7/97; HB 9–10/97; SLJ 9/97)

**1366** Arnold, Marsha Diane. *Heart of a Tiger* (PS–2). Illus. by Jamichael Henterly. 1995, Dial paper $14.89 (0-8037-1696-6). At an animal-naming ceremony, a small, gray housecat is afraid that he will be called "smallest of all." (Rev: SLJ 1/96)

**1367** Arnosky, Jim. *Rabbits and Raindrops* (PS–2). Illus. 1997, Putnam $15.99 (0-399-22635-4). 32pp. Five young rabbits explore the world outside their nest, until a rain shower interrupts their journey. (Rev: BCCB 3/97; BL 3/1/97; SLJ 3/97)

**1368** Aruego, Jose, and Ariane Dewey. *Rockabye Crocodile* (PS–1). Illus. by authors. 1988, Greenwillow $16.00 (0-688-06738-7); Morrow paper $4.95 (0-688-12333-3). 32pp. A retelling of a Philippine fable concerning 2 elderly boars, one kind, one mean, and their treatment from a mother crocodile. (Rev: BL 9/15/88; HB 9–10/88; SLJ 12/88)

**1369** Asch, Frank. *Bear Shadow* (PS–1). Illus. by author. 1988, Simon & Schuster paper $4.95 (0-671-66866-8). 32pp. Bear has a problem; every time he tries to catch a fish, his shadow scares it away! Also use: *Goodbye House* (1989). (Rev: BL 5/15/85; HB 7–8/85; SLJ 8/85)

**1370** Asch, Frank. *Bear's Bargain* (PS–K). Illus. by author. 1989, Simon & Schuster paper $4.95 (0-671-67838-8). Bear and Little Bird discover that there is more than one way to solve a problem when Bear wants to fly and Little Bird wants to grow big. Also use: *Skyfire* (1988). (Rev: BL 11/1/85; HB 1–2/86)

**1371** Asch, Frank. *Happy Birthday, Moon* (PS–1). Illus. by author. 1985, Simon & Schuster paper $4.95 (0-671-66455-7). 32pp. A little bear wants to give the moon a birthday present. Two sequels are: *Mooncake* (1986); *Moongame* (Scholastic 1992).

**1372** Asch, Frank. *Just Like Daddy* (PS–1). Illus. by author. 1984, Simon & Schuster paper $4.95 (0-671-66457-3). 32pp. Fatherhood is explained by a bear and his dad in this warm, humorous book. Another Bear story is: *Milk and Cookies* (Parents Magazine Pr. 1982).

**1373** Asch, Frank. *Moonbear's Pet* (PS–2). Illus. 1997, Simon & Schuster $15.00 (0-689-80794-5). 32pp. Bear and friend Little Bird find in a pond a pet they name Splash, and in time Splash becomes a frog. (Rev: BCCB 7–8/97; BL 6/1–15/97; SLJ 6/97*)

**1374** Asch, Frank. *Moondance* (PS–K). Illus. 1993, Scholastic $12.95 (0-590-45487-0). 32pp. Bear wants to dance with the moon, but doesn't feel worthy of the honor. (Rev: BL 2/15/93; SLJ 6/93)

**1375** Asch, Frank. *Sand Cake* (K–2). Illus. by author. 1979, Parents LB $5.95 (0-8193-0986-9). 48pp. On the beach, Papa Bear makes a sand cake.

**1376** Asch, Frank, and Vladimir Vagin. *Dear Brother* (K–3). Illus. 1992, Scholastic $13.95 (0-590-43107-2). 32pp. Two mice brothers read letters from 2 ancestors that prove how important a brother can be. (Rev: BCCB 2/92; BL 6/15/92; SLJ 4/92)

**1377** Asch, Frank, and Vladimir Vagin. *Insects from Outer Space* (PS–2). Illus. by Vladimir Vagin. 1995, Scholastic $14.95 (0-590-45489-7). 32pp. Insects from outer space and their earthling counterparts enjoy each other at the Bug Ball. (Rev: BL 2/1/95; SLJ 4/95)

**1378** Ashforth, Camilla. *Calamity* (PS–K). Illus. by author. 1993, Candlewick $15.95 (1-56402-252-8). Calamity, a racing donkey, invites Horatio, a tiny stuffed rabbit, to join him in a race. (Rev: SLJ 4/94)

**1379** Ashforth, Camilla. *Monkey Tricks* (PS–1). Illus. by author. 1993, Candlewick $15.95 (1-56402-170-X). 32pp. James the bear and Horatio the bunny are expecting a visit to the nursery from a mischievous monkey. (Rev: BL 1/15/93*; SLJ 5/93)

**1380** Auch, Mary Jane. *Bantam of the Opera* (K–3). Illus. 1997, Holiday LB $16.95 (0-8234-1312-8). 32pp. Luigi, a bantam rooster with a huge voice, gets his chance at the Cosmopolitan Opera Company. (Rev: BL 10/1/97; SLJ 10/97*)

**1381** Auch, Mary Jane. *Bird Dogs Can't Fly* (PS–1). Illus. 1993, Holiday LB $15.95 (0-8234-1050-1). 32pp. Blue, a bird dog, nurses an injured goose back to health. (Rev: BL 10/15/93; SLJ 12/93)

**1382** Auch, Mary Jane. *Eggs Mark the Spot* (PS–3). Illus. 1996, Holiday LB $16.95 (0-8234-1242-3). 32pp. A hen copies onto her eggs some portraits painted by famous artists. (Rev: BL 3/15/96; SLJ 5/96)

**1383** Auch, Mary Jane. *Hen Lake* (PS–3). Illus. 1995, Holiday LB $16.95 (0-8234-1188-5). 32pp. The hen Poulette stages her own ballet and also gets the best of snooty Mr. Peacock. (Rev: BL 8/95; SLJ 10/95)

**1384** Auch, Mary Jane. *Peeping Beauty* (PS–3). Illus. 1993, Holiday LB $16.95 (0-8234-1001-3). 32pp. Poulette the hen decides she wants to be a ballerina. (Rev: BL 3/1/93; SLJ 4/93*)

**1385** Axelrod, Amy. *Pigs in the Pantry: Fun with Math and Cooking* (PS–2). Illus. by Sharon McGinley-Nally. 1997, Simon & Schuster $13.00 (0-689-80665-5). 40pp. The story of Mr. Pig's disastrous cooking spree, with some added math facts about measuring ingredients. (Rev: BCCB 5/97; BL 3/1/97; SLJ 4/97)

**1386** Axelrod, Amy. *Pigs on a Blanket* (K–3). Illus. by Sharon McGinley-Nally. 1996, Simon & Schuster paper $13.00 (0-689-80505-5). 32pp. Unforeseen problems cause delays for a pig family that wants to spend a day at the beach. (Rev: BL 5/15/96; SLJ 6/96)

**1387** Axelrod, Amy. *Pigs Will Be Pigs* (K–3). Illus. by Sharon McGinley-Nally. 1994, Four Winds paper $14.00 (0-02-765415-X). 40pp. To finance a dinner out, the pig family engages in a money hunt around the house. (Rev: BCCB 2/94; BL 2/15/94; SLJ 5/94*)

**1388** Axworthy, Anni. *Along Came Toto* (PS–K). Illus. 1993, Candlewick $12.95 (1-56402-172-6). 32pp. Percy the dog has difficulty adjusting to a kit-

ten that arrives unexpectedly at his home. (Rev: BL 4/1/93; SLJ 4/93)

**1389** Babbitt, Natalie. *Nellie: A Cat on Her Own* (PS–2). Illus. 1989, Farrar $14.00 (0-374-35506-1). 32pp. The story of Nellie, a cat marionette. (Rev: BCCB 11/89; BL 10/15/89*; HB 1–2/90; SLJ 1/90)

**1390** Baker, Alan. *Benjamin's Balloon* (K–2). Illus. 1990, Smithmark $3.98 (0-8317-0902-2). A balloon that Benjamin the hamster blows up takes him on a ride. (Rev: SLJ 12/90)

**1391** Baker, Keith. *Cat Tricks* (PS–3). Illus. 1997, Harcourt $15.00 (0-15-292857-X). 44pp. An entertaining picture book that shows fictitious cat tricks while presenting a series of picture puzzles. (Rev: BL 12/15/97; SLJ 12/97)

**1392** Baker, Keith. *Who Is the Beast?* (K–2). Illus. 1990, Harcourt $14.95 (0-15-296057-0). 32pp. A tiger tries to make the other jungle animals less afraid of him. (Rev: BL 9/1/90; HB 11–12/90; SLJ 11/90)

**1393** Bancroft, Catherine, and Hannah C. Gruenberg. *Felix's Hat* (K–3). Illus. by Hannah C. Gruenberg. 1993, Macmillan LB $14.95 (0-02-708325-X). 32pp. Felix Frog cannot be consoled when he loses his favorite possession, an orange hat. (Rev: BL 3/15/93; SLJ 7/93)

**1394** Bang, Molly. *Goose* (PS–3). Illus. 1996, Scholastic $10.95 (0-590-89005-0). 40pp. After hatching from her egg, Duckling finds a surrogate family with a group of woodchucks. (Rev: BCCB 12/96; BL 9/15/96*; HB 11–12/96; SLJ 11/96*)

**1395** Barasch, Lynne. *Rodney's Inside Story* (PS–1). Illus. 1992, Smithmark $3.98 (0-831-76836-3). 32pp. Two small rabbits read about each other in their picture books. (Rev: BCCB 10/92; BL 10/1/92; HB 9–10/92; SLJ 9/92)

**1396** Barber, Antonia. *The Mousehole Cat* (K–3). Illus. by Nicola Bayley. 1996, Simon & Schuster $5.99 (0-689-80837-2). 40pp. A splendid retelling of a local fishing legend set in the Cornish village of Mousehole. (Rev: BL 10/1/90*; HB 11–12/90)

**1397** Barbot, Daniel. *A Bicycle for Rosaura* (PS–1). Illus. by Morella Fuenmayor. 1991, Kane/Miller $9.95 (0-916291-34-0). 24pp. A pet store owner is in a quandary when her hen Rosaura asks for a bicycle for her birthday. (Rev: BL 6/1/91; SLJ 10/91)

**1398** Baron, Alan. *Red Fox and the Baby Bunnies* (PS). Illus. 1997, Candlewick $9.99 (0-7636-0085-7). 24pp. Dan Dog and Tabby Cat rescue some bunnies from Red Fox. (Rev: BCCB 4/97; BL 2/1/97; SLJ 3/97)

**1399** Baron, Alan. *The Red Fox Monster* (PS–2). Illus. by author. 1996, Candlewick $9.99 (0-7636-0018-0). Dan Dog and Tabby Cat dress in Red Fox's clothing while he has a swim and frighten the other animals. (Rev: SLJ 11/96)

**1400** Barracca, Debra, and Sal Barracca. *The Adventures of Taxi Dog* (PS–3). Illus. by Mark Buehner. 1990, Dial LB $12.89 (0-8037-0672-3). Maxi recalls his days as a stray and his adoption by Jim, the taxi driver. (Rev: BL 5/15/90*; HB 5–6/90)

**1401** Barracca, Debra, and Sal Barracca. *Maxi, the Hero* (PS–3). Illus. by Mark Buehner. 1991, Dial paper $14.99 (0-8037-0939-0). 32pp. Maxi, a dog hero, catches the thief who stole a woman's purse. (Rev: BL 8/91; SLJ 10/91)

**1402** Barracca, Debra, and Sal Barracca. *Maxi, the Star* (PS–3). Illus. by Alan Ayers. 1993, Dial LB $13.89 (0-8037-1349-5). 32pp. Maxi, the taxi dog, is discovered by a producer of television commercials. (Rev: BL 5/1/93)

**1403** Bate, Lucy. *Little Rabbit's Loose Tooth* (PS–K). Illus. by Diane De Groat. 1975, Crown $18.00 (0-517-52240-3); paper $5.99 (0-517-55122-5). 32pp. Little Rabbit loses her first tooth and makes the most of it in this beguiling story.

**1404** Baumgart, Klaus. *Where Are You, Little Green Dragon?* (PS–2). Illus. by author. 1993, Hyperion $12.95 (1-56282-344-2); paper $4.95 (0-7868-1073-4). 32pp. The Little Green Dragon with his friendly fly share many adventures. (Rev: SLJ 8/93)

**1405** Bellows, Cathy. *The Grizzly Sisters* (PS–3). Illus. 1991, Macmillan $14.95 (0-02-709032-9). 32pp. Bear cubs decide to go out and scare the tourists; instead, they become frightened. (Rev: BL 12/15/91; SLJ 1/92)

**1406** Bender, Robert. *A Most Unusual Lunch* (PS–1). Illus. 1994, Dial paper $14.89 (0-8037-1711-3). 32pp. The food chain in nature is whimsically portrayed in this delightful picture book. (Rev: BL 9/15/94; SLJ 11/94)

**1407** Berends, Polly. *I Heard Said the Bird* (PS–1). Illus. by Brad Sneed. 1995, Dial paper $14.89 (0-8037-1224-3). 32pp. All the animals on a farm wonder who the newcomer will be that a bird maintains is about to arrive. (Rev: BL 12/15/95; SLJ 11/95)

**1408** Berenstain, Stan, and Jan Berenstain. *The Berenstain Bears in the Dark* (PS–2). Illus. by authors. 1982, Random paper $3.25 (0-394-85443-8). 32pp. Brother and Sister Bear in one of a very large series of books.

**1409** Berliner, Franz. *Wildebeest* (PS–1). Illus. by Lilian Brogger. 1991, Ideals $13.95 (0-8249-8488-9). 32pp. When a wildebeest changes his nature, he gets a new name — gnu. (Rev: BL 1/15/92)

**1410** Bianchi, John. *The Lab Rats of Doctor Eclair* (2–3). Illus. by author. 1997, Firefly $18.95 (0-921285-49-3); paper $6.95 (0-921285-48-5). Three

pampered lab rats join Doctor Eclair in his crusade to save animals by building a mechanical lab rat. (Rev: SLJ 8/97)

**1411** Bingham, Mindy. *Minou* (1–3). Illus. by Itoko Maeno. 1987, Advocacy $14.95 (0-911655-36-0). 64pp. When Minou loses her home in Paris, a smart cat named Celeste grooms her to become a mouser at Notre Dame. (Rev: BL 9/1/87; SLJ 6–7/87)

**1412** Birney, Betty G. *Tyrannosaurus Tex* (K–3). Illus. by John O'Brien. 1994, Houghton $14.95 (0-395-67648-7). 32pp. Everything is larger than life in this tall tale about a Texan cowboy who is really a dinosaur. (Rev: BL 6/1–15/94; HB 5–6/94; SLJ 5/94)

**1413** Bishop, Gavin. *Little Rabbit and the Sea* (PS–2). Illus. by author. 1997, North-South LB $15.88 (1-55858-810-8). Little Rabbit dreams of becoming a sailor and asks his family what the ocean is like. (Rev: SLJ 12/97)

**1414** Blackwood, Mary. *Derek the Knitting Dinosaur* (PS–2). Illus. by Kerry Argent. 1990, Carolrhoda LB $19.93 (0-87614-400-8); paper $5.95 (0-87614-540-3). 32pp. This dinosaur prefers to knit woolly socks and sweaters rather than terrorize the neighborhood like his uncivilized siblings. (Rev: BL 7/90; SLJ 7/90)

**1415** Blood, Charles L., and Martin Link. *The Goat in the Rug* (K–2). Illus. by Nancy Winslow Parker. 1990, Simon & Schuster paper $5.99 (0-689-71418-1). 40pp. How a Navajo rug is made, from the goat Geraldine's point of view.

**1416** Bloom, Suzanne. *We Keep a Pig in the Parlor* (PS–1). Illus. by author. 1988, Crown $13.95 (0-517-56829-2). 32pp. Piggy is bored with life in the barn, and longs for grander quarters. (Rev: BL 10/15/88; SLJ 1/89)

**1417** Blundell, Tony. *Beware of Boys* (1–5). Illus. 1992, Greenwillow LB $15.93 (0-688-10925-X). A funny tale in which a hungry wolf captures a boy who convinces the animal to try things like "Boy Soup" or "Boy Pie," but never seems to have all the ingredients. (Rev: BCCB 7–8/92; BL 4/1/92*; SLJ 5/92)

**1418** Boelts, Maribeth. *Dry Days, Wet Nights* (PS–K). Illus. by Kathy Parkinson. 1994, Albert Whitman $14.95 (0-8075-1723-2); paper $5.95 (0-8075-1724-0). 32pp. Little Bunny, who is out of diapers during the day is upset when he wets the bed at night. (Rev: BCCB 4/94; BL 5/1/94; SLJ 4/94)

**1419** Boelts, Maribeth. *Little Bunny's Cool Tool Set* (PS–K). Illus. by Kathy Parkinson. 1997, Albert Whitman LB $14.95 (0-8075-4584-8). 32pp. Little Bunny has trouble sharing when he brings his new tool set to school. (Rev: BL 9/15/97; SLJ 10/97)

**1420** Bogacki, Tomek. *Cat and Mouse* (PS–K). Illus. by author. 1996, Farrar $14.00 (0-374-31225-

7). A small mouse and a kitten play together, unaware of the roles that they should be playing. (Rev: SLJ 9/96)

**1421** Boggs, Cary. *W. D. the Wonder Dog* (PS–1). Illus. by Annora Spence. 1998, Simon & Schuster $16.00 (0-689-81376-7). 32pp. The dog W.D. wonders about everything and poses questions to himself like "Why do the birds sing in the morning?" (Rev: BL 3/1/98)

**1422** Boland, Janice. *Annabel* (PS–K). Illus. by Megan Halsey. 1993, Dial LB $12.89 (0-8037-1255-3). 32pp. Annabel, a pig, tries to become a different animal, but finds that being herself is best. (Rev: BL 1/15/93; SLJ 3/93)

**1423** Boland, Janice. *Annabel Again* (PS–K). Illus. by Megan Halsey. 1995, Dial paper $13.89 (0-8037-1757-1). 32pp. Annabel the pig searches for a new home but finally settles for her old one, a mud puddle. (Rev: BL 5/15/95; SLJ 8/95)

**1424** Bond, Felicia. *Poinsettia and Her Family* (PS–3). Illus. by author. 1981, HarperCollins LB $14.89 (0-690-04145-4); paper $4.95 (0-06-443076-6). 32pp. Poinsettia, a pig, resents her large family but misses them when they leave temporarily. Also use: *Poinsettia and the Firefighters* (1984).

**1425** Bond, Felicia. *Tumble Bumble* (PS–K). Illus. 1996, Front Street $13.95 (1-886910-15-4). 32pp. A simple rhyme about the adventures of a bug that goes for a walk. (Rev: BL 11/15/96; SLJ 10/96)

**1426** Bornstein, Ruth. *Little Gorilla* (PS). Illus. by author. 1986, Houghton $15.00 (0-395-28773-1); paper $5.95 (0-89919-421-4). 32pp. Even though Little Gorilla grows into a big gorilla, everyone still loves him.

**1427** Bornstein, Ruth. *Rabbit's Good News* (PS–1). Illus. 1995, Clarion $13.95 (0-395-68700-4). 32pp. A curious rabbit hops through a meadow awakening to spring to find the source of a strange sound she hears. (Rev: BL 5/1/95; SLJ 4/95)

**1428** Bos, Burny. *Leave It to the Molesons!* (2–4). Trans. by J. Alison James. Illus. by Hans de Beer. 1995, North-South LB $13.88 (1-55858-432-3). 46pp. Six episodes in the life of a mole family as told from the son's point of view. A sequel to *Meet the Molesons* (1994). (Rev: BL 3/1/96; SLJ 3/96)

**1429** Bourgeois, Paulette. *Franklin's Bad Day* (K–2). Illus. by Brenda Clark. 1997, Scholastic paper $3.95 (0-590-69332-8). Franklin the turtle misses his friend Otter so much that he makes a scrapbook to send to her. (Rev: SLJ 5/97)

**1430** Brandenberg, Franz. *Nice New Neighbors* (K–2). Illus. by Aliki. 1990, Greenwillow LB $13.88 (0-688-84105-8); Scholastic paper $2.75 (0-590-44117-5). 56pp. A family of mice children generously include their neighbors, who formerly spurned them, when they decide to give a play — The Three Blind Mice.

**1431** Breebaart, Joeri, and Piet Breebaart. *When I Die, Will I Get Better?* (K–3). Illus. by Piet Breebaart. 1993, Bedrick $11.95 (0-87226-375-4). 29pp. Using 2 rabbit brothers as central characters, this book tells how one adjusts to the death of the other. (Rev: SLJ 10/93)

**1432** Breese, Gillian, and Tony Langham. *The Amazing Adventures of Teddy Tum Tum* (PS–1). Illus. by Patrick Lowry. 1992, Arcade $11.95 (1-55970-185-4). 32pp. A teddy bear tells the other toys in the playroom about his adventures. (Rev: BL 6/15/92; SLJ 11/92)

**1433** Brenner, Barbara. *Group Soup* (PS–2). Illus. by Lynn Munsinger. 1999, NAL paper $4.99 (0-140-54093-8). Rhonda and her rabbit siblings decide to make soup. (Rev: SLJ 8/92)

**1434** Brett, Jan. *Annie and the Wild Animals* (K–3). Illus. by author. 1990, Houghton $15.00 (0-395-37800-1); paper $7.70 (0-395-53962-5). 32pp. Annie uses corn cakes to lure another animal to replace her pet cat, but they are all too big or fierce. (Rev: BL 5/1/85; HB 7–8/85; SLJ 4/85)

**1435** Brett, Jan. *Armadillo Rodeo* (PS–2). Illus. 1995, Putnam $15.95 (0-399-22803-9). 32pp. Near-sighted Bo, an armadillo, has fun when he wanders onto the Curly H Ranch. (Rev: BCCB 10/95; BL 9/15/95; SLJ 10/95)

**1436** Brett, Jan. *Berlioz Bear* (K–3). Illus. 1991, Putnam $14.95 (0-399-22248-0). 32pp. Berlioz, a bear, is mystified by a strange buzz coming from his bass fiddle. (Rev: BL 9/15/91; HB 11–12/91; SLJ 10/91*)

**1437** Brett, Jan. *Comet's Nine Lives* (PS–3). Illus. 1996, Putnam $16.95 (0-399-22931-0). 30pp. Comet, a white cat, has many adventures on Nantucket Island until finding a permanent home in a lighthouse. (Rev: BL 10/15/96; SLJ 12/96)

**1438** Brett, Jan. *Fritz and the Beautiful Horses* (K–3). Illus. by author. 1987, Houghton $16.00 (0-395-30850-X); paper $5.95 (0-395-45356-9). 32pp. The pony Fritz is ostracized from the other horses and leads a lonely life.

**1439** Brett, Jan. *The Hat* (PS–3). Illus. 1997, Putnam $16.95 (0-399-23101-3). 32pp. When a red wool stocking is blown onto the head of Hedgie the hedgehog, he maintains that it is his new hat. (Rev: BL 9/1/97*; SLJ 9/97)

**1440** Brett, Jan. *Town Mouse, Country Mouse* (PS–3). Illus. 1994, Putnam LB $15.95 (0-399-22622-2). 32pp. A town cat and a country owl, both of whom enjoy mice for dinner, decide to change places. (Rev: BL 9/1/94; SLJ 9/94)

**1441** Brewster, Patience. *Rabbit Inn* (PS–K). Illus. 1991, Little, Brown $14.95 (0-316-10747-6). Two rabbits run an inn and their guests help to spruce up the place. (Rev: SLJ 7/91)

**1442** Bridwell, Norman. *Clifford's Good Deeds* (PS–1). Illus. by author. 1985, Scholastic paper $2.99 (0-590-44292-9). 32pp. Clifford is a large shaggy dog whose efforts to be helpful result in comic mishaps. Also use: *Clifford Takes a Trip* (1985); *Clifford's Tricks* (1986); *Clifford the Big Red Dog* (1988); *Clifford the Small Red Puppy* (1990); *Clifford at the Circus* (1985); *Clifford Goes to Hollywood* (1986).

**1443** Brimner, Larry Dane. *If Dogs Had Wings* (PS–1). Illus. by Chris L. Demarest. 1996, Boyds Mills $14.95 (1-56397-146-1). In a dog's-eye view of the world, this fantasy describes what life would be like if dogs had wings. (Rev: SLJ 12/96)

**1444** Brock, Betty. *No Flying in the House* (2–4). Illus. by Wallace Tripp. 1970, HarperCollins paper $4.95 (0-06-440130-8). A small dog seeks shelter for herself and her human friends.

**1445** Brodzinsky, Anne Braff. *The Mulberry Bird: An Adoption Story*. Rev. ed. (K–4). Illus. by Diane Stanley. 1996, Perspectives $16.00 (0-944934-15-3). 47pp. The process of adoption is the subject of this book about a little bird whose mother can't care for him and so she allows another bird couple to take her place. (Rev: SLJ 11/96)

**1446** Brown, Ken. *Mucky Pup* (PS–1). Illus. 1997, Dutton paper $14.99 (0-525-45886-7). 32pp. A puppy gets so dirty that only a pig will play with him. (Rev: BL 12/15/97; SLJ 12/97)

**1447** Brown, Ken. *Nellie's Knot* (PS–K). Illus. 1993, Macmillan LB $13.95 (0-02-714930-7). 32pp. In order not to forget something, a young elephant ties a knot in her trunk, but now she can't remember why. (Rev: BL 4/15/93)

**1448** Brown, Marc. *Arthur Meets the President* (PS–3). Illus. 1991, Little, Brown $15.95 (0-316-11265-8). 32pp. Arthur the aardvark writes a prize-winning essay that takes him to Washington to meet the president. Also use: *Arthur's Pet Business* (1990); *Arthur Babysits* (1992). (Rev: BL 5/1/91; HB 7–8/91; SLJ 7/91)

**1449** Brown, Marc. *Arthur Writes a Story* (PS–3). Illus. 1996, Little, Brown $15.95 (0-316-10916-9). 32pp. Arthur's classmates embellish the simple story of how he got his pet puppy. (Rev: BL 9/15/96; SLJ 9/96)

**1450** Brown, Marc. *Arthur's Chicken Pox* (PS–3). Illus. by author. Series: Arthur Adventure. 1994, Little, Brown $15.95 (0-316-11384-0). When Arthur gets chicken pox, nobody can console him concern-

ing his lost trip to the circus. (Rev: HB 5–6/94; SLJ 6/94*)

**1451** Brown, Marc. *Arthur's Computer Disaster* (PS–1). Illus. 1997, Little, Brown $15.95 (0-316-11016-7). 32pp. Arthur disobeys his mother and plays with the computer, with unfortunate results. (Rev: BL 9/15/97; HB 11–12/97; SLJ 10/97)

**1452** Brown, Marc. *Arthur's Eyes* (K–3). 1979, Little, Brown $15.95 (0-316-11063-9); paper $5.95 (0-316-11069-8). 32pp. Some of aardvark Arthur's problems are solved when he gets glasses, but new problems are created. Two others are: *Arthur Goes to Camp* (1984); *Arthur's Nose* (1986).

**1453** Brown, Marc. *Arthur's Family Vacation* (PS–3). Illus. 1993, Little, Brown $15.95 (0-316-11312-3). 30pp. Arthur the aardvark reluctantly goes on a family vacation at the beach, and in spite of problems, he finally enjoys himself. (Rev: BL 5/15/93; HB 5–6/93; SLJ 5/93)

**1454** Brown, Marc. *Arthur's First Sleepover* (K–3). Illus. 1994, Little, Brown $15.95 (0-316-11445-6). 32pp. Arthur Aardvark and his friends are fooled into thinking that space aliens have landed. (Rev: BCCB 11/94; BL 10/1/94; SLJ 10/94)

**1455** Brown, Marc. *Arthur's New Puppy* (PS–1). Illus. 1993, Little, Brown $15.95 (0-316-11355-7). 32pp. Arthur the aardvark teaches his new puppy a few basic manners. (Rev: BL 12/1/93; SLJ 2/94)

**1456** Brown, Marc. *Arthur's Teacher Trouble* (1–3). Illus. by author. 1989, Little, Brown $15.95 (0-316-11244-5); paper $5.95 (0-316-11186-4). 32pp. Although Arthur is unhappy about having Mr. Ratburn for his third-grade teacher, he manages to win the spelling match. Also use: *Arthur's Tooth* (1985); *Arthur's Baby* (1990). (Rev: BL 11/1/86; SLJ 1/87)

**1457** Brown, Marc. *Arthur's TV Trouble* (PS–2). Illus. 1995, Little, Brown $15.95 (0-316-10919-3). 32pp. Arthur's purchase of a Treat Timer for his puppy, Pal, backfires when the device only frightens his pet. (Rev: BL 11/1/95; SLJ 2/96)

**1458** Brown, Marc. *D.W. Flips* (PS–K). Illus. by author. 1987, Little, Brown $15.95 (0-316-11239-9). D.W. and her first visit to a gymnastics class. Another story about Arthur's young sister is: *D.W. All Wet* (1988). (Rev: BCCB 6/87; BL 5/1/87; SLJ 6–7/87)

**1459** Brown, Marc. *D.W. Rides Again!* (PS–3). Illus. 1993, Little, Brown $14.95 (0-316-11356-5). 32pp. D.W. the aardvark learns how to ride a bike from her older brother, Arthur. (Rev: BL 11/1/93; HB 9–10/93; SLJ 12/93)

**1460** Brown, Marc. *D.W. the Picky Eater* (PS–2). Illus. 1995, Little, Brown $14.95 (0-316-10957-6). 32pp. The little aardvark, D.W., is a picky eater who gradually discovers what she is missing. (Rev: BL 2/1/95; HB 7–8/95; SLJ 3/95*)

**1461** Brown, Marc. *D.W. Thinks Big* (PS–3). Illus. 1993, Little, Brown $15.95 (0-316-11305-0). 24pp. An aardvark feels left out at the wedding where her brother is ring bearer and her cousin is the flower girl. (Rev: BL 3/15/93; HB 5–6/93; SLJ 5/93)

**1462** Brown, Marc, and Laurie Krasny Brown. *The Bionic Bunny Show* (2–3). Illus. by Marc Brown. 1984, Little, Brown $14.95 (0-316-11120-1); paper $5.95 (0-316-10992-4). 32pp. An ordinary rabbit becomes a super TV star thanks to makeup magic.

**1463** Brown, Marc, and Stephen Krensky. *Perfect Pigs: An Introduction to Manners* (K–2). Illus. by authors. 1983, Little, Brown paper $6.95 (0-316-11080-9). 32pp. Pig people show the basics of good manners.

**1464** Brown, Margaret Wise. *The Runaway Bunny* (PS–K). Illus. by Clement Hurd. 1972, Harper-Collins LB $14.89 (0-06-020766-3); paper $5.95 (0-06-443018-9). 40pp. With 9 colorful illustrations, this new edition of an old favorite is a charming story of mother bunny's love for her restless youngster, who keeps trying to escape but is always found.

**1465** Brown, Ruth. *Copycat* (PS–1). Illus. 1994, Dutton paper $14.99 (0-525-45326-1). 32pp. Buddy learns that there are some activities that cats shouldn't copy. (Rev: BL 10/1/94; SLJ 10/94)

**1466** Brown, Ruth. *A Dark Dark Tale* (PS–2). Illus. by author. 1981, Dial LB $12.89 (0-8037-1673-7); paper $3.95 (0-8037-0093-8). 32pp. An atmospheric tale about a black cat in a dark, dark house.

**1467** Browne, Anthony. *Gorilla* (K–3). Illus. 1985, Knopf LB $13.99 (0-394-97525-1); paper $6.99 (0-394-82225-0). 32pp. A little girl who adores gorillas receives a visit from one and the 2 go off on a great adventure. (Rev: BCCB 11/85; BL 1/15/86; SLJ 9/85)

**1468** Browne, Anthony. *Piggybook* (K–2). Illus. by author. 1990, Knopf LB $14.99 (0-394-98416-1); paper $7.99 (0-679-80837-X). 32pp. Mrs. Piggot walks out when her family turns into real pigs and takes her for granted. (Rev: BCCB 10/86; BL 10/1/86; SLJ 10/86)

**1469** Browne, Anthony. *Willy and Hugh* (PS–K). Illus. 1991, Knopf $13.00 (0-679-81446-9); Random paper $6.99 (0-679-87654-5). 32pp. Willy the chimp and Hugh the gorilla help each other in different situations. (Rev: BCCB 11/91; BL 10/15/91; SLJ 10/91)

**1470** Browne, Anthony. *Willy the Wimp* (K–2). Illus. by author. 1989, Knopf $5.99 (0-394-82610-8). 32pp. Willy the wimp is a chimp, but he sends away for a Charles Atlas-type book and takes on a gang of apes. (Rev: BCCB 4/85; BL 5/1/85; SLJ 5/85)

**1471** Browne, Anthony. *Willy the Wizard* (PS–3). Illus. 1996, Knopf $15.00 (0-679-87644-8). 32pp.

Willy the chimp receives a pair of magic boots to help his game of soccer. (Rev: BL 5/15/96; SLJ 2/96*)

**1472** Browne, Eileen. *No Problem* (PS–3). Illus. by David Parkins. 1993, Candlewick $14.99 (1-56402-200-5). 36pp. When Mouse receives a construction kit in the mail, all her friends have a try at putting it together. (Rev: BL 6/1–15/93; SLJ 7/93)

**1473** Browne, Eileen. *Tick-Tock* (PS–1). Illus. by David Parkins. 1994, Candlewick $14.95 (1-56402-300-1). 32pp. Owl helps young Skip Squirrel repair a cuckoo clock he has broken after disobeying his mother's instructions not to play too hard. (Rev: BL 6/1–15/94; SLJ 8/94)

**1474** Bryan, Ashley. *The Cat's Purr* (PS–2). Illus. by author. 1985, Macmillan $14.00 (0-689-31086-2). 48pp. Rat plays Cat's drum, and that's how the 2 got to be enemies. (Rev: BL 4/15/85; HB 5–6/85; SLJ 5/85)

**1475** Buehner, Caralyn, and Mark Buehner. *The Escape of Marvin the Ape* (PS–2). Illus. 1992, Dial LB $13.89 (0-8037-1124-7). 32pp. Marvin the ape has an exciting day in New York City when he escapes from the zoo. (Rev: BL 10/1/92; HB 9–10/92; SLJ 10/92)

**1476** Bullock, Kathleen. *It Chanced to Rain* (PS–1). Illus. by author. 1992, Simon & Schuster paper $3.95 (0-671-77820-X). The walk of several animal triplets is interrupted by the rain. (Rev: SLJ 8/89)

**1477** Burgess, Thornton W. *Old Mother West Wind* (2–3). Illus. by Michael Hague. 1990, Holt $18.95 (0-8050-1005-X). 90pp. This book contains 16 classic animal stories. First published in 1910. (Rev: BL 6/15/90)

**1478** Bush, John. *The Fish Who Could Wish* (PS–2). Illus. by Korky Paul. 1991, Kane/Miller $13.95 (0-916291-35-9); paper $6.95 (0-916291-48-0). The adventures of a fish whose wishes always come true. (Rev: SLJ 8/91)

**1479** Butterworth, Nick, and Mick Inkpen. *Jasper's Beanstalk* (PS–K). Illus. 1997, Simon & Schuster paper $5.99 (0-689-81540-9). 32pp. Jasper the cat becomes impatient when his bean seed doesn't grow into a beanstalk. (Rev: BL 1/15/93; SLJ 4/93)

**1480** Cain, Sheridan. *Why So Sad, Brown Rabbit?* (PS–1). Illus. by Jo Kelly. 1998, Dutton $14.99 (0-525-45963-4). 32pp. Brown Rabbit gets the family he longs for when 3 ducklings hatch and think that he is their mother. (Rev: BL 1/1–15/98; SLJ 2/98)

**1481** Calhoun, Mary. *Cross-Country Cat* (K–2). Illus. by Erick Ingraham. 1979, Morrow LB $16.93 (0-688-32186-0); paper $4.95 (0-688-06519-8). 40pp. A Siamese named Henry sets out on a cross-country skiing adventure.

**1482** Calhoun, Mary. *Henry the Sailor Cat* (PS–3). Illus. by Erick Ingraham. 1994, Morrow LB $15.93 (0-688-10841-5). 40pp. While on a sailboat, Henry the cat must take over steering the boat to save a man who has fallen overboard. (Rev: BL 5/1/94; HB 9–10/94; SLJ 5/94*)

**1483** Calhoun, Mary. *High-Wire Henry* (K–3). Illus. by Erick Ingraham. 1991, Morrow LB $15.93 (0-688-08984-4). 40pp. In order to regain the attention he lost when a puppy arrived in the household, Henry the cat takes up high-wire walking. (Rev: BL 4/1/91; HB 7–8/91; SLJ 4/91*)

**1484** Calhoun, Mary. *Hot-Air Henry* (PS–4). Illus. by Erick Ingraham. 1981, Morrow LB $15.93 (0-688-00502-0); paper $4.95 (0-688-04068-3). 40pp. Siamese cat Henry sneaks into the basket of a hot-air balloon and soon is afloat.

**1485** *The Candlewick Book of Animal Tales* (PS–3). Illus. 1996, Candlewick $19.99 (0-7636-0012-1). 96pp. An excellent collection of 20 animal picture books. (Rev: BL 10/1/96; SLJ 1/97)

**1486** *The Candlewick Book of Bear Stories* (PS–1). Illus. 1995, Candlewick $19.99 (1-56402-653-1). 96pp. An appealing anthology that reprints several well-known picture books whose subject is bears, including Alborough's *Where's My Teddy?* (1992). (Rev: BL 11/15/95; SLJ 12/95)

**1487** Cannon, Janell. *Stellaluna* (PS–3). Illus. 1993, Harcourt $16.00 (0-15-280217-7). 48pp. Stellaluna, a fruit bat, is separated from her mother and raised by regular birds. (Rev: BL 4/1/93; SLJ 6/93)

**1488** Cannon, Janell. *Trupp: A Fuzzhead Tale* (K–2). Illus. 1995, Harcourt $15.00 (0-15-200130-1). 48pp. After a narrow escape in the big city, Trupp, a catlike animal, decides to go back to his cave in the cliffs. (Rev: BCCB 5/95; BL 4/15/95; SLJ 7/95)

**1489** Cannon, Janell. *Verdi* (K–3). Illus. 1997, Harcourt $16.00 (0-15-201028-9). 48pp. A baby python named Verdi has fun and adventures when he travels alone in the rain forest. (Rev: BCCB 6/97; BL 4/15/97; SLJ 5/97)

**1490** Caple, Kathy. *The Coolest Place in Town* (K–2). Illus. 1990, Houghton $13.95 (0-395-51523-8). 32pp. Two brother hippos want to get even with their older sister. (Rev: BL 2/15/90; SLJ 5/90)

**1491** Caple, Kathy. *The Wimp* (PS–3). Illus. 1994, Houghton $14.95 (0-395-63115-7). 32pp. Arnold, a pig, tries to get even with some bullies who have been frightening him and his sister. (Rev: BL 6/1–15/94; SLJ 9/94)

**1492** Capucilli, Alyssa Satin. *Good Morning, Pond* (PS–2). Illus. by Cynthia Jabar. 1994, Hyperion LB $14.49 (1-56282-675-1). In this fantasy, 3 children watch all the different animals found in and around a pond greet the new day. (Rev: SLJ 11/94)

**1493** Carle, Eric. *The Grouchy Ladybug* (PS–K). Illus. by author. 1977, HarperCollins $15.00 (0-690-01391-4). 48pp. A grouchy ladybug, who is looking for a fight, challenges every insect and animal she meets regardless of size. Brilliantly illustrated in collage, the pages vary in size with the size of the animal.

**1494** Carle, Eric. *The Honeybee and the Robber* (PS–1). Illus. 1995, Putnam $18.95 (0-399-20767-8). 16pp. When tabs are pulled, creatures move in this story of a bear and a bee hive. (Rev: BL 2/1/96)

**1495** Carle, Eric. *The Mixed-Up Chameleon* (PS–2). Illus. by author. 1984, HarperCollins LB $15.89 (0-690-04397-X); paper $6.95 (0-06-443162-2). 32pp. A new edition of the story of a chameleon who finally decides to be himself.

**1496** Carle, Eric. *The Very Busy Spider* (PS–K). Illus. by author. 1989, Putnam $19.95 (0-399-21166-7). 32pp. A spider spins its web in this striking picture book. Also use the story of a crab that outgrows his shell in: *A House for Hermit Crab* (1991, Picture Book). (Rev: BCCB 5/85; BL 6/1/85; SLJ 5/85)

**1497** Carle, Eric. *The Very Lonely Firefly* (PS–1). Illus. 1995, Putnam $19.95 (0-399-22774-1). 32pp. A little firefly searches for some of his own kind but is confused by such lights as candles and fireworks. (Rev: BCCB 7–8/95; BL 5/15/95; HB 9–10/95; SLJ 8/95)

**1498** Carle, Eric. *The Very Quiet Cricket* (PS–1). Illus. 1990, Putnam $19.99 (0-399-21885-8). 48pp. A newly hatched cricket has a problem getting his wings to chirp. (Rev: BCCB 11/90; BL 10/1/90; HB 1–2/91; SLJ 12/90)

**1499** Carlson, Nancy. *Arnie and the Skateboard Gang* (PS–3). Illus. 1995, Viking paper $13.99 (0-670-85722-X). 32pp. Arnie, a skateboarding cat, decides caution is the better part of valor. (Rev: BL 6/1–15/95; SLJ 8/95)

**1500** Carlson, Nancy. *Harriet and the Garden* (PS–1). Illus. by author. 1982, Carolrhoda LB $17.27 (0-87614-184-X). 32pp. Harriet, a childlike dog, has several simple adventures. Others in the series are: *Harriet and the Roller Coaster; Harriet and Walt; Harriet's Recital* (all 1982).

**1501** Carlson, Nancy. *I Like Me!* (PS–K). Illus. by author. 1988, Puffin paper $4.99 (0-14-050819-8). 32pp. Learning to appreciate oneself. (Rev: BL 6/15/88; SLJ 9/88)

**1502** Carlson, Nancy. *Loudmouth George and the Cornet* (PS–2). Illus. by author. 1983, Carolrhoda LB $17.27 (0-87614-214-5). 32pp. George, a rabbit, gets dismissed from the school band. Others in the series are: *Loudmouth George and the Big Race; Loudmouth George and the Fishing Trip; Loudmouth*

*George and the New Neighbors; Loudmouth George and the Sixth-Grade Bully* (all 1983).

**1503**   Carlson, Nancy. *A Visit to Grandma's* (PS–3). Illus. 1991, Viking paper $13.95 (0-670-83288-X). 32pp. A family of beavers who visit Grandmother, now retired in Florida, are surprised at the changes they find. (Rev: BL 10/1/91; SLJ 11/91)

**1504**   Carlstrom, Nancy White. *Better Not Get Wet, Jesse Bear* (PS–K). Illus. by Bruce Degen. 1988, Macmillan LB $15.00 (0-02-717280-5). 32pp. Jesse Bear can't seem to stay away from water. Also use: *Jesse Bear, What Will You Wear?* (1986). (Rev: BL 4/15/88; HB 5–6/88)

**1505**   Carlstrom, Nancy White. *Guess Who's Coming, Jesse Bear* (PS–1). Illus. by Bruce Degen. Series: Jesse Bear. 1998, Simon & Schuster $15.00 (0-689-80702-3). 32pp. Jessie Bear dreads a visit from his bossy cousin, but he finds she is much better than expected. (Rev: BL 2/15/98; SLJ 4/98)

**1506**   Carlstrom, Nancy White. *How Do You Say It Today, Jesse Bear?* (PS–K). Illus. by Bruce Degen. 1992, Macmillan $15.00 (0-02-717276-7). 32pp. Throughout the year, Jesse Bear finds many ways to say "I Love You." (Rev: BL 9/15/92; SLJ 9/92)

**1507**   Carlstrom, Nancy White. *I'm Not Moving, Mama!* (K–2). Illus. by Thor Wickstrom. 1990, Macmillan LB $13.95 (0-02-717286-4). Little Mouse does not want to move his house, but Mama persuades him. (Rev: SLJ 1/91)

**1508**   Carlstrom, Nancy White. *Raven and River* (PS–3). Illus. by Jon Van Zyle. 1997, Little, Brown $15.95 (0-316-12894-5). 32pp. A picture book set in Alaska in which all the animals, beginning with Raven, notice the changes that spring brings to the river. (Rev: BCCB 6/97; BL 5/15/97; SLJ 4/97*)

**1509**   Carmichael, Clay. *Bear at the Beach* (1–3). Illus. by author. Series: Easy-to-Read Books. 1996, North-South LB $13.88 (1-55858-570-2). 45pp. Bear desperately wants a father and sets out to find one. (Rev: SLJ 7/96)

**1510**   Carrick, Carol. *What Happened to Patrick's Dinosaurs?* (K–2). Illus. by Donald Carrick. 1988, Houghton $16.00 (0-89919-406-0); paper $5.95 (0-89919-797-3). Patrick explains to his young brother his theory of how dinosaurs disappeared: they left by spaceship. (Rev: HB 8/86; SLJ 5/86)

**1511**   Carter, Penny. *A Big Trip for the Morrisons* (PS–2). Illus. 1997, Viking paper $13.99 (0-670-87022-6). 32pp. A picky dinosaur family takes a trip around the world but can't find any pleasure in all the wonderful sights. (Rev: BL 6/1–15/97; SLJ 8/97)

**1512**   Catalanotto, Peter. *Dylan's Day Out* (PS–2). Illus. 1989, Watts LB $16.99 (0-531-08429-9). 32pp. Dylan, a bored dalmatian, escapes for a day of freedom. (Rev: BL 10/1/89; SLJ 11/89)

**1513**   Cauley, Lorinda Bryan. *The Trouble with Tyrannosaurus Rex* (PS–2). Illus. by author. 1988, Harcourt paper $7.00 (0-15-290881-1). 32pp. The story of how Duckbill and Ankylosaurus scare away Tyrannosaurus Rex, the terror of the forest. (Rev: BL 4/1/88; SLJ 9/88)

**1514**   Caumartin, Francois. *Now You See Them, Now You Don't* (PS–2). Trans. from French by David Homel. Illus. by author. 1996, Firefly paper $4.95 (1-55209-007-8). 20pp. Whimsical illustrations show animals trying to disguise themselves in different ways to fool Simon the hunter. (Rev: SLJ 1/97)

**1515**   Cazet, Denys. *A Fish in His Pocket* (PS–2). Illus. by author. 1987, Orchard LB $16.99 (0-531-08313-6); paper $4.95 (0-531-07021-2). 32pp. Russell the bear causes the death of a fish — accidentally — in this story of who is responsible when an accident ends in death. (Rev: BL 8/87; SLJ 12/87)

**1516**   Cazet, Denys. *Nothing at All* (PS–1). Illus. 1994, Orchard LB $16.99 (0-531-08672-0). 32pp. A humorous picture book about silly farm animals and a scarecrow that has a mouse in his pants. (Rev: BCCB 7–8/94; BL 3/1/94; SLJ 5/94)

**1517**   Chadwick, Tim. *Cabbage Moon* (PS–1). Illus. by Piers Harper. 1994, Orchard $15.95 (0-531-06827-7). 32pp. A bunny travels to the moon and finds that it is a big, juicy, green cabbage. (Rev: BL 6/1–15/94; SLJ 4/94)

**1518**   Cherry, Lynne. *Archie, Follow Me* (PS–3). Illus. 1999, Dutton $12.95 (0-525-44647-8); paper $4.99 (0-140-55492-0). 32pp. A girl and her cat alternate in playing follow-the-leader roles. (Rev: BL 10/1/90; HB 9–10/90; SLJ 11/90)

**1519**   Cherry, Lynne. *The Armadillo from Amarillo* (K–3). Illus. 1994, Harcourt $16.00 (0-15-200359-2). 32pp. Sasparillo the armadillo wanders the earth and travels on a space shuttle to find out where he fits into the grand scheme of things. (Rev: BL 3/1/94; SLJ 4/94)

**1520**   Cherry, Lynne. *Who's Sick Today?* (PS–K). Illus. by author. 1998, Harcourt paper $6.00 (0-152-01886-7). 24pp. Showing such novelties as a "snake with an ache" or a "small red fox with chicken pox." (Rev: BL 5/15/88; HB 5–6/88; SLJ 7/88)

**1521**   Chorao, Kay. *Cathedral Mouse* (PS–1). Illus. by author. 1988, Dutton $12.95 (0-525-44400-9). 32pp. Mouse hopes to find a home in the cathedral, but it's not quite the sanctuary he had hoped for. (Rev: BL 9/1/88; SLJ 10/88)

**1522**   Christelow, Eileen. *Five Little Monkeys with Nothing to Do* (PS–1). Illus. 1996, Clarion $14.95 (0-395-75830-0). 36pp. Five little monkeys prepare for their Grandma Bessie's visit. (Rev: BCCB 12/96; BL 9/1/96; SLJ 11/96)

**1523** Christelow, Eileen. *The Great Pig Escape* (PS–1). Illus. 1994, Clarion $14.95 (0-395-66973-1). 32pp. On their way to be sold at market, some pigs escape and disguise themselves as humans. (Rev: BL 9/15/94; SLJ 11/94)

**1524** Christelow, Eileen. *The Robbery at the Diamond Dog Diner* (PS–1). Illus. by author. 1988, Houghton paper $6.95 (0-89919-722-1). 32pp. Some zany goings-on at the Diamond Dog Diner when Glenda Feathers announces that jewel thieves are in town. (Rev: BCCB 10/86; BL 11/1/86; SLJ 2/86)

**1525** Clifford, Eth. *Flatfoot Fox and the Case of the Missing Whoooo* (1–3). Illus. by Brian Lies. 1993, Houghton $13.95 (0-395-65364-9). 46pp. The great detective sets out to find the owl's missing "whoooo." (Rev: BCCB 11/93; BL 12/15/93; SLJ 8/93)

**1526** Cole, Babette. *Hurrah for Ethelyn* (K–3). Illus. 1991, Little, Brown $14.95 (0-316-15189-0). 32pp. A rat named Ethelyn bests the school bully, Tina Toerat. (Rev: BL 9/1/91; SLJ 3/92)

**1527** Collicott, Sharleen. *Seeing Stars* (PS–1). Illus. 1996, Dial paper $14.89 (0-8037-1523-4). 32pp. A toad and a squirrel travel by rocketship to the bottom of the ocean. (Rev: BL 8/96; SLJ 4/96)

**1528** Conover, Chris. *Mother Goose and the Sly Fox* (PS–K). Illus. 1989, Farrar $15.00 (0-374-35072-8). 32pp. A delightful look at a version of "The Wolf and the Seven Little Kids." (Rev: BCCB 2/90; BL 10/15/89; SLJ 12/89*)

**1529** Conrad, Pam. *The Rooster's Gift* (PS–3). Illus. by Eric Beddows. 1996, HarperCollins LB $15.89 (0-06-023604-3). 40pp. Young Rooster believes he has the power to command the sun to rise. (Rev: BL 9/15/96; HB 11–12/96; SLJ 9/96)

**1530** Coplans, Peta. *Dottie* (PS–2). Illus. by author. 1994, Houghton $14.95 (0-395-66788-7). Dot is an irresistible pup who has an urge to grow a garden in spite of her parents' objections. (Rev: SLJ 4/94)

**1531** Coplans, Peta. *Spaghetti for Suzy* (PS–3). Illus. 1993, Houghton $13.95 (0-395-65232-4). Suzy, who only eats spaghetti, is given some fruit by her animal friends. (Rev: SLJ 5/93)

**1532** Coursen, Valerie. *Mordant's Wish* (K–3). Illus. 1997, Holt $15.95 (0-8050-4374-8). 32pp. A mole named Mordant wishes for a turtle friend and eventually gets his wish. (Rev: BL 9/1/97; SLJ 9/97)

**1533** Cousins, Lucy. *Maisy Goes Swimming* (PS). Illus. 1990, Little, Brown $13.95 (0-316-15834-8). Maisy, a white mouse, goes to a swimming pool in this book that contains many flaps and tabs. Also use: *Maisy Goes to Bed* (1990). (Rev: BCCB 10/90*; SLJ 9/90)

**1534** Cousins, Lucy. *Maisy Goes to School* (PS–K). Illus. 1992, Candlewick $12.95 (1-56402-085-1).

Maisy, a little mouse, enjoys all the various activities when she attends preschool. Also use: *Maisy Goes to the Playground* (1992). (Rev: SLJ 11/92)

**1535** Cousins, Lucy. *Za-Za's Baby Brother* (PS). Illus. 1995, Candlewick $16.95 (1-56402-582-9). 32pp. At first, Za-Za, a young zebra, has problems adjusting to her mother's new baby. (Rev: BL 9/1/95; SLJ 10/95)

**1536** Cowley, Joy. *The Mouse Bride* (PS–1). Illus. by David Christiana. 1995, Scholastic $13.95 (0-590-47503-7). 32pp. A tiny mouse sets out to find a husband and after many rejections finds the mouse of her dreams. (Rev: BCCB 11/95; BL 1/1–15/96; SLJ 11/95)

**1537** Coxon, Michele. *The Cat Who Lost His Purr* (K–2). Illus. by author. 1996, Puffin paper $4.99 (0-140-55608-7). A tabby cat wakes up one morning to find that his purr has gone. (Rev: SLJ 3/92)

**1538** Crebbin, June. *Fly by Night* (PS–3). Illus. by Stephen Lambert. 1993, Candlewick $14.95 (1-56402-149-1). 32pp. A young owl waits impatiently through the day for the nighttime when he can fly. (Rev: BL 3/15/93; SLJ 4/93)

**1539** Crowe, Robert L. *Tyler Toad and the Thunder* (PS–2). Illus. by Kay Chorao. 1986, Dutton paper $4.95 (0-525-44243-X). 32pp. Tyler Toad finds that he is not the only animal afraid of thunder.

**1540** Crume, Marion. *Do You See Mouse?* (PS–2). Illus. by Normand Chartier. 1995, Silver Pr. LB $15.95 (0-382-24683-7); paper $5.95 (0-382-24685-3). Visual clues are used so the reader can enter into the animals' game of hide-and-seek. (Rev: SLJ 7/95)

**1541** Currey, Anna. *Tickling Tigers* (PS–K). Illus. 1996, Barron's $12.95 (0-8120-6594-8); paper $5.95 (0-8120-9594-4). 32pp. Hannibal, a little mouse, narrowly escapes capture by several tigers whom he has enraged. (Rev: BL 10/15/96)

**1542** Curtiss, A. B. *In the Company of Bears* (K–2). Illus. by Barbara Stone. 1994, Oldcastle LB $18.95 (0-932529-72-0). Humorous illustrations depict polar bears engaging in many human activities. (Rev: SLJ 9/94)

**1543** Cushman, Doug. *Mouse and Mole and the Year-Round Garden* (1–3). Illus. 1994, W. H. Freeman $11.20 (0-7167-6524-1). 32pp. Mouse and Mole enjoy good times together but only after tending their garden, in this book that explains how plants grow. (Rev: BL 4/1/94)

**1544** Dahl, Roald. *The Enormous Crocodile* (K–3). Illus. by Quentin Blake. 1978, Knopf LB $14.00 (0-394-93594-2); Puffin paper $3.99 (0-140-36556-7). 48pp. Animals band together to save a group of children from becoming a crocodile's lunch.

**1545** Daugherty, James. *Andy and the Lion* (1–4). Illus. by author. 1938, Viking $15.99 (0-670-12433-8); Puffin paper $4.99 (0-14-050277-7). 80pp. A popular, modern version of the story of Androcles and the lion.

**1546** Davenier, Christine. *Leon and Albertine* (PS–1). Illus. 1998, Orchard $15.95 (0-531-30072-2). 32pp. Leo, a pig, is attracted to Albertine, a chicken who is decidedly not interested. (Rev: BL 2/1/98; SLJ 3/98*)

**1547** Davol, Marguerite W. *Batwings and the Curtain of Night* (PS–4). Illus. by Mary Grandpre. 1997, Orchard $15.95 (0-531-30005-6). 32pp. In order to get more light, some nocturnal animals decide to pull back the curtain of night in this creation story. (Rev: BCCB 4/97; BL 4/15/97; SLJ 4/97)

**1548** Day, Alexandra. *Carl Goes to Daycare* (PS–2). Illus. 1993, Farrar $12.95 (0-374-31093-9). 32pp. In an emergency, Carl the rottweiler has to take care of youngsters at a day care center. (Rev: BCCB 11/93; BL 12/15/93; SLJ 12/93)

**1549** Day, Alexandra. *Carl's Afternoon in the Park* (2–6). Illus. 1991, Farrar $12.95 (0-374-31109-9). 32pp. Carl, a rottweiler, is placed in charge of a puppy and a toddler while Mom goes for tea with a friend in the park. (Rev: BCCB 11/91; BL 10/15/91; SLJ 11/91)

**1550** Day, Alexandra. *Carl's Christmas* (PS–K). Illus. 1990, Farrar $12.95 (0-374-31114-5). 32pp. On Christmas Eve, Carl, a big black dog, takes the baby he is caring for out to greet the world. (Rev: BCCB 10/90; BL 11/1/90)

**1551** Day, Alexandra. *Frank and Ernest on the Road* (PS–3). Illus. 1994, Scholastic $14.95 (0-590-45048-4). 48pp. Highway slang is introduced as Frank the bear and Ernest the elephant hit the road in a truck. (Rev: BCCB 3/94; BL 12/15/93*; SLJ 2/94*)

**1552** Day, Alexandra. *Frank and Ernest Play Ball* (K–4). Illus. 1990, Scholastic $12.95 (0-590-42548-X). 48pp. The intrepid bear and elephant temporarily manage a baseball team. (Rev: BCCB 6/90; BL 3/1/90; SLJ 2/90)

**1553** Day, David. *King of the Woods* (K–2). Illus. by Ken Brown. 1993, Four Winds LB $13.95 (0-02-726361-4). A little wren defeats all the stronger animals in the forest and claims as her own the golden apple she has found. (Rev: SLJ 3/94)

**1554** De Beer, Hans. *Bernard Bear's Amazing Adventure* (K–3). Illus. 1994, North-South LB $14.88 (1-55858-295-9). 32pp. Bernard the bear wants to spend the winter in Florida, but instead he must hibernate with some dormice. (Rev: BL 12/15/94; SLJ 7/95)

**1555** De Beer, Hans. *Little Polar Bear Finds a Friend* (PS–2). 1990, North-South $15.95 (1-55858-092-1). 32pp. A clever walrus is able to help Lars, a polar bear, escape captors. (Rev: BL 11/15/90; SLJ 2/91)

**1556** De Beer, Hans. *Little Polar Bear, Take Me Home!* (PS–2). Illus. 1996, North-South LB $15.88 (1-55858-631-8). 32pp. Sasha, a tiger cub, is helped home by Lars, a little polar bear. (Rev: BL 11/1/96; SLJ 11/96)

**1557** De Brunhoff, Jean. *The Story of Babar, the Little Elephant* (PS). Illus. by author. 1937, Random LB $13.99 (0-394-90575-X). A time-tested reading favorite about the little French elephant.

**1558** De Brunhoff, Jean. *The Travels of Babar* (PS–1). Illus. by author. 1967, Random LB $11.99 (0-394-90576-8). 48pp. Companion volume in over-size format to The Story of Babar, first published in 1934. Another oversize edition is: *Babar the King* (1989). (Rev: BL 10/1/85)

**1559** De Brunhoff, Jean, and Laurent De Brunhoff. *Babar's Anniversary Album: Six Favorite Stories* (K–1). Illus. by Jean De Brunhoff. 1981, Random LB $16.99 (0-394-94813-0). 144pp. A collection of 6 of the most popular Babar adventures.

**1560** De Brunhoff, Laurent. *Babar Loses His Crown* (PS–1). Illus. by author. 1967, Random LB $7.99 (0-394-90045-6). 72pp. Babar searches the tourist spots of Paris for his lost crown. Three others in this vast series are: *Meet Babar and His Family* (1973); *Babar Learns to Cook* (1979); *Babar and the Ghost* (1981).

**1561** De Brunhoff, Laurent. *Babar's Family Album* (PS–3). Illus. 1991, Random $17.00 (0-679-81167-2). 109pp. Five tales to charm young Babar fans. (Rev: BL 1/15/92)

**1562** De Brunhoff, Laurent. *Babar's Little Girl* (PS–2). Illus. by author. 1987, Random $11.00 (0-394-88689-5). 36pp. Isabelle — an "amazing baby" — joins the marvelous Babar family. Also use: *Babar's Little Circus Star* (1988). (Rev: BL 5/15/87; SLJ 9/87)

**1563** Degen, Bruce. *Jamberry* (PS–1). Illus. by author. 1983, HarperCollins LB $14.89 (0-06-021417-1). 32pp. A boy and a bear collect berries for jam.

**1564** Degen, Bruce. *Sailaway Home* (PS–K). Illus. 1996, Scholastic $14.95 (0-590-46443-4). 32pp. A little pig imagines all sorts of adventures that could take place aboard his toy boat. (Rev: BL 8/96; SLJ 3/96)

**1565** Demi. *Demi's Dragons and Fantastic Creatures* (PS–2). Illus. by author. 1993, Holt $19.95 (0-8050-2564-2). An interactive volume with foldout pages that depict an amazing array of fantastic animals. (Rev: SLJ 1/94)

**1566** Denim, Sue. *The Dumb Bunnies* (K–2). Illus. by Dav Pilkey. 1994, Scholastic $12.95 (0-590-47708-0). 32pp. The story of the 3 dumb bunnies and their hectic misadventures. (Rev: BL 1/15/94; SLJ 3/94)

**1567** Denim, Sue. *The Dumb Bunnies' Easter* (K–2). Illus. by Dav Pilkey. 1995, Scholastic $12.95 (0-590-20241-3). 32pp. The Dumb Bunnies have a very distorted view of what to expect from the Easter Bunny. (Rev: BL 2/1/95; SLJ 2/95)

**1568** Denim, Sue. *The Dumb Bunnies Go to the Zoo* (1–3). Illus. by Dav Pilkey. 1997, Scholastic $13.95 (0-590-84735-X). 32pp. The 3 Dumb Bunnies go to the zoo, where they create havoc. (Rev: BL 4/1/97; SLJ 3/97)

**1569** Denim, Sue. *Make Way for Dumb Bunnies* (1–3). Illus. by Dav Pilkey. 1996, Scholastic $12.95 (0-590-58286-0). 32pp. A slapstick tale about the misadventures of an unthinking rabbit family. (Rev: BL 2/1/96; SLJ 3/96)

**1570** dePaola, Tomie. *Bill and Pete Go Down the Nile* (K–3). Illus. by author. 1987, Putnam $15.95 (0-399-21395-3); paper $5.95 (0-698-11401-9). 32pp. A crocodile a bird in a delightful romp down the Nile. (Rev: BL 5/1/87; SLJ 9/87)

**1571** dePaola, Tomie. *Bonjour, Mr. Satie* (1–3). Illus. 1991, Putnam $15.95 (0-399-21782-7). 32pp. Mr. Satie, a cat, tells his niece and nephew about exciting experiences in the art salons of Paris. (Rev: BCCB 3/91; BL 3/1/93)

**1572** dePaola, Tomie. *Four Stories for Four Seasons* (2–3). Illus. by author. 1994, Simon & Schuster paper $6.95 (0-671-88633-9). 48pp. Dog, Cat, Frog, and Pig are involved in activities for each season in this reissued picture book. Also use: *Michael Bird Boy* (1987). (Rev: BL 4/1/90)

**1573** dePaola, Tomie. *The Knight and the Dragon* (1–3). Illus. by author. 1998, Putnam LB $15.95 (0-399-20707-4); paper $5.99 (0-698-11623-2). An inexperienced knight and an inexperienced dragon prepare themselves to do battle.

**1574** dePaola, Tomie. *Little Grunt and the Big Egg: A Prehistoric Fairy Tale* (PS–3). Illus. 1990, Holiday LB $15.95 (0-8234-0730-6). 32pp. Little Grunt adopts a pet dinosaur named George. (Rev: BL 4/1/90)

**1575** Derby, Sally. *The Mouse Who Owned the Sun* (PS–2). Illus. by Friso Henstra. 1993, Four Winds LB $14.95 (0-02-766965-3). A mouse who believes that he controls the sun sets out to explore the world. (Rev: SLJ 5/94)

**1576** DeSaix, Frank. *Hilary and the Lions* (K–3). Illus. by Deborah Durland DeSaix. 1990, Farrar $15.00 (0-374-33237-1). 32pp. The lions in front of the New York Public Library take Hilary on a tour of their town. (Rev: BL 12/1/90; SLJ 4/91)

**1577** De Vries, Anke. *My Elephant Can Do Almost Anything* (PS–1). Illus. by Ilja Walraven. 1996, Front Street $14.95 (1-886910-06-5). A boy's imaginary playmate, an elephant, is upset when the boy goes to school. (Rev: BCCB 6/96; HB 7–8/96; SLJ 6/96)

**1578** De Vries, Anke. *Piggy's Birthday Dream* (PS). Illus. by Jung-Hee Spetter. 1997, Front Street $14.95 (1-886910-21-9). 32pp. Piggy is so shy that she doesn't tell any of the barnyard animals it's her birthday, but they plan their own surprise for her. (Rev: BL 11/15/97; SLJ 11/97)

**1579** Dijs, Carla. *Are You My Daddy?* (PS). Illus. 1990, Simon & Schuster $6.95 (0-671-70227-0). This pop-up book features a tiger cub looking for his daddy. A companion volume is: *Are You My Mommy?* (1990). (Rev: SLJ 1/91)

**1580** Dodd, Lynley. *Hairy Maclary from Donaldson's Dairy* (PS–K). Illus. by author. 1988, Stevens LB $19.93 (0-918831-05-9). 38pp. A rhyming cumulative story about a small black dog; continued in *Hairy Maclary's Bone* (1990). Also use: *Hairy Maclary's Caterwaul Caper* (1989). (Rev: BL 11/15/85)

**1581** Dragonwagon, Crescent. *Alligators and Others All Year Long: A Book of Months* (PS–1). Illus. by Jose Aruego and Ariane Dewey. 1993, Macmillan $14.95 (0-02-733091-5). 32pp. For each of the months, a different animal engages in a suitable activity, such as a cat ice skating in January. (Rev: BL 10/15/93; SLJ 1/94)

**1582** Dubanevich, Arlene. *Pig William* (PS–1). Illus. by author. 1985, Simon & Schuster LB $14.95 (0-02-733200-4). 32pp. Pig William is such a dawdler that his brothers leave without him for a picnic. (Rev: BCCB 12/85; BL 1/15/86)

**1583** Duke, Kate. *Aunt Isabel Makes Trouble* (PS–2). Illus. 1996, Dutton paper $13.99 (0-525-45496-9). 32pp. Aunt Isabel, a mouse, tells her niece about the wonderful adventures of Lady Nell and the important birthday she forgot. A sequel to *Aunt Isabel Tells a Good One* (1992). (Rev: BL 10/15/96; SLJ 10/96)

**1584** Duke, Kate. *Aunt Isabel Tells a Good One* (PS–3). Illus. 1992, Dutton paper $14.99 (0-525-44835-7). 32pp. In this tale-within-a-tale, Aunt Isabel spins a "good story" for her mouse child niece. (Rev: BL 1/15/92; SLJ 3/92)

**1585** Dunbar, Joyce. *Seven Sillies* (PS–2). Illus. by Chris Downing. 1994, Artists & Writers Guild $13.95 (0-307-17504-9). While playing tricks on other animals, a frog reveals that he is also vulnerable. (Rev: SLJ 8/94)

**1586** Dunbar, Joyce. *The Spring Rabbit* (PS–2). Illus. by Susan Varley. 1994, Lothrop $13.00 (0-688-

13191-3). 32pp. An only child, the bunny Smudge waits for spring when his mother says he will have brothers and sisters. (Rev: BL 4/15/94; SLJ 5/94)

**1587** DuQuette, Keith. *Hotel Animal* (K–2). Illus. 1994, Viking paper $13.99 (0-670-85056-X). 32pp. Two married lizards take a vacation at a posh hotel but find they are too small to fit in until they find a dollhouse in the attic that is just right. (Rev: BL 3/15/94; SLJ 6/94)

**1588** Duvoisin, Roger. *Petunia* (K–2). Illus. by author. 1962, Knopf LB $13.99 (0-394-90865-1). Petunia, the silly goose, finds a book and carries it around believing this will make her wise, until her own foolishness proves her wrong.

**1589** Eduar, Gilles. *Jooka Saves the Day* (PS–2). Trans. by Dominic Barth. Illus. 1997, Orchard $15.95 (0-531-30036-6). 40pp. Jooka tries to be like all the crocodiles in the rain forest, but it is impossible because he is really a dragon. (Rev: BL 12/1/97; HB 9–10/97; SLJ 9/97)

**1590** Edwards, Pamela Duncan. *Dinorella: A Prehistoric Fairytale* (K–3). Illus. by Henry Cole. 1997, Hyperion LB $16.49 (0-7868-2249-X). 32pp. A raucous, exuberant reworking of the Cinderella story using dinosaurs. (Rev: BL 11/1/97; SLJ 11/97)

**1591** Edwards, Pamela Duncan. *Four Famished Foxes and Fosdyke* (K–3). Illus. by Henry Cole. 1995, HarperCollins LB $14.89 (0-06-024926-9). 32pp. The letter *F* figures prominently in this story about 4 foraging foxes. (Rev: BL 9/1/95; SLJ 12/95)

**1592** Edwards, Pamela Duncan. *Livingstone Mouse* (PS–2). Illus. by Henry Cole. 1996, HarperCollins LB $14.89 (0-06-025870-5). 32pp. A mouse decides that China would be a nice place for him to build his nest. (Rev: BL 10/1/96; SLJ 9/96)

**1593** Edwards, Pamela Duncan. *Some Smug Slug* (PS–3). Illus. by Henry Cole. 1996, HarperCollins LB $14.89 (0-06-024792-4). 32pp. Alliterations abound in this saga of a slug and a slippery slope. (Rev: BL 5/1/96; SLJ 6/96*)

**1594** Edwards, Richard. *Moles Can Dance* (PS–K). Illus. by Caroline Anstey. 1994, Candlewick $13.95 (1-56402-353-2). 32pp. A little mole learns to dance by watching a girl twirling to music in a deserted field. (Rev: BL 6/1–15/94; SLJ 9/94)

**1595** Edwards, Roland. *Tigers* (PS–K). Illus. by Judith Riches. 1992, Morrow LB $14.93 (0-688-11686-8). 32pp. A child imagines hearing a pride of playful tigers just beyond the bedroom door. (Rev: BL 2/1/93; SLJ 12/92)

**1596** Egan, Tim. *Burnt Toast on Davenport Street* (K–2). Illus. 1997, Houghton $14.95 (0-395-79618-0). 32pp. A fly — who has granted Arthur, a dog, 3 wishes — gets the wishes mixed up in this hilarious fantasy. (Rev: BL 4/15/97; SLJ 5/97*)

**1597** Egan, Tim. *Friday Night at Hodges' Cafe* (PS–1). Illus. 1994, Houghton $14.95 (0-395-68076-X). 32pp. "Hodges" is a cafe frequented by elephants with a no-tigers policy. (Rev: BL 10/1/94; SLJ 9/94*)

**1598** Egan, Tim. *Metropolitan Cow* (PS–2). Illus. 1996, Houghton $14.95 (0-395-73096-1). 32pp. The Gibbonses, an upper-crust cow family, are upset when Webster and his pig family move into their apartment building. (Rev: BL 3/1/96*; HB 7–8/96; SLJ 5/96*)

**1599** Ehlert, Lois. *Mole's Hill* (PS–2). Illus. 1994, Harcourt $15.00 (0-15-255116-6). 32pp. Fox demands that Mole move from her hill, but she is able to outwit him and remain. (Rev: BCCB 4/94; BL 3/15/94; HB 7–8/94; SLJ 5/94)

**1600** Ehlert, Lois. *Nuts to You!* (PS–2). Illus. 1993, Harcourt $16.00 (0-15-257647-9). A rural squirrel shows how he gathers food in the big city. (Rev: BL 3/1/93; HB 3–4/93; SLJ 4/93)

**1601** Ehrlich, Amy. *Parents in the Pigpen, Pigs in the Tub* (K–4). Illus. by Steven Kellogg. 1993, Dial LB $14.89 (0-8037-0928-5). 40pp. Farm animals and their owners exchange habitats with unfortunate but hilarious results. (Rev: BL 9/15/93*; SLJ 10/93)

**1602** Emberley, Michael. *Ruby* (PS–1). Illus. 1990, Little, Brown $14.95 (0-316-88859-1); paper $5.95 (0-316-23660-8). 32pp. In this variation on Red Riding Hood, a little mouse named Ruby treks across Boston to deliver goodies to her granny. (Rev: BL 11/1/90; HB 3–4/91; SLJ 10/90)

**1603** Enderle, Judith R., and Stephanie G. Tessler. *A Pile of Pigs* (4–6). Illus. by Charles Jordan. 1993, Boyds Mills $10.95 (1-878093-88-6). 32pp. Several pigs decide to form themselves into a pyramid similar to one they have seen on a circus poster. (Rev: BL 2/1/93; SLJ 3/93)

**1604** Enderle, Judith R., and Stephanie G. Tessler. *Six Sandy Sheep* (PS–1). Illus. by John O'Brien. 1997, Boyds Mills $14.95 (1-56397-582-3). This alliterative story tells how 6 sheep spend a day at the beach, where they swim, splash, surf, ski, snorkel, and collect shells. (Rev: SLJ 7/97)

**1605** Enderle, Judith R., and Stephanie G. Tessler. *What Would Mama Do?* (K–3). Illus. by Chris L. Demarest. 1995, Boyds Mills $14.95 (1-56397-418-5). 32pp. To outwit a clever Fox, Little Lilly, a goose, decides that she must do what her mama would do. (Rev: BL 10/1/95)

**1606** Ernst, Lisa Campbell. *Bubba and Trixie* (PS–2). Illus. 1997, Simon & Schuster paper $16.00 (0-689-81357-0). 32pp. Trixie, a ladybug, teaches a timid caterpillar how to enjoy life. (Rev: BL 8/97; SLJ 11/97)

**1607** Ernst, Lisa Campbell. *Duke the Dairy Delight Dog* (PS–1). Illus. 1996, Simon & Schuster paper $15.00 (0-689-80750-3). 32pp. Duke, a mangy dog, would like to find a home at the local ice cream parlor. (Rev: BCCB 1/97; BL 9/1/96; SLJ 9/96)

**1608** Ernst, Lisa Campbell. *Ginger Jumps* (PS–1). Illus. 1996, Simon & Schuster paper $5.99 (0-689-80652-3). 32pp. Ginger learns simple tricks at the circus but doesn't want to jump through hoops. (Rev: BCCB 6/90; BL 5/15/90*; SLJ 7/90*)

**1609** Ernst, Lisa Campbell. *Little Red Riding Hood: A Newfangled Prairie Tale* (K–3). Illus. 1995, Simon & Schuster paper $16.00 (0-689-80145-9). 32pp. The wolf is really after Grandma's recipe for muffins in this update of *Little Red Riding Hood*. (Rev: BCCB 10/95; BL 7/95; SLJ 9/95)

**1610** Ernst, Lisa Campbell. *Walter's Tail* (K–2). Illus. 1992, Macmillan paper $14.95 (0-02-733564-X). Walter the dog has a wildly waving tail that always gets him into trouble. (Rev: BCCB 5–6/92; SLJ 4/92*)

**1611** Ernst, Lisa Campbell. *When Bluebell Sang* (K–3). Illus. by author. 1989, Macmillan paper $5.99 (0-689-71584-6). 40pp. Bluebell the cow finds that life behind the footlights isn't all it's cracked up to be. (Rev: BL 3/1/89; SLJ 4/89)

**1612** Ernst, Lisa Campbell. *Zinnia and Dot* (PS–2). Illus. 1992, Viking paper $15.99 (0-670-83091-7). 32pp. Two fat, vain chickens who fight about everything learn to cooperate to save themselves from the tricky weasel. (Rev: BCCB 9/92; BL 7/92*; SLJ 7/92*)

**1613** Ets, Marie Hall. *In the Forest* (PS). Illus. by author. 1976, Puffin paper $5.99 (0-14-050180-0). A small boy's adventures with his forest friends.

**1614** Evans, Dilys, ed. *Monster Soup and Other Spooky Poems* (PS–1). Illus. by Jacquelin Rogers. 1992, Scholastic $14.95 (0-590-45208-8). 40pp. Watercolor paintings illustrate 16 poems that monster fans are sure to love. (Rev: BL 8/92; SLJ 10/92) [811]

**1615** Ezra, Mark. *The Frightened Little Owl* (PS–K). Illus. by Gavin Rowe. 1997, Interlink $14.95 (1-56656-264-3). 32pp. Fearful Little Owl takes her first flight in order to find her mother and discovers that she likes it. (Rev: BL 6/1–15/97; SLJ 7/97)

**1616** Ezra, Mark. *The Hungry Otter* (PS–2). Illus. by Gavin Rowe. 1996, Crocodile $14.95 (1-56656-216-3). When Little Otter saves a crow from a fox, the crow, in turn, helps the otter by breaking holes in the ice so that the animal can fish. (Rev: SLJ 4/97)

**1617** Ezra, Mark. *The Prickly Hedgehog* (K–3). Illus. by Gavin Rowe. 1995, Crocodile $14.95 (1-56656-189-2). A little hedgehog finds it hard to keep up with his family during a walk and gets lost. (Rev: SLJ 9/95)

**1618** Ezra, Mark. *The Sleepy Dormouse* (K–3). Illus. by Gavin Rowe. 1994, Interlink $14.95 (1-56656-153-1). 32pp. A dormouse is captured by a weasel who wants to fatten him for a tasty meal. (Rev: BL 1/1/95; SLJ 8/94)

**1619** Fair, David. *The Fabulous Four Skunks* (PS–2). Illus. by Bruce Koscielniak. 1996, Houghton $14.95 (0-395-73572-6). 32pp. Four smelly skunks, members of a band, find it difficult to attract an audience. (Rev: BL 2/1/96; SLJ 4/96)

**1620** Fanelli, Sara. *Wolf* (PS–3). Illus. 1997, Dial paper $14.99 (0-8037-2093-9). 40pp. Wolf travels to the city to make a friend, but only on the way home does he succeed. (Rev: BL 5/15/97; SLJ 7/97)

**1621** Faulkner, Keith. *The Long-Nosed Pig* (PS–K). Illus. by Jonathan Lambert. 1998, Dial paper $11.99 (0-8037-2296-6). An interactive pop-up book about a long-nosed pig that has an accident in which it is flattened. (Rev: BL 12/15/97)

**1622** Faulkner, Keith. *The Wide-Mouthed Frog* (PS–1). Illus. by Jonathan Lambert. 1996, Dial paper $10.95 (0-8037-1875-6). 14pp. An interactive book that pictures a variety of animals and their eating habits. (Rev: BL 2/1/96; SLJ 4/96)

**1623** Flack, Marjorie. *Ask Mr. Bear* (PS–1). Illus. by author. 1968, Macmillan $13.00 (0-02-735390-7); paper $4.95 (0-02-043090-6). 32pp. To find a present for his mother's birthday, Danny asks a variety of animals for suggestions, with little success until he meets Mr. Bear.

**1624** Fleming, Denise. *Lunch* (PS–K). Illus. 1992, Holt $14.95 (0-8050-1636-8). 30pp. A mouse samples all the goodies on a banquet table and gets fatter and fatter. (Rev: BCCB 12/92; BL 11/1/92; HB 1–2/93; SLJ 12/92*)

**1625** Fleming, Denise. *Time to Sleep* (PS–1). Illus. 1997, Holt $15.95 (0-8050-3762-4). 32pp. In this cumulative tale, Bear passes along the information that winter is on the way. (Rev: BL 10/1/97; SLJ 11/97)

**1626** Fox, Mem. *Hattie and the Fox* (PS–K). Illus. by Patricia Mullins. 1987, Macmillan $14.95 (0-02-735470-9); paper $5.99 (0-689-71611-7). 32pp. A cumulative tale about a big black hen who spies a fox in the farmyard. (Rev: BL 3/15/87; HB 5–6/87; SLJ 5/87)

**1627** Fox, Mem. *Koala Lou* (PS–2). Illus. by Pamela Lofts. 1989, Harcourt $13.95 (0-15-200502-1). 32pp. A young koala named Koala Lou finds that her mother is too busy with her younger children to shower the same affection on her as before. (Rev: BL 11/15/89; HB 11–12/89; SLJ 1/90)

**1628** Fox, Mem. *Possum Magic* (K–2). Illus. by Julie Vivas. 1990, Harcourt $14.00 (0-15-200572-2); paper $6.00 (0-15-263224-7). 32pp. Grandmother Opossum makes Hush invisible, and then forgets how she did it in this tale of "down under." (Rev: BL 12/1/87; SLJ 12/87)

**1629** Frascino, Edward. *Nanny Noony and the Dust Queen* (PS–3). Illus. 1990, Pippin LB $15.95 (0-945912-09-9). 32pp. Nanny Noony must grapple with a powerful sorceress, the Dust Queen. (Rev: BL 6/15/90; SLJ 9/90)

**1630** Freeman, Don. *Beady Bear* (K–2). Illus. by author. 1977, Puffin paper $4.99 (0-14-050197-5). 48pp. A toy bear is unhappy living in a cave like other bears and becomes happy when his young owner finds him.

**1631** Freeman, Don. *Bearymore* (K–3). Illus. by author. 1979, Puffin paper $4.99 (0-14-050279-3). 40pp. A circus bear must build a new act, but he hibernates instead.

**1632** Freeman, Don. *Corduroy* (PS–1). Illus. by author. 1968, Puffin paper $4.99 (0-14-050173-8). 32pp. The amusing story of a toy bear whose one missing button from his green corduroy overalls almost costs him the opportunity of belonging to someone. A sequel is: *A Pocket for Corduroy* (1978).

**1633** Freeman, Don. *Dandelion* (K–2). Illus. by author. 1964, Puffin paper $5.99 (0-14-050218-1). 48pp. A vain lion goes to a barber shop before a party and makes himself unrecognizable to his friends.

**1634** Freeman, Don. *Norman the Doorman* (PS–2). Illus. by author. 1989, Puffin paper $5.99 (0-14-050288-2). 64pp. Norman is the doorman at the basement of the art museum and enjoys showing his rodent friends through its treasures.

**1635** French, Vivian. *Little Tiger Goes Shopping* (PS–1). Illus. by Andy Cooke. 1994, Candlewick paper $3.99 (1-56402-263-3). 24pp. When a group of animals find their local store is closed, they pool their ingredients and bake a cake. (Rev: BL 2/1/94)

**1636** French, Vivian. *Red Hen and Sly Fox* (PS–2). Illus. by Sally Hobson. 1995, Simon & Schuster $15.00 (0-689-80010-X). 32pp. Sly Fox tries to make a meal of Red Hen, but justice triumphs. (Rev: BCCB 4/95; BL 5/1/95; HB 7–8/95; SLJ 6/95)

**1637** Froehlich, Margaret W. *That Kookoory!* (1–3). Illus. by Marla Frazee. 1995, Harcourt $15.00 (0-15-277650-8). 40pp. This picture book tells of the confrontation between a prideful rooster and his arch enemy the weasel. (Rev: BCCB 5/95; BL 4/15/95; HB 7–8/95; SLJ 5/95)

**1638** Fuchs, Diane M. *A Bear for All Seasons* (PS–1). Illus. by Kathryn Brown. 1995, Holt $14.95 (0-8050-2139-6). 32pp. During his winter sleep, Bear is awakened by Fox, who wants to chat. (Rev: BL 10/1/95; SLJ 12/95)

**1639** Gantos, Jack. *Not So Rotten Ralph* (PS–3). Illus. by Nicole Rubel. 1994, Houghton $15.00 (0-395-62302-2). 32pp. Sweet Sarah loses her patience and sends her cat, Rotten Ralph, to obedience school. (Rev: BL 3/1/94; HB 7–8/94; SLJ 4/94)

**1640** Gantos, Jack. *Rotten Ralph* (K–3). Illus. by Nicole Rubel. 1976, Houghton $15.00 (0-395-24276-2); paper $6.95 (0-395-29202-6). 48pp. Ralph is truly a nasty cat — mean and disruptive — until he is reformed under unusual circumstances. A sequel is: *Worse Than Rotten, Ralph* (1982).

**1641** Gantos, Jack. *Rotten Ralph's Show and Tell* (3–5). Illus. by Nicole Rubel. 1989, Houghton $15.00 (0-395-44312-1). 32pp. Rotten Ralph the cat makes a mess of show-and-tell at school. (Rev: BL 10/1/89; HB 11–12/89; SLJ 12/89)

**1642** Gantschev, Ivan. *Where Is Mr. Mole?* (PS–1). Adapted by Andrew Clements. Illus. 1990, Picture Book paper $15.95 (0-88708-109-6). 28pp. Mr. Mole disappears and his friends are worried until he reappears — with Mrs. Mole. (Rev: BL 3/15/90; SLJ 7/90)

**1643** Geisert, Arthur. *Oink* (PS–1). Illus. by author. 1991, Houghton $15.00 (0-395-55329-6). 32pp. The only word in this book is "oink," but the Pig family shows how much meaning can be expressed by a single word. (Rev: BL 6/1/91; HB 7–8/91*; SLJ 6/91)

**1644** Geraghty, Paul. *Solo* (PS–2). Illus. 1996, Crown $17.00 (0-517-70908-2). 32pp. Penguins Floe and Fin face difficulties in raising and feeding their baby, Solo. (Rev: BL 2/1/96; SLJ 3/96)

**1645** Gerstein, Mordicai, and Susan Y. Harris. *Daisy's Garden* (PS–3). Illus. 1995, Hyperion LB $15.49 (0-7868-2080-2). 32pp. A year in the life of a garden tended by rabbits, mice, groundhogs, goats, and other animals. (Rev: BL 7/95; SLJ 4/95)

**1646** Giannini, Enzo. *Zorina Ballerina* (PS–K). Illus. 1993, Simon & Schuster paper $14.00 (0-671-74776-2). 29pp. Zorina wants to dance with the other elephants, but she is too young. (Rev: BL 8/93)

**1647** Gill, Madeline. *The Spring Hat* (PS–1). Illus. 1993, Simon & Schuster paper $13.00 (0-671-75666-4). 32pp. When 3 bunnies accidentally lose their mother's hat, they make a new one out of flowers. (Rev: BL 3/1/93; SLJ 5/93)

**1648** Ginsburg, Mirra. *Across the Stream* (PS–2). Illus. by Nancy Tafuri. 1982, Greenwillow LB $15.93 (0-688-01206-X); Morrow paper $4.95 (0-688-10477-0). 24pp. Mother hen saves her 3 chicks from the fox.

**1649** Ginsburg, Mirra, trans. *The Chick and the Duckling* (PS–K). Adapted from the Russian by V.

Suteyev. Illus. by Jose Aruego and Ariane Dewey. 1988, Simon & Schuster paper $4.95 (0-689-71226-X). 32pp. A duck and a chick who hatch at the same time become constant companions.

**1650** Gliori, Debi. *Mr. Bear Says Peek-a-Boo* (PS). Illus. 1997, Simon & Schuster $4.99 (0-689-81516-6). 10pp. An interactive board book in which a bear and his baby play together. Also use *Mr. Bear Says I Love You* and *Mr. Bear Says Good Night* (both 1997). (Rev: BL 2/1/98)

**1651** Gliori, Debi. *Mr. Bear's Picnic* (PS–1). Illus. by author. 1995, Artists & Writers Guild $13.95 (0-307-17558-8). When Mr. Bear and his cub go on a picnic, they are accompanied by 3 constantly complaining neighbors. (Rev: BCCB 6/95; SLJ 8/95)

**1652** Goldsmith, Howard. *Sleepy Little Owl* (PS–1). Illus. by Denny Bond. 1997, McGraw-Hill $12.95 (0-07-024543-6). 30pp. Through a series of daytime adventures, a young owl realizes that he is a nocturnal creature. (Rev: SLJ 2/98)

**1653** Gomi, Taro. *The Crocodile and the Dentist* (PS–2). Illus. 1994, Millbrook LB $19.90 (1-56294-555-6). 32pp. A young crocodile has a toothache and is unhappy at the thought of visiting a dentist. (Rev: BL 1/1/95; SLJ 2/95)

**1654** Goodman, Joan E. *Bernard's Bath* (PS–K). Illus. by Dominic Catalano. 1996, Boyds Mills $14.95 (1-56397-323-5). 32pp. Baby elephant Bernard resists all efforts to get him to take a bath. (Rev: BL 2/1/96; SLJ 3/96)

**1655** Gordon, Jeffie R. *Six Sleepy Sheep* (PS–2). Illus. by John O'Brien. 1991, Boyds Mills $12.95 (1-878093-06-1). This fable about 6 sheep uses the sound "S" in captivating ways. (Rev: HB 1–2/92; SLJ 1/92)

**1656** Goss, Linda. *The Frog Who Wanted to Be a Singer* (K–3). Illus. by Cynthia Jabar. 1996, Orchard LB $16.99 (0-531-08745-X). 40pp. Scorned by both frogs and birds because he wants to sing, a young frog astounds everyone with his talent. (Rev: BCCB 4/96; BL 4/15/96*; SLJ 5/96)

**1657** Graham, Amanda. *Who Wants Arthur?* (PS–1). Illus. by Donna Gynell. 1987, Stevens LB $18.60 (1-55532-868-7). 32pp. Plain ordinary Arthur the dog thinks he has to imitate more desirable animals to get adopted. (Rev: BL 6/1/87; SLJ 11/87)

**1658** Graham, Margaret B. *Be Nice to Spiders* (PS–2). Illus. by author. 1967, HarperCollins LB $14.89 (0-06-022073-2). 32pp. Helen, Billy's pet spider, makes all the animals at the zoo happy when she spins webs and catches flies for them.

**1659** Graham, Thomas. *Mr. Bear's Boat* (PS–K). Illus. by author. 1991, Puffin paper $3.95 (0-525-44739-3). 32pp. Mr. Bear builds a sturdy little sailboat. (Rev: BCCB 4/88; BL 4/15/88)

**1660** Gray, Libba M. *Small Green Snake* (PS–1). Illus. by Holly Meade. 1994, Orchard LB $15.99 (0-531-08694-1). 32pp. A disobedient garter snake wanders away from home and finds himself a prisoner in a jelly jar. (Rev: BL 9/15/94*; SLJ 9/94)

**1661** Greene, Rhonda Gowler. *Barnyard Song* (PS–1). Illus. by Robert Bender. 1997, Simon & Schuster $13.00 (0-689-80758-9). 40pp. A variation of the "Old MacDonald" rhyme in which barnyard animals lose their voices because of bad cases of the flu. (Rev: BL 8/97; SLJ 9/97*)

**1662** Gretz, Susanna. *Duck Takes Off* (PS–K). Illus. 1991, Macmillan LB $12.95 (0-02-737472-6). 32pp. Duck tries to act like a schoolteacher with the result that she loses her friends. Also use in the same series: *Frog in the Middle* (1991). (Rev: BL 5/1/91; SLJ 5/91)

**1663** Gretz, Susanna. *Frog, Duck, and Rabbit* (PS–K). Illus. 1992, Macmillan LB $12.95 (0-02-737327-4). 32pp. Three animal friends have difficulty in completing a crocodile costume for a parade. Also use: *Rabbit Rambles On* (1992). (Rev: BL 2/15/92; SLJ 6/92)

**1664** Gretz, Susanna, and Alison Sage. *Teddy Bears Cure a Cold* (PS–K). Illus. by authors. 1986, Scholastic paper $4.99 (0-590-43495-0). 40pp. Five fuzzy bears nurse one of their own, William, through the flu. Another book featuring the Teddy Bears is: *Teddy Bears Stay Indoors* (1987). (Rev: BCCB 4/85; BL 4/15/85; SLJ 5/85)

**1665** Grindley, Sally. *Why Is the Sky Blue?* (PS–K). Illus. by Susan Varley. 1997, Simon & Schuster paper $16.00 (0-689-81486-0). The impatient, inquisitive Rabbit bombards poor Donkey with dozens of questions. (Rev: SLJ 6/97)

**1666** Grossman, Bill. *Tommy at the Grocery Store* (K–2). Illus. by Victoria Chess. 1991, HarperCollins paper $5.95 (0-06-443266-1). 32pp. Tommy, the little pig child, is left behind in the grocery store and customers mistake him for a salami among other things. (Rev: BCCB 11/89; BL 9/15/89; HB 9–10/89; SLJ 12/89*)

**1667** Guarino, Deborah. *Is Your Mama a Llama?* (PS–K). Illus. by Steven Kellogg. 1989, Scholastic $14.95 (0-590-41387-2). 32pp. A pleasing study of who belongs to whom, as a koala and her baby clutch each other or an opossum ambles off with babes aboard her back. (Rev: BCCB 11/89; BL 10/1/89; SLJ 10/89)

**1668** Gwynne, Fred. *Pondlarker* (PS–3). Illus. 1990, Simon & Schuster paper $14.00 (0-671-70846-5). 32pp. Remembering the fairy tale about the frog prince, a small frog acts like a member of royalty. (Rev: BCCB 11/90; BL 11/15/90; SLJ 11/90)

**1669** Hadithi, Mwenye. *Crafty Chameleon* (PS–1). Illus. by Adrienne Kennaway. 1987, Little, Brown paper $5.95 (0-316-33771-4). 32pp. This simple story with strong folklore roots tells of the triumph of brains over brawn. (Rev: BL 2/1/88; HB 11–12/87; SLJ 11/87)

**1670** Hadithi, Mwenye. *Hot Hippo* (PS–3). Illus. by Adrienne Kennaway. 1986, Little, Brown LB $14.95 (0-316-33722-6). A folktale-like story of Hot Hippo, who longed to live in the water, and the god of everything, who wanted him to live on land. (Rev: BL 12/1/86; HB 1–2/87; SLJ 2/87)

**1671** Hall, Donald. *I Am the Dog, I Am the Cat* (K–2). Illus. by Barry Moser. 1994, Dial LB $15.89 (0-8037-1505-6). 32pp. Dog and Cat reflect on their different natures, habits, and attitudes. (Rev: BCCB 12/94; BL 9/15/94*; HB 9–10/94; SLJ 9/94)

**1672** Hall, Martin. *Charlie and Tess* (PS–2). Illus. by Catherine Walters. 1996, Little Tiger $14.95 (1-888444-06-1). 28pp. An orphaned lamb that has been raised by a farmer's family later saves his flock on a snowy night. (Rev: BL 4/15/97; SLJ 3/97)

**1673** Harley, Bill. *Sitting Down to Eat* (K–3). Illus. by Kitty Harvill. 1996, August House $15.95 (0-87483-460-0). In this cumulative tale, a boy invites so many animals into his house that it explodes. (Rev: SLJ 1/97)

**1674** Harrison, David L. *When Cows Come Home* (PS–1). Illus. by Chris L. Demarest. 1994, Boyds Mills $15.95 (1-56397-143-7). 32pp. Cows have wonderful times dancing and playing games when the farmer isn't looking. (Rev: BL 5/1/94; SLJ 2/94)

**1675** Harrison, Joanna. *Dear Bear* (PS–2). Illus. 1994, Carolrhoda LB $19.93 (0-87614-839-9). 32pp. Katie is afraid of the bear that lives under the stairs and writes him a letter about her fear. (Rev: BCCB 1/95; BL 1/1/95; SLJ 2/95*)

**1676** Hassett, John, and Ann Hassett. *Charles of the Wild* (PS–K). Illus. 1997, Houghton $14.95 (0-395-78575-8). 32pp. A timid little dog has some tame encounters that he interprets as exciting adventures. (Rev: BL 4/1/97; SLJ 5/97)

**1677** Hayashi, Akiko. *Aki and the Fox* (PS–K). Illus. 1991, Doubleday LB $14.00 (0-385-41947-3). 40pp. In this Japanese picture book, Aki takes her stuffed fox to her grandmother's for repair. (Rev: BL 11/15/91; SLJ 12/91)

**1678** Hayes, Sarah. *The Grumpalump* (PS–K). Illus. by Barbara Firth. 1991, Houghton $15.95 (0-89919-871-6). 24pp. Several animals try to rouse the grumpalump, but only the gnu succeeds. (Rev: BCCB 6/91; BL 5/15/91; SLJ 9/91)

**1679** Hayes, Sarah. *This Is the Bear and the Bad Little Girl* (PS–K). Illus. by Helen Craig. 1995, Candlewick $14.99 (1-56402-648-5). 32pp. When a bad girl tries to steal a bear from a restaurant, a dog comes to his rescue. (Rev: BL 11/15/95; HB 11–12/95; SLJ 12/95)

**1680** Hayes, Sarah. *This Is the Bear and the Scary Night* (PS–K). Illus. by Helen Craig. 1998, Candlewick LB $5.99 (0-7636-0648-0). 28pp. This is a simple story about a gentle, fearless teddy bear and the scary night he spends alone in a park. (Rev: BL 3/1/92; HB 9–10/92; SLJ 4/92*)

**1681** Hayles, Karen, and Charles Fuge. *Whale Is Stuck* (PS–1). Illus. 1993, Simon & Schuster $14.00 (0-671-86587-0). 32pp. When Whale lands on an ice floe, even the other friendly sea creatures can't free him. (Rev: BL 9/1/93; SLJ 10/93)

**1682** Hazen, Barbara S. *The New Dog* (PS–1). Illus. by R. W. Alley. 1997, Dial paper $14.89 (0-8037-1813-6). 32pp. A pampered pup feels out of place and unwanted during his first day with a dog-walking group. (Rev: BL 8/97; SLJ 12/97)

**1683** Heal, Gillian. *Grandpa Bear's Fantastic Scarf* (K–3). Illus. 1997, Beyond Words $14.95 (1-885223-41-2). 30pp. A young bear learns about life's meaning through studying the colors in his grandpa's scarf, a visual record of his life. (Rev: BL 4/1/97; SLJ 7/97)

**1684** Hearn, Diane D. *Bad Luck Boswell* (K–3). Illus. by author. 1995, Simon & Schuster $15.00 (0-689-80303-6). Boswell the cat brings bad luck with him until he discovers he can neutralize a witch's curses. (Rev: SLJ 11/95)

**1685** Heine, Helme. *Friends* (PS–3). Illus. by author. 1982, Macmillan $16.00 (0-689-50256-7); paper $5.99 (0-689-71083-6). 32pp. A rooster, mouse, and pig share an outing on a bicycle.

**1686** Heine, Helme. *Friends Go Adventuring* (PS–2). Illus. 1995, Simon & Schuster paper $16.00 (0-689-80463-6). 32pp. Charlie Rooster, Johnny Mouse, and Fat Percy the pig encounter cutthroat pirates and a cannibal cook in this sequel to *Friends* (1982). (Rev: BCCB 1/96; BL 1/1–15/96; SLJ 2/96*)

**1687** Heine, Helme. *Mollywoop* (PS–1). Trans. by Ralph Manheim. Illus. 1991, Farrar $14.95 (0-374-35001-9). 32pp. A rooster, pig, and mouse share a group of adventures. (Rev: BL 9/15/91; SLJ 12/91)

**1688** Heine, Helme. *The Most Wonderful Egg in the World* (PS–2). Illus. by author. 1983, Macmillan paper $4.95 (0-689-71117-4). 32pp. Three quarrelsome chickens compete to see who will lay the most beautiful egg.

**1689** Heine, Helme. *The Pearl* (PS–3). Illus. 1985, Macmillan paper $3.95 (0-689-71262-6). 32pp. Beaver dreams that his friends envy the prize pearl he has found. (Rev: BL 5/1/85; HB 7–8/85; SLJ 9/85)

**1690** Heine, Helme. *The Pigs' Wedding* (PS–3). Illus. by author. 1986, Macmillan $16.00 (0-689-50409-8); paper $5.99 (0-689-71478-5). 32pp. Curly-tail and Porker say "I do." A reissue of a 1979 edition.

**1691** Heine, Helme. *Seven Wild Pigs: Eleven Picture Book Fantasies* (K–3). Illus. by author. 1988, Macmillan LB $18.95 (0-689-50439-X). 120pp. Poems, stories, and whimsical tales, mostly about unusual animals. (Rev: BCCB 5/88; BL 4/1/88; SLJ 8/88)

**1692** Hendra, Sue. *Oliver's Wood* (PS–1). Illus. 1996, Candlewick $15.99 (1-56402-932-8). 32pp. Oliver the owl has an unusual adventure when he wakes up while the sun is shining. (Rev: BL 7/96; SLJ 9/96)

**1693** Henkes, Kevin. *Chrysanthemum* (PS–1). Illus. 1991, Greenwillow LB $15.93 (0-688-09700-6). 32pp. Other mouse children make fun of Chrysanthemum's name until her music teacher helps out. (Rev: BCCB 10/92; BL 8/91; HB 9–10/91*; SLJ 9/91*)

**1694** Henkes, Kevin. *Julius, the Baby of the World* (PS–3). Illus. 1990, Greenwillow LB $15.93 (0-688-08944-5). 32pp. Lilly, a girl mouse, has a fit of jealousy when her baby brother gets all the attention in the family. (Rev: BCCB 11/90; BL 11/1/90; HB 1–2/91*; SLJ 10/90*)

**1695** Henkes, Kevin. *Owen* (PS). Illus. 1993, Greenwillow LB $15.93 (0-688-11450-4). 24pp. Owen, a mouse, loves his fuzzy yellow blanket more than anything. (Rev: BL 8/93*)

**1696** Henkes, Kevin. *Sheila Rae, the Brave* (PS–1). Illus. by author. 1987, Greenwillow LB $15.93 (0-688-07156-2); Puffin paper $3.95 (0-14-050835-X). 32pp. Sheila Rae, a mouse, fears nothing, until she takes the wrong way home. (Rev: BL 9/1/87; SLJ 9/87)

**1697** Henkes, Kevin. *A Weekend with Wendell* (PS–1). Illus. by author. 1986, Greenwillow LB $15.93 (0-688-06326-8); Morrow paper $4.95 (0-688-14024-6). 32pp. Wendell makes his weekend stay seem like a year to Sophie Mouse, until they have a meeting of the minds. (Rev: BCCB 10/86; BL 9/1/86; SLJ 10/86)

**1698** Herman, Gail. *The Littlest Duckling* (PS). Illus. by Ann Schweninger. 1996, Viking paper $13.99 (0-670-85113-2). 32pp. In this story for very young children, a duckling has trouble keeping up with his bigger brothers and sisters. (Rev: BL 1/1–15/96; SLJ 3/96)

**1699** Hest, Amy. *Baby Duck and the Bad Eyeglasses* (PS–1). Illus. by Jill Barton. 1996, Candlewick $16.99 (1-56402-680-9). 32pp. Baby Duck dislikes her new eyeglasses until Grandpa shows her how to accept them. (Rev: BCCB 10/96; BL 8/96*; HB 9–10/96; SLJ 10/96*)

**1700** Hest, Amy. *In the Rain with Baby Duck* (PS–1). Illus. by Jill Barton. 1995, Candlewick $16.95 (1-56402-532-2). 32pp. Grandpa helps Baby Duck adjust to the rain by supplying a red umbrella and boots. (Rev: BL 10/1/95)

**1701** Hest, Amy. *You're the Boss, Baby Duck!* (PS–K). Illus. by Jill Barton. Series: Baby Duck. 1997, Candlewick $16.99 (1-56402-667-1). 32pp. Baby Duck is unhappy about getting a baby sister, but Grandpa helps her adjust. (Rev: BL 9/1/97; SLJ 10/97)

**1702** Hill, Eric. *Spot at Home* (PS). Illus. by author. Series: Little Spot Board Books. 1991, Putnam $3.95 (0-399-21774-6). 14pp. This board book features the everyday adventures of the lovable dog Spot. (Rev: BL 6/15/91)

**1703** Hill, Eric. *Spot Goes to a Party* (PS–1). Illus. by author. 1992, Putnam $12.95 (0-399-22409-2). In this lift-the-flap book, Spot the dog dresses as a cowboy to go to a costume party. (Rev: SLJ 9/92)

**1704** Hill, Eric. *Spot Goes to the Park* (PS–1). Illus. by author. 1991, Putnam $12.95 (0-399-21833-5). In this book with easily lifted flaps, Spot the dog enjoys a day in the park playing with his friends. (Rev: SLJ 12/91)

**1705** Hill, Eric. *Spot Sleeps Over* (PS–K). Illus. by author. 1991, Putnam $11.95 (0-399-21815-7). A lift-the-flap book about Spot the dog and first-time sleeping over. (Rev: SLJ 3/91)

**1706** Hill, Eric. *Spot's Baby Sister* (PS). Illus. by author. 1989, Putnam $12.95 (0-399-21640-5). In a lift-the-flap format, this is the story of Spot and his little dog sister. (Rev: SLJ 11/89)

**1707** Hiskey, Iris. *Hannah the Hippo's No Mud Day* (3–6). Illus. by Karen L. Schmidt. 1991, Simon & Schuster paper $13.95 (0-671-69194-5). 32pp. Hannah, all dressed up, is warned to stay clean, but then she sees the biggest, muddiest puddle in the world! (Rev: BL 6/1/91; SLJ 10/91)

**1708** Hissey, Jane. *Little Bear Lost* (PS–K). Illus. 1994, Sandvick $9.48 (1-881445-44-5). 32pp. Just when the picnic is about to begin, Little Bear is missing. (Rev: BL 11/1/89)

**1709** Hissey, Jane. *Old Bear* (PS–1). Illus. by author. 1986, Putnam $15.00 (0-399-21401-1); paper $5.90 (0-399-22015-1). 32pp. Little Bear, Duck, and Rabbit decide it's time to rescue Old Bear from the attic — but how? Also use: *Little Bear's Trousers* (1987). (Rev: BCCB 2/87; BL 12/1/86; SLJ 2/87)

**1710** Hoban, Russell. *Dinner at Alberta's* (K–2). Illus. by James Marshall. 1980, HarperCollins $17.02 (0-690-23992-0); Bantam paper $1.25 (0-

440-41864-X). 40pp. Arthur, a really sloppy crocodile, valiantly practices his table manners in preparation for dinner at Alberta's, with whom he is smitten.

**1711** Hobbie, Holly. *Toot and Puddle* (PS–1). Illus. by author. 1997, Little, Brown $12.95 (0-316-36552-1). While one globe-trotting pig sees the world, his friend stays at home, enjoying life's simple pleasures. (Rev: SLJ 12/97)

**1712** Hoberman, Mary Ann. *Mr. and Mrs. Muddle* (K–2). Illus. by author. 1988, Little, Brown $13.95 (0-316-36735-4). 32pp. A horse couple can't decide on their means of transportation. (Rev: BL 12/1/88; HB 1–2/89; SLJ 2/89)

**1713** Hoberman, Mary Ann. *One of Each* (PS–2). Illus. by Marjorie Priceman. 1997, Little, Brown $15.95 (0-316-36731-1). 32pp. Oliver Tolliver, a dog, is happy that he has only one of everything, but his friend Peggoty Small, a cat, pursuades him that 2 is also nice. (Rev: BL 11/1/97*; SLJ 9/97*)

**1714** Hobson, Sally. *Chicken Little* (PS–K). Illus. 1994, Simon & Schuster $14.00 (0-671-89548-6). 32pp. The traditional story of Chicken Little is accompanied by bright, animated drawings. (Rev: BL 10/15/94; SLJ 11/94)

**1715** Hoff, Syd. *Duncan the Dancing Duck* (PS–2). Illus. by author. 1994, Clarion $14.95 (0-395-67400-X). 32pp. Duncan gains international fame as a dancing duck but is happy to return home, where he dances only for his mother. (Rev: SLJ 7/94)

**1716** Hogrogian, Nonny. *The Cat Who Loved to Sing* (PS–2). Illus. by author. 1988, Knopf LB $13.99 (0-394-99004-8). 40pp. A farm woman removes a thorn from a wandering cat's foot and begins to trade, eventually winding up with a mandolin for the cat. (Rev: BCCB 6/88; BL 4/1/88; SLJ 4/88)

**1717** Holabird, Katharine. *Angelina and Alice* (PS–1). Illus. by Helen Craig. 1988, Crown $16.00 (0-517-56074-7). 23pp. Angelina finds her new friendship with Alice becomes bumpy because of problems in gymnastics classes. Also use: *Angelina at the Fair; Angelina on Stage* (both 1988). (Rev: BL 1/1/88)

**1718** Holabird, Katharine. *Angelina and the Princess* (PS–K). Illus. by Helen Craig. 1984, Crown $16.00 (0-517-55273-6). 24pp. Angelina tries to do her best with her small part in the ballet troupe's performance for the Princess of Mouseland; then one of the leads sprains her ankle.

**1719** Holabird, Katharine. *Angelina Ballerina* (PS–2). Illus. by Helen Craig. 1988, Crown $16.00 (0-517-55083-0). 24pp. Angelina Mouseling enrolls in a ballet class.

**1720** Holabird, Katharine. *Angelina's Baby Sister* (PS–2). Illus. by Helen Craig. 1991, Crown $16.00 (0-517-58600-2). 28pp. Balletic mouse Angelina vows to be good to her new baby sister, but finds it's a hard task indeed. (Rev: BL 1/15/92)

**1721** Holder, Heidi. *Carmine the Crow* (PS–3). Illus. 1992, Farrar $16.00 (0-374-31119-6). 32pp. After helping a swan escape a trap, an ancient crow is given a box of magic stardust. (Rev: BCCB 1/93; BL 11/15/92)

**1722** Hoopes, Lyn Littlefield. *My Own Home* (PS–2). Illus. by Ruth Richardson. 1991, HarperCollins $13.95 (0-06-022570-X). A lost little owl is looking for his home. (Rev: SLJ 6/91)

**1723** Horse, Harry. *A Friend for Little Bear* (PS–2). Illus. by author. 1996, Candlewick $14.99 (1-56402-876-3). When he is stranded on an island, Little Bear tries to find happiness by collecting things. (Rev: SLJ 9/96)

**1724** Howe, Deborah, and James Howe. *Teddy Bear's Scrapbook* (2–3). Illus. by David S. Rose. 1994, Aladdin paper $3.95 (0-689-71812-8). 80pp. A teddy bear describes the pictures in his scrapbook to a little girl.

**1725** Howe, James. *The Day the Teacher Went Bananas* (K–3). Illus. by Lillian Hoban. 1984, Dutton paper $3.95 (0-525-44321-5). 32pp. The new teacher turns out to be a gorilla.

**1726** Howe, James. *Hot Fudge* (K–3). Illus. by Leslie Morrill. 1990, Morrow LB $13.88 (0-688-09701-4). 48pp. The dogs Harold and Howie and cat Chester track down the culprit who has stolen their fudge. (Rev: BL 9/15/90; SLJ 12/90)

**1727** Howe, James. *I Wish I Were a Butterfly* (PS–2). Illus. by Ed Young. 1987, Harcourt $17.00 (0-15-200470-X). 28pp. Cricket thinks he's ugly; then a butterfly hears his music and wishes he were a cricket. (Rev: BL 11/1/87; SLJ 11/87)

**1728** Hunter, Anne. *Possum and the Peeper* (K–2). Illus. by author. 1998, Houghton $15.00 (0-395-84631-5). Other animals join Possum in his search to find the origin of the peeping sound he hears. (Rev: SLJ 3/98*)

**1729** Hunter, Anne. *Possum's Harvest Moon* (PS–1). Illus. 1996, Houghton $15.00 (0-395-73575-0). 32pp. Possum is so inspired by the autumn that he throws a party for his animal friends. (Rev: BCCB 10/96; BL 9/1/96*; HB 9–10/96; SLJ 8/96*)

**1730** Hunter, Sara H. *Miss Piggy's Night Out* (K–2). Illus. by Tom Leigh. Series: Easy-to-Read. 1995, Viking paper $11.99 (0-670-86107-3). 32pp. Vain Miss Piggy tries to court the rich and famous while on a date with Kermit. (Rev: BCCB 10/95; SLJ 3/96)

**1731** Hurd, Thacher. *Art Dog* (PS–3). Illus. 1996, HarperCollins LB $14.89 (0-06-024425-9). 32pp. Arthur, a canine museum guard with artistic abilities, solves the mystery of the missing painting, the *Mona Woofa*. (Rev: BCCB 2/96; BL 1/1–15/96; SLJ 2/96)

**1732** Hurd, Thacher. *Little Mouse's Big Valentine* (PS–1). Illus. 1990, HarperCollins $13.95 (0-06-026192-7); paper $4.95 (0-06-443281-5). 32pp. Little Mouse makes a valentine so big that nobody wants it. (Rev: BL 1/1/90)

**1733** Hurd, Thacher. *Mama Don't Allow: Starring Miles and the Swamp Band* (PS–1). Illus. by author. 1984, HarperCollins LB $15.89 (0-06-022690-0); paper $5.95 (0-06-443078-2). 40pp. The Swamp Band finds that the only audience that likes them is the alligator.

**1734** Hurd, Thacher. *Mystery on the Docks* (1–3). Illus. by author. 1983, HarperCollins paper $5.95 (0-06-443058-8). 32pp. Ralph, an opera lover, rescues his favorite singer from rat-kidnappers.

**1735** Hurd, Thacher. *Tomato Soup* (PS–1). Illus. 1994, Random paper $4.99 (0-517-13538-8). 32pp. A cat-and-mouse game is played out by a clever mouse named Baby and his would-be nemesis, George. (Rev: BL 5/1/92; HB 3–4/92; SLJ 6/92)

**1736** Hutchins, Pat. *Good-Night, Owl!* (PS–K). Illus. by author. 1972, Macmillan LB $16.00 (0-02-745900-4). 32pp. Owl is kept awake by different animal noises, as various animals perch on a branch of his tree; but when darkness falls, owl has his turn and wakes everyone with his screeches.

**1737** Hutchins, Pat. *Little Pink Pig* (PS–1). Illus. 1994, Greenwillow $16.00 (0-688-12014-8). 32pp. Little Pig fails to heed his mother's call for bedtime because he is busy chasing a butterfly. (Rev: BL 4/1/94; HB 5–6/94; SLJ 5/94)

**1738** Hutchins, Pat. *Rosie's Walk* (K–2). Illus. by author. 1968, Macmillan LB $16.00 (0-02-745850-4); paper $5.99 (0-02-043750-1). 32pp. Rosie the hen miraculously escapes capture by a fox.

**1739** Hutchins, Pat. *The Surprise Party* (1–3). Illus. 1986, Macmillan LB $14.95 (0-02-745930-6). 32pp. A message about a party is passed from animal to animal, getting more confused each time. (Rev: BL 10/15/86)

**1740** Hutchins, Pat. *What Game Shall We Play?* (PS–K). Illus. 1995, Morrow paper $4.95 (0-688-13573-0). 24pp. Duck and Frog ask several of their animal friends what game they should play. (Rev: BCCB 10/90; BL 10/15/90; HB 11–12/90; SLJ 9/90*)

**1741** Ingman, Bruce. *When Martha's Away* (K–3). Illus. 1995, Houghton $14.95 (0-395-72360-4). 32pp. When humans are away, Lionel the cat has a great time talking on the phone, preparing lunch, and being friendly with Gladys, the neighbor's kitty. (Rev: BL 1/1–15/96; SLJ 12/95)

**1742** Inkpen, Mick. *Kipper's Snowy Day* (PS–K). Illus. by author. 1996, Harcourt $14.00 (0-15-201362-8). Two dogs enjoy a day's activities on a snowy day, including making a giant snow dog. (Rev: SLJ 12/96)

**1743** Irbinskas, Heather. *How Jackrabbit Got His Very Long Ears* (K–3). Illus. by Kenneth J. Spengler. 1994, Northland LB $14.95 (0-87358-566-6). 32pp. When Jackrabbit fails to follow the instructions of the Great Spirit, he is given big ears so that he can hear better. (Rev: BL 6/1–15/94)

**1744** Isenberg, Barbara, and Susan Wolf. *Albert the Running Bear Gets the Jitters* (2–4). Illus. by Diane De Groat. 1987, Houghton $13.95 (0-89919-517-2). 40pp. Albert, the marathon running bear, is challenged back at the zoo by a bully named Boris. (Rev: BCCB 9/87; BL 12/1/87; SLJ 10/87)

**1745** Isherwood, Shirley. *The Band over the Hill* (PS–3). Illus. by Reg Cartwright. 1997, Hutchinson $19.95 (0-09-176753-9). Two bears unearth some old band costumes and decide to join the marching band that they hear in the distance. (Rev: SLJ 1/98)

**1746** Isherwood, Shirley. *Something for James* (K–2). Illus. by Neil Reed. 1996, Dial paper $14.99 (0-8037-1914-0). 32pp. James and his friends, Elephant and Bear, can't determine what kind of animal has been left on James's doorstep. (Rev: BL 6/1–15/96; SLJ 4/96)

**1747** Jackson, Jean. *Thorndike and Nelson: A Monster Story* (K–2). Illus. by Vera Rosenberry. 1997, DK Publg. $15.95 (0-7894-2452-5). 32pp. Dot and Thorndike, appealing but ugly monsters, quarrel and insult each other terribly, but eventually they make up. (Rev: BL 10/1/97; SLJ 9/97)

**1748** Jacobs, Laurie A. *So Much in Common* (PS–3). Illus. by Valeri Gorbachev. 1994, Boyds Mills $14.95 (1-56397-115-1). Though seemingly direct opposites in tastes and interests, Philomena Midge, a hippo, and Horace Abercrombie, a goat, become fast friends. (Rev: SLJ 12/94)

**1749** Jaffrey, Madhur. *Robi Dobi: The Marvelous Adventures of an Indian Elephant* (K–3). Illus. by Amanda Hall. 1997, Dial paper $14.99 (0-8037-2193-5). 76pp. A friendly elephant helps a number of troubled animals, including a mouse painted orange by an evil witch. (Rev: HB 7–8/97; SLJ 9/97)

**1750** James, Simon. *Dear Mr. Blueberry* (PS–K). Illus. 1991, Macmillan $14.00 (0-689-50529-9). 32pp. Emily writes her teacher about a whale she believes she sees in her swimming pool. (Rev: BL 11/15/91; SLJ 10/91)

**1751** Janovitz, Marilyn. *Can I Help?* (PS–K). Illus. 1996, North-South LB $13.88 (1-55858-576-1). 24pp. A young wolf has only partial success helping his father work in their yard. (Rev: BL 5/1/96; SLJ 6/96)

**1752** Jarrell, Randall. *The Gingerbread Rabbit* (PS–2). Illus. by Garth Williams. 1996, HarperCollins $11.95 (0-06-205086-9); Macmillan paper $4.95 (0-06-205903-3). 56pp. A gingerbread rabbit escapes baking but is almost eaten by a fox.

**1753** Jennings, Linda. *The Brave Little Bunny* (PS–1). Illus. by Catherine Walters. 1995, Dutton paper $13.99 (0-525-45364-4). 32pp. Millie leaves her hutch and finds a mate in a wild rabbit named Seventy-six for his family birth order. (Rev: BL 2/15/95; SLJ 3/95)

**1754** Jennings, Linda. *Easy Peasy!* (PS–K). Illus. by Tanya Linch. 1997, Farrar $14.00 (0-374-31949-9). 24pp. Kitty decides on a daring scheme to reach the fish on the top of a kitchen cupboard. (Rev: BL 4/1/97; SLJ 5/97)

**1755** Jennings, Linda. *Scramcat* (PS–2). Illus. by Rhian N. James. 1994, Crocodile $13.95 (1-56656-137-X). A stray cat that is shunned by everyone suddenly becomes popular when it foils a robbery. (Rev: SLJ 11/94)

**1756** Jeram, Anita. *Bill's Belly Button* (PS–1). Illus. 1991, Little, Brown $14.95 (0-316-46114-8). 32pp. Bill, an elephant, becomes alarmed when he discovers he does not have a belly button. (Rev: BL 9/15/91; SLJ 10/91)

**1757** Jeram, Anita. *Daisy Dare* (PS–K). Illus. 1997, Candlewick paper $3.29 (1-56402-986-7). 24pp. Daisy Dare, a little mouse, shows great bravery when she tries to take the bell off a cat's collar. Also use *Contrary Mary* (1995). (Rev: BL 11/15/95; SLJ 1/96)

**1758** Jeschke, Susan. *Perfect the Pig* (K–2). Illus. by author. 1981, Holt $14.95 (0-8050-0704-0); Scholastic paper $5.95 (0-8050-4704-2). 40pp. The adventures of a winged pig named Perfect.

**1759** Johnson, Pamela. *A Mouse's Tale* (K–2). Illus. 1991, Harcourt $11.95 (0-15-256032-7). A small mouse collects bits and pieces of materials and makes a sailing craft. (Rev: SLJ 6/91)

**1760** Johnston, Tony. *The Iguana Brothers: A Tale of Two Lizards* (PS–2). Illus. by Mark Teague. 1995, Scholastic $14.95 (0-590-47468-5). 32pp. Dom and Tom, iguana brothers, have many differences but remain best friends. (Rev: BCCB 7–8/95; BL 1/15/95*; SLJ 4/95)

**1761** Johnston, Tony. *Little Wild Parrot* (PS–K). Illus. by Ora Eitan. 1995, Tambourine LB $14.93 (0-688-13536-6). A child and a pet parrot enjoy a day talking together and sharing small adventures. (Rev: SLJ 12/95)

**1762** Johnston, Tony. *Slither McCreep and His Brother* (PS–3). Illus. by Victoria Chess. 1996, Harcourt paper $5.00 (0-15-201387-3). 32pp. Two snake brothers, Slither and Joe, fight continually because Joe will not share his possessions. (Rev: BL 3/1/92; SLJ 4/92)

**1763** Joly, Fanny. *Mr. Fine, Porcupine* (PS–2). Illus. by Remi Saillard. 1997, Chronicle $12.95 (0-8118-1842-X). 32pp. A porcupine loses his contempt for his own body when he meets a beautiful female porcupine. (Rev: BL 12/1/97; SLJ 2/98)

**1764** Jones, Carol. *Town Mouse Country Mouse* (K–3). Illus. 1995, Houghton $14.95 (0-395-71129-0). 32pp. An imaginative retelling of the fable using modern urban and rural settings. (Rev: BL 4/15/95; HB 3–4/95; SLJ 6/95)

**1765** Jorgensen, Gail. *Crocodile Beat* (PS). Illus. by Patricia Mullins. 1994, Simon & Schuster paper $4.95 (0-689-71881-0). 32pp. An animal tale told in syncopated couplets, followed by a line of rhythmic animal sounds. (Rev: HB 11–12/89; SLJ 10/89)

**1766** Jorgensen, Gail. *Gotcha!* (PS–1). Illus. by Kerry Argent. 1997, Scholastic $15.95 (0-590-96208-6). 32pp. Bertha the bear creates mayhem when she chases a fly that has eyes on her birthday cake. (Rev: BCCB 4/97; BL 2/1/97; SLJ 3/97)

**1767** Joyce, William. *Bently and Egg* (PS–3). Illus. 1992, HarperCollins $15.00 (0-06-020385-4); paper $5.95 (0-06-443352-8). Bently, a frog, is asked to egg-sit for his friend the duck. (Rev: BCCB 3/92; BL 1/1/92; HB 3–4/92; SLJ 4/92*)

**1768** Joyce, William. *The Leaf Men and the Brave Good Bugs* (PS–3). Illus. 1996, HarperCollins LB $15.89 (0-06-027238-4). 40pp. The good bugs in a garden join to help restore an old woman's sickly rosebush. (Rev: BL 10/1/96; SLJ 10/96)

**1769** Jungman, Ann. *When the People Are Away* (K–3). Illus. by Linda Birch. 1993, Boyds Mills $12.95 (1-56397-202-6). 24pp. While their masters are away on vacation, 2 cats enjoy such activities as an all-night Tom and Jerry cartoon fest. (Rev: BL 9/1/93; SLJ 1/94)

**1770** Kaghan, Joan. *The Billy Goat Show* (PS–1). Illus. by author. 1993, Farrar $14.00 (0-374-30711-3). Using a series of 4-line rhymes, different holidays are introduced by animals at a festival hosted by Billy Goat. (Rev: SLJ 12/93)

**1771** Kalan, Robert. *Jump, Frog, Jump!* (PS–2). Illus. by Byron Barton. 1981, Scholastic paper $2.95 (0-590-71723-5). 32pp. A rhyming cumulative tale that ends "jump, frog, jump."

**1772** Kalan, Robert. *Moving Day* (PS–1). Illus. by Yossi Abolafia. 1996, Greenwillow LB $14.93 (0-688-13949-3). 32pp. A hermit crab sets out to find a new home. (Rev: BL 6/1–15/96; SLJ 7/96)

**1773** Kalman, Maira. *Max Makes a Million* (1–5). Illus. 1990, Viking paper $17.00 (0-670-83545-5). 40pp. In this delightfully zany book, a dog poet dreams of selling his poems and moving to Paris. A sequel is: *Max in Hollywood, Baby* (1992). (Rev: BL 10/1/90*; SLJ 12/90)

**1774** Kalman, Maira. *Ooh-La-La (Max in Love)* (PS–4). Illus. 1991, Viking paper $16.99 (0-670-84163-3). 32pp. Max, the dog, falls for Crepes Suzette, a dalmatian, in fascinating Paris. (Rev: BL 10/15/91; SLJ 11/91)

**1775** Kasza, Keiko. *Don't Laugh, Joe!* (PS–1). Illus. 1997, Putnam $15.95 (0-399-23036-X). 32pp. A young opossum has an unusual problem: He can't stop giggling while playing dead. (Rev: BL 8/97; SLJ 6/97)

**1776** Kasza, Keiko. *A Mother for Choco* (PS–1). Illus. 1992, Putnam LB $15.95 (0-399-21841-6). 32pp. A little bird sets out to find his mother and is adopted by a kindly bear. (Rev: BCCB 4/92; BL 3/15/92; HB 5–6/92; SLJ 4/92*)

**1777** Kasza, Keiko. *The Rat and the Tiger* (PS–3). Illus. 1993, Putnam LB $14.95 (0-399-22404-1). 32pp. Rat feels that he is always being taken advantage of by his friend Tiger. (Rev: BCCB 4/93; BL 1/15/93; HB 5–6/93; SLJ 4/93)

**1778** Kasza, Keiko. *The Wolf's Chicken Stew* (PS–K). Illus. by author. 1987, Putnam $15.95 (0-399-21400-3); paper $4.95 (0-698-11374-8). A hungry wolf finds out that he likes cooking for chickens better than eating them. (Rev: BCCB 5/87; BL 6/1/87)

**1779** Katz, Avner. *The Little Pickpocket* (K–2). Illus. by author. 1996, Simon & Schuster $15.00 (0-689-80494-6). A little kangaroo tries a series of different pouches but decides that his mother's is the best. (Rev: SLJ 7/96)

**1780** Katz, Avner. *Tortoise Solves a Problem* (K–3). Illus. 1993, HarperCollins LB $12.89 (0-06-020799-X). 32pp. While searching for a new house, the tortoise invents the tortoise shell. (Rev: BL 1/15/93)

**1781** Keller, Holly. *Brave Horace* (PS–1). Illus. 1998, Greenwillow $15.00 (0-688-15407-7). 32pp. Horace, a young leopard, builds up his courage to attend a monster-movie party. (Rev: BL 3/1/98; SLJ 4/98)

**1782** Keller, Holly. *Geraldine First* (PS–2). Illus. 1996, Greenwillow LB $14.93 (0-688-14150-1). 24pp. Geraldine the pig is annoyed when her young brother keeps copying all her actions. (Rev: BL 7/96; HB 5–6/96; SLJ 5/96)

**1783** Keller, Holly. *Geraldine's Big Snow* (PS–K). Illus. by author. 1988, Greenwillow LB $15.93 (0-688-07514-2). 24pp. Geraldine, a pig child, eagerly awaits the first snow. (Rev: BL 8/88; HB 11–12/88; SLJ 2/89)

**1784** Keller, Holly. *Geraldine's Blanket* (PS–2). Illus. by author. 1988, Morrow paper $4.95 (0-688-07810-9). 32pp. A little pig named Geraldine becomes extremely attached to a blanket her aunt gave her.

**1785** Keller, Holly. *Horace* (PS–1). Illus. 1991, Greenwillow LB $15.93 (0-688-09832-0). 32pp. Horace feels out of place because he is a spotted leopard being raised in a tiger family. (Rev: BL 2/1/91; HB 5–6/91; SLJ 4/91)

**1786** Kellogg, Steven, reteller. *Chicken Little* (1–3). Illus. by Steven Kellogg. 1985, Morrow paper $4.95 (0-688-07045-0). 32pp. A wacky version of the old favorite. (Rev: BCCB 11/85; BL 9/1/85; SLJ 10/85)

**1787** Kellogg, Steven. *The Island of the Skog* (1–3). Illus. by author. 1973, Dial paper $4.95 (0-8037-4122-7). 32pp. A new danger is found by mice who have sailed to a distant island to find safety.

**1788** Kellogg, Steven. *The Mysterious Tadpole* (K–3). Illus. by author. 1977, Dial paper $4.99 (0-8037-6244-5). 32pp. When a tadpole grows at an alarming rate, Louis discovers his new pet is really a baby Loch Ness Monster.

**1789** Kellogg, Steven. *Pinkerton, Behave!* (K–3). Illus. by author. 1979, Puffin paper $4.95 (0-8037-7250-5). 32pp. A mischievous Great Dane puppy foils a burglary attempt. A sequel is: *A Rose for Pinkerton* (1981).

**1790** Kellogg, Steven. *Prehistoric Pinkerton* (PS–3). Illus. by author. 1987, Dial paper $4.95 (0-8037-1053-4). 32pp. Enormous Great Dane puppy Pinkerton is teething and cannot be left alone, so he goes to the museum with his mistress for Dinosaur Day. (Rev: BL 10/1/87; SLJ 11/87)

**1791** Kent, Jack. *The Caterpillar and the Polliwog* (K–2). Illus. by author. 1985, Simon & Schuster paper $14.00 (0-671-66280-5). 32pp. The caterpillar and the polliwog become a butterfly and a frog.

**1792** Kent, Jack. *Joey* (PS–2). Illus. by author. 1987, Simon & Schuster $11.95 (0-671-66459-X). 32pp. Joey, a young kangaroo, is not allowed out of his mother's pouch, so he invites his friends in.

**1793** Kessler, Cristina. *Konte Chameleon Fine, Fine, Fine! A West African Folktale* (PS–2). Illus. by Christian Epanya. 1997, Boyds Mills $14.95 (1-56397-181-X). 32pp. An innocent young chameleon panics when he finds that he can change color. (Rev: BL 10/1/97; SLJ 9/97)

**1794** Kettner, Christine. *An Ordinary Cat* (PS–K). Illus. 1991, HarperCollins LB $13.89 (0-06-023173-4). 32pp. Inwardly, William is not the ordinary cat that everyone sees. (Rev: BL 1/1/91; SLJ 12/91)

**1795** King, Bob. *Sitting on the Farm* (PS–1). Illus. by Bill Slavin. n.d., Scholastic paper $7.99 (0-590-73979-2). 32pp. In successive verses of a silly song, a young girl calls on animals to remove a bug from her knee. (Rev: BL 2/1/92; SLJ 8/92)

**1796** King-Smith, Dick. *The Spotty Pig* (PS–1). Illus. by Mary Wormell. 1997, Farrar $15.00 (0-374-37154-7). 32pp. A young pig thinks his spots are ugly and tries to get rid of them. (Rev: BL 3/1/97; SLJ 5/97)

**1797** Kirby, David, and Allen Woodman. *The Cows Are Going to Paris* (K–3). Illus. by Chris L. Demarest. 1991, St. Martin's $15.95 (1-878093-11-8). 32pp. A group of cows decide to leave their countryside and travel to Paris. (Rev: BL 12/15/91; SLJ 3/92)

**1798** Kirby, Mansfield. *The Secret of Thut-Mouse III, or, Basil Beaudesert's Revenge* (2–4). Illus. by Mance Post. 1985, Farrar $14.00 (0-374-36677-2). 64pp. How some educated mice foil a prowling cat who enters the museum where 2 mice live in splendor. (Rev: BCCB 12/85; BL 11/15/85)

**1799** Kirk, David. *Miss Spider's New Car* (PS–2). Illus. 1997, Scholastic $16.95 (0-590-30713-4). 32pp. Miss Spider and her husband, Holley, go shopping for a car and become the victims of a nefarious car dealer. (Rev: BL 11/1/97; SLJ 1/98)

**1800** Kirk, David. *Miss Spider's Tea Party* (PS–3). Illus. 1994, Scholastic $15.95 (0-590-47724-2). 32pp. No one wants to accept Miss Spider's invitation to tea for fear of being eaten. (Rev: BL 1/15/94; SLJ 6/94)

**1801** Kirk, David. *Miss Spider's Wedding* (K–4). Illus. 1995, Scholastic $15.95 (0-590-56866-3). 40pp. Miss Spider finds she is very wrong when she thinks handsome Spiderus Reeves is "Mr. Right." A sequel to *Miss Spider's Tea Party* (1993). (Rev: BL 10/1/95; SLJ 10/95)

**1802** Kitamura, Satoshi. *Cat Is Sleepy* (PS). Illus. by author. 1996, Farrar $4.95 (0-374-31223-0). In this board book, a cat can't decide where to sleep. Also use *Dog Is Thirsty, Duck Is Dirty*, and *Squirrel Is Hungry* (all 1996). (Rev: SLJ 8/96)

**1803** Kitamura, Satoshi. *Sheep in Wolves' Clothing* (PS–2). Illus. 1996, Farrar $15.00 (0-374-36780-9). 32pp. Three sheep seek their revenge when wolves steal their woolly coats while they are swimming. (Rev: BL 5/1/96; HB 7–8/96; SLJ 8/96*)

**1804** Kleven, Elisa. *The Lion and the Little Red Bird* (PS–2). Illus. 1992, Dutton paper $14.99 (0-525-44898-5). 32pp. A little red bird is amazed when a friendly lion uses his tail as a paintbrush to create a picture just for her. (Rev: BL 5/15/92; SLJ 7/92*)

**1805** Kleven, Elisa. *The Puddle Pail* (PS–2). Illus. 1997, Dutton paper $14.99 (0-525-45803-4). 32pp. Ernst, a little crocodile, wants to have a collecting hobby, but he doesn't know what to collect. (Rev: BL 6/1–15/97; SLJ 6/97*)

**1806** Klinting, Lars. *Bruno the Carpenter* (PS–3). Illus. 1996, Holt $14.95 (0-8050-4501-5). 30pp. By making a wooden toolbox, Bruno, a beaver and carpenter, introduces his tools and their uses. (Rev: BCCB 6/96; BL 4/15/96; HB 11–12/96; SLJ 6/96)

**1807** Klinting, Lars. *Bruno the Tailor* (PS–3). Illus. 1996, Holt $14.95 (0-8050-4500-7). 32pp. Using a step-by-step approach, Bruno the beaver makes an apron in a way that can be copied by children. (Rev: BL 10/15/96; SLJ 12/96)

**1808** Knowles, Sheena. *Edwina the Emu* (PS–1). Illus. by Rod Clement. 1997, HarperTrophy paper $5.95 (0-06-443483-4). At the zoo, Edwina the emu leaves her husband to tend their eggs while she goes out looking for a job. (Rev: SLJ 9/97)

**1809** Knuppel, Helga. *Christabel Crocodile's Birthday Egg* (PS–K). 1992, Interlink $13.95 (1-56656-113-2). 32pp. Christabel Crocodile gets an egg for her birthday that hatches into a penguin. (Rev: BL 1/15/93)

**1810** Koci, Marta. *Sarah's Bear* (PS–1). Illus. by author. 1991, Picture Book paper $14.95 (0-88708-038-3). 28pp. Bear joins Sarah's home on a Greek island, which already includes Cat, Dog, Goat, Goose, Pig, and Crow. (Rev: BL 10/15/87; SLJ 12/87)

**1811** Koehler, Phoebe. *Making Room* (PS–1). Illus. 1993, Macmillan LB $14.95 (0-02-750875-7). 48pp. A large dog makes room in his household for a woman, a baby, and a cat. (Rev: BL 3/15/93; SLJ 8/93)

**1812** Kolar, Bob. *Stomp, Stomp! A Dino Romp* (PS–1). Illus. by author. 1997, North-South LB $15.88 (1-55858-633-4). A misbehaving young dinosaur is silenced by his mother. (Rev: SLJ 10/97)

**1813** Koller, Jackie F. *Fish Fry Tonight* (PS–2). Illus. by Catharine O'Neill. 1994, Random paper $3.99 (0-517-13540-X). 32pp. Although Mama Mouse's fish is large, it cannot feed all the animals that appear for dinner. (Rev: BL 4/15/92; HB 3–4/92; SLJ 8/92)

**1814** Komoda, Beverly. *The Too Hot Day* (PS–K). Illus. 1991, HarperCollins LB $14.89 (0-06-021612-3). 32pp. Mama and her bunny family try to escape the heat through a variety of activities. (Rev: BL 5/15/91; SLJ 8/91)

**1815** Komoda, Beverly. *The Winter Day* (PS–1). Illus. 1991, HarperCollins $13.95 (0-06-023301-X). 32pp. The Hopper children, a group of rabbits, are enjoying the snow until a bully named Spike spoils their fun. (Rev: BL 12/1/91; SLJ 1/92)

**1816** Koontz, Robin M. *Chicago and the Cat: The Family Reunion* (1–3). Illus. by author. Series: Little Chapter Books. 1996, Cobblehill paper $13.99 (0-525-65202-7). When Chicago brings his family to visit, the Cat is not very happy about the arrangements, including having to share his room. (Rev: SLJ 9/96)

**1817** Koscielniak, Bruce. *Geoffrey Groundhog Predicts the Weather* (PS–1). Illus. 1995, Houghton $13.95 (0-395-70933-4). 32pp. When Geoffrey Groundhog emerges from his hole on Groundhog Day, he finds he is part of a media event. (Rev: BCCB 11/95; BL 10/15/95; SLJ 10/95)

**1818** Kovalski, Maryann. *Brenda and Edward* (PS–2). Illus. 1997, Kids Can $14.95 (0-919964-77-X). 32pp. Two dogs who adore each other are separated until, years later, a series of coincidences brings them back together. (Rev: BL 10/15/97; SLJ 9/97)

**1819** Kraus, Robert. *Big Squeak, Little Squeak* (PS–1). Illus. by Kevin O'Malley. 1996, Orchard LB $15.99 (0-531-08774-3). 32pp. Two little mice outwit Mr. Kit Kat, the owner of the local cheese store, who is intent on capturing them. (Rev: BL 10/15/96; SLJ 10/96)

**1820** Kraus, Robert. *Come Out and Play, Little Mouse* (PS–K). Illus. by Jose Aruego and Ariane Dewey. 1987, Greenwillow LB $15.93 (0-688-05838-8). 32pp. Mouse is too busy to heed the voice calling him out to play; then he discovers that voice belongs to a wily cat. Also use: *Where Are You Going, Little Mouse?* (1986). (Rev: BL 3/15/87; HB 7–8/87; SLJ 4/87)

**1821** Kraus, Robert. *Herman the Helper* (PS–K). Illus. by Jose Aruego and Ariane Dewey. 1987, Simon & Schuster paper $6.99 (0-671-66270-8). Herman, a green octopus, helps his many friends with his many arms. A reissued title as are: *Another Mouse to Feed; Milton the Early Riser* (both 1987).

**1822** Kraus, Robert. *Leo the Late Bloomer* (PS–K). Illus. by Jose Aruego. 1971, HarperCollins LB $15.89 (0-87807-043-5). 32pp. Leo, a lion, is just a late bloomer, as Mother tells Father, but Father is worried. But finally Leo blooms — he can read, write, and eat neatly. A beguiling, humorous story.

**1823** Kraus, Robert. *Strudwick: A Sheep in Wolf's Clothing* (K–3). Illus. 1995, Viking paper $14.99 (0-670-85887-0). 32pp. Strudwick, a lamb, decides to fool people by wearing a wolf's suit. (Rev: BL 4/1/95; SLJ 4/95)

**1824** Kraus, Robert. *Whose Mouse Are You?* (PS–1). Illus. by Jose Aruego. 1970, Macmillan paper $4.95 (0-689-71142-5). 32pp. A young mouse is asked 8 questions by his family — which should delight young children who are asked similar questions by their families.

**1825** Kroll, Steven. *It's April Fools' Day!* (PS–2). Illus. by Jeni Bassett. 1990, Holiday LB $15.95 (0-8234-0747-0). 32pp. Alice the cat gets back at Horace the bully on April Fools' Day. (Rev: BL 3/15/90; SLJ 4/90)

**1826** Kroll, Steven. *Loose Tooth* (K–2). Illus. by Tricia Tusa. 1992, Scholastic paper $4.99 (0-590-45713-6). A boy bat loses his first tooth and his twin bat brother is jealous.

**1827** Kroll, Steven. *The Pigrates Clean Up* (K–3). Illus. by Jeni Bassett. 1995, Holt $14.95 (0-8050-2368-2). 32pp. A boatload of pig pirates clean up their ship and themselves for the captain's wedding. (Rev: BL 7/93; SLJ 5/93)

**1828** Kudrna, C. Imbior. *To Bathe a Boa* (PS). Illus. by author. 1986, Carolrhoda LB $14.96 (0-87614-306-0); paper $5.95 (0-87614-490-3). A little boy hunts high and low for his boa, who doesn't want a bath. (Rev: BL 1/1/87; SLJ 2/87)

**1829** Kvasnosky, Laura McGee. *See You Later, Alligator* (PS–K). Illus. 1995, Harcourt $9.00 (0-15-200301-0). 24pp. Popular sayings are used to describe a little alligator's day at school. (Rev: BL 9/15/95; SLJ 11/95)

**1830** Landstrom, Olof, and Lena Landstrom. *Boo and Baa at Sea* (PS). Illus. 1997, Farrar $7.95 (91-29-63921-2). 26pp. In this simple reading book, Boo and Baa get stuck when they take out a rowboat. Also use *Boo and Baa on a Cleaning Spree* (1997). (Rev: BL 7/97; SLJ 7/97)

**1831** Landstrom, Olof, and Lena Landstrom. *Boo and Baa in a Party Mood* (PS). Trans. by Joan Sandin. Illus. 1996, Farrar paper $7.95 (91-29-63918-2). 22pp. In this simple picture book, 2 young sheep, Boo and Baa, prepare for a friend's birthday party. Also use *Boo and Baa in Windy Weather* (1996). (Rev: BL 11/1/96)

**1832** Langreuter, Jutta. *Little Bear Brushes His Teeth* (PS–K). Illus. by Vera Sobat. 1997, Millbrook LB $21.40 (0-7613-0190-9); paper $6.95 (0-7613-0230-1). 32pp. Little Bear pretends he is a soldier fighting bacteria when he brushes his teeth. Also use *Little Bear Goes to Kindergarten* (1997). (Rev: BL 2/1/97; SLJ 7/97)

**1833** Lasky, Kathryn. *Lunch Bunnies* (K–3). Illus. by Marylin Hafner. 1996, Little, Brown $14.95 (0-316-51525-6). 32pp. During school lunchtime, Clyde is afraid that he will drop his tray. (Rev: BL 9/15/96; SLJ 9/96)

**1834** Latimer, Jim. *Going the Moose Way Home* (1–3). Illus. by Donald Carrick. 1988, Macmillan LB $15.00 (0-684-18890-2). 32pp. The adventures of Moose as he encounters others. (Rev: BL 12/1/88; SLJ 11/88)

**1835** Latimer, Jim. *Moose and Friends* (K–2). Illus. by Carolyn Ewing. 1993, Scribners $14.95 (0-684-19335-3). Three stories of friendship featuring kindhearted Moose, along with Fox, Skunk, and Barbary the sheep. (Rev: SLJ 9/93)

**1836** Leaf, Munro. *The Story of Ferdinand* (K–4). Illus. by Robert Lawson. 1936, Puffin paper $5.99 (0-14-050234-3). 72pp. The classic story of the bull who wants only to sit and smell flowers.

**1837** Lebrun, Claude. *Little Brown Bear Does Not Want to Eat* (PS). Illus. by Danièle Bour. Series: Little Brown Bear Books. 1996, Children's LB $12.00 (0-531-07823-2); paper $3.50 (0-531-17823-7). A simple book about a childhood problem and its solution. Also use *Little Brown Bear Is Growing Up* and *Little Brown Bear Wants to Be Read To* (both 1996). (Rev: SLJ 9/96)

**1838** Leedy, Loreen. *The Furry News: How to Make a Newspaper* (1–4). Illus. 1990, Holiday LB $15.95 (0-8234-0793-4). 32pp. Big Bear becomes disgusted with his local newspaper and decides to publish his own. (Rev: BCCB 5/90; BL 5/1/90)

**1839** Leedy, Loreen. *The Great Trash Bash* (K–2). Illus. 1991, Holiday LB $15.95 (0-8234-0869-8). Mayor Hippo discovers that his town has too much trash. (Rev: SLJ 5/91)

**1840** Leedy, Loreen. *The Monster Money Book* (2–4). Illus. 1992, Holiday LB $14.95 (0-8234-0922-8). 32pp. Sarah joins a monster club and learns about various denominations of money. (Rev: BCCB 3/92; BL 3/15/92; SLJ 6/92)

**1841** Leedy, Loreen. *Pingo the Plaid Panda* (PS–K). Illus. by author. 1989, Holiday LB $13.95 (0-8234-0727-6). 32pp. A panda whose fur is plaid feels he is not liked because he is different. (Rev: SLJ 7/89)

**1842** Leemis, Ralph. *Smart Dog* (K–2). Illus. by Chris L. Demarest. 1993, Boyds Mills $14.95 (1-56397-109-7). An old man expects great things from his dog who really wants to loaf. (Rev: SLJ 6/93)

**1843** Lerman, Rory S. *Charlie's Checklist* (PS–2). Illus. by Alison Bartlett. 1997, Orchard $14.95 (0-531-30001-3). 32pp. When Charlie the puppy places a want ad to find a new home in the city, his young country master is forlorn at the thought of him leaving. (Rev: BCCB 6/97; BL 6/1–15/97; SLJ 5/97)

**1844** Lester, Helen. *Listen, Buddy* (PS–3). Illus. by Lynn Munsinger. 1995, Houghton $14.95 (0-395-72361-2). 32pp. Buddy, a daydreaming rabbit, gets into serious trouble because he can't pay attention. (Rev: BL 10/15/95; SLJ 11/95)

**1845** Lester, Helen. *Me First* (PS–3). Illus. by Lynn Munsinger. 1992, Houghton $14.95 (0-395-58706-9). 32pp. Pinkerton the pig is so pushy that he will do anything to be first. (Rev: BL 10/1/92; HB 11–12/92; SLJ 10/92*)

**1846** Lester, Helen. *A Porcupine Named Fluffy* (PS–K). Illus. by Lynn Munsinger. 1986, Houghton $16.00 (0-395-36895-2); paper $6.95 (0-395-52018-5). Fluffy's ridiculous name leads to a friendship with a rhino, with another ridiculous name — Hippo. (Rev: BL 4/15/86; SLJ 8/86)

**1847** Lester, Helen. *Tacky the Penguin* (PS–3). Illus. by Lynn Munsinger. 1988, Houghton $15.00 (0-395-45536-7); paper $5.95 (0-395-56233-3). 32pp. Most penguins wear black, but Tacky prefers Hawaiian shirts and checkered bow ties. (Rev: BCCB 4/88; BL 4/1/88)

**1848** Lester, Helen. *Three Cheers for Tacky* (K–2). Illus. by Lynn Munsinger. 1994, Houghton $14.95 (0-395-66841-7). 32pp. Tacky the Penguin has the spirit but not the skill to function in a cheerleading competition. (Rev: BL 2/15/94; HB 9–10/94; SLJ 5/94)

**1849** Lester, Robin, and Helen Lester. *Wuzzy Takes Off* (PS). Illus. by Miko Imai. 1995, Candlewick $9.99 (1-56402-498-9). 32pp. Wuzzy, a teddy bear, confuses an ordinary playground with being on the moon. (Rev: BL 2/1/96)

**1850** Levine, Abby. *Ollie Knows Everything* (PS–2). Illus. by Lynn Munsinger. 1994, Albert Whitman LB $15.95 (0-8075-6020-0). 32pp. Ollie, a boastful hare, claims he knows everything about New York City but gets lost in the subway. (Rev: BCCB 5/94; BL 5/1/94; SLJ 5/94)

**1851** Lewin, Betsy. *Chubbo's Pool* (PS–2). Illus. 1996, Clarion $14.95 (0-395-72807-X). 32pp. A hippo learns to behave unselfishly toward other animals. (Rev: BCCB 10/96; BL 8/96; SLJ 9/96)

**1852** Lewin, Betsy. *What's the Matter, Habibi?* (PS–1). Illus. 1997, Clarion $15.00 (0-395-85816-X). 32pp. Habibi the camel won't budge when her owner wants her to give rides to some children. (Rev: BL 9/15/97; SLJ 9/97)

**1853** Lewison, Wendy C. *Shy Vi* (PS–K). Illus. by Stephen J. Smith. 1993, Simon & Schuster paper $14.00 (0-671-76968-5). 28pp. A little mouse named Violet is so shy that she can't speak above a whisper. (Rev: BL 5/1/93; SLJ 7/93)

**1854** Lidz, Jane. *Zak: The One-of-a-Kind Dog* (PS–2). Photos by author. 1997, Abrams paper $12.95 (0-8109-3995-9). Zak, a mixed-breed dog, wonders about his ancestors and concludes that whoever they were, he is one of a kind. (Rev: SLJ 3/98)

**1855** Lies, Brian. *Hamlet and the Enormous Chinese Dragon Kite* (K–3). Illus. 1994, Houghton $14.95 (0-395-68391-2). 26pp. Hamlet the pig is carried aloft during his first outing with a new Chinese dragon kite. (Rev: BCCB 10/94; BL 10/15/94; SLJ 8/94)

**1856** Lillegard, Dee. *Sitting in My Box* (PS–K). Illus. by Jon Agee. 1989, Dutton paper $12.95 (0-525-44528-5). 32pp. Wild animals ask to be let into a boy's cardboard box. (Rev: BL 11/15/89; SLJ 11/89)

**1857** Lillegard, Dee. *Tortoise Brings the Mail* (PS–1). Illus. by Jillian Lund. 1997, Dutton paper $14.99 (0-525-45156-0). 32pp. Although Tortoise is a slow mail deliverer, not one of the other animals can do it as well. (Rev: BL 5/15/97; SLJ 5/97)

**1858** Lindbergh, Reeve. *The Day the Goose Got Loose* (PS–1). Illus. by Steven Kellogg. 1990, Dial LB $12.89 (0-8037-0409-7). 32pp. A goose unlocks her pen and spends a day roaming the farm and causing problems. (Rev: BL 9/15/90*; HB 11–12/90; SLJ 9/90)

**1859** Lindgren, Astrid. *The Day Adam Got Mad* (PS–3). Trans. by Barbara Lucas. Illus. by Marit Tornqvist. 1993, R&S $13.00 (91-29-62064-3). 26pp. When Adam the bull who is usually placid gets angry, no one knows how to calm him. (Rev: BCCB 7–8/93; BL 4/1/93; SLJ 7/93)

**1860** Lionni, Leo. *Alexander and the Wind-Up Mouse* (K–2). Illus. by author. 1969, Knopf LB $18.99 (0-394-90914-3); Pantheon paper $5.99 (0-394-82911-5). 32pp. Alexander, a real mouse, envies Willy, a toy, windup mouse, who is loved and cuddled.

**1861** Lionni, Leo. *The Biggest House in the World* (PS–2). Illus. by author. 1968, Knopf paper $5.99 (0-394-82740-6). 32pp. A young snail, desiring a larger shell, receives fatherly advice and decides that small accommodations are an asset in regaining his mobility.

**1862** Lionni, Leo. *A Busy Year* (PS–1). Illus. 1992, Knopf LB $10.99 (0-679-92464-7). 28pp. Two mice develop a friendship with a talking tree and visit it every month. (Rev: BL 9/1/92; SLJ 6/92)

**1863** Lionni, Leo. *An Extraordinary Egg* (PS–2). Illus. 1994, Knopf $16.00 (0-679-85840-7). 32pp. After a frog helps hatch an egg, she thinks that a chicken emerges; but it is really an alligator. (Rev: BCCB 6/94; BL 6/1–15/94; HB 7–8/94; SLJ 6/94*)

**1864** Lionni, Leo. *Fish Is Fish* (K–2). Illus. by author. 1970, Pantheon LB $18.99 (0-394-90440-0); Knopf paper $5.99 (0-394-82799-6). 32pp. A fable about a fish who learns from a frog how to be happy just being himself.

**1865** Lionni, Leo. *Frederick* (PS–2). Illus. by author. 1967, Knopf LB $18.99 (0-394-91040-0); paper $5.99 (0-394-82614-0). 40pp. A field mouse appears to be ignoring the coming of winter, but actually he is not.

**1866** Lionni, Leo. *Frederick's Fables* (PS–2). Illus. by author. 1985, Pantheon $20.00 (0-394-87710-1). 144pp. Thirteen original Lionni tales such as "Swimmy" and "Alexander and the Wind-Up Mouse." (Rev: BL 2/1/86)

**1867** Lionni, Leo. *Inch by Inch* (PS–2). Illus. by author. 1962, Astor-Honor $15.95 (0-8392-3010-9).

When the birds demand that he measure the length of a nightingale's song, this clever, captive inchworm inches his way to freedom.

**1868** Lionni, Leo. *It's Mine!* (PS–1). Illus. by author. 1986, Knopf LB $15.99 (0-394-97000-4). 32pp. Three griping frogs realize that sharing is better than fighting when a storm almost causes their island to sink. (Rev: BCCB 4/86; BL 5/1/86; SLJ 3/86)

**1869** Lionni, Leo. *Matthew's Dream* (K–3). Illus. 1995, Random paper $5.99 (0-679-87318-X). With his imagination, Matthew, a little mouse, can turn his dismal home into something stunning. (Rev: BCCB 3/91; BL 1/1/91; SLJ 4/91*)

**1870** Lionni, Leo. *Mr. McMouse* (PS–1). Illus. 1992, Knopf $15.00 (0-679-83890-2). 32pp. Timothy, a city mouse, tries to find his true identity with some field mice. (Rev: BL 10/1/92; SLJ 10/92)

**1871** Lionni, Leo. *Six Crows: A Fable* (PS–3). Illus. by author. 1988, Knopf LB $16.99 (0-394-99572-4). 32pp. Life in the mountain valley is disturbed only by the noisy crows, which a farmer tries to frighten away. (Rev: BL 6/1/88; SLJ 7/88)

**1872** Lionni, Leo. *Swimmy* (PS–1). Illus. by author. 1963, Pantheon LB $18.99 (0-394-91713-8); Knopf paper $5.99 (0-394-82620-5). 40pp. A remarkable little fish instructs the rest of his school in the art of protection — swim in the formation of a gigantic fish! Beautiful, full-color illustrations.

**1873** Lionni, Leo. *Tillie and the Wall* (PS–3). Illus. by author. 1989, Knopf LB $13.99 (0-394-92155-0); paper $5.99 (0-679-81357-8). 32pp. Tillie, of all the mice, wonders what's on the other side of the wall. (Rev: BL 3/15/89; HB 7–8/89; SLJ 4/89)

**1874** Little, Jean. *Gruntle Piggle Takes Off* (PS–3). Illus. by Johnny Wales. 1997, Viking paper $13.99 (0-670-86340-8). 32pp. A little pig who is used to being in the city finds life on her grandfather's farm not to her liking. (Rev: BCCB 5/97; BL 4/15/97; SLJ 6/97)

**1875** Lobel, Arnold. *Fables* (2–4). Illus. by author. 1980, HarperCollins LB $14.89 (0-06-023974-3); paper $5.95 (0-06-443046-4). 48pp. An Americanized Aesop with excellent illustrations. Caldecott Medal winner, 1981.

**1876** Lodge, Bernard. *Tanglebird* (PS–1). Illus. 1997, Houghton $14.95 (0-395-84543-2). 32pp. Tanglebird searches for material so that he can make a nest as tidy as those of other birds. (Rev: BL 3/1/97; SLJ 4/97)

**1877** London, Jonathan. *Froggy Gets Dressed* (PS–1). Illus. by Frank Remkiewicz. 1992, Viking paper $13.99 (0-670-84249-4). Froggy gets so thrilled dressing and undressing to play in the snow that he decides to sleep for the winter. (Rev: SLJ 9/92)

**1878** London, Jonathan. *Froggy Goes to School* (PS–K). Illus. by Frank Remkiewicz. 1996, Viking paper $13.99 (0-670-86726-8). 32pp. Froggy is embarrassed to find himself at school in his underwear. (Rev: BL 6/1–15/96; SLJ 8/96)

**1879** London, Jonathan. *Froggy Learns to Swim* (PS–1). Illus. by Frank Remkiewicz. 1995, Viking paper $13.99 (0-670-85551-0). After his mother teaches him to swim and he learns how to use flippers and a snorkel, Froggy doesn't want to leave the water. (Rev: SLJ 1/96)

**1880** London, Jonathan. *Froggy's First Kiss* (PS–2). Illus. by Frank Remkiewicz. 1998, Viking $14.99 (0-670-87064-1). When Frogilina responds to Froggy's advances with a big kiss, the young swain retreats in panic. (Rev: SLJ 3/98)

**1881** London, Jonathan. *Hip Cat* (K–4). Illus. by Woodleigh Hubbard. 1993, Chronicle $14.95 (0-8118-0315-5). A saxophone-playing cat hits the big time when he goes to the city to seek his fortune. (Rev: SLJ 1/94*)

**1882** London, Jonathan. *Let's Go, Froggy!* (PS–2). Illus. by Frank Remkiewicz. 1994, Viking paper $14.99 (0-670-85055-1). Preparations for a picnic so exhaust Froggy and his father that they are too tired to travel and decide to have their picnic on the patio. (Rev: SLJ 5/94)

**1883** London, Jonathan. *Liplap's Wish* (PS–3). Illus. by Sylvia Long. 1994, Chronicle $13.95 (0-8118-0505-0). 32pp. Liplap, a bunny, finds comfort in the belief that his dead grandmother has become a star in the sky. (Rev: BL 1/15/95; SLJ 11/94)

**1884** London, Jonathan. *What Newt Could Do for Turtle* (PS–1). Illus. by Louise Voce. 1996, Candlewick $16.99 (1-56402-259-5). 40pp. Newt and Turtle, 2 swamp creatures, become friends. (Rev: BCCB 2/97; BL 12/15/96; SLJ 12/96)

**1885** Loomis, Christine. *Cowboy Bunnies* (PS–2). Illus. by Ora Eitan. 1997, Putnam $15.95 (0-399-22625-7). 32pp. In this easy-to-read book, rabbits engage in all sorts of cowboy activities. (Rev: BL 2/15/98; HB 11–12/97; SLJ 9/97*)

**1886** Lorenz, Lee. *A Weekend in the City* (PS–2). Illus. 1991, Pippin $15.95 (0-945912-15-3). 32pp. Pig and Duck search for some common ground with friend Moose when they propose a visit to the city for his birthday. (Rev: BCCB 11/91; BL 1/1/92; SLJ 12/91)

**1887** Low, Joseph. *Mice Twice* (K–3). Illus. by author. 1986, Macmillan paper $5.99 (0-689-71060-7). 32pp. Cat invites Mouse to dinner but Mouse brings along Dog. Reissue of 1980 publication.

**1888** Lowell, Susan. *The Three Little Javelings* (PS–3). Illus. by Jim Harris. 1992, Northland LB $15.95 (0-87358-542-9). 32pp. This Americanized version of the "Three Little Pigs" features a coyote instead of the wolf. (Rev: BL 1/1/93)

**1889** Lyon, David. *The Runaway Duck* (K–3). Illus. by author. 1985, Lothrop paper $4.95 (0-688-07334-4). 32pp. Egbert, a wooden duck, is tied to a car bumper, but when the string breaks his adventure really begins. (Rev: BCCB 5/85; BL 6/15/85; SLJ 5/85)

**1890** Macaulay, David. *Why the Chicken Crossed the Road* (K–3). Illus. by author. 1987, Houghton $16.00 (0-395-44241-9); paper $6.95 (0-395-58411-6). 32pp. Readers will enjoy the humor of this chain reaction set off when one chicken crosses the road. (Rev: BCCB 11/87; BL 10/15/87; SLJ 12/87)

**1891** McBratney, Sam. *The Caterpillow Fight* (PS–2). Illus. by Jill Barton. 1996, Candlewick $9.99 (1-56402-804-6). 24pp. Playful caterpillars engage in some unusual antics. (Rev: BL 5/15/96; SLJ 7/96)

**1892** McBratney, Sam. *The Dark at the Top of the Stairs* (PS–1). Illus. by Ivan Bates. 1996, Candlewick $15.99 (1-56402-640-X). 32pp. Young mice discover that the monster at the top of the stairs is actually a cat. (Rev: BL 2/15/96*; SLJ 3/96)

**1893** McBratney, Sam. *Just One!* (PS–1). Illus. by Ivan Bates. 1997, Candlewick paper $3.99 (0-7636-0223-X). 24pp. In this cumulative tale, a young squirrel is so generous that he gives away the lovely stack of berries that he and his friend have gathered. (Rev: BL 10/15/97)

**1894** McCaughrean, Geraldine. *Unicorns! Unicorns!* (K–2). Illus. by Sophie Windham. 1997, Holiday LB $15.95 (0-8234-1319-5). 32pp. Because they are busy helping other animals, 2 unicorns fail to get on Noah's ark. (Rev: BL 11/15/97; SLJ 10/97)

**1895** McCully, Emily Arnold. *First Snow* (PS–K). Illus. by author. 1985, HarperCollins $12.95 (0-06-024128-4). 32pp. The littlest girl mouse is afraid to join her siblings sledding on a steep hill in her first snow. (Rev: BL 9/15/85; HB 9–10/85; SLJ 10/85)

**1896** McCully, Emily Arnold. *My Real Family* (PS–2). Illus. 1994, Harcourt $14.00 (0-15-277698-2). 32pp. When Sarah, the youngest in a troupe of performing bears, feels that Blanche, a sheep, is getting too much attention, she decides to run away. (Rev: BL 4/1/94; HB 7–8/94; SLJ 6/94*)

**1897** McCully, Emily Arnold. *Speak Up, Blanche!* (K–3). Illus. 1991, HarperCollins LB $14.89 (0-06-024228-0). 32pp. The sheep Eva drops granddaughter Blanche off to apprentice at the theatrical bears theater. (Rev: BL 9/1/91*; SLJ 9/91)

**1898** MacDonald, Amy. *Little Beaver and the Echo* (PS–1). Illus. by Sarah Fox-Davies. 1990, Putnam $15.95 (0-399-22203-0). 32pp. A lonely little beaver mistakenly believes that his echo is a far-off friend. (Rev: BL 1/1/91; SLJ 3/91)

**1899** MacDonald, Amy. *The Spider Who Created the World* (PS–3). Illus. by G. Brian Karas. 1996, Orchard LB $16.99 (0-531-08855-3). 32pp. To find a place to lay her egg, Nobb the spider creates the earth with fire and water in this original creation story. (Rev: BCCB 5/96; BL 4/15/96; HB 9–10/96; SLJ 3/96)

**1900** MacDonald, Elizabeth. *The Wolf Is Coming!* (PS–K). Illus. by Ken Brown. 1998, Dutton $15.99 (0-525-45952-9). 32pp. A cumulative story about barnyard animals that look for shelter when they hear that the wolf is coming. (Rev: BL 2/1/98; SLJ 3/98)

**1901** MacDonald, Maryann. *Rosie and the Poor Rabbits* (K–2). Illus. by Melissa Sweet. 1994, Atheneum $13.95 (0-689-31832-4). 32pp. When Rosie, a rabbit, is asked to contribute gifts to needy rabbits, she finds it difficult to give up things she loves. (Rev: BCCB 3/94; BL 4/1/94; SLJ 6/94)

**1902** MacDonald, Maryann. *Rosie's Baby Tooth* (PS–2). Illus. by Melissa Sweet. 1991, Macmillan LB $12.95 (0-689-31626-7). 32pp. Rosie Rabbit resents losing one of her baby teeth and tells the Tooth Fairy how she feels. (Rev: BL 10/15/91; HB 9–10/91; SLJ 10/91)

**1903** McDonald, Megan. *Is This a House for Hermit Crab?* (PS–1). Illus. by S. D. Schindler. 1990, Watts LB $16.99 (0-531-08455-8). 32pp. When he outgrows his old shell, a hermit crab has difficulty finding a new home. (Rev: BL 3/1/90*; SLJ 4/90*)

**1904** McDonnell, Flora. *I Love Animals* (PS). Illus. 1994, Candlewick $14.95 (1-56402-387-7). 32pp. In double-page spreads, a host of farm animals gather to greet individually a young girl who visits them. (Rev: BL 10/15/94; SLJ 10/94)

**1905** McGuire, Leslie. *Brush Your Teeth, Please* (PS–K). Illus. by Jean Pidgeon. Series: Joshua Morris Books. 1993, Reader's Digest $10.99 (0-89577-474-7). A pop-up book with movable "toothbrushes" in an animal story designed to get kids to brush their teeth. (Rev: SLJ 9/93)

**1906** McGuire-Turcotte, Casey A. *How Honu the Turtle Got His Shell* (K–3). Illus. by Dick Sakahara. 1991, Raintree Steck-Vaughn LB $22.83 (0-8172-2783-0). 31pp. This story, written by a child, tells how the turtle got its shell. (Rev: SLJ 6/91)

**1907** McKee, David. *Elmer Again* (PS–2). Illus. 1992, Lothrop $15.00 (0-688-11596-9). 32pp. Elmer, a multicolored elephant, longs for the day he will turn plain gray. (Rev: BL 11/15/92; SLJ 1/93)

**1908** McKee, David. *Elmer and Wilbur* (PS). Illus. 1996, Lothrop $15.00 (0-688-14934-0). 32pp. Elmer, a patchwork elephant, sets out to find his cousin Wilbur. (Rev: BL 11/1/96; SLJ 11/96)

**1909** McKee, David. *Elmer in the Snow* (PS–1). Illus. by author. 1995, Lothrop $13.00 (0-688-14596-5). In this picture book, a patchwork elephant takes some other elephants to snow-covered mountains so they will appreciate the meaning of cold. (Rev: SLJ 12/95)

**1910** McKee, David. *I Can Too!* (PS). Illus. by author. 1997, Lothrop $15.95 (0-688-15547-2). In this pop-up book, an elephant takes a walk in the jungle and confronts different animals with different talents. (Rev: SLJ 1/98)

**1911** McKee, David. *Zebra's Hiccups* (PS–3). Illus. 1993, Simon & Schuster paper $14.00 (0-671-79440-X). Zebra begins to hiccup so violently that he begins to lose his stripes. (Rev: SLJ 6/93)

**1912** McKissack, Patricia. *Flossie and the Fox* (1–3). Illus. by Rachel Isadora. 1986, Dial LB $13.89 (0-8037-0251-5). 32pp. Flossie, a little black girl, outwits the fox who is trying to steal eggs by pretending she doesn't know he's a fox. (Rev: BCCB 9/86; BL 9/1/86; SLJ 10/86)

**1913** McKissack, Patricia. *A Million Fish . . . More or Less* (PS–3). Illus. 1992, Knopf LB $16.99 (0-679-90692-4). 36pp. A young boy, who learns to swap tall tales about his bayou home, has a real-life adventure when he captures 3 fish — and a million more. (Rev: BCCB 6/92; BL 1/1/92; SLJ 3/92)

**1914** McKissack, Patricia. *Nettie Jo's Friends* (PS–2). Illus. by Scott Cook. 1989, Knopf LB $15.99 (0-394-99158-3). 40pp. Nettie Jo wants a new dress for her favorite doll so that they can attend her cousin's wedding. (Rev: BCCB 2/89; BL 3/15/89; SLJ 5/89)

**1915** McLeod, Emilie W. *The Bear's Bicycle* (PS–2). Illus. by David McPhail. 1986, Little, Brown paper $5.95 (0-316-56206-8). 32pp. A small boy and his teddy bear have an exciting bicycle ride as he gives the bear safety lessons. When the bear, grown to grizzly bear proportions, does not follow the safety rules, the bear suffers the consequences.

**1916** McNaughton, Colin. *Boo!* (K–2). Illus. by author. 1996, Harcourt $14.00 (0-15-200834-9). A young pig enjoys frightening others until his father catches him. (Rev: SLJ 9/96)

**1917** McNaughton, Colin. *Oops!* (PS–1). Illus. 1997, Harcourt $14.00 (0-15-201588-4). 32pp. Preston Pig, dressed as Little Red Riding Hood, leads Mr. Wolf on a merry chase. (Rev: BL 10/1/97; SLJ 9/97)

**1918** McNaughton, Colin. *Suddenly!* (PS–2). Illus. 1995, Harcourt $14.00 (0-15-200308-8). 32pp. Preston the pig is unaware that he is being stalked by a big wolf. (Rev: BCCB 7–8/95; BL 5/15/95; SLJ 6/95*)

**1919** McNulty, Faith. *The Elephant Who Couldn't Forget* (1–3). Illus. by Marc Simont. 1980, HarperCollins $11.95 (0-06-024145-4). 64pp. A moral lesson about an elephant who was unable to forgive and forget.

**1920**  McPhail, David. *The Bear's Toothache* (PS–K). Illus. by author. 1972, Little, Brown $14.95 (0-316-56312-9); paper $5.95 (0-316-56325-0). 32pp. A very funny story of a little boy's attempt to help extract a bear's tooth and rid him of his toothache.

**1921**  McPhail, David. *Emma's Vacation* (PS–1). Illus. by author. 1987, Puffin paper $3.95 (0-525-44737-7). 24pp. Emma the little bear tells her parents how to spend a leisurely vacation. Also use: *Emma's Pet* (1985). (Rev: BCCB 5/87; BL 5/15/87; SLJ 5/87)

**1922**  McPhail, David. *First Flight* (PS–1). Illus. by author. 1991, Little, Brown paper $4.95 (0-316-56332-3). A young boy and his teddy bear go for an airplane ride, where the bear acts up. (Rev: BCCB 7–8/87; BL 6/1/87; SLJ 4/87)

**1923**  McPhail, David. *Fix-It* (PS–K). Illus. by author. 1984, Dutton paper $3.95 (0-525-44323-1). 24pp. Emma Bear is distraught when the television set won't work.

**1924**  McPhail, David. *The Glerp* (PS–3). Illus. 1994, Silver Burdett LB $15.95 (0-382-24668-3); paper $5.95 (0-382-24670-6). 32pp. The glerp, a snail-like animal that eats everything, meets its match when it tries to swallow an elephant. (Rev: BL 2/1/95; SLJ 4/95)

**1925**  McPhail, David. *Lost!* (PS–K). Illus. 1990, Little, Brown $14.95 (0-316-56329-3). 32pp. A young boy tries to help a bear get home from the big city. (Rev: BL 4/1/90; HB 5–6/90; SLJ 6/90)

**1926**  McPhail, David. *Pig Pig Gets a Job* (PS–1). Illus. 1990, Dutton paper $14.99 (0-525-44619-2). 32pp. Pig Pig thinks of exotic ways to make some money. (Rev: BL 11/15/90; HB 11–12/90)

**1927**  McPhail, David. *Pig Pig Grows Up* (PS–K). Illus. by author. 1980, Dutton paper $3.95 (0-525-44195-6). 32pp. Pig Pig refuses to stop being treated as a child. Two sequels are: *Pig Pig Rides* (1982); *Pig Pig Goes to Camp* (1983).

**1928**  McPhail, David. *Pigs Ahoy!* (PS–3). Illus. 1995, Dutton paper $14.99 (0-525-45334-2). 32pp. A very funny picture book about pigs on an ocean cruise. (Rev: BL 10/1/95*; SLJ 12/95)

**1929**  McPhail, David. *Pigs Aplenty, Pigs Galore!* (PS–3). Illus. 1993, Dutton paper $14.99 (0-525-45079-3). 32pp. An unsuspecting man is suddenly surrounded by hordes of pigs in various costumes engaged in a variety of activities. (Rev: BL 4/1/93*; SLJ 7/93*)

**1930**  McPhail, David. *Those Can-Do Pigs* (K–3). Illus. 1996, Dutton paper $14.99 (0-525-45495-0). 32pp. A group of energetic, overachieving pigs perform everyday tasks. (Rev: BL 6/1–15/96; SLJ 9/96)

**1931**  McQuade, Jacqueline. *Good Times with Teddy Bear* (PS). Illus. 1997, Dial paper $12.99 (0-8037-2076-9). 32pp. Teddy Bear spends a wonderful autumn day playing outdoors, baking cookies with his mother, and, finally, drifting off to sleep. (Rev: BL 10/15/97; SLJ 12/97)

**1932**  Maguire, Gregory. *Seven Spiders Spinning* (4–6). Illus. by Dirk Zimmer. 1994, Clarion $15.00 (0-395-68965-1). 144pp. In this farce, 7 tarantulas invade a classroom and go on their separate quests. (Rev: BCCB 10/94; BL 9/15/94; SLJ 10/94)

**1933**  Mahy, Margaret. *17 Kings and 42 Elephants* (K–3). Illus. by Patricia MacCarthy. 1987, Dial paper $4.95 (0-8037-0781-9). 32pp. Kings and elephants are off on a journey in jungle rhythm. (Rev: BL 9/15/87; HB 9–10/87; SLJ 11/87)

**1934**  Mahy, Margaret. *The Three-Legged Cat* (K–2). Illus. by Jonathan Allen. 1993, Viking paper $14.99 (0-670-85015-2). 32pp. A cat named Tom acts as a substitute hat for a traveling man named Danny in order to get his wish to see the world. (Rev: BL 5/1/93; HB 7–8/93*)

**1935**  Maitland, Barbara. *The Bear Who Didn't Like Honey* (PS–K). Illus. by Odilon Moraes. 1997, Orchard $14.95 (0-531-09546-0). 32pp. Little Bear hides his fears with a series of excuses but later demonstrates that he has unexpected courage. (Rev: BCCB 5/97; BL 2/15/97; SLJ 5/97)

**1936**  Mammano, Julie. *Rhinos Who Snowboard* (K–3). Illus. by author. 1997, Chronicle $11.95 (0-8118-1715-6). Snowboarding rhinos introduce the slang connected with the sport. (Rev: SLJ 3/98)

**1937**  Mammano, Julie. *Rhinos Who Surf* (PS–2). Illus. by author. 1996, Chronicle $11.95 (0-8118-1000-3). A group of rhinos go surfing in this action-packed, humorous picture book. (Rev: SLJ 7/96*)

**1938**  Marshall, James. *George and Martha* (PS–1). Illus. by author. 1972, Houghton $16.00 (0-395-16619-5); paper $6.95 (0-395-19972-7). 48pp. The friendship of 2 hippos leads to some very humorous situations. Also use the sequels: *George and Martha Encore* (1973); *George and Martha Rise and Shine* (1977); *George and Martha One Fine Day* (1982); *George and Martha Back in Town* (1984); *George and Martha Tons of Fun* (1986).

**1939**  Marshall, James. *George and Martha Round and Round* (K–2). Illus. by author. 1988, Houghton $13.95 (0-395-46763-2); paper $6.95 (0-395-58410-8). 48pp. Five stories about hippos George and Martha. (Rev: BCCB 9/88; BL 9/15/88; SLJ 9/88)

**1940**  Marshall, James. *Rats on the Roof: And Other Stories* (K–4). Illus. 1991, Dial paper $13.00 (0-8037-0834-3). 80pp. Funny stories in which animals triumph over enemies or succumb to their own vanities. (Rev: BCCB 6/91; BL 6/1/91; HB 7–8/91*; SLJ 7/91*)

**1941**  Marshall, James. *Wings: A Tale of Two Chickens* (PS–1). Illus. by author. 1988, Puffin paper $4.99 (0-14-050579-2). 32pp. Two plump chicken friends get into trouble when the somewhat dense one goes for a hot-air balloon ride with a suave fox. (Rev: BCCB 6/86; BL 3/15/86; SLJ 4/86)

**1942**  Marshall, James. *Yummers!* (PS–K). Illus. by author. 1973, Houghton $14.95 (0-395-14757-3); paper $5.95 (0-395-39590-9). 32pp. Emily Pig is worried about her weight, so she goes for a walk for exercise. Unfortunately, the walk is interrupted for several snacks, and the resulting stomachache, Emily Pig suggests, is due to the exercise, not the food!

**1943**  Marshall, James. *Yummers Too: The Second Course* (PS–1). Illus. by author. 1990, Houghton paper $5.95 (0-395-53967-6). 32pp. Emily Pig has trouble earning back the money when she eats the profits at Eugene's Popsicle business. (Rev: BL 10/1/86; SLJ 11/86)

**1944**  Martin, Bill, Jr. *The Happy Hippopotami* (PS–K). Illus. by Betsy Everitt. 1991, Harcourt $14.00 (0-15-233380-0). 32pp. A herd of happy hippos descends on a beach and has a grand time. (Rev: BL 5/15/91; SLJ 7/91)

**1945**  Martin, Bill, Jr., and John Archambault. *Barn Dance!* (PS–2). Illus. by Ted Rand. 1986, Holt $14.95 (0-8050-0089-5); paper $4.95 (0-8050-0799-7). 32pp. The animals are holding a lively barn dance on a full-moon night. (Rev: BL 1/15/87; SLJ 2/87)

**1946**  Martin, Linda. *When Dinosaurs Go Visiting* (PS–2). Illus. by author. 1993, Chronicle $11.95 (0-8118-0122-5). Rhyming couplets are used to describe dinosaurs as they engage in such everyday activities as dancing, playing chess, and gossiping. (Rev: SLJ 3/94)

**1947**  Mathers, Petra. *Sophie and Lou* (K–3). Illus. 1991, HarperCollins LB $14.89 (0-06-024072-5). 32pp. After learning on her own how to dance, mouse Sophie is invited to a dance by Lou. (Rev: BL 4/15/91; HB 5–6/91*; SLJ 6/91)

**1948**  Maxwell, William. *Mrs. Donald's Dog Bun and His Home Away from Home* (1–4). Illus. by James Stevenson. 1995, Knopf $16.00 (0-679-86053-3). 32pp. A dog named Bun decides that home is the best after he makes a try at independence. (Rev: BL 9/1/95; SLJ 10/95)

**1949**  Mayer, Marianna. *The Unicorn and the Lake* (K–4). Illus. by Michael Hague. 1990, Dial $17.99 (0-8037-0844-0); paper $4.95 (0-8037-0436-4). 32pp. A helpful unicorn purifies a lake so animals may use it.

**1950**  Mayne, William. *Lady Muck* (K–3). Illus. by Jonathan Heale. 1997, Houghton $15.95 (0-395-

75281-7). 32pp. Two pigs, Boark and Sowk, go to market to sell precious truffles that Boark has unearthed. (Rev: BCCB 4/97; BL 3/1/97*; SLJ 5/97*)

**1951**  Meddaugh, Susan. *Hog-Eye* (K–2). Illus. 1995, Houghton $14.95 (0-395-74276-5). 32pp. A female pig outwits a fox who has problems reading his recipe for pig soup. (Rev: BCCB 10/95; BL 9/1/95; SLJ 10/95*)

**1952**  Meddaugh, Susan. *Martha Calling* (PS–3). Illus. 1994, Houghton $14.95 (0-395-69825-1). 30pp. Martha, the talking dog, must disguise herself as a human to circumvent the "No Dogs Allowed" rule at the Come-On-Inn. (Rev: BCCB 9/94; BL 10/1/94*; HB 11–12/94; SLJ 11/94*)

**1953**  Meddaugh, Susan. *Martha Speaks* (PS–3). Illus. 1992, Houghton $15.00 (0-395-63313-3). 32pp. Helen feeds her dog alphabet soup, and suddenly she can talk! (Rev: BCCB 11/92*; BL 9/1/92*; HB 1–2/93*; SLJ 12/92)

**1954**  Meddaugh, Susan. *Tree of Birds* (PS–1). Illus. 1990, Houghton $16.00 (0-395-53147-0). 32pp. When Harry nurses Sally, an injured bird, back to health, her friends arrive to make sure Harry doesn't keep her as a pet. (Rev: BCCB 3/90; BL 4/1/90; HB 9–10/90; SLJ 4/90)

**1955**  Mennel, Wolfgang. *Henry and Horace Clean Up* (PS–1). Trans. by Marianne Martens. Illus. by Gisela Durr. 1996, North-South LB $15.88 (1-55858-659-8). 32pp. A story of friendship involving a neat, orderly elephant and a messy but likable pig. (Rev: BL 11/15/96; SLJ 12/96)

**1956**  Millais, Raoul. *Elijah and Pin-Pin* (PS–2). Illus. by author. 1992, Simon & Schuster paper $14.00 (0-671-75543-9). 40pp. Elijah the mole and Pin-Pin the hedgehog share many adventures in and around a castle. (Rev: SLJ 7/92)

**1957**  Miller, Edna. *Mousekin's Family* (1–3). Illus. by author. 1972, Prentice Hall LB $9.95 (0-13-604462-X). 32pp. Complications occur when a little white-footed mouse mistakenly believes she has found a relative. Other titles in the series are: *Mousekin's Close Call* (1980); *Mousekin's Fables* (1982).

**1958**  Miller, Virginia. *Be Gentle!* (PS–1). Illus. 1997, Candlewick $15.99 (0-7636-0251-5). 32pp. Ba Bear is brokenhearted when, after playing too hard with a kitten, his new friend runs away. (Rev: BL 8/97; SLJ 10/97)

**1959**  Miller, Virginia. *Eat Your Dinner!* (PS–1). Illus. 1992, Candlewick $14.95 (1-56402-121-1). 32pp. Stubborn Bartholomew is bribed into eating his dinner by big bear George. (Rev: BL 10/1/92; SLJ 12/92)

**1960** Modesitt, Jeanne. *Mama, If You Had a Wish* (PS–K). Illus. by Robin Spowart. 1993, Simon & Schuster $15.00 (0-671-75437-8). 30pp. When questioned by her son, a bunny mother says she only wants him to be his natural self. (Rev: BL 7/93; SLJ 8/93)

**1961** Mogensen, Jan. *The Tiger's Breakfast* (K–3). Illus. 1992, Crocodile $14.95 (0-940793-83-0). A wise mouse saves an elephant from becoming a tiger's breakfast. (Rev: SLJ 4/92)

**1962** Monsell, Mary Elise. *Underwear!* (PS–3). Illus. by Lynn Munsinger. 1988, Whitman LB $12.95 (0-8075-8308-1). 24pp. Zachary Zebra and Orfo Orangutan love underwear, and they take grumpy Bismark Buffalo to the World's Greatest Grassland Underwear Fair. (Rev: BL 4/1/88; SLJ 5/88)

**1963** Monson, A. M. *Wanted: Best Friend* (PS–2). Illus. by Lynn Munsinger. 1997, Dial paper $14.89 (0-8037-1485-8). 32pp. When Cat and Mouse quarrel, Cat unsuccessfully seeks a new friend. (Rev: BL 12/15/96; SLJ 1/97)

**1964** Moore, Inga. *Six-Dinner Sid* (PS–3). Illus. 1991, Simon & Schuster paper $15.00 (0-671-73199-8). 32pp. Sid the cat has 6 different homes, but eventually his secret is discovered. (Rev: BCCB 3/91; BL 5/1/91; SLJ 8/91)

**1965** Morgan, Michaela. *Helpful Betty Solves a Mystery* (PS–2). Illus. by Moira Kemp. Series: On My Own. 1994, Carolrhoda LB $18.60 (0-87614-832-1). While traveling through the jungle helping friends, Betty, a hippo, solves the mystery of a missing egg. Also use *Helpful Betty to the Rescue* (1994). (Rev: BCCB 9/94; SLJ 10/94)

**1966** Most, Bernard. *Cock-A-Doodle-Moo!* (PS–1). Illus. 1996, Harcourt $12.00 (0-15-201252-4). 32pp. When a rooster develops a voice problem, a cow tries to help out. (Rev: BL 9/1/96; SLJ 12/96)

**1967** Most, Bernard. *The Cow That Went Oink* (PS–1). Illus. 1990, Harcourt $13.00 (0-15-220195-5). A cow and a pig are ridiculed because they aren't the same as other farm animals. (Rev: HB 7–8/90; SLJ 12/90)

**1968** Most, Bernard. *If the Dinosaurs Came Back* (1–3). Illus. by author. 1978, Harcourt $15.00 (0-15-238020-5); paper $6.00 (0-15-238021-3). 32pp. All the things that might happen if dinosaurs came back to the world.

**1969** Muller, Robin. *Hickory, Dickory, Dock* (K–2). Illus. by Suzanne Duranceau. 1994, Scholastic $15.95 (0-590-47278-X). 32pp. A cat throws a party with unexpected guests in this book with a rhyme for each hour of the day. (Rev: BL 5/1/94; SLJ 5/94)

**1970** Muntean, Michaela. *Kermit and Robin's Scary Story* (K–2). Illus. by Tom Leigh. Series: Easy-to-Read. 1995, Viking paper $11.99 (0-670-86106-5). 32pp. When young Robin wants Kermit to read him a story, they decide to create their own instead. (Rev: BCCB 10/95; SLJ 3/96)

**1971** Murphy, Jill. *Peace at Last* (PS–2). Illus. by author. 1980, Dial paper $3.95 (0-8037-6964-4). 32pp. Mr. Bear finds many distractions keep him from sleeping. A sequel is: *What Next, Baby Bear?* (1984).

**1972** Murphy, Mary. *I Like It When . . .* (PS). Illus. 1997, Harcourt $10.95 (0-15-200039-9). 32pp. A small penguin tells her mother of her favorite things that they do together. (Rev: BL 4/1/97; SLJ 5/97)

**1973** Murphy, Pat. *Pigasus* (Ps–K). Illus. by Graham Percy. 1996, Dial paper $14.89 (0-8037-1588-9). 32pp. Pigasus, the flying pig, saves his mother's nose ring from wicked pirates. (Rev: BL 2/15/96; SLJ 4/96)

**1974** Myers, Walter Dean. *How Mr. Monkey Saw the Whole World* (PS–3). Illus. by Synthia Saint James. 1996, Doubleday $14.95 (0-385-32057-4). 32pp. Mr. Monkey turns the tables on the bullying Mr. Buzzard. (Rev: BCCB 6/96; BL 4/1/96; HB 7–8/96; SLJ 5/96)

**1975** Newton-John, Olivia, and Brian Seth Hurst. *A Pig Tale* (PS–1). Illus. by Sal Murdocca. 1993, Simon & Schuster paper $14.00 (0-671-78778-0). 28pp. Ziggy, a young pig, is unhappy at all the junk her father has collected and brought to their house. (Rev: BL 9/15/93; SLJ 10/93)

**1976** Noble, Trinka Hakes. *Jimmy's Boa and the Big Splash Birthday Bash* (K–3). Illus. by Steven Kellogg. 1989, Dial LB $13.89 (0-8037-0540-9). 32pp. The lovable orange-and-green spotted constrictor is involved in Jimmy's birthday escapade. (Rev: BL 8/89*; HB 11–12/89; SLJ 11/89*)

**1977** Nones, Eric Jon. *Wendell* (K–3). Illus. 1989, Farrar $13.95 (0-374-38266-2). 32pp. Wendell the cat gets blamed for all the mischief of the gnomelike creatures only he can see. (Rev: BL 11/15/89; SLJ 2/90)

**1978** Norac, Carl. *I Love You So Much* (PS–1). Illus. by Claude K. Dubois. 1998, Doubleday $9.95 (0-385-32512-6). Lola the hamster is looking for the proper occasion to tell her famiy that she loves them. (Rev: SLJ 2/98)

**1979** Norman, Philip R. *A Mammoth Imagination* (PS–2). Illus. 1992, Little, Brown $14.95 (0-316-61201-4). 32pp. A boar named Bonbon finds a herd of wooly mammoths to play with. (Rev: BL 2/1/93; SLJ 2/93)

**1980** Novak, Matt. *Gertie and Gumbo* (K–2). Illus. 1995, Orchard LB $15.99 (0-531-08778-6). 32pp. Gertie and her friend, a baby alligator named Gumbo, save the day when Gumbo's family lose their jobs in a wrestling show. (Rev: BL 9/1/95; SLJ 10/95)

**1981** Novak, Matt. *Mouse TV* (PS–3). Illus. 1994, Orchard LB $17.99 (0-531-08706-9). 32pp. When their TV breaks down, a mouse family, all of whom are TV addicts, must find new ways to amuse themselves. (Rev: BCCB 10/94; BL 9/1/94; SLJ 10/94*)

**1982** Novak, Matt. *Newt* (PS–2). Illus. by author. Series: I Can Read Books. 1996, HarperCollins LB $14.89 (0-06-024502-6). 48pp. A sportily dressed salamander has 3 easy-to-read adventures in this book about discovering friendship. (Rev: BCCB 2/96; SLJ 7/96)

**1983** Novak, Matt. *While the Shepherd Slept* (PS–1). Illus. n.d., Smithmark $3.98 (0-8317-6778-2). 32pp. When their shepherd goes to sleep, the sheep perform vaudeville turns in a local theater. (Rev: BL 2/1/91; HB 5–6/91; SLJ 7/91)

**1984** Numeroff, Laura. *The Chicken Sisters* (PS–2). Illus. by Sharleen Collicott. 1997, HarperCollins LB $14.89 (0-06-026680-5). 32pp. The 3 Chicken Sisters mistakenly believe that they have mastered many of the arts. (Rev: BL 5/1/97*; SLJ 5/97)

**1985** Numeroff, Laura. *Chimps Don't Wear Glasses* (PS–1). Illus. by Joe Mathieu. 1995, Simon & Schuster paper $14.00 (0-689-80150-5). 32pp. A humorous rhyme that points out how inept animals can be when they try various activities associated with humans. (Rev: BL 9/1/95; SLJ 11/95)

**1986** Numeroff, Laura. *Dogs Don't Wear Sneakers* (PS–K). Illus. by Joe Mathieu. 1993, Simon & Schuster paper $15.00 (0-671-79525-2). Through a series of zany illustrations, this book shows various examples of feats and accomplishments that are not possible for animals. (Rev: SLJ 1/94)

**1987** Numeroff, Laura. *If You Give a Moose a Muffin* (PS–2). Illus. by Felicia Bond. 1991, HarperCollins LB $14.89 (0-06-024406-2). 32pp. This circular tale begins with a moose being lured to a boy's house to receive a muffin. (Rev: BCCB 9/91; BL 7/91; SLJ 12/91*)

**1988** Numeroff, Laura. *If You Give a Mouse a Cookie* (PS–K). Illus. by Felicia Bond. 1985, HarperCollins LB $14.89 (0-06-024587-5). 32pp. A little mouse asks for a variety of things until the floor is a clutter of goods. (Rev: BCCB 7/85; BL 6/1/85; SLJ 5/85)

**1989** Oakley, Graham. *The Church Mice and the Ring* (PS–3). Illus. 1992, Macmillan $14.95 (0-689-31790-5). 32pp. The church mice help a young girl persuade her parents to let her adopt a dog. (Rev: BCCB 12/92; BL 11/15/92; HB 3–4/93; SLJ 1/93)

**1990** Oakley, Graham. *Hetty and Harriet* (K–3). Illus. by author. 1982, Macmillan $13.95 (0-689-30888-4). 32pp. Two chickens, Harriet and her sister Hetty, leave the barnyard to find a better place to live.

**1991** Oborne, Martine. *Juice the Pig* (PS–3). Illus. by Axel Scheffler. 1997, Holt $15.95 (0-8050-5172-4). A pig named Juice loves to collect hats, but other animals are always trying to snatch them away from him. (Rev: BL 7/97; SLJ 7/97)

**1992** O'Callahan, Jay. *Herman and Marguerite: An Earth Story* (K–3). Illus. by Laura O'Callahan. 1996, Peachtree $15.95 (1-56145-103-7). An earthworm that wants to explore aboveground is almost burned by the sun until a caterpillar rescues it. (Rev: SLJ 7/96)

**1993** Ogburn, Jacqueline K. *The Reptile Ball* (1–4). Illus. by John O'Brien. 1997, Dial LB $14.89 (0-8037-1732-6). 32pp. A humorous delight in which a group of lizards, crocodiles, and other reptiles have a fine time dancing at a very unusual party. (Rev: BCCB 7–8/97; BL 10/15/97; SLJ 10/97)

**1994** Oppenheim, Joanne. *Rooter Remembers: A Bank Street Book About Values* (PS–2). Illus. by Lynn Munsinger. 1991, Dutton paper $3.99 (0-14-054091-1). A book about farmyard animals that explores the concept of honesty. (Rev: SLJ 6/91)

**1995** Ormondroyd, Edward. *Broderick* (PS–3). Illus. by John Larrecq. 1969, Houghton LB $4.77 (0-686-86580-4). 40pp. Broderick, a mouse, loves to chew books, but one night he stops chewing and reads one. The book is on surfing, and it changes his life!

**1996** Oxenbury, Helen. *It's My Birthday* (PS). Illus. 1994, Candlewick $9.95 (1-56402-412-1). 24pp. A group of animal friends help a boy make a cake for his birthday by contributing ingredients. (Rev: BL 7/94; SLJ 11/94)

**1997** Packard, Mary. *We Are Monsters* (K–1). Illus. by John Magine. 1996, Scholastic $3.99 (0-590-68995-9). 32pp. At nighttime, terrible monsters are afraid that children are hiding under their beds in this book with removable flashcards. (Rev: BL 2/1/97)

**1998** Palatini, Margie. *Moosetache* (PS–2). Illus. by Henry Cole. 1997, Hyperion LB $16.49 (0-7868-2246-5). 32pp. A funny story about a moose that tries several ways to tame his uncontrollable mustache. (Rev: BL 4/15/97; SLJ 5/97)

**1999** Parkinson, Curtis. *Tom Foolery* (PS–2). Illus. by Cathy Bobak. 1993, Macmillan LB $13.95 (0-02-770025-9). A tiny cat goes overboard and has an adventure on a Caribbean island. (Rev: SLJ 5/93)

**2000** Paschkis, Julie. *So Happy/So Sad* (PS–1). Illus. by author. 1995, Holt $12.95 (0-8050-3862-0). A group of animals show a variety of emotions in an alliterative text. (Rev: SLJ 3/96)

**2001** Patz, Nancy. *Sarah Bear and Sweet Sidney* (K–2). Illus. by author. 1989, Macmillan LB $13.95

(0-02-770270-7). Sidney Bear thinks that winter and his time of hibernation are over, but Sarah Bear knows that spring has not yet arrived. (Rev: SLJ 9/89)

**2002** Paxton, Tom. *Engelbert Joins the Circus* (PS–2). Illus. by Roberta Wilson. 1997, Morrow LB $14.93 (0-688-09988-2). 32pp. Engelbert the Elephant joins a circus and dazzles the audience with his dancing and juggling. (Rev: BL 3/15/97; SLJ 3/97)

**2003** Payne, Emmy. *Katy No-Pocket* (PS–1). Illus. by H. A. Rey. 1973, Houghton $16.00 (0-395-17104-0); paper $5.95 (0-395-13717-9). 32pp. Until Katy finds an apron with pockets, she is very sad, for she has no way in which to carry her baby.

**2004** Pearson, Tracey Campbell. *The Howling Dog* (PS–K). Illus. 1991, Farrar $13.95 (0-374-33502-8). 32pp. A lonely dog collects a number of friends as he wanders through the night barking. (Rev: BL 9/15/91; HB 1–2/92; SLJ 10/91)

**2005** Peet, Bill. *Cock-a-Doodle Dudley* (PS–3). Illus. 1990, Houghton $14.95 (0-395-55331-8). 48pp. Dudley takes credit for making the sun rise. (Rev: BCCB 10/90; BL 9/15/90; HB 11–12/90; SLJ 11/90)

**2006** Peet, Bill. *Cowardly Clyde* (K–2). Illus. by author. 1984, Houghton paper $6.95 (0-395-36171-0). 48pp. A horse named Clyde quivers in fear at the thought of fighting a dragon with his master, Sir Galavant. Other titles by this author and publisher are: *Ant and the Elephant* (1980); *The Luckiest One of All* (1985); *No Such Things* (1985); *Pamela Camel* (1986); *Farewell to Shady Glade* (1991).

**2007** Peet, Bill. *Eli* (1–3). Illus. by author. 1984, Houghton paper $5.95 (0-395-36611-9). 48pp. An old lion is saved from hunters by playing dead. Others by Bill Peet and published by Houghton are: *Hubert's Hair-Raising Adventure* (1959); *Ella* (1964); *Chester the Worldly Pig* (1978); *Kermit the Hermit* (1980); *Cyrus the Unsinkable Sea Serpent* (1982).

**2008** Peet, Bill. *Encore for Eleanor* (K–3). Illus. by author. 1981, Houghton paper $3.95 (0-317-18520-9). 48pp. Eleanor the elephant must face retirement from her circus job. (Rev: HB 9–10/85)

**2009** Peet, Bill. *The Gnats of Knotty Pine* (K–3). Illus. by author. 1984, Houghton $14.95 (0-395-21405-X); paper $6.95 (0-395-36612-7). The tiny gnats help save the animals of Knotty Pine at hunting time.

**2010** Peet, Bill. *Whingdingdilly* (2–4). Illus. by author. 1977, Houghton $16.00 (0-395-24729-2); paper $6.95 (0-395-31381-3). Scamp, tired of leading a dog's life, is transformed by a witch. Some others by this author and publisher are: *The Spooky Tail of Prewitt Peacock* (1973); *Merle the High Flying Squirrel* (1974); *Fly, Homer, Fly* (1979); *Randy's*

*Dandy Lions* (1979); *Huge Harold* (1982); *How Droofus the Dragon Lost His Head* (1983); *The Pinkish, Purplish, Bluish Egg* (1984).

**2011** Peet, Bill. *Zella, Zack, and Zodiac* (PS–1). Illus. 1986, Houghton $14.95 (0-395-41069-X); paper $6.95 (0-395-52207-2). 32pp. The tale of Zack, an ostrich, adopted by Zella the zebra, and Zella's colt Zodiac, whom Zack saves. (Rev: BCCB 6/86; BL 3/16/86; SLJ 5/86)

**2012** Peguero, Leone. *Lionel and Amelia* (PS–1). Illus. by Adrian Peguero and Gerard Peguero. 1996, Mondo paper $4.95 (1-57255-197-6). 30pp. The mice, who want to be friends, copy each other's ways but decide it's best to be natural. (Rev: BL 1/1–15/97)

**2013** Percy, Graham. *24 Strange Little Animals: The Haunted House* (K–2). Illus. by author. 1996, Chronicle $12.95 (0-8118-1035-6). 35pp. When their bus breaks down, a number of little creatures must spend the night in a house they think is haunted. (Rev: SLJ 1/97)

**2014** Pfister, Marcus. *Dazzle the Dinosaur* (K–2). Illus. 1994, North-South LB $18.88 (1-55858-338-6). 32pp. Two young dinosaurs decide to chase away the giant Dragonsaurus, which has invaded their valley paradise. (Rev: BL 2/1/95; SLJ 1/95)

**2015** Pfister, Marcus. *Hopper's Treetop Adventure* (PS–1). Illus. 1997, North-South LB $15.88 (1-55858-681-4). 32pp. Hopper the rabbit meets a squirrel that teaches him to dig for nuts, climb trees, and swing from branch to branch. (Rev: BL 4/1/97; SLJ 3/97)

**2016** Pfister, Marcus. *How Leo Learned to Be King* (PS–1). Illus. 1998, North-South LB $15.88 (1-55858-914-7). 32pp. Leo, the deposed king of the beasts, learns to be helpful to others and is returned to the throne. (Rev: BL 3/1/98)

**2017** Pfister, Marcus. *Milo and the Magical Stones* (PS–2). Trans. by Marianne Martens. Illus. 1997, North-South $18.95 (1-55858-682-2). 28pp. A choose-your-own-ending book in which a group of mice on an island discover a nugget of gold. (Rev: BL 10/1/97; SLJ 9/97)

**2018** Pfister, Marcus. *Penguin Pete, Ahoy!* (PS–K). Trans. from German by Rosemary Lanning. Illus. by author. Series: Penguin Pete. 1993, North-South LB $15.88 (1-55858-221-5). Penguin Pete makes a new friend of Horatio, a mouse, and together they explore an abandoned ship. (Rev: SLJ 1/94)

**2019** Pfister, Marcus. *The Rainbow Fish* (PS–2). Trans. by J. Alison James. Illus. 1992, North-South LB $18.88 (1-55858-010-7). 28pp. Rainbow Fish feels superior to those plain fish that surround him until he finds that sharing brings happiness. (Rev: BL 1/1/93; SLJ 11/92)

**2020** Pfister, Marcus. *The Rainbow Fish Board Book* (PS). Illus. 1996, North-South $9.95 (1-55858-536-2). 12pp. A board book version of the tale first published in 1993 of the lovely rainbow fish and his quest for friends. (Rev: BL 3/15/96)

**2021** Pfister, Marcus. *Rainbow Fish to the Rescue!* (PS–1). Illus. 1995, North-South LB $18.88 (1-55858-487-0). 32pp. When Rainbow Fish and his friends face a shark attack, the group accepts a new striped fish into the circle. This is the sequel to *Rainbow Fish* (1992). (Rev: BL 9/15/95; SLJ 9/95)

**2022** Pilkey, Dav. *Dog Breath: The Horrible Trouble with Hally Tosis* (PS–2). Illus. 1994, Scholastic $12.95 (0-590-47466-9). 32pp. Hally Tosis, a dog with terrible breath, uses his affliction to capture 2 burglars. (Rev: BL 9/15/94; HB 11–12/94; SLJ 1/95)

**2023** Pilkey, Dav. *The Moonglow Roll-o-Rama* (PS–3). Illus. 1995, Orchard LB $15.99 (0-531-08726-3). 32pp. Some animals steal off at night to a magical roller skating rink, which is why they sleep during the day. (Rev: BCCB 3/95; BL 2/1/95; SLJ 3/95)

**2024** Pilkey, Dav. *The Silly Gooses* (PS–3). Illus. by author. 1998, Scholastic $13.95 (0-590-94733-8). 39pp. A slapstick story about 2 silly geese who marry and raise a silly family. (Rev: SLJ 2/98)

**2025** Polisar, Barry L. *The Trouble with Ben* (PS–3). Illus. by David Clark. 1992, Rainbow $14.95 (0-938663-13-5). 32pp. A young bear annoys his human classmates by indulging in bearlike activities. (Rev: BL 6/1/92; SLJ 7/92)

**2026** Pomerantz, Charlotte. *Here Comes Henny* (PS–K). Illus. by Nancy Winslow Parker. 1994, Greenwillow LB $13.93 (0-688-12356-2). 24pp. A catchy rhyme about what Henny the chicken puts in her backpack. (Rev: BL 10/15/94; SLJ 9/94)

**2027** Pomerantz, Charlotte. *The Piggy in the Puddle* (PS–K). Illus. by James Marshall. 1974, Macmillan LB $15.00 (0-02-774900-2). 32pp. Amusing story of the antics of a pig family enjoying a mud puddle.

**2028** Porter, Sue. *Little Wolf and the Giant* (K–3). Illus. 1990, Simon & Schuster paper $13.95 (0-671-70363-3). Little Wolf, on his way to Granny's, is sure there are monsters in the woods. (Rev: SLJ 10/90)

**2029** Porter, Sue. *My Little Rabbit Tale* (PS–K). Illus. 1994, DK Publg. $13.95 (1-56458-339-2). 32pp. Little Rabbit's active day includes time in a nursery school and a visit to the doctor. (Rev: BL 6/1–15/94; SLJ 8/94)

**2030** Potter, Beatrix. *The Complete Adventures of Peter Rabbit* (K–3). Illus. by author. 1982, Puffin paper $6.99 (0-14-050444-3). 96pp. An omnibus of the Peter Rabbit stories.

**2031** Potter, Beatrix. *Hill Top Tales: Four Original Peter Rabbit Stories* (PS–2). Illus. by author. 1989, Warne paper $8.95 (0-7232-3548-1). 128pp. Four familiar Potter tales about the Lake District. (Rev: BL 12/15/88)

**2032** Potter, Beatrix. *The Tale of Jemima Puddle-Duck and Other Farmyard Tales: The Tale of Mr. Jeremy Fisher, The Tale of Mrs. Tiggy-Winkle, The Tale of Pigling Bland* (PS–1). Illus. by author. 1987, Warne $13.00 (0-7232-3425-6). 80pp. This is a large-format edition of these classics, but the size of the illustrations is the same as the originals. (Rev: BL 5/15/87)

**2033** Potter, Beatrix. *The Tale of Mr. Jeremy Fisher* (K–4). Illus. by David Jorgensen. Series: Rabbit Ears Storybook Classics. 1989, Picture Book $14.95 (0-88708-095-2). This charming book can also be purchased with a cassette featuring Meryl Streep. (Rev: SLJ 2/90)

**2034** Potter, Beatrix. *The Tale of Peter Rabbit* (PS–3). Illus. by author. 1987, Warne paper $2.25 (0-7232-3485-X). Original illustrations are rephotographed in this edition of a classic tale. (Rev: BL 11/1/87)

**2035** Prelutsky, Jack. *The Baby Uggs Are Hatching* (K–4). Illus. by James Stevenson. 1982, Greenwillow LB $15.93 (0-688-00923-9); Morrow paper $3.95 (0-688-09239-X). 32pp. A collection of imaginary animals introduced in catchy verse.

**2036** Price, Mathew. *Lift-the-Flap Chick* (PS). Illus. by Moira Kemp. 1998, Lodestar paper $4.99 (0-525-67565-5). In this board book with flaps, a little chick is looking for its home. Also use *Lift-the-Flap Kitten, Lift-the-Flap Puppy* and *Lift-the-Flap Mouse* (all 1989). (Rev: SLJ 3/98)

**2037** Pryor, Bonnie. *Louie and Dan Are Friends* (K–3). Illus. by Elizabeth Miles. 1997, Morrow LB $15.93 (0-688-08561-X). 32pp. Because they are so different, 2 mice brothers wonder if they will always remain friends. (Rev: BL 10/1/97; SLJ 9/97)

**2038** Pryor, Bonnie. *The Porcupine Mouse* (PS–2). Illus. by Maryjane Begin. 1988, Morrow LB $15.93 (0-688-07154-6). 32pp. Louie and Dan don't heed Mama Mouse's warnings when they go off to find a home of their own. (Rev: BL 3/1/88; SLJ 9/88)

**2039** Quackenbush, Robert. *Batbaby* (PS–2). Illus. by author. Series: Little Dipper Books. 1997, Random LB $9.99 (0-679-98541-7). When a gust of wind blows Batbaby into Squirrel's treetop nest, Squirrel tries to accommodate his new guest. (Rev: SLJ 12/97)

**2040** Quackenbush, Robert. *Henry's Awful Mistake* (PS–2). Illus. by author. 1981, Parents LB $5.95 (0-8193-1040-9). 48pp. Henry, a duck, tries to rid his horse of an ant. A sequel is: *Henry's Important Date* (1982).

**2041** Quackenbush, Robert. *Lost in the Amazon: A Miss Mallard Mystery* (2–4). Illus. 1990, Pippin LB $15.95 (0-945912-11-0). Miss Mallard, the detective duck, is off on another case, this one in Brazil. (Rev: SLJ 1/91)

**2042** Radford, Derek. *Harry at the Garage* (PS–2). Illus. 1995, Candlewick $12.99 (1-56402-564-0). 32pp. Harry the Hippo learns what goes on in a garage when he takes his car in to be serviced. (Rev: BL 10/15/95; SLJ 1/96)

**2043** Ramirez, Michael Rose. *The Little Ant/La Hormiga Chiquita* (K–2). Illus. by Linda D. Sawaya. 1995, Rizzoli $12.95 (0-8478-1922-1). 31pp. When an ant slips on the snow, she looks around for someone to blame in this bilingual book. (Rev: SLJ 3/96)

**2044** Rand, Gloria. *Willie Takes a Hike* (1–3). Illus. by Ted Rand. 1996, Harcourt $15.00 (0-15-200272-3). 32pp. In spite of his elaborate preparations, Willie the mouse gets lost on a hiking trip. (Rev: BL 4/1/96; SLJ 6/96)

**2045** Rankin, Joan. *Scaredy Cat* (PS–1). Illus. 1996, Simon & Schuster $16.00 (0-689-80948-4). 30pp. A little kitten conquers his fears and takes on a dog many times his size. (Rev: BL 9/15/96; SLJ 11/96)

**2046** Rankin, Joan. *Wow! It's Great Being a Duck* (PS–1). Illus. by author. 1998, Simon & Schuster paper $16.00 (0-689-81756-8). A little duck learns her survival skills very quickly when she is confronted by a fox. (Rev: SLJ 3/98)

**2047** Raschka, Chris. *The Blushful Hippopotamus* (PS–K). Illus. by author. 1996, Orchard LB $15.99 (0-531-08882-0). Young Roosevelt Hippopotamus can't control his blushing and is ridiculed by his sister. (Rev: HB 9–10/96; SLJ 9/96)

**2048** Rathmann, Peggy. *Good Night, Gorilla* (PS–1). Illus. 1994, Putnam $14.99 (0-399-22445-9). 40pp. After the zookeeper says good-night to his animals, a playful gorilla lets them out of their cages. (Rev: BCCB 5/94; BL 7/94; HB 7–8/94; SLJ 7/94)

**2049** Ratz de Tagyos, Paul. *A Coney Tale* (PS–3). Illus. by author. 1992, Houghton $14.95 (0-395-58834-0). 32pp. A group of rabbits discover that the giant tree in town is really a carrot. (Rev: BL 5/1/92; SLJ 6/92)

**2050** Rayner, Mary. *Mrs. Pig Gets Cross and Other Stories* (2–3). Illus. by author. 1991, Puffin paper $5.95 (0-525-44705-9). 64pp. Seven short stories of Mrs. Pig, her untidy piglets, and other events. (Rev: BCCB 4/87; BL 4/1/87; SLJ 3/87)

**2051** Regan, Dian C. *Dear Dr. Sillybear* (PS–2). Illus. by Randy Cecil. 1997, Holt $15.95 (0-8050-5065-5). During a single day at the office, Dr. Sillybear and Nurse Rabbit encounter such medical mysteries as why a baby owl says "what" instead of "who." (Rev: SLJ 9/97)

**2052** Reich, Janet. *Gus and the Green Thing* (PS–2). Illus. by author. 1993, Walker LB $9.85 (0-8027-8253-1). A dog named Gus follows a leaf from the bleak city into the countryside and finds a new green world. (Rev: SLJ 10/93)

**2053** Reider, Katja. *Snail Started It!* (PS–2). Trans. by Rosemary Lanning. Illus. by Angela Von Roehl. 1997, North-South LB $15.88 (1-55858-707-1). A cumulative tale in which different animals exchange insults, for which they are sorry. (Rev: SLJ 6/97)

**2054** Reiser, Lynn. *Two Mice in Three Fables* (PS–1). Illus. 1995, Greenwillow LB $14.93 (0-688-13390-8). 32pp. A country mouse introduces an indoor mouse to the wonders of nature. (Rev: BL 3/1/95; SLJ 4/95)

**2055** Retan, Walter, ed. *Piggies, Piggies, Piggies: A Treasury of Stories, Songs, and Poems* (K–3). Illus. 1993, Simon & Schuster paper $15.00 (0-671-75244-8). 96pp. An anthology of nursery rhymes, poems, stories, and excerpts from novels, all having pigs as their subject. (Rev: BL 1/15/94; SLJ 1/94)

**2056** Rex, Michael. *The Painting Gorilla* (PS–2). Illus. 1997, Holt $15.95 (0-8050-5020-5). 32pp. A gorilla in a zoo becomes a millionaire by selling her paintings, but what should she do with the money? (Rev: BL 12/1/97; SLJ 9/97)

**2057** Rey, H. A. *Cecily G. and the Nine Monkeys* (K–2). Illus. by author. 1974, Houghton $14.95 (0-395-18430-4); paper $5.95 (0-395-50651-4). 32pp. A lonely giraffe and 9 homeless monkeys share some uproarious adventures.

**2058** Rey, H. A. *Curious George* (K–4). Illus. by author. 1941, Houghton $14.95 (0-395-15993-8); paper $5.95 (0-395-15023-X). 56pp. A small monkey finds himself in difficulties due to his mischievous curiosity. Also use by the same author: *Curious George Takes a Job* (1947); *Curious George Rides a Bike* (1952); *Curious George Gets a Medal* (1957).

**2059** Rey, Margaret. *Curious George Flies a Kite* (K–2). Illus. by H. A. Rey. 1973, Houghton $14.95 (0-395-16965-8); paper $5.95 (0-395-25937-1). 80pp. More predicaments are encountered by this fun-loving monkey. Also use by the same author: *Curious George Goes to the Hospital* (1973).

**2060** Riley, Linnea. *Mouse Mess* (PS–2). Illus. 1997, Scholastic $15.95 (0-590-10048-3). 32pp. While the human family is asleep upstairs, a messy mouse is creating havoc downstairs in a search for food. (Rev: BL 10/1/97; SLJ 11/97*)

**2061** Roberts, Bethany. *Monster Manners* (PS–2). Illus. by Andrew Glass. 1996, Clarion $15.00 (0-395-69850-2). 32pp. A rhyming book that explains basic manners with brilliantly colored illustrations and the antics of 3 often misbehaving monsters. (Rev: SLJ 4/96)

**2062**   Roberts, Bethany, and Patricia Hubbell. *Camel Caravan* (PS–1). Illus. by Cheryl M. Taylor. 1996, Morrow LB $15.93 (0-688-13940-X). 32pp. Five camels try out various forms of transportation and conclude that being beasts of burden isn't so bad after all. (Rev: BL 4/15/96; SLJ 4/96)

**2063**   Roche, Denis. *Brave Georgie Goat: Three Little Stories About Growing Up* (PS). Illus. by author. 1997, Crown LB $17.99 (0-517-70965-1). Three short stories about a little goat and how he conquers fears and achieves some independence. (Rev: SLJ 1/98)

**2064**   Rockwell, Anne. *Hugo at the Park* (PS–1). Illus. by author. 1990, Macmillan LB $13.95 (0-02-777301-9). Hugo, a pup, disobeys his young master and interrupts other people's activities in the park. (Rev: SLJ 3/90)

**2065**   Rockwell, Norman. *Willie Was Different* (1–3). Illus. by author. 1994, Berkshire House $16.95 (0-936399-61-9). After achieving world renown as a composer, Willie the wood thrush decides it is best to return to his forest home. (Rev: SLJ 12/94)

**2066**   Roddie, Shen. *Too Close Friends* (PS–1). Illus. by Sally Anne Lambert. 1998, Dial paper $14.99 (0-8037-2188-9). 32pp. Two close friends, Hippo and Pig, lose their sense of privacy when one cuts down a tall hedge that separates their properties. (Rev: BL 2/1/98; SLJ 3/98)

**2067**   Romanelli, Serena. *Little Bobo Saves the Day* (K–3). Illus. by Hans de Beer. 1997, North-South LB $15.88 (1-55858-787-X). 32pp. When his uncle gets very sick, Little Bobo, an orangutan, must go into the world to find some medicine. A sequel to *Little Bobo* (1995). (Rev: BL 2/1/98; SLJ 12/97)

**2068**   Root, Phyllis. *Coyote and the Magic Words* (PS–3). Illus. by Sandra Speidel. 1993, Lothrop LB $13.93 (0-688-10309-X). 32pp. Coyote creates such mayhem in the animal world that the Maker-of-all-things decides that all creatures must work for what they need. (Rev: BL 11/15/93; SLJ 1/94)

**2069**   Rosman, Steven M. *Deena the Damselfly* (K–2). Illus. by Giora Carmi. 1992, UAHC $10.95 (0-8074-0477-2). 31pp. A young damselfly nymph is changed into an adult damselfly. (Rev: SLJ 9/92)

**2070**   Ross, Tony. *The Treasure of Cozy Cove: or, The Voyage of the "Kipper"* (K–3). Illus. 1990, Farrar $14.00 (0-374-37744-8). 32pp. Two kittens share adventures aboard the Kipper with Cap'n Claws. (Rev: BCCB 5/90; BL 8/90; SLJ 7/90)

**2071**   Rowe, John. *Peter Piglet* (K–3). Illus. 1996, North-South LB $16.88 (1-55858-661-X). 32pp. A piglet is devastated when his magic golden slippers disappear. (Rev: BL 12/1/96; SLJ 11/96)

**2072**   Rowe, John. *Rabbit Moon* (PS–3). Illus. 1993, Picture Book paper $14.95 (0-88708-246-7). A rab-

bit mistakes a party decoration for the moon. (Rev: SLJ 6/93)

**2073**   Rowe, John. *Smudge* (PS–2). Illus. 1997, North-South LB $16.95 (1-55858-789-6). 36pp. Smudge, a rat, tries a number of surrogate animal families but finds his own is best. (Rev: BL 12/1/97; SLJ 2/98)

**2074**   Rowinski, Kate. *Ellie Bear and the Fly-Away Fly* (PS–2). Illus. by Dawn Peterson. 1993, Down East $14.95 (0-89272-335-1). On a fishing trip with her uncle, L. L. Bear, Ellie Bear catches a trout but decides to spare its life. (Rev: SLJ 4/94)

**2075**   Rubel, Nicole. *It Came from the Swamp* (PS–3). Illus. by author. 1988, Dial LB $10.89 (0-8037-0515-8); Puffin paper $3.99 (0-14-054541-7). 32pp. Alfie the alligator gets hit in the head with a baseball and flees the Everglades. (Rev: BL 10/15/88; HB 9–10/88; SLJ 1/89)

**2076**   Rudolph, Marguerita. *Grey Neck* (PS–3). Illus. by Leslie Shuman Kranz. 1988, Stemmer $13.95 (0-88045-068-1). 32pp. Grey Neck can't leave for the yearly journey south because of a broken wing. (Rev: BL 6/1/88; SLJ 9/88)

**2077**   Rush, Christopher. *Venus Peter Saves the Whale* (3–5). Illus. by Mairi Hedderwick. 1992, Pelican $14.95 (0-88289-928-7). 26pp. On an isolated Scottish island, seagulls want a young boy to save a stranded whale. (Rev: BL 6/1/92)

**2078**   Ryder, Joanne. *Winter White* (PS–2). Illus. by Carol Lacey. 1997, Morrow LB $15.93 (0-688-12993-5). 32pp. Fox and Lemming trade the sun for snow but later realize they have made a terrible bargain. (Rev: BL 12/1/97; SLJ 10/97)

**2079**   Sadler, Marilyn. *Elizabeth, Larry and Ed* (PS–1). Illus. by Roger Bollen. 1992, Simon & Schuster paper $14.00 (0-671-75956-6). 44pp. Elizabeth, an old lady, and her friend, the alligator Larry, are joined by a purple swamp creature. (Rev: BL 9/1/92; SLJ 2/93)

**2080**   Saller, Carol. *Pug, Slug, and Doug the Thug* (K–2). Illus. by Vicki Jo Redenbaugh. 1994, Carolrhoda LB $14.95 (0-87614-803-8). 32pp. In this Western tale, a young boy captures 3 outlaws when he accidentally starts a chain of events that prove to be their downfall. (Rev: BL 4/1/94)

**2081**   Saltzberg, Barney. *This Is a Great Place for a Hot Dog Stand* (1–3). Illus. 1995, Hyperion LB $15.49 (0-7868-2057-8). 32pp. The hot dog stand that the monster Izzy operates is threatened by the construction of a super shopping mall. (Rev: BL 4/15/95; SLJ 5/95)

**2082**   Sampson, Michael, and Mary Beth Sampson. *Star of the Circus* (PS–K). Illus. 1997, Holt $14.95 (0-8050-4284-9). 32pp. Each of a group of egocentric animals thinks that he or she is the star of the circus. (Rev: BL 4/1/97; SLJ 3/97)

**2083** Santore, Charles. *William the Curious: Knight of the Water Lilies* (K–2). Illus. 1997, Random $18.00 (0-679-88742-3). 32pp. The frog William was happy living in a castle moat until it became filled with junk, thanks to the queen's order that imperfect things were to be thrown out of the castle. (Rev: BL 12/15/97; SLJ 2/98)

**2084** Sardegna, Jill. *The Roly-Poly Spider* (PS–K). Illus. by Tedd Arnold. 1994, Scholastic $13.95 (0-590-47119-8). 32pp. A fat spider uses age-old devices like flattery to lure insect meals into its web. (Rev: BL 11/15/94; SLJ 1/95)

**2085** Saunders, Dave, and Julie Saunders. *Brave Jack* (K–3). Illus. by Dave Saunders. 1993, Macmillan $14.95 (0-02-781073-9). 32pp. In spite of warnings, a rabbit named Jack raids a cabbage patch. (Rev: BL 3/15/93; SLJ 6/93)

**2086** Saunders, Dave, and Julie Saunders. *Dibble and Dabble* (PS–1). Illus. by Dave Saunders. 1990, Macmillan $14.95 (0-02-781071-2). Two ducks tell their story of seeing a furry snake, which is really just a cat's tail. (Rev: HB 5–6/90; SLJ 4/90)

**2087** Saunders, Dave, and Julie Saunders. *Snowtime* (PS–1). Illus. by Dave Saunders. 1991, Macmillan LB $14.95 (0-02-781075-5). 32pp. Two ducks, Dibble and Dabble, become lost in a blizzard and wander into town. (Rev: BL 9/15/91; SLJ 12/91)

**2088** Scamell, Ragnhild. *Three Bags Full* (K–1). Illus. by Sally Hobson. 1993, Orchard $14.95 (0-531-05486-1). 26pp. Millie the sheep gives so much of her wool to her friends that she begins to feel the cold. (Rev: BL 7/93)

**2089** Scarry, Richard. *Pie Rats Ahoy!* (K–1). Illus. by author. Series: Step into Reading Books. 1994, Random LB $11.99 (0-679-94760-4); paper $3.99 (0-679-84760-X). 32pp. Uncle Willy hides inside a model of a crocodile to capture pirates who are frightening the residents of Busytown Bay. (Rev: SLJ 9/94)

**2090** Schlein, Miriam. *The Way Mothers Are* (PS–1). Illus. by Joe Lasker. 1993, Whitman LB $14.95 (0-8075-8691-9). 32pp. In this new edition of the 1963 book, the story is still of a mother cat's love for her young son. (Rev: BL 4/1/93)

**2091** Schmid, Eleonore. *The Squirrel and the Moon* (PS–2). Trans. from German by Rosemary Lanning. Illus. by author. 1996, North-South LB $15.88 (1-55858-531-1). The story of a year in the life of a squirrel and her love of the moon. (Rev: SLJ 9/96)

**2092** Schoenherr, John. *Bear* (K–3). Illus. 1991, Putnam $14.95 (0-399-22177-8). 32pp. In an Alaska setting, a young bear sets out to find his missing

mother. (Rev: BCCB 4/91; BL 4/1/91; HB 5–6/91; SLJ 5/91)

**2093** Schumaker, Ward. *Dance!* (PS–1). Illus. 1996, Harcourt $12.00 (0-15-200046-1). 32pp. In handsome 2-page spreads, various animals enjoy the freedom and exuberance of dancing. (Rev: BL 3/1/96; SLJ 5/96)

**2094** Schwartz, Henry. *How I Captured a Dinosaur* (PS–K). Illus. by Amy Schwartz. 1989, Orchard paper $5.95 (0-531-07028-X). 32pp. Liz discovers a dinosaur on a camping trip and takes him home. (Rev: BCCB 2/89; BL 2/1/89; SLJ 4/89)

**2095** Sebastian, John. *J.B.'s Harmonica* (K–3). Illus. by Garth Williams. 1993, Harcourt $13.95 (0-15-240091-5). 32pp. A young bear is so bad at playing the harmonica that the neighbors complain. (Rev: BL 3/15/93; SLJ 4/93)

**2096** Seibold, J. Otto, and Vivian Walsh. *Free Lunch* (K–3). Illus. 1996, Viking paper $15.99 (0-670-86988-0). 40pp. The dog Mr. Lunch finds that the quality of the Elephant Brand Bird Seed Company's product is declining. (Rev: BL 9/1/96; SLJ 11/96)

**2097** Seibold, J. Otto, and Vivian Walsh. *Mr. Lunch Borrows a Canoe* (K–3). Illus. by J. Otto Seibold. 1994, Viking paper $15.99 (0-670-85661-4). 32pp. Mr. Lunch, a dog who chases birds for a living, goes to Venice to chase the pigeons. (Rev: BL 10/15/94; SLJ 12/94)

**2098** Seibold, J. Otto, and Vivian Walsh. *Mr. Lunch Takes a Plane Ride* (PS–3). Illus. by J. Otto Seibold. 1993, Viking paper $15.99 (0-670-84775-5). 40pp. The dog Mr. Lunch has fun opening up everyone's luggage when he is confined to the baggage compartment on an airplane flight. (Rev: BCCB 1/94; BL 9/1/93; SLJ 9/93)

**2099** Selby, Jennifer. *Beach Bunny* (PS–1). Illus. 1996, Harcourt $14.00 (0-15-200840-3). 32pp. Harold the bunny spends a great day at the beach because he is well prepared. (Rev: BL 8/96; SLJ 6/96)

**2100** Selby, Jennifer. *The Seed Bunny* (PS–2). Illus. 1997, Harcourt $14.00 (0-15-201397-0). 32pp. A small bunny named Sam tries to get rid of a loose tooth so he can see the Seed Bunny, who takes teeth and leaves carrot seeds. (Rev: BCCB 4/97; BL 6/1–15/97; SLJ 4/97)

**2101** Selden, George. *Chester Cricket's Pigeon Ride* (2–4). Illus. by Garth Williams. 1983, Dell paper $3.50 (0-440-41389-3). 80pp. A friendly pigeon gives Chester Cricket a bird's-eye view of Manhattan. A sequel is: *Chester Cricket's New Home* (1983).

**2102** Seuss, Dr. *Horton Hears a Who!* (K–3). Illus. by author. 1954, Random LB $15.99 (0-394-90078-2). The children's favorite elephant discovers a whole town of creatures so small that they live on a speck of dust. Other titles by Dr. Seuss: *Horton Hatches the Egg* (1940); *If I Ran the Zoo* (1950); *If I Ran the Circus* (1956); *Yertle the Turtle and Other Stories* (1958).

**2103** Seuss, Dr. *Hunches in Bunches* (PS–3). Illus. by author. 1982, Random LB $15.99 (0-394-95502-1). 48pp. A rhyming story about the problems of making up one's mind. Three other titles by Dr. Seuss are: *Thidwick, the Big-Hearted Moose* (1948); *Scrambled Eggs Super!* (1953); *I Had Trouble in Getting to Solla Sollew* (1992).

**2104** Shannon, George. *April Showers* (PS–K). Illus. by Jose Aruego and Ariane Dewey. 1995, Greenwillow LB $14.93 (0-688-13122-0). 24pp. Five foolish frogs enjoy playing in the April rain. (Rev: BL 4/1/95; HB 5–6/95; SLJ 5/95)

**2105** Shannon, George. *Heart to Heart* (PS–3). Illus. by Steve Bjorkman. 1995, Houghton $14.00 (0-395-72773-1). 32pp. Squirrel prepares a unique valentine for his friend Mole that celebrates all the good times they have had together. (Rev: BL 11/15/95; SLJ 11/95)

**2106** Shannon, George. *Laughing All the Way* (PS–K). Illus. by Meg McLean. 1992, Houghton $13.95 (0-395-62473-8). 32pp. Duck is captured by Bear, who wants his feathers for a bed. (Rev: SLJ 10/92)

**2107** Sharmat, Marjorie W. *I'm Terrific* (PS–1). Illus. by Kay Chorao. 1977, Holiday LB $14.95 (0-8234-0282-7); paper $5.95 (0-8234-0955-4). 32pp. An amusing story of a bear cub who thinks he is marvelous and insists on telling everyone so.

**2108** Sharmat, Marjorie W. *Tiffany Dino Works Out* (PS–3). Illus. by Nate Evans. 1995, Simon & Schuster paper $15.00 (0-689-80309-5). 32pp. Tiffany Dino becomes upset with her weight and decides to do something about it. (Rev: BL 11/15/95; SLJ 12/95)

**2109** Sharmat, Mitchell. *Gregory, the Terrible Eater* (PS–3). Illus. by Jose Aruego and Ariane Dewey. 1980, Macmillan $15.00 (0-02-782250-8); Scholastic paper $4.99 (0-590-43350-4). 32pp. Gregory, a young goat, prefers a diet of fruit and vegetables to paper, shoes, and clothing.

**2110** Shaw, Nancy. *Sheep Take a Hike* (PS–1). Illus. by Margot Apple. 1994, Houghton $13.95 (0-395-68394-7). 32pp. When they get lost in the woods, a flock of sheep find their way home because of bits of wool left on bushes. (Rev: BL 9/15/94; HB 11–12/94; SLJ 9/94*)

**2111** Shields, Carol D. *Saturday Night at the Dinosaur Stomp* (PS–2). Illus. by Scott Nash. 1997, Candlewick $15.99 (1-56402-693-0). A group of friendly dinosaurs prepare for and later participate in a big dance called the Dinosaur Stomp. (Rev: SLJ 11/97)

**2112** Sierra, Judy. *Counting Crocodiles* (PS–1). Illus. by Will Hillenbrand. 1997, Harcourt $15.00 (0-15-200192-1). 40pp. A hungry monkey wants bananas from a neighboring island, but she is afraid that crocodiles will catch her if she tries to swim. (Rev: BL 9/1/97; SLJ 10/97)

**2113** Sierra, Judy. *The Elephant's Wrestling Match* (PS–2). Illus. by Brian Pinkney. 1992, Dutton paper $14.00 (0-525-67366-0). 32pp. A boastful elephant meets his match when he is challenged by a bat. (Rev: BCCB 2/92; BL 8/92; SLJ 9/92)

**2114** Sierra, Judy. *Good Night Dinosaurs* (PS–1). Illus. by Victoria Chess. 1996, Clarion $15.00 (0-395-65016-X). 32pp. Stylized drawings of dinosaurs portray them in humorous day-to-day activities, such as snoozing in the mud and sucking on baby bottles. (Rev: BCCB 3/96; BL 1/1–15/96; HB 7–8/96; SLJ 4/96)

**2115** Silverman, Erica. *Don't Fidget a Feather!* (PS–1). Illus. by S. D. Schindler. 1994, Macmillan paper $16.00 (0-02-782685-6). 32pp. Duck and Gander engage in contests to see who is the champion of champions. (Rev: BCCB 11/94; BL 11/15/94; SLJ 1/95*)

**2116** Silverstein, Shel. *Who Wants a Cheap Rhinoceros?* (K–2). Illus. by author. 1983, Macmillan paper $15.00 (0-02-782690-2). 56pp. All the advantages of owning a rhino.

**2117** Simont, Marc. *The Goose That Almost Got Cooked* (K–2). Illus. 1997, Scholastic $15.95 (0-590-69075-2). 40pp. A Canada goose is happy to leave the flock and join some white geese on a farm until she realizes that in this situation she might become somebody's dinner. (Rev: BL 11/1/97; SLJ 8/97*)

**2118** Siracusa, Catherine. *The Banana Split from Outer Space* (2–3). Illus. by author. Series: Hyperion Chapters. 1995, Hyperion $13.95 (0-7868-0040-2); paper $3.95 (0-7868-1062-9). 48pp. A wacky adventure that centers on a pig-operated roadside ice cream stand. (Rev: SLJ 4/96)

**2119** Slotboom, Wendy. *King Snake* (K–2). Illus. by John Manders. 1997, Houghton $14.95 (0-395-74680-9). Two mice named Henry and Tinkerton fall into the clutches of a talkative garter snake. (Rev: SLJ 5/97)

**2120** Slote, Elizabeth. *Nelly's Garden* (PS–K). Illus. 1991, Morrow LB $13.88 (0-688-10014-7). Nelly Dragon enjoys all the outdoor activities associated with each season. (Rev: SLJ 9/91)

**2121** Smith, Cara Lockhart. *Twenty-Six Rabbits Run Riot* (PS–3). Illus. 1990, Little, Brown $12.95 (0-316-80185-2). 32pp. When Mrs. Fitzwarren takes her baby rabbits for an outing, the youngest gets lost. (Rev: BL 10/1/90; SLJ 9/90)

**2122** Snape, Juliet, and Charles Snape. *Frog Odyssey* (PS–2). Illus. by authors. 1992, Simon & Schuster paper $14.00 (0-671-74741-X). Some frogs leave their polluted pond to find a new home in the city. (Rev: SLJ 7/92)

**2123** Snow, Alan. *The Truth About Cats* (K–4). Illus. 1996, Little, Brown $14.95 (0-316-80282-4). 32pp. With great daring, this book reveals that cats are really aliens from the Planet Nip. A companion to *How Dogs Really Work!* (1993). (Rev: BL 4/15/96; SLJ 3/96)

**2124** Solotareff, Gregoire. *Don't Call Me Little Bunny* (K–3). Illus. by author. 1988, Farrar $13.95 (0-374-35012-4). 32pp. Jack Carrot hates his nickname, but his size makes it stick. (Rev: BL 12/15/88; SLJ 3/89)

**2125** Soto, Gary. *Chato's Kitchen* (PS–3). Illus. by Susan Guevara. 1995, Putnam $15.95 (0-399-22658-3). 32pp. In his Los Angeles barrio home, the cat Chato extends an invitation to some mice to come to dinner. (Rev: BL 3/1/95; HB 9–10/95; SLJ 7/95*)

**2126** Speed, Toby. *Two Cool Cows* (PS–2). Illus. by Barry Root. 1995, Putnam $15.95 (0-399-22647-8). 32pp. Two adventurous cows jump to the moon, where they find many dozens of other cows enjoying themselves. (Rev: BL 6/1–15/95; SLJ 6/95)

**2127** Spohn, Kate. *Dog and Cat Make a Splash* (PS–2). Illus. by author. Series: Viking Easy-to-Read Book. 1997, Viking paper $11.99 (0-670-87178-8). 31pp. Four gentle stories about Dog and his best friend, Cat. (Rev: SLJ 6/97)

**2128** Spohn, Kate. *Ruth's Bake Shop* (K–2). Illus. 1990, Orchard LB $13.99 (0-531-08489-2). 32pp. Ruth, an octopus, spends a joyful day baking all kinds of goodies. (Rev: BL 8/90; SLJ 10/90)

**2129** Stadler, John. *Animal Cafe* (K–2). Illus. by author. 1986, Macmillan paper $3.95 (0-689-71063-1). 32pp. Maxwell wonders who is mysteriously buying from his food store. Reissue of a 1980 edition.

**2130** Stadler, John. *Hooray for Snail!* (K–2). Illus. by author. 1984, HarperCollins LB $14.89 (0-690-04413-5); paper $5.95 (0-06-443075-8). 32pp. Snail has a humorous journey around the bases in a baseball game.

**2131** Steig, William. *Doctor De Soto* (K–3). Illus. by author. 1982, Farrar $16.00 (0-374-31803-4). A mouse dentist outwits a fox.

**2132** Steig, William. *Doctor De Soto Goes to Africa* (PS–2). Illus. 1992, HarperCollins LB $14.89 (0-06-205003-6). 32pp. The mouse dentist, Dr. De Soto, travels to Africa to help an elephant with a rotten tooth. (Rev: BCCB 9/92; BL 7/92; SLJ 8/92)

**2133** Steig, William. *Farmer Palmer's Wagon Ride* (K–2). Illus. by author. 1992, Farrar paper $4.95 (0-374-42268-0). Farmer Palmer, a pig, and the hired hand, a donkey, have a disastrous ride home from the market in this engaging nonsensical bit of fun.

**2134** Steig, William. *Gorky Rises* (1–3). Illus. by author. 1986, Farrar paper $4.95 (0-374-42784-4). 32pp. A frog named Gorky concocts a formula that sends him on a magical journey.

**2135** Steig, William. *Solomon the Rusty Nail* (K–2). Illus. by author. 1985, Farrar $16.00 (0-374-37131-8); paper $5.95 (0-374-46903-2). 32pp. A rabbit's ability to change himself into a rusty nail whenever he wishes leads him to some interesting adventures and keeps him away from the prowling cat. (Rev: BCCB 3/86; BL 1/1/86; SLJ 2/86)

**2136** Steig, William. *Sylvester and the Magic Pebble* (K–3). Illus. by author. 1988, Simon & Schuster paper $5.95 (0-671-66269-4). 32pp. A donkey who collects pebbles finds a red stone that will grant wishes — and off Sylvester goes on a series of adventures. Caldecott Medal winner, 1970.

**2137** Steig, William. *Tiffky Doofky* (K–2). Illus. by author. 1978, Farrar paper $3.95 (0-374-47748-5). A canine garbage collector awaits a fortune-teller's prophecy to come true.

**2138** Steig, William. *Toby, Where Are You?* (PS). Illus. by Teryl Euvremer. 1997, HarperCollins LB $13.89 (0-06-205083-4). 32pp. A young rodent named Toby plays hide-and-seek with his parents in this clever picture book. (Rev: BL 12/15/96; SLJ 1/97*)

**2139** Stevens, Kathleen. *The Beast in the Bathtub* (PS–1). Illus. by Ray Bowler. 1985, Stevens LB $19.93 (0-91883-115-6). 32pp. Lewis claims he will be eaten if he has to take a bath, and indeed there is a big green creature in the tub, but the 2 get along just fine. (Rev: BL 12/1/85; SLJ 10/85)

**2140** Stevenson, James. *All Aboard!* (PS–3). Illus. 1995, Greenwillow LB $15.93 (0-688-12439-9). 32pp. An adventurous little mouse gets lost on his way to the 1939 World's Fair in New York. (Rev: BL 4/1/95*; HB 9–10/95; SLJ 6/95*)

**2141** Stevenson, James. *Heat Wave at Mud Flat* (K–2). Illus. 1997, Greenwillow LB $14.93 (0-688-14206-0). 32pp. During a very hot, dry period, a rainmaker visits Mud Flat and the animal inhabitants react in different ways. (Rev: BL 5/15/97; HB 7–8/97; SLJ 5/97*)

**2142** Stevenson, James. *The Worst Goes South* (K–3). Illus. 1995, Greenwillow LB $14.93 (0-688-13060-7). 32pp. The "Worst" leaves his home and travels to Florida, where he meets an equally dislikable grouch, his brother. (Rev: BL 9/1/95; SLJ 10/95)

**2143** Stickland, Paul. *One Bear, One Dog* (PS–1). Illus. 1997, Dutton paper $12.99 (0-525-45802-6). 32pp. A parade of different animals ends with the reader, because of a mirror on the last page. (Rev: BL 8/97; SLJ 9/97)

**2144** Stickland, Paul, and Henrietta Stickland. *Dinosaur Roar!* (PS–K). Illus. 1994, Dutton paper $12.99 (0-525-45276-1). 32pp. In this tale about 2 dinosaurs, several antonyms are introduced. (Rev: BL 10/1/94; SLJ 1/95)

**2145** Stimson, Joan. *Big Panda, Little Panda* (PS–1). Illus. by Meg Rutherford. 1994, Barron's paper $4.95 (0-8120-1691-2). 32pp. When a new panda arrives in the panda household, his older brother feels left out. (Rev: BL 5/1/94)

**2146** Stoeke, Janet Morgan. *A Friend for Minerva Louise* (PS–1). Illus. 1997, Dutton paper $13.99 (0-525-45869-7). 24pp. The hen Minerva is certain that her neighbors have a new bunny, but it turns out to be a baby. (Rev: BL 7/97; SLJ 11/97*)

**2147** Stoeke, Janet Morgan. *A Hat for Minerva Louise* (PS–K). Illus. 1994, Dutton paper $13.99 (0-525-45328-8). 24pp. A chicken named Minerva Louise ventures out on a winter morning, determined that she will somehow stay warm. (Rev: BL 10/15/94; SLJ 10/94*)

**2148** Stoeke, Janet Morgan. *Minerva Louise at School* (PS–1). Illus. 1996, Dutton paper $13.99 (0-525-45494-2). 24pp. A hen mistakes a school for a barn, with amusing results. (Rev: BCCB 9/96; BL 8/96; SLJ 8/96*)

**2149** Stone, Kazuko G. *Aligay Saves the Stars* (PS–1). Illus. 1991, Scholastic $13.95 (0-590-44382-8). An alligator is sent into space to retrieve the boomerang he threw too high. (Rev: SLJ 1/92)

**2150** Stow, Jenny. *Growing Pains* (PS–2). Illus. by author. 1995, BridgeWater paper $13.95 (0-8167-3500-X). A young rhinoceros, like the children of other animals he knows, is anxious to mature quickly. (Rev: SLJ 12/95)

**2151** Strasser, Todd. *Walt Disney's Lady and the Tramp* (3–5). Illus. by Franc Mateu. 1994, Disney LB $15.49 (1-56282-615-8). 96pp. An adaptation of the Disney movie about the high-class cocker spaniel and the mutt from the wrong side of town. (Rev: BL 3/15/94)

**2152** Strickland, Paul. *Dinosaur Stomp: A Monster Pop-up* (PS–K). Illus. 1996, Dutton paper $15.99 (0-525-45591-4). This pop-up book involves dancing dinosaurs. (Rev: BL 12/15/96; SLJ 2/97)

**2153** Summers, Kate. *Milly and Tilly: The Story of a Town Mouse and a Country Mouse* (PS–1). Illus. by Maggie Kneen. 1997, Dutton paper $14.99 (0-525-45801-8). 32pp. When they visit each other, the country mouse and the city mouse feel uncomfort-

able in their new surroundings. (Rev: BL 8/97; SLJ 7/97)

**2154** Sun, Chyng Feng. *Square Beak* (1–4). Illus. by Chihsien Chen. 1993, Houghton $13.95 (0-395-64567-0). 38pp. When a chick is born from a square egg and with a strangely shaped beak, she immediately becomes an outcast. (Rev: BL 4/1/93; SLJ 6/93)

**2155** Sundgaard, Arnold. *The Lamb and the Butterfly* (PS–K). Illus. by Eric Carle. 1988, Orchard LB $16.99 (0-531-08379-9). 32pp. A rhythmic story of a lamb and a butterfly who meet in a meadow. (Rev: BL 11/15/88; SLJ 1/89)

**2156** Suteyev, V. *Mushroom in the Rain* (K–2). Trans. by Mirra Ginsburg. Illus. by Jose Aruego and Ariane Dewey. 1987, Macmillan paper $5.99 (0-689-71441-6). 32pp. An ant huddled under a mushroom in the rain makes room for a variety of animals. A reissued 1974 book.

**2157** Sweeney, Joan. *Once upon a Lily Pad: Froggy Love in Monet's Garden* (PS–2). Illus. by Kathleen Fain. 1995, Chronicle $9.95 (0-8118-0868-8). 32pp. Two married frogs, Hector and Henrietta, play in Monet's lily pond at Giverny, France, and pose for the artist. (Rev: BL 1/1–15/96; SLJ 2/96)

**2158** Sykes, Julie. *Dora's Eggs* (PS). Illus. by Jane Chapman. 1997, Little Tiger $14.95 (1-888444-09-6). Dora the hen is disappointed when none of the animals pay attention to her first eggs; but when they hatch, it is a different matter. (Rev: SLJ 12/97)

**2159** Sykes, Julie. *I Don't Want to Take a Bath* (PS–1). Illus. by Tim Warnes. 1997, Little Tiger $14.95 (1-888444-20-7). 32pp. Little Tiger avoids taking a bath by running into the jungle to play with friends. (Rev: BL 12/1/97)

**2160** Sykes, Julie. *This and That* (PS). Illus. by Tanya Linch. 1996, Farrar $14.00 (0-374-37492-9). 32pp. Cat borrows objects from her farmyard friends to make a nest for her 2 newborn kittens. (Rev: BCCB 3/96; BL 5/1/96)

**2161** Szekeres, Cyndy. *Hide-and-Seek Duck* (PS). Illus. by author. Series: Golden Naptime Tales. 1991, Western $3.50 (0-307-12235-2). 18pp. Duck looks for his friend Little Bunny. (Rev: BL 12/1/85; SLJ 3/86)

**2162** Szekeres, Cyndy. *Nothing-to-Do Puppy* (PS). Illus. by author. Series: Golden Naptime Tales. 1991, Western $3.50 (0-307-12237-9). 18pp. Puppy is bored, but not after he visits his friends. (Rev: BL 12/1/85; SLJ 3/86)

**2163** Szekeres, Cyndy. *Puppy Too Small* (PS). Illus. by author. Series: Golden Naptime Tales. 1992, Western $3.50 (0-307-12201-8). 18pp. A puppy may not be big enough for some things, but he's just right for others.

**2164** Szekeres, Cyndy. *Suppertime for Frieda Fuzzy-paws* (PS). Illus. by author. Series: Golden Naptime Tales. 1991, Western $3.50 (0-307-12234-4). 18pp. A kitten can't have a cookie until she eats her supper. (Rev: BL 12/1/85; SLJ 3/86)

**2165** Szekeres, Cyndy. *Thumpity Thump Gets Dressed* (PS). Illus. by author. Series: Golden Naptime Tales. 1991, Western $4.95 (0-307-12203-4). 18pp. The weather ruins rabbit's day, but when bedtime comes his dreams let him play as he pleases.

**2166** Tafuri, Nancy. *Have You Seen My Duckling?* (PS–2). Illus. by author. 1984, Greenwillow LB $15.88 (0-688-02798-9); Morrow paper $4.95 (0-688-10994-2). 24pp. Mother Duck asks a number of animals if they have seen her missing duckling.

**2167** Takao, Yuko. *A Winter Concert* (K–2). Illus. by author. 1997, Millbrook LB $18.40 (0-7613-0301-4). As a mouse listens to a concert, his black-and-white world slowly becomes one of color. (Rev: SLJ 1/98)

**2168** Tallarico, Tony. *Find Freddie* (K–2). Illus. 1990, Troll LB $10.95 (0-8167-1955-1). In each of the picture puzzles in this book, the reader must find the central character and other objects. Also use: *Hunt for Hector; Look for Lisa;* and *Search for Sam* (all 1990). (Rev: SLJ 12/90)

**2169** Teague, Mark. *Pigsty* (PS–3). Illus. 1994, Scholastic $13.95 (0-590-45915-5). 32pp. Even messy Wendell, a pig, resents his friends creating chaos in his room. (Rev: BL 9/15/94; SLJ 10/94*)

**2170** Teckentrup, Britta. *Rumble in the Jungle* (PS–K). Illus. 1997, Viking paper $14.99 (0-670-87473-6). 32pp. Animals choose sides and engage in a wild tug-of-war in this joyous jungle tale. (Rev: BL 6/1–15/97)

**2171** Testa, Fulvio. *Time to Get Out* (PS–K). Illus. by author. 1993, Tambourine LB $13.93 (0-688-12908-9). A cumulative story about a boy and several animals that join forces to track down a loud noise they hear on a tropical island. (Rev: SLJ 10/93)

**2172** Tews, Susan. *Lizard Sees the World* (K–3). Illus. by George Crespo. 1997, Clarion $15.00 (0-395-72662-X). 32pp. Not content to sit around catching flies, Lizard sets out to see the world. (Rev: BL 11/1/97; SLJ 9/97)

**2173** Thaler, Mike. *What Could a Hippopotamus Be?* (PS–K). Illus. by Robert Grossman. 1990, Simon & Schuster paper $13.95 (0-671-70847-3). 32pp. A young hippo tries a variety of careers, including fireman and sailor, without success. (Rev: BL 9/15/90)

**2174** Tharlet, Eve. *Little Pig, Bigger Trouble* (K–2). Illus. 1992, Picture Book paper $14.95 (0-88708-237-8). Pierre and his friend, the pig Henri, share

adventures when they deliver a blackberry cake. (Rev: SLJ 8/92)

**2175** Tompert, Ann. *Just a Little Bit* (PS–K). Illus. by Lynn Munsinger. 1993, Houghton $14.95 (0-395-51527-0). 32pp. In this cumulative tale, several animals try to help Mouse balance the scales when he tries to seesaw with Elephant. (Rev: BL 11/1/93; HB 9–10/93; SLJ 12/93)

**2176** Tompert, Ann. *Little Fox Goes to the End of the World* (K–2). Illus. by John Wallner. 1984, Scholastic paper $2.95 (0-590-40439-3). 40pp. A fox cub pretends that she travels afar and outwits other animals.

**2177** Tompert, Ann. *Nothing Sticks Like a Shadow* (PS–3). Illus. by Lynn Munsinger. 1988, Houghton paper $6.95 (0-395-47950-9). 32pp. Rabbit tries to get rid of his shadow.

**2178** Torres, Daniel. *Tom* (K–3). Trans. by Julie Simmons-Lynch. Illus. 1996, Viking paper $15.99 (0-670-86665-2). 64pp. Tom, a friendly dinosaur, tries to make an impression on jaded New Yorkers. (Rev: BCCB 3/96; BL 3/15/96; SLJ 8/96)

**2179** Trivizas, Eugene. *The Three Little Wolves and the Big Bad Pig* (K–4). Illus. by Helen Oxenbury. 1993, Macmillan $17.00 (0-689-50569-8). 32pp. In this role-reversal story, 3 wolves are menaced by a big, bad pig who knocks their house down with a sledgehammer when huffing and puffing won't do the trick. (Rev: BCCB 9/93; BL 9/1/93; SLJ 12/93*)

**2180** Tryon, Leslie. *Albert's Field Trip* (PS–2). Illus. 1993, Atheneum $16.00 (0-689-31821-9). 32pp. Gary the skunk reports for the school paper what happened during the field trip his fellow animals take to an apple farm. (Rev: BCCB 10/93; BL 9/15/93; HB 9–10/93; SLJ 10/93)

**2181** Tryon, Leslie. *Albert's Play* (K–3). Illus. by author. 1992, Macmillan $13.95 (0-689-31525-2). Albert and other animal children put on a production of the Owl and the Pussycat. (Rev: BCCB 3/92; SLJ 5/92)

**2182** Turnbull, Ann. *Too Tired* (K–2). Illus. by Emma C. Clark. 1994, Harcourt $13.95 (0-15-200549-8). 32pp. There is a crisis on the ark when Noah discovers that the sloths are too tired to board. (Rev: BL 3/15/94; SLJ 4/94)

**2183** Turner, Charles. *The Turtle and the Moon* (PS–K). Illus. by Melissa Mathis. 1991, Dutton paper $14.99 (0-525-44659-1). 32pp. A lonely turtle finds a new playmate: the moon. (Rev: BL 5/15/91; SLJ 8/91)

**2184** Udry, Janice May. *Thump and Plunk* (PS–2). Illus. by Ann Schweninger. 1981, HarperCollins LB $13.89 (0-06-026150-1). 32pp. Two mouse children quarrel over their dolls.

**2185** Ungerer, Tomi. *Crictor* (PS–2). Illus. by author. 1958, HarperCollins paper $5.95 (0-06-443044-8). 32pp. A boa constrictor becomes the hero of a small French town after he captures a burglar.

**2186** Van Allsburg, Chris. *Two Bad Ants* (1–4). Illus. by author. 1988, Houghton $17.95 (0-395-48668-8). 32pp. The story of 2 adventuresome ants. (Rev: BCCB 12/88; BL 10/1/88; SLJ 11/88)

**2187** Van Laan, Nancy. *Possum Come a-Knockin'* (PS–2). Illus. by George Booth. 1990, Knopf LB $14.99 (0-394-92206-9). 28pp. In this cumulative story, many humans and animals ignore the possum when he comes knocking at their door. (Rev: BL 4/15/90; HB 7–8/90*; SLJ 7/90)

**2188** Van Leeuwen, Jean. *The Great Summer Camp Catastrophe* (4–6). Illus. by Diane De Groat. 1992, Dial paper $12.89 (0-8037-1107-7). 192pp. Marvin the mouse and rodent buddies Raymond and Fats end up at summer camp after hiding in a box that is shipped to Vermont. (Rev: BL 5/1/92; SLJ 4/92)

**2189** Van Leeuwen, Jean. *Tales of Oliver Pig* (K–2). Illus. by Arnold Lobel. 1979, Dial paper $4.95 (0-8037-8737-5). 64pp. Five charming stories about Oliver's adventures. Three sequels are: *More Tales of Oliver Pig* (1981); *Amanda Pig and Her Big Brother Oliver* (1982); *Tales of Amanda Pig* (1983).

**2190** Van Pallandt, Nicolas. *Troll's Search for Summer* (PS–2). Illus. 1994, Farrar $15.00 (0-374-36560-1). 32pp. Tired of winter, Troll sets out to find summer and instead meets some bizarre creatures. (Rev: BL 2/1/95; SLJ 12/94)

**2191** Varley, Susan. *Badger's Parting Gifts* (1–4). Illus. by author. 1984, Morrow paper $5.95 (0-688-11518-7). 32pp. After initial grief, the animals retain happy memories of their dead friend, Badger.

**2192** Vaughan, Marcia. *Snap!* (PS–2). Illus. by Sascha Hutchinson. 1996, Scholastic $14.95 (0-590-60377-9). 32pp. A young kangaroo plays with other Australian animals until a crocodile spoils their fun. (Rev: BL 7/96; SLJ 4/96)

**2193** Vaughan, Marcia. *Wombat Stew* (PS–1). Illus. by Pamela Lofts. 1986, Silver Burdett $8.95 (0-382-09211-2). 32pp. A fun introduction to Australia's animals that begins when a sly dingo catches a wombat and decides to make "wombat stew." (Rev: BL 7/86; SLJ 1/87)

**2194** Velthuijs, Max. *Crocodile's Masterpiece* (K–3). Illus. 1992, Farrar $14.00 (0-374-31658-9). 32pp. Though Crocodile gives Elephant only a blank canvas as a painting, Elephant is able to imagine some of the most beautiful pictures ever. (Rev: BL 3/15/92; SLJ 8/92)

**2195** Velthuijs, Max. *Elephant and Crocodile* (PS–K). Trans. by Anthea Bell. Illus. 1990, Farrar $12.95 (0-374-37675-1). 32pp. Elephant complains about the

noise that Crocodile makes when practicing the violin. (Rev: BL 12/15/90; HB 11–12/90; SLJ 2/91)

**2196** Velthuijs, Max. *Frog and the Birdsong* (PS–K). Illus. 1991, Farrar $13.95 (0-374-32467-0). 32pp. Frog is saddened by the death of a blackbird, but is consoled when he hears another blackbird singing. (Rev: BL 4/15/91; SLJ 10/91)

**2197** Velthuijs, Max. *Frog in Love* (PS–3). Trans. by Anthea Bell. Illus. 1988, Farrar $13.00 (0-374-32465-4); paper $4.95 (0-374-42470-5). 32pp. Frog sets out to impress Duck, with whom he has fallen in love. (Rev: BL 12/15/90; SLJ 12/89)

**2198** Velthuijs, Max. *Frog Is Frightened* (PS–2). Illus. 1995, Morrow $15.00 (0-688-14203-6). 32pp. Frog becomes frightened when he hears strange scratching sounds in his house. (Rev: BL 3/1/95; SLJ 10/95)

**2199** Verboven, Agnes. *Ducks Like to Swim* (PS). Illus. by Anne Westerduin. 1997, Orchard $13.95 (0-531-30054-4). 32pp. Mother Duck quacks for rain so that her babies can go swimming. (Rev: BL 9/1/97; SLJ 9/97)

**2200** Vincent, Gabrielle. *Ernest and Celestine at the Circus* (K–2). Illus. 1989, Greenwillow LB $15.93 (0-688-08685-3). 32pp. The beloved bear and mouse score a hit when they appear at the circus. (Rev: BL 8/89; SLJ 10/89)

**2201** Waber, Bernard. *An Anteater Named Arthur* (PS–2). Illus. by author. 1967, Houghton $14.95 (0-395-20336-8); paper $5.95 (0-395-25936-3). 48pp. A mother anteater despairs of her son Arthur, who has problems very much like those of a young boy.

**2202** Waber, Bernard. *Bearsie Bear and the Surprise Sleepover Party* (PS–K). Illus. 1997, Houghton $15.00 (0-395-86450-X). 40pp. A number of animals are given shelter for the night; but when the porcupine tries to bed down, everybody leaves. (Rev: BL 10/1/97; HB 9–10/97; SLJ 10/97)

**2203** Waber, Bernard. *Bernard* (K–3). Illus. by author. 1986, Houghton paper $7.95 (0-395-42648-0). 48pp. When his owners quarrel over his custody, Bernard leaves home.

**2204** Waber, Bernard. *Funny, Funny Lyle* (PS–1). Illus. by author. 1987, Houghton $16.00 (0-395-43619-2); paper $5.95 (0-395-60287-4). 40pp. Felicity, mother of Lyle the crocodile, is picked up for shoplifting, but finds her true calling as a nurse. (Rev: BL 8/87; SLJ 12/87)

**2205** Waber, Bernard. *The House on East 88th Street* (K–2). Illus. by author. 1973, Houghton $14.95 (0-395-18157-7); paper $5.95 (0-395-19970-0). 48pp. Adventures of a pet crocodile (Lyle) who lives with a family in a New York City brownstone. Other books about Lyle by the same author and publisher: *Lyle, Lyle, Crocodile* (1965); *Lyle and the Birthday*

*Party* (1966); *Lyle Finds His Mother* (1974); *Lovable Lyle* (1977).

**2206** Waber, Bernard. *I Was All Thumbs* (K–2). Illus. by author. 1975, Houghton paper $6.95 (0-395-53969-2). 48pp. The amusing adventures of Legs, a young octopus, who goes from a laboratory tank to sea, with its attendant dangers.

**2207** Waber, Bernard. *Ira Says Goodbye* (K–2). Illus. 1988, Houghton $15.00 (0-395-48315-8); paper $5.95 (0-395-58413-2). 40pp. Ira is sad because his best friend is moving away. (Rev: BCCB 10/88; BL 9/1/88; SLJ 9/88)

**2208** Waber, Bernard. *A Lion Named Shirley Williamson* (PS–2). Illus. 1996, Houghton $15.95 (0-395-80979-7). 40pp. The other lions in the zoo are jealous of the special attention given to the lion named Shirley Williamson. (Rev: BL 9/1/96*; SLJ 12/96*)

**2209** Waber, Bernard. *Lyle at the Office* (PS–3). Illus. 1994, Houghton $14.95 (0-395-70563-0). 46pp. Lyle becomes very popular when he spends a day helping out in Mr. Primm's office. (Rev: BL 6/1–15/94; SLJ 9/94*)

**2210** Waber, Bernard. *The Snake: A Very Long Love Story* (PS). Illus. by author. 1978, Houghton LB $7.95 (0-685-02310-9). A long trip brings the snake back home again.

**2211** Waber, Bernard. *You Look Ridiculous, Said the Rhinoceros to the Hippopotamus* (K–2). Illus. by author. 1973, Houghton $17.95 (0-395-07156-9); paper $5.95 (0-395-28007-9). 32pp. The hippopotamus is discontented with her shape and imagines herself with many of the appendages of neighboring animals.

**2212** Waddell, Martin. *Farmer Duck* (PS–1). Illus. by Helen Oxenbury. 1992, Candlewick $16.99 (1-56402-009-6). 40pp. Farmer Duck does all the work while the farmer stays in bed; then the farm animals decide to take over. (Rev: BCCB 6/92; BL 4/1/92*; SLJ 5/92)

**2213** Waddell, Martin. *The Happy Hedgehog Band* (PS–1). Illus. by Jill Barton. 1992, Candlewick $15.99 (1-56402-011-8). 32pp. As a member of the Hedgehog Band, Harry teaches other animals how to make music. (Rev: BL 5/15/92; SLJ 6/92)

**2214** Waddell, Martin. *Harriet and the Crocodiles* (3–4). Illus. by Mark Burgess. 1984, Little, Brown $11.95 (0-316-91622-6). Harriet loses her pet crocodile and sets out to find him.

**2215** Waddell, Martin. *Let's Go Home, Little Bear* (PS–K). Illus. by Barbara Firth. 1993, Candlewick $15.99 (1-56402-131-9). 32pp. Little Bear is frightened of the noises he hears in the woods, so Big Bear carries him home. (Rev: BL 5/1/93; HB 3–4/93; SLJ 3/93)

**2216** Waddell, Martin. *Little Mo* (PS–2). Illus. by Jill Barton. 1993, Candlewick $14.95 (1-56402-211-0). A small polar bear tries sliding on the ice but has problems keeping her balance. (Rev: SLJ 1/94)

**2217** Waddell, Martin. *Owl Babies* (PS–1). Illus. by Patrick Benson. 1992, Candlewick $15.99 (1-56402-101-7). 32pp. Three small owls, left alone by their mother, wonder if she is coming back. (Rev: BL 12/1/92; HB 3–4/93; SLJ 12/92)

**2218** Waddell, Martin. *Small Bear Lost* (PS–K). Illus. by Virginia Austin. 1996, Candlewick $15.99 (1-56402-871-2). 32pp. Because he is still a youngster, Small Bear must wait for hours at a crossing until someone accompanies him across the street. (Rev: BL 9/15/96; SLJ 9/96)

**2219** Waddell, Martin. *You and Me, Little Bear* (PS–K). Illus. by Barbara Firth. 1996, Candlewick $15.99 (1-56402-879-8). 32pp. Little Bear doesn't realize how tiring household chores can be when he volunteers to help Big Bear. (Rev: BL 10/1/96; SLJ 11/96)

**2220** Wagner, Jenny. *Motor Bill and the Lovely Caroline* (K–3). Illus. by Ron Brooks. 1995, Ticknor $14.95 (0-395-71547-4). 32pp. Bill, a donkey, is happy when Caroline, a goat, agrees to go riding with him. (Rev: BL 1/15/95; SLJ 4/95)

**2221** Wahl, Jan. *"I Remember!" Cried Grandma Pinky* (PS–1). Illus. by Arden Johnson. 1994, Troll paper $14.95 (0-8167-3456-9). 32pp. In this story about polar bears, Grandma is beginning to forget things except incidents that happened years ago. (Rev: BL 12/1/94; SLJ 12/94)

**2222** Wallace, Nancy E. *Snow* (PS–1). Illus. 1995, Artists & Writers Guild $11.95 (0-307-17562-6). 32pp. A father rabbit remembers the thrills and joys that the first snow of winter brings. (Rev: BL 11/15/95; SLJ 12/95)

**2223** Walsh, Ellen S. *Hop Jump* (PS–1). Illus. 1993, Harcourt $13.95 (0-15-292871-5). 32pp. Most of the other frogs enjoy hopping, but Betsy prefers to dance. (Rev: BL 11/1/93; HB 11–12/93; SLJ 10/93)

**2224** Walsh, Ellen S. *Mouse Paint* (PS–K). Illus. 1989, Harcourt $11.95 (0-15-256025-4). 32pp. Three mice paint themselves as camouflage and find they like their new look. (Rev: BL 5/15/89; HB 7–8/89; SLJ 9/89)

**2225** Walsh, Ellen S. *Pip's Magic* (PS–3). Illus. 1994, Harcourt $13.95 (0-15-292850-2). 32pp. By traveling through shadowy woods and a black night to visit a wizard for help, Pip, a salamander, cures himself of his fear of the dark. (Rev: BCCB 9/94; BL 10/15/94; SLJ 11/94)

**2226** Walsh, Ellen S. *Samantha* (PS–1). Illus. 1996, Harcourt $14.00 (0-15-252264-6). 32pp. Samantha, a mouse, doesn't want to become too dependent on the protection that her fairy godmother gives her. (Rev: BCCB 6/96; BL 2/15/96; SLJ 5/96)

**2227** Walsh, Ellen S. *You Silly Goose* (PS–1). Illus. by author. 1992, Harcourt $13.95 (0-15-299865-9). Lulu, a goose, mistakes George, a mouse, for the fox that has been reported in the neighborhood. (Rev: HB 1–2/93; SLJ 10/92)

**2228** Walters, Catherine. *When Will It Be Spring?* (PS–2). Illus. 1998, Dutton $14.99 (0-525-45881-6). 32pp. Alfie is a little bear who is so excited about the thoughts of the coming spring that he can't hibernate. (Rev: BL 1/1–15/98; SLJ 4/98)

**2229** Walton, Rick. *Once There Was a Bull . . . (frog)* (K–3). Illus. by Greg Hally. 1995, Gibbs Smith $15.95 (0-87905-652-5). 32pp. This clever story about a bullfrog searching for his lost hop uses the splitting of compound words to create different perceptions. (Rev: BL 12/15/95)

**2230** Waterton, Betty. *A Salmon for Simon* (K–3). Illus. by Ann Blades. 1991, Salem paper $4.95 (0-88899-107-X). 32pp. A small Canadian Indian has a great adventure with a live salmon.

**2231** Watkins, Will. *Sid Seal, Houseman* (3–5). Illus. by Toni Goffe. 1989, Orchard LB $13.99 (0-531-08384-5). 89pp. A proper Bostonian pig family finds a very active seal in their bathtub. (Rev: BCCB 7–8/89; BL 7/89; SLJ 9/89)

**2232** Watson, Wendy. *Tales for a Winter's Eve* (2–3). Illus. by author. 1988, Farrar $13.00 (0-374-37373-6); paper $4.95 (0-374-47419-2). 32pp. Freddie Fox breaks his skis, and family and friends cheer him with stories. (Rev: BCCB 11/88; BL 11/15/88; SLJ 2/89)

**2233** Watts, Bernadette. *Harvey Hare: Postman Extraordinaire* (PS–K). Illus. 1997, North-South LB $15.88 (1-55858-688-1). 32pp. Because Harvey Hare is such a devoted mail carrier, his friends give him a present to solve his problems with the weather. (Rev: BL 3/15/97; SLJ 3/97)

**2234** Weiss, Leatie. *My Teacher Sleeps in School* (K–2). Illus. by Ellen Weiss. 1985, Puffin paper $4.99 (0-14-050559-8). 32pp. Because their teacher is always there, 2 elephant children believe their teacher lives in school.

**2235** Wells, Rosemary. *Bunny Cakes* (PS–1). Illus. 1997, Dial paper $14.89 (0-8037-2144-7). 32pp. Max the bunny creates havoc in the kitchen when his baby sister begins making an angel cake for their grandmother. (Rev: BCCB 3/97; BL 1/1–15/97*; SLJ 1/97*)

**2236** Wells, Rosemary. *Bunny Money* (PS–1). Illus. 1997, Dial paper $14.89 (0-8037-2147-1). 32pp. Before bunnies Max and Ruby can buy a birthday present for Grandma, they spend their money in all

sorts of unforeseen ways. (Rev: BL 7/97*; SLJ 7/97*)

**2237** Wells, Rosemary. *Edward in Deep Water* (PS–K). Illus. Series: Edward the Unready. 1995, Dial paper $7.99 (0-8037-1882-9). 32pp. Edward, a little bear, is not prepared to attend his first pool party. He faces other crises in both *Edward Unready for School* and *Edward's Overwhelming Overnight* (both 1995). (Rev: BCCB 11/95; BL 9/1/95*; HB 11–12/95; SLJ 11/95)

**2238** Wells, Rosemary. *First Tomato* (PS–3). Illus. Series: Voyage to the Bunny Planet. 1992, Dial paper $12.89 (0-8037-1175-1). 32pp. When a bunny child is having a bad day, the child imagines escaping through a trip to the Bunny Planet. Two others in this series are: *The Island Light* and *Moss Pillows* (both 1992). (Rev: BCCB 12/92*; BL 12/1/92; HB 1–2/93*; SLJ 12/92)

**2239** Wells, Rosemary. *Fritz and the Mess Fairy* (K–2). Illus. 1991, Dial LB $13.89 (0-8037-0983-8). 32pp. A skunk named Fritz is such a slob that the Mess Fairy comes to give him some of his own medicine. (Rev: BCCB 11/91; BL 10/1/91; SLJ 1/92)

**2240** Wells, Rosemary. *Hazel's Amazing Mother* (PS–1). Illus. by author. 1985, Dial $3.95 (0-8037-0703-7). 32pp. Hazel the badger has her doll stolen by rowdies, but her mother comes to the rescue, routs the brats, and saves the doll. (Rev: BL 11/1/85; HB 11–12/85; SLJ 11/85)

**2241** Wells, Rosemary. *Max and Ruby's First Greek Myth: Pandora's Box* (K–2). Illus. 1993, Dial LB $11.89 (0-8037-1525-0). 32pp. When Max, a rabbit, enters his sister's room against her warning, she tells him the story of Pandora's box. (Rev: BL 7/93)

**2242** Wells, Rosemary. *Noisy Nora* (PS–1). Illus. 1997, Dial paper $15.89 (0-8037-1836-5). 32pp. Mouse Nora discovers that doing nothing is an excellent way of getting attention. (Rev: BL 8/97; SLJ 5/97*)

**2243** Wells, Rosemary. *Read to Your Bunny* (PS). Illus. by author. 1998, Scholastic $7.95 (0-590-30284-1). Using a cast of bunnies, the author shows that reading can be fun anywhere. (Rev: SLJ 3/98)

**2244** Wells, Rosemary. *Shy Charles* (PS–2). Illus. 1988, Dial LB $11.89 (0-8037-0564-6); Puffin paper $4.99 (0-14-054537-9). 32pp. Charles is too shy a mouse to speak to his shadow, but he finds his voice when his sitter needs help. (Rev: BCCB 9/88; BL 10/1/88; SLJ 10/88)

**2245** Wells, Rosemary. *Stanley and Rhoda* (PS–K). Illus. by author. 1978, Dial paper $4.95 (0-8037-7995-X). 40pp. Stanley copes with the problem of getting along with a difficult younger sister.

**2246** Weninger, Brigitte. *What Have You Done, Davy?* (PS–2). Trans. by Rosemary Lanning. Illus.

by Eve Tharlet. 1996, North-South LB $15.88 (1-55858-582-6). 32pp. Davy, a young rabbit, is having a terrible day and leaves a trail of destruction wherever he goes. (Rev: BL 4/15/96; SLJ 7/96)

**2247** Weninger, Brigitte. *What's the Matter, Davy?* (PS–1). Illus. by Eve Tharlet. 1998, North-South $15.95 (1-55858-900-7). 32pp. Davy, a little rabbit, is distraught when he loses his pet toy rabbit. (Rev: BL 3/15/98)

**2248** Weninger, Brigitte. *Where Have You Gone, Davy?* (PS–2). Trans. by Rosemary Lanning. Illus. by Eve Tharlet. 1996, North-South LB $15.88 (1-55858-665-2). 24pp. When bunny Davy is wrongfully accused of breaking a bowl, he decides to run away. (Rev: BL 12/1/96; SLJ 1/97)

**2249** Weninger, Brigitte. *Will You Mind the Baby, Davy?* (K–3). Illus. by Eve Tharlet. 1997, North-South LB $15.88 (1-55858-732-2). 32pp. Davy the bunny finds that his baby sister needs a strong older brother to help and protect her. (Rev: BL 5/15/97; SLJ 7/97)

**2250** West, Colin. *"Buzz, Buzz, Buzz," Went the Bumblebee* (PS–1). Illus. by author. 1996, Candlewick $9.99 (1-56402-681-7). A simple repetitive story featuring silly animals and a bee that journeys from one setting to another. (Rev: SLJ 4/96)

**2251** Weston, Martha. *Tuck in the Pool* (PS–1). Illus. 1995, Clarion $12.95 (0-395-65479-3). 32pp. Tuck, a little pig, doesn't enjoy being in the water and refuses to get dunked. (Rev: BCCB 11/95; BL 11/15/95; SLJ 2/96)

**2252** Whittle, Emily. *Sailor Cats* (PS–1). Illus. by Jeri Burdick. 1993, Simon & Schuster $14.00 (0-671-79933-9). 28pp. Two adventurous cats, Ping and Pong, are rescued at sea by friendly dolphins. (Rev: BL 9/1/93; SLJ 3/94)

**2253** Wickstrom, Lois. *Oliver: A Story About Adoption* (PS–3). Illus. by Priscilla Marden. 1991, Our Child Pr. $14.95 (0-9611872-5-5). When lizard Oliver receives a reprimand from his adoptive father, he thinks his real parents would behave differently. (Rev: SLJ 2/92)

**2254** Wiesner, David. *Tuesday* (PS–2). Illus. 1991, Houghton $15.95 (0-395-55113-7). 32pp. Frogs have a wonderful time on Tuesday. Will the pigs have as great a time one week later? Caldecott Medal winner, 1992. (Rev: BCCB 5/91; BL 5/1/91; SLJ 5/91*)

**2255** Wikler, Linda. *Alfonse, Where Are You?* (PS–1). Illus. by author. 1996, Crown LB $15.99 (0-517-70046-8). During a game of hide-and-seek, Alfonse the goose becomes so alarmed at not finding his friend the chicken that he sends out a search party. (Rev: SLJ 6/96*)

**2256** Wild, Margaret. *Old Pig* (PS–2). Illus. by Ron Brooks. 1996, Dial paper $14.99 (0-8037-1917-5).

40pp. A young pig faces the inevitable death of her beloved grandfather, Old Pig. (Rev: BCCB 3/96; BL 5/15/96*; SLJ 4/96)

**2257** Wildsmith, Brian. *Daisy* (K–2). Illus. by author. 1984, Pantheon LB $11.99 (0-394-95975-2). 48pp. The story of how fame in Hollywood changes a simple cow named Daisy.

**2258** Wildsmith, Brian. *The Hunter and His Dog* (K–2). Illus. by author. 1979, Oxford paper $11.95 (0-19-272147-X). 32pp. A hunter's dog protects a flock of wild ducks.

**2259** Wilhelm, Hans. *More Bunny Trouble* (PS–1). Illus. by author. 1989, Scholastic paper $4.99 (0-590-41590-5). 32pp. Ralph is tapped to baby-sit his bunny sister, but he lets her get out of sight and lost. (Rev: BL 3/1/89; SLJ 5/89)

**2260** Wilhelm, Hans. *The Royal Raven* (PS–3). Illus. 1996, Scholastic $15.95 (0-590-54337-7). 32pp. A raven named Crawford tries to become special by changing his appearance. (Rev: BL 3/15/96; SLJ 7/96)

**2261** Wilhelm, Hans. *Tyrone the Horrible* (PS–2). Illus. by author. 1988, Scholastic paper $4.99 (0-590-41472-0). 32pp. Tyrone the terrible bully dinosaur is making Boland's prehistoric life a misery. (Rev: BL 9/1/88; SLJ 12/88)

**2262** Willis, Jeanne. *The Pet Person* (K–3). Illus. by Tony Ross. 1996, Dial paper $13.99 (0-8037-2077-7). Rex is a dog who wants to adopt a person, but all of the members of his family have valid objections, like "It will ruin the furniture." (Rev: SLJ 1/97)

**2263** Wilson, Sarah. *Good Zap, Little Grog* (PS–2). Illus. by Susan Meddaugh. 1995, Candlewick $16.99 (1-56402-286-2). 32pp. In a strange new world, the reader is introduced to such creatures as the Ooglet, Froozel, and the Glipneep. (Rev: BCCB 12/95; BL 10/15/95; SLJ 1/96)

**2264** Wilson, Sarah. *Muskrat, Muskrat, Eat Your Peas!* (PS–1). Illus. by author. 1992, Simon & Schuster paper $3.95 (0-671-77822-6). 32pp. The smallest muskrat is the only family member who doesn't like peas. (Rev: BL 6/15/89)

**2265** Winch, Madeleine. *Come by Chance* (PS–2). Illus. 1990, Crown LB $11.99 (0-517-57667-8). 32pp. When bad weather comes, many different animals seek shelter in the house Bertha has renovated. (Rev: BL 5/15/90; HB 9–10/90; SLJ 7/90)

**2266** Winthrop, Elizabeth. *Bear and Mrs. Duck* (PS–K). Illus. by Patience Brewster. 1988, Holiday LB $15.95 (0-8234-0687-3). 32pp. Mrs. Duck comes to bear-sit when Teddy Bear has the sniffles. (Rev: BCCB 10/88; BL 9/15/88; HB 9–10/88)

**2267** Winthrop, Elizabeth. *Bear and Roly-Poly* (K–3). Illus. by Patience Brewster. 1996, Holiday LB

$15.95 (0-8234-1197-4). 32pp. Nora brings Bear a baby sister in the form of Roly-Poly panda. (Rev: BL 3/1/96; SLJ 5/96)

**2268** Wolf, Jake. *What You Do Is Easy, What I Do Is Hard* (2–3). Illus. by Anna Dewdney. 1996, Greenwillow $15.00 (0-688-13440-8). 24pp. Squirrel thinks his life is tougher than that of other animals, but in time he finds he is wrong. (Rev: BL 12/15/96; SLJ 12/96)

**2269** Wolkstein, Diane. *The Banza: A Haitian Story* (PS–3). Illus. by Marc Brown. 1984, Puffin paper $4.95 (0-8037-0058-X). 32pp. A tiger and a goat decide to be friends.

**2270** Wood, Audrey. *Little Penguin's Tale* (PS–2). Illus. 1989, Harcourt $13.95 (0-15-246475-1). 32pp. Little Penguin's escapades result in his being swallowed by a whale. (Rev: BL 11/15/89)

**2271** Wood, Audrey. *Oh My Baby Bear!* (PS–1). Illus. 1990, Harcourt $13.95 (0-15-257698-3). 32pp. Baby Bear gradually learns to take care of himself. (Rev: BL 11/1/90; SLJ 11/90)

**2272** Wood, Audrey. *Silly Sally* (PS). Illus. 1992, Harcourt $16.00 (0-15-274428-2). 32pp. This delightful nonsense book tells of Silly Sally and her trip into town walking backwards and upside down. (Rev: BCCB 6/92; BL 3/15/92*; SLJ 4/92)

**2273** Wood, Douglas. *Old Turtle* (K–4). Illus. by Cheng-Khee Chee. 1991, Pfeifer $17.95 (0-938586-48-3). 48pp. Wise Old Turtle asks people to save the world by experiencing "God in one another . . . and in the beauty of all the earth." (Rev: BL 8/92; SLJ 6/92)

**2274** Wormell, Mary. *Hilda Hen's Scary Night* (PS–K). Illus. 1996, Harcourt $14.00 (0-15-200990-6). 32pp. In the morning, Hilda Hen sets out to find the creatures that had frightened her the night before. (Rev: BL 9/15/96; SLJ 10/96)

**2275** Wormell, Mary. *Hilda Hen's Search* (PS–1). Illus. 1994, Harcourt $13.95 (0-15-200069-0). 32pp. Hilda Hen wanders the barnyard looking for a suitable place to lay her eggs. (Rev: BL 12/1/94; SLJ 11/94)

**2276** Wyllie, Stephen. *A Flea in the Ear* (PS–1). Illus. by Ken Brown. 1996, Dutton paper $14.99 (0-525-45648-1). 32pp. A dog who has been outwitted by a fox hopes to turn the tables. (Rev: BCCB 4/96; BL 6/1–15/96; SLJ 7/96)

**2277** Yee, Patrick. *Winter Rabbit* (PS). Illus. by author. 1994, Viking $13.99 (0-670-85353-6). A bear and a squirrel build a huge snow bunny before they begin their winter sleep. (Rev: SLJ 7/94)

**2278** Yee, Wong H. *Big Black Bear* (PS–K). Illus. 1993, Houghton $14.95 (0-395-66359-8). 32pp. An ill-mannered young bear who bullies a little girl gets

a severe bawling out from his mother. (Rev: BL 11/1/93; SLJ 10/93)

**2279** Yee, Wong H. *Mrs. Brown Went to Town* (PS–2). Illus. 1996, Houghton $14.95 (0-395-75282-5). 32pp. A group of domestic animals move into Mrs. Brown's house when the woman is sent to the hospital. (Rev: BL 4/1/96; SLJ 7/96)

**2280** Yee, Wong H. *The Officer's Ball* (PS–2). Illus. 1997, Houghton $14.95 (0-395-81182-1). 32pp. While carrying out his duties as a police officer, Sergeant Hippo practices his newly learned dance steps for the big officers ball. (Rev: BL 3/15/97; SLJ 5/97)

**2281** Yolen, Jane. *Picnic with Piggins* (K–3). Illus. by Jane Dyer. 1988, Harcourt paper $7.00 (0-15-261535-0). 32pp. Piggins, the pig butler, solves the mystery of the missing Rexy, one of the children of the house. Also use the first story about the Reynard butler, *Piggins* (1987); and *Piggins and the Royal Wedding* (1989). (Rev: BCCB 5/88; BL 4/1/88; HB 7–8/88)

**2282** Yorinks, Arthur. *Hey, Al* (2–4). Illus. 1986, Farrar $16.00 (0-374-33060-3); paper $4.95 (0-374-42985-5). 32pp. Eddie the dog wants to change his life, but when a bird takes him and Al the janitor to a bird-inhabited island, Eddie isn't quite so sure. Caldecott Medal winner, 1987. (Rev: BL 1/1/87; SLJ 3/87)

**2283** Young, Ed. *Cat and Rat: The Legend of the Chinese Zodiac* (1–4). Illus. 1995, Holt $15.95 (0-8050-2977-X). 32pp. The story of the 12 signs of the Chinese zodiac and how each animal achieved its place. (Rev: BCCB 11/95; BL 11/1/95*; SLJ 12/95) [133.5]

**2284** Zalben, Jane Breskin. *Miss Violet's Shining Day* (PS–1). Illus. 1995, Boyds Mills $14.95 (1-56397-234-4). 26pp. A timid bunny named Miss Violet blooms after she learns to play a trombone. (Rev: BL 8/95; SLJ 4/95)

**2285** Zalben, Jane Breskin. *Pearl Plants a Tree* (PS–2). Illus. 1995, Simon & Schuster paper $14.00 (0-689-80034-7). 32pp. A little lamb learns from her grandfather and plants an apple seed that later sprouts. (Rev: BL 11/15/95; SLJ 1/96)

**2286** Zelinsky, Paul O. *The Lion and the Stoat* (1–3). Illus. by author. 1984, Greenwillow LB $11.93 (0-688-02563-3). 40pp. A lion and a weasel vie for artistic supremacy.

**2287** Ziefert, Harriet. *Pete's Chicken* (PS–K). Illus. by Laura Rader. 1994, Morrow LB $14.93 (0-688-13257-X). 40pp. Even though his teacher and fellow students dislike Pete Rabbit's portrait of a chicken, Pete thinks it is a work of art. (Rev: BL 9/15/94; SLJ 9/94)

**2288** Ziefert, Harriet. *Pushkin Meets the Bundle* (PS–1). Illus. by Donald Saaf. 1998, Simon & Schuster $16.00 (0-689-81413-5). 40pp. The life of the dog Pushkin changes with the arrival of a new baby, also known as "the bundle." (Rev: BL 2/1/98)

**2289** Ziefert, Harriet. *Wee G* (PS–K). Illus. by Donald Saaf. 1997, Simon & Schuster $15.00 (0-689-81064-4). 32pp. In double-page spreads, this simple picture book tells how a little cat named Wee G. gets lost on the way home. (Rev: BL 4/15/97; SLJ 6/97)

**2290** Zolotow, Charlotte. *Mr. Rabbit and the Lovely Present* (PS–3). Illus. by Maurice Sendak. 1977, HarperCollins paper $4.95 (0-06-443020-0). 32pp. A little girl meets Mr. Rabbit, and together they find the perfect birthday gift for her mother.

## Realistic Stories

### ADVENTURE STORIES

**2291** Ackerman, Karen. *Bingleman's Midway* (1–4). Illus. by Barry Moser. 1995, Boyds Mills $14.95 (1-56397-366-9). 32pp. A boy becomes so intrigued with a traveling midway that he decides to run away from home and join it. (Rev: BL 10/15/95; SLJ 12/95)

**2292** Ahlberg, Allan. *It Was a Dark and Stormy Night* (K–3). Illus. by Janet Ahlberg. 1994, Viking paper $13.99 (0-670-85159-0). 32pp. A young captive of robbers escapes in the confusion caused by their acting out a story that he has told them. (Rev: BCCB 7–8/94; BL 5/1/94)

**2293** Alfredson, Hans. *The Night the Moon Came By* (K–3). Trans. from Swedish by Tiina Nunnally. Illus. by Per Ahlin. 1993, R&S $13.00 (91-29-62246-8). When 2 young girls hear strange sounds coming from their attic at night, they decide to investigate. (Rev: SLJ 3/94)

**2294** Aller, Susan Bivin. *Emma and the Night Dogs* (K–3). Illus. by Marni Backer. 1997, Albert Whitman LB $14.95 (0-8075-1993-6). 32pp. Emma is able to locate a boy who is lost in the woods. (Rev: BCCB 7–8/97; BL 9/15/97; SLJ 5/97)

**2295** Blades, Ann. *Back to the Cabin* (K–3). Illus. 1997, Orca $13.95 (1-55143-049-5); paper $6.95 (1-55143-051-7). 32pp. Activities like swimming and fishing take the place of TV watching when 2 brothers spend a summer in a cabin by a lake. (Rev: BL 6/1–15/97)

**2296** Bodkin, Odds. *The Banshee Train* (1–4). Illus. by Ted Rose. 1995, Clarion $14.95 (0-395-69426-4). 32pp. Engineer Mercer and his crew engage in a life-or-death race with a ghost train. (Rev: BCCB 4/95; BL 6/1–15/95; SLJ 8/95)

**2297** Brillhart, Julie. *When Daddy Took Us Camping* (PS–K). Illus. 1997, Albert Whitman LB $13.95 (0-8075-8879-2). 24pp. Two children learn about the outdoors when they go on a camping trip with their father. (Rev: BL 5/1/97; SLJ 5/97)

**2298** Brown, Don. *Alice Ramsey's Grand Adventure* (K–3). Illus. 1997, Houghton $15.00 (0-395-70127-9). 32pp. The story of Alice Ramsey's cross-country automobile trip in 1909. (Rev: BL 9/15/97; HB 11–12/97; SLJ 9/97*) [917.3]

**2299** Bunting, Eve. *Trouble on the T-Ball Team* (PS–2). Illus. by Irene Trivas. 1997, Clarion $13.95 (0-395-66060-2). 32pp. Members of Linda's T-ball team are mysteriously losing things. (Rev: BCCB 4/97; BL 3/1/97; SLJ 5/97)

**2300** Burningham, John. *Mr. Gumpy's Motor Car* (K–3). Illus. by author. 1976, HarperCollins LB $16.89 (0-690-00799-X). 48pp. Mr. Gumpy takes his daughter and an assortment of animals for a ride in the country in his old-fashioned touring car. Companion to: *Mr. Gumpy's Outing* (Holt 1995).

**2301** Caines, Jeannette. *Just Us Women* (PS–2). Illus. by Pat Cummings. 1984, HarperCollins paper $4.95 (0-06-443056-1). 32pp. A little black girl is looking forward to a car ride she is going to take with her aunt.

**2302** Carrick, Carol. *Left Behind* (PS–2). Illus. by Donald Carrick. 1988, Houghton $14.52 (0-89919-535-0). 32pp. On a class visit to the city aquarium, Christopher gets left behind at the subway stop. (Rev: BCCB 9/88; BL 9/15/88; HB 9–10/88)

**2303** Carrick, Carol. *Sleep Out* (K–2). Illus. by Donald Carrick. 1982, Houghton paper $6.95 (0-89919-083-9). 32pp. Christopher has an unsettling experience when he spends his first night outdoors in his sleeping bag. Another title by the same author: *Ben and the Porcupine* (1985).

**2304** Carter, David A. *In a Dark, Dark Wood: An Old Tale with a New Twist* (PS–1). 1991, Simon & Schuster $10.95 (0-671-74134-9). 24pp. A pop-up, oversized book with a spooky ghost at the end. (Rev: BCCB 12/92; BL 9/15/91)

**2305** Cleary, Beverly. *The Real Hole* (PS–1). Illus. by DyAnne DiSalvo-Ryan. 1986, Morrow LB $11.95 (0-688-05851-5); paper $4.95 (0-688-14741-0). 32pp. Four-year-old Jimmy digs a big hole and puts it to good use. A reissue of the 1960 edition.

**2306** Cohen, Miriam. *Lost in the Museum* (K–1). Illus. by Lillian Hoban. 1995, Bantam paper $4.99 (0-440-41095-9). Jim and his friends wander away from the group and get lost in the American Museum of Natural History.

**2307** Conrad, Pam. *The Lost Sailor* (2–4). 1995, Smithmark $4.98 (0-8317-2998-8). 32pp. A sea captain, washed ashore on an island, is finally rescued. (Rev: BCCB 10/92*; BL 9/1/92; HB 3–4/93; SLJ 9/92)

**2308** Crews, Donald. *Sail Away* (PS–3). Illus. 1995, Greenwillow LB $15.93 (0-688-11054-1). 32pp. A family weathers a storm in their sailboat. (Rev: BCCB 4/95; BL 4/1/95; HB 9–10/95; SLJ 5/95*)

**2309** Enderle, Judith R., and Stephanie G. Tessler. *Nell Nugget and the Cow Caper* (K–2). Illus. by Paul Yalowitz. 1996, Simon & Schuster paper $15.00 (0-689-80502-0). In this humorous Western tale, Nell Nugget sets out to find the culprit who has rustled her favorite cow, Goldie. (Rev: BCCB 5/96; HB 9–10/96; SLJ 7/96)

**2310** English, Karen. *Big Wind Coming!* (PS–2). Illus. by Cedric Lucas. 1996, Albert Whitman LB $14.95 (0-8075-0726-1). 32pp. A severe windstorm and its effects on an African American family as seen through the eye of the young daughter. (Rev: BCCB 1/97; BL 10/15/96; SLJ 11/96)

**2311** Feiffer, Jules. *I Lost My Bear* (PS–2). Illus. by author. 1998, Morrow LB $15.93 (0-688-15148-5). A young girl plays detective when she discovers that her favorite toy is missing. (Rev: SLJ 3/98)

**2312** Fox, Mem. *Tough Boris* (PS–3). Illus. by Kathryn Brown. 1994, Harcourt $15.00 (0-15-289612-0). 32pp. Boris is a rough and tough pirate, but when his parrot dies, he cries. (Rev: BL 3/1/94; HB 5–6/94; SLJ 5/94)

**2313** Franklin, Kristine L. *The Shepherd Boy* (PS–1). Illus. by Jill Kastner. 1994, Atheneum $14.95 (0-689-31809-X). 40pp. Ben, a young Navajo boy, and his dog search the mesa for a lost sheep. (Rev: BCCB 6/94; BL 7/94; SLJ 6/94)

**2314** Galef, David. *Tracks* (PS–2). Illus. by Tedd Arnold. 1996, Morrow LB $15.93 (0-688-13344-4). 32pp. Albert's job as a foreman of a track-laying crew gets botched when his glasses break. (Rev: BL 5/1/96; SLJ 4/96)

**2315** Gerrard, Roy. *Jocasta Carr: Movie Star* (K–3). Illus. 1992, Farrar $15.00 (0-374-33654-7). 32pp. A movie star flies around the world to rescue her sheepdog from a group of criminals. (Rev: BL 11/1/92; SLJ 11/92*)

**2316** Gerrard, Roy. *Rosie and the Rustlers* (K–3). Illus. 1989, Farrar $15.00 (0-374-36345-5). 32pp. Rosie sets out to catch the rustlers who have stolen her cattle. (Rev: BCCB 11/89; BL 11/15/89; HB 3–4/90; SLJ 2/90)

**2317** Gerrard, Roy. *Wagons West!* (K–2). Illus. 1996, Farrar $15.00 (0-374-38249-2). 32pp. A rollicking tall tale about Buckskin Dan, leader of a wagon train headed west in the 1840s. (Rev: BCCB 2/96; BL 3/15/96; SLJ 3/96*)

**2318** Gibbons, Faye. *Night in the Barn* (PS–1). Illus. by Erick Ingraham. 1995, Morrow LB $14.93 (0-688-13327-4). 32pp. A small boy is frightened when he spends a night in a barn with his brother and 2 cousins. (Rev: BL 9/1/95; HB 11–12/95; SLJ 1/96)

**2319** Gould, Deborah. *Camping in the Temple of the Sun* (PS–2). Illus. by Diane Paterson. 1992, Macmillan $13.95 (0-02-736355-4). 32pp. A family's first camping trip begins poorly, but when the sun comes out, things improve. (Rev: BL 2/15/92; SLJ 6/92)

**2320** Harrison, Troon. *Lavender Moon* (K–2). Illus. by Eugenie Fernandes. 1997, Annick LB $16.95 (1-55037-455-9); paper $6.95 (1-55037-454-0). Lavender Moon, a cafe owner, changes places with a bus driver and sets out to see the world. (Rev: SLJ 1/98)

**2321** Haynes, Max. *Dinosaur Island* (PS–2). Illus. 1991, Lothrop $13.95 (0-688-10329-4). 32pp. Maddy and Bing travel in a land where dinosaurs are hidden in the pictures. (Rev: BL 10/1/91; SLJ 1/92)

**2322** Hesse, Karen. *Lester's Dog* (PS–3). Illus. by Nancy Carpenter. 1993, Crown LB $16.99 (0-517-58358-5). 32pp. A boy and his hearing-impaired friend rescue an abandoned kitten. (Rev: BL 11/1/93; SLJ 10/93)

**2323** Hindley, Judy. *Into the Jungle* (PS–K). Illus. by Melanie Epps. 1994, Candlewick $14.95 (1-56402-423-7). 32pp. A boy and a girl take a walk through a jungle filled with animal life they can't see. (Rev: BL 8/94; SLJ 10/94)

**2324** Hopkinson, Deborah. *Birdie's Lighthouse* (PS–4). Illus. by Kimberly B. Root. 1997, Simon & Schuster $15.00 (0-689-81052-0). 32pp. A lighthouse story set in the 1850s about a girl who keeps the lamps burning when her father falls ill during a storm. (Rev: BL 6/1–15/97; HB 7–8/97; SLJ 6/97)

**2325** Jam, Teddy. *The Fishing Summer* (K–3). Illus. by Ange Zhang. 1997, Douglas & McIntyre $12.95 (0-88899-285-8). 32pp. A boys stows away on his uncle's fishing boat and works hard to learn the family trade. (Rev: BL 9/15/97; SLJ 2/98)

**2326** Jezek, Alisandra. *Miloli's Orchids* (K–3). Illus. by Yoshi Miyake. 1991, Raintree Steck-Vaughn LB $22.83 (0-8172-2784-9). 31pp. Written by a youngster, this story set in Hawaii tells of a young girl's attempts to save orchids from a volcano. (Rev: SLJ 6/91)

**2327** Johnson, Neil. *Fire and Silk: Flying in a Hot Air Balloon* (K–3). Illus. 1991, Little, Brown $15.95 (0-316-46959-9). 32pp. The facts and feel of ballooning in a nonfiction book that reads like an adventure story. (Rev: BCCB 4/91; BL 5/1/91; HB 7–8/91; SLJ 7/91) [797.5]

**2328** Johnson, Scott. *I Can't Wait Until I'm Old Enough to Hunt with Dad* (1–3). Illus. by Karen Johnson. 1995, Deer Pond $14.95 (1-887251-56-1). 32pp. A young boy accompanies his father on a bow-and-arrow deer hunt. (Rev: BL 2/1/96)

**2329** Keats, Ezra Jack. *Maggie and the Pirate* (1–3). Illus. by author. 1987, Scholastic paper $4.95 (0-590-44852-8). 32pp. Maggie tries to find the kidnapper of her pet cricket. A reissue of the 1979 edition.

**2330** Kimmel, Eric A. *Four Dollars and Fifty Cents* (2–4). Illus. by Glen Rounds. 1990, Holiday LB $16.95 (0-8234-0817-5). 32pp. To get out of paying a bad debt, cowboy Shorty Long pretends to be dead. (Rev: BL 9/15/90; HB 1–2/91*; SLJ 11/90)

**2331** Kinsey-Warnock, Natalie. *The Summer of Stanley* (PS–3). Illus. by Donald Gates. 1997, Dutton paper $14.99 (0-525-65177-2). 32pp. Stanley, the family goat, changes from pest to hero when he helps save a boy who has fallen into a river. (Rev: BL 7/97; SLJ 6/97)

**2332** Kotzwinkle, William. *The Million-Dollar Bear* (K–2). Illus. by David Catrow. 1995, Knopf LB $17.99 (0-679-95295-0). The first-ever teddy bear, who belongs to 2 millionaires, is accidentally found by a little boy who takes him home. (Rev: SLJ 1/96)

**2333** Kovacs, Deborah. *Moonlight on the River* (PS–3). Illus. by William Shattuck. 1996, Puffin paper $5.99 (0-14-054513-1). 32pp. Two brothers share a secret moonlit adventure on the river. (Rev: BL 5/1/93; SLJ 8/93)

**2334** Lasky, Kathryn. *Marven of the Great North Woods* (K–4). Illus. by Kevin Hawkes. 1997, Harcourt $16.00 (0-15-200104-2). 48pp. During the 1918 flu epidemic, 10-year-old Marven is sent to a logging camp in Minnesota, where he has to assume many adult responsibilities. (Rev: BL 12/15/97; HB 11–12/97; SLJ 10/97)

**2335** Lester, Alison. *Yikes! In Seven Wild Adventures, Who Would You Be?* (K–2). Illus. by author. 1995, Houghton $14.95 (0-395-71252-1). A reader-participation picture book in which 7 wild adventures are described. (Rev: BCCB 12/95; SLJ 11/95)

**2336** Lewis, Kim. *First Snow* (PS–K). Illus. 1993, Candlewick $14.95 (1-56402-194-7). 32pp. When Sara and her mother go to feed the sheep on the hill, there is a heavy snowfall and they have difficulty getting home. (Rev: BL 9/15/93)

**2337** Mahy, Margaret. *Beaten by a Balloon* (PS–3). Illus. by Jonathan Allen. 1998, Viking paper $15.99 (0-670-87697-6). Instead of the sword he wants for his birthday, Sam gets a balloon, a chocolate cake, and a sunflower in this tale about catching a bank robber. (Rev: SLJ 3/98)

**2338** Martin, Bill, Jr., and John Archambault. *The Ghost-Eye Tree* (K–3). Illus. by Ted Rand. 1985, Holt $13.95 (0-8050-0208-1); paper $5.95 (0-8050-0947-7). 32pp. A brother and sister are sent to fetch a pail of milk on a spooky night past the Ghost-Eye Tree. (Rev: BL 12/15/85; HB 1–2/86; SLJ 2/86)

**2339** Martin, Bill, Jr., and John Archambault. *White Dynamite and Curly Kidd* (1–3). Illus. by Ted Rand. 1986, Holt $12.95 (0-8050-0658-3); paper $5.95 (0-8050-1018-1). 48pp. A nervous fan carries on a conversation with a bull rider who is about to break out of the chute on White Dynamite. (Rev: BL 7/86; SLJ 4/86)

**2340** Martin, Bill, Jr., and Michael Sampson. *Swish!* (K–3). Illus. by Michael Chesworth. 1997, Holt $14.95 (0-8050-4498-1). 32pp. The excitement and energy of a girl's basketball game are captured in this picture book. (Rev: BL 12/15/97; SLJ 11/97)

**2341** Mott, Evelyn Clarke. *Balloon Ride* (K–3). Illus. 1991, Walker LB $14.85 (0-8027-8126-8). Megan takes her first trip in a hot-air balloon in this nonfiction account with photos by the author. (Rev: SLJ 10/91) [797.5]

**2342** Olson, Arielle North. *The Lighthouse Keeper's Daughter* (K–3). Illus. by Elaine Wentworth. 1987, Little, Brown $16.95 (0-316-65053-6). Young Miranda keeps the lamps in the lighthouse burning when her father is away, in this fictionalized account of a true story. (Rev: BCCB 11/87; BL 12/1/87; SLJ 10/87)

**2343** Paraskevas, Betty. *Monster Beach* (PS–2). Illus. by Michael Paraskevas. 1995, Harcourt $15.00 (0-15-292882-0). 32pp. A child thinks that the inflatable toy he sees on the beach is really a sea monster. (Rev: BL 6/1–15/95; SLJ 6/95)

**2344** Prater, John. *The Greatest Show on Earth* (PS–1). Illus. 1995, Candlewick $14.95 (1-56402-563-2). 32pp. Harry feels inept compared to other members of his family, each a circus star, but he finally finds his own niche. (Rev: BCCB 10/95; BL 10/15/95; SLJ 10/95)

**2345** Purdy, Carol. *Iva Dunnit and the Big Wind* (PS–3). Illus. by Steven Kellogg. 1988, Dial paper $4.99 (0-8037-0493-3). 32pp. Iva battles a tornado on the prairie and nearly loses until her 6 children come to the rescue. (Rev: BCCB 2/86; BL 11/1/85; SLJ 11/85)

**2346** Rockwell, Anne. *I Fly* (PS–2). Illus. by Annette Cable. 1997, Crown LB $17.99 (0-517-59684-9). 32pp. A young boy recounts his first airplane trip without his parents. (Rev: BL 8/97; SLJ 7/97)

**2347** Rosen, Michael J. *We're Going on a Bear Hunt* (PS–2). Illus. by Helen Oxenbury. 1989, Macmillan $17.00 (0-689-50476-4). 40pp. The storytelling favorite is re-created with expansive pictures that capture the enthusiasm of the story. (Rev: BCCB 9/89; BL 8/89*; HB 11–12/89*; SLJ 8/89*)

**2348** Roth, Susan L. *Creak, Thump, Bonk! A Very Spooky Mystery* (PS–K). Illus. 1995, Simon & Schuster $13.00 (0-689-80290-0). 34pp. Using only 45 words, the author tells the story of 3 boys who investigate strange nighttime noises. (Rev: BL 1/1–15/96; SLJ 12/95)

**2349** Rylant, Cynthia. *Tulip Sees America* (PS–3). Illus. by Lisa Desimini. 1998, Scholastic $16.95 (0-590-84744-9). 32pp. A young man and his dog travel across the United States and find a place by the sea in Oregon where they want to stay. (Rev: BL 3/15/98; SLJ 4/98)

**2350** Sampson, Michael. *The Football That Won . . .* (PS–2). Illus. by Ted Rand. Series: Bill Martin Books. 1996, Holt $14.95 (0-8050-3504-4). A cumulative romp that features players and spectators at a Super Bowl game between the Dallas Cowboys and the Kansas City Chiefs. (Rev: SLJ 10/96)

**2351** Schwartz, David M. *Supergrandpa* (1–3). Illus. by Bert Dodson. 1991, Lothrop LB $16.93 (0-688-09899-1). 32pp. This story of a grandfather who won the longest bike race in Sweden is based on fact. (Rev: BL 3/1/91; SLJ 6/91)

**2352** Scott, Ann H. *Cowboy Country* (1–3). Illus. by Ted Lewin. 1993, Clarion $14.95 (0-395-57561-3). 40pp. A hardworking cowhand takes a young boy on an overnight trip to show him what life on the range really is. (Rev: BCCB 11/93; BL 9/1/93; HB 11–12/93; SLJ 9/93*)

**2353** Seibert, Patricia. *Mush! Across Alaska in the World's Longest Sled-Dog Race* (2–4). Illus. 1992, Houghton paper $5.70 (0-395-64537-9). 32pp. Focusing on the work dogs of the 1,000-plus-mile Iditarod race from Anchorage to Nome. (Rev: BL 9/15/92; SLJ 11/92) [798.8]

**2354** Seymour, Tres. *We Played Marbles* (K–3). Illus. by Dan Andreasen. 1998, Orchard LB $16.99 (0-531-33074-5). 32pp. The Civil War battle that took place at Fort Craig, Kentucky, unfolds as 2 boys play an innocent game on its site. (Rev: BL 2/15/98; SLJ 3/98)

**2355** Slawski, Wolfgang. *Captain Jonathan Sails the Sea* (K–2). Trans. by Rosemary Lanning. Illus. by author. 1997, North-South LB $15.88 (1-55858-814-0). On his tugboat, Captain Jonathan gains self-esteem when he saves the cabin boy from drowning. (Rev: SLJ 1/98)

**2356** Steig, William. *Brave Irene* (K–2). Illus. by author. 1986, Farrar $17.00 (0-374-30947-7). 32pp. The incredible adventures of Irene, who sets out in a snowstorm to deliver the duchess's new dress for the ball. (Rev: BCCB 12/86; BL 11/1/86; HB 11–12/86)

**2357** Steiner, Barbara. *Desert Trip* (PS–3). Illus. by Ronald Himler. 1996, Sierra Club $16.95 (0-87156-581-1). 30pp. A young girl tells about an exciting overnight backpacking trek in a desert canyon taken by her and her mother. (Rev: BL 4/15/96; SLJ 6/96) [508]

**2358** Stevenson, James. *"Could Be Worse!"* (K–3). Illus. by author. 1977, Morrow paper $4.95 (0-688-07035-3). 32pp. Grandpa's response to minor catastrophes is always the same.

**2359** Stevenson, James. *Sam the Zamboni Man* (PS–2). Illus. by Harvey Stevenson. 1998, Greenwillow LB $14.93 (0-688-14485-3). 32pp. Grandfather, who operates the Zamboni that smooths the ice at the hockey stadium, invites young Matt to go to a real hockey game. (Rev: BL 2/1/98; SLJ 3/98)

**2360** Sullivan, Silky. *Grandpa Was a Cowboy* (K–3). Illus. by Bert Dodson. 1996, Orchard LB $16.99 (0-531-08861-8). 32pp. A young orphan is intrigued by the tales his grandfather spins about his career as a cowboy. (Rev: BL 4/1/96; SLJ 4/96)

**2361** Supraner, Robyn. *Sam Sunday and the Mystery at Ocean Beach* (1–3). Illus. by Will Hillenbrand. 1996, Viking paper $14.99 (0-670-84797-6). 32pp. Detective Sam Sunday spends a most unusual birthday. (Rev: BCCB 9/96; BL 8/96; SLJ 10/96)

**2362** Taylor, Mark. *Henry the Explorer* (K–2). Illus. by Graham Booth. 1988, Little, Brown paper $5.95 (0-316-83384-3). 48pp. Henry leaves home on an exploring expedition but finds at nightfall that he is hopelessly lost.

**2363** Teague, Mark. *How I Spent My Summer Vacation* (K–2). Illus. 1995, Crown $16.00 (0-517-59998-8). 32pp. Wallace surprises his teacher when he tells his class about the wild adventures he had out West during his summer vacation. (Rev: BL 9/1/95; SLJ 10/95)

**2364** Thomassie, Tynia. *Feliciana Feydra LeRoux: A Cajun Tall Tale* (1–3). Illus. by Cat B. Smith. 1995, Little, Brown $14.95 (0-316-84125-0). 32pp. A young Cajun girl joins the rest of her family in an old-fashioned alligator hunt. (Rev: BCCB 5/95; BL 4/1/95; HB 9–10/95; SLJ 4/95*)

**2365** Tucker, Kathy. *Do Pirates Take Baths?* (PS–2). Illus. by Nadine Bernard Westcott. 1994, Albert Whitman LB $15.95 (0-8075-1696-1). 32pp. A fanciful, humorous account that purports to be an exposé of how pirates really lived. (Rev: BCCB 10/94; BL 2/15/95; SLJ 1/95)

**2366** Van Allsburg, Chris. *The Garden of Abdul Gasazi* (K–3). Illus. by author. 1979, Houghton $17.95 (0-395-27804-X). 32pp. Young Alan wanders into the garden of a retired magician with unexpected results.

**2367** Wallace, Ian. *Morgan the Magnificent* (K–3). Illus. by author. 1988, Macmillan LB $13.95 (0-689-50441-1). 32pp. Morgan, who longs to be a high-wire acrobat, finds herself on the wire above the crowd — and scared to death. (Rev: BCCB 6/88; BL 3/15/88)

**2368** Wallace, Ian. *A Winter's Tale* (K–3). Illus. 1997, Douglas & McIntyre $15.95 (0-88899-286-6). 32pp. A gentle outdoor adventure in which Abigail is taken camping by her father and brother to celebrate her ninth birthday. (Rev: BL 10/15/97; SLJ 12/97)

**2369** Ward, Lynd. *The Biggest Bear* (K–3). Illus. by author. 1952, Houghton $16.00 (0-395-14806-5); paper $5.95 (0-395-15024-8). 88pp. Johnny wanted a bearskin on his barn so he went looking for the biggest bear. Caldecott Medal winner, 1953.

**2370** Weller, Frances W. *Madaket Millie* (2–4). Illus. by Marcia Sewall. 1997, Putnam $15.95 (0-399-22785-7). 32pp. A fictionalized account of the woman who was a legend on Nantucket because she patrolled the beaches helping people in trouble at sea. (Rev: BCCB 4/97; BL 3/15/97; SLJ 4/97)

**2371** Wiesner, David. *Hurricane* (1–3). Illus. 1990, Houghton $16.00 (0-395-54382-7). 32pp. Two boys take refuge in their hideout in a tree during a hurricane watch. (Rev: BCCB 11/90; BL 12/15/90; HB 1–2/91; SLJ 10/90*)

**2372** Williams, Vera B. *Three Days on a River in a Red Canoe* (K–3). Illus. by author. 1981, Greenwillow LB $15.93 (0-688-84307-7); Morrow paper $5.95 (0-688-04072-1). 32pp. A little girl describes a canoe trip with her cousins and their mother.

**2373** Wolff, Ashley. *Stella and Roy* (PS). Illus. 1993, Dutton paper $13.99 (0-525-45081-5). 32pp. Instead of the hare and the tortoise, this is the story of a race between 2 youngsters riding very different bicycles. (Rev: BCCB 7–8/93; BL 6/1–15/93)

## COMMUNITY AND EVERYDAY LIFE

**2374** Ackerman, Karen. *This Old House* (PS–2). Illus. by Sylvie Wickstrom. 1992, Macmillan LB $14.95 (0-689-31741-7). 40pp. People move out, but an owl sleeps in the rafters, rabbits nibble, and mice scamper about. (Rev: BL 10/15/92; SLJ 3/93)

**2375** Adams, Barbara J. *The Go-Around Dollar* (2–4). Illus. by Joyce A. Zarins. 1992, Macmillan LB $15.00 (0-02-700031-1). 32pp. The dollar is introduced within the framework of a story and the look of a picture book. (Rev: BCCB 2/92; BL 2/15/92; SLJ 5/92) [332.4]

**2376** Adorjan, Carol. *I Can! Can You?* (PS–K). Illus. by Miriam Nerlove. 1990, Whitman LB $12.95 (0-8075-3491-9). 24pp. A little girl tells about the skills she has mastered. (Rev: BL 12/15/90; SLJ 2/91)

**2377** Agell, Charlotte. *Dancing Feet* (PS–K). Illus. 1994, Harcourt $13.95 (0-15-200444-0). 36pp. In this joyous picture book, the various parts of the body are celebrated. (Rev: BL 7/94; SLJ 5/94)

**2378** Alexander, Martha. *How My Library Grew, by Dinah* (PS–K). Illus. by author. 1983, H.W. Wilson $18.00 (0-8242-0679-7). 32pp. Dinah and her teddy bear watch a library being built across the street.

**2379** Aliki. *Communication* (PS–4). Illus. 1993, Greenwillow LB $13.93 (0-688-11248-X). 32pp. This is a cleverly composed picture book that introduces ways by which we communicate with one another with emphasis placed on talking and listening. (Rev: BCCB 5/93; BL 4/15/93*; HB 5–6/93; SLJ 4/93) [302.2]

**2380** Aliki. *Hello! Good-bye!* (PS–2). Illus. 1996, Greenwillow LB $14.93 (0-688-14334-2). 32pp. The many ways of saying "hello" and "good-bye" around the world. (Rev: BCCB 12/96; BL 7/96; SLJ 9/96)

**2381** Aliki. *Manners* (K–3). Illus. 1990, Greenwillow LB $15.93 (0-688-09199-7). 32pp. Cartoon-style characters help make manners accessible to young readers. (Rev: BL 10/1/90; SLJ 11/90*) [395]

**2382** Allen, Thomas B. *On Granddaddy's Farm* (PS–2). Illus. 1989, Knopf LB $14.99 (0-394-99613-5). 40pp. Tom and his cousins spend their summers on Grandfather's Tennessee farm. (Rev: BCCB 1/90; BL 10/1/89; SLJ 2/90)

**2383** Anderson, Janet S. *Sunflower Sal* (PS–2). Illus. by Elizabeth Johns. 1997, Albert Whitman LB $15.95 (0-8075-7662-X). 32pp. A young girl plants sunflowers around her farm so that the rows will look like the stitches in a huge quilt. (Rev: BL 10/1/97; SLJ 9/97)

**2384** Anholt, Catherine, and Laurence Anholt. *Bear and Baby* (PS). Illus. 1993, Candlewick $5.95 (1-56402-235-8). 24pp. For the very young, this is the story of a child and her big protective teddy bear. Also use *Toddlers* (1993). (Rev: BL 11/1/93; SLJ 1/94)

**2385** Anholt, Catherine, and Laurence Anholt. *What I Like* (PS). Illus. 1998, Candlewick $5.99 (0-7636-0585-9). 32pp. Six children tell about the things they like and dislike. (Rev: BL 9/1/91; SLJ 12/91)

**2386** Anno, Mitsumasa. *All in a Day* (K–5). Illus. 1990, Putnam $15.99 (0-399-61292-0). 28pp. Includes the activities of children in 8 parts of the world. A reissue.

**2387** Antle, Nancy. *Staying Cool* (PS–3). Illus. by E. B. Lewis. 1997, Dial LB $14.99 (0-8037-1876-4). 32pp. Every day after school, Curtis goes to his grandfather's small gym because he hopes one day to become a famous boxer. (Rev: BL 6/1–15/97; SLJ 8/97)

**2388** Antoine, Héloïse. *Curious Kids Go to Preschool: Another Big Book of Words* (PS). Illus. by Ingrid Godon. 1996, Peachtree $13.95 (1-56145-129-0). An introduction to preschool experiences through defining such words as *school bus*, *backpack*, and *lunch box*. (Rev: SLJ 11/96)

**2389** Appelt, Kathi. *Watermelon Day* (PS–3). Illus. by Dale Gottlieb. 1996, Holt $14.95 (0-8050-2304-6). Young Jesse grows impatient waiting for her watermelon to grow sufficiently so that it can be eaten when her pappy declares it is a watermelon day. (Rev: BCCB 1/96; SLJ 6/96)

**2390** Asbury, Kelly. *Bonnie's Blue House* (PS). Illus. 1997, Holt $7.95 (0-8050-4022-6). 32pp. The color blue is explored in this book about Bonnie, her family, and their home. Two other titles in this series are *Rusty's Red Vacation* and *Yoland's Yellow School* (both 1997). (Rev: BL 3/1/97; SLJ 6/97)

**2391** *Baby's World: A First Picture Catalog* (PS). Illus. by Stephen Shott. 1990, Dutton paper $14.99 (0-525-44617-6). 48pp. In this picture book, a baby's toys, body parts, and everyday objects are pictured. (Rev: BL 1/1/91*; SLJ 3/91)

**2392** Baer, Edith. *This Is the Way We Eat Our Lunch: A Book About Children Around the World* (PS–3). Illus. by Steve Bjorkman. 1995, Scholastic $14.95 (0-590-46887-1). 32pp. A visit to lunchtime in 9 states, 2 Canadian provinces, and 11 other countries, with accompanying recipes and food facts. (Rev: BCCB 9/95; BL 9/15/95; SLJ 9/95)

**2393** Baer, Gene. *Thump, Thump, Rat-a-Tat-Tat* (PS–K). Illus. by Lois Ehlert. 1991, HarperCollins paper $4.95 (0-064-43265-3). 32pp. Re-creates the sights and sounds of a marching band. (Rev: BCCB 2/90; BL 11/1/89*; HB 9–10/89*; SLJ 1/90)

**2394** Ballard, Robin. *Good-bye, House* (PS–K). Illus. 1994, Greenwillow LB $13.93 (0-688-12526-3). 24pp. Before she moves, a little girl says good-bye to each room in her old home. (Rev: BL 3/15/94; HB 7–8/94; SLJ 6/94)

**2395** Bang, Molly. *Yellow Ball* (PS–1). Illus. 1991, Morrow LB $15.93 (0-688-06315-2). 24pp. The yellow ball over the sea on the jacket becomes the focus of a game of catch. (Rev: BCCB 4/91; BL 3/1/91*; SLJ 5/91)

**2396** Barber, Barbara E. *Allie's Basketball Dream* (PS–3). Illus. by Darryl Ligasan. 1996, Lee & Low $14.95 (1-880000-38-5). 32pp. When she receives her first basketball, Allie perseveres until she is able to shoot a basket. (Rev: BCCB 2/97; BL 1/1–15/97; SLJ 11/96)

**2397** Barber, Barbara E. *Saturday at The New You* (PS–3). Illus. by Anna Rich. 1994, Lee & Low $14.95 (1-880000-06-7). 32pp. Shauna, an African American girl, has fun on Saturdays helping at her mother's beauty shop. (Rev: BCCB 12/94; BL 12/1/94; SLJ 1/95)

**2398** Barton, Byron. *Building a House* (PS–2). Illus. by author. 1981, Greenwillow LB $16.93 (0-688-84291-7); Morrow paper $4.95 (0-688-09356-6).

32pp. The stages of building a house are simply presented.

**2399** Bartone, Elisa. *American Too* (PS–3). Illus. by Ted Lewin. 1996, Lothrop LB $15.93 (0-688-13279-0). 40pp. An Italian American girl dresses as the Statue of Liberty for the Festival of San Gennaro in New York City. (Rev: BCCB 12/96; BL 8/96; SLJ 12/96)

**2400** Bates, Artie Ann. *Ragsale* (PS–2). Illus. by Jeff Chapman-Crane. 1995, Houghton $14.95 (0-395-70030-2). 32pp. In an Appalachian setting, a family has fun searching for bargains at a tag sale. (Rev: BL 3/1/95; HB 9–10/95; SLJ 4/95)

**2401** Bauch, Patricia L. *Dance, Tanya* (PS–2). Illus. by Satomi Ichikawa. 1989, Putnam $15.95 (0-399-21521-2). 32pp. Tanya's mother says she's too young for ballet lessons, but Tanya proves her wrong. (Rev: BL 9/1/89; SLJ 10/89)

**2402** Baylor, Byrd. *The Best Town in the World* (2–4). Illus. by Ronald Himler. 1983, Macmillan $14.95 (0-684-18035-9); paper $3.95 (0-689-71086-0). A description of life in a small Texas town back when Father was a child.

**2403** Bennett, William J., ed. *The Children's Book of Virtues* (PS–3). Illus. by Michael Hague. 1995, Simon & Schuster $19.50 (0-684-81353-X). 111pp. Stories and poems and fables illustrate 10 virtues in this collection based on the concepts used in the adult *Book of Virtues*. (Rev: BL 1/1–15/96) [808.8]

**2404** Bernhard, Emery. *The Way of the Willow Branch* (PS–2). Illus. by Durga Bernhard. 1996, Harcourt $15.00 (0-15-200844-6). 32pp. A broken willow branch floats downstream and is finally found by a child. (Rev: BL 4/1/96; HB 7–8/96; SLJ 5/96)

**2405** Berry, Holly. *Busy Lizzie* (PS–1). Illus. 1994, North-South LB $14.88 (1-55858-324-6). 32pp. Lizzie is active all day long in this account of an energetic youngster others will want to copy. (Rev: BL 11/1/94; SLJ 11/94)

**2406** Best, Cari. *Red Light, Green Light, Mama and Me* (PS–2). Illus. by Niki Daly. 1995, Orchard LB $16.99 (0-531-08752-2). 32pp. Lizzie spends an exciting day with her mother, who is a children's librarian in a big downtown library. (Rev: BCCB 9/95; BL 9/1/95; SLJ 10/95)

**2407** Birdseye, Tom. *Airmail to the Moon* (K–2). Illus. by Stephen Gammell. 1988, Holiday LB $15.95 (0-8234-0683-0); paper $6.95 (0-8234-0754-3). 32pp. Motor-mouth Ora Mae vows to "send to the moon" the one who stole her tooth. (Rev: BL 3/15/88; HB 5–6/88; SLJ 5/88)

**2408** Blackstone, Stella. *Baby Rock, Baby Roll* (PS–1). Illus. by Denise Fraifeld and Fernando Azevedo. 1997, Holiday LB $13.95 (0-8234-1311-X). 32pp. Three children from different races bounce through a day's activities. (Rev: BL 9/1/97; SLJ 10/97)

**2409** Blos, Joan W. *Old Henry* (PS–1). Illus. by Stephen Gammell. 1987, Morrow $16.00 (0-688-06399-3). 32pp. A rhyming story about Henry, who moves into a house that has been vacant for a long time. (Rev: BCCB 5/87; BL 4/1/87; HB 5–6/87)

**2410** Boniface, William. *Welcome to Dinsmore, the World's Greatest Store* (K–3). Illus. by Tom Kerr. 1995, Andrews & McMeel $14.95 (0-8362-0743-2). 42pp. The amazing treasures found in a 9-floor department store are introduced in playful rhymes. (Rev: BL 2/1/96)

**2411** Borden, Louise. *Albie the Lifeguard* (PS–3). Illus. by Elizabeth Sayles. 1993, Scholastic $14.95 (0-590-44585-5). 32pp. Albie is not a confident swimmer, but in his backyard he fantasizes about being a lifeguard. (Rev: BL 3/15/93; SLJ 6/93)

**2412** Bourgeois, Paulette. *Big Sarah's Little Boots* (PS–1). Illus. by Brenda Clark. 1992, Scholastic paper $4.95 (0-590-42623-0). 32pp. Preschooler Sarah can't understand why her favorite yellow boots have shrunk. (Rev: BL 1/1/90; SLJ 11/89)

**2413** Bowdish, Lynea. *This Is Me, Laughing* (PS). Illus. by Walter Gaffney-Kessell. 1996, Farrar $16.00 (0-374-37489-9). 32pp. The power of laughter to spread joy to others is depicted in this picture book. (Rev: BL 4/15/96; SLJ 4/96)

**2414** Brandenberg, Alexa. *Chop, Simmer, Season* (PS–1). Illus. 1997, Harcourt $14.00 (0-15-200973-6). 32pp. Two restaurant workers cook a meal for their customers in this picture book that shows what goes on in a kitchen. (Rev: BL 4/15/97; SLJ 5/97)

**2415** Brandenberg, Alexa. *I Am Me!* (PS). Illus. by author. 1996, Harcourt $12.00 (0-15-200974-4). After toddlers mention a number of careers they are interested in, they engage in activities related to each. (Rev: SLJ 12/96)

**2416** Bravo, Olga. *Olga's Cup and Saucer* (PS–2). Illus. 1995, Holt $15.95 (0-8050-3301-7). 32pp. The dream of little Nickel Penny to become a baker comes true, and the reader learns about some of her special recipes. (Rev: BL 4/15/95; SLJ 6/95)

**2417** Brazelton, T. Berry. *Going to the Doctor* (PS–1). Illus. by Alfred Womack and Sam Ogden. 1996, Addison-Wesley $15.00 (0-201-40694-2). 48pp. Using photographs of real-life situations, visits to a doctor's office are explained. (Rev: BL 11/15/96) [618]

**2418** Brennan, Linda Crotta. *Flannel Kisses* (PS–2). Illus. by Mari Takabayashi. 1997, Houghton $16.00 (0-395-73681-1). 32pp. All the fun of a snowy day is pictured, from making a snowman and having hot soup for lunch to being tucked in at night between flannel sheets. (Rev: BL 10/15/97; SLJ 9/97)

**2419** Brisson, Pat. *Kate Heads West* (K–3). Illus. by Rick Brown. 1990, Macmillan LB $14.00 (0-02-714345-7). 40pp. In a series of letters, Kate describes her tour of the American West with her friend Lucy. Also use: *Kate on the Coast* (1992). (Rev: BL 9/1/90; SLJ 11/90)

**2420** Brisson, Pat. *The Summer My Father Was Ten* (PS–3). Illus. by Andrea Shine. 1998, Boyds Mills $15.95 (1-56397-435-5). A father tells his daughter while they plant a garden together of the guilt he felt when, as a child, he vandalized a neighbor's garden. (Rev: BL 2/1/98*; SLJ 4/98)

**2421** Brisson, Pat. *Wanda's Roses* (K–2). Illus. by Maryann Cocca-Leffler. 1994, Boyds Mills $14.95 (1-56397-136-4). When the plant she has been tending fails to bloom, Wanda attaches paper flowers to it. (Rev: SLJ 12/94)

**2422** Brown, Laurie Krasny, and Marc Brown. *Dinosaurs Alive and Well! A Guide to Good Health* (PS–3). Illus. 1990, Little, Brown $15.95 (0-316-10998-3); paper $5.95 (0-316-11009-4). 32pp. Using dinosaurs, the basic principles of nutrition and hygiene are covered. Also use *Dinosaurs Travel* (1990). (Rev: BCCB 5/90; BL 5/15/90; HB 5–6/90; SLJ 4/90*) [613]

**2423** Brown, Laurie Krasny, and Marc Brown. *Visiting the Art Museum* (K–3). Illus. 1992, Dutton paper $6.99 (0-140-54820-3). 32pp. An introduction to the art museum, sometimes an overpowering place for young children. (Rev: BCCB 10/86; BL 9/15/86; SLJ 10/86)

**2424** Brown, Marc, and Stephen Krensky. *Dinosaurs, Beware! A Safety Guide* (PS–2). Illus. by authors. 1984, Little, Brown paper $7.95 (0-316-11219-4). 32pp. Sixty safety tips are illustrated with drawings of dinosaurs.

**2425** Brown, Margaret Wise. *Red Light, Green Light* (PS–K). Illus. by Leonard Weisgard. 1994, Scholastic paper $4.95 (0-590-44559-6). 40pp. This introduction to traffic signs was first published in 1944.

**2426** Brownridge, William Roy. *The Final Game* (K–3). Illus. 1998, Orca $14.95 (1-55143-100-9). 32pp. After Danny and his friends join a hockey team, Travis, their star player, learns a lesson on teamwork. A sequel to *The Moccasin Goalie* (1995). (Rev: BL 3/1/98)

**2427** Bunting, Eve. *I Don't Want to Go to Camp* (PS–K). Illus. by Maryann Cocca-Leffler. 1996, Boyds Mills $14.95 (1-56397-393-6). 32pp. Lin loses her fear of going to camp when she helps her mother prepare to go to mothers' camp and later sees what fun there can be in camping. (Rev: BL 1/1–15/96; SLJ 3/96)

**2428** Bunting, Eve. *The Pumpkin Fair* (PS–2). Illus. by Eileen Christelow. 1997, Clarion $15.00 (0-395-

70060-4). 32pp. All of the activities and fun of an autumn pumpkin fair are here, including the pumpkin-judging contests. (Rev: BL 11/1/97; SLJ 9/97)

**2429** Bunting, Eve. *Smoky Night* (K–3). Illus. by David Diaz. 1994, Harcourt $15.00 (0-15-269954-6). 32pp. Two families, one Korean American and the other African American, reach out to one another during the terrible Los Angeles riots. Caldecott Medal winner, 1995. (Rev: BCCB 3/94; BL 3/1/94; HB 5–6/94; SLJ 5/94*)

**2430** Burke-Weiner, Kimberly. *The Maybe Garden* (K–3). Illus. by Fredrika Spillman. 1992, Beyond Words paper $7.95 (0-941831-57-4). 32pp. A little girl imagines that she has a magical garden complete with fairies instead of the ordinary one her mother tends. (Rev: BL 9/1/92)

**2431** Burton, Marilee Robin. *My Best Shoes* (PS–1). Illus. by James E. Ransome. 1994, Morrow $15.00 (0-688-11756-2). 32pp. A tribute to shoes as chanted by a multicultural group of children who wear a variety of footware. (Rev: BL 8/94; SLJ 7/94)

**2432** Burton, Virginia Lee. *The Little House* (1–3). Illus. by author. 1978, Houghton $14.95 (0-395-18156-9); paper $5.95 (0-395-25938-X). Story of a little house in the country that over the years witnesses change and progress. Caldecott Medal winner, 1943.

**2433** Butterworth, Nick. *Busy People* (1–4). Illus. 1994, Candlewick paper $3.99 (1-56402-365-6). 32pp. Many community helpers — such as a doctor, farmer, and baker — are introduced in this question-and-answer book. (Rev: BL 8/92; SLJ 11/92)

**2434** Caines, Jeannette. *I Need a Lunch Box* (PS–K). Illus. by Pat Cummings. 1988, HarperCollins LB $15.89 (0-06-020985-2); paper $5.95 (0-06-443341-2). 32pp. Mama says no to a lunch box for a little boy who hasn't yet started school. (Rev: BL 9/15/88; SLJ 12/88)

**2435** Caple, Kathy. *The Purse* (PS–1). Illus. by author. 1992, Houghton paper $6.95 (0-395-62981-0). 32pp. Her new purse doesn't "clunk" her hard-earned money the way her Band-Aid box did, decides Katie. (Rev: BL 9/15/86; HB 11–12/86; SLJ 1/87)

**2436** Carlson, Nancy. *Sit Still!* (K–3). Illus. 1996, Viking paper $13.99 (0-670-85721-1). 32pp. A boy has problems sitting still until his mother arrives at an unusual solution. (Rev: BL 4/15/96; SLJ 5/96)

**2437** Carlstrom, Nancy White. *The Snow Speaks* (3–7). Illus. by Jane Dyer. 1992, Little, Brown $15.95 (0-316-12861-9). 32pp. Children enjoy the various aspects of a snowstorm in the country from the first flakes to the coming of the snowplows. (Rev: BL 9/15/92)

**2438** Caseley, Judith. *Sophie and Sammy's Library Sleepover* (PS–2). Illus. 1993, Greenwillow LB $15.93 (0-688-10616-1). 32pp. Through the help of older sister Sophie, Sammy learns to love and respect books. (Rev: BCCB 6/93; BL 2/15/93; HB 7–8/93; SLJ 6/93)

**2439** Chapman, Cheryl. *Snow on Snow on Snow* (PS–K). Illus. by Synthia Saint James. 1994, Dial paper $14.89 (0-8037-1457-2). 32pp. Explores the use of prepositions in a story about a boy's activities with his dog on a snowy day. (Rev: BCCB 2/95; BL 9/1/94; SLJ 9/94)

**2440** Charlip, Remy, and Lillian Moore. *Hooray for Me!* (PS–2). Illus. by Vera B. Williams. 1996, Tricycle Pr. $14.95 (1-883672-43-0). 36pp. A new edition of an old favorite that explores a child's relationships. (Rev: BL 11/15/96)

**2441** Chinn, Karen. *Sam and the Lucky Money* (PS–2). Illus. by Cornelius Van Wright and Ying-Hwa Hu. 1995, Lee & Low $14.95 (1-880000-13-X). Sam decides that the money he has received at Chinese New Year would be best used by giving it to a poor stranger. (Rev: SLJ 12/95)

**2442** Christiansen, Candace. *The Mitten Tree* (K–3). Illus. by Elaine Greenstein. 1997, Fulcrum $16.95 (1-55591-349-0). 32pp. A lonely old woman endears herself to all when she knits mittens for needy children and places them on a tree to be taken. (Rev: BL 10/15/97; SLJ 2/98)

**2443** Clary, Margie Willis. *A Sweet, Sweet Basket* (K–4). Illus. by Dennis L. Brown. 1995, Sandlapper $15.95 (0-87844-127-1). 40pp. An older woman explains to her granddaughter how baskets are woven from the sweetgrass that grows in South Carolina. (Rev: BL 9/1/95)

**2444** Cole, Henry. *Jack's Garden* (PS–4). Illus. 1995, Greenwillow $16.00 (0-688-13501-3). 24pp. In this cumulative tale, the plants and insects found in Jack's garden are introduced. (Rev: BCCB 5/95; BL 4/1/95; HB 5–6/95; SLJ 5/95)

**2445** Coleman, Evelyn. *To Be a Drum* (K–3). Illus. by Aminah Robinson. 1998, Albert Whitman LB $16.96 (0-8075-8006-6). 32pp. Daddy Wes tells 2 children about the history of African Americans and their struggles as revealed in the earth rhythm of drumbeats. (Rev: BL 2/15/98)

**2446** Cooke, Trish. *When I Grow Bigger* (PS–1). Illus. by John Bendall-Brunello. 1994, Candlewick $13.95 (1-56402-430-X). 32pp. A baby looks up to everyone, except when Dad puts him on his shoulders. (Rev: BL 9/1/94; SLJ 9/94)

**2447** Cooper, Elisha. *Country Fair* (PS–2). Illus. 1997, Greenwillow $15.00 (0-688-15531-6). 40pp. The activities associated with a country fair are pictured. (Rev: BL 9/15/97; HB 9–10/97; SLJ 9/97)

**2448** Cooper, Melrose. *I Got Community* (K–3). Illus. by Dale Gottlieb. 1995, Holt $14.95 (0-8050-3179-0). 32pp. A book that shows kindnesses from all sorts of people — including firefighters, baby-sitters, and pizza makers — go into making a community. (Rev: BCCB 5/95; BL 6/1–15/95; SLJ 7/95)

**2449** Cousins, Lucy. *Maisy's Pop-up Playhouse* (2–5). Illus. 1995, Candlewick $19.99 (1-56402-635-3). 16pp. Pop-ups reveal the contents of Maisy's playhouse. (Rev: BL 2/1/96)

**2450** Cox, Judy. *Now We Can Have a Wedding!* (PS–2). Illus. by DyAnne DiSalvo-Ryan. 1998, Holiday LB $15.95 (0-8234-1342-X). 32pp. The narrator goes from apartment to apartment in her building and sees that everyone is making a different national dish to bring to her sister's wedding. (Rev: BL 2/15/98; SLJ 3/98)

**2451** Crebbin, June. *The Train Ride* (PS–1). Illus. by Stephen Lambert. 1995, Candlewick $14.95 (1-56402-546-2). 32pp. A young girl identifies the objects she sees through the window of her train coach. (Rev: BL 5/15/95; SLJ 10/95)

**2452** Crews, Donald. *Carousel* (PS–2). Illus. by author. 1982, Greenwillow LB $15.93 (0-688-00909-3). 32pp. A ride on a carousel is described in pictures and text.

**2453** Crews, Donald. *Night at the Fair* (K–2). Illus. 1998, Greenwillow LB $14.93 (0-688-11484-9). 24pp. Game booths, food concessions, and the Ferris wheel are only 3 of the attractions at a country fair that are highlighted in this engaging book. (Rev: BL 3/1/98; SLJ 4/98)

**2454** Crews, Donald. *Parade* (PS–2). Illus. by author. 1983, Greenwillow LB $15.93 (0-688-01996-X); Morrow paper $4.95 (0-688-06520-1). 32pp. A picture-book celebration of a parade — fire engine and all.

**2455** Crews, Donald. *Shortcut* (3–6). Illus. 1992, Greenwillow LB $15.93 (0-688-06437-X). 32pp. Seven children follow a railroad track back home as the train gets closer and closer. (Rev: BCCB 10/92*; BL 10/15/92*; HB 1–2/93*; SLJ 11/92)

**2456** Crews, Nina. *One Hot Summer Day* (PS–K). Illus. 1995, Greenwillow LB $14.93 (0-688-13394-0). 24pp. Using collages, the author illustrates the many activities associated with a hot summer's day. (Rev: BCCB 6/95; BL 6/1–15/95; HB 7–8/95; SLJ 6/95)

**2457** Crews, Nina. *Snowball* (PS–1). Illus. 1997, Greenwillow LB $14.93 (0-688-14929-4). 24pp. This is the story of an African American child in a city and how she gets her wish for snow. (Rev: BL 12/1/97; SLJ 9/97)

**2458** Crimi, Carolyn. *Outside, Inside* (PS–1). Illus. by Linnea A. Riley. 1995, Simon & Schuster paper $15.00 (0-671-88688-6). 32pp. While the rain is falling outside, Molly spends a comfortable time inside with her pets. (Rev: BCCB 5/95; BL 6/1–15/95; HB 9–10/95; SLJ 5/95)

**2459** Danis, Naomi. *Walk with Me* (PS). Illus. by Jacqueline Rogers. Series: Story Corner. 1995, Scholastic $6.95 (0-590-45855-8). A mother and her preschool daughter combine a pleasant outdoor walk with some nature study. (Rev: SLJ 8/95)

**2460** Davenport, Zoe. *Mealtime* (PS). Illus. 1995, Ticknor $5.95 (0-395-71536-9). 16pp. The parts of an egg and a sandwich are 2 of the foods discussed in this simple vocabulary book. (Rev: BL 2/1/95; SLJ 8/95) [641]

**2461** Delaney, A. *Pearl's First Prize Plant* (PS–2). Illus. by author. 1997, HarperCollins LB $14.89 (0-06-027357-7). Pearl is disappointed when her plant doesn't win a prize at the county fair, so she awards it her own blue ribbon. (Rev: SLJ 7/97)

**2462** Delton, Judy. *My Mom Made Me Go to Camp* (1–3). Illus. by Lisa McCue. 1993, Dell paper $2.99 (0-440-40838-5). 32pp. Archie, who does not want to attend summer camp, gradually changes his mind. (Rev: BL 1/1/91; SLJ 2/91)

**2463** Demuth, Patricia. *Busy at Day Care Head to Toe* (PS–K). Illus. by Jack Demuth. 1996, Dutton paper $14.99 (0-525-45603-1). 32pp. Activities in a Chicago suburban day care center are depicted in simple text and photos. (Rev: BCCB 6/96; BL 6/1–15/96; SLJ 7/96) [372.21]

**2464** Derby, Sally. *My Steps* (PS–1). Illus. by Adjoa J. Burrowes. 1996, Lee & Low $14.95 (1-880000-40-7). 32pp. An African American city child tells what a wonderful playground her front steps can be. (Rev: BL 10/15/96; SLJ 10/96)

**2465** Desimini, Lisa. *My House* (PS–1). Illus. 1994, Holt $15.95 (0-8050-3144-8). 32pp. With each season, a house takes on a different color and atmosphere. (Rev: BCCB 10/94; BL 11/15/94; HB 11–12/94; SLJ 10/94)

**2466** Diller, Harriet. *Big Band Sound* (PS–2). Illus. by Andrea Shine. 1996, Boyds Mills $14.95 (1-56397-129-1). 32pp. Everyday sounds and objects are used by Arlis to produce her own music. (Rev: BL 1/1–15/96; SLJ 3/96)

**2467** Diller, Harriet. *The Faraway Drawer* (K–3). Illus. by Andrea Shine. 1996, Boyds Mills $14.95 (1-56397-190-9). Each of the sweaters found by a young girl in a drawer sends her thoughts to a different place. (Rev: SLJ 11/96)

**2468** DiSalvo-Ryan, DyAnne. *City Green* (K–3). Illus. 1994, Morrow LB $15.93 (0-688-12787-8). 32pp. Marcy organizes her neighbors to turn a vacant lot into a community garden. (Rev: BCCB 9/94; BL 11/15/94; SLJ 9/94)

**2469** *Do Skyscrapers Touch the Sky? First Questions and Answers About the City* (PS–K). Illus. 1994, Time Life $14.95 (0-7835-0886-7). 48pp. Obvious questions about city life — like "What's under the street?" — are answered in well-illustrated double-page spreads. (Rev: BL 2/1/95) [307.76]

**2470** Dodd, Anne W. *Footprints and Shadows* (PS–1). Illus. by Henri Sorensen. 1994, Simon & Schuster paper $4.95 (0-671-89905-8). 36pp. This picture book tries to answer the question of where footprints and shadows go. (Rev: BL 12/1/92; SLJ 12/92)

**2471** Dooley, Norah. *Everybody Bakes Bread* (K–3). Illus. by Peter J. Thornton. 1996, Carolrhoda LB $19.93 (0-87614-864-X). 40pp. On an errand for her mother, Carrie sees her neighbors bake a variety of breads in this sequel to *Everybody Cooks Rice* (1991). (Rev: BL 3/1/96; SLJ 4/96)

**2472** Dowling, Paul. *The Night Journey* (PS–3). Illus. 1997, Doubleday $14.95 (0-385-32287-9). 10pp. Such nocturnal lights as stars and fireworks are revealed when tabs are pulled in this interactive book. (Rev: BL 12/15/96; SLJ 2/97)

**2473** Dragonwagon, Crescent. *Home Place* (1–3). Illus. by Jerry Pinkney. 1990, Macmillan $14.95 (0-02-733190-3). 40pp. A family out hiking comes on the remains of someone's home. (Rev: BCCB 12/90; BL 8/90; HB 11–12/90; SLJ 2/91)

**2474** Dragonwagon, Crescent. *The Itch Book* (K–3). Illus. by Joseph Mahler. 1990, Macmillan LB $13.95 (0-02-733121-0). 32pp. A rhyming text captures the fidgets of a hot summer day in the Ozarks. (Rev: BL 2/1/90)

**2475** Dragonwagon, Crescent. *This Is the Bread I Baked for Ned* (PS–2). Illus. by Isadore Seltzer. 1989, Macmillan paper $14.95 (0-02-733220-9). 32pp. A rhythmic story in which Ned gets a nice surprise. (Rev: BL 11/15/89; SLJ 12/89)

**2476** Duncan, Debbie. *When Molly Was in the Hospital: A Book for Brothers and Sisters of Hospitalized Children* (PS–2). Illus. by Nina Ollikainen. Series: MiniMed. 1994, Rayve $12.95 (1-877810-44-4). The experiences of a young girl whose younger sister faces major surgery and the many conflicting emotions she feels. (Rev: SLJ 3/95)

**2477** Edwards, Richard. *Fly with the Birds: A Word and Rhyme Book* (PS–K). Illus. by Satoshi Kitamura. 1996, Orchard $12.95 (0-531-09491-X). In this flap book, a child narrates her day, from waking up to bedtime and dreamland. (Rev: SLJ 3/96)

**2478** Edwards, Richard. *You're Safe Now, Waterdog* (PS–K). Illus. by Sophy Williams. 1997, Viking paper $14.99 (0-670-87385-3). 32pp. A stuffed dog named Watt is neglected by his first owner but later is cared for by a little girl. (Rev: BCCB 7–8/97; BL 7/97; SLJ 7/97)

**2479** Ehlert, Lois. *Circus* (PS–2). Illus. 1992, Harper-Collins $15.95 (0-060-20252-1). 40pp. The razzle-dazzle of the circus is translated into the relative quiet of the picture-book experience. (Rev: BL 1/1/92; HB 3–4/92; SLJ 4/92) [791.3]

**2480** Ehlert, Lois. *Growing Vegetable Soup* (PS–K). Illus. by author. 1987, Harcourt $15.00 (0-15-232575-1); paper $6.00 (0-15-232580-8). 40pp. Father and child plant seeds and sprouts "to grow vegetable soup." Also use: *Planting a Rainbow* (1988). (Rev: BL 3/1/87; SLJ 3/87)

**2481** Ehlert, Lois. *Hands* (K–2). Illus. 1997, Harcourt $13.00 (0-15-201506-X). 20pp. This picture book describes what hands can accomplish, their uses, and how they can bring people together. (Rev: BL 11/15/97*; HB 9–10/97; SLJ 12/97)

**2482** Evans, Lezlie. *Snow Dance* (PS–1). Illus. by Cynthia Jabar. 1997, Houghton $16.00 (0-395-77849-2). 32pp. Two bored sisters are successful when they engage in a snow dance because it soon begins to fall. (Rev: BL 10/1/97; SLJ 12/97)

**2483** Fair, Sylvia. *The Bedspread* (K–2). Illus. by author. 1982, Morrow $17.00 (0-688-00877-1). 32pp. Two old ladies decide to embroider their bedspreads.

**2484** Falwell, Cathryn. *P. J. and Puppy* (PS). Illus. 1997, Clarion $8.95 (0-395-56918-4). 23pp. A young boy and his new puppy both learn how to be toilet trained. (Rev: BL 2/15/97; SLJ 3/97)

**2485** Falwell, Cathryn. *Where's Nicky?* (PS). Illus. 1991, Houghton $5.95 (0-395-56936-2). 28pp. This is a hide-and-seek game featuring a one-year-old boy named Nicky. (Rev: BL 7/91)

**2486** Field, Rachel. *General Store* (PS–1). Illus. by Nancy Winslow Parker. 1988, Little, Brown $15.95 (0-316-28163-8). 24pp. A poem that extols the charms of the old-fashioned store. Another version has illustrations by Giles Laroche (1988, Little, Brown). (Rev: BCCB 5/88; BL 3/1/88; HB 5–6/88)

**2487** Flanagan, Alice K. *A Busy Day at Mr. Kang's Grocery Store* (1–2). Illus. by Christine Osinski. Series: Our Neighborhood. 1996, Children's LB $19.50 (0-516-20047-X). 32pp. Everyday activities in a neighborhood grocery store are pictured and introduced in a simple text. (Rev: BL 1/1–15/97) [381]

**2488** Flanagan, Alice K. *Call Mr. Vasquez, He'll Fix It!* (1–2). Illus. by Christine Osinski. Series: Our Neighborhood. 1996, Children's LB $19.50 (0-516-20045-3). 32pp. The activities of a neighborhood repairman are introduced in simple text and pictures. (Rev: BL 1/1–15/97) [647]

**2489** Flanagan, Alice K. *Ms. Davison, Our Librarian* (1–2). Illus. by Christine Osinski. Series: Our Neighborhood. 1996, Children's LB $19.50 (0-516-

20009-7); paper $6.95 (0-516-26060-X). 32pp. The activities and duties of a librarian are described and pictured. (Rev: BL 1/1–15/97; SLJ 2/97) [021]

**2490** Flanagan, Alice K. *Riding the Ferry with Captain Cruz* (1–2). Illus. by Christine Osinski. Series: Our Neighborhood. 1996, Children's LB $19.50 (0-516-20046-1); paper $6.95 (0-516-26059-6). 32pp. In text and pictures, the day-to-day work of a ferry captain is presented. (Rev: BL 1/1–15/97; SLJ 2/97) [386]

**2491** Flanagan, Alice K. *The Wilsons, a House-Painting Team* (1–2). Illus. by Christine Osinski. Series: Our Neighborhood. 1996, Children's LB $19.00 (0-516-20216-2); paper $6.95 (0-516-26063-4). 32pp. House painting, its importance, and difficulties encountered are portrayed in basic text with many pictures. (Rev: BL 1/1–15/97) [698]

**2492** Fleming, Denise. *Where Once There Was a Wood* (PS–2). Illus. 1996, Holt $15.95 (0-8050-3761-6). 32pp. A piece of land is described as it was before a housing development changed it. (Rev: BCCB 3/96; BL 5/1/96; SLJ 6/96)

**2493** Florian, Douglas. *A Chef* (PS–2). Illus. 1992, Greenwillow LB $13.93 (0-688-11109-2). 32pp. The hustle and bustle of a professional kitchen during a chef's workday are described. (Rev: BCCB 12/92; BL 10/15/92; HB 3–4/93; SLJ 10/92) [641]

**2494** Florian, Douglas. *City Street* (3–6). Illus. 1990, Greenwillow LB $15.93 (0-688-09544-5). 32pp. City scenes come to life with motion and moods. (Rev: BL 8/90; SLJ 2/91) [307]

**2495** Franklin, Kristine L. *Iguana Beach* (PS–2). Illus. by Lori Lohsoeter. 1997, Crown LB $18.99 (0-517-70901-5). On a beach in Central America, Little Reina finds a lagoon where she can swim without danger. (Rev: SLJ 8/97)

**2496** French, Vivian. *Oh No, Anna!* (PS). Illus. by Alex Ayliffe. 1997, Peachtree $14.95 (1-56145-125-8). A flap book that chronicles a number of minor household accidents that befall Anna. (Rev: SLJ 12/97)

**2497** Galbraith, Kathryn O. *Look! Snow!* (PS–2). Illus. by Nina S. Montezinos. 1992, Macmillan $13.95 (0-689-50551-5). 32pp. Children enjoy the season's first snowfall, particularly when they have the day off from school. (Rev: BL 11/1/92; SLJ 9/92)

**2498** Gardella, Tricia. *Casey's New Hat* (PS–1). Illus. by Margot Apple. 1997, Houghton $14.95 (0-395-72035-4). 32pp. Casey has trouble finding a new hat that she likes and finally settles for an old one the Grandpa no longer wants. (Rev: BL 4/15/97; SLJ 4/97)

**2499** Gardella, Tricia. *Just Like My Dad* (PS–2). Illus. by Margot Apple. 1996, HarperCollins paper $4.95 (0-064-43463-X). 32pp. On a ranch, a young boy dressed like a cowboy accompanies his father through the day's chores. (Rev: BL 5/1/93; HB 7–8/93)

**2500** Garland, Sherry. *The Summer Sands* (PS–1). Illus. by Robert J. Lee. 1995, Harcourt $15.00 (0-15-282492-8). 32pp. Children and their parents use their old Christmas trees to act as a windbreak to form new sand dunes. (Rev: BL 4/15/95; SLJ 6/95)

**2501** Gauch, Patricia L. *Tanya and the Magic Wardrobe* (PS–2). Illus. by Satomi Ichikawa. Series: Tanya. 1997, Putnam $16.95 (0-399-22940-X). 32pp. At a ballet performance of *Coppelia*, Tanya, a young dancer, meets an old woman who shows her costumes that are worn in different ballets. (Rev: BL 11/1/97; SLJ 10/97)

**2502** Gauch, Patricia L. *Tanya Steps Out* (PS–1). Illus. by Satomi Ichikawa. 1996, Putnam $13.95 (0-399-22936-1). 10pp. Ballet positions turn into animals when tabs are pulled in this interactive book. (Rev: BL 12/15/96; SLJ 12/96)

**2503** Gershator, David, and Phillis Gershator. *Bread Is for Eating* (PS–1). Illus. by Emma Shaw-Smith. 1995, Holt $14.95 (0-8050-3173-1). 32pp. This song with lyrics in both English and Spanish explains how bread is made. (Rev: BL 6/1–15/95; SLJ 8/95)

**2504** Gibbons, Gail. *Fire! Fire!* (PS–2). Illus. by author. 1984, HarperCollins LB $14.89 (0-690-04416-X); paper $5.95 (0-06-446058-4). 40pp. The various ways a fire is fought.

**2505** Gibbons, Gail. *How a House Is Built* (PS–K). Illus. 1990, Holiday LB $15.95 (0-8234-0841-8). 32pp. A good introduction to the construction of a wood frame house. (Rev: BL 10/15/90; SLJ 10/90) [690]

**2506** Gibbons, Gail. *Paper, Paper Everywhere* (PS–2). Illus. by author. 1997, Harcourt paper $5.00 (0-152-01491-8). 32pp. A picture book that shows how useful and ever-present is paper.

**2507** Gilchrist, Jan Spivey. *Madelia* (PS–3). Illus. 1997, Dial paper $14.89 (0-8037-2054-8). 32pp. Based on the author's experiences, this picture book describes how a child is moved and transported by the images taken from her preacher father's sermon. (Rev: BL 10/1/97; SLJ 12/97)

**2508** Glaser, Linda. *Compost! Growing Gardens from Your Garbage* (PS–1). Illus. by Anca Hariton. 1996, Millbrook LB $21.90 (1-56294-659-5). 32pp. A little girl explains how her family uses waste material to create a compost heap that eventually produces rich earth for spring planting. (Rev: BL 2/15/96; SLJ 4/96) [635]

**2509** Glaser, Linda. *Stop that Garbage Truck!* (PS–2). Illus. by Karen L. Schmidt. 1993, Albert Whitman LB $14.95 (0-8075-7626-3). Henry, who looks forward to watching the garbagemen do their job, is disappointed one morning when his mother forgets to put the garbage out. (Rev: SLJ 3/94)

**2510** Goennel, Heidi. *What I Eat* (PS). Illus. by author. Series: It's My World. 1995, Tambourine paper $3.95 (0-688-14145-5). Various items of food are identified, one per page, in this simple board book. Also use *What I See, What I Wear*, and *Where I Live* (all 1995). (Rev: SLJ 9/95)

**2511** Gomi, Taro. *Everyone Poops* (PS). Trans. by Amanda M. Stinchecum. Illus. Series: Can You Believe It! 1993, Kane/Miller $11.95 (0-916291-45-6). 28pp. This book shows that all animals poop and that this is a natural part of life. (Rev: BCCB 4/93; BL 5/15/93) [612]

**2512** Gomi, Taro. *My Friends* (PS–K). Illus. 1995, Chronicle paper $5.95 (0-811-81237-5). 36pp. A little girl talks about all the things she's learned from her friends, such as jumping from her dog. (Rev: BL 7/90; SLJ 7/90)

**2513** Gomi, Taro. *Who Ate It?* (PS–K). Illus. 1991, Millbrook LB $13.90 (1-56294-010-4). In this book from Japan, various items are hidden in pictures. A companion puzzle book is: *Who Hid It?* (1992). (Rev: SLJ 4/92)

**2514** Gould, Deborah. *Aaron's Shirt* (PS–1). Illus. by Cheryl Harness. 1989, Macmillan LB $13.95 (0-02-736351-1). 32pp. A deceptively simple tale about a boy who outgrows his shirt. (Rev: BCCB 4/89; BL 3/1/89; HB 7–8/89)

**2515** Graham, Bob. *The Red Woolen Blanket* (PS–K). Illus. by author. 1996, Candlewick paper $4.99 (1-564-02848-8). 32pp. Julia's bright red blanket stays with her from infancy until she enters school. (Rev: HB 5–6/88)

**2516** Graham, Bob. *Rose Meets Mr. Wintergarten* (PS–2). Illus. by author. 1992, Candlewick $14.95 (1-56402-039-8). 32pp. When her ball goes over Mr. Wintergarten's fence, Rose is able to find out what her neighbor is really like. (Rev: BCCB 7–8/92; BL 5/15/92; HB 5–6/92; SLJ 8/92)

**2517** Greenfield, Eloise. *Big Friend, Little Friend* (PS). Illus. by Jan S. Gilchrist. 1991, Writers & Readers $4.95 (0-86316-204-5). 12pp. This is one of a series of board books about the everyday activities of some African American children. Also use: *Daddy and I; I Make Music;* and *My Doll, Keshia* (all 1991). (Rev: BL 12/15/91; SLJ 12/91)

**2518** Greenfield, Eloise. *Night on Neighborhood Street* (K–3). Illus. by Jan S. Gilchrist. 1991, Dial LB $13.89 (0-8037-0778-9); paper $14.99 (0-8037-0777-0). 32pp. This picture book depicts life on the streets of an inner-city neighborhood. (Rev: BCCB 10/91; BL 8/91; HB 11–12/91*; SLJ 9/91*)

**2519** Gregory, Valiska. *Looking for Angels* (PS–2). Illus. by Leslie Baker. 1996, Simon & Schuster paper $17.00 (0-689-80500-4). 32pp. The wonders of everyday phenomena make Sarah realize that angels are everywhere. (Rev: BL 6/1–15/96; SLJ 3/96)

**2520** Grejniec, Michael. *What Do You Like?* (K–2). Illus. 1995, North-South paper $6.95 (1-55858-417-X). 32pp. A boy and a girl like the same things, but in different ways. (Rev: BL 8/92; SLJ 1/93)

**2521** Grey, Nigel. *A Country Far Away* (PS–2). Illus. by Philippe Dupasquier. 1989, Watts LB $16.99 (0-531-08392-6). 32pp. One boy in a Western city suburb and another in an African village show life-styles that are similar and different. (Rev: BL 11/15/89; SLJ 10/89)

**2522** Grimes, Nikki. *Come Sunday* (PS–3). Illus. by Michael Bryant. 1996, Eerdmans $15.00 (0-8028-5108-8); paper $7.50 (0-8028-5134-7). 32pp. Young Latasha finds that going to church on Sunday is an exciting adventure. (Rev: BCCB 3/97; BL 6/1–15/96*; SLJ 6/97)

**2523** Gundersheimer, Karen. *Find Cat, Wear Hat* (PS). Illus. 1995, Scholastic $5.95 (0-590-48061-8). 24pp. A beginner's book in which each page explains in 2 words the accompanying picture. Similar in scope is the author's *Splish Splash, Bang Crash* (1995). (Rev: BL 1/15/95; SLJ 9/95)

**2524** Hakkinen, Anita. *Summer Legs* (1–3). Illus. by Abby Carter. 1995, Holt $14.95 (0-8050-2262-7). 32pp. A rhyming story that celebrates all the things that legs can do in summer. (Rev: BL 5/15/95; SLJ 7/95)

**2525** Hamanaka, Sheila. *All the Colors of the Earth* (PS–2). Illus. 1994, Morrow LB $15.93 (0-688-11132-7). 32pp. A collection of paintings that show children of various ethnic backgrounds together having fun. (Rev: BCCB 10/94; BL 9/1/94; HB 11–12/94; SLJ 8/94*)

**2526** Hamm, Diane J. *Laney's Lost Momma* (PS–1). Illus. by Sally G. Ward. 1991, Whitman LB $14.95 (0-8075-4340-3). 32pp. Mother and daughter are reunited after Laney loses her mother in a department store. (Rev: BL 1/1/92; SLJ 12/91)

**2527** Harris, Peter. *Mouse Creeps* (PS–K). Illus. by Reg Cartwright. 1997, Dial paper $14.99 (0-8037-2183-8). 32pp. The actions of several animals affect the outcome of a battle in this simple picture book about the foolishness of war. (Rev: BCCB 3/97; BL 6/1–15/97; SLJ 6/97)

**2528** Hautzig, David. *At the Supermarket* (PS–2). Illus. 1994, Orchard LB $17.99 (0-531-08682-8). 32pp. An hour-by-hour account that describes in pictures and text what happens during a single day in a modern supermarket. (Rev: BL 3/15/94; SLJ 5/94) [381]

**2529** Havill, Juanita. *Jamaica's Find* (PS–1). Illus. by Anne S. O'Brien. 1986, Houghton $16.00 (0-395-

39376-0); paper $5.95 (0-395-45357-7). 32pp. Jamaica finds a stuffed dog, which she brings home, but her parents make her return to the park where she found it, and where she also finds its true owner. Also use: *Jamaica Tag-Along* (1989). (Rev: BCCB 5/86; BL 4/1/86; SLJ 8/86)

**2530** Hayes, Joe. *A Spoon for Every Bite* (PS–3). Illus. by Rebecca Leer. 1996, Orchard LB $16.99 (0-531-08799-9). 32pp. A poor couple fools a rich neighbor into spending his fortune for spoons. (Rev: BCCB 4/96; BL 3/15/96; SLJ 4/96)

**2531** Hayes, Sarah. *Eat Up, Gemma* (PS–1). Illus. by Jan Ormerod. 1988, Lothrop $16.00 (0-688-08149-5). 32pp. Gemma is at the stage where food is mostly a toy. (Rev: BCCB 9/88; BL 9/1/88; HB 11–12/88)

**2532** Hazen, Barbara S. *Good-bye Hello* (PS–K). Illus. by Michael Bryant. 1995, Simon & Schuster $15.00 (0-689-31665-8). 32pp. A picture book that tells how a young girl gradually adjusts to her new suburban home. (Rev: BL 5/15/95; SLJ 7/95)

**2533** Hazen, Barbara S. *Mommy's Office* (PS–1). Illus. by David Soman. 1992, Macmillan $13.95 (0-689-31601-1). 32pp. Emily spends an interesting day when her mother takes her to the office and shows her how she works. (Rev: BCCB 3/92; BL 3/1/92; SLJ 3/92)

**2534** Heap, Sue. *Cowboy Baby* (PS–K). Illus. 1998, Candlewick $15.99 (0-7636-0437-2). 32pp. A slight story set in the Southwest about an imaginative boy who would rather play cowboy than go to bed. (Rev: BL 3/1/98)

**2535** Hedlund, Carey. *Night Fell at Harry's Farm* (PS–K). Illus. 1997, Greenwillow $15.00 (0-688-14932-4). 24pp. The whole family piles into the car for an adventurous ride to Harry's for dinner. (Rev: BL 6/1–15/97; SLJ 5/97)

**2536** Heiligman, Deborah. *On the Move* (K–1). Illus. by Lizzy Rockwell. 1996, HarperCollins LB $14.89 (0-06-024742-8); paper $4.95 (0-06-445155-0). 32pp. Various kinds of movements — like running, walking, and dancing — are shown in cartoon-like drawings. (Rev: BL 5/1/96; SLJ 8/96)

**2537** Henderson, Kathy. *The Little Boat* (PS–1). Illus. by Patrick Benson. 1995, Candlewick $15.95 (1-56402-420-2). 32pp. The boat that a boy has made at his beach washes out to sea and is eventually found by a girl on another beach. (Rev: BL 9/1/95; SLJ 10/95)

**2538** Henkes, Kevin. *Clean Enough* (PS–2). Illus. by author. 1982, Greenwillow LB $11.93 (0-688-00829-1). 24pp. A young boy takes a bath.

**2539** Henkes, Kevin. *Good-bye, Curtis* (PS–K). Illus. by Marisabina Russo. 1995, Greenwillow LB $14.93 (0-688-12828-9). 24pp. After 42 years of ser-

vice, mailcarrier Curtis makes his last rounds. (Rev: BL 10/15/95; HB 11–12/95; SLJ 10/95)

**2540** Hennessy, B. G. *Jake Baked the Cake* (4–6). Illus. by Mary Morgan. 1990, Viking paper $12.95 (0-670-82237-X). 32pp. Wedding preparations go on while Jake bakes the cake. (Rev: BL 3/15/90; HB 5–6/90; SLJ 4/90)

**2541** Henwood, Simon. *The Hidden Jungle* (2–4). Illus. 1992, Farrar $14.00 (0-374-33070-0). 32pp. To help relieve the dullness of city life, Mr. Finn plants a tree on his windowsill. (Rev: BL 10/15/92; SLJ 1/93)

**2542** Heo, Yumi. *One Afternoon* (PS–1). Illus. 1994, Orchard $15.95 (0-531-06845-5). 32pp. A mother and her son discover on a big-city walk that everything from a jackhammer to a cash register makes its own distinctive sound. (Rev: BL 8/94; HB 11–12/94; SLJ 11/94)

**2543** Herold, Maggie R. *A Very Important Day* (PS–2). Illus. by Catherine Stock. 1995, Morrow LB $15.93 (0-688-13066-6). 40pp. Families from various racial backgrounds are excited because it is the day they will become U.S. citizens. (Rev: BL 9/1/95; SLJ 11/95)

**2544** Herron, Carolivia. *Nappy Hair* (K–4). Illus. by Joe Cepeda. 1997, Knopf LB $18.99 (0-679-97937-9). 32pp. This picture book about an African American girl also touches on slavery, Africa, and family. (Rev: BCCB 2/97; BL 2/1/97; SLJ 1/97)

**2545** Hest, Amy. *The Babies Are Coming!* (PS–1). Illus. by Chloe Cheese. 1997, Crown LB $18.99 (0-517-70944-9). 32pp. On a cold winter evening, parents are preparing to take their children to story hour, and the librarian is also preparing by choosing the perfect book to read to them. (Rev: BL 11/1/97; SLJ 1/98)

**2546** Hest, Amy. *How to Get Famous in Brooklyn* (K–3). Illus. by Linda D. Sawaya. 1995, Simon & Schuster paper $15.00 (0-689-80293-5). 32pp. A young girl faithfully records her experiences in her Brooklyn neighborhood. (Rev: BL 8/95; SLJ 9/95)

**2547** Hest, Amy. *The Purple Coat* (K–2). Illus. by Amy Schwartz. 1992, Macmillan paper $4.90 (0-689-71634-6). 32pp. This year Gabrielle wants a purple coat instead of the navy blue coat she always wears, and Grandpa the tailor comes up with an ingenious solution. (Rev: BL 9/1/86; HB 1–2/87; SLJ 11/86)

**2548** Hoban, Julia. *Amy Loves the Rain* (PS–K). Illus. by Lillian Hoban. 1989, HarperCollins $9.95 (0-06-022357-X). 24pp. Amy sits in her car seat as they go to pick up Daddy in the rain. Also use: *Amy Loves the Sun* (1988). (Rev: BL 4/15/89; HB 7–8/89)

**2549** Hoban, Julia. *Amy Loves the Snow* (PS). Illus. by Lillian Hoban. 1989, HarperCollins $9.95 (0-06-

022361-8). 24pp. A simple text that dramatizes the fun youngsters have in the snow. (Rev: BL 10/1/89; SLJ 10/89)

**2550** Hofsepian, Sylvia A. *Why Not?* (PS–3). Illus. by Friso Henstra. 1991, Macmillan LB $13.95 (0-02-743980-1). This cumulative tale begins with a lonely man bringing home a cat to keep him company. (Rev: SLJ 12/91)

**2551** Hooper, Meredith. *A Cow, a Bee, a Cookie, and Me* (PS–2). Illus. by Alison Bartlett. 1997, Kingfisher $14.95 (0-7534-5067-4). 32pp. While Ben is helping to make honey cookies, his grandmother tells him about the origin of each of the ingredients. (Rev: BL 6/1–15/97)

**2552** Hoopes, Lyn Littlefield. *The Unbeatable Bread* (PS–2). Illus. by Brad Sneed. 1996, Dial paper $14.89 (0-8037-1612-5). 32pp. Uncle Jon wants to create warmth and good feelings by baking the best bread ever. (Rev: BL 4/15/96; SLJ 3/96*)

**2553** Howard, Elizabeth F. *The Train to Lulu's* (PS–3). Illus. by Robert Casilla. 1994, Macmillan paper $4.95 (0-689-71797-0). 32pp. The story of the train journey of 2 little girls. (Rev: BCCB 7–8/88; BL 4/15/88; SLJ 5/88)

**2554** Hudson, Cheryl W., and Bernette G. Ford. *Bright Eyes, Brown Skin* (PS). Illus. by George Ford. 1990, Just Us $12.95 (0-940975-10-6). 24pp. This book features 4 African American children on a typical day in preschool. (Rev: BL 12/1/90*; SLJ 1/91)

**2555** Hughes, Shirley. *Being Together* (PS). Illus. by author. 1997, Candlewick $3.99 (0-7636-0399-6). In this board book, a little girl tells about the activities that she shares with her brother. Also use *Playing* (1997). (Rev: SLJ 2/98)

**2556** Hughes, Shirley. *Bouncing* (PS). Illus. 1993, Candlewick $12.95 (1-56402-128-9). 24pp. A preschooler shows how she spends the days with a number of bouncing activities. Also use: *Giving* (1993). (Rev: BL 5/1/93; SLJ 6/93)

**2557** Hughes, Shirley. *Chatting* (PS). Illus. 1994, Candlewick $13.95 (1-56402-340-0). 24pp. A small girl chats with all sorts of people as well as her pet cat. Also use *Hiding* (1994). (Rev: BL 7/94; HB 9–10/94; SLJ 9/94*)

**2558** Hughes, Shirley. *Tales of Trotter Street* (PS–2). Illus. 1997, Candlewick $17.99 (0-7636-0090-3). 64pp. An anthology of 4 Trotter Street books about people who live on the same street. (Rev: BL 2/1/97)

**2559** Hughes, Shirley. *Two Shoes, New Shoes* (PS). Illus. by author. 1986, Lothrop paper $4.95 (0-688-04207-4). 24pp. A rhyming board book about clothes. (Rev: BL 12/15/86; HB 1–2/87; SLJ 12/86)

**2560** Humphries, Tudor. *Hiding* (PS–K). Illus. 1997, Orchard $14.95 (0-531-30056-0). 32pp. After she

has been scolded by her mother, a little girl goes into hiding until she becomes lonely. (Rev: BL 12/1/97; SLJ 3/98)

**2561** Hurwitz, Johanna. *New Shoes for Silvia* (PS–3). Illus. by Jerry Pinkney. 1993, Morrow LB $15.93 (0-688-05287-8). 32pp. Silvia finds all sorts of uses for her new shoes until her feet are big enough for her to wear them. (Rev: BCCB 11/93; BL 10/15/93; HB 11–12/93; SLJ 10/93)

**2562** Hutchins, Pat. *The Doorbell Rang* (K–2). Illus. by author. 1986, Greenwillow LB $15.93 (0-688-05252-5); Morrow paper $3.95 (0-688-09234-9). 24pp. Every time the doorbell rings, it means more of Ma's cookies are eaten, which leaves less for Victoria and Sam — until Grandma arrives with a package. (Rev: BCCB 3/86; BL 6/15/86; SLJ 4/86)

**2563** Ichikawa, Satomi. *Nora's Roses* (PS–1). Illus. 1997, Putnam $6.95 (0-698-11566-X). 32pp. Nora, confined to her room with a cold, sees every passerby pick roses from her bush. (Rev: BL 3/15/93; SLJ 6/93)

**2564** *I'm Going to the Doctor: A Pop-Up Book* (PS–K). Illus. by Maxie Chambliss. 1997, Penguin paper $7.99 (0-7214-5715-0). Pop-ups of a mouth and a leg are used in this book that tries to reassure children about going to a doctor. (Rev: BL 12/15/97)

**2565** Intrater, Roberta G. *Smile!* (PS). Photos by author. Series: Babyfaces. 1997, Scholastic $4.95 (0-590-05899-1). In this board book, a toddler responds to a photographer's requests. Also use *Peek-a-Boo!* (1997). (Rev: SLJ 2/98)

**2566** Isaacs, Gwynne L. *While You Are Asleep* (PS–2). Illus. by Cathi Hepworth. 1991, Walker LB $13.85 (0-8027-6986-1). 32pp. This picture book describes the intersecting lives of several people who work at night. (Rev: BL 9/1/91; SLJ 8/91)

**2567** Isadora, Rachel. *Lili at Ballet* (K–3). Illus. 1993, Putnam LB $15.95 (0-399-22423-8). 32pp. A lovely picture book of a child's dance experiences. (Rev: BCCB 4/93; BL 2/1/93*; HB 5–6/93; SLJ 3/93)

**2568** Isadora, Rachel. *Lili on Stage* (PS–3). Illus. 1995, Putnam $15.95 (0-399-22637-0). 32pp. The story of Lili's experiences in a small part on opening night of the ballet *Nutcracker*. (Rev: BL 11/15/95; SLJ 12/95)

**2569** Jabar, Cynthia. *Bored Blue? Think What You Can Do!* (PS–1). Illus. 1991, Little, Brown $14.95 (0-316-43458-2). 32pp. This book suggests all sorts of activities for bored kids, some of them in the world of fantasy, in rhyming text. (Rev: BL 4/1/91; SLJ 6/91)

**2570** Jakob, Donna. *My Bike* (PS–2). Illus. by Nelle Davis. 1994, Hyperion LB $14.49 (1-56282-455-4).

32pp. A picture book poem about a boy and how he learns to ride his bicycle. (Rev: BL 8/94; SLJ 8/94)

**2571** Jakob, Donna. *My New Sandbox* (PS–1). Illus. by Julia Gorton. 1996, Hyperion LB $14.49 (0-7868-2144-2). In his sandbox, a young boy imitates the movements and activities of a number of animals. (Rev: SLJ 4/96)

**2572** Jakob, Donna. *Tiny Toes* (PS–1). Illus. by Mireille Levert. 1995, Hyperion LB $14.49 (0-7868-2009-8). 32pp. Toes engage in a variety of activities, including dancing. (Rev: BL 4/1/95; SLJ 6/95)

**2573** James, Betsy. *Flashlight* (PS–2). Illus. by Stacey Schuett. 1997, Knopf LB $18.99 (0-679-97970-0). 32pp. Marie is afraid of the dark until her grandfather gives her a flashlight. (Rev: BL 12/15/97; SLJ 1/98*)

**2574** Jenness, Aylette. *Come Home with Me: A Multicultural Treasure Hunt* (1–4). Photos by Max Belcher. Illus. by Laura DeSantis. Series: Kids Bridge. 1993, New Pr. $16.95 (1-56584-064-X). 48pp. A treasure hunt that introduces 4 cultural groups represented in various neighborhoods in Boston. (Rev: SLJ 4/94)

**2575** Johnson, Angela. *Daddy Calls Me Man* (PS–1). Illus. by Rhonda Mitchell. 1997, Orchard LB $16.99 (0-531-33042-7). 32pp. In these 4 short verses, a young boy marvels at his parents' artwork, enjoys his wonderful loving home, and longs for a pair of big athletic shoes. (Rev: BL 10/15/97; SLJ 10/97)

**2576** Johnson, Angela. *Joshua's Night Whispers* (PS). Illus. by Rhonda Mitchell. 1994, Orchard $4.95 (0-531-06847-1). 12pp. A little African American boy is afraid of noises at night in this fine board book. Also use *Joshua by the Sea* (1994). (Rev: BL 12/1/94; SLJ 1/95)

**2577** Johnson, Angela. *The Leaving Morning* (PS–2). Illus. by David Soman. 1996, Orchard paper $5.95 (0-531-07072-7). 32pp. All the sorrow and anticipation of a move are captured in this picture of a family saying good-bye to their home and friends. (Rev: BL 9/1/92; HB 9–10/92; SLJ 9/92)

**2578** Johnson, Angela. *Rain Feet* (PS). Illus. by Rhonda Mitchell. 1994, Orchard $4.95 (0-531-06849-8). 12pp. A little African American boy enjoys splashing through puddles in this board book. Also use *Mama Birds, Baby Birds* (1994). (Rev: BL 12/1/94; HB 9–10/94; SLJ 1/95)

**2579** Johnson, Angela. *Shoes like Miss Alice's* (PS–K). Illus. by Ken Page. 1995, Orchard LB $16.99 (0-531-08664-X). 32pp. Sally resents her baby-sitter Miss Alice until she sees her wide assortment of shoes. (Rev: BL 3/15/95; SLJ 7/95)

**2580** Johnson, Dolores. *What Kind of Baby-Sitter Is This?* (PS–2). Illus. 1991, Macmillan LB $15.00 (0-02-747846-7). 32pp. Kevin gets a big surprise when he discovers that his new baby-sitter, an elderly lady, loves baseball as much as he does. (Rev: BCCB 10/91; BL 1/1/91; HB 11–12/91; SLJ 12/91)

**2581** Johnson, Paul B. *Farmers' Market* (PS–2). 1997, Orchard LB $16.99 (0-531-33014-1). 32pp. On Saturdays during the summer, Laura and her family sell their produce at the Farmers' Market in Lexington, Kentucky. (Rev: BCCB 4/97; BL 3/15/97; SLJ 6/97)

**2582** Johnston, Tony. *The Quilt Story* (PS–2). Illus. by Tomie dePaola. 1996, Putnam paper $5.95 (0-698-11368-3). 32pp. The star of this book is the quilt, which gives fun, warmth, and comfort to 2 generations. (Rev: BCCB 7/85; BL 8/85; SLJ 9/85)

**2583** Jonas, Ann. *Reflections* (PS–2). Illus. by author. 1987, Greenwillow LB $15.93 (0-688-06141-9). 24pp. A book of seaside scenes told in 2 sets of pictures — one when the book is held upright; the other when it is held upside down. (Rev: BL 9/15/87; SLJ 10/87)

**2584** Jonas, Ann. *When You Were a Baby* (PS–1). Illus. by author. 1982, Greenwillow LB $15.93 (0-688-00864-X). 24pp. Simple text shows an infant's progress.

**2585** Jordan, June. *Kimako's Story* (K–3). Illus. by Kay Burford. 1991, Houghton paper $3.95 (0-395-60338-2). 42pp. Seven-year-old Kimako explores her neighborhood.

**2586** Kesselman, Wendy. *Sand in My Shoes* (PS–3). Illus. by Ronald Himler. 1995, Hyperion LB $15.49 (0-7868-2045-4). 32pp. At the end of summer, a little girl says good-bye to the beach she loves but still retains little remembrances like sand in her shoes. (Rev: BL 6/1–15/95; SLJ 7/95)

**2587** Ketteman, Helen. *I Remember Papa* (K–3). Illus. by Greg Shed. 1998, Dial LB $15.89 (0-8037-1849-7). 32pp. Audie remembers the summer in which he attended a Cincinnati Reds game with his father and the heartache he suffered when he lost the money he had saved to buy a baseball glove. (Rev: BL 3/15/98)

**2588** Kidd, Nina. *June Mountain Secret* (K–3). Illus. 1991, HarperCollins LB $14.89 (0-06-023168-8). A girl and her father enjoy a day fishing in a remote mountain stream. (Rev: SLJ 6/91)

**2589** Kirk, Daniel. *Lucky's 24-Hour Garage* (K–3). Illus. 1996, Hyperion LB $15.49 (0-7868-2168-X). 32pp. There are all kinds of different customers who use the services of Lucky's Garage. (Rev: BL 9/1/96; SLJ 9/96)

**2590** Konigsburg, E. L. *Amy Elizabeth Explores Bloomingdale's* (PS–2). Illus. 1992, Macmillan $14.95 (0-689-31766-2). 32pp. Amy visits her grandmother in New York City, and they set out to explore the sights. (Rev: BCCB 9/92; BL 9/1/92; SLJ 9/92)

**2591** Konigsburg, E. L. *Samuel Todd's Book of Great Inventions* (3–6). Illus. 1991, Macmillan $13.95 (0-689-31680-1). 32pp. Samuel Todd explains why certain inventions are his favorites, such as training wheels, step stools, and backpacks. (Rev: BL 8/91; HB 1–2/92; SLJ 10/91) [608]

**2592** Krasilovsky, Phyllis. *The Very Little Boy* (PS–1). Illus. by Karen Gundersheimer. 1992, Scholastic paper $4.95 (0-590-44762-9). In this book that describes development, a young boy grows physically and is able to accomplish more skills. (Rev: SLJ 12/92)

**2593** Kroll, Steven. *Gone Fishing* (2–4). Illus. by Harvey Stevenson. 1990, Crown LB $13.99 (0-517-57590-6). 48pp. Although he does not catch any fish on his first day out, Willie knows there is always tomorrow. (Rev: BCCB 9/90; BL 5/15/90)

**2594** Kruusval, Catarina. *No Clothes Today!* (PS). Illus. by author. 1995, R&S $6.95 (91-29-63074-6). Stubborn Ellen has trouble deciding what clothes to wear, so she puts them on her pets. Also use *Where's the Ball?* (1995). (Rev: SLJ 3/96)

**2595** Kunhardt, Edith. *I'm Going to Be a Police Officer* (PS–2). Illus. 1995, Scholastic paper $2.50 (0-590-25485-5). 32pp. An average day in a small-town police officer's day as seen through the eyes of his 2 children, who spend time with him at the police station. (Rev: BL 1/1–15/96)

**2596** Kuskin, Karla. *The Philharmonic Gets Dressed* (1–4). Illus. by Marc Simont. 1982, HarperCollins $14.95 (0-06-023622-1); paper $5.95 (0-06-443124-X). 48pp. One hundred and five musicians are across town getting ready for a big concert.

**2597** Landstrom, Olof, and Lena Landstrom. *Will Goes to the Beach* (PS–K). Illus. 1995, Farrar $13.00 (91-29-62914-4). 32pp. Will spends a memorable day at the beach that includes making his first swimming strokes. (Rev: BL 9/1/95)

**2598** Landstrom, Olof, and Lena Landstrom. *Will Goes to the Post Office* (PS–2). Trans. from Swedish by Elisabeth Dyssegaard. Illus. 1994, R&S $13.00 (91-29-62950-0). A simple story about a boy who goes to the post office to pick up a package from his uncle. (Rev: SLJ 12/94)

**2599** Leghorn, Lindsay. *Proud of Our Feelings* (PS–2). Illus. by author. 1995, Magination $11.95 (0-945354-68-1). A little girl demonstrates the various emotions that her friends feel, like friendliness, sadness, happiness, silliness, and anger. (Rev: SLJ 4/96)

**2600** Lent, Blair. *Bayberry Bluff* (1–3). Illus. by author. 1987, Houghton paper $4.95 (0-395-62984-5). 32pp. Readers follow the evolution of a town

from an island where nothing lives but bayberries, to the "summer people," and then to a town. (Rev: BCCB 5/87; BL 5/15/87; SLJ 4/87)

**2601** Lester, Alison. *Clive Eats Alligators* (PS–1). Illus. by author. 1986, Houghton paper $4.95 (0-395-58408-6). Seven children go about their day in different ways; Rosie has eggs and bacon for breakfast, Frank likes granola, but Clive eats alligators — Alligator Pops cereal; and other punch endings of each activity. (Rev: BL 4/1/86; HB 7–8/86; SLJ 5/86)

**2602** Lester, Alison. *When Frank Was Four* (PS–2). Illus. 1996, Houghton $15.00 (0-395-74275-7). 32pp. Double-page spreads reveal many activities that a group of Australian children engage in from infancy to school age. A sequel to *Clive Eats Alligators* (1986). (Rev: BL 2/15/96; HB 5–6/96; SLJ 4/96)

**2603** Lewin, Ted. *Market!* (K–3). Illus. 1996, Lothrop LB $15.93 (0-688-12162-4). 48pp. The excitement and color of market day are captured in 6 locales, like Uganda and Ecuador. (Rev: BCCB 9/96; BL 4/15/96; HB 7–8/98; SLJ 6/96*)

**2604** Lewis, Kim. *My Friend Harry* (PS–1). Illus. 1995, Candlewick $15.95 (1-56402-617-5). 32pp. James finds he has a great friend in his silent companion, a toy elephant named Harry. (Rev: BL 10/15/95; SLJ 9/95*)

**2605** Lewis, Kim. *The Shepherd Boy* (PS–2). Illus. 1990, Macmillan LB $13.95 (0-02-758581-6). 32pp. A young boy who longs to be a shepherd like his father practices on a toy lamb. (Rev: BL 12/1/90; SLJ 12/90)

**2606** Lewison, Wendy C. *The Princess and the Potty* (PS). Illus. by Rick Brown. 1994, Simon & Schuster paper $15.00 (0-671-87284-2). 32pp. A young princess gets potty trained because she wants a pair of pantalettes. (Rev: BL 4/15/94; SLJ 4/94)

**2607** Lillie, Patricia. *Everything Has a Place* (PS). Illus. by Nancy Tafuri. 1993, Greenwillow $14.00 (0-688-10082-1). 24pp. This oversized picture book explores the concept that everything has a proper place or home. (Rev: BL 5/1/93*; HB 5–6/93; SLJ 7/93)

**2608** Lindgren, Barbro. *Sam's Potty* (PS). Illus. by Eva Eriksson. 1986, Morrow paper $6.95 (0-688-06603-8). 32pp. Toddler Sam refuses to use his potty until he tries it with his dog on his lap. Also use: *Sam's Wagon* (1986). (Rev: BL 11/1/86; SLJ 12/86)

**2609** Lipniacka, Ewa. *Asleep at Last* (PS–K). Illus. by Basia Bogdanowicz. Series: Jamie and Luke. 1993, Crocodile $6.95 (1-56656-118-3). A charming, short book that tells about the everyday experiences of a mother, school-aged Luke, and toddler Jamie. Also use *It's Mine!*, *School Trip*, and *Tooth Fairy* (all 1993). (Rev: SLJ 5/94)

**2610** Lomas Garza, Carmen. *In My Family/En Mi Familia* (1–4). Illus. 1996, Children's Book Pr. $15.95 (0-89239-138-3). 32pp. In 13 paintings labeled bilingually, the artist portrays his childhood in Kingsville, Texas. (Rev: BL 11/1/96; HB 11–12/96)

**2611** London, Jonathan. *Like Butter on Pancakes* (PS–3). Illus. by G. Brian Karas. 1995, Viking paper $13.99 (0-670-85130-2). 32pp. A young boy enjoys his day on a farm. (Rev: BCCB 2/95; BL 4/1/95; SLJ 2/95*)

**2612** London, Jonathan. *Puddles* (PS–1). Illus. by G. Brian Karas. 1997, Viking paper $15.99 (0-670-87218-0). 32pp. The joys of playing in puddles is evoked through the actions of a brother and sister after a rainstorm. (Rev: BL 5/15/97; SLJ 5/97)

**2613** Loomis, Christine. *In the Diner* (PS–1). Illus. by Nancy Poydar. 1994, Scholastic $14.95 (0-590-46716-6). 32pp. Lots of action words in short sentences are used to describe the hustle and bustle of a diner. (Rev: BL 4/15/94; SLJ 5/94)

**2614** Loomis, Christine. *Rush Hour* (PS–2). Illus. by Mari Takabayashi. 1996, Houghton $15.95 (0-395-69129-X). 32pp. Catchy rhymes and lively illustrations show what working parents do after they leave home in the morning. (Rev: BL 7/96; SLJ 9/96)

**2615** Lowery, Linda. *Twist with a Burger, Jitter with a Bug* (PS–2). Illus. by Pat Dypold. 1995, Houghton $14.95 (0-395-67022-5). 32pp. Various kinds of dances are suggested in exuberant, rhythmic verses. (Rev: BL 9/1/95; SLJ 9/95)

**2616** Lunn, Janet. *Come to the Fair* (K–2). Illus. by Gilles Pelletier. 1997, Tundra $15.95 (0-88776-409-6). The Martin family prepares for a visit to the county fair and spends an enjoyable day there. (Rev: SLJ 2/98)

**2617** Lyon, George E. *Come a Tide* (PS–2). Illus. by Stephen Gammell. 1990, Orchard LB $16.99 (0-531-08454-X). 32pp. Grandma knows the tide will rise after a 4-day deluge. (Rev: BL 2/1/90*; HB 3–4/90; SLJ 6/90*)

**2618** Lyon, George E. *Who Came down That Road?* (K–3). Illus. by Peter Catalanotto. 1992, Orchard $16.95 (0-531-05987-1); paper $5.95 (0-531-07073-5). 32pp. The story of a road through history from the present and back to the beginning of time. (Rev: BL 9/1/92; SLJ 10/92)

**2619** Macaulay, David. *Shortcut* (K–4). Illus. 1995, Houghton $15.95 (0-395-52436-9). 64pp. The lives of 6 people cross in a series of different stories. The author also uses this method of overlapping storytelling in *Black and White* (1990). (Rev: BCCB 9/95; BL 10/15/95; HB 3–4/95; SLJ 9/95*)

**2620** MacDonald, Amy. *Let's Go* (PS). Illus. by Maureen Roffey. 1994, Candlewick $5.95 (1-56402-202-1). In this simple board book, children from dif-

ferent cultures engage in such activities as riding a rocking horse and playing patty-cake. Also use *Let's Pretend* (1994). (Rev: SLJ 5/94)

**2621** McDonald, Megan. *The Potato Man* (K–3). Illus. by Ted Lewin. 1991, Orchard LB $16.99 (0-531-08514-7). 32pp. Grampa recalls the time when his neighborhood was regularly visited by peddlers, including the potato man. (Rev: BCCB 2/91; BL 1/15/91*; HB 5–6/91)

**2622** McFarlane, Sheryl. *Going to the Fair* (K–3). Illus. by Sheena Lott. 1996, Orca paper $6.95 (1-55143-062-2). 32pp. Erin enjoys all the sights and sounds of a country fair, including the clowns and the food. (Rev: BL 11/1/96)

**2623** McGrath, Bob. *Uh Oh! Gotta Go! Potty Tales from Toddlers* (PS). Illus. by Shelley Dieterichs. 1996, Barron's $5.95 (0-8120-6564-6). About 20 children describe different potty experiences in this unusual book that will help in toilet training. (Rev: SLJ 1/97) [613]

**2624** McGregor, Merideth. *Cowgirl* (PS–1). Illus. 1992, Walker LB $15.85 (0-8027-8171-3). 32pp. Simple, direct text describes the routines of life on a present-day ranch. (Rev: BCCB 2/93; BL 10/1/92; SLJ 12/92) [636.2]

**2625** McGuire, Richard. *Night Becomes Day* (K–3). Illus. 1994, Viking paper $14.99 (0-670-85547-2). 32pp. Through a series of free-association thoughts, various phenomena are explored in a contemporary setting. (Rev: BCCB 12/94; BL 10/1/94*; SLJ 1/95)

**2626** Machotka, Hana. *Pasta Factory* (1–4). Illus. 1992, Houghton $14.95 (0-395-60197-5). 32pp. A group of children tour a pasta factory, with color photos. (Rev: BL 9/1/92; SLJ 12/92) [664]

**2627** MacKinnon, Debbie. *Billy's Boots* (PS). Photos by Anthea Sieveking. Series: First Lift-the-Flap Books. 1996, Dial paper $4.95 (0-8037-1905-1). In this board book with flaps, a child can't find his new red boots. Also use *Cathy's Cake, Ken's Kitten,* and *Meg's Monkey* (all 1996). (Rev: SLJ 7/96)

**2628** MacKinnon, Debbie. *Daniel's Duck* (PS). Photos by Anthea Sieveking. Series: A First Lift-the-Flap Book. 1997, Dial paper $4.99 (0-8037-2102-1). A toddler named Daniel is looking for his duck in this board book illustrated with photos. Also use *Sarah's Shovel, Tom's Train,* and *Pippa's Puppy.* (Rev: SLJ 3/97)

**2629** McLerran, Alice. *Roxaboxen* (K–3). Illus. by Barbara Cooney. 1991, Lothrop LB $15.93 (0-688-07593-2). 32pp. The story of children in the desert who fashion an imaginary town. (Rev: BCCB 3/91*; BL 2/15/91*; HB 3–4/91; SLJ 2/91*)

**2630** McMillan, Bruce. *One Sun: A Book of Terse Verse* (PS–1). 1992, Holiday paper $5.95 (0-8234-0951-1). 32pp. A day at the beach is described in verse. (Rev: BCCB 5/90*; BL 5/15/90; SLJ 7/90) [811]

**2631** McMillan, Bruce. *Play Day: A Book of Terse Verse* (PS–K). Illus. 1991, Holiday LB $14.95 (0-8234-0894-9). 32pp. Bright photos capture 2-year-olds playing in the yard. (Rev: BCCB 2/92; BL 10/1/91; HB 1–2/92) [811]

**2632** McPhail, David. *Annie & Co.* (PS–3). Illus. 1995, Holt $13.95 (0-8050-1596-5). 32pp. Six-year-old Annie, who has learned from her father, decides to go out in the world and fix things. (Rev: BL 6/1/91; SLJ 6/91)

**2633** McPhail, David. *Ed and Me* (1–3). Illus. 1990, Harcourt $13.95 (0-15-224888-9). 32pp. Ed, the family truck, performs all sorts of useful chores around the farm. (Rev: BL 1/1/91; SLJ 12/90)

**2634** McPhail, David. *Farm Morning* (PS–K). Illus. by author. 1985, Harcourt $15.95 (0-15-227299-2); paper $3.95 (0-15-227300-X). 32pp. A little girl and her father do early-morning farm chores. (Rev: BCCB 12/85; BL 11/15/85; HB 11–12/85)

**2635** Maestro, Betsy. *Taxi: A Book of City Words* (PS–1). Illus. by Giulio Maestro. 1989, Houghton $14.95 (0-89919-528-8); paper $6.95 (0-395-54811-X). A taxi picks up and drops off people over the city and introduces new words. (Rev: BL 4/15/89; SLJ 4/89)

**2636** Mahy, Margaret. *Keeping House* (PS–2). Illus. by Wendy Smith. 1991, Macmillan $13.95 (0-689-50515-9). 32pp. When Lizzie hires a man to clean her house, she is so ashamed to show him the mess that she cleans it up herself. (Rev: BL 3/1/91; SLJ 6/91)

**2637** Mansell, Dom. *My Old Teddy* (PS–K). Illus. 1992, Candlewick $12.95 (1-56402-035-5). 32pp. Even a brand new teddy bear can't replace the old worn-out one that a little girl loves. (Rev: BL 6/1/92; SLJ 7/92)

**2638** Manushkin, Fran. *Let's Go Riding in Our Strollers* (2–4). Illus. by Benrei Huang. 1993, Hyperion LB $14.49 (1-56282-391-4). 32pp. In a big city, 2 children enjoy all the excitement of being taken out for a ride by their mothers in their strollers. (Rev: BL 6/1–15/93)

**2639** Martin, Antoinette T. *Famous Seaweed Soup* (PS–2). Illus. by Nadine Bernard Westcott. 1993, Whitman LB $14.95 (0-8075-2263-5). 32pp. While the family is at the seashore, no one will help Sara make soup. (Rev: BL 5/15/93; SLJ 8/93)

**2640** Martin, Bill, Jr., and John Archambault. *Here Are My Hands* (PS). Illus. by Ted Rand. 1987, Holt $14.95 (0-8050-0328-2). 32pp. Children indicate body parts, such as a boy pointing to a bandaged knee, which is for "falling down." (Rev: BL 7/87; SLJ 6–7/87)

**2641** Martin, Bill, Jr., and John Archambault. *Listen to the Rain* (PS–2). Illus. by James Endicott. 1988, Holt $15.95 (0-8050-0682-6). 32pp. A rhyming story about rain with double-page watercolors. (Rev: SLJ 10/88)

**2642** Martin, Bill, Jr., and John Archambault. *Up and Down on the Merry-Go-Round* (PS–1). Illus. by Ted Rand. 1988, Holt $14.95 (0-8050-0681-8); paper $4.95 (0-8050-1638-4). 32pp. A full-color merry-go-round whirls its delighted passengers in rhyming cadence. (Rev: BL 6/15/88; HB 7–8/88)

**2643** Martin, Jacqueline B. *Green Truck Garden Giveaway: A Neighborhood Story and Almanac* (K–3). Illus. by Alec Gillman. 1997, Simon & Schuster paper $16.00 (0-689-80498-9). 32pp. This story about 2 modern Johnny Appleseeds who plant gardens for people they meet also contains information about plants, how they grow, and their characteristics. (Rev: BL 5/1/97; SLJ 6/97)

**2644** Marzollo, Jean. *Sun Song* (PS–2). Illus. by Laura Regan. 1995, HarperCollins LB $14.89 (0-06-020788-4). 32pp. The changes in everyday things caused by the earth's rotation are chronicled. (Rev: BL 6/1–15/95; SLJ 7/95)

**2645** Maynard, Bill. *Santa's Time Off* (K–3). Illus. by Tom Browning. 1997, Putnam $15.95 (0-399-23138-2). Lighthearted poems about Santa's activities when he has some time free from his duties. (Rev: SLJ 10/97)

**2646** Medearis, Angela Shelf. *Bye-Bye, Babies!* (PS). Illus. by Patrice Aggs. 1995, Candlewick $4.95 (1-56402-258-7). 14pp. A group of babies plays peekaboo and learns to wave good-bye. Also use *Eat, Babies, Eat!* (1995). (Rev: BL 10/15/95; SLJ 3/96)

**2647** Medearis, Angela Shelf. *Dancing with the Indians* (K–3). Illus. by Samuel Byrd. 1991, Holiday LB $15.95 (0-8234-0893-0). 32pp. A young black girl and her family attend a pow-wow of the Oklahoma Seminoles. (Rev: BCCB 11/91; BL 12/1/91; SLJ 1/92)

**2648** Medearis, Angela Shelf. *Poppa's New Pants* (K–3). Illus. by John Ward. 1995, Holiday LB $15.95 (0-8234-1155-9). 32pp. Shortening father's new pants to fit him causes a minor family crisis. (Rev: BCCB 7–8/95; BL 6/1–15/95; SLJ 6/95)

**2649** Meijer, Marie. *The Bake-a-Cake Book: Beat the Eggs, Measure the Flour — Come and Bake with the Cake-Bakers!* (PS–1). Illus. by Charlotte Ramel. 1994, Chronicle $16.95 (0-8118-0693-6). A delightful interactive book in which transparencies are used to explain how a cake is baked. (Rev: SLJ 10/94)

**2650** Merriam, Eve. *Bam Bam Bam* (PS–1). Illus. by Dan Yaccarino. 1995, Holt $14.95 (0-8050-3527-3). 32pp. The sounds caused by the demolition of a skyscraper are featured in text and pictures. (Rev: BL 4/1/95; HB 7–8/95; SLJ 7/95)

**2651** Merriam, Eve. *The Hole Story* (PS–1). Illus. by Ivan Chermayeff. 1995, Simon & Schuster paper $16.00 (0-671-88353-4). A delightful picture book that explores the world of holes in verse and pictures that combine collage art with photos. (Rev: SLJ 8/95)

**2652** Miller, Margaret. *Family Time* (PS). Photos by author. Series: Super Chubby Books. 1996, Simon & Schuster $4.99 (0-689-80051-7). This board book illustrated with photos shows toddlers having fun with a variety of relatives. Also use *At the Shore, Happy Days*, and *My Best Friends* (all 1996). (Rev: SLJ 8/96)

**2653** Miller, Margaret. *Who Uses This?* (PS–K). Illus. 1990, Greenwillow LB $14.93 (0-688-08279-3). 40pp. The uses of 9 tools, such as the hammer and scissors, are pictured. (Rev: BCCB 3/90; BL 3/1/90; HB 9–10/90; SLJ 5/90) [331.7]

**2654** Miranda, Anne. *Baby-Sit* (PS). Illus. by Dorothy Stott. 1990, Little, Brown $9.95 (0-316-57454-6). The activities of 2 children and their baby-sitter are portrayed. (Rev: SLJ 10/90)

**2655** Miranda, Anne. *To Market, To Market* (K–2). Illus. by Janet Stevens. 1997, Harcourt $16.00 (0-15-200035-6). 36pp. A wildly funny picture book about market day misunderstandings. (Rev: BL 11/1/97; HB 11–12/97; SLJ 1/98)

**2656** Moore, Elaine. *Good Morning, City* (K–3). Illus. by William Low. 1995, BridgeWater paper $14.95 (0-8167-3654-5). Early-morning activities in the city are pictured, e.g., subway workers starting their trains and bakers producing doughnuts. (Rev: SLJ 1/96)

**2657** Mora, Pat. *Tomas and the Library Lady* (PS–3). Illus. by Raul Colon. 1997, Knopf LB $18.99 (0-679-90401-8). 40pp. The story of a migrant boy who finds a special place that welcomes and helps him: the library. (Rev: BL 8/97; SLJ 10/97)

**2658** Morris, Ann. *Hats, Hats, Hats* (PS–1). Illus. by Ken Heyman. 1989, Lothrop LB $15.93 (0-688-06339-X); Morrow paper $4.95 (0-688-12274-4). 32pp. A full-color display of varieties of hats. Also use: *Bread, Bread, Bread* (1989). (Rev: BL 4/15/89; SLJ 5/89)

**2659** Morris, Ann. *Houses and Homes* (PS–1). Illus. 1992, Lothrop LB $16.93 (0-688-10169-0). 32pp. A fascinating look at how houses are built around the world. (Rev: BCCB 12/92; BL 10/1/92)

**2660** Morris, Ann. *Play* (PS–K). Photos by Ken Heyman. 1998, Lothrop LB $14.93 (0-688-14553-1). 29pp. A spare text and double-page spreads of photos introduce how people play. Also use *Work* (1998). (Rev: SLJ 3/98)

**2661** Morton, Christine. *Picnic Farm* (PS–K). Illus. by Sarah Barringer. 1998, Holiday LB $15.95 (0-8234-1332-2). After touring a farm, a little girl and boy have a picnic using some of its produce, like eggs, bread, butter, and fruit. (Rev: SLJ 3/98)

**2662** Moss, Marissa. *Mel's Diner* (PS–3). Illus. 1994, Troll paper $13.95 (0-8167-3460-7). 32pp. Mabel, an African American child, loves to help out at her parents' diner. (Rev: BL 10/1/94; SLJ 12/94)

**2663** Moss, Thylias. *I Want to Be* (K–4). Illus. by Jerry Pinkney. 1993, Dial LB $14.89 (0-8037-1287-1). 32pp. A young girl comes up with some imaginative answers when she is asked by several people what she wants to be. (Rev: BL 10/1/93; SLJ 9/93)

**2664** *My First Look at Home* (PS). Illus. Series: My First Look at. 1990, Random $7.00 (0-679-80622-9). 20pp. The concept of a home is introduced with color photos against a white background. (Rev: BL 10/15/90) [633]

**2665** Neitzel, Shirley. *The Bag I'm Taking to Grandma's* (PS–2). Illus. by Nancy Winslow Parker. 1995, Greenwillow LB $14.93 (0-688-12961-7). 32pp. A cumulative story about all the objects a boy wants to take on his visit to Grandma's house. (Rev: BL 6/1–15/95; HB 5–6/95; SLJ 4/95)

**2666** Neitzel, Shirley. *The House I'll Build for the Wrens* (PS–3). Illus. by Nancy Winslow Parker. 1997, Greenwillow LB $14.93 (0-688-14974-X). 32pp. This rebus uses carpentry tools in an ingenious way to tell the story of a boy building a wren house. (Rev: BL 8/97*; HB 9–10/97; SLJ 9/97)

**2667** Neitzel, Shirley. *The Jacket I Wear in the Snow* (PS–K). Illus. by Nancy Winslow Parker. 1989, Greenwillow LB $15.93 (0-688-08030-8). 32pp. Bit by bit, all the winter clothing that a girl wears in the snow is introduced in this cumulative tale. (Rev: BCCB 10/89; BL 9/1/89; HB 9–10/89; SLJ 11/89)

**2668** Nelson, Nan F. *My Day with Anka* (PS–2). Illus. by Bill Farnsworth. 1996, Lothrop LB $15.93 (0-688-11059-2). 24pp. Anka, the family domestic, makes all her chores fun for both herself and little Karrie. (Rev: BL 9/15/96; SLJ 9/96)

**2669** Newcome, Zita. *Toddlerobics* (PS). Illus. 1996, Candlewick $14.99 (1-56402-809-7). 32pp. Several youngsters engage in a variety of exercises when they go to their toddler gym. (Rev: BCCB 2/96; BL 4/1/96; SLJ 3/96)

**2670** Nikola-Lisa, W. *America: My Land, Your Land, Our Land* (K–3). Illus. 1997, Lee & Low $15.95 (1-880000-37-7). 32pp. A handsome picture book that shows many of the contrasts that are present in the United States. (Rev: BL 9/1/97; SLJ 7/97)

**2671** Nunes, Susan. *The Last Dragon* (PS–3). Illus. by Chris K. Soentpiet. 1995, Clarion $14.95 (0-395-67020-9). 32pp. A Chinese American boy named

Peter gets everyone in Chinatown to help him repair a 10-man dragon he has purchased. (Rev: BL 5/1/95; SLJ 5/95)

**2672** O'Malley, Kevin. *Roller Coaster* (K–3). Illus. 1995, Lothrop LB $15.93 (0-688-13972-8). 24pp. A child remembers last year's trip to an amusement park and looks forward to this year's, when he hopes to ride the roller coaster. (Rev: BL 6/1–15/95; SLJ 6/95*)

**2673** Oppenheim, Shulamith Levey. *I Love You, Bunny Rabbit* (PS–1). Illus. by Cyd Moore. 1995, Boyds Mills $14.95 (1-56397-322-7). 32pp. Even though most of its fur has been pulled out, Micah prefers her stuffed Bunny Rabbit above her other toys. (Rev: BCCB 2/95; BL 1/1/95; SLJ 2/95)

**2674** Osborne, Mary Pope. *Rocking Horse Christmas* (PS–3). Illus. by Ned Bittinger. 1997, Scholastic $15.95 (0-590-92955-0). 32pp. A young boy has many adventures on his favorite toy, a wooden rocking horse, but in time he outgrows it. (Rev: BL 10/1/97; SLJ 10/97)

**2675** Ovenell-Carter, Julie. *Adam's Daycare* (PS). Illus. by Ruth Ohi. 1997, Annick LB $15.95 (1-55037-445-1); paper $5.95 (1-55037-444-3). 32pp. Adam enjoys being dropped off at Ina's day care home because of the toys, musical instruments, and other children he finds there. (Rev: BL 1/1–15/98; SLJ 1/98)

**2676** Oxenbury, Helen. *Tom and Pippo Go Shopping* (PS). Illus. by author. 1989, Macmillan paper $5.95 (0-689-71278-2). 14pp. The toddler and his toy monkey on a new adventure. Also use: *Tom and Pippo in the Garden; Tom and Pippo See the Moon; Tom and Pippo's Day* (all 1989). (Rev: BL 3/15/89; HB 5–6/89)

**2677** Oxenbury, Helen. *Tom and Pippo Read a Story* (PS). Illus. by author. 1998, Simon & Schuster paper $4.99 (0-689-81958-7). 14pp. Tom wants daddy to read to his stuffed monkey but has to do it himself. (Rev: BL 1/1/89; HB 1–2/89; SLJ 4/89)

**2678** Page, Debra. *Orcas Around Me: My Alaskan Summer* (K–3). Illus. by Leslie Bowman. 1997, Albert Whitman LB $15.95 (0-8075-6137-1). 40pp. A boy observes the wildlife of the north Pacific coast while he helps on the salmon boats operated by his parents. (Rev: BL 8/97; SLJ 9/97) [639.2]

**2679** Pallotta, Jerry. *Going Lobstering* (PS–2). Illus. by Rob Bolster. 1990, Charlesbridge $15.95 (0-88106-475-0); paper $7.95 (0-88106-474-2). 32pp. A boy and his sister spend a fascinating day on a lobster boat. (Rev: BL 12/1/90)

**2680** Patrick, Denise Lewis. *The Car Washing Street* (PS–2). Illus. by John Ward. 1993, Morrow LB $13.93 (0-688-11453-9). 32pp. One Saturday morning while neighbors are washing their cars, a friend-

ly water fight breaks out and Matthew and his father join in. (Rev: BL 11/1/93; SLJ 1/94)

**2681** Patrick, Denise Lewis. *No Diapers for Baby!* (PS). Illus. by Sylvia Walker. 1996, Golden Bks. $3.95 (0-307-12870-9). 16pp. A toddler believes that she is potty trained but has an accident. (Rev: BL 5/15/96)

**2682** Paul, Ann W. *Shadows Are About* (3–6). Illus. by Mark Graham. 1992, Scholastic paper $13.95 (0-590-44842-0). 32pp. A brother and sister accompanied by their shadows explore the world around them. (Rev: BL 7/92; SLJ 4/92)

**2683** Paulsen, Gary. *Worksong* (PS–3). Illus. by Ruth W. Paulsen. 1997, Harcourt $15.00 (0-15-200980-9). 32pp. The world of work from blue-collar laborers to computer professionals is celebrated in a fascinating picture book that depicts many different fields of endeavor. (Rev: BL 5/1/97; SLJ 5/97)

**2684** Pilkey, Dav. *The Paperboy* (PS–1). Illus. 1996, Orchard LB $15.99 (0-531-08856-1). 32pp. This book reflects the thoughts of a young boy when he makes early-morning rounds on his paper route with his dog. (Rev: BCCB 3/96; BL 3/1/96*; HB 7–8/96; SLJ 3/96*)

**2685** Pinkney, Brian. *Max Found Two Sticks* (PS–3). Illus. 1994, Simon & Schuster paper $16.00 (0-671-78776-4). 32pp. A lonely boy sitting on the steps of his house is able to imitate the sounds of the big city. (Rev: BL 4/1/94*; HB 5–6/94; SLJ 7/94)

**2686** Pinkney, Gloria J. *Back Home* (K–4). Illus. by Jerry Pinkney. 1992, Dial LB $14.89 (0-8037-1169-7). 40pp. Ernestine discovers her roots when she visits her aunt and uncle in Lamberton, North Carolina. (Rev: BCCB 9/92; BL 6/15/92*; HB 1–2/93; SLJ 9/92)

**2687** Pluckrose, Henry. *Walls* (PS–K). Illus. by Stephen Shott. Series: New Look. 1996, Children's LB $15.60 (0-516-08239-6). 32pp. All kinds of walls are pictured and their uses explained. (Rev: BL 6/1–15/96)

**2688** Pocock, Rita. *Annabelle and the Big Slide* (PS). Illus. 1989, Harcourt $10.95 (0-15-200407-6). 32pp. Annabelle summons up her courage to climb the ladder and zoom down the playground slide. (Rev: BL 1/1/90; HB 11–12/89; SLJ 12/89)

**2689** Polacco, Patricia. *Aunt Chip and the Great Triple Creek Dam Affair* (K–3). Illus. 1996, Putnam $15.95 (0-399-22943-4). 32pp. Because of television, a whole town forgets how to read until Aunt Chip, the town librarian, intervenes. (Rev: BCCB 6/96; BL 4/15/96; SLJ 5/96*)

**2690** Pomeranc, Marion Hess. *The American Wei* (PS–3). Illus. by DyAnne DiSalvo-Ryan. 1998, Albert Whitman LB $15.95 (0-8075-0312-6). 32pp. Outside the courthouse where his parents are to be naturalized, a young Chinese American boy loses his tooth and is helped by people from all over the world. (Rev: BL 3/15/98)

**2691** Priddy, Roger. *Baby's Book of the Body* (PS). Illus. 1996, DK Publg. $9.95 (0-7894-0198-3). Color photos of children are used to point out body parts, emotions, sounds, actions, and food. (Rev: SLJ 8/96)

**2692** Quattlebaum, Mary. *Underground Train* (PS–1). Illus. by Cat B. Smith. 1997, Doubleday $14.95 (0-385-32204-6). 24pp. The fun and excitement of a subway ride is captured in this picture book about a girl and her mother taking a ride in Washington, D.C. (Rev: BL 12/1/97; SLJ 11/97)

**2693** Quinsey, Mary Beth. *Why Does That Man Have Such a Big Nose?* (PS–1). Illus. by Wilson Chan. 1986, Parenting Pr. LB $16.95 (0-943990-25-4); paper $5.95 (0-943990-24-6). 32pp. Explaining some of the physical differences among people and how or why they happen. (Rev: BL 1/1/87; SLJ 12/86)

**2694** Ransom, Candice. *The Big Green Pocketbook* (PS–1). Illus. by Felicia Bond. 1993, HarperCollins LB $15.89 (0-06-020849-X). 32pp. At every stop during a day of errands with her mother, a little girl is given something for her empty pocketbook. (Rev: BL 7/93; SLJ 7/93)

**2695** Raschka, Chris. *Charlie Parker Played Be Bop* (PS–2). Illus. 1992, Orchard LB $16.99 (0-531-08599-6). 32pp. A picture book that allows young readers to learn about Charlie Parker's music by "hearing" it with pictures and words. (Rev: BCCB 12/92; BL 6/15/92; HB 11–12/92; SLJ 10/92) [788.7]

**2696** Ray, Mary L. *Pianna* (PS–3). Illus. by Bobbie Henba. 1994, Harcourt $14.95 (0-15-261357-9). 32pp. A New England woman looks back on her long life and realizes how much music and her love of the piano have meant to her. (Rev: BL 3/15/94; SLJ 5/94)

**2697** Relser, Lynn. *Tomorrow on Rocky Pond* (PS–1). Illus. 1993, Greenwillow LB $13.93 (0-688-10673-0). 32pp. A young girl who has just arrived at her family's summer home thinks of all the wonderful things she will soon be able to do. (Rev: BL 8/93)

**2698** Rice, Eve. *City Night* (K–2). Illus. by Peter Sis. 1987, Greenwillow LB $12.93 (0-688-06857-X). 24pp. The life of a city at night is related in this poem. (Rev: BCCB 12/87; BL 9/1/87; HB 11–12/87)

**2699** Riddell, Edwina. *100 First Words to Say with Your Baby* (PS). Illus. by author. 1992, Barron's paper $4.95 (0-8120-4888-1). This book illustrates 100 common words that prereaders should become familiar with. (Rev: SLJ 9/92)

**2700** Ripley, Catherine. *Why Is Soap So Slippery? And Other Bathtime Stories* (PS–1). Illus. by Scot Ritchie. 1995, Firefly $14.95 (1-895688-34-5); paper $5.95 (1-895688-39-6). Through 12 questions about bathroom objects and activities, the reader learns such things as how hot and cold water come out of the same tap, why we brush our teeth, and what happens when the toilet is flushed. (Rev: SLJ 2/96) [394]

**2701** Robbins, Ken. *Make Me a Peanut Butter Sandwich (and a Glass of Milk)* (PS–3). Illus. 1992, Scholastic $14.95 (0-590-43550-7). 32pp. Photos and minimal text tell how a favorite snack for children gets to the table. (Rev: BCCB 10/92; BL 9/1/92) [641]

**2702** Robinson, Aminah B. *A Street Called Home* (2–5). Illus. 1997, Harcourt $18.00 (0-15-201465-9). 24pp. An accordian book with flaps that depicts the life on Mt. Vernon Avenue in the African American section of Columbus, Ohio. (Rev: BL 12/15/97; SLJ 2/98)

**2703** Roche, Denis. *Ollie All Over* (PS). Illus. 1997, Houghton $4.95 (0-395-81124-4). 14pp. A board book about a dog who finds all sorts of places to hide in the house. (Rev: BCCB 6/97; BL 4/15/97; SLJ 8/97)

**2704** Rockwell, Anne. *Once upon a Time This Morning* (PS). Illus. by Sucie Stevenson. 1997, Greeenwillow LB $14.93 (0-688-14707-0). 24pp. Ten short, simple stories in which toddlers engage in such everyday activities as going to a store or playing with a friend. (Rev: BCCB 4/97; BL 4/1/97; SLJ 3/97)

**2705** Rockwell, Anne. *Pots and Pans* (PS). Illus. by Lizzy Rockwell. 1993, Macmillan LB $13.95 (0-02-777631-X). Two tots identify the various pots and pans found in a kitchen. (Rev: BCCB 3/93; HB 5–6/93; SLJ 7/93)

**2706** Rockwell, Anne. *What We Like* (PS–K). Illus. 1992, Macmillan paper $13.95 (0-02-777274-8). 24pp. Simple pleasures for young ones, such as building a sand castle and baking cookies. (Rev: BL 10/15/92; SLJ 2/93) [428.1]

**2707** Roddie, Shen. *Toes Are to Tickle* (PS). Illus. by Kady M. Denton. 1997, Tricycle Pr. $13.95 (1-883672-49-X). 24pp. A playful picture book that gives pleasant definitions to common articles, like "A tree is to hide behind." (Rev: BL 6/1–15/97; SLJ 9/97)

**2708** Rogers, Jean. *Runaway Mittens* (PS–1). Illus. by Rie Munoz. 1988, Greenwillow LB $15.93 (0-688-07054-X). 24pp. Pica's mittens seem to have a life of their own — they always disappear. (Rev: BL 3/1/88; HB 5–6/88)

**2709** Rosa-Casanova, Sylvia. *Mama Provi and the Pot of Rice* (K–3). Illus. by Robert Roth. 1997, Simon & Schuster $16.00 (0-689-31932-0). 32pp.

Mama Provi barters some of her arroz con pollo for a variety of other national dishes in this multicultural story. (Rev: BL 5/15/97; SLJ 7/97)

**2710** Rose, Emma. *Ballet Magic: A Pop-up Book* (PS–1). Illus. by Jan Palmer. 1996, Scholastic $12.95 (0-590-26242-4). 12pp. Various ballet positions and movements are shown in this pop-up book. (Rev: BL 12/15/96)

**2711** Rotner, Shelley, and Ken Kreisler. *Citybook* (PS–K). Illus. by Shelley Rotner. 1994, Orchard LB $16.99 (0-531-08687-9). 32pp. Ken explains why he loves visiting the city in this picture book filled with color photos of big-city life and sights. (Rev: BL 2/15/94; HB 5–6/94; SLJ 3/94)

**2712** Rotner, Shelley, and Ken Kreisler. *Faces* (PS). Illus. 1994, Macmillan paper $14.95 (0-02-777887-8). 32pp. Multicultural children engage in common activities like smelling, thinking, and making faces in this picture book. (Rev: BL 11/15/94; SLJ 12/94) [153.7]

**2713** Rounds, Glen. *Cowboys* (PS–1). Illus. 1991, Holiday LB $15.95 (0-8234-0867-1). 32pp. A day in the life of a cowboy is described in sparse text and shown in complementary illustrations. (Rev: BCCB 4/91; BL 6/1/91; SLJ 5/91)

**2714** Russo, Marisabina. *Under the Table* (PS–1). Illus. 1997, Greenwillow LB $14.93 (0-688-14603-1). 32pp. A young girl creates her own world under a table, but she gets into trouble when she decides to use the table's underside as a drawing board. (Rev: BCCB 5/97; BL 4/1/97; SLJ 4/97)

**2715** Rylant, Cynthia. *Appalachia: The Voices of Sleeping Birds* (PS–3). Illus. by Barry Moser. 1991, Harcourt $16.00 (0-15-201605-8). 32pp. A loving book in simple text and art about remembering Appalachia. (Rev: BCCB 6/91; BL 2/1/91*; HB 9–10/91*; SLJ 4/91*) [974]

**2716** Rylant, Cynthia. *An Everyday Book* (PS–K). Illus. 1997, Simon & Schuster paper $12.95 (0-689-81255-8). 32pp. A collection of 5 previously released board books about everyday pets, a garden, children, a town, and a house. (Rev: BL 4/15/97)

**2717** Rylant, Cynthia. *Everyday Children* (PS). Illus. by author. Series: Everyday Books. 1993, Bradbury paper $4.95 (0-02-778022-8). The children in this board book engage in simple activities like loving different kinds of pets. Also use *Everyday Garden* (1993). (Rev: SLJ 10/93*)

**2718** Rylant, Cynthia. *Everyday House* (PS). Illus. by author. Series: Everyday Books. 1993, Bradbury paper $4.95 (0-02-778024-4). In this board book, it is pointed out that an everyday house contains a door, a porch, flowers, cookies, a dog, and a kitten. Also use *Everyday Pets* and *Everyday Town* (both 1993). (Rev: SLJ 10/93*)

**2719** Rylant, Cynthia. *Mr. Griggs' Work* (PS–2). Illus. by Julie Downing. 1989, Orchard paper $6.95 (0-531-07037-9). 32pp. Mr. Griggs, who works at the post office, loves his job. (Rev: BCCB 2/89; BL 2/1/89; HB 3–4/89)

**2720** Sabuda, Robert. *Cookie Count: A Tasty Pop-Up* (PS–1). Illus. 1997, Simon & Schuster paper $19.95 (0-689-81191-8). 12pp. Pop-ups involving food are featured in this book, including an amazing gingerbread house. (Rev: BL 12/15/97)

**2721** Sage, James. *The Little Band* (PS–2). Illus. by Keiko Narahashi. 1991, Macmillan $13.95 (0-689-50516-7). 32pp. A band of 6 children brings music and delight to a small town. (Rev: BCCB 7–8/91; BL 2/15/91; SLJ 5/91)

**2722** Sathre, Vivian. *On Grandpa's Farm* (PS). Illus. by Anne Hunter. 1997, Houghton $16.00 (0-395-76506-4). A day's activities on a farm end when Grandpa takes his young helper fishing. (Rev: SLJ 9/97)

**2723** Schotter, Roni. *Dreamland* (K–2). Illus. by Kevin Hawkes. 1996, Orchard LB $16.99 (0-531-08858-8). 40pp. Theo's fanciful drawings of strange inventions become real when his uncle creates an amusement park. (Rev: BL 4/1/96; SLJ 4/96*)

**2724** Schotter, Roni. *Nothing Ever Happens on 90th Street* (PS–2). Illus. by Kyrsten Brooker. 1997, Orchard LB $17.99 (0-531-08886-3). 32pp. Eva's writing assignment changes how her neighborhood acts and interacts. (Rev: BL 3/1/97; SLJ 3/97*)

**2725** Scott, Ann H. *Brave as a Mountain Lion* (K–3). Illus. by Glo Coalson. 1996, Clarion $14.95 (0-395-66760-7). 32pp. Spider, a Shoshone boy, gets help from his family to conquer his fears, but it is from watching a real spider that he gets real help. (Rev: BCCB 2/96; BL 3/15/96; SLJ 4/96)

**2726** Scott, Ann H. *Hi* (PS). Illus. by Glo Coalson. 1994, Putnam $15.95 (0-399-21964-1). 32pp. At the post office with her mother, little Margarita greets everyone, but no one pays attention until one of the workers smiles at her. (Rev: BL 5/15/94; HB 7–8/94; SLJ 7/94*)

**2727** *Secret Shapes: A Changing Picture Book* (PS). Illus. 1995, DK Publg. $6.95 (1-56458-962-5). 20pp. By pulling tabs, shapes turn into different objects in this interactive book. (Rev: BL 2/1/96)

**2728** Senisi, Ellen B. *Secrets* (PS–1). Illus. 1995, Dutton paper $13.99 (0-525-45393-8). 32pp. Explores all kinds of secrets — good and bad — and the behavior they cause. (Rev: BL 8/95; SLJ 1/96)

**2729** Serfozo, Mary. *Joe Joe* (PS–1). Illus. by Nina S. Montezinos. 1993, Simon & Schuster $15.95 (0-689-50578-7). Using only 16 words, the author describes a boy's outdoor walk and his encounter with a mud puddle. (Rev: SLJ 1/94)

**2730** Seuss, Dr. *Oh, the Places You'll Go!* (PS–3). Illus. 1990, Random LB $17.99 (0-679-90527-8). This book of advice for youngsters tells them that in spite of problems, they can succeed. (Rev: BL 1/1/90*; SLJ 3/90)

**2731** Seymour, Tres. *The Smash-up Crash-up Derby* (K–2). Illus. by S. D. Schindler. 1995, Orchard LB $16.99 (0-531-08731-X). 32pp. A boy and members of his family enjoy the fall fair, particularly the demolition derby. (Rev: BCCB 3/95; BL 2/1/95; SLJ 3/95)

**2732** Shelby, Anne. *Homeplace* (PS–2). Illus. by Wendy A. Halperin. 1995, Orchard LB $17.99 (0-531-08732-8). 32pp. A grandmother tells her grandchild about the history of her family and the old homestead. (Rev: BCCB 5/95; BL 2/15/95; SLJ 4/95*)

**2733** Shelby, Anne. *The Someday House* (PS–2). Illus. by Rosanne Litzinger. 1996, Orchard LB $15.99 (0-531-08860-X). 32pp. Three children imagine living in a variety of different houses and settings. (Rev: BL 3/1/96; SLJ 4/96)

**2734** Shulevitz, Uri. *Toddlecreek Post Office* (2–4). Illus. 1990, Farrar $14.95 (0-374-37635-2). 32pp. The inhabitants of a small village are told their post office must close. (Rev: BCCB 1/91; BL 11/15/90; SLJ 1/91)

**2735** Silverman, Erica. *Fixing the Crack of Dawn* (K–2). Illus. by Sandra Speidel. 1994, BridgeWater paper $13.95 (0-8167-3458-5). When Lisa hears that her mother will be home at the crack of dawn, she goes outdoors hoping to mend the crack. (Rev: SLJ 11/94)

**2736** Simon, Norma. *Wet World* (PS–2). Illus. by Alexi Natchev. 1995, Candlewick $12.95 (1-56402-190-4). 32pp. A wet, rainy day as experienced by a little girl. (Rev: BCCB 6/95; BL 6/1–15/95; SLJ 8/95)

**2737** Siomades, Lorianne. *A Place to Bloom* (PS). Illus. by author. 1997, Boyds Mills $7.95 (1-56397-656-0). A collection of random thoughts about attitudes, likes, dislikes, and emotions, all expressed in catchy rhymes. (Rev: SLJ 9/97)

**2738** Smalls-Hector, Irene. *Jonathan and His Mommy* (PS–K). Illus. by Michael Hays. 1992, Little, Brown $15.95 (0-316-79870-3). 32pp. A mother and child use a variety of steps as they take a walk around the city. (Rev: BCCB 1/92; BL 10/1/92; HB 11–12/92; SLJ 11/92)

**2739** Soentpiet, Chris K. *Around Town* (PS–2). Illus. 1994, Lothrop LB $15.93 (0-688-04573-1). 32pp. Big-city life is celebrated in this picture book about a young girl and her mother strolling around New York City. (Rev: BL 4/1/94; SLJ 5/94) [307.67]

**2740** Soto, Gary. *Snapshots from the Wedding* (K–3). Illus. by Stephanie Garcia. 1997, Putnam $15.95 (0-399-22808-X); paper $5.99 (0-698-11752-2). 32pp. A delightful picture book that chronicles the exciting and tearful moments during a Mexican American wedding. (Rev: BCCB 4/97; BL 2/15/97*; SLJ 5/97)

**2741** Spier, Peter. *People* (2–4). Illus. by author. 1980, Doubleday $16.95 (0-385-13181-X); paper $10.95 (0-385-24469-X). 48pp. A view of people's varying life-styles and ways of life.

**2742** Starr, Elizabeth. *Evan's Corner* (PS–2). Illus. by Sandra Speidel. 1991, Viking paper $13.99 (0-670-82830-0). Evan, who likes peace and quiet, finds his own little corner. (Rev: SLJ 3/91*)

**2743** Stevenson, James. *Fun/No Fun* (PS–3). Illus. 1994, Greenwillow LB $13.93 (0-688-11674-4). 32pp. Various everyday events taken from the author's life as he was growing up are classified as being either fun or no fun in this humorous but perceptive picture book. (Rev: BL 3/15/94; HB 7–8/94; SLJ 8/94) [813]

**2744** Stevenson, James. *July* (K–3). Illus. by author. 1990, Greenwillow LB $12.88 (0-688-08823-6). 32pp. The author recalls his childhood and the fun he had going to the beach with his grandparents. (Rev: BL 5/1/90; HB 5–6/90; SLJ 3/90*) [741]

**2745** Stewart, Sarah. *The Library* (K–3). Illus. by David Small. 1995, Farrar $15.00 (0-374-34388-8). 32pp. The life story of a woman who loved reading books so much that eventually a library was named after her. (Rev: BCCB 5/95; BL 3/15/95; HB 7–8/95; SLJ 9/95)

**2746** Tafuri, Nancy. *The Brass Ring* (PS–2). Illus. 1996, Greenwillow LB $15.93 (0-688-14169-2). 32pp. A young girl lists all the nice things about going on vacation, including grabbing the brass ring on the carousel. (Rev: BCCB 10/96; BL 10/1/96; SLJ 10/96)

**2747** Tarpley, Natasha A. *I Love My Hair!* (PS–1). Illus. by E. B. Lewis. 1998, Little, Brown $14.95 (0-316-52275-9). 32pp. A young African American girl has fun creating different styles with her hair. (Rev: BL 2/15/98; SLJ 2/98)

**2748** Temple, Charles. *Train* (PS–1). Illus. by Larry Johnson. 1996, Houghton $14.95 (0-395-69826-X). 32pp. An African American family experiences the excitement and fun of an overnight train trip. (Rev: BL 3/15/96; SLJ 4/96)

**2749** Thompson, Carol. *Baby Days* (PS). Illus. 1991, Macmillan $15.95 (0-02-789235-1). 48pp. Illustrates a number of activities that toddlers can engage in from waking to bedtime. (Rev: BL 12/1/91; SLJ 1/92)

**2750** Torres, Leyla. *Subway Sparrow* (PS–2). Illus. 1993, Farrar $15.00 (0-374-37285-3). 30pp. Four people who are riders in a New York City subway car try to help a sparrow that is trapped inside. (Rev: BL 1/15/94; SLJ 2/94)

**2751** Tresselt, Alvin. *Wake Up, City!* (PS–K). Illus. by Carolyn Ewing. 1990, Lothrop LB $13.88 (0-688-08653-5). 32pp. Pictures activities in the city from daybreak until the work day begins. (Rev: BCCB 9/90; BL 5/1/90; SLJ 8/90)

**2752** Tresselt, Alvin. *White Snow Bright Snow* (K–3). Illus. by Roger Duvoisin. 1988, Lothrop LB $15.93 (0-688-51161-9); Morrow paper $4.95 (0-688-08294-7). Small-town snowfall is chronicled in this reissued Caldecott Medal winner of 1948.

**2753** Tryon, Leslie. *Albert's Ballgame* (PS–1). Illus. 1996, Simon & Schuster $16.00 (0-689-80187-4). 32pp. There's lots of action and fun in this humorous description of a baseball game. (Rev: BL 5/1/96; SLJ 3/96*)

**2754** Van Leeuwen, Jean. *Emma Bean* (K–3). Illus. by Juan Wijngaard. 1993, Dial paper $13.89 (0-8037-1393-2). 40pp. Emma Bean is a stuffed rabbit that becomes Molly's prized possession during her childhood. (Rev: BL 7/93)

**2755** Vaughan, Marcia, and Patricia Mullins. *The Sea Breeze Hotel* (PS–2). Illus. 1992, HarperCollins LB $13.89 (0-06-020504-0). 32pp. The guests at the Sea Breeze Hotel find enjoyment in flying kites. (Rev: BL 7/92; SLJ 8/92)

**2756** Vizurraga, Susan. *Our Old House* (PS–3). Illus. by Leslie Baker. 1997, Holt $15.95 (0-8050-3911-2). 32pp. While her parents restore an old house, a young girl wonders about the people who used to live in it. (Rev: BL 12/1/97; SLJ 10/97)

**2757** Voetberg, Julie. *I Am a Home Schooler* (2–4). Illus. 1995, Albert Whitman LB $15.95 (0-8075-3441-2); paper $6.95 (0-8075-3442-0). 32pp. Nine-year-old Teigen describes why she is a home schooler and the educational routine she follows. Illustrated with photographs. (Rev: BCCB 12/95; BL 1/1–15/96; SLJ 2/96) [649]

**2758** Waddell, Martin. *Mimi's Christmas* (PS–K). Illus. by Leo Hartas. 1997, Candlewick paper $3.99 (0-7636-0413-5). A little mouse is comforted by his sister when he begins to worry that Santa Mouse won't bring him the drum he wants. (Rev: SLJ 10/97)

**2759** Waddell, Martin. *Once There Were Giants* (PS–1). Illus. by Penny Dale. 1989, Delacorte $13.95 (0-385-29806-4). 32pp. This book captures a child's view of growing up, where adults seem like giants. (Rev: BL 11/1/89; SLJ 12/89)

**2760** Wallace, John. *Little Bean's Friend* (PS–1). Illus. 1997, HarperFestival $10.95 (0-694-00973-3). 24pp. Little Bean and her dog Bouncer spend a fine

day playing indoors and outside. (Rev: BL 6/1–15/97; HB 9–10/97)

**2761** Watson, Nancy D. *Tommy's Mommy's Fish* (PS–3). Illus. by Thomas A. D. Watson. 1996, Viking paper $14.99 (0-670-85681-9). 32pp. Tommy decides to catch a fine fish as a gift for his mother on her birthday. (Rev: BL 5/1/96; SLJ 4/96)

**2762** Weidt, Maryann N. *Daddy Played Music for the Cows* (PS–3). Illus. by Henri Sorensen. 1995, Lothrop LB $14.93 (0-688-10058-9). 32pp. Life on a farm is recorded in this story of a girl who grows from baby to school age in this environment. (Rev: BL 10/1/95; SLJ 10/95)

**2763** Welch, Willy. *Playing Right Field* (PS–3). Illus. by Marc Simont. 1995, Scholastic $13.95 (0-590-48298-X). 32pp. An awkward boy inadvertently becomes a baseball hero. (Rev: BCCB 7–8/95; BL 1/15/95*; HB 9–10/95; SLJ 3/95*)

**2764** Wellington, Monica. *Baby at Home* (PS). Illus. 1997, Dutton paper $4.99 (0-525-45640-6). 12pp. A board book that introduces common objects found in the home. Also use *Baby Goes Shopping* (1997). (Rev: BL 9/1/97; SLJ 6/97)

**2765** Wellington, Monica. *Baby in a Buggy* (PS). Illus. 1995, Dutton paper $3.99 (0-525-45295-8). 12pp. Simple objects that a baby would see from its buggy are identified in this board book. Also use *Baby in a Car* (1995). (Rev: BL 6/1–15/95; SLJ 9/95)

**2766** Wellington, Monica. *Baby in a Car* (PS). Illus. by author. 1995, Dutton paper $3.99 (0-525-45296-6). A board book that pictures all the things a baby sees in a car. (Rev: SLJ 9/95)

**2767** Weninger, Brigitte. *Ragged Bear* (PS–2). Trans. from German by Marianne Martens. Illus. by Alan Marks. 1996, North-South LB $15.88 (1-55858-663-6). After poor Teddy is abused by his owner and left in the park, he is adopted by a more caring child. (Rev: SLJ 12/96)

**2768** Wilkes, Angela. *My First Word Board Book* (PS). Illus. 1997, DK Publg. $6.95 (0-7894-1514-3). For the very young, this board book identifies and labels common items. (Rev: SLJ 7/97)

**2769** Williams, Sherley A. *Working Cotton* (PS–2). Illus. by Carole Byard. 1992, Harcourt $14.95 (0-15-299624-9). 32pp. A migrant child laborer tells of her daylong work in the fields. (Rev: BCCB 10/92; BL 9/1/92*; HB 11–12/93; SLJ 11/92)

**2770** Williams, Sue. *I Went Walking* (PS–K). Illus. by Julie Vivas. 1990, Harcourt $16.00 (0-15-200471-8). 32pp. This book involves guessing the identity of animals hidden in pictures during a boy's afternoon walk. (Rev: BCCB 12/92; BL 9/1/90*; HB 11–12/90; SLJ 10/90*)

**2771** Williams, Vera B. *Cherries and Cherry Pits* (K–3). Illus. by author. 1986, Greenwillow LB $15.93 (0-688-05146-4); Morrow paper $4.95 (0-688-10478-9). 40pp. Three tales and pictures from young Bidemmi, a black girl, about giving, loving, and making art. (Rev: BL 10/15/86; HB 9–10/86; SLJ 10/86)

**2772** Williams, Vera B., and Jennifer Williams. *Stringbean's Trip to the Shining Sea* (2–4). Illus. by Vera B. Williams. 1988, Greenwillow LB $15.93 (0-688-07162-7); Scholastic paper $5.99 (0-590-44851-X). 48pp. A journey from Kansas to the West Coast, with Stringbean sending postcards along the way, which make up a kind of photo album. (Rev: BCCB 5/88; BL 3/1/88; SLJ 3/88)

**2773** Winthrop, Elizabeth. *Shoes* (PS–K). Illus. by William Joyce. 1986, HarperCollins LB $14.89 (0-06-026592-2); paper $4.95 (0-06-443171-1). 32pp. Rhyming verse about shoes and feet. (Rev: BL 10/1/86; HB 1–2/87; SLJ 12/86)

**2774** Wolff, Ferida. *A Weed Is a Seed* (K–2). Illus. by Janet Pedersen. 1996, Houghton $14.95 (0-395-72291-8). A family discovers that objects can be regarded in 2 ways, e.g., a breeze can bring refreshment or, to others, a sneeze. (Rev: SLJ 4/96)

**2775** Wolff, Ferida. *A Year for Kiko* (PS–1). Illus. by Joung Un Kim. 1997, Houghton $15.00 (0-395-77396-2). 32pp. This picture book shows the everyday activities that a little girl named Kiko engaged in during a year. (Rev: BL 12/15/97; SLJ 10/97)

**2776** Wong, Olive. *From My Window* (PS–K). Illus. by Anna Rich. 1995, Silver Pr. LB $15.95 (0-382-24665-9); paper $5.95 (0-382-24667-5). A young boy notices several changes in his neighborhood as snow falls. (Rev: SLJ 9/95)

**2777** Wood, Audrey. *The Napping House Wakes Up* (PS–2). Illus. by Don Wood. 1994, Harcourt $17.95 (0-15-200890-X). 20pp. All sorts of actions take place in this interactive version of the popular picture book. (Rev: BL 11/15/94; SLJ 11/94)

**2778** Yashima, Taro. *Umbrella* (PS–1). Illus. by author. 1958, Puffin paper $4.99 (0-14-050240-8). 32pp. A 3-year-old Japanese American girl, born in New York City, longs for a rainy day so she can use her new blue umbrella and red rubber boots.

**2779** Yee, Wong H. *Fireman Small* (PS–K). Illus. 1994, Houghton $15.00 (0-395-68987-2). 28pp. Every time Fireman Small tries to sleep, he must respond to another emergency. (Rev: BL 2/1/95; SLJ 12/94)

**2780** Young, Ruth. *Golden Bear* (PS). Illus. by Rachel Isadora. 1992, Viking paper $15.99 (0-670-82577-8). 32pp. Appealing pictures tell of a big, golden teddy bear and the little boy who loves him. (Rev: BCCB 7–8/92; BL 6/1/92*; SLJ 4/92)

**2781** Zolotow, Charlotte. *I Like to Be Little* (K–3). Illus. by Erik Blegvad. 1987, HarperCollins paper $4.95 (0-06-443248-3). 32pp. The advantages of being small are explored in this 1966 picture book originally titled I Want to Be Little.

## FAMILY STORIES

**2782** Ackerman, Karen. *By the Dawn's Early Light* (PS–2). Illus. by Catherine Stock. 1994, Atheneum $16.00 (0-689-31788-3). 40pp. Because mom works the night shift, grandmother must spend nights with the family's 2 young children. (Rev: BCCB 5/94; BL 4/1/94; SLJ 6/94)

**2783** Ackerman, Karen. *Song and Dance Man* (K–3). Illus. by Stephen Gammell. 1988, Knopf LB $16.99 (0-394-99330-6); paper $6.99 (0-679-81995-9). 32pp. Up in the attic, Grandpa shows 3 children what it's like to be a song-and-dance man. Caldecott Medal winner, 1989. (Rev: BCCB 11/88; BL 10/1/88; HB 11–12/88)

**2784** Addy, Sharon Hart. *A Visit with Great-Grandma* (K–2). Illus. by Lydia Halverson. 1989, Whitman LB $14.95 (0-8075-8497-5). 32pp. A little girl's visit to Great-grandma celebrates their Czechoslovakian heritage. (Rev: BL 4/15/89; SLJ 6/89)

**2785** Adoff, Arnold. *Black Is Brown Is Tan* (K–3). Illus. by Emily Arnold McCully. 1973, HarperCollins $15.00 (0-060-20083-9). 32pp. A story in rhyme, which needs to be read aloud for greater understanding, depicts the warmth and companionship of an interracial family.

**2786** Alexander, Martha. *Nobody Asked Me If I Wanted a Baby Sister* (PS–1). Illus. by author. 1977, Dial paper $3.95 (0-8037-6410-3). 32pp. A young boy discovers that he loves his baby sister in spite of the fact that he thinks there is too much fuss made over her.

**2787** Alexander, Martha. *Where Does the Sky End, Grandpa?* (PS). Illus. by author. 1992, Harcourt $12.95 (0-15-295603-4). In this gentle story, a young girl walks through the pastures with her grandfather. (Rev: SLJ 7/92)

**2788** Aliki. *Jack and Jake* (PS–1). Illus. by author. 1986, Greenwillow $12.95 (0-688-06099-4). 32pp. No one can ever tell Jack and Jake apart, except their sister, who sets everyone straight. (Rev: BCCB 4/86; BL 4/15/86; SLJ 8/86)

**2789** Aliki. *Welcome, Little Baby* (PS–K). Illus. by author. 1987, Greenwillow $16.00 (0-688-06810-3). 24pp. Addressed to the newborn child and celebrating the innocence of the infant. (Rev: BL 3/1/87; SLJ 6–7/87)

**2790** Anderson, Lena. *Stina* (K–2). Illus. 1989, Greenwillow LB $13.88 (0-688-08881-3). 40pp. Grandfather's house by the sea provides a wonderful summer for Stina. (Rev: BL 9/15/89; HB 9–10/89; SLJ 10/89)

**2791** Anderson, Lena. *Stina's Visit* (PS–1). Illus. 1989, Greenwillow $13.95 (0-688-08880-5). 32pp. Stina and her grandfather visit Stetcit, an old seaman who is a friend of grandfather's. (Rev: BCCB 5/91; BL 6/15/91; HB 7–8/91; SLJ 7/91)

**2792** Anholt, Catherine, and Laurence Anholt. *Here Come the Babies* (PS–K). Illus. 1993, Candlewick $13.95 (1-56402-209-9). 32pp. Through pictures and light verse, daily activities of babies are chronicled. (Rev: BL 10/15/93; HB 11–12/93; SLJ 1/94) [305.23]

**2793** Anholt, Laurence. *The Magpie Song* (K–3). Illus. by Dan Williams. 1996, Houghton $14.95 (0-395-75280-9). 40pp. In an exchange of letters, a grandmother and grandchild tell of their concerns and troubles. (Rev: BL 9/1/96)

**2794** Armstrong, Jennifer. *That Terrible Baby* (PS–1). Illus. by Susan Meddaugh. 1994, Morrow $14.00 (0-688-11832-1). 32pp. Two children continually get blamed for all the chaos caused by "speedy crawler," the baby of the house. (Rev: BL 4/1/94; SLJ 6/94)

**2795** Bahr, Mary. *The Memory Box* (K–3). Illus. by David Cunningham. 1992, Whitman LB $14.95 (0-8075-5052-3). 32pp. In this sensitive story, Zach shares a "memory box" with his Grandpa, who is fighting Alzheimer's disease. (Rev: BCCB 2/92; BL 2/15/92*; SLJ 9/92)

**2796** Ballard, Robin. *When I Am a Sister* (PS–K). Illus. 1998, Greenwillow $15.00 (0-688-15397-6). 24pp. Kate wonders if she will still be welcome when she visits her father and stepmother after their new baby arrives. (Rev: BL 3/1/98; SLJ 4/98)

**2797** Barbour, Karen. *Little Nino's Pizzeria* (PS–2). Illus. by author. 1990, Harcourt paper $6.00 (0-15-246321-6). 32pp. When his father's business turns big, Tony is only in the way. (Rev: BL 9/15/87; SLJ 11/87)

**2798** Barrett, John M. *Daniel Discovers Daniel* (2–3). Illus. by Joe Servello. 1980, Human Sciences $16.95 (0-87705-423-1). 32pp. Daniel tries to satisfy his father's need for a sports-minded son.

**2799** Bauer, Caroline Feller. *My Mom Travels a Lot* (K–2). Illus. by Nancy Winslow Parker. 1985, Puffin paper $4.99 (0-14-050545-8). 48pp. The best thing about Mom taking trips is the homecoming.

**2800** Baylor, Byrd. *Guess Who My Favorite Person Is* (1–3). Illus. by Robert Andrew Parker. 1992, Simon & Schuster $14.95 (0-684-19514-3). 32pp. A sensitive book that celebrates the joy and happiness in listing favorites. A reissue of the 1977 edition.

**2801** Baynton, Martin. *Why Do You Love Me?* (PS–1). Illus. 1990, Greenwillow LB $15.93 (0-688-09157-1). 32pp. A simple text about a boy asking his

father why he loves him. (Rev: BL 4/15/90; SLJ 7/90)

**2802** Behrens, June. *Fiesta!* (1–3). Illus. by Scott Taylor. 1978, Children's LB $17.80 (0-516-08815-7); paper $4.95 (0-516-48815-5). 32pp. The fun of celebrating a Mexican American family holiday — Cinco de Mayo.

**2803** Beil, Karen M. *Grandma According to Me* (PS–K). Illus. by Ted Rand. 1994, Dell paper $4.99 (0-440-40995-0). 32pp. What a grandmother thinks are her faults, a loving granddaughter turns into virtues. (Rev: BL 12/1/92; SLJ 2/93)

**2804** Bernhard, Emery. *A Ride on Mother's Back: A Day of Baby Carrying Around the World* (K–2). Illus. by Durga Bernhard. 1996, Harcourt $15.00 (0-15-200870-5). 40pp. Various ways of carrying babies reflect cultural differences around the world. (Rev: BL 10/15/96; SLJ 10/96) [392]

**2805** Bertrand, Diane Gonzales. *Sip, Slurp, Soup, Soup/Caldo, Caldo, Caldo* (K–3). Illus. by Alex P. DeLange. 1997, Piñata $14.95 (1-55885-183-6). A simple bilingual book about a family making soup. (Rev: SLJ 8/97)

**2806** Birdseye, Tom. *Waiting for Baby* (PS–K). Illus. by Loreen Leedy. 1991, Holiday LB $14.95 (0-8234-0892-2). 32pp. A young boy eagerly awaits an arrival in the family and later is happy with his baby brother. (Rev: BL 1/1/91; SLJ 11/91)

**2807** Bittner, Wolfgang. *Wake Up, Grizzly!* (PS–K). Illus. by Gustavo Rosemffet. 1996, North-South LB $15.88 (1-55858-519-2). 30pp. Like a papa and a baby grizzly bear, Toby and his dad share a snoozy Sunday. (Rev: BL 8/96; SLJ 7/96)

**2808** Blaine, Marge. *The Terrible Thing That Happened at Our House* (K–2). Illus. by John Wallner. 1991, Scholastic paper $3.95 (0-590-42371-1). 32pp. Chaos reigns when Mother decides to go back to work and the children have to learn to "cope."

**2809** Blake, Robert J. *The Perfect Spot* (PS–3). Illus. 1992, Putnam $15.95 (0-399-22132-8). 32pp. A boy and his father spend a wonderful day together in the woods. (Rev: BL 3/15/92; SLJ 7/92)

**2810** Blegvad, Lenore. *Once upon a Time and Grandma* (PS–3). Illus. by author. 1993, Macmillan $14.95 (0-689-50548-5). 32pp. Grandma shows her grandchildren the house she lived in when she was a girl and tells them of her many memories of growing up there. (Rev: BL 6/1–15/93; SLJ 8/93)

**2811** Bloom, Suzanne. *A Family for Jamie: An Adoption Story* (PS–K). Illus. 1991, Crown $13.00 (0-517-57492-6). 24pp. A young married couple makes preparations for adopting a baby. (Rev: BL 3/1/91; SLJ 7/91)

**2812** Blos, Joan W. *The Grandpa Days* (PS–1). Illus. by Emily Arnold McCully. 1994, Simon & Schuster paper $3.95 (0-671-88244-9). 32pp. The tender story of a little boy who spends a week with his grandfather. (Rev: BL 11/1/89; SLJ 11/89)

**2813** Blume, Judy. *The Pain and the Great One* (PS–1). Illus. by Irene Trivas. 1984, Simon & Schuster $16.00 (0-02-711100-8). 32pp. A brother and sister explain why they don't get along.

**2814** Bogart, Jo Ellen. *Gifts* (PS–2). Illus. by Barbara Reid. 1996, Scholastic $15.95 (0-590-55260-0). 44pp. A joyful picture book in which a grandmother presents her granddaughter with a variety of imaginative gifts. (Rev: BL 2/1/96; SLJ 3/96*)

**2815** Bolden, Tonya. *Just Family* (4–6). 1996, Dutton paper $14.99 (0-525-65192-6). 160pp. Beryl, who is growing up in East Harlem during the 1960s, discovers that her pesky older sister is really her half-sister. (Rev: BL 2/15/96; SLJ 5/96)

**2816** Bonners, Susan. *The Wooden Doll* (K–3). Illus. 1991, Lothrop LB $13.88 (0-688-08282-3). 32pp. While visiting her grandparents, Stephanie wants to play with a doll Grandfather brought from Poland. (Rev: BL 4/15/91; SLJ 4/91)

**2817** Bosak, Susan V. *Something to Remember Me By* (PS–3). Illus. by Laurie McGaw. 1997, Communication Project $15.95 (1-896232-01-9). 32pp. This touching story about the loving relationship between a girl and her grandmother that lasts until the girl is grown and the old lady dies. (Rev: BL 11/1/97; SLJ 12/97)

**2818** Bottner, Barbara. *Nana Hannah's Piano* (PS–3). Illus. by Diana C. Bluthenthal. 1996, Putnam $15.95 (0-399-22656-7). 32pp. Through the guidance of his grandmother, a boy learns that there is more to life than baseball. (Rev: BL 11/15/96; SLJ 12/96)

**2819** Brillhart, Julie. *When Daddy Came to School* (PS). Illus. 1995, Albert Whitman LB $12.95 (0-8075-8878-4). 32pp. On his third birthday, a little boy is delighted when his father visits his nursery school. (Rev: BL 3/1/95; SLJ 5/95)

**2820** Brooks, Ben. *Lemonade Parade* (PS–2). Illus. by Bill Slavin. 1992, Whitman LB $14.95 (0-8075-4432-9). 32pp. A father assumes many disguises to buy lemonade from Patty and her friends. (Rev: BL 6/15/92; SLJ 8/92)

**2821** Brown, Ruth. *Cry Baby* (PS–2). Illus. 1997, Dutton paper $14.99 (0-525-45902-2). 32pp. A girl hates to take her younger sister for a walk because she cries over the slightest misadventure. (Rev: BL 7/97; SLJ 2/98)

**2822** Buckley, Helen E. *Grandfather and I* (PS–1). Illus. by Jan Ormerod. 1994, Lothrop $16.00 (0-688-12533-6). 24pp. A young boy describes the fine times he has with his grandfather walking around the neighborhood. Also use *Grandmother and I* (1994). (Rev: BL 2/15/94; HB 7–8/94; SLJ 4/94*)

**2823** Buehner, Caralyn. *Fanny's Dream* (1–4). Illus. by Mark Buehner. 1996, Dial paper $14.89 (0-8037-1497-1). 40pp. With a few important differences, Fanny relives the Cinderella story. (Rev: BCCB 9/96; BL 3/15/96*; HB 7–8/96, 9–10/96; SLJ 4/96*)

**2824** Bunting, Eve. *A Day's Work* (K–3). Illus. by Ronald Himler. 1994, Clarion $15.00 (0-395-67321-6). 32pp. A young Mexican American boy must act as guardian and interpreter for his grandfather, newly arrived from Mexico and looking for work. (Rev: BCCB 10/94; BL 11/1/94; SLJ 1/95)

**2825** Bunting, Eve. *Flower Garden* (PS–1). Illus. by Kathryn Hewitt. 1994, Harcourt $15.00 (0-15-228776-0). 32pp. A girl and her father create a window box of flowers as a birthday present for her mother. (Rev: BL 2/15/94*; HB 5–6/94; SLJ 4/94*)

**2826** Bunting, Eve. *Sunshine Home* (K–3). Illus. by Diane De Groat. 1994, Clarion $14.95 (0-395-63309-5). 32pp. Timmie is unhappy when he visits his grandmother in her nursing home for the first time. (Rev: BCCB 4/94; BL 3/15/94; SLJ 4/94)

**2827** Bunting, Eve. *The Wall* (K–2). Illus. by Ronald Himler. 1990, Houghton $14.95 (0-395-51588-2). 32pp. A picture book on the subject of the Vietnam Veterans War Memorial. (Rev: BCCB 7–8/92; BL 4/1/90*; HB 7–8/90; SLJ 5/90*)

**2828** Bunting, Eve. *The Wednesday Surprise* (PS–2). Illus. by Donald Carrick. 1989, Houghton $15.00 (0-89919-721-3); paper $5.95 (0-395-54776-8). 32pp. Anna is proudest of Grandma's surprise — Grandma has learned to read, and Anna has taught her. (Rev: BCCB 3/89; BL 3/1/89; SLJ 6/89)

**2829** Burningham, John. *Granpa* (PS–1). Illus. by author. 1985, Crown $14.00 (0-517-55643-X). 32pp. In a series of pictures, this book portrays events shared by a little girl and her grandfather. (Rev: HB 7–8/85; SLJ 9/85)

**2830** Butterworth, Nick. *My Dad Is Awesome* (PS–2). Illus. by author. 1992, Candlewick paper $4.99 (1-56402-033-9). This father is accomplished in everything, but he still takes a bath with a rubber duck. (Rev: SLJ 10/92)

**2831** Butterworth, Oliver. *A Visit to the Big House* (PS–3). Illus. by Susan Avishai. 1993, Houghton $13.95 (0-395-52805-4). 48pp. Along with her mother and younger brother, Rose visits Dad in prison. (Rev: BL 3/1/93; SLJ 7/93)

**2832** Caines, Jeannette. *Abby* (PS–1). Illus. by Steven Kellogg. 1973, HarperCollins paper $4.95 (0-06-443049-9). 32pp. Abby, a little black girl, is adopted and enjoys hearing about the day she became part of her warm, loving family.

**2833** Campbell, Louisa. *Phoebe's Fabulous Father* (K–2). Illus. by Bridget S. Taylor. 1996, Harcourt $14.00 (0-15-200996-5). Phoebe has always respected her cello-playing father; but when she finds out how much of his music he has sacrificed for his family, she grows to love him more. (Rev: BCCB 11/96; SLJ 12/96)

**2834** Carle, Eric. *My Apron: A Story from My Childhood* (PS–1). Illus. 1994, Putnam $22.95 (0-399-22824-1). 32pp. Eric, a small boy, is given a tiny apron when he helps his Uncle Adam, who is a plasterer. (Rev: BL 12/1/94)

**2835** Carrick, Carol. *Valentine* (PS–2). Illus. by Paddy Bouma. 1995, Clarion $14.95 (0-395-66554-X). 29pp. In spite of a loving grandmother, Heather misses her mother when she goes to work. (Rev: BL 4/1/95; SLJ 5/95)

**2836** Carter, Alden R. *Big Brother Dustin* (PS–2). Illus. by Dan Young and Carol Carter. 1997, Albert Whitman LB $14.95 (0-8075-0715-6). 32pp. A young boy searches for the best name for the baby sister who is expected shortly. (Rev: BL 8/97; HB 5–6/97; SLJ 6/97)

**2837** Carter, Donna Renee. *Music in the Family* (K–2). Illus. by Cortrell J. Harris. 1995, Lindsey $15.95 (1-885242-01-8). 30pp. Oliver is crushed when the family tells him that he doesn't play his saxophone well enough to join them in an international music competition. (Rev: SLJ 2/96)

**2838** Caseley, Judith. *Apple Pie and Onions* (K–3). Illus. by author. 1987, Greenwillow $16.00 (0-688-06762-X). 32pp. Grandma embarrasses Rebecca when she talks in Yiddish, but Grandma understands. (Rev: BL 3/1/87; SLJ 2/87)

**2839** Caseley, Judith. *Dear Annie* (PS–2). Illus. 1991, Greenwillow LB $15.93 (0-688-10011-2). 32pp. In letters back and forth, a young girl and her grandfather keep in touch. (Rev: BCCB 9/91; BL 7/91; HB 9–10/91; SLJ 11/91)

**2840** Caseley, Judith. *Mama Coming and Going* (PS–1). Illus. 1994, Greenwillow $14.00 (0-688-11441-5). 32pp. A child realizes how busy her mother is after the arrival of a new baby. (Rev: BL 3/1/94; HB 5–6/94; SLJ 5/94)

**2841** Catalanotto, Peter. *The Painter* (PS–2). Illus. by author. Series: Richard Jackson Books. 1995, Orchard LB $16.99 (0-531-08765-4). A joyous picture book that celebrates a loving relationship between a girl and her artist-father. (Rev: SLJ 9/95*)

**2842** Cazet, Denys. *Dancing* (PS–1). Illus. 1995, Orchard LB $16.99 (0-531-08766-2). 32pp. The crying of his baby brother drives Alex out of the house onto the porch, where he is comforted by his father. (Rev: BL 9/15/95; SLJ 9/95)

**2843** Chocolate, Deborah M. *On the Day I Was Born* (PS–2). Illus. by Melodye Rosales. 1995, Scholastic $12.95 (0-590-47609-2). 32pp. An African American family greets a new baby in the home with welcoming rituals that go back to tribal Africa. (Rev: BL 12/15/95; SLJ 1/96)

**2844** Chocolate, Deborah M. *The Piano Man* (K–3). Illus. by Eric Velasquez. 1998, Walker $15.95 (0-8027-8646-4). 32pp. An African American girl recalls the importance of the piano in the life of her grandfather, who played in silent-movie theaters, medicine shows, and vaudeville. (Rev: BL 2/15/98; SLJ 2/98)

**2845** Choi, Sook N. *Halmoni and the Picnic* (K–3). Illus. by Karen M. Dugan. 1993, Houghton $14.95 (0-395-61626-3). 24pp. A grandmother newly arrived from Korea has difficulty adjusting to New York City. (Rev: BL 8/93)

**2846** Cole, Joanna. *How I Was Adopted: Samantha's Story* (PS–2). Illus. by Maxie Chambliss. 1995, Morrow LB $15.93 (0-688-11930-1). 48pp. Basic facts about adoption are given, plus a story of Samantha, a well-adjusted child living happily with adoptive parents. (Rev: BL 8/95; SLJ 9/95)

**2847** Cole, Joanna. *I'm a Big Brother* (PS–1). Illus. by Maxie Chambliss. 1997, Morrow $5.95 (0-688-14507-8). 32pp. Babies and their activities and needs are introduced in terms a big brother can understand. A companion volume that covers the same material is *I'm a Big Sister* (1997). (Rev: BL 3/1/97; SLJ 4/97)

**2848** Collins, Pat L. *Waiting for Baby Joe* (PS–2). Illus. by Joan W. Dunn. 1990, Whitman LB $12.95 (0-8075-8625-0). 28pp. When his baby brother is born prematurely, Joey is disappointed that the baby requires everyone's constant attention. (Rev: BCCB 11/90; BL 11/1/90; HB 11–12/90; SLJ 12/90)

**2849** Cook, Jean Thor. *Room for a Stepdaddy* (PS–K). Illus. by Martine Gourbault. 1995, Albert Whitman LB $14.95 (0-8075-7106-7). At first, Bill rejects his new stepfather in favor of his real father; but in time, he realizes that he has enough love for both of them. (Rev: SLJ 1/96)

**2850** Cooney, Barbara. *Island Boy* (2–4). Illus. by author. 1988, Puffin paper $5.99 (0-14-050756-6). 40pp. The life of Matthias Tibbetts of Tibbetts Island, Maine, who sails the world and returns home to raise his own family. (Rev: BCCB 10/88; BL 10/1/88; SLJ 10/88)

**2851** Cooper, Helen. *Little Monster Did It!* (PS–2). Illus. 1996, Dial paper $12.99 (0-8037-1993-0). 32pp. Amy blames her stuffed toy, Little Monster, for the many mishaps that occur around the house. (Rev: BCCB 5/96; BL 6/1–15/96; SLJ 7/96)

**2852** Cooper, Melrose. *I Got a Family* (K–3). Illus. by Dale Gottlieb. 1993, Holt $14.95 (0-8050-1965-0). 32pp. In a rhyming text, the young narrator introduces each member of his family. (Rev: BL 5/15/93*; SLJ 7/93)

**2853** Corey, Dorothy. *Will There Be a Lap for Me?* (PS–1). Illus. by Nancy Poydar. 1992, Whitman LB $12.95 (0-8075-9109-2). 24pp. When her mother's lap becomes smaller because she is expecting a baby, Lyle misses her favorite place to sit and be loved. (Rev: BL 3/1/92; SLJ 6/92)

**2854** Coville, Bruce. *The Lapsnatcher* (PS–2). Illus. by Marissa Moss. 1997, Troll paper $15.95 (0-8167-4233-2). 32pp. The thing that a boy dislikes most about the family's new baby is that it takes up all the room on his mother's lap. (Rev: BL 6/1–15/97; SLJ 7/97)

**2855** Cowen-Fletcher, Jane. *Mama Zooms* (PS–1). Illus. 1994, Scholastic $19.95 (0-590-72848-2); paper $3.95 (0-590-45775-6). 32pp. Mama's "zooming machine" turns out to be her wheelchair. (Rev: BL 4/15/93; SLJ 5/93)

**2856** Coy, John. *Night Driving* (PS–3). Illus. by Peter McCarty. 1996, Holt $14.95 (0-8050-2931-1). 28pp. A young boy takes his first long nighttime car ride with his father. (Rev: BCCB 12/96; BL 9/1/96; HB 9–10/96; SLJ 10/96)

**2857** Crews, Donald. *Bigmama's* (PS–2). Illus. 1991, Greenwillow LB $15.93 (0-688-09951-3). 32pp. A family's annual summer trip to grandparents' house in the country is a celebration of childhood memories. (Rev: BCCB 11/91*; BL 11/15/91*; HB 9–10/91; SLJ 10/91) [921]

**2858** Cross, Verda. *Great-Grandma Tells of Threshing Day* (1–3). Illus. by Gail Owens. 1992, Whitman LB $16.95 (0-8075-3042-5). 40pp. Great-Grandma tells of her childhood on a farm during threshing time. (Rev: BCCB 1/93; BL 10/1/92; SLJ 11/92)

**2859** Curtis, Jamie Lee. *Tell Me Again About the Night I Was Born* (PS–1). Illus. by Laura Cornell. 1996, HarperCollins LB $14.89 (0-06-024529-8). 40pp. A young girl gleefully fills in all the details about what happened on the night she was born. (Rev: BCCB 1/97; BL 10/15/96; SLJ 10/96*)

**2860** Curtis, Munzee. *When the Big Dog Barks* (PS–K). Illus. by Susan Avishai. 1997, Greenwillow LB $14.93 (0-688-09540-2). 24pp. A youngster conquers all her fears because she feels the security of her parent's love. (Rev: BL 3/1/97; SLJ 4/97)

**2861** Cutler, Jane. *Darcy and Gran Don't Like Babies* (PS–1). Illus. by Susannah Ryan. 1993, Scholastic $14.95 (0-590-44587-1). 32pp. Darcy dislikes babies, particularly her new baby sister, and finds comfort with her grandmother. (Rev: BCCB 10/93; BL 12/1/93; HB 11–12/93; SLJ 11/93*)

**2862** Dale, Penny. *Big Brother, Little Brother* (PS). Illus. 1997, Candlewick $15.99 (0-7636-0146-2). 32pp. A series of episodes show the strong bond between 2 young brothers. (Rev: BL 9/15/97; SLJ 11/97)

**2863** Daly, Niki. *Papa Lucky's Shadow* (4–6). Illus. 1992, Macmillan $16.00 (0-689-50541-8). 32pp. Sugar is thrilled when her grandfather, a real Mr. Bojangles, decides to put on his tap shoes once more. (Rev: BL 9/15/92*; SLJ 10/92)

**2864** D'Antonio, Nancy. *Our Baby from China: An Adoption Story* (PS–2). Illus. 1997, Albert Whitman LB $13.95 (0-8075-6162-2). 24pp. The story of a couple's journey to China, where they adopt a little girl, and their trip home with the baby. (Rev: BL 3/1/97; SLJ 6/97)

**2865** Darling, Benjamin. *Valerie and the Silver Pear* (K–3). Illus. by Daniel Lane. 1992, Macmillan paper $14.95 (0-02-726100-X). 32pp. Valerie and her grandfather search for the silver pear and find something more enduring in their relationship. (Rev: BL 9/1/92*; SLJ 9/92)

**2866** Davol, Marguerite W. *Black, White, Just Right!* (PS–1). Illus. by Irene Trivas. 1993, Albert Whitman LB $14.95 (0-8075-0785-7). 32pp. A child with mixed-race parentage enjoys the many differences she sees in her parents, not only their color. (Rev: BL 11/1/93)

**2867** Deedy, Carmen A. *Agatha's Feather Bed: Not Just Another Wild Goose Story* (PS–2). Illus. by Laura L. Seeley. 1991, Peachtree $14.95 (1-56145-008-1). 32pp. Agatha is ashamed when she learns that 6 geese are featherless so she could have a featherbed. (Rev: BL 6/1/91; SLJ 9/91)

**2868** dePaola, Tomie. *The Baby Sister* (PS–1). Illus. 1996, Putnam $15.95 (0-399-22908-6). 32pp. When Tommy's mother has a baby, his grandmother comes to stay. (Rev: BL 3/15/96; HB 5–6/96; SLJ 5/96)

**2869** dePaola, Tomie. *Tom* (K–2). Illus. 1993, Putnam LB $15.95 (0-399-22417-3). 32pp. A picture book about the special relationship between the author/artist and his grandfather. (Rev: BCCB 5/93; BL 1/15/93*; HB 7–8/93*; SLJ 4/93)

**2870** dePaola, Tomie. *Watch Out for the Chicken Feet in Your Soup* (K–2). Illus. by author. 1974, Simon & Schuster $12.95 (0-685-35587-X); paper $5.95 (0-685-35588-8). 32pp. Joey is a little embarrassed to take his friend Eugene to his old-fashioned Italian grandmother's for a visit, but in spite of her strange foreign ways, both boys pronounce the visit a great success.

**2871** Doro, Ann. *Twin Pickle* (PS–K). Illus. by Clare Mackie. 1996, Holt $14.95 (0-8050-3802-7). Energetic, amusing rhymes are used with cartoons to describe the antics of identical twin girls. (Rev: HB 7–8/96; SLJ 6/96)

**2872** Drescher, Joan. *My Mother's Getting Married* (K–3). Illus. by author. 1986, Dial LB $10.89 (0-8037-0176-4); Puffin paper $4.95 (0-8037-0642-1). 32pp. Katy is unhappy that her mother is getting married, right up until the wedding day. (Rev: BCCB 4/86; BL 5/1/86; SLJ 5/86)

**2873** Duncan, Alice Faye. *Willie Jerome* (PS–3). Illus. by Tyrone Geter. 1995, Simon & Schuster paper $15.00 (0-02-733208-X). 32pp. No one appreciates Willie's horn playing except his younger sister in this story that captures an inner-city environment. (Rev: BL 6/1–15/95; SLJ 6/95)

**2874** Eisenberg, Phyllis R. *You're My Nikki* (PS–1). Illus. by Jill Kastner. 1995, Puffin paper $5.99 (0-140-55463-7). 32pp. Nikki is afraid that her single-parent mother will forget her when she starts her new job. (Rev: BCCB 5/92; BL 5/1/92; SLJ 5/92)

**2875** Engel, Diana. *Fishing* (K–2). Illus. 1993, Smithmark $4.98 (0-765-10068-1). 32pp. When her family moves north, more than anything else Loretta misses fishing with her grandfather. (Rev: BL 6/1–15/93; SLJ 6/93)

**2876** Ericsson, Jennifer A. *The Most Beautiful Kid in the World* (PS–1). Illus. by Susan Meddaugh. 1996, Morrow LB $15.93 (0-688-13942-6). 32pp. Mom's ideas about what Annie should wear to Grandma's birthday party are different from those of her daughter. (Rev: BCCB 10/96; BL 9/15/96; SLJ 10/96)

**2877** Evans, Lezlie. *If I Were the Wind* (PS–1). Illus. by Victoria Lisi. 1997, Ideals $14.95 (1-57102-096-9). 32pp. A mother says that even if she is changed by enchantment into other objects she will still protect and love her young daughter. (Rev: BL 8/97; SLJ 6/97)

**2878** Falwell, Cathryn. *We Have a Baby* (PS). Illus. 1993, Clarion $15.00 (0-395-62038-4). 32pp. A picture book that shows how a toddler accepts and enjoys having a new baby in the house. (Rev: BCCB 6/96; BL 11/15/93; SLJ 10/93)

**2879** Farber, Norma. *How Does It Feel to Be Old?* (1–3). Illus. by Trina S. Hyman. 1988, Dutton paper $4.99 (0-525-44367-3). 32pp. Grandmother tries to explain to a young girl what it is like to be old.

**2880** Farber, Norma. *Without Wings, Mother, How Can I Fly?* (PS–1). Illus. by Keiko Narahashi. 1998, Holt $15.95 (0-8050-3380-7). 32pp. A mother reassures her child that in this modern world a child can do anything that an animal can. (Rev: BL 3/15/98)

**2881** Fazio, Brenda Lena. *Grandfather's Story* (PS–3). Illus. 1996, Sasquatch $15.95 (1-57061-028-2). 32pp. In a Japanese setting, this story tells how a grandfather teaches his young grandson about life. (Rev: BL 11/15/96; SLJ 3/97)

**2882** Ferguson, Alane. *The Practical Joke War* (3–6). 1993, Avon paper $3.50 (0-380-71721-2). 160pp. All-out war is declared when the Dillon children — lovers of practical jokes — are left to themselves one summer. (Rev: BCCB 7–8/91; BL 4/1/91; SLJ 6/91)

**2883** Fisher, Iris L. *Katie-Bo: An Adoption Story* (PS–3). Illus. by Miriam Schaer. 1988, Adama $12.95 (0-915361-91-4). The story of Katie-Bo, who is coming from Korea to join her new family, told through the eyes of a young boy. (Rev: BL 5/15/88; SLJ 8/88)

**2884** Flournoy, Valerie. *The Patchwork Quilt* (1–3). Illus. by Jerry Pinkney. 1985, Dial LB $14.89 (0-8037-0098-9). 32pp. A young black girl and her grandmother begin a patchwork quilt in this warm family story. (Rev: BCCB 4/85; BL 4/1/85; SLJ 4/85)

**2885** Fox, Mem. *Sophie* (K–3). Illus. by Aminah Robinson. 1994, Harcourt $13.95 (0-15-277160-3). 32pp. The story of the love shared by a girl and her grandfather from her birth to his death. (Rev: BCCB 11/94; BL 10/1/94; SLJ 11/94)

**2886** Fox, Mem. *Whoever You Are* (K–3). Illus. by Leslie Staub. 1997, Harcourt $16.00 (0-15-200787-3). 32pp. A reassuring book for children that tells them that regardless of their situations, there are toher like them all over the world. (Rev: BL 10/1/97; SLJ 10/97)

**2887** Friedman, Ina R. *How My Parents Learned to Eat* (2–4). Illus. by Allen Say. 1987, Houghton $15.00 (0-395-35379-3); paper $5.95 (0-395-44235-4). 32pp. John, an American, and Aiko, a Japanese girl, learn each other's eating habits.

**2888** Friend, David. *Baseball, Football, Daddy and Me* (K–3). Illus. 1992, Puffin paper $4.50 (0-140-50914-3). 32pp. This slice-of-life account centers around a father and son and sports events. (Rev: BL 2/15/90; SLJ 5/90)

**2889** Gackenbach, Dick. *Where Are Momma, Poppa, and Sister June?* (PS–1). Illus. by author. 1994, Clarion $13.95 (0-395-67323-2). 32pp. A young boy worries about the whereabouts of his family, not realizing that they have gone out to pick up pizza. (Rev: SLJ 9/94)

**2890** Gackenbach, Dick. *With Love from Gran* (PS–2). Illus. 1990, Houghton paper $6.95 (0-395-54775-X). 32pp. A grandmother takes a trip around the world and sends her grandson gifts. (Rev: BL 10/1/89; SLJ 11/89)

**2891** Galbraith, Kathryn O. *Laura Charlotte* (K–2). Illus. by Floyd Cooper. 1990, Putnam $15.95 (0-399-21613-8). Mama tells Laura the story of Charlotte, the stuffed elephant that is part of both their lives. (Rev: SLJ 4/90)

**2892** Gauch, Patricia L. *Christina Katerina and the Great Bear Train* (K–2). Illus. by Elise Primavera. 1990, Putnam $14.95 (0-399-21623-5). Christina decides to travel to the hospital by herself to visit her new sibling. (Rev: SLJ 11/90)

**2893** Gauch, Patricia L. *Christina Katerina and the Time She Quit the Family* (PS–2). Illus. by Elise Primavera. 1994, Putnam paper $5.95 (0-399-22405-X). 32pp. Christina Katerina divorces herself from the rest of the family, but discovers it's not much fun being alone. (Rev: BCCB 12/87; BL 11/15/87)

**2894** Gentieu, Penny. *Wow! Babies!* (PS). Photos by author. 1997, Crown $12.00 (0-517-70963-5). Using plenty of photos, this book shows different kinds of babies and their activities. (Rev: SLJ 10/97)

**2895** Gewing, Lisa. *Mama, Daddy, Baby and Me* (PS). Illus. by Donna Larimer. 1989, Spirit $14.95 (0-944296-04-1). 32pp. In simple rhymes, a youngster responds to a new baby in the house. (Rev: BL 12/1/89; SLJ 12/89)

**2896** Gilchrist, Jan Spivey. *Indigo and Moonlight Gold* (K–3). Illus. 1993, Black Butterfly $13.95 (0-86316-210-X). 32pp. A tender moment between a mother and child is described in moving prose and beautiful oil paintings. (Rev: BCCB 2/94; BL 3/1/94; SLJ 5/94)

**2897** Girard, Linda Walvoord. *Adoption Is for Always* (K–3). Illus. by Judith Friedman. 1991, Whitman LB $12.95 (0-8075-0185-9); paper $4.95 (0-8075-0187-5). 32pp. Celia is old enough to understand what adoption really means, and she isn't sure that she likes it. (Rev: BL 2/15/87; SLJ 4/87)

**2898** Gliori, Debi. *New Big House* (PS–1). Illus. 1992, Candlewick $13.95 (1-56402-036-3). 32pp. As the clutter mounts, a family finds that their house is just too small for them. (Rev: BCCB 4/92; BL 5/15/92; SLJ 8/93)

**2899** Good, Merle. *Reuben and the Blizzard* (K–3). Illus. by P. Buckley Moss. 1995, Good Books $14.95 (1-56148-184-X). 32pp. Young Reuben and his Amish family weather a blizzard and help a neighbor get to the hospital. (Rev: BL 1/1–15/96; SLJ 4/96)

**2900** Graham, Bob. *Spirit of Hope* (PS–3). Illus. 1996, Mondo $14.95 (1-57255-202-6). 30pp. The Fairweathers face a crisis when they are told to vacate their home. (Rev: BL 12/1/96; SLJ 3/97)

**2901** Gray, Libba M. *Dear Willie Rudd* (K–3). Illus. by Peter M. Fiore. 1993, Simon & Schuster paper $14.00 (0-671-79774-3). 28pp. Miss Elizabeth wishes she could make amends to the African American housekeeper who took care of her 50 years before. (Rev: BCCB 11/93; BL 9/1/93; SLJ 12/93)

**2902** Gray, Libba M. *My Mama Had a Dancing Heart* (PS–3). Illus. by Raul Colon. 1995, Orchard LB $16.99 (0-531-08770-0). 32pp. Evocative pic-

tures are used to illustrate a series of imaginative experiences shared by a mother and daughter in each of the seasons. (Rev: BL 9/15/95*; SLJ 9/95*)

**2903** Greenfield, Eloise. *First Pink Light* (PS–1). Illus. by Jan S. Gilchrist. 1991, Writers & Readers $13.95 (0-86316-207-X). A young African American boy waits in a rocking chair to greet his father, who has been away for a year. (Rev: BL 12/15/91; SLJ 1/92)

**2904** Greenfield, Eloise. *Grandmama's Joy* (2–5). Illus. by Carole Byard. 1980, Putnam $13.95 (0-399-21064-4). 32pp. The story of Rhondy and the grandmother who has raised her.

**2905** Greenfield, Eloise. *Grandpa's Face* (K–3). Illus. by Floyd Cooper. 1988, Philomel $15.95 (0-399-21525-5); Putnam paper $5.95 (0-698-11381-0). 32pp. Tamika worries about her grandfather's reactions. (Rev: BL 11/15/88; HB 3–4/89; SLJ 11/88)

**2906** Greenfield, Eloise. *She Come Bringing Me That Little Baby Girl* (K–2). Illus. by John Steptoe. 1990, HarperCollins paper $5.95 (0-06-443296-3). 32pp. Kevin resents all the attention the new baby is getting; most of all he resents the fact that she is a girl.

**2907** Greenfield, Eloise. *William and the Good Old Days* (K–3). Illus. by Jan S. Gilchrist. 1993, HarperCollins LB $15.89 (0-06-021094-X). 32pp. Young William is upset that his Grandma is now ill and someone else owns her diner, where everyone felt at home. (Rev: BL 9/15/93)

**2908** Griffith, Helen V. *Georgia Music* (1–3). Illus. by James Stevenson. 1986, Greenwillow $16.00 (0-688-06071-4); Morrow paper $4.95 (0-688-09931-9). 24pp. A quiet summer spent by a little girl at her grandfather's cabin in Georgia. A sequel is: *Grandaddy's Place* (1987). (Rev: BCCB 12/86; BL 10/1/86; SLJ 10/86)

**2909** Guback, Georgia. *Luka's Quilt* (PS–2). Illus. 1994, Greenwillow LB $13.93 (0-688-12155-1). 32pp. A Hawaiian girl is disappointed when the quilt her grandmother makes contains only 2 colors. (Rev: BCCB 7–8/94; BL 6/1–15/94*; HB 9–10/94; SLJ 7/94)

**2910** Guthrie, Donna. *Grandpa Doesn't Know It's Me: A Family Adjusts to Alzheimer's Disease* (K–3). Illus. by Katy K. Arnsteen. 1986, Human Sciences paper $10.95 (0-89885-308-7). The story of Lizzie, who adores her grandfather, and the tragedy of her grandfather's Alzheimer's disease. (Rev: BCCB 7–8/86; BL 8/86)

**2911** Hanrahan, Brendan. *My Sisters Love My Clothes* (PS–2). Illus. by Lise Stork. 1992, Perry Heights Pr. $12.95 (0-9630181-0-8). 32pp. Young Louie has a smart wardrobe, but his sisters keep borrowing his clothes. (Rev: BCCB 4/92; BL 9/1/92)

**2912** Harris, Robie H. *Happy Birth Day!* (PS–2). Illus. by Michael Emberley. 1996, Candlewick $16.99 (1-56402-424-5). 32pp. A baby's first day after birth is caught in text, narrated by the young parents, and paintings. (Rev: BL 5/1/96*; SLJ 12/96*)

**2913** Haskins, Francine. *I Remember "121"* (PS–3). Illus. 1991, Children's Book Pr. $14.95 (0-89239-100-6). 32pp. This is an autobiographical sketch of the artist growing up in an African American neighborhood in Washington, D.C. (Rev: BL 12/15/91; SLJ 3/92) [973]

**2914** Hassett, John, and Ann Hassett. *We Got My Brother at the Zoo* (PS). Illus. by authors. 1993, Houghton $14.95 (0-395-62429-0). 32pp. Mary Margaret resents having a new brother and remembers the good old days before he came. (Rev: SLJ 12/93)

**2915** Hausherr, Rosmarie. *Celebrating Families* (PS–2). Illus. 1997, Scholastic $16.95 (0-590-48937-2). 32pp. Different kinds of families are pictured in this photoessay. (Rev: BL 3/1/97; SLJ 3/97)

**2916** Havill, Juanita. *Treasure Map* (PS–2). Illus. by Elivia Savadier. 1992, Houghton $15.00 (0-395-57817-5). 32pp. Alicia hears the story of how her great-grandmother left Mexico and came to the United States. (Rev: BL 3/1/92; SLJ 6/92)

**2917** Hawxhurst, Joan C. *Bubbe and Gram: My Two Grandmothers* (PS–3). Illus. by Jane K. Bynum. 1996, Dovetail $12.95 (0-9651284-2-3). 32pp. From his 2 grandmothers — one Jewish, the other Christian — a young girl learns about and accepts 2 ways of worship. (Rev: BL 1/1–15/97)

**2918** Hazen, Barbara S. *Even If I Did Something Awful?* (K–2). Illus. by Nancy Kincade. 1992, Macmillan LB $13.95 (0-689-30843-4); paper $4.99 (0-689-71600-1). 32pp. Mother still loves you, even when you are bad.

**2919** Hazen, Barbara S. *If It Weren't for Benjamin (I'd Always Get to Lick the Icing Spoon)* (PS–2). Illus. by Laura Hartman. 1979, Human Sciences paper $9.95 (0-89885-172-6). 32pp. A younger sibling recounts the reasons for his sense of injustice.

**2920** Hearne, Betsy. *Seven Brave Women* (K–3). Illus. by Bethanne Andersen. 1997, Greenwillow LB $14.93 (0-688-14503-5). 24pp. The narrator introduces 7 creative, courageous women in her family who made their quiet but important marks on history, from the Revolutionary War to the present. (Rev: BL 6/1–15/97; HB 9–10/97; SLJ 9/97)

**2921** Henderickson, Karen. *Baby and I Can Play and Fun with Toddlers* (PS–K). Illus. by Marina Megale. 1990, Parenting Pr. LB $17.95 (0-943990-

57-2); paper $7.95 (0-943990-56-4). 56pp. This book tells preschoolers how to play safely with young babies. (Rev: BL 9/1/90) [649.64]

**2922** Henkes, Kevin. *Grandpa and Bo* (PS–K). Illus. by author. 1986, Greenwillow LB $15.93 (0-688-04957-5). 32pp. Grandpa and young Bo spend the summer together and even celebrate Christmas because they know they won't be together for the actual holiday. (Rev: BCCB 5/86; BL 3/1/86; SLJ 9/86)

**2923** Henkes, Kevin. *Shhhh* (PS–1). Illus. 1989, Greenwillow LB $11.88 (0-688-07986-5). 24pp. A little girl wakes up the whole household with her horn. (Rev: BL 8/89; SLJ 1/90)

**2924** Hennessy, B. G. *When You Were Just a Little Girl* (PS–2). Illus. by Jeanne Arnold. 1994, Puffin paper $4.99 (0-14-054172-1). Grandma tells her grandchildren that their interests are basically the same as she enjoyed as a child. (Rev: SLJ 12/91)

**2925** Heo, Yumi. *Father's Rubber Shoes* (PS–3). Illus. 1995, Orchard LB $16.99 (0-531-08723-9). 32pp. Yungsu's father tells his lonely son why the family has moved to the United States. (Rev: BL 9/15/95; HB 11–12/95; SLJ 11/95)

**2926** Hesse, Karen. *Poppy's Chair* (K–3). Illus. by Kay Life. 1993, Macmillan LB $14.95 (0-02-743705-1). 32pp. Leah learns from her grandmother how to accept her grandfather's death. (Rev: BL 3/15/93; SLJ 7/93)

**2927** Hest, Amy. *The Crack-of-Dawn Walkers* (PS–2). Illus. by Amy Schwartz. 1984, Simon & Schuster LB $13.95 (0-02-743710-8). 32pp. Sadie and her grandfather have lovely walks alone every other Sunday. A reissue of the 1984 edition.

**2928** Hest, Amy. *Jamaica Louise James* (PS–3). Illus. by Sheila W. Samton. 1996, Candlewick $15.99 (1-56402-348-6). 32pp. Through her drawings, Jamaica Louise tries to make her Granny's life happier. (Rev: BCCB 9/96; BL 9/1/96; HB 9–10/96; SLJ 12/96)

**2929** Hest, Amy. *The Mommy Exchange* (PS–2). Illus. by DyAnne DiSalvo-Ryan. 1988, Macmillan LB $13.95 (0-02-743650-0); paper $3.95 (0-689-71450-5). 32pp. Jason and Jessica, each fed up with home life, decide to trade moms and learn to appreciate their own. (Rev: BL 5/1/88; SLJ 10/88)

**2930** Hest, Amy. *Rosie's Fishing Trip* (PS–2). Illus. by Paul Howard. 1994, Candlewick $13.95 (1-56402-296-X). 32pp. While they wait for the fish to bite on their fishing excursion, Rosie's grandfather composes a poem. (Rev: BL 10/15/94; SLJ 2/95)

**2931** Hickman, Martha W. *Robert Lives with His Grandparents* (1–3). Illus. by Tim Hinton. 1995, Albert Whitman LB $14.95 (0-8075-7084-2). 32pp. Robert, who lives with his grandparents, is embarrassed at the thought that his grandmother will be coming to school on parents' day. (Rev: BL 2/1/96; SLJ 1/96)

**2932** Himmelman, John. *Wanted: Perfect Parents* (K–2). Illus. 1993, BridgeWater paper $13.95 (0-8167-3028-8). 32pp. Gregory realizes that perfect parents are those who can tuck him in lovingly at night. (Rev: BL 10/15/93; SLJ 8/93)

**2933** Hines, Anna Grossnickle. *Big Help!* (PS–1). Illus. 1995, Clarion $13.95 (0-395-68702-0). 32pp. Little sister Lucy always messes up Sam's pet projects when she tries to help. (Rev: BL 3/1/95; SLJ 4/95)

**2934** Hines, Anna Grossnickle. *Big Like Me* (PS–K). Illus. 1989, Greenwillow LB $15.93 (0-688-08355-2). 32pp. Big brother keeps telling baby sister all he'll show her when she grows up. (Rev: BL 10/1/89; HB 9–10/89; SLJ 12/89)

**2935** Hines, Anna Grossnickle. *Daddy Makes the Best Spaghetti* (PS–K). Illus. by author. 1986, Houghton $15.00 (0-89919-388-9); paper $5.95 (0-89919-794-9). The story of the warm relationship between a father and son as they spend time together doing things at home. (Rev: BL 3/1/86; HB 9–10/86; SLJ 5/86)

**2936** Hines, Anna Grossnickle. *Even If I Spill My Milk?* (PS–1). Illus. by author. 1994, Clarion $13.95 (0-395-65010-0). 32pp. Jamie tries every delaying tactic possible to prevent his parents' leaving him with a baby-sitter. (Rev: SLJ 6/94)

**2937** Hines, Anna Grossnickle. *Grandma Gets Grumpy* (PS–K). Illus. by author. 1988, Houghton paper $5.90 (0-395-52595-0). 32pp. When Lassen's 4 cousins show up, her normally "cool" Grandma actually gets annoyed. (Rev: BCCB 6/88; BL 5/1/88; HB 7–8/88)

**2938** Hines, Anna Grossnickle. *When We Married Gary* (PS–1). Illus. 1996, Greenwillow $15.00 (0-688-14276-1). 28pp. Two young sisters adjust to Gary, their new stepfather, when their mother remarries. (Rev: BL 3/1/96; HB 7–8/96; SLJ 5/96)

**2939** Hooks, William H. *The Mighty Santa Fe* (K–3). Illus. by Angela T. Thomas. 1993, Macmillan LB $14.95 (0-02-744432-5). 32pp. William is overjoyed to find that his grandmother shares his enthusiasm for model trains. (Rev: BL 11/15/93)

**2940** Houston, Gloria. *My Great-Aunt Arizona* (K–4). Illus. by Susan C. Lamb. 1992, HarperCollins LB $15.89 (0-06-022607-2). 32pp. The story of the author's great-aunt, who was born in the Appalachians and lived there until the age of 93. (Rev: BCCB 4/92; BL 1/1/92; SLJ 3/92) [371.1]

**2941** Howard, Elizabeth F. *Aunt Flossie's Hats (and Crab Cakes Later)* (PS–3). Illus. by James E. Ransome. 1991, Houghton $15.95 (0-395-54682-6).

32pp. Susan and Sarah visit Great-great Aunt Flossie to hear her tell stories about her hats. (Rev: BL 3/15/91*; HB 9–10/91; SLJ 5/91)

**2942** Howard, Elizabeth F. *What's in Aunt Mary's Room?* (PS–2). Illus. by Cedric Lucas. 1996, Clarion $14.95 (0-395-69845-6). 32pp. Aunt Flossie explains the importance in the life of this African American family of the book stored in Aunt Mary's room, the family Bible. A sequel to *Aunt Flossie's Hats (and Crab Cakes Later)* (1991). (Rev: BL 2/15/96; SLJ 5/96)

**2943** Hudson, Wade. *I Love My Family* (K–4). Illus. by Cal Massey. 1995, Scholastic paper $2.50 (0-590-45764-0). 32pp. A yearly reunion of a large, extended African American family. (Rev: BL 3/15/93; SLJ 4/93)

**2944** Hughes, Shirley. *The Big Alfie and Annie Rose Storybook* (2–3). Illus. by author. 1989, Lothrop $15.00 (0-688-07672-6). 64pp. Stories, poems, and eye-catching artwork featuring Alfie and his little sister. (Rev: BCCB 4/89; BL 3/15/89; HB 5–6/89)

**2945** Hughes, Shirley. *The Big Alfie Out of Doors Storybook* (PS–2). Illus. 1992, Lothrop $17.00 (0-688-11428-8). 64pp. Four-year-old Alfie has 4 happy experiences with different members of his family. (Rev: BCCB 10/92*; BL 10/15/92; HB 1–2/93; SLJ 10/92)

**2946** Hurd, Edith Thacher. *I Dance in My Red Pajamas* (PS–1). Illus. by Emily Arnold McCully. 1982, HarperCollins LB $15.89 (0-06-022700-1). 32pp. A little girl stays overnight at her grandparents' house.

**2947** Hutchins, Pat. *Tidy Titch* (PS–1). Illus. 1991, Greenwillow LB $15.93 (0-688-09964-5). 32pp. Tidy Titch helps his siblings clean up and soon has all their junk in his own room. (Rev: BL 1/15/92; HB 9–10/91; SLJ 10/91)

**2948** Hutchins, Pat. *Titch* (K–3). Illus. by author. 1971, Macmillan paper $5.95 (0-689-71688-5). 32pp. Titch, the youngest in the family, enjoys a moment of triumph. A sequel is: *You'll Soon Grow into Them, Titch* (1983, Greenwillow).

**2949** Igus, Toyomi. *Two Mrs. Gibsons* (K–3). Illus. by Daryl Wells. 1996, Children's Book Pr. $14.95 (0-89239-135-9). 32pp. The 2 Mrs. Gibsons in a young girl's life are her mother and her grandmother. (Rev: BCCB 5/96; BL 5/15/96; SLJ 10/96)

**2950** Igus, Toyomi. *When I Was Little* (K–3). Illus. by Higgins Bond. 1992, Just Us $14.95 (0-940975-32-7). 32pp. Noel finds it hard to believe there was no television and other things he takes for granted when his African American grandfather was growing up. (Rev: BL 3/1/93)

**2951** Isadora, Rachel. *Lili Backstage* (PS–3). Illus. 1997, Putnam $15.95 (0-399-23025-4). 32pp. Lili explores backstage life when she visits her grandfather, who plays the French horn in a theater orchestra. (Rev: BL 3/15/97; HB 7–8/97; SLJ 6/97)

**2952** Jacobs, Kate. *A Sister's Wish* (K–2). Illus. by Nancy Carpenter. 1996, Hyperion LB $15.49 (0-7868-2112-4). A little girl longs to have a sister of her own but later realizes that being a good sister to her brothers is nice, too. (Rev: SLJ 7/96)

**2953** Jam, Teddy. *The Year of Fire* (PS–3). Illus. by Ian Wallace. 1993, Macmillan paper $14.95 (0-689-50566-3). 48pp. A grandfather recalls a terrible fire that destroyed the maple grove where he and his granddaughter are now sugaring. (Rev: BCCB 7–8/93; BL 3/15/93; SLJ 5/93)

**2954** Johnson, Angela. *The Aunt in Our House* (PS–3). Illus. by David Soman. 1996, Orchard LB $16.99 (0-531-08852-9). 32pp. An aunt brings new life and interesting talents during a visit to her brother's biracial family. (Rev: BL 3/1/96; SLJ 4/96)

**2955** Johnson, Angela. *Do Like Kyla* (PS–1). Illus. by James E. Ransome. 1990, Orchard $15.95 (0-531-05852-2); paper $6.95 (0-531-07040-9). 32pp. The younger of 2 sisters imitates the older sibling all day long. (Rev: BL 2/15/90; SLJ 4/90)

**2956** Johnson, Angela. *One of Three* (PS–K). Illus. by David Soman. 1991, Orchard $15.95 (0-531-05955-3); paper $5.95 (0-531-07061-1). 32pp. A young black girl remembers the good times growing up with 2 older sisters. (Rev: BL 7/91; SLJ 10/91)

**2957** Johnson, Angela. *Tell Me a Story, Mama* (PS–1). Illus. by David Soman. 1989, Orchard paper $6.95 (0-531-07032-8). 32pp. A black mother and daughter reminisce about childhood. (Rev: BCCB 2/89; BL 4/1/89; SLJ 3/89)

**2958** Johnson, Angela. *When I Am Old with You* (PS–2). Illus. by David Soman. 1990, Orchard LB $16.99 (0-531-08484-1); paper $6.95 (0-531-07035-2). 32pp. A young black boy daydreams of all the things he and his grandfather can do when the youngster grows older. (Rev: BL 9/1/90; SLJ 9/90*)

**2959** Johnson, Dolores. *What Will Mommy Do When I'm at School?* (PS–1). Illus. 1990, Macmillan LB $15.00 (0-02-747845-9). 32pp. About to start school, a young girl worries about how her mother will cope. (Rev: BL 12/1/90; SLJ 1/91)

**2960** Johnson, Dolores. *Your Dad Was Just Like You* (K–3). Illus. 1993, Macmillan $13.95 (0-02-747838-6). 32pp. Peter understands his father better when his grandfather tells him about his dad's childhood. (Rev: BL 3/1/93; SLJ 8/93)

**2961** Johnston, Tony. *Fishing Sunday* (PS–4). Illus. by Barry Root. 1996, Morrow $16.00 (0-688-13458-0). 32pp. A young boy is embarrassed by his grandfather's eccentric behavior during a fishing expedition. (Rev: BL 5/15/96; SLJ 6/96)

**2962** Johnston, Tony. *Grandpa's Song* (PS–2). Illus. by Brad Sneed. 1991, Dial LB $12.89 (0-8037-0802-5). A grandfather who loves music teaches his grandchildren a song. (Rev: SLJ 7/91*)

**2963** Jolin, Dominique. *It's Not Fair!* (PS–3). Illus. by author. 1996, Crossing Pr. $12.95 (0-89594-780-3). A patient father listens as his daughter complains that her friends have more than she does and then reminds her that she has him. (Rev: SLJ 8/96)

**2964** Joosse, Barbara M. *I Love You the Purplest* (PS–1). Illus. by Mary Whyte. 1996, Chronicle $14.95 (0-8118-0718-5). 32pp. Two young brothers compete for the attention of their mother, who demonstrates that she loves them equally. (Rev: BL 10/15/96; SLJ 5/97)

**2965** Joosse, Barbara M. *Mama, Do You Love Me?* (PS–2). Illus. by Barbara Lavallee. 1991, Chronicle $14.95 (0-87701-759-X). An Eskimo girl asks her mother if she will still be loved even when she is naughty. (Rev: BCCB 12/91; HB 11–12/91; SLJ 11/91)

**2966** Joosse, Barbara M. *The Morning Chair* (K–3). Illus. by Marcia Sewall. 1995, Clarion $14.95 (0-395-62337-5). 32pp. The story of a young Dutch boy whose family emigrates to New York City in the 1950s. (Rev: BCCB 6/95; BL 6/1–15/95; HB 5–6/95; SLJ 6/95)

**2967** Jukes, Mavis. *Like Jake and Me* (2–3). Illus. by Lloyd Bloom. 1987, Knopf paper $7.99 (0-394-89263-1). 32pp. Alex and his stepfather explore the meaning of fear.

**2968** Jussek, Nicole. *Seymour and Opal* (PS–3). Illus. by Ana L. Escriva. 1996, Knopf $15.00 (0-679-86722-8). 32pp. Seymour wants to charge his sister a toll each time she walks through his room. (Rev: BL 12/1/96; SLJ 12/96)

**2969** Kaplan, John. *Mom and Me* (PS–1). Illus. 1996, Scholastic $10.95 (0-590-47294-1). 32pp. In photographs and text, 3 children talk about their mothers and what these maternal bonds mean to them. (Rev: BL 3/1/96; SLJ 4/96) [306]

**2970** Katz, Karen. *Over the Moon: An Adoption Tale* (PS–1). Illus. 1997, Holt $15.95 (0-8050-5013-2). 32pp. A husband and wife prepare for the baby they are going to adopt. (Rev: BL 9/1/97; SLJ 9/97)

**2971** Kaye, Marilyn. *The Real Tooth Fairy* (PS–3). Illus. by Helen Cogancherry. 1990, Harcourt $14.00 (0-15-265780-0). 21pp. Elsie is convinced that her mother is really the tooth fairy. (Rev: BCCB 10/92; BL 9/15/90; SLJ 10/90)

**2972** Keller, Holly. *Geraldine's Baby Brother* (PS–1). Illus. 1994, Greenwillow LB $14.93 (0-688-12006-7). 32pp. To prevent her young brother from getting all the attention, Geraldine begins to act up. (Rev: BL 8/94; HB 11–12/94; SLJ 8/94*)

**2973** Keller, Holly. *Harry and Tuck* (K–1). Illus. 1993, Greenwillow LB $13.93 (0-688-11463-6). 24pp. Only at school do twins gain sufficient independence to exist separately. (Rev: BL 7/93; HB 7–8/93; SLJ 7/93)

**2974** Kellerman, Jonathan. *Daddy, Daddy, Can You Touch the Sky? Poems for Children and Parents to Share* (PS–3). Illus. by author. 1994, Bantam $15.95 (0-553-07324-9). 102pp. Six short verses explore parent-child relationships and childhood fears. (Rev: SLJ 11/94)

**2975** Kellogg, Steven. *Can I Keep Him?* (K–2). Illus. by author. 1971, Dial $15.99 (0-8037-0988-9); Puffin paper $5.99 (0-14-054867-X). 32pp. Arnold, an incorrigible animal lover, constantly distresses his mother with a wide assortment of pets — real, imaginary, and human.

**2976** Ketner, Mary G. *Ganzy Remembers* (PS–2). Illus. by Barbara Sparks. n.d., Smithmark paper $4.98 (0-8317-2378-5). 32pp. A young girl and her grandmother visit Great-Grandmother in a nursing home. (Rev: BL 4/15/91; SLJ 6/91)

**2977** Khalsa, Dayal Kaur. *Tales of a Gambling Grandma* (K–3). Illus. by author. 1994, Crown paper $5.99 (0-517-88262-0). 32pp. Grandma, who escaped the Cossacks and came to America at age 3, has always been a gambler with life. (Rev: BCCB 11/86; SLJ 10/86)

**2978** Koehler, Phoebe. *The Day We Met You* (PS–2). Illus. 1990, Macmillan LB $15.00 (0-02-750901-X). 48pp. This book celebrates the great joy of welcoming an adopted baby into the household. (Rev: BL 5/15/90; SLJ 8/90)

**2979** Komaiko, Leah. *Just My Dad and Me* (K–3). Illus. by Jeffrey Greene. Series: Laura Geringer Books. 1995, HarperCollins LB $15.89 (0-06-024574-3). A young girl's dream of spending a day alone with her father is dashed when a carload of relatives arrives. (Rev: SLJ 7/95*)

**2980** Kraus, Robert. *Little Louie the Baby Bloomer* (PS–2). Illus. by Jose Aruego. 1998, HarperCollins LB $15.89 (0-06-026294-X). 32pp. Leo is worried about his younger brother, who can't do anything right. (Rev: BL 3/15/98)

**2981** Kroll, Virginia. *Beginnings: How Families Come to Be* (PS–3). Illus. by Stacey Schuett. 1994, Albert Whitman LB $14.95 (0-8075-0602-8). 34pp. Six children — some adopted, others not — discuss with their parents and other family members where they came from. (Rev: BL 3/15/94; SLJ 6/94)

**2982** Kroll, Virginia. *Butterfly Boy* (PS–3). Illus. by Gerardo Suzan. 1997, Boyds Mills $15.95 (1-56397-371-5). 32pp. Even though his grandfather can no longer talk, Emilio is certain that he is enjoying himself when they watch the butterflies together. (Rev: BL 11/1/97; SLJ 6/97)

**2983** Kuklin, Susan. *How My Family Lives in America* (PS–3). Illus. 1992, Macmillan $14.00 (0-02-751239-8). 40pp. Three children — an African American, a Hispanic American, and a Chinese American — talk about their families and their pride in their ancestors. (Rev: BCCB 4/92; BL 3/1/92; SLJ 3/92) [305.8]

**2984** Kurtis-Kleinman, Eileen. *When Aunt Lena Did the Rhumba* (PS–3). Illus. by Diane Greenseid. 1997, Hyperion LB $15.49 (0-7868-2067-5). 32pp. When theater-loving Aunt Lena is ill in bed, Sophie and other relatives put on a show for her. (Rev: BL 5/15/97; SLJ 6/97)

**2985** Lakin, Patricia. *Dad and Me in the Morning* (K–3). Illus. by Robert G. Steele. 1994, Albert Whitman LB $14.95 (0-8075-1419-5). 32pp. A deaf boy and his father communicate their feelings to each other as they watch a sunrise. (Rev: BL 4/1/94; SLJ 6/94)

**2986** Lasky, Kathryn. *My Island Grandma* (PS–2). Illus. by Amy Schwartz. n.d., Smithmark $3.98 (0-8317-1207-4). 32pp. A girl and her grandmother share simple experiences on an island in the ocean. (Rev: BL 3/15/93; SLJ 5/93)

**2987** Lasky, Kathryn, and Maxwell B. Knight. *A Baby for Max* (PS–2). Illus. by Christopher G. Knight. 1987, Macmillan paper $4.95 (0-689-71118-2). A book about a new addition to the family; illustrated with photographs.

**2988** Leedy, Loreen. *Who's Who in My Family?* (PS–1). Illus. 1995, Holiday LB $15.95 (0-8234-1151-6). 32pp. Family relationships and the words used to describe them are the subject of this book on all kinds of families. (Rev: BCCB 3/95; BL 3/1/95; SLJ 4/95)

**2989** Legge, David. *Bamboozled* (PS–3). Illus. 1995, Scholastic $14.95 (0-590-47989-X). 32pp. A surreal presentation of a girl's visit to her grandfather's house. (Rev: BCCB 3/95; BL 1/15/95; HB 11–12/95; SLJ 3/95*)

**2990** Leighton, Audrey O. *A Window of Time* (K–3). Illus. by Rhonda Kyrias. 1995, NADIA $15.95 (0-9636335-1-1). 32pp. Shawn is troubled by his grandfather's frequent loss of memory and mental confusion. (Rev: BL 2/1/96)

**2991** Lemieux, Margo. *The Fiddle Ribbon* (1–3). Illus. by Francis Livingston. 1996, Silver Burdett LB $15.95 (0-382-39096-2); paper $5.95 (0-382-39098-9). Jennie learns to play the fiddle and brother Jimmy enjoys folk dancing during the summer they spend on their grandparent's farm. (Rev: SLJ 9/96)

**2992** Levine, Abby. *What Did Mommy Do Before You?* (PS–K). Illus. by DyAnne DiSalvo-Ryan.

1988, Whitman LB $14.95 (0-8075-8819-9). 32pp. Children are fascinated with the fact that mothers weren't always mothers and were actually babies themselves. (Rev: BCCB 11/88; BL 9/1/88; SLJ 11/88)

**2993** Levinson, Riki. *Grandpa's Hotel* (PS–2). Illus. by David Soman. 1995, Orchard LB $16.99 (0-531-08775-1). 32pp. The narrator and her many cousins enjoy summer fun at her Jewish grandparents' hotel, supposedly in the New York Catskills. (Rev: BL 8/95; SLJ 10/95)

**2994** Levinson, Riki. *I Go with My Family to Grandma's* (PS–1). Illus. by Diane Goode. 1986, Dutton paper $3.95 (0-525-44557-9). 32pp. Turn-of-the-century New York is the setting as 5 children and their families go off on a trip to Grandma's. (Rev: BCCB 10/86; BL 9/1/86; SLJ 10/86)

**2995** Lewis, Rob. *Hide-and-Seek with Grandpa* (1–3). Illus. by author. 1997, Mondo paper $4.50 (1-57255-226-3). 48pp. Young Finley is always surprised at his Grandpa Bear's vim and vigor. Also use *Grandpa Comes to Stay* (1997). (Rev: SLJ 8/97)

**2996** Limmer, Milly J. *Where Do Little Girls Grow?* (PS–3). Illus. by Rosekrans Hoffman. 1993, Whitman LB $15.95 (0-8075-8924-1). 32pp. A little girl and her mother explore this age-old question, first with imagination, then with the truth, which seems just as magical as all of the other imagined possibilities. (Rev: BL 6/1–15/93; SLJ 8/93)

**2997** Lindbergh, Reeve. *Grandfather's Lovesong* (PS–2). Illus. by Rachel Isadora. 1993, Viking paper $15.99 (0-670-84842-5). 30pp. As a grandfather and his grandson roam through the season in a rural setting, the old man describes how much he loves the boy. (Rev: BL 1/15/93; SLJ 4/93)

**2998** Little, Jean. *Jess Was the Brave One* (PS–3). Illus. by Janet Wilson. 1992, Puffin paper $4.99 (0-14-054309-0). 32pp. Even though she is older, Claire has many more fears than her younger sister Jess. (Rev: BL 5/15/92; SLJ 7/92)

**2999** Little, Jean. *Revenge of the Small Small* (K–2). Illus. by Janet Wilson. 1993, Viking paper $14.00 (0-670-84471-3). 32pp. Patsy Small seeks revenge on her older brothers and sisters who won't let her play with them. (Rev: BL 2/1/93)

**3000** London, Jonathan. *A Koala for Katie* (PS–3). Illus. by Cynthia Jabar. 1993, Albert Whitman LB $13.95 (0-8075-4209-1). 32pp. Katie's adoptive parents use a trip to the zoo to explain how in nature substitute parents are often found to take care of orphans. (Rev: BL 11/15/93; SLJ 10/93)

**3001** London, Jonathan. *Old Salt, Young Salt* (K–2). Illus. by Todd L. W. Doney. 1996, Lothrop LB $15.93 (0-688-12976-5). 32pp. When Aaron and his father go fishing, it is the young boy who lands the salmon. (Rev: BL 10/15/96; SLJ 10/96)

**3002** Long, Earlene. *Gone Fishing* (PS–2). Illus. by Richard Brown. 1987, Houghton paper $5.95 (0-395-44236-2). 32pp. A loving story of a boy's fishing trip with his father.

**3003** Lyon, George E. *Five Live Bongos* (PS–1). Illus. by Jacqueline Rogers. 1994, Scholastic $15.95 (0-590-46654-2). 40pp. Five brothers and sisters make so much noise indoors that they are banished to the garage. (Rev: BL 10/15/94; SLJ 10/94)

**3004** Lyon, George E. *Mama Is a Miner* (K–3). Illus. by Peter Catalanotto. 1994, Orchard LB $16.99 (0-531-08703-4). 32pp. While a child is traveling to school, her mother is putting on miner's gear for her work underground in Appalachia. (Rev: BCCB 9/94; BL 6/1–15/94*; SLJ 9/94)

**3005** McCloskey, Robert. *One Morning in Maine* (1–3). Illus. by author. 1952, Puffin paper $4.99 (0-14-050174-6). An exciting day, the loss of Sal's first tooth, is realistically recaptured by this fine storyteller and in the large, extraordinary blue-pencil drawings of Penobscot Bay. Also use: *Blueberries for Sal* (1948).

**3006** McCutcheon, John. *Happy Adoption Day!* (PS–2). Illus. by Julie Paschkis. 1996, Little, Brown $15.95 (0-316-55455-3). 32pp. In simple rhymes, the story of an American family's adoption of an Asian child is told. (Rev: BL 12/1/96; SLJ 11/96) [782.42]

**3007** McDonald, Megan. *The Great Pumpkin Switch* (PS–3). Illus. by Ted Lewin. 1992, Orchard LB $16.99 (0-531-08600-3). 32pp. Grandpa shares growing-up experiences with his grandchildren. (Rev: BL 9/15/92*; SLJ 8/92*)

**3008** McElligott, Matthew. *The Truth About Cousin Ernie's Head* (PS–2). Illus. 1996, Simon & Schuster paper $15.00 (0-689-80179-3). 32pp. Ernie is able to settle a family squabble when he shows an old home movie. (Rev: BL 12/1/96; SLJ 11/96)

**3009** McFarlane, Sheryl. *Waiting for the Whales* (PS–3). Illus. by Ron Lightburn. 1991, Orca paper $7.95 (0-920501-96-6). 32pp. On his lonely island an old man and his granddaughter await the sighting of the summer whales. (Rev: BL 5/15/93; SLJ 6/93)

**3010** McKee, David. *The School Bus Comes at Eight O'Clock* (K–3). Illus. 1994, Hyperion $14.95 (1-56282-662-X). 32pp. Jennifer and Eric's parents decide it is time to buy a clock when the children start school. (Rev: BL 6/1–15/94; SLJ 8/94)

**3011** McKinley, Robin. *My Father Is in the Navy* (PS–1). Illus. by Martine Gourbault. n.d., Smithmark $3.98 (0-8317-3349-7). 24pp. Sara's father is in the navy, and she hasn't seen him for so long that she forgets what he looks like. (Rev: BCCB 4/92; BL 4/15/92; SLJ 5/92)

**3012** MacLachlan, Patricia. *Mama One, Mama Two* (1–3). Illus. by Ruth Bornstein. 1982, HarperCollins LB $15.89 (0-06-024082-2). 32pp. Maudie is told why she has 2 mothers in this gentle story of a foster home.

**3013** MacLachlan, Patricia. *Through Grandpa's Eyes* (1–3). Illus. by Deborah Kogan Ray. 1980, HarperCollins LB $14.89 (0-06-024043-1); paper $5.95 (0-06-443041-3). 48pp. John's blind grandfather shares with him the special way he sees and moves in the world.

**3014** McMillan, Bruce. *Grandfather's Trolley* (K–4). Illus. 1995, Candlewick $15.95 (1-56402-633-7). 32pp. A photoessay about a small girl who rides the trolley car that her grandfather operates. Two other photo-illustrated books by the author are *Eating Fractions* (Scholastic, 1991) and *Going on a Whale Watch* (Scholastic, 1992). (Rev: BCCB 12/95; BL 10/15/95; SLJ 12/95)

**3015** McMillan, Bruce. *Step by Step* (PS). Illus. by author. 1990, Apple Island LB $15.00 (0-688-07234-8). 28pp. Photos trace Evan from 4 months until he becomes a fast walker at 14 months. (Rev: BL 9/1/87; HB 11–12/87; SLJ 9/87)

**3016** McPhail, David. *Sisters* (PS–1). Illus. by author. 1984, Harcourt $14.00 (0-15-275319-2); paper $5.00 (0-15-275320-6). 32pp. Two loving sisters compare their similarities and differences.

**3017** Mahy, Margaret. *A Busy Day for a Good Grandmother* (PS–3). Illus. by Margaret Chamberlain. 1993, Macmillan $14.95 (0-689-50595-7). 32pp. Mrs. Oberon is an unconventional grandmother who rides skateboards and fights vultures and alligators. (Rev: BL 10/15/93; SLJ 9/93)

**3018** Mahy, Margaret. *The Rattlebang Picnic* (K–2). Illus. by Steven Kellogg. 1994, Dial paper $14.89 (0-8037-1319-3). 32pp. The adventures of the McTavish family — 7 children, mother, father, and Granny — on a fun-filled picnic in their rattlebang of a car. (Rev: BL 6/1–15/94*; HB 9–10/94; SLJ 10/94*)

**3019** Manning, Mick, and Brita Granström. *The World Is Full of Babies! How All Sorts of Babies Grow and Develop* (PS–1). Illus. by authors. 1996, Doubleday $14.95 (0-385-32258-5). 28pp. A simple picture book that compares the care and feeding of human babies with those of elephants, polar bears, seals, and other animals. (Rev: SLJ 10/96)

**3020** Markel, Michelle. *Gracias, Rosa* (K–3). Illus. by Diane Paterson. 1995, Albert Whitman LB $14.95 (0-8075-3024-7). 32pp. Kate learns about Guatemala and the sadness of leaving a daughter behind from the family's new baby-sitter, Rosa. (Rev: BL 6/1–15/95; SLJ 5/95)

**3021** Martin, C. L. G. *Three Brave Women* (K–2). Illus. by Peter Elwell. 1991, Macmillan paper $16.00 (0-02-762445-5). 32pp. Caitlin finds she is afraid of spiders, and her grandmother tells her of her private fears. (Rev: BL 5/1/91; SLJ 5/91)

**3022** Martin, Jane Read. *Now I Will Never Leave the Dinner Table* (K–3). Illus. by Roz Chast. 1996, HarperCollins LB $14.89 (0-06-024795-9). 32pp. Patty Jane defies her bossy older sister and refuses to eat her spinach. (Rev: BCCB 4/96; BL 4/1/96; HB 9–10/96; SLJ 5/96*)

**3023** Maslac, Evelyn Hughes. *Finding a Job for Daddy* (PS–3). Illus. by Kay Life. 1996, Albert Whitman LB $12.95 (0-8075-2437-9). 32pp. Laura tries to cheer up her father, who is out of work. (Rev: BL 4/1/96)

**3024** Mennen, Ingrid. *One Round Moon and a Star for Me* (PS–1). Illus. by Niki Daly. 1994, Orchard LB $16.99 (0-531-08654-2). 32pp. In this tale that takes place in Lesotho, a young boy needs reassurance when a new baby arrives in the family. (Rev: BCCB 4/94; BL 2/15/94; SLJ 9/94)

**3025** Michaels, William. *Clare and Her Shadow* (PS–1). Illus. by author. 1991, Shoe String LB $16.50 (0-208-02301-1). While on a walk with her grandmother, Clare discovers her shadow. (Rev: SLJ 2/92)

**3026** Miller, Margaret. *Now I'm Big* (PS–K). Illus. 1996, Greenwillow LB $14.93 (0-688-14078-5). 32pp. A group of primary-graders compare themselves with what they were as younger children. (Rev: BCCB 3/96; BL 4/15/96; HB 9–10/96; SLJ 5/96)

**3027** Miller, William. *A House by the River* (K–2). Illus. by Cornelius Van Wright. 1997, Lee & Low $15.95 (1-880000-48-2). 32pp. Belinda is afraid that her house will get flooded if heavy rains come, but her mother tells her about how the house has been a safe haven through the years. (Rev: BL 5/15/97; HB 7–8/97; SLJ 7/97)

**3028** Miller, William. *Zora Hurston and the Chinaberry Tree* (PS–3). Illus. by Cornelius Van Wright and Ying-Hwa Hu. 1994, Lee & Low $14.95 (1-880000-14-8); paper $5.95 (1-880000-33-4). 32pp. A picture book that explores the trauma experienced by the author Zora Hurston when her beloved mother died when the girl was only 9. (Rev: BL 10/15/94; SLJ 12/94) [813]

**3029** Mitchell, Barbara. *Down Buttermilk Lane* (K–3). Illus. by John Sandford. 1993, Lothrop LB $15.93 (0-688-10115-1). 32pp. Riding their horse-drawn buggy, an Amish family goes to spend a day in the village shopping and socializing. (Rev: BL 10/1/93; HB 11–12/93)

**3030** Mitchell, Barbara. *Waterman's Child* (K–3). Illus. by Daniel San Souci. 1997, Lothrop LB $15.93 (0-688-10862-8). 40pp. From her Chesapeake Bay island home, Annie describes the joys and sorrows her family has found from generation to generation trying to make a living from the sea. (Rev: BCCB 4/97; BL 6/1–15/97; SLJ 5/97)

**3031** Mitchell, Rhonda. *The Talking Cloth* (PS–2). Illus. 1997, Orchard LB $16.99 (0-531-33004-4). 32pp. When Amber drapes her aunt's cloth from Ghana around herself, she pretends she is an Ashanti princess. (Rev: BCCB 6/97; BL 2/15/97; SLJ 7/97)

**3032** Moon, Nicola. *Lucy's Picture* (PS–2). Illus. by Alex Ayliffe. 1995, Dial paper $15.99 (0-8037-1833-0). 32pp. Because her father is blind, Lucy decides not to paint a picture at school but instead make a collage that can be touched. (Rev: BL 1/15/95; SLJ 3/95)

**3033** Moore, Elaine. *Grandma's Smile* (PS–1). Illus. by Dan Andreasen. Series: Seasons With Grandma. 1995, Lothrop LB $15.93 (0-688-11076-2). 32pp. Kim and her grandmother share memorable experiences at an autumn fair. (Rev: BL 9/1/95; SLJ 10/95)

**3034** Mora, Pat. *Pablo's Tree* (PS–3). Illus. by Cecily Lang. 1994, Macmillan paper $16.00 (0-02-767401-0). 32pp. Ever since his daughter adopted young Pablo, grandfather decorates a tree on the anniversary of the boy's arrival. (Rev: BCCB 9/94; BL 11/1/94; HB 11–12/94)

**3035** Morris, Ann. *The Baby Book* (PS). Illus. Series: World's Family. 1995, Silver Burdett LB $15.95 (0-382-24698-5); paper $5.95 (0-382-24700-0). 32pp. Full-color photographs show infants from around the world, with ethnic backgrounds explained at the back of the book. (Rev: BL 2/15/96) [305.23]

**3036** Morris, Ann. *The Daddy Book* (PS). Illus. Series: The World's Family. 1995, Silver Burdett LB $15.95 (0-382-24695-0); paper $5.95 (0-382-24697-7). 32pp. In this photograph album, all kinds of daddies engage in everyday activities, like going fishing and telling stories. (Rev: BL 2/15/96; SLJ 5/96) [306]

**3037** Morris, Ann. *Loving* (PS–2). Illus. by Ken Heyman. 1990, Lothrop LB $15.93 (0-688-06341-1). 32pp. Clear photos focus on children, their families, and their pets. Also use: *On the Go* (1990). (Rev: BL 1/1/91; SLJ 1/91) [306.7]

**3038** Morris, Ann. *The Mommy Book* (PS). Illus. Series: The World's Family. 1995, Silver Burdett LB $15.95 (0-382-24693-4); paper $5.95 (0-382-24694-2). 32pp. Photographs from around the world depict mothers and children in a variety of shared experiences. (Rev: BL 2/15/96; SLJ 5/96) [306]

**3039** Muldoon, Kathleen M. *Princess Pooh* (K–4). Illus. by Linda Shute. 1989, Whitman LB $14.95 (0-8075-6627-6). A young girl is jealous of her wheelchair-bound older sister because of the attention she receives. (Rev: SLJ 11/89)

**3040** Newman, Leslea. *Heather Has Two Mommies* (PS–K). Illus. by Diana Souza. 1991, Alyson paper $8.95 (1-55583-180-X). 40pp. A child who has 2 lesbians as mothers realizes that her family does not include a daddy. (Rev: BCCB 2/90; BL 3/1/90)

**3041** Newman, Leslea. *Remember That* (PS–3). Illus. by Karen Ritz. 1996, Clarion $14.95 (0-395-66156-0). 32pp. A Jewish child recalls her grandmother Bubbe and the many joyful experiences they have shared. (Rev: BL 2/1/96; SLJ 3/96)

**3042** Nodar, Carmen Santiago. *Abuelita's Paradise* (K–2). Illus. by Diane Paterson. 1992, Whitman $14.95 (0-8075-0129-8). 32pp. Marita remembers the stories that her grandmother, now dead, told her about growing up in Puerto Rico. (Rev: BL 9/15/92; SLJ 9/92)

**3043** O'Callahan, Jay. *Orange Cheeks* (PS–2). Illus. by Patricia Raine. 1993, Peachtree $15.95 (1-56145-073-1). 40pp. A young boy tries not to create trouble when he visits his grandmother. (Rev: BL 7/93)

**3044** Oppenheim, Joanne. *Left and Right* (PS–3). Illus. by Rosanne Litzinger. 1989, Harcourt $13.95 (0-15-200505-6). 32pp. Two brothers who are shoemakers learn that they work best using each other's strengths. (Rev: BL 11/1/89; SLJ 12/89)

**3045** Oppenheim, Shulamith Levey. *Fireflies for Nathan* (PS–1). Illus. by John Ward. 1994, Tambourine LB $15.93 (0-688-12148-9). While visiting his grandparents in the country, a young African American boy engages in his father's favorite pastime: catching fireflies. (Rev: SLJ 10/94)

**3046** Ormerod, Jan. *101 Things to Do with a Baby* (PS–K). Illus. by author. 1984, Lothrop LB $15.93 (0-688-03802-6). 32pp. The whole family decides to amuse the baby.

**3047** Ormerod, Jan. *Who's Whose?* (K–3). Illus. 1998, Lothrop LB $15.93 (0-688-14679-1). 32pp. A delightful, breezy account of the members of 3 families, their activities, and how they help one another. (Rev: BL 3/15/98; SLJ 4/98)

**3048** Ostrow, Vivian. *My Brother Is from Outer Space: The Book of Proof* (K–3). Illus. by Eric Brace. 1996, Albert Whitman LB $14.95 (0-8075-5325-5). 32pp. Alex is convinced that his young brother is really an alien from outer space. (Rev: BCCB 5/96; BL 4/1/96; SLJ 6/96)

**3049** Otey, Mimi. *Blue Moon Soup Spoon* (PS–2). Illus. 1993, Farrar $15.00 (0-374-30851-9). 32pp. A young boy watches his mother prepare dinner while awaiting the arrival of his father. (Rev: BL 6/1–15/93)

**3050** Otey, Mimi. *Daddy Has a Pair of Striped Shorts* (PS–1). Illus. 1990, Farrar $13.95 (0-374-31675-9). 32pp. A little girl and her brother are embarrassed at their father's outlandish clothes. (Rev: BL 1/1/91; SLJ 1/91)

**3051** Patrick, Denise Lewis. *Red Dancing Shoes* (PS–2). Illus. by James E. Ransome. 1993, Morrow LB $15.93 (0-688-10393-6). Grandma gives her young granddaughter a new pair of dancing shoes. (Rev: BL 3/1/93; SLJ 3/93)

**3052** Paxton, Tom. *The Marvelous Toy* (PS–K). Illus. by Elizabeth Sayles. 1996, Morrow LB $15.93 (0-688-13880-2). This song tells of a boy's pleasure at receiving an unusual gift from his father and, much later, the happiness he gets passing it on to his son. (Rev: SLJ 8/96)

**3053** Pellegrini, Nina. *Families Are Different* (PS–3). Illus. 1991, Holiday LB $15.95 (0-8234-0887-6). 32pp. Two adopted Korean girls gradually adjust to their new American family. (Rev: BL 12/15/91; SLJ 10/91)

**3054** Perkins, Lynne Rae. *Clouds for Dinner* (K–2). Illus. by author. 1997, Greenwillow LB $14.93 (0-688-14904-9). 32pp. Because her parents are disorganized dreamers, Janet welcomes a chance to visit her efficient Aunt Peppy. (Rev: HB 9–10/97; SLJ 9/97)

**3055** Petersen, P. J. *Some Days, Other Days* (K–2). Illus. by Diane De Groat. 1994, Scribners paper $14.95 (0-684-19595-X). Jimmy is afraid that he is going to have one of his bad days until mother starts it off well with a big hug. (Rev: SLJ 12/94)

**3056** Peterson, Jeanne Whitehouse. *My Mama Sings* (PS–3). Illus. by Sandra Speidel. 1994, HarperCollins LB $15.89 (0-06-023859-3). 32pp. Depicts the role that all kinds of music play in the lives of an African American boy and his single mother. (Rev: BL 6/1–15/94; SLJ 8/94)

**3057** Pinkney, Gloria J. *The Sunday Outing* (PS–3). Illus. by Jerry Pinkney. 1994, Dial LB $14.89 (0-8037-1199-9). 32pp. Ernestine's waking hours are spent preparing for a trip to visit her aunt and uncle on their farm in North Carolina. (Rev: BCCB 7–8/94; BL 5/1/94; SLJ 7/94)

**3058** Polacco, Patricia. *The Keeping Quilt* (PS–2). Illus. by author. 1988, Simon & Schuster paper $16.00 (0-671-64963-9). 32pp. The quilt serves as a link between generations of a family. (Rev: BL 12/1/88; SLJ 10/88)

**3059** Polacco, Patricia. *My Ol' Man* (1–3). Illus. 1995, Putnam $15.95 (0-399-22822-5). 32pp. Two youngsters enjoy the stories that their traveling-salesman father tells when he comes home. (Rev: BL 4/1/95; SLJ 5/95)

**3060** Polacco, Patricia. *My Rotten Redheaded Older Brother* (K–3). Illus. 1994, Simon & Schuster paper $16.00 (0-671-72751-6). 30pp. A young girl engages in a fierce rivalry with her brother in spite of an underlying love. (Rev: BL 9/15/94; SLJ 10/94*)

**3061** Polacco, Patricia. *Thunder Cake* (PS–3). Illus. 1990, Putnam $15.95 (0-399-22231-6). 32pp. A grandmother helps her young granddaughter conquer her fears of electrical storms by eating Thunder Cake. (Rev: BCCB 3/90; BL 2/15/90*; HB 3–4/90; SLJ 3/90*)

**3062** Pomerantz, Charlotte. *The Chalk Doll* (PS–1). Illus. by Frane Lessac. 1989, HarperCollins paper $5.95 (0-06-443333-1). 32pp. Rose is sick, and Mother tells her stories of her Jamaican girlhood. (Rev: BL 5/15/89; HB 7–8/89)

**3063** Porter-Gaylord, Laurel. *I Love My Daddy Because . . .* (PS–K). Illus. by Ashley Wolff. 1991, Dutton paper $7.99 (0-525-44624-9). 24pp. Reasons for loving one's father are illustrated through both human and animal examples. A companion volume is *I Love My Mommy Because . . .* (Rev: BCCB 2/91; BL 4/15/91; SLJ 1/92)

**3064** Pryor, Bonnie. *The Dream Jar* (K–4). Illus. by Mark Graham. 1996, Morrow LB $15.93 (0-688-13062-3). 32pp. In turn-of-the-century New York City, a young immigrant girl helps her family by teaching them English. (Rev: BL 3/1/96; HB 7–8/96; SLJ 3/96)

**3065** Quinlan, Patricia. *My Dad Takes Care of Me* (PS–2). Illus. by Vlasta Van Kampen. 1987, Firefly LB $15.95 (0-920303-79-X); paper $4.95 (0-920303-76-5). 24pp. Although a little boy loves his father, he just can't get used to Dad's being home while Mother works. (Rev: BL 7/87; SLJ 9/87)

**3066** Rabe, Berniece. *Where's Chimpy?* (PS–2). Illus. by Diane Schmidt. 1988, Whitman LB $14.95 (0-8075-8928-4); paper $5.95 (0-8075-8927-6). 32pp. A little girl with Down's syndrome asks for Chimpy, her missing toy monkey, before she can go to sleep. (Rev: BCCB 10/88; BL 9/1/88; SLJ 12/88)

**3067** Rahaman, Vashanti. *Read for Me, Mama* (PS–1). Illus. 1997, Boyds Mills $14.95 (1-56397-313-8). 32pp. An African American boy hopes that his mother, a hotel maid, will have time to read a story to him. (Rev: BCCB 3/97; BL 2/15/97; SLJ 4/97)

**3068** Rand, Gloria. *The Cabin Key* (K–3). Illus. by Ted Rand. 1994, Harcourt $15.00 (0-15-213884-6). 32pp. A young girl tells about the wonderful things she loves about the family's log cabin in the mountains. (Rev: BCCB 10/94; BL 11/1/94; SLJ 11/94)

**3069** Ransom, Candice. *We're Growing Together* (PS–1). Illus. by Virginia Wright-Frierson. 1993, Bradbury LB $14.95 (0-02-775666-1). 32pp. Two young sisters face problems when they adjust to their new home in the country with a stepfather. (Rev: BL 10/1/93)

**3070** Regan, Dian C. *Daddies* (PS). Illus. by Mary Morgan. 1996, Scholastic $5.95 (0-590-47973-3). 32pp. Children engage in a variety of activities with their fathers. (Rev: BL 6/1–15/96; SLJ 7/96)

**3071** Reid, Margarette S. *The Button Box* (K–3). Illus. by Sarah Chamberlain. 1990, Dutton paper $14.99 (0-525-44590-0). 24pp. A boy imagines interesting stories behind the different buttons in his grandmother's button box. (Rev: BCCB 3/90; BL 4/15/90; SLJ 9/90)

**3072** Reiser, Lynn. *Cherry Pies and Lullabies* (PS–1). Illus. 1998, Greenwillow $16.00 (0-688-13391-6). 40pp. A girl shows how 4 generations in her family have given and received love while continuing treasured family traditions. (Rev: BL 3/1/98)

**3073** Rice, Eve. *Swim!* (PS–1). Illus. by Marisabina Russo. 1996, Greenwillow LB $14.93 (0-688-14275-3). 24pp. A young girl and her father spend Saturdays at the swimming pool. (Rev: BCCB 9/96; BL 8/96; SLJ 9/96)

**3074** Richardson, Jean. *Thomas's Sitter* (PS–1). Illus. by Dawn Holmes. 1991, Macmillan LB $13.95 (0-02-776146-0). 32pp. Thomas discourages all applicants for his family's baby-sitter job until Dan, a young poet, appears. (Rev: BL 7/91; SLJ 9/91)

**3075** Rochelle, Belinda. *When Jo Louis Won the Title* (K–3). Illus. by Larry Johnson. 1994, Houghton $14.95 (0-395-66614-7). 32pp. Jo Louis, a young African American girl, learns from her grandfather about the great boxer in whose honor she and her father were named. (Rev: BCCB 10/94; BL 7/94; SLJ 9/94)

**3076** Roe, Eileen. *Con Mi Hermano/With My Brother* (PS–K). Illus. by Robert Casilla. 1991, Macmillan LB $14.00 (0-02-777373-6). A bilingual book about the good times a boy spends with his older brother. (Rev: SLJ 4/91)

**3077** Rogers, Emma, and Paul Rogers. *Our House* (K–2). Illus. by Priscilla Lamont. 1993, Candlewick $14.95 (1-56402-134-3). 40pp. This picture book tells of 4 incidents that occurred in the same house over a period of 200 years. (Rev: BL 4/1/93; SLJ 8/93)

**3078** Rogers, Paul. *From Me to You* (PS–1). Illus. by Jane Johnson. 1988, Orchard LB $12.99 (0-531-08332-2). 32pp. Grandmother tells her granddaughter the story of her 80 years in an average English family. (Rev: BCCB 5/88; BL 12/15/88; HB 9–10/88)

**3079** Ross, Christine. *Lily and the Present* (PS–2). Illus. 1992, Houghton $13.95 (0-395-61127-X). Lily goes shopping for a present for her new baby brother. (Rev: SLJ 11/92)

**3080** Ross, Lillian. *Buba Leah and Her Paper Children* (1–4). Illus. by Mary Morgan. 1991, Jewish Publication Soc. $17.95 (0-8276-0375-4). 32pp. The "paper children" to which Great-Aunt Buba Leah refers turn out to be her real children, who sailed to America to build a better life. (Rev: BL 1/1/92; SLJ 1/92)

**3081** Roth, Susan L. *We'll Ride Elephants Through Brooklyn* (PS–2). Illus. by author. 1989, Farrar $13.95 (0-374-38258-1). A little girl imagines the great celebration that will take place when her grandfather gets better. (Rev: HB 3–4/90; SLJ 2/90)

**3082** Rotner, Shelley, and Sheila M. Kelly. *Lots of Moms* (PS). Illus. 1996, Dial paper $12.89 (0-8037-1892-6). 24pp. A number of multicultural families celebrate the important roles that mothers can play. (Rev: BL 4/1/96; SLJ 3/96)

**3083** Russo, Marisabina. *Grandpa Abe* (PS–3). Illus. 1996, Greenwillow LB $14.93 (0-688-14098-X). 32pp. Sarah adjusts to the death of her beloved grandfather-by-marriage. (Rev: BL 5/15/96; HB 5–6/96; SLJ 7/96)

**3084** Russo, Marisabina. *A Visit to Oma* (PS–2). Illus. 1991, Greenwillow LB $13.88 (0-688-09624-7). 32pp. Celeste visits her great-grandmother, who does not speak English. (Rev: BL 4/15/91; HB 3–4/91; SLJ 7/91)

**3085** Russo, Marisabina. *When Mama Gets Home* (PS–1). Illus. 1998, Greenwillow LB $14.93 (0-688-14986-3). 32pp. A young girl helps her brother and sister with the chores while all 3 await their single-parent mother to get home from work. (Rev: BL 3/1/98; SLJ 4/98)

**3086** Ryder, Joanne. *My Father's Hands* (PS–3). Illus. by Mark Graham. 1994, Morrow LB $15.93 (0-688-09190-3). 32pp. A little girl watches her father work the soil with his hands and is fascinated by the many tiny animals he finds in the garden. (Rev: BL 10/1/94; SLJ 9/94)

**3087** Rylant, Cynthia. *The Relatives Came* (K–2). Illus. by Stephen Gammell. 1985, Macmillan LB $16.00 (0-02-777220-9). 32pp. Details abound in this telling of the day the relatives came — in an old station wagon — hugs, fun, and laughter. (Rev: BCCB 12/85; BL 10/15/85; SLJ 10/85)

**3088** Rylant, Cynthia. *When I Was Young in the Mountains* (K–3). Illus. by Diane Goode. 1982, Dutton paper $3.99 (0-525-44198-0). 32pp. Two children live with their grandparents in this story of poverty in Appalachia.

**3089** Saint James, Synthia. *Sunday* (PS–1). Illus. 1996, Albert Whitman LB $15.95 (0-8075-7658-1). 30pp. Two African American sisters and their parents spend a quiet Sunday with their grandparents. (Rev: BCCB 10/96; BL 11/15/96; SLJ 1/97)

**3090** Say, Allen. *Grandfather's Journey* (PS–3). Illus. by author. 1993, Houghton $16.95 (0-395-57035-2). 32pp. An autobiographical story that chronicles the passages of generations of the author's family as they moved between Japan and the United States. Winner of the 1994 Caldecott Medal. (Rev: BL 7/93*)

**3091** Say, Allen. *The Lost Lake* (2–4). Illus. 1989, Houghton $14.95 (0-395-50933-5). 32pp. Realizing that he is not paying sufficient attention to his son, Dad takes him on a camping trip. (Rev: BCCB 1/90; BL 10/1/89; HB 1–2/90; SLJ 12/89*)

**3092** Schertle, Alice. *Down the Road* (PS–3). Illus. by E. B. Lewis. 1995, Harcourt $16.00 (0-15-276622-7). 40pp. Hetty accidentally breaks the eggs that she has been carefully carrying from the store for her family's breakfast. (Rev: BCCB 12/95; BL 9/15/95*; SLJ 4/96)

**3093** Schindel, John. *Dear Daddy* (K–3). Illus. by Dorothy Donohue. 1995, Albert Whitman LB $12.95 (0-8075-1531-0). 32pp. Jesse longs to see his dad, who lives miles away. Finally, in a telephone conversation, they plan for a summer visit. (Rev: BL 5/1/95; SLJ 5/95)

**3094** Schwartz, Amy. *A Teeny Tiny Baby* (PS–1). Illus. 1994, Orchard LB $16.99 (0-531-08668-2). 32pp. A teeny tiny baby tells about all the things he likes and dislikes about his status. (Rev: BCCB 9/94; BL 7/94*; SLJ 9/94*)

**3095** Seabrooke, Brenda. *Looking for Diamonds* (1–3). Illus. by Nancy Mantha. 1995, Dutton paper $14.99 (0-525-65173-X). 32pp. Amy gets an unexpected surprise when she visits her grandparents in the rural South. (Rev: BL 10/15/95; SLJ 10/95)

**3096** Segal, Lore. *Tell Me a Mitzi* (K–2). Illus. by Harriet Pincus. 1982, Farrar $17.00 (0-374-37392-2); paper $5.95 (0-374-47502-4). 40pp. Three hilarious stories about the antics of a city family: a mad trip to Grandma's house, coming down with a cold, and a meeting with the president.

**3097** Segal, Lore. *Tell Me a Trudy* (PS–3). Illus. by Rosemary Wells. 1977, Farrar $15.00 (0-374-37395-7); paper $4.95 (0-374-47504-0). 40pp. A zany family experiences ordinary situations that somehow become most unusual.

**3098** Selway, Martina. *Don't Forget to Write* (PS–2). Illus. 1992, Ideals $12.95 (0-8249-8543-5). 28pp. On a visit to Grandad's farm, Rosie writes letters daily to her mother. (Rev: BL 6/1/92; SLJ 8/92)

**3099** Shannon, George. *This Is the Bird* (K–3). Illus. by David Soman. 1997, Houghton $15.95 (0-395-72037-0). 32pp. Eight generations of the women in a family are connected to each other by a family heirloom: a wooden carving of a bird. (Rev: BL 2/15/97; SLJ 4/97)

**3100** Sharratt, Nick. *Snazzy Aunties* (PS). Illus. 1994, Candlewick $8.95 (1-56402-214-5). 24pp. A boy is visited by his 7 eccentric aunts. (Rev: BL 6/1–15/94; SLJ 9/94)

**3101** Sherkin-Langer, Ferne. *When Mommy Is Sick* (PS–2). Illus. by Kay Life. 1995, Albert Whitman $12.95 (1-8075-8894-6). 32pp. A first-person narrative about the emptiness a young girl feels when her mother is hospitalized. (Rev: BL 3/15/95; SLJ 5/95)

**3102** Showers, Paul. *The Listening Walk* (K–2). Illus. by Aliki. 1991, HarperCollins LB $14.89 (0-06-021638-7). A boy and his father listen to the sounds around them as they walk. (Rev: SLJ 7/91)

**3103** Shulevitz, Uri. *The Treasure* (K–2). Illus. by author. 1979, Farrar $16.00 (0-374-37740-5); paper $5.95 (0-374-47955-0). 32pp. A man discovers that the most valuable things in life are usually found at home.

**3104** Shute, Linda. *How I Named the Baby* (K–3). Illus. 1993, Whitman LB $14.95 (0-8075-3417-X). 32pp. During the 9-month wait for the baby to be born, all the members of the family suggest various names depending on the season. (Rev: BL 6/1–15/93; SLJ 7/93)

**3105** Simon, Norma. *The Baby House* (PS–1). Illus. by Barbara Samuels. 1995, Simon & Schuster paper $14.00 (0-671-87044-0). 32pp. A little girl is surrounded by expecting parents: her 2 cats and 2 dogs as well as her mother and father. (Rev: BL 4/15/95; SLJ 5/95)

**3106** Slier, Deborah. *Hello Baby* (PS). Illus. 1988, Checkerboard $2.95 (1-56288-087-X). 12pp. A board book that shows basic actions, such as sitting and crying, for the toddler. Also use: *Baby's Words; Busy Baby* (both 1988). (Rev: BCCB 7–8/88; BL 7/88)

**3107** Smalls, Irene. *Dawn and the Round To-It* (PS–1). Illus. by Tyrone Geter. 1994, Simon & Schuster paper $15.00 (0-671-87166-8). 28pp. When Dawn is promised by family members that they will play with her when they get around to it, she misunderstands and draws her own "round to-it." (Rev: BL 7/94; SLJ 9/94)

**3108** Smythe, Anne. *Islands* (K–2). Illus. by Laszlo Gal. 1996, Douglas & McIntyre $14.95 (0-88899-238-6). 32pp. A mother and a daughter skate across a frozen lake to 3 small islands and examine wildlife in this quiet picture book. (Rev: BL 12/1/96)

**3109** Snyder, Carol. *One Up, One Down* (PS–K). Illus. by Maxie Chambliss. 1995, Simon & Schuster $15.00 (0-689-31828-6). 32pp. A little girl helps her parents take care of twin baby brothers until they are able to walk. (Rev: BL 6/1–15/95; SLJ 5/95)

**3110** Steptoe, John. *Baby Says* (PS). Illus. by author. 1988, Lothrop LB $15.93 (0-688-07424-3). 32pp.

An almost wordless picture book catching the exchange between a baby and a big brother. (Rev: BL 4/1/88; HB 7–8/88; SLJ 3/88)

**3111** Steptoe, John. *Stevie* (PS–2). Illus. by author. 1969, HarperCollins paper $5.95 (0-06-443122-3). 32pp. A small African American boy eloquently expresses his resentment at having to share his possessions and mother with a temporary younger boarder who becomes "kinda like a little brother"; illustrated in bold line and color.

**3112** Stevenson, Harvey. *Grandpa's House* (PS–1). Illus. by author. 1994, Hyperion LB $15.49 (1-56282-589-5). A simple text is used with effective pictures to convey the fine time young Woody has during a visit with his grandfather. (Rev: SLJ 6/94)

**3113** Stevenson, James. *I Meant to Tell You* (K–4). Illus. 1996, Greenwillow LB $14.93 (0-688-14178-1). 24pp. The author recalls his daughter growing up and her interests when she was a child. (Rev: BL 4/1/96; SLJ 8/96) [813]

**3114** Stilz, Carol C. *Grandma Buffalo, May and Me* (K–3). Illus. by Constance R. Bergum. 1995, Sasquatch $14.95 (1-57061-015-0). 32pp. Poppy visits parts of Montana where her great-grandmother once lived and does the same things her ancestor did, like plant an apple tree and feed the buffalo. (Rev: BL 10/1/95; SLJ 12/95)

**3115** Straight, Susan. *Bear E. Bear* (PS–K). Illus. by Marisabina Russo. 1995, Hyperion LB $15.49 (1-56282-527-5). 32pp. Gaila loves her teddy bear even after her young sister drops him in the gutter. (Rev: BL 3/15/95; SLJ 6/95)

**3116** Temple, Charles. *On the River Bank* (PS–3). Illus. by Melanie Hall. 1992, Houghton $14.95 (0-395-61591-7). 32pp. At the end of school, a young boy and his parents take off on a fishing trip. (Rev: BL 11/15/92; SLJ 11/92)

**3117** Thomas, Elizabeth. *Green Beans* (PS–2). Illus. by Vicki Jo Redenbaugh. 1992, Carolrhoda LB $19.95 (0-87614-708-2). 32pp. Gramma, who is trying too hard to make her green beans grow, lets granddaughter Dorothea take over. (Rev: BCCB 2/93; BL 9/15/92; SLJ 1/93)

**3118** Thomas, Jane Resh. *Saying Good-bye to Grandma* (2–4). Illus. by Marcia Sewall. 1988, Houghton paper $6.95 (0-395-54779-2). 40pp. Seven-year-old Suzie attends Grandma's funeral. (Rev: BL 10/15/88; HB 9–10/88; SLJ 2/89)

**3119** Thomas, Naturi. *Uh-oh! It's Mama's Birthday!* (PS–3). Illus. by Keinyo White. 1997, Albert Whitman LB $12.95 (0-8075-8268-9). 24pp. An African American boy gives his mother what she really wants on her birthday: a big hug. (Rev: BL 2/15/97; HB 3–4/97; SLJ 5/97)

**3120** Thompson, Mary. *Gran's Bees* (PS–2). Illus. by Donna Peterson. 1996, Millbrook LB $21.90 (1-56294-652-8). 32pp. Jessie, her dad, and her grandmother harvest the summer's last honey on Gran's farm. (Rev: BL 2/15/96; SLJ 4/96)

**3121** Thompson, Mary. *My Brother Matthew* (K–4). Illus. 1992, Woodbine $14.95 (0-933149-47-6). 28pp. The family member who adjusts best to the baby who is born with physical problems is young David. (Rev: BL 2/15/93; SLJ 6/92)

**3122** Tiffault, Benette W. *A Quilt for Elizabeth* (1–4). Illus. by Mary McConnell. 1992, Centering paper $8.95 (1-56123-034-0). After Elizabeth accepts her father's death, she and her grandmother begin a quilt using patches of his clothing. (Rev: SLJ 8/92)

**3123** Titherington, Jeanne. *Where Are You Going, Emma?* (PS–K). Illus. 1988, Greenwillow LB $12.88 (0-688-07082-5). 24pp. Emma explores the orchard; but when she feels lost she is reassured by the sound of her grandfather's voice. (Rev: BL 9/1/88; SLJ 9/88)

**3124** Tompert, Ann. *Will You Come Back for Me?* (PS). Illus. by Robin Kramer. 1988, Whitman LB $14.95 (0-8075-9112-2); paper $5.95 (0-8075-9113-0). 32pp. Her mother must go to work and the little girl must go to day care, but she worries that her mother won't come back for her. (Rev: BCCB 12/88; BL 11/1/88; SLJ 1/89)

**3125** Tunnell, Michael O. *Mailing May* (K–3). Illus. by Ted Rand. 1997, Morrow LB $15.93 (0-688-12879-3). 32pp. Unable to afford a rail ticket, May's father sends her parcel post to visit her grandmother. (Rev: BL 8/97; HB 9–10/97; SLJ 9/97)

**3126** Turner, Ann. *Through Moon and Stars and Night Skies* (PS–2). Illus. by James G. Hale. 1990, HarperCollins LB $14.89 (0-06-026190-0). 32pp. An Asian boy recalls all of the steps in being adopted into his happy American home. (Rev: BL 5/15/90; HB 5–6/90; SLJ 5/90)

**3127** Turner, Barbara J. *A Little Bit of Rob* (1–3). Illus. by Marni Backer. 1996, Albert Whitman LB $14.95 (0-8075-4577-5). 32pp. A family tries unsuccessfully to forget the death of a son by going on a crabbing expedition. (Rev: BL 10/15/96; SLJ 12/96)

**3128** Vertreace, Martha M. *Kelly in the Mirror* (1–3). Illus. by Sandra Speidel. 1993, Whitman LB $14.95 (0-8075-4152-4). 32pp. Kelly wonders if she looks like any member of her family, and the discovery of a picture of her mother as a child supplies the answer. (Rev: BL 4/1/93)

**3129** Viorst, Judith. *Alexander and the Terrible, Horrible, No Good, Very Bad Day* (K–3). Illus. by Ray Cruz. 1972, Macmillan $14.00 (0-689-30072-7); paper $4.99 (0-689-71173-5). Alexander wakes up to a bad day and things get progressively worse as the hours wear on, until he thinks he may escape it all and go to Australia.

**3130** Viorst, Judith. *I'll Fix Anthony* (PS–3). Illus. by Arnold Lobel. 1969, Macmillan paper $4.99 (0-689-71202-2). 32pp. A young boy has a field day planning revenge on an older brother.

**3131** Waber, Bernard. *But Names Will Never Hurt Me* (PS–1). Illus. by author. 1976, Houghton $14.95 (0-395-24383-1). 32pp. Alison is teased about her last name, but after her family tells her the story of how she was named, she feels better and can even joke about it.

**3132** Waddell, Martin. *Grandma's Bill* (K–3). Illus. by Jane Johnson. 1991, Orchard LB $13.99 (0-531-08523-6). A boy gets to know his dead grandfather through photos in an album. (Rev: SLJ 5/91)

**3133** Waddell, Martin. *When the Teddy Bears Came* (PS–K). Illus. by Penny Dale. 1995, Candlewick $15.99 (1-56402-529-2). 32pp. When baby comes, all the friends and family bring teddy bears as gifts. (Rev: BL 8/95; SLJ 6/95*)

**3134** Walsh, Jill Paton. *When I Was Little Like You* (PS–K). Illus. by Stephen Lambert. 1997, Viking paper $13.99 (0-670-87608-9). 32pp. In this gentle story, a grandmother and her grandchild compare what life was like then with what it's like now. (Rev: BL 11/15/97; SLJ 12/97)

**3135** Walter, Mildred P. *My Mama Needs Me* (PS–1). Illus. by Pat Cummings. 1983, Lothrop LB $15.93 (0-688-01671-5). 32pp. Jason, a young black boy, wants to help his mother with his new baby sister.

**3136** Wells, Rosemary. *Night Sounds, Morning Colors* (PS–2). Illus. by David McPhail. 1994, Dial LB $14.89 (0-8037-1302-9). 32pp. In this story of a loving family, the young son takes delight in such simple pleasures as his father humming him to sleep. (Rev: BL 12/15/94; SLJ 10/94)

**3137** Wells, Rosemary. *Waiting for the Evening Star* (K–3). Illus. by Susan Jeffers. 1993, Dial LB $14.89 (0-8037-1399-1). 40pp. The story of brothers growing up as friends in a Vermont village and of the eventual decision of one to leave. (Rev: BCCB 12/93; BL 9/1/93; HB 11–12/93; SLJ 10/93)

**3138** Weston, Martha. *Apple Juice Tea* (PS–K). Illus. 1994, Clarion $14.95 (0-395-65480-7). 32pp. Polly scarcely remembers her grandmother; but when they are reunited, they have a great time together. (Rev: BL 11/1/94; SLJ 9/94)

**3139** Weston, Martha. *Bad Baby Brother* (K–2). Illus. 1997, Clarion $14.95 (0-395-72103-2). 32pp. In spite of all her overtures of friendship, Tessa finds that her new baby brother doesn't respond to her. (Rev: BL 4/15/97; SLJ 6/97)

**3140** Wickstrom, Sylvie. *Mothers Can't Get Sick* (K–2). Illus. by author. 1989, Crown $12.95 (0-517-57181-1). When Mama Jones gets sick, all the family pitches in to help to show Mama how much they love her. (Rev: HB 11–12/89; SLJ 9/89)

**3141** Wild, Margaret. *All the Better to See You With!* (K–3). Illus. by Pat Reynolds. 1993, Whitman LB $14.95 (0-8075-0284-7). 32pp. A girl who is always outshone by her 4 brothers and sisters gains attention when she needs glasses. (Rev: BL 7/93; SLJ 8/93)

**3142** Wild, Margaret. *Big Cat Dreaming* (K–3). Illus. by Anne Spudvilas. 1997, Annick $16.95 (1-55037-493-1). 32pp. Two grandchildren enjoy visiting their grandmother, partly because of her wonderful pets. (Rev: BL 2/1/98; SLJ 2/98)

**3143** Wild, Margaret. *Our Granny* (PS–1). Illus. by Julie Vivas. 1994, Ticknor $14.95 (0-395-67023-3). 32pp. All kinds of grandmothers from the glamorous and kinky to cuddly and plain are celebrated in this lively picture book. (Rev: BCCB 5/94; BL 1/15/94*; HB 5–6/94; SLJ 4/94*)

**3144** Wild, Margaret. *Remember Me* (PS–2). Illus. by Dee Huxley. 1995, Albert Whitman LB $14.95 (0-8075-6934-8). 32pp. In spite of her increasing forgetfulness, Grandma remembers the good times she spent with Ellie, her granddaughter. (Rev: BL 2/1/96; SLJ 1/96)

**3145** Wilhelm, Hans. *A Cool Kid — Like Me?* (PS–1). Illus. 1990, Crown LB $13.99 (0-517-57822-0). 32pp. A grandmother realizes that her small grandson needs a teddy bear for assurance. (Rev: BL 9/15/90; SLJ 12/90)

**3146** Willhoite, Michael. *Daddy's Roommate* (PS–2). Illus. 1990, Alyson $15.95 (1-55583-178-8); paper $9.95 (1-55583-118-4). 32pp. After his parents' divorce, a young boy finds that his father has a male partner and on weekends the boy enjoys visiting the 2 of them. (Rev: BCCB 2/91; BL 3/1/91; SLJ 4/91)

**3147** Willhoite, Michael. *Daddy's Wedding* (PS–3). Illus. 1996, Alyson $15.95 (1-55583-350-0). 32pp. Nick is best man when his father marries his male roommate. A sequel to *Daddy's Roommate* (1991). (Rev: BCCB 6/96; BL 7/96)

**3148** Willhoite, Michael. *Uncle What-Is-It Is Coming to Visit* (K–3). Illus. 1993, Alyson $12.95 (1-55583-205-9). 32pp. Two small kids discover that their gay uncle is a nice guy who doesn't live up to their stereotypic ideas. (Rev: BL 7/93)

**3149** Williams, Vera B. *A Chair for My Mother* (PS–2). Illus. by author. 1982, Greenwillow LB $15.93 (0-688-00915-8). 32pp. After fire destroys their home, Rose and her mother and grandmother save to buy a nice new chair. Two sequels are: *Something Special for Me* (1983); *Music, Music for Everyone* (1984).

**3150** Williams, Vera B. *Lucky Song* (PS–K). Illus. 1997, Greenwillow LB $14.93 (0-688-14460-8). 24pp. Evie is a lucky girl because all of her wants and needs are satisfied by her loving family. (Rev: BL 10/1/97*; HB 9–10/97; SLJ 8/97*)

**3151** Wing, Natasha L. *Jalapeno Bagels* (PS–2). Illus. by Robert Casilla. 1996, Simon & Schuster $15.00 (0-689-80530-6). 32pp. Pablo, who comes from a racially mixed family, finds his life is enriched by both cultures. (Rev: BL 6/1–15/96; SLJ 7/96)

**3152** Winter, Susan. *I Can* (PS–K). Illus. by author. 1993, DK Publg. $9.95 (1-56458-197-7). An older brother tells of his accomplishments and compares them to those of his younger sister. The sister's side of the story is told in a companion volume, *Me, Too* (1993). (Rev: SLJ 2/94)

**3153** Winthrop, Elizabeth. *I'm the Boss!* (PS–1). Illus. by Mary Morgan. 1994, Holiday LB $15.95 (0-8234-1113-3). 32pp. Julia is tired of being bossed around and wants her chance to be a dictator. (Rev: BL 5/1/94; SLJ 7/94)

**3154** Wittmann, Patricia. *Scrabble Creek* (1–3). Illus. by Nancy Poydar. 1993, Macmillan LB $14.95 (0-02-793225-7). 32pp. Too old to sleep with her parents, a young girl must move to the bunkhouse at her family's summer camp. (Rev: BCCB 3/93; BL 3/15/93; SLJ 5/93)

**3155** Wood, Audrey. *Weird Parents* (K–3). Illus. 1990, Dial LB $11.89 (0-8037-0649-9). 32pp. At first, a young boy is convinced that his parents are weird, but later he realizes they have saving graces. (Rev: BL 5/1/90; SLJ 7/90)

**3156** Woodtor, Dee Parmer. *Big Meeting* (K–3). Illus. by Dolores Johnson. 1996, Simon & Schuster $16.00 (0-689-31993-9). 32pp. A celebration of a down-home family reunion is chronicled in this joyous book. (Rev: BL 9/1/96; SLJ 9/96)

**3157** Wyeth, Sharon D. *Always My Dad* (K–2). Illus. by Raul Colon. 1995, Knopf LB $15.99 (0-679-93447-2). 32pp. While staying with her grandparents, a young African American girl receives an unexpected, joyous visit from her father. (Rev: BCCB 2/95; BL 2/15/95; SLJ 12/95)

**3158** Zalben, Jane Breskin. *Pearl's Marigolds for Grandpa* (PS–2). Illus. 1997, Simon & Schuster $15.00 (0-689-80448-2). 32pp. When her grandfather dies, Pearl decides that one way to remember him is to plant some marigold seeds as the two always did in the past. (Rev: BL 11/1/97; SLJ 9/97)

**3159** Zamorano, Ana. *Let's Eat!* (PS–2). Illus. by Julie Vivas. 1997, Scholastic $15.95 (0-590-13444-2). 32pp. A loving Spanish family enjoys Mama's food even more when she returns home from the hos-

pital with baby Rosa. (Rev: BCCB 4/97; BL 5/15/97; SLJ 4/97*)

**3160** Zapater, Beatriz M. *Fiesta!* (K–3). Illus. by Jose Ortega. 1993, Simon & Schuster paper $4.95 (0-671-79842-1). 26pp. Chucho and his family, from Colombia, plan a fiesta in their new home in America. (Rev: BL 3/15/93)

**3161** Zemach, Harve. *Mommy, Buy Me a China Doll* (K–3). Illus. by Margot Zemach. 1989, Farrar paper $4.95 (0-374-45286-5). 32pp. This adaptation of the Ozark song tells how Eliza Lou and her mother make plans to buy a doll. A reissue.

**3162** Ziefert, Harriet. *A New Coat for Anna* (K–3). Illus. by Anita Lobel. 1986, Knopf paper $6.99 (0-394-89861-3). 40pp. It's been a long time since Anna has had a new coat, and her mother vows to get one for her in this story of post-World War II Europe. (Rev: BCCB 3/87; BL 12/15/86; SLJ 12/86)

**3163** Zolotow, Charlotte. *The Quarreling Book* (K–2). Illus. by Arnold Lobel. 1963, HarperCollins paper $4.95 (0-06-443034-0). 32pp. Father's failure to kiss mother one morning triggers a series of quarrels, but the pet dog sets things right. Also use: *The Hating Book* (1969).

**3164** Zolotow, Charlotte. *This Quiet Lady* (PS–2). Illus. by Anita Lobel. 1992, Greenwillow LB $13.93 (0-688-09306-X). 24pp. In this celebration of life, a little girl looks at photos of her mother from babyhood to motherhood. (Rev: BCCB 6/92; BL 5/1/92*; SLJ 6/92)

**3165** Zolotow, Charlotte. *William's Doll* (PS–3). Illus. by William Pene du Bois. 1972, HarperCollins LB $14.89 (0-06-027048-9); paper $5.95 (0-06-443067-7). 32pp. William wanted a doll, much to his father's dismay; but when Grandma comes to visit she presents William with a doll, saying that now he will have an opportunity to practice being a good father.

### FRIENDSHIP STORIES

**3166** Aliki. *Best Friends Together Again* (PS–3). Illus. 1995, Greenwillow LB $14.93 (0-688-13754-7). 32pp. Peter and Robert, 2 dear friends, are reunited after Peter comes for a visit after he had to move. (Rev: BL 8/95; HB 9–10/95; SLJ 9/95)

**3167** Aliki. *Overnight at Mary Bloom's* (PS–1). Illus. by author. 1987, Greenwillow LB $15.93 (0-688-06765-4). 32pp. The activities and fun of staying overnight. (Rev: BCCB 11/87; BL 9/15/87; SLJ 9/87)

**3168** Aliki. *We Are Best Friends* (K–3). Illus. by author. 1982, Greenwillow LB $15.93 (0-688-00823-2); Morrow paper $4.95 (0-688-07037-X). 32pp. Robert is at a loss when his best friend moves away.

**3169**  Belton, Sandra. *May'naise Sandwiches and Sunshine Tea* (K–3). Illus. by Gail G. Carter. 1994, Four Winds paper $14.95 (0-02-709035-3). Big Mama recalls growing up in a poor but loving household and visiting friend Bettie Jean, who belonged to a middle-class African American family and lived in a much nicer neighborhood. (Rev: SLJ 12/94)

**3170**  Blegvad, Lenore. *Anna Banana and Me* (K–3). Illus. by Erik Blegvad. 1985, Macmillan $13.95 (0-689-50274-5); paper $3.95 (0-689-71114-X). 32pp. A young boy who is afraid of everything takes brave Anna Banana's advice when he is stranded alone. (Rev: BCCB 3/85; BL 7/85; HB 5–6/85)

**3171**  Bluthenthal, Diana Cain. *Matilda the Moocher* (PS–2). Illus. 1997, Orchard LB $16.99 (0-531-33003-6). 32pp. Libby gets tired of her friend Matilda's constant borrowing of her possessions and money. (Rev: BL 3/15/97; SLJ 5/97)

**3172**  Boelts, Maribeth. *Grace and Joe* (K–3). Illus. by Martine Gourbault. 1994, Albert Whitman LB $14.95 (0-8075-3019-0). Grace, a lonely preschooler, forms a friendship with Joe, a mail carrier, and follows him around on his route. (Rev: SLJ 12/94)

**3173**  Brown, Marc. *The True Francine* (1–3). Illus. by author. 1981, Little, Brown $15.95 (0-316-11212-7). Francine discovers the meaning of friendship when she is accused of cheating.

**3174**  Buckley, Helen E. *Moonlight Kite* (K–3). Illus. by Elise Primavera. 1997, Lothrop LB $15.93 (0-688-10932-2). 32pp. The 3 remaining monks in a monastery reestablish contact with the neighborhood children through a kite incident. (Rev: BL 3/15/97; SLJ 3/97)

**3175**  Carlson, Nancy. *How to Lose All Your Friends* (PS–2). Illus. 1994, Viking paper $14.99 (0-670-84906-5). 32pp. Cast in the framework of a self-help book, this account gives basic instructions on how to lose friends. (Rev: BL 9/1/94; SLJ 10/94)

**3176**  Carlstrom, Nancy White. *Blow Me a Kiss, Miss Lilly* (K–2). Illus. by Amy Schwartz. 1990, HarperCollins LB $14.89 (0-06-021013-3). 32pp. The story of a special friendship between an elderly lady and little Sara. (Rev: BCCB 5/90; BL 4/15/90; HB 5–6/90; SLJ 7/90)

**3177**  Caseley, Judith. *Slumber Party!* (PS–2). Illus. 1996, Greenwillow LB $14.93 (0-688-14016-5). 32pp. Zoe celebrates her birthday with a slumber party in which she and her 4 friends spend an eventful time. (Rev: BCCB 3/96; BL 3/1/96; HB 5–6/96; SLJ 6/96)

**3178**  Champion, Joyce. *Emily and Alice Again* (PS–2). Illus. by Sucie Stevenson. 1995, Harcourt $14.00 (0-15-200439-4). 32pp. Three episodes that tell of the everyday activities of 2 friends, Emily and Alice. (Rev: BL 3/15/95; HB 5–6/95; SLJ 5/95)

**3179**  Christiansen, C. B. *Sycamore Street* (1–3). Illus. by Melissa Sweet. 1993, Macmillan $13.95 (0-689-31784-0). 48pp. When best friend Angel goes on vacation, Chloe is forced to play with a newcomer. (Rev: BL 8/93)

**3180**  Clifton, Lucille. *Three Wishes* (PS–2). Illus. by Michael Hays. 1994, Doubleday $15.00 (0-385-30497-8); Dell paper $4.99 (0-440-40921-7). 32pp. When Zenobia finds a penny with her birth date on it, she is granted 3 wishes. (Rev: BL 4/15/92; SLJ 3/92)

**3181**  Cole, Joanna. *Don't Tell the Whole World!* (K–3). Illus. by Kate Duke. 1992, HarperCollins paper $4.95 (0-064-43292-0). 32pp. A husband tricks his wife into keeping secret the fact that they have found a buried treasure. (Rev: BL 11/1/90; HB 11–12/90; SLJ 12/90)

**3182**  Cote, Nancy. *Palm Trees* (PS–2). Illus. 1993, Macmillan LB $14.95 (0-02-724760-0). 32pp. Renne makes fun of Millie's hairstyle, but in time tries it herself. (Rev: BL 2/15/93; SLJ 7/93)

**3183**  DeClements, Barthe. *Spoiled Rotten* (1–3). Illus. by Jennifer Plecas. 1996, Hyperion paper $3.95 (0-7868-1145-5). 54pp. Some school chums get together to make their new friend realize that he is behaving in a spoiled, selfish way. (Rev: SLJ 7/96)

**3184**  Delton, Judy. *Teeny Weeny Zucchinis* (2–4). Illus. 1995, Dell paper $3.99 (0-440-40978-0). 88pp. The Pee Wee Scouts want to earn their harvest badge by helping at the annual Harvest Fest. (Rev: BL 1/1–15/96)

**3185**  Denslow, Sharon P. *Bus Riders* (PS–2). Illus. by Nancy Carpenter. 1993, Macmillan $14.95 (0-02-728682-7). 32pp. When their regular school bus driver becomes ill, the children cannot adjust to the substitute. (Rev: BL 3/15/93; HB 5–6/93; SLJ 7/93)

**3186**  Dionetti, Michelle. *Coal Mine Peaches* (PS–3). Illus. by Anita Riggio. 1991, Orchard LB $14.99 (0-531-08548-1). 32pp. This is the warm story of 3 generations of an Italian immigrant family. (Rev: BCCB 9/91; BL 9/1/91; HB 1–2/92; SLJ 9/91)

**3187**  Dugan, Barbara. *Loop the Loop* (1–3). Illus. by James Stevenson. 1992, Greenwillow LB $15.93 (0-688-09648-4). 32pp. Anne visits her old friend, Mrs. Simpson, who is now in a nursing home, in this engrossing book of intergenerational friendship. (Rev: BCCB 6/92*; BL 5/15/92; HB 5–6/92*; SLJ 5/92*)

**3188**  Edwards, Michelle. *Eve and Smithy* (K–3). Illus. 1994, Lothrop LB $14.93 (0-688-11826-7). 24pp. Gardener Smithy wants to give a gift to his neighbor, Miss Penny, for all her kindnesses throughout the years. (Rev: BL 6/1–15/94; SLJ 7/94)

**3189**  English, Karen. *Neeny Coming, Neeny Going* (PS–3). Illus. by Synthia Saint James. 1996, Troll paper $14.95 (0-8167-3796-7). 32pp. Two friends are reunited on an island off the coast of South Carolina but can't resume their relationship. (Rev: BL 5/15/96; HB 7–8/96; SLJ 7/96)

**3190** Farrell, Mame. *Marrying Malcolm Murgatroyd* (5–7). 1995, Farrar $14.00 (0-374-34838-3). 122pp. Hannah defends the class nerd because he has been kind to her handicapped younger brother. (Rev: BCCB 12/95; BL 11/1/95; SLJ 11/95)

**3191** Fleischman, Sid. *The Scarebird* (PS–2). Illus. by Peter Sis. 1988, Greenwillow LB $15.93 (0-688-07318-2). 32pp. An old farmer named Lonesome John puts up a headless scarecrow to scare the birds, but then decides to give the scarecrow a head. (Rev: BCCB 9/88; BL 9/15/88; SLJ 9/88)

**3192** Fox, Mem. *Wilfrid Gordon McDonald Partridge* (K–2). Illus. by Julie Vivas. 1989, Kane/Miller $13.95 (0-916291-04-9); paper $7.95 (0-916291-26-X). 32pp. The heartwarming story of the boy with 4 names who collects memorabilia in a box to take to his friend with 4 names in a nursing home because he has heard she is losing her memory. (Rev: BL 2/15/86; HB 1–2/86; SLJ 2/86)

**3193** Gauch, Patricia L. *Christina Katerina and Fats and the Great Neighborhood War* (PS–2). Illus. by Stacey Schuett. 1997, Putnam $15.95 (0-399-22651-6). 32pp. When friend Fats doesn't support Christina when she needs it, she begins a feud with him. (Rev: BCCB 6/97; BL 3/1/97; SLJ 3/97)

**3194** Gauch, Patricia L. *Tanya and Emily in a Dance for Two* (PS–3). Illus. by Satomi Ichikawa. 1994, Putnam $15.95 (0-399-22688-5). 32pp. Though they have different approaches to ballet, 2 young girls become friendly at dance class. (Rev: BCCB 1/95; BL 10/15/94*; HB 11–12/94; SLJ 9/94*)

**3195** Gray, Libba M. *Miss Tizzy* (K–4). Illus. by Jada Rowland. 1993, Simon & Schuster paper $15.00 (0-671-77590-1). 31pp. Miss Tizzy is the one person the neighborhood people can count on for kind acts and expressions of concern and love. (Rev: BL 6/1–15/93)

**3196** Greenfield, Eloise. *Honey, I Love* (PS–K). Illus. by Jan S. Gilchrist. 1995, HarperFestival $7.95 (0-694-00579-7). 20pp. With illustrations of African American children, this simple picture book describes various forms of love. Also use *On My Horse* (1995). (Rev: BL 2/1/95; HB 3–4/95; SLJ 2/95)

**3197** Guy, Rosa. *Billy the Great* (PS–1). Illus. by Caroline Binch. 1994, Dell paper $4.99 (0-440-40920-9). 32pp. Billy would like to be friends with Rod who lives next door, but his parents object. (Rev: BCCB 1/93; BL 9/1/92; HB 3–4/93)

**3198** Hamanaka, Sheila. *Bebop-A-Do-Walk!* (PS–3). Illus. 1995, Simon & Schuster $15.00 (0-689-80288-9). 32pp. A Japanese American girl and her best friend, an African American youngster, have fun exploring midtown Manhattan. (Rev: BL 9/1/95; SLJ 10/95)

**3199** Haseley, Dennis. *Crosby* (K–3). Illus. by Jonathan Green. 1996, Harcourt $15.00 (0-15-200829-2). While fixing a kite and flying it, a young African American boy finds a new friend. (Rev: SLJ 9/96)

**3200** Havill, Juanita. *Jamaica and Brianna* (PS–1). Illus. by Anne S. O'Brien. 1993, Houghton $16.00 (0-395-64489-5). 32pp. Jamaica is upset when her friend, Brianna, makes fun of her hand-me-down boots. (Rev: BCCB 11/93; BL 10/15/93; HB 11–12/93; SLJ 10/93)

**3201** Havill, Juanita. *Jamaica's Blue Marker* (PS–1). Illus. by Anne S. O'Brien. 1995, Houghton $15.00 (0-395-72036-2). 32pp. Jamaica feels annoyance toward a classmate until she finds out he is moving. (Rev: BCCB 10/95; BL 7/95; SLJ 1/96)

**3202** Henkes, Kevin. *Chester's Way* (PS–2). Illus. by author. 1988, Greenwillow LB $15.93 (0-688-07608-4). 32pp. Chester and Wilson are best friends and will have nothing to do with new girl Lilly, until she bails them out of trouble. (Rev: BL 9/1/88; HB 9–10/88; SLJ 9/88)

**3203** Hess, Debra. *Wilson Sat Alone* (K–3). Illus. by Diane Greenseid. 1994, Simon & Schuster paper $14.00 (0-671-87046-7). A boy with a reputation for being a loner responds to offers of friendship from a new girl in his class. (Rev: SLJ 11/94)

**3204** Hilton, Nette. *Andrew Jessup* (K–3). Illus. by Cathy Wilcox. 1993, Ticknor $13.95 (0-395-66900-6). 32pp. Andrew was a wonderful, considerate friend; and when he moves away, his buddy is convinced that no one can take his place. (Rev: BL 12/15/93; SLJ 10/93)

**3205** Himmelman, John. *Honest Tulio* (PS–2). Illus. 1997, Troll paper $14.95 (0-8167-3812-2). 32pp. People are so impressed with Tulio's honesty that they shower him with presents as a reward. (Rev: BL 6/1–15/97; SLJ 7/97)

**3206** Howard, Arthur. *When I Was Five* (PS–1). Illus. 1996, Harcourt $15.00 (0-15-200261-8). 40pp. A 6-year-old boy finds that he has changed a lot in a year, except that he still has the same best friend. (Rev: BL 5/1/96*; HB 9–10/96; SLJ 5/96*)

**3207** Hru, Dakari. *The Magic Moonberry Jump Ropes* (PS–3). Illus. by E. B. Lewis. 1996, Dial paper $14.89 (0-8037-1755-5). 32pp. The magic skipping ropes from Tanzania bring April and her sister new friends with whom to jump rope. (Rev: BCCB 2/96; BL 2/15/96; SLJ 3/96)

**3208** Hurwitz, Johanna. *Busybody Nora* (K–2). Illus. by Lillian Hoban. 1990, Puffin paper $3.99 (0-14-034592-2). Six-year-old Nora lives in an apartment building in New York City and wants to know all her neighbors. All of them are friendly, except for a woman who calls her a busybody.

**3209** Hurwitz, Johanna. *New Neighbors for Nora* (2–3). Illus. by Lillian Hoban. 1991, Morrow LB $12.88 (0-688-09948-3); Puffin paper $3.99 (0-14-034594-9). 80pp. Nora, hoping to make a new friend, is not too happy when Eugene Spencer Eastman moves into her building.

**3210** Hutchins, Pat. *My Best Friend* (PS–K). Illus. 1993, Greenwillow LB $15.93 (0-688-11486-5). 32pp. A little girl is pleased that the friend she admires is going to spend the night at her house. (Rev: BL 3/15/93; SLJ 5/93)

**3211** Jackson, Isaac. *Somebody's New Pajamas* (PS–3). Illus. by David Soman. 1996, Dial paper $14.89 (0-8037-1549-8). 32pp. Jerome and Robert are friends, but when Jerome is invited to sleep over at Robert's, he is embarrassed because he has no pajamas. (Rev: BCCB 2/96; BL 2/15/96*; SLJ 3/96)

**3212** James, Betsy. *Mary Ann* (PS–2). Illus. 1994, Dutton paper $14.99 (0-525-45077-7). 32pp. Amy misses her relocated best friend so much that she names her pet praying mantis Mary Ann, in her honor. (Rev: BL 1/1/94; SLJ 2/94*)

**3213** James, Simon. *Leon and Bob* (PS–1). Illus. 1997, Candlewick $15.99 (1-56402-991-3). 32pp. Leon loses his imaginary playmate when he forms a new, real friendship. (Rev: BCCB 3/97; BL 2/1/97; SLJ 4/97)

**3214** Johnston, Tony. *Amber on the Mountain* (PS–3). Illus. by Robert Duncan. 1994, Dial paper $14.89 (0-8037-1220-0). 32pp. A story of friendship between 2 girls, one of whom is living only temporarily in the area with her road-building father. (Rev: BL 9/1/94; SLJ 8/94)

**3215** Jones, Rebecca C. *Matthew and Tilly* (PS–2). Illus. by Beth Peck. 1995, Dutton $13.95 (0-525-44684-2); Puffin paper $4.99 (0-14-055640-0). 32pp. Matthew, a white boy, and Tilly, a black girl, resume their close friendship after an argument. (Rev: BL 1/15/91; SLJ 3/91)

**3216** Keats, Ezra Jack. *Apt. 3* (PS–3). Illus. by author. 1986, Macmillan paper $4.95 (0-689-71059-3). 32pp. Two brothers, investigating the various sounds of an apartment building, find a friend in Mr. Muntz, the blind man behind the door of Apt. 3.

**3217** Keats, Ezra Jack. *Goggles!* (K–3). Illus. by author. 1987, Macmillan paper $4.95 (0-689-71157-3). 40pp. Dachshund Willie outmaneuvers some neighborhood bullies trying to confiscate the motorcycle goggles found by Peter. Bold collage paintings perfectly capture inner-city neighborhood scenes.

**3218** Keats, Ezra Jack. *Whistle for Willie* (PS–1). Illus. by author. 1964, Puffin paper $4.99 (0-14-

050202-5). After many false starts, Peter at last learns to whistle.

**3219** Kellogg, Steven. *Best Friends* (K–3). Illus. by author. 1990, Dial paper $4.99 (0-8037-0829-7). 32pp. A story about Kathy and her best friend Louise: the highs and lows, jealousy and love of their friendship. (Rev: BCCB 4/86; BL 4/15/86; SLJ 5/86)

**3220** Khalsa, Dayal Kaur. *How Pizza Came to Queens* (K–2). Illus. by author. 1989, Crown $15.00 (0-517-57126-9). A warm story of how pizza came to one family's home. (Rev: BL 4/1/89; SLJ 5/89)

**3221** Kline, Suzy. *Horrible Harry and the Ant Invasion* (2–4). Illus. by Frank Remkiewicz. 1989, Viking paper $12.99 (0-670-82469-0). 64pp. Horrible Harry becomes class monitor for the ant farm. (Rev: BL 12/1/89; SLJ 3/90)

**3222** Kline, Suzy. *Horrible Harry's Secret* (K–2). Illus. by Frank Remkiewicz. 1990, Viking paper $11.99 (0-670-82470-4). 64pp. Horrible Harry falls in love with his classmate Song Lee. (Rev: BL 12/1/90; SLJ 2/91)

**3223** Komaiko, Leah. *Earl's Too Cool for Me* (K–2). Illus. by Laura Cornell. 1988, HarperCollins $14.00 (0-06-023281-1); paper $5.95 (0-06-443245-9). 40pp. A rhyming, outlandish story about Earl, the coolest kid around. (Rev: BL 12/1/88; HB 9–10/88; SLJ 11/88)

**3224** Kroll, Virginia. *Pink Paper Swans* (K–4). Illus. by Nancy L. Clouse. 1994, Eerdmans $15.00 (0-8028-5081-2). 32pp. In this account of how Janetta Jackson began helping Mrs. Tsujimoto, an origami expert, there are instructions for making a pink swan. (Rev: BCCB 10/94; BL 7/94; SLJ 8/94)

**3225** Lakin, Patricia. *Don't Forget* (K–3). Illus. by Ted Rand. 1994, Morrow $14.00 (0-688-12075-X). 32pp. While shopping for ingredients for her mother's birthday cake, Sarah meets the Singer family, who are survivers of a Nazi concentration camp. (Rev: BL 5/15/94; SLJ 6/94)

**3226** Lasky, Kathryn. *Double Trouble Squared* (5–7). 1991, Harcourt paper $8.00 (0-15-224127-2). 232pp. The first in a series concerning the lively Starbuck family, with youngsters who can read one another's minds. (Rev: BCCB 2/92; BL 1/15/92; SLJ 2/92)

**3227** Lester, Alison. *Tessa Snaps Snakes* (K–2). Illus. by author. 1991, Houghton paper $13.95 (0-685-52551-1). In double-page spreads, 7 little children reveal their secrets and pet dislikes. (Rev: HB 11–12/91; SLJ 12/91)

**3228** Lonborg, Rosemary. *Helpin' Bugs* (PS–2). Illus. by Diane R. Houghton. 1995, Little Friend $14.95 (0-9641285-2-7). 32pp. Lonely Hanna finds happiness helping her neighbor Douglas create a bug village. (Rev: BL 1/1–15/96; SLJ 2/96)

**3229** Lyon, George E. *Together* (PS–2). Illus. by Vera Rosenberry. 1989, Orchard $15.95 (0-531-05831-X); paper $6.95 (0-531-07047-6). 32pp. Short poems explore the meaning of togetherness and friendship. (Rev: BL 9/15/89; HB 11–12/89; SLJ 9/89) [811]

**3230** Martin, Ann M. *Rachel Parker, Kindergarten Show-Off* (PS–K). Illus. by Nancy Poydar. 1992, Holiday LB $15.95 (0-8234-0935-X). 40pp. Olivia's friendship with Rachel changes to rivalry, but an understanding teacher helps out. (Rev: BL 11/1/92; SLJ 11/92)

**3231** Mills, Claudia. *A Visit to Amy-Claire* (PS–K). Illus. by Sheila Hamanaka. 1992, Macmillan $14.95 (0-02-766991-2). 32pp. Rachel becomes jealous when her younger sister becomes cousin Amy-Claire's favorite. (Rev: BCCB 2/92; BL 2/1/92; SLJ 6/92*)

**3232** Pinkwater, Daniel. *Doodle Flute* (1–4). Illus. 1991, Macmillan LB $13.95 (0-02-774635-6). 32pp. Spoiled Kevin Spoon wants Mason Mintz's doodle flute in this story about sharing and friendship. (Rev: BL 2/1/91; HB 5–6/91; SLJ 6/91)

**3233** Polacco, Patricia. *The Bee Tree* (K–3). Illus. 1993, Putnam $15.95 (0-399-21965-X). 32pp. After gathering honey from the bee tree with his granddaughter, Grampa explains that sweet things also can be found in books. (Rev: BL 3/1/93; HB 5–6/93; SLJ 6/93*)

**3234** Polacco, Patricia. *Mrs. Katz and Tush* (K–4). Illus. 1992, Bantam $15.00 (0-553-08122-5). 32pp. A lonely Jewish widow is befriended by a black boy who brings her a kitten to love. (Rev: BCCB 7–8/92; BL 4/15/92; HB 11–12/92; SLJ 7/92)

**3235** Raschka, Chris. *Yo! Yes?* (K–4). Illus. 1993, Orchard LB $16.99 (0-531-08619-4). 32pp. This picture book consists of a conversation between 2 boys, one white, one African American. (Rev: BCCB 4/93; BL 3/15/93; HB 5–6/93; SLJ 5/93*)

**3236** Reiser, Lynn. *Best Friends Think Alike* (PS–3). Illus. 1997, Greenwillow LB $15.93 (0-688-15200-7). 32pp. Two independent girls can't agree on the role each will play when they start a game of horse and rider. (Rev: BL 6/1–15/97; HB 3–4/97; SLJ 5/97)

**3237** Reiser, Lynn. *Margaret and Margarita, Margarita y Margaret* (K–3). Illus. 1993, Greenwillow LB $15.93 (0-688-12240-X). 32pp. Though Margaret speaks English and Margarita speaks Spanish, the 2 girls get along well when they meet in a park. (Rev: BCCB 10/93; BL 9/15/93)

**3238** Ryan, Cheryl. *Sally Arnold* (K–3). Illus. by Bill Farnsworth. 1996, Dutton paper $14.99 (0-525-65176-4). 32pp. Jenny finds that the old lady who is gathering objects around her country home is using

them for her craft projects. (Rev: BL 5/1/96; SLJ 4/96)

**3239** Schick, Eleanor. *My Navajo Sister* (K–3). Illus. 1996, Simon & Schuster $16.00 (0-689-80529-2). 30pp. The author, as a child, and her friend Genni share some wonderful experiences on their Navajo land. (Rev: BL 12/1/96; SLJ 12/96)

**3240** Schotter, Roni. *Captain Snap and the Children of Vinegar Lane* (K–3). Illus. by Marcia Sewall. 1989, Orchard paper $5.95 (0-531-07038-7). 32pp. A bitter old man frightens the children away with his snapping fingers, until one day they discover he is ill. (Rev: BL 5/1/89; SLJ 5/89)

**3241** Schubert, Ingrid, and Dieter Schubert. *Wild Will* (K–2). Illus. 1994, Carolrhoda LB $14.95 (0-87614-816-X). 32pp. Gradually, young Frank breaks down the hostility that a retired pirate feels toward people. (Rev: BL 9/15/94; SLJ 8/94)

**3242** Shannon, George. *Seeds* (PS–2). Illus. by Steve Bjorkman. 1994, Houghton $13.95 (0-395-66990-1). 32pp. Little Warren enjoys being with his older buddy Bill and is crushed when Bill and his family move away. (Rev: BL 6/1–15/94; SLJ 4/94)

**3243** Slaughter, Hope. *A Cozy Place* (PS–K). Illus. by Susan Torrence. 1991, Red Hen LB $15.95 (0-931093-13-9). 32pp. Two girls discover that it is each other's presence that makes a place cozy. (Rev: BL 6/1/91)

**3244** Starkman, Neal. *The Riddle* (K–2). Illus. by Ellen Sasaki. 1990, Comprehensive Health paper $10.00 (0-935529-13-6). 50pp. When a class assignment matches them together, Maria and a shy boy named Pete become friends. (Rev: BL 9/1/90)

**3245** Steptoe, John. *Creativity* (PS–3). Illus. by E. B. Lewis. 1997, Clarion $15.95 (0-395-68706-3). 32pp. An African American boy wonders why a new class member who is as dark-skinned as himself can only speak Spanish. (Rev: BL 2/15/97; SLJ 4/97)

**3246** Strauss, Gwen. *The Night Shimmy* (PS–1). Illus. by Anthony Browne. 1992, Knopf LB $15.00 (0-679-82384-0). 32pp. Eric gives up an imaginary companion when he finds a real friend. (Rev: BCCB 6/92*; BL 2/1/92; HB 3–4/92; SLJ 5/92)

**3247** Stroud, Bettye. *Down Home at Miss Dessa's* (PS–3). Illus. by Felicia Marshall. 1996, Lee & Low $14.95 (1-880000-39-3). 32pp. When Miss Dessa is injured, neighborhood children help her in this story of African Americans in the South. (Rev: BCCB 12/96; BL 12/15/96; SLJ 1/97)

**3248** Turney-Zagwyn, Deborah. *Long Nellie* (PS–3). Illus. 1993, Orca $9.95 (0-920501-99-0). 32pp. Young Jeremy is determined to help Long Nellie, the town outcast and eccentric. (Rev: BL 1/1/94)

**3249** Tusa, Tricia. *Stay Away from the Junkyard* (PS–1). Illus. by author. 1988, Macmillan LB $14.95 (0-02-789541-6); paper $5.99 (0-689-71626-5). 32pp. Theodora is told to stay away from the junkyard because Old Man Crampton is "mad," but Theo discovers he isn't mad at all. (Rev: BL 5/1/88; SLJ 8/88)

**3250** Udry, Janice May. *Let's Be Enemies* (PS–2). Illus. by Maurice Sendak. 1961, HarperCollins LB $14.89 (0-06-026131-5). 32pp. John is tired of James and his bossiness and decides to tell him so, but things are patched up and they remain friends.

**3251** Viorst, Judith. *Rosie and Michael* (1–3). Illus. by Lorna Tomei. 1974, Macmillan $16.00 (0-689-30439-0); paper $4.99 (0-689-71272-3). 40pp. In spite of the many tricks they play on one another, Rosie and Michael are still friends.

**3252** Vulliamy, Clara. *Ellen and Penguin* (PS–K). Illus. by author. 1993, Candlewick $13.95 (1-56402-193-9). Ellen and her plush penguin conquer their fears and begin to play with a young girl who is accompanied by her toy monkey. (Rev: SLJ 12/93)

**3253** Waber, Bernard. *Gina* (PS–3). Illus. 1995, Houghton $14.95 (0-395-74279-X). 32pp. Gina's skill at baseball helps her make friends when she moves to a new neighborhood in Queens where there are just boys. (Rev: BL 9/15/95; SLJ 10/95)

**3254** Walter, Mildred P. *Ty's One-Man Band* (PS–2). Illus. by Margot Tomes. 1987, Macmillan LB $14.95 (0-02-792300-2). 32pp. Andro produces music from a collection of everyday objects. A reissue of the 1980 edition.

**3255** Widerberg, Siv. *Suddenly One Day* (K–2). Trans. from Swedish by Tiina Nunnally. Illus. by Anna Walfridson. 1993, R&S $13.00 (91-29-62248-4). The story of the blossoming of a friendship between and girl and a quiet young boy. (Rev: SLJ 3/94)

**3256** Wild, Margaret. *Mr. Nick's Knitting* (K–2). Illus. by Dee Huxley. 1989, Harcourt $12.95 (0-15-200518-8). 32pp. Mr. Nick and Mrs. Jolley always knit together on the morning train, but one day Mrs. Jolley doesn't appear. (Rev: BL 10/1/89; HB 11–12/89; SLJ 10/89)

**3257** Winthrop, Elizabeth. *Katharine's Doll* (K–3). Illus. by Marylin Hafner. 1991, Puffin paper $3.95 (0-525-44738-5). 32pp. Katharine and Molly quarrel when only one receives a new doll.

**3258** Yezerski, Thomas F. *Together in Pinecone Patch* (K–4). Illus. 1998, Farrar $16.00 (0-374-37647-6). 32pp. Two poor immigrant children, one from Poland and the other from Ireland, meet and fall in love and marry. (Rev: BL 2/1/98; SLJ 3/98)

**3259** Yolen, Jane. *Miz Berlin Walks* (K–4). Illus. by Floyd Cooper. 1997, Putnam $15.95 (0-399-22938-

8). 32pp. During her nightly walk, an older white woman tells stories to an African American girl who follows her. (Rev: BL 9/15/97; SLJ 10/97)

**3260** Zarin, Cynthia. *Rose and Sebastian* (PS–K). Illus. by Sarah Durham. 1997, Houghton $16.00 (0-395-75920-X). Rose meets her upstairs neighbor, a noisy, ill-mannered boy named Sebastian. (Rev: HB 9–10/97; SLJ 9/97)

**3261** Ziegler, Jack. *Mr. Knocky* (1–3). Illus. by author. 1993, Macmillan LB $14.95 (0-02-793725-9). All the kids think that Mr. Knocky is only a big bore until they begin to see him in a new light. (Rev: SLJ 12/93)

**3262** Zolotow, Charlotte. *I Know a Lady* (PS–2). Illus. by James Stevenson. 1984, Morrow paper $4.95 (0-688-11519-5). 24pp. Sally loves a kind old lady who lives in the neighborhood.

## HUMOROUS STORIES

**3263** Adam, Addie. *Hilda and the Mad Scientist* (K–2). Illus. by Lisa Thiesing. 1995, Dutton paper $14.99 (0-525-45386-5). 32pp. Hilda decides that the laboratory of Dr. Weinerstein, a mad scientist, needs housecleaning. (Rev: BCCB 7–8/95; BL 6/1–15/95; SLJ 8/95)

**3264** Adinolfi, JoAnn. *Tina's Diner* (PS–1). Illus. by author. 1997, Simon & Schuster paper $16.00 (0-689-80634-5). When the sink in Tina's diner gets clogged, an enterprising boy sets out to find the plumber. (Rev: SLJ 6/97)

**3265** Agee, Jon. *The Return of Freddy Legrand* (PS–1). Illus. 1992, Farrar $15.00 (0-374-36249-1). 32pp. The famous aviator Freddy Legrand is helped by Sophie and Albert when his plane crashes on their farm. (Rev: BL 11/1/92; HB 1–2/93; SLJ 11/92*)

**3266** Alarcon, Karen Beaumont. *Louella Mae, She's Run Away!* (PS–2). Illus. by Rosanne Litzinger. 1997, Holt $14.95 (0-8050-3532-X). 32pp. In this merry barnyard romp a farm family turns out in full force to have a search when the mysterious Louella Mae is missing. (Rev: BL 6/1–15/97; HB 5–6/97; SLJ 5/97)

**3267** Alexander, Lloyd. *The Fortune-Tellers* (PS–3). Illus. by Trina S. Hyman. 1992, Dutton paper $15.99 (0-525-44849-7). 32pp. In this cumulative disaster tale set in West Africa, a fortune-teller informs a young carpenter he will be rich. (Rev: BCCB 9/92*; BL 7/92*; HB 9–10/92*; SLJ 9/92)

**3268** Allard, Harry. *The Stupids Have a Ball* (K–3). Illus. by James Marshall. 1984, Houghton $14.95 (0-395-26497-9); paper $5.95 (0-395-36169-9). The whole Stupid family decides to celebrate when the children bring home terrible report cards from school. Two others in the series: *The Stupids Step Out* (1974); *The Stupids Die* (1981).

**3269** Allard, Harry. *The Stupids Take Off* (K–3). Illus. by James Marshall. 1989, Houghton $14.95 (0-395-50068-0). 32pp. The irresistible noodleheads set off on a fourth adventure, this time to avoid a visit from Uncle Carbuncle. (Rev: BCCB 10/89; BL 10/1/89; SLJ 10/89)

**3270** Allen, Pamela. *Belinda* (PS). Illus. by author. 1993, Viking paper $13.99 (0-670-84372-5). 32pp. Belinda is so used to being milked by Old Tom's wife that when she goes away the cow won't let anyone else touch her. (Rev: BL 5/1/93; HB 7–8/93)

**3271** Arnold, Tedd. *Parts* (K–3). Illus. 1997, Dial paper $14.89 (0-8037-2041-6). 32pp. A boy thinks he is falling apart when he loses a few hairs and he finds he has a loose tooth. (Rev: BL 8/97)

**3272** Arnold, Tedd. *The Signmaker's Assistant* (K–3). Illus. 1992, Dial paper $14.89 (0-8037-1011-9). A young sign maker's assistant creates havoc when he deliberately mixes up signs. (Rev: BL 5/15/92; HB 5–6/92; SLJ 5/92)

**3273** Aylesworth, Jim. *McGraw's Emporium* (K–3). Illus. by Mavis Smith. 1995, Holt $15.95 (0-8050-3192-8). 32pp. A nonsense book about all of the wonderful objects one can shop for at McGraw's Emporium. (Rev: BL 6/1–15/95; SLJ 6/95)

**3274** Baehr, Patricia. *Mouse in the House* (PS–1). Illus. by Laura Lydecker. 1994, Holiday LB $15.95 (0-8234-1102-8). When a mouse moves into Mrs. Teapot's house, she tries a number of unsuccessful ploys to get rid of it. (Rev: SLJ 9/94)

**3275** Baker, Keith. *Hide and Snake* (PS–K). Illus. 1991, Harcourt $12.95 (0-15-233986-8). 32pp. A snake hides in each of the double-page spreads depicting everyday life. (Rev: BL 11/15/91; SLJ 12/91*)

**3276** Barrett, Judith. *Animals Should Definitely Not Wear Clothing* (PS–1). Illus. by Ron Barrett. 1970, Macmillan $13.95 (0-689-20592-9); paper $5.99 (0-689-70807-6). 32pp. Humorous idea expressed in brief text and comic drawings. A sequel is: *Animals Should Definitely Not Act Like People* (1988, Simon & Schuster).

**3277** Barton, Byron. *Wee Little Woman* (PS–K). Illus. 1995, HarperCollins LB $14.89 (0-06-023388-5). 32pp. The milk that a wee woman gets from her wee cow is stolen by a cat. (Rev: BCCB 6/95; BL 7/95; SLJ 8/95*)

**3278** Birchman, David F. *The Raggly Scraggly No-Soap No-Scrub Girl* (PS–3). Illus. by Guy Porfirio. 1995, Lothrop LB $15.93 (0-688-11061-4). 32pp. A dirty little child disrupts a family's dinner when she makes an unexpected visit. (Rev: BCCB 9/95; BL 9/1/95; SLJ 10/95)

**3279** Birdseye, Tom, and Debbie H. Birdseye. *She'll Be Comin' Round the Mountain* (K–3). Illus. by Andrew Glass. 1994, Holiday LB $15.95 (0-8234-1032-3). 32pp. A variation on the old song that tells about a group of mountain folk who are awaiting Tootie's comin' round the mountain for a visit. (Rev: BL 7/94; SLJ 9/94)

**3280** Birney, Betty G. *Pie's in the Oven* (PS–1). Illus. by Holly Meade. 1996, Houghton $15.95 (0-395-76501-3). 32pp. A boy's family, friends, and neighbors line up to get a piece of his grandmother's famous pie. (Rev: BL 7/96; SLJ 9/96)

**3281** Bishop, Claire Huchet. *Five Chinese Brothers* (1–3). Illus. by Kurt Wiese. 1988, Putnam $12.95 (0-698-20044-6); paper $5.99 (0-698-11357-8). 64pp. Physically identical in every way, each of the 5 Chinese brothers has one distinguishing trait that saves the lives of all of them.

**3282** Borton, Lady. *Junk Pile!* (PS–3). Illus. by Kimberly B. Root. 1997, Putnam $15.95 (0-399-22728-8). 32pp. Jamie, who collects parts from her father's automobile junkyard, is able to repair the school bus when it gets stuck. (Rev: BCCB 5/97; BL 4/15/97; SLJ 4/97)

**3283** Bourgeois, Paulette. *Too Many Chickens!* (PS–3). Illus. by Bill Slavin. 1990, General Dist. Services paper $4.95 (1-550-74067-9). 32pp. A gift of chicken eggs to a class of elementary school children brings unexpected results. (Rev: BL 8/91; SLJ 6/91)

**3284** Bown, Deni. *Silly Heads* (K–3). Illus. 1996, DK Publg. $15.95 (0-7894-0219-X). 16pp. Mixing and matching facial parts create 3-D images in this interactive book. (Rev: BL 12/15/96)

**3285** Bradman, Tony. *Michael* (PS–3). Illus. by Tony Ross. 1998, Macmillan $13.95 (0-02-711850-9); Trafalgar paper $9.95 (0-86264-759-2). 32pp. Brainy Michael won't pay attention in class; he just wants to learn about spacecraft. (Rev: BL 1/15/91; SLJ 3/91)

**3286** Brillhart, Julie. *The Dino Expert* (K–3). Illus. 1993, Albert Whitman LB $14.95 (0-8075-1597-3). 32pp. Though only 5, Eric is considered the great expert on dinosaurs until one day he goofs. (Rev: BL 9/15/93; SLJ 2/94)

**3287** Brown, M. K. *Let's Go Camping with Mr. Sillypants* (PS–2). Illus. 1995, Crown LB $15.99 (0-517-59774-8). 32pp. Mr. Sillypants becomes lost in the woods but is eventually united with the campers of his Nature Club. Another book featuring this character is *Let's Go Swimming with Mr. Sillypants* (1992, Crown). (Rev: BL 9/15/95; SLJ 8/95)

**3288** Brown, Ruth. *The Big Sneeze* (PS–K). Illus. by author. 1997, Morrow paper $4.95 (0-688-15282-1). 32pp. A fly lands on a farmer's nose; he sneezes, and havoc breaks out in the barnyard. (Rev: BCCB 2/86; BL 9/15/85; SLJ 10/85)

**3289** Bunting, Eve. *My Backpack* (PS–K). Illus. 1997, Boyds Mills $14.95 (1-56397-433-9). 32pp. A young boy thinks he is doing everyone a favor when he gathers a lot of objects around the house and stores them in his backpack for safekeeping. (Rev: BL 5/1/97; SLJ 4/98)

**3290** Busser, Marianne, and Ron Schroder. *King Bobble* (K–3). Illus. by Hans de Beer. Series: Easy-to-Read. 1996, North-South LB $13.88 (1-55858-592-3). 62pp. Ten delightfully zany stories about the daffy King and Queen Bobble. (Rev: BL 5/15/96; SLJ 7/96)

**3291** Butler, Dorothy. *Another Happy Tale* (PS–2). Illus. by John Hurford. 1992, Crocodile $12.95 (0-940793-88-1). Mabel and Ned are so ill prepared to bring up their baby girl that they accidentally sell her as part of a litter of pigs. (Rev: SLJ 4/92)

**3292** Byars, Betsy. *The Golly Sisters Go West* (1–3). Illus. by Sue Truesdell. 1986, HarperCollins LB $15.89 (0-06-020884-8); paper $3.75 (0-06-444132-6). 64pp. In 6 stories, 2 adventurous women take on frontier life and the Wild West. (Rev: BCCB 11/86)

**3293** Cannon, Ann Edwards. *I Know What You Do When I Go to School* (K–3). Illus. by Jennifer Mazzucco. 1996, Gibbs Smith $14.95 (0-87905-743-2). Howie thinks he is missing good times at home when he goes to school, but his mother convinces him otherwise. (Rev: SLJ 12/96)

**3294** Carrick, Carol. *Big Old Bones: A Dinosaur Tale* (PS–3). Illus. by Donald Carrick. 1992, Houghton $13.95 (0-89919-734-5); paper $6.95 (0-395-61582-8). 32pp. Professor Potts finds a bunch of old bones to take back East to assemble. (Rev: BL 3/1/89; HB 5–6/89; SLJ 5/89)

**3295** Chesworth, Michael. *Archibald Frisby* (K–4). Illus. 1994, Farrar $15.00 (0-374-30392-4). 32pp. Archibald is so serious that he is sent to camp to learn how to have fun. (Rev: BL 4/1/94; SLJ 7/94)

**3296** Choldenko, Gennifer. *Moonstruck: The True Story of the Cow Who Jumped over the Moon* (K–2). Illus. by Paul Yalowitz. 1997, Hyperion LB $15.49 (0-7868-2130-2). 32pp. A horse supplies details about the amazing feat accomplished by a cow that jumped over the moon. (Rev: BL 3/1/97; SLJ 4/97)

**3297** Christelow, Eileen. *The Five-Dog Night* (PS–3). Illus. 1993, Clarion $14.95 (0-395-62399-5). 36pp. On cold nights, cranky old Ezra finds an unusual use for his 5 pet dogs. (Rev: BL 9/15/93; SLJ 10/93)

**3298** Cibula, Matt. *The Contrary Kid* (2–4). Illus. by Brian Strassburg. 1995, Zino $16.95 (1-55933-177-1). 32pp. Cartoons and rhymes are used to tell about the antics of a kooky kid who revels in being different. (Rev: BL 1/1–15/96; SLJ 7/96)

**3299** Clark, Emma C. *Across the Blue Mountains* (K–3). Illus. 1993, Harcourt $14.95 (0-15-201220-6). 32pp. Miss Bilberry sets out to find a new home but mistakenly moves back into her old house, which

she finds is "perfection." (Rev: BL 10/15/93; SLJ 1/94)

**3300** Clement, Rod. *Grandpa's Teeth* (PS–3). Illus. 1998, HarperCollins $14.95 (0-06-027671-1). 32pp. When Grandpa's false teeth are stolen, a nationwide search is begun. (Rev: BL 2/15/98; SLJ 3/98*)

**3301** Clements, Andrew. *Double Trouble in Walla Walla* (1–3). Illus. by Sal Murdocca. 1997, Millbrook LB $21.40 (0-7613-0306-5). A girl is sent to the principal's office when she can't stop speaking in hyphenated words, like mish-mash. (Rev: SLJ 1/98)

**3302** Cocca-Leffler, Maryann. *Clams All Year* (PS–3). Illus. 1996, Boyds Mills $14.95 (1-56397-469-X). 32pp. A family goes clamming and is so successful that soon their swimming pool is filled with clams. (Rev: BL 6/1–15/96; SLJ 7/96)

**3303** Cohen, Peter. *Olson's Meat Pies* (1–3). Trans. by Richard E. Fisher. Illus. by Olof Landstrom. 1989, R&S $12.95 (91-29-59180-5). When Olson's accountant runs off with the profits, the quality of the Olson Meat Pies declines. (Rev: SLJ 4/90)

**3304** Cole, Babette. *The Bad Good Manners Book* (K–3). Illus. 1996, Dial paper $13.99 (0-8037-2006-8). 32pp. A zany book of manners that, for example, maintains it is impolite to clog the toilet with paper. (Rev: BL 6/1–15/96; SLJ 7/96)

**3305** Crowe, Robert L. *Clyde Monster* (PS–2). Illus. by Kay Chorao. 1987, Dutton paper $3.95 (0-525-44289-8). 32pp. A humorous, reassuring story about an engaging monster named Clyde, who is afraid of the dark.

**3306** Cruickshank, Margrit. *Down by the Pond* (PS–K). Illus. by Dave Saunders. 1995, Simon & Schuster $15.00 (0-689-80205-6). 32pp. A cumulative animal tale that uses a pond as the center of humorous activities. (Rev: BL 2/15/96; SLJ 2/96)

**3307** Cuetara, Mittie. *Terrible Teresa and Other Very Short Stories* (PS–1). Illus. 1997, Dutton paper $14.99 (0-525-45768-2). 32pp. Using a series of double-page spreads, 14 very funny short stories are presented. (Rev: BL 10/15/97; SLJ 11/97)

**3308** Cummings, Pat. *Clean Your Room, Harvey Moon!* (PS–3). Illus. 1991, Macmillan $16.00 (0-02-725511-5). 32pp. Harvey's mother orders him to clean up his room in this humorous tale. (Rev: BL 2/15/91; SLJ 4/91)

**3309** Cuyler, Margery. *That's Good! That's Bad!* (PS–K). Illus. by David Catrow. 1993, Holt paper $6.95 (0-8050-2954-0). 32pp. A boy's red balloon wisks him aloft for a series of adventures. (Rev: BCCB 12/91; BL 12/1/91; SLJ 11/91)

**3310** Cyrus, Kurt. *Tangle Town* (PS–2). Illus. 1997, Farrar $16.00 (0-374-37384-1). 32pp. A fast-moving, humorous book about a series of misunderstandings that gradually involve an entire town. (Rev: BCCB 3/97; BL 5/1/97; SLJ 3/97)

**3311** Dale, Penny. *All About Alice* (PS–K). Illus. 1993, Candlewick $13.95 (1-56402-171-8). 32pp. In this book about a preschooler, the reader is able to participate by identifying familiar objects in the pictures. (Rev: BL 6/1–15/93; SLJ 7/93)

**3312** DeFelice, Cynthia. *Willy's Silly Grandma* (K–3). Illus. by Shelley Jackson. 1997, Orchard LB $16.99 (0-531-33012-5). Willy's Grandma spouts a lot of silly superstitions, but she is right in telling Willy not to go by the Old Swamp at night. (Rev: BCCB 6/97; HB 5–6/97; SLJ 4/97*)

**3313** Delton, Judy. *Blue Skies, French Fries* (2–3). Illus. by Alan Tiegreen. 1988, Dell paper $3.99 (0-440-40064-3). 80pp. The Pee Wee scouts earn badges. Also use: *Lucky Dog Days; Peanut Butter Pilgrims; Camp Ghost-Away* (all 1988). (Rev: BL 2/15/89)

**3314** dePaola, Tomie. *Helga's Dowry: A Troll Love Story* (K–2). Illus. by author. 1977, Harcourt paper $6.00 (0-15-640010-3). 32pp. Helga cannot marry Lars because she has no dowry, but this humorous account tells how she acquires one.

**3315** dePaola, Tomie. *Pancakes for Breakfast* (PS–2). Illus. by author. 1978, Harcourt $14.95 (0-15-259455-8); paper $5.00 (0-15-670768-3). 32pp. The trials and travails of a country woman who decides to make some pancakes.

**3316** Derby, Sally. *King Kenrick's Splinter* (K–3). Illus. by Leonid Gore. 1994, Walker LB $15.85 (0-8027-8323-6). 32pp. King Kenrick is afraid to have a splinter removed from his big toe. (Rev: BL 11/1/94; SLJ 1/95)

**3317** De Regniers, Beatrice S. *May I Bring a Friend?* (PS–2). Illus. by Beni Montresor. 1971, Macmillan LB $16.00 (0-689-20615-1); paper $4.95 (0-689-71353-3). 48pp. The king and queen invite a small boy to tea, and each time he goes, he takes a friend — a seal, a hippopotamus, and several lions. Caldecott Medal winner, 1965.

**3318** Dodds, Dayle Ann. *Sing, Sophie!* (PS–1). Illus. by Rosanne Litzinger. 1997, Candlewick $15.99 (0-7836-0131-4). 32pp. Everyone ignores Sophie's singing talent except her baby brother, who prefers it to the sound of thunder. (Rev: BL 5/15/97; SLJ 6/97)

**3319** Dodds, Dayle Ann. *Wheel Away!* (PS–K). Illus. by Thacher Hurd. 1991, HarperCollins paper $4.95 (0-06-443267-X). 32pp. A bicycle wheel goes on a journey of its own. (Rev: BL 3/1/89; HB 7–8/89)

**3320** Downey, Lynn. *Sing, Henrietta! Sing!* (PS–3). Illus. by Tony Sansevero. 1997, Ideals $14.95 (1-57102-103-5). George loves his dear friend Henrietta, but he finds her singing earsplitting. (Rev: SLJ 7/97)

**3321** Dragonwagon, Crescent. *The Bat in the Dining Room* (1–4). Illus. by S. D. Schindler. 1997, Marshall Cavendish LB $15.95 (0-7614-5007-6). 32pp. When a bat causes havoc after flying into the crowded dining room, Melissa gently coaxes the creature out. (Rev: BL 10/1/97; SLJ 9/97)

**3322** Drescher, Henrik. *Klutz* (PS–3). Illus. by author. 1996, Hyperion LB $16.49 (0-7868-2182-5). The accident-prone Klutz family finds its calling in a traveling circus. (Rev: SLJ 12/96)

**3323** Dunrea, Olivier. *Eppie M. Says . . .* (K–2). Illus. 1990, Macmillan LB $14.95 (0-02-733205-5). Little brother Ben believes everything his older sister tells him, even the preposterous parts. (Rev: BL 2/1/90*; HB 1–2/91; SLJ 10/90)

**3324** Dunrea, Olivier. *The Painter Who Loved Chickens* (PS–3). Illus. 1995, Farrar $15.00 (0-374-35729-3). 32pp. An artist who wants only to paint chickens moves to a farm where he can raise them. (Rev: BCCB 4/95; BL 3/1/95; HB 7–8/95; SLJ 6/95)

**3325** Egan, Tim. *Chestnut Cove* (PS–3). Illus. 1995, Houghton $14.95 (0-395-69823-5). 32pp. A once-happy community becomes divided when people compete to grow the biggest watermelon. (Rev: BL 3/15/95; HB 11–12/95; SLJ 3/95*)

**3326** English, Karen. *Just Right Stew* (PS–1). Illus. by Anna Rich. 1998, Boyds Mills $15.95 (1-56397-487-8). Friends and relatives offer advice concerning ingredients as Victoria's mother and aunt try to prepare oxtail soup. (Rev: BL 2/15/98; SLJ 3/98)

**3327** Ernst, Lisa Campbell. *The Luckiest Kid on the Planet* (K–2). Illus. 1994, Bradbury paper $14.95 (0-02-733566-6). 40pp. When Lucky finds out that this is not his real first name, he believes that his luck will change. (Rev: BL 9/1/94; HB 11–12/94; SLJ 11/94)

**3328** Ernst, Lisa Campbell. *Miss Penny and Mr. Grubbs* (PS–3). Illus. 1995, Simon & Schuster paper $4.95 (0-689-80035-5). 40pp. Mr. Grubbs decides to sabotage Miss Penny's garden by putting some rabbits in it. (Rev: BCCB 4/91; BL 3/15/91*; SLJ 6/91)

**3329** Evans, Nate. *The Mixed-Up Zoo of Professor Yahoo* (K–3). Illus. 1993, Junior League of Kansas City $14.95 (0-9607076-3-8). 32pp. In nonsense verse, this book describes a bumbling professor's attempts to create the best zoo in the land. (Rev: BL 7/93) [811]

**3330** Everett, Percival. *The One That Got Away* (1–3). Illus. by Dirk Zimmer. 1992, Houghton $14.95 (0-395-56437-9). 32pp. The number one figures prominently in this spoof of westerns. (Rev: BL 4/15/92; SLJ 4/92)

**3331** Everitt, Betsy. *Mean Soup* (PS–1). Illus. 1992, Harcourt $16.00 (0-15-253146-7). 32pp. Horace gets rid of his nasty thoughts and feelings by throwing them into a pot and making mean soup. (Rev: BL 3/15/92*; SLJ 7/92)

**3332** Fleming, Candace. *Madame La Grande and Her So High, to the Sky, Uproarious Pompadour* (PS–3). Illus. by S. D. Schindler. 1996, Knopf LB $16.99 (0-679-95835-5). 40pp. Trying to be on top of fashion, Madame La Grande has her hair coiffed into a huge pompadour. (Rev: BL 7/96; SLJ 7/96)

**3333** Fox, Mem. *Boo to a Goose* (PS–K). Illus. by David Miller. 1998, Dial paper $14.99 (0-8037-2274-5). 40pp. Wildly funny rhymes about a man's fantasies of being brave and courageous when, in reality, he wouldn't say boo to a goose. (Rev: BL 2/1/98; SLJ 3/98)

**3334** Fox, Mem. *Guess What?* (PS–2). Illus. by Vivienne Goodman. 1990, Harcourt $15.00 (0-15-200452-1). 32pp. Through a series of questions, a strange lady, who is a witch, is introduced. (Rev: BL 9/1/90; HB 11–12/91; SLJ 11/90)

**3335** Fox, Mem. *Shoes from Grandpa* (PS–K). Illus. by Patricia Mullins. 1992, Orchard paper $6.95 (0-531-07031-X). 32pp. A cumulative story about buying clothes for a growing Jessie. (Rev: BL 2/15/90; HB 3–4/90; SLJ 4/90*)

**3336** Freeman, Don. *Mop Top* (K–2). Illus. by author. 1978, Puffin paper $5.99 (0-14-050326-9). 48pp. Moppy changes his mind about a haircut after being mistaken for a floor mop by a nearsighted shopper.

**3337** French, Vivian. *Oliver's Vegetables* (PS–2). Illus. by Alison Bartlett. 1995, Orchard $13.95 (0-531-09462-6). 32pp. Longing for some French fries, Oliver promises to eat anything he finds in his Grandpa's vegetable garden, hoping to find potatoes. (Rev: BL 9/15/95; SLJ 10/95)

**3338** Gambrell, Jamey. *Telephone* (K–3). Illus. by Vladimir Radunsky. 1996, North-South LB $15.88 (1-55858-481-1). 28pp. A hilarious Russian poem about a telephone that won't stop ringing. (Rev: BL 12/15/96; SLJ 12/96)

**3339** Garrison, Susan. *How Emily Blair Got Her Fabulous Hair* (K–3). Illus. by Marjorie Priceman. 1995, Troll paper $14.95 (0-8167-3496-8). 32pp. Emily longs to have curly hair but settles for arranging her straight locks into braids. (Rev: BL 1/1–15/96; SLJ 1/96)

**3340** Gay, Marie-Louise. *Fat Charlie's Circus* (PS–2). Illus. by author. Series: A Cranky Nell Book. 1997, Kane/Miller $12.95 (0-916291-73-1). A circus-crazy youngster decides to dive into a cup of water from the top of a tall tree. (Rev: SLJ 6/97)

**3341** Geoghegan, Adrienne. *Dogs Don't Wear Glasses* (PS–1). Illus. 1996, Crocodile $14.95 (1-56656-208-2). 32pp. Nanny Needle discovers that it is her poor eyesight and not that of her dog's that is causing a series of mishaps. (Rev: BL 4/1/96; SLJ 5/96)

**3342** Geringer, Laura. *A Three Hat Day* (PS–1). Illus. by Arnold Lobel. 1985, HarperCollins LB $14.89 (0-06-021989-0); paper $5.95 (0-06-443157-6). 32pp. R. R. Pottle the Third is a gentleman who loves hats in this tale of loneliness and finding someone who cares. (Rev: BCCB 1/86; BL 9/15/85; HB 11–12/85)

**3343** Gibala-Broxholm, Janice. *Let Me Do It!* (PS). Illus. by Diane Paterson. 1994, Bradbury $14.95 (0-02-735827-5). 32pp. A youngster's desire to do things on her own creates chaos. (Rev: BL 1/15/94; SLJ 5/94)

**3344** Gibbons, Faye. *Mountain Wedding* (K–4). Illus. by Ted Rand. 1996, Morrow LB $15.93 (0-688-11349-4). 40pp. A series of humorous mishaps delay the wedding of widow Searcy and widower Long. (Rev: BCCB 9/96; BL 4/1/96; HB 5–6/96; SLJ 4/96)

**3345** Golembe, Carla. *Dog Magic* (PS–2). Illus. 1997, Houghton $15.00 (0-395-81662-9). 32pp. Molly Gail thinks that the new slippers she received for her birthday have magically cured her fear of dogs. (Rev: BL 11/1/97; SLJ 9/97)

**3346** Gottlieb, Dale. *Where Jamaica Go?* (PS–1). Illus. 1996, Orchard LB $15.99 (0-531-08875-8). 32pp. In Afro-Caribbean jargon, Jamaica travels downtown, to the beach, and on a trip in her father's van. (Rev: BL 10/1/96; SLJ 11/96)

**3347** Grambling, Lois G. *Can I Have a Stegosaurus, Mom? Can I? Please!?* (PS–1). Illus. by H. Lewis. 1995, Troll paper $15.95 (0-8167-3386-4). 32pp. A boy points out all the advantages of having a dinosaur for a pet, including eating all his distasteful vegetables. (Rev: BCCB 12/94; BL 1/15/95; SLJ 6/95)

**3348** Greene, Carol. *The Golden Locket* (K–3). Illus. by Marcia Sewall. 1992, Harcourt $13.95 (0-15-231220-X); paper $5.00 (0-15-201008-4). 32pp. Miss Teaberry's generosity leads to amusing complications in this picture book. (Rev: BCCB 7–8/92; BL 4/1/92; HB 5–6/92; SLJ 5/92)

**3349** Grossman, Bill. *Donna O'Neeshuck Was Chased by Some Cows* (K–3). Illus. by Sue Truesdell. 1988, HarperCollins paper $5.95 (0-06-443255-6). 40pp. A farcical rhyming story of a red-haired girl. (Rev: BL 11/15/88; HB 9–10/88; SLJ 2/89)

**3350** Hafner, Marylin. *Mommies Don't Get Sick* (PS–1). Illus. 1995, Candlewick $14.95 (1-56402-287-0). 32pp. Everything goes wrong when young Abby is left alone for a few minutes to take care of her baby brother. (Rev: BCCB 11/95; BL 9/1/95; SLJ 10/95)

**3351** Hafner, Marylin. *A Year with Molly and Emmett* (PS–1). Illus. 1997, Candlewick $15.99 (1-56402-966-2). 32pp. Through the seasons with Molly and her cat Emmett in this humorous picture book filled with delightful adventures. (Rev: BL 7/97; SLJ 6/97)

**3352** Halperin, Wendy A. *When Chickens Grow Teeth* (K–3). Illus. 1996, Orchard LB $16.99 (0-531-08876-6). 32pp. Confined to bed because of an accident, Toine makes himself useful by hatching some chicken eggs. (Rev: BL 10/15/96; SLJ 9/96)

**3353** Harper, Jo. *Outrageous, Bodacious Boliver Boggs!* (2–3). Illus. by JoAnn Adinolfi. 1996, Simon & Schuster paper $15.00 (0-689-80504-7). Boliver Boggs invents a number of outrageous stories to explain why he is late for school. (Rev: SLJ 4/96)

**3354** Hartmann, Wendy, and Niki Daly. *The Dinosaurs Are Back and It's All Your Fault Edward!* (PS–2). Illus. by Niki Daly. 1997, Simon & Schuster $16.00 (0-689-81152-7). 32pp. An older brother persuades Edward that the rock under his bed is really a dinosaur egg about to hatch. (Rev: BL 6/1–15/97; SLJ 6/97)

**3355** Hazen, Barbara S. *The Gorilla Did It* (PS–1). Illus. by Ray Cruz. 1974, Macmillan $13.95 (0-689-30138-3). 32pp. A boy keeps blaming an imaginary animal — a gorilla — for all the messes in his room.

**3356** Hazen, Barbara S. *The Knight Who Was Afraid of the Dark* (PS–2). Illus. by Tony Ross. 1989, Puffin paper $5.99 (0-14-054545-X). 32pp. Sir Fred, alas, is a knight afraid of the dark. (Rev: BL 5/15/89; SLJ 4/89)

**3357** Himmelman, John. *J.J. Versus the Baby-sitter* (K–2). Illus. by author. 1996, BridgeWater paper $13.95 (0-8167-3800-9). An entertaining read about a baby-sitter who doesn't realize that her charge has an identical twin. (Rev: SLJ 5/96)

**3358** Himmelman, John. *Lights Out!* (K–2). Illus. 1995, Troll paper $13.95 (0-8167-3450-X). 32pp. A humorous story about the terrible creatures the 6 Badger Scouts believe await them at summer camp. (Rev: BL 4/1/95; SLJ 8/95)

**3359** Hoberman, Mary Ann. *The Seven Silly Eaters* (PS–3). Illus. by Marla Frazee. 1997, Harcourt $15.00 (0-15-200096-8). 40pp. A humorous picture book about Mrs. Peters and her brood of picky eaters. (Rev: BCCB 5/97; BL 3/1/97; HB 5–6/97; SLJ 3/97)

**3360** Hoff, Syd. *Arturo's Baton* (PS–3). Illus. 1995, Clarion $13.95 (0-395-71020-0). 32pp. When a famous conductor loses his favorite baton, he no longer can perform. (Rev: BL 9/1/95; SLJ 9/95)

**3361** Hutchins, Pat. *Don't Forget the Bacon!* (K–3). Illus. by author. 1976, Greenwillow LB $15.93 (0-688-06788-3); Morrow paper $4.95 (0-688-08743-

4). 32pp. A young boy mixes up the shopping list on a trip to the grocery store.

**3362** Inkpen, Mick. *Billy's Beetle* (PS–2). Illus. 1992, Harcourt $13.95 (0-15-200427-0). 32pp. Even with the help of a trained dog, Billy is not able to find his lost beetle. (Rev: BL 4/15/92; SLJ 8/92)

**3363** Isaacs, Anne. *Swamp Angel* (K–4). Illus. by Paul O. Zelinsky. 1994, Dutton $15.99 (0-525-45271-0). 40pp. Angelica Longrider is a true tall-tale heroine because, among her many accomplishments, she is able to lasso a tornado. (Rev: BCCB 11/94; BL 10/15/94*; SLJ 12/94*)

**3364** Isadora, Rachel. *Max* (K–2). Illus. by author. 1976, Macmillan LB $13.95 (0-02-747450-X); paper $3.95 (0-02-043800-1). 32pp. Max, an avid baseball player, finds that joining his sister's dancing class makes an excellent warm-up for the game.

**3365** Jam, Teddy. *The Charlotte Stories* (1–3). Illus. by Harvey Chan. 1996, Groundwood $14.95 (0-88899-210-6). 48pp. Charlotte is a candid 7-year-old who can't avoid trouble because of her open, honest nature. (Rev: SLJ 12/96)

**3366** Johnson, Doug. *Never Ride Your Elephant to School* (PS–3). Illus. by Abby Carter. 1995, Holt $15.95 (0-8050-2880-3). 32pp. This cautionary tale describes all the catastrophes that can occur when you take an elephant to school. (Rev: BL 9/15/95; SLJ 12/95)

**3367** Jonas, Ann. *Round Trip* (PS–4). Illus. by author. 1983, Greenwillow LB $15.93 (0-688-01781-9); Morrow paper $3.95 (0-688-09986-6). 32pp. A book to read forward, backward, and then upside down.

**3368** Jonas, Ann. *Watch William Walk* (PS–K). Illus. 1997, Greenwillow LB $14.93 (0-688-14175-7). 24pp. An alphabet adventure in which the entire story is told with words that begin with *w*. (Rev: BL 4/1/97; HB 7–8/97; SLJ 4/97)

**3369** Jones, Rebecca C. *Great Aunt Martha* (K–3). Illus. by Shelley Jackson. 1995, Dutton paper $14.99 (0-525-45257-5). Things change when stern Great Aunt Martha arrives; the young narrator must start being neat and TV, pizza, and play are forbidden. (Rev: HB 9–10/95; SLJ 7/95*)

**3370** Kastner, Jill. *Barnyard Big Top* (PS–1). Illus. 1997, Simon & Schuster paper $16.00 (0-689-80484-9). 32pp. When Uncle Julius and his Two Ring Extravaganza suddenly arrive, young Ben's farm becomes a bustling circus. (Rev: BL 11/1/97; SLJ 11/97)

**3371** Keats, Ezra Jack. *Jennie's Hat* (K–2). Illus. by author. 1966, HarperCollins paper $6.95 (0-06-443072-3). 32pp. Jennie's drab new hat is decorated by her bird friends, who become its trimming.

**3372** Kellogg, Steven. *I Was Born About 10,000 Years Ago* (PS–4). Illus. 1996, Morrow LB $15.93 (0-688-13412-2). 48pp. Ageless youngsters tell about their pasts, which sometimes involves taming dinosaurs or voyaging with Columbus. (Rev: BCCB 10/96; BL 10/15/96*; HB 11–12/96; SLJ 9/96)

**3373** Kimmel, Eric A. *I Took My Frog to the Library* (PS–K). Illus. by Blanche Sims. 1992, Puffin paper $4.99 (0-14-050916-X). 32pp. A number of different animals create havoc when they visit the library. (Rev: BL 2/15/90; SLJ 3/90)

**3374** Knight, Joan. *Bon Appetit, Bertie!* (K–3). Illus. by Penny Dann. 1993, DK Publg. $13.95 (1-56458-195-0). 32pp. During a family trip to Paris, young Bertie sets out to see the sights alone. (Rev: BL 5/15/93; SLJ 7/93)

**3375** Kulman, Andrew. *Red Light Stop, Green Light Go* (PS–1). Illus. 1993, Simon & Schuster paper $15.00 (0-671-79493-0). A nonsense book about cars, people, and animals — all waiting for the green light. (Rev: SLJ 7/93)

**3376** Lacoe, Addie. *Just Not the Same* (PS–1). Illus. by Pau Estrada. 1992, Houghton $14.95 (0-395-59347-6). 32pp. Triplet girls who engage in sibling rivalry wonder how they will be able to share fairly their new dog. (Rev: BL 9/15/92; SLJ 11/92)

**3377** Landstrom, Olof, and Lena Landstrom. *Will Gets a Haircut* (K–2). Trans. from Swedish by Elisabeth Dyssegaard. Illus. by authors. 1993, R&S $13.00 (91-29-62075-9). Will's new hairdo, in the shape of a corkscrew, creates a sensation at school. (Rev: SLJ 2/94)

**3378** La Prise, Larry, et al. *The Hokey Pokey* (PS–3). Illus. by Sheila Hamanaka. 1997, Simon & Schuster $16.00 (0-689-80519-5). 32pp. A lively picture book about a variety of people caught in action dancing the hokey pokey. (Rev: BL 2/1/97*; SLJ 3/97)

**3379** Lattimore, Deborah N. *The Lady with the Ship on Her Head* (PS–2). Illus. 1990, Harcourt $14.95 (0-15-243525-5). 32pp. In 18th-century France, Madame Pompenstance is unaware that a ship has landed on her hair. (Rev: BL 3/15/90; SLJ 6/90)

**3380** Lester, Helen. *It Wasn't My Fault* (PS–1). Illus. by Lynn Munsinger. 1985, Houghton $16.00 (0-395-35629-6). 32pp. Nerdy Murdley Gurdson tries to discover why an ostrich laid an egg on his head. (Rev: BCCB 6/85; BL 3/1/85; SLJ 5/85)

**3381** Levitin, Sonia. *A Single Speckled Egg* (K–3). Illus. by John Larrecq. 1976, Houghton $6.95 (0-87466-074-2). 40pp. Three foolish farmers are outwitted by their wives in this ridiculous tale told in the folk tradition.

**3382** Lewis, J. Patrick. *The Boat of Many Rooms: The Story of Noah in Verse* (K–3). Illus. by Reg Cartwright. 1997, Simon & Schuster $16.00 (0-689-

80118-1). 28pp. A whimsical look at the overcrowding that existed on Noah's Ark. (Rev: BCCB 2/97; BL 2/1/97; SLJ 3/97)

**3383** Lindbergh, Anne. *Next Time, Take Care* (1–3). Illus. by Susan Ramsay Hoguet. 1988, Harcourt $13.95 (0-15-257200-7). 32pp. Ralph keeps losing the caps Aunt Mildred knits, until finally she fashions one he can't lose. (Rev: BL 10/1/88; SLJ 12/88)

**3384** Little, Jean, and Claire Mackay. *Bats About Baseball* (K–2). Illus. by Kim LaFave. 1995, Viking paper $12.99 (0-670-85270-8). 32pp. In spite of efforts to change her interests, Ryder's grandmother thinks about nothing but baseball. (Rev: BL 6/1–15/95; SLJ 8/95)

**3385** Lobel, Arnold. *Ming Lo Moves the Mountain* (PS–3). Illus. by author. 1982, Greenwillow LB $15.93 (0-688-00611-6); Morrow paper $4.95 (0-688-10995-0). 32pp. A humorous tale about a man's attempt to move a mountain away from his house.

**3386** London, Sara. *Firehorse Max* (PS–1). Illus. 1997, HarperCollins LB $14.89 (0-06-205095-8). 32pp. Grandpa Lev's new horse, a former horse at the firehouse, has a behavioral problem when fire bells ring. (Rev: BL 10/1/97; SLJ 10/97)

**3387** Lord, John Vernon. *The Giant Jam Sandwich* (PS–2). Illus. by author. 1987, Houghton $17.00 (0-395-16033-2); paper $5.95 (0-395-44237-0). A rhymed verse about the citizens of Itching Down who make a giant jam sandwich to attract wasps.

**3388** Lowell, Susan. *Little Red Cowboy Hat* (K–3). Illus. by Randy Cecil. 1997, Holt $14.95 (0-8050-3508-7). 32pp. A humorous retelling of *Little Red Riding Hood* using the Wild West as the setting. (Rev: BCCB 6/97; BL 4/15/97; SLJ 5/97*)

**3389** Lyon, George E. *A Regular Rolling Noah* (PS–1). Illus. by Stephen Gammell. 1986, Macmillan paper $4.95 (0-689-71449-1). 32pp. A farmhand tells how he once helped a family move its entire farm to Canada. (Rev: BL 9/1/86; HB 11–12/86; SLJ 11/86)

**3390** McCloskey, Robert. *Burt Dow, Deep-Water Man* (K–3). Illus. by author. 1963, Puffin paper $5.99 (0-14-050978-X). 64pp. The humorous tale of an old Maine fisherman who caught a whale by the tail and then used a multicolored Band-Aid to cover the hole.

**3391** McCloskey, Robert. *Lentil* (K–3). Illus. by author. 1940, Puffin paper $4.99 (0-14-050287-4). 64pp. Tale of a boy who can't carry a tune, yet learns to play the harmonica.

**3392** McCully, Emily Arnold. *Popcorn at the Palace* (K–3). Illus. 1997, Harcourt $16.00 (0-15-277699-0). 40pp. The Ferris family is considered odd by Illinois neighbors in the mid-1800s because they go to

England to demonstrate corn popping for the queen. (Rev: BL 9/15/97; SLJ 10/97)

**3393** MacDonald, Amy. *Cousin Ruth's Tooth* (PS–1). Illus. by Marjorie Priceman. 1996, Houghton $16.00 (0-395-71253-X). 32pp. When Ruth loses a tooth, the whole family mounts a search to find it. (Rev: BCCB 6/96; BL 4/1/96; SLJ 5/96)

**3394** MacDonald, Amy. *Rachel Fister's Blister* (PS–2). Illus. by Marjorie Priceman. 1990, Houghton $13.95 (0-395-52152-1); paper $4.95 (0-395-65744-X). 32pp. A doctor, pastor, rabbi, postman, and others have different suggestions to treat Rachel's blister. (Rev: BL 10/1/90; HB 11–12/90; SLJ 11/90)

**3395** MacDonald, Maryann. *The Pink Party* (2–3). Illus. by Abby Carter. 1994, Hyperion LB $11.49 (1-56282-621-2). 40pp. Two friends both love pink and compete with each to see who can acquire the most things in that color. (Rev: BL 10/15/94; SLJ 1/95)

**3396** McGuire, Richard. *What Goes Around Comes Around* (K–3). Illus. 1995, Viking paper $13.99 (0-670-86396-3). 32pp. A story about how one event causes another until a full circle has been reached. (Rev: BCCB 11/95; BL 9/1/95; SLJ 9/95)

**3397** McPhail, David. *Andrew's Bath* (PS–K). Illus. by author. 1996, Little, Brown paper $4.95 (0-316-56339-0). Andrew is finally old enough to take his own bath.

**3398** Mahy, Margaret. *The Boy Who Was Followed Home* (K–2). Illus. by Steven Kellogg. 1986, Puffin paper $4.95 (0-8037-0903-X). 32pp. Robert likes hippopotamuses and is delighted when one follows him home. A reissue.

**3399** Mangas, Brian. *Follow That Puppy!* (PS–2). Illus. by R. W. Alley. 1991, Simon & Schuster paper $12.95 (0-671-70780-9). When Puppy escapes his elderly owner while out for a walk, an exciting chase occurs. (Rev: SLJ 11/91)

**3400** Mantinband, Gerda. *The Blabbermouths* (PS–3). Illus. by Paul Borovsky. 1992, Greenwillow LB $13.93 (0-688-10604-8). 24pp. Neighbors can't keep quiet about their friend's discovery of a chest full of gold. (Rev: BCCB 9/92; BL 5/1/92; HB 7–8/92; SLJ 8/92)

**3401** Marshall, James. *The Cut-Ups* (K–3). Illus. by author. 1986, Puffin paper $4.99 (0-14-050637-3). 32pp. A pair of young boys gets into all sorts of trouble.

**3402** Marshall, James. *The Cut-Ups at Camp Custer* (K–3). Illus. 1991, Puffin paper $4.99 (0-14-050817-1). 32pp. Spud and Joe look forward to summer camp until they learn that the director is their school principal. (Rev: BL 10/1/89; HB 11–12/89; SLJ 11/89)

**3403** Marshall, James. *The Cut-Ups Carry On* (K–3). Illus. 1990, Viking paper $12.95 (0-670-81645-0). 32pp. Horrors — Spud and Joe have to go to dance class! (Rev: BL 3/15/90; HB 5–6/90; SLJ 6/90)

**3404** Marshall, James. *The Cut-Ups Crack Up* (K–3). Illus. 1992, Viking paper $14.00 (0-670-84486-1). 32pp. Spud and Joe get into trouble when they are videotaped in the school principal's new car. (Rev: BCCB 3/92; BL 6/1/92; HB 5–6/92; SLJ 5/92)

**3405** Marshall, James. *The Cut-Ups Cut Loose* (1–3). Illus. by author. 1987, Puffin paper $4.99 (0-14-050672-1). 32pp. Spud and Joe run into trouble on their first day back to school when they meet the new principal, who doesn't like cutups. (Rev: BL 9/15/87; HB 11–12/87; SLJ 10/87)

**3406** Martin, Bill, Jr. *The Maestro Plays* (PS–K). Illus. by Vladimir Radunsky. 1994, Holt $15.95 (0-8050-1746-1). 38pp. A circus setting is used to show all the different instruments the maestro plays. (Rev: BCCB 12/94; BL 11/1/94; SLJ 11/94*)

**3407** Martinez, Ruth. *Mrs. McDockerty's Knitting* (PS–1). Illus. by Catharine O'Neill. 1990, Houghton $13.95 (0-395-51591-2). 32pp. A series of visits by different animals interrupts the knitting of Mrs. McDockerty. (Rev: BL 2/15/90; HB 7–8/90; SLJ 6/90)

**3408** Marzollo, Jean. *I Spy Funhouse: A Book of Picture Riddles* (PS–3). Photos by Walter Wick. 1993, Scholastic $12.95 (0-590-46293-8). 40pp. This entertaining book consists of a series of picture puzzles involving an amusement park fun house and of a series of rhyming word clues. (Rev: BL 5/15/93; SLJ 4/93) [793]

**3409** Marzollo, Jean. *The Pizza Pie Slugger* (1–4). Illus. by Blanche Sims. 1989, Random LB $6.99 (0-394-92881-4); paper $3.99 (0-394-82881-X). 64pp. Billy blames his batting slump on his stepsister Lily. (Rev: BL 6/15/89)

**3410** Melmed, Laura K. *The Marvelous Market on Mermaid* (PS–K). Illus. by Maryann Kovalski. 1996, Lothrop LB $14.93 (0-688-13054-2). A humorous cumulative tale that features the pets, produce, and other articles found in an old-fashioned corner store. (Rev: SLJ 5/96)

**3411** Miller, Margaret. *Guess Who?* (PS–K). Illus. 1994, Greenwillow LB $14.93 (0-688-12784-3). 40pp. A series of simple questions get ridiculous answers, but finally the correct one is given. (Rev: BCCB 9/94; BL 8/94*; SLJ 10/94)

**3412** Miller, Margaret. *Whose Shoe?* (PS–2). Illus. 1991, Greenwillow LB $15.93 (0-688-10009-0). 40pp. A fun guessing game that asks who's wearing certain shoes. (Rev: BCCB 9/91; BL 1/1/91; HB 9–10/91; SLJ 11/91) [391]

**3413** Minters, Frances. *Sleepless Beauty* (K–4). Illus. by G. Brian Karas. 1996, Viking paper $14.99 (0-670-87033-1). 32pp. *Sleeping Beauty* is retold to a hip-hop beat. (Rev: BCCB 11/96; BL 11/1/96; HB 11–12/96; SLJ 9/96)

**3414** Modell, Frank. *Look Out, It's April Fools' Day* (K–2). Illus. by author. 1985, Greenwillow $16.00 (0-688-04016-0). 24pp. Marvin's sincere remarks are regarded by his friend Milton as an April Fools' Day trick. (Rev: BCCB 3/85; HB 5–6/85; SLJ 4/85)

**3415** Most, Bernard. *Whatever Happened to the Dinosaurs?* (1–3). Illus. by author. 1984, Harcourt $16.00 (0-15-295295-0); paper $4.95 (0-15-295296-9). 32pp. Fantastic explanations to the title question.

**3416** Munsch, Robert. *Alligator Baby* (PS–2). Illus. by Michael Martchenko. 1997, Scholastic $10.95 (0-590-21101-3). 29pp. An amusing story about overwrought parents who bring different baby animals home from the zoo, thinking each is their child. (Rev: SLJ 11/97)

**3417** Munsch, Robert. *Andrew's Loose Tooth* (1–2). Illus. by Michael Martchenko. 1998, Scholastic $10.95 (0-590-21102-1). 32pp. Even the Tooth Fairy who arrives on her motorcycle can't dislodge Andrew's stubborn loose tooth. (Rev: BL 3/15/98)

**3418** Munsch, Robert. *Stephanie's Ponytail* (1–3). Illus. by Michael Martchenko. 1996, Firefly $16.95 (1-55037-485-0); paper $5.95 (1-55037-484-2). Stephanie is annoyed when every one of her style changes is copied by class members and her teacher. (Rev: SLJ 11/96)

**3419** Murphy, Jill. *The Last Noo-Noo* (PS–1). Illus. 1995, Candlewick $15.99 (1-56402-581-0). 32pp. Members of his family finally convince Marlon that it is time to give up using his pacifier. (Rev: BL 11/1/95; SLJ 1/96)

**3420** Myers, Lynne B., and Christopher Myers. *Turnip Soup* (PS–2). Illus. by Katie Keller. 1994, Hyperion LB $14.49 (1-56282-446-5). 32pp. George is afraid that there is a Komodo dragon in his basement, and he is right. (Rev: BL 11/15/94; SLJ 2/95)

**3421** Naylor, Phyllis Reynolds. *"I Can't Take You Anywhere!"* (PS–2). Illus. by Jef Kaminsky. 1997, Simon & Schuster $15.00 (0-689-31966-5). 32pp. On every outing, Amy Audrey gets into so much trouble that everyone agrees they can't take her anywhere. (Rev: BL 10/1/97; SLJ 10/97)

**3422** Neitzel, Shirley. *We're Making Breakfast for Mother* (PS–1). Illus. by Nancy Winslow Parker. 1997, Greenwillow LB $14.93 (0-688-14576-0). 32pp. The breakfast that a family prepares for Mother is so bad that they all decide to go out to a cafe. (Rev: BCCB 5/97; BL 3/1/97; SLJ 4/97)

**3423** Nez, Redwing T. *Forbidden Talent* (PS–3). Illus. 1995, Northland LB $14.95 (0-87358-605-0).

32pp. In spite of his grandfather's objections, a young Navajo boy can't stop painting everything he sees. (Rev: BL 11/1/95; SLJ 12/95)

**3424** Nielsen, Laura F. *Jeremy's Muffler* (PS–3). Illus. by Christine M. Schneider. 1995, Simon & Schuster $15.00 (0-689-80319-2). 32pp. Jeremy's aunt knits him a muffler that is so long people make fun of it. (Rev: BL 12/15/95; SLJ 12/95)

**3425** Nims, Bonnie L. *Where Is the Bear in the City?* (PS–K). Illus. by Madelaine Gill. 1992, Whitman LB $12.95 (0-8075-8937-3). 24pp. A puzzle book in which the reader is asked to find the bear in a variety of city scenes. (Rev: BL 11/15/92; SLJ 11/92)

**3426** Noble, Trinka Hakes. *The Day Jimmy's Boa Ate the Wash* (PS–2). Illus. by Steven Kellogg. 1980, Dial LB $13.89 (0-8037-1724-5); Puffin paper $4.95 (0-8037-0094-6). 32pp. A hilarious story about a class trip to a farm. A sequel is: *Jimmy's Boa Bounces Back* (1984).

**3427** Noble, Trinka Hakes. *Meanwhile, Back at the Ranch* (PS–1). Illus. by Tony Ross. 1987, Dial LB $13.89 (0-8037-0354-6); Puffin paper $5.99 (0-14-054564-6). 32pp. A humorous Western adventure concerning Rancher Hicks and his drive into Sleepy Gulch for some excitement. (Rev: BL 4/1/87; SLJ 5/87)

**3428** Novak, Matt. *The Pillow War* (PS–2). Illus. 1998, Orchard LB $16.99 (0-531-33048-6). 32pp. Millie and Fred have a pillow fight over who will sleep with Sam the dog, but Sam has other plans. (Rev: BL 2/15/98; SLJ 3/98)

**3429** Numeroff, Laura. *Why a Disguise?* (PS–3). Illus. by David McPhail. 1996, Simon & Schuster $14.00 (0-689-80513-6). 32pp. A little boy dons a series of disguises to fool his parents. (Rev: BL 4/15/96*; SLJ 7/96)

**3430** Numeroff, Laura, and Barney Saltzberg. *Two for Stew* (1–3). Illus. by Sal Murdocca. 1996, Simon & Schuster $15.00 (0-689-80571-3). 32pp. A young woman and her poodle are disappointed at a restaurant when told there is no more stew. (Rev: BL 9/15/96; SLJ 12/96)

**3431** Oppenheim, Shulamith Levey. *What Is the Full Moon Full Of?* (PS–2). Illus. by Cyd Moore. 1997, Boyds Mills $14.95 (1-56397-479-7). 32pp. Every one of the animals has a different answer when Jonas asks what the moon is full of. (Rev: BL 12/1/97; SLJ 12/97)

**3432** Pearson, Tracey Campbell. *The Purple Hat* (PS–2). Illus. 1997, Farrar $16.00 (0-374-36153-3). 32pp. When Annie loses her new purple hat, the whole town turns out to help find it. (Rev: BCCB 3/97; BL 2/1/97; SLJ 4/97)

**3433** Peters, Lisa Westberg. *Purple Delicious Blackberry Jam* (PS–3). Illus. by Barbara McGregor.

1992, Arcade $14.95 (1-55970-167-6). 32pp. Two children persuade their grandmother to make blackberry jam, but the results are not as expected. (Rev: BL 12/1/92; SLJ 3/93)

**3434** Pinkwater, Daniel. *Author's Day* (1–4). Illus. 1993, Macmillan $14.00 (0-02-774642-9). 32pp. An author visits a school where a series of hilarious misadventures occurs. (Rev: BCCB 4/93; BL 3/15/93; SLJ 7/93)

**3435** Pinkwater, Daniel. *The Big Orange Splot* (K–2). Illus. by author. 1992, Hastings $12.95 (0-8038-9346-9); Scholastic paper $3.95 (0-590-44510-3). 32pp. A cumulative story about the effects of dropping a can of orange paint on the roof of Mr. Plumbean's house.

**3436** Plourde, Lynn. *Pigs in the Mud in the Middle of the Rud* (PS–2). Illus. by John Schoenherr. 1997, Scholastic $15.95 (0-590-56863-9). A farm family in their Model T Ford can't budge because of the animals in their way, including some pigs wallowing in the mud. (Rev: BCCB 2/97; SLJ 3/97*)

**3437** Polacco, Patricia. *In Enzo's Splendid Gardens* (1–4). Illus. 1997, Putnam $15.95 (0-399-23107-2). 32pp. A cumulative tale of chaos in an outdoor Italian restaurant begun by an innocent bee. (Rev: BL 8/97; SLJ 5/97)

**3438** Polisar, Barry L. *Don't Do That! A Child's Guide to Bad Manners, Ridiculous Rules, and Inadequate Etiquette.* Rev. ed. (K–4). Illus. by David Clark. 1995, Rainbow Morning Music $14.95 (0-938663-20-8). An irreverent book of manners that, for example, tells how to pick one's nose properly in public. (Rev: SLJ 8/95)

**3439** Pomerantz, Charlotte. *Serena Katz* (K–2). Illus. by R. W. Alley. 1992, Macmillan LB $13.95 (0-02-774901-0). 32pp. The Duncan family visits the amazing, multitalented Serena Katz of New York City. (Rev: BCCB 6/92; BL 4/15/92; SLJ 6/92)

**3440** Porte, Barbara Ann. *Chickens! Chickens!* (PS–2). Illus. by Greg Henry. 1995, Orchard LB $15.99 (0-531-08727-1). 32pp. A humorous tale of a man who achieves fame through his many paintings of chickens. (Rev: BCCB 4/95; BL 2/1/95; HB 3–4/95; SLJ 4/95)

**3441** Powell, Polly. *Just Dessert* (PS–1). Illus. 1996, Harcourt $15.00 (0-15-200383-5). 32pp. Patsy Apple creeps downstairs to eat the last piece of delicious yellow cake that is in the fridge. (Rev: BL 5/1/96; SLJ 8/96)

**3442** Poydar, Nancy. *Busy Bea* (PS–3). Illus. 1994, Macmillan paper $14.95 (0-689-50592-2). 32pp. Bea is always losing things, but she retrieves everything at the school's lost and found. (Rev: BL 11/1/94; SLJ 12/94)

**3443** Prelutsky, Jack, ed. *A Nonny Mouse Writes Again!* (PS–1). Illus. by Marjorie Priceman. 1993, Knopf $13.00 (0-679-83715-9). 30pp. A delightful collection of short, nonsense folk rhymes illustrated with brilliant watercolors. (Rev: BL 6/1–15/93; SLJ 7/93*) [811]

**3444** Priceman, Marjorie. *How to Make an Apple Pie and See the World* (PS–2). Illus. 1994, Knopf LB $16.99 (0-679-93705-6). 32pp. A young girl travels around the world gathering the ingredients for her luscious apple pie. (Rev: BCCB 2/94; BL 4/15/94; HB 9–10/94; SLJ 6/94)

**3445** Pulver, Robin. *Mrs. Toggle's Beautiful Blue Shoe* (PS–2). Illus. by R. W. Alley. 1994, Four Winds paper $13.95 (0-02-775456-1). 32pp. Members of Mrs. Toggle's class help her retrieve her shoe when she accidentally sends it flying into a tree. (Rev: BL 3/1/94; SLJ 5/94)

**3446** Pulver, Robin. *Mrs. Toggle's Zipper* (K–2). Illus. by R. W. Alley. 1990, Macmillan LB $13.95 (0-02-775451-0). 32pp. When Mrs. Toggle's zipper gets stuck, everyone at her school tries to help her out of her coat. (Rev: BCCB 3/90; BL 3/1/90; SLJ 5/90)

**3447** Radunsky, Vladimir, and Eugenia Radunsky. *Yucka Drucka Droni* (1–3). Illus. 1998, Scholastic $15.95 (0-590-09837-3). 40pp. A European tale that is a tongue twister about 3 brothers who marry 3 sisters and have children with strange names. (Rev: BL 2/1/98; SLJ 3/98*)

**3448** Rattigan, Jama Kim. *Truman's Aunt Farm* (PS–3). Illus. by G. Brian Karas. 1994, Houghton $14.95 (0-395-65661-3). 32pp. In a mix-up, Truman gets a colony of 50 aunts, not ants, from his mail order firm. (Rev: BCCB 3/94; BL 2/15/94; SLJ 6/94*)

**3449** Reay, Joanne. *Bumpa Rumpus and the Rainy Day* (PS–2). Illus. by Adriano Gon. 1995, Houghton $14.95 (0-395-71038-3). Bumpa Rumpas loves to make noise, particularly on a rainy day. (Rev: SLJ 3/96)

**3450** Riddell, Chris. *The Trouble with Elephants* (PS–1). Illus. by author. 1990, HarperCollins paper $6.95 (0-06-443170-3). 32pp. Elephants can cause trouble, a little girl relates, such as leaving pink rings in the bathtub. (Rev: BL 10/15/88; SLJ 3/89)

**3451** Robart, Rose. *The Cake That Mack Ate* (PS–K). Illus. by Maryann Kovalski. 1991, Little, Brown paper $4.95 (0-316-74891-9). A cumulative tale featuring a festive party table. (Rev: BL 3/1/87; SLJ 6–7/87)

**3452** Rodda, Emily. *Power and Glory* (PS–2). Illus. by Geoff Kelly. 1996, Greenwillow $15.00 (0-688-14214-1). 32pp. After a series of unwanted interruptions, a young boy, now accompanied by his whole family, plays his video game, "Power and Glory." (Rev: BL 4/15/96*; SLJ 5/96)

**3453** Rodda, Emily. *Yay!* (PS–2). Illus. by Craig Smith. 1997, Greenwillow $15.00 (0-688-15255-4). 40pp. A young boy manages to survive all the rides at an amusement park while members of his family drop out, one by one. (Rev: BL 9/1/97; SLJ 8/97)

**3454** Ross, Tony. *I Want a Cat* (PS–3). Illus. by author. 1989, Farrar $13.00 (0-374-33621-0); paper $4.95 (0-374-43544-8). 26pp. Jessy is so determined that she should have a cat as a pet that she begins acting like one. (Rev: HB 9–10/89; SLJ 7/89)

**3455** Ross, Tony. *I Want My Dinner* (PS). Illus. by author. 1996, Harcourt $12.00 (0-15-200972-8). A humorous look at an ill-mannered girl who throws temper tantrums when she doesn't get her way. (Rev: SLJ 5/96)

**3456** Ross, Tony. *I Want to Be* (PS–1). Illus. by author. 1993, Kane/Miller $11.95 (0-916291-46-4). A little princess seeks advice from others so that she will grow up to be a perfect adult. (Rev: SLJ 3/94)

**3457** Ross, Tony. *Super Dooper Jezebel* (K–2). Illus. by author. 1990, Farrar paper $3.95 (0-374-47342-0). Jezebel is the absolutely perfect child; the crocodile thinks so, too. (Rev: BL 10/15/88; SLJ 12/88)

**3458** Ryan-Lush, Geraldine. *Hairs on Bears* (K–3). Illus. by Normand Cousineau. 1994, Annick LB $14.95 (1-55037-351-X); paper $4.95 (1-55037-352-8). A humorous picture book about the problems caused when the family pooch begins to shed his hair. (Rev: SLJ 12/94)

**3459** Sadler, Marilyn. *Alistair's Time Machine* (K–2). Illus. by Roger Bollen. 1986, Simon & Schuster paper $5.95 (0-671-68493-0). 40pp. Alistair invents a time machine and has wondrous travels, but when he returns home and enters it in a science contest, he loses. (Rev: BL 7/86; SLJ 9/86)

**3460** Saltzberg, Barney. *Where, Oh, Where Is My Underwear? A Pop-up Book* (PS–K). Illus. 1994, Hyperion $9.95 (1-56282-694-8). 12pp. A search for underwear leads to great fun pulling tabs and lifting flaps in this interactive book. (Rev: BL 11/15/94)

**3461** Sanfield, Steve. *Bit by Bit* (PS–1). Illus. by Susan Gaber. 1995, Putnam $15.95 (0-399-22736-9). 32pp. Zundel the tailor continually recycles his beloved coat until it becomes only a button. (Rev: BCCB 5/95; BL 3/15/95; SLJ 8/95*)

**3462** Sant, Thomas. *The Amazing Adventures of Albert and His Flying Machine* (4–7). Illus. by Dee deRosa. 1990, Dutton paper $13.95 (0-525-67302-4). 160pp. To help him deliver newspapers, Albert buys a purple, saucer-shaped Zephyrcar. (Rev: BL 7/90; SLJ 9/90)

**3463** Saul, Carol P. *Someplace Else* (K–2). Illus. by Barry Root. 1995, Simon & Schuster $15.00 (0-689-80273-0). 32pp. Mrs. Tilby solves the problem of where to live by buying a trailer so she can move around. (Rev: BCCB 10/95; BL 11/15/95; HB 11–12/95; SLJ 1/96)

**3464** Schatell, Brian. *The McGoonys Have a Party* (2–3). Illus. by author. 1985, HarperCollins LB $12.89 (0-685-10299-8). 32pp. Mr. McGoony doesn't hear well and Mrs. McGoony is very absent-minded, so things usually go awry. (Rev: BL 12/15/85; SLJ 2/86)

**3465** Scheer, Julian. *Rain Makes Applesauce* (K–2). Illus. by Marvin Bileck. 1964, Holiday $16.95 (0-8234-0091-3). 36pp. A series of silly statements nonsensically presented and accompanied by humorous detailed pictures.

**3466** Scieszka, Jon. *The Stinky Cheese Man: And Other Fairly Stupid Tales* (2–6). Illus. by Lane Smith. 1992, Viking paper $16.99 (0-670-84487-X). 56pp. Lots of fun with fractured fairy tales. (Rev: BCCB 10/92*; BL 9/1/92; HB 11–12/92*; SLJ 9/92*)

**3467** Segal, Lore. *All the Way Home* (K–3). Illus. by James Marshall. 1988, Farrar paper $3.95 (0-374-40355-4). 32pp. Juliet's wailing attracts the attention of some animal friends in this amusing story of a day in the park.

**3468** Sendak, Maurice. *Chicken Soup with Rice: A Book of Months* (K–3). Illus. by author. 1962, HarperCollins LB $13.89 (0-06-025535-8). 48pp. A rhyming story that takes one through each of the months with the always suitable chicken soup with rice.

**3469** Seymour, Tres. *I Love My Buzzard* (K–3). Illus. by S. D. Schindler. 1994, Orchard LB $16.99 (0-531-08669-0). 32pp. Mom gives up and decides to leave when her young son's menagerie grows and grows. (Rev: BL 1/15/94; SLJ 4/94)

**3470** Seymour, Tres. *Too Quiet for These Old Bones* (PS–1). Illus. by Paul Johnson. 1997, Orchard LB $16.99 (0-531-33052-4). 32pp. To their surprise, 4 children discover that Granny doesn't really want the quiet they expect and instead would like to make a racket. (Rev: BL 11/15/97; SLJ 10/97)

**3471** Sharmat, Marjorie W. *Gila Monsters Meet You at the Airport* (PS–2). Illus. by Byron Barton. 1980, Macmillan $14.95 (0-02-782450-0); paper $4.95 (0-689-71383-5). 32pp. A young boy imagines all sorts of horrible things about his move from New York City.

**3472** Sharratt, Nick. *Mrs. Pirate* (PS–1). Illus. by author. 1994, Candlewick $8.95 (1-56402-249-8). In this small book, Mrs. Pirate goes off on a shopping spree to prepare for her sea journey. (Rev: SLJ 9/94)

**3473** Shortt, Tim. *The Babe Ruth Ballet School* (K–3). Illus. 1996, Firefly $14.95 (1-55209-030-2). 32pp. The last 9-year-old big-league baseball star wants to throw in her glove and attend ballet school. (Rev: BL 10/15/96; SLJ 1/97)

**3474** Silverman, Erica. *Mrs. Peachtree's Bicycle* (K–3). Illus. by Ellen Beier. 1996, Simon & Schuster $15.00 (0-689-80477-6). In turn-of-the-century New York, old Mrs. Peachtree masters the art of bicycle riding so well that she gets a speeding ticket. (Rev: SLJ 7/96)

**3475** Sloat, Teri. *The Thing That Bothered Farmer Brown* (PS–1). Illus. by Nadine Bernard Westcott. 1995, Orchard LB $16.99 (0-531-08733-6). 32pp. A pesky mosquito keeps Farmer Brown and all the farm animals awake. (Rev: BL 2/1/95; SLJ 3/95)

**3476** Slobodkina, Esphyr. *Caps for Sale* (K–3). Illus. by author. 1947, HarperCollins LB $14.89 (0-06-025778-4); paper $4.95 (0-06-443143-6). 48pp. When some monkeys engage in a bit of monkey business, the cap peddler must use his imagination to retrieve his wares.

**3477** Slyder, Ingrid. *The Fabulous Flying Fandinis* (PS–2). Illus. by author. 1996, Cobblehill paper $14.99 (0-525-65212-4). The Flying Fandinis, a circus act, move to a new neighborhood, where they live in a big-top tent and transform everyday activities into performances. (Rev: SLJ 9/96)

**3478** Spurr, Elizabeth. *The Long, Long Letter* (K–3). Illus. by David Catrow. 1996, Hyperion LB $15.49 (0-7868-2100-0). 32pp. Aunt Hetta longs to receive a letter, so her sister obliges with the longest one ever. (Rev: BL 4/15/96; SLJ 8/96)

**3479** Stadler, John. *The Cats of Mrs. Calamari* (PS–2). Illus. 1997, Orchard $15.95 (0-531-30020-X). 32pp. When Mrs. Calamari discovers that her new landlord hates cats, she must think of unusual ways to save her large brood. (Rev: BL 3/1/97*; SLJ 5/97)

**3480** Stanley, Diane. *Saving Sweetness* (PS–3). Illus. by G. Brian Karas. 1996, Putnam $15.95 (0-399-22645-1). 32pp. After she runs away from an orphanage, Sweetness must save the sheriff who has been trying to catch her. (Rev: BCCB 11/96; BL 1/1–15/97*; HB 9–10/96; SLJ 11/96*)

**3481** Steig, William. *The Amazing Bone* (K–2). Illus. by author. 1983, Farrar $17.00 (0-374-30248-0). 32pp. A bone that talks saves a piglet from being eaten by a fox in this nonsensical and witty story.

**3482** Stevens, Jan R. *Carlos and the Skunk: Carlos y el Zorrillo* (1–4). Illus. by Jeanne Arnold. 1997, Northland LB $14.95 (0-87358-591-7). 32pp. A bilingual book in which Carlos tangles with a skunk. (Rev: BL 5/15/97)

**3483** Stevens, Kathleen. *Aunt Skilly and the Stranger* (PS–3). Illus. by Robert Andrew Parker. 1994, Ticknor $14.95 (0-395-68712-8). 32pp. A stranger, whom Aunt Skilly helps, comes back at night to steal her valuable quilts in this story of Appalachian Mountain life. (Rev: BL 10/1/94; HB 11–12/94; SLJ 10/94)

**3484** Stevenson, James. *Worse Than the Worst* (K–3). Illus. 1994, Greenwillow LB $13.93 (0-688-12250-7). 32pp. Worst, the most cranky person ever, meets his match when his disagreeable grand-nephew Warren comes to stay. (Rev: BCCB 7–8/94; BL 3/1/94; HB 5–6/94; SLJ 7/94)

**3485** Stevenson, James. *Yard Sale* (2–4). Illus. 1996, Greenwillow LB $14.93 (0-688-14127-7). 32pp. All of the creatures of Mud Flat participate in an unusual yard sale. (Rev: BL 3/15/96; HB 7–8/96; SLJ 7/96*)

**3486** Stewart, Dianne. *Gift of the Sun* (PS–3). Illus. by Jude Daly. 1996, Farrar $15.00 (0-374-32425-5). 30pp. Thulani loves his wife but is too lazy to do the chores around their farm. (Rev: BCCB 12/96; BL 9/1/96; HB 11–12/96; SLJ 9/96*)

**3487** Stuart, Chad. *The Ballymara Flood* (PS–3). Illus. by George Booth. 1996, Harcourt $15.00 (0-15-205698-X). 40pp. A boy's innocent bath time ritual ends in a flood. (Rev: BL 4/1/96; SLJ 6/96)

**3488** Tafuri, Nancy. *This Is the Farmer* (PS). Illus. 1994, Morrow $15.00 (0-688-09468-6). 24pp. A series of amusing cause-and-effect situations begin when a farmer gives a good-morning kiss to his wife. (Rev: BL 5/15/94; HB 9–10/94; SLJ 5/94)

**3489** Teague, Mark. *Baby Tamer* (PS–3). Illus. 1997, Scholastic $15.95 (0-590-67712-8). 32pp. Amanda, the new baby-sitter, proves unflappable when tested by the Eggmont children. (Rev: BL 8/97; SLJ 10/97)

**3490** Tucker, Kathy. *Do Cowboys Ride Bikes?* (PS–2). Illus. by Nadine Bernard Westcott. 1997, Albert Whitman LB $15.95 (0-8075-1693-7). 32pp. A humorous picture book that explores cowboy behavior in a delightful series of questions and answers with droll illustrations. (Rev: BCCB 6/97; BL 4/1/97; SLJ 6/97)

**3491** Tusa, Tricia. *The Family Reunion* (1–3). Illus. 1993, Farrar $15.00 (0-374-32268-6). 28pp. A family reunion gets out of hand when 2 uninvited guests, Esther and Fester, arrive. (Rev: BL 1/15/94)

**3492** Tyler, Anne. *Tumble Tower* (PS–2). Illus. by Mitra Modarressi. 1993, Orchard LB $16.99 (0-531-08647-X). Princess Molly is the despair of her parents, King Clement the Clean and Queen Nellie the Neat, because of her untidy room. (Rev: SLJ 9/93)

**3493** Ungerer, Tomi. *Beast of Monsieur Racine* (K–3). Illus. by author. 1971, Farrar $15.95 (0-374-30640-0); paper $5.95 (0-374-40570-0). 32pp. Monsieur Racine catches the strange creature that was stealing the fruit from his prize pear tree; when the creature reveals his true identity, a surprise is in store.

**3494** Van Laan, Nancy. *Little Baby Bobby* (PS–1). Illus. by Laura Cornell. 1997, Knopf $17.00 (0-679-84922-X). 32pp. The whole town becomes involved when Bobby's baby buggy runs out of control. (Rev: BL 10/1/97; SLJ 11/97)

**3495** Van Laan, Nancy. *Round and Round Again* (PS–1). Illus. by Nadine Bernard Westcott. 1994, Hyperion LB $14.49 (0-7868-2005-5). 32pp. Mama is a collector of discarded objects that she plans to reuse in ingenious ways. (Rev: BL 10/1/94; SLJ 12/94)

**3496** Viorst, Judith. *Earrings!* (K–3). Illus. by Nola L. Malone. 1990, Macmillan $16.00 (0-689-31615-1). 32pp. A young heroine wants pierced ears so she can wear a wide variety of earrings. (Rev: BCCB 1/91; BL 10/1/90; HB 11–12/90; SLJ 11/90)

**3497** Viorst, Judith. *My Mama Says There Aren't Any Zombies, Ghosts, Vampires, Creatures, Demons, Monsters, Fiends, Goblins, or Things* (PS–1). Illus. by Kay Chorao. 1973, Macmillan $16.00 (0-689-30102-2); paper $5.99 (0-689-71204-9). 48pp. A humorous story concerned with a child's vivid description of imaginary monsters and his mother's reassurance that they don't exist.

**3498** Vivelo, Jackie. *Mr. Scatter's Magic Spell* (K–3). Illus. by Margaret Chamberlain. Series: Teachers' Secrets. 1993, DK Publg. $10.95 (1-56458-201-9). 32pp. Mr. Scatter is a zany teacher who practices amateur magic that leaves the principal sawed in half. (Rev: SLJ 3/94)

**3499** Waber, Bernard. *Do You See a Mouse?* (PS–1). Illus. 1995, Houghton $14.95 (0-395-72292-6). 32pp. Every one of the characters in this humorous picture book fails to see the mouse that is apparent to the reader. (Rev: BL 4/1/95; HB 7–8/95; SLJ 9/95)

**3500** Wahl, Jan. *Cats and Robbers* (PS–1). Illus. by Dolores Avendano. 1995, Morrow $16.00 (0-688-13042-9). 32pp. At night, Mrs. Mudge's quiet house is invaded first by mice and then by robbers. (Rev: BCCB 10/95; BL 9/1/95; SLJ 10/95)

**3501** Walsh, Melanie. *Do Pigs Have Stripes?* (PS–1). Illus. 1996, Houghton $12.95 (0-395-73976-4). 40pp. Nonsensical questions about animals (like the title) produce equally entertaining answers. (Rev: BL 3/1/96; HB 5–6/96; SLJ 4/96)

**3502** Walter, Virginia. *"Hi, Pizza Man!"* (PS–2). Illus. by Ponder Goembel. 1995, Orchard LB $16.99 (0-531-08735-2). 32pp. Vivian wonders what sort of messenger will deliver the pizza that she and her mother have ordered. (Rev: BL 1/15/95; HB 3–4/95; SLJ 3/95)

**3503** Watson, Pauline. *The Walking Coat* (PS–3). Illus. by Tomie dePaola. 1980, Walker LB $7.85 (0-8027-6351-0). 32pp. On the first cold day, Scott dons a huge coat that is much too big for him.

**3504** Westcott, Nadine Bernard. *Peanut Butter and Jelly: A Play Rhyme* (PS–K). Illus. by author. 1987, Puffin paper $4.99 (0-14-054852-1). 32pp. A play rhyme describes the making of this food that is a children's favorite. (Rev: BL 10/1/87; SLJ 9/87)

**3505** White, Linda. *Too Many Pumpkins* (PS–2). Illus. by Megan Lloyd. 1996, Holiday LB $15.95 (0-8234-1245-8). 28pp. Rebecca Estelle, who hates pumpkins, finds she has a bumper crop in her garden. (Rev: BCCB 12/96; BL 9/15/96; SLJ 11/96)

**3506** Willard, Nancy. *Simple Pictures Are Best* (PS–3). Illus. by Tomie dePaola. 1978, Harcourt paper $4.95 (0-15-682625-9). 32pp. Over a weary photographer's warnings, a couple insist on cluttering their anniversary portrait with all their worldly goods.

**3507** Williams, Barbara. *Albert's Toothache* (K–2). Illus. by Kay Chorao. 1974, Dutton paper $3.95 (0-525-44363-0). 32pp. Albert, a turtle, claims he has a toothache, but not until Grandma asks him where his tooth aches does Albert realize he is toothless.

**3508** Williams, Jay. *Everyone Knows What a Dragon Looks Like* (K–3). Illus. by Mercer Mayer. 1984, Macmillan paper $6.95 (0-02-045600-X). 32pp. In this humorous tale told in the folk tradition, the leaders argue about what a dragon looks like, but the people know — "a small, fat, bald old man."

**3509** Williams, Suzanne. *Library Lil* (PS–3). Illus. by Steven Kellogg. 1997, Dial paper $14.89 (0-8037-1699-0). 32pp. A happy story about a tough librarian who changes a bunch of TV couch potatoes into avid readers. (Rev: BL 10/15/97; SLJ 11/97*)

**3510** Williams, Suzanne. *My Dog Never Says Please* (K–3). Illus. by Tedd Arnold. 1997, Dial paper $14.89 (0-8037-1681-8). An ill-mannered girl decides that living like a dog would be better than being a human; however, after spending some time in the doghouse, she changes her mind. (Rev: SLJ 6/97)

**3511** Williams, Vera B. *"More More More," Said the Baby: 3 Love Stories* (PS). Illus. 1990, Greenwillow LB $15.93 (0-688-09174-1). 32pp. All the ways that parents and grandparents play with youngsters are portrayed in this humorous picture book. (Rev: BCCB 10/90; BL 10/1/90; HB 11–12/90; SLJ 10/90*)

**3512** Wolf, Jake. *Daddy, Could I Have an Elephant?* (PS–2). Illus. by Marylin Hafner. 1996, Greenwillow LB $14.93 (0-688-13295-2). 32pp. Tony wants a big animal like an elephant as a pet but finally settles for a puppy. (Rev: BCCB 10/96; BL 7/96; SLJ 9/96)

**3513** Wood, Audrey. *King Bidgood's in the Bathtub* (PS–2). Illus. by Don Wood. 1985, Harcourt $16.00 (0-15-242730-9). 32pp. No one can get the king out of his bathtub, until the young page thinks of pulling the plug. (Rev: BCCB 1/86; BL 10/1/85; SLJ 11/85)

**3514** Wood, Audrey. *The Napping House* (PS–2). Illus. by Don Wood. 1984, Harcourt $16.00 (0-15-256708-9). 32pp. A cumulative story about all the members of a household taking a nap except for a flea.

**3515** Wood, Audrey. *Red Racer* (PS–2). Illus. 1996, Simon & Schuster $15.00 (0-689-80553-5). 30pp. Nona tries unsuccessfully to get rid of her old bicycle so she can get a new red racer. (Rev: BCCB 7–8/96; BL 9/1/96; SLJ 9/96*)

**3516** Yaccarino, Dan. *An Octopus Followed Me Home* (PS–2). Illus. 1997, Viking paper $15.99 (0-670-87401-9). 32pp. After allowing his daughter to keep a menagerie of pets, a father draws the line at an octopus. (Rev: BL 8/97; SLJ 1/98)

**3517** Yee, Wong H. *Eek! There's a Mouse in the House* (PS–K). Illus. by author. 1992, Houghton $16.00 (0-395-62303-0). A young girl sends for larger and larger animals to rid her house of a mouse. (Rev: SLJ 10/92)

**3518** Yorinks, Arthur. *Oh, Brother* (K–3). Illus. by Richard Egielski. 1989, Farrar $15.95 (0-374-35599-1). 40pp. In this humorous tale, 2 orphan boys continue to quarrel regardless of what situation they are in. (Rev: BCCB 11/89; BL 10/15/89*; SLJ 12/89*)

**3519** Yorinks, Arthur. *Whitefish Will Rides Again!* (K–4). Illus. by Mort Drucker. 1994, HarperCollins LB $14.89 (0-06-205038-9). 32pp. Whitefish Will, a retired sheriff, is brought back to town to take care of evil Bart, who is terrorizing the citizenry. (Rev: BCCB 1/95; BL 11/15/94; SLJ 10/94)

**3520** Yorke, Malcolm. *Miss Butterpat Goes Wild!* (K–3). Illus. by Margaret Chamberlain. Series: Teachers' Secrets. 1993, DK Publg. $10.95 (1-56458-200-0). 32pp. A mousy little teacher spends an exciting summer in the Amazon region living with the Indians and consorting with bandits. (Rev: SLJ 3/94)

**3521** Zemach, Harve. *The Judge: An Untrue Tale* (1–3). Illus. by Margot Zemach. 1969, Farrar $17.00 (0-374-33960-0); paper $5.95 (0-374-43962-1). 48pp. A foolish judge, who would not believe the frantic reports of an unusual, threatening monster in the vicinity, gets his comeuppance in this rhyming tale with catchy refrain.

**3522** Zemach, Harve. *A Penny a Look: An Old Story Retold* (K–3). Illus. by Margot Zemach. 1971, Farrar $16.00 (0-374-35793-5); paper $4.95 (0-374-45758-1). 48pp. A rascal tries to exploit his brother in a wild money-making scheme.

**3523** Ziefert, Harriet. *I Swapped My Dog* (PS–1). Illus. by Emily Bolam. 1998, Houghton $15.00 (0-395-89159-0). 32pp. A cumulative story about a man who swaps each animal he receives for what he thinks is a better one, but ends up with his original faithful dog. (Rev: BL 3/1/98)

**3524** Zimelman, Nathan. *How the Second Grade Got $8,205.50 to Visit the Statue of Liberty* (K–3). Illus. by Bill Slavin. 1992, Whitman LB $14.95 (0-8075-3431-5). 32pp. Second-graders try to raise money for a field trip, with humorous results. (Rev: BL 9/15/92)

## NATURE AND SCIENCE

**3525** Albert, Burton. *Windsongs and Rainbows* (PS–2). Illus. by Susan Stillman. 1993, Simon & Schuster paper $14.00 (0-671-76004-1). Changes in the weather, including a rainstorm, are depicted. (Rev: SLJ 8/93)

**3526** Aldridge, Josephine Haskell. *A Possible Tree* (K–3). Illus. by Daniel San Souci. 1993, Macmillan LB $16.00 (0-02-700407-4). 32pp. All the pests around Joe Bracken's farm — like a blue jay, raccoon, and squirrel — take refuge in a small fir tree so that at Christmas it looks like a living Christmas wreath. (Rev: BL 10/1/93)

**3527** Allen, Marjorie. *Changes* (PS–K). Illus. by Shelley Rotner. 1991, Macmillan paper $14.00 (0-02-700252-7). This photoessay shows the changes that occur in nature, such as the opening of a flower. (Rev: BCCB 3/91; BL 6/15/91; SLJ 7/91)

**3528** Anderson, David A. *The Rebellion of Humans: An African Spiritual Journey* (K–4). Illus. by Claude Joachim. 1994, Sights $18.95 (0-9629978-6-2). 32pp. This ecological tale tells about an African tribe that forgets the lessons of the past and creates a wasteland by destroying the forests. A sequel to *The Origin of Life on Earth* (1992). (Rev: BL 10/1/94)

**3529** Anholt, Catherine, and Laurence Anholt. *Sun Snow Stars Sky* (PS–2). Illus. 1995, Viking paper $13.99 (0-670-86196-0). 32pp. A boy and a girl experience various kinds of weather. (Rev: BL 5/15/95; SLJ 7/95)

**3530** Arnosky, Jim. *Crinkleroot's Guide to Knowing the Birds* (K–4). Illus. 1992, Macmillan $15.00 (0-02-705857-3). 32pp. The lovable woodsman offers tips on all sorts of nature know-how. (Rev: BL 10/15/92; SLJ 11/92) [598]

**3531** Arnosky, Jim. *Crinkleroot's Guide to Walking in Wild Places* (1–3). Illus. 1990, Macmillan $15.00 (0-02-705842-5). 32pp. How-to for a leisurely walk through the woods. (Rev: BL 8/90; HB 11–12/90; SLJ 11/90) [796.5]

**3532** Asch, Frank. *The Earth and I* (PS–2). Illus. 1994, Harcourt $15.00 (0-15-200443-2). 32pp. A young boy shares many thoughts and activities with his friend the earth. (Rev: BL 1/15/95; SLJ 10/94)

**3533** Aschenbrenner, Gerald. *Jack, the Seal and the Sea* (1–4). Illus. by author. 1988, Silver Burdett LB $12.95 (0-382-09985-0); paper $4.95 (0-382-09986-9). 30pp. Jack rescues a seal who leads him to bountiful fishing grounds. (Rev: BL 1/15/89; SLJ 3/89)

**3534** Aylesworth, Jim. *Wake Up, Little Children: A Rise-and-Shine Rhyme* (PS–2). Illus. by Walter L. Krudop. 1996, Simon & Schuster $16.00 (0-689-31857-X). The flora and fauna of the countryside are pictured, with an invitation for children to come out and enjoy nature. (Rev: SLJ 4/96)

**3535** Baker, Sanna Anderson. *Mississippi Going North* (K–3). Illus. by Bill Farnsworth. 1996, Albert Whitman LB $15.95 (0-8075-5164-3). A picture book about a family that explores the northern part of the Mississippi River by canoe and sees many animals and birds. (Rev: SLJ 10/96)

**3536** Bang, Molly. *Common Ground: The Water, Earth, and Air We Share* (PS–3). Illus. 1997, Scholastic $12.95 (0-590-10056-4). 32pp. A parable in which villagers misuse their grazing areas points out the modern environmental problem of wasting the earth's resources. (Rev: BL 10/1/97*; HB 11–12/97; SLJ 10/97)

**3537** Barklem, Jill. *Autumn Story* (PS–3). Illus. by author. 1989, Putnam $10.95 (0-399-21754-1). The mice of Brambly Hedge celebrate the seasons. A reissue.

**3538** Baskwill, Jane. *Somewhere* (PS–1). Illus. by Trish Hill. 1996, Mondo $13.95 (1-57255-131-3). A simple rhyme and drawings of simple outdoor scenes are used to introduce the beauty and variety of nature. (Rev: SLJ 5/96)

**3539** Bauer, Marion Dane. *When I Go Camping with Grandma* (PS–2). Illus. by Allen Garns. 1995, Troll paper $15.95 (0-8167-3448-8). 32pp. A mood piece that lovingly describes a camping trip with a child and grandmother. (Rev: BL 1/1/95; SLJ 4/95)

**3540** Baylor, Byrd. *If You Are a Hunter of Fossils* (PS–1). Illus. by Peter Parnall. 1984, Simon & Schuster paper $4.95 (0-689-70773-8). 32pp. A story that introduces a sense of long ago.

**3541** Becker, Bonny. *The Quiet Way Home* (PS–K). Illus. by Benrei Huang. 1995, Holt $15.95 (0-8050-3530-3). 32pp. When grandfather takes his granddaughter home from school, he chooses a route where they can enjoy nature. (Rev: BL 12/1/95; SLJ 1/96)

**3542** Behn, Harry. *Trees* (1–3). Illus. by James Endicott. 1992, Holt $14.95 (0-8050-1926-X). 32pp. This short poem about trees is illustrated with colorful paintings. (Rev: BL 6/1/92; SLJ 5/92) [811]

**3543** Bess, Clayton. *The Truth About the Moon* (K–3). Illus. by Rosekrans Hoffman. 1983, Houghton $13.95 (0-395-34551-0); paper $6.95 (0-395-64371-6). 48pp. A young African boy hears both realistic and fanciful explanations for the moon.

**3544** Borden, Louise. *Caps, Hats, Socks, and Mittens: A Book About the Four Seasons* (PS–K). Illus. by Lillian Hoban. 1989, Scholastic paper $4.99 (0-590-44872-2). Children are introduced to the uniqueness of each season. (Rev: BL 2/15/89; SLJ 4/89)

**3545** Brady, Kimberley Smith. *Keeper for the Sea* (PS–1). Illus. by Peter M. Fiore. 1996, Simon & Schuster $16.00 (0-689-80472-5). 30pp. A boy and his grandfather creep out at night to catch bluefish on the seashore. (Rev: BL 10/15/96; SLJ 12/96)

**3546** Brandt, Keith. *Wonders of the Seasons* (1–3). Illus. by James Watling. 1982, Troll LB $12.95 (0-89375-580-X); paper $3.50 (0-89375-581-8). 32pp. A simple introduction to the 4 seasons and the characteristics of each.

**3547** Brinckloe, Julie. *Fireflies!* (PS–1). Illus. by author. 1986, Simon & Schuster paper $3.95 (0-689-71055-0). 32pp. A boy catches fireflies one evening, but when their light grows dim, he releases them. (Rev: BL 5/1/85; HB 9–10/85; SLJ 4/85)

**3548** Brown, Laurie Krasny, and Marc Brown. *Dinosaurs to the Rescue! A Guide to Protecting Our Planet* (PS–3). Illus. 1992, Little, Brown $14.95 (0-316-11087-6). 32pp. A crew of clever dinosaurs suggests some ways to save the earth. (Rev: BL 4/15/92; SLJ 3/92) [333.7]

**3549** Brown, Margaret Wise. *Wait Till the Moon Is Full* (PS–1). Illus. by Garth Williams. 1948, HarperCollins paper $4.95 (0-06-443222-X). 32pp. The fears of night are dispelled in this tender story about raccoons.

**3550** Buchanan, Ken. *This House Is Made of Mud* (PS–1). Illus. by Libba Tracy. 1994, Northland LB $14.95 (0-87358-593-3); paper $6.95 (0-87358-580-1). 32pp. A child describes his adobe house in the Sonoran Desert and the plants and animal life around it. (Rev: BL 9/15/91)

**3551** Bunting, Eve. *Secret Place* (K–3). Illus. by Ted Rand. 1996, Clarion $14.95 (0-395-64367-8). 32pp. A young boy finds a place in the city where wildlife still exists. (Rev: BL 9/1/96; SLJ 9/96)

**3552** Bunting, Eve. *Someday a Tree* (PS–3). Illus. by Ronald Himler. 1993, Houghton $15.00 (0-395-61309-4). 32pp. In spite of attention from friends, a sick tree continues to die. (Rev: BL 3/1/93; SLJ 5/93)

**3553** Bunting, Eve. *Sunflower House* (PS–2). Illus. by Kathryn Hewitt. 1996, Harcourt $15.00 (0-15-200483-1). 32pp. A boy plants some sunflower seeds and witnesses the dramatic miracle of plant growth. (Rev: BL 4/1/96; SLJ 5/96)

**3554** Burns, Kate. *Hide and Seek: In the Snow* (PS–K). Illus. by Dawn Apperley. 1996, Little, Brown $9.95 (0-316-11820-6). Pulling tabs in this book reveals various residents of Northern habitats. (Rev: BL 12/15/96; SLJ 1/97)

**3555** Cannon, Annie. *The Bat in the Boot* (PS–2). Illus. 1996, Orchard LB $16.99 (0-531-08795-6). 32pp. Two children nurture a baby bat until its mother comes to rescue it. (Rev: BL 4/1/96; SLJ 6/96)

**3556** Carle, Eric. *The Tiny Seed* (K–2). Illus. by author. 1991, Picture Book $16.00 (0-88708-015-4). 32pp. A tiny seed travels by the wind, survives all sorts of perils, and grows into a flower. A reissue.

**3557** Carlstrom, Nancy White. *Wild Wild Sunflower Child Anna* (PS–1). Illus. by Jerry Pinkney. 1987, Macmillan LB $14.95 (0-02-717360-7). 32pp. Watercolor illustrations highlight Little Anna's romp through a summer day. (Rev: BL 10/1/87; HB 11–12/87)

**3558** Carrier, Lark. *A Tree's Tale* (K–3). Illus. 1996, Dial paper $14.89 (0-8037-1203-0). 32pp. The history of the life and times of a giant oak tree that began its life 400 years ago on the East Coast of North America. (Rev: BCCB 6/96; BL 5/1/96; SLJ 4/96)

**3559** Cherry, Lynne. *The Great Kapok Tree: A Tale of the Amazon Rain Forest* (K–3). Illus. 1990, Harcourt $16.00 (0-15-200520-X). 32pp. A carefully researched picture book of the Amazon rain forest. (Rev: BL 3/15/90; HB 5–6/90; SLJ 5/90)

**3560** Clifton, Lucille. *The Boy Who Didn't Believe in Spring* (K–2). Illus. by Brinton Turkle. 1988, Dutton paper $4.95 (0-525-44365-7). 32pp. An account of a black child's determination to "get me some of this spring."

**3561** Condra, Estelle. *See the Ocean* (K–2). Illus. by Linda Crockett-Blassingame. 1994, Ideals $14.95 (1-57102-005-5). 32pp. A blind girl, using her inner feelings, is the first to detect the ocean. (Rev: BL 10/15/94; SLJ 10/94)

**3562** Cooner, Donna D. *The World God Made* (PS–K). Illus. by Kim Simons. 1994, Word $12.99 (0-8499-1162-1). 28pp. A cumulative book that describes some of the wonders that God created. (Rev: BL 12/1/94)

**3563** Cordova, Amy. *Abuelita's Heart* (K–3). Illus. 1997, Simon & Schuster paper $16.00 (0-689-80181-5). 32pp. A grandmother takes her granddaughter on a tour around their home in the Southwest to point out nature's beauty. (Rev: BL 8/97; SLJ 9/97)

**3564** Coucher, Helen. *Rain Forest* (K–2). Illus. by author. 1988, Farrar $15.00 (0-374-36167-3). 32pp.

A machine cuts down the trees in the rain forest, and when the rains come, with no trees to hold the soil in place, the river bursts its banks. (Rev: BL 1/15/89; SLJ 2/89)

**3565** Cunningham, David. *A Crow's Journey* (K–3). Illus. 1996, Albert Whitman LB $16.95 (0-8075-1356-3). 32pp. A crow's journey traces the flow of water from a trickle to becoming a stream and eventually a river flowing into the ocean. (Rev: BCCB 6/96; BL 5/1/96; SLJ 6/96)

**3566** Davies, Kay, and Wendy Oldfield. *My Balloon* (PS–1). Illus. by Fiona Pragoff. Series: Simple Science. 1990, Doubleday $7.99 (0-385-41199-5). Simple science principles are introduced. Also use: *My Mirror* (1990). (Rev: SLJ 10/90) [507]

**3567** Davol, Marguerite W. *The Heart of the Wood* (PS–1). Illus. by Sheila Hamanaka. 1992, Simon & Schuster paper $15.00 (0-671-74778-9). 32pp. A tree that is chopped down continues to give pleasure when it becomes a violin. (Rev: BCCB 2/93; BL 12/1/92; SLJ 10/92)

**3568** Denslow, Sharon P. *On the Trail with Miss Pace* (K–2). Illus. by G. Brian Karas. 1995, Simon & Schuster paper $15.00 (0-02-728688-6). 32pp. Two of her pupils join school teacher Miss Pace during her summer vacation out West. (Rev: BL 6/1–15/95; SLJ 6/95)

**3569** dePaola, Tomie. *Charlie Needs a Cloak* (PS–1). Illus. by author. 1982, Simon & Schuster paper $5.95 (0-671-66467-0). The facts about cloth making are humorously presented in this story of Charlie, a shepherd.

**3570** dePaola, Tomie. *The Cloud Book* (K–3). Illus. by author. 1975, Holiday LB $15.95 (0-8234-0259-2); paper $6.95 (0-8234-0531-1). 32pp. The 10 most common clouds, along with related myths and sayings.

**3571** dePaola, Tomie. *The Quicksand Book* (1–3). Illus. by author. 1977, Holiday LB $15.95 (0-8234-0291-6); paper $6.95 (0-8234-0532-X). 32pp. Science is both informative and entertaining in this story of Jungle Girl, who falls into a patch of quicksand.

**3572** Desimini, Lisa, et al. *All Year Round* (PS–1). Illus. 1997, Scholastic $15.95 (0-590-36097-3). 32pp. Four artists have contributed their illustrations and short poems to this book about the seasons. (Rev: BL 12/15/97)

**3573** Dorros, Arthur. *Feel the Wind* (PS–2). Illus. by author. 1989, HarperCollins LB $15.89 (0-690-04741-X); paper $4.95 (0-06-445095-3). 32pp. Defining what causes the wind to blow. (Rev: BL 4/1/89; SLJ 6/89)

**3574** Downing, Julie. *White Snow, Blue Feather* (PS–1). Illus. by author. 1989, Macmillan $14.95 (0-

02-732530-X). A little boy explores the countryside in the dead of winter. (Rev: SLJ 11/89)

**3575** Dunn, Judy. *The Little Rabbit* (K–2). Illus. by Phoebe Dunn. 1980, Random paper $3.25 (0-394-84377-0). 32pp. A real rabbit family is introduced in photographs.

**3576** Dunn, Phoebe. *Farm Animals* (PS). Illus. by author. 1984, Random $3.99 (0-394-86254-6). 28pp. An introduction to more than 15 farm animals.

**3577** Easwaran, Eknath. *The Monkey and the Mango: Stories of My Granny* (K–2). Illus. by Ilka Jerabek. 1996, Nilgiri Press $14.95 (0-915132-82-6). 29pp. In the southern Indian state of Kerala, a grandmother tells her grandson a number of stories that tell about the wonders of nature, creation, and humankind's relation to all creatures. (Rev: SLJ 8/96)

**3578** Edwards, Richard. *Ten Tall Oaktrees* (K–2). Illus. by Caroline Crossland. 1993, Tambourine LB $14.93 (0-688-04621-5). An ecological story about a grove of 10 oak trees that were destroyed one by one to accommodate the needs and whims of humans. (Rev: SLJ 10/93)

**3579** Ehlert, Lois. *Feathers for Lunch* (PS–2). Illus. 1990, Harcourt $15.00 (0-15-230550-5). 32pp. A wide variety of American birds are introduced by way of a cat's stalking activities. (Rev: BCCB 1/91; BL 9/1/90; HB 11–12/90*; SLJ 12/90)

**3580** Ehlert, Lois. *Red Leaf, Yellow Leaf* (4–6). Illus. 1991, Harcourt $16.00 (0-15-266197-2). 32pp. A child tells of buying, planting, and caring for a sugar maple tree. (Rev: BCCB 10/91; BL 10/1/91*; HB 11–12/91*; SLJ 11/91)

**3581** Evans, Lezlie. *Rain Song* (PS–1). Illus. by Cynthia Jabar. 1995, Houghton $14.95 (0-395-69865-0). 32pp. Two girls enjoy the sounds and the excitement of a rainstorm. (Rev: BCCB 3/95; BL 3/15/95; SLJ 7/95)

**3582** Eversole, Robyn. *Flood Fish* (PS–1). Illus. by Sheldon Greenberg. 1995, Crown $16.00 (0-517-59705-5). 32pp. An Australian boy is amazed at the sudden appearance of all kinds of fish after a dry riverbed is flooded. (Rev: BL 9/15/95; SLJ 12/95)

**3583** Fife, Dale H. *Empty Lot* (K–3). Illus. by Jim Arnosky. 1996, Sierra Club paper $6.95 (0-871-56859-4). Harry realizes that his empty country lot is actually alive with all kinds of wildlife. (Rev: SLJ 8/91)

**3584** Fleming, Denise. *In the Small, Small Pond* (PS–K). Illus. 1993, Holt $15.95 (0-8050-2264-3); paper $6.95 (0-8050-5983-0). 30pp. In a series of collages, a frog views a year of changing seasons in a small pond. (Rev: BL 9/1/93; HB 9–10/93; SLJ 9/93*)

**3585** Fletcher, Ralph. *Twilight Comes Twice* (K–2). Illus. by Kate Kiesler. 1997, Clarion $15.00 (0-395-84826-1). 32pp. In radiant illustrations, the author describes 2 times of day: the evening at twilight and dawn, when twilight colors are again present. (Rev: BL 10/15/97; SLJ 10/97)

**3586** Florian, Douglas. *Nature Walk* (PS–2). Illus. 1989, Greenwillow $12.95 (0-688-08266-1). 32pp. Mother and 2 children stroll through the woods. (Rev: BL 10/15/89; SLJ 1/90) [508]

**3587** Florian, Douglas. *A Summer Day* (PS–K). Illus. by author. 1988, Greenwillow LB $12.88 (0-688-07565-7). 24pp. A city family is on the way to the country for some fun. Also use: *A Winter Day* (1987). (Rev: BL 3/1/88; SLJ 5/88)

**3588** Florian, Douglas. *Vegetable Garden* (PS–1). Illus. 1991, Harcourt $13.95 (0-15-293383-2). 32pp. In simple verses, this book explains all the steps in cultivating a lovely garden. (Rev: BL 12/1/91; HB 1–2/92; SLJ 10/91)

**3589** Ford, Miela. *Sunflower* (PS). Illus. by Sally Noll. 1995, Greenwillow LB $15.93 (0-688-13302-9). 24pp. A young girl plants and cares for a single seed that grows into a massive sunflower. (Rev: BL 2/15/95; HB 5–6/95; SLJ 5/95)

**3590** Fowler, Allan. *What's the Weather Today?* (1–3). Illus. Series: Rookie Read-About Science. 1991, Children's LB $18.50 (0-516-04918-6). 32pp. Various kinds of weather are identified in a series of color photographs. (Rev: SLJ 2/92) [551.6]

**3591** Franklin, Kristine L. *When the Monkeys Came Back* (K–3). Illus. by Robert Roth. 1994, Atheneum $14.95 (0-689-31807-3). 32pp. When the Costa Rican forest in which Marta lives is destroyed by developers, she misses the monkeys who used to live there. (Rev: BL 1/1/95; SLJ 12/94)

**3592** Frasier, Debra. *On the Day You Were Born* (K–2). Illus. 1991, Harcourt $16.00 (0-15-257995-8). 32pp. The wonders of nature and the interdependence of all living things are celebrated in this book that introduces science in a personalized way. (Rev: BL 6/15/91; SLJ 6/91*)

**3593** Gackenbach, Dick. *Mighty Tree* (PS). Illus. 1992, Harcourt $13.95 (0-15-200519-6). 32pp. This large picture book presents the uses and wonder of trees. (Rev: BL 4/1/92; SLJ 6/92) [582.16]

**3594** Gage, Wilson. *My Stars, It's Mrs. Gaddy: The Three Mrs. Gaddy Stories* (1–4). Illus. by Marylin Hafner. 1991, Greenwillow $15.95 (0-688-10514-9). 96pp. Mrs. Gaddy has a number of humorous adventures on her farm. (Rev: BL 10/15/91)

**3595** George, Lindsay Barrett. *Around the Pond: Who's Been Here?* (PS–2). Illus. 1996, Greenwillow LB $15.93 (0-688-14377-6). 40pp. Creatures and objects around a pond are revealed through clues. (Rev: BL 9/15/96; SLJ 9/96)

**3596** George, Lindsay Barrett. *In the Snow: Who's Been Here?* (PS–1). Illus. 1995, Greenwillow LB $16.93 (0-688-12321-X). 40pp. On their way to go sledding, 2 children discover clues showing that various animals are present in this nature book that supplies interesting explanations. (Rev: BL 12/1/95; SLJ 12/95)

**3597** George, William T. *Box Turtle at Long Pond* (2–3). Illus. by Lindsay B. George. 1989, Greenwillow LB $15.93 (0-688-08185-1). 24pp. Box Turtle ambles out from a rotting log on Long Pond at the beginning of the day. (Rev: BL 9/1/89; SLJ 10/89*)

**3598** Gibbons, Gail. *The Reasons for Seasons* (K–3). Illus. 1995, Holiday LB $15.95 (0-8234-1174-5). 32pp. The seasons, their causes, and the changes they produce are introduced. (Rev: BL 4/1/95; SLJ 5/95) [525]

**3599** Gibbons, Gail. *The Seasons of Arnold's Apple Tree* (PS–1). Illus. by author. 1984, Harcourt $15.00 (0-15-271246-1); paper $6.00 (0-15-271245-3). 32pp. Arnold's apple tree is useful in all seasons.

**3600** Goble, Paul. *I Sing for the Animals* (PS–2). Illus. by author. 1991, Macmillan LB $9.95 (0-02-737725-3). 32pp. The relationship of humankind to the natural world and the creator. (Rev: BL 11/1/91; SLJ 10/91) [242.62]

**3601** Goldsen, Louise. *Weather* (K–2). Illus. by Sophie Kniffke. 1991, Scholastic $11.95 (0-590-45234-7). Various changes in the weather are illustrated through the use of overlays. (Rev: SLJ 5/92) [551.6]

**3602** Gomi, Taro. *Spring Is Here* (2–4). Illus. 1995, Chronicle paper $4.95 (0-811-81022-4). 32pp. For the very young, this is a delightful introduction to the spring season. (Rev: BL 8/89; HB 11–12/89; SLJ 10/89)

**3603** Griese, Arnold. *Anna's Athabaskan Summer* (K–3). Illus. by Charles Ragins. 1995, Boyds Mills $14.95 (1-56397-232-8). 32pp. A young Athabaskan Indian girl enjoys all the activities of being part of a summer fishing camp. (Rev: BL 6/1–15/95; SLJ 5/95)

**3604** Grindley, Sally. *Peter's Place* (PS–2). Illus. by Michael Foreman. 1996, Harcourt $15.00 (0-15-200916-7). 36pp. The creatures on Peter's favorite beach suffer as a result of an oil spill. (Rev: BL 3/1/96; HB 5–6/96; SLJ 5/96)

**3605** Guiberson, Brenda Z. *Cactus Hotel* (PS–3). Illus. by Megan Lloyd. 1991, Holt $15.95 (0-8050-1333-4). 32pp. The life cycle of the giant saguaro cactus. (Rev: BL 6/15/91; SLJ 7/91) [574.5]

**3606** Haas, Jessie. *Sugaring* (PS–2). Illus. by Joseph A. Smith. 1996, Greenwillow $15.00 (0-688-14200-1). 24pp. The stages of making maple sugar and syrup are examined when Nora decides to help her grandfather in this late winter ritual. A sequel to *Mowing* (1994) and *No Foal Yet* (1995). (Rev: BL 11/15/96; SLJ 10/96)

**3607** Hader, Berta, and Elmer Hader. *The Big Snow* (PS–3). Illus. by authors. 1972, Macmillan LB $16.00 (0-02-737910-8); paper $6.95 (0-689-71757-1). 48pp. How all the little animals of a country hillside survive a heavy winter storm. Caldecott Medal winner, 1949.

**3608** Hague, Kathleen. *Calendarbears: A Book of Months* (PS–1). Illus. by Michael Hague. 1997, Holt $14.95 (0-8050-3818-3). 32pp. Twelve engaging bears highlight activities associated with each of the months. (Rev: BL 3/15/97; SLJ 7/97)

**3609** Hall, Zoe. *The Apple Pie Tree* (PS–2). Illus. by Shari Halpern. 1996, Scholastic $13.95 (0-590-62382-6). 32pp. The changes that occur to an apple tree during one year are described by 2 sisters. (Rev: BCCB 12/96; BL 10/1/96; SLJ 12/96)

**3610** Hall, Zoe. *The Surprise Garden* (PS–1). Illus. by Shari Halpern. 1998, Scholastic $15.95 (0-590-10075-0). 32pp. A charming book in which children plant seeds and tend their gardens until the plants grow into marvelous vegetables. (Rev: BL 1/1–15/98; SLJ 3/98)

**3611** Helldorfer, M. C. *Gather Up, Gather In: A Book of Seasons* (1–4). Illus. by Judy Pedersen. 1994, Viking paper $14.99 (0-670-84752-6). 32pp. Each of the seasons is pictured with adults and children as a time of gathering up and gathering in, as in bringing in autumn's harvest. (Rev: BCCB 10/94; BL 11/15/94; SLJ 12/94*)

**3612** Heller, Ruth. *Chickens Aren't the Only Ones* (K–2). Illus. by author. 1981, Putnam $14.95 (0-448-01872-1). 48pp. All kinds of animals that lay eggs are introduced.

**3613** Henderson, Kathy. *A Year in the City* (PS–2). Illus. by Paul Howard. 1996, Candlewick $15.99 (1-56402-872-0). 32pp. A celebration of the seasons as experienced by a city child. (Rev: BL 1/1–15/97; HB 11–12/96; SLJ 1/97)

**3614** Henley, Claire. *Stormy Days* (PS–K). Illus. 1993, Hyperion $11.95 (1-56282-342-6). 32pp. This picture book describes a violent storm complete with black clouds, thunder, lightning, and rain. (Rev: BL 5/1/93)

**3615** Hines, Anna Grossnickle. *Miss Emma's Wild Garden* (PS–1). Illus. 1997, Greenwillow LB $14.93 (0-688-14693-7). 24pp. Chloe explores Miss Emma's overgrown garden and makes some amazing discoveries. (Rev: BCCB 5/97; BL 3/1/97; SLJ 5/97)

**3616** Hirschi, Ron. *Fall* (K–2). Illus. by Thomas D. Mangelsen. 1991, Dutton paper $15.99 (0-525-65053-9). 32pp. Fall comes to the meadow, woodland, and tundra. Also use: *Summer* (1991). (Rev: BL 8/91; SLJ 2/92) [508]

**3617** Hirschi, Ron. *Spring* (PS–K). Illus. by Thomas D. Mangelsen. 1990, Dutton paper $14.99 (0-525-65037-7). 32pp. Photos focus on spring as a time of renewal. (Rev: BL 10/15/90; HB 1–2/91; SLJ 11/90) [508]

**3618** Hirschi, Ron. *Winter* (PS–1). Illus. by Thomas D. Mangelsen. 1990, Dutton paper $14.99 (0-525-65026-1). 32pp. Full-color photos highlight wildlife in winter. (Rev: BL 11/15/90; HB 1–2/91; SLJ 11/90) [574.43]

**3619** Hiscock, Bruce. *The Big Tree* (K–3). Illus. 1991, Macmillan LB $14.95 (0-689-31598-8). 32pp. A tree in a neighbor's backyard is the focus of this book that discusses the life cycle of a tree. (Rev: BL 1/15/91; SLJ 3/91) [582.16]

**3620** Hiscock, Bruce. *When Will It Snow?* (PS–K). Illus. 1995, Simon & Schuster $15.00 (0-689-31937-1). 32pp. As a young boy awaits the year's first snowfall, animals and humans are making necessary preparations. (Rev: BL 12/1/95; SLJ 12/95)

**3621** *How Big Is the Ocean? First Questions and Answers About the Beach* (PS–3). Illus. Series: First Questions and Answers. 1994, Time Life $14.95 (0-7835-0897-2). 48pp. Basic questions about the ocean — such as "Why is it blue?" — are answered in this picture book. (Rev: BL 3/1/95) [508]

**3622** Hughes, Shirley. *Out and About* (PS–1). Illus. 1988, Lothrop $16.00 (0-688-07690-4). 48pp. A colorful journey through the seasons in a picture book of poems. (Rev: BCCB 6/88; BL 3/15/88; SLJ 5/88)

**3623** Intrater, Roberta G. *Two Eyes, a Nose, and a Mouth* (PS–1). Illus. 1995, Scholastic $12.95 (0-590-48247-5). 32pp. Text and color photos explore the uses, sizes, and shapes of such facial features as eyes, nose, and lips. (Rev: BCCB 3/95; BL 3/1/95; SLJ 4/95) [573]

**3624** Jackson, Ellen. *Brown Cow, Green Grass, Yellow Mellow Sun* (K–2). Illus. by Victoria Raymond. 1995, Hyperion LB $14.89 (0-7867-2006-3). 32pp. The process of getting milk from a cow and turning it into butter is the subject of this picture book illustrated with photos of objects made from modeling clay. (Rev: BL 6/1–15/95; SLJ 5/95)

**3625** Jones, Betty, comp. *A Child's Seasonal Treasury* (PS–2). Illus. by Betty Jones. 1997, Tricycle Pr. $22.95 (1-883672-30-9). 136pp. For each of the seasons, a collection of poems, songs, fingerplays, and activities. (Rev: SLJ 10/97)

**3626** Joosse, Barbara M. *Snow Day!* (K–2). Illus. by Jennifer Plecas. 1995, Clarion $14.95 (0-395-66588-4). 31pp. Activities to engage in on a snow day are pictured, including a family snow fight. (Rev: SLJ 9/95*)

**3627** Kalan, Robert. *Rain* (PS–1). Illus. by Donald Crews. 1978, Greenwillow LB $16.93 (0-688-84139-2); Morrow paper $5.95 (0-688-10479-7). 24pp. A rainstorm described in pictures and brief text.

**3628** Keats, Ezra Jack. *The Snowy Day* (PS–1). Illus. by author. 1962, Puffin paper $4.99 (0-14-050182-7). 40pp. A young black boy's delight during his first snowfall. Caldecott Medal winner, 1963.

**3629** Keister, Douglas. *Fernando's Gift/El Regalo de Fernando* (K–3). Illus. 1995, Sierra Club $16.95 (0-87156-414-9). 32pp. This Spanish-English story set in Costa Rica is about the dangers that development can bring to a rain forest as seen through the eyes of young Fernando. (Rev: BCCB 5/95; BL 6/1–15/95; SLJ 7/95)

**3630** Keller, Holly. *Island Baby* (1–3). Illus. 1992, Greenwillow LB $15.93 (0-688-10580-7). 32pp. A young Caribbean boy saves an injured flamingo, but after its recovery he must set it free. (Rev: BL 9/15/92; HB 11–12/92; SLJ 11/92)

**3631** Kerins, Tony. *Little Clancy's New Drum* (PS–K). Illus. by author. 1996, Candlewick $9.99 (0-7636-0061-X). Even when his new drum is taken away from him by people who want to sleep, Little Clancy goes around thumping and pounding on any object he can find. (Rev: SLJ 1/97)

**3632** Killion, Bette. *The Same Wind* (2–5). Illus. by Barbara B. Falk. 1992, HarperCollins LB $14.89 (0-06-021051-6). 32pp. The many kinds of winds and their uses are explored in this picture book. (Rev: BL 1/1/93)

**3633** King, Elizabeth. *Backyard Sunflower* (PS–3). Illus. 1993, Dutton paper $13.99 (0-525-45082-3). 32pp. With full-color photographs, this book shows the life cycle of a sunflower plant from seed to harvest. (Rev: BL 5/1/93; HB 7–8/93) [635.9]

**3634** Kinsey-Warnock, Natalie. *When Spring Comes* (K–2). Illus. by Stacey Schuett. 1993, Dutton paper $14.99 (0-525-45008-4). 32pp. Looking out on a winter landscape, a young girl remembers all the activities connected with spring. (Rev: BL 3/1/93; SLJ 4/93)

**3635** Koch, Michelle. *World Water Watch* (K–2). Illus. 1993, Greenwillow LB $15.93 (0-688-11465-2). 32pp. Simple prose and beautiful watercolors introduce 6 endangered aquatic animals, such as the Chilean fur seal and the Alaskan sea otter. (Rev: BL 6/1–15/93; SLJ 4/93*) [639.9]

**3636** Krauss, Ruth. *The Growing Story* (PS–2). Illus. by Phyllis Rowand. 1947, HarperCollins $11.95 (0-06-023380-X). 32pp. A little boy watches things grow but doesn't realize until fall that he, too, has grown.

**3637** Kroll, Virginia. *The Seasons and Someone* (K–3). Illus. by Tatsuro Kiuchi. 1994, Harcourt $15.00 (0-15-271233-X). 32pp. In this exquisite picture book, a little Eskimo girl watches the changes of seasons from her Northern home. (Rev: BL 12/1/94; SLJ 1/95*)

**3638** Laser, Michael. *The Rain* (K–3). Illus. by Jeffrey Greene. 1997, Simon & Schuster paper $16.00 (0-689-80506-3). 32pp. Three adults and 2 children react in various ways to being out in the rain. (Rev: BCCB 6/97; BL 4/1/97; SLJ 5/97)

**3639** Lasky, Kathryn. *Pond Year* (K–3). Illus. by Mike Bostock. 1995, Candlewick $14.99 (1-56402-187-4). 32pp. Two girls share fascinating experiences as they explore the life in a local pond. (Rev: BL 5/15/95; SLJ 9/95)

**3640** Leavitt, Melvin. *A Snow Story* (K–3). Illus. by JoEllen M. Stammen. 1995, Simon & Schuster $15.00 (0-689-80296-X). Even when he grows to adulthood and has his own children, Johnny writes poetry every winter, when it snows. (Rev: SLJ 12/95)

**3641** Leedy, Loreen. *Blast Off to Earth! A Look at Geography* (PS–3). Illus. 1992, Holiday LB $16.95 (0-8234-0973-2). 32pp. An alien teacher and his students take a class trip to Earth. (Rev: BL 11/1/92; SLJ 1/93) [910]

**3642** Lesser, Carolyn. *What a Wonderful Day to Be a Cow* (PS–1). Illus. by Melissa Mathis. 1995, Knopf LB $17.99 (0-679-92430-2). 32pp. The months of the year are celebrated by the activities of various farmyard animals. (Rev: BL 1/1/95; SLJ 1/95*)

**3643** Levine, Evan. *Not the Piano, Mrs. Medley!* (PS–2). Illus. by S. D. Schindler. 1991, Watts LB $16.99 (0-531-08556-2). 32pp. Mrs. Medley, Max, and Word the dog pack just about everything — except bathing suits — to go to the beach. (Rev: BL 7/91*; HB 9–10/91; SLJ 11/91*)

**3644** Lindbergh, Reeve. *North Country Spring* (K–2). Illus. by Liz Sivertson. 1997, Houghton $15.95 (0-395-82819-8). 32pp. Vivid rhyming couplets and expressive paintings evoke the changes that spring brings to the northern United States. (Rev: BL 5/15/97; SLJ 4/97)

**3645** Locker, Thomas. *Where the River Begins* (PS–3). Illus. by author. 1984, Dial LB $14.89 (0-8037-0090-3); Puffin paper $5.99 (0-14-054595-6). 32pp. Two boys hike with their grandfather to the source of a river.

**3646** LoMonaco, Palmyra. *Night Letters* (PS–2). Illus. by Normand Chartier. 1996, Dutton paper $14.99 (0-525-45387-3). 32pp. An observant young girl studies nature in her backyard. (Rev: BL 5/15/96; SLJ 3/96)

**3647** London, Jonathan. *I See the Moon and the Moon Sees Me* (PS–1). Illus. by Peter M. Fiore. 1996, Viking paper $14.99 (0-670-85918-4). 32pp. In simple rhymes, a boy greets a number of everyday objects during a day spent outdoors. (Rev: BL 2/1/96; HB 7–8/96; SLJ 3/96)

**3648** Lotz, Karen E. *Can't Sit Still* (PS–1). Illus. by Colleen Browning. 1993, Dutton paper $13.99 (0-525-45066-1). 48pp. A young African American girl is pictured enjoying each of the seasons in the big city. (Rev: BL 6/1–15/93)

**3649** Lotz, Karen E. *Snowsong Whistling* (PS–1). Illus. by Elisa Kleven. 1993, Dutton paper $14.99 (0-525-45145-5). 32pp. A simple verse and imaginative collages are used to evoke the activities that surround the coming of winter. (Rev: BL 10/15/93; SLJ 1/94)

**3650** Luenn, Nancy. *Mother Earth* (PS–3). Illus. by Neil Waldman. 1992, Macmillan $15.00 (0-689-31668-2). 32pp. The cycle of the seasons and their variety of life are celebrated in this tribute to Mother Earth. (Rev: BL 2/1/92; SLJ 3/92)

**3651** Maass, Robert. *When Autumn Comes* (PS–2). Illus. 1990, Holt paper $5.95 (0-8050-2349-6). 32pp. What people do as autumn progresses, with large, handsome photos. (Rev: BL 10/1/90; SLJ 9/90) [508]

**3652** Maass, Robert. *When Spring Comes* (PS–2). Illus. 1994, Holt $14.95 (0-8050-2085-3). 32pp. This photoessay celebrates spring, the changes that occur in nature, and many happy spring holidays and festivals. (Rev: BL 6/1–15/94; SLJ 6/94) [508]

**3653** Maass, Robert. *When Summer Comes* (K–2). Illus. 1993, Holt $14.95 (0-8050-2087-X); paper $5.95 (0-8050-4706-9). 30pp. In this tribute to the joys of summer, many of the activities associated with this season are pictured in photographs. (Rev: BL 6/1–15/93; SLJ 6/93) [508]

**3654** McCloskey, Robert. *Time of Wonder* (1–4). Illus. by author. 1957, Puffin paper $5.99 (0-14-050201-7). 64pp. Full-color watercolors illustrate this poetic text describing a summer on the Maine coast and the hurricane that hits it. Caldecott Medal winner, 1958.

**3655** McCurdy, Michael. *Hannah's Farm: The Seasons on an Early American Homestead* (1–3). Illus. by author. 1988, Holiday LB $12.95 (0-8234-0700-4). 32pp. The seasons are presented on this 19th-century farm in Massachusetts. (Rev: BL 11/15/88; SLJ 2/89)

**3656** MacGill-Callahan, Sheila. *And Still the Turtle Watched* (K–3). Illus. by Barry Moser. 1991, Dial LB $14.89 (0-8037-0932-3). 32pp. A stone turtle carved by an Indian years ago watches as the environment becomes polluted. (Rev: BCCB 12/91; BL 9/1/91; SLJ 9/91)

**3657** McNulty, Faith. *Orphan: The Story of a Baby Woodchuck* (K–3). Illus. by Darby Morrell. 1992, Scholastic $11.95 (0-590-43838-7). 48pp. The author befriends a baby woodchuck on her Rhode Island farm and then realizes she must teach it to return to the wild. (Rev: BL 4/15/92; SLJ 9/92) [599.32]

**3658** Maestro, Betsy. *Snow Day* (PS–2). Illus. by Giulio Maestro. 1992, Scholastic paper $4.95 (0-590-46083-8). 32pp. While families stay home because of the heavy snow, snow removal crews are doing their job. (Rev: BCCB 10/89; BL 11/1/89; SLJ 1/90) [628]

**3659** Magdanz, James. *Go Home, River* (K–2). Illus. by Dianne Widom. 1996, Alaska Northwest $15.95 (0-88240-476-8). 32pp. The place of a river in the life of a group of Inupiat people in Alaska is portrayed in this picture book set in 1875. (Rev: BL 11/1/96; SLJ 1/97)

**3660** Major, Beverly. *Over Back* (1–3). Illus. by Thomas B. Allen. 1993, HarperCollins LB $14.89 (0-06-020287-4). A young black girl takes the reader on a nature tour in back of her house. (Rev: BL 2/1/93; SLJ 3/93)

**3661** Malone, Peter. *Star Shapes* (PS–3). Illus. 1997, Chronicle $15.95 (0-8118-0726-6). 26pp. In this enchanting picture book, the shapes of many constellations are pictured with their earthly counterparts looking on. (Rev: BL 10/1/97; SLJ 11/97)

**3662** Marzollo, Jean. *Home Sweet Home* (PS–K). Illus. by Ashley Wolff. 1997, HarperCollins LB $14.89 (0-06-027353-4). 32pp. A simple poem that extols the beauty found in living things, from bees and tadpoles to snakes and whales. (Rev: BCCB 5/97; BL 4/1/97; SLJ 4/97) [811]

**3663** Michels, Tilde. *What a Beautiful Day!* (PS–2). Illus. by Thomas Muller. 1992, Carolrhoda LB $19.95 (0-87614-739-2). 32pp. On a beautiful summer morning, young Peter enjoys nature as he walks in the woods. (Rev: BL 1/15/93; SLJ 4/93)

**3664** Mora, Pat. *Listen to the Desert/Oye al Desierto* (PS–2). Illus. by Francisco Mora. 1994, Clarion $16.00 (0-395-67292-9). Using double-page spreads, this book in English and Spanish introduces the animals and sounds found in a Southwestern desert. (Rev: SLJ 10/94) [574.5]

**3665** Morris, Ann. *Tools* (PS–2). Illus. by Ken Heyman. 1992, Lothrop LB $15.93 (0-688-10171-2). A description of the functions of various tools, aided by color photos. (Rev: BCCB 12/92; BL 12/1/91) [621.9]

**3666** *My First Look at Seasons* (PS). Illus. Series: My First Look at. 1990, Random $7.00 (0-679-80621-0). 20pp. The concept of the changing seasons is introduced to the very young with bright photos. (Rev: BL 10/15/90) [508]

**3667** Nikola-Lisa, W. *Storm* (PS–1). Illus. by Michael Hays. 1993, Macmillan LB $14.95 (0-689-31704-2). 32pp. Two farm children are fascinated by the sights and sounds of a thunderstorm. (Rev: BL 2/15/93; SLJ 7/93)

**3668** Ormerod, Jan. *When We Went to the Zoo* (PS–1). Illus. 1991, Lothrop LB $13.88 (0-688-09879-7). 40pp. Two youngsters and their father travel around the zoo. (Rev: BL 2/15/91; HB 5–6/91; SLJ 6/91) [590]

**3669** Otten, Charlotte F. *January Rides the Wind: A Book of Months* (PS–2). Illus. by Todd L. W. Doney. 1997, Lothrop LB $15.93 (0-688-12557-3). 32pp. Short poems and evocative paintings capture the essence of the outdoor world during each month of the year. (Rev: BL 10/15/97*; SLJ 10/97)

**3670** Pearson, Susan. *Silver Morning* (PS–2). Illus. by David Christiana. 1998, Harcourt $16.00 (0-15-274786-9). 32pp. An atmospheric account of a boy and his mother taking a walk in the woods on a very foggy morning. (Rev: BL 3/15/98; SLJ 4/98)

**3671** Peet, Bill. *The Wump World* (1–3). Illus. by author. 1981, Houghton $16.00 (0-395-19841-0); paper $6.95 (0-395-31129-2). An animal parable in which pollution and the waste of natural resources are the main themes.

**3672** Perkins, Lynne Rae. *Home Lovely* (1–4). Illus. 1995, Greenwillow LB $14.93 (0-688-13688-5). 32pp. Tiffany, who is left alone while her mother works, learns a great deal about gardening, particularly from the friendly mail carrier. (Rev: BCCB 9/95; BL 1/1–15/96*; HB 11–12/95)

**3673** Peters, Lisa Westberg. *Meg and Dad Discover Treasure in the Air* (K–2). Illus. by Deborah Durland DeSaix. 1995, Holt $15.95 (0-8050-2418-2). 32pp. On a walk with her father, Meg learns a lot about rocks and fossils. (Rev: BL 12/1/95; SLJ 1/96)

**3674** Peters, Lisa Westberg. *October Smiled Back* (PS–2). Illus. by Ed Young. 1996, Holt $14.95 (0-8050-1776-3). 28pp. Each month is personified in this poem, accompanied by bold color illustrations. (Rev: BL 11/1/96; SLJ 10/96*)

**3675** Peters, Lisa Westberg. *The Sun, the Wind, and the Rain* (K–3). Illus. by Ted Rand. 1988, Holt $13.95 (0-8050-0699-0); paper $5.95 (0-8050-1481-0). 48pp. The creation and evolution of mountains using the analogy of a little girl at the beach. (Rev: BL 10/15/88; HB 11–12/88; SLJ 10/88)

**3676** Peters, Sharon. *Animals at Night* (PS–1). Illus. by Paul Harvey. 1996, Troll paper $3.50 (0-8167-1477-0). 32pp. A book about some animals that remain awake at night.

**3677** Petit, Genevieve. *The Seventh Walnut* (K–3). Illus. by Joelle Boucher. 1992, Wellington $13.95 (0-922984-10-7). 32pp. The story of how a walnut, dropped on the ground, grows into a tree; translated from the French. (Rev: BCCB 10/92; BL 12/1/92) [574]

**3678** Prelutsky, Jack. *It's Snowing! It's Snowing!* (1–4). Illus. by Jeanne Titherington. 1984, Greenwillow LB $17.93 (0-688-01513-1). 48pp. A few story poems on the experiences and joys of winter.

**3679** Priddy, Roger. *My Big Book of Everything* (PS–1). Illus. 1996, DK Publg. $14.95 (0-7894-0998-4). 61pp. A variety of subjects — like toys, concepts, and the body — are covered in more than 800 color photographs. (Rev: BL 12/15/96; SLJ 1/97) [413.1]

**3680** Ray, Mary L. *Mud* (PS–2). Illus. by Lauren Stringer. 1996, Harcourt $16.00 (0-15-256263-X). In the period between winter and spring, it is the season of mud, and this book joyfully explores it. (Rev: SLJ 6/96*)

**3681** Ripley, Catherine. *Why Do Stars Twinkle? and Other Nighttime Questions* (PS–3). Illus. by Scot Ritchie. Series: Question and Answer Storybook. 1996, Owl $17.95 (1-895688-41-8); paper $6.95 (1-895688-42-6). 32pp. In a question-and-answer format, facts about night, bedtime, and sleep are covered. (Rev: BL 12/1/96) [500]

**3682** Rockwell, Anne. *Ducklings and Pollywogs* (1–3). Illus. by Lizzy Rockwell. 1994, Macmillan paper $14.95 (0-02-777452-X). 32pp. A girl and her father visit a pond and watch all the changes that the 4 seasons bring. (Rev: BL 12/15/94; SLJ 1/95)

**3683** Rockwell, Anne. *The Storm* (K–3). Illus. by Robert Sauber. 1994, Hyperion LB $16.49 (0-7868-2013-6). The morning after a violent storm hits their coastal home, a young girl and her mother walk the beach and view all the accumulated debris. (Rev: SLJ 11/94)

**3684** Rockwell, Anne, and Harlow Rockwell. *The First Snowfall* (PS–1). Illus. by authors. 1987, Macmillan LB $13.95 (0-02-777770-7); paper $3.95 (0-689-71614-1). 24pp. The fun and beauty of the first snow as seen by a young girl. (Rev: BL 11/1/87; HB 11–12/87)

**3685** Romanova, Natalia. *Once There Was a Tree* (2–3). Illus. by Gennady Spirin. 1985, Dial paper $4.99 (0-8037-0705-3). 32pp. A decaying tree stump in the forest is used by many creatures, even humans, as a man out walking sits on it. (Rev: BCCB 1/86; BL 12/15/85; SLJ 1/86)

**3686** Rosenberg, Liz. *Moonbathing* (PS–3). Illus. by Stephen Lambert. 1996, Harcourt $14.00 (0-15-200945-0). 32pp. A young girl discovers that her favorite beach is transformed into a new world at night. (Rev: BL 10/15/96*; SLJ 10/96)

**3687** Rotner, Shelley, and Ken Kreisler. *Nature Spy* (2–6). Illus. by Shelley Rotner. 1992, Macmillan LB $14.95 (0-02-777885-1). 32pp. Vivid fall photos invite young readers to look closely at nature. (Rev: BL 9/15/92; SLJ 10/92) [508]

**3688** Rotner, Shelley, and Ken Kreisler. *Ocean Day* (PS–K). Illus. by Shelley Rotner. 1993, Macmillan $14.95 (0-02-777886-X). 32pp. In this photoessay, a young girl finds all sorts of sea life swelling in a tidal pool. (Rev: BL 4/1/93; SLJ 6/93)

**3689** Rucki, Ani. *When the Earth Wakes* (PS–1). Illus. 1998, Scholastic $15.95 (0-590-05951-3). 32pp. The text describes the changes that occur in the spring, and the pictures show a bear cub and its mother waking up and entering the world again. (Rev: BL 3/1/98; SLJ 3/98)

**3690** Ryder, Joanne. *Dancers in the Garden* (K–3). Illus. by Judith Lopez. 1992, Sierra Club $15.95 (0-87156-578-1). 32pp. The various activities of a hummingbird in a garden during a single day are pictured. (Rev: BL 11/15/92; SLJ 10/92)

**3691** Ryder, Joanne. *Earthdance* (K–4). Illus. by Norman Gorbaty. 1996, Holt $16.95 (0-8050-2678-9). 32pp. The earth and its wonders are celebrated in this brief poem with accompanying drawings. (Rev: BCCB 7–8/96; BL 4/1/96; SLJ 5/96*) [811]

**3692** Ryder, Joanne. *Shark in the Sea* (PS–3). Illus. by Michael Rothman. Series: Just for a Day. 1997, Morrow LB $15.93 (0-688-14910-3). 32pp. A boy changes into a shark and begins hunting for food. (Rev: BCCB 4/97; BL 3/1/97; SLJ 4/97)

**3693** Rylant, Cynthia. *This Year's Garden* (PS–K). Illus. by Mary Szilagyi. 1984, Macmillan paper $4.95 (0-689-71122-0). 32pp. A year in the garden in drawings and gentle text.

**3694** Rylant, Cynthia. *The Whales* (PS–3). Illus. 1996, Scholastic $14.95 (0-590-58285-2). 40pp. The behavior and thoughts of whales are depicted in words and illustrations. (Rev: BL 4/1/96; SLJ 3/96)

**3695** Salter, Mary Jo. *The Moon Comes Home* (K–2). Illus. by Stacey Schuett. 1989, Knopf LB $13.99 (0-394-99983-5). 32pp. The moon seems to follow a little girl and her family as they drive to visit Grandmother. (Rev: BL 11/1/89)

**3696** Sanders, Scott R. *Meeting Trees* (PS–2). Illus. by Robert Hynes. 1997, National Geographic $16.00 (0-7922-4140-1). During a walk in the woods with his father, a boy learns to identify a number of trees by their shapes, bark, and leaves. (Rev: SLJ 7/97)

**3697** Santrey, Louis. *Autumn* (PS–2). Illus. by Francene Sabin. 1983, Troll LB $11.50 (0-89375-905-8). 32pp. An introduction to what is happening during autumn. Other titles in this series are: *Spring; Summer; Winter* (all 1983).

**3698** Schoen, Mark. *Bellybuttons Are Navels* (PS–2). Illus. by M. J. Quay. 1990, Prometheus $17.95 (0-

87975-585-7). 40pp. While bathing naked, 2 pre-schoolers recite all the visible parts of their bodies. (Rev: BL 6/1/90; SLJ 11/90) [612]

**3699** Serfozo, Mary. *Rain Talk* (PS–K). Illus. by Keiko Narahashi. 1990, Macmillan LB $15.00 (0-689-50496-9). 32pp. An African-American girl and her dog enjoy listening to the various sounds that rain makes. (Rev: BL 10/1/90; SLJ 12/90*)

**3700** Seuss, Dr. *The Lorax* (K–3). Illus. by author. 1971, Random LB $15.99 (0-394-92337-5). 64pp. The Lorax, a little brown creature, has tried in vain to ward off pollution and ecological blight, but Onceler, who wanted the trees for his business, would not heed the warning.

**3701** Seymour, Tres. *Black Sky River* (K–2). Illus. by Dan Andreasen. 1996, Orchard LB $16.99 (0-531-08887-1). 32pp. A father remembers how the sky was once filled with migrating birds but now there are only small flocks. (Rev: BL 11/15/96; SLJ 9/96)

**3702** Shea, Pegi Deitz. *New Moon* (PS–1). Illus. by Cathryn Falwell. 1996, Boyds Mills $14.95 (1-56397-410-X). 24pp. Vinnie and her big brother explore the various phases of the moon. (Rev: BL 1/1–15/97; SLJ 10/96)

**3703** Shulevitz, Uri. *Dawn* (PS–2). Illus. by author. 1974, Farrar $16.00 (0-374-31707-0); paper $5.95 (0-374-41689-3). 32pp. A rare, beautiful book describing in simple poetic terms the coming of dawn.

**3704** Shulevitz, Uri. *Rain Rain Rivers* (PS–2). Illus. by author. 1969, Farrar $16.00 (0-374-36171-1); paper $3.95 (0-374-46195-3). 32pp. A little girl sits in her attic bedroom while the rain falls, and her imagination takes her to the places touched by the rain — the city, streams, and the sea.

**3705** Siddals, Mary M. *Tell Me a Season* (PS–K). Illus. by Petra Mathers. 1997, Clarion $12.95 (0-395-71021-9). 26pp. A cheerful picture book that explores the seasons and describes each in terms of colors. (Rev: BCCB 7–8/97; BL 4/1/97; SLJ 5/97)

**3706** Siebert, Diane. *Sierra* (K–3). Illus. by Wendell Minor. 1991, HarperCollins LB $15.89 (0-06-021640-9). 32pp. In pictures and text, evokes the beautiful Sierra Nevada range of mountains in California and Nevada. (Rev: BL 4/15/91; SLJ 4/91*)

**3707** Silsbe, Brenda. *Just One More Color* (PS–1). Illus. by Shawn Steffler. 1992, Firefly LB $14.95 (1-55037-133-9); paper $4.95 (1-55037-136-3). Mr. Hall tries to change the exterior of his house to suit each season. (Rev: SLJ 4/92)

**3708** Stynes, Barbara W. *Walking with Mama* (PS–K). Illus. 1997, Dawn $14.95 (1-883220-56-4); paper $6.95 (1-883220-57-2). 24pp. A nature walk through the forest with his mother is described by a toddler. (Rev: BL 9/15/97)

**3709** Sweetland, Nancy. *God's Quiet Things* (PS–K). Illus. by Rick Stevens. 1994, Eerdmans $15.00 (0-8028-5082-0). 32pp. Quiet things in nature, like butterflies flying, are celebrated in this thoughtful picture book. (Rev: BL 1/1/95; SLJ 1/95)

**3710** Tamar, Erika. *The Garden of Happiness* (PS–3). Illus. by Barbara Lambase. 1996, Harcourt $16.00 (0-15-230582-3). 40pp. Marisol's seed, planted in a New York City cracked sidewalk, grows into a huge sunflower. (Rev: BL 7/96*; SLJ 5/96)

**3711** Titherington, Jeanne. *Pumpkin Pumpkin* (PS–1). Illus. by author. 1986, Greenwillow LB $15.93 (0-688-05696-2); Morrow paper $3.95 (0-688-09930-0). 24pp. A simple, rhythmic picture book about the facts of plant life. (Rev: BCCB 3/86; BL 3/15/86; SLJ 4/86)

**3712** Tresselt, Alvin. *Hide and Seek Fog* (K–2). Illus. by Roger Duvoisin. 1965, Lothrop LB $15.93 (0-688-51169-4); Morrow paper $4.95 (0-688-07813-3). 32pp. Pastel watercolors quietly reflect obscure seashore scenes as the mysterious, deepening fog rolls in from the sea.

**3713** Tresselt, Alvin. *Rain Drop Splash* (K–3). Illus. by Leonard Weisgard. 1946, Morrow paper $4.95 (0-688-09352-3). 28pp. How the raindrops form a puddle that grows from pond to river and finally joins the sea.

**3714** Turner, Ann. *Apple Valley Year* (K–3). Illus. by Sandi W. Resnick. 1993, Macmillan $14.95 (0-02-789281-6). 32pp. A year on an apple farm as spent some time ago by the hardworking Clark family and an equally diligent family of foxes. (Rev: BL 9/1/93)

**3715** Udry, Janice May. *A Tree Is Nice* (PS). Illus. by Marc Simont. 1957, HarperCollins LB $14.89 (0-06-026156-0); paper $5.95 (0-06-443147-9). 32pp. The many delights to be had in, with, or under a tree: picking apples, raking leaves, swinging, or just sitting in the shade. Caldecott Medal winner, 1957.

**3716** Updike, John. *A Child's Calendar* (K–3). Illus. by Nancy E. Burkert. 1989, Knopf LB $12.99 (0-394-91059-1). 32pp. This is a collection of poems, one for each month of the year. A reissue. [811]

**3717** Van Leeuwen, Jean. *Touch the Sky Summer* (K–2). Illus. by Dan Andreasen. 1997, Dial paper $14.99 (0-8037-1819-5). 32pp. A little boy describes all the pleasures and activities that he and his family engage in when they visit his grandparents at their cabin by a lake. (Rev: BL 6/1–15/97; SLJ 7/97)

**3718** verDorn, Bethea. *Day Breaks* (PS–3). Illus. by Thomas Graham. 1992, Arcade $14.95 (1-55970-187-0). A gentle picture book that presents various scenes of morning as it is experienced across the United States. (Rev: SLJ 9/92)

**3719** Waboose, Jan B. *Morning on the Lake* (K–3). Illus. by Karen Reczuch. 1998, Kids Can $15.95 (1-55074-373-2). 32pp. Three stories about an Ojibwa grandfather and his young grandson, their walks in a forest, and the mystical bond they feel with nature. (Rev: BL 3/15/98)

**3720** Waddell, Martin. *The Big Big Sea* (PS–3). Illus. by Jennifer Eachus. 1994, Candlewick $15.95 (1-56402-066-5). 32pp. Under a full moon, a little girl and her mother take a walk by the sea. (Rev: BL 9/15/94; SLJ 9/94)

**3721** Wells, Rosemary. *Forest of Dreams* (PS–1). Illus. by Susan Jeffers. 1988, Puffin paper $4.99 (0-8037-1140-9). 32pp. A poem about a child who anticipates the coming of spring while walking in the woods in late winter. (Rev: BL 10/1/88; SLJ 11/88)

**3722** Widman, Christine. *The Willow Umbrella* (K–3). Illus. by Catherine Stock. 1993, Macmillan LB $14.95 (0-02-792760-1). 32pp. Two friends share a walk through a rainy countryside. (Rev: BL 3/15/93; SLJ 6/93)

**3723** Wildsmith, Brian. *Seasons* (PS–3). Illus. by author. 1980, Oxford paper $9.95 (0-19-272175-5). 32pp. A sense of the marvels of the seasons is conveyed in this picture book.

**3724** Wildsmith, Brian. *Wild Animals* (PS–2). Illus. by author. 1976, Oxford paper $11.95 (0-19-272103-8). A pride of lions, a skulk of foxes, and so on, parade across the pages.

**3725** Williams, David. *Walking to the Creek* (2–4). Illus. by Thomas B. Allen. 1990, Knopf LB $13.99 (0-394-90598-9). 32pp. Brothers explore the world of nature as they travel from their grandparents' house to a creek nearby. (Rev: BL 12/15/90; SLJ 12/90)

**3726** Wolff, Ashley. *A Year of Beasts* (PS–K). Illus. by author. 1986, Dutton paper $11.95 (0-525-44240-5). 32pp. Through the months, animals are described as they appear during the various seasons. (Rev: BCCB 7–8/86; BL 5/15/86; HB 9–10/86)

**3727** Wood, Audrey. *Birdsong* (PS–2). Illus. by Robert Florczak. 1997, Harcourt $15.00 (0-15-200014-3). 32pp. An impressive picture book that identifies a state bird and a flower through the experiences of children in different parts of the United States. (Rev: BL 10/1/97; SLJ 10/97)

**3728** Yerxa, Leo. *Last Leaf First Snowflake to Fall* (K–3). Illus. 1994, Orchard LB $17.99 (0-531-08674-7). 32pp. Two Indians explore the countryside and canoe across a pond in this picture book that explores the coming of winter. (Rev: BL 10/1/94; SLJ 12/94)

**3729** Yolen, Jane. *Letting Swift River Go* (K–4). Illus. by Barbara Cooney. 1992, Little, Brown $15.95 (0-316-96899-4). 32pp. A historically based story of the creation of the Quabbin Reservoir in Massachusetts is the background of this family story. (Rev: BCCB 9/92; BL 8/92; SLJ 9/92*)

**3730** Yolen, Jane. *Nocturne* (PS–2). Illus. by Anne Hunter. 1997, Harcourt $15.00 (0-15-201458-6). 32pp. Accompanied by his mother and his dog, a young boy explores the night sky and the world of nocturnal creatures. (Rev: BL 10/1/97; SLJ 11/97)

**3731** Yolen, Jane. *Welcome to the Green House* (PS–3). Illus. by Laura Regan. 1993, Putnam LB $15.95 (0-399-22335-5). 32pp. Through a simple text and double-page paintings, a rain forest is introduced with a plea to save this kind of habitat. (Rev: BL 4/1/93; SLJ 4/93) [574]

**3732** Zoehfeld, Kathleen W. *What's Alive?* (K–2). Illus. by Nadine Bernard Westcott. Series: Let's-Read-and-Find-Out Science. 1995, HarperCollins LB $14.89 (0-06-023444-X). 32pp. Explores the classification system used in biology, with a series of questions that differentiate between various plants, animals, and non-living things. (Rev: BCCB 2/96; BL 11/1/95; SLJ 3/96) [577]

## OTHER TIMES, OTHER PLACES

**3733** Ackerman, Karen. *Araminta's Paint Box* (K–3). Illus. by Betsy Lewin. 1998, Aladdin paper $5.99 (0-689-82091-7). 32pp. The Darling family is heading west to California by wagon. (Rev: BCCB 3/90; BL 2/1/90; SLJ 3/90)

**3734** Ackerman, Karen. *The Tin Heart* (1–3). Illus. by Michael Hays. 1990, Macmillan $13.95 (0-689-31461-2). 32pp. Even the Civil War cannot split the friendship of 2 girls from families of different sides. (Rev: BCCB 11/90; BL 12/15/90; SLJ 9/90)

**3735** Adams, Jeanie. *Going for Oysters* (K–3). Illus. by author. 1993, Albert Whitman LB $15.95 (0-8075-2978-8). A picture book that uses a simple story to introduce Australian aboriginal life by depicting life in a native outback community. (Rev: SLJ 1/94)

**3736** Alexander, Sue. *Sara's City* (PS–2). Illus. by Ronald Himler. 1995, Clarion $15.95 (0-395-64483-6). 32pp. City life in the 1940s is recalled in this series of incidents in a girl's everyday life. (Rev: BL 10/1/95; SLJ 12/95)

**3737** Ancona, George. *Fiesta Fireworks* (1–3). Photos by author. 1998, Lothrop LB $15.93 (0-688-14818-2). A photoessay describing a feast day in the city of Tultepec, Mexico, where some of the world's greatest fireworks are made. (Rev: SLJ 3/98)

**3738** Andrews, Jan. *Very Last First Time* (PS–1). Illus. by Ian Wallace. 1986, Macmillan $17.00 (0-689-50388-1). 32pp. Eva's first time alone under the ice searching for the shellfish that her Inuit people of northern Canada eat nearly turns into disaster when she dallies too long. (Rev: BCCB 9/86; BL 6/15/86; SLJ 5/86)

**3739** Angelou, Maya. *Kofi and His Magic* (1–4). Illus. by Margaret Courtney-Clarke. 1996, Crown $17.00 (0-517-70453-6). 48pp. A young West African boy uses his mental powers to move his family's home. (Rev: BL 3/1/97; SLJ 3/97)

**3740** Anholt, Laurence. *Camille and the Sunflowers: A Story About Vincent van Gogh* (PS–3). Illus. 1994, Barron's $14.95 (0-8120-6409-7). 32pp. Young Camille befriends the artist van Gogh when he comes to paint in his village in the Netherlands. (Rev: BL 12/1/94; SLJ 2/95)

**3741** Atwell, Debby. *Barn* (PS–3). Illus. 1996, Houghton $15.95 (0-395-78568-5). 32pp. Events in the life of a barn, from its erection in the late 1700s to the present day. (Rev: BL 10/1/96; SLJ 8/96*)

**3742** Avi. *Finding Providence: The Story of Roger Williams* (2–3). Illus. by James Watling. 1997, HarperCollins LB $14.89 (0-06-025294-4). 48pp. An easy-to-read book that tells, through the eyes of Roger Williams's daughter, the story of Williams's Boston trial and escape to the wilderness. (Rev: BCCB 3/97; BL 2/1/97; HB 5–6/97; SLJ 3/97)

**3743** Babbitt, Natalie. *Phoebe's Revolt* (K–3). Illus. by author. 1988, Farrar paper $3.95 (0-374-45792-1). 40pp. The story of a stubborn little girl set in the gaslight era.

**3744** Baker, Jeannie. *The Story of Rosy Dock* (K–3). Illus. 1995, Greenwillow LB $14.93 (0-688-11493-8). 32pp. In the outback of Australia, the plant ecology is disturbed when settlers introduce rosy dock, a plant with distinctive red seedpods. (Rev: BCCB 3/95; BL 4/1/95*; SLJ 5/95) [508.94]

**3745** Banim, Lisa. *American Dreams* (2–3). Illus. Series: Stories of the States. 1993, Silver Moon LB $13.95 (1-881889-34-3). 80pp. In this story set in California, the friendship between Jeannie and Amy, a Japanese American girl, is shattered when World War II breaks out. (Rev: SLJ 12/93)

**3746** Banks, Sara H. *A Net to Catch Time* (K–3). Illus. by Scott Cook. 1996, Knopf LB $17.99 (0-679-96673-0). 28pp. A typical day in the life of a boy living on the Sea Islands off Georgia. (Rev: BL 12/1/96; SLJ 1/97)

**3747** Barry, David. *The Rajah's Rice* (K–3). Illus. by Donna Perrone. 1994, W. H. Freeman $12.80 (0-7167-6568-3). 32pp. A girl in India outwits the rajah when she asks for a seemingly small reward of rice after she cures his elephants. (Rev: BCCB 2/95; BL 1/15/95)

**3748** Bartone, Elisa. *Peppe the Lamplighter* (2–4). Illus. by Ted Lewin. 1993, Lothrop LB $16.93 (0-688-10269-7); Morrow paper $4.95 (0-688-15469-7). 32pp. The story of an immigrant Italian boy who

is a lamplighter in turn-of-the-century New York City. (Rev: BCCB 5/93; BL 4/15/93; SLJ 7/93)

**3749** Baylor, Byrd. *One Small Blue Bead* (1–4). Illus. by Ronald Himler. 1992, Macmillan $16.00 (0-684-19334-5). 32pp. A story of an early tribe of cave dwellers in the American Southwest. First published in 1965. (Rev: BL 3/1/92; SLJ 4/92)

**3750** Bell, Lili. *The Sea Maidens of Japan* (K–4). Illus. by Erin M. Brammer. 1997, Ideals $14.95 (1-57102-095-0). 32pp. A Japanese girl who is afraid of diving is expected to become an ama — a woman who dives to the ocean floor to harvest seafood. (Rev: BCCB 5/97; BL 6/1–15/97; SLJ 6/97)

**3751** Bemelmans, Ludwig. *Madeline* (PS–3). Illus. by author. 1987, Viking paper $15.99 (0-670-81667-1). 32pp. The unforgettable Madeline in a pop-up-book format. (Rev: BL 11/15/87)

**3752** Bemelmans, Ludwig. *Madeline's Rescue* (K–3). Illus. by author. 1953, Puffin paper $4.99 (0-14-050207-6). 56pp. This Paris adventure of the inimitable Madeline won the 1954 Caldecott Medal. Also use: *Madeline and the Bad Hat* (1957); *Madeline* (1958); *Madeline and the Gypsies* (1959); *Madeline in London* (1961).

**3753** Benchley, Nathaniel. *George the Drummer Boy* (1–2). Illus. by Don Bolognese. 1977, HarperCollins LB $15.89 (0-06-020501-6). 64pp. The beginning of the American Revolution from the viewpoint of a young British soldier, told simply and dramatically.

**3754** Benchley, Nathaniel. *Sam the Minuteman* (2–4). Illus. by Arnold Lobel. 1969, HarperCollins LB $14.89 (0-06-020480-X); paper $3.75 (0-06-444107-5). 64pp. An easy-to-read book that gives information on the way of life at the beginning of the Revolution.

**3755** Beskow, Elsa. *Pelle's New Suit* (PS–3). Illus. by author. 1989, Gryphon $15.95 (0-86315-092-6). 16pp. A Swedish story of the steps in getting a new suit for a small boy, from shearing the lamb to tailoring.

**3756** Binch, Caroline. *Gregory Cool* (K–3). Illus. 1994, Dial paper $14.99 (0-8037-1577-3). 32pp. A story of an African American boy who visits his grandparents in their humble home in Tobago and has problems adjusting. (Rev: BCCB 9/94; BL 9/15/94; SLJ 9/94*)

**3757** Blos, Joan W. *The Heroine of the Titanic: A Tale Both True and Otherwise of the Life of Molly Brown* (1–4). Illus. by Tennessee Dixon. 1991, Morrow $16.00 (0-688-07546-0). 40pp. A picture-book biography of the boisterous survivor of the Titanic who later became a Colorado legend. (Rev: BCCB 9/91; BL 8/91; SLJ 9/91)

**3758** Blumberg, Rhoda. *Bloomers!* (K–4). Illus. by Mary Morgan. 1993, Macmillan LB $14.95 (0-02-711684-0). 32pp. A story that is based on fact of women who tried to become liberated by wearing balloon trousers, later called "bloomers." (Rev: BL 8/93) [305.42]

**3759** Booth, David. *The Dust Bowl* (K–4). Illus. by Karen Reczuch. 1997, Kids Can $16.95 (1-55074-295-7). 32pp. A story about a poor Canadian farm family living in a Western dust bowl during the 1930s. (Rev: BL 9/1/97; SLJ 12/97)

**3760** Borden, Louise. *Good-bye, Charles Lindbergh* (K–4). Illus. by Thomas B. Allen. 1998, Simon & Schuster paper $16.00 (0-689-81536-0). 40pp. Based on a true incident, this picture book tells of a young boy from Canton, Mississippi, and his encounter with the legendary Charles Lindbergh. (Rev: BL 3/1/98*; SLJ 3/98)

**3761** Boulton, Jane. *Only Opal: The Diary of a Young Girl* (1–4). Illus. by Barbara Cooney. 1994, Putnam $15.95 (0-399-21990-0). 32pp. This book is based on a real journal kept by a very young girl growing up in rural Oregon with a foster family at the turn of the century. (Rev: BCCB 6/94; BL 3/15/94*; HB 5–6/94; SLJ 5/94) [973]

**3762** Bradby, Marie. *More Than Anything Else* (K–3). Illus. by Chris K. Soentpiet. 1996, Orchard LB $16.99 (0-531-08764-6). 32pp. A fictionalized account of the childhood of Booker T. Washington, told in a picture book format. (Rev: BL 7/95; SLJ 11/95*)

**3763** Bresnick-Perry, Roslyn. *Leaving for America* (K–3). Illus. by Mira Reisberg. 1992, Children's Book Pr. LB $14.95 (0-89239-105-7). 32pp. Remembrances by the author, who left Russia in 1929 as a young child. (Rev: BCCB 2/93; BL 1/15/93; SLJ 2/93) [947]

**3764** *Brother Eagle, Sister Sky: A Message from Chief Seattle* (K–4). Illus. by Susan Jeffers. 1991, Dial LB $14.89 (0-8037-0963-3). 32pp. Striking drawings enhance the words of the leader of the Northwest Indian Nation in the 1850s. (Rev: BL 1/1/91; HB 11–12/91) [811.3]

**3765** Bunting, Eve. *Going Home* (K–3). Illus. by David Diaz. 1996, HarperCollins LB $14.89 (0-06-026297-4). 32pp. Carlos and his family leave their adopted home in California to visit their original home in Mexico. (Rev: BCCB 12/96; BL 10/1/96; SLJ 9/96)

**3766** Bunting, Eve. *Market Day* (PS–2). Illus. by Holly Berry. 1996, HarperCollins LB $14.89 (0-06-025368-1). 32pp. Market day in a small Irish town is an exciting event, particularly when the young narrator is given a penny by her father to spend. (Rev: BL 2/15/96*; SLJ 4/96)

**3767** Burke, Timothy R. *Tugboats in Action* (PS–2). Illus. 1993, Albert Whitman LB $15.95 (0-8075-8112-7). 32pp. Life aboard a tugboat on its journey on the Buffalo River to Lake Erie. (Rev: BCCB 12/93; BL 10/15/93; SLJ 1/94)

**3768** Carmi, Giora. *And Shira Imagined* (1–3). Illus. 1988, Jewish Publication Soc. $14.95 (0-8276-0288-X). 32pp. A young girl and her parents tour Israel.

**3769** Castaneda, Omar S. *Abuela's Weave* (K–3). Illus. by Enrique O. Sanchez. 1993, Lee $15.95 (1-880000-00-8). 32pp. In Guatemala, a young girl and her grandmother take their handicrafts to sell at a fiesta. (Rev: BL 8/93; SLJ 7/93)

**3770** Cech, John. *My Grandmother's Journey* (K–3). Illus. by Sharon McGinley-Nally. 1991, Macmillan LB $16.00 (0-02-718135-9). 40pp. A grandmother recalls the terrible life she had in Russia during the Revolution and World War II and how she came to freedom in the West. (Rev: BCCB 11/91; BL 8/91; SLJ 5/92)

**3771** Cherry, Lynne. *The Dragon and the Unicorn* (2–4). Illus. 1995, Harcourt $16.00 (0-15-224193-0). 40pp. The importance of conservation is shown in this medieval fantasy in which a dragon and a unicorn see their sacred forest destroyed by King Orlando and his men. (Rev: BL 1/1–15/96; SLJ 2/96)

**3772** Choi, Sook N. *Yunmi and Halmoni's Trip* (K–3). Illus. by Karen M. Dugan. 1997, Houghton $15.00 (0-395-81180-5). 32pp. Yunmi, a Korean American girl, goes to Korea for a visit with her grandmother. (Rev: BL 9/15/97; SLJ 10/97)

**3773** Claverie, Jean. *Little Lou* (2–3). Illus. 1990, Creative Ed. LB $16.95 (0-88682-329-3). 48pp. Little Lou describes how he was introduced to blues music when he was a child in the thirties. (Rev: BL 4/15/91)

**3774** Clements, Andrew. *Temple Cat* (K–3). Illus. by Kate Kiesler. 1996, Clarion $14.95 (0-395-69842-1). 32pp. A pampered temple cat in ancient Egypt finds happiness with a fisherman's family. (Rev: BCCB 2/96; BL 2/1/96; SLJ 3/96)

**3775** Coleman, Evelyn. *White Socks Only* (K–3). Illus. by Tyrone Geter. 1996, Albert Whitman LB $15.95 (0-8075-8955-1). 30pp. An elderly African American tells her granddaughter about her childhood in the segregated South. (Rev: BCCB 4/96; BL 2/15/96; SLJ 6/96)

**3776** Collier, Mary Jo, and Peter Collier. *The King's Giraffe* (1–3). Illus. by Stephane Poulin. 1996, Simon & Schuster $16.00 (0-689-80679-5). 40pp. In 1826, the pasha of Egypt sent the King of France an unusual gift: a giraffe. (Rev: BCCB 3/96; BL 6/1–15/96; SLJ 3/96)

**3777** Conway, Celeste. *Where Is Papa Now?* (1–3). Illus. by author. 1994, Boyds Mills $14.95 (1-56397-

130-5). This beautifully illustrated picture book follows the travels of a mid-19th-century New England sea captain. (Rev: BCCB 3/94; SLJ 3/94)

**3778** Cooney, Barbara. *Hattie and the Wild Waves: A Story from Brooklyn* (1–5). Illus. 1990, Viking paper $14.95 (0-670-83056-9). 40pp. A re-creation of a young girl's life growing up in turn-of-the-century Brooklyn and Manhattan. (Rev: BCCB 12/90*; BL 11/1/90*; HB 1–2/91*; SLJ 12/90)

**3779** Corpi, Lucha. *Where Fireflies Dance* (K–4). Illus. by Mira Reisberg. 1997, Children's Book Pr. $15.95 (0-89239-145-6). 32pp. The author remembers everyday incidents in her life growing up in a Mexican town. (Rev: BL 1/1–15/98; SLJ 12/97)

**3780** Covault, Ruth M. *Pablo and Pimienta/Pablo y Pimienta* (K–3). Illus. by Francisco Mora. 1994, Northland LB $14.95 (0-87358-588-7). 32pp. A bilingual story about the son of a Mexican migrant worker's family and how he gets lost in the desert. (Rev: BL 1/1/95)

**3781** Cowcher, Helen. *Whistling Thorn* (PS–3). Illus. 1993, Scholastic $14.95 (0-590-47299-2). 40pp. A nonfiction account of why the thorn trees of Africa's grasslands whistle when the wind blows through them. (Rev: BL 10/15/93; SLJ 10/93) [583]

**3782** Cowen-Fletcher, Jane. *It Takes a Village* (PS–1). Illus. 1994, Scholastic $15.95 (0-590-46573-2). 32pp. Yemi realizes that all the townspeople are concerned when her young brother wanders off at market time in this book that explores life in a West African village. (Rev: BL 1/1/94; SLJ 3/94)

**3783** Daly, Niki. *Not So Fast, Songololo* (PS–K). Illus. by author. 1986, Simon & Schuster $16.00 (0-689-50367-9); Puffin paper $4.95 (0-689-80154-8). 32pp. A South African boy who does everything slowly puts on a pair of red-striped sneakers and walks fast and proud. (Rev: BCCB 4/86; BL 4/1/86; SLJ 5/86)

**3784** Delacre, Lulu. *Vejigante Masquerader* (1–4). Illus. 1993, Scholastic $15.95 (0-590-45776-4). 40pp. In Puerto Rico, Ramon is looking forward to being a masquerader in the carnival. (Rev: BL 3/15/93)

**3785** Delgado, María Isabel. *Chave's Memories/Los Recuerdos de Chave* (PS–3). Illus. by Yvonne Symank. 1996, Piñata $14.95 (1-55885-084-8). A bilingual picture book in which a woman recalls her trips as a child from Brownsville, Texas, to her grandparents' ranch in northern Mexico. (Rev: SLJ 12/96)

**3786** Denslow, Sharon P. *Radio Boy* (K–3). Illus. by Alec Gillman. 1995, Simon & Schuster $15.00 (0-689-80295-1). 32pp. The childhood in Kentucky in the 1870s of Nathan B. Stubblefield, who later invented the radio. (Rev: BL 10/1/95; SLJ 9/95)

**3787** Dorros, Arthur. *This Is My House* (K–2). Illus. by author. 1992, Scholastic $15.95 (0-590-45302-5). Various houses from around the world that represent different peoples are pictured and identified in this book. (Rev: SLJ 9/92) [728]

**3788** Edwards, Pamela Duncan. *Barefoot: Escape on the Underground Railroad* (K–4). Illus. by Henry Cole. 1997, HarperCollins LB $14.89 (0-06-027138-8). 32pp. The birds and other animals in a forest seem to work together to help an escaped slave. (Rev: BL 2/15/97; SLJ 2/97*)

**3789** Emberley, Michael. *Welcome Back Sun* (K–3). Illus. 1993, Little, Brown $14.95 (0-316-23647-0). 32pp. During the long, dark Norwegian winter, a young girl sets out to find the sun. (Rev: BCCB 10/93; BL 10/15/93; SLJ 1/94*)

**3790** Emberley, Rebecca. *Taking a Walk/Caminando: A Book in Two Languages/Una Libra en Dos Lenguas* (1–3). Illus. 1994, Little, Brown paper $5.95 (0-316-23471-0). 32pp. Bright artwork and simple phrases introduce Spanish to English readers, and vice versa. Also use the bilingual *My House/Mi Casa* (1990). (Rev: BL 6/15/90; HB 9–10/90; SLJ 8/90)

**3791** Enderle, Judith R., and Stephanie G. Tessler. *Francis: The Earthquake Dog* (K–3). Illus. by Brooke Scudder. 1996, Chronicle $13.95 (0-8118-0630-8). 32pp. A pup is miraculously saved during the San Francisco earthquake of 1906. (Rev: BL 6/1–15/96; SLJ 7/96)

**3792** Ernst, Lisa Campbell. *Sam Johnson and the Blue Ribbon Quilt* (K–3). Illus. by author. 1983, Lothrop LB $15.93 (0-688-01517-4); Morrow paper $4.95 (0-688-11505-5). 32pp. The men and the women vie for honors in the quilting contest.

**3793** Ets, Marie Hall. *Gilberto and the Wind* (PS–1). Illus. by author. 1963, Puffin paper $4.99 (0-14-050276-9). 32pp. A small Mexican boy learns to play with and understand the moods of the wind.

**3794** Feder, Paula K. *The Feather-Bed Journey* (K–3). Illus. by Stacey Schuett. 1995, Albert Whitman LB $15.95 (0-8075-2330-5). 32pp. Grandma tells her grandchildren how her favorite feather pillow was once part of a large feather bed that kept her warm in a Jewish ghetto during World War II. (Rev: BCCB 12/95; BL 10/15/95; SLJ 11/95)

**3795** Feeney, Stephanie. *A Is for Aloha* (PS–K). Photos by Jeff Reese. 1985, Univ. of Hawaii Pr. $9.95 (0-8248-0722-7). A simple introduction to Hawaii and its many cultures.

**3796** Flack, Marjorie. *The Story About Ping* (PS–3). Illus. by Kurt Wiese. 1933, Puffin paper $4.99 (0-14-050241-6). 32pp. A little Peking duck spends a harrowing night on the Yangtze River after he is accidentally separated from his family.

**3797** Fleming, Candace. *Gabriella's Song* (PS–3). Illus. by Giselle Potter. 1997, Simon & Schuster $16.00 (0-689-80973-5). 40pp. The song that Gabriella hums on the streets of Venice, Italy, is so infectious that soon everyone is singing it. (Rev: BL 12/1/97; SLJ 11/97*)

**3798** Flora, James. *The Fabulous Firework Family* (K–2). Illus. 1994, Macmillan paper $14.95 (0-689-50596-5). 32pp. The Fabulous Firework Family makes fireworks for a village's saint's day in this happy picture book set in Mexico. (Rev: BL 5/1/94; SLJ 4/94)

**3799** Flournoy, Valerie. *Tanya's Reunion* (K–3). Illus. by Jerry Pinkney. 1995, Dial paper $15.89 (0-8037-1605-2). 40pp. Tanya visits the family farm with her grandmother and learns what it was like in the good old days. (Rev: BCCB 10/95; BL 9/1/95; HB 9–10/95; SLJ 9/95)

**3800** Franklin, Kristine L. *The Wolfhound* (K–3). Illus. by Kris Waldherr. 1996, Lothrop LB $15.93 (0-688-13675-3). 32pp. In czarist Russia, Pavel encounters problems when he rescues a wolfhound, a symbol of royalty. (Rev: BL 11/1/96; SLJ 2/97)

**3801** Friedrich, Elizabeth. *Leah's Pony* (K–3). Illus. by Michael Garland. 1996, Boyds Mills $14.95 (1-56397-189-5). 32pp. Conditions in the Dust Bowl are so bad for Leah's family that they must sell their stock and equipment to survive. (Rev: BL 3/1/96; SLJ 3/96*)

**3802** Garaway, Margaret K. *Ashkii and His Grandfather* (K–3). Illus. by Harry Warren. 1995, Old Hogan $14.95 (0-963-88517-0); paper $8.95 (0-963-88516-2). 33pp. A young Navajo boy helps his grandfather at summer sheep camp. (Rev: BL 3/1/90)

**3803** Garay, Luis. *The Long Road* (PS–4). Illus. 1997, Tundra $15.95 (0-88776-408-8). 32pp. The experiences of a Latin American boy and his mother, who are forced to flee their village and seek asylum in another country. (Rev: BL 11/1/97; SLJ 1/98)

**3804** Garay, Luis. *Pedrito's Day* (K–3). Illus. 1997, Orchard $14.95 (0-531-09522-3). 32pp. Pedrito, a Mexican boy, is heartbroken when he loses the money he had saved to buy a bicycle. (Rev: BL 3/1/97; SLJ 4/97)

**3805** George, Jean Craighead. *Arctic Son* (K–2). Illus. by Wendell Minor. 1997, Hyperion LB $15.49 (0-7868-2255-4). 32pp. Luke, whose Eskimo name is Kupaaq, participates in many of his people's activities during the period of the Arctic sun. (Rev: BL 9/1/97; SLJ 11/97)

**3806** Gerrard, Jean. *Matilda Jane* (K–3). Illus. by Roy Gerrard. 1983, Farrar $15.00 (0-374-34865-0). 32pp. A little Victorian girl spends a week at the seashore.

**3807** Gerrard, Roy. *Croco'Nile* (K–3). Illus. 1994, Farrar $15.00 (0-374-31659-7). 32pp. A picture book about 2 talented youngsters growing up in ancient Egypt. (Rev: BCCB 1/95; BL 10/15/94; SLJ 11/94)

**3808** Gerrard, Roy. *Mik's Mammoth* (K–3). Illus. 1990, Farrar $15.00 (0-374-31891-3). 32pp. Mik the caveman is called a coward, but he proves himself when he becomes separated from the others. (Rev: BCCB 11/90*; BL 12/1/90; SLJ 1/91)

**3809** Gerrard, Roy. *Sir Cedric* (1–4). Illus. by author. 1984, Farrar $14.95 (0-374-36959-3); paper $4.95 (0-374-46659-9). 32pp. A spoof on knights and the age of chivalry.

**3810** Gershator, Phillis. *Sweet, Sweet Fig Banana* (PS–1). Illus. by Fritz Millevoix. 1996, Albert Whitman LB $14.95 (0-8075-7693-X). 26pp. In this Caribbean tale, young Soto sells many of the bananas he has grown but saves some as gifts for his friends. (Rev: BL 2/15/96; SLJ 7/96)

**3811** Gershator, Phillis, and David Gershator. *Greetings, Sun* (PS–2). Illus. by Synthia Saint James. 1998, DK Publg. $15.95 (0-7894-2482-7). In this book set on a Caribbean island, 2 black children greet all of the things in life that they love. (Rev: BL 3/15/98)

**3812** Gerstein, Mordicai. *The Mountains of Tibet* (K–3). Illus. by author. 1989, HarperCollins paper $5.95 (0-06-443211-4). 32pp. A woodcutter spends his life in a Tibetan valley in this story of reincarnation. (Rev: BL 11/15/87; HB 11–12/87; SLJ 11/87)

**3813** Glass, Andrew. *Folks Call Me Appleseed John* (1–4). Illus. 1995, Doubleday $15.95 (0-385-32045-0). 42pp. A fictionalized account of how young Nathaniel is cared for by Indians when his half-brother Johnny Appleseed must go for provisions. (Rev: BL 9/1/95; SLJ 8/95*)

**3814** Glass, Andrew. *The Sweetwater Run: The Story of Buffalo Bill Cody and the Pony Express* (1–4). Illus. 1996, Doubleday $15.95 (0-385-32220-8). 48pp. Young Buffalo Bill saves the day when he takes the place of a stricken messenger boy. (Rev: BCCB 12/96; BL 12/15/96; SLJ 11/96)

**3815** Goble, Paul. *Death of the Iron Horse* (K–2). Illus. by author. 1993, Simon & Schuster paper $4.95 (0-689-71686-9). 32pp. Rail sabotage from the Indian point of view, set in 1867. (Rev: BCCB 4/87; BL 4/1/87; HB 5–6/87)

**3816** Goodall, John S. *The Story of a Farm* (2–5). Illus. by author. 1989, Macmillan $14.95 (0-689-50479-9). Detailing the changing centuries on an English farm. (Rev: BL 5/15/89; HB 5–6/89; SLJ 5/89)

**3817** Goodall, John S. *The Story of a Main Street* (K–3). Illus. by author. 1987, Macmillan $14.95 (0-

689-50436-5). 60pp. The history of "main street" in a town is chronicled without words. (Rev: BL 12/1/87; SLJ 9/87)

**3818**   Goode, Diane. *Mama's Perfect Present* (K–3). Illus. 1996, Dutton paper $15.99 (0-525-45493-4). 32pp. Two sisters and their pet dachshund, Zaza, search Paris for a present for their mother. (Rev: BL 7/96*; SLJ 9/96)

**3819**   Goode, Diane. *Where's Our Mama?* (PS–2). Illus. 1991, Dutton paper $13.95 (0-525-44770-9). 32pp. Two French children in Paris become alarmed when their mother runs off in search of her lost hat. (Rev: BCCB 9/91; BL 9/1/91; HB 11–12/91; SLJ 11/91*)

**3820**   Graham, Steve. *Dear Old Donegal* (PS–2). Illus. by John O'Brien. 1996, Clarion $15.95 (0-395-68187-1). 32pp. A colorful picture book version of the song about the Irishman who succeeded in the New World and later was welcomed back to his former home in Donegal. (Rev: BL 2/1/96; SLJ 4/96)

**3821**   Green, Norma B. *The Hole in the Dike* (K–2). Illus. by Eric Carle. 1975, Scholastic paper $4.95 (0-590-46146-X). 32pp. Brilliant illustrations accompany this simple retelling of the Mary Mapes Dodge story of the boy who put his finger in the dike and saved his Dutch town.

**3822**   Greenberg, Melanie H. *Aunt Lilly's Laundromat* (K–2). Illus. 1994, Dutton paper $13.99 (0-525-45211-7). 24pp. Lilly, a Haitian who has worked most of her life in Brooklyn, recalls her previous life on her island home. (Rev: BL 9/1/94; SLJ 2/95)

**3823**   Greenfield, Eloise. *Africa Dream* (K–3). Illus. by Carole Byard. 1989, HarperCollins LB $14.89 (0-690-04776-2); paper $4.95 (0-06-443277-7). 32pp. In this reissued picture book, a young black girl dreams about visiting her granddaddy's African village.

**3824**   Gregory, Valiska. *Kate's Giants* (PS–4). Illus. by Virginia Austin. 1995, Candlewick $15.99 (1-56402-299-4); paper $5.99 (0-7636-0151-9). 32pp. Kate believes that there are unfriendly monsters hiding behind the door that leads to the attic. (Rev: BL 10/15/95; SLJ 12/95)

**3825**   Grossman, Patricia. *Saturday Market* (K–3). Illus. by Enrique O. Sanchez. 1994, Lothrop LB $14.93 (0-688-12177-2). 32pp. Various people, like Miguel and his chile peppers, have articles to sell at the colorful Saturday market in a Mexican town. (Rev: BL 9/1/94; SLJ 9/94)

**3826**   Haddon, Mark. *The Sea of Tranquillity* (1–3). Illus. by Christian Birmingham. 1996, Harcourt $16.00 (0-15-201285-0). A man looks back at his childhood, when one night he stayed up late to watch the moon landing on TV. (Rev: SLJ 9/96)

**3827**   Hall, Donald. *Ox-Cart Man* (K–3). Illus. by Barbara Cooney. 1979, Puffin paper $5.99 (0-14-050441-9). 40pp. The cycle of production and sale of goods in 19th-century New England is pictured in human terms. Caldecott Medal winner, 1980.

**3828**   Hanson, Regina. *The Face at the Window* (1–3). Illus. by Linda Saport. 1997, Clarion $14.95 (0-395-78625-8). 32pp. A little girl in Jamaica is afraid of the old neighbor lady until her parents take the youngster to meet her. (Rev: BCCB 5/97; BL 6/1–15/97; SLJ 6/97)

**3829**   Harris, Christine. *The Silver Path* (K–3). Illus. by Helen Ong. 1994, Boyds Mills $14.95 (1-56397-338-3). This book is actually a letter in which Niko tells of the hardships his family has endured living under a savage dictatorship. (Rev: SLJ 8/94)

**3830**   Harvey, Brett. *My Prairie Year: Based on the Diary of Elenore Plaisted* (K–3). Illus. by Deborah Kogan Ray. 1986, Holiday LB $15.95 (0-8234-0604-0). 40pp. The story from the diary of the author's grandmother of her 1889 homesteading experience in the Dakota Territory. (Rev: BCCB 12/86; BL 11/1/86; SLJ 11/86)

**3831**   Hathorn, Libby. *Sky Sash So Blue* (K–3). Illus. by Benny Andrews. 1998, Simon & Schuster $16.00 (0-689-81090-3). 32pp. A slave secretly sews for her daughter a wedding dress made out of scraps. (Rev: BL 2/15/98)

**3832**   Heide, Florence Parry, and Judith Heide Gilliland. *The Day of Ahmed's Secret* (PS–3). Illus. by Ted Lewin. 1990, Lothrop LB $15.93 (0-688-08895-3). 32pp. Ahmed, a young boy in present-day Cairo, has a job delivering bottled gas. (Rev: BCCB 10/90; BL 9/1/90*; HB 11–12/90; SLJ 8/90*)

**3833**   Heide, Florence Parry, and Judith Heide Gilliland. *Sami and the Time of the Troubles* (1–4). Illus. by Ted Lewin. 1992, Houghton $15.95 (0-395-55964-2). 40pp. This compelling picture book shows a modern Beirut family caught up in the horrors of war. (Rev: BL 4/1/92*; HB 7–8/92; SLJ 5/92*)

**3834**   Hendershot, Judith. *In Coal Country* (1–3). Illus. by Thomas B. Allen. 1987, Knopf $16.00 (0-394-88190-7). 48pp. The story of life in the coal country during the 1930s. (Rev: BCCB 6/87; BL 4/1/87; HB 5–6/87)

**3835**   Hidaka, Masako. *Girl from the Snow Country* (K–2). Trans. by Amanda Mayer Stinchecum. Illus. 1986, Kane/Miller $13.95 (0-916291-06-5). 32pp. Her wish comes true when Mi-chan makes snow bunnies and needs something to make red eyes. (Rev: BL 2/1/87; SLJ 1/87)

**3836**   Hippely, Hilary H. *A Song for Lena* (PS–2). Illus. by Leslie Baker. 1996, Simon & Schuster paper $16.00 (0-689-80763-5). 32pp. In old Hungary, a mother gives a beggar a sample of her delicious strudel, with unforeseen consequences. (Rev: BL 11/1/96; SLJ 10/96)

**3837** Hirschi, Ron. *Seya's Song* (K–3). Illus. by Constance R. Bergum. 1992, Sasquatch $14.95 (0-912365-62-5); paper $7.95 (0-912365-91-9). 32pp. A young Native American girl tells of the salmon returning to the rivers in the nearly lost language of S'Kiallam. (Rev: BL 1/1/93; SLJ 5/93) [979]

**3838** Hodges, Margaret. *Brother Francis and the Friendly Beasts* (K–3). Illus. by Ted Lewin. 1991, Macmillan $14.95 (0-684-19173-3). 32pp. The story of the son of a merchant who rejected riches for prayer. (Rev: BCCB 11/91; BL 8/91; HB 9–10/91; SLJ 12/91) [271]

**3839** Hoffman, Mary. *Boundless Grace* (PS–3). Illus. by Caroline Binch. 1995, Dial paper $14.99 (0-8037-1715-6). 32pp. Grace's father sends airplane tickets for her to visit him in Gambia and meet his new family. (Rev: BCCB 6/95; BL 4/15/95; HB 7–8/95; SLJ 5/95*)

**3840** Hong, Lily T. *The Empress and the Silkworm* (PS–3). Illus. 1995, Albert Whitman LB $16.95 (0-8075-2009-8). 32pp. A Chinese empress uses the silk threads she finds when she discovers the cocoons of silkworms to make a robe for the emperor. (Rev: BCCB 12/95; BL 9/15/95; SLJ 11/95)

**3841** Hort, Lenny. *The Boy Who Held Back the Sea* (PS–2). Illus. by Thomas Locker. 1987, Dial $15.99 (0-8037-0406-2); Puffin paper $4.95 (0-8037-1049-6). 32pp. Commanding landscapes highlight this retelling of the little Dutch boy who saves Holland. (Rev: BL 9/15/87; SLJ 11/87)

**3842** Howard, Elizabeth F. *Papa Tells Chita a Story* (PS–1). Illus. by Floyd Cooper. 1995, Simon & Schuster paper $15.00 (0-02-744623-9). 28pp. Papa tells Chita of his experiences during the Spanish-American War. A sequel to *Chita's Christmas Tree* (1989). (Rev: BL 4/1/95; HB 9–10/95; SLJ 6/95)

**3843** Howard, Ellen. *The Log Cabin Quilt* (K–3). Illus. by Ronald Himler. 1996, Holiday LB $15.95 (0-8234-1247-4). 28pp. Quilting scraps help chink the holes in a log cabin in this story of Western pioneers. (Rev: BCCB 10/96; BL 12/15/96; SLJ 10/96)

**3844** Hughes, Monica. *A Handful of Seeds* (K–3). Illus. by Luis Garay. 1996, Orchard $14.95 (0-531-09498-7). 32pp. When Concepcion moves from the country to the city, she brings some seeds with her to start a garden in the barrio. (Rev: BCCB 6/96; BL 4/1/96; SLJ 3/96)

**3845** Isadora, Rachel. *At the Crossroads* (PS–3). Illus. 1991, Greenwillow LB $15.93 (0-688-05271-1). 32pp. Life in a black shanty town in South Africa is revealed in a story about fathers returning from the mines. (Rev: BCCB 5/91; BL 4/15/91*; HB 7–8/91; SLJ 6/91*)

**3846** Johnson, Angela. *The Rolling Store* (K–3). Illus. by Peter Catalanotto. 1997, Orchard LB $16.99 (0-531-33015-X). 32pp. A young African American girl tells her friend about the traveling store in a truck that used to visit their community during her grandfather's childhood. (Rev: BCCB 5/97; BL 2/15/97; SLJ 4/97)

**3847** Johnson, Dinah. *All Around Town: The Photographs of Richard Samuel Roberts* (K–4). Photos by Richard S. Roberts. 1998, Holt $15.95 (0-8050-5456-1). 32pp. This album of photos depicts the daily lives of African Americans living in Columbia, South Carolina, during the 1920s and 1930s. (Rev: BL 2/15/98; SLJ 3/98) [779]

**3848** Johnson, Dolores. *Now Let Me Fly: The Story of a Slave Family* (K–4). Illus. 1993, Macmillan LB $15.00 (0-02-747699-5). 32pp. The inhuman story of an African girl who is sold into slavery in the United States, where she raises a family. (Rev: BCCB 11/93; BL 10/15/93; SLJ 3/94)

**3849** Johnson, Dolores. *Seminole Diary: Remembrances of a Slave* (1–3). Illus. 1994, Macmillan paper $16.00 (0-02-747848-3). 32pp. Excerpts from a diary kept by a slave girl who escaped to southern Florida, where she lived with the Seminole Indians. (Rev: BCCB 10/94; BL 12/1/94; SLJ 11/94) [975.9]

**3850** Johnston, Tony. *How Many Miles to Jacksonville?* (PS–3). Illus. by Bart Forbes. 1996, Putnam $15.95 (0-399-22615-X). 32pp. Simple pleasures from bygone times are featured in this story set in the East Texas town of Jacksonville. (Rev: BL 10/15/96; SLJ 12/96)

**3851** Johnston, Tony. *The Magic Maguey* (PS–3). Illus. by Elisa Kleven. 1996, Harcourt $15.00 (0-15-250988-7). 32pp. Miguel tries to save from destruction the wonderful maguey tree, which supplies so many comforts for his family. (Rev: BL 10/15/96)

**3852** Johnston, Tony. *The Wagon* (2–3). Illus. by James E. Ransome. 1996, Morrow LB $15.93 (0-688-13537-4). 40pp. A boy born into slavery celebrates his freedom at the time of Lincoln's tragic death. (Rev: BCCB 9/96; BL 1/1–15/97; SLJ 3/97)

**3853** Kalman, Maira. *Sayonara, Mrs. Kackleman* (K–3). Illus. 1989, Viking paper $16.99 (0-670-82945-5). 40pp. Japan is introduced through the wild and woolly adventures of an American tourist. (Rev: BCCB 11/89; BL 11/15/89; SLJ 1/90)

**3854** Kerley, Barbara. *Songs of Papa's Island* (K–3). Illus. by Katherine Tillotson. 1995, Houghton $14.95 (0-395-71548-2). 59pp. A mother tells her child about the wildlife on the island in the Pacific where she lived while she was pregnant. (Rev: SLJ 10/95)

**3855** Khalsa, Dayal Kaur. *Cowboy Dreams* (K–3). Illus. 1990, Crown LB $18.99 (0-517-57491-8). 28pp. The story of a city girl's burning desire to be a cowgirl in the Old West. (Rev: BCCB 7–8/90; BL 6/1/90*; HB 9–10/90; SLJ 8/90)

**3856** Kidd, Richard. *Almost Famous Daisy!* (PS–3). Illus. 1996, Simon & Schuster paper $16.00 (0-689-80390-7). 32pp. Daisy visits the sites where painters like van Gogh and Monet found their inspiration so that she can begin work on her own masterpiece. (Rev: BL 4/15/96; SLJ 9/96)

**3857** Kinsey-Warnock, Natalie. *Wilderness Cat* (K–2). Illus. by Mark Graham. 1992, Dutton paper $14.99 (0-525-65068-7). 32pp. A cat travels 50 miles to rejoin the family that left him in Vermont when they moved to Canada. (Rev: BL 8/92; HB 3–4/93; SLJ 10/92)

**3858** Kirk, Daniel. *Breakfast at the Liberty Diner* (K–3). Illus. 1997, Hyperion LB $15.49 (0-7868-2243-0). 32pp. Bobby and his mother and baby brother have a meal at a busy diner during the 1940s and are surprised by a visit from President Roosevelt. (Rev: BL 11/1/97; SLJ 11/97)

**3859** Knight, Margy B. *Talking Walls* (3–5). Illus. by Anne S. O'Brien. 1992, Tilbury $17.95 (0-88448-102-6). 40pp. Prehistoric paintings on walls in Australia and notable walls from 6 continents introduce children to the world and its many cultures. (Rev: BL 8/92*; SLJ 9/92) [900]

**3860** Kroeger, Mary Kay, and Louise Borden. *Paperboy* (K–4). Illus. by Ted Lewin. 1996, Clarion $16.95 (0-395-64482-8). 32pp. In 1927 Cincinnati, a young paperboy has trouble selling his newspapers when boxing champ Jack Dempsey loses the prizefight. (Rev: BCCB 3/96; BL 3/15/96; HB 9–10/96; SLJ 8/96*)

**3861** Kroll, Virginia. *Africa Brothers and Sisters* (PS–2). Illus. by Vanessa French. 1992, Macmillan $15.00 (0-02-751166-9). 32pp. Father and son engage in a conservation/fact-finding game regarding contemporary Africa. (Rev: BL 2/15/93)

**3862** Kroll, Virginia. *A Carp for Kimiko* (PS–2). Illus. by Katherine Roundtree. 1993, Charlesbridge LB $15.88 (0-88106-413-0). 32pp. Although according to Japanese tradition girls can't fly kites, Kimiko gets a second-best present from her parents. (Rev: BL 12/1/93; SLJ 3/94)

**3863** Kroll, Virginia. *Sweet Magnolia* (1–3). Illus. by Laura Jacques. 1995, Charlesbridge LB $15.88 (0-88106-416-5); paper $6.95 (0-88106-414-9). When Denise visits her grandmother, a naturalist, in Louisiana, she learns about the flora and fauna of the swamps and tastes Cajun food. (Rev: SLJ 2/96)

**3864** Krull, Kathleen, and Enrique O. Sanchez. *Maria Molina and the Days of the Dead* (PS–2). Illus. 1994, Macmillan paper $15.95 (0-02-750999-0). 32pp. A Mexican family prepares for the celebra-

tion of the Day of the Dead and then participates in the festivities. (Rev: BL 10/15/94; SLJ 12/94)

**3865** Kurtz, Jane, and Christopher Kurtz. *Only a Pigeon* (PS–4). Illus. by E. B. Lewis. 1997, Simon & Schuster paper $16.00 (0-689-80077-0). 40pp. A little boy growing up in Addis Ababa, Ethiopia, takes pride in caring for some homing pigeons. (Rev: BCCB 7–8/97; BL 6/1–15/97; SLJ 6/97)

**3866** Lamorisse, Albert. *The Red Balloon* (1–3). Illus. by author. 1967, Doubleday $16.95 (0-385-00343-9); paper $10.95 (0-385-14297-8). 45pp. Pascal possesses a magic balloon that leads him on a tour of Paris, and he must defend the balloon from a gang of boys bent on bursting it.

**3867** Lattimore, Eleanor F. *Little Pear* (K–3). Illus. by author. 1992, Buccaneer LB $14.95 (0-89966-917-4); Harcourt paper $3.95 (0-15-652799-5). 106pp. A young boy growing up in China during the 1920s.

**3868** Lee, Jeanne M. *Silent Lotus* (K–3). Illus. 1991, Farrar $14.95 (0-374-36911-9). 32pp. Lotus, a deaf and mute Cambodian child, finds a method of communication through temple dancing. (Rev: BCCB 12/91; BL 11/15/91; HB 1–2/92; SLJ 12/91)

**3869** Lester, Alison. *My Farm* (K–4). Illus. 1994, Houghton $14.95 (0-395-68193-6). 32pp. The author recalls her childhood on an Australian farm — the chores, the cattle, and the joy of receiving a palomino pony at Christmas. (Rev: BCCB 7–8/94; BL 7/94; SLJ 9/94*) [630]

**3870** Levine, Ellen. *The Tree That Would Not Die* (1–4). Illus. by Ted Rand. 1995, Scholastic $14.95 (0-590-43724-0). 32pp. The story of the 400-year-old Treaty Oak in Texas and the important historical events that it witnessed. (Rev: BCCB 10/95; BL 11/1/95*; SLJ 12/95) [813]

**3871** Levinson, Riki. *Our Home Is the Sea* (PS–2). Illus. by Dennis Luzak. 1988, Puffin paper $4.99 (0-14-054552-2). 32pp. A young boy wants to be a fisherman like his father, in this story set off the shores of Hong Kong. (Rev: BCCB 1/89; HB 1–2/89; SLJ 11/88)

**3872** Levitin, Sonia. *Boom Town* (PS–3). Illus. by Cat B. Smith. 1998, Orchard LB $16.99 (0-531-33043-5). 40pp. In gold rush California, Amanda gets rich making wonderful gooseberry pies. A companion to *Nine for California* (1996). (Rev: BL 2/15/98; SLJ 3/98)

**3873** Levitin, Sonia. *Nine for California* (K–3). Illus. by Cat B. Smith. 1996, Orchard LB $17.99 (0-531-08877-4). Ma and her 5 children travel by stagecoach in the late 1800s to join their father in California's gold fields. (Rev: BCCB 12/96; SLJ 9/96*)

**3874** Levitin, Sonia. *A Piece of Home* (PS–3). Illus. by Juan Wijngaard. 1996, Dial paper $14.89 (0-

8037-1626-5). 32pp. In a contemporary setting, Gregor and his family leave Russia to live in the United States. (Rev: BCCB 1/97; BL 11/15/96; SLJ 12/96)

**3875** Lewin, Hugh. *Jafta* (K–3). Illus. by Lisa Kopper. 1983, Lerner paper $4.95 (0-87614-494-6). 24pp. There are 6 volumes in this set that are about a black South African child and his father. Others are: *Jafta's Father* (1983); *Jafta's Mother* (1983); *Jafta: The Journey* (1984); *Jafta: The Town* (1984); *Jafta and the Wedding* (1988).

**3876** Lieberman, Syd. *The Wise Shoemaker of Studena* (K–3). Illus. by Martin Lemelman. 1994, Jewish Publication Soc. $15.95 (0-8276-0509-9). 32pp. Samuel learns not to judge people by their appearances when he offends the disreputable-looking wise man Yossi. (Rev: BL 10/15/94)

**3877** Lied, Kate. *Potato: A Tale from the Great Depression* (K–3). Illus. by Lisa Campbell Ernst. 1997, National Geographic $16.00 (0-7922-3521-5). 32pp. A story about the Great Depression in which a family is forced to leave its home to pick potatoes in Idaho. (Rev: BL 4/1/97; HB 5–6, 9–10/97; SLJ 7/97)

**3878** Lindbergh, Reeve. *Johnny Appleseed* (1–3). Illus. by Kathy Jakobsen. 1990, Little, Brown $16.95 (0-316-52618-5). 32pp. Fact and fancy mingle in this story about Johnny Appleseed. (Rev: BCCB 10/90; BL 9/1/90*; HB 9–10/90*; SLJ 9/90*)

**3879** Lindgren, Astrid. *The Tomten* (PS–2). Illus. by Harald Wiberg. 1997, Putnam paper $5.99 (0-698-11591-0). 32pp. The friendly troll speaks in Tomten language only animals and children understand. By the same author, illustrator, and publisher: *The Tomten and the Fox* (1989).

**3880** Little, Mimi O. *Yoshiko and the Foreigner* (K–4). Illus. 1996, Farrar $16.00 (0-374-32448-4). 32pp. A love story about an African American soldier and the Japanese girl he meets in Tokyo. (Rev: BL 11/15/96; HB 11–12/96; SLJ 1/97)

**3881** Littlesugar, Amy. *Jonkonnu* (2–4). Illus. by Ian Schoenherr. 1997, Putnam $15.95 (0-399-22831-4). 32pp. A story, based on fact, about a trip the artist Winslow Homer took to Virginia to make studies of African Americans for a painting he was planning. (Rev: BL 1/1–15/98; SLJ 2/98)

**3882** Locker, Thomas. *The Land of Gray Wolf* (K–3). Illus. 1991, Dial LB $15.89 (0-8037-0937-4). 32pp. White men move in and spoil the natural paradise that the Indians once owned. (Rev: BL 5/15/91; SLJ 7/91)

**3883** London, Jonathan. *Ali, Child of the Desert* (K–4). Illus. by Ted Lewin. 1997, Lothrop LB $15.93 (0-688-12561-1). 32pp. Ali and his camel, Jabad, survive in the desert after a terrible dust storm separates them from the rest of their party. (Rev: BCCB 6/97; BL 3/1/97; SLJ 5/97)

**3884** London, Jonathan. *The Village Basket Weaver* (PS–3). Illus. by George Crespo. 1996, Dutton paper $14.99 (0-525-45314-8). 32pp. In Belize, a young boy learns about his people's traditions from his aged grandfather. (Rev: BL 8/96; SLJ 7/96)

**3885** Luenn, Nancy. *Nessa's Fish* (PS–3). Illus. by Neil Waldman. 1990, Macmillan $15.00 (0-689-31477-9). 32pp. When her grandmother becomes ill during an ice-fishing expedition, an Inuit girl must fight off the attacks of several animals. (Rev: BL 3/1/90*; SLJ 3/90)

**3886** Luenn, Nancy. *Nessa's Story* (K–3). Illus. by Neil Waldman. 1994, Atheneum $14.95 (0-689-31782-4). While walking in the tundra, an Eskimo girl uses her imagination and makes up a story similar to the ones that her grandmother frequently tells. (Rev: SLJ 4/94)

**3887** Lydon, Kerry Raines. *A Birthday for Blue* (K–3). Illus. by Michael Hays. 1989, Whitman LB $14.95 (0-8075-0774-1). 32pp. A pioneer boy spends his seventh birthday traveling in a covered wagon along the Cumberland Road. (Rev: BCCB 5/89; BL 4/1/89; SLJ 5/89)

**3888** Lyon, George E. *Cecil's Story* (K–2). Illus. by Peter Catalanotto. 1991, Watts LB $16.99 (0-531-08512-0). 32pp. A lonely boy does his farm work as a long blue-gray line of soldiers passes on the horizon in the Civil War. (Rev: BCCB 3/91; BL 1/1/91*; HB 5–6/91; SLJ 4/91*)

**3889** Lyon, George E. *Dreamplace* (K–4). Illus. by Peter Catalanotto. 1993, Orchard $15.95 (0-531-05466-7); paper $6.95 (0-531-07101-4). 32pp. A poetic text about a girl who sees the 800-year-old site of the Anasazi and dreams of when the tribe lived there long ago. (Rev: BCCB 3/93; BL 3/15/93*; HB 3–4/93; SLJ 3/93*)

**3890** McClintock, Barbara. *The Fantastic Drawings of Danielle* (PS–2). Illus. 1996, Houghton $17.00 (0-395-73980-2). 32pp. In 19th-century Paris, Danielle astounds everyone with her imaginative drawings. (Rev: BCCB 2/97; BL 10/15/96; SLJ 9/96)

**3891** McCully, Emily Arnold. *Beautiful Warrior: The Legend of the Nun's Kung Fu* (K–4). Illus. 1998, Scholastic $16.95 (0-590-37487-7). 40pp. In this beautiful picture book, 2 women learn kung fu and use it in different ways in 17th-century China. (Rev: BL 2/1/98; SLJ 2/98*)

**3892** McCully, Emily Arnold. *Mirette on the High Wire* (PS–2). Illus. 1992, Putnam $15.95 (0-399-22130-1). 32pp. Set in Paris 100 years ago, this is the story of how a young girl helps a high-wire performer regain his courage. Caldecott Medal winner, 1993. (Rev: BCCB 10/92*; BL 11/15/92; SLJ 10/92)

**3893** MacDonald, Suse. *Nanta's Lion: A Search and Find Adventure* (PS–1). Illus. 1995, Morrow $15.00

(0-688-13125-5). 24pp. An interactive book about an African girl who sets out to find the lion that has been stealing cattle from her village. (Rev: BL 4/15/95; SLJ 5/95)

**3894** McKay, Lawrence, Jr. *Caravan* (1–4). Illus. by Darryl Ligasan. 1995, Lee & Low $14.95 (1-880000-23-7). A boy tells about going on his first caravan through the mountains in Afghanistan to trade his family's furs for grain. (Rev: SLJ 12/95)

**3895** McKissack, Patricia. *Ma Dear's Aprons* (PS–3). Illus. by Floyd Cooper. 1997, Simon & Schuster $16.00 (0-689-81051-2). 32pp. During the early 1900s in Alabama, Ma Dear must support her family by doing domestic work. (Rev: BCCB 6/97; BL 2/15/97; HB 5–6/97; SLJ 6/97)

**3896** MacLachlan, Patricia. *Three Names* (K–3). Illus. by Alexander Pertzoff. 1991, HarperCollins LB $14.89 (0-06-024036-9). 32pp. A boy repeats the stories that his great-grandfather told him of growing up in pioneer days. (Rev: BCCB 1/92; BL 8/91; HB 9–10/91; SLJ 7/91)

**3897** MacLachlan, Patricia. *What You Know First* (K–3). Illus. by Barry Moser. Series: Joanna Cotler Books. 1995, HarperCollins LB $14.89 (0-06-024414-3). When a young girl is told that she will be leaving the prairie, she thinks of all the people and things she will miss, and gathers mementos to take with her. (Rev: BCCB 12/95; SLJ 11/95)

**3898** McLerran, Alice. *The Year of the Ranch* (K–4). Illus. by Kimberly B. Root. 1996, Viking paper $14.99 (0-670-85131-0). 32pp. In 1919, little Emily and her family hope to succeed as homesteaders on land outside Yuma, Arizona. (Rev: BCCB 4/96; BL 7/96; HB 7–8/96; SLJ 7/96)

**3899** Mandrell, Louise, and Ace Collins. *Sunrise over the Harbor: A Story About the Meaning of Independence Day* (1–3). Illus. by Mark Gale. Series: Children's Holiday Adventure. 1993, Summit $12.95 (1-56530-040-8). The circumstances surrounding the writing of the "Star Spangled Banner" are woven into an adventure story whose central character is a young cabin boy. (Rev: SLJ 10/93)

**3900** Manson, Ainslie. *A Dog Came, Too: A True Story* (1–3). Illus. by Ann Blades. 1993, Macmillan $13.95 (0-689-50567-1). 32pp. In a fictionalized format, this is the story of the dog that accompanied explorer Alexander Mackenzie across Canada to the Pacific Ocean. (Rev: BCCB 3/93; BL 5/1/93) [917.1]

**3901** Manson, Ainslie. *Just Like New* (1–4). Illus. by Karen Reczuch. 1996, Douglas & McIntyre $14.95 (0-88899-228-9). 32pp. During World War II, a Canadian girl sends her favorite doll to a deprived English youngster at Christmas. (Rev: BCCB 1/97; BL 11/15/96; SLJ 12/96)

**3902** Manuel, Lynn. *The Night the Moon Blew Kisses* (PS–2). Illus. by Robin Spowart. 1996, Houghton $14.95 (0-395-73979-9). An atmospheric tale of a walk through a nocturnal winter landscape by a girl and her grandmother. (Rev: SLJ 11/96)

**3903** Markun, Patricia M. *The Little Painter of Sabana Granda* (K–2). Illus. by Robert Casilla. 1993, Macmillan $14.95 (0-02-762205-3). 32pp. A young Panamanian boy paints pictures on the walls of his family's home. (Rev: BL 3/1/93; SLJ 7/93)

**3904** Martin, C. L. G. *The Blueberry Train* (PS–2). Illus. by Angela T. Thomas. 1995, Atheneum $15.00 (0-689-80304-4). This story set in Minnesota at the turn of the century tells about a boy who longs to make money so that he can buy his first long pants. (Rev: HB 11–12/95; SLJ 12/95)

**3905** Martin, Nora. *The Stone Dancers* (K–3). Illus. by Jill Kastner. 1995, Simon & Schuster $15.00 (0-689-80312-5). 32pp. A French grandfather tells his granddaughter how, many years ago, a king created a community for unwanted people. (Rev: BL 1/1–15/96; SLJ 12/95)

**3906** Marton, Jirina. *You Can Go Home Again* (K–3). Illus. by author. 1994, Annick LB $15.95 (1-55037-991-7); paper $5.95 (1-55037-990-9). Annie and her mother visit Prague, the city that had been the home of their family before World War II. (Rev: SLJ 11/94)

**3907** Medearis, Angela Shelf. *Rum-a-Tum-Tum* (PS–3). Illus. by James E. Ransome. 1997, Holiday LB $16.95 (0-8234-1143-5). 32pp. All the color, excitement, and sound of a market in the French Quarter of New Orleans at the turn of the century are captured in this picture book. (Rev: BCCB 7–8/97; BL 5/1/97; SLJ 7/97)

**3908** Melmed, Laura K. *Little Oh* (K–4). Illus. by Jim LaMarche. 1997, Lothrop LB $15.93 (0-688-14209-5). 32pp. In this story set in Japan, a potter makes an origami girl come to life. (Rev: BL 9/1/97; HB 9–10/97; SLJ 11/97*)

**3909** Mennen, Ingrid, and Niki Daly. *Somewhere in Africa* (K–3). Illus. by Nicolaas Maritz. 1992, Dutton paper $14.99 (0-525-44848-9). 32pp. A Malay boy growing up in Cape Town, South Africa, reads about the beasts that live in rural Africa. (Rev: BL 12/15/91; SLJ 1/92)

**3910** Millen, C. M. *A Symphony for the Sheep* (K–3). Illus. by Mary Azarian. 1996, Houghton $14.95 (0-395-76503-X). 32pp. The old-fashioned way of making woolen clothes is shown in this rhyme set in the Irish countryside. (Rev: BCCB 12/96; BL 8/96; SLJ 1/97)

**3911** Miller, William. *Richard Wright and the Library Card* (K–4). Illus. by Gregory Christie. 1997, Lee & Low $15.95 (1-880000-57-1). 32pp. In this story based on fact, African American Richard Wright, growing up in the segregated South, borrows books from the all-white library by pretending he is taking them to his white boss. (Rev: BL 12/1/97; SLJ 2/98)

**3912** Mitchell, Margaree King. *Granddaddy's Gift* (K–3). Illus. by Larry Johnson. 1997, Troll paper $14.95 (0-8167-4010-0). 32pp. Memories of a young girl growing up in segregated Mississippi and attending a school inferior to that of white children. (Rev: BL 2/15/97; SLJ 7/97)

**3913** Mollel, Tololwa M. *Big Boy* (PS–3). Illus. by E. B. Lewis. 1995, Clarion $14.95 (0-395-67403-4). 28pp. In Tanzania, a boy named Oli dreams of what it would be like to be a giant. (Rev: BCCB 3/95; BL 3/1/95; HB 7–8/95; SLJ 6/95)

**3914** Mollel, Tololwa M. *Kele's Secret* (K–3). Illus. by Catherine Stock. 1997, Dutton paper $14.99 (0-525-67500-0). 32pp. In this story set in Tanzania, Yoanes tries to find the place where one of his grandmother's hens lays her eggs. (Rev: BCCB 7–8/97; BL 6/1–15/97; SLJ 6/97)

**3915** Moore, Floyd C. *I Gave Thomas Edison My Sandwich* (K–3). Illus. by Donna Kae Nelson. 1995, Albert Whitman LB $14.95 (0-8075-3504-4). 32pp. An old man recalls how Edison years ago visited his hometown, Iron City, Tennessee, and he, then a fourth-grader, offered the inventor his lunch. (Rev: BL 6/1–15/95; SLJ 6/95)

**3916** Nakawatari, Harutaka. *The Sea and I* (PS–1). Trans. by Susan Matsui. Illus. 1992, Farrar $15.00 (0-374-36428-1). 31pp. In Japan, a young boy worries that his fisherman father will not return. (Rev: BCCB 12/92; BL 11/1/92; SLJ 11/92)

**3917** Namioka, Lensey. *The Loyal Cat* (K–3). Illus. by Aki Sogabe. 1995, Harcourt $15.00 (0-15-200092-5). 40pp. A wise cat tries to publicize the worth of her pious master, a Japanese priest. (Rev: BCCB 11/95; BL 9/15/95; SLJ 10/95)

**3918** Nerlove, Miriam. *Flowers on the Wall* (1–4). Illus. 1996, Simon & Schuster paper $16.00 (0-689-50614-7). 32pp. A Polish Jewish girl suffers persecution during World War II and ends up being deported to the Treblinka concentration camp. (Rev: BCCB 3/96; BL 4/15/96; HB 5–6/96; SLJ 4/96)

**3919** Nicholson, Nicholas B. A. *Little Girl in a Red Dress with Cat and Dog* (PS–3). Illus. by Cynthia Von Buhler. 1998, Viking paper $15.99 (0-670-87183-4). 32pp. After seeing a picture of a farm girl painted in New York State in 1835, the author imagines what her life was like. (Rev: BL 12/15/97; SLJ 2/98)

**3920** Nivola, Claire A. *Elisabeth* (K–4). Illus. 1997, Farrar $16.00 (0-374-32085-3). 32pp. Ruth's Jewish family flees pre-war Germany, leaving everything, including her doll, Elisabeth, behind. (Rev: BCCB 3/97; BL 2/1/97; HB 5–6/97; SLJ 4/97)

**3921** Nomura, Takaaki. *Grandpa's Town* (PS–3). Trans. by Amanda Mayer Stinchecum. Illus. 1991, Kane/Miller $13.95 (0-916291-36-7). 32pp. A story of rural Japan in which a family is afraid that their grandfather is very lonely after his wife's death. (Rev: BCCB 12/91*; HB 1–2/92; SLJ 1/92)

**3922** Nye, Naomi S. *Sitti's Secrets* (PS–3). Illus. by Nancy Carpenter. 1994, Four Winds paper $16.00 (0-02-768460-1). 32pp. A small American girl misses her sitti — Arabic for *grandmother* — who lives at home in her Palestinian village. (Rev: BCCB 3/94; BL 3/15/94; HB 5–6/94; SLJ 6/94*)

**3923** Oberman, Sheldon. *The Always Prayer Shawl* (1–4). Illus. by Ted Lewin. 1994, Boyds Mills $15.95 (1-878093-22-3). 32pp. Adam takes his grandfather's prayer shawl when he emigrates from Russia to the United States, where he wears it into manhood. (Rev: BL 12/15/93*; SLJ 3/94)

**3924** Olaleye, Isaac. *Bitter Bananas* (PS–3). Illus. by Ed Young. 1994, Boyds Mills $14.95 (1-56397-039-2). 32pp. Yusuf thinks of an ingenious scheme to deter the baboons from eating his palm sap in this story set in Nigeria. (Rev: BCCB 10/94; BL 9/15/94; SLJ 8/94*)

**3925** Onyefulu, Ifeoma. *Chidi Only Likes Blue: An African Book of Colors* (PS–3). Illus. 1997, Dutton paper $14.99 (0-525-65243-4). 30pp. The significance of various colors in the everyday life of a Nigerian village is shown in text and photos. (Rev: BL 9/15/97; HB 7–8/97; SLJ 8/97)

**3926** Orr, Katherine. *My Grandpa and the Sea* (K–3). Illus. 1990, Carolrhoda LB $19.95 (0-87614-409-1). 32pp. When Grandpa loses his fishing business to modern-day fishermen, he finds a new way of earning a living. (Rev: BCCB 11/90; BL 10/1/90)

**3927** Palacios, Argentina. *A Christmas Surprise for Chabelita* (K–3). Illus. by Lori Lohstoeter. 1993, Troll paper $14.95 (0-8167-3131-4). 32pp. When a little girl in Panama goes to live with her grandparents, her mother sends her a new red dress to wear to school. (Rev: BL 12/15/93)

**3928** Polacco, Patricia. *Babushka Baba Yaga* (PS–3). Illus. 1993, Putnam $15.95 (0-399-22531-5). 32pp. In this reversal of the traditional Russian folklore, the witch Baba Yaga is really a kindly grandmother named Babushka. (Rev: BL 8/93)

**3929** Pomeranc, Marion Hess. *The Hand-Me-Down Horse* (1–3). Illus. by Joanna Yardley. 1996, Albert Whitman LB $15.95 (0-8075-3141-3). Before a Jewish refugee boy can go to the United States after World War II, he makes the trip many times in his imagination on a rocking horse. (Rev: SLJ 1/97)

**3930** Pryor, Bonnie. *The House on Maple Street* (PS–1). Illus. by Beth Peck. 1987, Morrow paper $4.95 (0-688-12031-8). 32pp. Chris and Jenny find a small china cup and begin a kind of history exploration from the house on Maple Street. (Rev: BL 4/1/87; SLJ 5/87)

**3931** Rabin, Staton. *Casey Over There* (K–3). Illus. by Greg Shed. 1994, Harcourt $14.95 (0-15-253186-6). 32pp. In this picture book, Aubrey's brother is fighting in the trenches, while he is growing up in Brooklyn during World War I. (Rev: BL 3/15/94; SLJ 5/94)

**3932** Rael, Elsa O. *What Zeesie Saw on Delancey Street* (K–3). Illus. by Marjorie Priceman. 1996, Simon & Schuster $16.00 (0-689-80549-7). 28pp. Young Zeesie realizes the meaning of community while growing up in a Jewish American family on the Lower East Side of Manhattan in the early 1900s. (Rev: BCCB 12/96; BL 9/1/96; HB 11–12/96)

**3933** Rand, Gloria. *Baby in a Basket* (PS–3). Illus. by Ted Rand. 1997, Dutton paper $14.99 (0-525-65233-7). 32pp. Based on an event that occurred in Alaska in 1917, this picture book tells of the amazing rescue of a baby believed to be lost. (Rev: BL 11/15/97; SLJ 11/97)

**3934** Ray, Mary L. *Shaker Boy* (K–3). Illus. by Jeanette Winter. 1994, Harcourt $15.95 (0-15-276921-8). 48pp. The life story of a man who spent his life with the Shakers after being brought to them as a child after the Civil War. (Rev: BCCB 11/94; BL 11/15/94; SLJ 11/94)

**3935** Reddix, Valerie. *Dragon Kite of the Autumn Moon* (K–3). Illus. by Jean Tseng. 1992, Lothrop LB $13.93 (0-688-11031-2). 32pp. When Grandfather becomes sick, Tad-Tin must fly his kite alone in this tale set in Formosa. (Rev: BL 5/15/92; SLJ 8/92)

**3936** Reynolds, Marilyn. *The New Land: A First Year on the Prairie* (1–3). Illus. by Stephen McCallum. 1997, Orca $14.95 (1-55143-069-X). 32pp. A simple story about immigrants from Europe who settle on the prairie, build a home, plant a garden, and start a new life. (Rev: BL 10/15/97; SLJ 7/97)

**3937** Richardson, Jean. *The Courage Seed* (2–3). Illus. by Pat Finney. 1993, Eakin $14.95 (0-89015-902-5). 71pp. When her parents are killed, a young Navajo girl is fearful that she will lose her tribal ways when she goes to live with an aunt in Houston. (Rev: SLJ 2/94)

**3938** Rochelle, Belinda. *Jewels* (K–3). Illus. by Cornelius Van Wright and Ying-Hwa Hu. 1998, Dutton paper $15.99 (0-525-67502-7). 32pp. The stories about African Americans life and struggles that are told to Lea Mae by her grandparents become her "jewels." (Rev: BL 2/15/98; SLJ 3/98)

**3939** Roop, Peter, and Connie Roop. *Buttons for General Washington* (2–3). Illus. by Peter E. Hanson. 1986, Carolrhoda LB $18.60 (0-87614-294-3); paper $5.95 (0-87614-476-8). 48pp. Based on incidents from the life of John Darragh, this is the story of a 14-year-old boy who carries secret messages to George Washington hidden in his coat buttons during the Revolution. (Rev: BCCB 12/86; BL 12/1/86)

**3940** Rosenberg, Liz. *Grandmother and the Runaway Shadow* (K–3). Illus. by Beth Peck. 1996, Harcourt $15.00 (0-15-200948-5). 32pp. A young Jewish woman escapes persecution in Eastern Europe to find a new home in the United States. (Rev: BL 4/1/96; SLJ 5/96*)

**3941** Rosenblum, Richard. *Brooklyn Dodger Days* (1–4). Illus. 1991, Macmillan $13.95 (0-689-31512-0). 32pp. Re-creating a 1946 game between the Brooklyn Dodgers and the New York Giants. (Rev: BCCB 2/91; BL 1/1/91; SLJ 7/91) [796.357]

**3942** Rumford, James. *The Cloudmakers* (1–4). Illus. 1996, Houghton $15.95 (0-395-76505-6). 32pp. A Chinese grandfather and his grandson are commanded by a sultan to produce rain clouds. (Rev: BL 9/15/96; SLJ 9/96)

**3943** Rush, Ken. *The Seltzer Man* (PS–3). Illus. 1993, Macmillan LB $14.95 (0-02-777917-3). 32pp. Before he retires from his route in New York City, Eli, the friendly seltzer man, is accompanied on his route by 2 young girls. (Rev: BL 6/1–15/93; SLJ 7/93)

**3944** Ryder, Joanne. *Where Butterflies Grow* (PS–3). Illus. by Lynne Cherry. 1989, Dutton paper $15.99 (0-525-67284-2). 32pp. Detailed illustrations and poetic text explain the life cycle of a black swallowtail butterfly. (Rev: BL 11/1/89*; SLJ 9/89*) [595]

**3945** Saltzman, David. *The Jester Has Lost His Jingle* (1–3). Illus. 1995, Jester $20.00 (0-9644563-0-3). 64pp. A jester who is out of work because he isn't funny sets out to discover laughter in the world. (Rev: BL 10/15/95; SLJ 10/95)

**3946** Sanders, Scott R. *Aurora Means Dawn* (K–3). Illus. by Jill Kastner. 1989, Macmillan $15.00 (0-02-778270-0). 32pp. A pioneer family's journey westward is temporarily halted when a fallen tree blocks their path. (Rev: BCCB 12/89; BL 9/15/89*; HB 9–10/89; SLJ 11/89)

**3947** Sanders, Scott R. *The Floating House* (K–3). Illus. by Helen Cogancherry. 1995, Simon & Schuster paper $16.00 (0-02-778137-2). 32pp. The story of the McClure family, their trip by flatboat on the Ohio River in 1815, and their relocation to a farm in Indiana. (Rev: BL 6/1–15/95; SLJ 6/95)

**3948** Sanders, Scott R. *Here Comes the Mystery Man* (K–3). Illus. by Helen Cogancherry. 1993, Bradbury $15.95 (0-02-778145-3). 32pp. A pioneer family is delighted when a traveling peddler visits their log cabin. (Rev: BL 11/15/93; SLJ 10/93)

**3949** Sanders, Scott R. *A Place Called Freedom* (K–3). Illus. by Thomas B. Allen. 1997, Simon & Schuster $16.00 (0-689-80470-9). 32pp. Beginning with a single family of freed slaves who travel from the South to Indiana, others arrive and found a town called Freedom. (Rev: BCCB 7–8/97; BL 6/1–15/97; SLJ 8/97)

**3950** Sanders, Scott R. *Warm as Wool* (K–3). Illus. by Helen Cogancherry. 1992, Macmillan paper $16.00 (0-02-778139-9). 32pp. The mother of a pioneer family buys sheep so that she can make woolen clothing to keep her family warm in winter. (Rev: BL 11/15/92; SLJ 12/92)

**3951** Sandin, Joan. *The Long Way to a New Land* (1–3). Illus. by author. 1981, HarperCollins paper $3.75 (0-06-444100-8). 64pp. An easy-to-read account of a Swedish family's journey to New York in the late 1860s.

**3952** Sandoval, Dolores. *Be Patient, Abdul* (1–4). Illus. 1996, Simon & Schuster paper $15.00 (0-689-50607-4). 30pp. In Sierra Leone, 7-year-old Abdul saves his money so that he can go to school. (Rev: BL 9/15/96; SLJ 8/96)

**3953** Say, Allen. *The Bicycle Man* (K–3). Illus. by author. 1982, Houghton $11.95 (0-685-05704-6); paper $5.95 (0-395-50652-2). 48pp. Two American soldiers in Japan put on a show for a school.

**3954** Schroeder, Alan. *Carolina Shout!* (PS–3). Illus. by Bernie Fuchs. 1995, Dial paper $14.89 (0-8037-1678-8). 32pp. Street cries and other city noises create the atmosphere associated with pre–World War II African American life in Charleston, South Carolina. (Rev: BL 10/1/95*; SLJ 10/95)

**3955** Schuett, Stacey. *Somewhere in the World Right Now* (1–3). Illus. by author. 1995, Knopf LB $17.99 (0-679-96537-8). This picture book shows what is going on around the world at a particular moment. (Rev: SLJ 12/95)

**3956** Scott, Ann H. *On Mother's Lap* (PS–K). Illus. by Glo Coalson. 1992, Houghton $15.00 (0-395-58920-7); paper $5.95 (0-395-62976-4). 32pp. A warm, tender story of an Eskimo family and of a young boy's realization that there is enough room on mother's lap for both him and his sister.

**3957** Seabrooke, Brenda. *The Boy Who Saved the Town* (2–4). Illus. by Howard M. Burns. 1990, Tidewater $7.95 (0-87033-405-0). 28pp. This legend tells how the town of St. Michaels escaped bombardment by the British in the War of 1812. (Rev: BL 9/1/90)

**3958** Seed, Jenny. *Ntombi's Song* (5–8). Illus. by Anno Berry. 1989, Beacon $14.95 (0-8070-8318-6). 48pp. Six-year-old Ntombi, a Zulu girl, is sent to

market by her mother to buy sugar. (Rev: BL 3/1/90; SLJ 11/89)

**3959** Sisulu, Elinor B. *The Day Gogo Went to Vote* (PS–4). Illus. by Sharon Wilson. 1996, Little, Brown $14.95 (0-316-70267-6). 32pp. Thembi tells how her great-grandmother voted for the first time in Soweto, South Africa, in 1994. (Rev: BCCB 3/96; BL 2/15/96; SLJ 5/96*)

**3960** Smalls, Irene. *Irene Jennie and the Christmas Masquerade: The Johnkankus* (K–4). Illus. by Melodye Rosales. 1996, Little, Brown $15.95 (0-316-79878-9). 32pp. In the times of slavery, young Irene Jennie hopes her parents, on loan to another plantation, will return for Christmas. (Rev: BCCB 11/96; BL 9/15/96)

**3961** Smucker, Barbara. *Selina and the Bear Paw Quilt* (PS–3). Illus. by Janet Wilson. 1996, Crown $16.00 (0-517-70904-X). 30pp. During the Civil War, Selina and her grandmother are separated, but the quilt given to her by her grandmother brings comfort. (Rev: BL 6/1–15/96; HB 5–6/96; SLJ 7/96)

**3962** Sorensen, Henri. *New Hope* (PS–3). Illus. 1995, Lothrop LB $14.93 (0-688-13926-4). 32pp. A grandfather tells his grandson how his family came to the United States more than 100 years ago and of their problems as pioneers in the West. (Rev: BCCB 6/95; BL 6/1–15/95; HB 5–6/95; SLJ 7/95)

**3963** Soto, Gary. *The Old Man and His Door* (PS–2). Illus. by Joe Cepeda. 1996, Putnam $15.95 (0-399-22700-8). 32pp. In a Mexican setting, this fable tells of an old fool's adventures on the way to a barbeque. (Rev: BCCB 9/96; BL 4/1/96; HB 7–8/96; SLJ 6/96)

**3964** Steiner, Barbara. *Whale Brother* (K–3). Illus. by Gretchen Will Mayo. 1988, Walker LB $13.85 (0-8027-6805-9). The touching story of an Eskimo boy who wants to be an artist and his protective love for animals. (Rev: BCCB 1/89)

**3965** Stevens, Jan R. *Carlos and the Cornfield/Carlos y la Milpa de Maiz* (K–3). Illus. by Jeanne Arnold. 1995, Northland LB $14.95 (0-87358-596-8). 32pp. Carlos learns some truths about gardening when he plants corn to earn enough money to buy a pocketknife. (Rev: BL 9/1/95; SLJ 9/95)

**3966** Stevenson, James. *Don't You Know There's a War On?* (K–3). Illus. 1992, Greenwillow LB $13.93 (0-688-11384-2). 32pp. Remembrances of what it was like to be an American child growing up in a small town during World War II. (Rev: BCCB 11/92*; BL 11/1/92*; HB 1–2/93*; SLJ 10/92) [940.53]

**3967** Stevenson, James. *Higher on the Door* (5–7). Illus. by author. 1987, Greenwillow LB $12.88 (0-688-06637-2). 32pp. The warmth of growing up in a small town not far from New York City. (Rev: BCCB 4/87; BL 3/15/87; SLJ 4/87)

**3968** Stewart, Sarah. *The Gardener* (K–3). Illus. by David Small. 1997, Farrar $15.00 (0-374-32517-0). 40pp. During the Depression, a little girl is sent off to live with a cold, somber uncle, but gradually she wins him over. (Rev: BL 6/1–15/97; HB 11–12/97; SLJ 8/97*)

**3969** Tchana, Katrin H., and Louise T. Pami. *Oh, No, Toto!* (K–3). Illus. by Colin Bootman. 1997, Scholastic $15.95 (0-590-46585-6). 32pp. Toto, a young African boy, tastes exotic Cameroon food when his mother takes him to the market. (Rev: BCCB 3/97; BL 3/1/97; SLJ 3/97)

**3970** Thaxter, Celia. *Celia's Island Journal* (PS–3). Illus. by Loretta Krupinski. 1992, Little, Brown $15.95 (0-316-83921-3). 32pp. The author's life on White Island off the New England coast. (Rev: BL 12/1/92; HB 11–12/92; SLJ 10/92) [974.1]

**3971** Torres, Leyla. *Saturday Sancocho* (K–3). Illus. 1995, Farrar $15.00 (0-374-36418-4). 32pp. A South American girl and her grandmother visit a market with their eggs to barter for the ingredients of a chicken stew. (Rev: BL 4/15/95; SLJ 5/95)

**3972** Turner, Ann. *Dakota Dugout* (PS–1). Illus. by Ronald Himler. 1985, Macmillan $15.00 (0-02-789700-1); paper $4.50 (0-689-71296-0). 32pp. Rich images prevail as a lady tells of life on the prairie long ago. (Rev: BCCB 10/85; BL 12/1/85; HB 1–2/86)

**3973** Turner, Ann. *Katie's Trunk* (1–5). Illus. by Ronald Himler. 1992, Macmillan LB $15.00 (0-02-789512-2). When raiders attack Katie's house during the American Revolution, she tries to save her family's possessions. (Rev: BCCB 11–12/92; SLJ 11/92)

**3974** Van Laan, Nancy. *La Boda: A Mexican Wedding Celebration* (K–3). Illus. by Andrea Arroyo. 1996, Little, Brown $15.95 (0-316-89626-8). Using lively watercolors, this book celebrates a Zapotec wedding day in Oaxaca, Mexico. (Rev: BCCB 5/96; SLJ 5/96)

**3975** Van Leeuwen, Jean. *Going West* (K–3). Illus. by Thomas B. Allen. 1992, Doubleday LB $14.89 (0-8037-1028-3). 48pp. Seven-year-old Hannah and her family journey westward for a new life on the prairie. (Rev: BL 1/15/92*; HB 3–4/92; SLJ 3/92)

**3976** Von Ahnen, Katherine. *Charlie Young Bear* (2–3). Illus. by Paulette L. Lambert. Series: Council for Indian Education. 1994, Roberts Rinehart paper $4.95 (1-57098-001-2). 42pp. After the U.S. government agrees on a cash settlement with the Mesquakie Indians in 1955, Charlie Young Bear hopes his share will be a bike. (Rev: SLJ 4/95)

**3977** Waldman, Neil. *The Never-Ending Greenness* (1–4). Illus. 1997, Morrow LB $15.93 (0-688-14480-2). 40pp. After hiding in a forest to escape the Nazis when he was a child, a Jewish man plants trees

in his new homeland, Israel, as an act of rebirth and remembrance. (Rev: BCCB 6/97; BL 3/1/97; SLJ 4/97)

**3978** Ward, Leila. *I Am Eyes Ni Macho* (PS–1). Illus. by Nonny Hogrogian. 1987, Scholastic paper $3.95 (0-590-40990-5). 32pp. A new day and all of nature's wonders are greeted by a Kenyan child. A reissue of the 1978 edition.

**3979** Warner, Sunny. *The Magic Sewing Machine* (PS–3). Illus. 1997, Houghton $16.00 (0-395-82747-7). 32pp. Two orphaned children take their sewing machine to the orphanage in this story set in Dickensian London. (Rev: BL 9/15/97; SLJ 9/97)

**3980** Waterton, Betty. *Pettranella* (K–3). Illus. by Ann Blades. 1991, Firefly paper $4.95 (0-88899-108-8). 32pp. An immigrant girl grows flowers from seeds she brought from Europe.

**3981** Watkins, Sherrin. *Green Snake Ceremony* (PS–2). Illus. by Kim Doner. Series: The Greyfeather. 1996, Council Oak $17.95 (0-933031-89-0). Neither a Shawnee girl nor the green snake that lives under the porch want to participate in the traditional snake ceremony that involves the young girl putting the snake in her mouth. (Rev: SLJ 12/96)

**3982** Watson, Mary. *The Butterfly Seeds* (K–4). Illus. 1995, Morrow LB $15.93 (0-688-14133-1). 32pp. Jake, a new immigrant to the US, plants the seeds his grandfather back home gave him in a windowbox in his tenement building. (Rev: BL 9/1/95; SLJ 11/95)

**3983** Watson, Pete. *The Market Lady and the Mango Tree* (K–3). Illus. by Mary Watson. 1994, Morrow $14.00 (0-688-12970-6). 32pp. When Market Lady places nets around the mango tree so that children will have to buy the fruit rather than pick it from the ground, she realizes that this is an act of selfishness. (Rev: BL 2/15/94; SLJ 6/94)

**3984** Webb, Denise. *The Same Sun Was in the Sky* (1–4). Illus. by Walter Porter. 1995, Northland LB $14.95 (0-87358-602-6). 32pp. A boy and his grandfather think about the prehistoric Indians of the Southwest and the amazing rock paintings that they produced. (Rev: BL 8/95)

**3985** Weiss, Nicki. *Stone Men* (K–3). Illus. 1993, Greenwillow LB $13.93 (0-688-11016-9). 32pp. Isaac builds stone men to frighten off invading soldiers. (Rev: BL 3/1/93; SLJ 7/93)

**3986** Wells, Rosemary. *The Language of Doves* (K–2). Illus. by Greg Shed. 1996, Dial paper $14.89 (0-8037-1472-6). 48pp. Grandfather tells of an incident during World War II in which a pigeon saved the lives of 8 men. (Rev: BCCB 9/96; BL 8/96; SLJ 9/96*)

**3987** Wilder, Laura Ingalls. *Going to Town* (PS–1). Illus. by Renee Graef. Series: My First Little House

Books. 1995, HarperCollins LB $11.89 (0-06-023013-4). A picture book abridgment of a chapter from *Little House in the Big Woods* in which the Wilders prepare for a trip into town. (Rev: SLJ 12/95)

**3988** Williams, Karen L. *Galimoto* (K–2). Illus. by Catherine Stock. 1990, Lothrop LB $15.93 (0-688-08790-6). 32pp. A young Malawi boy has many adventures in his search for materials to build a toy. (Rev: BCCB 4/90; BL 3/1/90; HB 3–4/90; SLJ 6/90)

**3989** Williams, Karen L. *Tap-Tap* (PS–1). Illus. by Catherine Stock. 1994, Clarion $14.95 (0-395-65617-6). 34pp. After a day selling flowers in a Haitian market, young Sasifi treats herself to a ride home in a jitney. (Rev: BCCB 3/94; BL 4/15/94; HB 7–8/94; SLJ 6/94)

**3990** Williams, Karen L. *When Africa Was Home* (PS–2). Illus. by Floyd Cooper. 1991, Orchard LB $16.99 (0-531-08525-2). 32pp. A white boy is so at home in Africa with his black friends that he feels lost when he has to go to America. (Rev: BCCB 2/92; BL 1/15/91*; SLJ 4/91)

**3991** Willow, Diane. *At Home in the Rain Forest* (PS–3). Illus. by Laura Jacques. 1991, Charlesbridge $14.95 (0-88106-485-8). 32pp. The flora and fauna of the Amazon rain forest are explored in text and color paintings. (Rev: BL 6/1/91) [574]

**3992** Winnick, Karen B. *Mr. Lincoln's Whiskers* (1–3). Illus. 1996, Boyds Mills $15.95 (1-56397-485-1). 32pp. A young girl writes to Lincoln to suggest that he would gain votes if he grew whiskers. (Rev: BL 12/15/96; SLJ 1/97)

**3993** Winslow, Barbara. *Dance on a Sealskin* (1–3). Illus. by Teri Sloat. 1995, Alaska Northwest $15.95 (0-88240-443-1). 32pp. Annie is thrilled at being able to dance as a coming-of-age ritual at the Eskimos' potlatch. (Rev: BL 8/95; SLJ 12/95)

**3994** Winter, Jeanette. *Follow the Drinking Gourd* (K–3). Illus. by author. 1988, Knopf LB $17.99 (0-394-99694-1); paper $5.99 (0-679-81997-5). 48pp. The story of Peg Leg Pete who helps slaves escape to the North. (Rev: BCCB 1/89; BL 12/15/88; SLJ 5/89)

**3995** Wisniewski, David. *Rain Player* (K–3). Illus. 1991, Houghton $17.00 (0-395-55112-9). 32pp. Young Pik challenges the rain god in this story based on Mayan folklore. (Rev: BCCB 11/91; BL 10/15/91*; HB 1–2/92; SLJ 10/91)

**3996** Wittmann, Patricia. *Buffalo Thunder* (K–4). Illus. by Bert Dodson. 1997, Marshall Cavendish LB $15.95 (0-7614-5001-7). 32pp. A young boy and his family share many adventures when they travel west in their prairie schooner. (Rev: BL 9/15/97; SLJ 9/97)

**3997** Wright, Courtni C. *Jumping the Broom* (K–3). Illus. by Gershom Griffith. 1994, Holiday LB $15.95 (0-8234-1042-0). A picture book set in the days of slavery about the marriage celebration known as "jumping the broom." (Rev: BCCB 7–8/94; SLJ 4/94)

### PERSONAL PROBLEMS

**3998** Ada, Alma F. *The Gold Coin* (K–3). Trans. by Bernice Randall. Illus. by Neil Waldman. 1991, Macmillan $15.00 (0-689-31633-X). Juan, who has been a thief all his life, redeems himself in this gentle story translated from the Spanish. (Rev: BL 3/1/92; SLJ 4/91)

**3999** Alexander, Martha. *I'll Protect You from the Jungle Beasts* (PS–K). Illus. by author. 1983, Dial LB $8.89 (0-8037-4309-2). 32pp. A small boy and his teddy bear take a walk through the frightening woods.

**4000** Altman, Linda Jacobs. *Amelia's Road* (PS–3). Illus. by Enrique O. Sanchez. 1993, Lee & Low $15.95 (1-880000-04-0). 32pp. Amelia, the daughter of migrant workers, cries every time her father takes out a map because it means her family will move again. (Rev: BL 9/15/93; SLJ 12/93)

**4001** Arrington, Frances. *Stella's Bull* (PS–3). Illus. by Aileen Arrington. 1994, Houghton $14.95 (0-395-67345-3). 28pp. Mary is terrified of a bull that lives on a farm on her way to school even though she has never seen him. (Rev: BCCB 7–8/94; BL 9/15/94; HB 11–12/94; SLJ 9/94)

**4002** Babbitt, Natalie. *The Something* (PS–3). Illus. by author. 1970, Farrar $11.00 (0-374-37137-7). 40pp. Fear of the dark — common in childhood — underlies this fantasy in which the unusual-looking hero, Milo, comes face-to-face with the dreaded "something."

**4003** Barbour, Karen. *Mr. Bow Tie* (PS–3). Illus. 1991, Harcourt $13.95 (0-15-256165-X). 32pp. A family helps Mr. Bow Tie, a homeless man they see on the streets. (Rev: BL 9/1/91; SLJ 12/91)

**4004** Bat-Ami, Miriam. *Sea, Salt, and Air* (2–5). Illus. by Mary O. Young. 1993, Smithmark $4.98 (0-765-10095-9). 32pp. During a summer visit to her grandparents at the beach, a young girl ponders how she will develop in the future. (Rev: BL 5/15/93; SLJ 6/93)

**4005** Battle-Lavert, Gwendolyn. *Off to School* (K–3). Illus. by Gershom Griffith. 1995, Holiday LB $15.95 (0-8234-1185-0). 32pp. A migrant worker's child, Wezielee, longs to go to school but must stay at the camp and cook for the laborers. (Rev: BL 10/15/95; SLJ 1/96)

**4006** Bernatova, Eva. *The Wonder Shoes* (K–2). Illus. by Fiona Moodie. 1990, Farrar $13.95 (0-374-

38476-2). 32pp. Emma, who is an outsider in the village, learns how to dance from a ballerina who comes to town with a show. (Rev: BL 7/90; HB 9–10/90; SLJ 9/90)

**4007** Bernstein, Sharon C. *A Family That Fights* (PS–3). Illus. by Karen Ritz. 1991, Whitman LB $12.95 (0-8075-2248-1). 32pp. A quiet story that deals with 3 children who live in a family where the father hits their mother and threatens them when he is angry. (Rev: BL 11/15/91; SLJ 2/92)

**4008** Best, Cari. *Getting Used to Harry* (PS–3). Illus. by Diane Palmisciano. 1996, Orchard LB $16.99 (0-531-08794-8). 32pp. Cynthia gradually adjusts to her mother's new husband, Harry the shoe man. (Rev: BCCB 10/96; BL 11/1/96; SLJ 10/96)

**4009** Birchman, David F. *A Green Horn Blowing* (K–3). Illus. by Thomas B. Allen. 1997, Lothrop LB $14.93 (0-688-12389-9). 32pp. Unable to afford a horn, a musical boy practices on a long squash. (Rev: BL 9/15/97; SLJ 11/97)

**4010** Blegvad, Lenore. *A Sound of Leaves* (2–4). Illus. 1996, Simon & Schuster paper $15.00 (0-689-80038-X). 58pp. A 9-year-old is fearful of going to the beach for the first time but discovers that it is fun. (Rev: BCCB 5/96; BL 5/1/96; HB 9–10/96; SLJ 5/96)

**4011** Blumenthal, Deborah. *The Chocolate-Covered-Cookie Tantrum* (PS–K). Illus. by Harvey Stevenson. 1996, Clarion $15.00 (0-395-68699-7). 32pp. When she can't get the cookie she wants, a little girl stages a temper tantrum. (Rev: SLJ 9/96)

**4012** Bottner, Barbara. *Bootsie Barker Bites* (PS–3). Illus. by Peggy Rathmann. 1992, Putnam $15.95 (0-399-22125-5). 32pp. The young narrator stands just so much from bully Bootsie Barker and finally stands up for herself. (Rev: BCCB 9/92; BL 10/1/92*; HB 3–4/93; SLJ 2/93*)

**4013** Brown, Margaret Wise. *The Dead Bird* (PS–3). Illus. by Remy Charlip. 1979, Dell paper $1.50 (0-440-41775-9). After finding a dead bird, children give it a solemn burial in this book that introduces the concept of death to young people.

**4014** Brown, Tricia. *Someone Special, Just Like You* (PS–2). Photos by Fran Ortiz. 1984, Holt $15.95 (0-8050-0481-5). 64pp. A book that shows that children are children even if they are handicapped.

**4015** Bulla, Clyde Robert. *The Chalk Box Kid* (2–3). Illus. by Thomas B. Allen. 1987, Random LB $11.99 (0-394-99102-8); paper $3.99 (0-394-89102-3). 64pp. Miffed because Uncle Max is sharing his room, Gregory sets out to explore his new neighborhood. (Rev: BCCB 9/87; BL 12/1/87; SLJ 12/87)

**4016** Bunnett, Rochelle. *Friends in the Park* (PS–K). Illus. by Carl Sahlhoff. 1993, Checkerboard $7.95 (1-56288-347-X). 32pp. In this book of photographs

and text, disabled kids are shown enjoying all the activities that youngsters like. (Rev: BL 4/15/93) [305.9]

**4017** Bunting, Eve. *Fly Away Home* (K–3). Illus. by Ronald Himler. 1991, Houghton $16.00 (0-395-55962-6). 32pp. The airport serves as a home for 2 homeless people — a boy and his father. (Rev: BCCB 5/92; BL 4/1/91*; HB 7–8/91; SLJ 6/91*)

**4018** Bunting, Eve. *Ghost's Hour, Spook's Hour* (PS–2). Illus. by Donald Carrick. 1987, Houghton $16.00 (0-89919-484-2); paper $5.95 (0-395-51583-1). 32pp. A boy and his dog, Biff, search the house for Mom and Dad when they hear noises that frighten them. (Rev: BCCB 10/87; BL 8/87; SLJ 9/87)

**4019** Bunting, Eve. *On Call Back Mountain* (1–3). Illus. by Barry Moser. 1997, Scholastic $15.95 (0-590-25929-6). Two young brothers adjust to the death of an elderly man who has worked as a fire spotter in a tower close to their home. (Rev: SLJ 3/97)

**4020** Bunting, Eve. *Twinnies* (PS–1). Illus. by Nancy Carpenter. 1997, Harcourt $15.00 (0-15-291592-3). 32pp. A girl feels jealous when her twin sisters get all the attention. (Rev: BL 9/15/97; SLJ 10/97)

**4021** Cadnum, Michael. *The Lost and Found House* (K–3). Illus. by Steve Johnson and Lou Fancher. 1997, Viking paper $15.99 (0-670-84884-0). 32pp. The story of moving day as experienced by a young boy who is apprehensive about his new home. (Rev: BL 12/1/97; SLJ 11/97)

**4022** Canfield, Jack, and Mark V. Hansen. *Chicken Soup for Little Souls: The Best Night Out with Dad* (K–4). Illus. by Bert Dodson. Series: Chicken Soup for Little Souls. 1997, Health Communications $14.95 (1-55874-508-4). 32pp. This slight story teaches the value of being unselfish and giving to others. Also use *Chicken Soup for Little Souls: The Goodness Gorilla* and *Chicken Soup for Little Souls: The Never-Forgotten Doll* (1997). (Rev: BL 11/15/97; SLJ 1/98)

**4023** Carlson, Nancy. *Arnie and the New Kid* (PS–2). Illus. 1992, Puffin paper $4.99 (0-14-050945-3). 32pp. When Arnie has an accident, he realizes what life is like for newcomer Philip, who is confined to a wheelchair. (Rev: BCCB 5/90; BL 5/15/90)

**4024** Carr, Jan. *Dark Day, Light Night* (PS–2). Illus. by James E. Ransome. 1996, Hyperion LB $15.49 (0-7868-2014-4). 32pp. When 'Manda claims there is nothing in the world she really likes, Aunt Ruby compiles a list of her own favorite things. (Rev: BL 2/15/96; HB 5–6/96; SLJ 6/96)

**4025** Carrick, Carol. *The Accident* (K–3). Illus. by Donald Carrick. 1981, Houghton paper $6.95 (0-89919-041-3). 32pp. A story that deals sympathetically and realistically with a child's reaction to the death of his pet dog.

**4026** Carrick, Carol. *The Foundling* (PS–3). Illus. by Donald Carrick. 1986, Houghton paper $4.95 (0-89919-466-4). 32pp. Young Christopher has difficulty adjusting to his dog's death and getting a replacement.

**4027** Carrick, Carol. *Patrick's Dinosaurs* (PS–3). Illus. by Donald Carrick. 1983, Houghton $15.00 (0-89919-189-4); paper $5.95 (0-89919-402-8). 32pp. Patrick is frightened when his brother tells him about dinosaurs.

**4028** Carrier, Roch. *The Boxing Champion* (1–2). Trans. by Sheila Fischman. Illus. by Sheldon Cohen. 1991, Tundra $15.95 (0-88776-249-2). Young Rock wants to go into training so he can become a powerful boxer. (Rev: SLJ 7/91)

**4029** Carter, Dorothy. *Bye, Mis' Lela* (K–3). Illus. by Harvey Stevenson. 1998, Farrar $16.00 (0-374-31013-0). 32pp. An African American girl must cope with the death of her beloved baby-sitter, Mis' Lela. (Rev: BL 2/15/98; SLJ 3/98)

**4030** Caseley, Judith. *Harry and Willy and Carrothead* (PS–2). Illus. 1991, Greenwillow LB $15.93 (0-688-09493-7). 24pp. A young boy copes with being born with only one hand. (Rev: BCCB 4/91; BL 3/1/91; SLJ 7/91)

**4031** Caseley, Judith. *Hurricane Harry* (K–2). 1991, Greenwillow $13.95 (0-688-10027-9). 112pp. Harry and his family move and he has to face going to a new kindergarten. (Rev: BCCB 11/91; BL 10/15/91; SLJ 1/92)

**4032** Caseley, Judith. *Priscilla Twice* (K–2). Illus. 1995, Greenwillow LB $14.93 (0-688-13306-1). 32pp. After her parents divorce, Priscilla finds that she now has 2 of everything, including 2 sets of clothes. (Rev: BL 8/95; SLJ 9/95)

**4033** Cocca-Leffler, Maryann. *Missing: One Stuffed Rabbit* (K–3). Illus. 1998, Albert Whitman LB $14.95 (0-8075-5161-9). 32pp. Janine is frantic when she loses the class mascot, a stuffed rabbit named Coco, at a shopping mall. (Rev: BL 3/15/98)

**4034** Cohn, Janice. *I Had a Friend Named Peter: Talking to Children About the Death of a Friend* (K–3). Illus. by Gail Owens. 1987, Morrow LB $15.93 (0-688-06686-0). 32pp. Betsy's story about her friend Peter, who was killed in a car accident. (Rev: BL 11/15/87; SLJ 9/87)

**4035** Cohn, Janice. *Molly's Rosebush* (PS–2). Illus. by Gail Owens. 1994, Albert Whitman LB $14.95 (0-8075-5213-5). 32pp. Grandma helps Molly get over her grief at the loss of her mother's baby by miscarriage. (Rev: BL 1/15/95; SLJ 3/95)

**4036** Coman, Carolyn. *Losing Things at Mr. Mudd's* (K–2). Illus. by Lance Hidy. 1992, Farrar $14.00 (0-374-34657-7). While visiting Mr. Mudd's, Lucy loses a valuable ruby ring. (Rev: SLJ 5/92)

**4037** Cooney, Barbara. *Miss Rumphius* (PS–3). Illus. by author. 1982, Puffin paper $5.99 (0-14-050539-3). 32pp. Miss Rumphius wonders how she can make the world more beautiful.

**4038** Coville, Bruce. *My Grandfather's House* (K–3). Illus. by Henri Sorensen. 1996, Troll paper $14.95 (0-8167-3804-1). 32pp. A young boy painfully adjusts to his grandfather's death. (Rev: BL 6/1–15/96; SLJ 8/96)

**4039** Crary, Elizabeth. *I'm Frustrated* (PS–1). Illus. by Jean Whitney. 1992, Parenting Pr. LB $16.95 (0-943990-65-3). 30pp. In this slim book, a child is faced with a difficult situation and must work through his feelings. Others in this series are: *I'm Mad; I'm Proud* (both 1992). (Rev: SLJ 6/92)

**4040** Crew, Gary. *Bright Star* (1–3). Illus. by Anne Spudvilas. 1997, Kane/Miller $13.95 (0-916291-75-8). 32pp. In this Australian picture book, a young girl finds the freedom she wants when she develops an interest in astronomy. (Rev: BL 10/15/97; SLJ 2/98)

**4041** Cristaldi, Kathryn. *Samantha the Snob* (1–3). Illus. by Denise Brunkus. Series: Step into Reading Books. 1994, Random LB $11.99 (0-679-94640-3); paper $3.99 (0-679-84640-9). 48pp. Everyone thinks that the new girl in their class is a snob and showoff, but her birthday party shows that they are wrong. (Rev: SLJ 11/94)

**4042** Daly, Niki. *My Dad* (1–4). Illus. 1995, Simon & Schuster paper $16.00 (0-689-50620-1). 32pp. Two siblings react with embarrassment and fear when their father abuses alcohol. (Rev: BCCB 6/95; BL 5/1/95; SLJ 6/95)

**4043** Davies, Sally J. K. *Why Did We Have to Move Here?* (K–3). Illus. 1997, Carolrhoda $14.95 (1-57505-046-3). 32pp. After William and his family move to a new home, he has difficulty making friends. (Rev: BL 12/15/97)

**4044** Delton, Judy, and Dorothy Tucker. *My Grandma's in a Nursing Home* (K–2). Illus. by Charles Robinson. 1986, Whitman LB $12.95 (0-8075-5333-6). 32pp. Jason realizes that his grandmother, who suffers from Alzheimer's disease, needs the care of a nursing home. (Rev: BCCB 11/86; SLJ 2/87)

**4045** dePaola, Tomie. *Nana Upstairs and Nana Downstairs* (PS–2). Illus. 1998, Putnam $15.99 (0-399-23108-0); Puffin paper $4.99 (0-14-050290-4). 32pp. A reissue of the classic picture book about a boy's sorrow when his great-grandmother dies. (Rev: BL 2/15/98)

**4046** dePaola, Tomie. *Now One Foot, Now the Other* (K–3). Illus. by author. 1981, Putnam $13.95 (0-399-

20774-0). 48pp. Bobby helps his grandfather recover from a stroke.

**4047** dePaola, Tomie. *Oliver Button Is a Sissy* (K–3). Illus. by author. 1979, Harcourt $13.00 (0-15-257852-8); paper $6.00 (0-15-668140-4). 48pp. People think Oliver is a sissy until he shines in a talent show as a fine tap dancer.

**4048** De Regniers, Beatrice S. *Little House of Your Own* (PS). Illus. by Irene Haas. 1955, Harcourt $12.95 (0-15-245787-9). 32pp. An exploration of the many places in which a child can have a secret house.

**4049** DiSalvo-Ryan, DyAnne. *Uncle Willie and the Soup Kitchen* (2–4). 1991, Morrow $16.00 (0-688-09165-2). 32pp. Uncle Willie explains what goes on in a soup kitchen and tells of the people who are there. (Rev: BCCB 5/91; BL 3/1/91; SLJ 6/91)

**4050** Edwards, Michelle. *A Baker's Portrait* (PS–3). Illus. 1991, Smithmark paper $3.95 (0-831-73218-0). 32pp. Michelin has problems when she is commissioned to paint portraits of her aunt and uncle. (Rev: BCCB 2/92; BL 10/15/91; SLJ 10/91)

**4051** Ehrlich, Amy. *Lucy's Winter Tale* (K–4). Illus. by Troy Howell. 1999, Dial LB $13.89 (0-8037-0661-8); NAL paper $4.99 (0-140-55581-1). 32pp. A young girl runs away with a circus juggler who is looking for his lost love. (Rev: BCCB 1/93; BL 7/92; SLJ 9/92)

**4052** England, Linda. *The Old Cotton Blues* (PS–2). Illus. by Teresa Flavin. 1998, Simon & Schuster $16.00 (0-689-81074-1). 32pp. Dexter loves the sound of the clarinet, but his mother tells him that the little money they have must go for rent instead of musical instruments. (Rev: BL 2/15/98)

**4053** Falwell, Cathryn. *Dragon Tooth* (K–2). Illus. 1996, Clarion $14.95 (0-395-56916-8). 32pp. Sara gradually convinces herself that it is all right to have her father pull her loose tooth. (Rev: BL 4/15/96; SLJ 4/96)

**4054** Fiday, Beverly, and David Fiday. *Time to Go* (K–3). Illus. by Thomas B. Allen. 1990, Harcourt $14.95 (0-15-200608-7). A boy remembers his family farm when it was prosperous. (Rev: SLJ 9/90)

**4055** Fleming, Virginia. *Be Good to Eddie Lee* (K–3). Illus. by Floyd Cooper. 1993, Putnam $15.95 (0-399-21993-5). 30pp. Eddie Lee, a boy with Down's syndrome, teaches his neighbor, Christy, to look at the world differently. (Rev: BL 1/15/94; SLJ 2/94)

**4056** Foreman, Michael. *Seal Surfer* (K–4). Illus. 1997, Harcourt $16.00 (0-15-201399-7). 36pp. A disabled boy and his grandfather form an unusual bond between themselves and a seal pup. (Rev: BCCB 5/97; BL 5/1/97; SLJ 3/97*)

**4057** Gauch, Patricia L. *Bravo, Tanya* (PS–2). Illus. by Satomi Ichikawa. 1992, Putnam $15.95 (0-399-22145-X). 32pp. Young Tanya encounters difficulties when she begins taking ballet lessons. (Rev: BL 5/1/92; SLJ 3/92*)

**4058** Gehret, Jeanne. *The Don't-Give-Up-Kid and Learning Differences* (K–3). Illus. by Sandra A. DePauw. 1992, Verbal Images $13.95 (0-9625136-3-6); paper $9.95 (0-884-28110-9). 32pp. A first-grader receives special attention to help his dyslexia. (Rev: BL 6/1/90)

**4059** Giff, Patricia Reilly. *Adiós, Anna* (2–3). Illus. by DyAnne DiSalvo-Ryan. 1995, Dell paper $3.50 (0-440-41070-3). 65pp. When Anna goes to summer camp, her best friend must cope with spending a summer alone taking care of 2 younger children. (Rev: SLJ 10/95)

**4060** Giff, Patricia Reilly. *Ronald Morgan Goes to Bat* (PS–3). Illus. by Susanna Natti. 1988, Puffin paper $4.99 (0-14-050669-1). 32pp. Ronald is so bad a batter that he closes his eyes when the ball comes, but his spirit is unbeatable. Also use: *Watch Out, Ronald Morgan!* (1985). (Rev: BL 6/1/88; HB 9–10/88; SLJ 9/88)

**4061** Gray, Libba M. *Little Lil and the Swing-Singing Sax* (K–3). Illus. by Lisa Cohen. 1996, Simon & Schuster $16.00 (0-689-80681-7). 30pp. When Little Lil's mother gets sick, her uncle must pawn his beloved saxophone to buy medicine. (Rev: BCCB 2/97; BL 9/1/96; SLJ 11/96*)

**4062** Gray, Nigel. *Running Away from Home* (PS–2). Illus. by Gregory Rogers. 1996, Crown $16.00 (0-517-70923-6). 24pp. Sam resents his bossy father and decides to run away. (Rev: BL 8/96; SLJ 7/96)

**4063** Hamanaka, Sheila. *Peace Crane* (1–4). Illus. 1995, Morrow LB $15.93 (0-688-13816-0). 40pp. A poor African American girl tells her paper crane about her troubles and her hopes for the future. (Rev: BL 9/15/95; SLJ 9/95)

**4064** Hamilton, DeWitt. *Sad Days, Glad Days: A Story About Depression* (K–3). Illus. by Gail Owens. 1995, Albert Whitman LB $14.95 (0-8075-7200-4). 32pp. An honest account of a girl facing the problems caused by her mother's fits of depression. (Rev: BL 4/15/95; SLJ 5/95)

**4065** Hanson, Regina. *The Tangerine Tree* (PS–3). Illus. by Harvey Stevenson. 1995, Clarion $14.95 (0-395-68963-5). 32pp. Ida's Jamaican family is torn apart when her father must become a migrant worker in New York City. (Rev: BL 7/95; SLJ 9/95)

**4066** Harrison, Troon. *Aaron's Awful Allergies* (PS–1). Illus. by Eugenie Fernandes. 1998, Kids Can $12.95 (1-55074-299-X). Aaron is unhappy when he has to get rid of his pets because of his allergies. (Rev: SLJ 3/98)

**4067** Harshman, Marc. *The Storm* (K–3). Illus. by Mark Mohr. 1995, Dutton paper $15.99 (0-525-65150-0). 32pp. Wheelchair-bound Jonathan finds himself in the path of a deadly tornado. (Rev: BL 5/1/95; SLJ 7/95)

**4068** Hasler, Eveline. *The Giantess* (K–3). Trans. by Laura McKenna. Illus. by Renate Seelig. 1997, Kane/Miller $12.95 (0-916291-76-6). 24pp. A giantess named Emmeline finds happiness when she joins a traveling carnival. (Rev: BL 12/1/97; SLJ 12/97)

**4069** Heide, Florence Parry, and Roxanne H. Pierce. *Oh, Grow Up!* (K–4). Illus. by Nadine Bernard Westcott. 1996, Orchard LB $16.99 (0-531-08771-9). 32pp. Humorous verses and imaginative drawings illustrate everyday problems in growing up, such as dealing with brothers and sisters. (Rev: BCCB 3/96; BL 3/1/96; SLJ 4/96)

**4070** Heitler, Susan M. *David Decides About Thumbsucking: A Motivating Story for Children and an Informative Guide for Parents* (PS–3). Illus. by Paula Singer. 1996, Reading Matters paper $13.95 (0-9614780-2-0). 52pp. This photoessay concentrates on David and his decision to give up his thumb sucking. (Rev: BL 11/1/85; SLJ 2/86)

**4071** Henkes, Kevin. *Jessica* (PS–2). Illus. 1989, Greenwillow LB $15.93 (0-688-07830-3); Puffin paper $5.99 (0-14-054194-2). 24pp. The story of a little girl with an invisible friend. (Rev: BCCB 2/89; BL 3/15/89; HB 5–6/89)

**4072** Heron, Ann, and Meredith Maran. *How Would You Feel If Your Dad Was Gay?* (2–6). Illus. by Kris Kovick. 1994, Alyson paper $6.95 (1-55583-243-1). Jasmine faces problems with her schoolmates because she has 3 dads: her stepfather, her natural father, and his lover. (Rev: SLJ 2/92)

**4073** Hickman, Martha W. *When Andy's Father Went to Prison* (K–5). Illus. by Larry Raymond. 1990, Whitman LB $12.95 (0-8075-8874-1). Andy faces a personal crisis when he learns that his father has been sent to jail. (Rev: BCCB 1/91; SLJ 2/91)

**4074** Hoffman, Mary. *Henry's Baby* (PS–3). Illus. by Susan Winter. 1993, DK Publg. $13.95 (1-56458-196-9). 32pp. Henry, who wants to be part of the "in" crowd, is afraid his younger brother will hinder his social standing. (Rev: BL 11/15/93)

**4075** Holcomb, Nan. *Andy Finds a Turtle* (K–3). Illus. by Dot Yoder. Series: Turtle Books. 1992, Jason LB $13.95 (0-944727-13-1); paper $7.95 (0-944727-02-6). 32pp. The story of Andy, a young boy with cerebral palsy. Two other books about children with physical problems are: *Danny and the Merry-Go-Round* and *How about a Hug* (both 1992). All 3 are reissues.

**4076** Hru, Dakari. *Joshua's Masai Mask* (K–3). Illus. by Anna Rich. 1993, Lee & Low $15.95 (1-880000-02-4). 32pp. By playing the kalimba, an African musical instrument, in his school's talent show, Joshua gains self-esteem. (Rev: BL 4/1/93)

**4077** Hughes, Shirley. *Alfie and the Birthday Surprise* (PS–K). Illus. 1998, Lothrop $16.00 (0-688-15187-6). 32pp. Alfie, an English toddler, helps his neighbors adjust to the death of their pet cat, Smoky. (Rev: BL 3/1/98; SLJ 3/98)

**4078** Hughes, Shirley. *Dogger* (PS–K). Illus. by author. 1988, Lothrop LB $15.93 (0-688-07981-4); Morrow paper $4.95 (0-688-11704-X). 32pp. Dave's lost stuffed dog turns up at a fair booth, but Dave doesn't have the money to buy it back — until sister comes to the rescue. (Rev: BL 9/1/88)

**4079** Hutchins, Hazel. *Believing Sophie* (K–3). Illus. by Dorothy Donohue. 1995, Albert Whitman LB $14.95 (0-8075-0625-7). 32pp. Sophie is falsely accused of stealing cough drops from her local store. (Rev: BL 9/1/95; SLJ 1/96)

**4080** Hutchins, Pat. *Titch and Daisy* (PS). Illus. 1996, Greenwillow LB $14.93 (0-688-13960-4). 32pp. Titch feels uncomfortable attending a party with a lot of unknown children, but with the help of Daisy, who feels the same way, she conquers her fears. (Rev: BL 4/15/96; HB 5–6/96; SLJ 4/96)

**4081** Isadora, Rachel. *Ben's Trumpet* (K–3). Illus. by author. 1979, Greenwillow $16.00 (0-688-80194-3); Morrow paper $5.95 (0-688-10988-8). 32pp. A young black boy dreams of becoming a trumpet player and eventually is taken to a jazz club by a musician.

**4082** Johnson, Patricia P., and Donna R. Williams. *Morgan's Baby Sister: A Read-Aloud Book for Families Who Have Experienced the Death of a Newborn* (K–3). Illus. by Suzanne Schaffhausen. Series: Helping Children Who Hurt Books. 1993, Resource paper $10.95 (0-89390-257-8). 55pp. A young girl and her family adjust to the death of the baby they had been awaiting. (Rev: SLJ 3/94)

**4083** Joslin, Sesyle. *What Do You Say, Dear?* (1–3). Illus. by Maurice Sendak. 1958, HarperCollins LB $14.89 (0-06-023074-6); paper $5.95 (0-06-443112-6). 48pp. Humorous handbook on manners for young ladies and gentlemen of 6 to 8. Also use: *What Do You Do, Dear?* (1958).

**4084** Karas, G. Brian. *Home on the Bayou: A Cowboy's Story* (K–3). Illus. 1996, Simon & Schuster paper $15.00 (0-689-80156-4). 32pp. Ned has to contend with a new home on the bayou and Big Head Ed, the school bully. (Rev: BCCB 1/97; BL 9/15/96; SLJ 10/96*)

**4085** Karkowsku, Nancy. *Grandma's Soup* (PS–3). Illus. by Shelly O. Haas. 1989, Kar-Ben paper $4.95 (0-930494-99-7). Several grandchildren gradually adjust to the fact that their grandmother has Alzheimer's disease. (Rev: SLJ 12/89)

**4086** Keats, Ezra Jack. *Louie* (PS–K). Illus. by author. 1983, Greenwillow LB $14.93 (0-688-02383-5). 32pp. Louie, a silent child, makes his first friend, a puppet, and is allowed to keep it for his very own.

**4087** Kelley, True. *I've Got Chicken Pox* (PS–3). Illus. 1994, Dutton paper $13.99 (0-525-45185-4). 32pp. At first, Jess is excited at having chicken pox and missing school, but harsh reality sets in, in this exploration of the ups and downs of treating this illness. (Rev: BL 5/15/94; SLJ 6/94)

**4088** Kellogg, Steven. *Won't Somebody Play with Me?* (K–3). Illus. by author. 1976, Puffin paper $4.95 (0-8037-9612-9). 32pp. It's Kim's birthday, but no one is home to play with her.

**4089** Kibbey, Marsha. *My Grammy: A Book About Alzheimer's Disease* (1–3). Illus. by Karen Ritz. 1988, Carolrhoda paper $4.95 (0-87614-544-6). 32pp. Eight-year-old Amy and her family must cope with Grammy's worsening Alzheimer's disease. (Rev: BL 7/88; SLJ 10/88)

**4090** Kolbisen, Irene M. *Wiggle-Butts and Up-Faces* (PS–K). Illus. by Sandy D. Zmolek. 1989, I Think I Can LB $14.95 (1-877863-00-9). 32pp. Ingrid's young brother is afraid of taking beginner swimming lessons. (Rev: BL 12/1/89)

**4091** Krauss, Ruth. *A Very Special House* (PS–K). Illus. by Maurice Sendak. 1953, HarperCollins LB $16.89 (0-06-023456-3). 32pp. A little boy tells what it would be like in his very special house — no one would ever say "Stop, Stop."

**4092** Krisher, Trudy. *Kathy's Hats: A Story of Hope* (PS–3). Illus. by Nadine Bernard Westcott. 1992, Whitman LB $14.95 (0-8075-4116-8). 32pp. When Kathy undergoes chemotherapy for cancer, she finds a new reason to wear her hats. (Rev: BCCB 10/92; BL 10/1/92; SLJ 6/91)

**4093** Kroll, Virginia. *Can You Dance, Dalila?* (PS–3). Illus. by Nancy Carpenter. 1996, Simon & Schuster paper $15.00 (0-689-80551-9). 32pp. An African American child who can't master social dancing shines during a folk dance performance. (Rev: BL 11/15/96; SLJ 2/97)

**4094** Kroll, Virginia. *Fireflies, Peach Pies and Lullabies* (PS–3). Illus. by Nancy Cote. 1995, Simon & Schuster $15.00 (0-689-80291-9). 32pp. At Great-Granny Annabel's wake, Francie asks each family member to relate a remembrance of her. The list is read at the funeral service and becomes a celebration of Great-Granny's life. (Rev: BL 12/15/95; SLJ 4/96)

**4095** Lagercrantz, Rose, and Samuel Lagercrantz. *Is It Magic?* (K–3). Trans. by Paul Norlen. Illus. by Eva

Eriksson. 1991, R&S $13.95 (91-29-59182-1). Young Pete and Cilla are in love until the class bully steps in. (Rev: SLJ 3/91)

**4096** Lampert, Emily. *A Little Touch of Monster* (PS–1). Illus. by Melanie Kroupa. 1986, Little, Brown LB $12.95 (0-316-51287-7). 32pp. No one listens to Parker, so he turns into a bit of a monster; then they listen to him too much, granting almost his every wish. (Rev: BCCB 5/86; BL 3/15/86; HB 5–6/86)

**4097** Lanton, Sandy. *Daddy's Chair* (K–3). Illus. by Shelly O. Haas. 1991, Kar-Ben $12.95 (0-929371-51-8). Michael cannot believe that his now dead father will never sit in his favorite chair again. (Rev: SLJ 7/91)

**4098** Lasker, Joe. *Nick Joins In* (K–3). Illus. by author. 1980, Whitman LB $14.95 (0-8075-5612-2). 32pp. Wheelchair-bound Nicky wonders what will happen to him when he goes to a regular school.

**4099** Lasky, Kathryn. *The Tantrum* (PS–1). Illus. by Bobette McCarthy. 1993, Macmillan LB $13.95 (0-02-751661-X). 32pp. Gracie tells about her terrible temper tantrum and how everyone responded to it. (Rev: BL 4/1/93)

**4100** Leach, Norman. *My Wicked Stepmother* (PS–3). Illus. by Jane Browne. 1993, Macmillan LB $13.95 (0-02-754700-0). 32pp. At first, Tom hates his stepmother, but when he deliberately hurts her and she cries, his hate turns to love. (Rev: BCCB 7–8/93; BL 2/15/93; SLJ 3/93)

**4101** Lindgren, Barbro. *Sam's Ball* (PS). Illus. by Eva Eriksson. 1983, Morrow paper $6.95 (0-688-02359-2). 32pp. A book in which a toddler shares his toy with a kitty. Four others in this series are: *Sam's Car; Sam's Cookie; Sam's Teddy Bear* (all 1982); *Sam's Bath* (1983).

**4102** Litchfield, Ada B. *Words in Our Hands* (2–4). Illus. by Helen Cogancherry. 1980, Whitman LB $14.95 (0-8075-9212-9). Michael describes his life with his deaf parents.

**4103** Lobby, Ted. *Jessica and the Wolf: A Story for Children Who Have Bad Dreams* (PS–1). Illus. by Tennessee Dixon. 1990, Brunner $11.95 (0-945354-22-3); paper $8.95 (0-945354-21-5). 32pp. Parents help their daughter when she has a recurring nightmare about a wolf. (Rev: BL 9/1/90)

**4104** Locker, Thomas. *The Young Artist* (2–5). Illus. 1993, Puffin paper $4.99 (0-14-054923-4). 32pp. Adrian, a painter, has difficulties when he is commissioned to paint portraits of the royal family. (Rev: BCCB 1/90; BL 10/15/89; SLJ 12/89)

**4105** London, Jonathan. *The Lion Who Has Asthma* (PS–2). Illus. by Nadine Bernard Westcott. 1992, Whitman LB $14.95 (0-8075-4559-7). In his imagination, asthmatic Sean becomes a variety of animals to suit different situations. (Rev: SLJ 6/92)

**4106** London, Jonathan. *The Sugaring-Off Party* (K–3). Illus. by Gilles Pelletier. 1995, Dutton paper $15.99 (0-525-45187-0). 32pp. Paul's French Canadian grandmother describes the excitement of maple sugaring-off parties. (Rev: BL 1/1/95; SLJ 1/95)

**4107** Lottridge, Celia B. *Something Might Be Hiding* (PS–K). Illus. by Paul Zwolak. 1996, Douglas & McIntyre $14.95 (0-88899-176-2). 24pp. A child feels the stress of moving to a new house. (Rev: BL 8/96; SLJ 6/96)

**4108** McMahon, Patricia. *Listen for the Bus: David's Story* (K–4). Photos by John Godt. 1995, Boyds Mills $15.95 (1-56397-368-5). 48pp. In this photoessay, a blind boy who also has hearing problems nevertheless takes great joy in the simple things in life. (Rev: BL 11/1/95; SLJ 10/95) [362.41]

**4109** Magorian, Michelle. *Who's Going to Take Care of Me?* (PS–K). Illus. by James G. Hale. 1990, HarperCollins $13.95 (0-06-024105-5). 32pp. When Eric's older sister starts school, he wonders who will take care of him. (Rev: BL 11/15/90; HB 1–2/91; SLJ 12/90)

**4110** Martin, C. L. G. *Down Dairy Farm Road* (K–3). Illus. by Diane D. Hearn. 1994, Macmillan paper $14.95 (0-02-762450-1). 32pp. Junie Mae can't afford the beauty parlor curls her rich friend Lucinda has, so she settles for attractive braids instead. (Rev: BL 6/1–15/94; SLJ 5/94)

**4111** Mauser, Pat Rhoads. *Patti's Pet Gorilla* (2–4). Illus. by Diane Palmisciano. 1991, Avon paper $2.95 (0-380-71039-0). 64pp. Patti wants to impress her classmates at show-and-tell, so she tells them she has a pet gorilla. (Rev: BCCB 9/87; BL 3/15/87; SLJ 8/87)

**4112** Mayer, Mercer. *You're the Scaredy-Cat* (K–2). Illus. by author. 1991, Rain Bird paper $5.95 (1-879920-01-8). 40pp. Two young boys decide to spend the night camping out in the backyard.

**4113** Medearis, Angela Shelf. *Annie's Gifts* (K–3). Illus. by Anna Rich. 1995, Just Us $14.95 (0-940975-30-0); paper $6.95 (0-940975-31-9). Annie is upset because everyone in her family except her is musically talented. (Rev: BCCB 4/95; SLJ 9/95)

**4114** Miller, Kathryn Ann. *Did My First Mother Love Me? A Story for an Adopted Child* (K–3). Illus. by Jami Moffett. 1994, Morning Glory $12.95 (0-930934-85-7); paper $5.95 (0-930934-84-9). 47pp. A girl learns the reasons why her real mother put her up for adoption and is comforted by this knowledge. (Rev: SLJ 7/94)

**4115** Milstein, Linda. *Amanda's Perfect Hair* (PS–3). Illus. by Susan Meddaugh. 1993, Morrow LB $14.93 (0-688-11154-8). 32pp. Everyone loves Amanda's

blond hair so much that she is afraid that it is the only reason she is popular. (Rev: BL 11/1/93; HB 9–10/93; SLJ 1/94)

**4116** Mitchell, Rita P. *Hue Boy* (PS–3). Illus. by Caroline Binch. 1993, Dial paper $13.99 (0-8037-1448-3). 32pp. Hue Boy is so slow in growing that he worries about remaining small forever. (Rev: BL 5/1/93; HB 7–8/93)

**4117** Mochizuki, Ken. *Baseball Saved Us* (2–4). Illus. by Dom Lee. 1993, Lee & Low $15.95 (1-880000-01-6). 32pp. A Japanese American boy gains acceptance playing an excellent game of baseball learned while an internee during World War II. (Rev: BCCB 5/93; BL 4/15/93; HB 7–8/93; SLJ 6/93)

**4118** Moss, Deborah M. *Lee, the Rabbit with Epilepsy* (PS–1). Illus. by Carol Schwartz. 1989, Woodbine LB $12.95 (0-933149-32-8). 24pp. While fishing with her grandfather, Lee, a young rabbit, has her first epileptic seizure. A companion book is: *Shelley, the Hyperactive Turtle* (1989). (Rev: BL 12/1/89)

**4119** Munsch, Robert, and Saoussan Askar. *From Far Away* (K–3). Illus. by Michael Martchenko. 1995, Firefly LB $16.95 (1-55037-397-8); paper $5.95 (1-55037-396-X). 24pp. Saoussan, a war refugee, has problems adjusting to her new home in Canada. (Rev: BL 1/1–15/96; SLJ 3/96)

**4120** Naylor, Phyllis Reynolds. *King of the Playground* (K–3). Illus. by Nola L. Malone. 1991, Macmillan $16.00 (0-689-31558-9). 32pp. After some advice from his dad, Kevin is able to stand up to the playground bully. (Rev: BL 9/1/91; HB 9–10/91; SLJ 1/92)

**4121** Ness, Evaline. *Sam, Bangs and Moonshine* (K–2). Illus. by author. 1966, Holt $14.95 (0-8050-0314-2); paper $5.95 (0-8050-0315-0). 48pp. A little girl learns to distinguish truth from "moonshine" only after her cat and playmate nearly meet tragedy. Caldecott Medal winner, 1967.

**4122** Newman, Leslea. *Saturday Is Pattyday* (PS–3). Illus. by Annette Hegel. 1993, New Victoria LB $14.95 (0-934678-52-9); paper $6.95 (0-934678-51-0). 24pp. Frankie is unhappy when his 2 moms break up and one moves to her own apartment. (Rev: BCCB 11/93; BL 11/1/93)

**4123** Newman, Leslea. *Too Far Away to Touch* (K–4). Illus. by Catherine Stock. 1995, Clarion $14.95 (0-395-68968-6). 32pp. Uncle Leonard, who has AIDS, tries to prepare his young niece Zoe for his imminent death. (Rev: BCCB 5/95; BL 3/15/95; HB 5–6/95; SLJ 9/95)

**4124** Old, Wendie C. *Stacy Had a Little Sister* (PS–2). Illus. by Judith Friedman. 1995, Albert Whitman LB $14.95 (0-8075-7598-4). 32pp. When Stacy's baby sister dies of SIDS, she feels confused and guilty. (Rev: BCCB 5/95; BL 1/1/95; SLJ 2/95)

**4125** Paterson, Katherine. *The Smallest Cow in the World* (PS–2). Illus. by Jane Brown. 1991, Harper-Collins LB $14.89 (0-06-024691-X); paper $3.75 (0-06-444164-4). 64pp. When he and his family move to another farm, Marvin misses Rosie, the cow he left behind. (Rev: BCCB 1/92*; BL 9/15/91; HB 9–10/91; SLJ 1/92*)

**4126** Peterson, Jeanne Whitehouse. *I Have a Sister, My Sister Is Deaf* (1–3). Illus. by Deborah Kogan Ray. 1977, HarperCollins LB $14.89 (0-06-024702-9); paper $5.95 (0-06-443059-6). 32pp. About a young girl's adjustment to deafness.

**4127** Pinkney, Brian. *Jojo's Flying Side Kick* (K–4). Illus. 1995, Simon & Schuster $15.00 (0-689-80283-8). 32pp. Everyone offers advice to Jojo to help her win her yellow belt, which involves breaking a board with a flying side kick. (Rev: BCCB 12/95; BL 10/15/95; HB 9–10/95; SLJ 9/95)

**4128** Pollack, Eileen. *Whisper Whisper Jesse, Whisper Whisper Josh: A Story About AIDS* (K–4). Illus. by Bruce Gilfoy. 1992, Advantage LB $16.95 (0-9624828-4-6); paper $5.95 (0-9624828-3-8). 32pp. Jesse's uncle, Josh, who is dying of AIDS, comes to stay with Jesse's family. (Rev: BL 3/15/93)

**4129** Pulver, Robin. *Alicia's Tutu* (PS–3). Illus. by Mark Graham. 1997, Dial paper $14.89 (0-8037-1933-7). 32pp. Alicia is unhappy because she doesn't get the tutu she wants, but she learns that there are more important things in life. (Rev: BL 9/1/97; SLJ 10/97)

**4130** Purdy, Carol. *Least of All* (PS–1). Illus. by Tim Arnold. 1987, Macmillan LB $12.95 (0-689-50404-7); paper $3.95 (0-689-71681-8). 32pp. Raven Hannah is the youngest and the only girl in the family in turn-of-the-century Vermont, which means she is left out of everything. (Rev: BCCB 3/87; BL 3/1/87; SLJ 6–7/87)

**4131** Rabe, Berniece. *The Balancing Girl* (PS–3). Illus. by Lillian Hoban. 1988, Dutton paper $4.99 (0-525-44364-9). 32pp. A paraplegic girl named Margaret delights in balancing things.

**4132** Ransom, Candice. *When the Whippoorwill Calls* (K–3). Illus. by Kimberly B. Root. 1995, Morrow LB $15.93 (0-688-12730-4). 32pp. Polly's life changes when her parents' home and property are sold to the government to help create the Shenandoah National Park. (Rev: BCCB 12/95; BL 9/15/95; SLJ 11/95*)

**4133** Raskin, Ellen. *Spectacles* (K–3). Illus. by author. 1988, Macmillan paper $4.95 (0-689-71271-5). 48pp. A spectacle not to be missed is Iris Fogel's misinterpretation of everything she sees until her myopia is corrected. Cleverly illustrated.

**4134** Rathmann, Peggy. *Ruby the Copycat* (K–3). Illus. 1991, Scholastic $14.95 (0-590-43747-X).

32pp. At first, Angela is flattered when a new girl, Ruby, copies everything she does; then it becomes annoying. (Rev: BL 11/15/91; SLJ 1/92*)

**4135** Rheingrover, Jean S. *Veronica's First Year* (K–3). Illus. by Kay Life. 1996, Albert Whitman LB $13.95 (0-8075-8474-6). When Nathan's long-awaited sister arrives and is diagnosed as having Down's syndrome, his parents explain the situation to him and make plans for this special child. (Rev: BCCB 12/96; SLJ 10/96)

**4136** Riecken, Nancy. *Today Is the Day* (PS–3). Illus. by Catherine Stock. 1996, Houghton $14.95 (0-395-73917-9). 32pp. Yese awaits her father's return from the big city, where he has been working for 6 months, to their rural Mexican home. (Rev: BCCB 9/96; BL 9/15/96; SLJ 8/96)

**4137** Rockwell, Anne. *No! No! No!* (PS–K). Illus. 1995, Simon & Schuster paper $14.00 (0-02-777782-0). 32pp. Everything seems to go wrong for a young boy whose bad mood continues throughout a whole day. (Rev: BL 5/1/95; SLJ 7/95)

**4138** Rodell, Susanna. *Dear Fred* (PS–2). Illus. by Kim Gamble. 1995, Ticknor $14.95 (0-395-71544-X). 32pp. Grace writes to her half-brother, who has been separated from her because of divorce and relocation. (Rev: BL 8/95; SLJ 4/95)

**4139** Rodgers, Frank. *Who's Afraid of the Ghost Train?* (PS–K). Illus. by author. 1989, Harcourt $12.95 (0-15-200642-7). Robert uses his imagination to conquer his fears, including riding the carnival Ghost Train. (Rev: SLJ 10/89)

**4140** Rosen, Michael. *This Is Our House* (PS–2). Illus. by Bob Graham. 1996, Candlewick $15.99 (1-56402-870-4). 32pp. George learns to share when his friends exclude him because of his selfish ways. (Rev: BL 11/1/96; HB 7–8/96; SLJ 7/96)

**4141** Ross, Kent, and Alice Ross. *Cemetery Quilt* (K–3). Illus. by Rosanne Kaloustian. 1995, Houghton $14.95 (0-395-70948-2). 32pp. A young girl tries to avoid going to the funeral of the grandmother she loved dearly. (Rev: BL 9/15/95; SLJ 9/95)

**4142** Ross, Tony. *Happy Blanket* (PS–2). Illus. by author. 1990, Farrar $12.95 (0-374-32843-9). 32pp. Two stories about 2 children who have many fears. (Rev: SLJ 1/91)

**4143** Sakai, Kimiko. *Sachiko Means Happiness* (K–3). Illus. by Tomie Arai. 1990, Children's Book Pr. $14.95 (0-89239-065-4). 32pp. A young Japanese American girl has difficulty adjusting to the changes in her grandmother, who has Alzheimer's disease. (Rev: BCCB 1/91; BL 12/1/90; HB 1–2/91; SLJ 3/91)

**4144** Saltzberg, Barney. *Mrs. Morgan's Lawn* (K–3). Illus. 1993, Hyperion LB $14.49 (1-56282-424-4).

32pp. With an act of kindness, a boy melts the heart of mean old Mrs. Morgan. (Rev: BL 12/1/93)

**4145** Savageau, Cheryl. *Muskrat Will Be Swimming* (1–3). Illus. by Robert Hynes. 1996, Northland LB $14.95 (0-87358-604-2). 28pp. A legend told to a Native American girl by her grandfather helps her accept herself. (Rev: BL 6/1–15/96; SLJ 8/96)

**4146** Say, Allen. *Allison* (PS–3). Illus. 1997, Houghton $17.00 (0-395-85895-X). 32pp. Little Allison, an Asian girl, is upset when she learns that she has been adopted by her Caucasian parents. (Rev: BL 12/15/97*; SLJ 10/97)

**4147** Say, Allen. *Emma's Rug* (PS–3). Illus. 1996, Houghton $16.95 (0-395-74294-3). 32pp. Emma is inconsolable when she loses the rug that has been the inspiration for her art. (Rev: BCCB 11/96; BL 10/1/96; HB 9–10/96; SLJ 9/96)

**4148** Schories, Pat. *He's Your Dog!* (PS–2). Illus. 1993, Farrar $15.00 (0-374-32906-0). 32pp. After a young boy and his dog are chastised for misbehaving, the boy fantasizes about running away. (Rev: BL 1/1/94; SLJ 1/94)

**4149** Schwartz, Harriet B. *When Artie Was Little* (PS–3). Illus. by Thomas B. Allen. 1996, Knopf LB $16.99 (0-679-93236-4). 40pp. An old man named Artie recalls everyday incidents when he was growing up. (Rev: BL 5/15/96; SLJ 8/96)

**4150** Sendak, Maurice. *Pierre: A Cautionary Tale in Five Chapters and a Prologue* (K–3). Illus. by author. 1962, HarperCollins LB $14.89 (0-06-025965-5). 48pp. The story about a young boy whose motto is "I don't care."

**4151** Shannon, David. *A Bad Case of Stripes* (1–3). Illus. 1998, Scholastic $15.95 (0-590-92997-6). 32pp. Camilla's desire to please and be popular causes her some problems. (Rev: BL 1/1–15/98; SLJ 3/98)

**4152** Sharmat, Marjorie W. *A Big Fat Enormous Lie* (PS–1). Illus. by David McPhail. 1978, Puffin paper $3.99 (0-525-44242-1). 32pp. A small lie becomes a monster that haunts a youngster until he tells the truth.

**4153** Simon, Norma. *I Am Not a Crybaby* (K–3). Illus. by Helen Cogancherry. 1989, Whitman LB $14.95 (0-8075-3447-1). 40pp. A comforting book on emotions for primary grades. (Rev: BCCB 4/89; BL 4/15/89)

**4154** Simon, Norma. *I Was So Mad!* (K–3). Illus. by Dora Leder. 1974, Whitman LB $12.95 (0-8075-3520-6); paper $4.95 (0-8075-3519-2). 40pp. Children catalog the things that make them mad and learn that adults get angry too.

**4155** Simon, Norma. *I Wish I Had My Father* (2–4). Illus. by Arieh Zeldich. 1983, Whitman LB $12.95

(0-8075-3522-2). 32pp. A young boy wishes his divorced father was back with him.

**4156** Smalls, Irene. *Because You're Lucky* (PS–3). Illus. by Michael Hays. 1997, Little, Brown $15.95 (0-316-79867-3). 32pp. A young boy goes to live with his aunt's family and arouses the hostility of his cousin. (Rev: BL 9/1/97; SLJ 10/97)

**4157** Spelman, Cornelia. *After Charlotte's Mom Died* (K–2). Illus. by Judith Friedman. 1996, Albert Whitman LB $12.95 (0-8075-0196-4). 32pp. Charlotte feels conflicting emotions, such as anger and fear, as she adjusts to her mother's death. (Rev: BL 4/15/96; SLJ 8/96)

**4158** Spinelli, Eileen. *Somebody Loves You, Mr. Hatch* (K–3). Illus. by Paul Yalowitz. 1991, Macmillan LB $15.00 (0-02-786015-9). 32pp. An antisocial man receives a huge box of chocolates from an unknown admirer. (Rev: BL 11/15/91; HB 11–12/91; SLJ 2/92)

**4159** Stanek, Muriel. *All Alone After School* (2–3). Illus. by Gay Owens. 1985, Whitman LB $12.95 (0-8075-0278-2). 32pp. At first, Josh needs a lucky stone to help him cope with being alone after school while his mother works. (Rev: BCCB 4/85; BL 3/15/85; SLJ 9/85)

**4160** Stanek, Muriel. *Don't Hurt Me, Mama* (1–3). Illus. by Helen Cogancherry. 1983, Whitman LB $12.95 (0-8075-1689-9). 32pp. A simple story of child abuse as seen through the eyes of a child.

**4161** Steig, William. *Spinky Sulks* (K–3). Illus. 1988, Farrar $15.00 (0-374-38321-9); paper $4.95 (0-374-46990-3). 32pp. Spinky is a first-class sulker but is forced to reconsider his position. (Rev: BCCB 12/88; BL 1/15/89; HB 3–4/89)

**4162** Stein, Sara Bonnett. *About Dying* (1–3). Illus. by author. 1974, Walker $10.95 (0-8027-6172-0); paper $8.95 (0-8027-7223-4). 48pp. Sensitive portrayal of the death of a bird and of a grandfather. Also use: *About Handicaps* (1974); *Making Babies* (1974); *About Phobias; The Adopted One; On Divorce* (all 1979).

**4163** Stevenson, James. *I Had a Lot of Wishes* (PS–3). Illus. 1995, Greenwillow LB $14.93 (0-688-13706-7). 32pp. This autobiographical account tells of the wishes Stevenson had as a child, including going to summer camp. (Rev: BCCB 10/95; BL 10/15/95*; SLJ 2/96) [813]

**4164** Stolz, Mary. *Storm in the Night* (K–3). Illus. by Pat Cummings. 1988, HarperCollins LB $14.89 (0-06-025913-2); paper $5.95 (0-06-443256-4). 32pp. Grandfather tells Thomas, a young black boy, of a time when he was afraid, in order to calm the child's fears about a dark, stormy night. (Rev: BL 2/1/88; HB 7–8/88; SLJ 3/88)

**4165** Thomas, Marlo. *Free to Be . . . You and Me* (K–3). Illus. 1992, Peter Smith $21.00 (0-8446-6602-5). Twenty-five stories, poems, and songs to help children develop as individuals.

**4166** Thompson, Mary. *Andy and His Yellow Frisbee* (1–3). Illus. by author. 1996, Woodbine $14.95 (0-933149-83-2). The story of an autistic child as seen through the eyes of a young classmate. (Rev: SLJ 1/97)

**4167** Titherington, Jeanne. *A Place for Ben* (PS–K). Illus. by author. 1987, Greenwillow LB $15.93 (0-688-06494-9). 24pp. Ben has no place of his own since his baby brother arrived, but he finds his own spot in the garage. (Rev: BCCB 3/87; BL 3/1/87; HB 5–6/87)

**4168** Trottier, Maxine. *A Safe Place* (K–3). Illus. by Judith Friedman. 1997, Albert Whitman LB $13.95 (0-8075-7212-8). 24pp. At night, a little girl and her mother seek safety from an abusive daddy by going to a safe place, the white house on the hill. (Rev: BL 6/1–15/97; SLJ 5/97)

**4169** Trottier, Maxine. *The Tiny Kite of Eddie Wing* (PS–2). Illus. by Al Van Mil. 1996, Kane/Miller $13.95 (0-916291-66-9). 28pp. Eddie Wing's family is so poor that they can't afford to buy him a kite. (Rev: BL 11/15/96; SLJ 12/96)

**4170** Verniero, Joan C. *You Can Call Me Willy: A Story for Children About AIDS* (K–3). Illus. by Verdon Flory. Series: Books to Help Parents Help Their Children. 1995, Magination paper $8.95 (0-945354-60-6). A touching story of a third-grader who has AIDS and the intolerance and misunderstandings she faces at school. (Rev: SLJ 9/95)

**4171** Vigna, Judith. *Black Like Kyra, White Like Me* (PS). Illus. 1992, Whitman LB $14.95 (0-8075-0778-4). 32pp. Christy tells what happened after the family of her black friend Kyra Kirk moves into her all-white neighborhood. (Rev: BCCB 10/92; BL 11/15/92; SLJ 10/92)

**4172** Vigna, Judith. *I Wish Daddy Didn't Drink So Much* (PS). Illus. by author. 1988, Whitman LB $14.95 (0-8075-3523-0); paper $5.95 (0-8075-3526-5). 32pp. A Christmas story told by a little girl whose father is an alcoholic. (Rev: BL 10/1/88; SLJ 1/89)

**4173** Vigna, Judith. *Mommy and Me by Ourselves Again* (PS–2). Illus. by author. 1987, Whitman LB $14.95 (0-8075-5232-1). 32pp. Mother and daughter are alone after the divorce, and it's a lonely birthday until relatives arrive. (Rev: BCCB 11/87; BL 9/15/87; SLJ 12/87)

**4174** Vigna, Judith. *My Big Sister Takes Drugs* (K–3). Illus. 1990, Whitman LB $14.95 (0-8075-5317-4). 32pp. Young Paul becomes emotionally disturbed when he finds out that his sister is taking drugs. (Rev: BCCB 11/90; BL 10/15/90; SLJ 12/90)

**4175** Vigna, Judith. *My Two Uncles* (2–4). Illus. 1995, Albert Whitman LB $14.95 (0-8075-5507-X). 32pp. A little girl has difficulty understanding the hostility her grandfather feels toward her gay Uncle Ned and his partner, Phil. (Rev: BCCB 5/95; BL 4/15/95; SLJ 6/95)

**4176** Vigna, Judith. *Saying Goodbye to Daddy* (K–2). Illus. 1991, Whitman LB $14.95 (0-8075-7253-5). 32pp. When her father is killed in a car accident, Clare goes through the phases of grieving. (Rev: BL 2/1/91; SLJ 3/91)

**4177** Vigna, Judith. *When Eric's Mom Fought Cancer* (PS–3). Illus. 1993, Albert Whitman LB $14.95 (0-8075-8883-0). 32pp. Eric is frightened, confused, and, at times, angry when his mother undergoes various cancer treatments. (Rev: BL 10/1/93; SLJ 10/93)

**4178** Viorst, Judith. *The Good-bye Book* (PS–K). Illus. by Kay Chorao. 1988, Macmillan $16.00 (0-689-31308-X). A young boy is absolutely dead set against his parents going out — until they leave and the baby-sitter reads aloud. (Rev: BL 2/15/88; SLJ 8/88)

**4179** Viorst, Judith. *The Tenth Good Thing About Barney* (K–2). Illus. by Erik Blegvad. 1971, Macmillan $14.00 (0-689-20688-7); paper $4.99 (0-689-71203-0). 32pp. At a backyard funeral, a little boy tries to think of 10 good things to say about his cat, Barney — but can come up with only 9.

**4180** Waber, Bernard. *Ira Sleeps Over* (PS–2). Illus. by author. 1973, Houghton $15.00 (0-395-13893-0); paper $5.95 (0-395-20503-4). 48pp. When Ira is invited to sleep overnight at Reggie's house, he wants to go, but should he or shouldn't he take along his teddy bear?

**4181** Wainwright, Richard M. *Mountains to Climb* (3–5). Illus. by Jack Crompton. 1991, Family Life $18.00 (0-9619566-3-1). 56pp. During his 2-year stay in the United States, a young Ecuadoran boy gradually wins his classmates' acceptance. (Rev: BL 12/15/91; SLJ 1/92)

**4182** Wallace-Brodeur, Ruth. *Goodbye, Mitch* (PS–3). Illus. by Kathryn Miller. 1995, Albert Whitman LB $14.95 (0-8075-2996-6). 32pp. Michael sadly watches his pet cat Mitch waste away and die from the effects of a tumor. (Rev: BCCB 5/95; BL 6/1–15/95; SLJ 8/95)

**4183** Walsh, Jill Paton. *Connie Came to Play* (PS–K). Illus. by Stephen Lambert. 1996, Viking paper $12.99 (0-670-86210-X). 32pp. The importance of sharing is the concept explored in this story of selfish Robert and playmate Connie. (Rev: BL 1/1–15/96; HB 5–6/96; SLJ 2/96)

**4184** Watts, Jeri Hanel. *Keepers* (K–3). Illus. by Felicia Marshall. 1997, Lee & Low $15.95 (1-

880000-58-X). 32pp. Kenyon feels guilty because he has bought a baseball glove with the money intended for Grandmother's 90th birthday present. (Rev: BL 1/1–15/98; SLJ 1/98)

**4185** Yolen, Jane. *Grandad Bill's Song* (K–2). Illus. by Melissa Mathis. 1994, Putnam $15.95 (0-399-21802-5). 32pp. After his grandfather's death, a young boy asks different members of his family what they remember most about him. (Rev: BL 7/94; SLJ 7/94)

**4186** Zagwyn, Deborah T. *The Pumpkin Blanket* (PS–2). Illus. 1991, Celestial Arts $15.95 (0-89087-637-1). Through the help of her father, Clee learns to live without her comfort blanket. (Rev: SLJ 9/91)

**4187** Zolotow, Charlotte. *The Old Dog* (PS–2). Illus. by James E. Ransome. 1995, HarperCollins LB $14.89 (0-06-024412-7). 32pp. Ben has problems coping with the death of his beloved dog. (Rev: BL 9/1/95; HB 11–12/95; SLJ 12/95)

## REAL AND ALMOST REAL ANIMALS

**4188** Abercrombie, Barbara. *Charlie Anderson* (PS–3). Illus. by Mark Graham. 1990, Macmillan $16.00 (0-689-50486-1). 32pp. Sarah and Elizabeth discover that the cat that spends only the night with them is leading a double life. (Rev: BCCB 11/90; BL 10/15/90; SLJ 12/90)

**4189** Abercrombie, Barbara. *Michael and the Cats* (PS–2). Illus. by Mark Graham. 1993, Macmillan $13.95 (0-689-50543-4). 32pp. Michael has to use psychology to gain the friendship of his aunt's 2 cats. (Rev: BL 12/15/93; SLJ 10/93)

**4190** Adlerman, Daniel. *Africa Calling: Nighttime Falling* (PS–1). Illus. by Kimberly Adlerman. 1996, Whispering Coyote $15.95 (1-879085-98-4). 32pp. A young girl tries to imagine her stuffed animals in their native African habitats. (Rev: BL 10/1/96; SLJ 9/96)

**4191** Albert, Richard E. *Alejandro's Gift* (K–3). Illus. by Sylvia Long. 1994, Chronicle $14.95 (0-8118-0436-4). 26pp. An old man lives alone in the desert except for the animals that he helps feed. (Rev: BL 4/15/94; SLJ 7/94)

**4192** Aliki. *At Mary Bloom's* (K–2). Illus. by author. 1983, Greenwillow LB $15.93 (0-688-02481-5). 32pp. When her pet mouse has babies, a little girl shares the excitement with a neighbor's household.

**4193** Allen, Judy. *Seal* (K–3). Illus. by Tudor Humphries. 1994, Candlewick $14.95 (1-56402-145-9). 32pp. While vacationing on the coast of Greece, Jenny discovers a cave containing a colony of endangered Mediterranean monk seals. (Rev: BL 5/1/94; SLJ 4/94)

**4194** Ancona, George, and Mary Beth Ancona. *Handtalk Zoo* (1–4). Illus. 1989, Macmillan $14.95 (0-02-700801-0). 32pp. Children with hearing problems sign the names of various animals during a fun day at the zoo. (Rev: BCCB 1/90; BL 10/1/89*; HB 11–12/89; SLJ 10/89)

**4195** Anderson, Laurie Halse. *Ndito Runs* (PS–3). Illus. by Anita van der Merwe. 1996, Holt $15.95 (0-8050-3265-7). 32pp. A small girl in Kenya summons up the dreams of animals to speed her way to school. (Rev: BL 3/15/96; SLJ 5/96)

**4196** Anholt, Laurence. *The New Puppy* (PS–2). Illus. by Catherine Anholt. 1995, Western Artists & Writers $12.95 (0-307-17516-2). 32pp. Raising a puppy is harder than Anna ever expected. (Rev: BCCB 7–8/95; BL 8/95; SLJ 5/95)

**4197** *Animal Homes* (PS–2). Illus. Series: What's Inside? 1993, DK Publg. $8.95 (1-56458-218-3). 17pp. After seeing a picture of the exterior of an animal habitation, readers get an inside view by peeling back the diagram. (Rev: BL 8/93) [591]

**4198** Appelt, Kathi. *The Thunderherd* (PS–2). Illus. by Elizabeth Sayles. 1996, Morrow LB $15.93 (0-688-13264-2). 32pp. A lone mustang tries to join his herd during a severe electrical storm. (Rev: BL 5/15/96; SLJ 8/96)

**4199** Aragon, Jane C. *Salt Hands* (K–2). Illus. by Ted Rand. 1994, Puffin paper $5.99 (0-140-50321-8). 24pp. When a little girl sprinkles salt on her palm, a deer comes to her. (Rev: BL 9/15/89; SLJ 11/89)

**4200** Archambault, John. *The Birth of a Whale* (K–2). Illus. by Janet Skiles. 1996, Silver Burdett LB $15.95 (0-382-39566-2). 48pp. In rhythmic verse and watercolor illustrations, the birth of a humpback whale is chronicled. (Rev: BL 3/15/96; SLJ 3/96) [599.5]

**4201** Arnosky, Jim. *Little Lions* (PS). Illus. 1998, Putnam $15.99 (0-399-22944-2). 32pp. A simple picture book that reports on the playful activities of 2 mountain lion cubs and their ever-watchful mother. (Rev: BL 3/1/98; SLJ 3/98)

**4202** Arnosky, Jim. *Otters Under Water* (PS–1). Illus. 1992, Putnam $14.95 (0-399-22339-8). 32pp. Minimal text and full-color artwork tell of 2 young otters swimming in the pond with mother watching. (Rev: BL 9/1/92; SLJ 8/92) [599.74]

**4203** Arrigoni, Patricia. *Harpo: The Baby Harp Seal* (2–3). Illus. 1995, Travel Publishers $16.95 (0-9625468-8-7). 32pp. Harpo, a baby harp seal, is rescued by a little girl when he is separated from his mother. (Rev: BL 2/1/96)

**4204** Asch, Frank. *The Last Puppy* (PS–2). Illus. by author. 1989, Simon & Schuster LB $4.95 (0-671-66687-8). 32pp. An enchanting story of the puppy born last in a large litter.

**4205** Baker, Karen Lee. *Seneca* (PS–3). Illus. 1997l, Greenwillow $15.00 (0-688-14030-0). 32pp. In this picture book, a young girl tells how she has chosen her horse and how she rides him and takes care of him. (Rev: BCCB 3/97; BL 4/1/97; SLJ 4/97)

**4206** Balian, Lorna. *Amelia's Nine Lives* (PS–K). Illus. by author. 1986, Humbug LB $13.95 (0-687-01250-3). 32pp. Nora's black cat, Amelia, is missing, but when friends keep bringing black cats to replace it, Nora knows the difference. (Rev: BL 12/1/86; SLJ 2/87)

**4207** Banks, Kate. *Baboon* (PS–K). Illus. by Georg Hallensleben. 1997, Farrar $14.00 (0-374-30474-2). 32pp. A mother introduces her baby baboon to the intricacies of the great world. (Rev: BCCB 4/97; BL 3/1/97*; HB 5–6/97; SLJ 3/97)

**4208** Banks, Merry. *Animals of the Night* (PS–2). Illus. by Ronald Himler. 1990, Macmillan $13.95 (0-684-19093-1). 32pp. A parade of nocturnal animals is pictured in soft, dusky colors. (Rev: BCCB 6/90; BL 3/1/90; HB 3–4/90; SLJ 5/90) [599]

**4209** Barton, Byron. *Bones, Bones, Dinosaur Bones* (PS–K). Illus. 1990, HarperCollins LB $15.89 (0-690-04827-0). 32pp. Paleontologists collect a number of bones and reconstruct a dinosaur. (Rev: BL 10/15/90; HB 11–12/90*; SLJ 9/90)

**4210** Bernard, Robin. *Juma and the Honey Guide* (PS–3). Illus. by Nneka Bennett. 1996, Dillon LB $15.95 (0-382-39162-4); paper $5.95 (0-382-39164-0). 32pp. A young African boy and his father share a honeycomb with a small bird that has led them to the beehive. (Rev: BL 8/96; SLJ 8/96)

**4211** Blake, Robert J. *Akiak: A Tale from the Iditarod* (PS–3). Illus. 1997, Putnam $15.95 (0-399-22798-9). 32pp. An aging sled dog named Akiak participates in the Iditarod sled race for the last time. (Rev: BL 9/1/97; SLJ 9/97*)

**4212** Blake, Robert J. *Dog* (K–3). Illus. 1994, Putnam $14.95 (0-399-22019-4). 32pp. Gradually, a stray dog insinuates itself into the life of a grumpy old man in this story set in Ireland. (Rev: BL 3/15/94; SLJ 5/94)

**4213** Blanc, Esther S. *Berchick* (1–3). Illus. by Tennessee Dixon. 1989, Volcano $14.95 (0-912078-81-2). Mama takes care of a colt found beside its dead mother. (Rev: SLJ 11/89)

**4214** Boyle, Doe. *Gray Wolf Pup* (K–2). Illus. by Jeff Domm. Series: Wild Alaska. 1993, Soundprints $11.95 (1-56899-010-3). 31pp. Gray Wolf Pup learns to stay close to the pack after he gets lost one day and has trouble finding his way home. (Rev: SLJ 3/94)

**4215** Boyle, Doe. *Summer Coat, Winter Coat: The Story of a Snowshoe Hare* (K–2). Illus. by Allen Davis. Series: Wild Alaska. 1993, Soundprints $11.95 (1-56899-015-4). 31pp. Even though Snowshoe Hare changes coats seasonally for safety, she must still be on the lookout for danger. (Rev: SLJ 3/94)

**4216** Brenner, Barbara, and May Garelick. *Two Orphan Cubs* (PS–2). Illus. by Erika Kors. 1989, Walker LB $13.85 (0-8027-6869-5). 32pp. A wildlife researcher discovers 2 orphaned black bear cubs and introduces them to a new mother. (Rev: BL 6/1/89; SLJ 6/89)

**4217** Brenner, Barbara, and Julia Takaya. *Chibi: A True Story from Japan* (K–3). Illus. by June Otani. 1996, Clarion $14.95 (0-395-69623-2). 63pp. In this photographic essay, an actual wild duck family upsets daily life when it decides to change homes in downtown Tokyo. (Rev: BL 2/15/96; HB 7–8/96; SLJ 3/96*) [598.4]

**4218** Breslow, Susan, and Sally Blakemore. *I Really Want a Dog* (PS–3). Illus. by True Kelley. 1993, Puffin paper $4.99 (0-140-54941-2). 40pp. A youth confronts an enormous doglike cloud in the sky. (Rev: BL 6/1/90; HB 7–8/90; SLJ 7/90)

**4219** Brown, Alan. *The Windhover* (K–3). Illus. by Christian Birmingham. 1997, Harcourt $17.00 (0-15-201187-0). 32pp. Told from the falcon's, or windhover's, point of view, this story tells how the young bird is captured by a boy who wants to make him his pet. (Rev: BL 11/1/97; SLJ 1/98)

**4220** Brown, Craig. *In the Spring* (PS–K). Illus. 1994, Greenwillow LB $13.93 (0-688-10984-5). 24pp. In the spring, many farm animals give birth, as does the farmer's wife, who has twins. (Rev: BL 4/15/94; SLJ 7/94)

**4221** Brown, Craig. *Tractor* (PS–1). Illus. 1995, Greenwillow LB $15.93 (0-688-10500-9). 24pp. While a tractor is transporting a load of corn, the farm animals are going about their daily activities. (Rev: BCCB 10/95; BL 9/1/95; HB 11–12/95; SLJ 9/95)

**4222** Brown, Margaret Wise. *Baby Animals* (PS–K). Illus. by Susan Jeffers. 1989, Random $16.00 (0-394-82040-1). 32pp. Small farm animals in waking, eating, and nighttime activities. (Rev: BL 4/15/89)

**4223** Brown, Margaret Wise. *Big Red Barn* (PS–1). Illus. by Felicia Bond. 1989, HarperCollins LB $14.89 (0-06-020749-3). 32pp. The big red barn contains lots and lots of animals and their offspring. (Rev: BL 3/1/89; SLJ 6/89)

**4224** Brown, Margaret Wise. *The Old Mill* (K–3). Illus. by Philippe Harchy. 1994, Disney $12.95 (1-56282-644-1). 32pp. A fierce storm batters an old mill and frightens the animals that live in it. (Rev: BL 5/1/94)

**4225** Brown, Margaret Wise. *Wheel on the Chimney* (PS–3). Illus. by Tibor Gergely. 1954, HarperCollins

LB $13.89 (0-397-30296-7). 32pp. Hungarian storks return each spring from Africa to nest on farmers' chimneys. A 1955 Caldecott Honor Book.

**4226** Brown, Margaret Wise. *Young Kangaroo* (K–3). Illus. by Jennifer Dewey. 1993, Hyperion LB $15.49 (1-56282-410-4). 40pp. The experiences and feelings of a baby kangaroo prior to leaving his mother's pouch. (Rev: BL 10/15/93)

**4227** Brown, Ruth. *The Picnic* (K–1). Illus. 1993, Dutton paper $14.99 (0-525-45012-2). 32pp. Small forest animals are disturbed when a group of humans picnic too close to their homes. (Rev: BL 2/15/93; SLJ 3/93*)

**4228** Browne, Philippa-Alys. *Kangaroos Have Joeys* (PS–1). Illus. 1996, Simon & Schuster $15.00 (0-689-81040-7). 26pp. The offspring of animals — e.g., "moose have calves," "rabbits have kits" — are described and pictured. (Rev: BL 11/1/96; SLJ 11/96) [591.3]

**4229** Buck, Nola. *Oh, Cats!* (PS–1). Illus. by Nadine Bernard Westcott. 1997, HarperCollins LB $12.89 (0-06-025374-6). 32pp. A little girl tries to befriend 3 very independent cats. (Rev: BL 11/15/96; SLJ 2/97)

**4230** Bunting, Eve. *Jane Martin, Dog Detective* (PS–3). Illus. by Amy Schwartz. 1988, Harcourt paper $3.95 (0-15-239587-3). 44pp. For 25 cents a day, Jane Martin will solve your pet problem.

**4231** Bunting, Eve. *Red Fox Running* (PS–3). Illus. by Wendell Minor. 1993, Houghton $15.95 (0-395-58919-3). 30pp. A story about a hungry fox that hunts until it kills a bobcat to bring home to his family. (Rev: BL 11/15/93; SLJ 12/93)

**4232** Burningham, John. *Hey! Get Off Our Train* (K–3). Illus. 1990, Crown $16.00 (0-517-57638-4); paper $7.99 (0-517-88204-3). 48pp. A boy's dream takes him on a train trip around the world where he sees environmental dangers. (Rev: BCCB 4/90; BL 5/15/90; HB 5–6/90; SLJ 5/90)

**4233** Bushey, Jeanne. *A Sled Dog for Moshi* (K–3). Illus. by Germaine Arnaktauyok. 1994, Hyperion LB $15.49 (1-56282-632-8). 40pp. A sled dog saves 2 Inuit children during a storm. (Rev: BL 1/15/95; SLJ 1/95)

**4234** Bushnell, Jack. *Circus of the Wolves* (1–3). Illus. by Robert Andrew Parker. 1994, Lothrop $15.00 (0-688-12554-9). 32pp. The story of Kael, a timber wolf, and his life after being captured to become part of a traveling circus. (Rev: BL 4/1/94; SLJ 4/94)

**4235** Bushnell, Jack. *Sky Dancer* (K–3). Illus. by Jan Ormerod. 1996, Lothrop LB $15.93 (0-688-05289-4). 32pp. Jenny tries to save a red-tailed hawk from being shot by local farmers. (Rev: BL 9/15/96; SLJ 9/96)

**4236** Calhoun, Mary. *Tonio's Cat* (K–4). Illus. by Ed Martinez. 1996, Morrow LB $15.93 (0-688-13315-0). 32pp. New to California, Tonio befriends a stray cat. (Rev: BL 9/15/96; SLJ 9/96)

**4237** Cameron, Alice. *The Cat Sat on the Mat* (PS–K). Illus. by Carol Jones. 1994, Houghton $13.95 (0-395-68392-0). 32pp. In this interactive book, a restless cat has difficulty settling down. (Rev: BL 12/15/94; SLJ 10/94)

**4238** Campbell, Rod. *Dear Zoo* (PS). Illus. by author. 1983, Puffin paper $4.95 (0-317-62180-7). 22pp. A youngster keeps sending back the pets requested from a zoo until a puppy arrives.

**4239** Capucilli, Alyssa Satin. *Inside a Barn in the Country: A Rebus Read-Along Story* (PS–K). Illus. by Tedd Arnold. 1995, Scholastic $10.95 (0-590-46999-1). 32pp. Using simple verses, this game book also teaches the sounds that animals make. (Rev: BL 1/15/95; SLJ 4/95)

**4240** Carle, Eric. *Have You Seen My Cat?* (PS–2). Illus. by author. 1991, Picture Book $16.00 (0-88708-054-5). A small boy loses his cat, sees many other felines, and returns home to find that his cat has had kittens. A reissue of a 1973 title.

**4241** Carle, Eric. *The Very Hungry Caterpillar* (PS–2). Illus. by author. 1981, Putnam $19.99 (0-399-20853-4). 32pp. A caterpillar eats a great deal and then spins its cocoon.

**4242** Carrick, Carol. *Lost in the Storm* (K–3). Illus. by Donald Carrick. 1987, Houghton paper $6.95 (0-89919-493-1). 32pp. The story of a dog, lost overnight in a storm, who is found in the morning by his owner and safely sheltered under a flight of stairs.

**4243** Carson, Jo. *The Great Shaking: An Account of the Earthquakes of 1811 and 1812 by a Bear Who Was a Witness* (K–3). Illus. by Robert Andrew Parker. 1994, Orchard LB $16.99 (0-531-08659-3). 32pp. A bear narrates this story about how animals reacted to the earthquakes that shook Missouri in the early 1800s. (Rev: BCCB 5/94; BL 2/1/94; SLJ 3/94)

**4244** Caseley, Judith. *Mr. Green Peas* (PS–K). Illus. 1995, Greenwillow LB $14.93 (0-688-12860-2). 32pp. Norman's classmates won't believe him when he tells them he has a pet iguana at home. (Rev: BL 2/15/95; SLJ 4/95)

**4245** Chekhov, Anton. *Kashtanka* (K–3). Illus. by Gennady Spirin. 1995, Gulliver $16.00 (0-15-200539-0). In this story set in 19th-century Russia, a lost dog is found by a circus performer. (Rev: SLJ 12/95)

**4246** Christian, Peggy. *Chocolate, a Glacier Grizzly* (K–3). Illus. by Carol Cottone-Kolthoff. 1997, Benefactory $12.95 (1-882728-63-7). 32pp. The story of a female grizzly bear in Glacier National Park from her birth to the birth of her own cubs years later. (Rev: SLJ 11/97)

**4247** Climo, Lindee. *Chester's Barn* (2–4). Illus. by author. 1995, Tundra paper $6.95 (0-88776-351-0). The story in words and pictures of life in a Prince Edward Island barn on a winter afternoon.

**4248** Coffelt, Nancy. *Good Night, Sigmund* (PS–1). Illus. 1992, Harcourt $13.95 (0-15-200464-5). 40pp. The artwork is a show stealer in this story of a young boy and his pet cat. (Rev: BL 2/15/92; SLJ 5/92)

**4249** Cole, Joanna. *Daytime Animals* (K–3). Illus. by Kenneth Lilly. 1985, Knopf LB $12.99 (0-394-97188-4). 32pp. An oversized volume of life-size forms of animals. (Rev: BCCB 11/85; SLJ 2/86)

**4250** Cole, Joanna. *My New Kitten* (PS–1). Illus. by Margaret Miller. 1995, Morrow LB $14.93 (0-688-12902-1). 40pp. A photoessay about a young girl getting to know and love her new kitten. (Rev: BCCB 6/95; BL 3/1/95; HB 5–6/95; SLJ 4/95) [636.8]

**4251** Cole, William. *Have I Got Dogs!* (PS–1). Illus. by Margot Apple. 1996, Puffin paper $4.99 (0-140-54195-0). 32pp. Different dogs are introduced in rhyming couplets and engaging cartoonlike drawings. (Rev: BL 8/93)

**4252** Couture, Susan Arkin. *The Biggest Horse I Ever Did See* (PS–2). Illus. by Claire Ewart. 1997, HarperCollins LB $14.89 (0-06-023468-7). 32pp. A boy who enjoys watching a horse gallop over a mountain grows up and introduces his son to the same experience. (Rev: BL 7/97)

**4253** Cowcher, Helen. *Jaguar* (K–2). Illus. 1997, Scholastic $15.95 (0-590-29937-9). 32pp. When an armed hunter finally corners the jaguar that has been killing his cattle, he is so enthralled by its beauty that he cannot shoot it. (Rev: BL 10/15/97; SLJ 8/97)

**4254** Cowcher, Helen. *Tigress* (PS–1). Illus. 1991, Farrar $14.95 (0-374-37567-4). 40pp. A park ranger must do his best to save the life of a marauding tigress. (Rev: BCCB 11/91; BL 12/1/91; HB 1–2/92; SLJ 12/91*)

**4255** Cutler, Jane. *Mr. Carey's Garden* (K–3). Illus. by G. Brian Karas. 1996, Houghton $14.95 (0-395-68191-X). 32pp. Eveyone offers free advice on how Mr. Carey can rid his garden of snails. (Rev: BL 3/15/96; HB 5–6/96; SLJ 5/96)

**4256** Dabcovich, Lydia. *Sleepy Bear* (PS–1). Illus. by author. 1985, Dutton paper $4.95 (0-525-44196-4). 32pp. A bear's hibernation is illustrated in large pictures and a minimum of text.

**4257** Dalgliesh, Alice. *The Bears on Hemlock Mountain* (1–4). Illus. by Helen Sewell. 1990, Macmillan paper $4.95 (0-689-71604-4). 64pp. Jonathan ven-

tured over the mountain by himself after dark and discovered the reality of bear existence!

**4258** Damjan, Mischa. *Atuk* (PS–3). Illus. by Jozef Wilkon. 1996, North-South paper $6.95 (1-55858-590-7). 32pp. Atuk swears he will avenge the killing of his sled dog by a wolf. (Rev: SLJ 1/91)

**4259** Davenport, Zoe. *Animals* (PS). Illus. 1995, Ticknor $5.95 (0-395-71537-7). 16pp. A simple concept book that introduces vocabulary related to various animals. (Rev: BL 2/1/95; SLJ 8/95) [599]

**4260** Denslow, Sharon P. *Hazel's Circle* (PS–2). Illus. by Sharon McGinley-Nally. 1992, Macmillan $14.95 (0-02-728683-5). 32pp. A young girl named Hazel takes her pet rooster, Ike, for a walk to visit her neighbors. (Rev: BL 5/1/92; SLJ 1/93)

**4261** dePaola, Tomie. *The Kids' Cat Book* (1–3). Illus. by author. 1979, Holiday LB $15.95 (0-8234-0365-3); paper $5.95 (0-8234-0534-6). 32pp. Patrick learns about the care, feeding, and history of cats when he decides to adopt one.

**4262** DeSaix, Frank. *The Girl Who Danced with Dolphins* (K–2). Illus. by Deborah Durland DeSaix. 1991, Farrar $14.95 (0-374-32626-6). 32pp. After an exciting day exploring the life on the ocean reefs, Adrienne dreams of more adventures in the sea. (Rev: BL 10/15/91; SLJ 12/91)

**4263** Devlin, Wende, and Harry Devlin. *Cranberry Summer* (PS–2). Illus. 1992, Macmillan LB $13.95 (0-02-729181-2). 40pp. Maggie and Mr. Whiskers care for a donkey that has been left behind by a traveling circus. (Rev: BL 5/15/92; SLJ 6/92)

**4264** De Zutter, Hank. *Who Says a Dog Goes Bow-Wow?* (PS–K). Illus. by Suse MacDonald. 1997, Dell paper $5.99 (0-440-41338-9). 32pp. Various animal sounds as they are interpreted in various languages are presented. (Rev: BL 5/15/93; SLJ 8/93) [418]

**4265** Disher, Garry. *Switch Cat* (PS–2). Illus. by Andrew McLean. 1995, Ticknor $14.95 (0-395-71643-8). 32pp. Two very different girls have equally mismatched cats as pets. (Rev: BL 3/15/95; SLJ 3/95*)

**4266** Duffey, Betsy. *A Boy in the Doghouse* (2–4). Illus. by Leslie Morrill. 1993, Simon & Schuster paper $3.95 (0-671-86698-2). 56pp. George must train his dog, Lucky, or face having him be returned to the pound. (Rev: BL 12/1/91; SLJ 9/91)

**4267** Duffey, Betsy. *The Wild Things* (1–3). Illus. by Susanna Natti. Series: Duffey's Pet Patrol. 1995, Puffin paper $3.99 (0-140-34998-7). 80pp. Megan and Evie get involved in solving who or what is getting into the trash cans. (Rev: BL 3/1/93; SLJ 4/93)

**4268** Duffy, Dee Dee. *Barnyard Tracks* (PS–1). Illus. by Janet Marshall. 1992, Boyds Mills $14.95 (1-878093-66-5). 32pp. Common farm animals are introduced first by their footprints and then by full-color illustrations. (Rev: BL 4/15/92)

**4269** Dunbar, Joyce. *Four Fierce Kittens* (PS–K). Illus. by Jakki Wood. 1992, Scholastic $13.95 (0-590-45535-4). 32pp. Four kittens think they are fierce but cannot frighten the other farm animals. (Rev: BL 6/1/92; SLJ 4/92)

**4270** Dunn, Judy. *The Little Puppy* (PS–K). Illus. by Phoebe Dunn. 1984, Random LB $5.99 (0-394-96595-7); paper $3.25 (0-394-86595-2). 32pp. The story of a little boy who must care for his first puppy.

**4271** Eisler, Colin. *Cats Know Best* (K–2). Illus. by Lesley A. Ivory. 1988, Dial LB $13.89 (0-8037-0560-3); Puffin paper $4.99 (0-8037-1139-5). 32pp. Commenting on the wise ways of felines. (Rev: BL 11/15/88; SLJ 1/89)

**4272** Ellwand, David. *Emma's Elephant and Other Favorite Animal Friends* (K–3). Illus. 1997, Dutton paper $14.99 (0-525-45792-5). 32pp. A photo album in which youngsters pose with their favorite animals. (Rev: BL 7/97; SLJ 8/97)

**4273** Ericsson, Jennifer A. *No Milk!* (PS–2). Illus. by Ora Eitan. 1993, Morrow LB $15.93 (0-688-11307-9). A dairy cow refuses to be persuaded by a city boy to give milk. (Rev: SLJ 6/93*)

**4274** Erlbruch, Wolf. *Mrs. Meyer the Bird* (PS–2). Illus. 1997, Orchard LB $15.99 (0-531-33017-6). 32pp. Mrs. Meyer is a born worrier until she finds an injured bird to take care of and take her mind off her problems. (Rev: BCCB 5/97; BL 4/1/97; SLJ 4/97)

**4275** Ets, Marie Hall. *Just Me* (PS–K). Illus. by author. 1965, Puffin paper $4.99 (0-14-050325-0). 32pp. A little boy imagines he can match the antics of his animal friends as he spends an afternoon at solitary play.

**4276** Ets, Marie Hall. *Play with Me* (PS–K). Illus. by author. 1955, Puffin paper $4.99 (0-14-050178-9). 32pp. A little girl finds a playmate among the meadow creatures when she finally learns to sit quietly and not frighten them.

**4277** Evans, Katie. *Hunky Dory Ate It* (PS). Illus. by Janet M. Stoeke. 1996, Puffin paper $4.99 (0-140-55856-X). 32pp. A pup named Hunky Dory gets into trouble because of his uncontrollable appetite. (Rev: BL 2/1/92; SLJ 3/92)

**4278** Evans, Katie. *Hunky Dory Found It* (PS–K). Illus. by Janet M. Stoeke. 1994, Dutton paper $13.99 (0-525-45192-7). 32pp. An active puppy collects a number of objects and hides them under Julie's bed. (Rev: BL 1/15/94; SLJ 2/94)

**4279** Farjeon, Eleanor. *Cats Sleep Anywhere* (PS–1). Illus. by Anne Mortimer. 1996, HarperCollins LB $12.89 (0-06-027335-6). 24pp. Illustrations and rhyming text explore cats' sleep habits. (Rev: BL 9/1/96; SLJ 12/96) [821]

**4280** *Farm Animals* (PS). Illus. Series: Eye Openers. 1991, Macmillan $7.95 (0-689-71403-3). 24pp. In 8 double-page spreads, 8 farm animals are introduced with many smaller drawings and accompanying text. Also use in this series: *Zoo Animals* (1991). (Rev: BL 6/15/91) [636]

**4281** Faulkner, Keith. *David Dreaming of Dinosaurs* (K–2). Illus. by Jonathan Lambert. 1992, Fantasy $13.00 (1-56021-182-2). 12pp. David dreams of dinosaurs and they appear in foldout illustrations. (Rev: BL 11/15/92)

**4282** Flack, Marjorie. *Angus and the Ducks* (K–2). Illus. by author. 1997, Doubleday $12.95 (0-385-07213-9); Farrar paper $5.95 (0-374-40385-6). 40pp. Angus, the Scottish terrier, and his amusing adventures. Other titles in this series are: *Angus and the Cat* and *Angus Lost* (both 1989).

**4283** Fleming, Denise. *Barnyard Banter* (PS–1). Illus. 1994, Holt $15.95 (0-8050-1957-X). 32pp. All the farm animals greet Goose with their appropriate sounds as she tours the farmyard. (Rev: BCCB 5/94; BL 5/1/94; HB 5–6/94; SLJ 5/94*)

**4284** Fleming, Denise. *In the Tall, Tall Grass* (PS–1). Illus. 1991, Holt $15.95 (0-8050-1635-X). 32pp. An excellent story-hour book in which a caterpillar munches through the tall, tall grass, watching nature along the way. (Rev: BL 10/1/91*; HB 1–2/92*; SLJ 9/91*)

**4285** Florian, Douglas. *Turtle Day* (PS–2). Illus. 1989, HarperCollins LB $15.89 (0-690-04745-2). 32pp. A day in the life of a turtle. (Rev: BL 10/15/89; HB 11–12/89; SLJ 11/89)

**4286** Ford, Miela. *Bear Play* (PS–1). Illus. 1995, Greenwillow LB $14.93 (0-688-13833-0). 24pp. The antics of 2 playful polar bear cubs are captured in a simple text and large color photographs. (Rev: BL 1/1–15/96; SLJ 11/95)

**4287** Ford, Miela. *Follow the Leader* (PS–K). Illus. 1996, Greenwillow LB $14.93 (0-688-14655-4). 24pp. Two polar bear cubs engage in some creative play. (Rev: BL 7/96; SLJ 9/96)

**4288** Ford, Miela. *Little Elephant* (PS–K). Illus. by Tana Hoban. 1994, Greenwillow LB $14.93 (0-688-13141-7). 24pp. A baby zoo elephant decides to go into the pool in his cage by himself in this book illustrated with amazing color photos. (Rev: BL 6/1–15/94; HB 5–6/94; SLJ 7/94*)

**4289** Fox, Mem. *Zoo-Looking* (PS–1). Illus. by Candace Whitman. 1996, Mondo $14.95 (1-57255-010-4). 28pp. Flora is happy when the animals at the zoo seem to look back at her. (Rev: BCCB 7–8/96; BL 6/1–15/96; SLJ 7/96)

**4290** Fox-Davies, Sarah. *Little Caribou* (PS–2). Illus. 1996, Candlewick $15.99 (1-56402-923-9). 32pp. The first year in the life of a caribou is traced, with details on the behavior of the herd. (Rev: BL 12/1/96; SLJ 12/96)

**4291** Gackenbach, Dick. *A Bag Full of Pups* (PS–1). Illus. by author. 1983, Houghton paper $5.95 (0-89919-179-7). 32pp. A little boy would like one of the pups Mr. Mullen is giving away.

**4292** Gag, Wanda. *Millions of Cats* (PS–1). Illus. by author. 1996, Putnam paper $4.95 (0-698-11363-2). 112pp. A wonderful picture book about an old man looking for a cat who suddenly finds himself with millions.

**4293** Gammell, Stephen. *Once upon MacDonald's Farm . . .* (K–3). Illus. by author. 1990, Simon & Schuster paper $4.95 (0-689-71379-7). 32pp. MacDonald tries to populate his farm with circus animals. Originally published in 1981.

**4294** George, Jean Craighead. *Look to the North: A Wolf Pup Diary* (K–4). Illus. by Lucia Washburn. 1997, HarperCollins LB $14.89 (0-06-023640-X). 32pp. A description of a year in the lives of 3 wolf cubs and how they adjust to each of the seasons. (Rev: BL 4/15/97; SLJ 4/97)

**4295** Gill, Shelly. *Alaska's Three Bears* (PS–2). Illus. by Shannon Cartwright. 1990, Paws Four $15.95 (0-934007-10-1); paper $8.95 (0-934007-11-X). 32pp. In a folklike tale, 3 types of Alaskan bears — polar bears, black bears, and grizzlies — are introduced. (Rev: BL 3/1/91)

**4296** Gliori, Debi. *The Snow Lambs* (PS–3). Illus. 1996, Scholastic $15.95 (0-590-20304-5). 40pp. Young Sam worries about the safety of the family's sheepdog during severe winter weather. (Rev: BCCB 2/97; BL 11/15/96*; SLJ 10/96)

**4297** Goble, Paul. *The Girl Who Loved Wild Horses* (K–2). Illus. by author. 1982, Macmillan LB $16.00 (0-02-736570-0); paper $5.99 (0-689-71696-6). 32pp. A mystical story of a girl and her love for a black stallion. Caldecott Medal winner, 1979.

**4298** Gondosch, Linda. *Brutus the Wonder Poodle* (2–4). Illus. 1990, Random LB $5.99 (0-679-90573-1). 40pp. Ryan is disappointed when the dog Dad brings home is a toy poodle. (Rev: BCCB 6/90; BL 9/1/90; SLJ 9/90)

**4299** Gove, Doris. *One Rainy Night* (K–4). Illus. by Walter L. Krudop. 1994, Atheneum $14.95 (0-689-31800-6). 32pp. During a nocturnal walk in the Blue Ridge Mountains, a boy and his mother gather small animals, like a baby box turtle and salamanders, for her nature center. (Rev: BL 3/15/94; SLJ 6/94)

**4300** Graham, Bob. *Queenie, One of the Family* (PS–1). Illus. 1997, Candlewick $15.99 (0-7636-0359-7). 32pp. When Caitlin's dad rescues a hen

from the lake, the family doesn't realize that they have acquired a faithful pet. (Rev: BL 1/1–15/98*; SLJ 11/97*)

**4301** Graham, John. *I Love You, Mouse* (K–2). Illus. by Tomie dePaola. 1990, Harcourt paper $4.00 (0-15-644106-3). 32pp. A tender book about how a young boy would feel if he were several different animals.

**4302** Gregoire, Caroline. *Uglypuss* (K–3). Trans. by George Wen. Illus. 1994, Holt $14.95 (0-8050-3300-9). 32pp. Gradually, Marty realizes that his grotesque new dog, whom he calls Uglypuss, is really the best in the world. (Rev: BL 11/1/94; SLJ 3/95)

**4303** Griffith, Helen V. *"Mine Will," Said John* (PS–3). Illus. by Joseph A. Smith. 1992, Greenwillow LB $13.93 (0-688-10958-6). 32pp. John's parents try different pets until they hit on the perfect one, a puppy. (Rev: BL 10/1/92; SLJ 10/92)

**4304** Guthrie, Arlo. *Mooses Come Walking* (PS–K). Illus. by Alice M. Brock. 1995, Chronicle $11.95 (0-8118-1051-8). 32pp. A picture book that gives advice to youngsters when moose come visiting at night. (Rev: BL 12/15/95)

**4305** Haas, Jessie. *Chipmunk!* (PS–2). Illus. by Joseph A. Smith. 1993, Greenwillow LB $13.93 (0-688-11875-5). 24pp. When a chipmunk enters a household and wants to escape, mayhem results. (Rev: BL 10/15/93; SLJ 2/94)

**4306** Haas, Jessie. *Mowing* (PS–1). Illus. by Joseph A. Smith. 1994, Greenwillow $14.00 (0-688-11680-9). 32pp. While Gramp and Nora mow a field with a horse-drawn mower, they leave spaces uncut to protect a fawn and a killdeer nest. (Rev: BL 6/1–15/94; HB 5–6/94; SLJ 7/94)

**4307** Haas, Jessie. *No Foal Yet* (1–3). Illus. by Joseph A. Smith. 1995, Greenwillow LB $15.93 (0-688-12956-9). 24pp. Nora becomes impatient waiting for her horse Bonnie to give birth; but when it finally happens, no one is around. (Rev: BL 5/15/95; HB 5–6/95; SLJ 6/95)

**4308** Hale, Irina. *The Naughty Crow* (K–3). Illus. 1992, Macmillan LB $14.95 (0-689-50546-9). 32pp. In a story set in czarist Russia, a naughty crow is banished from the household that has adopted him. (Rev: BL 11/5/92; SLJ 10/92)

**4309** Hall, Derek. *Baby Animals: Five Stories of Endangered Species* (PS–1). Illus. by John Butler. 1992, Candlewick $14.95 (1-56402-004-5). 64pp. Each of the 5 stories in this volume features a young animal from a different habitat and tells how each is separated from and then reunited with its parents. (Rev: BL 3/15/92)

**4310** Hardy, Tad. *Lost Cat* (PS–2). Illus. by David Goldin. 1996, Houghton $14.95 (0-395-73574-2). A lost cat produces different reactions in the distraught master who has lost her and in the man who finds her. (Rev: HB 7–8/96; SLJ 6/96)

**4311** Harper, Isabelle. *My Cats Nick and Nora* (PS–1). Illus. by Barry Moser. 1995, Scholastic $14.95 (0-590-47620-3). 32pp. Isabelle and cousin Emmie spend every Sunday taking care of the family pets, Nick and Nora. A sequel to *My Dog Rosie* (1994). (Rev: BL 10/1/95; SLJ 10/95)

**4312** Harper, Isabelle. *Our New Puppy* (PS–1). Illus. by Barry Moser. 1996, Scholastic $14.95 (0-590-56926-0). 32pp. Rosie gradually grows to love the family's new puppy. (Rev: BL 9/1/96; SLJ 10/96)

**4313** Hazen, Barbara S. *Stay, Fang* (K–3). Illus. by Leslie Morrill. 1990, Macmillan LB $13.95 (0-689-31599-6). 32pp. Large, furry Fang can't bear to be parted from his young master. (Rev: BL 2/15/90; SLJ 6/90)

**4314** Hazen, Barbara S. *Tight Times* (2–3). Illus. by Trina S. Hyman. 1979, Puffin paper $3.99 (0-14-050442-7). 32pp. A child is allowed to keep a stray kitten even though there are hard times in the household.

**4315** Hendry, Diana. *Dog Donovan* (PS–2). Illus. by Margaret Chamberlain. 1995, Candlewick $13.95 (1-56402-537-3). 32pp. Members of the Donovan family conquer their fears when they find a dog they must protect. (Rev: BL 3/1/95; SLJ 4/95)

**4316** Herriot, James. *Blossom Comes Home* (1–3). Illus. by Ruth Brown. 1988, St. Martin's paper $6.95 (0-312-09131-1). 32pp. Farmer Dakin is sad to sell Blossom the cow, but happy when she escapes and returns home. (Rev: BL 12/1/88; HB 1–2/89)

**4317** Herriot, James. *Moses the Kitten* (PS–3). Illus. by Peter Barrett. 1984, St. Martin's paper $6.90 (0-312-06419-5). 32pp. The story of a stray black kitten and how it was saved.

**4318** Herriot, James. *Smudge, the Little Lost Lamb* (1–3). Illus. by Ruth Brown. 1991, St. Martin's $12.95 (0-312-06404-7). 32pp. Smudge, a new twin lamb, gets into trouble when he pushes under the fence and goes free. (Rev: BL 1/15/92)

**4319** Hilleary, Jane Kopper. *Fletcher and the Great Big Dog* (K–2). Illus. by Richard Brown. 1992, Houghton paper $4.95 (0-395-62982-9). 32pp. Fletcher flees a huge dog on his bike and is soon lost, with the dog following. (Rev: BCCB 12/88; BL 10/1/88; SLJ 12/88)

**4320** Hirschi, Ron. *What Is a Cat?* (PS–K). Illus. by Linda Q. Younker. 1991, Walker LB $14.85 (0-8027-8123-3). 32pp. An attractive book for young browsers to enjoy. (Rev: BL 1/15/92; SLJ 11/91) [599.7]

**4321** Hirschi, Ron. *What Is a Horse?* (PS–2). Illus. by Linda Q. Younker and Ron Hirschi. 1989, Walker LB $12.85 (0-8027-6877-6). 32pp. This introduction includes material on structure, habits, and uses of the horse. Also use: *Where Do Horses Live?* (1989). (Rev: BL 8/89; SLJ 1/90) [636.1]

**4322** Hirschi, Ron. *Where Do Cats Live?* (PS–K). Illus. by Linda Q. Younker. 1991, Walker LB $14.85 (0-8027-8110-1). 32pp. A visually appealing book that shows cats living alone, together, indoors, outdoors, everywhere. (Rev: BL 1/15/92; SLJ 11/91) [636.8]

**4323** Hoban, Tana. *One Little Kitten* (PS–1). Illus. by author. 1979, Greenwillow LB $15.00 (0-688-84222-4). 24pp. The activities of a kitten in text and unusual photographs.

**4324** Holsonback, Anita. *Monkey See, Monkey Do: An Animal Exercise Book for You!* (PS–K). Illus. by Leo Timmers. 1997, Millbrook LB $19.90 (0-7613-0260-3). Each page features an animal in its natural habitat along with a drawing of a boy and girl who mimic the way the creature moves and a verse. (Rev: SLJ 1/98)

**4325** Houk, Randy. *Chessie, the Travelin' Man* (K–3). Illus. by Paula Bartlett. 1997, Benefactory $12.95 (1-882728-56-4). 32pp. The story of a Florida manatee and his trips from the South to Port Judith, Rhode Island, in 1994 and 1995. (Rev: SLJ 11/97)

**4326** Inkpen, Mick. *Kipper* (PS–K). Illus. 1992, Talman $15.95 (1-85430-333-3). 32pp. When Kipper the dog cleans his basket and gets rid of his toys, he finds it is impossible to be as comfortable as he was before. (Rev: BL 4/1/92; SLJ 5/92)

**4327** Isadora, Rachel. *A South African Night* (PS–K). Illus. 1998, Greenwillow LB $14.93 (0-688-11390-7). 24pp. As the people of Johannesburg go home after a day's work and prepare for bed, many of the animals in the Kruger National Park begin their nocturnal activities. (Rev: BL 2/15/98)

**4328** Ivory, Lesley A. *Cats in the Sun* (K–3). Illus. by author. 1995, Puffin paper $5.99 (0-14-055338-X). 32pp. A book for cat lovers as the author muses on how cats all over the world love sunshine. (Rev: BL 5/1/91; SLJ 7/91) [636.8]

**4329** James, Shirley K. *Going to a Horse Farm* (1–3). Illus. by Laura Jacques. 1992, Charlesbridge $15.95 (0-88106-477-7). 32pp. Two children visit a horse farm to see a new foal. (Rev: BL 6/1/92) [636.1]

**4330** James, Simon. *The Wild Woods* (PS–1). Illus. 1993, Candlewick $13.95 (1-56402-219-6). 32pp. Jess realizes that the squirrel she would like to keep as a pet should remain free in the woods. (Rev: BL 10/15/93; SLJ 10/93)

**4331** Janovitz, Marilyn. *Bowl Patrol!* (PS). Illus. 1996, North-South LB $15.88 (1-55858-637-7). 30pp. In simple rhymes, a dog protects his water bowl from possible intruders. (Rev: BL 10/15/96; SLJ 12/96)

**4332** Johnson, Angela. *The Girl Who Wore Snakes* (PS–2). Illus. by James E. Ransome. 1993, Orchard LB $16.99 (0-531-08641-0). 32pp. Ali becomes so enamored of snakes that she purchases some from a pet store and wears them all day. (Rev: BL 11/1/93; SLJ 1/94)

**4333** Johnson, Herschel. *A Visit to the Country* (1–3). Illus. by Romare Bearden. 1989, Harper-Collins $13.95 (0-06-022849-0). 32pp. Mike nurses an injured cardinal back to health but knows he must return it to the wild. (Rev: BL 9/15/89; SLJ 12/89)

**4334** Johnson, Paul B., and Celeste Lewis. *Lost* (PS–2). Illus. by Paul Johnson. 1996, Orchard LB $16.99 (0-531-08851-0). 32pp. While camping out in Arizona's Tonto National Forest, a young girl's dog wanders off and gets lost. (Rev: BCCB 3/96; BL 4/1/96; SLJ 4/96*)

**4335** Johnston, Tony. *Lorenzo the Naughty Parrot* (PS–3). Illus. by Leo Politi. 1992, Harcourt $14.95 (0-15-249350-6). 32pp. In 4 separate stories, a family's daily activities are always supervised by their parrot, Lorenzo. (Rev: BL 11/15/92; SLJ 3/93)

**4336** Jonas, Ann. *Two Bear Cubs* (1–3). Illus. by author. 1982, Greenwillow LB $15.93 (0-688-01408-9). 24pp. A mother bear shepherds her 2 cubs through some everyday adventures.

**4337** Joosse, Barbara M. *Nugget and Darling* (K–3). Illus. by Sue Truesdell. 1997, Clarion $14.95 (0-395-64571-9). 32pp. The dog Nugget becomes jealous when his young mistress pays attention to a stray kitten. (Rev: BL 3/1/97; SLJ 4/97)

**4338** Kasperson, James. *Little Brother Moose* (PS–3). Illus. by Karlyn Holman. 1995, Dawn $16.95 (1-883220-34-3); paper $7.95 (1-883220-33-5). 32pp. A young moose who wanders into town finds his way home by following migrating geese. (Rev: BL 7/95; SLJ 10/95)

**4339** Kasza, Keiko. *When the Elephant Walks* (PS–K). Illus. 1997, Putnam paper $5.95 (0-698-11430-2). 32pp. In this cumulative tale, each animal has another bigger than himself to be frightened of. (Rev: BCCB 5/90; BL 3/1/90; HB 5–6/91; SLJ 6/90)

**4340** Ketteman, Helen. *Grandma's Cat* (PS–K). Illus. by Marsha Winborn. 1996, Houghton $14.95 (0-395-73094-5). 32pp. A little girl has trouble befriending her grandmother's independent cat. (Rev: BL 4/1/96; SLJ 5/96)

**4341** Khalsa, Dayal Kaur. *I Want a Dog* (PS–2). Illus. by author. 1988, Crown $15.00 (0-517-56532-3). 24pp. May is determined to have a dog, and she tries all sorts of enticements when her parents declare she is too young. (Rev: BL 12/1/87; HB 5–6/88)

**4342** Killilea, Maria. *Newf* (PS–3). Illus. by Ian Schoenherr. 1992, Putnam $14.95 (0-399-21875-0). 32pp. This picture book tells about a loving relationship between a kitten and a large Newfoundland dog. (Rev: BCCB 10/92; BL 12/1/92; SLJ 10/92)

**4343** King-Smith, Dick. *All Pigs Are Beautiful* (PS–3). Illus. by Anita Jeram. 1993, Candlewick $14.95 (1-56402-148-3). 32pp. In simple prose and watercolors, the habits and behavior of pigs are introduced. (Rev: BCCB 5/93; BL 5/1/93; HB 7–8/93*) [636.4]

**4344** Kinsey-Warnock, Natalie. *The Wild Horses of Sweetbriar* (3–4). Illus. by Ted Rand. 1990, Dutton paper $14.99 (0-525-65015-6). 32pp. At the turn of the century, a girl and her mother spend a summer on a Massachusetts island with a herd of wild horses as their only companions. (Rev: BL 11/1/90*; SLJ 12/90)

**4345** Kopper, Lisa. *Daisy Is a Mommy* (PS–1). 1997, Dutton paper $11.99 (0-525-45722-4). 24pp. Daisy the bull terrier cares for her 3 pups, just like the human baby's mother does on the opposite pages. (Rev: BL 12/1/96; SLJ 2/97)

**4346** Koralek, Jenny. *Cat and Kit* (PS–2). Illus. by Patricia MacCarthy. 1995, Hyperion LB $14.49 (0-7868-2030-6). 32pp. Cat rescues Kit, but in time the young kitten returns to the wild where he belongs. (Rev: BL 7/95; SLJ 9/95)

**4347** Kroll, Steven. *Andrew Wants a Dog* (2–4). Illus. by Molly Delaney. 1992, Little, Brown LB $12.49 (1-56282-119-9). 54pp. Seven-year-old Andrew wants a dog so much that he dresses up like one to get his parents to agree. (Rev: BL 5/15/92; SLJ 7/92)

**4348** Kvasnosky, Laura McGee. *Mr. Chips!* (PS–2). Illus. 1996, Farrar $15.00 (0-374-35092-2). 32pp. Ellie is distraught when her dog, Mr. Chips, gets lost and the family must move without him. (Rev: BCCB 11/96; BL 7/96; SLJ 8/96)

**4349** Leedy, Loreen. *Tracks in the Sand* (K–3). Illus. 1993, Doubleday $15.00 (0-385-30658-X). 32pp. The life cycle of a sea turtle is told in drawings and eloquent text. (Rev: BL 6/1–15/93*; SLJ 5/93) [597]

**4350** Lesser, Carolyn. *Dig Hole, Soft Mole* (K–3). Illus. by Laura Regan. 1996, Harcourt $15.00 (0-15-223491-8). 32pp. A marsh mole has many underground and underwater adventures and meets a number of other marshland creatures. (Rev: BL 10/1/96; SLJ 12/96)

**4351** Lesser, Carolyn. *Great Crystal Bear* (K–3). Illus. by William Noonan. 1996, Harcourt $15.00 (0-15-200667-2). 32pp. The author pictures how polar bears survive their hostile environment. (Rev: BL 5/1/96; SLJ 6/96)

**4352** Levy, Elizabeth. *Cleo and the Coyote* (PS–2). Illus. by Diana Bryer. 1996, HarperCollins LB

$14.89 (0-06-024272-8). The comfortable city life of a pup is upset when she is taken with her master to a sheep ranch in Utah, where she encounters a coyote. (Rev: SLJ 5/96)

**4353** Lewin, Betsy. *Booby Hatch* (PS–2). Illus. 1995, Clarion $14.95 (0-395-68703-9). 32pp. The life of the Galapagos Islands' booby is told in charming double-page spreads. (Rev: BL 3/1/95; SLJ 5/95*)

**4354** Lewis, Kim. *Emma's Lamb* (PS–K). Illus. 1998, Candlewick $15.99 (0-7636-0424-0). 32pp. Even though Emma showers her pet lamb with affection, she realizes he needs his mother. (Rev: BL 3/15/91; SLJ 7/91)

**4355** Lewis, Kim. *Floss* (PS–3). 1992, Candlewick $14.95 (1-56402-010-X). 32pp. A young Border collie has some trouble learning to be a sheep herder. (Rev: BL 2/15/92; SLJ 4/92)

**4356** Lindenbaum, Pija. *Boodil, My Dog* (K–3). 1992, Holt $14.95 (0-8050-1444-1); paper $5.95 (0-8050-3940-6). 48pp. Bull terrier Boodil is spoiled rotten, but to the young narrator, she can do no wrong. (Rev: BCCB 12/92*; BL 12/1/92; SLJ 2/93)

**4357** Lindgren, Barbro. *Rosa: Perpetual Motion Machine* (PS–2). Illus. by Eva Eriksson. 1996, Douglas & McIntyre $14.95 (1-55054-241-9). 32pp. A mischievous pup breaks her lease, runs away, and gets lost. (Rev: BL 6/1–15/96; SLJ 7/96)

**4358** Lipkind, William, and Nicolas Mordvinoff. *Finders Keepers* (K–3). Illus. by Nicolas Mordvinoff. 1951, Harcourt $14.95 (0-15-227529-0); paper $6.00 (0-15-630950-5). 32pp. Two dogs have a dispute over one bone but unite against a common enemy. Caldecott Medal winner, 1952.

**4359** Lobel, Arnold. *The Rose in My Garden* (PS–3). Illus. by Anita Lobel. 1984, Greenwillow LB $15.93 (0-688-02587-0); Morrow paper $5.95 (0-688-12265-5). 40pp. A cumulative tale that starts with a bee sleeping on a rose.

**4360** Locker, Thomas. *The Mare on the Hill* (1–3). Illus. by author. 1985, Dial LB $15.89 (0-8037-0208-6). 32pp. A mistreated white mare runs away from her new home as 2 boys try to tame her and see her through a bitter winter. (Rev: BCCB 11/85; BL 11/1/85; SLJ 11/85)

**4361** London, Jonathan. *Condor's Egg* (PS–3). Illus. by James Chaffee. 1994, Chronicle $14.95 (0-8118-0260-4). A picture book that tells how 2 condors hatch an egg in spite of a terrible thunderstorm. Material is appended about this bird's endangered status. (Rev: SLJ 12/94)

**4362** London, Jonathan. *Honey Paw and Lightfoot* (K–3). Illus. by Jon Van Zyle. 1995, Chronicle $14.95 (0-8118-0533-6). 40pp. The story of a female grizzly, Honey Paw, and the first year in the life of her cub, Lightfoot. (Rev: BL 3/15/95; HB 9–10/95)

**4363** London, Jonathan. *Jackrabbit* (PS–2). Illus. by Deborah Kogan Ray. 1996, Crown LB $17.99 (0-517-59658-X). 32pp. A woman rescues a baby jack rabbit from a construction site. (Rev: BCCB 9/96; BL 7/96; SLJ 7/96*)

**4364** London, Jonathan. *Red Wolf Country* (PS–2). Illus. by Daniel San Souci. 1996, Dutton paper $15.99 (0-525-45191-9). 32pp. She-Wolf and her mate search for a place to make a den so that she may safely have her litter. (Rev: BCCB 6/96; BL 1/1–15/96; SLJ 3/96*)

**4365** Longfellow, Layne. *Imaginary Menagerie* (PS–1). Illus. by Woodleigh Hubbard. 1997, Chronicle $10.95 (0-8118-0797-5). A puzzle book in which readers look through a cut-out square and guess what the animal is on the following page. (Rev: BL 1/1–15/98; SLJ 2/98)

**4366** Luenn, Nancy. *Otter Play* (PS–2). Illus. by Anna Vojtech. 1998, Simon & Schuster $16.00 (0-689-81126-8). 32pp. A family of otters and a human family seem to echo each other's actions in this gentle picture book. (Rev: BL 3/15/98)

**4367** Lyon, George E. *Ada's Pal* (PS–1). Illus. by Marguerite Casparian. 1996, Orchard LB $15.99 (0-531-08878-2). 32pp. Ada pines away when her companion, the other dog in the family, dies. (Rev: BL 9/15/96; SLJ 9/96)

**4368** McCloskey, Robert. *Make Way for Ducklings* (PS–3). Illus. by author. 1941, Viking $15.99 (0-670-45149-5); Puffin paper $4.99 (0-14-050171-1). 68pp. The Mallard family creates a commotion as it searches for and finds a permanent home in Boston. Caldecott Medal winner, 1942.

**4369** McClung, Robert M. *America's First Elephant* (2–4). Illus. by Marilyn Janovitz. n.d., Smithmark paper $4.98 (0-8317-0815-8). 40pp. A novel set in the 1790s and based on the actual exhibition of America's first elephant. (Rev: BL 8/91; SLJ 10/91)

**4370** McDonald, Megan. *Insects Are My Life* (PS–2). Illus. by Paul Johnson. 1995, Orchard LB $16.99 (0-531-08724-7). 32pp. No one seems to understand Amanda's fascination with insects. (Rev: BCCB 4/95; BL 3/1/95; HB 3–4/95; SLJ 3/95*)

**4371** McDonald, Megan. *Whoo-oo Is It?* (PS–1). Illus. by S. D. Schindler. 1992, Orchard LB $16.99 (0-531-08574-0). 32pp. A mother owl oversees the hatching of her egg in this book that explores the sounds of the night. (Rev: BL 2/1/92; HB 5–6/92; SLJ 4/92)

**4372** McGeorge, Constance W. *Boomer Goes to School* (PS–K). Illus. by Mary Whyte. 1996, Chronicle $13.95 (0-8118-1117-4). 32pp. Boomer, a golden retriever, becomes a hero during show-and-tell when he visits his young master's school. (Rev: BL 4/15/96; SLJ 7/96)

**4373** McGeorge, Constance W. *Boomer's Big Day* (PS–2). Illus. by Mary Whyte. 1994, Chronicle $13.95 (0-8118-0526-3). 32pp. Boomer, a dog, is a bystander as the family prepares to move, but eventually he is transported to his new home. (Rev: BL 7/94)

**4374** McKenna, Virginia. *Back to the Blue* (K–3). Illus. by Ian Andrew. Series: Born Free Wildlife Book/Templar Book. 1998, Millbrook LB $21.40 (0-7613-0409-6). Based on fact, these are accounts of real animal rescue and relocation projects run by the conservation charity Born Free Foundation. (Rev: SLJ 3/98)

**4375** McNeal, Tom, and Laura McNeal. *The Dog Who Lost His Bob* (K–2). Illus. by John Sandford. 1996, Albert Whitman LB $15.95 (0-8075-1662-7). 32pp. Phil, a dog that hates baths, escapes this ordeal but becomes lost as a result. (Rev: BCCB 10/96; BL 9/1/96; SLJ 11/96)

**4376** McNulty, Faith. *The Lady and the Spider* (K–3). Illus. by Bob Marstall. 1986, HarperCollins $15.00 (0-06-024191-8); paper $5.95 (0-06-443152-5). 48pp. The reader enters the small world of the spider, who lives on a head of lettuce in a garden and feels part of it. (Rev: BL 3/15/86; SLJ 9/86)

**4377** McNulty, Faith. *A Snake in the House* (K–4). Illus. by Ted Rand. 1994, Scholastic $14.95 (0-590-44758-0). 32pp. A captured garter snake escapes in a boy's house and eventually is successful in getting back to his pond. (Rev: BCCB 2/94; BL 5/1/94; SLJ 3/94)

**4378** Mahy, Margaret. *Making Friends* (K–4). Illus. by Wendy Smith. 1990, Macmillan $13.95 (0-689-50498-5). Two dogs bring their lonely owners together. (Rev: HB 5–6/90; SLJ 8/90)

**4379** Mantegazza, Giovanna. *The Hippopotamus* (PS–1). Illus. by Paola Marchi. 1992, Boyds Mills $6.95 (1-56397-033-3). 12pp. Absorbing facts about hippos for young readers in this Italian board book. (Rev: BL 6/15/92; SLJ 8/92) [599.734]

**4380** Marion, Jeff D. *Hello, Crow* (PS–3). Illus. by Leslie Bowman. n.d., Smithmark $3.98 (0-8317-6807-X). 32pp. Grandfather remembers when he brought a young crow to the farm and the many gifts the scavenger bird later brought him. (Rev: BL 10/1/92; HB 11–12/92; SLJ 3/93)

**4381** Maris, Ron. *Runaway Rabbit* (PS). Illus. 1989, Delacorte $12.95 (0-385-29764-5). 32pp. A rabbit escapes from its cage, but before it can get into serious trouble, its owner finds it. (Rev: BL 9/15/89; SLJ 12/89)

**4382** Marshak, Samuel. *The Pup Grew Up!* (K–3). Trans. by Richard Pevear. Illus. by Vladimir Radun-

sky. 1989, Holt $13.95 (0-8050-0952-3). 32pp. A lady boards a train loaded down with many bundles, including a tiny Pekingese, in this tale from Russia. (Rev: BCCB 3/89; BL 6/15/89; HB 3–4/89)

**4383** Martin, Ann M. *Leo the Magnificat* (K–3). Illus. by Emily Arnold McCully. 1996, Scholastic $15.95 (0-590-48498-2). 32pp. A nomadic cat finds a home in a community church. (Rev: BCCB 12/96; BL 9/1/96; SLJ 11/96)

**4384** Martin, Bill, Jr. *Polar Bear, Polar Bear, What Do You Hear?* (PS–K). Illus. by Eric Carle. 1991, Holt $15.95 (0-8050-1759-3). 32pp. Animal sounds from 10 different animals are featured in this picture book. (Rev: BCCB 12/91; BL 11/15/91; HB 1–2/92; SLJ 11/91*)

**4385** Martin, Jacqueline B. *Washing the Willow Tree Loon* (2–4). Illus. by Nancy Carpenter. 1995, Simon & Schuster $16.00 (0-689-80415-6). 40pp. A fictionalized account of how an oil-slicked loon is saved by a woman who, with others, tries to save animals after an oil barge hits a bridge. (Rev: BL 12/15/95; HB 9–10/95; SLJ 10/95)

**4386** Masurel, Claire. *No, No, Titus!* (PS–K). Illus. by Shari Halpern. 1997, North-South LB $15.88 (1-55858-726-8). 28pp. When the dog Titus wonders what his role will be on the farm his owners have moved to, he finds it is to frighten off the fox. (Rev: BL 6/1–15/97)

**4387** Mayne, William. *Pandora* (PS–3). Illus. by Dietlind Blech. 1996, Knopf LB $18.99 (0-679-94183-5). 32pp. Pandora the cat is miffed when a new baby in the family gets all the attention. (Rev: BL 9/15/96; HB 9–10/96; SLJ 6/96)

**4388** Mazer, Anne. *The Salamander Room* (PS–1). Illus. by Steve Johnson. 1991, Knopf LB $17.99 (0-394-92945-4). 32pp. A young boy tries to get permission from his mother to keep a salamander. (Rev: BL 2/15/91; SLJ 4/91)

**4389** Meeker, Clare Hodgson. *Who Wakes Rooster?* (PS). Illus. by Megan Halsey. 1996, Simon & Schuster $13.00 (0-689-80541-1). 32pp. Only when the rooster finally crows does the day officially begin and all the farm animals waken. (Rev: BL 11/1/96; SLJ 9/96)

**4390** Miller, Edna. *Patches Finds a New Home* (K–2). Illus. by author. 1989, Simon & Schuster paper $12.95 (0-671-66266-X). 40pp. A mother cat searches for a new home for herself and her kittens. (Rev: BL 6/15/89; SLJ 6/89)

**4391** Most, Bernard. *A Dinosaur Named After Me* (PS–2). Illus. 1991, Harcourt $12.95 (0-15-223494-2). 32pp. On each page is a dinosaur and a child who adds information about the beast. (Rev: BL 4/1/91; SLJ 5/91) [597.9]

**4392** Nethery, Mary. *Hannah and Jack* (PS–1). Illus. by Mary Morgan. 1996, Simon & Schuster $15.00 (0-689-80533-0). 32pp. Hannah misses her pet cat, Jack, so much when she visits Grandma that she sends him postcards. (Rev: BL 5/1/96; HB 7–8/96; SLJ 3/96)

**4393** Noll, Sally. *Watch Where You Go* (PS–1). Illus. 1993, Puffin paper $3.99 (0-14-054884-X). 32pp. A harried mouse miraculously averts danger on her trip back to the family nest. (Rev: BL 2/15/90*; HB 5–6/90*; SLJ 4/90*)

**4394** Okimoto, Jean D. *Blumpoe the Grumpoe Meets Arnold the Cat* (PS–3). Illus. by Howie Schneider. 1990, Little, Brown $13.95 (0-316-63811-0). 32pp. In an accommodating hotel, a grumpy old man is offered a cat to keep him company. (Rev: BL 5/15/90; HB 7–8/90; SLJ 7/90)

**4395** Orr, Katherine. *Story of a Dolphin* (K–4). Illus. 1993, Carolrhoda LB $14.95 (0-87614-777-5). 32pp. Tourists on a Caribbean island mistreat the dolphin that Laura and her father have grown to love and understand. (Rev: BL 9/15/93; SLJ 10/93)

**4396** Patent, Dorothy Hinshaw. *Baby Horses* (PS–1). Illus. by William Munoz. 1991, Carolrhoda LB $22.60 (0-87614-690-6). 56pp. A new edition presenting the first months of a foal's life in simple text and color photos. (Rev: BL 1/1/92) [636.1]

**4397** Paulsen, Gary. *Dogteam* (PS–2). Illus. by Ruth W. Paulsen. 1993, Delacorte $15.95 (0-385-30550-8). 32pp. The author and illustrator capture the joy, excitement, beauty, and danger of a dog sled run on a moonlit winter night. (Rev: BL 11/15/93; SLJ 10/93)

**4398** Penner, Lucille R. *Dinosaur Babies* (PS–1). Illus. by Peter Barrett. Series: Step into Reading Books. 1991, Random paper $3.99 (0-679-81207-5). 32pp. An easily read introduction to dinosaurs and their babies in large type with many illustrations. (Rev: BL 2/1/92; SLJ 1/92) [567.9]

**4399** Pilkey, Dav. *Dogzilla* (K–3). Illus. 1993, Harcourt $12.00 (0-15-223944-8); paper $7.00 (0-15-223945-6). 32pp. Using retouched photos of the author's pets as illustrations, this zany story tells of Dreadful Dogzilla, whose breath could send everyone running. Also use *Kat Kong* (1993). (Rev: BL 9/1/93; SLJ 12/93)

**4400** Pirotta, Saviour. *Turtle Bay* (PS–3). Illus. by Nilesh Mistry. 1997, Farrar $15.00 (0-374-37888-6). In this picture book set on a Japanese beach, 2 children witness the laying of eggs by sea turtles. Eight weeks later, they see the baby turtles hatch. (Rev: SLJ 11/97)

**4401** Politi, Leo. *Song of the Swallows* (K–3). Illus. by author. 1987, Macmillan LB $15.00 (0-684-18831-7); paper $4.95 (0-689-71140-9). 32pp. Juan

rings the mission's bells to welcome the swallows back to San Juan Capistrano. Caldecott Medal winner, 1950.

**4402** Pomerantz, Charlotte. *Where's the Bear?* (PS). Illus. by Byron Barton. 1984, Greenwillow LB $15.93 (0-688-01753-3); Morrow paper $3.95 (0-688-10999-3). 32pp. A picture book involving the search for a bear; the text uses only 7 words.

**4403** Porte, Barbara Ann. *Tale of a Tadpole* (PS–3). Illus. by Annie Cannon. 1997, Orchard LB $16.99 (0-531-33049-4). 32pp. Francine watches the changes that occur to a tadpole until it becomes a toad. (Rev: BL 8/97; SLJ 9/97)

**4404** Potter, Tessa. *Grayfur: The Story of a Rabbit in Summer* (PS–1). Illus. by Kenneth Lilly. Series: Animals Through the Year. 1997, Raintree Steck-Vaughn LB $21.40 (0-8172-4621-5). 32pp. A short book that tells of the danger that a little rabbit faces when he encounters a hungry weasel. Also use *Sarn: The Story of an Otter in Spring* (1997). (Rev: BL 6/1–15/97)

**4405** Potter, Tessa, and Donna Bailey. *Cows* (1–2). Illus. by Paula Chasty. 1990, Raintree Steck-Vaughn LB $21.40 (0-8114-2626-2). 32pp. A very simple text and many photos introduce cows. Also use *Goats; Hens* (both 1990). (Rev: SLJ 7/90)

**4406** Powell, Roxanne D. *Cat, Mouse and Moon* (PS–2). Illus. by Will Hillenbrand. 1994, Houghton $14.95 (0-395-59348-4). 32pp. Prowling the countryside at night for food, Cat almost catches Mouse. (Rev: BCCB 10/94; BL 1/1/95; SLJ 11/94)

**4407** Pringle, Laurence. *Naming the Cat* (K–3). Illus. by Katherine Potter. 1997, Walker LB $16.85 (0-8027-8622-7). 32pp. A family ponders what the best name would be for their new cat. After watching its escapades, they decide to call him Lucky. (Rev: BL 10/1/97; SLJ 11/97)

**4408** Radcliffe, Theresa. *Bashi, Elephant Baby* (PS–3). Illus. by John Butler. 1998, Viking paper $13.99 (0-670-87054-4). 32pp. When her baby gets stuck in a watering hole, a mother elephant must think fast to foil an attack by some hungry lionesses. (Rev: BL 2/1/98; SLJ 2/98)

**4409** Rand, Gloria. *Prince William* (PS–3). Illus. by Ted Rand. 1992, Holt $14.95 (0-8050-1841-7). 32pp. A young girl rescues a baby seal from an Alaskan oil spill. (Rev: BCCB 3/92; BL 6/1/92; SLJ 4/92)

**4410** Rathmann, Peggy. *Officer Buckle and Gloria* (PS–2). Illus. 1995, Putnam $15.99 (0-399-22616-8). 32pp. A police dog named Gloria steals the show when Officer Buckle gives a presentation on safety to local school children. Caldecott Medal winner, 1996. (Rev: BCCB 10/95; BL 11/1/95*; HB 11–12/95; SLJ 9/95*)

**4411** Reeves, Mona R. *The Spooky Eerie Night Noise* (K–2). Illus. by Paul Yalowitz. 1989, Macmillan LB $13.95 (0-02-775732-3). 32pp. At night a little girl hears a strange noise from outside and finds it is caused by skunks. (Rev: BL 8/89; SLJ 9/89)

**4412** Reiser, Lynn. *Dog and Cat* (PS–3). Illus. 1991, Greenwillow LB $13.88 (0-688-09893-2). 24pp. In this fight between a cat and a dog, the roles are reversed and the cat is the attacker. (Rev: BL 3/1/91; HB 5–6/91; SLJ 6/91)

**4413** Reiser, Lynn. *The Surprise Family* (PS–2). Illus. 1994, Greenwillow $16.00 (0-688-11671-X). 32pp. Despite obvious differences, a chicken loves the little ducks she has hatched. (Rev: BL 6/1–15/94; SLJ 7/94*)

**4414** Rice, Eve. *Sam Who Never Forgets* (PS–1). Illus. by author. 1977, Morrow paper $4.95 (0-688-07335-2). 32pp. Sam, the zookeeper, feeds all the animals each day, but one day there appears to be nothing for the elephant.

**4415** Robertus, Polly M. *The Dog Who Had Kittens* (PS–2). Illus. by Janet Stevens. 1991, Holiday LB $15.95 (0-8234-0860-4). 32pp. Baxter, a basset hound, decides that he can help raise the new family of Eloise the cat. (Rev: BL 3/15/91; SLJ 5/91)

**4416** Robinson, Marc. *Cock-A-Doodle-Doo! What Does It Sound Like to You?* (PS–1). Illus. by Steve Jenkins. 1993, Stewart, Tabori & Chang $6.50 (1-55670-267-1). 32pp. Animal sounds and some machine sounds are written as they sound in 12 languages. (Rev: BL 9/15/93; SLJ 9/93) [418]

**4417** Rockwell, Anne. *Our Yard Is Full of Birds* (PS–1). Illus. by Lizzy Rockwell. 1992, Macmillan LB $14.00 (0-02-777273-X). 32pp. A little boy observes and describes the birds that come into the yard. (Rev: BCCB 3/92; BL 1/15/92; SLJ 4/92) [598]

**4418** Rogers, Paul, and Emma Rogers. *Cat's Kittens* (PS–3). Illus. by Sophy Williams. 1997, Viking paper $13.99 (0-670-86255-X). 32pp. On each day of the week, one of a cat's kittens ventures out into the world to learn a lesson in independence. (Rev: BL 2/15/97; SLJ 3/97)

**4419** Rosen, Michael. *Moving* (K–3). Illus. by Sophy Williams. 1993, Viking paper $12.99 (0-670-84865-4). 32pp. A cat's comfortable routine is disrupted when the family moves from one household to another. (Rev: BL 12/15/93; SLJ 3/94)

**4420** Rosen, Michael J. *Bonesy and Isabel* (PS–4). Illus. by James E. Ransome. 1995, Harcourt $15.00 (0-15-209813-5). 32pp. A newly adopted girl from El Salvador feels a terrible loss when the farm dog she has grown to love dies. (Rev: BL 4/15/95; SLJ 6/95)

**4421** Rounds, Glen. *Once We Had a Horse* (K–2). Illus. 1996, Holiday LB $15.95 (0-8234-1241-5). 32pp. One summer, a boy and his sister learn to ride a gentle farm horse. (Rev: BL 6/1–15/96; SLJ 7/96*)

**4422** Rounds, Glen. *Wild Horses* (1–4). Illus. 1993, Holiday LB $14.95 (0-8234-1019-6). 32pp. The lives of wild horses in the West are explored in text and beautiful drawings. (Rev: BL 4/1/93) [599.72]

**4423** Roy, Ron. *Three Ducks Went Wandering* (PS–1). Illus. by Paul Galdone. 1987, Ticknor paper $5.20 (0-89919-494-X). Three ducks are oblivious to the dangers all around them when they take a walk.

**4424** Royston, Angela. *Baby Animals* (PS). Illus. by Andrew Aloof. Series: Eye Openers. 1992, Macmillan paper $7.95 (0-689-71563-3). 24pp. Numerous photographs in color help introduce a variety of baby animals to preschoolers. (Rev: BL 8/92; SLJ 10/92) [599]

**4425** Royston, Angela. *Jungle Animals* (PS–2). Illus. by Martine Blaney and Dave Hopkins. Series: Eye Openers. 1991, Macmillan $8.99 (0-689-71519-6). 21pp. A number of jungle animals are introduced. (Rev: BL 9/15/91; SLJ 1/92) [581]

**4426** Royston, Angela. *Sea Animals* (PS). Illus. by Stephen Shott. Series: Eye Openers. 1992, Macmillan $8.99 (0-689-71565-X). 32pp. In full-color photographs, a number of marine animals are identified for the very young. (Rev: BL 8/92; SLJ 10/92) [591]

**4427** Rush, Ken. *What About Emma?* (PS–3). Illus. 1996, Orchard LB $16.99 (0-531-08884-7). 32pp. Even though her farm family must sell their stock to survive, Sue is allowed to keep her favorite cow, Emma. (Rev: BL 9/1/96; SLJ 9/96)

**4428** Ryder, Joanne. *Jaguar in the Rain Forest* (K–4). Illus. by Michael Rothman. 1996, Morrow LB $15.93 (0-688-12991-9). 32pp. The home and habits of the graceful jaguar are explored in this sumptuous picture book. (Rev: BL 3/15/96; SLJ 3/96)

**4429** Rylant, Cynthia. *The Bookshop Dog* (PS–K). Illus. 1996, Scholastic $14.95 (0-590-54331-8). 40pp. A dog named Martha Jane becomes the mascot at her owner's bookshop. (Rev: BL 9/1/96; SLJ 9/96)

**4430** Rylant, Cynthia. *Dog Heaven* (PS–1). Illus. 1995, Scholastic $14.95 (0-590-41701-0). 32pp. In dog heaven, dogs run and play and wait for their absent friends. (Rev: BCCB 10/95; BL 8/95; SLJ 10/95)

**4431** Rylant, Cynthia. *The Old Woman Who Named Things* (PS–3). Illus. by Kathryn Brown. 1996, Harcourt $15.00 (0-15-257809-9). 32pp. An old lady who only names things that will outlive her doesn't name the pup she adopts. (Rev: BL 5/1/96*; HB 5–6/98; SLJ 10/96*)

**4432** Samuels, Barbara. *Duncan and Dolores* (K–2). Illus. by author. 1986, Macmillan paper $4.99 (0-689-71294-4). 32pp. Dolores learns a lesson when she smothers Duncan the cat with too much love and attention and he runs away from her. (Rev: BCCB 3/87; BL 10/15/86; HB 1–2/87)

**4433** Schoberle, Cecile. *Esmeralda and the Pet Parade* (PS–3). Illus. 1990, Simon & Schuster $14.95 (0-671-67958-9). 32pp. Juan's pet goat, Esmeralda, behaves so erratically that Juan is afraid to put her in the pet parade. (Rev: BL 6/1/90; SLJ 8/90)

**4434** Schoenherr, John. *Rebel* (K–2). Illus. 1995, Putnam $15.95 (0-399-22727-X). 32pp. A pair of wild geese raise a family, including a rebel gosling that tends to wander away from its family. (Rev: BCCB 12/95; BL 12/15/95*; SLJ 10/95*)

**4435** Sendak, Maurice, and Matthew Margolis. *Some Swell Pup, or Are You Sure You Want a Dog?* (PS–3). Illus. by Maurice Sendak. 1989, Farrar paper $5.95 (0-374-46963-6). 32pp. Two youngsters learn to have a good relationship with their new pup. A reissue.

**4436** Sewell, Anna. *Black Beauty* (1–3). Adapted by Robin McKinley. Illus. by Susan Jeffers. 1986, Random LB $20.99 (0-394-96575-2). 72pp. A smooth adaptation of the classic horse tale. (Rev: BCCB 1/87; BL 12/1/86; SLJ 12/86)

**4437** Seymour, Tres. *Hunting the White Cow* (PS–3). Illus. by Wendy A. Halperin. 1993, Orchard LB $17.99 (0-531-08646-1). 32pp. After a white cow has escaped from the farm, several people try unsuccessfully to catch her. (Rev: BCCB 10/93; BL 9/1/93; HB 11–12/93; SLJ 12/93*)

**4438** Shapiro, Arnold L. *Mice Squeak, We Speak* (PS–K). Illus. by Tomie dePaola. 1997, Putnam $13.99 (0-399-23202-8). 32pp. Three friends introduce the different sounds made by a variety of animals. (Rev: BL 9/15/97*; SLJ 10/97)

**4439** Sheehan, Patty. *Shadow and the Ready Time* (K–3). Illus. by Itoko Maeno. 1994, Advocacy $14.95 (0-911655-13-1). 38pp. A wolf cub is raised by an older, lame wolf when he is separated from his pack. (Rev: SLJ 12/94)

**4440** Sheppard, Jeff. *Splash, Splash* (PS–1). Illus. by Dennis Panek. 1994, Macmillan paper $15.00 (0-02-782455-1). 40pp. Different animals fall in the pond, make different sounds, and have different reactions. (Rev: BL 6/1–15/94; HB 5–6/94; SLJ 5/94)

**4441** Shub, Elizabeth. *The White Stallion* (1–3). Illus. by Rachel Isadora. 1982, Greenwillow LB $15.93 (0-688-01211-6). 56pp. In this story of pioneers, Gretchen is saved by a mysterious white stallion.

**4442** Simon, Norma. *Fire Fighters* (PS–K). Illus. by Pamela Paparone. 1995, Simon & Schuster $13.00 (0-689-80280-3). 32pp. A day in the life of firefighters who are actually dalmatians. (Rev: BL 9/15/95; SLJ 12/95)

**4443** Simon, Norma. *Mama Cat's Year* (PS–1). Illus. by Dora Leder. 1991, Whitman LB $15.95 (0-8075-4958-4). 32pp. The seasons of the year are described for Mama Cat and her owners in a cozy story of human and feline families. (Rev: BL 1/1/92; SLJ 1/92)

**4444** Simon, Norma. *Oh, That Cat!* (K–3). Illus. by Dora Leder. 1986, Whitman LB $12.95 (0-8075-5919-9). 32pp. Max may be obnoxious in some ways, but he's special too. (Rev: BL 4/15/86; SLJ 8/86)

**4445** Sis, Peter. *Komodo!* (PS–2). Illus. 1993, Greenwillow LB $15.93 (0-688-11584-5). 32pp. On a trip to Indonesia, a young boy encounters the animal he has been fascinated with, the Komodo dragon. (Rev: BCCB 6/93; BL 4/15/93*; HB 5–6/93*; SLJ 7/93*)

**4446** Sis, Peter. *An Ocean World* (PS–1). Illus. 1992, Greenwillow LB $15.93 (0-688-09068-0). 24pp. A young whale finds life is strange when he is released from the aquarium. (Rev: BCCB 11/92; BL 9/15/92; SLJ 10/92)

**4447** Slepian, Jan. *Lost Moose* (PS–2). Illus. by Ted Lewin. 1995, Putnam $15.95 (0-399-22749-0). 32pp. A small boy tracks a lost baby moose, and eventually both find their mothers. (Rev: BL 3/1/95; SLJ 8/95)

**4448** Slier, Deborah. *Farm Animals* (PS). Illus. 1988, Checkerboard $2.95 (1-56288-084-5). 12pp. Farm creatures for the toddler to admire. (Rev: BCCB 7–8/88; BL 7/88)

**4449** Sorensen, Henri. *Your First Step* (PS–K). Illus. 1996, Lothrop LB $14.93 (0-688-14668-6). 24pp. All sorts of interesting things happen on the day that a youngster takes his first steps. (Rev: BL 8/96; SLJ 6/96)

**4450** Stern, Maggie. *The Missing Sunflowers* (PS–2). Illus. by Donna Ruff. 1997, Greenwillow $15.00 (0-688-14873-5). 32pp. Simon wonders who has stolen the heads from his sunflower plants and finds that a hungry squirrel is the culprit. (Rev: BCCB 4/97; BL 5/15/97; SLJ 4/97)

**4451** Stock, Catherine. *Where Are You Going, Manyoni?* (PS–3). Illus. 1993, Morrow LB $14.93 (0-688-10353-7). 48pp. A little girl sees a variety of wildlife on her way to school in Zimbabwe. (Rev: BL 8/93)

**4452** Stockdale, Susan. *Some Sleep Standing Up* (PS–K). Illus. 1996, Simon & Schuster $13.00 (0-689-80509-8). 32pp. Two-page spreads illustrate the ways in which various animals sleep. (Rev: BL 9/1/96; SLJ 4/96) [591.52]

**4453** Strete, Craig Kee. *They Thought They Saw Him* (PS–1). Illus. by Jose Aruego and Ariane Dewey. 1996, Greenwillow LB $14.93 (0-688-14195-1). 32pp. A chameleon escapes many dangers by changing color in this clever picture book. (Rev: BL 4/15/96; HB 7–8/96; SLJ 5/96*)

**4454** Sturges, Philemon. *What's That Sound, Woolly Bear?* (PS–2). Illus. by Joan Paley. 1996, Little, Brown $14.95 (0-316-82021-0). 32pp. Woolly Bear, a caterpillar, is introduced, along with a number of other familiar insects that, unlike him, can make sounds. (Rev: BL 4/15/96; SLJ 8/96)

**4455** Swinburne, Stephen R. *Swallows in the Birdhouse* (K–3). Illus. by Robin Brickman. 1996, Millbrook LB $21.90 (1-56294-182-8). 32pp. Two tree swallows create a nest and raise a family after moving into a small birdhouse. (Rev: BL 6/1–15/96; SLJ 6/96) [598.2]

**4456** Tafuri, Nancy. *The Barn Party* (PS–1). Illus. 1995, Greenwillow $15.00 (0-688-04616-9). 32pp. At a memorable barn party, children enjoy petting the animals until the creatures are frightened away by a balloon popping. (Rev: BL 9/1/95; SLJ 10/95)

**4457** Tan, Amy. *The Chinese Siamese Cat* (1–4). Illus. by Gretchen Schields. 1994, Macmillan paper $16.95 (0-02-788835-5). 32pp. A Chinese tale that explains how cats got their markings. (Rev: BL 10/1/94; SLJ 11/94)

**4458** Taylor, Livingston. *Can I Be Good?* (PS–3). Illus. by Ted Rand. 1993, Harcourt $15.00 (0-15-200436-X). 32pp. Though he claims he is trying to be good, a golden retriever seems to be always causing confusion and disorder. (Rev: BL 9/15/93; SLJ 10/93)

**4459** Thornhill, Jan. *Wild in the City* (PS–3). Illus. 1996, Sierra Club $16.95 (0-87156-910-8). 32pp. During a prowl at night, Jenny's cat encounters such nocturnal wildlife as raccoons, moths, and bats. (Rev: BCCB 12/96; BL 12/1/96; SLJ 10/96) [574.526]

**4460** Tildes, Phyllis L. *Animals: Black and White* (PS–2). Illus. by author. 1996, Charlesbridge paper $6.95 (0-88106-959-0). This picture puzzle book consists of guessing games in which several black-and-white animals describe themselves and show parts of their bodies before their identities are revealed. (Rev: SLJ 1/97)

**4461** Timmel, Carol Ann. *Tabitha: The Fabulous Flying Feline* (PS–1). Illus. by Laura Kelly. 1996, Walker paper $16.85 (0-8027-8449-6). 32pp. Tabitha the cat remains undiscovered for 13 days in the cargo hold of a large airplane. (Rev: BL 10/15/96; SLJ 11/96)

**4462** Toriseva, JoNelle. *Rodeo Day* (1–3). Illus. by Robert Casilla. 1994, Bradbury paper $14.95 (0-02-789405-3). 32pp. Lacey is filled with fear and appre-

hension as she prepares herself and her horse for her first rodeo. (Rev: BL 11/1/94; SLJ 11/94)

**4463** Trapani, Iza. *What Am I? An Animal Guessing Game* (PS–1). Illus. 1992, Whispering Coyote LB $13.95 (1-879085-76-3). 30pp. An animal is described, and young readers must guess the identity. (Rev: BL 12/15/92; SLJ 1/93) [591.2]

**4464** Travers, Will. *The Elephant Truck* (K–3). Illus. by Lawrie Taylor. Series: Born Free Wildlife Book/Templar Book. 1998, Millbrook LB $21.40 (0-7613-0408-8). This picture book presents a fictionalized account of the first relocation of elephants in Kenya's translocation project. (Rev: SLJ 3/98)

**4465** Tregebov, Rhea. *The Big Storm* (PS–2). Illus. by Maryann Kovalski. 1993, Hyperion LB $14.49 (1-56282-462-7). 32pp. The promise of tasty latkes from a neighbor makes Jeanette forget about caring for her cat, Kitty Doyle. (Rev: BL 12/15/93; SLJ 1/94)

**4466** Vargo, Vanessa. *Zebra Talk* (PS–1). Illus. 1991, Child's Play paper $5.99 (0-85953-395-6). 20pp. A mother zebra explains how life was years ago when thousands of zebras roamed the plains of Africa. (Rev: BL 3/1/91)

**4467** Voake, Charlotte. *Ginger* (PS–3). Illus. 1997, Candlewick $16.99 (0-7636-0108-X). 40pp. Ginger the cat is upset when a new kitten is introduced into the household. (Rev: BCCB 4/97; BL 2/1/97; SLJ 4/97)

**4468** Wallace, Karen. *Imagine You Are a Crocodile* (PS–1). Illus. by Mike Bostock. 1997, Holt $14.95 (0-8050-4637-2). A picture book that gives the reader a crocodile's views of the world and its swampy habitat. (Rev: BL 5/1/97*; SLJ 7/97)

**4469** Walsh, Melanie. *Do Monkeys Tweet?* (PS). Illus. 1997, Houghton $15.00 (0-395-85081-9). 40pp. A funny picture book that answers such questions as "Do horses bark?" (Rev: BL 9/1/97; HB 11–12/97; SLJ 10/97) [591.59]

**4470** Weller, Frances W. *Riptide* (PS–3). Illus. by Robert J. Blake. 1990, Putnam $15.95 (0-399-21675-8). 32pp. A dog named Riptide acts as a lifeguard on Cape Cod. (Rev: BL 3/15/90*; HB 7–8/90; SLJ 4/90*)

**4471** Wellington, Monica. *Night Rabbits* (PS–K). Illus. 1995, Dutton paper $9.99 (0-525-45335-0). 32pp. Two rabbits enjoy a night of play and adventure leaping around the countryside. (Rev: BL 4/15/95; SLJ 3/95)

**4472** Wells, Rosemary. *Lucy Comes to Stay* (PS–3). Illus. by Mark Graham. 1994, Dial LB $14.89 (0-8037-1214-6). 32pp. A small girl and her family try to make their new puppy feel at home. (Rev: BL 6/1–15/94; SLJ 7/94*)

**4473** Wells, Rosemary. *McDuff and the Baby* (PS–1). Illus. by Susan Jeffers. 1997, Hyperion LB $12.89 (0-7868-2258-9). 24pp. McDuff, a terrier, loses status when a new baby arrives in his home. (Rev: BL 9/15/97; SLJ 10/97)

**4474** Wells, Rosemary. *McDuff Comes Home* (PS–K). Illus. by Susan Jeffers. 1997, Hyperion LB $13.49 (0-7868-2259-7). 32pp. McDuff the white terrier gets lost when he chases a rabbit but, through the help of matronly Mrs. Higgins, finds his way home again. (Rev: BL 6/1–15/97; HB 7–8/97; SLJ 7/97)

**4475** Wells, Rosemary. *McDuff Moves In* (PS–2). Illus. by Susan Jeffers. 1997, Hyperion LB $12.89 (0-7868-2257-0); paper $4.95 (0-7868-1190-0). 32pp. A little dog jumps out of a dog catcher's truck and finds himself a new home with a sympathetic couple. (Rev: BCCB 4/97; BL 4/1/97*; HB 7–8/97; SLJ 5/97*)

**4476** Wheeler, Cindy. *Bookstore Cat* (1–2). Illus. by author. Series: Step into Reading. 1994, Random LB $11.99 (0-394-94109-8); paper $3.99 (0-394-84109-3). 32pp. Mulligan, a cat that lives in a bookstore, is kept busy when a pigeon gets into the store. (Rev: SLJ 4/95)

**4477** Whelan, Gloria. *A Week of Raccoons* (PS–2). Illus. by Lynn Munsinger. 1988, Knopf LB $12.99 (0-394-98396-3). 40pp. The idyllic life of the Twerkles, who live in a cottage by a pond, is disrupted by raccoons. (Rev: BL 12/1/88; SLJ 12/88)

**4478** Wieler, Diana. *To the Mountains by Morning* (K–3). Illus. by Ange Zhang. 1996, Douglas & McIntyre $14.95 (0-88899-227-0). 32pp. Knowing she is going to be disposed of because of her age, Old Bailey the mare runs away. (Rev: BL 7/96; SLJ 6/96)

**4479** Wildsmith, Brian, and Rebecca Wildsmith. *Wake Up, Wake Up!* (PS–1). Illus. 1993, Harcourt $6.95 (0-15-200685-0). 16pp. One by one, the animals wake up until, finally, the farmer also wakes up to feed them. (Rev: BL 3/15/93)

**4480** Wilhelm, Hans. *I'll Always Love You* (PS–2). Illus. by author. 1988, Crown $17.00 (0-517-55648-0); paper $5.99 (0-517-57265-6). 32pp. The affection between boy and dog and the sadness when a beloved pet grows old and dies. (Rev: BCCB 1/86; BL 11/1/85)

**4481** Winters, Kay. *Wolf Watch* (K–3). Illus. by Laura Regan. 1997, Simon & Schuster paper $16.00 (0-689-80218-8). 32pp. Lyrical verses and striking paintings depict wolves and their pups engaging in many activities, including playing and searching for food. (Rev: BL 11/1/97; SLJ 11/97)

**4482** Wood, A. J. *Amazing Animals* (PS–K). Illus. 1991, Boyds Mills $8.95 (1-878093-46-0). With spare prose and double-page spreads, 10 different animals are introduced. (Rev: SLJ 11/91) [591]

**4483** Wood, A. J. *Beautiful Birds* (PS–K). Illus. 1991, Boyds Mills $8.95 (1-878093-47-9). In attactive pictures and short statements, 10 different birds are introduced. (Rev: SLJ 11/91) [591]

**4484** Wood, Jakki. *Animal Hullabaloo: A Wildlife Noisy Book* (PS–1). Illus. by author. 1995, Simon & Schuster $15.00 (0-689-80301-X). Double-page spreads are used to display a number of animals and describe the sounds they make. (Rev: SLJ 11/95) [591.51]

**4485** Yolen, Jane. *Owl Moon* (PS–2). Illus. by John Schoenherr. 1987, Putnam $16.99 (0-399-21457-7). 32pp. Winner of the 1988 Caldecott Medal, this the poetic story of a little girl and her father on an owl adventure in winter. (Rev: BL 12/15/87; SLJ 12/87)

## SCHOOL STORIES

**4486** Allard, Harry. *Miss Nelson Has a Field Day* (1–3). Illus. by James Marshall. 1985, Houghton $15.00 (0-395-36690-9); paper $5.95 (0-395-48654-8). 32pp. The plucky Miss Nelson gets a losing football team into shape. (Rev: BCCB 7/85; BL 5/15/85; HB 5–6/85)

**4487** Allard, Harry. *Miss Nelson Is Missing!* (K–2). Illus. by James Marshall. 1985, Houghton $16.00 (0-395-25296-2); paper $4.95 (0-395-40146-1). When Miss Nelson's students in Room 207 misbehave, she disappears and is replaced by a martinet. A sequel is: *Miss Nelson Is Back* (1985).

**4488** Aseltine, Lorraine. *First Grade Can Wait* (K–2). Illus. by Virginia Wright-Frierson. 1988, Whitman LB $12.95 (0-8075-2451-4). 32pp. At 6, Luke isn't mature enough to start school, so his parents decide to hold him out for a year. (Rev: BL 3/15/88; SLJ 7/88)

**4489** Ashley, Bernard. *Cleversticks* (PS–1). Illus. by Derek Brazell. 1995, Crown paper $6.99 (0-517-88332-5). 32pp. Ling Sung is a nobody at school until he reveals he can use chopsticks. (Rev: BCCB 7–8/92; BL 11/15/92; SLJ 3/93)

**4490** Baehr, Patricia. *School Isn't Fair* (PS). Illus. by R. W. Alley. 1989, Macmillan LB $13.95 (0-02-708130-3). Edward gets into trouble in his nursery school, mainly because of a bully. (Rev: SLJ 8/89)

**4491** Baker, Barbara. *Third Grade Is Terrible* (2–4). Illus. by Roni Shepherd. 1991, Pocket paper $3.50 (0-671-70379-X). 80pp. Lisa looked forward to third grade until she realized her teacher is mean Mrs. Rumford. (Rev: BCCB 5/89; BL 2/1/89)

**4492** Bianchi, John. *Welcome Back to Pokeweed Public School* (PS–1). Illus. 1996, Firefly $15.95 (0-

921285-45-0); paper $4.95 (0-921285-44-2). 24pp. The new computers at Pokeweed Public contain a few unexplained glitches. (Rev: BL 2/1/97)

**4493** Boelts, Maribeth. *Little Bunny's Preschool Countdown* (PS). Illus. by Kathy Parkinson. 1996, Albert Whitman LB $14.95 (0-8075-4582-1). 32pp. LB, a rabbit, begins to dread his first day at preschool. (Rev: BL 9/15/96; SLJ 11/96)

**4494** Boelts, Maribeth. *Summer's End* (K–3). Illus. by Ellen Kandoian. 1995, Houghton $14.95 (0-395-70559-2). 32pp. As summer draws to a close, a young girl becomes apprehensive about entering the second grade. (Rev: BCCB 3/95; BL 4/1/95; SLJ 4/95)

**4495** Bunting, Eve. *Our Teacher's Having a Baby* (K–2). Illus. by Diane De Groat. 1992, Houghton $14.95 (0-395-60470-2). 32pp. Mrs. Neal explains to her class that she is going to have a baby, and together they prepare for the event. (Rev: BL 9/15/92; SLJ 3/93)

**4496** Butterworth, Nick, and Mick Inkpen. *The School Trip* (K–3). Illus. 1990, Delacorte $13.95 (0-385-30242-8). The story of the field trip taken by Mrs. Jefferson's class to a natural history museum. (Rev: SLJ 3/91)

**4497** Caudill, Rebecca. *A Pocketful of Cricket* (1–3). Illus. by Evaline Ness. 1989, Holt LB $7.95 (0-03-089752-1); paper $5.95 (0-8050-1275-3). 48pp. A small boy delights in the countryside around his home, and one day his pet cricket goes to school in his pocket.

**4498** Chardiet, Bernice, and Grace Maccarone. *The Best Teacher in the World* (PS–2). Illus. by G. Brian Karas. 1991, Scholastic paper $2.50 (0-590-43307-5). 32pp. Bunny is selected by her favorite teacher to run an errand. (Rev: BL 1/1/90; SLJ 10/90)

**4499** Clements, Andrew. *Billy and the Bad Teacher* (K–3). Illus. by Elivia Savadier. 1993, Picture Book paper $15.00 (0-88708-244-0). In this humorous story, Billy is such a stickler for perfection that he writes a very critical report about his laid-back new teacher and sends it to his teacher's bosses. (Rev: SLJ 1/94)

**4500** Cohen, Miriam. *Best Friends* (PS–K). Illus. by Lillian Hoban. 1971, Macmillan LB $15.00 (0-02-722800-2); paper $4.95 (0-689-71334-7). 32pp. Kindergarten is the setting for this story of the friendship and disagreements between 2 boys. By the same author: *First Grade Takes a Test* (1983, Dell); *See You Tomorrow, Charles* (1989, Dell).

**4501** Cohen, Miriam. *Liar, Liar, Pants on Fire!* (K–2). Illus. by Lillian Hoban. 1995, Bantam paper $4.99 (0-440-41112-2). A new first-grade student boasts of owning a pony in this tale illustrating that children who tell fibs may be asking for attention.

Two other first-grade stories: *Starring First Grade* (1985); *It's George!* (1988). (Rev: BCCB 9/85; BL 9/15/85; HB 11–12/85)

**4502** Cohen, Miriam. *See You in Second Grade!* (1–2). Illus. by Lillian Hoban. 1990, Dell paper $2.95 (0-440-40303-0). 32pp. The famous first-graders of this author and artist are about to be promoted. (Rev: BCCB 3/89; BL 3/15/89; SLJ 4/89)

**4503** Cohen, Miriam. *Will I Have a Friend?* (PS–2). Illus. by Lillian Hoban. 1967, Macmillan paper $3.95 (0-689-71333-9). 32pp. Jim, a kindergartner, lives out the actual concern that small children have about finding a friend on the first day of school. By the same author and publisher: *No Good in Art* (1980); *So What?* (1982); *Jim's Dog Muffins* (1986); *Jim Meets the Thing* (1989).

**4504** Conlin, Susan, and Susan L. Friedman. *All My Feelings at Preschool: Nathan's Day* (PS–K). Illus. by Kathryn M. Smith. 1991, Parenting Pr. LB $16.95 (0-943990-61-0); paper $6.95 (0-943990-60-2). 32pp. This picture book describes a day in the life of Nathan at his nursery school. (Rev: BL 6/1/91)

**4505** Crebbin, June. *Danny's Duck* (PS–K). Illus. by Clara Vulliamy. 1995, Candlewick $13.95 (1-56402-536-5). 32pp. Danny secretly visits a duck's nest at the edge of the schoolyard and each time draws a picture of what he has seen. (Rev: BL 6/1–15/95; SLJ 5/95)

**4506** Davis, Gibbs. *The Other Emily* (K–2). Illus. by Linda Shute. 1990, Harcourt paper $4.95 (0-395-54947-7). 32pp. Emily loves her name until she encounters another Emily in her class.

**4507** Delton, Judy. *My Mom Made Me Go to School* (PS–2). Illus. by Lisa McCue. 1991, Delacorte $13.00 (0-385-30041-7). Although he goes along with all the preparations, Archie has no intention of going to school. (Rev: SLJ 4/92)

**4508** dePaola, Tomie. *The Art Lesson* (K–3). Illus. by author. 1989, Putnam $15.95 (0-399-21688-X). 32pp. Tommy just keeps on drawing and drawing and drawing. (Rev: BCCB 3/89; BL 3/1/89; SLJ 4/89)

**4509** Doherty, Berlie. *Snowy* (PS–3). Illus. by Keith Bowen. 1992, Smithmark $4.98 (0-8317-4559-2). 32pp. Rachel invites her entire class for a ride on the family barge pulled by Snowy, the horse. (Rev: BL 11/15/92)

**4510** Fain, Moira. *Snow Day* (K–3). Illus. 1996, Walker LB $16.85 (0-8027-8410-0). 32pp. Maggie Murphy escapes a school punishment when a snow day is declared the following day. (Rev: BCCB 10/96; BL 10/15/96; SLJ 10/96*)

**4511** Finchler, Judy. *Miss Malarkey Doesn't Live in Room 10* (K–3). Illus. by Kevin O'Malley. 1995, Walker LB $15.85 (0-8027-8387-2). 32pp. A young boy is convinced that his teacher lives at school until she moves into his apartment building. (Rev: BL 11/15/95; SLJ 12/95)

**4512** Flood, Nancy Bo. *I'll Go to School If . . .* (PS–K). Illus. by Ronnie W. Shipman. 1997, Fairview $14.95 (1-57749-024-X). 32pp. A fearful little boy panics at the thought of his first day of school and thinks of ways he can impress his school chums. (Rev: BL 6/1–15/97)

**4513** Giff, Patricia Reilly. *Next Year I'll Be Special* (1–3). Illus. by Marylin Hafner. 1993, Doubleday $13.95 (0-385-30903-1). Marilyn has a terrible first grade, but she is sure things will be better next year with Miss Lark as her teacher. (Rev: HB 7–8/93; SLJ 4/94)

**4514** Giff, Patricia Reilly. *Today Was a Terrible Day* (2–3). Illus. by Susanna Natti. 1980, Puffin paper $4.99 (0-14-050453-2). 32pp. Ronald is having a terrible day until his teacher writes him an understanding note.

**4515** Hathorn, Libby. *Freya's Fantastic Surprise* (1–3). Illus. by Sharon Thompson. 1989, Scholastic $12.95 (0-590-42442-4). 32pp. Freya makes up so many surprises at News Time in school that her classmates become hostile. (Rev: HB 3–4/89)

**4516** Henkes, Kevin. *Lilly's Purple Plastic Purse* (PS–K). Illus. 1996, Greenwillow LB $14.93 (0-688-12898-X). 32pp. Lilly runs afoul of her teacher, Mr. Slinger, whom she adores. A sequel to *Julius, the Baby of the World* (1990). (Rev: BCCB 10/96; BL 8/96*; HB 9–10/96, 1–2/97; SLJ 8/96*)

**4517** Hennessy, B. G. *School Days* (PS–3). Illus. by Tracey Campbell Pearson. 1990, Viking paper $13.95 (0-670-83025-9). 32pp. Everyday classroom life is interrupted when a rabbit gets loose. (Rev: BL 10/1/90; HB 11–12/90; SLJ 1/91)

**4518** Hinton, S. E. *Big David, Little David* (K–2). Illus. by Alan Daniel. 1995, Doubleday $15.95 (0-385-31093-5). 32pp. Nick finds that a boy in his kindergarten looks amazingly like his father. (Rev: BCCB 2/95; BL 1/15/95; SLJ 4/95)

**4519** Howe, James. *When You Go to Kindergarten* (PS–1). Photos by Betsy Imershein. 1994, Morrow LB $15.93 (0-688-12913-7). 48pp. With color photos and a simple text, this book tells what a child can expect when he or she goes to kindergarten. (Rev: BL 9/1/94; SLJ 9/94) [372.21]

**4520** Howlett, Bud. *I'm New Here* (K–4). Illus. 1993, Houghton $16.00 (0-395-64049-0). 32pp. A photoessay about a fifth-grader from El Salvador and her first experiences in an American school. (Rev: BL 10/1/93; SLJ 9/93)

**4521** Hutchins, Pat. *Three-Star Billy* (PS–K). Illus. 1994, Greenwillow LB $14.93 (0-688-13079-8). 32pp. Billy is so badly behaved that he wins plaudits

for being a good little monster. (Rev: BL 10/1/94; SLJ 8/94*)

**4522** Kline, Suzy. *Horrible Harry and the Kickball Wedding* (2–3). Illus. by Frank Remkiewicz. 1992, Viking paper $11.99 (0-670-83358-4). 64pp. Despite the typical second-grader attitude toward romantic love, Horrible Harry has a crush on Song Lee. (Rev: BL 10/1/92; SLJ 11/92)

**4523** Kline, Suzy. *Song Lee in Room 2B* (1–3). Illus. 1993, Viking paper $12.99 (0-670-84772-0). 64pp. This episodic story about the kids in Miss Mackle's Room 2B features a Korean-born girl, Song Lee. (Rev: BL 4/15/93)

**4524** Krensky, Stephen. *My Teacher's Secret Life* (PS–3). Illus. by JoAnn Adinolfi. 1996, Simon & Schuster paper $15.00 (0-689-80271-4). 28pp. A young school child discovers that his teacher really has a life outside of school. (Rev: BCCB 12/96; BL 11/15/96; SLJ 10/96)

**4525** Lawlor, Laurie. *How to Survive Third Grade* (2–4). Illus. by Joyce A. Zarins. 1988, Whitman LB $9.95 (0-8075-3433-1); Pocket paper $3.99 (0-671-67713-6). 72pp. Ernest isn't sure about third grade until he makes friends with Jomo from Kenya. (Rev: BCCB 11/88; BL 6/15/88; SLJ 9/88)

**4526** Lindgren, Astrid. *I Want to Go to School, Too!* (PS–1). Trans. by Barbara Lucas. Illus. by Ilon Wikland. 1987, Farrar $10.95 (91-29-58328-4). 32pp. Lena, at 5, visits school for a day with 7-year-old Peter and learns what it's all about. (Rev: BL 12/1/87)

**4527** Moon, Nicola. *Something Special* (K–2). Illus. by Alex Ayliffe. 1997, Peachtree $14.95 (1-56145-137-1). 32pp. Charlie decides to bring his new baby sister to school for a special show-and-tell. (Rev: BL 6/1–15/97; SLJ 6/97)

**4528** Moss, Marissa. *Regina's Big Mistake* (PS–2). Illus. 1990, Houghton $16.00 (0-395-55330-X). 32pp. At first, Regina is unable to get an inspiration for an art assignment, but gradually the drawing takes shape. (Rev: BCCB 10/90; BL 11/1/90; SLJ 1/91)

**4529** Mueller, Virginia. *Monster Goes to School* (PS–K). Illus. by Lynn Munsinger. 1992, Whitman LB $12.95 (0-8075-5264-X). 24pp. A scruffy kid monster paints a picture of his imaginary school clock. (Rev: BL 1/15/92)

**4530** Nims, Bonnie L. *Where Is the Bear at School?* (PS–K). Illus. by Madelaine Gill. 1989, Whitman LB $12.95 (0-8075-8935-7). 24pp. A solid message about school is combined with a clever puzzle. (Rev: BL 1/1/90)

**4531** Ormerod, Jan. *Ms. MacDonald Has a Class* (PS–2). Illus. 1996, Clarion $15.95 (0-395-77611-2). 32pp. After a visit to a farm, Ms. MacDonald's class prepares a pageant. (Rev: BCCB 10/96; BL 9/15/96; SLJ 8/96)

**4532** Poydar, Nancy. *Snip, Snip . . . Snow!* (PS–1). Illus. 1997, Holiday LB $15.95 (0-8234-1328-4). 32pp. Sophie is so disappointed at the lack of snow that she persuades her teacher to let the class make paper snowflakes. (Rev: BL 11/1/97; SLJ 10/97)

**4533** Pulver, Robin. *Nobody's Mother Is in Second Grade* (K–3). Illus. by G. Brian Karas. 1992, Dial paper $13.89 (0-8037-1211-1). 32pp. Cassandra's mother disguises herself so she can visit her daughter's second-grade classroom. (Rev: BL 6/15/92; SLJ 1/93)

**4534** Rockwell, Anne. *Show and Tell Day* (PS–K). Illus. by Lizzy Rockwell. 1997, HarperCollins LB $14.89 (0-06-027301-1). 32pp. In this show-and-tell story, 10 young boys and girls show their treasures to each other and a sympathetic teacher. (Rev: BL 4/1/97; SLJ 5/97)

**4535** Russo, Marisabina. *I Don't Want to Go Back to School* (PS–2). Illus. 1994, Greenwillow LB $14.93 (0-688-04602-9). 32pp. A little boy worries about his reception when he returns to school after summer vacation. (Rev: BL 9/1/94; SLJ 7/94*)

**4536** Saltzberg, Barney. *Phoebe and the Spelling Bee* (PS–2). Illus. 1997, Hyperion LB $15.49 (0-7868-2114-0). 32pp. Phoebe is an uninterested student who hates spelling bees, but in time she learns a new way to achieve success in the classroom. (Rev: BL 10/1/97)

**4537** Saltzberg, Barney. *Show-and-Tell* (K–3). Illus. 1994, Hyperion LB $15.49 (0-7868-2016-0). 32pp. Young Phoebe's parents always interfere with her school plans and create something grand out of a simple assignment. (Rev: BL 10/15/94; SLJ 10/94)

**4538** Schwartz, Amy. *Annabelle Swift, Kindergartner* (PS–K). Illus. by author. 1988, Orchard paper $5.95 (0-531-07027-1). 32pp. A good match of art and text tells the story of Annabelle, who finds that school isn't as much fun as she had thought — until it's time to count the milk money. (Rev: BCCB 5/88; BL 2/1/88; HB 3–4/88)

**4539** Scieszka, Jon. *Math Curse* (1–4). Illus. by Lane Smith. 1995, Viking paper $16.99 (0-670-86194-4). 32pp. All sorts of math problems and riddles, from the practical to the absurd are presented in this school story. (Rev: BCCB 10/95; BL 11/1/95*; HB 11–12/95; SLJ 9/95*)

**4540** Senisi, Ellen B. *Kindergarten Kids* (PS–K). Illus. 1994, Scholastic paper $2.50 (0-590-47614-9). 32pp. A photoessay that describes a typical day in a kindergarten class in Schenectady, New York. (Rev: BL 11/1/94) [372.21]

**4541** Serfozo, Mary. *Benjamin Bigfoot* (PS–2). Illus. by Joseph A. Smith. 1993, Macmillan $14.95 (0-689-50570-1). 32pp. Benjamin enjoys wearing his father's shoes so much that he wants to wear them when he starts kindergarten. (Rev: BL 4/15/93; SLJ 8/93)

**4542** Shipton, Jonathan. *No Biting, Horrible Crocodile!* (PS–K). Illus. by Claudio Munoz. 1995, Western Artists & Writers $12.95 (0-307-17521-9). 32pp. Flora gets the nickname "Horrible Crocodile" because she enjoys biting everything. (Rev: BL 10/15/95; SLJ 2/96)

**4543** Simon, Norma. *I'm Busy, Too* (PS–1). Illus. by Dora Leder. 1980, Whitman LB $12.95 (0-8075-3464-1). A day-care-center child realizes that every member of the family has an important role to play.

**4544** Tester, Sylvia Root. *We Laughed a Lot, My First Day of School* (PS–1). Illus. by Frances Hook. 1979, Child's World LB $14.95 (0-685-55556-9). A Mexican American boy has an unexpectedly pleasant first day at school.

**4545** Wells, Rosemary. *Timothy Goes to School* (PS–1). Illus. by author. 1981, Dial paper $15.99 (0-8037-8948-3). 32pp. Timothy's first day at school is almost ruined by a bully, but a friend helps him.

**4546** Willner-Pardo, Gina. *Natalie Spitzer's Turtles* (2–3). Illus. 1992, Whitman LB $14.95 (0-8075-5515-0). 32pp. In this story about second-graders, Jess deals with shifting friendships. (Rev: BL 9/1/92; SLJ 10/92)

**4547** Yashima, Taro. *Crow Boy* (K–3). Illus. by author. 1955, Puffin paper $4.99 (0-14-050172-X). 40pp. Distinguished picture book about a shy little Japanese boy who feels like an outsider at school.

## TRANSPORTATION AND MACHINES

**4548** *Around Town* (PS–K). Illus. 1995, DK Publg. $4.95 (1-56458-975-7). 10pp. Such city vehicles as taxis, cars, and trucks are featured in this simple picture book. Planes and trains are highlighted in *Going Places* (1995). (Rev: BL 8/95; SLJ 8/95)

**4549** Baer, Edith. *This Is the Way We Go to School* (PS–2). Illus. by Steve Bjorkman. 1994, Scholastic paper $4.99 (0-590-49443-0). 40pp. How children around the world go to school is told in rhyming couplets. (Rev: BCCB 10/90; BL 10/1/90; SLJ 7/90*) [629]

**4550** Bagenal, Elinor. *Tractor Factory: A Pop-up Book* (PS–K). Illus. by Steve Augarde. 1994, Golden Bks. $14.95 (0-307-17640-1). 10pp. Using pop-ups, the interior and exterior parts of a tractor and their uses are shown. (Rev: BL 11/15/94) [629]

**4551** Barton, Byron. *Airport* (PS–1). Illus. by author. 1982, HarperCollins LB $15.89 (0-690-04169-1); paper $5.95 (0-06-443145-2). 32pp. Common sights at an airport, reproduced in drawings and text.

**4552** *Bikes, Cars, Trucks and Trains* (PS–1). Illus. 1997, Scholastic $19.95 (0-590-47653-X). Overlays are used to explore the interiors of cars and other vehicles. Also use *Boats and Ships* (1997). (Rev: BL 12/15/97) [388.09]

**4553** Borden, Louise. *The Neighborhood Trucker* (PS–2). Illus. by Sandra Speidel. 1997, Scholastic paper $3.95 (0-590-46037-4). 32pp. A boy is entranced with trucks, particularly a cement truck driven by Slim. (Rev: BCCB 12/90; BL 9/1/90; SLJ 10/90)

**4554** Brown, Margaret Wise. *The Diggers* (PS–K). Illus. by Daniel Kirk. 1995, Hyperion LB $15.49 (0-7868-2001-2). 32pp. A newly illustrated edition of the book that deals with steam shovels and other earth movers in a set of poems. (Rev: BL 5/1/95; SLJ 7/95) [811]

**4555** Burton, Virginia Lee. *Mike Mulligan and His Steam Shovel* (1–3). Illus. by author. 1939, Houghton LB $11.95 (0-395-06681-6); paper $5.95 (0-395-25939-8). Thrilling race against time as Mike Mulligan and his steam shovel dig a cellar in one day. Also use: *Katy and the Big Snow* (1973).

**4556** *Cars* (K–3). Illus. Series: What's Inside? 1993, DK Publg. $8.95 (1-56458-219-1). 17pp. By using a peeled-back diagram, the exterior and interior of many autos are shown. Also use: *Great Inventions* (1993). (Rev: BL 8/93) [629.222]

**4557** Coulter, Hope N. *Uncle Chuck's Truck* (PS). Illus. by Rick Brown. 1993, Macmillan LB $13.95 (0-02-724825-9). 32pp. A youngster rides in a farm truck to feed the cows. (Rev: BL 1/15/93; SLJ 3/93)

**4558** Crews, Donald. *Bicycle Race* (PS–K). Illus. by author. 1985, Greenwillow LB $15.93 (0-688-05172-3). 24pp. A counting book that features 12 bicyclists in yellow numbered helmets, with a flat tire added for drama. (Rev: BL 9/15/85; SLJ 11/85)

**4559** Crews, Donald. *Flying* (PS). Illus. by author. 1986, Greenwillow LB $15.93 (0-688-04319-4); Morrow paper $4.95 (0-688-09235-7). 32pp. Brief text and full-color art highlight this study in movement as a plane takes off, flies over different landscapes, and lands. (Rev: BL 9/1/86; SLJ 10/86)

**4560** Crews, Donald. *Harbor* (K–2). Illus. by author. 1982, Greenwillow LB $15.93 (0-688-00862-3); Morrow paper $3.95 (0-688-07332-8). 32pp. The activities and objects associated with harbors and harbor activities are illustrated.

**4561** Crews, Donald. *School Bus* (PS–1). Illus. by author. 1984, Greenwillow LB $15.93 (0-688-02808-X); Morrow paper $4.95 (0-688-12267-1). 32pp. Many kinds of school buses pick up children for school.

**4562** Crowther, Robert. *Dump Trucks and Diggers* (PS–K). Illus. 1996, Candlewick $7.99 (0-7636-0008-3). 12pp. Dump trucks and other heavy machin-ery move in this book when tabs are pulled. (Rev: BL 12/15/96)

**4563** Demarest, Chris L. *Bus* (PS). Illus. 1996, Harcourt paper $4.95 (0-15-200810-1). 16pp. An appealing board book about a bus and its functions. (Rev: BL 4/1/96; SLJ 8/96)

**4564** Demarest, Chris L. *Train* (PS). Illus. 1996, Harcourt paper $4.95 (0-15-200809-8). 16pp. Trains and what they do are introduced in this attractive board book. (Rev: BL 4/1/96; SLJ 8/96)

**4565** *Emergency!* (PS–K). Illus. 1995, DK Publg. $4.95 (1-56458-974-9). 10pp. Police helicopters and patrol cars are 2 of the vehicles pictured. In *Giant Machines* (1995) tractors and trucks are featured. (Rev: BL 8/95; SLJ 8/95)

**4566** Gibbons, Gail. *Boat Book* (PS–1). Illus. by author. 1983, Holiday LB $16.95 (0-8234-0478-1); paper $5.95 (0-8234-0709-8). 32pp. An illustration of all sorts of boats in simple drawings.

**4567** Gibbons, Gail. *Emergency!* (PS–1). Illus. 1994, Holiday LB $15.95 (0-8234-1128-1). 32pp. This picture book shows how a number of people are saved through the use of such vehicles as fire engines, Coast Guard boats, and police cars. (Rev: BCCB 11/94; BL 10/15/94; SLJ 11/94) [363.3]

**4568** Gibbons, Gail. *New Road!* (K–2). Illus. by author. 1983, HarperCollins LB $14.89 (0-690-04343-0). 32pp. The process of road construction from start to finish.

**4569** Gramatky, Hardie. *Little Toot* (K–3). Illus. by author. 1939, Putnam $16.95 (0-399-22419-X); paper $6.95 (0-698-11576-7). 96pp. Little Toot, son of the mightiest tug in the harbor, had no ambition until he became a hero during a raging storm.

**4570** Gray, Libba M. *The Little Black Truck* (K–2). Illus. by Elizabeth Sayles. 1994, Simon & Schuster paper $15.00 (0-671-78105-7). 32pp. Left to rust after years of service, a little black truck named Mary Ann gets a new lease on life when a young man decides to restore her. (Rev: BL 6/1–15/94; SLJ 8/94)

**4571** Hennessy, B. G. *Road Builders* (PS–1). Illus. by Simms Taback. 1994, Viking paper $14.99 (0-670-83390-8). 32pp. A picture book that shows how different kinds of machines and vehicles are used in building a road. (Rev: BL 5/1/94; SLJ 9/94) [625.7]

**4572** Hindley, Judy. *The Big Red Bus* (PS). Illus. by William Benedict. 1995, Candlewick $15.99 (1-56402-639-6). 32pp. A simple picture book about a road jam caused by a big red bus that has a wheel caught in a large pothole. (Rev: BL 10/15/95; SLJ 1/96)

**4573** Hoban, Tana. *Construction Zone* (PS–1). Illus. 1997, Greenwillow LB $14.93 (0-688-12285-X).

32pp. Thirteen construction machines like the bulldozer, backhoe, and forklift are introduced in pictures and a simple text. (Rev: BCCB 4/97; BL 4/1/97; SLJ 3/97) [624]

**4574** Jennings, Dana A. *Me, Dad, and Number 6* (K–2). Illus. by Goro Sasaki. 1997, Harcourt $15.00 (0-15-200085-2). A reminiscence about a boy and his father who restore an old 1937 Pontiac coupe, which Dad later races at the stock car track. (Rev: BCCB 5/97; SLJ 4/97)

**4575** Katz, Bobbi. *Truck Talk: Rhymes on Wheels* (PS–1). Illus. 1997, Scholastic $10.95 (0-590-69328-X). 32pp. Each of the trucks pictured — e.g., tow trucks, ambulances, and garbage trucks — describes its function in its own words. (Rev: BL 4/1/97; SLJ 3/97) [811]

**4576** Kuklin, Susan. *Fighting Fires* (K–2). Illus. 1993, Macmillan LB $15.00 (0-02-751238-X). 32pp. In clear color photos, the daily life and equipment of fire fighters are described. (Rev: BL 7/93) [628.9]

**4577** Lyon, David. *The Biggest Truck* (PS–1). Illus. by author. 1988, Lothrop LB $13.88 (0-688-05514-1). 32pp. Jim the truck driver goes to work when everyone else is going to bed. (Rev: BL 11/1/88; SLJ 1/89)

**4578** Maccarone, Grace. *Cars! Cars! Cars!* (PS). Illus. by David A. Carter. 1995, Scholastic $6.95 (0-590-47572-X). 24pp. The concept of different styles, colors, and models of cars is introduced in this very simple picture book. (Rev: BL 1/15/95; SLJ 12/95)

**4579** McDonnell, Flora. *I Love Boats* (PS–1). Illus. 1995, Candlewick $15.95 (1-56402-539-X). 32pp. A picture book that introduces all kinds of boats, from a rowboat to a big ship. (Rev: BL 8/95; HB 7–8/95; SLJ 8/95)

**4580** McGough, Roger. *Until I Met Dudley: How Everyday Things Really Work* (K–4). Illus. by Chris Riddell. 1997, Walker $15.95 (0-8027-8623-5). An amusing story that explains how 5 common appliances, like a toaster, work. (Rev: SLJ 11/97)

**4581** Maestro, Betsy, and Ellen DelVecchio. *Big City Port* (PS–2). Illus. by Giulio Maestro. 1984, Macmillan LB $14.95 (0-02-762110-3); Scholastic paper $4.95 (0-590-41577-8). 32pp. A picture book that shows activities in a big-city port.

**4582** Micklethwait, Lucy. *I Spy a Freight Train: Transportation in Art* (K–3). Illus. Series: I Spy. 1996, Greenwillow LB $18.93 (0-688-14701-1). 32pp. Close inspection of a series of pictures reveals items connected to transportation. (Rev: BL 7/96; SLJ 8/96) [758]

**4583** Mott, Evelyn Clarke. *Steam Train Ride* (PS–K). Illus. 1991, Walker LB $14.85 (0-8027-6996-9). A delightful ride for train lovers on Engine 89. (Rev: BL 5/15/91; SLJ 8/91) [625.2]

**4584** Pienkowski, Jan. *Big Machines* (PS–K). Illus. 1997, Dutton paper $7.99 (0-525-45854-9). Pop-ups and a few words of text are used to show such machines as dump trucks and bulldozers. Also use *Boats* and *Planes* (both 1997). (Rev: BL 12/15/97; SLJ 8/97) [621.8]

**4585** Pienkowski, Jan. *Boats* (PS). Illus. by author. Series: Transportation Books. 1997, Dutton paper $7.99 (0-525-45851-4). Pop-ups that feature vehicles in action — for example, a tugboat towing an ocean liner. Others in this series are *Planes: And Other Things That Fly*, and *Trucks: And Other Working Wheels* (both 1997). (Rev: SLJ 8/97)

**4586** Piper, Watty. *The Little Engine That Could* (K–2). Illus. by George Hauman and Doris Hauman. 1930, Putnam $6.99 (0-448-40520-2). 48pp. Little Engine saves the day.

**4587** Relf, Patricia. *Tonka Big Book of Trucks* (PS–3). Illus. by Thomas La Padula. 1996, Scholastic $11.95 (0-590-84572-1). 48pp. Double-page spreads are used to describe a variety of trucks and their drivers. (Rev: BL 10/1/96; SLJ 9/96) [629.2]

**4588** Rockwell, Anne. *Fire Engines* (PS–K). Illus. by author. 1986, Puffin paper $4.99 (0-14-055250-2). 24pp. An introduction to fire trucks with dalmations performing all the duties. (Rev: BL 9/1/86; HB 3–4/87; SLJ 11/86)

**4589** Rotner, Shelley. *Wheels Around* (PS–1). Illus. 1995, Houghton $13.95 (0-395-71815-5). 32pp. All kinds of wheeled vehicles from fire and mail trucks to small trailers and wheelchairs are featured. (Rev: BL 11/1/95; SLJ 10/95) [621.8]

**4590** Royston, Angela. *Cars* (PS–2). Illus. by Jane Cradock-Watson and Dave Hopkins. Series: Eye Openers. 1991, Macmillan paper $7.95 (0-689-71517-X). 21pp. Double-page spreads introduce a variety of cars. Also use: *Diggers and Dump Trucks* (1991). (Rev: BL 9/15/91; SLJ 1/92) [629]

**4591** Siebert, Diane. *Plane Song* (PS–2). Illus. by Vincent Nasta. 1993, HarperCollins LB $14.89 (0-06-021467-8). 32pp. In rhyming verse and oil paintings, a variety of airplanes are introduced both on the ground and in flight. (Rev: BL 5/1/93; SLJ 6/93) [629]

**4592** Siebert, Diane. *Train Song* (PS–2). Illus. by Mike Wimmer. 1990, HarperCollins LB $15.89 (0-690-04728-2). 32pp. This poem portrays trains as they travel across America. (Rev: BCCB 12/90; BL 10/1/90; SLJ 9/90*)

**4593** Siebert, Diane. *Truck Song* (PS–1). Illus. by Byron Barton. 1984, HarperCollins LB $15.89 (0-690-04411-9); paper $6.95 (0-06-443134-7). 32pp. Simple rhymes tell of trucks traveling cross-country.

**4594** Swift, Hildegarde, and Lynd Ward. *Little Red Lighthouse and the Great Gray Bridge* (1–3). Illus.

by Lynd Ward. 1942, Harcourt $17.00 (0-15-247040-9); paper $8.00 (0-15-652840-1). 52pp. The beacon of the little red lighthouse at the base of the George Washington Bridge in New York City is still needed even after the bridge is built.

**4595** *Trucks* (PS). Illus. Series: Eye Openers. 1991, Macmillan $7.95 (0-689-71405-X). 24pp. Double-page spreads feature clear photos of a single object. (Rev: BL 6/15/91) [629.2]

**4596** Wilson-Max, Ken. *Little Green Tow Truck* (PS–2). Illus. 1997, Scholastic paper $14.95 (0-590-89802-7). 14pp. Tabs and flaps are featured in this book about the parts and uses of tow trucks. Also use *Big Red Fire Truck* (1997). (Rev: BL 12/15/97) [629]

**4597** Wilson-Max, Ken. *Little Red Plane* (PS–1). Illus. 1995, Scholastic $14.95 (0-590-43008-4). 14pp. By pulling tabs, the reader can make this airplane perform all sorts of stunts. (Rev: BL 2/1/96)

**4598** Wolf, Sallie. *Peter's Trucks* (PS–K). Illus. by Cat B. Smith. 1992, Whitman LB $14.95 (0-8075-6519-9). 24pp. A variety of trucks are introduced as Peter inquires about the contents of each. (Rev: BCCB 3/92; BL 3/1/92; SLJ 6/92)

**4599** Wood, Jakki. *Bumper to Bumper: A Traffic Jam* (PS). Illus. 1996, Simon & Schuster paper $14.00 (0-689-80391-5). 32pp. Various vehicles and their drivers are introduced during a traffic jam. (Rev: BL 6/1–15/96; SLJ 6/96)

## Stories about Holidays and Holy Days

### GENERAL AND MISCELLANEOUS

**4600** Barker, Margot. *What Is Martin Luther King, Jr. Day?* (K–2). Illus. by Matthew Bates. Series: Understanding Holidays. 1990, Children's LB $18.00 (0-516-03784-6); paper $4.95 (0-516-43784-4). 48pp. Two white classmates learn from their black friends who Martin Luther King, Jr., was and why we celebrate his birthday. (Rev: SLJ 2/91) [921]

**4601** Brown, Marc. *Arthur's April Fool* (PS–2). Illus. by author. 1985, Little, Brown $15.95 (0-316-11196-1); paper $5.95 (0-316-11234-8). 32pp. Arthur is afraid he will forget his magic tricks prepared for the April Fools' Day show.

**4602** Bunting, Eve. *The Mother's Day Mice* (PS–1). Illus. by Jan Brett. 1986, Houghton $15.00 (0-89919-387-0); paper $5.95 (0-89919-702-7). Three little mice go out to seek presents for Mother's Day; the smallest one brings home a song he heard a human sing. (Rev: BCCB 4/86; BL 4/1/86; SLJ 3/86)

**4603** Bunting, Eve. *A Perfect Father's Day* (PS–1). Illus. by Susan Meddaugh. 1993, Houghton paper $5.95 (0-395-66416-0). 32pp. Susie plans a perfect time for her father on Father's Day. (Rev: BL 4/15/91; SLJ 5/91)

**4604** Bunting, Eve. *St. Patrick's Day in the Morning* (PS–2). Illus. by Jan Brett. 1983, Houghton $15.00 (0-395-29098-8); paper $5.95 (0-89919-162-2). 32pp. Jamie is too small to parade to the top of the hill with the rest of his family, so he rises early and has a St. Patrick's Day adventure of his own.

**4605** Carrier, Roch. *A Happy New Year's Day* (2–4). Illus. by Gilles Pelletier. 1991, Tundra $14.95 (0-88776-267-0). This is a happy recollection of a New Year's Day spent in a French Canadian town during World War II. (Rev: SLJ 2/92)

**4606** Chin, Steven A. *Dragon Parade: A Chinese New Year Story* (PS–3). Illus. by Mou-Sien Tseng. 1993, Raintree Steck-Vaughn LB $22.83 (0-8114-7215-9). 32pp. This is a fictionalized account of the Chinese immigrant Noram Ah Sing, who started the first big New Year's Parade in San Francisco. (Rev: BL 5/1/93; SLJ 7/93) [394.2]

**4607** Chocolate, Deborah M. *My First Kwanzaa Book* (PS–2). Illus. by Cal Massey. 1992, Scholastic $10.95 (0-590-45762-4). 32pp. A celebration of African-American cultural heritage for the very young. (Rev: BCCB 2/93; BL 9/1/92) [394.2]

**4608** Demi. *Happy New Year! Kung-Hsi Fa-Ts' Ai!* (PS–3). Illus. 1997, Crown $16.00 (0-517-70957-0). 36pp. This joyous picture book shows all the preparations and celebrations that accompany the Chinese New Year festival. (Rev: BL 2/15/98; SLJ 3/98)

**4609** dePaola, Tomie. *The Lady of Guadalupe* (K–3). Illus. by author. 1980, Holiday LB $16.95 (0-8234-0373-4); paper $8.95 (0-8234-0403-X). 48pp. The legend of the patron saint of Mexico is retold in this excellent picture book.

**4610** *The 11th Commandment: Wisdom from Our Children* (PS–3). Illus. 1996, Jewish Lights $16.95 (1-879045-46-X). 48pp. The results of a survey of a group of children from different faiths who were asked to suggest an 11th commandment. (Rev: BL 10/1/96) [170]

**4611** Ford, Juwanda G. *K Is for Kwanzaa: A Kwanzaa Alphabet Book* (K–3). Illus. by Ken Wilson-Max. 1997, Scholastic $10.95 (0-590-92200-9). 32pp. Arranged alphabetically various objects, customs, and rituals connected with Kwanzaa are introduced. (Rev: BL 9/1/97; SLJ 10/97) [394.261]

**4612** Ghazi, Suhaib Hamid. *Ramadan* (K–4). Illus. by Omar Rayyan. 1996, Holiday $15.95 (0-8234-1254-7). 32pp. The Islamic month of Ramadan, with its fasting and prayers, as seen through the eyes of a young boy. (Rev: BCCB 12/96; BL 10/1/96; SLJ 10/96) [297]

**4613** Gilmore, Rachna. *Lights for Gita* (K–3). Illus. by Alice Priestley. 1995, Tilbury $9.95 (0-88448-150-6). 24pp. An Indian child celebrates the Hindu holiday of Divali in her new home in Canada. (Rev: BL 6/1–15/95)

**4614** Johnston, Tony. *Day of the Dead* (K–4). Illus. by Jeanette Winter. 1997, Harcourt $14.00 (0-15-222863-2). 56pp. A Mexican family makes preparations for the holiday Day of the Dead and celebrates it festively. (Rev: BL 9/15/97; SLJ 9/97)

**4615** Koller, Jackie F. *Mole and Shrew: All Year Through* (2–3). 1997, Random paper $3.99 (0-679-88666-4). 80pp. Best friends Mole and Shrew have great times celebrating such holidays as Christmas, Thanksgiving, New Year's Eve and Easter. (Rev: BL 2/1/98)

**4616** Kroll, Steven. *Happy Father's Day* (K–2). Illus. by Marylin Hafner. 1996, paper $3.99 (0-373-24033-3). 32pp. A healthy breakfast is the first of several special treats for Dad. (Rev: BCCB 6/88; BL 4/1/88; SLJ 5/88)

**4617** Kroll, Steven. *It's Groundhog Day!* (PS–2). Illus. by Jeni Bassett. 1987, Scholastic paper $2.99 (0-590-44669-X). 32pp. Godfrey Groundhog will not see his shadow come February 2, and this very much upsets Roland Raccoon, who owns a ski lodge. (Rev: BL 10/15/87; SLJ 11/87)

**4618** Kroll, Steven. *Mary McLean and the St. Patrick's Day Parade* (1–3). Illus. by Michael Dooling. 1991, Scholastic $15.95 (0-590-43701-1). 32pp. A young Irish girl newly arrived in the United States is visited by a leprechaun on St. Patrick's Day. (Rev: BCCB 2/91; BL 1/1/91; SLJ 6/91)

**4619** Levy, Janice. *The Spirit of Tío Fernando: A Day of the Dead Story/El Espíritu de Tío Fernando: Una Historia del Día de los Muertos* (1–3). Trans. by Teresa Mlawer. Illus. by Morella Fuenmayor. 1995, Albert Whitman $14.95 (0-8075-7585-2); paper $6.95 (0-8075-7586-0). 32pp. On the Day of the Dead, Nando remembers his Uncle Fernando, who died 6 months before. (Rev: BL 11/15/95; SLJ 11/95)

**4620** Low, William. *Chinatown* (K–1). Illus. 1997, Holt paper $15.95 (0-8050-4214-8). 32pp. At Chinese New Year's, a boy and his grandmother take a tour through their Chinatown. (Rev: BL 9/15/97; SLJ 9/97)

**4621** Lowery, Linda. *Earth Day* (2–3). Illus. by Mary Bergherr. 1991, Carolrhoda LB $18.60 (0-87614-662-0). 48pp. The significance of the 1990 Earth Day celebration is explained in simple terms. (Rev: BL 6/15/91; SLJ 8/91) [333.7]

**4622** Mills, Claudia. *Phoebe's Parade* (PS–1). Illus. by Carolyn Ewing. 1994, Macmillan paper $14.95 (0-02-767012-0). 32pp. Phoebe's plan to shine on the Fourth of July backfires. (Rev: BL 3/1/94; SLJ 6/94)

**4623** Mitchell, Barbara. *Red Bird* (K–3). Illus. by Todd L. W. Doney. 1996, Lothrop LB $15.93 (0-688-10860-1). 32pp. The traditional powwow is seen through the eyes of a contemporary Nanticoke girl who attends each year with her parents. (Rev: BCCB 9/96; BL 5/1/96; SLJ 6/96)

**4624** Moore, Elizabeth, and Alice Couvillon. *Mimi and Jean-Paul's Cajun Mardi Gras* (1–3). Illus. by Marilyn C. Rougelot. 1996, Pelican $14.95 (1-56554-069-7). The unique Courir (Run) de Mardi Gras celebrated in Cajun country is experienced by a young girl. (Rev: SLJ 3/96)

**4625** Moorman, Margaret. *Light the Lights! A Story About Celebrating Hanukkah and Christmas* (K–3). Illus. 1994, Scholastic $12.95 (0-590-47003-5). 32pp. This book celebrates the spirit of both Christmas and Hanukkah and shows similarities in these holidays and their traditions. (Rev: BL 8/94) [394.26]

**4626** Morris, Ann. *Weddings* (PS–2). Illus. 1995, Lothrop LB $14.93 (0-688-13273-1). 32pp. Different wedding customs and clothing from around the world are pictured and discussed. (Rev: BCCB 10/95; BL 10/1/95; SLJ 1/96) [391.5]

**4627** O'Donnell, Elizabeth Lee. *Patrick's Day* (K–2). Illus. by Jacqueline Rogers. 1994, Morrow $15.00 (0-688-07853-2). 32pp. When Patrick, who is growing up in an Irish village, realizes that St. Patrick's Day is not in his honor, he becomes very grumpy. (Rev: BL 4/1/94; SLJ 5/94)

**4628** Patrick, Diane. *Family Celebrations* (2–5). Illus. by Michael Bryant. 1993, Silver Moon LB $13.95 (1-881889-04-1). 62pp. Portrays a variety of family gatherings that are associated with such occasions as birth, marriage, and death as they are observed in many cultures. (Rev: BL 6/1–15/93) [392]

**4629** Pinkney, Andrea D. *Seven Candles for Kwanzaa* (K–4). Illus. by Brian Pinkney. 1993, Dial paper $14.89 (0-8037-1293-6). 32pp. Pictures and text describe the origins and customs surrounding the African American 7-day holiday. (Rev: BL 7/93*) [394.2]

**4630** Rattigan, Jama Kim. *Dumpling Soup* (PS–3). Illus. by Lillian Hsu-Flanders. 1993, Little, Brown $15.95 (0-316-73445-4). 32pp. Marisa attempts to make dumplings when her extended, multiracial family celebrates New Year's Eve in this story set in Hawaii. (Rev: BCCB 10/93; BL 9/15/93; HB 11–12/93; SLJ 12/93)

**4631** Riehecky, Janet. *Cinco de Mayo* (1–3). Illus. by Krystyna Stasiak. Series: Circle the Year with Holidays. 1993, Children's LB $19.00 (0-516-00681-9). 32pp. This picture book tells how a Mexican family celebrates this national holiday and of its significance in history. (Rev: SLJ 4/94)

**4632** Riehecky, Janet. *Kwanzaa* (K–3). Illus. by Lydia Halverson. 1993, Children's LB $19.00 (0-516-00686-X). 32pp. The rituals connected with Kwanzaa — like the candles, fruit, and special mat — are explained with full-color illustrations. (Rev: BL 12/15/93) [394.2]

**4633** Ross, Kathy. *Crafts for Kwanzaa* (1–3). Illus. by Sharon L. Holm. 1994, Millbrook LB $21.90 (1-56294-412-6). 48pp. A history of Kwanzaa is given, plus instructions for a number of projects using simple materials. (Rev: BL 10/15/94) [745]

**4634** Saint James, Synthia. *The Gifts of Kwanzaa* (PS–2). Illus. 1994, Albert Whitman LB $14.95 (0-8075-2907-9). 32pp. Explains the origins of Kwanzaa and identifies the Seven Principles as well as giving information about rituals. (Rev: BL 11/15/94) [394.2]

**4635** Sasso, Sandy Eisenberg. *A Prayer for the Earth: The Story of Naamah, Noah's Wife* (PS–2). Illus. by Bethanne Andersen. 1997, Jewish Lights $16.95 (1-879045-60-5). 32pp. Noah's wife, Naamah, is given the job of bringing samples of each of the earth's plants into Noah's Ark. (Rev: BCCB 7–8/97; BL 2/15/97; SLJ 6/97)

**4636** Thomas, Jane Resh. *Celebration!* (K–3). Illus. by Raul Colon. 1997, Hyperion LB $15.49 (0-7868-2160-4). 32pp. Everyone is celebrating the Fourth of July at Maggie's house, including a chagrined Maurice, who has been caught stealing candy from a drugstore. (Rev: BL 5/15/97; SLJ 7/97)

**4637** Van Leeuwen, Jean. *A Fourth of July on the Plains* (K–3). Illus. by Henri Sorensen. 1997, Dial paper $14.89 (0-8037-1772-5). 32pp. A pioneer story on how the Fourth of July was celebrated on the Oregon Trail in 1852. (Rev: BCCB 7–8/97; BL 5/15/97; SLJ 5/97)

**4638** Vaughan, Marcia. *The Dancing Dragon* (K–2). Illus. by Stanley Wong Hoo Foon. 1996, Mondo paper $5.95 (1-57255-134-8). In rhyming couplets, a Chinese American child describes preparations for Chinese New Year celebrations, including the dragon parade. (Rev: SLJ 12/96)

**4639** Walter, Mildred P. *Kwanzaa: A Family Affair* (PS–2). Illus. by Cheryl Carrington. 1995, Lothrop $15.00 (0-688-11553-5). 80pp. Background material, ways of celebrating the holiday, and crafts and gifts are all covered in this introduction to Kwanzaa. (Rev: BL 9/15/95) [394.2]

**4640** Waters, Kate, and Madeline Slovenz-Low. *Lion Dancer: Ernie Wan's Chinese New Year* (PS–3). 1990, Scholastic $14.95 (0-590-43046-7); paper $3.95 (0-590-43047-5). 32pp. This account describes how a Chinese-American family celebrates the lunar New Year. (Rev: HB 7–8/90; SLJ 2/90) [391.2]

**4641** Watson, Wendy. *Hurray for the Fourth of July* (PS–2). Illus. 1992, Houghton $14.95 (0-395-53627-8). 32pp. This picture book shows and tells how a New England family celebrates the Fourth of July in their village. (Rev: BL 4/1/92; SLJ 6/92)

**4642** Yolen, Jane. *The Three Bears Holiday Rhyme Book* (PS–2). Illus. by Jane Dyer. 1995, Harcourt $15.00 (0-15-200932-9). 32pp. Fifteen poems featuring Goldilocks and the Three Bears are used to introduce such holidays as Valentine's Day, Arbor Day, and Groundhog Day. (Rev: BL 3/15/95; SLJ 6/95) [811.54]

## BIRTHDAYS

**4643** Anholt, Catherine. *The Snow Fairy and the Spaceman* (PS–1). Illus. 1991, Delacorte $13.95 (0-385-30421-8). 24pp. A girl attends her birthday party dressed as a fairy and meets a guest in a spaceman's costume. (Rev: BL 12/15/91; SLJ 2/92)

**4644** Barker, Marjorie. *Magical Hands* (2–4). Illus. by Yoshi. 1989, Picture Book $16.00 (0-88708-103-7). 28pp. William does his friends' work, hoping they will think it is magic, and then finds that his work is done too! (Rev: BL 2/1/90)

**4645** Barrett, Judith. *Benjamin's 365 Birthdays* (K–2). Illus. by Ron Barrett. 1992, Simon & Schuster paper $4.95 (0-689-71635-4). 40pp. Benjamin the bear is so delighted with his birthday presents that he decides to rewrap them so that he can enjoy one each day throughout the ensuing months.

**4646** Brown, Marc. *Arthur's Birthday* (K–2). Illus. 1989, Little, Brown $15.95 (0-316-11073-6); paper $5.95 (0-316-11074-4). Muffy is upset to learn that Arthur's birthday is the same day as hers. (Rev: BL 4/15/89; HB 5–6/89)

**4647** Brown, Tricia. *Hello, Amigos!* (K–2). Illus. by Fran Ortiz. 1992, Holt $15.95 (0-8050-0090-9); paper $5.95 (0-8050-1891-3). 48pp. The anticipation and excitement of Frankie Valdez's birthday. (Rev: BCCB 1/87; BL 12/15/86; SLJ 4/87)

**4648** Cameron, Ann. *Julian, Dream Doctor* (2–4). Illus. by Ann Strugnell. Series: Stepping Stone. 1990, Random LB $11.99 (0-679-90524-3); paper $3.99 (0-679-80524-9). 40pp. In this warm story of a black family, Julian wants to discover Dad's idea of a dream birthday present. (Rev: BCCB 3/90; BL 5/15/90; HB 9–10/90; SLJ 7/90)

**4649** Carle, Eric. *The Secret Birthday Message* (PS–1). Illus. by author. 1972, HarperCollins LB $14.89 (0-690-72348-2); paper $5.95 (0-06-443099-5). 26pp. In a brightly illustrated picture book with intriguing cutouts, a little boy has to decipher the coded message to find his birthday present.

**4650** Carlstrom, Nancy White. *Happy Birthday, Jesse Bear!* (PS–K). Illus. by Bruce Degen. 1994,

Macmillan $15.00 (0-02-717277-5). 32pp. Jesse Bear arranges for his birthday party, which turns out to be a big success. (Rev: BL 11/1/94; SLJ 12/94)

**4651** Caseley, Judith. *Three Happy Birthdays* (PS–1). Illus. 1993, Morrow paper $4.95 (0-688-11699-X). This book about 3 different birthdays involves Benny, his sister Marla, and his dog Charlie. (Rev: SLJ 9/89)

**4652** Charlip, Remy, et al. *Handtalk Birthday: A Number and Story Book in Sign Language* (1–4). Illus. by George Ancona. 1987, Simon & Schuster $15.95 (0-02-718080-8). 48pp. A happy birthday book in sign language that tells about a surprise party for Mary Beth. (Rev: BL 3/15/87; HB 9–10/87; SLJ 5/87)

**4653** Cooke, Trish. *So Much* (PS–K). Illus. by Helen Oxenbury. 1994, Candlewick $16.99 (1-56402-344-3). 32pp. Relatives arrive for Daddy's surprise birthday party, but it is the baby who is the center of attention. (Rev: BCCB 1/95; BL 3/1/95*; HB 11–12/94; SLJ 1/95)

**4654** Corey, Dorothy. *Will It Ever Be My Birthday?* (PS–K). Illus. by Eileen Christelow. 1986, Whitman LB $14.95 (0-8075-9106-8). 32pp. Rabbit gets an invitation to Bear's birthday party and wonders if his will ever come. (Rev: BL 10/1/86; SLJ 3/86)

**4655** Day, Alexandra. *Carl's Birthday* (PS–2). Illus. 1995, Farrar $12.95 (0-374-31144-7). 32pp. In this almost wordless picture book, Madeline and her beloved Rottweiler, Carl, secretly help prepare a surprise birthday party for the dog. (Rev: BL 1/1–15/96; SLJ 12/95)

**4656** Dorflinger, Carolyn. *Tomorrow Is Mom's Birthday* (PS–1). Illus. by Iza Trapani. 1994, Whispering Coyote LB $14.95 (1-879085-84-4). 32pp. Tyler thinks of all sorts of things to give to his mother on her birthday, but he decides to paint a family portrait. (Rev: BCCB 4/94; BL 5/1/94)

**4657** Feldman, Eve B. *Birthdays! Celebrating Life Around the World* (K–3). Illus. 1996, BridgeWater paper $14.95 (0-8167-3494-1). 32pp. A celebration of birthdays around the world, illustrated with color drawings by children ages 9 to 13. (Rev: SLJ 8/96)

**4658** Fox, Mem. *Night Noises* (PS–2). Illus. by Terry Denton. 1989, Harcourt $15.00 (0-15-200543-9); paper $4.95 (0-15-257421-2). 32pp. An old lady's dog becomes agitated at the commotion he hears outside while the woman sleeps, which turns out to be relatives arriving for a surprise ninetieth birthday party. (Rev: BL 11/15/89; HB 11–12/89*; SLJ 9/89*)

**4659** Gantos, Jack. *Happy Birthday, Rotten Ralph* (PS–3). Illus. by Nicole Rubel. 1990, Houghton $13.95 (0-395-53766-5). 32pp. Rotten Ralph, a cat, is so rotten that even sweet Sarah decides he doesn't

deserve a birthday party. (Rev: BL 10/1/90; HB 1–2/90; SLJ 10/90)

**4660** Giff, Patricia Reilly. *Happy Birthday, Ronald Morgan!* (2–3). Illus. by Susanna Natti. 1988, Puffin paper $4.99 (0-14-050668-3). 32pp. The day goes from bad to worse for Ronald, but ends up delightfully with a surprise birthday party. (Rev: BL 10/15/86; SLJ 4/87)

**4661** Goldstein, Bobbye S., sel. *Birthday Rhymes, Special Times* (PS–3). Illus. by Jose Aruego and Ariane Dewey. 1995, Doubleday $15.00 (0-385-30419-6); Dell paper $5.99 (0-440-41018-5). 48pp. Poems that are amusingly illustrated deal with some aspect of birthdays. (Rev: SLJ 6/93) [811]

**4662** Hershenhorn, Esther. *There Goes Lowell's Party!* (K–3). Illus. by Jacqueline Rogers. 1998, Holiday LB $15.95 (0-8234-1313-6). In this tale set in the Ozarks, Lowell is afraid that rain will spoil his birthday party. (Rev: SLJ 3/98)

**4663** Hest, Amy. *Gabby Growing Up* (K–3). Illus. by Amy Schwartz. 1998, Simon & Schuster $16.00 (0-689-80573-X). 32pp. Gabby and her mother go to Manhattan, where they celebrate Grandpa's birthday with him at a skating rink. (Rev: BL 1/1–15/98; SLJ 3/98)

**4664** Hest, Amy. *Nana's Birthday Party* (K–4). Illus. by Amy Schwartz. 1993, Morrow $15.00 (0-688-07497-9). 32pp. Maggie wants to write a story for her grandmother for her birthday, but she lacks the inspiration. (Rev: BL 8/93*)

**4665** Hopkins, Lee Bennett, ed. *Happy Birthday* (K–4). Illus. by Hilary Knight. 1991, Simon & Schuster paper $11.95 (0-671-70973-9). This collection of poems about birthdays also contains a list of birthdays of famous people. (Rev: SLJ 10/91) [811]

**4666** Howe, James. *Creepy-Crawly Birthday* (PS–3). Illus. by Leslie Morrill. 1991, Morrow LB $13.88 (0-688-09688-3). 48pp. Toby's pet dog and cat have an unexpected surprise for him at his birthday party. (Rev: BL 11/15/91; SLJ 11/91)

**4667** Hutchins, Pat. *Happy Birthday, Sam* (1–3). Illus. by author. 1978, Morrow paper $4.95 (0-688-10482-7). 32pp. Sam is disappointed on his birthday morning to discover that he hasn't grown at all.

**4668** Jonas, Ann. *The Thirteenth Clue* (1–5). Illus. 1992, Greenwillow LB $15.93 (0-688-09743-X). 32pp. A young girl deciphers mysterious clues that finally lead her to a surprise birthday party. (Rev: BCCB 11/92; BL 11/15/92; HB 11–12/92)

**4669** Kellogg, Steven. *Much Bigger Than Martin* (K–2). Illus. by author. 1976, Dial paper $3.95 (0-8037-5811-1). 32pp. Henry is upset because his older brother is so much bigger than he is, and Henry tries many ways to overcome this.

**4670** Kleven, Elisa. *Hooray, A Piñata!* (PS–2). Illus. 1996, Dutton paper $15.99 (0-525-45605-8). 32pp. Clara doesn't want her piñata, the image of a small dog, to be destroyed. (Rev: BL 9/15/96*; SLJ 11/96)

**4671** Klinting, Lars. *Bruno the Baker* (PS–2). Illus. 1997, Holt $15.95 (0-8050-5506-1). In this step-by-step picture book, Bruno the beaver bakes his own birthday cake with the help of his friend Felix. (Rev: BL 1/1–15/98; SLJ 10/97)

**4672** Kulling, Monica. *Edgar Badger's Balloon Day* (K–3). Illus. by Carol O'Malia. 1997, Mondo paper $4.50 (1-57255-220-4). 46pp. Edgar Badger is afraid that his friends have forgotten that his birthday is approaching. (Rev: SLJ 1/98)

**4673** Lobe, Mira. *Christoph Wants a Party* (1–3). Retold by Marcia Lane. Illus. by Winfried Opgenoorth. 1995, Kane/Miller $15.95 (0-916291-59-6). In a 6-page foldout section, Christoph imagines an extravagant fifth birthday party. (Rev: SLJ 2/96)

**4674** Lopez, Loretta. *The Birthday Swap* (PS–3). Illus. 1997, Lee & Low $15.95 (1-880000-47-4). 32pp. A young Mexican American girl enjoys the annual reunion of family from both sides of the border, when everyone comes to celebrate her older sister's birthday. (Rev: BCCB 6/97; BL 5/1/97; SLJ 6/97)

**4675** Mora, Pat. *A Birthday Basket for Tia* (PS–1). Illus. by Cecily Lang. 1992, Macmillan LB $15.00 (0-02-767400-2). 32pp. Cecila decides on what is the perfect present for her great-aunt's ninetieth birthday. (Rev: BL 9/15/92; HB 1–2/93; SLJ 1/93)

**4676** Mueller, Virginia. *Monster's Birthday Hiccups* (PS–K). Illus. by Lynn Munsinger. 1992, Whitman LB $12.95 (0-8075-5267-4). 24pp. Monster cures his hiccups at his birthday party by blowing out the candles on his cake and granting his own wish. (Rev: BL 1/15/92)

**4677** Oram, Hiawyn. *Badger's Bring Something Party* (PS–2). Illus. by Susan Varley. 1995, Lothrop $15.00 (0-688-14082-3). 32pp. Mole feels out of place at Badger's birthday party because he didn't have a gift to bring. A prequel to *Badger's Parting Gifts* (1984). (Rev: BL 4/15/95; HB 5–6/95; SLJ 7/95)

**4678** Polacco, Patricia. *Some Birthday!* (K–3). Illus. 1991, Simon & Schuster paper $15.00 (0-671-72750-8). 32pp. Patricia thinks everyone has forgotten about her sixth birthday, until the surprise comes in the evening. (Rev: BL 1/1/92*; SLJ 10/91)

**4679** Rice, Eve. *Benny Bakes a Cake* (PS–3). Illus. 1993, Greenwillow LB $13.93 (0-688-11580-2). 32pp. On Benny's birthday, his mother allows him to bake a cake, but dog Ralph takes the biggest piece. A reissue.

**4680** Sathre, Vivian. *Three Kind Mice* (PS–2). Illus. by Rodger Wilson. 1997, Harcourt $13.00 (0-15-201266-4). Three mice bake a delicious cake to celebrate the birthday of their friend, a plump orange cat. (Rev: SLJ 3/97)

**4681** Shaw, Nancy. *Sheep in a Shop* (PS–1). Illus. by Margot Apple. 1991, Houghton $13.95 (0-395-53681-2). 32pp. Five sheep are a little short of cash when they shop for a present for a friend. (Rev: HB 5–6/91*; SLJ 2/91)

**4682** Spirn, Michele. *A Know-Nothing Birthday* (K–2). Illus. by R. W. Alley. Series: An I Can Read Book. 1997, HarperCollins LB $14.89 (0-06-027274-0). 48pp. An easy-to-read book about the Know-Nothings — Boris, Norris, Doris, and Morris — and the birthday party Boris gives himself. (Rev: SLJ 6/97)

**4683** Stock, Catherine. *Birthday Present* (PS–1). Illus. Series: Festive Year. 1991, Macmillan paper $11.95 (0-02-788401-5). 32pp. A boy takes special care in selecting a present for his friend Maria. (Rev: BCCB 3/91; BL 2/1/91; SLJ 9/91)

**4684** Turk, Hanne. *Philipp's Birthday Book* (PS–1). Illus. 1996, North-South $15.95 (1-55858-651-2). 24pp. Twelve poems celebrate the birthdays of Philipp the mouse and his friends. (Rev: BL 12/15/96; SLJ 11/96)

**4685** Wadsworth, Ginger. *Tomorrow Is Daddy's Birthday* (PS–1). Illus. by Maxie Chambliss. 1994, Boyds Mills $14.95 (1-56397-042-2). Rachel wants to surprise her father with a gift on his birthday, so she tells every living thing that she encounters not to give away her secret. (Rev: SLJ 11/94)

**4686** Wardlaw, Lee. *Bow-Wow Birthday* (PS–3). Illus. by Arden Johnson-Petrov. 1998, Boyds Mills $14.95 (1-56397-489-4). A humorous story about a group of children who hold a birthday party for an ancient dog who only wants to sleep in his favorite closet. (Rev: BL 3/1/98)

**4687** Whittington, Mary K. *The Patchwork Lady* (K–2). Illus. by Jane Dyer. 1991, Harcourt $13.95 (0-15-259580-5). A woman whose house and dress look like a patchwork quilt decides to hold a birthday party for herself. (Rev: SLJ 6/91)

**4688** Wormell, Mary. *Hilda Hen's Happy Birthday* (PS–K). Illus. 1995, Harcourt $14.00 (0-15-200299-5). 32pp. A hen finds presents in the most unusual places in this humorous picture book. (Rev: BL 4/1/95; HB 5–6/95; SLJ 4/95)

### CHRISTMAS

**4689** Ada, Alma F. *The Christmas Tree/El Arbol de Navidad* (1–3). Illus. by Terry Ybanez. 1997, Hyperion LB $15.49 (0-7868-2123-X). A bilingual book about the joy a Christmas tree brings to those who decorate it. (Rev: SLJ 10/97)

**4690** Adams, Adrienne. *The Christmas Party* (1–3). Illus. by author. 1978, Macmillan paper $3.95 (0-689-71630-3). 32pp. An Easter bunny helps prepare for a Christmas party.

**4691** Aliki. *Christmas Tree Memories* (PS–2). Illus. 1991, HarperCollins LB $14.89 (0-06-020008-1). 32pp. This is a remembrance of Christmases past and the activities associated with celebrations years ago. (Rev: BL 7/91; HB 11–12/91)

**4692** Ammon, Richard. *An Amish Christmas* (K–3). Illus. by Pamela Patrick. 1996, Simon & Schuster $17.00 (0-689-80377-X). 32pp. Many of the celebrations and holiday customs associated with an Amish Christmas are described. (Rev: BL 9/1/96)

**4693** Anaya, Rudolfo A. *The Farolitos of Christmas* (K–3). Illus. by Edward Gonzales. 1995, Hyperion LB $16.49 (0-7868-2047-0). 32pp. In a New Mexico setting, a Chicano family makes do in spite of the absence of their father, who has not yet returned from World War II. (Rev: BL 9/15/95; HB 11–12/95)

**4694** Barracca, Debra, and Sal Barracca. *A Taxi Dog Christmas* (PS–3). Illus. by Alan Ayers. 1994, Dial paper $14.89 (0-8037-1361-4). 40pp. After giving some stray kittens to fellow cabbies, Jim and Maxi, 2 dogs who are taxi drivers, help Santa deliver his presents when his sleigh crashes. (Rev: BL 8/94)

**4695** Bemelmans, Ludwig. *Madeline's Christmas* (PS–1). Illus. by author. 1985, Puffin paper $4.99 (0-14-050666-7). 32pp. Everyone's sick on Christmas Eve, but Madeline befriends a rug merchant who turns out to be a magician, and all the little girls get to go home for Christmas. (Rev: BCCB 10/85; HB 11–12/85; SLJ 10/85)

**4696** Berger, Barbara Helen. *The Donkey's Dream* (K–3). Illus. by author. 1985, Putnam $15.95 (0-399-21233-7). 32pp. The story of a donkey who at Christmas time carried "a lady full of heaven" to a stable. (Rev: HB 11–12/85; SLJ 10/85)

**4697** Bond, Michael. *Paddington Bear and the Christmas Surprise* (K–2). Illus. by R. W. Alley. 1997, HarperCollins $11.95 (0-694-00897-4). Paddington's visit with his family to a department store at Christmas is not the joyful occasion he had hoped for. (Rev: BL 9/15/97; SLJ 10/97)

**4698** Borden, Louise. *Just in Time for Christmas* (1–4). Illus. by Ted Lewin. 1994, Scholastic $14.95 (0-590-45355-6). 32pp. Christmas time for Will in Kentucky is a happy time except that he is fearful that Great Gram is becoming too forgetful. (Rev: BL 8/94)

**4699** Brett, Jan. *Christmas Trolls* (K–3). Illus. 1993, Putnam LB $15.95 (0-399-22507-2). 32pp. Treva discovers that the mysterious disappearance of

objects from her house is the work of trolls. (Rev: BL 7/93)

**4700** Brett, Jan. *The Wild Christmas Reindeer* (K–2). Illus. 1990, Putnam $15.95 (0-399-22192-1). 32pp. Santa has a whole new crew of wild reindeer that might not want to work on Christmas Eve. (Rev: BL 9/15/90*)

**4701** Briggs, Raymond. *Father Christmas* (K–3). Illus. by author. 1997, Random $18.99 (0-679-88776-8). 32pp. Christmas Eve, as Santa sees it, is pictured by the author-artist (winner of the Kate Greenaway Medal) in full-color, comic-strip style.

**4702** Brimner, Larry Dane. *Merry Christmas, Old Armadillo* (PS–2). Illus. by Dominic Catalano. 1995, Boyds Mills $14.95 (1-56397-354-5). 32pp. When Amadillo returns home, his friends plan a Christmas surprise to welcome him. (Rev: BL 9/15/95; SLJ 10/95*)

**4703** Brown, Marc. *Arthur's Christmas* (K–2). Illus. by author. 1984, Little, Brown $15.95 (0-316-11180-5). Arthur, an anteater, has a series of Christmas adventures.

**4704** Brown, Margaret Wise. *On Christmas Eve* (PS–3). Illus. by Nancy E. Calder. 1996, HarperCollins LB $14.89 (0-06-023649-3). 32pp. At Christmas, 3 children who can't sleep creep downstairs to see the Christmas tree. (Rev: BL 9/1/96; SLJ 10/96*)

**4705** Buck, Nola. *Santa's Short Suit Shrunk: and Other Christmas Tongue Twisters* (1–3). Illus. by Sue Truesdell. Series: I Can Read. 1997, HarperCollins LB $14.89 (0-06-026663-5). 32pp. A grab bag of tongue twisters about Christmas topics like shopping, feasting, and opening presents. (Rev: BL 9/15/97; HB 11–12/97; SLJ 10/97)

**4706** Bunting, Eve. *The Day Before Christmas* (1–3). Illus. by Beth Peck. 1992, Houghton $16.00 (0-89919-866-X). 32pp. Allie's grandfather takes her to see The Nutcracker, just as he had taken her deceased mother. (Rev: BL 11/1/92; HB 11–12/92)

**4707** Bunting, Eve. *December* (K–3). Illus. by David Diaz. 1997, Harcourt $15.00 (0-15-201434-9). 40pp. A miracle occurs when a homeless mother and her son allow an old lady to sleep in their cardboard home at Christmas time. (Rev: BL 9/1/97*; SLJ 10/97*)

**4708** Bunting, Eve. *Night Tree* (PS–3). Illus. by Ted Rand. 1991, Harcourt $16.00 (0-15-257425-5). 32pp. On the night before Christmas, a family drives into the woods and decorates a tree. (Rev: BCCB 10/91; BL 9/15/91; HB 11–12/91)

**4709** Carlstrom, Nancy White. *I Am Christmas* (K–2). Illus. by Lori McElrath-Eslick. 1995, Eerdmans $17.00 (0-8028-5075-8). 32pp. The story of Christmas and its significance today is retold. (Rev: BL 9/1/95) [232.92]

**4710** Carrier, Lark. *A Christmas Promise* (PS–2). Illus. by author. 1991, Simon & Schuster paper $15.95 (0-88708-032-4). 36pp. Amy nurtures her small tree, planning to bring it inside for Christmas, and then can't bear to cut it down. (Rev: BL 11/1/86)

**4711** Catalanotto, Peter. *Christmas Always . . .* (PS–2). Illus. 1991, Watts LB $16.99 (0-531-08546-5). 32pp. While awaiting Santa's arrival, Katie is visited by other guests — the Tooth Fairy and Jack Frost. (Rev: BL 9/15/91)

**4712** Chmielarz, Sharon. *Down at Angel's* (PS–3). Illus. by Jill Kastner. 1994, Ticknor $14.95 (0-395-65993-0). 32pp. At Christmas time, 2 children and their mother deliver a box of goodies to their friend, a woodcarver named Angel. (Rev: BCCB 12/94; BL 8/94; HB 11–12/94)

**4713** Chorao, Kay. *The Christmas Story* (PS–3). Illus. 1996, Holiday LB $15.95 (0-8234-1251-2). 28pp. The biblical account of Christmas from the King James version is illustrated in Renaissance-like paintings. (Rev: BL 9/1/96)

**4714** Christelow, Eileen. *Not Until Christmas, Walter!* (PS–2). Illus. 1997, Clarion $15.00 (0-395-82273-4). 40pp. Walter, a dog who has ruined a family's Christmas presents, redeems himself by tracking a lost person. (Rev: BL 9/1/97; SLJ 10/97)

**4715** Ciavonne, Jean. *Carlos, Light the Farolito* (PS–3). Illus. by Donna Clair. 1995, Clarion $14.95 (0-395-66759-3). 32pp. Carlos is a small boy who enjoys the tradition of lighting the farolito, a lantern that guides pilgrims at Christmas. (Rev: BL 9/15/95)

**4716** Clark, Elizabeth. *Father Christmas and the Donkey* (PS–3). Illus. by Jan Ormerod. 1994, Viking paper $13.99 (0-670-84811-5). 32pp. An old donkey is rewarded when he helps Father Christmas make his rounds on Christmas Eve. (Rev: BL 12/1/94)

**4717** Clements, Andrew. *Bright Christmas: An Angel Remembers* (PS–3). Illus. by Kate Kiesler. 1996, Clarion $16.00 (0-395-72096-6). 30pp. The Christmas story as seen through the eyes of an angel. (Rev: BCCB 11/96; BL 9/1/96)

**4718** Clifton, Lucille. *Everett Anderson's Christmas Coming* (PS–2). Illus. by Jan S. Gilchrist. 1991, HarperCollins $14.95 (0-8050-1549-3). 32pp. This book describes how Christmas comes for a young black boy, Everett Anderson. (Rev: BCCB 9/91; BL 10/1/91)

**4719** Climo, Shirley. *The Cobweb Christmas* (K–3). Illus. by Joe Lasker. 1982, HarperCollins LB $15.89 (0-690-04216-7); paper $4.95 (0-06-443110-X). 32pp. Spiders turn Tante's Christmas tree into a glistening thing of beauty.

**4720** Colle, Gisela. *The Star Tree* (K–2). Illus. 1997, North-South LB $15.88 (1-55858-742-X). 24pp. An

old man produces an old-fashioned Christmas tree for his neighbors. (Rev: BL 9/1/97; SLJ 10/97)

**4721** Collington, Peter. *On Christmas Eve* (PS–3). Illus. 1990, Knopf $14.95 (0-679-80830-2). 32pp. A wordless story of a little girl who writes to Santa but wonders how he will get into her chimneyless house. (Rev: BCCB 10/90; BL 9/15/90*; HB 11–12/90)

**4722** Cooper, Susan. *Danny and the Kings* (PS–1). Illus. by Joseph A. Smith. 1993, Macmillan $14.95 (0-689-50577-9). 32pp. Steve's tree, a gift to a poor friend at Christmas time, is ruined when a truck runs over it. (Rev: BCCB 2/94; BL 10/15/93; HB 11–12/93)

**4723** Corrin, Sara, and Stephen Corrin, eds. *Round the Christmas Tree* (K–4). Illus. by Jill Bennett. 1983, Puffin paper $3.95 (0-317-62263-3). Sixteen stories, many of them fairy tales, about Christmas.

**4724** Cushman, Doug. *Aunt Eater's Mystery Christmas* (1–2). Illus. 1995, HarperCollins LB $14.89 (0-06-023580-2). 64pp. Aunt Eater, an anteater, stops her Christmas shopping to solve some mysteries in this beginning reader. (Rev: BL 9/15/95)

**4725** Cuyler, Margery. *Fat Santa* (PS–1). Illus. by Marsha Winborn. 1989, Holt paper $4.95 (0-8050-1167-6). 32pp. Santa gets stuck in the chimney and resourceful Molly rescues him. (Rev: BCCB 11/87; BL 11/1/87)

**4726** Czernecki, Stefan, and Timothy Rhodes. *Pancho's Pinata* (PS–2). Illus. by Stefan Czernecki. 1992, Hyperion $14.95 (1-562-82277-2); paper $4.95 (0-786-81007-6). 40pp. The fanciful story of how the first pinata was invented, in the village of San Miguel. (Rev: BL 11/1/92) [398.2]

**4727** Day, Alexandra, and Cooper Edens. *The Christmas We Moved to the Barn* (PS–3). Illus. by Alexandra Day. 1997, HarperCollins $14.95 (0-06-205149-0). 32pp. A woman and her family get help from different animals when they are forced to move to a barn at Christmas. (Rev: BL 9/1/97; SLJ 10/97)

**4728** Delton, Judy. *The Perfect Christmas Gift* (PS–2). Illus. by Lisa McCue. 1992, Macmillan LB $13.95 (0-02-728471-9). 32pp. Bear has a difficult time finding a suitable Christmas present for her friend Duck. (Rev: BL 10/1/92)

**4729** dePaola, Tomie, ed. *The Clown of God* (K–3). Illus. by Tomie dePaola. 1978, Harcourt $15.00 (0-15-219175-5); paper $6.00 (0-15-618192-4). 45pp. On Christmas Eve, a juggler gives to a statue of Christ his only possession, the gift of his art.

**4730** dePaola, Tomie. *Country Angel Christmas* (PS–1). Illus. 1995, Putnam $16.95 (0-399-22817-9). 32pp. Three little angels think they have been forgotten in the preparations for Christmas, but St. Nicholas comes to the rescue. (Rev: BCCB 11/95; BL 9/15/95)

**4731** dePaola, Tomie. *An Early American Christmas* (K–2). Illus. by author. 1987, Holiday $16.95 (0-8234-0617-2); paper $6.95 (0-8234-0979-1). 32pp. What it might have been like for a German family of long ago to move to a New England village where most of the people did not celebrate Christmas. (Rev: BCCB 11/87; BL 9/1/87)

**4732** dePaola, Tomie, reteller. *The Legend of Old Befana* (PS–3). Illus. by Tomie dePaola. 1980, Harcourt $16.00 (0-15-243816-5); paper $6.00 (0-15-243817-3). 32pp. The legend of the old lady who is still searching for the Christ child.

**4733** dePaola, Tomie. *Merry Christmas, Strega Nona* (PS–3). Illus. by author. 1986, Harcourt $14.95 (0-15-253183-1); paper $7.00 (0-15-253184-X). 32pp. Strega Nona is worried because her helper Big Anthony doesn't seem to be helping her to prepare for Christmas at all. (Rev: BL 11/1/86; HB 11–12/86)

**4734** Donnelly, Liza. *Dinosaurs' Christmas* (PS–2). Illus. 1994, Scholastic paper $2.50 (0-590-44798-X). 32pp. Rex and his dog Bones travel by dinosaur to the North Pole just before Christmas. (Rev: BL 7/91)

**4735** Dunbar, Joyce. *This Is the Star* (K–3). Illus. by Gary Blythe. 1996, Harcourt $16.00 (0-15-200851-9). 36pp. A cumulative tale using the story of the Nativity as a framework. (Rev: BL 9/1/96)

**4736** Edens, Cooper. *Nicholi* (PS–2). Illus. by A. Scott Banfill. 1997, Simon & Schuster paper $16.00 (0-689-80495-4). 40pp. A mysterious stranger brings to life all the snow sculptures in a village in this Christmas story. (Rev: BL 9/1/97; SLJ 10/97)

**4737** Edens, Cooper. *Santa Cows* (1–4). Illus. by Daniel Lane. 1991, Simon & Schuster $14.00 (0-671-74863-7). 32pp. In this spoof, it is cows that come down the chimney at Christmastime. (Rev: BL 1/1/91)

**4738** Ets, Marie Hall, and Aurora Labastida. *Nine Days to Christmas* (K–2). Illus. by Marie Hall Ets. 1959, Viking $16.99 (0-670-51350-4); Puffin paper $4.99 (0-14-054442-9). 48pp. Kindergartner Ceci is old enough to have her first posada — one of the 9 special parties held in Mexico, one a day preceding the day of Christmas. Caldecott Medal winner, 1960.

**4739** Facklam, Margery. *Only a Star* (K–3). Illus. by Nancy Carpenter. 1996, Eerdmans $15.00 (0-8028-5122-3). 32pp. The Christmas star magically transforms all creatures and objects that it illuminates. (Rev: BL 10/15/96; SLJ 10/96*)

**4740** Fearrington, Ann. *Christmas Lights* (PS–2). Illus. 1996, Houghton $15.95 (0-395-71036-7). 32pp. On Christmas night, a family drives around the city to see all the Christmas lights. (Rev: BL 9/1/96)

**4741** Foreman, Michael. *The Little Reindeer* (PS–2). Illus. 1997, Dial $14.99 (0-8037-2184-6). 32pp. One of Santa's tiny reindeer is accidentally wrapped as a Christmas present and delivered to a boy. (Rev: BL 9/1/97; SLJ 10/97)

**4742** Forward, Toby. *Ben's Christmas Carol* (K–4). Illus. by Ruth Brown. 1996, Dutton paper $15.99 (0-525-45593-0). 48pp. A reworking of Dickens's famous tale using a miserly mouse that lives in Scrooge's house as the central character. (Rev: BL 9/1/96; HB 11–12/96; SLJ 10/96*)

**4743** Fox, Mem. *Wombat Divine* (PS–3). Illus. by Kerry Argent. 1996, Harcourt $15.00 (0-15-201416-0). 32pp. A sleepy wombat gets to play baby Jesus in the Christmas Nativity play. (Rev: BL 10/15/96; SLJ 10/96*)

**4744** French, Vivian. *A Christmas Star Called Hannah* (PS–3). Illus. by Anne Y. Gilbert. 1997, Candlewick $9.99 (0-7636-0397-X). 32pp. Hannah saves the day when she offers her brother as the Baby Jesus in the Christmas pageant. (Rev: BL 11/1/97; SLJ 10/97)

**4745** Gackenbach, Dick. *Claude the Dog: A Christmas Story* (K–3). Illus. by author. 1984, Houghton paper $5.95 (0-89919-124-X). 32pp. Claude gives away all his presents but gets an even better one from his master. A related title is: *What's Claude Doing?* (1984).

**4746** Gammell, Stephen. *Wake Up, Bear . . . It's Christmas!* (PS–1). Illus. by author. 1981, Lothrop LB $14.93 (0-688-00693-0); Morrow paper $4.95 (0-688-09934-3). 32pp. A bear is afraid he will sleep through Christmas.

**4747** Gantos, Jack. *Rotten Ralph's Rotten Christmas* (K–2). Illus. by Nicole Rubel. 1984, Houghton $15.00 (0-395-35380-7); paper $4.95 (0-395-45685-1). 32pp. This miserable cat is determined that Sarah's Christmas will also be miserable.

**4748** Gantschev, Ivan. *The Christmas Teddy Bear* (PS–2). Illus. 1994, North-South LB $14.88 (1-55858-348-3); paper $6.95 (1-55858-619-9). 26pp. When Grandpa goes to town to buy a teddy bear for his granddaughter at Christmas, he gets lost in a snowstorm. (Rev: BL 10/15/94)

**4749** Garland, Michael. *The Mouse Before Christmas* (PS–3). Illus. 1997, Dutton paper $15.99 (0-525-45578-7). 32pp. This version of "The Night Before Christmas" stars a little mouse that hitches a ride in Santa's sleigh. (Rev: BL 10/15/97; SLJ 10/97)

**4750** Gleeson, Brian. *The Savior Is Born* (K–3). Illus. by Robert Van Nutt. 1996, Simon & Schuster $19.95 (0-689-81098-9). 40pp. The Christmas story is retold using illustrations that resemble stained-glass windows. (Rev: BL 11/15/96) [232.92]

**4751** Godden, Rumer. *The Story of Holly and Ivy* (2–4). Illus. by Barbara Cooney. 1985, Puffin paper $5.99 (0-14-050723-X). 32pp. This is a new edition of the 1957 sentimental story about orphaned Ivy, a

Christmas doll named Holly, and a childless couple. (Rev: BCCB 10/85; BL 10/1/85; SLJ 10/85)

**4752** Greenfield, Monica. *Waiting for Christmas* (PS–1). Illus. by Jan S. Gilchrist. 1996, Scholastic $15.95 (0-590-52700-2). 32pp. An African American brother and sister look forward to the excitement of Christmas. (Rev: BL 9/1/96)

**4753** Hague, Michael. *The Perfect Present* (PS–1). Illus. 1996, Morrow $16.00 (0-688-10880-6). 48pp. Jack, a rabbit, goes to Big Bear's Toy Shoppe to find a Christmas present for his girlfriend. (Rev: BL 9/1/96)

**4754** Hall, Donald. *Lucy's Christmas* (K–3). Illus. by Michael McCurdy. 1994, Harcourt $14.95 (0-15-276870-X). 40pp. Everyday life of a New England family in 1909 from late fall through the celebration of Christmas. (Rev: BCCB 10/94; BL 8/94; HB 11–12/94)

**4755** Hall, Tom T. *Christmas and the Old House* (PS–3). Illus. by Laura L. Seeley. 1989, Peachtree $13.95 (0-934601-91-7). 48pp. Brenda and Bobby are so fascinated by a pine tree they find growing in an abandoned house that they decide to decorate it for Christmas. (Rev: BL 12/1/90)

**4756** Harvey, Brett. *My Prairie Christmas* (1–3). Illus. by Deborah Kogan Ray. 1990, Holiday LB $15.95 (0-8234-0827-2). 32pp. Young Eleanor wonders what sort of Christmas her pioneering family can have in their new Dakota home. (Rev: BCCB 11/90; BL 10/1/90)

**4757** Hayes, Sarah. *Happy Christmas, Gemma* (PS–1). Illus. by Jan Ormerod. 1986, Lothrop $16.00 (0-688-06508-2). 32pp. Christmas is warmly celebrated by this Jamaican immigrant family. (Rev: BCCB 11/86; BL 11/15/86; HB 11–12/86)

**4758** Heath, Amy. *Sofie's Role* (PS–2). Illus. 1992, Macmillan LB $14.95 (0-02-743505-9). 36pp. On the day before Christmas, a young girl helps her parents in their bakery. (Rev: BCCB 12/92; BL 7/92)

**4759** Helldorfer, M. C. *Daniel's Gift* (K–3). Illus. by Julie Downing. 1987, Macmillan paper $4.95 (0-689-71440-8). 32pp. The shepherd boy Daniel is the focus of this Nativity story set in the Middle Ages. (Rev: BL 11/1/87; SLJ 12/87)

**4760** Hennessy, B. G. *The First Night* (K–2). Illus. by Steve Johnson and Lou Fancher. 1993, Viking paper $13.99 (0-670-83026-7). 32pp. The Christmas story is told with beautiful illustrations and brief text. (Rev: BL 8/93)

**4761** High, Linda O. *A Christmas Star* (K–3). Illus. by Ronald Himler. 1997, Holiday LB $15.95 (0-8234-1301-2). 32pp. Stolen gifts are miraculously returned to a church in this Christmas tale set during the Depression. (Rev: BL 9/1/97; SLJ 10/97)

**4762** Hill, Susan. *King of Kings* (1–4). Illus. by John Lawrence. 1993, Candlewick $14.95 (1-56402-210-2). 32pp. On Christmas Eve, Mr. Hegarty, a recluse, discovers a baby on his doorstep. (Rev: BL 10/1/93)

**4763** Hoban, Lillian. *Arthur's Christmas Cookies* (1–2). Illus. by author. 1972, HarperCollins LB $14.89 (0-06-022368-5); paper $3.75 (0-06-444055-9). 64pp. What can Arthur give his parents for Christmas? Christmas cookies such as he learned to bake in Cub Scouts are the answer, but a hilarious mix-up occurs when salt is used instead of sugar.

**4764** Hodges, Margaret. *Silent Night: The Song and Its Story* (PS–3). Illus. by Tim Ladwig. 1997, Eerdmans $17.00 (0-8028-5138-X). 32pp. A dramatic retelling of the 1818 creation of this much-loved Christmas carol. (Rev: BL 9/1/97; SLJ 10/97)

**4765** Hoff, Syd. *Where's Prancer?* (PS–1). Illus. 1997, HarperCollins LB $13.89 (0-06-027601-0). 32pp. After making his rounds, Santa discovers that Prancer is missing. (Rev: BL 9/1/97)

**4766** Hoffman, Mary. *An Angel Just Like Me* (PS–2). Illus. by Cornelius Van Wright and Ying-Hwa Hu. 1997, Dial paper $14.99 (0-8037-2265-6). 32pp. When the Christmas tree angel breaks, a young African American boy named Tyler wants a replacement that looks like himself. (Rev: BL 11/1/97; SLJ 12/97)

**4767** Hogrogian, Nonny. *The First Christmas* (PS–3). Illus. 1995, Greenwillow LB $14.93 (0-688-13580-3). 32pp. Various passages from the King James version of the Bible are used to retell the Christmas story. (Rev: BCCB 11/95; BL 9/15/95) [232]

**4768** Holabird, Katharine. *Angelina's Christmas* (PS–1). Illus. by Helen Craig. 1985, Crown $16.00 (0-517-55823-8). 32pp. Angelina Mouse decides to cheer up Mr. Bell, the retired postman who is all alone at Christmas. (Rev: BCCB 1/86; BL 12/15/85; HB 11–12/85)

**4769** Hooper, Maureen B. *The Christmas Drum* (PS–1). Illus. by Diane Paterson. 1994, Boyds Mills $14.95 (1-56397-105-4). 28pp. Set in Romania, this Christmas story tells of a boy who wishes for his father's return so that he will not have to take his place as drum beater in the village rituals. (Rev: BL 10/1/94)

**4770** Houston, Gloria. *The Year of the Perfect Christmas Tree: An Appalachian Story* (K–3). Illus. by Barbara Cooney. 1988, Dial LB $14.89 (0-8037-0300-7). 32pp. The moving story of an Appalachian family in 1918 when Papa is away at war and Mama and Ruthie must keep his promise of providing the perfect Christmas tree for the town's celebration. (Rev: BCCB 10/88; BL 9/1/88; HB 11–12/88)

**4771** Howard, Elizabeth F. *Chita's Christmas Tree* (K–3). Illus. by Floyd Cooper. 1989, Macmillan LB

$14.95 (0-02-744621-2). 32pp. Set in turn-of-the-century Baltimore, this book celebrates the holiday season and family life. (Rev: BCCB 9/89; BL 9/1/89*)

**4772** Hudson, Cheryl W. *Hold Christmas in Your Heart: African-American Songs, Poems, and Stories for the Holidays* (K–2). Illus. 1995, Scholastic $10.95 (0-590-48024-3). 32pp. Poems, stories, and songs from African American authors are found in this fine anthology. (Rev: BL 9/15/95)

**4773** Impey, Rose. *A Letter to Santa Claus* (PS–2). Illus. by Sue Porter. 1989, Delacorte $12.95 (0-385-29714-9). 32pp. Charlotte mails the wrong letter to Santa Claus. (Rev: BCCB 11/89; BL 10/15/89; HB 11–12/89)

**4774** Janovitz, Marilyn. *What Could Be Keeping Santa?* (PS–1). Illus. 1997, North-South LB $15.88 (1-55858-820-5). 32pp. The sleigh is packed and the stockings are hung, but where's Santa? (Rev: BL 10/1/97; SLJ 10/97)

**4775** Jennings, Linda. *The Best Christmas Present of All* (K–2). Illus. by Catherine Walters. 1996, Dutton paper $13.99 (0-525-45692-9). 32pp. A dog named Buster is separated from his beloved master, but they are reunited on Christmas Day. (Rev: BL 9/1/96)

**4776** Johnston, Tony. *Pages of Music* (K–3). Illus. by Tomie dePaola. 1988, Putnam LB $13.95 (0-399-21436-4). 32pp. In Sardinia a shepherd fills Paolo with the joy of his music. (Rev: BL 10/15/88; SLJ 2/89)

**4777** Joseph, Daniel M., and Lydia J. Mendel. *All Dressed Up and Nowhere to Go* (PS–3). Illus. by Normand Chartier. 1993, Houghton $14.95 (0-395-60196-7). 32pp. Visiting at Christmas in Florida, a boy from Maine has to make a sandman instead of the usual snowman. (Rev: BL 1/15/94; HB 11–12/93)

**4778** Keller, Holly. *Merry Christmas, Geraldine* (PS–1). Illus. 1997, Greenwillow LB $14.93 (0-688-14501-9). 32pp. Two young pigs go out to choose the family Christmas tree. (Rev: BL 9/1/97; SLJ 10/97)

**4779** Kellogg, Steven. *The Christmas Witch* (K–3). Illus. 1992, Dial paper $14.89 (0-8037-1269-3). 40pp. Gloria, a witch in training, gets her chance to spread joy at Christmastime. (Rev: BCCB 9/92; BL 7/92; HB 3–4/93)

**4780** Kennedy, Pamela. *A Christmas Carol* (K–3). Illus. by Carol Heyer. 1995, Ideals $14.95 (1-57102-047-0). 32pp. With vibrant paintings and a simple text, the classic story is retold for a young audience. (Rev: BL 11/15/95)

**4781** Ketteman, Helen. *The Christmas Blizzard* (PS–3). Illus. by James Warhola. 1995, Scholastic $14.95 (0-590-45878-7). 32pp. When Santa is forced to move his workshop to Indiana, an elderly lady casts a spell so that snow will fall. (Rev: BL 9/15/95)

**4782** Kline, Suzy. *Horrible Harry and the Christmas Surprise* (K–2). Illus. by Frank Remkiewicz. 1991, Viking paper $13.99 (0-670-83357-6). 64pp. While reading a story to the class, Miss Mackle, the teacher in 2B, falls and is sent to the hospital. (Rev: BL 7/91)

**4783** Kroeber, Theodora. *A Green Christmas* (K–3). Illus. by John Larrecq. 1967, Houghton $6.95 (0-87466-047-5). Children new to California discover that Santa Claus will visit places without snow.

**4784** Kroll, Steven. *Santa's Crash-Bang Christmas* (K–3). Illus. by Tomie dePaola. 1977, Holiday LB $15.95 (0-8234-0302-5). 32pp. Santa's blunderings are graciously repaired by his faithful elf Gerald.

**4785** Kyte, Dennis. *Merry Christmas, Bigelow Bear* (PS–2). Illus. 1990, Doubleday paper $12.95 (0-385-26522-0). 32pp. When Bigelow Bear's Gramma comes for a Christmas visit, he forgets about his favorite friend, a truck named Ollie. (Rev: BL 11/1/90)

**4786** Lachner, Dorothea. *The Gift from Saint Nicholas* (K–3). Illus. by Maja Dusikov. 1995, North-South LB $15.88 (1-55858-457-9). 32pp. As the snow gets deeper, 2 children hope that Saint Nicholas will be able to blow a pathway to their house. (Rev: BL 11/1/95)

**4787** Leighton, Maxinne R. *An Ellis Island Christmas* (K–3). Illus. by Dennis Nolan. 1992, Viking paper $15.00 (0-670-83182-4). 32pp. A young Polish immigrant and her family arrive at Ellis Island on Christmas Eve. (Rev: BCCB 9/92; BL 7/92)

**4788** Lewis, J. Patrick. *The Christmas of the Reddle Moon* (PS–3). Illus. by Gary Kelley. 1994, Dial LB $15.89 (0-8037-1567-6). 32pp. On Christmas Eve, 2 children are helped by an old lady and St. Nicholas when they get lost on an English heath. (Rev: BL 8/94)

**4789** Lewis, J. Patrick. *Long Was the Winter Road They Traveled: A Tale of the Nativity* (PS–2). Illus. by Drew Bairley. 1997, Dial paper $14.89 (0-8037-1815-2). 32pp. A reverent retelling in poetic form of the Nativity story, with accompanying gentle paintings. (Rev: BL 10/1/97; SLJ 10/97) [811]

**4790** Lindgren, Astrid. *Christmas in Noisy Village* (K–2). 1981, Puffin paper $4.99 (0-14-050344-7). 32pp. Children of 3 neighboring farms share the joys of Christmas in a Swedish setting.

**4791** Lindgren, Astrid. *Christmas in the Stable* (PS–2). Illus. by Harald Wiberg. 1998, Putnam paper $5.99 (0-698-11664-X). 32pp. A mother tells her child the story of the birth of Jesus, and the child projects the tale into her own present-day farm-life setting.

**4792** Lindgren, Astrid. *Lotta's Christmas Surprise* (PS–2). Illus. by Ilon Wikland. 1990, R&S $13.95 (91-29-59782-X). 32pp. In this Christmas story, Lotta overcomes many trials and tribulations. (Rev: BL 12/1/90)

**4793** Lindgren, Astrid. *Pippi Longstocking's After-Christmas Party* (K–2). Illus. by Michael Chesworth. 1996, Viking paper $13.99 (0-670-86790-X). 32pp. An episodic story about Pippi's party in an igloo after Christmas. (Rev: BL 9/1/96)

**4794** Low, Alice, ed. *The Family Read-Aloud Christmas Treasury* (K–5). Illus. by Marc Brown. 1995, Little, Brown paper $12.95 (0-316-53284-3). 137pp. A rich compilation of Christmas read-aloud material. (Rev: BL 11/1/89*) [394.268]

**4795** Lussert, Anneliese. *The Christmas Visitor* (K–3). Illus. by Loek Koopmans. 1995, North-South LB $15.88 (1-55858-450-1). 24pp. Simon rebukes a beggar seeking shelter for himself and young son, but wife Sarah offers the stranger food and shelter. (Rev: BCCB 11/95; BL 9/15/95)

**4796** McCutcheon, Marc. *Grandfather's Christmas Camp* (K–3). Illus. by Kate Kiesler. 1995, Clarion $15.95 (0-395-69626-7). 32pp. In her search for an old, lost mongrel dog, Lizzie spends a Christmas sleeping in an igloo with her grandfather. (Rev: BCCB 11/95; BL 9/15/95; SLJ 10/95*)

**4797** McDonald, Megan. *Tundra Mouse: A Storyknife Tale* (PS–2). Illus. by S. D. Schindler. 1997, Orchard LB $16.99 (0-531-33047-8). 32pp. Tundra Mouse and House Mouse think they are doing people a favor when they tidy up by stripping a Christmas tree of its ornaments, little knowing it's the night before Christmas. (Rev: BL 1/1–15/98; SLJ 10/97)

**4798** McGovern, Ann. *The Lady in the Box* (K–3). Illus. by Marni Backer. 1997, Turtle $14.95 (1-890515-01-9). 32pp. At Christmas time, 2 youngsters help a homeless woman who is living over a hot-air vent. (Rev: BL 9/1/97; SLJ 10/97)

**4799** McPhail, David. *Santa's Book of Names* (K–3). Illus. 1993, Little, Brown $14.95 (0-316-56335-8). 27pp. Edward learns to read names while helping Santa deliver presents to other children. (Rev: BL 8/93)

**4800** McQuade, Jacqueline. *Christmas with Teddy Bear* (PS–K). Illus. 1996, Dial paper $13.99 (0-8037-2075-0). 32pp. Christmas traditions like carol singing are introduced through the activities of a teddy bear. (Rev: BL 9/1/96)

**4801** Mahy, Margaret. *The Christmas Tree Tangle* (PS–2). Illus. by Tony Kerins. 1994, Macmillan paper $16.00 (0-689-50616-3). 32pp. One animal after another gets stuck on the Christmas tree trying to rescue a kitten that has climbed to the top. (Rev: BL 8/94)

**4802** Maloney, Peter, and Felicia Zekauskas. *Redbird at Rockefeller Center* (1–4). Illus. 1997, Dial paper $14.89 (0-8037-2257-5). 32pp. Hundreds of toy birds that decorate the Christmas tree at Rockefeller Center come to life and fly the tree back to its original home. (Rev: BL 11/1/97; SLJ 12/97)

**4803** Manushkin, Fran. *The Perfect Christmas Picture* (PS–3). Illus. by Karen Ann Weinhaus. 1980, HarperCollins $11.95 (0-06-024068-7). 64pp. An easily read story of Mr. Green, who wants to photograph his family for a Christmas picture.

**4804** Marshall, James. *Merry Christmas, Space Case* (PS–3). Illus. by author. 1986, Dial paper $11.95 (0-8037-0215-9). 32pp. Will Buddy's extraterrestrial friends know where to find him on Christmas now that they're spending it at Grannie's? (Rev: BL 9/15/86; HB 11–12/86)

**4805** Marzollo, Jean. *I Spy Christmas: A Book of Picture Riddles* (PS–3). Illus. by Walter Wick. 1992, Scholastic $12.95 (0-590-45846-9). 40pp. Full-color photos illustrate 13 scenes of Christmas. (Rev: BCCB 11/92; BL 11/1/92) [793.73]

**4806** Matthews, Wendy. *The Gift of a Traveler* (1–3). Illus. by Robert Van Nutt. 1995, Troll paper $14.95 (0-8167-3656-1). 32pp. A Christmas story set in Romania that tells the story of a tree ornament given by a mysterious stranger to a child. (Rev: BL 9/15/95)

**4807** Mattingley, Christobel. *The Magic Saddle* (PS–3). Illus. by Patricia Mullins. 1996, Simon & Schuster $16.00 (0-689-80959-X). 32pp. An Australian Christmas story about a boy who receives a magical gingerbread horse that transports him to faraway places. (Rev: BL 9/1/96)

**4808** Mendez, Phil. *The Black Snowman* (K–4). Illus. by Carole Byard. 1989, Scholastic $15.95 (0-590-40552-7). 48pp. An African American learns a little about his heritage from a snowman that comes to life. (Rev: BCCB 11/89; BL 10/1/89; SLJ 9/89)

**4809** Menotti, Gian Carlo. *Amahl and the Night Visitors* (K–3). Illus. by Michele Lemieux. 1986, Morrow LB $19.88 (0-688-05427-7). 64pp. A lavish edition of the story of this touching opera. (Rev: BCCB 10/86; HB 11–12/86)

**4810** Mills, Claudia. *One Small Lost Sheep* (PS–3). Illus. by Walter L. Krudop. 1997, Farrar $16.00 (0-374-35649-1). 32pp. A lost sheep leads a young shepherd to the manger at the first Christmas. (Rev: BL 9/1/97; SLJ 10/97)

**4811** Moeri, Louise. *Star Mother's Youngest Child* (PS–2). Illus. by Trina S. Hyman. 1975, Houghton $14.95 (0-395-21406-8); paper $5.95 (0-395-29929-2). 48pp. An old woman and a star child celebrate Christmas.

**4812** Moore, Clement Clarke. *The Grandma Moses Night Before Christmas* (PS–3). Illus. by Grandma Moses. 1991, Random LB $15.99 (0-679-91526-5). 24pp. A full-color picture book of Moore's poem in a folk-art setting. (Rev: BL 11/15/91) [811]

**4813** Moses, Will. *Silent Night* (1–4). Illus. 1997, Putnam $16.95 (0-399-23100-5). 40pp. Using the words of the carol as chapter headings, this is the story of a family's exciting Christmas in rural Vermont. (Rev: BL 9/1/97; SLJ 10/97)

**4814** Naylor, Phyllis Reynolds. *Keeping a Christmas Secret* (PS–K). Illus. by Lena Shiffman. 1989, Macmillan $15.00 (0-689-31447-7). 32pp. Michael inadvertently tells Dad what the family has given him for Christmas. (Rev: BCCB 10/89; BL 9/1/89; HB 11–12/89)

**4815** Naylor, Phyllis Reynolds. *Old Sadie and the Christmas Bear* (K–3). Illus. by Patricia Montgomery Newton. 1984, Macmillan $15.00 (0-689-31052-8). 32pp. Amos, a hibernating bear, wakens to share a Christmas with Old Sadie.

**4816** Noble, Trinka Hakes. *Apple Tree Christmas* (K–3). Illus. by author. 1984, Dial paper $14.99 (0-8037-0102-0). 32pp. A 19th-century Christmas made special by the gift of an apple tree.

**4817** O'Brien, John. *Mother Hubbard's Christmas* (K–2). Illus. 1996, Boyds Mills $14.95 (1-56397-139-9). 28pp. This hilarious variation on the standard nursery rhyme tells how Mother Hubbard prepares for Christmas. (Rev: BL 10/15/96)

**4818** Olson, Arielle North. *Hurry Home, Grandma!* (K–2). Illus. by Lydia Dabcovich. 1990, Dutton paper $3.95 (0-525-44650-8). 32pp. An explorer-grandmother returns in time for Christmas.

**4819** Parish, Peggy. *Merry Christmas, Amelia Bedelia* (1–2). Illus. by Lynn Sweat. 1986, Greenwillow LB $15.93 (0-688-06102-8); Avon paper $3.99 (0-380-70325-4). 64pp. Christmas fun with silly Amelia Bedelia, the maid with nonsensical assumptions. (Rev: BCCB 10/86; BL 10/1/86)

**4820** Paterson, Katherine. *Marvin's Best Christmas Present Ever* (1–2). Illus. by Jane Brown. 1997, HarperCollins LB $14.89 (0-06-027160-4). 48pp. Marvin is so happy with the Christmas wreath he has made for the family's trailer door that he doesn't want to take it down. (Rev: BL 9/1/97; HB 11–12/97; SLJ 10/97*)

**4821** Pilkey, Dav. *Dragon's Merry Christmas* (1–2). Illus. 1991, Orchard LB $15.99 (0-531-08557-0). 48pp. The Christmas tree that Dragon finds in the forest is too perfect to cut down. (Rev: BL 7/91)

**4822** Polacco, Patricia. *The Trees of the Dancing Goats* (PS–3). Illus. 1996, Simon & Schuster $16.00 (0-689-80862-3). 32pp. A Jewish family delivers Christmas trees to needy Christian families. (Rev: BL 11/1/96; SLJ 2/97)

**4823** Polacco, Patricia. *Uncle Vova's Tree* (K–2). Illus. 1989, Putnam $15.95 (0-399-21617-0). 32pp. Old Christmas customs are described when a young girl spends Christmas with elderly Russian relatives. (Rev: BL 9/15/89; HB 11–12/89)

**4824** Price, Moe. *The Reindeer Christmas* (K–3). Illus. by Atsuko Morozumi. 1993, Harcourt $15.95 (0-15-266199-9). 32pp. A delightful Christmas story that tells why Santa decided that reindeer should be the animals to pull his sleigh. (Rev: BL 9/15/93)

**4825** Rahaman, Vashanti. *O Christmas Tree* (K–3). Illus. by Frane Lessac. 1996, Boyds Mills $14.95 (1-56397-237-9). 26pp. Anslem has problems believing in a traditional Christmas with snow and Christmas trees in his Caribbean home. (Rev: BCCB 11/96; BL 9/1/96*)

**4826** Ransom, Candice. *One Christmas Dawn* (K–3). Illus. by Peter M. Fiore. 1996, Troll paper $15.95 (0-8167-3384-8). 32pp. In 1917 Appalachia, a young girl awaits the promised arrival of her father for Christmas. (Rev: BL 10/15/96)

**4827** Repchuk, Caroline. *The Snow Tree* (PS–1). Illus. by Josephine Martin. 1997, Dutton paper $13.99 (0-525-45903-0). 32pp. Animals offer to a little bear many colorful objects to decorate his Christmas tree. (Rev: BL 9/1/97)

**4828** Riggio, Anita. *A Moon in My Teacup* (PS–2). Illus. 1993, Boyds Mills LB $14.95 (1-56397-008-2). 32pp. On a visit to her Italian American grandparents, a young girl sings "Silent Night" to the baby figure she finds in the stable of a miniature village that belongs to her grandfather. (Rev: BL 10/15/93)

**4829** Roberts, Bethany. *Waiting-for-Christmas Stories* (K–2). Illus. by Sarah Stapler. 1994, Clarion $13.95 (0-395-67324-0). 32pp. On Christmas Eve, Papa Rabbit reads 7 short stories about various activities centered around Christmas. (Rev: BCCB 11/94; BL 9/15/94)

**4830** Rosen, Michael J. *Elijah's Angel: A Story for Chanukah and Christmas* (K–3). Illus. by Aminah Robinson. 1992, Harcourt $13.95 (0-15-225394-7). 32pp. The story of an unusual friendship between an elderly black man and a 9-year-old Jewish boy. (Rev: BCCB 11/92; BL 8/92*; HB 11–12/92*)

**4831** Rylant, Cynthia. *Mr. Putter and Tabby Bake the Cake* (1–3). Illus. by Arthur Howard. 1994, Harcourt $12.00 (0-15-200205-7); paper $6.00 (0-15-200214-6). 44pp. Mr. Putter bakes a Christmas cake for his neighbor, Mrs. Teaberry, in this easily read book. (Rev: BL 10/15/94; HB 9–10/94; SLJ 12/94)

**4832** Rylant, Cynthia. *Silver Packages: An Appalachian Christmas Story* (K–3). Illus. by Chris K. Soentpiet. 1997, Orchard LB $17.99 (0-531-33051-

6). 32pp. At Christmas time, a young doctor tries to repay an Appalachian community for the gifts that were given to him in the past. (Rev: BL 9/1/97; SLJ 10/97)

**4833** Sawyer, Ruth. *The Remarkable Christmas of the Cobbler's Sons* (K–3). Illus. by Barbara Cooney. 1994, Viking paper $14.99 (0-670-84922-7). 32pp. King Laurin, disguised as a demanding beggar, helps a poor cobbler's family at Christmas. (Rev: BL 8/94) [394.26]

**4834** Say, Allen. *Tree of Cranes* (PS–3). Illus. 1991, Houghton $17.95 (0-395-52024-X). 32pp. A Japanese woman brings a tree indoors because it reminds her of the Christmas she spent years ago in California. (Rev: BCCB 9/91*; BL 9/15/91; HB 11–12/91*)

**4835** Schachner, Judith Byron. *Willy and May* (PS–3). Illus. 1995, Dutton paper $14.99 (0-525-45347-4). 32pp. May thinks of an unusual solution when a snowstorm prevents her great niece from visiting her at Christmas. (Rev: BL 11/1/95*; SLJ 10/95*)

**4836** Seuss, Dr. *How the Grinch Stole Christmas* (K–3). Illus. by author. 1957, Random LB $15.99 (0-394-90079-0). A rhyming book about a queer creature, the Grinch, who plans to do away with Christmas.

**4837** Shannon, David. *The Amazing Christmas Extravaganza* (K–3). Illus. 1995, Scholastic $15.95 (0-590-48090-1). 32pp. A parable about Mr. Merriweather and how he alienates his neighbors at Christmas time. (Rev: BL 9/15/95)

**4838** Shepard, Aaron. *The Baker's Dozen: A Saint Nicholas Tale* (PS–2). Illus. by Wendy Edelson. 1995, Simon & Schuster $15.00 (0-689-80298-6). 32pp. A baker learns the meaning of being generous at the same time he finds out what is meant by a baker's dozen in this story about a visit from Saint Nicholas. (Rev: BL 9/15/95) [398.2]

**4839** Soto, Gary. *Too Many Tamales* (PS–1). Illus. by Ed Martinez. 1993, Putnam $15.95 (0-399-22146-8). 32pp. A Hispanic child enthusiastically enters into the cooking and other rituals that surround her family's celebration of Christmas. (Rev: BCCB 10/93; BL 9/15/93; HB 11–12/93)

**4840** Stevenson, James. *The Night After Christmas* (K–3). Illus. 1981, Greenwillow LB $15.93 (0-688-00548-9). 32pp. Old toys, discarded after Christmas, find a new home.

**4841** Stevenson, James. *The Oldest Elf* (PS–1). Illus. 1996, Greenwillow LB $14.93 (0-688-13756-3). 32pp. One of Santa's elves, Elwyn, is too old to make modern toys. (Rev: BCCB 10/96; BL 9/1/96; SLJ 10/96*)

**4842** Stickland, Henrietta. *The Christmas Bear* (PS–2). Illus. by Paul Stickland. 1993, Dutton paper $15.99 (0-525-45062-9). 32pp. When a bear cub

accidentally falls into Santa's home, he is taken on a tour of the premises. (Rev: BL 10/1/93)

**4843** Sundvall, Viveca L. *Santa's Winter Vacation* (K–3). Trans. by Kjersti Board. Illus. by Olof Landstrom. 1995, Farrar $13.00 (91-29-62953-5). 32pp. At Christmas, Reuben Stormfoot becomes Santa Stormfoot and teaches a lesson to the loud, rude Sandworm children, whom he has encountered on his vacation. (Rev: BL 9/15/95)

**4844** Tews, Susan. *The Gingerbread Doll* (K–3). Illus. by Megan Lloyd. 1993, Clarion $14.95 (0-395-56438-7). 32pp. Starting as a poor youngster during the Great Depression when she gets a gingerbread doll, Rebecca finds that her Christmas presents change as her family gets more prosperous. (Rev: BL 9/1/93)

**4845** Thayer, Jane. *The Puppy Who Wanted a Boy* (1–3). Illus. by Lisa McCue. 1986, Morrow LB $13.93 (0-688-05945-7); paper $4.95 (0-688-08293-9). 48pp. Petey the puppy doesn't get a boy for Christmas as he wished, but he does find 50 boys in a Home for Boys to whom he can give his love. (Rev: BL 4/1/86; SLJ 5/86)

**4846** Thomson, Pat. *Beware of the Aunts!* (PS–2). Illus. by Emma C. Clark. 1992, Macmillan $14.95 (0-689-50538-8). Nine unusual aunts and Christmas gift giving are the subjects of this humorous book. (Rev: SLJ 7/92)

**4847** Tompert, Ann. *A Carol for Christmas* (K–3). Illus. by Laura Kelly. 1994, Macmillan paper $16.00 (0-02-789402-9). 32pp. A mouse witnesses the composition of the carol "Silent Night" from the comfort of a pastor's coat pocket. (Rev: BL 10/15/94)

**4848** Trivas, Irene. *Emma's Christmas* (PS–4). Illus. 1988, Orchard LB $16.99 (0-531-08380-2); paper $5.95 (0-531-07022-0). 32pp. When Emma, the farmer's daughter, declines the prince's offer of marriage, he begins to send her gifts. (Rev: BCCB 10/88; BL 9/15/88; HB 11–12/88)

**4849** Tryon, Leslie. *Albert's Christmas* (K–2). Illus. by author. 1997, Simon & Schuster $16.00 (0-689-81034-2). In this Christmas story, the animals of Pleasant Valley, led by Albert the duck, work hard to feed the reindeer, etc., when Santa makes a pit stop in their town. (Rev: SLJ 10/97)

**4850** Vainio, Pirkko. *The Christmas Angel* (K–2). Trans. by Anthea Bell. Illus. 1995, North-South LB $15.88 (1-55858-500-1); paper $6.95 (1-55858-774-8). 32pp. Through good works at Christmas time, a young girl helps a music box angel get her wings. (Rev: BL 12/15/95)

**4851** Van Allsburg, Chris. *The Polar Express* (K–2). Illus. by author. 1985, Houghton $18.95 (0-395-38949-6). 32pp. Whisked aboard the Polar Express to the North Pole on Christmas Eve, a young boy gets to receive the first gift of Christmas. Caldecott Medal winner, 1986. (Rev: BCCB 10/85; BL 10/1/85; SLJ 10/85)

**4852** Waldron, Jan L. *Angel Pig and the Hidden Christmas* (PS–2). Illus. by David McPhail. 1997, Dutton paper $14.99 (0-525-45744-5). 32pp. Six little pigs are getting excited about Christmas, but they have no money for presents. (Rev: BL 9/1/97*; SLJ 10/97)

**4853** Wallner, Alexandra. *An Alcott Family Christmas* (K–2). Illus. 1996, Holiday LB $15.95 (0-8234-1265-2). 30pp. A fictionalized account of how Louisa May Alcott's family might have observed Christmas as the March family did in *Little Women*. (Rev: BL 9/1/96)

**4854** Walsh, Vivian, and J. Otto Seibold. *Olive, the Other Reindeer* (1–3). Illus. 1997, Chronicle $12.95 (0-8118-1807-1). 32pp. A little dog believes that she is really a reindeer and heads to the North Pole to give Santa a hand. (Rev: BL 10/15/97)

**4855** Watson, Clyde. *How Brown Mouse Kept Christmas* (PS–3). Illus. by Wendy Watson. 1980, Farrar $10.00 (0-374-33494-3); paper $3.95 (0-374-43315-1). 32pp. When the people go to bed, mice come out to celebrate Christmas.

**4856** Wells, Rosemary. *Max's Christmas* (PS–1). Illus. by author. 1986, Dial paper $9.89 (0-8037-0290-6). 32pp. Max is determined to find out if Santa really exists and so he waits up to see him on Christmas Eve. (Rev: BCCB 11/86; BL 10/15/86; HB 11–12/86)

**4857** Wild, Margaret. *Thank You, Santa* (PS–3). Illus. by Kerry Argent. 1992, Scholastic $12.95 (0-590-45805-1). 32pp. After Christmas, a young girl in Australia begins a correspondence with Santa Claus. (Rev: BCCB 11/92; BL 11/1/92)

**4858** Winthrop, Elizabeth. *Bear's Christmas Surprise* (PS–2). Illus. by Patience Brewster. 1991, Holiday LB $14.95 (0-8234-0888-4). 32pp. While playing hide-and-seek, Bear accidentally discovers some Christmas presents hidden in a closet and opens them. (Rev: BL 9/15/91)

**4859** Wojciechowski, Susan. *The Christmas Miracle of Jonathan Toomey* (PS–4). Illus. by P. J. Lynch. 1995, Candlewick $17.99 (1-56402-320-6). 40pp. Mean old Jonathan Toomey is transformed at Christmas time when a widowed mother and her son ask him to build a Christmas creche for them. (Rev: BL 9/15/95; SLJ 10/95*)

**4860** Wright, Cliff. *Santa's Ark* (K–3). Illus. 1997, Millbrook LB $22.40 (0-7613-0314-6). 36pp. Different animals from around the world stow away in Santa's sleigh when he makes his stops. (Rev: BL 12/15/97; SLJ 10/97)

**4861** Zolotow, Charlotte. *The Beautiful Christmas Tree* (K–3). Illus. by Ruth Robbins. 1983, Houghton $13.95 (0-395-27676-4); paper $6.95 (0-395-34925-7). 32pp. With loving care, an old man nurtures a pine tree and brings to life the real spirit of Christmas.

### EASTER

**4862** Adams, Adrienne. *The Easter Egg Artists* (PS–2). 1991, Simon & Schuster paper $5.99 (0-689-71481-5). 32pp. A rabbit family paints 100 dozen eggs for Easter, helped greatly by the son's flair for comic design.

**4863** Bishop, Adela. *The Easter Wolf* (PS–2). Illus. by Carole Dzapla. 1991, Dot $12.95 (0-9625620-1-7). 28pp. When he is saved from drowning by the Easter Rabbit, a hungry wolf reforms. (Rev: BL 3/15/91)

**4864** Devlin, Wende, and Harry Devlin. *Cranberry Easter* (PS–3). Illus. by Harry Devlin. 1990, Macmillan LB $15.00 (0-02-729935-X). In the town of Cranberryport, friends help each other and the result is a happy Easter. (Rev: SLJ 3/90)

**4865** Friedrich, Priscilla, and Otto Friedrich. *The Easter Bunny That Overslept* (PS–1). Illus. by Adrienne Adams. 1983, Lothrop LB $15.93 (0-688-01541-7); Morrow paper $4.95 (0-688-07038-8). 40pp. Santa Claus helps a tardy Easter Bunny who has trouble getting up on time.

**4866** Gibbons, Gail. *Easter* (PS–2). Illus. by author. 1989, Holiday LB $15.95 (0-8234-0737-3); paper $6.95 (0-8234-0866-3). 32pp. Biblical, pagan, and modern aspects of the holiday are described. (Rev: BL 4/1/89; SLJ 3/89)

**4867** Heyward, DuBose. *The Country Bunny and the Little Gold Shoes* (K–3). Illus. by Marjorie Flack. 1939, Houghton $15.00 (0-395-15990-3); paper $5.95 (0-395-18557-2). 48pp. Cottontail, the mother of 21 bunnies, finally realizes her great ambition to be an Easter Bunny.

**4868** Houselander, Caryll. *Petook: An Easter Story* (K–3). Illus. by Tomie dePaola. 1988, Holiday LB $16.95 (0-8234-0681-4). 32pp. The rooster, Petook, and a simple story of Easter. (Rev: BL 4/15/88; SLJ 5/88)

**4869** Kroll, Steven. *The Big Bunny and the Magic Show* (PS–2). Illus. by Janet Stevens. 1986, Holiday LB $15.95 (0-8234-0589-3). 32pp. Wilbur decides to give up his career as the Easter Bunny and turn to magic shows, to the horror of his 4 young rabbit friends. (Rev: BCCB 4/86; BL 4/15/86; SLJ 9/86)

**4870** Lindgren, Astrid. *Lotta's Easter Surprise* (K–2). Trans. by Barbara Lucas. Illus. by Ilon Wikland. 1991, R&S $13.95 (91-29-59862-1). 32pp. When her local candy store goes out of business, Lotta must settle for Christmas candies at Easter. (Rev: BCCB 4/91; BL 3/15/91)

**4871** Nerlove, Miriam. *Easter* (PS–1). Illus. 1989, Whitman paper $4.95 (0-8075-1872-7). 24pp. This major religious holiday is described in rhyming text. (Rev: BL 1/15/90; SLJ 4/90)

**4872** Polacco, Patricia. *Chicken Sunday* (PS–3). Illus. 1992, Putnam $15.95 (0-399-22133-6). 32pp. Three youngsters of different races — black and white — and religions unite to help Miss Eula have a good Easter. (Rev: BCCB 7–8/92; BL 3/15/92*; SLJ 5/92*)

**4873** Stock, Catherine. *Easter Surprise* (PS–1). Illus. Series: Festive Year. 1991, Macmillan LB $13.00 (0-02-788371-X). 32pp. A girl and her older brother engage in such Easter activities as hunting for eggs. (Rev: BCCB 3/91; BL 2/1/91; SLJ 9/91)

**4874** Watson, Wendy. *Happy Easter Day!* (PS–2). Illus. 1993, Houghton $14.95 (0-395-53629-4). A family prepares for Easter by participating in such activities as baking hot-cross buns. (Rev: SLJ 4/93) [263]

**4875** Wells, Rosemary. *Max's Chocolate Chicken* (PS–K). Illus. by author. 1989, Dial LB $9.89 (0-8037-0586-7). 32pp. Max the rabbit covets the chocolate chicken left by the Easter Bunny, but so does his sister. (Rev: BCCB 3/89; BL 3/1/89; SLJ 3/89)

**4876** Zolotow, Charlotte. *The Bunny Who Found Easter* (PS–2). Illus. by Helen Craig. 1998, Houghton $15.00 (0-395-86265-5). 32pp. A new edition of the story about a bunny who wanders through a year searching for Easter so he can enjoy the company of other bunnies. The 1959 edition is illustrated by Betty Peterson. (Rev: BL 3/1/98)

## HALLOWEEN

**4877** Adams, Adrienne. *A Woggle of Witches* (PS–3). Illus. by author. 1971, Macmillan paper $4.95 (0-689-71050-X). 32pp. The activities of a group of witches on Halloween night as they go about their business of dining on bat stew and riding on a broom.

**4878** Andrews, Sylvia. *Rattlebone Rock* (PS–1). Illus. by Jennifer Plecas. 1995, HarperCollins LB $13.89 (0-06-023452-0). 32pp. A Halloween celebration of moans and rattling bones is joined by people in the neighborhood. (Rev: BL 9/15/95; SLJ 11/95)

**4879** Bauer, Marion Dane. *Alison's Fierce and Ugly Halloween* (2–4). Illus. 1997, Hyperion LB $14.49 (0-7868-2262-7); paper $3.95 (0-7868-1211-7). 48pp. In spite of her fierce pirate's costume, everyone still thinks Alison is pretty at Halloween. (Rev: BL 9/1/97; SLJ 10/97)

**4880** Beard, Darleen Bailey. *The Pumpkin Man from Piney Creek* (PS–3). Illus. by Laura Kelly. 1995, Simon & Schuster $15.00 (0-689-80315-X). 32pp. Hattie is sad because all of her father's pumpkins have been promised to the Pumpkin Man and she will not have one from which to carve a jack-o'-lantern. (Rev: BL 9/15/95; SLJ 10/95)

**4881** Bridwell, Norman. *Clifford's Halloween* (PS–1). Illus. by author. 1970, Scholastic paper $2.99 (0-590-44287-2). 32pp. Halloween adventures of a big red dog.

**4882** Brown, Marc. *Arthur's Halloween* (PS–2). Illus. by author. 1983, Little, Brown $15.95 (0-316-11116-3); paper $5.95 (0-316-11059-0). 32pp. Arthur must find courage to help his sister on Halloween.

**4883** Bunting, Eve. *In the Haunted House* (PS–2). Illus. by Susan Meddaugh. 1990, Houghton $14.95 (0-395-51589-0). 32pp. The identity of the 2 people wearing sneakers and touring a haunted house is kept a secret until the end of the book. (Rev: BL 9/1/90; HB 11–12/90; SLJ 9/90)

**4884** Bunting, Eve. *Scary, Scary Halloween* (PS–1). Illus. by Jan Brett. 1986, Houghton $15.00 (0-89919-414-1); paper $5.95 (0-89919-799-X). 32pp. A scary poem tells of a parade of creatures on Halloween night. (Rev: BCCB 9/86; BL 9/1/86; HB 11–12/86)

**4885** Carlson, Nancy. *Harriet's Halloween Candy* (PS–K). Illus. by author. 1982, Carolrhoda LB $17.50 (0-87614-182-3); Lerner paper $4.95 (0-87614-850-X). 32pp. A childlike dog overeats on Halloween candy.

**4886** Caseley, Judith. *Witch Mama* (PS–2). Illus. 1996, Greenwillow LB $14.93 (0-688-14458-6). 32pp. On Halloween, Mama becomes Witch Mama, but she still cares for her 2 children. (Rev: BL 9/1/96; SLJ 8/96)

**4887** Cassedy, Sylvia. *The Best Cat Suit of All* (1–2). Illus. by Rosekrans Hoffman. 1991, Dial LB $10.89 (0-8037-0517-4). 48pp. In this easy-to-read book, Matthew's Halloween becomes more lively when a cat appears at his door. (Rev: BCCB 10/91; BL 9/15/91; HB 11–12/91; SLJ 1/92)

**4888** Cohen, Miriam. *The Real-Skin Rubber Monster Mask* (PS–2). Illus. by Lillian Hoban. 1995, Bantam paper $4.99 (0-440-40949-7). 32pp. Second-graders prepare for the activities of Halloween. (Rev: BL 9/1/90; SLJ 11/90)

**4889** Coombs, Patricia. *Dorrie and the Halloween Plot* (2–4). Illus. 1976, Lothrop LB $12.93 (0-688-51764-1). 48pp. Dorrie foils a plot to kidnap the Great Sorceress.

**4890** Dodds, Dayle Ann. *Ghost and Pete* (K–3). Illus. by Matt Novak. Series: Step into Reading. 1995, Random LB $11.99 (0-679-96199-2); paper

$3.99 (0-679-86199-8). 48pp. When Pete moves into his new house, he becomes friendly with Ghost, who lives in the attic, in this Halloween story. (Rev: SLJ 3/96)

**4891** Enderle, Judith R., and Stephanie G. Tessler. *Six Creepy Sheep* (PS–1). Illus. by John O'Brien. 1992, Boyds Mills LB $12.95 (1-56397-092-9). 24pp. Six sheep go out on Halloween dressed as ghosts. (Rev: BL 9/1/92; HB 3–4/93; SLJ 10/92)

**4892** Gantos, Jack. *Rotten Ralph's Trick or Treat* (K–3). Illus. by Nicole Rubel. 1986, Houghton $15.00 (0-395-38943-7); paper $6.95 (0-395-48655-6). 32pp. Ralph the cat and waitress Sarah exchange identities at a Halloween party. (Rev: HB 9–10/86; SLJ 10/86)

**4893** Gordon, Lynn. *The Witch's Revenge* (K–4). Illus. by Val Martino. Series: Lights Out. 1997, Simon & Schuster $9.99 (0-689-81679-0). In this interactive book — which contains images that can be projected on walls using a flashlight — a witch plans to get even for a trick played on her at Halloween. (Rev: SLJ 1/98)

**4894** Hall, Zoe. *It's Pumpkin Time!* (K–3). Illus. by Shari Halpern. 1994, Scholastic $13.95 (0-590-47833-8). This picture book describes how 2 children plant a pumpkin seed and care for it so that it will be useful at Halloween. (Rev: SLJ 11/94)

**4895** Hautzig, Deborah. *Little Witch's Big Night* (1–2). Illus. by Marc Brown. 1984, Random LB $7.99 (0-394-96587-6); paper $3.99 (0-394-86587-1). 48pp. Little Witch has a better Halloween than she expected.

**4896** Heinz, Brian J. *The Monsters' Test* (K–2). Illus. by Sal Murdocca. 1996, Millbrook LB $23.90 (0-7613-0050-3). A group of scary monsters are frightened by some trick-or-treaters. (Rev: SLJ 10/96)

**4897** Hennessy, B. G. *Corduroy's Halloween: A Lift-the-Flap Book* (PS–K). Illus. by Lisa McCue. 1995, Viking paper $10.99 (0-670-86193-6). Flaps that lift add surprise to this story of how a little bear spends his Halloween. (Rev: SLJ 10/95)

**4898** Hines, Anna Grossnickle. *When the Goblins Came Knocking* (PS–K). Illus. 1995, Greenwillow LB $15.93 (0-688-13736-9). 24pp. A young boy decides that, unlike other Halloweens, this time he will be the one to frighten others. (Rev: BL 9/15/95; SLJ 9/95)

**4899** Hiser, Constance. *Ghosts in Fourth Grade* (2–4). Illus. by Cat B. Smith. 1991, Holiday $14.95 (0-8234-0865-5). 68pp. At Halloween, James and his friends decide to frighten the class bully. (Rev: BCCB 7–8/91; SLJ 6/91)

**4900** Hoban, Lillian. *Arthur's Halloween Costume* (1–3). Illus. by author. 1984, HarperCollins LB $14.89 (0-06-022391-X); paper $3.75 (0-06-444101-

6). 64pp. Arthur is annoyed because no one understands his Halloween costume.

**4901** Holub, Joan. *Boo Who? A Spooky Lift-the-Flap Book* (PS–1). Illus. by author. Series: Spooky Lift-the-Flap Book. 1997, Scholastic $6.95 (0-590-05905-X). Rhymes and flaps are used to introduce the objects and creatures associated with Halloween. (Rev: SLJ 10/97)

**4902** Howe, James. *Scared Silly: A Halloween Treat* (K–2). Illus. by Leslie Morrill. 1989, Morrow $16.00 (0-688-07666-1); paper $4.95 (0-688-16322-X). A really scary story featuring Chester and the crew from the Bunnicula series. (Rev: BL 8/89; SLJ 8/89*)

**4903** Hutchins, Pat. *Which Witch Is Which?* (PS–K). Illus. 1989, Greenwillow LB $15.93 (0-688-06358-6). 24pp. Identical twins dress as witches on Halloween. (Rev: BL 9/1/89; SLJ 8/89*)

**4904** Jane, Pamela. *Halloween Hide-and-Seek* (1–3). Illus. by Julie Durrell. Series: A Yearling First Choice Chapter Book. 1997, Delacorte paper $3.99 (0-440-41219-6). 48pp. Jonathan is unhappy because he has to wear last year's pirate costume to Leo's Halloween party. (Rev: SLJ 12/97)

**4905** Johnston, Tony. *The Soup Bone* (PS–3). Illus. by Margot Tomes. 1990, Harcourt $12.95 (0-15-277255-3). 32pp. A witch looking for a soup bone uncovers a whole skeleton. (Rev: BL 10/15/90; HB 11–12/90; SLJ 1/91)

**4906** Johnston, Tony. *The Vanishing Pumpkin* (PS–2). Illus. by Tomie dePaola. 1996, Putnam paper $5.99 (0-698-11414-0). 32pp. An old man and an old woman set out on Halloween to find their pumpkin.

**4907** Johnston, Tony. *Very Scary* (PS–K). Illus. by Douglas Florian. 1995, Harcourt $13.00 (0-15-293625-4). 32pp. When a girl carves a pumpkin into a jack-o'-lantern, it shouts "Boo" and frightens everyone. (Rev: BL 9/15/95; SLJ 11/95)

**4908** Keats, Ezra Jack. *The Trip* (1–3). Illus. by author. 1978, Greenwillow LB $15.93 (0-688-84123-6); Morrow paper $4.95 (0-688-07328-X). 32pp. Halloween proves to be a time when Louis isn't lonely anymore.

**4909** Kellogg, Steven. *The Mystery of the Flying Orange Pumpkin* (PS–2). Illus. by author. 1983, Puffin paper $3.50 (0-8037-0019-9). 32pp. Neighborhood children play a Halloween prank on mean Mr. King.

**4910** Kline, Suzy. *Mary Marony, Mummy Girl* (2–4). Illus. 1994, Putnam $13.95 (0-399-22609-5); Bantam paper $3.99 (0-440-41138-6). 80pp. Mary Marony, who stutters, wants to be a mummy at Halloween, and gets a bright idea when she sees a worn bed sheet. (Rev: BL 11/15/94; SLJ 12/94)

**4911** Kraus, Robert. *How Spider Saved Halloween* (K–3). Illus. by author. 1988, Scholastic paper $2.99 (0-590-42117-4). 32pp. Spider saves the fun of Halloween by creating an ingenious disguise.

**4912** Kroll, Steven. *The Biggest Pumpkin Ever* (PS–2). Illus. by Jeni Bassett. 1984, Holiday LB $15.95 (0-8234-0505-2); Scholastic paper $2.50 (0-590-41113-6). 32pp. Two mice hope to grow the largest pumpkin ever for Halloween.

**4913** Lattimore, Deborah N. *Cinderhazel: The Cinderella of Halloween* (PS–2). Illus. 1997, Scholastic $15.95 (0-590-20232-4). 32pp. A parody on the famous fairy tale, with a feminist twist and a Halloween setting. (Rev: BL 9/1/97; SLJ 10/97)

**4914** Leedy, Loreen. *The Dragon Halloween Party* (PS–2). Illus. by author. 1986, Holiday LB $15.95 (0-8234-0611-3); paper $5.95 (0-8234-0765-9). 32pp. Ten children and their mother Ma Dragon get ready for their Halloween party, in short rhyming verse. (Rev: BL 9/15/86; SLJ 12/86)

**4915** Leedy, Loreen. *2 x 2=Boo! A Set of Spooky Multiplication Stories* (1–4). Illus. 1995, Holiday LB $15.95 (0-8234-1190-7). 32pp. Halloween creatures and objects are used in a series of scary stories to demonstrate the principles of multiplication. (Rev: BL 9/15/95; SLJ 11/95)

**4916** Levine, Abby. *This Is the Pumpkin* (PS–K). Illus. by Paige Billin-Frye. 1997, Albert Whitman LB $13.95 (0-8075-7886-X). 24pp. All of the fun and excitement of Halloween, first at school then trick-or-treating, is captured in a catchy cumulative verse. (Rev: BL 9/1/97; SLJ 9/97)

**4917** Mangas, Brian. *You Don't Get a Carrot Unless You're a Bunny* (PS–2). Illus. by Sidney Levitt. 1989, Simon & Schuster paper $5.95 (0-671-67201-0). Two rabbits dressed as a duck and a bear go out trick-or-treating. (Rev: SLJ 2/90)

**4918** Marshall, Edward. *Space Case* (K–2). Illus. by James Marshall. 1980, Dial paper $4.99 (0-8037-8431-7). 32pp. Strange things happen when a space creature visits Earth on Halloween.

**4919** Martin, Bill, Jr. *Old Devil Wind* (K–3). Illus. by Barry Root. 1993, Harcourt $13.95 (0-15-257768-8). 32pp. A cumulative Halloween story about events in a haunted house. (Rev: BL 10/1/93)

**4920** Martin, Bill, Jr., and John Archambault. *The Magic Pumpkin* (PS–2). Illus. by Robert J. Lee. 1989, Holt $14.95 (0-8050-1134-X). 32pp. A carved pumpkin proves to be a menace to the young narrator in this scary story. (Rev: BL 9/1/89; SLJ 12/89)

**4921** Meddaugh, Susan. *The Witches' Supermarket* (PS–3). Illus. 1991, Houghton $13.95 (0-395-57034-4). 32pp. On Halloween, Helen finds herself in a strange supermarket offering such goodies as scum milk and bug bars. (Rev: BCCB 9/91; BL 8/91; SLJ 11/91)

**4922** Mooser, Stephen. *The Ghost with the Halloween Hiccups* (1–3). Illus. by Tomie dePaola. 1978, Avon paper $2.95 (0-380-40287-4). 32pp. Penny's hiccups are cured only by being frightened by 2 costumed kids.

**4923** Nerlove, Miriam. *Halloween* (PS–1). Illus. 1989, Whitman paper $4.95 (0-8075-3130-8). 24pp. A family gets ready for Halloween through such activities as carving a pumpkin. (Rev: BL 7/89; SLJ 9/89)

**4924** Nikola-Lisa, W. *Shake Dem Halloween Bones* (PS–2). Illus. by Mike Reed. 1997, Houghton $16.00 (0-395-73095-3). 32pp. Fairy tale characters shake, rattle, and roll at a super Halloween party. (Rev: BL 10/1/97)

**4925** O'Malley, Kevin. *Velcome* (2–4). Illus. 1997, Walker LB $16.95 (0-8027-8629-4). 32pp. A picture book of jokes and scary stories for Halloween that are narrated by a host who "velcomes" you into his house. (Rev: BL 9/1/97; SLJ 9/97)

**4926** Pilkey, Dav. *The Hallo-Wiener* (PS–2). Illus. 1995, Scholastic $12.95 (0-590-41703-7). 32pp. At Halloween, Oscar the dachshund earns a change in his nickname from Wiener Dog to Hero Sandwich. (Rev: BCCB 10/95; BL 9/15/95; SLJ 10/95*)

**4927** Polacco, Patricia. *Picnic at Mudsock Meadow* (K–3). Illus. 1992, Putnam $15.95 (0-399-21811-4). 32pp. During the Halloween festivities, William is a failure until he has courage enough to investigate a scary swamp. (Rev: BL 11/15/92; HB 11–12/92; SLJ 10/92)

**4928** Prager, Annabelle. *The Spooky Halloween Party* (1–3). Illus. by Tomie dePaola. 1981, Pantheon LB $7.99 (0-394-94370-8). 48pp. On Halloween, Albert finds himself surrounded by frightening creatures he doesn't know.

**4929** Regan, Dian C. *The Thirteen Hours of Halloween* (PS–3). Illus. by Lieve Baeten. 1993, Albert Whitman LB $14.95 (0-8075-7876-2). A takeoff for Halloween on "The Twelve Days of Christmas" that includes a "vulture in a dead tree." (Rev: SLJ 2/94)

**4930** Roberts, Bethany. *Halloween Mice!* (PS–1). Illus. by Doug Cushman. 1995, Clarion $12.95 (0-395-67064-0). 32pp. At Halloween, a group of mice turn the tables and frighten a cat. (Rev: BL 9/15/95; SLJ 9/95)

**4931** Rockwell, Anne. *Halloween Day* (PS–K). Illus. by Lizzy Rockwell. 1997, HarperCollins LB $14.89 (0-06-027568-5). 40pp. Nineteen children create Halloween costumes at home and come to school in their creations. (Rev: BL 9/1/97; SLJ 9/97)

**4932** Ross, Pat. *M & M and the Halloween Monster* (1–2). Illus. by Marylin Hafner. 1991, Viking paper $10.95 (0-670-83003-8). 48pp. While searching in their apartment house basement for Halloween costumes, Mandy and Mimi believe they see a monster. (Rev: BL 9/15/91; SLJ 12/91)

**4933** Roy, Ron. *The Bald Bandit* (2–4). Illus. by John S. Gurney. Series: A to Z Mysteries. 1997, Random LB $11.99 (0-679-98449-6); paper $3.99 (0-679-88449-1). 70pp. A short Halloween story about 3 youngsters who are trying to find a videotape of a bank robbery. (Rev: SLJ 1/98)

**4934** Shaw, Nancy. *Sheep Trick or Treat* (PS–1). Illus. by Margot Apple. 1997, Houghton $14.00 (0-395-84168-2). 32pp. Sheep in costumes go trick-or-treating at Halloween and have unexpected adventures. (Rev: BL 9/1/97; HB 9–10/97; SLJ 9/97)

**4935** Sierra, Judy. *The House That Drac Built* (K–2). Illus. by Will Hillenbrand. 1995, Harcourt $14.00 (0-15-200015-1). 40pp. Halloween misadventures occur to a number of animals in the house that Drac built. (Rev: BCCB 10/95; BL 9/15/95; SLJ 9/95)

**4936** Silverman, Erica. *The Halloween House* (PS–3). Illus. by Jon Agee. 1997, Farrar $15.00 (0-374-33270-3). 32pp. A counting book that uses monsters, vampires, bats, and other Halloween trappings as subjects. (Rev: BL 9/1/97; HB 9–10/97; SLJ 11/97)

**4937** Smalls, Irene. *Jenny Reen and the Jack Muh Lantern* (PS–3). Illus. by Keinyo White. 1996, Simon & Schuster $16.00 (0-689-31875-8). 32pp. Jenny Reen, a slave child, is frightened by a wild creature she sees in the woods in this Halloween tale. (Rev: BCCB 12/96; BL 9/1/96; SLJ 12/96)

**4938** Stevenson, James. *That Terrible Halloween Night* (PS–3). Illus. by author. 1980, Greenwillow LB $15.93 (0-688-84281-X). 32pp. Grampa tells how he was frightened one Halloween night.

**4939** Stock, Catherine. *Halloween Monster* (PS–K). Illus. 1990, Macmillan paper $13.00 (0-02-788404-X). 32pp. A young black boy is apprehensive about monsters he will meet on Halloween. (Rev: BCCB 11/90; BL 10/1/90; SLJ 10/90)

**4940** Stutson, Caroline. *By the Light of the Halloween Moon* (K–3). Illus. by Kevin Hawkes. 1993, Lothrop LB $15.93 (0-688-12046-6). 32pp. At Halloween, a tapping toe sets off a chain of funny events in this cumulative tale. (Rev: BL 7/93)

**4941** Updike, David. *An Autumn Tale* (2–4). Illus. by Robert Andrew Parker. 1988, Pippin $15.95 (0-945912-02-1). 40pp. A magical Halloween tale of young Homer and his dog Sophocles. (Rev: BCCB 5/89; BL 10/15/88; SLJ 11/88)

**4942** Van Leeuwen, Jean. *Oliver and Amanda's Halloween* (1–2). Illus. by Ann Schweninger. 1992, Dial LB $10.89 (0-8037-1238-3). 48pp. In this book for beginning readers, Oliver and Amanda Pig have differences on how to dress for the Halloween holiday. (Rev: BL 10/1/92; HB 11–12/92; SLJ 10/92)

**4943** Van Rynbach, Iris. *Five Little Pumpkins* (PS–K). Illus. 1995, Boyds Mills $7.95 (1-56397-452-5). 24pp. At Halloween, 5 little jack-o'-lanterns come alive and join in the holiday celebrations. (Rev: BL 9/15/95; SLJ 10/95)

**4944** Watson, Wendy. *Boo! It's Halloween* (PS–3). Illus. 1992, Houghton $14.95 (0-395-53628-6). 32pp. A family prepares for Halloween, and after the school party it's at last time for trick or treating. (Rev: BL 9/1/92)

**4945** Winters, Kay. *The Teeny Tiny Ghost* (PS–1). Illus. by Lynn Munsinger. 1997, HarperCollins LB $14.89 (0-06-025684-2). 32pp. A tiny ghost passes the test of not being frightened on Halloween. (Rev: BL 9/1/97; SLJ 11/97)

**4946** Wolff, Ferida, and Dolores Kozielski. *On Halloween Night* (PS–K). Illus. by Dolores Avendano. 1994, Morrow LB $15.93 (0-688-12973-0). 32pp. This counting book uses creatures associated with Halloween in a series of scary rhymes. (Rev: BL 8/94; SLJ 9/94*)

**4947** Yolen, Jane. *Child of Faerie, Child of Earth* (K–3). Illus. by Jane Dyer. 1997, Little, Brown $15.95 (0-316-96897-8). 32pp. On Halloween, a little girl is transported to a magical fairy land but, in time, realizes that she must go home. (Rev: BL 1/1–15/98; SLJ 1/98)

**4948** Ziefert, Harriet. *Two Little Witches: A Halloween Counting Story* (PS–K). Illus. by Simms Taback. 1996, Candlewick $9.99 (1-56402-621-3). 32pp. A counting book that uses Halloween symbols like pumpkins and witches. (Rev: BL 9/1/96; SLJ 12/96)

### JEWISH HOLY DAYS

**4949** Adler, David A. *Chanukah in Chelm* (K–3). Illus. by Kevin O'Malley. 1997, Lothrop LB $15.93 (0-688-09953-X). 32pp. A bumbling synagogue keeper is the central character in this story set at Hanukkah. (Rev: BL 9/1/97; HB 9–10/97; SLJ 10/97*)

**4950** Adler, David A. *The House on the Roof: A Sukkoth Story* (K–4). Illus. by Marilyn Hirsh. 1984, Kar-Ben paper $4.95 (0-930494-35-0). 32pp. An old man hauls all sorts of material into his apartment and builds a Sukkah to celebrate the holiday of Sukkoth.

**4951** Adler, David A. *One Yellow Daffodil: A Hanukkah Story* (K–3). Illus. by Lloyd Bloom. 1995, Harcourt $16.00 (0-15-200537-4). 32pp. A Holocaust survivor, who has lost all interest in life, is restored to concern for others by 2 children and their celebration of Hanukkah. (Rev: BCCB 12/95; BL 11/1/95)

**4952** Brodmann, Aliana. *The Gift* (K–3). Illus. by Anthony Carnabuci. 1993, Simon & Schuster paper $15.00 (0-671-75110-7). 32pp. At Hanukkah, a young girl discovers that giving can be better than receiving. (Rev: BL 7/93)

**4953** Drucker, Malka. *Grandma's Latkes* (PS–3). Illus. by Eve Chwast. 1992, Harcourt $13.95 (0-15-200468-8). 32pp. While Molly and her grandma make Hanukkah latkes, Grandmother explains some of the traditions connected with the holiday. (Rev: BL 8/92; HB 11–12/92)

**4954** Ehrlich, Amy. *The Story of Hanukkah* (PS–5). Illus. by Ori Sherman. 1989, Dial LB $14.89 (0-8037-0616-2). 32pp. This traditional story is told in poetic prose. (Rev: BCCB 12/89; BL 9/1/89*) [298.4]

**4955** Fishman, Cathy G. *On Passover* (PS–2). Illus. by Melanie Hall. 1997, Simon & Schuster $16.00 (0-689-80528-4). 40pp. Through the eyes of a young Jewish girl, the reader experiences the wonder and rituals of a traditional Passover. (Rev: BL 3/1/97; SLJ 4/97) [296.4]

**4956** Gelman, Rita G. *Queen Esther Saves Her People* (K–3). Illus. by Frane Lessac. 1998, Scholastic $15.95 (0-590-47025-6). 40pp. A personalized account of the Jewish girl Esther and how she saved her people at the court of the Persian king. (Rev: BL 3/1/98; SLJ 2/98) [222]

**4957** Glaser, Linda. *The Borrowed Hanukkah Latkes* (K–3). Illus. by Nancy Cote. 1997, Albert Whitman LB $15.95 (0-8075-0841-1). 32pp. Gradually, Rachel persuades the family's neighbor Mrs. Greenberg to join them for Hanukkah. (Rev: BL 9/1/97; SLJ 10/97)

**4958** Goldin, Barbara D. *Just Enough Is Plenty: A Hanukkah Tale* (PS–3). Illus. by Seymour Chwast. 1988, Puffin paper $4.99 (0-14-050787-6). 32pp. Although the family is poor, a stranger is welcomed to the table with assurances that Mama can make "just enough be plenty." (Rev: BL 9/15/88; HB 11–12/88)

**4959** Goldin, Barbara D. *The World's Birthday: A Rosh Hashanah Story* (PS–3). Illus. by Jeanette Winter. 1990, Harcourt $13.95 (0-15-299648-6). 32pp. On Rosh Hashanah, the celebration of the birth of the world, Daniel wants to invite the world over to its birthday party. (Rev: BL 9/1/90; HB 11–12/90; SLJ 2/91)

**4960** Greenberg, Melanie H. *Blessings: Our Jewish Ceremonies* (PS–3). Illus. 1995, Jewish Publication Soc. $16.95 (0-8276-0540-4). 32pp. Various ceremonies and rituals connected with the Jewish faith are explained. (Rev: BL 2/1/96) [296.4]

**4961** Hirsh, Marilyn. *Potato Pancakes All Around: A Hanukkah Tale* (1–3). Illus. 1982, Jewish Publication Soc. paper $7.95 (0-8276-0217-0). 34pp. A humorous story about making potato pancakes for Hanukkah.

**4962** Jaffe, Nina. *In the Month of Kislev: A Story for Hanukkah* (PS–3). Illus. by Louise August. 1992, Viking paper $15.00 (0-670-82863-7). 32pp. Unable to afford the potatoes for Hanukkah latkes, 3 poor sisters must content themselves with the delicious smell of a neighbor's cooking. (Rev: BCCB 11/92; BL 8/92; HB 11–12/92)

**4963** Kimmel, Eric A. *Asher and the Capmakers: A Hanukkah Story* (K–3). Illus. by Will Hillenbrand. 1993, Holiday LB $15.95 (0-8234-1031-5). 32pp. Asher has many adventures when he sets out to borrow an egg for the family's latkes. (Rev: BL 7/93)

**4964** Kimmel, Eric A. *The Chanukkah Guest* (PS–2). Illus. by Giora Carmi. 1990, Holiday LB $15.95 (0-8234-0788-8); paper $6.95 (0-8234-0978-3). 32pp. Bubba Brayna is making potato latkes for the rabbi. (Rev: BCCB 12/90; BL 9/15/90*)

**4965** Kimmel, Eric A. *Hershel and the Hanukkah Goblins* (K–3). Illus. by Trina S. Hyman. 1989, Holiday LB $16.95 (0-8234-0769-1). 32pp. In this tale set in Eastern Europe, Hershel is looking forward to Hanukkah until he finds that the synagogue is haunted by goblins. (Rev: BCCB 10/89; BL 9/1/89; HB 1–2/90)

**4966** Kimmel, Eric A. *The Magic Dreidels: A Hanukkah Story* (PS–3). Illus. by Katya Krenina. 1996, Holiday LB $15.95 (0-8234-1256-3). 28pp. In this Hanukkah story, Jacob receives a magic dreidel from a goblin. (Rev: BCCB 11/96; BL 9/1/96)

**4967** Kimmelman, Leslie. *Hanukkah Lights, Hanukkah Nights* (PS–K). Illus. by John Himmelman. 1995, HarperCollins $8.95 (0-694-00721-8). 32pp. Readers join in the warmth and fun of a family's Hanukkah celebration. (Rev: BL 9/1/92) [296.4]

**4968** Kobre, Faige. *A Sense of Shabbat* (PS–K). Illus. 1990, Torah $11.95 (0-933873-44-1). 32pp. This Jewish holiday is shown from a preschooler's sensory perspective. (Rev: BCCB 3/91; BL 1/1/91) [296.4]

**4969** Kress, Camille. *Tot Shabbat* (PS). Illus. 1996, UAHC $5.95 (0-8074-0607-4). 7pp. In this simple board book, the Jewish Sabbath is introduced. (Rev: BL 2/1/97; SLJ 9/97)

**4970** Lamstein, Sarah M. *Annie's Shabbat* (PS–3). Illus. by Cecily Lang. 1997, Albert Whitman LB $15.95 (0-8075-0376-2). 40pp. This first-person account describes the wonder and fun involved in the celebration of the Jewish Sabbath. (Rev: BL 10/1/97*; SLJ 12/97) [296.4]

**4971** Levine, Arthur A. *All the Lights in the Night* (K–3). Illus. by James E. Ransome. 1991, Morrow

LB $15.93 (0-688-10108-9). 32pp. Though it is Hanukkah, Moses and Benjamin are fearful that their home in Russia will be set afire. (Rev: BCCB 12/91; BL 12/1/91; HB 1–2/92; SLJ 3/92)

**4972** Manushkin, Fran. *The Matzah That Papa Brought Home* (PS–1). Illus. by Ned Bittinger. 1995, Scholastic $14.95 (0-590-47146-5). 32pp. A cumulative tale that introduces symbols associated with Passover. (Rev: BL 1/15/95; SLJ 2/95)

**4973** Manushkin, Fran. *Starlight and Candles: The Joys of the Sabbath* (K–3). Illus. by Jacqueline Chwast. 1995, Simon & Schuster paper $15.00 (0-689-80274-9). 32pp. Using one family's activities as examples, the traditions of the Jewish Sabbath are introduced. (Rev: BL 9/1/95; SLJ 12/95)

**4974** Nerlove, Miriam. *Hanukkah* (PS–1). Illus. 1989, Whitman paper $4.95 (0-8075-3142-1). 24pp. A brief history and explanation of the customs and activities of Hanukkah in verse. (Rev: BL 7/89; SLJ 9/89)

**4975** Nerlove, Miriam. *Passover* (PS–1). Illus. 1989, Whitman LB $12.95 (0-8075-6360-9). 24pp. A description of this Jewish holy day in rhyming text. (Rev: BL 1/15/90; SLJ 4/90)

**4976** Nerlove, Miriam. *Purim* (PS–1). Illus. 1992, Whitman LB $12.95 (0-8075-6682-9). 24pp. Watercolors and simple text explain the joyful observance of Purim. (Rev: BL 1/1/92; SLJ 9/92)

**4977** Oberman, Sheldon. *By the Hanukkah Light* (1–4). Illus. by Neil Waldman. 1997, Boyds Mills $15.95 (1-56397-658-7). 32pp. As Rachel and her grandfather polish the menorah at Hanukkah, he tells her about the Holocaust and its meaning for the Jewish people. (Rev: BL 9/1/97*; SLJ 10/97)

**4978** Peretz, I. L. *The Magician's Visit: A Passover Tale* (PS–3). Retold by Barbara D. Goldin. Illus. by Robert Andrew Parker. 1993, Viking paper $14.99 (0-670-84840-9). 32pp. A stranger appears at a poor Jewish couple's Passover seder and supplies a feast. (Rev: BCCB 3/93; HB 5–6/93; SLJ 7/93*)

**4979** Portnoy, Mindy A. *Matzah Ball: A Passover Story* (PS–3). Illus. by Katherine J. Kahn. 1994, Kar-Ben paper $6.95 (0-929371-69-0). While attending a baseball game during Passover, Aaron meets an elderly man (Elijah perhaps?) who tells him about Jewish fans going to games at Ebbets Field. (Rev: SLJ 8/94)

**4980** Rael, Elsa O. *When Zaydeh Danced on Eldridge Street* (PS–3). Illus. by Marjorie Priceman. 1997, Simon & Schuster $16.00 (0-689-80451-2). 40pp. Zeesie is taken to the synagogue by her grandfather in this explanation of the religious holiday of Simchas Torah. (Rev: BL 10/1/97; HB 11–12/97; SLJ 10/97)

**4981** Ross, Kathy. *The Jewish Holiday Craft Book* (PS–1). Illus. 1997, Millbrook LB $25.90 (0-7613-0055-4); paper $12.95 (0-7613-0175-5). 96pp. Using simple materials, craft projects, such as making a Yom Kippur doll, celebrate and explain Jewish traditions and holidays. (Rev: BL 3/1/97; SLJ 4/97) [296.4]

**4982** Rothenberg, Joan. *Inside-Out Grandma* (K–3). Illus. 1995, Hyperion LB $15.49 (0-7868-2092-6). 32pp. A circuitous story about the relationship between a grandmother wearing her clothes inside out and making potato pancakes at Hanukkah. (Rev: BCCB 11/95; BL 9/15/95)

**4983** Rouss, Sylvia A. *Sammy Spider's First Passover* (PS–K). Illus. by Katherine J. Kahn. 1995, Kar-Ben paper $5.95 (0-929371-82-8). A pleasant story about a little spider that watches the Shapiro family make preparations for Passover. (Rev: SLJ 7/95)

**4984** Rouss, Sylvia A. *Sammy Spider's First Rosh Hashanah* (PS–1). Illus. by Katherine J. Kahn. 1996, Kar-Ben paper $5.95 (0-929371-99-2). Mother Spider explains to her son Sammy the holiday customs and symbols associated with the Jewish New Year. (Rev: SLJ 5/97)

**4985** Schnur, Steven. *The Tie Man's Miracle: A Chanukah Tale* (K–3). Illus. by Stephen T. Johnson. 1995, Morrow LB $15.93 (0-688-13464-5). 32pp. Seth becomes impatient with the family's guest, old Mr. Hoffman, and wants to get on with the family's Hanukkah celebrations. (Rev: BCCB 12/95; BL 9/1/95*; HB 11–12/95)

**4986** Schotter, Roni. *Passover Magic* (PS–2). Illus. by Marylin Hafner. 1995, Little, Brown $15.95 (0-316-77468-5). 32pp. Diverse family members gather together for the traditional seder at Passover. (Rev: BL 3/1/95; SLJ 4/95)

**4987** Schotter, Roni. *Purim Play* (PS–3). Illus. by Marylin Hafner. 1998, Little, Brown $15.95 (0-316-77518-5). 32pp. In spite of illness, Fannie and her cousins put on the Purim play in which Queen Esther saves the Jewish people from wicked Haman. (Rev: BL 2/1/98; SLJ 4/98)

**4988** Schweiger-Dmi'el, Itzhak. *Hanna's Sabbath Dress* (PS–2). Trans. by Razi Dmi'el, et al. Illus. by Ora Eitan. 1996, Simon & Schuster $15.00 (0-689-80517-9). 30pp. In an act of unselfishness, Hanna helps an old man but ruins her special Sabbath dress. (Rev: BL 10/1/96; SLJ 11/96)

**4989** Silverman, Maida. *My First Book of Jewish Holidays* (K–4). Illus. by Barbara Garrison. 1994, Dial paper $14.89 (0-8037-1428-9). 32pp. Ten Jewish holidays, including Rosh Hashanah, Purim, Passover, and Shavuot, are explained in this well-illustrated book. (Rev: BL 10/1/94; SLJ 9/94) [296.4]

**4990** Simon, Norma. *The Story of Hanukkah* (K–3). Illus. by Leonid Gore. 1997, HarperCollins LB $14.89 (0-06-027420-4). 32pp. Legend and history are delineated in this book on the origins of Hanukkah. (Rev: BL 9/1/97; SLJ 10/97) [296.4]

**4991** Snyder, Carol. *God Must Like Cookies, Too* (PS–1). Illus. by Beth Glick. 1993, Jewish Publication Soc. $16.95 (0-8276-0423-8). 32pp. A young girl attends a Shabbat service at temple and looks forward to the 3 cookies she has been promised after the service. (Rev: BL 1/15/94; SLJ 10/93)

**4992** Topek, Susan Remick. *A Costume for Noah: A Purim Story* (PS–K). Illus. by Sally Springer. 1996, Kar-Ben $13.95 (0-929371-91-7); paper $5.95 (0-929371-90-9). Traditional terms and customs are introduced in this simple story of a boy preparing with his friends to celebrate Purim. (Rev: SLJ 5/96)

**4993** Wax, Wendy, ed. *Hanukkah, Oh, Hanukkah! A Treasury of Stories, Songs, and Games to Share* (PS–3). Illus. by John Speirs. 1993, Bantam $12.95 (0-553-09551-X). 64pp. A sparkling collection of readings and activities centered around Hanukkah and its traditions. (Rev: BL 10/15/93) [394.26]

**4994** Weilerstein, Sadie R. *K'tonton's Yom Kippur Kitten* (K–2). Illus. by Joe Boddy. 1995, Jewish Publication Soc. $12.95 (0-8276-0541-2). 36pp. K'tonton learns the true meaning of Yom Kippur when he tries to blame a kitten for the problems he has created. (Rev: BL 11/15/95; SLJ 3/96)

**4995** Zalben, Jane Breskin. *Beni's First Chanukah* (PS–K). Illus. by author. 1988, Holt $12.95 (0-8050-0479-3). 32pp. Beni Bear's first Hanukkah is filled with happy moments. (Rev: BL 12/15/88)

**4996** Zalben, Jane Breskin. *Happy New Year, Beni* (PS–3). Illus. 1993, Holt $13.95 (0-8050-1961-8). 28pp. A tender picture book showing an extended Jewish family celebrating the New Year. (Rev: BL 7/93)

**4997** Zalben, Jane Breskin. *Leo and Blossom's Sukkah* (PS–1). Illus. 1990, Holt $13.95 (0-8050-1226-5). 32pp. In spite of many problems, all ends well for 2 bears who decide to build their own sukkah. (Rev: BL 9/15/90; SLJ 2/92)

**4998** Zalben, Jane Breskin. *Papa's Latkes* (PS–1). Illus. 1996, Holt $13.95 (0-8050-4634-8). 32pp. When Beni the Bear's mother decides not to make latkes at Hanukkah, the rest of the family tries to prepare them instead. (Rev: BL 9/1/96)

**4999** Ziefert, Harriet. *Eight Days of Hanukkah* (PS–K). Illus. by Melinda Levine. 1997, Viking paper $10.99 (0-670-87326-8). 24pp. The traditions and significance of Hanukkah are explored in this picture book. (Rev: BL 9/15/97; SLJ 10/97)

## THANKSGIVING

**5000** Anderson, Laurie Halse. *Turkey Pox* (PS–2). Illus. by Dorothy Donohue. 1996, Albert Whitman LB $14.95 (0-8075-8127-5). 30pp. Charity's Thanksgiving is almost spoiled when it is discovered that she has chicken pox. (Rev: BCCB 11/96; BL 9/1/96; SLJ 10/96)

**5001** Borden, Louise. *Thanksgiving Is . . .* (1–2). Illus. by Steve Bjorkman. 1997, Scholastic $3.50 (0-590-33128-0). 32pp. In this easy reader, the story of the *Mayflower*, its passengers, and the first Thanksgiving are told in an interesting, fact-filled narrative. (Rev: BL 2/1/98; SLJ 3/98)

**5002** Brown, Marc. *Arthur's Thanksgiving* (K–3). Illus. by author. 1983, Little, Brown paper $5.95 (0-316-11232-1). 32pp. Arthur is made director of his class Thanksgiving play.

**5003** Bunting, Eve. *How Many Days to America? A Thanksgiving Story* (2–4). Illus. by Beth Peck. 1988, Houghton $16.00 (0-89919-521-0); paper $5.95 (0-395-54777-6). 32pp. A family flees oppression on a Caribbean island and heads for the United States. (Rev: BL 11/1/88; SLJ 10/88)

**5004** Bunting, Eve. *A Turkey for Thanksgiving* (PS–1). Illus. by Diane De Groat. 1991, Houghton $13.95 (0-89919-793-0). 32pp. After bringing a live turkey home at Thanksgiving, Mr. and Mrs. Moose decide to have a vegetarian meal. (Rev: BCCB 9/91; BL 10/1/91; SLJ 9/91)

**5005** Child, Lydia M. *Over the River and Through the Wood* (PS–2). Illus. by David Catrow. 1996, Holt $15.95 (0-8050-3825-6). 32pp. At Thanksgiving, a New York City family faces traffic jams on the way to Grandma's house. (Rev: BCCB 11/96; BL 9/1/96; SLJ 10/96)

**5006** Cowley, Joy. *Gracias, the Thanksgiving Turkey* (PS–2). Illus. by Joe Cepeda. 1996, Scholastic $15.95 (0-590-46976-2). 32pp. A New York City boy dreads Thanksgiving, when his pet turkey, Gracias, will be killed. (Rev: BCCB 11/96; BL 9/1/96; SLJ 12/96)

**5007** Cuyler, Margery. *Daisy's Crazy Thanksgiving* (2–4). Illus. by Robin Kramer. 1990, Holt $14.95 (0-8050-0559-5). 32pp. Daisy decides to visit her grandparents at Thanksgiving even though her mother warns her that their house is a "zoo." (Rev: BL 10/1/90; HB 11–12/90)

**5008** Dalgliesh, Alice. *The Thanksgiving Story* (K–3). Illus. by Helen Sewell. 1988, Macmillan $15.00 (0-684-18999-2); paper $5.99 (0-689-71053-4). 32pp. This reissued 1954 Caldecott Honor Book tells of the Hopkins family's experiences from the Mayflower voyage to the first Thanksgiving.

**5009** Grambling, Lois G. *Mrs. Tittle's Turkey Farm* (K–3). Illus. by Ellen Sasaki. 1994, Thomasson-

Grant paper $9.95 (1-56566-054-4). Turkey is able to escape becoming someone's Thanksgiving dinner by catching a would-be thief. (Rev: SLJ 12/94)

**5010** Hoban, Lillian. *Silly Tilly's Thanksgiving Dinner* (K–3). Illus. 1990, HarperCollins LB $15.89 (0-06-022423-1). 64pp. Forgetful Silly Tilly sends out recipe cards instead of invitations for Thanksgiving dinner. (Rev: BL 10/15/90; SLJ 9/90)

**5011** Jackson, Alison. *I Know an Old Lady Who Swallowed a Pie* (PS–2). Illus. by Judith Byron Schachner. 1997, Dutton paper $14.99 (0-525-45645-7). 32pp. This favorite folk song is given a new twist by using foods associated with Thanksgiving. (Rev: BL 9/1/97; SLJ 11/97)

**5012** Kroll, Steven. *Oh, What a Thanksgiving!* (K–2). Illus. by S. D. Schindler. 1988, Scholastic paper $3.95 (0-590-40616-7). 32pp. David imagines himself at Plymouth in 1620. (Rev: BL 9/15/88; SLJ 9/88)

**5013** Nerlove, Miriam. *Thanksgiving* (PS–1). Illus. 1990, Whitman LB $12.95 (0-8075-7818-5). 24pp. Discusses origins and customs of Thanksgiving in verse. (Rev: BL 7/90; SLJ 10/90)

**5014** Pilkey, Dav. *'Twas the Night Before Thanksgiving* (K–2). Illus. 1990, Orchard LB $16.99 (0-531-08505-8). 32pp. In this takeoff on Moore's famous Christmas poem, a busload of schoolchildren try to save some turkeys from becoming Thanksgiving dinner. (Rev: BL 8/90; SLJ 9/90)

**5015** Spinelli, Eileen. *Thanksgiving at the Tappletons'* (K–2). Illus. by Maryann Cocca-Leffler. 1992, HarperCollins LB $15.89 (0-06-020872-4). 32pp. Through a series of accidents, the Tappletons ruin their Thanksgiving dinner. (Rev: BL 10/1/92)

**5016** Stevenson, James. *Fried Feathers for Thanksgiving* (PS–2). Illus. by author. 1986, Greenwillow LB $15.93 (0-688-06676-3). 32pp. Two witches try to trick Emma Witch into making Thanksgiving dinner for them. (Rev: BL 9/15/86; HB 11–12/86; SLJ 9/86)

**5017** Stock, Catherine. *Thanksgiving Treat* (PS–K). Illus. 1990, Macmillan LB $13.00 (0-02-788402-3). 32pp. When a young boy tries to help out at Thanksgiving, he finds he is only in the way. (Rev: BCCB 11/90; BL 10/1/90; SLJ 10/90)

**5018** Tryon, Leslie. *Albert's Thanksgiving* (K–2). Illus. 1994, Atheneum $16.00 (0-689-31865-0). 32pp. Poor Albert the duck seems to be the only one who is working hard to prepare for the PTA Thanksgiving feast. (Rev: BL 8/94; SLJ 10/94)

### VALENTINE'S DAY

**5019** Adams, Adrienne. *The Great Valentine's Day Balloon Race* (K–3). Illus. by author. 1980, Macmillan $14.95 (0-684-16640-2); paper $4.95 (0-689-71847-0). 32pp. Two rabbits plus the Abbot family construct a balloon for a Valentine's Day race.

**5020** Balian, Lorna. *A Sweetheart for Valentine* (K–3). Illus. by author. 1988, Humbug $12.95 (0-687-37109-0). 32pp. An original, highly imaginative explanation of the origins of Valentine's Day.

**5021** Brown, Marc. *Arthur's Valentine* (K–3). Illus. by author. 1980, Little, Brown $15.95 (0-316-11062-0); Avon paper $5.95 (0-316-11187-2). 32pp. Who is sending Arthur valentines?

**5022** Bunting, Eve. *The Valentine Bears* (K–3). Illus. by Jan Brett. 1983, Houghton $14.95 (0-89919-138-X); paper $5.95 (0-89919-313-7). 32pp. Mr. and Mrs. Bear decide not to sleep through Valentine's Day this year.

**5023** Cohen, Miriam. *"Bee My Valentine!"* (1–3). Illus. by Lillian Hoban. 1983, Bantam paper $3.25 (0-440-40507-6). 32pp. George is dismayed when he doesn't receive as many valentines as his friends.

**5024** De Groat, Diane. *Roses Are Pink, Your Feet Really Stink* (PS–3). Illus. 1996, Morrow LB $14.93 (0-688-13605-2). 32pp. A chipmunklike youngster writes mean valentines to the people he dislikes; but in the end, all is forgiven. (Rev: BCCB 2/96; BL 3/1/96; SLJ 4/96)

**5025** Devlin, Wende, and Harry Devlin. *Cranberry Valentine* (PS–1). Illus. 1992, Simon & Schuster paper $5.99 (0-689-71509-9). 40pp. Mr. Whiskers, the town's bearded old salt, is surprised and at first dismayed to discover he's received so many valentines. (Rev: BL 10/15/86; SLJ 1/87)

**5026** Gantos, Jack. *Rotten Ralph's Rotten Romance* (PS–1). Illus. by Nicole Rubel. 1997, Houghton $14.95 (0-395-73978-0). 32pp. Rotten Ralph decides to be completely unlovable on Valentine's Day. (Rev: BL 11/15/96; SLJ 2/97)

**5027** Grambling, Lois G. *Happy Valentine's Day, Miss Hildy!* (2–3). Illus. by Bridget S. Taylor. 1997, Random LB $11.99 (0-679-98870-X); paper $3.99 (0-679-88870-5). 48pp. In this easily read story, Miss Hildy tries to determine who has sent her a gift of 12 pink flamingos for Valentine's Day. (Rev: BL 2/1/98)

**5028** Hoban, Lillian. *Arthur's Great Big Valentine* (1–2). Illus. by author. 1989, HarperCollins LB $15.89 (0-06-022407-X); paper $3.75 (0-06-444149-0). 64pp. Arthur wants to celebrate Valentine's Day, but he's mad at his best friend. (Rev: BL 3/1/89; HB 3–4/89)

**5029** Hoban, Lillian. *Silly Tilly's Valentine* (K–2). Illus. by author. Series: I Can Read Book. 1998, HarperCollins LB $14.89 (0-06-027401-8). 47pp. Tilly the mole is so excited about a snowfall that she forgets it is Valentine's Day. (Rev: SLJ 2/98)

**5030** Lexau, Joan M. *Don't Be My Valentine* (1–3). Illus. by Syd Hoff. 1985, HarperCollins LB $15.89 (0-06-023873-9). 64pp. Sam gets his valentines mixed up: the one that says you belong in a zoo goes to his teacher, and pesty Amy Lou gets the nice one. (Rev: BCCB 12/85; BL 10/15/85; SLJ 12/85)

**5031** Modell, Frank. *One Zillion Valentines* (PS–2). Illus. by author. 1987, Morrow paper $4.95 (0-688-07329-8). 32pp. Milton and Marvin distribute their homemade hearts to the neighborhood.

**5032** Nixon, Joan Lowery. *The Valentine Mystery* (1–3). Illus. by Jim Cummins. 1979, Whitman LB $8.95 (0-8075-8450-9). 32pp. Susan, with the help of her brothers, finds out who has sent her an anonymous valentine.

**5033** Roberts, Bethany. *Valentine Mice!* (PS–K). Illus. by Doug Cushman. 1998, Clarion $13.00 (0-395-77518-3). 32pp. A group of mice are so busy delivering valentines in a snowy forest that they don't realize the smallest one of them is missing. (Rev: BL 12/15/97; SLJ 1/98)

**5034** Schweninger, Ann. *Valentine Friends* (PS–1). Illus. 1988, Puffin paper $4.99 (0-14-050662-4). 32pp. Rabbit buddies Buttercup and Lucy do something special for Valentine's Day. (Rev: BL 2/1/88; SLJ 2/88)

**5035** Sharmat, Marjorie W. *The Best Valentine in the World* (K–3). Illus. by Lilian Obligado. 1982, Holiday LB $15.95 (0-8234-0440-4). 32pp. Ferdinand and Florette Fox celebrate Valentine's Day together.

**5036** Stevenson, James. *A Village Full of Valentines* (1–3). Illus. 1995, Greenwillow LB $15.93 (0-688-13603-6). 40pp. The way that different animals in a village celebrate Valentine's Day is described in a series of humorous short stories. (Rev: BCCB 2/95; BL 12/15/94; HB 3–4/95; SLJ 2/95)

## Books for Beginning Readers

**5037** Adler, David A. *Magic Money* (1–2). Illus. Series: First Stepping Stone Book. 1997, Random LB $11.99 (0-679-94699-3); paper $3.99 (0-679-84699-9). 68pp. The Houdini Club solves a mystery involving a shopping mall in this easy-to-read book. (Rev: BL 8/97)

**5038** Adler, David A. *My Dog and the Birthday Mystery* (1–2). Illus. by Dick Gackenbach. 1987, Holiday paper $5.95 (0-8234-0710-1). 32pp. Jenny and her dog named My Dog get involved in the mystery of the stolen bicycle — which is just a ploy to get Jenny to her surprise party. (Rev: BCCB 5/87; BL 6/1/87)

**5039** Adler, David A. *Wacky Jacks* (1–3). Illus. 1994, Random paper $3.99 (0-679-84696-4). 73pp. Herman Foster, also known as Houdini, is asked to solve the mystery of the missing hamster. (Rev: BL 11/15/94; SLJ 2/95)

**5040** Adler, David A. *Young Cam Jansen and the Dinosaur Game* (1–2). Illus. 1996, Viking paper $11.99 (0-670-86399-8). 32pp. Cam discovers that a boy has cheated in order to win a prize. (Rev: BCCB 5/96; BL 8/96; SLJ 7/96)

**5041** Adler, David A. *Young Cam Jansen and the Lost Tooth* (1–2). Illus. by Susanna Natti. Series: Viking Easy-to-Read. 1997, Viking paper $13.99 (0-670-87354-3). 32pp. Cam uses her photographic memory to locate a lost tooth in this easily read mystery. (Rev: BL 5/1/97; SLJ 7/97)

**5042** Adler, David A. *Young Cam Jansen and the Missing Cookie* (1–2). Illus. 1996, Viking paper $11.99 (0-670-86772-1). 32pp. Jason, Cam's friend, has a cookie stolen from his school lunchbox. (Rev: BL 8/96; SLJ 7/96)

**5043** Ahlberg, Allan. *Dinosaur Dreams* (PS–2). Illus. by Andre Amstutz. Series: Funnybones. 1991, Greenwillow LB $12.88 (0-688-09956-4). 24pp. Three skeletons dream about battling prehistoric animals. (Rev: BL 4/1/91; SLJ 7/91)

**5044** Ahlberg, Allan. *The Ghost Train* (1–2). Illus. by Andre Amstutz. Series: Funnybones. 1992, Morrow paper $3.95 (0-688-11659-0). 32pp. Three skeletons known as the Funnybones take a train ride to a ghost town. (Rev: BL 10/1/92)

**5045** Albee, Sarah. *I Can Do It!* (PS–K). Illus. by Larry DiFiori. Series: Step into Reading, Step 1. 1997, Random LB $11.99 (0-679-98687-1); paper $3.99 (0-679-88687-7). 30pp. A beginning reader featuring the Muppets, with the purpose of building self-confidence in children. (Rev: SLJ 2/98)

**5046** Albert, Shirley. *Doll Party* (1–2). Illus. by Amy Flynn. 1994, Putnam paper $3.99 (0-448-40182-7). 32pp. An easy-to-read book about Becky and her new doll. (Rev: BL 1/1/95)

**5047** Alexander, Sue. *Witch, Goblin, and Ghost Are Back* (1–3). Illus. by Jeanette Winter. 1985, Pantheon LB $9.99 (0-394-96296-6). 62pp. This trio of friends is back in 5 stories centered around Goblin. (Rev: SLJ 12/85)

**5048** Alexander, Sue. *World Famous Muriel and the Magic Mystery* (2–3). Illus. by Marla Frazee. 1990, HarperCollins LB $12.89 (0-690-04789-4). 32pp. Muriel, known for her tightrope walking and incredible smarts, is after a missing magician. (Rev: BL 3/15/90; SLJ 7/90)

**5049** Allen, Laura J. *Rollo and Tweedy and the Ghost at Dougal Castle* (1–2). Illus. Series: I Can Read Books. 1992, HarperCollins LB $14.89 (0-06-

020107-X). 64pp. A mouse detective and his assistant catch the ghost that is haunting a Scottish castle. (Rev: BCCB 9/92*; BL 6/15/92; HB 9–10/92; SLJ 10/92)

**5050** Alphin, Elaine M. *A Bear for Miguel* (1–3). Illus. 1996, HarperCollins LB $14.89 (0-06-024522-0). 64pp. On market day in El Salvador, Maria trades her stuffed bear for goods her family needs. (Rev: BCCB 2/96; BL 8/96; HB 5–6/96; SLJ 6/96)

**5051** Altman, Suzanne. *My Worst Days Diary* (2–3). Illus. by Diane Allison. 1995, Bantam paper $3.99 (0-553-37575-X). 48pp. Gradually, Mo's terrible days turn into good ones in this easy-to-read story. (Rev: BL 10/1/95; SLJ 1/96)

**5052** Anderson, Peggy Perry. *To the Tub* (PS–1). Illus. by author. 1996, Houghton $13.95 (0-395-77614-7). 32pp. In this easily read book, a young frog and his father enjoy a mud bath together. (Rev: SLJ 10/96)

**5053** Antle, Nancy. *Sam's Wild West Show* (1–3). Illus. by Simms Taback. Series: Dial Easy-to-Read. 1995, Dial paper $12.89 (0-8037-1533-1). 40pp. The good guys triumph over the bad guys in this easy-to-read Western adventure. (Rev: BCCB 4/95; BL 4/15/95; SLJ 8/95)

**5054** Armstrong, Jennifer. *Sunshine, Moonshine* (1–2). Illus. by Lucia Washburn. 1997, Random paper $3.99 (0-679-86442-3). 32pp. A busy day in the life of a young boy is chronicled in this easy-to-read book. (Rev: BL 5/1/97; SLJ 8/97)

**5055** Backstein, Karen. *The Blind Men and the Elephant* (1–2). Illus. by Annie Mitra. 1992, Scholastic paper $3.50 (0-590-45813-2). 48pp. The Indian folktale about the blind men who each see the nature of the elephant in a different way. (Rev: BL 3/1/93) [398.2]

**5056** Baker, Alan. *Little Rabbits' First Word Book* (PS). Illus. 1996, Kingfisher $9.95 (0-7534-5020-8). 40pp. For beginning readers, basic words are given for everyday objects. (Rev: BL 11/1/96) [428.1]

**5057** Baker, Barbara. *Digby and Kate and the Beautiful Day* (1–2). Illus. by Marsha Winborn. Series: Dutton Easy Reader. 1998, Dutton $13.99 (0-525-45855-7). 48pp. In this easy reader, dog Digby and cat Kate find that, like all true friends, they sometimes have their differences. (Rev: BL 2/1/98; SLJ 3/98*)

**5058** Baker, Barbara. *N-O Spells No!* (1–3). Illus. by Nola L. Malone. 1993, Scholastic paper $3.50 (0-590-44186-8). 64pp. In this book illustrated with cartoons, there are 5 short stories about Annie and her big brother. (Rev: BL 6/1/91; SLJ 8/91)

**5059** Baker, Barbara. *One Saturday Morning* (1–3). Illus. by Kate Duke. 1994, Dutton paper $12.99 (0-525-45262-1). 48pp. The Bear family has a busy Sat-

urday together in this easily read book. (Rev: BL 1/1/95; SLJ 11/94*)

**5060** Bauer, Marion Dane. *Alison's Wings* (1–2). Illus. 1996, Hyperion $13.95 (0-7868-0105-0); paper $3.95 (0-7868-1121-8). 48pp. Alison longs to grow wings and fly, and in her dreams she does. (Rev: BL 4/1/96; SLJ 8/96)

**5061** Bauer, Marion Dane. *Turtle Dreams* (1–2). Illus. by Diane D. Hearn. Series: Holiday House Reader. 1997, Holiday LB $14.95 (0-8234-1322-5). 48pp. In this easy reader, Turtle goes to sleep for the winter and finds that he has wonderful dreams. (Rev: BL 2/1/98; SLJ 1/98)

**5062** Benchley, Nathaniel. *A Ghost Named Fred* (1–3). Illus. by Ben Shecter. 1968, HarperCollins LB $14.89 (0-06-020474-5). 64pp. To get out of the rain, George enters an empty house and meets Fred, an absentminded ghost.

**5063** Benchley, Nathaniel. *Oscar Otter* (K–2). Illus. by Arnold Lobel. 1966, HarperCollins LB $14.89 (0-06-020472-9); paper $3.75 (0-06-444025-7). 64pp. Hilarious words and pictures describe Oscar's fun on the long and perilous slide he builds to get to his pool.

**5064** Benchley, Nathaniel. *Red Fox and His Canoe* (1–2). Illus. by Arnold Lobel. 1964, HarperCollins LB $15.89 (0-06-020476-1); paper $3.75 (0-06-444075-3). 64pp. Red Fox gets himself a large canoe and picks up so many unusual passengers that it capsizes. Also from the same author and publisher: *The Strange Disappearance of Arthur Cluck* (1967).

**5065** Berenstain, Stan, and Jan Berenstain. *Bears in the Night* (1–2). Illus. by authors. 1971, Random LB $11.99 (0-394-92286-7). Bear cubs go on a rampage after being put to bed. The lively cartoon style and simple phrases make this a good book for beginning readers. Also from the same authors and publisher: *Bears on Wheels* (1969).

**5066** Birnbaum, Bette. *My School, Your School* (1–3). Illus. Series: Ready-Set-Read. 1990, Raintree Steck-Vaughn LB $21.40 (0-8172-3583-3). 24pp. Common classroom activities are pictured and introduced. (Rev: BL 9/15/90)

**5067** Blocksma, Mary. *Yoo Hoo, Moon!* (1–3). Illus. by Patience Brewster. Series: Bank Street Ready-to-Read. 1992, Bantam paper $3.99 (0-553-35212-1). 32pp. Bear can't sleep because there is no moon visible. (Rev: BL 4/1/92; SLJ 3/92)

**5068** Boegehold, Betty. *A Horse Called Starfire* (2–4). Illus. by Neil Waldman. 1990, Bantam paper $3.99 (0-553-34853-1). 48pp. This historical novel tells how a horse is adopted by an Indian family after he wanders away from Spanish explorers. (Rev: BCCB 9/90; BL 6/1/90)

**5069** Boland, Janice. *A Dog Named Sam* (1–3). Illus. 1996, Dial paper $12.99 (0-8037-1530-7). 40pp. Three easily read stories focus on the antics of a mischievous dog. (Rev: BL 4/1/96; SLJ 4/96)

**5070** Bonsall, Crosby. *The Case of the Scaredy Cats* (1–2). Illus. by author. 1971, HarperCollins LB $15.89 (0-06-020566-0); paper $3.75 (0-06-444047-8). 64pp. What do you do when you find a bevy of girls in your secret clubhouse? Four other mysteries by the same author and publisher are: *The Case of the Hungry Stranger* (1963); *The Case of the Cat's Meow* (1965); *The Case of the Dumb Bells* (1966); *The Case of the Double Cross* (1980).

**5071** Bonsall, Crosby. *Mine's the Best* (1–2). Illus. by author. 1997, HarperCollins paper $3.75 (0-064-44213-6). 32pp. Two small boys discover they have identical balloons, and then begins the argument — whose is the best?

**5072** Bonsall, Crosby. *Piggle* (1–2). Illus. by author. 1973, HarperCollins LB $14.89 (0-06-020580-6). 64pp. Homer goes in search of someone to play games with and finds Bear, who enjoys "Piggle" with him. This rhyming spree of nonsense words will please beginning readers.

**5073** Bonsall, Crosby. *Tell Me Some More* (1–3). Illus. by Fritz Siebel. 1961, HarperCollins $14.89 (0-06-020601-2). 64pp. Andrew introduces his friend to the magic of the library.

**5074** Bonsall, Crosby. *What Spot?* (1–2). Illus. by author. 1963, HarperCollins LB $15.89 (0-06-020611-X). 64pp. Puffin says there is nothing in the snow, but walrus thinks otherwise.

**5075** Bonsall, Crosby. *Who's a Pest?* (1–3). Illus. by author. 1962, HarperCollins LB $14.89 (0-06-020621-7); paper $3.75 (0-06-444099-0). 64pp. Even though his 4 sisters, a lizard, a rabbit, and a chipmunk insist that he's a pest, Homer refuses to believe it.

**5076** Bonsall, Crosby. *Who's Afraid of the Dark?* (1–3). Illus. by author. 1980, HarperCollins LB $14.89 (0-06-020599-7); paper $3.75 (0-06-444071-0). 32pp. A little boy talks about how Stella, his dog, is afraid of the dark.

**5077** Bottner, Barbara. *Bootsie Barker Ballerina* (1–2). Illus. by G. Brian Karas. 1997, HarperCollins LB $14.89 (0-06-027101-9). 40pp. Bootsie Barker gets her comeuppance when she tries to bully everyone in her ballet class, including the teacher. (Rev: BL 5/1/97; SLJ 6/97)

**5078** Brenner, Barbara. *Beavers Beware!* (1–3). Illus. by Emily Arnold McCully. Series: Bank Street Ready-to-Read. 1992, Gareth Stevens $18.60 (0-8368-1769-9); Bantam paper $3.99 (0-553-35386-1). 32pp. A family who lives by a river discovers that beavers are constructing a lodge using their dock as a platform. (Rev: BL 4/1/92; SLJ 3/92)

**5079** Brenner, Barbara. *The Color Wizard* (1–3). Illus. by Leo Dillon and Diane Dillon. 1989, Bantam paper $3.99 (0-553-34690-3). 32pp. Wizard Gray forms a number of new colors from red, blue, and yellow. Also use: *Annie's Pet* (1989). (Rev: BL 9/15/89; SLJ 11/89)

**5080** Brenner, Barbara. *Moon Boy* (1–2). Illus. by J. Gaban. 1990, Bantam paper $3.99 (0-553-34851-5). 32pp. A young boy is surprised when a moonbeam turns into a tiny boy. (Rev: BL 6/1/90)

**5081** Brenner, Barbara. *Wagon Wheels* (1–3). Illus. by Don Bolognese. 1993, HarperCollins LB $14.89 (0-06-020669-1); paper $3.75 (0-06-444052-4). 64pp. The adventures of an African American family in Kansas in the 1870s.

**5082** Brill, Marlene T. *Allen Jay and the Underground Railroad* (1–2). Illus. by Janice L. Porter. Series: On My Own. 1993, Carolrhoda LB $18.60 (0-87614-776-7); paper $5.95 (0-87614-605-1). 48pp. This story, which is based on fact, tells how a young Quaker child helped a slave to freedom. (Rev: BL 7/93; SLJ 8/93)

**5083** Brisson, Pat. *Hot Fudge Hero* (1–3). Illus. by Diana C. Bluthenthal. 1997, Holt $14.95 (0-8050-4551-1). 73pp. A simple chapter book about the adventures of Bertie, a likable second-grade kid, who always gets a hot fudge sundae when he succeeds in his endeavors. (Rev: BCCB 6/97; BL 4/1/97; HB 7–8/97; SLJ 7/97)

**5084** Brown, Laurie Krasny. *Rex and Lilly Family Time* (1). Illus. by Marc Brown. Series: Dino Easy Reader. 1995, Little, Brown LB $12.95 (0-316-11385-9). 32pp. Dinosaur Lilly and brother Rex make a mess of their mother's birthday in this easy-to-read book. Also use *Rex and Lilly Playtime* (1995). (Rev: BL 4/15/95; SLJ 8/95)

**5085** Brown, Laurie Krasny. *Rex and Lilly Schooltime* (1–2). Illus. by Marc Brown. 1997, Little, Brown $12.95 (0-316-10920-7). 32pp. In this easy reader, dino Rex goes to school and participates in a show-and-tell exercise. (Rev: BL 5/1/97)

**5086** Brown, Marc. *There's No Place Like Home* (1–3). Illus. Series: Step into Reading. 1991, Parents $5.95 (0-8193-1125-1). 40pp. In this easy reader, various kinds of homes are introduced in verse. (Rev: BL 12/1/91)

**5087** Buck, Nola. *Sid and Sam* (PS–K). Illus. Series: My First I Can Read Book. 1996, HarperCollins LB $12.89 (0-06-025372-X). 32pp. Sid's song is so long that his friend Sam says, "So long." (Rev: BCCB 7–8/96; BL 8/96; SLJ 6/96)

**5088** Bulla, Clyde Robert. *Daniel's Duck* (1–3). Illus. by Joan Sandin. 1979, HarperCollins LB

$14.89 (0-06-020909-7); paper $3.75 (0-06-444031-1). 64pp. In this story for beginning readers, a young boy is hurt when people make fun of his wood carving of a duck.

**5089** Bulla, Clyde Robert. *Singing Sam* (2–3). Illus. by Susan Magurn. 1989, Random LB $11.99 (0-394-91977-7); paper $3.99 (0-394-81977-2). 48pp. Amy takes in Sam, a dog, when his owner, spoiled Rob, decides he wants a pony instead. (Rev: BL 6/1/89)

**5090** Buller, Jon, and Susan Schade. *Felix and the 400 Frogs* (2–3). Illus. 1996, Random LB $11.99 (0-679-96745-1); paper $3.99 (0-679-86745-7). 48pp. Felix helps a frog recapture a magic stone from a neighbor's yard. (Rev: BCCB 4/96; BL 9/15/96)

**5091** Buss, Nancy. *The Lobster and Ivy Higgins* (2–4). Illus. by Kim Mulkey. 1992, Boyds Mills $13.95 (1-56397-011-2). 54pp. Shy Ivy and a classmate scheme to save Captain Nemo, the 27-pound lobster at her father's fish market. (Rev: BL 7/92; SLJ 5/92)

**5092** Byars, Betsy. *Ant Plays Bear* (1–3). Illus. by Marc Simont. 1997, Viking paper $11.99 (0-670-86776-4). 32pp. An easy-to-read book that explores in 4 stories the relationship between a boy and his younger brother, Ant. (Rev: BL 9/1/97*; HB 7–8/97; SLJ 6/97)

**5093** Byars, Betsy. *The Golly Sisters Ride Again* (1–3). Illus. by Sue Truesdell. 1994, HarperCollins LB $14.89 (0-06-021564-X). 64pp. Easily read stories about the Golly sisters, who run a traveling show in the old West. (Rev: BCCB 6/94; BL 4/1/94; HB 7–8/94; SLJ 6/94*)

**5094** Byars, Betsy. *Hooray for the Golly Sisters!* (1–3). Illus. by Sue Truesdell. 1990, HarperCollins LB $15.89 (0-06-020899-6). 64pp. Five funny stories about the 2 fearless pioneer sisters and their adventures. (Rev: BCCB 10/90; BL 9/15/90; HB 1–2/91; SLJ 9/90*)

**5095** Byars, Betsy. *The Joy Boys* (1–3). Illus. by Frank Remkiewicz. Series: Yearling First Choice Chapter Books. 1996, Dell $13.95 (0-385-32164-3); paper $3.99 (0-440-41094-0). 48pp. Four brief, enjoyable adventures involving the Joy Boys, 2 brothers growing up with their dog, Bono, on a modern ranch. (Rev: BCCB 6/96; SLJ 6/96)

**5096** Byars, Betsy. *My Brother, Ant* (1–3). Illus. by Marc Simont. 1996, Viking paper $11.99 (0-670-86664-4). 32pp. A charming, amusing, easy chapter book in which a boy details some of the antics of his younger brother, Anthony — Ant, for short. (Rev: BL 1/1–15/96*; HB 7–8/96; SLJ 4/96)

**5097** Calmenson, Stephanie. *Marigold and Grandma on the Town* (1–2). Illus. by Mary Chalmers. Series: I Can Read. 1994, HarperCollins LB $14.89 (0-06-020813-9). 64pp. Marigold, a bunny, learns to make the wind her friend in this gentle, easy-to-read book. (Rev: BCCB 3/94; BL 2/1/94; HB 3–4/94; SLJ 4/94)

**5098** Calmenson, Stephanie. *My Dog's the Best!* (1–2). Illus. by Marcy Ramsey. 1997, Scholastic $3.50 (0-590-33072-1). 32pp. An easy-to-read book in which a number of children tell why they think their dog is best. (Rev: BL 2/1/98)

**5099** Calmenson, Stephanie. *Roller Skates!* (1–2). Illus. by True Kelley. 1992, Scholastic paper $3.50 (0-590-45716-0). 32pp. A young boy accidentally receives a shipment of 52 pairs of roller skates, so he decides to have a sale. (Rev: BL 3/1/93)

**5100** Cameron, Ann. *Julian's Glorious Summer* (2–3). Illus. by Dora Leder. 1987, Random LB $11.99 (0-394-99117-6); paper $3.99 (0-394-89117-1). 64pp. Troubles begin for Julian when he lies because he is afraid to ride a bike. Also use 2 other stories about the ups and downs of this warm African American family: *More Stories Julian Tells* (Knopf 1986); *Julian, Secret Agent* (Random 1988). (Rev: BCCB 12/87; BL 12/15/87; SLJ 12/87)

**5101** Capucilli, Alyssa Satin. *Biscuit* (K–1). Illus. 1996, HarperCollins LB $12.89 (0-06-026198-6). 32pp. A dog named Biscuit tries to make his wants known. (Rev: BL 8/96; SLJ 7/96)

**5102** Capucilli, Alyssa Satin. *Biscuit Finds a Friend* (1–2). Illus. by Pat Schories. 1997, HarperCollins LB $12.89 (0-06-027413-1). 24pp. In this easy reader, a puppy named Biscuit finds a lost baby duckling. (Rev: BL 5/1/97; SLJ 6/97)

**5103** Carle, Eric. *My Very First Book of Words* (PS–1). Illus. by author. 1985, HarperCollins $2.95 (0-690-57368-5). 10pp. A nicely illustrated beginning word book, printed on heavy stock cards.

**5104** Christian, Mary Blount. *The Toady and Dr. Miracle* (1–4). Illus. by Christine Jenny. Series: Ready-to-Read; Level 2. 1997, Simon & Schuster $15.00 (0-689-80890-9); paper $3.99 (0-689-80891-7). 40pp. A beginning reader in which Luther is able to trick Dr. Miracle, a phony medicine man. (Rev: SLJ 9/97)

**5105** Christopher, Matt. *The Lucky Baseball Bat* (3–4). Illus. by Dee deRosa. Series: Springboard Books. 1991, Little, Brown $13.95 (0-316-14073-2). 64pp. Martin loses confidence in his game when his favorite baseball bat breaks. Also use: *Centerfield Ballhawk* (1992). (Rev: BL 6/1/91; SLJ 7/91)

**5106** Cleary, Beverly. *Muggie Maggie* (2–3). Illus. by Kay Life. 1990, Morrow LB $15.93 (0-688-08554-7); Avon paper $4.50 (0-380-71087-0). 80pp. Third-grader Maggie decides that learning to write is not necessary for a girl who can use a computer. (Rev: BCCB 6/90; BL 3/15/90; HB 11–12/90; SLJ 6/90)

**5107** Clifford, Eth. *Flatfoot Fox and the Case of the Missing Schoolhouse* (2–3). Illus. by Brian Lies. 1997, Houghton $13.95 (0-395-81446-4). 48pp. An easy read in which Flatfoot Fox and sidekick Secretary Bird foil the schemes of Wacky Weasel. (Rev: BL 3/15/97; SLJ 4/97)

**5108** Clifford, Eth. *Flatfoot Fox and the Case of the Nosy Otter* (2–4). Illus. by Brian Lies. 1992, Houghton $13.95 (0-395-60289-0). 32pp. Flatfoot Fox is hot on the trail of Nosy, Mrs. Chatterbox Otter's missing son. Also use: *Flatfoot Fox and the Case of the Missing Eye* (1991). (Rev: BCCB 11/92; BL 9/1/92; SLJ 9/92)

**5109** Cobb, Annie. *Wheels!* (PS–K). Illus. Series: Early Step into Reading. 1996, Random LB $11.99 (0-679-96445-2); paper $3.99 (0-679-86445-8). 32pp. All sorts of wheels are shown in this beginning reader. (Rev: BL 8/96; SLJ 7/96)

**5110** Cocca-Leffler, Maryann. *Ice-Cold Birthday* (K–1). Illus. Series: All-Aboard Reading. 1992, Putnam paper $3.95 (0-448-40380-3). 32pp. A young girl has a delightful birthday in spite of a power blackout. (Rev: BL 10/1/92; SLJ 9/92)

**5111** Coerr, Eleanor. *The Big Balloon Race* (1–3). Illus. by Carolyn Croll. 1992, HarperCollins LB $14.89 (0-06-021353-1); paper $3.75 (0-06-444053-2). 64pp. Arill and her mother fly their balloon in a suspenseful race.

**5112** Coerr, Eleanor. *Buffalo Bill and the Pony Express* (2–4). Illus. by Don Bolognese. 1995, HarperCollins LB $14.89 (0-06-023373-7). 64pp. Billy outsmarts some Indians and scares off a pack of wolves in this easily read adventure. (Rev: BCCB 4/95; BL 4/15/95; HB 7–8/95; SLJ 5/95)

**5113** Coerr, Eleanor. *Chang's Paper Pony* (1–3). Illus. by author. 1988, HarperCollins LB $15.89 (0-06-021329-9); paper $3.75 (0-06-444163-6). 64pp. A young Chinese boy longs for a pony in the California Gold Rush days. (Rev: BL 7/88; SLJ 12/88)

**5114** Coerr, Eleanor. *The Josefina Story Quilt* (1–3). Illus. by Bruce Degen. 1986, HarperCollins LB $14.89 (0-06-021349-3); paper $3.75 (0-06-444129-6). 64pp. Faith's sorrow at the death of her pet hen during their trip west to California is softened by the quilt she sews in remembrance. (Rev: BCCB 5/86; BL 3/15/86; SLJ 5/86)

**5115** Cohen, Caron L. *How Many Fish?* (1–2). Illus. by S. D. Schindler. Series: My First I Can Read Book. 1998, HarperCollins $12.95 (0-06-027713-0). 32pp. A fish is trapped under a child's upside-down pail, but later it is freed in this easy-to-read adventure. (Rev: BL 2/1/98; SLJ 2/98)

**5116** Cohen, Miriam. *When Will I Read?* (1–2). Illus. by Lillian Hoban. 1977, Greenwillow LB $16.93 (0-688-84073-6); Bantam paper $3.25 (0-440-49333-1). 32pp. Jim, a first grader, experiences the joys of learning to read.

**5117** Cole, Joanna. *Bully Trouble* (1–3). Illus. by Marylin Hafner. 1989, Random LB $9.99 (0-394-94949-8); paper $3.99 (0-394-84949-3). 48pp. Two friends concoct a plan to get even with a bully. (Rev: BL 2/1/90; SLJ 2/90)

**5118** Cole, Joanna. *The Missing Tooth* (1–3). Illus. by Marylin Hafner. 1989, Random LB $7.99 (0-394-99279-2); paper $3.99 (0-394-89279-8). 48pp. Arlo is upset when best friend Robby loses a second tooth and he doesn't. (Rev: BL 3/1/89; SLJ 5/89)

**5119** Cole, Joanna. *Norma Jean, Jumping Bean* (1–3). Illus. 1987, Random LB $9.99 (0-394-98668-7); paper $3.99 (0-394-88668-2). 48pp. Norma Jean, a kangaroo child, stops jumping when her feelings are ruffled, until field day at school. (Rev: BCCB 6/87; BL 6/1/87; SLJ 6–7/87)

**5120** Cole, Joanna, and Stephanie Calmenson, eds. *Ready . . . Set . . . Read! The Beginning Reader's Treasury* (K–2). Illus. 1990, Doubleday $17.95 (0-385-41416-1). 144pp. This is an easily read collection of stories by such writers as Dr. Seuss and Maurice Sendak. (Rev: BL 12/1/90; SLJ 9/90*)

**5121** Coxe, Molly. *Big Egg* (1–2). Illus. 1997, Random LB $11.99 (0-679-98126-8); paper $3.99 (0-679-88126-3). 32pp. For the beginning reader, this story tells what happens after Hen finds a huge egg among her little ones. (Rev: BL 5/1/97)

**5122** Coxe, Molly. *R Is for Radish!* (1–2). Illus. 1997, Random LB $11.99 (0-679-98574-3); paper $3.99 (0-679-88574-9). 48pp. Three easily read stories about Radish Rabbit, who finds it is easy to remember spelling words if you invent a rap routine about them while you study. (Rev: BL 2/1/98)

**5123** Cristaldi, Kathryn. *Baseball Ballerina* (1–3). Illus. by Abby Carter. Series: Step into Reading. 1992, Random paper $3.99 (0-679-81734-4). 48pp. A young girl who loves baseball is afraid that her friends will find out she is taking ballet lessons. (Rev: BCCB 6/92; BL 6/1/92; SLJ 9/92)

**5124** Cristaldi, Kathryn. *Princess Lulu Goes to Camp* (1–2). Illus. by Heather H. Maione. 1997, Putnam paper $3.95 (0-448-41125-3). 48pp. An easy reader about the obnoxious Princess Lulu at a summer camp. (Rev: BL 8/97; SLJ 12/97)

**5125** Croll, Carolyn. *Too Many Babas* (PS–3). Illus. Series: I Can Read. 1994, HarperCollins LB $14.89 (0-06-021384-1). 64pp. Too many cooks spoil the broth in this easy-to-read book with a Russian setting. (Rev: BL 2/1/94)

**5126** Cushman, Doug. *Aunt Eater Loves a Mystery* (1–2). Illus. by author. 1987, HarperCollins LB $15.89 (0-06-021327-2); paper $3.75 (0-06-444126-1). 64pp. Grandmotherly Aunt Eater, an anteater, loves to solve mysteries. (Rev: BL 10/1/87; SLJ 12/87)

**5127** Cushman, Doug. *Aunt Eater's Mystery Vacation* (1–2). Illus. 1992, HarperCollins LB $15.89 (0-06-020514-8). 64pp. Amateur detective Aunt Eater finds mystery and adventure on what was promised to be a relaxing cruise. (Rev: BL 4/1/92; SLJ 6/92)

**5128** Delton, Judy. *Cookies and Crutches* (1–2). Illus. by Alan Tiegreen. 1988, Dell paper $3.99 (0-440-40010-4). 80pp. Molly and her friends find out that baking at home isn't quite as easy as it looks. (Rev: BL 6/1/88)

**5129** dePaola, Tomie. *Kit and Kat* (1–2). Illus. 1994, Putnam paper $3.99 (0-448-40748-5). 32pp. Three easily read stories about the everyday adventures of Kit and Kat, the Kitten Kids. (Rev: BL 1/1/95)

**5130** Dobkin, Bonnie. *Everybody Says* (1–2). Illus. by Keith Neely. 1993, Children's LB $17.00 (0-516-02019-6). 32pp. In this easy-to-read book, a young boy's opinions differ from those of everyone else. (Rev: BL 12/1/93)

**5131** Dodd, Lynley. *Slinky Malinki* (2–3). Illus. 1991, Stevens LB $19.93 (0-8368-0197-0). 32pp. By day, Slinky Malinki is perfectly behaved, but at night she becomes a thief. (Rev: BL 4/1/91; SLJ 7/91)

**5132** Dodds, Siobhan. *Words and Pictures* (PS–1). Illus. 1992, Candlewick $14.95 (1-56402-042-8). 32pp. This "first picture book dictionary" offers 12 well-known childhood experiences, explained in simple sentences. (Rev: BL 7/92; SLJ 8/92)

**5133** Donnelly, Judy. *The Titanic: Lost . . . and Found* (2–4). Illus. by Keith Kohler. 1987, Random LB $11.99 (0-394-98669-5); paper $3.99 (0-394-88669-0). 48pp. In a simple account the author describes the sinking of the *Titanic* and its rediscovery. (Rev: BCCB 6/87; BL 6/1/87; SLJ 6–7/87)

**5134** Donnelly, Judy. *Tut's Mummy: Lost . . . and Found* (2–3). Illus. by James Watling. 1988, Random LB $7.99 (0-394-99189-3); paper $3.99 (0-394-89189-9). 48pp. The story of the 20th-century discovery of King Tut's tomb. (Rev: BL 10/1/88; SLJ 10/88)

**5135** Dragonwagon, Crescent. *Annie Flies the Birthday Bike* (K–3). Illus. by Emily Arnold McCully. 1993, Macmillan $14.95 (0-02-733155-5). 32pp. Annie finally learns to ride her birthday present, a 2-wheel bike. (Rev: BL 3/1/93; SLJ 7/93)

**5136** Driscoll, Laura. *The Bravest Cat! The True Story of Scarlett* (K–2). Illus. by DyAnne DiSalvo-Ryan. Series: All Aboard Reading, Level 1. 1997, Grosset LB $13.89 (0-448-41720-0); paper $3.95 (0-448-41703-0). 32pp. Based on a true story, this easy reader tells how a mother cat saved her kittens from a fire in an old garage in 1996. (Rev: SLJ 2/98)

**5137** Dubowski, Cathy E. *Pirate School* (1–3). Illus. by Mark Dubowski. Series: All Aboard Reading. 1996, Grosset paper $3.95 (0-448-41132-6). 48pp. An easy-to-read adventure about a boy who attends pirate school. (Rev: SLJ 4/97)

**5138** Dubowski, Cathy E., and Mark Dubowski. *Snug Bug* (PS–1). Illus. 1995, Putnam paper $3.95 (0-448-40849-X). 32pp. An easily read book about a little bug that prepares for bed. (Rev: BL 7/95)

**5139** Duffey, Betsy. *How to Be Cool in the Third Grade* (1–3). Illus. by Janet Wilson. 1993, Viking paper $12.99 (0-670-84798-4). 80pp. Robbie wants to be a "cool dude" at school, but circumstances — including a run-in with the class bully — thwart his plans. (Rev: BCCB 10/93; BL 9/1/93; SLJ 9/93)

**5140** Eastman, P. D. *Are You My Mother?* (1–3). Illus. by author. 1960, Random LB $11.99 (0-394-90018-9). 64pp. A bird falls from the nest and looks for its mother.

**5141** Eastman, Patricia. *Sometimes Things Change* (K–1). Illus. by Seymour Fleishman. 1983, Children's LB $17.00 (0-516-02044-7); paper $4.95 (0-516-42044-5). 32pp. A story of how things in nature change.

**5142** Edwards, Roberta. *Five Silly Fishermen* (K–2). Illus. by Sylvie Wickstrom. 1989, Random LB $11.99 (0-679-90092-6); paper $3.99 (0-679-80092-1). 48pp. A simple version of the folktale about 5 fishermen who mistakenly believe one of them is missing. (Rev: BL 2/1/90; SLJ 4/90)

**5143** Ehrlich, Amy. *Leo, Zack, and Emmie* (1–3). Illus. by Steven Kellogg. 1997, Puffin paper $3.99 (0-140-36199-5). 64pp. An easily read story of the friendship shared by 3 people.

**5144** Ehrlich, Amy. *Leo, Zack, and Emmie Together Again* (1–2). Illus. by Steven Kellogg. 1990, Dial paper $3.95 (0-8037-0837-8). 64pp. Leo, Zack, and Emmie enjoy adventures in the second grade. (Rev: BL 10/1/87; SLJ 10/87)

**5145** Ehrlich, Fred. *A Class Play with Ms. Vanilla* (1–2). Illus. by Martha Gradisher. 1992, Puffin paper $3.50 (0-140-54580-8). 32pp. Primary graders put on their version of Red Riding Hood. (Rev: BL 12/1/92)

**5146** Elste, Joan. *True Blue* (2–3). Illus. by DyAnne DiSalvo-Ryan. 1996, Putnam paper $3.95 (0-448-41264-0). 48pp. J.D. worries when his faithful dog Blue disappears. (Rev: BL 11/15/96)

**5147** Etra, Jonathan, and Stephanie Spinner. *Aliens for Lunch* (2–4). Illus. by Steve Bjorkman. 1991, Random LB $6.99 (0-679-91056-5); paper $3.99 (0-679-81056-0). 39pp. Richard and Henry are called upon to help stop an evil planet's scheme to steal the dessert resources of the earth. (Rev: BL 6/1/91)

**5148** Farley, Walter. *Little Black, a Pony* (1–3). Illus. by James Schucker. 1961, Random LB $11.99 (0-394-90021-9). 62pp. The story of a boy and a pony who wishes it were big.

**5149** Feder, Paula K. *Where Does the Teacher Live?* (1–2). Illus. by Lillian Hoban. 1996, Viking paper $3.99 (0-14-038119-8). 48pp. Three young people try to find out where their teacher lives.

**5150** Fehlner, Paul. *Dog and Cat* (K–1). Illus. by Maxie Chambliss. Series: My First Reader. 1990, Children's LB $16.00 (0-516-05353-1). 30pp. Both dog and cat are becoming too old to chase each other as they used to. (Rev: BL 2/1/91; SLJ 10/90)

**5151** Galbraith, Kathryn O. *Roommates* (2–3). Illus. by Mark Graham. 1990, Macmillan LB $14.00 (0-689-50487-X). 48pp. Mimi and Beth must share a room because the new baby is coming, and they're not happy. A sequel is: *Roommates and Rachel* (1991). (Rev: BL 3/1/90; SLJ 3/90)

**5152** Giff, Patricia Reilly. *The Beast in Ms. Rooney's Room* (2–4). Illus. by Blanche Sims. 1984, Dell paper $3.99 (0-440-40485-1). 80pp. A volume in the Kids of the Polk Street School series. Another title is: *Fish Face* (1984).

**5153** Giff, Patricia Reilly. *Garbage Juice for Breakfast* (2–3). Illus. by Blanche Sims. 1989, Bantam paper $3.99 (0-440-40207-7). 156pp. Dawn hopes to beat her rival at finding the hidden treasure at summer camp. (Rev: BL 12/15/89)

**5154** Giff, Patricia Reilly. *Good Luck, Ronald Morgan!* (K–2). Illus. by Susanna Natti. 1996, Viking paper $13.99 (0-670-86303-3). 26pp. Ronald, who has just gotten a new dog, wonders if he can get along with his neighbor, who has a cat. (Rev: BCCB 10/96; SLJ 9/96)

**5155** Giff, Patricia Reilly. *In the Dinosaur's Paw* (2–4). Illus. by Blanche Sims. 1985, Dell paper $3.99 (0-440-44150-1). 80pp. The Polk Street School kids in the month of February. Also use: *The Candy Corn Contest* (1984); *December Secrets* (1984); *The Valentine Star* (1985); *All about Stacy* (1988). (Rev: BL 4/15/85)

**5156** Giff, Patricia Reilly. *The Powder Puff Puzzle* (1–2). Illus. by Blanche Sims. 1987, Dell paper $3.50 (0-440-47180-X). The class detective follows clues to find her missing cat. Also use: *The Riddle of the Red Purse; The Secret at the Polk Street School* (both 1987). (Rev: BL 4/1/88)

**5157** Giff, Patricia Reilly. *Purple Climbing Days* (1–3). Illus. by Blanche Sims. 1985, Bantam paper $3.99 (0-440-47309-8). 80pp. Richard "Beast" Best of the Polk Street School is afraid to climb the floor-to-ceiling rope in gym. Two others in this series are: *Lazy Lions, Lucky Lambs; Snaggle Doodles* (both 1985). (Rev: BL 8/85; SLJ 11/85)

**5158** Giff, Patricia Reilly. *Say Hola, Sarah* (1–3). Illus. by DyAnne DiSalvo-Ryan. Series: Friends and Amigos. 1995, Dell paper $3.50 (0-440-41077-0). 67pp. Sarah must work with pesky Benjamin on a school report while she is studying Spanish with her friend Anna in this charming school story. (Rev: SLJ 3/96)

**5159** Giff, Patricia Reilly. *Sunny-Side Up* (1–3). Illus. by Blanche Sims. 1986, Dell paper $3.99 (0-440-48406-5). 74pp. The Polk Street School kids are in summer school and have to deal with Matthew's announcement that he is moving away. Another in this series is: *Spectacular Stone Soup* (1989). (Rev: BL 10/1/86; SLJ 3/87)

**5160** Greene, Carol. *Hi, Clouds* (K–2). Illus. by Gene Sharp. 1983, Children's LB $16.00 (0-516-02036-6); paper $4.95 (0-516-42036-4). 32pp. Two children see many objects in clouds in this easy-to-read book. Two others in this series are: *Ice Is . . . Whee!; Shine, Sun!* (both 1983).

**5161** Greer, Gery, and Bob Ruddick. *Billy the Ghost and Me* (2–4). Illus. by Roger Roth. Series: I Can Read Chapter Book. 1997, HarperCollins LB $14.89 (0-06-026783-6). 48pp. Sarah and friend Billy the Ghost capture a gang of bank robbers. (Rev: BL 11/15/96; SLJ 3/97)

**5162** Griffith, Helen V. *Alex and the Cat* (2–3). Illus. 1997, Greenwillow $15.00 (0-688-15241-4). 56pp. Contains 7 charming short stories about the adventures of Alex the dog and his cat friend. (Rev: BL 10/15/97; SLJ 10/97)

**5163** Grimes, Nikki. *Wild, Wild Hair* (1–2). Illus. by George Ford. Series: Hello Reader! 1997, Scholastic $3.50 (0-590-26590-3). A young African American girl dreads Monday, when her hair is braided, in this easy-to-read book. (Rev: BL 5/1/97; SLJ 4/97)

**5164** Guilfoile, Elizabeth. *Nobody Listens to Andrew* (1–3). Illus. by Mary Stevens. 1957, Modern Curriculum paper $5.10 (0-8136-5959-0). The reaction of Andrew's elders when he tells them there is a bear in his bed.

**5165** Gurney, Nancy, and Eric Gurney. *The King, the Mice, and the Cheese* (1–3). Illus. 1989, Random LB $9.99 (0-394-90039-1). 72pp. The king calls on wise men to stop the mice from eating his cheese. A reissue.

**5166** Gutelle, Andrew. *Baseball's Best: Five True Stories* (2–4). Illus. by Cliff Spohn. 1990, Random LB $11.99 (0-394-90983-6); paper $3.99 (0-394-80983-1). 48pp. Special moments in the careers of 5 famous players. (Rev: BCCB 6/90; BL 6/1/90) [796.357]

**5167** Hall, Katy, and Lisa Eisenberg. *Bunny Riddles* (1–3). Illus. by Nicole Rubel. Series: Dial Easy to Read. 1997, Dial paper $12.89 (0-8037-1521-8).

48pp. Clever pictures accompany an easily read book of rabbit riddles. (Rev: BL 11/15/96; SLJ 2/97) [818]

**5168** Hall, Katy, and Lisa Eisenberg. *Chickie Riddles* (1–2). Illus. by Thor Wickstrom. Series: Dial Easy to Read. 1997, Dial paper $12.89 (0-8037-1779-2). 48pp. Chickens are the subject of these silly riddles. (Rev: BL 11/15/96; SLJ 2/97) [818]

**5169** Hall, Katy, and Lisa Eisenberg. *Snakey Riddles* (2–4). Illus. by Simms Taback. Series: Dial Easy-to-Read. 194, Puffin paper $3.50 (0-14-037141-9). 48pp. For the beginning reader, this is a book of catchy riddles. (Rev: BL 4/1/90; SLJ 4/90)

**5170** Hall, Kirsten. *At the Carnival* (K–1). Illus. by Laura Rader. 1996, Scholastic $3.99 (0-590-68994-0). 32pp. An easy reader that uses detachable pages and a trip to the carnival to introduce language. (Rev: BL 2/1/97)

**5171** Hall, Lynn. *Barry: The Bravest Saint Bernard* (2–4). Illus. by Antonio Castro. Series: Step into Reading. 1992, Random paper $3.50 (0-679-83054-5). 48pp. The true story of a Saint Bernard dog that saved 40 lives in Switzerland. (Rev: BL 3/1/93) [636.7]

**5172** Hanel, Wolfram. *Mia the Beach Cat* (1–3). Trans. from German by J. Alison James. Illus. by Kirsten Hocker. Series: Michael Neugebauer Books. 1994, North-South LB $12.88 (1-55858-315-7). 45pp. In this easy-to-read story, a little girl gradually persuades her parents to let her keep a kitten she has found on the beach. (Rev: BCCB 1/95; SLJ 12/94)

**5173** Hanel, Wolfram. *Old Mahony and the Bear Family* (1–3). Trans. by Rosemary Lanning. Illus. 1997, North-South LB $13.88 (1-55858-714-4). 46pp. Old Mahony enjoys salmon fishing with Big Bill the bear; but when Bill's family appears, he wonders about their future together. (Rev: BL 9/15/97; SLJ 7/97)

**5174** Harshman, Terry Webb. *Porcupine's Pajama Party* (1–3). Illus. by Doug Cushman. 1988, Harper-Collins $9.95 (0-06-022248-4); paper $3.75 (0-06-444140-7). 64pp. Porcupine, Otter, and Owl can't sleep after watching a scary movie. (Rev: BL 7/88; SLJ 10/88)

**5175** Hathorn, Elizabeth. *The Tram to Bondi Beach* (1–3). Illus. by Julie Vivas. 1989, Kane/Miller $12.95 (0-916291-20-0). 32pp. Paperboy Keiran decides that one day he will be the driver of the tram. (Rev: BL 6/1/89; HB 7–8/89)

**5176** Hautzig, Deborah. *Get Well, Granny Bird* (1–3). Illus. by Joe Mathieu. Series: Sesame Street Start-to-Read Books. 1989, Random LB $6.99 (0-394-92247-6). Big Bird's efforts to help Granny Bird

when she has a cold are never successful. (Rev: SLJ 8/89)

**5177** Hautzig, Deborah. *The Nutcracker Ballet* (1–3). Illus. by Carolyn Ewing. 1992, Random LB $9.99 (0-679-92385-3); paper $3.99 (0-679-82385-9). 48pp. In a simple narrative, this is the story of the Nutcracker. (Rev: BL 12/1/92)

**5178** Hayes, Geoffrey. *The Secret of Foghorn Island* (2–3). Illus. by author. 1988, Random LB $7.99 (0-394-99614-3); paper $3.99 (0-394-89614-9). 48pp. Otto and Uncle Tooth investigate 4 shipwrecks on the island. (Rev: BL 10/1/88; SLJ 12/88)

**5179** Hayes, Geoffrey. *Treasure of the Lost Lagoon* (2–3). Illus. Series: Step into Reading. 1992, Random LB $9.99 (0-679-91484-6); paper $3.99 (0-679-81484-1). 48pp. Otto tries to befriend sad Ducky Doodle by taking him on a picnic. (Rev: SLJ 4/92)

**5180** Haynes, Max. *In the Driver's Seat* (PS–1). Illus. by author. 1997, Doubleday $12.95 (0-385-32502-9). An easy-to-read story about a driving lesson that turns into an exciting race. (Rev: SLJ 10/97)

**5181** Hazen, Barbara S. *Digby* (1). Illus. by Barbara J. Phillips-Duke. Series: I Can Read. 1997, Harper-Collins LB $14.89 (0-06-026254-0). 32pp. A boy finds that the family dog is getting too old to play with him. (Rev: BL 11/15/96; SLJ 2/97)

**5182** Heilbroner, Joan. *Tom the TV Cat* (1–2). Illus. by Sal Murdocca. 1984, Random LB $7.99 (0-394-96708-9); paper $3.99 (0-394-86708-4). 48pp. Tom wants to do all the things he sees on TV.

**5183** Herman, Gail. *Double-Header* (1–2). Illus. by Jerry Smath. 1993, Putnam paper $3.95 (0-448-40157-6). 32pp. Monsters Bob and Rob, who share the same body, but with 2 heads, discuss their dilemma. (Rev: BL 12/1/93; SLJ 2/94)

**5184** Herman, Gail. *Flower Girl* (PS–2). Illus. by Paige Billin-Frye. Series: All Aboard Reading. 1996, Putnam LB $13.99 (0-448-41107-5); paper $3.99 (0-448-41108-3). 48pp. A beginning reader about an unsentimental girl who finds that her lucky ring saves her wedding day from being a disaster. (Rev: BCCB 9/96; SLJ 8/96)

**5185** Herman, Gail. *My Dog Talks* (PS–2). Illus. by Ron Fritz. Series: Hello Reader! Books. 1995, Scholastic paper $3.50 (0-590-22196-5). A beginning reader that describes the bond between a boy and his dog as so close that they seem to talk to each other. (Rev: SLJ 9/95)

**5186** Herman, R. A. *Pal the Pony* (1–2). Illus. 1996, Putnam paper $3.99 (0-448-41257-8). 32pp. A pony named Pal shows his true talents at a rodeo. (Rev: BL 8/96; SLJ 7/96)

**5187** Hill, Eric. *Spot Goes to School* (PS). Illus. by author. 1984, Putnam $12.95 (0-399-21073-3). 22pp.

A book that tells the story of a young dog. Two others in this series are: *Spot's First Walk* (1981); *Spot's Birthday Party* (1982).

**5188**   Hill, Eric. *Spot Goes to the Circus* (PS). Illus. by author. 1986, Putnam $12.95 (0-399-21317-1). 22pp. Spot loses his ball at the circus, and readers help him peer into the lion's jaws or the tiger's cage to find it. Also use: *Spot Goes to the Beach* (1985). (Rev: BL 8/86; HB 11–12/86; SLJ 12/86)

**5189**   Himmelman, John. *The Clover County Carrot Contest* (1–2). Illus. 1991, Silver Burdett paper $3.90 (0-671-69641-6). 48pp. Each member of a family of inventive bears tries to grow the best carrot. Also use: *The Super Camper Caper* (1991). (Rev: BL 6/1/91; SLJ 10/91)

**5190**   Himmelman, John. *The Ups and Downs of Simpson Snail* (1–3). Illus. 1997, Puffin paper $3.99 (0-14-038726-9). 48pp. In 4 easily read chapters, the innocent Simpson Snail has many adventures. (Rev: BL 12/1/89; SLJ 12/89)

**5191**   Hoban, Julia. *Quick Chick* (2–3). Illus. by Lillian Hoban. 1995, Puffin paper $3.50 (0-14-036664-4). 32pp. Quick Chick earns his name when the cat arrives. (Rev: BL 6/1/89)

**5192**   Hoban, Lillian. *Arthur's Back to School Day* (1–2). Illus. Series: I Can Read Book. 1996, HarperCollins LB $14.89 (0-06-024956-0). 48pp. Arthur and friends are confused by a lunch box mix-up on the first day at school. (Rev: BL 9/15/96; SLJ 9/96)

**5193**   Hoban, Lillian. *Arthur's Camp-Out* (1–2). Illus. 1993, HarperCollins LB $15.89 (0-06-020526-1). 64pp. Arthur the chimp camps out by himself with unfortunate results. (Rev: BL 3/1/93; SLJ 4/93)

**5194**   Hoban, Lillian. *Arthur's Honey Bear* (1–3). Illus. by author. 1974, HarperCollins LB $14.89 (0-06-022370-7); paper $3.75 (0-06-444033-8). 64pp. Arthur, a chimp, decides to sell all his old toys except his bear, but his sisters bribe him into parting with Honey Bear. Three others in the series are: *Arthur's Pen Pal* (1976); *Arthur's Prize Reader* (1978); *Arthur's Funny Money* (1981).

**5195**   Hoban, Lillian. *Arthur's Loose Tooth* (1–3). Illus. by author. 1985, HarperCollins LB $14.89 (0-06-022354-5); paper $3.95 (0-06-444093-1). 64pp. Brave Arthur the chimp is afraid of blood, so how does he get rid of his loose tooth in order to eat taffy apples? (Rev: BL 10/15/85; HB 11–12/85; SLJ 12/85)

**5196**   Hoban, Lillian. *Mr. Pig and Sonny Too* (1–3). Illus. by author. 1997, HarperCollins $8.86 (0-06-022340-5). 64pp. A dutiful son helps his father in this slapstick delight. Also use: *Mr. Pig and Family* (1980).

**5197**   Hoban, Lillian, and Phoebe Hoban. *Ready . . . Set . . . Robot!* (2–3). Illus. by Lillian Hoban. 1982, HarperCollins $11.95 (0-06-022345-6). 64pp. A robot, Sol-1, competes in a space race.

**5198**   Hoban, Russell. *Bedtime for Frances* (1–2). Illus. by Garth Williams. 1960, HarperCollins LB $13.89 (0-06-022351-0); paper $5.95 (0-06-443451-6). 32pp. Frances, a badger, tries every familiar trick to tease her way past bedtime. Others in the series: *Bread and Jam for Frances* (1965); *A Bargain for Frances* (1970).

**5199**   Hoban, Russell. *Best Friends for Frances* (1–2). Illus. by Lillian Hoban. 1969, HarperCollins LB $14.00 (0-06-022328-6); paper $5.90 (0-06-443008-1). 32pp. When friend Albert decides that he must exclude girls from his "wondering day" and baseball game, Frances chooses younger sister Gloria as a companion. Also use: *A Baby Sister for Frances* (1964).

**5200**   Hoff, Syd. *Albert the Albatross* (1–2). Illus. by author. 1961, HarperCollins LB $15.89 (0-06-022446-0). 32pp. A seabird's unsuccessful search for the ocean is rewarded by accompanying a lady who is going on an ocean trip.

**5201**   Hoff, Syd. *Barkley* (1–3). Illus. by author. 1975, HarperCollins LB $15.89 (0-06-022448-7). 32pp. An easily read story about a forcibly retired, aging circus dog.

**5202**   Hoff, Syd. *Barney's Horse* (1–3). Illus. by author. 1987, HarperCollins LB $14.89 (0-06-022450-9); paper $3.75 (0-06-444142-3). 32pp. Barney the peddler and his horse delight children, but elevated trains soon begin to rumble overhead. (Rev: BCCB 11/87; BL 10/1/87)

**5203**   Hoff, Syd. *Danny and the Dinosaur* (K–2). Illus. by author. 1958, HarperCollins LB $14.89 (0-06-022466-5); paper $3.75 (0-06-444002-8). 64pp. Danny wanted to play and so did the dinosaur. What could have been more natural than for them to leave the museum together? Also from the same author and publisher: *Sammy the Seal* (1959).

**5204**   Hoff, Syd. *Danny and the Dinosaur Go to Camp* (1–3). Illus. 1996, HarperCollins LB $14.89 (0-06-026440-3). 32pp. At summer camp, a dinosaur provides transportation for tired boys and girls. (Rev: BL 8/96; SLJ 6/96)

**5205**   Hoff, Syd. *Grizzwold* (1–2). Illus. by author. 1963, HarperCollins LB $14.89 (0-06-022481-9); paper $3.75 (0-06-444057-5). 64pp. After foresters have destroyed his home, a bear sets out to find a new one.

**5206**   Hoff, Syd. *Happy Birthday, Danny and the Dinosaur!* (1–3). Illus. 1995, HarperCollins LB $14.89 (0-06-026438-1). 32pp. Danny invites his friend the dinosaur to his birthday party in this easy-to-read book. (Rev: BCCB 10/95; BL 10/1/95; SLJ 9/95)

**5207** Hoff, Syd. *The Lighthouse Children* (1–2). Illus. Series: I Can Read. 1994, HarperCollins LB $15.89 (0-06-022959-4). 32pp. After a storm destroys their lighthouse, 2 children must leave the seagulls they feed in this easy-to-read book. (Rev: BL 2/1/94; SLJ 4/94)

**5208** Hoff, Syd. *Mrs. Brice's Mice* (PS–2). Illus. by author. 1988, HarperCollins LB $14.89 (0-06-022452-5); paper $3.75 (0-06-444145-8). 32pp. Mrs. Brice has 25 mice — one is an individualist. (Rev: BCCB 12/88; BL 12/1/88; SLJ 4/89)

**5209** Hoff, Syd. *Stanley* (1–3). Illus. by author. 1992, HarperCollins LB $15.89 (0-06-022536-X); paper $3.75 (0-06-444010-9). 64pp. A caveman finds a new home in this inventive tale.

**5210** Holland, Marion. *A Big Ball of String* (1–3). Illus. by Roy Mickie. 1958, Random LB $11.99 (0-394-90005-7). 72pp. A child dreams of what he would do with a ball of string and then receives one.

**5211** Hooks, William H., et al. *How Do You Make a Bubble?* (1). Illus. by Doug Cushman. Series: Ready to Read. 1992, Bantam paper $3.99 (0-553-35487-6). 32pp. Everyday activities are explained in this simple question-and-answer book told in rhyme. (Rev: BL 6/1/92)

**5212** Hooks, William H. *Lo-Jack and the Pirates* (PS–3). Illus. by Tricia Tusa. Series: Bank Street Ready-to-Read. 1992, Bantam paper $3.99 (0-553-35210-5). 48pp. Literal-minded Jack causes confusion when he is kidnapped by pirates. (Rev: SLJ 4/92)

**5213** Hooks, William H. *Mr. Baseball* (2–3). Illus. by Paul Meisel. 1998, Gareth Stevens LB $18.60 (0-8368-1765-6); Bantam paper $3.99 (0-553-35303-9). 48pp. Five-year-old Eddie wants to get involved in baseball, but can't find his niche. (Rev: BCCB 11/91; BL 12/1/91)

**5214** Hooks, William H. *Mr. Dinosaur* (2–3). Illus. by Paul Meisel. Series: Bank Street Ready-to-Read. 1994, Bantam paper $4.50 (0-553-37234-3). 32pp. Eli is tricked into believing that the lizard he is caring for is really a dinosaur. (Rev: BL 4/1/94; SLJ 4/94)

**5215** Hooks, William H. *Where's Lulu?* (1–2). Illus. by R. W. Alley. 1998, Gareth Stevens $18.60 (0-8368-1768-0); Bantam paper $3.99 (0-553-35211-3). 32pp. A little girl looks everywhere for Lulu to play with her. (Rev: BL 6/1/91)

**5216** Howe, James. *Pinky and Rex and the Mean Old Witch* (2–3). Illus. by Melissa Sweet. 1991, Macmillan $12.95 (0-689-31617-8). 40pp. Rex wants to get even with mean Mrs. Morgan, but Pinky thinks the old lady needs kindness. Also use: *Pinky and Rex and the Spelling Bee* (1991). (Rev: BL 4/15/91; SLJ 7/91)

**5217** Howe, James. *Pinky and Rex and the New Baby* (K–3). Illus. by Melissa Sweet. 1994, Avon paper $3.99 (0-380-12083-3). 48pp. Rex and her best friend are nervous about the new baby Rex's parents are planning to adopt. (Rev: BL 3/1/93; SLJ 6/93)

**5218** Howe, James. *Pinky and Rex and the New Neighbors* (1–3). Illus. by Melissa Sweet. 1997, Simon & Schuster $15.00 (0-689-80022-3); paper $3.99 (0-689-81296-5). 48pp. For beginning readers, this story tells how Rex worries about who will move next door when his beloved neighbor leaves. (Rev: BL 5/1/97; SLJ 6/97)

**5219** Howe, James. *Pinky and Rex Get Married* (K–3). Illus. by Melissa Sweet. 1990, Simon & Schuster LB $11.95 (0-685-58512-3). 48pp. Two young friends, a 7-year-old girl and a boy named Pinky, are so close that they decide to get married. Also use: *Pinky and Rex* (1990). (Rev: BCCB 4/90; BL 4/15/90*; HB 3–4/90; SLJ 5/90)

**5220** Howe, James. *Pinky and Rex Go to Camp* (2–3). Illus. by Melissa Sweet. 1992, Macmillan $15.00 (0-689-31718-2). 40pp. Pinky and Rex tackle the ups and downs of friendship when they get ready for sleep-away camp. (Rev: BL 4/1/92; SLJ 4/92)

**5221** Hudson, Wade. *Jamal's Busy Day* (PS–1). Illus. by George Ford. 1991, Just Us LB $12.95 (0-940975-21-1); paper $6.95 (0-940975-24-6). Jamal, an African-American boy, prepares with his parents for a busy day — he will spend his at school and they at work. (Rev: SLJ 2/92)

**5222** Hulbert, Jay. *Armando Asked, "Why?"* (1–3). Illus. by Sid Kantor. 1990, Raintree Steck-Vaughn LB $21.40 (0-8172-3576-0). 34pp. Armando asks so many tough questions that the family has to go to the library to find the answers. (Rev: BL 9/15/90)

**5223** Hurwitz, Johanna. *The Adventures of Ali Baba Bernstein* (2–4). Illus. 1985, Morrow $17.00 (0-688-04161-2); Avon paper $3.99 (0-380-72349-2). 96pp. Episodes in the life of David Bernstein, an 8-year-old who changes what he thinks is his boring name. Also use: *Hurray for Ali Baba Bernstein* (1989). (Rev: BCCB 6/85; BL 5/15/85; HB 5–6/85)

**5224** Hurwitz, Johanna. *Russell Sprouts* (1–3). Illus. by Lillian Hoban. 1987, Morrow $16.00 (0-688-07165-1); Puffin paper $3.99 (0-14-032942-0). 80pp. Six-year-old Russell worries about everything — including his Halloween costume and why his parents don't treat him better. Also use: *Russell Rides Again* (1985). (Rev: BL 10/1/87; HB 9–10/87; SLJ 9/87)

**5225** Hutchins, Pat. *The Tale of Thomas Mead* (1–3). Illus. by author. 1980, Greenwillow LB $15.93 (0-688-84282-8). 32pp. Thomas learns to read and suddenly becomes a bookworm.

**5226** Jacobs, Daniel. *What Does It Do? Inventions Then and Now* (1–2). Illus. Series: Ready-Set-Read. 1990, Raintree Steck-Vaughn LB $21.40 (0-8172-3586-8). 24pp. The stories behind the invention of the camera, the auto, and other items are featured. (Rev: BL 6/1/90) [609]

**5227** Jewell, Nancy. *Two Silly Trolls* (1–2). Illus. by Lisa Thiesing. Series: I Can Read Books. 1994, HarperCollins paper $3.75 (0-06-444173-3). 64pp. Four simple stories about the trolls Nip and Tuck. (Rev: BL 6/15/92; SLJ 2/93)

**5228** Johnson, Crockett. *Harold and the Purple Crayon* (K–2). Illus. by author. 1958, HarperCollins paper $5.95 (0-06-443022-7). 64pp. A little boy draws all of the things necessary for him to go for a walk. Three sequels are: *Harold's Trip to the Sky* (1957); *Harold's Circus* (1959); *A Picture for Harold's Room* (1960).

**5229** Johnston, Tony. *The Bull and the Fire Truck* (1–2). Illus. by R. W. Alley. 1996, Scholastic $3.50 (0-590-47597-5). 32pp. An easily read book about how a community accommodates a bull that hates the color red. (Rev: BL 2/1/97)

**5230** Johnston, Tony. *Sparky and Eddie: The First Day of School* (1–2). Illus. by Susannah Ryan. Series: Hello Reader! 1997, Scholastic $13.95 (0-590-47978-4); paper $3.99 (0-590-47979-2). 32pp. In this easy reader, friends Sparky and Eddie decide that they won't start school if they can't be in the same rooms. (Rev: BL 8/97; SLJ 9/97)

**5231** Karlin, Nurit. *The Fat Cat Sat on the Mat* (1–2). Illus. 1996, HarperCollins LB $14.89 (0-06-026674-0). 32pp. A witch's rat can't budge a cat from a favorite resting place, the mat. (Rev: BCCB 10/96; BL 9/15/96; SLJ 12/96)

**5232** Keenan, Sheila. *More or Less a Mess* (1–2). Illus. by Patrick Girouard. Series: Hello Math Reader. 1997, Scholastic $3.50 (0-590-60248-9). When a girl is told by her mother to tidy up her room, she doesn't know where to begin, so she puts everything under the covers of her bed. (Rev: BL 5/1/97)

**5233** Kessler, Ethel, and Leonard Kessler. *Stan the Hot Dog Man* (1–3). Illus. 1990, HarperCollins LB $14.89 (0-06-023280-3). 64pp. In all kinds of weather, Stan sells his hot dogs to satisfied customers. (Rev: BCCB 3/90; BL 4/1/90; SLJ 7/90)

**5234** Kessler, Leonard. *Here Comes the Strikeout* (1–2). Illus. by author. 1992, HarperCollins LB $14.89 (0-06-023156-4); paper $3.75 (0-06-444011-7). 64pp. Bobby always strikes out at bat until his friend Willie helps him to improve his game. Two other sports stories by the same author and publisher are: *Kick, Pass and Run* (1966); *Last One In Is a Rotten Egg* (1969). (Rev: BL 12/1/92)

**5235** Kessler, Leonard. *Old Turtle's Soccer Team* (1–2). Illus. by author. 1988, Greenwillow LB $14.93 (0-688-07158-9). 48pp. Old Turtle's team gets in shape to face the Big Raccoon's Rockets. (Rev: BCCB 10/88; BL 12/1/88; SLJ 10/88)

**5236** Kiser, SuAnn. *Hazel Saves the Day* (2). Illus. by Betsy Day. Series: Easy-to-Read. 1994, Dial paper $12.89 (0-8037-1489-0). 48pp. Newcomer Hazel Hen decides to throw a Friday-the-13th party to make new friends in this easy-to-read book. (Rev: BL 4/1/94; SLJ 7/94)

**5237** Kline, Suzy. *Horrible Harry in Room 2B* (2–4). Illus. by Frank Remkiewicz. 1988, Puffin paper $3.99 (0-14-032825-4). 64pp. The adventures of Harry, who is borderline obnoxious with redeeming qualities. Also use: *Horrible Harry and the Green Slime* (1989). (Rev: BL 10/15/88; SLJ 9/88)

**5238** Krensky, Stephen. *Lionel and His Friends* (2–3). Illus. by Susanna Natti. 1996, Dial paper $13.89 (0-8037-1751-2). 48pp. Four stories involving the amusing activities of Lionel and his friends. (Rev: BCCB 2/97; BL 9/15/96; SLJ 12/96)

**5239** Krensky, Stephen. *Lionel and Louise* (1–2). Illus. by Susanna Natti. Series: Easy-to-Read. 1991, Dial LB $10.89 (0-8037-1056-9). 48pp. Louise learns that in many ways she must be responsible for her younger brother, Lionel. (Rev: BL 12/1/91; HB 3–4/92; SLJ 4/92)

**5240** Krensky, Stephen. *Lionel at Large* (1–3). Illus. by Susanna Natti. Series: Easy-to-Read. 1986, Dial paper $4.95 (0-8037-0556-5). 56pp. Five vignettes about children's experiences, such as when Lionel discovers that getting a shot isn't as bad as he thought. A sequel is *Lionel in the Fall* (1987). (Rev: BCCB 4/86; BL 5/15/86; SLJ 5/86)

**5241** Krensky, Stephen. *Lionel in the Spring* (1–3). Illus. by Susanna Natti. Series: Easy-to-Read. 1997, Viking Penguin paper $3.50 (0-14-038463-4). In the spring of the year, Lionel engages in all sorts of activities. (Rev: BL 4/1/90; HB 7–8/90; SLJ 3/90)

**5242** Kuskin, Karla. *Soap Soup and Other Verses* (1–3). Illus. 1994, HarperCollins paper $3.75 (0-06-444174-1). 64pp. This easily read book contains simple poems about a variety of everyday objects and experiences. (Rev: BCCB 6/92; BL 4/1/92; SLJ 4/92) [811]

**5243** Kwitz, Mary D. *Gumshoe Goose, Private Eye* (2–3). Illus. by Lisa Campbell Ernst. 1996, Puffin paper $3.50 (0-14-036194-4). 48pp. Gumshoe Goose to the rescue of the kidnapped Baby Chick-Chick. (Rev: BL 12/1/88; SLJ 12/88)

**5244** Kwitz, Mary D. *Little Vampire and the Midnight Bear* (PS–3). Illus. by S. D. Schindler. 1995, Dial paper $12.89 (0-8037-1529-3). 48pp. Little Vampire, who still can't fly, is very afraid of the

Midnight Bear in this easy-to-read title. (Rev: BL 10/1/95; SLJ 9/95)

**5245** Larson, Kirby. *Cody and Quinn, Sitting in a Tree* (2–3). Illus. 1996, Holiday $14.95 (0-8234-1227-X). 64pp. Cody is teased by a bully because of his friendship with a girl, Quinn. (Rev: BCCB 9/96; BL 4/1/96; SLJ 4/96)

**5246** Le Sieg, Theo. *Ten Apples Up on Top* (K–2). Illus. 1961, Random LB $11.99 (0-394-90019-7). 72pp. Three bears try to pile apples on their heads in this nonsense story. Also from the same author and publisher: *I Wish That I Had Duck Feet* (1965); *Eye Book* (1968).

**5247** Leverich, Kathleen. *Best Enemies* (2–3). Illus. by Susan C. Lamb. 1989, Greenwillow $15.00 (0-688-08316-1); Knopf paper $3.99 (0-679-80156-1). 80pp. On her first day at school, Priscilla meets Felicity, who turns out to be a manipulator. Also use: *Best Enemies Again* (1991). (Rev: BL 4/15/89; SLJ 5/89)

**5248** Leverich, Kathleen. *Brigid Bewitched* (2–4). Illus. 1994, Random paper $2.99 (0-679-85433-9). 78pp. Like a fairy godmother, Brigid's new friend helps her overcome her fear of jumping off the new diving board in this easily read story. (Rev: BL 4/15/95)

**5249** Levinson, Nancy S. *Clara and the Bookwagon* (1–2). Illus. by Carolyn Croll. 1988, HarperCollins LB $15.89 (0-06-023838-0); paper $3.75 (0-06-444134-2). 64pp. A real-life story about a young girl who wants to read despite her father's objections. (Rev: BL 4/1/88; SLJ 7/88)

**5250** Levinson, Nancy S. *Snowshoe Thompson* (1–2). Illus. by Joan Sandin. 1992, HarperCollins LB $15.89 (0-06-023802-X). 64pp. Set in the pioneer West, this easy-to-read true story tells about a postman named Snowshoe Thompson and how he delivers a letter in spite of mountains of snow. (Rev: BL 12/1/91; HB 1–2/92; SLJ 1/92*) [979.4]

**5251** Levy, Elizabeth. *The Creepy Computer Mystery* (2–3). Illus. by Denise Brunkus. 1996, Scholastic paper $3.99 (0-590-60322-1). 48pp. The trio Invisible Ink solves the mystery of the online intruder. (Rev: BL 9/15/96)

**5252** Levy, Elizabeth. *The Karate Class Mystery* (2–4). Illus. by Denise Brunkus. 1996, Scholastic $3.99 (0-590-60323-X). 48pp. A mystery in which Justin's karate belt disappears and the culprit must be caught. (Rev: BL 2/1/97)

**5253** Levy, Elizabeth. *The Mystery of the Missing Dog* (2–3). Illus. 1995, Scholastic paper $3.50 (0-590-47484-7). 44pp. Invisible Chip loses his invisible dog, Max, but solves a mystery with the help of friends Justin and Charlene. (Rev: BL 1/1–15/96)

**5254** Lewis, Rob. *The White Bicycle* (2–3). Illus. by author. 1988, Farrar $12.00 (0-374-38384-7). 32pp. The travels of a rusty bike. (Rev: BL 10/15/88; SLJ 3/89)

**5255** Lexau, Joan M. *The Rooftop Mystery* (1–2). Illus. by Syd Hoff. 1968, HarperCollins LB $14.89 (0-06-023865-8). 64pp. Trying desperately to avoid transporting sister's doll on moving day, Sam and Albert lose it instead, and in the end prove their worth as junior detectives.

**5256** Lindgren, Barbro. *The Story of the Little Old Man* (1–2). Illus. by Eva Eriksson. 1992, R&S $6.00 (91-29-59942-3). 54pp. A solitary old man is befriended by a dog in this easily read story. (Rev: BL 12/1/92)

**5257** Lobel, Arnold. *Frog and Toad Are Friends* (K–2). Illus. by author. 1970, HarperCollins LB $14.89 (0-06-023958-1); paper $3.75 (0-06-444020-6). 64pp. Two new friends for the independent reader. Three sequels are: *Frog and Toad Together* (1972); *Frog and Toad All Year* (1976); *Days with Frog and Toad* (1979).

**5258** Lobel, Arnold. *Grasshopper on the Road* (1–2). Illus. by author. 1978, HarperCollins LB $14.89 (0-06-023962-X); paper $3.75 (0-06-444094-X). 64pp. A series of short stories, each with a vital message.

**5259** Lobel, Arnold. *Mouse Soup* (1–2). Illus. by author. 1977, HarperCollins LB $14.89 (0-06-023968-9); paper $3.75 (0-06-444041-9). 64pp. When Mouse is caught by Weasel, who plans to use him for soup, he convinces his captor that "mouse soup must be mixed with stones to make it taste really good."

**5260** Lobel, Arnold. *Mouse Tales* (1–2). Illus. by author. 1972, HarperCollins LB $14.89 (0-06-023942-5); paper $3.75 (0-06-444013-3). 64pp. Seven bedtime stories told by Papa Mouse to his 7 sons. Lively little drawings add to the humor.

**5261** Lobel, Arnold. *Owl at Home* (1–2). Illus. by author. 1975, HarperCollins LB $14.89 (0-06-023949-2); paper $3.75 (0-06-444034-6). 64pp. Five stories dealing with the humorous and bungling attempts of Owl to be helpful.

**5262** Lobel, Arnold. *Small Pig* (K–2). Illus. by author. 1969, HarperCollins LB $14.89 (0-06-023932-8); paper $3.75 (0-06-444120-2). 64pp. A dirty little pig in a search for mud ends up in cement.

**5263** Lobel, Arnold. *Uncle Elephant* (K–3). Illus. by author. 1981, HarperCollins LB $14.89 (0-06-023980-8); paper $3.75 (0-06-444104-0). 64pp. A nephew and uncle elephant form a friendship.

**5264** Lopshire, Robert. *Put Me in the Zoo* (1–3). Illus. by author. 1960, Beginner Books $7.99 (0-394-80017-6). 72pp. An unusual dog thinks he should be in the zoo, but his talents really mean he should be in a circus.

**5265** Lunn, Carolyn. *A Whisper Is Quiet* (1–2). Illus. by Clovis Martin. 1989, Children's LB $17.00 (0-516-02087-0); paper $4.95 (0-516-42087-9). 32pp. A concept book introduces opposites. (Rev: BL 3/1/89)

**5266** Luttrell, Ida. *The Bear Next Door* (1–2). Illus. by Sarah Stapler. 1991, HarperCollins LB $15.89 (0-06-024024-5). 64pp. In 3 different stories, Arlo Gopher tries to become friendly with his grouchy new neighbor, Vic Bear. (Rev: BL 4/1/91; SLJ 6/91)

**5267** Maccarone, Grace. *The Gym Day Winner* (PS–1). Illus. 1996, Scholastic paper $3.99 (0-590-26263-7). 32pp. A youngster finds a sport at which he excels. (Rev: BL 8/96; SLJ 1/97)

**5268** Maccarone, Grace. *The Lunch Box Surprise* (1). Illus. by Betsy Lewin. 1995, Scholastic paper $2.95 (0-590-26267-X). 32pp. First-grader Sam is surprised at school when he finds that his mother hasn't packed his lunch. (Rev: BL 1/1–15/96)

**5269** Maccarone, Grace. *My Tooth Is About to Fall Out* (1–2). Illus. by Betsy Lewin. 1995, Scholastic $3.50 (0-590-48376-5). 32pp. An easy-to-read book about the problems of having a loose tooth. (Rev: BL 7/95)

**5270** Maccarone, Grace. *Recess Mess* (1–2). Illus. by Betsy Lewin. Series: Hello Reader! 1996, Scholastic $3.50 (0-590-73878-X). 32pp. Sam has trouble determining which bathroom is for boys in this easily read school story. (Rev: BL 2/1/97)

**5271** Maccarone, Grace. *Sharing Time Troubles* (PS–1). Illus. by Betsy Lewin. Series: Hello Reader! 1997, Scholastic $3.50 (0-590-73879-8). For a school show-and-tell session, Sam gets a brilliant idea and brings his pesky younger brother. (Rev: BL 5/1/97; SLJ 7/97)

**5272** McClintock, Mike. *Stop That Ball!* (1–3). Illus. by Fritz Siebel. 1959, Beginner Books $7.99 (0-394-80010-9). Chasing a bouncing ball becomes a big adventure in this reissued picture book.

**5273** McCully, Emily Arnold. *The Grandma Mix-Up* (1–3). Illus. by author. 1988, HarperCollins LB $14.89 (0-06-024202-7); paper $3.75 (0-06-444150-4). 64pp. Two grandmothers with very different ways arrive to baby-sit. (Rev: BL 12/1/89; SLJ 3/89)

**5274** McCully, Emily Arnold. *Grandmas at Bat* (1–2). Illus. 1993, HarperCollins $14.00 (0-06-021031-1); paper $3.75 (0-06-444193-8). 64pp. Pip's 2 grandmothers, last-minute replacements, coach his baseball team. (Rev: BL 3/1/93; HB 7–8/93; SLJ 6/93)

**5275** McCully, Emily Arnold. *Grandma's at the Lake* (1–3). Illus. 1990, HarperCollins $10.95 (0-06-

024126-8); paper $3.75 (0-06-444177-6). 64pp. While sharing a lakeside cabin, Nan and Sal find it hard to accept their grandma's advice. (Rev: BCCB 5/90; BL 4/1/90; SLJ 6/90)

**5276** MacDonald, Maryann. *Hedgehog Bakes a Cake* (K–2). Illus. by Lynn Munsinger. Series: Bank Street Ready-to-Read. 1990, Bantam paper $3.99 (0-553-34890-6). There is mayhem when Hedgehog's friends help him bake a cake. (Rev: SLJ 5/91)

**5277** McDonald, Megan. *Beezy* (1–3). Illus. 1997, Orchard LB $14.99 (0-531-33046-X). 48pp. Three easy-to-read stories about Beezy, a dog she finds, and her friends. (Rev: BL 9/15/97; SLJ 11/97)

**5278** McGuire, Leslie. *This Farm Is a Mess* (1–3). Illus. by author. 1996, Gareth Stevens LB $18.60 (0-8368-0983-1). 48pp. The animals take over and clean up Farmer Wood's very messy farm.

**5279** McKissack, Patricia. *Monkey-Monkey's Trick: Based on an African Folk Tale* (1–3). Illus. by Paul Meisel. 1988, Random LB $7.99 (0-394-99173-7); paper $3.99 (0-394-89173-2). 48pp. Monkey-Monkey needs help building his new house in this amusing fable. (Rev: BL 3/1/89)

**5280** McKissack, Patricia, and Fredrick McKissack. *Bugs!* (1–2). Illus. by Clovis Martin. 1988, Children's LB $17.00 (0-516-02088-9); paper $4.95 (0-516-42088-7). 32pp. Multilegged and multicolored creatures are introduced. (Rev: BL 3/1/89)

**5281** McPhail, David. *Snow Lion* (PS–2). Illus. by author. 1983, Parents LB $5.95 (0-8193-1098-0). 48pp. A lion finds it's too hot for him to stay in the jungle.

**5282** Madsen, Ross Martin. *Perrywinkle's Magic Match* (2). Illus. by Dirk Zimmer. Series: An Easy-to-Read Book. 1997, Dial paper $12.89 (0-8037-1109-3). 40pp. A beginning reader in which a girl and a boy quarrel over who has the more powerful magic. (Rev: HB 9–10/97; SLJ 12/97)

**5283** Madsen, Ross Martin. *Stewart Stork* (1–2). Illus. by Megan Halsey. 1993, Dial LB $11.89 (0-8037-1326-6). 40pp. An easy-to-read book about a stork who wants to be different than he really is. (Rev: BL 12/1/93; SLJ 9/93)

**5284** Marshall, Edward. *Four on the Shore* (1–3). Illus. by James Marshall. 1985, Puffin paper $9.95 (0-8037-0155-1). 48pp. Three friends try to get rid of little Willie by telling scary stories, but he tells the scariest of all. (Rev: BL 3/15/85; HB 5–6/85; SLJ 5/85)

**5285** Marshall, Edward. *Fox and His Friends* (1–3). Illus. by James Marshall. 1982, Dial paper $4.95 (0-8037-2668-6). 56pp. Fox usually has his sister tagging along but finally gets together alone with his friends. Some sequels are: *Fox in Love* (1982); *Fox at*

*School* (1983); *Fox on Wheels* (1983); *Fox All Week* (1984).

**5286**   Marshall, Edward. *Three by the Sea* (1–3). Illus. by James Marshall. 1981, Puffin paper $3.99 (0-14-037004-8). 48pp. Three friends, Lolly, Spider, and Sam, tell stories by the seashore.

**5287**   Marshall, Edward. *Troll Country* (1–2). Illus. by James Marshall. 1980, Dial paper $4.95 (0-8037-6210-0). 56pp. Elsie Fay wanders into the woods and outsmarts a troll.

**5288**   Marshall, James. *Fox Be Nimble* (1–2). Illus. 1990, Dial LB $10.89 (0-8037-0761-4). 48pp. While baby-sitting, Fox plays the guitar and his charges float off on a bunch of balloons. (Rev: BCCB 9/90; BL 4/1/90; SLJ 5/90)

**5289**   Marshall, James. *Fox on Stage* (1–3). Illus. 1993, Dial paper $12.89 (0-8037-1357-6). 48pp. When Fox gets his friends to put on a play, he is unaware of all the problems it entails. (Rev: BCCB 1/93; BL 7/93; HB 3–4/93; SLJ 4/93)

**5290**   Marshall, James. *Fox on the Job* (1–2). Illus. by author. 1988, Dial LB $9.89 (0-8037-0351-1); Puffin paper $4.99 (0-8037-0746-0). 48pp. Work is a dirty word to Fox, but his mother tells him he has to earn his own money for a new bike. (Rev: BCCB 4/88; BL 4/1/88; SLJ 7/88)

**5291**   Marshall, James. *Fox Outfoxed* (2–3). Illus. 1992, Dial LB $11.89 (0-8037-1037-2); Viking paper $3.99 (0-14-038113-9). 48pp. Three easily read stories about Fox and how his careful plans misfire. (Rev: BCCB 4/92; BL 4/1/92; HB 7–8/92; SLJ 5/92*)

**5292**   Marshall, James. *Rats on the Range and Other Stories* (1–3). 1993, Dial LB $12.89 (0-8037-1385-1). 80pp. Eight stories involving such animals as pigs, which enjoy food and fast cars. (Rev: BL 6/1–15/93; HB 5–6/93*)

**5293**   Marzollo, Jean, et al. *Football Friends* (1–2). Illus. by True Kelley. Series: Hello Reader! 1997, Scholastic $3.50 (0-590-38395-7). 32pp. Freddy becomes so angry with his friend Mark when they choose teams for playing football that he begins using his fists and feet in this easy-to-read sports book. (Rev: BL 2/1/98; SLJ 3/98)

**5294**   Marzollo, Jean. *I Am an Apple* (PS–1). Illus. by Judith Moffatt. Series: Hello Reader, Level 1. 1997, Scholastic $3.50 (0-590-37223-8). A beginning reader that details the life of an apple from flower to fruit to market to table. (Rev: SLJ 1/98)

**5295**   Marzollo, Jean. *I'm a Caterpillar* (K–2). Illus. by Judith Moffatt. Series: Hello Reader! Science, Level 1. 1997, Scholastic $3.50 (0-590-84779-1). A beginning reader that presents, in story form, the life cycle of a caterpillar. (Rev: SLJ 11/97)

**5296**   Marzollo, Jean. *Soccer Cousins* (2–4). Illus. by Irene Trivas. Series: Hello Reader! 1997, Scholastic $3.99 (0-590-74254-X). 32pp. In this easy-to-read book David is afraid that he is not a good soccer player, but he is thrilled with the invitation to go to Mexico to see his cousin play. (Rev: BL 2/1/98)

**5297**   Marzollo, Jean. *Soccer Sam* (1–2). Illus. by Blanche Sims. 1987, Random LB $7.99 (0-394-98406-4); paper $3.99 (0-394-88406-X). 48pp. Marco from Mexico spends a year with his friend Sam in the United States, and the boys organize a soccer team. (Rev: BL 8/87; SLJ 9/87)

**5298**   Mason, Jane B. *Hellow, Two-Wheeler!* (1–2). Illus. by David Monteith. 1995, Putnam paper $3.95 (0-448-40853-8). 48pp. A boy accidentally learns to ride his bike without its training wheels. (Rev: BL 7/95)

**5299**   Matthias, Catherine. *I Love Cats* (K–1). Illus. by Tom Dunnington. 1983, Children's LB $17.00 (0-516-02041-2); paper $4.95 (0-516-42041-0). 32pp. The narrator likes many things, but cats are best.

**5300**   Medearis, Angela Shelf. *Here Comes the Snow* (1). Illus. 1996, Scholastic paper $3.50 (0-590-26266-1). 32pp. Kids enjoy all of the fun of a first snowfall. (Rev: BL 8/96; SLJ 9/96)

**5301**   Miles, Betty. *Hey! I'm Reading! An Exciting New Way to Get Started* (PS–2). Illus. by Sylvie Wickstrom. 1995, Knopf LB $16.99 (0-679-95644-1); paper $13.00 (0-679-85644-7). 59pp. After a brief discussion of the process of reading, this book gives a selection of easy poems and silly jokes, plus an alphabet and labeled diagrams, all to help the beginning reader. (Rev: SLJ 10/95)

**5302**   Milgrim, David. *Why Benny Barks* (1–2). Illus. Series: Step into Reading. 1994, Random LB $11.99 (0-679-96157-7); paper $3.99 (0-679-86157-2). 32pp. In this easily read book, a child tries to figure out why his dog barks. (Rev: BL 1/1/95)

**5303**   Miller, Sara S. *Three Stories You Can Read to Your Cat* (1–3). Illus. by True Kelley. 1997, Houghton $13.95 (0-395-78831-5). 48pp. An easy-to-read book about Kelley's playful, adventurous cat. (Rev: BL 3/1/97; SLJ 5/97)

**5304**   Miller, Sara S. *Three Stories You Can Read to Your Dog* (2–4). Illus. by True Kelley. 1995, Houghton $13.95 (0-395-69938-X). 42pp. Three easy-to-read stories that feature a muddle-headed dog that doesn't know how to behave. (Rev: BCCB 3/95; BL 4/15/95; SLJ 4/95)

**5305**   Mills, Claudia. *Gus and Grandpa* (1). Illus. by Catherine Stock. 1997, Farrar $13.00 (0-374-32824-2). 48pp. Three easily read stories about Gus, who is 6, and the fun he has with his grandfather. (Rev: BL 2/1/97; SLJ 4/97)

**5306** Mills, Claudia. *Gus and Grandpa and the Christmas Cookies* (1–2). Illus. by Catherine Stock. 1997, Farrar $13.00 (0-374-32823-4). 48pp. At Christmas time, Gus and his grandfather receive so many cookies that they decide to give some away. (Rev: BL 9/15/97; SLJ 10/97)

**5307** Milton, Joyce. *Whales: The Gentle Giants* (2–3). Illus. by Alton Langford. 1989, Random LB $7.99 (0-394-99809-X); paper $3.99 (0-394-89809-5). 48pp. A sailor named Brendan steps on the back of a whale. (Rev: BL 6/1/89)

**5308** Milton, Joyce. *Wild, Wild Wolves* (2–3). Illus. by Larry Schwinger. 1992, Random LB $11.99 (0-679-91052-2); paper $3.99 (0-679-81052-8). 48pp. This easy-to-read science book contains a wealth of information about wolves and how they live. (Rev: BCCB 5/92; BL 4/1/92; SLJ 8/92) [599.74]

**5309** Minarik, Else Holmelund. *Little Bear* (K–2). Illus. by Maurice Sendak. 1957, HarperCollins LB $14.89 (0-06-024241-8); paper $3.75 (0-06-444004-4). 64pp. Humorous adventure stories of Mother Bear and Little Bear. Others in the series: *Little Bear's Friend* (1960); *Little Bear's Visit* (1961); *A Kiss for Little Bear* (1968).

**5310** Minarik, Else Holmelund. *No Fighting, No Biting!* (PS–3). Illus. by Maurice Sendak. 1958, Harper-Collins LB $14.89 (0-06-024291-4); paper $3.75 (0-06-444015-X). 64pp. Light-foot and Quick-foot, 2 little alligators, teach Rosa and Willy a lesson.

**5311** Moffatt, Judith. *Who Stole the Cookies?* (1–2). Illus. 1996, Putnam paper $3.99 (0-448-41127-X). 32pp. A cast of animal characters ask who stole the cookies in this rhyming first reader. (Rev: BL 8/96; SLJ 9/96)

**5312** Neasi, Barbara J. *Just Like Me* (K–1). Illus. by Lois Axeman. 1984, Children's LB $17.00 (0-516-02047-1); paper $4.95 (0-516-42047-X). 32pp. Twins explore their similarities and differences.

**5313** Neitzel, Shirley. *The Dress I'll Wear to the Party* (PS–K). Illus. by Nancy Winslow Parker. 1992, Greenwillow LB $13.93 (0-688-09960-2). 32pp. A girl dresses up in her mother's clothes for a party, but later her mother has different ideas on what is suitable attire. (Rev: BL 10/15/92; SLJ 10/92)

**5314** Nodset, Joan L. *Come Here, Cat* (K–3). Illus. by Steven Kellogg. 1973, HarperCollins $10.00 (0-06-024557-3). 32pp. A young girl chases a cat around her house and onto the roof in this simple but enjoyable story.

**5315** Nodset, Joan L. *Go Away, Dog* (1–2). Illus. by Paul Meisel. 1997, HarperCollins LB $12.89 (0-06-027503-0). 32pp. A boy finds that he can't get rid of the dog that is following him in this easy-to-read book. (Rev: BL 8/97; SLJ 10/97)

**5316** Nodset, Joan L. *Who Took the Farmer's Hat?* (1–2). Illus. by Fritz Siebel. 1963, HarperCollins LB $14.89 (0-06-024566-2); paper $5.95 (0-06-443174-6). 32pp. When the wind blows away the farmer's hat, all of the animals think they saw it.

**5317** Nyul Choi, Sook. *The Best Older Sister* (1–3). Illus. by Cornelius Van Wright. 1997, Dell $13.95 (0-385-32208-9); paper $3.99 (0-440-41149-1). 48pp. Sunhi is jealous of all the attention her baby brother gets, but grandmother explains the importance of being a big sister in this easy-to-read book. (Rev: BL 5/1/97; SLJ 6/97)

**5318** O'Connor, Jane. *Kate Skates* (PS–1). Illus. by DyAnne DiSalvo-Ryan. 1995, Putnam paper $3.99 (0-448-40935-6). 48pp. Tiny Jen easily learns to skate on her double blades, but older sister Kate has problems with her grownup single blades. (Rev: BL 1/1–15/96; SLJ 5/96)

**5319** O'Connor, Jane. *Lulu and the Witch Baby* (1–2). Illus. by Emily Arnold McCully. 1986, HarperCollins LB $14.89 (0-06-024627-8). 64pp. In this witch family, the older sibling dislikes the new arrival. Also use: *Lulu Goes to Witch School* (1987). (Rev: BCCB 1/87; BL 10/1/86)

**5320** O'Connor, Jane. *Molly the Brave and Me* (1–3). Illus. by Sheila Hamanaka. 1990, Random LB $7.99 (0-394-94175-6); paper $3.99 (0-394-84175-1). 48pp. Molly seems fearless, but in time of trouble Beth leads the way. (Rev: BCCB 6/90; BL 6/1/90; SLJ 8/90)

**5321** O'Connor, Jane. *Nina, Nina Ballerina* (PS–1). Illus. by DyAnne DiSalvo-Ryan. 1993, Putnam paper $3.99 (0-448-40511-3). 32pp. When Nina breaks her arm, she worries that she will not be able to perform in her ballet class show. (Rev: BL 7/93; SLJ 8/93)

**5322** O'Connor, Jane. *Nina, Nina, Star Ballerina* (1–2). Illus. by DyAnne DiSalvo-Ryan. 1997, Putnam LB $13.89 (0-448-41611-5). 32pp. A young girl is playing a star but not *the* star in the ballet *Night Sky*. (Rev: BL 8/97)

**5323** O'Connor, Jane. *The Teeny Tiny Woman* (K–2). Illus. by R. W. Alley. 1986, Random LB $11.99 (0-394-98320-3); paper $3.99 (0-394-88320-9). 32pp. The familiar folktale retold. By the same author, another easy reader, *Sir Small and the Dragonfly* (1988). (Rev: BL 12/1/86)

**5324** O'Connor, Jim, and Jane O'Connor. *Slime Time* (2–4). Illus. by Pat G. Porter. 1990, Random paper $2.50 (0-679-80714-4). 48pp. Danny and friend Jeb enter a TV quiz program to win a skateboard. (Rev: BL 9/15/90)

**5325** Oechsli, Kelly. *Mice at Bat* (1–2). Illus. by author. 1986, HarperCollins $11.95 (0-06-024623-5); paper $3.75 (0-06-444139-3). 64pp. Two baseball teams (of mice) who are traditional rivals prepare for the big game. (Rev: BCCB 10/86; SLJ 5/86)

**5326** Oppenheim, Joanne. *The Show-and-Tell Frog* (1–2). Illus. by Kate Duke. Series: Ready-to-Read. 1998, Gareth Stevens LB $18.60 (0-8368-1762-1); Bantam paper $3.99 (0-553-35147-8). 32pp. A little green frog has some amazing adventures in this easily read book. (Rev: BL 6/1/92)

**5327** Orgel, Doris. *The Spaghetti Party* (1–3). Illus. by Julie Durrell. Series: Bank Street Ready-to-Read. 1995, Bantam $12.95 (0-553-09052-6); paper $3.99 (0-553-37571-7). 32pp. Keesha brings all her friends to Annie's for a spaghetti party in this easy-to-read book. (Rev: BL 1/1/95)

**5328** Osborne, Mary Pope. *Dinosaurs Before Dark* (1–2). Illus. by Sal Murdocca. 1992, Random LB $11.99 (0-679-92411-6). 68pp. Jack and his sister time-travel to the days of the dinosaurs. (Rev: BL 10/1/92; SLJ 9/92)

**5329** Parish, Herman. *Bravo, Amelia Bedelia!* (1–3). Illus. by Lynn Sweat. 1997, Greenwillow LB $11.88 (0-688-15155-8). 40pp. Literal-minded Amelia Bedelia creates havoc at a school concert in this beginning reader. (Rev: BL 5/1/97; SLJ 4/97)

**5330** Parish, Herman. *Good Driving, Amelia Bedelia* (1–2). Illus. by Lynn Sweat. 1995, Greenwillow LB $14.93 (0-688-13359-2). 40pp. The literal-minded Amelia Bedelia practices her driving with hilarious results. (Rev: BCCB 3/95; BL 4/15/95; SLJ 4/95)

**5331** Parish, Peggy. *Amelia Bedelia* (1–3). Illus. by Fritz Siebel. 1992, HarperCollins LB $14.89 (0-06-020187-8); paper $3.75 (0-06-444155-5). 64pp. The adventures of a literal-minded housekeeper, in a newly illustrated edition. Other series titles are: *Amelia Bedelia and the Surprise Shower* (1966); *Thank You, Amelia Bedelia* (1993).

**5332** Parish, Peggy. *Amelia Bedelia Goes Camping* (2–4). Illus. by Lynn Sweat. 1985, Greenwillow LB $15.93 (0-688-04057-8); Avon paper $3.99 (0-380-70067-0). 56pp. Amelia's camping trip is the occasion for all kinds of mistakes. Also use: *Amelia Bedelia's Family Album* (1988). (Rev: BCCB 7/85; BL 3/15/85; SLJ 5/85)

**5333** Parish, Peggy. *The Cats' Burglar* (1–2). Illus. by Lynn Sweat. 1983, Greenwillow LB $15.93 (0-688-01826-2); Avon paper $3.99 (0-380-72973-3). 64pp. Aunt Emma's 9 cats foil a burglary attempt.

**5334** Parish, Peggy. *Good Hunting, Blue Sky* (1–3). Illus. by James Watts. 1988, HarperCollins LB $14.89 (0-06-024662-6); paper $3.75 (0-06-444148-2). 64pp. Blue Sky intends to bring home some meat with his new bow and arrow. (Rev: BL 12/1/88)

**5335** Parish, Peggy. *No More Monsters for Me!* (K–3). Illus. by Marc Simont. 1981, HarperCollins LB $14.89 (0-06-024658-8); paper $3.75 (0-06-444109-1). 64pp. A young girl wants to keep a monster for a pet.

**5336** Parish, Peggy. *Play Ball, Amelia Bedelia* (1–3). Illus. by Wallace Tripp. 1972, HarperCollins LB $14.89 (0-06-024656-1); paper $3.75 (0-06-444205-5). 64pp. Amelia Bedelia has trouble with baseball lingo. Other series titles are: *Come Back, Amelia Bedelia* (1971); *Teach Us, Amelia Bedelia* (1977, Greenwillow); *Amelia Bedelia Helps Out* (1979, Greenwillow); *Amelia Bedelia and the Baby* (1981, Greenwillow).

**5337** Parish, Peggy. *Scruffy* (1–2). Illus. by Kelly Oechsli. 1988, HarperCollins LB $15.89 (0-06-024660-X); paper $3.75 (0-06-444137-7). 64pp. A small boy learns how to choose and care for his first pet — a kitten. (Rev: BL 2/1/88; SLJ 7/88)

**5338** Park, Barbara. *Junie B. Jones Has a Monster Under Her Bed* (2–3). Illus. by Denise Brunkus. Series: Stepping Stone Book. 1997, Random LB $11.99 (0-679-96697-8). 80pp. An easy reader in which little Junie is convinced that an invisible monster lives under her bed. Also use *Junie B. Jones Is Not a Crook* (1997). (Rev: HB 7–8/97; SLJ 11/97)

**5339** Park, Barbara. *Junie B. Jones Loves Handsome Warren* (1–2). Illus. by Denise Brunkus. 1996, Random LB $11.99 (0-679-96696-X); paper $3.99 (0-679-86696-5). 71pp. Junie falls in love with a new boy in her kindergarten class in this easy-to-read book. (Rev: BL 2/1/97)

**5340** Pearson, Susan. *Eagle-Eye Ernie Comes to Town* (2–3). Illus. by Gioia Fiammenghi. 1990, Simon & Schuster paper $11.95 (0-671-70564-4). 70pp. Ernestine earns the admiration of her classmates when she solves the mystery of items missing from lunch bags. (Rev: BCCB 12/92; BL 10/1/90; SLJ 4/91)

**5341** Pearson, Susan. *The Green Magician Puzzle* (1–3). Illus. by Gioia Fiammenghi. 1991, Simon & Schuster paper $11.95 (0-671-74054-7). 88pp. Ernie and her classmates must solve a series of riddles to become the Green Magicians of the Earth Day parade. (Rev: SLJ 12/91)

**5342** Peters, Lisa Westberg. *The Hayloft* (1–2). Illus. by K. D. Plum. 1995, Dial paper $12.89 (0-8037-1491-2). 48pp. A humorous, easy-to-read book about Caroline Rose, her sister Ivy, and a day spent on their farm. (Rev: BCCB 2/95; BL 1/1/95; SLJ 2/95*)

**5343** Petersen, P. J. *The Sub* (2–4). Illus. by Meredith Johnson. 1993, Dutton paper $13.99 (0-525-45059-9). 80pp. Two boys decide to trick their substitute teacher by switching places. (Rev: BL 6/1–15/93; SLJ 7/93*)

**5344** Petrie, Catherine. *Joshua James Likes Trucks* (PS–1). Illus. by Jerry Warshaw. 1982, Children's LB $17.00 (0-516-03525-8); paper $4.95 (0-516-

43525-6). 32pp. A description of all the trucks that Joshua likes.

**5345** Phillips, Joan. *My New Boy* (K–2). Illus. by Lynn Munsinger. 1986, Random LB $11.99 (0-394-98277-0); paper $3.99 (0-394-88277-6). 32pp. A pet store puppy searches for just the right owner. Also use: *Lucky Bear* (1986). (Rev: BCCB 1/87; BL 12/1/86)

**5346** Pinkney, Andrea D. *Solo Girl* (2–3). Illus. by Nneka Bennett. Series: Hyperion Chapters. 1997, Hyperion LB $14.49 (0-7868-2265-1); paper $3.95 (0-7868-1216-8). 56pp. A third-grader realizes that her superior math abilities can help her make friends when she moves to a new neighborhood. (Rev: SLJ 10/97)

**5347** Platt, Kin. *Big Max* (1–2). Illus. by Robert Lopshire. Series: I Can Read Book. 1992, Harper-Collins LB $12.89 (0-06-024751-7); paper $3.75 (0-06-444006-0). 64pp. A modest detective unravels the case of the king's missing elephant in this newly illustrated I Can Read Book.

**5348** Pomerantz, Charlotte. *The Outside Dog* (1–3). Illus. by Jennifer Plecas. 1993, HarperCollins LB $14.89 (0-06-024783-5). 64pp. An easy-reader that tells how Marisol gradually breaks down her grandfather's opposition to having a dog as a pet. (Rev: BCCB 10/93; BL 9/15/93*; SLJ 11/93*)

**5349** Poploff, Michelle. *Tea Party for Two* (2–3). Illus. by Maryann Cocca-Leffler. Series: Yearling First Choice Chapter Book. 1997, Delacorte paper $3.99 (0-440-41334-6). 41pp. Two girls plan a party and find that a boy and his dog have eaten all their food. (Rev: SLJ 2/98)

**5350** Porte, Barbara Ann. *Harry in Trouble* (1–3). Illus. by Yossi Abolafia. 1989, Greenwillow LB $15.93 (0-688-07722-6); Dell paper $4.99 (0-440-80210-5). 48pp. Harry's third library card has disappeared! (Rev: BCCB 2/89; BL 3/1/89; SLJ 3/89)

**5351** Porte, Barbara Ann. *Harry's Pony* (1–2). Illus. by Yossi Abolafia. 1997, Greenwillow LB $14.93 (0-688-14826-3). 56pp. Harry wins a pony in a contest, but his father won't let him keep it in this easily read book. (Rev: BL 8/97; HB 9–10/97; SLJ 8/97)

**5352** Prager, Annabelle. *The Baseball Birthday Party* (1–2). Illus. by Marilyn Mets. 1995, Random LB $11.99 (0-679-94171-1); paper $3.99 (0-679-84171-7). 48pp. A boy throws a baseball party, but none of his friends show up in this easily read story. (Rev: BL 7/95)

**5353** Prager, Annabelle. *The Surprise Party* (1–3). Illus. by Tomie dePaola. 1988, Random LB $7.99 (0-394-99596-1); paper $3.99 (0-394-89596-7). 48pp. Nicky plans his own surprise party but receives a real surprise in this easily read picture book.

**5354** *The Random House Book of Easy-to-Read Stories* (K–2). Illus. 1993, Random $18.00 (0-679-83438-9). 252pp. Easy-to-read stories from 16 authors, including Dr. Seuss, the Berenstains, and P. D. Eastman. (Rev: BCCB 1/94; BL 2/1/94; SLJ 3/94)

**5355** Rau, Dana Meachen. *A Box Can Be Many Things* (1–2). Illus. by Paige Billin-Frye. Series: Rookie Readers. 1997, Children's LB $17.00 (0-516-20317-7). 32pp. Two children rescue a big box from the garbage and use it in many imaginative ways in this beginning reader. (Rev: BL 5/1/97)

**5356** Reit, Seymour. *The Rebus Bears* (PS–2). Illus. by Kenneth Smith. Series: Bank Street Ready-to-Read. 1997, Gareth Stevens LB $18.60 (0-8368-1750-8); Bantam paper $3.99 (0-553-34689-X). Using pictures plus words, this simple rebus retells Goldilocks and the Three Bears. (Rev: SLJ 10/89)

**5357** Robins, Joan. *Addie Meets Max* (1–3). Illus. by Sue Truesdell. 1985, HarperCollins $9.95 (0-06-025063-1). 32pp. Addie is sure she won't like her new neighbor until mother invites him in for pizza. Also use: *Addie Runs Away* (1989). (Rev: BCCB 5/85; BL 4/15/85; SLJ 5/85)

**5358** Rockwell, Anne. *The Story Snail* (2–3). Illus. by Theresa Smith. 1997, Simon & Schuster $15.00 (0-689-81221-3); paper $3.99 (0-689-81220-5). 48pp. Unpopular John finds a magic snail that gives him interesting stories to tell in this easy reader. (Rev: BL 5/1/97; SLJ 9/97)

**5359** Rockwell, Anne. *Sweet Potato Pie* (PS–K). Illus. Series: Early Step into Reading. 1996, Random LB $11.99 (0-679-96440-1); paper $3.99 (0-679-86440-7). 32pp. Every member of a family stops what each is doing when Grandma bakes a sweet potato pie. (Rev: BL 8/96)

**5360** Roland, Timothy. *Come Down Now, Flying Cow!* (K–2). Illus. by author. Series: Beginner Books. 1997, Random LB $11.99 (0-679-98110-1). In this book for beginning readers, Beth the Cow and her bird companion share adventures during a trip in a hot-air balloon. (Rev: SLJ 10/97)

**5361** Roop, Peter, and Connie Roop. *Keep the Lights Burning, Abbie* (1–3). Illus. by Peter E. Hanson. 1985, Carolrhoda LB $18.60 (0-87614-275-7); paper $5.95 (0-87614-454-7). 40pp. The true story of Abbie Burgess, who keeps the lighthouse lights ablaze for 4 storm-filled weeks while her father is on the mainland. (Rev: BCCB 1/86; BL 1/15/86) [387.1]

**5362** Ross, Alice, and Kent Ross. *The Copper Lady* (1–3). Illus. by Leslie Bowman. 1997, Carolrhoda LB $18.60 (0-87614-934-4). 48pp. An easy-to-read book about a young Parisian who watches the construction of the Statue of Liberty and stows away on the ship that is taking it to the United States. (Rev: BCCB 7–8/97; BL 8/97; SLJ 9/97)

**5363** Ross, Pat. *M & M and the Haunted House* (K–3). Illus. by Marylin Hafner. 1990, Puffin paper $4.99 (0-14-034577-9). 64pp. Mimi and Mandy frighten themselves with their haunted house games. Also use: *M & M and the Bad News Babies* (1983).

**5364** Ruthstrom, Dorotha. *The Big Kite Contest* (1–3). Illus. by Lillian Hoban. 1980, Pantheon $6.95 (0-394-84430-0). 48pp. Stephen's kite crashes and so does his hope of winning the kite contest.

**5365** Rylant, Cynthia. *Henry and Mudge and the Careful Cousin* (1–3). Illus. by Sucie Stevenson. 1994, Bradbury $14.00 (0-02-778021-X). 48pp. At first, Annie finds lots to dislike about her cousin Henry and his dog Mudge, but gradually she comes around. (Rev: BL 2/1/94; HB 3–4/94; SLJ 4/94*)

**5366** Rylant, Cynthia. *Henry and Mudge and the Sneaky Crackers* (1–2). Illus. by Sucie Stevenson. 1998, Simon & Schuster $14.00 (0-689-81176-4). 40pp. Henry and his dog Mudge have fun with a new spy kit in this easily read book. (Rev: BL 2/1/98)

**5367** Rylant, Cynthia. *Henry and Mudge and the Wild Wind: The Twelfth Book of Their Adventures* (1–2). Illus. by Sucie Stevenson. 1993, Macmillan paper $13.00 (0-02-778014-7). 40pp. Henry and his dog don't like thunderstorms. (Rev: BL 7/93; HB 7–8/93; SLJ 6/93)

**5368** Rylant, Cynthia. *Henry and Mudge in the Family Trees* (1–2). Illus. by Sucie Stevenson. 1997, Simon & Schuster $14.00 (0-689-81179-9). 48pp. In this easy reader, Henry is afraid that his new relatives won't like his dog, Mudge. (Rev: BL 8/97; SLJ 9/97)

**5369** Rylant, Cynthia. *Mr. Putter and Tabby Fly the Plane* (1–2). Illus. by Arthur Howard. 1997, Harcourt $11.00 (0-15-256253-2); paper $5.00 (0-15-201060-2). 44pp. For beginning readers, this humorous story tells about Mr. Putter's purchase of a radio-controlled biplane. Also use *Mr. Putter and Tabby Row the Boat* (1997). (Rev: BL 4/1/97; SLJ 4/97)

**5370** Rylant, Cynthia. *Mr. Putter and Tabby Pick the Pears* (1–3). Illus. by Arthur Howard. 1995, Harcourt $12.00 (0-15-200245-6); paper $6.00 (0-15-200246-4). 44pp. Mr. Putter experiments with an alternative method to harvest pears from his tree. (Rev: BL 1/1–15/96; SLJ 10/95)

**5371** Rylant, Cynthia. *Mr. Putter and Tabby Pour the Tea* (1–2). Illus. by Arthur Howard. 1994, Harcourt $11.00 (0-15-256255-9); paper $6.00 (0-15-200901-9). 44pp. Lonely Mr. Putter finds a friend when he adopts a cat from the local pound. Also use *Mr. Putter and Tabby Walk the Dog* (1994). (Rev: BL 2/1/94; HB 5–6/94; SLJ 4/94)

**5372** Rylant, Cynthia. *Poppleton* (1–2). Illus. by Mark Teague. 1997, Scholastic $13.95 (0-590-84782-1). 48pp. Poppleton the pig has 3 adventures, including one in which he helps a friend take his medicine. (Rev: BL 2/1/97; SLJ 3/97)

**5373** Rylant, Cynthia. *Poppleton and Friends* (1–3). Illus. by Mark Teague. 1997, Scholastic $13.95 (0-590-84786-4). 48pp. Three stories about the friendship of Poppleton pig with his buddies Hudson and Cherry Sue. (Rev: BL 8/97; SLJ 9/97)

**5374** Sachar, Louis. *Marvin Redpost: Kidnapped at Birth?* (1–3). Illus. by Neal Hughes. Series: Stepping Stone. 1992, Random LB $11.99 (0-679-91946-5); paper $3.99 (0-679-81946-0). 68pp. Marvin Redpost secretly believes that he is the kidnapped son of the king. (Rev: BCCB 10/92; BL 12/1/92; SLJ 3/93)

**5375** Sadler, Marilyn. *It's Not Easy Being a Bunny* (PS–2). Illus. by Roger Bollen. 1983, Random LB $11.99 (0-394-96102-1). 48pp. A young rabbit tries to live with other animals. A sequel is: *The Very Bad Bunny* (1984).

**5376** Sadler, Marilyn. *The Parakeet Girl* (1–3). Illus. by Roger Bollen. Series: Step into Reading. 1997, Random paper $3.99 (0-679-87289-2). 48pp. Emma is happy with her parakeet until her brother also gets one in this easy reader. (Rev: BCCB 7–8/97; BL 5/1/97; SLJ 9/97)

**5377** Sandin, Joan. *Pioneer Bear* (2–3). Illus. Series: Step into Reading. 1995, Random LB $11.99 (0-679-96050-3); paper $3.99 (0-679-86050-9). 43pp. Using a pioneer setting, this is the story of a photographer who hopes to take pictures of a pet bear. (Rev: BCCB 7–8/95; BL 7/95; SLJ 10/95)

**5378** Sathre, Vivian. *Leroy Potts Meets the McCrooks* (2–3). Illus. Series: Yearling First Choice Chapter Book. 1997, Bantam $13.95 (0-385-32192-9); paper $3.99 (0-440-41137-8). 48pp. When Leroy gets struck by lightning, he loses his memory in this humorous beginning reader. (Rev: BL 5/1/97; SLJ 9/97)

**5379** Sathre, Vivian. *Mouse Chase* (PS–1). Illus. by Ward Schumaker. 1995, Harcourt $12.00 (0-15-200105-0). 40pp. A cat and mouse play together in this easy-to-read picture book. (Rev: BCCB 12/95; BL 1/1–15/96; SLJ 4/96)

**5380** Schade, Susan. *Space Rock* (2–3). Illus. 1989, Random paper $3.99 (0-394-89384-0). 48pp. Bob finds a purple rock that talks. (Rev: BL 3/1/89)

**5381** Schade, Susan, and Jon Buller. *Toad on the Road* (1). Illus. 1992, Random LB $7.99 (0-679-92689-5); paper $3.99 (0-679-82689-0). 32pp. Toad and his friends go out in his car for a series of pleasant experiences. (Rev: BL 6/15/92)

**5382** Schade, Susan, and Jon Buller. *Toad Takes Off* (1–2). Illus. 1997, Random paper $3.99 (0-679-

86935-2). 32pp. Toad takes his friends Pig and Cow on an airplane ride in this charming easy reader. (Rev: BL 5/1/97; SLJ 8/97)

**5383** Schecter, Ellen. *I Love to Sneeze* (K–1). Illus. by Gioia Fiammenghi. 1992, Bantam paper $3.99 (0-553-35159-1). 32pp. The effects of a little girl's giant sneeze include blowing the fleas off a dog. (Rev: BL 10/1/92)

**5384** Scherer, Jeffrey. *One Snowy Day* (1–2). Illus. 1997, Scholastic $3.50 (0-590-74240-X). 32pp. When snow arrives, a bear, kitten, and deer come together to build a snowman. (Rev: BL 2/1/98)

**5385** Schneider, Antonie. *The Birthday Bear* (PS–3). Trans. from German by J. Alison James. Illus. by Uli Waas. 1996, North-South LB $13.88 (1-55858-656-3). An easy-to-read book about a family camping trip that is interrupted by the arrival of a bear. (Rev: SLJ 12/96)

**5386** Schulman, Janet. *The Big Hello* (1–2). Illus. by Lillian Hoban. 1976, Greenwillow paper $3.95 (0-688-08405-2). 56pp. A good book for independent readers about a small girl who prattles to her doll, her dog, and her mother.

**5387** Schwartz, Alvin. *Busy Buzzing Bumblebees and Other Tongue Twisters* (1–3). Illus. by Paul Meisel. 1992, HarperCollins LB $14.89 (0-06-025269-3). 64pp. A collection of nonsensical tongue twisters, illustrated with watercolors, for beginning readers. (Rev: BL 4/1/92; SLJ 6/92) [818]

**5388** Schwartz, Alvin. *Ghosts! Ghostly Tales from Folklore* (K–2). Illus. by Victoria Chess. 1991, HarperCollins LB $15.89 (0-06-021797-9); paper $3.75 (0-06-444170-9). 64pp. Contains a number of suspenseful ghost stories written for the beginning reader. (Rev: BCCB 9/91; BL 9/15/91; HB 9–10/91; SLJ 9/91)

**5389** Schwartz, Alvin. *I Saw You in the Bathtub and Other Folk Rhymes* (1–3). Illus. by Syd Hoff. 1989, HarperCollins paper $3.75 (0-06-444151-2). 64pp. An amusing assortment of folk rhymes. Also use: *All of Our Noses Are Here and Other Noodle Tales* (1985). (Rev: BCCB 4/89; BL 3/1/89; SLJ 5/89)

**5390** Seixas, Judith S. *Water — What It Is, What It Does* (2–4). Illus. by Tom Huffman. 1987, Greenwillow LB $15.93 (0-688-06608-9). 56pp. Short, easy-to-read chapters describe properties and uses of water and its effects on the environment. (Rev: BL 12/1/87; SLJ 10/87)

**5391** Seuss, Dr. *The Cat in the Hat* (1–3). Illus. by author. 1957, Random LB $11.99 (0-394-90001-4). 72pp. The story of the fabulous cat that came to visit one rainy day when Mother was away. Also from the same author and publisher: *The Cat in the Hat Comes Back!* (1958); *Foot Book* (1968).

**5392** Seuss, Dr. *Green Eggs and Ham* (K–3). Illus. by author. 1960, Random LB $11.99 (0-394-90016-2). 72pp. A charming nonsense book.

**5393** Seuss, Dr. *Hop on Pop* (1–2). Illus. by author. 1963, Random LB $11.99 (0-394-90029-4). 72pp. One of the many entertaining, controlled vocabulary stories of Dr. Seuss. Also use: *One Fish, Two Fish, Red Fish, Blue Fish* (1960); *Fox in Socks* (1965).

**5394** Seuss, Dr. *I Am Not Going to Get Up Today!* (1–2). Illus. by James Stevenson. 1987, Random LB $11.99 (0-394-99217-2). 48pp. A rhyming story about a little boy who refuses to get up in the morning. (Rev: BL 12/1/87)

**5395** Seuss, Dr. *I Can Lick Thirty Tigers Today and Other Stories* (K–3). Illus. by author. 1969, Random $14.00 (0-394-80094-X). The Cat in the Hat tells 3 zany stories.

**5396** Seuss, Dr. *I Can Read with My Eyes Shut!* (1–2). Illus. by author. 1978, Random LB $11.99 (0-394-93912-3). The Cat in the Hat tells us of all the joys of reading.

**5397** Seuss, Dr. *Oh Say Can You Say?* (1–3). Illus. by author. 1979, Random LB $11.99 (0-394-94255-8). Tongue-twisting verses presented by a variety of imaginative creatures.

**5398** Sharmat, Marjorie W. *The Great Genghis Khan Look-Alike Contest* (2–4). Illus. by Mitchell Rigie. Series: Stepping Stone. 1993, Random paper $3.99 (0-679-85002-3). 76pp. Duz, an ugly dog, might become the replacement for the fierce TV dog, Genghis Khan. (Rev: BL 8/93)

**5399** Sharmat, Marjorie W. *Nate the Great* (1–3). Illus. by Marc Simont. 1986, Dell paper $3.99 (0-440-46126-X). 48pp. Nate, a boy detective, puts on his Sherlock Holmes outfit and sets out confidently to solve the mystery of the missing painting. Other titles in the series: *Nate the Great Goes Undercover* (1977); *Nate the Great and the Lost List* (1976); *Nate the Great and the Phony Clue* (1981); *Nate the Great and the Sticky Case* (1981); *Nate the Great and the Missing Key* (1981); *Nate the Great and the Snowy Trail* (1982).

**5400** Sharmat, Marjorie W. *Nate the Great and the Fishy Prize* (1–3). Illus. by Marc Simont. 1988, Dell paper $3.99 (0-440-40039-2). Nate the Great and his dog Sludge solve the mystery of the stolen prize. Also use: *Nate the Great Stalks Stupidweed* (1986); *Nate the Great Goes Down in the Dumps* (1989). (Rev: BL 8/85; SLJ 9/85)

**5401** Sharmat, Marjorie W. *Nate the Great Saves the King of Sweden* (1–3). Illus. by Marc Simont. 1997, Delacorte $14.95 (0-385-32120-1). 42pp. Although he doesn't leave home, Nate solves a crime in Sweden in this easy-to-read mystery story. (Rev: BL 2/1/98; SLJ 10/97)

**5402** Sharmat, Marjorie W., and Craig Sharmat. *Nate the Great and the Tardy Tortoise* (1–3). Illus. by Marc Simont. 1995, Delacorte $13.95 (0-385-32111-2). 48pp. Using a trail of half-eaten plants as a guide, Nate the Great is able to return a lost turtle to its owner. (Rev: BL 10/1/95; SLJ 10/95)

**5403** Sharmat, Marjorie W., and Rosalind Weinman. *Nate the Great and the Pillowcase* (1–3). Illus. by Marc Simont. 1993, Delacorte $12.95 (0-385-31051-X). 48pp. Nate follows a series of puzzling clues in his search for a cat's pillowcase that has been stolen from his friend Rosamond. (Rev: BL 11/15/93; SLJ 2/94)

**5404** Shaw, Nancy. *Sheep in a Jeep* (K–2). Illus. by Margot Apple. 1986, Houghton $14.00 (0-395-41105-X); paper $3.95 (0-395-47030-7). 32pp. Silly sheep in a silly tale; they fall down, Jeep and all, and land in a muddy pool. Also use: *Sheep on a Ship* (1989). (Rev: BL 9/15/86; HB 11–12/86)

**5405** Shaw, Nancy. *Sheep Out to Eat* (PS–1). Illus. by Margot Apple. 1992, Houghton $14.00 (0-395-61128-8). 32pp. Several sheep are asked to leave a tea shop after they misbehave in this amusing story in rhyme. (Rev: BL 9/15/92; SLJ 9/92)

**5406** Shea, George. *Amazing Rescues* (2–3). Illus. by Marshall H. Peck. 1992, Random paper $3.99 (0-679-81107-9). 48pp. There are 3 thrilling true-life rescue stories in this easily read book. (Rev: BCCB 11/92; BL 3/1/93; SLJ 4/93) [628.9]

**5407** Shea, George. *First Flight: The Story of Tom Tate and the Wright Brothers* (2–3). Illus. by Don Bolognese. Series: I Can Read Chapter Books. 1997, HarperCollins LB $14.89 (0-06-024504-2). 48pp. A fictional account of a boy who is a friend of Orville and Wilbur Wright and participates in their flights. (Rev: BL 11/15/96; HB 3–4/97; SLJ 1/97)

**5408** Simon, Charnan. *Come! Sit! Speak!* (PS–2). Illus. by Bari Weissman. Series: Rookie Readers. 1997, Children's LB $17.00 (0-516-20397-5). 32pp. A humorous beginning reader about a girl who wanted a puppy but got a baby sister instead. (Rev: SLJ 2/98)

**5409** Singer, Bill. *The Fox with Cold Feet* (K–2). Illus. by Dennis Kendrick. 1980, Parents LB $5.95 (0-8193-1022-0). 48pp. A fox sets out to get a pair of boots to help cure his cold feet.

**5410** Siracusa, Catherine. *No Mail for Mitchell* (K–1). Illus. 1990, Random LB $11.99 (0-679-90476-X); paper $3.99 (0-679-80476-5). 32pp. The postman, a dog named Mitchell, never gets any letters for himself. (Rev: BL 12/1/90)

**5411** Siracusa, Catherine. *The Peanut Butter Gang* (2). Illus. Series: Hyperion Chapters. 1996, Hyperion $13.95 (0-7868-0148-4); paper $3.95 (0-7868-

1115-3). 48pp. Billy proves that his love of bells and their sounds can have a practical use. (Rev: BL 4/1/96; SLJ 7/96)

**5412** Skofield, James. *Detective Dinosaur* (1–3). Illus. 1996, HarperCollins LB $14.89 (0-06-024908-0). 48pp. Three uncomplicated mysteries are included in this easily read book. (Rev: BL 8/96; SLJ 8/96)

**5413** Skofield, James. *Detective Dinosaur Lost and Found* (1–2). Illus. by R. W. Alley. Series: I Can Read Book. 1998, HarperCollins $14.95 (0-06-026784-4). 48pp. There are 3 humorous cases involving Detective Dinosaur in this easy-to-read book. (Rev: BL 2/1/98; SLJ 3/98)

**5414** Slaughter, Hope. *Buckley and Wilberta* (2–3). Illus. Series: I'm Reading Now. 1996, Red Hen LB $14.95 (0-931093-15-5). 64pp. Two friends, Buckley the Hedgehog and Wilberta Rabbit, are featured in 4 stories. (Rev: BL 4/1/96)

**5415** Smath, Jerry. *Pretzel and Pop's Closetful of Stories* (2–3). Illus. 1991, Silver Burdett LB $7.95 (0-671-72231-X). 64pp. Pop rabbit tells his daughter Pretzel stories about her relatives. (Rev: BL 12/1/91)

**5416** Smith, Janice Lee. *Wizard and Wart at Sea* (1–2). Illus. 1995, HarperCollins LB $13.89 (0-06-024755-X). 48pp. Though on a holiday, Wizard insists on casting spells on various animals in this easy-to-read story. (Rev: BCCB 9/95; BL 7/95; SLJ 12/95)

**5417** Spirn, Michele. *The Know-Nothings* (1–2). Illus. by R. W. Alley. Series: I Can Read Book. 1995, HarperCollins LB $14.89 (0-06-024500-X). 64pp. The Know-Nothings are featured in 4 humorous stories in this easily read book. (Rev: BCCB 7–8/95; BL 7/95; SLJ 11/95)

**5418** Spohn, Kate. *Dog and Cat Shake a Leg* (K–1). Illus. 1996, Viking paper $11.99 (0-670-86758-6). 32pp. Dog and Cat share many everyday activities and have good times in this easily read book. (Rev: BL 1/1–15/96; SLJ 4/96)

**5419** Stadler, John. *The Adventures of Snail at School* (1–2). Illus. 1993, HarperCollins LB $15.89 (0-06-021042-7). 64pp. Snail has an unexpected adventure when he volunteers to pick up books at the school library. (Rev: BL 9/15/93)

**5420** Stadler, John. *Ready, Set, Go!* (1–2). Illus. Series: I Can Read Book. 1996, HarperCollins LB $14.89 (0-06-024947-1). 32pp. Little Sasha, a dog, must contend with the scorn of her big cousin Oliver. (Rev: BL 9/15/96; SLJ 12/96)

**5421** Stamper, Judith B. *Five Goofy Ghosts* (2–3). Illus. by Tim Raglin. Series: Hello Reader! 1997, Scholastic $3.99 (0-590-92152-5). 32pp. Five horror stories that are also humorous are contained in this simple beginning reader. (Rev: BL 2/1/98)

**5422** Standiford, Natalie. *The Bravest Dog Ever: The True Story of Balto* (1–3). Illus. by Donald Cook. 1989, Random LB $11.99 (0-394-99695-X); paper $3.99 (0-394-89695-5). 48pp. In easy-to-read format, this is the true story of an amazing dog who guided a sled team carrying medicine to Nome, Alaska. (Rev: BCCB 1/90; BL 2/1/90; SLJ 2/90) [636.7]

**5423** Stevenson, James. *Mud Flat April Fool* (1–3). Illus. 1998, Greenwillow LB $14.93 (0-688-15164-7). 48pp. A humorous book for beginning readers in which the animal residents of Mud Flat have fun playing jokes on April Fools' Day. (Rev: BL 2/15/98; SLJ 3/98)

**5424** Stevenson, James. *Which One Is Whitney?* (K–3). Illus. 1990, Greenwillow LB $12.88 (0-688-09062-1). 40pp. Three tales about sea creatures known as dugongs. (Rev: BL 9/1/90; SLJ 1/91*)

**5425** Stevenson, Sucie. *The Twelve Dancing Princesses* (1–3). Illus. 1995, Bantam $13.95 (0-385-32167-8); paper $3.99 (0-440-41088-6). 48pp. A simple retelling of the Grimm Brothers' tale of the princesses who secretly dance away their nights. (Rev: BL 1/1–15/96; SLJ 3/96) [398.2]

**5426** Stolz, Mary. *Emmett's Pig* (1–3). Illus. by Garth Williams. 1959, HarperCollins LB $15.89 (0-06-025856-X). 64pp. Although he lives in a city apartment, Emmett's greatest wish is to own his own pig.

**5427** Swanson, June. *I Pledge Allegiance* (1–3). Illus. by Rick Hanson. 1990, Carolrhoda LB $17.95 (0-87614-393-1). 40pp. The difficult words in the Pledge of Allegiance are explained and its history is traced. (Rev: BCCB 6/90; BL 6/1/90; SLJ 7/90) [323.6]

**5428** Tafuri, Nancy. *Spots, Feathers, and Curly Tails* (PS). Illus. by author. 1988, Greenwillow LB $15.93 (0-688-07537-1). 32pp. A concept book that makes a mystery of identifying familiar animals from the barnyard. (Rev: BL 8/88; HB 11–12/88; SLJ 12/88)

**5429** Thaler, Mike. *Pack 109* (1–2). Illus. by Normand Chartier. 1988, Puffin paper $3.25 (0-14-036548-6). 48pp. The adventures of 5 rodents who make up Scout Pack 109. (Rev: BL 7/88; SLJ 9/88)

**5430** Turner, Ann. *Dust for Dinner* (1–2). Illus. by Robert Barrett. 1995, HarperCollins LB $14.89 (0-06-023377-X). 64pp. An easy-to-read book about an Oklahoma family ruined by drought and the Depression. (Rev: BCCB 9/95; BL 7/95; SLJ 10/95)

**5431** Uebe, Ingrid. *Melinda and Nock and the Magic Spell* (2–3). Trans. from German by J. Alison James. Illus. by Alex de Wolf. Series: Easy-to-Read Books. 1996, North-South LB $13.88 (1-55858-572-9). 62pp. An underwater fantasy about the adventures of a young mermaid and her water-sprite friend. (Rev: SLJ 7/96)

**5432** Van Leeuwen, Jean. *Amanda Pig, Schoolgirl* (K–1). Illus. by Ann Schweninger. Series: An Easy-to-Read Book. 1997, Dial paper $12.89 (0-8037-1981-7). 48pp. In this easy-to-read book, Amanda Pig spends her first day at school. (Rev: HB 5–6/97; SLJ 7/97*)

**5433** Van Leeuwen, Jean. *Oliver and Amanda and the Big Snow* (1–2). Illus. by Ann Schweninger. 1995, Dial paper $12.89 (0-8037-1763-6). 48pp. Oliver Pig and his little sister share many winter activities, like building a snow fort and sledding down a steep hill. (Rev: BCCB 1/96; BL 1/1–15/96; HB 9–10/95; SLJ 12/95*)

**5434** Viorst, Judith. *Alexander, Who Used to Be Rich Last Sunday* (K–2). Illus. by Ray Cruz. 1978, Macmillan $15.00 (0-689-30602-4); paper $3.95 (0-689-71199-9). 32pp. Alexander spends his dollar gift foolishly penny by penny.

**5435** Welch, Catherine A. *Danger at the Breaker* (1–4). Illus. by Andrea Shine. 1992, Carolrhoda LB $18.60 (0-87614-693-0); paper $5.95 (0-87614-564-0). 48pp. In the 1880s, 8-year-old Andrew must leave school to work in the coal mines. (Rev: BL 3/1/93; SLJ 9/92)

**5436** Wetterer, Margaret K. *Kate Shelley and the Midnight Express* (2–3). Illus. by Karen Ritz. 1990, Carolrhoda LB $18.60 (0-87614-425-3). 48pp. Based on a true story, the tale of a young girl who saved a train from disaster. (Rev: BCCB 11/90; BL 9/15/90; SLJ 1/91)

**5437** Wheeler, Cindy. *The Emperor's Birthday Suit* (1–3). Illus. by R. W. Alley. 1996, Random paper $3.99 (0-679-87424-0). 48pp. A hilarious variation on the familiar Hans Christian Andersen tale. (Rev: BL 9/15/96)

**5438** Wiseman, Bernard. *Barber Bear* (2–3). Illus. by author. 1987, Little, Brown paper $11.95 (0-316-94859-4). 48pp. Puns aplenty in this story of Barber Bear. (Rev: BL 8/87; SLJ 8/87)

**5439** Wiseman, Bernard. *Morris and Boris at the Circus* (1–2). Illus. by author. 1988, HarperCollins LB $15.89 (0-06-026478-0); paper $3.50 (0-06-444143-1). 64pp. Two friends, a moose and a bear, attend the circus. Also use: *Morris Goes to School* (1983). (Rev: BL 12/1/88; SLJ 2/89)

**5440** Wyeth, Sharon D. *Ginger Brown: The Nobody Boy* (2–3). Illus. by Cornelius Van Wright. 1997, Random paper $3.99 (0-679-85645-5). 71pp. Ginger Brown becomes friends with a boy who is sad because of his parents' separation in this easy-to-read book. (Rev: BL 5/1/97)

**5441** Ziefert, Harriet. *Dr. Cat* (K–1). Illus. by Suzy Mandel. Series: Hello Reading! 1989, Puffin paper $3.50 (0-14-050985-2). In this beginning reader, 3 kittens go to Dr. Cat for an examination. Others in this series are: *Harry Goes to Fun Land* and *When the TV Broke* (both 1989). (Rev: SLJ 10/89)

**5442** Ziefert, Harriet. *Harry Takes a Bath* (1–2). Illus. by Mavis Smith. 1987, Puffin paper $3.50 (0-14-050746-9). 32pp. Harry the hippo takes a fun, if messy bath, and cleans up afterward. (Rev: BL 8/87)

**5443** Ziefert, Harriet. *The Little Red Hen* (K–3). Illus. by Emily Bolam. 1995, Viking paper $11.99 (0-670-86050-6). 32pp. The familiar story retold in an easy-to-read format. (Rev: BL 10/1/95; SLJ 1/96)

**5444** Ziefert, Harriet. *Mike and Tony: Best Friends* (1–3). Illus. by Catherine Siracusa. 1987, Puffin paper $3.50 (0-14-050744-2). 32pp. Two young boys who share everything suddenly have a real fight. (Rev: BL 8/87)

**5445** Ziefert, Harriet. *Stitches* (1–3). Illus. by Amy Aitken. Series: Hello Reading! 1990, Puffin paper $3.50 (0-14-054224-8). 32pp. A little boy falls off his bike and needs stitches. (Rev: BL 9/1/90)

# Fiction for Older Readers

## Adventure and Mystery

**5446** Abbott, Kate. *Mystery at Echo Cliffs* (4–6). Illus. by Faith DeLong. 1994, Red Crane Bks. paper $11.95 (1-878610-37-6). 183pp. After the death of their parents, 2 Navajo youngsters move back to the reservation, where they help track down a gang of pottery thieves. (Rev: SLJ 12/94)

**5447** Abbott, Tony. *Danger Guys* (2–4). Illus. 1994, HarperCollins paper $3.95 (0-06-440519-2). 80pp. Zeek and Noodle have some wild adventures before they outwit thieves at a temple site. Also use *Danger Guys Blast Off!* (1994). (Rev: BL 8/94)

**5448** Adler, David A. *Cam Jansen and the Ghostly Mystery* (2–4). Illus. 1996, Viking paper $13.99 (0-670-86872-8). 64pp. Cam Jansen and her friend Eric are involved in the robbery of a ticket booth at a rock concert. (Rev: BL 1/1–15/97; SLJ 12/96)

**5449** Adler, David A. *Cam Jansen and the Mystery at the Haunted House* (2–4). Illus. by Susanna Natti. 1992, Viking paper $12.99 (0-670-83419-X). 58pp. Cam uses her photographic memory to uncover the thief who stole her aunt's wallet at an amusement park. (Rev: BL 4/1/92; SLJ 4/92)

**5450** Adler, David A. *Cam Jansen and the Mystery at the Monkey House* (2–4). Illus. 1985, Viking $9.95 (0-670-80782-6); Dell paper $2.50 (0-440-40047-3). 64pp. Cam, Eric, and new friend Billy are out to solve the disappearance of monkeys from the zoo in her tenth adventure. Also use: *Cam Jansen and the Mystery of the Circus Clown* (1983); *Cam Jansen and the Mystery of the Monster Movie* (1984). (Rev: BL 4/15/86)

**5451** Adler, David A. *Cam Jansen and the Mystery of Flight 54* (3–4). Illus. by Susanna Natti. 1989, Viking paper $11.99 (0-670-81841-0). 64pp. Cam uses her photographic memory to find a missing French girl. (Rev: BL 11/15/89; SLJ 11/89)

**5452** Adler, David A. *Cam Jansen and the Mystery of the Chocolate Fudge Sale* (2–4). Illus. by Susanna Natti. 1993, Viking LB $11.99 (0-670-84968-5). 64pp. Cam springs into action when she spots a suspicious woman around a vacant house. (Rev: BL 10/15/93; SLJ 9/93)

**5453** Adler, David A. *Cam Jansen and the Mystery of the Stolen Diamonds* (2–4). Illus. by Susanna Natti. 1980, Puffin paper $3.99 (0-14-034670-8). 64pp. Cam is captured by diamond thieves but still manages to keep in charge. Some sequels are: *Cam Jansen and the Mystery of the U.F.O.* (1980); *Cam Jansen and the Mystery of the Dinosaur Bones* (1981); *Cam Jansen and the Mystery of the Television Dog* (1981); *Cam Jansen and the Mystery of the Babe Ruth Baseball* (1982); *Cam Jansen and the Mystery of the Gold Coins* (1982).

**5454** Adler, David A. *Cam Jansen and the Scary Snake Mystery* (2–4). Illus. 1997, Viking $11.99 (0-670-87517-1). 64pp. Cam solves a mystery in which her mother's video camera is stolen after it had been used to photograph someone's pet snake. (Rev: BL 11/15/97; SLJ 12/97)

**5455** Adler, David A. *Cam Jansen and the Triceratops Pops Mystery* (2–4). Illus. 1995, Viking paper $12.99 (0-670-86027-1). 64pp. Cam and her friend Eric solve the mystery of the missing CDs. (Rev: BL 11/1/95; SLJ 12/95)

**5456** Adler, David A. *Lucky Stars* (2–4). Illus. 1996, Random LB $11.99 (0-679-94698-5); paper $3.99 (0-679-84698-0). 69pp. Harry "Houdini" Foster and cousin Janet solve the mystery of disappearing coats at the public library. (Rev: BL 8/96)

**5457** Adler, David A. *Onion Sundaes* (2–4). Illus. by Heather H. Maione. 1994, Random LB $11.99 (0-

679-94697-7). 72pp. Herman and his cousin Janet are determined to solve the mystery of the supermarket thief. (Rev: BL 9/1/94; SLJ 6/94)

**5458** Aiken, Joan. *Cold Shoulder Road* (5–8). Series: Wolves Chronicles. 1996, Delacorte $15.95 (0-385-32182-1). 283pp. In this continuation of the saga begun in *The Wolves of Willoughby Chase*, cousins Arun and Is Twite find danger and high adventure when they stumble on a smuggling ring. (Rev: BCCB 4/96; BL 4/1/96; HB 5–6/96; SLJ 3/96)

**5459** Aiken, Joan. *The Wolves of Willoughby Chase* (4–6). Illus. by Pat Marriott. 1987, Dell paper $3.99 (0-440-49603-9). 168pp. A Victorian melodrama about 2 little girls who outwit their wicked governess-guardian. A reissue of the 1963 edition. Two sequels are: *Black Hearts in Battersea* (1981) and *Nightbirds on Nantucket* (1969).

**5460** Alcock, Vivien. *The Trial of Anna Cotman* (5–8). 1990, Delacorte $13.95 (0-385-29981-8); Houghton paper $6.95 (0-395-81649-1). 160pp. Anna finds that the secret society to which she belongs is gradually becoming an instrument of terror. (Rev: SLJ 2/90)

**5461** Alexander, Lloyd. *The Drackenberg Adventure* (5–8). 1988, Dell paper $3.99 (0-440-40296-4). 160pp. This atypical heroine deals with villains and gypsies and attends the diamond jubilee of Maria-Sophia of Drackenberg. Part of series that includes: *The Illyrian Adventure* (1995, Bantam); *The El Dorado Adventure* (1990, Bantam). (Rev: BCCB 6/88)

**5462** Alexander, Lloyd. *The Jedera Adventure* (5–8). 1989, Dell paper $3.99 (0-440-40295-6). 208pp. Vesper decides to return a valuable library book borrowed by her late father, but the library is in the mythical kingdom of Jedera. (Rev: BL 6/1/89)

**5463** Anastasio, Dina. *The Case of the Glacier Park Swallow* (4–7). Illus. 1994, Roberts Rinehart paper $6.95 (1-879373-85-8). 80pp. Juliet, who wants to be a veterinarian, stumbles upon a drug-smuggling ring in this tightly knit mystery. (Rev: BL 12/1/94; SLJ 10/94)

**5464** Anastasio, Dina. *The Case of the Grand Canyon Eagle* (5–8). Series: Juliet Stone Environmental Mystery. 1994, Roberts Rinehart paper $6.95 (1-879373-84-X). 73pp. In this ecological mystery, 17-year-old Juliet Stone investigates the disappearance of eagle eggs.

**5465** Anderson, Mary. *Suzy's Secret Snoop Society* (4–6). 1990, Avon paper $2.95 (0-380-75917-9). 112pp. Two new friends accidentally uncover a criminal plot. (Rev: BL 12/15/90)

**5466** Andrews, Jean F. *The Secret in the Dorm Attic* (3–5). 1990, Gallaudet Univ. paper $4.95 (0-930323-66-1). 100pp. At a school for the deaf, some boys

uncover stolen jewels and become the victims of a kidnapping. (Rev: BL 10/1/90)

**5467** Avi. *Captain Grey* (5–8). 1993, Morrow paper $4.95 (0-688-12234-5). 160pp. In 1783, young Kevin is captured by pirates. A reissue.

**5468** Avi. *Man from the Sky* (4–6). Illus. by David Wiesner. 1992, Morrow paper $3.95 (0-688-11897-6). 96pp. Eleven-year-old Jamie spots a thief parachuting from an airplane.

**5469** Avi. *Something Upstairs: A Tale of Ghosts* (5–7). 1988, Orchard LB $16.99 (0-531-08382-9); Avon paper $4.50 (0-380-70853-1). 128pp. Kenny moves into a house in Rhode Island that is haunted by the ghost of a slave who was murdered in 1800. (Rev: BCCB 9/88; BL 11/1/88; SLJ 10/88)

**5470** Avi. *Who Stole the Wizard of Oz?* (4–6). Illus. by Derek James. 1990, McKay paper $4.99 (0-394-84992-2). 128pp. Several books disappear from the Chickertown Library book sale.

**5471** Avi. *Windcatcher* (4–7). 1991, Macmillan $15.00 (0-02-707761-6); Avon paper $4.50 (0-380-71805-7). 128pp. Eleven-year-old Tony dreads a summer by the sea, but ends up finding a sailing adventure. (Rev: BCCB 5/91; BL 3/1/91; HB 5–6/91; SLJ 4/91)

**5472** Babbitt, Natalie. *Goody Hall* (4–6). Illus. by author. 1986, Farrar paper $4.95 (0-374-42767-4). 176pp. Gothic mystery told with suspense and humor, centering around the magnificent home of the Goody family.

**5473** Babbitt, Natalie. *Kneeknock Rise* (4–7). Illus. by author. 1970, Farrar paper $3.95 (0-374-44260-6). 96pp. Young Egan sets out to see the people-eating Megrimum.

**5474** Bailey, Linda. *How Can I Be a Detective If I Have to Baby-Sit?* (4–6). 1996, Albert Whitman LB $13.95 (0-8075-3404-8); paper $4.50 (0-8075-3405-6). 157pp. Stevie and Jessie find that their baby-sitting charge is involved in a mystery. (Rev: BL 3/15/96; SLJ 7/96)

**5475** Bailey, Linda. *How Come the Best Clues Are Always in the Garbage?* (4–6). Series: Stevie Diamond Mystery. 1996, Albert Whitman LB $13.95 (0-8075-3409-9); paper $4.50 (0-8075-3410-2). 175pp. When Stevie's mother leads a crusade against a fast-food restaurant, their apartment is burglarized in this fast-moving mystery. (Rev: SLJ 5/96)

**5476** Bailey, Linda. *What's a Daring Detective Like Me Doing in the Doghouse?* (4–5). Series: Stevie Diamond Mystery. 1997, Albert Whitman LB $13.95 (0-8075-8834-2); paper $4.50 (0-8075-8835-0). 185pp. Stevie and her friend Jesse set out to find the culprit who has stolen the president's dog. (Rev: SLJ 1/98)

**5477** Baillie, Allan. *Adrift* (5–7). 1992, Viking paper $14.00 (0-670-84474-8). 128pp. Flynn finds courage and resourcefulness when he, his little sister, and her cat drift out to sea in an old crate. (Rev: BCCB 9/92; BL 3/15/92; HB 9–10/92; SLJ 5/92)

**5478** Baillie, Allan. *Little Brother* (5–8). Illus. by Elizabeth Honey. 1992, Viking paper $14.00 (0-670-84381-4). 144pp. Two brothers make their way through the Cambodian jungle as they try to escape from the Khmer Rouge. (Rev: BL 1/15/92; SLJ 3/92)

**5479** Baillie, Allan. *Secrets of Walden Rising* (5–7). 1997, Viking $13.99 (0-670-87351-9). 128pp. An adventure story set in Australia about a boy who finds a ghost town that is gradually rising from the bed of a reservoir. (Rev: BCCB 5/97; BL 4/1/97)

**5480** Barton, Byron. *I Want to Be an Astronaut* (2–4). Illus. by author. 1988, HarperCollins LB $14.89 (0-690-04744-4); paper $5.95 (0-06-443280-7). 32pp. Simple text explains a child's desire to go into outer space. (Rev: BCCB 10/88; BL 5/15/88; SLJ 5/88)

**5481** Base, Graeme. *The Eleventh Hour: A Curious Mystery* (4–6). Illus. 1989, Abrams $18.95 (0-8109-0851-4). 32pp. An elaborate picture book mystery written in verse. (Rev: BL 11/1/89; SLJ 2/90)

**5482** Bauer, Marion Dane. *On My Honor* (5–7). 1986, Houghton $15.00 (0-89919-439-7); Dell paper $4.50 (0-440-46633-4). 96pp. The powerful story of 12-year-old Joel who goes along with one of his friend Tony's schemes, which causes Tony's death, and how Joel realizes that he is responsible for his own choices. (Rev: BCCB 10/86; BL 9/1/86; SLJ 11/86)

**5483** Bellairs, John. *The Secret of the Underground Room* (5–7). 1990, Dial LB $13.89 (0-8037-0864-5). 128pp. Johnny Dixon, friend Fergie, and mentor are off to England in search of Father Higgins, who has disappeared. (Rev: BCCB 2/91; BL 12/15/90; SLJ 1/91)

**5484** Bellairs, John, and Brad Strickland. *The Drum, the Doll, and the Zombie* (5–7). 1994, Dial LB $14.89 (0-8037-1463-7). 176pp. Johnny Dixon and his friends battle zombies and voodoo demons in this weird, spooky story. (Rev: BL 7/94; SLJ 10/94)

**5485** Bethlen, Julianna. *The Ghost Pirate: A Spirited Hologram Book* (2–4). Illus. by Brian Lee. 1996, Dial paper $18.95 (0-8037-1958-2). 24pp. Holograms are used to illustrate this adventure story about pirates. (Rev: BL 12/15/96; SLJ 9/96)

**5486** Blades, Ann. *A Boy of Tache* (3–5). Illus. 1995, Tundra paper $5.95 (0-88776-350-2). A novel of life in Tache, an Indian reservation in northwest Canada, which focuses on a young boy and a trapping expedition.

**5487** Blatchford, Claire H. *Nick's Mission* (4–6). 1995, Lerner LB $19.95 (0-8225-0740-4). 144pp. A hearing-impaired boy happens on a gang of smugglers who are illegally bringing macaws into the United States from Mexico. (Rev: BL 11/15/95; SLJ 10/96)

**5488** Bledsoe, Lucy Jane. *Tracks in the Snow* (3–6). 1997, Holiday paper $14.95 (0-8234-1309-8). 96pp. A survival story about 2 girls caught in the woods during a violent snowstorm. (Rev: BL 8/97; SLJ 7/97)

**5489** Bonham, Frank. *Mystery of the Fat Cat* (5–7). Illus. by Alvin Smith. 1971, Bantam paper $1.25 (0-440-46226-6). 160pp. Four Oak Street Boys Club members set out to prove foul play in the death of a cat.

**5490** Brittain, Bill. *Dr. Dredd's Wagon of Wonders* (4–6). Illus. by Andrew Glass. 1987, HarperCollins LB $15.89 (0-06-020714-0). 160pp. Set in a remote New England town. Dr. Dredd comes to Coven Tree to cure the drought and causes havoc in this spooky tale. (Rev: SLJ 8/87)

**5491** Brittain, Bill. *Who Knew There'd Be Ghosts?* (4–6). Illus. by Michele Chessare. 1985, HarperCollins paper $4.50 (0-06-440224-X). 128pp. Tommy, the narrator, relates how he discovers ghosts Essie and Horace and how they help him solve a mystery. (Rev: BL 6/1/85; HB 7–8/85; SLJ 5/85)

**5492** Brontë, Charlotte. *Jane Eyre* (6–8). Illus. by Kathy Mitchell. 1983, Putnam $16.95 (0-448-06031-0); Bantam paper $3.95 (0-553-21140-4). 576pp. The immortal love story of Jane and Mr. Rochester.

**5493** Brown, Jane. *George Washington's Ghost* (3–5). Illus. by author. 1994, Houghton $13.95 (0-395-69452-3). 86pp. In this historical novel, Celinda, the youngest member of the Noodles family, who operate a traveling marionette theater, distinguishes herself by foiling a plot to take one of their best puppets. (Rev: BCCB 12/94; SLJ 11/94)

**5494** Bunting, Eve. *Coffin on a Case* (4–6). 1992, HarperCollins $13.95 (0-06-020273-4). 108pp. The daughter of a woman who has disappeared enlists the aid of a private detective's son to find her. (Rev: BCCB 11/92; BL 10/1/92; SLJ 10/92)

**5495** Bunting, Eve. *The Hideout* (5–7). 1991, Harcourt $14.95 (0-15-233990-6). 144pp. Andy decides to stage his own kidnapping so he can join his father in England. (Rev: BCCB 4/91; BL 4/1/91; SLJ 5/91)

**5496** Bunting, Eve. *Someone Is Hiding on Alcatraz Island* (5–8). 1986, Berkley paper $4.50 (0-425-10294-7). 144pp. A boy and a young woman ranger are trapped by a gang of thugs on Alcatraz.

**5497** Byars, Betsy. *The Dark Stairs: A Herculeah Jones Mystery* (4–6). 1994, Viking paper $13.99 (0-670-85487-5). 128pp. Pesky but brave Herculeah

Jones and her sidekick, Meat, solve the mystery surrounding a creepy old house. (Rev: BCCB 11/94; BL 8/94; HB 11–12/94; SLJ 9/94)

**5498** Byars, Betsy. *Dead Letter* (4–6). 1996, Viking paper $13.99 (0-670-86860-4). 128pp. Herculeah Jones finds a mysterious message in a coat she has bought in a used-clothing shop. (Rev: BCCB 7–8/96; BL 6/1–15/96; SLJ 7/96)

**5499** Byars, Betsy. *Death's Door* (4–6). 1997, Viking paper $13.99 (0-670-87423-X). 128pp. Herculeah Jones and her partner, Meat, try to find out who is trying to kill Meat's uncle Neiman. (Rev: BCCB 6/97; BL 3/1/97; SLJ 6/97)

**5500** Byars, Betsy. *Disappearing Acts* (4–6). 1998, Viking paper $14.99 (0-670-87735-2). 128pp. A Herculeah Jones mystery in which sidekick Meat finds a body at Funny Bonz comedy club. (Rev: BL 3/1/98; SLJ 3/98)

**5501** Byars, Betsy. *Tarot Says Beware* (4–6). Illus. 1995, Viking paper $13.99 (0-670-85575-8). 128pp. Herculeah and sidekick Meat discover a palmist's body with a knife in her chest and try to solve the mystery themselves. (Rev: BL 7/95; HB 11–12/95; SLJ 8/95)

**5502** Cadwallader, Sharon. *Cookie McCorkle and the Case of the Emerald Earrings* (3–5). Illus. by Patrick Chapin. 1991, Avon paper $2.95 (0-380-76098-3). 128pp. Ten-year-old Cookie and her dog Moriarity solve a mystery in the Holmesian manner. Followed by: *Cookie McCorkle and the Case of the Polka-Dot Safecracker* (1991). (Rev: BL 9/15/91)

**5503** Calhoun, B. B. *On the Right Track* (3–6). Illus. by Daniel Duffy. 1994, W. H. Freeman $10.40 (0-7167-6519-5); paper $3.20 (0-7167-6530-6). 128pp. Eleven-year-old Fenton solves a dinosaur puzzle with his father, a paleontologist, in Morgan, Wyoming. (Rev: BL 5/15/94; SLJ 6/94)

**5504** Calhoun, B. B. *Out of Place* (3–6). Illus. by Daniel Duffy. Series: Dinosaur Detective. 1994, W. H. Freeman $10.40 (0-7167-6543-8); paper $3.20 (0-7167-6551-9). 122pp. Max, a computer enthusiast, goes to Wyoming to visit his friend Fenton, whose main interest is paleontology. (Rev: SLJ 4/95)

**5505** Carey, Peter. *The Big Bazoohley* (4–6). Illus. 1995, Holt $14.95 (0-8050-3855-8). 115pp. Sam is kidnapped by 2 crooks who disguise him to look like their son in this adventure set in Toronto. (Rev: BCCB 12/95; BL 11/1/95; SLJ 10/95)

**5506** Carlyle, Carolyn. *Mercy Hospital: Crisis!* (5–8). 1993, Avon paper $3.50 (0-380-76846-1). 128pp. Three friends volunteer at a local hospital. (Rev: SLJ 7/93)

**5507** Casanova, Mary. *Moose Tracks* (4–6). 1995, Hyperion LB $15.49 (0-7868-2035-7). 128pp. During a moose hunt, Seth and friend Matt stumble onto

a pair of dangerous poachers. (Rev: BCCB 7–8/95; BL 7/95; SLJ 6/95)

**5508** Casanova, Mary. *Wolf Shadows* (5–7). 1997, Hyperion LB $15.49 (0-7868-2269-4). 192pp. In this outdoor story, a sequel to *Moose Tracks*, Seth and his friend Matt quarrel over wolf-protection programs but are brought together when a severe blizzard occurs on the first day of hunting season. (Rev: BL 10/1/97; SLJ 10/97)

**5509** Cavanagh, Helen. *The Last Piper* (4–7). 1996, Simon & Schuster paper $16.00 (0-689-80481-4). 123pp. While on a trip to Scotland, Christine comes to believe that her brother is the reincarnation of an innocent man executed years before. (Rev: BCCB 5/96; BL 7/96; SLJ 5/96)

**5510** Chocolate, Deborah M. *NEATE to the Rescue!* (4–7). 1992, Just Us paper $3.95 (0-940975-42-4). 98pp. A 13-year-old black girl and her friends help out when her mother's seat on the local council is put in doubt by a racist. (Rev: BCCB 3/93; BL 3/15/93)

**5511** Christian, Mary Blount. *Sebastian (Super Sleuth) and the Bone to Pick Mystery* (3–5). Illus. by Lisa McCue. 1983, Simon & Schuster $12.00 (0-02-718440-4). 64pp. Sebastian, an English sheepdog, and master John Jones at a fossil dig. Also use: *Sebastian (Super Sleuth) and the Crummy Yummies Caper* (1983).

**5512** Christian, Mary Blount. *Sebastian (Super Sleuth) and the Copycat Crime* (3–5). 1993, Macmillan LB $13.00 (0-02-718211-8). 64pp. Sebastian the dog detective once again comes to the rescue and this time solves the mystery of the stolen manuscript. (Rev: BL 1/1/94; SLJ 3/94)

**5513** Clark, Clara Gillow. *Willie and the Rattlesnake King* (5–7). 1997, Boyds Mills $14.95 (1-56397-654-4). 167pp. When 13-year-old Willie joins a traveling medicine show he finds that life on the road isn't as glamorous as expected. (Rev: BL 12/1/97; SLJ 11/97)

**5514** Clifford, Eth. *Harvey's Mystifying Raccoon Mix-Up* (3–5). 1994, Houghton $14.95 (0-395-68714-4). 112pp. Nora and Harvey solve the mystery of the prowler who is terrorizing a neighborhood. (Rev: BL 9/15/94; SLJ 10/94)

**5515** Clifford, Eth. *Help! I'm a Prisoner in the Library* (3–5). Illus. by George Hughes. 1979, Houghton $16.00 (0-395-28478-3); Scholastic paper $2.95 (0-590-44351-8). 112pp. Two youngsters are locked in a library after it closes. Two sequels are: *The Dastardly Murder of Dirty Pete* (1981); *Just Tell Me When We're Dead!* (1983).

**5516** Clifford, Eth. *Never Hit a Ghost with a Baseball Bat* (3–5). Illus. by George Hughes. 1993, Houghton $13.95 (0-395-61587-9). 111pp. Two girls find unexpected adventure and mystery when they visit a trolly car museum. (Rev: SLJ 6/93)

**5517** Clifford, Eth. *Scared Silly* (3–5). Illus. by George Hughes. 1989, Scholastic paper $2.75 (0-590-42382-7). 128pp. Mary Rose and Jo-Beth encounter a mysterious Walk-Your-Way-Around-the-World Museum. (Rev: BCCB 4/88; BL 4/1/88; SLJ 6–7/88)

**5518** Clymer, Eleanor. *The Horse in the Attic* (4–6). Illus. by Ted Lewin. 1985, Bantam paper $2.50 (0-440-43798-9). 96pp. In their new house, Caroline finds a painting of a horse in the attic.

**5519** Cohen, Daniel. *Great Ghosts* (3–6). Illus. by David Linn. 1990, Dutton paper $13.99 (0-525-65039-3). 48pp. Nine ghost stories, all concerning British-type haunted houses. (Rev: BL 10/1/90; SLJ 11/90)

**5520** Coleman, Michael. *Escape Key* (4–6). Illus. 1997, Bantam paper $3.99 (0-553-48621-7). 128pp. The Internet Detectives, 2 boys and a girl, solve the mystery of the criminal who is selling via the computer a chess game that doesn't exist. Also use *Net Bandits* (1997). (Rev: BL 3/1/98)

**5521** Conford, Ellen. *A Case for Jenny Archer* (2–4). Illus. by Diane Palmisciano. 1990, Little, Brown paper $4.50 (0-316-15352-4). Jenny, who longs to become a detective, inadvertently foils a burglary. (Rev: BL 1/15/89; SLJ 3/89)

**5522** Connell, David D., and Jim Thurman. *The Case of the Mystery Weekend* (5–8). Illus. by Danny O'Leary. Series: MathNet Casebook. 1995, Freeman $10.40 (0-7167-6554-3); paper $3.20 (0-7167-6555-1). 64pp. The Mathnet detectives find they are in the wrong house and in the middle of a puzzling mystery. Also use *The Case of the Smart Dummy* (1995). (Rev: SLJ 8/95)

**5523** Connell, David D., and Jim Thurman. *Despair in Monterey Bay* (3–5). Illus. 1993, Scientific American $8.80 (0-7167-6505-5); paper $3.20 (0-7167-6502-0). 64pp. The 2 Mathnet detectives use mathematical concepts to foil a jewel thief in this mystery story. Also use *The Case of the Unnatural* (1993). (Rev: BL 11/15/93; SLJ 12/93)

**5524** Cottonwood, Joe. *Quake!* (5–8). 1995, Scholastic $13.95 (0-590-22232-5). 112pp. Fran, her brother Sidney, and her friend Jennie survive the terrible California earthquake of 1989. (Rev: BCCB 4/95; BL 5/1/95; HB 9–10/95; SLJ 5/95)

**5525** Coville, Bruce. *The Ghost Wore Grey* (4–6). 1988, Bantam paper $3.99 (0-553-15610-1). 128pp. Sixth-graders unravel a 100-year-old mystery at a country inn. Also use: *The Ghost in the Third Row* (1987); *How I Survived My Summer Vacation* (1988, Pocket). (Rev: SLJ 9/88)

**5526** Cross, Gillian. *On the Edge* (5–8). 1985, Holiday $15.95 (0-8234-0559-1). 176pp. A suspenseful English novel about a terrorist's plot told from 2 points of view. (Rev: BCCB 6/85)

**5527** Curry, Jane L. *The Big Smith Snatch* (5–7). 1989, Macmillan LB $16.00 (0-689-50478-0). 192pp. The Smith children discover that they have been kidnapped. (Rev: BL 9/1/89; SLJ 10/89)

**5528** Curry, Jane L. *The Great Smith House Hustle* (4–7). 1993, Macmillan $14.95 (0-689-50580-9). 192pp. The Smith children uncover a real estate scam and help save their grandmother's house from being sold. (Rev: BL 5/1/93; SLJ 8/93)

**5529** Cushman, Doug. *The Mystery of King Karfu* (2–4). Illus. 1996, HarperCollins $14.95 (0-06-024796-7). 32pp. Wombat detective Seymour Sleuth and sidekick Abbott Muggs, a mouse, solve the mystery of a stolen stone chicken. (Rev: BL 1/1–15/97; SLJ 2/97*)

**5530** DeClements, Barthe. *Wake Me at Midnight* (4–6). 1993, Puffin paper $3.99 (0-140-36486-2). 154pp. Caitlin's problems include the responsibility for her baby brother, nasty neighbors, and the fact that the boy next door is acting strangely. (Rev: BCCB 9/91; BL 8/91; SLJ 11/91)

**5531** Deedy, Carmen A. *The Secret of Old Zeb* (2–3). Illus. by Michael P. White. 1997, Peachtree $16.95 (1-56145-115-0). An adventure novel in which Uncle Walter tells his niece about a summer when he found that his next-door neighbor was building a ship in his basement. (Rev: SLJ 3/98)

**5532** DeFelice, Cynthia. *Devil's Bridge* (4–6). 1992, Macmillan paper $14.00 (0-02-726465-3). 96pp. Ben and his mother's new boyfriend become involved in a plot to rig the Martha's Vineyard Striped Bass Derby. (Rev: BCCB 11/92; BL 12/1/92; SLJ 11/92)

**5533** DeFelice, Cynthia. *Lostman's River* (5–7). 1994, Macmillan paper $15.00 (0-02-726466-1). 160pp. Tyler's trust is betrayed when he takes an eccentric scientist to a secret rookery in the Everglades and the man reveals himself to be an unscrupulous plume hunter. (Rev: BCCB 6/94; BL 5/15/94; HB 9–10/94; SLJ 7/94)

**5534** Dexter, Catherine. *I Dream of Murder* (5–8). 1997, Morrow $15.00 (0-688-13182-4). 153pp. A strange-looking man who works at the zoo appears in a boy's recurring nightmare in this gripping mystery. (Rev: BCCB 3/97; SLJ 5/97)

**5535** Doyle, Brian. *Spud Sweetgrass* (5–8). 1996, Douglas & McIntyre $14.95 (0-88899-164-9). 128pp. Spud and 2 friends solve the mystery of who is dumping grease in the Ottawa River. A sequel to *Spud in Winter* (1996). (Rev: BCCB 7–8/96; BL 6/1–15/96; SLJ 9/96)

**5536** Draper, Sharon M. *Lost in the Tunnel of Time* (3–6). Illus. by Michael Bryant. Series: Ziggy and the Black Dinosaurs. 1996, Just Us paper $6.00 (0-940975-63-7). 96pp. While exploring tunnels used by the Underground Railroad, boys are trapped underground when one of the tunnels collapses. (Rev: SLJ 8/96)

**5537** Easley, Maryann. *I Am the Ice Worm* (4–6). 1996, Boyds Mills $15.95 (1-56397-412-6). 127pp. A California girl is rescued by Inupiats when she is stranded in Alaska after a plane crash. (Rev: BL 10/15/96; SLJ 11/96)

**5538** Easton, Patricia H. *A Week at the Fair: A Country Celebration* (2–5). Photos by Herb Ferguso. 1995, Millbrook LB $20.90 (1-56294-527-0). A week's activities at a county fair in western Pennsylvania are seen through the eyes of a 12-year-old girl. (Rev: SLJ 2/96)

**5539** Elmer, Robert. *Far from the Storm* (4–7). Series: Young Underground. 1995, Bethany paper $5.99 (0-55661-377-6). 174pp. At the end of World War II, Danish twins Peter and Elise set out to find the culprit who set their uncle's boat on fire. (Rev: BL 2/15/96)

**5540** Elmer, Robert. *Follow the Star* (5–8). Series: Young Underground Book. 1997, Bethany paper $5.99 (1-55661-660-0). 178pp. In post–World War II Denmark, Henrik believes that his mother is being held captive by the Russians, who believe she is a spy. (Rev: SLJ 2/98)

**5541** Emerson, Kathy L. *The Mystery of the Missing Bagpipes* (5–7). 1991, Avon paper $2.95 (0-380-76138-6). 128pp. Kim tries to find out who is the real culprit when a young boy is wrongfully accused of stealing a set of ancient bagpipes and some precious daggers. (Rev: BL 9/15/91)

**5542** Engh, M. J. *The House in the Snow* (4–6). Illus. 1990, Scholastic paper $2.75 (0-590-42658-3). 144pp. Orphan Benjamin lands in a house of robbers who have cloaks that make them invisible. With the help of the other boys, he plans to take over the house. (Rev: BL 11/1/87; SLJ 9/87)

**5543** Enright, Elizabeth. *Gone-Away Lake* (4–6). Illus. by Beth Krush and Joe Krush. 1990, Harcourt paper $6.00 (0-15-231649-3). 256pp. An abandoned summer colony bordering a swamp leads to a vacation of glorious exploration for Julian and Portia.

**5544** Farley, Carol. *The Case of the Haunted Health Club* (4–6). 1991, Avon paper $2.95 (0-380-75918-7). 112pp. Two sisters solve a mystery involving a health club. (Rev: BL 3/15/91)

**5545** Farley, Carol. *The Case of the Vanishing Villain* (5–6). Illus. 1986, Avon paper $2.95 (0-380-89959-0). 80pp. A 10-year-old solves the mystery of the escaped convict's disappearance. Also use: *Mystery of the Melted Diamonds* (1986); *The Case of the Lost Lookalike* (1988). (Rev: BL 9/15/86; SLJ 11/86)

**5546** Ferguson, Dwayne J. *Case of the Missing Ankh* (2–4). Series: Kid Caramel Private Investigator. 1997, Just Us paper $6.50 (0-940975-71-8). 59pp. Two junior detectives solve the mystery of the stolen museum treasure. (Rev: SLJ 9/97)

**5547** Fields, T. S. *Danger in the Desert* (5–7). 1997, Rising Moon $12.95 (0-87358-666-2); paper $6.95 (0-87358-664-6). 126pp. A survival story about 2 boys who endure great hardships when they are left without food or supplies in the desert. (Rev: SLJ 11/97)

**5548** Fleischman, Paul. *Finzel the Farsighted* (3–5). Illus. by Marcia Sewall. 1983, Dutton paper $11.95 (0-525-44057-7). 48pp. Finzel, the fortune-teller, is so near blindness that he becomes easy prey.

**5549** Fleischman, Paul. *The Half-a-Moon Inn* (5–7). Illus. by Kathryn Jacobi. 1991, HarperCollins LB $12.89 (0-06-021918-1); paper $3.95 (0-06-440364-5). 96pp. A young mute boy sets out to find his mother lost in a violent snowstorm.

**5550** Fleischman, Sid. *The Whipping Boy* (5–7). Illus. 1986, Greenwillow $16.00 (0-688-06216-4); Troll paper $4.95 (0-8167-1038-4). 96pp. Prince Brat and his whipping boy, Jemmy, who takes the blame for all the bad things the prince does, find their roles reversed when they meet up with CutWater and Hold-Your-Nose Billy. Newbery Medal winner, 1987. (Rev: BCCB 3/86; BL 3/1/86; SLJ 5/86)

**5551** Flora, James. *Grandpa's Ghost Stories* (2–4). Illus. by author. 1980, Macmillan $13.95 (0-689-50112-9). 32pp. Three grisly short stories told by an old man to his grandson.

**5552** Fowler, Anne B. *Ten-Minute Terrors: Camp Fear and Other Hideous Horrors* (5–7). Illus. by Eric Angeloch. 1995, Lowell House paper $4.95 (1-56565-321-1). 95pp. Ten stories in which the protagonists get into danger against their better judgment and pay a terrible price for their foolishness. (Rev: SLJ 3/96)

**5553** Fox, Paula. *How Many Miles to Babylon?* (4–6). Illus. by Paul Giovanopoulos. 1982, Macmillan $13.95 (0-02-735590-X). 128pp. Tension and suspense when 10-year-old James Douglas is kidnapped by teenage dog thieves and held captive in an abandoned Coney Island fun house.

**5554** Galbraith, Kathryn O. *Something Suspicious* (4–6). 1987, Avon paper $2.50 (0-380-70253-3). 128pp. Lizzie and her friend Ivy are on the trail of the bank robber known as the Green Pillowcase Bandit. (Rev: BCCB 1/86; BL 10/1/85)

**5555** Gantos, Jack. *Heads or Tails: Stories from the Sixth Grade* (5–8). 1994, Farrar $16.00 (0-374-32909-5). 176pp. A collection of 8 unusual short stories about a born survivor, a sixth-grader named Jack, who overcomes amazing obstacles in this book set in Fort Lauderdale. (Rev: BCCB 7–8/94; HB 7–8/94; SLJ 6/94*)

**5556** Gardiner, John Reynolds. *General Butterfingers* (4–6). Illus. by Cat B. Smith. 1993, Puffin $3.99 (0-14-036355-6). 96pp. Walter, at 11, outwits the nasty nephew who wants to evict the trio of elderly veterans of World War II. (Rev: BCCB 2/89; BL 1/15/87)

**5557** Garland, Sherry. *The Silent Storm* (4–7). 1993, Harcourt $14.95 (0-15-274170-4). 240pp. Alyssa, who has lost both of her parents in a violent storm and has become mute because of the trauma, hears that another hurricane is approaching. (Rev: BCCB 4/93; BL 6/1–15/93)

**5558** George, Jean Craighead. *The Case of the Missing Cutthroats: An Ecological Mystery* (4–8). 1996, HarperCollins LB $13.89 (0-06-025466-1). 145pp. A mystery-adventure involving a 13-year-old girl and the discovery of a cutthroat trout in an unusual habitat. (Rev: SLJ 6/96)

**5559** George, Jean Craighead. *Julie* (4–6). Illus. 1994, HarperCollins LB $14.89 (0-06-023529-2). 240pp. Julie must choose between her Eskimo ways and those of the white men in this sequel to *Julie of the Wolves* (1972). (Rev: BCCB 6/94, 10/94; BL 10/15/94*; HB 3–4/94, 11–12/94; SLJ 10/94)

**5560** George, Jean Craighead. *Julie of the Wolves* (5–8). Illus. by John Schoenherr. 1974, HarperCollins LB $15.89 (0-06-021944-0); paper $4.95 (0-06-440058-1). 180pp. Julie (Eskimo name, Miyax) begins a trek across frozen Alaska and is saved only by the friendship of a pack of wolves. Newbery Award winner, 1973.

**5561** George, Jean Craighead. *Julie's Wolf Pack* (5–7). Illus. Series: Julie of the Wolves. 1997, HarperCollins LB $15.89 (0-06-027407-7). 208pp. The life of Julie's wolf pack in the wild and how their lives become entwined with Julie's when Kapu, the leader, is captured by researchers. (Rev: BL 9/1/97; SLJ 9/97)

**5562** George, Jean Craighead. *The Missing 'Gator of Gumbo Limbo: An Ecological Mystery* (5–7). 1992, HarperCollins LB $14.89 (0-06-020397-8). 176pp. Liza and other homeless people try to protect Dajun, a 12-foot alligator in the Florida Everglades, from officials hired to eliminate him. (Rev: BCCB 4/92; BL 6/1/92; SLJ 6/92)

**5563** George, Jean Craighead. *My Side of the Mountain* (5–7). Illus. by author. 1988, Dutton paper $4.95 (0-525-44395-9). 176pp. Sam Gribley spends a winter alone in the Catskill Mountains.

**5564** George, Jean Craighead. *On the Far Side of the Mountain* (4–6). Illus. 1990, Dutton paper $15.00 (0-

525-44563-3). 170pp. In this continuation of the survival story *My Side of the Mountain,* Sam Bibley and his friend Bando try to find Sam's sister, who has disappeared. (Rev: BCCB 6/90; HB 7–8/90; SLJ 6/90)

**5565** George, Jean Craighead. *The Talking Earth* (6–8). 1983, HarperCollins LB $14.89 (0-06-021976-9); paper $4.95 (0-06-440212-6). 160pp. A young Seminole girl spends 3 months in the Everglades alone.

**5566** Gerson, Corrine. *My Grandfather the Spy* (5–7). 1990, Walker $14.95 (0-8027-6955-1). 120pp. When a man arrives on the family farm in Vermont with a briefcase full of money, Danny suspects his grandfather is a spy. (Rev: BL 6/15/90; SLJ 8/90)

**5567** Giff, Patricia Reilly. *Have You Seen Hyacinth Macaw?* (4–6). Illus. 1982, Bantam paper $3.99 (0-440-43450-5). 128pp. Abby Jones, a would-be detective, misunderstands clues and thinks her brother is a thief. A sequel is: *Loretta P. Sweeney, Where Are You?* (1983).

**5568** Gilson, Jamie. *Hobie Hanson: Greatest Hero of the Mall* (4–6). Illus. by Anita Riggio. 1989, Lothrop $16.00 (0-688-08968-2). 160pp. During a flood crisis, Hobie worries about what it takes to be a hero. (Rev: BL 9/1/89; SLJ 10/89)

**5569** Gilson, Jamie. *Soccer Circus: Featuring Hobie Hanson* (4–6). Illus. by Dee deRosa. 1993, Lothrop $15.00 (0-688-12021-0). 148pp. On a harmless overnight soccer trip, Hobie manages to get into a great deal of trouble. (Rev: BL 4/1/93; SLJ 6/93)

**5570** Gleitzman, Morris. *Misery Guts* (5–8). 1993, Harcourt $12.95 (0-15-254768-1). 122pp. When Keith and his family move from England to Australia, it isn't the paradise he expected. (Rev: SLJ 7/93)

**5571** Godden, Rumer. *The Rocking Horse Secret* (4–6). Illus. by Juliet Stanwell Smith. 1988, Puffin paper $3.95 (0-317-69650-5). 64pp. Tibby solves many problems when she finds a will hidden in a rocking horse.

**5572** Gorman, Carol. *Jennifer-the-Jerk Is Missing* (4–6). 1994, Simon & Schuster $15.00 (0-671-86578-1). 135pp. Amy wonders whether Malcolm, her baby-sitting charge, is telling the truth about seeing a kidnapping. (Rev: BCCB 5/94; BL 6/1–15/94; SLJ 6/94)

**5573** Gray, Patsey. *Barefoot a Thousand Miles* (5–7). 1984, Walker $11.95 (0-8027-6528-9). A young Apache boy sets out to retrieve his pet dog taken from the reservation.

**5574** Greenberg, Martin H., and Charles G. Waugh, eds. *A Newbery Halloween: A Dozen Scary Stories by Newbery Award-Winning Authors* (3–6). 1993, Delacorte LB $16.95 (0-385-31028-5). 208pp. Twelve spooky short stories or excerpts from longer works by such Newbery winners as Naylor, Cleary, and Konigsburg. (Rev: BL 9/1/93; SLJ 10/93)

**5575** Griffin, Peni R. *The Brick House Burglars* (4–6). 1994, Macmillan $14.95 (0-689-50579-5). 144pp. Four sixth-grade girls discover that someone is trying to burn down the abandoned building they are using as a club house. (Rev: BL 3/1/94; SLJ 6/94)

**5576** Griffin, Peni R. *The Treasure Bird* (4–6). 1992, Macmillan paper $14.00 (0-689-50554-X). 144pp. In this story set in Texas, 10-year-old Jessy thinks Goldie the parrot might have the clue to a jar of gold coins. (Rev: BCCB 2/93; BL 9/1/92; SLJ 11/92)

**5577** Grover, Wayne. *Dolphin Treasure* (3–5). Illus. 1996, Greenwillow $14.00 (0-688-14343-1). 48pp. Three veteran divers ignore warning signs in their exploration of a sunken Spanish galleon. (Rev: BL 8/96; SLJ 7/96)

**5578** Guiberson, Brenda Z. *Lobster Boat* (3–5). Illus. by Megan Lloyd. 1995, Holt $14.95 (0-8050-1756-9). 32pp. A real-life adventure about a day in the life of a lobsterman and his young nephew Tommy. (Rev: BL 4/15/93; SLJ 7/93)

**5579** Gutman, Dan. *The Million Dollar Shot* (4–6). 1997, Hyperion LB $14.49 (0-7868-2275-9). 120pp. Eddie gets a chance to earn a million dollars by sinking a free throw at an NBA finals game, but somebody is sabotaging his efforts. (Rev: BL 10/1/97; SLJ 12/97)

**5580** Guy, Rosa. *Paris, Pee Wee, and Big Dog* (3–5). Illus. by Caroline Binch. 1985, Delacorte $14.95 (0-385-29407-7); Dell paper $3.25 (0-440-40072-4). 112pp. Paris is supposed to be cleaning their new apartment in New York City, but when his friends show up from the old neighborhood, they are off on some fun adventures. (Rev: BL 12/1/85; HB 1–2/86; SLJ 11/85)

**5581** Hahn, Mary D. *Following the Mystery Man* (5–7). 1988, Avon paper $3.50 (0-380-70677-6). 192pp. Madigan is certain that her grandmother's new boarder is none other than her missing father. (Rev: BL 3/15/88; HB 7–8/88; SLJ 4/88)

**5582** Hahn, Mary D. *The Spanish Kidnapping Disaster* (5–7). 1991, Houghton $14.95 (0-395-55696-1); Avon paper $4.50 (0-380-71712-3). 132pp. Felix is tagging along on her mother's honeymoon in Spain and isn't having a good time. (Rev: BCCB 5/91; BL 3/15/91; SLJ 5/91)

**5583** Hall, Lynn. *The Tormentors* (5–8). 1990, Harcourt $14.95 (0-15-289470-5). 128pp. Sox Newman's beloved dog is mysteriously kidnapped. (Rev: BCCB 1/91; SLJ 1/91)

**5584** Hamilton, Virginia. *The House of Dies Drear* (5–8). Illus. by Eros Keith. 1984, Macmillan $17.00 (0-02-742500-2); paper $4.50 (0-02-043520-7). 256pp. First-rate suspense as history professor Small and his young son Thomas investigate their rented house, formerly a station on the Underground Railroad, unlocking the secrets and dangers from attitudes dating back to the Civil War.

**5585** Hamilton, Virginia. *The Mystery of Drear House* (5–7). 1987, Greenwillow $15.95 (0-688-04026-8); Scholastic paper $4.50 (0-590-95627-2). 224pp. The story of Thomas Small and the threat to the treasure of Drear House. The conclusion of the Dies Drear Chronicle. (Rev: BCCB 5/87; BL 6/15/87; SLJ 6–7/87)

**5586** Harding, Donal. *The Leaving Summer* (4–6). 1996, Morrow $15.00 (0-688-13893-4). 177pp. An 11-year-old boy and his aunt hide an injured escaped convict in their basement and nurse him back to health in this coming-of-age story. (Rev: BCCB 9/96; SLJ 4/96)

**5587** Harrison, Ted. *Children of the Yukon* (2–4). Illus. by author. 1977, Tundra paper $6.95 (0-88776-163-1). Life in present-day Yukon with a little historical material.

**5588** Hart, Alison. *Haunted Horseback Holiday* (4–6). Series: Super Special Riding Academy. 1996, Random paper $3.99 (0-679-88053-4). 212pp. In this mystery story, 4 girlfriends vacation at a working ranch in Colorado. (Rev: SLJ 9/96)

**5589** Hartas, Leo. *Haunted Castle: An Interactive Adventure Book* (4–7). Illus. by author. 1997, DK Publg. $14.95 (0-7894-2464-9). A choose-your-own-adventure tale in which the reader accompanies 2 boys as they explore tumbledown Grizzlemyst Castle. (Rev: SLJ 1/98)

**5590** Haugaard, Erik C. *Under the Black Flag* (5–7). 1994, Roberts Rinehart paper $8.95 (1-879373-63-7). 170pp. Fourteen-year-old William is captured by the pirate Blackbeard and held for ransom in this 18th-century yarn. (Rev: BL 4/1/94; HB 9–10/94; SLJ 5/94)

**5591** Hawks, Robert. *The Richest Kid in the World* (4–8). 1992, Avon paper $2.99 (0-380-76241-2). 136pp. Josh is kidnapped and taken to the estate of billionaire Grizzle Welch. (Rev: SLJ 5/92)

**5592** Hearne, Betsy. *Eli's Ghost* (5–7). Illus. by Ronald Himler. 1987, Macmillan $13.95 (0-689-50420-9). 112pp. Eli learns that his mother is not dead but has fled into the swamp, and he goes in search of her. (Rev: BCCB 3/87; BL 4/1/87; SLJ 4/87)

**5593** Heisel, Sharon E. *Wrapped in a Riddle* (4–6). 1993, Houghton $14.95 (0-395-65026-7). 140pp. When a series of unexplained events occur at her grandmother's bed-and-breakfast, Miranda becomes a sleuth intent on solving the mysteries. (Rev: BCCB 11/93; BL 10/1/93; SLJ 2/94)

**5594** Helldorfer, M. C. *Spook House* (5–7). 1989, Pocket paper $2.99 (0-671-72326-X). 160pp. Will and friends decide to give guided tours of an old abandoned house in their eastern shore Maryland town. (Rev: BL 10/1/89; HB 11–12/92; SLJ 10/89)

**5595** Henderson, Aileen K. *The Monkey Thief* (5–7). 1997, Milkweed $14.95 (1-57131-612-4). 144pp. While working with his uncle in the Costa Rican rain forest, Ron uncovers a plot to plunder ancient burial sites. (Rev: BL 11/1/97; SLJ 12/97)

**5596** Henderson, Aileen K. *The Summer of the Bonepile Monster* (3–5). Illus. 1995, Milkweed $15.95 (1-57131-603-5); paper $6.95 (1-57131-602-7). 140pp. Hollis changes into a self-reliant young man during a summer spent in the country during which he solves a community mystery. (Rev: BCCB 7–8/95; BL 5/1/95; SLJ 7/95)

**5597** Herman, Emily. *The Missing Fossil Mystery* (2–3). Illus. by Andrew Glass. 1996, Hyperion $13.95 (0-7868-0145-X); paper $3.95 (0-7868-1091-2). 56pp. When it disappears, Liza regrets taking her brother's fossil to school without his permission. (Rev: SLJ 12/96)

**5598** Herndon, Ernest. *The Secret of Lizard Island* (3–5). 1994, HarperCollins paper $5.99 (0-310-38251-3). 128pp. Through a misunderstanding, Eric, a typical 12-year-old, is sent to a South Pacific island where scientists are growing huge lizards. (Rev: BL 9/1/94)

**5599** Herzig, Alison C., and Jane L. Mali. *Mystery on October Road* (3–5). 1993, Puffin paper $3.99 (0-14-034614-7). 96pp. Casey wonders why his neighbor wears a bandanna over his face until he discovers that Mr. Smith has been disfigured in a fire. (Rev: BL 7/91; SLJ 9/91)

**5600** Hildick, E. W. *The Case of the Absent Author* (4–6). 1995, Macmillan paper $14.00 (0-02-743821-X). 144pp. McGurk and Co., young detectives, realize that the disappearance of the famous author William Le Grand has been staged. (Rev: BL 8/95; SLJ 7/95)

**5601** Hildick, E. W. *The Case of the Wiggling Wig* (4–6). 1996, Simon & Schuster paper $15.00 (0-689-80082-7). 154pp. A broken leg doesn't stop McGurk from his detective work. (Rev: BL 5/15/96; SLJ 5/96)

**5602** Hildick, E. W. *The Purloined Corn Popper* (4–6). 1997, Marshall Cavendish LB $14.95 (0-7614-5010-6). 160pp. In this new mystery series, Tim Kowalski and his friend investigate the disappearance of a corn popper that contained Mrs. Kowalski's money. Also use *Sneak Thief* (1997). (Rev: BL 1/1–15/98; SLJ 2/98)

**5603** Hilgartner, Beth. *A Murder for Her Majesty* (5–8). 1986, Houghton paper $5.95 (0-395-61619-0).

256pp. Alice disguises herself as a boy to escape her father's murderers. (Rev: BCCB 9/86; SLJ 10/86)

**5604** Hill, Kirkpatrick. *Toughboy and Sister* (4–6). 1990, Macmillan paper $15.00 (0-689-50506-X). 128pp. A survival story set in an Alaskan native village. (Rev: BCCB 11/90*; BL 9/15/90; HB 3–4/91*; SLJ 10/90)

**5605** Hill, Kirkpatrick. *Winter Camp* (4–6). 1993, Macmillan paper $15.00 (0-689-50588-4). 192pp. To teach them the ways of the wild, Natasha, an Athapascan Indian, and her 2 stepchildren spend a winter in an Alaskan bush camp. (Rev: BCCB 11/93; BL 10/1/93; SLJ 10/93)

**5606** Hitchcock, Alfred, ed. *Alfred Hitchcock's Daring Detectives* (6–8). Illus. by Arthur Shilstone. 1982, Random paper $4.99 (0-394-84902-7). Eleven thrillers from popular writers such as Agatha Christie and Ellery Queen. Also use: *Alfred Hitchcock's Supernatural Tales of Terror and Suspense* (1983).

**5607** Holman, Felice. *Slake's Limbo* (5–7). 1974, Macmillan $16.00 (0-684-13926-X); paper $3.95 (0-689-71066-6). 126pp. Thirteen-year-old Aremis Slake finds an ideal hideaway for 4 months in the labyrinth of the New York City subway.

**5608** Hopper, Nancy J. *Ape Ears and Beaky* (4–7). 1987, Avon paper $2.50 (0-380-70270-3). 112pp. Scott and Beaky solve the mystery of the robberies in a condominium.

**5609** Houston, James. *Frozen Fire* (6–8). Illus. by author. 1977, Macmillan $15.00 (0-689-50083-1); paper $4.95 (0-689-71612-5). 160pp. Two boys — one white and one Eskimo — set out on a rescue mission in the Far North.

**5610** Howard, Milly. *The Case of the Dognapped Cat* (2–4). Illus. 1997, Bob Jones Univ. paper $6.49 (0-89084-936-6). 144pp. Three Florida youngsters call themselves Crimebusters and, in this adventure, solve the mystery of a cat that has been kidnapped. (Rev: BL 1/1–15/98)

**5611** Howe, James. *Bunnicula Escapes! A Pop-up Adventure* (2–3). Illus. by Alan Daniel and Lea Daniel. 1994, Morrow paper $14.95 (0-688-13212-X). 12pp. In this Bunnicula adventure at a county fair, most of the fun comes from the amazing pop-ups. (Rev: BL 11/15/94)

**5612** Howe, James. *Dew Drop Dead: A Sebastian Barth Mystery* (4–7). 1990, Macmillan $15.00 (0-689-31425-6). 160pp. Sebastian Barth finds a body in the abandoned Dew Drop Inn, but before he can investigate, it disappears. (Rev: SLJ 4/90)

**5613** Hughes, Dean. *Nutty and the Case of the Ski-Slope Spy* (4–6). 1985, Macmillan $15.00 (0-689-31126-5). 144pp. Student council president Nutty Nutsell takes his show on the road this time as he organizes a student ski trip and runs into a case of stolen computer documents. (Rev: BL 11/1/85; SLJ 1/86)

**5614** Hutchins, Pat. *Follow That Bus!* (2–5). Illus. by Laurence Hutchins. 1988, Knopf paper $2.95 (0-394-80792-8). 112pp. A school picnic becomes a cops-and-robbers chase involving 2 holdup men in this fast-moving English story. A reissue of the 1977 edition.

**5615** Ingram, Scott. *Bloody Waters: Terrorizing Shark Tales* (4–7). Illus. 1995, Lowell House paper $5.95 (1-56565-225-8). 96pp. Five gory stories about young people involved in shark attacks. (Rev: BL 8/95)

**5616** Irwin, Hadley. *The Original Freddie Ackerman* (5–7). Illus. by James Hosten. 1992, Macmillan $15.00 (0-689-50562-0). 184pp. Twelve-year-old Trevor is dismayed to find himself on a Maine isle with 2 unknown great-aunts, no television, no theaters, and no malls. (Rev: BCCB 9/92; BL 1/1/92; SLJ 8/92*)

**5617** Jane, Pamela. *The Big Monkey Mix-up* (1–4). Illus. by Cathy Bobak. 1997, Avon paper $3.99 (0-380-78951-5). 65pp. A simple mystery that revolves around a missing monkey and Benjamin's desire to lose at least one of his baby teeth. (Rev: SLJ 1/98)

**5618** Johnson, Annabel, and Edgar Johnson. *The Grizzly* (5–7). Illus. by Gilbert Riswold. 1964, HarperCollins paper $4.95 (0-06-440036-0). 194pp. A perceptive story of a father-son relationship in which David, on a camping trip, saves his father's life when a grizzly bear attacks.

**5619** Karas, Phyllis. *For Lucky's Sake* (5–8). 1997, Avon paper $3.99 (0-380-78647-8). 153pp. In this mystery with an animal rights theme, Benjy investigates a mysterious fire in which 2 greyhounds, which have been rescued from a research lab, are killed. (Rev: BL 10/1/97)

**5620** Kehret, Peg. *Danger at the Fair* (5–8). 1995, Dutton $15.99 (0-525-65182-9); Pocket paper $3.99 (0-671-52939-0). 136pp. Ellen's brother Corey gets into trouble after he spots a pickpocket at a county fair. (Rev: BCCB 2/95; BL 12/1/94; SLJ 2/95)

**5621** Kehret, Peg. *Earthquake Terror* (4–7). 1996, Dutton paper $14.99 (0-525-65226-4). 144pp. A violent earthquake strikes the small island on which 12-year-old Jonathan is alone with his younger sister, Abby. (Rev: BCCB 3/96; BL 1/1–15/96; SLJ 2/96)

**5622** Kehret, Peg. *Frightmares: Don't Go Near Mrs. Tallie* (3–6). 1995, Pocket paper $3.99 (0-671-89191-X). 131pp. Rosie and Kayo suspect that their elderly neighbor, Mrs. Tallie, is slowly being poisoned. (Rev: BL 10/1/95; SLJ 12/95)

**5623** Kehret, Peg. *Nightmare Mountain* (4–6). 1989, Dutton paper $13.95 (0-525-65008-3). 176pp. Molly

and her cousin Glendon are trapped on a mountain by a mysterious intruder. (Rev: BL 9/15/89; SLJ 10/89)

**5624** Kehret, Peg. *Searching for Candlestick Park* (5–8). 1997, Dutton paper $14.99 (0-525-65256-6). 160pp. An adventure story about a boy who sets out from Seattle to find his father in San Francisco. (Rev: BL 8/97; SLJ 9/97)

**5625** Kehret, Peg. *Terror at the Zoo* (4–7). 1991, Dutton paper $14.99 (0-525-65083-0). 144pp. Twelve-year-old Ellen gets to camp out at the zoo for her birthday and runs into an escaped felon. (Rev: BL 12/1/91; SLJ 1/92)

**5626** Kelleher, D. V. *Defenders of the Universe* (3–6). Illus. by Jane Brown. 1993, Houghton $16.00 (0-395-60515-6). 128pp. Rachel is asked to join a crime-fighting club at her new school. (Rev: BL 3/15/93; SLJ 4/93)

**5627** King-Smith, Dick. *Harry's Mad* (4–6). Illus. 1990, Macmillan $15.95 (0-7451-1101-7); Knopf paper $4.99 (0-679-88688-5). Mad the talking parrot is stolen, but the sharp-witted bird finally makes it back home. (Rev: BCCB 5/87; BL 7/87; SLJ 5/87)

**5628** Kingman, Lee. *The Luck of the Miss L* (5–7). 1986, Houghton $12.95 (0-685-11813-4). 160pp. Alec faces obstacles at every turn as he practices rowing for the Junior Rowers Race. (Rev: BCCB 9/86; BL 8/86; HB 5–6/86)

**5629** Kline, Suzy. *Orp and the FBI* (3–6). 1995, Putnam $14.95 (0-399-22664-8). 112pp. The rival detective agencies formed by Orp and his sister Chloe compete to solve the mystery of strange sounds that come from a neighbor's house. (Rev: BL 4/15/95; SLJ 5/95)

**5630** Konigsburg, E. L. *Father's Arcane Daughter* (5–8). 1976, Macmillan $15.00 (0-689-30524-9). 128pp. When Caroline reappears after an absence of 17 years, everyone wonders if she is really an imposter in this complex suspense tale.

**5631** Konigsburg, E. L. *From the Mixed-Up Files of Mrs. Basil E. Frankweiler* (5–7). Illus. by author. 1967, Macmillan $16.00 (0-689-20586-4); Dell paper $4.99 (0-440-43180-8). 168pp. Adventure, suspense, detection, and humor are involved when 12-year-old Claudia and her younger brother elude the security guards and live for a week in New York's Metropolitan Museum of Art. Newbery Award winner, 1968.

**5632** Kotzwinkle, William. *Trouble in Bugland: A Collection of Inspector Mantis Mysteries* (6–8). Illus. by Joe Servello. 1996, Godine paper $14.95 (1-56792-070-5). 160pp. An all-insect cast in a takeoff on Sherlock Holmes mysteries. A reissue.

**5633** Krupinski, Loretta. *Lost in the Fog* (3–4). Illus. 1990, Little, Brown $14.95 (0-316-07462-4). 32pp. When their boat loaded with geese overturns, Mother Tipton thinks of a novel plan to save herself and Willie. (Rev: BL 5/1/90)

**5634** Lachtman, Ofelia Dumas. *Call Me Consuelo* (4–6). 1997, Arte Publico $14.95 (1-55885-188-7); paper $7.95 (1-55885-187-9). 147pp. Consuelo, a recent arrival in Los Angeles, becomes involved in finding the criminals who are committing mysterious local robberies. (Rev: SLJ 7/97)

**5635** Landon, Lucinda. *Meg Mackintosh and the Mystery at the Medieval Castle: A Solve-It-Yourself Mystery* (3–6). Illus. by author. 1989, Little, Brown paper $4.95 (0-316-51376-8). 64pp. While Meg and her class visit a castle, a jewel-encrusted chalice is stolen. Also use: *Meg Mackintosh and the Case of the Curious Whale Watch* (1987). (Rev: BL 6/15/89)

**5636** Landon, Lucinda. *Meg Mackintosh and the Mystery at the Soccer Match* (1–3). Illus. by author. Series: Solve-It-Yourself Mystery. 1997, Secret Passage paper $4.95 (1-888695-05-6). 48pp. Detective Meg and her soccer team are competing for a gold medal that suddenly disappears from the awards table. (Rev: SLJ 3/98)

**5637** Landon, Lucinda. *Meg Mackintosh and the Mystery in the Locked Library: A Solve-It-Yourself Mystery* (3–6). Illus. 1996, Secret Passage paper $4.95 (1-888695-04-8). 48pp. Along with Meg Mackintosh, readers are asked to solve the mystery of the stolen rare book. (Rev: BL 2/1/93; SLJ 3/93)

**5638** Lasky, Kathryn. *A Voice in the Wind: A Starbuck Family Adventure* (4–8). 1993, Harcourt $10.95 (0-15-294102-9); paper $6.00 (0-15-294103-7). 224pp. The 2 sets of Starbuck twins, who communicate through telepathy, uncover a plot to steal Native American artifacts during their trip west with their father. (Rev: SLJ 12/93)

**5639** Lehr, Norma. *The Secret of the Floating Phantom* (3–6). 1994, Lerner LB $19.95 (0-8225-0736-6). 192pp. Kathy's special psychic powers help her locate a buried treasure. (Rev: BL 12/1/94; SLJ 12/94)

**5640** Lehr, Norma. *The Shimmering Ghost of Riversend* (5–7). 1991, Lerner LB $19.95 (0-8225-0732-3). 168pp. An engaging mystery concerning an old family mansion in gold-rush country where Kathy has gone to spend the summer with her aunt. (Rev: BL 10/1/91)

**5641** Leroe, Ellen. *Racetrack Robbery* (2–4). Illus. 1996, Hyperion $13.95 (0-7868-0093-3); paper $3.95 (0-7868-1092-0). 64pp. With their invisible Ghost Dog, Artie and little sister Sarah solve the mystery of a missing coin. (Rev: BL 4/1/96; SLJ 5/96)

**5642** Leroux, Gaston. *The Phantom of the Opera* (3–6). Illus. by Paul Jennis. 1989, Random LB $5.99 (0-394-93847-X); paper $3.99 (0-394-83847-5).

48pp. An abridgment of this horror story about a defaced man who lives in the depths of an opera house. (Rev: SLJ 1/90)

**5643** Levin, Betty. *Fire in the Wind* (4–8). 1995, Greenwillow $15.00 (0-688-14299-0). 137pp. Meg, a self-sufficient girl who cares for her younger brother and backward cousin, faces a crisis when a raging fire threatens her home. (Rev: BCCB 1/96; SLJ 10/95)

**5644** Levin, Betty. *Island Bound* (5–7). Illus. 1997, Greenwillow $15.00 (0-688-15217-1). 224pp. Two teenagers uncover the truth behind a 150-year-old tragedy while they spend time on a tiny Maine island. (Rev: BL 7/97; SLJ 10/97)

**5645** Levy, Elizabeth. *Frankenstein Moved in on the Fourth Floor* (2–4). Illus. by Mordicai Gerstein. 1979, HarperCollins paper $3.95 (0-06-440122-7). 64pp. Is the strange Mr. Frank really Frankenstein? A sequel is: *Dracula Is a Pain in the Neck* (1983).

**5646** Levy, Elizabeth. *A Mammoth Mix-Up* (2–5). Illus. 1995, HarperCollins LB $12.89 (0-06-024815-7). 96pp. Brian and his sister Penny solve the mystery of the mammoth tusk they have found in their garden. (Rev: BL 9/15/95; SLJ 12/95)

**5647** Levy, Elizabeth. *Rude Rowdy Rumors* (2–4). Illus. 1994, HarperCollins LB $13.89 (0-06-023463-6). 96pp. Brian and his young sister set out to find the culprit who is spreading false rumors about him. (Rev: BL 1/1/95; SLJ 1/95)

**5648** Levy, Elizabeth. *Something Queer at the Library: A Mystery* (2–4). Illus. by Mordicai Gerstein. 1989, Dell paper $3.50 (0-440-48120-1). 48pp. Jill and Gwen try to track down the person who is mutilating books in the library. Sequels are: *Something Queer on Vacation* (1980, Delacorte); *Something Queer at the Haunted School* (1982, Delacorte); *Something Queer Is Going On* (1982); *Something Queer at the Ball Park* (1984).

**5649** Levy, Elizabeth. *Something Queer in Outer Space* (2–4). Illus. by Mordicai Gerstein. 1993, Hyperion paper $4.95 (1-56282-279-9). 48pp. Somebody is trying to sabotage the chances of Jill's pet basset hound becoming the first dog in space. (Rev: BL 10/15/93; SLJ 2/94)

**5650** Levy, Elizabeth. *Something Queer in the Cafeteria* (2–4). 1994, Hyperion $13.95 (0-7868-0001-1); paper $4.95 (0-7868-1000-9). 48pp. Strange happenings in the school cafeteria cause Gwen and Jill to begin investigating. (Rev: BL 10/1/94; SLJ 10/94)

**5651** Levy, Elizabeth. *Something Queer in the Wild West* (2–5). Illus. by Mordicai Gerstein. 1997, Hyperion $14.95 (0-7868-0258-8); paper $4.95 (0-7868-1117-X). 48pp. A lighthearted mystery in which friends Gwen and Jill visit a ranch in New Mexico and discover a haunted barn. (Rev: BL 4/15/97; SLJ 5/97)

**5652** Lindbergh, Anne. *The Worry Week* (5–7). Illus. by Kathryn Hewitt. 1985, Harcourt $12.95 (0-15-299675-3); Avon paper $2.95 (0-380-70394-7). 144pp. Left alone with her sisters for a week in Maine, 11-year-old "Legs" spends most of her time tending to and worrying about her siblings. (Rev: BL 6/1/85; HB 9–10/85; SLJ 8/85)

**5653** Lisle, Janet T. *A Message from the Match Girl* (4–6). Series: Investigators of the Unknown. 1995, Orchard LB $16.99 (0-531-08787-5). 128pp. Georgina and Poco wonder if the messages and mementos that Walter is receiving from the past are genuine. (Rev: BCCB 11/95; BL 10/1/95; SLJ 10/95*)

**5654** Lloyd, Emily. *Forest Slump: The Case of the Pilfered Pine Needles* (3–5). 1997, McGraw-Hill paper $4.25 (0-07-006388-5). 150pp. Using a message from science as a basis, this novel tells how 4 youngsters solve the mystery of who has stolen the pine needles from the forest floor. (Rev: BL 2/15/98; SLJ 4/98)

**5655** Lourie, Peter. *The Lost Treasure of Captain Kidd* (5–8). Illus. 1996, Shawangunk Pr. paper $10.95 (1-885482-03-5). 136pp. Friends Killian and Alex set out to discover Captain Kidd's treasure buried on the banks of the Hudson River centuries ago. (Rev: BL 2/15/96; SLJ 6/96)

**5656** McClain, Margaret S. *Bellboy: A Mule Train Journey* (4–6). Illus. by Sara Brown Stuart. 1989, New Mexico Publg. $17.95 (0-9622468-1-6). 192pp. A young boy takes a job leading a mule train into isolated towns in northern California in the 1870s. (Rev: BL 3/1/90)

**5657** MacGill-Callahan, Sheila. *To Capture the Wind* (3–5). Illus. 1997, Dial paper $14.99 (0-8037-1541-2). 32pp. Oonagh infiltrates a pirate's island in search of her kidnapped fiancé. (Rev: BL 9/1/97; SLJ 8/97)

**5658** McGraw, Eloise. *Tangled Webb* (5–7). 1993, Macmillan $13.95 (0-689-50573-6). 154pp. Twelve-year-old Juniper has the feeling that her new stepmother is hiding something from her past, and she sets out to find out what it is. (Rev: BCCB 6/93; BL 6/1–15/93)

**5659** Macken, Walter. *Island of the Great Yellow Ox* (4–7). 1991, Simon & Schuster paper $14.00 (0-671-73800-3). 192pp. Four boys are marooned on an Irish island where the golden ox of the Druids is hidden. (Rev: SLJ 10/91)

**5660** Mahy, Margaret. *Clancy's Cabin* (3–5). Illus. by Barbara Steadman. 1995, Overlook $14.95 (0-87951-592-9). 95pp. Two brothers and a sister spend a summer in a cabin in New Zealand and have great adventures, one of which involves finding a treasure. (Rev: SLJ 1/96)

**5661** Mahy, Margaret. *The Pirate Uncle* (3–6). Illus. 1995, Overlook $14.95 (0-87951-555-4). 128pp. Nick and sister Caroline vacation with Uncle Ludovic, a pirate who is trying to reform. (Rev: BCCB 5/95; BL 4/15/95; SLJ 5/95)

**5662** Mahy, Margaret. *Tangled Fortunes* (4–6). Illus. 1994, Delacorte $14.95 (0-385-32066-3). 105pp. The friendship between a brother and sister is explored in this mystery set in New Zealand. (Rev: BL 10/1/94; SLJ 11/94*)

**5663** Mahy, Margaret. *Tingleberries, Tuckertubs and Telephones* (3–5). Illus. 1996, Viking paper $12.99 (0-670-86331-9). 96pp. Young Saracen Hobday conquers both his shyness and a gang of villainous pirates. (Rev: BCCB 3/96; BL 1/1–15/96; HB 5–6/96; SLJ 2/96)

**5664** Mahy, Margaret. *Underrunners* (5–7). 1992, Viking paper $14.00 (0-670-84179-X). 192pp. A realistic look at life as Tris and his friend Winola are stalked by her violent father in rural New Zealand. (Rev: BCCB 3/92*; BL 2/1/92; HB 3–4/92)

**5665** Maifair, Linda Lee. *The Case of the Bashed-Up Bicycle* (2–4). 1996, Zondervan paper $3.99 (0-310-20736-3). 64pp. Tomboy Darcy solves the mystery of who stripped down her brother's new bicycle. Also use *The Case of the Nearsighted Neighbor* (1996). (Rev: BL 11/15/96)

**5666** Markham, Marion M. *The April Fool's Day Mystery* (2–4). Illus. by Pau Estrada. 1991, Houghton $13.95 (0-395-56235-X); Avon paper $3.50 (0-380-71716-6). 42pp. The detective twins Kate and Micky Dixon try to clear the name of Billy Wade, wrongfully accused of putting a snake in the school cafeteria's flour bin. (Rev: BL 7/91; SLJ 9/91)

**5667** Markham, Marion M. *The Halloween Candy Mystery* (2–4). Illus. by Emily Arnold McCully. 1982, Avon paper $2.95 (0-380-70965-1). 48pp. The Dixon twins and their brother solve the mystery of a Halloween thief. Another mystery is: *The Christmas Present Mystery* (1984).

**5668** Markham, Marion M. *The St. Patrick's Day Shamrock Mystery* (2–4). Illus. 1995, Houghton $15.00 (0-395-72137-7). 48pp. Someone has painted a large shamrock on their neighbor's front door, and the Dixon twins set out to find the culprit. (Rev: BL 9/15/95; SLJ 12/95)

**5669** Markham, Marion M. *The Thanksgiving Day Parade Mystery* (3–4). Illus. 1986, Avon paper $2.95 (0-380-70967-8). 48pp. Twins Kate and Mickey track down the disappearance of the school band on the way to the Macy's Thanksgiving Day Parade. Also use: *The Birthday Party Mystery* (1989). (Rev: BCCB 11/86; BL 9/15/86; SLJ 11/86)

**5670** Markham, Marion M. *The Valentine's Day Mystery* (2–4). Illus. by Karen A. Jerome. 1992,

Houghton $13.95 (0-395-61589-5). 48pp. The stage for this mystery is a Valentine's Day party, a missing heirloom, and suspicious guests. (Rev: BL 2/1/93; SLJ 12/92)

**5671** Martin, Les. *Humbug* (5–8). Series: The X-Files. 1996, HarperTrophy paper $3.95 (0-06-440627-X). 103pp. Even for veteran FBI agents Fox Mulder and Dana Scully, the murder of "The Alligator Man" is bizarre. (Rev: SLJ 6/96)

**5672** Mazer, Harry. *Snow Bound* (5–7). 1987, Dell $18.50 (0-8446-6240-2); paper $4.50 (0-440-96134-3). In this survival story, Tony and Cindy spend 11 days together snowbound.

**5673** Mazer, Norma Fox, and Harry Mazer. *The Solid Gold Kid* (5–8). 1989, Bantam paper $3.99 (0-553-27851-7). 224pp. Five adolescents are kidnapped, and each reacts differently to their harrowing situation.

**5674** Meacham, Margaret. *Oyster Moon* (3–6). Illus. by Marcy Ramsey. 1996, Cornell Maritime paper $9.95 (0-87033-459-X). 112pp. Anna, who is able to communicate through telepathy with her twin brother, Toby, receives messages indicating that he is in danger. (Rev: SLJ 11/96)

**5675** Medearis, Angela Shelf. *The Spray-Paint Mystery* (3–5). 1996, Scholastic paper $2.99 (0-590-48474-5). 102pp. A young African American third-grader sets out to find the culprit who is spray-painting a wall in his school. (Rev: BL 2/15/97; SLJ 4/97)

**5676** Miller, Dorothy R. *The Clearing: A Mystery* (4–6). 1996, Simon & Schuster $15.00 (0-689-80997-2). 119pp. An 11-year-old girl becomes involved in an unsolved mystery in rural Pennsylvania. (Rev: BCCB 11/96; BL 11/1/96; SLJ 10/96)

**5677** Monsell, Mary Elise. *The Mysterious Cases of Mr. Pin* (2–4). Illus. by Eileen Christelow. 1992, Pocket paper $3.50 (0-671-74084-9). 64pp. Mr. Pin is a penguin and he has come to Chicago from the South Pole to be a detective. (Rev: BL 5/15/89; SLJ 6/89)

**5678** Moore, Emily. *Just My Luck* (4–6). 1991, Puffin paper $3.99 (0-14-034790-9). 112pp. Olivia and Jeffery, 2 black children, set out to find Mrs. Dingle's lost dog.

**5679** Moss, Marissa. *Amelia Hits the Road* (3–4). Illus. Series: Amelia. 1997, Tricycle Pr. $14.95 (1-883672-57-0). 40pp. Amelia keeps a journal of a car trip she takes with her mother and older sister to the Southwest, where she visits the Grand Canyon and Death Valley. (Rev: BL 11/15/97; SLJ 11/97)

**5680** Murphy, Elspeth C. *The Mystery of the Dancing Angels* (2–5). Illus. 1995, Bethany paper $3.99 (1-55661-408-X). 64pp. The Three Cousins Detective Club sets out to solve the mystery involving a 4-

year-old distant cousin and a family riddle. (Rev: BL 10/1/95; SLJ 9/95)

**5681** Murphy, Elspeth C. *The Mystery of the Eagle Feather* (2–4). Illus. by Joe Nordstrom. Series: Three Cousins Detective Club. 1995, Bethany paper $3.99 (1-55661-413-6). 64pp. Timothy, Titus, and Sarah-Jane attend a powwow and solve the mystery of some missing feathers. (Rev: BL 2/15/96)

**5682** Murphy, Elspeth C. *The Mystery of the Haunted Lighthouse* (2–4). Illus. by Joe Nordstrom. Series: Three Cousins Detective Club. 1995, Bethany paper $3.99 (1-55661-411-X). 64pp. The Three Cousins Detective Club visits an abandoned lighthouse and decides it is haunted. (Rev: BL 12/15/95)

**5683** Murphy, Elspeth C. *The Mystery of the Hobo's Message* (2–4). Illus. 1995, Bethany paper $3.99 (1-55661-409-8). 64pp. Five youngsters use coded messages to foil a plot by developers to take over property dishonestly. (Rev: BL 10/15/95; SLJ 11/95)

**5684** Murrow, Liza Ketchum. *The Ghost of Lost Island* (4–6). 1991, Holiday $15.95 (0-8234-0874-4). 176pp. Gabe and his sister try to solve the mystery of a drowned dairymaid on Lost Island. (Rev: BCCB 5/91; BL 4/15/91; SLJ 5/91)

**5685** Myers, Edward. *Hostage* (5–7). 1996, Hyperion $15.95 (0-7868-0115-8). 192pp. During a hiking trip in Dinosaur National Monument, 2 youngsters are held hostage by a man who has stolen a dinosaur egg. (Rev: BCCB 2/96; BL 4/15/96; SLJ 4/96)

**5686** Myers, Walter Dean. *Smiffy Blue: Ace Crime Detective: The Case of the Missing Ruby and Other Stories* (2–4). Illus. by David J. A. Sims. 1996, Scholastic $14.95 (0-590-67665-2). 74pp. Four simple mysteries featuring detective Smiffy Blue, Dog, and assistant Jeremy Joe. (Rev: BCCB 5/96; SLJ 11/96)

**5687** Naylor, Phyllis Reynolds. *The Bodies in the Bessledorf Hotel* (4–6). 1986, Macmillan LB $15.00 (0-689-31304-7); Avon paper $2.99 (0-380-70485-4). 144pp. Bodies keep appearing in the hotel rooms, and Bernie is afraid his father will lose his manager's job. (Rev: BCCB 1/87; BL 10/1/86; SLJ 12/86)

**5688** Naylor, Phyllis Reynolds. *The Bomb in the Bessledorf Bus Depot* (4–6). 1996, Simon & Schuster $15.00 (0-689-80461-X). 136pp. Bernie and friends try to clear his sister from charges that she was involved in some local bombings. (Rev: BL 4/1/96; SLJ 5/96)

**5689** Naylor, Phyllis Reynolds. *The Face in the Bessledorf Funeral Parlor* (4–6). 1993, Atheneum $14.00 (0-689-31802-2). 144pp. A zany mystery that involves a new, improved funeral parlor, missing retirement funds, and a chuck roast. (Rev: BL 10/15/93; SLJ 10/93)

**5690** Naylor, Phyllis Reynolds. *The Fear Place* (5–7). 1994, Atheneum $16.00 (0-689-31866-9). 128pp. When 2 brothers are left alone in a remote mountain camp for a few days, their mounting dislike of each other explodes in this gripping survival story. (Rev: BCCB 1/95; BL 12/15/94; SLJ 12/94)

**5691** Naylor, Phyllis Reynolds. *One of the Third-Grade Thonkers* (4–6). Illus. 1988, Macmillan $15.00 (0-689-31424-8); Dell paper $3.99 (0-440-40407-X). 144pp. Jimmy and his third-grade pals form an elite macho club, but it takes a wreck on the Mississippi for them to learn what bravery is really about. (Rev: BL 10/1/88; SLJ 12/88)

**5692** Naylor, Phyllis Reynolds. *The Treasure of Bessledorf Hill* (3–5). 1998, Simon & Schuster $15.00 (0-689-81337-6). 136pp. In this Bessledorf mystery, Bernie decides to follow clues he hopes will lead to buried treasure. (Rev: BL 1/1–15/98; SLJ 3/98)

**5693** Newman, Robert. *The Case of the Baker Street Irregular: A Sherlock Holmes Story* (4–6). 1984, Macmillan paper $4.95 (0-689-70766-5). Young Andrew unexpectedly finds himself teamed up with Sherlock Holmes.

**5694** Nixon, Joan Lowery. *Search for the Shadowman* (4–6). 1996, Delacorte $15.95 (0-385-32203-8). 149pp. Using computer research, Andy tries to clear the name of a long-dead relative accused of treachery. (Rev: BCCB 1/97; BL 10/1/96; SLJ 11/96)

**5695** Nixon, Joan Lowery. *The Statue Walks at Night* (4–6). Illus. by Kathleen C. Howell. Series: Disney Adventures Casebusters. 1995, Disney paper $3.95 (0-7868-4018-8). 92pp. Two young brothers decide to solve the mystery of the valuable sketches that are missing from a museum. (Rev: SLJ 6/95)

**5696** Nones, Eric Jon. *Caleb's Friend* (2–4). Illus. by author. 1993, Farrar $15.00 (0-374-31017-3). After a strange sea creature he has befriended has been placed in a sideshow, Caleb plots to set him free. (Rev: SLJ 9/93)

**5697** O'Dell, Scott. *Black Star, Bright Dawn* (5–8). 1988, Houghton $16.00 (0-395-47778-6); Fawcett paper $4.50 (0-449-70340-1). 144pp. An Eskimo girl decides to run the 1,197-mile sled dog race called the Iditarod. (Rev: BCCB 6/88; BL 4/1/88; SLJ 5/88)

**5698** O'Dell, Scott. *Island of the Blue Dolphins* (5–8). 1960, Houghton $16.00 (0-395-06962-9); Dell paper $5.50 (0-440-43988-4). 192pp. An Indian girl spends 18 years alone on an island off the coast of California in the 1800s. Newbery Award winner, 1961. A sequel is: *Zia* (1976).

**5699** O'Malley, Kevin. *Who Killed Cock Robin?* (2–4). Illus. 1993, Lothrop LB $14.93 (0-688-12431-3). 32pp. In this complex mystery, Cock Robin fakes his own death to steal some precious jewels. (Rev: BL 11/15/93)

**5700** Osborne, Mary Pope. *Spider Kane and the Mystery Under the May-Apple* (3–5). Illus. by Victoria Chess. 1992, Knopf LB $11.99 (0-679-90855-2). 128pp. Nature details embellish the story of butterflies who seek the advice of sleuth Spider Kane. (Rev: BCCB 5/92; BL 5/1/92; SLJ 4/92)

**5701** Otis, James. *Toby Tyler: Or Ten Weeks with a Circus* (4–6). 1981, Buccaneer LB $25.95 (0-89966-363-X); Dover paper $2.00 (0-486-29349-1). 152pp. A perennial favorite about a subject popular with most children.

**5702** Page, Katherine H. *Christie and Company* (6–8). 1996, Avon $14.00 (0-380-97393-6). 148pp. In her new boarding school, Christie gets involved in a mystery involving someone who is sending her hate mail. (Rev: BL 12/1/96; SLJ 3/97)

**5703** Page, Katherine H. *Christie and Company Down East* (5–8). 1997, Avon paper $14.00 (0-380-97396-0). 160pp. Three girls spend a month at an inn on Maine's Little Bittern Island and become involved in a puzzling mystery. (Rev: BL 5/1/97; SLJ 7/97)

**5704** Parish, Peggy. *Pirate Island Adventure* (2–4). 1991, Dell paper $3.50 (0-440-47394-2). 176pp. Three children search for a long-lost family treasure.

**5705** Patneaude, David. *Someone Was Watching* (5–8). Illus. by Paul Micich. 1993, Whitman LB $14.95 (0-8075-7531-3). 221pp. Chris and his friend disobey parental orders and fly to Florida to rescue Chris's younger sister from kidnappers. (Rev: SLJ 7/93)

**5706** Paulsen, Gary. *Amos Binder, Secret Agent* (3–5). Series: Culpepper Adventures. 1997, Dell paper $3.99 (0-440-41050-9). 55pp. Through a mistake in the mail, 2 boys get a free trip to Arizona, where they become involved in a mystery and a series of adventures. (Rev: SLJ 4/97)

**5707** Paulsen, Gary. *Captive!* (4–6). Series: World of Adventure. 1995, Dell paper $3.99 (0-440-41042-8). 56pp. Roman Sanchez takes charge when he and his classmates are kidnapped by gunmen and held for ransom. (Rev: SLJ 2/96)

**5708** Paulsen, Gary. *The Case of the Dirty Bird* (4–6). Series: Culpepper Adventures. 1992, Dell paper $3.50 (0-440-40598-X). 84pp. Ten-year-old Dunc and klutzy Amos are on the trail of buried treasure. Also use: *Culpepper's Cannon; Dunc's Doll* (both 1992). (Rev: BL 11/1/92; SLJ 11/92)

**5709** Paulsen, Gary. *Escape from Fire Mountain* (4–6). Series: Culpepper Adventure. 1995, Dell paper $3.99 (0-440-41025-8). 67pp. An adventure story in which a young girl faces incredible challenges to rescue 2 lost children. (Rev: SLJ 7/95)

**5710** Paulsen, Gary. *The Legend of Red Horse Cavern* (4–6). Series: World of Adventure. 1994, Dell paper $3.50 (0-440-41023-1). 55pp. After 2 youngsters find a treasure chest, they become the targets of a gang of villains in this Western story. (Rev: SLJ 12/94)

**5711** Paulsen, Gary. *The Rock Jockeys* (4–6). Series: World of Adventure. 1995, Dell paper $3.99 (0-440-41026-6). 66pp. An adventure story in which 3 boys, the Rock Jockeys, set out to climb Devil's Wall to find the remains of a World War II bomber. (Rev: SLJ 10/95)

**5712** Paulsen, Gary. *The Treasure of El Patrón* (4–6). Series: World of Adventure. 1996, Dell paper $3.99 (0-440-41048-7). 70pp. Tag and his friend Cowboy run afoul of drug dealers in this adventure novel about 2 boys who are involved in underwater exploration. (Rev: SLJ 8/96)

**5713** Pearce, Philippa. *Who's Afraid? And Other Strange Stories* (5–7). 1987, Greenwillow $11.95 (0-688-06895-2). 160pp. Eleven ghost stories, mostly in the supernatural category. (Rev: BCCB 4/87; BL 4/1/87; HB 5–6/87)

**5714** Pepper, Dennis, ed. *The Oxford Book of Scary Tales* (5–8). Illus. 1992, Oxford $25.00 (0-19-278131-6). 160pp. A collection of ghost and monster stories that is meant for reading aloud and sharing. (Rev: BL 1/15/93; SLJ 1/93)

**5715** Petersen, P. J. *Liars* (5–8). 1992, Simon & Schuster paper $15.00 (0-671-75035-6). 146pp. Sam learns that he has the unusual ability to detect when people are not telling the truth. (Rev: SLJ 4/92*)

**5716** Petersen, P. J. *White Water* (4–6). 1997, Simon & Schuster paper $15.00 (0-689-80664-7). 112pp. When his father is bitten by a rattlesnake, timid Greg finds he is in charge in this white-water rafting adventure. (Rev: BCCB 6/97; BL 6/1–15/97; SLJ 5/97)

**5717** Peterson, Melissa. *Hasta La Vista, Blarney!* (3–6). Illus. 1997, HarperCollins paper $4.50 (0-06-440665-2). 144pp. Young detectives Ben and Maya globetrot while trying to follow clues left by Carmen Sandiego. (Rev: BL 2/1/97; SLJ 2/97)

**5718** Pfeffer, Susan Beth. *Justice for Emily* (4–7). 1997, Delacorte $14.95 (0-385-32259-3). 137pp. Emily witnesses 3 girls pushing another girl to her death in this sequel to *Nobody's Daughter* (1995). (Rev: BL 1/1–15/97; SLJ 2/97)

**5719** Polidori, John. *The Vampire* (3–6). Illus. by Paul Van Munching. 1989, Random LB $5.99 (0-394-93844-5); paper $3.50 (0-394-83844-0). 48pp. An adaptation of the adult story of the man who finds that his sister's fiancé is a vampire. (Rev: SLJ 1/90)

**5720** Pryor, Bonnie. *Marvelous Marvin and the Wolfman Mystery* (3–5). Illus. by Melissa Sweet.

1994, Morrow $15.00 (0-688-12866-1). 128pp. Marvin stumbles on some real crooks when he investigates the rumor that his new neighbor is a werewolf. (Rev: BL 3/15/94; SLJ 5/94)

**5721** Ransome, Arthur. *Swallows and Amazons* (4–7). Illus. by author. 1985, Godine paper $14.95 (0-87923-573-X). 352pp. These adventures of the 4 Walker children have been read for many years. A reissue. Others in the series: *Swallowdale* (1985); *Peter Duck* (1987).

**5722** Ransome, Arthur. *Winter Holiday* (4–7). Illus. by author. 1989, Godine paper $14.95 (0-87923-661-2). Further adventures of the Swallows and Amazons. A reissue. A sequel is: *Coot Club* (1989).

**5723** Raskin, Ellen. *The Westing Game* (5–8). 1978, Puffin paper $4.99 (0-14-034991-X). 192pp. A convoluted mystery that involves deciphering a will. Newbery Award winner, 1979.

**5724** Rau, Dana Meachen. *One Giant Leap* (3–5). Illus. by Thomas Buchs. Series: Odyssey. 1996, Smithsonian Institution $14.95 (1-56899-343-9); paper $5.95 (1-58899-344-7). 32pp. The first moon landing is described in a fictional account in which a young boy believes he is Neil Armstrong. (Rev: BL 10/15/96)

**5725** Riehecky, Janet. *The Mystery of the Missing Money* (4–6). Illus. 1996, Forest House LB $12.95 (1-56674-087-8); paper $5.95 (1-56674-701-2). 120pp. Twins Karen and Kyle investigate strange lights and noises in an empty old house. (Rev: BL 7/96; SLJ 7/96)

**5726** Riehecky, Janet. *The Mystery of the UFO* (4–6). Illus. 1996, Forest House LB $12.95 (1-56674-088-6); paper $6.95 (1-56674-702-3). 128pp. Rumors of UFO sightings bring twins Karen and Kyle to a campground to investigate. (Rev: BL 7/96; SLJ 7/96)

**5727** Roach, Marilynne K. *Encounters with the Invisible World* (5–7). Illus. by author. 1977, Amereon $18.95 (0-89190-874-9). For this reworking of traditional stories, there are 10 stories of ghosts, witches, and the devil.

**5728** Roberts, Willo Davis. *The Absolutely True Story: My Trip to Yellowstone Park with the Terrible Rupes (No Names Have Been Changed to Protect the Guilty) by Lewis Q. Dodge* (4–7). 1994, Atheneum $15.00 (0-689-31939-8). 160pp. A humorous mystery about a trip to Yellowstone Park by Lewis and sister Alison with the strange Rupes family. (Rev: BCCB 2/95; BL 1/15/95; SLJ 3/95)

**5729** Roberts, Willo Davis. *Baby-Sitting Is a Dangerous Job* (5–7). 1987, Fawcett paper $4.50 (0-449-70177-8). 192pp. Darcy tries to cope with 3 bratty children, but a kidnapping puts her and her charges in the hands of 3 dangerous men. (Rev: BCCB 3/85; BL 5/1/85; SLJ 5/85)

**5730** Roberts, Willo Davis. *Caught!* (4–7). 1994, Atheneum $16.00 (0-689-31903-7). 160pp. Vickie and her younger sister run away to join heir father in California, where they confront an intriguing mystery. (Rev: BL 4/1/94; SLJ 5/94)

**5731** Roberts, Willo Davis. *The Kidnappers* (4–7). 1998, Simon & Schuster $15.00 (0-689-81394-5). 144pp. Joel Bishop, a private-school student, can't get anyone to believe him when he witnesses a kidnapping. (Rev: BL 2/1/98; SLJ 3/98)

**5732** Roberts, Willo Davis. *Megan's Island* (5–7). 1988, Macmillan LB $14.95 (0-689-31397-7). 192pp. Eleven-year-old Megan and her brother are alarmed to discover that someone is following their family. (Rev: BCCB 4/88; BL 5/1/88; SLJ 4/88)

**5733** Roberts, Willo Davis. *The Pet-Sitting Peril* (4–6). 1990, Simon & Schuster paper $4.99 (0-689-71427-0). 176pp. Nick and friend Stan happen upon a gang of arsonists.

**5734** Roberts, Willo Davis. *Scared Stiff* (4–7). 1991, Macmillan $15.00 (0-689-31692-5). 160pp. Stories for middle readers set in an amusement park. (Rev: BCCB 2/91; BL 2/15/91)

**5735** Roberts, Willo Davis. *What Could Go Wrong?* (4–6). 1989, Macmillan $15.00 (0-689-31438-8); paper $3.95 (0-689-71690-7). 176pp. Three cousins find mystery and adventure on a plane trip to San Francisco. (Rev: HB 5–6/89)

**5736** Robinson, Mary. *The Amazing Valvano and the Mystery of the Hooded Rat* (4–6). 1990, Avon paper $2.75 (0-380-70713-6). 168pp. Maria's plans for her great magic act go astray when Lester the rat is stolen. (Rev: BL 6/15/88; SLJ 4/88)

**5737** Rocklin, Joanne. *Sonia Begonia* (4–6). Illus. by Julie Downing. 1986, Avon paper $2.50 (0-380-70307-6). 96pp. Sonia Begley wants to follow in her family's footsteps and open her own business, which she does with some amusing results. (Rev: BCCB 3/86; BL 3/15/86; SLJ 5/86)

**5738** Roos, Stephen. *My Favorite Ghost* (5–7). Illus. by Dee deRosa. 1988, Macmillan LB $13.95 (0-689-31301-2). 128pp. Thirteen-year-old Derek's money-making scheme involves the legend of a local ghost. A Plymouth Island story. (Rev: BL 4/15/88; HB 5–6/88; SLJ 4/88)

**5739** Rorby, Ginny. *Dolphin Sky* (5–7). 1996, Putnam $16.95 (0-399-22905-1). 240pp. Buddy, who suffers from dyslexia, plans to save some dolphins from a seedy aquashow. (Rev: BL 3/1/96; SLJ 4/96)

**5740** Ruckman, Ivy. *Night of the Twisters* (4–6). 1984, HarperCollins LB $14.89 (0-690-04409-7); paper $4.95 (0-06-440176-6). 160pp. An 11-year-old

boy witnesses a series of tornadoes that destroy his Nebraska town.

**5741** Ruckman, Ivy. *Spell It M-U-R-D-E-R* (4–6). 1994, Bantam paper $3.50 (0-553-48175-4). 160pp. Two girls stumble upon a murderer when they try to escape from a summer camp they detest. (Rev: BL 7/94; SLJ 8/94)

**5742** Saunders, Susan. *The Curse of the Cat Mummy* (2–4). Series: The Black Cat Club, No. 3. 1997, HarperTrophy paper $3.95 (0-06-442037-X). 73pp. When the children of the Black Cat Club visit an exhibit of artifacts from ancient Egypt, the cat Mittens falls under a mysterious spell. (Rev: SLJ 3/97)

**5743** Saunders, Susan. *The Ghost Who Ate Chocolate* (2–4). Illus. 1996, HarperCollins paper $3.95 (0-06-442035-3). 80pp. The 4 members of the Black Cat Club befriend the library ghost, Alice. A sequel is *The Haunted Skateboard* (1996). (Rev: BL 12/15/96; SLJ 11/96)

**5744** Scheffler, Ursel. *The Spy in the Attic* (2–4). Trans. by Marianne Martens. Illus. 1997, North-South $13.95 (1-55858-727-6). 62pp. In this mystery adventure, Martin and his friends think that their new neighbor is a spy. (Rev: BL 6/1–15/97; SLJ 4/97)

**5745** Schwartz, Alvin. *Scary Stories 3: More Tales to Chill Your Bones* (4–7). Illus. by Stephen Gammell. 1991, HarperCollins LB $14.89 (0-06-021795-2); paper $3.95 (0-06-440418-8). 128pp. A modernized version of spooky tales handed down through the years. (Rev: BL 8/91; HB 11–12/91; SLJ 11/91)

**5746** Scieszka, Jon. *Knights of the Kitchen Table* (3–5). Illus. by Lane Smith. 1991, Viking paper $11.99 (0-670-83622-2). 64pp. The Time Warp Trio hangs out with Lancelot and his pals. Also use: *The Not-So-Jolly Roger* (1991). (Rev: BCCB 7–8/91; BL 5/1/91; SLJ 8/91*)

**5747** Seidler, Tor. *The Tar Pit* (5–8). 1987, Farrar $14.00 (0-374-37383-3); paper $3.95 (0-374-47452-4). 160pp. Trying to skip math class, Edward retreats to an old tar pit and discovers a dinosaur jawbone. (Rev: BCCB 7–8/87; BL 8/87; SLJ 10/87)

**5748** Service, Pamela F. *Phantom Victory* (4–6). 1994, Scribners paper $16.00 (0-684-19441-4). 128pp. Two friends on South Bass Island in Ohio try to find a fabulous necklace that was hidden years ago. (Rev: BL 5/15/94; SLJ 7/94)

**5749** Sharpe, Susan. *Spirit Quest* (4–6). Illus. 1991, Macmillan LB $13.95 (0-02-782355-5). 128pp. As part of their spirit quests, 2 young Indian boys go on a 2-night camping trip. (Rev: BCCB 9/91; BL 9/1/91; SLJ 10/91)

**5750** Sharpe, Susan. *Waterman's Boy* (3–6). 1990, Macmillan paper $16.00 (0-02-782351-2). 96pp. Ten-year-old Ben helps an environmentalist track down the culprits who are polluting Chesapeake Bay. (Rev: BCCB 7–8/90; BL 5/1/90; SLJ 4/90)

**5751** Sherlock, Patti. *Four of a Kind* (4–6). 1991, Holiday $13.95 (0-8234-0913-9). 160pp. Eleven-year-old Andy has only one dream: to drive a draft horse team in a pulling contest. (Rev: SLJ 10/91)

**5752** Shreve, Susan. *Lucy Forever, Miss Rosetree, and the Stolen Baby* (3–6). Illus. 1994, Morrow $13.00 (0-688-12479-8). 144pp. Two girls who operate an imaginary psychiatric practice become involved in a mystery when a baby is kidnapped. (Rev: BCCB 10/94; BL 9/1/94; SLJ 9/94)

**5753** Shub, Elizabeth. *Cutlass in the Snow* (2–5). Illus. by Rachel Isadora. 1986, Greenwillow LB $14.93 (0-688-05928-7). 48pp. Sam and Grandpa are forced to spend the night stranded on Fire Island, where talk of pirates keeps them alert all night; in the morning, they find a cutlass in the snow, in this 19th-century tale based on a true incident. (Rev: BL 4/15/86; HB 5–6/86; SLJ 4/86)

**5754** Shura, Mary Francis. *Don't Call Me Toad!* (4–6). Illus. by Jacqueline Rogers. 1987, Avon paper $2.95 (0-380-70496-X). Jane and Dinah have a rocky relationship at first and become involved in a mystery about robberies that sweep a town. (Rev: BCCB 7–8/87; BL 5/15/87; SLJ 4/87)

**5755** Simon, Seymour. *The On-Line Spaceman and Other Cases* (3–6). Illus. 1997, Morrow $15.00 (0-688-14433-0). 96pp. Using deduction and an advanced knowledge of science, 12-year-old Einstein Anderson solves 10 short mysteries. (Rev: BL 5/1/97; SLJ 4/97)

**5756** Singer, Marilyn. *The Case of the Sabotaged School Play* (3–5). Illus. by Judy Glasser. 1984, HarperCollins paper $3.95 (0-06-440207-X). 64pp. The Bean brothers solve the mystery of who is trying to sabotage the school play.

**5757** Skurzynski, Gloria. *Lost in the Devil's Desert* (4–6). Illus. by Joseph M. Scrofani. 1993, Morrow paper $3.95 (0-688-04593-6). 96pp. In this adventure story, Kevin is trapped in an ex-con's getaway car. A reissue.

**5758** Skurzynski, Gloria, and Alane Ferguson. *Wolf Stalker* (4–6). Illus. 1997, National Geographic $15.00 (0-7922-7034-7). 154pp. Three youngsters solve the mystery of who is killing the wolves in Yellowstone Park. (Rev: BL 12/15/97; SLJ 1/98)

**5759** Smith, Roland. *Jaguar* (5–8). 1997, Hyperion LB $16.49 (0-7868-2226-0). 192pp. When Jake visits his zoologist father at a jaguar preserve in Brazil, he gets involved in a mystery and, at one point, must survive alone in the Amazon jungle. (Rev: BL 5/15/97; SLJ 6/97)

**5760** Smith, Roland. *Thunder Cave* (5–8). 1995, Hyperion $16.95 (0-7868-0068-2). 288pp. While

searching for his father in Kenya, Jacob encounters a gang of poachers. (Rev: BCCB 6/95; BL 5/1/95; SLJ 5/95)

**5761** Snyder, Zilpha Keatley. *The Headless Cupid* (4–7). 1971, Macmillan $17.00 (0-689-20687-9); Dell paper $4.50 (0-440-43507-2). 208pp. Amanda, a student of the occult, upsets her new family. A sequel is: *The Famous Stanley Kidnapping Case* (1985).

**5762** Snyder, Zilpha Keatley. *The Truth About Stone Hollow* (5–7). Illus. 1992, Peter Smith $16.00 (0-8446-6545-2). Although the ravine's past remains shrouded in mystery, Amy's and Jason's trips to the haunted hollow make a compelling excursion into the semisupernatural.

**5763** Sobol, Donald J. *Encyclopedia Brown and the Case of Pablo's Nose* (3–6). Illus. 1996, Doubleday $14.95 (0-385-32184-8). 80pp. The youthful, enterprising sleuth is back with more clever mysteries. (Rev: BL 1/1–15/97; SLJ 11/96)

**5764** Sobol, Donald J. *Encyclopedia Brown and the Case of the Disgusting Sneakers* (3–5). Illus. by Gail Owens. 1990, Morrow $15.95 (0-688-09012-5). 68pp. Ten new cases just as hard to solve and as much fun as previous brainteasers. (Rev: BCCB 12/90; BL 9/15/90; SLJ 1/91)

**5765** Sobol, Donald J. *Encyclopedia Brown and the Case of the Mysterious Handprints* (3–5). Illus. 1985, Morrow $16.00 (0-688-04626-6). 96pp. Matching wits with the 10-year-old sleuth in 10 more crime cases. Also use: *Encyclopedia Brown and the Case of the Secret Pitch* (1978, Bantam); *Encyclopedia Brown Lends a Hand* (1979, Dutton); *Encyclopedia Brown and the Case of the Treasure Hunt* (1988). (Rev: BL 11/15/85; SLJ 2/86)

**5766** Sobol, Donald J. *Encyclopedia Brown and the Case of the Two Spies* (3–6). Illus. by Eric Velasquez. Series: Encyclopedia Brown Books. 1994, Delacorte $13.95 (0-385-32036-1). 72pp. A series of short, baffling mysteries with the solutions at the back of the book, all featuring our favorite pint-size detective. (Rev: SLJ 3/94)

**5767** Sobol, Donald J. *Encyclopedia Brown, Boy Detective* (3–5). Illus. by Leonard Shortall and Lillian Brandi. 1979, Bantam paper $3.99 (0-553-15724-8). 96pp. Ten-year-old Leroy Brown opens his own detective agency and solves 10 crimes. Some sequels are: *Encyclopedia Brown and the Case of the Dead Eagles* (1977); *Encyclopedia Brown Finds the Clues; Encyclopedia Brown Gets His Man; Encyclopedia Brown Keeps the Peace* (all 1979); *Encyclopedia Brown Sets the Pace* (1984).

**5768** Sobol, Donald J. *Encyclopedia Brown Saves the Day* (3–5). Illus. by Leonard Shortall and Lillian Brandi. 1979, Dutton paper $13.99 (0-525-67210-9). 96pp. This title, as well as other titles in this popular series, consists of a number of short stories told with wit and suspense. Some sequels are: *Encyclopedia Brown Shows the Way; Encyclopedia Brown Takes the Case; Encyclopedia Brown Tracks Them Down; Encyclopedia Brown and the Case of the Midnight Visitor* (all 1979); *Encyclopedia Brown Carries On* (1981, Scholastic).

**5769** Soto, Gary. *Crazy Weekend* (4–7). 1994, Scholastic $13.95 (0-590-47814-1). 143pp. Two boys are being pursued by some crooks in this fast-moving adventure story. (Rev: BCCB 7–8/94; SLJ 3/94)

**5770** Sperry, Armstrong. *Call It Courage* (5–8). Illus. by author. 1968, Macmillan $16.00 (0-02-786030-2); paper $3.95 (0-689-71391-6). 96pp. The "Crusoe" theme is interwoven with this story of a Polynesian boy's courage in facing the sea he feared. Newbery Award winner, 1941.

**5771** Steiner, Barbara. *Foghorn Flattery and the Dancing Horses* (4–6). 1991, Avon paper $2.95 (0-380-76147-5). 108pp. Carly and brother Foghorn travel to Vienna and encounter a mystery. (Rev: BL 6/15/91)

**5772** Steiner, Barbara. *Ghost Cave* (4–7). 1990, Harcourt $13.95 (0-15-230752-4). 144pp. After discovering the hidden grave of an Indian boy in a cave, 2 youngsters find they are lost and can't get out. (Rev: BL 7/90; SLJ 7/90)

**5773** Stem, Jacqueline. *The Cellar in the Woods* (4–6). 1997, Eakin $14.95 (1-57168-115-9). 145pp. In East Texas, 3 cousins explore a deserted house and encounter danger. (Rev: SLJ 1/98)

**5774** Stevenson, Drew. *Terror on Cemetery Hill* (4–6). 1996, Dutton paper $14.99 (0-525-65217-5). 112pp. Sarah and her 2 sixth-grade friends encounter a monster in a graveyard. (Rev: BL 9/1/96; SLJ 9/96)

**5775** Stevenson, James. *The Bones in the Cliff* (4–7). 1995, Greenwillow $15.00 (0-688-13745-8). 128pp. Pete is sure that a hit man is stalking his father at their home on Cutlass Island. (Rev: BCCB 6/95; BL 5/1/95*; HB 7–8/95; SLJ 4/95)

**5776** Stevenson, James. *The Unprotected Witness* (4–7). 1997, Greenwillow $15.00 (0-688-15133-7). 176pp. In this sequel to *The Bones in the Cliff*, Pete and his friend Rootie try to unravel the mystery of where a treasure is buried by seeking cludes in a letter from Pete's dead father. (Rev: BL 10/1/97*; HB 11–12/97; SLJ 9/97)

**5777** Stevenson, William. *The Bushbabies* (5–8). Illus. by Victor G. Ambrus. 1984, Peter Smith $16.00 (0-8446-6167-8). In this reissue of a 1965 title set in South Africa, there is a search for a lost white girl last seen with an old native man.

**5778** Stone, G. H. *Rough Stuff* (4–6). Series: Three Investigators Crimebusters. 1989, Knopf paper $2.95 (0-394-80178-4). 140pp. The pilot of the Three Investigators plane mysteriously disappears after it crashes. (Rev: SLJ 12/89)

**5779** Stone, Tom B. *Don't Eat the Mystery Meat!* (3–6). 1994, Bantam paper $3.50 (0-553-48223-8). 128pp. At the same time a new lunchroom supervisor is hired at their school, students notice that pets begin disappearing all over town. (Rev: BL 9/15/94; SLJ 11/94)

**5780** Stray, P. J. *Secrets of the Mayan Ruins* (4–6). Series: Passport to Mystery. 1995, Silver Burdett LB $13.95 (0-382-24704-3); paper $4.95 (0-382-24705-1). 139pp. Three teenagers join forces to solve the mystery of the stolen Mayan artifacts in this mystery set in Mexico. (Rev: SLJ 9/95)

**5781** Strickland, Brad. *The Hand of the Necromancer* (4–6). 1996, Dial paper $14.89 (0-8037-1830-6). 176pp. In a continuation of the series begun by John Bellairs, Johnny Dixon and the Professor combat a wicked wizard, Mattheus Mergel. (Rev: BL 7/96; SLJ 9/96)

**5782** Talbott, Hudson, and Mark Greenberg. *Amazon Diary: The Jungle Adventures of Alex Winters* (4–6). Photos by Mark Greenberg. Illus. by Hudson Talbott. 1996, Putnam $15.95 (0-399-22916-7). While traveling in the Amazon rain forest, a young boy gets to know the Yanomami people and how they live. (Rev: BCCB 1/97; SLJ 9/96)

**5783** Tanaka, Shelley. *On Board the Titanic* (5–7). Illus. by Ken Marschall. 1996, Hyperion $16.95 (0-7868-0283-9). 48pp. Real-life characters are re-created in this story of 17-year-old Jack Thayer and his voyage on the *Titanic* with his parents. (Rev: BCCB 9/96; BL 9/1/96; SLJ 10/96)

**5784** Tate, Eleanora E. *The Secret of Gumbo Grove* (5–7). 1987, Bantam paper $4.50 (0-553-27226-8). 256pp. Raisin stirs up trouble in her black community in South Carolina when she investigates some local history. (Rev: BCCB 6/87; BL 5/15/87; SLJ 3/87)

**5785** Taylor, Theodore. *The Odyssey of Ben O'Neal* (6–8). Illus. by Richard Cuffari. 1991, Avon paper $3.50 (0-380-71026-9). 224pp. Action and humor are skillfully combined in this story of a trip by Ben and his friend Tee to England at the turn of the century. Two others in the series: *Teetoncey; Teetoncey and Ben O'Neal* (both 1981).

**5786** Taylor, Theodore. *Timothy of the Cay: A Prequel-Sequel* (5–7). 1993, Harcourt $13.95 (0-15-288358-4). 160pp. This tells what happened to the 2 main characters from the author's *The Cay* before their shipwreck on the Caribbean island and what happened after they were saved. (Rev: BCCB 11/93; BL 9/15/93; SLJ 10/93)

**5787** Taylor, William. *Numbskulls* (4–6). 1995, Scholastic $14.95 (0-590-22629-0). 144pp. To help his younger sister, Chas submits to the ordeal of being placed in evil Alice's learning machine. A sequel to *Knitwits* (1992). (Rev: BL 10/15/95; SLJ 10/95)

**5788** Thomas, Jane Resh. *Courage at Indian Deep* (5–7). 1984, Houghton paper $6.95 (0-395-55699-6). 128pp. A young boy must help save a ship caught in a sudden storm.

**5789** Thomas, Jane Resh. *Fox in a Trap* (3–5). Illus. by Troy Howell. 1987, Houghton paper $5.95 (0-395-54426-2). 96pp. Daniel changes his mind about trapping once he accompanies his Uncle Pete. (Rev: BCCB 4/87; BL 4/1/87; SLJ 6–7/87)

**5790** Tripp, Nathaniel. *Thunderstorm!* (4–6). Illus. by Juan Wijngaard. 1994, Dial paper $15.99 (0-8037-1365-7). 48pp. Farmer Ben is not the only one to sense that a storm is coming or to be affected by it when it arrives. (Rev: BCCB 4/94; BL 4/1/94; SLJ 3/95*)

**5791** Twain, Mark. *The Stolen White Elephant* (4–8). Illus. 1882, Ayer $19.95 (0-8369-3486-5). A tale of the elephant's guardian, who naively is impressed by a corrupt police detective. (Rev: BL 5/1/88; SLJ 2/88)

**5792** Updike, David. *A Spring Story* (3–5). Illus. by Robert Andrew Parker. 1989, Pippin LB $15.95 (0-945912-06-4). 40pp. When spring comes, the ice breaks up and 2 adventurous boys are stranded on an ice floe. (Rev: BCCB 3/90; BL 1/15/90; SLJ 1/90)

**5793** Valgardson, W. D. *Winter Rescue* (1–4). Illus. by Ange Zhang. 1995, Simon & Schuster paper $15.00 (0-689-80094-0). An adventure story that involves a young boy and the Icelandic-Canadian fishermen around Lake Winnipeg. (Rev: BCCB 12/95; SLJ 11/95)

**5794** Verne, Jules. *Around the World in Eighty Days* (5–8). Trans. by George Makepeace Towle. Illus. by Barry Moser. 1988, Morrow $22.00 (0-688-07508-8). 256pp. An 1829 world map as endpapers highlights this handsome edition of the classic. (Rev: BL 2/15/89)

**5795** Verne, Jules. *Twenty Thousand Leagues Under the Sea* (3–6). Illus. by Wayne Geehan. 1990, Troll LB $14.95 (0-8167-1879-2); paper $5.95 (0-8167-1880-6). 48pp. The fantastic adventures of Captain Nemo with a submarine in the 1860s.

**5796** Vigor, John. *Danger, Dolphins, and Ginger Beer* (5–7). 1993, Macmillan $16.00 (0-689-31817-0). 192pp. In the British Virgin Islands, Sally joins some island children to capture a gang of drug smugglers. (Rev: BL 8/93; SLJ 7/93)

**5797** Voigt, Cynthia. *The Callender Papers* (5–8). 1983, Fawcett paper $4.50 (0-449-70184-0). 224pp. Jean takes a summer job in the Berkshire hills of Massachusetts and finds adventure and mystery.

**5798** Wallace, Barbara Brooks. *Cousins in the Castle* (4–6). 1996, Simon & Schuster $15.00 (0-689-80637-X). 152pp. A thrilling mystery set in Victorian times about Amelia and her life in the United States and the danger she faces. (Rev: BCCB 4/96; BL 4/1/96*; SLJ 5/96)

**5799** Wallace, Barbara Brooks. *Peppermints in the Parlor* (4–6). 1993, Macmillan paper $3.95 (0-689-71680-X). 208pp. Emily encounters mystery and terror when she goes to her aunt's home in San Francisco.

**5800** Wallace, Barbara Brooks. *The Twin in the Tavern* (4–6). 1993, Atheneum $15.00 (0-689-31846-4). 192pp. In this mystery story, orphaned Taddy sets out to find his twin in Dickensian London. (Rev: BL 11/1/93; SLJ 10/93*)

**5801** Wallace, Bill. *Blackwater Swamp* (4–6). Illus. 1994, Holiday $15.95 (0-8234-1120-6). 185pp. A woman, known by all to be a witch, helps Ted catch a group of crooks responsible for some local robberies. (Rev: BCCB 5/94; BL 6/1–15/94; SLJ 4/94)

**5802** Wallace, Bill. *Danger in Quicksand Swamp* (4–7). 1989, Holiday $15.95 (0-8234-0786-1). 181pp. While searching for buried treasure, Ben and Jake become stranded on an island near Quicksand Swamp. (Rev: BL 1/1/90; SLJ 10/89)

**5803** Wallace, Bill. *Trapped in Death Cave* (5–8). 1984, Holiday $15.95 (0-8234-0516-8). 176pp. Gary is convinced his grandpa was murdered to secure a map indicating where some gold is buried.

**5804** Warner, Gertrude C. *The Mystery of the Hidden Painting* (3–5). Illus. by Charles Tang. Series: Boxcar Children Mystery. 1992, Whitman LB $13.95 (0-8075-5383-2). 117pp. Four children are determined to find the missing necklace once owned by their grandmother. (Rev: SLJ 9/92)

**5805** Waysman, Dvora. *Back of Beyond: A Bar Mitzvah Journey* (5–7). Illus. 1996, Pitspopany paper $4.95 (0-943706-54-8). 140pp. On his trip to Australia, a 12-year-old Jewish boy becomes involved in the Aborigine culture and witnesses a ritual of manhood similar to a bar mitzvah. (Rev: SLJ 5/96)

**5806** Weiss, Ellen, and Mel Friedman. *Color Me Criminal* (3–6). Illus. 1997, HarperCollins paper $4.50 (0-06-440663-6). 144pp. Based on the television show, 2 young detectives travel around the United States in search of Carmen Sandiego. (Rev: BL 2/1/97; SLJ 2/97)

**5807** Westall, Robert. *Stormsearch* (4–7). Illus. 1992, Farrar $14.00 (0-374-37272-1). 128pp. Tim finds a buried model ship and uncovers details of a romantic tragedy. (Rev: BL 10/15/92)

**5808** Whatley, Bruce, and Rosie Smith. *Whatley's Quest* (5–8). Illus. 1995, HarperCollins LB $14.89 (0-06-026292-3). 48pp. An oversize picture book that creates questing stories, each involving a letter of the alphabet and objects that begin with that letter. (Rev: BL 9/15/95; SLJ 1/96) [421]

**5809** Williams, Barbara. *Titanic Crossing* (4–8). 1995, Dial paper $15.89 (0-8037-1791-1). 160pp. Thirteen-year-old Albert and his mother, uncle, and sister are on the doomed *Titanic*. (Rev: BCCB 9/95; BL 5/15/95; SLJ 6/95)

**5810** Woodruff, Elvira. *Ghosts Don't Get Goose Bumps* (4–6). Illus. by Joel Iskowitz. 1993, Holiday $15.95 (0-8234-1035-8). 96pp. On her visit to West Virginia, Jenna befriends an impish girl and is soon involved in a haunted marble factory and a mysterious disappearance. (Rev: BL 11/15/93; SLJ 10/93)

**5811** Wright, Betty R. *The Dollhouse Murders* (4–7). 1983, Holiday $15.95 (0-8234-0497-8). 160pp. Dolls in a dollhouse come to life in this mystery about long-ago murders.

**5812** Wright, Betty R. *A Ghost in the Window* (5–7). 1987, Holiday $15.95 (0-8234-0661-X). 160pp. Meg wants her parents reunited, but during a summer with her father she learns that she is her own person and cannot be responsible for her parents. (Rev: BL 11/15/87; SLJ 10/87)

**5813** Wright, Betty R. *Nothing but Trouble* (3–5). Illus. 1995, Holiday $15.95 (0-8234-1175-3). 128pp. Vannie solves the mystery of local vandalism when she goes to live with her aged aunt. (Rev: BCCB 6/95; BL 2/15/95; SLJ 5/95)

**5814** Wright, Betty R. *Too Many Secrets* (3–5). 1997, Scholastic $14.95 (0-590-25235-6). 128pp. Chad and his friend Jeannie decide to investigate without telling others when they hear a prowler in a neighbor's house. (Rev: BL 10/1/97; HB 7–8/97; SLJ 8/97)

**5815** Wright, Susan K. *Dead Letters* (4–6). Series: Dead-End Road Mysteries. 1996, Herald Pr. paper $6.99 (0-8361-9036-X). 176pp. Nellie and her friends set out to catch the culprit who is stealing mail from the boxes outside the Lucky Clover trailer park. (Rev: SLJ 9/96)

**5816** Wright, Susan K. *The Secret of the Old Graveyard* (5–7). 1993, Herald Pr. paper $6.99 (0-8361-3627-6). 183pp. Nellie forgets the trouble she has accepting her hippielike parents when mysterious events occur in an old graveyard. (Rev: SLJ 11/93)

**5817** Wyeth, Sharon D. *The Dinosaur Tooth* (3–4). Illus. 1990, Bantam paper $2.75 (0-553-15815-5). 96pp. The loss of Gregory's tooth causes problems when 9-year-old Annie is rehearsing neighborhood kids in her play. (Rev: BL 10/1/90)

**5818** Wyss, Johann D. *Swiss Family Robinson* (5–8). Illus. by Lynd Ward. 1949, Putnam $16.95 (0-448-06022-1). 400pp. A family is shipwrecked in this classic story.

**5819** Yep, Laurence. *The Case of the Goblin Pearls* (5–7). 1997, HarperCollins LB $14.89 (0-06-024446-1). 192pp. Lily and her Auntie Tiger Lil, a former actress, solve the mystery of the stolen pearls. (Rev: BCCB 5/97; BL 1/1–15/97; SLJ 3/97)

**5820** Yolen, Jane. *The Ballad of the Pirate Queens* (3–5). Illus. by David Shannon. 1995, Harcourt $16.00 (0-15-200710-5). 32pp. This picture book recreates the careers of 2 female pirates, Anne Bonney and Mary Reade. (Rev: BCCB 4/95; BL 4/15/95; SLJ 6/95*)

**5821** York, Carol B. *Once upon a Dark November* (5–7). 1989, Holiday $12.95 (0-8234-0780-2). 98pp. In this fine, chilling novel, 14-year-old Katie is drawn into the murder of an elderly woman. (Rev: BL 12/1/89; SLJ 12/89)

**5822** Zambreno, Mary F. *Journeyman Wizard* (4–7). 1994, Harcourt $16.95 (0-15-200022-4); Hyperion paper $5.95 (0-7868-1127-7). 240pp. Student wizard Jeremy is studying the casting of spells with Lady Allons when an unfortunate death occurs and he is accused of murder. (Rev: BL 5/1/94; SLJ 6/94)

## Animal Stories

**5823** Adler, C. S. *More Than a Horse* (5–7). 1997, Clarion $14.95 (0-395-79769-1). 192pp. Leeann and her mother move to a dude ranch in Arizona, where the young girl develops a love of horses. (Rev: BCCB 3/97; BL 3/15/97; SLJ 4/97)

**5824** Albright, Molly. *The Mascot Mess* (3–5). Illus. by Eulala Conner. 1997, Troll paper $2.95 (0-8167-1485-1). 96pp. Missy thinks that her sheepdog Baby would be a good mascot for the soccer team. Also use from this series: *Video Stars* (Troll 1996). (Rev: SLJ 7/89)

**5825** Alter, Judith. *Maggie and a Horse Named Devildust* (5–7). 1989, Ellen C. Temple paper $5.95 (0-936650-08-7). 160pp. Maggie is determined to ride her spirited horse in the Wild West show in this historical horse story. (Rev: BL 4/15/89)

**5826** Alter, Judith. *Maggie and the Search for Devildust* (5–7). 1989, Ellen C. Temple paper $5.95 (0-936650-09-5). 159pp. Maggie, a gorgeous girl of the Old West, sets out to find her horse, which has been stolen. (Rev: BL 10/1/89)

**5827** Arnosky, Jim. *Long Spikes* (4–7). Illus. 1992, Houghton $13.00 (0-395-58830-8). 90pp. As spring turns to summer, a yearling buck and his twin sister travel together after the death of their mother. (Rev: BCCB 4/92; BL 5/1/92; SLJ 5/92)

**5828** Bagnold, Enid. *National Velvet* (5–8). Illus. by Ted Lewin. 1985, Avon paper $4.99 (0-380-71235-

0). 272pp. A reissue of one of the most famous horse stories ever written to celebrate its fiftieth anniversary. (Rev: BL 12/15/85)

**5829** Barber, Phyllis. *Legs: The Story of a Giraffe* (4–6). 1991, Macmillan $13.95 (0-689-50526-4). 80pp. The story of a giraffe born in Kenya that reveals much about the lives of these fascinating animals. (Rev: BL 12/15/91; SLJ 1/92)

**5830** Bauer, Marion Dane. *Alison's Puppy* (2–4). Illus. 1997, Hyperion LB $14.49 (0-7868-2237-6); paper $3.95 (0-7868-1140-4). 48pp. When a hoped-for puppy does not appear on her birthday, Alison settles for a kitten. (Rev: BL 5/1/97; SLJ 8/97)

**5831** Baylor, Byrd. *Hawk, I'm Your Brother* (3–5). Illus. by Peter Parnall. 1976, Macmillan $16.00 (0-684-14571-5); paper $4.95 (0-689-71102-6). 48pp. A desert boy captures a young hawk, hoping it will teach him how to fly.

**5832** Beales, Valerie. *Emma and Freckles* (3–6). Illus. by Jacqueline Rogers. 1992, Simon & Schuster paper $13.00 (0-671-74686-3). 176pp. Emma gets her wish with Freckles the pony, who turns out to be a little too much for an 11-year-old. (Rev: BCCB 5/92; BL 7/92; SLJ 6/92)

**5833** Berends, Polly. *The Case of the Elevator Duck* (3–5). Illus. by Diane Allison. 1989, Random paper $3.99 (0-394-82646-9). 64pp. In spite of the rule that no pets are allowed in his housing development, little Gilbert decides to keep a duck in an elevator.

**5834** Brandenburg, Jim. *Scruffy: A Wolf Finds His Place in the Pack* (2–4). Illus. 1996, Walker LB $16.85 (0-8027-8446-1). 32pp. A photoessay about an outcast wolf that gradually finds status in the pack. (Rev: BCCB 10/96; BL 9/1/96; SLJ 12/96)

**5835** Briggs-Bunting, Jane. *Laddie of the Light* (4–6). Illus. 1997, Black River Trading $17.00 (0-9649083-1-X). 43pp. Jessie adjusts to her parents' approaching divorce with the help of 2 dogs, one real and the other a fictitious one that her grandfather tells her about. (Rev: BL 7/97)

**5836** Brown, F. K. *Last Hurdle* (4–6). Illus. by Peter Spier. 1988, Shoe String LB $18.50 (0-208-02212-0). 202pp. Kathy spends her savings on a broken-down horse, but manages to restore him in this book originally published in 1953.

**5837** Brown, Ruth, reteller. *The Ghost of Greyfriar's Bobby* (1–4). Illus. by Ruth Brown. 1996, Dutton paper $14.99 (0-525-45581-7). The story of the faithful dog that refused to leave his master's grave in Edinburgh and died there in 1872 is told to 2 modern children. (Rev: BCCB 9/96; SLJ 8/96)

**5838** Bryant, Bonnie. *Horse Crazy* (4–6). 1996, Bantam paper $3.99 (0-553-48402-8). 144pp. Three girls become friends at a riding stable. Also use: *Horse Shy* (1996). (Rev: BL 2/15/89)

**5839** Bryant, Bonnie. *Pony Crazy* (3–5). Illus. 1995, Bantam paper $3.50 (0-553-48255-6). 104pp. This horse story also features 2 likable heroines and a mystery about strange occurrences in a new neighbor's house. (Rev: BL 7/95; SLJ 12/95)

**5840** Burgess, Melvin. *The Cry of the Wolf* (5–8). 1994, Morrow $16.00 (0-397-30693-8). 128pp. Young Ben Tilley insists that wolves run past his farm in rural Surrey, even though they have supposedly been gone from England for 500 years. (Rev: BL 10/15/92; SLJ 9/92)

**5841** Burnford, Sheila. *The Incredible Journey* (6–8). Illus. by Carl Burger. 1990, Bantam $14.95 (0-553-05874-6). The adventures of a Labrador retriever, a terrier, and a Siamese cat, who journey 250 miles through the Canadian wilderness to return home.

**5842** Byars, Betsy. *The Midnight Fox* (4–6). Illus. by Ann Grifalconi. 1968, Puffin paper $4.50 (0-14-031450-4). 160pp. When Tom spends 2 months on a farm with his aunt and uncle, he never expects that a black fox will become the focus of his life.

**5843** Byars, Betsy. *Tornado* (3–5). Illus. 1996, HarperCollins LB $13.89 (0-06-026452-7). 64pp. To pass the time during a tornado watch, Pete, a farmhand, tells about another Tornado, an unusual dog. (Rev: BCCB 11/96; BL 9/15/96; HB 11–12/96; SLJ 11/96)

**5844** Carlson, Nolan. *Summer and Shiner* (5–8). 1992, Hearth paper $6.95 (0-9627947-4-0). 160pp. In a small Kansas town in the 1940s, 12-year-old Carley adopts a raccoon called Shiner. (Rev: BL 9/15/92)

**5845** Carnell, Suzanne, ed. *A Treasury of Pet Stories* (3–5). Illus. 1997, Kingfisher $6.95 (0-7534-5074-7). 160pp. Some of the authors represented in this fine collection are Beverly Cleary, Joan Aiken, Betsy Byars, and Judy Blume. (Rev: BL 8/97; SLJ 12/97)

**5846** Carris, Joan. *Just a Little Ham* (4–6). Illus. by Dora Leder. 1993, Pocket paper $3.99 (0-671-74783-5). 144pp. The entire family soon becomes enamored of pet piglet Pandora. (Rev: BCCB 11/89; BL 1/15/90; SLJ 2/90)

**5847** Charbonnet, Gabrielle. *Snakes Are Nothing to Sneeze At* (3–4). Illus. by Abby Carter. 1990, Holt $13.95 (0-8050-1373-3). 70pp. Annabel decides that a small snake would be the perfect pet. (Rev: BL 8/90; SLJ 12/90)

**5848** Cole, Joanna, and Stephanie Calmenson, eds. *Give a Dog a Bone: Stories, Poems, Jokes, and Riddles About Dogs* (2–3). Illus. 1996, Scholastic $16.95 (0-590-46374-8). 96pp. An anthology of writings, anecdotes, and jokes about dogs. (Rev: BL 2/1/96; SLJ 3/96)

**5849** Cone, Molly. *Mishmash* (3–5). Illus. by Leonard Shortall. 1962, Houghton $16.00 (0-395-06711-1).

128pp. A dog, Mishmash, moves in, takes over, and then helps his owner to adjust to a new home. Other series titles are: *Mishmash and the Sauerkraut Mystery* (1974); *Mishmash and the Robot* (1991).

**5850** Coville, Bruce, ed. *Herds of Thunder, Manes of Gold: A Collection of Horse Stories and Poems* (4–7). Illus. by Ted Lewin. 1989, Doubleday $15.95 (0-385-24642-0). 192pp. An anthology of stories, poems, and excerpts from novels about real and imaginary horses. (Rev: BCCB 2/90; BL 12/15/89; HB 3–4/90; SLJ 12/89)

**5851** Dana, Barbara. *Zucchini Out West* (3–5). Illus. 1997, HarperCollins LB $14.89 (0-06-024898-X). 192pp. Ten-year-old Bill and his sister and pet ferret, Zucchini, travel west to spend time visiting ferret experts in Wyoming. (Rev: BL 7/97; SLJ 7/97)

**5852** Davis, Deborah. *The Secret of the Seal* (3–5). Illus. by Judy Labrasca. 1989, Crown $15.00 (0-517-56725-3). 57pp. Kyo, a young Eskimo boy, must save the seal pup he has befriended. (Rev: BL 6/15/89; SLJ 11/89)

**5853** DeJong, Meindert. *Along Came a Dog* (4–7). Illus. by Maurice Sendak. 1958, HarperCollins paper $4.95 (0-06-440114-6). 192pp. The friendship of a timid, lonely dog and a toeless little red hen is the basis for a very moving story, full of suspense.

**5854** DeJong, Meindert. *Hurry Home, Candy* (4–6). Illus. by Maurice Sendak. 1953, HarperCollins LB $14.89 (0-06-021486-4); paper $4.95 (0-06-440025-5). 244pp. Candy is a little dog who, after many adventures, finds a home.

**5855** Dickinson, Peter. *Chuck and Danielle* (3–6). Illus. 1996, Delacorte $14.95 (0-385-32188-0). 115pp. In a set of vignettes, Danielle and her pet whippet share some charming, often hilarious adventures. (Rev: BCCB 2/96; BL 3/1/96*; HB 9–10/96; SLJ 2/96)

**5856** Duffey, Betsy. *Puppy Love* (2–4). Illus. by Susanna Natti. Series: Pet Patrol. 1994, Puffin paper $3.99 (0-140-34997-9). 64pp. Evie and Megan have trouble placing Flea, the runt of the litter, in a good home. (Rev: BL 10/1/92; SLJ 9/92)

**5857** Eckert, Allan W. *Incident at Hawk's Hill* (6–8). Illus. by John Schoenherr. 1995, Bantam paper $5.95 (0-316-20948-1). 173pp. A 6-year-old boy wanders away from home and is nurtured and protected by a badger.

**5858** Estes, Eleanor. *Ginger Pye* (4–6). Illus. by author. 1951, Harcourt $17.00 (0-15-230930-6); paper $6.00 (0-15-230933-0). 306pp. Ginger is the Pye family's engaging puppy who mysteriously disappears. Newbery Award winner, 1952. Also use: *Pinky Pye* (1958).

**5859** Farley, Steven. *The Black Stallion's Shadow* (5–7). 1996, Random $16.00 (0-679-85004-X).

182pp. The Black Stallion develops a fear of shadows and trainer Alec Ramsay hopes for a cure. (Rev: BCCB 9/96; BL 9/15/96)

**5860** Farley, Walter. *Black Stallion* (5–8). Illus. by Keith Ward. 1944, Random LB $13.99 (0-394-90601-2). A wild Arabian stallion and the boy who trained him. Other series titles: *The Black Stallion Returns; Son of the Black Stallion* (both 1977).

**5861** Farley, Walter, and Steven Farley. *The Young Black Stallion* (4–7). 1989, Random $10.95 (0-394-84562-5). 163pp. In this prequel, the famous black stallion is a colt owned by an Arab sheik. (Rev: BL 2/15/90; SLJ 12/89)

**5862** Feldman, Eve B. *That Cat!* (2–4). Illus. 1994, Morrow $14.00 (0-688-13310-X). 112pp. Molly is devastated when her cat disappears, and she tries many tactics to get him home. (Rev: BL 10/1/94; SLJ 9/94)

**5863** Fenner, Carol. *A Summer of Horses* (4–6). 1989, Knopf LB $7.99 (0-394-90480-X). 120pp. Faith and her sister spend the summer in Michigan with a horsewoman friend of the girls' mother. (Rev: BL 8/89; SLJ 8/89)

**5864** Freeman, Martha. *Stink Bomb Mom* (5–8). 1996, Delacorte $15.95 (0-385-32219-4). 154pp. Rory is afraid that she is going to lose her dog because of a harmless accident, and her dippy mother isn't much help. (Rev: BCCB 2/97; SLJ 12/96)

**5865** George, Jean Craighead. *The Cry of the Crow* (5–7). 1980, HarperCollins paper $4.95 (0-06-440131-6). 160pp. Mandy finds a helpless baby crow in the woods and tames it.

**5866** George, Jean Craighead. *There's an Owl in the Shower* (3–5). Illus. 1995, HarperCollins $14.95 (0-06-024891-2). 144pp. Borden hates the spotted owl because his father lost his logging job through conservation efforts to save it, but later he finds himself caring for a young owl he has rescued. (Rev: BL 9/1/95; SLJ 11/95)

**5867** George, Twig C. *A Dolphin Named Bob* (2–5). Illus. 1996, HarperCollins LB $13.89 (0-06-025363-0). 64pp. Presents, in a fictional format, the life cycle of a dolphin at the Maryland State Aquarium. (Rev: BL 2/1/96; SLJ 5/96)

**5868** Gilbert, Suzie. *Hawk Hill* (3–5). Illus. by Sylvia Long. 1996, Chronicle $14.95 (0-8118-0839-4). 40pp. In this picture book, a young boy finds a new interest in caring for injured birds of prey. (Rev: BCCB 12/96; BL 11/1/96; SLJ 11/96)

**5869** Gipson, Fred. *Old Yeller* (6–8). Illus. by Carl Burger. 1956, HarperCollins $23.00 (0-06-011545-9); paper $4.95 (0-06-440382-3). 176pp. A powerful story set in the Texas hill country about a 14-year-old boy and the ugly stray dog he comes to love. Also use: *Savage Sam* (1976).

**5870** Graeber, Charlotte. *Fudge* (3–5). Illus. by Cheryl Harness. 1989, Pocket paper $3.50 (0-671-70288-2). 128pp. Chad Garcia's parents say he can have a puppy, but no one has time to train it, so Chad must prove himself responsible. (Rev: BCCB 7–8/87; BL 8/87)

**5871** Graeber, Charlotte. *Mustard* (3–5). Illus. by Donna Diamond. 1983, Bantam paper $2.25 (0-553-15384-6). 64pp. Eight-year-old Alex can't face the fact that his cat is getting old.

**5872** Griffith, Helen V. *Foxy* (4–6). 1984, Greenwillow $15.00 (0-688-02567-6). 144pp. Jeff believes his dog Foxy is dead, but his neighbor, Amber, knows this isn't true.

**5873** Haas, Jessie. *Be Well, Beware* (2–5). Illus. by Joseph A. Smith. 1996, Greenwillow $15.00 (0-688-14545-0). 72pp. Lily nurses her beloved horse, Beware, through a deadly attack of colic. (Rev: BCCB 3/96; BL 5/1/96; SLJ 4/96)

**5874** Haas, Jessie. *Beware the Mare* (2–4). 1993, Greenwillow $15.00 (0-688-11762-7). 64pp. Lily and her grandfather wonder why the horse they have just acquired is named Beware. (Rev: BCCB 7–8/93; BL 7/93; HB 5–6/93; SLJ 4/93)

**5875** Haas, Jessie. *A Blue for Beware* (2–4). Illus. 1995, Greenwillow $14.00 (0-688-13678-8). 64pp. Lily and her horse Beware compete in their first horse show. A sequel to *Beware the Mare* (1993). (Rev: BCCB 3/95; BL 5/15/95; HB 5–6/95; SLJ 5/95)

**5876** Haas, Jessie. *A Horse Like Barney* (4–6). 1993, Greenwillow $13.00 (0-688-12415-1). 176pp. When Sarah narrows her choice of a horse to 2, she must make some painful decisions. (Rev: BL 9/15/93; HB 11–12/93; SLJ 10/93)

**5877** Haas, Jessie. *Uncle Daney's Way* (4–7). 1994, Greenwillow $15.00 (0-688-12794-0). 128pp. Great-uncle Daney, his horse Nip, and young Cole engage in projects to help Cole's family, which has recently moved to the country. (Rev: BCCB 4/94; BL 4/15/94; HB 7–8/94; SLJ 4/94)

**5878** Hall, Elizabeth. *Child of the Wolves* (4–7). 1996, Houghton $16.00 (0-395-76502-1). 176pp. Granite, a Siberian husky pup, must survive in the wilderness when he is separated from his family. (Rev: BCCB 3/96; BL 4/1/96)

**5879** Hall, Lynn. *The Mystery of Pony Hollow* (3–5). Illus. by Ruth Sanderson. 1992, Random paper $3.99 (0-679-83052-9). 64pp. An entertaining story that also contains a baffling mystery.

**5880** Hall, Lynn. *Windsong* (4–6). 1992, Macmillan paper $12.95 (0-684-19439-2). 80pp. Looks like the only way Marty might be able to have a dog at home is if her parents divorce. (Rev: BCCB 2/93; BL 11/1/92)

**5881** Hanel, Wolfram. *Abby* (2–4). Illus. by Alan Marks. 1996, North-South LB $13.88 (1-55858-649-0). 60pp. Moira's beloved pet dog, Abby, becomes ill after eating poisoned meat in this story set on an island near Ireland. (Rev: BL 12/1/96*; SLJ 1/97)

**5882** Harper, Isabelle. *My Dog Rosie* (PS–K). Illus. by Barry Moser. 1994, Scholastic $13.95 (0-590-47619-X). 32pp. A youngster describes how she takes care of the family dog when her grandfather goes into his studio to work. (Rev: BCCB 12/94; BL 11/15/94; HB 11–12/94; SLJ 11/94)

**5883** Hawkins, Laura. *Figment, Your Dog, Speaking* (3–4). 1991, Houghton $13.95 (0-395-57032-8). 155pp. Lonely 10-year-old Marcella, who lies to get attention, finds companionship with a dog. (Rev: BCCB 11/91; BL 2/1/92; SLJ 3/92)

**5884** Hearne, Betsy. *Eliza's Dog* (3–5). 1996, Simon & Schuster paper $16.00 (0-689-80704-X). 151pp. Eliza shares many adventures with her sheepdog pup, Panda. (Rev: BCCB 3/96; BL 4/1/96; HB 9–10/96; SLJ 5/96)

**5885** Heinz, Brian J. *Kayuktuk: An Arctic Quest* (2–5). Illus. by Jon Van Zyle. 1996, Chronicle $14.95 (0-8118-0411-9). An Eskimo boy must find out what animal is stealing from his traps in this story set in the Alaskan Arctic. (Rev: SLJ 11/96)

**5886** Henkes, Kevin. *Protecting Marie* (5–7). 1995, Greenwillow $15.00 (0-688-13958-2). 208pp. Fanny is afraid that she will lose her pet dog if her temperamental father decides the dog must go. (Rev: BCCB 3/95; BL 3/15/95; HB 7–8/95; SLJ 5/95*)

**5887** Henry, Marguerite. *Brown Sunshine* (4–6). Illus. 1996, Simon & Schuster paper $16.00 (0-689-80364-8). 93pp. At first, Molly is unhappy with the old mare she has bought, but gradually she grows to love Lady Sue. (Rev: BCCB 10/96; BL 10/1/96; SLJ 9/96)

**5888** Henry, Marguerite. *King of the Wind* (5–8). Illus. by Wesley Dennis. 1990, Macmillan LB $15.00 (0-02-743629-2); Aladdin paper $3.95 (0-689-71486-6). 176pp. The horse Godolphin Arabian, ancestor of Man O'War and founder of the thoroughbred strain. Newbery Award winner, 1949. Also use: *Black Gold; Born to Trot* (both 1987).

**5889** Henry, Marguerite. *Misty of Chincoteague* (4–7). Illus. by Wesley Dennis. 1990, Simon & Schuster LB $15.00 (0-02-743622-5); paper $2.99 (0-689-82170-0). 176pp. A horse story. Two sequels are: *Sea Star; Stormy, Misty's Foal* (both 1991).

**5890** Henry, Marguerite. *Mustang, Wild Spirit of the West* (6–8). Illus. by Robert Lougheed. 1992, Macmillan paper $4.50 (0-689-71601-X). 224pp. An excellent horse story written by a master.

**5891** Henry, Marguerite. *San Domingo: The Medicine Hat Stallion* (4–6). Illus. by Robert Lougheed.

1992, Macmillan paper $4.50 (0-689-71631-1). 240pp. Set in the West during the mid-19th century, this is the story of a young man who rights a wrong inflicted on his father. Also from the same author and publisher: *Brighty of the Grand Canyon; Justin Morgan Had a Horse* (both 1991).

**5892** Herriot, James. *Only One Woof* (2–4). Illus. by Peter Barrett. 1985, St. Martin's $13.00 (0-312-58583-7); paper $6.95 (0-312-09129-X). 32pp. The sentimental story of 2 sheepdogs and the one and only time one of them barks. (Rev: BL 1/1/86; HB 3–4/86; SLJ 1/86)

**5893** Hess, Karen. *The Music of Dolphins* (4–7). 1996, Scholastic $14.95 (0-590-89797-7). 192pp. A young teen who has been raised by dolphins is returned to human society against her will. (Rev: BCCB 12/96; BL 10/15/96; SLJ 11/96*)

**5894** Hesse, Karen. *Sable* (2–4). Illus. by Marcia Sewall. 1994, Holt $14.95 (0-8050-2416-6). 60pp. Tate is sure that her dog, Sable, who has been given away for misbehaving, will return. (Rev: BCCB 5/94; BL 6/1–15/94; HB 7–8/94; SLJ 5/94*)

**5895** High, Linda O. *Hound Heaven* (5–7). 1995, Holiday $15.95 (0-8234-1195-8). 194pp. More than anything in the world, Silver Iris wants a dog, but her grandfather, with whom she lives, won't allow it. (Rev: BCCB 12/95; SLJ 11/95)

**5896** Howard, Ellen. *Murphy and Kate* (2–4). Illus. by Mark Graham. 1995, Simon & Schuster paper $15.00 (0-671-79775-1). 32pp. Kate and her dog, Murphy, grow up together; but when they were both age 14, death separates them and the young girl grieves the loss of her beloved friend. (Rev: BL 5/1/95; SLJ 6/95)

**5897** Hurwitz, Johanna. *A Llama in the Family* (2–4). Illus. 1994, Morrow $16.00 (0-688-13388-6). 96pp. Instead of the bike he has been hoping for as a surprise from his parents, Adam receives a llama. (Rev: BCCB 9/94; BL 9/1/94; SLJ 9/94)

**5898** Impey, Rose, and Jolyne Knox. *Desperate for a Dog* (2–4). Illus. 1991, Puffin paper $3.99 (0-14-034798-4). 94pp. Two sisters try some ingenious methods to get Dad to agree that they should have a dog. (Rev: BCCB 1/90; BL 12/15/89; SLJ 3/90)

**5899** Jimenez, Juan Ramon. *Platero y Yo/Platero and I* (5–7). Trans. by Myra Cohn Livingston and Joseph F. Dominguez. Illus. by Antonio Frasconi. 1994, Clarion $14.95 (0-395-62365-0). 47pp. Using both Spanish and English texts, this book contains excerpts from the prose poem about a writer and his donkey. (Rev: BL 6/1–15/94) [863]

**5900** Joyce, William. *Buddy* (4–6). Illus. 1997, HarperCollins LB $15.89 (0-06-027661-4). 96pp. Gertrude Lintz buys a gorilla and treats it like a human. (Rev: BL 8/97; SLJ 8/97)

**5901** Kamida, Vicki. *Night Mare* (5–8). 1997, Random $17.00 (0-679-88628-1). 208pp. In this horse story, Janet dreams of riding a magnificent white mare and one day the dream comes true. (Rev: BL 11/1/97; SLJ 11/97)

**5902** Kehret, Peg. *Frightmares: Bone Breath and the Vandals* (4–6). 1995, Pocket paper $3.50 (0-671-89189-8). 113pp. Rosie's dog, Bone Breath, is instrumental in capturing a gang of vandals who have been destroying school property. (Rev: BL 5/1/95; SLJ 5/95)

**5903** Kendall, Sarita. *Ransom for a River Dolphin* (5–8). 1993, Lerner LB $19.95 (0-8225-0735-8). 128pp. Carmenza nurses back to health a river dolphin wounded by her stepfather in this novel set on the banks of the Amazon River. (Rev: BL 2/1/94; SLJ 3/94)

**5904** King-Smith, Dick. *The Cuckoo Child* (3–6). Illus. by Leslie Bowman. 1995, Hyperion paper $3.95 (0-7868-1001-7). 128pp. Jack oversees the hatching of an ostrich egg and tends the offspring, Oliver, for 2 years in this humorous story. (Rev: BL 4/15/93; SLJ 4/93*)

**5905** King-Smith, Dick. *The Invisible Dog* (2–4). Illus. by Roger Roth. 1995, Random paper $4.99 (0-679-87041-5). Janie can't have a pet dog so she invents one. (Rev: BCCB 4/93; BL 3/1/93; HB 5–6/93; SLJ 5/93)

**5906** King-Smith, Dick. *Jenius: The Amazing Guinea Pig* (2–3). Illus. 1996, Hyperion $13.95 (0-7868-0243-X); paper $3.95 (0-7868-1135-8). 64pp. Judy is convinced that her pet guinea pig is a "Jenius." (Rev: BL 10/1/96; SLJ 11/96)

**5907** King-Smith, Dick. *Smasher* (2–4). Illus. 1997, Random LB $11.99 (0-679-98330-9); paper $3.99 (0-679-88330-4). 72pp. Smasher is a pup that causes so much trouble that Farmer Buzzard and his wife don't know how to control him. (Rev: BL 1/1–15/98)

**5908** King-Smith, Dick. *Sophie Hits Six* (2–4). Illus. by David Parkins. 1993, Candlewick $14.95 (1-56402-216-1). 128pp. Sophie hopes to become a farmer when she grows up and prepares for it by taking good care of her pets. (Rev: BL 11/1/93; SLJ 12/93)

**5909** King-Smith, Dick. *Sophie's Lucky* (3–4). Illus. 1996, Candlewick $14.99 (1-56402-869-0). 112pp. Sophie's dream of becoming a farmer comes closer to reality in this, Sophie's last book. (Rev: BCCB 2/96; BL 5/1/96; SLJ 4/96)

**5910** Kipling, Rudyard. *The Beginning of the Armadilloes* (1–5). Illus. by Lorinda Bryan Cauley. 1985, Harcourt $14.95 (0-15-206380-3); paper $6.00 (0-15-206381-1). 48pp. One of the lesser-known Just So Stories.

**5911**  Kipling, Rudyard. *The Jungle Book* (5–8). Illus. by Christian Broutin. Series: The Whole Story. 1996, Viking paper $22.99 (0-670-86919-8). 210pp. The original text is reprinted in this handsome edition, with period illustrations and newly commissioned paintings. (Rev: HB 1–2/96; SLJ 7/96)

**5912**  Kipling, Rudyard. *The Jungle Book: The Mowgli Stories* (4–7). Illus. by Jerry Pinkney. 1995, Morrow $20.00 (0-688-09979-3). 272pp. Eight stories about Mowgli are reprinted with 18 handsome watercolors. (Rev: BCCB 6/96; BL 10/15/95; SLJ 11/95)

**5913**  Kipling, Rudyard. *Just So Stories* (3–5). Illus. by David Frampton. 1991, HarperCollins $19.95 (0-06-023294-3). 128pp. Woodcuts enhance the retelling of these old favorites. (Rev: BL 11/15/91; HB 1–2/92; SLJ 11/91)

**5914**  Kipling, Rudyard. *Just So Stories* (4–6). Illus. by Barry Moser. 1996, Morrow $22.00 (0-688-13957-4). 160pp. Twelve classic stories are featured in this well-illustrated edition of Kipling favorites. (Rev: BL 11/1/96)

**5915**  Kipling, Rudyard. *Tales from the Jungle Book* (1–4). Adapted by Robin McKinley. Illus. by Joseph A. Smith. 1985, Random LB $8.99 (0-394-96940-5). 64pp. Three chapters from the Kipling classic describe the early years of Mowgli, the Indian boy raised by wolves. (Rev: BL 9/15/85)

**5916**  Kjelgaard, James A. *Big Red* (6–8). Illus. by Bob Kuhn. 1945, Holiday $17.95 (0-8234-0007-7); Bantam paper $4.50 (0-553-15434-6). 254pp. Adventures of a champion Irish setter and a trapper's son. Also use: *Irish Red: Son of Big Red* (1951); *Outlaw Red* (1953).

**5917**  Kjelgaard, James A. *Haunt Fox* (4–8). Illus. 1981, Bantam paper $3.99 (0-553-15743-4). 160pp. A fox is pursued by a boy and his dog; interest shifts from hunter to hunted.

**5918**  Knight, Dawn. *Mischief, Mad Mary, and Me* (2–4). Illus. 1997, Greenwillow $15.00 (0-688-14865-4). 112pp. Brit, who lives with her poor family in an underground house in Minnesota, befriends a dog that she hopes one day to own. (Rev: BL 5/15/97; SLJ 5/97)

**5919**  Knight, Eric. *Lassie Come Home* (4–7). Illus. by Marguerite Kirmse. 1940, Holt $16.95 (0-8050-0721-0); Bantam paper $4.95 (0-440-40136-4). 256pp. The classic that conveys the beautiful relationship between a boy and his loyal dog, and the lives of the people of Yorkshire as well.

**5920**  Lattimore, Deborah N. *Frida María: A Story of the Old Southwest* (2–4). Illus. by author. 1994, Harcourt $15.00 (0-15-276636-7). In this horse story set in Old California, Frida tries to be a conventional girl to please her mother, but her adventurous spirit prevails. (Rev: SLJ 5/94)

**5921**  Lawson, Julie. *Cougar Cove* (4–6). Illus. by David Powell. 1996, Orca paper $6.95 (1-55143-072-X). 138pp. An animal adventure involving a girl who is visiting relatives on Vancouver Island, Canada. (Rev: SLJ 9/96)

**5922**  Leitch, Patricia. *Cross-Country Gallop* (4–6). Series: Horseshoes. 1996, HarperTrophy LB $13.89 (0-06-027287-2). 114pp. Two friends, Sally and Thalia, share adventures as they try to win the show jumping and pairs cross-country competitions at the Tarent Horse Show. (Rev: SLJ 1/97)

**5923**  Leitch, Patricia. *Pony Club Rider* (4–6). Series: Horseshoes. 1996, HarperCollins LB $13.89 (0-06-027286-4). 116pp. Sally and her friend Thalia are chosen to compete with the Tarent Pony Club team at a horse show. (Rev: SLJ 12/96)

**5924**  Levin, Betty. *Away to Me, Moss* (5–7). 1994, Greenwillow $14.00 (0-688-13439-4). 192pp. When his master has a stroke, Moss, a border collie, runs out of control. (Rev: BCCB 12/94; BL 10/1/94; SLJ 10/94)

**5925**  Levin, Betty. *Gift Horse* (4–6). Illus. 1996, Greenwillow $15.00 (0-688-14698-8). 176pp. Uncle Oliver fulfills his promise and gives Matt a horse. (Rev: BCCB 11/96; BL 10/1/96; SLJ 11/96)

**5926**  Lewis, J. Patrick. *One Dog Day* (3–6). Illus. by Marcy Ramsey. 1993, Macmillan $12.95 (0-689-31808-1). 64pp. In spite of the derision of others, Jilly enters her pet collie in the county's annual coon dog contest. (Rev: BL 4/15/93; SLJ 6/93)

**5927**  Little, Jean. *Different Dragons* (4–6). Illus. 1987, Puffin paper $3.95 (0-14-031998-0). 144pp. Ben, who fears everything, especially his aunt's dog, learns that everyone sometimes has something to fear. (Rev: BCCB 7–8/87; BL 6/1/87; SLJ 6–7/87)

**5928**  London, Jack. *The Call of the Wild* (5–8). Illus. by Philippe Munch. Series: The Whole Story. 1996, Viking paper $21.99 (0-670-86918-X). 126pp. An unabridged edition of this classic, with newly commissioned paintings and period illustrations. (Rev: BCCB 6/96; SLJ 7/96)

**5929**  London, Jack. *White Fang* (5–8). 1964, Airmont paper $2.95 (0-8049-0036-1). The classic dog story in one of many editions available. A reissue of the 1935 edition.

**5930**  London, Jonathan. *The Eyes of Gray Wolf* (K–5). Illus. by Jon Van Zyle. 1993, Chronicle $14.95 (0-8118-0285-X). 32pp. After losing his mate to hunters, Grey Wolf is consoled when he encounters a wolf pack with a white wolf that will be his future mate. (Rev: BL 11/1/93*; SLJ 1/94)

**5931** London, Jonathan. *Voices of the Wild* (4–6). Illus. by Wayne McLoughlin. 1993, Crown $15.00 (0-517-59217-7). 32pp. A series of animals are identified as they intersect with the kayak of a man camping in a northern habitat. (Rev: BL 11/1/93)

**5932** McKay, Hilary. *Dog Friday* (4–6). 1995, Simon & Schuster paper $15.00 (0-689-80383-4). 134pp. In spite of his fear of dogs, Robin plans to nurse back to health a dog he has found on a beach. Also use by the same author: *The Exiles* (1993) and *The Exiles at Home* (1994). (Rev: BCCB 10/95; BL 11/15/95; SLJ 10/95*)

**5933** Malterre, Elona. *The Last Wolf of Ireland* (5–7). 1990, Houghton $15.00 (0-395-54381-9). 124pp. Devin and his friend Katey hide wolf pups when the pups are threatened. (Rev: BCCB 10/90; BL 9/15/90*; SLJ 10/90)

**5934** Maynard, Meredy. *Dreamcatcher* (5–7). 1995, Polestar paper $7.50 (1-896095-01-1). 137pp. With the help of an American Indian girl, a 13-year-old boy secretly raises a baby raccoon that was abandoned in the woods. (Rev: SLJ 5/96)

**5935** Monfried, Lucia, and Betsy James. *No More Animals!* (2–4). Illus. 1995, Dutton paper $12.99 (0-525-45390-3). 64pp. Mother is displeased when Charlie gets another pet and his existing menagerie escapes. (Rev: BL 11/15/95; SLJ 11/95)

**5936** Morehead, Debby. *A Special Place for Charlee: A Child's Companion Through Pet Loss* (3–6). Illus. by Karen Cannon. 1996, Partners in Publishing paper $6.95 (0-9654049-0-0). 36pp. Mark gets help and counseling when the dog he has grown up with dies. (Rev: BL 11/15/96)

**5937** Morey, Walt. *Gentle Ben* (5–7). Illus. by John Schoenherr. 1965, Puffin paper $4.99 (0-14-036035-2). 192pp. A warm story of the deep trust and friendship between a boy and an Alaskan bear.

**5938** Morey, Walt. *Runaway Stallion* (4–6). Illus. by Fredrika Spillman. 1989, Blue Heron paper $6.95 (0-936085-12-6). 176pp. Jeff Hunter solves personal problems through rescuing a race horse, in this reissued novel.

**5939** Morey, Walt. *Scrub Dog of Alaska* (4–8). 1989, Blue Heron paper $7.95 (0-936085-13-4). 160pp. A pup, abandoned because of his small size, turns out to be a winner. Also use: *Kavik the Wolf Dog* (1977, Dutton).

**5940** Morey, Walt. *Year of the Black Pony* (5–7). Illus. by Fredrika Spillman. 1989, Blue Heron paper $6.95 (0-936085-14-2). 160pp. A family story about a boy's love for his pony in rural Oregon at the turn of the century.

**5941** Morpurgo, Michael. *The Butterfly Lion* (4–6). 1997, Viking paper $14.99 (0-670-87461-2). 96pp. In this novel set in South Africa, a young boy is determined to find his pet white lion, which has been sold by his father. (Rev: BL 6/1–15/97; SLJ 8/97)

**5942** Morris, Judy K. *Nightwalkers* (4–6). Illus. 1996, HarperCollins $14.95 (0-06-027200-7). 144pp. James is doing a school report on elephants when Daisy, a pachyderm that has escaped from a zoo, adopts him. (Rev: BCCB 12/96; BL 12/1/96; SLJ 12/96)

**5943** Morrison, Dorothy Nafus. *Whisper Goodbye* (5–7). 1988, Troll paper $2.95 (0-8167-1045-7). 192pp. Thirteen-year-old Katie must decide whether to move away with her grandparents or stay in her hometown, living with friends and the horse she loves. (Rev: BCCB 5/85; BL 4/1/85; SLJ 5/85)

**5944** Mowat, Farley. *The Dog Who Wouldn't Be* (4–7). Illus. by Paul Galdone. 1957, Little, Brown $18.95 (0-316-58636-6); Bantam paper $4.50 (0-553-27928-9). 208pp. The humorous story of Mutt, a dog of character and personality, and his boy.

**5945** Mukerji, Dhan Gopal. *Gay-Neck: The Story of a Pigeon* (4–8). Illus. by Boris Artzybasheff. 1968, Dutton paper $15.99 (0-525-30400-2). 192pp. This Newbery Award winner, 1928, is the story of a boy from India and his brave carrier pigeon during World War I.

**5946** Myers, Anna. *Red-Dirt Jessie* (4–7). 1992, Walker $13.95 (0-8027-8172-1). 120pp. In this tale of the Depression era in Oklahoma, 12-year-old Jessie helps keep her family together. (Rev: BCCB 10/92; BL 1/15/93; HB 1–2/93; SLJ 11/92*)

**5947** Myers, Anna. *Spotting the Leopard* (4–6). 1996, Walker $15.95 (0-8027-8459-3). 160pp. In this sequel to *Red-Dirt Jessie* (1992), a young boy tries to save an escaped zoo leopard from recapture and possible death. (Rev: BCCB 2/97; BL 10/15/96; SLJ 11/96)

**5948** Napoli, Donna Jo. *The Bravest Thing* (4–6). 1995, Dutton paper $14.99 (0-525-45397-0). 160pp. Laurel is distressed when her pet rabbit refuses to nurse her litter and the young ones die. (Rev: BCCB 10/95; BL 10/1/95; SLJ 10/95)

**5949** Naylor, Phyllis Reynolds. *Saving Shiloh* (4–7). 1997, Simon & Schuster $15.00 (0-689-81460-7). 144pp. In this sequel to the Newbery Award–winning *Shiloh* and *Shiloh Season*, Marty again encounters the evil Judd Travers, who has been accused of murder. (Rev: BL 9/1/97*; HB 9–10/97; SLJ 9/97)

**5950** Naylor, Phyllis Reynolds. *Shiloh* (4–8). 1991, Macmillan $15.00 (0-689-31614-3); Dell paper $4.99 (0-440-40752-4). 144pp. When a beagle follows him home, Marty, from a West Virginia family with a strict code of honor, learns a painful lesson about right and wrong. Newbery Award winner, 1992. (Rev: BCCB 10/91; BL 12/1/91*; HB 1–2/92; SLJ 9/91)

**5951** Naylor, Phyllis Reynolds. *Shiloh Season* (4–8). 1996, Simon & Schuster $15.00 (0-689-80647-7). 120pp. The evil Judd Travers wants his dog back from the Prestons in this sequel to *Shiloh* (1991). (Rev: BCCB 12/96; BL 11/15/96*; HB 11–12/96; SLJ 11/96)

**5952** North, Sterling. *Rascal: A Memoir of a Better Era* (6–8). Illus. by John Schoenherr. 1984, Puffin paper $3.99 (0-14-034445-4). 192pp. Autobiographical memoir of the beauties of nature as experienced by an 11-year-old and his pet raccoon.

**5953** North, Sterling. *The Wolfling* (4–6). 1980, Scholastic paper $2.50 (0-590-41868-8). 256pp. A 13-year-old boy raises a wolf pup.

**5954** Parker, Cam. *A Horse in New York* (4–8). 1989, Avon paper $2.75 (0-380-75704-4). 135pp. To save Blue, the horse she rode at summer camp, from destruction, Tiffin has to convince her parents to board him for the winter. (Rev: BL 12/15/89)

**5955** Patent, Dorothy Hinshaw. *Return of the Wolf* (4–6). Illus. by Jared T. Williams. 1995, Clarion $15.95 (0-395-72100-8). 67pp. A female wolf banished from her pack finds a new mate and a territory where she can begin a new pack. (Rev: BCCB 7–8/95; SLJ 7/95)

**5956** Polikoff, Barbara G. *Riding the Wind* (5–7). 1995, Holt $14.95 (0-8050-3492-7). 131pp. With the help of some friends, Angie is able to nurse an injured horse back to health. A sequel to *Life's a Funny Proposition, Horatio* (1992). (Rev: BCCB 6/95; BL 6/1–15/95; SLJ 9/95)

**5957** Powell, Pamela. *The Turtle Watchers* (3–6). 1992, Viking paper $13.00 (0-670-84294-X). 128pp. Three turtle watchers protect the nest of more than 100 eggs from predators on a West Indies island. (Rev: BCCB 1/93; BL 10/1/92; SLJ 10/92)

**5958** Quattlebaum, Mary. *The Magic Squad and the Dog of Great Potential* (3–6). Illus. 1997, Delacorte $14.95 (0-385-32276-3). 117pp. Ten-year-old Calvin Hastings gets a new perspective on life when he tries to train a dog from the local humane society. (Rev: BCCB 2/97; BL 2/1/97; HB 5–6/97; SLJ 5/97)

**5959** Rawlings, Marjorie Kinnan. *The Yearling* (6–8). Illus. by N. C. Wyeth. 1985, Macmillan $27.00 (0-684-18461-3). 416pp. The contemporary classic of a boy and a fawn growing up together in the backwoods of Florida. A reissue of the 1938 edition.

**5960** Rawls, Wilson. *Summer of the Monkeys* (4–6). 1989, Doubleday $15.95 (0-385-11450-8); Bantam paper $4.99 (0-553-29818-6). 358pp. Jay and his dog spend a summer chasing 29 escaped monkeys.

**5961** Rounds, Glen. *The Blind Colt* (3–6). Illus. by author. 1989, Holiday $16.95 (0-8234-0010-7); paper $5.95 (0-8234-0758-6). 84pp. The story of the

colt that overcame his blindness and the boy who saved him. A reissue.

**5962** Rounds, Glen. *Wild Appaloosa* (3–6). Illus. by author. 1983, Holiday $13.95 (0-8234-0482-X). 96pp. The story of a wild filly and a boy who dreams of one day training such a horse.

**5963** Ruepp, Krista. *Horses in the Fog* (2–4). Trans. by Alison James. 1997, North-South $13.88 (1-55858-805-1). 58pp. A young girl living on an island gets to ride a neighbor's Arabian stallion and finds a new riding companion in Mona. A sequel to *Midnight Rider* (1995). (Rev: BL 2/1/98)

**5964** Ruepp, Krista. *Midnight Rider* (2–5). Trans. by J. Alison James. Illus. 1995, North-South LB $13.88 (1-55858-495-1). 62pp. Charlie has an accident while secretly riding her sullen neighbor's horse, Starbright. (Rev: BCCB 10/95; BL 12/1/95; SLJ 12/95)

**5965** Rylant, Cynthia. *Every Living Thing* (5–7). Illus. by S. D. Schindler. 1985, Macmillan LB $14.00 (0-02-777200-4); paper $3.95 (0-689-71263-4). 96pp. Twelve short stories that describe the effects that a bird or an animal has on disinterested humans. (Rev: HB 3–4/86)

**5966** Sachar, Louis. *Marvin Redpost: Alone in His Teacher's House* (2–4). 1994, Random LB $11.99 (0-679-91949-X); paper $3.99 (0-679-81949-5). 83pp. Marvin is upset and confused when the dog he is taking care of dies. (Rev: BL 6/1–15/94)

**5967** Sachs, Betsy. *The Boy Who Ate Dog Biscuits* (2–4). Illus. by Margot Apple. 1989, Random paper $3.99 (0-394-84778-4). 64pp. Billy, who helps out at the vet's office and likes dog biscuits, prefers dogs to his baby sister. (Rev: BL 1/15/90)

**5968** Salten, Felix. *Bambi: A Life in the Woods* (5–8). 1926, Pocket paper $3.99 (0-671-66607-X). The growing to maturity of an Austrian deer.

**5969** Sargent, Pat. *Barney the Bear Killer* (3–5). Illus. by Jane Lenoir. 1994, Ozark LB $18.95 (1-56763-054-5). 117pp. An abandoned hound dog proves he is worthy of being taken in and cared for by a farmer and his family. (Rev: BL 12/15/94)

**5970** Schecter, Ellen. *The Pet-Sitters* (2–4). Illus. by Bob Dorsey. Series: West Side Kids. 1996, Hyperion paper $3.95 (0-7868-1046-7). 74pp. When the West Side Kids want more pets than their apartments can hold, they decide on the next best thing: a pet-sitting service. (Rev: SLJ 3/97)

**5971** Schlein, Miriam. *The Year of the Panda* (3–5). Illus. by Kam Mak. 1990, HarperCollins LB $14.89 (0-690-04866-1). 96pp. A Chinese farm boy cares for an orphaned baby panda. (Rev: BCCB 11/90; BL 9/15/90; HB 11–12/90; SLJ 10/90)

**5972** Scott, Ann H. *A Brand Is Forever* (3–5). Illus. by Ronald Himler. 1993, Houghton $12.95 (0-395-60118-5). 48pp. Annie hates the idea of branding her pet calf named Doodle. (Rev: BCCB 4/93; BL 4/1/93; HB 5–6/93; SLJ 5/93)

**5973** Sewell, Anna. *Black Beauty* (4–6). Illus. by Fritz Eichenberg. 1945, Puffin paper $2.25 (0-14-035006-3). 320pp. One of several recommended editions of this classic horse story.

**5974** Shalant, Phyllis. *The Great Eye* (5–7). 1996, Dutton paper $15.99 (0-525-45695-3). 176pp. A seventh-grader gets comfort and gains maturity in training a labrador to become a guide dog. (Rev: BCCB 2/97; BL 11/1/96; SLJ 11/96)

**5975** Sharmat, Marjorie W. *Genghis Khan: A Dog Star Is Born* (2–4). Illus. by Mitchell Rigie. 1994, Random LB $9.99 (0-679-95406-1); paper $3.99 (0-679-85406-1). 74pp. When Fred's dog, Genghis Khan, a canine movie star, is kidnapped, the boy and his friend Pamela do some sleuthing. (Rev: BL 1/1/95; SLJ 9/94)

**5976** Silverstein, Shel. *Lafcadio, the Lion Who Shot Back* (3–6). Illus. by author. 1963, HarperCollins LB $14.89 (0-06-025676-1). 112pp. His marksmanship makes him a success, but Lafcadio discovers it's not to his liking.

**5977** Smith, Susan M. *The Booford Summer* (3–6). Illus. 1994, Clarion $13.95 (0-395-66590-6). 144pp. A girl takes pity on Booford, a neighbor's dog, and begins taking him for walks. (Rev: BL 9/15/94; SLJ 11/94)

**5978** Smucker, Barbara. *Incredible Jumbo* (4–6). 1991, Viking paper $12.95 (0-670-82970-6). 172pp. The story of the African elephant who joined Barnum's circus in America. (Rev: BCCB 5/91; BL 4/1/91; SLJ 4/91)

**5979** Stewart, Elisabeth J. *Bimmi Finds a Cat* (3–4). Illus. by James E. Ransome. 1996, Clarion $14.95 (0-395-64652-9). 32pp. A Creole boy tries to find the owner of the cat that he has befriended. (Rev: BL 10/15/96; SLJ 8/97)

**5980** Tamar, Erika. *Junkyard Dog* (5–7). 1995, Knopf $15.00 (0-679-87057-1). 185pp. Katie decides she must do something to help the pathetic junkyard dog she passes every day on her way to school. (Rev: BCCB 9/95; BL 5/1/95; SLJ 6/95)

**5981** Taylor, Theodore. *The Hostage* (5–8). 1988, Dell paper $3.99 (0-440-20923-4). 176pp. Fourteen-year-old Jamie in Canada is stunned when his efforts to capture a trapped whale are misinterpreted. (Rev: BL 2/15/88; SLJ 3/88)

**5982** Taylor, Theodore. *The Trouble with Tuck* (5–8). 1989, Doubleday $15.95 (0-385-17774-7). 96pp. The story of a golden Labrador retriever who becomes blind.

**5983** Taylor, Theodore. *Tuck Triumphant* (4–7). 1991, Avon paper $4.50 (0-380-71323-3). 150pp. A 1950s novel about a blind dog in a loving family and the deaf Korean boy they adopt. (Rev: BL 2/1/91)

**5984** Taylor, William. *Agnes the Sheep* (5–7). 1991, Scholastic $13.95 (0-590-43365-2). 132pp. A wild and woolly story about an ornery and ill-kempt sheep and the 2 middle-graders who must care for her. (Rev: BCCB 3/91*; BL 5/15/91*)

**5985** Terhune, Albert Payson. *Lad: A Dog* (6–8). Illus. by Sam Savitt. 1981, Harmony Raine LB $24.95 (0-89967-022-9); NAL paper $2.50 (0-451-14626-3). 189pp. One of the best-loved dog stories of all time.

**5986** Thomas, Jane Resh. *The Comeback Dog* (3–6). Illus. by Troy Howell. 1981, Houghton $16.00 (0-395-29432-0); Bantam paper $3.50 (0-553-15521-0). 64pp. Daniel, trying to forget the death of his dog, tries to train an English setter.

**5987** Thomas, Jane Resh. *Scaredy Dog* (1–3). Illus. by Marilyn Mets. 1996, Hyperion $13.95 (0-7868-0278-2); paper $3.95 (0-7868-1148-X). 43pp. In the pet shelter, Erin picks a fearful pup that has been mistreated and wins him over through love and attention. (Rev: SLJ 11/96)

**5988** Updike, David. *The Sounds of Summer* (3–5). Illus. by Robert Andrew Parker. 1993, Pippin $15.95 (0-945912-20-X). 40pp. After Homer's dog, Sophocles, dies, the boy remembers the good times they had together. (Rev: BCCB 10/93; BL 9/1/93; SLJ 10/93)

**5989** Wallace, Bill. *A Dog Called Kitty* (4–7). 1980, Holiday $15.95 (0-8234-0376-9); Pocket paper $3.99 (0-671-77081-0). 160pp. A boy tries to overcome his fear of dogs so he can help a stray.

**5990** Wells, Rosemary. *Lassie Come-Home: Eric Knight's Original 1938 Classic* (3–5). Illus. by Susan Jeffers. 1995, Holt $16.95 (0-8050-3794-2). 48pp. A simplified picture book version of Eric Knight's classic dog story set in the Scottish countryside. (Rev: BCCB 2/96; BL 12/1/95; SLJ 11/95*)

**5991** Whelan, Gloria. *Silver* (2–4). Illus. by Stephen Marchesi. 1988, Random LB $5.99 (0-394-99611-9); paper $3.99 (0-394-89611-4). 64pp. Rachel wants to compete in the Alaska Iditarod sled race, and she thinks she can win with her lead dog, Silver. (Rev: BCCB 7–8/88; BL 7/88; SLJ 10/88)

**5992** Wittbold, Maureen. *Mending Peter's Heart* (K–6). Illus. by Larry Salk. 1995, Portunus paper $8.95 (0-9641330-2-4). 32pp. Peter needs consolation when his pet husky, Mishka, dies. (Rev: SLJ 11/95)

**5993** Wright, Lynn F. *Flick* (3–5). Illus. by Tony Waters. 1995, Worry Wart $13.95 (1-881519-02-3); paper $7.95 (1-881519-03-1). 68pp. Jack nurses back to health a badly injured puppy he has found on the railroad tracks. (Rev: SLJ 2/96)

**5994** Yep, Laurence. *Later, Gator* (4–6). 1995, Hyperion LB $14.49 (0-7868-2083-7). 128pp. Teddy is surprised when his young brother is delighted at his birthday gift, a baby alligator. (Rev: BCCB 7–8/95; BL 5/1/95; HB 7–8/95; SLJ 7/95*)

# Ethnic Groups

**5995** Ada, Alma F. *My Name Is Maria Isabel* (3–5). Trans. by Ana M. Cerro. Illus. by K. Dyble Thompson. 1993, Macmillan $14.00 (0-689-31517-1). 64pp. A Puerto Rican girl in the United States resents the fact that her teacher calls her Mary instead of Maria. (Rev: BCCB 6/93; BL 6/1–15/93; SLJ 4/93)

**5996** Balgassi, Haemi. *Tae's Sonata* (5–8). 1997, Clarion $14.00 (0-395-84314-6). 122pp. When Tae, a Korean American, is given a school assignment on Korea she must come to terms with her native culture and the memories she has of her homeland. (Rev: BL 10/15/97; SLJ 9/97)

**5997** Blume, Judy. *Iggie's House* (4–7). 1970, Macmillan LB $14.00 (0-02-711040-0); Dell paper $3.99 (0-440-44062-9). 128pp. A black family moves into Iggie's old house.

**5998** Buss, Fran L. *Journey of the Sparrows* (5–8). 1993, Dell paper $4.50 (0-440-40785-0). 160pp. The plight of illegal aliens in the United States is the focus of this novel about 3 Salvadoran children. (Rev: BCCB 1/92; HB 11–12/91; SLJ 10/91)

**5999** Curtis, Christopher Paul. *The Watsons Go to Birmingham — 1963* (4–8). 1995, Delacorte $14.95 (0-385-32175-9); Dell paper $4.99 (0-440-41412-1). 210pp. An African American family returns to Alabama from Michigan to place their troubled son with his grandmother. (Rev: BL 8/95; SLJ 10/95*)

**6000** Fleischman, Paul. *Seedfolks* (4–8). Illus. by Judy Pedersen. 1997, HarperCollins LB $13.89 (0-06-027472-7). 69pp. Thirteen people from many cultures explain why they have planted their gardens in a vacant lot in Cleveland, Ohio. (Rev: BCCB 7–8/97; HB 5–6/97; SLJ 5/97*)

**6001** Gardiner, John Reynolds. *Stone Fox* (3–6). Illus. by Marcia Sewall. 1980, HarperCollins LB $14.89 (0-690-03984-0); paper $4.50 (0-06-440132-4). 96pp. Ten-year-old Willy competes against the Indian mountain man, Stone Fox, in the national dogsled races.

**6002** Garland, Sherry. *The Lotus Seed* (K–5). Illus. by Tatsuro Kiuchi. 1993, Harcourt $15.00 (0-15-249465-0). 32pp. A young narrator tells of fleeing

her Vietnamese homeland to settle with her family in America. (Rev: BL 3/15/93*; HB 5–6/93; SLJ 7/93)

**6003** Greenfield, Eloise. *Koya DeLaney and the Good Girl Blues* (4–6). 1995, Scholastic paper $2.95 (0-590-43299-0). 176pp. Sixth-grader Koya DeLaney, whose talent is a gift of laughter, has some growing up to do when family conflicts arise. (Rev: BCCB 3/92; BL 2/15/92; SLJ 3/92)

**6004** Harvey, Brett. *Immigrant Girl: Becky of Eldridge Street* (2–4). Illus. by Deborah Kogan Ray. 1987, Holiday LB $15.95 (0-8234-0638-5). 40pp. The life of Becky, an immigrant girl, and her family in New York City in 1910. (Rev: BCCB 5/87; BL 4/15/87; SLJ 5/87)

**6005** Hautzig, Esther. *Riches* (4–8). Illus. by Donna Diamond. 1992, HarperCollins LB $13.89 (0-06-022260-3). 44pp. In this beautiful book, a retiring Jewish shopkeeper learns that gifts from the heart bring the greatest joy. (Rev: BCCB 1/93; BL 12/1/92)

**6006** Hoffman, Mary. *Amazing Grace* (PS–2). Illus. by Caroline Binch. 1991, Dial paper $15.99 (0-8037-1040-2). 32pp. Grace is told she can't play Peter Pan in the class production because she's a girl and she's black. (Rev: BCCB 9/91*; BL 8/91*; HB 9–10/91*; SLJ 10/91*)

**6007** Hooks, William H. *Circle of Fire* (5–8). 1982, Macmillan LB $15.00 (0-689-50241-9). 144pp. Three friends — a white and 2 black boys — try to thwart an attack on some Irish gypsies by the Ku Klux Klan.

**6008** Hoyt-Goldsmith, Diane. *Day of the Dead: A Mexican-American Celebration* (4–6). Illus. 1994, Holiday LB $15.95 (0-8234-1094-3). 32pp. The Hispanic Day of the Dead celebration as seen through the experiences of an American family living in a Mexican American community. (Rev: BL 7/94; SLJ 9/94)

**6009** Kidd, Diana. *Onion Tears* (3–5). Illus. by Lucy Montgomery. 1991, Orchard LB $16.99 (0-531-08470-1); Morrow paper $3.95 (0-688-11862-3). 72pp. A Vietnamese girl tries to adjust to her new life with a foster mother. (Rev: BL 3/15/91; HB 5–6/91; SLJ 6/91)

**6010** Lee, Lauren. *Stella: On the Edge of Popularity* (5–7). 1994, Polychrome $10.95 (1-879965-08-9). 178pp. A Korean American girl has to choose between being popular and being loyal to her Korean culture. (Rev: BCCB 7–8/94; SLJ 9/94)

**6011** Lester, Julius. *Long Journey Home* (6–8). 1998, Viking paper $4.99 (0-14-038981-4). 160pp. Six based-on-fact stories concerning slaves, ex-slaves, and their lives in a hostile America.

**6012** Littlesugar, Amy. *A Portrait of Spotted Deer's Grandfather* (2–4). Illus. 1997, Albert Whitman LB

$15.95 (0-8075-6622-5). 32pp. Spotted Deer's grandfather, Moose Horn, is afraid that if he has his portrait painted he will lose his spirit. (Rev: BL 1/1–15/98; SLJ 9/97)

**6013** Lord, Bette Bao. *In the Year of the Boar and Jackie Robinson* (4–6). Illus. by Marc Simont. 1984, HarperCollins paper $4.95 (0-06-440175-8). 176pp. The story of a Chinese girl who leaves China to join her father in New York in 1947.

**6014** Martin, Bill, Jr., and John Archambault. *Knots on a Counting Rope* (PS–5). Illus. by Ted Rand. 1987, Holt $15.95 (0-8050-0571-4). 32pp. Each time his grandson asks him to repeat the story of Boy-Strength of Blue-Horses, Grandfather adds another knot in the counting rope, a metaphor for the passage of time. (Rev: BCCB 11/87; BL 11/15/87; SLJ 12/87)

**6015** Matthews, Mary. *Magid Fasts for Ramadan* (3–6). Illus. 1996, Clarion $15.95 (0-395-66589-2). 48pp. Eight-year-old Magid wants to fast as his family does during the holy month for Moslems, Ramadan. (Rev: BCCB 2/96; BL 3/1/96; HB 7–8/96; SLJ 7/96)

**6016** Mazer, Anne, ed. *America Street: A Multicultural Anthology of Stories* (5–8). 1993, Persea $14.95 (0-89255-190-9); paper $4.95 (0-89255-191-7). 160pp. A collection of 14 stories, each one dealing with a different American ethnic group. (Rev: BCCB 11/93; BL 9/1/93; SLJ 11/93)

**6017** Meyer, Carolyn. *Rio Grande Stories* (4–6). 1994, Harcourt $12.00 (0-15-200548-X); paper $6.00 (0-15-200066-6). 224pp. Twelve children in a middle school in Albuquerque, New Mexico, investigate their origins through oral histories and documents. (Rev: BCCB 9/94; BL 10/1/94; SLJ 6/94)

**6018** Mochizuki, Ken. *Heroes* (2–4). Illus. by Dom Lee. 1995, Lee & Low $15.95 (1-880000-16-4). 32pp. During the Vietnam War, a Japanese American child becomes the butt of other children's bullying. (Rev: BL 3/15/95; HB 5–6/95; SLJ 7/95)

**6019** Naidoo, Beverley. *Journey to Jo'burg: A South African Story* (4–6). Illus. by Eric Velasquez. 1986, HarperCollins LB $14.89 (0-397-32169-4); paper $4.95 (0-06-440237-1). 96pp. The story of Naledi, from a South African village, who travels to the city with her brother to seek their mother, who works in the home of whites, because their baby sister is dying. (Rev: BCCB 5/86; BL 3/25/86; SLJ 8/86)

**6020** Nelson, Vaunda M. *Mayfield Crossing* (4–6). Illus. by Leonard Jenkins. 1993, Putnam $14.95 (0-399-22331-2). 82pp. A group of children from Mayfield Crossing encounter racial prejudice when they enter a newer, bigger school at Parview. (Rev: BCCB 3/93; BL 4/1/93*)

**6021** Neufeld, John. *Edgar Allan* (5–8). Illus. by Loren Dunlap. 1968, Phillips $25.95 (0-87599-149-1); NAL paper $2.95 (0-451-15870-9). Three-year-old Edgar Allan is black and is adopted by a white minister's family.

**6022** Pinkney, Andrea D. *Hold Fast to Dreams* (5–8). 1995, Morrow $16.00 (0-688-12832-7). 112pp. A bright, resourceful African American girl faces problems when she finds she is the only black student in her new middle school. (Rev: BCCB 5/95; BL 2/15/95; HB 9–10/95; SLJ 4/95)

**6023** Pitts, Paul. *Racing the Sun* (5–7). 1988, Avon paper $4.50 (0-380-75496-7). 160pp. Brandon begins to understand his Navajo heritage after his grandfather comes to live with him. (Rev: BL 9/15/88; SLJ 2/89)

**6024** Roseman, Kenneth. *The Other Side of the Hudson: A Jewish Immigrant Adventure* (5–8). Illus. Series: Do-It-Yourself Adventure. 1993, UAHC paper $7.95 (0-8074-0506-X). 140pp. Using an interactive format, readers can choose various destinations for a young male Jewish immigrant after he arrives in New York City from Germany in 1851. (Rev: SLJ 6/94)

**6025** Schecter, Ellen. *The Big Idea* (2–5). Illus. 1996, Hyperion LB $14.49 (0-7868-2085-3); paper $3.95 (0-7868-1043-2). 80pp. Young Luzita wants to transform a vacant lot into a neighborhood garden. (Rev: BCCB 4/96; BL 1/1–15/97; SLJ 4/96)

**6026** Schroeder, Alan. *Ragtime Tumpie* (2–4). Illus. by Bernie Fuchs. 1989, Little, Brown $16.95 (0-316-77497-9). 32pp. Set in St. Louis in 1915, this fictional story is based on an incident in the childhood of Josephine Baker. (Rev: BCCB 10/89; BL 10/1/89; HB 1–2/90; SLJ 9/89*)

**6027** Sing, Rachel. *Chinese New Year's Dragon* (3–5). Illus. by Shao Wei Liu. 1994, Simon & Schuster LB $5.99 (0-671-88602-9). 23pp. A young girl works with her family to prepare for the Chinese New Year and then enjoys participating in the joyous festival. (Rev: BL 4/15/94)

**6028** Smothers, Ethel Footman. *Down in the Piney Woods* (5–8). 1992, Knopf $14.00 (0-679-80360-2). 144pp. The daily life of a black sharecropper family in Georgia in the 1950s. (Rev: BL 12/15/91; SLJ 1/92)

**6029** Smothers, Ethel Footman. *Moriah's Pond* (4–7). 1995, Knopf $16.00 (0-679-84504-6). 112pp. In this sequel to *In the Piney Woods* (1992), racial tensions surround African American youngsters growing up in rural Georgia in the 1950s. (Rev: BCCB 4/95; BL 1/15/95; SLJ 2/95)

**6030** Soto, Gary. *Baseball in April: And Other Stories* (4–7). 1990, Harcourt $16.00 (0-15-205720-X); paper $6.00 (0-15-205721-8). 109pp. The problems of teenagers, particularly Latinos growing up in California, are the focus of these 11 stories. (Rev: BCCB 4/90; HB 7–8/90*; SLJ 6/90)

**6031** Soto, Gary. *Local News* (4–7). 1993, Harcourt $14.00 (0-15-248117-6). 144pp. This collection of 13 short stories deals with a number of Mexican American youngsters at home, school, and play. (Rev: BL 4/15/93; HB 7–8/93*)

**6032** Soto, Gary. *Petty Crimes* (5–8). 1998, Harcourt $16.00 (0-15-201658-9). 176pp. Ten short stories about young Mexican American kids in California's Central Valley that deal with some humorous situations but more often, gangs, violence, and poverty. (Rev: BL 3/15/98)

**6033** Soto, Gary. *Taking Sides* (5–7). 1991, Harcourt $15.95 (0-15-284076-1). 160pp. An unhappy Hispanic American youngster, whose family has recently moved to a new neighborhood, meets problems on the basketball team. (Rev: SLJ 11/91)

**6034** Stanek, Muriel. *I Speak English for My Mom* (3–5). Illus. by Judith Friedman. 1989, Whitman LB $12.95 (0-8075-3659-8). 32pp. A young Mexican American translates for her mother, who can't read English. (Rev: BCCB 2/89; BL 3/1/89; SLJ 5/89)

**6035** Taylor, Mildred D. *The Friendship* (4–6). Illus. by Max Ginsburg. 1987, Dial LB $13.89 (0-8037-0418-6). 56pp. The story of Tom Bee, a black man, and what happens when he refuses to call a white man "mister." (Rev: BCCB 12/87; BL 12/15/87)

**6036** Taylor, Mildred D. *The Gold Cadillac* (3–5). Illus. by Michael Hays. 1987, Dial LB $12.89 (0-8037-0343-0). 48pp. A black family takes off in its new Cadillac for a dangerous journey south in 1950. (Rev: BL 8/87; HB 9–10/87; SLJ 9/87)

**6037** Taylor, Mildred D. *Mississippi Bridge* (5–7). Illus. by Max Ginsburg. 1990, Dial LB $13.89 (0-8037-0427-5). In this pre-civil rights era story, a bus tumbles off a bridge and kills all its white passengers. (Rev: BCCB 10/90; BL 9/15/90; HB 11–12/90; SLJ 11/90)

**6038** Uchida, Yoshiko. *Journey Home* (4–6). Illus. by Charles Robinson. 1978, Macmillan $16.00 (0-689-50126-9); paper $3.95 (0-689-71641-9). 144pp. Life of a Japanese American family after its release from a World War II internment camp.

**6039** Uchida, Yoshiko. *Journey to Topaz: A Story of the Japanese-American Evacuation* (4–7). Illus. by Donald Carrick. 1985, Creative Arts paper $9.95 (0-916870-85-5). 160pp. In this reissue of a 1971 title, 11-year-old Yuki and her family endure shameful treatment after Pearl Harbor.

**6040** Wyeth, Sharon D. *The World of Daughter McGuire* (4–6). 1994, Delacorte $14.95 (0-385-31174-5). 176pp. Daughter McGuire, an interracial child, is having trouble at her new school, where one

boy calls her "zebra" because she's neither black nor white. (Rev: BCCB 2/94; BL 5/1/94; SLJ 4/94)

**6041** Yep, Laurence. *Thief of Hearts* (5–8). 1995, HarperCollins LB $14.89 (0-06-025342-8). 197pp. Stacy, who is half Chinese, goes back to San Francisco's Chinatown to trace her family roots. (Rev: BCCB 9/95; BL 7/95; SLJ 8/95)

## Family Stories

**6042** Adler, C. S. *Her Blue Straw Hat* (4–7). 1997, Harcourt $16.00 (0-15-201466-7). 112pp. Rachel has an opportunity to meet her stepfather's daughter during a summer vacation. (Rev: BL 9/1/97; SLJ 9/97)

**6043** Adler, C. S. *One Sister Too Many* (5–7). 1989, Macmillan paper $3.95 (0-689-71521-8). 176pp. Casey and her reunited family are being driven crazy by the newest addition — a colicky baby. (Rev: BCCB 3/89; BL 3/15/89; SLJ 4/89)

**6044** Adler, C. S. *Youn Hee and Me* (4–6). 1995, Harcourt $11.00 (0-15-200073-9); paper $5.00 (0-15-200376-2). 192pp. Caitlin has difficulty adjusting to the different ways of her new adopted sister from Korea. (Rev: BCCB 3/95; BL 4/15/95; SLJ 5/95)

**6045** Alcott, Louisa May. *Eight Cousins* (5–8). 1985, Dell paper $3.99 (0-440-42231-0). 272pp. Further adventures of the March family, who also appears in *Rose in Bloom* (1976).

**6046** Alcott, Louisa May. *Little Women* (4–7). Illus. by Louis Jambor. 1947, Putnam $18.99 (0-448-06019-1). 656pp. One of the many fine editions of this enduring story. Two sequels are: *Little Men* (Knopf 1995); *Jo's Boys* (Viking 1996).

**6047** Aliki. *The Two of Them* (K–4). Illus. by author. 1987, Morrow paper $4.95 (0-688-07337-9). 32pp. A moving story of a tender relationship between a child and her grandfather and of the death of the old man.

**6048** Armstrong, William H. *Sounder* (6–8). Illus. by James Barkley. 1969, HarperCollins LB $14.89 (0-06-020144-4); paper $4.95 (0-06-440020-4). 128pp. Harsh customs and hard circumstances cripple the bodies of both the dog Sounder and his master. Newbery Award winner, 1970. A sequel is: *Sour Land* (1971).

**6049** Ayres, Katherine. *Family Tree* (4–6). 1996, Delacorte $15.95 (0-385-32227-5). 165pp. In studying her family tree, Tyler discovers that her father was originally Amish. (Rev: BCCB 2/97; BL 11/15/96; SLJ 11/96)

**6050** Babbitt, Natalie. *The Eyes of the Amaryllis* (4–6). 1977, Farrar $15.00 (0-374-32241-4); paper

$3.95 (0-374-42238-9). 160pp. In this story set in an Atlantic coastal village during the late 19th century, an 11-year-old girl is drawn into her grandmother's obsession.

**6051** Baker, Barbara. *Oh, Emma* (3–5). Illus. by Catherine Stock. 1993, Puffin paper $3.99 (0-140-36357-2). 96pp. When Emma learns that a fourth child is expected in their already cramped, low-income apartment, she becomes very upset. (Rev: BCCB 1/92; BL 11/15/91; SLJ 2/92)

**6052** Barnes, Joyce Annette. *The Baby Grand, the Moon in July, and Me* (4–6). 1994, Dial LB $14.89 (0-8037-1600-1). 130pp. Annie, who is growing up in a poor family during the 1960s, helps her older brother, who wants to become a jazz musician. (Rev: BCCB 1/94; SLJ 3/94)

**6053** Bawden, Nina. *Granny the Pag* (5–7). 1996, Clarion $14.95 (0-935-77604-X). 192pp. Catriona is embarrassed by her grandmother's eccentric ways, such as riding motorbikes and wearing leather jackets. (Rev: BCCB 3/96; BL 4/1/96; HB 9–10/96; SLJ 4/96*)

**6054** Bawden, Nina. *Humbug* (4–6). 1992, Houghton $13.95 (0-395-62149-6). 136pp. First there was her parents' trip to Japan, then her grandmother's trip to the hospital; it's all humbug, which Cora likes to think of as a magic word. (Rev: BCCB 11/92*; BL 10/1/92*; HB 3–4/93; SLJ 10/92*)

**6055** Bechard, Margaret. *My Mom Married the Principal* (5–8). 1998, Viking paper $14.99 (0-670-87394-2). 144pp. For Jonah the eighth grade is the pits and having his stepfather as principal doesn't help. (Rev: BL 3/1/98; SLJ 3/98)

**6056** Bertrand, Diane Gonzales. *Alicia's Treasure* (4–6). 1996, Arte Publico $14.95 (1-55885-085-6); paper $5.95 (1-55885-086-4). 125pp. Ten-year-old Alicia spends her first weekend at the beach, thanks to her brother's girlfriend. (Rev: BL 5/1/96; SLJ 7/96)

**6057** Blackman, Malorie. *Girl Wonder and the Terrific Twins* (2–4). Illus. by Lis Toft. 1993, Dutton paper $12.99 (0-525-45065-3). 72pp. Maxine and her younger twin brothers get into all sorts of innocent mischief in this story about an African American family. (Rev: BL 9/1/93; SLJ 1/94)

**6058** Boyd, Candy Dawson. *Daddy, Daddy, Be There* (3–6). Illus. by Floyd Cooper. 1995, Philomel $15.99 (0-399-22745-8). A picture book in which various youngsters hope that their daddies will be present at important events in their lives. (Rev: SLJ 11/95)

**6059** Brink, Carol Ryrie. *Caddie Woodlawn* (4–6). Illus. by Trina S. Hyman. 1973, Scholastic paper $2.50 (0-590-10121-8). 288pp. The delightful esca-

pades of a red-haired tomboy and her brothers in early Wisconsin. Newbery Award winner, 1936.

**6060** Burch, Robert. *Ida Early Comes over the Mountain* (4–7). 1990, Puffin paper $3.99 (0-14-034534-5). 140pp. Ida Early becomes the housekeeper for 4 motherless children.

**6061** Burnett, Frances Hodgson. *A Little Princess* (4–6). Illus. by Tasha Tudor. 1987, HarperCollins paper $3.95 (0-064-40187-1). 240pp. Sad story of a penniless orphan whose fortune is finally restored.

**6062** Byars, Betsy. *Beans on the Roof* (3–5). Illus. 1990, Bantam LB $14.95 (0-385-29855-2); Dell paper $3.99 (0-440-40314-6). 80pp. George's sister and the whole family are writing roof poems and George feels awful until he can write one too. (Rev: BCCB 11/88; BL 11/1/88; SLJ 11/88)

**6063** Byars, Betsy. *The Blossoms and the Green Phantom* (5–7). Illus. 1987, Delacorte $14.95 (0-385-29533-2); Dell paper $3.50 (0-440-40069-4). 160pp. Junior is about to launch his greatest invention — a hot-air balloon that he hopes will be mistaken for a flying saucer. The 3 other books about the Blossoms are: *The Blossoms Meet the Vulture Lady; The Not-Just-Anybody Family* (both 1987, Bantam); *A Blossom Promise* (1987, Delacorte). (Rev: BCCB 4/87; BL 3/15/87; HB 3–4/87)

**6064** Byars, Betsy. *The Glory Girl* (6–8). 1985, Puffin paper $3.99 (0-14-031785-6). 144pp. Anna is the nonsinging member of a family of gospel singers.

**6065** Byars, Betsy. *Wanted . . . Mud Blossom* (4–6). Illus. by Jacqueline Rogers. 1991, Delacorte $14.95 (0-385-30428-5). 148pp. Another story of the impossible antics of the zany Blossom family. (Rev: BCCB 10/91; BL 9/15/91; HB 9–10/91*; SLJ 7/91*)

**6066** Cameron, Ann. *The Most Beautiful Place in the World* (3–5). Illus. by Thomas B. Allen. 1988, Knopf LB $12.99 (0-394-99463-9). 64pp. Juan of Guatemala lives with his grandmother and is afraid she will not let him go to school. (Rev: BCCB 11/88; BL 1/1/89; SLJ 1/89)

**6067** Cameron, Ann. *The Stories Huey Tells* (2–3). Illus. 1995, Knopf LB $17.99 (0-679-96732-X). 102pp. Young Huey, a member of an African American family, has a series of amusing and affectionate stories to tell. (Rev: BCCB 12/95; BL 11/15/95; SLJ 1/96)

**6068** Cameron, Ann. *The Stories Julian Tells* (3–5). Illus. by Ann Strugnell. 1981, Pantheon LB $15.99 (0-394-94301-5); Knopf paper $4.99 (0-394-82892-5). 96pp. Six short stories chiefly about the home life of Julian and his family.

**6069** Canfield, Dorothy. *Understood Betsy* (4–6). Illus. by Martha Alexander. 1981, Buccaneer LB $21.95 (0-89966-342-7). 219pp. A new edition of the old favorite about Elizabeth Ann and the fearful new way of life that awaits her when she goes to live in the wilds of Vermont.

**6070** Caseley, Judith. *Harry and Arney* (2–4). 1994, Greenwillow $14.00 (0-688-12140-3). 144pp. An episodic story about Harry Kane growing up in a loving Jewish family that is adjusting to a new baby. (Rev: BL 9/1/94; SLJ 9/94)

**6071** Caseley, Judith. *Starring Dorothy Kane* (3–5). 1992, Greenwillow $13.00 (0-688-10182-8). 160pp. Dorothy does not want to move, does not want to go to a new school, and does not like being the middle child. (Rev: BCCB 5/92; BL 3/15/92; SLJ 5/92)

**6072** Christiansen, C. B. *I See the Moon* (5–7). 1994, Atheneum $14.95 (0-689-31928-2). 128pp. Grown-up Bitte looks back at being 12, the year her unmarried older sister became pregnant. (Rev: BCCB 1/95; BL 2/1/95; SLJ 1/95)

**6073** Cleary, Beverly. *Ramona the Brave* (3–5). Illus. by Alan Tiegreen. 1975, Morrow LB $15.93 (0-688-32015-5); Dell paper $2.95 (0-440-77351-2). 192pp. Our young heroine experiences the glories and difficulties of being in the first grade and of having a room of her own. Four other series titles are: *Ramona and Her Father* (1977); *Ramona and Her Mother* (1979); *Ramona Quimby, Age Eight* (1981); *Ramona Forever* (1985, Dell).

**6074** Cleary, Beverly. *Ramona the Pest* (3–5). Illus. by Louis Darling. 1968, Morrow LB $15.93 (0-688-31721-9). 192pp. The fine addition to this popular series follows spirited Ramona Quimby, sister to Beezus and neighbor to Henry, through her kindergarten escapades. Also use: *Beezus and Ramona* (1955); *Ribsy* (1964).

**6075** Cleary, Beverly. *Sister of the Bride* (6–8). Illus. by Beth Krush and Joe Krush. 1963, Morrow LB $16.93 (0-688-31742-1); Avon paper $4.50 (0-380-72807-9). 256pp. All the excitement and confusion an approaching wedding brings to a household.

**6076** Cleary, Beverly. *Socks* (4–6). Illus. by Beatrice Darwin. 1973, Morrow LB $15.93 (0-688-30067-7); Avon paper $4.50 (0-380-70926-0). 160pp. What happens when the family cat Socks realizes that his position of importance is threatened by the arrival of a baby.

**6077** Clifton, Lucille. *The Lucky Stone* (3–5). Illus. by Dale Payson. 1986, Bantam $6.46 (0-385-28600-7); Dell paper $3.50 (0-440-45110-8). 64pp. Several stories in the life of a girl's great-grandmother linked by the power of a stone.

**6078** Clough, B. W. *An Impossumble Summer* (4–6). 1992, Walker $14.95 (0-8027-8150-0). 146pp. Rianne and her siblings discover their grumpy opossum can speak and grant wishes. (Rev: BL 3/1/92; SLJ 4/92)

**6079** Clymer, Eleanor. *My Mother Is the Smartest Woman in the World* (4–6). Illus. by Nancy Kincade.

1982, Macmillan $13.95 (0-689-30916-3). 96pp. Kathleen's mom runs for mayor.

**6080** Cohen, Barbara. *The Carp in the Bathtub* (3–4). Illus. by Joan Halpern. 1972, Kar-Ben paper $5.95 (0-930494-67-9). 48pp. Two Jewish children decide that the carp in the bathtub should be rescued before it becomes Passover gefilte fish.

**6081** Conford, Ellen. *And This Is Laura* (4–6). 1992, Little, Brown paper $4.95 (0-316-15354-0). 192pp. A very ordinary girl discovers that she possesses psychic powers.

**6082** Conford, Ellen. *The Luck of Pokey Bloom* (4–6). Illus. by Bernice Lowenstein. 1975, Little, Brown $14.95 (0-316-15305-2). 144pp. The warm, sunny family story about a young girl, who has a compulsive interest in contests, and her brother, who is undergoing the pangs of first love.

**6083** Conrad, Pam. *Our House: The Stories of Levittown* (4–7). Illus. by Brian Selznick. 1995, Scholastic $14.95 (0-590-46523-6). 96pp. The history of the middle-class community Levittown, New York, is traced through a series of fictional vignettes. (Rev: BCCB 12/95; BL 1/1–15/96; HB 11–12/95; SLJ 11/95)

**6084** Corcoran, Barbara. *Family Secrets* (5–8). 1992, Macmillan LB $13.95 (0-689-31744-1). 136pp. After a move to New England with her family, 13-year-old Tracy discovers she is adopted. (Rev: BL 3/1/92; SLJ 2/92)

**6085** de Anda, Diane. *The Ice Dove and Other Stories* (3–5). 1997, Arte Publico paper $7.95 (1-55885-189-5). 72pp. In these 4 stories, 2 involving Christmas and 2 the classroom, Hispanic American youngsters gain the strength to face problems through help from their loving extended families. (Rev: BL 10/1/97)

**6086** DeGross, Monalisa. *Donavan's Word Jar* (2–3). Illus. 1994, HarperCollins LB $14.89 (0-06-020191-6). 80pp. Whereas his friends collect coins or comics, Donavan collects interesting words and puts them in a jar. (Rev: BL 6/1–15/94; SLJ 8/94)

**6087** Delton, Judy. *Angel's Mother's Baby* (4–6). Illus. by Margot Apple. 1989, Houghton $16.00 (0-395-50926-2). 112pp. Angel is content with her new stepfather in the family, but she had not counted on a new baby. (Rev: BL 9/15/89; HB 11–12/89; SLJ 10/89)

**6088** Delton, Judy. *Angel's Mother's Boyfriend* (3–5). Illus. by Margot Apple. 1986, Houghton $16.00 (0-395-39968-8). 176pp. Angel and brother Rags are dismayed to discover that their mother has a boyfriend, and doubly dismayed to discover that he is a clown — a real one! Also use: *Angel in Charge* (1985); *Angel's Mother's Wedding* (1987). (Rev: BL 4/1/86; HB 7–8/86; SLJ 8/86)

**6089** Delton, Judy. *Back Yard Angel* (3–5). Illus. by Leslie Morrill. 1983, Houghton $16.00 (0-395-33883-2). 112pp. Ten-year-old Angel O'Leary is saddled with taking care of her little brother.

**6090** Dewey, Jennifer O. *Cowgirl Dreams: A Western Childhood* (5–7). Illus. 1995, Boyds Mills $14.95 (1-56397-377-4). 141pp. In a fictionalized form, Dewey remembers her childhood on a New Mexico ranch and her many adventures, including finding a human skeleton. (Rev: BL 10/15/95; SLJ 12/95)

**6091** Duncan, Jane. *Brave Janet Reachfar* (4–6). Illus. by Mairi Hedderwick. 1975, Houghton $7.95 (0-8164-3130-2). 32pp. Scottish farm life is depicted through the adventures of young Janet and her relationship with her tyrannical grandmother.

**6092** Dunlop, Eileen. *Finn's Island* (4–6). 1992, Holiday $13.95 (0-8234-0910-4). 128pp. Bored and grieving, Finn takes a trip from Scotland to the Hebrides island of his grandfather's birth, where he learns to see the man more realistically. (Rev: BL 2/1/92; SLJ 6/92)

**6093** Engel, Diana. *Holding On* (4–6). 1997, Marshall Cavendish LB $14.95 (0-7614-5016-5). 96pp. Tommy is fearful about spending 2 weeks with his erratic great-uncle, but slowly they become friends. (Rev: BL 9/15/97; SLJ 11/97)

**6094** Enright, Elizabeth. *Thimble Summer* (4–6). Illus. by author. 1938, Holt $16.95 (0-8050-0306-1); Dell paper $3.99 (0-440-48681-5). 124pp. A small girl on a Wisconsin farm finds a magic thimble. Newbery Award winner, 1939.

**6095** Estes, Eleanor. *The Moffats* (4–6). Illus. by Louis Slobodkin. 1941, Harcourt $17.00 (0-15-255095-X); Dell paper $3.25 (0-440-70026-4). 32pp. Lively adventures of 4 Connecticut children, their family, and friends. Sequels are: *Rufus M* (1943); *The Moffat Museum* (1983); *The Middle Moffat* (1989).

**6096** Fakih, Kimberly O. *Grandpa Putter and Granny Hoe* (2–4). Illus. by Tracey Campbell Pearson. 1992, Farrar $13.00 (0-374-32762-9). 128pp. Quarrels make humorous stories as Grandpa Putter and Granny Hoe compete for the attention of their twin grandchildren. (Rev: BCCB 6/92; BL 2/15/92)

**6097** Fakih, Kimberly O. *High on the Hog* (4–7). 1994, Farrar $16.00 (0-374-33209-6). 166pp. A 12-year-old girl stays with her great-grandparents on a farm in Iowa and discovers a family secret. (Rev: BCCB 7–8/94; BL 6/1–15/94; SLJ 5/94*)

**6098** Fenner, Carol. *Yolonda's Genius* (4–6). 1995, Simon & Schuster paper $17.00 (0-689-80001-0). 153pp. African American Yolonda tries to prove that her young brother, who does poorly at school, is really a musical genius. (Rev: BL 6/1–15/95; SLJ 7/95)

**6099** Fine, Anne. *Step by Wicked Step* (4–6). 1996, Little, Brown $15.95 (0-316-28345-2). 138pp. Five children share stories about their stepfamilies. (Rev: BCCB 5/96; BL 5/15/96; HB 7–8/96; SLJ 6/96*)

**6100** Fitzhugh, Louise. *Nobody's Family Is Going to Change* (5–8). Illus. by author. 1986, Farrar paper $4.95 (0-374-45523-6). 221pp. There is considerable misunderstanding within a middle-class black family but also much humor and warmth.

**6101** Fletcher, Ralph. *Fig Pudding* (5–7). 1995, Clarion $15.00 (0-395-71125-8). 160pp. A year that brings both tragedy and hilarity in the life of a family of 6 children. (Rev: BCCB 5/95; BL 5/15/95; SLJ 7/95)

**6102** Fox, Paula. *Maurice's Room* (3–5). Illus. by Ingrid Fetz. 1985, Macmillan LB $13.95 (0-02-735490-3); paper $3.95 (0-689-71216-2). 64pp. An 8-year-old campaigns to protect his bedroom full of junk. A reissue.

**6103** Galbraith, Kathryn O. *Holding onto Sunday* (2–3). Illus. 1995, Simon & Schuster paper $14.00 (0-689-50623-6). 48pp. A child looks forward to Sundays, when she spends the whole day with her single-parent father. (Rev: BL 5/15/95; SLJ 9/95)

**6104** Gates, Doris. *Blue Willow* (4–6). Illus. by Paul Lantz. 1940, Puffin paper $4.99 (0-14-030924-1). 176pp. Janey, a child of migrant workers in the San Joaquin Valley of California, longs for a lasting home to "stay" in.

**6105** Giff, Patricia Reilly. *A Glass Slipper for Rosie* (3–4). Illus. Series: Ballet Slippers. 1997, Viking paper $13.99 (0-670-87469-8). 80pp. Rosie plans a special surprise for her Grandfather on his birthday involving a ballet in which she will be performing, but she discovers, to her disappointment, that he will be away on a trip. (Rev: BL 10/1/97; SLJ 12/97)

**6106** Greenfield, Eloise. *Sister* (5–7). Illus. by Moneta Barnett. 1974, HarperCollins $15.00 (0-690-00497-4); paper $4.50 (0-06-440199-5). 96pp. Four years in a black girl's life, as revealed through scattered diary entries, during which she shows maturation, particularly in her attitude toward her sister.

**6107** Griffith, Helen V. *Grandaddy's Stars* (2–4). Illus. by James Stevenson. 1995, Greenwillow LB $14.93 (0-688-13655-9). 32pp. Janetta is worried that the activities she has planned for her Grandaddy's visit to Baltimore will bore him. (Rev: BCCB 4/95; BL 4/15/95*; HB 5–6/95; SLJ 7/95*)

**6108** Hall, Donald. *Old Home Day* (3–6). Illus. by Emily Arnold McCully. 1996, Harcourt $16.00 (0-15-276896-3). 48pp. The changes in Blackwater Pond in New Hampshire from the Ice Age to the present, with emphasis on the time after the first settlers arrived in 1799. (Rev: BCCB 10/96; BL 9/1/96*; HB 11–12/96; SLJ 10/96)

**6109** Hamilton, Virginia. *Justice and Her Brothers* (6–8). 1992, Harcourt paper $3.95 (0-15-241640-4).

306

A slow-moving but compelling study of a young girl's relationship with her older twin brothers. Two sequels: *Dustland* (1980, Greenwillow); *The Gathering* (1989).

**6110** Hamilton, Virginia. *M. C. Higgins, the Great* (6–8). 1974, Macmillan LB $17.00 (0-02-742480-4); paper $4.50 (0-02-043490-1). 288pp. The Newbery Award winner (1975) about a 13-year-old black boy growing up in Appalachia as part of a loving family whose future is threatened by a possible mountain slide.

**6111** Harrison, Maggie. *Angels on Roller Skates* (2–4). Illus. 1992, Candlewick $14.95 (1-56402-003-7). 112pp. Bigun, Middlun, and Littun are the stars in 6 tales about family life in England. (Rev: BCCB 6/92; BL 5/1/92)

**6112** Harrison, Maggie. *Lizzie's List* (3–6). Illus. by Bethan Matthews. 1993, Candlewick $14.95 (1-56402-197-1). 112pp. Lizzie lacks the large family that her friends have, and so she sets out to create her own grandparents. (Rev: BL 10/1/93; SLJ 11/93)

**6113** Hautzig, Esther. *A Gift for Mama* (3–5). Illus. 1992, Peter Smith $18.00 (0-8446-6570-3); Puffin paper $3.99 (0-14-032384-8). 64pp. Sara works hard to earn enough money to buy Mama a Mother's Day gift. A reissue.

**6114** Henkes, Kevin. *The Zebra Wall* (4–6). 1988, Greenwillow $15.95 (0-688-07568-1); Puffin paper $4.99 (0-14-032969-2). 160pp. Adine and her sisters await the sixth child in the family. (Rev: BCCB 4/88; BL 4/15/88; SLJ 4/88)

**6115** Herzig, Alison C., and Jane L. Mali. *The Wimp of the World* (3–5). 1994, Viking paper $13.99 (0-670-85208-2). 130pp. Ten-year-old Bridget faces 2 crises: A new baby is expected in the family, and her 68-year-old aunt is getting engaged. (Rev: BL 4/1/94; HB 9–10/94; SLJ 9/94)

**6116** Hickman, Janet. *Jericho* (5–8). 1994, Greenwillow $15.00 (0-688-13398-3). 144pp. When Angela takes care of her grandmother during her last illness, she learns about the many disappointments the old lady faced during her life. (Rev: BCCB 11/94; BL 9/1/94; HB 11–12/94; SLJ 9/94)

**6117** Holl, Kristi D. *Just Like a Real Family* (4–6). 1997, Royal Fireworks paper $6.99 (0-88092-430-6). 132pp. June Finch, a 12-year-old, gets involved in a class project to adopt grandparents from a retirement home.

**6118** Holl, Kristi D. *No Strings Attached* (5–7). 1998, Royal Fireworks paper $6.99 (0-88092-434-9). 128pp. June finds some difficulties in adjustment when she and her mother move in with crabby old Franklin Cooper. (Rev: BCCB 5/88; BL 6/15/88; SLJ 4/88)

**6119** Holmes, Barbara W. *My Sister the Sausage Roll* (3–4). Illus. by Karen L. Schmidt. Series: Hyperion Chapters. 1997, Hyperion LB $14.49 (0-7868-2260-0); paper $3.95 (0-7868-1182-X). 59pp. An amusing book in which a young girl writes to her father, who is away on business, about her new baby sister. (Rev: BCCB 7–8/97; SLJ 8/97)

**6120** Howe, James. *Pinky and Rex and the Double-Dad Weekend* (2–4). Illus. by Melissa Sweet. 1995, Atheneum $14.00 (0-689-31871-5). 42pp. Pinky and Rex won't let a little rain spoil the camping trip they have planned with their dads. (Rev: BL 4/15/95; SLJ 8/95)

**6121** Hurwitz, Johanna. *The Down and Up Fall* (4–6). Illus. 1996, Morrow $15.00 (0-688-14568-X). 128pp. An 11-year-old girl adjusts to living with her great-aunt and -uncle while her parents are away. (Rev: BCCB 9/96; BL 10/15/96; SLJ 9/96)

**6122** Hurwitz, Johanna. *"E" Is for Elisa* (2–4). Illus. by Lillian Hoban. 1991, Morrow LB $12.88 (0-688-10440-1). 80pp. Episodes of everyday life with 8-year-old Russell who loves to tease his 4-year-old sister. (Rev: BCCB 9/91; BL 9/1/91*; HB 9–10/91; SLJ 8/91)

**6123** Hurwitz, Johanna. *Hurricane Elaine* (5–7). Illus. by Diane De Groat. 1986, Morrow $16.00 (0-688-06461-2). 112pp. Elaine, at 15 and the eldest of the Sossi children, can blame most of her typical teenage troubles on her impulsiveness. (Rev: BCCB 12/86; BL 9/1/86; SLJ 11/86)

**6124** Hurwitz, Johanna. *Make Room for Elisa* (2–4). Illus. by Lillian Hoban. 1993, Morrow $14.00 (0-688-12404-6); Puffin paper $3.99 (0-14-037034-X). 82pp. This beginning chapter book features a likable girl in 6 delightful, connected stories. (Rev: BL 8/93)

**6125** Hurwitz, Johanna. *Rip-Roaring Russell* (2–5). Illus. by Lillian Hoban. 1983, Morrow $16.00 (0-688-02347-9); Puffin paper $3.99 (0-14-032939-0). 96pp. The exploits of a self-willed 4-year-old.

**6126** Hurwitz, Johanna. *Roz and Ozzie* (2–4). Illus. by Eileen McKeating. 1992, Morrow $13.00 (0-688-10945-4). 128pp. Ozzie is 2 years younger than Roz and can't understand why she doesn't want him around all the time, even though he is her uncle. (Rev: BCCB 5/92; BL 2/15/92; SLJ 5/92)

**6127** Hurwitz, Johanna. *Russell and Elisa* (2–4). Illus. by Lillian Hoban. 1989, Puffin paper $3.99 (0-14-034406-3). 96pp. Through various episodes, the relationship between second-grader Russell and his young sister is explored. (Rev: BCCB 1/90; BL 9/1/89; HB 9–10/89; SLJ 8/89*)

**6128** Hurwitz, Johanna. *School's Out* (2–4). Illus. by Sheila Hamanaka. 1991, Morrow $12.95 (0-688-09938-6). 128pp. Lucas looks forward to the arrival of the French girl who has been hired to take care of his younger twin brothers. (Rev: BCCB 4/91; BL 1/15/91; HB 7–8/91; SLJ 5/91)

**6129** Irwin, Hadley. *I Be Somebody* (4–7). 1988, NAL paper $2.50 (0-451-15303-0). During the early 1900s, a black family relocates to northern Canada.

**6130** Jarrow, Gail. *If Phyllis Were Here* (5–7). 1989, Avon paper $2.75 (0-380-70634-2). 144pp. Libby, age 11, has to learn to adjust to living without her best friend — her grandmother who moves to Florida. (Rev: BL 10/15/87; SLJ 9/87)

**6131** Johnston, Tony. *Yonder* (2–4). Illus. by Lloyd Bloom. 1988, Dial LB $12.89 (0-8037-0278-7); Puffin paper $4.95 (0-8037-0987-0). 32pp. Three generations in a rural setting, following a farmer and his bride until they become grandparents. (Rev: BCCB 7–8/88; HB 7–8/88; SLJ 5/88)

**6132** Kehret, Peg. *Sisters Long Ago* (5–8). 1992, Pocket paper $3.99 (0-671-78433-4). 149pp. While surviving a near drowning, Willow has a glimpse of herself living another life in ancient Egypt. (Rev: SLJ 3/90)

**6133** Kennedy, Trish. *Baseball Card Crazy* (3–5). Illus. by Timothy Schodorf. 1993, Macmillan $11.95 (0-684-19536-4). 80pp. Oliver is obsessed with the idea of finding his dad's old baseball cards. (Rev: BL 3/15/93; SLJ 5/93)

**6134** King-Smith, Dick. *The Stray* (3–6). Illus. 1996, Crown LB $17.99 (0-517-70935-X). 128pp. At age 75, Henny leaves her old-folks home to find independence and freedom. (Rev: BL 9/15/96; SLJ 11/96)

**6135** Kinsey-Warnock, Natalie. *Sweet Memories Still* (3–6). Illus. 1997, Dutton paper $14.99 (0-525-65230-2). 80pp. An old box camera and its photographs have great meaning for Shelby's aging grandmother. (Rev: BL 2/15/97; SLJ 1/97)

**6136** Klein, Norma. *Mom, the Wolfman and Me* (5–8). 1972, Avon paper $3.50 (0-380-00791-6). 160pp. Brett has a most unusual mother and, therefore, doesn't mind the state of being fatherless, but the Wolfman changes things.

**6137** Klein, Robin. *The Sky in Silver Lace* (6–8). 1996, Viking $13.99 (0-670-86266-5). 184pp. The 4 Melling sisters and their mother move to a large city in Australia to find better times in this sequel to *All in the Blue Unclouded Weather* (1992). (Rev: BCCB 2/96; BL 2/15/96; HB 5–6/96; SLJ 2/96)

**6138** Konigsburg, E. L. *Journey to an 800 Number* (5–8). 1982, Macmillan $15.00 (0-689-30901-5). 144pp. Maximilian visits with his show biz father and his trained camel.

**6139** Lantz, Francess. *Mom, There's a Pig in My Bed!* (4–6). 1992, Avon paper $3.50 (0-380-76112-2). 144pp. Mr. Ewing, fired from his job, moves to

rural Kansas to raise seeing-eye pigs for blind people who are allergic to dogs, not realizing that pigs have poor eyesight too. (Rev: BL 4/15/92; SLJ 1/93)

**6140** L'Engle, Madeleine. *Meet the Austins* (5–7). 1997, Farrar $16.00 (0-374-34929-0); Dell paper $4.50 (0-440-95777-X). The story of a country doctor's family, told by the 12-year-old daughter, and their reaction to having Maggie, a spoiled orphan, come to live with them.

**6141** Levitin, Sonia. *Annie's Promise* (5–8). 1993, Macmillan $15.00 (0-689-31752-2). 192pp. In this third book about the Platt family that escaped from Nazi Germany to America, Annie, now 13, goes to a Quaker-run summer camp. (Rev: BCCB 3/93; SLJ 4/93*)

**6142** Levoy, Myron. *The Witch of Fourth Street and Other Stories* (4–7). Illus. 1991, Peter Smith $18.75 (0-8446-6450-2); HarperCollins paper $4.95 (0-06-440059-X). 128pp. Eight stories about growing up poor on the Lower East Side of New York City.

**6143** Levy, Elizabeth. *Wolfman Sam* (3–5). Illus. 1996, HarperCollins LB $13.89 (0-06-024817-3); paper $3.95 (0-06-442048-5). 128pp. Young Robert resents his older brother's entry into puberty. (Rev: BL 11/15/96; SLJ 4/97)

**6144** Lewis, Beverly. *The Chicken Pox Panic* (2–4). Illus. Series: Cul-de-Sac Kids. 1995, Bethany paper $3.99 (1-55661-626-0). 80pp. While recovering from chicken pox, Abby plans a birthday party for her Korean brother; but when he arrives, everyone has chicken pox. Also in the series: *The Double Dabble Surprise* (1995). (Rev: BL 9/1/95)

**6145** Lexau, Joan M. *Striped Ice Cream* (2–5). Illus. by John Wilson. 1968, HarperCollins LB $15.89 (0-397-31047-1). 96pp. The conquest of poverty is realistically portrayed in this warmly told story about a fatherless black family as they work together.

**6146** Lindquist, Jennie D. *The Little Silver House* (3–5). Illus. by Garth Williams. 1986, Peter Smith $16.00 (0-8446-6190-2). A 9-year-old girl is intrigued by a mysterious boarded-up house. A reissue of a 1959 title.

**6147** Loredo, Betsy. *Faraway Families* (2–4). Illus. by Monisha Raja. Series: Family Ties. 1995, Silver Moon LB $13.95 (1-881889-61-0). 56pp. Five short stories, each dealing with a different racial minority, explore the emotional problems that result after families are separated. (Rev: SLJ 8/95)

**6148** Lowry, Lois. *Us and Uncle Fraud* (4–6). 1984, Houghton $14.95 (0-395-36633-X). 192pp. Two children become disillusioned with their Uncle Claude.

**6149** MacDonald, Maryann. *No Room for Francie* (2–3). Illus. by Eileen Christelow. Series: Hyperion Chapters. 1995, Hyperion $13.95 (0-7868-0032-1);

paper $3.95 (0-7868-1081-5). 61pp. Family relationships are explored in this light story — a delightful beginning chapter book. (Rev: SLJ 4/96)

**6150** McKay, Hilary. *The Exiles* (4–7). 1992, Macmillan $16.00 (0-689-50555-8). 208pp. The 4 Conroe sisters are shipped off to Big Grandma's for the summer. She thinks they "read too much, answer back, and never do anything to help." (Rev: BCCB 11/92*; BL 1/1/93; HB 1–2/93*; SLJ 10/92)

**6151** McKay, Hilary. *The Exiles at Home* (4–7). 1994, Macmillan paper $15.95 (0-689-50610-4). 208pp. In this sequel to *The Exiles*, the 4 Conway sisters sponsor the schooling of a young African boy and must find the money to pay for their generosity. (Rev: BCCB 1/95; BL 1/15/95*; SLJ 2/95)

**6152** MacLachlan, Patricia. *All the Places to Love* (5–8). Illus. by Mike Wimmer. 1994, HarperCollins LB $15.89 (0-06-021099-0). 32pp. This picture book celebrates the love found in an extended rural family and the joy that a new arrival brings. (Rev: BCCB 7–8/94; BL 6/1–15/94*; SLJ 6/94)

**6153** MacLachlan, Patricia. *Cassie Binegar* (4–7). 1982, HarperCollins LB $14.89 (0-06-024034-2); paper $4.95 (0-06-440195-2). 128pp. Cassie is not happy with the disorder in her family situation.

**6154** MacLachlan, Patricia. *Seven Kisses in a Row* (2–4). Illus. by Maria Pia Marrella. 1983, HarperCollins LB $14.89 (0-06-024084-9); paper $4.50 (0-06-440231-2). 64pp. Seven stories about 2 youngsters who are cared for by an aunt and uncle.

**6155** Martin, Ann M. *Ten Kids, No Pets* (4–7). 1988, Scholastic paper $3.50 (0-590-43620-1). 184pp. The Rosso family — 12 strong — moves to New Jersey and a 100-year-old farmhouse. (Rev: BL 6/15/88; SLJ 5/88)

**6156** Mathis, Sharon Bell. *The Hundred Penny Box* (3–5). Illus. by Leo Dillon and Diane Dillon. 1975, Puffin paper $4.99 (0-14-032169-1). 48pp. Old and frail Aunt Dew tells Michael about her experiences through a box that contains a penny for each year of her life.

**6157** Meyer, Carolyn. *Jubilee Journey* (5–7). 1997, Harcourt $12.00 (0-15-201377-6). 256pp. A biracial girl finds her spiritual identity when she visits her African American relatives in Texas. (Rev: BL 9/1/97; SLJ 1/98)

**6158** Miles, Betty. *Just the Beginning* (4–7). 1978, Avon paper $2.50 (0-380-01913-2). 148pp. Being relatively poor in an upper-class neighborhood causes problems for 13-year-old Catherine Myers.

**6159** Napoli, Donna Jo. *When the Water Closes over My Head* (2–4). Illus. by Nancy Poydar. 1994, Dutton paper $13.99 (0-525-45083-1). 60pp. Mickey is going into the fourth grade, and his fear of the water is preventing him from learning to swim. (Rev: BCCB 9/95; BL 1/1/94; SLJ 3/94)

**6160** Naylor, Phyllis Reynolds, and Lura Schield Reynolds. *Maudie in the Middle* (3–5). Illus. by Judith G. Brown. 1988, Macmillan $16.00 (0-689-31395-0). 176pp. Eight-year-old Maudie, the middle of 7 children in the 1900s, longs to be "first" with someone. (Rev: BCCB 5/88; BL 4/1/88; SLJ 5/88)

**6161** Nesbit, Edith. *The Railway Children* (3–7). 1983, Puffin paper $2.95 (0-14-035005-5). 240pp. Bobbie, Peter, and Phyllis try to solve the mystery of their father's disappearance.

**6162** Paterson, Katherine. *Come Sing, Jimmy Jo* (5–7). 1985, Avon paper $3.99 (0-380-70052-2). 208pp. The family decides it's time to include James in their singing group. (Rev: BL 9/1/87)

**6163** Paterson, Katherine. *Jacob Have I Loved* (6–8). 1980, HarperCollins LB $14.89 (0-690-04079-2); paper $4.95 (0-06-440368-8). 228pp. A story set in the Chesapeake Bay region about the rivalry between 2 sisters. Newbery Award winner, 1981.

**6164** Pevsner, Stella. *And You Give Me a Pain, Elaine* (5–7). 1989, Pocket paper $2.99 (0-671-68838-3). 192pp. Andrea tries to get along with her older sister while trying to adjust to her mother's death.

**6165** Pfeffer, Susan Beth. *Kid Power* (4–6). Illus. by Leigh Grant. 1991, Scholastic paper $2.99 (0-590-42607-9). 121pp. A spunky young girl organizes an employment agency for herself and friends when her mother loses her job.

**6166** Porte, Barbara Ann. *Fat Fanny, Beanpole Bertha and the Boys* (4–6). Illus. by Maxie Chambliss. 1991, Orchard LB $16.99 (0-531-08528-7). 112pp. Fanny and Bertha are best friends despite their differences. (Rev: BCCB 4/91*; BL 3/1/91; HB 7–8/91; SLJ 2/91*)

**6167** Porte, Barbara Ann. *A Turkey Drive and Other Tales* (3–5). Illus. by Yossi Abolafia. 1993, Greenwillow $14.00 (0-688-11336-2). 48pp. An episodic look at an unusual family consisting of Abigail, brother Sam, dog Benton, artist Mother, and cab-driving Daddy. (Rev: BCCB 7–8/93; BL 4/15/93; HB 5–6/93; SLJ 5/93)

**6168** Pryor, Bonnie. *Toenails, Tonsils, and Tornadoes* (3–5). Illus. 1997, Morrow $15.00 (0-688-14885-9). 160pp. Fourth-grader Martin is not too happy when his Aunt Henrietta visits, principally because he has to give up his room. (Rev: BCCB 6/97; BL 5/15/97; SLJ 5/97)

**6169** Quirk, Anne. *Dancing with Great-Aunt Cornelia* (5–8). 1997, HarperCollins LB $14.89 (0-06-027333-X). 128pp. Connie discovers a family secret when she spends a few weeks with her super-rich Great Aunt Cornelia in Manhattan. (Rev: BCCB 6/97; BL 6/1–15/97; SLJ 5/97)

**6170** Robinson, Nancy K. *Angela and the Broken Heart* (3–5). 1991, Scholastic $12.95 (0-590-43212-5). 144pp. A warm story of family problems with Angela, who, in the second grade, wonders whether she is engaged or not, and her suddenly stuck-up brother. (Rev: BL 4/1/91; SLJ 4/91)

**6171** Rodowsky, Colby. *H, My Name Is Henley* (6–8). 1982, Farrar $14.00 (0-374-32831-5). 184pp. Henley's mother Patti is forever on the move.

**6172** Ross, Lillian. *Sarah, Also Known as Hannah* (4–6). Illus. by Helen Cogancherry. 1994, Albert Whitman LB $11.95 (0-8075-7237-3). 64pp. At age 12, Hannah is sent by her Jewish mother in the Ukraine to live in safety with her uncle in the United States. (Rev: BCCB 3/94; BL 4/1/94; SLJ 5/94)

**6173** Rylant, Cynthia. *The Blue Hill Meadows* (2–5). Illus. 1997, Harcourt $16.00 (0-15-201404-7). 48pp. Four gentle stories about everyday life with Willie and his family. (Rev: BL 9/1/97; SLJ 10/97)

**6174** Scheffler, Ursel. *Grandpa's Amazing Computer* (2–4). Illus. by Ruth Scholte van Mast. 1997, North-South LB $13.88 (1-55858-796-9). 46pp. Ollie's grandfather tells the young boy why a sunflower seed can perform more amazing feats than a computer. (Rev: BL 2/15/98)

**6175** Sendak, Philip. *In Grandpa's House* (4–6). Trans. by Seymour Barofsky. Illus. by Maurice Sendak. 1985, HarperCollins LB $9.89 (0-06-025463-7). 48pp. Translated from Yiddish, these are stories of an Eastern European Jewish immigrant and the family he created in America. (Rev: HB 1–2/86; SLJ 10/85)

**6176** Sheldon, Dyan. *My Brother Is a Superhero* (4–6). Illus. 1996, Candlewick $15.99 (1-56402-624-8). 128pp. Adam is reluctant to call on his overbearing older brother for help in fighting 3 teenage bullies. (Rev: BCCB 2/96; BL 5/1/96; SLJ 4/96)

**6177** Shreve, Susan. *Amy Dunn Quits School* (3–6). Illus. by Diane De Groat. 1993, Morrow $13.00 (0-688-10320-0). 86pp. Amy rebels at her mother's dominating attitudes and skips school the day her mother has planned a surprise visit. (Rev: BCCB 11/93; BL 9/1/93; SLJ 9/93)

**6178** Sidney, Margaret. *The Five Little Peppers and How They Grew* (4–6). 1981, Buccaneer LB $27.95 (0-89966-340-0). 302pp. The classic of 5 children growing up many decades ago.

**6179** Simon, Norma. *How Do I Feel?* (4–6). Illus. by Joe Lasker. 1970, Whitman LB $14.95 (0-8075-3414-5). A small boy has tangled, emotional problems with his twin and his older brother.

**6180** Slepian, Jan. *The Broccoli Tapes* (5–7). 1989, Putnam $14.95 (0-399-21712-6); Scholastic paper $3.50 (0-590-43473-X). Sara uses tapes during her stay in Hawaii to keep up with her class oral history project. (Rev: BCCB 4/89; SLJ 4/89)

**6181** Smith, Janice Lee. *The Monster in the Third Dresser Drawer and Other Stories About Adam Joshua* (3–5). Illus. by Dick Gackenbach. 1981, HarperCollins LB $15.89 (0-06-025739-3); paper $3.95 (0-06-440223-1). 96pp. Adam Joshua faces many everyday problems, including a new baby sister, in these 6 stories. A sequel is: *The Kid Next Door and Other Headaches: Stories about Adam Joshua* (1984).

**6182** Smith, Robert K. *The War with Grandpa* (4–6). Illus. by Richard Lauter. 1984, Dell paper $3.99 (0-440-49276-9). 128pp. Peter resents giving up his bedroom to his grandfather.

**6183** Sorensen, Virginia. *Miracles on Maple Hill* (4–6). 1990, Harcourt paper $6.00 (0-15-254561-1). 232pp. The story of a troubled family drawn together by the experience of a year of country living. Newbery Award winner, 1957.

**6184** Spinelli, Jerry. *Crash* (5–7). 1996, Knopf $16.00 (0-679-87957-9). 162pp. Athlete Crash Coogan changes his bullying ways after his grandfather suffers a stroke. (Rev: BCCB 5/96; BL 6/1–15/96; HB 9–10/96; SLJ 6/96*)

**6185** Springer, Nancy. *The Great Pony Hassle* (4–6). Illus. by Daniel Duffy. 1993, Dial LB $13.89 (0-8037-1308-8). 80pp. Two sets of twins united because of marriage face problems with one of the girls, Paisley, who not only is a pest but also demands a pony. (Rev: BL 6/1–15/93; SLJ 8/83)

**6186** Spurr, Elizabeth. *Mama's Birthday Surprise* (3–4). Illus. 1996, Hyperion $13.95 (0-7868-0265-0); paper $3.95 (0-7868-1124-2). 64pp. Three children discover that many of the stories about their mother's Mexican childhood are false. (Rev: BCCB 12/96; BL 11/1/96; HB 11–12/96; SLJ 11/96)

**6187** Spyri, Johanna. *Heidi* (4–6). Trans. from German by Eileen Hall. Illus. by Rozier-Gaudriault. Series: The Whole Story. 1996, Viking paper $22.99 (0-670-86986-4). 202pp. This unabridged text is accompanied by full-color illustrations: photos, drawings, and art reproductions. (Rev: SLJ 3/97)

**6188** Stolz, Mary. *Go Fish* (3–5). Illus. by Pat Cummings. 1991, HarperCollins LB $14.89 (0-06-025822-5). 80pp. Thomas and his grandfather spend warm times together. (Rev: BCCB 5/91; BL 5/15/91; HB 7–8/91; SLJ 5/91*)

**6189** Talbert, Marc. *A Sunburned Prayer* (4–6). 1995, Simon & Schuster paper $14.00 (0-689-80125-4). 112pp. Eloy knows that if he can make a pilgrimage to a local shrine he can save his grandmother from dying. (Rev: BCCB 7–8/95; BL 8/95; SLJ 7/95*)

**6190** Tashjian, Janet. *Tru Confessions* (5–7). 1997, Holt $15.95 (0-8050-5254-2). 160pp. Tru hatches a plan to get her own TV show and also help her mentally disabled twin brother. (Rev: BL 1/1–15/98; SLJ 12/97)

**6191** Taylor, Mildred D. *Roll of Thunder, Hear My Cry* (6–8). Illus. by Jerry Pinkney. 1976, Bantam paper $3.50 (0-553-25450-2). Set in rural Mississippi during the Depression, this Newbery Award winner (1977) continues the story about black Cassie Logan and her family. Begun in: *Song of the Trees* (1975); continued in: *Let the Circle Be Unbroken* (1981).

**6192** Taylor, Sydney. *All-of-a-Kind Family* (3–6). Illus. by Helen John. 1980, Peter Smith $18.50 (0-8446-6253-4); Dell paper $4.50 (0-440-40059-7). 192pp. Warm and moving stories of Jewish family life in New York City. Also use: *Ella of All-of-a-Kind Family* (1980, Dell paper).

**6193** Terris, Susan. *Octopus Pie* (4–6). 1983, Farrar $11.95 (0-374-35571-1). 166pp. Kristen and her sister Mari don't get along, particularly when father brings home an octopus.

**6194** Tomey, Ingrid. *Grandfather's Day* (3–5). Illus. by Robert A. McKay. 1992, Boyds Mills LB $12.95 (1-56397-022-8). 62pp. Nine-year-old Raydeen tries to mend grandfather's broken heart when he comes to live with them after the death of his wife. (Rev: BL 9/15/92; SLJ 10/92)

**6195** Uchida, Yoshiko. *The Happiest Ending* (4–6). 1985, Macmillan $15.00 (0-689-50326-1). 120pp. Twelve-year-old Rinko tries to stop an arranged marriage in this story of a Japanese-American family during the Great Depression. (Rev: SLJ 11/85)

**6196** Uchida, Yoshiko. *A Jar of Dreams* (4–7). 1981, Macmillan $15.00 (0-689-50210-9); paper $3.95 (0-689-71672-9). 144pp. A Japanese-American family is disillusioned until Aunt Waka arrives. A sequel is: *The Best Bad Thing* (1983).

**6197** Van Leeuwen, Jean. *Two Girls in Sister Dresses* (2–4). Illus. by Linda Benson. 1994, Dial paper $12.99 (0-8037-1230-8). 56pp. An episodic chapter book about a summer with a 7-year-old girl and her 2 younger siblings. (Rev: BL 4/1/94; HB 7–8/94; SLJ 6/94)

**6198** Van Steenwyk, Elizabeth. *Three Dog Winter* (5–8). 1987, Walker $13.95 (0-8027-6718-4). A story of dog racing, this family tale tells of 12-year-old Scott and his Malamute, Kaylah. (Rev: BL 2/1/88; SLJ 12/87)

**6199** Viorst, Judith. *Alexander, Who's Not (Do You Hear Me? I Mean It!) Going to Move* (4–8). Illus. by Robin P. Glasser. 1995, Simon & Schuster $15.00 (0-

689-31958-4). 42pp. Alexander of bad-day fame, faces another crisis when he adamantly refuses to move to the family's new home. (Rev: BCCB 11/95; BL 8/95*; SLJ 10/95*)

**6200** Voigt, Cynthia. *Dicey's Song* (5–8). 1982, Macmillan $17.00 (0-689-30944-9); Fawcett paper $4.50 (0-449-70276-6). 204pp. This story of Dicey's life with her "Gram" in Maryland won a Newbery Award (1983). Preceding it was: *Homecoming* (1981); a sequel is: *A Solitary Blue* (1983).

**6201** Wallace, Bill. *Beauty* (5–7). 1988, Holiday $15.95 (0-8234-0715-2). 192pp. Luke finds the adjustment difficult when he and his mother go to live on his grandfather's Oklahoma farm. (Rev: BCCB 11/88; BL 2/1/89; SLJ 10/88)

**6202** Wesley, Valerie W. *Freedom's Gifts: A Juneteenth Story* (3–6). Illus. by Sharon Wilson. 1997, Simon & Schuster paper $16.00 (0-689-80269-2). 32pp. Set in 1943, this novel about African Americans celebrating a holiday commemorating the end of slavery points out that the battle for civil rights isn't over. (Rev: BCCB 6/97; BL 5/1/97; SLJ 6/97)

**6203** Wiggin, Kate Douglas. *Rebecca of Sunnybrook Farm* (4–7). Illus. by Lawrence Beall Smith. 1986, Dell paper $3.99 (0-440-47533-3). Rebecca is a spunky, curious girl living in a quiet Maine community of the 19th century. One of many editions.

**6204** Wilder, Laura Ingalls. *Little House in the Big Woods* (4–7). Illus. by Garth Williams. 1953, HarperCollins LB $15.89 (0-06-026431-4); paper $3.95 (0-06-440001-8). 238pp. Outstanding story of a log-cabin family in Wisconsin in the late 1800s. Also use: *By the Shores of Silver Lake; Farmer Boy; Little House on the Prairie; Long Winter; On the Banks of Plum Creek; These Happy Golden Years* (all 1953); *Little Town on the Prairie* (1961); *The First Four Years* (1971).

**6205** Wilder, Laura Ingalls. *West from Home: Letters of Laura Ingalls Wilder, San Francisco, 1915* (6–8). 1974, HarperCollins paper $4.95 (0-06-440081-6). 176pp. Laura visited her daughter Rose in San Francisco in the year that the city was preparing a world's fair, and she wrote about her experiences to her husband.

**6206** Wilson, Jacqueline. *Double Act* (3–6). Illus. 1998, Delacorte $14.95 (0-385-32312-3). 185pp. In this English story, Ruby and Garnet are identical twins on the outside but very different inside, as their father's new girlfriend finds out. (Rev: BL 1/1–15/98*; SLJ 3/98)

**6207** Woodruff, Elvira. *"Dear Napoleon, I Know You're Dead, But . . ."* (3–5). Illus. 1992, Holiday $15.95 (0-8234-0962-7). 220pp. Marty is astounded when he receives a reply to his letter to Napoleon, after Gramps tells him about a courier at his nursing home who can deliver messages to the dead. (Rev: BCCB 12/92; BL 12/15/92; SLJ 10/92)

**6208** Young, Ronder T. *Learning by Heart* (5–7). 1993, Houghton $14.95 (0-395-65369-X). 172pp. Race relations and friendship become important to 10-year-old Rachel, who is growing up in a small Southern town in the 1960s with the family's African American maid, whom she adores. (Rev: BCCB 12/93; BL 12/15/93; SLJ 10/93*)

**6209** Zucker, David. *Uncle Carmello* (3–6). Illus. by Lyle Miller. 1993, Macmillan LB $14.95 (0-02-793760-7). 32pp. On one special day, David gets to know forbidding Uncle Carmello, who speaks with a thick Italian accent. (Rev: BL 3/15/93; SLJ 7/93)

---

# Fantasy and the Supernatural

**6210** Abbott, Donald. *How the Wizard Came to Oz* (4–6). Illus. by author. 1993, Books of Wonder $19.95 (0-929605-24-1); paper $9.95 (0-929605-15-2). 116pp. The story of how Oscar Diggs became the Wizard of Oz. A reissue.

**6211** Adams, Richard. *Watership Down* (6–8). Illus. 1974, Macmillan $40.00 (0-02-700030-3); Avon paper $12.00 (0-380-00428-3). 444pp. Rabbits, frightened by the coming destruction of their warren, journey across the English downs in search of a new home.

**6212** Adler, C. S. *Ghost Brother* (5–7). 1990, Houghton $15.00 (0-395-52592-6). 150pp. After his older brother dies in an accident, 11-year-old Wally finds comfort in his ghost. (Rev: BCCB 5/90; BL 5/15/90; SLJ 5/90)

**6213** Adler, C. S. *Good-bye Pink Pig* (5–7). 1986, Avon paper $2.75 (0-380-70175-8). 176pp. Shy Amanda takes comfort in the make-believe world of her miniature pink pig — away from the elegant world of her mother and easygoing life of her brother — until trouble enters her real and imaginary worlds and she learns to assert herself. (Rev: BCCB 2/86; BL 12/15/85)

**6214** Adler, C. S. *Help, Pink Pig!* (5–7). 1991, Avon paper $2.95 (0-380-71156-7). 176pp. Unsure of herself with her mother, Amanda retreats into the world of her miniature pink pig. (Rev: BL 5/1/90; SLJ 5/90)

**6215** Ahlberg, Allan. *The Giant Baby* (2–5). Illus. by Fritz Wegner. 1995, Viking paper $13.99 (0-670-84864-6). 155pp. Packed with excitement and humor, this is the story of a giant baby who is left on the doorstep of an unsuspecting family that grows to love its enormous charge. (Rev: SLJ 7/95*)

**6216** Alcock, Vivien. *The Haunting of Cassie Palmer* (5–8). 1997, Houghton paper $6.95 (0-395-81653-

X). 160pp. Cassie finds she is blessed with second sight.

**6217** Alcock, Vivien. *The Red-Eared Ghosts* (5–7). 1997, Houghton $15.95 (0-395-81660-2). 272pp. Mary Frewin travels through time to solve a mystery concerning her great-great-grandmother. (Rev: BL 3/1/97; SLJ 4/97)

**6218** Alcock, Vivien. *The Stonewalkers* (5–8). 1998, Houghton paper $4.95 (0-395-81652-1). 192pp. Statues come to life and begin stalking 2 girls.

**6219** Alexander, Lloyd. *The Book of Three* (5–8). 1964, Holt $16.95 (0-8050-0874-8); Dell paper $4.99 (0-440-40702-8). 224pp. Welsh legend and universal mythology are blended in the tale of an assistant pig keeper who becomes a hero. Newbery Award winner, 1969. Others in the Prydain cycle: *The Black Cauldron; The Castle of Llyr; Taran Wanderer; The High King* (all 1995, Holt).

**6220** Alexander, Lloyd. *The Cat Who Wished to Be a Man* (5–6). 1973, Dell paper $3.99 (0-440-40580-7). A cat named Lionel, turned into a man by a magician, begins combating the corrupt mayor of the town.

**6221** Alexander, Lloyd. *The First Two Lives of Lukas-Kasha* (5–7). 1998, Puffin paper $4.99 (0-141-30057-4). 224pp. Lukas awakens to find himself in a strange land.

**6222** Alexander, Lloyd. *Time Cat: The Remarkable Journeys of Jason and Gareth* (4–6). Illus. by Bill Sokol. 1996, Puffin paper $3.99 (0-140-37827-8). Jason's cat takes him to various times and places.

**6223** Alexander, Lloyd. *The Wizard in the Tree* (4–6). Illus. by Laszlo Kubinyi. 1998, Viking paper $4.50 (0-140-38801-X). 144pp. A delightful fantasy of a good-versus-evil struggle involving an orphan, Mallory, his wizard, and their battle against Mrs. Parsel and Squire Scrupnor.

**6224** Alphin, Elaine M. *The Ghost Cadet* (4–7). 1991, Holt $14.95 (0-8050-1614-7). 182pp. Benjy is in for a surprise when he spends the spring break with a grandmother he has never met. (Rev: BCCB 4/91; BL 5/1/91; SLJ 5/91)

**6225** Alphin, Elaine M. *Tournament of Time* (4–6). 1994, Bluegrass paper $3.95 (0-9643683-0-7). 125pp. A young American girl in York, England, solves a historic murder mystery with the help of ghosts. (Rev: BL 3/15/95)

**6226** Amoss, Berthe. *Lost Magic* (5–7). 1993, Hyperion $14.95 (1-56282-573-9). 192pp. Fantasy and history mingle in this story set in the Middle Ages about a young girl who knows how to use both healing herbs and magic. (Rev: BL 11/1/93)

**6227** Anderson, Janet S. *Going Through the Gate* (4–7). 1997, Dutton paper $15.99 (0-525-45836-0). 160pp. This mystery-fantasy deals with the transition that occurs in the young graduates of Miss Clough's one-room school when she takes them "through the gate." (Rev: BL 2/15/98; SLJ 11/97*)

**6228** Anderson, Margaret J. *The Ghost Inside the Monitor* (3–6). 1990, Knopf LB $11.99 (0-679-90359-3); Random paper $3.50 (0-679-80359-9). 119pp. When Sarah starts to write on the computer, it takes over and writes the story of a girl who lived at the turn of the century. (Rev: BL 1/1/91; SLJ 10/90)

**6229** Anzaldua, Gloria. *Prietita and the Ghost Woman* (3–6). Illus. by Christina Gonzalez. 1996, Children's Book Pr. $14.95 (0-89239-136-7). While looking for an herb to cure her mother, Prietita gets lost in the woods in this English-Spanish fantasy. (Rev: BCCB 4/96; SLJ 7/96)

**6230** Arkin, Alan. *The Lemming Condition* (4–7). Illus. by Joan Sandin. 1989, HarperCollins paper $9.00 (0-062-50048-1). 64pp. Bubber opposes the mass suicide of his companions in this interesting fable.

**6231** Atwood, Margaret. *Princess Prunella and the Purple Peanut* (3–5). Illus. by Maryann Kovalski. 1995, Workman $13.95 (0-7611-0166-7). 32pp. Words beginning with the letter P are used to tell this story of pampered Prunella and the purple peanut that grows on her nose. (Rev: BL 12/15/95)

**6232** Avi. *Poppy* (4–6). Illus. 1995, Orchard LB $16.99 (0-531-08783-2). 160pp. Tragedy occurs when a young deer mouse named Poppy disobeys her father and ventures out into the night with her boyfriend. (Rev: BCCB 1/96; BL 10/15/95*; SLJ 12/95*)

**6233** Avi. *Tom, Babette, and Simon: Three Tales of Transformation* (4–6). Illus. 1995, Simon & Schuster paper $15.00 (0-02-707765-9). 43pp. Three stories about the unusual consequences that occur when 3 youngsters are transformed into different beings. (Rev: BCCB 7–8/95; BL 5/15/95; SLJ 6/95)

**6234** Babbitt, Natalie. *The Devil's Other Storybook* (4–6). Illus. by author. 1987, Farrar $13.00 (0-374-31767-4); paper $4.95 (0-374-41704-0). 112pp. The devil generally fouls up things in these humorous tales, but sometimes does an unintentional good deed. (Rev: BCCB 7–8/87; BL 8/87; SLJ 8/87)

**6235** Babbitt, Natalie. *The Devil's Storybook* (4–6). Illus. by author. 1974, Farrar $13.00 (0-374-31770-4); paper $3.95 (0-374-41708-3). 102pp. Ten stories about outwitting the devil, in this case personified as a middle-aged, vain, but crafty adversary.

**6236** Babbitt, Natalie. *The Search for Delicious* (4–7). Illus. by author. 1969, Farrar $16.00 (0-374-36534-2). 176pp. The innocent task of polling the kingdom's subjects for personal food preferences

provokes civil war in a zestful spoof of taste and society.

**6237** Babbitt, Natalie. *Tuck Everlasting* (4–6). 1975, Farrar $15.00 (0-374-37848-7); paper $3.95 (0-374-48009-5). 160pp. Violence erupts when the Tuck family members discover that their secret about a spring that brings immortality has been discovered.

**6238** Bailey, Carolyn Sherwin. *Miss Hickory* (4–6). Illus. by Ruth Gannett. 1946, Puffin paper $4.99 (0-14-030956-X). 128pp. The adventures of a doll made from an apple branch with a hickory nut head. Newbery Award winner, 1947.

**6239** Baker, Jeannie. *Where the Forest Meets the Sea* (K–4). Illus. by author. 1988, Greenwillow LB $15.93 (0-688-06364-0). 32pp. A young boy travels through a reef and arrives in the rain forest in Australia and pretends he has gone back in time. (Rev: BCCB 5/88; BL 6/15/88; SLJ 7/88)

**6240** Ball, Duncan. *Selby: The Secret Adventures of a Talking Dog* (3–6). Illus. 1997, HarperCollins paper $4.50 (0-06-440673-3). 128pp. Thirteen adventures involving Selby, an Australian dog who can read, write, and speak English. (Rev: BL 2/1/97; SLJ 3/97)

**6241** Banks, Lynne Reid. *Angela and Diabola* (5–8). 1997, Avon paper $14.00 (0-380-97562-9). 164pp. A wicked romp that chronicles the lives of twin sisters, the angelic Angela and the truly horrible and destructive Diabola. (Rev: SLJ 7/97)

**6242** Banks, Lynne Reid. *Harry the Poisonous Centipede: A Story to Make You Squirm* (3–5). Illus. 1997, Morrow $15.00 (0-688-14711-9). 160pp. A fantasy about the many dangers facing Harry, a young centipede. (Rev: BL 9/15/97; SLJ 9/97)

**6243** Banks, Lynne Reid. *The Indian in the Cupboard* (3–5). Illus. by Brock Cole. 1985, Doubleday $15.95 (0-385-17051-3); Avon paper $4.50 (0-380-60012-9). 192pp. A magical cupboard turns toys into living things.

**6244** Banks, Lynne Reid. *The Mystery of the Cupboard* (5–8). Illus. by Tom Newsom. 1993, Morrow LB $15.93 (0-688-12635-9). 256pp. In this, the fourth of the Cupboard series, the young hero Omri uncovers a diary that reveals secrets about his magical cupboard. (Rev: BCCB 6/93; BL 4/1/93; HB 7–8/93; SLJ 6/93)

**6245** Banks, Lynne Reid. *The Return of the Indian* (5–7). Illus. by William Geldart. 1986, Doubleday $15.95 (0-385-23497-X); Avon paper $3.99 (0-380-70284-3). 192pp. Omri brings his plastic Indian figures to life and discovers that his friend Little Bear has been wounded and needs his help. (Rev: BL 9/15/86; HB 11–12/86; SLJ 11/86)

**6246** Banks, Lynne Reid. *The Secret of the Indian* (4–6). Illus. by Ted Lewin. 1989, Doubleday $15.95 (0-385-26292-2). 160pp. Once again, Omri's magic cupboard brings toy figures to life, and in this novel, friend Patrick travels back in time to the Old West. (Rev: BCCB 1/90; BL 9/15/89; HB 3–4/90; SLJ 10/89)

**6247** Barber, Antonia. *The Ghosts* (4–6). 1989, Pocket paper $3.50 (0-671-70714-0). Two youngsters meet ghosts from another country in their garden.

**6248** Barrie, J. M. *Peter Pan* (3–7). Illus. by Scott Gustafson. 1991, Viking paper $20.00 (0-670-84180-3). 184pp. A handsome edition of this classic, with more than 50 oil paintings. (Rev: SLJ 1/92)

**6249** Barrie, J. M. *Peter Pan* (4–6). Illus. by Michael Hague. 1987, Holt $19.95 (0-8050-0276-6). Color illustrations give the flavor of the Victorian era in this classic tale. (Rev: BL 12/15/87)

**6250** Barrie, J. M. *Peter Pan* (3–6). Illus. by Trina S. Hyman. 1995, Playmore $9.95 (0-86611-997-3); Penguin paper $2.99 (0-7214-5681-2). 192pp. The Darling family, Tinker Bell, and the whole beloved cast of characters in a recommended edition. Another recommended edition is illus. by Diane Goode (1983, Random).

**6251** Bauer, Marion Dane. *Ghost Eye* (3–6). Illus. by Trina S. Hyman. 1992, Scholastic $13.95 (0-590-45298-3). 64pp. Popcorn, a Cornish rex show cat who sees ghosts, leads a tantalizing cast of characters. (Rev: BL 9/15/92; SLJ 10/92)

**6252** Bauer, Marion Dane. *A Taste of Smoke* (5–7). 1993, Clarion $14.95 (0-395-64341-4). 106pp. On a camping trip with her sister, Caitlin encounters the ghost of a boy killed a century before. (Rev: BCCB 1/94; BL 10/15/93; SLJ 12/93)

**6253** Bauer, Marion Dane. *Touch the Moon* (5–7). Illus. by Alix Berenzy. 1987, Houghton $15.00 (0-89919-526-1). 96pp. Angry over not getting a real horse, Jennifer throws away her toy horse gift and learns a lesson in responsibility. (Rev: BCCB 9/87; BL 9/15/87; HB 9–10/87)

**6254** Baum, L. Frank. *The Marvelous Land of Oz* (4–6). Illus. by John R. Neill. 1985, Morrow $22.00 (0-688-05439-0). 288pp. This is a facsimile of the original 1904 edition with the illustrations in both color and black and white. Other titles in this series are published by Peter Smith and Amereon in hard cover and Dover and Puffin in paperback.

**6255** Baum, L. Frank. *The Wizard of Oz* (3–5). Illus. by Michael Hague. 1982, Holt $19.95 (0-8050-0221-9). 232pp. A new edition of this favorite. One of many editions.

**6256** Baum, L. Frank. *The Wizard of Oz* (PS–4). Illus. by Charles Santore. 1986, Ballantine paper $4.99 (0-345-33590-2). 96pp. For a younger audience than the original, this is an abridged, heavily

illustrated version of the Baum classic. (Rev: SLJ 12/91)

**6257** Baum, L. Frank. *The Wonderful Wizard of Oz* (4–8). Illus. by W. W. Denslow. 1987, Morrow $22.00 (0-688-06944-4). 316pp. A reissue of the 1900 classic with original colorplates. (Rev: BL 11/1/87)

**6258** Baum, Roger S. *Dorothy of Oz* (4–6). Illus. by Elizabeth Miles. 1989, Morrow $17.00 (0-688-07848-6). 176pp. A story true to the original in which Dorothy is called back to Oz because the Tin Woodman, the Scarecrow, and the Cowardly Lion need help. (Rev: BL 1/1/90; SLJ 10/89)

**6259** Bellairs, John. *The Curse of the Blue Figurine* (5–8). 1984, Bantam paper $3.50 (0-553-15540-7). 208pp. A boy steals an ancient book from a church and evil spells begin working. Two sequels are: *The Mummy, the Will, and the Crypt* (1985); *The Spell of the Sorcerer's Skull* (1997, Puffin).

**6260** Bellairs, John. *The Figure in the Shadows* (5–7). Illus. by Mercer Mayer. 1993, Puffin paper $4.50 (0-14-036337-8). 160pp. Excitement, magic, and suspense are combined in this story of a boy whose new-found ancient coin is actually an evil talisman. Two others in the series: *The House with a Clock in Its Walls; The Letter, the Witch and the Ring* (both 1993).

**6261** Bellairs, John. *The Ghost in the Mirror* (5–8). 1994, Puffin paper $4.50 (0-140-34934-0). 176pp. Fourteen-year-old Rose and white witch Mrs. Zimmerman are transported in time to 1828 on a secret mission. (Rev: SLJ 3/93)

**6262** Bellairs, John. *The Mansion in the Mist* (5–7). 1992, Dial LB $14.89 (0-8037-0846-7); Puffin paper $3.99 (0-140-34933-2). 176pp. Anthony Monday finds mystery and adventure on a remote island in northern Canada. (Rev: BL 8/92; SLJ 6/92)

**6263** Bellairs, John. *The Vengeance of the Witch-Finder* (4–6). 1993, Dial LB $14.89 (0-8037-1451-3). 176pp. During a visit to an old English home, Lewis accidentally releases a ghost that threatens to destroy him. (Rev: BL 10/15/93; SLJ 9/93)

**6264** Bellairs, John, and Brad Strickland. *The Doom of the Haunted Opera* (4–6). Illus. 1995, Dial paper $14.89 (0-8037-1465-3). 160pp. Lewis and his friend Rosa let loose an evil spirit that wants to take over the world. (Rev: BL 8/95; SLJ 9/95)

**6265** Bennett, David, ed. *A Treasury of Witches and Wizards* (4–6). Illus. 1996, Kingfisher paper $5.95 (1-85697-678-5). 160pp. A collection of supernatural tales by such writers as Diana Wynne Jones, Alan Garner, and Helen Cresswell. (Rev: BL 6/1–15/96)

**6266** Berger, Barbara Helen. *Gwinna* (4–8). Illus. 1990, Putnam $22.95 (0-399-21738-X). 126pp. A mystic coming-of-age fable when a couple's wish for a child is granted in the form of a daughter who grows wings. (Rev: BL 10/15/90; SLJ 12/90)

**6267**   Bethlen, Julianna. *Dracula Junior and the Fake Fangs: A 3-D Picture Book* (3–5). Illus. by Korky Paul. 1996, Dial paper $14.99 (0-8037-2008-4). 22pp. Closing caskets are featured in the 3-D interactive book about Dracula Jr. and his search for Grandma's fangs. (Rev: BL 12/15/96)

**6268**   Bial, Raymond. *The Fresh Grave: And Other Ghostly Stories* (5–7). 1997, Midwest Traditions $18.95 (1-883953-23-5); paper $13.95 (1-883953-22-7). 162pp. A series of 10 adventure stories featuring 2 teenage heroes and their escapades in a small midwestern town. (Rev: SLJ 12/97)

**6269**   Billingsley, Franny. *Well Wished* (5–8). 1997, Simon & Schuster $16.00 (0-689-81210-8). 176pp. An intriguing fantasy that involves a lonely girl and a wishing well that grants each person a single wish. (Rev: BCCB 4/97; BL 6/1–15/97; HB 5–6/97; SLJ 5/97*)

**6270**   Black, J. R. *My Teacher Ate My Homework* (3–6). Series: Shadow Zone. 1995, Random paper $3.99 (0-679-86929-8). 123pp. After Jesse buys a strange doll, it comes to life in the form of a teacher he dislikes. (Rev: SLJ 6/95)

**6271**   Blair, Margaret Whitman. *Brothers at War* (4–7). 1997, White Mane paper $7.95 (1-57249-049-7). 145pp. Two brothers and their friend Sarah find themselves transported back in time to the Battle of Antietam in 1862. (Rev: BL 8/97)

**6272**   Blankman, Lynn. *Green-Eyed Ghost* (4–6). 1997, Avon paper $3.99 (0-380-78616-8). 116pp. Charlotte learnes self-worth after she encounters a ghost while visiting her grandmother. (Rev: SLJ 1/98)

**6273**   Bliss, Corinne D. *Matthew's Meadow* (3–6). Illus. by Ted Lewin. 1997, Harcourt paper $7.00 (0-152-01500-0). 40pp. Nine-year-old Matthew returns each year to a meadow where he learns to communicate with a red-tailed hawk. (Rev: BL 3/15/92; SLJ 8/92)

**6274**   Bojunga-Nunes, Lygia. *The Companions* (2–4). Trans. by Ellen Watson. Illus. by Larry Wilkes. 1989, Farrar $11.95 (0-374-31465-9). 58pp. A delightful fantasy about the friendship of 3 animals. (Rev: BL 12/15/89; SLJ 1/90)

**6275**   Bomans, Godfried. *Eric in the Land of the Insects* (4–6). Illus. by Mark Richardson. 1994, Houghton $14.95 (0-395-65231-6). 197pp. Eric learns a great deal about the secret lives of insects when he enters their world in this fantasy. (Rev: BCCB 6/94; BL 3/15/94; SLJ 3/94)

**6276**   Bond, Adrienne. *Sugarcane House and Other Stories About Mr. Fat* (4–6). Illus. 1997, Harcourt $16.00 (0-15-201446-2). 80pp. Ma Minnie loves

telling stories about Mr. Fat, a.k.a. John Fortune, a Georgia trickster, and his strong-minded talking mule, Brownie. (Rev: BL 12/1/97; HB 11–12/97; SLJ 1/98)

**6277**   Bradshaw, Gillian. *The Land of Gold* (5–8). Illus. 1992, Greenwillow $14.00 (0-688-10576-9). 160pp. Prahotep, sidekick Baki, and Hathor the dragon save a Nubian princess in ancient Egypt. A sequel to *Dragon and the Thief* (1991). (Rev: BCCB 10/92; BL 9/15/92; HB 3–4/93; SLJ 10/92)

**6278**   Breathed, Berkeley. *The Last Basselope: One Ferocious Story* (4–7). Illus. 1992, Little, Brown $14.95 (0-316-10761-1). 32pp. In this imaginative picture book for older readers, Opus and his reluctant adventurers are after the nearly extinct basselope. (Rev: BCCB 1/93; BL 12/15/92; SLJ 1/93)

**6279**   Brittain, Bill. *All the Money in the World* (4–6). Illus. by Charles Robinson. 1992, HarperCollins paper $4.50 (0-06-440128-6). 160pp. A leprechaun grants Quentin Stowe his wish for all the money in the world.

**6280**   Brittain, Bill. *Devil's Donkey* (3–6). Illus. by Andrew Glass. 1981, HarperCollins LB $13.89 (0-06-020683-7). 128pp. Dan'l defies the witches and is turned into a donkey. A sequel is: *The Wish Giver: Three Tales of Coven Tree* (1983).

**6281**   Brittain, Bill. *The Ghost from Beneath the Sea* (4–6). Illus. by Michele Chessare. 1994, HarperCollins LB $13.89 (0-06-020828-7); paper $4.50 (0-064-40526-5). 128pp. Tommy, Books, and Harry must prove a poker game on the *Titanic* was rigged in order to save their ghost friends. (Rev: BL 12/1/92; HB 1–2/93; SLJ 1/93)

**6282**   Brittain, Bill. *The Mystery of the Several Sevens* (1–4). Illus. by James Warhola. 1994, HarperCollins LB $12.89 (0-06-024462-3). 96pp. Mr. Merlin, a substitute teacher, takes 2 of his pupils to a land where they must solve mysteries. (Rev: BL 11/15/94; SLJ 12/94)

**6283**   Brittain, Bill. *Wings* (5–7). 1995, HarperCollins paper $4.50 (0-064-40612-1). 144pp. Troubles really begin for 12-year-old Ian when he sprouts wings. (Rev: BCCB 11/91; BL 1/1/91; SLJ 10/91)

**6284**   Brown, Calef. *Polkabats and Octopus Slacks: 14 Stories* (3–5). Illus. 1998, Houghton $15.00 (0-395-85403-2). 32pp. Nonsense verses introduce some wacky characters, including Kansas City Octopus, who goes out on the town in four-legged bell bottoms. (Rev: BL 3/15/98)

**6285**   Brown, Marc. *Scared Silly! A Book for the Brave* (3–6). Illus. 1994, Little, Brown $18.95 (0-316-11360-3). 64pp. As well as containing a fine collection of spooky, but humorous, stories, this book provides suggestions for activities to frighten friends. (Rev: BL 10/1/94; HB 11–12/94; SLJ 9/94*)

**6286** Brown, Melanie, and Anthony Lawlor. *Frankie's Bau-Wau Haus* (2–4). Illus. by Elaine Arnold. 1995, Rizzoli $15.95 (0-8478-1918-3). 32pp. A dog gets a famous architect to design the perfect house for him and his friend, a mouse. (Rev: SLJ 5/96)

**6287** Buchwald, Emilie. *Gildaen: The Heroic Adventures of a Most Unusual Rabbit* (4–6). Illus. by Barbara Flynn. 1993, Milkweed paper $6.95 (0-915-94375-1). 184pp. This fantasy set in medieval times deals with the meek triumphing over might. A reissue.

**6288** Burgess, Melvin. *The Earth Giant* (3–6). 1997, Putnam $15.95 (0-399-23187-0). 160pp. After a terrible storm, an extraterrestrial giant is unearthed by Amy, who must protect it from being discovered by others. (Rev: BL 10/1/97)

**6289** Burnard, Damon. *Pork and Beef's Great Adventure* (2–4). Illus. 1998, Houghton $15.00 (0-395-86765-7). 48pp. Pork the pig and Beef the cow attach feathers to themselves and fly to the moon. (Rev: BL 3/1/98; SLJ 4/98)

**6290** Bush, Lawrence. *Emma Ansky-Levine and Her Mitzvah Machine* (4–6). Illus. by Joel Iskowitz. 1991, UAHC paper $7.95 (0-8074-0458-6). 115pp. Emma receives a machine from her uncle in Jerusalem that gives her personal guidance. (Rev: SLJ 7/91)

**6291** Byars, Betsy. *McMummy* (4–6). 1993, Viking paper $13.99 (0-670-84995-2). 176pp. A boy named Mozie believes he is being threatened by a giant, humming pea pod in this exciting fantasy. (Rev: BL 11/1/93; SLJ 9/93)

**6292** Byars, Betsy. *The Winged Colt of Casa Mia* (4–6). Illus. by Richard Cuffari. 1981, Avon paper $2.95 (0-380-00201-9). 132pp. In this fantasy, a young boy visits the Texas ranch of his uncle, an ex-stuntman, and encounters a colt with supernatural powers.

**6293** Calmenson, Stephanie, and Joanna Cole. *Rockin' Reptiles* (2–4). Illus. by Lynn Munsinger. 1997, Morrow LB $14.93 (0-688-12740-1). 80pp. The friendship of 2 alligators, Allie and Amy, is tested when an acquaintance can take only one of them to a rock concert. (Rev: BL 3/1/97; SLJ 4/97*)

**6294** Cameron, Eleanor. *The Court of the Stone Children* (5–7). 1990, Puffin paper $4.99 (0-14-034289-3). 192pp. Nina's move with her family to San Francisco is a disaster until she encounters a young ghost in a small museum.

**6295** Carroll, Lewis. *Alice's Adventures in Wonderland* (5–8). Illus. by Justin Todd. 1984, Outlet $3.99 (0-517-55591-3). 160pp. A well-designed addition to the Carroll shelf. (Rev: BL 7/85; SLJ 8/85)

**6296** Carroll, Lewis. *Alice's Adventures in Wonderland and Through the Looking Glass* (4–7). Illus. by John Tenniel. 1963, Putnam $15.99 (0-448-06004-

3). One of many recommended editions of these enduring fantasies.

**6297** Carroll, Lewis. *The Complete Works of Lewis Carroll* (4–7). Illus. by John Tenniel. 1979, Random $15.95 (0-394-60485-7). 1,293pp. Stories, short prose, poems, verse, puzzles, and games.

**6298** Carroll, Lewis. *Through the Looking Glass, and What Alice Found There* (4–7). Illus. by John Tenniel. 1977, St. Martin's $14.95 (0-312-80374-5). 224pp. Sequel to *Alice's Adventures in Wonderland.* One of many editions.

**6299** Carusone, Al. *Don't Open the Door After the Sun Goes Down* (3–6). Illus. 1994, Clarion $13.95 (0-395-65225-1); Hyperion paper $3.95 (0-7868-1086-6). 83pp. A collection of 9 scary stories, many of which deal with the supernatural. (Rev: BL 9/1/94; SLJ 9/94)

**6300** Cassedy, Sylvia. *Behind the Attic Wall* (6–8). 1983, HarperCollins LB $14.89 (0-690-04337-6). 320pp. Maggie Turner, a difficult girl, is contacted by ghosts in the large house where 2 great-aunts live.

**6301** Catling, Patrick Skene. *The Chocolate Touch* (3–5). Illus. by Margot Apple. 1979, Morrow LB $14.93 (0-688-32187-9); Bantam paper $2.99 (0-440-22796-8). 96pp. A Midas-story variation in which a boy turns his mother into chocolate.

**6302** Christian, Peggy. *The Bookstore Mouse* (4–6). Illus. by Gary Lippincott. 1995, Harcourt $16.00 (0-15-200203-0). 126pp. Cervantes, a bookstore mouse, is transported by a book to a medieval English monastery, where he meets Sigfried, a young scribe. (Rev: SLJ 11/95)

**6303** Clapp, Patricia. *Jane-Emily* (5–7). 1971, Bantam paper $1.75 (0-440-94185-7). 160pp. After seeing the image of a dead girl in a crystal ball, Jane becomes possessed by the ghost.

**6304** Clark, Margaret, comp. *A Treasury of Dragon Stories* (2–5). Illus. by Mark Robertson. Series: Treasury. 1997, Kingfisher paper $6.95 (0-7534-5114-X). 156pp. A collection of 15 previously published stories or excerpts from books that deal with dragons. (Rev: SLJ 1/98)

**6305** Clifford, Eth. *Flatfoot Fox and the Case of the Bashful Beaver* (2–4). Illus. by Brian Lies. 1995, Houghton $16.00 (0-395-70560-6). 47pp. Flatfoot Fox and Secretary Bird solve the mystery of strange thefts involving forest animals. (Rev: BL 3/1/95; SLJ 4/95)

**6306** Cohen, Daniel. *Dangerous Ghosts* (5–7). 1996, Putnam $14.95 (0-399-22913-2). 96pp. Seventeen ghost stories, many with historical backgrounds. (Rev: BL 11/15/96; SLJ 4/97)

**6307** Cohen, Daniel. *Ghostly Tales of Love and Revenge* (5–8). 1995, Pocket paper $3.50 (0-671-

79523-6). 95pp. An international collection of ghost stories that deal with vengeance and unhappy loves. (Rev: SLJ 7/92)

**6308** Cohen, Daniel. *Ghostly Warnings* (4–7). Illus. 1996, Dutton paper $14.99 (0-525-65227-2). 64pp. Some ghostly stories that the author claims are true. (Rev: BL 9/15/96; SLJ 10/96)

**6309** Cole, Joanna. *Doctor Change* (2–4). Illus. by Donald Carrick. 1986, Morrow LB $12.88 (0-688-06136-2). 32pp. Young Tom discovers that Doctor Change can turn himself into a variety of objects; he learns the man's secrets and confronts the evil magic. (Rev: BCCB 10/86; BL 9/15/86; SLJ 10/86)

**6310** Cole, Joanna. *The Magic School Bus Lost in the Solar System* (3–5). Illus. by Bruce Degen. 1990, Scholastic $15.95 (0-590-41428-3). 40pp. Basic facts about the cosmos are revealed in this fantasy. (Rev: BCCB 10/90; BL 11/15/90; HB 1–2/91; SLJ 8/90*)

**6311** Cole, Joanna, and Stephanie Calmenson. *The Gator Girls* (1–3). Illus. by Lynn Munsinger. 1995, Morrow LB $14.93 (0-688-12121-7). 64pp. Two alligator friends cram in many delightful activities before summer camp. (Rev: BL 4/15/95; SLJ 4/95*)

**6312** Coleman, Janet W. *Fast Eddie* (3–4). Illus. by Alec Gillman. 1993, Macmillan LB $13.95 (0-02-722815-0). 144pp. Eddie the raccoon faces danger when he plays tricks on humans. (Rev: SLJ 6/93)

**6313** Collodi, Carlo. *The Adventures of Pinocchio* (3–6). Illus. by Fritz Kredel. 1996, Putnam $15.95 (0-448-41479-1). 272pp. One of many recommended editions.

**6314** Collodi, Carlo. *Pinocchio* (4–7). Retold by James Riordan. Illus. by Victor G. Ambrus. 1996, Oxford $18.95 (0-19-279855-3); paper $11.95 (0-192-72287-5). 96pp. A lighthearted rendition of the classic tale. (Rev: BL 11/15/88)

**6315** Collodi, Carlo. *Pinocchio* (3–5). Illus. by Ed Young. 1996, Putnam $18.95 (0-399-22941-8). 48pp. An abridged version of this classic that nevertheless captures its flavor and excitement. (Rev: BL 11/15/96; SLJ 10/96)

**6316** Conly, Jane L. *R-T, Margaret, and the Rats of NIMH* (4–6). Illus. by Leonard Lubin. 1990, HarperCollins LB $15.89 (0-06-021364-7); paper $4.50 (0-06-440387-4). 288pp. The third installment of the brilliant rodents, in which 2 human children star. (Rev: BCCB 6/90; BL 5/15/90; SLJ 6/90)

**6317** Conly, Jane L. *Racso and the Rats of NIMH* (5–7). Illus. by Leonard Lubin. 1986, HarperCollins LB $15.89 (0-06-021362-0). 288pp. This sequel to the Newbery Medal winner involves once again the smart rodents who wish to live in peace in Thorn Valley. (Rev: BCCB 6/86; BL 6/1/86; SLJ 4/86)

**6318** Conrad, Pam. *Stonewords: A Ghost Story* (5–8). 1990, HarperCollins LB $14.89 (0-06-021316-7); paper $4.95 (0-06-440354-8). 144pp. Zoe moves to her grandparents' home and finds a playmate, from another century, already living there. (Rev: BCCB 5/90; BL 3/1/90; HB 7–8/90; SLJ 5/90*)

**6319** Conrad, Pam. *Zoe Rising* (4–7). 1996, HarperCollins LB $14.89 (0-06-027218-X). 128pp. In a sequel to *Stonewords* (1990), Zoe's time traveling brings her an experience that almost causes her death. (Rev: BCCB 10/96; BL 8/96; HB 11–12/96; SLJ 11/96)

**6320** Cooper, Susan. *The Boggart* (4–6). 1993, Macmillan $15.00 (0-689-50576-0). 200pp. An old desk unleashes the Boggart, a mischievous spirit who has lived in a Scottish castle for centuries. (Rev: BCCB 3/93; BL 1/15/93; HB 5–6/93*; SLJ 1/93)

**6321** Cooper, Susan. *The Boggart and the Monster* (4–6). 1997, Simon & Schuster paper $16.00 (0-689-81330-9). 192pp. The Boggart, a Scottish spirit-creature, wants to accompany young Jessup and Emily when they go to Loch Ness to find the monster. (Rev: BCCB 5/97; BL 3/1/97; HB 5–6/97; SLJ 5/97)

**6322** Cooper, Susan. *Seaward* (5–8). 1983, Macmillan LB $16.00 (0-689-50275-3); paper $3.95 (0-02-042190-7). 180pp. West follows his mother's dying words and heads seaward to his father.

**6323** Cooper, Susan. *Silver on the Tree* (5–7). 1980, Macmillan $17.00 (0-689-50088-2); paper $3.95 (0-689-71152-2). 256pp. The fifth and last volume of the series that tells of the final struggle waged by Will Stanton and his friends against the Dark, powers of evil. The first 4 volumes are: *Over Sea, Under Stone* (1966); *The Dark Is Rising* (1973); *The Grey King* (1975); *Greenwitch* (1985). *The Grey King* was the winner of the 1976 Newbery Medal.

**6324** Coville, Bruce. *The Dragonslayers* (4–6). Illus. 1994, Pocket $14.00 (0-671-89036-0); paper $3.99 (0-671-79832-4). 70pp. When a king promises the hand of his daughter to the person who kills a pesky dragon, his daughter disguises herself and joins the hunt. (Rev: BL 12/1/94; SLJ 2/95)

**6325** Coville, Bruce. *The Ghost in the Big Brass Bed* (4–6). 1991, Bantam LB $3.99 (0-553-15827-9). 184pp. Two ghosts appeal for help to Chris and Nina, who try to solve the mystery surrounding them. (Rev: SLJ 1/92)

**6326** Coville, Bruce. *Goblins in the Castle* (5–7). Illus. 1992, Pocket paper $3.99 (0-671-72711-7). 166pp. William, now 11, has grown up in Toad-in-a-Cage Castle and knows many of its secret passages. (Rev: BL 2/1/93)

**6327** Coville, Bruce. *Into the Land of the Unicorns* (4–6). 1994, Scholastic $12.95 (0-590-45955-4); paper $4.50 (0-590-45956-2). 176pp. A fantasy in which a girl, trying to escape pursuers, is helped by a unicorn. (Rev: BL 10/1/94; SLJ 10/94)

**6328** Coville, Bruce. *Jennifer Murdley's Toad* (3–5). Illus. by Gary Lippincott. 1992, Harcourt $16.95 (0-15-200745-8); Pocket paper $3.99 (0-671-79401-9). 160pp. Jennifer's magical adventures begin when she buys Bufo, a discounted toad, at a mysterious store. (Rev: BL 3/15/92; SLJ 9/92)

**6329** Coville, Bruce. *Jeremy Thatcher, Dragon Hatcher* (4–6). Illus. by Gary Lippincott. 1991, Harcourt $16.95 (0-15-200748-2); Pocket paper $3.99 (0-671-74782-7). 160pp. Jeremy buys a small ball that turns out to be a dragon egg. (Rev: BL 5/15/91; SLJ 5/91)

**6330** Coville, Bruce. *The Monster's Ring* (4–6). Illus. by Katherine Coville. 1989, Pocket paper $3.50 (0-671-69389-1). 96pp. A boy finds a ring that turns him into a monster.

**6331** Coville, Bruce. *The Skull of Truth* (5–7). Illus. Series: Magic Shop Books. 1997, Harcourt $17.00 (0-15-275457-1). 176pp. A fantasy in which compulsive liar Charlie learns to tell the truth through the efforts of a wisecracking skull. (Rev: BL 10/1/97; SLJ 10/97*)

**6332** Coville, Bruce. *The World's Worst Fairy Godmother* (3–5). Illus. 1996, Pocket $14.00 (0-671-00229-5); paper $3.99 (0-671-00228-7). 112pp. A klutz of a fairy godmother gets an unusual assignment to make a dislikable girl popular. (Rev: BL 1/1–15/97)

**6333** Creech, Sharon. *Pleasing the Ghost* (3–6). 1996, HarperCollins LB $14.89 (0-06-026986-3). 128pp. Dennis, who is visited by ghosts, has difficulty understanding the garbled language of the newest visitor, Uncle Arvie. (Rev: BCCB 10/96; BL 9/1/96; SLJ 11/96)

**6334** Cresswell, Helen. *The Secret World of Polly Flint* (5–7). Illus. by Shirley Felts. 1994, Peter Smith $18.00 (0-844-66760-9). 176pp. In this English fantasy, a young girl meets some inhabitants of a village that disappeared centuries ago.

**6335** Cresswell, Helen. *Time Out* (3–6). Illus. by Peter Elwell. 1997, Parkwest $12.95 (0-718-82658-2). 80pp. In 1887, a family is transported to 1987 for an unnerving vacation. (Rev: BL 2/1/90; SLJ 6/90)

**6336** Cresswell, Helen. *The Watchers* (4–6). 1994, Macmillan $15.95 (0-02-725371-6). 160pp. Katy and Josh run away from a children's home and hide out in an amusement park. (Rev: BCCB 2/95; BL 12/15/94; SLJ 2/95)

**6337** Cross, Gillian. *Pictures in the Dark* (5–8). 1996, Holiday $16.95 (0-8234-1267-9). 224pp. A boy whose life is miserable uses supernatural means to escape the pressures. (Rev: BCCB 1/97; BL 1/1–15/97)

**6338** Curry, Jane L. *Moon Window* (5–8). 1996, Simon & Schuster $16.00 (0-689-80945-X). 170pp. Joellen travels back in time and meets several of her ancestors. (Rev: BCCB 11/96; BL 10/15/96; SLJ 12/96)

**6339** Cuyler, Margery. *Weird Wolf* (3–6). Illus. by Dirk Zimmer. 1991, Holt paper $4.95 (0-8050-1643-0). 72pp. Nine-year-old Harry Walpole has to find out how to rid himself of being a werewolf, just like his grandfather. (Rev: BCCB 1/90; BL 12/1/89; SLJ 4/90)

**6340** Dadey, Debbie, and Marcia T. Jones. *Leprechauns Don't Play Basketball* (5–8). Illus. by John S. Gurney. 1992, Scholastic paper $2.99 (0-590-44822-6). 70pp. The Bailey Elementary third grade thinks the gym teacher is a leprechaun. (Rev: BL 9/15/92)

**6341** Dahl, Roald. *The BFG* (3–6). Illus. by Quentin Blake. 1982, Farrar $16.00 (0-374-30469-6); Puffin paper $4.99 (0-14-034019-X). 221pp. Sophie is saved by the BFG (Big Friendly Giant) and finds herself in a strange environment.

**6342** Dahl, Roald. *Charlie and the Chocolate Factory* (4–6). Illus. by Joseph Schindelman. 1964, Knopf LB $18.99 (0-394-91011-7); Puffin paper $4.99 (0-140-32869-6). A rather morbid tale of Charlie and 4 of his nasty friends who tour Willy Wonka's extraordinary chocolate factory. They all meet disaster except for Charlie, for he has obeyed orders. A sequel is: *Charlie and the Great Glass Elevator* (1984, Bantam).

**6343** Dahl, Roald. *Fantastic Mr. Fox* (4–6). Illus. by Donald Chaffin. 1986, Knopf LB $18.99 (0-394-90497-4); Bantam paper $2.50 (0-553-15390-0). 72pp. Mr. Fox outwits 3 rich, mean farmers.

**6344** Dahl, Roald. *George's Marvelous Medicine* (4–6). Illus. by Quentin Blake. 1998, Puffin paper $4.99 (0-14-130111-2). 96pp. George concocts medicine that shrinks his mean grandmother.

**6345** Dahl, Roald. *James and the Giant Peach* (3–5). Illus. by Lane Smith. 1996, Knopf LB $17.99 (0-679-98090-3). 144pp. James is unhappy living with his mean aunts until a magic potion produces an enormous peach, which becomes a home for him. (Rev: BL 5/1/96)

**6346** Dahl, Roald. *Magic Finger* (3–5). Illus. by William Pene du Bois. 1966, HarperCollins $15.00 (0-060-21381-7). 48pp. An 8-year-old girl mysteriously has the power to punish people for wrongdoing by pointing her finger at them.

**6347** Dahl, Roald. *The Witches* (3–6). Illus. by Quentin Blake. 1983, Farrar $16.00 (0-374-38457-6); Puffin paper $3.95 (0-14-031730-9). 208pp. A boy and his grandmamma save English children from being turned into mice by witches.

**6348** Dahl, Roald. *The Wonderful Story of Henry Sugar and Six More* (4–6). 1977, Knopf $17.00 (0-394-83604-9); Puffin paper $4.99 (0-14-032874-2). 224pp. Seven tales of fantasy and fun.

**6349** Dana, Barbara. *Zucchini* (3–5). Illus. by Eileen Christelow. 1982, HarperCollins LB $14.89 (0-06-021395-7); Bantam paper $3.99 (0-553-15608-X). 128pp. The story of a ferret and his escape from the Bronx Zoo.

**6350** Deary, Terry. *True Ghost Stories* (5–8). Illus. by David Wyatt. 1996, Puffin paper $3.99 (0-14-038224-0). 128pp. Nine true ghost stories from around the world are retold, each ending with a logical explanation. Also use *True Horror Stories* (1996). (Rev: SLJ 1/97)

**6351** Deem, James M. *The Very Real Ghost Book of Christina Rose* (4–6). Illus. 1996, Houghton $14.95 (0-395-76128-X). 176pp. Twins Christina and Danny feel they are being visited by their mother's ghost when they move to a new house in California. (Rev: BL 5/1/96; SLJ 5/96)

**6352** DeFelice, Cynthia. *The Ghost of Fossil Glen* (4–6). 1998, Farrar $16.00 (0-374-31787-9). 176pp. Allie has been chosen by the ghost of a young girl to avenge her death in this tense thriller. (Rev: BL 3/15/98)

**6353** Derby, Sally. *Jacob and the Stranger* (3–5). Illus. 1994, Ticknor $11.95 (0-395-66897-2). 32pp. Jacob takes care of a plant that sprouts miniature animals that become his companions. (Rev: BL 9/1/94; HB 9–10/94; SLJ 9/94)

**6354** Dexter, Catherine. *A Is for Apple, W Is for Witch* (3–5). Illus. by Capucine Mazille. 1996, Candlewick $14.99 (1-56402-541-1). 160pp. Apple learns a spell from her witch-mother and turns classmate Barnaby into a frog. (Rev: BCCB 2/96; BL 9/15/96; SLJ 7/96)

**6355** *Disney's The Little Mermaid: Tales from Under the Sea* (3–5). Illus. by Fred Marvin. 1991, Disney $10.95 (1-56282-014-1). 80pp. Twenty-two short stories and poems about Ariel of *The Little Mermaid.* (Rev: BL 4/1/92)

**6356** Dixon, Rachel. *The Witch's Ring* (3–6). Illus. 1994, Hyperion LB $15.49 (1-56282-546-1). 128pp. In this fantasy, Amy changes places with her look-alike, Castanetta. (Rev: BL 12/1/94; SLJ 1/95)

**6357** Doyle, Debra, and James D. MacDonald. *Knight's Wyrd* (5–8). 1992, Harcourt $16.95 (0-15-200764-4). 176pp. Young Will learns from a wizard that he will soon meet his death. (Rev: SLJ 11/92)

**6358** Duane, Diane. *Deep Wizardry* (5–8). 1996, Harcourt paper $6.00 (0-152-01240-0). 288pp. Nita and Kit, the 2 young wizards of *So You Want to Be a Wizard,* again use their powers to prevent a great catastrophe. (Rev: HB 5–6/85)

**6359** Duane, Diane. *So You Want to Be a Wizard* (5–8). 1996, Harcourt paper $6.00 (0-152-01239-7). 288pp. Nita and friends embark on a journey to retrieve the Book of Night with Moon.

**6360** du Bois, William Pene. *Gentlemen Bear* (4–7). Illus. 1985, Farrar $14.95 (0-374-32533-2); paper $5.95 (0-374-42536-1). 80pp. The lifelong relationship between Billy Browne-Browne and Bayard, his bear. (Rev: BL 3/15/86; SLJ 4/86)

**6361** Dunlop, Eileen. *The Ghost by the Sea* (4–6). 1996, Holiday $15.95 (0-8234-1264-4). 192pp. Robin uncovers details of a death that occurred 80 years ago and is haunted by a restless ghost. (Rev: BCCB 3/97; BL 1/1–15/97; SLJ 3/97)

**6362** Dunlop, Eileen. *Websters' Leap* (4–7). 1995, Holiday $15.95 (0-8234-1193-1). 160pp. In this time-slip fantasy, Jill gets involved with people who owned a Scottish castle 400 years before. (Rev: BL 10/1/95; SLJ 10/95)

**6363** Eager, Edward. *Knight's Castle* (4–6). Illus. by N. M. Bodecker. 1989, Peter Smith $16.75 (0-8446-6232-1); Harcourt paper $6.00 (0-15-243105-5). 198pp. Several children are introduced by an old lead soldier into the fantastic world peopled by characters in Scott's *Ivanhoe.*

**6364** Eager, Edward. *Magic by the Lake* (4–6). Illus. by Katie T. Treherne and N. M. Bodecker. 1989, Harcourt paper $6.00 (0-15-250444-3). 190pp. Four children on vacation have to learn how to tame a magic lake to find the treasure there.

**6365** Eager, Edward. *Seven-Day Magic* (5–6). Illus. by Katie T. Treherne and N. M. Bodecker. 1989, Harcourt paper $6.00 (0-15-272916-X). 190pp. Magic enters the lives of 5 children through a magic wishing book from the library. Also use: *Half Magic* (1954); *Magic or Not?* (1984).

**6366** Eager, Edward. *The Well Wishers* (3–6). Illus. by N. M. Bodecker. 1990, Harcourt paper $6.00 (0-15-294994-1). 220pp. Six children encounter magic powers in this reissue of a 1960 book. Also use: *The Time Garden* (1990).

**6367** Enright, Elizabeth. *Zeee* (2–5). Illus. by Susan Gaber. 1993, Harcourt $15.95 (0-15-299958-2). 48pp. A tiny fairy no larger than a bumblebee finds a permanent home in a child's dollhouse. (Rev: BL 6/1–15/93; SLJ 6/93)

**6368** Ephron, Delia. *The Girl Who Changed the World* (3–6). 1993, Ticknor $13.95 (0-395-66139-0). 160pp. Tired of being bullied by her older brother, Violet rebels and organizes other sibling victims to do the same. (Rev: BCCB 10/93; BL 11/15/93; SLJ 11/93)

**6369** Estes, Eleanor. *The Witch Family* (3–6). Illus. by Edward Ardizzone. 1990, Harcourt paper $7.00

319

(0-15-298572-7). 223pp. Amusing tale of 2 little girls, some fanciful witches, and a bumblebee.

**6370** Farmer, Nancy. *The Warm Place* (4–7). 1995, Orchard LB $16.99 (0-531-08738-7). 160pp. In this fantasy, the giraffe Ruva finds her way back to Africa from a zoo near San Francisco. (Rev: BCCB 5/95; BL 4/1/95; HB 9–10/95; SLJ 3/95)

**6371** Fawcett, Melissa Jayne, and Joseph Bruchac. *Makiawisug: The Gift of the Little People* (3–5). Illus. by David Wagner. 1997, Little People $19.95 (0-9656933-2-5). 28pp. The story of the antics of the American Indian "little people," the Makiawisug. (Rev: BL 9/15/97)

**6372** Field, Rachel. *Hitty: Her First Hundred Years* (4–6). Illus. by Dorothy P. Lathrop. 1969, Macmillan $16.00 (0-02-734840-7); Dell paper $4.50 (0-440-40337-5). 220pp. America 100 years ago seen through the adventures of a wooden doll. A reissue of the 1930 Newbery Award winner.

**6373** Fienberg, Anna. *Ariel, Zed and the Secret of Life* (4–7). Illus. 1994, Allen & Unwin paper $5.95 (1-86373-276-4). 184pp. Ariel and Zed are sent to an island inhabited by literary characters like Sleeping Beauty and Ali Baba. (Rev: BL 7/94; SLJ 6/94)

**6374** Fleischman, Sid. *The Midnight Horse* (3–6). Illus. by Peter Sis. 1990, Greenwillow $16.00 (0-688-09441-4). 84pp. An orphan boy named Touch, accompanied by a friendly ghost, is the center of this 19th-century tale. (Rev: BCCB 12/90; BL 8/90; HB 11–12/90; SLJ 9/90)

**6375** Fleischman, Sid. *The 13th Floor: A Ghost Story* (4–6). Illus. 1995, Greenwillow $15.00 (0-688-14216-8). 144pp. When a ghost who lived in the 17th century asks for his help, Bud obligingly travels back in time. (Rev: BL 10/1/95; HB 11–12/95; SLJ 10/95)

**6376** Fleming, Ian. *Chitty Chitty Bang Bang* (4–6). Illus. by John Burningham. 1964, Amereon LB $19.95 (0-88411-983-1). 159pp. Chitty Chitty Bang Bang, a magical racing car, flies, floats, and has a real talent for getting the Pott family in and out of trouble.

**6377** Fletcher, Susan. *Flight of the Dragon Kyn* (5–7). 1993, Atheneum $17.00 (0-689-31880-4). 224pp. A girl with a special talent to call down birds uses it to attract dragons for the king and his hunters. (Rev: BL 1/15/94; SLJ 11/93)

**6378** Fletcher, Susan. *Sign of the Dove* (5–7). 1996, Simon & Schuster $17.00 (0-689-80460-1). 214pp. Lyf tries to save some dragons from the evil queen, who wants to cut out their hearts. A sequel to *Dragon's Milk* (1989). (Rev: BL 5/1/96; HB 9–10/96; SLJ 5/96)

**6379** Foster, Elizabeth. *Gigi: The Story of a Merry-Go-Round Horse* (3–6). Illus. by Ilse Bischoff. 1983, North Atlantic paper $9.95 (0-913028-55-X). 124pp.

The beloved fantasy now reissued after many years. A sequel is: *Gigi in America: The Further Adventures of a Merry-Go-Round Horse* (1983).

**6380** Fremont, Eleanor. *Tales from the Crypt* (5–7). Illus. 1991, Random paper $2.99 (0-679-81799-9). 96pp. Old blood-and-guts standbys in smooth adaptations. (Rev: BL 9/1/91)

**6381** French, Jackie. *Somewhere Around the Corner* (5–7). 1995, Holt $14.95 (0-8050-3889-2). 230pp. Barbara time-travels to Australia in the 1930s and is adopted by a caring but very poor family. (Rev: BCCB 6/95; BL 5/15/95; HB 9–10/95; SLJ 7/95)

**6382** French, Vivian. *Under the Moon* (3–5). Illus. by Chris Fisher. 1994, Candlewick $14.95 (1-56402-330-3). 96pp. Three stories (one based on a folktale) that tell about fantastic beings and present timeless themes. (Rev: BL 3/15/94; SLJ 6/94)

**6383** Fromental, Jean-Luc. *Broadway Chicken* (5–8). Trans. by Suzi Baker. Illus. by Miles Hyman. 1995, Hyperion LB $15.49 (0-7868-2048-9). 40pp. After a leg operation, Charlie, the famous dancing chicken, finds that he will never dance again. (Rev: BL 12/15/95; SLJ 2/96)

**6384** Gale, David, ed. *Don't Give Up the Ghost: The Delacorte Book of Original Ghost Stories* (4–7). 1995, Bantam paper $3.99 (0-440-41098-3). 144pp. Several best writers of children's books have contributed to this collection of 12 modern ghost yarns. (Rev: BL 8/93)

**6385** Garden, Nancy. *Fours Crossing* (5–8). 1981, Farrar $15.00 (0-374-32451-4). 199pp. Melissa and new friend Jed think that their town and its inhabitants are under a spell. A sequel is: *Watersmeet* (1983).

**6386** Garden, Nancy. *Mystery of the Secret Marks* (5–8). 1989, Farrar $12.95 (0-374-35021-3). 240pp. A poltergeist gets vengeful at boarding school. (Rev: BL 12/15/89; SLJ 10/89)

**6387** Garland, Sherry. *Cabin 102* (5–8). 1995, Harcourt $11.00 (0-15-200663-X); paper $5.00 (0-15-200662-1). 224pp. On a cruise ship with his family, Dusty encounters a mysterious girl from the extinct Taino tribe. (Rev: BL 11/15/95; SLJ 12/95)

**6388** Gerstein, Mordicai. *The Giant* (3–5). Illus. 1995, Hyperion LB $14.49 (0-7868-2104-3). 40pp. When 3 children rebuff a giant's attempts to become friends with them, later that night they hear him sobbing. (Rev: BL 10/15/95; SLJ 11/95)

**6389** Gibbons, Faye. *Hook Moon Night: Spooky Stories from the Georgia Mountains* (3–6). Illus. 1997, Morrow $15.00 (0-688-14504-3). 128pp. In his Georgia home, Grandpa tells ghost stories, including one in which a sick woman is buried alive by her son-in-law. (Rev: BL 11/1/97; SLJ 10/97)

**6390** Godden, Rumer. *Four Dolls* (3–6). Illus. by Pauline Baynes. 1992, Lightyear LB $21.95 (0-899-68269-3); Dell paper $4.95 (0-440-42568-9). 144pp. Four stories that had previously been published in the 1950s about dolls.

**6391** Gogol, Nikolai. *The Nose* (3–8). Illus. by Gennady Spirin. 1993, Godine $17.95 (0-87923-963-8). In this novel of the absurd set in St. Petersburg, Kovaliov finds that his nose has disappeared. (Rev: SLJ 8/93)

**6392** Goldsmith, Howard. *The Twiddle Twins' Haunted House* (2–3). Illus. 1997, Mondo paper $4.50 (1-57255-222-0). 40pp. Hippo twins suspect a ghost when they are awakened one night by a tapping sound. Also use *Twiddle Twins' Music Box Mystery* (1997). (Rev: BL 2/1/98)

**6393** Gollub, Matthew. *The Twenty-Five Mixtec Cats* (4–6). Illus. by Leovigildo Martinez. 1993, Morrow LB $15.93 (0-688-11640-X). 32pp. Roughly based on a Mexican folktale, this is the amusing story of a healer in an Oaxacan village who returns from market with 25 cats. (Rev: BL 4/1/93; SLJ 6/93)

**6394** Goode, Diane. *Diane Goode's Book of Scary Stories and Songs* (3–6). Illus. 1994, Dutton paper $15.99 (0-525-45175-7). 64pp. This collection of eerie folktales also includes stories, poems, and songs. (Rev: BL 10/1/94; SLJ 9/94*)

**6395** Gormley, Beatrice. *Best Friend Insurance* (5–7). Illus. by Emily Arnold McCully. 1988, Avon paper $2.50 (0-380-69854-4). 160pp. Maureen finds that her mother has been transformed into a new friend named Kitty.

**6396** Gormley, Beatrice. *Fifth Grade Magic* (4–6). Illus. by Emily Arnold McCully. 1982, Avon paper $3.50 (0-380-67439-4). 128pp. Gretchen uses the help of an inept fairy godmother to get the lead in the school play.

**6397** Gormley, Beatrice. *The Ghastly Glasses* (4–6). Illus. by Emily Arnold McCully. 1985, Dutton paper $12.95 (0-525-44215-4). 128pp. Andrea learns that wishes can sometimes backfire when she gets a pair of remarkable glasses that allow her to manipulate people. (Rev: BCCB 3/86; BL 9/15/85; SLJ 1/86)

**6398** Gormley, Beatrice. *Mail-Order Wings* (3–5). Illus. by Emily Arnold McCully. 1984, Avon paper $2.95 (0-380-67421-1). 164pp. Andrea finds her Wonda-Wings are gradually transforming her into a bird.

**6399** Gormley, Beatrice. *More Fifth Grade Magic* (3–5). Illus. by Emily Arnold McCully. 1990, Avon paper $3.50 (0-380-70883-3). 128pp. Amy uses the magical powers she finds in a calendar to grant her wishes. (Rev: BL 8/89)

**6400** Gorog, Judith. *In a Messy, Messy Room* (4–6). Illus. by Kimberly B. Root. 1990, Putnam $14.95 (0-399-22218-9). 48pp. Eerie tales for the younger set. (Rev: BCCB 6/90; BL 6/1/90; SLJ 7/90)

**6401** Grahame, Kenneth. *The River Bank: And Other Stories from The Wind in the Willows* (2–4). Illus. by Inga Moore. 1996, Candlewick $19.99 (0-7636-0059-8). 93pp. A charming retelling of 5 stories from *The Wind in the Willows*, with rich-toned illustrations. (Rev: SLJ 1/97)

**6402** Grahame, Kenneth. *The Wind in the Willows* (4–7). Illus. by E. H. Shepard. 1983, Macmillan $19.00 (0-684-17957-1). 256pp. The classic that introduced Mole, Ratty, and Mr. Toad. Two of many other editions are: illus. by Michael Hague (1980, Henry Holt); illus. by John Burningham (1983, Viking).

**6403** Grahame, Kenneth. *The Wind in the Willows* (4–6). Illus. by Patrick Benson. 1995, St. Martin's $18.95 (0-312-13624-2). 272pp. A brilliantly illustrated edition of this classic, with pictures that rival the work of Ernest H. Shepard. (Rev: BL 2/1/96)

**6404** Gray, Luli. *Falcon's Egg* (3–5). 1995, Houghton $13.95 (0-395-71128-2). 144pp. A young girl hatches an egg she finds in Central Park and, as a result, is transported to a world of magical creatures. (Rev: BCCB 10/95; BL 9/15/95; SLJ 9/95*)

**6405** Greenberg, Martin H., et al., ed. *Great Writers and Kids Write Spooky Stories* (5–8). Illus. by Gahan Wilson. 1995, Random LB $18.99 (0-679-97662-0). 224pp. An anthology of 13 original horror stories by prominent writers who were given commissions for this collection. (Rev: SLJ 2/96)

**6406** Greenburg, Dan. *Dr. Jekyll, Orthodontist* (3–4). Illus. by Jack E. Davis. Series: The Zack Files. 1997, Grosset LB $11.99 (0-448-41584-4); paper $3.95 (0-448-41338-8). 57pp. Zack drinks some mouthwash at his dentist's office, and his teeth begin to grow. Also use *I'm Out of My Body . . . Please Leave a Message* (1996). (Rev: SLJ 3/97)

**6407** Greenburg, Dan. *A Ghost Named Wanda* (3–5). Illus. by Jack E. Davis. Series: Zack Files. 1996, Grosset paper $3.95 (0-448-41261-6). 59pp. The story of Zack, a 10-year-old with the knack of getting into unusual situations. Also use *Zap! I'm a Mind Reader* (1996). (Rev: SLJ 2/97)

**6408** Greenburg, Dan. *Great-Grandpa's in the Litter Box* (3–5). Illus. 1996, Putnam paper $3.95 (0-448-41260-8). 61pp. Zack adopts a cat that not only talks but also claims to be a relative. Zack has further adventures in *Through the Medicine Cabinet* (1996). (Rev: BL 1/1–15/97; SLJ 2/97)

**6409** Greer, Gery, and Bob Ruddick. *Max and Me and the Time Machine* (5–8). 1983, HarperCollins paper $4.95 (0-06-440222-3). 140pp. Steve and Max travel back in time to England during the Middle Ages.

**6410** Gregory, Valiska. *When Stories Fell Like Shooting Stars* (3–6). Illus. by Stefano Vitale. 1996, Simon & Schuster paper $16.00 (0-689-80012-6). 32pp. Two allegorical tales involving animals with supernatural powers. (Rev: BCCB 2/97; BL 1/1–15/97; SLJ 10/96)

**6411** Griffin, Peni R. *A Dig in Time* (4–7). 1991, Macmillan $14.95 (0-689-50525-6). 192pp. Twelve-year-old Nan and her brother spend the summer in San Antonio with their grandmother and find they can travel back in time to witness events in their family's history. (Rev: BCCB 10/91; BL 6/15/91; SLJ 6/91)

**6412** Griffin, Peni R. *Margo's House* (3–6). 1996, Simon & Schuster $16.00 (0-689-80944-1). 122pp. A girl and her father project themselves into the bodies of 2 dolls. (Rev: BCCB 11/96; BL 9/1/96; SLJ 10/96)

**6413** Griffith, Helen V. *Caitlin's Holiday* (3–5). Illus. by Susan C. Lamb. 1990, Greenwillow $12.95 (0-688-09470-8). 96pp. Caitlin's new doll talks, walks, and is just plain mean. (Rev: BCCB 10/90; BL 8/90; SLJ 10/90*)

**6414** Griffith, Helen V. *Dinosaur Habitat* (4–6). Illus. 1998, Greenwillow $15.00 (0-688-15324-0). 112pp. Through a freak accident, Nathan and his young brother land in a dinosaur terrarium where all the beasts suddenly come to life. (Rev: BL 3/15/98)

**6415** Grindley, Sally. *Breaking the Spell: Tales of Enchantment* (3–5). Illus. 1997, Kingfisher $17.95 (0-7534-5002-X). 80pp. Seven original folk and fairy tales set in exotic locales and written by both established and new writers. (Rev: BL 1/1–15/98; SLJ 12/97)

**6416** Gutman, Dan. *Honus and Me: A Baseball Card Adventure* (4–7). 1997, Avon paper $3.99 (0-380-78878-0). 160pp. Young Joe Stoshack finds a magical baseball card that allows him to travel through time and participate in the 1909 World Series. (Rev: BL 4/15/97; SLJ 6/97)

**6417** Haddix, Margaret P. *Running Out of Time* (4–7). 1995, Simon & Schuster paper $16.00 (0-689-80084-3). 185pp. Living in a historical site where the time is the 1840s, Jessie escapes into the present in this fantasy. (Rev: BCCB 11/95; BL 10/1/95; SLJ 10/95*)

**6418** Hague, Michael, ed. *The Book of Dragons* (4–7). Illus. by Michael Hague. 1995, Morrow $20.00 (0-688-10879-2). 160pp. Seventeen classic tales about dragons by such authors as Tolkien and Kenneth Grahame are included in this interesting anthology. (Rev: BL 10/1/95; SLJ 10/95)

**6419** Hahn, Mary D. *The Doll in the Garden: A Ghost Story* (4–6). Illus. 1989, Houghton $15.00 (0-89919-848-1). 160pp. Ten-year-old Ashley and her mother try to start a new life in a house owned by a grouchy octogenarian. (Rev: BCCB 3/89; BL 3/15/89; SLJ 5/89)

**6420** Hahn, Mary D. *Time for Andrew: A Ghost Story* (4–6). 1994, Clarion $15.00 (0-395-66556-6). 167pp. Drew changes places with his look-alike distant relative and travels back to 1910. (Rev: BCCB 4/94; BL 4/1/94; SLJ 5/94)

**6421** Hahn, Mary D. *Wait Till Helen Comes: A Ghost Story* (5–7). 1986, Houghton $15.00 (0-89919-453-2); Avon paper $4.50 (0-380-70442-0). 192pp. Things go from bad to worse for Molly and Michael and their stepsister Heather when Heather becomes involved in a frightening relationship with the ghost of a dead child. (Rev: BCCB 10/86; BL 9/1/86; SLJ 10/86)

**6422** Hall, Elizabeth, and Scott O'Dell. *Venus Among the Fishes* (4–6). 1995, Houghton $15.95 (0-395-70561-4). 143pp. A dolphin who is trained to rescue divers in trouble falls in love with a human. (Rev: BCCB 4/95; BL 4/15/95; SLJ 6/95)

**6423** Hamilton, Virginia. *The All Jahdu Storybook* (3–5). Illus. by Barry Moser. 1991, Harcourt $19.95 (0-15-239498-2). 108pp. A retelling of Jahdu stories about a shape-changing trickster. (Rev: BCCB 1/92; BL 12/1/91; SLJ 1/92)

**6424** Hamilton, Virginia. *Jaguarundi* (2–5). Illus. by Floyd Cooper. 1994, Scholastic $14.95 (0-590-47366-2). 40pp. A wildcat (jaguarundi) persuades a coati to flee across the river to find a new home. (Rev: BCCB 2/95; BL 12/15/94; SLJ 12/94)

**6425** Hansen, Brooks. *Caesar's Antlers* (5–7). Illus. 1997, Farrar $16.00 (0-374-31024-6). 224pp. In this animal fantasy, Caesar the reindeer and his friend Bette the sparrow and her 2 offspring set out to contact some human friends to get help for the winter. (Rev: BL 10/1/97; SLJ 11/97)

**6426** Hansen, Ron. *The Shadowmaker* (4–6). Illus. by Margot Tomes. 1987, HarperCollins paper $4.50 (0-06-440287-8). 80pp. Drizzle and her brother Soot save the day when they outwit Shadowmaker, who is selling the wrong shadows to everyone. (Rev: BL 5/15/87; HB 9–10/87; SLJ 8/87)

**6427** Haseley, Dennis. *Ghost Catcher* (3–5). Illus. by Lloyd Bloom. 1991, HarperCollins $15.95 (0-06-022244-1). 40pp. A man who can get close to ghosts without turning into one needs the help of his friends when he visits the shadow village. (Rev: BL 10/1/91; SLJ 11/91)

**6428** Hatrick, Gloria. *Masks* (4–6). 1996, Orchard LB $16.99 (0-531-08864-2). 128pp. In this fantasy, Pete uses animal masks to communicate with his paralyzed older brother. (Rev: BCCB 3/96; BL 4/15/96; SLJ 5/96)

**6429** Hayes, Sarah. *Crumbling Castle* (3–6). Illus. by Helen Craig. 1992, Candlewick $13.95 (1-56402-108-4). 80pp. A wizard moves into a castle that's been empty for 100 years, but it's his talkative crow who solves the mystery of why it's crumbling. (Rev: BL 12/15/92; SLJ 10/92)

**6430** Heidenreich, Elke. *Nero Corleone: A Cat's Story* (3–5). Trans. by Doris Orgel. Illus. 1997, Viking paper $15.99 (0-670-87395-0). 96pp. Don Nero is an amazing cat that dominates everybody and every situation in his home. (Rev: BL 9/15/97; SLJ 12/97)

**6431** Helprin, Mark. *A City in Winter* (5–8). Illus. by Chris Van Allsburg. 1996, Viking paper $22.50 (0-670-86843-4). 144pp. In this fantasy, a 10-year-old girl tries to fight the power of an evil usurper. (Rev: BCCB 2/97; BL 10/15/96; SLJ 11/96)

**6432** Helprin, Mark. *The Veil of Snows* (4–7). Illus. by Chris Van Allsburg. 1997, Viking paper $24.00 (0-670-87491-4). 128pp. This fantasy is also a political fable in which a reactionary queen tries to turn back the clock. (Rev: BL 11/15/97; SLJ 11/97)

**6433** Hill, Susan, ed. *The Random House Book of Ghost Stories* (4–6). Illus. by Angela Barrett. 1991, Random LB $23.99 (0-679-91234-7). 223pp. First published in Great Britain, this is an outstanding collection of gently haunting stories. (Rev: BCCB 12/91; BL 12/1/91)

**6434** Hiser, Constance. *The Missing Doll* (4–6). Illus. by Marcy Ramsey. 1993, Holiday $13.95 (0-8234-1046-3). 72pp. A girl's talking doll directs her to where her friend Julie is in danger. (Rev: BCCB 12/93; BL 11/15/93; SLJ 2/94)

**6435** Hiser, Constance. *Night of the Werepoodle* (2–4). Illus. 1994, Holiday $14.95 (0-8234-1116-8). 122pp. After being bitten by a poodle, Jonathan turns into a "werepoodle" and must find some wolfbane to become a boy again. (Rev: BL 6/1–15/94; SLJ 6/94)

**6436** Hoban, Russell. *The Trokeville Way* (5–8). 1996, Knopf $17.00 (0-679-88148-4). 128pp. A magical jigsaw puzzle leads Nick into a strange new universe. (Rev: BCCB 2/97; BL 11/15/96; SLJ 12/96)

**6437** Hodges, Margaret, ed. *Comus* (4–6). Illus. by Trina S. Hyman. 1996, Holiday LB $16.95 (0-8234-1146-X). 32pp. In this retelling of a work by John Milton, Alice resists the enchantment of the evil magician Comus. (Rev: BCCB 4/96; BL 3/1/96; SLJ 3/96)

**6438** Hodges, Margaret. *Gulliver in Lilliput: From Gulliver's Travels by Jonathan Swift* (4–7). Illus. by Kimberly B. Root. 1995, Holiday LB $16.95 (0-8234-1147-8). 32pp. The story of Gulliver in the land of the little people is retold with bright, detailed illus-

trations. (Rev: BCCB 6/95; BL 4/15/95; HB 7–8/95; SLJ 6/95*)

**6439** Hoffman, Mary. *The Four-Legged Ghosts* (3–5). Illus. by Laura L. Seeley. 1993, Dial LB $13.89 (0-8037-1645-1); Puffin paper $3.99 (0-14-037601-1). 96pp. Alex and his sister have a pet mouse that can conjure up the ghosts of animals that lived years ago. (Rev: BCCB 1/94; BL 9/1/93; SLJ 8/93)

**6440** Howe, James. *Morgan's Zoo* (4–6). Illus. by Leslie Morrill. 1984, Macmillan $16.00 (0-689-31046-3); Avon paper $3.99 (0-380-69994-X). 192pp. Morgan, a set of twins, and a number of animals band together to save a zoo.

**6441** Hughes, Carol. *Toots and the Upside-Down House* (4–6). Illus. 1997, Random LB $18.99 (0-679-98653-7). 141pp. In this fantasy, Toots is captured by fairies and reduced to their size. (Rev: BL 9/1/97; SLJ 10/97)

**6442** Hughes, Dean. *Nutty's Ghost* (5–7). 1993, Macmillan $13.95 (0-689-31743-3). 136pp. Nutty finds a ghost is sabotaging the completion of the movie in which he is appearing. (Rev: SLJ 5/93)

**6443** Hughes, Shirley. *Enchantment in the Garden* (3–5). Illus. 1997, Lothrop $18.00 (0-688-14597-3). 64pp. In this fantasy, a rich little girl in Italy during the 1920s brings to life the statue of a sea god's son. (Rev: BCCB 7–8/97; BL 5/15/97; HB 3–4/97; SLJ 5/97)

**6444** Hunter, Mollie. *The Mermaid Summer* (5–8). 1988, HarperCollins LB $14.89 (0-06-022628-5); paper $4.95 (0-06-440344-0). 160pp. Eric Anderson leaves his Scottish fishing village after his boat is dashed to pieces on the rocks, but he sends wonderful gifts back to his grandchildren. (Rev: BCCB 5/88; BL 6/1/88; SLJ 6–7/88)

**6445** Hunter, Mollie. *The Wicked One* (5–7). 1995, Peter Smith $18.00 (0-8446-6817-6). 128pp. A fantasy set in the Scottish Highlands in which a forester invokes the ire of a supernatural power.

**6446** Hurmence, Belinda. *A Girl Called Boy* (5–8). 1982, Houghton paper $4.70 (0-395-55698-8). 180pp. A contemporary black girl travels back to the time of slavery.

**6447** Hutchins, Hazel. *The Prince of Tarn* (3–5). Illus. 1997, Annick $14.95 (1-55037-439-7). 143pp. The spoiled prince created by his author mother in one of her fantasies comes to life and takes Fred to his kingdom. (Rev: BL 2/15/98; SLJ 2/98)

**6448** Hutchins, Hazel. *The Three and Many Wishes of Jason Reid* (2–4). Illus. by Julie Tennent. 1990, Puffin paper $3.99 (0-14-032178-0). 96pp. Eleven-year-old Jason stuns the leprechaun when his third magic wish is for "three more wishes." (Rev: BCCB 6/88; BL 8/88)

**6449** Ibbotson, Eva. *The Secret of Platform 13* (4–7). Illus. 1998, Dutton paper $15.99 (0-525-45929-4). 224pp. In this fantasy, 3 unusual creatures — a wizard, an ogre, and a hag — set out to rescue from their enchanted kingdom a prince who has been kidnapped. (Rev: BL 2/15/98; SLJ 3/98*)

**6450** Ingram, Scott. *More Scary Stories for Stormy Nights* (4–6). Illus. by Eric Angeloch. 1996, Lowell House paper $5.95 (1-56565-381-5). 95pp. The supernatural and science fiction are featured in these scary tales, all of which take place during violent weather. (Rev: SLJ 1/97)

**6451** Irving, Washington. *The Headless Horseman* (3–5). Retold by Tim Chadwick. Illus. by Emma Harding. 1995, Holt $15.95 (0-8050-3584-2). 28pp. A simple version of this classic story with powerful, brooding illustrations. (Rev: BL 12/1/95; SLJ 11/95)

**6452** Irving, Washington. *The Legend of Sleepy Hollow* (3–5). Retold by Robert D. San Souci. Illus. by Daniel San Souci. 1995, Bantam paper $5.99 (0-440-41074-6). 32pp. A retelling that retains the atmosphere and sense of character. (Rev: BL 1/15/87; SLJ 12/86)

**6453** Irving, Washington. *The Legend of Sleepy Hollow: Found Among the Papers of the Late Diedrich Knickerbocker* (5–8). Illus. by Michael Garland. 1992, Boyds Mills LB $15.95 (1-56397-027-9). 62pp. A lavishly illustrated version of the original text of this classic. (Rev: BL 11/1/92; SLJ 11/92)

**6454** Irving, Washington. *Rip Van Winkle* (3–5). Illus. by Thomas Locker. 1988, Dial LB $15.89 (0-8037-0521-2). 32pp. A formal version of the old classic with full-color paintings. (Rev: BL 10/15/88; SLJ 10/88)

**6455** Irving, Washington. *Rip Van Winkle* (5–7). Illus. by N. C. Wyeth. 1987, Morrow $22.00 (0-688-07459-6). 110pp. Distinguished illustrations highlight this 1921 edition. (Rev: BL 9/1/87)

**6456** Irving, Washington. *Rip Van Winkle* (3–5). Adapted and illus. by Rick Meyerowitz. 1995, Rabbit Ears $19.95 (0-689-80193-9). A delightful retelling of this classic tale, with illustrations of many historical occurrences of the era. (Rev: SLJ 12/95)

**6457** Irving, Washington. *Rip Van Winkle and the Legend of Sleepy Hollow* (5–7). Illus. by Felix O. Darley. 1980, Sleepy Hollow $19.95 (0-912882-42-5). 152pp. A handsome edition of these 2 classics.

**6458** Jacques, Brian. *The Bellmaker* (5–7). Illus. 1995, Putnam $21.95 (0-399-22805-5). 352pp. This seventh tale in the Redwall series of animal fantasies features Mariel, a courageous, outspoken mouse. (Rev: BCCB 4/95; BL 4/1/95; HB 5–6/95; SLJ 8/95)

**6459** Jacques, Brian. *The Great Redwall Feast* (4–6). Illus. by Christopher Denise. 1996, Putnam $18.95 (0-399-22707-5). 64pp. In this illustrated storybook,

the creatures of Redwall prepare a magnificent feast. (Rev: BL 10/15/96; SLJ 12/96)

**6460** Jacques, Brian. *The Long Patrol* (5–8). Illus. 1998, Putnam $21.99 (0-399-23165-X). 368pp. In this tenth Redwall adventure, the villainous Rapscallions decide to attack the peaceful Abbey of Redwall. (Rev: BL 12/15/97; SLJ 1/98)

**6461** Jacques, Brian. *Mariel of Redwall* (5–7). Illus. by Gary Chalk. 1992, Putnam $21.99 (0-399-22144-1). 400pp. Fourth in the saga of the animals of Redwall Abbey, this story tells how the great Joseph Bell is brought to the abbey. (Rev: BCCB 3/92; BL 1/15/92*; HB 9–10/92; SLJ 3/92)

**6462** Jacques, Brian. *Martin the Warrior* (5–7). Illus. by Gary Chalk. Series: Redwall. 1994, Putnam $21.99 (0-399-22670-2). 375pp. This Redwall book tells how the mouse Martin the Warrior became the bold, courageous fighter that he is. (Rev: BCCB 1/94; BL 3/1/94; HB 9–10/94; SLJ 1/94)

**6463** Jacques, Brian. *Mattimeo* (4–6). 1990, Putnam $21.99 (0-399-21741-X). 448pp. The son of Matthias, the hero of Redwall, overcomes the treachery of Slager, a sly fox. (Rev: BCCB 4/90; BL 4/15/90; SLJ 9/90)

**6464** Jacques, Brian. *Mossflower* (5–7). Illus. by Gary Chalk. 1988, Putnam $21.99 (0-399-21549-2); Avon paper $5.99 (0-380-70828-0). 432pp. How a brave and resourceful mouse took power from the evil wildcat. (Rev: BCCB 12/88; BL 11/1/88; SLJ 11/88)

**6465** Jacques, Brian. *Outcast of Redwall* (5–7). Illus. by Allan Curless. 1996, Putnam $21.99 (0-399-22914-0). 360pp. This episode in the Redwall saga involves the badger Sunflash the Mace and his enemy, the ferret Swartt Sixclaw. (Rev: BCCB 3/96; BL 3/1/96; SLJ 5/96)

**6466** Jacques, Brian. *The Pearls of Lutra* (5–8). 1997, Putnam $19.95 (0-399-22946-9). 408pp. The evil marten Mad Eyes threatens the peaceful Redwall Abbey in this book, the ninth in the series. (Rev: BCCB 4/97; BL 2/15/97; SLJ 3/97*)

**6467** Jacques, Brian. *Redwall* (5–7). Illus. 1987, Putnam $21.95 (0-399-21424-0); Avon paper $5.99 (0-380-70827-2). 352pp. The peaceful ways of Redwall Abbey, long a refuge for the mice, change as Cluny the Scourge, a one-eyed rat, takes over. (Rev: BCCB 7–8/87; BL 6/1/87)

**6468** Jacques, Brian. *Salamandastron* (5–7). Illus. by Gary Chalk. 1993, Putnam $21.95 (0-399-21992-7). 400pp. Tales centered on the badgers and hares of the castle of Salamandastron near the sea. (Rev: BCCB 7–8/93; BL 3/15/93; HB 5–6/93; SLJ 3/93)

**6469** Jacques, Brian. *Seven Strange and Ghostly Tales* (4–7). 1991, Putnam $15.99 (0-399-22103-4); Avon paper $3.99 (0-380-71906-1). 137pp. Seven genuinely scary stories with touches of humor. (Rev: BCCB 12/91; BL 1/1/91*; HB 5–6/92; SLJ 12/91)

**6470** James, Mary. *Shoebag* (3–7). 1990, Scholastic $13.95 (0-590-43029-7); paper $3.50 (0-590-43030-0). 144pp. Shoebag, a cockroach named after his place of birth, turns into a boy. (Rev: BCCB 3/90; BL 4/15/90; SLJ 6/90*)

**6471** James, Mary. *Shoebag Returns* (3–6). 1996, Scholastic $15.95 (0-590-48711-6). 176pp. Shoebag, the cockroach that can become a boy, decides to help Suart, the only male in an all-girl school. (Rev: BCCB 2/97; BL 2/1/97; SLJ 2/97)

**6472** James, Mary. *The Shuteyes* (4–7). 1994, Scholastic paper $3.25 (0-590-45070-0). 176pp. Chester has some unusual experiences when he journeys to Alert, a land where no one sleeps. (Rev: SLJ 4/93)

**6473** Jane, Pamela. *Noelle of the Nutcracker* (3–5). Illus. by Jan Brett. 1997, Houghton $17.00 (0-395-39969-6); Bantam paper $3.99 (0-440-41418-0). 64pp. Ilyana wants Noelle the ballerina doll, but her rich arch rival Mary Jane is bound to get her. (Rev: BCCB 10/86; BL 9/15/86)

**6474** Jarrell, Randall. *The Bat-Poet* (3–6). Illus. by Maurice Sendak. 1997, HarperCollins $11.95 (0-06-205084-2); paper $4.95 (0-06-205905-X). 44pp. A little-known bat makes up poems during the day to recite to his fellows.

**6475** Jennings, Patrick. *Faith and the Electric Dogs* (3–6). Illus. 1996, Scholastic $15.95 (0-590-69768-4). 128pp. Unhappy in Mexico and longing for the United States, Faith gets some comfort from a very unusual dog. (Rev: BCCB 1/97; BL 12/1/96*; SLJ 12/96)

**6476** Jennings, Paul. *Uncanny! Even More Surprising Stories* (4–8). 1991, Viking paper $13.95 (0-670-84174-9). 144pp. In each of these 9 short stories, there is a strange event that catches the reader off guard. (Rev: SLJ 1/92)

**6477** Jennings, Paul. *Uncovered! Weird, Weird Stories* (5–8). 1996, Viking paper $14.99 (0-670-86856-6). 134pp. A collection of spooky stories, each of which changes an everyday occurrence into a thing of horror. (Rev: BL 4/15/96; SLJ 4/96)

**6478** Jennings, Paul. *Undone! More Mad Endings* (5–8). 1995, Viking paper $14.99 (0-670-86005-0). 112pp. Eight stories that embody the weird, macabre, and horrific. (Rev: BCCB 2/95; BL 1/1/95; SLJ 1/95)

**6479** Jennings, Paul. *Unmentionable!* (5–8). 1995, Puffin paper $3.99 (0-14-037399-3). 120pp. Nine short stories about the supernatural, guaranteed to produce shudders. (Rev: SLJ 3/93)

**6480** Jensen, Dorothea. *The Riddle of Penncroft Farm* (5–7). 1989, Harcourt $16.00 (0-15-200574-9). 192pp. Lars finds a ghost from the American Revo-

lution when his family moves to rural Pennsylvania near Valley Forge. (Rev: BCCB 11/89; BL 10/1/89; SLJ 10/89)

**6481** Jocelyn, Marthe. *Invisible Day* (3–5). Illus. 1997, Dutton paper $14.99 (0-525-45908-1). 128pp. In Manhattan, a young girl uses a magic makeup kit that makes her invisible to get the privacy she longs for. (Rev: BL 1/1–15/98; SLJ 3/98)

**6482** Johansen, Hanna. *Dinosaur with an Attitude* (4–6). Trans. by Elisabetta Maccari. Illus. 1994, RDR Bks. $12.95 (1-57143-018-0). 144pp. In this fantasy, a boy faces problems caused by a dinosaur that hatched from one of his Easter eggs. (Rev: BL 8/94; SLJ 8/94)

**6483** Johnson, Annabel. *I Am Leaper* (3–5). Illus. by Stella Ormai. 1992, Scholastic paper $2.99 (0-590-43399-7). 128pp. A talking kangaroo mouse leaves her burrow to warn humans that a monster is destroying the desert. (Rev: BL 11/15/90; SLJ 1/91)

**6484** Johnson, Charles. *Pieces of Eight* (5–7). Illus. by Jennie Anne Nelson. 1989, Discovery $9.95 (0-944770-00-2). 110pp. David and Mitchell rouse a sea captain's ghost and get to meet Blackbeard the pirate. (Rev: BL 3/15/89)

**6485** Johnson, Venice, ed. *Voices of the Dream: African-American Women Speak* (4–8). Illus. 1996, Chronicle $12.95 (0-8118-1113-1). 108pp. Quotes from a wide range of black female authors and illustrations by important artists are the highlights of this anthology. (Rev: BL 2/15/96) [081]

**6486** Johnston, Tony. *The Ghost of Nicholas Greebe* (1–5). Illus. by S. D. Schindler. 1996, Dial paper $14.89 (0-8037-1649-4). 32pp. Nicholas Greebe arises from his grave to recover one of his bones stolen by a dog. (Rev: BCCB 10/96; BL 7/96; HB 11–12/96; SLJ 9/96*)

**6487** Jones, Diana Wynne. *Charmed Life* (4–6). 1998, Morrow paper $5.95 (0-688-15546-4). 224pp. Gwendole tries to obtain supernatural powers from her mysterious guardian. A sequel is: *Witch Week* (1988).

**6488** Jones, Terry. *The Saga of Erik the Viking* (4–6). Illus. by Michael Foreman. 1993, Puffin paper $3.99 (0-14-032261-2). 192pp. Erik and comrades set sail to find the land where the sun goes at night.

**6489** Joyce, William. *George Shrinks* (4–6). Illus. by author. 1985, HarperCollins LB $14.89 (0-06-023071-1); paper $4.95 (0-06-443129-0). 32pp. George wakes up to find he is small and must learn to cope with some strange situations. (Rev: BCCB 12/85; BL 1/15/86; SLJ 10/85)

**6490** Juster, Norton. *The Phantom Tollbooth* (4–6). Illus. by Jules Feiffer. 1972, Knopf $19.95 (0-394-81500-9); paper $4.99 (0-394-82037-1). 256pp. When Milo receives a tollbooth as a gift, he finds that it admits him to a land where many adventures take place. A favorite fantasy.

**6491** Kalman, Maira. *Swami on Rye: Max in India* (4–8). Illus. 1995, Viking $14.99 (0-670-84646-0). 40pp. A sophisticated comic novel about a dog who goes to India to find the meaning of life. (Rev: BL 10/15/95; SLJ 11/95)

**6492** Kassem, Lou. *A Summer for Secrets* (5–7). 1989, Avon paper $2.95 (0-380-75759-1). 105pp. Laura's ability to communicate with animals causes complications. (Rev: BL 10/1/89)

**6493** Keefauver, John. *The Three-Day Traffic Jam* (3–6). 1992, Simon & Schuster paper $13.00 (0-671-75599-4). 89pp. In the near future, when traffic jams around Los Angeles can last for months, Henry gets caught in one with his father's new car. (Rev: SLJ 6/92)

**6494** Keillor, Garrison. *Cat, You Better Come Home* (3–6). Illus. by Steve Johnson and Lou Fancher. 1995, Viking paper $15.99 (0-670-85112-4). When her master won't serve her the gourmet cat food she wants, Puff leaves her comfortable home to seek the high life. (Rev: BCCB 6/95; SLJ 7/95)

**6495** Kempton, Kate. *The World Beyond the Waves: An Environmental Adventure* (5–7). Illus. 1995, Portunus $14.95 (0-9641330-6-7); paper $8.95 (0-9641330-1-6). 88pp. After being washed overboard during a violent storm, Sam visits a land where she meets ocean animals that have been misused by humans. (Rev: BL 4/15/95; SLJ 3/95)

**6496** Kendall, Carol. *The Gammage Cup* (4–7). Illus. by Erik Blegvad. 1990, Harcourt paper $6.00 (0-15-230575-0). 283pp. Fantasy of the Minnipins, a small people of the "land between the mountains."

**6497** Kennedy, Richard. *Amy's Eyes* (5–6). Illus. by Richard Egielski. 1985, HarperCollins $15.00 (0-06-023219-6). 448pp. Amy's doll, Captain, comes alive and runs away to sea. Before he returns, Amy herself changes into a doll, and the Captain takes her with him for a journey of high adventure. (Rev: BCCB 4/85; BL 5/1/85; SLJ 5/85)

**6498** Kennedy, X. J. *The Eagle as Wide as the World* (3–6). 1997, Simon & Schuster $16.00 (0-689-81157-8). 173pp. A young boy is kidnapped by giant honeybees and taken to April Fool Isle, home of Meadea, queen of the bees. (Rev: SLJ 12/97)

**6499** King-Smith, Dick. *Ace: The Very Important Pig* (4–6). Illus. by Lynette Hemmant. 1990, Crown LB $13.99 (0-517-57833-6). 134pp. Ace, born with an ace-of-clubs marking on his thigh, is a pig who understands human speech. (Rev: BCCB 12/90; BL 10/15/90; HB 9–10/90*; SLJ 11/90*)

**6500** King-Smith, Dick. *Babe: The Gallant Pig* (4–5). Illus. by Mary Rayner. 1988, Crown $15.00 (0-517-55556-5); Dell paper $2.50 (0-440-40420-7).

176pp. Babe is destined for the dinner table at Farmer Hogget's until Fly the sheepdog begins coaching her in sheepherding. (Rev: BL 8/85; HB 7–8/85; SLJ 8/85)

**6501** King-Smith, Dick. *Martin's Mice* (4–6). Illus. by Jez Alborough. 1988, Crown $13.00 (0-517-57113-7). 128pp. Believe it or not, Martin, a farm cat, wants mice for friends! (Rev: BL 2/1/89; HB 3–4/89; SLJ 1/89)

**6502** King-Smith, Dick. *A Mouse Called Wolf* (2–4). Illus. 1997, Crown $16.00 (0-517-70973-2). 98pp. Mary Mouse is convinced that her son, whom she has named Wolfgang Amadeus, is a musical genius. (Rev: BL 10/1/97; SLJ 12/97)

**6503** King-Smith, Dick. *Mr. Potter's Pet* (2–4). Illus. 1996, Hyperion LB $14.49 (0-7868-2146-9). 64pp. When Mr. Potter acquires a talking mynah bird, he doesn't realize the consequences. (Rev: BCCB 3/96; BL 4/1/96; SLJ 4/96)

**6504** King-Smith, Dick. *Pigs Might Fly* (3–5). Illus. by Mary Rayner. 1990, Puffin paper $4.99 (0-14-034537-X). 168pp. A pig named Daggie Dogfoot saves the day because he can swim.

**6505** King-Smith, Dick. *The School Mouse* (3–5). Illus. 1995, Hyperion LB $14.49 (0-7868-2029-2). 124pp. Flora's ability to read saves her illiterate mouse parents from eating poison that has been placed around the school where they live. (Rev: BCCB 1/96; BL 10/15/95; SLJ 12/95*)

**6506** King-Smith, Dick. *Three Terrible Trins* (3–5). Illus. by Mark Teague. 1994, Crown LB $16.99 (0-517-59829-9). 128pp. Mrs. Gray, a mouse who lost her husband to a cat, swears that her 3 children will avenge his death. (Rev: BCCB 2/95; BL 11/15/94*; HB 11–12/94; SLJ 11/94*)

**6507** Kinsey-Warnock, Natalie. *As Long As There Are Mountains* (5–8). 1997, Dutton paper $14.99 (0-525-65236-1). 144pp. When her father is injured, Iris, age 13, wants to retain the family farm, but her older brother wants to sell it. (Rev: BL 8/97; SLJ 8/97*)

**6508** Kipling, Rudyard. *The Beginning of the Armadillos* (K–6). Illus. by John A. Rowe. Series: Michael Neugebauer Books. 1995, North-South LB $15.88 (1-55858-483-8). In this *Just-So* story, a hedgehog and a tortoise meld their characteristics to produce a new animal, the armadillo. (Rev: SLJ 1/96)

**6509** Kipling, Rudyard. *Rikki-Tikki-Tavi* (3–5). Illus. by Jerry Pinkney. 1997, Morrow LB $15.93 (0-688-14321-0). 40pp. In this classic tale, a mongoose repays a debt of kindness after he has been saved from drowning. (Rev: BL 9/1/97*; SLJ 8/97*)

**6510** Kline, Suzy. *Horrible Harry and the Purple People* (2–4). Illus. by Frank Remkiewicz. 1997, Viking paper $11.99 (0-670-87035-8). 64pp. Harry maintains that there are invisible purple people in the classroom and plans to invite one to a class tea party to prove it. (Rev: SLJ 9/97)

**6511** Koller, Jackie F. *Dragon Quest* (3–5). Illus. 1997, Pocket paper $3.50 (0-671-00193-0). 87pp. Darek's jealousy leads to a dragon hunt in this sequel to *The Dragonling* (1991) and *A Dragon in the Family* (1993). (Rev: BL 3/1/97)

**6512** Koller, Jackie F. *The Dragonling* (2–4). Illus. by Judith Mitchell. 1995, Pocket paper $3.99 (0-671-86790-3). 64pp. Darek befriends a young dragon that has been orphaned. (Rev: BL 1/1/91; SLJ 2/91)

**6513** Koller, Jackie F. *If I Had One Wish . . .* (5–8). 1991, Little, Brown $14.95 (0-316-50150-6). 161pp. Alex wishes that his pesky young brother had never been born; to his amazement, his wish is granted. (Rev: BCCB 12/91; SLJ 11/91)

**6514** Kortum, Jeanie. *Ghost Vision* (5–8). Illus. by Dugald Stermer. n.d., Scholastic paper $3.50 (0-614-19197-1). 160pp. A Greenland Eskimo realizes that his son has special mystical powers.

**6515** Kraan, Hanna. *Tales of the Wicked Witch* (3–5). Illus. by Annemarie van Haeringen. 1995, Front Street $13.95 (1-886910-04-9). 128pp. Fourteen short stories about several forest creatures who have problems with the resident witch. (Rev: BL 1/1–15/96; SLJ 1/96)

**6516** Kraan, Hanna. *The Wicked Witch Is at It Again* (3–5). Trans. by Wanda Boeke. Illus. 1997, Front Street $14.95 (1-886910-18-9). 128pp. Fourteen brief stories about the relationship between a wicked witch and the forest animals that live nearby. (Rev: BL 9/15/97; SLJ 7/97*)

**6517** Langton, Jane. *The Fledgling* (5–7). 1980, HarperCollins LB $14.89 (0-06-023679-5); paper $4.95 (0-06-440121-9). 192pp. A young girl learns to fly with her Goose Prince. A sequel is: *The Fragile Flag* (1984). Also use: *The Diamond in the Window* (1962).

**6518** Lansky, Bruce, ed. *Newfangled Fairy Tales, Book 1* (3–5). 1998, Meadowbrook Pr. LB $3.95 (0-671-57704-2). 110pp. These fractured fairy tales involve such characters as a backpacking Sleeping Beauty and King Midas as a workaholic banker. (Rev: BL 3/1/98)

**6519** Lasky, Kathryn. *Shadows in the Water: A Starbuck Family Adventure* (4–6). 1992, Harcourt $16.95 (0-15-273533-X); paper $8.00 (0-15-273534-8). 192pp. The Starbucks in a new adventure, this time investigating toxic waste dumping in the Florida Keys. (Rev: BL 1/15/93; SLJ 1/93)

**6520** Lassig, Jurgen. *Spiny* (2–4). Trans. by J. Alison James. Illus. 1995, North-South LB $13.88 (1-55858-402-1). 58pp. A young dinosaur's baby-sitter

saves him from being eaten by the dreaded tyrannosaurus. (Rev: BL 5/1/95; SLJ 6/95)

**6521** Lawson, Robert. *The Fabulous Flight* (4–6). Illus. by author. 1984, Little, Brown paper $5.95 (0-316-51731-3). 152pp. Peter becomes so small he can take a trip via a pet seagull.

**6522** Lawson, Robert. *Rabbit Hill* (4–7). Illus. by author. 1944, Puffin paper $4.50 (0-14-031010-X). 128pp. The small creatures of a Connecticut countryside — each with a distinct personality — create a warm and humorous story. Newbery Award winner, 1945.

**6523** Lee, Wendi, and Terry Beatty. *ElfQuest: Bedtime Stories* (4–6). Illus. by Gary Kato. 1994, Warp Graphics $19.95 (0-936861-37-1). 216pp. An anthology of stories for young people based on the concepts of the adult fantasy of ElfQuest tales. (Rev: BL 1/15/95)

**6524** Le Guin, Ursula K. *Catwings* (2–4). Illus. by S. D. Schindler. 1998, Orchard $14.95 (0-531-05759-3); Scholastic paper $2.95 (0-590-46072-2). 48pp. Four kittens are born with wings into a city neighborhood, but their mother urges them to strike out on their own for safety. Also use *Catwings Return* (1989). (Rev: BCCB 9/88; BL 8/88; HB 11–12/88)

**6525** Le Guin, Ursula K. *Wonderful Alexander and the Catwings* (2–4). Illus. Series: Catwings. 1994, Orchard LB $15.99 (0-531-08701-8). 48pp. Alexander the kitten helps Jane — one of the flying cats called Catwings — regain her power of speech. (Rev: BL 9/15/94; SLJ 9/94)

**6526** Leroe, E. W. *Monster Vision* (4–7). Series: Friendly Corners. 1996, Hyperion paper $3.95 (0-7868-1095-5). 125pp. Ghosts of people killed when a meteorite struck at Friendly Corners return to haunt the residents. Others in this series are *Nasty the Snowman*, *Pizza Zombies*, and *Hairy Horror* (all 1966). (Rev: SLJ 5/97)

**6527** Leroe, Ellen. *Ghost Dog* (3–5). Illus. by Bill Basso. 1993, Hyperion $12.95 (1-56282-268-3). 64pp. On a visit to his grandfather's, Artie encounters a ghost dog, and together they foil a thief intent on stealing a valuable baseball card. (Rev: BL 4/1/93; SLJ 6/93)

**6528** Leroe, Ellen. *H.O.W.L. High* (4–7). 1991, Pocket paper $2.95 (0-671-68568-6). 132pp. His classmates at H.O.W.L. Junior High do not realize that Drac is really a warlock. (Rev: SLJ 1/92)

**6529** Leverich, Kathleen. *Brigid the Bad* (2–4). Illus. by Dan Andreasen. 1995, Random paper $3.99 (0-679-87340-6). 72pp. With the help of her fairy godmother, Brigid becomes boss and doesn't like it. (Rev: BL 12/15/95; SLJ 3/96)

**6530** Levine, Arthur A., reteller. *The Boy Who Drew Cats: A Japanese Folktale* (2–6). Illus. by Frederic

Clement. 1994, Dial paper $15.89 (0-8037-1173-5). In this fantasy, the cats that young Kenji paints come to life and destroy an evil goblin. (Rev: BCCB 2/94; HB 3–4/94; SLJ 5/94)

**6531** Lewis, C. S. *A Book of Narnians: The Lion, the Witch and the Others* (3–7). Illus. by Pauline Baynes. 1995, HarperCollins LB $16.89 (0-06-025014-3). 88pp. An introduction to 33 of the chief characters, mostly nonhuman, that appear in the Narnia series. (Rev: SLJ 10/95)

**6532** Lewis, C. S. *The Lion, the Witch and the Wardrobe* (3–5). Illus. by Robin Lawrie. 1995, HarperCollins paper $8.95 (0-06-443399-4). 64pp. Using an elegant comic book format, the first of the Narnia books is abridged for young readers. (Rev: BCCB 6/95; SLJ 8/95)

**6533** Lewis, C. S. *The Lion, the Witch and the Wardrobe: A Story for Children* (4–7). Illus. by Pauline Baynes. 1988, Macmillan paper $7.95 (0-02-044490-7). 160pp. A beautifully written modern tale of the adventures of 4 children who go into the magical land of Narnia. A special edition with illustrations by Michael Hague was published in 1983. Some sequels are: *The Silver Chair; The Last Battle; Prince Caspian; The Voyage of the "Dawn Treader"; The Magician's Nephew* (all 1969); *The Horse and His Boy* (1986).

**6534** Lightfoot, D. J. *Trail Fever: The Life of a Texas Cowboy* (2–6). Illus. by John Bobbish. 1992, Lothrop $11.00 (0-688-11537-3). 72pp. Highlighting the life of a Texas trail driver born in the 1850s. (Rev: BL 11/1/92; SLJ 11/92)

**6535** Lindbergh, Anne. *Bailey's Window* (3–6). Illus. by Kinuko Craft. 1984, Harcourt $14.95 (0-15-205642-4); Avon paper $3.50 (0-380-70767-5). 115pp. A young boy paints a scene into which he enters.

**6536** Lindbergh, Anne. *The Hunky-Dory Dairy* (5–7). Illus. by Julie Brinckloe. 1986, Harcourt $14.95 (0-15-237449-3); Dell paper $2.75 (0-380-70320-3). 147pp. Zannah visits a community magically removed from the 20th century and enjoys introducing the people to bubble gum, tacos, and other "modern" things. (Rev: BCCB 9/86; BL 4/1/86; SLJ 8/86)

**6537** Lindbergh, Anne. *The People in Pineapple Place* (4–6). 1982, Harcourt $14.95 (0-15-260517-7); Avon paper $2.95 (0-380-70766-7). 153pp. August Brown is still adjusting to his parents' divorce when he meets some people only he can see.

**6538** Lindbergh, Anne. *The Prisoner of Pineapple Place* (5–7). 1988, Harcourt $13.95 (0-15-263559-9); Avon paper $2.95 (0-380-70765-9). 173pp. Pineapple Place is invisible to everyone except the inhabitants, and somehow finds itself landing in Connecticut. (Rev: BL 7/88; SLJ 8/88)

**6539** Lindbergh, Anne. *Three Lives to Live* (5–8). 1995, Pocket paper $3.50 (0-671-86732-6). 183pp. Garet is visited by Daisy, who is really her grandmother of 50 years before. (Rev: SLJ 6/92)

**6540** Lindgren, Astrid. *Ronia, the Robber's Daughter* (4–7). 1985, Puffin paper $4.99 (0-14-031720-1). 176pp. Ronia becomes friendly with the son of her father's rival in this fantasy.

**6541** Lisle, Janet T. *Afternoon of the Elves* (4–6). 1989, Orchard LB $16.99 (0-531-08437-X). 128pp. Hilary discovers that the strange girl named Sara-Kate has a garden inhabited by elves. (Rev: BCCB 10/89; BL 8/89*; HB 9–10/89; SLJ 9/89*)

**6542** Lisle, Janet T. *The Dancing Cats of Applesap* (4–6). Illus. by Joelle Shefts. 1993, Simon & Schuster paper $3.95 (0-689-71687-7). Melba discovers that the cats at Jigg's Drugstore have a special talent.

**6543** Lisle, Janet T. *The Gold Dust Letters* (4–6). 1994, Orchard LB $16.99 (0-531-08680-1). 128pp. Angela's father fools her into believing that she is receiving messages from a fairy in an effort to effect a reconciliation. (Rev: BCCB 7–8/94; BL 2/1/94; SLJ 4/94)

**6544** Lisle, Janet T. *The Lampfish of Twill* (4–8). Illus. by Wendy A. Halperin. 1991, Orchard $16.95 (0-531-05963-4). 176pp. Orphaned Eric faces forces of danger as he lives in the mysterious country of Twill. (Rev: BCCB 10/91; HB 1–2/92; SLJ 9/91*)

**6545** Lisle, Janet T. *Looking for Juliette* (4–6). 1994, Orchard LB $16.99 (0-531-08720-4). 128pp. Georgina and her friend Poco believe that the strange Miss Bone is responsible for running down their cat Juliette. (Rev: BCCB 12/94; BL 9/15/94; SLJ 8/94*)

**6546** Lively, Penelope. *The Ghost of Thomas Kempe* (4–6). Illus. by Antony Maitland. 1973, Dutton paper $14.95 (0-525-30495-9). 192pp. When his family moves into an old house in an English village, James is blamed when the resident ghost begins to act up.

**6547** Lofting, Hugh. *The Story of Doctor Dolittle* (3–6). Illus. by author. 1996, Dover paper $2.00 (0-486-29350-5). 144pp. Reissue of the 1970 edition, reedited to remove racially offensive passages. Also use the similarly edited 1923 Newbery Medal winner *The Voyages of Doctor Dolittle* (1988, Dell). (Rev: BL 7/88)

**6548** Lowry, Lois. *Stay! Keeper's Story* (5–8). Illus. 1997, Houghton $15.00 (0-395-87048-8). 128pp. A dog named Keeper narrates this story about his puppyhood and the 3 different masters he has had. (Rev: BL 11/1/97; SLJ 10/97)

**6549** Lunn, Janet. *The Root Cellar* (5–8). 1983, Macmillan LB $17.00 (0-684-17855-9); Puffin paper $3.99 (0-14-031835-6). 256pp. An unhappy girl is transported to Canada of 1860.

**6550** Macaulay, David. *BAAA* (5–7). Illus. by author. 1985, Houghton $13.95 (0-395-38948-8); paper $4.95 (0-395-39588-7). 64pp. A sophisticated fantasy about a world inhabited by humanlike sheep. (Rev: SLJ 10/85)

**6551** McCaughrean, Geraldine. *A Pack of Lies* (5–7). 1990, Macmillan $16.95 (0-7451-1154-8). 168pp. Stories told by mysterious M.C.C. Berkshire, who wanders into an antique store run by adolescent Ailsa and her mother. (Rev: BCCB 5/89)

**6552** MacDonald, Betty. *Hello, Mrs. Piggle-Wiggle* (3–5). Illus. by Hilary Knight. 1957, HarperCollins $14.95 (0-397-31715-8); paper $4.95 (0-06-440149-9). 132pp. Introducing the lady who loves all children, good or bad. Further adventures are: *Mrs. Piggle-Wiggle's Farm* (1954); *Mrs. Piggle-Wiggle* (1957); *Mrs. Piggle-Wiggle's Magic* (1957).

**6553** MacDonald, George. *At the Back of the North Wind* (4–7). Illus. by Jessie Willcox Smith. 1989, Morrow $22.00 (0-688-07808-7). 352pp. A facsimile edition of the 1919 printing of this classic fantasy.

**6554** MacDonald, George. *The Lost Princess: A Double Story* (4–6). Illus. by Bernhard Oberdieck. 1992, Eerdmans $22.00 (0-8028-5070-7). 148pp. With some help from a mysterious wise woman, little Princess Rosamond faces trials to help grow from a spoiled brat into a good child. (Rev: BL 1/15/93)

**6555** McGraw, Eloise. *The Moorchild* (4–6). 1996, Simon & Schuster paper $16.00 (0-689-80654-X). 242pp. Set in the Middle Ages, this fantasy tells of Moql, who is born half human and half fairy, and her difficulties fitting into either world. (Rev: BCCB 6/96; BL 3/1/96*; HB 9–10/96; SLJ 4/96*)

**6556** McHargue, Georgess. *Beastie* (5–7). 1992, Delacorte $14.00 (0-385-30589-3). 192pp. On an expedition to a Scottish loch, 12-year-old Mary is out to catch the monster and tame it. (Rev: BCCB 4/92; BL 2/1/92; SLJ 7/92)

**6557** McKay, Hilary. *The Amber Cat* (4–6). 1997, Simon & Schuster $15.00 (0-689-81360-0). 114pp. The supernatural is evoked in this story in which a mother tells about her childhood experiences and the mysterious girl named Harriet who would join her and her brothers from time to time. (Rev: BL 11/15/97*; HB 11–12/97; SLJ 11/97*)

**6558** McKean, Thomas. *The Secret of the Seven Willows* (4–6). 1991, Simon & Schuster paper $12.95 (0-671-72997-7). 160pp. Tad uses a magic ring to travel back in time to find out his family's past. (Rev: SLJ 10/91)

**6559** McKelvey, Douglas Kaine. *The Angel Knew Papa and the Dog* (3–5). 1996, Putnam $14.95 (0-399-23042-4). 96pp. An angel helps rescue Evangeline when she is threatened by rising flood waters. (Rev: BCCB 9/96; BL 9/15/96)

**6560** McKenzie, Ellen Kindt. *A Bowl of Mischief* (5–8). 1992, Holt $14.95 (0-8050-2090-X). 134pp. Ranjii, who cannot sit still long enough to be enlightened, goes on a mission in this Arabian Nights-type adventure. (Rev: BL 11/15/92; SLJ 11/92)

**6561** McKenzie, Ellen Kindt. *The King, the Princess, and the Tinker* (3–5). Illus. by William Low. 1992, Holt $14.95 (0-8050-1773-9); paper $4.95 (0-8050-2951-6). 70pp. The story of a king so self-absorbed that he looks in the mirror all day, his sweet daughter, and a pleasant tinker in this half-fable, half-nonsense story. (Rev: BCCB 3/92; BL 3/1/92; HB 5–6/92; SLJ 5/92)

**6562** MacLachlan, Patricia. *Tomorrow's Wizard* (3–5). Illus. by Kathryn Jacobi. 1982, HarperCollins LB $13.89 (0-06-024074-1). 96pp. Six short stories about a wizard, an apprentice, and their horse.

**6563** McMullan, Kate. *The New Kid at School* (3–6). Illus. 1997, Putnam LB $13.89 (0-448-41727-8); paper $3.95 (0-448-41592-5). 32pp. A clever fantasy about a boy who hates violence and his mission to kill the hated dragon Gorzil. (Rev: BL 12/1/97)

**6564** McMullan, Kate. *Under the Mummy's Spell* (4–8). 1992, Farrar $16.00 (0-374-38033-3). 224pp. An interweaving tale of a 12-year-old New Yorker and an Egyptian princess who lived 3 centuries ago. (Rev: BL 7/92; SLJ 7/92)

**6565** Mahy, Margaret. *The Blood-and-Thunder Adventure on Hurricane Peak* (4–6). Illus. by Wendy Smith. 1989, Macmillan $13.95 (0-689-50488-8). 132pp. Huxley and Zaza find fantastic adventures at Unexpected School on Hurricane Peak. (Rev: BCCB 10/89; BL 10/15/89; HB 11–12/89*; SLJ 10/89)

**6566** Mahy, Margaret. *The Five Sisters* (3–5). Illus. 1997, Viking paper $14.99 (0-670-87042-0). 80pp. Five paper dolls have a series of adventures that reveal their different personalities. (Rev: BCCB 5/97; BL 2/1/97; HB 3–4/97; SLJ 3/97*)

**6567** Mahy, Margaret. *A Tall Story and Other Tales* (3–5). Illus. by Jan Nesbitt. 1992, Macmillan $15.95 (0-689-50547-7). 96pp. Eleven stories combine witches and monsters and such with everyday life. (Rev: BL 2/1/92; SLJ 3/92)

**6568** Marks, Alan. *The Thief's Daughter* (2–4). Illus. by author. 1994, Farrar $11.00 (0-374-37481-3). 46pp. A mysterious woman gives Magpie a key that changes her life and the future of her family. (Rev: SLJ 4/94)

**6569** Marston, Elsa. *The Fox Maiden* (1–5). Illus. by Tatsuro Kiuchi. 1996, Simon & Schuster paper $16.00 (0-689-80107-6). An original fantasy set in ancient Japan about a fox who changes her shape to that of a human. (Rev: SLJ 12/96)

**6570** Matas, Carol, and Perry Nodelman. *Of Two Minds* (5–8). 1995, Simon & Schuster paper $16.00

(0-689-80138-6). 202pp. The adventure of Lenora, a princess with supernatural powers, and Coren, the shy prince who has been chosen to be her husband. (Rev: SLJ 10/95*)

**6571** Mather, Karen Trella. *Silas: The Bookstore Cat* (2–4). Illus. by Chris Van Dusen. 1994, Down East $14.95 (0-89272-352-2). 32pp. Silas, the bookstore cat, helps his master find books about his favorite subject, soccer. (Rev: BL 2/1/95; SLJ 3/95)

**6572** Mayne, William. *The Book of Hob Stories* (3–5). Illus. by Patrick Benson. 1997, Candlewick $17.99 (0-7636-0390-2). 93pp. This book includes all 20 of the previously published stories about Hob, the helpful household spirit. (Rev: BL 11/1/97; SLJ 11/97)

**6573** Mayne, William. *Hob and the Goblins* (3–5). Illus. by Norman Messenger. 1994, DK Publg. $12.95 (1-56458-713-4). 140pp. Hob, a spirit, must save the family he protects when they move into a house containing an evil force at work. (Rev: BCCB 12/94; BL 11/1/94; SLJ 11/94*)

**6574** Mayne, William. *Hob and the Peddler* (3–6). 1997, DK Publg. $15.95 (0-7894-2462-2). 128pp. Hob the helpful sprite finds something strange lurking in the pond behind the house where he lives. (Rev: BL 1/1–15/98; SLJ 12/97)

**6575** Mazer, Anne. *A Sliver of Glass and Other Uncommon Tales* (3–5). 1996, Hyperion LB $14.49 (0-7868-2165-5). 80pp. Eleven intriguing stories of horror and mystery. (Rev: BCCB 11/96; BL 9/15/96; SLJ 2/97)

**6576** Medearis, Angela Shelf. *Haunts: Five Hair-Raising Tales* (4–7). Illus. by Trina S. Hyman. 1996, Holiday LB $15.95 (0-8234-1280-6). 37pp. Five stories that contain elements of horror and the supernatural. (Rev: BL 2/1/97; SLJ 4/97)

**6577** Meeks, Arone R. *Enora and the Black Crane* (4–6). 1993, Scholastic $14.95 (0-590-46375-6). 32pp. Enora, growing up in a rain forest, spoils the mystical experiences he has had in the wilds by killing a crane. (Rev: BL 10/1/93)

**6578** Milne, A. A. *Pooh's Bedtime Book* (PS–3). Illus. by E. H. Shepard. 1980, Dutton paper $13.99 (0-525-44895-0). 48pp. Excerpts from *When We Were Very Young* and others.

**6579** Milne, A. A. *Winnie-the-Pooh* (K–5). Colored by Hilda Scott. Illus. by E. H. Shepard. 1961, Dutton $9.95 (0-525-43035-0); Bantam paper $3.50 (0-440-49571-7). The world-famous book that has become a classic. Also use: *The House at Pooh Corner* (1985); *The Pooh Story Book* (1965).

**6580** Milne, A. A. *The World of Pooh: The Complete Winnie-the-Pooh; and the House at Pooh Corner* (1–4). Illus. by E. H. Shepard. 1988, Dutton paper

$21.99 (0-525-44447-5). 320pp. A pleasing combination volume.

**6581** Monsell, Mary Elise. *Toohy and Wood* (3–5). Illus. 1992, Macmillan $12.95 (0-689-31721-2). 80pp. Toohy the lizard is devastated by the death of Pearl, a musical dove, in this story of a world inhabited by affectionate animals. (Rev: BCCB 12/92; BL 10/1/92; SLJ 10/92)

**6582** Moore, Lillian. *Don't Be Afraid, Amanda* (2–5). Illus. by Kathleen G. McCord. 1992, Macmillan $12.95 (0-689-31725-5). 80pp. Amanda Mouse is off to the country to see her pen pal, Adam Mouse. (Rev: BL 6/1/92; HB 7–8/92; SLJ 9/92)

**6583** Moore, Lillian. *I'll Meet You at the Cucumbers* (2–5). Illus. by Sharon Wooding. 1988, Macmillan $14.00 (0-689-31243-1); Bantam paper $2.50 (0-553-15705-1). 72pp. Country mouse visits city mouse in this age-old story. (Rev: BL 3/15/88; HB 7–8/88)

**6584** Morgan, Jill. *Blood Brothers* (4–6). 1996, HarperCollins paper $4.50 (0-06-440562-1). 144pp. A fast-paced adventure in which identical twins are turned into vampires. (Rev: BL 12/1/96; SLJ 1/97)

**6585** Moroney, Lynn. *Moontellers: Myths of the Moon from Around the World* (3–5). Illus. by Greg Shed. 1995, Northland LB $14.95 (0-87358-601-8). A collection of stories that reflect the attitudes of various cultures — such as the Aztecs and the Chinese — toward the moon, with a final section on modern astronomers. (Rev: SLJ 9/95)

**6586** Morris, Gilbert. *Vanishing Clues* (4–6). Series: Time Navigator. 1996, Bethany paper $5.99 (1-55661-396-2). 138pp. Danny and Dixie Fortune travel back to the time of the French and Indian Wars in this story that emphasizes religious principles. (Rev: BL 10/1/96)

**6587** Moses, Will. *The Legend of Sleepy Hollow* (3–5). Illus. 1995, Putnam $18.95 (0-399-22687-7). 48pp. A simple retelling of this classic tale, with paintings of various sizes and shapes. (Rev: BL 10/1/95; SLJ 10/95)

**6588** Murphy, Jill. *The Worst Witch* (4–6). 1982, Avon paper $2.50 (0-380-60665-8). 72pp. Mildred's first year at Miss Cackle's Academy for Witches is a disaster. A sequel is: *The Worst Witch Strikes Again* (1987).

**6589** Myers, Christopher A., and Lynne B. Myers. *Forest of the Clouded Leopard* (5–8). 1994, Houghton $13.95 (0-395-67408-5). 112pp. A 15-year-old boy growing up in the rain forest of Borneo enters the spirit world to rescue his father. (Rev: BCCB 7–8/94; SLJ 5/94)

**6590** Napoli, Donna Jo. *Jimmy, the Pickpocket of the Palace* (4–6). Illus. 1995, Dutton paper $14.99 (0-525-45357-1). 176pp. Jimmy the frog has trouble adjusting when he becomes a boy. (Rev: BCCB 6/95; BL 3/15/95; SLJ 6/95*)

**6591** Napoli, Donna Jo. *The Prince of the Pond: Otherwise Known as De Fawg Pin* (3–6). Illus. by Judith Byron Schachner. 1992, Dutton paper $14.99 (0-525-44976-0). 112pp. In this "different" telling of the frog prince tale, Jade, a female frog, meets the prince under his enchantment and never quite catches on that he really isn't a frog. (Rev: BCCB 1/93; BL 1/15/93; SLJ 10/92)

**6592** Naylor, Phyllis Reynolds. *Bernie and the Bessledorf Ghost* (4–6). 1990, Macmillan $15.00 (0-689-31499-X). 128pp. Bernie and his family discover that the hotel they operate has a ghost. (Rev: BL 4/15/90; SLJ 7/90)

**6593** Naylor, Phyllis Reynolds. *The Grand Escape* (5–7). Illus. 1993, Macmillan $15.00 (0-689-31722-0). 144pp. Two adventurous cats must solve 3 mysteries before they can join the Cats' Club of Mysteries. (Rev: BL 7/93; SLJ 8/93)

**6594** Naylor, Phyllis Reynolds. *The Healing of Texas Jake* (3–6). Illus. 1997, Simon & Schuster $15.00 (0-689-81124-1). 128pp. Each of the cats who are members of the Club of Mystery rally around their leader, Texas Jake, when he is injured in a brawl. (Rev: BL 5/1/97; SLJ 4/97)

**6595** Naylor, Phyllis Reynolds. *Witch's Sister* (4–6). Illus. by Gail Owens. 1988, Dell paper $2.95 (0-440-40028-7). Lynn is convinced that her sister Judith is becoming a witch. Two sequels are: *The Witch Herself; Witch Water* (both 1988).

**6596** Nesbit, Edith. *The Deliverers of Their Country* (3–5). Illus. by Lisbeth Zwerger. 1985, Picture Book paper $15.95 (0-88708-005-7). 32pp. Two children seek the advice of St. George, England's great dragon slayer, to rid the land of a plague of dragons. (Rev: BCCB 1/86; BL 1/15/86; HB 3–4/86)

**6597** Nesbit, Edith. *The Enchanted Castle* (4–6). Illus. by Paul O. Zelinsky. 1992, Morrow $20.00 (0-688-05435-8). 304pp. A handsome volume that showcases Nesbit's fantasy about 4 English children and their adventures with a magic ring, first published in 1907. (Rev: BL 12/15/92)

**6598** Nesbit, Edith. *Five Children and It* (4–6). Illus. by H. R. Miller. 1981, Buccaneer LB $25.95 (0-89966-362-1). 188pp. An enchanting story about a group of children who discover a Psammead, a sand fairy, who both enlivens and confuses their lives. Two more stories about the children: *The Phoenix and the Carpet* (1985); *The Story of the Amulet* (1986).

**6599** Newman, Robert. *Merlin's Mistake* (4–6). Illus. by Richard Lebenson. 1986, Peter Smith $16.25 (0-8446-6187-2). Sixteen-year-old Brian and his friend Tertius set out to find Merlin in this fantasy originally published in 1970. Followed by: *The Testing of Tertius* (1986).

**6600** Nimmo, Jenny. *Orchard of the Crescent Moon* (5–7). 1990, Troll paper $2.95 (0-8167-2265-X). 170pp. Nia has begun to believe it when her family says "Nia-can't-do-nothing." (Rev: BL 8/89)

**6601** Nodelman, Perry. *A Completely Different Place* (5–8). 1997, Simon & Schuster paper $16.00 (0-689-80836-4). 192pp. Johnny awakes from a nightmare and finds that he has shrunk in size and is in the land of the green-skinned Strangers. (Rev: BL 7/97; SLJ 6/97)

**6602** Noonan, R. A. *Enter at Your Own Risk* (4–5). Series: Monsterville. 1995, Simon & Schuster paper $3.95 (0-689-71863-2). 155pp. In this horror tale, Darcy and her 2 cousins discover Monsterville, a refuge for supernatural creatures. Also use *Don't Go into the Graveyard!* (1995). (Rev: SLJ 3/96)

**6603** Norton, Andre, and Phyllis Miller. *House of Shadows* (5–7). 1985, Tor paper $2.95 (0-8125-4743-8). 256pp. While staying with a great-aunt, 3 children learn about the family curse.

**6604** Norton, Mary. *Are All the Giants Dead?* (4–6). Illus. by Brian Froud. 1978, Harcourt paper $9.95 (0-15-607888-0). James journeys to the fairy-tale world of princes, giants, and witches.

**6605** Norton, Mary. *Bed-Knob and Broom-Stick* (4–6). 1990, Harcourt paper $6.00 (0-15-206231-9). 229pp. Charles, Carey, and Paul meet a woman who is studying to become a witch, and she takes them on many exciting but gruesome adventures.

**6606** Norton, Mary. *The Borrowers* (4–6). Illus. by Beth Krush and Joe Krush. 1953, Harcourt $17.00 (0-15-209987-5); paper $6.00 (0-15-209990-5). 180pp. Little people, no taller than a pencil, live in old houses and borrow what they need from humans. Some sequels are: *The Borrowers Afield* (1955); *The Borrowers Afloat* (1959); *The Borrowers Aloft* (1961); *The Borrowers Avenged* (1982).

**6607** Norton, Mary. *Poor Stainless: A New Story About the Borrowers* (2–4). Illus. by Beth Krush and Joe Krush. 1985, Harcourt $7.95 (0-15-263221-2). 32pp. The tiny people called The Borrowers are back in print.

**6608** O'Brien, Robert C. *Mrs. Frisby and the Rats of NIMH* (5–7). Illus. by Zena Bernstein. 1971, Macmillan $17.00 (0-689-20651-8); paper $4.50 (0-689-71068-2). 240pp. Saga of a group of rats made literate and given human intelligence by a series of experiments, who escape from their laboratory to found their own community. Newbery Award winner, 1972.

**6609** Ogburn, Jacqueline K. *Scarlett Angelina Wolverton-Manning* (4–6). Illus. by Brian Ajhar. 1994, Dial paper $14.89 (0-8037-1377-0). 32pp. When he abducts Scarlett Angelina, the kidnapper doesn't know she is a young werewolf. (Rev: BL 11/15/94; SLJ 11/94)

**6610** Oppel, Kenneth. *Silverwing* (4–6). 1997, Simon & Schuster paper $16.00 (0-689-81529-8). 217pp. The young hero Slade, who is an undersized bat, must save his colony from invaders. (Rev: HB 11–12/97; SLJ 10/97)

**6611** Oram, Hiawyn. *The Second Princess* (PS–2). Illus. by Tony Ross. 1994, Golden Bks. $13.95 (0-307-17513-8). 32pp. The Second Princess schemes to get rid of her sister and become First Princess. (Rev: BL 10/15/94; SLJ 1/95)

**6612** O'Rourke, Frank. *Burton and Stanley* (4–6). Illus. by Jonathan Allen. 1993, Godine $15.95 (0-87923-824-0). 56pp. Two talking birds from Africa are transported by a tornado to a small town in the Midwest. (Rev: BL 5/15/93; SLJ 5/93)

**6613** Osborne, Mary Pope. *Mummies in the Morning* (1–4). Illus. 1993, Random LB $11.99 (0-679-92424-8); paper $3.99 (0-679-82424-3). 72pp. Jack and Annie time-travel to ancient Egypt to help a queen find a copy of the Book of the Dead. (Rev: BL 4/1/94)

**6614** O'Shea, Pat. *The Hounds of the Morrigan* (5–8). 1986, Holiday $16.95 (0-8234-0595-8). 469pp. A fantasy about 10-year-old Pidge and his little sister, both of whom are drawn into a battle between Irish spirits. (Rev: BCCB 7–8/86; HB 7–8/86; SLJ 3/86)

**6615** Owen, Gareth. *Rosie No-Name and the Forest of Forgetting* (3–6). 1996, Holiday $15.95 (0-8234-1266-0). 109pp. Rose follows a mysterious girl into an enchanted land in this English fantasy. (Rev: BCCB 1/97; BL 11/1/96; SLJ 10/96)

**6616** Parish, Peggy. *Haunted House* (4–6). 1991, Peter Smith $17.75 (0-8446-6391-3); Dell paper $3.99 (0-440-43459-9). The Roberts family believes a ghost is loose and nearby.

**6617** Pascal, Francine. *Hangin' Out with Cici* (6–8). 1985, Bantam paper $2.50 (0-440-93364-1). 192pp. Victoria realizes that the girl she meets in Penn Station is really herself as she was in 1944.

**6618** Patneaude, David. *Dark Starry Morning: Stories of This World and Beyond* (5–8). 1995, Albert Whitman LB $13.95 (0-8075-1474-8). 128pp. Six eerie tales about encounters with the unknown and the supernatural. (Rev: BL 9/1/95; SLJ 9/95)

**6619** Pearce, Philippa. *Tom's Midnight Garden* (4–7). Illus. by Susan Einzig. 1959, HarperCollins LB $14.89 (0-397-30477-3); Dell paper $4.95 (0-06-440445-5). 240pp. When the clock strikes 13, Tom visits his garden and meets Hatty, a strange mid-Victorian girl.

**6620** Pearce, Q. L. *Super Scary Stories for Sleep-Overs, No. 5* (4–7). Illus. by Dwight Been. 1995, Price Stern Sloan paper $4.95 (0-8431-3915-3). 128pp. Ten scary stories that deal with subjects like Ouija boards, fetish dolls, extraterrestrials, and time warps. (Rev: SLJ 2/96)

**6621** Peck, Richard. *The Ghost Belonged to Me* (5–8). 1997, Viking paper $4.99 (0-14-038671-8). 184pp. Richard unwillingly receives the aid of his nemesis, Blossom Culp, in trying to solve the mystery behind the ghost of a young girl. Two sequels are: *Ghosts I Have Been* (1977); *The Dreadful Future of Blossom Culp* (1983).

**6622** Perez, L. King. *Ghoststalking* (3–6). Illus. 1995, Carolrhoda LB $19.93 (0-87614-821-6). 56pp. Chuy and Emilio camp outdoors to find the ghost of La Llorona, a woman who has drowned her children in this Latino tale of the supernatural. (Rev: BL 9/15/95; SLJ 12/95)

**6623** Perrin, Randy, et al. *Time Like a River* (5–7). 1997, RDR Bks. $14.95 (1-57143-061-X). 139pp. Margie travels back in time to find a cure for her mother's mysterious illness. (Rev: SLJ 3/98)

**6624** Peterson, Beth. *No Turning Back* (4–6). 1996, Simon & Schuster $14.00 (0-689-31914-2). 103pp. In an attempt to help his injured friend, Dillon travels through an enchanted forest filled with talking animals. (Rev: BL 5/1/96; SLJ 5/96)

**6625** Pfeffer, Susan Beth. *Sara Kate Saves the World* (2–4). Illus. Series: Sara Kate. 1995, Holt $14.95 (0-8050-3148-0). 58pp. Sara Kate's extraordinary powers, including X-ray vision, help her cope with the class bully. (Rev: BCCB 9/95; BL 9/1/95; SLJ 11/95)

**6626** Pfeffer, Susan Beth. *Sara Kate, Superkid* (1–3). Illus. 1994, Holt $14.95 (0-8050-3147-2). 58pp. Sara Kate is a perfectly ordinary girl except on Tuesdays, Thursdays, and some Saturdays, when she has magical powers. (Rev: BCCB 1/95; BL 12/1/94; SLJ 12/94)

**6627** Pfeffer, Susan Beth. *The Trouble with Wishes* (2–4). Illus. 1996, Holt $15.95 (0-8050-3826-4). 71pp. Katie has much to ponder when she obtains a magic lamp complete with 3 wishes. (Rev: BCCB 6/96; BL 5/1/96; SLJ 6/96)

**6628** Pipe, Jim. *The Werewolf* (4–7). Illus. Series: In the Footsteps Of. 1996, Millbrook LB $21.90 (0-7613-0450-9). 40pp. A horror story in which Bernard, a werewolf, commits terrible acts under the influence of a full moon. (Rev: SLJ 7/96)

**6629** Place, François. *The Last Giants* (4–6). Trans. from French by William Rodarmor. Illus. by author. 1993, Godine $15.95 (0-87923-990-5). 74pp. This novel tells of the fearless explorer Archibald Ruthmore and his journey into the Land of the Giants. It is part fable, part fantasy, and part exciting adventure story. (Rev: HB 11–12/93; SLJ 12/93)

**6630** Polacco, Patricia. *I Can Hear the Sun* (2–4). Illus. by author. 1996, Putnam $15.95 (0-399-22520-X). A fantasy in which a misunderstood, troubled boy accepts an invitation from the geese and flies away with them. (Rev: BL 11/1/96; SLJ 11/96)

**6631** Preussler, Otfried. *The Satanic Mill* (5–8). 1987, Peter Smith $19.50 (0-8446-6196-1). 256pp. A young apprentice outwits a strange magician in this fantasy first published in 1972.

**6632** Price, Susan. *The Ghost Drum: A Cat's Tale* (5–7). 1987, Farrar $12.95 (0-374-32538-3); paper $3.50 (0-374-42547-7). 176pp. Stories are related by a cat who spins memorable tales. (Rev: BCCB 10/87; BL 9/1/87; SLJ 9/87)

**6633** Priest, Robert. *The Town That Got Out of Town* (2–5). Illus. 1989, Godine $14.95 (0-87923-786-4). 48pp. One Labor Day, the city of Boston decides to pay a visit to Portland, Maine. (Rev: BL 1/1/90; SLJ 5/90)

**6634** Proysen, Alf. *Little Old Mrs. Pepperpot and Other Stories* (3–5). 1960, Astor-Honor $12.95 (0-8392-3021-4). The story of a woman who can shrink to the size of a pepper pot.

**6635** Pryor, Bonnie. *Marvelous Marvin and the Pioneer Ghost* (3–6). Illus. 1995, Morrow $15.00 (0-688-13886-1). 144pp. With the help of a ghost, Marvin and his friends find out who is polluting Liberty Creek. (Rev: BL 5/1/95; SLJ 7/95)

**6636** Pyle, Howard. *The Garden Behind the Moon: A Real Story of the Moon Angel* (4–6). Illus. by author. 1988, Parabola paper $10.95 (0-930407-22-9). 180pp. A boy follows the path of the moonlight and visits the Moon-Angel and the Man-in-the-Moon in this fantasy. A reissue of the 1895 edition.

**6637** Quindlen, Anna. *Happily Ever After* (2–4). Illus. by James Stevenson. 1997, Viking paper $13.99 (0-670-86961-9). 64pp. Spunky fourth-grader Kate reverses stereotypes when she magically becomes a fairytale princess. (Rev: BL 2/1/97; SLJ 3/97)

**6638** Raschka, Chris. *Elizabeth Imagined an Iceberg* (K–6). Illus. by author. Series: Richard Jackson Books. 1994, Orchard LB $15.99 (0-531-08667-4). Elizabeth meets an unusual, frightening woman and is able to repulse her advances in this unsettling picture book. (Rev: BCCB 5/94; SLJ 4/94)

**6639** Raskin, Ellen. *Figgs and Phantoms* (4–6). Illus. by author. 1989, Puffin paper $5.99 (0-14-032944-7). 160pp. The family of Figg-Newton has always dreamed of going to Capri, and in this fantasy, heroine Mona Lisa fulfills the wish.

**6640** Redmond, Shirley-Raye. *Grampa and the Ghost* (3–5). 1994, Avon paper $3.50 (0-380-77382-1). 82pp. When Mark and Sibyl advertise for a ghost writer, they get an assistant from beyond the grave named Tallulah. (Rev: SLJ 7/94)

**6641** Regan, Dian C. *Monsters in the Attic* (4–6). Illus. 1995, Holt $14.95 (0-8050-3709-8). 186pp. Life becomes complicated for Rilla when she joins the Monster of the Month Club. (Rev: BL 10/15/95; SLJ 11/95)

**6642** Rice, Bebe F. *The Year the Wolves Came* (5–8). 1994, Dutton paper $14.99 (0-525-45209-5). 160pp. A haunting book about a Canadian village in 1906 and how it is besieged by a pack of wolves looking for their leader. (Rev: BCCB 1/95; BL 1/15/95; SLJ 12/94)

**6643** Richemont, Enid. *The Glass Bird* (3–5). Illus. by Caroline Anstey. 1993, Candlewick $14.95 (1-56402-195-5). 112pp. Adam and Gary form a lasting friendship as a result of a magical glass bird that appears to Adam after he wishes on a chestnut. (Rev: BL 10/15/93; SLJ 10/93)

**6644** Richemont, Enid. *The Time Tree* (4–6). 1990, Little, Brown $12.95 (0-316-74452-2). 96pp. A girl from the 16th century visits the 20th and takes back the skills she has learned. (Rev: BCCB 5/90; BL 8/90; SLJ 6/90)

**6645** Robb, Jackie, and Berny Stringle. *Bat* (2–4). Illus. 1997, Price Stern Sloan $4.95 (0-8431-7930-9). 30pp. In this board book for older children, the reader is introduced to a funny creature named Bat, who dresses differently than other people. Other unusual beings can be found in the books *Brain Cell, Slug,* and *Spider* (all 1997). (Rev: BL 6/1–15/97)

**6646** Rodda, Emily. *The Pigs Are Flying* (4–6). Illus. by Noela Young. 1988, Greenwillow paper $2.95 (0-380-70555-9). 160pp. Rachel's friend Burt, who has come to cheer her when she has a cold, makes her believe in the impossible. (Rev: BL 10/1/88; HB 11–12/88)

**6647** Roden, Katie. *The Mummy* (3–6). Illus. Series: In the Footsteps Of. 1996, Millbrook LB $21.90 (0-7613-0451-7). 40pp. Fiction and fact mix in this account of mummification and a horror story about King Tut's tomb. (Rev: SLJ 5/96)

**6648** Rodowsky, Colby. *The Gathering Room* (5–8). 1981, Farrar $11.95 (0-374-32520-0). 186pp. Mudge is befriended by spirits that live in the cemetery where her parents are caretakers.

**6649** Ross, Gaby. *Damien the Dragon* (3–5). Illus. by Carla Daly. 1990, Poolbeg paper $6.95 (1-85371-078-4). 92pp. Alan and the residents of Gravellonia construct a companion for Lady Silk Dragon. (Rev: BL 12/15/90)

**6650** Rossi, Joyce. *The Gullywasher* (2–4). Illus. 1995, Northland LB $14.95 (0-87358-607-7). 32pp. In this tall tale, a grandfather tells his granddaughter about the most amazing rainstorm he ever experienced. (Rev: BL 12/15/95; SLJ 1/96)

**6651** Ruch, Sandi B. *Junkyard Dog* (2–4). Illus. 1990, Orchard LB $14.99 (0-531-08442-6). 96pp. Slobber, the new watchdog, and 5-year-old Huey establish a relationship. (Rev: BL 9/15/90; HB 7–8/90; SLJ 8/90)

**6652** Ruskin, John. *King of the Golden River or the Black Brother* (5–8). Illus. by Richard Doyle. 1974, Dover paper $3.50 (0-486-20066-3). 56pp. Two mean brothers incur the wrath of the South-West Wind, Esquire.

**6653** Russell, Barbara T. *Blue Lightning* (5–7). 1997, Viking paper $13.99 (0-670-87023-4). 128pp. When Rory dies, he comes back to haunt Cal Doogan, whom he met in a hospital emergency room. (Rev: BCCB 2/97; BL 2/15/97; HB 5–6/97; SLJ 2/97)

**6654** Rylant, Cynthia. *Gooseberry Park* (4–6). Illus. 1995, Harcourt $15.00 (0-15-232242-6). 144pp. A group of animals bands together to feed the squirrel Stumpy's babies after she disappears. (Rev: BCCB 2/96; BL 10/1/95; SLJ 12/95)

**6655** Rylant, Cynthia. *The Islander* (5–8). 1998, DK Publg. $14.95 (0-7894-2490-8). 97pp. Growing up on a lonely island off the coast of British Columbia with his grandfather, Daniel encounters a mermaid and, through her, learns about his family. (Rev: BL 2/1/98*; SLJ 3/98)

**6656** Rylant, Cynthia. *The Van Gogh Cafe* (4–6). 1995, Harcourt $14.00 (0-15-200843-8). 64pp. Seven vignettes about the people who frequent the Van Gogh Cafe situated off Highway 70 in Flowers, Kansas. (Rev: BCCB 9/95; BL 6/1–15/95; SLJ 7/95)

**6657** Saint-Exupery, Antoine de. *The Little Prince* (4–7). Trans. by Katherine Woods. Illus. by author. 1943, Harcourt $16.00 (0-15-246503-0); paper $10.00 (0-15-646511-6). 91pp. An original fantasy of a little prince who leaves his planet to discover great wisdom.

**6658** Salsitz, Rhoni V. *The Twilight Gate* (5–8). Illus. by Alan M. Clark. 1993, Walker $16.95 (0-8027-8213-2). 192pp. Siblings are being pursued by man-beasts called weevils in this unusual and complex fantasy. (Rev: SLJ 5/93)

**6659** San Souci, Robert D. *The Red Heels* (5–7). Illus. by Gary Kelley. 1996, Dial paper $15.89 (0-8037-1134-4). 32pp. When a cobbler makes new red shoes for Rebecca, she gains supernatural powers. (Rev: BCCB 10/96; BL 9/1/96; SLJ 10/96)

**6660** Sargent, Sarah. *Weird Henry Berg* (4–6). 1993, Knopf paper $3.50 (0-679-80703-9). 120pp. Henry,

his pet lizard Vincent, friend Millie, and a dragon named Aelf are the main characters in this fantasy.

**6661** Saunders, Susan. *Dorothy and the Magic Belt* (3–5). Illus. by David Rose. 1985, Random paper $1.95 (0-394-87067-0). 64pp. Another adventure for Dorothy and her friends in this "Land of Oz" spin-off. (Rev: BL 12/1/85; SLJ 11/85)

**6662** Say, Allen. *Stranger in the Mirror* (3–6). Illus. 1995, Houghton $16.95 (0-395-61590-9). 32pp. In this fantasy, Sam one morning discovers that he has the face of an old, wrinkled man. (Rev: BCCB 11/95; BL 10/1/95; SLJ 10/95*)

**6663** Schaeffer, Susan F. *The Dragons of North Chittendon* (5–7). Illus. by Darcy May. 1986, Simon & Schuster paper $2.95 (0-685-14462-3). The story of Arthur, an unruly dragon, and his ESP relationship with the boy Patrick in a story of humans and dragons in and above North Chittendon, Vermont. (Rev: BL 8/86; SLJ 9/86)

**6664** Scheidl, Gerda M. *Andy's Wild Animal Adventure* (1–3). Trans. by J. Alison James. Illus. 1997, North-South LB $13.88 (1-55858-798-5). 47pp. Andy draws pictures of a lion, an elephant, and a parrot, and miraculously they come to life. (Rev: BL 11/15/97)

**6665** Schmidt, Annie M. G. *Minnie* (3–6). Trans. by Lance Salway. Illus. 1994, Milkweed $14.95 (1-57131-601-9); paper $6.95 (1-57131-600-0). 164pp. Mr. Tibbs, a reporter, and Miss Minnie, formerly a cat, try to get a villain to confess to his crime. (Rev: BL 9/1/94; SLJ 9/94)

**6666** Schmidt, Gary D. *Pilgrim's Progress* (4–7). Illus. by Barry Moser. 1994, Eerdmans $25.00 (0-8028-5080-4). 88pp. A simple retelling of the classic in which Christian leaves his home to find the Celestial City. (Rev: BL 11/1/94; SLJ 12/94)

**6667** Schnur, Steven. *The Shadow Children* (4–7). Illus. by Herbert Tauss. 1994, Morrow LB $13.93 (0-688-13831-4). 86pp. The experiences of the Holocaust are relived by a boy when he visits an area in France where Jewish refugees lived before being sent to the death camps. (Rev: BCCB 12/94; BL 11/15/94; SLJ 10/94)

**6668** Scieszka, Jon. *The Time Warp Trio 2095* (3–5). Illus. by Lane Smith. 1995, Viking paper $11.99 (0-670-85795-5). 80pp. Joe, Fred, and Sam meet their great-grandchildren as they travel into the future. (Rev: BL 6/1–15/95; SLJ 7/95)

**6669** Scieszka, Jon. *Tut, Tut* (4–6). Illus. by Lane Smith. 1996, Viking paper $12.99 (0-670-84832-8). 80pp. The Time Warp Trio find themselves in ancient Egypt in the clutches of the pharaoh's evil priest. (Rev: BL 10/1/96)

**6670** Scieszka, Jon. *Your Mother Was a Neanderthal: The Time Warp Trio* (4–6). Illus. by Lane

Smith. 1993, Viking paper $12.99 (0-670-84481-0). 64pp. The Time Warp Trio travel back to the Stone Age, where they are discovered by some cavegirls. (Rev: BL 10/1/93; SLJ 10/93*)

**6671** Scott, Deborah. *The Kid Who Got Zapped Through Time* (4–7). 1997, Avon paper $14.00 (0-380-97356-1). 160pp. In this humorous time-travel fantasy, Flattop Kincaid is transported to England during the Middle Ages, where he becomes a serf. (Rev: BL 11/1/97; SLJ 9/97)

**6672** Seabrooke, Brenda. *The Care and Feeding of Dragons* (3–5). 1998, Dutton $15.99 (0-525-65252-3). 128pp. A humorous story about a young boy who has a pet dragon that he claims is really a rare dog. A sequel to *Seabrooke's Dragon That Ate Summer* (1992). (Rev: BL 2/1/98; SLJ 2/98)

**6673** Seidler, Tor. *Mean Margaret* (4–6). Illus. by Jon Agee. 1997, HarperCollins LB $14.89 (0-06-205091-5). 176pp. Two newly married woodchucks decide to adopt a human child who has made her parents' life miserable. (Rev: BL 12/1/97; SLJ 11/97*)

**6674** Seidler, Tor. *A Rat's Tale* (4–6). Illus. 1986, Farrar $16.00 (0-374-36185-1). 187pp. The rat community under New York City is threatened with extermination, but young Montague, looked down upon for working with his paws, offers to donate his pictures to help the cause. (Rev: BCCB 2/87; BL 1/15/87; HB 3–4/87)

**6675** Seidler, Tor. *The Wainscott Weasel* (4–6). Illus. by Fred Marcellino. 1993, HarperCollins LB $19.89 (0-06-205033-8). 200pp. Although his girl friend, a fish, spurns him, a weasel named Bagley Brown, Jr. is determined to help when her pond is threatened. (Rev: BCCB 11/93; BL 11/1/93*; HB 11–12/93; SLJ 12/93)

**6676** Selden, George. *The Cricket in Times Square* (3–6). Illus. by Garth Williams. 1960, Farrar $15.00 (0-374-31650-3); Dell paper $4.99 (0-440-41563-2). 160pp. A Connecticut cricket is transported in a picnic basket to New York's Times Square. Two sequels are: *Tucker's Countryside* (1969); *Harry Cat's Pet Puppy* (1974).

**6677** Selden, George. *The Genie of Sutton Place* (5–6). 1985, Farrar paper $4.95 (0-374-42530-2). The summer Tim lives with his Aunt Lucy on Sutton Place in New York City, he evokes his own magical genie who works not only miracles but mishaps.

**6678** Sendak, Maurice. *Higglety Pigglety Pop! or There Must Be More to Life* (K–4). Illus. by author. 1967, HarperCollins $15.00 (0-06-025487-4); paper $7.95 (0-06-443021-9). 80pp. Jennie, a Sealyham terrier who has everything but wants more, leaves home in search of experience.

**6679** Service, Pamela F. *Storm at the Edge of Time* (4–6). 1994, Walker $16.95 (0-8027-8306-6). 192pp.

Three children from different time periods are summoned to help Urkar, a Neolithic wise man. (Rev: BL 10/15/94; SLJ 12/94)

**6680** Service, Pamela F. *Vision Quest* (5–7). 1989, Fawcett paper $3.99 (0-449-70372-X). 160pp. Mourning the death of her father, Kate is changed by an ancient Indian charm-stone. (Rev: BCCB 5/89; BL 4/15/89; SLJ 3/89)

**6681** Shakespeare, William. *The Tempest* (3–6). Retold by Ann Keay Beneduce. Illus. by Gennady Spirin. 1996, Philomel $16.95 (0-399-22764-4). 32pp. A well-executed retelling of Shakespeare's play using paintings that suggest the Italian Renaissance. (Rev: BCCB 7–8/96; HB 5–6/96; SLJ 5/96)

**6682** Shulevitz, Uri. *The Strange and Exciting Adventures of Jeremiah Hash* (4–6). Illus. by author. 1986, Farrar $14.00 (0-374-33656-3). 96pp. Jeremiah the lonely monkey spends a disappointing evening in a singles' club. (Rev: BCCB 3/87; BL 2/1/87; SLJ 2/87)

**6683** Sims, J. Michael. *Young Claus: Legend of the Boy Who Became Santa* (2–4). 1995, Cygnet Trumpeter $12.95 (0-9645976-6-7). 112pp. A fantasy about a young orphan who encounters many adventures in his mission to be Santa. (Rev: BL 11/15/95)

**6684** Sincic, Alan. *Edward Is Only a Fish* (3–5). Illus. 1996, Holt paper $4.95 (0-8050-4906-1). 56pp. When the Billingsly home is flooded because of running bathwater, Edward the goldfish has a field day and a free tour of the house. (Rev: BL 1/15/95; SLJ 2/95)

**6685** Singer, Isaac Bashevis. *The Topsy-Turvy Emperor of China* (4–7). Illus. by Julian Jusim. 1996, Farrar $16.00 (0-374-37681-6). A new edition of the tale about a wicked emperor who inflicts his twisted values on his subjects. (Rev: SLJ 6/96)

**6686** Sleator, William. *The Beasties* (5–7). 1997, Dutton paper $15.99 (0-525-45598-1). 192pp. In this modern horror tale, Doug and his younger sister discover a hidden tunnel where a race of weird underground people live. (Rev: BL 10/1/97; HB 9–10/97; SLJ 12/97)

**6687** Slepian, Jan. *Back to Before* (5–7). 1994, Scholastic paper $3.25 (0-590-48459-1). 144pp. Cousins Linny and Hilary travel back to a time before Linny's mother's death and Hilary's parents' separation. (Rev: BCCB 9/93; BL 9/1/93*; SLJ 10/93)

**6688** Sloan, Carolyn. *The Sea Child* (5–7). 1988, Holiday $12.95 (0-8234-0723-3). 128pp. Ten-year-old Jessie and her father live alone on an island, and she has never seen another human being. (Rev: BCCB 11/88; HB 1–2/89; SLJ 10/88)

**6689** Small, David. *Fenwick's Suit* (4–8). Illus. 1996, Farrar $15.00 (0-374-32298-8). 30pp. Fenwick discovers that the new suit he has purchased has a life of its own. (Rev: BCCB 10/96; BL 9/15/96; SLJ 9/96)

**6690** Small, David. *George Washington's Cows* (3–4). Illus. 1994, Farrar $15.00 (0-374-32535-9). 32pp. Humorous rhymes that depict daily life of the animals at George Washington's Mount Vernon. (Rev: BL 11/1/94; SLJ 1/95*)

**6691** Smith, Dodie. *The Hundred and One Dalmatians* (3–5). 1981, Avon paper $2.95 (0-380-00895-5). 208pp. Pongo and Missis must save the Dalmatian puppies captured by Cruella de Vil.

**6692** Smith, L. J. *Heart of Valor* (5–7). 1990, Macmillan $14.95 (0-02-785861-8). 224pp. Claudia, in her third-grade classroom, realizes an earthquake is imminent. (Rev: BL 2/15/90; SLJ 12/90)

**6693** Smith, Sherwood. *Court Duel* (5–8). 1998, Harcourt $18.00 (0-15-201609-0). 256pp. In this fantasy, Meliara has problems at court when she can't distinguish friends from enemies. (Rev: BL 3/1/98; SLJ 4/98)

**6694** Smith, Sherwood. *Crown Duel* (5–8). 1997, Harcourt $17.00 (0-15-201608-2). 272 pp. Young Meliara and her brother Bran lead a small band of friends against the wicked King Galdran to protect their land. (Rev: BCCB 7–8/97; BL 4/15/97; SLJ 8/97)

**6695** Smith, Sherwood. *Wren to the Rescue* (5–7). 1990, Harcourt $15.95 (0-15-200975-2). 240pp. Wren discovers that Tess at the orphange is a princess. (Rev: BL 12/15/90; HB 3–4/91)

**6696** Smith, Sherwood. *Wren's War* (5–8). 1995, Harcourt $17.00 (0-15-200977-9). 208pp. Princess Teresa uses the help of Wren to prevent her kingdom from being taken over by evil forces. (Rev: BL 3/1/95*; SLJ 5/95)

**6697** Sneve, Virginia Driving Hawk. *The Trickster and the Troll* (3–6). 1997, Univ. of Nebraska Pr. $22.00 (0-8032-4261-1). 110pp. An American Indian trickster meets a Norwegian troll in this fantasy. (Rev: BL 9/15/97; SLJ 12/97)

**6698** Snyder, Zilpha Keatley. *The Trespassers* (5–7). 1995, Delacorte $15.95 (0-385-31055-2). 200pp. Grub, a 7-year-old, forms a friendship with a ghost after he and his older sister, Neely, explore a deserted mansion. (Rev: BCCB 10/95; BL 6/1–15/95; SLJ 8/95)

**6699** Sommer-Bodenburg, Angela. *My Friend the Vampire* (3–6). Illus. by Amelie Glienke. 1984, Dial LB $9.89 (0-8037-0046-6). 160pp. Tony finds he has problems when he befriends a vampire. A sequel is: *The Vampire Moves In* (1984).

**6700** Sonenklar, Carol. *Bug Boy* (3–6). Illus. 1997, Holt $14.95 (0-8050-4794-8). 100pp. Charlie, who is

nuts about bugs, gets a gift of a device that turns him into a number of different insects. (Rev: BCCB 5/97; BL 4/1/97; SLJ 7/97)

**6701** Soto, Gary. *The Cat's Meow* (2–5). Illus. 1995, Scholastic $13.95 (0-590-47001-9). 80pp. Graciela's cat, Pip, astounds everyone by suddenly speaking in Spanish. (Rev: BL 12/1/95; SLJ 10/95)

**6702** Spinner, Stephanie, and Ellen Weiss. *Born to Be Wild* (2–4). Series: Weebie Zone No. 3. 1997, HarperTrophy LB $13.89 (0-06-027338-0). 60pp. Garth and the gerbil with whom he communicates plan to help rescue a runaway bunny. (Rev: SLJ 2/97)

**6703** Springer, Nancy. *Red Wizard* (4–7). 1990, Macmillan $13.95 (0-689-31485-X). 138pp. In this fantasy, Ryan is summoned to an alternative world by a bumbling wizard. (Rev: SLJ 7/90)

**6704** Stanley, George E. *The Day the Ants Got Really Mad* (2–4). Illus. 1996, Simon & Schuster paper $3.99 (0-689-80858-5). 74pp. A colony of ants seeks revenge when Michael's family builds a house over their anthill. (Rev: BL 4/1/96; SLJ 8/96)

**6705** Steele, Mary Q. *Journey Outside* (5–8). Illus. by Rocco Negri. 1984, Peter Smith $18.50 (0-8446-6169-4); Puffin paper $4.99 (0-14-030588-2). 144pp. Young Dilar, believing that his Raft People in seeking a "Better Place" have been circling endlessly, sets out to discover the origin and fate of his kind.

**6706** Steiber, Ellen. *Shadow of the Fox* (3–6). 1994, Random paper $3.50 (0-679-86667-1). 106pp. A samurai warrior discovers that the woman he has taken as a bride changes into a fox at night. (Rev: BL 11/15/94)

**6707** Steig, William. *Abel's Island* (4–6). Illus. by author. 1976, Farrar $15.00 (0-374-30010-0); paper $4.95 (0-374-40016-4). 128pp. A tale of a pampered mouse who must fend for himself after being marooned on an isolated island.

**6708** Steig, William. *Dominic* (4–6). Illus. by author. 1984, Farrar paper $3.95 (0-374-41826-8). 160pp. A resourceful and engaging hound dog helps a group of animals overcome the wicked Doomsday Gang.

**6709** Steig, William. *The Real Thief* (4–5). Illus. by author. 1976, Farrar $12.95 (0-374-36217-3); paper $3.95 (0-374-46208-9). 64pp. Gawain, a goose, is disgraced when gold and jewels begin disappearing from the Royal Treasury where he is the guard.

**6710** Stephens, Michael. *Eddy the Great* (5–8). Illus. by Kim Gamble. 1994, Allen & Unwin paper $5.95 (1-86373-392-2). 136pp. A fantasy about a boy who has problems after he is sent to an English boarding school while his parents sort out their marriage difficulties. (Rev: BL 5/15/94)

**6711** Sterman, Betsy, and Samuel Sterman. *Backyard Dragon* (3–5). Illus. 1993, HarperCollins LB

$13.89 (0-06-020784-1). 192pp. In 20th-century New Jersey, Owen discovers a dragon that has been banished from Wales. (Rev: BL 10/1/93; SLJ 8/93)

**6712** Stevenson, James. *The Mud Flat Mystery* (2–4). Illus. 1997, Greenwillow LB $14.93 (0-688-14966-9). 56pp. All the animals of Mud Flat are curious to know about the contents of a large box delivered to Duncan. (Rev: BL 9/15/97; HB 9–10/97; SLJ 8/97)

**6713** Stevenson, James. *The Mud Flat Olympics* (2–4). Illus. 1994, Greenwillow LB $14.93 (0-688-12924-2). 56pp. A humorous look at animal Olympic games, including the smelliest-skunk contest. (Rev: BCCB 11/94; BL 9/1/94*; HB 11–12/94; SLJ 10/94)

**6714** Stevenson, Robert Louis. *The Bottle Imp* (4–7). Illus. by Jacqueline Mair. 1996, Clarion $16.95 (0-395-72101-6). 60pp. The classic story of the mixed blessings of owning a magic bottle that will grant wishes. (Rev: BCCB 2/96; BL 2/15/96; SLJ 5/96)

**6715** Strasser, Todd. *Help! I'm Trapped in Obedience School* (5–8). 1995, Scholastic paper $3.99 (0-590-54209-5). 126pp. Andy, trapped in a dog's body, must adjust to eating dog food and engaging in other typical canine activities. (Rev: BL 2/1/96; SLJ 2/96)

**6716** Strasser, Todd. *Hey Dad, Get a Life!* (5–8). 1996, Holiday $15.95 (0-8234-1278-4). 160pp. Kelly and Sasha train the ghost of their father to be helpful around the house. (Rev: BCCB 3/97; BL 2/15/97; SLJ 3/97)

**6717** Strickland, Brad. *The Bell, the Book, and the Spellbinder* (4–7). 1997, Dial $14.99 (0-8037-1831-4). 160pp. Fergie seems to fall under a strange spell when he opens an unusual book he has taken from the library. (Rev: BL 9/1/97; SLJ 8/97)

**6718** Swift, Jonathan. *Gulliver's Travels* (5–7). Adapted by James Riordan. Illus. by Victor G. Ambrus. 1992, Oxford $22.95 (0-19-279897-9). 94pp. Two of the most appealing of Gulliver's adventures: Lilliput, where the human is a giant among dwarves, and Brobdingnag, where the human is a dwarf among giants. (Rev: BL 11/15/92)

**6719** Tate, Eleanora E. *Don't Split the Pole: Tales of Down Home Folk Wisdom* (4–6). Illus. 1997, Delacorte $14.95 (0-385-32302-6). 131pp. These 7 tales mix humans and talking animals, and each elaborates on a proverb like "You can't teach an old dog new tricks." (Rev: BL 11/1/97; SLJ 11/97)

**6720** Thomas, Jane Resh. *The Princess in the Pigpen* (4–6). 1989, Houghton $15.00 (0-395-51587-4). 124pp. In a reverse time travel story, a girl is transported from 17th-century England to present-day America. (Rev: BL 9/15/89; SLJ 11/89)

**6721** Thompson, Colin. *Looking for Atlantis* (4–6). Illus. 1994, Knopf $16.00 (0-679-85648-X); paper $6.99 (0-679-88547-1). 32pp. A 10-year-old boy's

grandfather returns to the sea on his final voyage, but not before telling the boy that he must learn to look for Atlantis. (Rev: BL 4/1/94; SLJ 5/94)

**6722** Thompson, Kate. *Switchers* (5–7). 1998, Hyperion LB $15.49 (0-7868-2328-3). 224pp. A young shape-changing girl and her friend save the world from a new ice age in this fast-moving fantasy. (Rev: BL 3/15/98)

**6723** Thurber, James. *The Great Quillow* (3–5). Illus. by Steven Kellogg. 1994, Harcourt $17.95 (0-15-232544-1). 56pp. A little toy maker becomes a hero when he outwits a giant. (Rev: BL 12/1/94*; HB 11–12/94; SLJ 11/94)

**6724** Titus, Eve. *Basil of Baker Street* (4–6). Illus. by Paul Galdone. 1958, Pocket paper $2.50 (0-318-37408-0). A clever mystery about a mouse who moves to 221 Baker Street out of admiration for Mr. Holmes. Another in the series: *Basil in the Wild West* (1990).

**6725** Tolan, Stephanie S. *Who's There?* (5–8). 1994, Morrow $15.00 (0-688-04611-8); paper $4.95 (0-688-15289-9). 240pp. Fourteen-year-old Drew is convinced that there is a ghost in her crusty grandfather's house, where she and her brother Evan, who has been mute since their parents' deaths, are currently living. (Rev: BCCB 12/94; BL 9/1/94; SLJ 10/94)

**6726** Tolkien, J. R. R. *The Hobbit* (5–7). Illus. by author. 1938, Houghton $14.95 (0-395-07122-4); Ballantine paper $5.99 (0-345-33968-1). 320pp. A saga of dwarfs and elves, goblins and trolls in a far-off, long ago land. There is a special edition illustrated by Michael Hague (1984).

**6727** Tudor, Tasha. *The Great Corgiville Kidnapping* (4–6). Illus. 1997, Little, Brown $15.95 (0-316-85583-9). 48pp. Caleb Corgi, a dog detective, must save Babe the rooster when he is kidnapped by some no-good raccoons. (Rev: BL 10/15/97; SLJ 12/97)

**6728** Tunnell, Michael O. *School Spirits* (4–6). 1997, Holiday LB $15.95 (0-8234-1310-1). 201pp. Patrick and his new friend Nairen encounter a ghost that they believe wants to harm them. (Rev: BL 2/15/98; SLJ 3/98)

**6729** Turner, Ann. *Elfsong* (3–7). 1995, Harcourt $16.00 (0-15-200826-8). 208pp. Maddy and Grandpa discover a forest where elves live and they can hear birds and other animals speak. (Rev: BCCB 12/95; BL 10/1/95; SLJ 10/95)

**6730** Turner, Ann. *Finding Walter* (3–6). 1997, Harcourt $16.00 (0-15-200212-X). 176pp. While visiting their grandmother's house, 2 sisters investigate an old dollhouse in which the dolls are able to transmit thoughts. (Rev: BL 10/15/97; SLJ 10/97)

**6731** Turner, Megan W. *Instead of Three Wishes* (4–6). 1995, Greenwillow $15.00 (0-688-13922-1);

Viking paper $4.99 (0-14-038672-6). 144pp. Everyday lives of ordinary people and fairy tale situations intermingle in these 7 stories involving magic. (Rev: BCCB 10/95; BL 10/1/95*; SLJ 9/95)

**6732** Turner, Megan W. *The Thief* (5–8). 1996, Greenwillow $15.00 (0-688-14627-9). 224pp. To escape life imprisonment, Gen must steal a legendary stone in this historical novel. (Rev: BCCB 11/96; BL 1/1–15/97; HB 11–12/96; SLJ 10/96)

**6733** Twain, Mark. *A Connecticut Yankee in King Arthur's Court* (5–8). Illus. by Trina S. Hyman. 1988, Morrow $23.00 (0-688-06346-2). 384pp. A smooth talker finds himself time traveling to Arthurian England. A reissued edition.

**6734** Ure, Jean. *The Children Next Door* (4–6). 1996, Scholastic $14.95 (0-590-22293-7). 144pp. In this time-travel fantasy, Laura discovers the truth about 2 mysterious children who play in the garden next door. (Rev: BCCB 5/96; BL 1/1–15/96; SLJ 3/96)

**6735** Ure, Jean. *The Wizard in the Woods* (3–5). Illus. by David Amstey. 1992, Candlewick $14.95 (1-56402-110-6). 176pp. After a botched-up spell, Ben-Muzzy is transported to Three Penny Wood, near the home of twins Joel and Gemma. (Rev: BL 12/1/92; SLJ 10/92)

**6736** Ure, Jean. *Wizard in Wonderland* (3–5). Illus. by David Anstey. 1993, Candlewick $14.95 (1-56402-138-6). 176pp. Twins Joel and Gemma take a tour of Wonderland. (Rev: SLJ 7/93)

**6737** Van Allsburg, Chris. *The Sweetest Fig* (3–6). Illus. 1993, Houghton $17.95 (0-395-67346-1). 32pp. All of his wildest dreams come true when a cruel dentist eats the figs given him in payment by a poor woman. (Rev: BCCB 11/93; BL 10/1/93*; SLJ 11/93*)

**6738** Van Allsburg, Chris. *The Wreck of the Zephyr* (2–5). Illus. by author. 1983, Houghton $17.95 (0-395-33075-0). 32pp. The story behind the wreck of a sailboat.

**6739** Van Leeuwen, Jean. *The Great Rescue Operation* (3–5). Illus. by Margot Apple. 1982, Dial LB $10.89 (0-685-01456-8). 144pp. Two mice try to locate their friend who has disappeared in Macy's department store.

**6740** Vivelo, Jackie. *Chills in the Night: Tales That Will Haunt You* (5–8). 1997, DK Publg. $14.95 (0-7894-2463-0). 123pp. Everyday experiences become strange and fearsome in this collection of bizarre, sometimes scary, stories. (Rev: BL 1/1–15/98; SLJ 1/98)

**6741** Vivelo, Jackie. *Chills Run down My Spine* (4–6). Illus. 1994, DK Publg. $12.95 (1-56458-712-6). 125pp. A group of horror stories, many of them containing supernatural elements. (Rev: BL 11/15/94; SLJ 12/94)

**6742** Voigt, Cynthia. *Building Blocks* (5–8). 1984, Fawcett paper $3.99 (0-449-70130-1). 132pp. Inside a fortress his father built him, Braunn meets Kevin, his father as a child.

**6743** Wagener, Gerda. *The Ghost in the Classroom* (2–4). Trans. by J. Alison James. Illus. 1997, North-South LB $13.88 (1-55858-800-0). 46pp. A mischievous ghost named Otto helps Tina get the cat that she wants. (Rev: BL 1/1–15/98)

**6744** Wallace, Bill. *Snot Stew* (4–6). Illus. by Lisa McCue. 1989, Holiday $15.95 (0-8234-0745-4); Pocket paper $3.99 (0-671-69335-2). 96pp. The amusing tale of how Mama Cat moves her kittens out into the world. (Rev: BL 5/15/89; SLJ 4/89)

**6745** Wallace, Bill. *Totally Disgusting* (4–6). Illus. by Leslie Morrill. 1991, Holiday $15.95 (0-8234-0873-6); Pocket paper $3.50 (0-671-75416-5). 120pp. Feline Mewkiss wants to be brave and strong but isn't at all sure that he'll make it. (Rev: BCCB 6/91; BL 4/1/91; SLJ 6/91)

**6746** Wallace, Bill. *Watchdog and the Coyotes* (3–5). Illus. 1995, Pocket $14.00 (0-671-53620-6); paper $3.99 (0-671-89075-1). 105pp. A Great Dane learns to be more assertive when he becomes friends with an Irish setter and a beagle. (Rev: BL 12/15/95; SLJ 11/95)

**6747** Walsh, Jill Paton. *Birdy and the Ghosties* (1–4). Illus. by Alan Marks. 1989, Farrar $10.95 (0-374-30716-4). 48pp. Birdy's gift of second sight helps her and her family when 3 ghosties board her father's boat. (Rev: BCCB 2/90*; BL 2/1/90; SLJ 2/90)

**6748** Walsh, Jill Paton. *Matthew and the Sea Singer* (3–5). Illus. by Alan Marks. 1993, Farrar $13.00 (0-374-34869-3). 46pp. Matthew, a trained singer, is taken to the bottom of the sea to teach a sea queen's son to sing. (Rev: BCCB 5/93*; BL 4/15/93; SLJ 5/93)

**6749** Walsh, Jill Paton. *Pepi and the Secret Names* (3–5). Illus. by Fiona French. 1995, Lothrop $15.00 (0-688-13428-9). 32pp. In this fantasy set in ancient Egypt, Pepi gets animals to pose for her artist father by guessing their secret names. (Rev: BL 4/15/95; SLJ 4/95)

**6750** Waugh, Sylvia. *The Mennyms* (4–8). 1994, Greenwillow $16.00 (0-688-13070-4). 212pp. When their owner dies, a family of rag dolls comes to life and takes over her house in this beginning volume of an extensive series. (Rev: BCCB 5/94; HB 7–8/94; SLJ 4/94)

**6751** Waugh, Sylvia. *Mennyms Alive* (4–6). 1997, Greenwillow $16.00 (0-688-15201-5). 224pp. The last book about the Mennyms, rag dolls who have problems finding a permanent home. (Rev: BL 9/15/97; HB 11–12/97; SLJ 9/97)

**6752**   Waugh, Sylvia. *Mennyms Alone* (4–6). 1996, Greenwillow $16.00 (0-688-14702-X). 208pp. The rag doll creatures known as the Mennyms prepare for the end of their existence. (Rev: BCCB 11/96; BL 9/15/96; SLJ 9/96)

**6753**   Waugh, Sylvia. *Mennyms in the Wilderness* (4–6). 1995, Greenwillow $15.00 (0-688-13820-9). 256pp. The Mennyms, a family of lively rag dolls, fight the highway construction that threatens to destroy their home. A sequel to *The Mennyms* (1994). (Rev: BCCB 3/95; BL 5/1/95; HB 7–8/95; SLJ 5/95)

**6754**   Waugh, Sylvia. *Mennyms Under Siege* (4–6). 1996, Greenwillow $16.00 (0-688-14372-5). 224pp. The Mennyms, rag dolls that have come to life, courageously guard their precarious existence as humans. A sequel to *The Mennyms* (1994) and *Mennyms in the Wilderness* (1995). (Rev: BCCB 3/96; BL 3/15/96; SLJ 6/96)

**6755**   Weinberg, Karen. *Window of Time* (5–7). Illus. by Annelle W. Ratcliffe. 1991, White Mane paper $9.95 (0-942597-18-4). 166pp. Ben climbs through a window and finds himself 125 years back in time. (Rev: SLJ 7/91)

**6756**   Welch, R. C. *Scary Stories for Stormy Nights* (5–7). Illus. 1995, Lowell House paper $5.95 (1-56565-262-2). 128pp. Ten contemporary horror stories that involve such characters as a werewolf and some pirates. (Rev: BL 5/1/95)

**6757**   Wesley, Mary. *Haphazard House* (5–7). 1993, Overlook $14.95 (0-87951-470-1). 150pp. An artist's magic hat enables him to make money betting on the Derby race during a visit to England. (Rev: BCCB 10/93; BL 1/1/94)

**6758**   West, Tracey. *Voyage of the Half Moon* (3–5). Illus. Series: Stories of the States. 1993, Silver Moon LB $13.95 (1-881889-18-1). 55pp. When Gwen is sent to live with a new foster family, she is haunted by a ghost that no one else can see. (Rev: SLJ 9/93)

**6759**   Westall, Robert. *Ghost Abbey* (5–7). 1989, Scholastic paper $3.25 (0-590-41693-6). Twelve-year-old Maggi is in charge of her small English household since her mother died. (Rev: BCCB 2/89; BL 2/1/89; SLJ 3/89)

**6760**   Whatley, Bruce, and Rosie Smith. *Detective Donut and the Wild Goose Chase* (3–4). Illus. by authors. 1997, HarperCollins LB $14.89 (0-06-026607-4). Detective Donut, a bear, solves a crime involving a famous archaeologist and a masked goose posing as his assistant. (Rev: SLJ 12/97)

**6761**   White, E. B. *Charlotte's Web* (3–5). Illus. by Garth Williams. 1952, HarperCollins LB $14.89 (0-06-026386-5); paper $4.95 (0-06-440055-7). 184pp.

Classic, whimsical barnyard fable about a spider who saves the life of Wilbur the pig. Read about the ever-engaging mouse in *Stuart Little* (1945).

**6762**   White, E. B. *The Trumpet of the Swan* (3–6). Illus. by Edward Frascino. 1970, HarperCollins LB $14.89 (0-06-026398-9); paper $4.95 (0-06-440048-4). 222pp. Louis, a voiceless trumpeter swan, is befriended by Sam, learns to play a trumpet, and finds fame, fortune, and fatherhood.

**6763**   Willard, Nancy. *Beauty and the Beast* (4–8). Illus. by Barry Moser. 1992, Harcourt $19.95 (0-15-206052-9). 68pp. A clever reworking of the folktale using New York City at the turn of the century as a setting. (Rev: BCCB 11/92; HB 11–12/92; SLJ 10/92)

**6764**   Willard, Nancy. *The High Rise Glorious Skittle Skat Roarious Sky Pie Angel Food Cake* (3–5). Illus. by Richard J. Watson. 1990, Harcourt $15.95 (0-15-234332-6). 64pp. Grandma's cake has mysterious ingredients — an odd spell and the special help of angels. (Rev: BCCB 12/90; BL 9/1/90; SLJ 11/90*)

**6765**   Willard, Nancy. *The Marzipan Moon* (4–5). Illus. by Marcia Sewall. 1981, Harcourt paper $3.95 (0-15-252963-2). 46pp. A cracked pot given to a parish priest has miraculous powers.

**6766**   Willard, Nancy. *The Tortilla Cat* (3–5). Illus. by Jeanette Winter. 1998, Harcourt $16.00 (0-15-289587-6). 48pp. Dr. Romero is convinced that the little cat that helps his children get better when they are ill is only a dream. (Rev: BL 3/1/98; SLJ 3/98)

**6767**   Willard, Nancy. *Uncle Terrible: More Adventures of Anatole* (4–6). Illus. by David McPhail. 1985, Harcourt paper $5.95 (0-15-292794-8). 120pp. A boy's visit to Uncle Terrible, so named because he is so terribly nice.

**6768**   Williams, Margery. *The Velveteen Rabbit* (2–4). Illus. by David Jorgensen. 1985, Knopf $12.00 (0-394-87711-X). 48pp. Fifty full-color pictures highlight this famous story. (Rev: BCCB 11/85; BL 12/15/85; SLJ 1/86)

**6769**   Williams, Margery. *The Velveteen Rabbit: Or, How Toys Become Real* (2–4). Illus. by Michael Hague. 1983, Holt $13.95 (0-8050-0209-X). 48pp. Love brings a toy rabbit to life. One of many fine editions.

**6770**   Winthrop, Elizabeth. *The Battle for the Castle* (4–7). 1993, Holiday $15.95 (0-8234-1010-2). 216pp. William and friend Jason time-travel to the Middle Ages, where they become involved in a struggle to prevent the return of evil as a ruling power. A sequel to *The Castle in the Attic* (1985). (Rev: BL 9/1/93; HB 7–8/93; SLJ 5/93)

**6771**   Winthrop, Elizabeth. *The Castle in the Attic* (5–7). 1985, Holiday $15.95 (0-8234-0579-6). 192pp. In an effort to keep his sitter from returning to England, William miniaturizes her and then must find a way to undo the deed. (Rev: BCCB 10/85; BL 1/15/86; SLJ 2/86)

**6772** Wiseman, David. *Jeremy Visick* (5–8). 1981, Houghton paper $6.95 (0-395-56153-1). Matthew helps the ghost of young Jeremy find rest.

**6773** Wojciechowski, Susan. *Beany (Not Beanhead) and the Magic Crystal* (2–4). Illus. 1997, Candlewick $15.99 (0-7636-0052-0). 96pp. In this lighthearted story, Beany thinks that a crystal from a chandelier might be magical and wonders what would be the perfect wish. (Rev: BL 7/97; SLJ 7/97)

**6774** Woodruff, Elvira. *Awfully Short for the Fourth Grade* (3–6). Illus. by Will Hillenbrand. 1989, Holiday $14.95 (0-8234-0785-3). 112pp. Noah's toy soldiers and superheroes come to life and he becomes their size when he uses a special dust from his magic kit. (Rev: BL 1/1/90; SLJ 11/89)

**6775** Woodruff, Elvira. *Orphan of Ellis Island* (4–7). 1997, Scholastic $14.95 (0-590-48245-9). 192pp. Left alone on Ellis Island, Dominic finds himself transported in time to the village in Italy his family came from. (Rev: BCCB 3/97; BL 6/1–15/97; SLJ 5/97)

**6776** Woodruff, Elvira. *The Summer I Shrank My Grandmother* (4–6). Illus. by Katherine Coville. 1992, Bantam paper $3.99 (0-440-40640-4). 160pp. Nelly finds an ancient chemistry set and changes her grandmother into a gorgeous 30-year-old who keeps getting younger. (Rev: BL 1/1/91; SLJ 12/90)

**6777** Wrede, Patricia C. *Book of Enchantments* (5–8). 1996, Harcourt $17.00 (0-15-201255-9). 240pp. A collection of stories with various settings, each dealing with an enchantment. (Rev: BCCB 5/96; BL 5/15/96; SLJ 6/96)

**6778** Wright, Betty R. *Christina's Ghost* (4–6). 1985, Holiday $15.95 (0-8234-0581-8). 128pp. Dismayed at having to spend the summer with grumpy Uncle Ralph in his Victorian mansion, Christina is even more dismayed to discover a ghost in the house. (Rev: BCCB 2/86; BL 2/1/86)

**6779** Wright, Betty R. *The Ghost Comes Calling* (3–6). 1994, Scholastic $14.95 (0-590-47353-0). 128pp. When Chad encounters the ghost that built the shabby log cabin his father has just bought, he sets out to right a wrong and let the ghost rest. (Rev: BCCB 3/94; BL 2/15/94; HB 9–10/94; SLJ 4/94)

**6780** Wright, Betty R. *The Ghost in Room 11* (2–4). 1997, Holiday $15.95 (0-8234-1318-7). 112pp. Matt can't convince his classmates that he is being visited by the ghost of an old school teacher. (Rev: BL 3/1/98; SLJ 3/98)

**6781** Wright, Betty R. *A Ghost in the House* (5–7). 1991, Scholastic $13.95 (0-590-43606-6). 160pp. Bizarre happenings take place when Sarah's elderly

aunt moves in. (Rev: BCCB 11/91; BL 1/1/91; SLJ 11/91)

**6782** Wright, Betty R. *The Ghost of Popcorn Hill* (2–4). Illus. by Karen Ritz. 1993, Holiday $15.95 (0-8234-1009-9). 96pp. Martin and Peter are frightened by the ghost who visits their bedroom each night in their rustic home on Popcorn Hill. (Rev: BCCB 6/93; BL 2/15/93; HB 7–8/93; SLJ 5/93)

**6783** Wright, Betty R. *The Ghost Witch* (3–5). Illus. by Ellen Eagle. 1993, Holiday $15.95 (0-8234-1036-6). 103pp. When Jenny and her mother move into a new house, the young girl is unnerved when she is welcomed by a ghost. (Rev: BCCB 12/93; BL 1/15/94; SLJ 12/93)

**6784** Wright, Betty R. *The Ghosts of Mercy Manor* (4–7). 1993, Scholastic $13.95 (0-590-43601-5). 160pp. Gwen's happiness in her foster home is upset when she is visited by the ghost of a young girl. (Rev: BCCB 9/93; BL 9/15/93; SLJ 9/93*)

**6785** Wright, Betty R. *Haunted Summer* (4–6). 1996, Scholastic $13.95 (0-590-47355-7). 128pp. Abby discovers that a wicked witch wants possession of a music box that Abby's aunt has sent as a gift. (Rev: BCCB 4/96; BL 4/1/96; HB 7–8/96; SLJ 5/96)

**6786** Wright, Betty R. *Out of the Dark* (4–6). 1995, Scholastic $13.95 (0-590-43598-1). 128pp. Jessica's stay in her grandmother's home in the country becomes unexpectedly horrifying when she encounters a ghost. (Rev: BCCB 2/95; BL 12/1/94; SLJ 1/95)

**6787** Wright, Jill. *The Old Woman and the Jar of Uums* (2–5). Illus. by Glen Rounds. 1990, Putnam $14.95 (0-399-21736-3). 32pp. An old woman discovers that the strange-looking green jar she has taken home has magical powers. (Rev: BL 5/15/90; SLJ 6/90)

**6788** Wyeth, Sharon D. *Vampire Bugs: Stories Conjured from the Past* (4–6). Illus. 1995, Delacorte $14.95 (0-385-32082-5). 80pp. Six unusual, often macabre tales inspired by folktales and legends. (Rev: BCCB 4/95; BL 1/1/95; SLJ 3/95*)

**6789** Wynne Jones, Diana. *Fantasy Stories* (4–8). Illus. 1994, Kingfisher paper $6.95 (1-85697-982-2). 256pp. A selection of fantasies from such authors as Kipling, C. S. Lewis, and Jane Yolen. (Rev: BL 3/1/95; SLJ 11/94)

**6790** Wynne-Jones, Tim. *Some of the Kinder Planets* (5–8). 1995, Orchard LB $16.99 (0-531-08751-4). 144pp. Nine imaginative stories about young people in unusual situations. (Rev: BCCB 5/95; BL 3/1/95*; HB 1–2/95, 5–6/95, 9–10/95; SLJ 4/95*)

**6791** Yee, Paul. *Ghost Train* (3–5). Illus. by Harvey Chan. 1996, Douglas & McIntyre $15.95 (0-88899-257-2). 32pp. In this historical fantasy, a Chinese girl comes to the United States and discovers that her father has been killed while working as a railroad construction laborer. (Rev: BCCB 2/97; BL 11/1/96)

**6792** Yep, Laurence. *Dragon of the Lost Sea* (5–8). 1982, HarperCollins paper $4.95 (0-06-440227-4). 224pp. Shimmer, a dragon, in the company of a boy, Thorn, sets out to destroy the villain Civet.

**6793** Yep, Laurence. *The Imp That Ate My Homework* (3–7). Illus. 1998, HarperCollins LB $13.89 (0-06-027689-4). 96pp. A 6-foot-tall, 4-armed ancient creature enters Jim's life and creates havoc in this novel set in San Francisco's Chinatown. (Rev: BL 12/15/97; SLJ 3/98)

**6794** Yolen, Jane. *Here There Be Angels* (4–7). Illus. 1996, Harcourt $18.00 (0-15-200938-8). 112pp. Original poetry and stories dealing with various aspects of angels. (Rev: BL 10/15/96; SLJ 11/96)

**6795** Yolen, Jane. *Here There Be Dragons* (3–8). Illus. by David Wilgus. Series: Jane Yolen Books. 1993, Harcourt $16.95 (0-15-209888-7); paper $10.00 (0-15-201705-4). 160pp. This original collection of pieces about dragons contains 8 stories and 5 poems. (Rev: SLJ 12/93)

**6796** Yolen, Jane. *Merlin* (5–8). 1997, Harcourt $15.00 (0-15-200814-4). 112pp. In this concluding volume of the Young Merlin trilogy, Hawk-Hobby, alias Merlin, escapes from his enemies with a young friend who will later become King Arthur. (Rev: BL 4/15/97; SLJ 5/97)

**6797** Yolen, Jane. *Merlin and the Dragons* (3–8). Illus. by Li Ming. 1995, Dutton paper $16.99 (0-525-65214-0). 40pp. A troubled young King Arthur gets solace in hearing the story told by Merlin of Emrys and his dream of 2 dragons. (Rev: BL 9/15/95; SLJ 3/96)

**6798** Yolen, Jane. *Passager: The Young Merlin Trilogy, Book One* (4–7). 1996, Harcourt $15.00 (0-15-200391-6). 96pp. In medieval England, an abandoned 8-year-old boy named Merlin is taken in by a friendly man who becomes his master. (Rev: BL 5/1/96; HB 7–8/96; SLJ 5/96*)

**6799** Yolen, Jane. *Wizard's Hall* (4–6). 1991, Harcourt $13.95 (0-15-298132-2). 144pp. Henry, an 11-year-old novice wizard, can't seem to get anything right. (Rev: BCCB 7–8/91; BL 3/15/91; SLJ 7/91)

**6800** Yoshi. *The Butterfly Hunt* (5–8). Illus. 1991, Picture Book paper $14.95 (0-88708-137-1). In this fantasy, a young boy releases a butterfly and forevermore it becomes his own. (Rev: SLJ 6/91)

**6801** Zadrzynska, Ewa. *The Peaceable Kingdom* (4–6). Illus. by Tomek Olbinski. 1994, M.M. Art Bks. $14.95 (0-9638904-0-9). 32pp. In this fantasy, visitors to Brooklyn find that the 3 animals pictured in Hicks's painting "The Peaceable Kingdom," hanging in the Brooklyn Museum, are sitting in the park. (Rev: BL 7/94; SLJ 9/94)

# Friendship Stories

**6802** Adler, C. S. *Always and Forever Friends* (5–7). 1990, Avon paper $3.99 (0-380-70687-3). 176pp. Wendy, at 11, is having a painful struggle making new friends after Meg moves away until she meets Honor, who is black and very hesitant about accepting Wendy. (Rev: BCCB 4/88; BL 4/1/88; SLJ 4/88)

**6803** Adler, C. S. *The Magic of the Glits* (5–7). Illus. by Ati Forberg. 1987, Avon paper $2.50 (0-380-70403-X). 96pp. Jeremy, age 12, takes care of 7-year-old Lynette for the summer. A reissue of the 1979 edition. Also use: *Some Other Summer* (1988).

**6804** Angell, Judie. *The Buffalo Nickel Blues Band* (5–8). 1991, Macmillan paper $3.95 (0-689-71448-3). 192pp. Five youngsters join together to form a band.

**6805** Appelbaum, Diana. *Cocoa Ice* (2–5). Illus. by Holly Meade. 1997, Orchard LB $17.99 (0-531-33040-0). 56pp. Two girls, one in Santo Domingo and the other in Maine, are linked by world trade, which brings chocolate to one and ice to the other. (Rev: BL 11/1/97*; SLJ 1/98*)

**6806** Auch, Mary Jane. *Kidnapping Kevin Kowalski* (4–6). 1990, Holiday $15.95 (0-8234-0815-9). 128pp. Kevin's friends think his slow recovery from an accident is caused by his overprotective mother, so they kidnap him to bolster his self-confidence. (Rev: BL 6/15/90; HB 5/90; SLJ 5/90)

**6807** Bauer, Marion Dane. *A Dream of Queens and Castles* (4–6). 1990, Houghton $13.95 (0-395-51330-8). 103pp. Except for the fact that she can meet the Princess of Wales, Diana is not happy to be going to England for a year. (Rev: BCCB 6/90; BL 2/15/90; HB 7–8/90; SLJ 5/90)

**6808** Bedard, Michael. *Emily* (3–5). Illus. by Barbara Cooney. 1992, Doubleday $16.95 (0-385-30697-0). A young girl visits her neighbor, the reclusive Emily Dickinson. (Rev: BCCB 1/93; BL 2/1/93; HB 1–2/93; SLJ 11/92)

**6809** Belton, Sandra. *Ernestine and Amanda* (4–6). 1996, Simon & Schuster $16.00 (0-689-80848-8). 150pp. Two young African American girls tell of their misunderstandings in alternating chapters. (Rev: BL 1/1–15/97; SLJ 11/96)

**6810** Belton, Sandra. *Ernestine and Amanda: Summer Camp, Ready or Not!* (4–6). 1997, Simon & Schuster $16.00 (0-689-80846-1). 176pp. Two African American girls, who are friends, are sent to different summer camps and report on their experiences. (Rev: BCCB 1/97; BL 8/97; SLJ 8/97)

**6811** Belton, Sandra. *Members of the C.L.U.B.* (4–7). 1997, Simon & Schuster paper $16.00 (0-689-81611-1). 176pp. The friendship of Ernestine and

Amanda, 2 African American girls from different backgrounds, seems to have ended permanently when one forms a club and excludes the other. (Rev: BL 11/15/97; SLJ 11/97)

**6812** Blair, I. E. *Welcome to Junior High!* (5–8). Series: Girl Talk. 1990, Western paper $2.95 (0-307-22001-X). 121pp. Four seventh-grade girls become friends while working on a homecoming dance committee. (Rev: BL 10/1/90)

**6813** Bonners, Susan. *The Silver Balloon* (3–5). Illus. 1997, Farrar $14.00 (0-374-36913-5). 80pp. Two pen pals reveal facts about each other through a series of mystery gifts they exchange. (Rev: BL 9/15/97; SLJ 10/97)

**6814** Briggs, Raymond. *The Man* (3–5). Illus. 1995, Random $22.00 (0-679-87643-X). 64pp. In this picture book, John is both annoyed by and attracted to a filthy old man who accosts him. (Rev: BCCB 2/96; BL 2/1/96)

**6815** Bunting, Eve. *Summer Wheels* (3–5). Illus. by Thomas B. Allen. 1992, Harcourt $14.95 (0-15-207000-1). 48pp. Lawrence and Brady are annoyed by the new kid, who signs out a bike from the Bicycle Man with the clear intention of not returning it. (Rev: BCCB 3/92; BL 4/15/92; HB 7–8/92; SLJ 8/92)

**6816** Burnett, Frances Hodgson. *The Secret Garden* (4–6). Illus. by Tasha Tudor. 1987, HarperCollins paper $3.50 (0-06-440188-X). 256pp. Three children find a secret garden and make it bloom again; the garden, in turn, changes the children. One of many fine editions.

**6817** Buscaglia, Leo. *A Memory for Tino* (4–6). Illus. by Carol Newsom. 1988, Slack $12.95 (1-556-42020-X). 50pp. Tino becomes friends with elderly Mrs. Sunday, and gives her his family's TV set. (Rev: BL 4/1/88; SLJ 5/88)

**6818** Byars, Betsy. *The Animal, the Vegetable and John D. Jones* (5–8). Illus. by Ruth Sanderson. 1983, Dell paper $3.50 (0-440-40356-1). 160pp. Clara and Deanie must share their vacation with the brainy John D.

**6819** Byars, Betsy. *The Pinballs* (5–7). 1977, HarperCollins LB $14.89 (0-06-020918-6). 144pp. Three misfits in a foster home band together to help lessen their problems.

**6820** Calhoun, Mary. *Katie John* (4–6). Illus. by Paul Frame. 1960, HarperCollins LB $13.80 (0-06-020951-8). 128pp. In spite of her worst fears, Katie John has a pleasant time and makes new friends during a summer in a small Southern town. Two sequels are: *Depend on Katie John; Katie John and Heathcliff* (both 1981).

**6821** Carlson, Natalie Savage. *The Family Under the Bridge* (3–5). Illus. by Garth Williams. 1958, Harper-

Collins LB $14.89 (0-06-020991-7); paper $4.95 (0-06-440250-9). 112pp. Old Armand, a Paris hobo, finds 3 children huddled in his hideaway under the bridge and befriends them.

**6822** Carrick, Carol. *Some Friend!* (3–5). Illus. by Donald Carrick. 1987, Houghton paper $5.95 (0-89919-525-3). 112pp. It is difficult for Mike to accept his friend Rob's overbearing behavior.

**6823** Christiansen, C. B. *A Snowman on Sycamore Street* (2–4). Illus. 1996, Simon & Schuster $15.00 (0-689-31927-4). 30pp. In this sequel to *Sycamore Street* (1993), the 3 friends — Angel, Chloe, and Rupert — continue to have good times together. (Rev: BL 10/1/96; SLJ 11/96)

**6824** Cohen, Barbara. *The Orphan Game* (4–6). Illus. by Diane De Groat. 1989, Bantam paper $2.75 (0-553-15706-X). 160pp. Twins Sally and Emily must put up with stuck-up cousin Miranda during a summer at the Jersey shore. (Rev: BCCB 7–8/88; BL 6/15/88)

**6825** Cooper, Ilene. *Queen of the Sixth Grade* (4–6). 1990, Puffin paper $3.95 (0-140-34028-9). 128pp. Robin and Veronica, acknowledged leader of the sixth grade, fight, and Robin learns about being an outsider. (Rev: BCCB 11/88; BL 9/1/88; SLJ 11/88)

**6826** Cooper, Ilene. *Star-Spangled Summer* (4–7). 1996, Viking paper $14.99 (0-670-85655-X). 120pp. Five sixth-grade girls struggle to make sure their plans for summer camp are not spoiled. (Rev: BL 4/15/96; SLJ 5/96)

**6827** Cooper, Ilene. *Stupid Cupid* (4–7). Series: Holiday Five. 1995, Viking paper $14.99 (0-670-85059-4). 128pp. Maddy worries about her weight in this book in the Holiday Five series. (Rev: BL 1/1/95; SLJ 2/95)

**6828** Cooper, Susan. *Dawn of Fear* (5–6). Illus. by Margery Gill. 1989, Simon & Schuster paper $4.50 (0-689-71327-4). 157pp. Reality must be faced by a group of English boys when one of their friends is killed in an air raid during World War II.

**6829** Cosby, Bill. *The Best Way to Play* (2–4). Illus. 1997, Scholastic $13.95 (0-590-13756-5); paper $3.99 (0-590-95617-5). 40pp. Little Bill wants a $50 video game but finds that he can have more fun making up a game with his friends. Also use *The Meanest Thing To Say* and *The Treasure Hunt* (both 1997). (Rev: BL 2/15/98; SLJ 12/97)

**6830** DeFelice, Cynthia. *The Light on Hogback Hill* (4–8). 1993, Macmillan paper $14.00 (0-02-726453-X). 144pp. Two friends explore the haunted Hogback Hill and make a friend of the recluse they find living there. (Rev: BCCB 12/93; BL 11/1/93; SLJ 11/93)

**6831** Dorros, Arthur. *Radio Man/Don Radio: A Story in English and Spanish* (1–5). Illus. 1993, Harper-Collins LB $15.89 (0-06-021548-8). 40pp. Two young friends, Diego and David, the sons of migrant workers, keep in touch through the farm worker's radio in this bilingual book. (Rev: BCCB 1/94; BL 1/15/94*)

**6832** Duffy, James. *Uncle Shamus* (4–6). 1992, Macmillan LB $13.95 (0-684-19434-1). 144pp. Two children form an unusual friendship with an elderly black man, returned after 30 years in prison. (Rev: BCCB 5/92; BL 3/1/92; SLJ 7/92)

**6833** Dunlop, Eileen. *Finn's Search* (4–7). 1994, Holiday $14.95 (0-8234-1099-4). 128pp. Two Scottish boys try to save a gravel pit from local developers. (Rev: BCCB 12/94; BL 10/1/94; SLJ 10/94)

**6834** Ellis, Sarah. *Next-Door Neighbors* (4–6). 1990, Simon & Schuster LB $15.00 (0-689-50495-0); Dell paper $3.25 (0-440-40620-X). 160pp. Peggy is nervous about attending a new school after her minister father moves the family to western Canada. (Rev: BCCB 3/90; BL 3/1/90*; HB 5–6/90; SLJ 3/90)

**6835** England, Linda. *3 Kids Dreamin'* (2–5). Illus. by Dena Schutzer. 1997, Simon & Schuster paper $16.00 (0-689-80866-6). Three youngsters form a rap group and become a big success. (Rev: SLJ 6/97)

**6836** Feuer, Elizabeth. *Lost Summer* (5–8). 1995, Farrar $16.00 (0-374-31020-3). 185pp. Lydia has difficulties adjusting to her cabinmates at summer camp. (Rev: BCCB 4/95; BL 5/15/95; SLJ 5/95)

**6837** Fields, Julia. *The Green Lion of Zion Street* (4–6). Illus. by Jerry Pinkney. 1988, Simon & Schuster $14.95 (0-689-50414-4). 32pp. A group of black children cautiously approach a stone lion in a fog-shrouded park. (Rev: BCCB 6/88; BL 4/15/88; SLJ 5/88)

**6838** Gabhart, Ann. *Two of a Kind* (3–6). 1992, Avon paper $3.50 (0-380-76153-X). 170pp. Birdie decides it's better to be aloof, even with her likable aunt and uncle, so she won't feel so bad when she's sent to another foster home. (Rev: BL 8/92)

**6839** Galbraith, Kathryn O. *Roommates Again* (2–4). Illus. 1994, Macmillan paper $13.00 (0-689-50597-3). 48pp. Two sisters go to summer camp together and find they each must conquer private fears involving new situations. (Rev: BL 8/94; SLJ 8/94)

**6840** Giff, Patricia Reilly. *The Girl Who Knew It All* (3–5). Illus. by Leslie Morrill. 1989, Bantam paper $3.25 (0-440-42855-6). 128pp. Tracy faces up to the fact that she has reading problems.

**6841** Giff, Patricia Reilly. *Love, from the Fifth-Grade Celebrity* (4–6). Illus. by Leslie Morrill. 1998, Bantam paper $3.99 (0-440-44948-0). 144pp. Casey and Tracy get involved in tattling on each other and realize the error of their ways. (Rev: BL 9/1/86)

**6842** Giff, Patricia Reilly. *Ronald Morgan Goes to Camp* (2–3). Illus. by Susanna Natti. 1995, Viking

paper $13.99 (0-670-86195-2). 32pp. Ronald wins an unusual medal at summer camp, that of being a good friend. (Rev: BL 7/95; SLJ 6/95)

**6843** Giff, Patricia Reilly. *Rosie's Big City Ballet* (2–4). Illus. 1998, Viking $13.99 (0-670-87792-1). 80pp. Rosie is torn between practicing ballet and helping her friend Murphy build a tree house. (Rev: BL 2/15/98)

**6844** Giff, Patricia Reilly. *Shark in School* (2–5). Illus. 1994, Delacorte $14.95 (0-385-32029-9). 96pp. At school, Matthew deserts his friend J.P. when she needs him, and he regrets it. A companion to *Matthew Jackson Meets the Wall* (1990). (Rev: BL 7/94; HB 9–10/94; SLJ 9/94)

**6845** Gilson, Jamie. *Hello, My Name Is Scrambled Eggs* (5–7). Illus. by John Wallner. 1985, Lothrop $16.00 (0-688-04095-0). 160pp. Harvey looks forward to the arrival of a Vietnam refugee family and their son, but runs into trouble with the prejudice of his American friend Quint. (Rev: BCCB 7/85; BL 4/14/85; SLJ 8/85)

**6846** Greenberg, Jan. *The Iceberg and Its Shadow* (5–7). 1980, Farrar $13.00 (0-374-33624-5); paper $3.50 (0-374-43550-2). 132pp. Anabeth's position as class leader is jeopardized by the arrival of arrogant Mindy.

**6847** Greene, Bette. *Philip Hall Likes Me, I Reckon Maybe* (4–6). Illus. by Charles Lilly. 1975, Dell paper $4.50 (0-440-45755-6). 144pp. Beth finds that letting Philip Hall get first place in their class turns out not to be the best way to gain his affection.

**6848** Greene, Carol. *The Jenny Summer* (2–4). Illus. by Ellen Eagle. 1988, HarperCollins $11.95 (0-06-022208-5). 80pp. Robin learns a lot about friendship during one summer. (Rev: BL 6/15/88; SLJ 8/88)

**6849** Greene, Constance C. *A Girl Called Al* (5–7). Illus. by Byron Barton. 1991, Puffin paper $4.99 (0-14-034786-0). 128pp. The friendship between 2 seventh graders and their apartment building superintendent is humorously and deftly recounted.

**6850** Grove, Vicki. *The Crystal Garden* (5–8). 1995, Putnam $15.95 (0-399-21813-0). 217pp. When she moves to a small town in Missouri, Eliza is determined to become part of the rich girls' clique. (Rev: BCCB 6/95; BL 9/1/95; SLJ 5/95*)

**6851** Hahn, Mary D. *Daphne's Book* (6–8). 1983, Houghton $13.45 (0-89919-183-5); Avon paper $4.50 (0-380-72355-7). 192pp. The story of a friendship between 2 very different girls.

**6852** Hahn, Mary D. *The Sara Summer* (4–6). 1995, Avon paper $4.50 (0-380-72354-9). 160pp. Two young girls, Sara and Emily, form a friendship one summer. A reissue of the 1978 edition.

**6853** Hansen, Joyce. *The Gift-Giver* (4–7). 1980, Houghton paper $6.95 (0-89919-852-X). 128pp. Doris forms a friendship with a quiet boy, Amir.

**6854** Hansen, Joyce. *Yellow Bird and Me* (4–6). 1986, Houghton paper $6.95 (0-395-55388-1). 128pp. The continuing story of the growing up of Doris, a black girl in the Bronx, New York, and her friendship with Yellow Bird, who suffers from dyslexia. (Rev: BCCB 4/86; BL 4/1/86; SLJ 5/86)

**6855** Haynes, David. *Business as Usual/The Gumma Wars* (4–6). Illus. 1997, Milkweed paper $6.95 (1-57131-608-6). 122/108pp. The 2 novels in this volume deal with the Wildcats, a group of boys growing up in a working-class neighborhood in St. Paul, Minnesota, and their adventures at home, school, and on the streets. (Rev: BL 10/15/97; SLJ 3/98)

**6856** Herman, Charlotte. *Max Malone Makes a Million* (3–5). Illus. 1991, Holt $13.95 (0-8050-1374-1); paper $4.95 (0-8050-2328-3). 77pp. Max wants to make a fortune, but learns a lesson in generosity instead. Also use: *Max Malone and the Great Cereal Rip-Off* (1990). (Rev: BCCB 6/91; BL 3/1/91; SLJ 6/91)

**6857** Herman, Charlotte. *Millie Cooper and Friends* (2–4). Illus. by Helen Cogancherry. 1995, Viking paper $13.99 (0-670-86043-3). 96pp. In this novel set in Chicago in the 1940s, Millie is hurt when her friend Sandy seems to prefer a new girl in their class. (Rev: BL 9/15/95; SLJ 9/95)

**6858** Hermes, Patricia. *Friends Are Like That* (5–8). 1984, Harcourt $14.95 (0-15-229722-7). 128pp. Tracy must make a choice between unconventional Kelly and the popular crowd.

**6859** Hermes, Patricia. *I Hate Being Gifted* (5–8). 1992, Pocket paper $3.50 (0-671-74786-X). 144pp. Everybody says it's an honor to be in the Learning Enrichment Activity Program, but KT thinks it can ruin her entire sixth-grade year. (Rev: BL 12/1/90)

**6860** Hest, Amy. *Pajama Party* (2–4). Illus. by Irene Trivas. 1992, Morrow LB $13.93 (0-688-07870-2). 48pp. Casey plans a sleep-over party with 2 of her friends. (Rev: BCCB 7–8/92; BL 3/1/92; SLJ 4/92)

**6861** Hirsch, Karen. *Ellen Anders on Her Own* (4–6). 1994, Macmillan paper $15.00 (0-02-743975-5). 96pp. Ellen learns about friendship through reading a journal kept by her mother years before she died. (Rev: BL 5/1/94; SLJ 6/94)

**6862** Honeycutt, Natalie. *Josie's Beau* (5–7). 1988, Avon paper $2.95 (0-380-70524-9). 128pp. Beau's mother doesn't want him fighting, so Josie offers to say she's the one who fights — but the lie backfires. (Rev: BCCB 12/87; BL 12/1/87; SLJ 12/87)

**6863** Hossack, Sylvie A. *The Flying Chickens of Paradise Lane* (3–6). 1994, Avon paper $3.50 (0-380-72201-1). 144pp. Ten-year-old Brenda, who desperately wants to learn to fly, forms a secret club with friends and practices jumping from ever-increasing heights. (Rev: BL 3/1/93; SLJ 3/93)

**6864** Hurwitz, Johanna. *The Cold and Hot Winter* (4–6). Illus. by Carolyn Ewing. 1988, Morrow $12.95 (0-688-07839-7). 144pp. The relationship of 3 children is strained because one may be a thief. (Rev: BCCB 11/88; BL 10/15/88; SLJ 9/88)

**6865** Hurwitz, Johanna. *The Hot and Cold Summer* (4–6). Illus. by Gail Owens. 1984, Morrow $13.00 (0-688-02746-6); Scholastic paper $3.99 (0-590-42858-6). 176pp. Roddy and Derek wonder about their neighbor's niece, who is spending the summer with her aunt.

**6866** Hurwitz, Johanna. *Ozzie on His Own* (2–4). Illus. by Eileen McKeating. 1995, Morrow $15.00 (0-688-13742-3). 128pp. When Ozzie finds an abandoned chicken coop, he soon forms a club and makes new friends. (Rev: BCCB 3/95; BL 3/1/95; SLJ 6/95)

**6867** Hurwitz, Johanna. *Spring Break* (3–5). Illus. 1997, Morrow $15.00 (0-688-14937-5). 144pp. An appealing novel about Cricket and her adventures when she is unable to go with her class to Washington, D.C., during spring break because of a broken ankle. (Rev: BCCB 4/97; BL 4/15/97; SLJ 5/97)

**6868** Hurwitz, Johanna. *The Up and Down Spring* (3–6). Illus. by Gail Owens. 1993, Morrow $14.00 (0-688-11922-0). 112pp. On a trip to Ithaca, New York, Roddy has trouble keeping his fear of flying a secret in this sequel to *The Hot and Cold Summer* (1984). (Rev: BCCB 4/93; BL 2/15/93; SLJ 7/93)

**6869** Hyppolite, Joanne. *Seth and Samona* (3–5). Illus. 1995, Bantam $18.95 (0-385-44630-6); Dell paper $3.99 (0-440-41272-2). 121pp. Seth, a Haitian American boy, secretly enjoys his friendship with the pesky, often obnoxious Samona. (Rev: BCCB 7–8/95; BL 5/1/95; SLJ 5/95)

**6870** Jukes, Mavis. *Getting Even* (5–7). 1988, Knopf LB $12.99 (0-394-99594-5); paper $3.99 (0-679-86570-5). 160pp. Maggie seems unable to stop the nasty pranks of classmate Corky, and receives differing advice from her divorced parents. (Rev: BCCB 5/88; BL 4/1/88; SLJ 5/88)

**6871** Kaye, Marilyn. *Cabin Six Plays Cupid* (4–6). 1989, Avon paper $2.95 (0-380-75701-X). 116pp. Five friends in Cabin 6 at Camp Sunnyside try to help their counselor's love life. Also use: *No Boys Allowed* (1989). (Rev: BL 7/89; SLJ 9/89)

**6872** Kaye, Marilyn. *A Friend Like Phoebe* (4–6). 1989, Harcourt $13.95 (0-15-200450-5). 144pp. Phoebe's best friend is chosen for an honor that Phoebe wanted, which causes a crisis in their friendship. A sequel to *Phoebe* (1987). (Rev: BL 8/89; SLJ 11/89)

**6873** Kehret, Peg. *The Richest Kids in Town* (4–6). 1994, Dutton paper $13.99 (0-525-65166-7). 128pp. Peter and his friend Wishbone embark on several ill-fated money-making schemes but discover they have something more precious than money: their friendship. (Rev: BL 9/1/94; HB 11–12/94; SLJ 9/94)

**6874** Keillor, Garrison, and Jenny L. Nilsson. *The Sandy Bottom Orchestra* (5–8). 1996, Hyperion LB $15.49 (0-7868-2145-0). 263pp. Rachel, age 14, faces some problems in growing up, including the ending of a treasured friendship. (Rev: BCCB 2/97; BL 1/1–15/97; SLJ 1/97)

**6875** Kline, Suzy. *Herbie Jones and the Dark Attic* (3–5). Illus. by Richard Williams. 1992, Putnam $13.95 (0-399-21838-6). 112pp. Herbie is not sure he can go through with it when he volunteers to sleep in the attic when Grandpa comes. (Rev: BL 11/15/92; SLJ 12/92)

**6876** Koller, Jackie F. *Impy for Always* (2–4). Illus. by Carol Newsom. 1989, Little, Brown $9.95 (0-316-50147-6); paper $3.95 (0-316-50149-2). 64pp. Eight-year-old Imogene's thoughts of another fun summer are dashed when 12-year-old cousin Christina arrives all grown up. (Rev: BL 6/15/59)

**6877** Konigsburg, E. L. *Jennifer, Hecate, Macbeth, William McKinley, and Me, Elizabeth* (4–6). Illus. by author. 1971, Macmillan $15.00 (0-689-30007-7); Dell paper $3.99 (0-440-44162-5). 128pp. Black Jennifer hazes white newcomer Elizabeth, her apprentice witch, and their amusing amateur sorcery leads to the magic of a firm friendship for 2 loners.

**6878** Konigsburg, E. L. *The View from Saturday* (5–7). 1996, Simon & Schuster $16.00 (0-689-80993-X). 163pp. A complicated tale about 4 sixth-graders who are contestants in an Academic Bowl competition. Newbery Medal winner, 1997. (Rev: BCCB 11/96; BL 10/15/96; SLJ 9/96*)

**6879** Kroll, Steven. *Patrick's Tree House* (3–4). Illus. by Roberta Wilson. 1994, Macmillan paper $13.95 (0-02-751005-0). 64pp. Patrick and Sarah don't know what to do when 2 older children take over their treehouse. (Rev: BL 5/1/94; SLJ 8/94)

**6880** Lamb, Nancy. *The Great Mosquito, Bull, and Coffin Caper* (3–5). Illus. by Frank Remkiewicz. 1994, Morrow paper $4.95 (0-688-12944-7). 120pp. To make sure they will not forget each other when one moves away, 2 friends face 3 dares, each tougher than the last. (Rev: BL 10/15/92; SLJ 11/92)

**6881** Leverich, Kathleen. *Best Enemies Forever* (2–4). Illus. 1995, Greenwillow $14.00 (0-688-13963-9). 100pp. Rivals Priscilla and Felicity clash over a do-gooders club that Priscilla has founded. (Rev: BL 8/95; SLJ 10/95)

**6882** Levin, Betty. *Starshine and Sunglow* (3–5). Illus. by Joseph A. Smith. 1994, Greenwillow $14.00 (0-688-12806-8). 96pp. In this picture book, neighbors "adopt" 2 scarecrows and help 3 children in their battle to save corn plants from raiders like birds and raccoons. (Rev: BL 5/1/94*; HB 9–10/94; SLJ 6/94)

**6883** Lewis, Beverly. *Holly's First Love* (4–6). Series: Holly's Heart. 1993, Zondervan paper $6.99 (0-310-38051-0). 160pp. Holly and Andie's friendship is strained when they both find they are attracted to the new boy in town. Also use *Secret Summer Dreams* (1993). (Rev: SLJ 12/93)

**6884** Lindberg, Becky T. *Chelsea Martin Turns Green* (3–4). Illus. by Nancy Poydar. 1993, Whitman LB $12.95 (0-8075-1134-X). 123pp. Chelsea is afraid that Abigail is trying to steal her best friend. (Rev: SLJ 7/93)

**6885** Lindberg, Becky T. *Speak Up, Chelsea Martin!* (2–5). Illus. by Nancy Poydar. 1992, Whitman LB $12.95 (0-8075-7552-6). 157pp. Third-grader Chelsea takes her mother's advice and stands up for herself, then has to face the consequences. (Rev: BCCB 10/91; BL 5/1/92; SLJ 11/91)

**6886** McGuigan, Mary Ann. *Where You Belong* (5–8). 1997, Simon & Schuster $16.00 (0-689-81250-7). 176pp. In 1963 in the Bronx, a lonely white girl growing up in poverty forms a friendship with a black girl. (Rev: BCCB 5/97; BL 6/1–15/97; SLJ 7/97)

**6887** McKenna, Colleen O'Shaughnessy. *Camp Murphy* (5–7). 1993, Scholastic $13.95 (0-590-45807-8). 160pp. It's harder than it looks when Collette and friends decide to run a week-long day camp for the neighborhood kids. (Rev: BCCB 3/93; BL 3/15/93; SLJ 4/93)

**6888** Maguire, Gregory. *Six Haunted Hairdos* (4–6). Illus. 1997, Clarion $15.00 (0-395-78626-6). 148pp. A funny story about 2 rival school groups, the boys' Copycats and the girls' Tattletales, and how they amuse themselves by telling ghost stories. The sequel to *Seven Spiders Spinning* (1994). (Rev: BL 11/1/97; SLJ 9/97)

**6889** Makris, Kathryn. *The Five Cat Club* (4–6). Series: Eco-Kids. 1994, Avon paper $3.50 (0-380-77049-0). 156pp. Three junior high girls find homes for 5 abandoned kittens and become interested in animal rights and environmental issues. Also use *The Green Team* and *The Clean-up Crew* (both 1994). (Rev: SLJ 9/94)

**6890** Mazer, Norma Fox. *Mrs. Fish, Ape and Me, the Dump Queen* (5–7). 1981, Avon paper $3.50 (0-380-69153-1). 144pp. Three misfits band together in friendship.

**6891** Medearis, Angela Shelf. *The Adventures of Sugar and Junior* (2–3). Illus. by Nancy Poydar. 1995, Holiday LB $15.95 (0-8234-1182-6). 32pp. A simple story of a friendship between a Hispanic American and an African American youngster and their happy times together. (Rev: BL 10/15/95; SLJ 12/95)

**6892** Miller, Judi. *My Crazy Cousin Courtney* (5–7). 1993, Pocket paper $2.99 (0-671-73821-6). Cathy is shocked to discover how much she and her California cousin are alike. (Rev: BL 3/1/93)

**6893** Modarressi, Mitra. *The Beastly Visits* (PS–2). Illus. 1996, Orchard LB $16.99 (0-531-08880-4). 32pp. A strange-looking monster boy named Newton helps his friend Miles when he is attacked by a bully. (Rev: BL 10/1/96; SLJ 9/96)

**6894** Moore, Martha. *Under the Mermaid Angel* (5–8). 1995, Delacorte $14.95 (0-385-32160-0). 168pp. Thirteen-year-old Jesse is fascinated by her new neighbor, fast-talking, brash Roxanne. (Rev: BCCB 12/95; BL 8/95; SLJ 10/95)

**6895** Mosher, Richard. *The Taxi Navigator* (5–7). 1996, Putnam $15.95 (0-399-23104-8). 144pp. Nine-year-old Kyle shares many adventures with his taxi-driving Uncle Hank. (Rev: BL 9/15/96; SLJ 1/97)

**6896** Moss, Marissa. *Amelia Writes Again* (3–5). Illus. 1996, Tricycle Pr. $14.00 (1-883672-42-2). 32pp. In this sequel to *Amelia's Notebook* (1995), Amelia writes in her journal about friendships and everyday occurrences. (Rev: BL 11/1/96; SLJ 10/96)

**6897** Naylor, Phyllis Reynolds. *Josie's Troubles* (3–5). 1992, Macmillan $13.95 (0-689-31659-3). 112pp. Josephine discovers that if your relationship is strong enough, there's room for other friends in it. (Rev: BL 9/1/92; SLJ 11/92)

**6898** Nicholson, Peggy, and John F. Warner. *The Case of the Furtive Firebug* (3–5). 1994, Lerner LB $13.27 (0-8225-0709-9). 120pp. Halley and her little brother Jason try to help a Vietnamese American girl who is falsely accused of arson. (Rev: BL 3/1/95)

**6899** O'Connor, Jane. *Amy's (Not So) Great Camp-Out* (1–3). Illus. by Laurie S. Long. 1993, Putnam paper $4.95 (0-448-40166-5). 64pp. A superactive girl gets sick when her Brownie troop goes on a camping trip. Also use *Corrie's Secret Pal* (1993). (Rev: BL 1/1/94)

**6900** O'Connor, Jane. *Sarah's Incredible Idea* (1–3). Illus. by Laurie S. Long. 1993, Putnam paper $4.95 (0-448-40162-2). 64pp. A shy girl gets up the nerve to suggest a service project for her Brownie troop. Also use *Make Up Your Mind, Marsha!* (1993). (Rev: BL 1/1/94)

**6901** O'Connor, Jane. *Yours Till Niagara Falls, Abby* (4–6). Illus. by Margot Apple. 1997, Putnam paper $5.95 (0-698-11597-X). 128pp. Abby's summer at camp proves to be unexpectedly rewarding.

**6902** Park, Barbara. *Buddies* (5–8). 1986, Avon paper $2.95 (0-380-69992-3). 144pp. Dinah's 2 weeks in camp are the subject of this first-person narrative. (Rev: BCCB 5/85; SLJ 5/85)

**6903** Paterson, Katherine. *Bridge to Terabithia* (6–8). Illus. by Donna Diamond. 1977, HarperCollins LB $15.89 (0-690-04635-9); paper $4.95 (0-06-440184-7). 144pp. Jess becomes a close friend of Leslie, a new girl in his school, and suffers agony after her accidental death. Newbery Award winner, 1978.

**6904** Patneaude, David. *The Last Man's Reward* (5–8). 1996, Albert Whitman LB $14.95 (0-8075-4370-5). 185pp. In this adventure, a group of boys agree to a pact rewarding the last to leave the neighborhood. (Rev: BL 6/1–15/96; SLJ 7/96)

**6905** Paulsen, Gary. *The Schernoff Discoveries* (5–7). 1997, Delacorte $15.95 (0-385-32194-5). 103pp. A humorous novel about the misadventures of 2 friends, both self-confessed geeks. (Rev: BCCB 7–8/97; BL 6/1–15/97; SLJ 7/97)

**6906** Peck, Robert Newton. *Soup* (5–7). Illus. by Charles C. Gehm. 1974, Knopf LB $15.99 (0-394-92700-1); Dell paper $3.99 (0-440-48186-4). 104pp. Rural Vermont in the 1920s is re-created in these reminiscences of the author of the times he spent with his friend Soup. Also use: *Soup for President* (1978); *Soup in the Saddle* (1983).

**6907** Peck, Robert Newton. *Soup on Fire* (4–6). Illus. by Charles Robinson. 1987, Delacorte $13.95 (0-385-29580-4). 112pp. Narrator Rob Peck tells of his friend Soup's hilarious brush with show business in this addition to a lively series. (Rev: BL 1/1/88; SLJ 12/87)

**6908** Peck, Robert Newton. *Soup on Ice* (4–6). Illus. by Charles Robinson. 1985, Knopf LB $13.99 (0-394-97613-4). 128pp. Rob and Soup get a big surprise on Christmas Eve in Vermont when the meanest man in town plays Santa Claus. Also use: *Soup's Goat* (1984). (Rev: BL 9/15/85; SLJ 10/85)

**6909** Peck, Robert Newton. *Soup 1776* (4–7). Illus. Series: Soup. 1995, Knopf $16.00 (0-679-87320-1). 160pp. In this slapstick comedy, Soup and Rob are writing the script for a Fourth of July pageant. (Rev: BL 9/1/95; SLJ 10/95)

**6910** Peck, Robert Newton. *Soup's Hoop* (4–6). Illus. by Charles Robinson. 1992, Dell paper $3.99 (0-440-40589-0). 112pp. Soup and Rob hope that they can enlist basketball star Piffle Shootensinker to play in their game against the Pratt Falls Wombats. Also use: *Soup in Love* (1992). (Rev: BL 4/15/90; SLJ 4/90)

**6911** Peters, Julie A. *How Do You Spell G-E-E-K?* (4–7). 1996, Little, Brown $12.95 (0-316-70266-8). 112pp. Kim feels left out when her best friend, Ann, befriends Lurlene, a new student. (Rev: BCCB 10/96; BL 9/15/96; SLJ 10/96)

**6912** Petersen, P. J. *I Hate Camping* (4–6). Illus. by Frank Remkiewicz. 1991, Dutton paper $13.00 (0-525-44673-7). 96pp. Dan is not thrilled about a camping trip with his mother's boyfriend, Mike, and his children. (Rev: BL 6/15/91; SLJ 5/91)

**6913** Pryor, Bonnie. *The Plum Tree War* (2–5). Illus. by Dora Leder. 1989, Morrow $11.95 (0-688-08142-8). 128pp. Nine-year-old Robert isn't happy when a cousin comes to stay for a year. (Rev: BL 6/15/89; SLJ 4/89)

**6914** Radin, Ruth Yaffe. *Tac's Island* (3–6). Illus. by Gail Owens. 1989, Troll paper $2.95 (0-8167-1320-0). 80pp. The growing friendship between Tac, a year-round island boy, and Steve, vacationing on the coastal Virginia island. (Rev: BL 5/1/86; SLJ 8/86)

**6915** Radley, Gail. *Odd Man Out* (4–6). 1995, Simon & Schuster paper $14.00 (0-02-775792-7). 144pp. The deep friendship of sixth-grader twins is tested when they differ about the friends each has made. (Rev: BCCB 9/95; BL 8/95; SLJ 6/95)

**6916** Rosner, Ruth. *I Hate My Best Friend* (2–4). Illus. 1997, Hyperion $14.49 (0-7868-2079-9); paper $3.95 (0-7868-1169-2). 64pp. When Nina begins to act cruelly toward Annie, the 2 best friends become enemies. (Rev: BL 4/15/97; SLJ 8/97)

**6917** Ruckman, Ivy. *This Is Your Captain Speaking* (5–7). 1987, Walker $14.95 (0-8027-6734-6). Adrift in junior high, Tom finds a friend in an old sea captain. (Rev: BL 11/15/87; SLJ 10/87)

**6918** Sachar, Louis. *Sixth Grade Secrets* (4–6). 1987, Scholastic paper $3.99 (0-590-46075-7). 208pp. Laura starts a club called Pig City, which eventually ends up by telling everyone's secrets. (Rev: BL 11/1/87; SLJ 9/87)

**6919** Shura, Mary Francis. *The Josie Gambit* (5–7). 1986, Avon paper $2.50 (0-380-70497-8). 160pp. Josie's friend Tory behaves in an inexplicable way to his new friend Greg. (Rev: BCCB 5/86; SLJ 9/86)

**6920** Skurzynski, Gloria. *Good-bye, Billy Radish* (5–7). Illus. 1992, Macmillan LB $15.00 (0-02-782921-9). 176pp. Vignettes set against the backdrop of World War I Pennsylvania describe the friendship between 2 boys of different backgrounds. (Rev: BL 10/15/92; HB 11–12/92; SLJ 12/92*)

**6921** Snyder, Zilpha Keatley. *The Egypt Game* (5–7). Illus. by Alton Raible. 1967, Macmillan $17.00 (0-689-30006-9); Dell paper $4.99 (0-440-42225-6). 224pp. Humor and suspense mark an outstanding story of city children whose safety, while playing at an unsupervised re-creation of an Egyptian ritual, is threatened by a violent lunatic.

**6922** Snyder, Zilpha Keatley. *The Gypsy Game* (4–6). 1997, Delacorte $15.95 (0-385-32266-6). 217pp. In this sequel to *The Egypt Game* (1967), 5 friends decide to become gypsies, but their plans change when one of them disappears. (Rev: BCCB 2/97; BL 2/1/97; HB 3–4/97; SLJ 2/97)

**6923** Steele, Mary. *Featherbys* (4–6). 1996, Peachtree paper $6.95 (1-56145-135-5). 180pp. Sixthgraders Jess and Vicky befriend 2 elderly sisters and help them fight a menacing relative. (Rev: BL 12/15/96)

**6924** Stolz, Mary. *The Bully of Barkham Street* (4–8). Illus. by Leonard Shortall. 1963, HarperCollins paper $4.95 (0-06-440159-6). 224pp. Eleven-year-old Martin goes through a typical phase of growing up — feeling misunderstood. Also use: *A Dog on Barkham Street* (1960).

**6925** Stolz, Mary. *The Explorer of Barkham Street* (4–6). Illus. by Emily Arnold McCully. 1985, HarperCollins paper $3.95 (0-06-440210-X). 192pp. Martin the underachiever fantasizes about heroic adventures and finally proves his dependability in baby-sitting. (Rev: BCCB 10/85; BL 9/15/85; SLJ 11/85)

**6926** Stolz, Mary. *The Noonday Friends* (4–6). Illus. by Louis Glanzman. 1965, HarperCollins LB $14.89 (0-06-025946-9); paper $4.95 (0-06-440009-3). 192pp. Eleven-year-old Franny's unskilled father is out of work, and the demanded family teamwork leaves her free from chores only during lunch periods.

**6927** Taylor, Theodore. *The Cay* (5–8). 1987, Doubleday $15.95 (0-385-07906-0); Avon paper $4.50 (0-380-00142-X). 160pp. Themes of growing up and survival — black versus white, innocence and distrust versus wisdom and respect — are deftly woven into the saga of a young blind American boy and an old West Indian native, both stranded on a Caribbean cay.

**6928** Waggoner, Karen. *Dad Gummit and Ma Foot* (2–4). Illus. by Anita Riggio. 1990, Orchard LB $14.99 (0-531-08491-4). 32pp. Cantankerous Thomas and Clara have a spat just before the wedding. (Rev: BL 9/15/90; SLJ 9/90)

**6929** Waggoner, Karen. *Partners* (3–5). Illus. 1995, Simon & Schuster paper $14.00 (0-671-86466-1). 95pp. Jamie balks at being partners with his brother in a scheme to raise mice for snake food. (Rev: BCCB 9/95; BL 5/15/95; HB 11–12/95; SLJ 6/95)

**6930** Walsh, Jill Paton. *Gaffer Samson's Luck* (4–6). Illus. by Brock Cole. 1984, Farrar $11.95 (0-374-32498-0); paper $3.50 (0-374-42513-2). 112pp. Out to retrieve a good luck stone for his elderly friend Gaffer, James runs into the school bully and learns about different kinds of friendship.

**6931** Warner, Sally. *Some Friend* (4–7). 1996, Knopf $15.00 (0-679-87620-0). 128pp. Case faces a difficult choice when a friend, who has run away from a foster home, asks for help. (Rev: BCCB 9/96; BL 6/1–15/96; SLJ 5/96)

**6932** Williams, Suzanne. *Edwin and Emily* (2–3). Illus. by Abby Carter. Series: Hyperion Chapters. 1995, Hyperion $13.95 (0-7868-0129-8); paper $3.95 (0-7868-1065-3). 48pp. A simple chapter book that deals with friendship and the inevitable disagreements. (Rev: SLJ 4/96)

**6933** Williams, Vera B. *Scooter* (4–6). Illus. 1993, Greenwillow LB $14.93 (0-688-09377-9). 160pp. Elana Rose explores her new urban neighborhood and finds that it is filled with new friends and new experiences. (Rev: BCCB 10/93; BL 11/15/93; SLJ 10/93)

**6934** Willner-Pardo, Gina. *When Jane-Marie Told My Secret* (3–4). Illus. 1995, Clarion $14.95 (0-395-66382-2). 40pp. Carolyn can't forgive her dear friend Jane-Marie after she has given away one of their secrets. (Rev: BL 8/95; SLJ 9/95)

**6935** Wilson, Nancy H. *Old People, Frogs, and Albert* (3–4). Illus. 1997, Farrar $14.00 (0-374-35625-4). 64pp. Albert loses his fear of a nursing home when he has to visit a friend there who has had a stroke. (Rev: BL 9/15/97; SLJ 11/97)

**6936** Wright, Betty R. *The Summer of Mrs. Mac-Gregor* (5–8). 1986, Holiday $15.95 (0-8234-0628-8). 160pp. Caroline becomes disillusioned with her new friend, "Mrs. MacGregor," a 17-year-old sophisticate from New York. (Rev: BCCB 12/86; SLJ 11/86)

**6937** York, Carol B. *The Key to the Playhouse* (2–4). Illus. by John Speirs. 1994, Scholastic $13.95 (0-590-46258-X). 69pp. Cousins Alice Ann and Megan behave cruelly toward their neighbor Cissie and later regret their actions. (Rev: BCCB 4/94; HB 9–10/94; SLJ 6/94)

# Growing into Maturity

## Family Problems

**6938** Ackerman, Karen. *The Leaves in October* (4–6). 1991, Macmillan $13.95 (0-689-31583-X). 128pp. A docunovel about 9-year-old Livvy, her little brother, and unemployed father. (Rev: BL 2/1/91)

**6939** Adler, C. S. *The Silver Coach* (4–6). 1988, Avon paper $2.50 (0-380-75498-3). 112pp. Chris and her sister adjust to their parents' imminent divorce during a summer with their grandmother. A reissue.

**6940** Auch, Mary Jane. *Out of Step* (5–7). 1992, Holiday $13.95 (0-8234-0985-6). 124pp. Jeremy's biggest problem is not his new stepmother but his new stepsister, who is a natural and talented athlete. (Rev: BCCB 2/93; BL 1/15/93; SLJ 9/92)

**6941** Bauer, Marion Dane. *A Question of Trust* (5–7). 1994, Scholastic $14.95 (0-590-47915-6). 128pp. Brad transfers the anguish he feels about his mother's departure into caring for a young kitten. (Rev: BCCB 2/94; BL 1/15/94*; HB 7–8/94; SLJ 3/94*)

**6942** Bawden, Nina. *The Real Plato Jones* (5–8). 1993, Clarion $13.95 (0-395-66972-3). 166pp. Plato Jones discovers that his Greek grandfather might have been a coward during World War II. (Rev: BCCB 11/93; BL 10/15/93; SLJ 11/93*)

**6943** Betancourt, Jeanne. *Puppy Love* (5–6). Illus. 1986, Avon paper $2.50 (0-380-89958-2). Aviva is having trouble dealing with her divorced parents' new lives and her own crush on Bob Hanley. (Rev: BL 8/86; SLJ 12/86)

**6944** Birdseye, Tom. *Just Call Me Stupid* (4–6). 1993, Holiday $15.95 (0-8234-1045-5). 128pp. Patrick's reading problems are complicated by an unfortunate home situation and his feelings of unworthiness. (Rev: BL 1/15/94; SLJ 10/93)

**6945** Birdseye, Tom. *Tucker* (4–6). 1990, Holiday $15.95 (0-8234-0813-2). 112pp. Tucker's 9-year-old sister comes to live with him and his father after an absence of 7 years. (Rev: BL 7/90; SLJ 6/90)

**6946** Blume, Judy. *It's Not the End of the World* (4–7). 1982, Macmillan LB $15.00 (0-02-711050-8); Dell paper $4.50 (0-440-44158-7). 176pp. Twelve-year-old Karen's world seems to end when her parents are divorced and her older brother runs away.

**6947** Bohlmeijer, Arno. *Something Very Sorry* (4–6). 1996, Houghton $13.95 (0-395-74679-5). 176pp. A terrible automobile accident in which Rose and her family are involved changes the young girl's life forever. (Rev: BCCB 3/96; BL 4/1/96; SLJ 7/96*)

**6948** Bowdish, Lynea. *Living with My Stepfather Is like Living with a Moose* (3–5). Illus. 1997, Farrar $14.00 (0-374-34630-5). 64pp. Matt finds that he and his new stepfather have little in common. (Rev: BL 3/1/97; SLJ 4/97)

**6949** Boyd, Candy Dawson. *Charlie Pippin* (5–7). 1988, Puffin paper $4.99 (0-14-032587-5). 192pp. A daughter tries to find out why her father is so embittered about his war experiences in Vietnam. (Rev: BCCB 5/87; BL 4/15/87; SLJ 4/87)

**6950** Boyd, Candy Dawson. *Fall Secrets* (5–7). 1994, Penguin paper $3.99 (0-14-036583-4). 224pp. Jessie has many family worries as she enters a middle school for the performing arts. (Rev: BL 9/15/94; SLJ 12/94)

**6951** Broome, Errol. *Rockhopper* (3–5). Illus. by Ann James. 1995, Allen & Unwin paper $6.95 (1-86373-678-6). 92pp. Bullied at school and overly protected at home, young Quentin is taught to be brave by a mysterious stranger in this story set in Australia. (Rev: BL 1/1–15/96)

**6952** Brown, Susan M. *You're Dead, David Borelli* (5–7). 1995, Simon & Schuster $15.00 (0-689-31959-2). 155pp. From a sheltered rich-kid life, David is suddenly thrown into a foster home in a rough neighborhood when his mother dies and his father disappears. (Rev: BL 6/1–15/95; SLJ 7/95)

**6953** Bunting, Eve. *The In-Between Days* (4–6). Illus. 1994, HarperCollins LB $13.89 (0-06-023612-4). 96pp. George is afraid that young Caroline is becoming too friendly with his Dad and tries to derail a possible romance. (Rev: BL 10/1/94; SLJ 10/94)

**6954** Bunting, Eve. *Is Anybody There?* (4–7). 1990, HarperCollins paper $3.95 (0-06-440347-5). 176pp. His latchkey disappears and things are stolen, and Marcus is both scared and angry. (Rev: BCCB 10/88; BL 12/15/88; SLJ 12/88)

**6955** Bunting, Eve. *Sharing Susan* (5–7). 1994, HarperCollins paper $3.95 (0-064-40430-7). 128pp. The nightmarish story of 2 families whose daughters were switched in the hospital at birth. (Rev: BL 9/15/91; HB 1–2/92; SLJ 10/91)

**6956** Byars, Betsy. *Cracker Jackson* (5–6). 1986, Puffin paper $4.50 (0-14-031881-X). 168pp. Eleven-year-old Cracker proves a caring friend to his ex-baby-sitter when he suspects she is a victim of wife beating. (Rev: BL 4/1/85; HB 5–6/85; SLJ 5/85)

**6957** Byars, Betsy. *The Two-Thousand-Pound Goldfish* (4–6). 1982, HarperCollins LB $14.89 (0-06-020890-2). 160pp. Warren can't accept the fact that his mother has rejected him.

**6958** Calvert, Patricia. *Glennis, Before and After* (5–8). 1996, Simon & Schuster $16.00 (0-689-80641-8). 150pp. Glennis must face many harsh realities when her father is sent to prison for white-collar crime and her mother has a nervous breakdown. (Rev: BCCB 10/96; SLJ 9/96)

**6959** Clifford, Eth. *Family for Sale* (3–5). 1996, Houghton $14.95 (0-395-73571-8). 112pp. Four young siblings, left in the charge of a 17-year-old sister, quarrel over who should make decisions. (Rev: BCCB 3/96; BL 2/1/96; SLJ 4/96)

**6960** Clifford, Eth. *The Remembering Box* (4–6). Illus. 1985, Houghton $15.95 (0-395-38476-1); Morrow paper $4.95 (0-688-11777-5). 64pp. Joshua enjoys a special relationship with his grandmother, who shortly before her death gives him a "remembering box" in which she places a girlhood picture of herself. (Rev: BCCB 12/85; BL 12/1/85; HB 3–4/86)

**6961** Coman, Carolyn. *What Jamie Saw* (5–8). 1995, Front Street $13.95 (1-886910-02-2). 128pp. In this novel seen through the eyes of a young boy, a mother and her family flee her physically abusive husband. (Rev: BCCB 12/95; BL 12/15/95*; SLJ 12/95*)

**6962** Crew, Linda. *Nekomah Creek* (4–6). Illus. by Charles Robinson. 1991, Delacorte $14.00 (0-385-30442-0). 191pp. Robby begins to wonder if his family life is normal when a guidance counselor starts to interrogate him. (Rev: BCCB 9/91; BL 10/15/91; SLJ 8/91)

**6963** Cullen, Lynn. *The Three Lives of Harris Harper* (5–7). 1996, Clarion $14.95 (0-395-73680-3). 160pp. Harris Harper's family is an embarrassment to him, unlike the seemingly perfect Benya family for whom he works. (Rev: BCCB 4/96; BL 4/1/96; SLJ 3/96)

**6964** Cummings, Priscilla. *Autumn Journey* (4–8). 1997, Cobblehill paper $14.99 (0-525-65238-8). 128pp. Tensions in the family mount when Will's father loses his job and the family has to move to Grampa's farm in Pennsylvania. (Rev: SLJ 10/97)

**6965** Danziger, Paula. *Amber Brown Wants Extra Credit* (3–5). Illus. 1996, Putnam $13.95 (0-399-22900-0). 112pp. Troubled by her parents' divorce, Amber begins having problems with her schoolwork. (Rev: BCCB 10/96; BL 6/1–15/96; SLJ 8/96)

**6966** Danziger, Paula. *Can You Sue Your Parents for Malpractice?* (6–8). 1979, Delacorte $11.95 (0-385-28112-9); Bantam paper $3.99 (0-440-91066-8). 266pp. Quarreling parents and a strong-willed father are only 2 of 14-year-old Lauren's problems.

**6967** Danziger, Paula. *The Divorce Express* (6–8). 1983, Delacorte $5.95 (0-385-28217-6); Bantam paper $3.99 (0-440-92062-0). 144pp. Phoebe commutes between divorced parents.

**6968** Danziger, Paula. *Forever Amber Brown* (2–4). Illus. 1996, Putnam $13.95 (0-399-22932-9). 101pp. Amber's divorced mother is being courted by Max, and the young girl is concerned. (Rev: BL 11/15/96; SLJ 2/97)

**6969** Danziger, Paula. *The Pistachio Prescription* (6–8). 1978, Bantam paper $3.99 (0-440-96895-X). 168pp. A 13-year-old talks about her school problem and possible divorce in the family.

**6970** DeClements, Barthe. *The Fourth Grade Wizards* (3–5). 1990, Puffin paper $3.99 (0-14-032760-6). 144pp. A fourth-grader and her father adjust to a new life after the death of her mother. (Rev: BCCB 10/88; BL 1/1/89; SLJ 10/88)

**6971** Doren, Marion. *Nell of Blue Harbor* (4–6). 1990, Harcourt $15.95 (0-15-256889-1). 160pp. From a commune in Vermont, 11-year-old Nell finds it difficult to adjust to life in Maine. (Rev: BCCB 1/91; BL 9/1/90; SLJ 11/90)

**6972** Duffey, Betsy. *Coaster* (4–8). 1994, Viking paper $13.99 (0-670-85480-8). 128pp. Hart is not too happy about his parents' divorce and that his father doesn't come around much anymore. (Rev: BCCB 10/94; BL 8/94; SLJ 9/94)

**6973** Duncan, Lois. *A Gift of Magic* (5–8). Illus. by Arvis Stewart. 1990, Pocket paper $3.99 (0-671-72649-8). A young girl, gifted with extrasensory perception, adjusts to her parents' divorce.

**6974** Ellis, Sarah. *Out of the Blue* (5–7). Illus. 1995, Simon & Schuster paper $15.00 (0-689-80025-8). 120pp. Twelve-year-old Megan discovers that she has a 24-year-old half-sister whom her mother gave up for adoption years ago. (Rev: BCCB 4/95; BL 5/1/95; HB 7–8/95; SLJ 5/95)

**6975** Fletcher, Susan. *The Stuttgart Nanny Mafia* (4–6). 1991, Macmillan LB $14.95 (0-689-31709-3). 160pp. When her mother marries a dentist, Aurora realizes that her life is about to be "taken over." (Rev: BCCB 9/91; BL 12/15/91; SLJ 10/91)

**6976** Foggo, Cheryl. *One Thing That's True* (5–8). 1998, Kids Can $14.95 (1-55074-411-9). 128pp. Roxanne is heartbroken when her older brother runs away after learning that he is adopted. (Rev: BL 2/15/98; SLJ 4/98)

**6977** Fox, Paula. *One-Eyed Cat* (6–8). Illus. by Irene Trivas. 1984, Macmillan $14.95 (0-02-735540-3); Dell paper $4.50 (0-440-46641-5). 192pp. A story about a boy growing up in upstate New York and a gift of an air rifle.

**6978** Franklin, Kristine L. *Lone Wolf* (4–7). 1997, Candlewick $16.99 (1-56402-935-2). 224pp. Perry has problems with his father when the 2 move to the north woods of Minnesota and Perry faces a life of isolation. (Rev: BCCB 5/97; BL 7/97; SLJ 6/97*)

**6979** French, Simon. *Change the Locks* (5–7). 1993, Scholastic $13.95 (0-590-45593-1). 112pp. Steven wants to know about his past, but his single-parent mother remains silent on the topic. (Rev: BCCB 5–6/93; BL 5/1/93)

**6980** Giff, Patricia Reilly. *Rat Teeth* (4–6). Illus. by Leslie Morrill. 1989, Bantam paper $3.99 (0-440-47457-4). 144pp. Radcliffe can't adjust to both his parents' divorce and a new school.

**6981** Gilliland, Hap, and William Walters. *Flint's Rock* (5–7). 1996, Roberts Rinehart paper $8.95 (1-879373-82-3). 144pp. Flint, a young Cheyenne, faces problems when he moves with his parents from the reservation to Butte, Montana. (Rev: BCCB 5/96; BL 5/1/96)

**6982** Gleitzman, Morris. *Puppy Fat* (5–7). 1996, Harcourt $11.00 (0-15-200047-X); paper $5.00 (0-15-200052-6). 144pp. Beset by quarreling parents, Keith discovers that his father is attracted to his friend's mother. A sequel to *Misery Guts* and *Worry Worts* (both 1993). (Rev: BCCB 7–8/96; BL 6/1–15/96; SLJ 5/96)

**6983** Gold, Carolyn J. *Dragonfly Secret* (3–6). 1997, Simon & Schuster $15.00 (0-689-31938-X). 144pp. Even though Gramps has his faults, the family rallies around to prevent Aunt Louise from sending him to a retirement home. (Rev: BL 7/97; SLJ 7/97)

**6984** Goodman, Joan E. *Songs from Home* (5–7). Illus. 1994, Harcourt paper $4.95 (0-15-203591-5). 224pp. Anna discovers the truth about her father, who has become a drifter in Italy singing for tips in restaurants. (Rev: BCCB 12/94; BL 9/1/94; SLJ 10/94)

**6985** Green, Connie J. *Emmy* (5–8). 1992, Macmillan $13.95 (0-689-50556-6). 160pp. This is the story of 11-year-old Emmy and her family after her father is injured in a Kentucky mine cave-in in 1924. (Rev: BCCB 2/92; BL 12/1/92; HB 1–2/93; SLJ 12/92)

**6986** Griffin, Adele. *Sons of Liberty* (4–6). 1997, Hyperion LB $15.49 (0-7868-2292-9). 176pp. Two brothers differ on how they should cope with an abusive, domineering father. (Rev: BL 9/15/97; SLJ 11/97)

**6987** Griffin, Adele. *Split Just Right* (5–8). 1997, Hyperion LB $15.49 (0-7868-2288-0). 160pp. Even though Danny's father has been gone as long as she can remember, she still wonders about him. (Rev: BL 6/1–15/97; HB 7–8/97; SLJ 6/97)

**6988** Hahn, Mary D. *Following My Own Footsteps* (5–8). 1996, Clarion $14.00 (0-395-76477-7). 192pp. Living with a grandmother to escape a drunken father, William has problems adjusting. (Rev: BCCB 10/96; BL 9/15/96; HB 9–10/96; SLJ 11/96)

**6989** Hahn, Mary D. *The Jellyfish Season* (5–7). 1992, Avon paper $3.99 (0-380-71635-6). 176pp. Kathleen must learn to cope with change: a move to Chesapeake Bay, a hostile cousin, her father's drinking, and her mother's pregnancy. (Rev: BCCB 2/86; BL 10/1/85; SLJ 10/85)

**6990** Hahn, Mary D. *Tallahassee Higgins* (5–7). 1987, Avon paper $3.50 (0-380-70500-1). 192pp. With her mother gone to Hollywood with a boyfriend, 12-year-old Tallahassee is stuck in her mother's hometown, where she finds out a lot about her mother's childhood. (Rev: BCCB 4/87; BL 3/1/87; HB 5–6/87)

**6991** Hamilton, Virginia. *Plain City* (5–7). 1993, Scholastic $13.95 (0-590-47364-6). 194pp. Buhlaire's life changes dramatically when the father she believed to be dead unexpectedly arrives in town. (Rev: BCCB 11/93; BL 9/15/93*; SLJ 11/93*)

**6992** Henkes, Kevin. *Two Under Par* (4–6). Illus. by author. 1987, Greenwillow $16.00 (0-688-06708-5). 128pp. Wedge doesn't like his new stepfather — the miniature golf king! — and he's doubly unhappy with the prospect of a new baby. (Rev: BL 6/1/87; HB 7–8/87; SLJ 6–7/87)

**6993** Hermes, Patricia. *Heads, I Win* (4–7). Illus. 1988, Pocket paper $2.99 (0-671-67408-0). 132pp. Bailey is foster-home smart; she always leaves before someone can dump her. (Rev: BL 6/15/88; SLJ 8/88)

**6994** Hermes, Patricia. *Mama, Let's Dance* (5–7). 1991, Little, Brown $15.95 (0-316-35861-4). 176pp. After being placed in foster homes when their mother runs off, 3 sisters decide to fend for themselves. (Rev: BCCB 12/91; BL 12/1/92; HB 1–2/92*; SLJ 9/91*)

**6995** Hermes, Patricia. *You Shouldn't Have to Say Good-bye* (5–8). 1982, Harcourt $11.95 (0-15-299944-2); Scholastic paper $3.25 (0-590-43174-9). 117pp. Sarah's mother is dying of cancer.

**6996** High, Linda O. *Maizie* (4–8). 1995, Holiday $14.95 (0-8234-1161-3). 177pp. Maizie, a survivor, succeeds in spite of being abandoned by her mother and left with an alcoholic father. (Rev: BCCB 4/95; BL 4/15/95; HB 5–6/95; SLJ 4/95)

**6997** High, Linda O. *A Stone's Throw from Paradise* (4–6). 1997, Eerdmans $15.00 (0-8028-5147-9); paper $5.00 (0-8028-5142-8). 128pp. Lizzie, whose parents were excommunicated from an Amish community, is spending a summer with her Amish Granny Zook. (Rev: BL 6/1–15/97; SLJ 12/97)

**6998** Holl, Kristi D. *Hidden in the Fog* (5–7). 1997, Royal Fireworks paper $6.99 (0-88092-436-5). 144pp. Set on a Mississippi steamboat, this story tells how Nikki worries that a fading tourist season will bring back her father's depression. (Rev: BCCB 3/89)

**6999** Honeycutt, Natalie. *Twilight in Grace Falls* (5–8). 1997, Orchard LB $17.99 (0-531-33007-9). 192pp. A moving novel about the closing of a lumber mill that brings unemployment to the father of 11-year-old Dasie Jenson. (Rev: BCCB 6/97; BL 3/15/97*; HB 7–8/97; SLJ 5/97)

**7000** Hunter, Evan. *Me and Mr. Stenner* (5–8). 1976, HarperCollins $11.95 (0-397-31689-5). 128pp. Abby's attitudes toward her new stepfather gradually change from resentment to love.

**7001** Hurwitz, Johanna. *DeDe Takes Charge!* (5–7). Illus. by Diane De Groat. 1984, Morrow $16.00 (0-688-03853-0). 128pp. DeDe's life is not the same A.D. (after divorce).

**7002** Hutchins, Hazel. *Tess* (3–5). Illus. by Ruth Ohi. 1995, Annick LB $16.95 (1-55037-395-1); paper $5.95 (1-55037-394-3). 32pp. Set during the Great

Depression in western Canada, this story tells how Tess and her family cope with extreme poverty. (Rev: BL 12/15/95)

**7003** James, Mary. *Frankenlouse* (5–8). 1994, Scholastic $13.95 (0-590-46528-7). 176pp. Nick and his father clash at the military academy where Nick is a student and his father a teacher. (Rev: BCCB 11/94; BL 10/15/94; SLJ 11/94)

**7004** Johnson, Angela. *Songs of Faith* (5–8). 1998, Orchard LB $16.99 (0-531-33023-0). 112pp. Doreen is a child of divorce who is particularly upset at seeing her younger brother's problems in adjusting after their father moves away. (Rev: BL 2/15/98; SLJ 3/98)

**7005** Jordan, Mary K. *Losing Uncle Tim* (2–4). Illus. by Judith Friedman. 1989, Whitman LB $14.95 (0-8075-4756-5). 32pp. A little boy remembers the fine times he had with Uncle Tim, who died of AIDS. (Rev: BCCB 11/89; BL 12/1/89; HB 1–2/90; SLJ 1/90)

**7006** Karr, Kathleen. *The Cave* (4–7). 1994, Farrar $16.00 (0-374-31230-3). 165pp. Christine, who is living on the family South Dakota farm during the Depression, finds and explores an amazing cave. (Rev: BL 9/15/94; SLJ 9/94)

**7007** Kaye, Marilyn. *Happily Ever After* (4–6). 1992, Avon paper $3.50 (0-380-76555-1). 116pp. When 2 friends become stepsisters, adjustment problems begin. (Rev: SLJ 4/92)

**7008** Lantz, Francess. *Stepsister from the Planet Weird* (5–8). 1997, Random LB $11.99 (0-679-97330-3); paper $3.99 (0-679-87330-9). 170pp. Megan and her almost-stepsister Ariel conspire to prevent their parents from marrying. (Rev: SLJ 2/98)

**7009** Lasky, Kathryn. *Memoirs of a Bookbat* (5–8). 1994, Harcourt $10.95 (0-15-215727-1). 192pp. A young girl who has to stifle her true nature from her strict, puritanical parents finds release through the friendship of a boy from a liberal family. (Rev: BCCB 4/94; BL 4/15/94; HB 9–10/94; SLJ 7/94)

**7010** Levinson, Marilyn. *No Boys Allowed* (5–8). 1993, Troll paper $13.95 (0-8167-3135-7). 128pp. Cassie, her father's pet, is crushed when he divorces her mother and moves to Kentucky. (Rev: BL 10/1/93; SLJ 11/93)

**7011** Lewis, Beverly. *Whispers down the Lane* (5–8). Series: Summerhill Secrets. 1995, Bethany paper $5.99 (1-55661-476-4). 144pp. An Amish girl agrees to hide Lissa, who has run away from her father's abusive treatment. (Rev: BL 9/1/95; SLJ 2/96)

**7012** Lindbergh, Anne. *Nobody's Orphan* (4–6). 1983, Avon paper $2.95 (0-380-70395-5). Martha believes that she is adopted, though she has no proof.

**7013** Little, Kimberley G. *Breakaway* (4–6). 1997, Avon paper $14.00 (0-380-97488-6). 160pp. Luke's hopes that his divorced father will reappear and help him with his soccer skills are dashed, but the boy learns to cope and survive. (Rev: BL 10/1/97; HB 5–6/97; SLJ 12/97)

**7014** Locker, Thomas. *Family Farm* (2–4). Illus. by author. 1988, Dial paper $16.99 (0-8037-0489-5). 32pp. A family works extra hard to save its farm. (Rev: BCCB 5/88; BL 4/15/88)

**7015** Loftis, Chris. *The Boy Who Sat by the Window* (3–6). Illus. by Catharine Gallagher. 1997, New Horizon Pr. paper $12.95 (0-88282-147-4). 52pp. Using free verse, the author tells the story of a boy who has been randomly shot while riding his bike to school. (Rev: BL 6/1–15/97; SLJ 8/97)

**7016** London, Jonathan. *Where's Home?* (5–7). 1995, Viking paper $13.99 (0-670-86028-X). 96pp. Impoverished Adrian and his Vietnam veteran dad hitchhike to San Francisco in the hope of finding a better life. (Rev: BCCB 10/95; BL 6/1–15/95; SLJ 8/95)

**7017** Lowery, Linda. *Laurie Tells* (4–6). 1994, Carolrhoda LB $19.95 (0-87614-790-2). 40pp. Eleven-year-old Laurie is ignored by her mother when she tells her of being sexually abused by her father. (Rev: BL 6/1–15/94; SLJ 7/94)

**7018** Luger, Harriett. *Bye, Bye, Bali Kai* (5–7). 1996, Harcourt $11.00 (0-15-200862-4); paper $5.00 (0-15-200863-2). 192pp. Suzie's family hits rock bottom when they are evicted and forced to live in an abandoned building. (Rev: BCCB 3/96; BL 6/1–15/96; SLJ 6/96)

**7019** McDonald, Joyce. *Comfort Creek* (5–8). 1996, Delacorte $15.95 (0-385-32232-1). 194pp. Quinn faces family problems when her father loses his job and her mother leaves to become a country singer. (Rev: BCCB 2/97; BL 11/15/96; SLJ 11/96*)

**7020** McKenzie, Ellen Kindt. *Under the Bridge* (5–7). 1994, Holt $14.95 (0-8050-3398-X). 140pp. Ritchie, who is devastated when his mother disappears, discovers she is suffering mental problems. (Rev: BCCB 2/95; BL 12/1/94; SLJ 3/95)

**7021** MacLachlan, Patricia. *Journey* (5–7). Illus. by Barry Moser. 1991, Delacorte $14.95 (0-385-30427-7). 83pp. A boy named Journey and his sister Cat must make a new life for themselves on their grandparents' farm. (Rev: BCCB 10/91; BL 9/15/91; HB 11–12/91*; SLJ 9/91)

**7022** McLean, Susan. *Pennies for the Piper* (5–7). 1981, Farrar paper $4.50 (0-374-45754-9). A moving story of a young girl alone facing the death of her mother.

**7023** Marino, Jan. *For the Love of Pete* (5–8). 1994, Avon paper $3.50 (0-380-72281-X). 197pp. Three

devoted servants take Olivia on a journey to find the father she has never met. (Rev: BCCB 7–8/93; SLJ 5/93*)

**7024** Martin, Ann M. *Me and Katie (the Pest)* (3–6). Illus. by Blanche Sims. 1985, Holiday $13.95 (0-8234-0580-X). 160pp. Ten-year-old Wendy thinks she can finally outdo her younger sister at horseback riding, until Katie starts taking lessons. (Rev: BCCB 2/86; BL 11/1/85; HB 3–4/86)

**7025** Martin, Patricia A. *Travels with Rainie Marie* (5–7). 1997, Hyperion LB $16.49 (0-7868-2212-0). 192pp. When there is no one to care for her and her 5 brothers and sisters, Rainie Marie is afraid that her bossy aunt will try to split up the family among various relatives. (Rev: BL 5/15/97; SLJ 7/97)

**7026** Mead, Alice. *Junebug* (4–7). 1995, Farrar $14.00 (0-374-33964-3). 112pp. Junebug, a young boy, realizes that the only hope for his family is to move from the city project where they live. (Rev: BCCB 12/95; BL 9/15/95; SLJ 11/95)

**7027** Mead, Alice. *Walking the Edge* (5–8). 1995, Albert Whitman LB $14.95 (0-8075-8649-8). 190pp. Scott escapes the abuse of his drunken father by throwing himself into his 4-H science project. (Rev: SLJ 12/95)

**7028** Metzger, Lois. *Barry's Sister* (4–7). 1992, Macmillan $15.95 (0-689-31521-X). 227pp. When Ellen's new brother develops cerebral palsy, she blames herself because she didn't want a baby brother. (Rev: SLJ 6/92)

**7029** Meyer, Carolyn. *Gideon's People* (5–7). 1996, Harcourt $12.00 (0-15-200303-7); paper $6.00 (0-15-200304-5). 320pp. Similarities and differences in religious practices become apparent when an Orthodox Jewish boy spends time on an Amish farm in 1911. (Rev: BCCB 5/96; BL 5/1/96; SLJ 4/96)

**7030** Miller, Dorothy R. *Home Wars* (5–8). 1997, Simon & Schuster $16.00 (0-689-81411-9). 176pp. Halley has misgivings when her father brings home 3 rifles, one for himself and the others for her 2 brothers. (Rev: BL 9/1/97; SLJ 10/97)

**7031** Myers, Anna. *Rosie's Tiger* (4–8). 1994, Walker $14.95 (0-8027-8305-8). 128pp. Rosie is filled with jealousy when her beloved brother returns home from the Korean War with a wife and child. (Rev: BL 9/15/94; SLJ 11/94)

**7032** Namioka, Lensey. *Yang the Third and Her Impossible Family* (4–7). Illus. by Kees de Kiefte. 1996, Bantam paper $3.99 (0-440-41231-5). 144pp. Mary, part of a Chinese family newly arrived in Seattle, is embarrassed by her parents' old-country ways in this humorous story. (Rev: BCCB 5/95; BL 4/15/95; SLJ 8/95)

**7033** Naylor, Phyllis Reynolds. *Being Danny's Dog* (4–7). 1995, Simon & Schuster $15.00 (0-689-

31756-5). 150pp. T.R.'s strong bond with his older brother, Danny, is tested when he discovers that Danny is involved in an unsavory plot. (Rev: BCCB 1/96; BL 10/1/95; SLJ 10/95)

**7034** Naylor, Phyllis Reynolds. *Reluctantly Alice* (5–8). 1991, Macmillan $15.00 (0-689-31681-X). 192pp. Alice's life in the seventh grade seems full of embarrassment. (Rev: BCCB 4/91*; BL 2/1/91; HB 7–8/91)

**7035** Nixon, Joan Lowery. *Maggie Forevermore* (5–7). 1987, Harcourt $13.95 (0-15-250345-5). 112pp. Maggie spends Christmas with her father and his new bride at their beach house in Malibu. Two other Maggie stories are: *Maggie, Too* (1985); *And Maggie Makes Three* (1986). (Rev: BCCB 4/87; BL 3/1/87; SLJ 3/87)

**7036** O'Connor, Barbara. *Beethoven in Paradise* (5–8). 1997, Farrar $16.00 (0-374-30666-4). 176pp. Martin, who wants to be a musician, clashes with his father, who prefers to see him play baseball. (Rev: BCCB 5/97; BL 4/15/97; SLJ 4/97)

**7037** Park, Barbara. *Don't Make Me Smile* (4–6). 1981, Knopf LB $10.99 (0-394-84978-7); Avon paper $2.95 (0-380-61994-6). Charles refuses to face the fact of his parents' divorce.

**7038** Park, Barbara. *Mick Harte Was Here* (5–7). 1995, Knopf LB $16.99 (0-679-97088-6). 96pp. Phoebe Harte recalls her unusual brother and the effect his death had on her family. (Rev: BCCB 6/95; BL 3/1/95; SLJ 5/95*)

**7039** Park, Barbara. *My Mother Got Married (and Other Disasters)* (4–6). 1989, Knopf LB $13.99 (0-394-92149-6). 128pp. Charlie is just getting used to his parents' divorce when his mother suddenly has a suitor. (Rev: BCCB 2/89; BL 3/1/89; SLJ 3/89)

**7040** Paterson, Katherine. *Park's Quest* (4–7). 1989, Puffin paper $3.99 (0-14-034262-1). 160pp. A boy searches for the cause of his father's death in Vietnam. (Rev: BCCB 4/88; HB 7–8/88; SLJ 5/88)

**7041** Pearson, Kit. *Awake and Dreaming* (4–7). 1997, Viking paper $13.99 (0-670-86954-6). 228pp. A girl who is abused by her unwed mother is determined to meet the family of her dreams. (Rev: BCCB 5/97; BL 6/1–15/97; SLJ 6/97)

**7042** Pearson, Kit. *A Handful of Time* (4–7). 1988, Puffin paper $6.99 (0-14-032268-X). 192pp. Patricia is ill at ease staying with her aunt and cousins while her parents work out a divorce. (Rev: HB 7–8/88)

**7043** Petersen, P. J. *I Want Answers and a Parachute* (4–6). Illus. by Anna DiVito. 1993, Simon & Schuster paper $13.00 (0-671-86577-3). 112pp. Jason and older brother Matt are apprehensive about meeting their father's new wife and her young daughter. (Rev: BCCB 9/93; BL 10/1/93; SLJ 12/93)

**7044** Pevsner, Stella. *I'm Emma: I'm a Quint* (4–7). 1993, Clarion $13.95 (0-395-64166-7). 186pp. A set of quintuplets are now in the eighth grade and face problems of becoming individuals rather than being just part of a famous family. A sequel to *Sister of the Quints* (1987). (Rev: BCCB 11/93; BL 10/1/93; SLJ 12/93)

**7045** Pevsner, Stella. *Would My Fortune Cookie Lie?* (5–8). 1996, Clarion $14.95 (0-395-73082-1). 192pp. Alexis, already upset by her parents' separation, learns a shattering secret from a mysterious stranger. (Rev: BCCB 3/96; BL 2/15/96; SLJ 4/96)

**7046** Philbrick, Rodman. *The Fire Pony* (5–8). 1996, Scholastic $14.95 (0-590-55251-1). 175pp. Rescued from a foster home by his half-brother Joe, Roy hopes that life will be better on the ranch where Joe finds work. (Rev: BCCB 7–8/96; BL 5/1/96; HB 7–8/96; SLJ 9/96)

**7047** Polikoff, Barbara G. *Life's a Funny Proposition, Horatio* (4–7). 1992, Holt $13.95 (0-8050-1972-3). 103pp. When his father dies, Horatio and his mother move to Wisconsin. (Rev: SLJ 8/92*)

**7048** Roberts, Willo Davis. *What Are We Going to Do About David?* (5–8). 1993, Macmillan $16.00 (0-689-31793-X). 176pp. A realistic story about 11-year-old David and what happens when his parents prepare to separate. (Rev: BL 3/15/93; SLJ 4/93)

**7049** Rodowsky, Colby. *Hannah in Between* (5–8). 1994, Farrar $15.00 (0-374-32837-4). 158pp. Hannah slowly realizes that her mother is sinking into alcoholism and wonders what to do about it. (Rev: BL 4/1/94; HB 9–10/94; SLJ 5/94)

**7050** Ross, Ramon R. *The Dancing Tree* (5–7). 1995, Simon & Schuster $14.00 (0-689-80072-X). 59pp. Zeenie's grandmother helps her cope with the sudden disappearance of her mother, who hopes to sort out her life. (Rev: BL 9/1/95; SLJ 2/96)

**7051** Sachs, Marilyn. *Another Day* (4–7). 1997, Dutton paper $15.99 (0-525-45787-9). 178pp. Olivia's problems begin when her grandfather dies and her mother walks out on the family, leaving her father no choice but to move her to her grandmother's. (Rev: BCCB 7–8/97; SLJ 6/97)

**7052** Sachs, Marilyn. *Fran Ellen's House* (4–6). 1989, Avon paper $2.75 (0-380-70583-4). Although her family is back together, Fran Ellen's baby sister won't talk to her and their house is in a shambles. A sequel to: *The Bears' House* (1987). (Rev: BCCB 11/87; BL 11/1/87; SLJ 10/87)

**7053** Sachs, Marilyn. *Ghosts in the Family* (5–8). 1995, Dutton paper $15.99 (0-525-45421-7). 144pp. Gabriella discovers some disturbing news about her family after her mother's death and a stay with her aunt. (Rev: BCCB 12/95; BL 1/1–15/96; SLJ 12/95)

**7054** Sachs, Marilyn. *Thirteen Going on Seven* (5–7). 1993, Dutton paper $14.99 (0-525-45096-3). 112pp. Dezzy, a girl with a learning disability, clashes with her honor-roll twin sister Dee. (Rev: BCCB 6/93; BL 5/1/93; SLJ 6/93)

**7055** Shawver, Margaret. *What's Wrong with Grandma? A Family's Experience with Alzheimer's* (3–6). Illus. 1996, Prometheus $14.95 (1-57392-107-6). 63pp. Ellen is confused and sometimes terrified when her grandmother begins to exhibit the erratic behavior associated with Alzheimer's disease. (Rev: BL 4/15/97)

**7056** Shreve, Susan. *The Formerly Great Alexander Family* (3–5). Illus. by Chris Cart. 1995, Tambourine $13.00 (0-688-13551-X). 91pp. The security and happiness of 10-year-old Liam Alexander come to an end when his parents announce they're divorcing. (Rev: HB 1–12/95; SLJ 9/95)

**7057** Smith, Doris Buchanan. *Best Girl* (4–6). 1993, Viking paper $13.99 (0-670-83752-0). 144pp. When the city tries to cut down a 100-year-old tree, Nealy climbs to the top and won't come down. (Rev: BCCB 3/93; BL 1/15/93)

**7058** Snyder, Zilpha Keatley. *Cat Running* (4–6). 1994, Delacorte $15.95 (0-385-31056-0). 168pp. To spite her father, Cat Kinsey, a fast runner, refuses to participate in the annual school sports fair. (Rev: BCCB 1/95; BL 9/1/94; SLJ 11/94*)

**7059** Stevenson, Laura C. *Happily After All* (4–7). 1990, Houghton $16.00 (0-395-50216-0). 256pp. Becca goes to live with her mother, who she believes abandoned her when she was young. (Rev: BCCB 5/90; BL 4/15/90; HB 5–6/90; SLJ 6/90)

**7060** Stowe, Cynthia. *Not-So-Normal Norman* (3–5). 1995, Albert Whitman LB $12.95 (0-8075-5767-6). 127pp. Anthony's first client in the pet-sitting service he has started is a tarantula named Norman. (Rev: BL 1/15/95; SLJ 3/95)

**7061** Strete, Craig Kee. *The World in Grandfather's Hands* (5–7). 1995, Clarion $13.95 (0-395-72102-4). 135pp. An 11-year-old American Indian boy faces problems when he and his mother leave their pueblo and move to the city. (Rev: BCCB 10/95; SLJ 9/95*)

**7062** Sussman, Susan. *Casey the Nomad* (4–6). Illus. 1985, Whitman $9.95 (0-8075-1068-8). 128pp. Casey awaits the return of his father after a month's business trip, only to find that Dad will be called away for the next 2 years. (Rev: BL 12/1/85; SLJ 3/86)

**7063** Tamar, Erika. *Alphabet City Ballet* (3–6). 1996, HarperCollins $15.00 (0-06-027328-3). 176pp. Marisol longs to become a ballet dancer, while her older brother seems headed for a life of crime. (Rev: BCCB 1/97; BL 9/15/96; SLJ 3/97)

**7064** Tate, Eleanora E. *A Blessing in Disguise* (5–8). 1995, Delacorte $14.95 (0-385-32103-1). 184pp. Zambia is tired of living with her conventional aunt and uncle and longs to join her fast-living father. (Rev: BCCB 2/95; BL 1/1/95; SLJ 2/95)

**7065** Terris, Susan. *The Latchkey Kids* (5–7). 1986, Farrar $15.00 (0-374-34363-2). 167pp. The loss of her father's job has forced a change to a smaller apartment and in 10-year-old Callie's life as a latchkey kid in charge of her 6-year-old brother. (Rev: BCCB 3/86; BL 3/1/86; SLJ 4/86)

**7066** Terris, Susan. *No Scarlet Ribbons* (5–8). 1981, Farrar $11.95 (0-374-35532-0). 154pp. Rachel is determined to ruin her mother's new marriage when she feels rejected.

**7067** Thesman, Jean. *Nothing Grows Here* (4–6). 1994, HarperCollins LB $14.89 (0-06-024458-5). 192pp. Maryanne resents having to live in an apartment after her father's death and also objects to her mother's new boyfriend. (Rev: BCCB 11/94; BL 11/1/94; SLJ 11/94)

**7068** Thesman, Jean. *When the Road Ends* (5–8). 1992, Houghton $14.95 (0-395-59507-X). 184pp. Mary tells how she and other foster children spend a summer in a remote cabin with a sick adult. (Rev: BCCB 4/92; HB 5–6/92; SLJ 4/92)

**7069** Thomas, Jane Resh. *Daddy Doesn't Have to Be a Giant Anymore* (2–4). Illus. 1996, Clarion $14.95 (0-395-69427-2). 46pp. A young girl's beloved father becomes her enemy when he begins abusing alcohol. (Rev: BL 10/15/96; SLJ 1/97)

**7070** Tolan, Stephanie S. *Save Halloween!* (4–7). 1993, Morrow $16.00 (0-688-12168-3). 176pp. Johnna, the daughter of a preacher, is forbidden to take part in any of the rituals and parties connected with Halloween. (Rev: BCCB 10/93; BL 9/1/93*; SLJ 10/93)

**7071** Van Leeuwen, Jean. *Blue Sky, Butterfly* (4–7). 1996, Dial paper $14.99 (0-8037-1972-8). 128pp. Twig's life becomes barren after her parents' divorce and her father's departure. (Rev: BCCB 2/96; BL 6/1–15/96; SLJ 6/96*)

**7072** Van Leeuwen, Jean. *Dear Mom, You're Ruining My Life* (4–6). Illus. 1989, Puffin paper $4.99 (0-14-034386-5). 160pp. Samantha's sixth-grade year is filled with ups and downs. (Rev: BCCB 5/89; BL 5/1/89; HB 6/89)

**7073** Viglucci, Patricia C. *Sun Dance at Turtle Rock* (5–7). 1996, Patri/Stone Pine paper $4.95 (0-9645914-9-9). 128pp. The child of a racially mixed marriage feels uncomfortable when he visits his white grandfather. (Rev: BL 4/15/96)

**7074** Wallace, Bill. *True Friends* (4–7). 1994, Holiday $14.95 (0-8234-1141-9). 160pp. Everything in Courtney's life becomes a shambles and she must rely on her new friend Judy to help her. (Rev: BCCB 11/94; BL 10/15/94; SLJ 10/94)

**7075** Walter, Mildred P. *Mariah Keeps Cool* (3–6). 1990, Macmillan LB $15.00 (0-02-792295-2). 140pp. Mariah, who is preoccupied with an upcoming swimming meet, finds she has new problems when her half-sister moves in. (Rev: BCCB 4/90; BL 4/15/90; SLJ 6/90)

**7076** Ware, Cheryl. *Catty-Cornered* (4–6). Illus. by Paul Yalowitz. 1998, Orchard LB $16.99 (0-531-33067-2). 106pp. A smart, curious, and funny girl keeps a journal of the 2 months she had to spend with her grandmother in a trailer park. (Rev: SLJ 3/98)

**7077** Whitelaw, Nancy. *A Beautiful Pearl* (3–5). Illus. by Judith Friedman. 1991, Whitman $14.95 (0-8075-0599-4). 32pp. Now that Grandmother has Alzheimer's disease, will Lisa continue to get a pearl each year on her birthday? (Rev: BCCB 12/91; BL 12/15/91; SLJ 2/92)

**7078** Willner-Pardo, Gina. *Jason and the Losers* (4–7). 1995, Clarion $14.95 (0-395-70160-0). 112pp. Jason takes out his resentment at his parents' divorce by excelling in sports and being mean to the crowd of losers that includes his cousin Everett. (Rev: BCCB 6/95; BL 4/15/95; HB 9–10/95; SLJ 4/95)

**7079** Willner-Pardo, Gina. *Spider Storch's Carpool Catastrophe* (2–4). Illus. by Nick Sharratt. 1997, Albert Whitman LB $11.95 (0-8075-7575-5); paper $3.95 (0-8075-7576-3). 60pp. Joey, nicknamed Spider, is afraid that his mother's friendship with Mrs. Brennerman will mean that he will have to get involved with her unpopular daughter. (Rev: SLJ 11/97)

**7080** Wilson, Jacqueline. *Elsa, Star of the Shelter* (4–6). Illus. 1996, Albert Whitman LB $14.95 (0-8075-1981-2). 208pp. The grim life of a homeless English family as seen through the eyes of courageous 10-year-old Elsa. (Rev: BCCB 2/96; BL 1/1–15/96; SLJ 2/96)

**7081** Wilson, Jacqueline. *The Suitcase Kid* (4–6). Illus. 1997, Delacorte $15.95 (0-385-32311-5). 140pp. On weekends, Andrea lives out of a suitcase because it is then that she alternately visits each of her divorced parents. (Rev: BCCB 7–8/97; BL 10/15/97; SLJ 9/97)

**7082** Wilson, Nancy H. *Becoming Felix* (4–6). 1996, Farrar $16.00 (0-374-30664-8). 184pp. Twelve-year-old JJ makes sacrifices to help save the family farm. (Rev: BCCB 1/97; BL 10/15/96; SLJ 10/96)

**7083** Wilson, Nancy H. *The Reason for Janey* (5–7). Illus. 1994, Macmillan paper $15.00 (0-02-793127-7). 176pp. A mentally disabled woman helps Janie adjust to her parents' divorce and her father's departure. (Rev: BCCB 6/94; BL 4/15/94; HB 7–8/94; SLJ 5/94*)

**7084** Wolitzer, Hilma. *Wish You Were Here* (5–8). 1984, Farrar paper $3.45 (0-374-48412-0). Bernie does not want to live with his stepfather and decides to move to Florida with his grandfather.

**7085** Wyeth, Sharon D. *Ginger Brown: Too Many Houses* (1–3). Illus. 1996, Random LB $11.99 (0-679-95437-6); paper $3.99 (0-679-85437-1). 80pp. Six-year-old Ginger, who is from an interracial family, is confused by her parents' divorce and by seeing that both sets of grandparents have different skin colors than she. (Rev: BCCB 7–8/96; BL 4/15/96; SLJ 6/96)

**7086** Yarbrough, Camille. *Tamika and the Wisdom Rings* (3–5). Illus. 1994, Random paper $3.99 (0-679-82749-8). 104pp. Tamika and her family are forced to move after their father is murdered by drug dealers in this grim novel set in an inner city. (Rev: BL 9/15/94)

**7087** Yep, Laurence. *Ribbons* (5–7). 1996, Putnam $15.95 (0-399-22906-X). 192pp. Robin begins to understand and sympathize with her Chinese grandmother after she learns the woman's secret. (Rev: BCCB 2/96; BL 1/1–15/96; SLJ 2/96)

**7088** Young, Ronder T. *Moving Mama to Town* (5–8). 1997, Orchard LB $18.99 (0-531-33025-7). 224pp. Although his father is a gambler and a failure, Fred never loses faith in him in this story of a boy who must help support his family though he's only 13. (Rev: BL 6/1–15/97; HB 7–8/97; SLJ 6/97)

## Personal Problems

**7089** Adler, C. S. *Daddy's Climbing Tree* (5–7). 1993, Houghton $13.95 (0-395-63032-0). 134pp. Jessica cannot adjust to the death of her father in a hit-and-run accident. (Rev: BCCB 7–8/93; BL 6/1–15/93; HB 7–8/93; SLJ 5/93)

**7090** Adler, C. S. *The Lump in the Middle* (5–7). 1991, Avon paper $3.50 (0-380-71176-1). 160pp. Kelsey, the middle child, struggles for her identity after dad loses his job. (Rev: BL 10/1/89; SLJ 10/89)

**7091** Adler, C. S. *What's to Be Scared Of, Suki?* (4–7). 1996, Clarion $13.95 (0-395-77600-7). 176pp. A neighbor's handsome 13-year-old son helps Suki overcome her fears. (Rev: BL 11/1/96; SLJ 10/96)

**7092** Adler, C. S. *Willie, the Frog Prince* (4–7). 1994, Clarion $15.00 (0-395-65615-X). 163pp. Willie's inability to accept responsibility almost causes the loss of his dog, Booboo. (Rev: BL 4/15/94; SLJ 6/94)

**7093** Angell, Judie. *Dear Lola: Or, How to Build Your Own Family* (4–6). 1982, Bantam paper $2.50 (0-440-91787-5). Six children run away from their orphanage and form their own family.

**7094** Armstrong, Robb. *Drew and the Bub Daddy Showdown* (3–5). 1996, HarperCollins paper $3.95 (0-06-442030-2). 96pp. Drew Taylor finds he has artistic ability and soon creates his own comic book hero. (Rev: BL 9/15/96; SLJ 8/96)

**7095** Auch, Mary Jane. *Seven Long Years Until College* (4–7). 1991, Holiday $13.95 (0-8234-0901-5). 160pp. Unhappy at home, Natalie runs away to join her older sister at college. (Rev: BCCB 1/92; SLJ 10/91)

**7096** Avi. *What Do Fish Have to Do with Anything?* (5–8). Illus. 1997, Candlewick $17.99 (0-7636-0329-5); paper $4.99 (0-7636-0412-7). 208pp. Seven excellent stories about youngsters facing the first pangs of adolescence. (Rev: BL 11/15/97; HB 11–12/97; SLJ 12/97*)

**7097** Barnes, Joyce Annette. *Promise Me the Moon* (5–8). 1997, Dial paper $14.99 (0-8037-1798-9). 176pp. Annie faces many problems in eighth grade, including being labeled an egghead, in this sequel to *The Baby Grand, the Moon in July, and Me* (1994). (Rev: BCCB 2/97; BL 11/15/96; SLJ 2/97)

**7098** Barrie, Barbara. *Lone Star* (5–8). 1990, Delacorte $13.95 (0-385-30156-1). 182pp. Jane struggles to keep her Jewish faith when her family moves to a predominately Christian town in Texas. (Rev: BCCB 1/91; SLJ 1/91)

**7099** Bechard, Margaret. *Really No Big Deal* (5–7). 1994, Viking paper $13.99 (0-670-85444-1). 144pp. It is difficult enough coping with his parent's divorce for Jonah, but now his mother is dating his school principal. (Rev: BL 3/15/94; HB 7–8/94; SLJ 5/94*)

**7100** Benjamin, Carol Lea. *The Wicked Stepdog* (4–7). Illus. by author. 1982, Avon paper $2.50 (0-380-70089-1). Louise is in the midst of puberty problems and her father's remarriage.

**7101** Birdseye, Tom. *Tarantula Shoes* (3–6). 1995, Holiday $15.95 (0-8234-1179-6); Puffin paper $4.50 (0-14-037955-X). 96pp. With the help of a new friend and his pet tarantula, Ryan is able to buy the basketball shoes of his dreams. (Rev: BL 4/15/95; SLJ 5/95)

**7102** Blades, Ann. *Mary of Mile 18* (2–4). Illus. by author. 1971, Tundra paper $8.95 (0-88776-059-7). Mile 18 is in reality a Mennonite community in Canada, and Mary was a student in the school where the author taught.

**7103** Blume, Judy. *Are You There God? It's Me, Margaret* (4–6). 1990, Macmillan $16.00 (0-02-710991-7); Dell paper $4.50 (0-440-40419-3). 156pp. Eleven-year-old Margaret is the daughter of a Jewish father and a Catholic mother.

**7104** Blume, Judy. *Blubber* (4–6). 1982, Macmillan LB $16.00 (0-02-711010-9); Dell paper $3.99 (0-440-40707-9). 160pp. Jill finds out what it's like to be an outsider when she defends Linda, a classmate who is teased because of her obesity.

**7105** Blume, Judy. *Otherwise Known as Sheila the Great* (4–6). 1972, Dell paper $4.50 (0-440-46701-2). 128pp. During a summer in New York, Sheila learns a great deal about herself and how to overcome her feelings of inferiority.

**7106** Blume, Judy. *Then Again, Maybe I Won't* (5–7). 1971, Dell paper $4.50 (0-440-48659-9). 176pp. Thirteen-year-old Tony adjusts with difficulty to his family's move to a home in the affluent suburbs of Long Island, New York.

**7107** Blume, Judy. *Tiger Eyes: A Novel* (6–8). 1981, Dell paper $4.99 (0-440-98469-6). 256pp. Davey must deal with reactions to her father's murder.

**7108** Boyd, Candy Dawson. *A Different Beat* (4–6). 1996, Penguin paper $4.99 (0-14-036582-6). 182pp. In this sequel to *Fall Secrets* (1994), Jessie suffers discrimination even within the African American community because of her dark skin. (Rev: BL 11/15/96)

**7109** Buck, Pearl. *The Big Wave* (4–6). 1973, HarperCollins LB $15.89 (0-381-99923-8); paper $4.50 (0-06-440171-5). 88pp. The loss of family and home in a tidal wave reveals the courage of a little Japanese boy.

**7110** Bulla, Clyde Robert. *Shoeshine Girl* (3–5). Illus. by Leigh Grant. 1975, HarperCollins LB $14.89 (0-690-04830-0); paper $4.50 (0-06-440228-2). 80pp. A somewhat indolent 10-year-old girl matures during a summer working for Al at his shoeshine stand.

**7111** Bunting, Eve. *Your Move* (2–5). Illus. by James E. Ransome. 1998, Harcourt $16.00 (0-15-200181-6). 32pp. A 10-year-old boy and his young brother are caught up in the violence that accompanies the rivalry between street gangs. (Rev: BL 2/15/98)

**7112** Burch, Robert. *Queenie Peavy* (4–7). Illus. by Jerry Lazare. 1987, Puffin paper $4.50 (0-14-032305-8). 160pp. A defiant 13-year-old rescues her future from reform school in a Georgia town of the 1930s.

**7113** Byars, Betsy. *After the Goat Man* (5–7). Illus. by Ronald Hunter. 1982, Puffin paper $4.50 (0-14-031533-0). 128pp. The effects on a number of people of an old man's vehement refusal to sell his home for the building of a superhighway are explored in this convincing novel.

**7114** Byars, Betsy. *The Cartoonist* (4–6). Illus. by Richard Cuffari. 1978, Puffin paper $3.99 (0-14-032309-0). 128pp. Alfie's refuge in his attic room with his cartoons is disrupted by his brother's return.

**7115** Byars, Betsy. *The House of Wings* (4–6). Illus. by Daniel Schwartz. 1972, Puffin paper $4.99 (0-14-

031523-3). 148pp. Sammy is distraught when he is left alone with his grandfather, but things get better when a wounded crane is found and must be taken care of.

**7116** Byars, Betsy. *The Night Swimmers* (5–6). Illus. by Troy Howell. 1983, Bantam paper $3.99 (0-440-45857-9). 160pp. An enterprising girl tries to be a housekeeper and to take care of her 2 brothers.

**7117** Calhoun, Mary. *Flood* (PS–3). Illus. by Erick Ingraham. 1997, Morrow LB $15.93 (0-688-13920-5). 40pp. A story set during the Mississippi River flood of 1993 that tells how a family lost its home. (Rev: BCCB 4/97; BL 3/15/97*; SLJ 5/97)

**7118** Calvert, Patricia. *The Stone Pony* (5–8). 1982, NAL paper $2.99 (0-451-13729-9). 160pp. Jo Beth seems unable to cope with the death of her older sister.

**7119** Calvert, Patricia. *Writing to Richie* (4–6). Illus. 1994, Scribners $13.95 (0-684-19764-2). 128pp. With the help of an ill-tempered young girl who has come to his foster home, David learns to grieve for his dead younger brother. (Rev: BL 12/15/94; SLJ 1/95)

**7120** Capote, Truman. *The Thanksgiving Visitor* (5–7). Illus. by Beth Peck. 1996, Knopf $19.00 (0-679-83898-8). 32pp. Buddy conquers his loneliness and fear of a bully, Odd Henderson, through his friendship with Miss Sook. (Rev: BL 10/15/96; SLJ 12/96)

**7121** Casanova, Mary. *Riot* (5–8). 1996, Hyperion LB $14.49 (0-7868-2204-X). 128pp. Young Bryan is caught up in his father's conflict concerning the hiring of nonunion workers at his workplace. (Rev: BCCB 1/97; BL 11/1/96; SLJ 10/96)

**7122** Caseley, Judith. *Chloe in the Know* (3–5). 1993, Greenwillow $14.00 (0-688-11055-X). 144pp. In this sequel to *Hurricane Harry* (1991) and *Starring Dorothy Kane* (1992), Chloe, big sister to Harry and Dorothy, is upset when she finds out that her mother is pregnant again. (Rev: BCCB 4/93; BL 4/15/93; SLJ 4/93)

**7123** Caseley, Judith. *Dorothy's Darkest Days* (2–4). Illus. 1997, Greenwillow $15.00 (0-688-13422-X). 144pp. Dorothy is filled with guilt when her disliked classmate is killed in a car accident. (Rev: BL 8/97; SLJ 8/97)

**7124** Caseley, Judith. *Jorah's Journal* (2–4). Illus. 1997, Greenwillow $15.00 (0-688-14879-4). 64pp. Jorah has problems adjusting to her family's move to a different city and becoming the new girl in her class. (Rev: BL 5/1/97; SLJ 6/97)

**7125** Cavanagh, Helen. *Panther Glade* (4–6). 1993, Simon & Schuster paper $16.00 (0-671-75617-6). 147pp. Bill gains a little self-confidence during a summer with an aunt who is an archaeologist. (Rev: SLJ 6/93)

**7126** Charbonnet, Gabrielle. *Tutu Much Ballet* (3–5). Illus. by Abby Carter. 1994, Holt $14.95 (0-8050-3063-8). 69pp. Having to take ballet lessons and a long visit from her grandmother are spoiling Charlotte's summer. (Rev: BL 5/15/94; SLJ 6/94)

**7127** Cleary, Beverly. *Dear Mr. Henshaw* (4–7). Illus. by Paul O. Zelinsky. 1983, Morrow LB $15.93 (0-688-02406-8); Dell paper $4.50 (0-440-41794-5). 144pp. A Newbery Award winner (1984) about a boy who pours out his problems in letters to a writer he greatly admires.

**7128** Cleary, Beverly. *Lucky Chuck* (2–4). Illus. by J. Winslow Higginbottom. 1984, Morrow LB $15.93 (0-688-02738-5). 40pp. Through bitter experience, Chuck learns the principles of bicycle safety.

**7129** Cleary, Beverly. *Strider* (4–8). Illus. by Paul O. Zelinsky. 1991, Morrow LB $15.93 (0-688-09901-7). 192pp. In this sequel to the 1984 Newbery winner *Dear Mr. Henshaw,* Leigh Botts is beginning high school and finding himself, aided by his beloved dog Strider. (Rev: BCCB 10/91; BL 7/91*; HB 9–10/91; SLJ 9/91)

**7130** Cleaver, Vera, and Bill Cleaver. *Grover* (4–7). Illus. by Fred Marvin. 1970, HarperCollins $13.95 (0-397-31118-4). 128pp. After his mother's suicide and his father's resultant breakdown, 10-year-old Grover must face the hard reality of death and trouble.

**7131** Colman, Hila. *Diary of a Frantic Kid Sister* (4–6). 1973, Archway paper $2.95 (0-671-61926-8). Sarah has trouble communicating with her family, so she pours out her soul to her diary.

**7132** Conford, Ellen. *Hail, Hail Camp Timberwood* (5–7). Illus. by Gail Owens. 1978, Little, Brown $14.95 (0-316-15291-9). Thirteen-year-old Melanie's first summer at camp.

**7133** Conly, Jane L. *Crazy Lady!* (5–8). 1993, HarperCollins LB $13.89 (0-06-021360-4). 196pp. In a city slum Vernon forms a friendship with an eccentric lady who cares for her disabled teenage son. (Rev: BCCB 7–8/93; BL 5/15/93*; SLJ 4/93*)

**7134** Conrad, Pam. *Prairie Songs* (5–8). Illus. by Darryl S. Zudeck. 1985, HarperCollins $17.02 (0-060-21336-1); paper $4.50 (0-06-440206-1). 176pp. Louise's family thrives despite the harshness of the prairie land, but the life there is unendurable for others. (Rev: SLJ 10/85)

**7135** Conrad, Pam. *Staying Nine* (4–6). Illus. by Mike Wimmer. 1988, HarperCollins paper $3.95 (0-06-440377-7). 80pp. A private few days in the life of a young girl who doesn't want to be 10. (Rev: BCCB 10/88; BL 11/15/88; SLJ 12/88)

**7136** Coolidge, Susan. *What Katy Did* (4–6). 1988, Buccaneer LB $19.95 (0-899-66585-3). Tomboy Katy Carr overcomes a tragic accident in this classic story.

**7137** Cooper, Ilene. *My Co-Star, My Enemy* (5–8). 1993, Puffin paper $3.25 (0-14-036156-1). 149pp. Alison discovers that her costar on a TV series is out to sabotage her. (Rev: SLJ 6/93)

**7138** Cooper, Melrose. *Life Magic* (4–6). 1996, Holt $14.95 (0-8050-4114-1). 116pp. Crystal, who is facing her own problems at school, discovers that her uncle is dying of AIDS. (Rev: BL 10/15/96; SLJ 2/97)

**7139** Cooper, Melrose. *Life Riddles* (5–8). 1994, Holt $14.95 (0-8050-2613-4). 90pp. The story of a lonely young African American girl and how she turned to writing as an outlet. (Rev: BCCB 4/94; SLJ 4/94)

**7140** Corbin, William. *Me and the End of the World* (5–7). 1991, Simon & Schuster paper $15.00 (0-671-74223-X). 256pp. Fearful that the world is soon ending, 13-year-old-Tom decides to do things he has always wanted to do. (Rev: SLJ 9/91)

**7141** Corcoran, Barbara. *The Potato Kid* (5–8). 1993, Macmillan $13.95 (0-689-31589-9); Avon paper $3.50 (0-380-71213-X). 192pp. In spite of her protests, Ellis is chosen to take care of an underprivileged girl her mother takes in for the summer. (Rev: BCCB 11/89; HB 1–2/90; SLJ 10/89)

**7142** Cottonwood, Joe. *Danny Ain't* (5–8). 1992, Scholastic $13.95 (0-590-45067-0). 240pp. When Danny's father, a Vietnam War vet, is taken to a VA hospital, the boy tries to survive on his own. (Rev: SLJ 10/92)

**7143** Creech, Sharon. *Absolutely Normal Chaos* (5–8). 1995, HarperCollins LB $14.89 (0-06-026992-8). 208pp. Mary Lou keeps a journal during her 13th absolutely normal summer and chronicles such events as her first kiss and her summer reading assignments. (Rev: BCCB 11/95; BL 10/1/95; SLJ 11/95)

**7144** Creech, Sharon. *Chasing Redbird* (5–8). 1997, HarperCollins LB $15.89 (0-06-026988-X). 261pp. Thirteen-year-old Zinny, who lives in Appalachia, is trying to understand herself while adjusting to the death of her beloved Aunt Jessie. (Rev: HB 5–6/97; SLJ 4/97*)

**7145** Cullen, Lynn. *Meeting the Make-out King* (5–7). 1994, Clarion $13.95 (0-395-67889-7). 132pp. Seventh-grader Nora is ashamed of her lack of experience when it comes to boys. (Rev: SLJ 10/94)

**7146** Cutler, Jane. *Family Dinner* (3–5). Illus. by Philip Caswell. 1992, Farrar $14.00 (0-374-32267-8). 126pp. Through a friendship with her great-uncle, Rachel learns about life and living. (Rev: HB 3–4/92; SLJ 5/92)

**7147** DeClements, Barthe. *Five-Finger Discount* (4–6). 1989, Delacorte $14.95 (0-385-29705-X). 130pp. Jerry, whose father is in prison for robbery, himself has a tendency to steal. (Rev: BCCB 4/89; BL 5/1/89; SLJ 4/89)

**7148** DeClements, Barthe. *The Pickle Song* (4–6). 1993, Viking paper $13.99 (0-670-85101-9). 151pp. Paula befriends a difficult girl who, she discovers, is homeless. (Rev: BCCB 9/93; BL 10/15/93; SLJ 8/93)

**7149** Dorman, N. B. *Petey and Miss Magic* (3–5). 1993, Shoe String LB $16.00 (0-208-02345-3). 99pp. A lonely boy who longs for a pet finds a worm that he begins to care for. (Rev: SLJ 3/93)

**7150** Dragonwagon, Crescent. *Winter Holding Spring* (3–6). Illus. by Ronald Himler. 1990, Macmillan paper $15.00 (0-02-733122-9). 32pp. Father and daughter talk about their feelings over the death of their wife and mother. (Rev: BL 4/1/90)

**7151** Duffey, Betsy. *Utterly Yours, Booker Jones* (5–7). Illus. 1995, Viking paper $13.99 (0-670-86007-7). 128pp. Twelve-year-old Booker faces many problems: finishing his science fiction novel, having to sleep under the dining room table, and coping with an impossible older sister. (Rev: BCCB 10/95; BL 9/15/95; HB 11–12/95; SLJ 9/95)

**7152** Durant, Penny R. *When Heroes Die* (5–8). 1992, Macmillan $15.00 (0-689-31764-6). 144pp. Gary learns that the uncle he loves has AIDS. (Rev: SLJ 11/92)

**7153** Enderle, Judith R., and Stephanie G. Tessler. *What's the Matter, Kelly Beans?* (2–4). 1996, Candlewick $14.99 (1-56402-534-9). 112pp. Eight-year-old Kelly is unhappy after the family moves and she has to share her room with her kid sister, Erin. (Rev: BL 10/1/96; SLJ 10/96)

**7154** Evans, Douglas. *So What Do You Do?* (4–6). 1997, Front Street $14.95 (1-886910-20-0). 124pp. Two middle-schoolers try to help their beloved former teacher, who has become a hopeless drunk. (Rev: BL 11/1/97; SLJ 1/98)

**7155** Fenner, Carol. *Randall's Wall* (3–6). 1991, Macmillan $15.00 (0-689-50518-3). 96pp. Fifth-grader Randall Lord is so dirty that no one wants to sit near him, so he imagines himself behind an invisible wall that keeps others out. (Rev: BCCB 7–8/91; BL 4/1/91; HB 7–8/91; SLJ 4/91)

**7156** Ferguson, Alane. *Stardust* (4–6). 1993, Macmillan LB $14.00 (0-02-734527-0). 160pp. A former television child star returns to a normal life in her small hometown. (Rev: BCCB 4/93; BL 5/15/93; SLJ 6/93)

**7157** Fletcher, Ralph. *Spider Boy* (5–8). 1997, Clarion $15.00 (0-395-77606-6). 192pp. Bobby — whose nickname is Spider Boy because he knows so much about spiders — has problems adjusting to his new life in New Paltz, New York. (Rev: BCCB 4/97; BL 6/1–15/97; HB 7–8/97; SLJ 7/97)

**7158** Ford, Barbara. *The Most Wonderful Movie in the World* (4–6). 1996, Dutton paper $14.99 (0-525-45455-1). 160pp. Eleven-year-old Moira Flynn faces problems of growing up — e.g., making difficult decisions and dealing with boys. (Rev: BCCB 6/96; BL 5/15/96; SLJ 7/96)

**7159** Fox, Paula. *Monkey Island* (5–8). 1991, Watts LB $16.99 (0-531-08562-7). 160pp. At age 11, Clay finds himself homeless in New York City and struggles for the basics of life. (Rev: BCCB 10/91*; BL 9/1/91; HB 9–10/91*; SLJ 8/91)

**7160** Fox, Paula. *Radiance Descending* (4–7). 1997, DK Publg. $14.95 (0-7894-2467-3). 101pp. Paul learns the true meaning of love when he gradually accepts his younger brother, who has Down's syndrome. (Rev: BL 9/1/97; HB 9–10/97; SLJ 9/97)

**7161** Fox, Paula. *The Stone-Faced Boy* (4–7). Illus. by Donald MacKay. 1982, Simon & Schuster LB $13.95 (0-02-735570-5). 112pp. Gus, a sensitive and timid middle child in a family of 5, learns to mask his feelings and present a "stone face" to the world.

**7162** Fox, Paula. *The Village by the Sea* (5–8). 1988, Orchard $15.95 (0-531-05788-7); Dell paper $3.99 (0-440-40299-9). Emma is staying with an aunt and uncle while her father has heart surgery, and the 3 interact in complex ways. Also use the reissued *A Likely Place* (1997, Simon & Schuster). (Rev: BCCB 7–8/88; HB 9–10/88; SLJ 8/88)

**7163** Fox, Paula. *Western Wind* (5–8). Series: Richard Jackson Books. 1993, Orchard LB $17.99 (0-531-08652-6). 201pp. At first resentful of being sent to spend a summer with her grandmother on a Maine island, Elizabeth gradually adjusts and learns a great deal about herself. (Rev: BCCB 9/93; SLJ 12/93*)

**7164** Freeman, Suzanne. *The Cuckoo's Child* (5–8). 1996, Greenwillow $15.00 (0-688-14290-7). 256pp. Because her parents are missing, Mia leaves Lebanon to live with her aunt in Tennessee. (Rev: BCCB 3/96; BL 3/15/96*; HB 7–8/96; SLJ 4/96*)

**7165** Friedman, Aileen. *A Cloak for the Dreamer* (3–5). Illus. by Kim Howard. 1995, Scholastic $14.95 (0-590-48987-9). 15pp. Misha sets out to find his fortune in an amazing cloak designed by his father and brothers. (Rev: BL 2/1/95; SLJ 4/95)

**7166** Fromm, Pete. *Monkey Tag* (4–7). 1994, Scholastic $14.95 (0-590-46525-2). 352pp. When his twin is paralyzed from an accident, Eli feels partly responsible. (Rev: BCCB 12/94; BL 10/15/94; SLJ 10/94)

**7167** George, Jean Craighead. *The Summer of the Falcon* (5–8). 1992, Peter Smith $18.50 (0-8446-6503-7); HarperCollins paper $4.95 (0-06-440095-6). 153pp. June learns to take responsibility and discipline when she trains her own falcons.

**7168** Geras, Adele. *Little Swan* (2–4). Illus. 1995, Random LB $11.99 (0-679-97000-2); paper $3.99 (0-679-87000-8). 63pp. Seven-year-old Louisa is delighted when she is picked to dance the role of a little swan in *Swan Lake*. (Rev: BL 7/95)

**7169** Gifaldi, David. *Toby Scudder, Ultimate Warrior* (4–6). 1993, Clarion $14.00 (0-395-66400-4). 201pp. A new teacher helps overweight Toby find the self-esteem he lacks. (Rev: BCCB 11/93; BL 10/15/93; SLJ 10/93*)

**7170** Giff, Patricia Reilly. *Dance with Rosie* (2–5). Illus. Series: Ballet Slippers. 1996, Vikin paper $13.99 (0-670-86864-7). 64pp. Rosie seems to face insurmountable problems in reaching her goal to be a ballerina. Also use *Rosie's Nutcracker Dreams* (1996). (Rev: BCCB 12/96; BL 9/1/96; SLJ 1/97)

**7171** Giff, Patricia Reilly. *The Gift of the Pirate Queen* (4–6). Illus. by Jenny Rutherford. 1983, Dell paper $3.99 (0-440-43046-1). 160pp. Grace is looking forward to the arrival of Fiona from Ireland to take care of her family.

**7172** Giff, Patricia Reilly. *Matthew Jackson Meets the Wall* (2–5). Illus. by Blanche Sims. 1990, Delacorte $13.95 (0-385-29972-9); Dell paper $3.50 (0-440-40547-5). 104pp. Matthew misses his friends in New York City when he moves to Deposit, Ohio. (Rev: BL 6/1/90; SLJ 7/90)

**7173** Giff, Patricia Reilly. *Poopsie Pomerantz, Pick Up Your Feet* (3–5). Illus. by Leslie Morrill. 1998, Bantam paper $3.99 (0-440-40287-5). 147pp. Poopsie's self-confidence really fades when she's chosen to play the pig in a performance of The Ugly Duckling. (Rev: BL 3/1/89; HB 5–6/89)

**7174** Giff, Patricia Reilly. *Starring Rosie* (2–4). Illus. by Julie Durrell. 1997, Viking paper $13.99 (0-670-86967-8). 96pp. Rosie is crushed when she is cast as the wicked fairy in the class production of *Sleeping Beauty*. (Rev: BL 12/15/96; SLJ 3/97)

**7175** Gilson, Jamie. *Do Bananas Chew Gum?* (4–6). 1980, Lothrop paper $16.00 (0-671-42690-7). 160pp. Sam still can't read, and he is in the sixth grade.

**7176** Girard, Linda Walvoord. *Alex, the Kid with AIDS* (3–5). 1991, Whitman LB $14.95 (0-8075-0245-6). 32pp. Alex, who has AIDS, gets special treatment in class and uses the sympathy of adults to manipulate them. (Rev: BL 4/1/91; SLJ 6/91)

**7177** Girard, Linda Walvoord. *At Daddy's on Saturdays* (1–4). Illus. by Judith Friedman. 1987, Whitman LB $14.95 (0-8075-0475-0); paper $5.95 (0-8075-0473-4). 32pp. The emotions and concerns of young Katie as her father moves out one Saturday after the divorce and returns for their outing the next. (Rev: BL 11/15/87; SLJ 12/87)

**7178** Glaser, Linda. *Tanya's Big Green Dream* (3–5). Illus. 1994, Macmillan paper $13.95 (0-02-735994-8). 48pp. Tanya overcomes many obstacles to have a tree planted in a public park on Earth Day. (Rev: BL 5/15/94; SLJ 8/94)

**7179** Glassman, Miriam. *Box Top Dreams* (4–7). 1998, Delacorte $14.95 (0-385-32532-0). 184pp. Ari is devastated when her best friend moves away; but through this experience she learns independence. (Rev: BL 2/1/98; SLJ 3/98)

**7180** Godden, Rumer. *Listen to the Nightingale* (4–6). Illus. 1994, Puffin paper $3.99 (0-140-36091-3). 192pp. Finding a puppy alters the plans of 10-year-old Lottie to become a ballerina. (Rev: BCCB 11/92; BL 12/15/92*; HB 11–12/92; SLJ 12/92)

**7181** Gosselin, Kim. *Smoking Stinks!!* (2–4). Illus. by Thom Buttner. 1997, JayJo $16.95 (0-9639449-5-9). When Maddie's grandfather comes to school to tell her class why he smokes, he agrees that smoking stinks. (Rev: SLJ 1/98)

**7182** Greenberg, Jan. *Just the Two of Us* (5–7). 1988, Farrar $14.00 (0-374-36198-3); paper $3.95 (0-374-43982-6). 128pp. Holly tries to think of ways to prevent her mother from making them leave New York City for Iowa. (Rev: BL 1/15/89; HB 1–2/89; SLJ 12/88)

**7183** Greene, Constance C. *Beat the Turtle Drum* (4–6). Illus. by Donna Diamond. 1994, Puffin paper $4.99 (0-14-036850-7). 128pp. A young girl must adjust to the accidental death of her beloved younger sister.

**7184** Greenwald, Sheila. *My Fabulous New Life* (4–6). 1993, Harcourt $10.95 (0-15-277693-1); paper $3.95 (0-15-276716-9). 160pp. Shocked by all the poor people she sees around her new home in Manhattan, Alison tries to find a way to help them. (Rev: BL 10/1/93; SLJ 10/93)

**7185** Groth, B. L., and Thomas Wray, eds. *Home Is Where We Live* (3–5). Illus. 1995, Cornerstone paper $7.95 (0-940895-34-X). 32pp. A simple story told in photos and narrative of a homeless child in a Chicago shelter. (Rev: BL 10/15/95; SLJ 12/95)

**7186** Hamilton, Virginia. *Cousins* (5–8). 1990, Putnam $15.95 (0-399-22164-6). 125pp. Cammy faces both guilt and grief when her cousin Patty Ann drowns. (Rev: BCCB 11/90*; HB 3–4/91; SLJ 12/90)

**7187** Hamilton, Virginia. *Drylongso* (3–5). Illus. by Jerry Pinkney. 1992, Harcourt $18.95 (0-15-224241-4). 64pp. During a great duststorm on the prairie in 1975, a tall boy appears who helps Lindy and her

family find water. (Rev: BCCB 10/92*; BL 7/92*; HB 9–10/92; SLJ 1/93)

**7188** Hamilton, Virginia. *Zeely* (4–6). Illus. by Symeon Shimin. 1967, Macmillan $16.00 (0-02-742470-7); paper $3.95 (0-689-71695-8). 128pp. An 11-year-old black city girl is lightly guided from her daydreams to reality by Zeely, who is as kind as she is tall and beautiful.

**7189** Harrah, Madge. *The Nobody Club* (4–6). 1989, Avon paper $2.50 (0-380-75631-5). 166pp. Three misunderstood girls form a club to help solve one another's problems. (Rev: SLJ 8/89)

**7190** Hartling, Peter. *Ben Loves Anna* (4–6). Trans. by J. H. Auerbach. Illus. by Ellen Weinstein. 1990, Overlook $12.95 (0-87951-401-9). 96pp. The feelings of a lovestruck 10-year-old boy are captured by one of Germany's most distinguished children's writers. (Rev: BCCB 4/91; BL 6/15/91; SLJ 5/91)

**7191** Haseley, Dennis. *Shadows* (3–5). Illus. by Leslie Bowman. 1991, Farrar $12.95 (0-374-36761-2). 80pp. The mystery concerning the death of Jamie's father is somewhat relieved when his grandfather begins to teach him how to make shadow figures. (Rev: BCCB 7–8/91; BL 7/91; HB 7–8/91; SLJ 6/91)

**7192** Henkes, Kevin. *Sun and Spoon* (3–5). 1997, Greenwillow $15.00 (0-688-15232-5). 144pp. Spoon takes his dead grandmother's solitaire cards as a memento, but later he regrets his action. (Rev: BL 8/97; HB 9–10/97; SLJ 7/97*)

**7193** Hermes, Patricia. *The Cousins Club: Everything Stinks* (4–6). 1995, Pocket paper $3.50 (0-671-87967-7). 147pp. Jennifer and twin Amy are in the fifth grade and facing the problems of becoming adolescents. (Rev: BL 1/15/95; SLJ 3/95)

**7194** Hest, Amy. *The Private Notebook of Katie Roberts, Age 11* (4–6). Illus. 1995, Candlewick $14.95 (1-56402-474-1). 80pp. Katie confides in her diary about problems adjusting to her new Texas home and about her many questions concerning the difficulties of growing up. (Rev: BL 7/95*; HB 9–10/95; SLJ 9/95)

**7195** High, Linda O. *The Summer of the Great Divide* (5–8). 1996, Holiday $15.95 (0-8234-1228-8). 176pp. During the summer of 1969, 13-year-old Wheezie sorts herself out at her relative's farm. (Rev: BCCB 7–8/96; BL 6/1–15/96; SLJ 4/96)

**7196** Holden, Dwight. *Grand-Gran's Best Trick* (3–5). Illus. by Michael Chesworth. 1989, Brunner paper $8.95 (0-945354-16-9). 48pp. A young girl faces the sad experience of her beloved grandfather's death. (Rev: BL 12/1/89)

**7197** Holl, Kristi D. *First Things First* (5–7). 1997, Royal Fireworks paper $6.99 (0-88092-432-2). Informed that the family can't afford to send her to camp this year, Shelley decides to earn her own money. (Rev: BL 5/1/86; SLJ 5/86)

**7198** Hopper, Nancy J. *I Was a Fifth-Grade Zebra* (3–5). 1993, Dial LB $13.89 (0-8037-1595-1). 144pp. Chelsea doesn't know what to do when she receives an invitation to a party where she must bring a boy. (Rev: BCCB 4/93; BL 7/93)

**7199** Howe, James. *A Night Without Stars* (5–7). 1983, Macmillan $16.00 (0-689-30957-0); Avon paper $2.95 (0-380-69877-3). 192pp. A novel about a young girl's hospitalization and serious operation.

**7200** Howe, James. *Pinky and Rex and the Bully* (2–4). Illus. 1996, Simon & Schuster $15.00 (0-689-80021-5); paper $3.99 (0-689-80834-8). 40pp. When the local bully calls him a sissy, Pinky wonders if he should change his ways. (Rev: BL 4/1/96; SLJ 4/96)

**7201** Hughes, Dean. *Family Pose* (5–8). 1989, Macmillan LB $14.95 (0-689-31396-9). 192pp. A novel of an 11-year-old runaway and his growing attachment to a "new family." (Rev: BL 4/1/89; SLJ 4/89)

**7202** Hunt, Irene. *No Promises in the Wind* (5–8). 1987, Berkley paper $4.50 (0-425-09969-5). 100pp. During the Great Depression, Josh Grondowski is forced to make his own way in life.

**7203** Hunt, Irene. *Up a Road Slowly* (5–8). 1993, Silver Burdett $10.95 (0-382-24336-8); Scholastic paper $1.95 (0-590-03171-6). 192pp. Julie goes to live with Aunt Cordelia after her mother's death and finds the adjustment very difficult. Newbery Award winner, 1967.

**7204** Hurwitz, Johanna. *Once I Was a Plum Tree* (4–5). Illus. by Ingrid Fetz. 1992, Morrow paper $3.95 (0-688-11848-8). 160pp. In spite of her parents' indifference, Geraldine becomes aware of her Jewish inheritance.

**7205** Hurwitz, Johanna. *Yellow Blue Jay* (3–5). Illus. by Donald Carrick. 1986, Morrow paper $3.95 (0-688-12278-7). 128pp. Shy city-boy Jay finds that 2 weeks at a Vermont cabin is not as bad as he feared. (Rev: BCCB 6/86; BL 6/15/86; SLJ 8/86)

**7206** Hyppolite, Joanne. *Ola Shakes It Up* (4–8). Illus. 1998, Delacorte $14.95 (0-385-32235-6). 166pp. A spunky girl tries to prevent her parents from moving to a neighborhood where she will be the only African American in school. (Rev: BL 2/15/98; SLJ 2/98)

**7207** Irwin, Hadley. *The Lilith Summer* (6–8). 1979, Feminist Pr. $8.95 (0-912670-52-5). 126pp. Twelve-year-old Ellen learns about old age when she "lady sits" with 77-year-old Lilith Adams.

**7208** Jarrow, Gail. *Beyond the Magic Sphere* (4–6). 1994, Harcourt $15.95 (0-15-200193-X). 192pp. S. B.'s only ray of hope during the summer she is

spending with her unsympathetic cousin is meeting Cally, who plays a strange fantasy game. (Rev: BL 10/15/94; SLJ 11/94)

**7209** Joosse, Barbara M. *Anna and the Cat Lady* (3–6). Illus. by Gretchen Will Mayo. 1992, Harper-Collins LB $13.89 (0-06-020243-2). 176pp. Two third-graders rescue a kitten and meet an elderly eccentric woman who they later realize needs their help to survive. (Rev: BCCB 2/92; BL 1/1/92; SLJ 3/92)

**7210** Joosse, Barbara M. *Pieces of the Picture* (5–8). 1989, HarperCollins LB $12.89 (0-397-32343-3); paper $3.50 (0-06-440310-6). 144pp. Emily finds life unhappy when she and her mother move to Wisconsin from Chicago after her father's death. (Rev: BL 6/1/89; SLJ 4/89)

**7211** Jukes, Mavis. *Blackberries in the Dark* (3–4). Illus. 1993, Knopf $15.00 (0-394-87599-0). 48pp. Austin's first visit to his grandparents' house after his grandfather's death feels lonely and strange, until he and his grandmother express their sorrow together and go fishing. (Rev: BCCB 1/86; BL 1/1/86; HB 3–4/86)

**7212** Katz, Welwyn W. *Out of the Dark* (5–8). 1996, Simon & Schuster $16.00 (0-689-80947-6). 176pp. A young boy escapes the painful present by imagining himself as a Viking shipbuilder. (Rev: BL 10/15/96; HB 11–12/96; SLJ 9/96)

**7213** Kaye, Marilyn. *Real Heroes* (5–7). 1993, Harcourt $13.95 (0-15-200563-3); Avon paper $3.50 (0-380-72283-6). 144pp. Kevin finds he is in the middle of a situation involving quarrels between parents and between best friends, and a controversy about a teacher who is HIV positive. (Rev: BCCB 5/93; BL 4/1/93)

**7214** Keene, Carolyn. *Love Times Three* (5–8). Series: River Heights. 1991, Pocket paper $3.50 (0-671-96703-7). 156pp. Nikki has a crush on Tim, but Brittany wants him too. (Rev: BL 12/15/89)

**7215** Killien, Christi. *Artie's Brief: The Whole Truth, and Nothing But* (5–7). 1989, Avon paper $2.95 (0-380-71108-7). 112pp. Sixth-grader Artie deals with the suicide of his older brother. (Rev: BL 5/15/89)

**7216** King-Smith, Dick. *Sophie Is Seven* (2–4). Illus. 1995, Candlewick $14.95 (1-56402-542-X). 123pp. A classroom unit on life helps promote Sophie's determination to own a farm one day. (Rev: BCCB 5/95; BL 7/95; SLJ 7/95)

**7217** Kinsey-Warnock, Natalie. *The Canada Geese Quilt* (4–6). Illus. by Leslie Bowman. 1989, Dutton paper $14.99 (0-525-65004-0). 64pp. Ariel and her grandmother adjust to the elderly woman's stroke and to a new baby in the family. (Rev: BCCB 1/90; BL 10/1/89*; SLJ 11/89*)

**7218** Kinsey-Warnock, Natalie. *In the Language of Loons* (4–7). 1998, Cobblehill $15.99 (0-525-65237-X). 105pp. During a summer on his grandfather's farm, Arlis gains self-confidence and learns how to tap his potential. (Rev: SLJ 3/98)

**7219** Klass, Sheila S. *Kool Ada* (5–7). 1991, Scholastic $13.95 (0-590-43902-2). 176pp. Ada reacts only with her fists when she is sent to live in inner-city Chicago. (Rev: BL 10/15/91; SLJ 8/91*)

**7220** Kline, Suzy. *Marvin and the Mean Words* (2–4). Illus. 1997, Putnam $14.95 (0-399-23009-2). 80pp. Marvin, the second-grade class bully, gets a taste of his own medicine. (Rev: BL 4/1/97; SLJ 5/97)

**7221** Kline, Suzy. *Mary Marony and the Chocolate Surprise* (2–4). Illus. 1995, Putnam $13.95 (0-399-22829-2). 86pp. Mary Marony cheats to become a contest winner and later wonders if it was worth it. (Rev: BL 12/1/95; SLJ 12/95)

**7222** Konigsburg, E. L. *Altogether, One at a Time* (4–6). Illus. by Gail E. Haley. 1971, Macmillan paper $3.99 (0-689-71290-1). 88pp. Four short stories by the Newbery Medal-winning writer, each of which explores the theme that compromise is often necessary to appreciate life fully.

**7223** Konigsburg, E. L. *T-Backs, T-Shirts, Coat, and Suit* (5–8). Series: Jean Karl Books. 1993, Atheneum $14.00 (0-689-31855-3). 160pp. When Chloé goes to visit her former flower-child sister, she becomes part of a struggle for individual rights in the workplace. (Rev: BCCB 11/93; SLJ 10/93*)

**7224** Korman, Gordon. *Liar, Liar, Pants on Fire* (2–4). Illus. by JoAnn Adinolfi. 1997, Scholastic $14.95 (0-590-27142-3). 84pp. Third-grader Zoe lies so much that no one believes her when she tells the truth. (Rev: SLJ 9/97)

**7225** Krumgold, Joseph. *Onion John* (5–8). Illus. by Symeon Shimin. 1959, HarperCollins LB $14.89 (0-690-04698-7); paper $4.95 (0-06-440144-8). 248pp. A Newbery Medal winner (1960) about a boy's friendship with an old man. Also use the Newbery Award winner . . . *And Now Miguel* (1954).

**7226** Layton, George. *The Swap* (5–8). 1997, Putnam $16.95 (0-399-23148-X). 192pp. A series of stories narrated by an 11-year-old working-class boy in the north of England, who is troubled by bullying and growing up without a father. (Rev: BL 10/1/97; SLJ 9/97)

**7227** LeMieux, A. C. *Dare to Be, M.E.!* (5–7). Illus. 1997, Avon paper $14.00 (0-380-97496-7). 224pp. Mary Ellen must help her friend Justine cope with bulimia. (Rev: BL 6/1–15/97; SLJ 7/97)

**7228** LeMieux, A. C. *Fruit Flies, Fish and Fortune Cookies* (4–6). Illus. by Diane De Groat. 1994, Morrow $15.00 (0-688-13299-5). 192pp. Everything

seems to go wrong for sixth-grader Mary Ellen, including being sprayed by a skunk. (Rev: BL 11/1/94; SLJ 10/94)

**7229** Leverich, Kathleen. *Daisy* (2–4). Illus. 1997, HarperCollins paper $4.25 (0-06-442019-1). 96pp. Daisy is unhappy when she discovers she will be only one of several flower girls at an upcoming wedding. Other stories about flower girls are *Violet, Rose*, and *Heather* (all 1997). (Rev: BL 7/97; HB 5–6/97; SLJ 4/97)

**7230** Levinson, Marilyn. *The Fourth-Grade Four* (2–4). Illus. by Leslie Bowman. 1989, Holt paper $4.95 (0-8050-1640-6). 57pp. Alex gets into trouble because he refuses to wear glasses. (Rev: BCCB 1/90; BL 12/1/89; SLJ 2/90)

**7231** Levitin, Sonia. *Adam's War* (4–6). Illus. 1994, Dial paper $12.89 (0-8037-1507-2). 96pp. Adam leads his gang, the Angels, effectively until a rival gang interferes. (Rev: BL 7/94; SLJ 6/94)

**7232** Levy, Elizabeth. *My Life as a Fifth-Grade Comedian* (4–6). Illus. 1997, HarperCollins $14.95 (0-06-026602-3). 128pp. Jimmy, a born joker, has problems at home and finds that his grades are slipping at school. (Rev: BL 8/97; SLJ 9/97)

**7233** Lewis, Beverly. *Catch a Falling Star* (5–8). 1995, Bethany paper $5.99 (1-55661-478-0). 144pp. An Amish boy faces excommunication when he begins paying too much attention to a non-Amish girl. (Rev: BL 3/15/96)

**7234** Lewis, Beverly. *Night of the Fireflies* (5–8). 1995, Bethany paper $5.99 (1-55661-479-9). 144pp. In this sequel to *Catch a Falling Star* (1995), Levi, an Amish boy, tries to save his young sister, who has been struck by a car. (Rev: BL 3/15/96)

**7235** Little, Jean. *The Belonging Place* (4–6). 1997, Viking paper $13.99 (0-670-87593-7). 144pp. Already uprooted once because of the death of her parents, Elspet Mary is upset when her aunt and uncle with whom she has been living decide to move up to the Canadian wilderness. (Rev: BL 11/15/97; SLJ 11/97)

**7236** Lorbiecki, Marybeth. *Just One Flick of a Finger* (3–6). Illus. by David Diaz. 1996, Dial paper $14.89 (0-8037-1949-3). 40pp. Jack steals his father's gun to confront Reebo, who is bullying him. (Rev: BL 6/1–15/96; SLJ 9/96)

**7237** Love, D. Anne. *My Lone Star Summer* (4–6). 1996, Holiday $15.95 (0-8234-1235-0). 192pp. Jill experiences the first problems of adolescence when she spends her twelfth summer visiting her grandmother's ranch. (Rev: BCCB 7–8/96; BL 5/1/96; SLJ 3/96)

**7238** Lowery, Linda. *Somebody Somewhere Knows My Name* (3–5). Illus. by John E. Karpinski. 1995, Carolrhoda LB $14.95 (0-87614-946-8). 40pp. Grace and her 8-year-old brother are abandoned by their mother and taken to a shelter for the homeless. (Rev: BL 12/1/95; SLJ 11/95)

**7239** McCutcheon, Elsie. *The Rat War* (5–7). 1986, Farrar $10.95 (0-374-36182-7). 111pp. In postwar Britain, a shy, lonely boy makes a pet of a rat. (Rev: BL 8/86; SLJ 10/86)

**7240** McKenna, Colleen O'Shaughnessy. *Fifth Grade: Here Comes Trouble* (4–6). 1991, Scholastic paper $3.25 (0-590-41734-7). 128pp. Collette feels insecure when her rich friend invites her to her first boy-girl party. (Rev: BCCB 10/89; SLJ 9/89)

**7241** McKenzie, Ellen Kindt. *Stargone John* (3–5). Illus. by William Low. 1990, Holt $13.95 (0-8050-1451-9). 68pp. Shy John can't adjust to a one-room school. (Rev: BCCB 12/90*; BL 11/15/90; SLJ 12/90)

**7242** MacLachlan, Patricia. *The Facts and Fictions of Minna Pratt* (5–7). 1988, HarperCollins LB $14.89 (0-06-024117-9); paper $4.50 (0-06-440265-7). 144pp. A budding young cellist on the verge of adolescence experiences her first boyfriend. (Rev: BCCB 4/88; BL 6/15/88; SLJ 6–7/88)

**7243** MacLachlan, Patricia. *Unclaimed Treasures* (5–8). 1984, HarperCollins paper $3.95 (0-06-440189-8). 128pp. A romantic story of a young girl finding herself.

**7244** Mathis, Sharon Bell. *Sidewalk Story* (3–5). Illus. 1986, Puffin paper $3.99 (0-14-032165-9). 64pp. A reissue of the story about a young black girl and her family and their eviction from their apartment.

**7245** Miles, Betty. *The Trouble with Thirteen* (4–6). 1979, Knopf LB $12.99 (0-394-93930-1); paper $2.95 (0-394-82043-6). 112pp. Annie's life is disrupted by many changes, including a move to New York City.

**7246** Miles, Miska. *Annie and the Old One* (2–5). Illus. by Peter Parnall. 1972, Little, Brown $16.95 (0-316-57117-2); paper $7.95 (0-316-57120-2). Annie, a young Navajo girl, realizes her wonderful grandmother is dying and tries to put off the inevitable.

**7247** Miles, Miska. *Gertrude's Pocket* (3–5). Illus. by Emily Arnold McCully. 1984, Peter Smith $15.75 (0-8446-6164-3). A reissue of a 1970 title in which Gertrude's tormentor gets his comeuppance in a story about poor folk in Appalachia.

**7248** Miller, Mary Jane. *Fast Forward* (4–7). 1993, Viking paper $14.99 (0-670-84339-3). 144pp. A sixth-grade girl who cheated on an exam wishes she could fast forward her life. (Rev: BL 7/93; SLJ 8/93)

**7249** Mills, Claudia. *Cally's Enterprise* (4–6). 1989, Avon paper $2.75 (0-380-70693-8). 128pp. Cally, the daughter of overachievers, breaks her foot and can't go to ballet and gym, and to her surprise learns that

she likes being a businesswoman when her friend Chuck gets her to sell magazines. (Rev: BCCB 4/88; BL 6/1/88; SLJ 5/88)

**7250** Mills, Claudia. *Dinah Forever* (5–7). 1995, Farrar $14.00 (0-374-31788-7). 144pp. Dinah, who is a competitive achiever, questions her values when an elderly friend dies. (Rev: BCCB 11/95; BL 10/1/95; SLJ 11/95*)

**7251** Mills, Lauren. *The Rag Coat* (3–5). Illus. 1991, Little, Brown $16.95 (0-316-57407-4). 32pp. A picture book that celebrates Appalachia. (Rev: BCCB 1/92; BL 10/15/91; HB 11–12/91; SLJ 11/91*)

**7252** Mohr, Nicholasa. *The Magic Shell* (2–4). Illus. 1995, Scholastic $13.95 (0-590-47110-4). 112pp. A young boy is not happy in his new home in New York City and misses his native land, the Dominican Republic. (Rev: BCCB 12/95; BL 8/95; SLJ 10/95)

**7253** Montgomery, L. M. *Anne of Green Gables* (5–8). Illus. by Jody Lee. 1983, Putnam $25.95 (0-448-06030-2). 384pp. The old-fashioned story of an orphan girl and her adventures. Others in this series are available in paperback from Bantam.

**7254** Mooney, Bel. *The Voices of Silence* (5–8). 1997, Delacorte $14.95 (0-385-32326-3). 180pp. A novel about contemporary Romania and a 13-year-old girl's adjustment to the political chaos. (Rev: BCCB 4/97; HB 3–4/97; SLJ 3/97*)

**7255** Moore, Emily. *Whose Side Are You On?* (5–7). 1988, Farrar $14.00 (0-374-38409-6); paper $3.95 (0-374-48373-6). 128pp. Barbra is dismayed to find out that her math tutor is none other than T.J., the class pest. (Rev: BCCB 10/88; BL 1/15/89; SLJ 10/88)

**7256** Moran, George. *Imagine Me on a Sit-Ski!* (2–5). Illus. by Nadine Bernard Westcott. 1995, Albert Whitman LB $14.95 (0-8075-3618-0). 32pp. Wheelchair-bound Billy gets an opportunity to ski with special equipment at Snow Valley. (Rev: BL 3/1/95; SLJ 2/95)

**7257** Moss, Marissa. *Amelia's Notebook* (3–5). Illus. 1995, Tricycle Pr. $14.00 (1-883672-18-X). 32pp. The secret writings and drawings of a 9-year-old girl as she faces problems in growing up are the focus of this novel. (Rev: BL 4/1/95; SLJ 7/95)

**7258** Myers, Walter Dean. *Darnell Rock Reporting* (4–6). 1994, Delacorte $14.95 (0-385-32096-5). 106pp. When Darnell interviews a homeless Vietnam veteran for the school newspaper, his life changes. (Rev: BCCB 10/94; BL 8/94; SLJ 9/94)

**7259** Napoli, Donna Jo. *On Guard* (3–4). 1997, Dutton paper $15.99 (0-525-45759-3). 160pp. Mikey learns about sportsmanship when he takes up fencing. (Rev: BCCB 2/97; BL 12/15/96; SLJ 5/97)

**7260**  Naylor, Phyllis Reynolds. *The Agony of Alice* (5–7). 1985, Macmillan $16.00 (0-689-31143-5); Dell paper $3.99 (0-689-81672-3). 144pp. Sixth-grader Alice is motherless and longing for a female model, which she finally finds in her teacher, Mrs. Plotkin, whom she hates. (Rev: BL 10/1/85; SLJ 1/86)

**7261**  Naylor, Phyllis Reynolds. *Alice in April* (5–8). 1993, Macmillan $15.00 (0-689-31805-7). Al faces problems at school and at home, all related to her growing up. (Rev: SLJ 6/93)

**7262**  Naylor, Phyllis Reynolds. *Alice the Brave* (5–7). 1995, Simon & Schuster $15.00 (0-689-80095-9); paper $3.99 (0-689-80598-5). 131pp. Alice conquers her fear of deep water and also feels the pangs of growing up in this amusing continuation of a popular series. (Rev: BCCB 4/95; BL 5/1/95; HB 7–8/95; SLJ 5/95)

**7263**  Naylor, Phyllis Reynolds. *All But Alice* (5–8). 1992, Macmillan $14.00 (0-689-31773-5). 128pp. Alice, now a seventh-grader and still motherless, looks for guidance by joining in the activities of her peer group. (Rev: BCCB 5/92; HB 7–8/92; SLJ 5/92)

**7264**  Naylor, Phyllis Reynolds. *Eddie, Incorporated* (4–6). Illus. by Blanche Sims. 1980, Macmillan $15.00 (0-689-30754-3). After many tries, a sixth-grader finally finds a way to make money.

**7265**  Naylor, Phyllis Reynolds. *Night Cry* (5–8). 1984, Macmillan $16.00 (0-689-31017-X); Dell paper $3.99 (0-440-40017-1). 168pp. A 13-year-old Mississippi girl lives alone in the backwoods.

**7266**  Nelson, Vaunda M. *Possibles* (4–8). 1995, Putnam $15.95 (0-399-22823-3). 192pp. After her father's death from cancer, 12-year-old Sheppy must take a summer job to help her family. (Rev: BL 2/1/96; SLJ 10/95)

**7267**  Nilsson, Ulf. *If You Didn't Have Me* (3–5). Trans. by George Blecher. Illus. by Eva Eriksson. 1987, Macmillan $15.00 (0-689-50406-3). While his parents are building a house in town, a Swedish boy spends a lonely summer on his grandparents' farm. (Rev: BCCB 4/87; BL 4/15/87; HB 5–6/87)

**7268**  Orgel, Doris. *Don't Call Me Slob-o* (2–5). Illus. 1996, Hyperion LB $14.49 (0-7868-2086-1); paper $3.95 (0-7868-1044-0). 80pp. Shrimp, once the target of the neighborhood kids' jokes, loses that status when a new kid, Slob-o, comes to town. (Rev: BL 1/1–15/97; SLJ 7/96)

**7269**  Palatini, Margie. *The Wonder Worm Wars* (4–6). 1997, Hyperion LB $15.49 (0-7868-2295-3). 144pp. Elliot faces a dismal summer after he breaks his arm and discovers that his next-door neighbor, a girl, is a better athlete than he is. (Rev: BL 10/1/97; SLJ 12/97)

**7270**  Paterson, Katherine. *The Great Gilly Hopkins* (4–6). 1978, HarperCollins LB $14.89 (0-690-03838-0); paper $4.95 (0-06-440201-0). 192pp. Precocious Gilly bounces from one foster home to another.

**7271**  Patron, Susan. *Maybe Yes, Maybe No, Maybe Maybe* (3–5). Illus. by Dorothy Donahue. 1993, Orchard LB $16.99 (0-531-08632-1). 96pp. P.K. thinks that being the middle sister is no picnic. (Rev: BCCB 7–8/93; BL 3/15/93; SLJ 3/93*)

**7272**  Patterson, Nancy R. *The Shiniest Rock of All* (3–5). Illus. by Karen A. Jerome. 1991, Farrar $13.00 (0-374-36805-8). 80pp. Robert Reynolds cannot pronounce — of all things — the letter R. (Rev: BCCB 9/91; BL 9/15/91; HB 11–12/91; SLJ 11/91)

**7273**  Paulsen, Gary. *The Cookcamp* (5–7). 1991, Orchard $15.95 (0-531-05927-8). 128pp. After a 5-year-old boy discovers his mother is having an affair, he is sent off to northern Minnesota in this World War II story. (Rev: BCCB 3/91; BL 3/1/91; HB 3–4/91; SLJ 2/91*)

**7274**  Pearson, Gayle. *The Secret Box* (5–8). 1997, Simon & Schuster $15.00 (0-689-81379-1). 128pp. Five short stories about the pangs of growing up, set in Oakland, California. (Rev: BCCB 7–8/97; BL 8/97; SLJ 6/97)

**7275**  Peterseil, Tehila. *The Safe Place* (5–8). 1996, Pitspopany $16.95 (0-943706-71-8); paper $12.95 (0-943706-72-6). 136pp. A moving story of an Israeli girl and the problems she faces at school because of a learning disability. (Rev: SLJ 12/96)

**7276**  Petersen, P. J. *I Hate Company* (2–4). 1994, Dutton paper $12.99 (0-525-45329-6). 96pp. Dan is horrified when his mother invites guests to stay with them; but when they leave, he misses them just a little. (Rev: BCCB 11/94; BL 11/1/94; SLJ 10/94)

**7277**  Porter, Tracey. *Treasures in the Dust* (5–7). 1997, HarperCollins LB $14.89 (0-06-027564-2). 160pp. With alternating points of view, 2 girls from poor families in Oklahoma's Dust Bowl tell their stories. (Rev: BL 8/97; HB 9–10/97; SLJ 12/97*)

**7278**  Radin, Ruth Yaffe. *All Joseph Wanted* (3–7). Illus. by Deborah Kogan Ray. 1991, Macmillan $14.00 (0-02-775641-6). 80pp. When 11-year-old Joseph persuades his mother to learn to read at a literacy program at the public library, he is freed from adult responsibilities and reclaims time for friends and school work. (Rev: BCCB 11/91; BL 1/1/91; SLJ 1/92)

**7279**  Ransom, Candice. *More Than a Name* (3–5). 1995, Macmillan $14.00 (0-02-775795-1). 115pp. When her mother remarries, Cammie has many adjustments to make, including living with her stepfather's large family. (Rev: BCCB 9/95; BL 7/95; SLJ 7/95)

**7280** Regan, Dian C. *The Curse of the Trouble Dolls* (3–5). Illus. by Michael Chesworth. 1992, Holt $14.95 (0-8050-1944-8). 64pp. The Guatemalan Trouble Dolls sent by Aunt Li escalate Angie's problems instead of solving them. (Rev: BCCB 5/92; BL 3/15/92; SLJ 8/92)

**7281** Richardson, Judith B. *David's Landing* (4–6). Illus. by Molly Bang. 1984, Woods Hole $10.95 (0-9611374-1-X). 150pp. A boy troubled by his parents' divorce is healed in this old-fashioned story of life in a small town. (Rev: BL 8/85; HB 9–10/85)

**7282** Richardson, Judith B. *First Came the Owl* (4–6). 1996, Holt $14.95 (0-8050-4547-3). 153pp. Nita gradually begins to see that life in her family resembles the situation in the fairy tale *Snow White*. (Rev: BCCB 7–8/96; BL 7/96; HB 9–10/96; SLJ 7/96)

**7283** Richardson, Sandy. *The Girl Who Ate Chicken Feet* (4–6). 1998, Dial paper $15.99 (0-8037-2254-0). 144pp. The story of Sissy and her problems being an adolescent in a Southern town during the 1960s. (Rev: BL 3/1/98; SLJ 3/98)

**7284** Roberts, Willo Davis. *Don't Hurt Laurie!* (4–6). Illus. by Ruth Sanderson. 1977, Macmillan $16.00 (0-689-30571-0); paper $3.95 (0-689-71206-5). 176pp. Seen from the viewpoint of 11-year-old Laurie, this is a harrowing story of child abuse.

**7285** Roberts, Willo Davis. *Secrets at Hidden Valley* (5–7). 1997, Simon & Schuster $16.00 (0-689-81166-7). 160pp. Gradually, 11-year-old Steffi learns to fit in when she is sent to northern Michigan to live with a grandfather she has never met. (Rev: BL 3/15/97; SLJ 6/97)

**7286** Robinson, Nancy K. *Countess Veronica* (4–6). 1994, Scholastic $13.95 (0-590-44485-9). 176pp. Pesky Veronica Schmidt tries to marry off her father to the local librarian. (Rev: BL 2/1/94; SLJ 4/94)

**7287** Rodowsky, Colby. *The Turnabout Shop* (4–6). 1998, Farrar $16.00 (0-374-37889-4). 135pp. Livvy has a difficult time fitting in when, after her mother's death, she is sent to live with her mother's old college friend, whom the girl has never met. (Rev: SLJ 3/98*)

**7288** Rosen, Michael J. *The Heart Is Big Enough* (5–7). Illus. 1997, Harcourt $16.00 (0-15-201402-0). 208pp. In each of these 5 stories, disabled or troubled youngsters gain inspiration and help from bonding with nature. (Rev: BL 3/1/97; SLJ 7/97)

**7289** Rottman, S. L. *Hero* (5–7). 1997, Peachtree $14.95 (1-56145-159-2). 144pp. When his home life becomes unbearable, Sean is sent to Carbondale Ranch, where his sense of self-worth gradually grows. (Rev: BL 12/1/97; SLJ 12/97)

**7290** Russell, Barbara T. *Last Left Standing* (5–7). 1996, Houghton $14.95 (0-395-71037-5). 144pp.

Gradually, Josh is able to accept the reality of his brother's death. (Rev: BL 11/15/96; SLJ 10/96)

**7291** Ryan, Mary C. *The Voice from the Mendelsohns' Maple* (5–7). Illus. by Irena Roman. 1990, Little, Brown $13.95 (0-316-76360-8). 132pp. Penny tries to cope with many problems, including finding out who the woman is who is hiding in the neighbor's maple tree. (Rev: SLJ 12/89)

**7292** Ryan, Mary E. *Me, My Sister, and I* (4–7). 1992, Simon & Schuster paper $15.00 (0-671-73851-8). 160pp. Mattie is in a dilemma about whom to ask to the Sadie Hawkins dance in this story of the ups and downs of being twins. (Rev: BL 12/15/92)

**7293** Ryan, Mary E. *The Trouble with Perfect* (5–8). 1995, Simon & Schuster $15.00 (0-689-80276-5). 175pp. Trying to please his father, Kyle is tempted to cheat on the exam to get on the Knowledge Bowl team. (Rev: BCCB 11/95; BL 10/1/95; SLJ 11/95)

**7294** Ryden, Hope. *Wild Horse Summer* (5–8). Illus. 1997, Clarion $15.00 (0-395-77519-1). 155pp. During a summer on her relatives' Wyoming ranch, Alison overcomes her anxieties and fears. (Rev: BL 8/97; SLJ 9/97)

**7295** Rylant, Cynthia. *A Blue-Eyed Daisy* (5–7). 1985, Macmillan LB $15.00 (0-02-777960-2); Dell paper $3.25 (0-440-40927-6). 112pp. One year in the rather sad and troubled world of 11-year-old Ellie. (Rev: BCCB 9/85; HB 7–8/85; SLJ 4/85)

**7296** Rylant, Cynthia. *A Fine White Dust* (5–7). 1986, Macmillan LB $16.00 (0-02-777240-3); Dell paper $3.50 (0-440-42499-2). 120pp. Peter falls under the spell of the traveling Preacher Man and decides to journey with him. (Rev: BCCB 9/86; SLJ 9/86)

**7297** Rylant, Cynthia. *Missing May* (5–8). 1992, Orchard LB $15.99 (0-531-08596-1); Dell paper $3.99 (0-440-40865-2). 96pp. Caring about each other is the tender message in this story of 12-year-old Summer, who, along with her uncle, must cope with the death of her beloved aunt. Newbery Award winner, 1993. (Rev: BCCB 3/92*; BL 2/15/92*; HB 3–4/92; SLJ 3/92*)

**7298** Sachar, Louis. *Dogs Don't Tell Jokes* (5–7). 1991, Knopf LB $14.99 (0-679-92017-X). 184pp. Gary thinks he's funny, but his friends think he's a dweeb in this story that deals with popularity and growing up. (Rev: BCCB 10/91; BL 7/91; SLJ 9/91)

**7299** Sachar, Louis. *Marvin Redpost: Why Pick on Me?* (2–4). Illus. by Barbara Sullivan. 1993, Random LB $11.99 (0-679-91947-3); paper $3.99 (0-679-81947-9). 40pp. Marvin becomes a social outcast after he is wrongfully accused of picking his nose. (Rev: BCCB 2/93; BL 5/1/93)

**7300** Scarboro, Elizabeth. *Phoenix, Upside Down* (3–5). 1996, Viking paper $14.99 (0-670-86335-1).

128pp. Jamie has problems adjusting to her new home in Phoenix, Arizona. (Rev: BL 6/1–15/96; SLJ 6/96)

**7301** Shreve, Susan. *The Bad Dreams of a Good Girl* (3–4). Illus. by Diane De Groat. 1993, Morrow paper $3.95 (0-688-12113-6). 96pp. A fourth grader faces all sorts of family problems.

**7302** Shreve, Susan. *The Goalie* (4–6). 1996, Morrow $15.00 (0-688-14379-2). 96pp. After her mother's death, Julie hides her grief by taking over management of the household and playing soccer. (Rev: BL 12/1/96; SLJ 2/97)

**7303** Shreve, Susan. *Wait for Me* (3–5). Illus. by Diane De Groat. 1992, Morrow $13.00 (0-688-11120-3). 96pp. Fifth-grader Molly Lottmann feels alone because her brother and sister seem to have suddenly grown up and left her behind. (Rev: BCCB 10/92; BL 9/1/92; SLJ 9/92)

**7304** Shreve, Susan. *Zoe and Columbo* (3–4). Illus. 1995, Morrow $15.00 (0-688-13552-8). 96pp. When he moves to a new school, Columbo won't admit to his classmates that he is adopted. (Rev: BL 12/15/95; SLJ 1/96)

**7305** Shura, Mary Francis. *The Search for Grissi* (4–6). Illus. by Ted Lewin. 1987, Avon paper $3.50 (0-380-70305-X). Eleven-year-old Peter has difficulty adjusting to life in Peoria until his little sister involves him in a search for her lost cat. (Rev: BCCB 7/85; BL 3/15/85; SLJ 5/85)

**7306** Shura, Mary Francis. *The Sunday Doll* (5–7). 1988, Avon paper $2.95 (0-380-70618-0). 112pp. Thirteen-year-old Emmy is miffed when the family won't tell her what has happened to upset her older sister Jayne, until she learns that Jayne's boyfriend has committed suicide. (Rev: BCCB 7–8/88; BL 7/88; SLJ 8/88)

**7307** Slepian, Jan. *The Mind Reader* (5–7). 1997, Putnam $15.95 (0-399-23150-1). 208pp. A 12-year-old clairvoyant runs away from vaudeville and a drunken father to live with a cousin he has never met. (Rev: BL 9/15/97; HB 9–10/97; SLJ 9/97)

**7308** Smith, Doris Buchanan. *A Taste of Blackberries* (4–6). Illus. by Charles Robinson. 1973, HarperCollins LB $13.89 (0-690-80512-8); paper $4.95 (0-06-440238-X). 64pp. Young Jamie dies unexpectedly of a bee sting, and his friends adjust to this loss.

**7309** Smith, Robert K. *Jelly Belly* (4–6). Illus. by Bob Jones. 1982, Dell paper $3.99 (0-440-44207-9). 160pp. A boy is sent to a weight-loss camp by his parents.

**7310** Snyder, Zilpha Keatley. *The Diamond War* (4–6). Series: Castle Court. 1995, Dell paper $3.50 (0-440-40985-3). 119pp. It's the boys versus the girls in this story about whether the trees in the only vacant lot in the area should be chopped down to

make a baseball diamond. (Rev: BL 9/1/95; SLJ 8/95)

**7311** Sommers, Beverly. *The Uncertainty Principle* (5–8). 1990, Fawcett paper $3.50 (0-449-14608-1). 155pp. Kathy is a gifted teenager who has some problems. (Rev: SLJ 4/91)

**7312** Sorensen, Virginia. *Plain Girl* (4–6). Illus. by Charles Geer. 1988, Harcourt paper $7.00 (0-15-262437-6). An Amish girl finds it difficult to accept both her cultural heritage and the world around her.

**7313** Sorenson, Jody. *The Secret Letters of Mama Cat* (5–8). 1988, Walker LB $13.85 (0-8027-6791-5). 122pp. Grandma died, and 12-year-old Meredith is not ready to let go. (Rev: BCCB 6/88; BL 9/15/88; SLJ 6–7/88)

**7314** Soto, Gary. *The Pool Party* (4–7). Illus. by Robert Casilla. 1992, Delacorte $13.95 (0-385-30890-6). 112pp. Rudy, part of a Mexican-American family, has growing-up problems. (Rev: SLJ 6/93)

**7315** Speregen, Devra. *Phone Call from a Flamingo* (5–7). Series: Full House. 1993, Pocket paper $3.99 (0-671-88004-7). 134pp. Stephanie decides that the price of being popular with the in crowd is too high when it involves hurting others. Based on the TV series *Full House*. (Rev: SLJ 11/93)

**7316** Spinelli, Jerry. *Maniac Magee* (5–7). 1990, Little, Brown $15.95 (0-316-80722-2). 192pp. This Newbery Medal winner (1991) tells of an amazing boy who can help others but needs help himself. (Rev: BL 6/1/90*)

**7317** Spinelli, Jerry. *Wringer* (4–7). 1997, HarperCollins LB $14.89 (0-06-024914-5). 192pp. A sensitive boy must participate in the massacre of thousands of pigeons released at an annual fair. (Rev: BL 9/1/97*; HB 9–10/97; SLJ 9/97*)

**7318** Spurr, Elizabeth. *Lupe and Me* (3–4). Illus. by Enrique O. Sanchez. 1995, Harcourt $13.00 (0-15-200522-6). 40pp. Susan is upset when her mother's housekeeper, 16-year-old Lupe, has to return to Mexico because she is an illegal alien. (Rev: BL 6/1–15/95; SLJ 6/95)

**7319** Stiles, Martha Bennett. *Sarah the Dragon Lady* (4–6). 1986, Avon paper $2.75 (0-380-70471-4). 96pp. Sarah tries to adjust to life in a small Kentucky town and face the fact of trouble in her parents' marriage. (Rev: BCCB 2/87; BL 1/1/87; SLJ 12/86)

**7320** Testa, Maria. *Nine Candles* (3–5). Illus. 1996, Carolrhoda LB $19.93 (0-87614-940-9). 32pp. Raymond is looking forward to visiting his mother, who is in prison. (Rev: BCCB 9/96; BL 7/96; SLJ 9/96)

**7321** Testa, Maria. *Someplace to Go* (3–5). Illus. 1996, Albert Whitman LB $14.95 (0-8075-7524-0). 32pp. Unlike his classmates, Davey has no home to return to after school. (Rev: BCCB 3/96; BL 4/15/96; SLJ 5/96)

**7322** Tolliver, Ruby C. *I Love You, Daisy Phew* (4–6). 1994, Hendrick-Long LB $13.95 (0-937460-86-9). 168pp. Blake finds an unusual pet in a goat named Daisy Phew when the troubled boy goes to live with his grandfather in Texas. (Rev: BL 1/15/95)

**7323** Toriseva, JoNelle. *Becoming Ballet* (4–6). 1995, Simon & Schuster $15.00 (0-689-80289-7). 152pp. Alexandra's dream of studying ballet at a summer camp is dashed when she has to remain at home on the farm. (Rev: BCCB 11/95; BL 12/15/95; SLJ 1/96)

**7324** Towne, Mary. *Steve the Sure* (4–6). 1990, Macmillan LB $13.95 (0-689-31646-1). 144pp. During his stay in Vermont one summer, know-it-all Steve arranges a talent show. (Rev: SLJ 12/90)

**7325** Vail, Rachel. *Daring to Be Abigail* (4–6). 1996, Orchard LB $16.99 (0-531-08867-7). 144pp. At summer camp, Abigail deliberately misbehaves so she won't be considered an outsider by the in-crowd. (Rev: BCCB 2/96; BL 3/1/96; HB 5–6/96; SLJ 3/96*)

**7326** Vail, Rachel. *Ever After* (5–8). 1994, Orchard LB $16.99 (0-531-08688-7). 176pp. Fourteen-year-old Molly is trying to act maturely but always seems to mess things up. (Rev: BCCB 4/94; BL 3/1/94; HB 5–6/94, 7–8/94; SLJ 5/94*)

**7327** Van Oosting, James. *The Last Payback* (5–8). 1997, HarperCollins $14.95 (0-06-027491-3). 144pp. The story of how Dimple gradually accepts the death of her twin brother, who has died of a gunshot wound. (Rev: BCCB 6/97; BL 6/1–15/97; HB 7–8/97; SLJ 7/97)

**7328** Wagner, Jane. *J.T.* (4–6). Photos by Gordon Parks. 1972, Dell paper $3.99 (0-440-44275-3). 128pp. J. T. Gamble lives in Harlem, and his most prized possessions are a tiny portable radio and a stray cat, for whom he has made a home.

**7329** Walker, Alice. *To Hell with Dying* (4–7). Illus. 1988, Harcourt paper $5.95 (0-15-289074-2). The Walker family won't let old Mr. Sweet die. (Rev: BCCB 4/88; BL 4/15/88; HB 7–8/88)

**7330** Walter, Mildred P. *Justin and the Best Biscuits in the World* (3–5). Illus. by Catherine Stock. 1986, Lothrop $16.00 (0-688-06645-3); Knopf paper $3.25 (0-679-80346-7). 128pp. Justin thinks some things are "women's work" until his grandfather shows him differently. (Rev: BCCB 12/86; BL 10/15/86; SLJ 11/86)

**7331** Warner, Sally. *Ellie and the Bunheads* (4–6). 1997, Knopf $16.00 (0-679-88229-4). 156pp. Twelve-year-old Ellie is torn between continuing her ballet classes or living the life of a normal adolescent. (Rev: BL 6/1–15/97; SLJ 9/97)

**7332** White Deer of Autumn. *The Great Change* (3–5). Illus. by Carol Grigg. 1992, Beyond Words $14.95 (0-941831-79-5). After Grandfather's death, a Native American woman explains the circle of life to her granddaughter. (Rev: SLJ 12/92)

**7333** Willis, Patricia. *Out of the Storm* (4–7). 1995, Clarion $15.00 (0-395-68708-X). 160pp. In 1946, Mandy's family moves in with her difficult Aunt Bess, who makes her tend a flock of sheep. (Rev: BCCB 5/95; BL 4/15/95; SLJ 4/95)

**7334** Willner-Pardo, Gina. *Daphne Eloise Slater, Who's Tall for Her Age* (3–5). Illus. 1997, Clarion $15.00 (0-395-73080-5). 40pp. After a cruel classmate calls her a giraffe, Daphne becomes painfully aware of her height. (Rev: BL 8/97; HB 9–10/97; SLJ 10/97)

**7335** Willner-Pardo, Gina. *Hunting Grandma's Treasures* (3–5). Illus. 1996, Clarion $14.95 (0-395-68190-1). 42pp. After his grandmother dies, Kevin experiences all the stages of grief until reaching acceptance. (Rev: BL 2/1/96; SLJ 6/96)

**7336** Wilson, Johnniece M. *Poor Girl* (5–7). 1992, Scholastic $13.95 (0-590-44732-7). 176pp. A first-person story about Miranda, who spends the summer trying to earn money for contact lenses before the fall. (Rev: BCCB 4/92; BL 8/92; SLJ 4/92)

**7337** Wilson, Johnniece M. *Robin on His Own* (4–6). 1992, Scholastic paper $2.95 (0-590-41809-2). 144pp. Watusi the cat comforts a young black boy when his mother dies. (Rev: BL 10/15/90; SLJ 1/91)

**7338** Wohl, Lauren L. *Christopher Davis's Best Year Yet* (2–4). Illus. 1995, Hyperion paper $3.95 (0-7868-1083-1). 64pp. Second-grader Christopher solves a series of minor personal problems in the course of a year. (Rev: BL 4/1/96; SLJ 4/96)

**7339** Wojciechowska, Maia. *Shadow of a Bull* (5–7). Illus. by Alvin Smith. 1964, Macmillan $16.00 (0-689-30042-5); paper $3.95 (0-689-71567-6). 160pp. Manolo, surviving son of a great bullfighter, has his own "moment of truth" when he faces his first bull. Newbery Award winner, 1965.

**7340** Wolitzer, Hilma. *Toby Lived Here* (5–7). 1986, Farrar paper $3.45 (0-374-47924-0). Two sisters adjust in different ways to a foster home.

**7341** Wood, June R. *The Man Who Loved Clowns* (5–8). 1992, Putnam $15.95 (0-399-21888-2). 192pp. When Delrita's parents are killed in an auto accident, she grows close to her uncle, an adult with Down's syndrome. (Rev: BL 11/15/92; SLJ 9/92)

**7342** Wood, June R. *Turtle on a Fence Post* (5–8). 1997, Putnam $16.95 (0-399-23184-6). 260pp. After the deaths of her parents and an uncle, Delrita, now living with an aunt and her husband, is so emotionally upset that it seems she will never love anyone again. A sequel to *The Man Who Loved Clowns* (1992). (Rev: BL 11/15/97; SLJ 9/97)

**7343**    Wood, June R. *When Pigs Fly* (5–8). 1995, Putnam $16.95 (0-399-22911-6). 240pp. In a family-living project, Buddy and her classmates are assigned hard-boiled eggs to take care of as though they were their parents. (Rev: BCCB 11/95; BL 12/1/95; SLJ 10/95)

**7344**    Woodruff, Elvira. *The Secret Funeral of Slim Jim the Snake* (4–5). 1993, Holiday $15.95 (0-8234-1014-5). 144pp. Nick lives over a funeral home and faces some problems with humorous solutions. (Rev: SLJ 3/93)

**7345**    Wright, Betty R. *The Scariest Night* (5–7). 1991, Holiday $15.95 (0-8234-0904-X). 144pp. Erin is furious at having to spend the summer in Milwaukee until she discovers that her new neighbor is a medium. (Rev: BCCB 12/91; BL 1/15/92; HB 9–10/91; SLJ 10/91)

## Physical and Emotional Problems

**7346**    Abbott, Deborah, and Henry Kisor. *One TV Blasting and a Pig Outdoors* (3–5). Illus. 1994, Albert Whitman LB $14.95 (0-8075-6075-8). 40pp. A book that describes what it's like to live in a household where the father is deaf. (Rev: BL 9/15/94; SLJ 12/94)

**7347**    Banks, Jacqueline T. *Egg-Drop Blues* (4–6). 1995, Houghton $15.00 (0-395-70931-8). 128pp. Judge Jenkins, a dyslexic, faces problems when his mother threatens to send him to a different school if he doesn't do better where he is. A sequel to Banks' *Project Wheels* (1993) and *The New One* (1994). (Rev: BCCB 5/95; BL 4/15/95; HB 7–8/95; SLJ 8/95)

**7348**    Bantle, Lee F. *Diving for the Moon* (4–7). 1995, Simon & Schuster paper $14.00 (0-689-80004-5). 78pp. Bird watches her best friend Josh slowly change from being HIV positive to a person with AIDS. (Rev: BL 9/1/95; SLJ 10/95)

**7349**    Betancourt, Jeanne. *My Name Is Brain/Brian* (4–6). 1993, Scholastic $14.95 (0-590-44921-4). 176pp. Brian, a sixth-grader who is dyslexic, matures and changes his attitudes toward his friends and teachers. (Rev: BCCB 4/93; BL 4/1/93; SLJ 4/93)

**7350**    Blue, Rose. *Me and Einstein: Breaking Through the Reading Barrier* (4–6). Illus. by Peggy Luks. 1984, Human Sciences $16.95 (0-87705-388-X); paper $10.95 (0-89885-185-8). Bobby, a dyslexic youngster, tries to hide the fact that he can't read.

**7351**    Blume, Judy. *Deenie* (5–7). 1982, Macmillan LB $14.95 (0-02-711020-6); Dell paper $4.50 (0-440-93259-9). 192pp. Instead of becoming a model, as her mother wishes, Deenie must cope with scoliosis and wearing a spinal brace.

**7352**    Brooks, Bruce. *Everywhere* (5–8). 1990, HarperCollins LB $14.89 (0-06-020729-9). 80pp. Eleven-year-old Dooley, who is black, helps a 10-year-old white boy live through the emotional trauma of waiting to see if his beloved grandfather will recover from a heart attack. (Rev: BCCB 10/90; BL 10/15/90*; SLJ 9/90*)

**7353**    Butts, Nancy. *Cheshire Moon* (5–7). 1996, Front Street $14.95 (1-886910-08-1). 105pp. A friendless deaf girl grieves for a cousin who has drowned at sea in this novel in an island setting. (Rev: BL 10/15/96; SLJ 11/96)

**7354**    Byars, Betsy. *The Summer of the Swans* (5–7). Illus. by Ted Coconis. 1970, Puffin paper $4.50 (0-14-031420-2). 144pp. The story of a 14-year-old named Sara — moody, unpredictable, and on the brink of womanhood — and how her life changes when her younger, mentally retarded brother disappears. Newbery Award winner, 1971.

**7355**    Byars, Betsy. *The TV Kid* (3–4). Illus. by Richard Cuffari. 1987, Puffin paper $3.99 (0-14-032308-2). 128pp. In his loneliness, a young boy escapes into the world of television watching and soon has difficulty distinguishing fact from fancy.

**7356**    Cunningham, Julia. *Burnish Me Bright* (4–6). 1980, Peter Smith $18.75 (0-8446-6252-6). An imaginative mute boy named Auguste is scorned by the inhabitants of the French village where he lives.

**7357**    Cutler, Jane. *Spaceman* (4–6). 1997, Dutton paper $14.99 (0-525-45636-8). 144pp. Gary, who has a learning disability, is about to give up when he is sent to a special school. (Rev: BCCB 5/97; BL 3/15/97; SLJ 5/97)

**7358**    Fassler, Joan. *Howie Helps Himself* (2–4). Illus. by Joe Lasker. 1975, Whitman LB $14.95 (0-8075-3422-6). 32pp. Howie adjusts to cerebral palsy and the use of his wheelchair.

**7359**    Fine, Anne. *The Tulip Touch* (4–8). 1997, Little, Brown $15.95 (0-316-28325-8). 160pp. Natalie forms a dangerous friendship with Tulip, a girl going completely out of control. (Rev: BL 9/15/97*; HB 9–10, 11–12/97; SLJ 9/97*)

**7360**    Garfield, James B. *Follow My Leader* (4–6). Illus. 1994, Puffin paper $4.99 (0-140-36485-4). 192pp. With the aid of friends and a guide dog, an 11-year-old boy resumes his life.

**7361**    Gleitzman, Morris. *Sticky Beak* (4–6). 1995, Harcourt $11.00 (0-15-200366-5); paper $5.00 (0-15-200367-3). 160pp. Rowena, a mute from birth, faces having a new sibling and caring for a foul-mouthed cockatoo in this humorous novel from Australia. (Rev: BCCB 4/95; BL 6/1–15/95; SLJ 6/95)

**7362** Gould, Marilyn. *Golden Daffodils* (5–7). 1991, Allied Crafts paper $10.95 (0-9632305-1-4). 17pp. Janis adjusts to her handicap resulting from cerebral palsy.

**7363** Hermes, Patricia. *What If They Knew?* (4–6). 1981, Dell paper $2.25 (0-440-79515-X). 128pp. Jeremy has epilepsy and must adjust to living with her grandparents.

**7364** Hesse, Karen. *Wish on a Unicorn* (4–6). 1991, Holt $13.95 (0-8050-1572-8). 108pp. In a single-parent family, Maggie finds it's sometimes hard to care for her younger brother and brain-injured sister. (Rev: BL 3/15/91; HB 7–8/91; SLJ 5/91)

**7365** Howard, Ellen. *Edith, Herself* (5–7). 1987, Macmillan $15.00 (0-689-31314-4). 144pp. In the 1890s, young Edith is sent to live with her married sister when their mother dies; there her life is complicated by epileptic seizures. (Rev: BCCB 5/87; BL 4/1/87; SLJ 4/87)

**7366** Janover, Caroline. *The Worst Speller in Jr. High* (4–7). 1994, Free Spirit paper $4.95 (0-915793-76-8). 208pp. Katie finds her new junior high school particularly difficult because of her dyslexia. (Rev: BL 2/1/95; SLJ 2/95)

**7367** Janover, Caroline. *Zipper: The Kid with ADHD* (4–7). Illus. 1997, Woodbine paper $11.95 (0-933149-95-6). 164pp. Zipper Wilson suffers from attention deficit hyperactivity disorder and gradually learns to cope with it. (Rev: BL 2/1/98; SLJ 3/98)

**7368** Kachur, Wanda G. *The Nautilus* (5–7). 1997, Peytral paper $7.95 (0-9644271-5-X). 171pp. A compassionate novel about a girl's rehabilitation after receiving spinal cord injuries in an automobile accident. (Rev: SLJ 9/97)

**7369** Konigsburg, E. L. *[George]* (5–8). Illus. by author. 1985, Dell paper $3.50 (0-440-42847-5). 160pp. George lives inside Ben and in times of mental stress emerges as the dark side of Ben's personality.

**7370** Lasker, Joe. *He's My Brother* (2–4). Illus. by author. 1974, Whitman LB $14.95 (0-8075-3218-5). 40pp. A family's attitudes and their wonderful treatment of their retarded family member, Jamie, are told by his older brother.

**7371** Levine, Edna S. *Lisa and Her Soundless World* (3–5). Illus. by Gloria Kamen. 1984, Human Sciences $18.95 (0-87705-104-6); paper $10.95 (0-89885-204-8). The plight of a deaf girl is explored in this gripping, realistic story of Lisa and her problems.

**7372** Litchfield, Ada B. *A Cane in Her Hand* (2–4). Ed. by Caroline Rubin. Illus. by Eleanor Mill. 1977, Whitman LB $14.95 (0-8075-1056-4). A partially sighted girl must adjust to using a cane.

**7373** Little, Jean. *From Anna* (4–6). Illus. by Joan Sandin. 1972, HarperCollins paper $4.95 (0-06-440044-1). 208pp. Anna's family emigrates to Canada to escape Nazi persecution, and this opens up a new world and a wonderful change for the partially sighted girl.

**7374** Little, Jean. *Mine for Keeps* (4–6). Illus. by Lewis Parker. 1995, Viking $13.99 (0-670-85967-2); Little, Brown paper $4.95 (0-316-52800-5). The exceptionally well-handled story of Sal, a cerebral palsy victim, who must adjust to her family after being in a special school.

**7375** McMahon, Patricia. *Summer Tunes: A Martha's Vineyard Vacation* (3–6). Photos by Peter Simon. 1996, Boyds Mills $16.95 (1-56397-572-6). 47pp. A photoessay about Conor, a 10-year-old physically handicapped boy, and his family, who go to Martha's Vineyard for a vacation. (Rev: SLJ 10/96)

**7376** Marino, Jan. *Eighty-Eight Steps to September* (5–7). 1989, Avon paper $2.95 (0-380-71001-3). 162pp. Amy and Robbie have the usual sibling rivalry, until Robbie develops leukemia. (Rev: BCCB 5/89; BL 8/89)

**7377** Morpurgo, Michael. *The Ghost of Grania O'Malley* (4–6). 1996, Viking paper $14.99 (0-670-86861-2). 144pp. On an island close to Ireland, Jessie, who has cerebral palsy, witnesses 2 factions quarrel over custody of a beautiful hill. (Rev: BL 6/1–15/96; SLJ 7/96)

**7378** Osofsky, Audrey. *My Buddy* (3–6). Illus. by Ted Rand. 1992, Holt $14.95 (0-8050-1747-X). 32pp. A boy with muscular dystrophy talks of his best friend, Buddy, a golden retriever service dog. (Rev: BCCB 10/92; BL 2/1/93)

**7379** Riskind, Mary. *Apple Is My Sign* (5–6). 1995, Houghton paper $5.95 (0-395-65747-4). 160pp. A deaf and mute boy is sent to a special school in the early 1900s.

**7380** Roberts, Willo Davis. *Sugar Isn't Everything* (4–6). 1987, Macmillan $16.00 (0-689-31316-0); paper $4.95 (0-689-71225-1). 192pp. A story that presents the facts of diabetes for young readers. (Rev: BCCB 4/87; BL 3/1/87; SLJ 5/87)

**7381** Shyer, Marlene Fanta. *Welcome Home, Jellybean* (5–7). 1978, Macmillan paper $3.95 (0-689-71213-8). 160pp. Twelve-year-old Neil encounters a near-tragic situation when his older retarded sister comes home to stay.

**7382** Slote, Alfred. *Hang Tough, Paul Mather* (4–7). 1973, HarperCollins paper $4.50 (0-06-440153-7). 160pp. Paul recollects from his hospital bed the details of his struggle with leukemia. Told candidly and without sentimentality.

**7383** Smith, Mark. *Pay Attention, Slosh!* (3–4). Illus. 1997, Albert Whitman LB $11.95 (0-8075-6378-1).

54pp. Using a fictional format, this is the story of a boy who is suffering from attention deficit disorder and how his condition is treated. (Rev: BL 12/1/97; SLJ 10/97)

**7384** Snyder, Zilpha Keatley. *The Witches of Worm* (5–8). Illus. by Alton Raible. 1972, Macmillan $16.00 (0-689-30066-2); Dell paper $4.50 (0-440-49727-2). 192pp. A deeply disturbed girl believes that her selfish and destructive acts are caused by bewitchment.

**7385** Strachan, Ian. *The Flawed Glass* (5–8). 1990, Little, Brown $14.95 (0-316-81813-5). 208pp. Physically disabled Shona makes friends with an American boy on an island off the Scottish coast. (Rev: BCCB 11/90; BL 12/1/90; SLJ 1/91)

**7386** Testa, Maria. *Thumbs Up, Rico!* (3–4). Illus. 1994, Albert Whitman LB $14.95 (0-8075-7906-8). 40pp. Rico, a boy with Down's syndrome, tells about his trials and triumphs in this simple chapter book. (Rev: BL 4/15/94; SLJ 7/94)

**7387** Wanous, Suzanne. *Sara's Secret* (2–4). Illus. by Shelly O. Haas. 1995, Carolrhoda LB $14.95 (0-87614-856-9). 40pp. Sara's secret is that she has a brother who is a victim of cerebral palsy and is mentally retarded. (Rev: BL 7/95; SLJ 8/95)

**7388** Welch, Sheila K. *Don't Call Me Marda* (4–6). Illus. 1991, Our Child Pr. $16.95 (0-9611872-3-9); paper $12.95 (0-9611872-4-7). 138pp. Marsha is disappointed when the girl her parents adopt is mentally handicapped. (Rev: SLJ 3/91)

**7389** Werlin, Nancy. *Are You Alone on Purpose?* (5–8). 1994, Houghton $16.00 (0-395-67350-X). 176pp. When Harry Roth, a rabbi's son, is confined to a wheelchair after an accident, Alison becomes interested in being a friend of this overbearing boy. (Rev: BCCB 12/94; BL 8/94; SLJ 9/94)

**7390** Whelan, Gloria. *Hannah* (3–5). Illus. by Leslie Bowman. 1991, Knopf LB $11.99 (0-679-91397-1). 42pp. In northern Michigan in 1887, 9-year-old Hannah is encouraged by the new teacher to attend school despite her blindness. (Rev: BCCB 6/91; BL 3/1/91; HB 5–6/91; SLJ 6/91)

**7391** Wilson, Nancy H. *Bringing Nettie Back* (5–7). 1992, Macmillan $15.00 (0-02-793075-0). 160pp. The story of a friendship between 2 "opposites" and of Nettie's illness. (Rev: BL 1/1/93; SLJ 10/92)

**7392** Wright, Betty R. *Rosie and the Dance of the Dinosaurs* (4–6). 1989, Holiday $15.95 (0-8234-0782-9). 112pp. Rosie, who has only 9 fingers, is worried about the piano recital in which she must perform. (Rev: BCCB 2/90; BL 11/15/89; HB 3–4/90)

# Historical Fiction and Foreign Lands

## General and Miscellaneous

**7393** Conrad, Pam. *Pedro's Journal: A Voyage with Christopher Columbus* (3–5). Illus. by Peter Koeppen. 1991, Boyds Mills $15.95 (1-878093-17-7). 81pp. The journal of a "ship boy" aboard the Santa Maria, dated August 3, 1492, to February 14, 1493. (Rev: BCCB 2/92; BL 10/15/92; SLJ 2/92)

**7394** Durbin, William. *The Broken Blade* (5–8). 1997, Delacorte $14.95 (0-385-32224-0). 163pp. To help his family, 13-year-old Pierre becomes a *voyageur*, a fur trader in old Quebec. (Rev: BCCB 2/97; BL 3/1/97; SLJ 2/97)

**7395** Hammer, Loretta J., and Gail L. Karwoski. *The Tree That Owns Itself: And Other Adventure Tales from Out of the Past* (3–6). Illus. by James Watling. 1996, Peachtree paper $8.95 (1-56145-120-7). 149pp. In these 12 stories, famous characters associated with the history of Georgia come to life and interact with fictitious young heroes and heroines. (Rev: SLJ 7/96)

**7396** Hill, Anthony. *The Burnt Stick* (4–7). Illus. 1995, Houghton $12.95 (0-395-73974-8). 64pp. The moving story of a boy who, at age 5, is taken from his Aborigine mother in Australia and raised in a white missionary community. (Rev: BCCB 9/95; BL 7/95; HB 11–12/95; SLJ 10/95)

**7397** Holeman, Linda. *Promise Song* (5–8). 1997, Tundra paper $7.95 (0-88776-387-1). 264pp. In 1900, Rosetta, an English orphan who has been sent to Canada, becomes an indentured servant. (Rev: BL 6/1–15/97; SLJ 10/97)

**7398** Lisle, Janet T. *The Great Dimpole Oak* (5–7). Illus. by Stephen Gammell. 1987, Orchard LB $16.99 (0-531-08316-0). 144pp. The majestic oak is the focus of this look at how different people relate to the tree. (Rev: BL 9/15/87; SLJ 12/87)

**7399** Lottridge, Celia B. *Ticket to Canada* (4–6). Illus. 1995, Silver Burdett LB $13.95 (0-382-39145-4). 144pp. In 1915, Sam and his family relocate from Iowa to rural Alberta and must build their own house. (Rev: BL 2/1/96; SLJ 2/96)

**7400** Lottridge, Celia B. *Wings to Fly* (4–7). Illus. 1997, Douglas & McIntyre $15.95 (0-88899-293-9). 176pp. This Canadian novel describes homesteading in Canada as seen through the eyes and experiences of a bright, adventurous 11-year-old girl. A sequel to *Ticket to Canada* (1996). (Rev: BL 11/15/97)

**7401** Merrill, Linda, and Sarah Ridley. *The Princess and the Peacocks: Or, The Story of the Room* (4–6). Illus. by Tennessee Dixon. 1993, Hyperion LB

$15.49 (1-56282-328-0). 32pp. For older readers, this fictionalized account tells how the painter Whistler decorated his famous Peacock Room. (Rev: BL 6/1–15/93; SLJ 8/93)

**7402** Napoli, Donna Jo. *Trouble on the Tracks* (5–7). 1997, Scholastic $14.95 (0-590-13447-7). 190pp. Zach and his younger sister are embroiled in an Australian adventure involving smugglers and survival in a desert. (Rev: BCCB 3/97; BL 2/1/97; SLJ 3/97)

**7403** Nunes, Susan. *To Find the Way* (4–6). Illus. by Cissy Gray. 1992, Univ. of Hawaii Pr. $12.95 (0-8248-1376-6). 48pp. A picture story of the amazing voyage by the ancient Polynesians from Tahiti to Hawaii, seen through a child's eyes. (Rev: BL 1/15/93)

**7404** Schneider, Mical. *Between the Dragon and the Eagle* (5–8). 1997, Carolrhoda LB $21.27 (0-87614-649-3). 151pp. A historical novel that follows a piece of silk from China to Rome. (Rev: BCCB 3/97; BL 2/1/97; SLJ 4/97)

**7405** Speare, Elizabeth G. *The Bronze Bow* (6–8). 1961, Houghton $16.00 (0-395-07113-5); paper $6.95 (0-395-13719-5). 256pp. A Jewish boy seeks revenge against the Romans who killed his parents, but he finally loses his hatred after he hears the messages and teachings of Jesus. Newbery Medal winner, 1962.

**7406** Valgardson, W. D. *Sarah and the People of Sand River* (3–5). Illus. by Ian Wallace. 1996, Douglas & McIntyre $16.95 (0-88899-255-6). 56pp. An Icelandic family, now relocated in Manitoba, Canada, is helped by Cree Indians. (Rev: BCCB 12/96; BL 11/1/96*; SLJ 12/96) [398.2]

**7407** Wheatley, Nadia. *My Place* (3–8). Illus. by Donna Rawlins. 1992, Kane/Miller $14.95 (0-916291-42-1). 24pp. A glimpse of life on an Australian piece of land over a 100-year period. (Rev: BCCB 7–8/90; SLJ 8/90)

## Prehistory

**7408** Caselli, Giovanni. *An Ice Age Hunter* (3–5). 1992, Bedrick LB $12.95 (0-87226-103-4). 30pp. The story of a year in the life of an ice-age family as experienced by a young girl. (Rev: SLJ 7/92)

**7409** Cowley, Marjorie. *Dar and the Spear-Thrower* (5–7). 1994, Clarion $14.00 (0-395-68132-4). 118pp. This is the story of Dar, a boy growing up in the Cro-Magnon period, and the problems he faces when beginning to accept adult responsibilities. (Rev: BL 8/94; SLJ 9/94)

**7410** Craig, Ruth. *Malu's Wolf* (4–6). 1995, Orchard LB $16.99 (0-531-08784-0). 192pp. Set in Stone Age Europe, this novel tells how Malu domesticated a wolf cub named Kono. (Rev: BL 12/15/95; SLJ 10/95)

**7411** Denzel, Justin. *Boy of the Painted Cave* (5–7). 1988, Putnam $14.95 (0-399-21559-X). 160pp. The story of a boy who longs to be a cave artist, set in Cro Magnon times. (Rev: BL 11/1/88; SLJ 11/88)

**7412** Denzel, Justin. *Return to the Painted Cave* (5–8). 1997, Putnam $16.95 (0-399-23117-X). 208pp. In this adventure story set in the Stone Age, Tao, a 14-year-old boy, faces the mad shaman Zugor in a deadly power struggle. (Rev: BL 11/1/97; SLJ 11/97)

**7413** Hughes, Ted. *Tales of the Early World* (5–8). Illus. by Andrew Davidson. 1991, Farrar $15.00 (0-374-37377-9). 128pp. This handsome volume contains 10 creation stories by England's famous poet. (Rev: BL 4/15/91*; SLJ 5/91*)

**7414** Nolan, Dennis. *Wolf Child* (3–5). Illus. 1989, Macmillan paper $16.00 (0-02-768141-6). 40pp. A young boy's affection for an orphaned wolf cub is the focus of this prehistoric tale. (Rev: BL 12/15/89; SLJ 12/89)

**7415** Turnbull, Ann. *Maroo of the Winter Caves* (4–7). 1984, Houghton paper $6.95 (0-395-54795-4). 144pp. A story centered on seminomadic people who lived in southern Europe during the last Ice Age.

## Africa

**7416** Bunting, Eve. *I Am the Mummy Heb-Nefert* (3–6). Illus. by David Christiana. 1997, Harcourt $15.00 (0-15-200479-3). 32pp. A touching picture book in which a female mummy tells of her life as the wife of the pharaoh's brother and of her death and how her body was preserved. (Rev: BCCB 5/97; BL 5/15/97; SLJ 8/97)

**7417** Ellis, Veronica F. *Afro-Bets First Book About Africa* (2–5). Illus. by George Ford. 1990, Just Us LB $13.95 (0-940975-12-2); paper $6.95 (0-940975-03-3). 32pp. A classroom of African Americans learns about the history and culture of Africa. (Rev: BL 3/1/90*; SLJ 5/90)

**7418** Farmer, Nancy. *Do You Know Me?* (4–6). Illus. by Shelley Jackson. 1993, Orchard LB $16.99 (0-531-08624-0). 112pp. There are culture clashes (many amusing) when 9-year-old Tapiwa's uncle comes from rural Mozambique to live with her family in the city. (Rev: BL 4/1/93; SLJ 4/93)

**7419** Fourie, Corlia. *Ganekwane and the Green Dragon: Four Stories from Africa* (3–5). Illus. by Christian Epanya. 1994, Albert Whitman LB $14.95 (0-8075-2744-0). 40pp. Four original folktales that imitate the original African models. (Rev: BL 10/15/94; SLJ 12/94)

**7420** Gordon, Sheila. *The Middle of Somewhere: A Story of South Africa* (4–7). 1990, Watts LB $16.99 (0-531-08508-2). 160pp. The story of a black child whose home is destroyed to make way for land reserved for whites in South Africa. (Rev: BCCB 10/90; BL 10/1/90; HB 11–12/90; SLJ 10/90)

**7421** Havill, Juanita. *Sato and the Elephants* (2–4). Illus. by Jean Tseng and Mou-Sien Tseng. 1993, Lothrop LB $14.93 (0-688-11156-4). 32pp. A young ivory carver realizes that animals must be killed to supply him with material and therefore decides to try working in stone the next time. (Rev: BL 10/15/93; SLJ 4/94)

**7422** Kroll, Virginia. *Masai and I* (2–4). Illus. by Nancy Carpenter. 1992, Macmillan LB $16.00 (0-02-751165-0). A young African American girl contrasts her life with the life of the Masai in Africa. (Rev: SLJ 10/92)

**7423** Lattimore, Deborah N. *The Winged Cat: A Tale of Ancient Egypt* (3–6). Illus. 1992, HarperCollins $15.00 (0-06-023635-3). 32pp. A serving girl witnesses the killing of the sacred cat Bast in this handsomely illustrated tale of ancient Egypt. (Rev: BL 9/1/92; SLJ 4/92)

**7424** Marie, D. *Tears for Ashan* (3–6). Illus. by Norman Childers. 1989, Creative $11.95 (0-9621681-0-6). 32pp. Set in Africa years ago. Kumasi sees his best friend taken captive by slave traders. (Rev: BL 12/1/89)

**7425** Naidoo, Beverley. *No Turning Back* (5–8). 1997, HarperCollins LB $14.89 (0-06-027506-5). 160pp. Jaabu, a homeless African boy, looks for shelter in contemporary Johannesburg. (Rev: BCCB 2/97; BL 12/15/96*; HB 3–4/97; SLJ 2/97)

**7426** Posner, Mitch. *Kai, a Big Decision: Africa, 1440* (4–6). Illus. 1997, Simon & Schuster paper $5.99 (0-689-80990-5). 72pp. Kai must decide if she can face leaving her Nigerian village to become an honored member of a craft guild. (Rev: BL 5/1/97)

**7427** Rubalcaba, Jill. *A Place in the Sun* (3–6). 1997, Clarion $13.95 (0-395-82645-4). 96pp. Set in 13th-century-B.C. Egypt, this fast-moving novel describes the fate of a boy who is exiled to the gold mines of Nubia. (Rev: BL 4/1/97; SLJ 4/97)

**7428** Rupert, Rona. *Straw Sense* (K–3). Illus. by Michael Dooling. 1993, Simon & Schuster paper $14.00 (0-671-77047-0). 32pp. In this story set in South Africa, young Goolam-Habib finds the courage to speak through the friendship he develops with an old man. (Rev: BCCB 1/94; BL 11/15/93; SLJ 2/94)

**7429** Schur, Maxine R. *When I Left My Village* (2–4). Illus. by Brian Pinkney. 1996, Dial paper $14.89 (0-8037-1562-5). 64pp. A fictionalized account

of the hardships of a Jewish African family in their flight from Ethiopia through Sudan to Israel. (Rev: BCCB 2/96; BL 2/15/96; HB 5–6/96; SLJ 3/96)

**7430** Stolz, Mary. *Zekmet, the Stone Carver: A Tale of Ancient Egypt* (1–4). Illus. by Deborah Nourse. 1988, Harcourt $14.95 (0-15-299961-2). 32pp. The story of how the Sphinx may have come to be, with illustrations that tell the story in hieroglyphics. (Rev: BCCB 5/88; BL 5/15/88; SLJ 5/88)

**7431** Thomas, Dawn C. *Kai: A Mission for Her Village* (3–6). Illus. by Vanessa Holley. Series: Girlhood Journeys. 1996, Simon & Schuster $13.00 (0-689-81140-3). 71pp. This novel, set in 15th-century Africa, features a young girl who longs to become an artisan, even though women were banned from this work. (Rev: SLJ 3/97)

## Asia

**7432** Atkins, Jeannine. *Aani and the Tree Huggers* (2–5). Illus. by Venantius J. Pinto. 1995, Lee & Low $14.95 (1-880000-24-5). In this tale set in India, a village woman tries to save a tree from big-city developers by throwing her arms around it. (Rev: SLJ 12/95)

**7433** Axworthy, Anni. *Anni's India Diary* (3–5). Illus. 1992, Whispering Coyote $14.95 (1-879085-59-3). 32pp. In diary form, an account of a girl's 3-month trip through India. (Rev: BL 11/1/92; SLJ 12/92)

**7434** Balgassi, Haemi. *Peacebound Trains* (3–5). Illus. by Chris K. Soentpiet. 1996, Clarion $14.95 (0-395-72093-1). 47pp. Sumi's grandmother tells about the perilous journey she took to escape the Communists during the Korean War. (Rev: BCCB 10/96; BL 9/15/96; SLJ 1/97)

**7435** Bond, Ruskin. *Binya's Blue Umbrella* (2–5). Illus. by Vera Rosenberry. 1995, Boyds Mills $12.95 (1-56397-135-6). 68pp. In this novel set in India, Binya acquires a wonderful umbrella that everyone envies. (Rev: BL 3/15/95; SLJ 3/95)

**7436** Breckler, Rosemary K. *Sweet Dried Apples: A Vietnamese Wartime Childhood* (3–5). Illus. by Deborah Kogan Ray. 1996, Houghton $15.95 (0-395-73570-X). 32pp. Using a picture book format, a childhood in war-torn Vietnam is examined. (Rev: BL 9/1/96; SLJ 3/97)

**7437** Choi, Sook N. *Echoes of the White Giraffe* (5–8). 1993, Houghton $14.95 (0-395-64721-5). 144pp. In this sequel to *Year of Impossible Goodbyes* (1991), Sookan and her family once again are separated, this time by the Korean War. (Rev: SLJ 5/93)

**7438** Chrisman, Arthur B. *Shen of the Sea* (4–6). Illus. by Else Hasselriis. 1968, Dutton paper $16.99 (0-525-39244-0). 224pp. These engaging short stories of Chinese life received the Newbery Award, 1926.

**7439** Coerr, Eleanor. *Mieko and the Fifth Treasure* (4–7). 1993, Putnam $14.95 (0-399-22434-3). 78pp. A Japanese girl believes that she will never draw again after she is injured during the atomic bomb attack on Nagasaki. (Rev: BCCB 4/93; BL 4/1/93*; SLJ 7/93)

**7440** Crofford, Emily. *Born in the Year of Courage* (5–8). 1992, Carolrhoda LB $21.27 (0-87614-679-5). 160pp. Based on fact, this story tells of a Japanese fisherman, educated in America, who participated in the California Gold Rush. (Rev: SLJ 12/92)

**7441** Curtis, Chara M. *No One Walks on My Father's Moon* (4–8). Illus. by Rebecca Hyland. 1996, Voyage LB $16.95 (0-9649454-1-X). 26pp. A Turkish boy is accused of blasphemy when he states that a man has walked on the moon. (Rev: BL 11/15/96)

**7442** Disher, Garry. *The Bamboo Flute* (3–6). 1993, Ticknor $12.00 (0-395-66595-7). 96pp. Growing up in terrible poverty in rural Australia during 1932, young Paul forms a friendship with a drifter named Eric the Red. (Rev: BL 9/1/93; SLJ 9/93*)

**7443** Giles, Gail. *Breath of the Dragon* (4–7). Illus. 1997, Clarion $14.95 (0-395-76476-9). 112pp. In this story set in Thailand, Malila faces rejection and loneliness because her father was a thief. (Rev: BCCB 4/97; BL 4/1/97; SLJ 6/97)

**7444** Glass, Tom. *Even a Little Is Something: Stories of Nong* (4–6). Illus. by Elena Gerard. 1997, Linnet LB $16.95 (0-208-02457-3). 119pp. Accurately depicts the daily struggle of peasants living hand-to-mouth in northeastern Thailand. (Rev: SLJ 2/98)

**7445** Godden, Rumer. *Premlata and the Festival of Lights* (4–6). Illus. by Ian Andrew. 1997, Greenwillow $15.00 (0-688-15136-1). 58pp. The story of a poor family in the Bengal region of India and how they plan to celebrate the festival of light, Diwali, to honor the goddess Kali. (Rev: HB 5–6/97; SLJ 5/97)

**7446** Huynh, Quang Nhuong. *The Land I Lost: Adventures of a Boy in Vietnam* (5–8). Illus. by Mai Vo-Dinh. 1990, HarperCollins LB $14.89 (0-397-32448-0); paper $4.95 (0-06-440183-9). 128pp. The story of a boy's growing up in rural Vietnam before the war.

**7447** Kamal, Aleph. *The Bird Who Was an Elephant* (3–5). Illus. by Frane Lessac. 1990, HarperCollins LB $14.89 (0-397-32446-4). 32pp. The story of what a bird sees as it flies over an Indian village. (Rev: BCCB 7–8/90; BL 4/15/90; SLJ 8/90)

**7448** Lattimore, Deborah N. *Fool and the Phoenix: A Tale of Ancient Japan* (3–6). Illus. 1997, HarperCollins LB $14.89 (0-06-026211-7). 40pp. Hideo, a mute, falls in love with the phoenix bird of Japan and catches her in a net. (Rev: BL 8/97; SLJ 9/97)

**7449** Lewis, Elizabeth Foreman. *Young Fu of the Upper Yangtze* (5–8). Illus. by Ed Young. 1973, Dell paper $4.50 (0-440-49043-X). 268pp. Young Fu must pay back a debt of $5 or face public shame. Newbery Medal winner, 1933.

**7450** McKibbon, Hugh William. *The Token Gift* (3–5). Illus. by Scott Cameron. 1996, Annick $16.95 (1-55037-499-0); paper $6.95 (1-55037-498-2). 32pp. Set in ancient India, this is the story of Mohan, the boy who invented chess. (Rev: BL 2/1/97; SLJ 1/97)

**7451** Neuberger, Anne E. *The Girl-Son* (3–6). Illus. 1994, Carolrhoda LB $21.27 (0-87614-846-1). 132pp. Based on fact, this is the story of a Korean girl born in 1896 and her fight for women's rights. (Rev: BCCB 2/95; BL 1/1/95; SLJ 2/95)

**7452** Paterson, Katherine. *The Master Puppeteer* (4–7). Illus. by Haru Wells. 1989, HarperCollins paper $4.95 (0-06-440281-9). 192pp. Feudal Japan is the setting for this story about a young apprentice puppeteer and his search for a mysterious bandit.

**7453** Paterson, Katherine. *Of Nightingales That Weep* (4–7). Illus. by Haru Wells. 1974, HarperCollins $14.00 (0-690-00485-0); paper $4.50 (0-06-440282-7). 192pp. A story set in feudal Japan tells of Takiko, a samurai's daughter, who is sent to the royal court when her mother remarries.

**7454** Paterson, Katherine. *The Sign of the Chrysanthemum* (5–7). Illus. by Peter Landa. 1973, HarperCollins LB $14.89 (0-690-04913-7); paper $4.95 (0-06-440232-0). 128pp. At the death of his mother, a young boy sets out to find his samurai father in 12th-century Japan.

**7455** Pevsner, Stella, and Fay Tang. *Sing for Your Father, Su Phan* (4–6). 1997, Clarion $14.00 (0-395-82267-X). 112pp. A fictional memoir of a North Vietnamese girl's experience and hardships during the Vietnam War. (Rev: BL 1/1–15/98; SLJ 12/97)

**7456** Russell, Ching Yeung. *First Apple* (3–5). Illus. 1994, Boyds Mills $13.95 (1-56397-206-9). 127pp. In this tale set in China, Ying is determined to buy her grandmother a birthday gift that she has never had before, an apple. (Rev: BCCB 1/95; BL 11/1/94; SLJ 9/94)

**7457** Russell, Ching Yeung. *Lichee Tree* (4–7). 1997, Boyds Mills $14.95 (1-56397-629-3). 182pp. Growing up in China during the 1940s, Ying dreams of selling lichee nuts and visiting Canton. (Rev: BCCB 4/97; BL 3/15/97; SLJ 6/97)

**7458** Russell, Ching Yeung. *Water Ghost* (3–5). Illus. 1995, Boyds Mills $14.95 (1-56397-413-4). 192pp. Ying, age 10 and growing up in China, faces the scorn of her family when she helps an aged grandmother. (Rev: BL 10/15/95; SLJ 12/95)

**7459** Spivak, Dawnine. *Grass Sandals: The Travels of Basho* (3–5). Illus. by Demi. 1997, Simon &

Schuster $16.00 (0-689-80776-7). 40pp. An outstanding picture book about the 17th-century poet and his travels around Japan. (Rev: BCCB 7–8/97; BL 5/1/97*; SLJ 4/97) [895.6]

**7460** Sreenivasan, Jyotsna. *Aruna's Journeys* (4–7). Illus. 1997, Smooth Stone paper $6.95 (0-9619401-7-4). 136pp. Aruna denies her Indian heritage until she spends a summer in Bangalore, India. (Rev: BL 7/97)

**7461** Tan, Amy. *The Moon Lady* (4–6). Illus. by Gretchen Schields. 1992, Macmillan LB $16.95 (0-02-788830-4). 32pp. A grandmother in the United States remembers her childhood in China in this story adapted from the adult best-seller The Joy Luck Club. (Rev: BCCB 11/92; BL 9/1/92; SLJ 9/92)

**7462** Wartski, Maureen C. *A Boat to Nowhere* (4–5). 1981, NAL paper $4.99 (0-451-16285-4). 160pp. An adventure story about the Vietnamese "boat people."

**7463** Whelan, Gloria. *Goodbye, Vietnam* (5–7). 1992, Knopf LB $13.99 (0-679-92263-6). 136pp. The wrenching story of Mai and her family and their escape from Vietnam to Hong Kong and a new life. (Rev: BCCB 10/92*; BL 1/1/93; HB 1–2/93; SLJ 9/92)

**7464** Wu, Priscilla. *The Abacus Contest: Stories from Taiwan and China* (5–8). Illus. 1996, Fulcrum $15.95 (1-55591-243-5). 55pp. Six simple short stories explore life in a city on Taiwan. (Rev: BL 7/96; SLJ 6/96)

**7465** Yumoto, Kazumi. *The Friends* (5–7). Trans. by Cathy Hirano. 1996, Farrar $15.00 (0-374-32460-3). 176pp. Three young friends witness the gradual death of their dear friend, an old man, in this novel set in Japan. (Rev: BCCB 2/97; BL 10/15/96; HB 11–12/96; SLJ 12/96)

## Europe

**7466** Alcock, Vivien. *Singer to the Sea God* (5–8). 1995, Dell paper $3.99 (0-440-41003-7). 208pp. This historical tale, which is set in Greece during mythological times, tells of the adventurous escape from King Polydectes' court. (Rev: BCCB 2/93; HB 7–8/93; SLJ 3/93)

**7467** Anderson, Margaret J. *Children of Summer: Henri Fabre's Insects* (4–7). Illus. 1997, Farrar $14.00 (0-374-31243-5). 112pp. A fictionalized biography of the French naturalist Jean Henri Fabre and his work with insects. (Rev: BCCB 6/97; BL 3/1/97; HB 7–8/97; SLJ 9/97)

**7468** DeJong, Meindert. *Wheel on the School* (4–7). Illus. by Maurice Sendak. 1954, HarperCollins LB $14.89 (0-06-021586-0); paper $4.95 (0-06-440021-2). 256pp. The storks are brought back to their island

by the schoolchildren in a Dutch village. Newbery Medal winner, 1955.

**7469** de Trevino, Elizabeth. *I, Juan de Pareja* (5–8). 1965, Farrar $16.00 (0-374-33531-1); paper $3.95 (0-374-43525-1). 192pp. Through the eyes of his devoted black slave, Juan de Pareja, the character of the artist Velasquez is revealed. Newbery Medal winner, 1966.

**7470** Deverell, Catherine. *Stradivari's Singing Violin* (3–5). Illus. by Andrea Shine. 1992, Carolrhoda LB $13.95 (0-87614-732-5). 48pp. A fictional account of the historical figure behind what is perhaps the world's best-known musical instrument. (Rev: BL 2/15/93)

**7471** Dexter, Catherine. *Safe Return* (5–7). 1996, Candlewick $15.99 (0-7636-0005-9). 96pp. On her island home in the Baltic Sea in 1824, an orphan anxiously awaits the return of her aunt, who has sailed to Stockholm, Sweden. (Rev: BCCB 11/96; BL 10/15/96; HB 11–12/96; SLJ 12/96)

**7472** Elmer, Robert. *Chasing the Wind* (4–7). Series: Young Underground. 1996, Bethany paper $5.99 (1-55661-658-9). 187pp. Three Danish children discover that after the Germans surrender some Nazis are still in their town diving for sunken treasure. (Rev: BL 5/1/96)

**7473** Gray, Elizabeth Janet. *Adam of the Road* (5–8). Illus. by Robert Lawson. 1942, Puffin paper $4.99 (0-14-032464-X). 320pp. Adventures of a 13th-century minstrel boy. Newbery Medal winner, 1943.

**7474** Greene, Jacqueline D. *One Foot Ashore* (4–6). 1994, Walker $16.95 (0-8027-8281-7). 208pp. To escape servitude in Brazil, Maria stows away on a boat bound for Amsterdam, where she finds work in the home of Rembrandt. (Rev: BCCB 6/94; BL 4/1/94; HB 7–8/94; SLJ 6/94)

**7475** Harrison, Michael. *Don Quixote* (4–6). Illus. by Victor G. Ambrus. 1995, Oxford LB $22.95 (0-19-274165-9). 95pp. Important episodes from the Cervantes work are abridged to a readable form for youngsters. (Rev: BL 2/1/96; SLJ 2/96)

**7476** Hest, Amy. *When Jessie Came Across the Sea* (2–4). Illus. by P. J. Lynch. 1997, Candlewick $16.99 (0-7636-0094-6). 40pp. A Jewish girl living in an Eastern European shtetl gets an opportunity to come to the United States, but she will have to leave her wonderful grandmother behind. (Rev: BL 2/1/98; SLJ 11/97)

**7477** Hodges, Margaret, ed. *Don Quixote and Sancho Panza* (4–6). Illus. by Stephen Marchesi. 1992, Macmillan $16.95 (0-684-19235-7). 80pp. Abridged episodes from the Cervantes novel suitable for young readers. (Rev: BCCB 2/93; BL 12/1/92; HB 3–4/93; SLJ 11/92)

**7478** Hunt, Jonathan. *Leif's Saga: A Viking Tale* (3–5). Illus. by author. 1996, Simon & Schuster paper $16.00 (0-689-80492-X). In this novel set in Viking times, Sigrid hears her father tell of Leif Eriksson's famed Voyage to North America. (Rev: BCCB 3/96; SLJ 5/96)

**7479** Jackson, Dave, and Neta Jackson. *The Betrayer's Fortune* (3–6). Illus. 1994, Bethany paper $5.99 (1-55661-467-5). 144pp. During the persecution of the Anabaptists in the 16th century, a young boy discovers he possesses great reserves of courage. (Rev: BL 4/1/95)

**7480** Juster, Norton. *Alberic the Wise* (4–8). Illus. by Leonard Baskin. 1992, Picture Book $16.95 (0-88708-243-2). 32pp. In this picture book set in the Renaissance, Alberic becomes an apprentice to a stained-glass maker. (Rev: BCCB 2/93; BL 1/15/93; SLJ 3/93)

**7481** Kelly, Eric P. *The Trumpeter of Krakow* (5–8). Illus. by Janina Domanska. 1966, Macmillan LB $17.00 (0-02-750140-X); paper $4.50 (0-689-71571-4). 224pp. Mystery surrounds a precious jewel and the youthful patriot who stands watch over it in a church tower in this novel of 15th-century Poland. Newbery Medal winner, 1929.

**7482** Kimmel, Eric A. *Count Silvernose: A Story from Italy* (3–6). Illus. by Omar Rayyan. 1996, Holiday LB $15.95 (0-8234-1216-4). 30pp. Set in the late Renaissance, this adventure story tells how Assunta sets out to find her sisters, who have been abducted by Count Silvernose. (Rev: BCCB 7–8/96; BL 3/15/96*; HB 7–8/96; SLJ 3/96)

**7483** Kramer, Stephen. *Theodoric's Rainbow* (4–6). Illus. by Daniel Duffy. 1995, Scientific American $14.40 (0-7167-6603-5). 32pp. A picture book for middle-graders that tells the story of Theodoric, a 13th-century monk who experiments with the wonders of rainbows. (Rev: BCCB 2/96; BL 1/1–15/96)

**7484** Krasnopolsky, Fara Lynn. *I Remember* (4–6). Illus. 1995, Clarion $15.95 (0-395-67401-8). 124pp. The story of a poor Jewish girl growing up in Czarist Russia at the turn of the century. (Rev: BL 6/1–15/95; SLJ 7/95)

**7485** Lasky, Kathryn. *The Night Journey* (4–7). Illus. by Trina S. Hyman. 1986, Puffin paper $4.99 (0-14-032048-2). 152pp. Nana tells her great-granddaughter about her escape from Czarist Russia.

**7486** Liorente, Pilar M. *The Apprentice* (5–7). Trans. by Robin Longshaw. Illus. by Juan R. Alonso. 1993, Farrar $13.00 (0-374-30389-4). 99pp. In Renaissance Florence, Arduino finds that being an apprentice to a famous painter is not as wonderful as expected. (Rev: BL 8/93)

**7487** Littlesugar, Amy. *Marie in Fourth Position: The Story of Degas' "The Little Dancer"* (1–3). Illus.

by Ian Schoenherr. 1996, Philomel $15.99 (0-399-22794-6). The story of a young ballet student who modeled for Degas to get money for her poor parents. (Rev: SLJ 10/96*)

**7488** Lorbiecki, Marybeth. *My Palace of Leaves in Sarajevo* (3–7). Illus. by Herbert Tauss. 1997, Dial paper $14.89 (0-8037-2034-3). 53pp. Through fictitious letters to her friend in Minnesota, Nadja describes the terrible effect of the war in Bosnia on herself and her Serbian/Muslim family during the early 1990s. (Rev: BCCB 3/97; SLJ 6/97)

**7489** Macaulay, David. *Rome Antics* (4–8). Illus. 1997, Houghton $17.00 (0-395-82289-3). 80pp. The reader gets a pigeon-eye view of vistas and building as the bird flies over Rome. (Rev: BL 9/15/97; SLJ 11/97*)

**7490** Morrison, Taylor. *The Neptune Fountain: The Apprenticeship of a Renaissance Sculptor* (3–6). Illus. 1997, Holiday LB $15.95 (0-8234-1293-8). 32pp. The creation of a marble sculpture is described in this novel about an apprentice to a famous sculptor in 17th-century Rome. (Rev: BL 6/1–15/97; SLJ 6/97)

**7491** Nichol, Barbara. *Beethoven Lives Upstairs* (3–6). Illus. by Scott Cameron. 1994, Orchard $15.95 (0-531-06828-5). 48pp. When Beethoven moves into his house, young Christoph gradually learns to sympathize with the agonies suffered by Beethoven because of his deafness. (Rev: BCCB 2/94; BL 1/1/94*; HB 7–8/94; SLJ 4/94)

**7492** Pernoud, Regine. *A Day with a Miller* (4–7). Trans. by Dominique Clift. Illus. by Giorgio Bacchin. 1997, Runestone LB $22.60 (0-8225-1914-3). 48pp. A description of the life of a miller and his family in the 12th century and how hydraulic energy was being introduced at that time. (Rev: SLJ 3/98)

**7493** Pyle, Howard. *Otto of the Silver Hand* (6–8). Illus. by author. 1967, Dover paper $7.95 (0-486-21784-1). 173pp. Life in feudal Germany, the turbulence and cruelty of robber barons, and the peaceful, scholarly pursuits of the monks are presented in the story of the kidnapped son of a robber baron.

**7494** Schur, Maxine R. *The Circlemaker* (5–7). 1994, Dial paper $14.99 (0-8037-1354-1). 192pp. In 1852, a young Jewish boy and the town bully flee from their small Ukrainian town to find safety in the New World. (Rev: BCCB 2/94; SLJ 2/94)

**7495** Seredy, Kate. *The Good Master* (4–6). Illus. by author. 1986, Puffin paper $4.99 (0-14-030133-X). 196pp. Warm and humorous story of a city girl on her uncle's farm in prewar Hungary.

**7496** Skurzynski, Gloria. *The Minstrel in the Tower* (3–4). Illus. by Julek Heller. 1988, Random paper $3.99 (0-394-89598-3). 64pp. Alice and Roger search for their uncle after their father has been killed in the Crusades, in this story of life in the Middle Ages. (Rev: BCCB 7–8/88; BL 7/88)

**7497** Vos, Ida. *Dancing on the Bridge at Avignon* (5–8). Trans. by Terese Edlstein and Inez Smidt. 1995, Houghton $14.95 (0-395-72039-7). 144pp. Rosa, a Jewish girl in the Netherlands during World War II, lives in constant fear that the Nazis will deport her and her family. (Rev: BCCB 2/96; BL 10/15/95; SLJ 10/95)

**7498** Wild, Margaret. *Let the Celebrations Begin!* (3–6). Illus. by Julie Vivas. 1991, Watts LB $16.99 (0-531-08537-6). 32pp. A picture book for older children about a group of Polish women in the Belsen death camp who organized a party for the surviving children after liberation. (Rev: BCCB 9/91; BL 8/91; SLJ 7/91)

**7499** Williams, Laura E. *Behind the Bedroom Wall* (5–8). Illus. 1996, Milkweed $15.95 (1-57131-607-8); paper $6.95 (1-57131-606-X). 176pp. Korinna, a young Nazi, discovers that her parents are hiding a Jewish couple. (Rev: BL 8/96; SLJ 9/96)

## Great Britain and Ireland

**7500** Borden, Louise. *The Little Ships: The Heroic Rescue at Dunkirk in World War II* (3–5). Illus. by Michael Foreman. 1997, Simon & Schuster $15.00 (0-689-80827-5). 32pp. A young English girl and her father help during the evacuation of Dunkirk (Dunkerque), France during World War II. (Rev: BCCB 4/97; BL 3/1/97; HB 5–6/97; SLJ 4/97*)

**7501** Branford, Henrietta. *Fire, Bed, and Bone* (5–8). 1998, Candlewick $15.99 (0-7636-0338-4). 128pp. This unusual novel, narrated from a dog's point of view, tells about the oppression of the peasants in late 14th-century England and of the revolt led by Wat Tyler and the preacher John Ball. (Rev: BL 3/15/98)

**7502** Bulla, Clyde Robert. *The Sword in the Tree* (2–5). Illus. by Paul Galdone. 1962, HarperCollins LB $14.89 (0-690-79909-8). 128pp. A simply written account of knighthood at the time of King Arthur.

**7503** Chaucer, Geoffrey. *Canterbury Tales* (4–8). Adapted by Barbara Cohen. Illus. by Trina S. Hyman. 1988, Lothrop $20.00 (0-688-06201-6). 96pp. Beautiful edition of selected stories including: The Pardoner's Tale and The Wife of Bath's Tale. (Rev: BL 9/1/88; SLJ 8/88)

**7504** Cole, Sheila. *The Dragon in the Cliff: A Novel Based on the Life of Mary Anning* (5–8). Illus. by T. C. Farrow. 1991, Lothrop $13.95 (0-688-10196-8). 176pp. A story based on the life of the spunky English girl who discovered the first complete dinosaur fossil ever found. (Rev: BCCB 5/91; BL 3/1/91; SLJ 9/91)

**7505** Conlon-McKenna, Marita. *Fields of Home* (5–7). Illus. by Donald Teskey. 1997, Holiday paper $15.95 (0-8234-1295-4). 189pp. The story of the effects of the 19th-century potato famine in Ireland and the grinding poverty it produced on the young daughter of one of the survivers. (Rev: BCCB 7–8/97; SLJ 6/97)

**7506** Conlon-McKenna, Marita. *Under the Hawthorn Tree* (4–6). 1990, Holiday $13.95 (0-8234-0838-8). 153pp. This story is set during the Great Famine in Ireland in the late 1840s. A sequel is: *Wildflower Girl* (1992). (Rev: BCCB 12/90; BL 11/15/90; SLJ 12/90)

**7507** De Angeli, Marguerite. *The Door in the Wall* (5–7). Illus. by author. 1990, Dell paper $4.50 (0-440-40283-2). Crippled Robin proves his courage in plague-ridden 19th-century London. Newbery Medal winner, 1950.

**7508** Dickens, Charles. *Oliver Twist* (5–7). Illus. by Christian Birmingham. 1996, Dial paper $19.99 (0-8037-1995-7). 144pp. A concise retelling of Dickens's work that retains the major story elements and characters. (Rev: BL 9/1/96; SLJ 5/97)

**7509** Doherty, Berlie. *Street Child* (5–7). 1994, Orchard LB $16.99 (0-531-08714-X). 160pp. The story of a street urchin in Victorian London who is forced to work on a river barge until he escapes. (Rev: BCCB 11/94; BL 9/1/94; SLJ 10/94)

**7510** Goodman, Joan E. *The Winter Hare* (4–8). Illus. 1996, Houghton $15.95 (0-395-78569-3). 240pp. In 12th-century England, Will becomes a page to the wicked Earl Aubrey. (Rev: BCCB 2/97; BL 11/15/96; SLJ 11/96)

**7511** Graham, Harriet. *A Boy and His Bear* (4–6). 1996, Simon & Schuster $16.00 (0-689-80943-3). 196pp. In Elizabethan England, Dickon is determined to save his pet bear from being killed in a bear-baiting competition. (Rev: BCCB 2/97; BL 10/15/96; SLJ 11/96*)

**7512** Graves, Robert. *An Ancient Castle* (4–6). Illus. by Elizabeth Graves. 1991, Michael Kesend paper $8.95 (0-935576-33-9). 72pp. A novel of heroes, villains, and buried treasures set in pre-World War I Britain.

**7513** Haugaard, Erik C. *A Boy's Will* (4–6). Illus. by Troy Howell. 1983, Houghton paper $5.95 (0-395-54962-0). A novel set on a coastal Irish island during the American Revolution.

**7514** Howe, John, reteller. *The Knight with the Lion: The Story of Yvain* (3–6). Illus. by John Howe. 1996, Little, Brown $15.95 (0-316-37583-7). A beautifully illustrated medieval romance about the exploits of Yvain, one of King Arthur's knights. (Rev: BCCB 2/97; SLJ 9/96)

**7515** Kirwan, Anna. *Juliet: A Dream Takes Flight* (3–6). Illus. by Lynne Marshall. Series: Girlhood Journeys. 1996, Simon & Schuster $13.00 (0-689-81137-3); paper $5.99 (0-689-80983-2). 71pp. Set in England in 1339, this story tells of the place of women and their difficulties as seen through the experiences of young Juliet. (Rev: BCCB 11/96; SLJ 9/96)

**7516** McCully, Emily Arnold. *Little Kit; or, the Industrious Flea Circus Girl* (5–8). Illus. 1995, Dial paper $14.89 (0-8037-1674-5). 32pp. In Victorian London, young Kit disguises herself as a boy and joins a flea circus. (Rev: BCCB 2/95; BL 1/1/95*; SLJ 10/95)

**7517** MacDonald, George. *Sir Gibbie* (4–6). 1987, Sunrise $27.50 (0-940652-55-2). The story of a Scottish waif and the triumph of love over hardship.

**7518** Morpurgo, Michael. *The Wreck of the Zanzibar* (4–6). Illus. 1995, Viking paper $14.99 (0-670-86360-2). 80pp. A man reads the diary that his great-aunt kept of an eventful year of life at home on Scilly Islands, off the coast of southwest England. (Rev: BCCB 12/95; BL 11/15/95; SLJ 11/95)

**7519** Pyle, Howard. *Men of Iron* (5–8). Adapted by Earle Hitchner. Illus. 1930, Troll paper $3.95 (0-8167-1872-5). 48pp. Brave deeds and knightly adventure in England — an old favorite.

**7520** Rosen, Sidney, and Dorothy S. Rosen. *The Magician's Apprentice* (5–8). 1994, Carolrhoda LB $19.95 (0-87614-809-7). 155pp. An orphaned 15-year-old boy is sent by the Inquisition to spy on the English scientist Roger Bacon to see if he is performing black magic. (Rev: BL 5/1/94; SLJ 6/94)

**7521** Wallace, Barbara Brooks. *Sparrows in the Scullery* (5–7). 1997, Simon & Schuster $15.00 (0-689-81585-9). 160pp. Without explanation, Colley finds himself in an orphan home in this novel set in the London of Dickens. (Rev: BL 9/15/97; SLJ 11/97)

## Latin America

**7522** Baden, Robert. *And Sunday Makes Seven* (2–5). Illus. by Michelle Edwards. 1990, Whitman $14.95 (0-8075-0356-8). Poor Carlos and Ana live across the street from rich Ricardo in this funny tale from Costa Rica that also teaches the days of the week in Spanish. (Rev: BCCB 6/90; BL 4/15/90; SLJ 6/90) [398.2]

**7523** Belpré, Pura. *Firefly Summer* (5–7). 1996, Piñata $14.95 (1-55885-174-7); paper $7.95 (1-55885-180-1). 205pp. In this novel set in turn-of-the-century Puerto Rico, 2 girls uncover the identity of an orphaned boy who has grown up on their finca (estate). (Rev: SLJ 2/97)

**7524** Clark, Ann Nolan. *Secret of the Andes* (4–8). Illus. by Jean Charlot. 1976, Puffin paper $4.99 (0-14-030926-8). 136pp. Cusi, a young Inca boy, tends a precious llama herd high in the Peruvian mountains and ponders his future. Newbery Medal winner, 1953.

**7525** de Trevino, Elizabeth. *El Guero: A True Adventure Story* (4–6). Illus. by Leslie Bowman. 1989, Farrar $14.00 (0-374-31995-2). 99pp. A century ago a boy and his family embarked on a dangerous journey from Mexico City to the Baja peninsula. (Rev: BL 9/1/89; HB 9–10/89; SLJ 9/89)

**7526** Gantos, Jack. *Jack's New Power: Stories from a Caribbean Year* (5–8). 1995, Farrar $16.00 (0-374-33657-1); paper $4.95 (0-374-43715-7). 214pp. Eight stories about the interesting people Jack meets when his family moves to the Caribbean. A sequel to *Heads or Tails* (1994). (Rev: BCCB 12/95; BL 12/1/95; SLJ 11/95*)

**7527** Head, Judith. *Culebra Cut* (4–6). 1995, Carolrhoda LB $21.27 (0-87614-878-X). 153pp. William witnesses the building of the Panama Canal when his doctor father is transferred to the area in 1911. (Rev: BCCB 12/95; BL 11/1/95; SLJ 1/96)

**7528** Lattimore, Deborah N. *The Flame of Peace: A Tale of the Aztecs* (4–6). Illus. 1987, HarperCollins paper $5.95 (0-06-443272-6). 48pp. Details about Aztec life are compiled in this folklorelike story. (Rev: BL 11/15/87; SLJ 11/87)

**7529** McColley, Kevin. *The Walls of Pedro Garcia* (4–7). 1993, Delacorte $15.00 (0-385-30806-X). 112pp. Pedro, a poor Mexican boy, learns about life and its struggles working in the fields on an estate. (Rev: SLJ 2/93)

**7530** O'Dell, Scott. *My Name Is Not Angelica* (5–7). 1989, Houghton $18.00 (0-395-51061-9). 144pp. A fictionalized account of the slave revolt that occurred in the Virgin Islands in 1733-34. (Rev: BL 11/15/89*)

**7531** Pico, Fernando. *The Red Comb* (2–4). Trans. from Spanish by Argentina Palacios. Illus. by Maria Antonia Ordonez. 1994, BridgeWater paper $14.95 (0-8167-3539-5). In this story set in Puerto Rico in the 1850s, Rosa and her friend Vitita try to hide an escaped slave. (Rev: BCCB 11/94; SLJ 11/94)

**7532** Robinet, Harriette G. *If You Please, President Lincoln* (4–6). 1995, Simon & Schuster $15.00 (0-689-31969-X). 147pp. In 1863, Moses, an escaped slave, is shanghaied to Haiti by a madman who plans to form his own colony there. (Rev: BCCB 9/95; BL 8/95; SLJ 6/95)

**7533** Rohmer, Harriet. *Uncle Nacho's Hat* (3–6). Illus. by Mira Reisberg. 1993, Children's Book Pr. $14.95 (0-89239-043-3); paper $6.95 (0-89239-112-X). 32pp. This bilingual book tells a Nicaraguan tale about how hard it is to break habits. A reissue.

**7534** Stanley, Diane. *Elena* (3–5). Illus. 1996, Hyperion LB $14.49 (0-7868-2211-2). 56pp. A daughter recalls the life of her Mexican mother, who defied authority and took her family on a dangerous journey to the United States. (Rev: BCCB 3/96; BL 4/1/96; SLJ 6/96)

**7535** Yolen, Jane. *Encounter* (2–5). Illus. by David Shannon. 1992, Harcourt $16.00 (0-15-225962-7). 32pp. From the viewpoint of a Taino Indian boy, this picture book tells of the first meeting between Native Americans and Columbus. (Rev: BCCB 5/92; BL 3/1/92; SLJ 5/92)

# United States

### INDIANS OF NORTH AMERICA

**7536** Armstrong, Nancy M. *Navajo Long Walk* (4–7). Illus. 1994, Roberts Rinehart paper $8.95 (1-879373-56-4). 120pp. The story of the Long Walk of the Navajo in 1864 and their confinement in an internment camp are vividly told. (Rev: BL 10/1/94; SLJ 1/95)

**7537** Bird, E. J. *The Rainmakers* (4–6). Illus. 1993, Carolrhoda LB $15.95 (0-87614-748-1). 120pp. This novel about a young Indian boy and his pet bear is centered around the life of the Anasazi Indians, who disappeared from the Southwest around A.D. 1300. (Rev: BL 6/1–15/93)

**7538** Bruchac, Joseph. *A Boy Called Slow: The True Story of Sitting Bull* (5–8). Illus. by Rocco Baviera. 1995, Putnam $15.95 (0-399-22692-3). 32pp. The story of the boyhood of Sitting Bull, who, because of his sluggishness, had been called Slow. (Rev: BCCB 4/95; BL 3/15/95; HB 9–10/95; SLJ 10/95)

**7539** Bruchac, Joseph. *Eagle Song* (2–4). Illus. 1997, Dial paper $14.89 (0-8037-1919-1). 80pp. The story of an Iroquois boy and the adjustments he makes to life with his family in Brooklyn. (Rev: BCCB 3/97; BL 2/1/97; SLJ 3/97)

**7540** Bunting, Eve. *Cheyenne Again* (3–5). Illus. by Irving Toddy. 1995, Clarion $14.95 (0-395-70364-6). 32pp. In the 1880s, a young Cheyenne boy is taken from the reservation and sent to a white boarding school. (Rev: BCCB 9/95; BL 8/95; SLJ 12/95)

**7541** Chandonnet, Ann. *Chief Stephen's Parky: One Year in the Life of an Athapascan Girl* (4–7). Illus. by Janette Kasl. 1993, Roberts Rinehart paper $7.95 (1-879373-39-4). 81pp. In turn-of-the-century Alaska, a young wife tries to make a parka suitable for her husband, an Athapascan chief. (Rev: BL 9/1/93; SLJ 8/93)

**7542** Chanin, Michael. *Grandfather Four Winds and Rising Moon* (3–5). Illus. by Sally J. Smith. 1994, H. J. Kramer $14.95 (0-915811-47-2). Grandfather Four Winds introduces young Rising Moon to the sacred

"Tree of Our People" to help him stop worrying about the future. (Rev: SLJ 12/94)

**7543** Cooper, James Fenimore. *Last of the Mohicans* (3–5). Adapted by Les Martin. Illus. by Shannon Stirnweis. Series: Step-Up Classics. 1993, Random paper $3.99 (0-679-84706-5). 96pp. A simplified version of the Cooper classic that illuminates details and abridges the plot for young readers. (Rev: SLJ 10/93)

**7544** Curry, Jane L. *Back in the Beforetime: Tales of the California Indians* (4–6). Illus. by James Watts. 1987, Macmillan $15.00 (0-689-50410-1). 144pp. A loose narrative containing traditional tales from many native tribes of California. (Rev: BCCB 5/87; BL 6/15/87; SLJ 4/87)

**7545** Dorris, Michael. *Morning Girl* (5–8). 1992, Little, Brown $12.95 (1-56282-284-5). 76pp. A story for reading aloud of a brother and sister who grow up on an island and spend their time quarreling and coming together. (Rev: BCCB 10/92; BL 8/92; HB 11–12/92*; SLJ 10/92)

**7546** Dorris, Michael. *Sees Behind Trees* (3–6). 1996, Hyperion LB $15.49 (0-7868-2215-5). 128pp. Set in 16th-century America, this story tells about a young Indian boy who earned the name Sees Behind Trees. (Rev: BCCB 1/97; BL 9/15/96*; HB 9–10/96; SLJ 10/96*)

**7547** Grutman, Jewel H., and Gay Matthaei. *The Ledgerbook of Thomas Blue Eagle* (4–8). Illus. by Adam Cvijanovic. 1994, Thomasson-Grant $17.95 (1-56566-063-3). 72pp. A young Native American boy attends a white man's school but tries to retain his own identity and culture in this story that takes place in the West 100 years ago. (Rev: SLJ 12/94)

**7548** Hamm, Diane J. *Daughter of Suqua* (3–6). 1997, Albert Whitman LB $14.95 (0-8075-1477-2). 153pp. In 1905, Ida's life in the Puget Sound area is changed when the government forces her Indian family to relocate. (Rev: BL 9/1/97; SLJ 10/97)

**7549** Hirschfelder, Arlene, and Beverly R. Singer, eds. *Rising Voices: Writings of Young Native Americans* (5–8). 1992, Macmillan $14.00 (0-684-19207-1). 115pp. This anthology of poems, stories, songs, and essays presents the writings of modern young Native Americans. (Rev: BCCB 9/92; SLJ 12/92*)

**7550** Hudson, Jan. *Sweetgrass* (5–8). 1989, Scholastic paper $3.99 (0-590-43486-1). 160pp. A description of the culture of the Dakota Indians in the 1830s. (Rev: BCCB 4/89; BL 4/1/89; SLJ 4/89)

**7551** Hunter, Sara H. *The Unbreakable Code* (2–4). Illus. by Julia Miner. 1996, Northland LB $14.95 (0-87358-638-7). A Navajo man reassures his grandson that he will adjust successfully to a move off the reservation with his mother and new stepfather. (Rev: SLJ 8/96)

**7552** Keehn, Sally M. *I Am Regina* (5–8). 1991, Putnam $15.95 (0-399-21797-5). 219pp. Set in the mid-18th century, this is the story of a young girl's years of captivity by Indians. (Rev: SLJ 6/91)

**7553** Kesey, Ken. *The Sea Lion: A Story of the Sea Cliff People* (4–6). Illus. by Neil Waldman. 1991, Viking paper $14.95 (0-670-83916-7). 48pp. The story of Eemook, an orphan with a crooked back and a withered leg, in Northwest Coast Indian territory. (Rev: BCCB 12/91; BL 10/1/91*; SLJ 11/91)

**7554** Kudlinski, Kathleen V. *Night Bird: A Story of the Seminole Indians* (3–6). Illus. by James Watling. 1993, Viking paper $12.99 (0-670-83157-3). 64pp. A story of 11-year-old Night Bird and the Seminoles' time of sadness in the 1850s when they were moved to Oklahoma. (Rev: BL 1/15/93; SLJ 5/93)

**7555** McLain, Gary. *The Indian Way: Learning to Communicate with Mother Earth* (3–6). Illus. by Michael Taylor. 1990, John Muir paper $9.95 (0-945465-73-4). 114pp. Stories told by an Indian grandfather, all with ecological themes. (Rev: BCCB 3/91; BL 12/1/90)

**7556** Marchand, Peter. *What Good Is a Cactus?* (3–5). Illus. by Craig Brown. 1994, Roberts Rinehart paper $7.95 (1-879373-83-1). Through talking to a wise Native American and observing nature, a scientist realizes the importance of all living things and the role each plays. (Rev: SLJ 11/94)

**7557** Mead, Alice. *Crossing the Starlight Bridge* (3–5). 1994, Bradbury LB $15.00 (0-02-765950-X). 128pp. Rayanne, a young Penobscot girl, gets inspiration from her Gram when the youngster leaves the reservation on a Maine Island and goes to live on the mainland. (Rev: BCCB 6/94; BL 6/1–15/94*; HB 9–10/94; SLJ 6/94)

**7558** Richter, Conrad. *Light in the Forest* (6–8). Illus. by Warren Chappell. 1966, Knopf $23.00 (0-394-43314-9); Fawcett paper $4.99 (0-449-70437-8). A young white boy is captured by Indians and, after becoming a true tribe member, is suddenly returned to his parents.

**7559** Rodolph, Stormy. *Quest for Courage* (4–7). Illus. by Paulette L. Lambert. 1993, Roberts Rinehart paper $8.95 (1-879373-57-2). 104pp. A boy nicknamed Lame Bear because of the injury that made him a cripple is not able to join hunting parties with his friends. (Rev: BL 3/15/94)

**7560** Roop, Peter. *The Buffalo Jump* (1–4). Illus. by Bill Farnsworth. 1996, Northland LB $14.95 (0-87358-616-6). Little Blaze, an American Indian boy, saves his older brother's life during a buffalo hunt. (Rev: SLJ 2/97)

**7561** Roop, Peter, and Connie Roop. *Ahyoka and the Talking Leaves* (3–5). Illus. by Yoshi Miyake. 1992, Lothrop $15.00 (0-688-10697-8). 56pp. Six-year-old Ahyoka, daughter of Sequoyah of the Cherokee, follows her father in his goal of developing a written language — "talking leaves." (Rev: BL 4/1/92; HB 7–8/92; SLJ 7/92)

**7562** Stewart, Elisabeth J. *On the Long Trail Home* (5–7). 1994, Clarion $13.95 (0-395-68361-0). 106pp. A Cherokee girl escapes from the Trail of Tears and makes her way back to the Appalachian Mountains during the 1830s. (Rev: BCCB 12/94; BL 10/15/94; SLJ 12/94)

**7563** Strasser, Todd. *The Diving Bell* (4–7). Illus. 1992, Scholastic $13.95 (0-590-44620-7). 192pp. When Spanish ships ladened with gold sink close to their island, some natives try to salvage them in this story set in the New World during the Spanish conquest. (Rev: SLJ 6/92)

**7564** Von Ahnen, Katherine. *Heart of Naosaqua* (4–6). Illus. 1996, Roberts Rinehart paper $9.95 (1-57098-010-1). 160pp. In 1823, Naosaqua and her people, the Mesquakie Indians, must find a new home. (Rev: BL 7/96)

## COLONIAL PERIOD

**7565** Bowen, Gary. *Stranded at Plimoth Plantation, 1626* (3–6). Illus. 1994, HarperCollins LB $19.89 (0-06-022542-4). 88pp. Using a fictional diary as a framework, this well-researched account describes the arduous living conditions in the Pilgrims' Massachusetts colony. (Rev: BCCB 10/94; BL 9/15/94; HB 11–12/94; SLJ 11/94) [973.2]

**7566** Bulla, Clyde Robert. *A Lion to Guard Us* (3–6). Illus. by Michele Chessare. 1981, HarperCollins LB $14.89 (0-690-04097-0); paper $4.95 (0-06-440333-5). 128pp. Three motherless children sail for America to be united with their father in the Jamestown, Virginia, colony.

**7567** Dalgliesh, Alice. *Courage of Sarah Noble* (3–5). Illus. by Leonard Weisgard. 1954, Macmillan $15.00 (0-684-18830-9); paper $4.95 (0-689-71540-4). 64pp. The true story of a brave little girl who in 1707 went with her father into the wilds of Connecticut.

**7568** Duey, Kathleen. *Sarah Anne Hartford* (4–7). Series: American Diaries. 1996, Simon & Schuster paper $3.99 (0-689-80384-2). 137pp. A story set in Puritan New England about 2 girls who are placed in a pillory for playing on the Sabbath. (Rev: BCCB 5/96; BL 5/15/96; HB 9–10/96; SLJ 6/96)

**7569** Edmonds, Walter. *The Matchlock Gun* (5–7). Illus. by Paul Lantz. 1941, Putnam $16.95 (0-399-21911-0). 64pp. Exciting, true story of a courageous boy who protected his mother and sister from the Indians of the Hudson Valley. Newbery Medal winner, 1942.

**7570** Field, Rachel. *Calico Bush* (5–7). Illus. by Allen Louis. 1987, Macmillan $16.00 (0-02-734610-2); Bantam paper $4.99 (0-440-40368-5). 224pp. This 1932 Newbery Honor Book is an adventure story of a French girl "loaned" to a family of American pioneers in Maine in the 1740s.

**7571** Harness, Cheryl. *Three Young Pilgrims* (3–5). Illus. by author. 1992, Macmillan paper $16.00 (0-02-742643-2). 40pp. This is a fictionalized account of the voyage of the Pilgrims as experienced by 3 children. (Rev: SLJ 9/92)

**7572** Hildick, E. W. *Hester Bidgood: Investigatrix of Evill Deedes* (4–6). 1994, Macmillan paper $15.00 (0-02-743966-6). 160pp. Two young residents in a 17th-century New England village set out to find who branded a cat with the sign of the cross. (Rev: BCCB 12/94; BL 11/15/94; SLJ 12/94)

**7573** Hoobler, Dorothy, and Thomas Hoobler. *Priscilla Foster: The Story of a Salem Girl* (3–6). Illus. 1997, Silver Burdett LB $14.95 (0-382-39640-5); paper $4.95 (0-382-39641-3). 128pp. A grandmother takes her granddaughter to Salem, Massachusetts, and tells her about the witch trials of 1692. (Rev: BL 8/97; SLJ 8/97)

**7574** Jacobs, Paul S. *James Printer: A Novel of Rebellion* (5–8). 1997, Scholastic $15.95 (0-590-16381-7). 224pp. During colonial times, an Indian boy who was raised in Cambridge, Massachusetts, agonizes over his divided loyalties when the English and the Indians go to war. (Rev: BCCB 3/97; BL 4/15/97; SLJ 6/97)

**7575** Lasky, Kathryn. *A Journey to the New World: The Diary of Remember Patience Whipple* (4–7). Series: Dear America. 1996, Scholastic $9.95 (0-590-50214-X). 144pp. Using diary entries as a format, this is the story of 12-year-old Mem Whipple, her journey on the *Mayflower*, and her first year in the New World. (Rev: BCCB 10/96; HB 9–10/96; SLJ 8/96)

**7576** Littlesugar, Amy. *The Spinner's Daughter* (3–5). Illus. 1994, Pippin LB $14.95 (0-945912-22-6). 32pp. In her strict Puritan community in Connecticut, Elspeth is considered sinful because she has a cornhusk doll. (Rev: BL 9/1/94; SLJ 9/94)

**7577** Luttrell, Wanda. *Home on Stoney Creek* (4–6). 1995, Chariot paper $5.99 (0-7814-0901-2). 208pp. Eleven-year-old Sarah relocates with her family to Virginia from Kentucky in 1775. (Rev: BL 5/15/95)

**7578** Martin, Jacqueline B. *Grandmother Bryant's Pocket* (2–4). Illus. by Petra Mathers. 1996, Houghton $14.95 (0-395-68984-8). 48pp. Set in Maine during 1787, this is the story of how a young girl's grandmother helps her adjust to the death of her dog. (Rev: BCCB 7–8/96; BL 5/15/96; HB 7–8/96; SLJ 6/96*)

**7579** Ovecka, Janice. *Cave of Falling Water* (4–8). Illus. by David K. Fadden. 1992, New England Pr. paper $10.95 (0-933050-98-4). 116pp. A cave in the hills of Vermont plays a part in the lives of 3 girls, one an Indian and one white, both from colonial times, and the last, a contemporary adolescent. (Rev: BL 5/1/93)

**7580** Petry, Ann. *Tituba of Salem Village* (6–8). 1988, HarperCollins paper $4.95 (0-06-440403-X). 254pp. The story of the slave Tituba and her husband, John Indian, from the day they were sold in the Barbados until the tragic Salem witchcraft trials.

**7581** Rue, Nancy N. *The Rescue* (4–6). Series: Christian Heritage. 1995, Focus on the Family paper $5.99 (1-56179-346-9). 185pp. In Salem Village of the 1690s, young Hope gets to know a woman who is shunned because she is friendly with the Indians. Also part of the series is *The Stowaway* (1995). (Rev: BL 9/1/95)

**7582** Speare, Elizabeth G. *The Sign of the Beaver* (6–8). 1983, Houghton $16.00 (0-395-33890-5); Dell paper $4.50 (0-440-47900-2). 144pp. In Maine in 1768, Matt, though only 12, must protect his family.

**7583** Speare, Elizabeth G. *The Witch of Blackbird Pond* (6–8). 1958, Houghton $16.00 (0-395-07114-3); Dell paper $4.99 (0-440-99577-9). 256pp. Historical romance set in Puritan Connecticut with the theme of witchcraft. Newbery Medal winner, 1959. Also use: *Calico Captive* (1957).

**7584** Tripp, Valerie. *Changes for Felicity: A Winter Story* (2–5). Illus. by Dan Andreasen. Series: American Girl. 1992, Pleasant LB $12.95 (1-56247-038-8); paper $5.95 (1-56247-037-X). 34pp. In this story of a girl who lives in colonial Williamsburg, the father of her best friend is jailed as a Loyalist. Also use: *Felicity Saves the Day: A Summer Story;* and *Happy Birthday, Felicity* (both 1992). (Rev: BL 5/1/92)

**7585** Tripp, Valerie. *Felicity Learns a Lesson: A School Story* (3–5). Illus. by Dan Andreasen. Series: American Girl. 1991, Pleasant paper $5.95 (1-56247-007-8). 69pp. Felicity learns to control her temper in this story set in colonial Williamsburg. (Rev: BL 1/1/91; SLJ 1/92)

**7586** Tripp, Valerie. *Felicity's Surprise: A Christmas Story* (3–5). Illus. by Dan Andreasen. Series: American Girl. 1991, Pleasant paper $5.95 (1-56247-010-8). 69pp. The family must depend more on Felicity when her mother is ill, in this story of colonial Williamsburg. (Rev: BL 1/1/91; SLJ 1/92)

**7587** Wisler, G. Clifton. *This New Land* (5–8). 1987, Walker LB $14.85 (0-8027-6727-3). Twelve-year-old Richard and his family begin a new life in Plymouth, Massachusetts, in 1620. (Rev: BL 3/15/88)

## THE REVOLUTION

**7588**   Avi. *The Fighting Ground* (5–7). Illus. by Ellen Thompson. 1984, HarperCollins LB $14.89 (0-397-32074-4); paper $4.95 (0-06-440185-5). 160pp. Thirteen-year-old Jonathan marches off to fight the British.

**7589**   Banim, Lisa. *Drums at Saratoga* (3–5). Series: Stories of the States. 1993, Silver Moon LB $13.95 (1-881889-20-3). 58pp. Young Nathaniel Phillips and a black servant are captured by the American forces during the Revolutionary War. (Rev: SLJ 10/93)

**7590**   Banim, Lisa. *The Hessian's Secret Diary* (3–5). Illus. 1997, Silver Moon LB $13.95 (1-881889-86-6). 80pp. In 1776, a young Brooklyn resident helps a wounded Hessian soldier, even though this endangers her family's safety. (Rev: BL 5/1/97; SLJ 4/97)

**7591**   Banim, Lisa. *A Spy in the King's Colony* (3–5). Illus. by Tatyana Yuditskaya. Series: Mysteries in Time. 1994, Silver Moon $13.95 (1-881889-54-8). 76pp. In 1775, 11-year-old Emily Parker is living in British-occupied Boston, where spies for both sides abound. (Rev: SLJ 7/94)

**7592**   Berleth, Richard. *Samuel's Choice* (4–6). Illus. by James Watling. 1990, Whitman LB $14.95 (0-8075-7218-7). 40pp. Samuel, 14, is a young black slave in Brooklyn who plays a heroic role in the Battle of Long Island during the American Revolution. (Rev: BCCB 1/91; BL 1/1/91; SLJ 4/91)

**7593**   Bruchac, Joseph. *The Arrow over the Door* (4–7). Illus. 1998, Dial paper $15.99 (0-8037-2078-5). 96pp. Two boys, one a Quaker and the other an American Indian, share the narration of this story that takes place immediately before the Battle of Saratoga in 1777. (Rev: BL 2/15/98; SLJ 4/98)

**7594**   Collier, James Lincoln, and Christopher Collier. *My Brother Sam Is Dead* (6–8). 1984, Simon & Schuster $17.00 (0-02-722980-7); Scholastic paper $4.50 (0-590-42792-X). 224pp. The story, based partially on fact, of a Connecticut family divided in loyalties during the Revolutionary War.

**7595**   Fleming, Candace. *The Hatmaker's Sign: A Story by Benjamin Franklin* (3–5). Illus. by Robert Andrew Parker. 1998, Orchard $15.95 (0-531-30075-7). 40pp. When Jefferson complains to Dr. Franklin about the mutilation of his Declaration of Independence by Congress, the good doctor tells him a comforting parable. (Rev: BL 2/15/98; SLJ 4/98)

**7596**   Forbes, Esther. *Johnny Tremain: A Novel for Old and Young* (6–8). Illus. by Lynd Ward. 1943, Houghton $15.00 (0-395-06766-9); Dell paper $4.99 (0-440-94250-0). 272pp. Story of a young silversmith's apprentice, who plays an important part in the American Revolution. Newbery Medal winner, 1944.

**7597**   Fritz, Jean. *The Cabin Faced West* (3–6). Illus. by Feodor Rojankovsky. 1958, Putnam $14.95 (0-399-23223-0); Puffin paper $3.99 (0-14-032256-6). 128pp. The western Pennsylvania territory of 1784 is a very lonely place for Ann until General Washington comes to visit.

**7598**   Fritz, Jean. *George Washington's Breakfast* (3–5). Illus. by Paul Galdone. 1998, Putnam paper $5.99 (0-698-11611-9). 43pp. George W. Allen knows all there is to know about our first president — except what he had for breakfast.

**7599**   Gauch, Patricia L. *Aaron and the Green Mountain Boys* (4–6). Illus. 1988, Betterway paper $5.95 (1-55870-220-2). 64pp. A reissue of a fine 1972 historical novel set in Revolutionary times.

**7600**   Gauch, Patricia L. *This Time, Tempe Wick?* (2–5). 1992, Putnam $13.95 (0-399-21880-7). 48pp. Tempe (Temperance) Wick helped the Revolutionary soldiers who camped on her farm in New Jersey in 1780, until they tried to steal her horse, and then she got mad.

**7601**   Gregory, Kristiana. *The Winter of Red Snow: The Revolutionary War Diary of Abigail Jane Stewart* (5–8). Series: Dear America. 1996, Scholastic $9.95 (0-590-22653-3). 176pp. The hardships faced by the Revolutionary Army at Valley Forge in 1777–1778 are seen through the eyes of young girl who lives close to the encampment. (Rev: BCCB 10/96; HB 9–10/96; SLJ 9/96)

**7602**   Harrah, Madge. *My Brother, My Enemy* (4–7). 1997, Simon & Schuster paper $16.00 (0-689-80968-9). 144pp. Using Bacon's Rebellion in 1676 as a background, this novel involves a 14-year-old whose family is killed during an Indian raid on their cabin. (Rev: BCCB 7–8/97; BL 5/1/97; SLJ 7/97)

**7603**   Massie, Elizabeth. *Patsy's Discovery* (3–5). 1997, Pocket paper $3.99 (0-671-00132-9). 135pp. Thirteen-year-old Patsy Black is growing up in Philadelphia during the Continental Congress meetings of 1776. (Rev: BL 12/1/97; SLJ 8/97)

**7604**   Moore, Ruth Nulton. *Distant Thunder* (5–8). Illus. by Allan Eitzen. 1991, Herald Pr. paper $6.99 (0-8361-3557-1). 160pp. During the Revolution, when wounded Americans are sent to Pennsylvania to recover, young Kate experiences the horrors of war. (Rev: BCCB 1/92; SLJ 1/92)

**7605**   Myers, Anna. *The Keeping Room* (4–7). 1997, Walker $15.95 (0-8027-8641-3). 144pp. In this tale set during the Revolutionary War, Joseph's home is taken over by the Redcoats after his father goes off to war. (Rev: BL 11/1/97; SLJ 12/97)

**7606**   O'Dell, Scott. *Sarah Bishop* (5–8). 1980, Houghton $16.00 (0-395-29185-2); Scholastic paper $4.50 (0-590-44651-7). 240pp. A first-person narrative of a girl who lived through the American Revolution and its toll of suffering and misery.

**7607** Reit, Seymour. *Guns for General Washington: A Story of the American Revolution* (4–7). 1990, Harcourt $15.95 (0-15-200466-1). 144pp. A novel of the Revolution about taking cannons to Washington from Fort Ticonderoga. (Rev: SLJ 1/91)

**7608** Walker, Sally M. *The 18 Penny Goose* (1–3). Illus. by Ellen Beier. Series: I Can Read. 1998, HarperCollins LB $14.89 (0-06-027557-X). 64pp. In this easy reader based on fact, a little girl is afraid that the British army raiders will eat her pet goose during the Revolutionary War. (Rev: BL 2/1/98; SLJ 3/98)

**7609** Waters, John F. *Night Raiders Along the Cape* (3–5). Illus. 1998, Silver Moon LB $13.95 (1-881889-85-8). 96pp. Asa rows from his island home to warn the mainlanders of a British plot in this novel set in Massachusetts during the American Revolution. (Rev: BL 2/15/98)

### THE YOUNG NATION, 1789–1861

**7610** Arbuckle, Scott. *Zeb, the Cow's on the Roof Again! And Other Tales of Early Texas Dwellings* (3–7). Illus. by author. 1996, Eakin $14.95 (1-57168-102-7). 128pp. Four youngsters tell about their dwellings in stories that take place at various times in Texas history. (Rev: SLJ 4/97)

**7611** Armstrong, Jennifer. *Steal Away* (5–8). 1992, Orchard LB $14.99 (0-531-08583-X); Scholastic paper $3.99 (0-590-46921-5). 224pp. Susannah, who hates slavery, is given a slave when she moves to Virginia to live with her uncle and his family. (Rev: SLJ 2/92)

**7612** Auch, Mary Jane. *Journey to Nowhere* (4–7). 1997, Holt $15.95 (0-8050-4922-3). 202pp. In 1815, 11-year-old Mem and her family relocate from Connecticut to Genesee County in western New York. (Rev: BCCB 6/97; BL 4/15/97; HB 7–8/97; SLJ 5/97)

**7613** Berleth, Richard. *Mary Patten's Voyage* (4–6). Illus. by Ben Otero. 1994, Albert Whitman LB $14.95 (0-8075-4987-8). 40pp. Based on facts involving an 1856 clipper ship race, this is the story of Mary Patten, who took command when her captain husband became ill. (Rev: BCCB 12/94; BL 1/1/95; SLJ 12/94)

**7614** Blos, Joan W. *A Gathering of Days: A New England Girl's Journal, 1830–32* (6–8). 1979, Macmillan $15.00 (0-684-16340-3); paper $3.95 (0-689-71419-X). 144pp. A fictional diary kept by 13-year-old Catherine Cabot, who is growing up in the town of Meredith, New Hampshire. Newbery Medal winner, 1980.

**7615** Bryant, Louella. *The Black Bonnet* (5–7). 1996, New England Pr. paper $12.95 (1-881535-22-3). 160pp. Two sisters are smuggled out of the South via the Underground Railroad to Burlington, Vermont. (Rev: BL 2/1/97; SLJ 2/97)

**7616** Carrick, Carol. *Stay Away from Simon!* (4–6). Illus. by Donald Carrick. 1985, Houghton paper $5.95 (0-89919-849-X). 64pp. Mentally handicapped Simon has a reputation of being dangerous, but Lucy discovers he also has a generous heart in this story set in Martha's Vineyard in the 1830s. (Rev: BCCB 11/85; BL 8/85; SLJ 4/85)

**7617** Coleman, Evelyn. *The Foot Warmer and the Crow* (2–5). Illus. by Daniel Minter. 1994, Macmillan paper $14.95 (0-02-722816-9). With the help of a crow, the slave Nezekiah outwits his cruel master and gains his freedom. (Rev: BCCB 12/94; SLJ 11/94)

**7618** Collier, James Lincoln, and Christopher Collier. *The Clock* (5–7). Illus. by Maddox Kelly. 1995, Delacorte $15.00 (0-385-30037-9); Dell paper $3.99 (0-440-40999-3). 176pp. Fifteen-year-old Annie Steele contends with the harsh life of mill work in Connecticut in 1810. (Rev: BCCB 4/92; BL 2/1/92; HB 3–4/92)

**7619** Connelly, Bernardine. *Follow the Drinking Gourd: A Story of the Underground Railroad* (3–7). Illus. by Yvonne Buchanan. 1997, Simon & Schuster paper $22.00 (0-689-80242-0). The infamous days of slavery and the heroism and courage involved in the operation of the Underground Railroad are combined in this story about Mary Prentice and her escape to freedom with her family. (Rev: SLJ 3/98)

**7620** Curry, Jane L. *What the Dickens!* (4–6). 1991, Macmillan LB $13.95 (0-689-50524-8). 160pp. It is Pennsylvania in 1842 and 11-year-old Cherry and her twin brother are chasing Charles Dickens to recover a stolen manuscript. (Rev: BL 10/1/91; SLJ 9/91)

**7621** DeFelice, Cynthia. *The Apprenticeship of Lucas Whitaker* (5–8). 1996, Farrar $15.00 (0-374-34669-0). 152pp. In the mid-1800s, orphan Lucas becomes an apprentice to the local dentist/barber/undertaker, Dr. Uriah M. Beecher. (Rev: BCCB 10/96; BL 10/1/96; SLJ 8/96*)

**7622** Duey, Kathleen. *Evie Peach: St. Louis, 1857* (3–6). Series: American Diaries. 1997, Simon & Schuster paper $3.99 (0-689-81621-9). 144pp. In pre–Civil War St. Louis, freed slaves Evie Peach and her father are saving money to buy the freedom of Evie's mother. (Rev: BL 2/15/98; SLJ 3/98)

**7623** Fox, Paula. *The Slave Dancer* (6–8). Illus. by Eros Keith. 1982, Macmillan $16.00 (0-02-735560-8); Dell paper $4.50 (0-440-96132-7). 192pp. Fourteen-year-old Jessie is kidnapped and press-ganged aboard an American slave ship bound for Africa. Newbery Medal winner, 1974.

**7624** Fritz, Jean. *Brady* (4–7). Illus. by Lynd Ward. 1960, Puffin paper $4.99 (0-14-032258-2). 224pp. When Brady discovers his father is an Underground Railroad agent, he learns to control his tongue and form his own opinion about slavery.

**7625** Gaeddert, Louann. *Breaking Free* (5–8). 1994, Atheneum $16.00 (0-689-31883-9). 144pp. In upstate New York in 1800, orphaned Richard is upset that there are slaves on his uncle's farm and is determined to help one escape. (Rev: BL 4/1/94; HB 9–10/94; SLJ 5/94)

**7626** Givens, Steven J. *Levi Dust: A Tale from the Kerry Patch* (2–4). 1997, New Canaan paper $4.25 (1-889658-07-3). 56pp. Ten-year-old twins get lost on the streets of St. Louis in the 1850s and are brought home by a kindly bell ringer. (Rev: BL 2/1/98)

**7627** Gregory, Kristiana. *The Stowaway: A Tale of California Pirates* (4–6). 1995, Scholastic $3.99 (0-590-48822-8). 144pp. Carlito must endure the squalid life of being a pirate's captive in this tale set on the California coast during the early 1800s. (Rev: BCCB 10/95; BL 9/15/95; SLJ 9/95)

**7628** Hansen, Joyce. *The Captive* (5–8). 1994, Scholastic $13.95 (0-590-41625-1). 195pp. The exciting story based on fact of a young African boy sold into slavery in Massachusetts and how he eventually escaped. (Rev: BCCB 3/94; HB 1–2/94, 5–6/94; SLJ 1/94)

**7629** Hilts, Len. *Timmy O'Dowd and the Big Ditch: A Story of the Glory Days on the Old Erie Canal* (5–7). 1988, Harcourt $13.95 (0-15-200606-0). 91pp. Timmy and his cousin Dennis don't get along, but when the canals threaten to flood, they realize each other's strengths and stamina. (Rev: BCCB 12/88; BL 10/1/88; SLJ 12/88)

**7630** Holland, Isabelle. *The Promised Land* (4–6). 1996, Scholastic $15.95 (0-590-47176-7). 156pp. Orphaned Maggie and Annie, who have been happily living with the Russell family on the Kansas frontier, are visited by an uncle who wants them to come home with him. A sequel to *The Journey Home* (1990). (Rev: BCCB 4/96; BL 4/15/96; SLJ 8/96)

**7631** Hooks, William H. *The Ballad of Belle Dorcas* (3–5). Illus. by Brian Pinkney. 1990, Knopf LB $14.99 (0-394-94645-6). 32pp. A story of true love and the conflicts of slaves who had no power over their lives. (Rev: BCCB 12/92; BL 9/1/90*; HB 3–4/91; SLJ 10/90)

**7632** Hooks, William H. *Freedom's Fruit* (2–4). Illus. by James E. Ransome. 1995, Knopf LB $17.99 (0-679-92438-8). 42pp. Using her sorcery and spells,

Mama Marina plots to free several slaves, including her daughter, Sheba. (Rev: BL 2/15/96; SLJ 2/96)

**7633** Hopkinson, Deborah. *Sweet Clara and the Freedom Quilt* (3–5). Illus. by James E. Ransome. 1993, Knopf LB $16.99 (0-679-92311-X). 36pp. In this picture book for older readers, a slave girl maps out her escape to Canada on a brightly colored quilt. (Rev: BCCB 7–8/93; BL 4/15/93; HB 5–6/93*; SLJ 6/93)

**7634** Jackson, Dave, and Neta Jackson. *The Runaway's Revenge* (4–6). Series: Trailblazer Books. 1995, Bethany paper $5.99 (1-55661-471-3). 144pp. A novel about the life of John Newton, a slave trader who later became a minister and wrote such hymns as "Amazing Grace." (Rev: BL 1/1–15/96)

**7635** Jackson, Dave, and Neta Jackson. *The Thieves of Tyburn Square* (3–6). Series: Trailblazer Books. 1995, Bethany paper $5.99 (1-55661-470-5). 144pp. In this fictionalized account set in the early 1800s, the Quaker Elizabeth Fry helps 2 youngsters caught picking pockets. (Rev: BL 3/15/96)

**7636** Jakes, John. *Susanna of the Alamo: A True Story* (3–5). Illus. by Paul Bacon. 1986, Harcourt $13.95 (0-15-200592-7); paper $7.00 (0-15-200595-1). 32pp. Only women, children, and slaves were spared by the Mexicans at the battle of the Alamo in 1836, and one, Susanna Dickinson, was spared to inform Sam Houston of the outcome. (Rev: BCCB 6/86; BL 6/15/86; SLJ 8/86)

**7637** Johnson, Lois W. *Escape into the Night* (4–6). Illus. 1995, Bethany paper $5.99 (1-55661-351-2). 160pp. On a Mississippi River steamboat, young Libby must rethink her attitudes toward slavery when she encounters a conductor on the Underground Railroad. (Rev: BL 11/15/95; SLJ 10/95)

**7638** Johnson, Lois W. *Midnight Rescue* (4–6). 1996, Bethany paper $5.99 (1-55661-353-9). 160pp. Twelve-year-old Libby, a riverboat captain's daughter, becomes involved with the Underground Railroad and an escaped slave. (Rev: BL 1/1–15/97)

**7639** Johnston, Norma. *Lotta's Progress* (5–7). 1997, Avon paper $14.00 (0-380-97367-7). 155pp. A family of German immigrants to Boston in the late 1840s gets help from the Alcotts, including Louisa May, and a fictitious neighboring Irish family. (Rev: SLJ 9/97)

**7640** Karr, Kathleen. *The Great Turkey Walk* (4–8). 1998, Farrar $16.00 (0-374-32773-4). 199pp. A good-humored tale about a pioneer entrepreneur who decides to buy turkeys in the Midwest to sell in Denver, where the price is sky-high. (Rev: SLJ 3/98*)

**7641** Lottridge, Celia B. *The Wind Wagon* (2–4). Illus. by Daniel Clifford. 1995, Silver Burdett LB $12.95 (0-382-24927-5); paper $4.95 (0-382-24929-1). 56pp. A fictionalized account of Sam Peppard and his invention of a wagon powered by the wind in Kansas in 1860. (Rev: SLJ 8/95)

**7642** McCaughrean, Geraldine, adapt. *Moby Dick* (5–8). Illus. by Victor G. Ambrus. 1997, Oxford $22.95 (0-19-274156-X). 100pp. A shortened version of this classic that does not sacrifice the quality of the original. (Rev: SLJ 5/97*)

**7643** McCully, Emily Arnold. *The Bobbin Girl* (3–5). Illus. 1996, Dial paper $14.89 (0-8037-1828-4). 40pp. To help her mother, who runs a boarding house, 10-year-old Rebecca goes to work in a textile mill in Lowell, Massachusetts, during he 1830s. (Rev: BCCB 3/96; BL 4/15/96; HB 9–10/96; SLJ 4/96)

**7644** McKissack, Patricia. *A Picture of Freedom: The Diary of Clotee, a Slave Girl* (4–6). 1997, Scholastic paper $9.95 (0-614-25386-1). 208pp. Using a diary format, this novel describes the life of slaves on a Southern plantation as seen through the eyes of a young slave girl. (Rev: BL 4/15/97; SLJ 9/97)

**7645** Minahan, John A. *Abigail's Drum* (2–5). Illus. 1995, Pippin $14.95 (0-945912-25-0). 64pp. During the War of 1812, Rebecca and Abigail try to save their father, who has been captured by the British. (Rev: BCCB 2/96; BL 2/15/96; SLJ 2/96)

**7646** Monjo, F. N. *The Drinking Gourd* (2–4). Illus. by Fred Brenner. 1970, HarperCollins LB $14.89 (0-06-024330-9); paper $3.75 (0-06-444042-7). 64pp. A New England white boy helps a black family escape on the Underground Railroad.

**7647** Paterson, Katherine. *Jip, His Story* (5–8). 1996, Dutton paper $15.99 (0-525-67543-4). 208pp. An orphan boy who works on a poor farm in Vermont in the 1850s finds a stranger is stalking him. (Rev: BCCB 12/96; BL 9/1/96*; HB 11–12/96; SLJ 10/96*)

**7648** Patrick, Denise Lewis. *The Adventures of Midnight Son* (5–8). 1997, Holt $15.95 (0-8050-4714-X). 152pp. Fleeing slavery on a horse given to him by his parents, Midnight rides to Mexico and freedom. (Rev: BL 12/15/97; SLJ 12/97)

**7649** Rinaldi, Ann. *The Blue Door* (5–8). 1996, Scholastic $15.95 (0-590-46051-X). 272pp. In this, the third volume of the Quilt trilogy — following *A Stitch in Time* (1994) and *Broken Days* (1995) — Amanda is forced to take a mill job in Lowell, Massachusetts, because of an identity misunderstanding. (Rev: BL 11/1/96)

**7650** Robinet, Harriette G. *The Twins, the Pirates, and the Battle of New Orleans* (4–6). 1997, Simon & Schuster $15.00 (0-689-81208-6). 144pp. Twins Andrew and Pierre, who have been rescued from slavery, are left alone in a Louisiana swamp, where

they battle alligators, pirates, and bounty hunters. (Rev: BL 11/15/97; SLJ 12/97)

**7651** Robinet, Harriette G. *Washington City Is Burning* (5–7). 1996, Simon & Schuster $16.00 (0-689-80773-2). 149pp. In this historical novel set in the Washington, D.C., of James and Dolley Madison, young Virginia helps slaves escape. (Rev: BCCB 12/96; BL 11/1/96; SLJ 11/96)

**7652** Rosen, Michael J. *A School for Pompey Walker* (4–6). Illus. 1995, Harcourt $16.00 (0-15-200114-X). 48pp. This story, based on fact, tells about a slave who sold himself several times into slavery to get the money to open a school for black children. (Rev: BCCB 1/96; BL 10/15/95; SLJ 11/95)

**7653** Rosenburg, John. *William Parker: Rebel Without Rights* (5–7). 1996, Millbrook LB $21.90 (1-56294-139-9). 144pp. A fictionalized account of William Parker, an escaped slave, who led the Christiana Riot in Pennsylvania in 1851 to prevent the return of slaves to the South. (Rev: BL 2/15/96; SLJ 5/96)

**7654** Smucker, Barbara. *Runaway to Freedom* (3–5). Illus. by Charles Lilly. 1978, HarperCollins paper $4.95 (0-06-440106-5). 160pp. Two slave girls try to reach Canada and freedom.

**7655** Thomas, Velma M. *Lest We Forget: The Passage from Africa to Slavery and Emancipation* (5–8). Illus. 1997, Crown $29.95 (0-609-60030-3). An interactive book about slavery based on material from the Black Holocaust Museum. (Rev: BL 12/15/97) [973.6]

**7656** Turkle, Brinton. *Rachel and Obadiah* (3–4). Illus. by author. 1978, Dutton paper $15.00 (0-525-38020-5). 32pp. Obadiah and his sister, Rachel, vie to be first with the news of a ship's arrival in port. Also use: *Thy Friend, Obadiah* (1982, Puffin).

**7657** Turner, Glennette Tilley. *Running for Our Lives* (5–7). Illus. 1994, Holiday $16.95 (0-8234-1121-4). 198pp. A thoroughly researched novel about a boy and his family who escape slavery in the 1850s and traveled on the Underground Railroad to Canada. (Rev: BCCB 6/94; BL 6/1–15/94; SLJ 4/94)

**7658** Weitzman, David. *Old Ironsides* (3–6). Illus. 1997, Houghton $15.95 (0-395-74678-7). 32pp. A fictionalized account of the building of the ship in President Washington's time that would protect merchant ships from pirates. (Rev: BCCB 6/97; BL 5/1/97; HB 5–6/97; SLJ 4/97*)

**7659** West, Tracey. *Mr. Peale's Bones* (4–6). Series: Stories of the States. 1994, Silver Moon LB $13.95 (1-881889-50-5). 63pp. In this novel, set in upstate New York in 1801, Will and his estranged father find a new bond when they help Charles Willson Peale and his excavation of mammoth bones. (Rev: SLJ 7/94)

**7660** Whelan, Gloria. *Once on This Island* (4–7). 1995, HarperCollins LB $14.89 (0-06-026249-4). 224pp. In 1812, Mary and her older brother and sister must tend the family farm on Mackinac Island when their father goes off to war. (Rev: BCCB 11/95; BL 10/1/95; SLJ 11/95)

**7661** Wisler, G. Clifton. *Caleb's Choice* (5–8). 1996, Dutton paper $14.99 (0-525-67526-4). 160pp. During 1858 in northern Texas, 13-year-old Caleb helps 2 escaped slaves. (Rev: BCCB 9/96; BL 8/96; SLJ 8/96)

**7662** Wright, Courtni C. *Journey to Freedom: A Story of the Underground Railroad* (3–5). Illus. by Griffith Gershom. 1994, Holiday LB $16.95 (0-8234-1096-X). 28pp. A picture book that tells of 8-year-old Joshua and his flight to freedom on the Underground Railroad. (Rev: BL 11/15/94; SLJ 1/95)

## PIONEERS AND WESTWARD EXPANSION

**7663** Anderson, Joan. *Pioneer Children of Appalachia* (4–6). Illus. 1986, Houghton paper $6.95 (0-395-54792-X). The Davis family is shown in everyday life in Appalachia of the early 1800s. (Rev: BCCB 12/86; BL 11/1/86; SLJ 10/86)

**7664** Armstrong, Jennifer. *Black-Eyed Susan* (3–5). 1995, Crown $15.00 (0-517-70107-3). 107pp. Explores the mind of a 10-year-old homesteader and the joys and hardships of pioneer life in the Dakota Territory. (Rev: BCCB 10/95; SLJ 10/95)

**7665** Avi. *The Barn* (3–6). Series: Richard Jackson Books. 1994, Orchard LB $15.99 (0-531-08711-5). 106pp. In this novel set in 1855 Oregon, 3 motherless children try to run the family farm after their father becomes sick. (Rev: SLJ 10/94)

**7666** Bailer, Darice. *The Last Rail* (3–5). Illus. by Bill Farnsworth. Series: Odyssey. 1996, Smithsonian Institution $14.95 (1-56899-362-5); paper $5.95 (1-56899-363-3). 32pp. Using a fictional format, this book tells about a young girl who witnesses the building of the first transcontinental railroad. (Rev: BL 10/15/96)

**7667** Bird, E. J. *Chuck Wagon Stew* (3–5). Illus. by author. 1988, Carolrhoda $8.95 (0-87614-313-3). 72pp. Folk stories from old Matt Warner, "a genuine reformed outlaw." (Rev: BL 3/1/88; SLJ 3/88)

**7668** Blakeslee, Ann R. *A Different Kind of Hero* (5–7). 1997, Marshall Cavendish $14.95 (0-7614-5000-9). 144pp. In 1881 Colorado, Renny is criticized for befriending and helping a Chinese boy new to town. (Rev: BL 9/1/97; SLJ 1/98)

**7669** Buchanan, Jane. *Gratefully Yours* (3–6). 1997, Farrar $15.00 (0-374-32775-0). 128pp. After her parents die in a fire, Hattie rides the Orphan Train west to find a new family. (Rev: BL 10/15/97; SLJ 12/97)

**7670** Bunting, Eve. *Train to Somewhere* (2–5). Illus. by Ronald Himler. 1996, Clarion $15.00 (0-395-71325-0). 32pp. The story of the Orphan Train as seen from the point of view of Marianne, a homeless girl who travels west in 1878 to find an adoptive family. (Rev: BCCB 3/96; BL 2/1/96*; SLJ 3/96*)

**7671** Byars, Betsy. *Trouble River* (3–6). Illus. by Rocco Negri. 1989, Puffin paper $4.50 (0-14-034243-5). 160pp. Dewey uses his canoe to escape Indians.

**7672** Calvert, Patricia. *Bigger* (5–8). 1994, Scribners paper $16.00 (0-684-19685-9). 144pp. After the Civil War, 12-year-old Tyler travels from Missouri to the Rio Grande in search of his soldier-father. (Rev: BCCB 3/94; BL 4/1/94; HB 7–8/94; SLJ 4/94)

**7673** Calvert, Patricia. *The Snowbird* (5–8). 1982, NAL paper $1.95 (0-451-13353-6). 160pp. Orphaned Willana and her brother travel to the Dakota Territory to join their uncle and his wife.

**7674** Coville, Bruce. *Fortune's Journey* (5–8). 1995, Troll paper $13.95 (0-8167-3650-2). 256pp. A historical novel about a troupe of actors heading west in pioneer days, led by feisty Fortune Plunkett, age 16. (Rev: BL 10/15/95; SLJ 11/95)

**7675** Cushman, Karen. *The Ballad of Lucy Whipple* (5–8). 1996, Clarion $15.00 (0-395-72806-1). 208pp. Lucy hates being stuck in the California wilderness with an overbearing mother who runs a boarding house. (Rev: BCCB 9/96; BL 8/96; HB 9–10/96; SLJ 8/96*)

**7676** DeFelice, Cynthia. *Weasel* (4–6). 1990, Macmillan paper $15.00 (0-02-726457-2). 112pp. A stranger appears at the cabin door of Nathan and his sister Molly with a locket that could have come only from their missing father. (Rev: BCCB 5/90; BL 5/15/90; SLJ 5/90*)

**7677** Duey, Kathleen. *Anisett Lundberg: California, 1851* (4–7). Series: American Diaries. 1996, Simon & Schuster paper $3.99 (0-689-80386-9). 139pp. An adventure story featuring Anisett and her family, who live in the fold-mining region of California in 1851. (Rev: HB 9–10/96; SLJ 12/96)

**7678** Duey, Kathleen. *Willow Chase: Kansas Territory, 1847* (4–6). 1997, Simon & Schuster paper $3.99 (0-689-81355-4). 144pp. When accidently swept down the Platte River, Willow Chase must find her way back to the family's wagon train. (Rev: BL 3/1/97; SLJ 4/97)

**7679** Fleischman, Paul. *The Borning Room* (5–8). 1991, HarperCollins paper $4.95 (0-06-447099-7). 80pp. In Georgina's family house in Ohio, there is a room for birthing and a room for dying as the images of life unfold. (Rev: BCCB 9/91; BL 10/1/91*; HB 11–12/91*)

**7680** Fleischman, Sid. *Jim Ugly* (4–6). Illus. by Joseph A. Smith. 1992, Greenwillow $16.00 (0-688-10886-5). 144pp. In the time of the Old West, Jake — accompanied by his dad's mongrel dog — sets off in search of his missing father. (Rev: BCCB 3/92*; BL 5/15/92; SLJ 4/92)

**7681** Gaeddert, Louann. *Hope* (5–7). 1995, Simon & Schuster $14.00 (0-689-80128-9). 165pp. While their father is panning for gold in California, Hope and brother John move to a Shaker community. (Rev: BL 12/15/95; SLJ 11/95)

**7682** Glass, Andrew. *A Right Fine Life: Kit Carson on the Santa Fe Trail* (3–5). Illus. 1997, Holiday LB $16.95 (0-8234-1326-8). 48pp. This tall tale tells about 16-year-old Kit Carson's first journey west and his many adventures along the way. (Rev: BL 2/1/98; SLJ 2/98)

**7683** Gregory, Kristiana. *Across the Wide and Lonesome Prairie: The Oregon Trail Diary of Hattie Campbell* (4–7). Illus. Series: Dear America. 1997, Scholastic $9.95 (0-590-22651-7). 149pp. In a diary format, this novel chronicles the hardships that pioneers endured during a trip west on the Oregon Trail. (Rev: SLJ 3/97)

**7684** Gutman, Bill. *Along the Dangerous Trail* (4–7). 1993, HarperCollins paper $3.50 (0-06-106152-2). 176pp. These exciting adventures of the Gregg family on the Oregon Trail in 1848 are continued in *Across the Wild River* (1993). (Rev: BL 3/1/94)

**7685** Hahn, Mary D. *The Gentleman Outlaw and Me-Eli: A Story of the Old West* (5–8). 1996, Clarion $14.95 (0-395-73083-X). 224pp. In frontier days, Eliza, masquerading as a boy, travels west in search of her father. (Rev: BCCB 4/96; BL 4/1/96; HB 9–10/96; SLJ 5/96)

**7686** Harvey, Brett. *Cassie's Journey: Going West in the 1860s* (2–4). Illus. by Deborah Kogan Ray. 1988, Holiday LB $15.95 (0-8234-0684-9). 40pp. Cassie and her pioneer family travel to California from Illinois. (Rev: BCCB 7–8/88; BL 5/15/88; HB 7–8/88)

**7687** Henry, Joanne L. *A Clearing in the Forest: A Story About a Real Settler Boy* (3–5). Illus. by Charles Robinson. 1992, Macmillan $14.95 (0-02-743671-3). 44pp. Action highlights this historical novel about growing up in Indianapolis in the 1830s. (Rev: BCCB 6/92; BL 3/1/92; SLJ 3/92)

**7688** Hoff, Carol. *Johnny Texas* (4–6). Illus. by Bob Meyers. 1992, Hendrick-Long paper $12.00 (0-937460-81-8). 160pp. Texas history is interwoven into this story of a pioneer German family. A reissue.

**7689** Holland, Isabelle. *The Journey Home* (4–6). 1990, Scholastic $13.95 (0-590-43110-2). 192pp. Two orphaned girls start life anew in the second half

of the 19th century when they are adopted by a couple in Kansas. (Rev: BCCB 12/90; SLJ 12/90)

**7690** Holling, Holling C. *Tree in the Trail* (4–7). Illus. by author. 1942, Houghton $17.95 (0-395-18228-X); paper $8.95 (0-395-54534-X). 64pp. The history of the Santa Fe Trail, described through the life of a cottonwood tree, a 200-year-old landmark to travelers and a symbol of peace to the Indians.

**7691** Hooks, William H. *Pioneer Cat* (2–4). Illus. by Charles Robinson. 1988, Random LB $6.99 (0-394-92038-4); paper $3.99 (0-394-82038-X). 64pp. Kate smuggles a cat aboard the prairie schooner as the family heads west on the Oregon Trail. (Rev: BCCB 12/88; BL 1/15/89; SLJ 3/89)

**7692** Howard, Ellen. *The Chickenhouse House* (3–5). Illus. by Nancy Oleksa. 1991, Macmillan LB $13.00 (0-689-31695-X). 64pp. A pioneer family builds a home on the prairie. (Rev: BCCB 5/91; BL 5/15/91; HB 7–8/91; SLJ 7/91)

**7693** Irwin, Hadley. *Jim-Dandy* (5–7). 1994, Macmillan LB $15.00 (0-689-50594-9). 144pp. When his father sells his horse to the army, Caleb joins Custer's Cavalry to be near his pet in this story set in the Kansas frontier. (Rev: BCCB 4/94; BL 4/15/94; HB 7–8/94; SLJ 5/94)

**7694** Jackson, Dave, and Neta Jackson. *Abandoned on the Wild Frontier* (4–6). 1995, Bethany paper $5.99 (1-55661-468-3). 144pp. Based on fact, this is the story of a young boy's search for his mother, who has been carried off by Indians after the War of 1812. (Rev: BL 9/1/95)

**7695** Karr, Kathleen. *Go West, Young Women!* (4–6). Series: The Petticoat Party. 1996, HarperCollins LB $14.89 (0-06-027152-3). 202pp. A pioneer story about being on the Oregon Trail in 1845, as told by 12-year-old Phoebe Brown. (Rev: BCCB 2/96; SLJ 5/96)

**7696** Kent, Peter. *Quest for the West: In Search of Gold* (3–6). Illus. 1997, Millbrook LB $21.40 (0-7613-0302-2). 32pp. The Hornik family leave their Czech homeland in 1849 to find a new life in the United States in this novel with excellent pen-and-ink and watercolor illustrations. (Rev: BL 12/1/97)

**7697** Kerr, Rita. *Texas Footprints* (4–7). Illus. 1988, Eakin $12.95 (0-89015-676-X). 80pp. A tale of the author's great-great-grandparents who went to Texas in 1823. (Rev: BL 3/1/89)

**7698** Kramer, Sydelle. *Wagon Train* (1–3). Illus. by Deborah Kogan Ray. Series: All Aboard Reading. 1997, Putnam paper $3.95 (0-448-41334-5). 48pp. This easy-to-read book follows a family as it crosses the United States wagon in 1848. (Rev: BL 2/1/98)

**7699** Kudlinski, Kathleen V. *Facing West: A Story of the Oregon Trail* (3–5). Series: Once upon America. 1994, Viking paper $12.99 (0-670-85451-4). 49pp.

Overprotected Ben learns self-reliance on the trail when his family moves west in 1845. (Rev: SLJ 8/94)

**7700** Laurgaard, Rachel K. *Patty Reed's Doll: The Story of the Donner Party* (3–6). Illus. by Elizabeth Michaels. 1989, Tomato Enterprises paper $7.95 (0-9617357-2-4). 144pp. A fantasy seen through the eyes of a doll about a survivor of the Donner Party. A reissue. (Rev: SLJ 11/89)

**7701** Lawlor, Laurie. *Addie Across the Prairie* (3–5). Illus. 1986, Whitman $12.95 (0-8075-0165-4); Pocket paper $3.99 (0-671-70147-9). 128pp. Nine-year-old Addie learns about sod houses and curious Indians as her family travels cross-country to the Dakota Territory. (Rev: BL 8/86; SLJ 10/86)

**7702** Lawlor, Laurie. *Addie's Dakota Winter* (3–5). Illus. by Toby Gowing. 1989, Whitman LB $12.95 (0-8075-0171-9). 160pp. Addie is disappointed when her only possibility for a friend turns out to be a boastful immigrant child. (Rev: BCCB 12/89; BL 11/15/89; SLJ 1/90)

**7703** Lawlor, Laurie. *Addie's Long Summer* (5–7). Illus. by Toby Gowing. 1992, Whitman LB $12.95 (0-8075-0167-0). 174pp. Addie is disappointed to find that her cousins do not fit into pioneer farm life. (Rev: BCCB 11/92; BL 8/92; SLJ 11/92)

**7704** Lawlor, Laurie. *George on His Own* (4–6). Illus. by Toby Gowing. 1993, Albert Whitman LB $12.95 (0-8075-2823-4). 192pp. In frontier days in South Dakota, young George is so angry when his father threatens to sell his trombone that he leaves home and joins a traveling theater troupe. (Rev: BCCB 6/93; BL 9/1/93; SLJ 7/93)

**7705** Lawlor, Laurie. *Gold in the Hills* (4–6). 1995, Walker $15.95 (0-8027-8371-6). 152pp. When their father sets out to find gold, Hattie and her brother must stay with bitter, tyrannical cousin Tirzah in this novel set in Colorado during frontier days. (Rev: BCCB 7–8/95; BL 6/1–15/95; SLJ 8/95)

**7706** Leland, Dorothy K. *Sallie Fox: The Story of a Pioneer Girl* (4–6). 1995, Tomato Enterprises paper $8.95 (0-9617357-6-7). 115pp. A fictionalized account of the trek of 12-year-old Sallie Fox by wagon train with her family from Iowa to California in the mid 1800s. (Rev: SLJ 2/96)

**7707** Love, D. Anne. *Bess's Log Cabin Quilt* (2–5). Illus. by Ronald Himler. 1995, Holiday $15.95 (0-8234-1178-8). 72pp. In frontier Oregon, Bess hopes that by winning a quilt contest she can help ease her family's financial problems. (Rev: BCCB 6/95; BL 2/15/95; SLJ 6/95)

**7708** Love, D. Anne. *Dakota Spring* (3–5). Illus. 1995, Holiday $14.95 (0-8234-1189-3). 64pp. Caroline's stiff, unbending grandmother comes to help on their Dakota prairie farm in this novel set in the late 1800s. (Rev: BL 11/15/95; SLJ 11/95)

**7709** Loveday, John. *Goodbye, Buffalo Sky* (5–8). 1997, Simon & Schuster $16.00 (0-689-81370-8). 176pp. Two girls are kidnapped by a vengeful Sioux warrior in this exciting adventure set in the Great Plains during the 1870s. (Rev: BL 1/1–15/98; SLJ 11/97)

**7710** MacBride, Roger L. *In the Land of the Big Red Apple* (3–7). Illus. by David Gilleece. 1995, Harper-Collins LB $14.89 (0-06-024964-1). 352pp. In the mid-1890s, the farm at Rocky Ridge, where Rose Wilder Lane is growing up, gradually prospers. (Rev: BL 5/15/95; SLJ 9/95)

**7711** MacBride, Roger L. *Little Farm in the Ozarks* (3–6). Illus. 1994, HarperCollins LB $15.89 (0-06-024246-9); paper $4.95 (0-06-440510-9). 304pp. Based on the journals of Rose Wilder Lane, this novel tells about the Wilder family's first spring and summer in Mansfield, Missouri. (Rev: BL 5/1/94)

**7712** MacBride, Roger L. *Little House on Rocky Edge* (3–7). Illus. by David Gilleece. 1993, Harper-Collins paper $4.95 (0-06-440478-1). 304pp. This reworking of Laura Ingalls Wilder's material tells the story from Rose's perspective of the Wilder family's move from South Dakota to Missouri. This is the first part of a projected 5-part series. (Rev: BL 6/1–15/93)

**7713** MacBride, Roger L. *New Dawn on Rocky Ridge* (4–7). Illus. Series: Rocky Ridge. 1997, HarperCollins $15.95 (0-06-024971-4); paper $4.95 (0-06-440581-8). 320pp. This part of the Wilder family story covers 1900–1903 and focuses on Rose's difficult early teen years. (Rev: BL 11/1/97; SLJ 2/98)

**7714** MacBride, Roger L. *On the Other Side of the Hill* (3–5). Series: Rocky Ridge Years. 1995, Harper-Collins LB $14.89 (0-06-024968-4). 347pp. In this story about Rose Wilder's childhood on a farm, she has many experiences, some dramatic — like surviving a cyclone — and others very ordinary — like a cider pressing. (Rev: SLJ 12/95)

**7715** McGugan, Jim. *Josepha: A Prairie Boy's Story* (2–5). Illus. by Murray Kimber. 1994, Chronicle $11.95 (0-8118-0802-5). 32pp. An immigrant boy is ridiculed by his much younger classmates when he goes to school to learn English in the turn-of-the-century West. (Rev: BCCB 11/94; BL 10/1/94; SLJ 11/94)

**7716** McKissack, Patricia. *Run Away Home* (4–7). 1997, Scholastic $14.95 (0-590-46751-4). 176pp. In 1888 rural Alabama, a young African American girl helps shelter a fugitive Apache boy. (Rev: BL 10/1/97; HB 11–12/97; SLJ 11/97)

**7717** MacLachlan, Patricia. *Sarah, Plain and Tall* (3–5). Illus. by Marcia Sewall. 1985, HarperCollins LB $14.89 (0-06-024102-0); paper $4.95 (0-06-440205-3). 64pp. Two children wait on the prairie for the arrival of their new stepmother, who has answered their father's ad for a wife. Newbery Medal winner, 1986. (Rev: BCCB 5/85; BL 5/1/89; SLJ 5/85)

**7718** MacLachlan, Patricia. *Skylark* (4–6). 1994, HarperCollins LB $12.89 (0-06-023333-8). 64pp. In this sequel to *Sarah, Plain and Tall* (1985), Sarah goes back east with her children, leaving Jacob, her husband, to take care of the farm. (Rev: BCCB 2/94; BL 1/1/94; HB 7–8/94; SLJ 3/94)

**7719** Miller, Robert H. *A Pony for Jeremiah* (3–6). Illus. by Nneka Bennett. 1996, Silver Burdett LB $12.95 (0-382-39459-3); paper $4.95 (0-382-39460-7). 64pp. A historial novel about a runaway slave and his family who settle in Nebraska. (Rev: BL 2/15/97; SLJ 3/97)

**7720** Milligan, Bryce. *With the Wind, Kevin Dolan: A Novel of Ireland and Texas* (5–7). Illus. 1987, Corona paper $7.95 (0-931722-45-4). 194pp. The story of Kevin and Tom, brothers who leave the famine in Ireland in the 1830s and head for America. (Rev: BL 8/87; SLJ 9/87)

**7721** Moeri, Louise. *Save Queen of Sheba* (5–7). 1990, Avon paper $3.50 (0-380-71154-0). 112pp. Young David survives a wagon train massacre and must take care of his young sister.

**7722** Nixon, Joan Lowery. *Circle of Love* (4–6). 1997, Delacorte $15.95 (0-385-32280-1). 176pp. While waiting for her boyfriend to marry her, Frances agrees to chaperone 30 children to the West, where they hope to find families. (Rev: BL 4/1/97; SLJ 5/97)

**7723** Nixon, Joan Lowery. *A Family Apart* (4–5). 1987, Bantam $13.95 (0-553-05432-5); paper $4.50 (0-553-27478-3). 176pp. The story of Frances Mary and the other Kelly children sent to St. Louis in the mid-19th century to live with frontier families. A sequel is: *Caught in the Act* (1988). (Rev: BCCB 10/87; BL 9/15/87; SLJ 11/87)

**7724** Nixon, Joan Lowery. *Lucy's Wish* (3–6). 1998, Delacorte $9.95 (0-385-32293-3). 104pp. Ten-year-old Lucy faces disappointment when she is put on the Orphan Train to find a new family in the West during the 1850s. (Rev: BL 12/15/97)

**7725** O'Dell, Scott. *Streams to the River, River to the Sea: A Novel of Sacagawea* (5–8). 1986, Houghton $16.00 (0-395-40430-4); Fawcett paper $4.50 (0-449-70244-8). 191pp. A fictionalized portrait of the real-life Indian woman who traveled west with Lewis and Clark on their famous journey. (Rev: BL 3/15/86; HB 9–10/86)

**7726** Paulsen, Gary. *Call Me Francis Tucket* (5–8). 1995, Delacorte $15.95 (0-385-32116-3). 97pp. Fifteen-year-old Francis becomes separated from the wagon train to Oregon that he has joined and later becomes hopelessly lost in the wilderness. (Rev: BL 7/95; SLJ 6/95)

**7727** Paulsen, Gary. *Tucket's Ride* (4–7). 1997, Delacorte $15.95 (0-385-32199-6). 86pp. Fifteen-year-old Francis Tucket faces hair-raising dangers while traveling into the Old West with orphans Lottie and Billy. (Rev: BL 12/15/96; SLJ 3/97)

**7728** Rinaldi, Ann. *The Second Bend in the River* (5–8). 1997, Scholastic $15.95 (0-590-74258-2). 288pp. A novel set in colonial Ohio in which the Indian chief Tecumseh falls in love with a white settler, Rebecca Galloway. (Rev: BCCB 3/97; BL 2/15/97; SLJ 6/97)

**7729** Roberts, Willo Davis. *Jo and the Bandit* (4–6). 1992, Macmillan $15.00 (0-689-31745-X). 192pp. Jo's life is in danger when the bandits who robbed the stagecoach in which she was a passenger find out she can draw accurate likenesses of them. (Rev: BL 6/1/92; SLJ 7/92)

**7730** Rounds, Glen. *Sod Houses on the Great Plains* (K–3). Illus. 1995, Holiday LB $15.95 (0-8234-1162-1). 32pp. An illustrated account of the construction and utilization of a sod house, home of many prairie pioneers. (Rev: BCCB 3/95; BL 3/1/95*; HB 5–6/95; SLJ 3/95*) [693]

**7731** Ryan, Pam M. *Riding Freedom* (3–6). Illus. 1998, Scholastic $15.95 (0-590-95766-X). 144pp. Based on fact, this is the story of a girl who lived her life as a man in mid-19th-century America. (Rev: BL 1/1–15/98; SLJ 3/98)

**7732** Shaw, Janet. *Happy Birthday Kirsten!* (3–5). Illus. 1987, Pleasant LB $12.95 (0-937295-88-4); paper $5.95 (0-937295-33-7). 72pp. It is 1854 in Minnesota and Kirsten looks forward to the gift of a day off from household chores. Also use: *Changes for Kirsten; Kirsten Saves the Day* (both 1988). (Rev: BL 4/1/88)

**7733** Shaw, Janet. *Kirsten Learns a Lesson: A School Story* (3–5). Illus. 1986, Pleasant LB $12.95 (0-937295-82-5); paper $5.95 (0-937295-10-8). 72pp. Kirsten, a young immigrant girl, lives with her Swedish family in 1854 Minnesota. Others in this series are: *Kirsten's Surprise: A Christmas Story; Meet Kirsten: An American Girl* (both 1986). (Rev: BL 12/1/86)

**7734** Stevens, Carla. *Trouble for Lucy* (4–6). Illus. by Ronald Himler. 1979, Houghton paper $5.95 (0-89919-523-7). 80pp. Lucy's pup Finn causes trouble during a wagon trip to the Oregon Territory.

**7735** Thomas, Joyce C. *I Have Heard of a Land* (3–6). Illus. by Floyd Cooper. 1998, HarperCollins LB $14.89 (0-06-023478-4). 32pp. This tribute to the pioneer spirit tells, through the eyes of a black woman, what it was like to come to the untamed frontier, build a home, and put down roots. (Rev: BL 2/15/98*)

**7736** Travis, Lucille. *Redheaded Orphan* (4–7). 1995, Baker Book House paper $5.99 (0-8010-4023-X). 152pp. In 1864, Ben Abee and his family move from New York City to Minnesota, where Ben befriends orphaned Jamie. (Rev: BL 2/15/96)

**7737** Tripp, Valerie. *Meet Josefina: An American Girl* (3–5). Illus. Series: American Girls. 1997, Pleasant paper $5.95 (1-56247-515-0). 85pp. In this story set in 1824 on a Mexican ranch in present-day New Mexico, the young heroine helps manage the ranch after her mother's death. Also use *Josefina Learns a Lesson: A School Story* (1997). (Rev: BL 10/1/97; SLJ 12/97)

**7738** Turner, Ann. *Grasshopper Summer* (4–6). 1989, Troll paper $3.95 (0-8167-2262-5). 144pp. Sam's father moves his family from Kentucky to the Dakota Territory. (Rev: BCCB 4/89; BL 6/15/89)

**7739** Van Leeuwen, Jean. *Bound for Oregon* (4–6). Illus. 1994, Dial paper $14.89 (0-8037-1527-7). 176pp. Based on an actual journal, this novel tells of a family's adventures on the Oregon Trail in 1852. (Rev: BCCB 11/94; BL 10/1/94; SLJ 10/94)

**7740** Waddell, Martin. *Little Obie and the Flood* (3–6). Illus. 1992, Candlewick $13.95 (1-56402-106-8). 80pp. The story of Obie and his grandparents, who have little worldly goods but always room for one more. (Rev: BL 9/1/92; SLJ 11/92)

**7741** Waddell, Martin. *Little Obie and the Kidnap* (3–5). Illus. by Elsie Lennox. 1994, Candlewick $14.95 (1-56402-352-4). 79pp. A pioneer story in which a community unites to care for 2 orphan boys who are found with their dead mother in a stranded wagon. (Rev: SLJ 10/94)

**7742** Wallace, Bill. *Red Dog* (4–6). 1987, Holiday $15.95 (0-8234-0650-4); Pocket paper $3.99 (0-671-70141-X). 192pp. Adam and his dog Ruff defy gold speculators in this story of the Wyoming Territory in the 1860s. (Rev: BL 6/1/87; SLJ 6–7/87)

**7743** Welch, Catherine A. *Clouds of Terror* (2–4). Illus. by Laurie K. Johnson. 1994, Carolrhoda LB $18.60 (0-87614-771-6). 48pp. The harm caused by hordes of grasshoppers is depicted in this story set on a Minnesota farm during the 1870s. (Rev: BL 9/15/94; SLJ 8/94)

**7744** Whalen, Sharla S. *Friends on Ice* (3–5). Illus. 1997, ABDO paper $5.95 (1-56239-901-2). 64pp. This is a story about 4 friends growing up on the Illinois prairie in the 1890s and of their preparations for the Winter Entertainment festivities. (Rev: BL 2/1/98)

**7745** Whelan, Gloria. *The Indian School* (3–5). Illus. 1996, HarperCollins LB $13.89 (0-06-027078-0). 80pp. In frontier days, a young girl learns about Indian culture when she helps her aunt and uncle operate a mission school. (Rev: BL 10/15/96; SLJ 11/96)

**7746** Whelan, Gloria. *Next Spring an Oriole* (2–4). Illus. 1987, Random LB $6.99 (0-394-99125-7); paper $3.99 (0-394-89125-2). 64pp. The story of 10-year-old Libby who journeys to Michigan from Virginia in a covered wagon with her family in 1837. (Rev: BCCB 10/87; BL 10/1/87)

**7747** Wilkes, Maria D. *Little House in Brookfield* (3–6). Illus. by Dan Andreasen. Series: The Brookfield Years. 1996, HarperCollins LB $14.89 (0-06-026462-4); paper $4.95 (0-06-440610-5). 298pp. This spinoff from the *Little House* books tells of the childhood in Brookfield, Wisconsin, of Caroline Quiner, who much later would become the mother of Laura Ingalls Wilder. (Rev: SLJ 8/96)

**7748** Wilkes, Maria D. *Little Town at the Crossroads* (3–6). Illus. 1997, HarperCollins LB $14.89 (0-06-026996-0). 368pp. The fictionalized story of Laura Ingalls Wilder's mother and her growing up in Brookfield, Wisconsin, in 1846–1847. (Rev: BL 4/15/97; SLJ 7/97)

**7749** Wills, Patricia. *Danger Along the Ohio* (4–7). 1997, Clarion $15.00 (0-395-77044-0). 192pp. This action-packed historical novel set in Ohio in 1795 tells how Amos and his younger brother and sister are captured by Indians. (Rev: BCCB 5/97; BL 5/1/97; SLJ 5/97)

**7750** Wisler, G. Clifton. *Jericho's Journey* (4–6). 1993, Dutton paper $13.99 (0-525-67428-4). 144pp. Young Jericho tells of his family's adventures relocating from Tennessee to Texas in pioneer days. (Rev: BL 9/1/93; SLJ 10/93)

**7751** Woodruff, Elvira. *Dear Levi: Letters from the Overland Trail* (4–6). Illus. 1994, Knopf $15.00 (0-679-84641-7). 119pp. In his letters home, Austin chronicles the dangers and disasters that were part of traveling with a wagon train on the Oregon Trail in the 1850s. (Rev: BCCB 9/94; BL 7/94; HB 9–10/94; SLJ 8/94)

### THE CIVIL WAR

**7752** Beatty, Patricia. *Who Comes with Cannons?* (5–7). 1992, Morrow $15.00 (0-688-11028-2). 192pp. The Civil War brings danger to Truth Hopkins and her Quaker family because they are pacifists. (Rev: BCCB 10/92; BL 1/1/93; HB 1–2/93; SLJ 10/92)

**7753** Brill, Marlene T. *Diary of a Drummer Boy* (4–7). 1998, Millbrook LB $21.90 (0-7613-0118-6). 48pp. Using a diary format, this novel tells of a 12-year-old's experiences as a drummer in the Union Army during the Civil War. (Rev: BL 3/1/98)

**7754** Bunting, Eve. *The Blue and the Gray* (3–5). Illus. by Ned Bittinger. 1996, Scholastic $14.95 (0-590-60197-0). 32pp. Using free verse, the author recreates a Civil War battle and points out what we have learned from this terrible conflict. (Rev: BCCB 2/97; BL 11/15/96; SLJ 12/96)

**7755** Donahue, John. *An Island Far from Home* (4–7). 1994, Carolrhoda LB $21.27 (0-87614-859-3). 180pp. Joshua, a Union supporter, forms an unusual friendship through corresponding with a young Southern soldier who is a prisoner of war. (Rev: BCCB 2/95; BL 2/15/95; SLJ 2/95)

**7756** Forman, James D. *Becca's Story* (5–8). 1992, Macmillan LB $15.00 (0-684-19332-9). 192pp. The story of the courtship between Becca, in Michigan, and Alex, in the Union Army, during the Civil War. (Rev: BL 12/1/92)

**7757** Freedman, Florence B. *Two Tickets to Freedom: The True Story of Ellen and William Craft, Fugitive Slaves* (4–8). Illus. by Ezra Jack Keats. 1971, Bedrick $12.95 (0-87226-330-4); paper $5.95 (0-87226-221-9). 96pp. An exciting story of slavery, escape, and pursuit that is based on fact. A reissue.

**7758** Hoobler, Thomas, and Dorothy Hoobler. *Sally Bradford: The Story of a Rebel Girl* (4–7). Illus. 1997, Silver Burdett LB $14.95 (0-382-39258-2); paper $4.95 (0-382-39259-0). 128pp. The Civil War changes the lives of Sally Bradford and her family, who operate a farm without slaves in Norfolk, Virginia. (Rev: BL 6/1–15/97; SLJ 8/97)

**7759** Houston, Gloria. *Mountain Valor* (4–7). Illus. by Thomas B. Allen. 1994, Putnam $15.95 (0-399-22519-6). 224pp. In this Civil War novel, Valor lives up to her name by recovering the family's supplies after they have been stolen by Yankee soldiers. (Rev: BCCB 6/94; BL 4/1/94; SLJ 6/94)

**7760** Hunt, Irene. *Across Five Aprils* (6–8). 1993, Silver Burdett paper $5.45 (0-8136-7202-3). 100pp. A young boy's experiences during the Civil War in the backwoods of southern Illinois. One brother joins the Union forces, the other the Confederacy, and the family is divided.

**7761** Karr, Kathleen. *Spy in the Sky* (2–4). Illus. by Thomas F. Yezerski. Series: Hyperion Chapters. 1997, Hyperion LB $14.49 (0-7868-2239-2); paper $3.95 (0-7868-1165-X). 60pp. An exciting, simple novel that uses as background the exploits of Thaddeus Lowe and his Balloon Corps on the Union side of the Civil War. (Rev: SLJ 8/97)

**7762** Keith, Harold. *Rifles for Watie* (6–8). 1991, HarperCollins LB $14.89 (0-690-04907-2); paper $4.95 (0-06-447030-X). 332pp. Life of a Union soldier and spy fighting the Civil War in the West. Newbery Medal winner, 1958.

**7763** O'Dell, Scott. *Sing Down the Moon* (5–8). 1970, Houghton $16.00 (0-395-10919-1); Dell paper $3.99 (0-440-97975-7). 138pp. The tragic forced march of the Indians to Fort Sumter in 1864, told by a young Navajo girl.

**7764** Polacco, Patricia. *Pink and Say* (K–5). Illus. 1994, Putnam $15.95 (0-399-22671-0). 32pp. Based on a true incident during the Civil War, this book tells of the friendship of 2 Union soldiers: Say, a white man who is rescued by a black man, Pinkus, known as Pink. (Rev: BCCB 9/94; BL 9/1/94; HB 11–12/94; SLJ 10/94*)

**7765** Porter, Connie. *Addy Learns a Lesson* (3–6). Illus. by Melodye Rosales. Series: American Girls Collection. 1993, Pleasant LB $12.95 (1-56247-078-7); paper $5.95 (1-56247-077-9). 70pp. In the year 1864, young Addy and her mother try to escape slavery by fleeing to the North after her father is sold again and they are separated. (Rev: BL 8/93; SLJ 1/94)

**7766** Reeder, Carolyn. *Across the Lines* (4–7). 1997, Simon & Schuster $16.00 (0-689-81133-0). 224pp. Edward and his slave friend, Simon, are separated when Yankees capture their Virginia plantation in this Civil War novel. (Rev: BCCB 6/97; BL 4/1/97*; SLJ 6/97)

**7767** Reeder, Carolyn. *Shades of Gray* (4–7). 1989, Macmillan LB $15.00 (0-02-775810-9). 152pp. The story of 12-year-old Will, the last surviving member of his family from the South during the Civil War. (Rev: BCCB 1/90; BL 1/15/90; HB 3–4/90; SLJ 1/90)

**7768** Stolz, Mary. *A Ballad of the Civil War* (4–6). Illus. 1997, HarperCollins LB $13.89 (0-06-027363-1). 64pp. Based on a Civil War ballad, this is the story of 2 Southern brothers who enlist on opposite sides. (Rev: BL 10/1/97; SLJ 2/98)

**7769** Wisler, G. Clifton. *The Drummer Boy of Vicksburg* (4–6). 1997, Dutton paper $15.99 (0-525-67537-X). 144pp. The story of a drummer boy who is in the Union Army during the Civil War. (Rev: BL 12/1/96; SLJ 3/97)

**7770** Wisler, G. Clifton. *Mr. Lincoln's Drummer* (5–7). 1994, Dutton paper $15.99 (0-525-67463-2). 144pp. Eleven-year-old Willie, a Vermonter, joins the Union Army as a drummer boy when his father enlists. (Rev: BCCB 1/95; BL 1/15/95)

**7771** Wisler, G. Clifton. *Mustang Flats* (5–8). 1997, Dutton paper $14.99 (0-525-67544-2). 128pp. Abby wants to help his family when his father returns from the Civil War a broken, bitter man. (Rev: BL 8/97; SLJ 7/97)

### RECONSTRUCTION TO WORLD WAR II, 1865–1941

**7772** Adler, Susan S. *Meet Samantha: An American Girl* (3–5). Illus. 1986, Pleasant LB $12.95 (0-937295-80-9); paper $5.95 (0-937295-04-3). 72pp. Samantha is an orphan living with her wealthy grandmother in the America of 1904. Two others in the series are: *Samantha Learns a Lesson; Samantha's Surprise* (both 1986). (Rev: BL 12/1/86)

**7773** Alter, Judith. *Luke and the Van Zandt County War* (5–8). Illus. 1984, Christian Univ. $10.95 (0-912646-88-8). 132pp. Life in Reconstruction Texas as seen through the eyes of 2 14-year-olds. (Rev: SLJ 3/85)

**7774** Bader, Bonnie. *East Side Story* (3–5). Series: Stories of the States. 1993, Silver Moon LB $13.95 (1-881889-22-X). 72pp. The story of an 11-year-old Jewish immigrant girl and her sister, both of whom work in the Triangle Shirtwaist Factory in New York City during the early 1900s. (Rev: SLJ 2/94)

**7775** Bartoletti, Susan Campbell. *Dancing with Dziadziu* (3–6). Illus. by Annika Nelson. 1997, Harcourt $15.00 (0-15-200675-3). 40pp. Gabriella's grandmother, now in failing health, remembers her experiences as an immigrant in this country and the joys of dancing with her husband. (Rev: BCCB 5/97; BL 3/15/97*; SLJ 5/97)

**7776** Beatty, Patricia. *Sarah and Me and the Lady from the Sea* (4–6). Illus. 1989, Morrow $11.95 (0-688-08045-6). 192pp. The focus is on the younger members of the Kimball family, who live on a peninsula in Washington State during the 1890s. (Rev: BCCB 1/90; BL 9/1/89*; HB 1–2/90; SLJ 11/89)

**7777** Blos, Joan W. *Brooklyn Doesn't Rhyme* (5–7). Illus. 1994, Scribners $15.00 (0-684-19694-8). 96pp. A young girl narrates this episodic story about a Polish-Jewish family new to New York City in the early 1900s. (Rev: BCCB 11/94; BL 9/15/94; HB 9–10/94; SLJ 9/94)

**7778** Bradley, Kimberly Brubaker. *Ruthie's Gift* (3–5). Illus. 1998, Delacorte $14.95 (0-385-32525-8). 143pp. This honest, moving novel describes a girl's feelings and actions as she grows up on a farm in Indiana around 1915. (Rev: BL 1/1–15/98; SLJ 2/98*)

**7779** Bunting, Eve. *Dandelions* (2–4). Illus. by Greg Shed. 1995, Harcourt $16.00 (0-15-200050-X). 48pp. Zoe compares the dandelions she sees growing wild in a meadow to her family, which has just traveled west to the Nebraska Territory by covered wagon. (Rev: BCCB 9/95; BL 9/15/95; SLJ 11/95*)

**7780** Burandt, Harriet, and Shelley Dale. *Tales from the Homeplace: Adventures of a Texas Farm Girl* (4–8). 1997, Holt $14.95 (0-8050-5075-2). 158pp. A family story that takes place on a Texas cotton farm during the Depression and features a spunky heroine, 12-year-old Irene, and her 6 brothers and sisters. (Rev: BCCB 7–8/97; HB 5–6/97; SLJ 4/97*)

**7781** Christiansen, Candace. *The Ice Horse* (3–5). Illus. by Thomas Locker. 1993, Dial paper $15.89 (0-8037-1401-7). 32pp. Jack recalls that, during his boyhood in the Hudson River Valley, he participated in the winter's ice harvest and escaped death when he fell through the ice. (Rev: BL 11/15/93; SLJ 10/93)

**7782** Cochrane, Patricia A. *Purely Rosie Pearl* (5–7). 1996, Delacorte $14.95 (0-385-32193-7). 136pp. The story of the hardships and heartbreak suffered by Rosie Pearl and her family, who are migrant workers during the Great Depression. (Rev: BCCB 5/96; BL 1/1–15/96; SLJ 3/96)

**7783** Crofford, Emily. *A Place to Belong* (5–7). Illus. 1994, Carolrhoda LB $19.95 (0-87614-808-9). 160pp. During the Depression, clubfooted Talmadge and his family lose their home and must become cotton pickers in Arkansas. (Rev: BCCB 7–8/94; BL 5/15/94; SLJ 6/94)

**7784** Cross, Gillian. *The Great American Elephant Chase* (5–8). 1993, Holiday $15.95 (0-8234-1016-1). 194pp. A heartwarming story of a lonely orphan and his journey with an elephant in 1881 America. (Rev: BCCB 6/93; BL 3/15/93*; SLJ 5/93*)

**7785** De Angeli, Marguerite. *Copper-Toed Boots* (3–6). Illus. by author. 1996, Wayne State Univ. Pr. paper $15.95 (0-814-32654-4). 96pp. American family life in the early 20th century.

**7786** DeClements, Barthe. *The Bite of the Gold Bug: A Story of the Alaskan Gold Rush* (3–6). Illus. by Dan Andreasen. Series: Once upon America. 1994, Puffin paper $4.99 (0-140-36081-6). 64pp. The story of 12-year-old Bucky who spends 6 months in the gold fields with his father and uncle. (Rev: BCCB 5/92; BL 5/15/92; SLJ 8/92)

**7787** Denenberg, Barry. *So Far from Home: The Diary of Mary Driscoll, an Irish Mill Girl* (4–8). 1997, Scholastic $9.95 (0-590-92667-5). 176pp. Using a diary format, this novel tells the story of Mary Driscoll's journey to the United States from Ireland and her ordeals as a worker in a Massachusetts textile mill in the 1800s. (Rev: BL 12/15/97; SLJ 10/97)

**7788** Ducey, Jean Sparks. *The Bittersweet Time* (4–6). 1995, Eerdmans $13.00 (0-8028-5096-0). 115pp. At the beginning of the Great Depression, a seventh-grade girl must get a job to help support her family. (Rev: BL 6/1–15/95; SLJ 5/95)

**7789** Duey, Kathleen. *Ellen Elizabeth Hawkins: Mobeetie, Texas, 1886* (4–7). Series: American Diaries, Book 6. 1997, Simon & Schuster paper $3.99 (0-689-81409-7). 141pp. In this novel set on a Texas cattle ranch in 1886, young Ellen wants to be a rancher in spite of her father's objections. (Rev: SLJ 8/97)

**7790** Duffy, James. *Radical Red* (5–8). 1993, Scribners $15.00 (0-684-19533-X). 160pp. Connor O'Shea joins a demonstration for women's rights when Susan B. Anthony comes to Albany in 1894. (Rev: BCCB 1/94; BL 12/1/93; SLJ 1/94)

**7791** Gregory, Kristiana. *Orphan Runaways* (5–7). 1998, Scholastic $15.95 (0-590-60366-3). 160pp. Two brothers run away from a San Francisco orphanage in 1879 to look for an uncle in the gold fields. (Rev: BL 2/15/98; SLJ 3/98)

**7792** Gross, Virginia T. *The Day It Rained Forever: A Story of the Johnstown Flood* (3–5). Illus. by Ronald Himler. Series: Once upon America. 1991, Viking paper $11.95 (0-670-83552-8). 64pp. The experiences of a family living in the mountains above Johnstown. (Rev: BCCB 4/91; BL 5/1/91; SLJ 8/91)

**7793** Hall, Donald. *The Milkman's Boy* (3–5). Illus. 1997, Walker LB $16.85 (0-8027-8465-8). 32pp. Around the time of World War I, Paul's father, a milkman, does not believe in the necessity of pasteurization. (Rev: BL 9/1/97; SLJ 9/97)

**7794** Hansen, Joyce. *I Thought My Soul Would Rise and Fly: The Diary of Patsy, a Freed Girl* (4–8). 1997, Scholastic $9.95 (0-590-84913-1). 208pp. In this novel in the form of a diary, a freed slave girl wonders what to do with her life after leaving the plantation. (Rev: BL 12/15/97; SLJ 11/97)

**7795** Hesse, Karen. *Letters from Rifka* (4–8). 1992, Holt $14.95 (0-8050-1964-2). 148pp. The harrowing story of a young Russian Jew's journey to America in 1919. (Rev: BCCB 10/92; HB 9–10/92*; SLJ 8/92*)

**7796** Hesse, Karen. *A Time of Angels* (5–8). 1995, Hyperion LB $16.49 (0-7868-2072-1). 224pp. Through the experience of Hannah and her sisters in New England, the terrible effects of the flu epidemic of 1918 are re-created. (Rev: BCCB 1/96; BL 12/1/95; SLJ 12/95)

**7797** Hoobler, Dorothy, and Thomas Hoobler. *Florence Robinson: The Story of a Jazz Age Girl* (3–6). Illus. by Robert Sauber. Series: Her Story. 1997, Silver Burdett LB $14.95 (0-382-39644-8); paper $4.95 (0-382-39645-6). 123pp. In the 1920s, an African American family moves north to Chicago in pursuit of freedom and a better life. (Rev: SLJ 8/97)

**7798** Houston, Gloria. *Littlejim* (4–6). Illus. by Thomas B. Allen. 1990, Putnam $14.95 (0-399-22220-0). 176pp. In this story of Appalachia, sensitive Littlejim tries to gain attention from his macho father. (Rev: BL 11/1/90; SLJ 2/91)

**7799** Houston, Gloria. *Littlejim's Dreams* (5–8). Illus. by Thomas B. Allen. 1997, Harcourt $16.00 (0-15-201509-4). 231pp. Littlejim wants to become a writer, but his father thinks he should be a farmer and logger like himself, in this novel set in Appalachia in 1920. A sequel to *Littlejim* (1990). (Rev: SLJ 7/97)

**7800** Hurwitz, Johanna. *Faraway Summer* (5–7). Illus. by Mary Azarian. 1998, Morrow $15.00 (0-688-15334-8). 112pp. In 1910, a Jewish orphan who lives in a tenement in New York City is thrilled at the

thought of spending 2 weeks on a farm in Vermont, thanks to the Fresh Air Fund. (Rev: BL 3/1/98)

**7801** Hyatt, Patricia Rusch. *Coast to Coast with Alice* (3–6). Illus. 1995, Carolrhoda LB $21.27 (0-87614-789-9). 72pp. A fictionalized account of the first automobile cross-country trip by a woman in 1909. (Rev: BCCB 9/95; BL 7/95; HB 11–12/95; SLJ 8/95)

**7802** Isaacs, Anne. *Treehouse Tales* (3–5). Illus. 1997, Dutton paper $14.99 (0-525-45611-2). 96pp. This book, set in Pennsylvania in the 1880s, contains 3 stories, one for each of the Barrett children. (Rev: BL 9/15/97; HB 9–10/97; SLJ 7/97)

**7803** Jones, J. Sydney. *Frankie* (5–7). 1997, Dutton paper $16.99 (0-525-67574-4). 192pp. At the time of the coal miners' strike in Ludlow, Colorado, a strange girl shows up in a novel that uses historical figures like Mother Jones as characters. (Rev: BL 12/15/97; SLJ 11/97)

**7804** Kalman, Esther. *Tchaikovsky Discovers America* (3–5). Illus. by Laura Fernandez and Rick Jacobson. 1995, Orchard $14.98 (0-531-06894-3). 32pp. Through a diary kept by 11-year-old Eugenia, the reader learns about Tchaikovsky's trip to the United States in 1891. (Rev: BL 3/15/95; HB 1–2/95; 5–6/95; SLJ 4/95)

**7805** Karr, Kathleen. *It Ain't Always Easy* (5–7). 1990, Farrar $14.95 (0-374-33645-8). 240pp. Eleven-year-old orphan Jack cares for a small runaway in the New York City slums in the 1880s. (Rev: BCCB 2/91; BL 10/15/90; HB 3–4/90; SLJ 12/90)

**7806** Kinsey-Warnock, Natalie. *The Night the Bells Rang* (4–7). Illus. by Leslie Bowman. 1991, Dutton paper $13.99 (0-525-65074-1). 80pp. Mason is tormented by a bully in rural Vermont during World War I. (Rev: BCCB 11/91; BL 11/15/91; HB 1–2/92; SLJ 2/92)

**7807** Klass, Sheila S. *A Shooting Star: A Novel About Annie Oakley* (5–7). 1996, Holiday $15.95 (0-8234-1279-2). 192pp. A fictionalized biography of the woman who rose from poverty to become a famous show business sharpshooter. (Rev: BL 12/15/96; SLJ 5/97)

**7808** Koller, Jackie F. *Nothing to Fear* (5–7). 1991, Harcourt $14.95 (0-15-200544-7); paper $8.00 (0-15-257582-0). 288pp. The focus is on Danny Garvey, first-generation Catholic Irish American, growing up in New York City in the 1930s. (Rev: BCCB 3/91; BL 3/1/91; SLJ 5/91)

**7809** Kudlinski, Kathleen V. *Shannon: A Chinatown Adventure* (3–6). Illus. by Bill Farnsworth. Series: Girlhood Journeys. 1996, Simon & Schuster $13.00 (0-689-81138-1); paper $5.99 (0-689-80984-0). 71pp. Set in San Francisco in 1880, this novel tells about a lonely Irish American girl and her efforts to help another girl she has seen in Chinatown. (Rev: BCCB 11/96; SLJ 9/96)

**7810** Kudlinski, Kathleen V. *Shannon, Lost and Found: San Francisco, 1880* (4–6). Illus. 1997, Simon & Schuster paper $5.99 (0-689-80988-3). 72pp. In 1880, Shannon and her friend Mi Ling become involved in collecting books for the new San Francisco Public Library. (Rev: BCCB 11/96; BL 5/1/97)

**7811** Lasky, Kathryn. *She's Wearing a Dead Bird on Her Head!* (3–5). Illus. by David Catrow. 1995, Hyperion LB $15.49 (0-7868-2052-7). 40pp. Two Boston ladies of the 1890's are so shocked by the fashion of wearing stuffed birds on hats that their protests result in the founding of the Massachusetts Audubon Society. (Rev: BL 10/15/95; SLJ 12/95)

**7812** Lawlor, Laurie. *Addie's Forever Friend* (2–4). Illus. Series: Addie. 1997, Albert Whitman LB $13.95 (0-8075-0164-6). 126pp. While Addie's father is out west looking for a homestead, she lives with an aunt and forms a friendship that changes her life. (Rev: BL 11/15/97; SLJ 2/98)

**7813** Lawlor, Laurie. *Come Away with Me: Book 1* (3–6). Series: Heartland. 1996, Pocket paper $3.99 (0-671-53716-4). 184pp. In the early 1900s in a small Wisconsin town, Moe has trouble growing up in a household with a controlling mother and older sister. Also use *Take to the Sky: Book 2* (1996). (Rev: SLJ 11/96)

**7814** Lehrman, Robert. *The Store That Mama Built* (4–7). 1992, Macmillan LB $13.95 (0-02-754632-2). 128pp. The story of a Russian immigrant family in Pennsylvania in 1917. (Rev: BCCB 5/92; BL 4/15/92; SLJ 7/92)

**7815** Lenski, Lois. *Strawberry Girl* (4–6). Illus. by author. 1945, HarperCollins LB $16.89 (0-397-30110-3); paper $4.95 (0-06-440585-0). 192pp. Lively adventures of a little girl, full of the flavor of the Florida lake country. Newbery Medal winner, 1946.

**7816** Littlefield, Holly. *Fire at the Triangle Factory* (4–6). Illus. 1996, Carolrhoda LB $18.60 (0-87614-868-2); paper $5.95 (0-87614-970-0). 48pp. Two young workers — Jewish Minnie and Catholic Tessa — work at the Triangle Shirtwaist Company at the time of the fire of 1911. (Rev: BL 8/96; SLJ 10/96)

**7817** Lowell, Susan. *I Am Lavina Cumming* (5–7). Illus. by Paul Mirocha. 1993, Milkweed $14.95 (0-915943-39-5); paper $6.95 (0-915943-77-8). 198pp. Ten-year-old Lavina encounters a number of challenging adjustments when she is sent to live with an aunt in San Francisco at the time of the earthquake. (Rev: BCCB 2/94; SLJ 1/94)

**7818** Marvin, Isabel R. *A Bride for Anna's Papa* (5–7). 1994, Milkweed paper $6.95 (0-915943-93-X). 136pp. In this novel set in Minnesota in 1907, 13-year-old Anna takes over managing the household after her mother's death and tries to find a new bride for her father. (Rev: SLJ 7/94)

**7819** Mayerson, Evelyn Wilde. *The Cat Who Escaped from Steerage* (4–6). 1990, Macmillan $15.00 (0-684-19209-8). 64pp. The story of a 2-week steerage voyage to the United States by Polish immigrants. (Rev: BL 10/1/90; HB 1–2/91; SLJ 2/91)

**7820** Medearis, Angela Shelf, reteller. *Treemonisha* (2–6). Illus. by Michael Bryant. 1995, Holt $15.95 (0-8050-1748-8). 37pp. Set in Arkansas in 1884, this book, based on Scott Joplin's opera, tells about the lives and hopes of former slaves. (Rev: BCCB 2/96; SLJ 1/96)

**7821** Miles, Betty. *I Would If I Could* (3–6). 1983, Avon paper $2.95 (0-380-63438-4). 128pp. During 1930, a 10-year-old girl spends a summer visiting her grandmother in rural Ohio.

**7822** Mills, Judith C. *The Stonehook Schooner* (2–4). Illus. by author. 1997, Firefly $14.95 (1-55013-653-4); paper $4.95 (1-55013-719-0). In this story, set on a ship in Lake Ontario in the early 1900s, young Matthew ties himself to the mast to help sight land during a violent storm. (Rev: SLJ 8/97)

**7823** Mitchell, Margaree King. *Uncle Jed's Barber Shop* (2–5). Illus. by James E. Ransome. 1993, Simon & Schuster $16.00 (0-671-76969-3); paper $5.99 (0-689-81913-7). 40pp. Uncle Jed, an African American barber in the 1920s, hopes to open his own shop, but his generosity always prevents him from saving enough money. (Rev: BCCB 9/93; BL 9/1/93; HB 11–12/93; SLJ 10/93)

**7824** Myers, Anna. *Graveyard Girl* (5–8). 1995, Walker $14.95 (0-8027-8260-4). 125pp. During the yellow-fever epidemic in Memphis in 1878, young Eli, whose family has been decimated, forms a friendship with Grace, who rings the bell for the dead at the graveyard. (Rev: SLJ 10/95)

**7825** Oneal, Zibby. *A Long Way to Go* (3–5). Illus. by Michael Dooling. 1992, Puffin paper $4.99 (0-14-032950-1). 64pp. Lila's life changes when her grandmother is jailed for fighting for women's rights in 1917 America. (Rev: BCCB 9/90; BL 3/1/90; HB 7–8/90; SLJ 9/90)

**7826** Partridge, Elizabeth. *Clara and the Hoodoo Man* (3–6). 1996, Dutton paper $14.99 (0-525-45403-9). 128pp. In turn-of-the-century mountain country, Clara must fetch the Hoodoo Man to help her sick sister. (Rev: BCCB 9/96; BL 9/1/96; HB 11–12/96; SLJ 7/96)

**7827** Peck, Robert Newton. *A Day No Pigs Would Die* (6–8). 1972, Knopf $24.00 (0-394-48235-2).

144pp. A gentle story about a 12-year-old Vermont farm boy.

**7828** Perez, N. A. *Breaker* (4–6). 1988, Houghton $16.00 (0-395-45537-5). 216pp. The story of a 14-year-old slate picker in a Pennsylvania coal-mining town. (Rev: BCCB 7–8/88; SLJ 8/88)

**7829** Porter, Connie. *Addy Saves the Day: A Summer Story* (2–4). Illus. by Bradford Brown. 1994, Pleasant paper $5.95 (1-56247-083-3). 59pp. In this novel set in Philadelphia in 1864, Addy, a former slave, and her family try to make money to search for relatives lost in the Civil War. Also use *Happy Birthday, Addy!* (1994). (Rev: BL 11/1/94; SLJ 11/94)

**7830** Rabe, Berniece. *Hiding Mr. McMulty* (5–8). 1997, Harcourt $18.00 (0-15-201330-X). 256pp. This novel, set in southeast Missouri in 1937, tells of both race and class conflicts as experienced by 11-year-old Rass. (Rev: BL 10/15/97; SLJ 12/97)

**7831** Ransom, Candice. *Fire in the Sky* (3–5). Illus. 1997, Carolrhoda LB $19.93 (0-87614-867-4). 72pp. In the late 1930s in New Jersey, Stenny becomes involved in the flight of the dirigible *Hindenburg* and the rescue operation after it burns. (Rev: BL 5/1/97; SLJ 8/97)

**7832** Ransom, Candice. *Jimmy Crack Corn* (3–5). Illus. 1994, Carolrhoda LB $19.95 (0-87614-786-4). 56pp. The beginning of the Great Depression as seen through the experiences of a farm family sinking into poverty with no hope for the future. (Rev: BCCB 6/94; BL 7/94; SLJ 6/94)

**7833** Raven, Margot T. *Angels in the Dust* (3–6). Illus. by Roger Essley. 1997, Troll paper $15.95 (0-8167-3806-8). 32pp. Based on a true story, this picture book describes the hardships of an Oklahoma family living in the 1930s Dust Bowl. (Rev: BL 4/15/97; SLJ 6/97)

**7834** Robinet, Harriette G. *Children of the Fire* (4–7). 1991, Macmillan $16.00 (0-689-31655-0). 144pp. Hallelujah, born into slavery, escapes to Chicago, where she spends one night following the path of the Great Fire. (Rev: BCCB 9/91; BL 10/15/91; SLJ 10/91)

**7835** Rodowsky, Colby. *Fitchett's Folly* (5–7). 1987, Farrar $15.00 (0-374-32342-9). 160pp. Sarey cannot accept Faith, the waif she feels is responsible for her father's death, in this story set in the 1870s. (Rev: BCCB 6/87; BL 6/1/87; SLJ 6–7/87)

**7836** Rose, Deborah L. *The Rose Horse* (3–4). Illus. 1995, Harcourt $16.00 (0-15-200068-2). 80pp. The story of the Jewish immigrant community in Coney Island, Brooklyn, at the turn of the century. (Rev: BCCB 11/95; BL 9/1/95; SLJ 1/96)

**7837** Ross, Pat. *Hannah's Fancy Notions* (3–6). Illus. by Bert Dodson. 1992, Puffin paper $3.99 (0-14-032389-9). 64pp. The story of Hannah and the folk art of making band boxes. (Rev: BL 10/1/88; SLJ 1/89)

**7838** Rossiter, Phyllis. *Moxie* (4–7). 1990, Macmillan $14.95 (0-02-777831-2). 185pp. The story of a gallant family's fight against drought and foreclosure in the Dust Bowl of the 1930s. (Rev: SLJ 12/90)

**7839** Sandin, Joan. *The Long Way Westward* (2–4). Illus. 1989, HarperCollins paper $3.75 (0-06-444198-9). 64pp. In this continuation of *A Long Way to a New Land* (1981), the immigrant Swedish family continues its journey to Minnesota. (Rev: BCCB 11/89; BL 9/15/89; HB 9–10/89; SLJ 9/89)

**7840** Sawyer, Ruth. *Roller Skates* (4–6). Illus. by Valenti Angelo. 1988, Peter Smith $18.75 (0-8446-6343-3). 192pp. A little girl explores New York City on roller skates in the 1890s. Newbery Honor book, 1937.

**7841** Sebestyen, Ouida. *Words by Heart* (5–7). 1979, Little, Brown $15.95 (0-316-77931-8). 144pp. Race relations are explored when a black family moves to an all-white community during the Reconstruction Era.

**7842** Sherman, Eileen B. *Independence Avenue* (5–8). 1990, Jewish Publication Soc. $14.95 (0-8276-0367-3). 145pp. A 14-year-old Jewish boy from Russia is all alone in the United States of 1907. (Rev: SLJ 1/91)

**7843** Snyder, Zilpha Keatley. *Gib Rides Home* (5–8). 1998, Delacorte $15.95 (0-385-32267-4). 246pp. Set in post–World War I America, this is the story of an orphan boy and how he conquered hardships and deprivations. (Rev: BL 1/1–15/98; SLJ 1/98*)

**7844** Stevens, Carla. *Anna, Grandpa, and the Big Storm* (2–4). Illus. by Margot Tomes. 1982, Puffin paper $3.99 (0-14-031705-8). 48pp. A family story that takes place during the famous blizzard of 1888 in New York City.

**7845** Taylor, Mildred D. *The Well: David's Story* (5–7). 1995, Dial paper $14.89 (0-8037-1803-9). 96pp. This part of the Logan family saga about a family of poor black landowners in the South during the Depression is told by David Logan, the father. (Rev: BCCB 2/95; BL 12/15/94; HB 7–8/95; SLJ 2/95*)

**7846** Tolliver, Ruby C. *Boomer's Kids* (4–6). Illus. by Lyle Miller. 1992, Hendrick-Long paper $10.95 (0-885777-22-1). 128pp. Teenagers Andy and Ellie are tired of moving, as the family follows their father, a "boomer" in the oil fields in 1901. (Rev: BL 8/92)

**7847** Tripp, Valerie. *Changes for Samantha: A Winter Story* (3–5). Illus. by Robert Grace and Nancy Niles. 1988, Pleasant LB $12.95 (0-937295-95-7); paper $5.95 (0-937295-47-7). 72pp. Wealthy New Yorker Samantha now lives with her aunt and uncle in a series that takes place in 1904 and includes:

*Happy Birthday Samantha* (1987); *Samantha Saves the Day* (1988). (Rev: BL 1/1/89; SLJ 2/89)

**7848** Uchida, Yoshiko. *Samurai of Gold Hill* (5–8). Illus. by Ati Forberg. 1984, Creative Arts paper $9.95 (0-916870-86-3). 128pp. In this reissue of a 1972 title, a group of Japanese colonists try to farm an arid stretch of California in 1869.

**7849** West, Tracey. *Fire in the Valley* (3–5). Illus. Series: Stories of the States. 1993, Silver Moon LB $13.95 (1-881889-32-7). 80pp. Eleven-year-old Sarah becomes involved in mob violence concerning water rights in this novel set in 1905 California. (Rev: SLJ 12/93)

**7850** Whalen, Sharla S. *Meet the Friends* (3–5). Illus. 1997, ABDO paper $5.95 (1-56239-900-4). 64pp. Set in 1896, this is the story of 4 very different girlfriends. (Rev: BL 5/15/97)

**7851** Whitmore, Arvella. *The Bread Winner* (4–6). 1990, Houghton $16.00 (0-395-53705-3). 144pp. In this Depression-era story, the Pucketts are forced to sell their farm. (Rev: BCCB 1/91; BL 11/1/90; SLJ 10/90)

**7852** Wyman, Andrea. *Red Sky at Morning* (5–7). 1991, Holiday $15.95 (0-8234-0903-1). 230pp. Twelve-year-old Callie, her sister, and grandfather must cope with the death of the girls' mother and a runaway father on their Indiana farm in 1909. (Rev: BCCB 1/92; BL 12/1/91; SLJ 9/91)

## World War II and After

**7853** Ackerman, Karen. *The Night Crossing* (2–5). Illus. by Elizabeth Sayles. 1994, Knopf $14.00 (0-679-83169-X). 36pp. A novel based on fact about an Austrian Jewish family that escaped the Nazis in 1938 and fled to Switzerland. (Rev: BCCB 4/94; BL 3/15/94; SLJ 7/94)

**7854** Avi. *Who Was That Masked Man, Anyway?* (5–7). 1992, Orchard LB $16.99 (0-531-08607-0). 176pp. In a story told through dialogue, sixth-grader Frankie lives through World War II by immersing himself in his beloved radio serials. (Rev: BCCB 10/92*; BL 8/92*; HB 3–4/93; SLJ 10/92*)

**7855** Banks, Sara H. *Under the Shadow of Wings* (4–8). 1997, Simon & Schuster $15.00 (0-689-81207-8). 147pp. In this novel set in rural Alabama near the end of World War II, 11-year-old Tattnall is filled with grief and guilt when his 15-year-old brain-damaged cousin dies. (Rev: SLJ 6/97)

**7856** Bishop, Claire Huchet. *Twenty and Ten* (4–6). Illus. by William Pene du Bois. 1984, Peter Smith $18.00 (0-8446-6168-6); Puffin paper $3.99 (0-14-031076-2). A nun and 20 French children hide 10 young refugees from the Nazis.

**7857** Chang, Margaret, and Raymond Chang. *In the Eye of War* (5–7). 1990, Macmillan $14.95 (0-689-50503-5). 224pp. A novel based on true experiences of growing up in Shanghai during World War II. (Rev: BCCB 4/90; BL 3/15/90; SLJ 8/90)

**7858** Charyn, Jerome. *Back to Bataan* (5–7). 1993, Farrar $14.00 (0-374-30476-9). 101pp. During World War II, 11-year-old Jack Dalton is so disturbed by news of his father's death that he runs away from home. (Rev: BL 6/1–15/93)

**7859** Cutler, Jane. *My Wartime Summers* (5–7). 1994, Farrar $15.00 (0-374-35111-2). 158pp. This novel contrasts home front life during World War II with the story of a girl's older brother, who is a soldier. (Rev: BCCB 11/94; BL 10/1/94*; SLJ 11/94)

**7860** DeJong, Meindert. *The House of Sixty Fathers* (6–8). Illus. by Maurice Sendak. 1956, Harper-Collins LB $15.89 (0-06-021481-3); paper $4.95 (0-06-440200-2). 192pp. Tien Pao and his pig, Glory-of-the-Republic, journey to find his parents in Japanese-occupied China.

**7861** Douglas, Kirk. *The Broken Mirror* (5–8). 1997, Simon & Schuster paper $13.00 (0-689-81493-3). 96pp. This short novel by the famous actor depicts the despair and loss of faith that occurs to a Jewish child who has lost all his loved ones in the Holocaust. (Rev: BL 10/1/97; SLJ 9/97)

**7862** Drucker, Malka, and Michael Halperin. *Jacob's Rescue* (5–8). 1993, Bantam $15.00 (0-553-08976-5). 128pp. In a Passover setting, a Jewish father tells how he and his brother were saved during the Holocaust. (Rev: SLJ 5/93)

**7863** Elmer, Robert. *Into the Flames* (5–7). Series: Young Underground. 1995, Bethany paper $5.99 (1-55661-376-8). 144pp. Danish twins are captured by the Gestapo while trying to rescue their uncle during World War II. (Rev: BL 5/15/95; SLJ 8/95)

**7864** Garrigue, Sheila. *The Eternal Spring of Mr. Ito* (4–6). 1994, Simon & Schuster paper $3.95 (0-689-71809-8). 176pp. This sequel to *All the Children Were Sent Away* (o.p.) continues the story of a young girl evacuated from London to Vancouver, British Columbia, during World War II. (Rev: BCCB 12/85; HB 1–2/86; SLJ 11/85)

**7865** Giff, Patricia Reilly. *Lily's Crossing* (5–8). 1997, Delacorte $14.95 (0-385-32142-2). 180pp. During World War II, motherless Lily must say good-bye to her father when he is sent to fight in France. (Rev: BCCB 4/97; BL 2/1/97; HB 3–4/97, 9–10/97; SLJ 2/97)

**7866** Hahn, Mary D. *Stepping on the Cracks* (5–8). 1991, Houghton $16.00 (0-395-58507-4); Avon paper $4.50 (0-380-71900-2). 218pp. The compelling story of a sixth-grade girl during World War II and her painful decision to help a pacifist deserter.

(Rev: BCCB 12/91*; BL 10/15/91*; HB 11–12/91; SLJ 12/91*)

**7867** Heneghan, James. *Wish Me Luck* (5–8). 1997, Farrar $16.00 (0-374-38453-3). 208pp. When Jamie is evacuated to Canada from England during World War II, the ship he is on is sunk by a German U-boat. (Rev: BCCB 4/97; BL 6/1–15/97; HB 9–10/97; SLJ 6/97)

**7868** Hest, Amy. *Love You, Soldier* (4–6). 1993, Puffin paper $3.99 (0-14-036174-X). 48pp. It is New York City during World War II and 7-year-old Katie tells of the changes in her family. (Rev: BCCB 9/91; BL 9/15/91; HB 9–10/91; SLJ 8/91)

**7869** Hoestlandt, Jo. *Star of Fear, Star of Hope* (2–4). Trans. by Mark Polizzotti. Illus. by Johanna Kang. 1995, Walker LB $16.85 (0-8027-8374-0). 32pp. In World War II–occupied France, Helen witnesses the growing persecution of her Jewish friend Lydia. (Rev: BCCB 6/95; BL 5/1/95; HB 9–10/95; SLJ 8/95)

**7870** Holm, Anne. *North to Freedom* (6–8). 1984, Harcourt paper $6.00 (0-15-257553-7). 239pp. A boy who has never known anything except life in a concentration camp makes his way across Europe alone and escapes to freedom.

**7871** Innocenti, Roberto, and Christophe Gallaz. *Rose Blanche* (5–7). Illus. 1986, Creative Ed. LB $16.95 (0-87191-994-X). 32pp. A German girl discovers a concentration camp near her home during World War II, aids the children there, and is later killed in cross fire. (Rev: BL 11/1/85; HB 9–10/85)

**7872** Kerr, Judith. *When Hitler Stole Pink Rabbit* (4–7). Illus. by author. 1987, Dell paper $3.99 (0-440-49017-0). Based on incidents in the author's life, this is an exciting story of a German-Jewish family and their escape from Nazi Germany.

**7873** Kogawa, Joy. *Naomi's Road* (4–6). Illus. by Matt Gould. 1988, Oxford paper $9.95 (0-19-540547-1). 88pp. The World War II internment of a Japanese-Canadian girl. (Rev: BCCB 7–8/88; BL 6/1/88; SLJ 5/88)

**7874** Kudlinski, Kathleen V. *Pearl Harbor Is Burning! The Story of World War II* (4–6). Illus. by Ronald Himler. 1993, Puffin paper $4.99 (0-14-034509-4). 64pp. Historical events are brought into perspective in a fictional framework as Frank, a newcomer to Hawaii, must learn to adjust to island living. (Rev: BCCB 10/91; BL 11/15/91; SLJ 2/92)

**7875** Lee, Milly. *Nim and the War Effort* (2–5). Illus. by Yangsook Choi. 1997, Farrar $16.00 (0-374-35523-1). 32pp. Nim, who is growing up in San Francisco's Chinatown during World War II, wants to help in the war effort. (Rev: BCCB 3/97; BL 2/1/97; HB 3–4/97; SLJ 3/97)

**7876** Levitin, Sonia. *Journey to America* (5–8). Illus. by Charles Robinson. 1970, Macmillan $16.00 (0-689-31829-4); paper $3.95 (0-689-71130-1). 160pp. A Jewish mother and her 3 daughters flee Nazi Germany in 1938 for a long and difficult journey to join their father in America. (Rev: BL 9/1/93)

**7877** Lowry, Lois. *Number the Stars* (5–7). 1989, Houghton $14.95 (0-395-51060-0); Dell paper $4.99 (0-440-40327-8). 160pp. The story of war-torn Denmark and best friends Annemarie Johansen and Ellen Rosen. Newbery Medal winner, 1990. (Rev: BCCB 3/89; BL 3/1/89; SLJ 3/89)

**7878** McSwigan, Marie. *Snow Treasure* (4–7). Illus. by Andre Le Blanc. 1986, Scholastic paper $3.50 (0-590-42537-4). 156pp. Children smuggle gold out of occupied Norway on their sleds.

**7879** Mathers, Petra. *Kisses from Rosa* (2–4). Illus. 1995, Knopf $16.00 (0-679-82686-6). 42pp. In post–World War II Germany, Rosa is sent to live with her aunt and cousin on a farm in the Black Forest. (Rev: BCCB 1/96; BL 11/1/95; HB 11–12/95; SLJ 11/95*)

**7880** Michener, James A. *South Pacific* (5–8). Illus. by Michael Hague. 1992, Harcourt $16.95 (0-15-200618-4). 40pp. The famous author retells the story of his Tales from the South Pacific, on which the musical and movie South Pacific were based. (Rev: BCCB 11/92; BL 9/1/92; SLJ 11/92)

**7881** Mori, Hana. *Jirohattan* (3–6). Trans. from Japanese by Tamiko Kurosaki and Elizabeth Crowe. Illus. by Elizabeth Crowe. 1993, Bess Pr. paper $6.95 (1-880188-69-4). 76pp. In this tale set in World War II Japan, a slow-witted boy named Jirohattan helps others but is unable to comprehend death. (Rev: BCCB 2/94; SLJ 5/94)

**7882** Napoli, Donna Jo. *Stones in Water* (5–8). 1997, Dutton paper $15.99 (0-525-45842-5). 154pp. The exciting story of 2 Italian boys, one of whom is Jewish, who have been transported to work camps by the Nazis during World War II. (Rev: BL 10/1/97; SLJ 11/97*)

**7883** Orlev, Uri. *The Island on Bird Street* (5–7). 1984, Houghton $16.00 (0-395-33887-5); paper $5.95 (0-395-61623-9). 176pp. A young Jewish boy inside the Warsaw ghetto during World War II.

**7884** Orlev, Uri. *Lydia, Queen of Palestine* (4–6). Trans. from Hebrew by Hillel Halkin. 1993, Houghton $13.95 (0-395-65660-5). 168pp. Lydia, a holy terror, leaves her native Romania during World War II to stay at a kibbutz in Palestine. (Rev: BCCB 11/93; BL 10/1/93*; SLJ 10/93)

**7885** Reiss, Johanna. *The Upstairs Room* (5–8). 1972, HarperCollins $15.00 (0-690-85127-8); paper $4.95 (0-06-440370-X). 196pp. Two young Jewish girls are hidden for over 2 years in the home of a simple Dutch peasant during the German occupation. A sequel is: *The Journey Back* (1976).

**7886** Rinaldi, Ann. *Keep Smiling Through* (4–6). 1996, Harcourt $12.00 (0-15-200768-7); paper $6.00 (0-15-201072-6). 208pp. Life on the home front during World War II as seen through the eyes of Kay, a lonely 10-year-old. (Rev: BCCB 4/96; BL 7/96*; SLJ 6/96)

**7887** Serraillier, Ian. *The Silver Sword* (6–8). Illus. by C. Walter Hodges. 1959, Phillips $31.95 (0-87599-104-1). A World War II story of Polish children who are separated from their parents and finally reunited.

**7888** Shemin, Margaretha. *The Little Riders* (4–6). Illus. by Peter Spier. 1988, Morrow paper $4.95 (0-688-12499-2). 80pp. An 11-year-old girl is trapped in German-occupied Netherlands during World War II. A reissue.

**7889** Sim, Dorrith M. *In My Pocket* (3–6). Illus. by Gerald Fitzgerald. 1997, Harcourt $16.00 (0-15-201357-1). 32pp. A picture book about a small girl who is one of the 10,000 Jewish children taken from Nazi Europe to Great Britain. (Rev: BCCB 6/97; BL 4/15/97; SLJ 5/97)

**7890** Tripp, Valerie. *Meet Molly: An American Girl* (3–5). Illus. by C. F. Payne. 1986, Pleasant LB $12.95 (0-937295-81-7); paper $5.95 (0-937295-07-8). 72pp. Molly is growing up without a father during World War II in America. Others in the series are: *Molly Learns a Lesson* (1986); *Molly's Surprise* (1986); *Molly Saves the Day* (1988); *Happy Birthday, Molly!* (1987); *Changes for Molly* (1988). (Rev: BL 12/1/86)

**7891** Uchida, Yoshiko. *The Bracelet* (1–5). Illus. by Joanna Yardley. 1993, Putnam $15.95 (0-399-22503-X). 32pp. Emi, a Japanese American girl, is confused and frightened when she is interned in a prison camp during World War II. (Rev: BCCB 9/93; BL 9/15/93; HB 11–12/93; SLJ 12/93)

**7892** Vander Els, Betty. *The Bombers' Moon* (5–7). 1992, Farrar paper $4.50 (0-374-30877-7). 168pp. Missionary children Ruth and Simeon are evacuated to escape the Japanese invasion of China; they will not see their parents for 4 years. A sequel is: *Leaving Point* (1987). (Rev: BCCB 9/85; BL 11/1/85; HB 9–10/85)

**7893** Vos, Ida. *Anna Is Still Here* (5–7). Trans. by Terese Edelstein and Inez Smidt. 1993, Houghton $13.95 (0-395-65368-1). 144pp. The story of a survivor of the Holocaust and her adjustment to freedom after years of solitude and terror. (Rev: BL 4/15/93*; HB 7–8/93; SLJ 5/93)

**7894** Vos, Ida. *Hide and Seek* (4–8). Trans. by Terese Edelstein and Inez Smidt. 1991, Houghton $15.00 (0-395-56470-0). 144pp. A first-person narrative of a Jewish girl in Holland during the Nazi occupation. (Rev: BCCB 3/91; BL 3/15/91*; HB 5–6/91; SLJ 5/91)

**7895** Walsh, Jill Paton. *Fireweed* (5–8). 1970, Farrar paper $3.50 (0-374-42316-4). 144pp. Teenagers Bill and Julie meet during a London blitz.

**7896** Winkler, Allan M. *Cassie's War* (4–6). 1994, Royal Fireworks LB $15.00 (0-88092-107-2); paper $5.00 (0-88092-106-4). 94pp. Cassie is growing up in California during World War II, which brings internment to her Japanese American friend and death to her soldier father. (Rev: BL 2/1/95)

**7897** Yep, Laurence. *Hiroshima* (4–7). 1995, Scholastic $9.95 (0-590-20832-2). 64pp. A powerful fiction work that explores the bombing of Hiroshima in 1945 and its aftermath. (Rev: BCCB 6/95; BL 3/15/95*; HB 9–10/95; SLJ 5/95)

**7898** Yolen, Jane. *The Devil's Arithmetic* (4–8). 1988, Puffin paper $4.99 (0-14-034535-3). 160pp. This time-warp story transports a young Jewish girl back to Poland in the 1940s, conveying the horrors of the Holocaust. (Rev: SLJ 8/88)

# Holidays and Holy Days

**7899** Alcott, Louisa May. *An Old Fashioned Thanksgiving* (4–5). Illus. by Jody Wheeler. 1990, Applewood paper $5.95 (1-55709-135-8). 40pp. The happenings in a New Hampshire farm family in the 1820s, first published in 1881. (Rev: BL 10/1/89; SLJ 10/89)

**7900** Aleichem, Sholem. *Holiday Tales of Sholem Aleichem* (4–6). Illus. by Thomas Di Grazia. 1994, Peter Smith $19.25 (0-8446-6767-6). 145pp. Seven diverse tales that deal with Jewish holidays.

**7901** Allan, Nicholas. *Jesus' Christmas Party* (3–6). Illus. 1997, Bantam $7.95 (0-385-32521-5). 32pp. The nativity story, as told from the point of view of the innkeeper. (Rev: BL 7/92)

**7902** Ames, Mildred. *Grandpa Jake and the Grand Christmas* (3–5). 1990, Macmillan $15.00 (0-684-19241-1). 96pp. Long-lost Grandpa Jake turns up for a Christmas visit. (Rev: BCCB 11/90; BL 11/15/90; SLJ 3/91*)

**7903** Axelrod, Amy. *Pigs Go to Market: Halloween Fun with Math and Shopping* (2–4). Illus. by Sharon McGinley-Nally. 1997, Simon & Schuster $13.00 (0-689-81069-5). At Halloween, the Pig family eats all the candy before the guests arrive. (Rev: SLJ 9/97)

**7904** Bat-Ami, Miriam. *Dear Elijah* (4–6). 1995, Farrar $14.00 (0-374-31755-0). 106pp. Eleven-year-old Rebecca, a young Jewish girl, addresses personal concerns in her diary to the prophet Elijah, hoping he can help her. (Rev: BCCB 5/95; BL 4/1/95; SLJ 5/95)

**7905** Bauer, Caroline Feller, ed. *Halloween: Stories and Poems* (3–6). Illus. by Peter Sis. 1989, Harper-Collins LB $14.89 (0-397-32301-8). 96pp. An anthology with spooky happenings for reading on Halloween, although not directly related to the holiday. (Rev: BL 9/1/89; SLJ 10/89)

**7906** Bauer, Caroline Feller. *Thanksgiving: Stories and Poems* (4–6). Illus. 1994, HarperCollins LB $14.89 (0-06-023327-3). 96pp. Stories, poems, and songs are included in this rich Thanksgiving anthology. (Rev: BL 8/94; HB 11–12/94; SLJ 7/95)

**7907** Bradbury, Ray. *The Halloween Tree* (5–7). Illus. 1988, Knopf LB $13.99 (0-394-92409-6); Bantam paper $3.95 (0-553-25823-0). 160pp. Boys visit a deserted house and find a pumpkin tree.

**7908** Burch, Robert. *Christmas with Ida Early* (5–7). 1985, Puffin paper $4.99 (0-14-031971-9). 144pp. A preacher involves Ida in a Christmas pageant in this amusing story.

**7909** Burden-Patmon, Denise. *Imani's Gift at Kwanzaa* (3–5). Illus. by Floyd Cooper. 1993, Simon & Schuster LB $4.95 (0-671-79841-3). 26pp. Imani isn't sure she wants a new girl to join her family's Kwanzaa celebration. (Rev: BL 1/15/93)

**7910** Burton, Tim. *The Nightmare Before Christmas* (3–5). Illus. 1993, Hyperion $15.95 (1-56282-411-2). 40pp. Based on the movie of the same name, this book tells of Jack Skellington's diabolical decision to trade places with Santa. (Rev: BL 10/1/93)

**7911** Capote, Truman. *A Christmas Memory* (3–6). Illus. by Beth Peck. 1989, Knopf $19.00 (0-679-80040-9). A tender story about Christmas preparations in a parentless, poor household. (Rev: HB 3–4/90; SLJ 12/89)

**7912** Caudill, Rebecca. *A Certain Small Shepherd* (3–6). Illus. by William Pene du Bois. 1997, Holt paper $6.95 (0-805-05392-1). A mute boy gets an opportunity to play one of the shepherds in a Christmas pageant.

**7913** Cohen, Barbara. *The Christmas Revolution* (4–6). 1993, Dell paper $3.50 (0-440-40871-7). 96pp. Jewish twins Emily and Sally find themselves ostracized when Emily refuses to participate in Christmas celebrations at school. (Rev: BL 9/1/87)

**7914** Cohen, Barbara. *Molly's Pilgrim* (2–5). Illus. by Michael J. Deraney. 1983, Lothrop $16.00 (0-688-02103-4). 32pp. At Thanksgiving time, Molly begins to feel proud of her Jewish heritage.

**7915** Collington, Peter. *A Small Miracle* (2–5). Illus. 1997, Knopf $18.00 (0-679-88725-3). 32pp. An old woman who has rescued Nativity scene figures from

the hands of a thief is in turn helped by them when she collapses in the snow. (Rev: BL 10/15/97*; HB 11–12/97; SLJ 10/97)

**7916** Cooper, Ilene. *No-Thanks Thanksgiving* (4–7). 1996, Viking paper $14.99 (0-670-85657-6). 128pp. Five friends spend a less-than-successful Thanksgiving weekend in New York. (Rev: BL 9/1/96)

**7917** Davies, Valentine. *Miracle on 34th Street* (3–6). Illus. by Tomie dePaola. 1987, Harcourt paper $11.00 (0-15-254528-X). 120pp. An old man named Kris Kringle is hired as the Macy's Santa Claus.

**7918** Delton, Judy. *Halloween Helpers* (2–4). Illus. by Alan Tiegreen. Series: Pee Wee Scouts /Yearling Book. 1997, Bantam paper $3.99 (0-440-41330-3). 115pp. When their leader leaves temporarily, the Pee Wee Scouts are afraid that they won't have their usual Halloween party. (Rev: SLJ 1/98)

**7919** Delton, Judy. *Tricks and Treats* (2–3). Illus. 1994, Dell paper $3.99 (0-440-40976-4). 87pp. In this story set at Halloween, young Molly worries about what will happen to her family because her father has unexpectedly lost his job. (Rev: BL 9/15/94)

**7920** Dickens, Charles. *A Christmas Carol* (6–8). Illus. by Trina S. Hyman. 1983, Holiday $18.95 (0-8234-0486-2). 128pp. A handsome edition of this classic.

**7921** Dickens, Charles. *A Christmas Carol* (3–6). Illus. by Lisbeth Zwerger. 1991, Picture Book $19.95 (0-88708-069-3). 60pp. The classic tale with distinctive illustrations. (Rev: HB 11–12/88)

**7922** Dickens, Charles. *A Christmas Carol* (5–8). Illus. by Carter Goodrich. 1996, Morrow $18.00 (0-688-13606-0). 64pp. An abridged version of Dickens's performance text, with excellent illustrations. (Rev: BL 9/1/96; HB 1–2/96)

**7923** Dickens, Charles. *A Christmas Carol* (4–8). Illus. by Quentin Blake. 1995, Simon & Schuster paper $19.95 (0-689-80213-7). 144pp. The classic Christmas story illustrated by a master. (Rev: BL 10/15/95)

**7924** Giff, Patricia Reilly. *Turkey Trouble* (2–4). Illus. 1994, Dell paper $3.99 (0-440-40955-1). 31pp. Emily is preparing for a school Thanksgiving party and also preparing her younger sister for the arrival of a new baby in their household. (Rev: BL 12/1/94)

**7925** Goldin, Barbara D. *While the Candles Burn: Eight Stories for Hanukkah* (3–6). Illus. 1996, Viking paper $15.99 (0-670-85875-7). 64pp. Eight short stories highlight the various traditions of Hanukkah. (Rev: BCCB 11/96; BL 9/15/96)

**7926** Greenberg, Martin H., and Charles G. Waugh, eds. *A Newbery Christmas: Fourteen Stories of Christmas* (4–6). 1991, Delacorte $16.95 (0-385-

30485-4). 194pp. Newbery Award winners offer stories about the holiday. (Rev: BCCB 12/91; BL 11/15/91)

**7927** Hague, Michael. *Michael Hague's Family Christmas Treasury* (4–6). Illus. 1995, Holt $19.95 (0-8050-1011-4). 32pp. A selection of the author's favorite stories, poems, and carols about Christmas. (Rev: BL 11/1/95) [394]

**7928** Hall, Lynn. *Here Comes Zelda Claus and Other Holiday Disasters* (4–6). 1989, Harcourt $16.00 (0-15-233790-3). 144pp. Each of the 5 stories about Zelda Claus in this collection deals with a different holiday. (Rev: BL 10/1/89; HB 3–4/90; SLJ 10/89)

**7929** Hamilton, Virginia. *The Bells of Christmas* (3–5). Illus. by Lambert Davis. 1989, Harcourt $17.95 (0-15-206450-8). 60pp. A century ago a young boy celebrates the holiday with his family in Ohio. (Rev: BCCB 11/89; BL 10/1/89*; HB 11–12/89)

**7930** Hamilton, Virginia. *Willie Bea and the Time the Martians Landed* (5–8). 1983, Greenwillow LB $16.00 (0-688-02390-8). 224pp. A story built around the Halloween night on which Orson Welles made his famous invasion-from-Mars broadcast.

**7931** Hardy, Sian. *A Treasury of Christmas Stories* (3–5). Illus. 1994, Kingfisher paper $6.95 (1-85697-985-7). 160pp. A fine collection of stories by such writers as Cleary, Andersen, and Aiken. (Rev: BL 10/1/94)

**7932** Henry, O. *The Gift of the Magi* (5–8). Illus. by Carol Heyer. 1994, Ideals LB $14.95 (1-57102-003-9). 32pp. The classic story of unselfish love at Christmas gets some handsome illustrations. Another fine edition is illus. by Kevin King (1988, Simon & Schuster). (Rev: BL 8/94)

**7933** Hill, Susan. *The Christmas Collection* (4–7). Illus. by John Lawrence. 1994, Candlewick $19.95 (1-56402-341-9). 96pp. Four moving Christmas stories and a poem comprise this holiday anthology. (Rev: BL 10/15/94)

**7934** Hill, Susan. *The Glass Angels* (3–6). Illus. by Valerie Littlewood. 1992, Candlewick $17.95 (1-56402-111-4). 96pp. A sentimental story of post-World War II England and the life of Tilly and her widowed mother. (Rev: BCCB 11/92; BL 9/15/92*)

**7935** Houston, Gloria. *Littlejim's Gift: An Appalachian Christmas Story* (2–4). Illus. by Thomas B. Allen. 1994, Putnam $15.95 (0-399-22696-6). 32pp. Set in Appalachia in 1917, this novel explores father-son relationships and tells how Littlejim uses his hard-earned money to buy a doll for his sister at Christmas. A sequel to *Littlejim* (1990). (Rev: BL 8/94; HB 11–12/94)

**7936** Jewell, Nancy. *Christmas Lullaby* (2–5). Illus. by Stefano Vitale. 1994, Clarion $14.95 (0-395-

66586-8). 32pp. In this Christmas lullaby, all the animals bring gifts to the Baby Jesus. (Rev: BL 10/1/94; HB 11–12/94)

**7937** Joseph, Lynn. *An Island Christmas* (2–6). Illus. by Catherine Stock. 1992, Houghton $14.95 (0-395-58761-1). 32pp. Memories of island life in the Caribbean are enhanced by muted watercolors. (Rev: BCCB 11/92; BL 9/15/92)

**7938** Kertes, Joseph. *The Gift* (3–5). Illus. 1996, Douglas & McIntyre $12.95 (0-88899-235-1). 48pp. An immigrant Jewish boy gives an inappropriate Christmas gift to a friend. (Rev: BL 11/1/96)

**7939** Kimmel, Eric A. *The Spotted Pony: A Collection of Hanukkah Stories* (3–6). Illus. by Leonard Everett Fisher. 1992, Holiday $15.95 (0-8234-0936-8). 70pp. A collection of wonderfully earthy and joyous Jewish folktales. (Rev: BL 11/15/92)

**7940** Kingman, Lee. *The Best Christmas* (3–5). Illus. by Barbara Cooney. 1984, Peter Smith $17.00 (0-8446-6160-0). 96pp. First published in 1949, this reissue is about a Finnish family and their concerns over an absent son at Christmas time.

**7941** L'Engle, Madeleine. *The Twenty-Four Days Before Christmas: An Austin Family Story* (3–5). Illus. by Joe DeVelasco. 1984, Harold Shaw $11.99 (0-87788-843-4); Dell paper $3.99 (0-440-40105-4). 48pp. Things work out for 7-year-old Vicky, who worries that she will be an awkward angel in the play and that her mother will be in the hospital having a baby on Christmas Day.

**7942** Lewis, Beverly. *The Crazy Christmas Angel Mystery* (2–4). Series: Cul-de-Sac Kids. 1995, Bethany paper $3.99 (1-55661-627-9). 62pp. Eric is convinced that his strange new neighbor is dancing with angels in this holiday mystery story. (Rev: BL 9/15/95)

**7943** Lovelace, Maud H. *The Trees Kneel at Christmas* (4–6). Illus. by Marie-Claude Monchaux. 1994, ABDO LB $16.98 (1-56239-999-3). 110pp. Afify and her young brother go to a Brooklyn park to see if trees really bow down on Christmas Eve, as the legend says. (Rev: BL 8/94)

**7944** Montgomery, L. M. *Christmas with Anne and Other Holiday Stories* (4–7). 1996, Delacorte paper $16.95 (0-385-32288-7). 214pp. A collection of 16 short pieces and stories (2 from the Anne books) that deal with Christmas. (Rev: BL 9/1/96)

**7945** Moore, Miriam, and Penny Taylor. *The Kwanzaa Contest* (2–4). Illus. by Laurie Spencer. 1996, Hyperion $13.95 (0-7868-0261-8); paper $3.95 (0-7868-1122-6). 64pp. Ronald, a third-grader, is determined to win a Kwanzaa contest. (Rev: BL 9/15/96)

**7946** Moser, Barry. *Good and Perfect Gifts: An Illustrated Retelling of O. Henry's The Gift of the Magi* (3–6). Illus. 1997, Little, Brown $14.95 (0-316-

58543-2). 32pp. Set in a modern Appalachian community, this is a retelling of O. Henry's story, with a number of fresh twists. (Rev: BL 9/1/97; SLJ 10/97)

**7947** Nettell, Stephanie. *A Christmas Treasury* (3–8). Illus. 1997, Dutton paper $20.00 (0-525-67560-4). 160pp. A Christmas compendium of poems and stories by such authors as Milne, Cleary, and Dickens. (Rev: BL 9/1/97)

**7948** Paterson, Katherine. *Angels and Other Strangers: Family Christmas Stories* (5–8). 1991, Harper-Collins LB $13.89 (0-690-04911-0); paper $3.95 (0-06-440283-5). 128pp. Nine stories that explore various meanings of Christmas and what it should represent to people.

**7949** Paterson, Katherine. *A Midnight Clear: Stories for the Christmas Season* (5–8). 1995, Dutton paper $16.00 (0-525-67529-9). 192pp. A collection of the author's Christmas stories, each with a contemporary setting. (Rev: BCCB 11/95; BL 9/15/95; HB 11–12/95)

**7950** Paulsen, Gary. *A Christmas Sonata* (4–7). Illus. 1992, Delacorte $14.95 (0-385-30441-2). 78pp. At Christmastime in 1943, a boy and his mother spend the holiday in northern Minnesota in this poignant story. (Rev: BL 9/1/92*)

**7951** Pearl, Sydelle. *Elijah's Tears: Stories for the Jewish Holidays* (3–5). Illus. 1996, Holt $14.95 (0-8050-4627-5). 62pp. These stories feature 4 Jewish holidays in which the prophet Elijah appears. (Rev: BCCB 11/96; BL 9/15/96; SLJ 1/97)

**7952** Penn, Malka. *The Hanukkah Ghosts* (3–5). 1995, Holiday $14.95 (0-8234-1145-1). 88pp. Susan — who is living with an elderly aunt on an English moor during Hanukkah — is visited by children who lived there during World War II. (Rev: BL 9/15/95)

**7953** Robinson, Barbara. *The Best Christmas Pageant Ever* (4–6). Illus. by Judith G. Brown. 1972, Harper-Collins LB $14.89 (0-06-025044-5); paper $4.95 (0-06-440275-4). 96pp. When a family of unrestrained children takes over the church Christmas pageant, the results are hilarious.

**7954** Rock, Gail. *The House Without a Christmas Tree* (4–6). Illus. by Charles C. Gehm. 1974, Knopf LB $9.99 (0-394-92833-4). 96pp. A conflict between a father and daughter about having a Christmas tree.

**7955** Russell, Ching Yeung. *Moon Festival* (3–5). Illus. by Christopher Zhong-Yuan. 1997, Boyds Mills $15.95 (1-56397-596-3). 32pp. Ying and her friends celebrate the summer Moon Festival in many ways, including making paper lanterns. (Rev: BL 9/15/97)

**7956** Rylant, Cynthia. *Children of Christmas: Stories for the Season* (4–6). Illus. by S. D. Schindler. 1987, Orchard paper $5.95 (0-531-07042-5). 48pp. Six quiet stories about the emotions of Christmas. (Rev: BCCB 10/87; BL 9/1/87)

**7957** Singer, Isaac Bashevis. *The Power of Light* (4–7). Illus. by Irene Lieblich. 1980, Avon paper $2.50 (0-380-60103-6). 80pp. A collection of 8 charming, original stories celebrating Hanukkah, the Festival of Lights.

**7958** *A Small Treasury of Christmas: Poems and Prayers* (1–3). Illus. by Susan Spellman. 1997, Boyds Mills $8.95 (1-56397-680-3). 32pp. A collection of 26 poems and prayers dealing with Christmas. (Rev: SLJ 10/97) [811]

**7959** Sussman, Susan. *Hanukkah, Eight Lights Around the World* (2–8). Illus. by Judith Friedman. 1988, Whitman LB $12.95 (0-8075-3145-6). 40pp. Celebrating the Festival of Lights with stops around the world. (Rev: BL 5/1/88)

**7960** Sussman, Susan. *There's No Such Thing as a Chanukah Bush, Sandy Goldstein* (3–5). Illus. by Charles Robinson. 1983, Whitman LB $8.95 (0-8075-7862-2). 48pp. The difference between believing in a holiday and helping others celebrate is brought out in this story.

**7961** Taylor, Theodore. *Maria Taylor: A Christmas Story* (5–7). 1992, Harcourt $15.00 (0-15-217763-9). 112pp. Maria wants desperately to enter a float in the annual Christmas parade, but her family can budget only $10.00. (Rev: BCCB 10/92; BL 9/15/92; SLJ 1/93)

**7962** Van Leeuwen, Jean. *The Great Christmas Kidnapping Caper* (3–5). Illus. by Steven Kellogg. 1975, Dial $12.95 (0-685-01454-1). 144pp. A group of mice who live in a dollhouse at Macy's solve the mystery of the disappearance of Santa Claus.

**7963** Walter, Mildred P. *Have a Happy . . .* (3–5). Illus. by Carole Byard. 1989, Avon paper $3.99 (0-380-71314-4). 144pp. In this story set during Kwanzaa, a week after Christmas, the fortunes of a struggling black family are told. (Rev: BCCB 12/89; BL 9/1/89; HB 11–12/89)

**7964** Weatherford, Carole Boston. *Juneteenth Jamboree* (2–4). Illus. by Yvonne Buchanan. 1995, Lee & Low $15.95 (1-880000-18-0). Two youngsters, new to Texas, celebrate Juneteenth, which commemorates the day Texas slaves learned that the Emancipation Proclamation freed them. (Rev: SLJ 1/96)

**7965** Westall, Robert. *Christmas Spirit* (5–7). Illus. 1994, Farrar $15.00 (0-374-31260-5). 154pp. These 2 Christmas stories — one a ghost story and the other about 2 children adopting a cat — take place in the north of England during the Depression. (Rev: BCCB 10/94; BL 10/1/94; HB 11–12/94)

**7966** Wiggin, Kate Douglas. *The Birds' Christmas Carol* (3–5). Illus. by Jessie Gillespie. 1941, Houghton $9.95 (0-395-07205-0). A beautiful edition of a story first published in 1888.

**7967** Williams, Karen L. *A Real Christmas This Year* (5–8). 1995, Clarion $13.95 (0-395-70115-5). 164pp. Megan hopes for a "real" Christmas in spite of the many problems she faces both at home and at school. (Rev: BCCB 11/95; BL 9/15/95; HB 11–12/95)

**7968** Wolf, Winfried. *Christmas with Grandfather* (5–8). Trans. by J. Alison James. Illus. by Eugen Sopko. 1994, North-South LB $14.88 (1-55858-297-5). 26pp. Thomas and his mother are still mourning the death of the boy's father when they visit Grandfather's place at Christmas. (Rev: BL 10/15/94)

# Humorous Stories

**7969** Adler, David A. *Eaton Stanley and the Mind Control Experiment* (4–6). Illus. by Joan Drescher. 1995, Bantam paper $3.50 (0-440-41115-7). 96pp. Precocious Eaton decides to take control of his sixth-grade teacher's mind for his science project. (Rev: BL 10/1/85; HB 7–8/85; SLJ 8/85)

**7970** Ahlberg, Allan. *The Better Brown Stories* (3–5). Illus. 1996, Viking paper $14.99 (0-670-85894-3). 112pp. When the fictional members of the Brown family tell their author that they want to be depicted differently, the action gets out of hand. (Rev: BCCB 2/96; BL 1/1–15/96; HB 9–10/96; SLJ 2/96*)

**7971** Alford, Jan. *I Can't Believe I Have to Do This* (4–7). 1997, Putnam $16.95 (0-399-23130-7). 192pp. When Dean turns 12, his mother gives him a diary, and the entries he makes are funny, terse, and authentic. (Rev: BL 10/15/97; SLJ 9/97)

**7972** Atwater, Richard, and Florence Atwater. *Mr. Popper's Penguins* (4–6). Illus. by Robert Lawson. 1938, Little, Brown $16.95 (0-316-05842-4). 144pp. Mr. Popper has to get a penguin from the zoo to keep his homesick penguin company; soon there are 12.

**7973** Auch, Mary Jane. *I Was a Third Grade Science Project* (2–4). Illus. by Herm Auch. 1998, Holiday $15.95 (0-8234-1357-8). 94pp. Brian tries to hypnotize his dog into believing he's a cat, but the spell works on one of Brian's classmates instead. (Rev: BL 3/15/98)

**7974** Base, Graeme. *The Discovery of Dragons* (5–8). Illus. 1996, Abrams $16.95 (0-8109-3237-7). 32pp. A humorous account of the 3 pioneers in dragon research. (Rev: BL 11/15/96; SLJ 11/96)

**7975** Bateman, Teresa. *The Ring of Truth* (3–6). Illus. by Omar Rayyan. 1997, Holiday $15.95 (0-8234-1255-5). 32pp. In this picture book with an Irish flavor, a famous fibber, who is also a car salesman, is denied the right to lie. (Rev: BCCB 5/97; BL 7/97; SLJ 5/97)

**7976** Beard, Darleen Bailey. *The Flimflam Man* (2–4). Illus. 1998, Farrar $15.00 (0-374-32346-1). 96pp. On a hot day in 1950, an advance man for a circus begins selling tickets for future performances, but some townspeople think that he is a fraud. (Rev: BL 2/15/98; SLJ 3/98)

**7977** Belloc, Hilaire. *Jim, Who Ran Away from His Nurse, and Was Eaten by a Lion* (3–5). Illus. by Victoria Chess. 1987, Little, Brown $4.95 (0-316-13816-9). Spoiled young Jim runs away from nanny at the zoo — with dire consequences. (Rev: BL 5/1/87; HB 5–6/87; SLJ 6–7/87)

**7978** Birchman, David F. *Jigsaw Jackson* (4–6). Illus. by Daniel San Souci. 1996, Lothrop LB $15.93 (0-688-11633-7). 32pp. In this tall tale, J. Jupiter Jackson, a jigsaw puzzle genius, is exploited by a con artist. (Rev: BL 4/15/96; SLJ 7/96)

**7979** Birdseye, Tom. *I'm Going to Be Famous* (4–6). 1986, Holiday $15.95 (0-8234-0630-X). 144pp. Fifth-grader Arlo Moore is going to break the Guinness Book of World Records' time for eating bananas. (Rev: BCCB 1/87; BL 12/1/86)

**7980** Birdseye, Tom. *A Regular Flood of Mishap* (PS–3). Illus. by Megan Lloyd. 1994, Holiday LB $15.95 (0-8234-1070-6). 32pp. In spite of accidentally causing a number of disasters, Ima Bean finds she is still wanted by her family. (Rev: BL 3/15/94; SLJ 3/94)

**7981** Bliss, Corinne D. *Electra and the Charlotte Russe* (2–4). Illus. by Michael Garland. 1997, Boyds Mills $15.95 (1-56397-436-3). When she trips and upsets the cream on the pastries she is taking home, Electra tries to reshape them with her tongue. (Rev: SLJ 10/97)

**7982** Blume, Judy. *Freckle Juice* (2–5). Illus. by Sonia O. Lisker. 1971, Macmillan $15.00 (0-02-711690-5); Dell paper $3.99 (0-440-42813-0). 40pp. A gullible second-grader pays 50¢ for a recipe to grow freckles.

**7983** Blume, Judy. *Fudge-a-Mania* (4–6). 1990, Dutton paper $13.99 (0-525-44672-9). 128pp. Brother Peter and Fudge must spend the summer with the dreaded Sheila the Great. (Rev: BCCB 11/90; BL 10/15/90; HB 1–2/91; SLJ 12/90)

**7984** Blume, Judy. *Starring Sally J. Freedman as Herself* (4–7). 1977, Macmillan LB $17.00 (0-02-711070-2); Dell paper $4.50 (0-440-48253-4). 296pp. A story of a fifth-grader's adventures in New Jersey and Florida in the late 1940s.

**7985** Blume, Judy. *Tales of a Fourth Grade Nothing* (3–4). Illus. by Roy Doty. 1972, Dell paper $3.99 (0-440-48474-X). 128pp. Peter Hatcher's trials and tribulations, most of which are caused by his 2-year-old pesky brother, Fudge. A sequel is: *Superfudge* (1994, Bantam).

**7986** Bond, Michael. *A Bear Called Paddington* (3–6). Illus. by Peggy Fortnum. 1960, Houghton $14.95 (0-395-06636-0); Dell paper $3.99 (0-440-40483-5). 128pp. An endearing bear with a talent for getting into trouble. Some sequels (published by Houghton and Dell) are: *More about Paddington* (1979); *Paddington at Work* (1967); *Paddington Goes to Town* (1977); *Paddington Abroad* (1973); *Paddington Helps Out* (1973).

**7987** Bond, Michael. *Paddington on Screen* (3–5). Illus. by Barry Macey. 1992, Bantam paper $2.75 (0-440-40029-5). Further adventures of Paddington, everyone's favorite bear. Four other Paddington stories: *Paddington at Large* (1988); *Paddington Marches On* (1965); *Paddington Takes to TV* (1991, Dell); *Paddington Takes the Test* (1980).

**7988** Bond, Michael. *Paddington's Storybook* (3–5). Illus. by Peggy Fortnum. 1984, Houghton $21.95 (0-395-36667-4). 160pp. A selection of some of the very best stories published over the past 25 years.

**7989** Bunting, Eve. *Nasty, Stinky Sneakers* (4–6). Illus. 1994, HarperCollins LB $14.89 (0-06-024237-X). 128pp. Colin thinks his sneakers are so smelly that they will win a prize, and then they suddenly disappear. (Rev: BL 5/1/94; SLJ 6/94)

**7990** Butterworth, Oliver. *The Enormous Egg* (3–6). Illus. by Louis Darling. 1995, Houghton $9.00 (0-395-73249-2). The story of a boy whose hen lays a large egg, which hatches a triceratops!

**7991** Butterworth, Oliver. *The Trouble with Jenny's Ear* (4–6). Illus. by Julian de Miskey. 1993, Little, Brown paper $4.95 (0-316-11922-9). 288pp. A humorous tale of 2 boys and a sister they discover has extrasensory perception. A reissue.

**7992** Byars, Betsy. *Bingo Brown* (5–8). 1990, Viking paper $12.95 (0-670-83322-3). 160pp. In this third book about Bingo, he encounters both love problems and a new arrival in the family. (Rev: SLJ 6/90*)

**7993** Byars, Betsy. *Bingo Brown and the Language of Love* (5–8). 1989, Viking paper $12.95 (0-670-82791-6). 160pp. Bingo must produce 36 dinners to pay for the phone bills for long distance calls to his girlfriend. Also use: *Bingo Brown's Guide to Romance* (1992). (Rev: HB 9–10/89*; SLJ 7/89)

**7994** Byars, Betsy. *The Cybil War* (4–6). Illus. by Gail Owens. 1981, Puffin paper $3.99 (0-14-034356-3). 144pp. A humorous story about the relationship between 2 boys and a girl, Cybil.

**7995** Byars, Betsy. *The Seven Treasure Hunts* (3–5). Illus. by Jennifer Barrett. 1992, HarperCollins paper $3.95 (0-06-440435-8). 80pp. Readers giggle and guess their way through the story of Jackson and friend Goat who are into treasure hunts. (Rev: BCCB 4/91; BL 3/15/91; HB 7–8/91; SLJ 6/91)

**7996** Callen, Larry. *Who Kidnapped the Sheriff? Tales from Tickfaw* (4–6). Illus. by Stephen Gammell. 1985, Little, Brown $14.95 (0-316-12499-0). 176pp. The small town of Tickfaw has lots of characters, who are introduced in these related short stories. (Rev: BL 6/1/85; HB 5–6/85; SLJ 8/85)

**7997** Cameron, Ann. *More Stories Huey Tells* (2–4). Illus. 1997, Farrar $13.00 (0-374-35065-5). 128pp. Some humorous everyday adventures experienced by a bright, eager 7-year-old named Huey. (Rev: BCCB 7–8/97; BL 4/15/97; HB 7–8/97; SLJ 6/97)

**7998** Cleary, Beverly. *Ellen Tebbits* (3–5). Illus. by Louis Darling. 1951, Morrow LB $15.93 (0-688-31264-0); Avon paper $4.50 (0-380-70913-9). 160pp. Eight-year-old Ellen has braces on her teeth, takes ballet lessons, and, worst of all, wears long woolen underwear.

**7999** Cleary, Beverly. *Emily's Runaway Imagination* (3–6). Illus. by Beth Krush and Joe Krush. 1961, Morrow LB $15.93 (0-688-31267-5); Avon paper $4.50 (0-380-70923-6). 224pp. Emily's imagination helps get a library for Pitchfork, Oregon, in the 1920s.

**8000** Cleary, Beverly. *Henry Huggins* (3–5). Illus. by Louis Darling. 1950, Morrow LB $15.93 (0-688-31385-X); Avon paper $4.50 (0-380-70912-0). 160pp. Henry is a small boy with a knack for creating hilarious situations. Others in the series: *Henry and Beezus* (1952); *Henry and Ribsy* (1954); *Henry and the Paper Route* (1957); *Henry and the Clubhouse* (1962).

**8001** Cleary, Beverly. *Otis Spofford* (3–6). Illus. by Louis Darling. 1953, Morrow LB $14.93 (0-688-31720-0); Avon paper $4.50 (0-380-70919-8). 192pp. This story of Otis stirring up a little excitement at school is full of humor.

**8002** Cleary, Beverly. *Runaway Ralph* (3–5). Illus. by Louis Darling. 1970, Morrow LB $16.00 (0-688-31701-4). 176pp. A motorcyclist mouse finds family life too stifling so he takes to his wheels, only to find that freedom is an evasive thing. Two others in the series: *The Mouse and the Motorcycle* (1965); *Ralph S. Mouse* (1982).

**8003** Clements, Bruce. *I Tell a Lie Every So Often* (5–8). 1984, Farrar paper $3.50 (0-374-43539-1). 160pp. The adventures of the 14-year-old narrator, an imaginative bender of the truth, and his older brother on a trip up the Missouri River in 1848.

**8004** Clifford, Eth. *Harvey's Horrible Snake Disaster* (3–5). 1984, Houghton $15.00 (0-395-35378-5). 128pp. Harvey tries to disguise the fact that he is petrified of snakes.

**8005** Conford, Ellen. *The Frog Princess of Pelham* (5–7). 1997, Little, Brown $15.95 (0-316-15246-3). 112pp. When Chandler is turned into a frog after kissing the local heartthrob, she tries all sorts of ways to solve this problem. (Rev: BCCB 7–8/97; BL 3/15/97; SLJ 6/97)

**8006** Conford, Ellen. *Get the Picture, Jenny Archer?* (2–4). Illus. 1994, Little, Brown $13.95 (0-316-15247-1). 64pp. Jenny Archer takes pictures of what she thinks are mysterious happenings, but they are really only everyday occurrences. (Rev: BL 12/1/94; SLJ 12/94)

**8007** Conford, Ellen. *Jenny Archer to the Rescue* (3–5). Illus. by Diane Palmisciano. 1992, Little, Brown paper $4.50 (0-316-15369-9). 64pp. Jenny wants to be a hero, so she hunts for someone to save. Also use: *Can Do, Jenny Archer* (1991). (Rev: BL 11/1/90; SLJ 12/90)

**8008** Conford, Ellen. *A Job for Jenny Archer* (2–4). Illus. by Diane Palmisciano. 1990, Little, Brown paper $4.50 (0-316-15349-4). Jenny's plans for an expensive present for her mother's birthday backfire, but she learns that small gifts can be precious, too. (Rev: BL 4/1/88; HB 7–8/88; SLJ 4/88)

**8009** Conford, Ellen. *My Sister the Witch* (3–5). Illus. by Tim Jacobus. Series: Norman Newman. 1996, Troll LB $15.35 (0-8167-3815-7). 92pp. Norman mistakes his sister's readings from *Macbeth* as proof that she is practicing witchcraft. (Rev: SLJ 6/96)

**8010** Conford, Ellen. *Nibble, Nibble, Jenny Archer* (2–4). Illus. by Diane Palmisciano. 1993, Little, Brown $14.95 (0-316-15371-0). 62pp. Jenny's enthusiasm and pride in being part of a TV commercial fades when she sees the final ad. (Rev: BCCB 7–8/93; BL 9/15/93; SLJ 7/93)

**8011** Conford, Ellen. *What's Cooking, Jenny Archer?* (2–4). Illus. by Diane Palmisciano. 1991, Little, Brown paper $3.95 (0-316-15357-5). 80pp. Jenny is inspired to make her own lunches after watching a cooking show. (Rev: BL 1/15/90; SLJ 1/90)

**8012** Corbett, Scott. *The Lemonade Trick* (3–5). Illus. by Paul Galdone. 1988, Scholastic paper $2.99 (0-590-32197-8). 96pp. Kirby and his wonderful chemistry change good boys into bad boys and vice versa.

**8013** Corrin, Sara, comp. *A Time to Laugh: Funny Stories for Children* (3–5). Illus. by Gerald Rose. 1991, Faber paper $3.95 (0-571-15499-9). 142pp. An international collection of humorous stories.

**8014** Cresswell, Helen. *Posy Bates, Again!* (3–5). 1994, Macmillan paper $13.95 (0-02-725372-4). 112pp. Posy is determined to keep the stray dog left behind after her pet show. (Rev: BL 5/15/94; HB 7–8/94; SLJ 6/94)

**8015** Cutler, Jane. *No Dogs Allowed* (3–5). Illus. by Tracey Campbell Pearson. 1992, Farrar $14.00 (0-374-35526-6). 112pp. Edward and his older brother

cannot have a dog because they are allergic, so Edward decides that he is a dog. (Rev: BL 10/15/92*; HB 1–2/93*; SLJ 12/92)

**8016** Cutler, Jane. *Rats!* (3–5). Illus. 1996, Farrar $14.00 (0-374-36181-9). 114pp. Two brothers, one in the fourth grade and the other in the first grade, face everyday crises with amusing results in this sequel to *No Dogs Allowed* (1992). (Rev: BL 2/1/96; HB 5–6/96; SLJ 4/96*)

**8017** Dahl, Roald. *Danny: The Champion of the World* (3–5). Illus. by Jill Bennett. 1975, Knopf LB $16.99 (0-394-93103-3); Puffin paper $4.99 (0-14-032873-4). 208pp. Nine-year-old Danny helps his father on a poaching expedition to wealthy Mr. Hazell's woods.

**8018** Dahl, Roald. *Esio Trot* (3–5). Illus. by Quentin Blake. 1990, Viking paper $15.99 (0-670-83451-3). 64pp. Mr. Hoppy is smitten with Mrs. Silver, whose main concern is her tortoise. (Rev: BCCB 12/90; BL 10/15/90; SLJ 11/90)

**8019** Dahl, Roald. *The Vicar of Nibbleswicke* (4–6). Illus. by Quentin Blake. 1991, Viking paper $12.50 (0-670-84384-9). 24pp. The tale of a shy vicar who suffers from "back-to-front dyslexia," which makes him speak important words backward. (Rev: BL 1/15/92)

**8020** Danziger, Paula. *Amber Brown Goes Fourth* (2–4). Illus. 1995, Putnam $13.99 (0-399-22849-7). 112pp. Amber Brown, a fourth-grader unsure of herself, doesn't know how to react to her divorced mother's new boyfriend. (Rev: BCCB 11/95; BL 10/15/95; HB 11–12/95; SLJ 10/95*)

**8021** Danziger, Paula. *Amber Brown Is Not a Crayon* (2–4). Illus. by Tony Ross. 1994, Putnam $13.99 (0-399-22509-9). 80pp. Amber Brown's close friendship with Justin Daniels will end soon because Justin's family is moving. (Rev: BCCB 6/94; BL 4/15/94; HB 7–8/94; SLJ 5/94*)

**8022** Danziger, Paula. *Amber Brown Sees Red* (2–4). Illus. 1997, Putnam $13.99 (0-399-22901-9). 120pp. Amber Brown is now in the fourth grade and is increasingly upset with her parents' custody battles involving her. (Rev: BL 5/15/97; SLJ 7/97)

**8023** Danziger, Paula. *Make Like a Tree and Leave* (4–6). 1992, Delacorte $13.95 (0-385-30151-0); Dell paper $3.99 (0-440-40577-7). 118pp. Matthew Martin has his problems as chairman of the mummy committee. (Rev: BCCB 11/90; BL 8/90; SLJ 10/90)

**8024** Danziger, Paula. *Not for a Billion Gazillion Dollars* (4–6). 1992, Delacorte $14.95 (0-385-30819-1); Dell paper $3.99 (0-440-40919-5). 128pp. Matthew just has to make money for that expensive computer program. A sequel to *Everyone Else's Parents Said Yes* (1989); *Earth to Matthew* (1991). (Rev: BL 9/1/92; SLJ 9/92)

**8025** Danziger, Paula. *You Can't Eat Your Chicken Pox, Amber Brown* (2–4). Illus. by Tony Ross. 1995, Putnam $13.95 (0-399-22702-4). 112pp. Amber visits London with her aunt while her parents are getting a divorce. A sequel to *Amber Brown Is Not a Crayon* (1994). (Rev: BCCB 4/95; BL 3/15/95; SLJ 6/95*)

**8026** Davol, Marguerite W. *Papa Alonzo Leatherby: A Collection of Tall Tales from the Best Storyteller in Carroll County* (3–6). 1995, Simon & Schuster $14.00 (0-689-80278-1). 70pp. Tall tales from New England that involve the Alonzo family, Papa, his wife Lulie, and 9 children. (Rev: SLJ 10/95)

**8027** Delaney, Michael. *Deep Doo-Doo* (4–6). 1996, Dutton paper $14.99 (0-525-45647-3). 165pp. Bennet and his friend Pete discover that their short-wave set can disrupt local TV programming. (Rev: BCCB 2/97; BL 1/1–15/97; SLJ 12/96)

**8028** Dewey, Ariane. *The Narrow Escapes of Davy Crockett* (2–4). Illus. 1993, Morrow paper $4.95 (0-688-12269-8). 48pp. Stories from The Crockett Almanacs provide wild escapades for young readers. (Rev: BCCB 6/90; BL 3/1/90; SLJ 5/90)

**8029** du Bois, William Pene. *Twenty-One Balloons* (4–6). Illus. by author. 1947, Puffin paper $4.99 (0-14-032097-0). 184pp. Truth and fiction are combined in the adventures of a professor who sails around the world in a balloon. Newbery Medal winner, 1948.

**8030** Duffey, Betsy. *Cody's Secret Admirer* (2–3). Illus. 1998, Viking paper $13.99 (0-670-87400-0). 80pp. A humorous story about 9-year-old Cody, who regards getting a valentine from a secret admirer as "gross." (Rev: BL 2/1/98)

**8031** Duffey, Betsy. *The Gadget War* (2–4). Illus. by Janet Wilson. 1991, Viking paper $12.99 (0-670-84152-8). 64pp. When Albert Einstein Jones comes to third grade, it is hate at first sight for Kelly, undisputed gadget champ. (Rev: BCCB 9/91; BL 10/1/91*; SLJ 11/91)

**8032** Duffey, Betsy. *Hey, New Kid!* (2–4). Illus. 1996, Viking paper $13.99 (0-670-86760-8). 80pp. When third-grader Cody and his family move, the boy decides that it is a perfect time to create a new image. (Rev: BL 4/1/96; HB 7–8/96; SLJ 4/96)

**8033** Duffey, Betsy. *Virtual Cody* (2–4). Illus. 1997, Viking paper $13.99 (0-670-87470-1). 80pp. When Cody learns he was named after a dog, he is fearful that people, particularly P.J. and her friends, will make fun of him. (Rev: BCCB 6/97; BL 6/1–15/97; HB 7–8/97; SLJ 7/97)

**8034** Feiffer, Jules. *The Man in the Ceiling* (5–7). Illus. 1993, HarperCollins $15.00 (0-06-205035-4); paper $5.95 (0-06-205907-6). 192pp. Jimmy turns to cartooning in an effort to gain some recognition in a family that is intent on ignoring him. (Rev: BCCB 12/93; BL 11/15/93; SLJ 2/94*)

**8035** Fitzgerald, John D. *The Great Brain* (4–7). Illus. by Mercer Mayer. 1985, Dial LB $11.89 (0-803-73076-4); Dell paper $3.99 (0-440-43071-2). 192pp. A witty and tender novel in which narrator John recalls the escapades of older brother Tom whose perceptive and crafty schemes set him apart. Some sequels are: *More Adventures of the Great Brain* (1969); *Me and My Little Brain* (1971); *The Great Brain at the Academy* (1972); *The Great Brain Reforms* (1973); *The Return of the Great Brain* (1974); *The Great Brain Does It Again* (1975).

**8036** Fitzgerald, John D. *The Great Brain Is Back* (3–6). Illus. by Diane De Groat. Series: Great Brain. 1995, Dial paper $14.89 (0-8037-1347-9). 128pp. The eighth and last of the series about J.D. and his scheming older brother, Tom. (Rev: BL 1/1/95; SLJ 3/95)

**8037** Fleischman, Sid. *By the Great Horn Spoon* (4–6). Illus. by Eric Von Schmidt. 1988, Little, Brown $16.95 (0-316-28577-3); paper $5.95 (0-316-28612-5). Accompanied by Praiseworthy, the butler, an orphan boy named Jack Fogg runs away and becomes involved in the California gold rush of 1849 in this hilarious adventure story.

**8038** Fleischman, Sid. *Chancy and the Grand Rascal* (5–7). Illus. by Eric Von Schmidt. 1966, Little, Brown $14.95 (0-316-28575-7); paper $4.95 (0-316-26012-6). 190pp. The boy and his uncle, the grand rascal, combine hard work and quick wits to outsmart a scoundrel, hoodwink a miser, and capture a band of outlaws.

**8039** Fleischman, Sid. *The Ghost in the Noonday Sun* (5–7). Illus. by Warren Chappell. 1989, Greenwillow $16.00 (0-688-08410-9); Scholastic paper $3.50 (0-590-43662-7). 144pp. Pirate story with all the standard ingredients of shanghaied boy, villainous captain, and buried treasure.

**8040** Fleischman, Sid. *The Ghost on Saturday Night* (3–5). Illus. by Eric Von Schmidt. 1974, Little, Brown $14.95 (0-316-28583-8). 64pp. Ten-year-old Opie's efforts to raise money for a saddle involve him in a ghost-raising session and the recovery of money stolen from a bank.

**8041** Fleischman, Sid. *Humbug Mountain* (4–6). Illus. by Eric Von Schmidt. 1998, Bantam paper $4.50 (0-440-41403-2). A madcap tall tale adventure in the wild West.

**8042** Fleischman, Sid. *McBroom Tells the Truth* (3–5). Illus. by Walter Lorraine. 1981, Little, Brown $12.45 (0-316-28550-1). 48pp. A tall tale about a New England farmer named McBroom. Also use: *McBroom and the Great Race* (1980).

**8043** Fleischman, Sid. *Mr. Mysterious and Company* (3–5). Illus. by Eric Von Schmidt. 1997, Greenwillow $15.00 (0-688-14921-9); paper $4.95 (0-688-14922-7). A traveling magic show during the 1880s makes for an entertaining family story that is also an excellent historical novel.

**8044** Foley, June. *Susanna Siegelbaum Gives Up Guys* (5–8). 1992, Scholastic paper $3.25 (0-590-43700-3). 160pp. Susanna, a flirt, makes a bet that she can give up guys for 3 months. (Rev: SLJ 8/91)

**8045** Franklin, Kristine L. *Nerd No More* (4–6). 1996, Candlewick $15.99 (1-56402-674-4). 144pp. Wiggie sets out to correct his nerdish image by changing his personality. (Rev: BCCB 10/96; BL 10/15/96; HB 11–12/96; SLJ 10/96)

**8046** Gannett, Ruth. *My Father's Dragon* (4–6). Illus. by author. 1986, Random $14.95 (0-394-88460-4); Knopf paper $4.99 (0-394-89048-5). 88pp. Hilarious adventures of Elmer Elevator. Also use: *The Dragons of Blueland* (1963); *Elmer and the Dragon* (1987).

**8047** Gardiner, John Reynolds. *Top Secret* (4–6). Illus. by Marc Simont. 1995, Little, Brown paper $3.95 (0-316-30363-1). 129pp. Allen is convinced he can solve the world's hunger problem, and when no one believes him he goes to the president of the United States. (Rev: BCCB 11/85; BL 1/15/86; SLJ 11/85)

**8048** Garland, Sarah. *Tex the Cowboy* (K–4). Illus. by author. 1995, Dutton paper $12.99 (0-525-45418-7). Helped by his faithful horse, Gloria, Tex is able to defend the West from a series of villains. (Rev: BCCB 9/95; SLJ 8/95)

**8049** Getz, David. *Almost Famous* (3–5). Illus. 1994, Holt paper $5.95 (0-805-03464-1). 182pp. Overbearing Maxine knows she's destined to be an inventor, but for now, she has to team up with Toni the troublemaker for an invention contest partner. (Rev: BL 12/15/92*; SLJ 2/93)

**8050** Giff, Patricia Reilly. *Meet the Lincoln Lions Band* (2–4). Illus. by Emily Arnold McCully. 1992, Dell paper $3.25 (0-440-40516-5). 72pp. Chrissie, who often feels inadequate compared to her siblings, longs to become a member of the Lincoln Lions band. (Rev: BL 1/15/93)

**8051** Giff, Patricia Reilly. *Not-So-Perfect Rosie* (2–4). Illus. 1997, Viking paper $13.99 (0-670-86968-6). 80pp. Rosie's summer is a busy one, with her planned ballet performance and a visit with a cousin from Ireland. (Rev: BL 5/1/97; SLJ 10/97)

**8052** Gondosch, Linda. *The Monsters of Marble Avenue* (2–4). Illus. by Cat B. Smith. 1988, Little, Brown $10.95 (0-316-31991-0). 64pp. Luke learns the meaning of "the show must go on" when the pup-

pets for his upcoming show are given away by mistake. (Rev: BL 4/1/87; SLJ 8/88)

**8053** Gormley, Beatrice. *The Magic Mean Machine* (4–6). Illus. by Emily Arnold McCully. 1989, Avon paper $2.95 (0-380-75519-X). 128pp. Marvin invents a special machine to ensure that friend Alison will beat bully Spencer at chess. (Rev: BL 7/89)

**8054** Graham, Alastair. *Full Moon Soup: Or the Fall of the Hotel Splendide* (4–8). Illus. by author. 1991, Dial paper $15.00 (0-8037-1045-3). In this wordless book, a series of rooms in the grand Hotel Splendide are pictured at various times of the day. (Rev: SLJ 2/92)

**8055** Graves, Bonnie. *Mystery of the Tooth Gremlin* (2–4). Illus. by Paige Billin-Frye. 1997, Hyperion LB $14.49 (0-7868-2238-4); paper $3.95 (0-7868-1158-7). 64pp. Jessie Stone has 2 problems: Someone has stolen his tooth, and he must read 3 books so that his class can go on a field trip. (Rev: BL 5/15/97; SLJ 8/97)

**8056** Greene, Constance C. *Isabelle the Itch* (4–6). Illus. by Emily Arnold McCully. 1992, Puffin paper $4.50 (0-14-036028-X). 128pp. Isabelle is a hyperactive fifth-grader who expends her energies in many directions, not getting much of anywhere.

**8057** Greenwald, Sheila. *Mariah Delany's Author-of-the-Month Club* (4–6). 1990, Troll paper $2.95 (0-8167-3000-8). 124pp. Mariah is back in business with an author-of-the-month club. (Rev: BL 12/1/90; SLJ 12/91)

**8058** Greenwald, Sheila. *Rosy Cole: She Grows and Graduates* (3–5). Illus. 1997, Orchard LB $15.99 (0-531-33022-2). 92pp. This sunny, gentle comedy centers on Rosy Cole and the choice she must make concerning which high school to attend. (Rev: BL 11/1/97; SLJ 11/97)

**8059** Greenwald, Sheila. *Rosy Cole: She Walks in Beauty* (3–5). Illus. 1994, Little, Brown $14.95 (0-316-32743-3). 83pp. Rosy decides to transform herself into a beauty and goes to an art museum to look for role models. (Rev: BCCB 1/95; BL 12/15/94; SLJ 1/95)

**8060** Greer, Gery, and Bob Ruddick. *This Island Isn't Big Enough for the Four of Us!* (4–6). 1987, HarperCollins paper $3.95 (0-06-440203-7). 160pp. It's boys against girls in this tale of too many camping out on Turtle Island. (Rev: BCCB 9/87; BL 7/87; SLJ 8/87)

**8061** Gutman, Dan. *The Kid Who Ran for President* (4–6). 1996, Scholastic $15.95 (0-590-93987-4). 144pp. A 12-year-old boy runs an outrageous campaign when he decides to run for U.S. president. (Rev: BCCB 11/96; BL 11/1/96; SLJ 11/96)

**8062** Haas, Dorothy. *Burton and the Giggle Machine* (3–6). Illus. by Cathy Bobak. 1996, Pocket paper

$3.50 (0-671-79897-9). 160pp. Can the scion of the famous family of inventors produce a giggle machine that will make his friends happy enough to forget their problems? (Rev: BCCB 4/92; BL 2/15/92; SLJ 4/92)

**8063** Haas, Jessie. *Clean House* (2–4). 1996, Greenwillow $15.00 (0-688-14079-3). 56pp. When relatives visit Tess's newly cleaned house, she makes them feel at home by returning it to its usual state. (Rev: BCCB 3/96; BL 4/15/96; HB 5–6/96; SLJ 5/96)

**8064** Hall, Lynn. *The Secret Life of Dagmar Schultz* (4–6). 1988, Macmillan $13.95 (0-684-18915-1). 96pp. Dagmar, oldest of 6, longs for something of her own, so when best friend Shelly gets a boyfriend, Dagmar makes up one for herself. (Rev: BL 6/1/88; HB 7–8/88; SLJ 4/88)

**8065** Hayes, Daniel. *Eye of the Beholder* (5–8). 1998, Fawcett paper $4.99 (0-449-00235-7). 192pp. Two eighth-graders, looking for the lost work of a famous sculptor, try their hand at the art. (Rev: BL 2/1/93; SLJ 12/92)

**8066** Heide, Florence Parry. *The Shrinking of Treehorn* (2–5). Illus. by Edward Gorey. 1971, Holiday $12.95 (0-8234-0189-8); paper $4.95 (0-8234-0975-9). 64pp. Treehorn has a special talent — he can become smaller by the moment — but nobody notices. A sequel is: *The Adventures of Treehorn* (1983).

**8067** Heide, Florence Parry. *Tales for the Perfect Child* (3–6). Illus. by Victoria Chess. 1985, Dell paper $2.99 (0-440-40463-0). 80pp. Seven "wicked morality" tales, including one in which Gertrude and Gloria get to help mother with the dishes; Gertrude is careful, but Gloria drops the plates, so Gertrude gets to help every day and Gloria gets to go out and play. (Rev: BL 10/1/85; HB 11–12/85; SLJ 10/85)

**8068** Herman, Charlotte. *Max Malone, Superstar* (3–5). Illus. by Cat B. Smith. 1992, Holt $14.95 (0-8050-1375-X). 68pp. In this adventure, Max decides that he wants to become a TV star. (Rev: BCCB 6/92; BL 2/15/92; SLJ 8/92)

**8069** Herman, Charlotte. *Max Malone the Magnificent* (3–5). Illus. by Cat B. Smith. 1993, Holt $14.95 (0-8050-2282-1); paper $4.95 (0-8050-3548-6). 64pp. After learning simple tricks, Max goes to the magic shop for more "sophisticated" illusions. (Rev: BL 2/15/93)

**8070** Hermes, Patricia. *Kevin Corbett Eats Flies* (4–6). Illus. 1986, Harcourt $13.00 (0-15-242290-0); Pocket paper $3.90 (0-671-69183-X). 160pp. Kevin and his father move around whenever the mood strikes; now Kevin doesn't want to move anymore and thinks that if his father fell in love, he wouldn't want to either. (Rev: BCCB 9/86; BL 8/86; SLJ 5/86)

**8071** Hermes, Patricia. *Nothing but Trouble* (4–6). 1994, Scholastic $13.95 (0-590-43499-3). 160pp. A humorous story about a fifth-grader who wants to prove herself as a baby-sitter. (Rev: BL 3/15/94; SLJ 4/94)

**8072** Hodgman, Ann. *My Babysitter Is a Vampire* (3–6). Illus. by John Pierard. 1991, Pocket paper $3.50 (0-671-64751-2). 121pp. Meg and Trevor do research on how to get rid of Vincent Graver, their baby-sitter, who they believe is a vampire. (Rev: SLJ 12/91)

**8073** Horvath, Polly. *The Happy Yellow Car* (5–7). 1994, Farrar $15.00 (0-374-32845-5). 150pp. In a small Missouri town, where this humorous story takes place, 12-year-old Betty Grunt must find a dollar if she wants to be elected Pork-Fry Queen. (Rev: BCCB 11/94; BL 8/94; SLJ 9/94)

**8074** Horvath, Polly. *No More Cornflakes* (4–6). 1990, Farrar $14.00 (0-374-35530-4). 134pp. Ten-year-old Hortense has come up with a weird plan to get the eccentric Hemple family closer together. (Rev: BCCB 10/90; BL 10/1/90; HB 1–2/91)

**8075** Horvath, Polly. *An Occasional Cow* (4–6). Illus. by Gioia Fiammenghi. 1989, Farrar $13.95 (0-374-35559-2); paper $3.95 (0-374-45573-2). 112pp. Imogene's camp burns down, so she is shipped off to Iowa to stay with relatives. (Rev: BCCB 5/89; BL 5/15/89; HB 6/89)

**8076** Horvath, Polly. *When the Circus Came to Town* (5–8). 1996, Farrar $15.00 (0-374-38308-1). 144pp. Ivy witnesses her town develop divided loyalties when a circus troupe decides to relocate there. (Rev: BCCB 12/96; BL 11/15/96; SLJ 12/96*)

**8077** Howe, Deborah, and James Howe. *Bunnicula: A Rabbit Tale of Mystery* (4–6). Illus. by Alan Daniel. 1979, Macmillan $15.00 (0-689-30700-4); Avon paper $3.99 (0-380-51094-4). 112pp. A dog named Harold tells the story of a rabbit many believe to be a vampire. Two sequels by James Howe are: *Howliday Inn* (1982); *The Celery Stalks at Midnight* (1983).

**8078** Howe, James. *The New Nick Kramer; or, My Life as a Baby-sitter* (5–8). 1995, Hyperion LB $14.49 (0-7868-2053-5). 120pp. Nick and rival Mitch make an unusual bet on who will win the affections of newcomer Jennifer. (Rev: BL 12/15/95; SLJ 1/96)

**8079** Howe, James. *Nighty-Nightmare* (3–6). Illus. by Leslie Morrill. 1987, Macmillan $15.00 (0-689-31207-5); Avon paper $3.99 (0-380-70490-0). 128pp. Harold the canine and friends set out on a camping trip. (Rev: BCCB 4/87; BL 3/1/87; SLJ 4/87)

**8080** Howe, James. *Return to Howliday Inn* (3–6). Illus. by Alan Daniel. 1992, Macmillan $14.00 (0-689-31661-5). 174pp. With the vampire bunny off with friends, the focus is on the Chateau Bow-Wow where the family boards their cat and dogs. (Rev: BL 5/1/92; HB 7–8/92; SLJ 5/92)

**8081** Hughes, Dean. *Nutty, the Movie Star* (4–6). 1989, Macmillan $15.00 (0-689-31509-0); paper $3.95 (0-689-71524-2). 144pp. Friend William gets Nutty a job in Hollywood. (Rev: BL 10/15/89; SLJ 10/89)

**8082** Hughes, Shirley. *Here Comes Charlie Moon* (4–5). Illus. 1990, Chivers $17.95 (0-7451-1067-3). 144pp. Charlie has many adventures in Wales, where his aunt owns a joke-and-novelty shop; many Briticisms. (Rev: BCCB 6/86; BL 7/86; SLJ 12/86)

**8083** Hurwitz, Johanna. *Aldo Applesauce* (3–5). Illus. by John Wallner. 1979, Morrow LB $15.93 (0-688-32199-2); Puffin paper $3.99 (0-14-034083-1). 128pp. Aldo moves to New York City and acquires a new nickname and a strange friend. Two others in the series are: *Much Ado About Aldo* (1978); *Aldo Ice Cream* (1981).

**8084** Hurwitz, Johanna. *Ali Baba Bernstein, Lost and Found* (3–5). Illus. by Karen Milone. 1992, Morrow LB $13.93 (0-688-11455-5). 96pp. Ali Baba finds a hundred-dollar bill and gets to claim it. (Rev: BCCB 9/92; BL 10/15/92; SLJ 11/92)

**8085** Hurwitz, Johanna. *Elisa in the Middle* (2–4). Illus. by Lillian Hoban. Series: Russell and Elisa. 1995, Morrow $15.00 (0-688-14050-5). 64pp. In her efforts to help members of her family, Elisa often causes mayhem and catastrophe in this humorous beginning chapter book. (Rev: BCCB 10/95; BL 9/1/95; HB 11–12/95; SLJ 10/95)

**8086** Jones, Rebecca C. *Germy Blew the Bugle* (4–6). 1990, Arcade $14.95 (1-55970-088-2). 144pp. Germy wants to start a school newspaper. (Rev: BL 8/90; SLJ 9/90)

**8087** Joosse, Barbara M. *Wild Willie and King Kyle Detectives* (2–4). Illus. by Sue Truesdell. 1993, Houghton $12.95 (0-395-64338-4). 66pp. After Kyle's best friend and next-door neighbor moves away, Lucy moves in. (Rev: BL 5/1/93; SLJ 6/93)

**8088** Keller, Beverly. *Desdemona: Twelve Going on Desperate* (5–7). 1986, Lothrop $13.00 (0-688-06076-5); HarperCollins paper $4.95 (0-06-440226-6). 160pp. Mishap after mishap befalls Desdemona, including running into the handsomest boy in school. A sequel is: *Fowl Play, Desdemona* (1989). (Rev: BCCB 12/86; BL 10/1/86; SLJ 11/86)

**8089** Keller, Holly. *I Am Angela* (2–4). Illus. 1997, Greenwillow $15.00 (0-688-14967-7). 64pp. In a short chapter book, Angela thinks about the recent important events in her life, like visiting a zoo and setting up a class exhibit. (Rev: BL 5/15/97; SLJ 5/97)

**8090** Kerr, M. E. *Dinky Hocker Shoots Smack!* (6–8). 1972, HarperCollins paper $4.50 (0-06-447006-7). 204pp. Dinky, a compulsive eater, tries many ways to gain her parents' attention.

**8091** Kidd, Ronald. *Sammy Carducci's Guide to Women* (5–7). 1995, Dramatic Publishing $3.50 (0-87129-522-9). 112pp. A somewhat sexist sixth-grader discovers that, where women are concerned, perhaps he is not as irresistible as he thinks he is. (Rev: BCCB 1/92; BL 1/1/92; SLJ 1/92)

**8092** Kline, Suzy. *Orp* (4–6). 1989, Putnam $13.95 (0-399-21639-1); Avon paper $3.50 (0-380-71038-2). 94pp. Orville is so discontented with his name that he forms the I Hate My Name Club. (Rev: BL 7/89)

**8093** Kline, Suzy. *Orp and the Chop Suey Burgers* (4–6). 1990, Putnam $13.95 (0-399-22185-9); Avon paper $3.50 (0-380-71359-4). 94pp. Orville Rudemeyer Pyugenski, Jr., enters a cooking contest for a trip to Disney World. (Rev: BL 6/1/90; SLJ 9/90)

**8094** Kline, Suzy. *Orp Goes to the Hoop* (5–7). 1993, Avon paper $3.50 (0-380-71829-4). 109pp. Seventh-grader Orp gets a chance to play a big part in the basketball team's big game. (Rev: BCCB 7–8/91; BL 7/91; SLJ 7/91)

**8095** Kline, Suzy. *Who's Orp's Girlfriend?* (5–7). 1993, Putnam $13.95 (0-399-22431-9). 94pp. Orp, who is attracted to 2 girls, makes a date with both of them for the same night. (Rev: BL 8/93; SLJ 7/93)

**8096** Konigsburg, E. L. *About the B'nai Bagels* (3–6). Illus. by author. 1971, Dell paper $3.99 (0-440-40034-1). 176pp. Poor Mark — his mother is the manager of the Little League baseball team on which he plays, and his older brother is the coach.

**8097** Korman, Gordon. *The Chicken Doesn't Skate* (4–6). 1996, Scholastic $14.95 (0-590-85300-7). 192pp. As part of his science fair project on food chains, Milo plans to eat Henrietta, a chicken who has become the school mascot. (Rev: BL 11/15/96; SLJ 11/96)

**8098** Kraus, Robert. *Fables Aesop Never Wrote: But Robert Kraus Did* (3–5). Illus. 1994, Viking paper $14.99 (0-670-85630-4). 32pp. Humorous variations of Aesop's originals, e.g., *The City Moose and the Country Moose* and *The Wolf Who Cried Boy*. (Rev: BL 1/1/95; SLJ 2/95)

**8099** Kraus, Robert. *Near Myths: Dug Up and Dusted Off* (3–5). Illus. 1996, Viking paper $14.99 (0-670-85751-3). 32pp. With tongue in cheek, several myths are retold. For example, in one, the greatest of Hercules' labors is to clean his room. (Rev: BCCB 7–8/96; BL 5/1/96; SLJ 6/96)

**8100** Lawson, Robert. *Ben and Me* (5–8). Illus. by author. 1939, Little, Brown $16.95 (0-316-51732-1); paper $5.95 (0-316-51730-5). The events of Benjamin Franklin's life, as told by his good mouse Amos, who lived in his old fur cap.

**8101** Lawson, Robert. *Captain Kidd's Cat* (3–5). Illus. by author. 1984, Little, Brown paper $7.95 (0-316-51735-6). A narrative recount by McDermot, faithful cat of Captain William Kidd.

**8102** Lawson, Robert. *Mr. Revere and I* (5–8). Illus. by author. 1953, Little, Brown paper $5.95 (0-316-51729-1). 152pp. A delightful account of certain episodes in Revere's life, as revealed by his horse Scheherazade.

**8103** Levoy, Myron. *The Magic Hat of Mortimer Wintergreen* (4–6). 1988, HarperCollins $11.95 (0-06-023841-0). 224pp. Joshua and Amy escape from creepy Aunt Vootch with a magician and search for their grandparents. (Rev: BL 2/15/88; SLJ 3/88)

**8104** Lexau, Joan M. *Trouble Will Find You* (3–5). Illus. by Michael Chesworth. 1994, Houghton $14.95 (0-395-64380-5). 68pp. Diz promises to keep out of trouble for a day, but it is difficult with jewel thieves all around. (Rev: BL 4/1/94; SLJ 4/94)

**8105** Lindgren, Astrid. *Pippi Longstocking* (4–6). Trans. by Florence Lamborn. Illus. by Louis Glanzman. 1950, Puffin paper $3.99 (0-14-030957-8). 158pp. A little Swedish tomboy who has a monkey and a horse for companions. Also use: *Pippi Goes on Board* (1957); *Pippi in the South Seas* (1959).

**8106** Lowry, Lois. *Anastasia, Absolutely* (4–6). Series: Anastasia Krupnik. 1995, Houghton $13.95 (0-395-74521-7); Bantam paper $3.99 (0-440-41222-6). 176pp. Anastasia absentmindedly throws a bag filled with her dog's poop into a mailbox and incurs an investigation by the police. (Rev: BCCB 9/95; BL 10/1/95; HB 11–12/95; SLJ 10/95)

**8107** Lowry, Lois. *Anastasia at This Address* (5–8). 1991, Houghton $15.00 (0-395-56263-5). 112pp. Seventh-grader Anastasia Krupnik answers a personal ad, using her mother's picture instead of her own. (Rev: BCCB 3/91; BL 4/1/91; SLJ 8/91)

**8108** Lowry, Lois. *Anastasia Krupnik* (4–6). 1979, Houghton $15.00 (0-395-28629-8); Bantam paper $2.99 (0-440-22784-4). 160pp. A lively romp with an intelligent and articulate 10-year-old girl leading the way. Three sequels are: *Anastasia Again!* (1981); *Anastasia at Your Service* (1982); *Anastasia, Ask Your Analyst* (1984).

**8109** Lowry, Lois. *Anastasia on Her Own* (5–7). Illus. 1985, Houghton $16.00 (0-395-38133-9); Dell paper $3.99 (0-440-40291-3). 131pp. Seventh-grader Anastasia Krupnik must face both domestic crisis and romance. Another chapter in Anastasia's busy life is recounted in *Anastasia Has the Answers* (1986). (Rev: BL 5/15/85; HB 9–10/85; SLJ 8/85)

**8110** Lowry, Lois. *Anastasia's Chosen Career* (5–7). 1987, Houghton $16.00 (0-395-42506-9); Bantam

paper $3.99 (0-440-40100-3). Thirteen-year-old Anastasia gets some surprises when she begs to go to charm school to change her freaky looks. Anastasia's baby brother is featured in *All About Sam* (1988). (Rev: BCCB 9/87; BL 9/1/87; SLJ 9/87)

**8111** Lowry, Lois. *Attaboy, Sam!* (2–5). Illus. by Diane De Groat. 1992, Houghton $14.95 (0-395-61588-7). 116pp. Anastasia Krupnik's little brother, Sam, decides to make perfume for his mother's birthday. (Rev: BCCB 4/92; BL 2/15/92*; HB 7–8/92*; SLJ 5/92*)

**8112** Lowry, Lois. *The One Hundredth Thing About Caroline* (5–7). 1983, Houghton $16.00 (0-395-34829-3); Dell paper $3.99 (0-440-46625-3). 160pp. Caroline tries everything and anything to break up her mother's new romance.

**8113** Lowry, Lois. *See You Around, Sam!* (3–6). Illus. by Diane De Groat. 1996, Houghton $15.00 (0-395-81664-5). 144pp. Sam decides to run away to Alaska because his mother won't let him wear his plastic fangs. (Rev: BCCB 11/96; BL 10/1/96*; HB 9–10/96; SLJ 10/96*)

**8114** Lowry, Lois. *Switcharound* (5–7). 1985, Houghton $16.00 (0-395-39536-4); Dell paper $3.50 (0-440-48415-4). Caroline and her nemesis brother J.P. must spend the summer with their divorced father's new family in Des Moines. A sequel to: *The One Hundredth Thing about Caroline* (1983). (Rev: BCCB 1/86; BL 10/1/85; HB 1–2/86)

**8115** Lynch, Chris. *Babes in the Woods* (5–7). 1997, HarperCollins paper $4.50 (0-06-440656-3). 128pp. Thirteen-year-old Stephen and 3 unusual colleagues go on a wilderness trip in this funny adventure of the He-Man Women Haters Club. Also from the series: *Johnny Chesthair* (1997). (Rev: BL 2/15/97; HB 5–6/97; SLJ 3/97)

**8116** Lynch, Chris. *Scratch and the Sniffs* (5–7). 1997, HarperCollins paper $4.50 (0-06-440657-1). 128pp. The members of the He-Man Woman Haters Club, under the leadership of wheelchair-bound Wolf, decide to form their own rock band. (Rev: BL 4/15/97; HB 5–6/97; SLJ 8/97)

**8117** McCloskey, Robert. *Homer Price* (3–6). Illus. by author. 1943, Puffin paper $3.99 (0-14-030927-6). 160pp. Popular and preposterous adventures of a Midwestern boy. Continued in: *Centerburg Tales* (1951).

**8118** MacDonald, Amy. *No More Nice* (4–7). Illus. 1996, Orchard LB $15.99 (0-531-08892-8). 128pp. A humorous story about a spring vacation spent by a boy with his eccentric great-aunt and -uncle. (Rev: BCCB 10/96; BL 9/1/96; SLJ 9/96)

**8119** Mackay, Claire, sel. *Laughs* (5–8). 1997, Tundra paper $6.95 (0-88776-393-6). 199pp. An anthology of humorous stories from well-known Canadian writers. (Rev: SLJ 9/97)

**8120** McKenna, Colleen O'Shaughnessy. *Mother Murphy* (5–7). 1993, Scholastic paper $2.95 (0-590-44856-0). 160pp. With her mother confined to bed, 12-year-old Collette volunteers as mother-for-a-day with disasterous and funny results. (Rev: BCCB 2/92; BL 2/1/92; SLJ 2/92)

**8121** MacLachlan, Patricia. *Arthur, for the Very First Time* (4–6). Illus. by Lloyd Bloom. 1980, Harper-Collins LB $14.89 (0-06-024047-4); paper $4.95 (0-06-440288-6). 128pp. Arthur spends a summer on the farm of his aunt and uncle.

**8122** Mahy, Margaret. *The Birthday Burglar and a Very Wicked Headmistress* (5–7). Illus. by Margaret Chamberlain. 1991, Chivers $15.95 (0-7451-1407-5). 144pp. Humorous tales about a boy who lives on an island with his butler, and the story of a head-mistress who opens a school for rich kids and then saves money by being various teachers. (Rev: BCCB 10/88; BL 11/15/88; SLJ 10/88)

**8123** Manes, Stephen. *Be a Perfect Person in Just Three Days!* (4–6). Illus. by Tom Huffman. 1982, Houghton $16.00 (0-89919-064-2); Bantam paper $2.99 (0-440-22790-9). 64pp. Milo Crinkley decides to change his ways via a book he has found in the library.

**8124** Manes, Stephen. *Chocolate-Covered Ants* (4–6). 1993, Scholastic paper $2.95 (0-590-40961-1). 128pp. Max bets his brother that people do eat chocolate-covered ants. (Rev: BCCB 12/92; BL 9/1/90; SLJ 12/90)

**8125** Manes, Stephen. *The Great Gerbil Roundup* (3–5). Illus. by John McKinley. 1988, Harcourt $13.95 (0-15-232490-9); paper $4.50 (0-06-440375-0). 105pp. Industry takes over the Gerbil town, and tourists flock to the Great Gerbil Roundup. (Rev: BL 12/15/88; SLJ 1/89)

**8126** Manes, Stephen. *Make Four Million Dollars by Next Thursday!* (3–6). Illus. by George Ulrich. 1996, Bantam paper $3.99 (0-440-41370-2). 112pp. Would-be millionaire Jazon Nozzle finds a book that tells him how to do it. (Rev: BCCB 2/91; BL 2/15/91; SLJ 6/91)

**8127** Merrill, Jean. *The Pushcart War* (5–7). Illus. by Ronni Solbert. 1987, Dell paper $4.99 (0-440-47147-8). 224pp. Mack, driving a Mighty Mammoth, runs down a pushcart belonging to Morris the Florist, and a most unusual war is on!

**8128** Merrill, Jean. *The Toothpaste Millionaire* (4–6). Illus. by Jan Palmer. 1974, Houghton $16.00 (0-395-18511-4). 96pp. Kate tells the delightful story of a black boy, Rufus, who challenges the entire business community by marketing a product called simply "toothpaste."

**8129** Mills, Claudia. *Dinah in Love* (4–7). 1993, Macmillan LB $14.00 (0-02-766998-X). 148pp. Dinah can't believe that boorish Nick, who continually insults her, really likes her. (Rev: BL 11/15/93; SLJ 12/93)

**8130** Murphy, Jill. *Jeffrey Strangeways* (3–5). Illus. 1992, Candlewick $14.95 (1-56402-018-5). 140pp. Eleven-year-old Jeffrey, who unfortunately is very clumsy, wants nothing more than to become a knight. (Rev: BCCB 9/92; BL 6/15/92; SLJ 5/92)

**8131** Myers, Laurie. *Garage Sale Fever* (2–4). Illus. by Kathleen C. Howell. 1993, HarperCollins LB $12.89 (0-06-022908-X). 86pp. Will must retrieve a plaque that he has put in a garage sale before the girl who gave it to him discovers that it has been sold. (Rev: BL 11/15/93; SLJ 5/94)

**8132** Naylor, Phyllis Reynolds. *Alice In-Between* (5–7). 1994, Atheneum $15.00 (0-689-31890-1). 160pp. Alice, now 13, along with her friends, is becoming very aware of her changing body and of boys in this humorous look at early adolescence. (Rev: BCCB 5/94; BL 5/1/94; HB 7–8/94; SLJ 6/94)

**8133** Naylor, Phyllis Reynolds. *Alice in Rapture, Sort Of* (4–7). 1989, Macmillan $16.00 (0-689-31466-3); Dell paper $3.50 (0-440-40462-2). 176pp. Alice and her friends vow to find boyfriends before summer's end. (Rev: HB 5–6/89; SLJ 4/89)

**8134** Naylor, Phyllis Reynolds. *Beetles, Lightly Toasted* (4–6). 1987, Macmillan $16.00 (0-689-31355-1). 144pp. Andy must test his essay premise that beetles are good eating. (Rev: BCCB 11/87; BL 9/1/87; SLJ 10/87)

**8135** Naylor, Phyllis Reynolds. *Boys Against Girls* (4–6). 1994, Delacorte $14.95 (0-385-32081-7). 147pp. Boys and girls try to trick each other into believing that a strange monster exists, and maybe they are right. (Rev: BCCB 11/94; BL 9/1/94; SLJ 11/94)

**8136** Naylor, Phyllis Reynolds. *The Boys Start the War* (4–6). 1993, Delacorte $15.95 (0-385-30814-0). 144pp. Four brothers torment a group of girls who have moved where their favorite chums used to live. (Rev: SLJ 3/93)

**8137** Naylor, Phyllis Reynolds. *The Girls Get Even* (3–5). 1993, Delacorte $14.95 (0-385-31029-3). 144pp. The Malloy girls try to outwit the Hartford boys in this humorous novel set in a West Virginia town. (Rev: BL 8/93)

**8138** Naylor, Phyllis Reynolds. *Outrageously Alice* (5–8). Series: A Jean Karl Book. 1997, Simon & Schuster $15.00 (0-689-80354-0). 133pp. Thirteen-year-old Alice, now in the eighth grade, decides that she is too ordinary and wants to do something about it. (Rev: BCCB 7–8/97; HB 7–8/98; SLJ 6/97)

**8139** Park, Barbara. *Junie B. Jones and a Little Monkey Business* (2–3). Illus. by Denise Brunkus. 1993, Random paper $3.99 (0-679-83886-4). 46pp. Junie is amazed to learn that her new brother is a monkey after grandmother declares, "He's the cutest monkey I've ever seen!" (Rev: BL 3/1/93)

**8140** Park, Barbara. *Junie B. Jones and Some Sneaky Peeky Spying* (2–4). Illus. 1994, Random LB $11.99 (0-679-95101-6); paper $3.99 (0-679-85101-1). 66pp. Junie's flair for sleuthing and misinterpreting ordinary occurrences gets her into trouble. (Rev: BL 11/15/94; SLJ 10/94)

**8141** Park, Barbara. *Junie B. Jones and the Stupid Smelly Bus* (2–3). Illus. by Denise Brunkus. 1992, Random LB $11.99 (0-679-92642-9); paper $3.99 (0-679-82642-4). 70pp. Junie B. is a cross between Lily Tomlin's Edith Ann and Eloise in this funny story of a youngster on her way to kindergarten. (Rev: BL 12/1/92; SLJ 11/92)

**8142** Park, Barbara. *The Kid in the Red Jacket* (4–6). 1988, Knopf paper $3.99 (0-394-80571-2). 128pp. Ten-year-old Howard is having some trouble adjusting to life in Massachusetts when his family moves from Arizona. (Rev: BCCB 3/87; BL 2/15/87; SLJ 3/87)

**8143** Park, Barbara. *Operation: Dump the Chump* (3–6). Illus. by Robert Sauber. 1989, Knopf paper $4.99 (0-394-82592-6). 128pp. Oscar Winkle devises a plan to get rid of his young brother.

**8144** Peck, Richard. *Bel-Air Bambi and the Mall Rats* (5–7). 1993, Delacorte $15.95 (0-385-30823-X). 192pp. The Babcock family has a series of zany adventures when, after losing their wealth, they are forced to live as ordinary folk in a small town. (Rev: BCCB 10/93; BL 9/1/93; SLJ 9/93*)

**8145** Peck, Robert Newton. *Higbee's Halloween* (5–7). 1990, Walker LB $14.85 (0-8027-6969-1). 101pp. Higbee decides something must be done about the unruly Striker children. (Rev: SLJ 10/90)

**8146** Pilkey, Dav. *The Adventures of Captain Underpants* (2–4). Illus. 1997, Scholastic $16.95 (0-590-84627-2). 128pp. A superhero spoof in which 2 boys capture their principal and turn him into Captain Underpants. (Rev: BL 7/97; SLJ 12/97)

**8147** Pinkwater, Daniel. *Fat Men from Space* (3–6). Illus. by author. 1977, Dell paper $3.25 (0-440-44542-6). 64pp. Among other adventures, William encounters raiders of junk food from outer space in this nutrition-conscious farce.

**8148** Pinkwater, Daniel. *The Hoboken Chicken Emergency* (3–7). 1977, Simon & Schuster LB $4.95 (0-671-66447-6). 94pp. A young boy buys a 6-foot, 260-pound chicken in this humorous story.

**8149** Pinkwater, Daniel. *The Snarkout Boys and the Avocado of Death* (5–8). 1983, NAL paper $2.50 (0-451-15852-0). 160pp. In this zany adventure, Walter and Winston search for Rat Face's missing uncle. A sequel is: *The Snarkout Boys and the Baconburg Horror* (1985).

**8150** Pollack, Pamela, ed. *The Random House Book of Humor for Children* (4–6). Illus. by Paul O. Zelinsky. 1988, Random LB $16.99 (0-394-98049-2). 320pp. Excerpts from popular humor writers. (Rev: BCCB 1/89; BL 11/15/88; SLJ 12/88)

**8151** Poploff, Michelle. *Busy O'Brien and the Great Bubble Gum Blowout* (3–5). Illus. by Abby Carter. 1990, Walker LB $13.85 (0-8027-6984-5). 80pp. Ten-year-old Busy O'Brien wishes she had more time to spend with her mom so she devises a plan. (Rev: BL 12/15/90; SLJ 10/90)

**8152** Pryor, Bonnie. *Vinegar Pancakes and Vanishing Cream* (2–4). Illus. by Gail Owens. 1987, Morrow $16.00 (0-688-06728-X). 128pp. The ups and downs of life for Martin Elwood Snodgrass, who has too-successful older siblings and a too-cute baby brother. (Rev: BL 6/15/87; SLJ 6–7/87)

**8153** Quigley, James. *Johnny Germ Head* (2–5). Illus. 1997, Holt $14.95 (0-8050-5395-6). 72pp. After his parents buy him a microscope and books about the human body, Johnny becomes a hypochondriac. (Rev: BL 12/1/97; SLJ 12/97)

**8154** Raskin, Ellen. *The Mysterious Disappearance of Leon (I Mean Noel)* (4–6). Illus. by author. 1989, Puffin paper $4.99 (0-14-032945-5). 160pp. Humorous saga of Mrs. Carillon's search for her husband Leon (or Noel), who is the joint heir to a soup fortune.

**8155** Regan, Dian C. *Monster of the Month Club* (3–5). Illus. by Laura Cornell. 1994, Holt $14.95 (0-8050-3443-9). 143pp. Rilla's life becomes chaotic when she begins receiving pets from the Monster of the Month Club. (Rev: BCCB 1/95; BL 1/1/95; SLJ 3/95)

**8156** Richler, Mordecai. *Jacob Two-Two's First Spy Case* (4–5). Illus. 1997, Farrar $16.00 (0-374-33659-8). 152pp. Jacob Two-Two and a friend discover that the new headmaster at their school has his hands in the till in this humorous adventure. (Rev: BL 8/97; HB 7–8/97; SLJ 8/97)

**8157** Robertson, Keith. *Henry Reed, Inc.* (5–7). Illus. by Robert McCloskey. 1989, Puffin paper $4.99 (0-14-034144-7). 240pp. Told deadpan in diary form, this story of Henry's enterprising summer in New Jersey presents one of the most amusing boys since Tom and Huck. Others in the series: *Henry Reed's Journey* (1963); *Henry Reed's Baby-Sitting Service* (1966); *Henry Reed's Big Show* (1970).

**8158** Robinson, Barbara. *The Best School Year Ever* (3–5). 1994, HarperCollins LB $14.89 (0-06-023043-

6). 128pp. Beth has to write a complimentary composition about a classmate who appears to have no redeeming qualities. (Rev: BL 10/15/94; HB 11–12/94; SLJ 10/94)

**8159** Robinson, Barbara. *My Brother Louis Measures Worms and Other Louis Stories* (3–6). 1988, HarperCollins LB $14.89 (0-06-025083-6); paper $4.50 (0-06-440362-9). 160pp. Events in 10 stories of the wild Lawson family. (Rev: BCCB 12/88; BL 11/1/88; SLJ 12/88)

**8160** Rockwell, Thomas. *How to Eat Fried Worms* (4–6). Illus. by Emily Arnold McCully. 1973, Watts LB $24.00 (0-531-02631-0); Dell paper $4.99 (0-440-44545-0). 128pp. In this very humorous story, Billy takes on a bet — he will eat 15 worms in 15 days. His family and friends help devise ways to cook them.

**8161** Rodgers, Mary. *Freaky Friday* (4–7). 1972, HarperCollins LB $15.89 (0-06-025049-6); paper $4.95 (0-06-440046-8). 156pp. Thirteen-year-old Annabel learns some valuable lessons during the day she becomes her mother. Two sequels are: *A Billion for Boris* (1974); *Summer Switch* (1982).

**8162** Rodowsky, Colby. *Dog Days* (3–5). Illus. by Kathleen C. Howell. 1990, Farrar $14.00 (0-374-36342-0). 144pp. It looks like Rosie is in for a dull summer until a famous author and her golden retriever move in next door. (Rev: BCCB 3/91; BL 1/1/91; HB 3–4/91; SLJ 2/91)

**8163** Roos, Stephen. *Twelve-Year-Old Vows Revenge After Being Dumped by Extraterrestrial on First Date* (5–6). Illus. 1991, Dell paper $3.25 (0-440-40465-7). 119pp. The rivalry between 2 girls reaches such a point that they take the matter to court. (Rev: BL 5/15/90; SLJ 7/90)

**8164** Ross, Rhea Beth. *The Bet's On, Lizzie Bingman!* (4–7). 1988, Houghton paper $4.95 (0-395-64375-9). 192pp. If Tom Sawyer had a sister, it would be Lizzie, because she has a genius for getting into trouble. (Rev: HB 7–8/88)

**8165** Ryan, Mary C. *My Friend, O'Connell* (3–5). Illus. by Patrick Chapin. 1991, Avon paper $2.95 (0-380-76145-9). 104pp. In this humorous story, Bradley and friend O'Connell get involved in such situations as running a golf tournament and organizing a school cafeteria boycott. (Rev: BL 6/15/91)

**8166** Sachar, Louis. *Marvin Redpost: Is He a Girl?* (2–4). Illus. by Barbara Sullivan. 1993, Random LB $11.99 (0-679-91948-1); paper $3.99 (0-679-81948-7). 74pp. Marvin wonders if he is turning into a girl because he seems to be developing feminine interests. (Rev: BCCB 6/94; BL 11/15/93)

**8167** Sachar, Louis. *Sideways Arithmetic from Wayside School* (4–8). Series: Wayside School. 1992, Scholastic paper $2.99 (0-590-45726-8). 89pp. Sue

learns a new kind of math and encounters some humorous brainteasers when she transfers to Wayside School. (Rev: BL 12/15/89)

**8168** Sandburg, Carl. *Rootabaga Stories* (4–6). Illus. by Michael Hague. 1988, Harcourt paper $7.00 (0-15-269065-4). 192pp. A reissued collection of modern tales from Rootabaga country.

**8169** Sandburg, Carl. *Rootabaga Stories: Part Two* (3–6). Illus. by Michael Hague. 1989, Harcourt $19.95 (0-15-269062-X); paper $6.00 (0-15-269063-8). 179pp. Twenty-four nonsense stories first published in 1923. A companion volume to Part One (1988). (Rev: BL 8/89; SLJ 6/89)

**8170** Schwartz, Alvin. *Tales of Trickery from the Land of Spoof* (4–6). Illus. 1985, Farrar $14.00 (0-374-37378-7); paper $3.50 (0-374-47426-5). 87pp. Tales from Americana, including April Fool tricks, fun from the Old West, and a prank by Abraham Lincoln. (Rev: BCCB 3/86; BL 3/1/86; SLJ 1/86)

**8171** Shalant, Phyllis. *Beware of Kissing Lizard Lips* (4–6). 1995, Dutton paper $14.99 (0-525-45199-4). 160pp. The pangs of pre-adolescence as experienced by Zach in this richly humorous novel. (Rev: BL 5/15/95*; SLJ 7/95)

**8172** Smith, Lane. *Glasses: Who Needs 'Em?* (3–4). Illus. 1991, Viking paper $15.99 (0-670-84160-9). 32pp. A nutty optometrist uses extreme measures to get a young boy to wear his glasses. (Rev: BL 9/1/91; HB 11–12/91; SLJ 10/91)

**8173** Smith, Robert K. *Chocolate Fever* (4–6). Illus. by Gioia Fiammenghi. 1989, Putnam $11.99 (0-399-61224-6); Dell paper $3.99 (0-440-41369-9). 96pp. Henry Green develops the first recorded case of chocolate fever in this reissued story.

**8174** Snow, Alan. *How Dogs Really Work!* (3–5). Illus. 1993, Little, Brown $15.95 (0-316-80261-1). 30pp. This is a spoof of dog-training manuals that gives an irreverent picture of dogs and their habits. (Rev: BL 12/15/93) [636.7]

**8175** Soto, Gary. *Summer on Wheels* (5–8). 1995, Scholastic $13.95 (0-590-48365-X). 144pp. In this sequel to *Crazy Weekend* (1994), Hector and Mando take a bike ride from their barrio home in Los Angeles to Santa Monica. (Rev: BL 1/15/95; SLJ 4/95)

**8176** Spinelli, Eileen. *Lizzie Logan Gets Married* (2–4). 1997, Simon & Schuster paper $15.00 (0-689-81066-0). 96pp. A humorous novel about Lizzie Logan, her friends, and her mother's upcoming wedding. (Rev: BL 8/97; SLJ 6/97)

**8177** Spinelli, Eileen. *Lizzie Logan Wears Purple Sunglasses* (2–4). Illus. 1995, Simon & Schuster paper $14.00 (0-671-74685-5). 122pp. The rocky friendship between 8-year-old Heather and Lizzie, a bossy 10-year-old, is re-created in this humorous novel. (Rev: BL 5/15/95; HB 9–10/95; SLJ 6/95)

**8178** Spinelli, Jerry. *The Bathwater Gang* (2–4). Illus. by Meredith Johnson. 1990, Little, Brown $10.95 (0-316-80720-6). 59pp. Bertie is bored, so she forms a Girls Only gang, and the boys retaliate. (Rev: BCCB 9/90; BL 6/15/90; SLJ 5/90)

**8179** Spinelli, Jerry. *The Library Card* (5–7). 1997, Scholastic $15.95 (0-590-46731-X). 160pp. Four humorous, poignant stories about how books changed the lives of several youngsters. (Rev: BCCB 3/97; BL 2/1/97; HB 3–4/97; SLJ 3/97)

**8180** Spinelli, Jerry. *Tooter Pepperday* (3–5). Illus. 1995, Random LB $11.99 (0-679-94702-7); paper $3.99 (0-679-84702-2). 85pp. Tooter has some hilarious adventures while adjusting to life on a farm far from her beloved city. (Rev: BCCB 6/95; BL 5/1/95; HB 9–10/95; SLJ 7/95)

**8181** Stanley, George E. *Hershell Cobwell and the Miraculous Tattoo* (4–8). 1991, Avon paper $2.95 (0-380-75897-0). 128pp. A junior high boy decides to gain popularity by getting a tattoo. (Rev: BL 3/15/91)

**8182** Steiner, Barbara. *Oliver Dibbs to the Rescue!* (4–6). Illus. 1985, Avon paper $2.50 (0-380-70465-X). 96pp. To save threatened wildlife, Oliver paints his dog Dolby as a tiger and exhibits him in a shopping mall. When Dolby "escapes," Oliver lands in the police station. Also use: *Oliver Dibbs and the Dinosaur Cause* (1986). (Rev: BL 12/1/85; SLJ 3/86)

**8183** Strasser, Todd. *Kidnap Kids* (5–7). 1998, Putnam $15.99 (0-399-23111-0). 208pp. Because 2 brothers rarely see their busy parents, they hatch a plan to kidnap them. (Rev: BL 1/1–15/98; SLJ 3/98)

**8184** Trahey, Jane. *The Clovis Caper* (5–8). 1990, Avon paper $2.95 (0-380-75914-4). 138pp. Martin is so upset at leaving his dog, Clovis, when going to England that Aunt Hortense plots to smuggle the dog out of the country. (Rev: BL 7/90)

**8185** Twain, Mark. *Adventures of Huckleberry Finn* (6–8). 1993, Random $16.50 (0-679-42470-9). One of many editions.

**8186** Twain, Mark. *The Adventures of Tom Sawyer* (5–7). Illus. by Claude Lapointe. Series: The Whole Story. 1996, Viking paper $23.99 (0-670-86984-8). 284pp. Key scenes from *Tom Sawyer* are illustrated with accompanying passages from the novel and good background information on the author and life in the United States at that time. (Rev: SLJ 1/97)

**8187** Voigt, Cynthia. *Bad, Badder, Baddest* (5–8). 1997, Scholastic $16.95 (0-590-60136-9). 272pp. A hilarious mix of funny situations and outrageous dialogue is featured in this novel about 2 sixth-grade outsiders who deserve their reputation for being bad. A sequel to *Bad Girls* (1996). (Rev: BL 11/1/97; SLJ 11/97)

**8188** Voigt, Cynthia. *Bad Girls* (4–6). 1996, Scholastic $16.95 (0-590-60134-2). 256pp. Mikey and Margalo, 2 fifth-graders with reputations for causing trouble, test their limits. (Rev: BCCB 4/96; BL 4/1/96; HB 7–8/96; SLJ 5/96)

**8189** Wallace, Bill. *The Biggest Klutz in Fifth Grade* (4–6). 1992, Holiday $15.95 (0-8234-0984-8). 148pp. Klutzy Pat takes a bet that he can go through the entire summer without a scratch. (Rev: BCCB 1/93; BL 12/1/92; SLJ 12/92)

**8190** Wallace, Bill. *Ferret in the Bedroom, Lizards in the Fridge* (4–6). 1986, Holiday $15.95 (0-8234-0600-8). 144pp. Liz would certainly win the sixth-grade presidency if it weren't that her zoology teacher-father keeps so many unusual animals around the house and scares away her friends. (Rev: BCCB 7–8/86; BL 6/15/86)

**8191** Wardlaw, Lee. *101 Ways to Bug Your Parents* (3–6). 1996, Dial paper $14.99 (0-8037-1901-9). 208pp. Sneeze Wyatt uses a summer session at school to compile a book on how to annoy parents. (Rev: BCCB 11/96; BL 10/1/96; SLJ 10/96)

**8192** Weiss, Ellen, and Mel Friedman. *The Adventures of Ratman* (2–4). Illus. by Dirk Zimmer. 1990, Random paper $3.99 (0-679-80531-1). 62pp. When he dons his rat costume, 8-year-old Tod Watson becomes the superhero Ratman. (Rev: BCCB 9/90; BL 8/90)

**8193** Wisniewski, David. *The Secret Knowledge of Grown-ups* (3–5). Illus. 1998, Lothrop LB $15.93 (0-688-15340-2). 48pp. A zany book that explores the truth behind such parental directives as "Drink your milk" and "Don't bite your fingernails." (Rev: BL 3/1/98; SLJ 3/98)

**8194** Wojciechowski, Susan. *Don't Call Me Beanhead!* (3–5). Illus. 1994, Candlewick $14.95 (1-56402-319-2). 80pp. Five humorous stories about a little worrywart named Beany. (Rev: BL 10/15/94; SLJ 10/94)

**8195** Yep, Laurence. *The Cook's Family* (4–6). 1998, Putnam $15.95 (0-399-22907-8). 192pp. In order to get a Chinese cook to do his work, Robin and her grandmother must pretend to be the man's relatives. (Rev: BL 1/1–15/98; SLJ 4/98)

**8196** Yorinks, Arthur. *Bravo, Minski* (3–5). Illus. by Richard Egielski. 1988, Farrar $15.00 (0-374-30951-5). 32pp. Young Minski is a brilliant inventor but longs to be a singer. (Rev: BCCB 12/88; BL 12/15/88; SLJ 12/88)

**8197** Zalben, Jane Breskin. *Earth to Andrew O. Blechman* (4–6). Illus. 1989, Farrar $14.00 (0-374-31916-2). 160pp. Andrew's upstairs neighbor teaches the boy how to become a vaudeville comedian in exchange for Hebrew lessons. (Rev: BL 12/15/89; SLJ 11/89)

# School Stories

**8198** Asch, Frank. *Hands Around Lincoln School* (4–6). 1994, Scholastic $13.95 (0-590-44149-3). 217pp. Amy, a sixth-grader, decides to start a Save the Earth Club in her school to fight pollution and help save the environment. (Rev: BL 1/15/94; SLJ 3/94)

**8199** Bechard, Margaret. *My Sister, My Science Report* (5–7). 1990, Puffin paper $4.99 (0-14-034408-X). 96pp. In this humorous novel, Tess's sister becomes the object of a scientific study for a school project. (Rev: BL 5/15/90; HB 5/90 & 9–10/90; SLJ 5/90)

**8200** Benjamin, Saragail Katzman. *My Dog Ate It* (4–6). 1994, Holiday $14.95 (0-8234-1047-1). 166pp. Danny dislikes homework so much that he decides to go on strike, but his teacher comes up with a novel solution. (Rev: SLJ 5/94)

**8201** Byars, Betsy. *The Burning Questions of Bingo Brown* (6–8). 1990, Puffin paper $4.50 (0-14-032479-8). 160pp. During Bingo's sixth-grade year, he falls in love 3 times for starters. (Rev: BCCB 4/88; BL 4/15/88; SLJ 5/88)

**8202** Byars, Betsy. *The 18th Emergency* (4–6). Illus. by Robert Grossman. 1981, Puffin paper $4.50 (0-14-031451-2). 128pp. A young boy, nicknamed Mousi, incurs the wrath of the school bully and awaits his inevitable punishment with fear.

**8203** Caudill, Rebecca. *Did You Carry the Flag Today, Charley?* (2–5). Illus. by Nancy Grossman. 1966, Holt $16.95 (0-8050-1201-X); Dell paper $3.50 (0-440-40092-9). 96pp. Contemporary Appalachia is the setting for the activities of Charley, an irrepressibly curious kindergartner, who finally achieves the honor of carrying the school flag for his class.

**8204** Cleary, Beverly. *Mitch and Amy* (3–5). Illus. by Bob Marstall. 1991, Morrow $13.95 (0-688-10806-7); Avon paper $4.50 (0-380-70925-2). 224pp. Twins Mitch and Amy squabble their way through fourth grade.

**8205** Clements, Andrew. *Frindle* (3–6). Illus. 1996, Simon & Schuster $15.00 (0-689-80669-8). 105pp. Nick's desire to get even with a teacher gets out of hand. (Rev: BL 9/1/96; HB 11–12/96; SLJ 9/96)

**8206** Cohen, Barbara. *Two Hundred Thirteen Valentines* (3–5). Illus. by Wil Clay. 1993, Holt paper $4.95 (0-805-02627-4). 55pp. Two black children who transfer to a school for the gifted must rethink their attitudes. (Rev: BCCB 1/92; BL 9/1/91; HB 3–4/92; SLJ 11/91)

**8207** Conford, Ellen. *Dear Lovey Hart, I Am Desperate* (6–7). 1975, Little, Brown $14.95 (0-316-15306-0). 224pp. Freshman reporter Carrie Wasserman gets into trouble with her advice column in the school newspaper.

**8208** Coville, Bruce. *Aliens Ate My Homework* (4–6). Illus. by Katherine Coville. 1993, Pocket $14.00 (0-671-87249-4). 180pp. No one believes Ron when he maintains that an alien ate his homework, even though it is the truth. (Rev: BL 1/15/94)

**8209** Cullen, Lynn. *Stink Bomb* (4–6). 1998, Avon $14.00 (0-380-97647-1). 120pp. When Kenny breaks wind during gym class, he blames it on the class nerd, Alice Glowers, who becomes known as "Stink Bomb." (Rev: SLJ 3/98)

**8210** Dahl, Roald. *Matilda* (4–8). Illus. by Quentin Blake. 1988, Puffin paper $4.99 (0-14-034294-X). 224pp. Superbright first-grader Matilda deals with the evil school principal Miss Trunchbutt. (Rev: BCCB 10/88; HB 1–2/89; SLJ 10/88)

**8211** Danziger, Paula. *The Cat Ate My Gymsuit* (6–8). 1974, Dell $14.95 (0-440-50223-3); Bantam paper $3.99 (0-440-91612-7). 128pp. Marcy will go to any length to get out of going to gym and to defend an English teacher she feels has been wrongly dismissed. A sequel is: *There's a Bat in Bunk Five* (1980).

**8212** DeClements, Barthe. *Nothing's Fair in Fifth Grade* (4–6). 1981, Puffin paper $3.99 (0-14-034443-8). 144pp. Overweight Elsie steals lunch money to feed her habits. A sequel is: *Seventeen and In-Between* (1984).

**8213** DeClements, Barthe. *Sixth Grade Can Really Kill You* (4–6). 1995, Puffin paper $3.99 (0-140-37130-3). 146pp. "Bad Helen" acts up to cover her embarrassment about her reading problem in this portrayal of life for a learning-disabled child. (Rev: BCCB 12/85; BL 11/1/85; SLJ 11/85)

**8214** Delton, Judy. *Kitty from the Start* (4–6). 1987, Houghton $16.00 (0-395-42847-5). 141pp. The story of Kitty, a Catholic girl growing up in the 1940s, and her life in third grade. (Rev: BL 4/1/87; HB 5–6/87; SLJ 5/87)

**8215** Demuth, Patricia. *In Trouble with Teacher* (2–4). Illus. 1995, Dutton paper $13.99 (0-525-45286-9). 80pp. Montgomery is a terrible speller and dreads the test that he knows he will flunk. (Rev: BCCB 5/95; BL 4/1/95; SLJ 5/95)

**8216** Duffey, Betsy. *The Math Wiz* (3–5). Illus. by Janet Wilson. 1990, Viking $12.00 (0-670-83422-X); Puffin paper $3.99 (0-14-034477-2). 64pp. Marty the math wiz has trouble in gym class. (Rev: BL 9/15/90; SLJ 12/90)

**8217** Dugan, Barbara. *Good-bye, Hello* (4–6). 1994, Greenwillow $13.00 (0-688-12447-X). 160pp. Bobbie thinks she has more than her share of problems at school until she discovers that her grandmother is dying. (Rev: BL 4/1/94; HB 7–8/94; SLJ 5/94)

**8218** Duncan, Lois. *Wonder Kid Meets the Evil Lunch Snatcher* (2–4). Illus. 1990, Little, Brown paper $4.50 (0-316-19561-8). 76pp. Brian and his friend Robbie devise Wonder Kid, who can take care of any bully at school. (Rev: BL 6/1/88; SLJ 5/88)

**8219** Estes, Eleanor. *The Hundred Dresses* (3–5). Illus. by Louis Slobodkin. 1944, Harcourt $16.00 (0-15-237374-8); paper $6.00 (0-15-642350-2). 32pp. A little Polish girl in an American school finally wins acceptance by her classmates.

**8220** Feuer, Elizabeth. *One Friend to Another* (5–8). 1987, Farrar $15.00 (0-374-35642-4). 192pp. The agonies of junior high are suffered by brainy Nicole, who wants to be like popular Rhonda but is unable to see Rhonda's cruel nature. (Rev: BL 1/15/88; SLJ 12/87)

**8221** Fine, Anne. *Flour Babies* (5–8). 1994, Little, Brown $15.95 (0-316-28319-3). 178pp. Simon discovers hidden truths about himself when he participates in a class project in which he has to care for a 6-pound flour baby. (Rev: BCCB 6/94; BL 4/1/94; HB 9–10/94, 11–12/94; SLJ 6/94*)

**8222** Fitzhugh, Louise. *Harriet the Spy* (4–6). Illus. by author. 1964, HarperCollins LB $15.89 (0-06-021911-4); paper $4.50 (0-064-40660-1). 224pp. Precocious, overprivileged Harriet darts around her Manhattan neighborhood ferreting out and writing down the worst and best on her scene, sparing no one. A provocative sequel, primarily about Harriet's friend Beth, is: *The Long Secret* (1965).

**8223** Floca, Brian. *The Frightful Story of Harry Walfish* (2–4). Illus. 1997, Orchard LB $16.99 (0-531-33008-7). 32pp. When Ms. Leonard-Brakhurst's class misbehaves at the natural-history museum, she tells them a cautionary tale that quiets them down. (Rev: BL 4/1/97; SLJ 3/97)

**8224** Getz, David. *Thin Air* (5–7). 1990, Holt $14.95 (0-8050-1379-2). 120pp. Jacob tries to behave normally, but he is prone to terrible asthma attacks. (Rev: BCCB 1/91; SLJ 1/91)

**8225** Giff, Patricia Reilly. *Fourth Grade Celebrity* (3–5). Illus. by Leslie Morrill. 1989, Bantam paper $3.50 (0-440-42676-6). 128pp. Casey decides that she wants to become famous, and she does, in a most surprising way. Two sequels are: *The Girl Who Knew It All* (1979); *The Winter Worm Business* (1981).

**8226** Giff, Patricia Reilly. *Look Out, Washington, D.C.!* (2–4). Illus. 1995, Dell paper $3.99 (0-440-40934-9). 118pp. A series of setbacks dull Emily's enthusiasm for the field trip the Polk Street School class is taking to Washington, D.C. (Rev: BCCB 7–8/95; BL 6/1–15/95; SLJ 10/95)

**8227** Giff, Patricia Reilly. *Next Stop, New York City! The Polk Street Kids on Tour* (1–3). Illus. by Blanche Sims. Series: Polk Street Special. 1997, Dell paper $3.99 (0-440-41362-1). 119pp. When Ms. Rooney and the Polk Street crowd visit New York City, Emily Arrow is upset because she has been dubbed an expert on the Big Apple, but she really knows nothing about it. (Rev: SLJ 10/97)

**8228** Giff, Patricia Reilly. *Pet Parade* (1–3). Illus. 1996, Dell paper $3.99 (0-440-41232-3). 100pp. Ms. Rooney's class prepares for the day each child can bring a pet to school. (Rev: BL 9/15/96; SLJ 8/96)

**8229** Gilson, Jamie. *It Goes Eeeeeeeeeeeee!* (2–4). Illus. by Diane De Groat. 1994, Clarion $15.00 (0-395-67063-2). 68pp. Patrick, a conceited new boy in school, is put in his place when he spreads misinformation about bats in class and is corrected by Dawn Marie. (Rev: BCCB 5/94; BL 4/1/94; SLJ 6/94)

**8230** Gilson, Jamie. *Thirteen Ways to Sink a Sub* (4–7). Illus. by Linda Strauss Edwards. 1982, Lothrop $16.00 (0-688-01304-X). 144pp. The girls in Room 4A challenge the boys to see who can first make their substitute teacher cry. A sequel is: *4B Goes Wild* (1983).

**8231** Gilson, Jamie. *Wagon Train 911* (4–6). 1996, Lothrop $15.00 (0-688-14550-7). 160pp. The tallest girl and the shortest boy in the class are teamed in a project on American pioneers. (Rev: BCCB 1/97; BL 9/1/96; SLJ 9/96)

**8232** Granger, Michele. *Fifth Grade Fever* (3–5). 1995, Dutton paper $14.99 (0-525-45279-6). 128pp. Both Marty and her friend Nina have a crush on "gorgeous" Mr. Truesdale, their fifth-grade teacher. (Rev: BCCB 5/95; BL 5/15/95; SLJ 7/95)

**8233** Graves, Bonnie. *The Best Worst Day* (2–3). Illus. by Nelle Davis. 1996, Hyperion $13.95 (0-7868-0167-0); paper $3.95 (0-7868-1090-4). 64pp. During a typical school day, Lucy tries to make friends with the new girl in her class. (Rev: SLJ 7/96)

**8234** Greenberg, David. *The Great School Lunch Rebellion* (2–5). Illus. by Maxie Chambliss. 1989, Bantam paper $3.25 (0-553-15551-2). 48pp. A rhyming account of an extraordinary food fight. (Rev: BL 4/15/89)

**8235** Greene, Stephanie. *Owen Foote, Second Grade Strongman* (2–3). Illus. 1996, Clarion $14.95 (0-395-72098-2). 96pp. When Owen openly criticizes the school nurse, Mrs. Jackson, he gets into trouble with the principal and his parents. (Rev: BCCB 3/96; BL 4/15/96; HB 5–6/96; SLJ 4/96)

**8236** Guthrie, Donna. *Frankie Murphy's Kiss List* (5–7). 1993, Simon & Schuster paper $15.00 (0-671-75624-9). 144pp. Frankie Murphy accepts a bet that he can kiss all 6 girls in his sixth-grade class. (Rev: SLJ 9/93)

**8237** Hall, Katy, and Lisa Eisenberg. *The Paxton Cheerleaders: Go for It, Patti!* (4–7). 1994, Simon & Schuster paper $3.50 (0-671-89490-X). 137pp. Four seventh-grade girls from different backgrounds make the cheerleading team in their junior high school. (Rev: BL 2/1/95)

**8238** Harding, William H. *Alvin's Famous No-Horse* (2–4). Illus. by Michael Chesworth. 1995, Holt $4.95 (0-8050-2227-9). 58pp. Third-grader Alvin is a good student, but he just can't draw. His horses always look like blobs. (Rev: BL 12/15/92; SLJ 12/92)

**8239** Haywood, Carolyn. *"B" Is for Betsy* (3–4). Illus. by author. 1939, Harcourt $15.00 (0-15-204975-4); paper $5.00 (0-15-204977-0). 159pp. Betsy's adventures in the first grade. Others in the series: *Betsy and Billy* (1941); *Back to School with Betsy* (1943); *Betsy and the Boys* (1945).

**8240** Holmes, Barbara W. *Charlotte Shakespeare and Annie the Great* (4–6). Illus. by John Himmelman. 1989, HarperCollins $12.95 (0-06-022614-5); paper $3.95 (0-06-440385-8). 126pp. Charlotte writes a Halloween school play and gets jealous because of all the attention the leading lady receives. (Rev: BCCB 11/89; BL 11/15/89; SLJ 11/89)

**8241** Honeycutt, Natalie. *The All New Jonah Twist* (4–6). Illus. 1987, Avon paper $3.50 (0-380-70317-3). 128pp. Jonah is determined to change his image at the start of third grade — he'll no longer be inattentive in class, and he'll prove himself responsible enough for a pet. A sequel is: *The Best-Laid Plans of Jonah Twist* (1988). (Rev: BL 5/15/86; SLJ 8/86)

**8242** Honeycutt, Natalie. *Invisible Lissa* (4–6). Illus. 1986, Avon paper $2.75 (0-380-70120-0). 192pp. Lissa challenges the student power structure in her fifth-grade class. (Rev: BCCB 7/85; BL 4/1/85; SLJ 8/85)

**8243** Hopper, Nancy J. *What Happened in Mr. Fisher's Room* (4–7). 1995, Dial paper $14.99 (0-8037-1841-1). 144pp. Lanie faces several problems in eighth grade, including dealing with a boy who has a crush on her and an inept science teacher. (Rev: BL 9/1/95; SLJ 8/95)

**8244** Hughes, Dean. *Re-Elect Nutty!* (4–6). 1995, Simon & Schuster $14.00 (0-671-31862-6). 122pp. In this humorous novel, Nutty decides to run for reelection even though he was considered the worst student council president his school has ever had. (Rev: BL 5/1/95; SLJ 6/95)

**8245** Hurwitz, Johanna. *Class Clown* (3–5). Illus. by Sheila Hamanaka. 1987, Morrow $16.00 (0-688-06723-9); Scholastic paper $2.99 (0-590-41821-1). 112pp. Lucas the class clown learns that there is a right and wrong way to use his humor. A sequel is: *Teacher's Pet* (1988). (Rev: BCCB 4/87; BL 5/15/87; HB 5–6/87)

**8246** Hurwitz, Johanna. *Class President* (3–5). Illus. by Sheila Hamanaka. 1990, Morrow $16.00 (0-688-09114-8); Scholastic paper $3.50 (0-590-44064-0). 160pp. Julio works to get his friend elected class president, but discovers that he's the one with leadership qualities. (Rev: BCCB 5/90; BL 4/1/90; HB 7–8/90; SLJ 5/90)

**8247** Hurwitz, Johanna. *Ever-Clever Elisa* (2–4). Illus. by Lillian Hoban. 1997, Morrow $15.00 (0-688-15189-2). 64pp. Six short episodes about Elisa in first grade, including one in which she gives her mother's engagement ring to her teacher as a sign of love. (Rev: BL 7/97; HB 9–10/97; SLJ 11/97)

**8248** Hurwitz, Johanna. *School Spirit* (3–5). Illus. by Karen M. Dugan. 1994, Morrow $14.00 (0-688-12825-4). 144pp. Julio is annoyed when another boy hogs the spotlight as leader of a protest to save their school from being closed. (Rev: BL 5/1/94; HB 7–8/94; SLJ 5/94)

**8249** Hurwitz, Johanna. *Tough-Luck Karen* (4–6). Illus. by Diane De Groat. 1982, Morrow $12.95 (0-688-01485-2). 160pp. Karen prefers housework to homework.

**8250** Johnston, Janet. *Ellie Brader Hates Mr. G.* (4–7). 1991, Houghton $13.95 (0-395-58195-8). 131pp. Ellie is unhappy because her beloved fifth-grade teacher is replaced. (Rev: BCCB 11/91; BL 11/15/91; SLJ 12/91)

**8251** Kline, Suzy. *Herbie Jones* (3–5). Illus. 1985, Putnam $13.95 (0-399-21183-7); Puffin paper $3.99 (0-14-032071-7). 96pp. Herbie and Raymond are determined to get out of the lowest reading group in the third grade. Other books about Herbie are: *What's the Matter with Herbie Jones?* (1986); *Herbie Jones and the Class Gift* (1987); *Herbie Jones and the Monster Ball* (1988). (Rev: BCCB 9/85; BL 8/85; SLJ 10/85)

**8252** Kline, Suzy. *Horrible Harry and the Drop of Doom* (2–4). Illus. 1998, Viking paper $13.99 (0-670-85849-8). 64pp. When he visits an amusement park with friends, Harry doesn't want them to know he is afraid of going into the haunted house. (Rev: BL 2/15/98)

**8253** Kline, Suzy. *Horrible Harry and the Dungeon* (2–3). Illus. by Frank Remkiewicz. 1996, Viking paper $12.99 (0-670-86862-0). 64pp. Unusual doings in Miss Mackle's 2B classroom involve Horrible Harry and a new teacher. (Rev: BL 8/96; SLJ 8/96)

**8254** Kline, Suzy. *Mary Marony Hides Out* (2–3). Illus. by Blanche Sims. 1993, Putnam $13.95 (0-399-22433-5). 80pp. Mary Marony longs to meet her favorite author when he comes to her school, but she is ashamed of her stuttering. (Rev: BL 9/1/93)

**8255** Kline, Suzy. *Song Lee and the Hamster Hunt* (1–3). Illus. 1994, Viking paper $12.99 (0-670-

84773-9). 64pp. Song Lee brings her pet hamster to school, and it escapes. (Rev: BL 7/94; SLJ 9/94)

**8256** Kline, Suzy. *Song Lee and the Leech Man* (2–3). Illus. 1995, Viking paper $11.99 (0-670-85848-X). 64pp. During a class field trip to a pond, Sidney falls in the water and comes out covered with leeches. (Rev: BL 10/1/95; SLJ 12/95)

**8257** Koehler-Pentacoff, Elizabeth. *Louise the One and Only* (3–5). Illus. 1996, Troll LB $10.50 (0-8167-3756-8); paper $2.95 (0-8167-3757-6). 64pp. In kindergarten, Louise longs to be the best at something. (Rev: BL 7/96; SLJ 8/96)

**8258** Komaiko, Leah. *Annie Bananie Best Friends to the End* (2–4). Illus. by Abby Carter. 1997, Delacorte $14.95 (0-385-32112-0). 63pp. In this school story, Annie is supposed to have lunch at friend Libby's home, but Grandma takes them to a fast-food restaurant instead. (Rev: BCCB 10/87; BL 6/1/87; SLJ 5/97)

**8259** Korman, Gordon. *Something Fishy at Macdonald Hall* (4–6). 1995, Scholastic $14.95 (0-590-25521-5). 198pp. At Macdonald Hall School, Boots and Bruno are accused of pranks they didn't commit and so they set out to find the real culprit. (Rev: BL 8/95; SLJ 9/95)

**8260** Korman, Gordon. *The Twinkle Squad* (5–7). 1992, Scholastic $13.95 (0-590-45249-5). 160pp. A bossy, insecure sixth-grader and a defender of weaker kids are sentenced to the school's Special Discussion Group. (Rev: BCCB 11/92; BL 9/15/92; SLJ 9/92)

**8261** Korman, Gordon. *The Zucchini Warriors* (4–6). 1991, Scholastic paper $4.50 (0-590-44174-4). 208pp. The boys at a Canadian boarding school have a wild and woolly adventure. (Rev: BL 1/1/89; SLJ 9/88)

**8262** Larson, Kirby. *Second-Grade Pig Pals* (2–4). Illus. 1994, Holiday $14.95 (0-8234-1107-9). 96pp. Quinn is at a loss to know what to bring to class for its Pig Patch. (Rev: BCCB 12/94; BL 11/1/94; SLJ 11/94)

**8263** Lauture, Denizé. *Running the Road to ABC* (1–5). Illus. by Reynold Ruffins. 1996, Simon & Schuster paper $16.00 (0-689-80507-1). A joyous picture book about a group of Haitian children happily going to school, where they hope to learn to read. (Rev: BCCB 3/96; HB 5–6/96; SLJ 6/96)

**8264** Levy, Elizabeth. *Keep Ms. Sugarman in the Fourth Grade* (3–5). 1991, HarperCollins LB $13.89 (0-06-020427-3). 96pp. Smart-alecky and disruptive Jackie meets her match in Ms. Sugarman, a gifted teacher. (Rev: BL 12/1/91; SLJ 1/92)

**8265** Lewis, Beverly. *Frog Power* (2–5). Illus. 1995, Bethany paper $3.99 (1-55661-645-7). 80pp. Stacy, who is afraid of frogs, is dismayed when she learns

that Jason has brought his pet frog to school. (Rev: BL 10/1/95)

**8266** Lindberg, Becky T. *Thomas Tuttle, Just in Time* (2–4). Illus. 1994, Albert Whitman LB $12.95 (0-8075-7898-3). 112pp. Thomas, a third-grader, might do a little better if he would only get organized. (Rev: BL 11/15/94; SLJ 10/94)

**8267** Lovelace, Maud H. *Betsy-Tacy* (3–4). Illus. by Lois Lenski. 1940, HarperCollins paper $4.95 (0-06-440096-4). 113pp. Two 5-year-olds are inseparable at school and at play. One of a popular series. Five sequels are: *Betsy-Tacy and Tib* (1941); *Betsy and Tacy Go over the Big Hill* (1942); *Betsy and Tacy Go Downtown* (1943); *Heaven to Betsy* (1945); *Betsy in Spite of Herself* (1946).

**8268** Low, Alice, ed. *Stories to Tell a Six-Year-Old* (K–3). Illus. 1997, Little, Brown paper $8.95 (0-316-53418-8). 192pp. A delightful anthology of 20 folktales, short stories, picture book texts, and chapters from books like *Mary Poppins*. (Rev: BL 3/1/98; SLJ 10/97)

**8269** Lurie, Jon. *Allison's Story: A Book About Homeschooling* (2–4). Illus. by Rebecca Dallinger. 1996, Lerner LB $15.95 (0-8225-2579-8). 40pp. A photoessay about an 8-year-old's experiences with home schooling. (Rev: BL 11/1/96; SLJ 12/96) [649]

**8270** MacDonald, Maryann. *Secondhand Star* (2–5). Illus. by Eileen Christelow. 1994, Hyperion $11.95 (1-56282-616-6). 64pp. Francie, who is cast as Toto in the school production of "The Wizard of Oz," becomes a last-minute replacement for an ill Dorothy. (Rev: BL 7/94; SLJ 7/94)

**8271** McKenna, Colleen O'Shaughnessy. *Live from the Fifth Grade* (4–6). Illus. 1994, Scholastic $13.95 (0-590-46684-4). 145pp. Practical joker Roger Friday becomes serious when a friendly custodian at his school is accused of theft. (Rev: BL 11/15/94; SLJ 10/94)

**8272** McMullan, Kate. *The Great Eggspectations of Lila Fenwick* (4–6). Illus. by Diane De Groat. 1991, Farrar $13.95 (0-374-32774-2). 148pp. Lila gets involved with a project in which each sixth-grader must take care of an egg as though it were a newborn. (Rev: BCCB 7–8/91; BL 6/15/91; SLJ 8/91)

**8273** Masters, Susan R. *Libby Bloom* (2–4). Illus. 1995, Holt $14.95 (0-8050-3374-2). 86pp. After a series of musical failures, Libby hopes to excel as the tuba player in the school band. (Rev: BCCB 7–8/95; BL 7/95; SLJ 9/95)

**8274** Miles, Betty. *Maudie and Me and the Dirty Book* (5–7). 1989, Knopf paper $3.99 (0-394-82595-0). 144pp. Kate, a sixth-grader, becomes involved in a censorship case involving a first-grade book about birth.

**8275** Mills, Claudia. *Dinah for President* (3–6). 1992, Macmillan LB $14.00 (0-02-766999-8). 128pp. Conflicting emotions in a middle schooler form the basis of this believable story. (Rev: BCCB 4/92; BL 7/92; HB 7–8/92; SLJ 5/92*)

**8276** Mills, Claudia. *Losers, Inc.* (5–7). 1997, Farrar $16.00 (0-374-34661-5). 160pp. Ethan develops a crush on his new student teacher and tries every way possible to impress her. (Rev: BCCB 4/97; BL 3/1/97; SLJ 4/97)

**8277** Morris, Judy K. *The Kid Who Ran for Principal* (4–6). 1989, HarperCollins LB $12.89 (0-397-32360-3). 212pp. Sixth-grader Gail persuades Bonnie to be a candidate for interim principal in their school. (Rev: BCCB 1/90; BL 11/15/89; SLJ 10/89)

**8278** Myers, Laurie. *Earthquake in the Third Grade* (2–4). Illus. by Karen Ritz. 1993, Clarion $15.00 (0-395-65360-6). 63pp. John and his friends try to reverse their teacher's decision to move away. (Rev: BL 12/1/93)

**8279** Myers, Laurie. *Guinea Pigs Don't Talk* (2–4). Illus. 1994, Clarion $13.95 (0-395-68967-8). 68pp. Two students play pranks on Lisa, the new student in class, but she retaliates. (Rev: BL 10/15/94; SLJ 10/94)

**8280** Park, Barbara. *Junie B. Jones and her Big Fat Mouth* (2–4). Illus. by Denise Brunkus. 1993, Random LB $11.99 (0-679-94407-9); paper $3.99 (0-679-84407-4). 72pp. In this hilarious story of kindergartner Junie B. Jones, the little girl has trouble with the Pledge of Allegiance, keeping quiet in class, and deciding what to be on Job Day. (Rev: BL 11/15/93)

**8281** Park, Barbara. *Junie B. Jones and the Yucky Blucky Fruitcake* (2–4). Illus. by Denise Brunkus. Series: Junie B. Jones. 1995, Random paper $3.99 (0-679-86694-9). 71pp. A young kindergartner tells about her many troubles at school, where she is always a loser. (Rev: BL 12/15/95)

**8282** Peck, Robert Newton. *Arly* (5–8). 1989, Walker $16.95 (0-8027-6856-3). 151pp. In this story set in 1927 in Florida, Arly has few hopes of learning to read until a teacher named Miss Binie appears. (Rev: BL 7/89)

**8283** Petersen, P. J. *Can You Keep a Secret?* (3–5). Illus. 1997, Dutton paper $15.99 (0-525-45840-9). 80pp. Mike, who has a reputation for not being able to keep a secret, finds he is being made a confidant by his friend Amy and wonders if he can keep her trust. (Rev: BL 10/1/97; SLJ 1/98)

**8284** Pinkwater, Jill. *Mister Fred* (4–6). 1994, Dutton paper $15.99 (0-525-44778-4). 160pp. A substitute teacher challenges his students to find out if he is really from outer space. (Rev: BCCB 1/95; BL 12/15/94; SLJ 1/95)

**8285** Pryor, Bonnie. *Poison Ivy and Eyebrow Wigs* (3–5). Illus. by Gail Owens. 1993, Morrow $15.00 (0-688-11200-5). 156pp. Martin's problems in the fourth grade include wanting to be popular and having a crush on his teacher. (Rev: BL 4/15/93; SLJ 6/93)

**8286** Ragz, M. M. *French Fries up Your Nose* (5–8). 1994, Pocket paper $3.99 (0-671-88410-7). 74pp. Though most people think it is a joke, Iggy Sands really wants to win the election and become student council president. (Rev: BL 3/15/94)

**8287** Regan, Dian C. *The Class with the Summer Birthdays* (3–5). Illus. by Susan Guevara. 1991, Holt $13.95 (0-8050-1657-0). 52pp. All the birthday parties next door are driving Brittany and her classmates crazy until she comes up with a solution. (Rev: BCCB 5/91; BL 3/1/91; SLJ 4/91)

**8288** Rocklin, Joanne. *For Your Eyes Only* (4–6). 1997, Scholastic $14.95 (0-590-67447-1). 144pp. Sixth-grader Lucy blossoms under the attention of Mr. Moffat, a substitute teacher. (Rev: BCCB 4/97; BL 3/1/97; SLJ 3/97*)

**8289** Sachar, Louis. *Wayside School Is Falling Down* (3–6). Illus. by Joel Schick. 1989, Lothrop $16.00 (0-688-07868-0); Avon paper $4.50 (0-380-75484-3). 192pp. Episodes with the children who inhabit the world's wackiest elementary school. (Rev: BL 5/1/89; SLJ 5/89)

**8290** Sachs, Marilyn. *The Bears' House* (4–7). Illus. by Louis Glanzman. 1987, Avon paper $2.99 (0-380-70582-6). 80pp. A poor girl escapes from reality by living in a fantasy in her classroom. A reissue of the 1971 edition.

**8291** Sathre, Vivian. *J. B. Wigglebottom and the Parade of Pets* (3–5). Illus. by Catharine O'Neill. 1993, Macmillan $12.95 (0-689-31811-1). 96pp. J. B. gets back at Buddy the bully. (Rev: BL 3/1/93; SLJ 7/93)

**8292** Schlieper, Anne. *The Best Fight* (3–5). Illus. 1995, Albert Whitman LB $10.95 (0-8075-0662-1). 63pp. Jamie, who has a reading disability and often gets into fights at school, gets good advice from his principal. (Rev: BL 3/15/95; SLJ 7/95)

**8293** Schurfranz, Vivian. *Amanda, the Cut-up* (4–6). 1990, Scholastic paper $2.75 (0-590-42555-2). 154pp. Amanda bids for popularity by performing magic tricks. (Rev: BL 3/15/90)

**8294** Sharmat, Marjorie W. *Getting Something on Maggie Marmelstein* (3–5). Illus. by Ben Shecter. 1971, HarperCollins LB $14.89 (0-06-025552-8). 110pp. When Thad's mortal enemy, Maggie, sees him cooking and begins teasing him, Thad must find some way of blackmailing her into silence. Two sequels are: *Maggie Marmelstein for President*

(1975); *Mysteriously Yours, Maggie Marmelstein* (1982).

**8295** Shreve, Susan. *The Flunking of Joshua T. Bates* (3–5). Illus. by Diane De Groat. 1984, Knopf LB $13.99 (0-394-96380-6). 96pp. Joshua must face the fact that he flunked the third grade.

**8296** Shreve, Susan. *Joshua T. Bates in Trouble Again* (3–5). Illus. 1997, Knopf $17.00 (0-679-88520-X). 90pp. At school, Joshua has trouble with bullies, but he decides that standing up to them is the only solution. A sequel to *The Flunking of Joshua T. Bates* (1984) and *Joshua T. Bates Takes Charge* (1993). (Rev: BL 2/1/98; SLJ 1/98)

**8297** Shreve, Susan. *Joshua T. Bates Takes Charge* (3–5). Illus. by Dan Andreasen. 1993, Knopf $15.00 (0-394-84362-2). 102pp. When bully Tommy begins tormenting newcomer Sean, Joshua must take some action. (Rev: BCCB 7–8/93; BL 7/93; SLJ 8/93)

**8298** Smith, Janice Lee. *Serious Science* (2–4). Illus. by Dick Gackenbach. 1993, HarperCollins LB $12.89 (0-06-020782-5). 74pp. When Adam Smith's class decides to hold a science fair, there are many humorous complications. (Rev: BL 6/1–15/93; SLJ 6/93)

**8299** Soto, Gary. *Off and Running* (3–5). Illus. 1996, Delacorte $15.95 (0-385-32181-3). 136pp. Miata Ramirez is running for school president against Rudy Herrera in this humorous story set in a Mexican American community in Fresno, California. (Rev: BCCB 10/96; BL 10/1/96; SLJ 9/96)

**8300** Warner, Sally. *Dog Years* (3–6). 1995, Knopf $13.00 (0-679-87147-0). 160pp. In his new school, Case gets some status by inventing a comic strip called "Dog Years". (Rev: BCCB 5/95; BL 4/15/95; SLJ 4/95)

**8301** Wilkinson, Brenda. *Definitely Cool* (4–7). 1992, Scholastic $13.95 (0-590-46186-9). 176pp. Traveling with a crowd isn't quite what Roxanne, new to junior high, expected. (Rev: BL 2/15/93)

**8302** Williams, Suzanne. *Emily at School* (1–3). Illus. by Abby Carter. Series: Hyperion Chapters. 1996, Hyperion $13.95 (0-7868-0149-2); paper $3.95 (0-7868-1133-1). 39pp. Each of the 3 short stories in this book tell how Emily and her 2 friends manage during their first few days at school. (Rev: SLJ 12/96)

**8303** Willis, Meredith S. *Marco's Monster* (3–5). 1996, HarperCollins LB $13.89 (0-06-027196-5). 128pp. Marco faces a number of crises at school, including losing a part in the class play to his best friend. (Rev: BL 11/15/96; SLJ 1/97)

**8304** Willner-Pardo, Gina. *Spider Storch's Teacher Torture* (2–4). Illus. 1997, Albert Whitman LB $11.95 (0-8075-7577-1); paper $3.95 (0-8075-7578-X). 60pp. Spider Storch thinks up some wild

schemes to prevent his beloved teacher from retiring. (Rev: BL 1/1–15/98; SLJ 11/97)

**8305** Winslow, Vicki. *Follow the Leader* (4–7). 1997, Delacorte $14.95 (0-385-32285-2). 207pp. When schools in Winston, North Carolina, are desegregated in 1971 Amanda feels out of place when she discovers that she is one of only a few white girls in her sixth-grade class. (Rev: BL 11/1/97; SLJ 12/97)

**8306** Wyman, Andrea. *Faith, Hope, and Chicken Feathers* (4–6). 1994, Holiday $15.95 (0-8234-1117-6). 208pp. Three new students become close friends when they join Mrs. Ten Broeck's sixth-grade class in a West Virginia town. (Rev: BCCB 7–8/94; BL 7/94; SLJ 4/94)

**8307** Zindel, Paul. *Attack of the Killer Fishsticks* (4–6). 1993, Bantam paper $3.50 (0-553-48084-7). 117pp. The 4 members of the Lunch Bunch team up to help a new fifth-grader. (Rev: BL 10/1/93; SLJ 10/93)

## Science Fiction

**8308** Anderson, Kevin J., and Ralph McQuarrie. *Stars Wars: Jabba's Palace Pop-up Book* (2–4). Illus. 1996, Little, Brown $19.95 (0-316-53513-3). 14pp. A pop-up book using sound and pictures to illustrate parts of the *Star Wars* films. (Rev: BL 12/15/96)

**8309** Archer, Chris. *Alien Blood* (4–6). 1997, Pocket paper $3.99 (0-671-01483-8). 118pp. A chilling story narrated by a 13-year-old who is experiencing strange and frightening events. Also use *Alien Terror* (1997). (Rev: BL 12/15/97; SLJ 3/98)

**8310** Asimov, Janet. *Norby and the Terrified Taxi* (3–5). Illus. 1997, Walker $15.95 (0-8027-8642-1). 144pp. Using time travel and brains, Norby the Robot and Jeff are able to foil the nasty Garc the Great. (Rev: BL 1/1–15/98; SLJ 12/97)

**8311** Asimov, Janet. *The Package in Hyperspace* (5–7). Illus. 1988, Walker LB $14.85 (0-8027-6823-7). 84pp. Two space-wrecked children must fend for themselves as they try to reach Merkina. (Rev: BL 1/1/89; SLJ 11/88)

**8312** Asimov, Janet, and Isaac Asimov. *Norby and the Court Jester* (4–6). 1991, Walker LB $14.95 (0-8027-8132-2); Ace paper $5.50 (0-441-00341-9). 118pp. Jeff, his robot Norby, and the head of a space academy travel to the planet Izz. (Rev: SLJ 2/92)

**8313** Asimov, Janet, and Isaac Asimov. *Norby and the Invaders* (5–8). 1985, Walker LB $10.85 (0-8027-6607-2). 138pp. In a fast-paced adventure, Jeff and his robot, Norby, are off to the planet Jamya to the rescue of Norby's ancestor. (Rev: BL 3/1/86; SLJ 2/86)

**8314** Asimov, Janet, and Isaac Asimov. *Norby and the Oldest Dragon* (3–5). 1990, Walker LB $15.85 (0-8027-6910-1). 110pp. When Jeff visits the planet Jamyn, he finds that a mysterious vapor surrounds him and other residents. (Rev: SLJ 7/90)

**8315** Asimov, Janet, and Isaac Asimov. *Norby Down to Earth* (4–7). 1989, Walker LB $13.85 (0-8027-6867-9). 107pp. Robot Norby and human friend Jeff encounter a bizarre adventure when they research the life of the roboticist who constructed Norby. Also use: *Norby and Yobo's Great Adventure* (1989). (Rev: BL 7/89)

**8316** Asimov, Janet, and Isaac Asimov. *Norby Finds a Villain* (4–8). 1987, Walker LB $13.85 (0-8027-6711-7). 102pp. Norby the robot and his human friends set out to free Pera, who has been robotnapped by the traitor Ing, in this sixth book of the Norby series. Also use: *Norby and the Queen's Necklace* (1986). (Rev: BL 1/1/88; SLJ 11/87)

**8317** Asimov, Janet, and Isaac Asimov. *Norby, the Mixed-up Robot* (4–6). 1984, Walker LB $10.85 (0-8027-6496-7). 96pp. Jeff, his brother Fargo, and a robot named Norby combat Ing the Ingrate. A sequel is: *Norby's Other Secret* (1984).

**8318** Bechard, Margaret. *Star Hatchling* (4–7). 1995, Viking paper $13.99 (0-670-86149-9). 160pp. When Hanna accidentally lands on an alien planet, she encounters strange creatures and an unusual culture. (Rev: BCCB 1/96; BL 9/15/95; SLJ 8/95*)

**8319** Brennan, Herbie. *The Mystery Machine* (3–5). 1995, Simon & Schuster paper $14.00 (0-689-50615-5). 52pp. Herbie discovers that his neighbor is actually an alien preparing to take over the world. (Rev: BL 5/1/95; HB 9–10/95; SLJ 7/95)

**8320** Brittain, Bill. *Shape-Changer* (4–8). 1994, HarperCollins LB $13.89 (0-06-024239-6). 128pp. Frank and his school friends search for a villainous alien that can assume any convenient shape. (Rev: BL 4/15/94; HB 7–8/94; SLJ 6/94)

**8321** Byars, Betsy. *The Computer Nut* (4–6). 1984, Puffin paper $4.50 (0-14-032086-5). 144pp. Through her computer, Kate encounters an extraterrestrial being.

**8322** Cameron, Eleanor. *Mr. Bass's Planetoid* (4–6). Illus. by Louis Darling. 1958, Little, Brown $14.95 (0-316-12525-3). A further story about the Mushroom Planet, Mr. Bass, and 2 young heroes. Also use: *Stowaway to the Mushroom Planet* (1956).

**8323** Cameron, Eleanor. *The Wonderful Flight to the Mushroom Planet* (4–6). Illus. by Robert Henneberger. 1988, Little, Brown paper $6.95 (0-316-12540-7). Science fiction combined with magic in the story of 2 boys who take off on a spaceship with a magical man named Tyco Bass.

**8324** Christopher, John. *When the Tripods Came* (5–8). 1990, Macmillan paper $3.95 (0-02-042575-9). 160pp. How the Tripods came to Earth and imposed a new order. (Rev: BCCB 7–8/88; BL 7/88; HB 9–10/88)

**8325** Christopher, John. *The White Mountains* (6–8). 1967, Simon & Schuster LB $16.00 (0-02-718360-2); Macmillan paper $3.95 (0-02-042711-5). 192pp. The first volume of a trilogy in which a young boy escapes from a futuristically mechanized tyranny. The other volumes are: *City of Gold and Lead* (1967); *Pool of Fire* (1968).

**8326** Coville, Bruce. *I Left My Sneakers in Dimension X* (4–6). Illus. by Katherine Coville. 1994, Pocket $14.00 (0-671-89072-7); paper $3.99 (0-671-79833-2). 180pp. Rod is kidnapped by an alien monster and must save the universe from destruction. This is a sequel to *Aliens Ate My Homework* (1993). (Rev: BL 1/15/95; SLJ 3/95)

**8327** Coville, Bruce. *My Teacher Fried My Brains* (3–6). Illus. by John Pierard. 1991, Pocket paper $3.99 (0-671-72710-9). 136pp. Duncan is convinced his teacher is an alien when he finds a fake hand in a dumpster. (Rev: BL 9/15/91)

**8328** Coville, Bruce. *Space Brat 4: Planet of the Dips* (3–5). Illus. Series: Space Brat. 1995, Pocket $14.00 (0-671-50090-2); paper $3.99 (0-671-50092-9). 72pp. Lunk's spaceship goes off course, and he finds himself on the loony planet of the Dips. (Rev: BL 11/1/95; SLJ 12/95)

**8329** DeFelice, Cynthia. *The Strange Night Writing of Jessamine Colter* (4–6). Illus. 1988, Macmillan paper $13.95 (0-02-726451-3). 56pp. Jessie feels compelled to write things she knows nothing about, and realizes that her strange writing predicts the future. (Rev: BCCB 9/88; BL 10/1/88; SLJ 11/88)

**8330** Dexter, Catherine. *Alien Game* (5–8). 1995, Morrow $15.00 (0-688-11332-X). 208pp. Zoe is convinced that the new girl in the eighth grade is really an alien. (Rev: BCCB 3/95; BL 5/1/95; HB 9–10/95; SLJ 4/95)

**8331** Doyle, Debra, and James D. MacDonald. *Groogleman* (5–8). 1996, Harcourt $15.00 (0-15-200235-9). 112pp. A science fiction novel about a boy who is pitted against the groogleman, the person who collects the heads of plague victims. (Rev: BCCB 12/96; SLJ 12/96)

**8332** Etra, Jonathan, and Stephanie Spinner. *Aliens for Breakfast* (3–5). Illus. 1988, Random LB $11.99 (0-394-92093-7); paper $3.99 (0-394-82093-2). 64pp. Richard meets an alien who needs help to find a secret weapon. (Rev: BCCB 12/88; BL 1/15/89; SLJ 3/89)

**8333** Evans, Douglas. *The Classroom at the End of the Hall* (2–4). Illus. 1996, Front Street $14.95 (1-

886910-07-3). 128pp. Typical third-graders have some atypical adventures in these 11 stories. (Rev: BCCB 9/96; BL 8/96; SLJ 10/96)

**8334** Follett, Ken. *The Power Twins* (4–8). 1991, Scholastic paper $2.75 (0-590-42507-2). 90pp. Three youngsters travel to a planet where large, gentle worms live. (Rev: SLJ 1/91)

**8335** Gauthier, Gail. *My Life Among the Aliens* (3–6). 1996, Putnam $14.95 (0-399-22945-0). 104pp. In this episodic book, Will and his friends encounter aliens in a variety of situations. (Rev: BCCB 6/96; SLJ 6/96)

**8336** Gilden, Mel. *Outer Space and All That Junk* (5–7). Illus. 1989, HarperCollins LB $12.89 (0-397-32307-7). 176pp. Myron's uncle is collecting junk, which he believes will help aliens return to their home in outer space. (Rev: BL 12/1/89; SLJ 12/89)

**8337** Gilden, Mel. *The Pumpkins of Time* (4–7). 1994, Harcourt $10.95 (0-15-276603-0); paper $4.95 (0-15-200889-6). 192pp. Myron, his friend Princess, and their cat do some stylish time-traveling. (Rev: BL 10/15/94; SLJ 10/94)

**8338** Gormley, Beatrice. *Paul's Volcano* (4–6). Illus. 1988, Avon paper $2.50 (0-380-70562-1). 143pp. Adam and new kid Paul tangle over a science-fair volcano model that seems to have a mind of its own. (Rev: BL 5/15/87; SLJ 3/87)

**8339** Gormley, Beatrice. *Wanted: UFO* (3–6). Illus. by Emily Arnold McCully. 1992, Dutton $12.95 (0-525-44593-5); Avon paper $2.99 (0-380-71313-6). 128pp. Elise and Nick discover 2 aliens in the backyard. (Rev: BCCB 6/90; BL 7/90; SLJ 7/90)

**8340** Greenburg, Dan. *My Son, the Time Traveler* (2–4). Illus. by Jack E. Davis. Series: Zack Files. 1997, Grosset LB $12.99 (0-448-41587-9); paper $3.95 (0-448-41341-8). 57pp. In this time-travel story, Zack, a fifth-grader, meets his future son. (Rev: SLJ 10/97)

**8341** Greer, Gery, and Bob Ruddick. *Max and Me and the Wild West* (4–6). 1988, Harcourt $12.95 (0-15-253136-X). 138pp. Professor Flybender's time machine once more lands Steve and Max in the middle of an adventure — this time in 1882 Arizona Territory. (Rev: BL 2/15/88)

**8342** Griffin, Peni R. *Switching Well* (5–8). 1993, Macmillan $16.00 (0-689-50581-7). 224pp. Two girls from different centuries trade places. (Rev: BCCB 7–8/93; SLJ 6/93*)

**8343** Heintze, Ty. *Valley of the Eels* (5–8). Illus. 1993, Eakin $14.95 (0-89015-904-1). 156pp. In the Gulf of Mexico, Billy and Shawn discover an underwater station where aliens live in this novel about pollution and scuba diving. (Rev: BL 3/1/94)

**8344** Hill, William. *The Magic Bicycle* (5–8). 1998, Otter Creek paper $13.95 (1-890611-00-X). 326pp. For helping an alien escape, Danny receives a magical bicycle that is capable of transporting him through time and space. (Rev: BL 1/1–15/98; SLJ 3/98)

**8345** Hooks, William H. *The Girl Who Could Fly* (3–4). Illus. by Kees de Kiefte. 1995, Macmillan paper $14.00 (0-02-744433-3). 53pp. Tom, a girl, is actually an alien from outer space who can perform amazing feats like stopping a ball in midair. (Rev: BCCB 7–8/95; BL 8/95; SLJ 7/95)

**8346** Hoover, H. M. *Only Child* (4–7). 1992, Dutton paper $13.99 (0-525-44865-9). 128pp. Gody, who has lived all of his 12 years on a spaceship, is captured by alien creatures on the earthlike planet of Patma. (Rev: BCCB 7–8/92; BL 5/15/92; SLJ 7/92)

**8347** Hughes, Monica. *The Golden Aquarians* (4–6). 1995, Simon & Schuster paper $15.00 (0-671-50543-2). 186pp. Walt is sent by his father to the planet Aqua with the hope of making a man of him. (Rev: BCCB 10/95; BL 5/1/95; HB 9–10/95; SLJ 8/95)

**8348** Kahn, Sharon. *Kacy and the Space Shuttle Secret: A Space Adventure for Young Readers* (4–6). Illus. by Mark Mitchell. 1996, Eakin $14.95 (1-57168-025-X). 128pp. An exciting science fiction adventure in which a young would-be scientist helps launch a space shuttle. (Rev: SLJ 4/96)

**8349** Katz, Welwyn W. *Time Ghost* (4–6). 1995, Simon & Schuster paper $16.00 (0-689-80027-4). 171pp. In a heavily polluted 21st-century environment, Sara time-travels to the 1990s, when the world was still green. (Rev: BCCB 5/95; BL 5/1/95; SLJ 5/95)

**8350** Key, Alexander. *The Forgotten Door* (5–7). 1986, Scholastic paper $3.99 (0-590-43130-7). 144pp. When little Jon falls to earth from another planet, he encounters suspicion and hostility as well as sympathy.

**8351** King-Smith, Dick. *Harriet's Hare* (2–4). Illus. 1995, Crown LB $16.99 (0-517-59831-0). 128pp. Harriet shares an adventurous summer with a hare who is actually a space alien. (Rev: BCCB 6/95; BL 4/15/95*; SLJ 6/95)

**8352** Klause, Annette Curtis. *Alien Secrets* (5–8). 1993, Delacorte $15.95 (0-385-30928-7). 240pp. On a spaceship to see her parents, Robin finds herself involved in a murder and a mystery involving an alien named Hush. (Rev: BL 6/1–15/93*)

**8353** Kurts, Charles. *These Are the Voyages: A Three-Dimensional Star Trek Album* (4–7). Illus. 1996, Simon & Schuster $35.00 (0-671-55139-6). Pop-ups are used to re-create the Starfleet ships, including the U.S.S. *Enterprise*. (Rev: BL 12/15/97)

**8354** L'Engle, Madeleine. *A Wrinkle in Time* (6–8). 1962, Farrar $17.00 (0-374-38613-7); Dell paper $5.50 (0-440-49805-8). 224pp. A provocative fantasy-science fiction tale of a brother and sister in search of their father, who is lost in the fifth dimension. Newbery Medal winner, 1963. Also use: *Wind in the Door* (1973); *A Swiftly Tilting Planet* (1978); *A Ring of Endless Light* (1981).

**8355** Levy, Robert. *Escape from Exile* (4–8). 1993, Houghton $16.00 (0-395-64379-1). 176pp. After being knocked unconscious by a strange bolt of lightning, Daniel wakes up in a strange land. (Rev: SLJ 5/93)

**8356** Lindbergh, Anne. *The Shadow on the Dial* (5–7). 1988, Avon paper $2.75 (0-380-70545-1). 160pp. Dawn and Marcus get into all sorts of adventures when they discover a way to take them backward and forward in time. (Rev: BL 7/87; HB 7–8/87; SLJ 6–7/87)

**8357** Lisle, Janet T. *Angela's Aliens* (4–6). Series: Unknown. 1996, Orchard LB $15.99 (0-531-08891-X). 128pp. Angela is abducted by mysterious aliens in the fourth and final volume of the Unknown series. (Rev: BL 11/1/96; SLJ 11/96)

**8358** MacGrory, Yvonne. *The Secret of the Ruby Ring* (4–6). Illus. by Terry Myler. 1994, Milkweed paper $6.95 (0-915943-92-1). 192pp. A fantasy about a young Irish girl who time-travels to live in a nearby castle over a century ago. (Rev: BCCB 5/94; BL 3/1/94; SLJ 3/94)

**8359** Mahy, Margaret. *Raging Robots and Unruly Uncles* (4–6). Illus. by Peter Stevenson. 1993, Overlook $13.95 (0-87951-469-8). 94pp. Twin uncles — one bad, one good — are saddled with children they regard as unsatisfactory. (Rev: BL 3/1/93; SLJ 3/93)

**8360** Morris, Gilbert. *The Dangerous Voyage* (4–6). Series: Time Navigators. 1995, Bethany paper $5.99 (1-55661-395-4). 160pp. In order to help their ailing young brother, twins Danny and Dixie volunteer to travel through time in this book, the first of the series. (Rev: BL 1/1–15/96; SLJ 1/96)

**8361** Orr, Wendy. *A Light in Space* (5–6). Series: Young Novels. 1994, Annick paper $5.95 (1-55037-975-5). 188pp. Andrew makes contact with a space alien who plans to use Earth as a colony for her people. (Rev: SLJ 2/95)

**8362** Peck, Richard. *The Great Interactive Dream Machine* (4–6). 1996, Dial paper $14.99 (0-8037-1989-2). 160pp. In this sequel to *Lost in Cyberspace* (1995), Josh and his friend Aaron travel again through time and space. (Rev: BCCB 9/96; BL 9/1/96; SLJ 9/96)

**8363** Peck, Richard. *Lost in Cyberspace* (4–7). 1995, Dial paper $14.99 (0-8037-1931-0). 160pp. When Josh's friend Aaron converts 2 computers into a time machine, they are visited by strangers from the past. (Rev: BCCB 9/95; BL 10/15/95*; SLJ 9/95)

**8364** Pinkwater, Daniel. *Borgel* (5–7). 1990, Macmillan $15.00 (0-02-774671-2). 160pp. An unusual visitor takes young Melvin on a trip to the stars. (Rev: BCCB 7–8/90; BL 5/1/90; SLJ 3/90)

**8365** Pinkwater, Daniel. *Mush, a Dog from Space* (2–5). Illus. 1995, Simon & Schuster $15.00 (0-689-80317-6). 40pp. In spite of her parents, Kelly is determined to keep the dog from outer space that she has found. (Rev: BL 10/1/95; HB 11–12/95; SLJ 11/95)

**8366** Pinkwater, Daniel. *Ned Feldman, Space Pirate* (3–5). Illus. 1994, Macmillan paper $14.95 (0-02-774633-X). 48pp. Captain Bugbeard takes Ned on a galactic trip to a planet where giant chickens live. (Rev: BCCB 10/94; BL 11/1/94; SLJ 12/94)

**8367** Pinkwater, Daniel. *Wallpaper from Space* (2–4). Illus. by Jill Pinkwater. 1996, Simon & Schuster $15.00 (0-689-80764-3). 32pp. A spaceship on Steven's new wallpaper takes him on a zany space trip. (Rev: BCCB 10/96; BL 9/1/96; SLJ 10/96)

**8368** Regan, Dian C. *Monsters in Cyberspace* (4–6). Illus. 1997, Holt $14.95 (0-8050-4677-1). 178pp. A 13-year-old girl and her Monster of the Month enjoy running up bills surfing the Net. (Rev: BCCB 7–8/97; BL 6/1–15/97; SLJ 9/97)

**8369** Regan, Dian C. *Princess Nevermore* (5–7). 1995, Scholastic $14.95 (0-590-47582-6). 232pp. A princess from another world gets her wish to visit Earth, where she is befriended by 2 teenagers, Sarah and Adam. (Rev: BCCB 11/95; SLJ 9/95)

**8370** Rodda, Emily. *Finders Keepers* (4–7). Illus. by Noela Young. 1991, Greenwillow $12.95 (0-688-10516-5). 192pp. Patrick is transported onto the set of a quiz show in a parallel world beyond the "great barrier." (Rev: BCCB 12/91; BL 11/15/91; SLJ 8/91)

**8371** Service, Pamela F. *Stinker from Space* (3–6). 1988, Macmillan $12.95 (0-684-18910-1); Fawcett paper $4.50 (0-449-70330-4). 96pp. When his spaceship crashes to earth, Tsyng Tyr from the Sylon Confederacy takes over the body of a skunk. (Rev: BL 3/1/88; HB 9–10/88)

**8372** Service, Pamela F. *Stinker's Return* (4–6). 1993, Macmillan $12.95 (0-684-19542-9). 96pp. In this sequel to *Stinker from Space* (1990), alien Tsyng Yr again returns to earth as a skunk, and with Jonathan and Karen has many adventures in Washington, D.C. (Rev: BCCB 6/93; BL 4/1/93; SLJ 5/93)

**8373** Sheldon, Dyan. *Harry the Explorer* (4–6). Illus. by Sue Heap. 1992, Candlewick $13.95 (1-56402-109-2). 80pp. Adventures of the girl Chicken and Harry, her cat, who is really a visitor from another planet. (Rev: BL 10/15/92; SLJ 9/92)

421

**8374** Slote, Alfred. *My Robot Buddy* (4–6). Illus. by Joel Schick. 1975, HarperCollins paper $4.50 (0-06-440165-0). 80pp. For his tenth birthday, Jack's parents get him his very own Robot Buddy. Sequels are: *My Trip to Alpha I* (1978); *Omega Station* (1983).

**8375** Slote, Alfred. *The Trouble on Janus* (3–5). Illus. 1985, HarperCollins LB $14.89 (0-397-32159-7). 192pp. Jack and his robot Danny are off on a mission to the planet Janus. (Rev: BCCB 2/86; BL 9/1/85; SLJ 11/85)

**8376** Sobol, Donald J. *My Name Is Amelia* (4–8). 1994, Atheneum $14.00 (0-689-31970-3). 128pp. Lisa is cast ashore on a strange island governed by a mad scientist with plans to inhabit a distant galaxy. (Rev: BCCB 2/95; BL 1/1/95; SLJ 1/95)

**8377** Standiford, Natalie. *Space Dog and the Pet Show* (3–4). Illus. by Kelly Oechsli. 1990, Avon paper $2.95 (0-380-75954-3). 76pp. A literate dog from outer space is entered into a competition by his new owner. Further adventures of Space Dog are found in *Space Dog in Trouble* (1991). (Rev: BL 12/15/90)

**8378** Walsh, Jill Paton. *The Green Book* (4–7). Illus. by Lloyd Bloom. 1982, Farrar $13.00 (0-374-32778-5); paper $3.95 (0-374-42802-6). 80pp. The exodus of a group of Britons from dying earth to another planet.

**8379** Wells, H. G. *The Time Machine* (3–5). Adapted by Les Martin. Illus. by John Edens. 1990, Random paper $3.99 (0-679-80371-8). 93pp. A clever adaptation of a classic science fiction story about a time traveler and his friends. (Rev: SLJ 4/91)

**8380** Whitman, John. *Star Wars: The Death Star* (2–5). Illus. by Barbara Gibson. 1997, Little, Brown $15.95 (0-316-93592-1). 12pp. Action-packed science fiction is featured in this pop-up book. Also use *Millennium Falcon* (1997). (Rev: BL 12/15/97)

**8381** Wismer, Donald. *Starluck* (6–8). 1982, Ultramarine $20.00 (0-89366-255-0). 186pp. Paul becomes a threat to the Emperor of the Three Hundred Suns.

# Short Stories and Anthologies

**8382** Baylor, Byrd. *I'm in Charge of Celebrations* (4–6). Illus. 1986, Macmillan $14.95 (0-684-18579-2). 32pp. Poetic prose about rainbows, cactus greens, and desert browns. (Rev: BL 11/1/86; HB 1–2/87)

**8383** Bennett, William J., ed. *The Book of Virtues for Young People: A Treasury of Great Moral Stories* (4–6). 1995, Silver Burdett LB $16.95 (0-382-24923-2). 384pp. A book of readings organized under such themes as friendship, self-discipline, work, and honesty. (Rev: BL 8/95; SLJ 8/95) [808.8]

**8384** Castor, Harriet, ed. *Ballet Stories* (4–6). Illus. 1997, Kingfisher $6.95 (0-7534-5073-9). 224pp. Fifteen stories (2 from autobiographies) tell about the joys, sorrows, and conflicts that young people face when they study ballet seriously. (Rev: BL 7/97; SLJ 1/98)

**8385** Dahl, Roald. *The Roald Dahl Treasury* (4–6). Illus. 1997, Viking paper $35.00 (0-670-87769-7). 448pp. An omnibus volume that features a generous selection of excerpts from Dahl's novels, autobiographies, and poetry, all handsomely illustrated by well-known artists. (Rev: BL 12/1/97) [820]

**8386** Durell, Ann, and Marilyn Sachs. *The Big Book for Peace* (4–6). Illus. 1990, Dutton paper $17.50 (0-525-44605-2). 128pp. Contributions from 32 writers and illustrations on the subject of peace. (Rev: BCCB 10/90; BL 9/15/90; HB 11–12/90; SLJ 10/90*)

**8387** Harrison, Michael, and Christopher Stuart-Clark, eds. *The Oxford Treasury of Children's Stories* (3–5). Illus. 1995, Oxford $25.00 (0-19-278133-2). 161pp. An excellent collection of 26 stories, chiefly by such British writers as Kipling and Wilde and contemporaries like Joan Aiken and Philippa Pierce. (Rev: BL 7/95; SLJ 9/95)

**8388** Highlights for Children, eds. *Ashanti Festival* (3–5). 1996, Boyds Mills paper $3.95 (1-56397-608-0). 96pp. Sixteen excellent short stories taken from the pages of *Highlights for Children*. (Rev: SLJ 1/97)

**8389** Hurwitz, Johanna, ed. *Birthday Surprises: Ten Great Stories to Unwrap* (4–6). 1995, Morrow $16.00 (0-688-13194-8). 128pp. Ten short stories by such writers as Richard Peck and Ellen Conford deal with presents in containers that are empty. (Rev: BCCB 5/95; BL 4/15/95; SLJ 4/95*)

**8390** Jennings, Paul. *Unbearable! More Bizarre Stories* (4–6). 1995, Viking paper $14.99 (0-670-86262-2). 116pp. A group of stories about youngsters in unusual, often humorous situations. (Rev: BCCB 7–8/95; BL 6/1–15/95; SLJ 7/95)

**8391** Jennings, Paul. *Unreal! Eight Surprising Stories* (4–8). 1995, Puffin paper $3.99 (0-14-037577-5). 112pp. A good assortment of short stories from an Australian writer. (Rev: BCCB 9/91; BL 8/91; SLJ 12/91*)

**8392** Maccaulay, David. *Black and White* (2–6). Illus. 1990, Houghton $16.95 (0-395-52151-3). 32pp. With thought-provoking illustrations, 4 short stories are presented. Caldecott Medal winner, 1991. (Rev: BCCB 5/90; BL 4/1/90*; HB 9–10/90)

**8393** *My Wish for Tomorrow: Words and Pictures from Children Around the World* (K–5). Illus. 1995, Morrow LB $15.93 (0-688-14456-X). 48pp. To celebrate the 50th birthday of the United Nations, this is a collection of writing and art by children ages 4 to

14 from around the world. (Rev: BL 10/15/95; SLJ 10/95)

**8394** Pilling, Ann, comp. *Love Stories* (4–7). Illus. by Aafke Brouwer. Series: Story Library. 1997, Kingfisher paper $6.95 (0-7534-5117-4). 223pp. This collection of 20 stories and book excerpts — many by well-known writers like Oscar Wilde and Betsy Byars — explores various facets of love. (Rev: SLJ 12/97)

**8395** Speed, Toby. *Water Voices* (2–4). Illus. by Julie Downing. 1998, Putnam $15.95 (0-399-22631-1). 32pp. A group of verses that are riddles describing the nature of water in various places and situations. (Rev: BL 2/1/98; SLJ 4/98)

**8396** Valgardson, W. D. *Garbage Creek and Other Stories* (4–6). Illus. 1997, Douglas & McIntyre $15.95 (0-88899-297-1). 132pp. These 8 short stories deal with such themes as moving, poverty, absent fathers, and protecting nature. (Rev: BL 1/1–15/98)

**8397** *The Viking Treasury of Children's Stories* (3–6). Illus. 1997, Viking paper $19.99 (0-670-87303-9). 320pp. This excellent anthology contains 36 complete stories and excerpts from children's classics. (Rev: BL 6/1–15/97; SLJ 7/97)

## Sports Stories

**8398** Alter, Judith. *Callie Shaw, Stable Boy* (4–6). 1996, Eakin $15.95 (1-57168-092-6). 188pp. During the Great Depression, Callie, disguised as a boy, works in a stable and uncovers a race-fixing racket. (Rev: BL 2/1/97; SLJ 8/97)

**8399** Alvord, Douglas. *Sarah's Boat: A Young Girl Learns the Art of Sailing* (3–6). Illus. 1994, Tilbury $16.95 (0-88448-117-4). 44pp. Sarah learns how to sail from her grandfather and enters her *Bluejay* sloop in the Labor Day race. (Rev: BL 7/94)

**8400** Armstrong, Jennifer. *Patrick Doyle Is Full of Blarney* (2–4). Illus. 1996, Random LB $17.99 (0-679-97285-4). 80pp. In the Hell's Kitchen section of New York City in 1915, Patrick Doyle secures access to a baseball diamond through his skill and the help of the Giants hitter Larry Doyle. (Rev: BCCB 4/96; BL 5/1/96; SLJ 8/96)

**8401** Auch, Mary Jane. *Angel and Me and the Bayside Bombers* (2–4). Illus. by Cat B. Smith. 1989, Little, Brown $9.95 (0-316-05914-5); paper $2.95 (0-316-05915-3). 60pp. A poor soccer player, Brian bribes his way onto the team. (Rev: BL 1/15/90; HB 3–4/90; SLJ 3/90)

**8402** Avi. *S.O.R. Losers* (5–7). 1984, Macmillan $15.00 (0-02-793410-1). 112pp. The most inept soc-

cer team in the history of the South Orange River Middle School is formed.

**8403** Baker, Carin G. *Fight for Honor* (4–6). Series: Karate Club. 1992, Puffin paper $4.99 (0-14-036024-7). 138pp. Lee, an adopted Vietnamese boy and karate expert, must cope with school bullies. (Rev: SLJ 6/92)

**8404** Bauer, Joan. *Sticks* (4–6). 1996, Delacorte $15.95 (0-385-32165-1). 182pp. Ten-year-old Mickey gets an old family friend to teach him pool tricks so that he has a chance of winning the Pool Hall Youth Championship. (Rev: BCCB 5/96; BL 5/1/96; SLJ 6/96)

**8405** Bledsoe, Lucy Jane. *The Big Bike Race* (2–4). 1995, Holiday $14.95 (0-8234-1206-7). 80pp. Though disappointed that he did not receive the bike of his dreams for his birthday, Ernie trains for the Citywide Cup race. (Rev: BCCB 12/95; BL 10/1/95; SLJ 11/95)

**8406** *The Blue Darter and Other Sports Stories* (4–6). 1995, Boyds Mills paper $2.95 (1-56397-446-0). 96pp. A collection of 11 sports stories from *Highlights for Children* that deals with various sports. (Rev: BL 10/1/95)

**8407** Bowen, Fred. *Playoff Dreams* (3–5). Illus. 1997, Peachtree paper $4.95 (1-56145-155-X). 112pp. When Brendan begins to feel that he is the only salvation open to his baseball team, Uncle Jack steps in with some good advice. (Rev: BL 11/1/97; SLJ 3/98)

**8408** Bowen, Fred. *T.J.'s Secret Pitch* (3–5). Illus. by Jim Thorpe. Series: Allstar SportStory. 1996, Peachtree paper $4.95 (1-56145-119-3). 104pp. A young Little Leaguer copies the famous pitch of the legendary Truett "Rip" Sewell and achieves fame. (Rev: SLJ 7/96)

**8409** Bowman, Crystal. *Ivan and the Dynamos* (4–6). 1997, Eerdmans $15.00 (0-8028-5087-1); paper $5.00 (0-8028-5090-1). 140pp. An 11-year-old boy is unhappy about being traded to a new hockey team, particularly when he learns that the coach is eccentric. (Rev: SLJ 9/97)

**8410** Brooks, Bruce. *Boot* (4–7). Series: The Wolfbay Wings. 1998, HarperCollins LB $14.89 (0-06-027569-3); paper $4.50 (0-06-440680-6). 122pp. In this hockey story, a foster child named The Boot is reluctant to "hit" his opponents. (Rev: SLJ 3/98)

**8411** Brooks, Bruce. *Cody* (4–6). Series: The Wolfbay Wings. 1997, HarperCollins LB $14.89 (0-06-027541-3); paper $4.50 (0-06-440599-0). 101pp. In this hockey story, Cody must defy his father, the coach, for the good of the team. (Rev: SLJ 12/97)

**8412** Brooks, Bruce. *Woodsie* (4–6). 1997, HarperCollins paper $4.50 (0-06-440597-4). 144pp. In this sports novel about the Wolfbay Wings Squirt A hockey team, Woodsie finds he is in a no-win situation. Also use *Zip* (1997). (Rev: BL 1/1–15/98; SLJ 12/97)

**8413** Charbonnet, Gabrielle. *Competition Fever* (5–7). 1996, Bantam paper $3.50 (0-553-48295-5). 138pp. In this novel, rivalry between 2 girls endangers a team's chances of victory in gymnastics competitions. (Rev: BL 9/1/96; SLJ 6/96)

**8414** Christopher, Matt. *Baseball Turnaround* (4–6). 1977, Little, Brown $15.95 (0-316-14275-1); paper $3.95 (0-316-14264-6). 160pp. After Sandy has had a brush with the law, he tries to keep this part of his past a secret from his teammates. (Rev: BL 6/1–15/97; SLJ 8/97)

**8415** Christopher, Matt. *The Comeback Challenge* (4–6). Illus. 1996, Little, Brown $15.95 (0-316-14090-2); paper $3.95 (0-316-14152-6). 160pp. Twelve-year-old Mark has problems with Vince, the captain of his soccer team. (Rev: BL 1/1–15/96; SLJ 1/96)

**8416** Christopher, Matt. *Dirt Bike Racer* (3–5). Illus. by Barry Bomzer. 1986, Little, Brown $15.95 (0-316-13977-7); paper $3.95 (0-316-14053-8). Ron finds a bike at the bottom of a lake and begins dirt bike racing. Another sports story from the same author is: *Dirt Bike Runaway* (1989).

**8417** Christopher, Matt. *The Dog That Pitched a No-Hitter* (2–4). Illus. by Daniel Vasconcellos. 1993, Little, Brown paper $3.95 (0-316-14103-8). 42pp. Mike's dog Harry has powers of ESP and helps Mike with his pitching game. (Rev: BL 5/15/88; SLJ 8/88)

**8418** Christopher, Matt. *Double Play at Short* (3–6). Illus. 1995, Little, Brown $15.95 (0-316-14267-0). 160pp. Danny is convinced that the shortstop on a rival baseball team is actually his twin. (Rev: BL 5/1/95; SLJ 6/95)

**8419** Christopher, Matt. *The Hit-Away Kid* (2–5). Illus. 1988, Little, Brown $12.95 (0-316-13995-5); paper $4.50 (0-316-14007-4). 55pp. Barry McGee, left fielder for the Peach Street Mudders, learns a lesson in sportsmanship and telling the truth. Two other baseball stories are: *Supercharged Infield* (1985); *The Spy on Third Base* (1988). (Rev: BCCB 5/88; BL 4/1/88; SLJ 5/88)

**8420** Christopher, Matt. *The Hockey Machine* (3–5). Illus. 1986, Little, Brown $15.95 (0-316-14055-4); paper $3.95 (0-316-14087-2). 137pp. Thirteen-year-old Steve Crandall finds himself kidnapped and spirited away to a secluded camp because of his hockey skills. (Rev: BCCB 12/86; BL 1/1/87)

**8421** Christopher, Matt. *Penalty Shot* (3–5). Illus. 1997, Little, Brown $15.95 (0-316-13787-1); paper $3.95 (0-316-14190-9). 134pp. Kevin is thrown off the hockey team for bad grades but is determined to get back on. (Rev: BL 1/1–15/97; SLJ 2/97)

**8422** Christopher, Matt. *Pressure Play* (3–5). Illus. by Karin Lidbeck. 1990, Little, Brown $15.95 (0-316-14098-8). 154pp. Travis deals with a growing lack of self-confidence in this novel with plenty of baseball action. (Rev: BL 8/93; SLJ 7/93)

**8423** Christopher, Matt. *Red-Hot Hightops* (4–6). Illus. 1992, Little, Brown $14.95 (0-316-14056-2); paper $3.95 (0-316-14089-9). 128pp. Shyness prevents Kelly from showing off her basketball skills or speaking to a boy she likes until she finds a pair of red sneakers in her locker. (Rev: BL 1/15/88)

**8424** Christopher, Matt. *Return of the Home Run Kid* (4–7). Illus. by Paul Casale. 1994, Little, Brown $3.95 (0-316-14273-5). 176pp. In this sequel to *The Kid Who Only Hit Homers* (1972), Sylvester learns to be more aggressive on the field but gets criticism from his friends. (Rev: BL 4/15/92; SLJ 5/92)

**8425** Christopher, Matt. *Shadow over Second* (2–4). Illus. by Anna Dewdney. Series: Peach Tree Mudders Story. 1996, Little, Brown $13.95 (0-316-14078-3). 64pp. Nicky Chong's superstitious nature gets in the way of continuing his winning record with the Peach Street Mudders baseball team. (Rev: SLJ 6/96)

**8426** Christopher, Matt. *Shortstop from Tokyo* (3–5). Illus. by Harvey Kidder. 1988, Little, Brown paper $3.95 (0-316-13992-0). Stogie feels resentment when a Japanese boy takes his place on the baseball team. Also from the same author and publisher: *The Kid Who Only Hit Homers* (1972); *The Fox Steals Home* (1985); *The Year Mom Won the Pennant* (1986); *No Arm in Left Field* (1987).

**8427** Christopher, Matt. *Skateboard Tough* (4–6). 1991, Little, Brown $15.95 (0-316-14247-6). 168pp. Brett finds a skateboard and is able to do tricks he has never done before. (Rev: BCCB 5/91; BL 5/15/91; SLJ 6/91)

**8428** Christopher, Matt. *Snowboard Maverick* (4–7). 1997, Little, Brown $15.95 (0-316-14261-1); paper $3.95 (0-316-14203-4). 152pp. Dennis overcomes his fears and begins snowboarding. (Rev: SLJ 3/98)

**8429** Christopher, Matt. *Soccer Halfback* (4–6). Illus. by Larry Johnson. 1985, Little, Brown $15.95 (0-316-13946-7); paper $3.95 (0-316-13981-5). Everyone wants Jabber to play football, but his favorite sport is soccer.

**8430** Christopher, Matt. *Soccer Scoop* (3–6). 1998, Little, Brown $15.95 (0-316-14206-9). 160pp. A soccer story in which the team's star goalie becomes the target of a series of unflattering cartoons. (Rev: BL 2/15/98)

**8431** Christopher, Matt. *Stranger in Right Field* (2–4). Illus. 1997, Little, Brown $13.95 (0-316-14111-9). 61pp. Alfie is afraid that a new player on his baseball team is being groomed to take his place. (Rev: BL 9/1/97; SLJ 10/97)

**8432** Christopher, Matt. *Tackle Without a Team* (4–7). Illus. 1989, Little, Brown $15.95 (0-316-14067-8). 128pp. Scott vows to find whoever framed him with marijuana and got him kicked off the team. (Rev: BL 3/1/89; SLJ 3/89)

**8433** Christopher, Matt. *Takedown* (4–7). Illus. by Margaret Sanfilippo. 1990, Little, Brown $15.95 (0-316-13930-0). 147pp. Sean takes up wrestling and finds he has a rival in a bigger, better wrestler. (Rev: SLJ 1/90)

**8434** Christopher, Matt. *Undercover Tailback* (3–7). Illus. by Paul Casale. 1992, Little, Brown $15.95 (0-316-14251-4). 145pp. Parker Nolan, great with a football but short on telling the truth, tries to convince his coach and team members that someone has stolen game plays. (Rev: BL 1/15/93; SLJ 12/92)

**8435** Christopher, Matt. *The Winning Stroke* (4–8). Illus. 1994, Little, Brown $15.95 (0-316-14266-2). 168pp. As part of his physical therapy after breaking a leg, Jerry takes up swimming and learns a lesson in sportsmanship. (Rev: BL 5/1/94; SLJ 6/94)

**8436** Cohen, Barbara. *Thank You, Jackie Robinson* (4–6). Illus. by Richard Cuffari. 1989, Scholastic paper $3.99 (0-590-42378-9). A memoir written by Sam about his friendship with an old man and his devotion as a boy to the Brooklyn Dodgers and Ebbets Field.

**8437** Cooper, Ilene. *Choosing Sides* (4–6). 1990, Morrow $15.00 (0-688-07934-2). 224pp. Jonathan wants to quit the basketball team but does not want to disappoint his dad. (Rev: BCCB 9/90; BL 2/15/90; SLJ 5/90)

**8438** Davis, Gibbs. *Tony's Double Play* (2–4). Illus. by George Ulrich. 1992, Bantam $3.50 (0-553-15996-8). 80pp. Recovered from a broken leg, Tony gets to play shortstop. (Rev: BL 7/92)

**8439** DeClements, Barthe. *Tough Loser* (4–6). 1994, Viking paper $13.99 (0-670-85619-3). 128pp. Young Mark is a fine hockey player, but his temper is out of control. (Rev: BCCB 12/94; BL 10/1/94; SLJ 10/94)

**8440** Drumtra, Stacy. *Face-Off* (4–8). 1992, Avon paper $3.50 (0-380-76863-1). 118pp. T.J. and his twin Brad become rivals both for friends and for status on the hockey team. (Rev: BL 4/1/93)

**8441** Dygard, Thomas J. *Quarterback Walk-On* (5–8). 1998, Morrow paper $3.99 (0-688-16368-8). 192pp. Denny, a fourth-string quarterback, must save the day for his college team.

**8442** Fenner, Carol. *The Skates of Uncle Richard* (3–4). Illus. by Ati Forberg. 1978, Random LB $9.99 (0-394-93553-5). 48pp. Nine-year-old Marsha tries to ice-skate on hand-me-down skates from Uncle Richard.

**8443** Giff, Patricia Reilly. *Left-Handed Shortstop* (4–6). Illus. by Leslie Morrill. 1997, Bantam paper $3.99 (0-440-44672-4). 128pp. Walter tries everything possible not to play baseball.

**8444** Greenberg, Martin H., and Charles G. Waugh, eds. *A Newbery Zoo: A Dozen Animal Stories by Newbery Award-Winning Authors* (4–7). 1995, Delacorte $16.95 (0-385-32263-1). 143pp. Twelve animal stories by such Newbery winners as Beverly Cleary, Betsy Byars, and Jean Craighead George. (Rev: BL 1/15/95; SLJ 4/95)

**8445** Greene, Stephanie. *Owen Foote, Soccer Star* (1–3). Illus. 1998, Clarion $14.00 (0-395-86143-8). 88pp. When Owen joins a local soccer team, he is not prepared for the powerhouse players he meets. A sequel to *Owen Foote, Second Grade Strongman* (1996). (Rev: BL 3/15/98)

**8446** Hall, Donald. *When Willard Met Babe Ruth* (4–6). Illus. by Barry Moser. 1996, Harcourt $16.00 (0-15-200273-1). 48pp. A young New Hampshire farm boy and his father have a chance meeting with Babe Ruth. (Rev: BCCB 6/96; BL 3/15/96*; HB 9–10/96; SLJ 5/96)

**8447** Hest, Amy. *Party on Ice* (2–4). Illus. by Irene Trivas. 1995, Morrow LB $14.93 (0-688-14268-0). 48pp. Casey invites her 2 friends to a skating birthday party, which is a success until one falls and breaks her arm. A sequel to *Pajama Party* (1992) and *Nannies for Hire* (1994). (Rev: BL 10/15/95; SLJ 12/95)

**8448** Heymsfeld, Carla. *Coaching Ms. Parker* (3–5). Illus. by Jane O'Connor. 1992, Macmillan LB $13.00 (0-02-743715-9). 96pp. Fourth-graders face the challenge of teaching Ms. Parker baseball in time for the faculty versus sixth-grade game. (Rev: BCCB 6/92; BL 6/15/92; SLJ 7/92)

**8449** Hiser, Constance. *Dog on Third Base* (2–4). Illus. by Carolyn Ewing. 1991, Holiday $13.95 (0-8234-0898-1). 128pp. James and baseball-playing dog Tag help tame bully Mean Mitchell. (Rev: BL 10/15/91; SLJ 10/91)

**8450** Hite, Sid. *An Even Break* (5–7). 1995, Holt $14.95 (0-8050-3837-X). 92pp. Twelve-year-old Frisk tries to help his mother financially by taking a job in the local billiard parlor. (Rev: BCCB 1/96; BL 11/1/95; SLJ 12/95)

**8451** Hughes, Dean. *End of the Race* (5–7). 1993, Atheneum $13.95 (0-689-31779-4). 160pp. Both Jared and his African American track team competitor, Davin, are pressured by their parents to win. (Rev: BL 11/1/93; SLJ 12/93)

**8452** Hughes, Dean. *The Trophy* (4–6). Illus. 1994, Knopf $13.00 (0-679-84368-X). 135pp. Danny's desire to play basketball and his father's alcoholism collide in this story of family tensions and problems. (Rev: BL 2/15/95; SLJ 12/94)

**8453** Hurwitz, Johanna. *Baseball Fever* (3–6). Illus. by Ray Cruz. 1981, Morrow paper $3.95 (0-688-10495-9). 128pp. Mr. Feldman loathes baseball, but his son Ezra loves it.

**8454** Joosse, Barbara M. *The Losers Fight Back* (3–6). Illus. 1994, Clarion $13.95 (0-395-62335-9). 128pp. When the Bruisers, a losing soccer team, bribe Chuckie to join them, they find that he takes over their games. (Rev: BL 9/15/94; SLJ 11/94)

**8455** Knudson, R. R. *Rinehart Lifts* (4–6). 1982, Avon paper $1.95 (0-380-57059-9). 88pp. A failure at all sports, Rinehart finds he can excel in weight lifting.

**8456** Kroll, Steven. *New Kid in Town* (2–4). Illus. 1992, Avon paper $3.50 (0-380-76407-5). 80pp. Phil finally makes the Raymondtown Rockets baseball team, only to find his happiness threatened because his father may be transferred. (Rev: BL 3/15/92)

**8457** Lowell, Melissa. *Breaking the Ice* (4–6). 1993, Bantam paper $3.50 (0-553-48134-7). 135pp. A novel that uses the Silver Blades Skating Club, for Olympic hopefuls, in Seneca Falls, New York, as its setting and an aspiring figure skater as its heroine. (Rev: BL 1/1/94; SLJ 2/94)

**8458** Mackel, Kathy. *A Season of Comebacks* (4–7). 1997, Putnam $15.95 (0-399-23026-2). 112pp. Molly is jealous of her sister Allie, who plays a better game of baseball than she does. (Rev: BCCB 4/97; BL 8/97; SLJ 7/97)

**8459** Maifair, Linda Lee. *Batter Up, Bailey Benson!* (3–5). 1997, Zondervan paper $3.99 (0-310-20705-3). 64pp. Bailey faces jealousy problems when she finds that she is on a different baseball team than her friend Nicole. (Rev: BL 3/15/97)

**8460** Maifair, Linda Lee. *Go Figure, Gabriella Grant!* (3–5). 1997, Zondervan paper $3.99 (0-310-20702-9). 64pp. Gabriella has problems budgeting her time when she takes up figure skating. (Rev: BL 3/15/97)

**8461** Manes, Stephen. *An Almost Perfect Game* (4–7). 1995, Scholastic $14.95 (0-590-44432-8). 163pp. Jake and Randy enjoy visiting their grandparents each summer because all of them are avid baseball fans. (Rev: BL 6/1–15/95; SLJ 6/95)

**8462** Marzollo, Jean. *Slam Dunk Saturday* (2–4). Illus. 1994, Random LB $11.99 (0-679-92366-7); paper $3.99 (0-679-82366-2). 79pp. Billy is nervous about the outcome of a basketball-shooting contest he has entered. (Rev: BL 1/1/95)

**8463** Mathis, Sharon Bell. *Running Girl: The Diary of Ebonee Rose* (3–5). Illus. 1997, Harcourt $17.00

(0-15-200674-5). 64pp. Ebonee Rose, a star runner, looks forward to the All-City Track Meet. (Rev: BL 9/1/97; SLJ 10/97)

**8464** Myers, Walter Dean. *Me, Mop, and the Moondance Kid* (5–7). Illus. 1988, Delacorte $13.95 (0-440-50065-6); Dell paper $3.99 (0-440-40396-0). 128pp. The efforts of T.J. and Moondance to get their friend Mop adopted. (Rev: BCCB 12/88; BL 2/1/89; SLJ 1/88)

**8465** Myers, Walter Dean. *Mop, Moondance and the Nagasaki Knights* (4–6). 1992, Delacorte $14.00 (0-385-30687-3). 152pp. Mop, Moondance, and T.J. are involved in a Little League playoff with a foreign team. (Rev: BL 6/15/92; HB 11–12/92; SLJ 9/92)

**8466** Park, Barbara. *Skinnybones* (4–6). 1982, Knopf LB $13.99 (0-394-94988-9); paper $3.99 (0-394-82596-9). 128pp. The story of a Little League misfit.

**8467** Schnur, Steven. *The Koufax Dilemma* (4–6). Illus. 1997, Morrow $15.00 (0-688-14221-4). 192pp. Danny faces problems because of his parents' divorce and the fact that his mother won't let him play baseball in the big game on Passover. (Rev: BCCB 5/97; BL 3/15/97; SLJ 5/97)

**8468** Scholz, Jackson. *The Football Rebels* (5–7). 1993, Morrow paper $4.95 (0-688-12643-X). 256pp. Clint does his best on the intramural football team when he doesn't make the varsity. Also use: *Rookie Quarterback* (1993). Both are reissues.

**8469** Shannon, David. *How Georgie Radbourn Saved Baseball* (1–5). Illus. 1994, Scholastic $14.95 (0-590-47410-3). 32pp. A rich and powerful wheeler-dealer decides to ban baseball, and it's up to young Georgie Radbourn to save it. (Rev: BL 1/15/94; SLJ 4/94*)

**8470** Slote, Alfred. *Finding Buck McHenry* (4–6). 1991, HarperCollins LB $15.89 (0-06-021653-0). 256pp. Is Jason's baseball coach really the former great player he sees on a baseball card? (Rev: BCCB 5/91; BL 3/15/91; SLJ 5/91)

**8471** Slote, Alfred. *The Trading Game* (4–6). 1990, HarperCollins LB $15.89 (0-397-32398-0). 208pp. Andy's grandfather, a former baseball star, comes to town and offers to coach Andy's team. (Rev: BCCB 4/90; BL 3/15/90*; SLJ 5/90)

**8472** Spinelli, Jerry. *There's a Girl in My Hammerlock* (5–8). 1991, Simon & Schuster paper $14.00 (0-671-74684-7). 200pp. At 105 pounds, Maisie Potter is going out for junior high wrestling. (Rev: BCCB 9/91; BL 10/15/91; HB 9–10/91; SLJ 9/91*)

**8473** Stolz, Mary. *Coco Grimes* (3–5). 1995, HarperCollins paper $4.50 (0-06-440512-5). 96pp. Young Thomas is told about the Negro Baseball Leagues by one of the veteran players, Coco Grimes. (Rev: BCCB 7–8/94; BL 5/1/94; HB 7–8/94; SLJ 6/94)

**8474** Sullivan, Ann. *Molly Maguire: Wide Receiver* (4–6). 1992, Avon paper $2.99 (0-380-76114-9). 104pp. Molly wants to show a certain bully that she can play football, with the help of her next-door neighbor, who played for Notre Dame. (Rev: BL 10/1/92)

**8475** Tamar, Erika. *Soccer Mania!* (2–4). Illus. by Dee deRosa. 1993, Random LB $11.99 (0-679-93396-4); paper $3.99 (0-679-83396-X). 63pp. Pete and his friends are happy that parents are going to sponsor their soccer team, but they are dismayed at the rules they impose. (Rev: BL 9/15/93)

**8476** Tunis, John R. *The Kid from Tomkinsville* (5–8). 1990, Harcourt $14.95 (0-15-242568-3); paper $3.95 (0-15-242567-5). "Kid" Tucker's rookie year with the 1940 Brooklyn Dodgers. Other Tunis classics are: *Rookie of the Year; Keystone Kids* (both 1990). (Rev: BL 8/87)

**8477** Wallace, Bill. *Never Say Quit* (5–7). 1993, Holiday $15.95 (0-8234-1013-7). 212pp. A group of misfits who don't make the soccer team decide to form one of their own. (Rev: BL 4/15/93)

**8478** Webster-Doyle, Terrence. *Breaking the Chains of the Ancient Warrior: Tests of Wisdom for Young Martial Artists* (5–8). Illus. by Rod Cameron. 1995, Martial Arts for Peace $25.00 (0-942941-33-0); paper $14.95 (0-942941-32-2). 176pp. A collection of karate parables and tests that promote ethical behavior, with accompanying follow-up questions for the reader and a message for adults. (Rev: SLJ 1/96)

**8479** Wyeth, Sharon D. *The Winning Stroke* (4–7). 1996, Bantam paper $3.99 (0-553-48394-3). 155pp. Kristy hopes to prove that she is as good a swimmer as her brother. (Rev: BL 9/1/96; SLJ 6/96)

**8480** Zirpoli, Jane. *Roots in the Outfield* (5–7). 1988, Houghton $15.00 (0-395-45184-1). 133pp. Josh spends a summer with his newly married father in Wisconsin and discovers some baseball memorabilia that help him overcome his own fears and ineptness in right field. (Rev: BL 4/1/88; SLJ 5/88)

# Fairy Tales

**8481** Andersen, Hans Christian. *Eighty Fairy Tales* (4–7). 1983, Pantheon paper $17.00 (0-394-71055-X). 394pp. An excellent collection of Andersen's best.

**8482** Andersen, Hans Christian. *The Emperor and the Nightingale* (K–6). Illus. by Meilo So. 1995, Simon & Schuster paper $10.95 (0-689-80363-X). This is a streamlined but very effective retelling of the Andersen tale. (Rev: SLJ 10/92)

**8483** Andersen, Hans Christian. *The Emperor's New Clothes* (K–3). Retold by Anthea Bell. Illus. by Dorothee Duntze. 1986, North-South $16.95 (1-55858-036-0). 32pp. A formal, slightly oversize rendition of the famous tale. (Rev: BL 10/15/86; SLJ 1/87)

**8484** Andersen, Hans Christian. *The Emperor's New Clothes* (PS–2). Adapted and illus. by Janet Stevens. 1985, Holiday LB $15.95 (0-8234-0566-4). 32pp. The classic tale with new trappings — the emperor is a finely dressed pig and the unscrupulous weavers are 2 sly foxes. (Rev: BL 10/15/85; SLJ 11/85)

**8485** Andersen, Hans Christian. *The Emperor's New Clothes* (1–3). Trans. by Naomi Lewis. Illus. by Angela Barrett. 1997, Candlewick $15.99 (0-7636-0119-5). 32pp. In this version of the Andersen tale, 2 con men persuade the emperor to order a magical suit that will expose the incompetence of those who can't see it. (Rev: BL 12/15/97; HB 11–12/97; SLJ 11/97*)

**8486** Andersen, Hans Christian. *Fairy Tales of Hans Christian Andersen* (4–6). Ed. by Neil Philip. Illus. 1995, Viking paper $19.99 (0-670-85930-3). 144pp. A collection of 12 tales (some not well known) retold in a conversational, appealing style. (Rev: BL 11/15/95; SLJ 12/95)

**8487** Andersen, Hans Christian. *The Fir Tree* (2–4). Illus. by Bernadette Watts. 1990, North-South $14.95

(1-55858-093-X). 32pp. A large-format edition of the classic tale. (Rev: BL 1/1/91)

**8488** Andersen, Hans Christian. *Hans Christian Andersen Fairy Tales* (1–5). Trans. by Anthea Bell. Illus. by Lisbeth Zwerger. 1992, Picture Book $19.95 (0-88708-182-7). 70pp. This is a collection of 8 of Andersen's tales, some familiar, others not. (Rev: BL 11/15/92)

**8489** Andersen, Hans Christian. *The Little Match Girl* (4–6). Illus. by Blair Lent. 1975, Houghton paper $1.95 (0-685-02294-3). The touching story of the lonely, shivering little match girl who sees visions in the flames of the matches she cannot sell.

**8490** Andersen, Hans Christian. *The Little Mermaid* (3–6). Illus. by Charles Santore. 1993, JellyBean $14.00 (0-517-06495-2). 48pp. A new edition of this classic fairy tale that retains almost all of Andersen's original language. (Rev: BL 9/15/93; SLJ 10/93)

**8491** Andersen, Hans Christian. *The Snow Queen* (K–3). Trans. and retold by Anthea Bell. Illus. by Bernadette Watts. 1987, North-South $14.95 (1-55858-053-0). 32pp. A large-format edition of this beloved fairy tale. (Rev: BL 11/1/87; SLJ 10/87)

**8492** Andersen, Hans Christian. *The Snow Queen* (3–6). Illus. by P. J. Lynch. 1994, Harcourt $16.95 (0-15-200874-8). 48pp. In this Andersen tale, Gerda saves Kay after he is captured by the Snow Queen. (Rev: BL 9/15/94; SLJ 11/94)

**8493** Andersen, Hans Christian. *The Steadfast Tin Soldier* (K–4). Retold by Tor Seidler. Illus. by Fred Marcellino. 1997, HarperCollins paper $5.95 (0-062-05900-9). 32pp. This version of the popular tale sticks to the traditional story and acknowledges the author. (Rev: BL 12/1/92*; HB 3–4/93; SLJ 2/93)

**8494** Andersen, Hans Christian. *The Steadfast Tin Soldier* (K–3). Retold by Adrian Mitchell. Illus. by Jonathan Heale. 1996, DK Publg. $14.95 (1-56458-

310-4). 32pp. A retelling of Andersen's tale of unrequited love, with lovely illustrations that bring out the poignant nature of the story. (Rev: SLJ 1/97)

**8495** Andersen, Hans Christian. *Stories from Hans Christian Andersen* (2–4). Retold by Andrew Matthews. Illus. by Alan Snow. 1993, Orchard $18.95 (0-531-05463-2). 96pp. Eleven popular Andersen fairy tales, like *The Steadfast Tin Soldier* and *The Little Mermaid*, are retold in a simplified, conversational manner. (Rev: SLJ 12/93) [398.2]

**8496** Andersen, Hans Christian. *The Swan's Stories* (3–5). Trans. by Brian Alderson. Illus. by Chris Riddell. 1997, Candlewick $22.99 (1-56402-894-1). 144pp. A handsome, large-format book in which there are graceful retellings of 13 of Andersen's tales, some of which are widely known. (Rev: BL 12/15/97; HB 11–12/97; SLJ 9/97)

**8497** Andersen, Hans Christian. *Thumbelina* (1–3). Trans. by Erik Haugaard. Illus. by Arlene Graston. Series: Children's Classics. 1997, Delacorte $16.95 (0-385-32251-8). 32pp. With captivating illustrations, this book includes the complete text of the engaging fairy tale. (Rev: BL 11/15/97; SLJ 9/97*)

**8498** Andersen, Hans Christian. *Thumbeline* (PS–2). Illus. by Lisbeth Zwerger. 1986, Simon & Schuster paper $16.00 (0-88708-006-5). 28pp. Adventures of a girl no bigger than a thumb and her animal friends. (Rev: BL 1/1/86; SLJ 2/86)

**8499** Andersen, Hans Christian. *The Tinderbox* (1–4). Illus. by Warwick Hutton. 1988, Macmillan paper $14.95 (0-689-50458-6). 32pp. The tale of a soldier and how power and prosperity come to him through a witch's tinderbox. (Rev: BL 10/1/88; HB 11–12/88; SLJ 12/88)

**8500** Andersen, Hans Christian. *The Tinderbox* (PS–3). Retold by Peggy Tomson. Illus. by James Warhola. 1991, Simon & Schuster paper $14.95 (0-671-70546-6). A retelling that omits some of the violence but keeps the flavor of the tale. (Rev: BL 9/1/91; SLJ 11/91)

**8501** Andersen, Hans Christian. *The Top and the Ball* (K–2). Illus. by Elisabeth Nyman. 1992, Ideals LB $15.00 (0-8249-8583-4). 32pp. In the 19th century, a wooden top loves a ball in a boy's toy box. (Rev: BL 10/15/92)

**8502** Andersen, Hans Christian. *The Ugly Duckling* (PS–1). Adapted by Joel Tuber and Clara Stites. Illus. by Robert Van Nutt. 1986, Knopf $12.95 (0-394-88403-5). 48pp. A modestly updated, strikingly illustrated edition of the classic. Another edition is: Illus. by Lorinda Bryan Cauley (1979, Harcourt). (Rev: BL 1/1/87; SLJ 2/87)

**8503** Andersen, Hans Christian. *The Wicked Prince* (3–6). Illus. by Georges Lemoine. 1995, Harcourt $18.00 (0-15-200958-2). A wicked, arrogant prince is so sure of his power that he tries to conquer God. (Rev: SLJ 1/96)

**8504** Andersen, Hans Christian. *The Wild Swans* (K–2). Retold by Amy Ehrlich. Illus. by Susan Jeffers. 1981, Dial paper $5.95 (0-8037-0451-8). 40pp. The purity of a gentle princess triumphs over evil.

**8505** Balcells, Jacqueline. *The Enchanted Raisin* (3–6). Trans. by Elizabeth G. Miller. Illus. 1989, Latin American Literary Review Pr. paper $11.00 (0-935480-38-2). 103pp. Ten contemporary fairy stories by a noted Chilean writer for children. (Rev: BL 12/1/89)

**8506** Banks, Lynne Reid. *The Fairy Rebel* (4–6). Illus. by William Geldart. 1989, Avon paper $4.50 (0-380-70650-4). 128pp. A modern-day fairy tale of a woman who wants to have a child and a fairy who grants her wish and offends the all-powerful fairy queen. (Rev: BL 12/1/88; SLJ 10/88)

**8507** Barber, Antonia. *Catkin* (K–3). Illus. by P. J. Lynch. 1994, Candlewick $17.99 (1-56402-485-7). 48pp. When Carrie is kidnapped by the Little People, her faithful cat sets out to find her in this modern fairy tale. (Rev: BL 1/1/95; SLJ 1/95) [398.2]

**8508** Bazilian, Barbara. *The Red Shoes* (K–2). Illus. 1997, Whispering Coyote $15.95 (1-879085-56-9). 40pp. This attractive retelling of Andersen's story has been changed to make it less preachy and gory. (Rev: BL 11/1/97; SLJ 10/97)

**8509** Bender, Robert. *Toads and Diamonds* (K–3). Illus. 1995, Dutton paper $13.99 (0-525-67509-4). 32pp. Two sisters, one good and the other evil, encounter a 3-headed troll in the forest in this obscure Perrault tale. (Rev: BL 6/1–15/95; SLJ 6/95) [398.2]

**8510** Berenzy, Alix. *A Frog Prince* (K–3). Illus. 1989, Holt $14.95 (0-8050-0426-2). 32pp. This classic tale is told from the frog's point of view. (Rev: BCCB 10/89; BL 12/1/89; SLJ 10/89*)

**8511** Bull, Emma. *The Princess and the Lord of Night* (1–5). Illus. by Susan Gaber. 1994, Harcourt $14.95 (0-15-263543-2). 32pp. A young princess sets out to break the spell placed on her by the evil Lord of the Night. (Rev: BL 6/1–15/94; SLJ 5/94) [398.2]

**8512** Campbell, Ann. *Once upon a Princess and a Pea* (PS–3). Illus. by Kathy O. Young. 1993, Stewart, Tabori & Chang $13.95 (1-55670-289-2). 32pp. In a modern version of this fairy tale, a runaway princess must prove her sensitivity. (Rev: BL 8/93)

**8513** Charles, Veronika M. *The Crane Girl* (K–2). Illus. 1995, paper $6.95 (0-773-75718-X). 32pp. After she feels rejected by her parents, Yoshiko begs the cranes to transform her into one of them so she can fly away. (Rev: BL 5/1/93; SLJ 7/93)

**8514** Coady, Christopher. *Red Riding Hood* (1–3). Illus. 1995, Smithmark $4.98 (0-8317-6215-2). 32pp. A foreboding rendition of Perrault's original fairy tale. (Rev: BL 6/1/92; SLJ 6/92) [398.2]

**8515** Coatsworth, Elizabeth. *The Cat Who Went to Heaven* (4–6). Illus. by Lynd Ward. 1990, Simon & Schuster $16.00 (0-02-719710-7); Macmillan paper $3.95 (0-689-71433-5). 72pp. A charming legend of a Japanese artist, his cat, and a Buddhist miracle. Newbery Medal winner, 1931.

**8516** Cole, Brock. *The Giant's Toe* (K–2). Illus. by author. 1986, Farrar $15.00 (0-374-32559-6); paper $3.95 (0-374-42557-4). 32pp. A "revisionist" version of Jack and the Beanstalk, with a grandfatherly giant and a teeny boy. (Rev: BCCB 7–8/86; BL 8/86; SLJ 10/86)

**8517** Curry, Jane L. *Little Little Sister* (K–3). Illus. by Erik Blegvad. 1989, Macmillan $12.95 (0-689-50459-4). A Thumbelina-size girl saves the day when she brings her brother back home. (Rev: BCCB 11/89; BL 12/1/89; HB 11–12/89; SLJ 11/89)

**8518** Edens, Cooper, and Harold Darling. *Favorite Fairy Tales: A Classic Illustrated Edition* (1–4). Illus. 1991, Chronicle $17.95 (0-87701-848-0). 117pp. This collection of 14 favorite folktales includes *Cinderella, Jack and the Beanstalk,* and *Hansel and Gretel.* (Rev: SLJ 12/91) [398.2]

**8519** *Fairy Tales of Oscar Wilde* (5–8). Illus. by P. Craig Russell. 1992, Nantier $15.95 (1-56163-056-X). 46pp. Cartoon art enlivens the retelling of 2 of Wilde's short stories. (Rev: BL 1/15/93)

**8520** Falloon, Jane. *Thumbelina* (PS–3). Illus. by Emma C. Clark. 1997, Simon & Schuster $16.00 (0-689-81181-0). 48pp. A charming retelling of the Andersen fairy tale about a tiny girl who marries the King of the Flowers. (Rev: BL 4/15/97; SLJ 6/97)

**8521** Geras, Adele. *Beauty and the Beast and Other Stories* (4–7). Illus. by Louise Brierley. 1996, Viking paper $16.99 (0-670-86652-0). 32pp. Eight well-known fairy tales, including *Hansel and Gretel,* accompanied by haunting paintings. (Rev: BL 11/15/96; SLJ 2/97) [398.2]

**8522** Grahame, Kenneth. *The Reluctant Dragon* (2–4). Illus. by E. H. Shepard. 1938, Holiday $14.95 (0-8234-0093-X); paper $6.95 (0-8234-0755-1). 58pp. Tongue-in-cheek story of a boy who makes friends with a peace-loving dragon. Another fine edition is: Illus. by Michael Hague (1983, Holt).

**8523** Greaves, Margaret. *Sarah's Lion* (PS–3). 1995, Barron's paper $5.95 (0-812-09272-4). 32pp. A spirited princess rebels at always being staid and proper. (Rev: BL 12/1/92; SLJ 5/93)

**8524** Gregory, Philippa. *Florizella and the Wolves* (4–6). Illus. by Patrice Aggs. 1993, Candlewick $14.95 (1-56402-126-2). 80pp. A princess adopts 4 orphaned wolf cubs, and eventually one of them saves her life. (Rev: BL 5/1/93; SLJ 5/93)

**8525** Harness, Cheryl. *The Queen with Bees in Her Hair* (K–3). Illus. 1995, Smithmark $3.98 (0-8317-5243-2). 32pp. Vain Queen Ruby banishes all the honeybees and songbirds in her kingdom. (Rev: BL 3/1/93; SLJ 6/93)

**8526** Hautzig, Deborah. *Beauty and the Beast* (2–3). Illus. by Kathy Mitchell. 1995, Random LB $11.99 (0-679-95296-9); paper $3.99 (0-679-85296-4). 48pp. A simple version of this familiar fairy tale prepared for beginning readers. (Rev: BL 7/95) [398.2]

**8527** Hayes, Sarah. *The Candlewick Book of Fairy Tales* (K–4). Illus. by P. J. Lynch. 1993, Candlewick $16.95 (1-56402-260-9). 92pp. Ten famous fairy tales from Perrault and the Grimm Brothers, like *Cinderella* and *Rapunzel,* are retold in an abridged format with attractive illustrations. (Rev: SLJ 12/93) [398.2]

**8528** Helldorfer, M. C. *Cabbage Rose* (K–3). Illus. by Julie Downing. 1993, Macmillan $14.95 (0-02-743513-X). 32pp. Cabbage, a serving girl, is given a magic paintbrush that can bring to life everything it paints. (Rev: BL 2/1/93)

**8529** Helldorfer, M. C. *The Mapmaker's Daughter* (K–3). Illus. by Jonathan Hunt. 1991, Macmillan LB $15.95 (0-02-743515-6). 40pp. In this fairy tale with an Eastern setting, an attractive girl rescues a prince from an evil witch. (Rev: BCCB 4/91; BL 4/15/91; SLJ 7/91)

**8530** Impey, Rose. *Read Me a Fairy Tale: A Child's Book of Classic Fairy Tales* (3–6). Illus. by Ian Beck. 1993, Scholastic $16.95 (0-590-49431-7). 128pp. A collection of 14 favorite fairy tales told in an informal style. (Rev: BL 1/15/94; SLJ 2/94)

**8531** Isadora, Rachel, reteller. *The Steadfast Tin Soldier* (PS–2). Illus. by Rachel Isadora. 1996, Putnam $15.95 (0-399-22676-1). 32pp. After a series of adventures, a one-legged tin soldier returns home to his beloved ballerina in this story based on the Hans Christian Andersen's original. (Rev: BCCB 1/97; BL 4/15/96*; SLJ 4/96) [398.2]

**8532** Jackson, Ellen. *Cinder Edna* (PS–3). Illus. by Kevin O'Malley. 1994, Lothrop $16.00 (0-688-12322-8). 32pp. Whereas Cinderella is a passive wimp, Cinder Edna is a spirited girl who mows lawns to make money so she can attend the ball. In this book, the 2 stories are told side by side. (Rev: BL 3/15/94; SLJ 4/94)

**8533** Johnston, Tony. *The Cowboy and the Black-Eyed Pea* (PS–3). Illus. by Warren Ludwig. 1992, Putnam $15.95 (0-399-22330-4). 32pp. Farethee Well decides to try a reversal of the "princess and the pea" story to find a suitably sensitive husband. (Rev: BL 11/15/92; SLJ 12/92)

**8534** Jones, Terry. *Fantastic Stories* (K–3). Illus. by Michael Foreman. 1993, Viking paper $16.99 (0-670-84899-9). 128pp. Twenty-one original fairy tales written with humor and zest by a former member of the Monty Python group. (Rev: BCCB 5/93; BL 8/93)

**8535** Kaye, M. M. *The Ordinary Princess* (3–5). Illus. by author. 1998, Dell paper $3.50 (0-440-40880-6). As the seventh daughter of the king and queen, Amy should be the prettiest, but a fairy god-mother decides that she will be ordinary; unhappiness follows until Amy finds someone who likes her just that way.

**8536** Kroll, Steven. *Queen of the May* (PS–3). Illus. by Patience Brewster. 1993, Holiday LB $15.95 (0-8234-1004-8). 32pp. Sylvie becomes Queen of the May in spite of her meddling stepmother and step-sister. (Rev: BL 4/1/93; SLJ 7/93)

**8537** Lang, Andrew, ed. *Blue Fairy Book* (4–6). 1965, Dover paper $7.95 (0-486-21437-0). 390pp. A fine edition of this classic collection. There are 11 other "color" Fairy Books. Some are: *Green Fairy Book* (1965); *Yellow Fairy Book* (1966); *Grey Fairy Book; Orange Fairy Book; Red Fairy Book* (all 1968).

**8538** Lang, Andrew, ed. *The Rainbow Fairy Book* (4–6). Illus. by Michael Hague. 1993, Morrow $20.00 (0-688-10878-4). 288pp. A selection of 31 folktales and fairy tales taken from various volumes of Lang's colored fairy books, illustrated by the award-winning artist. (Rev: BL 11/1/93; SLJ 10/93) [398.21]

**8539** Langton, Jane. *The Queen's Necklace: A Swedish Folktale* (3–5). Illus. by Ilse Plume. 1994, Hyperion LB $16.49 (0-7868-2007-1). 40pp. When a queen gives away pearls to help the poor, her cruel king demands her life. (Rev: BL 10/1/94; SLJ 10/94)

**8540** Lattimore, Deborah N. *The Dragon's Robe* (K–3). Illus. 1990, HarperCollins $15.00 (0-06-023719-8). 32pp. A story about an orphan and a poor weaver set in 13th-century China. (Rev: BCCB 6/90; BL 4/1/90; SLJ 5/90)

**8541** Levine, Gail C. *Ella Enchanted* (5–8). 1997, HarperCollins LB $14.89 (0-06-027511-1). 240pp. A spirited retelling of the Cinderella story in which Ella is finally paired with the Prince Charmant. (Rev: BCCB 5/97; BL 4/15/97*; HB 5/6/97; SLJ 4/97*)

**8542** Levinson, Riki, reteller. *The Emperor's New Clothes* (K–3). Illus. by Robert Byrd. 1991, Dutton paper $14.95 (0-525-44611-7). 40pp. In this retelling of the Andersen tale, the main characters are depicted as animals. (Rev: BL 12/15/91; SLJ 11/91)

**8543** Levitin, Sonia. *The Man Who Kept His Heart in a Bucket* (K–3). Illus. by Jerry Pinkney. 1995, Puffin paper $5.99 (0-14-055461-0). 32pp. A tin man

must solve a riddle in order to regain his heart, which has been stolen by an enchanted maiden. (Rev: BCCB 1/92; HB 9–10/91; SLJ 9/91)

**8544** Little, Jean, and Maggie De Vries. *Once upon a Golden Apple* (PS–2). Illus. by Phoebe Gilman. 1991, Viking paper $12.95 (0-670-82963-3). 32pp. Father reads a fairy tale that is a combination of many of the standard ones but thoroughly mixed up. (Rev: BL 7/91; SLJ 8/91)

**8545** Lobel, Anita. *The Dwarf Giant* (1–3). Illus. 1996, Greenwillow $16.00 (0-688-14407-1); Morrow paper $4.95 (0-688-14408-X). 32pp. The life of a bored prince becomes more interesting when a dwarf arrives. (Rev: BCCB 4/91; BL 4/1/91)

**8546** McDermott, Gerald. *Tim O'Toole and the Wee Folk* (PS–5). Illus. 1992, Puffin paper $4.99 (0-14-050675-6). 32pp. When given by the wee folk a magic goose that lays golden eggs, Tim loses his prize to the wily McGoons. (Rev: BL 3/1/90; HB 7–8/90; SLJ 2/90*)

**8547** MacDonald, George. *The Golden Key* (2–6). Illus. by Maurice Sendak. 1993, Farrar $15.00 (0-374-32706-8); paper $4.95 (0-374-42590-6). 96pp. In this classic fairy tale, 2 young people search for a keyhole where their golden key will fit.

**8548** MacDonald, George. *The Light Princess* (3–6). Illus. by Maurice Sendak. 1984, Farrar paper $4.95 (0-374-44458-7). 120pp. The story of the princess without gravity and the prince who saves her.

**8549** MacDonald, George. *The Light Princess* (1–6). Adapted by Robin McKinley. Illus. by Katie T. Treherne. 1988, Harcourt $13.95 (0-15-245300-8). 44pp. A prince breaks the spell of a princess who has been deprived of gravity. (Rev: BL 7/88)

**8550** MacDonald, George. *The Princess and the Goblin* (4–7). Illus. by Jessie Willcox Smith. 1986, Morrow $22.00 (0-688-06604-6). 208pp. Full-color edition of the 1920 classic about the princess who is protected by the goblins beneath the castle. (Rev: BL 10/15/86)

**8551** MacDonald, Margaret Read. *The Old Woman Who Lived in a Vinegar Bottle: A British Fairy Tale* (PS–2). Illus. by Nancy D. Fowlkes. 1995, August House $15.95 (0-87483-415-5). 32pp. In this English folktale, a fairy discovers that there is no pleasing some people when she supplies better housing for an old woman who had been living in a vinegar bottle. (Rev: BL 10/1/95; SLJ 1/96) [398.2]

**8552** McKinley, Robin. *The Door in the Hedge* (6–8). 1981, Greenwillow $15.00 (0-688-00312-5). 224pp. A sensitive retelling of 4 fairy tales.

**8553** Mahy, Margaret. *The Chewing-Gum Rescue* (3–4). Illus. by Jan Ormerod. 1992, Overlook $12.95 (0-87951-424-8). 141pp. A collection of 11 short stories, most of which are fairy tales or contain elements of fantasy. (Rev: SLJ 2/92)

**8554** Melmed, Laura K. *The Rainbabies* (PS–2). Illus. by Jim LaMarche. 1992, Lothrop LB $15.93 (0-688-10756-7). 32pp. An elderly couple care for 12 teeny babies they find in the grass. (Rev: BL 11/1/92; HB 3–4/93; SLJ 12/92)

**8555** Mills, Lauren. *The Book of Little Folk: Faery Stories and Poems from Around the World* (3–6). Illus. 1997, Dial paper $23.99 (0-8037-1458-0). 144pp. A collection of 13 fairy tales from around the world, interspersed with connecting poems. (Rev: BL 8/97; SLJ 11/97)

**8556** Minters, Frances. *Cinder-Elly* (K–3). Illus. by G. Brian Karas. 1994, Viking paper $14.99 (0-670-84417-9). 32pp. A present-day version of Cinderella, with the heroine living in New York City and her godmother changing a garbage can into a bicycle so that Elly can go to an important basketball game. (Rev: BCCB 4/94; BL 1/15/94; SLJ 6/94) [398.2]

**8557** Mitchell, Adrian, reteller. *The Steadfast Tin Soldier* (PS–3). Illus. by Jonathan Heale. 1996, DK Publg. $14.95 (1-56458-310-4). 30pp. The retelling of the favorite fairy tale, with woodcut and watercolor illustrations. (Rev: BL 11/1/96)

**8558** Mitchell, Adrian. *The Ugly Duckling: Hans Christian Andersen* (1–3). Retold by Adrian Mitchell. Illus. by Jonathan Heale. 1994, DK Publg. $14.95 (1-56458-557-3). 32pp. A retelling of the Andersen fairy tale that retains the quality of the original. (Rev: BL 7/94; SLJ 7/94)

**8559** Nesbit, Edith. *Melisande* (K–3). Illus. by P. J. Lynch. 1989, Harcourt $13.95 (0-15-253164-5). 48pp. The fairies take their revenge when a royal family excludes them from the daughter's christening party. (Rev: BL 10/1/89*; HB 11–12/89; SLJ 1/90)

**8560** Nones, Eric Jon. *The Canary Prince* (1–3). Illus. 1991, Farrar $14.95 (0-374-31029-7). 32pp. A princess is locked in a tower by her wicked stepmother in this little-known tale from Italy. (Rev: BL 8/91)

**8561** Opie, Iona, and Peter Opie, eds. *The Classic Fairy Tales* (4–8). Illus. 1992, Oxford $35.00 (0-19-211559-6); paper $14.95 (0-19-520219-8). 256pp. Contains the earliest published text of these tales.

**8562** Perlman, Janet. *Cinderella Penguin: Or, The Little Glass Flipper* (PS–2). Illus. 1993, Viking paper $14.99 (0-670-84753-4). 32pp. A humorous retelling of the Cinderella story in which the central characters are all penguins. (Rev: BL 5/15/93; SLJ 8/93)

**8563** Perlman, Janet, reteller. *The Emperor Penguin's New Clothes* (K–3). Illus. by Janet Perlman. 1995, Viking paper $14.99 (0-670-85864-1). A humorous variation on the Andersen story about the

pompous getting their comeuppance. (Rev: SLJ 8/95)

**8564** Philip, Neil, ed. *Christmas Fairy Tales* (4–6). 1996, Viking paper $19.99 (0-670-86805-1). 144pp. Twelve stories about Christmas and the spirit that it represents. (Rev: BL 9/1/96; SLJ 10/96*)

**8565** Philip, Neil, ed. *The Fairy Tales of Oscar Wilde* (4–6). Illus. by Isabelle Brent. 1994, Viking paper $19.99 (0-670-85585-5). 144pp. A splendid edition of these fairy tales with 2 or 3 illustrations per story. (Rev: BL 12/1/94; SLJ 3/95)

**8566** Philip, Neil. *Fairy Tales of the Brothers Grimm* (4–6). Illus. by Isabelle Brent. 1997, Viking paper $19.99 (0-670-87290-3). 144pp. A masterful retelling of several classic Grimm fairy tales, with the inclusion of some of their short comic stories. (Rev: BL 10/15/97; SLJ 2/98) [398.2]

**8567** Prokofiev, Sergei. *Peter and the Wolf* (1–4). Illus. by Barbara Cooney. 1986, Viking paper $18.99 (0-670-80849-0). 10pp. A 3-dimensional celebration of the famous tale. (Rev: BL 6/1/86; SLJ 5/86)

**8568** Pyle, Howard. *The Swan Maiden* (K–3). Illus. by Robert Sauber. 1994, Holiday LB $15.95 (0-8234-1088-9). 28pp. In this fairy tale, one of the king's sons discovers that a swan maiden is stealing pears from his father's pear tree. (Rev: BL 10/15/94; SLJ 1/95)

**8569** Pyle, Howard. *The Wonder Clock: Or Four and Twenty Marvelous Tales* (4–6). Illus. by author. 1915, Dover paper $8.95 (0-486-21446-X). 319pp. Tales for each hour in the day, told by figures on a clock.

**8570** Rackham, Arthur, ed. *The Arthur Rackham Fairy Book* (2–5). Illus. by Arthur Rackham. 1991, Outlet $3.99 (0-517-24213-3). 271pp. Twenty-three favorite fairy and folk tales.

**8571** Riggio, Anita. *Beware the Brindlebeast* (K–2). Illus. 1994, Boyds Mills $16.95 (1-56397-133-X). 32pp. A courageous old lady finds a cast-iron kettle that changes into the fierce Brindlebeast in this English fairy tale. (Rev: BL 9/15/94; SLJ 10/94) [398.2]

**8572** Sand, George. *The Castle of Pictures and Other Stories: A Grandmother's Tale*, vol. 1 (4–6). Trans. by Holly Erskine Hirko. Illus. 1995, Feminist Pr. $19.95 (1-55861-091-X); paper $9.95 (1-55861-092-8). 176pp. Four fairy tales written in the 19th century by this distinguished French novelist for her grandchildren. (Rev: BL 5/15/95; SLJ 5/95)

**8573** Sanderson, Ruth. *Papa Gatto: An Italian Fairy Tale* (4–6). Illus. 1995, Little, Brown $15.95 (0-316-77073-6). 32pp. A male cat advertises for a nanny to take care of his brood with mixed results. (Rev: BCCB 12/95; BL 12/1/95*; SLJ 10/95) [398.2]

**8574** Sanderson, Ruth. *Rose Red and Snow White: A Grimms Fairy Tale* (1–3). Illus. 1997, Little, Brown

$15.95 (0-316-77094-9). 32pp. A handsome edition of the Grimm Brothers' tale about 2 loving sisters, their enchanted forest, and the dwarf that brings evil into their lives. (Rev: BL 4/15/97; SLJ 5/97)

**8575** San Jose, Christine, reteller. *Cinderella* (3–4). Illus. by Debrah Santini. 1994, Boyds Mills $15.95 (1-56397-152-6). This well-written, imaginative version of Cinderella is set in Manhattan during the Gay Nineties. (Rev: SLJ 9/94)

**8576** San Jose, Christine. *The Little Match Girl* (K–3). Illus. by Anastassija Archipowa. 1995, Boyds Mills $14.95 (1-56397-470-3). 32pp. A retelling of Andersen's fairy tale about the poor match girl who sees visions in the flames of her matches but dies alone in the snow. (Rev: BL 9/15/95; SLJ 11/95) [398.2]

**8577** San Jose, Christine. *Sleeping Beauty* (K–3). Illus. by Dominic Catalano. 1997, Boyds Mills $14.95 (1-56397-636-6). 32pp. Dormouse characters are used in this successful retelling of the traditional fairy tale. (Rev: BL 10/15/97; SLJ 9/97) [398]

**8578** San Souci, Robert D. *Nicholas Pipe* (K–4). Illus. by David Shannon. 1997, Dial paper $14.99 (0-8037-1764-4). 32pp. A fisherman's daughter loves a merman who must touch the sea every day or he will die. (Rev: BCCB 7–8/97; BL 6/1–15/97; SLJ 5/97*)

**8579** San Souci, Robert D., reteller. *The White Cat: An Old French Fairy Tale* (3–4). Illus. by Gennady Spirin. 1990, Orchard LB $17.99 (0-531-08409-4). 32pp. The retelling of the story of 3 princes who vie for their father's kingdom. (Rev: BCCB 11/90; BL 9/1/90; HB 11–12/90; SLJ 10/90)

**8580** Schami, Rafik. *Fatima and the Dream Thief* (1–4). Trans. by Anthea Bell. Illus. by Els Cools and Oliver Streich. 1996, North-South LB $15.88 (1-55858-654-7). 32pp. Fatima outwits a giant who enslaves people by collecting their dreams in this original fairy tale. (Rev: BCCB 2/97; BL 12/15/96; SLJ 1/97)

**8581** Schroeder, Alan. *Smoky Mountain Rose: An Appalachian Cinderella* (3–6). Illus. by Brad Sneed. 1997, Dial paper $14.89 (0-8037-1734-2). 32pp. In this Appalachian version of Cinderella, young Rose is at the mercy of her father's mean second wife and 2 stepsisters. (Rev: BCCB 7–8/97; BL 5/15/97; SLJ 6/97) [398.2]

**8582** Scieszka, Jon. *The Frog Prince Continued* (1–4). Illus. by Steve Johnson. 1991, Viking paper $14.95 (0-670-83421-1). 32pp. After the princess and the former frog are married, he still keeps hopping about and wonders if he should change back into a frog. (Rev: BCCB 5/91; BL 6/1/91; HB 7–8/91; SLJ 5/91)

**8583** Singer, Marilyn. *In the Palace of the Ocean King* (K–3). Illus. by Ted Rand. 1995, Simon & Schuster $15.00 (0-689-31755-7). 32pp. Roles are reviewed in this modern fairy tale about a gallant girl who dives to the Ocean King's realm to rescue her true love, a prince. (Rev: BL 7/95; SLJ 8/95)

**8584** Stanley, Diane. *Rumpelstiltskin's Daughter* (K–4). Illus. 1997, Morrow LB $14.93 (0-688-14328-8). 32pp. Like her mother, Rumpelstiltskin's daughter must spin straw into gold, but her solutions to this problem are unique. (Rev: BCCB 7–8/97; BL 3/1/97I; SLJ 3/97*)

**8585** Stewig, John W. *Princess Florecita and the Iron Shoes: A Spanish Fairy Tale* (4–7). Illus. by K. Wendy Popp. 1995, Knopf $16.95 (0-679-84775-8). 32pp. In this Spanish fairy tale, princess Florecita saves the life of a sleeping prince. (Rev: BL 10/1/95; SLJ 1/96) [398.2]

**8586** Thurber, James. *Many Moons* (2–4). Illus. by Marc Simont. 1990, Harcourt $14.95 (0-15-251872-X). 48pp. A sick princess asks her father for the moon to help her get better. The original edition, illustrated by Louis Slobodkin, was the 1944 Caldecott Medal winner. (Rev: BL 9/15/90; HB 1–2/90*; SLJ 1/91)

**8587** Thurber, James. *The White Deer* (6–7). Illus. by author. 1968, Harcourt paper $7.00 (0-15-696264-0). 115pp. Three princes, a princess, and magic occurrences in this modern fairy tale.

**8588** Treherne, Katie T., reteller. *The Little Mermaid* (1–5). Illus. by Katie T. Treherne. 1989, Harcourt $15.95 (0-15-246320-8). 48pp. A retelling of Andersen's familiar story of the mermaid who falls in love with a prince. (Rev: BL 1/1/90; SLJ 11/89)

**8589** *Twelve Tales: Hans Christian Andersen* (4–6). Illus. by Erik Blegvad. 1994, Macmillan paper $19.95 (0-689-50584-1). 96pp. A newly translated and illustrated collection of a dozen of Andersen's tales, some familiar, others not. (Rev: BL 10/1/94; HB 11–12/94; SLJ 10/94)

**8590** Wallis, Diz, reteller. *Something Nasty in the Cabbages* (2–6). Illus. by Diz Wallis. 1991, Boyds Mills $15.95 (1-878093-10-X). 32pp. This adaptation of the Chanticleer and the Fox story contains many new variations and stunning illustrations. (Rev: BCCB 2/92; SLJ 12/91)

**8591** Walsh, Ellen S. *Jack's Tale* (PS–2). Illus. 1997, Harcourt $15.00 (0-15-200323-1). 32pp. While an author ponders what he will write about, a fairy tale about a frog who escapes from trolls gradually takes shape. (Rev: BL 12/1/97; SLJ 11/97)

**8592** Wegman, William. *Cinderella* (PS–2). Illus. 1993, Hyperion $16.95 (1-56282-348-5). 38pp. The characters in this reworking of the Cinderella story are all dogs, but the story remains the same. (Rev: BCCB 7–8/93; BL 5/15/93; SLJ 4/93)

**8593** Wenzel, David, and Doug Wheeler. *Fairy Tales of the Brothers Grimm* (4–6). Illus. 1995, NBM $15.95 (1-56163-130-2). 48pp. Using a comic book format, some of the best-known tales of the Grimm Brothers are retold, with an emphasis on story-telling pictures. (Rev: BL 4/15/96) [398.2]

**8594** Wilde, Oscar. *Happy Prince* (3–5). Illus. by Ed Young. 1992, Simon & Schuster paper $5.95 (0-671-77819-6). 32pp. The lovely story of the prince-statue and the swallow who gives his life for the Happy Prince. (Rev: BL 6/15/89)

**8595** Wilde, Oscar. *The Happy Prince* (K–2). Illus. by Jane Ray. 1995, Dutton paper $15.99 (0-525-45367-9). 32pp. A presentation of this classic fairy tale in a picture book format. (Rev: BL 12/15/94; SLJ 3/95)

**8596** Wisniewski, David. *The Warrior and the Wise Man* (3–5). Illus. by author. 1989, Lothrop LB $15.93 (0-688-07890-7). 32pp. Twin sons of the emperor of Japan search for 5 magical elements of the world. (Rev: BL 5/1/89; HB 7–8/89; SLJ 4/89)

**8597** Wood, Audrey. *Heckedy Peg* (PS–2). Illus. by Don Wood. 1987, Harcourt $16.00 (0-15-233678-8); paper $6.00 (0-15-233679-6). 32pp. Mother promises gifts to her 7 children, all named for days of the week, taken from a 16th-century game still played in England. (Rev: BCCB 12/87; BL 9/15/87; SLJ 11/87)

**8598** Yep, Laurence. *The Ghost Fox* (3–5). Illus. by Jean Tseng and Mou-Sien Tseng. 1994, Scholastic $13.95 (0-590-47204-6). 70pp. In this Chinese fairy tale, Little Lee must save his mother from a dangerous ghost fox that is stealing her soul. (Rev: BCCB 3/94; BL 11/15/93; SLJ 5/94)

**8599** Ziefert, Harriet, reteller. *The Princess and the Pea* (K–1). Illus. by Emily Bolam. Series: Easy-to-Read Books. 1996, Viking paper $11.99 (0-670-86054-9). An easy-to-read version of the classic fairy tale by Andersen about a supersensitive princess. (Rev: SLJ 8/96)

# Folklore

**8600** Adler, Naomi. *The Dial Book of Animal Tales from Around the World* (2–4). Illus. 1996, Dial paper $19.99 (0-8037-2063-7). 80pp. Animal tales, such as "The Musicians of Bremen," are retold with attractive illustrations. (Rev: BCCB 11/96; BL 10/1/96; SLJ 10/96) [398.2]

**8601** Brusca, Maria C., and Tona Wilson. *When Jaguars Ate the Moon* (2–4). Illus. by Maria C. Brusca. 1995, Holt $16.95 (0-8050-2797-1). 44pp. A collection of folktales from North and South American Indian cultures. (Rev: BCCB 4/95; BL 4/1/95; SLJ 6/95) [398.2]

**8602** Carle, Eric. *Eric Carle's Treasury of Classic Stories for Children by Aesop, Hans Christian Andersen, and the Brothers Grimm* (2–4). Illus. by author. 1988, Orchard $24.95 (0-531-05742-9). 160pp. Familiar stories with Carle's distinctive mark. (Rev: BCCB 6/88; BL 3/1/88; SLJ 4/88) [398.2]

**8603** Chorao, Kay. *The Baby's Story Book* (PS). Illus. by author. 1985, Dutton $15.99 (0-525-44200-6); Puffin paper $5.99 (0-14-055738-5). 64pp. "Goldilocks" and "Little Red Riding Hood" are among the familiar tales in this full-color illustrated presentation. (Rev: BCCB 12/85; BL 9/15/85; SLJ 11/85) [398.2]

**8604** Climo, Shirley. *King of the Birds* (PS–3). Illus. by Ruth Heller. 1991, HarperCollins paper $4.95 (0-06-443273-4). 32pp. The long-ago legend of how the birds chose a king. (Rev: BL 2/15/88; SLJ 8/88) [398.2]

**8605** Climo, Shirley. *A Treasury of Mermaids: Mermaid Tales from Around the World* (4–8). Illus. by Jean Tseng and Mou-Sien Tseng. 1997, HarperCollins LB $16.95 (0-06-023876-3). 80pp. A fine retelling of 8 folktales from around the world about mermaids and other enchanted sea creatures. (Rev: BL 11/15/97; SLJ 10/97) [398.2]

**8606** Climo, Shirley, col. and reteller. *A Treasury of Princesses: Princess Tales from Around the World* (2–5). Illus. by Ruth Sanderson. 1996, HarperCollins LB $16.89 (0-06-024533-6). 76pp. Seven folktales about princesses from such sources as the Arabian Nights, the Brothers Grimm, and the folklore of China, Russia, Guatemala, and Greece. (Rev: SLJ 10/96) [398.2]

**8607** Cook, Joel. *The Rats' Daughter* (K–3). Illus. 1992, Boyds Mills $14.95 (1-56397-140-2). 32pp. The lovely daughter of a prominent rat family is torn between her parents' wishes and her love for a handsome rat boy. (Rev: BL 1/15/93; SLJ 5/93) [398.2]

**8608** dePaola, Tomie, ed. *Tomie dePaola's Favorite Nursery Tales* (PS–3). Illus. by Tomie dePaola. 1986, Putnam $24.95 (0-399-21319-8). 128pp. The artist's favorite childhood remembrances in an attractive package. (Rev: BCCB 2/87; BL 11/1/86; SLJ 1/87) [398.2]

**8609** DeSpain, Pleasant, reteller. *Thirty-Three Multicultural Tales to Tell* (3–7). Illus. by Joe Shlichta. Series: American Folklore and Storytelling. 1993, August House paper $15.00 (0-87483-266-7). 126pp. An interesting international collection of folktales that span a number of subjects and moods. (Rev: SLJ 6/94) [398.2]

**8610** Forest, Heather. *Wisdom Tales from Around the World* (4–7). 1996, August House $27.95 (0-87483-478-3); paper $17.95 (0-87483-479-1). 160pp. Fifty fables, folktales, and myths from around the world. (Rev: BCCB 2/97; BL 3/1/97) [398.2]

**8611** Forest, Heather. *Wonder Tales from Around the World* (4–6). Illus. 1995, August House $26.95 (0-87483-421-X); paper $16.95 (0-87483-422-8). 160pp.

A collection of 27 traditional stories, some familiar and others never anthologized before. (Rev: BL 11/15/95; SLJ 4/96) [398.2]

**8612** Garner, Alan. *Once upon a Time: Though It Wasn't in Your Time, and It Wasn't in My Time, and It Wasn't in Anybody Else's Time . . .* (K–3). Illus. by Norman Messenger. 1993, DK Publg. $12.95 (1-56458-381-3). 32pp. Three traditional tales told with simplicity, with evocative watercolors. (Rev: BCCB 1/94; BL 12/1/93; SLJ 3/94) [398.21]

**8613** Goode, Diane. *Diane Goode's Book of Giants and Little People* (K–4). Illus. 1997, Dutton paper $17.99 (0-525-45660-0). 64pp. A collection of tales and poetry, each with the theme of how the small and vulnerable triumph over the big and powerful. (Rev: BL 9/15/97; SLJ 11/97) [398.2]

**8614** Hadley, Eric, and Tessa Hadley. *Legends of the Sun and Moon* (2–6). Illus. by Jan Nesbitt. 1989, Cambridge Univ. Pr. $16.95 (0-521-25227-X); paper $9.95 (0-521-37912-1). 32pp. A collection of folktales on the moon and sun from all over the world. [398.2]

**8615** Hamilton, Virginia. *A Ring of Tricksters: Animal Tales from North America, the West Indies, and Africa* (3–6). Illus. by Barry Moser. 1997, Scholastic $19.95 (0-590-47374-3). 112pp. This is a stunning collection of trickster tales, many from Africa and others that were adapted by slaves to reflect conditions in the West Indies and the United States. (Rev: BL 1/1–15/98; SLJ 11/97) [398.2]

**8616** Hodges, Margaret, ed. *Hauntings: Ghosts and Ghouls from Around the World* (5–8). Illus. by David Wenzel. 1991, Little, Brown $16.95 (0-316-36796-6). 144pp. Sixteen meaty retellings of stories of the supernatural. (Rev: BL 11/15/91; HB 11–12/91; SLJ 11/91) [398.2]

**8617** Hutchinson, Duane. *The Gunny Wolf and Other Fairy Tales* (4–6). Illus. 1993, Foundation paper $6.95 (0-934988-29-3). 88pp. A total of 7 folktales, including Tom Thumb and The Six Swans, are included in this collection. (Rev: BL 5/15/93) [398.2]

**8618** Knapp, Toni. *Ordinary Splendors: Tales of Virtues and Wisdoms* (4–6). Illus. 1995, Roberts Rinehart $15.95 (1-57098-003-9). 48pp. Seventeen folktales from around the world are presented with the moral lesson each teaches. (Rev: BL 7/95; SLJ 8/95) [398.2]

**8619** Kneen, Maggie. *"Too Many Cooks . . ." and Other Proverbs* (PS–3). Illus. by author. 1992, Simon & Schuster $13.00 (0-671-78120-0). 32pp. Twenty-five proverbs, most of them familiar to older readers, are attractively presented. (Rev: BL 9/15/92; SLJ 10/92) [398.2]

**8620** Krishnaswami, Uma. *Stories of the Flood* (4–6). Illus. 1994, Roberts Rinehart $15.95 (1-57098-007-1). 41pp. In a picture book format, 9 flood myths from such places as ancient Sumeria and Hawaii are retold. (Rev: BL 2/1/95; SLJ 2/95) [291.13]

**8621** Lansky, Bruce, sel. *Girls to the Rescue: Tales of Clever, Courageous Girls from Around the World* (3–6). 1995, Meadowbrook Pr. paper $3.95 (0-88166-215-1). 100pp. A collection of stories about resourceful young women, many of which originated in the world's folklore. (Rev: SLJ 12/95) [398.2]

**8622** Lansky, Bruce, ed. *Girls to the Rescue Book 2: Tales of Clever, Courageous Girls from Around the World* (3–6). 1996, Meadowbrook Pr. LB $3.95 (0-671-57375-6). 103pp. In each of the folktales gathered from around the world, young women must rely on their ingenuity to overcome obstacles. (Rev: SLJ 2/97) [398.2]

**8623** Lottridge, Celia B. *Ten Small Tales* (PS–K). Illus. by Joanne Fitzgerald. 1994, Macmillan paper $15.95 (0-689-50568-X). 64pp. These simple folktales move quickly, have simple dialogue, and use rhyme and repetition effectively. (Rev: BCCB 5/94; BL 3/15/94; HB 1–2/94; SLJ 6/94) [398.2]

**8624** McCaughrean, Geraldine. *The Silver Treasure: Myths and Legends of the World* (5–8). Illus. by Bee Willey. 1997, Simon & Schuster paper $19.95 (0-689-81322-8). 144pp. A collection of 23 myths and legends, some well known, like *Rip Van Winkle*, and others unfamiliar, like a Bolivian legend on how the natives outsmarted their Spanish conquerors. (Rev: BCCB 6/97; BL 4/15/97; SLJ 4/97*) [398.2]

**8625** MacDonald, Margaret Read. *Peace Tales: World Folktales to Talk About* (5–7). Illus. 1992, Shoe String LB $25.00 (0-208-02328-3); paper $15.95 (0-208-02329-1). 114pp. Stories and proverbs directed toward achieving world peace. (Rev: BL 6/15/92; SLJ 10/92) [398.2]

**8626** Martin, Rafe. *Mysterious Tales of Japan* (4–7). Illus. by Tatsuro Kiuchi. 1996, Putnam $18.95 (0-399-22677-X). 80pp. Ten haunting folktales about the spiritual powers in nature, such as the story of a priest who lived 3 days as a carp. (Rev: BL 3/15/96; HB 9–10/96; SLJ 4/96*) [398.2]

**8627** Matthews, Andrew. *Marduk the Mighty and Other Stories of Creation* (4–6). Illus. by Sheila Moxley. 1997, Millbrook LB $22.40 (0-7613-0204-2). 96pp. A collection of 24 creation stories, beginning with Genesis and ending with a Norse myth about the fall of the gods. (Rev: BCCB 6/97; BL 6/1–15/97; SLJ 7/97) [291.1]

**8628** Mayo, Margaret, reteller. *Magical Tales from Many Lands* (3–6). Illus. by Jane Ray. 1993, Dutton paper $19.99 (0-525-45017-3). 128pp. A collection of 14 traditional tales, each from a different culture. (Rev: BL 11/1/93; SLJ 9/93) [398.2]

**8629** Mayo, Margaret. *Mythical Birds and Beasts from Many Lands* (4–6). Illus. by Jane Ray. 1997, Dutton paper $19.99 (0-525-45788-7). 112pp. From the world's mythology and folklore, this is a collection of stories about such beasts as the minotaur. (Rev: BCCB 7–8/97; BL 5/1/97*; SLJ 6/97) [398.2]

**8630** Mayo, Margaret. *Tortoise's Flying Lesson* (2–4). Illus. by Emily Bolam. 1995, Harcourt $17.00 (0-15-200332-0). 72pp. A collection of short international folktales, each dealing with an animal. (Rev: BCCB 6/95; BL 5/1/95; SLJ 5/95) [398.2]

**8631** Mayo, Margaret. *When the World Was Young: Creation and Pourquoi Tales* (4–7). Illus. by Louise Brierley. 1996, Simon & Schuster paper $19.95 (0-689-80867-4). 75pp. Age-old questions are answered in this collection of folktales that give explanations for natural phenomena. (Rev: BCCB 2/97; BL 9/1/96; SLJ 12/96) [398.2]

**8632** Milord, Susan. *Tales Alive! Ten Multicultural Folktales with Activities* (4–6). Illus. 1995, Williamson paper $15.95 (0-913589-79-9). 128pp. This book contains 19 folktales plus such related material as riddles, puzzles, and craft projects. (Rev: BL 4/15/95; SLJ 3/95) [398.2]

**8633** Milord, Susan, reteller. *Tales of the Shimmering Sky: Ten Global Folktales with Activities* (3–6). Illus. by JoAnn E. Kitchel. Series: A Williamson Tales Alive! Book. 1996, Williamson paper $15.95 (1-885593-01-5). 128pp. Ten folktales from different cultures explore such topics as the sky, wind, seasons, colors, and the weather, with additional background material and many suggested projects. (Rev: SLJ 2/97) [398.2]

**8634** Minard, Rosemary, ed. *Womenfolk and Fairy Tales* (4–6). Illus. by Suzanna Klein. 1975, Houghton $18.00 (0-395-20276-0). 176pp. In each of these 18 stories, the female characters triumph because of wit, spunk, and courage. [398.2]

**8635** Osborne, Mary Pope, ed. *Mermaid Tales from Around the World* (3–6). Illus. by Troy Howell. 1993, Scholastic $16.95 (0-590-44377-1). 96pp. Twelve stories about mermaids collected from the world's folklore. (Rev: BCCB 2/94; BL 10/15/93; SLJ 11/93) [398.21]

**8636** Passes, David. *Dragons: Truth, Myth, and Legend* (4–6). Illus. by Wayne Anderson. 1993, Western Artists & Writers $12.95 (0-307-17500-6). 42pp. Classic tales involving dragons and heroes like Beowulf and St. George are well retold and elegantly illustrated. (Rev: BL 12/15/93; SLJ 12/93) [398.2]

**8637** Pearson, Maggie. *The Fox and the Rooster and Other Tales* (K–3). Illus. by Joanne Moss. 1997, Little Tiger $14.95 (1-888444-17-7). 77pp. Fourteen countries — e.g., Norway, Japan, and Ireland — are represented in this collection of folktales. (Rev: BL 2/15/98) [398.2]

**8638** Peters, Andrew F. *Strange and Spooky Stories* (3–6). Illus. 1997, Millbrook LB $23.90 (0-7613-0321-9). 80pp. Nine unusual but appealing tales from North America, the British Isles, Central Europe, and the Czech Republic. (Rev: BL 2/1/98) [398.2]

**8639** Phelps, Ethel Johnston. *The Maid of the North: Feminist Folk Tales from Around the World* (2–6). 1981, Holt paper $9.95 (0-8050-0679-6). 196pp. A collection of folktales from around the world. [398.2]

**8640** Phelps, Ethel Johnston. *Tatterhood and Other Tales* (3–6). Illus. by Pamela Baldwin-Ford. 1978, Feminist Pr. paper $9.95 (0-912670-50-9). 192pp. Tales in which women play a vital and decisive role. [398.2]

**8641** Pilling, Ann. *Creation: Read-Aloud Stories from Many Lands* (3–5). Illus. 1997, Candlewick $19.99 (1-56402-888-7). 96pp. A retelling of 16 creation stories that come from such sources as the Bible, Greek mythology, and Chinese and Norse folklore. (Rev: BL 9/1/97; SLJ 10/97) [291.2]

**8642** Polacco, Patricia. *Babushka's Mother Goose* (PS–1). Illus. 1995, Putnam $17.95 (0-399-22747-4). 64pp. A retelling of the stories and legends told by a babushka (grandmother) to her granddaughter. (Rev: BL 10/15/95; SLJ 10/95) [398.8]

**8643** Rosen, Michael J. *How the Animals Got Their Colors* (5–8). Illus. by John Clemenston. 1992, Harcourt $14.95 (0-15-236783-7). 48pp. Tales from around the world that explain such things as a leopard's spots and the green on a frog's back. (Rev: BCCB 7–8/92; BL 6/15/92; SLJ 9/91) [398.2]

**8644** Rosen, Michael J., ed. *South and North, East and West: The Oxfam Book of Children's Stories* (K–8). Illus. 1992, Candlewick $19.95 (1-56402-117-3). 96pp. Around the world in 25 stories showing the lore and wisdom of the native peoples. (Rev: BCCB 12/92; BL 9/15/92; SLJ 12/92) [398.2]

**8645** San Souci, Robert D. *Even More Short and Shivery: Thirty Spine-Tingling Stories* (5–8). Illus. by Jacqueline Rogers. 1997, Delacorte $14.95 (0-385-32252-6). 140pp. A collection of 30 scary stories, mostly folktales from around the world, that are great for reading or giving presentations before a group. (Rev: BL 7/97; SLJ 10/97) [398.2]

**8646** Shannon, George. *Still More Stories to Solve: Fourteen Folktales from Around the World* (4–6). Illus. 1994, Greenwillow $15.00 (0-688-04619-3). 64pp. Each of these folktales from around the world also contains the answer to a riddle. (Rev: BL 10/1/94; HB 11–12/94; SLJ 9/94) [398.2]

**8647** Shannon, George. *Stories to Solve: Folktales from Around the World* (4–6). Illus. by Peter Sis. 1985, Morrow paper $4.95 (0-688-10496-7). 56pp. Fourteen stories combine puzzles and folklore asking readers how the problem was figured out or the mystery solved. (Rev: BL 12/1/85; HB 9–10/85; SLJ 9/85) [398.2]

**8648** Shannon, George. *True Lies: 18 Tales for You to Judge* (4–6). Illus. 1997, Greenwillow $15.00 (0-688-14483-7). 48pp. Short folktales are used to explore the various meanings of truth. (Rev: BL 5/15/97; HB 7–8/97; SLJ 6/97) [398.2]

**8649** Sherman, Josepha. *Told Tales: Nine Folktales from Around the World* (4–6). Illus. 1995, Silver Moon LB $13.95 (1-881889-64-5). 80pp. A general introduction for beginning storytellers that uses a question-and-answer technique and supplies 9 folktales from around the world. (Rev: BL 2/1/96; SLJ 1/96) [398.2]

**8650** Shulevitz, Uri. *The Secret Room* (PS–2). Illus. 1993, Farrar $15.00 (0-374-34169-9). 32pp. A jealous chief counselor to the king tries to get rid of a wise old man who seems to be taking his place. (Rev: BCCB 2/94; BL 11/15/93; HB 1–2/93; SLJ 1/94) [398.2]

**8651** Sierra, Judy, ed. *Nursery Tales Around the World* (4–6). Illus. by Stefano Vitale. 1996, Clarion $20.00 (0-395-67894-3). 114pp. This fascinating work retells folktales with similar themes as they exist in different cultures. (Rev: BCCB 2/96; BL 3/1/96; HB 5–6/96; SLJ 4/96) [398.2]

**8652** Thompson, Stith, ed. *One Hundred Favorite Folktales* (5–8). Illus. by Franz Altschuler. 1968, Indiana Univ. Pr. $39.95 (0-253-15940-7); paper $18.95 (0-253-20172-1). 456pp. A selection from an international store of folktales. [398.2]

**8653** Walker, Paul R. *Giants! Stories from Around the World* (3–6). Illus. 1995, Harcourt $17.00 (0-15-200883-7). 80pp. A collection of 7 stories about giants, some obscure and others as familiar as "Jack and the Beanstalk." (Rev: BL 11/1/95; SLJ 2/96) [398.2]

**8654** Walker, Paul R. *Little Folk: Stories from Around the World* (K–4). Illus. by James Bernardin. 1997, Harcourt $17.00 (0-15-200327-4). 80pp. The retelling of 8 tales about pixies, including *Rumpelstiltskin* and a story about a leprechaun. (Rev: BCCB 7–8/97; BL 3/15/97; SLJ 4/97) [398.2]

**8655** Ward, Helen. *The King of the Birds* (PS–3). Illus. 1997, Millbrook LB $23.90 (0-7613-0313-8). 40pp. In this folktale about determining who is the king of the birds, it is the humble wren and not the eagle who wins. (Rev: BL 10/15/97; SLJ 1/98) [398.2]

**8656** Williams, Rose. *The Book of Fairies: Nature Spirits from Around the World* (5–7). Illus. 1997, Beyond Words $18.95 (1-885223-56-0). 80pp. Fairies play a major role in these 8 stories from such countries as France, Ireland, and India. (Rev: BL 1/1–15/98; SLJ 1/98) [398.2]

**8657** Yep, Laurence. *Tree of Dreams: Ten Tales from the Garden of Night* (3–6). Illus. by Isadore Seltzer. 1995, Troll paper $13.95 (0-8167-3498-4). 96pp. Folktales from China, Greece, Brazil, and other countries explore the world of sleep. (Rev: BCCB 4/95; BL 1/15/95; HB 11–12/95; SLJ 3/95) [398.2]

**8658** Yolen, Jane. *Once upon a Bedtime Story* (K–3). Illus. by Ruth T. Councell. 1997, Boyds Mills $17.95 (1-57397-484-3). 96pp. This is a charming collection of 16 folktales, fairy tales, and fables, chiefly from Europe. (Rev: BL 11/15/97; SLJ 9/97) [398.2]

**8659** Young, Ed. *Donkey Trouble* (PS–3). Illus. 1995, Simon & Schuster $16.00 (0-689-31854-5). 32pp. A man and his grandson eventually find that the advice offered by people to them on their journey to market with their donkey is not helpful. (Rev: BL 11/15/95*; SLJ 12/95) [392.2]

**8660** Young, Richard, and Judy D. Young, eds. *Stories from the Days of Christopher Columbus* (5–8). 1992, August House paper $8.95 (0-87483-198-9). 160pp. This collection of folktales comes from a variety of sources, including Italian, Spanish, Portuguese, and North and South American Indians. (Rev: SLJ 7/92)

**8661** Zerner, Amy, and Jessie S. Zerner, retellers. *Scheherazade's Cat: And Other Fables from Around the World* (3–6). Illus. by Amy Zerner and Jessie S. Zerner. 1994, Tuttle $16.95 (0-8048-1807-X). 115pp. A collection of 9 folktales, including one originally in the *1001 Nights* anthology about a wise cat. (Rev: SLJ 4/94) [398.2]

# Africa

**8662** Aardema, Verna. *Anansi Does the Impossible!* (K–4). Illus. by Lisa Desimini. 1997, Simon & Schuster $16.00 (0-689-81092-X). 32pp. In this Ashanti tale, Anansi the spider performs 3 difficult tasks to get stories from the Sky God. (Rev: BL 12/1/97; SLJ 9/97*) [398.2]

**8663** Aardema, Verna. *Anansi Finds a Fool: An Ashanti Tale* (PS–3). Illus. by Bryna Waldman. 1992, Dial LB $13.89 (0-8037-1165-4). 32pp. Anansi, in human form, is tricked by Bonsu when they go fishing. (Rev: BCCB 1/93; BL 9/1/92; SLJ 9/92) [398.2]

**8664** Aardema, Verna. *Bimwili and the Zimwi: A Tale from Zanzibar* (K–3). Illus. by Susan Meddaugh. 1985, Dial LB $12.89 (0-8037-0213-2); Puffin paper $4.99 (0-14-054608-1). 32pp. The story of little Bimwili, who finds a shell, loses it, is captured by the ogrelike Zimwi, and then outwits him to escape. (Rev: BL 12/1/85; SLJ 11/85) [398.2]

**8665** Aardema, Verna, reteller. *Bringing the Rain to Kapiti Plain: A Nandi Tale* (PS–2). Illus. by Beatriz Vidal. 1981, Dial LB $15.89 (0-8037-0807-6); Puffin paper $5.99 (0-14-054616-2). 32pp. A rhyming book on how the rain was brought to an African plain. [398.2]

**8666** Aardema, Verna. *How the Ostrich Got Its Long Neck: A Tale from the Akamba of Kenya* (PS–3). Illus. by Marcia Brown. 1995, Scholastic $14.95 (0-590-48367-6). 32pp. Ostrich gets its long neck while in a tug-of-war trying to get its head out of a crocodile's mouth. (Rev: BL 6/1–15/95; SLJ 11/95) [398.2]

**8667** Aardema, Verna. *The Lonely Lioness and the Ostrich Chicks* (PS–2). Illus. by Yumi Heo. 1996, Knopf LB $18.99 (0-679-96934-0). 32pp. In this Masai story, a lonely lioness is determined to raise an ostrich's 4 chicks. (Rev: BCCB 2/97; BL 11/15/96; SLJ 12/96*) [398.2]

**8668** Aardema, Verna, reteller. *Misoso: Once upon a Time Tales from Africa* (2–6). Illus. by Reynold Ruffins. 1994, Knopf LB $19.99 (0-679-93430-8). 88pp. A fine collection of African tales, with each story preceded by a map showing its locale and a glossary of unfamiliar words. (Rev: SLJ 12/94*) [398.2]

**8669** Aardema, Verna. *Oh, Kojo! How Could You!* (K–3). Illus. by Marc Brown. 1984, Dial LB $12.89 (0-8037-0007-5); Puffin paper $4.99 (0-8037-0449-6). 32pp. Humor and colorful artwork add to this tale of Kojo, who squanders her gold dust at the urgings of the trickster Ananse. [398.2]

**8670** Aardema, Verna. *Princess Gorilla and a New Kind of Water* (PS–2). Illus. by Victoria Chess. 1988, Dial LB $10.89 (0-8037-0413-5); Puffin paper $3.95 (0-8037-0914-5). 32pp. A monkey cheats to marry the king's daughter; he and his friends are banished to the trees, where they've lived ever since. (Rev: BL 4/1/88; HB 7–8/88; SLJ 6–7/88) [398.2]

**8671** Aardema, Verna. *Rabbit Makes a Monkey of Lion* (K–1). Illus. by Jerry Pinkney. 1989, Puffin paper $5.99 (0-14-054593-X). 32pp. A Swahili tale of a wily little rabbit outwitting the big brawny lion. (Rev: BL 3/1/89; HB 5–6/89; SLJ 6/89) [398.2]

**8672** Aardema, Verna. *Sebgugugu the Glutton: A Bantu Tale from Rwanda, Africa* (4–6). Illus. by Nancy L. Clouse. 1993, Africa World Pr. $14.95 (0-86543-377-1). 32pp. In this Rwandian folktale, a foolish man loses everything because of his greed. (Rev: BL 4/1/93; SLJ 6/93) [398.2]

**8673** Aardema, Verna. *This for That: A Tonga Tale* (PS–3). Illus. by Victoria Chess. 1997, Dial paper $14.89 (0-8037-1554-4). 32pp. In this African tale, Rabbit lies in order to get some berries to eat; but in time, justice prevails. (Rev: BCCB 3/97; BL 3/15/97; SLJ 12/97) [398.24]

**8674** Aardema, Verna. *Traveling to Tondo: A Tale of the Nkundo of Zaire* (PS–2). Illus. by Will Hillenbrand. 1991, Knopf LB $14.99 (0-679-90081-0). 32pp. In this funny Central African tale, a civet cat and his companions go to fetch his bride in Tondo. (Rev: BL 2/1/91; HB 7–8/91*; SLJ 3/91*) [398.2]

**8675** Aardema, Verna, reteller. *What's So Funny, Ketu? A Nuer Tale* (K–3). Illus. by Marc Brown. 1989, Dial paper $4.95 (0-8037-0646-4). A secret joke almost leads to disaster in this comic Sudanese folktale. [398.2]

**8676** Aardema, Verna, ed. *Who's in Rabbit's House? A Masai Tale* (K–3). Illus. by Leo Dillon and Diane Dillon. 1977, Dial paper $4.99 (0-8037-9549-1). 32pp. Rabbit's friends try to evict a mysterious Long One who has moved into her house. [398.2]

**8677** Aardema, Verna, ed. *Why Mosquitoes Buzz in People's Ears: A West African Tale* (K–3). Illus. by Leo Dillon and Diane Dillon. 1992, Puffin paper $4.99 (0-14-054905-6). 32pp. Bold, stylized paintings illustrate this tale of a mosquito who tells a whopping lie, thus setting off a chain of events. Caldecott Medal winner, 1976. [398.2]

**8678** *African Tales: Folklore of the Central African Republic* (3–5). Illus. by Rodney Wilmer. 1992, Telecraft $10.95 (1-878893-15-7); paper $6.95 (1-878893-14-9). 95pp. Twelve interesting tales collected from the peoples of the Central African Republic. (Rev: SLJ 2/92) [398.2]

**8679** Anderson, David A. *The Origin of Life on Earth: An African Creation Myth* (2–6). Illus. by Kathleen A. Wilson. 1991, Sights LB $18.95 (0-9629978-5-4). This African myth tells how earthly creatures were formed and how the world began spinning. (Rev: SLJ 7/92) [398.2]

**8680** Appiah, Peggy. *Tales of an Ashanti Father* (2–7). Illus. by Mora Dickson. 1989, Beacon paper $7.95 (0-8070-8313-5). 160pp. Twenty-two stories about trickster Ananse. [398.2]

**8681** Araujo, Frank P. *The Perfect Orange: A Tale from Ethiopia* (K–3). Illus. by Xiao Jun Li. Series: Toucan Tales. 1994, Rayve $16.95 (1-877810-94-0). In this Ethiopian folktale, a simple girl impresses a king with her generosity, and he rewards her with gold and jewels. (Rev: SLJ 3/95) [398.2]

**8682** Arkhurst, Joyce Cooper. *The Adventures of Spider: West African Folktales* (4–7). Illus. by Jerry Pinkney. 1992, Little, Brown $7.95 (0-316-05107-1). Six humorous stories featuring the crafty spider. [398.2]

**8683** Ashabranner, Brent, and Russell Davis. *The Lion's Whiskers and Other Ethiopian Tales* (4–7). Illus. 1997, Linnet LB $19.95 (0-208-02429-8). 96pp. A classic collection of 16 Ethiopian folktales originally published in 1995. (Rev: BL 10/1/97; SLJ 5/97*) [398.2]

**8684** Barbosa, Rogerio Andrade. *African Animal Tales* (4–6). Trans. by Feliz Guthrie. Illus. by Cica Fittipaldi. 1993, Volcano $17.95 (0-912078-96-0). 63pp. Weak, small animals outwit stronger animals in this collection of 10 African folktales. (Rev: BL 2/15/94) [398.2]

**8685** Berry, James. *Don't Leave an Elephant to Go and Chase a Bird* (PS–1). Illus. by Ann Grifalconi. 1996, Simon & Schuster $16.00 (0-689-80464-4). 32pp. A group of elephants conspire to out-trick the cunning Anancy Spiderman in this folktale from Ghana. (Rev: BCCB 1/96; BL 2/15/96; SLJ 3/96) [398.2]

**8686** Berry, James. *First Palm Trees* (PS–4). Illus. by Greg Couch. 1997, Simon & Schuster $17.00 (0-689-81060-1). 40pp. In this West African tale, Anansi the spider seeks help to make palm trees so that he can collect a reward from the king. (Rev: BL 12/15/97; SLJ 12/97) [398.2]

**8687** Bryan, Ashley. *Beat the Story-Drum, Pum-Pum* (K–4). Illus. by author. 1987, Macmillan paper $8.95 (0-689-71107-7). 80pp. A retelling of 5 Nigerian folktales. [398.2]

**8688** Bryan, Ashley. *Lion and the Ostrich Chicks and Other African Folk Tales* (3–5). Illus. 1996, Simon & Schuster $6.95 (0-689-80713-9). 96pp. Spirited retelling of African folktales involving the triumph of the underdog. (Rev: BCCB 2/87; BL 2/1/87; SLJ 1/87) [398.2]

**8689** Bryan, Ashley. *The Story of Lightning and Thunder* (3–6). Illus. 1993, Atheneum $15.00 (0-689-31836-7). 32pp. In this African folktale, Thunder, a sheep, and her son Lightning are banished to the sky when Lightning becomes too destructive. (Rev: BCCB 10/93; BL 9/15/93; SLJ 9/93*) [398.2]

**8690** Butler, Andrea. *Mr. Sun and Mr. Sea* (1–2). Illus. by Lily Toy Hong. 1994, Scott Foresman/GoodYear $2.95 (0-673-36198-5). 16pp. An easy-to-read version of the African folktale that tells why Mr. Sun went to the sky to live. (Rev: BL 1/1/95) [398.3]

**8691** Chocolate, Deborah M. *Imani in the Belly* (PS–3). Illus. by Alex Boies. 1994, Troll paper $14.95 (0-8167-3466-6). 32pp. Imani sets out to catch Simba the lion, who has taken her children. (Rev: BL 10/15/94; SLJ 12/94) [398.2]

**8692** Climo, Shirley. *The Egyptian Cinderella* (1–4). Illus. by Ruth Heller. 1989, HarperCollins LB $14.89 (0-690-04824-6). 32pp. A tale based on fact about a Greek girl who was kidnapped and brought to Egypt is one of the world's first Cinderella stories. (Rev: BCCB 10/89; BL 9/1/89; SLJ 10/89*) [398.2]

**8693** Courlander, Harold, and George Herzog. *The Cow-Tail Switch: And Other West African Stories* (4–6). Illus. by Madye Lee Chastain. 1988, Holt $13.95 (0-8050-0288-X); paper $7.95 (0-8050-0298-7). 160pp. Originally published in 1947, this is a fine collection of folktales about foolish and wise men and animals. [398.2]

**8694** Day, Nancy Raines. *The Lion's Whiskers: An Ethiopian Folktale* (PS–2). Illus. by Ann Grifalconi. 1995, Scholastic $14.95 (0-590-45803-5). 32pp. A stepmother seeks the aid of a medicine man in her efforts to win the affection of the stepson who rejects her. (Rev: BCCB 3/95; BL 2/15/95; SLJ 4/95*) [398.2]

**8695** Dee, Ruby. *Two Ways to Count to Ten: A Liberian Folktale* (PS–1). Illus. by Susan Meddaugh. 1990, Holt paper $5.95 (0-8050-1314-8). 32pp. The antelope outsmarts them all when the king advertises for a successor. (Rev: BL 7/88; SLJ 6–7/88) [398.2]

**8696** Diakite, Baba Wague. *The Hunterman and the Crocodile: A West African Folktale* (K–3). Illus. 1997, Scholastic $15.95 (0-590-89828-0). 32pp. A West African folktale about the Hunterman who runs afoul of Bamba the Crocodile and is helped by Rabbit. (Rev: BCCB 2/97; BL 3/15/97; SLJ 3/97) [398.2]

**8697** Fairman, Tony. *Bury My Bones but Keep My Words* (K–2). Illus. by Meshack Asare. 1993, Holt $15.95 (0-8050-2333-X). 192pp. Stories about Africa retold by the author, who once taught and lived there. (Rev: BCCB 4/93; BL 2/15/93; SLJ 3/93*) [398.2]

**8698** Farris, Pamela J. *Young Mouse and Elephant: An East African Folktale* (PS–2). Illus. by Valeri Gorbachev. 1996, Houghton $14.95 (0-395-73977-2). 32pp. Young Mouse believes he is the strongest animal alive and sets off across the African plains to prove to Elephant that he is right. (Rev: BL 5/1/96; SLJ 4/96) [398.2]

**8699** Gerson, Mary-Joan. *Why the Sky Is Far Away: A Nigerian Folktale* (K–3). Illus. by Carla Golembe. 1992, Little, Brown $15.95 (0-316-30852-8). 36pp. In this Nigerian folktale, when peasants misuse the sky it decides to move farther away. (Rev: BCCB 10/92; BL 8/92; HB 9–10/92; SLJ 9/92*) [398.2]

**8700** Greaves, Nick. *When Hippo Was Hairy: And Other Tales from Africa* (4–8). Illus. 1988, Barron's paper $11.95 (0-8120-4548-3). 144pp. Thirty-one traditional African tales, a combination of folklore and fact. (Rev: BL 2/15/89; SLJ 2/89) [398.2]

**8701** Greaves, Nick. *When Lion Could Fly and Other Tales from Africa* (4–8). Illus. by Rod Clement. 1993, Barron's $13.95 (0-8120-6344-9); paper $8.95 (0-8120-1625-4). 144pp. In addition to the folktales about various African animals, the author gives factual information about the actual traits of each animal. (Rev: BL 1/1/94; SLJ 4/94) [398.24]

**8702** Green, Roger L. *Tales of Ancient Egypt* (6–8). Illus. by Elaine Raphael. 1996, Viking paper $3.99 (0-14-036716-0). 192pp. Some of the oldest stories known. [398.2]

**8703** Greger, C. Shana. *Cry of the Benu Bird: An Egyptian Creation Story* (4–6). Illus. Series: 398.2. 1996, Houghton $14.95 (0-395-73573-4). 32pp. In this book based on an Egyptian creation myth, an enchanted bird fights the darkness of Chaos to help the beginnings of human life. (Rev: BL 3/15/96; SLJ 4/96) [398.2]

**8704** Grifalconi, Ann. *The Village of Round and Square Houses* (PS–2). Illus. by author. 1986, Little, Brown $16.95 (0-316-32862-6). 32pp. This blend of fiction, anthropology, and folklore centers around the central African remote village of Tos. (Rev: BCCB 6/86; BL 6/15/86; SLJ 8/86) [398.2]

**8705** Guy, Rosa, adapt. *Mother Crocodile: "Maman-Caiman"* (K–3). Illus. by John Steptoe. 1981, Delacorte $10.42 (0-385-30803-5). A folktale from Senegal told by Uncle Amadou about Mother Crocodile, whose children ignored her when she said they should learn from past experience. [398.2]

**8706** Haley, Gail E. *A Story, a Story* (1–4). Illus. by author. 1970, Macmillan LB $17.00 (0-689-20511-2); paper $4.95 (0-689-71201-4). 36pp. How African "spider stories" began is traced back to the time when Ananse, the Spider Man, made a bargain with the Sky God. Caldecott Medal winner, 1971. [398.2]

**8707** *The Honey Hunters* (PS–3). Illus. by Francesca Martin. 1992, Candlewick $14.95 (1-56402-086-X). 32pp. The tale of a time long ago when all earth animals were friends and they all liked honey. (Rev: BL 11/15/92) [398.2]

**8708** Hull, Robert, reteller. *Egyptian Stories* (4–6). Illus. by Noel Bateman and Barbara Loftus. Series: Tales from Around the World. 1994, Thomson Learning LB $24.26 (1-56847-155-6). 48pp. Introduces 7 traditional tales, including a creation story, as well as life in ancient Egypt. (Rev: SLJ 8/94) [398.2]

**8709** Kimmel, Eric A. *Anansi and the Moss-Covered Rock* (PS–3). Illus. by Janet Stevens. 1988, Holiday LB $15.95 (0-8234-0689-X); paper $6.95 (0-8234-0798-5). 32pp. Anansi the trickster discovers a magic rock that knocks animals out, and then he steals their food. (Rev: BCCB 10/88; BL 10/1/88; SLJ 11/88) [398.2]

**8710** Kimmel, Eric A. *Anansi and the Talking Melon* (PS–3). Illus. by Janet Stevens. 1994, Holiday LB $15.95 (0-8234-1104-4). 32pp. Hiding inside a melon, Anansi the Spider tricks all the animals into believing that the melon can speak in this African folktale. (Rev: BCCB 6/94; BL 2/15/94; SLJ 3/94*) [398.2]

**8711** Kimmel, Eric A. *Anansi Goes Fishing* (K–3). Illus. by Janet Stevens. 1992, Holiday LB $15.95 (0-8234-0918-X). 32pp. Lazy but lovable trickster Anansi is outwitted by the clever turtle in this contemporary rendition of an old tale. (Rev: BL 3/15/92; SLJ 5/92) [398.2]

**8712** Kimmel, Eric A. *Rimonah of the Flashing Sword: A North African Tale* (K–3). Illus. by Omar Rayyan. 1995, Holiday LB $15.95 (0-8234-1093-5). 32pp. An Egyptian folktale that is a variation on the Snow White story about a princess fleeing the wrath of a wicked stepmother. (Rev: BL 3/1/95; SLJ 3/95) [398.2]

**8713** Knutson, Barbara. *How the Guinea Fowl Got Her Spots: A Swahili Tale of Friendship* (PS–2). Illus. 1990, Carolrhoda LB $19.95 (0-87614-416-4). 24pp. Cow returns a favor given by Nganga the Guinea Fowl by giving her spots that can help her hide from enemies. (Rev: BCCB 7–8/90*; BL 6/15/90; HB 9–10/90; SLJ 9/90) [398.2]

**8714** Kurtz, Jane. *Fire on the Mountain* (1–4). Illus. by E. B. Lewis. 1994, Simon & Schuster paper $16.00 (0-671-88268-6). 32pp. A young boy and his sister trick a wealthy man into paying his debts in this Ethiopian folktale. (Rev: BCCB 10/94; BL 10/15/94; HB 11–12/94; SLJ 12/94*) [398.2]

**8715** Kurtz, Jane. *Pulling the Lion's Tail* (PS–3). Illus. by Floyd Cooper. 1995, Simon & Schuster paper $15.00 (0-689-80324-9). 32pp. A child's grandfather gives an unusual prescription for gaining her stepmother's love in this Ethiopian folktale. (Rev: BL 9/1/95; SLJ 12/95) [398.2]

**8716** Kurtz, Jane. *Trouble* (4–7). Illus. by Durga Bernhard. 1997, Harcourt $15.00 (0-15-200219-7). 40pp. An Eritrean story about a young goatherd who has a knack for getting into trouble. (Rev: BL 3/15/97; SLJ 4/97) [398.2]

**8717** Lake, Mary D., reteller. *The Royal Drum: An Ashanti Tale* (K–2). Illus. by Carol O'Malia. 1996, Mondo $14.95 (1-57255-140-2). Using a rebus approach, this tale from Ghana tells how Anansi the spider gets all of the animals to participate in making a drum for Lion the king. (Rev: SLJ 11/96) [398.2]

**8718** Larungu, Rute. *Myths and Legends from Ghana for African-American Cultures* (4–7). Illus. by Lou Turechek. 1992, Telcraft LB $14.95 (1-878893-21-1); paper $8.95 (1-878893-20-3). 96pp. Fast-paced tales from 2 distinct African cultures — the Hausa and the Ashanti. (Rev: BL 12/1/92) [398.2]

**8719** Lester, Julius. *How Many Spots Does a Leopard Have?* (K–5). Illus. by David Shannon. 1994, Scholastic paper $5.95 (0-590-41972-2). 72pp. This is a splendid retelling of 12 folktales, 10 of which are African and the other 2 Jewish. (Rev: BCCB 9/89; BL 11/15/89; HB 1–2/90; SLJ 11/89) [398.2]

**8720** Lottridge, Celia B., reteller. *The Name of the Tree* (K–5). Illus. by Ian Wallace. 1990, Macmillan $16.00 (0-689-50490-X). This Bantu tale begins with hungry animals finding a tree laden with every fruit imaginable. (Rev: BCCB 4/90; SLJ 3/90) [398.2]

**8721** McDermott, Gerald. *Anansi, the Spider: A Tale from the Ashanti* (K–3). Illus. by author. 1972, Holt LB $15.95 (0-8050-0310-X); paper $5.95 (0-8050-0311-8). 48pp. Because Anansi and his sons quarrel, the moon remains in the sky. [398.2]

**8722** McDermott, Gerald. *Zomo the Rabbit: A Trickster Tale from West Africa* (PS–3). Illus. 1992, Harcourt $14.95 (0-15-299967-1). 32pp. An enduring Nigerian tale of a trickster who is cunning but not always wise. (Rev: BCCB 9/92*; BL 9/15/92*; SLJ 11/92*) [398.2]

**8723** Mama, Raouf. *Why Goats Smell Bad and Other Stories from Benin* (4–6). Illus. 1998, Linnet LB $19.95 (0-208-02469-7). 138pp. This interesting collection of African folktales from Benin contains stories about children, spirits, animals, and tricksters. (Rev: BL 2/15/98; SLJ 4/98) [398.2]

**8724** Medearis, Angela Shelf. *The Singing Man* (PS–3). Illus. by Terea D. Shaffer. 1994, Holiday LB $16.95 (0-8234-1103-6). 36pp. Banzar is scorned in his Nigerian village because he wants to become a musician, but eventually he returns to his home in triumph. (Rev: BL 7/94; SLJ 9/94) [398.2]

**8725** Medearis, Angela Shelf. *Too Much Talk* (PS–2). Illus. by Stefano Vitale. 1995, Candlewick $15.95 (1-56402-323-0). 32pp. A cumulative West African folktale about a group of people who discover that inanimate objects and animals can speak their language. (Rev: BCCB 12/95; BL 1/1–15/96; HB 11–12/95; SLJ 12/95) [398.2]

**8726** Medlicott, Mary, ed. and sel. *The River That Went to the Sky: Twelve Tales by African Storytellers* (4–7). Illus. by Ademola Akintola. 1995, Kingfisher $16.95 (1-85697-608-4). 90pp. Twelve excellent folktales represent 11 geographical areas of Africa. (Rev: SLJ 4/96) [398.2]

**8727** Mollel, Tololwa M. *Ananse's Feast: An Ashanti Tale* (K–3). Illus. by Andrew Glass. 1997, Clarion $14.95 (0-395-67402-6). 32pp. Akye the turtle gets revenge on Ananse the spider in this gentle Ashanti tale. (Rev: BL 4/15/97; SLJ 5/97) [398.2]

**8728** Mollel, Tololwa M. *The Flying Tortoise* (3–5). Illus. by Barbara Spurll. 1994, Clarion $14.95 (0-395-68845-0). 32pp. A Nigerian folktale about how a crafty tortoise gets his cracked shell. (Rev: BCCB 10/94; BL 11/15/94; SLJ 9/94) [398.2]

**8729** Mollel, Tololwa M. *The King and the Tortoise* (K–3). Illus. by Kathy Blankley. 1993, Houghton $14.95 (0-395-64480-1). 32pp. In this folktale from Cameroon, a clever tortoise is able to make a robe of smoke for a proud king. (Rev: BL 4/1/93) [398.2]

**8730** Mollel, Tololwa M. *The Orphan Boy* (K–3). Illus. by Paul Morin. 1991, Houghton $15.95 (0-89919-985-2). 32pp. In this Masai folktale, an old man takes in an orphan boy who is actually the planet Venus. (Rev: BCCB 4/91*; BL 5/1/91; SLJ 7/91*) [398.2]

**8731** Moodie, Fiona, reteller. *Nabulela* (K–3). Illus. by Fiona Moodie. 1997, Farrar $15.00 (0-374-35486-3). In this South African folktale, several girls are given a seemingly hopeless task because they have behaved cruelly toward the chieftain's daughter. (Rev: BCCB 7–8/97; SLJ 3/97) [398.2]

**8732** Onyefulu, Obi, reteller. *Chinye: A West African Folk Tale* (K–3). Illus. by Evie Safarewicz. 1994, Viking paper $14.99 (0-670-85115-9). This African version of Cinderella features a heroine who must labor endlessly for a wicked stepmother and her lazy stepsister. (Rev: SLJ 9/94) [398.2]

**8733** Rappaport, Doreen. *The New King* (K–4). Illus. by E. B. Lewis. 1995, Dial paper $14.99 (0-8037-1460-2). 32pp. A Wise Woman helps a young prince accept the death of his father in this tale from Madagascar. (Rev: BL 5/1/95; SLJ 7/95*) [398.2]

**8734** Savory, Phyllis. *Zulu Fireside Tales* (4–6). Illus. by Sylvia Baxter. 1993, Carol Publg. paper $9.95 (0-8065-1380-2). 240pp. This is an authentic collection of 10 Zulu tales that originated in the area now known as Kwazulu. (Rev: BL 5/1/93) [398.2]

**8735** Seeger, Pete, adapt. *Abiyoyo: Based on a South African Lullaby and Folk Story* (PS–1). Illus. by Michael Hays. 1986, Macmillan LB $16.00 (0-02-781490-4). 48pp. An ostracized father and little boy who plays the ukelele find a way to best the giant Abiyoyo. (Rev: BCCB 6/86; BL 5/1/86; SLJ 8/86) [398.2]

**8736** Serwadda, W. Moses. *Songs and Stories from Uganda* (3–5). Illus. by Leo Dillon and Diane Dillon. 1987, World Music paper $12.95 (0-937203-16-5). A mixture of folk materials from Uganda, including songs in the native language (with translations) and a description of accompanying dance steps. [398.2]

**8737** Sierra, Judy. *The Mean Hyena* (2–4). Illus. 1997, Dutton paper $15.99 (0-525-67510-8). 32pp. A tortoise who delights in painting spots, stripes, etc. on animals encounters a nasty hyena in this African folktale. (Rev: BL 9/1/97; SLJ 10/97*) [398.2]

**8738** Steptoe, John. *Mufaro's Beautiful Daughters: An African Tale* (PS–2). Illus. by author. 1987, Lothrop LB $15.93 (0-688-04046-2). 32pp. Two sisters of opposite natures vie for the hand of the king. (Rev: BCCB 4/87; BL 4/15/87; SLJ 6–7/87) [398.2]

**8739** Wisniewski, David. *Sundiata: Lion King of Mali* (K–5). Illus. 1992, Houghton $17.00 (0-395-

61302-7). 32pp. The dying king gives his kingdom to a sickly prince who cannot walk or speak, but in time, he becomes a great and brave leader. (Rev: BL 12/1/92*; HB 3–4/93; SLJ 10/92*) [398.2]

**8740** Wolfson, Margaret O. *Marriage of the Rain Goddess: A South African Myth* (4–6). Illus. by Clifford Alexander Parms. 1996, Marlowe $14.95 (1-56924-774-9). 28pp. In this South African myth, the rain goddess devises a test to determine if a mortal is worthy of her affections. (Rev: BL 8/96; SLJ 8/96) [398.2]

# Asia

## General and Miscellaneous

**8741** Asian Cultural Center for Unesco, ed. *Folk Tales from Asia for Children Everywhere: Book Three* (2–5). Illus. 1976, Weatherhill $6.50 (0-8348-1034-4). 60pp. Nine tales with a wide range of folk themes. [398.2]

**8742** Choi, Yangsook. *The Sun Girl and the Moon Boy* (PS–3). Illus. 1997, Random $17.00 (0-679-88386-X). 32pp. In this Korean folktale, a variation on the Little Red Riding Hood story, it is a fierce tiger that eats the Mother. (Rev: BL 12/15/97; SLJ 4/98) [398.2]

**8743** Climo, Shirley. *The Korean Cinderella* (K–3). Illus. by Ruth Heller. 1993, HarperCollins $15.00 (0-06-020432-X). 48pp. After Pear Blossom's mother dies and her father remarries, she is mistreated by her stepmother and stepsister. (Rev: BCCB 6/93; BL 5/1/93; SLJ 8/93) [398.2]

**8744** Davison, Katherine. *Moon Magic: Stories from Asia* (3–5). Illus. 1994, Carolrhoda LB $19.95 (0-87614-751-1). 56pp. A retelling of 4 Asian myths that deal with the moon and its phases. (Rev: BL 5/15/94; SLJ 6/94) [398.2]

**8745** Farley, Carol. *Mr. Pak Buys a Story* (K–3). Illus. by Benrei Huang. 1997, Albert Whitman LB $15.95 (0-8075-5178-3). 32pp. A Korean folktale about a servant who is sent by a wealthy couple to buy a story in the big city. (Rev: BCCB 5/97; BL 4/15/97; HB 7–8/97; SLJ 4/97) [398.2]

**8746** Froese, Deborah. *The Wise Washerman: A Folktale from Burma* (K–3). Illus. by Wang Kui. 1996, Hyperion LB $15.49 (0-7868-2232-5). A jealous neighbor tries to get an industrious washerwoman into trouble in this Burmese folktale. (Rev: BCCB 12/96; SLJ 1/97) [398.2]

**8747** Ginsburg, Mirra. *The Chinese Mirror* (1–3). Illus. by Margot Zemach. 1991, Harcourt paper $6.00 (0-15-217508-3). 26pp. An old folktale from Korea tells of a man who brings home a mirror — unknown to his fellow villagers — from a trip to China. (Rev: BCCB 5/88; BL 4/15/88; SLJ 4/88) [398.2]

**8748** Han, Oki S., and Stephanie H. Plunkett. *Kongi and Potgi: A Cinderella Story from Korea* (PS–3). Illus. 1996, Dial paper $14.89 (0-8037-1572-2). 32pp. From Korea, a variation on the Cinderella story that retains the prince's ball and the magic slipper. (Rev: BCCB 2/97; BL 11/15/96; SLJ 12/96) [398.2]

**8749** Han, Suzanne C. *The Rabbit's Escape* (PS–3). Illus. by Yumi Heo. 1995, Holt $15.95 (0-8050-2675-4). 32pp. A Korean folktale in English and Korean about the origin of using ginsing roots for medicinal purposes. (Rev: BCCB 5/95; BL 5/15/95; HB 9–10/95; SLJ 6/95*) [398.2]

**8750** Han, Suzanne C. *The Rabbit's Judgment* (K–3). Illus. by Yumi Heo. 1994, Holt $15.95 (0-8050-2674-6). 32pp. A wily rabbit saves a man from becoming a tiger's dinner in this Korean folktale told in both Korean and English. (Rev: BCCB 5/94; BL 6/1–15/94; SLJ 6/94) [398.2]

**8751** Heo, Yumi. *The Green Frogs* (K–3). Illus. 1996, Houghton $14.95 (0-395-68378-5). 32pp. Two disobedient frogs decide to honor their mother's last wish in this Korean folktale. (Rev: BCCB 10/96; BL 7/96; HB 11–12/96) [398.2]

**8752** Jaffe, Nina. *Older Brother, Younger Brother: A Korean Folktale* (PS–3). Illus. by Wenhai Ma. 1995, Viking paper $14.99 (0-670-85645-2). 32pp. Using double-page illustrations, this Korean folktale about a good brother and his evil sibling is retold. (Rev: BCCB 9/95; BL 6/1–15/95; SLJ 7/95) [398.2]

**8753** O'Brien, Anne S. *The Princess and the Beggar: A Korean Folktale* (K–3). Illus. 1993, Scholastic $14.95 (0-590-46092-7). 32pp. In this Korean folktale, a princess is banished from her father's castle because she refuses to marry a man she doesn't love. (Rev: BCCB 6/93; BL 4/15/93; SLJ 5/93) [398.2]

**8754** Rhee, Nami. *Magic Spring: A Korean Folktale* (K–3). Illus. 1993, Putnam LB $15.95 (0-399-22420-3). 32pp. A Korean folktale about an elderly couple who find a magical spring that returns their youth. (Rev: BCCB 6/93; BL 4/1/93; SLJ 7/93*) [398.2]

**8755** Riordan, James, reteller. *Korean Folk-Tales* (4–8). Series: Oxford Myths and Legends. 1995, Oxford paper $12.95 (0-19-274160-8). 133pp. A clear and interesting retelling of 20 well-known Korean folktales. (Rev: SLJ 3/95) [398.2]

**8756** Seros, Kathleen, adapt. *Sun and Moon: Fairy Tales from Korea* (2–5). Illus. by Norman Sibley and Robert Krause. 1983, Hollym $16.50 (0-930878-25-6). 61pp. A collection of 7 stories from Korea. [398.2]

**8757** Yep, Laurence. *The Khan's Daughter* (K–3). Illus. by Jean Tseng and Mou-Sien Tseng. 1997, Scholastic $16.95 (0-590-48389-7). 32pp. A Mongolian folktale in which the hero's most formidable opponent is the khan's daughter. (Rev: BCCB 3/97; BL 2/1/97*; HB 3–4/97; SLJ 2/97*) [398.2]

## China

**8758** Birdseye, Tom. *A Song of Stars* (3–5). Illus. by Ju-Hong Chen. 1990, Holiday LB $14.95 (0-8234-0790-X). 32pp. A retelling of the Chinese myth about the stars Vega and Altair, which lead to the Festival of the Milky Way. (Rev: BL 4/15/90; HB 5–6/90; SLJ 5/90) [398.2]

**8759** Bouchard, David. *The Great Race* (3–6). Illus. by Zhong-Yang Huang. 1997, Millbrook LB $21.40 (0-7613-0305-7). 32pp. This folktale tells that the order of the animals in the Chinese zodiac was determined by a great race. (Rev: BL 2/1/98; SLJ 1/98) [398.2]

**8760** Carpenter, F. R. *Tales of a Chinese Grandmother* (5–7). Illus. by Malthe Hasselriis. 1973, Amereon LB $24.95 (0-89190-481-6); Tuttle paper $8.95 (0-8048-1042-7). 293pp. A boy and a girl listen to 30 classic Chinese tales. [398.2]

**8761** Chang, Margaret, and Raymond Chang. *The Beggar's Magic* (1–3). Illus. by David Johnson. 1997, Simon & Schuster paper $16.00 (0-689-81340-6). 32pp. In this Chinese folktale, when a wise man is denied a pear by a stingy farmer, he plants a tree that will bear enough fruit to feed a village. (Rev: BL 10/15/97; HB 11–12/97; SLJ 12/97*) [398.2]

**8762** Chang, Margaret, and Raymond Chang. *The Cricket Warrior: A Chinese Tale* (K–4). Illus. by Warwick Hutton. 1994, Macmillan paper $14.95 (0-689-50605-8). 32pp. A boy is transformed into a cricket and saves his family in this Chinese folktale. (Rev: BCCB 10/94; BL 11/1/94; SLJ 1/95) [398.2]

**8763** Chin, Charlie. *China's Bravest Girl: The Legend of Hua Mu Lan* (1–3). Illus. by Tomie Arai. 1993, Children's Book Pr. $14.95 (0-89239-120-0). 31pp. A Chinese girl disguised as a man becomes a distinguished warrior in this folktale told in both English and Mandarin Chinese. (Rev: BL 3/1/94; SLJ 3/94) [398.21]

**8764** Chin, Yin-lien C., ed. *Traditional Chinese Folktales* (5–8). Illus. by Lu Wang. 1989, East Gate $39.95 (0-87332-507-9). 180pp. This is a collection of 12 Chinese folktales that express a variety of themes and genres from faithful lovers to trickster tales. (Rev: SLJ 8/89) [398.2]

**8765** Czernecki, Stefan. *The Cricket's Cage: A Chinese Folktale* (1–4). Illus. 1997, Hyperion LB $15.49 (0-7868-2234-1). 32pp. In this Chinese folktale, a

cricket helps a kindly carpenter design the watchtowers in the Forbidden City. (Rev: BCCB 6/97; BL 4/15/97; SLJ 6/97) [398.2]

**8766** Demi. *The Dragon's Tale and Other Animal Fables of the Chinese Zodiac* (3–6). Illus. 1996, Holt $16.95 (0-8050-3446-3). 26pp. A collection of 12 fables that involve the animals in the Chinese zodiac. (Rev: BCCB 1/97; BL 9/15/96; SLJ 10/96) [398.2]

**8767** Demi. *The Empty Pot* (K–2). Illus. by author. 1990, Holt $15.95 (0-8050-1217-6). 32pp. Young Ping finds out that honesty pays when the emperor gives seeds to each child in the kingdom to produce the best flower. (Rev: BL 4/1/90; HB 5–6/90 & 1-2/91; SLJ 7/90) [398.2]

**8768** Fang, Linda. *The Ch'i-lin Purse: A Collection of Ancient Chinese Stories* (3–5). Illus. by Jeanne M. Lee. 1995, Farrar $16.00 (0-374-31241-9). 127pp. Nine folktales from ancient China are dramatically retold, each with an accompanying illustration. (Rev: BCCB 4/95; BL 1/15/95*; HB 5–6/95; SLJ 3/95) [398.2]

**8769** Gao, R. L. *Adventures of Monkey King* (PS–2). Illus. by Marylys Barton. 1997, Victory paper $6.95 (0-9620765-1-1). 132pp. An action-packed story of Monkey King's journey from China to India, translated from a Chinese folktale that is over 400 years old. (Rev: BL 3/1/90) [398.2]

**8770** Greene, Ellin. *Ling-Li and the Phoenix Fairy: A Chinese Folktale* (4–6). Illus. by Zong-Zhou Wang. 1996, Clarion $14.95 (0-395-71528-8). 32pp. This picture book for older readers retells the Chinese folktale about Ling-Li and the beautiful robe she has embroidered. (Rev: BL 2/15/96; SLJ 3/96) [398.2]

**8771** Han, Carolyn. *Why Snails Have Shells: Minority and Han Folktales from China* (4–6). Trans. by Jay Han. Illus. 1994, Univ. of Hawaii Pr. $14.95 (0-8248-1505-X). 73pp. Attractive paintings accompany this splendid collection of 20 folktales from China. (Rev: BL 8/94) [398.2]

**8772** Heyer, Marilee. *The Weaving of a Dream: A Chinese Folktale* (3–5). Illus. by author. 1989, Puffin paper $5.99 (0-14-050528-8). 32pp. The third of an old widow's sons retrieves her precious brocade, from whence steps the Red Fairy, and all 3 live happily ever after. (Rev: BL 4/15/86; SLJ 4/86) [398.2]

**8773** Hong, Lily T. *How the Ox Star Fell from Heaven* (PS–3). Illus. 1995, Whitman paper $6.95 (0-8075-3429-3). 32pp. A retelling of the Chinese folktale of how oxen first lolled about the celestial home of the emperor of All the Heavens. (Rev: BL 4/1/91; SLJ 7/91*) [398.2]

**8774** Hong, Lily T. *Two of Everything: A Chinese Folktale* (K–3). Illus. 1993, Whitman LB $15.95 (0-8075-8157-7). 32pp. Elderly Mr. Haktak finds a magical brass pot in his garden. (Rev: BL 3/15/93*; HB 7–8/93*; SLJ 6/93*) [398.2]

**8775** Hume, Lotta Carswell. *Favorite Children's Stories from China and Tibet* (3–6). Illus. by Lo Koon-Chiu. 1962, Tuttle paper $16.95 (0-8048-1605-0). 120pp. An enjoyable retelling of 19 tales from the East, many with an uncanny resemblance to Western counterparts. [398.2]

**8776** Kendall, Carol, and Li Yao-wen. *Sweet and Sour: Tales from China* (5–7). Illus. 1990, Houghton paper $7.95 (0-395-54798-9). 112pp. A choice collection of some enchanting Chinese folktales. [398.2]

**8777** Lawson, Julie. *The Dragon's Pearl* (PS–3). Illus. by Paul Morin. 1993, Houghton $15.95 (0-395-63623-X). 36pp. Fearful that robbers will steal his magic pearl, a young boy swallows it and turns into a dragon. (Rev: BCCB 5/93; BL 4/15/93; SLJ 7/93) [398.2]

**8778** Lee, Jeanne M., reteller. *Legend of the Milky Way* (K–3). 1982, Holt paper $5.95 (0-8050-1361-X). 32pp. The Chinese legend of how the stars Vega and Altair were born. [398.2]

**8779** Lee, Jeanne M. *The Song of Mu Lan* (5–8). Illus. 1995, Front Street $15.95 (1-886910-00-6). 32pp. Mu Lan disguises herself as a boy and joins the emperor's army in this traditional Chinese tale. (Rev: BL 11/15/95; SLJ 12/95) [398.2]

**8780** Louie, Ai-Ling, reteller. *Yeh-Shen: A Cinderella Story from China* (2–6). Illus. by Ed Young. 1982, Putnam $15.95 (0-399-20900-X). 32pp. A Chinese story about a poor girl living with her cruel stepmother and stepsisters. [398.2]

**8781** Mahy, Margaret. *The Seven Chinese Brothers* (K–3). Illus. by Jean Tseng. 1992, Scholastic paper $4.99 (0-590-42057-7). 40pp. Each of 7 Chinese brothers has an amazing gift, used to help one another. (Rev: BCCB 7–8/90; BL 4/1/90; HB 7–8/90; SLJ 3/90*) [398.2]

**8782** Mosel, Arlene. *Tikki Tikki Tembo* (K–2). Illus. by Blair Lent. 1968, Holt $14.95 (0-8050-0662-1); paper $5.95 (0-8050-1166-8). 32pp. Explains why the Chinese no longer honor their firstborn with an unusually long name. [398.2]

**8783** Rappaport, Doreen. *The Long-Haired Girl: A Chinese Legend* (PS–3). Illus. by Yang Ming-Yi. 1995, Dial paper $14.89 (0-8037-1412-2). 32pp. A Chinese girl decides to risk her life to help save her people in this folktale. (Rev: BL 1/15/95; SLJ 3/95) [398.2]

**8784** Sanfield, Steve. *Just Rewards, or Who Is That Man in the Moon and What's He Doing Up There Anyway?* (PS–3). Illus. by Emily Lisker. 1996, Orchard LB $15.99 (0-531-08885-5). 32pp. The origin of the belief that there is a man in the moon is retold in this Chinese folktale. (Rev: BL 10/1/96; HB 11–12/96; SLJ 9/96*) [398.2]

**8785** San Souci, Robert D. *The Enchanted Tapestry: A Chinese Folktale* (1–3). Illus. by Laszlo Gal. 1987, Dial paper $4.95 (0-8037-0862-9). 32pp. Gravely ill, a woman sends her sons to retrieve her tapestry, but only the youngest succeeds. (Rev: BL 5/15/87; SLJ 6–7/87) [398.2]

**8786** Torre, Betty L. *The Luminous Pearl: A Chinese Folktale* (PS–3). Illus. by Carol Inouye. 1990, Watts LB $14.99 (0-531-08490-6). 32pp. In this Chinese folktale, only the man who can retrieve a magic pearl will marry the princess. (Rev: BL 10/1/90; SLJ 11/90) [398.2]

**8787** Wang, Rosalind C. *The Magical Starfruit Tree: A Chinese Folktale* (K–2). Illus. by Shao Wei Liu. 1994, Beyond Words $14.95 (0-941831-89-2). 30pp. In this Chinese tale, a stranger rewards a young acrobat for his kindness and punishes a miser for his nastiness. (Rev: BL 7/94) [398.2]

**8788** Wang, Rosalind C. *The Treasure Chest: A Chinese Tale* (PS–3). Illus. by Will Hillenbrand. 1995, Holiday LB $15.95 (0-8234-1114-1). 32pp. In this Chinese tale, a humble peasant gets help from the Ocean King to fight an evil despot. (Rev: BL 6/1–15/95; SLJ 6/95) [398.2]

**8789** Whitfield, Susan. *The Animals of the Chinese Zodiac* (K–3). Illus. by Philippa-Alys Browne. 1998, Crocodile $16.00 (1-56656-236-8). 39pp. This book retells the Buddhist legend of how the order of animals in the Chinese zodiac was detemined. (Rev: SLJ 2/98) [398.2]

**8790** Wilson, Barbara K., reteller. *Wishbones* (K–6). Illus. by Meilo So. 1993, Bradbury paper $14.95 (0-02-793125-0). In this Chinese folktale, a wicked stepmother kills and eats a young girl's magical fish, but its bones continue to help her. (Rev: SLJ 3/94) [398.2]

**8791** Wolkstein, Diane. *The Magic Wings: A Tale from China* (K–3). Illus. by Robert Andrew Parker. 1983, Dutton paper $4.95 (0-525-44275-8). 32pp. A folktale about a group of girls who long to fly in the spring. [398.2]

**8792** Wolkstein, Diane. *White Wave: A Chinese Tale* (K–3). Illus. by Ed Young. 1996, Harcourt $16.00 (0-15-200293-6). In this Chinese folktale, the moon goddess, White Wave, comes to earth as a moon snail to care for a poor farmer. (Rev: SLJ 1/97) [398.2]

**8793** Ye, Ting-xing. *Three Monks, No Water* (K–3). Illus. by Harvey Chan. 1997, Annick LB $16.95 (1-55037-443-5); paper $6.95 (1-55037-442-7). 32pp. This story supposedly explains the origin of the Chinese expression "Three monks, no water," which is used when children try to avoid chores. (Rev: BL 2/1/98; SLJ 12/97) [398.2]

**8794** Yep, Laurence. *The Dragon Prince: A Chinese Beauty and the Beast Tale* (4–6). Illus. by Kam Mak. 1997, HarperCollins LB $14.89 (0-06-024393-7). 32pp. A Chinese fairy tale in which a farmer's life can be saved only if one of his daughters marries a dragon. (Rev: BL 7/97; SLJ 10/97) [398.2]

**8795** Yep, Laurence. *The Junior Thunder Lord* (K–3). Illus. by Robert Van Nutt. 1994, Troll paper $15.95 (0-8167-3454-2). 32pp. Yue's chance kindness toward a stranger helps saves his village from drought in this Chinese folktale. (Rev: BCCB 12/94; BL 11/1/94; SLJ 10/94) [398.2]

**8796** Yep, Laurence. *The Man Who Tricked a Ghost* (K–3). Illus. by Isadore Seltzer. 1993, Troll paper $15.95 (0-8167-3030-X). 32pp. In ancient China, a fearless boy encounters a ghost. (Rev: BL 6/1–15/93*) [398.2]

**8797** Yep, Laurence. *The Shell Woman and the King: A Chinese Folktale* (K–3). Illus. by Yang Ming-Yi. 1993, Dial paper $13.89 (0-8037-1395-9). 32pp. This Chinese fairy tale tells the story of a woman who has the magical powers to turn herself into a seashell. (Rev: BL 7/93) [398.2]

**8798** Yep, Laurence. *Tiger Woman* (PS–4). Illus. by Robert Roth. 1995, BridgeWater paper $15.95 (0-8167-3464-X). In this version of a Shantung folk song, a selfish old woman won't share her food with a beggar. (Rev: SLJ 2/96) [398.2]

**8799** Yolen, Jane. *The Emperor and the Kite* (K–3). Illus. by Ed Young. 1988, Putnam $15.95 (0-399-21499-2). 32pp. Oriental-like paper cuts illustrate this Chinese legend about the unshakable loyalty of the emperor's smallest daughter. First published in 1967. [398.2]

**8800** Young, Ed. *Lon Po Po: A Red-Riding-Hood Story from China* (2–4). Illus. 1989, Putnam $15.95 (0-399-21619-7). 32pp. In this variation of the Red Riding Hood story, Mother visits Grandmother, leaving her 3 children in danger from a marauding wolf. Caldecott Medal winner, 1990. (Rev: BCCB 11/89*; BL 11/15/89; HB 1–2/90*; SLJ 12/89*) [398.2]

**8801** Young, Ed. *The Lost Horse: A Chinese Folktale* (K–3). Illus. 1998, Harcourt $18.00 (0-15-201016-5). 32pp. Every sad or happy event in a Chinese peasant's life brings the same response in this Chinese folktale about a man who accepts his fate stoically. (Rev: BL 3/15/98; SLJ 4/98) [398.2]

**8802** Young, Ed. *Mouse Match: A Chinese Folktale* (PS–2). Illus. 1997, Harcourt $20.00 (0-15-201453-5). 26pp. In this Chinese folktale, a young mouse waits for her doting parents to decide who is the best choice in a husband for her. (Rev: BL 10/15/97*; HB 11–12/97; SLJ 10/97*) [398.2]

**8803** Young, Ed. *Night Visitors* (PS–3). Illus. 1995, Putnam $15.95 (0-399-22731-8). 32pp. Ho Kuan dreams that he has become part of an ant colony in this Chinese folktale. (Rev: BCCB 1/96; BL 9/15/95; SLJ 10/95*) [398.2]

## India

**8804** Beach, Milo Cleveland. *The Adventures of Rama* (4–6). Illus. 1983, Smithsonian Institution $15.00 (0-934686-51-3). 64pp. Tales from the Hindu epic Ramayana. [398.2]

**8805** Birch, David. *The King's Chessboard* (3–5). Illus. by Devis Grebu. 1988, Dial LB $10.89 (0-8037-0367-8); Puffin paper $5.99 (0-14-054880-7). 32pp. A wise man outsmarts a vain king when he is offered a reward. (Rev: BL 5/15/88; SLJ 4/88) [398.2]

**8806** Demi. *One Grain of Rice* (3–6). Illus. 1997, Scholastic $19.95 (0-590-93998-X). 40pp. Rani outwits the rajah to gain food for her people in this Indian folktale. (Rev: BCCB 2/97; BL 3/1/97*; SLJ 3/97*) [398.2]

**8807** Ernst, Judith, reteller. *The Golden Goose King: A Tale Told by the Buddha* (3–6). Illus. by Judith Ernst. 1995, Parvardigar $19.95 (0-9644362-0-5). A Jataka tale about a queen who captures the Golden Goose King, who is actually Buddha. (Rev: BL 9/1/95; SLJ 9/95) [398.2]

**8808** Galdone, Paul. *The Monkey and the Crocodile: A Jataka Tale from India* (K–3). Illus. by author. 1969, Houghton paper $6.95 (0-89919-524-5). 32pp. A crocodile decides he will catch a monkey. [398.2]

**8809** *Heart of Gold* (2–4). Illus. by Rosalyn White. 1989, Dharma paper $6.95 (0-89800-193-5). In this retelling of a Jataka story, a wealthy man gives away all his possessions. Another Jataka story is: *The Rabbit in the Moon* (1989). (Rev: BL 8/89) [294.3]

**8810** Jacobs, Joseph. *Indian Fairy Tales* (3–6). Illus. by John D. Batten. 1969, Dover paper $6.95 (0-486-21828-7). 255pp. A standard collection by the well-known authority. [398.2]

**8811** Jaffrey, Madhur. *Seasons of Splendor: Tales, Myths, and Legends from India* (5–8). Illus. by Michael Foreman. 1985, Puffin paper $7.95 (0-317-62172-6). 128pp. Folktales and family stories as well as accounts of Rama and Krishna. (Rev: BCCB 1/86; BL 1/15/86) [398.2]

**8812** Kajpust, Melissa. *The Peacock's Pride* (PS–2). Illus. by Jo'Anne Kelly. 1997, Hyperion LB $15.49 (0-7868-2233-3). 32pp. In this Indian folktale, a proud, strutting peacock is put in his place by a little bird. (Rev: BL 1/1–15/98) [398.2]

**8813** Martin, Rafe. *The Brave Little Parrot* (K–3). Illus. by Susan Gaber. 1998, Putnam $15.99 (0-399-22825-X). 32pp. As a reward for trying to put out a forest fire, a little parrot is given colored plumage in this Indian jataka tale. (Rev: BL 2/15/98) [298.2]

**8814** Martin, Rafe. *Foolish Rabbit's Big Mistake* (PS–2). Illus. by Ed Young. 1985, Putnam $16.95 (0-399-21178-0). 32pp. A tale from India reminiscent of Chicken Little, about a little rabbit who fears the end of the world and tells everyone that the earth is breaking up. A Jataka tale. (Rev: BCCB 12/85; BL 12/15/85; HB 3–4/86) [398.2]

**8815** Martin, Rafe. *The Monkey Bridge* (1–4). Illus. by Fahimeh Amiri. 1997, Knopf $17.00 (0-679-88106-9). 32pp. A Buddhist tale from India that tells how the monkey king gave his life to protect his tribe from human invaders. (Rev: BL 5/15/97; SLJ 7/97) [398.2]

**8816** Ness, Caroline. *The Ocean of Story: Fairy Tales from India* (4–6). Illus. 1996, Lothrop $17.00 (0-688-13584-6). 128pp. Eighteen fairy tales from India that have been collected from unusual and often obscure source materials. (Rev: BCCB 5/96; BL 4/15/96; SLJ 4/96) [398.2]

**8817** Shepard, Aaron. *The Gifts of Wali Dad* (1–3). Illus. by Daniel San Souci. 1995, Atheneum paper $16.00 (0-684-19445-7). 32pp. Although Wali Dad gains great wealth, he only wants to remain a simple grass cutter in this folktale from India. (Rev: BL 5/1/95; SLJ 8/95) [398.2]

**8818** Shepard, Aaron, reteller. *Savitri: A Tale of Ancient India* (3–6). Illus. by Vera Rosenberry. 1992, Whitman LB $16.95 (0-8075-7251-9). 40pp. In picture book format, the retelling of India's epic poem, the Mahabharata. (Rev: BCCB 3/92; BL 3/15/92; SLJ 5/92) [398.2]

**8819** Souhami, Jessica, reteller. *Rama and the Demon King: An Ancient Tale from India* (K–3). Illus. by Jessica Souhami. 1997, DK Publg. $14.95 (0-7894-2450-9). A retelling of the important incidents in this Hindu epic about the journeys of the exiled Prince Rama, who was accompanied by his wife, Sita, and brother, Lakshman. (Rev: SLJ 9/97) [398.2]

**8820** Wolf, Gita. *The Very Hungry Lion: A Folktale* (PS–1). Illus. by Indrapramit Roy. 1996, Annick $24.95 (1-55037-461-3). 32pp. In this folktale from western India, a lion is too lazy to go out to hunt. (Rev: BL 11/1/96; SLJ 1/97) [398.24]

**8821** Young, Ed. *Seven Blind Mice* (PS–3). Illus. 1992, Putnam $17.99 (0-399-22261-8). 44pp. A stunning picture book illustrating a version of the old Indian folktale about 7 blind men and one elephant. (Rev: BCCB 3/92*; BL 4/1/92*; HB 3–4/92; SLJ 4/92) [398.2]

## Japan

**8822** Bang, Molly. *Dawn* (3–5). Illus. 1983, Morrow paper $3.95 (0-688-10989-6). 32pp. A variation on the Orpheus story via a Japanese tale. [398.2]

**8823** Edmonds, I. G. *Ooka the Wise: Tales of Old Japan* (3–6). Illus. by Sanae Yamazaki. 1994, Linnet LB $16.00 (0-208-02379-8). 96pp. A collection of 17 Japanese folktales featuring the legendary judge Ooka Tadasuke, who is devoted to the cause of justice. (Rev: BL 5/15/94) [398.2]

**8824** Garrison, Christian. *The Dream Eater* (K–2). Illus. by Diane Goode. 1978, Macmillan paper $4.95 (0-689-71058-5). 32pp. Yukio meets a creature who eats bad dreams in this Japanese folktale. [398.2]

**8825** Hamanaka, Sheila. *Screen of Frogs* (K–3). Illus. 1993, Orchard LB $13.99 (0-531-08614-3). 32pp. Rich, spoiled Koji learns a lesson from a huge green frog. (Rev: BL 3/15/93; SLJ 6/93*) [398.2]

**8826** Hamilton, Morse. *Belching Hill* (1–3). Illus. by Forest Rogers. 1997, Greenwillow $15.00 (0-688-14561-2). 32pp. A variation on the Japanese folktale about a little old woman who outsmarts some disgusting monsters. (Rev: BL 4/15/97; SLJ 4/97) [398.2]

**8827** Hedlund, Irene. *Mighty Mountain and the Three Strong Women* (PS–3). Trans. by Judith Elkin. Illus. 1990, Volcano $14.95 (0-912078-86-3). 32pp. A sumo wrestler meets 3 women who surpass him in strength. (Rev: BL 6/1/90; SLJ 10/90) [398.2]

**8828** Hooks, William H. *Peach Boy* (1–3). Illus. by June Otani. 1996, Gareth Stevens LB $18.60 (0-8368-1662-5); Bantam paper $4.50 (0-553-35429-9). 48pp. An easy-to-read version of the Japanese folktale about a boy, born from a peach, who becomes the son of a childless couple. (Rev: BL 2/1/92; SLJ 3/92) [398.2]

**8829** Johnston, Tony. *The Badger and the Magic Fan: A Japanese Folktale* (PS–3). Illus. by Tomie dePaola. 1990, Putnam $13.95 (0-399-21945-5). 32pp. A greedy badger steals the Japanese goblin's magic fan. (Rev: BCCB 4/90; BL 5/1/90*; HB 9–10/90; SLJ 6/90) [398.2]

**8830** Kimmel, Eric A. *The Greatest of All: A Japanese Folktale* (PS–3). Illus. by Giora Carmi. 1991, Holiday LB $15.95 (0-8234-0885-X). 32pp. The father of Chuko Mouse is not happy when she tells him she wants to marry a humble, but handsome, field mouse. (Rev: BL 10/15/91; SLJ 10/91) [398.2]

**8831** Kudler, David. *The Seven Gods of Luck* (PS–3). Illus. by Linda Finch. 1997, Houghton $15.00 (0-395-78830-7). 32pp. In this traditional Japanese tale, as a reward for cleaning the snow off the statues of the Seven Gods of Luck, 2 girls are rewarded with a feast. (Rev: BL 12/15/97; SLJ 10/97) [398.2]

**8832** *Lady Kaguya's Secret: A Japanese Folktale* (3–7). Illus. by Jirina Marton. 1997, Annick $19.95 (1-55037-441-9). 48pp. A foundling grows into a beautiful, bright young woman, but she wonders about her origins in this Japanese folktale. (Rev: BL 1/1–15/98; SLJ 2/98) [398.2]

**8833** Langston, Laura. *The Magic Ear* (2–6). Illus. by Victor Bosson. 1995, Orca $14.95 (1-55143-035-5). Based on a Japanese folktale, this is the story of a simple, honest gardener who is given a magic conch shell with which he can understand the language of animals. (Rev: SLJ 1/96) [398.2]

**8834** Long, Jan F. *The Bee and the Dream: A Japanese Tale* (PS–3). Illus. by Kaoru Ono. 1996, Dutton paper $15.99 (0-525-45287-7). 40pp. In this Japanese folktale, Shin believes that because a bee has flown out of his nose, good fortune will follow. (Rev: BL 7/96; SLJ 7/96) [398.2]

**8835** McCarthy, Ralph F. *The Inch-High Samurai* (K–3). Illus. by Shiro Kasamatsu. 1993, Kodansha $19.95 (4-7700-1758-8). 48pp. Pint-sized Inchy Bo performs some mighty deeds, including fighting an ogre, in this Japanese folktale. (Rev: BL 12/15/93; SLJ 2/94) [398.2]

**8836** McCarthy, Ralph F. *The Moon Princess* (3–6). Illus. by Kancho Oda. Series: Children's Classics. 1993, Kodansha $19.95 (4-7700-1756-1). 48pp. Retellings in verse of 3 Japanese folktales, one about a virtuous old man and his dog, another a Tom Thumb–like character, and another, the title story, about a couple who find a tiny girl inside a bamboo. (Rev: SLJ 2/94) [398.2]

**8837** McDermott, Gerald. *The Stonecutter: A Japanese Folk Tale* (K–3). Illus. by author. 1975, Puffin paper $5.99 (0-14-050289-0). 32pp. The familiar tale of the stonecutter who kept demanding greater power is brilliantly illustrated with colorful, stylized collage paintings. [398.2]

**8838** Merrill, Jean. *The Girl Who Loved Caterpillars: A Twelfth-Century Tale from Japan* (5–8). Illus. by Floyd Cooper. 1992, Putnam $15.95 (0-399-21871-8). 32pp. The story of a young Izumi who has no interest in lute playing or writing poetry but is fascinated with "creepy crawlies" instead. (Rev: BCCB 11/92; BL 9/1/92*; SLJ 9/92) [398.2]

**8839** Mosel, Arlene. *The Funny Little Woman* (PS–4). Illus. by Blair Lent. 1972, Dutton paper $4.95 (0-525-45036-X). 40pp. A Japanese folktale about a little woman whose pursuit of a rice dumpling that falls from her table leads to her capture by wicked people. Caldecott Medal winner, 1973. [398.2]

**8840** Paterson, Katherine. *The Tale of the Mandarin Ducks* (K–4). Illus. by Leo Dillon and Diane Dillon. 1990, Dutton paper $15.99 (0-525-67283-4). 36pp. Because they have helped free a caged duck, a Japanese girl and her beloved are rewarded with freedom from a sentence of death. (Rev: BCCB 9/90*; BL 9/1/90*; HB 11–12/90*; SLJ 10/90*) [398.2]

**8841** Sakade, Florence, ed. *Japanese Children's Favorite Stories* (2–4). Illus. by Yoshio Kurosaki. 1958, Tuttle $16.95 (0-8048-0284-X). 120pp. Twenty folktales traditionally told to Japanese children. [398.2]

**8842** Schroeder, Alan. *Lily and the Wooden Bowl* (1–4). Illus. by Yoriko Ito. 1994, Doubleday $14.95 (0-385-30792-6). In this Japanese folktale, Lily obeys her dying grandmother's request that she always wear a wooden bowl over her head. (Rev: SLJ 12/94) [398.2]

**8843** Snyder, Dianne. *The Boy of the Three-Year Nap* (K–3). Illus. by Allen Say. 1988, Houghton $16.95 (0-395-44090-4). 32pp. In this Japanese folktale adaptation, Taro, who does nothing but eat and sleep, schemes to marry his rich neighbor's daughter. (Rev: BCCB 4/88; BL 4/1/88; HB 5–6/88) [398.2]

**8844** Uchida, Yoshiko. *Magic Listening Cap* (4–6). Illus. by author. 1987, Creative Arts paper $8.95 (0-88739-016-1). 160pp. Japanese folktales retold with charm and simplicity. [398.2]

**8845** Uchida, Yoshiko. *The Magic Purse* (K–3). Illus. by Keiko Narahashi. 1993, Macmillan $15.95 (0-689-50559-0). 32pp. A poor Japanese farmer is rewarded when he carries a message to the parents of a girl who is held captive by the lord of the Black Swamp. (Rev: BL 10/1/93) [398.2]

**8846** Uchida, Yoshiko. *The Wise Old Woman* (K–3). Illus. by Martin Springett. 1994, Macmillan paper $14.95 (0-689-50582-5). 32pp. The wisdom of an old lady, who has been condemned to die because of her age, saves the people of her village in this Japanese folktale. (Rev: BL 11/15/94; SLJ 7/95*) [398.2]

**8847** Waite, Michael P. *Jojofu* (K–2). Illus. by Yoriko Ito. 1996, Lothrop LB $15.93 (0-688-13661-3). 32pp. In this Japanese tale, a dog named Jojofu protects his master during a hunting trip. (Rev: BCCB 10/96; BL 11/15/96; SLJ 10/96) [398.2]

**8848** Watkins, Yoko K. *Tales from the Bamboo Grove* (4–7). Illus. by Jean Tseng and Mou-Sien Tseng. 1992, Macmillan $16.00 (0-02-792525-0). 50pp. Six Japanese folktales heard by the author as a child while living in Korea are retold. (Rev: BCCB 12/92; BL 9/15/92; SLJ 11/92) [398.2]

**8849** Wells, Ruth. *The Farmer and the Poor God: A Folktale from Japan* (PS–2). Illus. by Yoshi. 1996, Simon & Schuster $16.00 (0-689-80214-5). 32pp. A Japanese folktale in which a family blames the Poor God, who lives with them, for their plight. (Rev: BL 4/1/96; SLJ 5/96*) [398.2]

**8850** Williams, Carol Ann. *Tsubu the Little Snail* (K–3). Illus. by Tatsuro Kiuchi. 1995, Simon & Schuster paper $15.00 (0-671-87167-6). 24pp. Love transforms a snail into a handsome young man in this Japanese folktale. (Rev: BL 6/1–15/95) [398.2]

## Southeast Asia

**8851** Coburn, Jewell Reinhart, and Tzexa Cherta Lee, adapt. *Jouanah: A Hmong Cinderella* (K–3). Illus. by Anne S. O'Brien. 1996, Shen's $15.95 (1-885008-01-5). This version of the Cinderella story from the Hmong of Southeast Asia takes place in a peasant village. (Rev: BCCB 12/96; SLJ 3/97) [398.2]

**8852** Ho, Minfong, and Saphan Ros. *Brother Rabbit* (1–4). Illus. by Jennifer Hewitson. 1997, Lothrop LB $15.93 (0-688-12553-0). 32pp. After Brother Rabbit tricks a crocodile into ferrying him across a river, the croc seeks revenge in this Cambodian folktale. (Rev: BCCB 5/97; BL 5/1/97; SLJ 5/97) [398.2]

**8853** Lee, Jeanne M., reteller. *Toad Is the Uncle of Heaven: A Vietnamese Folk Tale* (4–7). Illus. by Jeanne M. Lee. 1985, Holt paper $5.95 (0-8050-1147-1). 32pp. This book tells the story of Toad who collects companions on his way to see the King of Heaven, who makes rain. (Rev: BL 11/1/85; HB 3–4/86) [398.2]

**8854** Meeker, Clare Hodgson. *A Tale of Two Rice Birds: A Folktale from Thailand* (4–8). Illus. by Christine Lamb. 1994, Sasquatch $14.95 (1-57061-008-8). 32pp. Two rice birds are reincarnated as a princess and a farmer's son in this Thai folktale. (Rev: BL 1/15/95; SLJ 11/94) [398.2]

**8855** Spagnoli, Cathy. *Judge Rabbit and the Tree Spirit: A Folktale from Cambodia* (PS–2). Illus. by Nancy Hom. 1991, Children's Book Pr. $14.95 (0-89239-071-9). 32pp. A tree spirit takes the shape of an absent husband. (Rev: BL 9/15/91; SLJ 8/91) [398.2]

**8856** Vuong, Lynette Dyer. *The Brocaded Slipper and Other Vietnamese Tales* (5–7). Illus. by Vo-Dinh Mai. 1982, HarperCollins paper $4.50 (0-06-440440-4). 96pp. Five Vietnamese fairytales, some of which are similar to our own. [398.2]

**8857** Xiong, Blia. *Nine-in-One, Grr! Grr!* (3–6). Adapted by Cathy Spagnoli. Illus. by Nancy Hom. 1993, Children's Book Pr. $14.95 (0-89239-048-4); paper $6.95 (0-89239-110-3). 32pp. In this folktale from Laos, Bird comes up with a trick to prevent the earth from being overpopulated with tigers. A reissue. [398.2]

## Australia and the Pacific Islands

**8858** Bishop, Gavin. *Maui and the Sun: A Maori Tale* (K–3). Illus. 1996, North-South LB $15.88 (1-

55858-578-8). 32pp. A Maori tale about trickster Maui and how he captured the sun. (Rev: BL 5/1/96; SLJ 7/96) [398.]

**8859** Galdone, Paul. *The Turtle and the Monkey: A Philippine Tale* (K–2). Illus. by author. 1990, Houghton paper $6.95 (0-395-54425-4). 32pp. Turtle asks monkey to help him save a banana tree. [398.2]

**8860** Gittins, Anne. *Tales from the South Pacific Islands* (4–6). Illus. by Frank Rocca. 1977, Stemmer $12.95 (0-916144-02-X). 96pp. Twenty-two folktales from such places as Fiji and Samoa in which the sea and its creatures play prominent roles. [398.3]

**8861** Lattimore, Deborah N. *Punga: The Goddess of Ugly* (K–3). Illus. 1993, Harcourt $14.95 (0-15-292862-6). 32pp. In this Maori legend, a girl tricks the Goddess of Ugly to free her twin sister. (Rev: BL 12/1/93; SLJ 12/93) [398.2]

**8862** Morin, Paul. *Animal Dreaming: An Aboriginal Dreamtime Story* (3–6). Illus. by author. 1998, Harcourt $16.00 (0-15-200054-2). A folktale from Australia that tells how 3 animals — a kangaroo, a turtle, and an emu — try to bring peace to a warring world. (Rev: SLJ 3/98) [398.2]

**8863** Roth, Susan L. *The Biggest Frog in Australia* (K–2). Illus. 1996, Simon & Schuster paper $15.00 (0-689-80490-3). 30pp. A parched frog swallows all the water on the continent and in the rain clouds to slake his great thirst. (Rev: BL 6/1–15/96; SLJ 6/96*) [398.2]

**8864** Trezise, Percy, and Dick Roughsey. *Turramulh the Giant Quinkin* (3–6). Illus. 1988, Stevens LB $12.95 (1-55532-947-0). 32pp. An evil giant blunders when he pursues 2 children in this Australian aboriginal tale. (Rev: BL 2/15/89; SLJ 2/89) [398.2]

**8865** Wardlaw, Lee. *Punia and the King of Sharks: A Hawaiian Folktale* (K–3). Illus. by Felipe Davalos. 1997, Dial paper $14.89 (0-8037-1683-4). 32pp. A Polynesian boy is able to outwit a school of sharks in this Hawaiian folktale. (Rev: BCCB 2/97; BL 12/1/96; SLJ 1/97) [398.2]

## Europe

### Central and Eastern Europe

**8866** Bodnar, Judit Z. *A Wagonload of Fish* (PS–2). Illus. by Alexi Natchev. 1996, Lothrop LB $14.93 (0-688-12173-X). 32pp. In this Hungarian folktale, a nagging wife demands that her husband bring her some fish to eat. (Rev: BL 4/1/96; SLJ 5/96) [398.21]

**8867** Brett, Jan. *The Mitten* (PS–2). Illus. 1990, Putnam $15.95 (0-399-21920-X). In this Ukrainian folktale, Nicki loses in the snow one of the mittens that his grandmother knit him. (Rev: BCCB 12/89; BL 9/15/89*; HB 11–12/89; SLJ 11/89) [398.2]

**8868** Early, Margaret. *William Tell* (K–4). Illus. 1991, Abrams $17.95 (0-8109-3854-5). 32pp. An enchanting, full-color retelling of the story of this famous and good man who triumphed over evil. (Rev: BCCB 2/92; BL 11/15/91*; HB 1–2/92; SLJ 1/91*) [398.2]

**8869** Fisher, Leonard Everett. *Kinderdike* (K–3). Illus. 1994, Macmillan paper $15.95 (0-02-735365-6). 32pp. A Dutch folktale about how villagers found the strength to rebuild after a flood destroyed their homes. (Rev: BL 1/1/94; SLJ 4/94) [398.2]

**8870** Fisher, Leonard Everett. *William Tell* (1–3). Illus. 1996, Farrar $16.00 (0-374-38436-3). 32pp. The legend of William Tell and his struggle against tyranny are well retold in this attractive picture book. (Rev: BL 2/15/96; SLJ 3/96*) [398]

**8871** Hogrogian, Nonny. *One Fine Day* (K–3). Illus. by author. 1971, Macmillan $16.00 (0-02-744000-1); paper $5.99 (0-02-043620-3). 32pp. Based on an Armenian folktale, this cumulative story is ideal for reading aloud. Caldecott Medal winner, 1972. [398.2]

**8872** Kimmel, Eric A. *Sirko and the Wolf* (K–3). Illus. by Robert Sauber. 1997, Holiday LB $15.95 (0-8234-1257-1). 32pp. When a dog grows too old to be useful, he strikes a bargain with a wolf in this Ukrainian folktale. (Rev: BL 9/15/97; SLJ 11/97) [398.2]

**8873** Kimmel, Eric A. *The Valiant Red Rooster* (K–3). Illus. by Katya Arnold. 1995, Holt $15.95 (0-8050-2781-5). 32pp. A rooster threatens to crow nonstop until a greedy sultan returns his diamond button in this Hungarian folktale. (Rev: BCCB 5/95; BL 6/1–15/95; SLJ 5/95) [398.2]

**8874** Olson, Arielle North. *Noah's Cats and the Devil's Fire* (PS–3). Illus. by Barry Moser. n.d., Smithmark $3.98 (0-8317-2469-2). 32pp. A cheerful variation on the biblical story telling of how a devil sneaks onto the ark disguised as a mouse. (Rev: BCCB 3/92; BL 2/1/92; SLJ 5/92) [333.91]

**8875** Peters, Andrew. *Salt Is Sweeter Than Gold* (1–3). Illus. by Zdenka Kabatova-Taborska. 1994, Shambhala $16.00 (1-56957-933-4). 32pp. A Czech folktale in which a king asks his 3 daughters how much they love him. (Rev: BL 1/1/95) [398.2]

**8876** San Souci, Robert D., reteller. *A Weave of Words* (2–5). Illus. by Raul Colon. 1998, Orchard LB $16.99 (0-531-33053-2). In this Armenian tale, an imprisoned king uses his weaving skills to communicate with his wife. (Rev: SLJ 3/98) [398.2]

**8877** Seredy, Kate. *The White Stag* (5–8). Illus. by author. 1937, Puffin paper $4.99 (0-14-031258-7). 96pp. A legendary account of the westward migration of the Hungarians to new lands. Newbery Medal, 1938. [398.2]

**8878** Tresselt, Alvin, ed. *The Mitten* (K–2). Illus. by Yaroslava Mills. 1964, Lothrop LB $14.93 (0-688-51053-1); paper $4.95 (0-688-09238-1). 30pp. An old Ukrainian folktale about a little boy and his lost mitten. [398.2]

**8879** Vojtech, Anna, and Philemon Sturges. *Marushka and the Month Brothers* (K–3). Illus. 1996, North-South LB $15.88 (1-55858-629-6). 32pp. In this Czech folktale, a young girl outwits her wicked stepmother and stepsister with the help of the 12 Month Brothers. (Rev: BCCB 3/97; BL 10/15/96; SLJ 11/96) [398.2]

**8880** Walker, Barbara K., ed. *A Treasury of Turkish Folktales for Children* (4–7). 1988, Shoe String LB $22.50 (0-208-02206-6). 155pp. A witty collection interspersed with riddles. (Rev: BL 10/15/88; SLJ 10/88) [398.2]

## France

**8881** Brett, Jan, reteller. *Beauty and the Beast* (PS–3). Illus. 1989, Houghton $16.00 (0-89919-497-4). 32pp. A smooth, brief retelling of the old classic. (Rev: BCCB 12/89; BL 10/1/89; SLJ 11/89) [398.2]

**8882** Brown, Marcia. *Stone Soup* (1–4). Illus. by author. 1979, Macmillan $16.00 (0-684-92296-7); paper $5.99 (0-689-71103-4). 48pp. An old French tale about 3 soldiers who make soup from stones. [398.2]

**8883** DeFelice, Cynthia, and Mary DeMarsh. *Three Perfect Peaches* (K–2). Illus. by Irene Trivas. 1995, Orchard LB $16.99 (0-531-08722-0). 32pp. In this French folktale, a young farmboy claims the hand of a princess he helped save from death. (Rev: BCCB 4/95; BL 1/15/95; SLJ 4/95) [398.2]

**8884** Early, Margaret. *Sleeping Beauty* (1–4). Illus. 1993, Abrams $17.95 (0-8109-3835-9). 32pp. A retelling of the Perrault classic, with dramatic illustrations. (Rev: BL 12/1/93; SLJ 1/94) [398]

**8885** Huck, Charlotte. *Toads and Diamonds* (K–3). Illus. by Anita Lobel. 1996, Greenwillow LB $15.93 (0-688-13681-8). 32pp. A downtrodden girl is rewarded for her kindness in this retelling of a folktale. (Rev: BCCB 1/97; BL 11/1/96*; HB 11–12/96; SLJ 9/96) [398.2]

**8886** Kimmel, Eric A. *Three Sacks of Truth: A Story from France* (PS–3). Illus. by Robert Rayevsky. 1993, Holiday LB $15.95 (0-8234-0921-X). 32pp. In this French folktale, a king promises his daughter to the man who can bring him the perfect peach. (Rev: BCCB 7–8/93; BL 4/15/93; SLJ 7/93) [398.2]

**8887** Kirsten, Lincoln, adapt. *Puss in Boots* (K–3). Illus. by Alain Vaes. 1994, Little, Brown paper $6.95 (0-316-89501-6). 32pp. Full-color paintings highlight this retelling of Perrault's classic tale. (Rev: BCCB 4/92*; BL 5/15/92; SLJ 4/92*) [398.2]

**8888** McGovern, Ann, adapt. *Stone Soup* (PS–1). Illus. by Winslow Pels. 1986, Scholastic paper $2.99 (0-590-41602-2). 32pp. The old story of the young man who asks for food and is refused by the old woman, then he asks her for a stone. (Rev: BCCB 2/87; BL 10/15/86; SLJ 11/86) [398.2]

**8889** Mayer, Marianna. *Beauty and the Beast* (3–5). Illus. by author. 1987, Simon & Schuster paper $6.95 (0-689-71151-4). 48pp. A fine retelling made memorable by dazzling pictures. Another version is: *Beauty and the Beast* by Deborah Apy, illus. by Michael Hague (1995, Henry Holt). [398.2]

**8890** Perrault, Charles. *Cinderella* (2–3). Retold by Amy Ehrlich. Illus. by Susan Jeffers. 1993, Puffin paper $4.95 (0-8037-0830-0). 32pp. Another interpretation of the famous classic. (Rev: BCCB 10/85; BL 10/15/85) [398.2]

**8891** Perrault, Charles. *Cinderella* (PS–3). Retold by Barbara Karlin. Illus. by James Marshall. 1992, Little, Brown paper $5.95 (0-316-48303-6). 32pp. This rendition is filled with earthy humor. (Rev: BCCB 4/89; BL 5/1/89; SLJ 5/89) [398.2]

**8892** Perrault, Charles. *The Complete Fairy Tales of Charles Perrault* (4–6). Trans. by Neil Philip and Nicoletta Simborowski. Illus. by Sally Holmes. 1993, Clarion $18.95 (0-395-57002-6). 156pp. Eleven tales by Perrault, newly translated and illustrated with watercolors and printed with fine historical notes. (Rev: BL 11/1/93; SLJ 9/93) [398]

**8893** Perrault, Charles. *Perrault's Fairy Tales* (4–6). Illus. by Gustave Dore. 1969, Dover paper $6.95 (0-486-22311-6). 117pp. A classic edition with illustrations by the French master. [398.2]

**8894** Perrault, Charles. *Puss in Boots* (PS–1). Illus. by Lorinda Bryan Cauley. 1986, Harcourt $13.95 (0-15-264227-7). 32pp. Sly Puss comes to life in this old tale. (Rev: BCCB 12/86; BL 9/15/86; SLJ 12/86) [398.2]

**8895** Perrault, Charles. *Puss in Boots* (K–3). Illus. by Paul Galdone. 1983, Houghton paper $6.95 (0-89919-192-4). 32pp. A favorite French folktale. [398.2]

**8896** Perrault, Charles. *Puss in Boots* (K–4). Illus. by Fred Marcellino. 1990, Farrar $16.00 (0-374-36160-6). 32pp. A handsomely illustrated version of this classic tale. (Rev: BCCB 12/90; BL 12/1/90*; HB 3–4/91*; SLJ 1/91) [398.2]

**8897** Perrault, Charles. *The Sleeping Beauty* (K–2). Adapted by Jane Yolen. Illus. by Ruth Sanderson. 1986, Knopf $12.95 (0-394-55433-7). 240pp. An ornate appearance distinguishes this rendition of the classic tale. (Rev: BL 1/1/87) [398.2]

**8898** Roth, Susan L. *Brave Martha and the Dragon* (PS–3). Illus. 1996, Dial paper $14.89 (0-8037-1853-5). 32pp. A reworking of a French folktale concerning a confrontation between young Martha and a dragon. (Rev: BL 8/96; SLJ 8/96) [398.2]

## Germany

**8899** Bell, Anthea. *Jack in Luck* (PS–2). Illus. by Eve Tharlet. 1992, Picture Book paper $14.95 (0-88708-249-1). 32pp. Winsome watercolors highlight this retelling of the classic tale about a simple lad who starts with a fortune and goes downhill from there. (Rev: BL 1/15/93; SLJ 4/93) [398]

**8900** Berenzy, Alix. *Rapunzel* (K–3). Illus. 1995, Holt $15.95 (0-8050-1283-4). 32pp. The classic story of the fair-haired beauty imprisoned in a tower is retold with handsome illustrations. (Rev: BL 10/15/95; SLJ 12/95) [398.2]

**8901** de la Mare, Walter. *The Turnip* (1–4). Illus. by Kevin Hawkes. 1992, Godine $18.95 (0-87923-934-4). 32pp. Based on a Grimm brothers tale, the story of a good but poor man with an enormous turnip and his greedy, rich half-brother. (Rev: BL 11/15/92; HB 1–2/93; SLJ 12/92) [398.2]

**8902** Gay, Marie-Louise, adapt. *Rumpelstiltskin* (PS–2). Illus. by Marie-Louise Gay. 1997, Groundwood $15.95 (0-88899-279-3). This childlike version of the tale will appeal to youngsters. (Rev: SLJ 11/97) [389.2]

**8903** Geringer, Laura. *The Seven Ravens* (1–4). Illus. by Edward S. Gazsi. 1994, HarperCollins LB $15.89 (0-06-023553-5). 32pp. A new version of the Grimm tale about a girl who tries to rescue her 7 brothers, who have been turned into ravens. (Rev: BL 9/1/94; SLJ 12/94) [398.21]

**8904** Grimm Brothers. *The Brave Little Tailor* (K–4). Retold by Anthea Bell. Illus. by Eve Tharlet. 1989, Picture Book paper $14.95 (0-88708-091-X). A charming retelling of the folktale about a fearless tailor and his encounter with a giant. (Rev: SLJ 9/89) [398.2]

**8905** Grimm Brothers. *The Classic Grimm's Fairy Tales* (K–3). Retold by Louise B. Egan. Illus. 1989, Courage Books $10.98 (0-89471-768-5). 56pp. Ten of the most famous tales from Grimm, including *Snow White, Rapunzel,* and *Rumpelstiltskin,* are retold in this handsome volume. (Rev: SLJ 3/90) [398.2]

**8906** Grimm Brothers. *The Complete Grimm's Fairy Tales* (4–6). Illus. by Josef Scharl. 1974, Pantheon paper $18.00 (0-394-70930-6). Based on Margaret Hunt's translation, this has become the standard edition of these perennial favorites. [398.2]

**8907** Grimm Brothers. *Dear Mili* (1–3). Illus. by Maurice Sendak. 1988, Farrar $16.95 (0-374-31762-3). 40pp. A mother sends her only child into the forest to escape the war that is raging. (Rev: BCCB 11/88; BL 11/1/88; SLJ 11/88) [398.2]

**8908** Grimm Brothers. *The Devil with the Three Golden Hairs* (K–5). Illus. by Nonny Hogrogian. 1983, Knopf LB $10.99 (0-394-95560-9). 40pp. In order to keep his princess bride, a young man must collect 3 golden hairs from the devil's head. [398.2]

**8909** Grimm Brothers. *The Elves and the Shoemaker* (PS–K). Retold and illus. by Paul Galdone. 1984, Houghton paper $6.95 (0-89919-422-2). 32pp. A poor shoemaker is visited by elves at night. [398.2]

**8910** Grimm Brothers. *The Fisherman and His Wife* (2–4). Adapted by Eric Metaxas. Illus. by Diana Bryan. 1991, Rabbit Ears $19.95 (0-88708-123-1). Unusual illustrations with cutout silhouettes adorn this age-old story. (Rev: SLJ 9/91) [398.2]

**8911** Grimm Brothers. *The Fisherman and His Wife* (K–3). Illus. by Alan Marks. 1987, Farrar paper $6.95 (0-374-42326-1). 28pp. A lyrical translation of the well-known tale of the simple fisherman and his demanding wife. (Rev: BL 6/15/89) [398.2]

**8912** Grimm Brothers. *The Fisherman and His Wife* (2–3). Retold by John Warren Stewig. Illus. by Margot Tomes. 1988, Holiday LB $13.95 (0-8234-0714-4). 32pp. The old tale of the fisherman who must face his wife's demands. Another recommended edition is: Illus. by Margot Zemach (1987, Farrar). (Rev: BL 11/1/88; SLJ 12/88) [398.2]

**8913** Grimm Brothers. *The Frog Prince: Or, Iron Henry* (2–3). Trans. by Naomi Lewis. Illus. by Binette Schroeder. 1989, North-South $15.95 (1-55858-015-8). 32pp. Fancy special effects highlight this retelling of the classic tale. (Rev: BL 1/15/90; HB 1–2/90; SLJ 12/89) [398.2]

**8914** Grimm Brothers. *Hansel and Gretel* (K–3). Illus. by Susan Jeffers. 1980, Dial LB $14.89 (0-8037-3491-3); Puffin paper $4.95 (0-8037-0318-X). 32pp. A fine retelling of the classic tale. [398.2]

**8915** Grimm Brothers. *Household Stories of the Brothers Grimm* (4–7). Illus. by Walter Crane. n.d., Dover paper $6.95 (0-486-21080-4). 269pp. First published in the United States in 1883. [398.2]

**8916** Grimm Brothers. *King Grisly-Beard* (K–3). Illus. by Maurice Sendak. 1973, Farrar $14.00 (0-374-34133-8); paper $2.95 (0-374-44049-2). Lovely humorous pictures make this a delightful picture book version of the folktale. [398.2]

**8917** Grimm Brothers. *Little Brother and Little Sister* (K–3). Trans. by Anthea Bell. Illus. by Bernadette Watts. 1996, North-South LB $15.88 (1-55858-589-3). 26pp. A variation on the Hansel and Gretel story that features a wicked stepmother and her ugly one-eyed daughter. (Rev: BL 5/15/96; SLJ 5/96) [398.2]

**8918** Grimm Brothers. *Nibble Nibble Mousekin* (K–3). Illus. by Joan Walsh Anglund. 1962, Harcourt $10.95 (0-15-257400-X); paper $4.95 (0-15-665588-8). 32pp. A version of the Hansel and Gretel story. [398.2]

**8919** Grimm Brothers. *Rapunzel* (1–4). Illus. by Trina S. Hyman. 1982, Holiday LB $16.95 (0-8234-0454-4); paper $5.95 (0-8234-0652-0). 32pp. The famous tale of the captive princess and her fabulous hair. Another version is: Illus. by Michael Hague (1984, Creative Ed.). [398.2]

**8920** Grimm Brothers. *Rapunzel* (K–3). Trans. by Anthea Bell. Illus. by Maja Dusikov. 1997, North-South LB $15.88 (1-55858-685-7). 25pp. A fine retelling of the classic fairy tale, with exquisite artwork. (Rev: BL 8/97) [398.2]

**8921** Grimm Brothers. *Rumpelstiltskin* (PS–1). Illus. by Paul Galdone. 1985, Houghton $16.00 (0-89919-266-1); paper $5.95 (0-395-52599-3). 32pp. Bold drawings highlight this straightfoward version of the little man who spins straw into gold. Another fine edition is: Illus. by John Wallner (1984, Prentice). (Rev: BL 6/1/ 5; SLJ 8/85) [398.2]

**8922** Grimm Brothers. *Rumpelstiltskin* (PS–2). Retold and illus. by Paul O. Zelinsky. 1986, Dutton paper $15.99 (0-525-44265-0). 40pp. Closeups and much detail in the illustrations highlight the retelling of this old favorite. (Rev: BCCB 10/86; BL 9/1/86; SLJ 10/86) [398.2]

**8923** Grimm Brothers. *The Seven Ravens* (K–4). Trans. by Anthea Bell. Illus. by Henriette Sauvant. 1995, North-South LB $15.88 (1-55858-459-5). 28pp. In this classic story from the Grimm Brothers, a young girl tries to break the enchantment that has turned her brothers into ravens. (Rev: BCCB 1/96; BL 2/1/96; SLJ 2/96) [398.2]

**8924** Grimm Brothers. *The Shoemaker and the Elves* (K–2). Illus. by Adrienne Adams. 1982, Evanescent $60.00 (0-945303-04-1). 16pp. A favorite German tale illustrated with soft watercolors. [398.2]

**8925** Grimm Brothers. *The Shoemaker and the Elves* (K–2). Retold and illus. by Ilse Plume. 1991, Harcourt $14.95 (0-15-274050-3). This folktale is relocated to Renaissance Italy, but the plot is the same except that the elves now number 4. (Rev: SLJ 1/92) [398.2]

**8926** Grimm Brothers. *The Six Servants* (1–3). Trans. by Anthea Bell. Illus. by Sergei Goloshapov. 1996, North-South LB $15.88 (1-55858-476-5). 32pp. A prince uses 6 men with magical powers to help him win the hand of a princess. (Rev: BCCB 6/96; BL 6/1–15/96; SLJ 6/96) [398.2]

**8927** Grimm Brothers. *Snow White and Rose Red* (2–3). Retold and illus. by Bernadette Watts. 1988, North-South $14.95 (1-55858-054-9). 32pp. An oversize format for this retelling of the story of 2 good sisters and how they free a prince from enchantment. (Rev: BL 4/1/88; SLJ 9/88) [398.2]

**8928** Grimm Brothers. *Snow White and the Seven Dwarves* (1–4). Trans. and adapted by Anthea Bell. Illus. by Chihiro Iwasaki. 1991, Picture Book $15.95 (0-88708-012-X). 40pp. A good translation and light-hearted artwork highlight this interpretation of the classic tale. (Rev: BL 1/1/86; SLJ 3/86) [398.2]

**8929** Grimm Brothers. *The Three Feathers* (5–8). Illus. by Eleonore Schmid. 1984, Creative Ed. LB $13.95 (0-87191-941-9). 32pp. A version for older readers that is faithful to the original. [398.2]

**8930** Grimm Brothers. *The Three Languages* (3–5). Illus. by Ivan Chermayeff. 1984, Creative Ed. LB $13.95 (0-87191-940-0). 32pp. The tale of the seemingly foolish son who ends up as Pope of Rome. [398.2]

**8931** Grimm Brothers. *Twelve Dancing Princesses* (PS–4). Retold by Marianna Mayer. Illus. by Kinuko Craft. 1989, Morrow LB $15.93 (0-688-02026-7). 40pp. A graceful retelling of the classic tale. (Rev: BL 3/15/89) [398.2]

**8932** Grimm Brothers. *The Twelve Dancing Princesses* (3–5). Trans. by Anthea Bell. Illus. by Dorothee Duntze. 1995, North-South LB $16.88 (1-55858-217-7). 32pp. A delightful translation of the story about the princesses who dance the night away. (Rev: BL 2/1/96; SLJ 1/96) [398.2]

**8933** Grimm Brothers. *The Water of Life: A Tale from the Brothers Grimm* (PS–3). Retold by Barbara Rogasky. Illus. by Trina S. Hyman. 1986, Holiday LB $15.95 (0-8234-0552-4). 40pp. Three brothers journey to find the water of life for their ailing father. (Rev: BCCB 11/86; BL 9/15/86; HB 3–4/87) [398.2]

**8934** Grimm Brothers. *The Wolf and the Seven Little Kids* (PS–3). Illus. by Bernadette Watts. 1995, North-South LB $15.88 (1-55858-446-3). 28pp. Even though her kids have been eaten by the wicked wolf, ingenious Mother Goat is able to save them. (Rev: BL 1/1–15/96; SLJ 1/96) [398.2]

**8935** Hodges, Margaret. *The Hero of Bremen* (3–6). Illus. by Charles Mikolaycak. 1993, Holiday LB $16.95 (0-8234-0934-1). 32pp. In this German folktale, a disabled cobbler is helped by the ghost of Roland, the legendary knight who saved the city of Bremen centuries before. (Rev: BCCB 10/93; BL 10/15/93; HB 11–12/93; SLJ 10/93) [398.2]

**8936** Hoffman, E. T. A. *The Nutcracker* (4–6). Trans. by Ralph Manheim. Illus. by Maurice Sendak. 1984, Crown paper $20.00 (0-517-58659-2). 120pp. A brilliant, new rendition of this favorite story. [398.2]

**8937** Hoffman, E. T. A. *The Strange Child* (3–5). Adapted by Anthea Bell. Illus. by Lisbeth Zwerger. 1984, Picture Book paper $16.95 (0-907234-60-7). 28pp. A reworking of the Hoffman story of 2 children who fall under magic spells. [398.2]

**8938** Holden, Robert. *The Pied Piper of Hamelin* (PS–4). Illus. by Drahos Zak. 1998, Houghton $15.00 (0-395-89918-4). 32pp. A brilliant version of this folktale in which both the rats and the residents of Hamelin, Germany are equally ugly. (Rev: BL 3/1/98*) [398.2]

**8939** Kajpust, Melissa. *A Dozen Silk Diapers: A Christmas Story* (PS–2). Illus. by Veselina Tomova. 1993, Hyperion LB $14.49 (1-56282-457-0). 32pp. In this German folktale, a young spider who has come to visit the child Jesus falls into the manger. (Rev: BL 9/1/93) [598.2]

**8940** Kimmel, Eric A. *The Four Gallant Sisters* (PS–3). Illus. by Tatyana Yuditskaya. 1992, Holt $15.95 (0-8050-1901-4). 32pp. Adapted from the Grimm brothers stories, this is a feminist fairy tale about sisters who disguise themselves as men to find work and independence. (Rev: BL 5/1/92; SLJ 5/92) [398.2]

**8941** Kimmel, Eric A. *The Goose Girl: A Story from the Brothers Grimm* (4–6). Illus. by Robert Sauber. 1995, Holiday LB $15.95 (0-8234-1074-9). 32pp. A retelling of the Brothers Grimm tale of the young princess who is cheated out of her birthright by a greedy serving girl. (Rev: BL 10/15/95; SLJ 10/95) [398.2]

**8942** Kimmel, Eric A. *Iron John* (K–4). Illus. by Trina S. Hyman. 1994, Holiday LB $16.95 (0-8234-1073-0). 32pp. An adaptation of a Grimms tale about Prince Walter, who was Iron John in the forest and breaks a spell that has been cast over him. (Rev: BCCB 12/94; BL 11/1/94; SLJ 12/94) [398.2]

**8943** Latimer, Jim. *The Irish Piper* (3–5). Illus. by John O'Brien. 1991, Macmillan $13.95 (0-684-19130-X). 32pp. A retelling of this legend combines fantasy and contemporary nonsense in a medieval setting. (Rev: BCCB 1/92; BL 1/1/91*; SLJ 12/91) [398.2]

**8944** Marshall, James, reteller. *Hansel and Gretel* (K–3). Illus. 1990, Puffin paper $5.99 (0-14-050836-8). A retelling of the famous story with innovative, often humorous, illustrations. (Rev: SLJ 12/90*) [398.2]

**8945** Marshall, James. *Red Riding Hood* (PS–2). Illus. by author. 1987, Dial LB $10.89 (0-8037-0345-7); Puffin paper $4.95 (0-8037-1054-2). 32pp. A rather homely Red Riding Hood and the wolf are comic figures in this rendition. (Rev: BL 9/1/87; HB 11–12/87; SLJ 9/87) [398.2]

**8946** Ray, Jane, reteller. *Hansel and Gretel* (K–3). Illus. by Jane Ray. 1997, Candlewick $15.99 (0-7636-0358-9). A graceful retelling of this familiar German folktale. (Rev: BL 12/1/97; SLJ 11/97) [398.2]

**8947** Ray, Jane. *The Twelve Dancing Princesses* (K–3). Illus. 1996, Dutton paper $15.99 (0-525-45595-7). 32pp. A delightful, richly illustrated retelling of the classic Grimms' fairy tale. (Rev: BL 10/1/96*; SLJ 10/96) [398.2]

**8948** Ross, Tony, reteller. *Hansel and Gretel* (K–3). Illus. 1990, Trafalgar $15.95 (0-86264-210-8). Humorous, imaginative details are added to the famous tale. (Rev: SLJ 8/90) [398.2]

**8949** Sanderson, Ruth. *The Twelve Dancing Princesses* (K–4). Illus. 1990, Little, Brown $15.95 (0-316-77017-5). 32pp. The mystery of how slippers are worn to shreds each night is retold in this fine version of the German folktale. (Rev: BL 3/1/90; SLJ 6/90) [398.2]

**8950** Shulevitz, Uri. *The Golden Goose* (PS–3). Illus. 1995, Farrar $16.00 (0-374-32695-9). 32pp. When he aids an old man that his brothers have shunned, a simpleton is rewarded with the gift of a gold-feathered goose in this tale from the Grimm Brothers. (Rev: BCCB 1/96; BL 11/15/95; SLJ 12/95) [398.2]

**8951** Vande Velde, Vivian. *Tales from the Brothers Grimm and the Sisters Weird* (4–8). Illus. by Brad Weinman. Series: Jane Yolen Books. 1995, Harcourt $17.00 (0-15-200220-0). 128pp. Using a role-reversal technique, the author examines the nature of good and evil in some of the standard tales from the Brothers Grimm. (Rev: BCCB 10/95; SLJ 1/96) [398.2]

**8952** Vozar, David. *Rapunzel: A Happenin' Rap* (PS–2). Illus. by Betsy Lewin. 1998, Doubleday $15.95 (0-385-32314-X). 32pp. The Rapunzel story is told as rap using an urban setting and contemporary characters. (Rev: BL 1/1–15/98) [398.2]

**8953** Wallace, Ian. *Hansel and Gretel* (2–4). Illus. 1996, Douglas & McIntyre $14.95 (0-88899-212-2). 32pp. A scary retelling in a contemporary setting of the famous Grimms' folktale. (Rev: BL 6/1–15/96; SLJ 5/96) [398.2]

**8954** Wegman, William, et al. *Little Red Riding Hood* (2–4). Illus. 1993, Hyperion LB $17.49 (1-56282-417-1). 40pp. The famous fairy tale is retold with some new plot twists and using the author's weimaraners dressed in clothes as models. (Rev: BL 12/1/93; SLJ 3/94) [398.21]

**8955** Yolen, Jane. *The Musicians of Bremen: A Tale from Germany* (PS–2). Illus. by John Segal. 1996, Simon & Schuster paper $14.00 (0-689-80501-2). 32pp. The popular German folktale is retold with some humorous twists. (Rev: BL 7/96; HB 5–6/96; SLJ 7/96) [398.2]

**8956** Zelinsky, Paul O. *Rapunzel* (3–5). Illus. 1997, Dutton $16.99 (0-525-45607-4). 48pp. Rich oil paintings illustrate this tale of the enduring power of love. Caldecott Medal winner, 1998. (Rev: BL 11/15/97*; SLJ 11/97*) [398.2]

**8957** Zemach, Margot. *The Three Wishes: An Old Story* (PS–2). Illus. by author. 1986, Farrar $16.00 (0-374-37529-1). 32pp. The story of a poor woodcutter and his wife who are granted 3 wishes — and squander them. (Rev: BCCB 3/87; BL 1/1/87; SLJ 12/86) [398.2]

## Great Britain and Ireland

**8958** Barton, Byron. *The Little Red Hen* (PS–2). Illus. 1993, HarperCollins LB $14.89 (0-06-021676-X). 32pp. A new interpretation of this favorite story of the industrious hen, with appealing illustrations. (Rev: BL 5/1/93; SLJ 7/93) [398.2]

**8959** Barton, Byron. *The Three Bears* (PS). Illus. 1991, HarperCollins LB $14.89 (0-06-020424-9). 32pp. For the very young, this is a retelling of the story of Goldilocks and the Three Bears. (Rev: BL 1/1/91; SLJ 11/91) [398.2]

**8960** Behan, Brendan. *The King of Ireland's Son* (3–5). Illus. by P. J. Lynch. 1997, Orchard $16.95 (0-531-09549-5). 32pp. A rich retelling of the Irish folktale about 3 princes who set out to find the origin of the heavenly music that is heard in their land. (Rev: BCCB 4/97; BL 4/15/97; SLJ 6/97) [398.2]

**8961** Briggs, Katharine. *An Encyclopedia of Fairies, Hobgoblins, Brownies, Bogies, and Other Supernatural Creatures* (4–8). Illus. 1978, Pantheon paper $20.00 (0-394-73467-X). An eclectic encyclopedia of British fairy lore. [398.2]

**8962** Brown, Marcia. *Dick Whittington and His Cat* (K–3). Illus. by author. 1988, Macmillan $16.00 (0-684-18998-4). 32pp. A reissue of a Caldecott Honor Book published in 1950 about the boy who went to London to seek his fortune. [398.2]

**8963** *The Cock, the Mouse, and the Little Red Hen* (PS–2). Illus. by Graham Percy. 1992, Candlewick $14.95 (1-56402-008-8). 32pp. The little red hen story retold with the added ingredient of 5 foxes. (Rev: BL 2/1/92) [398.2]

**8964** Cohen, Barbara. *Robin Hood and Little John* (1–4). Illus. by David Ray. 1995, Putnam $15.95 (0-399-22732-6). 32pp. The story of how Robin Hood made friends with the giant Little John, who later became his second-in-command. (Rev: BL 12/15/95; SLJ 11/95) [398.2]

**8965** Colum, Padraic, ed. *A Treasury of Irish Folk-lore* (6–8). 1969, Outlet $12.99 (0-517-42046-5). 640pp. A marvelous collection of traditional Irish tales. [398.2]

**8966** Cooper, Susan, reteller. *The Selkie Girl* (3–5). Illus. by Warwick Hutton. 1986, Macmillan paper $4.95 (0-689-71467-X). 32pp. A Scottish tale about a seal who sheds its skin and takes human form on land. (Rev: BL 9/15/86; HB 11–12/86; SLJ 11/86) [398.2]

**8967** Cooper, Susan, reteller. *The Silver Cow: A Welsh Tale* (K–4). Illus. by Warwick Hutton. 1991, Simon & Schuster paper $5.99 (0-689-71512-9). 32pp. A greedy farmer inherits a silver cow from his son, who received it for his harp playing. [398.2]

**8968** Cooper, Susan. *Tam Lin* (3–6). Illus. by Warwick Hutton. 1991, Macmillan $14.95 (0-689-50505-1). 32pp. A retelling of the old Scottish ballad with ethereal illustrations. (Rev: BL 2/15/91; HB 5–6/91; SLJ 5/91) [398.2]

**8969** Creswick, Paul. *Robin Hood* (6–8). Illus. by N. C. Wyeth. 1984, Macmillan $28.00 (0-684-18162-2). 362pp. A classic edition now reissued. [398.2]

**8970** Crossley-Holland, Kevin, trans. *Beowulf* (6–8). Illus. by Charles Keeping. 1988, Oxford paper $9.95 (0-19-272184-4). 48pp. The English epic folktale retold in prose form. [398.2]

**8971** Crossley-Holland, Kevin, reteller. *British Folk Tales: New Versions* (5–8). Illus. 1987, Orchard $24.95 (0-531-05733-X). 384pp. Old folktales are re-created by combining them with introductions, changing from prose to poetry, and shifting from third to first person. (Rev: BL 1/5/88) [398.2]

**8972** Curry, Jane L. *The Christmas Knight* (K–4). Illus. by DyAnne DiSalvo-Ryan. 1993, Macmillan $14.95 (0-689-50572-8). 32pp. Sir Cleges so pleases King Uther that he is given a castle in Wales where he can distribute food to the poor each Christmas. (Rev: BL 9/15/93) [398.2]

**8973** Curry, Jane L. *Robin Hood and His Merry Men* (3–5). Illus. by John Lytle. 1994, Macmillan paper $13.95 (0-689-50609-0). 48pp. The traditional tales of Robin Hood, Little John, the Sheriff of Nottingham, et al., told in a modern version. (Rev: BL 1/15/95; SLJ 4/95) [398.2]

**8974** Curry, Jane L. *Robin Hood in the Greenwood* (3–5). Illus. 1995, Simon & Schuster paper $15.00 (0-689-80147-5). 50pp. Seven traditional stories about Robin Hood that end with him going to London to live at the court of his king. (Rev: BL 11/15/95; SLJ 1/96) [398.2]

**8975** dePaola, Tomie, reteller. *Fin M'Coul: The Giant of Knockmany Hill* (PS–3). Illus. by Tomie dePaola. 1981, Holiday LB $16.95 (0-8234-0384-X); paper $6.95 (0-8234-0385-8). 32pp. Fin's wife saves him from the most feared giant in Ireland. [398.2]

**8976** dePaola, Tomie. *Jamie O'Rourke and the Big Potato: An Irish Folktale* (PS–3). Illus. 1992, Putnam $15.95 (0-399-22257-X). 32pp. Lazy Jamie gets a seed from a leprechaun and produces an enormous potato. (Rev: BL 2/15/92; SLJ 4/92) [398.2]

**8977** Dunlop, Eileen. *Stones of Destiny* (4–7). 1994, Poolbeg paper $7.95 (1-85371-307-4). 142pp. A collection of Scottish and Irish folktales that has the stones from these countries as their subject. (Rev: BL 11/15/94) [398.2]

**8978** Early, Margaret. *Robin Hood* (3–5). Illus. 1996, Abrams $17.95 (0-8109-4428-6). 32pp. A lavishly illustrated edition of 14 of the most popular stories about Robin Hood and his Merry Men. (Rev: BL 6/1–15/96; SLJ 8/96) [398.22]

**8979** Egielski, Richard. *The Gingerbread Boy* (PS–4). Illus. 1997, HarperCollins LB $14.89 (0-06-026031-9). 32pp. This traditional folktale is transported to the streets of New York City, and the chase now involves the subway, among other landmarks. (Rev: BL 10/15/97; HB 9–10/97; SLJ 9/97*) [398.2]

**8980** Eisen, Armand, reteller. *Goldilocks and the Three Bears* (PS–K). Illus. by Lynn Bywaters Ferris. 1987, Knopf $9.95 (0-394-55882-0). 24pp. With brief text and intricate illustrations, this is a comical retelling of the old folktale for very young children. (Rev: BL 1/1/88) [398.2]

**8981** Forest, Heather. *The Woman Who Flummoxed the Fairies: An Old Tale from Scotland* (K–3). Illus. by Susan Gaber. 1990, Harcourt $14.95 (0-15-299150-6). In this retelling of a tale from Scotland, the fairies kidnap a baker so she will make cakes only for them. (Rev: BL 4/1/90; SLJ 6/90) [398.2]

**8982** Foster, Joanna. *The Magpies' Nest* (K–3). Illus. by Julie Downing. 1995, Clarion $15.95 (0-395-62155-0). 32pp. An English folktale that compares how various birds build their nests. (Rev: BL 2/1/96; SLJ 3/96) [398.2]

**8983** Francois, Andre, illus. *Jack and the Beanstalk: English Fairy Tale* (3–6). 1983, Creative Ed. LB $13.95 (0-87191-947-8). 32pp. For an older audience, this is a faithful version of the original. [398.2]

**8984** Galdone, Paul. *The Gingerbread Boy* (PS–1). Illus. by author. 1983, Houghton $16.00 (0-395-28799-5); paper $5.95 (0-89919-163-0). 40pp. Humorous and vigorous illustrations enhance this favorite folktale of the adventures of a runaway gingerbread boy. [398.2]

**8985** Galdone, Paul. *Henny Penny* (K–2). Illus. by author. 1979, Houghton $16.00 (0-395-28800-2); paper $5.95 (0-89919-225-4). 32pp. A retelling of the favorite cumulative folktale of the hen who thought the sky was falling. [398.2]

**8986** Galdone, Paul. *The Little Red Hen* (K–2). Illus. by author. 1979, Houghton $15.00 (0-395-28803-7); paper $5.95 (0-89919-349-8). A little hen works for her lazy housemates in this reworking of the old tale. Another fine edition is: *The Little Red Hen: An Old Story,* illus. by Margot Zemach (1983, Farrar). [398.2]

**8987** Galdone, Paul. *The Three Bears* (K–2). Illus. by author. 1979, Houghton $15.00 (0-395-28811-8); paper $5.95 (0-89919-401-X). 32pp. The illustrations for this familiar story are large, colorful, and humorous; excellent to use with a group. [398.2]

**8988** Galdone, Paul. *The Three Little Pigs* (PS–1). Illus. by author. 1979, Houghton $15.00 (0-395-28813-4). The old folktale told in verse. Another recommended edition is: Illus. by Erik Blegvad (1980, Macmillan). [398.2]

**8989** Garner, Alan, reteller. *The Little Red Hen* (PS–2). Illus. by Norman Messenger. 1997, DK Publg. $8.95 (0-7894-1171-7). 32pp. A retelling of this folktale by one of England's great writers for children. (Rev: BL 11/1/97; SLJ 12/97) [398.2]

**8990** *The Gingerbread Boy* (PS). Illus. by Kathy Wilburn. 1984, Putnam $3.99 (0-448-10217-X). 18pp. A favorite folktale with color illustrations in sturdy books for thumbing by toddlers. [398.2]

**8991** Gleeson, Brian. *Finn McCoul: The Legendary Irish Folk Hero* (1–4). Illus. by Peter de Seve. 1995, Simon & Schuster $19.95 (0-689-80201-3). The exploits of the legendary Irish giant as told by his wife, Oonagh, who appears to be his match in every way. (Rev: SLJ 3/96) [398.2]

**8992** Green, Roger L. *Adventures of Robin Hood* (4–6). 1995, Puffin paper $3.99 (0-140-36700-4). 256pp. A classic retelling of stories involving Robin and his merry men. [398.2]

**8993** Green, Roger L. *King Arthur and His Knights of the Round Table* (5–7). 1974, Puffin paper $2.95 (0-14-030073-2). 288pp. The famous deeds of this worthy king and his knights. [398.2]

**8994** Greene, Ellin. *Billy Beg and His Bull* (K–3). Illus. by Kimberly B. Root. 1994, Holiday LB $15.95 (0-8234-1100-1). 32pp. Using gifts he has received from a magic bull, Billy Beg defeats giants and wins a princess in this Irish folktale. (Rev: BCCB 4/94; BL 3/1/94; SLJ 7/94) [398.21]

**8995** Gross, Gwen, ed. *Knights of the Round Table* (2–5). Illus. by Norman Green. 1992, Random paper $3.99 (0-394-87579-6). 112pp. A retelling of many of the most popular Arthurian legends. (Rev: BCCB 9/85; SLJ 2/86) [398.2]

**8996** Hastings, Selina, reteller. *Sir Gawain and the Green Knight* (3–7). Illus. by Juan Wijngaard. 1981, Lothrop $16.00 (0-688-00592-6). 32pp. A nicely illustrated retelling of the Arthurian legend. [398.2]

**8997** Hastings, Selina, reteller. *Sir Gawain and the Loathly Lady* (5–8). Illus. by Juan Wijngaard. 1987, Lothrop paper $4.95 (0-688-07046-9). 32pp. Noble Sir Gawain agrees to honor a pledge for a husband to a deformed old hag and discovers that he has broken an old spell and released a beautiful woman. (Rev: BCCB 11/85; BL 11/15/85) [398.2]

**8998** Hewitt, Kathryn, adapt. *The Three Sillies* (K–3). Illus. by Kathryn Hewitt. 1989, Harcourt paper $3.95 (0-15-286856-9). A suitor sets out to find 3 sillier people than his betrothed's family. (Rev: BCCB 5/86; BL 4/1/86; SLJ 5/86) [398.2]

**8999** Heyer, Carol, reteller. *Robin Hood* (2–4). Illus. by Carol Heyer. 1993, Ideals LB $15.00 (0-8249-8648-2). This handsome book retells the most famous of Robin Hood's exploits, culminating in the King's pardon. (Rev: SLJ 11/93) [398.2]

**9000** Hodges, Margaret, reteller. *The Kitchen Knight: A Tale of King Arthur* (3–6). Illus. by Trina S. Hyman. 1990, Holiday LB $15.95 (0-8234-0787-X). A lavishly illustrated version of the story of the king who hides his identity to work in the kitchen at King Arthur's court. (Rev: BCCB 11/90*; HB 3–4/91; SLJ 1/91) [398.2]

**9001** Hodges, Margaret. *St. George and the Dragon: A Golden Legend* (2–5). Illus. by Trina S. Hyman. 1984, Little, Brown $16.95 (0-316-36789-3). A reworking of the English tale as it appeared in Edmund Spenser's Fairie Queen. Caldecott Medal winner, 1985. [398.2]

**9002** Hodges, Margaret, and Margery Evernden, retellers. *Of Swords and Sorcerers: The Adventures of King Arthur and His Knights* (4–8). Illus. by David Frampton. 1993, Macmillan $15.00 (0-684-19437-6). 96pp. From Merlin as a young boy to the last battle, this is the story of King Arthur and the knights and ladies connected with his court. (Rev: SLJ 8/93) [398.2]

**9003** Howe, John. *Jack and the Beanstalk* (K–2). Illus. 1998, Little, Brown $15.95 (0-316-37579-9); paper $5.95 (0-316-37562-4). 32pp. This fine retelling includes realistic paintings. (Rev: BCCB 11/89; BL 10/15/89; HB 11–12/89; SLJ 2/90) [398.2]

**9004** Huck, Charlotte. *Princess Furball* (PS–2). Illus. by Anita Lobel. 1989, Greenwillow LB $15.93 (0-688-07838-9). 40pp. In this Cinderella variation, a princess runs away from home to escape an arranged marriage. (Rev: BCCB 10/89; BL 9/1/89*; HB 11–12/89; SLJ 9/89*) [398.2]

**9005** Hunter, Mollie. *Gilly Martin the Fox* (PS–1). Illus. by Dennis McDermott. 1994, Hyperion $15.95 (1-56282-517-8). 40pp. A Scottish folktale about a fox that helps a young prince win the hand of a beautiful princess. (Rev: BL 4/1/94; SLJ 6/94) [398.2]

**9006** Jacobs, Joseph. *Celtic Fairy Tales* (3–6). Illus. by John D. Batten. 1968, Peter Smith $20.25 (0-8446-2302-4); Dover paper $6.95 (0-486-21826-0). 267pp. A classic collection. Followed by: *More Celtic Fairy Tales* (1969, Dover). [398.2]

**9007** Jacobs, Joseph. *English Fairy Tales* (3–6). Illus. by John D. Batten. 1969, Peter Smith $20.25 (0-8446-2303-2); Dover paper $6.95 (0-486-21818-X). A standard collection by a master storyteller. [398.2]

**9008** Kellogg, Steven. *Jack and the Beanstalk* (PS–2). Illus. 1991, Morrow LB $15.93 (0-688-10251-4). 40pp. A well-known artist's version of the classic folktale. (Rev: BL 10/15/91; HB 1–2/92; SLJ 12/91*) [398.2]

**9009** Kellogg, Steven. *The Three Little Pigs* (K–3). Illus. 1997, Morrow LB $15.93 (0-688-08732-9). 32pp. A humorous retelling of the old story, with inventive new details sure to please. (Rev: BL 8/97*; SLJ 9/97) [398.2]

**9010** Kimmel, Eric A. *The Gingerbread Man* (PS–K). Illus. by Megan Lloyd. 1993, Holiday LB $15.95 (0-8234-0824-8). 32pp. This is a modern version of a classic tale about the cookie that says he can't be caught. (Rev: BL 3/15/93; SLJ 6/93*) [398.2]

**9011** Kimmel, Eric A. *The Old Woman and Her Pig* (PS–3). Illus. by Giora Carmi. 1992, Holiday LB $15.95 (0-8234-0970-8). 32pp. An excellent retelling of the classic British folktale. (Rev: BL 1/1/93; SLJ 10/92) [398.2]

**9012** Leavy, Una. *Irish Fairy Tales and Legends* (4–8). Illus. 1997, Roberts Rinehart $17.95 (1-57098-177-9). 96pp. An attractive book that contains 10 Irish legends, some going back 2,000 years. (Rev: BL 2/1/98; SLJ 2/98) [398.2]

**9013** Litzinger, Rosanne. *The Old Woman and Her Pig: An Old English Tale* (PS–2). Illus. 1993, Harcourt $13.95 (0-15-257802-1). 32pp. This is the classic folktale about the woman who can't get her new-bought pig to climb over a stile. (Rev: BL 5/1/93; SLJ 6/93) [398.2]

**9014** McDermott, Gerald. *Daniel O'Rourke: An Irish Tale* (PS–3). Illus. by author. 1986, Puffin paper $4.99 (0-14-050673-X). 32pp. Introducing a familiar figure in Irish folklore, this is the story of Daniel O'Rourke's run in with an equine spirit and other unearthly creatures. (Rev: BL 5/1/86; SLJ 5/86) [398.2]

**9015** MacDonald, Margaret Read. *Slop! A Welsh Folktale* (K–2). Illus. by Yvonne Davis. 1997, Fulcrum $15.95 (1-55591-352-0). 24pp. In this Welsh folktale, fairies become annoyed when their neighbor continually empties his slop bucket on top of their cottage. (Rev: BL 11/1/97; SLJ 11/97) [398.2]

**9016** MacGill-Callahan, Sheila. *The Children of Lir* (K–3). Illus. by Gennady Spirin. 1993, Dial LB $14.99 (0-8037-1122-0). 32pp. This Irish folktale tells of an evil stepmother who turns her 4 stepdaughters into swans. (Rev: BL 6/1–15/93*; HB 5–6/93*; SLJ 4/93) [398.2]

**9017** McGovern, Ann. *Too Much Noise* (K–3). Illus. by Simms Taback. 1967, Houghton $16.00 (0-395-18110-0); paper $5.95 (0-395-62985-3). 48pp. An old man follows the advice of the village wise man when he complains that his house is too noisy. [398.2]

**9018** Marshall, James. *Goldilocks and the Three Bears* (PS–2). Illus. by author. 1988, Dial LB $13.89 (0-8037-0543-3). 32pp. A slightly wacky interpretation of the classic tale. (Rev: BL 10/1/88; HB 11–12/88; SLJ 10/88) [398.2]

**9019** Marshall, James, reteller. *The Three Little Pigs* (PS–2). Illus. 1989, Dial LB $12.89 (0-8037-0594-8). 32pp. A comic rendering of the classic story. (Rev: BCCB 1/90; BL 9/1/89; HB 11–12/89; SLJ 12/89*) [398.2]

**9020** Moodie, Fiona. *The Boy and the Giants* (K–3). Illus. 1993, Farrar $15.00 (0-374-30927-2). 30pp. In this Scottish folktale, Thomas is able to secure Kate's freedom from a giant only by securing a string of pearls from the sea kingdom. (Rev: BL 6/1–15/93; SLJ 8/93) [398.2]

**9021** Morpurgo, Michael. *Arthur: High King of Britain* (4–7). Illus. by Michael Foreman. 1995, Harcourt $22.00 (0-15-200080-1). 144pp. King Arthur tells 9 stories of his exploits to a 12-year-old boy. (Rev: BCCB 5/95; BL 8/95; SLJ 7/95)

**9022** Morpurgo, Michael. *Robin of Sherwood* (4–6). Illus. by Michael Foreman. 1996, Harcourt $22.00 (0-15-201315-6). 128pp. The tales of Robin Hood are retold through the dreams of a young boy. (Rev: BCCB 1/97; BL 10/1/96*; SLJ 2/97*) [398.2]

**9023** Muller, Robin, reteller. *Mollie Whuppie and the Giant* (K–2). Illus. by Robin Muller. 1995, Firefly $14.95 (1-895565-84-7); paper $5.95 (1-895565-79-0). 36pp. In this English folktale, Mollie Whuppie fools a giant and secures a bright future for herself and her 2 sisters. (Rev: SLJ 1/96) [398.2]

**9024** Paterson, Katherine. *Parzival: The Quest of the Grail Knight* (5–8). Illus. 1998, Dutton $15.99 (0-525-67579-5). 128pp. A retelling of the epic poem about the quest for the Holy Grail and the sin that caused the knight Parzival to wander the world looking for peace. (Rev: BL 3/1/98; SLJ 2/98*) [398.2]

**9025** Pyle, Howard. *The Merry Adventures of Robin Hood* (5–8). Illus. by author. 1968, Dover paper $7.95 (0-486-22043-5). 296pp. Stories about Robin Hood and the inhabitants of Sherwood Forest. [398.2]

**9026** Pyle, Howard. *The Story of King Arthur and His Knights* (6–8). Illus. by author. 1966, Dover paper $8.95 (0-486-21445-1). One of the most famous editions of these classic stories. A sequel is: *The Story of the Champions of the Round Table* (1968). [398.2]

**9027** Pyle, Howard. *The Story of the Grail and the Passing of Arthur* (5–8). Illus. by author. 1985, Macmillan paper $8.95 (0-486-27361-X). 340pp. The last title of a 4-volume King Arthur series, first published in 1910. (Rev: BL 12/15/85) [398.2]

**9028** Ross, Tony, reteller. *Goldilocks and the Three Bears* (K–3). Illus. 1992, Viking $13.95 (0-87951-453-1). 28pp. An enjoyable retelling of the old classic with modern updating. (Rev: BL 2/15/93) [398.2]

**9029** Rounds, Glen. *Three Little Pigs and the Big Bad Wolf* (PS–1). Illus. 1992, Holiday LB $15.95 (0-8234-0923-6). 32pp. This version of the classic tale presents the animals as animals, without human clothing. (Rev: BL 6/1/92; HB 7–8/92; SLJ 6/92) [398.2]

**9030** Sabuda, Robert. *Arthur and the Sword* (2–5). Illus. 1995, Simon & Schuster $16.00 (0-689-31987-8). 32pp. The story of young King Arthur and how he pulled the sword Excalibur from the anvil. (Rev: BL 11/1/95; SLJ 11/95)

**9031** San Souci, Robert D. *Young Arthur* (1–3). Illus. by Jamichael Henterly. 1997, Doubleday $16.95 (0-385-32268-2). 32pp. This account of the youth of King Arthur ends after he has received the sword Excalibur and has won his first battle. (Rev: BL 11/1/97; SLJ 10/97) [398.2]

**9032** San Souci, Robert D. *Young Guinevere* (3–5). Illus. by Jamichael Henterly. 1993, Doubleday $16.95 (0-385-41623-7). A large picture book that tells about the childhood of Guinevere. (Rev: SLJ 5/93) [398.2]

**9033** San Souci, Robert D. *Young Lancelot* (3–5). Illus. by Jamichael Henterly. 1996, Doubleday $15.95 (0-385-32171-6). 32pp. The story of the Arthurian knight who gained renown after learning to feel compassion for others. (Rev: BL 11/15/96; SLJ 11/96) [398.2]

**9034** Scieszka, Jon. *The True Story of the Three Little Pigs: By A. Wolf* (PS–2). Illus. 1989, Viking paper $15.99 (0-670-82759-2). 32pp. A hip and funny version, from the wolf's point of view. (Rev: BCCB 9/89*; BL 9/1/89; HB 1–2/90; SLJ 10/89) [398.2]

**9035** Seuling, Barbara. *The Teeny Tiny Woman: An Old English Ghost Tale* (K–3). Illus. by author. 1978, Puffin paper $4.99 (0-14-050266-1). 32pp. A picture book version of the classic story about the little woman and her soup bone. Another edition is: Illus. by Paul Galdone (1986, Houghton). [398.2]

**9036** Singer, Marilyn. *The Maiden on the Moor* (1–3). Illus. by Troy Howell. 1995, Morrow LB $14.93 (0-688-08765-6). 40pp. In this English ballad, 2 shepherd brothers discover a young woman lying unconscious and must decide if they should care for her. (Rev: BL 4/15/95; SLJ 4/95) [398.2]

**9037** Stevens, Janet. *How the Manx Cat Lost Its Tail* (K–3). Illus. 1990, Harcourt $14.95 (0-15-236765-9). 32pp. Based on a folktale, this story of how the Manx cat lost its tail goes back to the time of Noah. (Rev: BCCB 10/90; BL 3/1/90*; SLJ 5/90) [398.2]

**9038** Sutcliff, Rosemary, reteller. *Beowulf* (5–8). Illus. by Charles Keeping. 1984, Smith $22.50 (0-8446-6165-1). This is a reissue of the Anglo-Saxon tale published originally in 1962. Also use the King Arthur story, *The Sword and the Circle* (1981, Dutton). [398.2]

**9039** Talbott, Hudson. *Excalibur* (3–6). Illus. 1996, Morrow LB $15.93 (0-688-13381-9). 48pp. The story of King Arthur is retold, from his glory days at Camelot to his defeat in battle and death. (Rev: BL 11/15/96; SLJ 9/96) [398.2]

**9040** Talbott, Hudson, reteller. *King Arthur and the Round Table* (2–4). Illus. by Hudson Talbott. Series: Tales of King Arthur. 1995, Morrow LB $15.93 (0-688-11341-9). Three stories about King Arthur in which he forms the Round Table and marries Guinevere. (Rev: SLJ 12/95) [398.2]

**9041** Thomas, Gwyn, and Kevin Crossley-Holland. *Tales from the Mabinogion* (5–8). Illus. by Margaret Jones. 1985, Overlook $19.95 (0-87951-987-8). 88pp. A translation of Welsh hero tales. (Rev: BCCB 6/85; BL 4/1/85) [398.2]

**9042** Wells, Rosemary, reteller. *Jack and the Beanstalk* (PS–2). Illus. by Norman Messenger. 1997, DK Publg. $8.95 (0-7894-1170-9). 32pp. In this version of the folktale, Jack not only confronts the giant but also frees his father from his captors. (Rev: BL 11/1/97; SLJ 12/97) [398.2]

**9043** White, Carolyn. *Whuppity Stoorie: A Scottish Folktale* (PS–2). Illus. by S. D. Schindler. 1997, Putnam $15.95 (0-399-22903-5). 32pp. In this Scottish folktale, a mysterious woman asks a high price for nursing a pig back to health. (Rev: BCCB 7–8/97; BL 9/1/97; SLJ 7/97) [398.2]

**9044** Williams, Marcia. *The Adventures of Robin Hood* (3–5). Illus. 1995, Candlewick $17.95 (1-56402-535-7); paper $7.99 (0-7636-0275-2). 32pp. Eleven of the most famous exploits of Robin Hood are retold using a bold comic strip style. (Rev: BL 3/15/95; SLJ 4/95) [398.22]

**9045** Yolen, Jane, ed. *Camelot* (4–7). Illus. 1995, Putnam $19.95 (0-399-22540-4). 198pp. Ten stories and one song explore various facets of the life of King Arthur and the circle of friends and enemies that surrounded him. (Rev: BL 2/1/96; SLJ 1/96) [398.2]

**9046** Yolen, Jane. *Tam Lin* (4–6). Illus. by Charles Mikolaycak. 1990, Harcourt $14.95 (0-15-284261-6). 32pp. How a headstrong Scottish lass rescues her love from his faerie captors. (Rev: BL 9/15/90*; HB 1–2/91; SLJ 1/91) [398.2]

**9047** Zemach, Harve. *Duffy and the Devil: A Cornish Tale Retold* (1–3). Illus. by Margot Zemach. 1973, Farrar $17.00 (0-374-31887-5); paper $4.95 (0-374-41897-7). 40pp. A variant of "Rumpelstilt-skin," this folktale is told with humor and verve and boldly illustrated. Caldecott Medal winner, 1974. [398.2]

**9048** Zemach, Margot. *The Three Little Pigs: An Old Story* (PS–1). Illus. by author. 1988, Farrar $14.00 (0-374-37527-5). 32pp. In this version the wolf eats the first 2 pigs and the third pig eats wolf soup. (Rev: BL 2/15/89; HB 3–4/89; SLJ 3/89) [398.2]

**9049** Ziefert, Harriet. *Henny-Penny* (1–2). Illus. by Emily Bolam. 1997, Viking paper $11.99 (0-670-86810-8). 32pp. The familiar nursery rhyme is retold in an easily read format. (Rev: BL 11/15/96; SLJ 3/97) [398.2]

## Greece and Italy

**9050** Aesop. *The Aesop for Children* (3–5). Illus. by Milo Winter. 1984, Checkerboard $12.95 (1-56288-039-X); paper $5.99 (0-590-47977-6). This edition, reissued with the original artwork, includes 126 tales. [398.2]

**9051** Aesop. *Aesop's Fables* (3–5). Illus. by Charles Santore. 1988, Outlet $14.00 (0-517-64115-1). 48pp. Oversize, illustrated volume of 27 fables. (Rev: BL 1/1/89; SLJ 12/88) [398.2]

**9052** Aesop. *Aesop's Fables* (3–5). Illus. by Fulvio Testa. 1989, Barron's $12.95 (0-8120-5958-1). 48pp. Twenty familiar tales illustrated with paintings that use a Middle East oasis as a setting. (Rev: BCCB 5/89; HB 7–8/89) [398.2]

**9053** Aesop. *Aesop's Fables* (1–3). Illus. by Lisbeth Zwerger. 1989, Picture Book $16.00 (0-88708-108-8). 28pp. Twelve familiar tales are interpreted with watercolor paintings. (Rev: BCCB 2/90; BL 11/15/89; SLJ 12/89) [398.2]

**9054** Aesop. *Fables of Aesop* (4–6). Illus. by David Levine. 1984, Harvard Common $13.95 (0-87645-074-5); paper $8.95 (0-87645-116-4). 108pp. One of many recommended editions of this classic. [398.2]

**9055** Aesop. *The Tortoise and the Hare: An Aesop Fable* (PS–K). Illus. by Janet Stevens. 1984, Holiday LB $15.95 (0-8234-0510-9); paper $6.95 (0-8234-

0564-8). 32pp. An updated, charming retelling of the classic fable. [398.2]

**9056** Aesop. *The Town Mouse and the Country Mouse* (PS–1). Illus. by T. R. Garcia. 1979, Troll LB $11.89 (0-89375-131-6); paper $2.95 (0-89375-109-X). 32pp. The classic story faithfully and entertainingly retold. [398.2]

**9057** Aesop. *The Town Mouse and the Country Mouse* (1–3). Retold by Ellen Schecter. Illus. by Holly Hannon. Series: Bank Street Ready-to-Read. 1995, Bantam paper $3.99 (0-553-37572-5). 47pp. A fast-paced, poetic retelling of this fable, with charming illustrations. (Rev: SLJ 4/95) [398.2]

**9058** Aesop. *The Town Mouse and the Country Mouse: An Aesop Fable* (PS–1). Adapted and illus. by Janet Stevens. 1987, Holiday paper $5.95 (0-8234-0733-0). 32pp. A comic romp of the classic tale of 2 mice. (Rev: BCCB 7–8/87; BL 5/1/87) [398.2]

**9059** Ash, Russell, and Bernard A. Higton, eds. *Aesop's Fables* (3–6). Illus. 1991, Chronicle $17.95 (0-87701-780-8). 95pp. More than 50 fables reprinted and illustrated with artists from the past. (Rev: SLJ 3/91) [398.2]

**9060** Bader, Barbara. *Aesop and Company* (4–6). Illus. by Arthur Geisert. 1991, Houghton $16.95 (0-395-50597-6). 64pp. A background book that traces the origins of Aesop's fables and their use through the centuries, plus a collection of 19 famous tales. (Rev: BCCB 1/92; BL 1/1/92; SLJ 1/92) [398.2]

**9061** Barnes-Murphy, Frances. *The Fables of Aesop* (3–5). Illus. 1994, Lothrop $19.95 (0-688-07051-5). 96pp. An extensive collection of more than 100 fables with lively illustrations. (Rev: BL 12/1/94; SLJ 10/94) [398.2]

**9062** Caduto, Michael J. *The Crimson Elf: Italian Tales of Wisdom* (4–8). Illus. 1997, Fulcrum $15.95 (1-55591-323-7). 64pp. Six folktales from Italy, the first of which tells of Donatella's adventures in the lair of the crimson elf. (Rev: BL 8/97; SLJ 8/97) [398.2]

**9063** Craig, Helen. *The Town Mouse and the Country Mouse* (K–3). Illus. 1992, Candlewick $13.95 (1-56402-102-5). 32pp. A refreshing variation on the Aesop fable with embellishments that add a new flavor. (Rev: BCCB 1/93; BL 11/15/92; HB 1–2/93; SLJ 3/93)

**9064** dePaola, Tomie. *Days of the Blackbird: A Tale of Northern Italy* (K–3). Illus. 1997, Putnam $15.99 (0-399-22929-9). 32pp. An Italian tale about a faithful bird that stays through the winter to sing for an ailing duke. (Rev: BL 3/15/97; HB 3–4/97; SLJ 3/97*)

**9065** dePaola, Tomie. *The Mysterious Giant of Barletta: An Italian Folktale* (K–3). Illus. by author. 1988, Harcourt paper $6.00 (0-15-256349-0). 32pp.

A statue of an old lady saves the town from marauders. [398.2]

**9066** dePaola, Tomie. *Strega Nona* (PS–2). Illus. by author. 1979, Simon & Schuster paper $6.95 (0-671-66606-1). 32pp. The old Italian folktale retold. Also use: *Big Anthony and the Magic Ring* (1979) and *Strega Nona's Magic Lessons* (1982). [398.2]

**9067** dePaola, Tomie. *Strega Nona: Her Story* (PS–3). Illus. 1996, Putnam $15.95 (0-399-22818-7). 32pp. This book supplies background information on the birth and youth of Nona and how she became the village strega. (Rev: BL 9/15/96; HB 11–12/96; SLJ 10/96) [398.2]

**9068** dePaola, Tomie. *Tony's Bread: An Italian Folktale* (K–3). Illus. 1989, Putnam $15.95 (0-399-21693-6). 32pp. A Milano nobleman hopes to win Serafina by setting her father up in business in the city. (Rev: BL 10/1/89; HB 1–2/90; SLJ 11/89) [398.2]

**9069** Fox, Paula. *Amzat and His Brothers: Three Italian Tales* (3–5). Illus. by Emily Arnold McCully. 1993, Orchard $16.95 (0-531-05462-4). 80pp. Tales retold from a grandfather who lived in a small Italian village. (Rev: BCCB 3/93*; BL 3/15/93; HB 7–8/93; SLJ 7/93) [398.2]

**9070** Gal, Laszlo, and Raffaella Gal. *The Parrot* (K–3). Illus. 1997, Douglas & McIntyre $16.95 (0-88899-287-4). 32pp. In this Italian folktale, a prince assumes the identity of a parrot to help a princess. (Rev: BL 9/15/97; SLJ 10/97) [398.2]

**9071** Jones, Carol. *The Hare and the Tortoise* (K–3). Illus. 1996, Houghton $13.95 (0-395-81368-9). 32pp. Peepholes and detailed illustrations are used in this retelling of the famous Aesop fable. (Rev: BL 9/1/96; SLJ 9/96) [398.24]

**9072** Lowell, Susan. *The Tortoise and the Jackrabbit* (PS–2). Illus. by Jim Harris. 1994, Northland LB $14.95 (0-87358-586-0). 32pp. This favorite Aesop fable is retold with the tortoise an aged grandmother and the hare a conceited egocentric. (Rev: BL 1/15/95; SLJ 2/95)

**9073** McClintock, Barbara. *Animal Fables from Aesop* (4–6). Illus. 1991, Godine $18.95 (0-87923-913-1). 48pp. The text is an expansion of 9 fables complete with dialogue and dramatic situations. (Rev: BCCB 1/92; BL 1/1/92; HB 1–2/92; SLJ 1/92) [398.2]

**9074** Manna, Anthony L., and Christodoula Mitakidou. *Mr. Semolina-Semolinus: A Greek Folktale* (1–4). Illus. by Giselle Potter. 1997, Simon & Schuster $15.00 (0-689-81093-8). 40pp. Areti creates the perfect man for herself, but he is stolen by an evil queen. (Rev: BCCB 7–8/97; BL 4/15/97; HB 5–6/97; SLJ 4/97) [398.2]

**9075** Peterson, Julienne. *Caterina, the Clever Farm Girl* (K–3). Illus. by Enzo Giannini. 1996, Dial paper $14.89 (0-8037-1182-4). 32pp. In this Tuscan folktale, a king is so impressed with Caterina's ingenuity that he marries her. (Rev: BL 4/1/96; SLJ 6/96) [398.2]

**9076** Stevens, Janet, reteller. *Androcles and the Lion* (K–3). Illus. 1989, Holiday LB $14.95 (0-8234-0768-3). 32pp. A retelling of a young slave and the lion he helps. (Rev: BL 11/1/89; SLJ 11/89) [398.2]

**9077** Vittorini, Domenico. *The Thread of Life* (3–7). Illus. by Mary Grandpre. 1995, Crown $20.00 (0-517-59594-X). 80pp. A collection of 12 Italian tales, including a different version of Cinderella. (Rev: BCCB 11/95; BL 11/1/95; SLJ 12/95) [398.2]

## Russia

**9078** Afanasyev, Alexander, ed. *Russian Fairy Tales* (4–7). Illus. by Alexander Alexeieff. 1976, Pantheon paper $18.00 (0-394-73090-9). The definitive collection of folktales reissued in the 1945 edition. [398.2]

**9079** Arnold, Katya. *Baba Yaga* (PS–3). Illus. 1993, North-South LB $14.88 (1-55858-209-6). 32pp. A child outwits the fierce witch Baba Yaga in this colorful retelling of the Russian folktale. (Rev: BL 10/1/93; SLJ 1/94) [398.2]

**9080** Ayres, Becky. *Matreshka* (K–3). Illus. by Alexi Natchev. 1996, Dell paper $4.99 (0-440-41288-9). 32pp. An original retelling of the Russian folktale about Baba Yaga, the ugly witch who's always looking for children to eat. (Rev: BCCB 11/92; BL 1/15/93; SLJ 2/93) [398.2]

**9081** Beck, Ian. *Peter and the Wolf* (PS–3). Illus. 1995, Simon & Schuster $13.00 (0-689-80336-2). 32pp. The story of Prokofiev's musical tale is retold with illustrations that recapture the setting of old Russia. (Rev: BL 12/15/95; SLJ 11/95) [398.2]

**9082** Cech, John. *First Snow, Magic Snow* (K–3). Illus. by Sharon McGinley-Nally. 1992, Macmillan LB $14.95 (0-02-717971-0). In this Russian folktale, a childless woodsman makes a baby from snow. (Rev: BCCB 11/92; HB 11–12/92; SLJ 12/92) [398.2]

**9083** Cecil, Laura. *The Frog Princess* (PS–3). Illus. by Emma C. Clark. 1995, Greenwillow $16.00 (0-688-13506-4). 32pp. In this variation on a Russian folktale, a young prince falls in love with a little green frog. (Rev: BCCB 4/95; BL 2/1/95; SLJ 4/95*) [398.2]

**9084** Cole, Joanna. *Bony-Legs* (1–4). Illus. by Dirk Zimmer. 1983, Macmillan $16.00 (0-02-722970-X); Scholastic paper $3.99 (0-590-40516-0). 48pp. A simply read story based on the Russian Baba Yaga. [398.2]

**9085** Crouch, Marcus. *Ivan: Stories of Old Russia* (3–5). Illus. by Bob Dewar. 1989, Oxford $20.00 (0-19-274135-7). 80pp. Simple Ivan wins in the end in these Russian tales. (Rev: BCCB 5/89; BL 7/89; SLJ 9/89) [398.2]

**9086** Demi. *The Firebird* (2–4). Illus. 1994, Holt $16.95 (0-8050-3244-4). 32pp. A beautiful retelling of the Russian tale about Dimitri and his hunt for the elusive Firebird. (Rev: BL 11/15/94; SLJ 12/94) [398.2]

**9087** De Regniers, Beatrice S. *Little Sister and the Month Brothers* (K–3). Illus. by Margot Tomes. 1976, Houghton $8.95 (0-8164-3147-7). 48pp. A delightful retelling of an old Slavic tale reminiscent of the Cinderella theme. [398.2]

**9088** Gal, Laszlo, reteller. *Prince Ivan and the Firebird* (2–5). Illus. by Laszlo Gal. 1992, Firefly $14.95 (0-920668-98-4). 40pp. A lavish retelling of one of Russia's most popular folk legends. (Rev: SLJ 7/92) [398.2]

**9089** Ginsburg, Mirra. *Clay Boy* (PS–3). Illus. by Joseph A. Smith. 1997, Greenwillow LB $15.93 (0-688-14410-1). 32pp. In this Russian folktale, a grandpa makes a clay boy who comes to life and has a voracious appetite. (Rev: BL 4/15/97*; HB 3–4/97; SLJ 5/97) [398.2]

**9090** Ginsburg, Mirra. *Good Morning, Chick* (PS–K). Illus. by Byron Barton. 1980, Greenwillow LB $15.93 (0-688-84284-4); Morrow paper $4.95 (0-688-08741-8). 32pp. A Russian folktale about a chick who must learn his identity. [398.2]

**9091** Heins, Ethel. *The Cat and the Cook and Other Fables of Krylov* (3–5). Illus. by Anita Lobel. 1995, Greenwillow LB $14.93 (0-688-12311-2). 32pp. The retelling of 12 Russian fables from the pen of Ivan Krylov, with charming artwork. (Rev: BCCB 5/95; BL 3/15/95; HB 7–8/95; SLJ 4/95) [398.2]

**9092** Hogrogian, Nonny. *The Contest* (3–5). Illus. by author. 1976, Greenwillow LB $15.93 (0-688-84042-6). 32pp. Adaptation of the folktale about 2 robbers who discover that they are engaged to the same girl. [398.2]

**9093** Jackson, Ellen. *The Impossible Riddle* (K–3). Illus. by Alison Winfield. 1995, Whispering Coyote $14.95 (1-879085-93-3). 32pp. In this Russian folktale, a czar hopes to prevent his daughter's marriage by demanding that prospective suitors answer an impossible riddle. (Rev: BL 1/1–15/96) [398.2]

**9094** Kimmel, Eric A. *Baba Yaga: A Russian Folktale* (K–3). Illus. by Megan Lloyd. 1991, Holiday LB $15.95 (0-8234-0854-X). 32pp. A traditional Russian folktale about Marina, whose wicked stepmother sends her to the forest witch. (Rev: BL 5/1/91; SLJ 6/91) [398.2]

**9095** Kimmel, Eric A. *Bearhead: A Russian Folktale* (K–3). Illus. by Charles Mikolaycak. 1991, Holiday LB $16.95 (0-8234-0902-3). 32pp. A peasant woman finds an odd-looking foundling with the body of a human and the head of a bear. (Rev: BCCB 12/91; BL 9/1/91; SLJ 10/91) [398.2]

**9096** Kimmel, Eric A. *I Know Not What, I Know Not Where: A Russian Tale* (4–6). Illus. by Robert Sauber. 1994, Holiday LB $16.95 (0-8234-1020-X). 64pp. In this Russian fairy tale, a hunter is rewarded for saving an enchanted dove's life by getting help to perform tasks demanded by the czar. (Rev: BCCB 7–8/94; BL 3/1/94; SLJ 6/94) [398.2]

**9097** Kimmel, Eric A. *One Eye, Two Eyes, Three Eyes: A Hutzul Tale* (PS–3). Illus. by Dirk Zimmer. 1996, Holiday LB $15.95 (0-8234-1183-4). 32pp. A traveler unwittingly bargains away his daughter in this Ukrainian tale. (Rev: BL 11/1/96; SLJ 1/97) [398.2]

**9098** Langton, Jane. *Salt: From a Russian Folktale* (K–3). Trans. by Alice Plume. Illus. by Ilse Plume. 1992, Hyperion $14.95 (1-56282-178-4). 48pp. A Russian folktale about 3 brothers who go to sea to seek their fortunes. (Rev: BCCB 1/93; BL 10/15/92; SLJ 12/92) [398.2]

**9099** Lemieux, Michele. *Peter and the Wolf* (PS–2). Illus. 1991, Morrow LB $13.88 (0-688-09847-9). 32pp. This is a handsome retelling of the fairy tale on which Prokofiev based his musical composition. (Rev: BL 10/1/91) [398.2]

**9100** Lewis, J. Patrick. *The Frog Princess: A Russian Folktale* (K–3). Illus. by Gennady Spirin. 1994, Dial paper $15.89 (0-8037-1624-9). 32pp. A Russian folktale about a prince who marries a frog and finds that she is actually the beautiful Vasilisa the Wise under a spell. (Rev: BL 9/15/94; SLJ 9/94) [398.2]

**9101** Marshak, Samuel, reteller. *The Month-Brothers: A Slavic Tale* (K–4). Illus. by Diane Stanley. 1983, Morrow LB $15.93 (0-688-01510-7). 32pp. A folktale involving such familiar elements as a girl and a mean stepmother. [398.2]

**9102** Mayer, Marianna. *Baba Yaga and Vasilisa the Brave* (PS–3). Illus. by Kinuko Craft. 1994, Morrow $16.00 (0-688-08500-8). 40pp. Vasilisa survives both the schemes of her wicked stepmother and a visit to the witch Baba Yaga and finally marries the czar. (Rev: BL 6/1–15/94; SLJ 7/94*) [398.2]

**9103** Mikolaycak, Charles. *Babushka: An Old Russian Folktale* (PS–2). Illus. by author. 1984, Holiday LB $15.95 (0-8234-0520-6); paper $5.95 (0-8234-0712-8). 32pp. Babushka refuses to leave her home to search for the Christ child. [398.2]

**9104** Oram, Hiawyn. *Baba Yaga and the Wise Doll: A Traditional Russian Folktale* (PS–1). Illus. by Ruth Brown. 1998, Dutton $15.99 (0-525-45947-2). 32pp.

Too Nice Child, a little doll, outwits both her horrible sisters and the witch Baba Yaga in this Russian folktale. (Rev: BL 1/1–15/98; SLJ 3/98) [398.2]

**9105** Pushkin, Aleksandr. *The Tale of Tsar Saltan* (2–4). Illus. by Gennady Spirin. 1996, Dial paper $16.99 (0-8037-2001-7). 32pp. A Russian folktale about a young prince who is able to reunite his estranged parents. (Rev: BCCB 11/96; BL 10/15/96; SLJ 10/96*) [398.2]

**9106** Ransome, Arthur. *The Fool of the World and the Flying Ship* (1–4). Illus. by Uri Shulevitz. 1968, Farrar $16.00 (0-374-32442-5); paper $6.95 (0-374-42438-1). 48pp. Colorful, panoramic scenes extend this retelling of a popular Russian folktale about a simple peasant boy who acquires a flying ship. Caldecott Medal winner, 1969. [398.2]

**9107** Reyher, Becky. *My Mother Is the Most Beautiful Woman in the World* (2–5). Illus. by Ruth Gannett. 1945, Lothrop LB $16.93 (0-688-51251-8). 40pp. A girl tries to find her mother in this Russian setting. [398.2]

**9108** Robbins, Ruth. *Baboushka and the Three Kings* (2–4). Illus. by Nicholas Sidjakov. 1960, Houghton $16.00 (0-395-27673-X); paper $6.95 (0-395-42647-2). 32pp. The Russian legend of the old woman who refused to follow the 3 kings in search of the Holy Child. Caldecott Medal winner, 1961. [398.2]

**9109** Shepard, Aaron. *The Sea King's Daughter: A Russian Legend* (4–6). Illus. by Gennady Spirin. 1997, Simon & Schuster $17.00 (0-689-80759-7). 40pp. In this Russian folktale Sadko, a talented musician, must decide whether he loves the daughter of the King of the Sea enough to remain in the underwater kingdom for the rest of his life. (Rev: BL 11/15/97; SLJ 12/97) [398.2]

**9110** Sherman, Josepha. *Vassilisa the Wise: A Tale of Medieval Russia* (K–3). Illus. by Daniel San Souci. 1988, Harcourt $16.00 (0-15-293240-2). 26pp. Staver, a merchant, brags that his wife, Vassilisa, is more clever than any woman at the royal court, which makes the prince angry. (Rev: BL 4/15/88; HB 7–8/88; SLJ 9/88) [398.2]

**9111** Winthrop, Elizabeth. *The Little Humpbacked Horse: A Russian Tale* (4–6). Illus. by Alexander Koshkin. 1997, Clarion $14.95 (0-395-65361-4). 24pp. A retelling of the Russian tale about a boy whose mentor is a humpbacked colt. (Rev: BCCB 5/97; BL 3/1/97; SLJ 4/97*) [398.2]

**9112** Ziefert, Harriet. *The Turnip* (K–1). Illus. 1996, Viking paper $11.99 (0-670-86053-0). 32pp. The familiar Russian folktale is retold in this easy reader. (Rev: BL 8/96; SLJ 8/96)

## Scandinavia

**9113** Arnold, Tim. *The Three Billy Goats Gruff* (PS–1). Illus. 1993, Macmillan LB $14.95 (0-689-50575-2). 32pp. This Norwegian folktale is retold with a Rocky Mountain setting and a few modern touches. (Rev: BL 12/1/93; HB 7–8/93; SLJ 10/93) [398.2]

**9114** Asbjornsen, Peter C. *Tatterhood and the Hobgoblins: A Norwegian Folktale* (K–3). Retold by Lauren Mills. Illus. 1993, Little, Brown $15.95 (0-316-57406-6). 32pp. Tatterhood has grown up "wild as a weed" in this Norwegian tale. (Rev: BL 3/1/93; SLJ 6/93) [398.2]

**9115** Asbjornsen, Peter C. *The Three Billy Goats Gruff* (PS–2). Retold by Glen Rounds. Illus. 1993, Holiday LB $15.95 (0-8234-1015-3). 32pp. This veteran illustrator noted for animal drawings illustrates and retells this famous Norweigan folktale. (Rev: BL 4/15/93; HB 7–8/93; SLJ 6/93*) [398.2]

**9116** Asbjornsen, Peter C., and Jorgen Moe. *The Man Who Kept House* (PS–3). Illus. by Otto S. Svend. 1992, Macmillan $13.95 (0-689-50560-4). 32pp. A farmer and his wife swap jobs for the day; he never again complains about his wife's housekeeping. (Rev: BL 2/1/93; HB 1–2/93; SLJ 1/93) [398.2]

**9117** Asbjornsen, Peter C., and Jorgen Moe. *Norwegian Folk Tales* (3–6). Illus. by Erik Werenskiold and Theodor Kittelsen. 1978, Pantheon paper $14.00 (0-394-71054-1). This edition retains the original illustrations from the 1845 edition. [398.2]

**9118** DeGerez, Toni, reteller. *Louhi, Witch of North Farm: A Finnish Tale* (K–2). Illus. by Barbara Cooney. 1986, Viking paper $13.95 (0-670-80556-4). 32pp. Louhi is bored so she steals the sun and the moon and locks them behind 9 doors. (Rev: BCCB 10/86; BL 10/1/86; HB 11–12/86) [398.2]

**9119** *East o' the Sun and West o' the Moon* (3–6). Trans. by George Webbe. Illus. by P. J. Lynch. 1992, Candlewick $15.95 (1-56402-049-5). 48pp. A striking picture-book version of a beloved Norwegian folktale. (Rev: BL 9/15/92*; SLJ 9/92) [398.2]

**9120** Emberley, Rebecca. *Three Cool Kids* (K–3). Illus. 1995, Little, Brown $15.95 (0-316-23666-7). 32pp. A variation on "The Three Billy Goats Gruff" featuring 3 sibling goats who live in an inner-city area. (Rev: BCCB 4/95; BL 3/1/95; SLJ 3/95*) [398.2]

**9121** French, Vivian. *Why the Sea Is Salty* (K–3). Illus. by Patrice Aggs. 1993, Candlewick $14.95 (1-56402-183-1). 32pp. In this Norwegian folktale, the misuse of wishes by a miser produces enough salt to make the oceans salty. (Rev: BL 6/1–15/93; SLJ 8/93) [398.2]

**9122** Galdone, Paul. *The Three Billy Goats Gruff* (PS–3). Illus. by author. 1973, Houghton $15.00 (0-395-28812-6). 32pp. A troll meets his match. [398.2]

**9123** Kimmel, Eric A. *Boots and His Brothers: A Norwegian Tale* (PS–3). Illus. by Kimberly B. Root. 1992, Holiday LB $14.95 (0-8234-0886-8). 32pp. In this Norwegian folktale, 3 brothers set out to seek their fortunes, but only the youngest, Boots, succeeds. (Rev: BCCB 3/92; BL 3/1/92) [398.2]

**9124** Mayer, Mercer. *East of the Sun and West of the Moon* (3–5). Illus. by author. 1980, Macmillan paper $6.99 (0-689-71113-1). 48pp. A poor farmer gives his daughter to a strange white bear in this Norwegian folktale. [398.2]

**9125** Shepard, Aaron. *The Maiden of Northland: A Hero Tale of Finland* (3–7). Illus. by Carol Schwartz. 1996, Simon & Schuster $16.00 (0-689-80485-7). In this tale from the Finnish epic the Kalevala, Aila, the maiden of Northland, is courted by 2 suitors. (Rev: SLJ 4/96) [398.2]

**9126** Shepard, Aaron. *Master Maid: A Tale of Norway* (K–3). Illus. by Pauline Ellison. 1997, Dial $14.99 (0-8037-1821-7). 32pp. In this Norwegian folktale, young Leif goes to work for a troll, who gives him difficult tasks. (Rev: BL 6/1–15/97; SLJ 6/97) [398.2]

**9127** Wisniewski, David. *Elfwyn's Saga* (4–5). Illus. 1990, Viking LB $13.88 (0-688-09590-9). 32pp. Boldly colored dramatic artwork provides the scene for these Icelandic sagas. (Rev: BL 11/1/90; HB 11–12/90; SLJ 10/90*) [398.2]

## Spain and Portugal

**9128** Araujo, Frank P. *Nekane, the Lamina and the Bear: A Tale of the Basque Pyrenees* (K–2). Illus. by Xiao Jun Li. 1993, Rayve $16.95 (1-877810-01-0). 32pp. In this Basque version of the standard fairy tale, Red Riding Hood becomes Nekane, who is stopped by a forest spirit on her way to her uncle's home. (Rev: BCCB 3/94; BL 2/1/94; SLJ 5/94) [398.2]

**9129** Cruz Martinez, Alejandro. *The Woman Who Outshone the Sun: The Legend of Lucia Zenteno* (K–3). Trans. by Rosalma Zubizarreta. Illus. by Fernando Olivera. 1991, Children's Book Pr. $14.95 (0-89239-101-4). 30pp. This Hispanic folktale in English and Spanish tells about a woman who is misunderstood because of her great bond with nature. (Rev: BCCB 2/92; SLJ 3/92) [398.2]

**9130** Heyer, Marilee, adapt. *The Girl, the Fish, and the Crown: A Spanish Folktale* (2–4). Illus. by Marilee Heyer. 1995, Viking paper $14.99 (0-670-85409-3). A Spanish folktale about a spoiled girl who, after being turned into a fish, sets out to restore human

form to a beautiful mermaid under an enchantment. (Rev: BCCB 9/95; SLJ 10/95) [398.2]

**9131** Kimmel, Eric A. *Bernal and Florinda: A Spanish Tale* (K–3). Illus. by Robert Rayevsky. 1994, Holiday LB $15.95 (0-8234-1089-7). 32pp. A comic fairy tale about 2 Spanish lovers who are united in marriage despite the objections of the bride's father. (Rev: BCCB 9/94; BL 9/15/94; SLJ 11/94) [398.2]

**9132** Kimmel, Eric A. *Squash It! A True and Ridiculous Tale* (3–5). Illus. by Robert Rayevsky. 1997, Holiday LB $15.95 (0-8234-1299-7). 32pp. The Spanish tale of the king who adopted a louse as his favorite pet. (Rev: BL 6/1–15/97; HB 7–8/97; SLJ 7/97) [398.2]

**9133** Robbins, Sandra. *The Firefly Star: A Hispanic Folk Tale* (PS–3). Illus. by Iku Oseki. 1995, See-More's Workshop paper $6.95 (1-882601-23-8). 32pp. In this Spanish folktale, the important holiday Three Kings' Day almost doesn't take place until a mouse and a ladybug intervene. (Rev: BL 12/1/95; SLJ 2/96) [398.2]

## Jewish Folklore

**9134** Aroner, Miriam. *The Kingdom of Singing Birds* (K–5). Illus. by Shelly O. Haas. 1993, Kar-Ben $13.95 (0-929371-43-7); paper $5.95 (0-929371-44-5). In this Jewish folktale, a rabbi tells a king that the only way to get his birds to sing is to set them free. (Rev: SLJ 9/93) [398.2]

**9135** Brodmann, Aliana, reteller. *Such a Noise! A Jewish Folktale* (K–3). Trans. by Aliana Brodmann and David Filingham. Illus. by Hans Poppel. 1989, Kane/Miller $11.95 (0-916291-25-1). A man tries to drown out the noise in his household by bringing farm animals inside. (Rev: SLJ 12/89) [398.2]

**9136** Clement, Gary. *Just Stay Put: A Chelm Story* (K–4). Illus. 1996, Douglas & McIntyre $14.95 (0-88899-239-4). 32pp. A resident of Chelm, Poland, mistakes his hometown for Warsaw. (Rev: BL 9/15/96; SLJ 6/96) [398.2]

**9137** Davis, Aubrey. *Bone Button Borscht* (K–3). Illus. by Dusan Petricic. 1997, Kids Can $15.95 (1-55074-224-8). 32pp. An Eastern European version of *Stone Soup*, in which a beggar persuades the synagogue caretaker to let him make borscht from his coat buttons. (Rev: BL 11/1/97; SLJ 11/97) [398.2]

**9138** Forest, Heather. *A Big Quiet House: A Yiddish Folktale from Eastern Europe* (PS–3). Illus. by Susan Greenstein. 1996, August House $15.95 (0-87483-462-7). 32pp. A rollicking retelling of the Yiddish tale *It Could Always Be Worse*, in which a man accepts the advice of a wise woman and invites all sorts of animals into his house. (Rev: BL 10/1/96; SLJ 11/96) [398.2]

**9139** Freedman, Florence B. *It Happened in Chelm: A Story of the Legendary Town of Fools* (K–4). Illus. by Nik Krevitsky. 1990, Shapolsky paper $9.95 (0-933503-22-9). A retelling of one of the Jewish folktales about the fools who live in Chelm. (Rev: SLJ 3/91) [398.2]

**9140** Gershator, Phillis, reteller. *Honi's Circle of Trees* (K–2). Illus. by Mim Green. 1995, Jewish Publication Soc. $13.95 (0-8276-0511-0). The adventures of the Talmudic hero noted for his selflessness, his planting of carob trees in Israel, and his ability to communicate with God. (Rev: SLJ 9/95) [398.2]

**9141** Gerstein, Mordicai. *The Shadow of a Flying Bird: A Legend from the Kurdistani Jews* (1–5). Illus. 1994, Hyperion LB $16.49 (0-7868-2012-8). 32pp. God comes to earth to claim the life of his faithful servant Moses in this Jewish folktale. (Rev: BL 10/1/94; SLJ 9/94) [398.2]

**9142** Gilman, Phoebe. *Something from Nothing* (PS–3). Illus. 1993, Scholastic $15.95 (0-590-47280-1). 32pp. This folktale tells how a frugal grandfather recycles the material from a jacket to ever smaller objects, ending with the covering for a button. (Rev: BCCB 2/94; BL 9/1/93; HB 11–12/93; SLJ 1/94) [398.2]

**9143** Gordon, Ruth. *Feathers* (K–4). Illus. by Lydia Dabcovich. 1993, Macmillan LB $14.95 (0-02-736511-5). 32pp. The foolish men of Chelm botch the plan to collect money for a new bathhouse in this Jewish folktale. (Rev: BCCB 12/93; BL 10/15/93) [398.21]

**9144** Harber, Frances. *The Brothers' Promise* (4–6). Illus. by Thor Wickstrom. 1998, Albert Whitman LB $15.95 (0-8075-0900-0). 32pp. In this traditional Jewish tale, 2 brothers secretly sacrifice to help each other and fulfill their father's wishes. (Rev: BL 3/15/98) [398.2]

**9145** Jaffe, Nina, and Steve Zeitlin. *While Standing on One Foot: Puzzle Stories and Wisdom Tales from the Jewish Tradition* (4–7). Illus. by John Segal. 1993, Holt $14.95 (0-8050-2594-4). 80pp. Seventeen Jewish folktales in which the reader is asked to suggest an appropriate ending before the real one is revealed. (Rev: BCCB 12/93; BL 1/1/94*; SLJ 1/94) [296.1]

**9146** Kimmel, Eric A. *The Adventures of Hershel of Ostropol* (K–4). Illus. by Trina S. Hyman. 1995, Holiday $15.95 (0-8234-1210-5). 64pp. Ten Jewish folktales that use as a locale a village community in the Ukraine during the 19th century. (Rev: BL 10/15/95; SLJ 11/95) [398.2]

**9147** Kimmel, Eric A. *Days of Awe: Stories for Rosh Hashanah and Yom Kippur* (4–6). Illus. by Erika Weihs. 1991, Viking paper $14.50 (0-670-82772-X). 48pp. Three tales that show how repentance, prayer, and charity are the soul of the Jewish High Holy Days. (Rev: BL 8/91*; HB 11–12/91; SLJ 9/91) [398.2]

**9148** Kimmel, Eric A. *Onions and Garlic* (PS–3). Illus. by Katya Arnold. 1996, Holiday LB $15.95 (0-8234-1222-9). 32pp. In this Hebrew folktale, young Getzel is able to use a sackful of onions to obtain a fortune in diamonds. (Rev: BCCB 6/96; BL 4/1/96; SLJ 7/96) [398.2]

**9149** Patterson, Jose. *Angels, Prophets, Rabbis and Kings: From the Stories of the Jewish People* (3–6). Illus. by Claire Bushe. 1991, Bedrick LB $24.95 (0-87226-912-4). 144pp. A treasure chest of stories and parables. (Rev: BL 9/15/91; SLJ 8/91) [398.2]

**9150** Podwal, Mark. *Golem: A Giant Made of Mud* (K–4). Illus. 1995, Greenwillow LB $14.93 (0-688-13812-X). 32pp. A collection of stories about the mysterious shape-changing creature that is associated with Prague. (Rev: BL 10/1/95; SLJ 11/95) [398.2]

**9151** Prose, Francine. *The Angel's Mistake: Stories of Chelm* (PS–4). Illus. by Mark Podwal. 1997, Greenwillow LB $14.93 (0-688-14906-5). 24pp. A series of anecdotes about the city of Chelm — where fools reside — its creation and eventual destruction. (Rev: BCCB 7–8/97; BL 3/1/97; HB 7–8/97; SLJ 4/97) [398.2]

**9152** Prose, Francine. *Dybbuk: A Story Made in Heaven* (PS–3). Illus. by Mark Podwal. 1996, Greenwillow LB $15.93 (0-688-14308-3). 24pp. In this Jewish folktale, the angel's choice of a mate for Leah is thwarted by interfering parents. (Rev: BL 4/15/96; SLJ 4/96) [398.2]

**9153** Rogasky, Barbara. *The Golem* (4–6). Illus. by Trina S. Hyman. 1996, Holiday $18.95 (0-8234-0964-3). 96pp. The story of the giant monster of the 16th century and its use to help protect the Jewish people in Prague from persecution. (Rev: BCCB 9/96; BL 10/1/96*; HB 1–2/96; SLJ 10/96) [398.2]

**9154** Rossel, Seymour. *Sefer Ha-Aggadah: The Book of Legends for Young Readers* (4–7). Illus. by Judy Dick. 1996, UAHC paper $14.00 (0-8074-0603-1). 67pp. A collection of legends based on stories about the Jewish people from the Old Testament. (Rev: SLJ 3/97) [398.2]

**9155** Rothenberg, Joan. *Yettele's Feathers* (PS–3). Illus. 1995, Hyperion LB $15.49 (0-7868-2081-0). 40pp. A rabbi makes Yettele realize how harmful her gossiping can be. (Rev: BL 5/1/95; SLJ 4/95) [398.2]

**9156** Sanfield, Steve. *Strudel, Strudel, Strudel* (2–4). Illus. by Emily Lisker. 1995, Orchard LB $16.99 (0-531-08729-8). 32pp. In this Jewish folktale from Poland, a teacher and his wife devise a plan to get all the strudel they can eat. (Rev: BCCB 2/95; BL 4/1/95; HB 3–4/95; SLJ 4/95) [398.2]

**9157** Schwartz, Amy. *Yossel Zissel and the Wisdom of Chelm* (PS–2). Illus. by author. 1986, Jewish Publication Soc. $14.95 (0-8276-0258-8). 32pp. How Yossel Zissel spreads Chelm's wisdom throughout the world. (Rev: BCCB 1/87; BL 1/15/87) [398.2]

**9158** Schwartz, Howard. *Next Year in Jerusalem: 3000 Years of Jewish Stories* (3–6). Illus. by Neil Waldman. 1996, Viking paper $16.99 (0-670-86110-3). 64pp. A collection of Jewish tales and legends related to the city of Jerusalem. (Rev: BCCB 1/96; BL 2/1/96; HB 7–8/96; SLJ 1/96) [296.4]

**9159** Schwartz, Howard, and Barbara Rush. *The Diamond Tree: Jewish Tales from Around the World* (PS–4). Illus. by Uri Shulevitz. 1991, HarperCollins $17.00 (0-06-025239-1). 120pp. Fifteen stories reflect the history of the Jews and their common tradition. (Rev: BCCB 12/91; BL 12/15/91; HB 1–2/92; SLJ 3/92*) [398.2]

**9160** Sherman, Josepha. *Rachel the Clever and Other Jewish Folktales* (4–6). Illus. 1993, August House $18.95 (0-87483-306-X); paper $10.95 (0-87483-307-8). 176pp. Jewish tales gathered from many lands. (Rev: BL 3/15/93) [398.2]

**9161** Singer, Isaac Bashevis. *Elijah the Slave* (PS–3). Illus. by Antonio Frasconi. 1970, Farrar $16.00 (0-374-32084-5); paper $4.95 (0-374-42047-5). 32pp. Retelling of a Hebrew legend. [398.2]

**9162** Singer, Isaac Bashevis. *The Fools of Chelm and Their History* (5–6). Illus. by Uri Shulevitz. 1973, Farrar $14.00 (0-374-32444-1). 64pp. Nonsense stories about the village that is the setting of other Singer tales. [398.2]

**9163** Singer, Isaac Bashevis. *Stories for Children* (4–7). 1984, Farrar $22.95 (0-374-37266-7); paper $13.00 (0-374-46489-8). 338pp. A collection of stories that draw on Yiddish folklore. [398.2]

**9164** Singer, Isaac Bashevis. *When Shlemiel Went to Warsaw and Other Stories* (4–7). Illus. by Margot Zemach. 1986, Farrar paper $4.95 (0-374-48365-5). 161pp. Illustrations and the 8 stories retold here delightfully reveal the distinctive people of Chelm and their extraordinary, universally exportable wisdom. [398.2]

**9165** Singer, Isaac Bashevis. *Zlateh the Goat and Other Stories* (4–6). Illus. by Maurice Sendak. 1966, HarperCollins $16.00 (0-06-025698-2); paper $5.95 (0-06-440147-2). 96pp. Warm, humorous, and ironical stories based on middle European Jewish folklore and on the author's childhood memories. [398.2]

**9166** Wisniewski, David. *Golem* (3–6). Illus. 1996, Clarion $15.95 (0-395-72618-2). 30pp. The terrifying story of the golem, who was created by Rabbi Loew in the 16th century to help protect his people

in the Prague ghetto. Caldecott Medal winner, 1997. (Rev: BCCB 9/96; BL 10/1/96*; SLJ 10/96) [398.2]

**9167** Zemach, Margot. *It Could Always Be Worse: A Yiddish Folktale* (K–3). Illus. by author. 1976, Farrar $17.00 (0-374-33650-4); Scholastic paper $4.95 (0-374-43636-3). 32pp. A Yiddish version of an old tale with colorful, humorous illustrations. [398.2]

**9168** Ziefert, Harriet. *The Cow in the House* (1–3). Illus. by Emily Bolam. 1997, Viking paper $11.99 (0-670-86779-9). 32pp. An easy-to-read version of the classic Jewish tale of a man who is advised to bring animals into his house when he finds it is too noisy. (Rev: BL 8/97) [398.2]

# Middle East

**9169** Alderson, Brian. *The Arabian Nights; or, Tales Told by Sheherezade During a Thousand Nights and One Night* (4–8). Illus. by Michael Foreman. 1995, Morrow $20.00 (0-688-14219-2). 192pp. A fine collection of more than 30 tales that includes parts from the stories of Sinbad, Ali Baba, and Aladdin. (Rev: BL 10/15/95; SLJ 9/95) [398.22]

**9170** Ben-Ezer, Ehud. *Hosni the Dreamer: An Arabian Tale* (K–3). Illus. by Uri Shulevitz. 1997, Farrar $16.00 (0-374-33340-8). 32pp. This old Arabian folktale about a young shepherd who buys a life-changing verse from a wise man. (Rev: BL 11/1/97; HB 9–10/97; SLJ 12/97*) [398.2]

**9171** dePaola, Tomie. *The Legend of the Persian Carpet* (K–3). Illus. by Claire Ewart. 1993, Putnam $14.95 (0-399-22415-7). 32pp. When his prize diamond is stolen and shattered, a Persian king finds solace in a beautiful new carpet woven for him. (Rev: BL 10/1/93; SLJ 1/94) [398.2]

**9172** Kherdian, David. *The Rose's Smile: Farizad of the Arabian Nights* (3–6). Illus. by Stefano Vitale. 1997, Holt $15.95 (0-8050-3912-0). 32pp. Two children grow up not knowing that their father is the sultan in this tale from the *Arabian Nights*. (Rev: BL 9/1/97; SLJ 11/97) [398.2]

**9173** Kimmel, Eric A. *The Tale of Aladdin and the Wonderful Lamp: A Story from the Arabian Nights* (PS–3). Illus. by Ju-Hong Chen. 1992, Holiday LB $14.95 (0-8234-0938-4). 32pp. A humorous retelling of the famous story. (Rev: BL 11/1/92; SLJ 12/92) [398.2]

**9174** Kimmel, Eric A. *The Three Princes* (K–3). Illus. by Leonard Everett Fisher. 1994, Holiday LB $15.95 (0-8234-1115-X). 30pp. A beautiful princess shows great wisdom in choosing her husband from the 3 noble cousins who are her suitors in this Middle Eastern folktale. (Rev: BCCB 4/94; BL 3/1/94*; SLJ 3/94) [398.2]

**9175** Lang, Andrew, ed. *The Arabian Nights Entertainments* (5–8). Illus. 1969, Dover paper $7.95 (0-486-22289-6). 424pp. Fairy tales, folktales, and legends of Arabia and the East. [398.2]

**9176** Lattimore, Deborah N. *Arabian Nights: Three Tales* (1–5). Illus. 1995, HarperCollins LB $16.89 (0-06-024734-7). 64pp. The 3 stories masterfully retold are "Aladdin," "The Queen of the Serpents," and "Ubar, the Lost City of Brass." (Rev: BL 10/15/95; SLJ 9/95) [398.2]

**9177** McVilly, Walter, reteller. *Ali Baba and the Forty Thieves* (K–4). Illus. by Margaret Early. 1989, Abrams $17.95 (0-8109-1888-9). 32pp. Vivid re-creation of the most famous story of the Thousand and One Nights. (Rev: BL 5/15/89; HB 7–8/89) [398.2]

**9178** Moore, Christopher. *Ishtar and Tammuz: A Babylonian Myth of the Seasons* (4–7). Illus. by Christina Balit. 1996, Kingfisher $15.95 (0-7534-5012-7). 32pp. The goddess Ishtar rescues her dead son from the underworld in this Babylonian fertility myth. (Rev: BCCB 12/96; BL 9/1/96; SLJ 12/96) [398.2]

**9179** Oppenheim, Shulamith Levey. *Iblis* (1–4). Illus. by Ed Young. 1994, Harcourt $15.95 (0-15-238016-7). 32pp. In this Islamic version of Adam and Eve's expulsion from Eden, the devil is called Iblis. (Rev: BCCB 4/94; BL 3/15/94; SLJ 4/94) [297]

**9180** Philip, Neil. *The Arabian Nights* (4–6). Illus. by Sheila Moxley. 1994, Orchard $19.95 (0-531-06868-4). 160pp. With lovely paintings and colorful prose, this is an excellent retelling of 16 of the Arabian Nights stories, including Ali Baba, Scheherazade, and Aladdin. (Rev: BL 12/15/94; HB 5–6/94; SLJ 12/94*) [398.2]

**9181** Shepard, Aaron. *The Enchanted Storks: A Tale of Bagdad* (K–3). Illus. by Alisher Dianov. 1995, Clarion $14.95 (0-395-65377-0). 32pp. A Calif and his Vizier magically turn themselves into storks but don't know how to reverse the spell. (Rev: BL 6/1–15/95; SLJ 4/95) [398.2]

**9182** Yeoman, John. *The Seven Voyages of Sinbad the Sailor* (4–7). Illus. by Quentin Blake. 1997, Simon & Schuster $19.95 (0-689-81368-6). 128pp. In these adaptations of stories from *Arabian Nights*, Sinbad tells about the 7 amazing voyages that brought him horror, disaster, adventure, and eventually wealth. (Rev: BL 1/1–15/98; SLJ 12/97) [398.2]

# North America

## Eskimos

**9183** Bernhard, Emery, and Durga Bernhard. *How Snowshoe Hare Rescued the Sun: A Tale from the Arctic* (K–3). Illus. 1993, Holiday LB $15.95 (0-8234-1043-9). 32pp. Snowshoe Hare is sent to rescue the Sun, which has been captured by evil demons in this Eskimo legend. (Rev: BCCB 10/93; BL 11/1/93; SLJ 10/93) [398.2]

**9184** Bierhorst, John, ed. *The Dancing Fox: Arctic Folktales* (4–6). Illus. 1997, Morrow $15.00 (0-688-14406-3). 192pp. After an introduction to the land and people of the American Arctic, the author presents 18 Eskimo folktales. (Rev: BCCB 7–8/97; BL 4/15/97; HB 5–6/97; SLJ 6/97) [398.2]

**9185** Dabcovich, Lydia, reteller. *The Polar Bear Son: An Inuit Tale* (K–2). Illus. by Lydia Dabcovich. 1997, Clarion $14.95 (0-395-72766-9). 37pp. In this Eskimo tale, the men of a village want to kill the polar bear that one of their women had adopted when it was an orphaned cub. (Rev: SLJ 6/97) [398.2]

**9186** De Armond, Dale. *The Seal Oil Lamp* (1–4). Illus. 1997, Sierra Club paper $7.95 (0-87156-858-6). 48pp. According to Eskimo law, the blind child of a hunter and his wife cannot be allowed to live if he cannot grow up to take care of himself. (Rev: BL 11/1/88; SLJ 12/88) [398.2]

**9187** Houston, James. *Tikta'liktak: An Eskimo Legend* (4–6). Illus. by author. 1990, Harcourt paper $10.00 (0-15-287748-7). 63pp. Legend of a young Eskimo hunter who is carried out to sea on a drifting ice floe with only his bow and arrows and a harpoon. Also use: *The White Archer: An Eskimo Legend* (1990). [398.2]

**9188** Martin, Rafe. *The Eagle's Gift* (K–4). Illus. by Tatsuro Kiuchi. 1997, Putnam $15.95 (0-399-22923-X). 32pp. An eagle transformed into a man helps Marten learn the gift of joy in this Eskimo folktale. (Rev: BL 9/15/97; SLJ 2/98) [398.2]

**9189** Norman, Howard. *The Girl Who Dreamed Only Geese and Other Stories of the Far North* (4–8). Illus. by Leo Dillon and Diane Dillon. 1997, Harcourt $22.00 (0-15-230979-9). 164pp. A fine collection of Eskimo tales, enhanced by illustrations resembling stone carvings. (Rev: BL 9/15/97*; SLJ 11/97*) [398.2]

**9190** Sloat, Teri. *The Hungry Giant of the Tundra* (K–3). Illus. by Robert Sloat and Teri Sloat. 1993, Dutton paper $14.99 (0-525-45126-9). 32pp. In this

Eskimo legend, a group of children escape being a giant's dinner with the help of a chickadee and a crane. (Rev: BL 12/1/93; SLJ 1/94) [398.2]

## Indians of North America

**9191**   Ata, Te. *Baby Rattlesnake* (PS–K). Adapted by Lynn Moroney. Illus. by Veg Reisberg. 1990, Children's Book Pr. $14.95 (0-89239-049-2); paper $6.95 (0-89239-111-1). 32pp. A baby rattlesnake doesn't know how to behave when he is given a rattle before reaching maturity. (Rev: BL 3/1/90; SLJ 4/90) [398.2]

**9192**   Baylor, Byrd. *Moon Song* (1–3). Illus. by Ronald Himler. 1982, Macmillan LB $13.95 (0-684-17463-4). 24pp. Why the coyote and descendants gather in the night and sing to the moon. [398.2]

**9193**   Bierhorst, John, ed. *The Naked Bear: Folktales of the Iroquois* (4–7). Illus. 1987, Morrow $16.00 (0-688-06422-1). 144pp. Sixteen stories of the Iroquois tribe of New York State and Ontario Province. (Rev: BCCB 4/87; BL 8/87; SLJ 6–7/87) [398.2]

**9194**   Bierhorst, John, sel. *On the Road of Stars: Native American Night Poems and Sleep Charms* (2–6). Illus. by Judy Pedersen. 1994, Macmillan paper $15.95 (0-02-709735-8). An unusual, charming collection of more than 50 night songs and lullabies from different North American Indian cultures. (Rev: BCCB 3/94; HB 7–8/94; SLJ 5/94) [398.2]

**9195**   Bierhorst, John. *The Woman Who Fell from the Sky: The Iroquois Story of Creation* (K–4). Illus. by Robert Andrew Parker. 1993, Morrow LB $14.93 (0-688-10681-1). 32pp. Sky Woman, with the help of her 2 sons, creates the earth. (Rev: BCCB 5/93; BL 3/15/93; HB 5–6/93; SLJ 4/93) [398.2]

**9196**   Bruchac, Joseph. *Between Earth and Sky: Legends of Native American Sacred Places* (2–5). Illus. by Thomas Locker. 1996, Harcourt $16.00 (0-15-200042-9). 32pp. A retelling of 10 legends dealing with sacred places from various Native American tribes. (Rev: BL 4/1/96; HB 5–6/96; SLJ 7/96) [398.2]

**9197**   Bruchac, Joseph. *Dog People: Native Dog Stories* (3–6). Illus. by Murv Jacob. 1995, Fulcrum $14.95 (1-55591-228-1). 63pp. This book contains 5 very readable stories about the Abenaki Indian children and their dogs. (Rev: SLJ 1/96) [398.2]

**9198**   Bruchac, Joseph. *The First Strawberries: A Cherokee Story* (PS–3). Illus. by Anna Vojtech. 1993, Dial paper $14.89 (0-8037-1332-0). In this folktale,

the first woman on earth leaves her husband when he gets angry because she picked flowers instead of making his dinner. (Rev: BL 7/93) [398.2]

**9199**   Bruchac, Joseph. *Flying with the Eagle, Racing the Great Bear: Stories from Native North America* (5–8). Illus. 1993, Troll paper $13.95 (0-8167-3026-1). 144pp. Sixteen stories, arranged geographically, introduce coming-of-age rites for males in Native American cultures. (Rev: BL 12/15/93; SLJ 9/93) [398.2]

**9200**   Bruchac, Joseph. *Four Ancestors: Stories, Songs, and Poems from Native North America* (4–6). Illus. 1996, Troll paper $18.95 (0-8167-3843-2). 96pp. Folktales from various Native American peoples deal with the elements: fire, earth, water, and air. (Rev: BL 7/96; SLJ 5/96) [398.2]

**9201**   Bruchac, Joseph. *Gluskabe and the Four Wishes* (PS–3). Illus. by Christine N. Shrader. 1995, Dutton paper $15.99 (0-525-65164-0). 32pp. An Indian legend that explains why Gluskabe is considered a hero by the Abnaki Indians of New England. (Rev: BCCB 2/95; BL 12/15/94; HB 3–4/95; SLJ 2/95) [398.2]

**9202**   Bruchac, Joseph. *The Great Ball Game: A Muskogee Story* (PS–3). Illus. by Susan L. Roth. 1994, Dial LB $14.89 (0-8037-1540-4). 32pp. When the birds lose a contest against the beasts, they are banished to the South for half of each year in this Creek Indian folktale. (Rev: BCCB 9/94; BL 9/15/94; HB 11–12/94; SLJ 12/94) [398.2]

**9203**   Bruchac, Joseph. *Native American Animal Stories* (1–5). Illus. by John K. Fadden and David K. Fadden. 1992, Fulcrum paper $12.95 (1-55591-127-7). 160pp. Includes 24 engrossing animal tales from tribes across North America. (Rev: SLJ 11/92) [398.2]

**9204**   Bruchac, Joseph. *Native Plant Stories* (4–8). Illus. 1995, Fulcrum paper $12.95 (1-55591-212-5). 128pp. A collection of stories about plants that come from various Indian cultures in North and Central America. (Rev: BL 9/1/95) [398.24]

**9205**   Bruchac, Joseph, and Gayle Ross. *The Story of the Milky Way: A Cherokee Tale* (PS–3). Illus. by Virginia A. Stroud. 1995, Dial paper $14.89 (0-8037-1738-5). 32pp. This Cherokee legend tells how a giant spirit dog created the Milky Way. (Rev: BL 9/1/95; SLJ 9/95) [398.2]

**9206**   Cohen, Caron L. *The Mud Pony: A Traditional Skidi Pawnee Tale* (K–3). Illus. by Shonto Begay. 1988, Scholastic $15.95 (0-590-41525-5). 32pp. The moving story of a boy too poor to have a pony of his own who grows up to become chief of his people. (Rev: BCCB 12/88; BL 12/1/88; SLJ 1/89) [398.2]

**9207** Connolly, James E. *Why the Possum's Tail Is Bare: And Other North American Indian Nature Tales* (4–7). Illus. 1992, Stemmer $15.95 (0-88045-069-X); paper $7.95 (0-88045-107-6). 64pp. Nature and folklore are combined in 13 Native American animal tales. (Rev: BL 9/1/85; SLJ 10/85) [398.2]

**9208** Dengler, Marianna. *The Worry Stone* (3–5). Illus. by Sibyl G. Gerig. 1996, Northland LB $14.95 (0-87358-642-5). 34pp. When her grandfather dies, Amanda finds that she gets comfort from rubbing a stone that the old man had given to her. (Rev: BL 12/15/96; SLJ 1/97) [398.2]

**9209** dePaola, Tomie, reteller. *The Legend of the Bluebonnet: An Old Tale of Texas* (K–3). Illus. by Tomie dePaola. 1983, Putnam $15.95 (0-399-20937-9). 32pp. This book retells the Comanche Indian story of the origin of the Texas bluebonnet flower. [398.2]

**9210** dePaola, Tomie. *The Legend of the Indian Paintbrush* (PS–2). Illus. by author. 1988, Putnam $15.95 (0-399-21534-4); paper $5.99 (0-698-11360-8). 40pp. Little Gopher discovers his true calling as the recorder of his tribe's stories, but he cannot find the right colors to use. (Rev: BL 3/15/88; HB 7–8/88; SLJ 6–7/88) [398.2]

**9211** Dominic, Gloria, adapt. *Brave Bear and the Ghosts: A Sioux Legend* (2–4). Illus. by Charles Reasoner. Series: Native American Lore and Legends. 1996, Rourke LB $16.95 (0-86593-429-0). 47pp. A charming trickster tale with a surprise ending from the Sioux. Also use *Coyote and the Grasshoppers: A Pomo Legend* and *Song of the Hermit Thrush: An Iroquois Legend* (both 1996). (Rev: SLJ 3/97) [398.2]

**9212** Duncan, Lois. *The Magic of Spider Woman* (K–3). Illus. by Shonto Begay. 1996, Scholastic $14.95 (0-590-46155-9). 32pp. In this Navajo legend, a shepherdess learns how to weave wool blankets from the Spider Woman. (Rev: BCCB 6/96; BL 3/1/96; HB 7–8/96; SLJ 3/96*) [398.2]

**9213** Dwyer, Mindy, reteller. *Coyote in Love* (PS–3). Illus. by Mindy Dwyer. 1997, Alaska Northwest $15.95 (0-88240-485-7). This American Indian tale of how Crater Lake was formed tells of Coyote's unrequited love for a star. (Rev: SLJ 7/97) [398.2]

**9214** Eagle Walking Turtle. *Full Moon Stories: Thirteen Native American Legends* (3–6). Illus. 1997, Hyperion LB $16.49 (0-7868-2175-2). 48pp. A wonderful collection of legends that were told to the author by his grandfather years ago. (Rev: BL 6/1–15/97; SLJ 7/97) [398.2]

**9215** Esbensen, Barbara J. *Ladder to the Sky: How the Gift of Healing Came to the Ojibway Nation* (K–3). Illus. by Helen K. Davie. 1989, Little, Brown $15.95 (0-316-24952-1). 32pp. Although the Ojibway (Chippewa) lost their direct connection to the Great Spirit, they were granted healing powers. (Rev: BCCB 2/90; BL 11/1/89; SLJ 10/89) [398.2]

**9216** Esbensen, Barbara J. *The Star Maiden: An Ojibway Tale* (3–5). Illus. by Helen K. Davie. 1991, Little, Brown paper $5.95 (0-316-24955-6). 32pp. A star appears in a dream to a young brave, falls to earth, and becomes a water lily. (Rev: BCCB 4/88; BL 4/1/88; SLJ 6–7/88) [398.2]

**9217** French, Fiona. *Lord of the Animals: A Miwok Indian Creation Myth* (PS–3). Illus. 1997, Millbrook $15.95 (0-7613-0112-7). 32pp. In this American Indian myth, Coyote creates man to be Lord of the Animals. (Rev: BCCB 6/97; BL 6/1–15/97; SLJ 9/97) [398.2]

**9218** Goble, Paul. *Adopted by the Eagles* (3–5). Illus. 1994, Bradbury paper $15.95 (0-02-736575-1). 40pp. One friend betrays another when they both fall in love with the same maiden in this Dakota Indian folktale. (Rev: BL 11/1/94; SLJ 1/95) [398.2]

**9219** Goble, Paul. *Buffalo Woman* (4–6). Illus. by author. 1984, Macmillan $14.95 (0-02-737720-2); paper $5.99 (0-689-71109-3). 32pp. A legend from the Plains Indians about a buffalo that turns into a beautiful girl. [398.2]

**9220** Goble, Paul. *Crow Chief: A Plains Indian Story* (K–3). Illus. by author. 1992, Orchard LB $17.99 (0-531-08547-3). 32pp. This Plains Indian legend explains why crows have black feathers. (Rev: BCCB 4/92; BL 2/15/92; HB 3–4/92; SLJ 3/92) [398.2]

**9221** Goble, Paul. *The Gift of the Sacred Dog* (2–4). Illus. by author. 1982, Macmillan LB $15.00 (0-02-736560-3). 32pp. A boy brings to his starving people the gift of horses. [398.2]

**9222** Goble, Paul. *The Great Race: Of the Birds and Animals* (K–3). Illus. by author. 1991, Simon & Schuster paper $5.99 (0-689-71452-1). 32pp. The story of the great race between the animals and humans in which the people won and now have responsibility to care for animals. (Rev: BCCB 9/85; BL 9/15/85; SLJ 9/85) [398.2]

**9223** Goble, Paul. *Her Seven Brothers* (K–3). Illus. by author. 1988, Macmillan $14.95 (0-02-737960-4); paper $5.99 (0-689-71730-X). 32pp. The Cheyenne legend that tells of the origin of the Big Dipper. (Rev: BCCB 4/88; BL 4/15/88; SLJ 6–7/88) [398.2]

**9224** Goble, Paul. *Iktomi and the Berries: A Plains Indian Story* (K–2). Illus. by author. 1992, Orchard paper $6.95 (0-531-07029-8). 32pp. A witty Indian folktale about a disreputable hero. (Rev: BCCB 12/89*; BL 9/15/89; HB 11–12/89; SLJ 9/89*) [398.2]

**9225** Goble, Paul. *Iktomi and the Boulder: A Plains Indian Story* (3–5). Illus. by author. 1988, Orchard $16.95 (0-531-05760-7); paper $6.95 (0-531-07023-9). 32pp. Iktomi, a trickster, is the hero of many humorous adventures in these Sioux tales. (Rev: BCCB 7–8/88; BL 8/88; HB 9–10/88) [398.2]

**9226** Goble, Paul. *Iktomi and the Buffalo Skull: A Plains Indian Story* (K–3). Illus. by author. 1996, Orchard $16.95 (0-531-05911-1); paper $5.95 (0-531-07077-8). 32pp. Iktomi the trickster tries to impress girls but ends up with his head stuck in a buffalo skull. (Rev: BL 2/1/91; HB 5–6/91; SLJ 3/91) [398.2]

**9227** Goble, Paul. *Iktomi and the Buzzard: A Plains Indian Story* (K–3). Illus. 1994, Orchard LB $17.99 (0-531-08662-3). 32pp. Smart-talking Iktomi gets Buzzard angry by making fun of him, but later the bird gets his revenge. (Rev: BCCB 6/94; BL 3/1/94; HB 7–8/94; SLJ 3/94) [398.2]

**9228** Goble, Paul. *Iktomi and the Ducks: A Plains Indian Story* (K–2). Illus. by author. 1990, Orchard LB $17.99 (0-531-08483-3). 32pp. Another lively tale about the traditional Indian trickster. (Rev: BL 11/1/90; HB 9–10/90; SLJ 8/90 & 3/91) [398.2]

**9229** Goble, Paul. *The Legend of the White Buffalo Woman* (4–8). Illus. 1998, National Geographic $16.95 (0-7922-7074-6). 32pp. After a great flood, an earth woman and an eagle mate to produce a new people in his Lakota Indian tale. (Rev: BL 3/15/98) [398.2]

**9230** Goble, Paul. *The Lost Children* (3–5). Illus. 1993, Macmillan $14.95 (0-02-736555-7). An Indian legend about 6 orphaned boys who journey to the sky and become the Pleiades. (Rev: BCCB 6/93; SLJ 5/93) [398.2]

**9231** Goble, Paul. *Love Flute* (3–8). Illus. by author. 1992, Macmillan $16.00 (0-02-736261-2). 32pp. From the legends of the Plains Indians, this is a love story about a young man too shy to woo the woman he loves. (Rev: BCCB 12/92; BL 8/92*; HB 3–4/93; SLJ 10/92) [398.2]

**9232** Goble, Paul. *Remaking the Earth: A Creation Story from the Great Plains of North America* (3–6). Illus. 1996, Orchard LB $16.99 (0-531-08874-X). 32pp. In this creation myth, Earth Maker re-creates the land after a destructive flood. (Rev: BL 9/15/96; SLJ 10/96) [398.2]

**9233** Goble, Paul. *The Return of the Buffaloes: A Plains Indian Story About Famine and Renewal of the Earth* (K–3). Illus. 1996, National Geographic $15.95 (0-7922-2714-X). 32pp. A Lakota myth about a woman with magical powers who saves her people. (Rev: BL 6/1–15/96; HB 7–8/96; SLJ 7/96) [398.2]

**9234** Goble, Paul, reteller. *Star Boy* (2–4). 1991, Simon & Schuster paper $5.99 (0-689-71499-8).

32pp. An Indian legend on how Star Boy was able to rid himself of a disfiguring scar. [398.2]

**9235** Goldin, Barbara D. *Coyote and the Fire Stick: A Pacific Northwest Indian Tale* (3–5). Illus. by Will Hillenbrand. 1996, Harcourt $15.00 (0-15-200438-6). 40pp. In this Pacific Northwest tale, a coyote sets out to steal fire from 3 ugly evil spirits. (Rev: BL 10/1/96; HB 11–12/96; SLJ 10/96) [398.2]

**9236** Goldin, Barbara D. *The Girl Who Lived with the Bears* (4–6). Illus. by Andrew Plewes. 1997, Harcourt $15.00 (0-15-200684-2). 40pp. A folktale from the Pacific Northwest Indians about a chief's daughter who insulted the bear people and was later forced to live with them as their slave. (Rev: BL 4/15/97; SLJ 4/97) [398.2]

**9237** Gregg, Andy. *Great Rabbit and the Long-Tailed Wildcat* (2–4). Illus. by Cat B. Smith. 1993, Whitman LB $14.95 (0-8075-3047-6). 32pp. This Indian folktale explains why the wildcat has a stubby tail. (Rev: BCCB 6/93; BL 5/1/93; SLJ 7/93) [398.2]

**9238** Haley, Gail E., reteller. *Two Bad Boys: A Very Old Cherokee Tale* (3–6). Illus. by Gail E. Haley. 1996, Dutton paper $14.99 (0-525-45311-3). In this folktale, a Cherokee lad and the Wild Boy he befriends cause a situation that results in all their descendants having to work for their food. (Rev: BCCB 6/96; SLJ 8/96) [398.2]

**9239** Harrell, Beatrice O. *How Thunder and Lightning Came to Be* (K–3). Illus. by Susan L. Roth. 1995, Dial paper $14.89 (0-8037-1749-0). 32pp. The Choctaw legend of how 2 silly birds created thunder and lightning. (Rev: BL 8/95; SLJ 8/95) [398.2]

**9240** Hausman, Gerald. *How Chipmunk Got Tiny Feet* (3–5). Illus. by Ashley Wolff. 1995, Harper-Collins LB $14.89 (0-06-022907-1). 48pp. Seven pourquoi tales from various North American Indian peoples, each involving animals. (Rev: BL 9/1/95; HB 9–10/95; SLJ 6/95) [398.2]

**9241** Highwater, Jamake. *Anpao: An American Indian Odyssey* (5–8). Illus. by Fritz Scholder. 1993, HarperCollins paper $6.95 (0-06-440437-4). 256pp. A young hero encounters great danger on his way to meet his father, the Sun, in this dramatic American Indian folktale. [398.2]

**9242** Hillerman, Tony, ed. *The Boy Who Made Dragonfly: A Zuni Myth* (5–7). Illus. by Laszlo Kubinyi. 1986, Univ. of New Mexico Pr. paper $8.95 (0-8263-0910-0). 85pp. A Zuni boy and his little sister are left behind by their tribe and survive hunger and deprivation through the intervention of the Cornstalk Being. [398.2]

**9243** Jackson, Ellen. *The Precious Gift: A Navaho Creation Myth* (1–3). Illus. by Woodleigh Hubbard. 1996, Simon & Schuster paper $16.00 (0-689-

80480-6). In this part of the creation myth of the Navajo, water is brought to the arid earth. (Rev: BCCB 6/96; SLJ 5/96) [398.2]

**9244** Jones, Jennifer B. *Heetunka's Harvest: A Tale of the Plains Indians* (K–3). Illus. by Shannon Keegan. 1995, Roberts Rinehart $15.95 (1-879373-17-3). 32pp. Nature takes revenge on a thieving Dakota Indian woman who steals from Heetunka the bean mouse. (Rev: BL 1/1/95; SLJ 4/95) [398.2]

**9245** Larrabee, Lisa. *Grandmother Five Baskets* (2–4). Illus. by Lori Sawyer. 1993, Harbinger paper $9.95 (0-943173-90-6). 60pp. Using 5 baskets that have been made by a Poarch Creek Indian woman as a metaphor, different stages of life are explained. (Rev: SLJ 3/94)

**9246** Larry, Charles. *Peboan and Seegwun* (1–4). Illus. 1993, Farrar $16.00 (0-374-35773-0). 32pp. This Ojibwa folktale tells how spring comes and takes the place of winter. (Rev: BL 12/1/93) [398.2]

**9247** Lasky, Kathryn. *Cloud Eyes* (K–4). Illus. by Barry Moser. 1994, Harcourt $14.95 (0-15-219168-2). In this folklike story, a young Native American is able to subdue both a hiveful of bees and some greedy bears to provide honey for his people. (Rev: SLJ 10/94) [398.2]

**9248** Lavitt, Edward, and Robert E. McDowell. *Nihancan's Feast of Beaver: Animal Tales of the North American Indians* (2–6). Illus. by Bunny P. Huffman. 1990, Museum of New Mexico paper $12.95 (0-89013-211-9). 120pp. This handsome book contains 36 tales from 9 different cultural areas in North America. (Rev: BL 3/1/91) [398.2]

**9249** Lelooska, Chief. *Echoes of the Elders: The Stories and Paintings of Chief Lelooska* (1–4). Illus. by author. 1997, DK Publg. $24.95 (0-7894-2455-X). 38pp. Five American Indian tales that reveal a profound respect for nature and the role of the supernatural in everyday life. (Rev: HB 11–12/97; SLJ 11/97*) [398.2]

**9250** Lewis, Paul O. *Frog Girl* (K–3). Illus. 1997, Beyond Words $14.95 (1-885223-57-9). 32pp. In this Pacific Northwest Indian tale, a young girl helps save the frogs that have been captured by a group of boys. (Rev: BL 11/1/97; SLJ 11/97) [398.2]

**9251** Lewis, Paul O. *Storm Boy* (1–4). Illus. 1995, Beyond Words $14.95 (1-885223-12-9). 32pp. A West Coast Indian tale of the adventures of a young man who ventures into a strange village. (Rev: BL 9/15/95; SLJ 7/95*) [398.24]

**9252** London, Jonathan, and Lanny Pinola. *Fire Race: A Karuk Coyote Tale About How Fire Came to the People* (K–3). Illus. by Sylvia Long. 1993, Chronicle $13.95 (0-8118-0241-8). 32pp. Wise Coyote and some animal friends, who are suffering through a cold winter, steal fire from the Yellow Jacket sisters. (Rev: BL 7/93; SLJ 8/93) [398.2]

**9253** Luenn, Nancy. *The Miser on the Mountain: A Nisqually Legend of Mount Rainier* (3–6). Illus. by Pierr Morgan. 1997, Sasquatch $15.95 (1-57061-082-7). 32pp. An Indian legend set on Ta-co-bet, or Mount Rainier, in which greed leads to a man's downfall. (Rev: BL 9/15/97; SLJ 1/98) [398.2]

**9254** McDermott, Gerald. *Arrow to the Sun: A Pueblo Indian Tale* (K–4). Illus. by author. 1991, Viking $16.99 (0-670-13369-8); Puffin paper $5.99 (0-14-050211-4). 48pp. Brilliant colors effectively highlight this adaptation of a Pueblo myth — the search by a young Indian boy for his father, the Sun. Caldecott Medal winner, 1975. [398.2]

**9255** McDermott, Gerald. *Coyote: A Trickster Tale from the American Southwest* (PS–K). Illus. 1994, Harcourt $15.00 (0-15-220724-4). 32pp. Obnoxious Coyote has a comedown when he tries to fly with the crows. (Rev: BCCB 11/94; BL 8/94*; SLJ 11/94) [398.2]

**9256** McDermott, Gerald. *Raven: A Trickster Tale from the Pacific Northwest* (K–4). Illus. by author. 1993, Harcourt $14.95 (0-15-265661-8). 32pp. A traditional tale told by the tribes of the area and illustrated by a Caldecott Medal winner. (Rev: BCCB 6/93*; BL 3/1/93*; HB 7–8/93*; SLJ 5/93*) [398]

**9257** Malotki, Ekkehart, comp. *The Magic Hummingbird: A Hopi Folktale* (2–4). Illus. by Michael Lacapa. 1996, Kiva $15.95 (1-885772-04-1). In this Hopi tale, a boy makes a toy hummingbird that comes to life and helps end a drought by taking the boy and his sister to the fertility god. (Rev: SLJ 11/96) [398.2]

**9258** Manitonquat. *The Children of the Morning Light: Wampanoag Tales* (3–5). Illus. 1994, Macmillan paper $16.95 (0-02-765905-4). 80pp. Several creation stories and 4 other legends from the Wampanoag Indians of Massachusetts are retold. (Rev: BCCB 6/94; BL 4/15/94; HB 7–8/94; SLJ 4/94) [398.2]

**9259** Martin, Rafe. *The Boy Who Lived with the Seals* (4–6). Illus. by David Shannon. 1993, Putnam LB $15.95 (0-399-22413-0). 32pp. A boy vanishes and goes to live with the seals, becoming one of them. (Rev: BCCB 6/93; BL 3/15/93*; HB 7–8/93; SLJ 4/93) [398.2]

**9260** Martin, Rafe. *The Rough-Face Girl* (1–4). Illus. by David Shannon. 1992, Putnam LB $15.95 (0-399-21859-9). 32pp. This variation on the Cinderella tale takes place in an Algonquin village on the shores of Lake Ontario. (Rev: BL 4/15/92; HB 7–8/92; SLJ 5/92) [398.2]

**9261** Max, Jill, ed. *Spider Spins a Story: Fourteen Legends from Native America* (3–6). Illus. 1997,

Northland $16.95 (0-87358-611-5). 72pp. Spider plays a prominent role in these folktales, illustrated by 6 American Indian artists. (Rev: BL 12/15/97; SLJ 1/98) [398.2]

**9262** Mayo, Gretchen Will, reteller. *Big Trouble for Tricky Rabbit!* (2–4). Illus. by Gretchen Will Mayo. Series: Native American Trickster Tales. 1994, Walker LB $13.85 (0-8027-8276-0). 38pp. Using simple vocabulary and short sentences, the author retells 5 trickster tales from Native American folklore, all involving Rabbit. (Rev: BCCB 6/94; SLJ 7/94) [398.2]

**9263** Mayo, Gretchen Will. *Earthmaker's Tales: North American Indian Stories About Earth Happenings* (4–6). Illus. 1989, Walker LB $13.85 (0-8027-6840-7). 96pp. Legends that center on the earth itself. (Rev: BL 3/1/89) [398.2]

**9264** Mayo, Gretchen Will. *Here Comes Tricky Rabbit!* (2–4). Illus. Series: Native American Trickster Tales. 1994, Walker LB $13.85 (0-8027-8274-4). 48pp. These 5 folktales reveal Rabbit to be a wily trickster. (Rev: BCCB 6/94; BL 8/94; SLJ 7/94) [398.2]

**9265** Mayo, Gretchen Will, reteller. *Meet Tricky Coyote!* (2–5). Illus. by Gretchen Will Mayo. Series: Native American Trickster Tales. 1993, Walker LB $13.85 (0-8027-8199-3). 36pp. A retelling of some short, humorous American Indian stories about the clever trickster coyote. Companion volumes are *That Tricky Coyote!* and *Magical Tales from Many Lands* (both 1993). (Rev: SLJ 9/93) [398.2]

**9266** Mayo, Gretchen Will. *Star Tales: North American Indian Stories About the Stars* (4–7). Illus. by author. 1987, Walker LB $13.85 (0-8027-6673-0). 96pp. Fourteen tales, each introduced by a one-page commentary on a constellation. (Rev: BL 6/15/87; SLJ 5/87) [398.2]

**9267** Mayo, Gretchen Will. *That Tricky Coyote!* (PS–3). Illus. 1993, Walker LB $13.85 (0-8027-8201-9). 32pp. Five short stories from different tribes that deal with the escapades of the trickster Coyote. (Rev: BL 9/1/93; SLJ 9/93) [398.2]

**9268** Monroe, Jean Guard, and Ray A. Williamson. *They Dance in the Sky: Native American Star Myths* (4–8). Illus. 1987, Houghton $15.00 (0-395-39970-X). 130pp. Numerous Native American legends about stars. (Rev: BL 9/1/87; SLJ 9/87) [398.2]

**9269** Morgan, Pierr, reteller. *Supper for Crow: A Northwest Coast Indian Tale* (1–4). Illus. by Pierr Morgan. 1995, Crown LB $15.99 (0-517-59379-3). A folktale about greed and trust that features a mischievous raven that delights in tricking other birds. (Rev: SLJ 8/95) [398.2]

**9270** Murphy, Claire R. *The Prince and the Salmon People* (3–5). Illus. by Duane Pasco. 1993, Rizzoli $19.95 (0-8478-1662-1). 48pp. The son of an Indian chief in the Northwest reminds his people of the importance of performing the rituals honoring the salmon. (Rev: BL 6/1–15/93) [398.2]

**9271** Neitzel, Shirley. *From the Land of the White Birch* (K–4). Illus. by Daniel Powers. 1997, River Road $14.95 (0-938682-44-X). 30pp. Three stories from the Ojibwa Indians explain such phenomena as the beaver's hairless tail and the bear's black nose. (Rev: SLJ 2/98) [398.2]

**9272** Oliviero, Jamie. *The Day Sun Was Stolen* (K–3). Illus. by Sharon Hitchcock. 1995, Hyperion LB $15.49 (0-7868-2026-8). 32pp. In this Haida Indian story, Bear, who is hot in his heavy coat, hides the sun in his cave to keep cool. (Rev: BL 11/1/95; SLJ 12/95) [398.2]

**9273** Oughton, Jerrie. *How the Stars Fell into the Sky: A Navajo Legend* (PS–3). Illus. by Lisa Desimini. 1992, Houghton $14.95 (0-395-58798-0). 32pp. In this Navajo legend, the trickster coyote brings chaos to the night sky. (Rev: BCCB 6/92; BL 3/15/92*; SLJ 5/92) [398.2]

**9274** Oughton, Jerrie. *The Magic Weaver of Rugs: A Tale of the Navajo* (2–5). Illus. by Lisa Desimini. 1994, Houghton $14.95 (0-395-66140-4). 32pp. This Navajo folktale explains how the gift of weaving came to the tribe through the help of the Spider Woman. (Rev: BL 3/1/94; SLJ 8/94) [398.2]

**9275** Pohrt, Tom. *Coyote Goes Walking* (PS–3). Illus. 1995, Farrar $16.00 (0-374-31628-7). 32pp. Different aspects of Coyote's personality are explored in these 4 tales from the Plains Indians. (Rev: BCCB 12/95; BL 12/15/95; SLJ 12/95) [398.2]

**9276** Pollock, Penny. *The Turkey Girl: A Zuni Cinderella Story* (4–6). Illus. by Ed Young. 1996, Little, Brown $16.95 (0-316-71314-7). 32pp. In this Zuni folktale, Turkey Girl's magical transformation ends in disaster when she forgets her promise to return to her flock of birds. (Rev: BCCB 4/96; BL 4/15/96; HB 5–6/96; SLJ 5/96) [398.2]

**9277** Renner, Michelle. *The Girl Who Swam with the Fish* (K–3). Illus. by Christine Cox. 1995, Alaska Northwest $15.95 (0-88240-442-3). 32pp. In this fantasy, a curious girl gets to run with the salmon. (Rev: BL 10/15/95; SLJ 10/95) [398.2]

**9278** Riordan, James. *The Songs My Paddle Sings* (2–5). Illus. 1998, Pavilion paper $16.95 (1-86205-076-7). 128pp. An anthology of 20 legends from various American Indian peoples, including creation stories, hero legends, and cautionary tales. (Rev: BL 3/15/98) [398.2]

**9279** Rodanas, Kristina, adapt. *The Dragonfly's Tale* (PS–3). Illus. 1992, Houghton $14.95 (0-395-57003-4). 28pp. The Ashiwi's waste of food causes the Corn Maiden to bring famine to the village, but a boy and his sister find a way to harvest a successful crop. (Rev: BCCB 6/92; BL 4/1/92; SLJ 7/92) [398.2]

**9280** Rodanas, Kristina. *The Eagle's Song: A Tale from the Pacific Northwest* (2–5). Illus. 1995, Little, Brown $15.95 (0-316-75375-0). 32pp. An American Indian folktale that describes how, through music, Ermine brought his people out of self-imposed isolation. (Rev: BL 12/15/95; SLJ 1/96) [398.2]

**9281** Rosen, Michael. *Crow and Hawk* (PS–3). Illus. by John Clementson. 1995, Harcourt $15.00 (0-15-200257-X). 32pp. In this Pueblo Indian folktale, a hawk demands custody of the crows that she has helped hatch. (Rev: BL 4/15/95; SLJ 7/95) [398.2]

**9282** Rosen, Michael J. *The Dog Who Walked with God* (K–4). Illus. by Stan Fellows. 1998, Candlewick $16.99 (0-7636-0470-4). 40pp. An Indian creation story that tells how the Great Traveler, accompanied by his dog, reshapes the world after a devastating flood. (Rev: BL 3/15/98) [398.2]

**9283** Ross, Gayle. *How Turtle's Back Was Cracked: A Traditional Cherokee Tale* (K–3). Illus. by Murv Jacob. 1995, Dial paper $14.89 (0-8037-1729-6). 32pp. This Cherokee tale explains how the Turtle got cracks on his back when he is thrown into a river. (Rev: BCCB 2/95; BL 1/15/95; HB 3–4/95; SLJ 4/95) [398.2]

**9284** Ross, Gayle. *The Legend of the Windigo: A Tale from Native North America* (3–6). Illus. by Murv Jacob. 1996, Dial paper $14.89 (0-8037-1898-5). 32pp. A fast-paced version of the story of the first mosquitoes and the monster Windigo. (Rev: BCCB 11/96; BL 9/15/96; SLJ 11/96) [398.2]

**9285** Rubalcaba, Jill. *Uncegila's Seventh Spot: A Lakota Legend* (3–5). Illus. 1995, Clarion $14.95 (0-395-68970-8). 32pp. After killing a monster that has terrorized their people, 2 Indian brothers continue to heed the demands made by the monster's heart. (Rev: BL 9/15/95; SLJ 1/96) [398]

**9286** Sage, James. *Coyote Makes Man* (PS–3). Illus. by Britta Teckentrup. 1995, Simon & Schuster $15.00 (0-689-80011-8). 32pp. In this Crow Indian tale, Coyote sets out to create the first human. (Rev: BCCB 7–8/95; BL 5/15/95; SLJ 6/95) [398.2]

**9287** San Souci, Robert D. *Sootface: An Ojibwa Cinderella Story* (K–4). Illus. by Daniel San Souci. 1994, Doubleday $16.95 (0-385-31202-4). 32pp. In this Ojibwa tale, the humble Sootface is chosen to be the bride of an invisible warrior. (Rev: BL 10/15/94; SLJ 11/94) [398.2]

**9288** San Souci, Robert D. *Two Bear Cubs* (K–4). Illus. by Daniel San Souci. 1997, Yosemite $14.95 (0-939666-87-1). Two bear cubs fall asleep on a rock that grows into a mountain in this American Indian folktale that explains the rock formation known as El

Capitan in Yosemite National Park. (Rev: BL 1/1–15/98; SLJ 4/98) [398.2]

**9289** Siberell, Anne. *Whale in the Sky* (PS–2). Illus. by author. 1982, Puffin paper $3.95 (0-525-44197-2). 32pp. Thunderbird removes Whale from the sea to save the salmon for the Indians. [398.2]

**9290** Sierra, Judy. *Wiley and the Hairy Man* (K–3). Illus. by Brian Pinkney. 1996, Dutton paper $15.99 (0-525-67477-2). 32pp. This popular African American folktale has been given a successful treatment by a good retelling and vibrant illustrations. (Rev: BCCB 3/96; BL 3/1/96; HB 5–6/96; SLJ 3/96) [398.2]

**9291** Simms, Laura. *The Bone Man* (2–4). Illus. by Michael McCurdy. 1997, Hyperion LB $15.49 (0-7868-2074-8). 32pp. This is the story of a young American Indian who must fulfill his grandmother's prediction and confront a horrible monster, the Bone Man. (Rev: BL 11/1/97; SLJ 11/97) [398.2]

**9292** Spooner, Michael, and Lolita Taylor. *Old Meshikee and the Little Crabs* (K–3). Illus. by John Hart. 1996, Holt $15.95 (0-8050-3487-0). 32pp. The sand crabs take revenge on Old Meshikee the turtle because of his loud drumming. (Rev: BL 6/1–15/96; SLJ 6/96) [398.2]

**9293** Steptoe, John, reteller. *The Story of Jumping Mouse: A Native American Legend* (1–4). 1984, Morrow paper $4.95 (0-688-08740-X). 40pp. The legend of the mouse who, because of good acts, is transformed into an eagle. [398.2]

**9294** Stevens, Janet. *Coyote Steals the Blanket: A Ute Tale* (4–6). Illus. 1993, Holiday LB $15.95 (0-8234-0996-1). 32pp. In this amusing Indian legend, a rock chases a coyote after the animal steals a blanket that had covered it. (Rev: BCCB 5/93*; BL 4/1/93; SLJ 6/93) [398.2]

**9295** Stevens, Janet. *Old Bag of Bones: A Coyote Tale* (K–4). Illus. 1996, Holiday LB $15.95 (0-8234-1215-6). 32pp. Coyote, who resents growing old, persuades Young Buffalo to share his youth with him in this Shoshone tale. (Rev: BCCB 5/96; BL 5/1/96; HB 7–8/96; SLJ 5/96*) [398.24]

**9296** Strauss, Susan. *Coyote Stories for Children* (2–7). Illus. by Gary Lund. 1992, Beyond Words paper $7.95 (0-941831-62-0). A collection of 4 stories from Native American cultures that tell about the trickster coyote. (Rev: SLJ 4/92) [398.2]

**9297** Swamp, Chief Jake. *Giving Thanks: A Native American Good Morning Message* (PS–1). Illus. by Erwin Printup. 1995, Lee & Low $15.95 (1-880000-15-6). 24pp. A Mohawk chieftain gives thanks for Mother Earth and the universe that surrounds her. (Rev: BL 10/15/95; SLJ 11/95) [299]

**9298** Taylor, C. J. *The Ghost and Lone Warrior: An Arapaho Legend* (2–5). Illus. by author. 1991, Tundra $13.95 (0-88776-263-8). When he is injured, Lone Warrior is left behind by his hunting party and must survive in the wilderness alone. (Rev: BCCB 2/92; SLJ 2/92) [398.2]

**9299** Taylor, C. J. *How We Saw the World: Nine Native Stories of the Way Things Began* (4–6). Illus. 1993, Tundra $17.95 (0-88776-302-2). 32pp. These 9 stories from various Indian tribes explain the origin of several animals, like horses, and geographical landmarks, like Niagara Falls. (Rev: BL 11/1/93; SLJ 2/94) [398.3]

**9300** Taylor, C. J. *The Secret of the White Buffalo* (K–3). Illus. 1993, Tundra $13.95 (0-88776-321-9). 24pp. Two Indian scouts encounter a beautiful woman when they set out to track buffalo in this Oglala Indian folktale. (Rev: BL 1/1/94) [398.2]

**9301** Taylor, Harriet P. *Brother Wolf: A Seneca Tale* (PS–3). Illus. 1996, Farrar $15.00 (0-374-30997-3). 32pp. A Seneca folktale concerning the consequences of a rivalry between Wolf and Raccoon. (Rev: BL 11/1/96; SLJ 10/96) [398.24]

**9302** Taylor, Harriet P. *Coyote and the Laughing Butterflies* (1–3). Illus. 1995, Simon & Schuster paper $15.00 (0-02-788846-0). 32pp. Butterflies always carry Coyote home before he can gather the bag of salt he sets out to get. (Rev: BL 7/95; SLJ 8/95) [398.2]

**9303** Taylor, Harriet P. *Coyote Places the Stars* (K–2). Illus. 1993, Bradbury LB $16.00 (0-02-788845-2). 32pp. A clever coyote rearranges the stars in the sky so they resemble the shapes of his animal friends in this Wasco Indian folktale. (Rev: BL 11/15/93; SLJ 12/93) [398.2]

**9304** Taylor, Harriet P. *When Bear Stole the Chinook* (K–3). Illus. 1997, Farrar $16.00 (0-374-30589-7). 32pp. In this Blackfoot Indian folktale, an orphan boy and his animal friends investigate why the spring warm winds don't come. (Rev: BL 1/1–15/98; SLJ 10/97) [398.2]

**9305** Toye, William. *The Loon's Necklace* (K–3). Illus. by Elizabeth Cleaver. 1990, Oxford paper $7.95 (0-19-540675-3). 24pp. In this reissue of a 1977 picture book of an Indian legend, an old man rewards a loon with a necklace for helping him regain his sight. [398.2]

**9306** Van Laan, Nancy. *In a Circle Long Ago: A Treasury of Native Lore from North America* (3–5). Illus. 1995, Knopf LB $21.99 (0-679-95807-5). 128pp. Nature is explored in 25 tales from North American Indian peoples, geographically arranged, with an introduction to their cultures. (Rev: BL 11/15/95; SLJ 11/95) [392.2]

**9307** Van Laan, Nancy. *Shingebiss: An Ojibwe Legend* (3–4). Illus. by Betsy Bowen. 1997, Houghton $16.00 (0-395-82745-0). 32pp. In this Ojibwa (Chip-

pewa) legend, it appears that Shingebiss, a duck, will freeze during the winter because he has only 4 logs to heat his lodge. (Rev: BL 7/97; HB 11–12/97; SLJ 10/97) [398.2]

**9308** Wisniewski, David. *The Wave of the Sea-Wolf* (3–6). Illus. by author. 1994, Clarion $17.00 (0-395-66478-0). This Tlingit Indian legend tells how Princess Kchokeen saves her people by luring destructive white traders to their death. (Rev: BCCB 11/94; SLJ 10/94) [398.2]

**9309** Wood, Audrey. *The Rainbow Bridge: Inspired by a Chumash Tale* (1–4). Illus. by Robert Florczak. 1995, Harcourt $16.00 (0-15-265475-5). 32pp. In this Chumash tale, earth goddess Hutash turns some of her people into dolphins to save them from drowning. (Rev: BCCB 12/95; BL 12/1/95; SLJ 10/95) [398.24]

**9310** Wood, Douglas. *Rabbit and the Moon* (PS–3). Illus. by Leslie Baker. 1998, Simon & Schuster $15.00 (0-689-80769-4). 40pp. In this Cree Indian tale, Rabbit persuades Crane to take him on a flight so that he can get a moon's eye view of the world. (Rev: BL 2/15/98) [398.2]

**9311** Wood, Douglas. *The Windigo's Return: A North Woods Story* (3–6). Illus. by Greg Couch. 1996, Simon & Schuster paper $16.00 (0-689-80065-7). 32pp. An exciting, imaginative version of the Indian legend of how the first mosquitoes came to be. (Rev: BCCB 11/96; BL 9/15/96; SLJ 11/96) [398.2]

**9312** Wood, Nancy. *The Girl Who Loved Coyotes: Stories of the Southwest* (K–4). Illus. by Diana Bryer. 1995, Morrow $16.00 (0-688-13981-7). 48pp. Twelve stories about the coyote who manages to survive in its native habitat in spite of the invasions of strangers of many cultures. (Rev: BL 9/15/95; SLJ 12/95) [398.2]

**9313** Yolen, Jane. *Sky Dogs* (PS–3). Illus. by Barry Moser. 1990, Harcourt $15.95 (0-15-275480-6). 32pp. This picture book, based on Indian stories, tells how the Blackfeet first acquired horses. (Rev: BCCB 2/91; BL 10/15/90; HB 1–2/90; SLJ 11/90) [398.2]

**9314** Young, Richard, and Judy D. Young, eds. *Race with Buffalo: And Other Native American Stories for Young Readers* (3–7). Illus. by Wendell E. Hall. 1994, August House $19.95 (0-87483-343-4); paper $12.95 (0-87483-342-6). 175pp. This collection of 32 American Indian folktales includes such genres as creation and trickster stories. (Rev: SLJ 8/94) [398.2]

## United States

**9315** Bang, Molly. *Wiley and the Hairy Man* (2–4). Illus. by author. 1996, Simon & Schuster $14.00 (0-689-81141-1); paper $3.99 (0-689-81142-X). 64pp.

In this story from Alabama, Wiley's mother helps him outwit the Hairy Man, a terrible swamp creature. Adapted from an American folktale. [398.2]

**9316** Birdseye, Tom. *Soap! Soap! Don't Forget the Soap! An Appalachian Folktale* (3–6). Illus. by Andrew Glass. 1993, Holiday LB $15.95 (0-8234-1005-6). 32pp. An adaptation of a familiar story about a forgetful hero sent to the store by his mother. (Rev: BCCB 6/93; BL 3/15/93; HB 5–6/93) [398.2]

**9317** Brown, Marcia. *Backbone of the King: The Story of Paka'a and His Son Ku* (5–7). Illus. by author. 1984, Univ. of Hawaii Pr. $9.95 (0-8248-0963-7). 180pp. A reissue of the book based on a Hawaiian legend of a boy who wants to help his exiled father. [398.2]

**9318** Cech, John. *Django* (K–3). Illus. by Sharon McGinley-Nally. 1994, Four Winds paper $15.95 (0-02-765705-1). 40pp. A fiddler named Django saves the animals of a Florida swamp when he warns them by playing his instrument during a hurricane. (Rev: BL 12/1/94; SLJ 12/94) [398.21]

**9319** Chase, Richard. *Grandfather Tales* (4–6). Illus. by Berkeley Williams. 1948, Houghton $17.95 (0-395-06692-1); paper $7.95 (0-395-56150-7). 240pp. Folktales gathered from the South. Also use: *The Jack Tales* (1943). [398.2]

**9320** Cohen, Daniel. *Railway Ghosts and Highway Horrors* (3–5). Illus. by Stephen Marchesi. 1993, Scholastic paper $2.95 (0-590-45423-4). 112pp. Phantom hitchhikers and accident victims fill this anthology of American and British travelers' lore. (Rev: BL 11/15/91) [133.1]

**9321** Cohen, Daniel. *Southern Fried Rat and Other Gruesome Tales* (6–8). Illus. by Peggy Brier. 1989, Avon paper $3.50 (0-380-70655-5). 128pp. Grisly folktales — some funny, some gruesome. [398.2]

**9322** Compton, Joanne, reteller. *Ashpet: An Appalachian Tale* (1–3). Illus. by Kenn Compton. 1994, Holiday LB $15.95 (0-8234-1106-0). An Appalachian version of the Cinderella story with some clever twists. (Rev: SLJ 6/94) [398.2]

**9323** Compton, Joanne. *Sody Sallyratus* (PS–3). Illus. by Kenn Compton. 1995, Holiday LB $15.95 (0-8234-1165-6). 32pp. In this Appalacian folktale, Jack tries to outsmart a bear that has swallowed his family. (Rev: BL 2/1/95; SLJ 4/95) [398.2]

**9324** Davis, Aubrey. *Sody Salleratus* (PS–2). Illus. by Alan Daniel and Lea Daniel. 1998, Kids Can $14.95 (1-55074-281-7). 32pp. In this American folktale, a wise squirrel solves the problem of having a bear in town that delights in eating everyone. (Rev: BL 3/15/98; SLJ 4/98) [398.2]

**9325** Davis, Donald. *Jack and the Animals* (PS–2). Illus. by Kitty Harvill. 1995, August House $15.95

(0-87483-413-9). 32pp. Jack and a group of unhappy animals outwit a gang of robbers in this Appalachian tale. (Rev: BL 10/1/95; SLJ 1/96)

**9326** DeFelice, Cynthia. *The Dancing Skeleton* (1–3). Illus. by Robert Andrew Parker. 1996, Simon & Schuster $5.99 (0-689-80453-9). 32pp. Old Aaron refuses to stay in his coffin until he "feels dead." (Rev: BCCB 10/89; BL 9/1/89; HB 1–2/90; SLJ 9/89*) [398.2]

**9327** Doucet, Sharon Arms. *Why Lapin's Ears Are Long and Other Tales from the Louisiana Bayou* (4–6). Illus. by David Catrow. 1997, Orchard LB $19.99 (0-531-33041-9). 64pp. Three entertaining folktales from Cajun country that feature the trickster rabbit. (Rev: BL 8/97; HB 9–10/97; SLJ 9/97) [398.2]

**9328** Durell, Ann, sel. *The Diane Goode Book of American Folk Tales and Songs* (2–5). Illus. by Diane Goode. 1989, Dutton paper $15.95 (0-525-44458-0). 63pp. This is a fetching collection of 9 tales and several poems that come from America's folk tradition. (Rev: BCCB 11/89; BL 9/1/89; HB 1–2/90; SLJ 10/89) [398.2]

**9329** Faulkner, William J. *Brer Tiger and the Big Wind* (K–4). Illus. by Roberta Wilson. 1995, Morrow LB $14.93 (0-688-12986-2). 32pp. Brer Rabbit tricks Brer Tiger so that the other animals can secure drinking water. (Rev: BCCB 11/95; BL 4/1/95; HB 5–6/95; SLJ 4/95) [398.2]

**9330** Forest, Heather. *The Baker's Dozen: A Colonial American Tale* (PS–2). Illus. by Susan Gaber. 1993, Harcourt paper $5.00 (0-152-05687-4). 28pp. A baker in colonial New York State cuts back on his cookie recipe, and when a woman demands 13 cookies for the dozen and he refuses, his baking is cursed. (Rev: BCCB 10/88; BL 9/15/88; SLJ 4/89) [398.2]

**9331** Galdone, Joanna. *The Tailypo: A Ghost Story* (1–3). Illus. by Paul Galdone. 1984, Houghton paper $6.95 (0-395-30084-3). In this ghostly story, a mysterious creature returns to retrieve his tail, cut off by an old man. [398.2]

**9332** Hamilton, Virginia. *Her Stories: African American Folktales, Fairy Tales, and True Tales* (5–8). Illus. by Leo Dillon and Diane Dillon. 1995, Scholastic $19.95 (0-590-47370-0). 144pp. A collection of 19 folktales about African American women. (Rev: BL 11/1/95*; SLJ 11/95*) [398.2]

**9333** Hamilton, Virginia. *The People Could Fly: American Black Folk Tales* (4–8). Illus. by Leo Dillon and Diane Dillon. 1985, Knopf LB $18.99 (0-394-96925-1); paper $13.00 (0-679-84336-1). 192pp. These 24 folktales include such familiar titles as Tar Baby and lesser-known stories from Africa. (Rev: BCCB 7/85; BL 7/85; SLJ 11/85) [398.2]

**9334** Hamilton, Virginia. *When Birds Could Talk and Bats Could Sing: The Adventures of Bruh Sparrow, Sis Wren, and Their Friends* (4–6). Illus. by Barry Moser. 1996, Scholastic $17.95 (0-590-47372-7). 72pp. Each of these 8 tales from the American South deals with unpleasant, often foolish birds, and each ends with an important moral. (Rev: BCCB 6/96; BL 4/15/96*; HB 9–10/96; SLJ 5/96*) [398.2]

**9335** Harris, Jim. *Jack and the Giant: A Story Full of Beans* (K–4). Illus. 1997, Northland LB $15.95 (0-87358-680-8). 32pp. This version of "Jack and the Beanstalk" had Jack living on a ranch in Arizona with his mother, Annie Okey-Dokey. (Rev: BL 2/1/98; SLJ 2/98) [398.2]

**9336** Harris, Joel Chandler. *Brer Rabbit and Boss Lion* (PS–4). Retold by Brad Kessler. Illus. by Bill Mayer. 1996, Simon & Schuster paper $10.95 (0-689-80606-X). When a lion begins to eat the inhabitants of Brer Village, Brer Rabbit decides to take on the beast. (Rev: SLJ 1/97) [398.2]

**9337** Harris, Joel Chandler. *Jump! The Adventures of Brer Rabbit* (3–5). Adapted by Van Dyke Parks and Malcolm Jones. Illus. by Barry Moser. 1986, Harcourt $15.95 (0-15-241350-2); paper $7.00 (0-15-201493-4). 40pp. An edition with tracings of the stories' roots in oral tradition. (Rev: BCCB 11/86; BL 1/1/87; SLJ 11/86) [398.2]

**9338** Harris, Joel Chandler. *The Tales of Uncle Remus: The Adventures of Brer Rabbit* (4–8). Retold by Julius Lester. Illus. by Jerry Pinkney. 1987, Dial paper $16.89 (0-8037-0272-8). 176pp. A landmark collection resurrecting these biting tales. (Rev: BL 4/15/87; HB 7–8/87; SLJ 4/87) [398.2]

**9339** Hayward, Linda. *All Stuck Up* (1–3). Illus. by Normand Chartier. 1990, Random LB $7.99 (0-679-90216-3); paper $3.99 (0-679-80216-9). 32pp. The tar baby story featuring Brer Rabbit is retold. (Rev: BCCB 7–8/92; BL 6/1/90; SLJ 8/90) [398.2]

**9340** Hayward, Linda. *Hello, House!* (1–2). Illus. by Lynn Munsinger. 1988, Random LB $6.99 (0-394-98864-7); paper $3.99 (0-394-88864-2). 32pp. The Uncle Remus tale in which Brer Rabbit outsmarts sly Brer Wolf. (Rev: BL 10/1/88) [398.2]

**9341** Helldorfer, M. C. *Jack, Skinny Bones, and the Golden Pancakes* (K–3). Illus. by Elise Primavera. 1996, Viking paper $14.99 (0-670-86006-9). 32pp. Jack and his dog, Skinny Bones, outwit the devil in this original folktale set in the Southwest. (Rev: BCCB 12/96; BL 10/15/96; SLJ 10/96) [398]

**9342** Hoberman, Mary Ann. *Miss Mary Mack: A Hand-Clapping Rhyme* (K–3). Illus. by Nadine Bernard Westcott. 1998, Little, Brown $14.95 (0-316-93118-7). 32pp. A catchy hand-clapping rhyme that uses appropriate cartoon illustrations. (Rev: BL 3/15/98) [398.2]

**9343** Hooks, William H. *Snowbear Whittington: An Appalachian Beauty and the Beast* (1–4). Illus. by Victoria Lisi. 1994, Macmillan paper $15.95 (0-02-744355-8). 56pp. To save her father, a young girl agrees to accompany a large white bear to his castle in this American folktale. (Rev: BL 10/15/94; SLJ 11/94) [398.2]

**9344** Hooks, William H. *The Three Little Pigs and the Fox* (PS–2). Illus. by S. D. Schindler. 1997, Simon & Schuster paper $5.95 (0-689-80962-X). 32pp. A refreshing version drawn from Appalachian sources. (Rev: BCCB 1/90*; BL 9/1/89; HB 3–4/90; SLJ 10/89) [398.2]

**9345** Hunt, Angela E. *The Tale of Three Trees: A Traditional Folktale* (K–2). Illus. by Tim Jonke. 1989, Lion $14.95 (0-7459-1743-7). 32pp. A folktale about 3 trees — a manger for the Christ child, a fishing boat that carries Jesus, and timbers that become the cross. (Rev: BL 11/1/89) [398.2]

**9346** Keats, Ezra Jack. *John Henry: An American Legend* (1–3). Illus. by author. 1965, Knopf LB $12.99 (0-394-99052-8); paper $5.99 (0-394-89052-3). 32pp. Large, bold figures capture the spirit of the hero who died with a hammer in his hand. [398.2]

**9347** Kellogg, Steven. *Mike Fink* (PS–4). Illus. 1992, Morrow LB $15.93 (0-688-07004-3). 48pp. The old tall tale about Mike Fink, who ran away from home as a 2-day-old babe, is illustrated with humor. (Rev: BL 9/15/92; HB 11–12/92; SLJ 10/92) [398.2]

**9348** Kellogg, Steven. *Paul Bunyan* (K–4). Illus. by author. 1984, Morrow LB $15.93 (0-688-03850-6); paper $5.95 (0-688-05800-0). 40pp. Several stories about Paul and the blue ox Babe, all wittily illustrated. [398.2]

**9349** Kellogg, Steven, reteller. *Pecos Bill* (K–3). Illus. by Steven Kellogg. 1986, Scholastic paper $5.95 (0-688-09924-6). 32pp. Humor permeates these tall tales of the American folk hero. (Rev: BCCB 11/86; BL 9/1/86; SLJ 9/86) [398.2]

**9350** Kellogg, Steven. *Sally Ann Thunder Ann Whirlwind Crockett* (PS–3). Illus. 1995, Morrow LB $16.93 (0-688-14043-2). 48pp. A humorous look at the life of Davy Crockett's wife and her equally amazing exploits. (Rev: BCCB 9/95; BL 8/95; SLJ 10/95) [398.2]

**9351** Kidd, Ronald, ed. *On Top of Old Smoky: A Collection of Songs and Stories from Appalachia* (4–6). Illus. by Linda Anderson. 1992, Ideals $13.95 (0-8249-8569-9). 38pp. A handsome collection of songs and stories from Appalachia with distinctive illustrations. (Rev: BL 12/1/92) [782]

**9352** Kimmel, Eric A. *Billy Lazroe and the King of the Sea: A Tale of the Northwest* (2–4). Illus. by Michael Steirnagle. 1996, Harcourt $16.00 (0-15-200108-5). 40pp. A Russian folktale reset in Oregon, about Billy's love of the sea and its consequences. (Rev: BCCB 12/96; BL 12/15/96; SLJ 12/96) [398.2]

**9353** Lester, Julius. *Further Tales of Uncle Remus* (4–8). Illus. by Jerry Pinkney. 1990, Dial LB $14.89 (0-8037-0611-1). In this third volume of Julius Lester's collected tales of Uncle Remus, we meet such characters as Niz Cricket and Brer Turtle. (Rev: BCCB 5/90; BL 4/15/90*; HB 7–8/90; SLJ 5/90) [398.2]

**9354** Lester, Julius. *John Henry* (PS–4). Illus. by Jerry Pinkney. 1994, Dial paper $16.89 (0-8037-1607-9). 40pp. A glowing retelling of the John Henry story and his legendary contest with a steam drill. (Rev: BCCB 10/94; BL 6/1–15/94*; HB 11–12/94; SLJ 11/94) [398.2]

**9355** Lester, Julius. *The Knee-High Man and Other Tales* (K–2). Illus. by Ralph Pinto. 1972, Puffin paper $3.95 (0-8037-0234-5). 32pp. Six black American folktales concerned with animals make this an appealing selection for reading aloud or storytelling to younger readers. [398.2]

**9356** Lester, Julius. *The Last Tales of Uncle Remus* (4–8). Illus. by Jerry Pinkney. 1994, Dial paper $18.89 (0-8037-1304-5). 176pp. Tall tales, ghost stories, and trickster tales are all represented in these 39 selections of African American folktales. (Rev: BCCB 2/94; BL 12/15/93*; HB 5–6/94; SLJ 1/94) [398.2]

**9357** Lester, Julius. *More Tales of Uncle Remus: Further Adventures of Brer Rabbit, His Friends, Enemies, and Others* (3–6). Illus. by Jerry Pinkney. 1988, Dial LB $15.89 (0-8037-0420-8). 160pp. Thirty-seven tales of the famous trickster. (Rev: BL 6/15/88; HB 9–10/88; SLJ 7/88) [398.2]

**9358** Liddell, Janice. *Imani and the Flying Africans* (2–5). Illus. by Linda Nickens. 1994, African World Pr. $14.95 (0-86543-365-8); paper $6.95 (0-86543-366-6). After hearing about the Flying Africans, who could rise into the air and escape slavery, young Imani dreams that he is captured by kidnappers and uses the same method to achieve freedom. (Rev: SLJ 11/94) [398.2]

**9359** Lyons, Mary E., ed. *Raw Head, Bloody Bones: African-American Tales of the Supernatural* (5–7). 1991, Macmillan $15.00 (0-684-19333-7). 112pp. A bone-chiller full of ghosts, devils, and ogres as well as less familiar demons such as Plat-Eye and the monstrous night doctor. (Rev: BCCB 2/92; BL 1/1/92; HB 1–2/92; SLJ 12/91*) [398.2]

**9360** McCormick, Dell J. *Paul Bunyan Swings His Axe* (4–6). Illus. by author. 1936, Caxton $15.95 (0-87004-093-6). The stories of the giant woodsman and his great blue ox named Babe are favorites among American folktales. [398.2]

**9361** McKissack, Patricia. *The Dark-Thirty: Southern Tales of the Supernatural* (4–8). Illus. by Brian Pinkney. 1992, Knopf LB $17.99 (0-679-91863-9). 124pp. Ten tales "rooted in African-American history and the oral storytelling tradition." (Rev: BCCB 12/92; BL 12/15/92; HB 3–4/93; SLJ 12/92) [398.2]

**9362** Mathews, Judith, and Fay Robinson. *Nathaniel Willy, Scared Silly* (PS–2). Illus. by Alexi Natchev. 1994, Bradbury paper $15.00 (0-02-765285-8). 32pp. Gramma brings in a variety of animals to comfort young Nathaniel who can't get to sleep because of a squeaky door. (Rev: BCCB 2/94; BL 5/15/94; SLJ 5/94) [398.2]

**9363** Medearis, Angela Shelf. *Tailypo: A Newfangled Tall Tale* (K–3). Illus. by Sterling Brown. 1996, Holiday LB $15.95 (0-8234-1249-0). 32pp. A variation on the folktale about a monster that leaves its tail behind in the cabin of an African American boy. (Rev: BL 11/1/96; SLJ 1/97) [398.2]

**9364** Metaxas, Eric. *Stormalong: The Legendary Sea Captain* (1–4). Illus. by Don Vanderbeek. 1995, Rabbit Ears paper $19.95 (0-689-80194-7). An amusing retelling of the tall tale about the legendary New England sea captain. (Rev: SLJ 12/95) [398.2]

**9365** Osborne, Mary Pope. *American Tall Tales* (4–7). Illus. by Michael McCurdy. 1991, Knopf LB $23.99 (0-679-90089-6). 115pp. Nine tall tales perfect for telling to all ages. (Rev: BCCB 1/92; BL 3/15/92; SLJ 12/91*) [398.2]

**9366** Rattigan, Jama Kim. *The Woman in the Moon: A Story from Hawai'i* (2–5). Illus. by Carla Golembe. 1996, Little, Brown $15.95 (0-316-73446-2). 32pp. In this Hawaiian story, an overworked woman escapes to the moon. (Rev: BL 11/1/96; SLJ 12/96) [398.2]

**9367** Reneaux, J. J. *Haunted Bayou: And Other Cajun Ghost Stories* (4–8). 1994, August House $19.95 (0-87483-384-1); paper $9.95 (0-87483-385-X). 158pp. Thirteen scary, entertaining folktales from Cajun country are retold effectively. (Rev: SLJ 12/94) [398.2]

**9368** Reneaux, J. J. *Why Alligator Hates Dog* (1–3). Illus. by Donnie Lee Green. 1995, August House $15.95 (0-87483-412-0). 32pp. Dog loves to torment Alligator, but the wily reptile plots his revenge. (Rev: BL 10/15/95; SLJ 1/96) [398.3]

**9369** Rounds, Glen. *Ol' Paul, the Mighty Logger* (3–6). Illus. by author. 1976, Holiday $16.95 (0-8234-0269-X); paper $5.95 (0-8234-0713-6). 96pp. An account of the incredible exploits of one of our national folk heroes. [398.2]

**9370** Rumford, James. *The Island-Below-the-Star* (1–3). Illus. 1998, Houghton $15.00 (0-395-85159-9). 32pp. A folk-like story about 5 adventurous brothers who set out to find a new island home. (Rev: BL 3/15/98) [398.2]

**9371** Sanfield, Steve. *A Natural Man: The True Story of John Henry* (4–6). Illus. 1990, Godine paper $9.95 (0-87923-844-5). 32pp. The tall tale of the steel driving man "who died with a hammer in his hand." (Rev: BCCB 2/87; BL 2/1/87; SLJ 4/87) [398.2]

**9372** San Souci, Robert D. *Cut from the Same Cloth: American Women of Myth, Legend and Tall Tale* (4–6). Illus. by Brian Pinkney. 1993, Putnam $19.99 (0-399-21987-0). 142pp. This is a lively collection of folktales retold by the author, each of which features a female central character. (Rev: BCCB 6/93*; BL 4/15/93; SLJ 6/93) [398.2]

**9373** San Souci, Robert D. *The Hired Hand: An African-American Folktale* (K–4). Illus. by Jerry Pinkney. 1997, Dial paper $15.89 (0-8037-1297-9). 40pp. Young Sam's exploitation of the New Hand in the family's sawmill leads to disaster in this folktale. (Rev: BCCB 4/97; BL 2/15/97; SLJ 5/97) [398.2]

**9374** San Souci, Robert D. *The Little Seven-Colored Horse: A Spanish American Folktale* (4–6). Illus. by Jan T. Dicks. 1995, Chronicle $14.95 (0-8118-0412-7). 40pp. In this folktale, Juanito forms a special relationship with a 7-colored horse. (Rev: BL 12/1/95; SLJ 1/96) [398.2]

**9375** San Souci, Robert D., reteller. *Sukey and the Mermaid* (K–3). Illus. by Brian Pinkney. 1992, Macmillan LB $15.00 (0-02-778141-0). 32pp. Drawing from African tradition, this is the story of a rare black mermaid and how she saves a poor unhappy girl. (Rev: BCCB 3/92*; BL 2/1/92; SLJ 5/92*) [398.2]

**9376** San Souci, Robert D. *The Talking Eggs: A Folktale from the American South* (K–3). Illus. by Jerry Pinkney. 1989, Dial paper $15.89 (0-8037-0620-0). 32pp. Blanche runs away to the woods to escape her harsh mother's assignments in this Creole folktale. (Rev: BL 8/89; SLJ 9/89) [398.2]

**9377** Sawyer, Ruth. *Journey Cake, Ho!* (K–3). Illus. by Robert McCloskey. 1978, Puffin paper $4.99 (0-14-050275-0). 56pp. Retelling of the old folktale of Johnny and his chase after a journey cake that rolls away singing a taunting verse. [398.2]

**9378** Schwartz, Alvin, ed. *Kickle Snifters and Other Fearsome Critters* (3–5). Illus. by Glen Rounds. 1976, HarperCollins paper $4.95 (0-06-446129-7). 64pp. A dictionary of beasts found chiefly in American tall tales with descriptions and amusing illustrations. [398.2]

**9379** Schwartz, Alvin. *More Scary Stories to Tell in the Dark* (4–7). Illus. by Stephen Gammell. 1984, HarperCollins LB $14.89 (0-397-32082-5); paper $4.95 (0-06-440177-4). 128pp. Brief tales from folk stories and hearsay with a scary bent. [398.2]

**9380** Schwartz, Alvin, ed. *Scary Stories to Tell in the Dark* (3–8). Illus. by Stephen Gammell. 1981, HarperCollins LB $14.89 (0-397-31927-4); paper $4.95 (0-06-440170-7). 128pp. Ghost stories collected from American folklore. [398.2]

**9381** Schwartz, Alvin, ed. *Whoppers: Tall Tales and Other Lies* (3–5). Illus. 1975, HarperCollins paper $5.95 (0-06-446091-6). 128pp. A collection of long and short humorous tales from a number of sources. [398.2]

**9382** Shapiro, Irwin. *Joe Magarac and His U.S.A. Citizen Papers* (5–7). Illus. by James Daugherty. 1979, Univ. of Pittsburgh Pr. paper $7.95 (0-8229-5305-6). 58pp. Tall tale of the Hungarian-born hero to the steel mills of Pennsylvania. [398.2]

**9383** Shepard, Aaron. *The Legend of Slappy Hooper: An American Tall Tale* (K–3). Illus. by Toni Goffe. 1993, Scribners $14.95 (0-684-19535-6). 32pp. Slappy Hooper's paintings of animals and plants are so realistic that they come to life. (Rev: BL 11/1/93) [398.21]

**9384** Sloat, Teri. *Sody Sallyratus* (K–3). Illus. 1997, Dutton paper $15.99 (0-525-45609-0). 32pp. In this Appalachian tale, the Big Black Bear attacks family members as they go, one by one, to the store for sody sallyratus — baking soda. (Rev: BL 12/15/96; SLJ 1/97) [398.2]

**9385** Stevens, Janet. *Tops and Bottoms* (PS–2). Illus. 1995, Harcourt $16.00 (0-15-292851-0). 32pp. An African American folktale about how Hare takes unfair advantage of Bear in a garden project. (Rev: BCCB 4/95; BL 3/15/95*; HB 5–6/95; SLJ 5/95) [398.2]

**9386** Vagin, Vladimir. *The Enormous Carrot* (K–2). Illus. 1998, Scholastic $15.95 (0-590-45491-9). 32pp. A reworking of the old folktale "The Enormous Turnip," with an engaging cast of animal characters. (Rev: BL 3/1/98; SLJ 3/98) [398.2]

**9387** Van Laan, Nancy. *With a Whoop and a Holler: A Bushel of Lore from Way Down South* (3–6). Illus. 1998, Simon & Schuster $19.95 (0-689-81061-X). 112pp. A priceless collection of rhymes, folktales, superstitions, and riddles from the South. (Rev: BL 3/1/98*; SLJ 4/98) [398]

**9388** Wahl, Jan. *Little Eight John* (PS–3). Illus. 1992, Dutton paper $14.99 (0-525-67367-9). 32pp. Mean Little Eight John, who does everything his mother warns him not to do, gets his comeuppance from Old Raw Head Bloody Bones. (Rev: BL 7/92; SLJ 11/92) [398.2]

**9389** Wahl, Jan. *The Singing Geese* (PS–1). Illus. by Sterling Brown. 1998, Dutton paper $15.99 (0-525-67499-3). 32pp. In this tall tale, a flock of geese swoop down and save a goose that has been shot by a hunter. (Rev: BL 2/15/98; SLJ 2/98) [398.2]

**9390** Wahl, Jan. *Tailypo!* (1–4). Illus. by Wil Clay. 1991, Holt $14.95 (0-8050-0687-7). 32pp. A folktale of a black man in Tennessee who whacks off the tail of a strange creature and eats it for supper. (Rev: BL 6/1/91; SLJ 6/91) [398.2]

**9391** Walker, Paul R. *Big Men, Big Country: A Collection of American Tall Tales* (4–6). Illus. by James Bernardin. 1993, Harcourt $18.00 (0-15-207136-9). 80pp. After an introduction on the origins of American tales, there is a rollicking, retelling of the exploits of such characters as Davy Crockett, Paul Bunyan, and lesser-known figures like Gib Morgan and Big Mose. (Rev: BCCB 6/93; BL 4/1/93; SLJ 5/93) [398.2]

**9392** Wooldridge, Connie N. *Wicked Jack* (K–3). Illus. by Will Hillenbrand. 1995, Holiday LB $15.95 (0-8234-1101-X). 32pp. A retelling of the Southern tale about a mean blacksmith who outwits the Devil and his young sons. (Rev: BCCB 12/95; BL 11/1/95; SLJ 12/95*) [398.2]

## South and Central America

### Mexico and Other Central American Lands

**9393** Aardema, Verna. *Borreguita and the Coyote: A Tale from Ayutla, Mexico* (PS–1). Illus. by Petra Mathers. 1991, Knopf LB $17.99 (0-679-90921-4). 32pp. A small animal outwits a more powerful one in this Mexican tale. (Rev: BCCB 12/91; BL 9/15/91; HB 9–10/91*; SLJ 8/91*) [398.2]

**9394** Ada, Alma F. *The Lizard and the Sun* (K–3). Illus. by Felipe Davalos. 1997, Doubleday $16.95 (0-385-32121-X). 40pp. In this Mexican tale told in both English and Spanish, a lizard, with the help of an emperor and a woodpecker, frees the sun that is trapped inside a rock. (Rev: BL 12/15/97; SLJ 8/97) [398.2]

**9395** Ada, Alma F. *Mediopollito: Half-Chicken* (PS–3). Trans. by Rosalma Zubizarreta. Illus. by Kim Howard. 1995, Doubleday $10.50 (0-385-32044-2). 46pp. The story of how weathercocks came into being is told in this Mexican folktale. (Rev: BL 9/15/95; HB 11–12/95; SLJ 11/95) [398.2]

**9396** Anaya, Rudolfo A. *Maya's Children: The Story of La Llorona* (1–4). Illus. by Maria Baca. 1997, Hyperion LB $15.49 (0-7868-2124-8). 32pp. A retelling of the Latin American tale of Maya, the daughter of the sun god, who has been given the gift of immortality. (Rev: BCCB 7–8/97; BL 5/1/97; SLJ 6/97) [398.2]

**9397** Bernhard, Emery. *The Tree That Rains: The Flood Myth of the Huichol Indians of Mexico* (K–3). Illus. by Durga Bernhard. 1994, Holiday LB $15.95 (0-8234-1108-7). 32pp. A myth from the Indians of Mexico that tells of a miraculous fig tree that spouts water. (Rev: BCCB 7–8/94; BL 7/94; SLJ 5/94) [398.2]

**9398** Bierhorst, John. *Doctor Coyote: A Native American Aesop's Fables* (3–5). Illus. by Wendy Watson. 1987, Macmillan LB $15.95 (0-02-709780-3). 48pp. Aesop's fables as they were translated into Spanish in the New World. (Rev: BCCB 3/87; BL 3/15/87; SLJ 5/87) [398.2]

**9399** Bierhorst, John, ed. *The Monkey's Haircut: And Other Stories Told by the Maya* (4–6). Illus. by Robert Andrew Parker. 1986, Morrow $16.00 (0-688-04269-4). 160pp. Forms of folklore in a collection of Maya legends, most from the early 1900s. (Rev: BCCB 5/86; BL 7/86; SLJ 8/86) [398.2]

**9400** Brenner, Anita. *The Boy Who Could Do Anything and Other Mexican Folk Tales* (3–8). Illus. by Jean Charlot. 1992, Shoe String LB $18.50 (0-208-02353-4). 134pp. A fine collection of 26 spirited tales from pre-Columbian Indian folklore and mythology, first published 50 years ago. (Rev: BL 11/15/92) [398.2]

**9401** Climo, Shirley, reteller. *The Little Red Ant and the Great Big Crumb* (PS–2). Illus. by Francisco Mora. 1995, Clarion $14.95 (0-395-70732-3). 39pp. A tiny ant seeks help in vain from other animals to move a heavy crumb in this Mexican tale. (Rev: SLJ 11/95) [398.2]

**9402** Czernecki, Stefan, and Timothy Rhodes. *The Sleeping Bread* (1–3). Illus. by Stefan Czernecki. 1992, Hyperion $14.95 (1-562-82183-0). 40pp. In this Central American folktale, the tears of a beggar who is driven out of town change the village's bread when they are added to the dough. (Rev: BCCB 9/92; BL 4/15/92; SLJ 8/92) [398.2]

**9403** dePaola, Tomie. *The Legend of the Poinsettia* (K–4). Illus. 1994, Putnam LB $15.95 (0-399-21692-8). 32pp. Lucinda is unhappy because she has ruined the blanket that was intended for use in a Christmas procession. (Rev: BL 8/94; HB 11–12/94) [398.2]

**9404** de Sauza, James. *Brother Anansi and the Cattle Ranch/El Hermano Anansi y el Rancho de Ganada* (3–6). Adapted by Harriet Rohmer. Illus. by Stephen Von Mason. 1989, Children's Book Pr. $14.95 (0-89239-044-1). 32pp. A bilingual retelling of the ancient folktale about the trickster spider, now transplanted to Nicaragua. Two others in this dual-language series are: *Mr. Sugar Came to Town/La Visita del Señor Azucar* (1989); *Uncle Nacho's Hat/El Sombrero de Tío Nacho* (1989). (Rev: BL 11/15/89) [398.2]

**9405** Ehlert, Lois. *Cuckoo/Cucu* (PS–2). Trans. by Gloria de Aragon Andujar. Illus. 1997, Harcourt $16.00 (0-15-200274-X). 40pp. In this Mayan tale, Cuckoo saves the annual harvest of seeds on which the other birds live during the winter. (Rev: BCCB 6/97; BL 4/1/97*; SLJ 3/97) [398.2]

**9406** Gerson, Mary-Joan. *People of Corn: A Mayan Story* (1–4). Illus. by Carla Golembe. 1995, Little, Brown $15.95 (0-316-30854-4). 32pp. A picture book that recounts the creation myth that originated with the Mayans of Guatemala concerning the beginnings of life and the cultivation of corn. (Rev: BL 1/1–15/96; SLJ 12/95*) [398.2]

**9407** Gollub, Matthew. *Uncle Snake* (1–4). Illus. by Leovigildo Martinez. 1996, Morrow LB $15.93 (0-688-13945-0). 32pp. An original folktale in which a boy exchanges his face with that of a snake. (Rev: BCCB 10/96; BL 10/1/96; SLJ 10/96) [398.2]

**9408** Greger, C. Shana, reteller. *The Fifth and Final Sun: An Ancient Aztec Myth of the Sun's Origin* (1–4). Illus. by C. Shana Greger. 1994, Houghton $14.95 (0-395-67438-7). This Aztec creation myth tells about the origin of our sun and moon. (Rev: BCCB 10/94; SLJ 12/94) [398.2]

**9409** Johnston, Tony. *The Tale of Rabbit and Coyote* (PS–3). Illus. by Tomie dePaola. 1994, Putnam $15.95 (0-399-22258-8). 32pp. Trickster Rabbit always is able to get the best of foolish Coyote in this tale from Mexico. (Rev: BCCB 7–8/94; BL 5/15/94*; HB 5–6/94; SLJ 6/94) [398.2]

**9410** Lewis, Richard. *All of You Was Singing* (PS–3). Illus. by Ed Young. 1991, Macmillan $13.95 (0-689-31596-1). 32pp. This creation myth from the Aztecs is retold in simple text and mystical illustrations. (Rev: BCCB 7–8/91; BL 1/15/91) [398.2]

**9411** McDermott, Gerald. *Musicians of the Sun* (PS–3). Illus. 1997, Simon & Schuster paper $17.00 (0-689-80706-6). 40pp. In this Aztec creation story, Wind is sent to free the colors Red, Yellow, Blue, and Green, who are being held prisoner by the Sun. (Rev: BL 11/1/97*; SLJ 12/97*) [389.2]

**9412** Madrigal, Antonio H. *The Eagle and the Rainbow: Timeless Tales from México* (4–7). Illus. by Tomie dePaola. 1997, Fulcrum $15.95 (1-55591-317-2). 56pp. A collection of wise, wonderful, but little-known folktales from Mexico. (Rev: BL 7/97) [398.2]

**9413** Mora, Pat. *The Race of Toad and Deer* (PS–2). Illus. by Maya I. Brooks. 1995, Orchard LB $15.99 (0-531-08777-8). 32pp. In this Guatemalan folktale, a toad, Sapo, and his friends outwit the swiftest deer in the jungle. (Rev: BL 10/15/95; SLJ 12/95) [398.2]

**9414** Ober, Hal. *How Music Came to the World: An Ancient Mexican Myth* (1–4). Illus. by Carol Ober. 1994, Houghton $16.00 (0-395-67523-5). 32pp. How music came to the world is the subject of this folktale dating to pre-Columbian times. (Rev: BL 3/15/94; SLJ 10/94) [398.2]

**9415** Patent, Dorothy Hinshaw. *Quetzal: Sacred Bird of the Cloud Forest* (3–6). Illus. by Neil Waldman. 1996, Morrow LB $15.93 (0-688-12663-4). 40pp. Mythology and natural history merge in this study of the beautifully plumed quetzal. (Rev: BL 8/96; SLJ 10/96) [398.2]

**9416** Shetterly, Susan Hand. *The Dwarf-Wizard of Uxmal* (4–6). Illus. by Robert Shetterly. 1990, Macmillan LB $13.95 (0-689-31455-8). 32pp. This Mayan legend tells how the great temple at Uxmal originated as a large tortilla pyramid. (Rev: BL 3/15/90; SLJ 4/90) [398.2]

## Puerto Rico and Other Caribbean Islands

**9417** Bryan, Ashley. *Turtle Knows Your Name* (K–3). Illus. 1989, Macmillan $14.95 (0-689-31578-3). 32pp. A fine retelling of a West Indies folktale that points out the importance of names in this culture. (Rev: BCCB 2/90; BL 10/1/89; HB 1–2/90; SLJ 10/89) [398.2]

**9418** Comissiong, Lynette. *Mind Me Good Now!* (PS–3). Illus. by Marie Lafrance. 1997, Annick $16.95 (1-55037-483-4); paper $6.95 (1-55037-482-6). 32pp. A Hansel and Gretel–like Caribbean folktale about Tina, her brother Dalby, and a wicked witch, Cocoya, who loves eating boys. (Rev: BL 1/1–15/98) [398.2]

**9419** Gershator, Phillis. *Tukama Tootles the Flute* (PS–3). Illus. by Synthia Saint James. 1994, Orchard LB $16.99 (0-531-08661-5). 32pp. A flute-playing youngster uses his music to escape the clutches of a giant in this folktale from the Virgin Islands. (Rev: BCCB 4/94; BL 5/1/94; HB 5–6/94; SLJ 4/94) [398.2]

**9420** Gonzalez, Lucia M. *The Bossy Gallito* (K–3). Illus. by Lulu Delacre. 1994, Scholastic $15.95 (0-590-46843-X). 32pp. In this cumulative tale from Cuba, a rooster must involve a great number of animals in order to get his beak cleaned. (Rev: BCCB 7–8/94; BL 5/15/94; HB 9–10/94; SLJ 4/94) [398.2]

**9421** Hausman, Gerald. *Duppy Talk: West Indian Tales of Mystery and Magic* (4–8). Illus. 1994, Simon & Schuster $14.00 (0-671-89000-X). 102pp. Six tales brought from Africa to Jamaica are included in this anthology. (Rev: BL 1/15/95; SLJ 1/95) [398.2]

**9422** Izcoa, Carmen Rivera, adapt. *Mediopollito/Half-a-Chick* (K–3). Illus. by Nívea O. Montáñez. 1996, Ediciones Huracan $10.50 (0-929157-43-5). A Puerto Rican folktale about a bird that punishes the king for being mean and selfish. (Rev: SLJ 11/97) [398.2]

**9423** Jaffe, Nina. *The Golden Flower: A Taino Myth from Puerto Rico* (K–3). Illus. by Enrique O. Sanchez. 1996, Simon & Schuster $16.00 (0-689-

80469-5). 32pp. The creation of the island of Puerto Rico is told in this Taino myth about a magical pumpkin. (Rev: BCCB 6/96; BL 6/1–15/96; SLJ 7/96) [398.2]

**9424** Joseph, Lynn. *The Mermaid's Twin Sister: More Stories from Trinidad* (3–7). Illus. 1994, Clarion $13.95 (0-395-64365-1). 65pp. A retelling in the native patois of some folktales from Trinidad, many of them scary. (Rev: BCCB 6/94; BL 4/15/94; HB 7–8/94; SLJ 6/94) [398.2]

**9425** Joseph, Lynn. *A Wave in Her Pocket: Stories from Trinidad* (3–5). Illus. by Brian Pinkney. 1991, Houghton $14.95 (0-395-54432-7). 50pp. Traditional folklore is combined with a child's view of island life in these 6 stories. (Rev: BCCB 7–8/91; BL 5/15/91*; SLJ 7/91*) [398.2]

**9426** Mohr, Nicholasa. *The Song of El Coqui and Other Tales of Puerto Rico* (PS–3). Illus. by Antonio Martorell. 1995, Viking paper $15.99 (0-670-85837-4). 40pp. Three Puerto Rican folktales (one a creation story), impressively illustrated. (Rev: BCCB 9/95; BL 6/1–15/95; SLJ 8/95) [398.2]

**9427** Moreton, Daniel. *La Cucaracha Martina: A Caribbean Folktale* (PS–2). Illus. 1997, Turtle $14.95 (1-890515-03-5). 32pp. A refined cockroach finally finds her mate, a handsome cricket, in this Caribbean folktale. (Rev: BL 1/1–15/98; SLJ 11/97) [398.2]

**9428** Pitre, Felix. *Juan Bobo and the Pig: A Puerto Rican Folktale* (1–4). Illus. by Christy Hale. 1993, Dutton paper $13.99 (0-525-67429-2). 32pp. When the family pig won't keep quiet, Juan Bobo dresses it in clothes and sends it off to church in this Puerto Rican tale. (Rev: BL 10/15/93) [398.2]

**9429** Pitre, Felix. *Paco and the Witch: A Puerto Rican Folktale* (PS–3). Illus. by Christy Hale. 1995, Dutton paper $13.99 (0-525-67501-9). 32pp. In this Puerto Rican version of *Rumpelstiltskin*, a boy is captured by a wicked witch who wants him to guess her name. (Rev: BCCB 5/95; BL 5/15/95; SLJ 8/95) [398.2]

**9430** Rahaman, Vashanti. *A Little Salmon for Witness: A Story from Trinidad* (K–3). Illus. by Sandra Speidel. 1997, Lodestar paper $15.99 (0-525-67521-3). In this story set in Trinidad, a young boy tries to get a tin of salmon as a special gift for his grandmother on her birthday. (Rev: SLJ 2/97) [398.2]

**9431** San Souci, Robert D. *The Faithful Friend* (K–4). Illus. by Brian Pinkney. 1995, Simon & Schuster paper $16.00 (0-02-786131-7). 40pp. On the island of Martinique, Hippolyte tries to save his friend's wedding from destruction by the bride's evil uncle. (Rev: BCCB 9/95; BL 4/15/95*; HB 9–10/95; SLJ 6/95) [398.2]

**9432** San Souci, Robert D. *The House in the Sky* (K–3). Illus. by Wil Clay. 1996, Dial paper $14.89 (0-8037-1285-5). 32pp. Rabby's greed leads to his downfall in this Caribbean folktale. (Rev: BCCB 2/96; BL 2/1/96; SLJ 2/96) [398.2]

**9433** Sherlock, Philip M., ed. *West Indian Folk Tales* (3–6). Illus. by Joan Kiddell-Monroe. 1978, Oxford paper $12.95 (0-19-274127-6). 151pp. Tales from the Caribbean including those about the spider, Anansi. [398.2]

**9434** Temple, Frances. *Tiger Soup: An Anansi Story from Jamaica* (K–3). Illus. 1994, Orchard $15.95 (0-531-06859-5). 32pp. Anansi tricks Tiger into thinking it was monkeys and not he who ate Tiger's sweet soup. (Rev: BCCB 9/94; BL 8/94; SLJ 8/94*) [398.2]

**9435** Wolkstein, Diane. *Bouki Dances the Kokioko: A Comical Tale from Haiti* (K–3). Illus. by Jesse Sweetwater. 1997, Harcourt $15.00 (0-15-200034-8). 32pp. In this Haitian trickster tale, a king invents a dance and offers a large reward for anyone who can master it. (Rev: BL 9/15/97; SLJ 11/97) [398.2]

## South America

**9436** Ada, Alma F. *The Rooster Who Went to His Uncle's Wedding: A Latin American Folktale* (PS–2). Illus. by Kathleen Kuchera. 1998, Putnam paper $5.99 (0-698-11682-8). 32pp. A cumulative tale about a well-groomed rooster on his way to his uncle's wedding. (Rev: BL 3/1/93; SLJ 5/93) [398.2]

**9437** Aldana, Patricia, ed. *Jade and Iron: Latin American Tales from Two Cultures* (5–8). Trans. by Hugh Hazelton. Illus. 1996, Douglas & McIntyre $18.95 (0-88899-256-4). 64pp. Fourteen folktales on a variety of subjects and from many regions in Latin America are retold in this large-format picture book. (Rev: BCCB 1/97; BL 12/1/96) [398.2]

**9438** Brusca, Maria C., and Tona Wilson. *Pedro Fools the Gringo and Other Tales of a Latin American Trickster* (3–5). Illus. 1995, Holt $14.95 (0-8050-3827-2). 37pp. A collection of 12 trickster tales from Latin America that features the wily Pedro Urdemales. (Rev: BL 10/1/95; SLJ 11/95) [39.82]

**9439** Crespo, George, reteller. *How Iwariwa the Cayman Learned to Share: A Yanomami Myth* (2–4). Illus. by George Crespo. 1995, Clarion $14.95 (0-395-67162-0). The animals of the Amazon rain forest come to life in this folktale about the sharing of life-giving fire. (Rev: SLJ 7/95) [398.2]

**9440** Delacre, Lulu. *Golden Tales: Myths, Legends and Folktales from Latin America* (4–6). Illus. 1996, Scholastic $18.95 (0-590-48186-X). 80pp. Twelve important Latin American folktales from before and after the time of Columbus are clearly presented. (Rev: BCCB 1/97; BL 12/15/96; SLJ 9/96) [398.2]

**9441** Dorson, Mercedes, and Jeanne Wilmot. *Tales from the Rain Forest: Myths and Legends from the Amazonian Indians of Brazil* (5–8). Illus. 1997, Ecco $18.00 (0-88001-567-5). 133pp. Ten entertaining folktales from the Amazonian Indians of Brazil. (Rev: BL 2/15/98) [398.2]

**9442** Ehlert, Lois. *Moon Rope: A Peruvian Folktale* (4–8). Illus. 1992, Harcourt $17.00 (0-15-255343-6). 40pp. In both English and Spanish, this is the story of Fox, who wants to go to the moon and persuades his friend Mole to go along. (Rev: BCCB 12/92; BL 10/15/92*; HB 11–12/92; SLJ 10/92*) [398.2]

**9443** Finger, Charles J. *Tales from Silver Lands* (4–6). Illus. by Paul Honore. 1996, Doubleday $16.95 (0-385-07513-8). 225pp. Folklore from South America. Newbery Medal winner, 1925. [398.2]

**9444** Gonzalez, Lucia M. *Señor Cat's Romance and Other Favorite Stories from Latin America* (1–3). Illus. by Lulu Delacre. 1997, Scholastic $17.95 (0-590-48537-7). 48pp. Six enchanting folktales popular in Latin America. (Rev: BCCB 4/97; BL 2/1/97; HB 3–4/97; SLJ 2/97) [398.2]

**9445** Hickox, Rebecca. *Zorro and Quwi: Tales of a Trickster Guinea Pig* (PS–2). Illus. by Kim Howard. 1997, Doubleday $14.95 (0-385-32122-8). 32pp.

Based on Peruvian folklore, this is the tale of Zorro the fox and how he is tricked by Quwi the guinea pig. (Rev: BCCB 2/97; BL 12/15/96; SLJ 2/97) [398.2]

**9446** Jendresen, Erik, and Alberto Villoldo. *The First Story Ever Told* (1–3). Illus. by Yoshi. 1996, Simon & Schuster $16.00 (0-689-80515-2). 32pp. An explorer dreams about the creation of the earth and life in this tale from the Incas. (Rev: BL 12/15/96; SLJ 12/96) [398.2]

**9447** Kurtz, Jane. *Miro in the Kingdom of the Sun* (2–4). Illus. by David Frampton. 1996, Houghton $15.95 (0-395-69181-8). 32pp. A young girl searches for magic lake water to save her brother's life in this Inca legend. (Rev: BCCB 4/96; BL 5/1/96; HB 11–12/96; SLJ 5/96) [398.2]

**9448** Metaxas, Eric. *The Monkey People* (K–3). Illus. by Diana Bryan. 1995, Simon & Schuster paper $19.95 (0-689-80191-2). 32pp. A group of rain forest people become too dependent on monkeys to perform all their chores in this Colombian folktale. (Rev: BL 2/1/96; SLJ 2/96) [398.2]

**9449** Weiss, Jacqueline Shachter. *Young Brer Rabbit: And Other Trickster Tales from the Americas* (4–6). Illus. 1985, Stemmer $14.95 (0-88045-037-1); paper $9.95 (0-88045-138-6). 80pp. Fifteen stories translated from Spanish, French, and Portuguese. (Rev: BCCB 1/86; BL 3/1/86; SLJ 1/86) [398.2]

# Mythology

## General and Miscellaneous

**9450** Harris, Geraldine. *Gods and Pharaohs from Egyptian Mythology* (5–8). Illus. by David O'Connor and John Sibbick. 1992, Bedrick LB $24.95 (0-87226-907-8). 132pp. A collection of myths and legends from ancient Egypt. [398.2]

**9451** McCaughrean, Geraldine. *The Golden Hoard: Myths and Legends of the World* (4–6). Illus. by Bee Willey. 1996, Simon & Schuster $19.95 (0-689-80741-4). 130pp. Twenty-two myths from around the world are retold in imaginative, often colloquial prose. (Rev: BCCB 7–8/96; BL 5/1/96; HB 5–6/96; SLJ 3/96*) [883]

**9452** O'Neill, Cynthia, ed. *Goddesses, Heroes and Shamans: The Young People's Guide to World Mythology* (5–8). Illus. 1997, Kingfisher paper $15.95 (0-7534-5058-5). 160pp. Using a geographical arrangement, this book introduces world mythology, with coverage on characters, purpose, and significance. (Rev: BL 10/1/97) [291.1]

**9453** Philip, Neil. *The Illustrated Book of Myths: Tales and Legends of the World* (5–8). Illus. by Nilesh Mistry. 1995, DK Publg. $19.95 (0-7894-0202-5). 192pp. Ancient myths from both the Old World and the New World have been collected under such headings as creation, destruction, and fertility. (Rev: BL 12/1/95; SLJ 12/95) [291.1]

**9454** Waldherr, Kris. *The Book of Goddesses* (4–7). Illus. 1996, Beyond Words $17.95 (1-885223-30-7). 64pp. In an oversize volume, 26 goddesses from mythology are profiled. (Rev: BL 4/1/96; SLJ 5/96) [291.2]

## Classical

**9455** Climo, Shirley. *Atalanta's Race: A Greek Myth* (3–5). Illus. by Alexander Koshkin. 1995, Clarion $16.00 (0-395-67322-4). 32pp. A retelling of the Greek myth about Atalanta, who, abandoned at birth, becomes the world's fastest runner. (Rev: BCCB 6/95; BL 4/15/95; SLJ 4/95*) [398.21]

**9456** Colum, Padraic. *The Children's Homer: The Adventures of Odysseus and the Tale of Troy* (4–6). Illus. by Willy Pogany. 1982, Macmillan paper $9.95 (0-02-042520-1). 256pp. First published in 1918, the engrossing tales of Homer. [398.2]

**9457** Colum, Padraic. *The Golden Fleece and the Heroes Who Lived Before Achilles* (5–7). Illus. by Willy Pogany. 1983, Macmillan LB $17.00 (0-02-723620-X); paper $9.95 (0-02-042260-1). 320pp. Jason's search for the Golden Fleece incorporates some of the best-known myths and legends of ancient Greece. [398.2]

**9458** Coolidge, Olivia. *Greek Myths* (4–7). Illus. by Eduard Sandoz. 1949, Houghton $16.00 (0-395-06721-9). 256pp. Twenty-seven well-known myths dramatically retold with accompanying illustrations. [398.2]

**9459** Craft, M. Charlotte. *Cupid and Psyche* (3–5). Illus. by Kinuko Craft. 1996, Morrow LB $15.93 (0-688-13164-6). 40pp. The Greek myth retold with 40 full-page paintings. (Rev: BCCB 9/96; BL 7/96; SLJ 4/96) [398.2]

**9460** D'Aulaire, Ingri, and Edgar D'Aulaire. *D'Aulaire's Book of Greek Myths* (3–6). Illus. by authors. 1962, Bantam LB $14.95 (0-385-07108-6); Dell paper $16.95 (0-440-40694-3). Full-color pictures highlight these brief stories, which are excellent for first readers in mythology. [398.2]

**9461** Fisher, Leonard Everett. *Cyclops* (1–6). Illus. 1991, Holiday LB $15.95 (0-8234-0891-4); paper $5.95 (0-8234-1062-5). 32pp. The retelling of this classical tale inspires pity and terror in the reader. (Rev: BCCB 12/91; BL 1/1/91*; SLJ 1/92) [398.2]

**9462** Fisher, Leonard Everett. *The Olympians: Great Gods and Goddesses of Ancient Greece* (3–5). Illus. by author. 1984, Holiday LB $15.95 (0-8234-0522-2); paper $6.95 (0-8234-0740-3). 32pp. The stories behind 12 of the gods and goddesses of ancient Greece. [398.2]

**9463** Fisher, Leonard Everett. *Theseus and the Minotaur* (3–6). Illus. by author. 1988, Holiday paper $5.95 (0-8234-0954-6). 32pp. The story of the birth of Theseus, his adventures, and his killing of the Minotaur. (Rev: BCCB 10/88; BL 10/15/88; SLJ 10/88) [398.2]

**9464** Galloway, Priscilla. *Aleta and the Queen: A Tale of Ancient Greece* (4–7). Illus. 1995, Annick LB $29.95 (1-55037-400-1); paper $14.95 (1-55037-462-1). 158pp. Told from the standpoint of a 12-year-old girl, this novel traces the story of Penelope and the final weeks of her wait for Odysseus. (Rev: BL 1/1–15/96; SLJ 1/96)

**9465** Galloway, Priscilla. *Daedalus and the Minotaur* (4–6). Illus. Series: Tales of Ancient Lands. 1997, Annick LB $27.95 (1-55037-459-1); paper $14.95 (1-55037-458-3). 112pp. This account explands and embellishes the story of Daedalus; his son, Icarus; and the king's monstrous son, Minotaur, who is held captive in a giant labyrinth. (Rev: BL 1/1–15/98; SLJ 2/98) [813.54]

**9466** Gates, Doris. *A Fair Wind for Troy* (5–8). 1976, Puffin paper $4.99 (0-14-031718-X). 96pp. A retelling of legends connected with the Trojan War. [398.2]

**9467** Gates, Doris. *Lord of the Sky: Zeus* (3–6). Illus. by Robert Handville. 1982, Puffin paper $4.99 (0-14-031532-2). 128pp. In the first of a series, the author has retold simply and directly myths in which Zeus plays a central part. [398.2]

**9468** Gates, Doris. *Mightiest of Mortals: Heracles* (4–6). Illus. by Richard Cuffari. 1984, Puffin paper $4.99 (0-14-031531-4). 96pp. All of the tales of Heracles are presented in logical order in a breezy, informal style. [398.2]

**9469** Gates, Doris. *The Warrior Goddess: Athena* (4–6). Illus. by Don Bolognese. 1982, Puffin paper $4.99 (0-14-031530-6). 128pp. A spirited retelling of the myths associated with Athena. [398.2]

**9470** Geringer, Laura. *The Pomegranate Seeds: A Classic Greek Myth* (2–4). Illus. by Leonid Gore. 1995, Houghton $15.95 (0-395-68192-8). 48pp. Adapted from one of Hawthorne's *Tanglewood Tales*, this is the story of the kidnapping of Persephone and her eventual return to Demeter, her mother. (Rev: BL 2/1/96; SLJ 3/96) [398.21]

**9471** Green, Roger L. *Tales of Greek Heroes* (4–6). 1989, Puffin paper $2.99 (0-14-035099-3). 208pp. Stories in this volume include those about Prometheus, Dionysus, Perseus, and Heracles. Also use: *The Tale of Troy* (1974). [398.2]

**9472** Hawthorne, Nathaniel. *Wonder Book and Tanglewood Tales* (5–7). 1972, Ohio State Univ. Pr. $60.00 (0-8142-0158-X). 476pp. This is a highly original retelling of the Greek myths, originally published in 1853. [398.2]

**9473** Hutton, Warwick. *Odysseus and the Cyclops* (K–4). Illus. 1995, Simon & Schuster paper $15.00 (0-689-80036-3). 32pp. A retelling of the encounter between Odysseus and his men and the one-eyed monster. (Rev: BCCB 11/95; BL 10/1/95; SLJ 11/95) [398.2]

**9474** Hutton, Warwick. *Persephone* (1–4). Illus. 1994, Macmillan paper $14.95 (0-689-50600-7). 32pp. The story of Persephone and her mother, Demeter, whose bargain with the god Hades caused the seasons. (Rev: BL 2/1/94; HB 5–6/94; SLJ 4/94) [398.21]

**9475** Hutton, Warwick. *Perseus* (2–4). Illus. 1993, Macmillan $14.95 (0-689-50565-5). 32pp. A retelling of the myth of Perseus and the monsters he encounters. (Rev: BL 3/1/93; SLJ 6/93) [398.2]

**9476** Hutton, Warwick. *Theseus and the Minotaur* (3–5). Illus. 1989, Macmillan paper $14.95 (0-689-50473-X). 32pp. A retelling of the Athenian hero's journey to Crete to slay the Minotaur. (Rev: BCCB 10/89; BL 11/1/89; HB 1–2/90; SLJ 10/89*) [398.2]

**9477** Lasky, Kathryn. *Hercules: The Man, the Myth, the Hero* (3–5). Illus. by Mark Hess. 1997, Hyperion LB $16.49 (0-7868-2274-0). 32pp. In 15 double-page spreads in this large-format picture book, Hercules tells his own story. (Rev: BL 6/1–15/97; SLJ 7/97) [292.2]

**9478** Low, Alice. *The Macmillan Book of Greek Gods and Heroes* (4–6). Illus. by Arvis Stewart. 1985, Macmillan LB $17.00 (0-02-761390-9). 192pp. Well-known myths and legends from ancient Greece in a large-format edition. (Rev: BCCB 11/85; BL 11/15/85; SLJ 1/86) [398.2]

**9479** McCaughrean, Geraldine. *Greek Myths* (4–6). Illus. by Emma C. Clark. 1993, Macmillan $20.00 (0-689-50583-3). 96pp. Sixteen epic stories of heroes and monsters, gods and warriors. (Rev: BL 2/1/93*; SLJ 4/93) [883]

**9480**  McLean, Mollie, and Ann S. Wiseman. *Adventures of Greek Heroes* (4–6). Illus. by W. T. Mars. 1973, Houghton $16.95 (0-395-06913-0); paper $5.95 (0-685-42189-9). 192pp. Easily read version of myths involving such heroes as Jason, Hercules, and Theseus. [398.2]

**9481**  Mayer, Marianna. *Pegasus* (3–6). Illus. by Kinuko Craft. 1998, Morrow $16.00 (0-688-13382-7). 40pp. A retelling of the Greek myth about the winged horse Pegasus and how it helped Bellerophon kill Chimera the monster. (Rev: BL 3/15/98; SLJ 4/98) [398.2]

**9482**  Moore, Robin. *Hercules* (2–5). Illus. 1997, Simon & Schuster $14.00 (0-689-81228-0); paper $3.99 (0-689-81229-9). 80pp. An easily read paperback that tells of Hercules' exploits in short, nicely illustrated chapters. (Rev: BL 6/1–15/97; SLJ 7/97) [292.2]

**9483**  Naden, Corinne J. *Jason and the Golden Fleece* (2–4). Illus. by Robert Baxter. 1980, Troll LB $13.95 (0-89375-360-2). 32pp. One of a series of retold myths. Others by the same author and publisher are: *Pegasus, the Winged Horse; Perseus and Medusa; Theseus and the Minotaur* (all 1980). [398.2]

**9484**  Nolan, Dennis. *Androcles and the Lion* (PS–3). Illus. 1997, Harcourt $15.00 (0-15-203355-6). 32pp. A bright retelling of the Roman story of the slave Androcles and how his life was saved by a lion he had helped years before. (Rev: BL 10/15/97; SLJ 11/97) [398.2]

**9485**  Osborne, Mary Pope. *Favorite Greek Myths* (3–6). Illus. by Troy Howell. 1989, Scholastic paper $17.95 (0-590-41338-4). 96pp. This large-format book contains 13 of the best-known stories from classical mythology. (Rev: BL 8/89) [398.2]

**9486**  Philip, Neil, reteller. *The Adventures of Odysseus* (3–6). Illus. by Peter Malone. 1997, Orchard $17.95 (0-531-30000-5). 72pp. A fine retelling of the epic journey home by Odysseus and his encounters with such creatures as Cyclops, Circe, and the Sirens. (Rev: SLJ 5/97*) [292.1]

**9487**  Richardson, I. M. *The Adventures of Eros and Psyche* (3–6). Illus. by Robert Baxter. 1983, Troll LB $13.95 (0-89375-861-2); paper $2.95 (0-89375-862-0). 32pp. How Psyche is able to prove her love for Eros in this retelling of the Greek myth. Others by this author and publisher are: *The Adventures of Hercules; Demeter and Persephone: The Seasons of Time; Prometheus and the Story of Fire* (all 1983). [398.2]

**9488**  Riordan, James. *The Twelve Labors of Hercules* (4–6). Illus. 1997, Millbrook LB $22.40 (0-

7613-0315-4). 64pp. Each of the 12 tasks performed by Hercules for King Eurystheus gets a separate chapter in the large-format book. (Rev: BL 1/1–15/98; SLJ 2/98) [398.2]

**9489**  Rockwell, Anne. *The One-Eyed Giant and Other Monsters from the Greek Myths* (1–4). Illus. 1996, Greenwillow LB $15.93 (0-688-13810-1). 32pp. Several Greek myths about monsters like Medusa and the minotaur are retold. (Rev: BCCB 4/96; BL 4/1/96; SLJ 4/96) [398.2]

**9490**  Rockwell, Anne. *The Robber Baby: Stories from the Greek Myths* (1–4). Illus. 1994, Greenwillow LB $17.93 (0-688-09741-3). 80pp. Fifteen familiar stories from Greek mythology are retold with expressive illustrations. (Rev: BL 6/1–15/94; SLJ 6/94) [398.2]

**9491**  Rockwell, Anne, reteller. *Romulus and Remus* (1–2). Illus. by Anne Rockwell. Series: A Ready-to-Read Book; Level 2. 1997, Simon & Schuster $15.00 (0-689-81291-4); paper $3.99 (0-689-81290-6). 40pp. An admirable retelling of the myth of the 2 brothers who were cared for by a wolf and later, when one stayed with the pack, the other founded the city of Rome. (Rev: SLJ 9/97) [292]

**9492**  Strachan, Ian. *The Iliad* (5–8). Illus. 1997, Kingfisher $17.95 (0-7534-5107-7). 96pp. This large, handsome volume gives an exciting account of the main events in the siege and fall of Troy. (Rev: BL 1/1–15/98; SLJ 11/97) [292]

**9493**  Sutcliff, Rosemary. *Black Ships Before Troy: The Story of the Iliad* (5–8). Illus. by Alan Lee. 1993, Delacorte $19.95 (0-385-31069-2). 128pp. The story of the *Iliad* and the 10-year siege of Troy are retold by a master writer of historical fiction. (Rev: BCCB 1/94; BL 10/15/93) [883]

**9494**  Sutcliff, Rosemary. *The Wanderings of Odysseus: The Story of the Odyssey* (5–8). Illus. by Alan Lee. 1996, Delacorte $22.50 (0-385-32205-4). 120pp. An oversize volume that retells Homer's *Odyssey* and all the adventures of Odysseus on his homeward journey from the Trojan Wars. (Rev: BCCB 9/96; BL 9/1/96; HB 5–6/96; SLJ 6/96*) [883]

**9495**  Usher, Kerry. *Heroes, Gods and Emperors from Roman Mythology* (5–8). Illus. by John Sibbick. 1992, Bedrick LB $24.95 (0-87226-909-4). 132pp. The story of the Aeneid plus those of the Tarquino and Romulus and Remus are 3 of the legends retold here. [398.2]

**9496**  Vautier, Ghislaine. *The Shining Stars: Greek Legends of the Zodiac* (4–6). Illus. by Jacqueline Bezencon. 1981, Cambridge Univ. Pr. paper $9.95 (0-521-37914-8). The Greek legends of the origin of each sign of the zodiac are retold. [398.2]

**9497**  Waldherr, Kris. *Persephone and the Pomegranate: A Myth from Greece* (K–3). Illus. 1993, Dial paper $14.89 (0-8037-1192-1). 32pp. Brilliant, lavish paintings are used to retell the Greek myth about the creation of the seasons. (Rev: BL 7/93) [398.2]

**9498** Williams, Marcia. *Greek Myths for Young Children* (1–6). Illus. by author. 1992, Candlewick $17.95 (1-56402-115-7). Eight famous Greek myths are retold in a pseudo comic-strip format. (Rev: BCCB 11/92; SLJ 10/92) [291.1]

**9499** Williams, Marcia, reteller. *The Iliad and the Odyssey* (3–5). Illus. by Marcia Williams. 1996, Candlewick $17.99 (0-7636-0053-9). Using a comic strip format, the highlights of these 2 Greek epics are retold. (Rev: BCCB 2/97; HB 1–2/97; SLJ 5/97) [938]

# Scandinavian

**9500** Climo, Shirley. *Stolen Thunder: A Norse Myth* (3–5). Illus. by Alexander Koshkin. 1994, Clarion $15.95 (0-395-64368-6). 32pp. In this Norse myth, Thor's magic hammer is stolen by Thrym, the Frost King, and he sends Loki to retrieve it. (Rev: BL 5/1/94; SLJ 7/94) [293.1]

**9501** D'Aulaire, Ingri, and Edgar D'Aulaire. *D'Aulaire's Norse Gods and Giants* (4–6). Illus. by authors. 1967, Doubleday paper $17.95 (0-385-23692-1). 168pp. A vigorous retelling of many of the Norse myths, illustrated with bold, colorful lithographs. [398.2]

**9502** Green, Richard L. *The Myths of the Norsemen* (4–6). Illus. by Brian Wildsmith. 1970, Puffin paper $3.50 (0-14-035098-5). 208pp. The great Norse myths woven into a continuous narrative. [398.2]

**9503** Osborne, Mary Pope. *Favorite Norse Myths* (4–6). Illus. by Troy Howell. 1996, Scholastic $17.95 (0-590-48046-4). 96pp. A masterful retelling of Norse myths, with a thorough glossary of names, places, events, and symbols connected with these tales. (Rev: BL 3/1/96; SLJ 4/96*) [293]

**9504** Philip, Neil, reteller. *Odin's Family: Myths of the Vikings* (3–6). Illus. by Maryclare Foa. 1996, Orchard $19.95 (0-531-09531-2). 124pp. Fifteen Viking myths — including "Thor's Hammer" and "The Death of Balder" — are retold with vivid illustrations. (Rev: BCCB 10/96; SLJ 11/96*) [398.2]

# Poetry

## General

**9505** Ada, Alma F. *Gathering the Sun: An Alphabet in Spanish and English* (K–3). Trans. by Rosa Zubizarreta. Illus. by Simon Silva. 1997, Lothrop LB $15.93 (0-688-13904-3). 40pp. Using the Spanish alphabet as a framework, this volume contains 27 poems about Mexican life. (Rev: BCCB 6/97; BL 4/15/97; SLJ 3/97) [861]

**9506** Adoff, Arnold. *All the Colors of the Race* (4–7). Illus. by John Steptoe. 1982, Lothrop LB $15.93 (0-688-00880-1). 56pp. Poems that deal with the many races of mankind.

**9507** Adoff, Arnold. *Eats* (4–6). Illus. by Susan Russo. 1992, Morrow paper $3.95 (0-688-11695-7). 48pp. A joyous collection that praises such morsels as apple pie and newly baked bread.

**9508** Adoff, Arnold. *Love Letters* (1–4). Illus. by Lisa Desimini. 1997, Scholastic $15.95 (0-590-48478-8). 32pp. All sorts and conditions of love are the subjects of this delightful work with outstanding illustrations. (Rev: BCCB 3/97; BL 1/1–15/97; SLJ 3/97*) [811]

**9509** Adoff, Arnold. *Street Music: City Poems* (K–4). Illus. by Karen Barbour. 1995, HarperCollins LB $15.89 (0-06-021523-2). 32pp. Fourteen poems that deal realistically with city life, its noises, squalor, and beauty. (Rev: BCCB 3/95; BL 2/1/95; HB 5–6/95; SLJ 3/95*) [811]

**9510** Alarcon, Francisco X. *Laughing Tomatoes and Other Spring Poems/Jitomates Risueños y Otros Poemas de Primavera* (K–3). Illus. by Maya C. Gonzalez. 1997, Children's Book Pr. $15.95 (0-89239-139-1). 32pp. A bilingual collection of short poems, many about California, by the Chicano poet Alarcon. (Rev: BCCB 6/97; BL 6/1–15/97; SLJ 5/97) [811]

**9511** Bagert, Brod. *Chicken Socks: And Other Contagious Poems* (2–5). Illus. by Tim Ellis. 1993, Boyds Mills $15.95 (1-56397-292-1). 32pp. A collection of 22 poems that depict, usually in a comic way, typical activities of children. (Rev: SLJ 3/94) [811]

**9512** Bauer, Caroline Feller, ed. *Rainy Day: Stories and Poems* (3–5). Illus. by Michele Chessare. 1986, HarperCollins LB $15.89 (0-397-32105-8). 96pp. Poems and stories from mostly well-known children's poets such as John Ciardi and Langston Hughes. Also use: *Snowy Day: Stories and Poems* (1986). (Rev: BCCB 9/86; BL 7/86; SLJ 9/86)

**9513** Baylor, Byrd. *The Way to Start a Day* (3–5). Illus. by Peter Parnall. 1978, Macmillan $14.95 (0-684-15651-2); paper $4.95 (0-689-71054-2). 32pp. A poetic tribute to the many ways people have greeted a new day.

**9514** Benet, Rosemary, and Stephen Vincent Benet. *A Book of Americans* (4–8). Illus. by Charles Child. 1987, Holt paper $5.95 (0-8050-0297-9). 128pp. A collection of poetry portraying 56 famous Americans from Columbus to Woodrow Wilson. A reissue. (Rev: BL 4/15/87)

**9515** Bennett, Jill, ed. *A Cup of Starshine: Poems and Pictures for Young Children* (PS–1). Illus. by Graham Percy. 1991, Harcourt $16.95 (0-15-220982-4). 64pp. These include the traditional rhymes with modern verse and full-color drawings. (Rev: BL 10/15/91; SLJ 12/91) [811]

**9516** Bennett, Jill, ed. *Spooky Poems* (1–5). Illus. by Mary Rees. 1990, General Dist. Services $14.95 (0-7737-2350-1). 32pp. From a variety of poets comes a collection of scary poems about ghosts, monsters, and other supernatural beings. (Rev: BL 12/1/89; HB 1–2/90; SLJ 1/90) [811]

**9517** Berry, James, ed. *Classic Poems to Read Aloud* (4–8). Illus. 1995, Kingfisher $16.95 (1-85697-987-

3); paper $7.95 (0-7534-5069-0). 256pp. A fine collection of standard poems, chiefly English, that are arranged by theme. (Rev: BL 5/1/95; SLJ 5/95) [811]

**9518** Blake, Quentin. *All Join In* (PS–2). Illus. 1991, Little, Brown $14.95 (0-316-09934-1). 32pp. The theme of cooperation is explored in 6 bright poems. (Rev: BCCB 5/91; BL 4/15/91; SLJ 7/91) [821]

**9519** Booth, David, ed. *'Til All the Stars Have Fallen: A Collection of Poems for Children* (3–5). Illus. by Kady M. Denton. 1994, Puffin paper $6.99 (0-14-034438-1). 96pp. The more than 70 poems in this collection are mainly from Canadian poets. (Rev: BL 1/1/91; SLJ 12/90*) [808]

**9520** Bouchard, David. *If Sarah Will Take Me* (4–8). Illus. by Robb T. Dunfield. 1997, Orca $16.95 (1-55143-081-9). The author, who is paralyzed from the neck down, recalls his love of nature and his many inspiring experiences outdoors. (Rev: SLJ 8/97) [811]

**9521** Brown, Marc, ed. *Party Rhymes* (K–3). Illus. by Marc Brown. 1994, Puffin paper $4.99 (0-140-50318-8). 48pp. Vignettes filled with humorous touches including verses like "Farmer in the Dell." (Rev: HB 1–2/89)

**9522** Bryan, Ashley. *Sing to the Sun: Poems and Pictures* (K–8). Illus. 1996, HarperCollins paper $4.95 (0-064-43437-0). Short poems with a Caribbean lilt. (Rev: BCCB 10/92; BL 10/15/92; HB 3–4/93; SLJ 10/92) [811.54]

**9523** Carlson, Lori M. *Sol a Sol* (2–5). Illus. by Emily Lisker. 1998, Holt $15.95 (0-8050-4373-X). A bilingual anthology of poems that describe the daily activities of a Hispanic family. (Rev: SLJ 3/98) [808]

**9524** Chandra, Deborah. *Balloons and Other Poems* (3–5). Illus. by Leslie Bowman. 1990, Farrar $12.95 (0-374-30509-9). 48pp. A collection of 24 short poems that leave clear, memorable images. (Rev: BL 2/1/91; SLJ 2/91) [811]

**9525** Clarke, Gillian, comp. *The Whispering Room: Haunted Poems* (3–6). Illus. by Justin Todd. 1996, Kingfisher $15.95 (0-7534-5024-0). 72pp. An anthology of more than 50 poems about supernatural beings from both prominent and less well known poets. (Rev: BCCB 1/97; SLJ 12/96) [811]

**9526** Cooney, Barbara, reteller. *Chanticleer and the Fox* (1–4). Illus. by Barbara Cooney. 1958, HarperCollins LB $16.89 (0-690-18562-6); paper $3.95 (0-690-04318-X). 36pp. Chaucer's Nun's Priest Tale retold by the illustrator. Caldecott Medal winner, 1959.

**9527** Cullinan, Bernice E., ed. *A Jar of Tiny Stars: Poems by NCTE Award-Winning Poets* (3–5). Illus. 1995, Boyds Mills $16.95 (1-56397-087-2). 94pp. A collection of more than 50 poems chosen by children from the works of the 10 winners of the National

Council of Teachers of English Award for Poetry for Children, including poems by Karla Kuskin, Myra Cohn Livingston, and Eve Merriam. (Rev: BCCB 2/96; BL 1/1–15/96; SLJ 2/96) [811.54]

**9528** Dakos, Kalli. *The Goof Who Invented Homework: And Other School Poems* (3–6). Illus. 1996, Dial paper $14.89 (0-8037-1928-0). 80pp. A group of original poems that deal with everyday occurrences at school. (Rev: BL 9/15/96; SLJ 9/96) [811]

**9529** Dakos, Kalli. *Mrs. Cole on an Onion Roll and Other School Poems* (1–3). Illus. by JoAnn Adinolfi. 1995, Simon & Schuster paper $14.00 (0-02-725583-2). 40pp. A collection of 32 poems about the behavior and concerns of elementary school children. (Rev: BL 6/1–15/95; SLJ 8/95) [811]

**9530** Daniel, Mark, ed. *A Child's Treasury of Poems* (3–5). Illus. 1986, Dial paper $18.99 (0-8037-0330-9). 160pp. A collection of poems from the Victorian and Edwardian eras with paintings to match. (Rev: BL 11/1/86; SLJ 12/86)

**9531** de la Mare, Walter. *Peacock Pie* (3–6). Illus. by Louise Brierley. 1988, Faber paper $8.95 (0-571-14963-4). 128pp. Dancing rhymes of fairies, witches, and farmers.

**9532** De Regniers, Beatrice S., ed. *Sing a Song of Popcorn: Every Child's Book of Poems* (PS–6). Illus. by Marcia Brown. 1988, Scholastic $18.95 (0-590-43974-X). 160pp. A treasure from highly regarded poets, with exciting artwork. (Rev: BCCB 10/88; BL 8/88; SLJ 8/88)

**9533** De Regniers, Beatrice S. *The Way I Feel . . . Sometimes* (2–4). Illus. 1988, Houghton $14.95 (0-89919-647-0). 48pp. Short poems about feelings — feeling better, feeling mean, and so on. (Rev: BL 5/15/88; SLJ 6–7/88)

**9534** Dickinson, Emily. *A Brighter Garden* (4–6). Illus. by Tasha Tudor. 1990, Putnam $17.95 (0-399-21490-9). 64pp. Lovely paintings complement this edition of Dickinson's first volume of poetry. (Rev: BL 10/1/90; SLJ 10/90) [811]

**9535** Dickinson, Emily. *Poems for Youth* (4–6). Illus. by Thomas B. Allen. 1996, Little, Brown $15.95 (0-316-18435-7). 111pp. A handsome collection of Dickinson's poems, best suited for a young audience. (Rev: BL 7/96; SLJ 9/96) [811]

**9536** Dotlich, Rebecca. *Lemonade Sun and Other Summer Poems* (PS–3). Illus. by Jan S. Gilchrist. 1998, Boyds Mills $15.95 (1-56397-660-9). 32pp. This book of poems shows children in everyday situations and depicts their sense of wonder. (Rev: BL 2/15/98; SLJ 3/98) [811]

**9537** Dunning, Stephen, et al., eds. *Reflections on a Gift of Watermelon Pickle and Other Modern Verse* (6–8). Illus. 1967, Lothrop LB $20.00 (0-688-41231-9). 144pp. An attractive volume of 114 expressive poems by recognized modern poets, illustrated with striking photographs.

**9538** Eccleshare, Julia, ed. *First Poems* (PS–3). Illus. by Selina Young. 1994, Bedrick $8.99 (0-87226-373-8). 64pp. A collection of happy, often humorous poems, including a number of old favorites and several by contemporary poets. (Rev: BL 7/94; SLJ 8/94) [821]

**9539** Esbensen, Barbara J. *Who Shrank My Grandmother's House? Poems of Discovery* (1–3). Illus. by Eric Beddows. 1992, HarperCollins $15.00 (0-060-21827-4). 48pp. This book presents a celebration of everything in a collection of 23 poems. (Rev: BCCB 4/92; BL 6/1/92; HB 5–6/92; SLJ 4/92*) [811]

**9540** Ferris, Helen, ed. *Favorite Poems Old and New* (4–6). Illus. by Leonard Weisgard. 1957, Doubleday $23.95 (0-385-07696-7). 598pp. A book brimming with all kinds of poetry — lyrics, rhymes, doggerel, songs.

**9541** Fletcher, Ralph. *Buried Alive: The Elements of Love* (5–8). 1996, Simon & Schuster $14.00 (0-689-80593-4). 46pp. A series of free-verse poems explore various aspects of love — puppy and otherwise. (Rev: BCCB 6/96; BL 5/1/96; SLJ 5/96) [811]

**9542** Fletcher, Ralph. *I Am Wings: Poems About Love* (5–7). Illus. by Joe Baker. 1994, Macmillan paper $14.00 (0-02-735395-8). 48pp. Thirty-three simple, short poems depict a boy's falling in and out of love. (Rev: BCCB 6/94; BL 3/15/94; HB 7–8/94; SLJ 6/94*) [811]

**9543** Frank, Josette, ed. *Poems to Read to the Very Young* (PS). Illus. by Eloise Wilkin. 1982, Random $10.00 (0-394-85188-9); paper $3.25 (0-394-89768-4). 48pp. A collection of short simple verses, many of them old favorites.

**9544** Frost, Robert. *Stopping by Woods on a Snowy Evening* (K–4). Illus. by Susan Jeffers. 1978, Dutton paper $15.99 (0-525-40115-6). A richly illustrated version of Frost's most famous poem.

**9545** Frost, Robert. *A Swinger of Birches: Poems of Robert Frost for Young People* (4–7). Illus. by Peter Koeppen. 1982, Stemmer $21.95 (0-916144-92-5); paper $14.95 (0-916144-93-3). 80pp. A collection of 38 poems suitable for young people.

**9546** Frost, Robert. *You Come Too* (5–7). Illus. by Thomas W. Nason. 1959, Holt $14.95 (0-8050-0299-5). 96pp. A collection of some of the best-loved Frost poems illustrated with wood engravings.

**9547** Glaser, Isabel Joshlin, et al., ed. *Dreams of Glory: Poems Starring Girls* (2–5). Illus. 1995, Simon & Schuster $15.00 (0-689-31891-X). 48pp. A collection of 30 poems about girls, many of which tell about dreams of the future. (Rev: BL 11/15/95; SLJ 12/95) [811]

**9548** Goldstein, Bobbye S., ed. *Inner Chimes: Poems on Poetry* (2–6). Illus. by Jane Breskin Zalben. 1992, Boyds Mills LB $16.95 (1-56397-040-6). 24pp. This collection presents 20 poems that are inspirational, opening up a wealth of ideas and language in an entertaining manner. (Rev: BL 1/15/93; SLJ 10/92) [808.81]

**9549** Graham, Joan B. *Splish Splash* (K–5). Illus. by Steve Scott. 1994, Ticknor $15.00 (0-395-70128-7). 32pp. Several whimsical poems about water in its various states, including hail and ice cubes. (Rev: BCCB 10/94; BL 9/1/94*; SLJ 8/94*) [813]

**9550** Granfield, Linda. *In Flanders Fields: The Story of the Poem by John McCrae* (4–6). Illus. 1996, Doubleday $15.95 (0-385-32228-3). 32pp. Recalls the experiences during World War I that led the Canadian poet John McCrae to write "In Flanders Fields." (Rev: BL 11/1/96*; SLJ 12/96) [811]

**9551** Greenfield, Eloise. *Under the Sunday Tree* (2–5). Illus. by Amos Ferguson. 1988, HarperCollins paper $5.95 (0-06-443257-2). 48pp. Poems of life in the Bahamas. (Rev: BCCB 12/88; HB 11–12/88)

**9552** Grimes, Nikki. *It's Raining Laughter* (K–2). Illus. by Myles C. Pinkney. 1997, Dial paper $14.89 (0-8037-2004-1). 32pp. Illustrated with photos of African American children, this poetry book introduces everyday experiences of youngsters. (Rev: BL 10/1/97; SLJ 12/97) [811]

**9553** Gunning, Monica. *Under the Breadfruit Tree* (3–6). Illus. 1998, Boyds Mills $15.95 (1-56397-539-4). 48pp. These 38 poems describe the Caribbean peoples and their culture from the standpoint of a young Jamaican girl. (Rev: BL 2/15/98; SLJ 4/98) [811]

**9554** Hall, Donald. *The Man Who Lived Alone* (4–7). Illus. 1998, Godine paper $11.95 (1-56792-050-0). 36pp. A narrative poem concerning a man who ran away from abuse to see the world and returns in later life.

**9555** Hall, Donald, ed. *The Oxford Book of Children's Verse in America* (3–7). Illus. 1985, Oxford $35.00 (0-19-503539-9); paper $14.95 (0-19-506761-4). Poems adopted by or written for American children during certain periods. (Rev: BCCB 9/85; HB 9–10/85; SLJ 8/85)

**9556** Harrison, David L. *The Boy Who Counted Stars* (K–3). Illus. by Betsy Lewin. 1994, Boyds Mills $14.95 (1-56397-125-9). 30pp. A collection of imaginative poems that deal with a variety of subjects and moods. (Rev: SLJ 11/94) [811]

**9557** Harrison, David L. *A Thousand Cousins: Poems of Family Life* (2–4). Illus. by Betsy Lewin. 1996, Boyds Mills $14.95 (1-56397-131-3). 32pp. Short poems and cartoonlike drawings portray some of the humorous aspects of family life. (Rev: BL 1/1–15/96; SLJ 3/96) [811.54]

**9558** Harrison, Michael, and Christopher Stuart-Clark. *The New Oxford Treasury of Children's Poems* (3–6). Illus. 1997, Oxford $25.00 (0-19-276137-4). 170pp. This excellent well-illustrated collection of both old favorites and contemporary poems emphasizes British poets. (Rev: BL 1/1–15/98; SLJ 11/97) [821]

**9559** Harrison, Michael, and Christopher Stuart-Clark, eds. *The Oxford Book of Story Poems* (4–7). Illus. 1990, Oxford $25.00 (0-19-276087-4). 176pp. A smorgasbord of narrative poems by both British and American poets in a large volume. (Rev: BL 2/1/91) [821]

**9560** Harrison, Michael, and Christopher Stuart-Clark, eds. *The Oxford Treasury of Children's Poems* (4–6). Illus. 1994, Oxford paper $14.95 (0-19-276134-X). 174pp. A variety of verse, from Victorian to modern. (Rev: BCCB 2/89; BL 11/15/88; SLJ 1/89)

**9561** Hoberman, Mary Ann, ed. *My Song Is Beautiful: Poems and Pictures in Many Voices* (PS–3). Illus. 1994, Little, Brown $16.95 (0-316-36738-9). 32pp. An anthology of 14 poems that celebrate diversity in cultures and attitudes. (Rev: BCCB 4/94; BL 6/1–15/94; SLJ 6/94*) [808]

**9562** Hopkins, Lee Bennett, ed. *April Bubbles Chocolate: An ABC of Poetry* (PS–1). Illus. by Barry Root. 1994, Simon & Schuster paper $14.00 (0-671-75911-6). 40pp. An enjoyable anthology of poems arranged from A to Z. (Rev: BCCB 6/94; BL 5/1/94; HB 7–8/94; SLJ 9/94) [811]

**9563** Hopkins, Lee Bennett. *Been to Yesterdays* (4–7). Illus. 1995, Boyds Mills $14.95 (1-56397-467-3). 64pp. Through 28 simple but moving poems, the author chronicles the pleasures and pains of his middle years. (Rev: BL 1/1–15/96; SLJ 9/95*) [811.54]

**9564** Hopkins, Lee Bennett, et al., eds. *Blast Off! Poems About Space* (1–3). Illus. by Melissa Sweet. Series: I Can Read. 1995, HarperCollins LB $13.89 (0-06-024261-2). 48pp. An easily read book of poems about space and the wonders of the universe. (Rev: BCCB 4/95; BL 4/15/95; HB 7–8/95; SLJ 8/95) [811]

**9565** Hopkins, Lee Bennett, ed. *Click, Rumble, Roar: Poems About Machines* (3–6). Illus. 1987, HarperCollins LB $14.89 (0-690-04589-1). 48pp. Cars, trucks, trains, and all sorts of machines are featured in these 18 selections. Also use others of his collections: *Creatures* (1985, Harcourt); *Dinosaurs* (1987, Harcourt). (Rev: BL 7/87; HB 9–10/87; SLJ 9/87)

**9566** Hopkins, Lee Bennett, ed. *Good Books, Good Times* (K–3). Illus. by Harvey Stevenson. 1990, HarperCollins LB $16.89 (0-06-022528-9). 32pp. Fourteen short poems celebrate book reading. (Rev: BL 11/15/90; HB 1–2/91; SLJ 10/90*) [811]

**9567** Hopkins, Lee Bennett, ed. *Hand in Hand* (4–8). Illus. 1994, Simon & Schuster paper $20.00 (0-671-73315-X). 144pp. An overview of the history of American poetry, with an interesting selection of poems arranged chronologically. (Rev: BCCB 1/95; BL 1/1/95; SLJ 12/94) [811]

**9568** Hopkins, Lee Bennett. *Marvelous Math: A Book of Poems* (3–5). Illus. by Karen Barbour. 1997, Simon & Schuster paper $17.00 (0-689-80658-2). 31pp. A collection of simple poems by well-known writers that deal with math and numbers. (Rev: SLJ 10/97) [811]

**9569** Hopkins, Lee Bennett, ed. *School Supplies: A Book of Poems* (PS–1). Illus. by Renee Flower. 1996, Simon & Schuster paper $17.00 (0-689-80497-0). 37pp. Pencils, crayons, and books are some of the school supplies highlighted in 16 short poems. (Rev: BL 8/96; SLJ 11/96) [811]

**9570** Hopkins, Lee Bennett, ed. *Song and Dance* (1–3). Illus. by Cheryl M. Taylor. 1997, Simon & Schuster paper $16.00 (0-689-80159-9). 32pp. A collection of 16 poems that celebrate the sounds of the language in verses that deal with songs and dancing. (Rev: BL 4/15/97; SLJ 6/97) [811]

**9571** Hopkins, Lee Bennett, ed. *Surprises* (K–4). Illus. by Megan Lloyd. 1984, HarperCollins paper $3.75 (0-06-444105-9). 64pp. A collection of simple poems for beginning readers.

**9572** Huck, Charlotte, ed. *Secret Places* (PS–3). Illus. by Lindsay B. George. 1993, Greenwillow LB $14.93 (0-688-11670-1). 32pp. A collection of 19 poems about secret places that children love, like hideouts and containers for keeping secret things. (Rev: BL 10/1/93; SLJ 8/93) [811]

**9573** Hughes, Shirley. *Rhymes for Annie Rose* (PS–K). Illus. 1995, Lothrop $16.00 (0-688-14220-6). 48pp. In simple poems, daily occurrences in a young child's life are celebrated. (Rev: BCCB 11/95; BL 8/95; SLJ 9/95*) [821]

**9574** Janeczko, Paul B. *Home on the Range: Cowboy Poetry* (3–6). Illus. by Bernie Fuchs. 1997, Dial paper $15.89 (0-8037-1911-6). 40pp. A series of short poems showing many sides of the cowboy's way of life. (Rev: BL 10/15/97; SLJ 12/97) [811]

**9575** Janeczko, Paul B. *The Place My Words Are Looking For: What Poets Say About and Through Their Work* (4–8). Illus. 1990, Macmillan paper $16.00 (0-02-747671-5). 128pp. A collection by some of the best contemporary poets. (Rev: BCCB 7–8/90; BL 5/1/90; HB 5–6/90*; SLJ 5/90) [811]

**9576** Johnston, Tony. *My Mexico/México Mío* (K–3). Illus. by F. John Sierra. 1996, Putnam $15.95 (0-399-22275-8). 36pp. Mexican scenes are presented in double-page spreads with 18 poems in both English and Spanish. (Rev: BCCB 7–8/96; HB 5–6/96; SLJ 4/96) [811]

**9577** Johnston, Tony. *Once in the Country: Poems of a Farm* (K–3). Illus. by Thomas B. Allen. 1996, Putnam $15.95 (0-399-22644-3). 32pp. The joys of rural life are celebrated in this collection of 18 charming poems. (Rev: SLJ 12/96) [811]

**9578** Joseph, Lynn. *Coconut Kind of Day: Island Poems* (K–2). Illus. by Sandra Speidel. 1990, Lothrop LB $13.88 (0-688-09120-2). 32pp. A portrait of a young black girl in the West Indies. (Rev: BCCB 1/91; BL 9/15/90; SLJ 11/90) [811]

**9579** Kennedy, Dorothy M., ed. *I Thought I'd Take My Rat to School: Poems for September to June* (2–5). Illus. by Abby Carter. 1993, Little, Brown $16.95 (0-316-48893-3). 64pp. An anthology of 57 poems about the agony and ecstasy of attending school. (Rev: BCCB 11/93; BL 11/1/93; HB 11–12/93; SLJ 9/93) [811]

**9580** Kennedy, X. J., and Dorothy M. Kennedy. *Knock at a Star: A Child's Introduction to Poetry* (4–6). Illus. by Karen Ann Weinhaus. 1982, Little, Brown paper $10.95 (0-316-48854-2). 160pp. A collection of 150 poems, plus advice on writing one's own.

**9581** Kennedy, X. J., and Dorothy M. Kennedy, eds. *Talking Like the Rain: A First Book of Poems* (PS–3). Illus. by Jane Dyer. 1992, Little, Brown $19.95 (0-316-48889-5). 96pp. This is a cheerful collection of 100 well-illustrated poems in a variety of subjects and moods. (Rev: BCCB 7–8/92; BL 3/15/92; HB 7–8/92; SLJ 6/92) [821]

**9582** Kipling, Rudyard. *Gunga Din* (5–8). Illus. by Robert Andrew Parker. 1987, Harcourt $12.95 (0-15-200456-4). 28pp. A vibrantly illustrated edition of the classic poem about the life of an Indian water carrier, Gunga Din. (Rev: BCCB 10/87; BL 11/1/87)

**9583** Kuskin, Karla. *Dogs and Dragons, Trees and Dreams: A Collection of Poems* (3–6). Illus. by author. n.d., HarperCollins $7.66 (0-06-023543-8). 96pp. A welcome reissue of poems that had appeared previously in the author's works.

**9584** Lansky, Bruce, ed. *No More Homework! No More Tests! Kids' Favorite Funny School Poems* (2–6). Illus. 1997, Meadowbrook Pr. LB $8.00 (0-671-57702-6). 80pp. Humorous, often outrageous, poems that deal with real and fantastic school situations. (Rev: BL 9/15/97) [811]

**9585** Larrick, Nancy, ed. *Piping down the Valleys Wild* (1–5). Illus. by Ellen Raskin. 1985, Dell paper $5.50 (0-440-46952-X). 256pp. Animals, children,

and the seasons are represented in this fine collection culled from a variety of sources.

**9586** Levy, Constance. *When Whales Exhale and Other Poems* (3–5). Illus. 1996, Simon & Schuster $15.00 (0-689-80946-8). 42pp. A group of poems about the wonders of small things that are part of larger objects or events. (Rev: BL 12/15/96; SLJ 12/96) [811]

**9587** Lewis, Claudia. *Long Ago in Oregon* (3–7). Illus. by Joel Fontaine. 1987, HarperCollins $11.95 (0-06-023839-9). 64pp. Short poems that recall the nostalgia of childhood in Oregon in the early 1900s. (Rev: BCCB 5/87; BL 7/87; SLJ 9/87)

**9588** Liatsos, Sandra O. *Bicycle Riding: And Other Poems* (1–4). Illus. by Karen M. Dugan. 1997, Boyds Mills $15.95 (1-56397-235-2). A collection of 22 poems that deal with the everyday activities of children. (Rev: SLJ 5/97) [811]

**9589** Lillegard, Dee. *The Wild Bunch* (PS–1). Illus. by Rex Barron. 1997, Putnam $15.95 (0-399-22826-8). In 30 short poems, various fruits and vegetables are introduced. (Rev: SLJ 10/97) [811]

**9590** Livingston, Myra Cohn. *Flights of Fancy and Other Poems* (3–5). 1994, Macmillan paper $13.95 (0-689-50613-9). 48pp. Some of the 40 short poems in this collection deal with airplanes, but most deal with flights of the imagination. (Rev: BCCB 1/95; BL 11/15/94; SLJ 12/94) [811]

**9591** Livingston, Myra Cohn, ed. *I Am Writing a Poem About . . . a Game of Poetry* (4–6). 1997, Simon & Schuster $15.00 (0-689-81156-X). 72pp. A collection of poems that came from a master class taught by Myra Cohn Livingston. (Rev: BL 9/1/97; SLJ 10/97) [811]

**9592** Livingston, Myra Cohn, ed. *I Like You, If You Like Me: Poems of Friendship* (4–8). 1987, Macmillan $14.95 (0-689-50408-X). 160pp. Ninety short poems on the theme of friendship, from many cultures and time periods. (Rev: BL 4/1/87; HB 5–6/87; SLJ 4/87)

**9593** Livingston, Myra Cohn. *I Never Told and Other Poems* (3–6). 1992, Macmillan $12.95 (0-689-50544-2). 44pp. Forty-two short poems highlight flight — in an airplane and in the imagination. (Rev: BCCB 4/92; BL 6/1/92; SLJ 4/92) [811]

**9594** Livingston, Myra Cohn. *Light and Shadow* (3–6). Illus. by Barbara Rogasky. 1992, Holiday LB $14.95 (0-8234-0931-7). 32pp. Fourteen short blank-verse poems illustrated with color photos. (Rev: BCCB 5/92*; BL 5/15/92; SLJ 4/92) [811]

**9595** Livingston, Myra Cohn. *Remembering and Other Poems* (3–6). 1989, Macmillan LB $13.95 (0-689-50489-6). 64pp. Thoughts and emotions from a variety of childhood activities. (Rev: BCCB 1/90; BL 12/1/89; SLJ 12/89*) [811]

**9596** Livingston, Myra Cohn, ed. *Roll Along: Poems on Wheels* (3–5). 1993, Macmillan $11.95 (0-689-50585-X). 72pp. An anthology of poems about wheels on various kinds of vehicles, from skateboards and bicycles to garbage trucks and trains. (Rev: BL 9/15/93; SLJ 8/93) [811]

**9597** Longfellow, Henry Wadsworth. *The Children's Hour* (K–2). Illus. by Glenna Lang. 1993, Godine $17.95 (0-87923-971-9). 32pp. The classic poem is illustrated with paintings depicting Longfellow spending time with his children. (Rev: BL 11/15/93) [811]

**9598** Longfellow, Henry Wadsworth. *The Children's Own Longfellow* (5–8). Illus. 1908, Houghton $20.00 (0-395-06889-4). 109pp. Eight selections from the best-known and best-loved of Longfellow's poems.

**9599** Longfellow, Henry Wadsworth. *Hiawatha* (K–3). Illus. by Susan Jeffers. 1983, Dial paper $16.99 (0-8037-0013-X). 32pp. A beautifully illustrated version of sections of Longfellow's poem.

**9600** Longfellow, Henry Wadsworth. *Paul Revere's Ride* (2–4). Illus. by Nancy Winslow Parker. 1985, Greenwillow LB $14.93 (0-688-04015-2); Morrow paper $4.95 (0-688-12387-2). 48pp. Soft illustrations relieve the suspense of this famous ride. (Rev: BCCB 5/85; BL 3/1/85; HB 5–6/85)

**9601** Longfellow, Henry Wadsworth. *Paul Revere's Ride* (PS–3). Illus. by Ted Rand. 1990, Dutton paper $16.99 (0-525-44610-9). 40pp. The poem's essential drama is captured in a series of paintings. (Rev: BCCB 12/90; BL 9/15/90*; HB 1–2/91; SLJ 11/90*) [811]

**9602** Lyne, Sandford, comp. *Ten-Second Rainshowers: Poems by Young People* (4–8). Illus. by Virginia Halstead. 1996, Simon & Schuster paper $16.00 (0-689-80113-0). 124pp. A variety of subjects — including nature, home, and family — are touched on in this collection of free verse written by 130 children from ages 8 to 18. (Rev: SLJ 12/96) [811]

**9603** McCord, David. *All Day Long: Fifty Rhymes of the Never Was and Always Is* (4–7). Illus. by Henry B. Kane. 1975, Little, Brown paper $6.95 (0-316-55532-0). A collection of poems on a variety of subjects, chiefly times that are important in childhood.

**9604** McCord, David. *One at a Time: His Collected Poems for the Young* (3–8). Illus. by Henry B. Kane. 1986, Little, Brown $18.95 (0-316-55516-9). All 7 of the poet's anthologies in one handsome volume.

**9605** *Maples in the Mist: Children's Poems from the Tang Dynasty* (K–5). Trans. by Minfong Ho. Illus. by Jean Tseng and Mou-Sien Tseng. 1996, Lothrop LB $14.93 (0-688-14723-2). 32pp. Sixteen rhymes from the Tang Dynasty in modern language, each accompanied by a watercolor. (Rev: BCCB 9/96; BL 10/1/96; SLJ 9/96) [895.1]

**9606** Marshak, Samuel. *Hail to Mail* (1–4). Trans. by Richard Pevear. Illus. by Vladimir Radunsky. 1995, Holt paper $5.95 (0-8050-3124-3). 32pp. A zesty tribute to mail carriers. (Rev: BCCB 12/92; BL 12/1/90; HB 1–2/91; SLJ 2/91) [891]

**9607** Mavor, Salley, ed. *You and Me: Poems of Friendship* (PS–3). Illus. 1997, Orchard LB $17.99 (0-531-33045-1). 32pp. An anthology of 19 enjoyable poems that celebrate the joys and problems that come with friendships. (Rev: BL 7/97; SLJ 9/97) [811]

**9608** Milne, A. A. *The World of Christopher Robin* (K–3). Illus. by E. H. Shepard. 1958, Dutton paper $19.99 (0-525-44448-3). 256pp. Original illustrations have been retained in this edition that combines the poems from *When We Were Very Young* and *Now We Are Six.*

**9609** Moore, Lillian. *I Never Did That Before* (PS–K). Illus. by Lillian Hoban. 1995, Simon & Schuster $15.00 (0-689-31889-8). 32pp. Fourteen simple poems about the joys of such childhood accomplishments as learning to skip rope. (Rev: BL 11/1/95; SLJ 10/95) [811]

**9610** Mora, Pat. *Confetti* (1–4). Illus. by Enrique O. Sanchez. 1996, Lee & Low $14.95 (1-880000-25-3). 32pp. A series of poems that mingle Spanish expressions with basic English. (Rev: BL 11/15/96; SLJ 11/96) [811]

**9611** Morninghouse, Sundaira. *Nightfeathers* (PS–K). Illus. by Jody Kim. 1990, Open Hand $9.95 (0-940880-27-X); paper $4.95 (0-940880-28-8). 32pp. In 24 short poems, a typical day in the life of an African American child is portrayed. (Rev: BL 6/1/90) [811]

**9612** Moss, Jeff. *Bone Poems* (3–5). Illus. by Tom Leigh. 1997, Workman $14.95 (0-7611-0884-X). 78pp. A group of rhymes that explore facts about dinosaurs and make paleontology fun. (Rev: SLJ 12/97*) [811]

**9613** Moss, Jeff. *The Butterfly Jar* (2–5). Illus. by Chris L. Demarest. 1989, Bantam $16.95 (0-553-05704-9). 128pp. Upbeat poetry, including the silly and the serious. (Rev: BL 2/1/90; SLJ 7/90) [811]

**9614** Moss, Jeff. *The Dad of the Dad of the Dad of Your Dad: Stories About Kids and Their Fathers* (4–8). Illus. by Chris L. Demarest. 1997, Ballantine $18.00 (0-345-38591-8). 88pp. Eight humorous poems trace the history of families, from a prehistoric father and his boy to a futuristic dad with his family. (Rev: SLJ 7/97) [811]

**9615** Myers, Walter Dean. *Glorious Angels* (1–4). Illus. 1995, HarperCollins LB $15.89 (0-06-024823-8). 48pp. A collection of turn-of-the-century photos of children from many cultures. (Rev: BCCB 10/95; BL 9/1/95; SLJ 9/95) [811]

**9616** Noyes, Alfred. *The Highwayman* (5–8). Illus. by Charles Mikolaycak. 1987, Oxford paper $10.95 (0-19-272133-X). 32pp. An exciting narrative poem, nicely illustrated on laminated boards.

**9617** O'Neill, Mary. *Hailstones and Halibut Bones* (PS–3). Illus. by Leonard Weisgard. 1973, Doubleday paper $7.95 (0-385-41078-6). Imaginative poems about color.

**9618** Paraskevas, Betty. *Junior Kroll* (2–4). Illus. by Michael Paraskevas. 1993, Harcourt $13.95 (0-15-241497-5). Fifteen poems about a mischievous boy and his adventures. (Rev: BCCB 5/93; SLJ 6/93) [822]

**9619** Philip, Neil, ed. *Songs Are Thoughts: Poems of the Inuit* (K–4). Illus. by Maryclare Foa. 1995, Orchard $15.95 (0-531-06893-5). 32pp. Short Inuit poems are featured in double-page spreads, each containing a poem and an illustration. (Rev: BCCB 5/95; BL 4/15/95; SLJ 4/95) [897]

**9620** Pomerantz, Charlotte. *Halfway to Your House* (PS–1). Illus. by Gabrielle Vincent. 1993, Greenwillow LB $13.93 (0-688-11805-4). 32pp. The thoughts and feelings of different children at play are explored in watercolors and short poems. (Rev: BL 10/15/93) [811]

**9621** Pomerantz, Charlotte. *If I Had a Paka: Poems in Eleven Languages* (PS–3). Illus. by Nancy Tafuri. 1993, Morrow paper $4.95 (0-688-12510-7). 32pp. In each of these poems, English is interspersed with one of 11 languages. A reissue. [811]

**9622** Pooley, Sarah. *It's Raining, It's Pouring: A Book for Rainy Days* (PS–3). Illus. 1993, Greenwillow $18.00 (0-688-11803-8). 80pp. This book is filled with poems, songs, and ideas for all kinds of activities just perfect for a rainy day. (Rev: BL 5/1/93; SLJ 7/93) [808]

**9623** Prelutsky, Jack. *Monday's Troll* (4–6). Illus. by Peter Sis. 1996, Greenwillow LB $15.93 (0-688-14373-3). 40pp. Seventeen original poems that deal with supernatural beings like witches, trolls, wizards, and ogres. (Rev: BCCB 3/96; BL 4/15/96; HB 5–6/96; SLJ 4/96*) [811]

**9624** Prelutsky, Jack. *Nightmares: Poems to Trouble Your Sleep* (5–8). Illus. by Arnold Lobel. 1976, Greenwillow LB $15.93 (0-688-84053-1). 38pp. Shuddery, macabre poems that will frighten but amuse a young audience. A sequel is: *The Headless Horseman Rides Tonight: More Poems to Trouble Your Sleep* (1980).

**9625** Prelutsky, Jack. *A Pizza the Size of the Sun* (3–6). Illus. by James Stevenson. 1996, Greenwillow LB $17.93 (0-688-13236-7). 160pp. Humorous, imaginative light verses explore a variety of subjects. (Rev: BCCB 9/96; BL 9/15/96*; HB 9–10/96; SLJ 9/96*) [811]

**9626** Prelutsky, Jack, ed. *The Random House Book of Poetry for Children* (2–6). Illus. by Arnold Lobel. 1983, Random LB $21.99 (0-394-95010-0). 248pp. Old standbys and new gems are included in this fine anthology of 572 poems.

**9627** Prelutsky, Jack. *Read-Aloud Rhymes for the Very Young* (PS–1). Illus. by Marc Brown. 1986, Knopf LB $21.99 (0-394-97218-X). 112pp. An oversize book of lighthearted verse. (Rev: BL 12/15/86; HB 1–2/87; SLJ 12/86)

**9628** Ridlon, Marci. *Sun Through the Window: Poems for Children* (3–6). Illus. 1996, Boyds Mills paper $7.95 (1-56397-454-1). 64pp. A collection of 54 poems dealing with everyday experiences and emotions. (Rev: SLJ 10/96) [811]

**9629** Robb, Laura, ed. *Music and Drum: Voices of War and Peace, Hope and Dream* (3–6). Illus. by Debra Lill. 1997, Putnam $16.95 (0-399-22024-0). 32pp. An anthology of war poems that are strikingly illustrated with photos reflecting the power and emotion of the poems. (Rev: BCCB 5/97; BL 4/1/97) [808]

**9630** Robinson, Fay, ed. *A Frog Inside My Hat: A First Book of Poems* (PS–2). Illus. by Cyd Moore. 1993, BridgeWater paper $16.95 (0-8167-3129-2). 62pp. This book of 37 poems by well-known writers is divided into topics like animals, nonsense verse, food, and weather. (Rev: SLJ 10/93) [811]

**9631** Rosen, Michael. *The Best of Michael Rosen* (3–5). Illus. by Quentin Blake. 1995, Wetlands paper $16.95 (1-57143-046-6). 136pp. Sixty-five insightful, often lighthearted poems by the popular English poet. (Rev: BL 2/1/96) [808.81]

**9632** Rosen, Michael, ed. *Poems for the Very Young* (PS–2). Illus. by Bob Graham. 1993, Kingfisher $15.95 (1-85697-908-3). 80pp. A delightful collection of rhymes for young children, chiefly from American and British sources and illustrated with charming cartoonlike drawings. (Rev: BL 1/1/94*; SLJ 1/94) [821]

**9633** Rosen, Michael J., ed. *Food Fight: Poets Join the Fight Against Hunger with Poems to Favorite Foods* (3–6). Illus. by Michael J. Rosen. 1996, Harcourt $17.00 (0-15-201065-3). 56pp. Thirty-five children's book writers share their impressions of food and eating in this delightful collection of poems. (Rev: BL 10/1/96; SLJ 4/97) [811]

**9634** Rossetti, Christina. *Sing Song: A Nursery Rhyme Book* (K–3). Illus. by Arthur Hughes. 1969, Dover paper $4.95 (0-486-22107-5). 130pp. Many of the poems are about small creatures and familiar objects and have a singing quality that young children enjoy.

**9635** Roth, Susan L. *Gypsy Bird Song* (1–4). Illus. 1991, Farrar $14.95 (0-374-32825-0). 32pp. A long free-verse poem that provides a glimpse into many aspects of gypsy life. (Rev: BL 12/15/91; SLJ 12/91) [811]

**9636** Sandburg, Carl. *Grassroots* (3–6). Illus. by Wendell Minor. 1998, Harcourt $18.00 (0-15-200082-8). 34pp. Fourteen poems by Sandburg that describe the Midwest are reprinted, with handsome framed pictures. (Rev: BL 3/15/98) [811]

**9637** Sandburg, Carl. *The Sandburg Treasury: Prose and Poetry for Young People* (5–8). Illus. 1970, Harcourt $25.95 (0-15-270180-X). 480pp. Sandburg's whimsical stories, poetry, and portions of his autobiography.

**9638** Schertle, Alice. *Keepers* (1–4). Illus. by Ted Rand. 1996, Lothrop LB $15.93 (0-688-11635-3). 32pp. A collection of original poems in which everyday objects become transformed through one's imagination. (Rev: BL 10/15/96; SLJ 12/96) [811]

**9639** Schmidt, Gary D., ed. *Robert Frost* (5–7). Illus. by Henri Sorensen. Series: Poetry for Young People. 1994, Sterling $14.95 (0-8069-0633-2). 48pp. An anthology of 25 poems suitable for young people, with watercolor illustrations that picture the New England landscape that Frost loved. (Rev: BL 12/1/94; SLJ 2/95) [811]

**9640** Seabrooke, Brenda. *Under the Pear Tree* (4–6). Illus. 1997, Dutton paper $13.99 (0-525-65213-2). 96pp. An illustrated narrative poem that describes 3 girls growing up in a small town in Georgia during the 1950s. (Rev: BL 8/97; HB 7–8/97; SLJ 9/97) [811]

**9641** Service, Robert W. *The Cremation of Sam McGee* (5–8). Illus. by Ted Harrison. 1987, Greenwillow $18.00 (0-688-06903-7). 32pp. Poems for young readers who like a touch of the bizarre and macabre. (Rev: BL 4/15/87; HB 5–6/87; SLJ 3/87)

**9642** Shields, Carol D. *Lunch Money and Other Poems About School* (1–3). Illus. by Paul Meisel. 1995, Dutton paper $14.99 (0-525-45345-8). 48pp. Daily events at school are celebrated in this charming group of poems. (Rev: BL 11/15/95; SLJ 1/96) [811]

**9643** Siebert, Diane. *Heartland* (K–4). Illus. by Wendell Minor. 1989, HarperCollins paper $6.95 (0-06-443287-4). 32pp. A lyrical celebration of the Midwest. (Rev: BL 3/1/89; SLJ 5/89)

**9644** Silverstein, Shel. *Falling Up* (3–6). Illus. 1996, HarperCollins LB $17.89 (0-06-024803-3). 176pp. More than 150 delightful original poems that amuse and amaze. (Rev: BCCB 6/96; BL 7/96*; HB 9–10/96; SLJ 7/96) [811]

**9645** Silverstein, Shel. *Where the Sidewalk Ends* (3–6). Illus. by author. 1974, HarperCollins LB $16.89 (0-06-025668-0). 176pp. The author explores various facets and interests of children, with appro-

priate cartoonlike drawings. Also use: *A Light in the Attic* (1981).

**9646** Simon, Seymour, ed. *Star Walk* (4–8). Illus. 1995, Morrow LB $14.93 (0-688-11887-7). 32pp. Simple poems and outstanding photographs create an impressive introduction to stars and outer space. (Rev: BL 3/1/95; SLJ 4/95) [811]

**9647** Singer, Marilyn. *All We Needed to Say: Poems About School from Tanya and Sophie* (PS–3). Illus. by Lorna Clark. 1996, Simon & Schuster $15.00 (0-689-80667-1). 28pp. Two girls compare their school experiences in a series of short monologues. (Rev: BCCB 9/96; BL 8/96; SLJ 9/96) [811]

**9648** Singer, Marilyn. *Family Reunion* (K–3). Illus. by R. W. Alley. 1994, Macmillan paper $14.95 (0-02-782883-2). 32pp. Fourteen poems that celebrate a family reunion, ending with Dad receiving photos of the proceedings. (Rev: BL 9/1/94; SLJ 11/94) [811]

**9649** Singer, Marilyn. *The Morgans Dream* (1–6). Illus. by Gary Drake. 1995, Holt $15.95 (0-8050-3004-2). The poems in this collection describe the dreams of each of the 7 Morgan children, their parents, their dog and cat, and a set of grandparents. (Rev: SLJ 11/95*) [811]

**9650** Soto, Gary. *Canto Familiar* (4–6). Illus. 1995, Harcourt $17.00 (0-15-200067-4). 88pp. Simple poems, many involving Mexican Americans, celebrate experiences at school, home, and in the street. A companion to *Neighborhood Odes* (1992). (Rev: BL 10/1/95; SLJ 12/95*) [811]

**9651** Soto, Gary. *Neighborhood Odes* (4–6). Illus. by David Diaz. 1992, Harcourt $15.95 (0-15-256879-4). 80pp. Unrhymed verses celebrate such items in a Mexican-American neighborhood as pinatas, weddings, libraries, and tennis shoes. (Rev: BL 6/15/92; HB 5–6/92*; SLJ 5/92) [811]

**9652** Spinelli, Eileen. *Where Is the Night Train Going?* (PS–3). Illus. by Cyd Moore. 1996, Boyds Mills $14.95 (1-56397-171-2). 32pp. Everyday concerns and activities are portrayed in this group of well-illustrated, evocative poems. (Rev: BL 1/1–15/96; SLJ 4/96) [811]

**9653** Standiford, Natalie. *Astronauts Are Sleeping* (1–3). Illus. by Allen Garns. 1996, Knopf LB $18.99 (0-679-96999-3). Poems that explore the dreams of astronauts as they circle the earth in orbit. (Rev: BCCB 2/97; SLJ 12/96) [811]

**9654** Stevenson, James. *Sweet Corn* (3–5). Illus. 1995, Greenwillow $15.00 (0-688-12647-2). 64pp. A collection of poems that deal with everyday occurrences in a realistic way. (Rev: BCCB 3/95; BL 2/15/95; HB 7–8//95; SLJ 3/95*) [811]

**9655** Stevenson, Robert Louis. *Block City* (PS–K). Illus. by Ashley Wolff. 1988, Puffin paper $4.99 (0-14-054551-4). 32pp. Picture-book version of the poem from *A Child's Garden of Verses*. (Rev: BL 9/1/88; HB 1–2/89; SLJ 9/88)

**9656** Stevenson, Robert Louis. *A Child's Garden of Verses* (K–4). Illus. 1989, Chronicle $17.95 (0-87701-608-9). 121pp. A handsome edition of the old favorite, using some 100 19th-century illustrations. (Rev: BL 11/1/89*; SLJ 2/90) [821]

**9657** Stevenson, Robert Louis. *A Child's Garden of Verses* (K–4). Illus. by Tasha Tudor. 1988, Macmillan $13.95 (0-02-689093-3). 72pp. Verses known and loved by generations of young people, brilliantly illustrated.

**9658** Stevenson, Robert Louis. *A Child's Garden of Verses* (PS). Illus. by Joanna Isles. 1994, Abrams $14.95 (0-8109-3196-6). 87pp. A freshly illustrated edition of this classic, published to commemorate the centenary of the author's death. (Rev: SLJ 10/94) [821]

**9659** Strickland, Michael R. *Poems That Sing to You* (3–7). Illus. by Alan Leiner. 1993, Boyds Mills $14.95 (1-56397-178-X). 55pp. A collection of poems that suggest music and dancing, some from well-known writers and others from pop lyrics and age-old chants. (Rev: HB 11–12/93; SLJ 10/93) [811]

**9660** Swanson, Susan M. *Getting Used to the Dark: 26 Night Poems* (2–5). Illus. by Peter Catalanotto. Series: Richard Jackson Book. 1997, DK Publg. $14.95 (0-7894-2468-1). 45pp. The nature of night, darkness, and dreams is explored in this book of poetry. (Rev: SLJ 1/98) [811]

**9661** Swenson, May. *The Complete Poems to Solve* (5–8). Illus. by Christy Hale. 1993, Macmillan LB $13.95 (0-02-788725-1). 128pp. From simple riddles to more complex questions, each of these poems contains a puzzle. (Rev: HB 3–4/93; SLJ 5/93) [811]

**9662** Sword, Elizabeth Hauge, and Victoria McCarthy, eds. *A Child's Anthology of Poetry* (4–7). Illus. 1995, Ecco $22.00 (0-88001-378-8). 336pp. A collection of traditional favorites (with a few from contemporary poets) that includes all the standard children's choices. (Rev: BL 11/15/95) [808]

**9663** Taberski, Sharon, ed. *Morning, Noon, and Night: Poems to Fill Your Day* (PS–3). Illus. by Nancy Doniger. 1996, Mondo $14.95 (1-57255-128-3). 32pp. The day's activities are traced in 29 poems by well-known writers. (Rev: BL 12/15/96; SLJ 5/96) [811]

**9664** Tagore, Rabindranath. *Paper Boats* (PS–3). Illus. by Grayce Bochak. 1992, Boyds Mills $14.95 (1-878093-12-6). 32pp. After launching a set of paper boats in a stream, an Indian boy thinks of where the fragile fleet may carry his dreams. (Rev: BL 1/1/92; HB 3–4/92; SLJ 2/92) [891.44]

**9665** Turner, Ann. *Mississippi Mud: Three Prairie Journals* (4–8). Illus. by Robert J. Blake. 1997, HarperCollins LB $15.89 (0-06-024433-X). 48pp. Through a series of poems, one family's experiences are chronicled as they journey from Kentucky to Oregon in the 19th century. (Rev: BCCB 6/97; BL 4/15/97; SLJ 6/97*) [811]

**9666** Turner, Ann. *Street Talk* (2–4). Illus. by Catherine Stock. 1988, Houghton paper $3.95 (0-395-61625-5). 47pp. A total of 29 original poems about everyday subjects like teachers and pizza. (Rev: BCCB 6/86; SLJ 9/86)

**9667** Viorst, Judith. *If I Were in Charge of the World and Other Worries: Poems for Children and Their Parents* (5–8). Illus. by Lynne Cherry. 1981, Macmillan $16.00 (0-689-30863-9); paper $4.95 (0-689-70770-3). 64pp. Situations that vex are explored in these 41 poems.

**9668** Wallace, Daisy, ed. *Ghost Poems* (4–7). Illus. by Tomie dePaola. 1979, Holiday paper $4.95 (0-8234-0849-3). 32pp. New and old poems to delight and frighten young readers.

**9669** Wallace, Daisy, ed. *Witch Poems* (3–6). Illus. by Trina S. Hyman. 1976, Holiday LB $14.95 (0-8234-0281-9); paper $4.95 (0-8234-0850-7). 32pp. Eighteen poems chosen from several different sources on a wide variety of witches.

**9670** Whipple, Laura. *Eric Carle's Dragons Dragons and Other Creatures That Never Were* (2–6). Illus. by Eric Carle. 1991, Putnam $18.95 (0-399-22105-0). 69pp. This is a collection of poems about dragons and other mythological creatures illustrated by Eric Carle. (Rev: BCCB 12/91; BL 11/1/91; HB 11–12/91; SLJ 10/91) [811]

**9671** Wilbur, Richard. *Runaway Opposites* (4–6). Illus. by Henrik Drescher. 1995, Harcourt $15.00 (0-15-258722-5). 32pp. An intriguing, involved book of poems that deal with synonyms and antonyms. (Rev: BCCB 4/95; BL 4/15/95; SLJ 5/95) [811]

**9672** Willard, Nancy. *The Ballad of Biddy Early* (4–8). Illus. by Barry Moser. 1989, Knopf LB $14.99 (0-394-98414-5). 48pp. In original poetry, Willard tells about an Irish woman who lived in the 19th century and could see into the future. (Rev: BCCB 1/90; BL 12/15/89; SLJ 3/90) [811]

**9673** Willard, Nancy. *A Visit to William Blake's Inn: Poems for Innocent and Experienced Travelers* (2–5). Illus. by Alice Provensen and Martin Provensen. 1981, Harcourt $16.00 (0-15-293822-2); paper $7.00 (0-15-293823-0). 44pp. A collection of poems that won the Newbery Award, 1982.

**9674** Willard, Nancy. *The Voyage of the Ludgate Hill: Travels with Robert Louis Stevenson* (1–4). Illus. by Alice Provensen and Martin Provensen. 1987, Harcourt $14.95 (0-15-294464-8). A poem told through the poet's eyes of his 1887 journey across the Atlantic. (Rev: BCCB 4/87; BL 6/1/87; SLJ 5/87)

**9675** Winters, Kay. *Did You See What I Saw? Poems About School* (PS–1). Illus. by Martha Weston. 1996, Viking paper $13.99 (0-670-87118-4). 32pp. Everyday experiences in school are the subject of these 23 short poems. (Rev: BCCB 9/96; BL 8/96; SLJ 10/96) [811]

**9676** Wong, Janet S. *A Suitcase of Seaweed and Other Poems* (4–7). 1996, Simon & Schuster $15.00 (0-689-80788-0). 42pp. Personal poems that deal with the author's cultural backgrounds — Korean, Chinese, and American. (Rev: BCCB 4/96; BL 4/1/96; HB 7–8/96; SLJ 9/96) [811]

**9677** Worth, Valerie. *All the Small Poems and Fourteen More* (PS–3). Illus. by Natalie Babbitt. 1994, Farrar $18.00 (0-374-30211-1). 194pp. A collection of all 113 poems in the Small People series. (Rev: BCCB 2/95; BL 1/15/95) [811]

**9678** Worth, Valerie. *Still More Small Poems* (4–7). Illus. by Natalie Babbitt. 1978, Farrar $11.00 (0-374-37258-6). Simple poems about everyday things that reveal the poet's skill and fertile imagination. Also use: *Small Poems Again* (1986).

**9679** Yolen, Jane. *O Jerusalem* (4–6). Illus. by John Thompson. 1996, Scholastic $15.95 (0-590-48426-5). A group of original poems that explore the importance of Jerusalem in Judaism, Christianity, and Islam. (Rev: BL 2/1/96*; SLJ 3/96*) [811]

**9680** Yolen, Jane. *Sacred Places* (4–6). Illus. by David Shannon. 1996, Harcourt $16.00 (0-15-269953-8). 40pp. A worldwide collection of informational poems about the places sacred to various faiths. (Rev: BCCB 7–8/96; BL 10/1/96; HB 1–2/96; SLJ 3/96) [811]

**9681** Yolen, Jane, ed. *Sky Scrape/City Scape: Poems of City Life* (1–4). Illus. by Ken Condon. 1996, Boyds Mills $15.95 (1-56397-179-8). 32pp. An anthology of 25 poems that deal with life in a big city. (Rev: BL 5/15/96*; SLJ 6/96) [808.81]

**9682** Yolen, Jane, ed. *Street Rhymes Around the World* (1–3). Illus. 1992, Boyds Mills $16.95 (1-878093-53-3). 40pp. An offering of short rhymes, in both English and the native language, is used for counting, tag, jumping rope, and so on. (Rev: BL 5/15/92; SLJ 5/92) [398.8]

# African American Poetry

**9683** Adedjouma, Davida, ed. *The Palm of My Heart: Poetry by African American Children* (1–4). Illus. by Gregory Christie. 1996, Lee & Low $15.95

(1-880000-41-5). 32pp. Twenty poems by African American children about the beauty and joy of being black. (Rev: BCCB 12/96; BL 2/15/97; SLJ 1/97) [811]

**9684** Adoff, Arnold, ed. *My Black Me: A Beginning Book of Black Poetry* (3–6). 1974, Dutton $12.95 (0-525-35460-3). 96pp. An anthology by black writers, stressing the positive aspects of blackness, pride, and joy. Also use: *I Am the Darker Brother: An Anthology of Modern Poems by Negro Americans* (1997, Simon & Schuster).

**9685** Brooks, Gwendolyn. *Bronzeville Boys and Girls* (2–5). Illus. by Ronni Solbert. 1956, Harper-Collins LB $15.89 (0-06-020651-9). 48pp. Everyday experiences of black children growing up in Chicago are revealed in these simple poems.

**9686** Bryan, Ashley. *Ashley Bryan's ABC of African American Poetry* (PS–4). Illus. 1997, Simon & Schuster $16.00 (0-689-81209-4). 32pp. A collection of charming African American poetry using the alphabet as a framework. (Rev: BL 9/1/97; SLJ 9/97) [811]

**9687** Clifton, Lucille. *Everett Anderson's Goodbye* (K–2). Illus. by Ann Grifalconi. 1983, Holt $15.95 (0-8050-0235-9); paper $5.95 (0-8050-0800-4). 32pp. Poems about a young black boy.

**9688** Clifton, Lucille. *Some of the Days of Everett Anderson* (K–2). Illus. by Evaline Ness. 1987, Holt paper $5.95 (0-8050-0289-8). 32pp. A black 6-year-old boy has a poem for each day of the week — and 2 for Friday. Also use: *Everett Anderson's Nine Month Long* (1978).

**9689** Giovanni, Nikki. *Ego-Tripping and Other Poems for Young People* (5–8). Illus. by George Ford. 1994, Chicago Review $14.95 (1-55652-188-X). 53pp. This well-known book of verse has been reissued with 10 new poems. (Rev: BL 4/15/94) [811]

**9690** Giovanni, Nikki. *Knoxville, Tennessee* (PS–3). Illus. by Larry Johnson. 1994, Scholastic $14.95 (0-590-47074-4). 32pp. Nikki Giovanni re-creates the summers she spent growing up in Knoxville and the simple pleasures she enjoyed. (Rev: BCCB 7–8/94; BL 2/15/94; HB 9–10/94; SLJ 4/94) [811]

**9691** Giovanni, Nikki. *The Sun Is So Quiet* (K–2). Illus. by Ashley Bryan. 1996, Holt $14.95 (0-8050-4119-2). 32pp. Thirteen poems that depict everyday occurrences, with illustrations that feature African American children in many cultures. (Rev: BL 10/15/96; SLJ 1/97) [811]

**9692** Greenfield, Eloise. *Honey, I Love, and Other Love Poems* (2–4). Illus. by Diane Dillon and Leo Dillon. 1978, HarperCollins $13.95 (0-690-01334-5); paper $4.95 (0-06-443097-9). 48pp. Sixteen poems on family love and friendship as experienced by a black girl.

**9693** Greenfield, Eloise. *Nathaniel Talking* (2–5). Illus. by Jan S. Gilchrist. 1988, Writers & Readers $12.95 (0-86316-200-2). 32pp. Simple poems on a black American's recollection of childhood. (Rev: BL 12/15/89; HB 9–10/90; SLJ 8/89) [811]

**9694** Grimes, Nikki. *Meet Danitra Brown* (PS–3). Illus. by Floyd Cooper. 1994, Lothrop $16.00 (0-688-12073-3). 32pp. In a series of simple poems, the friendship between 2 African American children is explored. (Rev: BCCB 7–8/94; BL 2/15/94; HB 7–8/94; SLJ 5/94) [811]

**9695** Grimes, Nikki. *Something on My Mind* (3–5). Illus. by Tom Feelings. 1986, Dial paper $4.95 (0-8037-0273-6). 32pp. A collection of poems about the black experience.

**9696** Hudson, Wade, ed. *Pass It On: African-American Poetry for Children* (PS–3). Illus. by Floyd Cooper. 1993, Scholastic $15.95 (0-590-45770-5). 32pp. A fine anthology with contributions by such writers as Langston Hughes and Gwendolyn Brooks. (Rev: BL 1/15/93*) [811]

**9697** *In Daddy's Arms I Am Tall: African Americans Celebrating Fathers* (3–5). Illus. by Javaka Steptoe. 1997, Lee & Low $15.95 (1-880000-31-8). 32pp. An impressively illustrated book of poems about African American fathers and their many roles. (Rev: BL 2/15/98*; SLJ 2/98) [811]

**9698** Lawrence, Jacob. *Harriet and the Promised Land* (1–4). Illus. 1993, Simon & Schuster paper $16.00 (0-671-86673-7). 32pp. The story of Harriet Tubman, an escaped slave, who ventured into the South 19 times to help others escape. (Rev: BL 10/1/93*) [811]

**9699** Myers, Walter Dean. *Angel to Angel: A Mother's Gift of Love* (4–7). Illus. 1998, HarperCollins LB $15.89 (0-06-027722-X). 40pp. This picture book of poems and old photos shows African American mothers and grandmothers in loving poses with their children. (Rev: BL 2/15/98) [811]

**9700** Myers, Walter Dean. *Brown Angels: An Album of Pictures and Verse* (3–6). Illus. 1993, HarperCollins LB $15.89 (0-06-022918-7). 40pp. Photographs of African American children from the beginning of this century are reproduced with short verses that evoke the spirit of African American culture. (Rev: BCCB 10/93; BL 10/15/93; HB 11–12/93; SLJ 10/93) [811]

**9701** Nikola-Lisa, W. *Bein' with You This Way* (PS–2). Illus. by Michael Bryant. 1994, Lee & Low $15.95 (1-880000-05-9). 32pp. A rap poem led by an African American girl talks about racial tolerance. (Rev: BL 7/94; SLJ 7/94) [811]

**9702** Shine, Deborah S., ed. *Make a Joyful Sound: Poems for Children by African-American Poets* (2–7). Illus. by Cornelius Van Wright and Ying-Hwa

Hu. 1996, Scholastic $13.95 (0-590-67432-3). 107pp. More than 60 well-illustrated poems by 23 poets are found in this collection celebrating life in general and African American life in particular. (Rev: BL 6/1/91; SLJ 10/96) [811]

**9703** Strickland, Dorothy S., and Michael R. Strickland, eds. *Families: Poems Celebrating the African American Experience* (K–3). Illus. by John Ward. 1994, Boyds Mills $14.95 (1-56397-288-3); paper $7.95 (1-56397-560-2). 32pp. Poems by such writers as Gwendolyn Brooks and Langston Hughes are featured with large acrylic paintings. (Rev: BL 2/15/95; SLJ 10/94) [811]

## Animals

**9704** Albert, Burton. *Journey of the Nightly Jaguar* (3–6). Illus. by Robert Roth. 1996, Simon & Schuster $16.00 (0-689-31905-3). Watercolor illustrations enhance this poem about the daily activities of a jaguar and the Mayan culture. (Rev: HB 5–6/96; SLJ 6/96) [811]

**9705** Andreae, Giles. *Rumble in the Jungle* (PS). Illus. by David Wojtowycz. 1997, Little Tiger $14.95 (1-888444-08-8). A collection of poems about the animals that a small group of ants encounter as they march through the jungle. (Rev: SLJ 11/97) [811]

**9706** Baylor, Byrd. *Desert Voices* (3–6). Illus. by Peter Parnall. 1981, Macmillan $14.95 (0-684-16712-3); paper $5.95 (0-689-71691-5). 32pp. A series of poems written from the viewpoint of various desert creatures.

**9707** Blake, William. *The Tyger* (1–6). Illus. by Neil Waldman. 1993, Harcourt $15.95 (0-15-292375-6). 36pp. Acrylic paintings reinforce the sense of wonder created by Blake in his poem. (Rev: BL 11/15/93*; SLJ 1/94) [821]

**9708** Bouchard, David. *Voices from the Wild: An Animal Sensagoria* (3–5). Illus. by Ron Parker. 1996, Chronicle $17.95 (0-8118-1462-9). 72pp. A collection of poems on how and why animals use their senses. (Rev: BL 12/1/96) [811]

**9709** Chandra, Deborah. *Rich Lizard and Other Poems* (4–6). Illus. by Leslie Bowman. 1993, Farrar $14.00 (0-374-36274-2). 35pp. In these 24 poems, each of the ordinary animals and objects described becomes items of special beauty. (Rev: BL 6/1–15/93; SLJ 8/93) [811]

**9710** Chandra, Deborah. *Who Comes?* (PS–2). Illus. by Katie Lee. 1995, Sierra Club $16.95 (0-87156-407-6). 32pp. At an African watering hole, a lion watches as each animal comes to drink until he attacks a zebra. (Rev: BL 12/1/95) [811]

**9711** Chorao, Kay, comp. *Jumpety-Bumpety Hop: A Parade of Animal Poems* (PS–2). Illus. by Kay Chorao. 1997, Dutton paper $16.99 (0-525-45825-5). 40pp. A collection of approximately 50 poems about animals, many by well-known writers, representing such genres as nursery rhymes, lullabies, and haiku. (Rev: HB 11–12/97; SLJ 11/97) [811]

**9712** Cole, William, ed. *An Arkful of Animals: Poems for the Very Young* (3–5). Illus. by Lynn Munsinger. 1992, Houghton paper $3.95 (0-395-61618-2). 128pp. A fine collection of humorous poems about animals.

**9713** Cole, William, ed. *A Zooful of Animals* (K–4). Illus. by Lynn Munsinger. 1992, Houghton $17.95 (0-395-52278-1). 96pp. This large-size volume offers animal nonsense verse and appealing watercolors. (Rev: BCCB 7–8/92; BL 6/1/92; HB 7–8/92*; SLJ 9/92) [811]

**9714** Day, David. *Aska's Animals* (3–6). Illus. by Warabe Aska. 1991, Doubleday $15.00 (0-385-25315-X). 32pp. A prose poem about the nature of animals is accompanied by full-color oil paintings. (Rev: BCCB 2/92; SLJ 3/92) [811]

**9715** Edwards, Richard. *Moon Frog: Animal Poems for Young Children* (PS–3). Illus. by Sarah Fox-Davies. 1993, Candlewick $16.95 (1-56402-116-5). 48pp. Lively poems describe the sounds and shapes of various animals. (Rev: BL 1/15/93; SLJ 4/93) [811]

**9716** Eliot, T. S. *Growltiger's Last Stand: And Other Poems* (3–6). Illus. by Errol LeCain. 1987, Farrar $14.00 (0-374-32809-9); paper $4.95 (0-374-42811-5). 32pp. Three poems excerpted from Old Possum's Book of Practical Cats and made popular by the musical *Cats*. (Rev: BL 12/1/87)

**9717** Eliot, T. S. *Mr. Mistoffelees with Mungojerrie and Rumpelteazer* (3–6). Illus. by Errol LeCain. 1991, Harcourt $13.95 (0-15-256230-3). These 2 poems by Eliot concern very unusual cats. (Rev: SLJ 5/91*) [811]

**9718** Evans, Dilys, ed. *Weird Pet Poems* (PS–3). Illus. by Jacqueline Rogers. 1997, Simon & Schuster paper $16.00 (0-689-80734-1). 40pp. An anthology of 14 poems about pets, common and otherwise. (Rev: BL 9/15/97; SLJ 11/97) [811]

**9719** Fleischman, Paul. *I Am Phoenix: Poems for Two Voices* (3–8). Illus. by Ken Nutt. 1985, Harper-Collins paper $4.95 (0-06-446092-4). 64pp. Poems about birds, designed to be read aloud by 2 voices; the focus is on the pleasure of sharing poetry. (Rev: BL 12/1/85; SLJ 11/85)

**9720** Fleischman, Paul. *Joyful Noise: Poems for Two Voices* (3–6). Illus. by Eric Beddows. 1988, Harper-Collins LB $14.89 (0-06-021853-3); paper $4.95 (0-06-446093-2). 64pp. Poems for reading aloud that explore the lives of insects. Newbery Medal winner, 1989. (Rev: BL 2/15/88; HB 5–6/88; SLJ 2/88)

**9721** Florian, Douglas. *Beast Feast* (PS–3). Illus. 1994, Harcourt $16.00 (0-15-295178-4). 48pp. Twenty-one animals are featured, with a humorous poem for each. (Rev: BCCB 7–8/94; BL 2/15/94; SLJ 5/94*) [811]

**9722** Florian, Douglas. *In the Swim* (1–4). Illus. 1997, Harcourt $15.00 (0-15-201307-5). 48pp. A collection of 21 original poems about freshwater and saltwater creatures. (Rev: BCCB 5/97; BL 3/15/97; HB 7–8/97; SLJ 5/97*) [811]

**9723** Florian, Douglas. *Insectlopedia* (3–5). Illus. 1998, Harcourt $16.00 (0-15-201306-7). 56pp. A well-designed book of poems about insects and spiders. (Rev: BL 3/15/98; SLJ 4/98) [811]

**9724** Florian, Douglas. *On the Wing* (3–5). Illus. 1996, Harcourt $16.00 (0-15-200497-1). 48pp. Twenty-one poems celebrate a wide variety of birds, from hummingbirds to vultures. (Rev: BCCB 4/96; BL 3/15/96; SLJ 6/96) [811]

**9725** Fyleman, Rose. *A Fairy Went a-Marketing* (PS–1). Illus. by Jamichael Henterly. 1986, Dutton paper $3.95 (0-525-44556-0). 24pp. A fairy who likes little animals goes about releasing them from captivity. (Rev: BCCB 10/86; BL 10/1/86; SLJ 1/87)

**9726** Giovanni, Nikki. *The Genie in the Jar* (K–3). Illus. by Chris Raschka. 1996, Holt $15.95 (0-8050-4118-4). 32pp. In this lilting poem, a young African American girl always returns to her mother's loving arms after each of her independent actions. (Rev: BCCB 5/96; BL 4/1/96; SLJ 5/96*) [811]

**9727** Greenberg, David T. *Bugs!* (K–3). Illus. by Lynn Munsinger. 1997, Little, Brown $14.95 (0-316-32574-0). 32pp. In humorous verses, a number of insects and their distinctive characteristics are introduced. (Rev: BL 9/1/97; SLJ 9/97) [811]

**9728** Hoberman, Mary Ann. *A Fine Fat Pig* (K–5). Illus. by Malcah Zeldis. 1991, HarperCollins $14.95 (0-06-022425-8). These 14 poems deal with animals, their characteristics, and habits. (Rev: HB 5–6/91; SLJ 4/91) [811]

**9729** Hulme, Joy N. *What If? Just Wondering Poems* (K–3). Illus. by Valeri Gorbachev. 1993, Boyds Mills $14.95 (1-56397-186-0). 32pp. In 29 poems, questions about animals and their behavior are answered. (Rev: SLJ 8/93) [811]

**9730** Levy, Constance. *I'm Going to Pet a Worm Today and Other Poems* (3–5). Illus. by Ronald Himler. 1991, Macmillan $14.00 (0-689-50535-3). 48pp. This book of original poems celebrates such creatures of nature as spiders, worms, and beetles. (Rev: BCCB 2/92*; BL 11/15/92; SLJ 10/91) [811]

**9731** Lewis, J. Patrick. *A Hippopotamusn't and Other Animal Verses* (K–4). Illus. by Victoria Chess. 1994, Puffin paper $4.99 (0-14-055273-1). 40pp. Witty verse describing 35 animals. (Rev: BCCB 7–8/90; BL 5/1/90*; HB 5–6/90*; SLJ 5/90*) [811]

**9732** Livingston, Myra Cohn, ed. *Cat Poems* (3–6). Illus. by Trina S. Hyman. 1987, Holiday LB $15.95 (0-8234-0631-8). 32pp. Poems that reflect the many moods of felines. (Rev: BCCB 6/87; BL 6/1/87; SLJ 5/87)

**9733** Livingston, Myra Cohn, ed. *If the Owl Calls Again: A Collection of Owl Poems* (4–7). Illus. by Antonio Frasconi. 1990, Macmillan $13.95 (0-689-50501-9). 128pp. A wide range of owl poems from various sources. (Rev: BCCB 1/91; BL 10/1/90; SLJ 1/91) [808.81]

**9734** Livingston, Myra Cohn, ed. *If You Ever Meet a Whale* (1–4). Illus. by Leonard Everett Fisher. 1992, Holiday LB $14.95 (0-8234-0940-6). 32pp. Seventeen whale poems with full-color paintings. (Rev: BL 11/15/92) [811]

**9735** McLoughland, Beverly. *A Hippo's a Heap and Other Animal Poems* (PS–3). Illus. by Laura Rader. 1993, Boyds Mills $14.95 (1-56397-017-1). 32pp. A collection of nonsense poems and chirpy illustrations. (Rev: BL 1/15/93; SLJ 3/93) [811]

**9736** Munsterberg, Peggy. *Beastly Banquet: Tasty Treats for Animal Appetites* (K–3). Illus. by Tracy Gallup. 1997, Dial paper $14.99 (0-8037-1481-5). 32pp. The eating habits of several kinds of fish, birds, and other animals are described in 20 poems. (Rev: BL 1/1–15/97; SLJ 1/97) [811]

**9737** Nichol, Barbara. *Biscuits in the Cupboard* (K–4). Illus. by Philippe Beha. 1998, Stoddart $12.95 (0-7737-3025-7). 32pp. A delightful collection of poems about dogs, written entirely from their point of view. (Rev: SLJ 3/98) [808]

**9738** Nichols, Grace. *Asana and the Animals* (PS–1). Illus. by Sarah Adams. 1997, Candlewick $16.99 (0-7636-0145-4). 32pp. A collection of 17 simple verses about all the animals that Asana likes, including a spider and a giraffe. (Rev: BL 6/1–15/97; SLJ 7/97) [811]

**9739** O'Huigin, Sean. *Ghost Horse of the Mounties* (5–7). Illus. by Barry Moser. 1991, Godine $14.95 (0-87923-721-X). 72pp. A long poem about a black midsummer night in 1874 on the empty plains of the Northwest Territories in Canada. (Rev: BCCB 7–8/91; BL 5/1/91) [811]

**9740** Patterson, Elizabeth B. *Whose Eyes Are These?* (K–2). Illus. 1997, Thomas Nelson $14.99 (0-8499-1464-7). 32pp. Short poems introduce a guessing game to identify different animals. (Rev: BL 9/1/97; SLJ 10/97) [811]

**9741** Prelutsky, Jack, ed. *The Beauty of the Beast: Poems from the Animal Kingdom* (3–7). Illus. by Meilo So. 1997, Knopf $25.00 (0-679-87058-X). 101pp. A wonderful, beautifully illustrated collection of more than 200 animal poems by 20th-century writers whose works are arranged by animal genus. (Rev: BL 9/15/97; SLJ 1/98*) [811]

**9742** Prelutsky, Jack. *The Dragons Are Singing Tonight* (K–4). Illus. by Peter Sis. 1993, Greenwillow LB $15.93 (0-688-12511-5). 40pp. These 17 poems all deal with the pastimes and problems that dragons face in their everyday life. (Rev: BL 9/1/93*; HB 9–10/93; SLJ 10/93*) [811]

**9743** Prelutsky, Jack. *The Snopp on the Sidewalk and Other Poems* (3–6). Illus. by Byron Barton. 1977, Greenwillow LB $15.93 (0-688-84084-1). 32pp. Twelve wildly imaginative poems about strange imaginary beasts that bring to mind the Jabberwocky.

**9744** Prelutsky, Jack. *Tyrannosaurus Was a Beast* (2–5). Illus. by Arnold Lobel. 1988, Greenwillow $16.00 (0-688-06442-6); Morrow paper $4.95 (0-688-11569-1). 32pp. Poems and watercolor portraits bring dinosaurs to life. (Rev: BCCB 9/88; BL 8/88; HB 9–10/88)

**9745** Prelutsky, Jack. *Zoo Doings: Animal Poems* (3–6). Illus. by Paul O. Zelinsky. 1983, Greenwillow LB $14.93 (0-688-01784-3). 80pp. A collection of animal verses previously published by this poet.

**9746** Robb, Laura, ed. *Snuffles and Snouts* (PS–3). Illus. by Steven Kellogg. 1995, Dial paper $14.89 (0-8037-1598-6). 40pp. A collection of 24 poems about pigs, with joyously madcap illustrations. (Rev: BL 9/15/95; SLJ 11/95) [811]

**9747** Schertle, Alice. *Advice for a Frog* (1–4). Illus. by Norman Green. 1995, Lothrop LB $15.93 (0-688-13487-4). Each of the 14 poems in this collection deals with an animal — in most cases, an exotic or endangered one. (Rev: SLJ 9/95*) [811]

**9748** Singer, Marilyn. *Please Don't Squeeze Your Boa, Noah!* (K–3). Illus. by Clement Oubrerie. 1995, Holt $15.95 (0-8050-3277-0). 24pp. A collection of humorous poems, each dealing with different pets. (Rev: BL 4/15/95; SLJ 5/95) [811]

**9749** Singer, Marilyn. *Turtle in July* (K–3). Illus. by Jerry Pinkney. 1989, Macmillan paper $14.95 (0-02-782881-6). 32pp. This book contains animal poems arranged by season of the year. (Rev: BCCB 9/89*; BL 10/15/89*; HB 1–2/90; SLJ 11/89) [811]

**9750** Tiller, Ruth. *Cats Vanish Slowly* (K–3). Illus. by Laura L. Seeley. 1995, Peachtree $16.95 (1-56145-106-1). 32pp. Twelve poems about the cats (including B.P., for "bad penny") that are found on the farm of the author's grandmother. (Rev: BL 1/1–15/96; SLJ 1/96) [811]

**9751** Whipple, Laura, ed. *Eric Carle's Animals Animals* (PS–3). Illus. by Eric Carle. 1989, Putnam $21.95 (0-399-21744-4). Eric Carle's collages illustrate various writers' poems, each dealing with an animal. (Rev: BCCB 10/89*; BL 9/1/89*; HB 11–12/89; SLJ 11/89) [811]

**9752** Yolen, Jane, ed. *Alphabestiary: Animal Poems from A to Z* (2–4). Illus. by Allan Eitzen. 1995, Boyds Mills $16.95 (1-56397-222-0). 64pp. A collection of animal poems, mostly nonsense verse. (Rev: BL 12/15/94; SLJ 4/95) [808]

**9753** Yolen, Jane. *The Originals* (3–6). Illus. by Ted Lewin. 1998, Putnam $15.95 (0-399-23007-6). 32pp. In poetry and painting, this account celebrates animals that have hardly changed through time, like the red jungle fowl and the Exmoor pony. (Rev: BL 2/1/98; SLJ 3/98) [811]

**9754** Yolen, Jane. *Sea Watch* (3–5). Illus. by Ted Lewin. 1996, Putnam $15.95 (0-399-22734-2). 32pp. Unusual sea creatures are pictured in watercolors and poetry. (Rev: BCCB 6/96; BL 6/1–15/96; SLJ 6/96) [811]

# Haiku

**9755** *In the Eyes of the Cat: Japanese Poetry for All Seasons* (PS–3). Trans. by Tze-si Huang. Illus. by Demi. 1994, Holt paper $5.95 (0-8050-3383-1). 80pp. These short Japanese poems, known as haiku, use words and images appreciated by young readers. (Rev: BCCB 5/92; BL 4/15/92; SLJ 5/92) [895.6]

**9756** Lewis, J. Patrick. *Black Swan/White Crow* (K–4). Illus. by Christopher Manson. 1995, Simon & Schuster $15.00 (0-689-31899-5). 32pp. Thirteen haiku poems accompanied by dramatic woodcuts. (Rev: BL 10/15/95; SLJ 11/95) [811]

**9757** Livingston, Myra Cohn. *Cricket Never Does: A Collection of Haiku and Tanka* (5–8). Illus. 1997, Simon & Schuster $15.00 (0-689-81123-3). 48pp. Seasonal changes are explored in more than 60 short haiku and tanka. (Rev: BL 3/1/97; SLJ 4/97) [811]

**9758** Shannon, George. *Spring: A Haiku Story* (K–3). Illus. by Malcah Zeldis. 1996, Greenwillow $16.00 (0-688-13888-8). 32pp. Incidents that occur during a spring walk are depicted in 14 translated Japanese haiku. (Rev: BL 4/15/96; HB 3–4/96; SLJ 5/96) [895.6]

# Holidays

**9759** Carlstrom, Nancy White. *Who Said Boo? Halloween Poems for the Very Young* (PS–1). Illus. by R. W. Alley. 1995, Simon & Schuster $14.00 (0-689-80308-7). 32pp. Scary poems that celebrate the mystery and menace of Halloween. (Rev: BL 9/15/95; SLJ 9/95) [811]

**9760** *Christmas in the Stable* (2–4). Illus. by Beverly Duncan. 1990, Harcourt $14.95 (0-15-217758-2). 32pp. Friendly beasts of all kinds appear in these poems and songs. (Rev: BL 10/1/90) [811]

**9761** Coatsworth, Elizabeth. *Song of the Camels: A Christmas Poem* (PS–3). Illus. by Anna Vojtech. 1997, North-South LB $15.88 (1-55858-812-4). 24pp. This is a Christmas poem narrated by the camels that carry the 3 kings to Bethlehem. (Rev: BL 11/15/97; SLJ 10/97) [811]

**9762** Foster, John, comp. *Let's Celebrate: Festival Poems* (3–6). Illus. 1997, Oxford paper $11.95 (0-192-76085-8). 111pp. This collection of 85 poems celebrates a variety of holidays around the world. (Rev: SLJ 7/90) [811]

**9763** Harness, Cheryl. *Papa's Christmas Gift: Around the World on the Night Before Christmas* (1–3). Illus. 1995, Simon & Schuster paper $15.00 (0-689-80344-3). 32pp. In this poem, Christmas activities around the world are described on the night that "A Visit from Saint Nicholas" took place. (Rev: BL 9/15/95) [811]

**9764** Hopkins, Lee Bennett, ed. *Hey-How for Halloween!* (3–6). Illus. by Janet McCaffery. 1974, Harcourt $12.95 (0-15-233900-0). 32pp. A varied and appealing selection of poems about happenings and creatures associated with Halloween.

**9765** Kennedy, X. J. *The Beasts of Bethlehem* (2–6). Illus. by Michael McCurdy. 1992, Macmillan $13.95 (0-689-50561-2). 48pp. It is Christmas Eve and 19 animals gather in the manger to witness a miracle. (Rev: BCCB 12/92*; BL 9/15/92; HB 11–12/92) [811]

**9766** Livingston, Myra Cohn, ed. *Celebrations* (1–4). Illus. by Leonard Everett Fisher. 1985, Holiday LB $16.95 (0-8234-0550-8); paper $6.95 (0-8234-0654-7). 32pp. A handsome book of verse illustrating 16 celebrations, such as Valentine's Day, birthdays, and Easter. (Rev: BCCB 4/85; BL 4/1/85; HB 5–6/85)

**9767** Livingston, Myra Cohn, ed. *Christmas Poems* (PS–3). Illus. by Trina S. Hyman. 1984, Holiday LB $15.95 (0-8234-0508-7). 32pp. A collection of 18 poems, half of which were commissioned for the volume.

**9768** Livingston, Myra Cohn, ed. *Easter Poems* (2–4). Illus. by John Wallner. 1985, Holiday LB $15.95 (0-8234-0546-X). 32pp. A collection of varied distinguished poems, most of them new. (Rev: BCCB 6/85; SLJ 9/85)

**9769** Livingston, Myra Cohn. *Halloween Poems* (3–6). Illus. by Stephen Gammell. 1989, Holiday LB

$14.95 (0-8234-0762-4). 32pp. Spooky verses and illustrations with a sense of humor. (Rev: BCCB 10/89; BL 9/15/89; HB 11–12/89; SLJ 9/89) [811]

**9770** Livingston, Myra Cohn, ed. *Poems for Jewish Holidays* (K–6). Illus. by Lloyd Bloom. 1986, Holiday LB $14.95 (0-8234-0606-7). 32pp. Poems that contain the essence of major Jewish holidays. (Rev: BCCB 2/87; BL 11/1/86; HB 1–2/87)

**9771** Livingston, Myra Cohn, ed. *Thanksgiving Poems* (2–4). Illus. by Stephen Gammell. 1985, Holiday LB $14.95 (0-8234-0570-2). 32pp. New and traditional poems for the holiday season. (Rev: BCCB 10/85; BL 10/1/85; SLJ 9/85)

**9772** Livingston, Myra Cohn, ed. *Valentine Poems* (3–6). Illus. 1987, Holiday LB $15.95 (0-8234-0587-7). 32pp. Sprightly poems from established names and modern ones, too. (Rev: BL 1/15/87; SLJ 12/86)

**9773** Moore, Clement Clarke. *The Night Before Christmas* (PS–3). Illus. by Tomie dePaola. 1980, Holiday LB $16.95 (0-8234-0414-5); paper $6.95 (0-8234-0417-X). 32pp. A lovely edition of this popular and loved Christmas poem. Another edition is: Illus. by Anita Lobel (1996, Knopf).

**9774** Moore, Clement Clarke. *The Night Before Christmas* (PS–1). Illus. by Cheryl Harness. 1990, Random $8.99 (0-394-82698-1). 40pp. A traditional treatment of the classic holiday poem. (Rev: BL 11/1/90; HB 11–12/90) [811]

**9775** Moore, Clement Clarke. *The Night Before Christmas* (PS–3). Illus. by Ted Rand. 1995, North-South LB $16.88 (1-55858-466-8). 32pp. A large-format picture book with new illustrations for the classic poem, each using a double-page spread. (Rev: BL 10/15/95) [871]

**9776** Moore, Clement Clarke. *The Night Before Christmas* (PS–3). Illus. by Ruth Sanderson. 1997, Little, Brown $12.95 (0-316-57963-7). 32pp. An old-fashioned version of this classic poem. (Rev: BL 9/15/97; SLJ 10/97) [811]

**9777** Moore, Clement Clarke. *The Night Before Christmas: Or, a Visit of St. Nicholas* (PS–3). Illus. 1989, Putnam $17.95 (0-399-21614-6). 32pp. This handsomely produced edition of the famous poem was illustrated years ago by a now-forgotten artist. (Rev: BL 9/15/89) [811]

**9778** Prelutsky, Jack. *It's Christmas* (2–4). Illus. by Marylin Hafner. 1981, Greenwillow LB $15.93 (0-688-00440-7). 48pp. A group of simple original poems that celebrate the joys of Christmas.

**9779** Prelutsky, Jack. *It's Halloween* (1–3). Illus. by Marylin Hafner. 1977, Greenwillow LB $15.93 (0-688-84102-3). 48pp. An easy-to-read book of 12 illustrated poems about the traditions of Halloween.

**9780** Prelutsky, Jack. *It's Thanksgiving* (PS–4). Illus. by Marylin Hafner. 1982, Greenwillow LB $15.93 (0-688-00442-3). 48pp. Twelve poems covering various aspects of Thanksgiving.

**9781** Prelutsky, Jack. *It's Valentine's Day* (1–4). Illus. by Yossi Abolafia. 1985, Scholastic paper $2.50 (0-590-40979-4). 48pp. Bright, humorous poems in celebration of love and Valentine's Day.

**9782** *A Small Treasury of Easter: Poems and Prayers* (K–4). Illus. by Susan Spellman. 1997, Boyds Mills $8.95 (1-56397-647-1). 32pp. An illustrated collection of secular and religious Easter poems, divided into 2 parts: "A Time to Play" and "A Time to Pray." (Rev: SLJ 7/97) [811]

**9783** Thomas, Dylan. *A Child's Christmas in Wales* (5–8). Illus. by Trina S. Hyman. 1985, Holiday LB $16.95 (0-8234-0565-6). 48pp. A prose poem about the poet's childhood in a small Welsh village. Another edition is: Illus. by Edward Ardizzone (1980, Godine).

## Humorous Poetry

**9784** Ahlberg, Allan. *The Mysteries of Zigomar: Poems and Stories* (4–6). Illus. 1997, Candlewick $17.99 (0-7636-0352-X). 64pp. A collection of zany poems and stories sure to delight readers who enjoy the absurd and whimsical. (Rev: BL 12/1/97; SLJ 11/97) [828]

**9785** Base, Graeme. *Lewis Carroll's Jabberwocky: A Book of Brillig Dioramas* (3–5). Illus. 1996, Abrams $19.95 (0-8109-3520-1). 14pp. Three-dimensional dinosaurs are used to illustrate Lewis Carroll's *Jabberwocky*. (Rev: BL 12/15/96) [811]

**9786** Billings, John. *My Pet Crocodile and Other Slightly Outrageous Verse* (PS–3). Illus. by Janette Todd. 1993, Chokecherry $16.95 (1-884035-55-8). 128pp. Humorous poems on such subjects as bungee jumping, nose picking, and bubble gum. (Rev: BL 1/1/94) [811]

**9787** Bodecker, N. M. *Hurry, Hurry, Mary Dear!* (3–6). Illus. by author. 1987, Macmillan $14.00 (0-689-50066-1). 128pp. An appealing collection of nonsense poems with accompanying droll illustrations in a picture book first published in 1976.

**9788** Brewton, Sara, et al., eds. *Of Quarks, Quasars and Other Quirks: Quizzical Poems for the Supersonic Age* (5–8). Illus. by Quentin Blake. 1977, HarperCollins LB $13.89 (0-690-04885-8). 128pp. Contemporary poems that poke fun at such modern innovations as transplants and water beds.

**9789** Burgess, Gelett. *The Little Father* (1–3). Illus. by Richard Egielski. 1985, Farrar $14.00 (0-374-

34596-1). 32pp. Michael Master's father drinks so much india ink that he shrinks to his son's size and then smaller and smaller, until the boy almost loses his tiny father. (Rev: BCCB 12/85; BL 1/1/86; SLJ 1/86)

**9790** Carroll, Lewis. *Jabberwocky* (1–4). Illus. by Graeme Base. 1989, Abrams $16.95 (0-8109-1150-7). 32pp. Carroll's nonsense poem is given a fresh treatment with illustrations picturing a medieval locale. (Rev: SLJ 8/89) [821]

**9791** Carroll, Lewis. *The Walrus and the Carpenter* (4–5). Illus. by Jane Breskin Zalben. 1990, Holt paper $4.95 (0-8050-1482-9). 32pp. Full-color edition of the popular poem. (Rev: BL 10/15/86; SLJ 2/87)

**9792** Carryl, Charles E. *The Walloping Window-Blind* (K–2). Illus. by Jim LaMarche. 1994, Lothrop $16.00 (0-688-12517-4). 24pp. A nonsense verse about a fantastic sea voyage illustrated in double-page spreads. (Rev: BL 5/1/94; SLJ 7/94) [811]

**9793** Ciardi, John. *Doodle Soup* (3–6). Illus. by Merle Macht. 1992, Houghton paper $5.95 (0-395-61617-4). 64pp. The gentle wit of the poet shows up in these 38 tongue-in-cheek verses. (Rev: BCCB 10/85; BL 2/1/86; SLJ 1/86)

**9794** Ciardi, John. *The Hopeful Trout and Other Limericks* (2–6). Illus. by Susan Meddaugh. 1992, Houghton paper $5.95 (0-395-61616-6). 52pp. Forty-one humorous limericks with wacky drawings. (Rev: BL 3/15/89; SLJ 3/89)

**9795** Ciardi, John. *You Read to Me, I'll Read to You* (4–6). Illus. by Edward Gorey. 1987, HarperCollins paper $6.95 (0-06-446060-6). 64pp. A collection of original verse for both adults and children.

**9796** Cole, Joanna, and Stephanie Calmenson. *Yours till Banana Splits: 201 Autograph Rhymes* (3–5). Illus. by Alan Tiegreen. 1995, Morrow LB $14.93 (0-688-13186-7). 64pp. An amusing collection of rhymes from autograph albums and school yearbooks. (Rev: BL 2/15/95; SLJ 4/95) [811]

**9797** Cole, William, ed. *Poem Stew* (2–6). Illus. by Karen Ann Weinhaus. 1981, HarperCollins $7.66 (0-397-31963-0); paper $4.95 (0-06-440136-7). 96pp. A collection of 57 witty poems about food.

**9798** Coltman, Paul. *Tog the Ribber, or Granny's Tale* (4–6). Illus. by Gillian McClure. 1985, Farrar $15.00 (0-374-37630-1). 32pp. A Gothic tale of shivery terror about a skeleton that jumps down from a tree and chases Granny when she was young. (Rev: BL 7/85; HB 9–10/85; SLJ 9/85)

**9799** Dakos, Kalli. *Don't Read This Book, Whatever You Do! More Poems About School* (2–4). Illus. by G. Brian Karas. 1993, Macmillan LB $15.00 (0-02-725582-4). 64pp. Classroom sketches in quick, easy lines. (Rev: BL 2/15/93; SLJ 4/93) [811]

**9800** Florian, Douglas. *Bing Bang Boing* (4–6). Illus. 1994, Harcourt $16.00 (0-15-233770-9). 144pp. A lighthearted, imaginative collection of short, humorous verses. (Rev: BCCB 11/94; BL 12/1/94; SLJ 11/94) [811]

**9801** Harrison, David L. *Somebody Catch My Homework* (2–4). Illus. by Betsy Lewin. 1993, Boyds Mills $14.95 (1-878093-87-8). 36pp. Light comic verse about grade-school mayhem. (Rev: BL 1/15/93; SLJ 1/93) [811]

**9802** Kennedy, X. J. *Brats* (3–5). Illus. by James Watts. 1986, Macmillan $14.00 (0-689-50392-X). Short poems showing bratty kids getting their just desserts. (Rev: BCCB 7–8/86; BL 7/86; SLJ 8/86)

**9803** Kennedy, X. J. *Fresh Brats* (3–5). Illus. by James Watts. 1990, Macmillan $14.00 (0-689-50499-3). 48pp. Short, snappy poems about bratty kids. (Rev: BCCB 3/90; BL 5/1/90*; HB 3–4/90; SLJ 7/90) [811]

**9804** Kennedy, X. J. *Uncle Switch: Loony Limericks* (1–3). Illus. by John O'Brien. 1997, Simon & Schuster $15.00 (0-689-80967-0). 32pp. Twenty-two funny limericks involving the dimwitted Uncle Switch. (Rev: BCCB 4/97; BL 5/1/97; SLJ 4/97) [811]

**9805** Korman, Gordon, and Bernice Korman. *The D-Poems of Jeremy Bloom: A Collection of Poems About School, Homework, and Life (Sort of)* (4–6). 1992, Scholastic paper $3.50 (0-590-44819-6). 98pp. The engaging and funny poems of rambunctious sixth-grader Jeremy Bloom. (Rev: BL 1/15/93; SLJ 2/93) [811]

**9806** Lansky, Bruce, ed. *A Bad Case of the Giggles: Kids' Favorite Funny Poems* (2–5). Illus. by Stephen Carpenter. 1994, Meadowbrook Pr. $14.00 (0-88166-213-5). 132pp. A great collection of humorous poems that includes puns, tongue twisters, and parodies, many by well-known writers. (Rev: BL 11/15/94; SLJ 2/95) [811]

**9807** Lear, Edward. *A Was Once an Apple Pie* (PS–2). Illus. by Julie Lacome. 1997, Candlewick paper $5.99 (0-7636-0103-9). 32pp. This book of nonsense verse is complemented by buoyant illustrations. (Rev: BL 1/15/92; SLJ 3/92) [821]

**9808** Lear, Edward. *Complete Nonsense Book of Edward Lear* (4–6). Illus. by author. n.d., Dover paper $6.95 (0-486-20167-8). 287pp. Verse, prose, drawings, alphabets, and other amusing absurdities.

**9809** Lear, Edward. *Daffy Down Dillies* (PS–3). Illus. by John O'Brien. 1992, Boyds Mills $14.95 (1-56397-007-4). 32pp. An edition that captures in drawings the irreverence that Lear's limericks demand. (Rev: BL 1/15/92; SLJ 3/92) [821]

**9810** Lear, Edward. *Nonsense Songs* (K–3). Illus. by Bee Willey. 1997, Simon & Schuster $16.00 (0-689-81369-4). 40pp. Imaginative illustrations accompany

4 of Lear's most famous nonsense poems, including "The Owl and the Pussycat" and "The Jumblies." (Rev: BL 4/1/97; SLJ 6/97) [811]

**9811** Lear, Edward. *The Owl and the Pussycat* (PS–1). Illus. by Jan Brett. 1991, Putnam $15.95 (0-399-21925-0). 32pp. Beautiful double-page spreads enhance the enchantment of this retelling. (Rev: BL 3/1/91*; SLJ 2/91*) [821]

**9812** Lear, Edward. *The Owl and the Pussycat* (PS–2). Illus. by Louise Voce. 1997, Candlewick paper $5.99 (0-7636-0336-8). 32pp. Cartoon-style illustrations adorn this retelling of the classic Lear poem. (Rev: BL 1/1/91; SLJ 12/91) [821]

**9813** Lear, Edward. *Owl and the Pussycat* (PS–1). Illus. by Ian Beck. 1996, Simon & Schuster $13.00 (0-689-81032-6). 30pp. Full and double-page spreads are used to illustrate this classic poem. (Rev: BL 10/1/96; SLJ 12/96) [821]

**9814** Lear, Edward. *The Quangle Wangle's Hat* (PS–1). Illus. by Janet Stevens. 1988, Harcourt $12.95 (0-15-264450-4); paper $6.00 (0-15-201478-0). 32pp. This classic nonsense poem is illustrated in sassy full color. (Rev: BL 10/1/88)

**9815** Lear, Edward. *There Was an Old Man: A Gallery of Nonsense Rhymes* (3–5). Illus. by Michele Lemieux. 1994, Morrow $15.00 (0-688-10788-5). 80pp. An illustrated edition of 53 of Lear's most charming and humorous limericks. (Rev: BL 9/15/94; SLJ 9/94) [821]

**9816** Lee, Dennis. *Dinosaur Dinner with a Slice of Alligator Pie: Favorite Poems* (PS–1). Ed. by Jack Prelutsky. Illus. by Debbie Tilley. 1997, Knopf $17.00 (0-679-87009-1). 32pp. An anthology of 40 of the most famous humorous poems of the Canadian poet Dennis Lee. (Rev: BCCB 6/97; BL 4/1/97; SLJ 4/97) [811]

**9817** Lee, Dennis. *The Ice Cream Store* (PS–3). Illus. by David McPhail. 1992, Scholastic $14.95 (0-590-45861-2). 64pp. A collection of sassy and bright poems, with occasional flashes of schoolyard humor. (Rev: BCCB 12/92; BL 11/15/92; SLJ 9/92*) [811]

**9818** Lewis, J. Patrick. *The La-di-da Hare* (K–4). Illus. by Diana C. Bluthenthal. 1997, Simon & Schuster $16.00 (0-689-31925-8). In this nonsense rhyme, Honeypot Bear and Commodore Mouse journey to an island where they meet the La-di-da Hare. (Rev: SLJ 5/97) [811]

**9819** Lewis, J. Patrick. *Ridicholas Nicholas* (PS–4). Illus. by Victoria Chess. 1995, Dial paper $14.89 (0-8037-1328-2). 40pp. This volume contains several nonsense verses, many using word play and rhyming jokes. (Rev: BL 12/1/95; SLJ 11/95) [811]

**9820** Livingston, Myra Cohn, ed. *Lots of Limericks* (5–8). Illus. by Rebecca Perry. 1991, Simon &

Schuster $15.00 (0-689-50531-0). 128pp. Nonsense limericks and wordplay abound in this collection. (Rev: BL 10/1/91; SLJ 1/92) [821]

**9821** McNaughton, Colin. *Making Friends with Frankenstein: A Book of Monstrous Poems and Pictures* (2–4). Illus. 1994, Candlewick $19.99 (1-56402-308-7). 90pp. Nonsense verses that make fun of monsters and the macabre with puns, word play, and outrageous rhymes. (Rev: BCCB 4/94; BL 5/15/94*; SLJ 5/94) [821]

**9822** Mahy, Margaret. *Bubble Trouble and Other Poems and Stories* (3–6). Illus. 1992, Macmillan $13.95 (0-689-50557-4). 70pp. Nonsense poems and stories made for reading aloud. (Rev: BL 12/1/92; SLJ 10/92) [828]

**9823** Manley, Molly. *Talkaty Talker* (PS–2). Illus. by Janet Marshall. 1994, Boyds Mills $9.95 (1-56397-195-X). Zany limericks and attractive cut-paper collages are used to introduce a number of humorous animals. (Rev: SLJ 3/94) [811]

**9824** Marshall, James. *Pocketful of Nonsense* (PS–3). Illus. 1993, Western $12.95 (0-307-17552-9). 24pp. A collection of 20 cleverly illustrated nonsense rhymes and limericks. (Rev: BL 11/15/93) [811]

**9825** Michelson, Richard. *Animals That Ought to Be: Poems About Imaginary Pets* (K–3). Illus. by Leonard Baskin. 1996, Simon & Schuster paper $16.00 (0-689-80635-3). 24pp. Poems about imaginary animals, like the Nightmare Scarer who protects one from under the bed. (Rev: BCCB 10/96; BL 10/15/96; HB 11–12/96; SLJ 9/96) [811]

**9826** Milne, A. A. *When We Were Very Young* (PS–3). Illus. by E. H. Shepard. 1988, Dutton $10.99 (0-525-44445-9); Dell paper $3.50 (0-440-49485-0). 112pp. Whimsical nonsense verses that have enchanted 3 generations. Also use: *Now We Are Six* (1988).

**9827** Morrison, Lillian. *I Scream, You Scream: A Feast of Food Rhymes* (3–5). Illus. 1997, August House $12.95 (0-87483-495-3). 96pp. Food is the subject of this humorous collection of rhymes, autograph-book verses, tongue twisters, and jokes. (Rev: BL 11/15/97; SLJ 11/97) [811]

**9828** Nash, Ogden. *Custard the Dragon and the Wicked Knight* (PS–3). Illus. by Lynn Munsinger. 1996, Little, Brown $14.95 (0-316-59882-8). 32pp. In this nonsense poem, a shy dragon saves Belinda from the clutches of Sir Garagoyle. (Rev: BCCB 4/96; BL 4/1/96; SLJ 4/96) [811]

**9829** Opie, Iona, and Peter Opie, eds. *I Saw Esau: The Schoolchild's Pocket Book* (2–5). Illus. by Maurice Sendak. 1992, Candlewick $19.95 (1-56402-046-0). 160pp. Schoolyard folk rhymes that are absurd, fierce, vulgar, and compelling. (Rev: BCCB 5/92*; BL 4/15/92*; SLJ 6/92*) [811]

**9830** Paraskevas, Betty. *Gracie Graves and the Kids from Room 402* (1–3). Illus. by Michael Paraskevas. 1995, Harcourt $15.00 (0-15-200321-5). 40pp. A collection of 30 silly poems, each related to Miss Graves and her crazy classroom. (Rev: BL 12/1/95; SLJ 11/95) [811]

**9831** Paraskevas, Betty. *Junior Kroll and Company* (K–3). Illus. by Michael Paraskevas. 1994, Harcourt $13.95 (0-15-292855-3). 40pp. A mischievous, shrewd toddler has a series of adventures, like learning to waltz with Cousin Blanche. (Rev: BL 4/15/94; SLJ 5/94) [811]

**9832** Prelutsky, Jack, ed. *For Laughing Out Loud: Poems to Tickle Your Funnybone* (K–5). Illus. by Marjorie Priceman. 1991, Knopf LB $15.99 (0-394-92144-5). 32pp. Nonsense poems by different poets cover everything physical — food, animals, family members, and messiness, to name a few. (Rev: BL 5/1/91*; HB 7–8/91; SLJ 7/91*) [811]

**9833** Prelutsky, Jack, ed. *For Laughing Out Louder: More Poems to Tickle Your Funnybone* (PS–3). Illus. by Marjorie Priceman. 1995, Knopf $15.00 (0-679-87063-6). 39pp. This is an excellent anthology of silly, catchy poems illustrated with hilarious pictures. (Rev: BL 1/1–15/96; SLJ 5/96) [811]

**9834** Prelutsky, Jack. *The New Kid on the Block: Poems* (3–6). Illus. by James Stevenson. 1984, Greenwillow LB $17.93 (0-688-02272-3). 160pp. A collection of over 100 humorous poems by this prolific master.

**9835** Prelutsky, Jack. *Ride a Purple Pelican* (PS–2). Illus. by Garth Williams. 1986, Greenwillow $17.95 (0-688-04031-4). 64pp. New verses that sound like old favorites. (Rev: BL 10/1/86; HB 1–2/87; SLJ 11/86)

**9836** Prelutsky, Jack. *Rolling Harvey Down the Hill* (1–3). Illus. by Victoria Chess. 1980, Greenwillow LB $15.93 (0-688-84258-5). 40pp. Humorous verses about everyday mischief, illustrated with black-and-white drawings.

**9837** Prelutsky, Jack. *The Sheriff of Rottenshot* (2–4). Illus. by Victoria Chess. 1982, Greenwillow LB $14.93 (0-688-00198-X). 32pp. A collection of the author's humorous poetry, with many a well-turned rhyme.

**9838** Prelutsky, Jack. *Something Big Has Been Here* (4–6). Illus. by James Stevenson. 1990, Greenwillow $17.95 (0-688-06434-5). 160pp. A bountiful collection of witty poems. (Rev: BCCB 12/90; BL 9/1/90*; HB 11–12/90*; SLJ 10/90*) [811]

**9839** Schertle, Alice. *How Now, Brown Cow?* (K–4). Illus. by Amanda Schaffer. 1994, Harcourt $14.95 (0-15-276648-0). 32pp. Clever, imaginative poems dealing with cows, real and invented. (Rev: BCCB 12/94; BL 9/15/94*; HB 11–12/94; SLJ 4/95) [811]

**9840** Smith, William J. *Laughing Time: Collected Nonsense* (3–5). Illus. by Fernando Krahn. 1990, Farrar $14.00 (0-374-34366-7); paper $3.50 (0-374-44315-7). 176pp. New poems have been added to this satisfyingly silly collection. Revision of the 1980 edition. (Rev: BL 2/15/90; SLJ 3/91) [811]

**9841** Spilka, Arnold. *Bumples, Fumdidlers, and Jellybeans* (K–3). Illus. by author. 1996, Houghton $15.95 (0-395-74522-5). 31pp. The humorous, imaginative poetry in this collection is accompanied by appealing, childlike drawings. (Rev: SLJ 2/97) [811]

**9842** Steig, Jeanne. *Consider the Lemming* (2–5). Illus. by William Steig. 1988, Farrar $9.00 (0-374-31536-1); paper $3.50 (0-374-41361-4). 48pp. Poems that offer a lighthearted tour through the animal kingdom. (Rev: BCCB 10/88; HB 9–10/88; SLJ 9/88)

**9843** Tripp, Wallace, ed. *A Great Big Ugly Man Came Up and Tied His Horse to Me: A Book of Nonsense Verse* (K–3). Illus. by Wallace Tripp. 1974, Little, Brown LB $14.95 (0-316-85280-5). 48pp. The hilarious drawings that accompany this selection of nonsense verses make this an especially entertaining book.

**9844** Viorst, Judith. *Sad Underwear and Other Complications* (4–7). Illus. 1995, Atheneum $16.00 (0-689-31929-0). 78pp. A series of imaginative poems, some humorous, some contemplative. (Rev: BCCB 4/95; BL 4/1/95; SLJ 5/95) [811]

**9845** Westcott, Nadine Bernard. *The Lady with the Alligator Purse* (PS–1). Illus. by author. 1988, Little, Brown $15.95 (0-316-93135-7); paper $5.95 (0-316-93136-5). The lady with the alligator purse chooses pizza instead of penicillin in this jump-rope rhyme. (Rev: BL 3/15/88; HB 5–6/88)

**9846** Westcott, Nadine Bernard, ed. *Never Take a Pig to Lunch and Other Poems About the Fun of Eating* (PS–3). Illus. 1994, Orchard $18.95 (0-531-06834-X). 64pp. A collection of poems — mostly humorous, many nonsensical — about the joy and crises caused by eating. (Rev: BCCB 6/94; BL 2/1/94; HB 5–6/94; SLJ 3/94*) [811]

**9847** Yolen, Jane. *Animal Fare* (3–5). Illus. by Janet Street. 1994, Harcourt $14.95 (0-15-203550-8). 32pp. Tricks with words and outlandish puns highlight this collection of 16 nonsense poems about imaginary animals. (Rev: BCCB 7–8/94; BL 6/1–15/94; SLJ 4/94) [811]

**9848** Yolen, Jane. *How Beastly! A Menagerie of Nonsense Poems* (K–3). Illus. by James Marshall. 1994, Boyds Mills $14.95 (1-56397-086-4). 48pp. Twenty-two rhymes, charmingly illustrated, about such creatures as the Edgehog, Pythong, and Crocodial. (Rev: BL 2/15/94) [811]

## Indians of North America

**9849** Bruchac, Joseph, and Jonathan London. *Thirteen Moons on Turtle's Back: A Native American Year of Moons* (1–5). Illus. by Thomas Locker. 1992, Putnam $15.95 (0-399-22141-7). 32pp. For each of the 13 moon cycles in a year, this book contains a poem and an oil painting illustrating it. (Rev: BL 3/1/92; SLJ 7/92) [811.54]

**9850** Philip, Neil. *Earth Always Endures: Native American Poems* (4–8). Illus. 1996, Viking paper $19.99 (0-670-86873-6). 96pp. Beautiful photographs of Native Americans accompany this collection of poetry from many tribal groups. (Rev: BL 10/1/96; SLJ 11/96) [897]

**9851** Sneve, Virginia Driving Hawk, ed. *Dancing Teepees: Poems of American Indian Youth* (3–8). Illus. by Stephen Gammell. 1989, Holiday LB $16.95 (0-8234-0724-1); paper $8.95 (0-8234-0879-5). 32pp. A collection of traditional tribal prayers, songs, and short poems. (Rev: BCCB 5/89; BL 5/15/89; SLJ 6/89)

**9852** Turcotte, Mark. *Songs of Our Ancestors: Poems About Native Americans* (3–6). Illus. by Kathleen S. Presnell. 1995, Children's LB $23.00 (0-516-05154-7). In 22 poems about American Indians, the author gives short biographies of individuals important as heroes and preservers of their culture. (Rev: SLJ 12/95) [811]

## Nature and the Seasons

**9853** Adoff, Arnold. *In for Winter, Out for Spring* (K–4). Illus. by Jerry Pinkney. 1991, Harcourt $14.95 (0-15-238637-8). 48pp. Big and small moments in the life of a young black girl, with radiant illustrations. (Rev: BCCB 5/91; BL 2/1/91*; SLJ 4/91) [398.2]

**9854** Asch, Frank. *Cactus Poems* (3–6). Illus. by Ted Levin. 1998, Harcourt $18.00 (0-15-200676-1). 48pp. A poet and a nature photographer combine talents to explore the desert and the animals and plants that live there. (Rev: BL 3/15/98) [811]

**9855** Asch, Frank. *Sawgrass Poems: A View of the Everglades* (3–6). Illus. by Ted Levin. 1996, Harcourt $18.00 (0-15-200180-8). 52pp. In 20 illustrated poems, the Florida Everglades and the life it supports are explored. (Rev: BL 4/1/96; SLJ 6/96) [811]

**9856** Berry, James. *Rough Sketch Beginning* (3–6). Illus. by Robert Florczak. 1996, Harcourt $18.00 (0-15-200112-3). 32pp. A poem about the work of a landscape artist is accompanied by expressive drawings and a concluding painting of the outdoors. (Rev: BL 5/1/96; SLJ 5/96*) [821]

**9857** Brenner, Barbara, ed. *The Earth Is Painted Green: A Garden of Poems About Our Planet* (3–5). Illus. by S. D. Schindler. 1994, Scholastic $16.95 (0-590-45134-0). 96pp. An excellent collection of poetry about nature and the environment that includes many by contemporary poets but also old favorites like "Daffodils." (Rev: BL 1/15/94; SLJ 4/94) [808.81]

**9858** Brown, Margaret Wise. *Under the Sun and the Moon and Other Poems* (K–2). Illus. by Tom Leonard. 1993, Hyperion LB $15.49 (1-56282-355-8). 32pp. Eighteen poems that deal with animals and nature. (Rev: SLJ 6/93) [811]

**9859** Buchanan, Ken, and Debby Buchanan. *It Rained on the Desert Today* (2–4). Illus. by Libba Tracy. 1994, Northland LB $14.95 (0-87358-575-5). 32pp. A rainstorm in the desert is evoked in free verse and evocative watercolors. (Rev: BL 10/15/94; SLJ 8/94) [811]

**9860** Chorao, Kay. *The Book of Giving: Poems of Thanks, Praise and Celebration* (PS–2). Illus. 1995, Dutton paper $17.99 (0-525-45409-8). 64pp. Of the more than 60 poems in this collection, most deal with the wonders of nature, selected from writings as varied as prayers from American Indians to the work of contemporary poets. (Rev: BL 11/15/95; SLJ 1/96) [811]

**9861** Coleman, Mary Ann. *The Dreams of Hummingbirds: Poems from Nature* (4–6). Illus. by Robert Masheris. 1993, Whitman LB $14.95 (0-8075-1720-8). 32pp. A poetic nature hike through the changing seasons. (Rev: BCCB 4/93; BL 3/15/93; SLJ 6/93) [811]

**9862** Daniel, Mark, comp. *A Child's Treasury of Seaside Verse* (4–8). Illus. 1991, Dial paper $16.95 (0-8037-0889-0). 137pp. There are 75 poems in this fine collection dealing with the seaside. (Rev: BL 6/1/91; SLJ 7/91) [811]

**9863** Esbensen, Barbara J. *Dance with Me* (3–6). Illus. by Megan Lloyd. 1995, HarperCollins LB $14.89 (0-06-022823-7). 32pp. Fifteen delightful poems that describe dances in nature, from those performed by trees to others by raindrops. (Rev: SLJ 10/95) [811]

**9864** Esbensen, Barbara J. *Echoes for the Eye: Poems to Celebrate Patterns in Nature* (3–5). Illus. by Helen K. Davie. 1996, HarperCollins LB $14.89 (0-06-024399-6). 32pp. Various shapes found in the natural world are explored in poetry and paintings. (Rev: BL 5/1/96; SLJ 5/96) [811]

**9865** Field, Rachel. *If Once You Have Slept on an Island* (PS–3). Illus. by Iris Van Rynbach. 1993, Boyds Mills $14.95 (1-56397-106-2). 32pp. An enchanting book that evokes the sights, sounds, and experiences of an island. (Rev: BL 1/15/93; SLJ 2/93) [811]

**9866** Fletcher, Ralph. *Ordinary Things: Poems from a Walk in Early Spring* (4–6). Illus. 1997, Simon & Schuster $15.00 (0-689-81035-0). 48pp. A fine collection of poems by Fletcher involving the thoughts and emotions that come with spring. (Rev: BL 4/15/97; SLJ 5/97*) [811]

**9867** Frank, Josette, sel. *Snow Toward Evening: A Year in a River Valley* (2–6). Illus. by Thomas Locker. 1990, Dial LB $15.89 (0-8037-0811-4). This includes 13 short nature poems by various authors. (Rev: SLJ 11/90) [811]

**9868** Frost, Robert. *Birches* (4–8). Illus. 1988, Holt $13.95 (0-8050-0570-6); paper $5.95 (0-8050-1316-4). 32pp. Frost's 1916 poem still entices new readers. (Rev: BL 10/1/88; SLJ 10/88)

**9869** Geis, Jacqueline. *Where the Buffalo Roam* (PS–3). Illus. 1992, Ideals LB $14.00 (0-8249-8584-2). 32pp. With illustrations and verses to the familiar cowboy tune, the American Southwest is celebrated. (Rev: BL 11/15/92; SLJ 1/93) [811]

**9870** George, Kristine O'Connell. *The Great Frog Race and Other Poems* (4–6). Illus. by Kate Kiesler. 1997, Clarion $15.00 (0-395-77607-4). 40pp. A richly atmospheric picture book that captures some of the outdoor activities of children, including watching captured frogs race. (Rev: BCCB 6/97; BL 3/15/97*; SLJ 4/97*) [811]

**9871** Harvey, Anne, ed. *Shades of Green* (4–8). Illus. by John Lawrence. 1992, Smithmark $4.98 (0-8317-3263-6). 192pp. A fine anthology that includes Dickinson, Whitman, Wordsworth, and others. (Rev: BL 6/15/92) [821]

**9872** Hazeltine, Alice I., and Elva Smith, eds. *The Year Around: Poems for Children* (4–6). Illus. by Paula Hutchison. 1973, Ayer $18.95 (0-8369-6403-9). A collection of seasonal poems.

**9873** Highwater, Jamake. *Songs for the Seasons* (PS–4). Illus. by Sandra Speidel. 1995, Lothrop LB $14.93 (0-688-10659-0). 32pp. A gentle look at the changes that occur with plants and animals during the cycle of the 4 seasons. (Rev: BL 4/15/95; SLJ 4/95) [811]

**9874** Hopkins, Lee Bennett, ed. *Small Talk: A Book of Short Poems* (2–4). Illus. by Susan Gaber. 1995, Harcourt $14.00 (0-15-276577-8). 48pp. Short poems by distinguished authors are arranged according to seasonal changes. (Rev: BCCB 5/95; BL 8/95; HB 5–6/95; SLJ 5/95*) [811]

**9875** Hopkins, Lee Bennett, ed. *Weather* (1–2). Illus. by Melanie Hall. Series: I Can Read. 1994, HarperCollins LB $14.89 (0-06-021462-7). 64pp. Simple, easy-to-read poems are found in this collection that explores weather, fair and foul. (Rev: BCCB 3/94; BL 2/1/94; HB 7–8/94; SLJ 3/94) [811]

**9876** *Imaginary Gardens: American Poetry and Art for Young People* (3–7). Illus. by Charles Sullivan. 1989, Abrams $19.95 (0-8109-1130-2). 111pp. A number of garden poems are matched with beautiful color reproductions of famous paintings. (Rev: HB 1–2/90; SLJ 2/90) [811]

**9877** Levy, Constance. *A Tree Place and Other Poems* (3–5). Illus. 1994, Macmillan paper $15.00 (0-689-50599-X). 48pp. Forty short poems that show a keen observation of common phenomena in nature. (Rev: BCCB 3/94; BL 9/1/94; HB 5–6/94, 11–12/94; SLJ 4/94) [811]

**9878** Lewis, J. Patrick. *Earth Verses and Water Rhymes* (2–5). Illus. by Robert Sabuda. 1991, Simon & Schuster LB $13.95 (0-689-31693-3). 128pp. The moods of the natural world are evoked with warm illustrations. (Rev: BCCB 1/92; BL 10/1/91; SLJ 9/91*) [811.54]

**9879** Lewis, J. Patrick. *July Is a Mad Mosquito* (K–3). Illus. by Melanie Hall. 1994, Atheneum $14.95 (0-689-31813-8). 32pp. Each poem in this collection tells about the sights, sounds, and activities of a different month of the year. (Rev: BCCB 2/94; BL 7/94; SLJ 4/94) [811]

**9880** Lindbergh, Reeve. *The Midnight Farm* (PS–1). Illus. by Susan Jeffers. 1987, Dial $15.99 (0-8037-0331-7); Puffin paper $5.99 (0-14-055668-0). 32pp. A child's fears of the dark are soothed when he is taken on a trip of the barnyard by night. (Rev: BCCB 12/87; BL 9/1/87; SLJ 10/87)

**9881** Livingston, Myra Cohn. *A Circle of Seasons* (3–5). Illus. by Leonard Everett Fisher. 1982, Holiday LB $15.95 (0-8234-0452-8); paper $5.95 (0-8234-0656-3). 32pp. A group of poems that brings the seasons to life.

**9882** Livingston, Myra Cohn. *Sky Songs* (3–6). Illus. by Leonard Everett Fisher. 1984, Holiday LB $14.95 (0-8234-0502-8). 32pp. Fourteen poems about the sky and the universe.

**9883** Livingston, Myra Cohn. *Up in the Air* (3–5). Illus. by Leonard Everett Fisher. 1989, Holiday LB $14.95 (0-8234-0736-5). 32pp. A celebration of flight begins as an airliner takes off. (Rev: BCCB 5/89; BL 5/15/89)

**9884** Merriam, Eve. *The Singing Green: New and Selected Poems for All Seasons* (3–7). Illus. by Kathleen C. Howell. 1992, Morrow $14.00 (0-688-11025-8). 112pp. The wordplay romps and frolics in this celebration of sun, trees, and the child in us all. (Rev: BCCB 2/93; BL 12/1/92; HB 1–2/93; SLJ 12/92) [811]

**9885** Moore, Lillian. *Adam Mouse's Book of Poems* (2–5). Illus. by Kathleen G. McCord. 1992, Macmillan $12.95 (0-689-31765-4). 48pp. Poems from the natural world, written by a country mouse. (Rev: BCCB 3/93; BL 9/15/92; SLJ 10/92) [811]

**9886** Moore, Lillian. *Poems Have Roots* (3–6). Illus. 1997, Simon & Schuster $15.00 (0-689-80029-0). 48pp. Seventeen short nature poems that explore the joy and wonder of land, sky, and water. (Rev: BL 9/1/97; SLJ 12/97) [811]

**9887** Mora, Pat. *The Desert Is My Mother/El Desierto Es Mi Madre* (PS–3). Illus. by Daniel Lechon. 1994, Arte Publico $14.95 (1-55885-121-6). 32pp. In this bilingual book of poems, everyday life in the desert is seen through the eyes of a child. (Rev: BL 1/15/95) [811]

**9888** Mora, Pat. *This Big Sky* (K–2). Illus. by Steve Jenkins. 1998, Scholastic $15.95 (0-590-37120-7). 32pp. Through poems and dynamic illustrations, the spirit and beauty of the American Southwest are captured. (Rev: BL 2/15/98) [811]

**9889** Morrison, Lillian. *Whistling the Morning In* (4–6). Illus. by Joel Cook. 1992, Boyds Mills LB $16.95 (1-56397-035-X). 34pp. In spirited free verse, the quiet blessings of a new day are created. (Rev: BL 1/15/93; SLJ 1/93) [811]

**9890** Olaleye, Isaac. *The Distant Talking Drum* (2–4). Illus. by Frane Lessac. 1995, Boyds Mills $14.95 (1-56397-095-3). 32pp. Through a series of short poems and colorful illustrations, the flora and fauna of the Nigerian rain forest are covered. (Rev: BL 1/1/95; HB 3–4/95; SLJ 2/95) [896]

**9891** Rogasky, Barbara. *Winter Poems* (3–6). Illus. by Trina S. Hyman. 1994, Scholastic $15.95 (0-590-42872-1). 40pp. An anthology of poems that deal with winter around the world and activities associated with it. (Rev: BCCB 1/95; BL 9/15/94; HB 11–12/94; SLJ 10/94*) [811]

**9892** Shaw, Alison. *Until I Saw the Sea: A Collection of Seashore Poems* (PS–3). Illus. 1995, Holt $15.95 (0-8050-2755-6). 32pp. Many great poets are represented in this anthology on such subjects as oceans, sandcastles, seaweed, and fog. (Rev: BL 7/95; SLJ 6/95) [811]

**9893** Siebert, Diane. *Mojave* (4–6). Illus. by Wendell Minor. 1988, HarperCollins LB $15.89 (0-690-04569-7); paper $5.95 (0-06-443283-1). 32pp. A lyrical poem that describes the desert, its history, and the animals that live in it. (Rev: BCCB 4/88; BL 2/1/88)

**9894** Singer, Marilyn. *Sky Words* (K–3). Illus. by Deborah Kogan Ray. 1994, Macmillan paper $14.95 (0-02-782882-4). 32pp. Fifteen poems about the sky and topics related to it are beautifully illustrated with multimedia artwork. (Rev: BL 2/15/94; HB 5–6/94; SLJ 5/94) [811]

**9895** Smith, William J., and Carol Ra, comp. *The Sun Is Up: A Child's Year of Poems* (K–3). Illus. by Jane C. Wright. 1996, Boyds Mills $15.95 (1-56397-029-5). A poetic trip through the seasons by the 2 authors and several classic poets, like Robert Louis Stevenson and Sara Teasdale. (Rev: SLJ 12/96) [811]

**9896** Turner, Ann. *A Moon for Seasons* (3–6). Illus. by Robert Noreika. 1994, Macmillan paper $14.95 (0-02-789513-0). 40pp. Using a rural setting and double-page spreads with exciting watercolors, the seasons of the year are presented. (Rev: BL 3/1/94; SLJ 7/94) [811]

**9897** Weil, Zaro. *Mud, Moon and Me* (K–3). Illus. by Jo Burroughes. 1992, Houghton $13.95 (0-395-58038-2). A collection of 44 short poems about the weather and the seasons. (Rev: SLJ 7/92) [811]

**9898** Windham, Sophie. *The Mermaid and Other Sea Poems* (3–5). Illus. 1996, Scholastic $16.95 (0-590-20898-5). 32pp. Sea creatures from mermaids to fish are featured in 18 poems by well-known writers. (Rev: BL 2/1/96; SLJ 5/96) [821]

**9899** Yolen, Jane, ed. *Mother Earth, Father Sky* (5–8). Illus. 1995, Boyds Mills $15.95 (1-56397-414-2). 54pp. An anthology of 40 poems that celebrate the wonders of nature, chiefly from well-known English and American writers. (Rev: BL 2/1/96; SLJ 3/96) [808.81]

**9900** Yolen, Jane, ed. *Once upon Ice* (3–6). Illus. by Jason Stemple. 1997, Boyds Mills $17.95 (1-56397-408-8). 32pp. A collection of poems from different writers, each of whom has reacted to photographs of ice formations. (Rev: BL 2/1/97; SLJ 3/97) [811]

**9901** Yolen, Jane. *Ring of Earth* (3–6). Illus. by John Wallner. 1986, Harcourt $14.95 (0-15-267140-4). 32pp. In a picture book for older children, the seasons are described in poems and paintings. (Rev: BCCB 3/87; SLJ 12/86) [811]

**9902** Yolen, Jane. *Water Music* (3–5). Photos by Jason Stemple. 1995, Boyds Mills $16.95 (1-56397-336-7). 40pp. Seventeen short poems that explore water and its various forms and uses. (Rev: BL 11/15/95; SLJ 11/95) [811]

**9903** Yolen, Jane, ed. *Weather Report* (3–5). Illus. by Annie Gusman. 1993, Boyds Mills $16.95 (1-56397-101-1). 64pp. An anthology including classic, contemporary, adult, and children's poems on rain, snow, sun, wind, and fog. (Rev: BCCB 5/93; BL 1/15/93; HB 3–4/93; SLJ 3/93) [808]

## Sports

**9904** Adoff, Arnold. *Sports Pages* (3–6). Illus. 1986, HarperCollins LB $14.89 (0-397-32103-1); paper

$6.95 (0-06-446098-3). 80pp. A thought, feeling, or movement of an athlete is chronicled in these free-verse poems dealing with sports. (Rev: BCCB 6/86; BL 5/1/86; SLJ 5/86)

**9905** Burleigh, Robert. *Hoops* (4–8). Illus. by Stephen T. Johnson. 1997, Harcourt $16.00 (0-15-201450-0). 32pp. A poem that expresses the joy, exhilaration, and excitement of basketball, as seen from the player's point of view. (Rev: BL 11/15/97*; SLJ 11/97*) [811]

**9906** Greenfield, Eloise. *For the Love of the Game: Michael Jordan and Me* (PS–4). Illus. by Jan S. Gilchrist. 1997, HarperCollins LB $14.89 (0-06-027299-6). 32pp. The basketball moves made by Michael Jordan are used as a metaphor for the game of life in this inspiring poem. (Rev: BCCB 3/97; BL 2/15/97; HB 3–4/97; SLJ 3/97) [811]

**9907** Hopkins, Lee Bennett, ed. *Extra Innings: Baseball Poems* (4–6). Illus. by Scott Medlock. 1993, Harcourt $16.00 (0-15-226833-2). 48pp. Nineteen poems about baseball. (Rev: BL 3/15/93; SLJ 4/93) [811]

**9908** Hopkins, Lee Bennett, ed. *Opening Days: Sports Poems* (3–6). Illus. by Scott Medlock. 1996, Harcourt $16.00 (0-15-200270-7). 48pp. There are 18 poems in this collection dealing with a variety of

sports, each accompanied by a full-page painting. (Rev: BL 2/15/96; HB 5–6/96; SLJ 5/96) [811]

**9909** Korman, Gordon, and Bernice Korman. *The Last-Place Sports Poems of Jeremy Bloom: A Collection of Poems About Winning, Losing, and Being a Good Sport (Sometimes)* (3–6). 1996, Scholastic paper $3.50 (0-590-25516-9). 92pp. A book that explores the world of sports by using different kinds of poetry, from haiku to narrative verse. (Rev: SLJ 4/97) [811]

**9910** Morrison, Lillian, ed. *At the Crack of the Bat* (4–6). Illus. by Steve Cieslawski. 1992, Little, Brown LB $15.49 (1-56282-177-6). 64pp. Full-color paintings add to the hero-loving glory of this all-American sport. (Rev: BCCB 5/92; BL 8/92; SLJ 6/92) [811]

**9911** Morrison, Lillian, ed. *Slam Dunk: Poems About Basketball* (4–6). Illus. 1995, Hyperion LB $16.49 (0-7868-2042-X). 64pp. An anthology of 42 short poems about basketball, many by important writers like Walter Dean Myers and Jack Prelutsky. (Rev: BL 10/1/95; SLJ 11/95) [811]

**9912** Thayer, Ernest Lawrence. *Casey at the Bat* (K–3). Illus. by Gerald Fitzgerald. 1995, Atheneum $15.00 (0-689-31945-2). 32pp. An entertaining version of the perennial favorite, with fresh, humorous drawings. (Rev: BL 4/15/95; SLJ 6/95) [811]

# Plays

## General

**9913** Adorjan, Carol, and Yuri Rasovsky. *WKID: Easy Radio Plays* (3–7). Illus. 1988, Whitman LB $10.95 (0-8075-9155-6). 80pp. Four scripts for radio plays for young people to act in and produce. (Rev: BL 10/1/88; SLJ 11/88)

**9914** Alexander, Sue. *Small Plays for Special Days* (2–4). Illus. by Tom Huffman. 1988, Houghton paper $6.95 (0-89919-798-1). 64pp. Short 2-character plays for many holidays.

**9915** Boiko, Claire. *Children's Plays for Creative Actors: A Collection of Royalty-Free Plays for Boys and Girls* (3–6). 1985, Plays paper $16.95 (0-8238-0267-1). 384pp. Thirty-one playlets, comedies, holiday plays, and one-act plays.

**9916** Bradley, Alfred, and Michael Bond. *Paddington on Stage* (3–5). Illus. by Peggy Fortnum. 1977, Houghton $14.95 (0-395-25155-9); Dell paper $3.25 (0-440-46846-9). Seven short plays about the adventures of the bear who always gets in and out of trouble.

**9917** Butterfield, Moira. *Hansel and Gretel* (2–4). Photos by Trever Clifford. Illus. by Frances Cony. Series: Playtales. 1997, Heinemann $19.92 (1-57572-648-3). 24pp. Contains the script of a play based on this folktale plus direction on how to stage it, from casting and making props to the actual performance. Also use *Sleeping Beauty* (1997). (Rev: SLJ 2/98) [809]

**9918** Butterfield, Moira. *Little Red Riding Hood* (2–4). Photos by Trever Clifford. Illus. by Frances Cony. Series: Playtales. 1997, Heinemann LB $19.92 (1-57572-650-5). 24pp. Provides a script based on this fairy tale, as well as a list of parts, directions for production of the play, and instructions for making

costumes and sets. Also use *Puss-in-Boots* (1997). (Rev: SLJ 3/98) [809]

**9919** Dahl, Roald. *James and the Giant Peach: A Play* (3–5). 1983, Puffin paper $4.50 (0-14-031464-4). 128pp. A condensed version of the story about James, who has fantastic adventures.

**9920** Fisher, Aileen. *Year-Round Programs for Young Players* (2–8). Illus. 1985, Plays paper $14.95 (0-8238-0266-3). 334pp. Twenty holidays and special occasions are covered in 100 skits, plays, poems, and recitations. (Rev: BL 2/1/86; SLJ 4/86)

**9921** Fredericks, Anthony D. *Tadpole Tales and Other Totally Terrific Treats for Readers Theatre* (4–8). 1997, Libraries Unlimited paper $18.50 (1-56308-547-X). 139pp. A delightful collection of scripts for young performers that are spin-offs from folktales, fables, and nursery rhymes. (Rev: BL 3/1/98) [372.67]

**9922** Gerke, Pamela. *Multicultural Plays for Children Grades K–3* (K–3). 1996, Smith & Kraus paper $19.95 (1-57525-005-5). 159pp. Ten entertaining plays, each of which deals with a different racial group. Also use volume 2 (1996), which contains 10 plays for grades 4 to 6. (Rev: BL 12/1/96; SLJ 9/96) [812]

**9923** Jennings, Coleman A., and Aurand Harris, eds. *Plays Children Love, Volume II: A Treasury of Contemporary and Classic Plays for Children* (5–8). Illus. by Susan Swan. 1988, St. Martin's $19.95 (0-312-01490-2). 512pp. A group of 20 plays requiring royalties based on such stories as *Charlotte's Web, The Wizard of Oz,* and *The Wind in the Willows.*

**9924** Kamerman, Sylvia E., ed. *Christmas Play Favorites for Young People* (1–7). 1982, Plays paper $13.95 (0-8238-0257-4). Eighteen plays from the pages of *Plays* magazine.

**9925** Kamerman, Sylvia E., ed. *Great American Events on Stage: 15 Plays to Celebrate America's Past* (5–8). 1996, Plays paper $15.95 (0-8238-0305-8). 231pp. A collection of 15 short plays on events in American history, mostly featuring such personalities as Nathan Hale, Molly Pitcher, and Martin Luther King, Jr. (Rev: SLJ 5/97) [808]

**9926** Kamerman, Sylvia E., ed. *Plays from Favorite Folk Tales: 25 One-Act Dramatizations of Stories Children Love* (3–5). 1987, Plays paper $13.95 (0-8238-0280-9). 293pp. Includes plays about Robin Hood, Finn McCool, and King Midas. Also use: *Plays of Black Americans* (1987); *The Big Book of Christmas Plays* (1988). (Rev: BL 1/1/88)

**9927** Kamerman, Sylvia E., ed. *Thirty Plays from Favorite Stories: Royalty-Free Dramatizations of Myths, Folktales, and Legends from Around the World* (2–4). 1997, Plays paper $15.95 (0-8238-0306-6). 291pp. Thirty short plays based loosely on folktales from around the world. (Rev: SLJ 12/97) [809]

**9928** McCullough, L. E. *Plays of America from American Folklore for Children Grades K–6* (3–6). Series: Young Actors. 1996, Smith & Kraus paper $14.95 (1-57525-038-1). 161pp. A collection of 15 plays from American folklore and history that represent many cultural backgrounds. (Rev: SLJ 8/96) [808.82]

**9929** McCullough, L. E. *Plays of the Wild West* (3–7). 1997, Smith & Kraus paper $19.95 (1-57525-105-1). 224pp. Both serious and slapstick views of the Wild West are reflected in these 12 plays, mostly musicals. A companion volume is *Plays of the Wild West: Grades K–3* (1997). (Rev: BL 11/1/97; SLJ 1/98) [812]

**9930** MacDonald, Margaret Read. *The Skit Book: 101 Skits from Kids* (3–6). Illus. by Marie-Louise Scull. 1990, Shoe String LB $25.00 (0-208-02258-9); paper $16.50 (0-208-02283-X). 160pp. Funny, silly skits from kids that kids will like. (Rev: BL 6/1/90; SLJ 6/90) [812]

**9931** Miller, Helen L. *Everyday Plays for Boys and Girls* (3–5). 1986, Plays paper $12.95 (0-8238-0274-4). 198pp. Fifteen one-act plays suitable for school performances. Also use: *Special Plays for Holidays* (1986). (Rev: BCCB 2/87; BL 11/15/86; SLJ 3/87)

**9932** Miller, Helen L. *First Plays for Children* (3–7). 1985, Plays paper $12.95 (0-8238-0268-X). 295pp. A useful collection of nonroyalty plays.

**9933** Nolan, Paul T. *Folk Tale Plays Round the World: A Collection of Royalty-Free, One-Act Plays About Lands Far and Near* (4–7). 1982, Plays paper $13.95 (0-8238-0253-1). Johnny Appleseed and Robin Hood are heroes featured in 2 of the 17 plays in this collection.

**9934** Smith, Marisa, ed. *The Seattle Children's Theatre: Six Plays for Young Audiences* (5–8). Series: Young Actors. 1997, Smith & Kraus $16.95 (1-57525-008-X). 308pp. Six plays that contain young adolescents as characters, adapted from books like *Afternoon of the Elves* and *Anne of Green Gables*. (Rev: SLJ 6/97) [809]

**9935** Soto, Gary. *Novio Boy: A Play* (5–8). 1997, Harcourt paper $7.00 (0-15-201531-0). 96pp. A play about Chicanos in which Rudy, a ninth-grader, asks an eleventh-grade girl out on a date. (Rev: BL 4/15/97; SLJ 6/97) [812]

**9936** Vigil, Angel. *¡Teatro! Hispanic Plays for Young People* (4–8). Illus. 1996, Teacher Ideas paper $25.00 (1-56308-371-X). 220pp. This collection contains 14 scripts that contain elements of the Hispanic traditions of the Southwest. (Rev: BL 3/1/97) [812]

**9937** Willard, Nancy. *East of the Sun and West of the Moon: A Play* (3–5). Illus. by Barry Moser. 1989, Harcourt $14.95 (0-15-224750-5). 64pp. A Norse myth about a poor woodcutter in play form. (Rev: BCCB 4/89; BL 3/15/89)

**9938** Winther, Barbara. *Plays from African Tales* (3–6). 1992, Plays paper $13.95 (0-8238-0296-5). 145pp. This book consists of a series of one-act plays based on folktales from all parts of Africa. (Rev: SLJ 9/92) [812.08]

# Shakespeare

**9939** Birch, Beverley. *Shakespeare's Stories: Comedies* (5–8). Illus. 1988, Bedrick $12.95 (0-87226-191-3); paper $6.95 (0-87226-225-1). 126pp. Retelling Shakespeare's best-known comedies. (Rev: BL 2/15/89; SLJ 2/89)

**9940** Birch, Beverley. *Shakespeare's Stories: Histories* (5–8). Illus. 1988, Bedrick paper $6.95 (0-87226-226-X). 126pp. Retelling the classic stories of Shakespeare. (Rev: BL 2/15/89; SLJ 2/89)

**9941** Birch, Beverley. *Shakespeare's Stories: Tragedies* (5–8). Illus. 1988, Bedrick paper $6.95 (0-87226-227-8). 126pp. Retelling the great tragedies. (Rev: BL 2/15/89; SLJ 2/89)

**9942** Coville, Bruce. *William Shakespeare's Macbeth* (4–8). Illus. by Gary Kelley. 1997, Dial paper $16.89 (0-8037-1900-0). 48pp. Using a picture book format, the story of Macbeth is retold, with emphasis on the supernatural aspects. (Rev: BL 11/1/97; SLJ 12/97) [822.3]

**9943** Lamb, Charles, and Mary Lamb. *Tales from Shakespeare* (4–8). Illus. by Elinore Blaisdell. 1988, Puffin paper $3.99 (0-14-035088-8). 352pp. The classic retelling of several of Shakespeare's most popular plays.

**9944** Nesbit, Edith. *The Best of Shakespeare* (4–6). Illus. 1997, Oxford $16.95 (0-19-511689-5). 128pp. E. Nesbit has retold the plots of 10 of Shakespeare's most popular plays, illustrated with photos from English productions. (Rev: BL 10/15/97) [822.3]

**9945** Ross, Stewart. *Shakespeare and Macbeth: The Story Behind the Play* (5–8). Illus. by Tony Karpinski. 1994, Viking paper $16.99 (0-670-85629-0). 48pp. The story of the writing and first production of Shakespeare's *Macbeth*, with material on the playwright's source material. (Rev: BCCB 1/95; BL 3/15/95; SLJ 1/95) [822.3]

# Biography

# Adventurers and Explorers

## Collective

**9946** Baird, Anne. *The U.S. Space Camp Book of Astronauts* (4–6). Illus. 1996, Morrow LB $15.93 (0-688-12227-2). 48pp. Profiles of 14 astronauts, representing various stages in the development of the space program. (Rev: BL 3/15/96; SLJ 7/96) [920]

**9947** Collins, James L. *The Mountain Men* (4–6). Illus. 1996, Watts LB $21.00 (0-531-20229-1). 59pp. Brief biographies of mountain men like Jim Bridger and Kit Carson, all of whom explored the Far West. (Rev: BL 6/1–15/96; SLJ 7/96) [920]

**9948** Fradin, Dennis B. *Explorers* (2–4). Illus. 1984, Children's LB $21.00 (0-516-01926-0). 48pp. Easy text and clear photos tell the story of explorations, from the earliest civilizations to the space program. 

**9949** Fritz, Jean. *Around the World in a Hundred Years: From Henry the Navigator to Magellan* (4–6). Illus. 1994, Putnam $18.99 (0-399-22527-7); paper $6.99 (0-698-11638-0). 128pp. A history of exploration and explorers, from 1421 to 1522, in a series of short biographies. (Rev: BCCB 6/94; BL 5/15/94; HB 7–8/94; SLJ 8/94) [920]

**9950** MacDonald, Fiona. *Exploring the World* (3–6). Illus. by Gerald Wood. Series: Voyages of Discovery. 1996, Bedrick $18.95 (0-87226-487-4). 48pp. With superb illustrations and many maps, this book tells of the voyages of Magellan and Drake. (Rev: SLJ 1/97) [920]

**9951** Mason, Antony. *Peary and Amundsen: Race to the Poles* (5–8). Illus. Series: Beyond the Horizons. 1995, Raintree Steck-Vaughn LB $24.26 (0-8114-3977-1). 46pp. Gives extensive historical information about transportation used by explorers and their equipment, including epic polar races. (Rev: SLJ 5/95) [920]

**9952** Masters, Anthony. *Heroic Stories* (4–8). Illus. Series: Story Library. 1994, Kingfisher paper $6.95 (1-85697-983-0). 256pp. Various kinds of courage are explored in the lives of 23 people, including Charles Lindbergh and Anne Frank. (Rev: BL 3/1/95) [920]

**9953** Matthews, Rupert. *Explorer* (4–8). Illus. Series: Eyewitness Books. 1991, Knopf LB $20.99 (0-679-91460-9). 64pp. Covers the world's greatest explorers and their discoveries in a series of double-page spreads. (Rev: BL 12/1/91) [920]

**9954** Morris, Deborah. *Real Kids, Real Adventures, Book 4* (3–7). 1995, Broadman & Holman paper $4.99 (0-8054-4054-2). 98pp. True adventures experienced by 3 courageous, thoughtful young people are retold, such as one in which a young man risks his life to save a girl dangling from a ski lift. (Rev: SLJ 12/95) [920]

**9955** Rozakis, Laurie. *Dick Rutan and Jena Yeager: Flying Non-Stop Around the World* (3–4). Illus. by Jerry Harston. Series: Partners. 1994, Blackbirch LB $13.95 (1-56711-087-8). 47pp. The story of this pair of adventurers and their nonstop flight around the world. (Rev: SLJ 1/95) [920]

**9956** Rozakis, Laurie. *Matthew Henson and Robert Peary: The Race for the North Pole* (2–6). Illus. by Tom Foty. Series: Partners. 1994, Blackbirch LB $13.95 (1-56711-066-5). 47pp. The story of the North Pole expedition that describes the contributions of each man while supplying good historical information on polar exploration. (Rev: SLJ 7/94) [920]

**9957** Schraff, Anne. *American Heroes of Exploration and Flight* (5–7). Illus. Series: Collective Biographies. 1996, Enslow LB $19.95 (0-89490-619-4). 112pp. From the Wright Brothers, Lindbergh, and Earhart to Neil Armstrong and Sally Ride, this is a history of 12 Americans who dared the unknown. (Rev: BL 4/15/96; SLJ 5/96) [920]

**9958** Twist, Clint. *Gagarin and Armstrong: The First Steps in Space* (5–8). Illus. Series: Beyond the Horizons. 1995, Raintree Steck-Vaughn LB $24.26 (0-8114-3978-X). 46pp. A history of space exploration and the development of related technology precedes the biographies of these 2 space pioneers. (Rev: SLJ 5/95) [920]

**9959** Twist, Clint. *Magellan and da Gama: To the Far East and Beyond* (4–7). Illus. Series: Beyond the Horizons. 1994, Raintree Steck-Vaughn LB $24.26 (0-8114-7254-X). 48pp. Describes the period in which these 2 explorers lived, as well as their voyages and accomplishments. (Rev: BL 8/94) [920]

**9960** Twist, Clint. *Stanley and Livingstone: Expeditions Through Africa* (5–8). Illus. Series: Beyond the Horizons. 1995, Raintree Steck-Vaughn LB $24.26 (0-8114-3976-3). 46pp. An attractive book that tells about foreign influences in Africa as well as introducing these 2 very different adventurer-explorers. (Rev: SLJ 5/95) [920]

**9961** Wright, Rachel. *Pirates* (3–5). Illus. 1991, Watts LB $20.00 (0-531-14156-X). 32pp. This book gives a brief history of piracy, followed by short biographies of famous men and women. (Rev: SLJ 3/92) [920]

# Individual

## ARMSTRONG, NEIL

**9962** Kramer, Barbara. *Neil Armstrong: The First Man on the Moon* (5–7). Illus. Series: People to Know. 1997, Enslow LB $19.95 (0-89490-828-6). 112pp. This biography covers Armstrong's public and private life, with details on his specialized training and many space missions. (Rev: SLJ 12/97) [921]

## BAILEY, REX

**9963** Greenberg, Keith E. *Test Pilot: Taking Chances in the Air* (4–7). Illus. Series: Risky Business. 1996, Blackbirch LB $14.95 (1-56711-158-0). 32pp. The story of Major Rex Bailey, who faces death in his many exploits as a test pilot. (Rev: BL 2/1/97) [921]

## BLANCHARD, JEAN-PIERRE

**9964** Wallner, Alexandra. *The First Air Voyage in the United States: The Story of Jean-Pierre Blanchard* (K–4). Illus. 1996, Holiday LB $15.95 (0-8234-1224-5). 32pp. The story of the man who participated in 1793 in the first air flight in the United States. (Rev: BCCB 5/96; BL 5/15/96; SLJ 6/96) [921]

## BLUFORD, GUION

**9965** Haskins, Jim, and Kathleen Benson. *Space Challenger: The Story of Guion Bluford* (4–7). Illus. 1984, Carolrhoda LB $16.95 (0-87614-259-5). 64pp. The story of the first black man to have ridden in space.

## BOONE, DANIEL

**9966** Brandt, Keith. *Daniel Boone: Frontier Adventures* (3–5). Illus. by John Lawn. 1983, Troll LB $12.95 (0-89375-843-4); paper $3.95 (0-89375-844-2). 48pp. A readable account about the famous wilderness scout.

**9967** Lawlor, Laurie. *Daniel Boone* (5–8). Illus. by Bert Dodson. 1989, Whitman LB $13.95 (0-8075-1462-4). 160pp. A powerful biography of the famous American frontier hero. (Rev: BL 2/1/89)

**9968** Raphael, Elaine, and Don Bolognese. *Daniel Boone: Frontier Hero* (3–5). Series: Drawing America. 1996, Scholastic $14.95 (0-590-47900-8). An attractive book that presents the salient events in this frontiersman's life. (Rev: SLJ 3/96) [921]

**9969** Sanford, William R., and Carl R. Green. *Daniel Boone: Wilderness Pioneer* (4–6). Illus. Series: Legendary Heroes of the Wild West. 1997, Enslow LB $15.95 (0-89490-674-7). 48pp. This short biography of the colorful frontiersman who promoted the settlement of Kentucky tries to separate fact from legend. (Rev: BL 3/15/97; SLJ 4/97) [921]

## BOWDITCH, NATHANIEL

**9970** Latham, Jean Lee. *Carry On, Mr. Bowditch* (6–8). Illus. by John O'Hara Cosgrove. 1955, Houghton $15.95 (0-395-06881-9); paper $6.95 (0-395-13713-6). 256pp. This fictionalized biography of the great American navigator is enlivened by fascinating material on sailing ships and the romance of old Salem. Newbery Medal winner, 1956.

## BYRD, ADMIRAL

**9971** Burleigh, Robert. *Black Whiteness: Admiral Byrd Alone in the Antarctic* (4–8). Illus. by Walter L. Krudop. 1998, Simon & Schuster $16.00 (0-689-81299-X). 40pp. An outstanding picture biography, with generous quotes from Byrd's diary that tell of his great endurance and his lonely vigil in a small underground structure in the Antarctic. (Rev: BL 1/1–15/98*; SLJ 3/98) [921]

## CARSON, KIT

**9972** Sanford, William R., and Carl R. Green. *Kit Carson: Frontier Scout* (4–6). Illus. Series: Legendary Heroes of the Wild West. 1996, Enslow LB $15.95 (0-89490-650-X). 48pp. A lively biography of the frontier scout and mountain man, with details on how he survived in the wilderness. (Rev: SLJ 7/96) [921]

### CHAMPLAIN, SAMUEL DE

**9973** Jacobs, William J. *Champlain: A Life of Courage* (4–6). Illus. Series: First Books. 1994, Watts LB $21.00 (0-531-20112-0). 63pp. A brief, attractively illustrated biography of this French explorer and colonizer who is one of the heroes of Canadian history. (Rev: SLJ 8/94) [921]

### COCHRAN, JACQUELINE

**9974** Smith, Elizabeth Simpson. *Coming Out Right: The Story of Jacqueline Cochran, the First Woman Aviator to Break the Sound Barrier* (5–8). Illus. 1991, Walker LB $15.85 (0-8027-6989-6). 114pp. From her impoverished childhood to her triumphs in the air and later, this is the story of a female aviation pioneer. (Rev: SLJ 5/91) [921]

### COLEMAN, BESSIE

**9975** Fisher, Lillian M. *Brave Bessie: Flying Free* (4–7). Illus. 1995, Hendrick-Long $13.95 (0-937460-94-X). 88pp. This biography tells of the struggles of Bessie Coleman, who became the first African American aviatrix in the United States. (Rev: BL 2/15/96; SLJ 2/96) [921]

**9976** Hart, Philip S. *Up in the Air: The Story of Bessie Coleman* (4–6). Illus. 1996, Carolrhoda LB $16.95 (0-87614-949-2); paper $6.95 (0-87614-978-6). 80pp. Forced by restrictions at home to get her training in France in the 1920s, Coleman became the first African American female airplane pilot. (Rev: BL 8/96; SLJ 8/96) [921]

**9977** Lindbergh, Reeve. *Nobody Owns the Sky* (PS–3). Illus. by Pamela Paparone. 1996, Candlewick $15.99 (1-56402-533-0). 32pp. A poem that commemorates the life of African American aviator Bessie Coleman. (Rev: BL 1/1–15/97; SLJ 11/96) [921]

### COLUMBUS, CHRISTOPHER

**9978** Adler, David A. *Christopher Columbus: Great Explorer* (3–5). Illus. by Lyle Miller. Series: First Biography. 1991, Holiday LB $15.95 (0-8234-0895-7). 48pp. This account covers the entire life of Columbus, from his childhood through his last unhappy years. (Rev: SLJ 5/92) [921]

**9979** Adler, David A. *A Picture Book of Christopher Columbus* (K–3). Illus. by John Wallner. Series: Picture Book Biography. 1991, Holiday LB $15.95 (0-8234-0857-4); paper $6.95 (0-8234-0949-X). 32pp. The life of this famous explorer is described in sim-

ple text and many illustrations. (Rev: BL 6/1/91; SLJ 5/91) [921]

**9980** Clare, John D., ed. *The Voyages of Christopher Columbus* (5–8). Illus. Series: Living History. 1992, Harcourt $16.95 (0-15-200507-2). 64pp. Using actors and backdrops of the period, this account reconstructs each of Columbus's New World voyages. (Rev: SLJ 11/92) [921]

**9981** Columbus, Christopher. *The Log of Christopher Columbus' First Voyage to America in the Year 1492 as Copied Out in Brief by Bartholomew Las Casas* (4–6). Illus. by John O'Hara Cosgrove. 1989, Shoe String LB $17.00 (0-208-02247-3). 84pp. An abridged log by the explorer giving day-to-day events on his sea journey. A reissue.

**9982** Fritz, Jean. *Where Do You Think You're Going, Christopher Columbus?* (3–5). Illus. by Margot Tomes. 1980, Putnam $13.95 (0-399-20723-6); paper $5.95 (0-698-11580-5). 80pp. A fresh, interesting account of Columbus and his voyages.

**9983** Pelta, Kathy. *Discovering Christopher Columbus: How History Is Invented* (5–7). Illus. 1991, Lerner LB $21.27 (0-8225-4899-2). 112pp. After telling what we do know about Columbus, the author examines how myths and legends about him have grown over the years. (Rev: BL 10/1/91) [921]

**9984** Yue, Charlotte, and David Yue. *Christopher Columbus: How He Did It* (4–8). 1992, Houghton $14.95 (0-395-52100-9). 136pp. Besides basic history, this book concentrates on the technology of the times that allowed Columbus to succeed. (Rev: BL 6/15/92*; SLJ 7/91) [921]

### CORTÉS, HERNANDO

**9985** Lilley, Stephen R. *Hernando Cortes* (4–8). Illus. Series: The Importance Of. 1996, Lucent LB $22.45 (1-56006-066-2). 112pp. A biography of this Spanish conquistador and the effects of his invasion on the New World. (Rev: BL 3/15/96; SLJ 1/96) [921]

### CROCKETT, DAVY

**9986** Adler, David A. *A Picture Book of Davy Crockett* (K–3). Illus. by John Wallner. Series: Picture Book Biography. 1996, Holiday LB $15.95 (0-8234-1212-1). 32pp. With simple, brief text and many illustrations, this is a beginning biography of a frontier hero. (Rev: BL 4/15/96; SLJ 5/96) [921]

**9987** Sanford, William R., and Carl R. Green. *Davy Crockett: Defender of the Alamo* (4–6). Illus. Series: Legendary Heroes of the Wild West. 1996, Enslow LB $15.95 (0-89490-648-8). 48pp. A brief action-filled biography of Davy Crockett that tries to sort out fact from fiction. (Rev: BL 7/96; SLJ 7/96) [921]

**9988** Santrey, Laurence. *Davy Crockett: Young Pioneer* (4–6). Illus. 1983, Troll paper $3.95 (0-89375-848-5). 48pp. All sorts of stories about Davy Crockett, one of the most interesting frontier scouts.

DAVIS, JAN

**9989** Greenberg, Keith E. *Stunt Woman: Daredevil Specialist* (4–7). Illus. Series: Risky Business. 1996, Blackbirch LB $14.95 (1-56711-159-9). 32pp. The story of Jan Davis who, for fun and profit, engages in such activities as jumping from airplanes. (Rev: BL 2/1/97; SLJ 1/97) [921]

DRAKE, SIR FRANCIS

**9990** Gerrard, Roy. *Sir Francis Drake: His Daring Deeds* (2–5). Illus. by author. 1988, Farrar $15.00 (0-374-36962-3). 32pp. In rhyming verse, the story of young Drake in the England of long ago. (Rev: BCCB 7–8/88; BL 8/88; SLJ 8/88)

EARHART, AMELIA

**9991** Chadwick, Roxane. *Amelia Earhart: Aviation Pioneer* (4–6). Illus. 1987, Lerner LB $18.60 (0-8225-0484-7); paper $4.95 (0-8225-9515-X). 56pp. The life of the young daredevil who lived to fly. (Rev: BCCB 6/87; BL 6/15/87; SLJ 8/87)

**9992** Davies, Kath. *Amelia Earhart Flies Around the World* (3–6). Illus. Series: Great 20th Century Expeditions. 1994, Dillon LB $13.95 (0-87518-531-2). 32pp. This is a lively biography that clearly summarizes Amelia Earhart's exciting and rebellious life. (Rev: SLJ 11/94) [921]

**9993** Landsman, Susan. *What Happened to Amelia Earhart?* (3–5). Illus. 1991, Avon paper $3.50 (0-380-76221-8). 96pp. While giving background information on Amelia Earhart, this book focuses on her disappearance. (Rev: BL 9/15/91) [921]

**9994** Lauber, Patricia. *Lost Star: The Story of Amelia Earhart* (5–7). Illus. 1988, Scholastic paper $3.50 (0-590-41159-4). 96pp. A candid biography of the famed lost aviator. (Rev: BL 10/1/88; SLJ 12/88)

**9995** Parr, Jan. *Amelia Earhart: First Lady of Flight* (5–8). Illus. Series: Book Report Biographies. 1997, Watts $22.00 (0-531-11407-4). 112pp. A short, useful biography that tells about the public and private life of this adventurer who broke many records and helped open up the world of flight for women. (Rev: BL 11/15/97; SLJ 11/97) [921]

**9996** Sabin, Francene. *Amelia Earhart: Adventure in the Sky* (3–5). Illus. by Karen Milone. 1983, Troll LB $12.95 (0-89375-839-6); paper $3.95 (0-89375-840-X). 48pp. A biography that shows this amazing woman's courage and endurance.

**9997** Szabo, Corinne. *Sky Pioneer: A Photobiography of Amelia Earhart* (4–8). Illus. 1997, National Geographic $16.00 (0-7922-3737-4). 64pp. A lavishly illustrated biography of Earhart that concentrates more on her accomplishments than her disappearance. (Rev: BL 2/15/97; SLJ 4/97) [921]

EXQUEMELIN

**9998** Exquemelin, A. O. *Exquemelin and the Pirates of the Caribbean* (5–8). Ed. by Jane Shuter. Illus. Series: History Eyewitness. 1995, Raintree Steck-Vaughn LB $24.26 (0-8114-8282-0). 48pp. An edited version of the exciting journal of the 17th-century Frenchman who joined a pirate gang as a barber-surgeon. (Rev: BL 4/15/95) [921]

FREMONT, JOHN C.

**9999** Sanford, William R., and Carl R. Green. *John C. Fremont: Soldier and Pathfinder* (4–6). Illus. Series: Legendary Heroes of the Wild West. 1996, Enslow LB $15.95 (0-89490-649-6). 48pp. A biography of the soldier and politician who also participated in many explorations that opened up the West, including California. (Rev: BL 7/96; SLJ 7/96) [921]

HALL, DANIEL

**10000** Stanley, Diane. *The True Adventure of Daniel Hall* (4–6). Illus. 1995, Dial paper $15.89 (0-8037-1469-6). 40pp. A brief picture book that deals with the life of Daniel Hall, who, at 14, signed on to the whaling ship *Condor* in 19th-century New England. (Rev: BCCB 11/95; BL 9/15/95; HB 11–12/95; SLJ 9/95) [921]

HENSON, MATTHEW

**10001** Dolan, Sean. *Matthew Henson* (4–7). Illus. Series: Junior World Biographies. 1991, Chelsea LB $15.95 (0-7910-1568-8). 80pp. An upbeat biography of the arctic explorer with well-captioned photos. (Rev: BL 9/1/91) [921]

**10002** Ferris, Jeri. *Arctic Explorer: The Story of Matthew Henson* (3–6). Illus. 1989, Carolrhoda LB $22.60 (0-87614-370-2). 80pp. Robert Peary described his black assistant as "a most nearly indispensable man." (Rev: BL 6/1/89; HB 7–8/89)

HILLARY, EDMUND

**10003** Hacking, Sue M. *Mount Everest and Beyond: Sir Edmund Hillary* (3–6). Illus. Series: Biographies. 1996, Benchmark LB $21.36 (0-7614-0491-0). 48pp. A biography of this multifaceted man who gained fame for climbing Mount Everest but has been equally accomplished in other fields. (Rev: SLJ 2/97) [921]

**10004** Stewart, Whitney. *Sir Edmund Hillary: To Everest and Beyond* (5–8). Photos by Anne B. Keiser. Illus. Series: Newsmakers. 1996, Lerner LB $23.95 (0-8225-4927-1). 128pp. The life of this famous mountain climber is presented with interesting details about his other interests, like bee keeping, conservation, and helping the Sherpa people. (Rev: SLJ 9/96) [921]

### LAW, RUTH

**10005** Brown, Don. *Ruth Law Thrills a Nation* (1–3). Illus. 1993, Ticknor $15.00 (0-395-66404-7). 32pp. A simple biography about the woman flier who broke a nonstop cross-country record. (Rev: BL 8/93) [921]

### LEWIS AND CLARK

**10006** Kroll, Steven. *Lewis and Clark: Explorers of the American West* (1–5). Illus. by Richard Williams. 1994, Holiday LB $16.95 (0-8234-1034-X). 32pp. An appealing picture book that dramatically describes the famous journey of Lewis and Clark. (Rev: BCCB 11/94; BL 11/1/94; SLJ 9/94) [921]

**10007** Stein, R. Conrad. *Lewis and Clark* (3–5). Series: Cornerstones of Freedom. 1997, Children's LB $19.50 (0-516-20461-0). 32pp. A well-illustrated, attractive introduction to the famous Western expedition and the men who carried it out. (Rev: BL 12/15/97) [921]

### LINDBERGH, CHARLES

**10008** Burleigh, Robert. *Flight: The Journey of Charles Lindbergh* (2–4). Illus. by Mike Wimmer. 1991, Putnam $15.95 (0-399-22272-3). 32pp. A picture book that uses Lindbergh's autobiography as a basis for the text. (Rev: BCCB 11/91; BL 9/1/91*; HB 11–12/91*; SLJ 10/91) [921]

### MCAULIFFE, CHRISTA

**10009** Naden, Corinne J., and Rose Blue. *Christa McAuliffe: Teacher in Space* (3–5). Illus. Series: Gateway Biography. 1991, Millbrook LB $20.90 (1-56294-046-5). 48pp. Personal anecdotes about America's "first private citizen in space" are crisscrossed with space program information. (Rev: BL 1/1/92; SLJ 1/92) [921]

### MACCREADY, PAUL B.

**10010** Taylor, Richard L. *The First Human-Powered Flight: The Story of Paul B. MacCready and His Airplane, the Gossamer Condor* (4–8). Illus. Series: First Books on Aviation History. 1995, Watts LB $22.00 (0-531-20185-6). 63pp. After an introduction to the history of human-powered flight, this account focuses on MacCready's amazing flight in 1977. (Rev: SLJ 11/95) [921]

### MCNAIR, RONALD

**10011** Naden, Corinne J. *Ronald McNair* (5–7). Illus. Series: Black Americans of Achievement. 1991, Chelsea LB $19.95 (0-7910-1133-X). 109pp. The story of the second African-American astronaut, who died in the Challenger disaster. (Rev: SLJ 3/91) [921]

**10012** Shaw, Dena. *Ronald McNair: Challenger Astronaut* (5–8). Illus. Series: Junior World Biographies. 1994, Chelsea LB $15.95 (0-7910-2110-6); paper $4.95 (0-7910-2116-5). 79pp. The life story of the African American physicist who was killed in the 1986 Challenger explosion. (Rev: SLJ 12/94) [921]

### O'GRADY, SCOTT

**10013** O'Grady, Scott, and Michael French. *Basher Five-Two: The True Story of F-16 Fighter Pilot Captain Scott O'Grady* (5–8). Illus. 1997, Doubleday $16.95 (0-385-32300-X). 133pp. The true story of Scott O'Grady's survival ordeal after his F-16 fighter plane was shot down by the Serbs in Bosnia. (Rev: BCCB 7–8/97; HB 7–8/97; SLJ 7/97) [921]

### O'MALLEY, GRANIA

**10014** McCully, Emily Arnold. *The Pirate Queen* (1–3). Illus. 1995, Putnam $16.95 (0-399-22657-5). 32pp. The story of the Irish pirate queen Grania O'Malley, who was born in 1530 and later met England's Queen Elizabeth. (Rev: BCCB 10/95; BL 11/15/95; SLJ 11/95*) [921]

### PEARY, ROBERT E.

**10015** Anderson, Madelyn K. *Robert E. Peary and the Fight for the North Pole* (5–8). 1992, Watts LB $23.60 (0-531-13004-5). 120pp. This account has been assembled from Peary's writings and letters home to his wife. (Rev: SLJ 3/92) [921]

**10016** Charleston, Gordon. *Peary Reaches the North Pole* (4–6). Illus. Series: Great 20th Century Expeditions. 1993, Dillon LB $13.95 (0-87518-535-5). 32pp. Focuses on Peary's last expedition in 1910, in which he reached the North Pole. (Rev: BL 9/15/93; SLJ 9/93) [921]

### PIKE, ZEBULON

**10017** Sanford, William R., and Carl R. Green. *Zebulon Pike: Explorer of the Southwest* (4–6). Illus. Series: Legendary Heroes of the Wild West. 1996, Enslow LB $15.95 (0-89490-671-2). 48pp. The story of the Western explorer who, on one of his expeditions, traveled up the Arkansas River and sighted a peak later named after him. (Rev: BL 10/15/96; SLJ 9/96) [921]

## PIZARRO, GONZALO

**10018**  Jacobs, William J. *Pizarro: Conqueror of Peru* (4–6). Illus. Series: First Books. 1994, Watts LB $21.00 (0-531-20107-4). 63pp. The story of this Spanish explorer and his conquest of Peru is covered, with a brief, readable text and attractive illustrations. (Rev: SLJ 8/94) [921]

## POLO, MARCO

**10019**  Twist, Clint. *Marco Polo: Overland to Medieval China* (4–7). Illus. Series: Beyond the Horizons. 1994, Raintree Steck-Vaughn LB $24.26 (0-8114-7251-5). 48pp. This book concentrates on Marco Polo's journey to China, his reception, and the wonders he saw. (Rev: BL 8/94) [921]

## PONCE DE LEON, JUAN

**10020**  Dolan, Sean. *Juan Ponce de Leon* (5–8). Illus. Series: Hispanics of Achievement. 1995, Chelsea LB $19.95 (0-7910-2023-1). 112pp. The story of the conqueror and governor of Puerto Rico who also discovered Florida. (Rev: BL 10/15/95) [921]

## POST, WILEY

**10021**  Taylor, Richard L. *The First Solo Flight Around the World: The Story of Wiley Post and His Airplane, the Winnie Mae* (4–7). Illus. 1993, Watts LB $21.00 (0-531-20160-0). 64pp. In this exciting biography, we relive the triumphs of pioneer airplane pilot Wiley Post and his flights around the world. (Rev: BL 4/15/94; SLJ 2/94) [921]

## POWELL, JOHN WESLEY

**10022**  Bruns, Roger A. *John Wesley Powell: Explorer of the Grand Canyon* (5–8). Illus. Series: Historical American Biographies. 1997, Enslow LB $19.95 (0-89490-783-2). 128pp. This biography tells about Powell's youth, education, and Civil War days, as well as his many expeditions and research activities. (Rev: SLJ 10/97) [921]

## RODGERS, CALBRAITH PERRY

**10023**  Taylor, Richard L. *The First Flight Across the United States: The Story of Calbraith Perry Rodgers and His Airplane, the Vin Fiz* (4–7). Illus. 1993, Watts LB $21.00 (0-531-20159-7). 64pp. This is the exciting story of Calbraith Perry Rodgers, the first man to fly across the United States. (Rev: BL 4/15/94; SLJ 2/94) [921]

## VAN METER, VICKI

**10024**  Van Meter, Vicki, and Dan Gutman. *Taking Flight: My Story* (4–6). 1995, Viking paper $14.99 (0-670-86260-6). 96pp. The autobiography of the young girl who learned to fly at age 10 and 2 years later piloted a plane across the Atlantic. (Rev: BCCB 11/95; BL 6/1–15/95; SLJ 8/95) [921]

## YEAGER, CHUCK

**10025**  Stein, R. Conrad. *Chuck Yeager Breaks the Sound Barrier* (3–5). Illus. Series: Cornerstones of Freedom. 1997, Children's LB $19.50 (0-516-20294-4). 32pp. A well-organized, illustrated account of this historical aviation event that also gives details of Yeager's life, before and after breaking the sound barrier. (Rev: BL 6/1–15/97) [921]

# Artists, Composers, Entertainers, and Writers

## Collective

**10026** Bredeson, Carmen. *American Writers of the 20th Century* (5–8). Illus. 1996, Enslow LB $19.95 (0-89490-704-2). 104pp. Ten writers for adults, like Toni Morrison and F. Scott Fitzgerald, are profiled briefly. (Rev: BL 6/1–15/96; SLJ 9/96) [920]

**10027** Ehrlich, Amy, ed. *When I Was Your Age* (5–8). 1996, Candlewick $15.99 (1-56402-306-0). 160pp. Ten well-known writers — e.g., Avi, Susan Cooper, and Nicholasa Mohr — recall incidents from their childhood. (Rev: BCCB 4/96; BL 4/15/96; SLJ 8/96) [810.9]

**10028** Glubok, Shirley. *Great Lives: Painting* (5–8). 1994, Scribners $24.95 (0-684-19052-4). 256pp. Brief biographies of 23 artists, including 5 Americans: Homer, Whistler, Church, Cassatt, and O'Keeffe. Illustrated with reproductions and photos of the artists at work. (Rev: SLJ 7/94) [920]

**10029** Hacker, Carlotta. *Great African Americans in Jazz* (3–5). Series: Outstanding African Americans. 1997, Crabtree LB $21.28 (0-86505-804-0); paper $8.95 (0-86505-818-0). 64pp. Seven portraits of great African American jazz musicians are given, among them Louis Armstrong, Duke Ellington, Billie Holiday, and Bessie Smith, plus 7 other mini profiles. (Rev: BL 9/15/97) [920]

**10030** Hacker, Carlotta. *Great African Americans in the Arts* (3–5). Series: Outstanding African Americans. 1997, Crabtree LB $21.28 (0-86505-807-5); paper $8.95 (0-86505-821-0). 64pp. Seven African Americans — e.g., Gordon Parks, Alvin Ailey, and Marion Anderson — are given lengthy coverage, with 7 others introduced in shorter profiles. (Rev: BL 9/15/97; SLJ 12/97) [920]

**10031** Hudson, Wade, and Cheryl W. Hudson, comps. *In Praise of Our Fathers and Our Mothers: A Black Family Treasury by Outstanding Authors and Artists* (4–7). Illus. 1997, Just Us $29.95 (0-940975-59-9). 131pp. A collection of reminiscences of family life told by 40 African American writers and illustrators, e.g., Virginia Hamilton and Walter Dean Myers. (Rev: HB 3–4/97; SLJ 6/97) [920]

**10032** Jackson, Nancy. *Photographers: History and Culture Through the Camera* (5–8). Illus. Series: American Profiles. 1997, Facts on File $19.95 (0-8160-3358-7). 134pp. Short biographies of 8 famous photographers are given, including Matthew Brady, Alfred Stieglitz, Edward Steichen, and Gordon Parks. (Rev: SLJ 7/97) [920]

**10033** Krull, Kathleen. *Lives of the Artists: Masterpieces, Messes (and What the Neighbors Thought)* (4–6). Illus. by Kathryn Hewitt. 1995, Harcourt $20.00 (0-15-200103-4). 96pp. Nineteen thumbnail sketches on such artists as van Gogh, O'Keeffe, and Warhol. (Rev: BCCB 11/95; BL 11/1/95; SLJ 10/95) [920]

**10034** Krull, Kathleen. *Lives of the Musicians: Good Times, Bad Times (and What the Neighbors Thought)* (3–6). 1993, Harcourt $20.00 (0-15-248010-2). 96pp. This book contains lively biographies of 19 composers, including Bach, Beethoven, Chopin, Gershwin, and Joplin. (Rev: BCCB 4/93; BL 4/1/93*; SLJ 5/93*) [920]

**10035** Krull, Kathleen. *Lives of the Writers: Comedies, Tragedies (and What the Neighbors Thought)* (3–6). Illus. by Kathryn Hewitt. 1994, Harcourt $18.95 (0-15-248009-9). 96pp. Twenty profiles of authors, some well known, like E. B. White and Shakespeare, and others more obscure. (Rev: BCCB 10/94; BL 9/15/94; SLJ 10/94*) [920]

**10036** Press, Skip. *Candice and Edgar Bergen* (4–8). Illus. Series: Star Families. 1995, Silver Burdett paper $7.95 (0-382-24940-2). 48pp. The story of a father and daughter who had vastly different talents, yet each became a star. (Rev: SLJ 9/95) [920]

**10037** Press, Skip. *Natalie and Nat King Cole* (4–8). Illus. Series: Star Families. 1995, Silver Burdett LB $15.95 (0-89686-879-6); paper $4.95 (0-382-24942-9). 48pp. A short book that describes the upbringing and home life of Natalie Cole and her father's influence on her career. (Rev: SLJ 9/95) [920]

**10038** Rediger, Pat. *Great African Americans in Entertainment* (4–6). Illus. Series: Outstanding African Americans. 1996, Crabtree LB $21.28 (0-86505-799-0); paper $8.95 (0-86505-813-X). 64pp. Bill Cosby, Spike Lee, and Whoopi Goldberg are 3 of the 13 African Americans profiled. (Rev: BL 9/15/96) [920]

**10039** Rediger, Pat. *Great African Americans in Literature* (4–6). Illus. Series: Outstanding African Americans. 1996, Crabtree LB $21.28 (0-86505-802-4); paper $8.95 (0-86505-816-4). 64pp. Some of the 13 African Americans profiled are Maya Angelou, Toni Morrison, James Baldwin, and Alex Haley. (Rev: BL 9/15/96; SLJ 8/96) [920]

**10040** Rediger, Pat. *Great African Americans in Music* (4–6). Illus. Series: Outstanding African Americans. 1996, Crabtree LB $21.28 (0-86505-800-8); paper $8.95 (0-86505-814-8). 64pp. Ray Charles, Nat King Cole, Ella Fitzgerald, and the rapper Hammer are profiled, along with 9 others. (Rev: BL 9/15/96) [920]

**10041** Rylant, Cynthia. *Margaret, Frank, and Andy: Three Writers' Stories* (3–6). Illus. 1996, Harcourt $15.00 (0-15-201083-1). 56pp. Three writers for children — Margaret Wise Brown, L. Frank Baum, and E. B. White — are lovingly introduced. (Rev: BL 1/1–15/97; SLJ 11/96) [920]

**10042** Sills, Leslie. *Inspirations: Stories About Women Artists* (5–7). Illus. 1989, Whitman LB $17.95 (0-8075-3649-0). 56pp. The stories of 4 talented women who followed their career dreams to success. (Rev: BCCB 1/89; BL 2/1/89; SLJ 1/89)

**10043** Sills, Leslie. *Visions: Stories About Women Artists* (5–8). Illus. 1993, Whitman LB $18.95 (0-8075-8491-6). 58pp. The lives of 4 women artists — Cassatt, Saar, Carrington, and Frank — are covered in text and reproductions of their art. (Rev: BCCB 3/93; HB 7–8/93; SLJ 5/93) [920]

**10044** Sullivan, George. *Black Artists in Photography, 1840–1940* (5–8). Illus. 1996, Dutton paper $16.99 (0-525-65208-6). 112pp. Features 7 African American photographers of importance who worked between 1840 and 1940. (Rev: BL 10/15/96; SLJ 10/96) [920]

**10045** Ventura, Piero. *Great Composers* (5–8). 1989, Putnam $25.95 (0-399-21746-0). 124pp. Thumbnail

profiles of the world's greatest composers are given in this large-format book. (Rev: SLJ 4/90) [920]

**10046** Wolf, Sylvia. *Focus: Five Women Photographers* (5–8). Illus. 1994, Albert Whitman LB $18.95 (0-8075-2531-6). 64pp. Biographies of 5 women photographers, 2 from the past (e.g., Margaret Bourke-White) and 3 from the present (e.g., Lorna Simpson), all accompanied by excellent reproductions of their work. (Rev: BCCB 11/94; BL 10/15/94; HB 11–12/94; SLJ 11/94) [920]

# Artists

## ADAMS, ANSEL

**10047** Dunlap, Julie. *Eye on the Wild: A Story About Ansel Adams* (3–6). Illus. Series: Creative Minds Books. 1995, Carolrhoda LB $19.93 (0-87614-944-1). 64pp. A brief biography about the great nature photographer Ansel Adams. (Rev: BL 10/15/95; SLJ 12/95) [921]

## AUDUBON, JOHN JAMES

**10048** Kastner, Joseph. *John James Audubon* (5–8). Illus. Series: First Impressions. 1992, Abrams $19.95 (0-8109-1918-4). 92pp. A lively account of the adventurous life of Audubon, with many fine art reproductions. (Rev: HB 3–4/93; SLJ 12/92) [921]

**10049** Roop, Peter, and Connie Roop, eds. *Capturing Nature* (5–7). Illus. by Rick Farley. 1993, Walker LB $17.85 (0-8027-8205-1). 48pp. Audubon's prints and original paintings and excerpts from his journals are combined to produce a stunning biography. (Rev: BCCB 12/93; BL 12/15/93; SLJ 1/94) [921]

## BOURKE-WHITE, MARGARET

**10050** Welch, Catherine A. *Margaret Bourke-White* (2–4). Illus. 1997, Carolrhoda LB $18.60 (0-87614-890-9). 56pp. The life of this outstanding photographer reveals the excitement and danger involved in her work. (Rev: BL 9/1/97; SLJ 8/97) [921]

## CALDER, ALEXANDER

**10051** Lipman, Jean, and Margaret Aspenwall. *Alexander Calder and His Magical Mobiles* (5–8). Illus. 1981, Hudson Hills $19.95 (0-933920-17-2). 96pp. An exciting biography of this controversial sculptor.

## CARLE, ERIC

**10052** Carle, Eric. *Flora and Tiger: 19 Very Short Stories from My Life* (4–8). Illus. 1997, Putnam $17.95 (0-399-23203-6). 57pp. An autobiography of the famous picture book artist who was born in Germany but who has lived in the United States since 1952. (Rev: BL 12/15/97; SLJ 2/98) [921]

## CASSATT, MARY

**10053** Brooks, Philip. *Mary Cassatt: An American in Paris* (4–7). Illus. Series: First Books. 1995, Watts LB $22.00 (0-531-20183-X). 64pp. A biography of the American artist who found fulfillment painting in Paris. (Rev: BL 10/1/95; HB 1–2/95; SLJ 10/95) [921]

**10054** Meyer, Susan E. *Mary Cassatt* (4–8). Illus. Series: First Impressions. 1991, Abrams $19.95 (0-8109-3154-0). 92pp. The story of the American artist who spent her most productive painting years in France. (Rev: SLJ 5/91) [921]

## CATLIN, GEORGE

**10055** Plain, Nancy. *The Man Who Painted Indians: George Catlin* (3–6). Series: Biographies. 1996, Benchmark LB $21.36 (0-7614-0486-4). 48pp. The story of the artist, born in 1796, who left his law career to live in the American wilderness and paint its people and places. (Rev: SLJ 2/97) [921]

## CÉZANNE, PAUL

**10056** Sellier, Marie. *Cézanne from A to Z* (4–8). Trans. from French by Claudia Zoe Bedrick. Illus. Series: Artists from A to Z. 1996, Bedrick LB $14.95 (0-87226-476-9). 59pp. An imaginative, well-executed account that covers the life and works of Cézanne. (Rev: SLJ 5/96) [921]

## CHANG, WAH MING

**10057** Riley, Gail B. *Wah Ming Chang: Artist and Master of Special Effects* (4–8). Illus. Series: Multicultural Junior Biographies. 1995, Enslow LB $18.95 (0-89490-639-9). 112pp. A thorough, well-documented biography of this Chinese American, who has gained prominence in the field of special effects. (Rev: BL 2/15/96; SLJ 2/96) [921]

## CLOSE, CHUCK

**10058** Greenberg, Jan, and Sandra Jordan. *Chuck Close, Up Close* (3–6). Illus. 1998, DK Publg. $19.95 (0-7894-2486-X). 48pp. The inspiring story of the contemporary artist who suffered a learning disability as a youngster, became a famous artist, and had to start over after an attack of paralysis. (Rev: SLJ 3/98*) [921]

## DAY, TOM

**10059** Lyons, Mary E. *Master of Mahogany: Tom Day, Free Black Cabinetmaker* (5–8). Illus. 1994, Scribners paper $15.95 (0-684-19675-1). 48pp. The

story of a free black in the 18th century who excelled as a woodcarver in North Carolina. (Rev: BL 10/1/94; HB 11–12/94; SLJ 10/94*) [921]

## DEGAS, EDGAR

**10060** Skira-Venturi, Rosabianca. *A Weekend with Degas* (3–8). Illus. Series: A Weekend With. 1992, Rizzoli $19.95 (0-8478-1439-4). 64pp. This account, told through the voice of the artist, introduces the reader to Degas, his art, and his life. (Rev: BL 8/92; HB 7–8/92; SLJ 6/92) [921]

## DESJARLAIT, PATRICK

**10061** Williams, Neva. *Patrick DesJarlait: Conversations with a Native American Artist* (5–7). Illus. 1994, Lerner LB $22.60 (0-8225-3151-8). 56pp. A beautifully illustrated biography of the Native American artist who worked at the Red Lake Indian Reservation in Minnesota. (Rev: BL 1/1/95; SLJ 1/95) [921]

## DISNEY, WALT

**10062** Cole, Michael D. *Walt Disney: Creator of Mickey Mouse* (4–7). Illus. Series: People to Know. 1996, Enslow LB $19.95 (0-89490-694-1). 112pp. A thoughtful biography of the great animator, perfectionist, and founder of an entertainment empire. (Rev: BL 6/1–15/96; SLJ 8/96) [921]

**10063** Ford, Barbara. *Walt Disney* (4–8). Illus. 1989, Walker LB $16.85 (0-8027-6865-2). 160pp. The story of Disney's youth and his struggle to fulfill his dreams. (Rev: BL 5/15/89)

**10064** Schroeder, Russell, ed. *Walt Disney: His Life in Pictures* (4–6). Illus. 1996, Disney LB $14.89 (0-7868-5043-4). 64pp. This pictorial biography of Walt Disney uses quotes from interviews, films, and articles. (Rev: BCCB 11/96; SLJ 10/96) [921]

**10065** Selden, Bernice. *The Story of Walt Disney, Maker of Magical Worlds* (4–6). Illus. Series: Yearling Biographies. 1989, Dell paper $3.99 (0-440-40240-9). 92pp. A balanced account of the genius who established the art of animation in Hollywood. (Rev: BL 3/15/90; SLJ 4/90) [921]

## EL GRECO

**10066** Venezia, Mike. *El Greco* (2–4). Series: Getting to Know the World's Greatest Artists/Composers. 1997, Children's LB $21.00 (0-516-20586-2). 32pp. This appealing introduction to El Greco and his works contains several color reproductions plus the author's playful cartoons. (Rev: BL 10/15/97) [921]

## EVANS, MINNIE

**10067** Lyons, Mary E. *Painting Dreams: Minnie Evans, Visionary Artist* (5–7). Illus. 1996, Houghton $14.95 (0-395-72032-X). 48pp. The life of the deeply religious African American folk artist Millie Evans. (Rev: BCCB 9/96; BL 7/96; SLJ 7/96) [921]

## FOREMAN, MICHAEL

**10068** Foreman, Michael. *After the War Was Over* (4–8). Illus. 1996, Arcade $18.95 (1-55970-329-6). 95pp. A memoir by a British artist about growing up in an English coastal village after World War II. A sequel to *War Game* (1990). (Rev: BL 5/15/96) [921]

## GOGH, VINCENT VAN

**10069** Dionetti, Michelle. *Painting the Wind* (1–4). Illus. by Kevin Hawkes. 1996, Little, Brown $15.95 (0-316-18602-3). 32pp. Van Gogh's last tormented years in Arles, France, as seen through the eyes of his housekeeper's daughter. (Rev: BL 10/1/96; SLJ 10/96) [921]

**10070** Harrison, Peter. *Vincent van Gogh* (5–7). Illus. Series: Art for Young People. 1996, Sterling $14.95 (0-8069-6156-2). 32pp. This book gives a multifaceted view of van Gogh and his work through good biographical coverage, fine reproductions, incisive critical comments, and interesting asides. (Rev: BL 3/15/97; SLJ 8/96) [921]

**10071** Lucas, Eileen. *Vincent van Gogh* (2–4). Illus. 1997, Carolrhoda LB $13.13 (1-57505-038-2). 56pp. A simple biography that captures the life and anxieties of the artist, with a good commentary on his work. (Rev: BCCB 9/96; BL 9/1/97; SLJ 9/97) [921]

## GORMAN, R. C.

**10072** Hermann, Spring. *R. C. Gorman: Navajo Artist* (4–8). Illus. Series: Multicultural Junior Biographies. 1995, Enslow LB $19.95 (0-89490-638-0). 104pp. The story of this contemporary Native American artist, who reflects his heritage in his work. (Rev: BL 2/15/96; SLJ 3/96) [921]

## GOYA, FRANCISCO

**10073** Venezia, Mike. *Francisco Goya* (2–5). Illus. Series: Getting to Know the World's Greatest Artists. 1991, Children's LB $21.00 (0-516-02292-X). 32pp. This is an introduction to the life and work of the great Spanish portrait artist who was also a bitter social satirist. (Rev: BL 8/91; SLJ 12/91) [921]

**10074** Waldron, Ann. *Francisco Goya* (5–8). Illus. Series: First Impressions. 1992, Abrams $19.95 (0-8109-3368-3). 92pp. Covers the stormy life of Goya and the many intrigues at court, along with many reproductions. (Rev: SLJ 12/92) [921]

## HOMER, WINSLOW

**10075** Beneduce, Ann Keay. *A Weekend with Winslow Homer* (3–8). Illus. Series: Weekend With. 1993, Rizzoli $19.95 (0-8478-1622-2). 64pp. An introduction to the famous New England painter of landscapes and the sea, with an explanation of his importance and a sampling of his work. (Rev: BL 12/15/93; SLJ 11/93) [921]

## KAHLO, FRIDA

**10076** Frazier, Nancy. *Frida Kahlo: Mysterious Painter* (5–7). Illus. Series: Library of Famous Women. 1993, Rosen LB $15.95 (1-56711-012-6). 64pp. A biography of this enigmatic artist with examples of her work. (Rev: BL 2/15/93) [921]

**10077** Garza, Hedda. *Frida Kahlo* (5–8). Illus. Series: Hispanics of Achievement. 1994, Chelsea LB $19.95 (0-7910-1698-6); paper $8.95 (0-7910-1699-4). 120pp. The life story of the famous and colorful Mexican artist and her many accomplishments. (Rev: BL 3/1/94) [921]

**10078** Turner, Robyn Montana. *Frida Kahlo* (3–6). Illus. Series: Portraits of Women Artists for Children. 1993, Little, Brown $16.95 (0-316-85651-7). 32pp. With many color reproductions of her paintings, this is the fascinating life of the fine painter whose accomplishments are often overshadowed by the work of her husband, Diego Rivera. (Rev: BL 4/1/93; HB 5–6/93; SLJ 5/93) [921]

## KEATS, EZRA JACK

**10079** Engel, Dean, and Florence B. Freedman. *Ezra Jack Keats: A Biography with Illustrations* (3–6). Illus. 1995, Silver Moon $21.95 (1-881889-65-3). 96pp. Using first-hand sources, including interviews, this is the story of the artist/author best known for *The Snowy Day*. (Rev: BCCB 9/95; BL 4/15/95; HB 5–6/95, 9–10/95; SLJ 6/95) [921]

## KLEE, PAUL

**10080** Venezia, Mike. *Paul Klee* (2–5). Illus. Series: Getting to Know the World's Greatest Artists. 1991, Children's LB $21.00 (0-516-02294-6). 32pp. An informal, simple biography of this Swiss artist, as well as many examples of his work and comments on his style. (Rev: BL 1/15/92) [921]

## KURELEK, WILLIAM

**10081** Kurelek, William. *A Prairie Boy's Summer* (3–5). Illus. by author. 1975, Houghton $7.95 (0-395-20280-9); Tundra paper $7.95 (0-88776-116-X). 48pp. Each of this Canadian artist's paintings depicts a farm activity, which the accompanying text describes in this companion piece to the author's earlier *A Prairie Boy's Winter* (1984).

## LANGE, DOROTHEA

**10082** Turner, Robyn Montana. *Dorothea Lange* (3–6). Illus. Series: Portraits of Women Artists for Children. 1994, Little, Brown $16.95 (0-316-85656-8). 32pp. The life story of the artist who pioneered the field of documentary photography. (Rev: BL 9/1/94; SLJ 10/94) [921]

## LEONARDO DA VINCI

**10083** Hart, Tony. *Leonardo da Vinci* (3–5). Illus. by Susan Hellard. Series: Famous Children. 1994, Barron's paper $5.95 (0-8120-1828-1). This biography focuses on the childhood of Leonardo and how his genius was shown at an early age. (Rev: SLJ 8/94) [921]

**10084** Mason, Antony. *Leonardo da Vinci* (4–8). Illus. 1994, Barron's $10.95 (0-8120-6460-7); paper $6.95 (0-8120-1997-0). 32pp. A brief biography that chronicles the achievements of this multifaceted genius and supplies pictures of some of his great triumphs. (Rev: BL 12/1/94) [921]

**10085** Provensen, Alice, and Martin Provensen. *Leonardo da Vinci: The Artist, Inventor, Scientist in Three-Dimensional, Movable Pictures* (3–5). Illus. by authors. 1984, Viking paper $19.95 (0-670-42384-X). 12pp. Pop-up or movable paintings show some of Leonardo's great inventions and creations.

**10086** Stanley, Diane. *Leonardo da Vinci* (3–7). Illus. 1996, Morrow LB $15.93 (0-688-10438-X). 48pp. Both the life of the artist and an introduction to the Italian Renaissance are contained in this beautifully illustrated book. (Rev: BCCB 9/96; BL 9/15/96*; SLJ 9/96*) [921]

**10087** Venezia, Mike. *Da Vinci* (2–5). Illus. by author. Series: Getting to Know the World's Greatest Artists. 1989, Children's LB $21.00 (0-516-02275-X). 32pp. Using text, cartoons, and the artist's paintings, this is an introduction to the life and work of Leonardo da Vinci. (Rev: SLJ 3/90) [921]

## LIN, MAYA

**10088** Italia, Bob. *Maya Lin: Honoring Our Forgotten Heroes* (3–5). Illus. Series: Everyone Contributes. 1993, ABDO LB $13.98 (1-56239-234-4). 32pp. A biography of the architect who designed the Vietnam Veterans Memorial in Washington, D.C. (Rev: BL 12/1/93; SLJ 12/93) [921]

**10089** Ling, Bettina. *Maya Lin* (5–7). Illus. Series: Contemporary Asian Americans. 1997, Raintree Steck-Vaughn LB $24.26 (0-8172-3992-8). 48pp. A profile of the Asian American architect and an introduction to many of her projects, including the Vietnam War Memorial in Washington, D.C. (Rev: BL 5/1/97) [921]

**10090** Malone, Mary. *Maya Lin: Architect and Artist* (4–6). Illus. Series: People to Know. 1995, Enslow LB $19.95 (0-89490-499-X). 112pp. The life story of the renowned architect best known for her Vietnam Veterans Memorial. (Rev: BL 4/15/95; SLJ 5/95) [921]

## MARTINEZ, MARIA

**10091** Anderson, Peter. *Maria Martinez: Pueblo Potter* (3–5). Illus. Series: Picture-Story Biographies. 1992, Children's LB $18.20 (0-516-04184-3). 32pp. The story of the nationally acclaimed Indian potter who developed her craft from her people's traditions. (Rev: BL 1/1/93; SLJ 1/93) [921]

**10092** Morris, Juddi. *Tending the Fire: The Story of Maria Martinez* (5–8). 1997, Northland LB $12.95 (0-87358-665-4); paper $6.95 (0-87358-654-9). 120pp. The life story of New Mexico's most famous potter, who was born in an Indian pueblo in 1887. (Rev: BL 12/1/97; SLJ 1/98) [921]

## MATISSE, HENRI

**10093** Venezia, Mike. *Henri Matisse* (2–4). Illus. Series: Getting to Know the World's Greatest Artists/Composers. 1997, Children's LB $20.30 (0-516-20311-8). 32pp. A light but realistic overview of Matisse and his work, with many color reproductions, clever cartoon illustrations, and an interesting story line. (Rev: BL 7/97) [921]

## MICHELANGELO

**10094** Hart, Tony. *Michelangelo* (3–5). Illus. by Susan Hellard. Series: Famous Children. 1994, Barron's paper $5.95 (0-8120-1827-3). An attractive biography that focuses on the boyhood of Michelangelo and how he revealed his genius as a young apprentice. (Rev: SLJ 8/94) [921]

## MILLER, TOM

**10095** Miller, Tom, and Camay C. Murphy. *Can a Coal Scuttle Fly?* (2–5). Illus. 1996, Maryland Historical Soc. $14.00 (0-938420-55-0). 32pp. Baltimore artist Tom Miller tells about his life and the great joy that can be found in art. (Rev: BL 10/15/96) [921]

## MONET, CLAUDE

**10096** Harrison, Peter. *Claude Monet* (5–7). Illus. Series: Art for Young People. 1996, Sterling $14.95 (0-8069-6158-9). 32pp. Double-page spreads act as chapters in this book that combines biographical material with good reproductions of paintings and interesting critical comments. (Rev: BCCB 9/96; BL 3/15/97; SLJ 8/96) [921]

**10097** Koja, Stephan, and Katja Miksovsky. *Claude Monet: The Magician of Color* (3–7). Trans. by Andrea Belloli. Illus. Series: Adventures in Art. 1997, Prestel $14.95 (3-7913-1812-8). A straightforward biography of Monet that is enlivened by drawings, paintings, and photos. (Rev: SLJ 1/98) [921]

**10098** Venezia, Mike. *Monet* (2–5). Illus. Series: Getting to Know the World's Greatest Artists. 1990, Children's LB $21.00 (0-516-02276-8). 32pp. Using many paintings by Monet, this book introduces the reader to impressionism. (Rev: SLJ 11/90) [921]

MOORE, HENRY

**10099** Gardner, Jane M. *Henry Moore: From Bones and Stones to Sketches and Sculptures* (2–4). Illus. 1993, Macmillan $15.95 (0-02-735812-7). 32pp. A simple biography told mainly through photographs of the great British 20th-century sculptor, Henry Moore. (Rev: BCCB 4/93; BL 4/15/93; HB 7–8/93; SLJ 6/93) [921]

MOSES, GRANDMA

**10100** Oneal, Zibby. *Grandma Moses: Painter of Rural America* (5–7). Illus. by Donna Ruff. 1987, Puffin paper $4.99 (0-14-032220-5). 64pp. The story of Anna Mary Robertson, who became famous as Grandma Moses. (Rev: BCCB 10/86; BL 11/1/86; SLJ 10/86)

MOUNT, WILLIAM SIDNEY

**10101** Howard, Nancy S. *William Sidney Mount: Painter of Rural America* (4–7). Illus. 1994, Sterling $14.95 (1-87192-275-4). 48pp. An interactive book that explores the work and paintings of the 19th-century American painter William Sidney Mount. (Rev: BL 1/15/95) [921]

O'KEEFFE, GEORGIA

**10102** Ball, Jacqueline A., and Catherine Conant. *Georgia O'Keeffe: Painter of the Desert* (5–8). Illus. Series: Library of Famous Women. 1991, Blackbirch LB $15.95 (1-56711-033-9). 64pp. The focus is on O'Keeffe's life, stressing her independence and artistic talents. (Rev: BL 3/15/91) [921]

**10103** Brooks, Philip. *Georgia O'Keeffe: An Adventurous Spirit* (4–7). Illus. Series: First Books. 1995, Watts $21.00 (0-531-20182-1). 64pp. An insightful portrait of the American artist and her internal struggle to paint what, how, and where she chose. (Rev: BL 10/1/95; SLJ 10/95) [921]

**10104** Lowery, Linda. *Georgia O'Keeffe* (2–4). Illus. 1996, Carolrhoda LB $18.60 (0-87614-860-7); paper $5.95 (0-87614-898-4). 48pp. A simple account of the life and work of this amazing painter of the Southwest. (Rev: BL 9/1/96; SLJ 8/96) [921]

PEALE, CHARLES WILLSON

**10105** Wilson, Janet. *The Ingenious Mr. Peale: Painter, Patriot and Man of Science* (5–8). Illus. 1996, Simon & Schuster $16.00 (0-689-31884-7). 122pp. A profile of the famous portrait painter of the colonial period, with details about his varied interests. (Rev: BCCB 6/96; BL 5/15/96; SLJ 6/96*) [921]

PEET, BILL

**10106** Peet, Bill. *Bill Peet: An Autobiography* (2–5). Illus. 1989, Houghton $20.00 (0-395-50932-7). 192pp. The autobiography of the author/illustrator who worked at the Disney Studio for many years. (Rev: BL 7/89; HB 7–8/89*; SLJ 7/89) [921]

PICASSO, PABLO

**10107** Hart, Tony. *Picasso* (3–5). Illus. by Susan Hellard. Series: Famous Children. 1994, Barron's paper $5.95 (0-8120-1826-5). Visually attractive, this biography limits its coverage to the childhood of Picasso, who was the son of rich, indulgent parents. (Rev: SLJ 8/94) [921]

**10108** Meadows, Matthew. *Pablo Picasso* (5–7). Illus. Series: Art for Young People. 1996, Sterling $14.95 (0-8069-6160-0). 32pp. In double-page spreads, presents the life and work of this multitalented Spanish artist. (Rev: BL 2/1/97; HB 5–6/96; SLJ 3/97) [921]

**10109** Selfridge, John W. *Pablo Picasso* (5–8). Illus. Series: Hispanics of Achievement. 1993, Chelsea LB $19.95 (0-7910-1777-X). 120pp. A colorful biography of this great Spanish painter, who lived most of his life as a political exile in France. (Rev: BL 3/1/94) [921]

**10110** Venezia, Mike. *Picasso* (PS–4). Illus. 1988, Children's LB $21.00 (0-516-02271-7); paper $6.95 (0-516-42271-5). 32pp. Amusing facts are tucked in with information about the artist and his work. (Rev: BL 10/1/88; SLJ 9/88)

PIPPIN, HORACE

**10111** Lyons, Mary E. *Starting Home: The Story of Horace Pippin, Painter* (5–7). Illus. Series: African-American Artists and Artisans. 1993, Scribners $15.95 (0-684-19534-8). 48pp. The story of this self-taught African American painter who depicted the horrors of World War I in his work. (Rev: BL 11/15/93; SLJ 2/94) [921]

POWERS, HARRIET

**10112** Lyons, Mary E. *Stitching Stars: The Story Quilts of Harriet Powers* (5–7). Illus. Series: African-American Artists and Artisans. 1993, Scribners

$17.00 (0-684-19576-3). 48pp. After Emancipation, this former slave created 2 huge story quilts that hang today in the Smithsonian and Boston's Museum of Fine Arts. (Rev: BCCB 12/93; BL 11/15/93; SLJ 2/94) [921]

### REMBRANDT VAN RIJN

**10113** Bonafoux, Pascal. *A Weekend with Rembrandt* (3–8). Illus. Series: A Weekend With. 1992, Rizzoli $19.95 (0-8478-1441-6). 64pp. Lavish illustrations introduce Rembrandt, his training, technique, and creative style. (Rev: BL 8/92; HB 1–2/93; SLJ 6/92) [921]

**10114** Venezia, Mike. *Rembrandt* (PS–4). Illus. 1988, Children's LB $20.30 (0-516-02272-5); paper $6.95 (0-516-42272-3). 32pp. Learning about art and great artists can be fun. (Rev: BL 10/1/88; SLJ 9/88)

### RENOIR, AUGUSTE

**10115** Parsons, Tom. *Pierre Auguste Renoir* (5–7). Illus. Series: Art for Young People. 1996, Sterling $14.95 (0-8069-6162-7). 32pp. The life and work of this prolific French artist are examined in a series of double-page spreads. (Rev: BL 2/1/97; SLJ 3/97) [921]

**10116** Venezia, Mike. *Pierre Auguste Renoir* (2–4). Illus. Series: Getting to Know the World's Greatest Artists/Composers. 1996, Children's LB $21.00 (0-516-02225-3). 32pp. This biography includes examples of Renoir's paintings and an introduction to Impressionism. (Rev: BL 9/15/96; SLJ 12/96) [921]

### RIVERA, DIEGO

**10117** Braun, Barbara. *A Weekend with Diego Rivera* (3–8). Illus. Series: Weekend With. 1994, Rizzoli $19.95 (0-8478-1749-0). 64pp. A well-researched introduction to the life and work of this Mexican artist, best known as a muralist. (Rev: BL 9/15/94; SLJ 5/94) [921]

### ROCKWELL, NORMAN

**10118** Cohen, Joel H. *Norman Rockwell: America's Best-Loved Illustrator* (4–6). Illus. 1997, Watts LB $21.00 (0-531-20266-6). 64pp. Using 16 full-color reproductions, this book introduces the life of this all-American artist who lived in small towns in New England and painted their inhabitants. (Rev: BL 11/1/97; SLJ 8/97) [921]

**10119** Durrett, Deanne. *Norman Rockwell* (4–8). Illus. Series: The Importance Of. 1997, Lucent LB $22.45 (1-56006-080-8). 95pp. An introduction to the life and work of this beloved New England artist whose paintings glorified everyday American life. (Rev: BL 1/1–15/97) [921]

### ROUSSEAU, HENRI

**10120** Plazy, Gilles. *A Weekend with Rousseau* (3–8). Illus. Series: Weekend With. 1993, Rizzoli $19.95 (0-8478-1717-2). 64pp. Using the format of a visit, the life and work of this great French primitive painter are presented. (Rev: BL 1/15/94; SLJ 11/93) [921]

### RUSSELL, CHARLES

**10121** Winter, Jeanette. *Cowboy Charlie: The Story of Charles M. Russell* (K–4). Illus. 1995, Harcourt $15.00 (0-15-200857-8). 32pp. Chronicles Russell's lifelong love of the West and his career immortalizing it in paintings. (Rev: BCCB 10/95; BL 11/1/95; SLJ 12/95) [921]

### SIMMONS, PHILIP

**10122** Lyons, Mary E. *Catching the Fire: Philip Simmons, Blacksmith* (3–6). Illus. 1997, Houghton $16.00 (0-395-72033-8). 48pp. A biography of a master craftsman and blacksmith, the African American Philip Simmons. (Rev: BL 9/1/97*; HB 9–10/97; SLJ 9/97) [921]

### STEIFF, MARGARETE

**10123** Greene, Carol. *Margarete Steiff: Toy Maker* (2–4). Illus. Series: Rookie Biography. 1993, Children's LB $19.00 (0-516-04257-2). 48pp. The inspiring story of a woman who conquered physical handicaps to become a famous toy maker. (Rev: BL 2/15/94; SLJ 2/94) [921]

### TOULOUSE-LAUTREC, HENRI DE

**10124** Hart, Tony. *Toulouse-Lautrec* (3–5). Illus. by Susan Hellard. Series: Famous Children. 1994, Barron's paper $5.95 (0-8120-1825-7). This visually attractive biography is limited in scope to the childhood of Toulouse-Lautrec, when he suffered a crippling disease. (Rev: SLJ 8/94) [921]

### WARHOL, ANDY

**10125** Venezia, Mike. *Andy Warhol* (2–4). Illus. Series: Getting to Know the World's Greatest Artists/Composers. 1996, Children's LB $21.00 (0-516-20053-4); paper $6.95 (0-516-26075-8). 32pp. An appealing introduction to this pop artist's life and work, with many fine art reproductions. (Rev: BL 12/15/96; HB 5–6/96) [921]

### WILLIAMS, PAUL R.

**10126** Hudson, Karen E. *The Will and the Way: Paul R. Williams, Architect* (5–7). Illus. 1994, Rizzoli $14.95 (0-8478-1780-6). 64pp. The story of this African American architect who, in his career from the 1920s to the 1970s, designed more than 3,000 buildings. (Rev: BL 2/15/94; SLJ 3/94) [921]

## WOOD, GRANT

**10127** Duggleby, John. *Artist in Overalls: The Life of Grant Wood* (5–7). Illus. 1996, Chronicle $15.95 (0-8118-1242-1). 48pp. The life of this American artist tells of his difficult struggle with poverty and his great attachment to the Midwest. (Rev: BCCB 6/96; BL 4/15/96; HB 7–8/96; SLJ 5/96) [921]

## WOOD, MICHELE

**10128** Igus, Toyomi. *Going Back Home: An Artist Returns to the South* (4–8). Illus. by Michele Wood. 1996, Children's Book Pr. $15.95 (0-89239-137-5). 32pp. The author tries to re-create the family history of the African American illustrator Michele Wood. (Rev: BCCB 12/96; BL 9/15/96; SLJ 7/97) [921]

## WRIGHT, FRANK LLOYD

**10129** Thorne-Thomsen, Kathleen. *Frank Lloyd Wright for Kids* (4–6). Illus. 1994, Chicago Review paper $14.95 (1-55652-207-X). 144pp. In addition to providing a life of this famous architect, this book contains many projects related to his work and a recipe for his favorite breakfast. (Rev: BL 4/15/94; SLJ 7/94) [921]

## YANI, WANG

**10130** Zhensun, Zheng. *A Young Painter: The Life and Paintings of Wang Yani — China's Extraordinary Young Artist* (5–8). Illus. 1991, Scholastic $17.95 (0-590-44906-0). 80pp. Teenager Wang Yani is hailed as a national treasure in China. (Rev: BCCB 9/91; BL 10/1/91*; SLJ 8/91) [921]

## ZHANG, SONG NAN

**10131** Zhang, Song Nan. *A Little Tiger in the Chinese Night: An Autobiography in Art* (5–8). Illus. 1993, Tundra $19.95 (0-88776-320-0). 48pp. The biography of a Chinese artist who endured many hardships before he was able to relocate in Montreal. (Rev: BCCB 3/94; BL 1/1/94*; SLJ 5/94) [921]

# Composers

## BEETHOVEN, LUDWIG VAN

**10132** Balcavage, Dynise. *Ludwig Van Beethoven: Composer* (4–8). Illus. Series: Great Achievers: Lives of the Physically Challenged. 1997, Chelsea LB $19.95 (0-7910-2082-7). 119pp. A well-rounded biography of Beethoven that covers both his profes-

sional career and his personal life and problems. (Rev: SLJ 7/97) [921]

**10133** Venezia, Mike. *Ludwig Van Beethoven* (2–4). Illus. Series: Getting to Know the World's Greatest Artists/Composers. 1996, Children's LB $21.00 (0-516-04542-3). 32pp. An informal portrait of Beethoven and an introduction to his music. (Rev: BL 9/15/96) [921]

## BERLIN, IRVING

**10134** Streissguth, Thomas. *Say It with Music: A Story About Irving Berlin* (3–5). Illus. 1994, Carolrhoda LB $14.95 (0-87614-810-0). 64pp. This biography of the great American songwriter concentrates on his first 30 years, from childhood in Russia to success on Broadway. (Rev: BL 5/1/94; SLJ 8/94) [921]

## BERNSTEIN, LEONARD

**10135** Hurwitz, Johanna. *Leonard Bernstein: A Passion for Music* (4–8). Illus. by Sonia O. Lisker. 1993, Jewish Publication Soc. $12.95 (0-8276-0501-3). 80pp. The career of this amazing conductor and composer who was also a gifted pianist and teacher. (Rev: BL 2/15/94; SLJ 12/93) [921]

**10136** Venezia, Mike. *Leonard Bernstein* (2–4). Series: Getting to Know the World's Greatest Artists/Composers. 1997, Children's LB $21.00 (0-516-20492-0). 32pp. A brief profile of this great American composer, who also excelled as a conductor and pianist. (Rev: BL 10/15/97) [921]

## GERSHWIN, GEORGE

**10137** Mitchell, Barbara. *America, I Hear You: A Story About George Gershwin* (3–5). Illus. 1987, Carolrhoda LB $19.93 (0-87614-309-5). 64pp. The life, times, and career of one of America's great musicians. (Rev: BCCB 11/87; BL 10/1/87; SLJ 12/87)

**10138** Venezia, Mike. *George Gershwin* (2–4). Illus. by author. Series: Getting to Know the World's Greatest Composers. 1994, Children's LB $21.00 (0-516-04536-9). 32pp. A breezy retelling of the life and times of this multitalented American composer of both classical and popular music. (Rev: SLJ 4/95) [921]

**10139** Vernon, Roland. *Introducing Gershwin* (5–7). Illus. 1996, Silver Burdett LB $14.95 (0-382-39161-6); paper $8.95 (0-382-39160-8). 32pp. This oversize volume with copious illustrations re-creates the life and times of George Gershwin. (Rev: BL 5/1/96; SLJ 9/96) [921]

## JOPLIN, SCOTT

**10140** Mitchell, Barbara. *Raggin': A Story About Scott Joplin* (3–5). Illus. 1987, Carolrhoda LB $14.95

(0-87614-310-9); paper $5.95 (0-87614-589-6). 64pp. The story of a great American musician whose genius was not recognized until after his death. (Rev: BL 10/1/87; SLJ 12/87)

## MENDELSSOHN, FANNY

**10141** Kamen, Gloria. *Hidden Music: The Life of Fanny Mendelssohn* (4–6). Illus. 1996, Simon & Schuster $15.00 (0-689-31714-X). 82pp. Fanny Mendelssohn, the sister of Felix, was also a talented musician and composer, but being a woman, she was denied the same opportunities as her brother. (Rev: BCCB 5/96; BL 3/15/96; HB 9–10/96) [921]

## MOZART, WOLFGANG AMADEUS

**10142** Downing, Julie. *Mozart Tonight* (2–4). Illus. 1991, Macmillan LB $15.95 (0-02-732881-3). 40pp. In picture-book format, the life of the young Mozart is presented. (Rev: BCCB 4/91; BL 4/15/91; SLJ 4/91) [921]

**10143** Greene, Carol. *Wolfgang Amadeus Mozart: Musical Genius* (2–4). Illus. Series: Rookie Biographies. 1993, Children's LB $19.00 (0-516-04256-4). 48pp. A succinct treatment for beginning readers about this great composer. (Rev: BL 8/93) [921]

**10144** Isadora, Rachel. *Young Mozart* (PS–3). Illus. 1997, Viking $14.99 (0-670-87120-6). 32pp. A picture book biography that focuses on Mozart's childhood as an amazing prodigy who performed for royalty in Europe. (Rev: BL 5/1/97; SLJ 7/97) [921]

**10145** Vernon, Roland. *Introducing Mozart* (5–7). Illus. 1996, Silver Burdett LB $14.95 (0-382-39159-4); paper $8.95 (0-382-39158-6). 32pp. The life and times of Mozart are covered in the oversize, heavily illustrated volume. (Rev: BL 5/1/96; SLJ 1/97) [921]

## SCHUMANN, CLARA

**10146** Allman, Barbara. *Her Piano Sang: A Story About Clara Schumann* (4–7). Illus. 1996, Carolrhoda LB $19.95 (1-57505-012-9). 64pp. The story of this groundbreaking composer and pianist who also championed her husband's music. (Rev: BL 1/1–15/97; SLJ 1/97) [921]

## SOUSA, JOHN PHILIP

**10147** Greene, Carol. *John Philip Sousa: The March King* (2–4). Illus. Series: Rookie Biographies. 1992, Children's LB $19.00 (0-516-04226-2). 48pp. The life of the famous band master and composer of marches is introduced. (Rev: BL 6/15/92; SLJ 8/92) [921]

## STRAVINSKY, IGOR

**10148** Venezia, Mike. *Igor Stravinsky* (2–4). Illus. Series: Getting to Know the World's Greatest Artists/Composers. 1996, Children's LB $21.00 (0-516-20054-2). 32pp. The life of this great 20th-century composer and his work are briefly presented, with many illustrations. (Rev: BCCB 7–8/96; BL 12/15/96) [921]

## TCHAIKOVSKY, PETER

**10149** Venezia, Mike. *Peter Tchaikovsky* (2–4). Illus. by author. Series: Getting to Know the World's Greatest Composers. 1994, Children's LB $21.00 (0-516-04537-7). 32pp. An introduction to the life, times, and music of this Russian composer, in a visually pleasing format. (Rev: SLJ 4/95) [921]

# Entertainers

## ABDUL, PAULA

**10150** Ford, M. Thomas. *Paula Abdul: Straight Up* (3–6). Illus. Series: Taking Part. 1992, Macmillan LB $13.95 (0-87518-508-8). 72pp. The life story of the pop entertainer, who takes special interest in a young audience. (Rev: BL 11/15/92; SLJ 7/92) [921]

## ANDERSON, MARIAN

**10151** Ferris, Jeri. *What I Had Was Singing: The Story of Marian Anderson* (3–6). Illus. 1994, Carolrhoda LB $21.50 (0-87614-818-6); paper $6.95 (0-87614-634-5). 96pp. The story of this African American contralto's struggles and triumphs, including her appearances at the Lincoln Memorial in 1939 and the Metropolitan Opera in the 1950s. (Rev: BL 7/94) [921]

**10152** Livingston, Myra Cohn. *Keep on Singing: A Ballad of Marian Anderson* (K–3). Illus. by Samuel Byrd. 1994, Holiday LB $15.95 (0-8234-1098-6). 32pp. In a narrative poem, the life and career of Marian Anderson is celebrated. (Rev: BL 11/1/94; SLJ 3/95) [921]

**10153** McKissack, Patricia, and Fredrick McKissack. *Marian Anderson: A Great Singer* (2–4). Illus. Series: Great African Americans. 1991, Enslow LB $13.95 (0-89490-303-9). 32pp. A biography of the great American concert singer, the first African American to sing with the Metropolitan Opera in New York City. (Rev: SLJ 11/91) [921]

## ARMSTRONG, LOUIS

**10154** McKissack, Patricia, and Fredrick McKissack. *Louis Armstrong: Jazz Musician* (2–4). Illus. Series: Great African Americans. 1991, Enslow LB

$13.95 (0-89490-307-1). 32pp. A simple biography of this well-loved American musician. (Rev: BL 1/1/92; SLJ 2/92) [921]

**10155** Medearis, Angela Shelf. *Little Louis and the Jazz Band: The Story of Louis "Satchmo" Armstrong* (3–4). Illus. by Anna Rich. Series: Rainbow Biography. 1994, Lodestar paper $13.99 (0-525-67424-1). 42pp. A simple biography with black-and-white photos that tell of Louis Armstrong's childhood and rise to fame. (Rev: SLJ 11/94) [921]

**10156** Orgill, Roxane. *If I Only Had a Horn: Young Louis Armstrong* (K–8). Illus. by Leonard Jenkins. 1997, Houghton $16.00 (0-395-75919-6). 32pp. This lively retelling of key events in jazz musician Louis Armstrong's life is made exciting by the use of dynamic color paintings. (Rev: BL 11/1/97; SLJ 9/97) [921]

### BALANCHINE, GEORGE

**10157** Kristy, Davida. *George Balanchine: American Ballet Master* (5–8). Illus. Series: Biographies. 1996, Lerner LB $23.93 (0-8225-4951-4). 128pp. The story of the Russian émigré choreographer and how he changed the history of American ballet. (Rev: SLJ 8/96) [921]

### BALL, LUCILLE

**10158** Krohn, Katherine E. *Lucille Ball: Pioneer of Comedy* (4–6). Illus. Series: Achievers. 1992, Lerner LB $18.60 (0-8225-0543-6). 64pp. A biography that tries to capture the hilarity that was the "I Love Lucy" show. (Rev: BL 6/15/92; SLJ 7/92) [921]

### BARNUM, P. T.

**10159** Fleming, Alice. *P. T. Barnum: The World's Greatest Showman* (5–8). Illus. 1993, Walker LB $15.85 (0-8027-8235-3). 128pp. This biography of a master showman gives a rundown on his many careers before show business. (Rev: BL 1/15/94; SLJ 12/93) [921]

### BEATLES

**10160** Venezia, Mike. *The Beatles* (2–4). Illus. Series: Getting to Know the World's Greatest Artists/Composers. 1997, Children's LB $21.00 (0-516-20310-X). 32pp. Color photos, humorous cartoons, and a clever text are used to re-create the fabulous careers of these boys from Liverpool. (Rev: BL 5/15/97) [920]

**10161** Woog, Adam. *The Beatles* (4–8). Series: Importance Of. 1997, Lucent LB $22.45 (1-56006-088-3). 128pp. Outlines the lives and careers of these 4 Liverpool natives and their many achievements. (Rev: BL 10/15/97; SLJ 12/97) [921]

### BLADES, RUBÉN

**10162** Cruz, Barbara C. *Rubén Blades: Salsa Singer and Social Activist* (4–7). Illus. Series: Hispanic Biographies. 1997, Enslow LB $19.95 (0-89490-893-6). 128pp. A biography of this Panamanian entertainer who has become famous as a singer, actor, and activist. (Rev: SLJ 1/98) [921]

### BROOKS, GARTH

**10163** Tallman, Edward. *Garth Brooks* (3–6). Illus. Series: Taking Part. 1993, Dillon LB $13.95 (0-87518-595-9). 64pp. The story of the country music superstar. (Rev: BL 10/15/93; SLJ 2/94) [921]

### CHARLES, RAY

**10164** Turk, Ruth. *Ray Charles: Soul Man* (5–8). Illus. Series: Newsmakers. 1996, Lerner LB $23.93 (0-8225-4928-X). 112pp. This candid biography of the great blind entertainer gives compelling details about Ray Charles's childhood. (Rev: SLJ 8/96) [921]

### COSBY, BILL

**10165** Conord, Bruce W. *Bill Cosby: Family Man* (3–5). Series: Junior World Biography. 1993, Chelsea LB $12.95 (0-7910-1761-3). 76pp. A biography of this famous actor and comedian. (Rev: SLJ 6/93) [921]

**10166** Haskins, Jim. *Bill Cosby: America's Most Famous Father* (5–7). Illus. 1988, Walker LB $14.85 (0-8027-6786-9). 128pp. The childhood and career of this famous entertainer. (Rev: BL 6/1/88) [921]

**10167** Schuman, Michael A. *Bill Cosby: Actor and Comedian* (4–6). Illus. Series: People to Know. 1995, Enslow LB $19.95 (0-89490-548-1). 128pp. The life of this multitalented African American entertainer is told in a highly readable style. (Rev: BL 9/15/95; SLJ 2/96) [921]

**10168** Woods, Harold, and Geraldine Woods. *Bill Cosby: Making America Laugh and Learn* (4–7). Illus. 1988, Macmillan LB $13.95 (0-87518-240-2). 48pp. A biography of the outstanding black comedian, educator, and humanitarian. [921]

### DUNCAN, ISADORA

**10169** O'Connor, Barbara. *Barefoot Dancer: The Story of Isadora Duncan* (5–7). Illus. 1994, Carolrhoda LB $22.60 (0-87614-807-0). 96pp. The story of this eccentric individualist who influenced and liberated a generation of dancers. (Rev: BCCB 10/94; BL 7/94) [921]

## ESTEFAN, GLORIA

**10170** Gonzalez, Fernando. *Gloria Estefan: Cuban-American Singing Star* (3–6). Illus. Series: Hispanic Heritage. 1993, Millbrook LB $14.90 (1-56294-371-5). 32pp. The story of the Cuban singer who has become one of America's musical superstars. (Rev: BL 11/15/93) [921]

**10171** Rodriguez, Janel. *Gloria Estefan* (4–8). Illus. Series: Contemporary Hispanic Americans. 1995, Raintree Steck-Vaughn LB $24.26 (0-8172-3982-0). 48pp. A fine biography of this Hispanic American entertainer, who has shown the power of music and of self-determination. (Rev: BL 3/15/96; SLJ 1/96) [921]

**10172** Shirley, David. *Gloria Estefan* (4–7). Illus. Series: Hispanics of Achievement. 1994, Chelsea LB $15.95 (0-7910-2114-4); paper $4.95 (0-7910-2117-3). 80pp. A nicely illustrated biography of the Cuban-born rock star. (Rev: BL 11/15/94; SLJ 10/94) [921]

**10173** Stefoff, Rebecca. *Gloria Estefan* (5–8). Illus. 1991, Chelsea LB $19.95 (0-7910-1244-1). 104pp. The story of the singer who broke her back in a 1990 bus accident and her eventual triumph. (Rev: BL 8/91) [921]

**10174** Strazzabosco, Jeanne M. *Learning About Determination from the Life of Gloria Estefan* (2–5). Illus. Series: A Character Building Book. 1996, Rosen LB $13.95 (0-8239-2416-5). 24pp. The life story of this important entertainer, emphasizing that her success came from the determination to overcome obstacles. (Rev: BL 10/15/96; SLJ 12/96) [921]

## FONDA, JANE

**10175** Shorto, Russell. *Jane Fonda: Political Activist* (4–6). Series: New Directions. 1991, Millbrook LB $21.90 (1-56294-045-7); Houghton paper $5.70 (0-395-63564-0). 101pp. Covers Jane Fonda's public and private life, her acting career, and her devotion to a number of causes. (Rev: SLJ 10/91) [921]

## GISH, LILLIAN

**10176** Gish, Lillian, and Selma G. Lanes. *An Actor's Life for Me!* (4–8). Illus. 1987, Viking paper $15.00 (0-670-80416-9). 64pp. A fascinating autobiography of the famous early-20th-century vaudeville star who began her career at the age of 6. (Rev: BCCB 11/87; BL 1/15/88) [921]

## GOLDBERG, WHOOPI

**10177** Adams, Mary A. *Whoopi Goldberg: From Street to Stardom* (4–6). Illus. Series: Taking Part. 1993, Macmillan LB $13.95 (0-87518-562-2). 64pp. An easily read biography of this talented comedian, actress, and talk-show hostess. (Rev: BL 5/1/93; SLJ 7/93) [921]

## GRAHAM, MARTHA

**10178** Pratt, Paula B. *Martha Graham* (4–8). Illus. Series: The Importance Of. 1995, Lucent LB $22.45 (1-56006-056-5). 112pp. The life of this amazing dancer, choreographer, and dance company founder and how she changed the course of modern dance in the United States and the world. (Rev: BL 1/15/95; SLJ 1/95) [921]

**10179** Probosz, Kathilyn S. *Martha Graham* (5–8). Illus. Series: People in Focus Books. 1995, Dillon paper $7.95 (0-382-24961-5). 184pp. A biography that tells of this dancer's many accomplishments while also giving details of her youth and the influences on her work. (Rev: SLJ 10/95) [921]

## GRANT, AMY

**10180** Italia, Bob. *Amy Grant: From Gospel to Pop* (4–6). Illus. Series: Leading Lady. 1992, ABDO LB $12.94 (1-56239-145-3). 32pp. An engaging biography with high-low interest. (Rev: BL 2/1/93; SLJ 4/93) [921]

## HAMMER, M. C.

**10181** Saylor-Marchant, Linda. *Hammer: 2 Legit 2 Quit* (3–6). Illus. Series: Taking Part. 1992, Macmillan LB $13.95 (0-87518-522-3). 64pp. The life of the popular African-American rap musician and his struggle to succeed. (Rev: BL 1/15/93; SLJ 2/93) [921]

## HENSON, JIM

**10182** Durrett, Deanne. *Jim Henson* (4–8). Illus. Series: The Importance Of. 1994, Lucent LB $22.45 (1-56006-048-4). 112pp. The life of this puppeteer and how he changed this art through the creation of the Muppets and his work in animation and films. (Rev: BL 8/94) [921]

## HOUDINI, HARRY

**10183** Woog, Adam. *Harry Houdini* (4–8). Illus. Series: The Importance Of. 1995, Lucent LB $22.45 (1-56006-053-0). 112pp. The story of the escape artist who amazed and baffled the world with his incredible stunts. (Rev: BL 1/15/95; SLJ 1/95) [921]

## IGLESIAS, JULIO

**10184** Martino, Elizabeth. *Julio Iglesias* (5–8). Illus. Series: Hispanics of Achievement. 1994, Chelsea LB $19.95 (0-7910-2017-7). 112pp. The life and accomplishments of this internationally popular singer. (Rev: BL 9/15/94) [921]

## JACKSON, MICHAEL

**10185** Nicholson, Lois. *Michael Jackson* (4–8). Illus. Series: Black Americans of Achievement. 1994, Chelsea LB $19.95 (0-7910-1929-2); paper $8.95 (0-7910-1930-6). 104pp. A life of this popular singer that ends before the sexual abuse charges of 1993. (Rev: BL 10/15/94; SLJ 10/94) [921]

## LENNON, JOHN

**10186** Wright, David K. *John Lennon: The Beatles and Beyond* (4–6). Illus. Series: People to Know. 1996, Enslow LB $19.95 (0-89490-702-6). 112pp. The story of the famous Beatle, his rise to fame, his activities outside music, and his tragic death. (Rev: BL 10/15/96; SLJ 12/96) [921]

## MARSALIS, WYNTON

**10187** Awmiller, Craig. *Wynton Marsalis: Gifted Trumpet Player* (3–6). Illus. Series: Picture-Story Biographies. 1996, Children's LB $18.20 (0-516-04196-7). 32pp. The talented musician and his multifaceted career are introduced. (Rev: BL 8/96; SLJ 8/96) [921]

**10188** Ellis, Veronica F. *Wynton Marsalis* (4–6). Illus. Series: Contemporary African Americans. 1997, Raintree Steck-Vaughn LB $24.26 (0-8172-3998-X). 48pp. A fine biography of this Grammy award–winning musician who is equally at home with jazz and classical music. (Rev: BL 5/15/97; SLJ 2/98) [921]

## MONK, THELONIOUS

**10189** Raschka, Chris. *Mysterious Thelonious* (3–7). Illus. 1997, Orchard LB $14.99 (0-531-33057-5). 32pp. In a lively mixture of color and motion, this book presents an unusual handling of an unusual subject, a tribute to jazz musician Thelonious Monk. (Rev: BL 11/1/97; SLJ 9/97*) [921]

## NEW KIDS ON THE BLOCK

**10190** McGibbon, Robin. *New Kids on the Block: The Whole Story* (5–8). Illus. 1990, Avon paper $6.95 (0-380-76344-3). 120pp. Stories about members of this band have been collected from a variety of sources, including the members themselves. (Rev: BL 10/1/90) [921]

## NIMOY, LEONARD

**10191** Micklos, John. *Leonard Nimoy: A Star's Trek* (3–6). Illus. 1988, Macmillan LB $13.95 (0-87518-376-X). 64pp. A simple biography of the man best known as Mr. Spock on "Star Trek." (Rev: BL 7/88; SLJ 10/88)

## OLMOS, EDWARD JAMES

**10192** Carrillo, Louis. *Edward James Olmos* (4–8). Illus. Series: Contemporary Hispanic Americans. 1997, Raintree Steck-Vaughn LB $24.26 (0-8172-3989-8). 48pp. Along with a time line and glossary, this account traces the life of this contemporary human rights activist and actor. (Rev: BL 4/15/97) [921]

**10193** Martinez, Elizabeth Coonrod. *Edward James Olmos: Mexican American Actor* (3–5). Illus. 1994, Millbrook LB $19.90 (1-56294-410-X). 32pp. A biography of this acclaimed Hispanic American actor who has justifiably become a role model for young people. (Rev: BL 1/1/95; SLJ 1/95) [921]

## OZAWA, SEIJI

**10194** Tan, Sheri. *Seiji Ozawa* (5–7). Illus. Series: Contemporary Asian Americans. 1997, Raintree Steck-Vaughn LB $24.26 (0-8172-3993-6). 48pp. A profile of the Asian American musician who has been the chief conductor of the Boston Symphony for more than 20 years. (Rev: BL 5/1/97; SLJ 9/97) [921]

## PAVLOVA, ANNA

**10195** Levine, Ellen. *Anna Pavlova: Genius of the Dance* (5–7). 1995, Scholastic $14.95 (0-590-44304-6). 128pp. The life and career of this legendary ballerina, with coverage on the famous ballets in which she danced. (Rev: BCCB 5/95; BL 1/1/95; SLJ 4/95*) [921]

## PERLMAN, ITZHAK

**10196** Behrman, Carol H. *Fiddler to the World: The Inspiring Life of Itzhak Perlman* (5–8). Illus. 1992, Betterway paper $5.95 (1-55870-238-5). 128pp. The life of the premier violinist, who began playing at the age of 3 and contracted polio at the age of 4. (Rev: BL 5/1/92) [921]

## PICKETT, BILL

**10197** Pinkney, Andrea D. *Bill Pickett: Rodeo-Ridin' Cowboy* (PS–3). Illus. by Brian Pinkney. 1996, Harcourt $16.00 (0-15-200100-X). 32pp. The story of Bill Pickett, African American rodeo superstar and superb horseman. (Rev: BCCB 11/96; BL 11/1/96; HB 11–12/96; SLJ 10/96) [921]

**10198** Sanford, William R., and Carl R. Green. *Bill Pickett: African-American Rodeo Star* (4–6). Illus. Series: Legendary Heroes of the Wild West. 1997, Enslow LB $15.95 (0-89490-676-3). 48pp. This is a short biography of the colorful rodeo star who is considered one of the legends of the Wild West. (Rev: BL 3/15/97) [921]

## PRESLEY, ELVIS

**10199** Krohn, Katherine E. *Elvis Presley: The King* (5–7). Illus. 1994, Lerner LB $18.60 (0-8225-2877-0). 64pp. A somewhat sanitized biography of Elvis Presley that highlights important events in his career. (Rev: BL 7/94; SLJ 7/94) [921]

**10200** Woog, Adam. *Elvis Presley* (4–8). Illus. Series: The Importance Of. 1997, Lucent LB $22.45 (1-56006-084-0). 112pp. The life of this great rocker and his lasting influence on popular music. (Rev: BL 1/1–15/97) [921]

## PRICE, LEONTYNE

**10201** Steins, Richard. *Leontyne Price: Opera Star* (4–6). Illus. Series: The Library of Famous Women. 1993, Blackbirch LB $15.95 (1-56711-009-6). 64pp. A candid view of the singer who, while thrilling millions, broke color barriers in the world of opera. (Rev: BL 6/1–15/93; SLJ 8/93) [921]

## QUINN, ANTHONY

**10202** Amdur, Melissa. *Anthony Quinn* (5–8). Illus. Series: Hispanics of Achievement. 1993, Chelsea LB $19.95 (0-7910-1251-4). 104pp. The life of this Mexican American actor is told with many interesting asides concerning his career and black-and-white stills from his movies. (Rev: BL 9/15/93) [921]

## ROBESON, PAUL

**10203** Holmes, Burnham. *Paul Robeson: A Voice of Struggle* (5–8). Illus. Series: American Troublemakers. 1995, Raintree Steck-Vaughn LB $27.11 (0-8114-2381-6). 128pp. The story of the great African American singer-actor who became an outcast in his own country because of his outspoken search for justice for his people. (Rev: SLJ 7/95) [921]

**10204** McKissack, Patricia, and Fredrick McKissack. *Paul Robeson: A Voice to Remember* (2–4). Illus. by Michael D. Blegel. Series: Great African Americans. 1992, Enslow LB $13.95 (0-89490-310-1). 32pp. The story of the great singer and actor who spoke out against discrimination. (Rev: BL 9/15/92; SLJ 10/92) [921]

## ROGERS, WILL

**10205** Bennett, Cathereen L. *Will Rogers: Quotable Cowboy* (4–6). Illus. 1995, Lerner LB $19.95 (0-8225-3155-0). 96pp. The exciting life of Will Rogers — noted actor, writer, humorist, and humanitarian. (Rev: BL 3/1/96; SLJ 12/95) [921]

**10206** Malone, Mary. *Will Rogers: Cowboy Philosopher* (4–7). Illus. Series: People to Know. 1996, Enslow LB $19.95 (0-89490-695-X). 128pp. A lively look at the life and accomplishments of this cow-

boy and show business idol. (Rev: BL 5/15/96; SLJ 6/96) [921]

## RONSTADT, LINDA

**10207** Amdur, Melissa. *Linda Ronstadt* (5–8). Illus. Series: Hispanics of Achievement. 1993, Chelsea LB $19.95 (0-7910-1781-8). 112pp. This biography of the popular singer focuses on her Mexican American heritage and how she became aware of it. (Rev: BL 9/15/93; SLJ 10/93) [921]

## SPIELBERG, STEVEN

**10208** Meachum, Virginia. *Steven Spielberg: Hollywood Filmmaker* (4–6). Illus. Series: People to Know. 1996, Enslow LB $19.95 (0-89490-697-6). 112pp. The creator of such movie hits as *ET, Jaws,* and *Schindler's List,* is profiled in this easily read biography. (Rev: BL 8/96; SLJ 10/96) [921]

**10209** Powers, Tom. *Steven Spielberg: Master Storyteller* (5–7). Illus. 1997, Lerner LB $23.93 (0-8225-4929-8). 128pp. A candid biography of this successful film maker, illustrated with stills from many of his most famous pictures, e.g., *Jaws* and *Schindler's List.* (Rev: BL 6/1–15/97) [921]

## TALLCHIEF, MARIA

**10210** Erdrich, Heidi E. *Maria Tallchief* (4–6). Illus. by Rick Whipple. Series: American Indian Stories. 1993, Raintree Steck-Vaughn LB $21.40 (0-8114-6577-2). 32pp. A biography of the famous ballet dancer whose Native American origins caused problems in furthering her career. (Rev: BL 7/93) [921]

## WASHINGTON, DENZEL

**10211** Simmons, Alex. *Denzel Washington* (4–6). Illus. Series: Contemporary African Americans. 1997, Raintree Steck-Vaughn LB $24.26 (0-8172-3986-3). 48pp. In this biography of actor Denzel Washington, he claims that his mother and the Boys Club saved him from a life of crime. (Rev: BL 5/15/97; SLJ 2/98) [921]

## WINFREY, OPRAH

**10212** Otfinoski, Steven. *Oprah Winfrey: Television Star* (4–6). Illus. Series: Library of Famous Women. 1993, Blackbirch LB $15.95 (1-56711-015-0). 64pp. Accurately portrays the personal and public life of this influential superstar. (Rev: BL 11/15/93; SLJ 2/94) [921]

**10213** Woods, Geraldine. *The Oprah Winfrey Story: Speaking Her Mind* (3–6). Series: Taking Part. 1991, Macmillan LB $13.95 (0-87518-463-4). 79pp. From dire poverty and abuse to talk show stardom, this is the story of Oprah Winfrey. (Rev: SLJ 3/92) [921]

# Writers

## AARDEMA, VERNA

**10214** Aardema, Verna. *A Bookworm Who Hatched* (2–5). Illus. by Dede Smith. Series: Meet the Author. 1993, Richard C. Owen $14.95 (1-878450-39-5). 32pp. In this autobiographical account, the noted author reveals stories about her life, writing techniques, and how she interacts with her reading audience. (Rev: BL 9/1/93; HB 9–10/93) [921]

## ANDERSEN, HANS CHRISTIAN

**10215** Brust, Beth Wagner. *The Amazing Paper Cuttings of Hans Christian Andersen* (3–6). Illus. 1994, Ticknor $17.00 (0-395-66787-9). 80pp. The story of Hans Christian Andersen's life is told and illustrated with many examples of his famous paper cuttings. (Rev: BCCB 3/94; BL 3/1/94; HB 7–8/94; SLJ 3/94) [921]

**10216** Burch, Joann J. *A Fairy-Tale Life: A Story About Hans Christian Andersen* (3–5). Illus. 1994, Carolrhoda LB $19.93 (0-87614-829-1). 64pp. A biography that concentrates on Andersen's childhood and his development as a writer. (Rev: BL 9/1/94) [921]

## ANGELOU, MAYA

**10217** King, Sarah E. *Maya Angelou Greeting the Morning* (3–5). Illus. Series: Gateway Biographies. 1994, Millbrook LB $20.90 (1-56294-431-2). 48pp. The inspiring story of the great African American writer and the terrible difficulties she has overcome. (Rev: BL 8/94; SLJ 4/94) [921]

**10218** Pettit, Jayne. *Maya Angelou: Journey of the Heart* (5–7). Illus. 1996, Dutton paper $14.99 (0-525-67518-3). 70pp. Drawing on Angelou's autobiographical writing, the author has created a moving portrait of this famous African American woman. (Rev: BL 2/15/96; SLJ 4/96) [921]

**10219** Spain, Valerie. *Meet Maya Angelou* (3–5). Illus. Series: Bullseye Biography. 1995, Knopf paper $3.99 (0-679-86542-X). 92pp. A short, simple biography that gives details of the personal and professional life of this great African American writer, with details taken from her autobiographical writings. (Rev: BL 2/15/95) [921]

## ASCH, FRANK

**10220** Asch, Frank. *One Man Show* (1–4). Photos by Jan Asch. Illus. Series: Meet the Author. 1997, Richard C. Owen $14.95 (1-57274-095-7). 32pp. In this autobiography, author Asch introduces himself and his family, interests, and writing techniques. (Rev: SLJ 9/97) [921]

## AVI

**10221** Markham, Lois. *Avi* (5–7). Illus. 1996, Learning Works paper $6.95 (0-88160-280-9). 128pp. The life and writing techniques of Avi, a very successful writer of books for young people. (Rev: BL 4/1/96; SLJ 8/96) [921]

## BALDWIN, JAMES

**10222** Tackach, James. *James Baldwin* (4–8). Illus. Series: The Importance Of. 1997, Lucent LB $22.45 (1-56006-070-0). 95pp. Covers the life and accomplishments of this important African American writer. (Rev: BL 1/1–15/97) [921]

## BAUER, MARION DANE

**10223** Bauer, Marion Dane. *A Writer's Story from Life to Fiction* (5–8). 1995, Clarion $14.95 (0-395-72094-X); paper $6.95 (0-395-75053-9). 133pp. This famous author explains how she has taken her own experiences and used them as the beginning of many of her books. (Rev: BL 9/15/95; SLJ 10/95) [921]

## BRONTË, CHARLOTTE

**10224** Ross, Stewart. *Charlotte Brontë and Jane Eyre* (5–8). Illus. 1997, Viking paper $16.99 (0-670-87486-8). 48pp. A picture book biography of Charlotte Brontë that focuses on the writing of *Jane Eyre* with a detailed plot summary. (Rev: BL 1/1–15/98; SLJ 1/98) [921]

## BROWN, HELEN GURLEY

**10225** Falkof, Lucille. *Helen Gurley Brown: The Queen of Cosmopolitan* (5–8). Illus. Series: Wizards of Business. 1992, Garrett LB $17.26 (1-56074-013-2). 60pp. This life story of the magazine magnate includes excellent tips for aspiring entrepreneurs. (Rev: BL 6/15/92; SLJ 7/92) [921]

## BROWN, MARGARET WISE

**10226** Blos, Joan W. *The Days Before Now: An Autobiographical Note by Margaret Wise Brown* (K–3). Illus. by Thomas B. Allen. 1994, Simon & Schuster paper $15.00 (0-671-79628-3). 32pp. A picture book biography of the famous children's author using her own words to tell her story. (Rev: BCCB 1/95; BL 12/15/94; SLJ 3/95) [921]

**10227** Greene, Carol. *Margaret Wise Brown: Author of Goodnight Moon* (1–3). Illus. 1993, Children's LB $19.00 (0-516-04254-8). 48pp. A beginning reader that tells of this great writer of children's books and her untimely death at age 42. (Rev: BL 12/1/93) [921]

## BUCK, PEARL S.

**10228** Mitchell, Barbara. *Between Two Worlds: A Story About Pearl Buck* (3–6). Illus. by Karen Ritz. 1988, Carolrhoda LB $19.93 (0-87614-332-X). 56pp. The life of this child of American missionaries in China, who grew up to become a famous novelist. (Rev: BL 3/1/89; SLJ 2/89)

## BUNTING, EVE

**10229** Bunting, Eve. *Once upon a Time* (2–5). Illus. 1995, Richard C. Owen $14.95 (1-878450-59-X). 32pp. An autobiography of the prolific writer of children's books, who spent her childhood in Ireland. (Rev: BCCB 7–8/95; BL 8/95; HB 7–8/95) [921]

## BURNETT, FRANCES HODGSON

**10230** Carpenter, Angelica S., and Jean Shirley. *Frances Hodgson Burnett: Beyond the Secret Garden* (4–8). Illus. 1990, Lerner LB $23.93 (0-8225-4905-0). 128pp. The story of the well-known English-born writer who came to America at the age of 15. (Rev: BCCB 12/90; BL 1/1/91; SLJ 3/91) [921]

## BYARS, BETSY

**10231** Byars, Betsy. *The Moon and I* (4–7). Illus. 1996, Morrow paper $4.95 (0-688-13704-0). 96pp. A memoir from this well-known children's author, which gives her the opportunity to tell how she likes both writing and snakes. (Rev: BCCB 3/92*; BL 5/15/92; SLJ 4/92) [921]

## CATHER, WILLA

**10232** Bedard, Michael. *The Divide* (K–4). Illus. by Emily Arnold McCully. 1997, Doubleday $16.95 (0-385-32124-4). 32pp. This partial biography tells about the move that Willa Cather made with her family when she was 9 to the plains of Nebraska in 1883 and the painful adjustment she had to make. (Rev: BL 10/1/97; SLJ 9/97) [921]

**10233** Streissguth, Thomas. *Writer of the Plains: A Story About Willa Cather* (4–7). Illus. 1997, Carolrhoda LB $14.95 (1-57505-015-3). 64pp. A simple introduction to the works of Willa Cather and the places where she lived and wrote. (Rev: BL 6/1–15/97; SLJ 10/97) [921]

## CERVANTES, MIGUEL DE

**10234** Goldberg, Jake. *Miguel de Cervantes* (5–8). Illus. Series: Hispanics of Achievement. 1993, Chelsea LB $19.95 (0-7910-1238-7). 112pp. The biography of the creator of *Don Quixote*, whose life, including time spent as a slave in Algiers, also reads like a novel. (Rev: BL 9/15/93) [921]

## COLE, JOANNA

**10235** Cole, Joanna, and Wendy Saul. *On the Bus with Joanna Cole* (2–6). Illus. Series: Creative Sparks. 1996, Heinemann $16.95 (0-435-08131-4). 61pp. The creator of the Magic School Bus series talks about her life and writing. (Rev: HB 9–10/96; SLJ 6/96*) [921]

## DAHL, ROALD

**10236** Dahl, Roald. *Boy: Tales of Childhood* (5–8). Illus. 1984, Farrar $16.00 (0-374-37374-4); Puffin paper $5.99 (0-14-031890-9). 176pp. Beginning with a family history, the author recounts vignettes of memorable experiences in his childhood.

## DICKENS, CHARLES

**10237** Collins, David R. *Tales for Hard Times: A Story About Charles Dickens* (4–8). Illus. by David Mataya. Series: Creative Minds. 1991, Carolrhoda LB $14.95 (0-87614-433-4). 64pp. The life of Charles Dickens, including his poverty-ridden childhood. (Rev: SLJ 3/91) [921]

**10238** Stanley, Diane, and Peter Vennema. *Charles Dickens: The Man Who Had Great Expectations* (3–8). Illus. by Diane Stanley. 1993, Morrow LB $14.93 (0-688-09111-3). 48pp. A candid retelling of the author's life, which was often as dramatic as his novels. (Rev: BCCB 11/93; BL 9/1/93; HB 11–12/93; SLJ 8/93) [921]

## DORRIS, MICHAEL

**10239** Weil, Ann. *Michael Dorris* (4–7). Illus. Series: Contemporary Native Americans. 1997, Raintree Steck-Vaughn LB $24.26 (0-8172-3994-4). 48pp. The life story of the late Native American writer and teacher and his crusade to fight alcohol abuse. (Rev: BL 6/1–15/97) [921]

## EHLERT, LOIS

**10240** Ehlert, Lois. *Under My Nose* (3–5). Illus. 1996, Richard C. Owen $14.95 (1-57274-027-2). 32pp. A simple autobiography of this artist whose children's books are widely read. (Rev: BL 9/1/96; HB 9–10/96; SLJ 12/96) [921]

## FAVERSHAM, CHARLES

**10241** Gerrard, Roy. *The Favershams* (1–4). Illus. by author. 1983, Farrar $15.00 (0-374-32292-9); paper $3.95 (0-374-42293-1). 32pp. Rhyming verses tell the story of the Favershams in Victorian England and Charles, the famous writer.

## FRITZ, JEAN

**10242** Fritz, Jean. *Homesick: My Own Story* (5–7). Illus. by Margot Tomes. 1982, Putnam $15.95 (0-399-20933-6); Dell paper $4.99 (0-440-43683-4). 160pp. Growing up in the troubled China of the 1920s.

**10243** Fritz, Jean. *Surprising Myself* (2–5). Illus. by Andrea F. Pfleger. Series: Meet the Author. 1993, Richard C. Owen $14.95 (1-878450-37-9). 32pp. As well as telling the reader about her life, Fritz explains how she does research for her many historical biographies. (Rev: BL 9/1/93; HB 9–10/93) [921]

## GEISEL, THEODOR

**10244** Weidt, Maryann N. *Oh, the Places He Went: A Story About Dr. Seuss* (3–6). Illus. by Kerry Maguire. Series: Creative Minds Biographies. 1994, Carolrhoda LB $19.95 (0-87614-823-2); paper $5.95 (0-87614-627-2). 64pp. The life story of the famous children's author that tells of his many hardships and of some of his most important books. (Rev: BCCB 2/95; SLJ 1/95) [921]

## GEORGE, JEAN CRAIGHEAD

**10245** Cary, Alice. *Jean Craighead George* (4–6). Illus. 1996, Learning Works paper $6.95 (0-88160-283-3). 136pp. A lively re-creation of the life of this renowned nature writer and Newbery Award winner. (Rev: BL 11/15/96; SLJ 9/96) [921]

**10246** George, Jean Craighead. *The Tarantula in My Purse* (4–6). Illus. 1996, HarperCollins LB $14.89 (0-06-023627-2). 128pp. The author describes the many wild pets that her family had sheltered while her children were growing up. (Rev: BCCB 12/96; BL 11/15/96; SLJ 10/96) [921]

## GOBLE, PAUL

**10247** Goble, Paul. *Hau Kola Hello Friend* (2–4). Illus. by Gerry Perrin. Series: Meet the Author. 1994, Richard C. Owen $14.95 (1-878450-44-1). 32pp. This dedicated author, who has specialized in American Indian folk material, tells about his life and writing. (Rev: BL 8/94; SLJ 8/94) [921]

## HANSBERRY, LORRAINE

**10248** Tripp, Janet. *Lorraine Hansberry* (4–8). Series: Importance Of. 1997, Lucent LB $22.45 (1-56006-081-6). 112pp. Tells of the short life of this playwright and of her amazing achievements. (Rev: BL 10/15/97; SLJ 1/98) [921]

## HELLER, RUTH

**10249** Heller, Ruth. *Fine Lines* (3–5). Illus. 1996, Richard C. Owen $14.95 (1-878450-76-X). 32pp. In

this autobiography, the author tells about her childhood, training, writing, and artwork. (Rev: BL 9/1/96; HB 9–10/96; SLJ 1/97) [921]

## HERRERA, JUAN FILIPE

**10250** Herrera, Juan Felipe. *Calling the Doves/El Canto de las Palomas* (3–6). Illus. by Elly Simmons. 1995, Children's $14.95 (0-89239-132-4). 32pp. In this bilingual autobiography, the Mexican American poet Juan Felipe Herrera describes his childhood in California as the son of migrant workers. (Rev: BCCB 12/95; BL 1/1–15/96; SLJ 12/95) [921]

## HOPKINS, LEE BENNETT

**10251** Hopkins, Lee Bennett. *The Writing Bug* (2–5). Illus. by Diane Rubinger. Series: Meet the Author. 1993, Richard C. Owen $14.95 (1-878450-38-7). 32pp. The acclaimed poet, author, and anthologist tells about his life and the experiences that inspire him to write. (Rev: BL 9/1/93; HB 9–10/93) [921]

## HOWE, JAMES

**10252** Howe, James. *Playing with Words* (1–4). Photos by Michael Craine. Series: Meet the Author. 1994, Richard C. Owen $14.95 (1-878450-40-9). 32pp. People who love this author's zany mysteries will enjoy reading about how he writes, gets his inspiration, and spends a typical day. (Rev: BL 8/94; SLJ 8/94) [921]

## HUGHES, LANGSTON

**10253** Cooper, Floyd. *Coming Home: From the Life of Langston Hughes* (3–6). Illus. 1994, Putnam $15.95 (0-399-22682-6). 32pp. A sensitive retelling of Langston Hughes's unhappy childhood and his search for a permanent home. (Rev: BCCB 1/95; BL 10/1/94; HB 9–10/94; SLJ 11/94) [921]

**10254** McKissack, Patricia, and Fredrick McKissack. *Langston Hughes: Great American Poet* (2–4). Illus. by Michael D. Blegel. Series: Great African Americans. 1992, Enslow LB $13.95 (0-89490-315-2). 32pp. The sounds and language of Harlem were incorporated into the poems of this black writer. (Rev: BL 1/15/92; SLJ 1/93) [921]

## HURSTON, ZORA NEALE

**10255** Calvert, Roz. *Zora Neale Hurston* (5–8). Illus. Series: Black Americans of Achievement. 1993, Chelsea LB $15.95 (0-7910-1766-4). 80pp. A lively account of the life of the famous American writer and folklorist. (Rev: BL 5/1/93; SLJ 6/93) [921]

**10256** McKissack, Patricia, and Fredrick McKissack. *Zora Neale Hurston: Writer and Storyteller* (2–4). Illus. by Michael Bryant. Series: Great African Americans. 1992, Enslow LB $13.95 (0-89490-316-

0). 32pp. Zora Hurston, anthropologist and story-teller, was an active writer during the Harlem Renaissance. (Rev: BL 10/15/92; SLJ 12/92) [921]

### JUANA DE LA GUZ, SISTER

**10257** Martinez, Elizabeth Coonrod. *Sor Juana: A Trailblazing Thinker* (3–6). Illus. Series: Hispanic Heritage. 1994, Millbrook $19.90 (1-56294-406-1). 32pp. The story of the 17th-century Mexican-born poet who is considered the finest writer of Mexico's colonial period. (Rev: BL 6/1–15/94; SLJ 4/94) [921]

### KEY, FRANCIS SCOTT

**10258** Whitcraft, Melissa. *Francis Scott Key* (4–7). Illus. 1995, Watts LB $21.00 (0-531-20163-5). 64pp. A biography of this famous poet that supplies good background information on the creation of "The Star Spangled Banner." (Rev: BL 2/15/95; SLJ 6/95) [921]

### KIPLING, RUDYARD

**10259** Kamen, Gloria. *Kipling: Storyteller of East and West* (3–5). Illus. 1985, Macmillan $15.00 (0-689-31195-8). 80pp. A lively biography centering on the writer's childhood and role as a father. (Rev: BCCB 3/86; BL 1/1/86; SLJ 2/86)

### KUSKIN, KARLA

**10260** Kuskin, Karla. *Thoughts, Pictures, and Words* (2–5). Illus. Series: Meet the Author. 1995, Richard C. Owen $14.95 (1-878450-41-7). 32pp. This renowned writer discusses her prose, poetry, and illustrations, and discusses how she approaches writing. (Rev: BCCB 7–8/95; BL 8/95; HB 7–8/95; SLJ 9/95) [921]

### LESTER, HELEN

**10261** Lester, Helen. *Author: A True Story* (2–4). Illus. 1997, Houghton $10.95 (0-395-82744-2). 32pp. A delightful autobiography illustrated with her own cartoons. (Rev: BCCB 4/97; BL 3/15/97; HB 5–6/97; SLJ 5/97*) [921]

### LOWRY, LOIS

**10262** Markham, Lois. *Lois Lowry* (5–8). Illus. Series: Meet the Author. 1995, Learning Works paper $6.95 (0-88160-278-7). 128pp. This biography of the Newbery Award–winning author tells how she became a writer and what personal experiences can be found in her books. (Rev: SLJ 1/96) [921]

### LYON, GEORGE ELLA

**10263** Lyon, George E. *A Wordful Child* (3–5). Illus. 1996, Richard C. Owen $14.95 (1-57274-016-7). 32pp. The author tells about her life and the stories

she heard as a child that influenced her work. (Rev: BL 9/1/96; HB 9–10/96; SLJ 1/97) [921]

### MCKISSACK, PATRICIA

**10264** McKissack, Patricia. *Can You Imagine?* (2–5). Illus. Series: Meet the Author. 1997, Richard C. Owen $14.95 (1-878450-61-1). 32pp. An autobiographical account of this fantasy writer in which she tells of the importance of imagination in her life. (Rev: BL 6/1–15/97; SLJ 9/97) [921]

### MCPHAIL, DAVID

**10265** McPhail, David. *In Flight with David McPhail* (2–6). Illus. by author. Series: Creative Sparks. 1996, Heinemann $15.95 (0-435-08132-2). 45pp. This famous artists talks about his life and the processes involved in illustrating a book. (Rev: HB 9–10/96; SLJ 6/96*) [921]

### MAHY, MARGARET

**10266** Mahy, Margaret. *My Mysterious World* (2–5). Illus. Series: Meet the Author. 1995, Richard C. Owen $14.95 (1-878450-58-1). 32pp. The New Zealand writer describes her many interests and how she approaches writing. (Rev: BCCB 7–8/95; BL 8/95; HB 7–8/95; SLJ 9/95) [921]

### MARTÍ, JOSÉ J.

**10267** West, Alan. *José Martí: Man of Poetry, Soldier of Freedom* (5–8). Illus. Series: Hispanic Heritage. 1994, Millbrook LB $19.90 (1-56294-408-8). 32pp. The life story of the famous 19th-century Cuban poet, with excerpts from his work in both Spanish and English. (Rev: SLJ 1/95) [921]

### MARTIN, RAFE

**10268** Martin, Rafe. *A Storyteller's Story* (3–6). Illus. by Jill Krementz. Series: Meet the Author. 1992, Owen $14.95 (0-913461-03-2). 32pp. The author takes readers to his home to meet family and friends. (Rev: BCCB 9/92; BL 8/92; SLJ 8/92) [921]

### MORRISON, TONI

**10269** Patrick-Wexler, Diane. *Toni Morrison* (4–6). Illus. Series: Contemporary African Americans. 1997, Raintree Steck-Vaughn LB $24.26 (0-8172-3987-1). 48pp. A fine biography of this influential writer, who has won both the Nobel and Pulitzer prizes. (Rev: BL 5/15/97; SLJ 2/98) [921]

### MYERS, WALTER DEAN

**10270** Patrick-Wexler, Diane. *Walter Dean Myers* (4–6). Illus. Series: Contemporary African Americans. 1995, Raintree Steck-Vaughn LB $24.26 (0-

8172-3979-0). 48pp. The life of the popular African American author is covered, with emphasis on the hardships he has overcome. (Rev: BL 2/15/96; SLJ 1/96) [921]

### PATERSON, KATHERINE

**10271** Cary, Alice. *Katherine Paterson* (5–8). Illus. Series: Meet the Author. 1997, Learning Works paper $6.95 (0-88160-281-7). 136pp. A biography of the 2-time Newbery winner, with many quotes from interviews and autobiographical essays. (Rev: BL 5/1/97; SLJ 7/97) [921]

### POTTER, BEATRIX

**10272** Aldis, Dorothy. *Nothing Is Impossible: The Story of Beatrix Potter* (3–6). Illus. by Richard Cuffari. 1988, Peter Smith $19.25 (0-8446-6359-X). The story of a remarkable woman whose lonely childhood in London was relieved only by her pets, her reading, and her drawings.

**10273** Collins, David R. *The Country Artist: A Story About Beatrix Potter* (3–5). Illus. by Karen Ritz. 1989, Carolrhoda LB $19.93 (0-87614-344-3); paper $5.95 (0-87614-509-8). 56pp. The story of the creator of Peter Rabbit and other famous creatures. (Rev: BL 5/1/89)

**10274** Wallner, Alexandra. *Beatrix Potter* (K–3). Illus. 1995, Holiday LB $15.95 (0-8234-1181-8). 32pp. A fascinating account of the life of this children's book author who was also an expert on mushrooms and an early conservationist. (Rev: BL 9/1/95; SLJ 10/95) [921]

### PRINGLE, LAURENCE

**10275** Pringle, Laurence. *Nature! Wild and Wonderful* (2–5). Illus. Series: Meet the Author. 1997, Richard C. Owen $14.95 (1-57274-071-X). 32pp. An autobiographical account of this writer of more than 80 books that tells how he became interested in nature study and in writing about it. (Rev: BL 6/1–15/97; SLJ 9/97) [921]

### PYLE, ERNIE

**10276** O'Connor, Barbara. *The Soldiers' Voice: The Story of Ernie Pyle* (4–7). Illus. 1996, Carolrhoda $16.95 (0-87614-942-5). 80pp. The story of the renowned World War II correspondent who died in the South Pacific while covering the war. (Rev: BCCB 10/96; BL 9/1/96; SLJ 8/96) [921]

### RYLANT, CYNTHIA

**10277** Rylant, Cynthia. *Best Wishes* (3–6). Illus. by Carlo Ontal. 1992, Owen $14.95 (1-878450-20-4). 32pp. The author takes her readers to her home in

Ohio, then travels back to her childhood in West Virginia. (Rev: BCCB 9/92; BL 8/92; SLJ 8/92) [921]

### SANDBURG, CARL

**10278** Mitchell, Barbara. *"Good Morning Mr. President": A Story About Carl Sandburg* (3–6). 1988, Carolrhoda LB $19.93 (0-87614-329-X). 56pp. The story of Sandburg's growing up and the experiences that were later reflected in his poetry. (Rev: BL 3/1/89; SLJ 2/89)

### SHAKESPEARE, WILLIAM

**10279** Stanley, Diane, and Peter Vennema. *Bard of Avon: The Story of William Shakespeare* (3–8). Illus. by Diane Stanley. 1992, Morrow $16.00 (0-688-09108-3). 48pp. A handsome volume on the life of Shakespeare. (Rev: BCCB 12/92; BL 9/1/92*; HB 11–12/92*; SLJ 11/92) [921]

### SINGER, ISAAC BASHEVIS

**10280** Perl, Lila. *Isaac Bashevis Singer: The Life of a Storyteller* (5–7). Illus. 1994, Jewish Publication Soc. $12.95 (0-8276-0512-9). 95pp. The life story of the Nobel Prize–winning author, his years in Poland and in the United States, and the nature of his writing for children and adults. (Rev: BL 5/1/94; SLJ 3/95) [921]

**10281** Singer, Isaac Bashevis. *A Day of Pleasure: Stories of a Boy Growing Up in Warsaw* (6–8). Illus. by Roman Vishniac. 1969, Farrar paper $5.95 (0-374-41696-6). 160pp. A Hasidic Jew's fond remembrances of the world in which he grew up.

### SLEATOR, WILLIAM

**10282** Sleator, William. *Oddballs* (4–6). 1993, Dutton paper $14.99 (0-525-45057-2). 176pp. Scenes from the childhood of an irreverent writer-to-be. (Rev: BCCB 5/93; HB 5–6/93) [921]

### STEINBECK, JOHN

**10283** Ito, Tom. *John Steinbeck* (4–8). Illus. Series: The Importance Of. 1994, Lucent LB $22.45 (1-56006-049-2). 112pp. The biography of the great novelist who immortalized the common people of the Great Depression and some coastal towns in California. (Rev: BL 8/94; SLJ 6/94) [921]

### STEVENSON, ROBERT LOUIS

**10284** Carpenter, Angelica S., and Jean Shirley. *Robert Louis Stevenson: Finding Treasure Island* (5–8). Illus. 1997, Lerner LB $23.93 (0-8225-4955-7). 144pp. A lively narrative of this great writer, who was a disappointment to his family because he did not become a minister. (Rev: BL 11/15/97; SLJ 12/97) [921]

**10285** Gherman, Beverly. *Robert Louis Stevenson: Teller of Tales* (5–8). Illus. 1996, Simon & Schuster $16.00 (0-689-31985-1). 136pp. The story of the author of *Treasure Island,* who though always in poor health lived a full, adventurous life. (Rev: BL 9/15/96; SLJ 2/97) [921]

**10286** Greene, Carol. *Robert Louis Stevenson: Author of a Child's Garden of Verses* (2–3). Illus. by Steven Dobson. Series: Rookie Biographies. 1994, Children's LB $19.00 (0-516-04265-3). 47pp. An attractive beginner's biography of the writer whom many children know through his poems. (Rev: SLJ 1/95) [921]

### STINE, R. L.

**10287** Stine, R. L., and Joe Arthur. *It Came From Ohio! My Life as a Writer* (4–6). Illus. 1997, Scholastic $9.95 (0-590-36674-2). 144pp. An autobiography of the creator of the hugely successful Fear Street and Goosebumps series. (Rev: BCCB 6/97; BL 8/97; HB 7–8/97; SLJ 7/97) [921]

### STOWE, HARRIET BEECHER

**10288** Ash, Maureen. *The Story of Harriet Beecher Stowe* (3–5). Illus. Series: Cornerstones of Freedom. 1990, Children's paper $5.95 (0-516-44746-7). 32pp. A brief biography of the woman who wrote Uncle Tom's Cabin and changed many people's attitudes toward slavery. (Rev: BL 7/90; SLJ 10/90) [921]

**10289** Bland, Celia. *Harriet Beecher Stowe: Anti-slavery Author* (3–5). Illus. Series: Junior World Biographies. 1993, Chelsea LB $15.95 (0-7910-1773-7). 79pp. The story of the renowned writer and her courageous stand against slavery. (Rev: SLJ 10/93) [921]

**10290** Fritz, Jean. *Harriet Beecher Stowe and the Beecher Preachers* (5–8). Illus. 1994, Putnam $16.95 (0-399-22666-4). 144pp. In addition to covering *Uncle Tom's Cabin,* this biography gives a full account of Harriet Beecher's private life, marriage, and extended family. (Rev: BCCB 10/94; BL 8/94; HB 9–10/94; SLJ 9/94*) [921]

### THOREAU, HENRY DAVID

**10291** Burleigh, Robert. *A Man Named Thoreau* (4–6). Illus. 1985, Macmillan $15.00 (0-689-31122-2). 48pp. A profile of the 19th-century thinker in prose that makes him available to the younger grades. (Rev: BCCB 12/85; BL 3/15/86; SLJ 1/86)

**10292** Murphy, Jim. *Into the Deep Forest with Henry David Thoreau* (4–6). Illus. 1995, Clarion $14.95 (0-395-60522-9). 32pp. An introduction to the life and work of Thoreau, including a description of a hiking trip he took in Maine using quotes from the naturalist's journals. (Rev: BL 4/15/95; SLJ 7/95) [921]

### TOLKIEN, J. R. R.

**10293** Neimark, Anne E. *Myth Maker: J. R. R. Tolkien* (4–6). Illus. by Brad Weinman. 1996, Harcourt $17.00 (0-15-298847-5). 111pp. A brief biography that covers the important events in the life of the writer who created Hobbits and other fantastic beings. (Rev: SLJ 10/96) [921]

### TWAIN, MARK

**10294** Collins, David R. *Mark T-W-A-I-N! A Story About Samuel Clemens* (3–5). Illus. by Vicky Carey. 1994, Carolrhoda LB $19.95 (0-87614-801-1). 64pp. Beginning with his boyhood in Hannibal, Missouri, through his many jobs as a youth, to his distinguished career as a writer, this is a lively biography of Clemens. (Rev: BL 3/1/94; SLJ 3/94) [921]

**10295** Press, Skip. *Mark Twain* (4–8). Illus. 1994, Lucent LB $22.45 (1-56006-043-3). 112pp. A biography that reports on Clemens's intriguing personal and public lives and his prolific literary output. (Rev: BL 5/15/94; SLJ 4/94) [921]

### VERNE, JULES

**10296** Teeters, Peggy. *Jules Verne: The Man Who Invented Tomorrow* (5–7). Illus. 1993, Walker LB $14.85 (0-8027-8191-8). 128pp. The life of the famous writer of science fiction, including his childhood in France. (Rev: BL 3/15/93; SLJ 5/93) [921]

### WALKER, ALICE

**10297** Kramer, Barbara. *Alice Walker: Author of the Color Purple* (4–6). Illus. Series: People to Know. 1995, Enslow LB $19.95 (0-89490-620-8). 128pp. The life, struggles, and work of this celebrated African American writer are covered concisely in a conversational style. (Rev: BL 9/15/95; SLJ 11/95) [921]

### WARNER, GERTRUDE C.

**10298** Ellsworth, Mary Ellen. *Gertrude Chandler Warner and the Boxcar Children* (3–5). Illus. 1997, Albert Whitman LB $14.95 (0-8075-2837-4). 61pp. The life story of the author who created the Boxcar Children and lived her entire life in Connecticut. (Rev: BL 8/97; HB 7–8/97; SLJ 7/97) [921]

### WATSON, LYALL

**10299** Watson, Lyall. *Warriors, Warthogs, and Wisdom: Growing Up in Africa* (4–7). Illus. 1997, Kingfisher $16.95 (0-7534-5066-6). 80pp. This well-known nature writer descibes his childhood in the

South African bush and how, at an early age, he learned to live off the land with his Zulu friend. (Rev: BL 10/1/97; SLJ 8/97) [921]

## WHEATLEY, PHILLIS

**10300**  Sherrow, Victoria. *Phillis Wheatley: Poet* (4–7). Illus. Series: Junior World Biographies. 1992, Chelsea LB $12.95 (0-7910-1753-2). 80pp. The biography of the poet who is considered to be the first important African American writer. (Rev: BL 8/92; SLJ 8/92) [921]

**10301**  Weidt, Maryann N. *Revolutionary Poet: A Story About Phillis Wheatley* (3–6). Illus. Series: Creative Minds. 1997, Carolrhoda LB $14.95 (1-57505-037-4); paper $5.95 (1-57505-059-5). 64pp. The story of the poetry-writing slave girl who was the first African American to have a book published. (Rev: BL 2/15/98) [921]

## WHITE, E. B.

**10302**  Collins, David R. *To the Point: A Story About E. B. White* (3–5). Illus. by Amy Johnson. 1989, Carolrhoda LB $14.95 (0-87614-345-1); paper $5.95 (0-87614-508-X). 56pp. The story of a writer who made a great impact on children's reading. (Rev: BL 5/1/89)

## WHITMAN, WALT

**10303**  Loewen, Nancy, ed. *Walt Whitman* (5–8). Illus. by Rob Day. 1994, Creative Ed. LB $17.95 (0-88682-608-X). 45pp. With generous quotes from *Leaves of Grass* and color photos, various vignettes from Whitman's life are retold. (Rev: SLJ 7/94*) [921]

## WIESEL, ELIE

**10304**  Lazo, Caroline. *Elie Wiesel* (4–7). Illus. 1994, Dillon paper $7.95 (0-382-24715-9). 64pp. The story of the distinguished writer and spokesman on the Holocaust who won the Nobel Peace Prize in 1986. (Rev: BL 2/15/95; SLJ 7/95) [921]

**10305**  Pariser, Michael. *Elie Wiesel: Bearing Witness* (4–6). Illus. Series: Gateway Biographies. 1994, Millbrook LB $21.90 (1-56294-419-3). 48pp. A slim biography of the Nobel Prize winner, who at age 15 was sent to Auschwitz. (Rev: SLJ 4/95) [921]

## WILDER, LAURA INGALLS

**10306**  Anderson, William. *Pioneer Girl: The Story of Laura Ingalls Wilder* (2–4). Illus. by Dan Andreasen. 1998, HarperCollins LB $15.89 (0-06-027244-9). This biography of the author covers the significant events in her life. (Rev: SLJ 3/98) [921]

**10307**  Giff, Patricia Reilly. *Laura Ingalls Wilder: Growing Up in the Little House* (3–6). Illus. by Eileen McKeating. 1988, Puffin paper $4.99 (0-14-032074-1). 64pp. Stories of growing up in the Big Woods of Wisconsin, long, long ago. (Rev: BCCB 9/87; BL 8/87; SLJ 4/87) [921]

**10308**  Wadsworth, Ginger. *Laura Ingalls Wilder: Storyteller of the Prairie* (4–6). Illus. 1997, Lerner LB $23.93 (0-8225-4950-6). 128pp. A solid, factual biography of the creator of the "Little House" books. (Rev: BL 3/1/97; HB 11–12/97; SLJ 4/97) [921]

**10309**  Wallner, Alexandra. *Laura Ingalls Wilder* (K–3). Illus. 1997, Holiday LB $15.95 (0-8234-1314-4). 32pp. A concise biography that traces Wilder's life from childhood to her emergence as a juvenile book author. (Rev: BL 10/1/97; SLJ 11/97) [921]

## YOLEN, JANE

**10310**  Yolen, Jane. *A Letter from Phoenix Farm* (3–6). Illus. by Jason Stemple. 1992, Owen $14.95 (1-878450-36-0). 32pp. Spending a day with this writer of children's books. (Rev: BCCB 9/92; BL 8/92; SLJ 8/92) [921]

# Contemporary and Historical Americans

## Collective

**10311**   Allen, Paula Gunn, and Patricia C. Smith. *As Long As the Rivers Flow: The Stories of Nine Native Americans* (5–8). Illus. 1996, Scholastic $15.95 (0-590-47869-9). 328pp. Profiles of 9 Native Americans, including Geronimo, Will Rogers, and Maria Tallchief. (Rev: BL 12/1/96) [920]

**10312**   Altman, Susan. *Extraordinary Black Americans: From Colonial to Contemporary Times* (5–8). Illus. 1989, Children's LB $37.00 (0-516-00581-2). 240pp. A collection of 85 short biographies, valuable as a resource. (Rev: BL 6/15/89; SLJ 6/89)

**10313**   Blassingame, Wyatt. *The Look-It-Up Book of Presidents* (3–6). Illus. 1990, Random LB $14.99 (0-679-90353-4); paper $8.99 (0-679-80358-0). There is good coverage on each of our presidents and on their terms of office.

**10314**   Blue, Rose, and Corinne J. Naden. *The White House Kids* (4–7). Illus. 1995, Millbrook LB $24.90 (1-56294-447-9). 96pp. An overview of the children of presidents who have called the White House their home. (Rev: BCCB 9/95; BL 6/1–15/95; SLJ 8/95) [920]

**10315**   Burleigh, Robert. *Who Said That? Famous Americans Speak* (5–8). Illus. by David Catrow. 1997, Holt $15.95 (0-8050-4394-2). 45pp. Using quotes from 33 famous personalities, from Benjamin Franklin to Marilyn Monroe, brief profiles of the subjects are presented. (Rev: BL 3/1/97*; SLJ 5/97) [920]

**10316**   Calvert, Patricia. *Great Lives: The American Frontier* (4–8). Illus. 1997, Simon & Schuster $25.00 (0-689-80640-X). 400pp. A large book that contains profiles of 27 individuals who played a significant role in the opening up of the West. (Rev: BL 2/15/98; SLJ 1/98) [920]

**10317**   Colman, Penny. *United States of America* (5–8). Illus. Series: Women in Society. 1994, Marshall Cavendish LB $19.95 (1-85435-560-0). 128pp. Brief biographies are used to introduce the many contributions that women have made to the United States throughout history. (Rev: SLJ 10/94) [921]

**10318**   Davidson, Sue. *Getting the Real Story: Nellie Bly and Ida B. Wells* (4–6). 1992, Seal Pr. paper $8.95 (1-878067-16-8). 152pp. The story of 2 gallant women news reporters, both of whom fought for justice and against corruption. (Rev: SLJ 7/92) [920]

**10319**   Davis, Burke. *Black Heroes of the American Revolution* (4–6). Illus. 1992, Harcourt paper $5.00 (0-15-208561-0). 80pp. A look at American blacks who performed key roles in the American Revolution.

**10320**   Delisle, Jim. *Kidstories: Biographies of 20 Young People You'd Like to Know* (PS–3). Illus. 1991, Free Spirit paper $9.95 (0-915793-34-2). 168pp. This collection of short biographies tells about young people from different life-styles and locales. (Rev: BCCB 1/92; BL 12/15/91; SLJ 1/92) [920]

**10321**   Drimmer, Frederick. *Incredible People: Five Stories of Extraordinary Lives* (4–7). Illus. 1997, Simon & Schuster $16.00 (0-689-31921-5). 192pp. The stories of 5 people who were considered outsiders, like seven-and-a-half-foot-tall Jack Earle and conjoined twins Daisy and Violet Hilton. (Rev: BCCB 7–8/97; BL 6/1–15/97; SLJ 5/97) [920]

**10322**   Dudley, Karen. *Great African Americans in Government* (3–5). Series: Outstanding African Americans. 1997, Crabtree LB $21.28 (0-86505-806-7); paper $8.95 (0-86505-820-2). 64pp. In-depth profiles of 7 African Americans in government — e.g., Adam Clayton Powell, Colin Powell, and

Shirley Chisolm — with 7 shorter sketches that include Julian Bond and David Dinkins. (Rev: BL 9/15/97; SLJ 1/98) [920]

**10323** Gormley, Beatrice. *First Ladies: Women Who Called the White House Home* (4–6). Illus. 1997, Scholastic paper $6.99 (0-590-25518-5). 96pp. A collection of short profiles of U.S. presidents' wives, from Martha Washington to Hillary Clinton. (Rev: BL 3/15/97) [920]

**10324** Green, Carl R. *The Younger Brothers* (4–6). Illus. Series: Outlaws and Lawmen of the Wild West. 1995, Enslow LB $15.95 (0-89490-592-9). 48pp. The story of the interesting characters who were involved with Jesse James in the old West. (Rev: SLJ 9/95) [920]

**10325** Hacker, Carlotta. *Great African Americans in History* (3–5). Illus. Series: Outstanding African Americans. 1997, Crabtree LB $21.28 (0-86505-805-9); paper $8.95 (0-86505-819-9). 64pp. Brief biographies of such historically important African Americans as Sojourner Truth, W. E. B. Du Bois, and Booker T. Washington. (Rev: BL 9/15/97; SLJ 1/98) [920]

**10326** Haskins, Jim. *One More River to Cross: The Stories of Twelve Black Americans* (4–8). Illus. 1992, Scholastic $13.95 (0-590-42896-9). 160pp. Eight men and 4 women who defied the odds to achieve prominence in their fields are introduced, including Ralph Bunche, Shirley Chisolm, and Ron McNair. (Rev: BCCB 4/92; BL 2/1/92; SLJ 4/92) [920]

**10327** Hudson, Wade, and Valerie Wesley Wilson. *Afro-Bets Book of Black Heroes from A to Z: An Introduction to Important Black Achievers* (4–7). Illus. 1988, Just Us paper $7.95 (0-940975-02-5). 64pp. Forty-nine black men and women of outstanding accomplishment. (Rev: BL 1/1/89; SLJ 12/88)

**10328** Igus, Toyomi, ed. *Great Women in the Struggle* (3–6). Illus. Series: Book of Black Heroes. 1992, Just Us LB $17.95 (0-940975-27-0); paper $10.95 (0-940975-26-2). 107pp. More than 80 contemporary African American women are profiled. (Rev: SLJ 8/92) [920]

**10329** Jeffrey, Laura S. *Great American Businesswomen* (4–7). Illus. 1996, Enslow LB $19.95 (0-89490-706-9). 112pp. Profiles of 10 successful American businesswomen, e.g., Maggie L. Walker and Katherine Graham. (Rev: BL 9/1/96; SLJ 9/96) [920]

**10330** Katz, William L. *Black People Who Made the Old West* (6–8). Illus. 1992, Africa World $35.00 (0-86543-363-1); paper $14.95 (0-86543-364-X). Sketches of 35 black explorers, pioneers, etc., who helped open up the West.

**10331** Katz, William L., and Paula A. Franklin. *Proudly Red and Black: Stories of Native and African*

*Americans* (4–7). Illus. 1993, Atheneum $15.00 (0-689-31801-4). 96pp. A collective biography of famous people of mixed Native American and African ancestry. (Rev: BL 12/1/93) [920]

**10332** King, David C. *First Facts About American Heroes* (3–6). Illus. 1995, Blackbirch LB $24.95 (1-56711-165-3). 112pp. The lives and accomplishments of 42 famous Americans are presented, each with a full-page photograph or painting and a single page of facts. (Rev: SLJ 2/96) [920]

**10333** Lawson, Robert. *They Were Strong and Good* (4–6). Illus. by author. 1940, Viking paper $16.99 (0-670-69949-7). 72pp. The author has drawn word-and-pen portraits of his grandparents, typical Americans of their time. Caldecott Medal winner, 1941.

**10334** Lindop, Edmund. *Dwight D. Eisenhower, John F. Kennedy, Lyndon B. Johnson* (4–7). Illus. Series: Presidents Who Dared. 1996, Twenty-First Century LB $18.90 (0-8050-3404-8). 64pp. The highlights of these 3 administrations are presented, preceded by an introduction to the American presidency. (Rev: BL 4/15/96; SLJ 6/96) [920]

**10335** Lindop, Edmund. *George Washington, Thomas Jefferson, Andrew Jackson* (4–7). Illus. Series: Presidents Who Dared. 1995, Twenty-First Century LB $18.90 (0-8050-3401-3). 64pp. After a general introduction on the duties of the president, brief biographies of 3 are given, with emphasis on their accomplishments in office. (Rev: BL 1/1–15/96; SLJ 11/95) [920]

**10336** Lindop, Edmund. *James K. Polk, Abraham Lincoln, Theodore Roosevelt* (4–7). Illus. Series: Presidents Who Dared. 1995, Twenty-First Century LB $18.90 (0-8050-3402-1). 64pp. Highlights and evaluations of the presidencies of Polk, Lincoln, and Theodore Roosevelt. (Rev: BL 1/1–15/96; SLJ 11/95) [920]

**10337** Lindop, Edmund. *Richard M. Nixon, Jimmy Carter, Ronald Reagan* (4–7). Illus. Series: Presidents Who Dared. 1996, Twenty-First Century LB $18.90 (0-8050-3405-6). 64pp. The office of the U.S. presidency is introduced, followed by important events and decisions involving these 3 presidents. (Rev: BL 4/15/96; SLJ 6/96) [920]

**10338** Lindop, Edmund. *Woodrow Wilson, Franklin D. Roosevelt, Harry S. Truman* (4–7). Illus. Series: Presidents Who Dared. 1995, Twenty-First Century LB $18.90 (0-8050-3403-X). 64pp. After an overview of the presidency, this account briefly tells about the accomplishments of Wilson, FDR, and Truman. (Rev: BL 1/1–15/96; SLJ 11/95) [920]

**10339** Marvis, Barbara J. *Famous People of Asian Ancestry*, vol. 4 (4–7). Illus. Series: Contemporary American Success Stories. 1994, Mitchell Lane paper $10.95 (1-883845-09-2). 96pp. A collective biography of Asian Americans, including actor

Dustin Nguyen, novelist Amy Tan, and businessman Rocky Aoki. Also use volumes 1 through 3 (2nd ed., 1997). (Rev: BL 10/1/94; SLJ 11/94) [920]

**10340** Marvis, Barbara J. *Famous People of Hispanic Heritage*, vol. 1 (4–7). Illus. Series: Contemporary American Success Stories. 1995, Mitchell Lane LB $21.95 (1-883845-21-1); paper $12.95 (1-883845-20-3). 96pp. This is the first of 3 volumes that give brief biographies of Hispanic Americans from all walks of life who have made significant contributions to our country. Also use volumes 2 through 10 (1995–1998). (Rev: BL 11/15/95; SLJ 1/96) [920]

**10341** Mayberry, Jodine. *Business Leaders Who Built Financial Empires* (5–8). Illus. Series: 20 Events. 1995, Raintree Steck-Vaughn LB $24.26 (0-8114-4934-3). 48pp. The biographies of 19 financial wizards and entrepreneurs, beginning with Levi Strauss and Andrew Carnegie and ending with Steven Jobs and Anita Roddick. (Rev: SLJ 7/95) [920]

**10342** Morin, Isobel V. *Women Chosen for Public Office* (5–7). Illus. 1995, Oliver LB $16.95 (1-881508-20-X). 160pp. Nine biographies of women who are involved in the federal government from the superintendent of army nurses to Supreme Court justice Ruth Bader Ginsburg. (Rev: BL 5/1/95; SLJ 6/95) [920]

**10343** Parker, Janice. *Great African Americans in Film* (3–5). Illus. Series: Outstanding African Americans. 1997, Crabtree LB $21.28 (0-86505-808-3); paper $8.95 (0-86505-822-9). 64pp. Among the 13 important African Americans highlighted here are Dorothy Dandridge, Richard Pryor, and Denzel Washington. (Rev: BL 9/15/97; SLJ 12/97) [920]

**10344** Pascoe, Elaine. *First Facts About the Presidents* (4–8). Illus. Series: First Facts About . . . 1996, Blackbirch LB $24.95 (1-56711-167-X). 112pp. Divided into 4 historical periods, this book covers the major historical events of the time, introduces each of the presidents, and briefly describes his presidency. (Rev: SLJ 5/96) [920]

**10345** Pelz, Ruth. *Black Heroes of the Wild West* (3–5). Illus. by Leandro Della Piana. 1989, Open Hand $12.95 (0-940880-25-3); paper $6.95 (0-940880-26-1). 56pp. The stories of 5 black men and 4 black women who contributed to the history of the Old West. (Rev: BL 6/1/90) [920]

**10346** Pelz, Ruth. *Women of the Wild West: Biographies from Many Cultures* (3–5). Illus. 1995, Open Hand $12.95 (0-940880-49-0); paper $6.95 (0-940880-50-4). 64pp. The biographies of 8 women — e.g., Sacajawea and exslave Biddy Mason — who played important roles in the history of the American West. (Rev: BL 3/1/95) [921]

**10347** Phillips, Louis. *Ask Me Anything About the Presidents* (5–8). Illus. by Valeria Costantino. 1992, Avon paper $4.50 (0-380-76426-1). 130pp. A collec-

tion of many unusual facts about various aspects of the U.S. presidency, in a question-and-answer format. (Rev: BL 4/15/92) [920]

**10348** Potter, Joan, and Constance Claytor. *African Americans Who Were First* (4–8). Illus. 1997, Dutton paper $15.99 (0-525-65246-9). 128pp. A brief introduction to 65 African Americans who earned "firsts" in a variety of fields. (Rev: BL 9/1/97; SLJ 9/97) [920]

**10349** Provensen, Alice. *My Fellow Americans: A Family Album* (4–6). Illus. 1995, Harcourt $19.95 (0-15-276642-1). 64pp. Hundreds of prominent Americans grouped by fields of accomplishment are pictured and identified. (Rev: BCCB 1/96; BL 12/1/95; SLJ 12/95*) [920]

**10350** Rediger, Pat. *Great African Americans in Business* (4–6). Illus. Series: Outstanding African Americans. 1996, Crabtree LB $21.28 (0-86505-803-2); paper $8.95 (0-86505-817-2). 64pp. Such people as John H. Johnson and Oprah Winfrey are profiled. (Rev: BL 9/15/96; SLJ 8/96) [920]

**10351** Rediger, Pat. *Great African Americans in Civil Rights* (4–6). Illus. Series: Outstanding African Americans. 1996, Crabtree LB $21.28 (0-86505-798-2); paper $8.95 (0-86505-812-1). 64pp. In short chapters, such civil rights leaders as Thurgood Marshall, Rosa Parks, and Jesse Jackson are introduced. (Rev: BL 9/15/96; SLJ 8/96) [920]

**10352** Ringgold, Faith. *Dinner at Aunt Connie's House* (K–4). Illus. 1993, Hyperion LB $15.49 (1-56282-426-0). 32pp. Twelve African American women of importance, such as Rosa Parks and Fannie Lou Hamer, are introduced through portraits that 2 youngsters discover in their Aunt Connie's attic. (Rev: BL 9/15/93; SLJ 10/93) [920]

**10353** Rubel, David. *Scholastic Encyclopedia of the Presidents and Their Times*. Rev. ed. (4–8). Illus. 1997, Scholastic $17.95 (0-590-49366-3). 232pp. This fine reference book not only introduces each of the presidents and his administration but also supplies material on other historical events, movements, and personalities. (Rev: SLJ 5/97) [920]

**10354** St. George, Judith. *Dear Dr. Bell . . . Your Friend, Helen Keller* (5–7). Illus. 1992, Morrow paper $4.95 (0-688-12814-9). 172pp. A joint biography about the friendship between Alexander Graham Bell and Helen Keller. (Rev: BCCB 11–12/92 & 2/93; SLJ 12/92) [920]

**10355** Sinnott, Susan. *Extraordinary Asian Pacific Americans* (4–6). Illus. 1993, Children's LB $37.00 (0-516-03152-X). 270pp. A history of the Chinese and Japanese in this country, plus brief biographies of such notables as Kristi Yamaguchi and Seiji Ozawa. (Rev: BL 1/15/94; SLJ 2/94) [920]

**10356** Sinnott, Susan. *Extraordinary Hispanic Americans* (5–8). Illus. Series: Extraordinary People. 1991, Children's LB $37.00 (0-516-00582-0). 260pp. This book answers the demand for multicultural role models, including bios of Spanish-speaking peoples of the United States. (Rev: BL 2/1/92) [920]

**10357** Turner, Glennette Tilley. *Take a Walk in Their Shoes* (4–6). Illus. by Elton C. Fax. 1989, Dutton paper $15.99 (0-525-65006-7). 160pp. Sketches of 14 prominent African Americans with skits about each subject. (Rev: BL 12/15/89; SLJ 11/89) [920]

## African Americans

### ABERNATHY, DAVID

**10358** Reef, Catherine. *Ralph David Abernathy* (5–8). Illus. Series: People in Focus Books. 1995, Dillon $13.95 (0-87518-653-X); paper $7.95 (0-382-24965-8). 167pp. A biography that describes this civil rights leader's youth and many accomplishments. (Rev: SLJ 10/95) [921]

### ALLEN, RICHARD

**10359** Klots, Steve. *Richard Allen* (5–8). Illus. Series: Black Americans of Achievement. 1990, Chelsea LB $19.95 (1-55546-570-6). 112pp. Born a slave in 1780, this convert to Christianity founded the first black Methodist Church. (Rev: SLJ 2/91) [921]

### BETHUNE, MARY MCLEOD

**10360** Greenfield, Eloise. *Mary McLeod Bethune* (2–4). Illus. by Jerry Pinkney. 1994, HarperCollins paper $5.95 (0-06-446168-8). 40pp. Bethune was the only one of 17 children in her family to go to school. Through courage and hard work, she became an educator of national importance.

**10361** Kelso, Richard. *Building a Dream: Mary Bethune's School* (2–4). Illus. by Debbe Heller. Series: Stories of America. 1993, Raintree Steck-Vaughn LB $24.26 (0-8114-7217-5). 46pp. The story of Mary Bethune and how she realized her dream of building a school for poor African American children. (Rev: SLJ 7/93) [921]

**10362** McKissack, Patricia, and Fredrick McKissack. *Mary McLeod Bethune: A Great Teacher* (2–4). Illus. Series: Great African Americans. 1991, Enslow LB $13.95 (0-89490-304-7). 32pp. The life and times of an extraordinary black American. (Rev: BL 1/1/92; SLJ 12/91) [921]

**10363** Meltzer, Milton. *Mary McLeod Bethune: Voice of Black Hope* (4–7). Illus. 1988, Puffin paper $4.99 (0-14-032219-1). 64pp. An effective profile of the black educator. (Rev: BCCB 5/87; BL 3/15/87; SLJ 3/87)

**10364** Wolfe, Rinna E. *Mary McLeod Bethune* (3–6). Illus. 1992, Watts LB $21.00 (0-531-20103-1). 64pp. The story of the daughter of slaves who dedicated her life to the education of black people. (Rev: BL 8/92; SLJ 9/92) [921]

### CARMICHAEL, STOKELY

**10365** Cwiklik, Robert. *Stokely Carmichael and Black Power* (4–6). Illus. Series: Gateway Civil Rights. 1993, Millbrook LB $20.90 (1-56294-276-X). 32pp. The life of the controversial civil rights leader who coined the term "black power." (Rev: BCCB 5/93; BL 8/93) [921]

### CHERRY, FRED V.

**10366** Myers, Walter Dean. *A Place Called Heartbreak* (3–6). Illus. by Frederick Porter. 1993, Raintree Steck-Vaughn LB $25.68 (0-8114-7237-X). 72pp. This is a biography of the African American pilot who was shot down during the Vietnam War and spent over 7 years as a prisoner of war. (Rev: BCCB 7–8/93; BL 9/1/93; HB 5/93; SLJ 6/93) [921]

### CHISHOLM, SHIRLEY

**10367** Pollack, Jill S. *Shirley Chisholm* (3–5). Illus. Series: First Books. 1994, Watts LB $21.00 (0-531-20168-6). 64pp. An interesting biography of this African American, with emphasis on her political career in Washington, D.C. (Rev: BL 1/15/95) [921]

### CUFFE, PAUL

**10368** Diamond, Arthur. *Paul Cuffe: Merchant and Abolitionist* (5–8). 1989, Chelsea LB $19.95 (1-55546-579-X). 111pp. The story of the half-black half-Indian who tried to challenge the racial prejudice of America in the early 1800s. (Rev: SLJ 1/90) [921]

### DOUGLASS, FREDERICK

**10369** Adler, David A. *A Picture Book of Frederick Douglass* (K–3). Illus. by Samuel Byrd. Series: Headliners. 1993, Holiday LB $15.95 (0-8234-1002-1). 32pp. A simple life story of the famous African American abolitionist who died in 1895. (Rev: BL 4/1/93; SLJ 8/93) [921]

**10370** Bennett, Evelyn. *Frederick Douglass and the War Against Slavery* (3–5). Series: Gateway Civil Rights. 1993, Millbrook LB $20.90 (1-56294-341-3). 32pp. A brief biography of the man who began life as a slave and later became a presidential advisor. (Rev: BL 10/1/93; SLJ 10/93) [921]

**10371** Girard, Linda Walvoord. *Young Frederick Douglass: The Slave Who Learned to Read* (3–5). Illus. by Colin Bootman. 1994, Albert Whitman LB $14.95 (0-8075-9463-6). 40pp. A brief biography based on Douglass's autobiography that is gripping in its use of dialogue and descriptions of inner feelings. (Rev: SLJ 11/94) [921]

**10372** Kerby, Mona. *Frederick Douglass* (4–6). Illus. Series: First Books. 1995, Watts LB $21.00 (0-531-20173-2). 64pp. A dramatic biography of the famous abolitionist writer and speaker who suffered the cruelty of slavery. (Rev: BL 2/15/95; HB 7–8/95, 9–10/95; SLJ 7/95) [921]

**10373** McKissack, Patricia, and Fredrick McKissack. *Frederick Douglass: Leader Against Slavery* (2–4). Illus. Series: Great African Americans. 1991, Enslow LB $13.95 (0-89490-306-3). 32pp. Fine documentary photographs highlight this biography. (Rev: BL 1/1/92; SLJ 2/92) [921]

**10374** Marlowe, Sam. *Learning About Dedication from the Life of Frederick Douglass* (2–5). Illus. Series: Character Building. 1996, Rosen LB $13.95 (0-8239-2425-4). 24pp. Both slavery and the life of the man who fought against it are covered in this short book. (Rev: BL 10/15/96; SLJ 1/97) [921]

**10375** Miller, William. *Frederick Douglass: The Last Day of Slavery* (2–4). Illus. by Cedric Lucas. 1995, Lee & Low $14.95 (1-880000-17-2). 32pp. A picture book biography of this freedom fighter who suffered the cruelty of slavery. (Rev: BL 3/15/95; SLJ 6/95) [921]

**10376** Santrey, Laurence. *Young Frederick Douglass: Fight for Freedom* (3–5). Illus. by Bert Dodson. 1983, Troll LB $12.95 (0-89375-857-4); paper $3.50 (0-89375-858-2). 48pp. The story of the slave who became a leader of the abolitionist movement.

**10377** Schomp, Virginia. *He Fought for Freedom: Frederick Douglass* (3–6). Illus. Series: Biographies. 1996, Benchmark LB $21.36 (0-7614-0488-0). 48pp. A brief but thorough account of the former slave who led the antislavery movement, with quotes from his autobiography. (Rev: HB 11–12/96; SLJ 2/97) [921]

### DU BOIS, W. E. B.

**10378** Cavan, Seamus. *W. E. B. Du Bois and Racial Relations* (3–5). Illus. Series: Gateway Civil Rights. 1993, Millbrook LB $20.90 (1-56294-288-3). 32pp. The story of the life and contributions of this great African American civil rights leader and author who died in 1963. (Rev: BL 10/1/93; SLJ 10/93) [921]

**10379** Cryan-Hicks, Kathryn. *W. E. B. Du Bois: Crusader for Peace* (3–6). Illus. by David Huckins. 1991, Discovery $14.95 (1-878668-05-6); paper $7.95 (1-878668-09-9). 48pp. The life story of the writer and leader who devoted his life to rights for African Americans and world peace. (Rev: SLJ 10/91) [921]

### FARMER, JAMES

**10380** Jakoubek, Robert E. *James Farmer and the Freedom Rides* (3–5). Illus. Series: Gateway Civil Rights. 1994, Millbrook LB $20.90 (1-56294-381-2). 32pp. The story of the Freedom Riders and their leader, James Farmer, who dedicated his life to the struggle for civil rights. (Rev: BL 4/15/94; SLJ 6/94) [921]

### FIELDS, MARY

**10381** Miller, Robert H. *The Story of Stagecoach Mary Fields* (1–4). Illus. by Cheryl Hanna. 1995, Silver Burdett LB $14.95 (0-382-24390-0); paper $5.95 (0-382-24394-3). 32pp. In the late 1800s, Mary Fields, a freed slave, was the first African American woman letter carrier. (Rev: BL 4/15/95; SLJ 5/95) [921]

### FLIPPER, HENRY O.

**10382** Pfeifer, Kathryn B. *Henry O. Flipper* (4–8). Illus. Series: African-American Soldiers. 1993, Twenty-First Century LB $17.90 (0-8050-2351-8). 80pp. The story of Henry Flipper, the first African American graduate of West Point, who lived from 1856 to 1940. (Rev: BL 2/15/94; SLJ 4/94) [921]

### FORTUNE, AMOS

**10383** Yates, Elizabeth. *Amos Fortune, Free Man* (6–8). Illus. by Nora S. Unwin. 1950, Puffin paper $4.99 (0-14-034158-7). 181pp. The simplicity and dignity of the human spirit and its triumph over degradation are movingly portrayed in this portrait of a slave who bought his freedom. Newbery Medal winner, 1951.

### HAMER, FANNIE LOU

**10384** Colman, Penny. *Fannie Lou Hamer and the Fight for the Vote* (3–5). Illus. Series: Gateway Civil Rights. 1993, Millbrook LB $20.90 (1-56294-323-5). 32pp. A biography of the civil rights activist who fought for African American voter registration. (Rev: BL 10/1/93; SLJ 10/93) [921]

### HILL, ANITA

**10385** Italia, Bob. *Anita Hill: Speaking Out Against Harassment* (4–6). Illus. Series: Everyone Contributes. 1993, ABDO LB $12.94 (1-56239-259-X). 32pp. This biography concentrates on the Clarence Thomas hearings and Anita Hill's role in them. (Rev: BL 12/1/93; SLJ 1/94) [921]

### JACKSON, JESSE

**10386** Celsi, Teresa. *Jesse Jackson and Political Power* (4–6). Illus. Series: Gateway Civil Rights.

1991, Millbrook paper $4.95 (1-878-84170-X). 32pp. A short, basic biography that covers highlights of Jackson's life in text and both color and black-and-white illustrations. (Rev: BL 1/1/92; SLJ 1/92) [921]

### JACOBS, HARRIET

**10387** Fleischner, Jennifer. *I Was Born a Slave: The Story of Harriet Jacobs* (4–7). Illus. 1997, Millbrook LB $24.90 (0-7613-0111-9). 96pp. An adaptation of the slave narrative that tells of the tragedies and triumphs of a plucky woman who finally escaped slavery. (Rev: BL 9/15/97; SLJ 1/98) [921]

### JAMES, DANIEL

**10388** Super, Neil. *Daniel "Chappie" James* (4–8). Series: African American Soldiers. 1992, Twenty-First Century LB $17.90 (0-8050-2138-8). 80pp. An inspiring story of the African American boy, growing up in Florida in the 1920s and 1930s, who would one day become a 4-star general. (Rev: BL 12/15/92; SLJ 11/92) [921]

### JOHNSON, ISAAC

**10389** Marston, Hope I. *Isaac Johnson: From Slave to Stonecutter* (5–8). Illus. 1995, Dutton paper $14.99 (0-525-65165-9). 80pp. The story of an escaped slave who, after the Civil War, went back to Kentucky in search of his family. (Rev: BL 9/15/95; SLJ 9/95) [976.9]

### JOHNSON, JOHN H.

**10390** Falkof, Lucille. *John H. Johnson: The Man from "Ebony"* (5–8). Illus. Series: Wizards of Business. 1992, Garrett LB $17.26 (1-56074-018-3). 60pp. The life story of the most successful black entrepreneur in America. (Rev: BL 6/15/92; SLJ 7/92) [921]

### JORDAN, BARBARA

**10391** Patrick-Wexler, Diane. *Barbara Jordan* (4–6). Illus. Series: Contemporary African Americans. 1995, Raintree Steck-Vaughn LB $24.26 (0-8172-3976-6). 48pp. The story of the famous African American congresswoman from childhood through her later career as an educator. (Rev: BL 2/15/96; SLJ 4/96) [921]

### KING, CORETTA SCOTT

**10392** Henry, Sondra, and Emily Taitz. *Coretta Scott King: Keeper of the Dream* (4–8). 1992, Enslow LB $19.95 (0-89490-334-9). 128pp. This is the story of the widow of Martin Luther King, Jr., from birth to her present-day activities with the Center for Nonviolent Change. (Rev: SLJ 10/92) [921]

**10393** Medearis, Angela Shelf. *Dare to Dream: Coretta Scott King and the Civil Rights Movement* (3–5). Illus. by Anna Rich. 1994, Dutton paper $13.99 (0-525-67426-8). 64pp. A sensitive biography that uses Coretta Scott King's autobiography as its principal source. (Rev: BL 1/1/95; SLJ 2/95) [921]

**10394** Wheeler, Jill C. *Coretta Scott King* (4–6). Illus. Series: Leading Ladies. 1992, ABDO LB $13.98 (1-56239-116-X). 32pp. The life of the civil rights leader, emphasizing her activities since her husband's death. (Rev: BL 2/1/93; SLJ 3/93) [921]

### KING, MARTIN LUTHER, JR.

**10395** Adler, David A. *Martin Luther King, Jr.: Free at Last* (3–6). Illus. 1986, Holiday LB $15.95 (0-8234-0618-0); paper $5.95 (0-8234-0619-9). 48pp. The events of the civil rights movement become part of King's life story in this account aimed at older children with some reading problems. (Rev: BL 11/15/86; HB 3–4/87; SLJ 10/86)

**10396** Adler, David A. *A Picture Book of Martin Luther King, Jr.* (PS–2). Illus. by Robert Casilla. Series: Picture Book Biography. 1989, Holiday LB $15.95 (0-8234-0770-5); paper $6.95 (0-8234-0847-7). 32pp. The life of the civil rights leader is presented in picture book format. (Rev: BCCB 2/90; BL 11/1/89; SLJ 9/89) [921]

**10397** Bray, Rosemary L. *Martin Luther King* (2–4). Illus. by Malcah Zeldis. 1995, Greenwillow LB $15.93 (0-688-13132-8); paper $5.95 (0-688-15219-8). 48pp. A large-format biography that supplies basic information with dramatic paintings on each page. (Rev: BL 2/15/95; HB 5–6/95; SLJ 2/95*) [921]

**10398** Darby, Jean. *Martin Luther King, Jr.* (4–8). Illus. Series: Lerner Biography. 1990, Lerner LB $23.96 (0-8225-4902-6). 144pp. An in-depth look at King's life and the civil rights movement. (Rev: BL 7/90; SLJ 11/90) [921]

**10399** De Kay, James T. *Meet Martin Luther King, Jr.* (2–5). Illus. 1989, Random LB $6.99 (0-394-91962-9); paper $2.99 (0-394-81962-4). 72pp. Focusing on Dr. King's philosophy of civil disobedience, this is a valuable biography.

**10400** Greene, Carol. *Martin Luther King, Jr.: A Man Who Changed Things* (2–4). Series: Rookie Biographies. 1989, Children's LB $19.00 (0-516-04205-X). 48pp. A simple biography that includes interesting material on Martin Luther King, Jr.'s family and his childhood. (Rev: SLJ 11/89) [921]

**10401** Hakim, Rita. *Martin Luther King, Jr. and the March Toward Freedom* (4–6). Illus. Series: Gateway Civil Rights. 1991, Millbrook LB $20.90 (1-878841-13-0). 32pp. Good photographs add appeal to this basic short biography of the famed civil rights leader. (Rev: BL 1/1/92; SLJ 8/91) [921]

**10402** Haskins, Jim. *I Have a Dream* (4–6). Illus. 1992, Millbrook LB $27.40 (1-56294-087-2). 112p. A well-researched biography, supported by excerpts from King's writings and speeches. (Rev: BL 2/15/93) [921]

**10403** Haskins, Jim. *The Life and Death of Martin Luther King, Jr.* (5–7). Illus. 1992, Morrow paper $4.95 (0-688-11690-6). 176pp. Covering the life and career of the black leader, with focus on the civil rights movement.

**10404** Lambert, Kathy K. *Martin Luther King, Jr.* (4–7). Illus. Series: Junior World Biographies. 1992, Chelsea LB $15.95 (0-7910-1759-1). 82pp. A well-designed biography using many photos to re-create the life of the great civil rights leader. (Rev: BL 11/1/92) [921]

**10405** Lowery, Linda. *Martin Luther King Day* (2–4). Illus. by Hetty Mitchell. 1987, Carolrhoda LB $18.60 (0-87614-299-4); Lerner paper $5.95 (0-87614-468-7). 56pp. Origins of the holiday and high points of Dr. King's life. (Rev: BL 4/1/87; SLJ 6–7/87)

**10406** McKissack, Patricia, and Fredrick McKissack. *Martin Luther King, Jr.: Man of Peace* (2–4). Illus. Series: Great African Americans. 1991, Enslow LB $13.95 (0-89490-302-0). 32pp. An easily read biography of the black leader whose dream was civil rights for all Americans. (Rev: SLJ 11/91) [921]

**10407** Marzollo, Jean. *Happy Birthday, Martin Luther King* (PS–3). Illus. by Brian Pinkney. 1992, Scholastic $14.95 (0-590-44065-9). 32pp. The focus is on King's ability to bring people together in this simple biography. (Rev: BL 12/15/92; SLJ 3/93) [921]

**10408** Milton, Joyce. *Marching to Freedom: The Story of Martin Luther King, Jr.* (5–7). Illus. 1987, Dell paper $3.50 (0-440-45433-6). 92pp. The biography of a famous black American from childhood to civil rights leader. (Rev: BL 6/15/87; SLJ 10/87)

**10409** Patrick, Diane. *Martin Luther King, Jr.* (4–8). Illus. 1990, Watts LB $21.00 (0-531-10892-9). 144pp. A colorful format helps to make this look at King's life accessible to middle-grade readers. (Rev: BL 7/90; SLJ 9/90) [921]

**10410** Ringgold, Faith. *My Dream of Martin Luther King* (1–4). Illus. 1995, Crown $18.00 (0-517-59976-7). 32pp. Through the author's dream, key events in the life of Martin Luther King, Jr., are recalled in this picture book, which also explains the impact of his life on humanity. (Rev: BCCB 1/96; BL 2/15/96; SLJ 2/96) [921]

**10411** Roop, Peter, and Connie Roop. *Martin Luther King, Jr.* (2–3). Series: Lives and Times. 1997,

Heinemann $12.95 (1-57572-560-6). 24pp. A simple picture book biography that gives a very brief introduction to the life and contributions of Martin Luther King, Jr. (Rev: BL 3/15/98; HB 5–6/97) [921]

**10412** Schuman, Michael A. *Martin Luther King, Jr.: Leader for Civil Rights* (5–8). Illus. Series: African-American Biographies. 1996, Enslow LB $19.95 (0-89490-687-9). 128pp. A straightforward biography that covers the main events of King's life. (Rev: SLJ 12/96) [921]

**10413** Stein, R. Conrad. *The Assassination of Martin Luther King, Jr.* (3–5). Illus. Series: Cornerstones of Freedom. 1996, Children's LB $19.50 (0-516-20004-6). 32pp. After a brief introduction to the life and work of Martin Luther King, Jr., the assassination is described and its significance explored. (Rev: BL 12/15/96; SLJ 4/97) [921]

**10414** Strazzabosco, Jeanne M. *Learning About Dignity from the Life of Martin Luther King, Jr.* (2–5). Illus. Series: A Character Building Book. 1996, Rosen $13.95 (0-8239-2415-7). 24pp. This brief biography describes King's many virtues, above all his innate dignity. (Rev: BL 10/15/96; SLJ 12/96) [921]

### LOVE, NAT

**10415** Miller, Robert, and Michael Bryant. *The Story of Nat Love* (K–3). Illus. 1994, Silver Burdett LB $14.95 (0-382-24389-7); paper $5.95 (0-382-24393-5). 32pp. A picture book biography of the cowboy of the Old West, Nat Love, who began his life as a slave. (Rev: BL 1/1/95; SLJ 1/95) [921]

### MALCOLM X

**10416** Adoff, Arnold. *Malcolm X* (3–5). Illus. by John Wilson. 1970, HarperCollins LB $14.89 (0-690-51414-X). 40pp. A realistic portrayal of this spokesman for the black cause in the United States until his assassination in 1965.

**10417** Cwiklik, Robert. *Malcolm X and Black Pride* (4–6). Illus. Series: Gateway Civil Rights. 1991, Millbrook LB $20.90 (1-56294-042-2). 32pp. This clear overview of this important civil rights leader contains many excellent color and black-and-white photos. (Rev: BL 1/1/92; SLJ 4/92) [921]

**10418** Myers, Walter Dean. *Malcolm X: By Any Means Necessary* (5–8). Illus. 1993, Scholastic $13.95 (0-590-46484-1). 210pp. Malcolm X's life dealt with in 4 parts. (Rev: BCCB 3/93; SLJ 2/93) [921]

**10419** Stine, Megan. *The Story of Malcolm X, Civil Rights Leader* (4–7). Illus. 1994, Dell paper $3.50 (0-440-40900-4). 112pp. A clear, straightforward biography with black-and-white photos. (Rev: BL 2/15/94; SLJ 8/94) [921]

## MARSHALL, THURGOOD

**10420** Adler, David A. *A Picture Book of Thurgood Marshall* (3–4). Illus. by Robert Casilla. Series: Picture Book Biography. 1997, Holiday LB $15.95 (0-8234-1308-X). 32pp. The life of this Supreme Court justice is well re-created in simple language that chronicles his battles against segregation and discrimination. (Rev: BL 11/15/97; SLJ 1/98) [921]

**10421** Carpenter, Eric. *Young Thurgood Marshall: Fighter for Equality* (2–4). Illus. Series: Troll First Start. 1996, Troll paper $3.50 (0-8167-3771-1). 32pp. A beginning biography that stresses the childhood and early influences as well as the adult accomplishments of this Supreme Court justice. (Rev: BL 2/15/96) [921]

**10422** Greene, Carol. *Thurgood Marshall: First African-American Supreme Court Justice* (2–4). Illus. Series: Rookie Biographies. 1991, Children's LB $19.00 (0-516-04225-4). 48pp. For beginning readers, this is the biography of the black judge who changed the history of both the Supreme Court and the entire United States. (Rev: BL 3/15/92; SLJ 3/92) [921]

**10423** Hitzeroth, Deborah, and Sharon Leon. *Thurgood Marshall* (4–8). Illus. Series: Importance Of. 1997, Lucent LB $22.45 (1-56006-061-1). 112pp. As well as tracing the career of this Supreme Court justice, this account pinpoints Marshall's lasting contributions to his country and his race. (Rev: BL 6/1–15/97; SLJ 9/97) [921]

**10424** Kallen, Stuart A. *Thurgood Marshall: A Dream of Justice for All* (3–5). Illus. Series: I Have a Dream. 1993, ABDO LB $15.98 (1-56239-258-1). 40pp. The story of the first African American to serve on the Supreme Court and his contributions to the struggle for civil rights. (Rev: BL 2/1/94) [921]

**10425** Kent, Deborah. *Thurgood Marshall and the Supreme Court* (3–5). Illus. Series: Cornerstones of Freedom. 1997, Children's LB $18.70 (0-516-20297-9). 32pp. The life story of this Supreme Court justice, who served from 1967 through 1991, and his struggle to bring equal rights to African Americans. (Rev: BL 6/1–15/97) [921]

**10426** Prentzas, G. S. *Thurgood Marshall: Champion of Justice* (4–8). Illus. Series: Junior World Biographies. 1993, Chelsea LB $15.95 (0-7910-1769-9); paper $4.95 (0-7910-1969-1). 79pp. An interesting biography of Thurgood Marshall that touches on his civil rights work but focuses on his years as a Supreme Court justice. (Rev: SLJ 11/93) [921]

## MATZELIGER, JAN

**10427** Mitchell, Barbara. *Shoes for Everyone: A Story About Jan Matzeliger* (3–5). Illus. 1986, Carol-rhoda LB $14.95 (0-87614-290-0); Lerner paper $5.95 (0-87614-473-3). 64pp. The life of the black inventor who changed the industry with his shoe-lasting machine. (Rev: BCCB 7–8/86; BL 8/86; SLJ 9/86)

## MEREDITH, JAMES

**10428** Elish, Dan. *James Meredith and School Desegregation* (3–5). Illus. Series: Gateway Civil Rights. 1994, Millbrook LB $20.90 (1-56294-379-0). 32pp. The biography of the young African American man who was a pioneer in integrating institutions of higher education in Mississippi. (Rev: BL 4/15/94; SLJ 5/94) [921]

## PARKS, ROSA

**10429** Adler, David A. *A Picture Book of Rosa Parks* (2–4). Illus. by Robert Casilla. Series: Picture Book Biography. 1993, Holiday LB $15.95 (0-8234-1041-2). 30pp. The life story of the civil rights leader who refused to give up her bus seat to a white passenger. (Rev: BL 10/15/93; SLJ 12/93) [921]

**10430** Benjamin, Anne. *Young Rosa Parks: Civil Rights Heroine* (2–4). Illus. Series: First Start Biography. 1996, Troll paper $3.50 (0-8167-3775-4). 32pp. Attractive color illustrations are included in this account of the life of a civil rights activist that emphasizes her childhood. (Rev: BL 2/15/96) [921]

**10431** Celsi, Teresa. *Rosa Parks and the Montgomery Bus Boycott* (4–6). Illus. Series: Gateway Civil Rights. 1991, Millbrook LB $20.90 (1-878841-14-9). 32pp. In clear text and many color photos, the story of the Montgomery, Alabama, bus boycott is outlined in relation to its modest leader. (Rev: BL 1/1/92; SLJ 8/91) [921]

**10432** Greenfield, Eloise. *Rosa Parks* (2–4). Illus. by Eric Marlow. 1996, HarperCollins LB $14.89 (0-06-027110-8); paper $3.95 (0-06-442025-6). 40pp. A convincing sketch of the woman whose brave stand precipitated the Montgomery bus strike and her ensuing involvement with the civil rights struggle.

**10433** Holland, Gini. *Rosa Parks* (2–4). Illus. by David Price. Series: First Biographies. 1997, Raintree Steck-Vaughn LB $21.40 (0-8172-4451-4). 32pp. A simple account of Rosa Parks's life, covering her childhood, civil rights work, imprisonment, and release. (Rev: SLJ 2/98) [921]

**10434** Parks, Rosa, and Jim Haskins. *I Am Rosa Parks* (2–4). Illus. Series: Dial Easy-to-Read Book. 1997, Dial LB $12.89 (0-8037-1206-5). 48pp. An easy-to-read version of the civil rights leader's autobiography that retains its message and honesty. (Rev: BCCB 6/97; BL 5/1/97; HB 5–6/97; SLJ 5/97) [921]

POWELL, COLIN

**10435** Blue, Rose, and Corinne J. Naden. *Colin Powell: Straight to the Top* (3–5). Illus. Series: Gateway Biographies. 1997, Millbrook LB $20.90 (0-7613-0256-5). 48pp. A balanced biography of Colin Powell that focuses on his adult life and his stint as chairman of the Joint Chiefs of Staff. (Rev: BL 9/15/97; SLJ 1/98) [921]

**10436** Finlayson, Reggie. *Colin Powell: People's Hero* (5–8). Illus. Series: Achievers Biographies. 1997, Lerner LB $19.93 (0-8225-2891-6). 64pp. From his birth in Harlem to his distinguished military career, this is a fine biography of Colin Powell. (Rev: SLJ 4/97) [921]

**10437** Patrick-Wexler, Diane. *Colin Powell* (4–6). Illus. Series: Contemporary African Americans. 1995, Raintree Steck-Vaughn LB $24.26 (0-8172-3977-4). 48pp. A simple biography of the man who grew up in the Bronx and rose to be a 4-star general and chairman of the Joint Chiefs of Staff. (Rev: BL 2/15/96; SLJ 1/96) [921]

**10438** Reef, Kristensen. *Colin Powell* (4–8). Illus. Series: African American Soldiers. 1992, Twenty-First Century LB $17.90 (0-8050-2136-1). 80pp. This is a simple but comprehensive biography of the first African American to become chairman of the Joint Chiefs of Staff. (Rev: BL 11/15/92) [921]

**10439** Senna, Carl. *Colin Powell: A Man of War and Peace* (4–8). Illus. 1992, Walker LB $16.85 (0-8027-8181-0). 192pp. The life of the general who became the first African American chairman of the Joint Chiefs of Staff. (Rev: BL 3/15/93) [921]

**10440** Strazzabosco, Jeanne M. *Learning About Responsibility from the Life of Colin Powell* (2–4). Illus. Series: Character Building Book. 1996, Rosen/Power Kids Pr. LB $15.93 (0-8239-2414-9). 24pp. This biography emphasizes the many important responsibilities that Colin Powell faced in his various positions in the U.S. government. (Rev: SLJ 5/97) [921]

RANDOLPH, A. PHILIP

**10441** Cwiklik, Robert. *A. Philip Randolph and the Labor Movement* (3–5). Series: Gateway Civil Rights. 1993, Millbrook LB $20.90 (1-56294-326-X). 32pp. The story of the African American who organized the sleeping-car porters into a union and later directed a march on Washington, D.C., in 1941, to protest unfair labor practices. (Rev: BL 10/1/93; SLJ 10/93) [921]

**10442** Hanley, Sally. *A. Philip Randolph* (5–8). 1988, Chelsea LB $19.95 (1-55546-607-9); paper $8.95 (0-7910-0222-5). 112pp. Biography of the man who became a great labor leader and civil rights activist. (Rev: BL 10/1/88)

SMALLS, ROBERT

**10443** Cooper, Michael L. *From Slave to Civil War Hero: The Life and Times of Robert Smalls* (5–8). Illus. Series: Rainbow Biography. 1994, Lodestar paper $13.99 (0-525-67489-6). 73pp. The life story of the slave who commandeered the cotton steamer on which he was the pilot and escaped to freedom. (Rev: SLJ 12/94) [921]

TAYLOR, MARSHALL B.

**10444** Scioscia, Mary. *Bicycle Rider* (2–5). Illus. by Ed Young. 1983, HarperCollins paper $5.95 (0-06-443295-5). 48pp. The fictionalized biography of the black man who at one time was the fastest bicyclist in the world.

TAYLOR, SUSIE KING

**10445** Jordan, Denise. *Susie King Taylor: Destined to Be Free* (3–5). Illus. by Higgins Bond. 1994, Just Us paper $5.00 (0-940975-50-5). 42pp. The story of the freed slave who, after the Civil War, became a teacher of African American children and adults and wrote an account of her life. (Rev: SLJ 7/95) [921]

TERRELL, MARY CHURCH

**10446** McKissack, Patricia, and Fredrick McKissack. *Mary Church Terrell: Leader for Equality* (2–4). Illus. by Ned Ostendorf. Series: Great African Americans. 1991, Enslow LB $13.95 (0-89490-305-5). 32pp. This educator and social reformer was the first president of the National Association of Colored Women. (Rev: SLJ 2/92) [921]

THOMAS, CLARENCE

**10447** Halliburton, Warren J. *Clarence Thomas: Supreme Court Justice* (4–6). Illus. Series: People to Know. 1993, Enslow LB $19.95 (0-89490-414-0). 104pp. This straightforward account covers Judge Thomas's life from childhood and education to his professional life and confirmation to the Supreme Court. (Rev: BL 6/1–15/93; SLJ 5/93) [921]

TRUTH, SOJOURNER

**10448** Adler, David A. *A Picture Book of Sojourner Truth* (2–4). Illus. by Gershom Griffith. Series: Picture Book Biographies. 1994, Holiday LB $15.95 (0-8234-1072-2). In an easily read format, the life and works of Sojourner Truth are introduced. (Rev: SLJ 6/94) [921]

**10449** Ferris, Jeri. *Walking the Road to Freedom: A Story About Sojourner Truth* (3–6). Illus. 1988, Carolrhoda LB $14.95 (0-87614-318-4); Lerner paper $5.95 (0-87614-505-5). 64pp. The story of the woman born into slavery who vowed to travel the land singing of its evils. (Rev: BL 3/1/88; SLJ 3/88)

**10450** Macht, Norman L. *Sojourner Truth* (4–7). Illus. Series: Junior World Biographies. 1992, Chelsea LB $15.95 (0-7910-1754-0). 80pp. The story of the freed slave who traveled through the North preaching emancipation and women's rights. (Rev: BL 10/1/92; SLJ 12/92) [921]

**10451** McKissack, Patricia, and Fredrick McKissack. *Sojourner Truth: A Voice for Freedom* (2–4). Illus. by Michael D. Blegel. Series: Great African Americans. 1992, Enslow LB $13.95 (0-89490-313-6). 32pp. Through her life as a freed slave, Sojourner Truth traveled in the Northeast preaching against slavery. (Rev: BCCB 1/93; BL 11/15/92; HB 3–4/93; SLJ 1/93) [921]

## TUBMAN, HARRIET

**10452** Adler, David A. *A Picture Book of Harriet Tubman* (2–4). Illus. by Samuel Byrd. Series: Picture Book Biography. 1992, Holiday LB $15.95 (0-8234-0926-0). 32pp. Easy-to-read text describes the life of this famous American who helped slaves gain freedom. (Rev: BCCB 7–8/92; BL 6/15/92; SLJ 6/92) [921]

**10453** Burns, Bree. *Harriet Tubman* (4–7). Illus. Series: Junior World Biographies. 1992, Chelsea LB $14.95 (0-7910-1751-6). 80pp. This is a straightforward account of the escaped slave who helped free more than 300 slaves via the Underground Railroad. (Rev: BL 10/1/92; SLJ 12/92) [921]

**10454** Elish, Dan. *Harriet Tubman and the Underground Railroad* (4–6). Illus. Series: Gateway Civil Rights. 1993, Millbrook LB $20.90 (1-56294-273-5). 32pp. The story of the slave who led the organization that helped slaves escape via the Underground Railroad. (Rev: BL 8/93) [921]

**10455** Ferris, Jeri. *Go Free or Die: A Story About Harriet Tubman* (3–6). Illus. 1988, Carolrhoda LB $19.93 (0-87614-317-6); Lerner paper $5.95 (0-87614-504-7). 64pp. The story of the former slave and her fight to rid the country of slavery. (Rev: BL 3/1/88; SLJ 3/88)

**10456** Mosher, Kiki. *Learning About Bravery from the Life of Harriet Tubman* (2–5). Illus. Series: A Character Building Book. 1996, Rosen LB $13.95 (0-8239-2424-6). 24pp. This short biography shows how the element of courage was paramount in the life of this leader of the Underground Railroad. (Rev: BL 10/15/96; SLJ 1/97) [921]

**10457** Rowley, John. *Harriet Tubman* (2–3). Illus. Series: Lives and Times. 1997, Heinemann LB $12.95 (1-57572-558-4). 24pp. A simple picture book biography that talks about slavery and tells of the life, courage, and endurance of this leader on the Underground Railroad. (Rev: BL 3/15/98) [921]

**10458** Schroeder, Alan. *Minty: A Story of Young Harriet Tubman* (K–4). Illus. by Jerry Pinkney. 1996, Dial LB $16.89 (0-8037-1889-6). 40pp. The daily life of Harriet Tubman when she was young and a slave is re-created in this partially fictionalized biography. (Rev: BL 2/15/96; HB 9–10/96; SLJ 5/96) [921]

**10459** Taylor, M. W. *Harriet Tubman* (5–8). Illus. Series: Black Americans of Achievement. 1990, Chelsea LB $19.95 (1-55546-612-5). 111pp. The story of the famous conductor on the Underground Railroad. (Rev: SLJ 1/91) [921]

## TURNER, NAT

**10460** Hendrickson, Ann-Marie. *Nat Turner: Rebel Slave* (4–7). Illus. Series: Junior World Biographies. 1995, Chelsea $15.95 (0-7910-2386-9). 77pp. An attractive biography of this slave who led a revolution and became a symbol of heroism for his people. (Rev: BL 10/15/95) [921]

## WALKER, MADAM C. J.

**10461** Colman, Penny. *Madam C. J. Walker: Building a Business Empire* (3–6). Illus. 1994, Millbrook LB $21.90 (1-56294-338-3). 48pp. The success story of the African American woman who rose from extreme poverty to found a beauty preparation empire. (Rev: BL 6/1–15/94; SLJ 9/94) [921]

**10462** McKissack, Patricia, and Fredrick McKissack. *Madam C. J. Walker: Self-Made Millionaire* (2–4). Illus. by Michael Bryant. Series: Great African Americans. 1992, Enslow LB $13.95 (0-89490-311-X). 32pp. The story of the black woman who built a cosmetics empire and became the first self-made black woman millionaire. (Rev: BL 10/15/92; SLJ 12/92) [921]

## WALKER, MAGGIE

**10463** Branch, Muriel Miller, and Dorothy M. Rice. *Pennies to Dollars: The Story of Maggie Lena Walker* (4–7). Illus. 1997, Linnet LB $17.95 (0-208-02453-0); paper $13.95 (0-208-02455-7). 128pp. Maggie Walker, the daughter of a former slave, helped African Americans through her financial schemes, including founding the Penny Savings Bank. (Rev: BL 11/1/97; SLJ 10/97) [921]

## WASHINGTON, BOOKER T.

**10464** McKissack, Patricia, and Fredrick McKissack. *Booker T. Washington: Leader and Educator* (2–4). Illus. by Michael Bryant. Series: Great African Americans. 1992, Enslow LB $13.95 (0-89490-314-4). 32pp. This book tells how Booker T. Washington created a school for African Americans at Tuskegee

Institute in Alabama. (Rev: BL 9/15/92; SLJ 10/92) [921]

**10465** Roberts, Jack L. *Booker T. Washington: Educator and Leader* (3–5). Illus. Series: Gateway Civil Rights. 1995, Millbrook LB $20.90 (1-56294-487-8). 32pp. The story of this pioneering civil rights leader and how this African American has been an inspiration to all races. (Rev: BL 10/15/95) [921]

## WELLS-BARNETT, IDA B.

**10466** Freedman, Suzanne. *Ida B. Wells-Barnett and the Anti-Lynching Crusade* (3–5). Illus. Series: Gateway Civil Rights. 1994, Millbrook LB $20.90 (1-56294-377-4). 32pp. The biography of the African American journalist who fought for civil rights and justice in the South. (Rev: BL 4/15/94; SLJ 5/94) [921]

**10467** McKissack, Patricia, and Fredrick McKissack. *Ida B. Wells-Barnett: A Voice Against Violence* (2–4). Illus. Series: Great African Americans. 1991, Enslow LB $13.95 (0-89490-301-2). 32pp. A simple biography of the founder of the NAACP. (Rev: SLJ 11/91) [921]

**10468** Medearis, Angela Shelf. *Princess of the Press: The Story of Ida B. Wells-Barnett* (3–5). Illus. Series: Rainbow Biography. 1997, Dutton $14.99 (0-525-67493-4). 32pp. This daughter of slaves went on to become one of the founders of the NAACP and a co-owner of several African American journals. (Rev: BL 12/1/97; SLJ 12/97) [921]

## WHITE, WALTER

**10469** Jakoubek, Robert E. *Walter White and the Power of Organized Protest* (3–5). Illus. Series: Gateway Civil Rights. 1994, Millbrook LB $20.90 (1-56294-378-2). 32pp. Background material on the NAACP is given through the life story of one of its leaders, Walter White. (Rev: BL 4/15/94; SLJ 6/94) [921]

## WOODSON, CARTER G.

**10470** McKissack, Patricia, and Fredrick McKissack. *Carter G. Woodson: The Father of Black History* (2–4). Illus. by Ned Ostendorf. Series: Great African Americans. 1991, Enslow LB $13.95 (0-89490-309-8). 32pp. This famous African American, who died in 1950, tried to educate people about the accomplishments of his people. (Rev: SLJ 2/92) [921]

## YOUNG, ANDREW

**10471** Roberts, Naurice. *Andrew Young: Freedom Fighter* (2–4). Illus. 1990, Children's paper $3.95 (0-516-43450-0). 32pp. A simple-to-read biography of the prominent black politician.

# Hispanic Americans

## ANTONNETTY, EVELINA LOPEZ

**10472** Mohr, Nicholasa. *All for the Better: A Story of El Barrio* (2–5). Illus. by Rudy Gutierrez. 1993, Raintree Steck-Vaughn LB $24.26 (0-8114-7220-5). 56pp. The story of Evelina Lopez Antonnetty and the difference she made in Spanish Harlem, New York. (Rev: BCCB 7–8/93; SLJ 5/93) [921]

## CHAVEZ, CESAR

**10473** Altman, Linda Jacobs. *Cesar Chavez* (4–8). Illus. Series: The Importance Of. 1996, Lucent LB $22.45 (1-56006-071-9). 111pp. The life of this great union organizer, with emphasis on his lasting contributions to helping farm workers in the United States. (Rev: BL 3/15/96) [921]

**10474** Cedeno, Maria E. *Cesar Chavez: Labor Leader* (3–6). Illus. Series: Hispanic Heritage. 1993, Millbrook LB $19.90 (1-56294-280-8). 32pp. The story of the leader who helped organize migrant workers to demand their rights. (Rev: BL 5/15/93; SLJ 7/93) [921]

**10475** Collins, David R. *Farmworker's Friend: The Story of Cesar Chavez* (3–5). Illus. 1996, Carolrhoda LB $22.60 (0-87614-982-4). 80pp. The story of this champion of poor farm workers is retold from a variety of original sources. (Rev: BL 12/15/96) [921]

**10476** Conord, Bruce W. *Cesar Chavez: Union Leader* (4–7). Illus. Series: Junior World Biographies. 1993, Chelsea paper $4.95 (0-791-01999-3). 80pp. The life of the Mexican American who helped organize the farm workers of California is told in text and pictures. (Rev: BL 10/1/92; SLJ 12/92) [921]

**10477** Franchere, Ruth. *Cesar Chavez* (2–5). Illus. by Earl Thollander. 1970, HarperCollins LB $14.89 (0-690-18384-4). 42pp. An inspiring story of the man who rose from poverty to become the union organizer of his people.

## CISNEROS, EVELYN

**10478** Simon, Charnan. *Evelyn Cisneros: Prima Ballerina* (2–4). Illus. Series: Picture-Story Biographies. 1990, Children's LB $18.20 (0-516-04276-9). 32pp. A biography of the Mexican American who danced her way to the top of the ballet world. (Rev: BL 1/1/91) [921]

## CISNEROS, HENRY

**10479** Bredeson, Carmen. *Henry Cisneros: Building a Better America* (5–8). Illus. Series: People to Know. 1995, Enslow LB $19.95 (0-89490-546-5). 128pp. A straightforward biography of this important

American that uses many quotations and material from original sources. (Rev: SLJ 7/95) [921]

**10480** Martinez, Elizabeth Coonrod. *Henry Cisneros: Mexican-American Leader* (3–6). Illus. Series: Hispanic Heritage. 1993, Millbrook LB $19.90 (1-56294-368-5). 32pp. A biography of the Mexican American who was once a mayor and is still an important politician. (Rev: BL 11/15/93) [921]

### DE LA RENTA, OSCAR

**10481** Carrillo, Louis. *Oscar de la Renta* (4–8). Illus. Series: Contemporary Hispanic Americans. 1995, Raintree Steck-Vaughn LB $24.26 (0-8172-3980-4). 48pp. Focuses on the professional life of the renowned fashion designer. (Rev: BL 3/15/96; SLJ 1/96) [921]

### GALAN, NELY

**10482** Rodriguez, Janel. *Nely Galan* (4–8). Illus. Series: Contemporary Hispanic Americans. 1997, Raintree Steck-Vaughn LB $24.26 (0-8172-3991-X). 48pp. The life of this contemporary Hispanic American who, as a Hollywood producer, is responsible for developing TV and video projects for other Hispanic Americans. (Rev: BL 4/15/97) [921]

### HUERTA, DOLORES

**10483** Perez, Frank. *Dolores Huerta* (4–8). Illus. Series: Contemporary Hispanic Americans. 1995, Raintree Steck-Vaughn LB $24.26 (0-8172-3981-2). 48pp. The accomplishments of Dolores Huerta, an organizer of farm workers, is highlighted in this informative biography. (Rev: BL 3/15/96) [921]

### JULIA, RAUL

**10484** Perez, Frank, and Ann Well. *Raul Julia* (4–8). Illus. Series: Contemporary Hispanic Americans. 1995, Raintree Steck-Vaughn LB $24.26 (0-8172-3984-7). 48pp. The story of the brilliant stage and film actor who gained fame in *The Addams Family* and on *Sesame Street*. (Rev: BL 3/15/96; SLJ 1/96) [921]

### MARTINEZ, VILMA

**10485** Codye, Corinn. *Vilma Martinez* (2–5). Illus. by Susi Kilgore. Series: Hispanic Stories. 1989, Raintree Steck-Vaughn LB $21.40 (0-8172-3382-2). 32pp. With English and Spanish text, the life of the brilliant lawyer who won the civil rights case allowing bilingual education is given. (Rev: BL 2/1/90) [921]

### QUINTANILLA, GUADALUPE

**10486** Wade, Mary D. *Guadalupe Quintanilla: Leader of the Hispanic Community* (4–8). Illus. Series: Multicultural Junior Biographies. 1995, Enslow LB $18.95 (0-89490-637-2). 104pp. An inspiring story of a woman who once was considered mentally disabled and now is a leader in her Spanish American community. (Rev: BL 3/1/96; SLJ 2/96) [921]

### RODRIGUEZ, LUIS

**10487** Schwartz, Michael. *Luis Rodriguez* (4–8). Illus. Series: Contemporary Hispanic Americans. 1997, Raintree Steck-Vaughn LB $24.26 (0-8172-3990-1). 48pp. The life of this contemporary Hispanic American who went from gang leader and drug addict to writer, journalist, publisher, speaker, and youth activist. (Rev: BL 4/15/97; SLJ 6/97) [921]

## Historical Figures and Important Contemporary Americans

### ADAMS, SAMUEL

**10488** Farley, Karin C. *Samuel Adams: Grandfather of His Country* (5–8). Series: American Troublemakers. 1995, Raintree Steck-Vaughn LB $27.11 (0-8114-2379-4). 128pp. A biography of this outspoken American, who gained the reputation of being a troublemaker. (Rev: SLJ 7/95) [921]

**10489** Fritz, Jean. *Why Don't You Get a Horse, Sam Adams?* (3–5). Illus. by Trina S. Hyman. 1974, Putnam $14.95 (0-698-20292-9); paper $5.95 (0-698-11416-7). 48pp. How Sam Adams was finally persuaded to ride a horse is told in this humorous re-creation of Revolutionary times.

### ALBRIGHT, MADELEINE

**10490** Maass, Robert. *UN Ambassador: A Behind-the-Scenes Look at Madeleine Albright's World* (3–5). Illus. 1995, Walker LB $17.85 (0-8027-8356-2). 48pp. A biography of Madeleine Albright, who, at the time of writing, was U.S. ambassador to the United Nations. (Rev: BL 11/15/95; SLJ 11/95) [921]

### APPLESEED, JOHNNY

**10491** Aliki. *The Story of Johnny Appleseed* (K–3). Illus. by author. 1971, Simon & Schuster paper $5.95 (0-671-66746-7). A picture story of the man who wandered through the Midwest spreading love and apple seeds.

**10492** Demuth, Patricia. *Johnny Appleseed* (K–2). Illus. by Michael Montgomery. Series: All Aboard Reading. 1996, Grosset LB $13.89 (0-448-41131-8); paper $3.99 (0-448-41130-X). 32pp. An easy-to-read biography that covers the most appealing events in the life of Johnny Appleseed. (Rev: SLJ 4/97) [921]

**10493** Greene, Carol. *John Chapman: The Man Who Was Johnny Appleseed* (2–4). Illus. Series: Rookie Biographies. 1991, Children's LB $19.00 (0-516-04223-8). 48pp. In an easily read text and an appealing layout, the story of this pioneer apple grower is told. (Rev: BL 3/15/92; SLJ 4/92) [921]

**10494** Hodges, Margaret. *The True Tale of Johnny Appleseed* (K–3). Illus. by Kimberly B. Root. 1997, Holiday LB $15.95 (0-8234-1282-2). 32pp. A biography that tells about John Chapman's childhood in Massachusetts and his relocation in the West, where he was noted for planting and caring for apple trees. (Rev: BL 7/97; SLJ 9/97) [921]

**10495** Kellogg, Steven. *Johnny Appleseed* (2–4). Illus. by author. 1988, Morrow LB $15.93 (0-688-06418-3). 48pp. The story of the famed John Chapman, who traveled the country in the 1700s spreading good cheer and apple seeds. (Rev: BCCB 11/88; BL 9/1/88; SLJ 10/88)

**10496** Lawlor, Laurie. *The Real Johnny Appleseed* (4–6). Illus. 1995, Albert Whitman LB $13.95 (0-8075-6909-7). 64pp. A well-researched biography of John Chapman, with details on his character and contributions to society. (Rev: BCCB 11/95; BL 9/1/95; SLJ 1/96) [921]

### BEAN, JUDGE ROY

**10497** Green, Carl R., and William R. Sanford. *Judge Roy Bean* (4–6). Illus. Series: Outlaws and Lawmen of the Wild West. 1995, Enslow LB $15.95 (0-89490-591-0). 48pp. A biography of this colorful, many-sided character from the old Wild West. (Rev: SLJ 9/95) [921]

### BILLY THE KID

**10498** Green, Carl R., and William R. Sanford. *Billy the Kid* (4–8). Illus. Series: Outlaws and Lawmen of the Wild West. 1992, Enslow LB $15.95 (0-89490-364-0). 48pp. The life story of the outlaw William H. Bonney, who lived from 1859 to 1881. (Rev: BL 7/92; SLJ 8/92) [921]

### BRADY, MATHEW

**10499** Van Steenwyk, Elizabeth. *Mathew Brady: Civil War Photographer* (4–6). Illus. Series: First Books. 1997, Watts LB $21.00 (0-531-20264-X). 64pp. The life and work of the famous Civil War photographer are covered, with many reproductions of his pictures. (Rev: BL 9/1/97) [921]

### BROWN, JOHN

**10500** Collins, James L. *John Brown and the Fight Against Slavery* (4–6). Illus. Series: Gateway Civil Rights. 1991, Millbrook LB $20.90 (1-56294-043-0). 32pp. This volume gives an excellent overview of the life and accomplishments of this important leader in the Abolitionist movement. (Rev: BL 1/1/92; SLJ 1/92) [921]

**10501** Everett, Gwen. *John Brown: One Man Against Slavery* (4–8). Illus. by Jacob Lawrence. 1993, Rizzoli $15.95 (0-8478-1702-4). 32pp. This story of John Brown and his raid on Harper's Ferry is told from the standpoint of his 16-year-old daughter. (Rev: BL 6/1–15/93*; SLJ 8/93) [921]

**10502** Potter, Robert R. *John Brown: Militant Abolitionist* (5–8). Illus. Series: American Troublemakers. 1995, Raintree Steck-Vaughn LB $27.11 (0-8114-2378-6). 128pp. A biography of the abolitionist, his controversial ideas, and his outspoken, courageous nature. (Rev: SLJ 7/95) [921]

### BURK, MARTHA JANE

**10503** Sanford, William R., and Carl R. Green. *Calamity Jane* (4–6). Illus. Series: Legendary Heroes of the Wild West. 1996, Enslow LB $15.95 (0-89490-647-X). 48pp. The life of the legendary Western belle is presented with historical photos. (Rev: BL 7/96; SLJ 7/96) [921]

### BUTCHER, SOLOMON

**10504** Conrad, Pam. *Prairie Visions: The Life and Times of Solomon Butcher* (4–6). Illus. by Darryl S. Zudeck. 1994, HarperCollins paper $9.95 (0-064-46135-1). 85pp. Through the life of Solomon Butcher and his neighbors, life on the American frontier comes alive. (Rev: BCCB 4/91; BL 3/15/91; HB 5–6/91; SLJ 5/91) [921]

### CASSIDY, BUTCH

**10505** Green, Carl R., and William R. Sanford. *Butch Cassidy* (4–8). Series: Outlaws and Lawmen of the Wild West. 1995, Enslow LB $15.95 (0-89490-587-2). 48pp. The wild West is re-created in this brief account of the life of this colorful outlaw, whose death remains a mystery. (Rev: BL 6/1–15/95; SLJ 7/95) [921]

### CODY, BUFFALO BILL

**10506** Sanford, William R., and Carl R. Green. *Buffalo Bill Cody: Showman of the Wild West* (4–6). Illus. Series: Legendary Heroes of the Wild West. 1996, Enslow LB $15.95 (0-89490-646-1). 48pp. The life of the Wild West hero in brief text and many black-and-white photos. (Rev: BL 7/96; SLJ 7/96) [921]

**10507** Spies, Karen B. *Buffalo Bill Cody: Western Legend* (5–8). Series: Historical American Biographies. 1998, Enslow LB $19.95 (0-7660-1015-5). 128pp. An in-depth look at this legendary frontiersman and the Wild West show he later founded. (Rev: BL 3/15/98) [921]

### DOLE, BOB

**10508** Lisandrelli, Elaine S. *Bob Dole, Legendary Senator* (4–6). Series: People to Know. 1997, Enslow LB $19.95 (0-89490-825-1). 128pp. An illustrated biography of this senator and unsuccessful presidential candidate. (Rev: BL 10/15/97) [921]

### EARP, WYATT

**10509** Green, Carl R., and William R. Sanford. *Wyatt Earp* (4–8). Illus. Series: Outlaws and Lawmen of the Wild West. 1992, Enslow LB $15.95 (0-89490-367-5). 48pp. With maps and authentic illustrations, this biography tells the story of the deputy marshal who tried to clean up Tombstone, Arizona. (Rev: BL 10/1/92; SLJ 11/92) [921]

### EISNER, MICHAEL

**10510** Tippins, Sherill. *Michael Eisner: Fun for Everyone* (5–8). Illus. Series: Wizards of Industry. 1992, Garrett LB $17.26 (1-56074-014-0). 64pp. The life of Walt Disney Productions' chief executive officer. (Rev: BL 6/15/92; SLJ 9/92) [921]

### FARRAGUT, DAVID

**10511** Shorto, Russell. *David Farragut and the Great Naval Blockade* (4–7). Illus. Series: The Story of the Civil War. 1991, Silver Burdett paper $7.95 (0-382-24050-2). 135pp. The story of the outstanding naval commander who closed the Gulf ports to Confederate blockade-running during the Civil War. (Rev: BL 9/1/91) [921]

### FRANKLIN, BENJAMIN

**10512** Adler, David A. *Benjamin Franklin: Printer, Inventor, Statesman* (3–5). Illus. by Lyle Miller. 1992, Holiday LB $15.95 (0-8234-0929-5). 48pp. Amusing anecdotes bring fresh life to another biography of Benjamin Franklin. (Rev: BL 5/15/92; SLJ 7/92) [921]

**10513** Adler, David A. *A Picture Book of Benjamin Franklin* (K–3). Illus. by John Wallner and Alexandra Wallner. Series: Picture Book Biography. 1990, Holiday LB $15.95 (0-8234-0792-6); paper $6.95 (0-8234-0882-5). 32pp. Glimpses of personality and family are interwoven in this simple biography. (Rev: BL 4/15/90; HB 5–6/90; SLJ 5/90) [921]

**10514** Cousins, Margaret. *Ben Franklin of Old Philadelphia* (6–8). 1981, Random paper $5.99 (0-394-84928-0). 160pp. A well-rounded portrait of this major figure in American history.

**10515** D'Aulaire, Ingri, and Edgar D'Aulaire. *Benjamin Franklin* (3–5). Illus. by authors. 1987, Doubleday paper $12.95 (0-385-24103-8). 48pp. A story biography enriched with full-page color lithographs.

**10516** Foster, Leila M. *Benjamin Franklin: Founding Father and Inventor* (5–8). Illus. Series: Historical American Biographies. 1997, Enslow LB $19.95 (0-89490-784-0). 128pp. An admiring biography that describes Franklin's many talents — as a printer, businessman, scientist, inventor, and statesman. (Rev: SLJ 11/97) [921]

**10517** Fritz, Jean. *What's the Big Idea, Ben Franklin?* (3–5). Illus. by Margot Tomes. 1996, Putnam paper $5.95 (0-698-11372-1). 48pp. Franklin's life told in the clever, lively manner associated with this author.

**10518** Greene, Carol. *Benjamin Franklin: A Man with Many Jobs* (2–3). Illus. 1988, Children's paper $4.95 (0-516-44202-3). 48pp. Introducing the important points in the life of this multitalented, multifaceted American. (Rev: BL 2/15/89; SLJ 4/89)

**10519** Quackenbush, Robert. *Benjamin Franklin and His Friends* (2–3). Illus. 1991, Pippin $14.95 (0-945912-14-5). 40pp. A friend is described in each chapter, emphasizing the influence on Franklin's life. (Rev: BL 12/1/91; SLJ 11/91) [921]

### GALLAUDET, THOMAS

**10520** Bowen, Andy Russell. *A World of Knowing: A Story About Thomas Hopkins Gallaudet* (3–5). Illus. Series: Creative Minds Biographies. 1995, Carolrhoda LB $14.95 (0-87614-871-2). 64pp. The story of the man who empathized with deaf persons and developed sign language to enable them to communicate with others. (Rev: BL 1/1–15/96; SLJ 1/96) [921]

### GALVEZ, BERNARDO DE

**10521** De Varona, Frank. *Bernardo de Galvez* (2–5). Illus. by Tom Redman. Series: Hispanic Stories. 1988, Raintree Steck-Vaughn LB $21.40 (0-8172-3379-2). 32pp. With English and Spanish text, this is the biography of the Spanish governor who drove the British from the Mississippi Valley during the American Revolution. (Rev: BL 2/1/90) [921]

### GARNER, JOHN NANCE, IV

**10522** Liles, Maurine. *Boy of Blossom Prairie Who Became Vice President* (4–6). Illus. by Pat Finney. 1993, Eakin $14.95 (0-89015-913-0). 118pp. Based on fact, this is the story of the adventurous boyhood of a future vice president under FDR: John Nance Garner IV. (Rev: SLJ 2/94) [921]

## GATES, BILL

**10523** Dickinson, Joan D. *Bill Gates* (4–6). Series: People to Know. 1997, Enslow LB $19.95 (0-89490-824-3). 104pp. A brief, interesting biography of this billionaire computer giant. (Rev: BL 10/15/97; SLJ 12/97) [921]

## GINSBURG, RUTH BADER

**10524** Ayer, Eleanor. *Ruth Bader Ginsburg: Fire and Steel on the Supreme Court* (5–8). Illus. 1995, Dillon $13.95 (0-87518-651-3); paper $7.95 (0-382-24721-3). 128pp. A biography of the second woman Supreme Court justice, with emphasis on the many obstacles she had to overcome. (Rev: BL 5/15/95; SLJ 4/95) [921]

**10525** Bredeson, Carmen. *Ruth Bader Ginsburg: Supreme Court Justice* (4–6). Illus. Series: People to Know. 1995, Enslow LB $19.95 (0-89490-621-6). 128pp. The life and struggles of the second female Supreme Court Justice are told in an attractive format. (Rev: BL 9/15/95; SLJ 12/95) [921]

**10526** Henry, Christopher. *Ruth Bader Ginsburg* (4–6). Illus. 1994, Watts LB $21.00 (0-531-20174-0). 64pp. A brief biography of the Brooklyn-born lawyer who is now a Supreme Court justice. (Rev: BL 2/1/95) [921]

## GORE, ALBERT

**10527** Italia, Bob. *Al Gore: The Vice President of the United States* (4–6). Illus. Series: All the President's Men and Women. 1993, ABDO LB $14.98 (1-56239-253-0). 32pp. This biography of Gore covers his personality and interests, as well as his public life. (Rev: SLJ 3/94) [921]

**10528** Stefoff, Rebecca. *Al Gore: Vice President* (3–5). Illus. Series: Gateway Biographies. 1994, Millbrook LB $20.90 (1-56294-433-9). 48pp. The life story of the vice president and his climb to high political office. (Rev: BL 8/94; SLJ 4/94) [921]

## HAMILTON, ALEXANDER

**10529** Whitelaw, Nancy. *More Perfect Union: The Story of Alexander Hamilton* (4–7). Illus. Series: Notable Americans. 1997, Morgan Reynolds LB $18.95 (1-883846-20-X). 112pp. This biography traces the dramatic story of Hamilton's life from his birth in Nevis (British West Indies) to his death after the duel with Aaron Burr. (Rev: BL 7/97; SLJ 10/97) [921]

## HANCOCK, JOHN

**10530** Fritz, Jean. *Will You Sign Here, John Hancock?* (3–5). Illus. by Trina S. Hyman. 1997, Putnam paper $5.95 (0-698-11440-X). 48pp. Under the sprightly title is a delightful, well-researched biography of this signer of the Declaration of Independence.

## HENRY, PATRICK

**10531** Adler, David A. *A Picture Book of Patrick Henry* (K–3). Illus. by John Wallner and Alexandra Wallner. Series: Picture Book Biographies. 1995, Holiday LB $15.95 (0-8234-1187-7). 32pp. The story of the famous patriot who served 5 terms as governor of Virginia. (Rev: BL 9/15/95; SLJ 12/95) [921]

## HERSHEY, MILTON S.

**10532** Burford, Betty. *Chocolate by Hershey: A Story About Milton S. Hershey* (3–6). Illus. by Loren Chantland. Series: Creative Minds. 1994, Carolrhoda LB $19.93 (0-87614-830-5); paper $5.95 (0-87614-641-8). 64pp. An engrossing biography of the candy-making entrepreneur and his many philanthropies. (Rev: SLJ 1/95) [921]

## HICKOK, WILD BILL

**10533** Green, Carl R., and William R. Sanford. *Wild Bill Hickok* (4–8). Illus. Series: Outlaws and Lawmen of the Wild West. 1992, Enslow LB $15.95 (0-89490-366-7). 48pp. The life story of the famous frontier marshal in Kansas is retold in text and pictures. (Rev: BL 7/92; SLJ 8/92) [921]

## HINE, LEWIS

**10534** Freedman, Russell. *Kids at Work: Lewis Hine and the Crusade Against Child Labor* (5–8). Photos by Lewis Hine. 1994, Clarion $16.95 (0-395-58703-4). 104pp. This photoessay describes child labor in the United States at the beginning of the century and how Lewis Hine fought for reforms. (Rev: BCCB 10/94; BL 8/94; HB 11–12/94; SLJ 9/94*) [921]

## HOLLIDAY, DOC

**10535** Green, Carl R., and William R. Sanford. *Doc Holliday* (4–8). Series: Outlaws and Lawmen of the Wild West. 1995, Enslow LB $15.95 (0-89490-589-9). 48pp. The life and exploits of this colorful Western character are reproduced with photos and maps. (Rev: BL 6/1–15/95) [921]

## HOUSTON, SAM

**10536** Fritz, Jean. *Make Way for Sam Houston* (4–7). Illus. by Elise Primavera. 1986, Putnam paper $7.95 (0-399-21304-X). 112pp. Houston, a larger-than-life Texan, lived a fascinating life well captured in this biography. (Rev: HB 5–6/86; SLJ 5/86)

**10537** Wade, Mary D. *I Am Houston* (3–5). Illus. 1993, Colophon $11.95 (1-882539-05-2); paper $5.95 (1-882539-06-0). 64pp. The biography of the soldier and politician who has become one of Texas's favorite heroes. (Rev: BL 4/15/93) [921]

### IACOCCA, LEE

**10538** Collins, David R. *Lee Iacocca: Chrysler's Good Fortune* (5–8). Illus. Series: Wizards of Business. 1992, Garrett LB $17.26 (1-56074-017-5). 64pp. The life of Lee Iacocca, top manager in the auto industry, is retold in simple text and many photos. (Rev: BL 6/15/92; SLJ 7/92) [921]

### JACKSON, STONEWALL

**10539** Bennett, Barbara J. *Stonewall Jackson: Lee's Greatest Lieutenant* (4–7). Illus. Series: The History of the Civil War. 1990, Silver Burdett paper $7.95 (0-382-24048-0). 135pp. The story of the Confederate general who gained his nickname beause he stood "like a stone wall." (Rev: BL 9/1/91) [921]

**10540** Pflueger, Lynda. *Stonewall Jackson: Confederate General* (5–8). Illus. 1997, Enslow LB $19.95 (0-89490-781-6). 128pp. This sympathetic biography of Jackson provides good material on his personal life and beliefs while quoting generously from firsthand sources. (Rev: BL 10/1/97) [921]

### JAMES, JESSE

**10541** Green, Carl R., and William R. Sanford. *Jesse James* (4–8). Illus. Series: Outlaws and Lawmen of the Wild West. 1992, Enslow LB $15.95 (0-89490-365-9). 48pp. In this easy-to-read text, the authentic as well as the legendary Jesse James is discussed. (Rev: BL 3/1/92; SLJ 5/92) [921]

**10542** Wukovits, John. *Jesse James* (5–8). Illus. Series: Legends of the West. 1996, Chelsea $15.95 (0-7910-3876-9). 60pp. An action-packed biography that tries to probe the complex nature of the famous Western outlaw. (Rev: SLJ 4/97) [921]

### JONES, JOHN PAUL

**10543** Brandt, Keith. *John Paul Jones: Hero of the Seas* (3–5). Illus. by Susan Swan. 1983, Troll LB $12.95 (0-89375-849-3); paper $3.50 (0-89375-850-7). 48pp. The U.S. naval hero is introduced in an account that does not ignore either his strengths or his weaknesses.

### KELLEY, FLORENCE

**10544** Saller, Carol. *Florence Kelley* (2–4). Illus. by Ken Green. Series: On My Own Biographies. 1997, Carolrhoda LB $18.60 (1-57505-016-1). 48pp. The story of the labor leader and her fight against child

labor. (Rev: BCCB 7–8/97; BL 6/1–15/97; SLJ 11/97) [921]

### KENNEDY, ROBERT

**10545** Harrison, Barbara, and Daniel Terris. *A Ripple of Hope: The Life of Robert F. Kennedy* (5–8). Illus. 1997, Dutton paper $16.99 (0-525-67506-X). 144pp. The story of the seventh of the Kennedy children, who grew up in the shadow of his older brothers but later found his own path to greatness. (Rev: BCCB 7–8/97; BL 6/1–15/97; SLJ 8/97) [921]

### KING, RICHARD

**10546** Sanford, William R., and Carl R. Green. *Richard King: Texas Cattle Rancher* (4–6). Illus. Series: Legendary Heroes of the Wild West. 1997, Enslow LB $15.95 (0-89490-673-9). 48pp. This short biography of the colorful Texan tells how he was able to amass the land that became one of the largest ranches in the world. (Rev: BL 3/15/97; SLJ 4/97) [921]

### KNIGHT, PHILIP

**10547** Collins, David R. *Philip H. Knight: Running with Nike* (5–8). Illus. Series: Wizards of Business. 1992, Garrett LB $17.26 (1-56074-020-5). 64pp. The life story of the man who originated and operated the sportswear firm of Nike. (Rev: BL 6/15/92; SLJ 9/92) [921]

### KOREMATSU, FRED

**10548** Chin, Steven A. *When Justice Failed: The Fred Korematsu Story* (3–6). Illus. by David Tamura. 1993, Raintree Steck-Vaughn LB $25.68 (0-8114-7236-1). 105pp. The biography of the Japanese American whose rights were continually violated during World War II. (Rev: SLJ 7/93) [921]

### LAUREN, RALPH

**10549** Canadeo, Anne. *Ralph Lauren: Master of Fashion* (5–8). Illus. Series: Wizards of Business. 1992, Garrett LB $17.26 (1-56074-021-3). 64pp. This book introduces one of the most influential fashion designers working today. (Rev: BL 6/15/92) [921]

### LAZARUS, CHARLES P.

**10550** Koopman, Anne. *Charles P. Lazarus: The Titan of Toys "R" Us* (5–8). Illus. Series: Wizards of Business. 1992, Garrett LB $17.26 (1-56074-022-1). 64pp. The success story of the Toys "R" Us retail chain is told through the life of the founder. (Rev: BL 6/15/92; SLJ 7/92) [921]

## LEE, ROBERT E.

**10551** Adler, David A. *A Picture Book of Robert E. Lee* (3–4). Illus. by Alexandra Wallner and John Wallner. Series: Picture Book Biographies. 1994, Holiday LB $15.95 (0-8234-1111-7). Using a story format, this simple account covers the highlights of Lee's life and military career. (Rev: SLJ 5/94) [921]

**10552** Cannon, Marian G. *Robert E. Lee* (4–6). Illus. Series: First Book. 1993, Watts LB $21.00 (0-531-20120-1). 64pp. A biography that concentrates on Lee's public career more than his personal life. (Rev: BL 2/15/94; SLJ 2/94) [921]

**10553** Dubowski, Cathy E. *Robert E. Lee: The Rise of the South* (4–7). Illus. Series: The History of the Civil War. 1990, Silver Burdett paper $7.95 (0-382-24051-0). 135pp. The life of the Confederate general who was a stirring commander and a man of great character. (Rev: BL 9/1/91) [921]

**10554** Kerby, Mona. *Robert E. Lee: Southern Hero of the Civil War* (5–8). Illus. Series: Historical American Biographies. 1997, Enslow LB $19.95 (0-89490-782-4). 128pp. This thorough, sympathetic biography of Lee points out that he did not approve of slavery or the South's secession from the Union. (Rev: BL 10/1/97; SLJ 9/97) [921]

## LILIUOKALANI, QUEEN

**10555** Guzzetti, Paula. *The Last Hawaiian Queen: Liliuokalani* (3–5). Illus. Series: Biographies. 1996, Benchmark LB $21.36 (0-7614-0490-2). 48pp. A history of Hawaii with special emphasis on the life of its last queen, the fascinating Liliuokalani. (Rev: SLJ 3/97) [921]

## LYON, MARY

**10556** Rosen, Dorothy S. *A Fire in Her Bones: The Story of Mary Lyon* (5–7). Illus. 1995, Carolrhoda LB $22.60 (0-87614-840-2). 88pp. A biography of the woman who defied social barriers and founded Mount Holyoke Female Seminary, now known as Mount Holyoke College. (Rev: BL 6/1–15/95; SLJ 4/95) [921]

## MACARTHUR, DOUGLAS

**10557** Darby, Jean. *Douglas MacArthur* (4–7). Illus. Series: Lerner Biography. 1989, Lerner LB $23.93 (0-8225-4901-8). 112pp. This biography highlights the general's leadership during World War II and his later dismissal by Truman. (Rev: BL 11/15/89) [921]

**10558** Finkelstein, Norman H. *The Emperor General: A Biography of Douglas MacArthur* (5–7). Illus. 1989, Macmillan LB $13.95 (0-87518-396-4). 128pp. The life of this famous 5-star general of World War II. (Rev: BL 3/1/89; SLJ 4/89)

## MARIN, DON LUIS MONEZ

**10559** Bernier-Grand, Carmen T. *Poet and Politician of Puerto Rico: Don Luis Munoz Marin* (5–8). Illus. 1995, Orchard LB $16.99 (0-531-08737-9). 128pp. Through this story of the life of the man who helped make Puerto Rico a commonwealth, a history of the island is chronicled. (Rev: BL 5/15/95; SLJ 4/95) [921]

## NEWTON, JOHN

**10560** Haskins, Jim. *Amazing Grace: The Story Behind the Song* (5–7). Illus. 1992, Millbrook LB $20.90 (1-56294-117-8). 48pp. A profile of John Newton, the man behind one of the most popular of all songs. (Rev: BL 11/1/92) [921]

## OLMSTED, FREDERICK LAW

**10561** Dunlap, Julie. *Parks for the People: A Story About Frederick Law Olmsted* (3–6). Illus. by Susan F. Lieber. Series: Creative Minds Biographies. 1994, Carolrhoda LB $19.93 (0-87614-824-0). 63pp. The life story of America's first landscape architect, his masterpiece — Central Park in New York City — and how he tried to save Yosemite from commercial exploitation. (Rev: SLJ 2/95) [921]

## PATTON, GEORGE

**10562** Peifer, Charles. *Soldier of Destiny: A Biography of George Patton* (4–7). Illus. 1988, Macmillan LB $13.95 (0-87518-395-6). 128pp. The life and times of the colorful general who commanded the Third Army in Europe during World War II. (Rev: BL 3/1/89)

## PEROT, ROSS

**10563** Bredeson, Carmen. *Ross Perot: Billionaire Politician* (4–6). Illus. Series: People to Know. 1995, Enslow LB $18.95 (0-89490-545-7). 128pp. An engrossing biography that gives details of Perot's early years and his political aspirations. (Rev: BL 4/15/95; SLJ 5/95) [921]

**10564** Italia, Bob. *Ross Perot: The Man Who Woke Up America* (4–6). Illus. Series: Everyone Contributes. 1993, ABDO LB $13.98 (1-56239-236-0). 40pp. The story of Perot's childhood and business success, with emphasis on his run for the presidency. (Rev: BL 12/1/93; SLJ 1/94) [921]

## PINKERTON, ALAN

**10565** Green, Carl R., and William R. Sanford. *Allan Pinkerton* (4–8). Illus. Series: Outlaws and Lawmen. 1995, Enslow LB $15.95 (0-89490-590-2). 48pp. A simple biography that presents the highlights of the life of the creator of the famous detective agency. (Rev: BL 11/15/95) [921]

**10566** Josephson, Judith P. *Allan Pinkerton: The Original Private Eye* (5–8). Illus. 1996, Lerner LB $17.21 (0-8225-2923-9). 128pp. The story of the famed criminal-catcher who founded the world-famous detective agency. (Rev: BL 10/15/96; SLJ 10/96) [921]

### RENO, JANET

**10567** Hamilton, John. *The Attorney General Through Janet Reno* (4–6). Illus. Series: All the President's Men and Women. 1993, ABDO LB $14.98 (1-56239-251-4). 32pp. The biography of Janet Reno also supplies material on the components of the Department of Justice. (Rev: SLJ 3/94) [921]

**10568** Meachum, Virginia. *Janet Reno: United States Attorney General* (4–6). Illus. Series: People to Know. 1995, Enslow LB $19.95 (0-89490-549-X). 128pp. This attractive account tells of this amazing woman's career in law and her gradual rise to becoming attorney general. (Rev: BL 7/95; SLJ 8/95) [921]

**10569** Simon, Charnan. *Janet Reno: First Woman Attorney General* (2–4). Illus. Series: Picture-Story Biographies. 1994, Children's LB $18.20 (0-516-04191-6). 32pp. Large type and many black-and-white photographs are used to present a brief biography of this important lawyer and scholar. (Rev: BL 8/94; SLJ 9/94) [921]

### REVERE, PAUL

**10570** Adler, David A. *A Picture Book of Paul Revere* (K–3). Illus. Series: Picture Book Biographies. 1995, Holiday LB $15.95 (0-8234-1144-3). 42pp. A simple biography of this Revolutionary War hero, with an emphasis on colorful illustrations. (Rev: BL 3/15/95; SLJ 4/95) [921]

**10571** Sakurai, Gail. *Paul Revere* (3–5). Series: Cornerstones of Freedom. 1997, Children's LB $19.50 (0-516-20463-7). 32pp. The life of this early patriot is traced, with emphasis on his role during the Revolutionary War. (Rev: BL 12/15/97) [921]

### SHERBURNE, ANDREW

**10572** Zeinert, Karen, ed. *The Memoirs of Andrew Sherburne: Patriot and Privateer of the American Revolution* (5–8). Illus. 1993, Shoe String LB $17.50 (0-208-02354-2). 96pp. An action-filled, first-person narrative about a colonialist who served in the navy during the American Revolution. (Rev: SLJ 7/93) [921]

### SHERMAN, WILLIAM T.

**10573** Whitelaw, Nancy. *William Tecumseh Sherman: Defender and Destroyer* (5–8). 1996, Morgan Reynolds LB $18.95 (1-883846-12-9). 112pp. Both the personal and public life of this Civil War gener-

al, who brought destruction to the South, is retold using many quotes. (Rev: BL 3/15/96; SLJ 6/96) [921]

### STRAUSS, LEVI

**10574** Henry, Sondra, and Emily Taitz. *Everyone Wears His Name: A Biography of Levi Strauss* (5–8). Illus. 1990, Macmillan $13.95 (0-87518-375-1). 128pp. The man who started out as a peddler in 1853 and changed the clothes of America. (Rev: BL 4/1/90; SLJ 7/90) [921]

**10575** Weidt, Maryann N. *Mr. Blue Jeans: A Story About Levi Strauss* (3–5). Illus. 1990, Carolrhoda LB $19.95 (0-87614-421-0). 64pp. The story of the phenomenal blue jeans and of their phenomenal creator. (Rev: BL 12/1/90; SLJ 1/91) [921]

### YOUNG, BRIGHAM

**10576** Sanford, William R., and Carl R. Green. *Brigham Young: Pioneer and Mormon Leader* (4–6). Illus. Series: Legendary Heroes of the Wild West. 1996, Enslow LB $15.95 (0-89490-672-0). 48pp. A simple account that chronicles the life and career of the great Mormon leader Brigham Young. (Rev: BL 10/15/96; SLJ 9/96) [921]

## Indians of North America

### GERONIMO

**10577** Hermann, Spring. *Geronimo: Apache Freedom Fighter* (4–6). Illus. Series: Native American Biographies. 1997, Enslow LB $19.95 (0-89490-864-2). 128pp. The story of the great Apache chieftain who led his people first against the Mexicans and then against the Americans. (Rev: BL 4/15/97; SLJ 6/97) [921]

**10578** Jeffery, David. *Geronimo* (3–5). Illus. by Tom Redman. Series: American Indian Stories. 1990, Raintree Steck-Vaughn LB $21.40 (0-8172-3404-7). 32pp. The story of the Apache chief who terrorized the West. (Rev: SLJ 10/90) [921]

**10579** Sanford, William R. *Geronimo: Apache Warrior* (4–6). Illus. Series: Native American Leaders of the Wild West. 1994, Enslow LB $15.95 (0-89490-510-4). 48pp. A concise treatment of the long life of this Apache leader and of his lasting contributions. (Rev: SLJ 10/94) [921]

### HARRIS, LA DONNA

**10580** Schwartz, Michael. *La Donna Harris* (4–7). Illus. Series: Contemporary Native Americans. 1997, Raintree Steck-Vaughn LB $24.26 (0-8172-3995-2). 48pp. The life story and accomplishments of this

Native American, who has openly championed her people's rights before the Senate. (Rev: BL 6/1–15/97) [921]

### HENIO, KATIE

**10581** Thomson, Peggy. *Katie Henio: Navajo Sheepherder* (4–6). Photos by Paul Conklin. 1995, Dutton paper $16.99 (0-525-65160-8). 64pp. A Navajo great-grandmother tends her flock of sheep and upholds the ancient customs of her people. (Rev: BCCB 4/95; BL 1/15/95; HB 9–10/95; SLJ 3/95) [921]

### HIAWATHA

**10582** Fradin, Dennis B. *Hiawatha: Messenger of Peace* (4–7). Illus. 1992, Macmillan $16.00 (0-689-50519-1). 48pp. Distinguishing between fact and fiction about the Iroquois leader is the premise of this book. (Rev: BL 9/15/92; HB 1–2/93; SLJ 7/92*) [921]

### ISHI

**10583** Kroeber, Theodora. *Ishi, Last of the Tribe* (5–7). Illus. by Ruth Robbins. 1973, Bantam paper $4.99 (0-553-24898-7). 224pp. A California Yahi Indian, the last of his tribe, leaves his primitive life and enters the modern world.

### JOSEPH (NEZ PERCE CHIEF)

**10584** Sanford, William R. *Chief Joseph: Nez Perce Warrior* (4–6). Illus. Series: Native American Leaders of the Wild West. 1994, Enslow LB $15.95 (0-89490-509-0). 48pp. A clearly written introduction to the life of this leader of the Nez Perce Indians. (Rev: SLJ 12/94) [921]

### MANKILLER, WILMA

**10585** Glassman, Bruce. *Wilma Mankiller: Chief of the Cherokee Nation* (5–7). Illus. Series: Library of Famous Women. 1992, Blackbirch LB $15.95 (1-56711-032-0). 64pp. This is an inspiring biography of the amazing woman who led her Cherokee Indians through difficult crises. (Rev: BL 6/1/92; SLJ 4/92) [921]

**10586** Lazo, Caroline. *Wilma Mankiller* (4–7). Illus. Series: Peacemakers. 1995, Silver Burdett paper $7.95 (0-382-24716-7). 64pp. The dramatic story of the woman who contributed to peace within the American Indian community. (Rev: BL 7/95; SLJ 7/95) [921]

**10587** Lowery, Linda. *Wilma Mankiller* (2–4). Illus. 1996, Carolrhoda LB $13.95 (0-87614-880-1); paper $5.95 (0-87614-953-0). 56pp. The great hardships that were faced by the Native American woman are

the focus of this inspiring, simple biography. (Rev: BCCB 9/96; BL 9/1/96; SLJ 9/96) [921]

### OSCEOLA (SEMINOLE CHIEF)

**10588** Sanford, William R. *Osceola: Seminole Warrior* (4–6). Illus. Series: Native American Leaders of the Wild West. 1994, Enslow LB $15.95 (0-89490-535-X). 48pp. Material is presented on Osceola's boyhood and his military and political accomplishments as leader of the Seminoles. (Rev: SLJ 12/94) [921]

### PARKER, QUANAH (COMANCHE CHIEF)

**10589** Sanford, William R. *Quanah Parker: Comanche Warrior* (4–6). Illus. Series: Native American Leaders of the Wild West. 1994, Enslow LB $15.95 (0-89490-512-0). 48pp. A clearly written, concise biography of this Comanche leader's life and accomplishments. (Rev: SLJ 12/94) [921]

### PHILIP (SACHEM OF THE WAMPANOAGS)

**10590** Averill, Esther. *King Philip: The Indian Chief* (5–8). Illus. by Vera Belsky. 1993, Shoe String LB $18.50 (0-208-02357-7). 148pp. The story of the Wampanoag chief who befriended the Pilgrims and later waged war against the settlers. (Rev: BL 7/93) [921]

**10591** Cwiklik, Robert. *King Philip and the War with the Colonists* (4–7). Illus. Series: Biography Series of American Indians. 1989, Silver Burdett LB $12.95 (0-382-09573-1); paper $7.95 (0-382-09762-9). 144pp. A biography of the Wampanoag Indian chief who led his people in the most important Indian War in New England. (Rev: BL 1/1/90) [921]

### POCAHONTAS

**10592** D'Aulaire, Ingri, and Edgar D'Aulaire. *Pocahontas* (2–4). Illus. by authors. 1985, Doubleday $13.95 (0-385-07454-9). 48pp. The story of the Indian girl who saved the life of John Smith.

**10593** Fritz, Jean. *The Double Life of Pocahontas* (4–7). Illus. 1987, Puffin paper $3.99 (0-14-032257-4). 128pp. A biography of the Indian maiden now chiefly associated with Captain John Smith.

**10594** Holler, Anne. *Pocahontas: Powhatan Peacemaker* (5–8). Illus. Series: North American Indians of Achievement. 1993, Chelsea $19.95 (0-7910-1705-2); paper $8.95 (0-7910-1952-7). 103pp. A brief biography of the woman who helped the English settlers survive at Jamestown. (Rev: SLJ 4/93) [921]

**10595** Iannone, Catherine. *Pocahontas* (4–7). Illus. Series: Junior World Biographies. 1995, Chelsea LB $15.95 (0-7910-2496-2); paper $4.95 (0-7910-2497-0). 80pp. The fascinating story of the Indian princess who eventually married a white man and was received by English royalty. (Rev: BL 10/15/95; SLJ 10/95) [921]

**10596** Raphael, Elaine, and Don Bolognese. *Pocahontas: Princess of the River Tribes* (1–3). Illus. by authors. Series: Drawing America. 1993, Scholastic $12.95 (0-590-44371-2). Important episodes in the life of Pocahontas are retold in this brief picture book biography. (Rev: SLJ 10/93) [921]

### RED CLOUD

**10597** Sanford, William R. *Red Cloud: Sioux Warrior* (4–8). Illus. 1994, Enslow LB $15.95 (0-89490-513-9). 48pp. The story of the great 19th-century Oglala Indian leader and his struggle with the U.S. government. (Rev: BL 12/15/94; SLJ 2/95) [921]

### SACAGAWEA

**10598** Raphael, Elaine, and Don Bolognese. *Sacajawea: The Journey West* (1–3). Illus. by authors. Series: Drawing America. 1994, Scholastic $12.95 (0-590-47898-2). A brief biography about Sacajawea's life and her journey west with Lewis and Clark. (Rev: SLJ 12/94) [921]

**10599** Rowland, Della. *The Story of Sacajawea: Guide to Lewis and Clark* (4–6). Illus. by Richard Leonard. 1989, Dell paper $3.99 (0-440-40215-8). 96pp. In brief text, this account tells of the courage and daring of the Shoshone woman who guided Lewis and Clark. (Rev: BCCB 9/89; BL 12/15/89; SLJ 12/89) [921]

**10600** St. George, Judith. *Sacagawea* (4–6). 1997, Putnam $16.95 (0-399-23161-7). 128pp. A sympathetic account of the life of this Shoshone Indian woman and her exciting adventures while helping in the Lewis and Clark expedition. (Rev: BL 8/97; SLJ 3/98) [921]

**10601** Sanford, William R., and Carl R. Green. *Sacagawea: Native American Hero* (4–6). Illus. Series: Legendary Heroes of the Wild West. 1997, Enslow LB $15.95 (0-89490-675-5). 48pp. A short biography of the gallant Shoshone Indian woman who accompanied Lewis and Clark west during 1805–1806. (Rev: BL 3/15/97; SLJ 3/97) [921]

**10602** White, Alana J. *Sacagawea: Westward with Lewis and Clark* (4–6). Illus. Series: Native American Biographies. 1997, Enslow LB $19.95 (0-89490-867-7). 128pp. A well-written account of this gallant woman's life. Also includes a further-reading list, chapter notes, and chronology. (Rev: BL 4/15/97; SLJ 8/97) [921]

### SEQUOYAH

**10603** Cwiklik, Robert. *Sequoyah and the Cherokee Alphabet* (4–7). Illus. Series: Biography Series of American Indians. 1989, Silver Burdett LB $11.98 (0-382-09570-7). 144pp. The story of the great Cherokee leader who was able to translate the language of his people to written form. (Rev: BL 1/1/90; SLJ 4/90) [921]

**10604** Klausner, Janet. *Sequoyah's Gift: A Portrait of the Cherokee Leader* (4–7). Illus. 1993, HarperCollins LB $14.89 (0-06-021236-5). 128pp. The life of this Cherokee leader is retold, with material on his invention of a written alphabet and his behavior during the Trail of Tears journey. (Rev: BL 9/1/93; HB 9–10/93; SLJ 11/93) [921]

### SITTING BULL (SIOUX CHIEF)

**10605** Black, Sheila. *Sitting Bull and the Battle of the Little Bighorn* (4–7). Illus. Series: Biography Series of American Indians. 1989, Silver Burdett LB $12.95 (0-382-09572-3); paper $7.95 (0-382-09761-0). 144pp. A biography of the Sioux leader who defeated Custer at the Little Bighorn. (Rev: BL 1/1/90; SLJ 4/90) [921]

**10606** Eisenberg, Lisa. *The Story of Sitting Bull, Great Sioux Chief* (5–7). Illus. by David Rickman. 1991, Dell paper $3.99 (0-440-40508-4). 108pp. This is the story of the gallant Sioux leader from birth to death in 1890. (Rev: SLJ 1/92) [921]

**10607** Sanford, William R. *Sitting Bull: Sioux Warrior* (4–6). Illus. Series: Native American Leaders of the Wild West. 1994, Enslow LB $15.95 (0-89490-514-7). 48pp. A concise, basic biography that introduces the Sioux Indians and gives details on the life of their most important leader. (Rev: SLJ 12/94) [921]

**10608** Schleichert, Elizabeth. *Sitting Bull: Sioux Leader* (4–6). Illus. Series: Native American Biographies. 1997, Enslow LB $19.95 (0-89490-868-5). 112pp. As well as describing the life of this great leader who fought to save the lands occupied by the Sioux, there is information on the life and culture of the Sioux. (Rev: BL 4/15/97; SLJ 6/97) [921]

**10609** Viola, Herman J. *Sitting Bull* (3–5). Illus. Series: American Indian Stories. 1990, Raintree Steck-Vaughn LB $21.40 (0-8172-3401-2). 32pp. The story of the Sioux Indian chief associated with the Battle of Little Bighorn. (Rev: SLJ 10/90) [921]

### SQUANTO

**10610** Bulla, Clyde Robert. *Squanto, Friend of the Pilgrims* (3–6). Illus. by Peter Burchard. 1990, Scholastic paper $3.50 (0-590-44055-1). 112pp. The first American Indian to reach Europe.

**10611** Kessel, Joyce K. *Squanto and the First Thanksgiving* (2–3). Illus. by Lisa Donze. 1983, Carolrhoda LB $13.95 (0-87614-199-8); paper $5.95 (0-87614-452-0). 48pp. An easily read story of an Indian sold into slavery but eventually freed close to the Plymouth Colony.

### TECUMSEH (SHAWNEE CHIEF)

**10612** Fleischer, Jane. *Tecumseh: Shawnee War Chief* (3–4). Illus. by Hal Frenck. 1979, Troll LB $11.89 (0-89375-153-7); paper $3.50 (0-89375-143-X). 48pp. A basic account of this Indian chief and his fight to prevent a territorial takeover by the white settlers.

**10613** Immell, Myra H., and William H. Immell. *Tecumseh* (4–8). Illus. Series: Importance Of. 1997, Lucent LB $22.45 (1-56006-087-5). 112pp. The story of the great Shawnee Indian leader who tried to unify American Indians against white domination and who was killed during the War of 1812. (Rev: BL 5/15/97; SLJ 8/97) [921]

### WINNEMUCCA, SARAH

**10614** Morrow, Mary Frances. *Sarah Winnemucca* (3–5). Illus. by Ken Bronikowski. Series: American Indian Stories. 1990, Raintree Steck-Vaughn LB $21.40 (0-8172-3402-0); paper $4.95 (0-8114-4095-8). 32pp. The life story of the Paiute woman who stood for Indian rights and education. (Rev: SLJ 10/90) [921]

## Presidents

### ADAMS, JOHN

**10615** Brill, Marlene T. *John Adams: Second President of the United States* (4–6). Illus. 1986, Children's LB $23.00 (0-516-01384-X). 100pp. Crisply written biography of the second U.S. president. (Rev: BL 3/15/87; SLJ 5/87)

### ADAMS, JOHN QUINCY

**10616** Harness, Cheryl. *Young John Quincy* (3–5). Illus. 1994, Bradbury paper $15.95 (0-02-742644-0). 48pp. Through the childhood of John Quincy Adams, the reader is told about the Declaration of Independence, the American Revolution, and the amazing Adams family. (Rev: BL 3/1/94; SLJ 4/94) [921]

**10617** Kent, Zachary. *John Quincy Adams: Sixth President of the United States* (4–7). Illus. 1987, Children's LB $23.00 (0-516-01386-6). 100pp. This son of the second president spent 50 years serving his country. (Rev: BL 10/15/87)

### ARTHUR, CHESTER A.

**10618** Simon, Charnan. *Chester A. Arthur* (4–6). Illus. Series: Encyclopedia of Presidents. 1989, Children's LB $24.00 (0-516-01369-6). 100pp. The story

of the honest, efficient president who reached office after Garfield's assassination. (Rev: BL 1/15/90) [921]

**10619** Stevens, Rita. *Chester A. Arthur: 21st President of the United States* (5–7). Illus. 1989, Garrett LB $19.93 (0-944483-05-4). 122pp. Life story of a former Vermont teacher. (Rev: BL 5/1/89)

### BUCHANAN, JAMES

**10620** Brill, Marlene T. *James Buchanan: Fifteenth President of the United States* (4–7). Illus. 1988, Children's LB $24.00 (0-516-01358-0). 120pp. Biography of the man who was president just prior to the Civil War. (Rev: BL 3/15/89; SLJ 5/89)

### BUSH, GEORGE

**10621** Kent, Zachary. *George Bush: Forty-First President of the United States* (4–6). Illus. Series: Encyclopedia of Presidents. 1989, Children's LB $24.00 (0-516-01374-2). 100pp. A lively account of the life of the former president and of his wife, Barbara. (Rev: BL 1/15/90) [921]

**10622** Spies, Karen B. *George Bush: Power of the President* (3–6). Illus. Series: Taking Part. 1991, Macmillan LB $13.95 (0-87518-487-1). 64pp. A profile of the former president, with references to Gorbachev and Iran-Contra. (Rev: BL 3/15/92; SLJ 3/92) [921]

**10623** Stefoff, Rebecca. *George H. W. Bush: 41st President of the United States* (K–2). Illus. Series: Presidents of the United States. 1992, Garrett LB $19.93 (1-56074-033-7). 124pp. The political career of George Bush minus the last 2 years of his presidency. (Rev: BL 8/90) [921]

### CARTER, JAMES E.

**10624** Carrigan, Mellonee. *Jimmy Carter: Beyond the Presidency* (4–6). Illus. 1995, Children's LB $18.20 (0-516-04193-2). 32pp. After covering Carter's life through the presidential years, this book focuses on his many present-day humanitarian efforts. (Rev: BL 6/1–15/95) [921]

**10625** Lazo, Caroline. *Jimmy Carter: On the Road to Peace* (4–7). Illus. 1996, Dillon LB $13.95 (0-382-39262-0); paper $7.95 (0-382-39263-9). 112pp. A biography of the president that also gives good coverage of his career since leaving office. (Rev: BL 8/96; SLJ 8/96) [921]

**10626** Richman, Daniel A. *James E. Carter* (5–8). Series: Presidents of the United States. 1989, GEC LB $19.93 (0-944483-24-0). 121pp. The story of this former U.S. president, his political career, family, and present charitable activities. (Rev: SLJ 9/89) [921]

**10627** Slavin, Ed. *Jimmy Carter* (4–8). Illus. 1989, Chelsea LB $19.95 (1-55546-828-4). 112pp. Introducing the thirty-ninth president of the United States. (Rev: BL 7/89)

**10628** Smith, Betsy. *Jimmy Carter, President* (5–7). Illus. 1986, Walker LB $13.85 (0-8027-6652-8). 128pp. A profile of Jimmy Carter and his one-term presidency. (Rev: BL 2/15/87; SLJ 12/86)

**10629** Wade, Linda R. *James Carter: Thirty-Ninth President of the United States* (4–6). Illus. Series: Encyclopedia of Presidents. 1989, Children's LB $23.00 (0-516-01372-6). 100pp. This account includes coverage on the early life, influences, and career of Jimmy Carter. (Rev: BL 1/15/90) [921]

CLEVELAND, GROVER

**10630** Kent, Zachary. *Grover Cleveland: Twenty-Second and Twenty-Fourth President of the United States* (4–7). Illus. 1988, Children's LB $24.00 (0-516-01360-2). 100pp. Biography of the only president to serve 2 nonconsecutive terms. (Rev: BL 3/15/89)

CLINTON, BILL

**10631** Cwiklik, Robert. *Bill Clinton: President of the 90's* (3–5). Illus. Series: Gateway Biographies. 1997, Millbrook LB $20.90 (0-7613-0129-1). 48pp. A readable biography that concentrates on Clinton's career as governor of Arkansas and his early years as president. (Rev: BL 9/15/97; SLJ 7/97) [921]

**10632** Greenberg, Keith E. *Bill and Hillary: Working Together in the White House* (2–6). Illus. by Jerry Harston. Series: Partners. 1994, Blackbirch LB $13.95 (1-56711-067-3). 47pp. Deals with the cooperative and joint creative efforts that have made the Clintons the successful couple they are. (Rev: SLJ 7/94) [921]

**10633** Landau, Elaine. *Bill Clinton and His Presidency* (4–6). Illus. 1997, Watts LB $22.00 (0-531-20295-X). 64pp. A concise biography with good coverage of the years Clinton has been in politics. (Rev: BL 9/15/97; SLJ 9/97) [921]

**10634** Martin, Gene L., and Aaron Boyd. *Bill Clinton: President from Arkansas* (5–8). Illus. 1993, Tudor LB $17.95 (0-936389-31-1). 112pp. This biography, which contains good anecdotal material, only covers Clinton's life through his first election. (Rev: BL 9/1/93; SLJ 6/93) [921]

**10635** Sherrow, Victoria. *Bill Clinton* (3–6). Illus. Series: Taking Part. 1993, Dillon LB $13.95 (0-87518-620-3). 72pp. A biography of the president that ends shortly after his first national election. (Rev: BL 10/15/93; SLJ 12/93) [921]

COOLIDGE, CALVIN

**10636** Kent, Zachary. *Calvin Coolidge: Thirtieth President of the United States* (4–7). Illus. 1988, Children's LB $24.00 (0-516-01362-9). 100pp. Biography of the man known as Silent Cal. (Rev: BL 3/15/89)

EISENHOWER, DWIGHT D.

**10637** Darby, Jean. *Dwight D. Eisenhower: A Man Called Ike* (4–7). Illus. Series: Lerner Biography. 1989, Lerner LB $23.93 (0-8225-4900-X). 112pp. The story of the World War II general who later became president of the United States. (Rev: BL 11/15/89) [921]

**10638** Deitch, Kenneth, and Joanne B. Weisman. *Dwight D. Eisenhower: Man of Many Hats* (5–7). Illus. by Jay Connolly. 1990, Discovery LB $14.95 (1-878668-02-1). 48pp. Each stage of Eisenhower's multifaceted career is represented. (Rev: SLJ 2/91) [921]

**10639** Ellis, Rafaela. *Dwight D. Eisenhower: 34th President of the United States* (5–7). Illus. 1989, Garrett LB $19.93 (0-944483-13-5). 122pp. Compact biography of the World War II hero and president. (Rev: BL 5/1/89)

**10640** Hargrove, Jim. *Dwight D. Eisenhower: Thirty-Fourth President of the United States* (4–7). Illus. 1987, Children's LB $24.00 (0-516-01389-0). 100pp. The life of the World War II hero who became a loved president. (Rev: BL 12/15/87)

**10641** Van Steenwyk, Elizabeth. *Dwight David Eisenhower, President* (5–8). Illus. 1987, Walker LB $13.85 (0-8027-6671-4). 128pp. The focus is on the career of this war-hero president. (Rev: BL 5/15/87) [921]

FILLMORE, MILLARD

**10642** Casey, Jane C. *Millard Fillmore: Thirteenth President of the United States* (4–7). Illus. 1988, Children's LB $24.00 (0-516-01353-X). 100pp. A biography of a little-known president. (Rev: BL 8/88)

FORD, GERALD

**10643** Sipiera, Paul P. *Gerald Ford: Thirty-Eighth President of the United States* (4–6). Illus. Series: Encyclopedia of Presidents. 1989, Children's LB $24.00 (0-516-01371-8). 100pp. The story of the man who succeeded Nixon and an account of the times in which he served. (Rev: BL 1/15/90) [921]

GARFIELD, JAMES A.

**10644** Lillegard, Dee. *James A. Garfield* (4–7). Illus. 1988, Children's LB $24.00 (0-516-01394-7). 100pp. The life and career of the twentieth U.S. president, who was assassinated. (Rev: BL 5/15/88; SLJ 6–7/88)

## GRANT, ULYSSES S.

**10645** Kent, Zachary. *Ulysses S. Grant* (4–7). Illus. Series: Encyclopedia of Presidents. 1989, Children's LB $24.00 (0-516-01364-5). 100pp. The troubled years of the Civil War and after are reflected in the life of Grant as soldier and statesman. (Rev: BL 7/89) [921]

**10646** Rickarby, Laura A. *Ulysses S. Grant and the Strategy of Victory* (4–7). Illus. Series: The Story of the Civil War. 1991, Silver Burdett paper $7.95 (0-382-24053-7). 160pp. This book focuses mainly on Grant's role in the winning of the Civil War for the North. (Rev: BL 9/1/91) [921]

## HARDING, WARREN G.

**10647** Wade, Linda R. *Warren G. Harding* (4–7). Illus. Series: Encyclopedia of Presidents. 1989, Children's LB $24.00 (0-516-01368-8). 100pp. The life of the president who served from 1921 to 1923 and died suddenly in San Francisco. (Rev: BL 7/89; SLJ 2/90) [921]

## HARRISON, BENJAMIN

**10648** Clinton, Susan. *Benjamin Harrison: Twenty-Third President of the United States* (4–6). Illus. Series: Encyclopedia of Presidents. 1989, Children's LB $24.00 (0-516-01370-X). 100pp. The story of the Republican president who defeated Cleveland through the electoral college process. (Rev: BL 1/15/90) [921]

## HARRISON, WILLIAM H.

**10649** Fitz-Gerald, Christine Maloney. *William Henry Harrison* (4–7). Illus. 1988, Children's LB $24.00 (0-516-01392-0). 100pp. The biography of the man who was president for 31 days. (Rev: BL 5/15/88; SLJ 6–7/88)

## HAYES, RUTHERFORD B.

**10650** Kent, Zachary. *Rutherford B. Hayes* (4–7). Illus. Series: Encyclopedia of Presidents. 1989, Children's LB $24.00 (0-516-01365-3). 100pp. The story of the president whose term ended the Reconstruction era. (Rev: BL 7/89; SLJ 2/90) [921]

## HOOVER, HERBERT

**10651** Clinton, Susan. *Herbert Hoover: Thirty-First President of the United States* (4–7). Illus. 1988, Children's LB $23.00 (0-516-01355-6). 100pp. Biography of the president associated with the Stock Market Crash of 1929. (Rev: BL 8/88)

## JACKSON, ANDREW

**10652** Osinski, Alice. *Andrew Jackson: Seventh President of the United States* (4–7). Illus. 1987, Children's LB $23.00 (0-516-01387-4). 100pp. A frontier lawyer and backwoods judge, Jackson was a strong believer in the common people. (Rev: BL 10/15/87)

## JEFFERSON, THOMAS

**10653** Adler, David A. *A Picture Book of Thomas Jefferson* (K–3). Illus. by John Wallner and Alexandra Wallner. Series: Picture Book Biography. 1990, Holiday LB $15.95 (0-8234-0791-8); paper $6.95 (0-8234-0881-7). 32pp. Basic facts and personal glimpses make up this simple biography of the third U.S. president. (Rev: BL 4/15/90; SLJ 5/90) [921]

**10654** Barrett, Marvin. *Meet Thomas Jefferson* (2–4). Illus. by Pat Fogarty. 1967, Random paper $3.99 (0-394-81964-0). 72pp. A simple, informal story of the third president.

**10655** Giblin, James Cross. *Thomas Jefferson: A Picture Book Biography* (4–6). Illus. by Michael Dooling. 1994, Scholastic $16.95 (0-590-44838-2). 48pp. This handsome, historically accurate biography of Thomas Jefferson covers his presidency and his accomplishments. (Rev: BCCB 10/94; BL 10/15/94; SLJ 9/94) [921]

**10656** Greene, Carol. *Thomas Jefferson: Author, Inventor, President* (2–4). Illus. Series: Rookie Biographies. 1991, Children's LB $19.00 (0-516-04224-6). 48pp. The many facets of Jefferson's genius are touched on in simple text with interesting photos and watercolors. (Rev: BL 3/15/92) [921]

**10657** Hargrove, Jim. *Thomas Jefferson: Third President of the United States* (4–6). Illus. 1986, Children's LB $23.00 (0-516-01385-8). 100pp. A biography of the third U.S. president, a most creative, intelligent person. (Rev: BL 3/15/87; SLJ 5/87)

**10658** Morris, Jeffrey. *The Jefferson Way* (5–8). Illus. Series: Great Presidential Decisions. 1994, Lerner LB $23.93 (0-8225-2926-2). 128pp. This book on Jefferson focuses on his terms as president, particularly the troubled second term. (Rev: BL 12/15/94; SLJ 12/94) [921]

**10659** Old, Wendie C. *Thomas Jefferson* (4–6). Illus. Series: United States Presidents. 1997, Enslow LB $19.95 (0-89490-837-5). 112pp. This account of the life and presidency of Jefferson contains a number of reproductions of portraits and documents. (Rev: BL 2/1/98; SLJ 3/98) [921]

## JOHNSON, ANDREW

**10660** Kent, Zachary. *Andrew Johnson* (4–7). Illus. Series: Encyclopedia of Presidents. 1989, Children's LB $24.00 (0-516-01363-7). 100pp. The story of the post-Civil War president who narrowly escaped impeachment. (Rev: BL 7/89) [921]

**10661** Stevens, Rita. *Andrew Johnson: 17th President of the United States* (5–7). Illus. 1989, Garrett LB $19.93 (0-944483-16-X). 122pp. Story of the man who became president on Lincoln's assassination. (Rev: BL 5/1/89)

### JOHNSON, LYNDON B.

**10662** Falkof, Lucille. *Lyndon B. Johnson: 36th President of the United States* (5–7). Illus. 1989, Garrett LB $19.93 (0-944483-20-8). 120pp. Life story of the man from Texas. (Rev: BL 5/1/89)

**10663** Hargrove, Jim. *Lyndon B. Johnson* (4–7). Illus. 1988, Children's LB $24.00 (0-516-01396-3). 100pp. The life and times of the thirty-sixth president, who took office after the assassination of John F. Kennedy. (Rev: BL 5/15/88; SLJ 6–7/88)

### KENNEDY, JOHN F.

**10664** Adler, David A. *A Picture Book of John F. Kennedy* (2–4). Illus. by Robert Casilla. Series: Picture Book Biography. 1991, Holiday LB $15.95 (0-8234-0884-1). A straightforward account in an attractive format that provides basic information about President John F. Kennedy. (Rev: SLJ 12/91) [921]

**10665** Cole, Michael D. *John F. Kennedy: President of the New Frontier* (4–7). Illus. Series: People to Know. 1996, Enslow LB $19.95 (0-89490-693-3). 128pp. A profile of the life and accomplishments of this charismatic president. (Rev: BL 5/15/96; SLJ 6/96) [921]

**10666** Donnelly, Judy. *Who Shot the President? The Death of John F. Kennedy* (3–4). Illus. 1989, Random LB $7.99 (0-394-99944-4); paper $3.99 (0-394-89944-X). 48pp. An overview of the JFK presidency and assassination. (Rev: BL 3/1/89)

**10667** Graves, Charles P. *John F. Kennedy* (2–5). Illus. by Paul Frame. 1981, Bantam paper $2.95 (0-440-44242-7). 80pp. The life of our thirty-fifth president.

**10668** Hampton, Wilborn. *Kennedy Assassinated! The World Mourns* (5–8). Illus. 1997, Candlewick $17.99 (1-56402-811-9). 96pp. A first-person account of the death of President Kennedy and of its devastating effects. (Rev: BL 9/15/97*; SLJ 10/97) [921]

**10669** Kent, Zachary. *John F. Kennedy: Thirty-Fifth President of the United States* (4–7). Illus. 1987, Children's LB $23.00 (0-516-01390-4). 99pp. The life of the young idealized president who died by an assassin's bullet. (Rev: BL 12/15/87)

### LINCOLN, ABRAHAM

**10670** Adler, David A. *A Picture Book of Abraham Lincoln* (PS–3). Illus. by John Wallner and Alexandra Wallner. 1989, Holiday LB $15.95 (0-8234-0731-4); paper $6.95 (0-8234-0801-9). 32pp. The life of perhaps our most famous president told in a profusely illustrated format. (Rev: BL 6/1/89; SLJ 5/89)

**10671** Bial, Raymond. *Where Lincoln Walked* (3–6). Illus. 1998, Walker $16.95 (0-8027-8630-8). 48pp. This unusual biography of Lincoln concentrates on the years before he became president and on the sight and people he knew at that time. (Rev: BL 3/1/98; SLJ 2/98) [921]

**10672** Brenner, Martha. *Abe Lincoln's Hat* (1–3). Illus. by Donald Cook. 1994, Random paper $3.99 (0-679-84977-7). 48pp. A simple biography of Lincoln that makes him a believable person through the retelling of simple anecdotes. (Rev: BL 9/15/94; SLJ 11/94) [921]

**10673** D'Aulaire, Ingri, and Edgar D'Aulaire. *Abraham Lincoln* (2–5). Illus. by authors. 1957, Doubleday $12.95 (0-385-07669-X); paper $9.95 (0-385-24108-9). Lincoln's life from boyhood to a tired war president. Caldecott Medal winner, 1940.

**10674** Freedman, Russell. *Lincoln: A Photobiography* (4–8). Illus. 1987, Houghton $17.00 (0-89919-380-3); paper $7.95 (0-395-51848-2). 160pp. A no-nonsense, unromanticized look at this beloved president. Newbery Medal winner, 1988. (Rev: BL 12/15/87; SLJ 12/87)

**10675** Gross, Ruth Belov. *True Stories About Abraham Lincoln* (2–5). Illus. by Jill Kastner. 1991, Scholastic paper $2.50 (0-590-43879-4). 48pp. This is a collection of anecdotes about Lincoln. Originally published in 1973. (Rev: BCCB 3/90; BL 3/1/90; SLJ 4/90) [921]

**10676** Hargrove, Jim. *Abraham Lincoln: Sixteenth President of the United States* (4–7). Illus. 1988, Children's LB $17.27 (0-516-01359-9). 100pp. Biography of the man forever associated with freedom. (Rev: BL 3/15/89; SLJ 5/89)

**10677** Harness, Cheryl. *Abe Lincoln Goes to Washington, 1837–1865* (1–4). Illus. 1997, National Geographic $18.00 (0-7922-3736-6). 48pp. In this sequel to *Young Abe Lincoln* (1996), Lincoln's life from his arrival in Springfield, Illinois, to his assassination is covered. (Rev: BL 1/1–15/97; SLJ 3/97*) [921]

**10678** Harness, Cheryl. *Young Abe Lincoln* (1–4). Illus. 1996, National Geographic $15.95 (0-7922-2713-1). 32pp. A picture book that traces Lincoln's early life until he leaves for Springfield, Illinois. (Rev: BL 9/1/96; SLJ 6/96) [921]

**10679** Ito, Tom. *Abraham Lincoln* (5–8). Illus. Series: Mysterious Deaths. 1996, Lucent LB $22.45 (1-56006-259-2). 96pp. This book explores the various conspiracy theories that surround Lincoln's death. (Rev: SLJ 5/97) [921]

**10680** Kunhardt, Edith. *Honest Abe* (PS–3). Illus. by Malcah Zeldis. 1993, Greenwillow LB $15.93 (0-688-11190-4). 32pp. Folk art helps to create this picture book version of Lincoln's life. (Rev: BL 12/1/92*; SLJ 3/93*) [921]

**10681** Livingston, Myra Cohn. *Abraham Lincoln: A Man for All the People* (1–4). Illus. by Samuel Byrd. 1993, Holiday LB $15.95 (0-8234-1049-8). 32pp. In rhyming quatrains, the life and accomplishments of this great president are retold. (Rev: BL 11/1/93; SLJ 10/93) [921]

**10682** Mosher, Kiki. *Learning About Honesty from the Life of Abraham Lincoln* (2–5). Illus. Series: A Character Building Book. 1996, Rosen LB $13.95 (0-8239-2420-3). 24pp. A brief biography of Lincoln that emphasizes his belief in honesty and truth. (Rev: BL 10/15/96; SLJ 12/96) [921]

**10683** Sandburg, Carl. *Abe Lincoln Grows Up* (6–8). Illus. by James Daugherty. 1975, Harcourt paper $7.00 (0-15-602615-5). 222pp. Classic account of Lincoln's boyhood based on Volume I of *The Prairie Years.*

**10684** Stefoff, Rebecca. *Abraham Lincoln: 16th President of the United States* (5–7). Illus. 1989, Garrett LB $19.93 (0-944483-14-3). 122pp. Compact biography of a president much respected and admired. (Rev: BL 5/1/89)

### MCKINLEY, WILLIAM

**10685** Kent, Zachary. *William McKinley: Twenty-Fifth President of the United States* (4–7). Illus. 1988, Children's LB $24.00 (0-516-01361-0). 100pp. Biography of an assassinated president. (Rev: BL 3/15/89)

### MADISON, JAMES

**10686** Clinton, Susan. *James Madison: Fourth President of the United States* (4–6). Illus. 1986, Children's LB $23.00 (0-516-01382-3). 100pp. Depicting the important events in the life of the fourth U.S. president. (Rev: BL 3/15/87; SLJ 5/87)

**10687** Fritz, Jean. *The Great Little Madison* (5–8). 1989, Putnam $15.95 (0-399-21768-1). 160pp. The story of the fourth president of the United States, James Madison, and of the people and events that surrounded his political career. (Rev: BCCB 10/89; HB 3–4/90*; SLJ 11/89) [921]

**10688** Malone, Mary. *James Madison* (4–6). Illus. 1997, Enslow LB $19.95 (0-89490-834-0). 128pp. This interesting, well-researched biography of James Madison focuses on his presidency. (Rev: BL 9/15/97; SLJ 9/97) [921]

**10689** Quackenbush, Robert. *James Madison and Dolley Madison and Their Times* (3–6). Illus. 1992, Pippin $14.95 (0-945912-18-8). 40pp. A fact-filled short biography of James and Dolley Madison with many interesting bits about their personal lives. (Rev: BL 1/15/93; SLJ 1/93) [921]

### NIXON, RICHARD M.

**10690** Lillegard, Dee. *Richard Nixon: Thirty-Seventh President of the United States* (4–7). Illus. 1988, Children's LB $24.00 (0-516-01356-4). 100pp. Ups and downs in the turbulent career of our thirty-seventh president. (Rev: BL 8/88; SLJ 10/88)

### PIERCE, FRANKLIN

**10691** Brown, Fern G. *Franklin Pierce* (5–8). Series: Presidents of the United States. 1989, GEC LB $19.93 (0-944483-25-9). 121pp. The story of Pierce, his political life and presidency, plus material on his personal life. (Rev: SLJ 9/89) [921]

**10692** Simon, Charnan. *Franklin Pierce: Fourteenth President of the United States* (4–7). Illus. 1988, Children's LB $24.00 (0-516-01357-2). 100pp. Biography of the New Hampshire lawyer elected president. (Rev: BL 3/15/89; SLJ 5/89)

### POLK, JAMES K.

**10693** Lillegard, Dee. *James K. Polk: Eleventh President of the United States* (4–7). Illus. 1988, Children's LB $24.00 (0-516-01351-3). 100pp. Includes chronological events in the life and career of the eleventh president. (Rev: BL 8/88)

### REAGAN, RONALD

**10694** Kent, Zachary. *Ronald Reagan: Fortieth President of the United States* (4–6). Illus. Series: Encyclopedia of Presidents. 1989, Children's LB $24.00 (0-516-01373-4). 100pp. A dramatic account of the movie star who became a 2-term president. (Rev: BL 1/15/90) [921]

**10695** Robbins, Neal. *Ronald W. Reagan: 40th President of the United States* (K–2). Illus. Series: Presidents of the United States. 1990, Garrett LB $19.93 (0-944483-66-6). 124pp. The life of Ronald Reagan is presented. (Rev: BL 8/90) [921]

**10696** Sullivan, George. *Ronald Reagan* (5–8). Illus. 1991, Simon & Schuster $14.98 (0-671-74537-9). 142pp. Revised edition adds new material on Reagan's second term. (Rev: BL 1/15/92) [921]

### ROOSEVELT, FRANKLIN D.

**10697** Freedman, Russell. *Franklin Delano Roosevelt* (5–8). Illus. 1990, Houghton $16.95 (0-89919-379-X). 200pp. A carefully researched and well-illustrated account of the man and the times. (Rev: HB 3–4/90; SLJ 12/90*) [921]

**10698** Greenblatt, Miriam. *Franklin D. Roosevelt: 32nd President of the United States* (5–7). Illus. 1989, Garrett LB $19.93 (0-944483-06-2). 122pp. Biography of the man who guided the country through World War II. (Rev: BL 5/1/89)

**10699** Morris, Jeffrey. *The FDR Way* (5–8). Illus. Series: Great Presidential Decisions. 1996, Lerner LB $23.93 (0-8225-2929-7). 136pp. In a straightforward style, this is an incisive analysis of the decisions, many of them painful, that FDR made and of their consequences. (Rev: BL 3/15/96) [921]

**10700** Osinski, Alice. *Franklin D. Roosevelt* (4–7). Illus. 1988, Children's LB $23.00 (0-516-01395-5). 100pp. The life and career of the thirty-second president, who led the nation through World War II. (Rev: BL 5/15/88; SLJ 6–7/88)

**10701** Schuman, Michael A. *Franklin D. Roosevelt: The Four-Term President* (4–7). Illus. Series: People to Know. 1996, Enslow LB $19.95 (0-89490-696-8). 128pp. A thoughtful, serious biography of this great president, his important decisions, and his significance in history. (Rev: BL 6/1–15/96; SLJ 8/96) [921]

### ROOSEVELT, THEODORE

**10702** DeStefano, Susan. *Theodore Roosevelt: Conservation President* (2–5). Illus. by Antonio Castro. Series: Earth Keepers. 1993, Holt LB $14.95 (0-8050-2122-1). 80pp. This biography of Teddy Roosevelt concentrates on his work as a naturalist and environmentalist. (Rev: BL 5/1/93; SLJ 6/93) [921]

**10703** Fritz, Jean. *Bully for You, Teddy Roosevelt!* (5–8). Illus. by Mike Wimmer. 1991, Putnam $15.95 (0-399-21769-X). 103pp. An affectionate portrait of the president who considered himself a "true American." (Rev: BL 4/15/91; HB 7–8/91; SLJ 7/91) [921]

**10704** Harness, Cheryl. *Young Teddy Roosevelt* (3–5). Illus. 1998, National Geographic $17.95 (0-7922-7094-0). 48pp. Illustrated with lavish watercolors, this picture book biography tells of Roosevelt's sickly childhood and ends with him becoming president of the United States. (Rev: BL 3/15/98) [921]

**10705** Kent, Zachary. *Theodore Roosevelt: Twenty-Sixth President of the United States* (4–7). Illus. 1988, Children's LB $23.00 (0-516-01354-8). 100pp. The life and career of Teddy Roosevelt. (Rev: BL 8/88)

**10706** Schuman, Michael A. *Theodore Roosevelt* (4–6). Illus. Series: United States Presidents. 1997, Enslow LB $19.95 (0-89490-836-7). 128pp. This well-illustrated account of the life and presidency of Theodore Roosevelt includes fascinating details of

his very adventurous life. (Rev: BL 2/1/98; SLJ 2/98) [921]

### TAFT, WILLIAM H.

**10707** Casey, Jane C. *William Howard Taft* (4–7). Illus. Series: Encyclopedia of Presidents. 1989, Children's LB $24.00 (0-516-01366-1). 100pp. The story of the president who served from 1909 to 1913. (Rev: BL 7/89) [921]

### TAYLOR, ZACHARY

**10708** Collins, David R. *Zachary Taylor: 12th President of the United States* (5–7). Illus. 1989, Garrett LB $19.93 (0-944483-17-8). 121pp. Life story of a military man elected president in 1848. (Rev: BL 5/1/89)

**10709** Kent, Zachary. *Zachary Taylor: Twelfth President of the United States* (4–7). Illus. 1988, Children's LB $24.00 (0-516-01352-1). 100pp. A look at the life and career of the president in a young nation. (Rev: BL 8/88)

### TRUMAN, HARRY S.

**10710** Hargrove, Jim. *Harry S. Truman: Thirty-Third President of the United States* (4–7). Illus. 1987, Children's LB $24.00 (0-516-01388-2). 100pp. The life of the president no one thought would win and few thought would do the job. (Rev: BL 12/15/87)

### TYLER, JOHN

**10711** Lillegard, Dee. *John Tyler* (4–7). Illus. 1988, Children's LB $24.00 (0-516-01393-9). 100pp. The life and career of the tenth president. (Rev: BL 5/15/88)

### VAN BUREN, MARTIN

**10712** Ellis, Rafaela. *Martin Van Buren: 8th President of the United States* (5–7). Illus. 1989, Garrett LB $19.93 (0-944483-12-7). 120pp. Story of a New York governor who became president. (Rev: BL 5/1/89)

**10713** Hargrove, Jim. *Martin Van Buren* (4–7). Illus. 1988, Children's LB $24.00 (0-516-01391-2). 100pp. Life during the administration of Van Buren, eighth U.S. president. (Rev: BL 5/15/88)

### WASHINGTON, GEORGE

**10714** Adler, David A. *A Picture Book of George Washington* (PS–3). Illus. by John Wallner and Alexandra Wallner. 1989, Holiday LB $15.95 (0-8234-0732-2); paper $6.95 (0-8234-0800-0). 32pp. A picture biography of America's first president for young readers. (Rev: BL 6/1/89; SLJ 5/89)

**10715** D'Aulaire, Ingri, and Edgar D'Aulaire. *George Washington* (2–3). Illus. by authors. 1936, Doubleday paper $13.95 (0-385-07306-2). 64pp. A simple recounting of the life of the first president.

**10716** Falkof, Lucille. *George Washington: 1st President of the United States* (5–7). Illus. 1989, Garrett LB $19.93 (0-944483-19-4). 120pp. Compact life story of the first president. (Rev: BL 5/1/89)

**10717** Kent, Zachary. *George Washington: First President of the United States* (4–6). Illus. 1986, Children's LB $23.00 (0-516-01381-5). 100pp. The events in the life of the first U.S. president. (Rev: BL 3/15/87; SLJ 5/87)

**10718** Morris, Jeffrey. *The Washington Way* (5–8). Illus. Series: Great Presidential Decisions. 1994, Lerner LB $23.93 (0-8225-2928-9). 128pp. This biography focuses on Washington's term of office as president and on his problems and accomplishments. (Rev: BL 12/15/94) [921]

**10719** Mosher, Kiki. *Learning About Leadership from the Life of George Washington* (2–5). Illus. Series: A Character Building Book. 1996, Rosen LB $13.95 (0-8239-2421-1). 24pp. A brief biography of Washington that emphasizes his leadership qualities. (Rev: BL 10/15/96; SLJ 12/96) [921]

**10720** Old, Wendie C. *George Washington* (5–8). Illus. 1997, Enslow LB $19.95 (0-89490-832-4). 128pp. Both Washington's personal and public lives are dealt with equally in this thoughtful biography. (Rev: BL 9/15/97; SLJ 12/97) [921]

**10721** Rosenburg, John. *Young George Washington: The Making of a Hero* (6–8). Illus. 1997, Millbrook LB $22.40 (0-7613-0043-0). 128pp. The biography of Washington's life from his teens through his military career to age 27. (Rev: BL 2/15/97; SLJ 4/97) [921]

### WILSON, WOODROW

**10722** Collins, David R. *Woodrow Wilson: 28th President of the United States* (5–7). Illus. 1989, Garrett LB $19.93 (0-944483-18-6). 121pp. Compact biography of a Nobel Peace Prize–winning president. (Rev: BL 5/1/89)

**10723** Osinski, Alice. *Woodrow Wilson* (4–7). Illus. Series: Encyclopedia of Presidents. 1989, Children's LB $24.00 (0-516-01367-X). 100pp. The life story of the president who saw this country through World War I. (Rev: BL 7/89) [921]

# Women

### ADDAMS, JANE

**10724** McPherson, Stephanie S. *Peace and Bread: The Story of Jane Addams* (5–8). Illus. 1993, Carolrhoda LB $22.60 (0-87614-792-9). 96pp. A brief biography of the woman noted for her work with the poor people of Chicago. (Rev: BL 1/15/94; SLJ 2/94) [921]

**10725** Wheeler, Leslie. *Jane Addams* (4–7). Illus. Series: Pioneers in Change. 1990, Silver Burdett LB $13.95 (0-382-09962-1); paper $6.95 (0-382-09968-0). 138pp. The story of the famous social worker who also worked for woman suffrage. (Rev: SLJ 4/91) [921]

### ANTHONY, SUSAN B.

**10726** Levin, Pamela. *Susan B. Anthony: Fighter for Women's Rights* (3–5). Illus. Series: Junior World Biographies. 1993, Chelsea LB $15.95 (0-7910-1762-1). 79pp. An informative, interesting biography of the great fighter for social causes, including women's right to vote. (Rev: SLJ 10/93) [921]

**10727** Mosher, Kiki. *Learning About Fairness from the Life of Susan B. Anthony* (2–5). Illus. Series: A Character Building Book. 1996, Rosen LB $13.95 (0-8239-2422-X). 24pp. The spirit of fairness and justice is shown in the life of this leader for women's rights. (Rev: BL 10/15/96; SLJ 12/96) [921]

**10728** Roop, Peter, and Connie Roop. *Susan B. Anthony* (2–3). Series: Lives and Times. 1997, Heinemann LB $12.95 (1-57572-563-0). 24pp. A simple picture book biography that gives a short introduction to the life and times of this fighter for women's rights. (Rev: BL 3/15/98) [921]

### ASH, MARY KAY

**10729** Stefoff, Rebecca. *Mary Kay Ash: A Beautiful Business* (5–8). Illus. Series: Wizards of Business. 1992, Garrett LB $17.26 (1-56074-012-4). 64pp. The story behind the great cosmetics empire and the woman who founded it, with tips for those who would like to be successful in the same business. (Rev: BL 6/15/92) [921]

### BAKER, S. JOSEPHINE

**10730** Ptacek, Greg. *Champion for Children's Health: A Story About Dr. S. Josephine Baker* (3–5). Illus. by Lydia M. Anderson. 1994, Carolrhoda LB $19.93 (0-87614-806-2). 64pp. The story of the woman who pioneered public-health standards for children at the turn of the century. (Rev: BL 3/1/94; SLJ 3/94) [921]

## BARTON, CLARA

**10731** Rose, Mary Catherine. *Clara Barton: Soldier of Mercy* (3–5). Illus. 1991, Chelsea LB $14.95 (0-7910-1403-7). A simply written account of this courageous nurse who founded the Red Cross.

**10732** Sonneborn, Liz. *Clara Barton* (4–7). Illus. Series: Junior World Biographies. 1991, Chelsea LB $15.95 (0-7910-1565-3). 80pp. A straightforward account of this famous, dedicated nurse. (Rev: BL 9/1/91) [921]

## BLY, NELLIE

**10733** Carlson, Judy. *"Nothing Is Impossible," Said Nellie Bly* (2–4). Illus. by Mike Eagle. Series: Real Readers. 1989, Raintree Steck-Vaughn LB $21.40 (0-8172-3521-3). 32pp. An easily read introduction to the newspaper woman and her famous trip around the world. (Rev: BL 2/1/90) [921]

**10734** Emerson, Kathy L. *Making Headlines: A Biography of Nellie Bly* (4–6). Illus. 1989, Macmillan LB $13.95 (0-87518-406-5). 112pp. The life of this journalist and outspoken reformer is presented. (Rev: BCCB 12/89; BL 7/89; SLJ 9/89) [921]

**10735** Kendall, Martha E. *Nellie Bly: Reporter for the World* (3–5). Illus. Series: Gateway Biography. 1992, Millbrook LB $21.90 (1-56294-061-9); paper $4.80 (0-395-64538-7). 48pp. The life story of the famous woman journalist whose real name was Elizabeth Seaman. (Rev: BL 8/92; SLJ 11/92) [921]

## BRIDGMAN, LAURA DEWEY

**10736** Hunter, Edith Fisher. *Child of the Silent Night* (3–5). Illus. 1963, Houghton $16.00 (0-395-06835-5). 128pp. The story of a blind-deaf child who paved the way for the successes of Helen Keller.

## BUSH, BARBARA

**10737** Spies, Karen B. *Barbara Bush: Helping America Read* (3–6). Illus. Series: Taking Part. 1991, Macmillan LB $13.95 (0-87518-488-X). 64pp. A look at the former First Lady, with some data on her interest in the literacy campaign. (Rev: BL 3/15/92; SLJ 3/92) [921]

## CARTER, ROSALYNN

**10738** Turk, Ruth. *Rosalynn Carter: Steel Magnolia* (4–6). Illus. Series: First Book: Monarchs. 1997, Watts $21.00 (0-531-20312-3). 64pp. From her childhood in Plains, Georgia, to the White House and her current interests, this is the story of Rosalynn Carter. (Rev: BL 12/1/97) [921]

## CLINTON, HILLARY RODHAM

**10739** Bach, Julie. *Hillary Rodham Clinton* (3–5). Illus. Series: Leading Ladies. 1993, ABDO LB $13.98 (1-56239-221-2). 32pp. An account of the First Lady's life, from childhood in a Chicago suburb to her arrival in Washington, D.C., for her husband's first term. (Rev: SLJ 3/94) [921]

**10740** Boyd, Aaron. *First Lady: The Story of Hillary Rodham Clinton* (5–8). 1994, Morgan Reynolds LB $17.95 (1-883846-02-1). 124pp. A biography of the first lady and her accomplishments that ends during Clinton's first term. (Rev: BL 4/15/94; SLJ 3/94) [921]

**10741** Guernsey, JoAnn B. *Hillary Rodham Clinton: A New Kind of First Lady* (4–7). Illus. 1993, Lerner LB $19.93 (0-8225-2875-4); paper $6.95 (0-8225-9650-4). 80pp. A behind-the-scenes biography of the first lady that ends with her attempts to reform health care. (Rev: BL 11/1/93; SLJ 12/93) [921]

**10742** LeVert, Suzanne. *Hillary Rodham Clinton: First Lady* (3–5). Illus. Series: Gateway Biographies. 1994, Millbrook LB $20.00 (1-56294-432-0); paper $7.95 (1-56294-726-5). 48pp. A biography of the first lady that ends with her beginning to work on health care in 1993. (Rev: BL 7/94) [921]

**10743** Sherrow, Victoria. *Hillary Rodham Clinton* (3–6). Illus. Series: Taking Part. 1993, Dillon LB $13.95 (0-87518-621-1). 64pp. A biography of the first lady that focuses on her schooling and law career. (Rev: BL 10/15/93; SLJ 12/93) [921]

## DE PASSE, SUZANNE

**10744** Mussari, Mark. *Suzanne De Passe: Motown's Boss Lady* (5–8). Illus. Series: Wizards of Business. 1992, Garrett LB $17.26 (1-56074-026-4). 64pp. The story of the woman who helped make Motown the great name in the music industry. (Rev: BL 6/15/92) [921]

## DIX, DOROTHEA

**10745** Schleichert, Elizabeth. *The Life of Dorothea Dix* (4). Illus. by Antonio Castro. Series: Pioneers in Health and Medicine. 1992, Century LB $13.95 (0-941477-68-1). 80pp. The story of the woman who spoke out against the neglect and abuse of the mentally ill. (Rev: SLJ 3/92) [921]

## EDELMAN, MARIAN WRIGHT

**10746** Burch, Joann J. *Marian Wright Edelman: Children's Champion* (4–6). Illus. Series: Gateway Biographies. 1994, Millbrook LB $20.90 (1-56294-457-6). 48pp. The engrossing life story of the founder of the Children's Defense Fund, who has devoted her life to protecting children's rights. (Rev: SLJ 2/95) [921]

**10747** Old, Wendie C. *Marian Wright Edelman: Fighting for Children's Rights* (4–6). Illus. Series: People to Know. 1995, Enslow LB $19.95 (0-89490-623-2). 112pp. The story of this 20th-century American and her fight for the rights of children. (Rev: BL 10/15/95; SLJ 12/95) [921]

### EDMONDS, EMMA

**10748** Reit, Seymour. *Behind Rebel Lines: The Incredible Story of Emma Edmonds, Civil War Spy* (5–8). 1988, Harcourt $12.95 (0-15-200416-5); paper $6.00 (0-15-200424-6). 144pp. The remarkable Canadian-born spy who helped to defend the Union in the Civil War. (Rev: BL 3/1/88; SLJ 3/88)

**10749** Stevens, Bryna. *Frank Thompson: Her Civil War Story* (5–7). Illus. 1992, Macmillan LB $14.00 (0-02-788185-7). 144pp. The life of Emma Edmonds, a Canadian woman who dressed as a man to join the U.S. Union Army. (Rev: BCCB 12/92; BL 12/15/92; HB 1–2/93; SLJ 10/92) [921]

### FIELDS, DEBBI

**10750** Spiesman, Harriet. *Debbi Fields: The Cookie Lady* (5–8). Illus. Series: Wizards of Business. 1992, Garrett LB $17.26 (1-56074-015-9). 64pp. Simple text and many pictures tell the life story of the woman who amazed herself with her success in the cookie industry. (Rev: BL 6/15/92) [921]

### GOLDMAN, EMMA

**10751** Gay, Kathlyn, and Martin Gay. *Emma Goldman* (4–8). Illus. Series: Importance Of. 1997, Lucent LB $22.45 (1-56006-024-7). 128pp. An introduction to the life of this 20th-century American activist and agitator whose activities resulted in her deportation to Russia. (Rev: BL 1/1–15/97) [921]

### GORE, TIPPER

**10752** Guernsey, JoAnn B. *Tipper Gore: Voice for the Voiceless* (4–6). Illus. 1994, Lerner LB $21.27 (0-8225-2876-2); paper $6.95 (0-8225-9651-2). 64pp. This biography of the vice president's wife reveals her to be an independent, determined woman who champions a number of worthy causes. (Rev: BL 9/15/94; SLJ 7/94) [921]

### HALE, CLARA

**10753** Italia, Bob. *Clara Hale: Mother to Those Who Needed One* (3–5). Illus. Series: Everyone Contributes. 1993, ABDO LB $13.98 (1-56239-235-2). 32pp. The biography of the woman whose work with foster children has become a model for others. (Rev: BL 12/1/93) [921]

### HOOVER, LOU

**10754** Colbert, Nancy A. *Lou Hoover: The Duty to Serve* (5–8). Illus. 1997, Morgan Reynolds LB $18.95 (1-883846-22-6). 112pp. As well as being the wife of an unpopular president, Mrs. Hoover was also a most interesting person, who, among other accomplishments, was the first woman to get a degree in geology in this country. (Rev: BL 2/15/98; SLJ 3/98) [921]

### HUTCHINSON, ANNE

**10755** Ilgenfritz, Elizabeth. *Anne Hutchinson* (5–8). Illus. Series: American Women of Achievement. 1990, Chelsea LB $19.95 (1-55546-660-5). 111pp. The story of the woman in pre-Revolutionary days who stood trial to defend religious liberty. (Rev: SLJ 4/91) [921]

### JONES, MOTHER

**10756** Colman, Penny. *Mother Jones and the March of the Mill Children* (3–6). Illus. 1994, Millbrook LB $21.90 (1-56294-402-9). 48pp. The story of the activist against child labor who led a protest march to President Theodore Roosevelt's home in Oyster Bay, New York in 1903. (Rev: BL 5/1/94) [921]

**10757** Horton, Madelyn. *The Importance of Mother Jones* (4–8). Illus. Series: The Importance Of. 1996, Lucent LB $22.45 (1-56006-057-3). 95pp. The life of the legendary American labor organizer who was active in the United States before and after the turn of the century. (Rev: BL 5/15/96; SLJ 7/96) [921]

**10758** Kraft, Betsy Harvey. *Mother Jones: One Woman's Fight for Labor* (5–8). Illus. 1995, Clarion $16.95 (0-395-67163-9). 116pp. The story of the woman who became a leader in the American labor movement from 1870 to 1930. (Rev: BCCB 9/95; SLJ 7/95*) [921]

### KARAN, DONNA

**10759** Tippins, Sherill. *Donna Karan: Designing an American Dream* (5–8). Illus. Series: Wizards of Business. 1992, Garrett LB $17.26 (1-56074-019-1). 64pp. Along with the life story of one of America's top fashion designers is advice for those who wish to enter the field. (Rev: BL 6/15/92) [921]

### KELLER, HELEN

**10760** Adler, David A. *A Picture Book of Helen Keller* (2–4). Illus. by John Wallner and Alexandra Wallner. Series: Picture Book Biography. 1990, Holiday LB $15.95 (0-8234-0818-3); paper $6.95 (0-8234-0950-3). 32pp. This account focuses on Keller's personality, stamina, and accomplishments. (Rev: BL 12/15/90; SLJ 11/90) [921]

**10761** Graff, Stewart, and Polly Graff. *Helen Keller: Toward the Light* (3–5). Illus. 1992, Chelsea LB $14.95 (0-7910-1412-6). 80pp. A simply written biography of the woman who overcame the handicaps of blindness and deafness.

**10762** Markham, Lois. *Helen Keller* (4–6). Illus. Series: First Books Biographies. 1993, Watts LB $21.00 (0-531-20104-X). 64pp. A well-written biography that includes little-known details of Keller's life. (Rev: SLJ 6/93) [921]

LOW, JULIETTE GORDON

**10763** Brown, Fern G. *Daisy and the Girl Scouts: The Story of Juliette Gordon Low* (4–6). Illus. 1996, Albert Whitman LB $14.95 (0-8075-1440-3). 112pp. Juliette Gordon Low led a pampered young life but went on to found what became the Girl Scouts. (Rev: BL 5/1/96; SLJ 5/96) [921]

LUDINGTON, SYBIL

**10764** Brown, Drollene P. *Sybil Rides for Independence* (3–5). Illus. by Margot Apple. 1985, Whitman $12.95 (0-8075-7684-0). 48pp. The story of 16-year-old Sybil Ludington who rode the countryside to bring her father's regiment to muster to ward off a British attack during the Revolution. (Rev: BL 11/15/85; SLJ 2/86)

O'CONNOR, SANDRA DAY

**10765** Deegan, Paul J. *Sandra Day O'Connor* (4–6). Illus. Series: Supreme Court Justices. 1992, ABDO LB $14.98 (1-56239-089-9). 40pp. This biography includes material on Judge O'Connor's position on various issues and quotes from her written opinions. (Rev: BL 6/1–15/93) [921]

**10766** Gherman, Beverly. *Sandra Day O'Connor: Justice for All* (3–5). Illus. by Robert Masheris. Series: Women of Our Time. 1991, Viking paper $10.95 (0-670-82756-8). 54pp. This concise biography includes good material on the justice's childhood and education. (Rev: BCCB 3/91; BL 3/1/91; SLJ 7/91) [921]

**10767** Henry, Christopher. *Sandra Day O'Connor* (4–6). Illus. 1994, Watts LB $21.00 (0-531-20175-9). 64pp. The story of the Supreme Court justice and the obstacles she overcame to achieve stature in the legal profession. (Rev: BL 2/1/95) [921]

**10768** Macht, Norman L. *Sandra Day O'Connor: Supreme Court Justice* (4–7). Illus. Series: Junior World Biographies. 1992, Chelsea paper $8.95 (0-7910-0448-1). 80pp. In clear text with many photographs, this is a simple account of the first female Supreme Court Justice. (Rev: BL 8/92; SLJ 8/92) [921]

OAKLEY, ANNIE

**10769** Dadey, Debbie. *Shooting Star: Annie Oakley, the Legend* (K–3). Illus. by Scott Goto. 1997, Walker LB $16.85 (0-8027-8485-2). 32pp. Fact and fiction mingle in this tall tale about the famous Western sharp shooter. (Rev: BCCB 6/97; BL 3/15/97; HB 5–6/97; SLJ 4/97*) [921]

**10770** Kunstler, James Howard. *Annie Oakley: The American Legend* (K–3). Illus. by Fred Warter. 1996, Simon & Schuster paper $19.95 (0-689-80605-1). The life of the female sharpshooter, of her partnership and marriage to Frank Butler, and her career with Buffalo Bill Cody's Wild West Show. (Rev: SLJ 8/96) [921]

**10771** Spinner, Stephanie. *Little Sure Shot: The Story of Annie Oakley* (2–3). Illus. by Jose Miralles. 1993, Random paper $3.99 (0-679-83432-X). 48pp. An interesting portrait of Annie Oakley (real name, Phoebe Ann Moses) and her remarkable career as a markswoman. (Rev: BL 2/1/94; SLJ 2/94) [921]

ONASSIS, JACKIE KENNEDY

**10772** Anderson, Catherine C. *Jackie Kennedy Onassis* (4–7). Illus. 1995, Lerner LB $19.93 (0-8225-2885-1); paper $6.95 (0-8225-9714-4). 88pp. An adoring biography of the former First Lady, who was a model of courage and dignity. (Rev: BL 2/1/96) [921]

RICHARDS, ANN

**10773** Siegel, Dorothy S. *Ann Richards: Politician, Feminist, Survivor* (4–7). Illus. Series: People to Know. 1996, Enslow LB $19.95 (0-89490-497-3). 112pp. In a conversational style, this biography covers the important events in the life of this Texas politician. (Rev: BL 5/15/96; SLJ 10/96) [921]

ROOSEVELT, ELEANOR

**10774** Adler, David A. *A Picture Book of Eleanor Roosevelt* (K–3). Illus. by Robert Casilla. Series: Picture Book Biography. 1991, Holiday LB $15.95 (0-8234-0856-6). 32pp. The life of this well-known First Lady is described in simple text and many illustrations. (Rev: BCCB 4/91; BL 6/1/91; SLJ 5/91) [921]

**10775** Cooney, Barbara. *Eleanor* (K–3). Illus. 1996, Viking paper $15.99 (0-670-86159-6). 40pp. A picture book biography that supplies details on Eleanor Roosevelt's life, particularly her lonely childhood. (Rev: BCCB 11/96; BL 9/15/96*; HB 9–10/96; SLJ 9/96*) [921]

**10776** Faber, Doris. *Eleanor Roosevelt: First Lady to the World* (5–7). Illus. by Donna Ruff. 1986, Puffin paper $4.99 (0-14-032103-9). 64pp. Eleanor Roosevelt's life before and after FDR is discussed. (Rev: BL 9/1/85; HB 9–10/85; SLJ 8/85)

**10777** Gottfried, Ted. *Eleanor Roosevelt: First Lady of the Twentieth Century* (5–8). Illus. Series: Book Report Biographies. 1997, Watts $22.00 (0-531-11406-6). 112pp. A short, useful biography that traces Eleanor Roosevelt's life and her lasting achievements. (Rev: BCCB 7–8/97; BL 11/15/97; SLJ 12/97) [921]

**10778** Lazo, Caroline. *Eleanor Roosevelt* (4–7). Illus. Series: Peacemakers. 1993, Dillon $13.95 (0-87518-594-0). 64pp. A biography of the famous first lady that focuses on her many lasting contributions, particularly in promoting world peace. (Rev: BL 12/15/93; SLJ 1/94) [921]

**10779** Morey, Eileen. *Eleanor Roosevelt* (4–8). Series: Importance Of. 1997, Lucent LB $22.45 (1-56006-086-7). 96pp. The career of this famous First Lady and her many achievements fighting for world peace. (Rev: BCCB 7–8/97; BL 10/15/97; SLJ 12/97) [921]

**10780** Schuman, Michael A. *Eleanor Roosevelt: First Lady and Humanitarian* (5–8). Illus. Series: People to Know. 1995, Enslow LB $19.95 (0-89490-547-3). 128pp. A straightforward account that covers the basic facts of Eleanor Roosevelt's life and objectively discusses her accomplishments. (Rev: HB 1–2/95; SLJ 7/95) [921]

**10781** Weidt, Maryann N. *Stateswoman to the World: A Story About Eleanor Roosevelt* (4–6). Illus. by Lydia M. Anderson. 1991, Carolrhoda LB $14.95 (0-87614-663-9). 64pp. A frank biography of the First Lady so admired and respected throughout the world. (Rev: BL 12/15/91; SLJ 12/91) [921]

### ROSS, BETSY

**10782** St. George, Judith. *Betsy Ross: Patriot of Philadelphia* (3–6). Illus. 1997, Holt $15.95 (0-8050-5439-1). 118pp. A biography of Betsy Ross that tells of her childhood as a Quaker in Philadelphia as well as the meeting with George Washington that led to making our first flag. (Rev: BL 1/1–15/98; SLJ 2/98) [921]

**10783** Wallner, Alexandra. *Betsy Ross* (K–3). Illus. 1994, Holiday LB $15.95 (0-8234-1071-4). 32pp. A biography of the famous seamstress who advised General Washington on the nature of the nation's first flag and ran the family business until her death in 1836. (Rev: BCCB 3/94; BL 2/15/94; SLJ 4/94) [92]

### SAMPSON, DEBORAH

**10784** McGovern, Ann. *The Secret Soldier: The Story of Deborah Sampson* (4–6). Illus. by Ann Grifalconi. 1987, Macmillan paper $2.99 (0-590-43052-1). 64pp. The story of the woman who disguised herself as a man and joined the Continental army. A reissue.

### SHELLEY, KATE

**10785** San Souci, Robert D. *Kate Shelley: Bound for Legend* (3–5). Illus. by Max Ginsburg. 1995, Dial paper $14.89 (0-8037-1290-1). 32pp. The life story of the fabled heroine who overcame tremendous obstacles to prevent a possibly deadly railroad accident. (Rev: BCCB 12/95; BL 7/95; SLJ 9/95*) [921]

### STANTON, ELIZABETH CADY

**10786** Fritz, Jean. *You Want Women to Vote, Lizzie Stanton?* (4–7). Illus. 1995, Putnam $15.95 (0-399-22786-5). 96pp. An exciting, witty re-creation of the life of Elizabeth Cady Stanton, fighter for women's rights, including suffrage. (Rev: BCCB 10/95; BL 8/95*; SLJ 9/95*) [921]

**10787** McCully, Emily Arnold. *The Ballot Box Battle* (2–5). Illus. 1996, Knopf LB $18.99 (0-679-97938-7). 32pp. Elizabeth Cady Stanton tells the story of her struggle for women's rights to Cordelia, an eager listener. (Rev: BCCB 9/96; BL 9/1/96; SLJ 9/96*) [921]

**10788** Swain, Gwenyth. *The Road to Seneca Falls* (3–6). Illus. Series: Creative Minds. 1996, Carolrhoda LB $14.95 (0-87614-947-6); paper $5.95 (1-57505-025-0). 64pp. This biography of Elizabeth Cady Stanton chronicles the birth of the women's rights movement. (Rev: BL 2/15/97; SLJ 3/97) [921]

### STEINEM, GLORIA

**10789** Hoff, Mary. *Gloria Steinem: The Women's Movement* (4–6). Illus. Series: New Directions. 1991, Millbrook LB $21.90 (1-878841-19-X). 96pp. The life story of this journalist who questioned women's roles in modern society. (Rev: SLJ 4/91) [921]

### STONE, LUCY

**10790** McPherson, Stephanie S. *I Speak for the Women: A Story About Lucy Stone* (4–6). Illus. by Brian Liedahl. Series: Creative Minds Book. 1992, Carolrhoda LB $19.95 (0-87614-740-6). 64pp. The life of a dedicated abolitionist and champion of women's rights in 19th-century America. (Rev: BCCB 3/93; BL 3/15/93; SLJ 2/93) [921]

### WASHINGTON, MARY BALL

**10791** Fritz, Jean. *George Washington's Mother* (2–3). Illus. by DyAnne DiSalvo-Ryan. 1992, Putnam paper $3.95 (0-448-40384-6). 48pp. A simple biography of Mary Ball Washington, the mother of our first president. (Rev: BL 10/1/92; SLJ 10/92) [921]

## WILSON, EDITH

**10792** Giblin, James Cross. *Edith Wilson: The Woman Who Ran the United States* (4–7). Illus. by Michele Laporte. 1992, Viking paper $11.00 (0-670-83005-4). 64pp. The life of Edith Wilson, wife of President Woodrow Wilson, and her role in government after her husband suffered a stroke. (Rev: BCCB 4/92; BL 6/1/92; SLJ 5/92) [921]

# Scientists, Inventors, and Naturalists

## Collective

**10793** Camp, Carole Ann. *American Astronomers: Searchers and Wonderers* (5–7). Illus. Series: Collective Biographies. 1996, Enslow LB $19.95 (0-89490-631-3). 104pp. Profiles with accompanying photos of 9 important American astronomers, including Maria Mitchell, Edwin Hubble, and Carl Sagan. (Rev: BL 4/15/96; SLJ 5/96) [920]

**10794** Clements, Gillian. *The Picture History of Great Inventors* (4–6). Illus. by author. 1994, Knopf paper $13.00 (0-679-84787-1). 77pp. A series of thumbnail sketches of some of the great inventors of the Western world and their inventions. (Rev: SLJ 7/94) [920]

**10795** Faber, Doris, and Harold Faber. *Nature and the Environment* (5–8). Series: Great Lives. 1991, Macmillan $22.95 (0-684-19047-8). 288pp. This book explores the lives of some of the great naturalists and conservationists. (Rev: BL 6/1/91; HB 7–8/91; SLJ 10/91) [920]

**10796** Fradin, Dennis B. *"We Have Conquered Pain": The Discovery of Anesthesia* (5–8). Illus. 1996, Simon & Schuster paper $16.00 (0-689-50587-6). 145pp. The story of 4 19th-century doctors, each of whom claimed to have developed anesthesia. (Rev: BCCB 6/96; BL 5/15/96; HB 9–10/96; SLJ 5/96) [920]

**10797** Keene, Ann T. *Earthkeepers: Observers and Protectors of Nature* (4–8). Illus. 1993, Oxford $35.00 (0-19-507867-5). 222pp. Profiles are given for more than 40 people throughout history who have worked to preserve the environment, beginning with the self-educated botanist John Bartram, who worked in the 1700s. (Rev: HB 11–12/93; SLJ 8/94*) [920]

**10798** Krensky, Stephen. *Four Against the Odds: The Struggle to Save Our Environment* (5–8). 1992, Scholastic paper $2.99 (0-590-44743-2). 112pp. The work of conservationists John Muir, Chico Mendes, Rachel Carson, and Lois Gibb is discussed. (Rev: BL 6/1/92; SLJ 10/92) [920]

**10799** Mulcahy, Robert. *Medical Technology: Inventing the Instruments* (5–8). Illus. Series: Innovators. 1997, Oliver LB $16.95 (1-881508-34-X). 144pp. Seven short biographies of scientists who were responsible for such inventions as the X-ray, stethoscope, thermometer, and electrocardiograph. (Rev: BCCB 7–8/97; SLJ 7/97) [920]

**10800** Pflaum, Rosalynd. *Marie Curie and Her Daughter Irene* (4–6). Illus. 1993, Lerner LB $23.93 (0-8225-4915-8). 144pp. A biography outlining the splendid teamwork of mother and daughter that resulted in 3 Nobel prizes. (Rev: SLJ 6/93) [920]

**10801** Stanley, Phyllis M. *American Environmental Heroes* (4–7). Illus. 1996, Enslow LB $19.95 (0-89490-630-5). 128pp. John Muir, Barry Commoner, Sylvia Earle, and 7 other environmentalists are profiled. (Rev: BL 9/1/96; SLJ 7/96) [920]

**10802** Stille, Darlene R. *Extraordinary Women Scientists* (5–8). Illus. 1995, Children's LB $37.00 (0-516-00585-5). 208pp. Garnered from 200 years of science history, this book briefly profiles 49 important women scientists. (Rev: BL 10/1/95; SLJ 12/95) [920]

**10803** Weitzman, David. *Great Lives: Human Culture* (4–6). Illus. Series: Great Lives. 1994, Scribners $22.95 (0-684-19438-4). 294pp. An exhilarating collective biography of 27 archaeologists and anthropologists including Ruth Benedict, Franz Boas, Jane Goodall, and Zora Neale Hurston. (Rev: SLJ 4/95) [920]

**10804** Wilkinson, Philip, and Michael Pollard. *Scientists Who Changed the World* (3–5). Illus. by Robert Ingpen. Series: Turning Points in History. 1994, Chelsea LB $19.95 (0-7910-2763-5). 93pp. Twenty brief biographies of scientists, including Galileo, Marie Curie, DNA decoders, and the first men on the moon. (Rev: BL 12/1/94) [920]

# Individual

### ALVAREZ, LUIS W.

**10805** Codye, Corinn. *Luis W. Alvarez* (2–5). Illus. by Robert Masheris. Series: Hispanic Stories. 1989, Raintree Steck-Vaughn LB $21.40 (0-8172-3376-8). 32pp. This dual English and Spanish text tells the story of the 1968 Nobel Prize for Physics winner. (Rev: BL 2/1/90) [921]

### BANNEKER, BENJAMIN

**10806** Ferris, Jeri. *What Are You Figuring Now? A Story About Benjamin Banneker* (3–6). Illus. 1988, Lerner LB $14.95 (0-87614-331-1); Carolrhoda paper $5.95 (0-87614-521-7). 56pp. The life of this black American who was a math whiz. (Rev: BL 1/1/89; SLJ 2/89)

**10807** Pinkney, Andrea D. *Dear Benjamin Banneker* (1–4). Illus. by Brian Pinkney. 1994, Harcourt $16.00 (0-15-200417-3). 32pp. Born into a family of freed slaves, Banneker became an important astronomer and corresponded with Thomas Jefferson. (Rev: BCCB 11/94; BL 9/15/94; SLJ 11/94) [921]

### BELL, ALEXANDER GRAHAM

**10808** Lewis, Cynthia C. *Hello, Alexander Graham Bell Speaking* (4–7). Illus. Series: Taking Part. 1991, Macmillan LB $13.95 (0-87518-461-8). 64pp. This inventor studied human speech and created one of the greatest means of communication, the telephone. (Rev: BL 9/1/91; SLJ 12/91) [921]

### BLACKWELL, ELIZABETH

**10809** Schleichert, Elizabeth. *The Life of Elizabeth Blackwell* (4–6). Illus. by Antonio Castro. Series: Pioneers in Health and Medicine. 1992, Century LB $13.95 (0-941477-66-5). 80pp. America's first woman doctor, Elizabeth Blackwell also fought for the rights of women, children, and the poor. (Rev: SLJ 3/92) [921]

### BURROUGHS, JOHN

**10810** Wadsworth, Ginger. *John Burroughs: The Sage of Slabsides* (5–8). Illus. 1997, Clarion $16.95 (0-395-77830-1). 95pp. A biography of the American naturalist and essayist who lived in a cabin in the Catskill Mountains and wrote about his observations. (Rev: BCCB 5/97; BL 3/15/97; HB 7–8/97; SLJ 5/97) [921]

### CARAS, ROGER

**10811** Caras, Roger A. *A World Full of Animals: The Roger Caras Story* (3–5). Illus. 1994, Chronicle $13.95 (0-8118-0654-5). 45pp. The autobiography of the famous writer and ABC correspondent, who tells about his life with animals from all over the world. (Rev: BL 9/1/94; SLJ 9/94) [921]

### CARSON, BEN

**10812** Simmons, Alex. *Ben Carson* (4–6). Illus. Series: Contemporary African Americans. 1995, Raintree Steck-Vaughn LB $24.26 (0-8172-3975-8). 48pp. A simple biography of the African American who became chief of pediatric neurosurgery at Johns Hopkins University Hospital. (Rev: BL 2/15/96; SLJ 4/96) [921]

### CARSON, RACHEL

**10813** Greene, Carol. *Rachel Carson: Friend of Nature* (2–4). Illus. by Steven Dobson. Series: Rookie Biographies. 1992, Children's LB $19.00 (0-516-04229-7); paper $4.95 (0-516-44229-5). 48pp. With easily read short sentences, interesting photos, and other illustrations, the life story of the naturalist who made America conservation conscious is retold. (Rev: BL 1/1/93) [921]

**10814** Harlan, Judith. *Sounding the Alarm: A Biography of Rachel Carson* (5–7). Illus. Series: People in Focus. 1989, Macmillan LB $13.95 (0-87518-407-3). 128pp. A good account of this founder of the modern ecology movement. (Rev: BL 10/1/89; SLJ 11/89) [921]

**10815** Henricksson, John. *Rachel Carson: The Environmental Movement* (4–6). Illus. Series: New Directions. 1991, Millbrook paper $5.95 (1-56294-833-4). 96pp. A well-researched account of the life of the woman who opened up the topic of conservation. (Rev: SLJ 5/91) [921]

**10816** Kudlinski, Kathleen V. *Rachel Carson: Pioneer of Ecology* (3–6). Illus. 1988, Puffin paper $4.99 (0-14-032242-6). 64pp. The life of the famous nature writer and environmentalist, born in 1907. (Rev: BL 3/15/88; SLJ 8/88)

**10817** Presnall, Judith J. *Rachel Carson* (4–8). Illus. Series: The Importance Of. 1995, Lucent LB $22.45 (1-56006-052-2). 96pp. The life of this innovative scientist whose writings, including *Silent Spring*, made the world aware of conservation and the erosion of our environment. (Rev: BL 1/15/95; SLJ 1/95) [921]

**10818** Ransom, Candice. *Listening to Crickets: A Story About Rachel Carson* (3–5). Illus. by Shelly O. Haas. 1993, Carolrhoda LB $19.95 (0-87614-727-9). 64pp. Beginning with her childhood, this account traces the life of the woman who helped make millions aware of the destruction of their environment. (Rev: BL 5/15/93; SLJ 7/93) [921]

**10819** Reef, Catherine. *Rachel Carson: A Wonder of Nature* (2–5). Illus. Series: Earth Keepers. 1991, Twenty-First Century LB $14.95 (0-941477-38-X). 72pp. The life and writings of the biologist who warned the public of the dangers of pesticides. (Rev: BL 3/15/92) [921]

**10820** Ring, Elizabeth. *Rachel Carson: Caring for the Earth* (3–5). Illus. Series: Eyewitness Juniors. 1992, Millbrook LB $19.90 (1-56294-056-2). 48pp. The story of the pioneer conservationist whose book Silent Spring influenced a whole generation. (Rev: BL 8/92; SLJ 11/92) [921]

**10821** Wadsworth, Ginger. *Rachel Carson: Voice for the Earth* (5–7). Illus. Series: Lerner Biographies. 1992, Lerner LB $23.93 (0-8225-4907-7). 128pp. The life and work of the conservationist and author, best known for Silent Spring. (Rev: BL 6/1/92; HB 7–8/92; SLJ 7/92) [921]

### CARTER, HOWARD

**10822** Ford, Barbara. *Howard Carter: Searching for King Tut* (4–7). Illus. by Janet Hamlin. Series: Science Superstars. 1995, W. H. Freeman $12.00 (0-7167-6587-X); paper $4.00 (0-7167-6588-8). 64pp. The story of the famous British Egyptologist and his discovery of King Tut's tomb. (Rev: BL 7/95; SLJ 9/95) [921]

### CARVER, GEORGE WASHINGTON

**10823** Benge, Janet, and Geoff Benge. *George Washington Carver, What Do You See?* (3–4). Illus. by Kennon James. Series: Another Great Achiever. 1997, Advance Publg. LB $14.95 (1-57537-102-2). 48pp. This biography stresses Carver's humanity, inventiveness, and deep religious faith. (Rev: SLJ 8/97) [921]

**10824** McKissack, Patricia, and Fredrick McKissack. *George Washington Carver: The Peanut Scientist* (2–4). Illus. by Ned Ostendorf. Series: Great African Americans. 1991, Enslow LB $13.95 (0-89490-308-X). 32pp. More than the inventor of peanut butter, this scientist helped revive the economy of the South after the Civil War. (Rev: SLJ 2/92) [921]

**10825** Mitchell, Barbara. *A Pocketful of Goobers: A Story About George Washington Carver* (3–5). Illus. 1986, Carolrhoda LB $19.95 (0-87614-292-7); Lerner paper $5.95 (0-87614-474-1). 64pp. An introductory biography partly fictionalized, with much infor-

mation on Carver's research with peanuts. (Rev: BL 8/86; SLJ 9/86)

**10826** Nicholson, Lois. *George Washington Carver: Botanist and Ecologist* (4–7). Illus. Series: Junior World Biographies. 1994, Chelsea LB $14.95 (0-7910-1763-X); paper $4.95 (0-7910-2114-9). 80pp. A brief, richly illustrated biography of this renowned African American scientist whose discoveries involving the peanut brought a living to many poor farmers. (Rev: BL 11/15/94) [921]

**10827** Rogers, Teresa. *George Washington Carver: Nature's Trailblazer* (2–5). Illus. by Antonio Castro. Series: Earth Keepers. 1992, Twenty-First Century LB $14.95 (0-8050-2115-9). 72pp. The life of the great black American agricultural chemist who discovered many new uses for peanuts, soybeans, and sweet potatoes. (Rev: BL 5/1/92; SLJ 7/92) [921]

### CHINN, MAY

**10828** Butts, Ellen R., and Joyce R. Schwartz. *May Chinn: The Best Medicine* (4–7). Illus. by Janet Hamlin. Series: Science Superstars. 1995, W. H. Freeman $12.00 (0-7167-6589-6); paper $4.00 (0-7167-6590-X). 48pp. The story of the famous woman physician and her accomplishments. (Rev: BL 7/95; SLJ 9/95) [921]

### CURIE, MARIE

**10829** Brandt, Keith. *Marie Curie: Brave Scientist* (3–5). Illus. by Karen Milone. 1983, Troll LB $12.95 (0-89375-855-8); paper $3.50 (0-89375-856-6). 48pp. An account that emphasizes the struggle before eventual success.

**10830** Fisher, Leonard Everett. *Marie Curie* (3–6). Illus. 1994, Macmillan paper $14.95 (0-02-735375-3). 32pp. This biography tells of Madame Curie's childhood and her struggle for recognition and the honors bestowed on her in later life. (Rev: BL 9/15/94; SLJ 10/94) [921]

**10831** Poynter, Margaret. *Marie Curie: Discoverer of Radium* (4–7). Illus. Series: Great Minds of Science. 1994, Enslow LB $19.95 (0-89490-477-9). 128pp. The life and significance of this discoverer of radium are covered, with a chapter of suggested activities. (Rev: BL 1/1/95; SLJ 10/94) [921]

### DARWIN, CHARLES

**10832** Anderson, Margaret J. *Charles Darwin: Naturalist* (4–7). Illus. Series: Great Minds of Science. 1994, Enslow LB $19.95 (0-89490-476-0). 128pp. In addition to a biography of this controversial naturalist, there is a chapter on activities for the reader. (Rev: BL 1/1/95; SLJ 10/94) [921]

**10833** Ventura, Piero. *Darwin: Nature Reinterpreted* (4–7). Illus. 1995, Houghton $16.95 (0-395-70738-

2). 76pp. A picture book that explores the life and revolutionary theories of Darwin. (Rev: BL 3/1/95; SLJ 5/95) [921]

## DOUGLAS, MARJORY STONEMAN

**10834** Sawyer, Kem Knapp. *Marjory Stoneman Douglas: Guardian of the Everglades* (6–8). Illus. by Leslie Carow. 1993, Discovery Enterprises LB $14.95 (1-878668-20-X). 72pp. The life story of the courageous woman who spent years fighting to preserve the Florida Everglades. (Rev: SLJ 12/93) [921]

## DREW, CHARLES R.

**10835** Talmadge, Katherine S. *The Life of Charles Drew* (5–8). Illus. Series: Pioneers in Health and Medicine. 1992, Twenty-First Century LB $13.95 (0-941477-65-7). 84pp. This African-American medical researcher is best known as the father of the modern blood bank. (Rev: SLJ 4/92) [921]

## EASTMAN, CHARLES

**10836** Ross, Michael E. *Wildlife Watching with Charles Eastman* (4–6). Illus. by Laurie A. Caple. Series: Naturalist's Apprentice Biographies. 1997, Carolrhoda LB $14.95 (1-57505-004-8). 48pp. Charles Eastman, who was born in 1858 in the Dakota Nation, became a physician and later used his childhood experiences to teach children to love and respect nature. (Rev: SLJ 3/98) [921]

## EASTWOOD, ALICE

**10837** Ross, Michael E. *Flower Watching with Alice Eastwood* (3–5). Illus. Series: Naturalist's Apprentice. 1997, Carolrhoda LB $19.93 (1-57505-005-6). 46pp. This account of the life of Alice Eastwood — an African American who became an expert on the wildflowers of the Rockies and the West Coast — also gives tips to the amateur flower watcher. (Rev: BL 3/1/98; SLJ 3/98) [921]

## EDISON, THOMAS ALVA

**10838** Anderson, Kelly C. *Thomas Edison* (4–8). Illus. Series: The Importance Of. 1994, Lucent LB $22.45 (1-56006-041-7). 112pp. The story of Edison's life, with emphasis on his importance in the history of science and technology. (Rev: BL 8/94; SLJ 4/94) [921]

**10839** Cousins, Margaret. *The Story of Thomas Alva Edison* (4–6). Illus. 1981, Random paper $5.99 (0-394-84883-7). 160pp. An account that emphasizes his work with the light bulb, motion pictures, and photography.

**10840** Mitchell, Barbara. *The Wizard of Sound: A Story About Thomas Edison* (4–6). Illus. by Hetty Mitchell. Series: Creative Minds. 1991, Carolrhoda

LB $14.95 (0-87614-445-8). 64pp. The story of how a shy, inept youngster became the inventor of wonders. (Rev: SLJ 1/92) [921]

**10841** Sabin, Louis. *Thomas Alva Edison: Young Inventor* (3–5). Illus. by George Ulrich. 1983, Troll LB $12.95 (0-89375-841-8); paper $3.50 (0-89375-842-6). 48pp. An account that concentrates on Edison's childhood.

## EINSTEIN, ALBERT

**10842** McPherson, Stephanie S. *Ordinary Genius: The Story of Albert Einstein* (4–7). Illus. 1995, Carolrhoda LB $22.60 (0-87614-788-0). 96pp. Good historical background information is given on the life of Einstein plus a clear explanation of his discoveries. (Rev: BL 6/1–15/95; SLJ 9/95) [921]

**10843** Reef, Catherine. *Albert Einstein: Scientist of the 20th Century* (4–7). Illus. Series: Taking Part. 1991, Macmillan LB $13.95 (0-87518-462-6). 64pp. Einstein gave the world a new way of looking at time, space, gravity, and the nature of light. (Rev: BL 9/1/91; SLJ 12/91) [921]

## ERICSSON, JOHN

**10844** Brophy, Ann. *John Ericsson: The Inventions of War* (4–7). Illus. Series: The History of the Civil War. 1990, Silver Burdett paper $7.95 (0-382-24052-9). 135pp. In clear text, this is the life story of the Swedish engineer who designed and constructed the Monitor. (Rev: BL 9/1/91) [921]

## FARNSWORTH, PHILO

**10845** McPherson, Stephanie S. *TV's Forgotten Hero: The Story of Philo Farnsworth* (4–7). Illus. 1996, Carolrhoda LB $16.95 (1-57505-017-X). 96pp. The biography of the genius who invented electronic television when he was only 14. (Rev: BL 2/1/97; SLJ 2/97) [921]

## FINLAY, CARLOS

**10846** Sumption, Christine, and Kathleen Thompson. *Carlos Finlay* (2–5). Illus. by Les Didier. Series: Hispanic Stories. 1989, Raintree Steck-Vaughn LB $21.40 (0-8172-3378-4). 32pp. The story of the Cuban doctor's medical discoveries that helped curb yellow fever, in Spanish and English texts. (Rev: BL 2/1/90) [921]

## FLEMING, ALEXANDER

**10847** Kaye, Judith. *The Life of Alexander Fleming* (5–7). Illus. 1993, Twenty-First Century LB $13.95 (0-8050-2300-3). 80pp. An exciting description of this famous scientist and his work, such as developing penicillin. (Rev: SLJ 7/93) [921]

## FORD, HENRY

**10848** Mitchell, Barbara. *We'll Race You, Henry: A Story About Henry Ford* (3–5). Illus. 1986, Carolrhoda LB $14.95 (0-87614-291-9); Lerner paper $5.95 (0-87614-471-7). 64pp. The focus is on race-car ventures in this partly fictionalized biography. (Rev: BL 8/86; SLJ 9/86)

## FULTON, ROBERT

**10849** Bowen, Andy Russell. *A Head Full of Notions: A Story About Robert Fulton* (4–6). Illus. 1997, Carolrhoda LB $19.95 (0-87614-876-3); paper $5.95 (1-57505-026-9). 64pp. A brief biography of the life and times of the man who worked first on plans for a submarine and then on his famous steamboat. (Rev: BL 4/15/97; SLJ 3/97) [921]

**10850** Landau, Elaine. *Robert Fulton* (4–6). Illus. Series: First Books. 1991, Watts LB $21.00 (0-531-20016-7). 62pp. The story of the inventor and engineer whose *Clermont* steamboat made history. (Rev: SLJ 9/91) [921]

## GALDIKAS, BIRUTE

**10851** Gallardo, Evelyn. *Among the Orangutans: The Birute Galdikas Story* (4–7). Illus. Series: Great Naturalists. 1993, Chronicle paper $7.95 (0-8118-0408-9). 48pp. The story of this important primate specialist who began studying orangutans in 1971. (Rev: BL 4/1/93; SLJ 6/93) [921]

## GALILEO

**10852** Fisher, Leonard Everett. *Galileo* (3–6). Illus. 1992, Macmillan LB $16.00 (0-02-735235-8). 32pp. A narrative that stresses Galileo's genius as a mathematician and physicist as well as his contributions to astronomy. (Rev: BL 6/1/92; HB 7–8/92; SLJ 6/92) [921]

**10853** Hightower, Paul. *Galileo: Astronomer and Physicist* (4–7). Illus. Series: Great Minds of Science. 1997, Enslow LB $19.95 (0-89490-787-5). 128pp. This biography not only includes material on the life and accomplishments of this courageous scientist but also contains several activities that give an understanding of his work. (Rev: BL 6/1–15/97) [921]

**10854** Rosen, Sidney. *Galileo and the Magic Numbers* (6–8). Illus. by Harve Stein. 1958, Little, Brown $13.95 (0-316-75704-7). The Italian astronomer who was persecuted for his beliefs concerning the earth's relationship to the sun.

**10855** Sis, Peter. *Starry Messenger* (4–6). Illus. 1996, Farrar $16.00 (0-374-37191-1). 32pp. The world of Galileo and his amazing life and accomplishments are re-created in this unusual picture book. (Rev: BCCB 11/96; BL 10/15/96*; SLJ 10/96*) [921]

## GODDARD, ROBERT

**10856** Streissguth, Thomas. *Rocket Man: The Story of Robert Goddard* (5–7). Illus. Series: Trailblazer. 1995, Carolrhoda LB $16.95 (0-87614-863-1). 88pp. A history of rocketry, with emphasis on the life and accomplishments of Goddard. (Rev: BL 10/15/95; SLJ 9/95) [921]

## GOODALL, JANE

**10857** Fromer, Julie. *Jane Goodall: Living with the Chimps* (2–5). Illus. by Antonio Castro. Series: Earth Keepers. 1992, Twenty-First Century LB $14.95 (0-8050-2116-7). 72pp. An easily read biography of the zoologist who studied chimpanzee societies in Africa. (Rev: BL 5/1/92; SLJ 6/92) [921]

**10858** Goodall, Jane. *My Life with the Chimpanzees* (3–6). Illus. 1992, Houghton paper $11.04 (0-395-61849-5). The famed ethologist talks about her life studying the chimps of Africa. (Rev: BCCB 5/88; BL 7/88; SLJ 4/88)

**10859** Pratt, Paula B. *Jane Goodall* (4–8). Illus. Series: The Importance Of. 1997, Lucent LB $22.45 (1-56006-082-4). 112pp. The story of the great naturalist who studied and protected the primates of Africa. (Rev: BL 1/1–15/97) [921]

**10860** Sean, J. A. *Jane Goodall: Naturalist* (4–6). Illus. Series: Library of Famous Women. 1993, Blackbirch LB $15.95 (1-56711-010-X). 64pp. An accurate, engrossing account of the life of this great naturalist, who produced landmark studies on apes and their society. (Rev: BL 11/15/93; SLJ 2/94) [921]

## GUTENBERG, JOHANN

**10861** Burch, Joann J. *Fine Print: A Story About Johann Gutenberg* (3–6). Illus. by Kent A. Aldrich. 1991, Carolrhoda LB $19.93 (0-87614-682-5). 64pp. An account of the man who changed world history by inventing the process of printing books from movable type. (Rev: BL 1/1/92; SLJ 3/92) [686.2]

**10862** Fisher, Leonard Everett. *Gutenberg* (1–5). Illus. 1993, Macmillan $14.95 (0-02-735238-2). 32pp. This is a picture book about the life and accomplishments of the early printer Johann Gutenberg. (Rev: BL 6/1–15/93; SLJ 8/93) [921]

**10863** Willard, Nancy. *Gutenberg's Gift* (PS–6). Illus. by Bryan Leister. 1995, Wild Honey $20.00 (0-15-200783-0). 12pp. Pop-up pictures and a rhyming text tell the story of Gutenberg. (Rev: BCCB 11/95; BL 2/1/96) [921]

## HAMILTON, ALICE

**10864** McPherson, Stephanie S. *The Workers' Detective: A Story About Dr. Alice Hamilton* (3–6). Illus. by Janet Schulz. Series: Creative Minds. 1992, Carolrhoda LB $14.95 (0-87614-699-X). 64pp. Introducing the woman who studied the effects of lead and other lethal materials on workers' health and changed industrial medicine. (Rev: BL 1/15/93; SLJ 10/92) [921]

### HARVEY, WILLIAM

**10865** Yount, Lisa. *William Harvey: Discoverer of How Blood Circulates* (4–8). Illus. Series: Great Minds of Science. 1994, Enslow LB $19.95 (0-89490-481-7). 128pp. A biography of the 17th-century scientist that describes early theories about the blood system and the importance of Harvey's discoveries. (Rev: SLJ 2/95) [921]

### HAWKING, STEPHEN

**10866** Henderson, Harry. *Stephen Hawking* (4–8). Illus. Series: The Importance Of. 1995, Lucent LB $22.45 (1-56006-050-6). 96pp. A lively account of this amazing scientist's life, his physical handicaps, and the effects of his theories on modern thought. (Rev: BL 1/15/95) [921]

### HOPPER, GRACE

**10867** Whitelaw, Nancy. *Grace Hopper: Programming Pioneer* (3–6). Illus. 1995, W. H. Freeman paper $4.80 (0-7167-6599-3). 64pp. The story of the navy rear admiral and computer pioneer who became known as the grandmother of the computer language COBOL. (Rev: BL 3/15/96; SLJ 4/96) [921]

### HORNER, JOHN R.

**10868** Lessem, Don. *Jack Horner: Living with Dinosaurs* (4–7). Illus. Series: Scientific American Science Superstars. 1994, W. H. Freeman $12.00 (0-7167-6546-2). 48pp. In this biography, a young man with dyslexia becomes one of the world's greatest paleontologists. (Rev: BCCB 12/94; BL 11/15/94) [921]

### HUBBLE, EDWIN

**10869** Datnow, Claire. *Edwin Hubble: Discoverer of Galaxies* (4–8). Illus. Series: Great Minds of Science. 1997, Enslow LB $19.95 (0-89490-934-7). 128pp. A biography of the great astronomer, noted for his amazing scientific abilities and quirky pretentions. (Rev: BL 12/1/97; SLJ 3/98) [921]

### JONES, FREDERICK MCKINLEY

**10870** Swanson, Gloria M., and Margaret V. Ott. *I've Got an Idea! The Story of Frederick McKinley Jones* (3–6). Illus. 1994, Lerner LB $17.50 (0-8225-3174-7); paper $7.95 (0-8225-9662-8). 112pp. Jones was an amazing African American inventor credited with devising refrigeration units for trucks and box office

ticket machines. (Rev: BL 6/1–15/94; SLJ 7/94) [921]

### KENNY, ELIZABETH

**10871** Crofford, Emily. *Healing Warrior: A Story About Sister Elizabeth Kenny* (3–6). Illus. by Steve Michaels. Series: Creative Minds. 1989, Carolrhoda LB $19.95 (0-87614-382-6). 64pp. The story of the Australian nurse renowned for her revolutionary therapy and rehabilitation work with polio patients. (Rev: BL 2/15/90; SLJ 3/90) [921]

### LAVOISIER, ANTOINE

**10872** Yount, Lisa. *Antoine Lavoisier: Founder of Modern Chemistry* (4–7). Illus. Series: Great Minds of Science. 1997, Enslow LB $19.95 (0-89490-785-9). 128pp. In addition to providing an assessment of the life and works of Lavoisier, called the Father of Chemistry, this book includes several hands-on activities that depend on an understanding of his work. (Rev: BL 6/1–15/97) [921]

### LEAKEY, LOUIS AND MARY

**10873** Poynter, Margaret. *The Leakeys: Uncovering the Origins of Humankind* (5–8). Illus. Series: Great Minds of Science. 1997, Enslow LB $19.95 (0-89490-788-3). 128pp. The story of the famous husband-and-wife team of scientists, Louis and Mary Leakey, and how they expanded our knowledge of evolution. (Rev: BL 12/1/97; SLJ 12/97) [921]

### LEAKEY, MARY

**10874** Heiligman, Deborah. *Mary Leakey: In Search of Human Beginnings* (4–6). Illus. 1995, W. H. Freeman $12.80 (0-7167-6612-4); paper $4.80 (0-7167-6613-2). 64pp. A lively telling of the life of the anthropologist who contributed greatly to our knowledge of evolution. (Rev: BL 12/1/95; SLJ 12/95) [921]

### LEEUWENHOEK, ANTONI VAN

**10875** Yount, Lisa. *Antoni van Leeuwenhoek: First to See Microscopic Life* (4–7). Illus. Series: Great Minds of Science. 1996, Enslow LB $19.95 (0-89490-680-1). 128pp. A brief biography of the Dutch maker of microscopes, who was the first to closely examine bacteria and blood cells. (Rev: BL 10/15/96; SLJ 12/96) [921]

### LEOPOLD, ALDO

**10876** Dunlap, Julie. *Aldo Leopold: Living with the Land* (4–6). Illus. 1993, Twenty-First Century LB $14.95 (0-8050-2501-4). 80pp. The life story of the naturalist who, in the early 20th century, worked on the creation of nature preserves. (Rev: BL 2/15/94; SLJ 2/94) [921]

**10877** Lorbiecki, Marybeth. *Of Things Natural, Wild, and Free: A Story About Aldo Leopold* (4–7). Illus. 1993, Carolrhoda LB $19.95 (0-87614-797-X). 64pp. The story of a man who was a great hunter until he realized the importance of the balance in nature, and then turned a tract of farmland into a nature refuge. (Rev: BL 11/1/93; SLJ 11/93) [921]

### LINNAEUS, CARL

**10878** Anderson, Margaret J. *Carl Linnaeus: Father of Classification* (5–7). Illus. Series: Great Minds of Science. 1997, Enslow LB $19.95 (0-89490-786-7). 128pp. Discusses the personal life of Linnaeus, including his explorations in Lapland, but it focuses on the development of his important biological classification system. (Rev: BL 12/1/97; SLJ 9/97) [921]

### LOVELACE, ADA KING

**10879** Wade, Mary D. *Ada Byron Lovelace: The Lady and the Computer* (5–8). Illus. 1995, Silver Burdett LB $13.95 (0-87518-598-3); paper $7.95 (0-382-24717-5). 128pp. A biography of the poet Byron's amazing daughter, who was a distinguished mathematician and pioneer computer programmer. (Rev: BL 5/1/95) [921]

### MCCLINTOCK, BARBARA

**10880** Heiligman, Deborah. *Barbara McClintock: Alone in Her Field* (4–7). Illus. Series: Scientific American Science Superstars. 1994, W. H. Freeman $12.00 (0-7167-6536-5). 64pp. This pioneer geneticist won the Nobel Prize in 1983 at age 81. (Rev: BL 11/15/94) [921]

### MAYO, WILLIAM AND CHARLES

**10881** Crofford, Emily. *Frontier Surgeons: A Story About the Mayo Brothers* (3–6). Illus. by Karen Ritz. Series: Creative Minds Biographies. 1989, Carolrhoda LB $19.93 (0-87614-381-8); paper $5.95 (0-87614-553-5). 56pp. The fascinating story of the brothers, William and Charles, who started what became a world-class medical facility. (Rev: BL 2/15/90; SLJ 3/90) [921]

### MEAD, MARGARET

**10882** Ziesk, Edra. *Margaret Mead* (5–8). Illus. Series: American Women of Achievement. 1990, Chelsea $17.95 (1-55546-667-2). 109pp. A useful book covering the career and personal life of this unconventional anthropologist. (Rev: SLJ 9/90) [921]

### MENDEL, GREGOR

**10883** Klare, Roger. *Gregor Mendel: Father of Genetics* (5–7). Illus. Series: Great Minds of Science. 1997, Enslow LB $19.95 (0-89490-789-1). 128pp. The science of genetics is introduced through the life of Mendel and his experimentation with peas. (Rev: BL 12/1/97; SLJ 12/97) [921]

### MENDES, CHICO

**10884** Burch, Joann J. *Chico Mendes: Defender of the Rain Forest* (3–5). Illus. Series: Gateway Biographies. 1994, Millbrook LB $20.90 (1-56294-413-4). 48pp. The life story of the conservationist who has courageously tried to stop the destruction of the Amazon rain forest. (Rev: BL 8/94; SLJ 4/94) [921]

### MITCHELL, MARIA

**10885** McPherson, Stephanie S. *Rooftop Astronomer: A Story About Maria Mitchell* (4–6). 1990, Carolrhoda LB $14.95 (0-87614-410-5). 64pp. The woman who became the first professional female astronomer in the United States. (Rev: BCCB 11/90; BL 11/15/90; SLJ 1/91) [921]

### MOSS, CYNTHIA

**10886** Pringle, Laurence. *Elephant Woman: Cynthia Moss Explores the World of Elephants* (3–6). Illus. 1997, Simon & Schuster $16.00 (0-689-80142-4). 48pp. Through this biography of Cynthia Moss, who has studied elephants in Kenya's Amboseli National Park for 25 years, the reader learns about the habits of elephants, why they are endangered, and how they can be saved. (Rev: BL 11/15/97; SLJ 12/97*) [921]

### MUIR, JOHN

**10887** Greene, Carol. *John Muir: Man of the Wild Places* (2–4). Illus. Series: Rookie Biographies. 1991, Children's LB $19.00 (0-516-04220-3). 48pp. The story of the great naturalist and traveler who discovered the glacier in Alaska later named after him. (Rev: BL 8/91) [921]

**10888** Ito, Tom. *The Importance of John Muir* (4–8). Illus. Series: The Importance Of. 1996, Lucent LB $22.45 (1-56006-054-9). 110pp. A short biography of the naturalist who pioneered the U.S. conservation movement. (Rev: BL 5/15/96) [921]

**10889** Naden, Corinne J., and Rose Blue. *John Muir: Saving the Wilderness* (3–5). Illus. Series: Gateway Biographies. 1992, Millbrook LB $19.90 (1-56294-110-0). 48pp. The life and work of this well-known conservationist, especially his role in founding the national parks. (Rev: BL 5/1/92; SLJ 6/92)

**10890** Talmadge, Katherine S. *John Muir: At Home in the Wild* (3–5). Illus. by Antonio Castro. Series:

Earth Keepers. 1993, Holt LB $14.95 (0-8050-2123-X). 80pp. Muir was an explorer, naturalist, conservationist, and writer — and this is his life. (Rev: BL 5/1/93; SLJ 7/93) [921]

**10891** Wadsworth, Ginger. *John Muir: Wilderness Protector* (4–6). Illus. 1992, Lerner LB $23.93 (0-8225-4912-3). 144pp. From his childhood in Scotland to adulthood in California, this biography focuses on why Muir became a conservationist and his efforts in this area. (Rev: SLJ 9/92) [921]

### NAVY, CARYN

**10892** Verheyden-Hilliard, Mary Ellen. *Mathematician and Computer Scientist, Caryn Navy* (2–4). Illus. 1988, Equity paper $5.00 (0-932469-12-4). 32pp. Brief biography of a woman scientist who is blind. (Rev: BL 2/15/89; SLJ 1/89)

### NEWTON, ISAAC

**10893** Anderson, Margaret J. *Isaac Newton: The Greatest Scientist of All Time* (4–7). Illus. Series: Great Minds of Science. 1996, Enslow LB $19.95 (0-89490-681-X). 128pp. The life of the great English mathematician and physicist who formulated the laws of motion and gravity. (Rev: BL 10/15/96; SLJ 12/96) [921]

**10894** Hitzeroth, Deborah, and Sharon Leon. *Sir Isaac Newton* (4–8). Illus. Series: The Importance Of. 1994, Lucent LB $22.45 (1-56006-046-8). 96pp. The life of this great mathematician and physicist, whose work on gravity and allied subjects changed our way of looking at the world. (Rev: BL 8/94; SLJ 7/94) [921]

### NICE, MARGARET MORSE

**10895** Dunlap, Julie. *Birds in the Bushes: A Story About Margaret Morse Nice* (3–5). Illus. by Ralph L. Ramstad. Series: Creative Minds. 1996, Carolrhoda LB $19.93 (1-57505-006-4). 63pp. A biography of the noted American ornithologist and conservationist who died in 1974. (Rev: SLJ 10/96) [921]

**10896** Ross, Michael E. *Bird Watching with Margaret Morse Nice* (4–6). Illus. by Laurie A. Caple. Series: Naturalist's Apprentice Biographies. 1997, Carolrhoda LB $19.93 (1-57505-002-1). 48pp. At the turn of the century, Margaret Morse Nice raised her family while pursuing her hobby of bird watching. (Rev: SLJ 3/98) [921]

### PACHCIARZ, JUDITH

**10897** Verheyden-Hilliard, Mary Ellen. *Scientist and Physician, Judith Pachciarz* (2–4). Illus. 1988, Equity paper $5.00 (0-932469-13-2). 32pp. Biography of an M.D. and microbiologist who is deaf. (Rev: BL 2/15/89; SLJ 4/89)

### PASTEUR, LOUIS

**10898** Newfield, Marcia. *The Life of Louis Pasteur* (5–8). Illus. Series: Pioneers in Health and Medicine. 1992, Twenty-First Century LB $13.95 (0-941477-67-3). 80pp. A well-rounded biography of this famous French scientist. (Rev: SLJ 4/92) [921]

**10899** Sabin, Francene. *Louis Pasteur: Young Scientist* (3–5). Illus. by Susan Swan. 1983, Troll LB $12.95 (0-89375-853-1); paper $3.50 (0-89375-854-X). 48pp. A simple biography that concentrates on the boyhood of Pasteur.

**10900** Smith, Linda W. *Louis Pasteur: Disease Fighter* (4–8). Illus. Series: Great Minds of Science. 1997, Enslow LB $19.95 (0-89490-790-5). 128pp. The story of the "father of microbiology," who discovered pasteurization while working on a wine problem for Napoleon. (Rev: BL 12/1/97; SLJ 12/97) [921]

**10901** Yount, Lisa. *Louis Pasteur* (4–8). Illus. Series: The Importance Of. 1995, Lucent LB $22.45 (1-56006-051-4). 96pp. The life and accomplishments of this great French scientist and of his lasting effects on the world of hygiene and preventive medicine. (Rev: BL 1/15/95) [921]

### PAULING, LINUS

**10902** White, Florence Meiman. *Linus Pauling: Scientist and Crusader* (5–7). Illus. 1980, Walker LB $9.85 (0-8027-6390-1). 96pp. A biography that stresses Pauling's contributions to science and humanity.

### PICOTTE, SUSAN LAFLESCHE

**10903** Ferris, Jeri. *Native American Doctor: The Story of Susan LaFlesche Picotte* (4–6). Illus. 1991, Carolrhoda LB $22.60 (0-87614-443-1). The story of the first Native American woman to earn a medical degree. (Rev: BCCB 12/91; BL 1/1/91; HB 1–2/92) [921]

### PLOTKIN, MARK

**10904** Pascoe, Elaine, adapt. *Mysteries of the Rain Forest: 20th Century Medicine Man* (4–8). Illus. Series: New Explorers. 1997, Blackbirch LB $16.95 (1-56711-229-3). 48pp. Describes the work and findings of Mark Plotkin, an ethnobotanist, who has worked for years in the rain forest of the Amazon. (Rev: SLJ 2/98) [921]

### RAMSAY, KATHLEEN

**10905** Dewey, Jennifer O. *Wildlife Rescue: The Work of Dr. Kathleen Ramsay* (4–7). Illus. 1994, Boyds Mills $19.95 (1-56397-045-7). 63pp. Describes the work of Dr. Kathleen Ramsay, who takes care of injured wild animals at the National Wildlife Center in New Mexico. (Rev: BL 9/1/94; SLJ 9/94*) [921]

## RICHARDS, ELLEN

**10906** Vare, Ethlie A. *Adventurous Spirit: A Story About Ellen Swallow Richards* (3–6). Illus. by Jennifer Hagerman. Series: Creative Minds Book. 1992, Carolrhoda LB $19.93 (0-87614-733-3). 64pp. The life of the first woman accepted at M.I.T. (Rev: BL 1/15/93) [921]

## ROENTGEN, WILHELM

**10907** Gherman, Beverly. *The Mysterious Rays of Dr. Roentgen* (2–5). Illus. by Stephen Marchesi. 1994, Atheneum LB $14.95 (0-689-31839-1). 32pp. An engrossing biography of the man who discovered X-rays and won a Nobel Prize in 1901. (Rev: BCCB 10/94; BL 12/1/94; SLJ 9/94) [921]

## ROOKS, JUNE

**10908** Verheyden-Hilliard, Mary Ellen. *Scientist and Strategist, June Rooks* (2–4). Illus. 1988, Equity paper $5.00 (0-932469-14-0). 32pp. Polio victim and black woman, June Rooks has a career at the China Lake Naval Research Base in California. (Rev: BL 2/15/89; SLJ 1/89)

## SABIN, FLORENCE

**10909** Kaye, Judith. *The Life of Florence Sabin* (4–7). Illus. 1993, Twenty-First Century LB $13.95 (0-8050-2299-6). 80pp. A biography of the American medical doctor who was a trail blazer in tuberculosis research. (Rev: BL 8/93) [921]

## SCULLEY, JOHN

**10910** Spiesman, Harriet. *John Sculley: Building the Apple Dream* (5–8). Illus. Series: Wizards of Industry. 1992, Garrett LB $17.26 (1-56074-023-X). 64pp. The life story of the computer genius who was once behind the Apple computer empire. (Rev: BL 6/15/92; SLJ 7/92) [921]

## SPOCK, BENJAMIN

**10911** Kaye, Judith. *The Life of Benjamin Spock* (5–8). Illus. Series: Pioneers in Health and Medicine. 1993, Twenty-First Century LB $13.95 (0-8050-2301-1). 80pp. The life story of the author of *Baby and Child Care* and of his later career as a political activist. (Rev: SLJ 1/94) [921]

## STEARNER, PHYLLIS

**10912** Verheyden-Hilliard, Mary Ellen. *Scientist and Activist, Phyllis Stearner* (2–4). Illus. 1988, Equity paper $5.00 (0-932469-15-9). 32pp. Biography of an

expert in radiation biology who has cerebral palsy. (Rev: BL 2/15/89; SLJ 1/89)

## STRONG, MAURICE

**10913** Westrup, Hugh. *Maurice Strong: Working for Planet Earth* (3–6). Illus. 1994, Millbrook LB $20.90 (1-56294-414-2). 48pp. A biography of the Canadian environmentalist who organized the Rio de Janeiro Earth Summit. (Rev: BL 12/1/94; SLJ 12/94) [921]

## SWANSON, ANNE BARRETT

**10914** Verheyden-Hilliard, Mary Ellen. *Scientist and Teacher, Anne Barrett Swanson* (2–4). Illus. 1988, Equity paper $5.00 (0-932469-16-7). 32pp. Biography of a scientist who overcame a brittle bone condition that hampered her physical growth. (Rev: BL 2/15/89; SLJ 4/89)

## TOMBAUGH, CLYDE

**10915** Wetterer, Margaret K. *Clyde Tombaugh and the Search for Planet X* (2–5). Illus. by Laurie A. Caple. 1996, Carolrhoda LB $18.60 (0-87614-893-3); paper $5.95 (0-87614-969-7). 56pp. The life story of Tombaugh, whose interest in astronomy led to the discovery of Pluto. (Rev: BL 12/15/96; SLJ 1/97) [921]

## TURNER, HENRY

**10916** Ross, Michael E. *Bug Watching with Charles Henry Turner* (3–5). Illus. Series: Naturalist's Apprentice. 1997, Carolrhoda $19.93 (1-57505-003-X). 48pp. As well as providing many hints on bug watching, this book is a biography of the important African American zoologist who studied insects for many years. (Rev: BL 3/1/98; SLJ 3/98) [921]

## WILLIAMS, DANIEL HALE

**10917** Kaye, Judith. *The Life of Daniel Hale Williams* (5–8). Illus. Series: Pioneers in Health and Medicine. 1993, Twenty-First Century LB $13.95 (0-8050-2302-X). 80pp. The life story of the famous doctor who pioneered heart surgery and also helped open up the medical profession to African Americans. (Rev: SLJ 1/94) [921]

## WOZNIAK, STEVE

**10918** Gold, Rebecca. *Steve Wozniak: A Wizard Called Woz* (3–5). Illus. Series: Achievers. 1994, Lerner LB $19.95 (0-8225-2881-9). 72pp. The biography of the math whiz and multimillionaire who founded the Apple Computer Company. (Rev: BL 12/1/94) [921]

WRIGHT, WILBUR AND ORVILLE

**10919** Reynolds, Quentin. *The Wright Brothers* (4–7). Illus. 1981, Random paper $5.99 (0-394-84700-8). 160pp. The lives of 2 mechanical geniuses.

**10920** Taylor, Richard L. *The First Flight: The Story of the Wright Brothers* (K–3). Illus. Series: First Books. 1990, Watts LB $22.00 (0-531-10891-0). 64pp. Explains the problems that the Wright brothers faced and the solutions they devised in making a functioning airplane. (Rev: BL 4/15/90; SLJ 10/90) [921]

# Sports Figures

## Collective

**10921** Bjarkman, Peter C. *Top 10 Baseball Base Stealers* (3–6). Illus. Series: Sports Top 10. 1995, Enslow LB $18.95 (0-89490-609-7). 48pp. Short biographies of 10 famous baseball players, past and present, known statistically as the top base stealers. (Rev: BL 9/15/95) [920]

**10922** Bjarkman, Peter C. *Top 10 Basketball Slam Dunkers* (3–6). Illus. Series: Sports Top 10. 1995, Enslow LB $18.95 (0-89490-608-9). 48pp. Full-page photos and a 2-page biography are given for each of these 10 basketball stars. (Rev: BL 9/15/95) [920]

**10923** Christopher, Andre. *Top 10 Men's Tennis Players* (4–7). Series: Sports Top 10. 1998, Enslow LB $17.95 (0-7600-1009-0). 48pp. Brief biographies of past and present tennis greats, with fact boxes, career statistics, and chapter notes. (Rev: BL 3/15/98) [920]

**10924** Deane, Bill. *Top 10 Baseball Home Run Hitters* (4–7). Illus. Series: Sports Top 10. 1997, Enslow LB $17.95 (0-89490-804-9). 48pp. Ten brief biographies of baseball hitters, e.g., Hank Aaron, Mickey Mantle, Jimmie Foxx, and Frank Thomas. (Rev: BL 9/15/97) [920]

**10925** Deane, Bill. *Top 10 Men's Baseball Hitters* (4–7). Series: Sports Top 10. 1998, Enslow LB $17.95 (0-7600-1007-4). 48pp. Brief biographies of great past and present baseball hitters, with fact boxes, career statistics, and chapter notes. (Rev: BL 3/15/98) [920]

**10926** Devaney, John. *Winners of the Heisman Trophy* (5–8). Illus. 1990, Walker LB $15.85 (0-8027-6907-1). 167pp. Profiles of 15 winners of this highest college football award. (Rev: SLJ 6/90) [920]

**10927** Dolin, Nick, et al. *Basketball Stars* (4–8). Illus. 1997, Black Dog & Leventhal $24.98 (1-884822-61-4). 128pp. This oversize book contains 50 2-page profiles with statistics of today's star basketball players. (Rev: BL 8/97) [920]

**10928** Golenbock, Peter. *Teammates* (1–3). Illus. by Paul Bacon. 1990, Harcourt $16.00 (0-15-200603-6). 32pp. Segregated life in the United States of the 1940s introduces the reader to the Negro leagues. (Rev: BCCB 4/90; BL 4/1/90; HB 5–6/90; SLJ 6/90) [796.357]

**10929** Harrington, Denis J. *Top 10 Women Tennis Players* (3–6). Illus. Series: Sports Top 10. 1995, Enslow LB $18.95 (0-89490-612-7). 48pp. Biographies of the top 10 women tennis players of all time, with a photograph of each and accompanying statistics. (Rev: BL 7/95; SLJ 11/95) [921]

**10930** Hunter, Shaun. *Great African Americans in the Olympics* (3–5). Series: Outstanding African Americans. 1997, Crabtree LB $21.28 (0-86505-809-1); paper $8.95 (0-86505-823-7). 64pp. In-depth profiles of 7 African Americans — e.g., Gail Devers, George Foreman, Sugar Ray Leonard — and additional shorter profiles of 6 others. (Rev: BL 9/15/97) [920]

**10931** Knapp, Ron. *Top 10 Basketball Centers* (3–6). Illus. Series: Sports Top 10. 1994, Enslow LB $18.95 (0-89490-515-5). 48pp. For each basketball star, there are about 2 pages of text and photographs. (Rev: BL 1/15/95; SLJ 6/95) [920]

**10932** Knapp, Ron. *Top 10 Basketball Scorers* (3–6). Illus. Series: Sports Top 10. 1994, Enslow LB $18.95 (0-89490-516-3). 48pp. Ten short biographies of basketball's top scorers, past and present, with tables of comparative statistics. (Rev: BL 1/15/95; SLJ 6/95) [920]

**10933** Knapp, Ron. *Top 10 Hockey Scorers* (3–6). Illus. Series: Sports Top 10. 1994, Enslow LB $18.95 (0-89490-517-1). 48pp. Statistics, a brief biography, and 2 photographs are given for each hockey player highlighted. (Rev: BL 1/15/95) [920]

**10934** Kramer, S. A. *Baseball's Greatest Hitters* (2–4). Illus. Series: Step into Reading. 1995, Random LB $11.99 (0-679-95307-8); paper $3.99 (0-679-85307-3). 48pp. Five great hitters — Honus Wagner, Ty Cobb, Babe Ruth, Ted Williams, and Hank Aaron — are introduced, each with a simple biography and career statistics. (Rev: BL 7/95) [920]

**10935** Kramer, S. A. *Baseball's Greatest Pitchers* (3–5). Illus. by Jim Campbell. 1992, Random paper $3.99 (0-679-82149-X). 48pp. Black-and-white photos and watercolor paintings add flavor to this collection of profiles of great pitchers. (Rev: BL 4/1/92; SLJ 7/92) [796.357]

**10936** Kramer, S. A. *Wonder Women of Sports* (2–3). Illus. by Jim Campbell. Series: All Aboard Reading. 1997, Putnam LB $13.89 (0-448-41722-7); paper $3.95 (0-448-41589-5). 48pp. A beginning reader that profiles some women athletes, like Gail Devers, Dominique Moceanu, and Rebecca Lobo. (Rev: BL 2/1/98) [920]

**10937** Krull, Kathleen. *Lives of the Athletes* (4–7). Illus. by Kathryn Hewitt. 1997, Harcourt $19.00 (0-15-200806-3). 96pp. A collective biography that describes the public and private lives of 20 famous athletes, including Johnny Weissmuller, Red Grange, Babe Didrikson Zaharias, Sonja Henie, and Bruce Lee. (Rev: BCCB 6/97; BL 3/15/97; HB 5–6/97; SLJ 5/97) [920]

**10938** Lace, William W. *Top 10 Football Quarterbacks* (3–6). Illus. Series: Sports Top 10. 1994, Enslow LB $18.95 (0-89490-518-X). 48pp. Star quarterbacks both past and present are highlighted in 10 brief biographies, each with a photograph and a record of achievements. (Rev: BL 1/15/95) [920]

**10939** Lace, William W. *Top 10 Football Rushers* (3–6). Illus. Series: Sports Top 10. 1994, Enslow LB $18.95 (0-89490-519-8). 48pp. Each of the 10 featured stars gets a 2-page biography, a photograph, and coverage of important statistics. (Rev: BL 1/15/95) [920]

**10940** O'Connor, Jim. *Comeback! Four True Stories* (2–4). Illus. by Jim Campbell. 1992, Random LB $9.99 (0-679-92666-6); paper $3.99 (0-679-82666-1). 48pp. Stories about 4 athletes who overcame physical adversity to succeed. (Rev: BL 6/15/92; SLJ 8/92) [920]

**10941** Rappoport, Ken. *Guts and Glory: Making It in the NBA* (4–7). Illus. 1997, Walker LB $16.85 (0-8027-8431-3). 160pp. Ten short biographies of star players, like John Lucas and Isiah Thomas, who over-came obstacles to success in the NBA. (Rev: BL 8/97; SLJ 7/97) [920]

**10942** Rappoport, Ken. *Top 10 Basketball Legends* (3–6). Illus. Series: Sports Top 10. 1995, Enslow LB $18.95 (0-89490-610-0). 48pp. Biographies of the top 10 basketball players of the past, with statistics to prove the unique contribution of each. (Rev: BL 7/95; SLJ 11/95) [920]

**10943** Rediger, Pat. *Great African Americans in Sports* (4–6). Illus. Series: Outstanding African Americans. 1996, Crabtree LB $21.28 (0-86505-801-6); paper $8.95 (0-86505-815-6). 64pp. Three of the 13 sports heroes profiled are Michael Jordan, Jackie Joyner-Kersee, and Carl Lewis. (Rev: BL 9/15/96) [920]

**10944** Rennert, Richard, ed. *Book of Firsts: Sports Heroes* (5–8). Illus. Series: Profiles of Great Black Americans. 1993, Chelsea LB $15.95 (0-7910-2055-X); paper $5.95 (0-7910-2056-8). 63pp. Contains profiles of these great African American athletes: Arthur Ashe, Chuck Cooper, Althea Gibson, Jesse Owens, Jackie Robinson, Jack Johnson, Frank Robinson, and Bill Russell. (Rev: SLJ 12/93) [920]

**10945** Riley, Gail B. *Top 10 NASCAR Drivers* (3–4). Illus. Series: Sports Top 10. 1995, Enslow LB $18.95 (0-89490-611-9). 48pp. Ten of the top race car drivers are highlighted in these short biographies. (Rev: BL 9/15/95) [796.7]

**10946** Savage, Jeff. *Top 10 Basketball Point Guards* (4–7). Series: Sports Top 10. 1997, Enslow LB $18.95 (0-89490-807-3). 48pp. Each of the athletes is presented in 4 pages containing a biography, statistics, and 2 photographs. Also use *Top 10 Basketball Power Forwards* (1997). (Rev: BL 9/15/97) [920]

**10947** Savage, Jeff. *Top 10 Football Sackers* (4–7). Series: Sports Top 10. 1997, Enslow LB $18.95 (0-89490-805-7). 48pp. Each of the 10 football stars highlighted is covered in 4 pages that include a short biography, 2 photos, and a statistics table. (Rev: BL 9/15/97) [920]

**10948** Schwabacher, Martin. *Superstars of Women's Tennis* (4–6). Illus. Series: Female Sports Stars. 1997, Chelsea LB $15.95 (0-7910-4393-2). 64pp. Profiles tennis greats Billie Jean King, Chris Evert, Martina Navratilova, Steffi Graff, and Monica Seles. (Rev: SLJ 8/97) [920]

**10949** Sehnert, Chris W. *Top 10 Sluggers* (5–8). Illus. Series: Top 10 Champions. 1997, ABDO LB $16.95 (1-56239-797-4). 48pp. An overview of the careers of such notable hitters as Babe Ruth, Hank Aaron, and Roberto Clemente. (Rev: BL 1/1–15/98) [920]

**10950** Smith, Pohla. *Superstars of Women's Figure Skating* (4–6). Illus. Series: Female Sports Stars. 1997, Chelsea LB $15.95 (0-7910-4392-4). 64pp. A clear easy reader that includes profiles of Sonja Henie, Peggy Fleming, Dorothy Hamill, Katarina Witt, Kristi Yamaguchi, and Oksana Baiul. (Rev: SLJ 8/97) [920]

**10951** Sullivan, George. *Great Lives: Sports* (5–7). Illus. 1988, Macmillan $24.00 (0-684-18510-5). 288pp. Introducing 27 sports stars from all fields. (Rev: BL 1/1/89; HB 3–4/89)

**10952** Sullivan, George. *Sluggers!* (4–7). Illus. 1991, Macmillan $18.00 (0-689-31566-X). 74pp. Profiles of the careers of 27 of baseball's best hitters. (Rev: SLJ 1/92) [920]

**10953** Sullivan, Michael J. *Top 10 Baseball Pitchers* (3–6). Illus. Series: Sports Top 10. 1994, Enslow LB $18.95 (0-89490-520-1). 48pp. Star pitchers from both the past and present are featured, each receiving a 2-page biography and color photograph. (Rev: BL 1/15/95) [920]

**10954** Thornley, Stew. *Top 10 Football Receivers* (3–6). Illus. Series: Sports Top 10. 1995, Enslow LB $18.95 (0-89490-607-0). 48pp. The position of receiver is highlighted in the biographies of 10 of the greatest, past and present. (Rev: BL 7/95; SLJ 11/95) [920]

**10955** Young, Ken. *Cy Young Award Winners* (4–6). Illus. 1994, Walker LB $15.85 (0-8027-8301-5). 160pp. Profiles of 10 winners of the Cy Young Award for pitching, e.g., Whitey Ford, Sandy Koufax, Fernando Valenzuela, and Dwight Gooden. (Rev: BL 9/1/94; SLJ 8/94) [920]

## Automobile Racing

### ST. JAMES, LYN

**10956** Olney, Ross R. *Lyn St. James: Driven to Be First* (4–6). Illus. 1997, Lerner LB $19.93 (0-8225-2890-8); paper $5.95 (0-8225-9749-7). 64pp. The biography of one of the few women who has succeeded in the world of race car driving. (Rev: BL 2/15/97; SLJ 3/97) [921]

## Baseball

### AARON, HANK

**10957** Margolies, Jacob. *Hank Aaron: Home Run King* (4–6). Illus. Series: First Books. 1992, Watts LB $21.00 (0-531-20075-2). 64pp. The all-time baseball great who beat Babe Ruth's 714 home run mark. (Rev: BL 6/15/92) [921]

**10958** Tackach, James. *Hank Aaron* (4–6). Illus. Series: Baseball Legends. 1991, Chelsea LB $15.95 (0-7910-1165-8). 64pp. In addition to the life of base-ball legend Aaron, this biography includes sections of statistics, a chronology, and numerous photographs. (Rev: BL 12/1/91) [921]

### ABBOTT, JIM

**10959** Johnson, Rick L. *Jim Abbott: Beating the Odds* (4–7). Illus. Series: Taking Part. 1991, Macmillan LB $13.95 (0-87518-459-6). 64pp. This account re-creates the life of the baseball pitcher who overcame a severe disability. (Rev: BL 9/1/91) [921]

**10960** White, Ellen E. *Jim Abbott: Against All Odds* (3–5). Illus. Series: Scholastic Biography. 1990, Scholastic paper $2.99 (0-590-43503-5). 86pp. The amazing pitcher for the California Angels, who once pitched a no-hitter for the New York Yankees, who has only one hand. (Rev: SLJ 10/90) [921]

### ALEXANDER, GROVER CLEVELAND

**10961** Kavanagh, Jack. *Grover Cleveland Alexander* (4–6). Illus. Series: Baseball Legends. 1990, Chelsea LB $15.95 (0-7910-1166-6). 63pp. A fine profile of one of the greats of the baseball game. (Rev: BL 6/1/90) [921]

### BENCH, JOHNNY

**10962** Shannon, Mike. *Johnny Bench* (4–6). Illus. Series: Baseball Legends. 1990, Chelsea LB $15.95 (0-7910-1168-2). 64pp. Biographical data plus background statistics, a chronology, and many photos. (Rev: BL 10/1/90; SLJ 1/91) [921]

### BONDS, BARRY

**10963** Savage, Jeff. *Barry Bonds: Mr. Excitement* (4–8). Illus. Series: Sports Achievers. 1997, Lerner LB $19.93 (0-8225-2889-4). 64pp. The story of this fantastic baseball player who has won the Most Valuable Player award 3 times and who grew up in the shadow of a famous father. (Rev: BL 4/15/97; SLJ 2/97) [921]

### BONILLA, BOBBY

**10964** Knapp, Ron. *Bobby Bonilla* (5–8). Illus. Series: Sports Great. 1993, Enslow LB $16.95 (0-89490-417-5). 64pp. Using easy-to-read prose and a number of action photos, this is a lively introduction to baseball star Bobby Bonilla. (Rev: BL 9/15/93) [921]

**10965** Rappoport, Ken. *Bobby Bonilla* (5–8). Illus. 1993, Walker LB $15.85 (0-8027-8256-6). 144pp. A well-written sports biography on the New York Mets–Baltimore Orioles–Florida Marlins player. (Rev: SLJ 5/93) [921]

## CAMPANELLA, ROY

**10966** Tackach, James. *Roy Campanella* (4–6). Illus. Series: Baseball Legends. 1990, Chelsea LB $15.95 (0-7910-1170-4). 64pp. Covers not only the life and career of Roy Campanella, but also the most important games in which he played. (Rev: BL 4/15/91) [921]

## CANSECO, JOSÉ

**10967** Aaseng, Nathan. *Jose Canseco: Baseball's Forty-Forty Man* (4–7). Illus. 1989, Lerner LB $18.60 (0-8225-0493-6); paper $4.95 (0-8225-9586-9). 56pp. The ups and downs of this sometimes controversial baseball star of the Oakland A's. (Rev: BCCB 9/89; BL 7/89; SLJ 8/89) [921]

## CLEMENTE, ROBERTO

**10968** Bjarkman, Peter C. *Roberto Clemente* (4–6). Illus. Series: Baseball Legends. 1991, Chelsea LB $14.95 (0-7910-1171-2). 64pp. The inspiring career of the Puerto Rican baseball legend. (Rev: BL 3/1/91) [921]

**10969** Gilbert, Tom. *Roberto Clemente* (5–8). Illus. 1991, Chelsea LB $19.95 (0-7910-1240-9). 112pp. The life of the first Hispanic in the Baseball Hall of Fame. (Rev: BL 8/91) [921]

**10970** Greene, Carol. *Roberto Clemente: Baseball Superstar* (2–4). Illus. Series: Rookie Biographies. 1991, Children's LB $19.00 (0-516-04222-X). 48pp. In an appealing format and easily read text, the life of this Puerto Rican baseball superstar is covered. (Rev: BL 2/15/92) [921]

**10971** Walker, Paul R. *Pride of Puerto Rico: The Life of Roberto Clemente* (4–7). 1988, Harcourt $14.00 (0-15-200562-5); paper $6.00 (0-15-263420-7). 132pp. The life of a baseball star and hero who died trying to help others. (Rev: BL 10/1/88; HB 9–10/88; SLJ 1/89)

**10972** West, Alan. *Roberto Clemente: Baseball Legend* (3–6). Illus. Series: Hispanic Heritage. 1993, Millbrook LB $19.90 (1-56294-367-7). 32pp. A biography of the Puerto Rican baseball superstar. (Rev: BL 11/15/93) [921]

## COBB, TY

**10973** Macht, Norman L. *Ty Cobb* (4–6). Illus. Series: Baseball Legends. 1992, Chelsea LB $15.95 (0-685-48322-3). 64pp. The life of this baseball great is recalled in a text that gives coverage of pivotal games, plus statistics and a chronology. (Rev: BL 4/1/93) [921]

## DEAN, DIZZY

**10974** Kavanagh, Jack. *Dizzy Dean* (4–6). Illus. Series: Baseball Legends. 1991, Chelsea LB $15.95 (0-7910-1173-9). 64pp. The story of the famous pitcher for the St. Louis Cardinals. (Rev: BL 2/1/91) [921]

## DIMAGGIO, JOE

**10975** Appel, Marty. *Joe DiMaggio* (4–6). Illus. Series: Baseball Legends. 1990, Chelsea LB $15.95 (0-7910-1164-X). 63pp. A biography of the ultimate baseball hero. (Rev: BL 6/1/90; SLJ 10/90) [921]

**10976** Sanford, William R., and Carl R. Green. *Joe DiMaggio* (4–6). Illus. Series: Sports Immortals. 1993, Macmillan LB $11.95 (0-89686-738-2). 48pp. The biography of Joe DiMaggio, alias "The Yankee Clipper," who was given the Greatest Living Player Award in the 1969 Summer Olympics. (Rev: BL 4/15/93; SLJ 8/93) [921]

## FELLER, BOB

**10977** Eckhouse, Morris. *Bob Feller* (4–6). Illus. Series: Baseball Legends. 1990, Chelsea LB $15.95 (0-7910-1174-7). 64pp. The life and career of the legendary baseball pitcher are re-created. (Rev: BL 10/1/90) [921]

## FOXX, JIMMIE

**10978** Macht, Norman L. *Jimmie Foxx* (4–6). Illus. Series: Baseball Legends. 1990, Chelsea LB $15.95 (0-7910-1175-5). 64pp. A lively account that focuses on Foxx's life and top games. (Rev: BL 11/15/90) [921]

## GEHRIG, LOU

**10979** Adler, David A. *Lou Gehrig: The Luckiest Man* (3–5). Illus. by Terry Widener. 1997, Harcourt $15.00 (0-15-200523-4). 32pp. An excellent biography of the "Iron Horse," the baseball legend who was a model of sportsmanship and courage. (Rev: BCCB 4/97; BL 5/15/97; HB 7–8/97, 9–10/97; SLJ 5/97) [921]

**10980** Macht, Norman L. *Lou Gehrig* (4–6). Illus. Series: Baseball Legends. 1993, Chelsea LB $15.95 (0-7910-1176-3). 64pp. The story of this baseball great and gallant American is told with particular attention to his most important games. (Rev: BL 4/1/93) [921]

## GONZALEZ, JUAN

**10981** Gutman, Bill. *Juan Gonzalez: Outstanding Outfielder* (4–6). Illus. Series: Sports World. 1995, Millbrook LB $19.90 (1-56294-567-X). 48pp. A brief, well-illustrated biography of this baseball star. (Rev: BL 9/15/95; SLJ 1/96) [921]

### GOODEN, DWIGHT

**10982** Aaseng, Nathan. *Dwight Gooden: Strikeout King* (4–7). Illus. 1988, Lerner LB $18.60 (0-8225-0478-2). 56pp. The early stunning feats of "Dr. K," his drug problem and rehabilitation, and his fight to regain his form and reputation. (Rev: BL 8/88)

### GRIFFEY, KEN (FATHER AND SON)

**10983** Gutman, Bill. *Ken Griffey, Sr., and Ken Griffey, Jr.* (4–6). Illus. Series: Millbrook Sports World. 1993, Millbrook LB $19.90 (1-56294-226-3). 48pp. An account of the father and son who made baseball history playing together for the Seattle Mariners. (Rev: BL 3/15/93) [921]

### GRIFFEY, KEN, JR.

**10984** Macnow, Glen. *Ken Griffey, Jr.: Star Outfielder* (4–6). Series: Sports Reports. 1997, Enslow LB $19.95 (0-89490-802-2). 104pp. The life and career of this baseball star are covered, with action photos and behind-the-scenes coverage. (Rev: BL 2/15/98) [921]

### HERSHISER, OREL

**10985** Knapp, Ron. *Sports Great Orel Hershiser* (5–8). Illus. Series: Sports Greats. 1993, Enslow LB $16.95 (0-89490-389-6). 64pp. This easily read biography of this current sports favorite re-creates Orel Hershiser's life and his most exciting sports moments. (Rev: BL 4/1/93) [921]

### HORNSBY, ROGERS

**10986** Kavanagh, Jack. *Rogers Hornsby* (4–6). Illus. Series: Baseball Legends. 1991, Chelsea LB $15.95 (0-7910-1178-X). 64pp. A well-illustrated biography of this baseball great. (Rev: BL 2/1/91) [921]

### JACKSON, BO

**10987** Devaney, John. *Bo Jackson: A Star for All Seasons* (5–7). Illus. 1992, Walker LB $15.85 (0-802-78179-9). 110pp. Biography of the Kansas City Royals baseball star, who also played pro football for the Los Angeles Raiders. (Rev: BL 2/15/89; SLJ 1/89)

### JACKSON, REGGIE

**10988** Woods, Andrew. *Young Reggie Jackson: Hall of Fame Champion* (2–4). Illus. Series: Troll First Start. 1996, Troll paper $3.50 (0-8167-3763-0). 32pp. With emphasis on his early life, this is an eas-

ily read biography of this baseball legend. (Rev: BL 2/15/96) [921]

### JOHNSON, WALTER

**10989** Kavanagh, Jack. *Walter Johnson* (4–8). Illus. Series: Baseball Legends. 1991, Chelsea LB $15.95 (0-7910-1179-8). 144pp. A biography of a baseball giant, including coverage of important games and many black-and-white photos. (Rev: BL 1/15/92) [921]

### KOUFAX, SANDY

**10990** Grabowski, John. *Sandy Koufax* (4–6). Illus. Series: Baseball Legends. 1991, Chelsea LB $15.95 (0-7910-1180-1). The life of this great baseball pitcher is portrayed through many illustrations and good background information. (Rev: BL 1/15/92) [921]

**10991** Sanford, William R., and Carl R. Green. *Sandy Koufax* (4–6). Illus. Series: Sports Immortals. 1993, Macmillan LB $11.95 (0-89686-780-3). 48pp. A short biography of this baseball immortal that contains many photos, recollections of friends, and trivia questions. (Rev: BL 10/1/93) [921]

### MADDUX, GREG

**10992** Christopher, Matt. *On the Mound with . . . Greg Maddux* (4–7). Illus. 1997, Little, Brown paper $4.50 (0-316-14191-7). 144pp. The life of the famous player with the Chicago Cubs and Atlanta Braves, who has been called the best pitcher in baseball. (Rev: BL 7/97) [921]

**10993** Thornley, Stew. *Sports Great Greg Maddux* (5–8). Illus. Series: Sports Great. 1997, Enslow LB $16.95 (0-89490-873-1). 64pp. The life of this baseball great is traced, supplemented by career statistics and many action photos. (Rev: BL 2/15/97) [921]

### MATHEWSON, CHRISTY

**10994** Macht, Norman L. *Christy Mathewson* (4–6). Illus. Series: Baseball Legends. 1991, Chelsea LB $15.95 (0-7910-1182-8). 64pp. The life of the great pitcher, including important games in his career. (Rev: BL 9/15/91) [921]

### MAYS, WILLIE

**10995** Grabowski, John. *Willie Mays* (4–6). Illus. Series: Baseball Legends. 1990, Chelsea LB $15.95 (0-7910-1183-6). 63pp. A profile of one of baseball's greatest hitters. (Rev: BL 6/1/90) [921]

### NOMO, HIDEO

**10996** Rodman, Edmon J. *Nomo: The Tornado Who Took America by Storm* (4–7). Illus. 1996, Lowell House paper $5.95 (1-56565-394-7). 111pp. The story of the life and career of the Japanese pitcher for the Los Angeles Dodgers, Hideo Nomo. (Rev: SLJ 8/96) [921]

## PAIGE, SATCHEL

**10997** Macht, Norman L. *Satchel Paige* (4–6). Illus. Series: Baseball Legends. 1991, Chelsea LB $15.95 (0-7910-1185-2). 64pp. The story of the great African-American baseball player and popular hero, with special attention to key games in which he played. (Rev: BL 9/15/91) [921]

**10998** McKissack, Patricia, and Fredrick McKissack. *Satchel Paige: The Best Arm in Baseball* (2–4). Illus. by Michael D. Blegel. Series: Great African Americans. 1992, Enslow LB $13.95 (0-89490-317-9). 32pp. The life story of the Hall of Famer who was the first African American pitcher in the American League. (Rev: BL 10/15/92; SLJ 1/93) [921]

## PUCKETT, KIRBY

**10999** Puckett, Kirby, and Greg Brown. *Kirby Puckett: Be the Best You Can Be* (2–4). Illus. by Tim Houle. 1993, Waldman $14.95 (0-931674-20-4). A picture book autobiography of the star of the Minnesota Twins, filled with advice on how to achieve one's potential. (Rev: BL 8/93; SLJ 2/94) [921]

## RIPKEN, CAL, JR.

**11000** Macnow, Glen. *Sports Great Cal Ripken, Jr.* (5–8). Illus. Series: Sports Greats. 1993, Enslow LB $16.95 (0-89490-387-X). 64pp. The life of this current baseball star is created in text and pictures that concentrate on the sports action that has made him famous. (Rev: BL 4/1/93) [921]

**11001** Savage, Jeff. *Cal Ripken, Jr.: Star Shortstop* (4–6). Illus. Series: Sports Reports. 1994, Enslow LB $19.95 (0-89490-485-X). 104pp. A book about the star baseball player who gained fame as an all-star shortstop for the Baltimore Orioles. (Rev: SLJ 2/95) [921]

## ROBINSON, BROOKS

**11002** Wolff, Rick. *Brooks Robinson* (4–6). Illus. Series: Baseball Legends. 1990, Chelsea LB $15.95 (0-7910-1186-0). 64pp. This biography tells the life of Brooks Robinson and his most important games. (Rev: BL 10/1/90) [921]

## ROBINSON, FRANK

**11003** Macht, Norman L. *Frank Robinson* (4–6). Illus. Series: Baseball Legends. 1991, Chelsea LB $15.95 (0-7910-1187-9). 64pp. This account gives good coverage of Robinson's crucial games. (Rev: BL 2/1/91) [921]

## ROBINSON, JACKIE

**11004** Adler, David A. *Jackie Robinson: He Was the First* (3–5). Illus. by Robert Casilla. 1989, Holiday LB $14.95 (0-8234-0734-9). 48pp. A profile of the first black player in the major leagues. (Rev: BL 7/89) [921]

**11005** Adler, David A. *A Picture Book of Jackie Robinson* (K–3). Illus. by Robert Casilla. Series: Picture Book Biography. 1994, Holiday LB $15.95 (0-8234-1122-2). 32pp. This simple biography of the baseball giant reads like a story for young children. (Rev: BL 11/15/94; SLJ 12/94) [921]

**11006** Coombs, Karen Mueller. *Jackie Robinson: Baseball's Civil Rights Legend* (5–7). Illus. Series: African American Biographies. 1997, Enslow LB $19.95 (0-89490-690-9). 128pp. The story of the baseball great who stood up to racism in athletics. (Rev: BL 6/1–15/97) [921]

**11007** Davidson, Margaret. *The Story of Jackie Robinson: Bravest Man in Baseball* (3–7). Illus. 1988, Dell paper $3.50 (0-440-40019-8). 92pp. The life of the man who broke the baseball color barrier. (Rev: BL 6/1/88; SLJ 5/88)

**11008** Denenberg, Barry. *Stealing Home: The Story of Jackie Robinson* (4–6). Illus. 1997, Scholastic paper $3.99 (0-590-42560-9). 116pp. A biography that balances Robinson's life and significance on and off the baseball diamond. (Rev: SLJ 1/91) [921]

**11009** Grabowski, John. *Jackie Robinson* (4–6). Illus. Series: Baseball Legends. 1990, Chelsea LB $15.95 (0-7910-1188-7). 64pp. The life story of the pro baseball player who broke the color line. (Rev: BL 11/15/90) [921]

**11010** O'Connor, Jim. *Jackie Robinson and the Story of All-Black Baseball* (3–5). Illus. by Jim Butcher. 1989, Random LB $7.99 (0-394-92456-8); paper $3.99 (0-394-82456-3). 48pp. The story of Jackie Robinson and the Negro Leagues, preceding his entry into pro ball. (Rev: BCCB 9/89; BL 7/89) [921]

**11011** Reiser, Howard. *Jackie Robinson: Baseball Pioneer* (4–8). Illus. Series: First Books. 1992, Watts LB $21.00 (0-531-20095-7). 64pp. Attractive layout and photos highlight the career of the man who broke the pro baseball color barrier. (Rev: BL 10/1/92) [921]

**11012** Sanford, William R., and Carl R. Green. *Jackie Robinson* (4–6). Illus. Series: Sports Immortals. 1992, Macmillan LB $11.95 (0-89686-743-9). 48pp. Basic biographical data plus many photos tell the life of the man who broke the color barrier in pro baseball. (Rev: BL 2/1/93; SLJ 1/93) [921]

**11013** Santella, Andrew. *Jackie Robinson Breaks the Color Line* (3–5). Illus. Series: Cornerstones of Freedom. 1996, Children's LB $19.50 (0-516-06637-4). 32pp. Discusses the career of Jackie Robinson and its significance in the history of baseball and for the civil rights movement. (Rev: BL 4/15/96; SLJ 11/96) [921]

### RUTH, BABE

**11014** Macht, Norman L. *Babe Ruth* (4–6). Illus. Series: Baseball Legends. 1991, Chelsea LB $15.95 (0-7910-1189-5). 64pp. The life of the legendary left-handed pitcher, outfielder, and slugger is re-created. (Rev: BL 4/15/91) [921]

**11015** Nicholson, Lois. *Babe Ruth: Sultan of Swat* (5–8). Illus. 1995, Goodwood $17.95 (0-9625427-1-7). 119pp. This well-written account of the famous slugger explains his lasting influence on baseball. (Rev: SLJ 7/95) [921]

**11016** Sanford, William R., and Carl R. Green. *Babe Ruth* (4–6). Illus. Series: Sports Immortals. 1992, Macmillan LB $11.95 (0-89686-741-2). 48pp. Numerous photos enhance this bio of the great Yankee star for middle-grade readers. (Rev: BL 2/1/93; SLJ 1/93) [921]

### RYAN, NOLAN

**11017** Lace, William W. *Sports Great Nolan Ryan* (5–8). Illus. Series: Sports Great. 1993, Enslow LB $16.95 (0-89490-394-2). 64pp. The life story and important games are covered in this biography of the exciting baseball star, Nolan Ryan. (Rev: BL 6/1–15/93) [921]

**11018** Rappoport, Ken. *Nolan Ryan: The Ryan Express* (3–6). Illus. Series: Taking Part. 1992, Macmillan LB $13.95 (0-87518-524-X). 64pp. The life story of the amazing baseball player who has developed a large following. (Rev: BL 1/15/93) [921]

### SNIDER, DUKE

**11019** Bjarkman, Peter C. *Duke Snider* (4–6). Illus. Series: Baseball Legends. 1994, Chelsea LB $15.95 (0-7910-1190-9). 63pp. A biography of the superstar from the golden age of baseball. (Rev: BL 10/15/94) [921]

### STARGELL, WILLIE

**11020** Shannon, Mike. *Willie Stargell* (4–6). Illus. Series: Baseball Legends. 1992, Chelsea LB $15.95 (0-7910-1192-5). 64pp. A biography of the star baseball player, with an emphasis on the pivotal games in his career. (Rev: BL 12/1/92) [921]

### STRAWBERRY, DARRYL

**11021** Torres, John A., and Michael J. Sullivan. *Darryl Strawberry* (4–6). Illus. Series: Sports Greats. 1990, Enslow LB $16.95 (0-89490-291-1). 64pp. The story of the fine but controversial baseball play-

er, with good coverage of his childhood. (Rev: SLJ 11/90) [921]

### THOMAS, FRANK

**11022** Gutman, Bill. *Frank Thomas: Power Hitter* (4–6). Illus. Series: Sports World. 1996, Millbrook LB $19.90 (1-56294-569-6). 48pp. This biography of the baseball superstar tells about his life and his talent. (Rev: BL 5/15/96; SLJ 6/96) [921]

**11023** Spiros, Dean. *Frank Thomas: Star First Baseman* (4–6). Illus. Series: Sports Reports. 1996, Enslow LB $19.95 (0-89490-659-3). 104pp. The life of this baseball hero is covered, with emphasis on key games and important career decisions. (Rev: BL 11/15/96) [921]

**11024** Thornley, Stew. *Frank Thomas: Baseball's Big Hurt* (4–8). Series: Sports Achievers. 1997, Lerner $19.93 (0-8225-3651-X); paper $5.95 (0-8225-9759-4). 64pp. As well as being a big-time hitter in baseball, this star — nicknamed "The Big Hurt" — devotes much of his spare time to the fight against leukemia. (Rev: BL 1/1–15/98) [921]

### TOPORCER, GEORGE

**11025** Motomora, Mitchell. *Specs: The True Story of Baseball Player George Toporcer* (2–3). Illus. by Nina Barbaresi. Series: Ready Set Read. 1990, Raintree Steck-Vaughn LB $21.40 (0-8172-3585-X). 24pp. As a youngster, Specs was determined to play ball even though he wore glasses. (Rev: BL 6/1/90; SLJ 11/90) [921]

### YOUNG, CY

**11026** Macht, Norman L. *Cy Young* (4–6). Illus. Series: Baseball Legends. 1991, Chelsea LB $15.95 (0-7910-1196-8). 144pp. The story of this legendary pitcher, with interesting background and team information. (Rev: BL 1/15/92) [921]

## Basketball

### ABDUL-JABBAR, KAREEM

**11027** Margolies, Jacob. *Kareem Abdul-Jabbar: Basketball Great* (4–7). Illus. 1992, Watts LB $21.00 (0-531-20076-0). 64pp. The story of the New York-born athlete whose career lasted longer than that of any other professional basketball player. (Rev: BL 8/92) [921]

**11028** Sanford, William R., and Carl R. Green. *Kareem Abdul-Jabbar* (4–6). Illus. Series: Sports Immortals. 1993, Macmillan LB $11.95 (0-89686-737-4). 48pp. The life and career of Lew Alcindor, better known as Kareem Abdul-Jabbar, who was named the NBA Most Valuable Player 6 times. (Rev: BL 4/15/93; SLJ 8/93) [921]

## BARKLEY, CHARLES

**11029** Dolan, Sean. *Charles Barkley* (5–7). Illus. Series: Basketball Legends. 1996, Chelsea LB $14.95 (0-7910-2433-4). 62pp. The life of this basketball superstar, with details on his record on the court. (Rev: BL 7/96) [921]

**11030** Knapp, Ron. *Charles Barkley: Star Forward* (4–6). Illus. Series: Sports Reports. 1996, Enslow LB $19.95 (0-89490-655-0). 104pp. A short biography of this basketball star, with career statistics and many action photos. (Rev: BL 8/96; SLJ 8/96) [921]

## BIRD, LARRY

**11031** Kavanagh, Jack. *Sports Great Larry Bird* (4–8). Illus. Series: Sports Great Books. 1992, Enslow LB $16.95 (0-89490-368-3). 64pp. The extraordinary story of the basketball player who drove his team, the Boston Celtics, to 5 NBA finals. (Rev: BL 7/92; SLJ 10/92) [921]

## EWING, PATRICK

**11032** Kavanagh, Jack. *Sports Great Patrick Ewing* (5–8). Illus. Series: Sports Great Books. 1992, Enslow LB $16.95 (0-89490-369-1). 64pp. An easily read, candid look at the basketball great from Jamaica. (Rev: BL 9/1/92) [921]

**11033** Wiener, Paul. *Patrick Ewing* (4–6). Illus. Series: Basketball Legends. 1996, Chelsea LB $15.95 (0-7910-2434-2). 64pp. The story of this New York Knicks center and his quest for an NBA championship. (Rev: BL 7/96) [921]

## HARDAWAY, ANFERNEE

**11034** Gutman, Bill. *Anfernee Hardaway: Super Guard* (4–6). Illus. Series: Sports World. 1997, Millbrook LB $19.90 (0-7613-0062-7). 48pp. This basketball star's life story is given, with plenty of sports action and summary career statistics. (Rev: BL 4/15/97) [921]

**11035** Rekela, George R. *Sports Great Anfernee Hardaway* (5–8). Illus. Series: Sports Great. 1996, Enslow LB $16.95 (0-89490-758-1). 64pp. An interesting biography illustrated with black-and-white photos of this basketball star. (Rev: BL 3/15/96) [921]

## HILL, GRANT

**11036** Christopher, Matt. *On the Court with . . . Grant Hill* (3–7). Illus. Series: Matt Christopher Sports Biography. 1996, Little, Brown paper $4.50 (0-316-13790-1). 144pp. A fine biography of this

basketball hero whose rise to fame involved personal determination and courage. (Rev: BL 2/15/97; SLJ 6/97) [921]

**11037** Gutman, Bill. *Grant Hill: Basketball's High Flier* (3–6). Illus. Series: Sports World. 1996, Millbrook LB $19.90 (0-7613-0038-4); paper $6.95 (0-7613-0133-X). 48pp. A brief biography that concentrates on Hill's basketball career, particularly at Duke University and with the Detroit Pistons. (Rev: SLJ 2/97) [921]

**11038** Savage, Jeff. *Grant Hill: Humble Hotshot* (4–8). Illus. Series: Sports Achievers. 1997, Lerner LB $19.93 (0-8225-2893-2). 64pp. The story of the humble basketball star who has been a mainstay of the Detroit Pistons. (Rev: BL 4/15/97; SLJ 6/97) [921]

## JOHNSON, MAGIC

**11039** Greenberg, Keith E. *Magic Johnson: Champion with a Cause* (4–7). Illus. Series: Achievers. 1992, Lerner LB $18.60 (0-8225-0546-0). 64pp. The story of the gifted athlete for the L.A. Lakers, whose career was cut short when he discovered he was HIV-positive. (Rev: BL 8/92; SLJ 7/92) [921]

**11040** Gutman, Bill. *Magic Johnson: Hero on and off the Court* (4–6). Illus. Series: Sports World. 1992, Millbrook paper $5.95 (1-56294-825-3). 48pp. This story of the life of the basketball superstar emphasizes that hard work and dedication lead to success. (Rev: BL 11/1/92; SLJ 12/92) [921]

**11041** Haskins, Jim. *Sports Great Magic Johnson* (4–8). Illus. 1992, Enslow LB $16.95 (0-89490-348-9). 80pp. The story of the great "great" of the Los Angeles Lakers pro basketball team. (Rev: BL 6/15/89)

**11042** Schwabacher, Martin. *Magic Johnson: Basketball Wizard* (4–6). Illus. Series: Junior World Biographies. 1993, Chelsea LB $15.95 (0-7910-2037-1). 79pp. A fine biography of this superstar that covers his life through the revelation of his HIV status, but not his comeback. (Rev: SLJ 1/94) [921]

## JORDAN, MICHAEL

**11043** Aaseng, Nathan. *Sports Great Michael Jordan* (5–8). Illus. Series: Sports Greats. 1992, Enslow LB $16.95 (0-89490-370-5). 64pp. Michael Jordan's life, his successes as guard of the Chicago Bulls, and his commercials for TV are discussed in this easily read book. (Rev: BL 10/15/92) [921]

**11044** Berger, Phil, and John Rolfe. *Michael Jordan* (4–7). Illus. 1990, Little, Brown paper $4.95 (0-316-09229-0). 124pp. This account covers Jordan's childhood and his career development. (Rev: BL 12/15/90; SLJ 4/91) [921]

**11045** Christopher, Matt. *On the Court with . . . Michael Jordan* (3–7). Illus. Series: Matt Christopher Sports Biography. 1996, Little, Brown paper $4.50 (0-316-13792-8). 144pp. The life of this pro basketball legend whose self-determination and family support helped him rise to the top. (Rev: BL 2/15/97; SLJ 6/97) [921]

**11046** Gutman, Bill. *Michael Jordan: A Biography* (5–8). 1995, Pocket paper $3.99 (0-671-51972-7). 133pp. This readable book contains good coverage on the formative years as well as the current accomplishments of this basketball hero. (Rev: SLJ 5/92) [921]

**11047** Gutman, Bill. *Michael Jordan: Basketball Champ* (4–6). Illus. Series: Sports World. 1992, Houghton paper $4.80 (0-395-64545-X). The life and dedication to hard work of one of basketball's greatest stars. (Rev: BL 11/1/91; SLJ 12/92) [921]

KEMP, SHAWN

**11048** Thornley, Stew. *Shawn Kemp: Star Forward* (4–6). Series: Sports Reports. 1998, Enslow LB $19.95 (0-89490-929-0). 104pp. An account that stresses this fine basketball player's good character traits and strong athletic abilities. (Rev: BL 2/15/98) [921]

LUCAS, JOHN

**11049** Simmons, Alex. *John Lucas* (4–6). Illus. Series: Contemporary African Americans. 1995, Raintree Steck-Vaughn LB $24.26 (0-8172-3978-2). 48pp. An inspiring story of the man who conquered drug addiction and became the first African American coach of the San Antonio Spurs. (Rev: BL 2/15/96; SLJ 4/96) [921]

MILLER, REGGIE

**11050** Thornley, Stew. *Sports Great Reggie Miller* (5–8). Illus. Series: Sports Great. 1996, Enslow LB $16.95 (0-89490-874-X). 64pp. The life of this basketball star is traced, with special emphasis on key games. (Rev: BL 9/15/96) [921]

MOURNING, ALONZO

**11051** Fortunato, Frank. *Sports Great Alonzo Mourning* (5–8). Illus. Series: Sports Great. 1997, Enslow LB $16.95 (0-89490-875-8). 64pp. An easily read biography of this amazing basketball star. (Rev: BL 2/15/97) [921]

**11052** Gutman, Bill. *Alonzo Mourning: Center of Attention* (4–6). Illus. Series: Sports World. 1997, Millbrook LB $19.90 (0-7613-0061-9). 48pp. This action-filled biography of the basketball star supplies good career statistics. (Rev: BL 4/15/97) [921]

MULLIN, CHRIS

**11053** Morgan, Terri, and Shmuel Thaler. *Chris Mullin: Sure Shot* (4–8). Illus. Series: Sports Achievers. 1994, Lerner LB $10.13 (0-8225-2887-7). 64pp. The story of this amazing basketball star who overcame many obstacles, including alcoholism. (Rev: BL 1/1/95; SLJ 1/95) [921]

O'NEAL, SHAQUILLE

**11054** Macnow, Glen. *Shaquille O'Neal: Star Center* (4–6). Illus. Series: Sports Reports. 1996, Enslow LB $19.95 (0-89490-656-9). 104pp. An account of this pro basketball star, with career statistics and a behind-the-scenes look at his life and interests. (Rev: BL 11/15/96) [921]

**11055** Tallman, Edward. *Shaquille O'Neal* (3–6). Illus. 1994, Silver Burdett $13.95 (0-87518-637-8). 72pp. The life of the NBA star who is also known as an actor and a rap artist. (Rev: BL 2/1/95) [921]

**11056** Townsend, Brad. *Shaquille O'Neal: Center of Attention* (3–5). Illus. Series: Sports Achievers. 1994, Lerner LB $19.95 (0-8225-2879-7); paper $5.95 (0-8225-9655-5). 56pp. This life story tells about O'Neal's childhood, his school basketball career, and his first year in the NBA. (Rev: BL 5/15/94; SLJ 9/94) [921]

**11057** Ungs, Tim. *Shaquille O'Neal* (5–7). Illus. Series: Basketball Legends. 1996, Chelsea LB $15.95 (0-7910-2437-7). 64pp. An interesting portrait of the unstoppable Lakers basketball superstar. (Rev: BL 7/96) [921]

OLAJUWON, HAKEEM

**11058** Gutman, Bill. *Hakeem Olajuwon: Superstar Center* (4–6). Illus. Series: Sports World. 1995, Millbrook LB $19.90 (1-56294-568-8). 64pp. A fast-moving, well-illustrated biography of this basketball star. (Rev: BL 9/15/95; SLJ 1/96) [921]

**11059** McMane, Fred. *Hakeem Olajuwon* (5–7). Series: Basketball Legends. 1997, Chelsea LB $15.95 (0-7910-4385-1). 64pp. The story of this basketball star of the Houston Rockets, his boyhood in Nigeria, and his role as part of the U.S. Olympic "Dream Team." (Rev: BL 9/15/97) [921]

**11060** Rekela, George R. *Hakeem Olajuwon: Tower of Power* (3–6). Illus. Series: Sports Achievers. 1993, Lerner LB $18.60 (0-8225-0518-5); paper $4.95 (0-8225-9637-7). 64pp. The life story of the Nigerian native who changed from soccer to basketball and created an amazing one-game record. (Rev: SLJ 12/93) [921]

**11061** Torres, John A. *Hakeem Olajuwon: Star Center* (4–6). Series: Sports Reports. 1997, Enslow LB $19.95 (0-89490-803-0). 104pp. This biography of the star basketball player also contains career statistics, action photos, and chapter notes. (Rev: BL 11/15/97) [921]

### PIPPEN, SCOTTIE

**11062** Bjarkman, Peter C. *Sports Great Scottie Pippen* (5–8). Illus. Series: Sports Great. 1996, Enslow LB $16.95 (0-89490-755-7). 64pp. Action photos, career statistics, and an account of important games are highlights of this basketball biography. (Rev: BL 9/15/96) [921]

**11063** McMane, Fred. *Scottie Pippen* (5–7). Illus. Series: Basketball Legends. 1996, Chelsea LB $15.95 (0-7910-2498-9). 64pp. The life of this basketball star, highlighting his special abilities and his court record. (Rev: BL 7/96) [921]

**11064** Pippen, Scottie, and Greg Brown. *Reach Higher* (4–7). 1997, Taylor $14.95 (0-87833-981-7). 40pp. The story of the famous Chicago Bulls basketball star, who came from a family of 12 and whose original sports were baseball and football. (Rev: BL 10/1/97) [921]

### ROBINSON, DAVID

**11065** Aaseng, Nathan. *Sports Great David Robinson* (5–8). Illus. Series: Sports Greats. 1992, Enslow LB $16.95 (0-89490-373-X). 64pp. This easily read biography highlights David Robinson of the San Antonio Spurs, the 1990 Rookie of the Year. (Rev: BL 10/15/92) [921]

**11066** Bock, Hal. *David Robinson* (5–7). Series: Basketball Legends. 1997, Chelsea LB $15.95 (0-7910-4387-8). 64pp. The story of this star of the San Antonio Spurs, who was a brilliant student and an officer in the U.S. Navy before turning to professional sports. (Rev: BL 9/15/97) [921]

**11067** Green, Carl R., and Roxanne Ford. *David Robinson* (4–8). Illus. Series: Sports Headliners. 1994, Silver Burdett $13.95 (0-89686-839-7); paper $7.95 (0-382-24808-2). 48pp. A slim biography of this basketball star, who gained fame during the 1987 Navy–Duke game. (Rev: BL 10/1/94) [921]

**11068** Gutman, Bill. *David Robinson: NBA Super Center* (4–6). Illus. Series: Millbrook Sports World. 1993, Millbrook LB $19.90 (1-56294-228-X). 48pp. A brief biography about Robinson's contributions to basketball and his career with the San Antonio Spurs. (Rev: BL 3/15/93) [921]

**11069** Macnow, Glen. *David Robinson: Star Center* (4–6). Illus. Series: Sports Reports. 1994, Enslow LB $19.95 (0-89490-483-3). 104pp. The life of this sports hero who gained fame as an all-pro center for the San Antonio Spurs. (Rev: SLJ 2/95) [921]

**11070** Miller, Dawn M. *David Robinson: Backboard Admiral* (3–5). Illus. Series: The Achievers. 1991, Lerner LB $18.60 (0-8225-0494-4). 64pp. Story of

the basketball star, including his Pan American and Olympic games. (Rev: SLJ 9/91) [921]

### RODMAN, DENNIS

**11071** Thornley, Stew. *Sports Great Dennis Rodman* (5–8). Illus. Series: Sports Great. 1996, Enslow LB $16.95 (0-89490-759-X). 64pp. The life story of this controversial basketball star discusses his often outrageous behavior and his amazing accomplishments. (Rev: BL 31596) [921]

### STOCKTON, JOHN

**11072** Aaseng, Nathan. *Sports Great John Stockton* (5–8). Illus. Series: Sports Great. 1995, Enslow LB $16.95 (0-89490-598-8). 64pp. A short biography of the basketball great John Stockton, with sports action and lively photographs. (Rev: BL 9/15/95) [921]

### THOMAS, ISIAH

**11073** Knapp, Ron. *Sports Great Isiah Thomas* (5–8). Illus. Series: Sports Great Books. 1992, Enslow LB $16.95 (0-89490-374-8). 64pp. Using a standard chronological approach and many photographs, this is an accurate, appealing biography of this great black basketball player. (Rev: BL 9/1/92) [921]

### WEBBER, CHRIS

**11074** Knapp, Ron. *Chris Webber: Star Forward* (4–6). Illus. Series: Sports Reports. 1997, Enslow LB $19.95 (0-89490-799-9). 104pp. Complete with career statistics and action photos, this is the story of the star basketball player and his rise to the top. (Rev: BL 8/97) [921]

### WILKINS, DOMINIQUE

**11075** Bjarkman, Peter C. *Sports Great Dominique Wilkins* (5–8). Illus. Series: Sports Great. 1996, Enslow LB $16.95 (0-89490-754-9). 64pp. The story of this basketball star, with profiles of his most exciting games and career statistics. (Rev: BL 9/15/96) [921]

## Boxing

### ALI, MUHAMMAD

**11076** Conklin, Tim. *Muhammad Ali: The Fight for Respect* (5–8). Illus. Series: New Directions. 1992, Millbrook LB $21.90 (1-56294-112-7). 101pp. A well-documented biography of this boxing great. (Rev: SLJ 4/92) [921]

**11077** Diamond, Arthur. *Muhammad Ali* (4–8). Illus. Series: The Importance Of. 1995, Lucent LB $22.45

(1-56006-060-3). 112pp. The life story of this colorful boxer is outlined, with emphasis on his contributions to the sport of boxing and to the betterment of African Americans. (Rev: BL 1/15/95) [921]

**11078** Sanford, William R., and Carl R. Green. *Muhammad Ali* (4–6). Illus. Series: Sports Immortals. 1993, Macmillan LB $11.95 (0-89686-739-0). 48pp. The story of the boxer who won the heavyweight title 3 times and made headlines for his opinions and for caring for others. (Rev: BL 4/15/93; SLJ 8/93) [921]

### CHAVEZ, JULIO CESAR

**11079** Dolan, Terrance. *Julio Cesar Chavez* (5–8). Illus. Series: Hispanics of Achievement. 1994, Chelsea LB $19.95 (0-7910-2021-5). 128pp. A biography of the fighting boxer and his struggle to get to the top. (Rev: BL 9/15/94) [921]

# Football

### AIKMAN, TROY

**11080** Gutman, Bill. *Troy Aikman: Super Quarterback* (4–6). Illus. Series: Sports World. 1996, Millbrook LB $19.90 (1-56294-570-X). 48pp. A colorful biography that tells about the life, talent, and drive of this football hero. (Rev: BL 5/15/96; SLJ 6/96) [921]

**11081** Macnow, Glen. *Sports Great Troy Aikman* (5–8). Illus. Series: Sports Great. 1995, Enslow LB $16.95 (0-89490-593-7). 64pp. The life story of the football great Troy Aikman, with good action photographs and sports statistics. (Rev: BL 9/15/95) [921]

**11082** Spiros, Dean. *Troy Aikman: Star Quarterback* (4–6). Series: Sports Reports. 1997, Enslow LB $19.95 (0-89490-927-4). 104pp. An in-depth look at this star quarterback, with career statistics, action photos, and a behind-the-scenes look at this colorful player. (Rev: BL 12/15/97) [921]

### BETTIS, JEROME

**11083** Majewski, Stephen. *Sports Great Jerome Bettis* (5–8). Illus. Series: Sports Great. 1997, Enslow LB $16.95 (0-89490-872-3). 64pp. The great football hero Jerome Bettis is highlighted in this easily read biography. (Rev: BL 2/15/97) [921]

### BRYANT, PAUL W.

**11084** Smith, E. S. *Bear Bryant: Football's Winning Coach* (6–8). Illus. 1984, Walker $11.95 (0-8027-6526-2). 128pp. The story of one of the most famous coaches in football history.

### ESIASON, BOOMER

**11085** Esiason, Boomer. *A Boy Named Boomer* (1–2). Illus. by Jacqueline Rogers. 1995, Scholastic paper $3.50 (0-590-52835-1). 46pp. Boomer Esiason, a former NFL quarterback, recalls several incidents from his childhood in this easy reader. (Rev: BL 1/1–15/96; SLJ 3/96) [921]

### FAVRE, BRETT

**11086** Mooney, Martin. *Brett Favre* (5–7). Illus. Series: Football Legends. 1997, Chelsea LB $15.95 (0-7910-4396-7). 64pp. The story of the famous quarterback who took the Green Bay Packers to victory in the 1997 Super Bowl. (Rev: BL 1/1–15/98) [921]

**11087** Savage, Jeff. *Sports Great Brett Favre* (5–8). Series: Sports Greats. 1998, Enslow LB $16.95 (0-7660-1000-7). 64pp. An exciting biography of the star quarterback of the Green Bay Packers. (Rev: BL 3/15/98) [921]

### JACKSON, BO

**11088** Gutman, Bill. *Bo Jackson: A Biography* (4–7). Illus. 1991, Pocket paper $2.99 (0-671-73363-X). 120pp. This account covers such topics as Jackson's winning the Heisman trophy and recent injuries. (Rev: BL 6/15/91) [921]

**11089** Knapp, Ron. *Sports Great Bo Jackson* (5–8). Illus. Series: Sports Great Books. 1990, Enslow LB $16.95 (0-89490-281-4). 64pp. A standard biography that includes unexpected aspects of Jackson's personality. (Rev: BL 10/15/90; SLJ 3/91) [921]

### KELLY, JIM

**11090** Harrington, Denis J. *Sports Great Jim Kelly* (5–8). Illus. Series: Sports Great. 1996, Enslow LB $16.95 (0-89490-670-4). 64pp. A short, action-filled biography of this former star quarterback, complete with career statistics. (Rev: BL 3/15/96) [921]

### MONTANA, JOE

**11091** Kavanagh, Jack. *Sports Great Joe Montana* (4–8). Illus. Series: Sports Great Books. 1992, Enslow LB $16.95 (0-89490-371-3). 64pp. In simple text, this is the story of the quarterback who led his San Francisco 49ers to 4 Super Bowl championships. (Rev: BL 7/92; SLJ 10/92) [921]

**11092** Raber, Thomas R. *Joe Montana: Comeback Quarterback* (4–6). Illus. 1989, Lerner LB $18.60 (0-8225-0486-3). 64pp. A career-oriented biography of the great pro quarterback. (Rev: BL 12/1/89; SLJ 1/90) [921]

## NAMATH, JOE

**11093** Sanford, William R., and Carl R. Green. *Joe Namath* (4–6). Illus. Series: Sports Immortals. 1993, Macmillan LB $11.95 (0-89686-782-X). 48pp. The life and career of this remarkable football player is told using many black-and-white photos, trivia questions, and a concise text. (Rev: BL 10/1/93) [921]

## RICE, JERRY

**11094** Dickey, Glenn. *Jerry Rice* (5–8). Illus. Series: Sports Great. 1993, Enslow LB $16.95 (0-89490-419-1). 64pp. A brief biography of the star football player who gained fame with the San Francisco 49ers. (Rev: BL 9/15/93) [921]

**11095** Thornley, Stew. *Jerry Rice: Star Wide Receiver* (4–6). Series: Sports Reports. 1998, Enslow LB $19.95 (0-89490-928-2). 104pp. A biography of the football player for the San Francisco 49ers that tells about both his athletic abilities and his good character traits. (Rev: BL 2/15/98) [921]

## SANDERS, BARRY

**11096** Aaseng, Nathan. *Barry Sanders: Star Running Back* (4–7). Illus. Series: Sports Reports. 1994, Enslow LB $19.95 (0-89490-484-1). 104pp. This biography of the football star of the Detroit Lions contains many quotes about him from his associates. (Rev: SLJ 8/94) [921]

**11097** Gutman, Bill. *Barry Sanders: Football's Rushing Champ* (4–6). Illus. Series: Millbrook Sports World. 1993, Millbrook LB $19.90 (1-56294-227-1). 48pp. The life and career of one of the stars of the Detroit Lions. (Rev: BL 3/15/93) [921]

**11098** Knapp, Ron. *Barry Sanders* (5–8). Illus. Series: Sports Great. 1993, Enslow LB $16.95 (0-89490-418-3). 64pp. This brief biography of the star football player contains many action photos and a separate section on his career statistics. (Rev: BL 9/15/93) [921]

## SANDERS, DEION

**11099** Savage, Jeff. *Deion Sanders: Star Athlete* (4–6). Illus. Series: Sports Reports. 1996, Enslow LB $19.95 (0-89490-652-6). 104pp. An in-depth look at this football hero, with black-and-white photos. (Rev: BL 4/15/96) [921]

## SEAU, JUNIOR

**11100** Morgan, Terri. *Junior Seau: High-Voltage Linebacker* (4–8). Illus. Series: Sports Achievers. 1996, Lerner $14.96 (0-8225-2896-7); paper $5.95 (0-8225-9746-2). 56pp. This biography traces Junior Seau's career in football and highlights his important games. (Rev: BL 12/15/96) [921]

**11101** Savage, Jeff. *Junior Seau: Star Linebacker* (4–6). Illus. Series: Sports Reports. 1997, Enslow LB $19.95 (0-89490-800-6). 104pp. A biography of this famous football player, complete with career statistics and action photos. (Rev: BL 8/97) [921]

## SMITH, EMMITT

**11102** Savage, Jeff. *Emmitt Smith: Star Running Back* (4–6). Illus. Series: Sports Reports. 1996, Enslow LB $19.95 (0-89490-653-4). 104pp. The professional life of one of the stars of the Dallas Cowboys is highlighted in this biography, which also covers Smith's childhood and character traits. (Rev: BL 4/15/96) [921]

**11103** Thornley, Stew. *Emmitt Smith: Relentless Rusher* (4–8). Illus. Series: Sports Achievers. 1997, Lerner LB $19.93 (0-8225-2897-5). 64pp. This biography of the famous football star also contains career statistics and many action photos. (Rev: BL 4/15/97; SLJ 8/97) [921]

## THOMAS, THURMAN

**11104** Savage, Jeff. *Thurman Thomas: Star Running Back* (4–7). Illus. Series: Sports Reports. 1994, Enslow LB $19.95 (0-89490-445-0). 104pp. This life story of the football hero also contains action photos, fact boxes, and professional-career statistics. (Rev: SLJ 8/94) [921]

## WALKER, HERSCHEL

**11105** Benagh, Jim. *Sports Great Herschel Walker* (5–8). Illus. Series: Sports Great Books. 1990, Enslow LB $16.95 (0-89490-207-5). 64pp. This account tells how Walker grew up in Georgia and went on to a career in professional football. (Rev: BL 10/15/90; SLJ 3/91) [921]

## YOUNG, STEVE

**11106** Christopher, Matt. *In the Huddle with . . . Steve Young* (3–7). Illus. Series: Matt Christopher Sports Biography. 1996, Little, Brown paper $4.50 (0-316-13793-6). 144pp. A solid biography of this gridiron hero whose self-determination led to stardom. (Rev: BL 2/15/97; SLJ 2/97) [921]

**11107** Gutman, Bill. *Steve Young: NFL Passing Wizard* (3–6). Illus. Series: Sports World. 1996, Millbrook LB $19.90 (1-56294-184-4); paper $6.95 (0-7613-0134-8). 48pp. An absorbing biography that describes Young's career at Brigham Young University, his short stint with the Tampa Bay Buccaneers, and his career as quarterback with the San Francisco 49ers. (Rev: SLJ 2/97) [921]

**11108** Knapp, Ron. *Steve Young: Star Quarterback* (4–6). Illus. Series: Sports Reports. 1996, Enslow LB $19.95 (0-89490-654-2). 104pp. A profile of the San

Francisco 49ers quarterback, his professional career, character traits, and outside interests. (Rev: BL 4/15/96) [921]

**11109** Morgan, Terri, and Shmuel Thaler. *Steve Young: Complete Quarterback* (4–8). Illus. Series: Sports Achievers. 1995, Lerner LB $19.95 (0-8225-2886-X); paper $5.95 (0-8225-9716-0). 64pp. A short, easy-to-read biography of the star quarterback Steve Young, with a color photograph and career statistics. (Rev: BL 11/15/95) [921]

# Tennis

## AGASSI, ANDRE

**11110** Christopher, Matt. *On the Court with . . . Andre Agassi* (3–6). Illus. 1997, Little, Brown paper $4.50 (0-316-14202-6). 120pp. This biography begins with Agassi's childhood and ends in 1996, when he won the gold medal at the Summer Olympics. (Rev: SLJ 12/97) [921]

**11111** Knapp, Ron. *Andre Agassi: Star Tennis Player* (4–6). Illus. Series: Sports Reports. 1997, Enslow LB $19.95 (0-89490-798-0). 104pp. An in-depth look at the life and career of this amazing tennis star. (Rev: BL 8/97; SLJ 8/97) [921]

**11112** Rambeck, Richard. *Andre Agassi* (2–5). Illus. Series: Sports Superstars. 1995, Child's World LB $21.36 (1-56766-202-1). 23pp. A simple biography of this flamboyant tennis star that covers his accomplishments and career highlights. (Rev: SLJ 4/96) [921]

**11113** Savage, Jeff. *Andre Agassi: Reaching the Top — Again* (4–8). Series: Sports Achievers. 1997, Lerner LB $19.93 (0-8225-2894-0); paper $5.95 (0-8225-9750-0). 64pp. A short, easily read biography of this volatile tennis star. (Rev: BL 1/1–15/98) [921]

## ASHE, ARTHUR

**11114** Dexter, Robin. *Young Arthur Ashe: Brave Champion* (2–4). Illus. by R. W. Alley. Series: First Start Biography. 1996, Troll paper $3.50 (0-8167-3773-8). 32pp. The life and death of this courageous tennis champion are dealt with in simple text and numerous color illustrations. (Rev: BL 2/15/96) [921]

**11115** Wright, David K. *Arthur Ashe: Breaking the Color Barrier in Tennis* (4–7). Illus. Series: African-American Biographies. 1996, Enslow LB $19.95 (0-89490-689-5). 128pp. The story of the groundbreaking tennis star and his battle with AIDS. (Rev: SLJ 10/96) [921]

## GARRISON, ZINA

**11116** Porter, A. P. *Zina Garrison: Ace* (4–6). Series: Sports Achievers. 1992, Lerner LB $19.95 (0-8225-0499-5); paper $4.95 (0-8225-9596-6). 64pp. The life of the tennis star who became the first African American to play a singles final at famed Wimbledon, England. (Rev: BCCB 6/92; BL 12/15/92) [921]

## KING, BILLIE JEAN

**11117** Sanford, William R., and Carl R. Green. *Billie Jean King* (4–6). Illus. Series: Sports Immortals. 1993, Macmillan LB $11.95 (0-89686-781-1). 48pp. Illustrated with many black-and-white photos, this slim biography of tennis star Billie Jean King also contains several trivia questions. (Rev: BL 10/1/93) [921]

## SAMPRAS, PETE

**11118** Rambeck, Richard. *Pete Sampras* (2–5). Illus. 1996, Child's World LB $21.36 (1-56766-262-5). 23pp. A very brief biography, with more photos than text, about this tennis wonder. (Rev: SLJ 6/97) [921]

**11119** Sherrow, Victoria. *Sports Great Pete Sampras* (5–8). Illus. Series: Sports Great. 1996, Enslow LB $16.95 (0-89490-756-5). 64pp. The story of this amazing tennis star, his accomplishments, and his career statistics, with a number of black-and-white photos. (Rev: BL 3/15/96) [921]

## SELES, MONICA

**11120** Rambeck, Richard. *Monica Seles* (2–5). Illus. 1996, Child's World LB $21.36 (1-56766-312-5). 23pp. A short biography of the tennis star, with coverage on her tragic stabbing and her comeback. (Rev: SLJ 6/97) [921]

# Track and Field

## DEVERS, GAIL

**11121** Gutman, Bill. *Gail Devers* (3–6). Illus. Series: Overcoming the Odds. 1996, Raintree Steck-Vaughn LB $24.26 (0-8172-4122-1). 48pp. The story of this track star who was largely self-trained, her childhood in San Diego, and her participation in the 1993 World Championships. (Rev: SLJ 11/96) [921]

## JOYNER, FLORENCE GRIFFITH

**11122** Aaseng, Nathan. *Florence Griffith Joyner: Dazzling Olympian* (4–6). Illus. Series: Sports Achievers. 1989, Lerner LB $18.60 (0-8225-0495-2); paper $4.95 (0-8225-9587-7). 56pp. A profile of this gold medalist in the 1988 Summer Olympics. (Rev: BCCB 1/90; BL 12/15/89; SLJ 3/90) [921]

**11123** Koral, April. *Florence Griffith Joyner: Track and Field Star* (3–5). Illus. Series: First Books. 1992, Watts LB $22.00 (0-531-20061-2). 64pp. The life and career of this great athlete who won 4 gold medals in the 1988 Olympics. (Rev: BL 10/1/92; SLJ 8/92) [921]

JOYNER-KERSEE, JACKIE

**11124** Cohen, Neil. *Jackie Joyner-Kersee* (3–7). Illus. 1992, Sports Illustrated for Kids paper $4.95 (0-316-15047-9). 124pp. From East Saint Louis to 2 gold medals in the 1988 Olympics, the inspiring story of a great athlete. (Rev: BL 8/92; SLJ 7/92) [921]

**11125** Goldstein, Margaret J., and Jennifer Larson. *Jackie Joyner-Kersee: Superwoman* (3–5). Illus. Series: Sports Achievers. 1994, Lerner LB $18.60 (0-8225-0524-X); paper $4.95 (0-8225-9653-9). 56pp. The story of this famous track star's youth in Illinois, her training, and her Olympic successes. (Rev: BL 5/15/94; SLJ 9/94) [921]

**11126** Green, Carl R. *Jackie Joyner-Kersee* (4–8). Illus. Series: Sports Headliners. 1994, Macmillan LB $13.95 (0-89686-838-9). 48pp. This biography of the African American track and field star highlights her winning the 1986 heptathlon at the Goodwill Games. (Rev: BL 10/1/94) [921]

LEWIS, CARL

**11127** Aaseng, Nathan. *Carl Lewis: Legend Chaser* (4–8). Illus. 1985, Lerner LB $18.60 (0-8225-0496-0). 56pp. Childhood, college, and Olympic performances are covered in this biography, including both praise and criticism about Lewis's attempt at the long-jump record. (Rev: BCCB 11/85; BL 7/85; SLJ 8/85)

OWENS, JESSE

**11128** Adler, David A. *A Picture Book of Jesse Owens* (K–3). Illus. by Robert Casilla. Series: Picture Book Biography. 1992, Holiday LB $15.95 (0-8234-0966-X); paper $5.95 (0-8234-1066-8). 32pp. Relying heavily on illustrations to supply details, this is an introduction to the famous track and field star. (Rev: BL 11/15/92; SLJ 12/92) [921]

**11129** McKissack, Patricia, and Fredrick McKissack. *Jesse Owens: Olympic Star* (2–4). Illus. by Michael D. Blegel. Series: Great African Americans. 1992, Enslow LB $13.95 (0-89490-312-8). 32pp. The story of the black athlete whose 4 gold medals in the 1936 Olympics embarrassed Hitler. (Rev: BL 10/15/92; SLJ 1/93) [921]

**11130** Rennert, Rick. *Jesse Owens* (4–7). Illus. Series: Junior World Biographies. 1991, Chelsea LB $12.95 (0-7910-1570-X). 80pp. An attractive, well-illustrated account of this famous track and field star

who embarrassed Hitler by winning 4 gold medals at the 1936 Olympic Games. (Rev: BL 9/1/91; SLJ 9/91) [921]

**11131** Sanford, William R., and Carl R. Green. *Jesse Owens* (4–6). Illus. Series: Sports Immortals. 1992, Macmillan LB $11.95 (0-89686-742-0). 48pp. A biography of the outstanding track and field athlete who helped break the color barrier in sports. (Rev: BL 2/1/93; SLJ 1/93) [921]

RUDOLPH, WILMA

**11132** Krull, Kathleen. *Wilma Unlimited: How Wilma Rudolph Became the World's Fastest Woman* (2–5). Illus. by David Diaz. 1996, Harcourt $16.00 (0-15-201267-2). 48pp. A biography of the amazing Wilma Rudolph, who overcame incredible obstacles to become a track star. (Rev: BL 5/1/96*; HB 9–10/96; SLJ 6/96*) [921]

**11133** Sherrow, Victoria. *Wilma Rudolph: Olympic Champion* (4–6). Illus. Series: Junior World Biographies. 1995, Chelsea LB $15.95 (0-7910-2290-0). 79pp. The life of this great track star and of the poverty, bad health, and emotional challenges she faced and overcame in her desire to succeed. (Rev: BCCB 4/96; SLJ 8/95) [921]

THORPE, JIM

**11134** Coffey, Wayne. *Jim Thorpe* (3–6). Illus. by David Taylor. Series: Olympic Gold! 1993, Blackbirch LB $15.95 (1-56711-005-3). 64pp. This biography of the great sports hero describes Thorpe being stripped of his Olympic medals and his later problems, including alcoholism. (Rev: SLJ 9/93) [921]

**11135** Lipsyte, Robert. *Jim Thorpe: 20th-Century Jock* (4–8). Illus. 1993, HarperCollins LB $13.89 (0-06-022989-6). 103pp. The story of Jim Thorpe, the Native American who suffered from racial discrimination but triumphed at the Olympics. (Rev: BL 2/1/94; SLJ 5/94) [921]

**11136** Long, Barbara. *Jim Thorpe: Legendary Athlete* (5–7). Illus. Series: Native American Biographies. 1997, Enslow LB $19.95 (0-89490-865-0). 128pp. The story of the Amazing Native American athlete whose career had tremendous highs and lows. (Rev: BL 6/1–15/97) [921]

**11137** Nardo, Don. *Jim Thorpe* (4–8). Illus. Series: The Importance Of. 1994, Lucent LB $22.45 (1-56006-045-X). 95pp. The biography of the man whom many consider to be the greatest all-around athlete that the United States has produced. (Rev: BL 8/94) [921]

**11138** Rivinus, Edward F. *Jim Thorpe* (3–5). Illus. by Robert Masheris. Series: American Indian Stories. 1990, Raintree Steck-Vaughn LB $21.40 (0-8172-3403-9). 32pp. The story of the Native American who excelled in a number of sports. (Rev: SLJ 10/90) [921]

**11139** Sanford, William R., and Carl R. Green. *Jim Thorpe* (4–6). Illus. Series: Sports Immortals. 1992, Macmillan LB $11.95 (0-89686-740-4). 48pp. This biography of the multitalented Native American is enhanced by many photos. (Rev: BL 2/1/93; SLJ 1/93) [921]

**11140** Santrey, Laurence. *Jim Thorpe: Young Athlete* (4–6). Illus. 1983, Troll LB $12.95 (0-89375-845-0); paper $3.95 (0-89375-846-9). 48pp. An account that details his Indian heritage and his emerging athletic abilities.

---

# Miscellaneous Sports

### BAIUL, OKSANA

**11141** Baiul, Oksana. *Oksana: My Own Story* (4–6). Illus. 1997, Random $16.99 (0-679-88382-7). 46pp. An autobiography of the figure-skating champion who won the Olympic gold medal in 1994. (Rev: BL 5/1/97; SLJ 5/97) [921]

### BLAIR, BONNIE

**11142** Blair, Bonnie, and Greg Brown. *A Winning Edge* (3–5). Illus. 1996, Taylor $14.95 (0-87833-931-0). 40pp. The autobiography of the Olympic medal-winning speed skater, with insights into her life off the ice. (Rev: BL 5/15/96) [921]

**11143** Breitenbucher, Cathy. *Bonnie Blair: Golden Streak* (4–8). Illus. Series: Sports Achievers. 1994, Lerner LB $19.93 (0-8225-2883-5). 64pp. A worthy biography of the U.S. speed skater and winner of many Olympic medals. (Rev: BL 1/1/95; SLJ 1/95) [921]

**11144** Rambeck, Richard. *Bonnie Blair* (2–5). Illus. Series: Sports Superstars. 1995, Child's World LB $21.36 (1-56766-186-6). 23pp. A simple biography of this speed skater that focuses on her quiet determination and career accomplishments. (Rev: SLJ 4/96) [921]

### BOITANO, BRIAN

**11145** Boitano, Brian, and Suzanne Harper. *Boitano's Edge: Inside the Real World of Figure Skating* (4–8). Illus. 1997, Simon & Schuster paper $25.00 (0-689-81915-3). 144pp. In this autobiography, Boitano tells about his life, the 1988 Olympics, his training program, touring, and his preparation for competitions. (Rev: BL 2/15/98; SLJ 4/98) [921]

### BUTCHER, SUSAN

**11146** Wadsworth, Ginger. *Susan Butcher: Sled Dog Racer* (4–7). Illus. Series: Sports Achievers. 1994, Lerner LB $18.60 (0-8225-2878-9). 63pp. This exciting biography brings to life the 4-time Iditarod winner and the rigors and courage each race involved. (Rev: SLJ 6/94) [921]

### EL CHINO

**11147** Say, Allen. *El Chino* (3–6). Illus. 1990, Houghton $14.95 (0-395-52023-1). 32pp. The first-person narrative of a Chinese-American civil engineer who becomes a matador. (Rev: BCCB 9/90*; BL 9/1/90*; HB 1–2/91; SLJ 11/90) [921]

### GRETZKY, WAYNE

**11148** Christopher, Matt. *On the Ice with . . . Wayne Gretzky* (3–7). Illus. Series: Matt Christopher Sports Biography. 1996, Little, Brown paper $4.50 (0-316-13789-8). 144pp. The life story of this hockey superstar details both the highs and lows of his career. (Rev: BL 2/15/97) [921]

**11149** Fortunato, Frank. *Wayne Gretzky: Star Center* (4–6). Series: Sports Reports. 1998, Enslow LB $19.95 (0-89490-930-4). 104pp. An in-depth look at the life and career of this amazing hockey player. (Rev: BL 2/15/98) [921]

**11150** Rappoport, Ken. *Sports Great Wayne Gretzky* (5–8). Illus. Series: Sports Great. 1996, Enslow LB $16.95 (0-89490-757-3). 64pp. A brief biography of this hockey phenomenon, illustrated with black-and-white action photos. (Rev: BL 3/15/96) [921]

### HAMILL, DOROTHY

**11151** Sanford, William R., and Carl R. Green. *Dorothy Hamill* (4–6). Illus. Series: Sports Immortals. 1993, Macmillan LB $11.95 (0-89686-799-X). 48pp. The life and career of this remarkable ice skater is told in this slim volume filled with many black-and-white photos. (Rev: BL 10/1/93) [921]

### HULL, BRETT

**11152** Goldstein, Margaret J. *Brett Hull: Hockey's Top Gun* (3–6). 1992, Lerner LB $18.60 (0-8225-0544-4); paper $4.95 (0-8225-9599-0). 48pp. A behind-the-scenes look at the St. Louis Blues' star scorer. (Rev: BCCB 7–8/92; SLJ 10/92) [921]

### KERRIGAN, NANCY

**11153** Morrissette, Mikki. *Nancy Kerrigan: Heart of a Champion* (4–7). Illus. 1994, Bantam paper $3.99 (0-553-48254-8). 100pp. This book on the life of the figure skater was published before she won a silver medal at the Olympics. (Rev: BL 5/1/94) [921]

## KRONE, JULIE

**11154** Callahan, Dorothy. *Julie Krone: A Winning Jockey* (4–6). Illus. 1990, Macmillan LB $13.95 (0-87518-425-1). 64pp. A biography of the woman who became the leading female jockey at the age of 25. (Rev: BCCB 9/90; BL 7/90; SLJ 9/90) [921]

**11155** Gutman, Bill. *Julie Krone* (3–6). Illus. Series: Overcoming the Odds. 1996, Raintree Steck-Vaughn LB $24.26 (0-8172-4121-3). 48pp. An absorbing biography of this female jockey, her participation in more than 16,000 races, and the 1993 accident that left her seriously injured. (Rev: SLJ 2/97) [921]

**11156** Savage, Jeff. *Julie Krone, Unstoppable Jockey* (2–5). Illus. 1996, Lerner LB $19.93 (0-8225-2888-6). 56pp. The story of a top female jockey and her unique accomplishments. (Rev: BL 8/96; SLJ 9/96) [921]

## KWAN, MICHELLE

**11157** James, Laura. *Michelle Kwan: Heart of a Champion* (4–8). Illus. 1997, Scholastic $14.95 (0-590-76340-7). 176pp. A highly personal account of this figure-skating champion's life and feelings that shows a maturity beyond her years. (Rev: BL 11/15/97; SLJ 11/97) [921]

## LEMIEUX, MARIO

**11158** Hughes, Morgan E. *Mario Lemieux: Beating the Odds* (4–6). Illus. Series: Sports Achievers. 1996, Lerner LB $19.93 (0-8225-2884-3); paper $5.95 (0-8225-9717-9). 64pp. A biography of the star hockey player, with a section on career statistics. (Rev: SLJ 9/96) [921]

## LEMOND, GREG

**11159** Porter, A. P. *Greg LeMond: Premier Cyclist* (4–7). Illus. Series: Sports Achievers. 1990, Lerner LB $18.60 (0-8225-0476-6). 64pp. Although he suffered severe injuries in a hunting accident, LeMond won the Tour de France bicycle race. (Rev: BL 6/15/90; SLJ 9/90) [921]

## LINDROS, ERIC

**11160** Rappoport, Ken. *Sports Great Eric Lindros* (5–8). Series: Sports Great. 1997, Enslow LB $16.95 (0-89490-871-5). 64pp. A biography of the famous hockey star that includes career statistics and several action photos. (Rev: BL 10/15/97) [921]

## LIPINSKI, TARA

**11161** Lipinski, Tara, and Emily Costello. *Triumph on Ice* (4–6). Illus. 1997, Bantam $15.95 (0-553-09775-X). 116pp. The life story of the famous ath-

lete, from her childhood in New Jersey to winning both the U.S. and world figure-skating championship in 1997. (Rev: BL 1/1–15/98; SLJ 4/98) [921]

## LOUIS, JOE

**11162** Campbell, Jim. *Joe Louis* (4–8). Illus. Series: Importance Of. 1997, Lucent LB $22.45 (1-56006-085-9). 128pp. The fabulous life and career of the Brown Bomber are traced, with emphasis on his lasting contributions to boxing and his race. (Rev: BL 5/15/97) [921]

## MESSIER, MARK

**11163** Sullivan, Michael J. *Mark Messier: Star Center* (4–6). Series: Sports Reports. 1997, Enslow LB $19.95 (0-89490-801-4). 104pp. This biography of Messier contains career statistics, action photos, and a behind-the-scenes look at this hockey star. (Rev: BL 12/15/97) [921]

## MILLER, SHANNON

**11164** Green, Septima. *Shannon Miller: American Gymnast from Girlhood Dreams to Olympic Glory* (3–5). Illus. Series: Going for the Gold. 1996, Avon paper $4.50 (0-380-78680-X). 86pp. A simple biography of the famous gymnast that tells of her setbacks and accomplishments. (Rev: SLJ 8/96) [921]

## MOCEANU, DOMINIQUE

**11165** Quiner, Krista. *Dominique Moceanu: A Gymnastics Sensation* (4–7). Illus. 1997, Bradford paper $12.95 (0-9643460-3-6). 191pp. The story of the United States' youngest gold-medal winner in gymnastics, with a special 24-page insert of photos. (Rev: SLJ 3/97) [921]

## PELE

**11166** Arnold, Caroline. *Pele: The King of Soccer* (4–8). Illus. Series: First Books. 1992, Watts LB $21.00 (0-531-20077-9). 64pp. The career of one of the world's greatest soccer players is traced from early promise to superstar. (Rev: BL 10/1/92) [921]

## SIFFORD, CHARLIE

**11167** Britt, Grant. *Charlie Sifford* (4–7). Illus. 1998, Morgan Reynolds LB $17.95 (1-883846-27-7). 64pp. This biography of the African American golfer stresses the problems he faced breaking the color barrier when he entered the sport after World War II. (Rev: BL 2/15/98) [921]

## WITT, KATARINA

**11168** Coffey, Wayne. *Katarina Witt* (4–7). Illus. 1992, Blackbirch LB $15.95 (1-56711-001-0). 64pp. This biography highlights the 1988 Olympic Games, where this figure skater became a star. (Rev: SLJ 11/92) [921]

## WOODS, TIGER

**11169** Boyd, Aaron. *Tiger Woods* (5–7). Illus. 1997, Morgan Reynolds LB $17.95 (1-883846-19-6). 64pp. A brief, straightforward biography of this amazing golfer who was a prodigy. (Rev: BL 5/1/97; SLJ 8/97) [921]

**11170** Teague, Allison L. *Prince of the Fairway: The Tiger Woods Story* (4–7). Illus. 1997, Avisson LB $18.50 (1-888105-22-4). 106pp. A biography that emphasizes the wholesome behavioral traits of this golf phenomenon, the youngest professional player to win the Masters Tournament in Augusta, Georgia. (Rev: SLJ 10/97) [921]

## YAMAGUCHI, KRISTI

**11171** Donohue, Shiobhan. *Kristi Yamaguchi: Artist on Ice* (3–6). Illus. 1993, Lerner LB $18.60 (0-8225-0522-3). 64pp. A biography of the figure skater that stresses her dedication and hard work. (Rev: BL 2/15/94; SLJ 3/94) [921]

**11172** Savage, Jeff. *Kristi Yamaguchi* (3–6). Illus. Series: Taking Part. 1993, Dillon LB $13.95 (0-87518-583-5). 64pp. A biography of the Japanese American ice skater and her triumph at the Olympic Games. (Rev: BL 10/15/93; SLJ 2/94) [921]

## ZAHARIAS, BABE DIDRIKSON

**11173** Sanford, William R., and Carl R. Green. *Babe Didrikson Zaharias* (4–6). Illus. Series: Sports Immortals. 1993, Macmillan LB $11.95 (0-89686-736-6). 48pp. The story of the amazing woman who excelled in basketball, baseball, and track and who won 2 gold medals at the 1932 Summer Olympics. (Rev: BL 4/15/93; SLJ 8/93) [921]

# World Figures

## Collective

**11174** Aaseng, Nathan. *The Peace Seekers: The Nobel Peace Prize* (5–8). Illus. 1987, Lerner LB $18.60 (0-8225-0654-8); paper $5.95 (0-8225-9604-0). 80pp. Martin Luther King, Jr., and Lech Walesa are among those whose lives and works are introduced. (Rev: BL 2/1/88)

**11175** Blue, Rose, and Corinne J. Naden. *People of Peace* (4–7). Illus. 1994, Millbrook LB $25.90 (1-56294-409-6). 80pp. Brief biographies of 10 people in modern history who have made great sacrifices for world peace, including Mohandas Gandhi and Desmond Tutu. (Rev: BL 12/15/94; SLJ 2/95) [920]

**11176** Harris, Laurie L., ed. *Biography Today: Profiles of People of Interest to Young Readers* (4–7). Illus. Series: Scientists and Inventors. 1996, Omnigraphics LB $36.00 (0-7808-0068-0). 194pp. Profiles of 14 important contemporaries like Carl Sagan and Jane Goodall with some lesser-known figures like geneticist and AIDS fighter Mathilde Krim. (Rev: SLJ 2/97) [920]

**11177** Hazell, Rebecca. *Heroes: Great Men Through the Ages* (4–6). Illus. 1997, Abbeville $19.95 (0-7892-0289-1). 80pp. From Socrates to Martin Luther King, Jr., this collection of 12 biographies of famous men also includes Shakespeare, Mozart, Leonardo da Vinci, and Jorge Luis Borges. (Rev: BL 7/97; HB 5–6/97; SLJ 6/97) [920]

**11178** Hoobler, Dorothy, and Thomas Hoobler. *South American Portraits* (5–8). Illus. by Stephen Marchesi. Series: Images Across the Ages. 1994, Raintree Steck-Vaughn LB $27.11 (0-8114-6383-4). 96pp. Profiles of 12 important South Americans past and present, including Simón Bolívar, Eva Perón,

Pel, and Gabriel García Márquez. (Rev: SLJ 8/94) [920]

**11179** Leon, Vicki. *Outrageous Women of Ancient Times* (4–7). Illus. 1997, Wiley paper $12.95 (0-471-17006-2). 128pp. Fifteen unusual women from ancient cultures in Europe, Asia, and Africa are profiled, including Cleopatra and Sappho. (Rev: BL 11/1/97; SLJ 12/97) [920]

**11180** Marzollo, Jean. *My First Book of Biographies: Great Men and Women Every Child Should Know* (2–4). Illus. by Irene Trivas. 1994, Scholastic $14.95 (0-590-45014-X). 80pp. Brief profiles of 45 famous people whom youngsters have heard about, from Cleopatra to Beatrix Potter. (Rev: BL 12/1/94; SLJ 9/94) [920]

**11181** Pollard, Michael. *People Who Care* (4–6). Series: Pioneers in History. 1992, Garrett LB $19.93 (1-56074-035-3). 48pp. Nineteen individuals who devoted their lives to helping others are profiled in this book. People who participated in revolutions are covered in *Revolutionary Power* (1992) and great philosophers in *Thinkers* (1992). (Rev: SLJ 9/92) [920]

**11182** Schraff, Anne. *Women of Peace: Nobel Peace Prize Winners* (5–8). Illus. 1994, Enslow LB $19.95 (0-89490-493-0). 112pp. Biographies of the 8 women who have won the Nobel Peace Prize, including Jane Addams and Mother Teresa. (Rev: BL 1/1/95; SLJ 9/94) [920]

**11183** Sullivan, George. *In the Line of Fire* (3–6). Illus. 1996, Scholastic paper $3.99 (0-590-48294-7). 118pp. From the American Revolution through World War II, the stories of 8 female spies are retold. (Rev: BL 6/1–15/96) [920]

**11184** Wilkinson, Philip, and Jacqueline Dineen. *People Who Changed the World* (3–5). Illus. by Robert Ingpen. Series: Turning Points in History.

1994, Chelsea $19.95 (0-7910-2764-3). 93pp. Includes brief biographies of religious leaders, philosophers, and explorers like Pericles, Jesus Christ, Karl Marx, and Martin Luther King, Jr. Also use *Statesmen Who Changed the World* (1994). (Rev: BL 12/15/94) [920]

**11185** Wilkinson, Philip, and Michael Pollard. *Generals Who Changed the World* (4–6). Illus. by Robert Ingpen. Series: Turning Points in History. 1994, Chelsea LB $19.95 (0-7910-2761-9). 93pp. A profile of 20 important military men and how their accomplishments changed the course of history. (Rev: SLJ 11/94) [920]

# Individual

## ALEXANDER THE GREAT

**11186** Green, Robert. *Alexander the Great* (4–6). Illus. Series: First Books: Ancient Biographies. 1996, Watts LB $22.00 (0-531-20230-5). 64pp. The life, conquests, and legacy of Alexander are well covered. (Rev: BL 7/96; SLJ 9/96) [921]

**11187** Stewart, Gail B. *Alexander the Great* (4–8). Illus. Series: The Importance Of. 1994, Lucent LB $22.45 (1-56006-047-6). 127pp. A brief biography of the conqueror whose great importance lay in introducing the East to Western culture. (Rev: BL 8/94; SLJ 7/94) [921]

## BADEN-POWELL, SIR ROBERT

**11188** Brower, Pauline. *Baden-Powell: Founder of the Boy Scouts* (2–4). Illus. Series: Picture-Story Biographies. 1989, Children's LB $18.20 (0-516-04173-8). 32pp. The life of the man who developed the scouting program for boys in Britain. (Rev: BL 1/15/90; SLJ 3/90) [921]

## BOLIVAR, SIMON

**11189** Adler, David A. *A Picture Book of Simon Bolivar* (3–5). Illus. by Robert Casilla. Series: Picture Book Biography. 1992, Holiday LB $15.95 (0-8234-0927-9). 32pp. A biography of the "George Washington" of many South American nations. (Rev: BL 4/15/92; SLJ 7/92) [921]

**11190** De Varona, Frank. *Simon Bolivar: Latin American Liberator* (3–6). Illus. Series: Hispanic Heritage. 1993, Millbrook LB $19.90 (1-56294-278-6). 32pp. Simon Bolivar, in spite of all odds, led much of South and Central America to overthrow Spanish rule. (Rev: BL 5/15/93; SLJ 7/93) [921]

## BRAILLE, LOUIS

**11191** Adler, David A. *A Picture Book of Louis Braille* (2–4). Illus. by John Wallner and Alexandra

Wallner. Series: Picture Book Biography. 1997, Holiday $16.95 (0-8234-1291-1). 34pp. For young readers, this is a simple, well-illustrated biography that also includes a page of the braille raised-dot alphabet and numbers. (Rev: BL 4/15/97; SLJ 6/97) [921]

**11192** Bryant, Jennifer. *Louis Braille: Inventor* (5–7). Illus. 1994, Chelsea LB $19.95 (0-7910-2077-0). 112pp. This well-researched biography of Braille tells about the horror of his own blindness as well as the development of the alphabet that allows blind people to read. (Rev: BL 7/94; SLJ 8/94) [921]

**11193** Fradin, Dennis B. *Louis Braille: The Blind Boy Who Wanted to Read* (2–4). Illus. 1997, Silver Burdett LB $15.95 (0-382-39468-2); paper $5.95 (0-382-39469-0). 32pp. A picture book biography of the amazing blind Frenchman who invented his famous reading system when he was only 15. (Rev: BL 5/1/97; SLJ 7/97) [921]

**11194** Freedman, Russell. *Out of Darkness: The Story of Louis Braille* (4–8). Illus. 1997, Clarion $15.95 (0-395-77516-7). 81pp. The story of the blind Frenchman who, more than 170 years ago, invented a system of reading using raised dots. (Rev: BCCB 5/97; BL 3/1/97; HB 5–6/97; SLJ 3/97*) [921]

**11195** O'Connor, Barbara. *The World at His Fingertips: A Story About Louis Braille* (3–5). Illus. by Rochelle Draper. Series: Creative Minds Biographies. 1997, Carolrhoda LB $14.95 (1-57505-052-8). 64pp. A fast-paced biography that reveals many interesting facts about this inventor of a writing system for the blind. (Rev: SLJ 10/97) [921]

**11196** Woodhouse, Jayne. *Louis Braille* (2–3). Series: Lives and Times. 1997, Heinemann $12.95 (1-57572-559-2). 24pp. The life and contributions of this famous French blind man are told in this simple picture book biography with a brief text. (Rev: BL 3/15/98) [921]

## CAESAR, JULIUS

**11197** Green, Robert. *Julius Caesar* (5–8). Illus. Series: First Books: Ancient Biographies. 1996, Watts LB $21.00 (0-531-20241-0). 63pp. The story of Caesar's political and military careers, how he expanded the Roman Empire, and his lasting importance. (Rev: SLJ 2/97) [921]

**11198** Nardo, Don. *Julius Caesar* (4–8). Illus. Series: The Importance Of. 1997, Lucent LB $22.45 (1-56006-083-2). 112pp. An introductory biography that stresses the lasting importance of this great leader, who expanded the Roman Empire significantly. (Rev: BL 1/1–15/97) [921]

## CAROLINE, PRINCESS OF MONACO

**11199** Wheeler, Jill C. *Princess Caroline of Monaco* (4–6). Illus. Series: Leading Ladies. 1992, ABDO LB

$13.98 (1-56239-117-8). 32pp. A simple biography of the princess who is the daughter of the late Grace Kelly. (Rev: BL 2/1/93; SLJ 3/93) [921]

### CHARLEMAGNE

**11200** Biel, Timothy. *Charlemagne* (4–8). Illus. Series: Importance Of. 1997, Lucent LB $22.45 (1-56006-074-3). 127pp. The story of the king of the Franks, his empire, and his lasting importance in European history. (Rev: BL 6/1–15/97; SLJ 9/97) [921]

### CHENG, NIEN

**11201** Sommer, Robin L. *Nien Cheng: Prisoner in China* (5–7). Illus. Series: Library of Famous Women. 1993, Rosen LB $15.95 (1-56711-011-8). 64pp. The story of the Chinese woman who influenced the Cultural Revolution and became a political prisoner in her homeland. (Rev: BL 2/15/93) [921]

### CHRISTOPHER, SAINT

**11202** dePaola, Tomie. *Christopher: The Holy Giant* (K–3). Illus. 1994, Holiday LB $16.95 (0-8234-0862-0). 32pp. The story of Saint Christopher and how Jesus gave him that name for his good works. (Rev: BL 5/1/94; HB 5–6/94; SLJ 3/94*) [398.22]

### CHURCHILL, WINSTON

**11203** Driemen, J. E. *Winston Churchill: An Unbreakable Spirit* (5–8). Illus. Series: People in Focus. 1990, Macmillan LB $13.95 (0-87518-434-0). 128pp. A biography of this amazing statesman, leader, and writer. (Rev: SLJ 8/90) [921]

**11204** Severance, John B. *Winston Churchill: Soldier, Statesman, Artist* (5–8). Illus. 1996, Clarion $17.95 (0-395-69853-7). 144pp. A well-organized, clearly written account of the life and works of Britain's great statesman. (Rev: BL 4/15/96; HB 7–8/96; SLJ 4/96*) [921]

### CID, EL

**11205** Koslow, Philip. *El Cid* (5–8). Illus. Series: Hispanics of Achievement. 1993, Chelsea LB $19.95 (0-7910-1239-5). 112pp. The story of Spain's national hero, who gained fame fighting the Moors. (Rev: BL 9/15/93) [921]

### CLEOPATRA

**11206** Green, Robert. *Cleopatra* (4–6). Illus. Series: First Books: Ancient Biographies. 1996, Watts LB $22.00 (0-531-20231-3). 64pp. In a male-dominated world, this Egyptian queen wielded great power, but she lost her kingdom and life in a love affair with Mark Antony. (Rev: BL 7/96; SLJ 9/96) [921]

**11207** Stanley, Diane, and Peter Vennema. *Cleopatra* (3–6). Illus. by Diane Stanley. 1994, Morrow LB $15.93 (0-688-10414-2). 48pp. With stunning illustrations, this biography covers Cleopatra's life from the time she became Queen of Egypt until her death at 39. (Rev: BCCB 10/94; BL 9/15/94*; HB 11–12/94; SLJ 10/94) [921]

### DALAI LAMA

**11208** Demi. *The Dalai Lama* (3–6). Illus. by author. 1998, Holt $16.95 (0-8050-5443-X). This biography of the current, now-exiled, Dalai Lama also supplies details on his functions, mission, and responsibilities. (Rev: SLJ 3/98) [921]

**11209** Stewart, Whitney. *The 14th Dalai Lama: Spiritual Leader of Tibet* (5–8). Illus. Series: Newsmakers. 1996, Lerner LB $17.95 (0-8225-4926-3). 128pp. As well as describing the life and spiritual beliefs of the current Dalai Lama, this account describes the current political situation in Tibet. (Rev: SLJ 6/96) [921]

**11210** Stewart, Whitney. *To the Lion Throne: The Story of the Fourteenth Dalai Lama* (2–6). Illus. 1990, Snow Lion paper $8.95 (0-937938-75-0). 64pp. This is the fascinating biography of the fourteenth Dalai Lama and how he was chosen. (Rev: BL 12/1/90) [921]

### DALOKAY, VEDAT

**11211** Dalokay, Vedat. *Sister Shako and Kolo the Goat: Memories of My Childhood in Turkey* (5–7). Trans. by Guner Ener. 1994, Lothrop $14.00 (0-688-13271-5). 96pp. A memoir by the former mayor of Ankara about growing up Muslim in rural Turkey in the 1930s and of his friendship with an indomitable widow named Sister Shako. (Rev: BCCB 4/94; BL 5/1/94; SLJ 6/94) [921]

### DAVID, KING OF ISRAEL

**11212** Cohen, Barbara. *David: A Biography* (5–8). 1995, Clarion $15.95 (0-395-58702-6). 108pp. Recreates the events in the life of the biblical David, who began as a simple shepherd and ended as a warrior king. (Rev: BCCB 9/95; SLJ 7/95) [921]

### DIANA, PRINCESS OF WALES

**11213** Cerasini, Marc. *Diana: Queen of Hearts* (5–7). Illus. 1997, Random paper $4.99 (0-679-89214-1). 94pp. A breezy, easily read account of the life of this fairy tale princess. (Rev: BL 12/1/97) [921]

**11214** Licata, Renora. *Princess Diana: Royal Ambassador* (4–6). Illus. Series: The Library of Famous Women. 1993, Blackbirch LB $16.95 (1-56711-013-4). 64pp. Princess Diana comes alive in this account that covers her celebrity status and her public service work. (Rev: BL 6/1–15/93; SLJ 8/93) [921]

## ELIZABETH I, QUEEN OF ENGLAND

**11215** Green, Robert. *Queen Elizabeth I* (4–7). Illus. Series: First Book: Monarchs. 1997, Watts LB $21.00 (0-531-20302-6). 64pp. This account of the life of Elizabeth I also includes material on the religious conflicts of the day, her suitors, and the war with Spain. (Rev: BL 2/1/98; SLJ 1/98) [921]

**11216** Stanley, Diane, and Peter Vennema. *Good Queen Bess: The Story of Elizabeth of England* (4–6). Illus. 1990, Macmillan LB $16.95 (0-02-786810-9). 40pp. An excellent biography of Elizabeth I, with emphasis on understanding the reasons for her actions in the context of the time. (Rev: BCCB 10/90; BL 9/1/90*; HB 1–2/91*; SLJ 12/90) [921]

## ELIZABETH II, QUEEN OF ENGLAND

**11217** Green, Robert. *Queen Elizabeth II* (4–6). Illus. Series: First Book: Monarchs. 1997, Watts LB $21.00 (0-531-20303-4). 64pp. This account tells about Elizabeth's childhood during World War II, how she came to the throne, and changes that have occurred during her reign. (Rev: BL 12/1/97; SLJ 12/97) [921]

## EQUIANO, OLAUDAH

**11218** Cameron, Ann. *The Kidnapped Prince: The Life of Olaudah Equiano* (5–8). 1995, Knopf $16.00 (0-679-85619-6). 133pp. Adapted from his autobiography, this is the story of Olaudah Equiano, an African prince sold into slavery in the 18th century. (Rev: BCCB 4/95; BL 1/1/95; SLJ 2/95) [921]

## FRANCIS OF ASSISI, SAINT

**11219** dePaola, Tomie. *Francis: The Poor Man of Assisi* (4–7). Illus. by author. 1982, Holiday LB $18.95 (0-8234-0435-8); paper $8.95 (0-8234-0812-4). 48pp. A simple retelling of the life of St. Francis with fine pictures by dePaola.

**11220** Wildsmith, Brian. *Saint Francis* (1–3). Illus. 1996, Eerdmans $20.00 (0-8028-5123-1). 36pp. A large-size picture book that tells the story of St. Francis as a first-person narrative with a biographical note following the story. (Rev: BCCB 7–8/96; BL 1/1–15/96; SLJ 2/96) [921]

## FRANK, ANNE

**11221** Adler, David A. *A Picture Book of Anne Frank* (2–4). Illus. by Karen Ritz. 1993, Holiday LB $15.95 (0-8234-1003-X). 32pp. A simple biography for young readers. (Rev: BCCB 3/93; BL 3/1/93; SLJ 5/93) [921]

**11222** Brown, Gene. *Anne Frank: Child of the Holocaust* (3–6). Series: The Library of Famous Women. 1993, Blackbirch LB $15.95 (1-56711-030-4); paper $7.95 (1-56711-049-5). 64pp. In this biography of Anne Frank, important background information about Holland and the Nazis is supplied. (Rev: BL 1/15/92; SLJ 5/92) [921]

**11223** Epstein, Rachel. *Anne Frank* (3–6). Illus. 1997, Watts $22.00 (0-531-20298-4). 64pp. A forthright and personal account of the life and death of this young Jewish girl, with quotes from her diary and from people who knew her. (Rev: BL 12/1/97; SLJ 11/97) [921]

**11224** Frank, Anne. *Anne Frank: The Diary of a Young Girl* (5–8). 1967, Doubleday $24.95 (0-385-04019-9); Pocket paper $3.95 (0-685-05466-7). 312pp. A moving diary of a young Jewish girl hiding from the Nazis in World War II Amsterdam.

**11225** Gold, Alison L. *Memories of Anne Frank: Reflections of a Childhood Friend* (4–8). Illus. 1997, Scholastic $16.95 (0-590-90722-0). 160pp. Anne Frank's story as told through recollections of her best friend in Amsterdam, Hannah Goslar, a survivor of the Holocaust. (Rev: BL 9/1/97; SLJ 11/97) [921]

**11226** Hurwitz, Johanna. *Anne Frank: Life in Hiding* (4–7). Illus. by Vera Rosenberry. 1989, Jewish Publication Soc. $13.95 (0-8276-0311-8). 64pp. Describing the 25 months of a family's hiding from the Nazis in the 1940s. (Rev: BL 4/15/89)

## GANDHI, MAHATMA

**11227** Barraclough, John. *Mohandas Gandhi* (2–3). Illus. Series: Lives and Times. 1997, Heinemann LB $12.95 (1-57572-561-4). 24pp. A simple picture book biography that tells of Gandhi's work in South Africa and his struggle against British rule in India. (Rev: BL 3/15/98) [921]

**11228** Fisher, Leonard Everett. *Gandhi* (5–7). Illus. 1995, Simon & Schuster paper $16.00 (0-689-80337-0). 32pp. In powerful black-and-white drawings and simple text, this is a handsome addition to the life of the Indian leader. (Rev: BL 10/1/95; SLJ 10/95) [921]

## GEORGE III, KING OF ENGLAND

**11229** Green, Robert. *King George III* (4–6). Series: First Books: Monarchs. 1997, Watts LB $21.00 (0-531-20333-6). 64pp. An objective account of the life of the troubled monarch whose policies toward his colonies caused the American Revolution. (Rev: BL 12/15/97; SLJ 12/97) [921]

## GHENGIS KHAN

**11230** Demi. *Chingis Khan* (3–5). Illus. by author. 1991, Holt $19.95 (0-8050-1708-9). 56pp. Highly readable portrait of the great king of the Mongols. (Rev: BCCB 1/92; BL 10/1/91*; SLJ 10/91) [950.2]

## GORBACHEV, MIKHAIL

**11231** Selfridge, John W. *Mikhail Gorbachev* (4–7). Illus. Series: Junior World Biographies. 1991, Chelsea $12.95 (0-7910-1567-X). 80pp. This biography of the former leader of the U.S.S.R. has many well-captioned illustrations. (Rev: BL 9/1/91) [921]

## HANNIBAL

**11232** Green, Robert. *Hannibal* (5–8). Illus. Series: First Books: Ancient Biographies. 1996, Watts LB $22.00 (0-531-20240-2). 63pp. Although some material is given on Hannibal's formative years, most of this account deals with his military career and the significance of his life. (Rev: SLJ 2/97) [921]

## HEROD OF JUDEA

**11233** Green, Robert. *Herod the Great* (4–6). Illus. Series: First Books: Ancient Biographies. 1996, Watts LB $22.00 (0-531-20232-1). 64pp. The life of the notorious Roman ruler of Judea and the political and religious conditions during his life. (Rev: BL 7/96; SLJ 9/96) [921]

## HIDALGO Y COSTILLA, MIGUEL

**11234** De Varona, Frank. *Miguel Hidalgo y Costilla: Father of Mexican Independence* (3–6). Illus. Series: Hispanic Heritage. 1993, Millbrook LB $19.90 (1-56294-370-7); paper $4.95 (1-56294-863-6). 32pp. The story of the Mexican priest and revolutionary who became a martyr in the pursuit of his country's freedom. (Rev: BL 11/15/93) [921]

## HITLER, ADOLF

**11235** Ayer, Eleanor. *Adolf Hitler* (4–8). Illus. Series: The Importance Of. 1996, Lucent LB $22.45 (1-56006-072-7). 128pp. A biography of this dictator that discusses the impact of his life on Germany and the world. (Rev: BL 3/15/96; SLJ 1/96) [921]

## JOAN OF ARC

**11236** Bunson, Margaret, and Matthew Bunson. *St. Joan of Arc* (4–6). Illus. Series: Saints You Should Know. 1992, Sunday Visitor $7.95 (0-87973-784-0); paper $5.95 (0-87973-558-9). 56pp. A clear, unsentimental portrait of the saint who lost her life trying to save her country. (Rev: BL 1/1/93) [921]

## JOHN PAUL II, POPE

**11237** Mohan, Claire J. *The Young Life of Pope John Paul II* (4–6). Illus. 1995, Young Sparrow $14.95 (0-943135-11-7); paper $7.95 (0-943135-12-5). 64pp.

The story of Pope John Paul II when he was Karol Wojtyla growing up in Poland. (Rev: BL 9/1/95; SLJ 11/95) [921]

**11238** Sullivan, George. *Pope John Paul II: The People's Pope* (4–7). Illus. 1984, Walker $11.95 (0-8027-6523-8). 120pp. A brief retelling of the life of this controversial pope.

## JUAREZ, BENITO

**11239** De Varona, Frank. *Benito Juarez: President of Mexico* (3–6). Illus. Series: Hispanic Heritage. 1993, Millbrook LB $19.90 (1-56294-279-4). 32pp. The story of the rise to greatness of a native Indian who became president of Mexico. (Rev: BL 5/15/93; SLJ 7/93) [921]

**11240** Palacios, Argentina. *Viva Mexico! A Story of Benito Juarez and Cinco de Mayo* (2–4). Illus. by Howard Berelson. 1993, Raintree Steck-Vaughn LB $22.83 (0-8114-7214-0). 32pp. For very young readers, this is a simple biography of the man often referred to as the architect of modern Mexico. (Rev: BL 5/15/93; SLJ 7/93) [921]

## KAIULANI, PRINCESS OF HAWAII

**11241** Stanley, Fay. *The Last Princess: The Story of Princess Ka'iulani of Hawaii* (4–6). Illus. by Diane Stanley. 1991, Macmillan LB $18.00 (0-02-786785-4). 40pp. The ill-fated princess who never achieved her goal of being queen of Hawaii. (Rev: BL 3/15/91*) [921]

## KHERDIAN, JERON

**11242** Kherdian, Jeron. *The Road from Home: The Story of an Armenian Girl* (6–8). 1979, Greenwillow LB $13.88 (0-688-84205-4); Morrow paper $4.95 (0-688-14425-X). 256pp. A memoir of a survivor of the Turkish slaughter of Armenians.

## KOLLEK, TEDDY

**11243** Rabinovich, Abraham. *Teddy Kollek: Builder of Jerusalem* (5–8). Illus. 1996, Jewish Publication Soc. $14.95 (0-8276-0559-5); paper $9.95 (0-8276-0561-7). 124pp. The story of the former mayor of Jerusalem, who supervised the city's unification after the Six Days War in 1967. (Rev: BL 5/15/96) [921]

## KOSSMAN, NINA

**11244** Kossman, Nina. *Behind the Border* (5–7). 1994, Lothrop $14.00 (0-688-13494-7). 128pp. This book contains 12 episodes that tell about the author's childhood in Communist Russia before emigrating to the United States. (Rev: BCCB 10/94; BL 8/94; SLJ 10/94) [921]

## L'OUVERTURE, TOUSSAINT

**11245** Myers, Walter Dean. *Toussaint L'Ouverture: The Fight for Haiti's Freedom* (4–8). Illus. by Jacob Lawrence. 1996, Simon & Schuster paper $16.00 (0-689-80126-2). 32pp. Powerful paintings highlight this story of the liberator of the people of Haiti. (Rev: BCCB 1/97; BL 9/1/96; SLJ 11/96*) [921]

## MANDELA, NELSON

**11246** Cooper, Floyd. *Mandela: From the Life of the South African Statesman* (2–4). Illus. 1996, Putnam $15.95 (0-399-22942-6). 40pp. A picture book biography that focuses on Mandela's childhood and youth. (Rev: BL 9/15/96; SLJ 11/96*) [921]

**11247** Dell, Pamela. *Nelson Mandela: Freedom for South Africa* (3–5). Illus. 1994, Children's LB $19.00 (0-516-04192-4). 32pp. A simple photoessay on the life of Mandela and his struggle against apartheid. (Rev: BL 2/1/95) [921]

**11248** Feinberg, Brian. *Nelson Mandela* (4–7). Illus. Series: Junior World Biographies. 1991, Chelsea LB $15.95 (0-7910-1569-6). 80pp. This straightforward biography of the South African leader includes many illustrations. (Rev: BL 9/1/91; SLJ 8/91) [921]

**11249** Holland, Gini. *Nelson Mandela* (2–4). Illus. by Mike White. Series: First Biographies. 1997, Raintree Steck-Vaughn LB $21.40 (0-8172-4454-9). 32pp. A simple retelling of Nelson Mandela's life from his childhood as the son of a black chieftain to his release from prison in 1990 and resumption of his political career. (Rev: SLJ 2/98) [921]

**11250** Roberts, Jack L. *Nelson Mandela: Determined to Be Free* (2–4). Illus. Series: Gateway Biographies. 1995, Millbrook LB $21.90 (1-56294-558-0). 48pp. A short, direct biography illustrated by numerous photographs. (Rev: BL 5/1/95) [921]

**11251** Stefoff, Rebecca. *Nelson Mandela: A Voice Set Free* (5–8). Series: Great Lives Biography. 1990, Fawcett paper $5.99 (0-449-90570-5). 128pp. Details about Mandela's personal life plus history and politics of the times. (Rev: BL 10/1/90) [921]

**11252** Strazzabosco, Jeanne M. *Learning About Forgiveness from the Life of Nelson Mandela* (2–5). Illus. Series: Character Building. 1996, Rosen LB $13.95 (0-8239-2413-0). 24pp. Covers, in a small-format book, the life of this South African hero and politician who fought successfully against apartheid. (Rev: BL 10/15/96; SLJ 11/96) [921]

## MENCHU, RIGOBERTA

**11253** Brill, Marlene T. *Journey for Peace: The Story of Rigoberta Menchu* (3–5). Illus. Series: Rainbow Biography. 1996, Dutton paper $14.99 (0-525-67524-8). 64pp. The story of the 1992 Nobel Prize winner who helped fight oppression in her native Guatemala. (Rev: BL 9/1/96; SLJ 9/96) [921]

## MONTESSORI, MARIA

**11254** O'Connor, Barbara. *Mammolina: A Story About Maria Montessori* (3–6). Illus. by Sara Campitelli. Series: Creative Minds. 1993, Carolrhoda LB $19.95 (0-87614-743-0). 64pp. This is a story of the educational philosopher who developed revolutionary ideas on child development and their application in schools. (Rev: BCCB 4/93; BL 4/1/93; SLJ 4/93) [921]

**11255** Shephard, Marie T. *Maria Montessori: Teacher of Teachers* (5–7). Illus. 1996, Lerner LB $23.93 (0-8225-4952-2). 128pp. A biography of the Italian educator and her unusual teaching methods for the young. (Rev: BL 8/96; SLJ 9/96) [921]

## MORRIS, SAMUEL

**11256** Jackson, Dave, and Neta Jackson. *Quest for the Lost Prince* (3–6). Illus. by Julian Jackson. Series: Trailblazer Books. 1996, Bethany paper $5.99 (1-55661-472-1). 144pp. The true story of an African prince, born in 1872, who became a Christian and came to the United States. (Rev: BL 10/1/96) [921]

## MUGABE, ROBERT

**11257** Worth, Richard. *Robert Mugabe of Zimbabwe* (5–8). Illus. Series: In Focus Biographies. 1990, Silver Burdett LB $13.95 (0-671-68987-8); paper $7.95 (0-671-70684-5). 111pp. Tells the story of Zimbabwe's first prime minister, along with a history of this emerging country. (Rev: SLJ 2/91) [921]

## NAPOLEON BONAPARTE

**11258** Carroll, Bob. *Napoleon Bonaparte* (4–8). Illus. Series: The Importance Of. 1994, Lucent LB $22.45 (1-56006-021-2). 112pp. From humble beginnings on the island of Corsica to becoming Emperor of the French and his final wartime defeat and exile, this is the story of France's hero Napoleon. (Rev: BL 5/15/94; SLJ 4/94) [921]

## NIGHTINGALE, FLORENCE

**11259** Adler, David A. *A Picture Book of Florence Nightingale* (K–3). Illus. by John Wallner. Series: Picture Book Biography. 1992, Holiday LB $15.95 (0-8234-0965-1). 32pp. Through simple text and illustrations that supply details of time and place, the life of this gallant nurse is introduced. (Rev: BL 11/15/92; SLJ 10/92) [921]

## PATRICK, SAINT

**11260** dePaola, Tomie. *Patrick: Patron Saint of Ireland* (PS–3). Illus. 1992, Holiday LB $16.95 (0-8234-0924-4). 32pp. With simple text and glowing pictures, the life of Ireland's saint is portrayed. (Rev: BCCB 4/92; BL 3/15/92; HB 9–10/92; SLJ 5/92) [921]

## PULASKI, CASIMIR

**11261** Collins, David R. *Casimir Pulaski: Soldier on Horseback* (4–8). Illus. 1995, Pelican $14.95 (1-56554-082-4). 96pp. The stirring biography of the Polish patriot who organized Washington's cavalry during the American Revolutionary War. (Rev: BL 2/15/96) [921]

## RABIN, ITZHAK

**11262** Sofer, Barbara. *Shalom, Haver: Goodbye, Friend* (2–5). Illus. 1996, Kar-Ben $16.95 (0-929371-97-6). 48pp. A biography of the Israeli prime minister, Itzhak Rabin, with details on his peacemaking activities. (Rev: BL 8/96*; SLJ 7/96) [921]

## SADAT, ANWAR

**11263** Rosen, Deborah Nodler. *Anwar el-Sadat: A Man of Peace* (5–7). Illus. 1986, Children's LB $18.60 (0-516-03214-3). 152pp. A biography of Egypt's man of peace. (Rev: BL 2/15/87; SLJ 2/87)

**11264** Sullivan, George. *Sadat: The Man Who Changed Mid-East History* (5–8). Illus. 1981, Walker LB $9.85 (0-8027-6435-5). 99pp. The life story of the man who shaped modern Egypt's destiny.

## SAN MARTÍN, JOSÉ DE

**11265** Fernandez, Jose B. *Jose de San Martin: Latin America's Quiet Hero* (3–6). Illus. Series: Hispanic Heritage. 1994, Millbrook $19.90 (1-56294-383-9). 32pp. The life story of the South American revolutionary who rivaled Bolívar in importance but who died in obscurity in Europe. (Rev: BL 6/1–15/94; SLJ 4/94) [921]

## SASAKI, SADAKO

**11266** Coerr, Eleanor. *Sadako and the Thousand Paper Cranes* (3–5). Illus. by Ronald Himler. 1977, Putnam $14.95 (0-399-20520-9); Dell paper $3.99 (0-440-47465-5). 64pp. The moving biography of a young Japanese girl who dies of leukemia that developed as a result of radiation sickness from the bombing of Hiroshima.

## SAUTUOLA, MARIA DE

**11267** Fradin, Dennis B. *Maria de Sautuola: The Bulls in the Cave* (3–5). Illus. Series: Remarkable Children. 1997, Silver Burdett LB $15.95 (0-382-39470-4); paper $5.95 (0-382-39471-2). 32pp. The story of the young Spanish girl who discovered the first known prehistoric cave paintings in 1879. (Rev: BL 6/1–15/97; SLJ 7/97) [921]

## SCHINDLER, OSKAR

**11268** Roberts, Jack L. *Oskar Schindler* (4–8). Illus. Series: The Importance Of. 1996, Lucent LB $22.45 (1-56006-079-4). 111pp. The story of one man's fight to save some Jews from Nazi death camps during World War II. (Rev: BL 3/15/96; SLJ 1/96) [921]

## SHAKA (ZULU CHIEF)

**11269** Stanley, Diane, and Peter Vennema. *Shaka: King of the Zulus* (2–4). Illus. by Diane Stanley. 1988, Morrow LB $15.93 (0-688-07343-3). 40pp. The life story of a Zulu military genius who became king of his people in the 19th century. (Rev: BCCB 11/88; BL 11/1/88; HB 1–2/89)

## TERESA, MOTHER

**11270** Barraclough, John. *Mother Teresa* (2–3). Series: Lives and Times. 1997, Heinemann $12.95 (1-57572-562-2). 24pp. A simple picture book biography that gives a very brief introduction to the life and contributions of Mother Teresa. (Rev: BL 3/15/98) [921]

**11271** Giff, Patricia Reilly. *Mother Teresa: Sister to the Poor* (3–5). Illus. 1987, Puffin paper $4.99 (0-14-032225-6). 64pp. Beginning with her childhood in Macedonia, this is the story of the woman who has won the Nobel Peace Prize for her work to better thousands of lives. (Rev: BCCB 4/86; BL 8/86; SLJ 9/86)

**11272** Jacobs, William J. *Mother Teresa: Helping the Poor* (3–5). Illus. Series: Gateway Biographies. 1991, Millbrook LB $20.90 (1-56294-020-1). 48pp. An admiring portrait of this woman of compassion and peace, including an overview of her work with the poor. (Rev: BL 1/1/92; SLJ 1/92) [921]

**11273** Johnson, Linda C. *Mother Teresa: Protector of the Sick* (5–8). Illus. Series: Library of Famous Women. 1991, Blackbirch LB $16.95 (1-56711-034-7). 64pp. Tracing Mother Teresa's life from her childhood in Yugoslavia to her renowned efforts to aid the sick around the world. (Rev: BL 3/15/93) [921]

**11274** Mohan, Claire J. *The Young Life of Mother Teresa of Calcutta* (4–6). Illus. by Jane Robbins. 1996, Young Sparrow $14.95 (0-943135-26-5); paper $7.95 (0-943135-25-7). 64pp. This biography concentrates on Mother Teresa's life from when she was called to serve God at age 12 to her leaving the convent to go to Calcutta. (Rev: SLJ 1/97) [921]

**11275** Pond, Mildred. *Mother Teresa: A Life of Charity* (4–7). Illus. Series: Junior World Biographies. 1992, Chelsea LB $15.95 (0-7910-1755-9). 80pp. The inspiring life story of the nun who has given her life to serve and help the poor, particularly in India. (Rev: BL 8/92; SLJ 7/92) [921]

### THATCHER, MARGARET

**11276** Hughes, Libby. *Madam Prime Minister* (5–7). Illus. 1989, Macmillan LB $13.95 (0-87518-410-3). 144pp. This solid biography shows both the public and the private sides of the former British prime minister. (Rev: BL 11/1/89*; SLJ 1/90) [921]

### TUTANKHAMEN, KING

**11277** Green, Robert. *Tutankhamun* (4–6). Illus. Series: First Books: Ancient Biographies. 1996, Watts LB $21.00 (0-531-20233-X). 64pp. The opening of his tomb in the 20th century brought fame and importance to this little-known Egyptian monarch. (Rev: BL 7/96; SLJ 7/96) [921]

**11278** Sabuda, Robert. *Tutankhamen's Gift* (K–4). Illus. 1994, Atheneum $17.00 (0-689-31818-9). 32pp. A fictionalized account of the boyhood of Tutankhamen and how he became pharaoh at an early age. (Rev: BL 4/15/94; SLJ 5/94) [921]

### VICTORIA, QUEEN

**11279** Netzley, Patricia. *The Importance of Queen Victoria* (4–8). Illus. Series: The Importance Of. 1996, Lucent LB $22.45 (1-56006-063-8). 128pp. A biography of the long-reigning British monarch who gave her name to an age of British eminence. (Rev: BL 5/15/96; SLJ 7/96) [921]

### VILLA, PANCHO

**11280** Carroll, Bob. *Pancho Villa* (4–8). Illus. Series: The Importance Of. 1996, Lucent LB $22.45 (1-56006-069-7). 112pp. The story of this colorful fighter against tyranny and of his lasting influence on Mexico's history. (Rev: BL 3/15/96; SLJ 2/96) [921]

**11281** O'Brien, Steven. *Pancho Villa* (5–8). Illus. Series: Hispanics of Achievement. 1994, Chelsea LB $19.95 (0-7910-1257-3). 112pp. The life and accomplishments of this Mexican freedom fighter. (Rev: BL 9/15/94) [921]

### WALESA, LECH

**11282** Lazo, Caroline. *Lech Walesa* (4–7). Illus. Series: Peacemakers. 1993, Dillon LB $13.95 (0-87518-525-8). 64pp. The story of the Polish Solidarity labor movement leader is told with generous quotes from Walesa's autobiography and speeches. (Rev: BL 12/15/93; SLJ 1/94) [921]

### WALLENBERG, RAOUL

**11283** Linnea, Sharon. *Raoul Wallenberg: The Man Who Stopped Death* (5–7). Illus. 1993, Jewish Publication Soc. $17.95 (0-8276-0440-8); paper $9.95 (0-8276-0448-3). 120pp. This Swedish architect saved thousands of Jews in Hungary from the Nazi Holocaust. (Rev: BL 6/1–15/93) [940]

### YELTSIN, BORIS

**11284** Lambroza, Shlomo. *Boris Yeltsin* (5–8). Illus. Series: World Leaders. 1993, Rourke $19.93 (0-86625-482-X). 110pp. After describing recent events and the emergence of Russia from the Soviet Union, this biography outlines Yeltsin's life and accomplishment through 1993. (Rev: SLJ 12/93) [921]

# The Arts and Language

# Art and Architecture

## General and Miscellaneous

**11285**  *A Is for Artist* (PS–1). Illus. 1997, J. Paul Getty Museum $16.95 (0-89236-377-0). 60pp. Using an alphabetical approach, this book introduces 26 glorious paintings from the Getty Museum. (Rev: BL 10/15/97) [708.194]

**11286**  Angelou, Maya. *My Painted House, My Friendly Chicken, and Me* (PS–3). Illus. by Margaret Courtney-Clarke. 1994, Crown $16.00 (0-517-59667-9). 36pp. The customs and beautifully decorated houses of the Ndebele people of South Africa are featured in this picture book. (Rev: BCCB 12/94; BL 10/1/94; SLJ 10/94*) [704]

**11287**  Björk, Christina. *Linnea in Monet's Garden* (1–4). Trans. by Joan Sandin. Illus. by Lena Anderson. 1987, Farrar $13.00 (91-29-58314-4). 56pp. Linnea, a young French girl, learns about flowers, the painter Monet, and impressionism from her friend Mr. Bloom. (Rev: BL 12/1/87)

**11288**  Blanquet, Claire-Helene. *Miró: Earth and Sky* (5–7). Trans. from French by John Goodman. Illus. Series: Art for Children. 1994, Chelsea LB $15.95 (0-7910-2813-5). 59pp. Using a conversational style and some fictitious characters, the life and works of the famous 20th-century French painter Miró are introduced. (Rev: SLJ 12/94) [709]

**11289**  Blizzard, Gladys S. *Come Look with Me: Enjoying Art with Children* (1–4). Illus. 1991, Thomasson-Grant $13.95 (0-934738-76-9). 32pp. Readers are urged to examine 12 paintings of children by famous artists. (Rev: BCCB 5/91; BL 6/1/91) [750.1]

**11290**  Blizzard, Gladys S. *Come Look with Me: Exploring Landscape Art with Children* (1–4). Illus. 1992, Thomasson-Grant $13.95 (0-934738-95-5).

32pp. For primary-grade youngsters, this is an introduction to different styles of landscape painting as seen through the work of 12 important artists. (Rev: BL 3/1/92; HB 9–10/92) [758.1]

**11291**  Blizzard, Gladys S. *Come Look with Me: World of Play* (1–4). Illus. 1993, Thomasson-Grant $13.95 (1-56566-031-5). 32pp. This art appreciation book reproduces 11 paintings and one sculpture that depict various ways in which children play. (Rev: BL 9/1/93) [701.1]

**11292**  Capek, Michael. *Artistic Trickery: The Tradition of Trompe l'Oeil Art* (5–8). Illus. 1995, Lerner LB $22.60 (0-8225-2064-8). 64pp. The art of creating images so perfect that the viewer thinks they are real is introduced, with many historical and contemporary examples. (Rev: BCCB 7–8/95; BL 6/1–15/95; SLJ 7/95) [758]

**11293**  Capek, Michael. *Murals: Cave, Cathedral, to Street* (5–8). Illus. 1996, Lerner LB $23.93 (0-8225-2065-6). 80pp. The history of mural painting from cave painting to such modern masters as Diego Rivera. (Rev: BL 6/1–15/96; SLJ 10/96) [751.7]

**11294**  Davidson, Rosemary. *Take a Look: An Introduction to the Experience of Art* (5–8). Illus. 1994, Viking paper $18.99 (0-670-84478-0). 128pp. In 11 chapters that cover all aspects of the creative experience, the author relates art to everyday life in a lively text with many reproductions. (Rev: BCCB 2/94; BL 3/1/94; SLJ 2/94) [801.1]

**11295**  Delafosse, Claude. *Animals* (PS–2). Illus. by Tony Ross. Series: First Discovery Art. 1995, Scholastic $11.95 (0-590-55202-3). 26pp. Youngsters are introduced to art through a series of laminated pages that alternate with transparencies and give the impression of change and motion. (Rev: BL 1/1–15/96; SLJ 1/96) [701]

**11296** Delafosse, Claude. *Landscapes* (4–7). Illus. Series: First Discovery Art. 1996, Scholastic $11.95 (0-590-50216-6). 24pp. The art and techniques of landscape painting are introduced, with many examples from the masters in various historical periods. (Rev: BL 6/1–15/96; SLJ 7/96) [750]

**11297** Delafosse, Claude. *Paintings* (4–7). Illus. Series: First Discovery Art. 1996, Scholastic $11.95 (0-590-55201-5). 28pp. A general introduction to painting, with many reproductions and lessons in art appreciation. (Rev: BL 6/1–15/96; SLJ 7/96) [750]

**11298** Delafosse, Claude. *Portraits* (PS–2). Illus. by Tony Ross. Series: First Discovery Art. 1995, Scholastic $11.95 (0-590-55200-7). 26pp. Objects gain new dimensions when seen through transparencies in this introduction to art appreciation. (Rev: BL 1/1–15/96; SLJ 1/96) [701]

**11299** Fisher, Leonard Everett. *Alphabet Art: Thirteen ABCs from Around the World* (5–8). Illus. 1984, Macmillan $16.95 (0-02-735230-7). 64pp. Thirteen alphabets — from Arabic to Tibetan — are pictured with their English equivalents.

**11300** Gogerty, Clare. *Conflict in Art* (5–7). Illus. Series: Let's Investigate Art. 1996, Marshall Cavendish LB $22.14 (0-7614-0011-7). 47pp. An interesting account of how war has been portrayed in art and how artists have often shaped public opinion. (Rev: SLJ 2/97) [709]

**11301** Gogerty, Clare. *Feelings in Art* (4–7). Illus. Series: Let's Investigate Art. 1996, Marshall Cavendish LB $15.50 (1-85435-771-9). 48pp. The world of emotions and feelings as expressed in painting, drawings, and other art works is presented from many cultures and periods. (Rev: BL 1/15/95; SLJ 1/95) [701]

**11302** Gogerty, Clare. *People in Art* (4–7). Illus. Series: Let's Investigate Art. 1994, Marshall Cavendish $13.95 (1-85435-768-9). 48pp. In text and excellent reproductions, portraits and other depictions of people in art are explored. (Rev: BL 1/15/95; SLJ 1/95) [701]

**11303** Gogerty, Clare. *Places in Art* (4–7). Illus. Series: Let's Investigate Art. 1996, Marshall Cavendish LB $22.14 (1-85435-769-7). 48pp. An art appreciation book that explores representations of places from many different countries and time periods, along with suggestions for examining other art works creatively. (Rev: BL 1/15/95; SLJ 1/95) [701]

**11304** Gogerty, Clare. *Stories in Art* (4–7). Illus. Series: Let's Investigate Art. 1994, Marshall Cavendish LB $22.14 (1-85435-770-0). 48pp. How pictures tell stories and re-create history are explored in words and pictures from many times and cultures. (Rev: BL 1/15/95) [701]

**11305** *Groom Your Room: Terrific Touches to Brighten Your Bedroom!* (3–8). Photos by Michael Walker and Fritz Geiger. Series: American Girl Library. 1997, Pleasant paper $7.95 (1-56247-531-2). 48pp. A beginning decorating book that also gives tips on cleaning and organizing possessions. (Rev: SLJ 3/98) [745]

**11306** *The History of Printmaking* (3–6). Illus. Series: Voyages of Discovery. 1996, Scholastic $19.95 (0-590-47649-1). 48pp. Overlays and foldouts are used to present a history of prints and print images, including computer images. (Rev: BL 12/15/97) [769]

**11307** Isaacson, Philip M. *Round Buildings, Square Buildings, and Buildings That Wiggle* (4–6). Illus. 1988, Knopf $22.00 (0-394-89382-4); paper $13.00 (0-679-80649-0). 128pp. The beauty in all kinds of buildings is explored in text and photographs. (Rev: HB 1–2/89)

**11308** Isaacson, Philip M. *A Short Walk Around the Pyramids and Through the World of Art* (5–8). Illus. 1993, Knopf LB $20.99 (0-679-91523-0). 120pp. Through examination of a number of objects and structures, the author shows how art and its elements — like form and color — form part of our daily life. (Rev: BCCB 10/93; BL 9/15/93; HB 9–10/93; SLJ 8/93*) [700]

**11309** Kalman, Bobbie. *The Victorian Home* (3–5). Illus. by Barbara Bedell. Series: Historic Communities. 1997, Crabtree LB $19.16 (0-86505-431-2); paper $7.95 (0-86505-461-4). 32pp. Examines 19th-century homes, their exteriors, interior rooms, and furnishings. (Rev: SLJ 7/97) [690]

**11310** King, Penny, and Clare Roundhill. *Animals* (2–4). Illus. Series: Artists' Workshop. 1996, Crabtree $19.96 (0-86505-851-2); paper $8.95 (0-86505-861-X). 32pp. Readers learn how animals are depicted in art, examine 6 appropriate art works, and are given tips on how to create their own pictures. Also use *Landscapes, Portraits,* and *Stories* (all 1996). (Rev: SLJ 1/97) [709]

**11311** Kutschbach, Doris. *The Blue Rider: The Yellow Cow Sees the World in Blue* (3–7). Trans. by Andrea Belloli. Illus. Series: Adventures in Art. 1997, Prestel $14.95 (3-7913-1811-X). 35pp. This art appreciation volume explores a group of painters — including Klee and Kandinsky — who freed color and form from reality. (Rev: SLJ 1/98) [709]

**11312** Le Tord, Bijou. *A Blue Butterfly: A Story About Claude Monet* (K–3). Illus. 1995, Doubleday $15.95 (0-385-31102-8). 32pp. An account of how Monet painted, with illustrations that seem to be by the master himself. (Rev: BL 10/15/95; SLJ 11/95) [759.4]

**11313** Lewis, J. D. *Journeys in Art* (5–8). Illus. Series: Let's Investigate Art. 1996, Marshall Cavendish LB $22.14 (0-7614-0009-5). 47pp. Examines works of art that portray great journeys from Greek mythology and the Vikings to our own Western pioneers. (Rev: SLJ 1/97) [709]

**11314** Loumaye, Jacqueline. *Chagall: My Sad and Joyous Village* (4–8). Trans. from French by John Goodman. Illus. by Veronique Boiry. Series: Art for Children. 1994, Chelsea LB $15.95 (0-7910-2807-0). 57pp. A youngster learns about Chagall and his paintings from a violinist who grew up in the artist's home town in Russia. (Rev: SLJ 8/94) [709]

**11315** Loumaye, Jacqueline. *Degas: The Painted Gesture* (4–8). Trans. from French by John Goodman. Illus. by Nadine Massart. Series: Art for Children. 1994, Chelsea LB $15.95 (0-7910-2809-7). 57pp. Using a series of workshops for children at the Orsay Museum (Paris) as a focus, the life and works of Degas are introduced. (Rev: SLJ 8/94) [709]

**11316** Loumaye, Jacqueline. *Van Gogh: The Touch of Yellow* (4–8). Trans. from French by John Goodman. Illus. by Claudine Roucha. Series: Art for Children. 1994, Chelsea LB $15.95 (0-7910-2817-8). 57pp. Two youngsters visit the museums in Amsterdam to learn about van Gogh, his tragic life, and his paintings. (Rev: SLJ 8/94) [709]

**11317** Mallat, Kathy, and Bruce McMillan. *The Picture That Mom Drew* (2–4). Illus. 1997, Walker LB $15.85 (0-8027-8618-9). 24pp. Using "The House That Jack Built" as a framework, the materials and techniques used by an artist are introduced. (Rev: BL 1/1–15/97*; SLJ 4/97) [741.2]

**11318** Manning, Mick, and Brita Granström. *Art School* (2–5). Illus. by authors. 1996, Kingfisher paper $6.95 (0-7534-5000-3). 47pp. Various art techniques are covered, as well as topics like scale, color theory, and light and shadow plus a number of art activities. (Rev: SLJ 12/96) [709]

**11319** Micklethwait, Lucy. *A Child's Book of Art: Great Pictures, First Words* (1–4). Illus. 1993, DK Publg. $16.95 (1-56458-203-5). 64pp. Combines a word book with art appreciation by showing how common concepts like work and numbers are shown in great works of art. (Rev: BL 1/15/94; SLJ 2/94) [701]

**11320** Micklethwait, Lucy. *A Child's Book of Play in Art* (PS–4). Illus. 1996, DK Publg. $16.95 (0-7894-1003-6). 45pp. Using a variety of paintings from many ages and places, this volume will help stimulate a child's interest in art. (Rev: BL 10/1/96*; SLJ 11/96*) [372.5]

**11321** Micklethwait, Lucy. *I Spy a Lion* (2–4). Illus. 1994, Greenwillow LB $18.93 (0-688-13231-6). 48pp. Animals are hidden in this collection of reproductions of paintings that are used to develop art appreciation. (Rev: BL 9/15/94; HB 11–12/94; SLJ 10/94) [758.3]

**11322** Micklethwait, Lucy. *Spot a Cat* (PS–2). Illus. 1995, DK Publg. $9.95 (0-7894-0144-4). 32pp. In this collection of paintings by famous artists, cats are featured, often where it is difficult to find them. A companion volume is *Spot a Dog* (1995). (Rev: BL 10/1/95; SLJ 2/96) [750]

**11323** Pekarik, Andrew. *Painting: Behind the Scenes* (4–7). Illus. 1992, Hyperion LB $19.49 (1-56282-297-7). 64pp. Exploring the art of painting, including basic elements involved in each process. (Rev: BL 2/1/93; SLJ 2/93) [750]

**11324** Platt, Richard. *Stephen Biesty's Incredible Cross-Sections* (4–7). 1992, Knopf $22.00 (0-679-81411-6). 48pp. Intricately drawn illustrations feature models of vehicles and buildings. (Rev: BL 9/1/92) [741.6]

**11325** Richardson, Joy. *Inside the Museum: A Children's Guide to the Metropolitan Museum of Art* (4–7). Illus. 1993, Abrams paper $12.95 (0-8109-2561-3). 72pp. A guide to some of the treasures in the Metropolitan Museum of Art in New York City, with a peek behind the scenes. (Rev: BL 1/1/94; SLJ 2/94) [708.13]

**11326** Richardson, Joy. *Looking at Pictures: An Introduction to Art for Young People* (5–8). Illus. 1997, Abrams $17.95 (0-8109-4252-6). 80pp. A large-size volume that introduces art appreciation to middle-graders and describes different types of pictures and techniques. (Rev: BCCB 7–8/97; BL 4/15/97; SLJ 6/97*) [750]

**11327** Richmond, Robin. *Children in Art: The Story in a Picture* (4–6). Illus. by author. 1992, Ideals LB $16.00 (0-8249-8588-5). 48pp. Children are introduced to art by the use of pictures with children as subjects. (Rev: BL 12/15/92; SLJ 2/93) [750]

**11328** Roalf, Peggy. *Cats* (5–8). Illus. Series: Looking at Paintings. 1992, Hyperion paper $6.95 (1-56282-091-5). 48pp. In this history of art, the subject of cats is featured as portrayed through the ages. Others in this series are: *Dancers; Families;* and *Seascapes* (all 1992). (Rev: SLJ 8/92) [709]

**11329** Roalf, Peggy. *Dogs* (5–8). Illus. Series: Looking at Paintings. 1993, Hyperion paper $6.95 (1-56282-530-5). 48pp. Various ways that dogs have been represented in paintings are reproduced, with explanations, in this attractive book on art appreciation. (Rev: BL 2/15/94; SLJ 2/94) [758.3]

**11330** Roalf, Peggy. *Musicians* (5–8). Illus. Series: Looking at Paintings. 1993, Hyperion paper $6.95 (1-56282-532-1). 48pp. Traces art movements and styles by using examples of how musicians have been painted through the years. (Rev: BL 2/15/94; SLJ 2/94) [758]

**11331** Rohmer, Harriet, ed. *Just Like Me: Stories and Self-Portraits by Fourteen Artists* (3–6). Illus.

1997, Children's Book Pr. $15.95 (0-89239-149-9). 32pp. In 2-page spreads, 14 artists, all of whom have produced books for children, talk about themselves and their inspirations. (Rev: BL 9/1/97; SLJ 12/97) [704.9]

**11332** Scott, Elaine. *Funny Papers: Behind the Scenes of the Comics* (3–6). Photos by Margaret Miller. 1993, Morrow LB $14.93 (0-688-11576-4). 96pp. A richly illustrated history of comic strips, their different forms, and how they are created, sold, and distributed. (Rev: BCCB 1/94; BL 11/15/93; SLJ 11/93) [741.5]

**11333** Sellier, Marie. *Matisse from A to Z* (3–7). Trans. from French by Claudia Zoe Bedrick. Illus. 1995, Bedrick LB $14.95 (0-87226-475-0). 59pp. The subjects used by Matisse in his paintings and events in his life are used in this unusual alphabet book containing many reproductions of his work. (Rev: SLJ 12/95) [759.4]

**11334** Somerville, Louisa. *Animals in Art* (5–8). Illus. Series: Let's Investigate Art. 1996, Marshall Cavendish LB $15.50 (0-7614-0012-5). 47pp. Beginning with cave art, this account traces the history of the depiction of animals in art while also giving many suggestions for art projects. (Rev: SLJ 1/97) [709]

**11335** Taylor, George. *Imagination in Art* (5–7). Illus. Series: Let's Investigate Art. 1996, Marshall Cavendish LB $22.14 (0-7614-0010-9). 47pp. How the world of the imagination — including fantasy, dreams, mythology, religion, and optical illusions — have influenced the choice of subjects that a number of important artists have used. (Rev: SLJ 2/97) [709]

**11336** Terzian, Alexandra M. *The Kids' Multicultural Art Book: Art and Craft Experiences from Around the World* (3–6). Illus. 1993, Williamson paper $12.95 (0-913589-72-1). 160pp. Using a walking tour across the continents as a framework, this book introduces the cultures of many areas in Africa, Asia, and Central America, with a section on the Indians of North America. (Rev: BL 9/1/93; SLJ 8/93) [745]

**11337** Voss, Gisela. *Museum Colors* (PS–1). Illus. 1994, Museum of Fine Arts, Boston $14.00 (0-87846-369-0). 20pp. Works of art are used to point out different colors in this board book. Also use *Museum Numbers* and *Museum Shapes* (both 1994). (Rev: BL 5/1/94; SLJ 8/94) [701.8]

**11338** Waters, Elizabeth, and Annie Harris. *Painting: A Young Artist's Guide* (4–8). Illus. Series: Young Artist. 1993, DK Publg. $14.95 (1-56458-348-1). 48pp. Concepts in art — like color, shape, texture, rhythm, and pattern — are explained through a series of color reproductions of famous paintings. (Rev: BL 1/15/94; SLJ 3/94) [751.4]

# The Ancient World

**11339** Avi-Yonah, Michael. *Piece by Piece! Mosaics of the Ancient World* (5–8). Illus. Series: Buried Worlds. 1993, Runestone LB $23.93 (0-8225-3204-2). 64pp. Using archaeological methods to determine facts, describes the creation of mosaics in various parts of the ancient world and how they differed among cultures. (Rev: BL 1/15/94; SLJ 3/94) [738.5]

**11340** Gonen, Rivka. *Fired Up! Making Pottery in Ancient Times* (5–8). Illus. Series: Buried Worlds. 1993, Runestone LB $23.93 (0-8225-3202-6). 72pp. A heavily illustrated account that traces the manufacture, designs, and uses of pottery in various civilizations of the ancient world. (Rev: BL 1/15/94; SLJ 4/94) [738.3]

**11341** Lauber, Patricia. *Painters of the Caves* (4–8). Illus. 1998, National Geographic $16.95 (0-7922-7095-9). 48pp. A description of cave paintings and the people responsible for it is given, with information on the most famous caves and their discovery. (Rev: SLJ 3/98*) [709]

**11342** Wilkinson, Philip, and Michael Pollard. *The Master Builders* (4–7). Illus. by Robert Ingpen. Series: Mysterious Places. 1994, Chelsea LB $19.95 (0-7910-2753-8). 92pp. Such extraordinary sites as Stonehenge, Skara Brae, Troy, and Machu Picchu are examined, and, from these ruins, facts are determined about the people who built them. (Rev: BL 1/15/94; SLJ 5/94) [930.3]

# Indian Arts and Crafts

**11343** Arnold, Caroline. *Stories in Stone: Rock Art Pictures by Early Americans* (4–6). Illus. by Richard Hewitt. 1996, Clarion $15.95 (0-395-72092-3). 48pp. Highlights of the rock art of Native Americans found in the Coso Range in California. (Rev: BL 12/15/96; SLJ 12/96) [709]

**11344** Baylor, Byrd. *When Clay Sings* (2–5). Illus. by Tom Bahti. 1987, Macmillan $16.00 (0-684-18829-5); paper $5.99 (0-689-71106-9). 32pp. An exploration of the designs that originally appeared on the pottery of the Indians of the Southwest.

**11345** Presilla, Maricel E. *Mola: Cuna Life Stories and Art* (5–7). Illus. 1996, Holt $16.95 (0-8050-3801-9). 32pp. Through an examination of their folk art, the life of the Cuna Indians, who live on islands off the coast of Panama, is presented. (Rev: BCCB 1/97; BL 10/1/96; SLJ 10/96) [305.48]

**11346** Whiteford, Andrew Hunter. *North American Indian Arts* (5–8). Illus. by Vern Schaffer. 1990,

Western paper $5.50 (0-307-24032-0). 160pp. A presentation of the arts and crafts of North American Indians.

## Middle Ages and the Renaissance

**11347** Beckett, Wendy. *The Duke and the Peasant: Life in the Middle Ages* (4–6). Illus. Series: Adventures in Art. 1997, Prestel $14.95 (3-7913-1813-6). 30pp. The 12 calendar paintings from the Duc de Berry's *Book of Hours* are reproduced, with explanations of each and an introduction to the art of the Middle Ages. (Rev: BL 8/97; SLJ 10/97) [940.1]

**11348** Macaulay, David. *Cathedral: The Story of Its Construction* (6–8). Illus. by author. 1973, Houghton $18.00 (0-395-17513-5). 80pp. Gothic architecture as seen through a detailed examination of the construction of an imaginary cathedral.

**11349** Morrison, Taylor. *Antonio's Apprenticeship: Painting a Fresco in Renaissance Italy* (3–6). Illus. 1996, Holiday LB $15.95 (0-8234-1213-X). 32pp. A step-by-step description of how a fresco was created in 15th-century Florence as seen through the eyes of an apprentice. (Rev: BL 4/15/96; SLJ 5/96) [759.5]

**11350** Perdrizet, Marie-Pierre. *The Cathedral Builders* (5–8). Trans. by Mary Beth Raycraft. Illus. by Eddy Krahenbuhl. Series: People of the Past. 1992, Millbrook LB $22.40 (1-56294-162-3). 64pp. This book introduces a Gothic cathedral and the people who built it. (Rev: SLJ 8/92) [726]

## United States

**11351** Adelstein, Amy. *The Arts* (4–6). Illus. Series: African American Life. 1995, Rourke LB $23.93 (1-57103-028-X). 48pp. A volume that tells of the various contributions that have been made to the arts by African Americans, with an annotated list of important people. (Rev: SLJ 3/96) [700]

**11352** Cummings, Pat, ed. *Talking with Artists*, vol. 2 (3–7). Illus. 1995, Simon & Schuster $19.95 (0-689-80310-9). 96pp. Thirteen artists describe how they work and the media they use, with examples of their art work as children. Also use volume 1 (1992). (Rev: BCCB 10/95; BL 9/1/95; HB 11–12/95; SLJ 10/95) [741.6]

**11353** Esterman, M. M. *A Fish That's a Box: Folk Art*

*from the National Museum of American Art, Smithsonian Institution* (4–6). Illus. 1990, Great Ocean $12.95 (0-915556-21-9). 32pp. An eye-pleasing introduction to American folk art. (Rev: BCCB 2/91; BL 12/15/90; SLJ 3/91) [745]

**11354** Gilbert, Alma, ed. *Maxfield Parrish: A Treasury of Art and Children's Literature* (3–6). Illus. 1995, Simon & Schuster $23.00 (0-689-80300-1). 88pp. A sampling of Maxfield Parrish's splendid illustrations for children's books, with the texts that inspired them. (Rev: BL 2/1/96; SLJ 11/95) [759.13]

**11355** Howard, Nancy S. *Jacob Lawrence: American Scenes, American Struggles* (4–7). Illus. 1996, Davis $16.95 (0-87192-302-5). 48pp. The narrative paintings of this contemporary African American artist are featured, with several suggested follow-up activities. (Rev: BL 11/1/96) [759.13]

**11356** Joyce, William. *The World of William Joyce Scrapbook* (4–7). Illus. 1997, HarperCollins $16.95 (0-06-027432-8). 48pp. A scrapbook collected by the author-artist that contains handwritten memoirs, sketches, finished artwork, and personal photos. (Rev: BL 1/1–15/98; SLJ 2/98) [813]

**11357** Porte, Barbara Ann. *Black Elephant with a Brown Ear (in Alabama)* (3–6). Illus. by Bill Traylor. 1996, Greenwillow $16.00 (0-688-14374-1). 48pp. Using 10 of the primitive paintings of former slave Bill Traylor, the author weaves stories about each one. (Rev: BCCB 6/96; BL 5/15/96; SLJ 5/96) [813]

**11358** Seltzer, Isadore. *The House I Live In: At Home in America* (2–5). Illus. by author. 1992, Macmillan $14.95 (0-02-781801-2). 32pp. Describes 12 American house designs, from log cabins to apartment buildings. (Rev: BCCB 4/92; BL 3/15/92; SLJ 5/92) [728]

**11359** Thomson, Peggy, and Barbara Moore. *The Nine-Ton Cat: Behind the Scenes at an Art Museum* (4–8). Illus. 1997, Houghton $21.95 (0-395-81655-1); paper $14.95 (0-395-82683-7). 96pp. An inside look at the workings of the National Gallery in Washington, D.C., that gives descriptions of the work of a variety of personnel, from curators and conservators to gardeners. (Rev: BCCB 4/97; BL 3/15/97*; HB 5–6/97; SLJ 4/97) [708.153]

**11360** Zelver, Patricia. *The Wonderful Towers of Watts* (K–3). Illus. by Frane Lessac. 1994, Morrow $15.00 (0-688-12649-9). 32pp. The story of the construction of the Watts Tower in Los Angeles over a period of 33 years by Old Sam, the nickname of Simon Rodia. (Rev: BCCB 7–8/94; BL 5/1/94; SLJ 9/94) [725]

# Communication

## Codes and Ciphers

**11361** Huckle, Helen. *The Secret Code Book* (3–6). Illus. 1995, Dial paper $14.99 (0-8037-1725-3). 64pp. An explanation of 19 important codes, with instructions on how to apply and decipher them. (Rev: BL 8/95) [652]

## Flags

**11362** Armbruster, Ann. *The American Flag* (4–6). Illus. 1991, Watts LB $22.00 (0-531-20045-0). 64pp. In addition to a history of the American flag, this illustrated account covers such subjects as the flag as a symbol, the saluting custom, and modern flag manufacturing. (Rev: BL 1/1/92; SLJ 1/92) [929.9]

**11363** Ayer, Eleanor. *Our Flag* (4–6). Illus. Series: I Know America. 1992, Millbrook paper $8.95 (1-878841-86-6). 48pp. This volume gives a colorfully illustrated introduction to the U.S. flag, its parts, and their meaning. (Rev: BL 5/15/92) [929.9]

**11364** Brandt, Sue R. *State Flags* (3–5). Illus. Series: Our State Symbols. 1992, Watts LB $23.00 (0-531-20001-9). 64pp. Each state flag is pictured and its significance explained in brief text. (Rev: BL 2/1/93) [929.9]

**11365** Crampton, William. *Flag* (4–6). Illus. Series: Eyewitness Books. 1989, Knopf LB $16.99 (0-394-92255-7). 64pp. The meaning behind flags is explored and various types are covered, with many illustrations. (Rev: BL 10/15/89; SLJ 1/90) [929.9]

**11366** Fisher, Leonard Everett. *Stars and Stripes: Our National Flag* (1–3). Illus. 1993, Holiday LB $16.95 (0-8234-1053-6). 32pp. A brief history of the American flag from 1775 to the present. (Rev: BL 10/15/93; SLJ 10/93) [973.7]

**11367** Fradin, Dennis B. *The Flag of the United States* (2–3). Illus. 1989, Children's paper $5.50 (0-516-41158-6). 48pp. How this important symbol of America came to be. (Rev: BL 5/15/89)

**11368** Haban, Rita D. *How Proudly They Wave: Flags of the Fifty States* (5–8). Illus. 1989, Lerner LB $23.93 (0-8225-1799-X). 111pp. Pictures and information on the background history of the state flags. (Rev: BL 12/15/89; SLJ 3/90) [929.9]

**11369** Oxlade, Chris. *Flags* (3–6). Illus. Series: Craft Topics. 1996, Watts LB $20.00 (0-531-14386-4). 32pp. Discusses the origins of flags and their various uses. Activities include a 3-D coat of arms and making a flag. (Rev: BL 4/15/96) [929.9]

**11370** Radlauer, Ruth. *Honor the Flag: A Guide to Its Care and Display* (4–7). Illus. by J. J. Smith-Moore. 1992, Forest LB $12.95 (1-878363-61-1). 48pp. Lots of information about the American flag and its care. (Rev: BL 10/15/92) [929.92]

**11371** Rollo, Vera F. *The American Flag* (3–6). Illus. by Alvin C. Jasper. 1990, Maryland $12.95 (0-917882-28-8). 78pp. The history of the U.S. flag plus myths that have grown up about its origins. (Rev: BL 6/1/90) [929.9]

**11372** Ryan, Pam M. *The Flag We Love* (2–4). Illus. by Ralph Masiello. 1996, Charlesbridge $15.95 (0-88106-845-4). 32pp. The origins of the American flag, its history, and its uses are described in this colorful picture book. (Rev: BL 1/1–15/96; SLJ 5/96) [929.9]

**11373** Spencer, Eve. *A Flag for Our Country* (K–3). Illus. by Mike Eagle. Series: Stories of America. 1993, Raintree Steck-Vaughn LB $22.83 (0-8114-7211-6). The story of how Betsy Ross made the first American flag. (Rev: SLJ 5/93) [929.9]

**11374** Williams, Earl P. *What You Should Know About the American Flag* (4–8). Illus. 1989, Thomas Publns. paper $4.95 (0-939631-10-5). 68pp. A comprehensive guide to facts and legends, history and traditions concerning the U.S. flag. (Rev: BL 11/15/87)

## Language and Languages

**11375** Cooper, Kay. *Why Do You Speak as You Do? A Guide to World Languages* (5–8). Illus. by Brandon Kruse. 1992, Children's LB $14.85 (0-8027-8165-9). 66pp. A simple yet lively presentation of linguistics. (Rev: BCCB 2/93; BL 1/15/93) [400]

**11376** Elya, Susan Middleton. *Say Hola to Spanish* (PS–4). Illus. by Loretta Lopez. 1996, Lee & Low $15.95 (1-880000-29-6). 32pp. More than 70 common Spanish words are introduced in delightful rhymes with pencil illustrations. (Rev: BL 5/1/96; SLJ 6/96) [468.1]

**11377** Feder, Jane. *Table, Chair, Bear: A Book in Many Languages* (PS–2). Illus. 1997, Houghton paper $5.95 (0-395-85075-4). 32pp. The names of common objects in 13 different languages, including Korean, French, Spanish, and Chinese. (Rev: BL 3/1/95; HB 5–6/95; SLJ 3/95) [413]

**11378** Johnson, Stephen T. *Alphabet City* (4–7). Illus. 1995, Viking paper $14.99 (0-670-85631-2). 32pp. A sophisticated alphabet book that consists of a series of paintings, each of which represents a letter. (Rev: BCCB 11/95; BL 1/1–15/96; HB 11–12/95; SLJ 1/96*) [421]

**11379** Lee, Huy Voun. *In the Snow* (PS–4). Illus. 1995, Holt $15.95 (0-8050-3172-3). 32pp. A Chinese mother writes 10 Chinese characters in the snow in this introduction to simple Chinese writing for youngsters. (Rev: BL 10/15/95; SLJ 12/95)

**11380** Leventhal, Debra. *What Is Your Language?* (PS–1). Illus. by Monica Wellington. 1994, Dutton paper $12.99 (0-525-45133-1). 32pp. A small child visits various countries, where he gets different answers to the question "What's your language?" (Rev: BCCB 1/94; BL 12/15/93; SLJ 3/94) [400]

**11381** Schwartz, Alvin. *The Cat's Elbow and Other Secret Languages* (4–7). Illus. by Margot Zemach. 1982, Farrar $15.00 (0-374-31224-9). 96pp. Several secret languages are explained.

**11382** Voun Lee, Huy. *At the Beach* (PS–3). Illus. 1994, Holt $14.95 (0-8050-2768-8). 32pp. Introduces 10 Mandarin Chinese characters and the object each suggests. (Rev: BL 6/1–15/94; SLJ 7/94) [495.1]

**11383** Young, Ed. *Voices of the Heart* (4–8). Illus. 1997, Scholastic $17.95 (0-590-50199-2). 32pp. Twenty-six emotions and their corresponding modern Chinese characters are described. (Rev: BCCB 4/97; BL 4/15/97; HB 5–6/97; SLJ 6/97) [179]

## Reading, Speaking, and Writing

### Books, Printing, and Libraries

**11384** Aliki. *How a Book Is Made* (K–3). Illus. by author. 1986, HarperCollins LB $15.89 (0-690-04498-4); paper $5.95 (0-06-446085-1). 32pp. Cat people play all the parts in this minimal text account of how picture books are made. (Rev: BCCB 11/86; BL 9/15/86; SLJ 9/86)

**11385** Brookfield, Karen. *Book* (4–8). Illus. Series: Eyewitness Books. 1993, Knopf LB $20.99 (0-679-94012-X). 64pp. A history of books and printing that also explains how books are currently written and produced. (Rev: BL 10/1/93; SLJ 11/93) [002]

**11386** Chapman, Gillian, and Pam Robson. *Making Shaped Books* (4–6). Illus. 1995, Millbrook LB $19.90 (1-56294-560-2). 32pp. Clear directions and many illustrations highlight this project book on how to create several books of different shapes. (Rev: BL 11/15/95; SLJ 12/95) [736]

**11387** Cummins, Julie. *The Inside-Outside Book of Libraries* (1–4). Illus. by Roxie Munro. 1996, Dutton paper $15.99 (0-525-45608-2). 40pp. All sorts of libraries — big and small; public, school, and special — are visited in this introduction. (Rev: BCCB 10/96; BL 10/15/96; HB 9–10/96; SLJ 8/96*) [027]

**11388** Falwell, Cathryn. *The Letter Jesters* (2–4). Illus. 1994, Ticknor $14.95 (0-395-66898-0). 48pp. Using the activities of 2 jesters as a framework, a number of different typefaces are introduced. (Rev: BCCB 12/94; BL 11/15/94; HB 11–12/94; SLJ 9/94) [686.224]

**11389** Fowler, Allan. *The Dewey Decimal System* (3–5). Illus. 1996, Children's LB $21.00 (0-516-20132-8). 47pp. An explanation of the Dewey Decimal System, using clear text and many examples. (Rev: BL 2/1/97; SLJ 4/97) [025.4]

**11390** Fowler, Allan. *The Library of Congress* (2–6). Illus. Series: True Books: Books and Libraries. 1996, Children's LB $21.00 (0-516-20137-9). 48pp. An information-packed account that describes the history, contents, and functions of the Library of Congress. (Rev: SLJ 2/97) [027]

**11391** Ganeri, Anita. *The Story of Writing and Printing* (3–6). Illus. Series: Signs of the Times. 1997, Oxford LB $14.95 (0-19-521256-8). 30pp. In a series of double-page spreads, presents the story of writing in many cultures, as well as a history of printing up to desktop publishing. (Rev: BL 2/1/97; SLJ 2/97) [652]

**11392** Guthrie, Donna, et al. *The Young Author's Do-It-Yourself Book* (3–4). Illus. 1994, Millbrook LB $21.90 (1-56294-350-2). 64pp. This simple guide on how to make a book explains each stage from writing the manuscript to binding the finished product. (Rev: BL 4/15/94; SLJ 4/94) [070.5]

**11393** Jaspersohn, William. *My Hometown Library* (K–3). Illus. 1994, Houghton $14.95 (0-395-55723-2). 48pp. From an examination of the floor plans to checking out materials, this is an introduction to all aspects of a functioning public library, with special emphasis on the children's room. (Rev: BCCB 2/94; BL 3/1/94; SLJ 5/94) [027.4]

**11394** Kehoe, Michael. *A Book Takes Root: The Making of a Picture Book* (4–7). Illus. 1993, Carolrhoda LB $16.95 (0-87614-756-2). 40pp. Covers the birth of a picture book from the first ideas to the finished product. (Rev: BL 8/93) [070]

**11395** Knowlton, Jack. *Books and Libraries* (2–5). Illus. by Harriett Barton. 1991, HarperCollins LB $14.89 (0-06-021610-7). 48pp. The history of books and libraries is traced from cave paintings to the present. (Rev: BCCB 3/91; BL 4/1/91; SLJ 4/91) [002]

**11396** Krensky, Stephen. *Breaking into Print: Before and After the Invention of the Printing Press* (2–5). Illus. by Bonnie Christensen. 1996, Little, Brown $15.95 (0-316-50376-2). 32pp. Beginning with the writing of manuscripts, this account traces the birth of printing and the contributions of Gutenberg. (Rev: BCCB 1/97; BL 10/15/96; SLJ 10/96*) [686.2]

**11397** McInerney, Claire. *Find It! The Inside Story at Your Library* (4–6). Illus. by Harry Pulver. 1989, Lerner LB $15.93 (0-8225-2425-2). 56pp. An introduction to libraries and their uses, including computers. (Rev: BL 11/15/89; SLJ 1/90) [025]

**11398** Madama, John. *Desktop Publishing: The Art of Communication* (5–8). Illus. Series: Media Workshop. 1993, Lerner LB $21.27 (0-8225-2303-5). 64pp. The history of desktop publishing, the equipment used, and the production of a newsletter. (Rev: SLJ 6/93) [686.2]

**11399** Stowell, Charlotte. *Step-by-Step Making Books* (4–6). Illus. Series: Step by Step. 1994, Kingfisher paper $6.95 (1-85697-518-5). 40pp. Provides the supplies needed and the basic procedures for creating a number of different books, including pop-ups and flap books. (Rev: BL 3/15/95) [741.6]

**11400** Swain, Gwenyth. *Bookworks: Making Books by Hand* (4–7). Illus. 1995, Carolrhoda LB $16.00 (0-87614-858-5). 64pp. After a brief history of books and printing, this account gives directions for making

paper and various kinds of books. (Rev: BL 7/95; SLJ 8/95*) [745.5]

**11401** Thomson, Ruth. *Printing* (K–3). Illus. 1994, Children's LB $16.00 (0-516-07992-1). 24pp. This book contains simple step-by-step instructions for a number of projects involving printing. (Rev: BL 3/15/95) [761]

## Signs and Symbols

**11402** Charlip, Remy, and Mary Beth Ancona. *Handtalk: An ABC of Finger Spelling and Sign Language* (3–6). Illus. by George Ancona. 1984, Simon & Schuster LB $15.95 (0-02-718130-8). 48pp. This is a beginning book on finger spelling and sign language.

**11403** Fain, Kathleen. *Handsigns: A Sign Language Alphabet* (2–5). Illus. by author. 1993, Chronicle $13.95 (0-8118-0310-4). Full-page paintings of animals are used to introduce each letter in the sign language alphabet. (Rev: SLJ 12/93) [419]

**11404** Gross, Ruth Belov. *You Don't Need Words! A Book About Ways People Talk Without Words* (1–4). Illus. by Susannah Ryan. 1991, Scholastic $14.95 (0-590-43897-2). 48pp. A demonstration of how people talk nonverbally. (Rev: BL 12/15/91; SLJ 1/92) [302]

**11405** Gryski, Camilla. *Hands On, Thumbs Up: Secret Handshakes, Fingerprints, Sign Languages and More Handy Ways to Have Fun with Hands* (3–6). Illus. by Pat Cupples. 1991, Addison-Wesley paper $8.95 (0-201-56756-3). 112pp. All about the human hand — facts, trivia, superstitions, jokes, and more. (Rev: BL 12/15/91) [611.97]

**11406** Hofsinde, Robert. *Indian Sign Language* (4–7). Illus. by author. 1956, Morrow LB $13.93 (0-688-31610-7). A brief history of Indian sign language and its meanings.

**11407** Klove, Lars. *I See a Sign* (PS–2). Photos by author. Series: Ready-to-Read Books. 1996, Simon & Schuster $14.00 (0-689-80800-3); paper $3.99 (0-689-80799-6). 32pp. This account pictures and explains a number of signs, like stop signs and railroad-crossing signs. (Rev: SLJ 9/96) [133]

**11408** Miller, Mary Beth, and George Ancona. *Handtalk School* (PS–3). Illus. by George Ancona. 1991, Macmillan $14.95 (0-02-700912-2). At a school for the deaf, children use sign language as they prepare for Thanksgiving. (Rev: BCCB 11/91; SLJ 9/91)

**11409** Rankin, Laura. *The Handmade Alphabet* (PS–6). Illus. 1991, Dial paper $15.99 (0-8037-0974-9). 32pp. Hands do the talking in this sign-language alphabet book. (Rev: BCCB 9/91; BL 8/91*; HB 11–12/91; SLJ 10/91*) [419]

**11410** Samoyault, Tiphaine. *Give Me a Sign! What Pictograms Tell Us Without Words* (4–7). Trans. by Esther Allen. Illus. 1997, Viking paper $13.99 (0-670-87466-3). 32pp. Explains a number of road signs and travelers' information signage, as well as other pictograms. (Rev: BL 10/15/97; SLJ 1/98) [302.23]

**11411** Wheeler, Cindy. *More Simple Signs* (1–4). Illus. 1998, Viking paper $14.99 (0-670-87477-9). 32pp. Simple words that children would use are translated into sign language using drawings that show the hand positions. (Rev: BL 1/1–15/98; SLJ 1/98) [419]

**11412** Wheeler, Cindy. *Simple Signs* (PS–1). Illus. 1995, Viking paper $12.99 (0-670-86282-7). 32pp. Twenty-eight basic words are converted into sign language in this introduction to communicating with hand movements. (Rev: BCCB 12/95; BL 9/1/95; SLJ 10/95) [419]

## Words and Grammar

**11413** Agee, Jon. *So Many Dynamos! And Other Palindromes* (3–6). Illus. 1994, Farrar $13.31 (0-374-22473-0). 80pp. A collection of humorous, inventive palindromes illustrated by amusing cartoons. (Rev: BCCB 1/95; BL 12/15/94) [818]

**11414** Asimov, Isaac. *Words from the Myths* (5–8). Illus. by William Barss. 1969, NAL paper $3.95 (0-451-14097-4). 224pp. Excellent essays on modern words derived from classical myths, with emphasis on scientific vocabulary.

**11415** Brown, Marc. *Arthur's Really Helpful Word Book* (PS–1). Illus. by author. 1997, Random LB $14.99 (0-679-98735-5). An entertaining word book that illustrates and identifies hundreds of common words. (Rev: SLJ 11/97) [400]

**11416** Burstein, Chaya M. *The Jewish Kids' Hebrew-English Wordbook* (1–4). Illus. by author. 1994, Jewish Publication Soc. $16.95 (0-8276-0381-9). 39pp. A picture dictionary that contains definitions of 500 words in English and Hebrew, with a pronunciation guide. (Rev: SLJ 5/94) [492.4]

**11417** Cole, Joanna, and Stephanie Calmenson. *Bug in a Rug: Reading Fun for Just-Beginners* (PS–1). Illus. by Alan Tiegreen. 1996, Morrow LB $15.93 (0-688-12209-4). 48pp. Activities, puzzles, and stories painlessly teach language and reading skills. (Rev: BL 9/1/96; SLJ 11/96) [818]

**11418** Cox, James A. *Put Your Foot in Your Mouth and Other Silly Sayings* (3–5). Illus. by Sam Q. Weissman. 1980, Random $3.95 (0-394-84503-X). 72pp. The origins of such expressions as "pay through the nose" are described in this board book.

**11419** Dobkin, Bonnie. *Go-With Words* (1–2). Illus. by Tom Dunnington. Series: Rookie Readers. 1993, Children's LB $17.00 (0-516-02016-1). 32pp. An easy-to-read book that explores the concept of vocabulary and the value of words. (Rev: BL 3/1/94) [428.1]

**11420** Eastman, P. D. *The Cat in the Hat Beginner Book Dictionary* (K–3). Illus. 1964, Random LB $9.99 (0-394-91009-5). 144pp. Explains word meanings with sentences and pictures.

**11421** Gonzalez, Ralfka, and Ana Ruiz. *My First Book of Proverbs/Mi Primer Libro de Dichos* (2–5). Illus. by authors. 1995, Children's Book Pr. $15.95 (0-89239-134-0). A bilingual book of 27 Mexican dichos (proverbs) illustrated in bright, glowing colors. (Rev: SLJ 2/96) [398.9]

**11422** Heller, Ruth. *Behind the Mask: A Book About Prepositions* (2–4). Illus. 1995, Putnam $17.99 (0-448-41123-7). 48pp. Using rhymes, a variety of prepositions are introduced and used. (Rev: BL 12/15/95) [428.2]

**11423** Heller, Ruth. *Kites Sail High: A Book About Verbs* (2–4). Illus. by author. 1988, Putnam LB $17.95 (0-448-10480-6); paper $5.99 (0-698-11389-6). 48pp. Romping through an explanation of verbs with various moods of verbs graphically illustrated. (Rev: BCCB 1/89)

**11424** Heller, Ruth. *Many Luscious Lollipops* (1–4). Illus. by author. 1989, Putnam $17.99 (0-448-03151-5). In a series of rhymes, a variety of adjectives are introduced and identified. (Rev: BCCB 11/89; SLJ 1/90) [415]

**11425** Heller, Ruth. *Merry-Go-Round: A Book About Nouns* (3–5). Illus. 1990, Putnam $17.95 (0-448-40085-5). 48pp. This picture book in verse explores the different types of nouns. (Rev: BCCB 1/91; BL 1/1/91; HB 1–2/91; SLJ 12/90) [425]

**11426** Heller, Ruth. *Mine, All Mine: A Book About Pronouns* (2–5). Illus. 1997, Putnam $17.95 (0-448-41606-9). 48pp. Using large, colorful illustrations and a direct text, the world of pronouns and their uses is covered in an entertaining way. (Rev: BL 11/15/97; SLJ 2/98*) [428.2]

**11427** Heller, Ruth. *Up, Up and Away: A Book About Adverbs* (2–5). Illus. 1991, Putnam $17.99 (0-448-40249-1); paper $6.99 (0-698-11663-1). 32pp. In color drawings and catchy rhymes, Heller explains how adverbs answer precisely the questions of how, how often, when, and where. Also use by Heller: *A Cache of Jewels and Other Collective Nouns* (on collective nouns) and *Kites Sail High* (on verbs) (both 1998). (Rev: BCCB 1/92; BL 1/15/92; SLJ 2/92) [418]

**11428** Hill, Eric. *Spot's Big Book of Words* (PS). Illus. by author. 1988, Putnam $10.95 (0-399-21563-

8). 28pp. Lovable Spot teaches young readers the words of their everyday world. (Rev: BL 10/1/88; SLJ 11/88)

**11429** Hoban, Tana. *All About Where* (PS–1). Illus. 1991, Greenwillow LB $13.88 (0-688-09698-0). 32pp. A book that teaches spatial relationships and location words. (Rev: BCCB 4/91; BL 3/15/91; HB 5–6/91; SLJ 4/91*) [428.2]

**11430** Juster, Norton. *As: A Surfeit of Similes* (2–5). Illus. by David Small. 1989, Morrow LB $15.93 (0-688-08140-1). 80pp. A long list of similes enter the conversation of 2 funny little men. (Rev: BCCB 5/89; BL 5/15/89; SLJ 4/89)

**11431** Leigh, Tom, illus. *The Sesame Street Word Book* (PS–1). 1990, Western $9.95 (0-307-15549-8). 72pp. Over 1,000 words are introduced in cartoon-like illustrations.

**11432** Levey, Judith, ed. *The Macmillan Picture Wordbook* (PS–K). Illus. 1990, Simon & Schuster LB $8.95 (0-02-754641-1). 64pp. Several common words are introduced under broad headings. (Rev: BL 6/15/91)

**11433** Root, Betty. *My First Dictionary* (PS–2). Illus. by Jonathan Langley. Series: My First Reference. 1993, DK Publg. $16.95 (1-56458-277-9). 96pp. Definitions and illustrations are given for 1,000 words commonly used by children plus an appended collection of word games. (Rev: SLJ 1/94) [423]

**11434** Scarry, Richard. *Richard Scarry's Best Word Book Ever* (PS–2). Illus. by author. 1963, Western $10.95 (0-307-15510-2). 72pp. A diverse, unorthodox picture dictionary for children who like lots of little pictures.

**11435** Schneider, R. M. *Add It, Dip It, Fix It: A Book of Verbs* (PS–1). Illus. 1995, Houghton $13.95 (0-395-72771-5). 32pp. Action verbs arranged alphabetically are introduced by handsome collages. (Rev: BL 8/95; SLJ 9/95) [428]

**11436** Shiffman, Lena. *My First Book of Words: 1,000 Words Every Child Should Know* (PS). Illus. by author. 1992, Scholastic $13.95 (0-590-45142-1). 62pp. Through a series of illustrations, many objects, actions, and emotions are identified in this basic word book. (Rev: SLJ 3/92)

**11437** Terban, Marvin. *The Dove Dove: Funny Homograph Riddles* (4–7). Illus. by Tom Huffman. 1988, Houghton paper $6.95 (0-89919-810-4). 64pp. Making homographs less puzzling. Also use: *Mad As a Wet Hen! and Other Funny Idioms* (1987). (Rev: BL 1/1/89)

**11438** Terban, Marvin. *Eight Ate: A Feast of Homonym Riddles* (2–3). Illus. by Giulio Maestro. 1982, Houghton paper $6.95 (0-89919-086-3). 64pp. A question-and-answer approach to introducing a variety of homonyms.

**11439** Terban, Marvin. *Guppies in Tuxedos: Funny Eponyms* (3–6). Illus. by Giulio Maestro. 1988, Houghton paper $6.95 (0-89919-770-1). 64pp. Telling the story behind 100 eponyms arranged by categories. (Rev: BL 7/88; SLJ 8/88)

**11440** Terban, Marvin. *In a Pickle and Other Funny Idioms* (3–6). Illus. by Giulio Maestro. 1983, Houghton paper $6.95 (0-89919-164-9). 64pp. Common idioms are explained, and their origins are given.

**11441** Terban, Marvin. *Punching the Clock: Funny Action Idioms* (3–6). Illus. by Tom Huffman. 1990, Houghton paper $6.95 (0-89919-865-1). 64pp. Such expressions as "playing possum" and "batting a thousand" are among the nearly 100 explained and illustrated with amusing drawings. (Rev: BL 6/15/90; SLJ 7/90) [428.1]

**11442** Terban, Marvin. *Scholastic Dictionary of Idioms* (4–7). Illus. 1996, Scholastic $15.95 (0-590-27549-6). 256pp. More than 600 idioms are listed with their origins and meanings. (Rev: BCCB 7–8/96; BL 3/15/96) [423]

**11443** Terban, Marvin. *Too Hot to Hoot: Funny Palindrome Riddles* (3–6). Illus. by Giulio Maestro. 1985, Houghton paper $6.95 (0-89919-320-X). 64pp. A wordplay book exploring palindromes: words, phrases, sentences, and numbers that are the same read forward and backward. (Rev: BCCB 6/85; BL 5/15/85; SLJ 9/85)

**11444** Terban, Marvin. *Your Foot's on My Feet! And Other Tricky Nouns* (3–5). Illus. by Giulio Maestro. 1986, Houghton paper $6.95 (0-89919-413-3). 64pp. A lively look at sometimes confusing singular and plural nouns. (Rev: BL 7/86; SLJ 9/86)

**11445** Van Allsburg, Chris. *The Z Was Zapped: A Play in Twenty-Six Acts* (3–8). Illus. 1987, Houghton $17.95 (0-395-44612-0). 56pp. The 26 acts turn out to be a new way to introduce the alphabet. (Rev: BL 11/1/87; SLJ 11/87)

**11446** Wildsmith, Brian. *Brian Wildsmith's Amazing World of Words* (K–4). Illus. by author. 1997, Millbrook LB $23.90 (0-7613-0045-7). Many environments — like jungles, playgrounds, and farms — are pictured, with labels for each of the objects. (Rev: SLJ 5/97) [401]

**11447** Wittels, Harriet, and Joan Greisman. *A First Thesaurus* (4–6). Illus. 1985, Western paper $7.50 (0-307-15835-7). 144pp. Simple entry words are in boldface with synonyms and antonyms for more than 2,000 words. (Rev: BL 11/1/85; SLJ 2/86)

**11448** Ziefert, Harriet. *Baby Buggy, Buggy Baby* (PS–2). Illus. by Richard Brown. Series: Word Play Flap Book. 1997, Houghton $10.95 (0-395-85161-

0). Using flaps, this word book shows how phrases change meaning if one reverses the word order. Homonyms are introduced in *Night, Knight* (1997). (Rev: BCCB 4/97; SLJ 7/97)

## Writing and Speaking

**11449** Asher, Sandy. *Where Do You Get Your Ideas? Helping Young Writers Begin* (5–7). Illus. 1987, Walker LB $13.85 (0-8027-6691-9). 96pp. Keeping a journal and other interesting ideas for would-be journalists. (Rev: BCCB 12/87; BL 9/15/87; SLJ 9/87)

**11450** Asher, Sandy. *Wild Words and How to Tame Them* (5–7). Illus. by Dennis Kendrick. 1989, Walker LB $14.85 (0-8027-6888-1). 112pp. Advice for beginning writers on putting words together. (Rev: BL 1/1/90; SLJ 1/90) [372.6]

**11451** Bailly, Sharon. *Pass It On!* (3–5). Illus. 1995, Millbrook LB $23.40 (1-56294-588-2). 64pp. Hints on how to perk up the writing and sending of notes, including secret codes. (Rev: BL 2/1/96; SLJ 2/96) [652]

**11452** Bedard, Michael. *Glass Town* (3–5). Illus. by Laura Fernandez and Rick Jacobson. 1997, Simon & Schuster $16.00 (0-689-81185-3). 40pp. An unusual picture book that explores the secret world of the Brontë children, their fantasies, and their vast output of children's stories. (Rev: BL 8/97; SLJ 10/97) [652]

**11453** Bentley, Nancy, and Donna Guthrie. *Putting On a Play* (4–6). Illus. 1997, Millbrook LB $22.40 (0-7613-0011-2). 64pp. A guide to all aspects of playwriting and production, with practical tips for those on stage and behind the scenes. (Rev: BL 2/1/97; SLJ 3/97) [792]

**11454** Bruchac, Joseph. *Tell Me a Tale* (4–8). 1997, Harcourt $16.00 (0-15-201221-4). 144pp. A master storyteller reveals tricks of the trade, tells where to find stories, and explores their origins and effects, with many examples from various cultures. (Rev: BL 3/15/97; SLJ 8/97) [808.5]

**11455** Burns, Peggy. *News* (3–5). Illus. Series: Stepping Through History. 1995, Thomson Learning LB $22.83 (1-56847-342-7). 32pp. A history of journalism and the distribution of news from ancient times to the present. (Rev: BL 7/95) [070.4]

**11456** Burns, Peggy. *Writing* (3–5). Illus. Series: Stepping Through History. 1995, Raintree Steck-Vaughn $22.83 (1-56847-341-9). 32pp. A history of writing from ancient forms like hieroglyphics to the many languages of today. (Rev: BL 7/95) [411]

**11457** Christelow, Eileen. *What Do Authors Do?* (3–5). Illus. 1995, Clarion $15.00 (0-395-71124-X). 32pp. Using cartoonlike drawings, the process of

writing a book is traced using the experiences of 2 imaginary authors. (Rev: BCCB 11/95; BL 9/15/95; HB 11–12/95; SLJ 12/95*) [808.06]

**11458** Curry, Barbara K., and James Michael Brodie. *Sweet Words So Brave: The Story of African American Literature* (5–8). Illus. by Jerry Butler. 1996, Zino $24.95 (1-55933-179-8). 64pp. An outline of African American literature, from slave narratives to the great writers of today — e.g., Nikki Giovanni and Toni Morrison. (Rev: BL 2/15/97*; SLJ 4/97) [810.9]

**11459** Detz, Joan. *You Mean I Have to Stand Up and Say Something?* (4–8). Illus. 1986, Macmillan LB $13.95 (0-689-31221-0). 96pp. A chatty guide to effective speaking before an audience. (Rev: BCCB 2/87; BL 2/1/87)

**11460** Dubrovin, Vivian. *Storytelling Adventures: Stories Kids Can Tell* (4–7). Illus. by Bobbi Shupe. 1997, Storycraft paper $14.95 (0-9638339-2-8). 64pp. This book not only includes a selection of stories to tell but also suggests appropriate props to use, with directions on how to make them. (Rev: SLJ 5/97) [808.5]

**11461** Dubrovin, Vivian. *Storytelling for the Fun of It* (4–8). Illus. by Bobbi Shupe. 1994, Storycraft paper $16.95 (0-9638339-0-1). 160pp. This useful guide is divided into 3 parts that give general information, where and what kinds of stories to tell, and how to learn and perform them. (Rev: SLJ 4/94) [808.5]

**11462** Feller, Ron, and Marsha Feller. *Fanciful Faces and Handbound Books: Fairy Tales* (3–6). Illus. by Kathryn K. Hastings. 1989, Arts Factory paper $9.95 (0-9615873-1-8). 72pp. How to make fairy tale figures and write stories about them. (Rev: BL 7/89) [808]

**11463** Gibbons, Gail. *Deadline! From News to Newspaper* (K–3). 1987, HarperCollins LB $15.89 (0-690-04602-2). 32pp. With a small-town newspaper as a backdrop, readers can follow the workings of the press. (Rev: BL 6/15/87; HB 5–6/87; SLJ 6–7/87)

**11464** Goldstein, Peggy. *Long Is a Dragon: Chinese Writing for Children* (2–5). Illus. 1991, China Books $17.95 (1-881896-01-3). 32pp. This introduction to Chinese writing gives a brief history and 75 simple characters, including the numbers 1 to 12. (Rev: BCCB 5/91; BL 6/1/91; SLJ 7/91) [495.1]

**11465** Hackman, Peggy, and Don Oldenburg, eds. *Dear Mr. President* (4–7). 1993, Avon paper $4.00 (0-380-77473-9). 130pp. A selection of letters from children giving advice to President Clinton. (Rev: BL 1/15/94) [816]

**11466** Hamilton, Martha, and Mitch Weiss. *Stories in My Pocket: Tales Kids Can Tell* (4–7). Illus. 1997, Fulcrum paper $15.95 (1-55591-957-X). 184pp. This handbook of storytelling for young storytellers includes 30 tales to begin with. (Rev: BL 1/1–15/97) [372.6]

**11467** Hulme, Joy N., and Donna Guthrie. *How to Write, Recite, and Delight in All Kinds of Poetry* (3–6). 1996, Millbrook LB $24.90 (1-56294-576-9). 96pp. Using examples of poetry written by grade school children, this book introduces different types of poetry and gives help in writing and reciting poems. (Rev: SLJ 12/96) [811]

**11468** James, Elizabeth, and Carol Barkin. *How to Write a Great School Report* (4–6). Illus. 1983, Lothrop LB $11.93 (0-688-02283-9). 167pp. A simple, well-organized account that starts with choosing the topic and ends with the final presentation.

**11469** James, Elizabeth, and Carol Barkin. *How to Write Your Best Book Report* (4–6). Illus. by Roy Doty. 1998, Lothrop paper $4.95 (0-688-16140-5). 80pp. A chatty account of dos and don'ts that can make book report writing seem almost painless. (Rev: BL 11/15/86)

**11470** James, Elizabeth, and Carol Barkin. *Sincerely Yours: How to Write Great Letters* (4–7). 1993, Houghton $14.95 (0-395-58831-6). 146pp. A practical guide to writing both personal and business letters with plenty of samples that can be used as guides. (Rev: BL 5/1/93; SLJ 5/93) [808.6]

**11471** Janeczko, Paul B. *Poetry from A to Z: A Guide for Young Writers* (5–7). Illus. 1994, Bradbury paper $16.00 (0-02-747672-3). 176pp. Poets speak about their work and give examples, but the core of this book is the author's encouraging tips to youngsters who might give poetry writing a try. (Rev: BCCB 3/95; BL 12/15/94) [808.1]

**11472** Leedy, Loreen. *Messages in the Mailbox: How to Write a Letter* (2–4). Illus. 1991, Holiday LB $15.95 (0-8234-0889-2). 32pp. In this cheery guide, an alligator teacher shows the class of children and animals how to write a letter. (Rev: BCCB 12/91; BL 1/1/91; SLJ 9/91*) [295.4]

**11473** Lewis, Amanda. *Writing: A Fact and Fun Book* (4–6). Illus. by Heather Collins. 1992, Kids Can paper $8.95 (1-55074-052-0). 96pp. A lively book packed with information on all aspects of writing. (Rev: BL 1/15/93; SLJ 1/93) [411]

**11474** Nixon, Joan Lowery. *If You Were a Writer* (3–5). Illus. by Bruce Degen. 1988, Macmillan LB $15.00 (0-02-768210-2). 32pp. A re-creation of what goes on in a writer's mind, as Melia thinks she might like to be like her writer-mother. (Rev: BL 10/1/88; SLJ 11/88)

**11475** Otfinoski, Steven. *Speaking Up, Speaking Out: A Kid's Guide to Making Speeches, Oral Reports, and Conversation* (5–8). Illus. 1996, Millbrook LB $23.90 (1-56294-345-6). 96pp. All kinds

of public-speaking situations are introduced, with suggestions on how to be a success at each. (Rev: BL 1/1–15/97; SLJ 1/97) [808.5]

**11476** Pellowski, Anne. *The Storytelling Handbook* (4–6). Illus. 1995, Simon & Schuster $16.00 (0-689-80311-7). 122pp. A fine practical guide for the young storyteller, with several good stories as examples. (Rev: BL 2/1/96; SLJ 12/95) [372.64]

**11477** *Scrawl! Writing in Ancient Times* (5–8). Illus. Series: Buried Worlds. 1994, Lerner LB $23.93 (0-8225-3209-3). 72pp. Using text, many illustrations, and sidebars, the development of writing in ancient civilizations is traced. (Rev: BL 1/15/95) [411.7]

**11478** Seuling, Barbara. *To Be a Writer: A Guide for Young People Who Want to Write and Publish* (4–8). Illus. 1997, Twenty-First Century LB $16.98 (0-8050-4692-5). 128pp. A well-organized how-to book that gives good advice to budding writers, including how to outline a book and define characters. (Rev: BL 6/1–15/97; SLJ 8/97) [808]

**11479** Stevens, Carla. *A Book of Your Own: Keeping a Diary or Journal* (5–8). 1993, Clarion $14.95 (0-89919-256-4). 94pp. A useful manual on how to keep a journal, with tips on writing expressively, along with samples from diaries by notables like Anne Frank. (Rev: BL 1/15/94; SLJ 11/93) [808]

**11480** Stevens, Janet. *From Pictures to Words: A Book About Making a Book* (2–4). Illus. 1995, Holiday LB $15.95 (0-8234-1154-0). 42pp. This manual for youngsters who want to create their own picture books deals with such topics as setting, plot, and characterization. (Rev: BCCB 6/95; BL 4/15/95; SLJ 7/95*) [741.6]

**11481** Terban, Marvin. *Checking Your Grammar* (5–8). Series: Scholastic Guides. 1993, Scholastic $10.95 (0-590-49454-6). 144pp. An attractive, witty guide to effective writing of all sorts of letters, book reports, essays, and reviews. (Rev: BL 10/1/93; SLJ 2/94) [428.2]

**11482** Terban, Marvin. *It Figures! Fun Figures of Speech* (4–6). Illus. by Giulio Maestro. 1993, Clarion $13.95 (0-395-61584-4); paper $6.95 (0-395-66591-4). 62pp. Six figures of speech — including similes, alliteration, hyperbole, and personification — are explained, with examples from literature and folklore plus exercises on their use. (Rev: BL 12/1/93; SLJ 11/93) [808]

**11483** Vinton, Ken. *Alphabet Antics: Hundreds of Activities to Challenge and Enrich Letter Learners of All Ages* (5–8). Illus. by author. 1996, Free Spirit paper $19.95 (0-915793-98-9). 135pp. For each letter of the alphabet, there is a history, how it appears in different alphabets, important words that begin with that letter, a quotation from someone whose name starts with it, and a number of interesting related projects. (Rev: SLJ 1/97) [411]

**11484** Warburton, Lois. *The Beginning of Writing* (5–8). Illus. 1991, Lucent LB $22.45 (1-56006-113-8). 112pp. The author traces prealphabetic communication through history and explains how our present-day alphabet evolved. [652.1]

**11485** Young, Sue. *Writing with Style* (4–6). Series: Scholastic Guides. 1997, Scholastic paper $12.95 (0-590-50977-2). 144pp. A guide for the novice writer, with chapters on planning, presenting, and publishing one's work. (Rev: BL 3/1/97; SLJ 5/97) [372.6]

**11486** Zeman, Anne, and Kate Kelly. *Everything You Need to Know About American History Homework: A Desk Reference for Students and Parents* (4–6). Illus. Series: Scholastic Homework Reference. 1994, Scholastic $18.95 (0-590-49362-0). 136pp. This book helps youngsters understand concepts in American history and how to apply them while doing homework assignments. Also use *Everything You Need to Know About Math Homework* and *Everything You Need to Know About Science Homework* (both 1994). (Rev: SLJ 1/95) [372.13]

# Music

## General

**11487** Ardley, Neil. *A Young Person's Guide to Music* (5–8). Illus. 1995, DK Publg. $24.95 (0-7894-0313-7). 80pp. With an accompanying CD, this book introduces instruments of the orchestra and supplies a concise history of classical music. (Rev: BL 12/15/95; SLJ 1/96) [780]

**11488** Englander, Roger. *Opera! What's All the Screaming About?* (6–8). Illus. 1983, Walker $12.95 (0-8027-6491-6). 192pp. History and explanation of different parts of the opera.

**11489** Gatti, Anne, reteller. *The Magic Flute* (4–7). Illus. by Peter Malone. 1997, Chronicle $17.95 (0-8118-1003-8). An elegant retelling of the Mozart opera, with each scene given a full-color painting and a page of text. The accompanying CD has 16 selections coded to each page. (Rev: SLJ 1/98*) [782.1]

**11490** Igus, Toyomi. *I See the Rhythm* (5–8). Illus. by Michele Wood. 1998, Children's Book Pr. $15.95 (0-89239-151-0). 32pp. Using a timeline and a succinct text, this title traces African American contributions to such musical forms as the blues, big band, jazz, bebop, gospel, and rock. (Rev: BL 2/15/98) [780]

**11491** Medearis, Angela Shelf, and Michael R. Medearis. *Music* (5–7). Illus. Series: African American Arts. 1997, Twenty-First Century LB $16.98 (0-8050-4482-5). 64pp. This book on African Americans and music covers those African instruments, chants, and rhythms that evolved into ragtime, blues, jazz, soul, and rock. (Rev: BL 7/97; SLJ 7/97) [780]

**11492** Price, Leontyne, reteller. *Aida* (4–8). Illus. by Leo Dillon and Diane Dillon. 1990, Harcourt $19.00 (0-15-200405-X). The story of one of the grandest of operas retold by one of opera's grandest divas. (Rev: BCCB 10/90; HB 3–4/91; SLJ 11/90*) [782.1]

**11493** Raschka, Chris. *Simple Gifts: A Shaker Hymn* (PS–4). Illus. 1998, Holt $15.95 (0-8050-5143-0). 32pp. A brilliantly original treatment of the old Shaker hymn, with dynamic illustrations. (Rev: BL 3/1/98*; SLJ 4/98) [294]

**11494** Rowe, Julian. *Music* (4–7). Illus. Series: Science Encounters. 1997, Rigby $13.95 (1-57572-091-4). 32pp. This book shows how scientific principles are used in music, musical instruments, hearing, and recording devices. (Rev: SLJ 10/97) [780]

**11495** Sommer, Elyse. *The Kids' World Almanac of Music: From Rock to Bach* (3–8). 1992, Pharos paper $7.95 (0-88687-521-8). 276pp. Facts and anecdotes about all kinds of music. (Rev: BL 7/92) [780]

**11496** Woodyard, Shawn. *Music and Song* (4–6). Illus. Series: African American Life. 1995, Rourke LB $23.93 (1-57103-029-8). 48pp. The contributions of African Americans to musical entertainment are chronicled, with an annotated list of famous composers and performers. (Rev: SLJ 3/96) [780]

## Ballads and Folk Songs

**11497** Axelrod, Alan, ed. *Songs of the Wild West* (3–6). Illus. 1991, Simon & Schuster paper $19.95 (0-671-74775-4). 128pp. Through paintings and songs, this volume tells of the American West. (Rev: BL 12/15/91; SLJ 1/92*) [784.7]

**11498** Berger, Melvin. *The Story of Folk Music* (6–8). Illus. 1976, Phillips LB $28.95 (0-87599-215-3). How and why American folk music evolved, with biographical information on singers from Woody Guthrie to John Denver.

**11499** Bryan, Ashley, ed. *All Night, All Day: A Child's First Book of African-American Spirituals* (PS–3). Illus. by Ashley Bryan. 1991, Macmillan $16.00 (0-689-31662-3). 48pp. Contains 20 African American spirituals, with musical notations for each. (Rev: BCCB 7–8/91; BL 10/1/91; HB 7–8/91*; SLJ 5/91) [783.6]

**11500** Bullock, Kathleen. *She'll Be Comin' Round the Mountain* (PS–4). Illus. 1993, Simon & Schuster paper $14.00 (0-671-79153-2). 32pp. An exuberant version of this folk song, with humorous paintings filled with amazing details. (Rev: BL 9/1/93; SLJ 12/93) [811]

**11501** Burgie, Irving. *Caribbean Carnival: Songs of the West Indies* (1–8). Illus. by Frane Lessac. 1992, Morrow LB $15.93 (0-688-10780-X). 32pp. A collection of 13 original and traditional songs of the West Indies. (Rev: BCCB 1/93; BL 10/1/92; SLJ 11/92) [782.42]

**11502** *The Cat Came Back* (K–2). Illus. by Bill Slavin. 1992, Whitman LB $14.95 (0-8075-1097-1). 32pp. From a Canadian tale; Old Mister Johnson's home really belongs to his cat. (Rev: BL 9/15/92; SLJ 3/93) [782.42]

**11503** Chalk, Gary. *Mr. Frog Went a-Courting* (1–4). Illus. 1994, DK Publg. $13.95 (1-56458-622-7). 32pp. A fresh twist to this familiar song that uses a setting of 17th-century England. (Rev: BL 11/1/94; SLJ 2/95) [782.42]

**11504** Chalk, Gary. *Yankee Doodle* (1–4). Illus. 1993, DK Publg. $14.95 (1-56458-202-7). 32pp. Using a series of new verses for the familiar folk tune, the American Revolution is introduced. (Rev: BL 6/1–15/93) [782]

**11505** Clarke, Gus. *E I E I O: The Story of Old Mac-Donald Who Had a Farm* (PS–K). Illus. 1993, Lothrop $14.00 (0-688-12215-9). 32pp. With cartoonlike illustrations, this is an old favorite folk song with a surprise ending. (Rev: BL 5/1/93) [782.42]

**11506** Cohn, Amy L., ed. *From Sea to Shining Sea: A Treasury of American Folklore and Folk Songs* (PS–8). Illus. 1993, Scholastic $29.95 (0-590-42868-3). 416pp. A rich, vibrant collection of more than 140 folk songs and tales, illustrated by 15 distinguished artists, many of them Caldecott winners. (Rev: BCCB 1/94; BL 9/15/93*; HB 11–12/93; SLJ 11/93*) [810.8]

**11507** Collins, Judy. *My Father* (3–6). Illus. by Jane Dyer. 1997, Little, Brown paper $4.95 (0-316-15238-2). 32pp. A picture-book treatment of the nostalgic song of the 1960s sung by folksinger Collins. (Rev: BL 11/1/89; SLJ 10/89) [784]

**11508** Cooper, Floyd. *Cumbayah* (PS–3). Illus. 1998, Morrow $16.00 (0-688-13543-9). 32pp. The illustrations that accompany this folk song show a

multiracial group enjoying themselves. (Rev: BL 2/15/98) [782.42]

**11509** Engvick, William. *Lullabies and Night Songs* (K–3). Illus. by Maurice Sendak. 1965, Harper-Collins $26.00 (0-06-021820-7). A collection of the poet's verses and those of others set to music by Alec Wilder.

**11510** Fox, Dan, ed. *Go in and out the Window: An Illustrated Song Book for Young People* (1–8). Illus. 1987, Holt $25.95 (0-8050-0628-1). 144pp. Sixty-one favorite songs — from "Amazing Grace" to "Yankee Doodle" — listed alphabetically and well illustrated. (Rev: BL 12/15/87)

**11511** Goode, Diane. *Diane Goode's Book of Silly Stories and Songs* (PS). Illus. by author. 1992, Dutton paper $15.00 (0-525-44967-1). 64pp. A book that emphasizes the helpful ability to laugh at oneself. (Rev: BL 10/1/92; HB 9–10/92; SLJ 9/92) [808]

**11512** Granfield, Linda. *Amazing Grace: The Story of the Hymn* (4–8). Illus. by Janet Wilson. 1997, Tundra $15.95 (0-88776-389-8). This account tells about the life of John Newton; his rejection of slavery, even though he once transported slaves; and his later ministry, when he wrote hymns like "Amazing Grace." (Rev: SLJ 8/97) [264]

**11513** Higginsen, Vy. *This Is My Song! A Collection of Gospel Music for the Family* (4–7). Illus. by Brenda Joysmith. 1995, Crown LB $26.99 (0-517-59493-5). 96pp. This beautifully illustrated volume includes the words and music for 30 gospel songs and interesting background information on the history of this genre. (Rev: BL 1/1–15/96; SLJ 1/96) [782.27]

**11514** *An Illustrated Treasury of Songs* (PS–8). Illus. 1994, Rizzoli paper $15.95 (0-8478-1835-7). 128pp. Double-page spreads include musical notation for voice and piano and 55 songs in all, from "Clementine" to "When the Saints Go Marching In." (Rev: BL 1/15/92; SLJ 1/92) [784.6]

**11515** Johnson, James W. *Lift Ev'ry Voice and Sing* (PS–4). Illus. by Jan S. Gilchrist. 1995, Scholastic $14.95 (0-590-46982-7). 32pp. Using the lyrics of this beautiful anthem as a framework, the history and culture of African Americans are traced in touching illustrations. (Rev: BL 2/15/95*; SLJ 2/95) [782]

**11516** Karas, G. Brian. *I Know an Old Lady* (PS–1). Illus. 1995, Scholastic $14.95 (0-590-46575-9). 32pp. An uproarious version of the traditional cumulative nonsense rhyme. (Rev: BCCB 2/95; BL 1/15/95*; SLJ 3/95) [782]

**11517** Kovalski, Maryann. *Take Me Out to the Ballgame* (PS–2). Illus. 1993, Scholastic $14.95 (0-590-45638-5). 32pp. Jenny and Joanna go to the ball game with their wacky and fun-loving grandmother. (Rev: BL 1/15/93; SLJ 4/93) [811]

**11518** Kroll, Steven. *By the Dawn's Early Light: The Story of the Star Spangled Banner* (2–4). Illus. by Dan Andreasen. 1994, Scholastic $15.95 (0-590-45054-9). 40pp. The circumstances of writing our national anthem are re-created, along with a history of the Battle of Baltimore, in this handsomely illustrated book. (Rev: BL 12/15/93; SLJ 3/94) [349.73]

**11519** Krull, Kathleen, ed. *Gonna Sing My Head Off!* (2–8). Illus. by Allen Garns. 1995, Knopf paper $12.00 (0-679-87232-9). 146pp. A collection of 62 contemporary and traditional singing favorites. (Rev: BCCB 10/92*; BL 10/15/92*; HB 3–4/93; SLJ 10/92*) [784.7]

**11520** Langstaff, John. *Frog Went A-Courtin'* (K–3). Illus. by Feodor Rojankovsky. 1955, Harcourt $16.00 (0-15-230214-X); paper $7.00 (0-15-633900-5). 32pp. A rollicking folk song with matching illustrations. Caldecott Medal winner, 1956.

**11521** Langstaff, Nancy, and John Langstaff. *Sally Go Round the Moon* (K–4). Illus. by Jan Pienkowski. 1986, Revels paper $14.95 (0-9640836-3-9). 127pp. A collection of folk songs and singing games originally published in 1970.

**11522** McNeil, Keith, and Rusty McNeil. *Colonial and Revolution Songbook: With Historical Commentary* (4–7). 1996, WEM Records paper $11.95 (1-878360-08-6). 71pp. This songbook contains 39 traditional songs from the 17th century through the War of 1812, with brief historical comments for each. (Rev: SLJ 12/96) [973]

**11523** Mallett, David. *Inch by Inch: The Garden Song* (PS–1). Illus. by Ora Eitan. 1995, Harper-Collins $14.95 (0-06-024303-1). 32pp. This folk song describes all of the work and activities necessary to make a garden grow. (Rev: BCCB 7–8/95; BL 5/15/95; HB 11–12/95; SLJ 8/95) [781.62]

**11524** Mattox, Cheryl W., ed. *Shake It to the One That You Love the Best: Play Songs and Lullabies from Black Musical Traditions* (PS–6). Illus. by Varnette P. Honeywood. 1990, Warren-Mattox paper $7.95 (0-9623381-0-9). 56pp. Music and lyrics for 16 songs and 10 lullabies. (Rev: BL 12/1/90*) [781.62]

**11525** Nic Leodhas, Sorche. *Always Room for One More* (K–3). Illus. by Nonny Hogrogian. 1965, Holt $14.95 (0-8050-0331-2); paper $5.95 (0-8050-0330-4). 32pp. From the Scottish folk song about Machie MacLachlan, who had so many people into his house that it burst. Caldecott Medal winner, 1966.

**11526** *Old MacDonald Had a Farm* (PS–1). Illus. by Carol Jones. 1989, Houghton $15.00 (0-395-49212-2). Detailed watercolors on one page and the words to the old song on the opposite. (Rev: BL 5/1/89) [784.4]

**11527** *Old MacDonald Had a Farm* (PS–1). Illus. by Glen Rounds. 1989, Holiday LB $15.95 (0-8234-0739-X); paper $5.95 (0-8234-0846-9). 32pp. A laugh-filled version of the old classic. (Rev: BCCB 4/89; BL 5/1/89; SLJ 5/89) [784.4]

**11528** *Old MacDonald Had a Farm* (PS–2). Illus. by Holly Berry. 1994, North-South LB $14.88 (1-55858-282-7). 26pp. A delightful rendition of the traditional song, with all of the barnyard animals playing musical instruments. (Rev: BL 6/1–15/94; SLJ 6/94) [782]

**11529** Rogers, Sally. *Earthsong* (PS–1). Illus. by Melissa Mathis. 1998, Dutton $15.99 (0-525-45873-5). 32pp. A reworking of the traditional song "Over in the Meadow" in which 11 endangered animals from around the world are introduced. (Rev: BL 3/1/98; SLJ 3/98) [782]

**11530** Rounds, Glen, ed. *I Know an Old Lady Who Swallowed a Fly* (PS–3). Illus. by Glen Rounds. 1990, Holiday LB $16.95 (0-8234-0814-0). 32pp. This humorous folksong is cleverly illustrated with mottled colors. (Rev: BCCB 9/90; BL 5/15/90; SLJ 8/90) [782]

**11531** Seeger, Ruth C. *American Folk Songs for Children* (2–6). Illus. by Barbara Cooney. 1980, Doubleday paper $14.95 (0-385-15788-6). 192pp. All types of songs, including chants and ballads, that will delight and amuse children.

**11532** Siegen-Smith, Nikki, comp. *Songs for Survival: Songs and Chants from Tribal Peoples Around the World* (4–7). Illus. by Bernard Lodge. 1996, Dutton paper $18.99 (0-525-45564-7). 80pp. These chants and songs gathered from around the world speak of primitive people's concerns about the land and its future. (Rev: BCCB 9/96; SLJ 7/96) [782]

**11533** Silverman, Jerry. *Children's Songs* (4–6). Illus. 1993, Chelsea LB $18.95 (0-7910-1831-8); paper $7.95 (0-7910-1847-4). 64pp. This collection of 31 African American songs includes church songs, slave songs, and folk songs. (Rev: BL 2/15/94; SLJ 12/93) [782]

**11534** Souhami, Jessica. *Old MacDonald* (PS–K). Illus. 1996, Orchard $11.95 (0-531-09493-6). 24pp. Old MacDonald uses a variety of vehicles to transport all of the animals he has on his farm. (Rev: BL 4/1/96; HB 5–6/96; SLJ 5/96) [784.4]

**11535** Spier, Peter. *London Bridge Is Falling Down* (K–3). Illus. by author. 1985, Doubleday paper $3.99 (0-440-40710-9). 48pp. The Mother Goose rhyme set to music with accompanying historical sketch.

**11536** Staines, Bill. *All God's Critters Got a Place in the Choir* (PS–K). Illus. by Margot Zemach. 1989, Puffin paper $5.99 (0-14-054838-6). 32pp. Lyrics and illustrations for this famous folk tune. (Rev: BL 4/1/89; HB 7–8/89; SLJ 6/89)

**11537** Taback, Simms. *There Was an Old Lady Who Swallowed a Fly* (PS–2). Illus. 1997, Viking paper $14.99 (0-670-86939-2). 32pp. A very funny version of the song in which each of the animals makes separate asides. (Rev: BL 11/15/97; SLJ 12/97*) [782]

**11538** *This Old Man* (PS–1). Illus. by Carol Jones. 1990, Houghton $15.00 (0-395-54699-0). An attractively designed edition of this well-loved children's song. (Rev: SLJ 1/91) [784.7]

**11539** Trapani, Iza. *The Itsy Bitsy Spider* (K–1). Illus. 1993, Whispering Coyote LB $15.95 (1-879085-77-1). 32pp. Building on the popular song, this book continues the adventures of the tiny spider. (Rev: BL 3/1/93)

**11540** Weeks, Sarah. *Crocodile Smile* (PS–2). Illus. by Lois Ehlert. 1994, HarperCollins $15.95 (0-06-022867-9). 48pp. Charming songs that are sung by animals that are either extinct, like the dinosaur, or endangered, like the Komodo dragon. Includes audio cassette. (Rev: BL 12/1/94; SLJ 11/94*) [782]

**11541** Weiss, Nicki. *If You're Happy and You Know It: Eighteen Story Songs Set to Pictures* (PS–2). Illus. 1987, Greenwillow $16.00 (0-688-06444-2). 40pp. Songs familiar to preschoolers and early elementary audiences "set to pictures." (Rev: BL 9/15/87; SLJ 11/87)

**11542** Westcott, Nadine Bernard. *I Know an Old Lady Who Swallowed a Fly* (2–4). Illus. by author. 1980, Little, Brown $14.95 (0-316-93128-4); paper $6.95 (0-316-93127-6). 32pp. A newly illustrated edition of this outrageously funny song.

**11543** Westcott, Nadine Bernard. *I've Been Working on the Railroad* (PS–1). Illus. 1996, Hyperion LB $14.49 (0-7868-2041-1). 32pp. This familiar folk song is seen through the eyes of a small boy who, with his dog, have adventures on a train. (Rev: BL 4/1/96; SLJ 6/96) [782]

**11544** *Yankee Doodle* (PS–3). Illus. by Steven Kellogg. 1996, Simon & Schuster paper $5.99 (0-689-80726-0). 32pp. In a large format, the words of this song are illustrated, with background notes on its origin. (Rev: BL 7/96) [782]

**11545** Yolen, Jane, ed. *Jane Yolen's Songs of Summer* (K–2). Illus. by Cyd Moore. 1993, Boyds Mills $12.95 (1-56397-110-0). 32pp. Of the 16 songs included in this collection with their lyrics and music, 13 are folk songs from a number of countries, including the United States. (Rev: BL 6/1–15/93; SLJ 8/93) [782.42]

**11546** Yolen, Jane, and Adam Stemple. *Jane Yolen's Old MacDonald Songbook* (PS–1). Illus. by Rosekrans Hoffman. 1994, Boyds Mills $16.95 (1-56397-281-6). 96pp. A spirited collection of 43 songs featuring animals on the farm. (Rev: BL 11/15/94; SLJ 10/94) [784.6]

**11547** Ziefert, Harriet. *Sleepy-O!* (PS–2). Illus. by Laura Rader. 1997, Houghton $15.00 (0-395-87369-X). 32pp. A song that explains what to do with a baby who won't go to sleep at a barn dance. (Rev: BL 9/1/97; SLJ 1/98) [782.4]

## Holidays

**11548** Delacre, Lulu. *Las Navidades: Popular Christmas Songs from Latin America* (K–4). Illus. 1990, Scholastic $13.95 (0-590-43548-5). 32pp. Christmas traditions of Latin America through seasonal songs. (Rev: BL 11/15/90) [782.42]

**11549** Downes, Belinda. *Silent Night: A Christmas Carol Sampler* (3–7). Illus. 1995, Knopf $18.00 (0-679-86959-X). 32pp. A collection of Christmas carols, with outstanding illustrations. (Rev: BL 9/15/95; SLJ 10/95*) [782.281]

**11550** *The Friendly Beasts: A Traditional Christmas Carol* (3–7). Illus. by Sarah Chamberlain. 1991, Dutton paper $13.95 (0-525-44773-3). 24pp. Glowing illustrations complement this tender carol about animals from the Christmas stable. (Rev: BL 10/15/91) [782]

**11551** Granfield, Linda. *Silent Night: The Song from Heaven* (2–4). Illus. by Nelly Hofer and Ernst Hofer. 1997, Tundra $15.95 (0-88776-395-2). The story of the writing and first performance of this hymn, as experienced by 2 children who are helping in the church in Obendorf, Austria, where it was written in 1818. (Rev: SLJ 10/97)

**11552** Ivory, Lesley A. *Cats and Carols* (3–6). Illus. 1995, Little, Brown $16.95 (0-8212-2136-1). 32pp. Paintings of cats are used to illustrate this collection of 15 traditional Christmas carols. (Rev: BL 11/15/95) [759.13]

**11553** Jeffers, Susan, illus. *Silent Night* (2–5). 1984, Dutton paper $4.99 (0-525-44431-9). 32pp. A lush setting of the Christmas carol.

**11554** Keats, Ezra Jack, illus. *The Little Drummer Boy* (2–4). 1987, Macmillan paper $4.95 (0-689-71158-1). 32pp. The lyrics of this popular Christmas song are well illustrated.

**11555** Knight, Hilary. *Hilary Knight's the Twelve Days of Christmas* (K–3). Illus. by author. 1987, Macmillan paper $4.95 (0-689-71150-6). 34pp. The traditional folk song with animals as participants.

**11556** Langstaff, John, ed. *What a Morning! The Christmas Story in Black Spirituals* (2–7). Illus. by Ashley Bryan. 1987, Macmillan $14.95 (0-689-50422-5). 32pp. Five black spirituals that celebrate the Christmas story are joyously presented. (Rev: BCCB 12/87; BL 9/1/87)

**11557** McCullough, L. E. *Stories of the Songs of Christmas* (3–5). Illus. by Irene Kelly. 1997, Smith & Kraus $19.95 (1-57525-116-7). 149pp. Background material on such Christmas carols and songs as "Silent Night," "Jingle Bells," and "The Twelve Days of Christmas." (Rev: SLJ 10/97) [782]

**11558** Pearson, Tracey Campbell, illus. *We Wish You a Merry Christmas: A Traditional Christmas Carol* (K–3). 1983, Dial paper $3.95 (0-8037-0310-4). 32pp. A humorous rendition of this popular carol.

**11559** *Raffi's Christmas Treasury: Fourteen Illustrated Songs and Musical Arrangements* (PS–4). Illus. by Nadine Bernard Westcott. 1988, Crown $17.95 (0-517-56806-3). Pen-and-ink drawings illustrate popular tunes. (Rev: BL 11/15/88)

**11560** Riley, Linnea. *The 12 Days of Christmas* (PS–2). Illus. 1995, Simon & Schuster $15.00 (0-689-80275-7). 32pp. A version of the Christmas carol in which a young lord tries to impress his beloved by giving her some unusual gifts. (Rev: BL 9/15/95; SLJ 10/95*) [782.42]

**11561** Sabuda, Robert. *The Twelve Days of Christmas: A Pop-up Celebration* (K–4). Illus. 1996, Simon & Schuster paper $19.95 (0-689-80865-8). 12pp. A delightful pop-up version of the popular Christmas carol. (Rev: BCCB 9/96; BL 9/1/96*; HB 11–12/96) [782]

**11562** *The Twelve Days of Christmas* (PS–3). Illus. by John O'Brien. 1993, Boyds Mills $14.95 (1-56397-142-9). 32pp. In this version of the Christmas carol, a gentleman is the receiver of 12 days of unusual gifts. (Rev: BL 9/15/93) [783]

**11563** *The Twelve Days of Christmas: A Song Rebus* (PS–3). Illus. by Emily Bolam. 1997, Simon & Schuster $16.00 (0-689-81101-2). 32pp. A happy version of the traditional Christmas carol using a rebus format. (Rev: BL 9/1/97; SLJ 10/97) [782.42]

**11564** Tyrrell, Frances. *Woodland Christmas: Twelve Days of Christmas in the North Woods* (PS–2). Illus. 1996, Scholastic $15.95 (0-590-86367-3). 32pp. Woodland creatures portray the "true love's" gifts on each of the 12 days of Christmas. (Rev: BL 9/1/96) [782]

## Musical Instruments

**11565** Ardley, Neil. *Music* (4–8). Illus. Series: Eyewitness. 1989, Knopf LB $20.99 (0-394-92259-X). 64pp. An introduction to the types of musical instruments, a history of music, and famous musicians. (Rev: BL 7/89*; SLJ 8/89) [781.91]

**11566** Corbett, Sara. *Shake, Rattle, and Strum* (3–7). Illus. Series: A World of Difference. 1995, Children's

LB $21.00 (0-516-08194-2). 32pp. The world of musical instruments is explored, with examples from various cultures and explanations of how they related to the traditions and customs of each land. (Rev: BL 7/95) [784.19]

**11567** Davis, Wendy. *From Metal to Music* (PS–2). Illus. Series: Changes. 1997, Children's LB $23.00 (0-516-20707-5). 32pp. Explains how horns are made from mining the ore to producing sheets of metal and to the attachment of valves and testing the final product. (Rev: BL 10/15/97) [788.9]

**11568** Drew, Helen. *My First Music Book* (2–5). Illus. 1993, DK Publg. $12.95 (1-56458-215-9). 48pp. For young readers, this book describes and gives instructions on how to make a number of musical instruments with common household objects. (Rev: BL 6/1–15/93; SLJ 8/93) [784]

**11569** Ganeri, Anita. *The Young Person's Guide to the Orchestra: Benjamin Britten's Composition on CD* (4–6). Illus. 1996, Harcourt $25.00 (0-15-201304-0). 64pp. The text explains and illustrates the various instruments of the orchestra, with an accompanying CD of Britten's music. (Rev: BL 10/1/96; SLJ 10/96) [784.2]

**11570** Hayes, Ann. *Meet the Marching Smithereens* (K–3). Illus. by Karmen Thompson. 1995, Harcourt $15.00 (0-15-253158-0). 32pp. Several musical instruments are introduced through a description of an animal marching band called the Smithereens. (Rev: BCCB 6/95; BL 7/95; SLJ 5/95) [784.3]

**11571** Hayes, Ann. *Meet the Orchestra* (4–7). Illus. by Karmen Thompson. 1991, Harcourt $15.00 (0-15-200526-9). 32pp. Animals in evening dress introduce young readers to the orchestra. (Rev: BCCB 3/91; BL 4/15/91; SLJ 5/91) [784.19]

**11572** Miles, J. C. *First Book of the Keyboard* (5–8). Illus. by Kim Blundell. Series: First Music. 1993, EDC paper $10.95 (0-7460-0962-3). 64pp. A beginner's guide to the electronic keyboard. (Rev: SLJ 7/93) [786]

**11573** Moss, Lloyd. *Zin! Zin! Zin! A Violin* (1–3). Illus. by Marjorie Priceman. 1995, Simon & Schuster paper $16.00 (0-671-88239-2). 28pp. Ten instruments of the orchestra are introduced in rhyming couplets. (Rev: BL 5/15/95; SLJ 5/95*)

**11574** Oates, Eddie Herschel. *Making Music: Six Instruments You Can Create* (3–5). Illus. 1995, HarperCollins LB $14.89 (0-06-021479-1). 32pp. After an introduction to various kinds of musical instruments, this project book tells you how to make 6 instruments from easy-to-find supplies. (Rev: BL 7/95) [783]

**11575** Rubin, Mark. *The Orchestra* (2–4). Illus. by Alan Daniel. 1992, Firefly paper $8.95 (0-920668-99-2). After a general introduction to music, this book introduces each of the instruments of the orchestra. (Rev: SLJ 6/92) [781.91]

**11576** Sabbeth, Alex. *Rubber-Band Banjos and a Java Jive Bass: Projects and Activities on the Science of Music and Sound* (4–7). Illus. 1997, Wiley paper $12.95 (0-471-15675-2). 112pp. Describes the basic elements of music while giving directions for making a variety of homemade instruments. (Rev: BL 3/15/97; SLJ 6/97) [781]

**11577** Thyacott, Louise. *Musical Instruments* (5–7). Illus. Series: Traditions Around the World. 1995, Thomson Learning LB $24.26 (1-56847-228-5). 48pp. A continent-by-continent survey of the many kinds of musical instruments found in various cultures. (Rev: BCCB 11/94; BL 9/15/95) [784.3]

**11578** Turner, Barrie C. *The Living Clarinet* (4–8). Illus. 1996, Knopf $25.00 (0-679-88179-4). 48pp. A book/CD combination that gives a history of the clarinet and introduces some of the major compositions written for it. Also use *The Living Violin* (1996). (Rev: BL 12/15/96; SLJ 4/97) [788.62]

**11579** Turner, Barrie C. *The Living Flute* (4–8). Illus. Series: Complete Companion to Listening, Learning, and Playing. 1996, Knopf $25.00 (0-679-88178-6). 48pp. After a history of the development of the flute, there is an introduction to composers who wrote for this instrument plus a CD of flute music. (Rev: BL 12/15/96; SLJ 4/97) [788]

**11580** Turner, Barrie C. *The Living Piano* (4–8). Illus. Series: Complete Companion to Listening, Learning, and Playing. 1996, Knopf $25.00 (0-679-88180-8). 46pp. The development of the piano is traced, with profiles of 10 composers who wrote important works for the piano plus a CD of piano music. (Rev: BL 12/15/96; SLJ 4/97) [786.2]

## National Anthems and Patriotic Songs

**11581** Bates, Katherine L. *America the Beautiful* (K–4). Illus. by Neil Waldman. 1993, Macmillan $16.00 (0-689-31861-8). 32pp. An effective picture book illustrating the first verse of "America the Beautiful." (Rev: BL 7/93) [811]

**11582** St. Pierre, Stephanie. *Our National Anthem* (4–6). Illus. Series: I Know America. 1992, Millbrook LB $20.90 (1-56294-106-2). 48pp. A heavily illustrated history of the U.S. national song. (Rev: BL 5/15/92; SLJ 7/92) [782.42]

## Singing Games and Songs

**11583** Boy Scouts of America. *Cub Scout Songbook* (4–6). Illus. 1969, Boy Scouts of America paper $2.55 (0-8395-3222-9). 80pp. Words to 150 songs that are sung to popular tunes.

**11584** Carle, Eric. *Today Is Monday* (PS–K). Illus. 1992, Putnam $15.95 (0-399-21966-8). 32pp. A picture book that bursts with food, animals, and energy, and also includes music and lyrics, so everyone can sing along. (Rev: BL 1/1/93*; SLJ 4/93) [782]

**11585** Craver, Mike. *Beaver Ball at the Bug Club* (PS–1). Illus. by Joan Kaghan. 1992, Farrar $12.00 (0-374-30662-1). 32pp. Woodsy animals prance across the pages of this illustrated version of a new song. (Rev: BL 5/15/92; SLJ 8/92) [782]

**11586** Delacre, Lulu, ed. *Arroz con Leche: Popular Songs and Rhymes from Latin America* (PS–1). Trans. by Elena Paz. Illus. by Lulu Delacre. 1989, Scholastic paper $4.95 (0-590-41886-6). A bilingual collection of folk rhymes, chants, and fingerplays. (Rev: BCCB 5/89)

**11587** Emberley, Barbara. *Drummer Hoff* (K–3). Illus. by Ed Emberley. 1967, Simon & Schuster $15.00 (0-671-66248-1); paper $5.95 (0-671-66245-X). 32pp. The classic song about the assembling of a cannon. Caldecott Medal winner, 1968.

**11588** Farjeon, Eleanor. *Morning Has Broken* (PS–3). Illus. by Tim Ladwig. 1996, Eerdmans $15.00 (0-8028-5127-4); paper $7.50 (0-8028-5132-0). 32pp. An illustrated version of the hymn that was once recorded by Cat Stevens. (Rev: BL 10/1/96; SLJ 12/96) [782]

**11589** *For Our Children: A Book to Benefit the Pediatric AIDS Foundation* (PS–3). Illus. 1991, Disney LB $16.89 (1-56282-112-1). 72pp. An album of 20 songs by Carol King, Little Richard, and other artists. (Rev: BL 10/1/91; SLJ 10/91) [782.42]

**11590** Girl Scouts of the U.S.A. *Sing Together: Girl Scout Songbook* (4–8). Illus. 1973, Girl Scouts of the U.S.A. paper $8.25 (0-88441-309-8). 192pp. More than 140 songs of all types.

**11591** Glazer, Tom. *Eye Winker, Tom Tinker, Chin Chopper* (1–3). Illus. by Ronald Himler. 1987, Doubleday paper $8.00 (0-385-13344-8). 64pp. Fifty wonderful songs complete with finger plays.

**11592** Glazer, Tom. *The Mother Goose Songbook* (PS–2). Illus. by David McPhail. 1990, Doubleday paper $12.95 (0-385-24631-5). 95pp. A collection of 44 nursery rhymes set to music. (Rev: SLJ 12/90) [784]

**11593** Goodhart, Pippa. *Row, Row, Row Your Boat* (PS–2). Illus. by Stephen Lambert. 1997, Crown

$16.00 (0-517-70970-8). A boy, a girl, and their toy rabbit reenact this traditional song. (Rev: SLJ 12/97) [782]

**11594** Guthrie, Woody, and Marjorie M. Guthrie. *Woody's 20 Grow Big Songs* (2–8). Illus. 1992, HarperCollins LB $16.00 (0-06-020283-1). 22pp. Music and lyrics are complete for each song in this collection that was "lost" for 40 years. (Rev: BL 6/15/92; SLJ 7/92*) [782]

**11595** Halpern, Shari. *What Shall We Do When We All Go Out? A Traditional Song* (PS–K). Illus. 1995, North-South LB $14.88 (1-55858-425-0). 32pp. The text of the song forms the basis of this lively picture book. (Rev: BL 4/1/95; SLJ 7/95) [782.42]

**11596** Hart, Jane, ed. *Singing Bee! A Collection of Favorite Children's Songs* (PS–3). Illus. by Anita Lobel. 1989, Lothrop $22.95 (0-688-41975-5). 160pp. A collection of 125 simple songs with piano and guitar arrangements.

**11597** Hudson, Wade, and Cheryl W. Hudson. *How Sweet the Sound: African-American Songs for Children* (PS–3). Illus. by Floyd Cooper. 1995, Scholastic $15.95 (0-590-48030-8). 48pp. A collection of the words of African American songs, from spirituals and work songs to jazz and the works of Stevie Wonder. (Rev: BL 9/15/95; SLJ 11/95) [844]

**11598** Johnson, James W. *Lift Every Voice and Sing* (PS–8). Illus. by Elizabeth Catlett. 1993, Walker LB $15.85 (0-8027-8251-5). 36pp. Dramatic linecut prints highlight the song known as the African American national anthem. (Rev: BCCB 4/93; BL 2/15/93*; SLJ 3/93) [782.42]

**11599** Kennedy, Jimmy. *The Teddy Bears' Picnic* (PS–1). Illus. by Michael Hague. 1995, Holt $16.95 (0-8050-1008-4); paper $5.95 (0-8050-5349-2). 32pp. Large-size format and drawings complement this popular song about teddy bears gathering for a picnic. (Rev: BL 4/15/92; SLJ 6/92) [782]

**11600** Kovalski, Maryann. *The Wheels on the Bus* (PS–2). Illus. by author. 1987, Little, Brown paper $4.95 (0-316-50259-6). 32pp. Grandmother takes her lookalike granddaughters shopping and teaches them a silly song while waiting for the bus. (Rev: BL 12/15/87; SLJ 11/87)

**11601** Moreillon, Judi. *Sing Down the Rain* (2–5). Illus. by Michael Chiago. 1997, Kiva $14.95 (1-885772-07-6). This choral reading in 8 parts celebrates the Saguaro Wine Ceremony of the Tohono O'odham tribe of the Sonoran desert. (Rev: SLJ 1/98) [811]

**11602** Near, Holly. *The Great Peace March* (4–6). Illus. by Lisa Desimini. 1993, Holt $15.95 (0-8050-1941-3). 32pp. Lyrics to the title song about the Great Peace March for Nuclear Disarmament in 1986. (Rev: BCCB 4/93; BL 3/1/93; SLJ 5/93) [782]

**11603** Oram, Hiawyn, and Carl Davis. *A Creepy Crawly Song Book* (PS–3). Illus. by Satoshi Kitamura. 1993, Farrar $17.00 (0-374-31639-2). 54pp. Seventeen tunes with words that pay tribute to a variety of bugs, including head lice and the common housefly. (Rev: BCCB 11/93; BL 12/15/93; SLJ 1/94) [782.42]

**11604** Paxton, Tom. *Going to the Zoo* (PS–1). Illus. by Karen L. Schmidt. 1996, Morrow LB $14.93 (0-688-13801-2). 40pp. Three children and their dad go to a zoo in this picture book that illustrates Tom Paxton's popular song. (Rev: BL 6/1–15/96; SLJ 3/96) [782.42]

**11605** Raffi. *One Light, One Sun* (PS–1). Illus. by Eugenie Fernandes. 1988, Crown LB $9.95 (0-517-56785-7). 32pp. Based on the thought that rhyme and repetition prompt children to sing along. (Rev: BL 4/1/88; SLJ 6–7/88)

**11606** Raffi. *Raffi's Top 10 Songs to Read* (PS–1). Illus. 1995, Crown $15.00 (0-517-70907-4). 45pp. A collection of 10 of Raffi's most popular songbooks, complete with words, music, and illustrations. (Rev: BL 2/15/96; SLJ 3/96) [782.42]

**11607** Raffi. *Rise and Shine* (PS–2). Illus. by Eugenie Fernandes. 1996, Crown $16.00 (0-517-70939-2). 32pp. The excitement of facing a new day is conveyed in this song by Raffi. (Rev: BL 1/1–15/97; SLJ 1/97) [782.42]

**11608** Raffi. *Wheels on the Bus* (PS–1). Illus. by Sylvie Wickstrom. 1988, Crown LB $13.00 (0-517-56784-9). 32pp. Humor and culture are shown in this rhyme of a bus journeying through the French countryside. (Rev: BL 4/1/88; HB 7–8/88)

**11609** Sullivan, Arthur. *I Have a Song to Sing, O! An Introduction to the Songs of Gilbert and Sullivan* (4–8). Ed. by John Langstaff. Illus. by Emma C. Clark. 1994, Macmillan $17.95 (0-689-50591-4). 80pp. Sixteen famous songs from Gilbert and Sullivan's operettas are handsomely presented with arrangements for both piano and guitar. (Rev: BL 12/1/94; SLJ 10/94) [782]

**11610** Tashjian, Virginia A., sel. *Juba This and Juba That: Stories to Tell, Songs to Sing, Rhymes to Chant, Riddles to Guess, and More!* (PS–5). Illus. by Nadine Bernard Westcott. 1995, Little, Brown $15.95 (0-316-83234-0). 106pp. A favorite source of rhymes, stories, riddles, games, and poetry. (Rev: SLJ 7/95) [782]

**11611** Trapani, Iza, reteller. *How Much Is That Doggie in the Window?* (PS–3). Score and lyrics by Bob Merrill. Illus. by Iza Trapani. 1997, Whispering Coyote $15.95 (1-879085-74-7). This expanded version of the once-popular song tells about a little boy who wants a spotted puppy in a pet shop but can't afford to buy it. (Rev: SLJ 3/98) [782]

**11612**  Weiss, George D., and Bob Thiele. *What a Wonderful World* (PS–3). Illus. by Ashley Bryan. 1995, Simon & Schuster $16.00 (0-689-80087-8). 32pp. Children use a puppet stage to introduce this song. (Rev: BL 5/15/95; SLJ 5/95)

**11613**  *Who Built the Ark?* (PS–1). Illus. by Pamela Paparone. 1994, Simon & Schuster paper $15.00 (0-671-87129-3). 32pp. An illustrated version of the African American spiritual about the building of Noah's Ark and bringing the animals into it. (Rev: BL 7/94; SLJ 6/94) [782]

**11614**  Winn, Marie. *The Fireside Book of Fun and Game Songs* (2–6). Illus. by Whitney Darrow. 1974, Simon & Schuster $14.95 (0-671-65213-3). 224pp. All sorts of playful songs are included, such as question-and-answer songs and riddles.

**11615**  Winn, Marie, and Allan Miller. *The Fireside Book of Children's Songs* (K–5). Illus. by John Alcorn. 1966, Simon & Schuster $12.95 (0-671-25820-6). More than 100 songs in this collection, including nursery songs and games.

**11616**  Zelinsky, Paul O., adapt. *The Wheels on the Bus* (PS–1). Illus. 1990, Dutton paper $15.99 (0-525-44644-3). A pop-up edition with pull tabs of the familiar song. (Rev: BCCB 10/90; SLJ 10/90) [784]

# Performing Arts

## Circuses, Fairs, and Parades

**11617** Alter, Judith. *Amusement Parks, Roller Coasters, Ferris Wheels, and Cotton Candy* (4–6). Illus. 1997, Watts $22.00 (0-531-20304-2). 64pp. The author traces the history of amusement parks, starting with the Columbian Exposition of 1893, and then describes some current favorites, like Coney Island and Disney World. Also use *Meet Me at the Fair! County, State, and World's Fairs and Expositions* (1997). (Rev: BL 12/15/97) [791.06]

**11618** Alter, Judith. *Beauty Pageants: Tiaras, Roses, and Runways* (4–8). Illus. 1997, Watts LB $21.00 (0-531-20253-4). 64pp. After introducing various kinds of pageants, this book describes in detail the Miss America pageant, its history and organization. (Rev: BL 12/1/97; SLJ 9/97) [791.6]

**11619** Alter, Judith. *Wild West Shows: Rough Riders and Sure Shots* (4–7). Illus. 1997, Watts LB $21.00 (0-531-20274-7). 63pp. A brief photoessay that covers the history of the Wild West show, with a special focus on the contributions of Buffalo Bill to this form of entertainment. (Rev: BL 10/1/97; SLJ 8/97) [791.8]

**11620** Granfield, Linda. *Circus: An Album* (4–8). Illus. 1998, DK Publg. $19.95 (0-7894-2453-3). 96pp. Following a history of the circus from ancient times to the present, this title describes famous people connected with the circus and gives details on its problems and scandals. (Rev: BL 3/1/98; SLJ 3/98*) [791.3]

**11621** Helldorfer, M. C. *Carnival* (PS–K). Illus. by Dan Yaccarino. 1996, Viking paper $14.99 (0-670-86687-3). All the action, sights, smells, sounds, and tastes of a carnival are captured in this picture book. (Rev: HB 5–6/96; SLJ 3/96) [394]

**11622** Johnson, Neil. *Big-Top Circus* (1–3). Illus. 1995, Dial paper $14.89 (0-8037-1603-6). 32pp. This account follows the circus rituals from setting up the big tent to the actual performance. (Rev: BL 1/15/95; SLJ 3/95) [791.3]

**11623** Lewin, Ted. *Fair!* (K–3). Illus. 1997, Lothrop LB $15.93 (0-688-12851-3). 40pp. The excitement and fun of a county fair and its midway are captured in this picture book. (Rev: BL 7/97; SLJ 7/97*) [394]

**11624** Presnall, Judith J. *Circuses: Under the Big Top* (4–7). Illus. Series: First Books: Performances and Entertainment. 1996, Watts LB $22.00 (0-531-20235-6). 63pp. A history of circuses from ancient times to today with material on star performers. (Rev: SLJ 3/97) [791.3]

**11625** Wildsmith, Brian. *The Circus* (PS–3). Illus. by author. 1970, Oxford paper $9.95 (0-19-272102-X). Bold and brilliant colors create a wonderful world of an imaginary circus.

## Dance

**11626** Barber, Antonia. *Shoes of Satin, Ribbons of Silk: Tales from the Ballet* (4–6). Illus. 1995, Kingfisher $18.95 (1-85697-693-2). 96pp. In dramatic retellings, the stories of 9 ballets (several less well known) are presented. (Rev: BL 11/15/95; SLJ 1/96) [792.8]

**11627** Bell, Anthea. *Swan Lake: A Traditional Folktale* (2–4). Illus. by Chihiro Iwasaki. 1991, Picture Book paper $15.95 (0-88708-028-6). 28pp. Picture book version of the Swan Lake ballet. (Rev: BL 12/1/86; SLJ 12/86) [792.8]

**11628** Berger, Melvin. *The World of Dance* (6–8). Illus. 1978, Phillips $28.95 (0-87599-221-8). An overview of the subject that begins in prehistoric times and ends with today's social dancing and ballet.

**11629** Bussell, Darcey, and Patricia Linton. *The Young Dancer* (3–6). Illus. 1994, DK Publg. $15.95 (1-56458-468-2). 64pp. Two ballet practitioners explain the basic steps and movements and provide a history of ballet and its traditions. (Rev: BL 9/1/94; SLJ 8/94) [792.8]

**11630** Castle, Kate. *Ballet* (4–6). Illus. 1996, Kingfisher $15.95 (0-7534-5001-1). 64pp. A well-illustrated introduction to the world of ballet, with material on the composer, choreographer, designer, famous dancers, and stories of well-known ballets. (Rev: SLJ 12/96) [792.8]

**11631** Dufort, Antony. *Ballet Steps: Practice to Performance* (4–8). Illus. by author. 1990, Crown $18.00 (0-517-57770-4). 176pp. In text, drawings, and photographs, the author explains basic and advanced ballet movements. (Rev: SLJ 4/86)

**11632** Elliott, Donald. *Frogs and Ballet* (4–6). Illus. by Clinton Arrowood. 1979, Harvard Common paper $8.95 (0-87645-119-9). Familiar ballet steps and how they are woven into the classical ballet.

**11633** Fonteyn, Margot. *Swan Lake* (3–7). Illus. by Trina S. Hyman. 1989, Harcourt $16.00 (0-15-200600-1). 32pp. Large-format picture book based on the ballet. (Rev: BCCB 5/89; BL 3/1/89; SLJ 4/89)

**11634** Hayden, Melissa, ed. *The Nutcracker Ballet* (K–4). Illus. by Stephen T. Johnson. 1992, Andrews & McMeel $14.95 (0-8362-4501-6). 32pp. This retelling is based on Balanchine's version of the ballet. (Rev: BL 2/1/93) [792]

**11635** Hollyer, Belinda. *Stories from the Classical Ballet* (4–7). Illus. 1995, Viking paper $15.99 (0-670-86605-9). 128pp. A well-illustrated, attractive volume that tells the story of 8 popular ballets, including *The Nutcracker, Swan Lake*, and *Coppelia*. (Rev: BCCB 2/96; BL 1/1–15/96) [792.84]

**11636** Horosko, Marian. *Sleeping Beauty: The Ballet Story* (3–6). Illus. by Todd L. W. Doney. 1994, Atheneum $14.95 (0-689-31885-5). 32pp. A scene-by-scene description of the Petipa — choreographed ballet, with noteworthy explanations and lush illustrations. (Rev: BL 1/1/95; SLJ 11/94) [792.8]

**11637** Isadora, Rachel. *My Ballet Class* (1–3). Illus. by author. 1980, Greenwillow $16.00 (0-688-80253-2). 32pp. The first-person account that traces a young girl's actions during a ballet class.

**11638** McCaughrean, Geraldine. *The Random House Book of Stories from the Ballet* (4–6). Illus. 1995, Random $20.00 (0-679-87125-X). 112pp. A delightful retelling of 10 stories of full-length ballets like *Cinderella* and *The Sleeping Beauty.* (Rev: BL 10/1/95; SLJ 12/95) [792.8]

**11639** Medearis, Angela Shelf, and Michael R. Medearis. *Dance* (5–7). Illus. Series: African American Arts. 1997, Twenty-First Century LB $16.98 (0-8050-4481-7). 64pp. The contributions of African Americans to dance is covered, including their roles in jazz, tap, and modern dance. (Rev: BL 7/97; SLJ 7/97) [793.3]

**11640** Medova, Marie-Laure. *Ballet for Beginners* (4–6). Illus. 1996, Sterling $19.95 (0-8069-3876-5). 112pp. Many facets of ballet are covered in this introductory account, including history, the content of classes, exercises, steps, and the life of a dancer. (Rev: BL 2/15/96) [792.8]

**11641** Newman, Barbara. *The Illustrated Book of Ballet Stories* (4–6). Illus. 1997, DK Publg. $19.95 (0-7894-2225-5). 64pp. This book not only gives the stories of 5 popular ballets, but also explains the dance elements that are found in each. (Rev: BL 12/15/97) [792.8]

**11642** Riordan, James. *Favorite Stories of the Ballet* (4–6). Illus. by Victor G. Ambrus. 1993, Checkerboard $14.95 (1-56288-252-X). These ballet stories include *The Nutcracker, Swan Lake, Sleeping Beauty,* and *Cinderella.*

**11643** San Souci, Robert D., reteller. *The Firebird* (PS–3). Illus. by Kris Waldherr. 1992, Doubleday LB $13.89 (0-8037-0800-9). 32pp. Beautiful illustrations help tell the story of this dramatic ballet. (Rev: BL 12/15/91) [398.2]

**11644** Sorine, Stephanie Riva. *Our Ballet Class* (2–4). Illus. by Daniel S. Sorine. 1981, Knopf LB $8.99 (0-394-94821-1). 48pp. A photoessay about a weekly ballet class.

**11645** Spatt, Leslie E. *Behind the Scenes at the Ballet* (4–6). Illus. 1995, Viking paper $13.99 (0-670-86162-6). 48pp. A look at a ballet company in England as it prepares for and executes a performance of *The Sleeping Beauty.* (Rev: BL 11/15/95) [792]

**11646** *Step-by-Step Ballet Class: The Official Illustrated Guide* (4–6). Illus. 1994, Contemporary paper $14.95 (0-8092-3499-8). 144pp. This guide developed by the Royal Academy of Dancing in England gives material for various levels of development, including positions, movements, and advice on appearance. (Rev: BL 12/1/94) [792.8]

**11647** Tythacott, Louise. *Dance* (5–7). Illus. Series: Traditions Around the World. 1995, Thomson Learning LB $24.26 (1-56847-275-7). 48pp. The ways people dance around the world and the reasons they do are presented with many color photos. (Rev: BL 6/1–15/95; SLJ 9/95) [793.3]

**11648** Vagin, Vladimir. *The Nutcracker Ballet* (K–3). Illus. 1995, Scholastic $14.95 (0-590-47220-8).

32pp. All the characters in the *Nutcracker*, including Clara and Herr Drosselmeier, come to life in this retelling of the ballet story with effective, detailed illustrations. (Rev: BL 9/15/95)

## Marionettes and Puppets

**11649** Buetter, Barbara MacDonald. *Simple Puppets from Everyday Materials* (PS–3). Illus. by Barbara M. Buetter and George Buetter. 1997, Sterling $19.95 (1-895569-05-2). 80pp. Features easy-to-make puppets like a dragon, frog, and Humpty Dumpty, using readily available materials. (Rev: SLJ 3/97) [745.592]

**11650** Doney, Meryl. *Puppets* (4–6). Illus. Series: World Crafts. 1996, Watts LB $20.00 (0-531-14399-6). 32pp. An impressive number of puppets are introduced from different cultures, with full instructions on how to make them. (Rev: SLJ 7/96) [745.5]

**11651** Lade, Roger. *The Most Excellent Book of How to Be a Puppeteer* (3–5). Illus. Series: Most Excellent Book Of. 1996, Millbrook $5.95 (0-7613-0505-X). 32pp. This how-to book tells how to make puppets and how to use them to give a brilliant performance. (Rev: BL 10/15/96; SLJ 2/97) [791.5]

**11652** Renfro, Nancy. *Puppet Show Made Easy!* (3–6). Illus. 1984, Renfro $16.95 (0-931044-13-8). 96pp. Creating puppets and how to stage a show.

**11653** Supraner, Robyn, and Lauren Supraner. *Plenty of Puppets to Make* (1–3). Illus. by Renzo Barto. 1981, Troll LB $12.50 (0-89375-432-3); paper $3.95 (0-89375-433-1). 48pp. A book about 11 easy-to-make puppets.

**11654** Wallace, Mary. *I Can Make Puppets* (2–5). Photos by author. 1994, Greey de Pencier Bks. $14.95 (1-895688-24-8); paper $5.95 (1-895688-20-5). 32pp. Directions for making different puppets and marionettes are given using everyday materials. (Rev: SLJ 12/94) [745]

## Motion Pictures, Radio, and Television

**11655** Dowd, Ned. *That's a Wrap: How Movies Are Made* (5–7). Illus. 1991, Silver Burdett paper $4.95 (0-382-24376-5). 62pp. Lots of information about movie-making is contained in this behind-the-scenes movie shoot. (Rev: BCCB 1/92; BL 1/1/92) [791.43]

**11656** Gleasner, Diana C. *The Movies (Inventions That Changed Our Lives)* (4–6). Illus. 1983, Walker LB $8.85 (0-8027-6483-5). A history of moviemaking.

**11657** Hautzig, Esther. *On the Air: Behind the Scenes at a TV Newscast* (4–6). Illus. by David Hautzig. 1991, Macmillan $15.95 (0-02-743361-7). 48pp. A straightforward look at the workings of a TV newscast, with background information and job descriptions. (Rev: BCCB 3/92; BL 2/1/92; SLJ 2/92) [070.1]

**11658** *The History of Moviemaking* (3–6). Illus. 1995, Scholastic $19.95 (0-590-47645-9). 47pp. A history of film is enlivened by transparencies, flaps, and other interactive devices. (Rev: BL 2/1/96; SLJ 5/96) [791]

**11659** Hitzeroth, Deborah, and Sharon Heerboth. *Movies: The World on Film* (5–8). Illus. Series: Encyclopedia of Discovery and Invention. 1992, Lucent LB $23.70 (1-56006-210-X). 96pp. A brief history of movies and their effects on society. (Rev: SLJ 4/92) [791]

**11660** Krauss, Ronnie. *Take a Look, It's in a Book: How Television Is Made at Reading Rainbow* (2–4). Illus. by Christopher Hornsby. 1997, Walker LB $16.85 (0-8027-8489-5). 32pp. A behind-the-scenes look at the television program *Reading Rainbow* and how it is put together. (Rev: BL 3/1/97; SLJ 6/97*) [791.45]

**11661** Miller, Marilyn. *Behind the Scenes at the TV News Studio* (PS–3). Illus. Series: Behind the Scenes. 1996, Raintree Steck-Vaughn LB $21.40 (0-8172-4089-6). 32pp. A fascinating inside look at the inner workings of a TV news station. (Rev: BL 4/15/96; SLJ 12/96) [070.1]

**11662** Morley, Jacqueline. *Entertainment: Screen, Stage and Stars* (3–6). Illus. Series: Timelines. 1994, Watts LB $24.00 (0-531-14311-2). 48pp. Using color diagrams, cutaways, and reconstructions, this is a history of different types of entertainment, from the Greek theater to present-day television. (Rev: BL 7/94) [790]

## Theater and Play Production

**11663** Bany-Winters, Lisa. *On Stage: Theater Games and Activities for Kids* (4–7). Illus. 1997, Chicago Review paper $14.95 (1-55652-324-6). 160pp. This book provides a number of theater games involving improvisation, creating characters, using and becoming objects, and ideas for pantomime and puppetry. (Rev: BL 2/1/98; SLJ 3/98) [327.12]

**11664** Morin, Alice. *Newspaper Theatre: Creative Play Production for Low Budgets and No Budgets*

(5–8). Illus. 1989, Fearon paper $8.99 (0-8224-6349-0). 80pp. No-nonsense tips on play production. (Rev: BL 6/1/89)

**11665** Morley, Jacqueline. *Shakespeare's Theater* (4–6). Illus. Series: Inside Story. 1995, Bedrick LB $18.95 (0-87226-309-6). 48pp. Details on Shakespeare's Globe Theatre and performances that took place there are preceded by a brief history of Euro-

pean theater. (Rev: BL 4/15/95) [792]

**11666** Slaight, Craig, and Jack Sharrar, eds. *Great Scenes and Monologues for Children* (5–8). Series: Young Actors. 1993, Smith & Kraus paper $11.95 (1-880399-15-6). 172pp. A collection of scenes and monologues from children's stories and fairy tales, and from adult plays like Thornton Wilder's *The Skin of Our Teeth*. (Rev: BL 10/1/93; SLJ 11/93) [808.82]

# History and Geography

# History and Geography in General

## Miscellaneous

**11667**  Ajmera, Maya K., and Anna R. Versola. *Children from Australia to Zimbabwe: A Photographic Journey Around the World* (3–6). Illus. 1997, Charlesbridge $18.95 (0-88106-999-X). 64pp. A photographic journey around the globe that introduces 25 countries and gives basic fact about each. (Rev: BL 1/1–15/98; SLJ 7/97) [305.23]

**11668**  *Atlas of Countries* (1–3). Illus. by Donald Grant. Series: First Discovery Atlases. 1996, Scholastic $11.95 (0-590-58282-8). This atlas explains maps and globes, landforms, the earth's evolution and rotation, while also supplying maps of the world's countries. (Rev: SLJ 9/96) [912]

**11669**  Bell, Neill. *The Book of Where: Or How to Be Naturally Geographic* (4–7). Illus. by Richard Wilson. 1982, Little, Brown paper $12.95 (0-316-08831-5). 140pp. A collection of activities that make one aware of the study of geography.

**11670**  Brooks, Susan. *The Geography of the Earth* (4–6). Illus. 1996, Oxford $18.95 (0-19-521232-0). 64pp. A large-format book that introduces world geography, basic concepts, and each of the 7 continents. (Rev: BL 10/15/96; SLJ 8/96) [910]

**11671**  Burger, Leslie, and Debra L. Rahm. *Sister Cities in a World of Difference* (4–8). Illus. 1996, Lerner LB $22.60 (0-8225-2697-2). 93pp. The pairing of cities internationally and its many positive results are introduced. (Rev: BL 9/1/96; SLJ 9/96) [303.48]

**11672**  Chiarelli, Brunetto. *The Atlas of World Cultures* (4–6). Illus. by Paola Ravaglia. 1997, Bedrick $19.95 (0-87226-499-8). 61pp. Arranged by geo-

graphical area, this book examines various peoples and their religion, language, food, dress, and arts. (Rev: SLJ 10/97) [910]

**11673**  Gold, John C. *Environments of the Western Hemisphere* (5–8). Illus. Series: Comparing Continents. 1997, Twenty-First Century $21.40 (0-8050-5601-7). 96pp. Compares the climates of South, North, and Central America and shows how these affect the environment and the way people live and work. (Rev: BL 2/1/98; SLJ 3/98) [363.7]

**11674**  Kindersley, Barnabas, and Anabel Kindersley. *Children Just Like Me: A Unique Celebration of Children Around the World* (3–6). Illus. 1995, DK Publg. $18.95 (0-7894-0201-7). 79pp. An attractive book that views children around the world, arranged by continents. (Rev: BCCB 2/95; SLJ 1/96) [305]

**11675**  Knowlton, Jack. *Geography from A to Z: A Picture Glossary* (2–5). Illus. by Harriett Barton. 1988, HarperCollins $15.95 (0-690-04616-2); paper $6.95 (0-06-446099-1). 48pp. Each entry describes the earth's physical geography. (Rev: BL 11/1/88)

**11676**  Llewellyn, Claire. *Our Planet Earth* (K–3). Illus. Series: Scholastic First Encyclopedia. 1997, Scholastic paper $14.95 (0-590-87929-4). 77pp. An introductory book on the Earth's origins, physical geography, and the life forms that inhabit our planet. (Rev: SLJ 2/98) [910]

**11677**  Maisner, Heather. *The Magic Globe: An Around-the-World Adventure Game* (4–6). Illus. by Alan Baron. 1995, Candlewick $12.95 (1-56402-445-8). 29pp. A game book that takes the reader through a number of countries where they get a glimpse of the culture and geography of each. A companion volume is *The Magic Hourglass: A Time-*

*Travel Adventure Game* (1995). (Rev: SLJ 9/95) [910]

**11678** Perham, Molly, and Julian Rowe. *Landscapes* (4–6). Illus. Series: Mapworlds. 1996, Watts LB $19.30 (0-531-14373-2). 32pp. Using an atlaslike approach and many illustrations, the world's basic landscapes are identified and defined. (Rev: BL 10/15/96; SLJ 1/97) [551.4]

**11679** Reid, Struan. *Cultures and Civilizations* (5–8). Illus. Series: Silk and Spice Routes. 1994, Silver Burdett LB $15.95 (0-02-726315-0). 48pp. In a handsome, oversize book with stunning illustrations, the many historic cultures that thrived along the ancient trade route to the East are introduced. (Rev: BL 12/15/94; SLJ 12/94) [909]

**11680** Rosenthal, Paul. *Where on Earth? A Geografunny Guide to the Globe* (4–7). Illus. by Marc Rosenthal. 1992, Knopf LB $15.99 (0-679-90833-1); paper $11.00 (0-679-80833-7). 106pp. An informative tongue-in-cheek guide to world geography. (Rev: BCCB 2/93; BL 1/15/93; SLJ 1/93) [910]

**11681** Stienecker, David L. *The World* (2–5). Series: Discovering Geography. 1997, Marshall Cavendish LB $21.36 (0-7614-0543-7). 32pp. The geography of the world is introduced, with material on land formations, climate, and various environments. (Rev: BL 2/15/98) [910]

**11682** Tivers, Jacqueline, and Michael Day. *The Viking Children's World Atlas* (3–4). Illus. 1983, Puffin paper $5.99 (0-14-031874-7). 48pp. A clearly presented atlas with maps of products and topography as well as political divisions.

**11683** Wood, Robert W. *Easy Geography Activities* (3–6). Illus. by John D. Wood. 1991, TAB $16.95 (0-8306-2493-7); paper $9.95 (0-8306-2492-9). 141pp. Helping to understand the principles and vocabulary of geography through such activities as reading road maps, making a compass, and understanding continental drift. (Rev: BL 2/1/92) [910]

**11684** Zeman, Anne, and Kate Kelly. *Everything You Need to Know About Geography Homework: A Desk Reference for Students and Parents* (4–6). Illus. by Moffit Cecil. Series: Scholastic Homework Reference. 1997, Scholastic $18.95 (0-590-53851-9). 133pp. Explains such basic concepts in geography as maps and globes, the Earth, water, biomes, and the geography of people and places. (Rev: SLJ 5/97) [910]

## Maps and Globes

**11685** Baicker-McKee, Carol. *Mapped Out! The Search for Snookums* (4–6). Illus. by Traci O. Covey. 1997, Gibbs Smith $19.95 (0-87905-788-2). 32pp. Using map-reading skills and other references techniques, the reader is able to find the "petnapper" of a rare iguana. (Rev: SLJ 1/98) [912]

**11686** Berger, Melvin, and Gilda Berger. *The Whole World in Your Hands: Looking at Maps* (2–3). Illus. by Robert Quackenbush. Series: Discovery Readers. 1993, Ideals LB $12.00 (0-8249-8646-6); paper $4.50 (0-8249-8609-1). 48pp. This book for beginning readers introduces maps from simple to complex. (Rev: BCCB 4/93; BL 7/93) [912]

**11687** Ganeri, Anita. *The Story of Maps and Navigation* (3–6). Series: Signs of the Times. 1998, Oxford LB $14.95 (0-19-521410-2). 32pp. A history of maps and navigational devices is given, with brief coverage on their uses during the age of exploration. (Rev: BL 3/15/98) [912]

**11688** Haslam, Andrew. *Maps* (3–6). Illus. Series: Make It Work! 1996, World Book $11.95 (0-7166-1753-6); paper $6.95 (0-7166-1754-4). 48pp. The concept of maps and important terminology connected with them are covered, with accompanying projects. (Rev: BL 11/15/96) [526]

**11689** Knowlton, Jack. *Maps and Globes* (2–4). Illus. 1985, HarperCollins paper $5.95 (0-06-446049-5). 48pp. This is a clear introduction to maps and globes and how to read them. (Rev: BCCB 3/86; BL 12/15/85)

**11690** Smith, A. G. *Where Am I? The Story of Maps and Navigation* (4–8). Illus. 1997, Stoddart paper $13.95 (0-7737-5836-4). 96pp. Each of the important discoveries and innovations involved in the history of map making are explained. (Rev: BL 9/1/97) [910]

**11691** Stienecker, David L. *Maps* (2–5). Series: Discovering Geography. 1997, Marshall Cavendish LB $21.36 (0-7614-0538-0). 32pp. The evolution of maps is traced, and basic map-reading skills are introduced. (Rev: BL 2/15/98; SLJ 4/98) [912]

**11692** Sweeney, Joan. *Me on the Map* (K–3). Illus. by Annette Cable. 1996, Crown $12.00 (0-517-70095-6). 32pp. The concept of maps is introduced, from a floor plan of a room to a representation of the earth. (Rev: BL 4/1/96; SLJ 6/96) [912]

# Paleontology and Dinosaurs

**11693** Aliki. *Digging Up Dinosaurs* (2–4). Illus. by author. 1989, HarperCollins LB $14.89 (0-690-04716-9); paper $4.95 (0-06-445078-3). 32pp. This book answers the question "How do dinosaurs get into museums?"

**11694** Aliki. *Dinosaur Bones* (PS–3). Illus. by author. 1988, HarperCollins paper $4.95 (0-06-445077-5). 32pp. In this book, her fourth on dinosaurs, Aliki discusses the discovery of fossils and the many theories that emerged about their meaning. (Rev: BCCB 1/88; BL 2/1/88; SLJ 4/88)

**11695** Aliki. *Fossils Tell of Long Ago* (2–4). Illus. Series: Let's Read-and-Find-Out Science Books. 1990, HarperCollins LB $15.89 (0-690-04829-7); paper $4.95 (0-06-445093-7). 32pp. A handsome revision of the original 1972 title with full-color artwork. (Rev: BL 4/15/90; SLJ 7/90) [560]

**11696** Aliki. *My Visit to the Dinosaurs* (PS–3). Illus. by author. 1985, HarperCollins LB $15.89 (0-690-04423-2); paper $4.95 (0-06-445020-1). 32pp. Revision of the 1969 book, including new material. Also use: *Dinosaurs Are Different* (1985). (Rev: BCCB 10/85; BL 9/15/85; SLJ 1/86)

**11697** Aliki. *Wild and Woolly Mammoths*. Rev. ed. (K–3). Illus. 1996, HarperCollins LB $14.89 (0-06-026277-X). 32pp. An expanded, updated edition of the excellent introduction to various types of mammoths. (Rev: BL 2/1/96; SLJ 2/96*) [569]

**11698** Arnold, Caroline. *Dinosaur Mountain: Graveyard of the Past* (4–7). Illus. 1990, Ticknor $15.95 (0-89919-693-4). A visit to the Dinosaur National Monument quarry in Utah. (Rev: BL 5/15/89)

**11699** Arnold, Caroline. *Dinosaurs All Around: An Artist's View of the Prehistoric World* (3–6). Photos by Richard Hewett. 1993, Houghton $14.95 (0-395-62363-4). 48pp. This book concentrates on the art of creating dinosaur models from miniature and life-sized ones. (Rev: BCCB 4/93; BL 4/15/93; HB 7–8/93; SLJ 5/93) [567.9]

**11700** Arnold, Caroline. *Trapped in Tar: Fossils from the Ice Age* (3–5). Illus. 2000, Houghton paper $6.95 (0-395-54783-0). 64pp. Photos highlight the story of California's La Brea pits, where bones and plant life trapped in tar make up a record of life long ago. (Rev: BCCB 6/87; BL 6/1/87; SLJ 8/87)

**11701** Asimov, Isaac. *Death from Space: What Killed the Dinosaurs?* (3–5). Illus. Series: Isaac Asimov's New Library of the Universe. 1994, Gareth Stevens LB $19.93 (0-8368-1129-1). 32pp. Explores the theory that dinosaurs became extinct because of a cosmic collision. (Rev: BL 2/15/95) [567.9]

**11702** Barton, Byron. *Dinosaurs, Dinosaurs* (PS–1). Illus. 1989, HarperCollins LB $14.89 (0-690-04768-1); paper $5.95 (0-06-443298-X). 40pp. Dinosaur characteristics in splashy colors. (Rev: BL 3/15/89; HB 5–6/89; SLJ 4/89)

**11703** Bennett, S. Christopher. *Pterosaurs: The Flying Reptiles* (5–8). Illus. by Brian Franczak, et al. Series: Prehistoric Life. 1995, Watts LB $25.90 (0-531-11181-4). 64pp. The evolution of this flying reptile, its body structure, and its behavior. (Rev: SLJ 10/95) [567.9]

**11704** Benton, Michael. *Dinosaur and Other Prehistoric Animal Factfinder* (3–6). Illus. 1992, Kingfisher paper $13.95 (1-85697-802-8). 256pp. A quick reference source about prehistoric life, including profiles of dinosaurs and other animals. (Rev: BL 12/15/92) [560]

**11705** Benton, Michael. *Dinosaurs* (3–6). Illus. Series: Make It Work. 1996, World Book $11.95 (0-7166-1755-2); paper $6.95 (0-7166-1756-0). 48pp. Facts about dinosaurs are conveyed in a series of projects, including model making and other activities. (Rev: BL 11/15/96) [567.91]

**11706** Berger, Melvin. *Mighty Dinosaurs* (4–8). Illus. 1990, Avon paper $2.95 (0-380-76052-5). 128pp. Covers various kinds of dinosaurs and includes the latest research on their extinction. (Rev: BL 12/15/90) [567.9]

**11707** Bishop, Roma. *My First Pop-up Book of Prehistoric Animals* (K–3). Illus. 1994, Simon & Schuster $12.95 (0-671-86556-7). An engaging text and a series of pop-ups introduce the world of the dinosaur to primary graders. (Rev: BL 11/15/94) [560]

**11708** Branley, Franklin M. *What Happened to the Dinosaurs?* (1–3). Illus. by Marc Simont. 1989, HarperCollins LB $14.89 (0-690-04749-5). 32pp. A good discussion of what might have happened to cause the end of the dinosaurs. (Rev: BL 9/1/89; HB 11–12/89; SLJ 10/89) [567.9]

**11709** Cohen, Daniel. *Prehistoric Animals* (4–6). Illus. 1988, Doubleday $9.95 (0-385-23416-3). 48pp. An oversize edition of prehistoric birds and animals. (Rev: BL 7/88; SLJ 9/88)

**11710** Cohen, Daniel, and Susan Cohen. *Where to Find Dinosaurs Today* (5–7). Illus. 1992, Dutton paper $15.00 (0-525-65098-9). 210pp. A necessary guide for any serious dinosaur lover. (Rev: BL 9/1/92) [567.9]

**11711** Cole, Joanna. *Dinosaur Story* (K–3). Illus. by Mort Kunstle. 1974, Morrow LB $13.93 (0-688-31826-6). 32pp. Ten different species are introduced with beginning coverage on paleontology.

**11712** Cole, Joanna. *The Magic School Bus in the Time of the Dinosaurs* (K–4). Illus. by Bruce Degen. 1994, Scholastic $15.95 (0-590-44688-6). 46pp. Through time travel, Ms. Frizzle takes her students to various geological periods when dinosaurs lived in this fact-filled book about prehistoric life. (Rev: BCCB 10/94; BL 8/94; HB 11–12/94; SLJ 9/94) [567.9]

**11713** Cutts, David. *More About Dinosaurs* (K–2). Illus. by Greg Wenzel. 1982, Troll LB $12.95 (0-89375-668-7); paper $3.50 (0-89375-669-5). 32pp. A simple introduction to this fascinating subject for primary grades.

**11714** Dal Sasso, Cristiano. *Animals: Origins and Evolution* (4–8). Illus. Series: Beginnings — Origins and Evolution. 1995, Raintree Steck-Vaughn LB $24.26 (0-8114-3333-1). 48pp. This well-illustrated account traces the development of animals from bacteria to the invertebrates and then fish, amphibians, reptiles, birds, and mammals. (Rev: BL 5/1/95; SLJ 6/95) [591]

**11715** Dingus, Lowell. *What Color Is That Dinosaur? Questions, Answers, and Mysteries* (4–6). Illus. by Stephen C. Quinn. 1994, Millbrook LB $23.90 (1-56294-365-0). 79pp. Unusual facts about dinosaurs, including their color, are covered in this fascinating volume. (Rev: SLJ 7/94) [567.9]

**11716** Dingus, Lowell, and Mark A. Norell. *Searching for Velociraptor* (4–6). Illus. 1996, HarperCollins LB $15.89 (0-06-025894-2). 32pp. A first-person account of discovering raptor fossils in Mongolia. (Rev: BL 9/1/96; SLJ 2/97) [567.9]

**11717** *Dinosaurs* (1–3). Illus. by James Prunier and Henri Galeron. Series: First Discovery. 1993, Scholastic $11.95 (0-590-46358-6). With cutaway illustrations and transparencies, different dinosaurs and their anatomy are shown. (Rev: SLJ 8/93) [567.9]

**11718** Dixon, Dougal. *Be a Dinosaur Detective* (1–4). Illus. 1988, Lerner paper $6.95 (0-8225-9538-9). 32pp. The author explains how all evidence for dinosaurs is deduced from fossils. (Rev: BL 5/1/88; SLJ 8/88)

**11719** Dixon, Dougal. *Dougal Dixon's Dinosaurs* (4–6). Illus. 1993, Boyds Mills $17.95 (1-56397-261-1). 160pp. A description in text and double-page spreads of 26 dinosaurs, with material on their anatomy and living habits. (Rev: BL 9/15/93; SLJ 10/93*) [567.9]

**11720** Dixon, Dougal. *Questions and Answers About Dinosaurs* (3–6). Illus. Series: Questions and Answers About. 1995, Kingfisher paper $5.95 (1-85697-553-3). 40pp. In a question-and-answer format, basic information about dinosaurs is covered, as well as some unusual facts like "Which were the deadliest?" (Rev: SLJ 4/95) [567.9]

**11721** Dixon, Dougal. *The Search for Dinosaurs* (4–7). Illus. Series: Digging Up the Past. 1995, Thomson Learning LB $24.26 (1-56847-396-6). 48pp. A history of the various discoveries that paleontologists have made about dinosaurs and other prehistoric beasts. (Rev: SLJ 2/96) [567.9]

**11722** Dodson, Peter. *An Alphabet of Dinosaurs* (2–4). Illus. by Wayne D. Barlowe. 1995, Scholastic $14.95 (0-590-46486-8). 64pp. Twenty-six kinds of dinosaurs are introduced in text and drawings in this unusual alphabet book. (Rev: BL 1/15/95; SLJ 3/95*) [567.9]

**11723** Eastman, David. *Story of Dinosaurs* (K–2). Illus. by Joel Snyder. 1997, Troll paper $2.95 (0-89375-649-0). Simple material presented in short sentences with many illustrations.

**11724** Eldredge, Niles, et al. *The Fossil Factory: A Kid's Guide to Digging Up Dinosaurs, Exploring Evolution, and Finding Fossils* (4–8). Illus. by True Kelley and Steven Lindblom. 1990, Addison-Wesley paper $9.95 (0-201-18599-7). 112pp. A broad overview with fully illustrated text. (Rev: BL 3/1/90; SLJ 5/90) [560]

**11725** Facklam, Margery. *Tracking Dinosaurs in the Gobi* (5–8). Illus. 1997, Twenty-First Century $21.40

(0-8050-5165-1). 96pp. The story of the paleontologist Roy Chapman Andrews and his amazing dinosaur finds in the Gobi Desert beginning in the 1920s. (Rev: BL 2/1/98; SLJ 2/98*) [567.9]

**11726** Farlow, James O. *On the Tracks of Dinosaurs* (4–8). Illus. by Doris Tischler. 1991, Watts LB $25.90 (0-531-10991-7). 72pp. The importance of dinosaur footprints is the focus of this book. (Rev: BL 5/1/91; SLJ 7/91) [567.9]

**11727** Farlow, James O., and Ralph E. Molnar. *The Great Hunters: Meat-Eating Dinosaurs and Their World* (5–8). Illus. by Bob Walters and Brian Franczak. Series: Prehistoric Life. 1995, Watts LB $24.00 (0-531-11180-6). 64pp. This book on carnivorous dinosaurs shows how their facial muscles, skeletons, and eyes helped in their search for food. (Rev: SLJ 10/95) [567.9]

**11728** Fowler, Allan. *It Could Still Be a Dinosaur* (1–2). Illus. Series: Rookie Readers. 1993, Children's LB $18.50 (0-516-06002-3). 32pp. For beginning readers, this is a very simple book about dinosaurs. (Rev: BL 3/1/94) [567.9]

**11729** Freedman, Russell. *Dinosaurs and Their Young* (1–3). Illus. by Leslie Morrill. 1983, Holiday LB $14.95 (0-8234-0496-X). 32pp. The story of how paleontology has helped us understand how young dinosaurs were raised.

**11730** Gibbons, Gail. *Dinosaurs* (2–4). Illus. 1987, Holiday LB $15.95 (0-8234-0657-1); paper $6.95 (0-8234-0708-X). 32pp. Giant reptiles explained in simple terms for the young set. (Rev: BL 12/15/87; SLJ 11/87)

**11731** Gibbons, Gail. *Prehistoric Animals* (K–2). Illus. 1988, Holiday LB $15.95 (0-8234-0707-1). 32pp. A brief overview of a subject that fascinates young readers. (Rev: BL 9/1/88; SLJ 10/88)

**11732** Gillette, J. Lynett. *Dinosaur Ghosts: The Mystery of Coelophysis* (3–5). Illus. by Douglas Henderson. 1997, Dial LB $15.99 (0-8037-1721-0). 32pp. The author, a paleontologist, explains the mystery of the mass grave of tiny dinosaur skeletons found at Ghost Ranch, New Mexico. (Rev: BCCB 7–8/97; BL 4/1/97; HB 7–8/97; SLJ 4/97*) [567.9]

**11733** Gillette, J. Lynett. *The Search for Seismosaurus: The World's Longest Dinosaur* (3–6). Illus. by Mark Hallett. 1994, Dial $14.89 (0-8037-1359-2). 40pp. The story of the discovery of the world's largest dinosaur, Seismosaurus, and of the work of paleontologists. (Rev: BCCB 3/94; BL 3/15/94; SLJ 3/94) [567.9]

**11734** Granger, Judith. *Amazing World of Dinosaurs* (1–3). Illus. by Pamela Baldwin Ford. 1982, Troll LB $12.95 (0-89375-562-1); paper $2.95 (0-89375-563-X). 32pp. This book describes many plant and meat-eating dinosaurs.

**11735** Granowsky, Alvin. *The Dinosaurs' Last Days* (PS–1). Illus. by Paul Lopez. Series: World of Dinosaurs. 1992, Raintree Steck-Vaughn LB $21.40 (0-8114-3250-5). 32pp. An easy book that explores theories of why the dinosaurs disappeared. Also use: *Meat-Eating Dinosaurs* (1992). (Rev: SLJ 9/92) [567.9]

**11736** Halls, Kelly M. *Dino-Trekking: The Ultimate Dinosaur Lover's Travel Guide* (4–8). Illus. by Rick Spears. 1996, Wiley paper $14.95 (0-471-11498-7). 199pp. This dinosaur directory describes sites, museums, and theme parks in the United States and Canada. (Rev: SLJ 3/96) [567.9]

**11737** Horner, John R., and Don Lessem. *Digging Up Tyrannosaurus Rex* (4–7). Illus. 1992, Crown LB $15.99 (0-517-58784-X). 36pp. Describing the discovery and excavation of the first complete skeleton of Tyrannosaurus Rex in 1990. (Rev: BL 1/15/93) [567.9]

**11738** Krueger, Richard. *The Dinosaurs* (2–5). Illus. Series: Prehistoric North America. 1996, Millbrook LB $21.90 (1-56294-548-3). 48pp. With plenty of color illustrations, this chatty overview tells about North American dinosaurs. (Rev: BL 5/15/96; SLJ 4/96) [567.9]

**11739** Kurokawa, Mitsuhiro. *Dinosaur Valley* (K–4). Illus. 1992, Chronicle $14.95 (0-8118-0257-4). 50pp. Readers go on a trip to Dinosaur Valley millions of years ago. (Rev: BL 2/1/93; SLJ 3/93) [567.9]

**11740** Lauber, Patricia. *Dinosaurs Walked Here: And Other Stories Fossils Tell* (3–5). Illus. 1987, Macmillan LB $16.95 (0-02-754510-5); paper $5.95 (0-689-71603-6). 64pp. More about fossils and what they tell us than about dinosaurs. (Rev: BCCB 9/87; BL 9/1/87; SLJ 9/87)

**11741** Lauber, Patricia. *How Dinosaurs Came to Be* (4–6). Illus. 1996, Simon & Schuster $17.00 (0-689-80531-4). 48pp. The ancestors of dinosaurs are described in this account that traces the evolution of these giant reptiles. (Rev: BL 4/15/96; SLJ 5/96) [567.9]

**11742** Lauber, Patricia. *Living with Dinosaurs* (3–6). Illus. by Douglas Henderson. 1991, Macmillan $16.95 (0-02-754521-0). 49pp. Re-creating what life was like in Montana 75 million years ago. (Rev: BL 3/1/91*; HB 5–6/91; SLJ 5/91*) [567.9]

**11743** Lauber, Patricia. *The News About Dinosaurs* (3–7). Illus. 1989, Macmillan LB $17.00 (0-02-754520-2); paper $6.95 (0-689-71870-5). 48pp. Recent thinking about the extinction of these giant beasts. (Rev: BCCB 3/89; BL 3/1/89; HB 5–6/88) [567.9]

**11744** Lessem, Don. *Bigger Than T. Rex* (4–6). Illus. by Robert F. Walters. 1997, Crown LB $19.99 (0-

517-70931-7). 32pp. A fascinating science book that supplies information about Gigantosaurus, the newly discovered dinosaur in Argentina that is larger than a Tyrannosaurus rex. (Rev: SLJ 12/97*) [567.9]

**11745** Lessem, Don. *Dinosaur Worlds: New Dinosaurs, New Discoveries* (5–8). Illus. 1996, Boyds Mills $19.95 (1-56397-597-1). 192pp. The reader visits various dinosaur digs worldwide in a review of what we know about these amazing creatures. (Rev: BL 11/15/96; SLJ 12/96*) [567.9]

**11746** Lessem, Don. *Ornithomimids: The Fastest Dinosaur* (3–6). Illus. Series: Special Dinosaurs. 1996, Carolrhoda LB $19.95 (0-87614-813-5). 40pp. How the remains of these speedy dinosaurs were discovered and how our knowledge of them was collected highlight this well-illustrated volume. (Rev: BL 2/15/96; SLJ 4/96) [567.9]

**11747** Lessem, Don. *Raptors! The Nastiest Dinosaurs* (4–6). Illus. 1996, Little, Brown $14.95 (0-316-52119-1). 32pp. Raptors and their savage relatives are introduced, as well as dinosaur digs that have uncovered information on them. (Rev: BL 9/1/96; SLJ 10/96) [567.9]

**11748** Lessem, Don. *Seismosaurus: The Longest Dinosaur* (3–5). Illus. by Donna Braginetz. Series: Special Dinosaurs. 1996, Carolrhoda LB $14.95 (0-87614-987-5). 40pp. This account introduces the seismosaurus and its characteristics and explains how we have determined these facts from fossils. (Rev: SLJ 9/96) [567.9]

**11749** Lessem, Don. *Supergiants! The Biggest Dinosaurs* (4–6). Illus. by David Peters. 1997, Little, Brown $14.95 (0-316-52118-3). 32pp. Current information about gigantic dinosaurs is given in this well-organized book, which includes the latest theories and discoveries concerning them. (Rev: SLJ 9/97) [567.9]

**11750** Lessem, Don. *Troodon: The Smartest Dinosaur* (3–6). Illus. Series: Special Dinosaurs. 1996, Carolrhoda LB $14.96 (0-87614-798-8). 40pp. The role of paleontologists in piecing together bits of information about this dinosaur is covered, along with information on its appearance, habits, and intelligence. (Rev: BL 2/15/96; SLJ 4/96) [567.9]

**11751** Lindsay, William. *Barosaurus* (4–7). Illus. 1993, DK Publg. $12.95 (1-56458-123-3). 30pp. This book introduces one of the biggest dinosaurs — its characteristics, habits, and habitats. (Rev: BL 4/15/93) [567.9]

**11752** Lindsay, William. *Triceratops* (3–6). Illus. 1993, DK Publg. $12.95 (1-56458-226-4). 32pp. The daily life of the plant-eating triceratops is re-created through models, fossil findings, and research. (Rev: BL 12/1/93) [567.9]

**11753** Lindsay, William. *Tyrannosaurus* (4–7). Illus. 1993, DK Publg. $12.95 (1-56458-124-1). 30pp. The life and world of one of the most ferocious dinosaurs is re-created with color photographs of scale models and actual fossils. (Rev: BL 4/15/93) [567.9]

**11754** Llamas, Andreu. *The Era of the Dinosaurs* (4–8). Illus. by Luis Rizo. Series: Development of the Earth. 1996, Chelsea LB $15.95 (0-7910-3452-6). 32pp. Various kinds of dinosaurs are introduced in this account that emphasizes their evolution. Also use *The First Amphibians* (1996). (Rev: SLJ 7/96) [567.9]

**11755** McGowan, Christopher. *Discover Dinosaurs* (4–6). Illus. by Tina Holdcroft. 1993, Addison-Wesley paper $9.95 (0-201-62267-X). 96pp. This is a concise introduction to the basic known facts about the large animals that once ruled the earth, with many accompanying experiments and projects. (Rev: BL 5/15/93) [567.9]

**11756** MacLeod, Elizabeth. *Dinosaurs: The Fastest, the Fiercest, the Most Amazing* (3–5). Illus. by Gordon Sauve. 1995, Viking paper $11.99 (0-670-86026-3). A Guinness-type book that explores record holders in the world of the dinosaur. (Rev: SLJ 8/95) [567/9]

**11757** McMullan, Kate. *Dinosaur Hunters* (2–4). Illus. by John R. Jones. 1989, Random LB $7.99 (0-394-91150-4); paper $3.99 (0-394-81150-X). 46pp. An easy reader on how fossils are found and studied, with coverage on new theories about dinosaurs. (Rev: BCCB 12/89; SLJ 9/89) [567.9]

**11758** Mannetti, William. *Dinosaurs in Your Backyard* (5–7). Illus. by author. 1982, Macmillan $15.00 (0-689-30906-6). 160pp. The latest discoveries and theories concerning dinosaurs and their history are incorporated into this account.

**11759** Massare, Judy A. *Prehistoric Marine Reptiles: Sea Monsters During the Age of Dinosaurs* (5–8). Illus. 1991, Watts LB $25.90 (0-531-11022-2). 64pp. A competent survey of sea life during the Mesozoic Era, with many photos, drawings, and maps. (Rev: BL 2/15/92; SLJ 2/92) [567.9]

**11760** Milner, Angela, ed. *Dinosaurs* (4–6). Illus. Series: Nature Company Discoveries. 1995, Time Life LB $16.00 (0-7835-4765-X). 64pp. A brief introduction to the world of dinosaurs, with colorful illustrations and an 8-page foldout. (Rev: BL 1/1–15/96; SLJ 1/96) [567.9]

**11761** Moody, Richard. *Over 65 Million Years Ago: Before the Dinosaurs Died* (4–6). Illus. Series: History Detective. 1992, Macmillan LB $13.95 (0-02-767270-0). 32pp. How paleontologists have found out about dinosaurs and a summary of how they lived. (Rev: SLJ 12/92) [567.92]

**11762** Most, Bernard. *Dinosaur Cousins?* (1–3). Illus. by author. 1987, Harcourt $13.95 (0-15-223497-7); paper $6.00 (0-15-223498-5). 40pp. Musing about whether a rhinoceros, for instance, could be a dinosaur's cousin leads to facts about prehistoric animals. (Rev: BL 2/15/87; SLJ 5/85)

**11763** Most, Bernard. *Dinosaur Questions* (PS–2). Illus. 1995, Harcourt $15.00 (0-15-292885-5). 40pp. Common questions about dinosaurs are answered, with many asides to test the reader. (Rev: BL 10/1/95; SLJ 2/96) [567.9]

**11764** Most, Bernard. *How Big Were the Dinosaurs?* (PS–2). Illus. 1994, Harcourt $16.00 (0-15-236800-0). 32pp. The size of 20 different dinosaurs is shown by comparisons with everyday modern objects, like a school bus or a bowling alley. (Rev: BL 3/1/94; SLJ 4/94) [567.9]

**11765** Most, Bernard. *Where to Look for a Dinosaur* (1–4). Illus. 1993, Harcourt $13.00 (0-15-295616-6). 32pp. An actual geographical guidebook pinpointing the remains of more than 25 beasts. (Rev: BL 2/15/93; SLJ 6/93) [567.9]

**11766** Murphy, Jim. *Dinosaur for a Day* (K–3). Illus. by Mark A. Weatherby. 1992, Scholastic $15.95 (0-590-42866-7). 40pp. A mother dinosaur and her 8 children search for food on a lush island. (Rev: BL 10/15/92; SLJ 10/92) [567.9]

**11767** Nardo, Don. *The Extinction of the Dinosaurs* (3–6). Illus. 1994, Lucent LB $22.45 (1-56006-154-5). 48pp. Several of the current theories on the cause of dinosaur extinction are presented. (Rev: BL 3/1/94) [567.9]

**11768** Norman, David, and Angela Milner. *Dinosaur* (4–8). Illus. Series: Eyewitness. 1989, Knopf LB $20.99 (0-394-92253-0). 64pp. Rich illustrations highlight various dinosaurs, with details on structure and habits. (Rev: BL 10/15/89; SLJ 1/90) [567.9]

**11769** Parish, Peggy. *Dinosaur Time* (K–2). Illus. by Arnold Lobel. 1974, HarperCollins LB $14.89 (0-06-024654-5); paper $3.75 (0-06-444037-0). 32pp. Eleven dinosaurs are introduced in this book for the beginning reader.

**11770** Pascoe, Elaine, adapt. *New Dinosaurs: Skeletons in the Sand* (4–6). Illus. Series: New Explorers. 1997, Blackbirch LB $16.95 (1-56711-231-5). 48pp. An account of the hardships and eventual success of a group of paleontologists who went to the Sahara in 1993 to find evidence of new dinosaurs. (Rev: SLJ 2/98) [567.9]

**11771** Pope, Joyce. *Fossil Detective* (3–6). Illus. by Chris Forsey. Series: Nature Club. 1993, Troll LB $12.95 (0-8167-2781-3); paper $4.95 (0-8167-2782-1). 31pp. This introduction to paleontology as a hobby contains material on what fossils are, how

they were formed, and how young people can collect them. (Rev: SLJ 3/94) [560]

**11772** Pringle, Laurence. *Dinosaurs! Strange and Wonderful* (K–3). Illus. by Carol Heyer. 1995, Boyds Mills $15.95 (1-878093-16-9). 32pp. With a brief text and striking illustrations, 11 dinosaurs are described. (Rev: BL 3/15/95; SLJ 3/95) [567.9]

**11773** Rhodes, Frank H. *Fossils* (5–8). Illus. 1962, Western paper $5.50 (0-307-24411-3). This volume contains a history of fossil formation, plus tips on identification.

**11774** Roberts, Allan. *Fossils* (1–4). Illus. 1983, Children's LB $20.00 (0-516-01678-4). 48pp. An introduction to paleontology for the very young, with fine color photographs. [560]

**11775** Royston, Angela. *Dinosaurs* (PS–2). Illus. by Jane Cradock-Watson and Dave Hopkins. Series: Eye Openers. 1991, Macmillan $7.95 (0-689-71518-8). 24pp. Many of the most important kinds of dinosaurs are introduced. (Rev: BL 9/15/91; SLJ 1/92) [567.9]

**11776** Sattler, Helen R. *Tyrannosaurus Rex and Its Kin: The Mesozoic Monsters* (4–6). Illus. by Joyce Powzyk. 1989, Lothrop LB $15.93 (0-688-07748-X). 48pp. An account of the largest land-dwelling predators that ever lived. (Rev: BCCB 2/89; BL 4/1/89; SLJ 3/89)

**11777** Schlein, Miriam. *Discovering Dinosaur Babies* (2–4). Illus. by Margaret Colbert. 1991, Macmillan LB $14.95 (0-02-778091-0). 40pp. Explaining what is known about dinosaur babies and how mothers cared for them. (Rev: BL 3/1/91; SLJ 7/91) [567.9]

**11778** Schlein, Miriam. *The Puzzle of the Dinosaur-Bird: The Story of Archaeopteryx* (4–6). Illus. by Mark Hallett. 1996, Dial paper $15.89 (0-8037-1283-9). 40pp. The scientific controversy to determine whether Archaeopteryx was a bird or a dinosaur is explored, with different viewpoints presented fairly. (Rev: SLJ 9/96) [567.9]

**11779** Senior, Kathryn. *Dinosaurs and Other Prehistoric Creatures* (3–8). Illus. by Carolyn Scrace. Series: X-Ray Picture Books. 1995, Watts LB $24.00 (0-531-14352-X). 48pp. In this general introduction to dinosaurs, 2 of the many topics discussed are survival techniques and reproduction. (Rev: SLJ 12/95) [567.9]

**11780** Simon, Seymour. *New Questions and Answers About Dinosaurs* (2–5). Illus. by Jennifer Dewey. 1990, Morrow LB $15.93 (0-688-08196-7). 48pp. Using a question-and-answer approach, covers interesting facts and figures about dinosaurs. (Rev: BCCB 5/90; BL 2/15/90; HB 7–8/90; SLJ 5/90) [567.9]

**11781** Simon, Seymour. *The Smallest Dinosaurs* (2–4). Illus. by Anthony Rao. 1988, Crown paper

$4.95 (0-517-56550-1). An easy-to-read book that gives basic facts and introduces 7 small species.

**11782** Simpson, Judith. *Mighty Dinosaurs* (2–4). Illus. Series: Nature Company Young Discoveries. 1996, Time Life $10.00 (0-7835-4837-0). 32pp. Some of the most noteworthy dinosaurs are pictured and described in this brief introduction. (Rev: BL 12/15/96) [567.9]

**11783** Taylor, Barbara. *The Really Deadly and Dangerous Dinosaur: And Other Monsters of the Prehistoric World* (PS–4). Illus. Series: The Really Horrible Guides. 1997, DK Publg. $9.95 (0-7894-2051-1). This account explores the various ways — like teeth, claws, horns, and stingers — that prehistoric animals defended themselves. (Rev: SLJ 12/97) [567.79]

**11784** Taylor, Paul D. *Fossil* (4–8). Illus. Series: Eyewitness Books. 1990, Knopf LB $20.99 (0-679-90440-9). 64pp. This book tells how fossils are formed and what stories they reveal. (Rev: SLJ 9/90) [560.9]

**11785** Thompson, Sharon E. *Death Trap: The Story of the La Brea Tar Pits* (4–8). Illus. 1995, Lerner LB $23.93 (0-8225-2851-7). 72pp. A history of the 40,000-year-old tar pits in Los Angeles and of the many species of prehistoric animals that were trapped in them. (Rev: BL 6/1–15/95; SLJ 5/95) [560]

**11786** Unwin, David. *The New Book of Dinosaurs* (3–6). Illus. 1997, Millbrook LB $23.90 (0-7613-0568-8); paper $9.95 (0-7613-0589-0). 32pp. Computer-generated illustrations bring different dinosaurs alive, with lucid accompanying text. (Rev: BL 9/15/97; SLJ 9/97) [567.9]

**11787** VanCleave, Janice. *Dinosaurs for Every Kid: Easy Activities That Make Learning Science Fun* (4–7). Illus. Series: Science for Every Kid. 1994, Wiley $27.95 (0-471-30813-7); paper $10.95 (0-471-

30812-9). 224pp. With accompanying activities, this book explores the world of dinosaurs and how paleontology has discovered, through fossils, how they lived. (Rev: BL 4/1/94; SLJ 7/94) [567.9]

**11788** Weishampel, David B. *Plant-Eating Dinosaurs* (4–6). Illus. by Brian Franczak. 1992, Watts LB $25.90 (0-531-11021-4). 64pp. What did these big vegetarians eat and how did they live for more than 160 million years? (Rev: BL 6/15/92; SLJ 7/92) [567.9]

**11789** Westrup, Hugh. *The Mammals* (3–5). Illus. Series: Prehistoric North America. 1996, Millbrook LB $21.90 (1-56294-546-7). 48pp. The woolly mammoth and saber-toothed tiger are 2 of the prehistoric mammals described in words and pictures. (Rev: BL 5/15/96; SLJ 4/96) [569]

**11790** Whitfield, Philip. *Macmillan Children's Guide to Dinosaurs and Other Prehistoric Animals* (3–6). Illus. 1992, Macmillan LB $18.95 (0-02-762362-9). 96pp. A handsome guide to prehistoric animal life. (Rev: BL 10/15/92; SLJ 12/92) [567.9]

**11791** Wilkes, Angela. *The Big Book of Dinosaurs: A First Book for Young Children* (PS–2). Illus. 1994, DK Publg. $12.95 (1-56458-718-5). 32pp. An oversize book that contains double-page spreads introducing a wide variety of dinosaurs, including some that are little known. (Rev: BL 11/15/94; SLJ 1/95) [567.9]

**11792** Zallinger, Peter. *Dinosaurs and Other Archosaurs* (4–6). Illus. 1986, Random LB $9.99 (0-394-94421-6). 96pp. A solid overview of these fascinating creatures, era by era, group by group. (Rev: BL 9/1/86)

**11793** Zallinger, Peter. *Prehistoric Animals* (1–3). Illus. by author. 1981, Random paper $3.25 (0-394-83737-1). A brief guide to prehistoric animals — chiefly dinosaurs — and their habits.

# Anthropology and Prehistoric Life

**11794** *Atlas of People* (PS–2). Illus. Series: First Discovery. 1996, Scholastic $11.95 (0-590-58281-X). 24pp. A basic introduction to the various races of humankind, with attractive visuals. (Rev: BL 10/15/96; SLJ 2/97) [305.8]

**11795** Branigan, Keith. *Stone Age People* (3–6). Illus. Series: Make It Work. 1996, World Book $13.95 (0-7166-1725-0); paper $7.95 (0-7166-1726-9). 48pp. The life and accomplishments of prehistoric people are covered through a series of activities and projects. (Rev: BL 11/15/96) [768]

**11796** Buell, Janet. *Bog Bodies* (5–8). Illus. Series: Time Travelers. 1997, Twenty-First Century $20.40 (0-8050-5164-3). 64pp. This account tells of the discovery of Lindow Man, a Celtic man preserved by an English bog, with details on his life and information on how scientists use carbon dating, X-rays, and other forensic techniques. (Rev: BL 2/1/98; SLJ 3/98) [599.9]

**11797** Buell, Janet. *Ice Maiden of the Andes* (5–8). Illus. Series: Time Travelers. 1997, Twenty-First Century $20.40 (0-8050-5185-6). 64pp. The story of the discovery of the frozen body of a young Inca girl who died 500 years ago and of how forensic methods like DNA testing have revealed details of Inca society, its religion, and gender roles. (Rev: BL 2/1/98; SLJ 3/98) [985]

**11798** Childress, Diana. *Prehistoric People of North America* (3–5). Illus. Series: Junior Library of American Indians. 1996, Chelsea $15.95 (0-7910-2481-4); paper $8.95 (0-7910-2482-2). 80pp. The story of the people who inhabited America in prehistoric times, with material on how they survived. (Rev: BL 11/15/96; SLJ 12/96) [970.01]

**11799** Cole, Joanna. *Evolution* (2–3). Illus. by Aliki. 1989, HarperCollins paper $4.50 (0-06-445086-4). 32pp. The story of evolution beginning with fossils

and on to the theory of Darwin. (Rev: BCCB 10/87; BL 11/1/87; HB 11–12/87)

**11800** Cole, Joanna. *The Human Body: How We Evolved* (4–6). Illus. 1987, Morrow LB $12.88 (0-688-06720-4). 64pp. The human body examined from the viewpoint of evolutionary development. (Rev: BCCB 11/87; BL 9/1/87; HB 11–12/87)

**11801** Corbishley, Mike. *What Do We Know About Prehistoric People?* (4–7). Illus. Series: What Do We Know About . . .? 1996, Bedrick LB $18.95 (0-87226-383-5). 40pp. Using double-page spreads, this book explores the known facts about human prehistoric life around the world. (Rev: BL 6/1–15/96) [930.1]

**11802** Denny, Sidney, and Ernest L. Schusky. *The Ancient Splendor of Prehistoric Cahokia* (4–8). Illus. 1997, Ozark $12.95 (1-56763-271-8); paper $3.45 (1-56763-272-6). 41pp. Using the findings from the Cahokia Mounds in southern Illinois as a beginning, the author re-creates the life and culture of these prehistoric American Indians. (Rev: BL 5/1/97) [977.3]

**11803** Facchini, Fiorenzo. *Humans: Origins and Evolution* (4–8). Illus. Series: Beginnings. 1995, Raintree Steck-Vaughn LB $24.26 (0-8114-3336-6). 48pp. Theories and facts involving human evolution are presented in a straightforward way, with extensive art work and diagrams. (Rev: BL 4/15/95; SLJ 6/95) [573.2]

**11804** Gamlin, Linda. *Evolution* (3–6). Illus. Series: Eyewitness Science. 1993, DK Publg. $15.95 (1-56458-233-7). 64pp. A very attractive book that begins with early theories about life, continues through the work of Darwin and Mendel, and ends with a discussion about DNA and its implications for the future. (Rev: SLJ 9/93) [575]

**11805** Garassino, Alessandro. *Life: Origins and Evolution* (4–8). Illus. Series: Beginnings — Origins and Evolution. 1995, Raintree Steck-Vaughn LB $24.26 (0-8114-3335-8). 48pp. Discusses the structure of plant and animal cells plus how organisms evolve and are classified. (Rev: BL 5/1/95) [575]

**11806** Getz, David. *Frozen Man* (4–6). Illus. 1994, Holt $14.95 (0-8050-3261-4). 68pp. An account of the discovery of the Copper Age man frozen in the Italian Alps, how his age was determined, and the facts that could be deduced from examining the body. (Rev: BCCB 1/95; BL 11/15/94; SLJ 12/94) [937.3]

**11807** Lindsay, William. *Prehistoric Life* (4–8). Illus. Series: Eyewitness Books. 1994, Knopf LB $20.99 (0-679-96001-5). 64pp. Prehistoric life is described, as well as the process of evolution and the methods used by anthropologists. (Rev: BL 10/15/94; SLJ 8/94) [560]

**11808** Martell, Hazel M. *Over 6,000 Years Ago: In the Stone Age* (3–6). Illus. by Chris Rothero. 1992, Macmillan LB $13.95 (0-02-762429-3). 32pp. A look at life in the Stone Age, with watercolor drawings and photos. (Rev: BL 9/15/92; SLJ 12/92) [930.12]

**11809** Merriman, Nick. *Early Humans* (4–8). Illus. Series: Eyewitness. 1989, Knopf LB $20.99 (0-394-92257-3). A well-illustrated account of prehistoric people, including Ice Age hunters and Bronze Age warriors. (Rev: BL 7/89; SLJ 8/89) [930.1]

**11810** Perham, Molly, and Julian Rowe. *People* (4–6). Illus. Series: Mapworlds. 1996, Watts LB $19.30 (0-531-14362-7). 32pp. The important races of the world and their homelands are identified in an atlaslike format with many illustrations. (Rev: BL 10/15/96; SLJ 1/97) [306]

**11811** Pickering, Robert. *The People* (3–5). Illus. Series: Prehistoric North America. 1996, Millbrook LB $21.90 (1-56294-550-5). 48pp. An account of the people who lived in prehistoric North America, with

details on how they lived. (Rev: BL 5/15/96; SLJ 4/96) [973.01]

**11812** Place, Robin. *Bodies from the Past* (4–7). Illus. Series: Digging Up the Past. 1995, Thomson Learning LB $24.26 (1-56847-397-4). 48pp. Explores the preserved remains of people around the world from burial sites in China and mummies in peat bogs to the Ice Man recently discovered in the Alps. (Rev: SLJ 2/96) [567.9]

**11813** Ruiz, Andres L. *Evolution* (3–5). Illus. Series: Cycles of Life. 1997, Sterling $12.95 (0-8069-9329-4). 32pp. A step-by-step explanation of evolution, beginning with single-cell organisms and ending with the appearance of humans. (Rev: SLJ 6/97) [575]

**11814** Sattler, Helen R. *Hominids: A Look Back at Our Ancestors* (5–7). Illus. 1988, Lothrop $15.95 (0-688-06061-7). Tracing long-ago humans. (Rev: BL 7/88; HB 9–10/88; SLJ 6–7/88)

**11815** Tanaka, Shelley. *Discovering the Iceman: What Was It Like to Find a 5,300-Year-Old Mummy?* (4–7). Illus. 1997, Hyperion $16.95 (0-7868-0284-7). 48pp. The story of discovering the 5,300-year-old Iceman in the Swiss Alps in 1991 and his importance to science. (Rev: BCCB 5/97; BL 4/15/97; SLJ 6/97) [937]

**11816** Unwin, David. *Prehistoric Life* (5–8). Illus. Series: Mysteries Of . . . 1996, Millbrook LB $22.90 (0-7613-0535-1). 40pp. In addition to discussing dinosaurs, this book gives a history of the evolution of both animals and humans. (Rev: SLJ 1/97) [575]

**11817** Wood, Marion. *The World of Native Americans* (2–5). Illus. 1998, Bedrick LB $19.95 (0-87226-280-4). 48pp. Traces the journey to North America of prehistoric people from across the Bering Strait, tells where they settled, and describes the 8 cultural groups of American Indians. (Rev: BL 3/15/98) [970]

# Archaeology

**11818** Avi-Yonah, Michael. *Dig This! How Archaeologists Uncover Our Past* (5–8). Illus. Series: Buried Worlds. 1993, Lerner LB $23.93 (0-8225-3200-X). 96pp. As well as explaining what archaeologists do, this book gives a history of the profession, a glimpse at their techniques, and a look at some ancient civilizations. (Rev: BL 1/15/94; SLJ 2/94) [930.1]

**11819** Barber, Nicola. *The Search for Lost Cities* (4–6). Illus. Series: Treasure Hunters. 1997, Raintree Steck-Vaughn LB $24.97 (0-8172-4840-4). 46pp. Using double-page spreads for each site, this account covers such places as Troy, Knossos, Pompeii, and Ankor Wat. (Rev: BL 11/15/97; SLJ 1/98) [909]

**11820** Barber, Nicola, and Anita Ganeri. *The Search for Sunken Treasure* (4–6). Series: Treasure Hunters. 1997, Raintree Steck-Vaughn LB $24.97 (0-8172-4838-2). 46pp. This overview covers such topics as the lost treasures in sunken ships and the sacred well of Chichén Itzá, with additional material on how ancient artifacts have been recovered and what they tell us about other times. (Rev: BL 11/15/97) [930]

**11821** Corbishley, Mike. *How Do We Know Where People Came From?* (5–8). Illus. Series: How Do We Know. 1995, Raintree Steck-Vaughn LB $24.26 (0-8114-3880-5). 41pp. The rudiments of archaeology are introduced, with discussion of such topics as Stonehenge, the Great Wall of China, and Easter Island. (Rev: SLJ 1/96) [930]

**11822** Donnelly, Judy. *True-Life Treasure Hunts* (2–4). Illus. by Thomas La Padula. 1993, Random paper $3.99 (0-679-83980-1). 48pp. True stories of finding hidden treasure in all sorts of places, like sunken ships. (Rev: BL 4/1/94) [930.1]

**11823** Duke, Kate. *Archaeologists Dig for Clues* (1–4). Series: Let's-Read-and-Find-Out Science. 1997, HarperCollins LB $14.89 (0-06-027057-8). 32pp. Archaeologist Sophie describes how her col-

leagues collect information and analyze their findings. (Rev: BL 12/1/96; SLJ 2/97*) [930]

**11824** Fradin, Dennis B. *Archaeology* (1–4). Illus. 1993, Children's paper $5.50 (0-516-41691-X). 48pp. A very broad topic competently introduced for primary grades.

**11825** Ganeri, Anita. *The Search for Tombs* (4–6). Illus. Series: Treasure Hunters. 1997, Raintree Steck-Vaughn LB $24.97 (0-8172-4839-0). 46pp. This fascinating account covers such burial places as the Egyptian pyramids, the royal tombs of China, and the Roman catacombs. (Rev: BL 11/15/97; SLJ 2/98) [393]

**11826** Goldenstern, Joyce. *Lost Cities* (3–6). Illus. Series: Weird and Wacky Science. 1996, Enslow LB $18.95 (0-89490-615-1). 48pp. The history and rediscovery of such lost cities as Troy, Machu Picchu, Mohenjo-daro, and Herculaneum are covered. (Rev: SLJ 6/96) [930]

**11827** Hoobler, Dorothy. *Lost Civilizations* (5–7). Illus. by Thomas Hoobler. 1992, Walker LB $15.85 (0-8027-8153-5). 176pp. Interesting discussion of Stonehenge, the Mound Builders, and other lost ancient civilizations. (Rev: BL 5/1/92; SLJ 9/92) [930]

**11828** Jameson, W. C. *Buried Treasures of the Atlantic Coast: Legends of Sunken Pirate Treasures, Mysterious Caches, and Jinxed Ships* (4–8). Series: Buried Treasure. 1997, August House paper $11.95 (0-87483-484-8). 192pp. Describes how buried treasures were acquired and lost and the modern attempts to retrieve them. Also use *Buried Treasures of New England* (1997). (Rev: SLJ 10/97) [910.4]

**11829** Kent, Peter. *A Slice Through a City* (4–8). Illus. by author. 1996, Millbrook LB $23.90 (0-7613-0039-2). 29pp. This introduction to archaeology shows cutaway views of a European city from the Stone Age to the present. (Rev: SLJ 3/97) [930]

**11830** Knapp, Ron. *Mummies* (3–6). Illus. Series: Weird and Wacky Science. 1996, Enslow LB $18.95 (0-89490-618-6). 48pp. Describes how bodies have been preserved in different cultures and situations, ending with the recent discovery of the Ice Man in the Alps. (Rev: SLJ 6/96) [930]

**11831** Lauber, Patricia. *Tales Mummies Tell* (5–8). Illus. 1985, HarperCollins LB $16.89 (0-690-04389-9). 128pp. How people and animals were mummified and what mummies can tell scientists. (Rev: BCCB 7/85; HB 5–6/85; SLJ 8/85)

**11832** Lessem, Don. *The Iceman* (4–7). Illus. 1994, Crown $16.00 (0-517-59596-6). 32pp. Chronicles the discovery in 1991 of a Copper Age man frozen in an alpine glacier. (Rev: BCCB 9/94; BL 11/1/94; HB 5–6/94; SLJ 7/94) [937]

**11833** Maynard, Christopher. *Incredible Buried Treasure* (1–3). Illus. 1994, DK Publg. paper $4.95 (1-56458-728-2). 32pp. Pictures dominate this book about all forms of buried treasure and their discoverers. (Rev: BL 1/15/95) [930.1]

**11834** Reid, Struan. *The Children's Atlas of Lost Treasures* (4–7). Illus. Series: Children's Atlases. 1997, Millbrook LB $27.40 (0-7613-0219-0); paper $14.95 (0-7613-0240-9). 96pp. Using a double-page spread for each site, this book supplies a survey of the world-famous discoveries of treasures that began as religious offerings, pirate booty, and items lost in war or by natural disasters. (Rev: SLJ 3/98) [930.1]

**11835** Schultz, Ron. *Looking Inside Sunken Treasure* (4–6). Illus. by Nick Gadbois and Peter Aschwanden. Series: X-ray Vision. 1993, John Muir paper $6.95 (1-56261-074-0). 43pp. This oversized paperback describes the world of underwater archaeology. (Rev: SLJ 8/93) [930.1]

**11836** Sullivan, George. *Slave Ship: The Story of the Henrietta Marie* (5–8). Illus. 1994, Dutton paper $15.99 (0-525-65174-8). 80pp. While giving details on the underwater archaeological exploration of the slave ship *Henrietta Marie* that sunk off Florida in the 1700s, the author supplies many details on the slave trade. (Rev: BL 11/1/94; SLJ 12/94) [975.9]

**11837** *Sunk! Exploring Underwater Archaeology* (5–8). Illus. Series: Buried World. 1994, Lerner LB $23.93 (0-8225-3205-0). 72pp. An introduction to underwater archaeology that explains the methods of examining artifacts to re-create the past. (Rev: BL 10/15/94; SLJ 9/94) [930.1]

# World History

## General

**11838** Adams, Simon, et al. *Junior Chronicle of the 20th Century: Month-by-Month History of Our Amazing Century* (5–8). Illus. 1997, DK Publg. $39.95 (0-7894-2033-3). 336pp. A collection of articles, photos, and other illustrations that cover the important events of the 20th century, with double-page spreads and a month-by-month arrangement. (Rev: SLJ 1/98) [909.82]

**11839** Barber, Nicola. *The Search for Gold* (4–6). Series: Treasure Hunters. 1997, Raintree Steck-Vaughn LB $24.97 (0-8172-4837-4). 46pp. This overview covers such topics as the Spanish destruction of the Aztec and Inca cultures, the African gold trade, and the California Gold Rush. (Rev: BL 11/15/97) [900]

**11840** Cooper, Kay. *Who Put the Cannon in the Courthouse Square?* (5–8). Illus. 1984, Walker LB $12.85 (0-8027-6561-0). Advice on how to become a local historian. (Rev: BL 7/85; SLJ 9/85)

**11841** Garwood, Val. *The World of the Pirate* (3–6). Illus. 1998, Bedrick LB $19.95 (0-87226-281-2). 48pp. The lives of pirates are explored through history, with material on famous pirates and topics like their food and weapons. (Rev: BL 2/1/98; SLJ 1/98) [910.4]

**11842** Gelber, Carol. *Masks Tell Stories* (5–7). Illus. Series: Beyond Museum Walls. 1993, Millbrook LB $23.90 (1-56294-224-7). 62pp. Explores the nature, meaning, and uses of masks in different cultures at various times. (Rev: BL 8/93) [391]

**11843** Gibbons, Gail. *Pirates: Robbers of the High Seas* (2–4). Illus. 1993, Little, Brown $15.95 (0-316-30975-3). 32pp. A fascinating account that re-creates the world of pirates, their swashbuckling fights, and

their hidden treasures. (Rev: BCCB 9/93; BL 11/15/93; SLJ 10/93) [910.5]

**11844** Gold, Susan D. *Governments of the Western Hemisphere* (5–8). Illus. Series: Comparing Continents. 1997, Twenty-First Century $21.40 (0-8050-5602-5). 96pp. Examines the struggle for independence in the United States, Canada, Mexico, Central America, and South America and the different directions each area moved toward once independence was achieved. (Rev: BL 2/1/98; SLJ 3/98) [320.3]

**11845** Jungrels, Abigail. *Know Your Hometown History: Projects and Activities* (4–6). Illus. 1992, Watts LB $21.00 (0-531-11124-5). 62pp. Explains how to investigate hometowns and describes projects for doing it. (Rev: BL 2/15/93) [973]

**11846** Knight, Margy B. *Talking Walls: The Stories Continue* (3–7). Illus. by Anne S. O'Brien. 1996, Tilbury House $17.95 (0-88448-164-6). Double-page spreads are used to introduce some famous walls, like the dikes in the Netherlands, Hadrian's Wall, the Belfast Peace Lines, and prayer-wheel walls in India and Tibet. (Rev: SLJ 10/96) [900]

**11847** Lincoln, Margarette. *The Pirate's Handbook: How to Become a Rogue of the High Seas* (4–6). Illus. 1995, Dutton paper $12.99 (0-525-65209-4). 36pp. The daily life of pirates, including their clothing and food, is covered, with some interesting related projects. (Rev: BCCB 10/95; BL 9/15/95; SLJ 9/95) [910.45]

**11848** Morgan, Kate. *The Story of Things* (3–5). Illus. by Joyce A. Zarins. 1991, Walker LB $15.85 (0-8027-6919-5). 32pp. A history of civilization in a slim volume that will attract a child's interest. (Rev: BL 6/15/91; SLJ 7/91) [523.4]

**11849** Nott, Valerie. *Great Disasters* (4–6). Illus. Series: What Happened Next? 1995, Watts LB $23.60 (0-531-14360-0). 48pp. Readers consider several different explanations for such historical events as the destruction of Pompeii, the Black Death, and the sinking of the *Titanic*. (Rev: BL 9/15/95) [904]

**11850** Pirotta, Saviour. *Pirates and Treasure* (4–5). Illus. Series: Remarkable World. 1995, Thomson Learning LB $24.26 (1-56847-366-4). 47pp. A history of piracy from the days of the Phoenicians onward, with full-color art reproductions, maps, and many sidebars. (Rev: SLJ 1/96) [910.4]

**11851** Platt, Richard. *In the Beginning: The Nearly Complete History of Almost Everything* (3–7). Illus. 1995, DK Publg. $19.95 (0-7894-0206-8). 76pp. A basic history of the world from the big bang theory to the present in a lavishly illustrated volume. (Rev: BL 12/1/95; SLJ 1/96) [909]

**11852** Platt, Richard. *Pirate* (4–8). Illus. Series: Eyewitness Books. 1995, Knopf $17.00 (0-679-87255-8). 64pp. A history of piracy, with profiles of some of the major bucaneers of the past, in an account that separates truth from myth. (Rev: BL 8/95; SLJ 8/95) [364.1]

**11853** Ross, Stewart. *Conquerors and Explorers* (5–7). Illus. Series: Fact or Fiction. 1996, Millbrook LB $24.90 (0-7613-0532-7). 48pp. The subtitle of this work is "The Greed, Cunning, and Bravery of the Travelers and Plunderers Who Opened Up the World." (Rev: BL 10/15/96; SLJ 4/97) [910]

**11854** Ross, Stewart. *Pirates* (5–7). Illus. Series: Fact or Fiction. 1995, Millbrook LB $24.90 (1-56294-619-6). 48pp. A good overview of pirates, including details of the various regions where they roamed. (Rev: BL 7/95; SLJ 5/95) [904.7]

**11855** Sammis, Fran. *Measurements* (2–5). 1997, Marshall Cavendish LB $21.36 (0-7614-0539-9). 32pp. Explains how geographical distances are measured and how these systems began. (Rev: BL 2/15/98) [910]

**11856** Steele, Philip. *Pirates* (3–5). Illus. 1997, Kingfisher $15.95 (0-7534-5052-6). 64pp. A chronologically arranged history of piracy from Roman times through the Vikings to modern highjackings. (Rev: SLJ 5/97) [910]

**11857** Stienecker, David L. *Countries* (2–5). Series: Discovering Geography. 1997, Marshall Cavendish LB $21.36 (0-7614-0542-9). 32pp. Basic geographical concepts are explored in a question-and-answer format. (Rev: BL 2/15/98) [910]

**11858** Weitzman, David. *My Backyard History Book* (4–7). Illus. by James Robertson. 1975, Little, Brown $16.95 (0-316-92901-8); paper $12.95 (0-316-92902-6). 128pp. A guide to re-creating history that occurred close to home by interviewing, for example, family and friends.

**11859** Williams, Brian. *The Modern World: From the French Revolution to the Computer Age* (5–8). Illus. by James Field. Series: Timelink. 1994, Bedrick LB $18.95 (0-87226-312-6). 64pp. An overview of the 200 years of world history that outlines major events, with useful timelines and maps. (Rev: SLJ 1/95) [909]

**11860** Williams, Brian, and Brenda Williams. *The Age of Discovery: From the Renaissance to American Independence* (5–8). Illus. by James Field. Series: Timelink. 1994, Bedrick LB $18.95 (0-87226-311-8). 64pp. An overview of world history from the Renaissance through the American Revolution presented in 50-year segments. (Rev: SLJ 1/95) [909]

# Ancient History

## General and Miscellaneous

**11861** Burrell, Roy. *Oxford First Ancient History* (4–7). Illus. 1994, Oxford $37.95 (0-19-521058-1). 320pp. A survey of ancient civilizations, particularly those of the Mediterranean but also including the Chinese and Assyrians. (Rev: BL 7/94) [930]

**11862** Gregory, Tony. *The Dark Ages* (4–7). Illus. 1993, Facts on File $19.95 (0-8160-2787-0). 78pp. Beginning with human evolution, this account traces the history of early settlements to about 200 B.C. (Rev: SLJ 7/93) [938]

**11863** Jessop, Joanne. *The X-Ray Picture Book of Big Buildings of the Ancient World* (2–6). Illus. 1994, Watts LB $24.00 (0-531-14286-8). 48pp. This handsomely illustrated book shows cutaway views of such structures as the Great Pyramid, the Parthenon, the Coliseum, Notre Dame, Mont St. Michel, and the Taj Mahal. (Rev: BL 6/1–15/94; SLJ 7/94) [720]

**11864** Martell, Hazel M. *The Kingfisher Book of the Ancient World: From the Ice Age to the Fall of Rome* (4–8). Illus. 1995, Kingfisher $22.95 (1-85697-565-7). 160pp. Presents ancient civilizations from 11 areas, like the Americas, Africa, and the Mediterranean. (Rev: BL 2/1/96; SLJ 1/96) [930]

**11865** Odijk, Pamela. *The Phoenicians* (4–7). Illus. Series: Ancient World. 1989, Silver Burdett LB $14.95 (0-382-09891-9). 48pp. The ancient traders of the Mediterranean Sea are introduced. (Rev: BL 1/15/90; SLJ 5/90) [939.44]

**11866** Stille, Darlene R. *Ice Age* (1–3). Illus. Series: New True Books. 1990, Children's paper $5.50 (0-516-41107-1). 48pp. With minimum text and many illustrations, the ice age is introduced to the very young reader. (Rev: BL 1/1/91) [551.7]

**11867** Wilkinson, Philip, and Jacqueline Dineen. *The Mediterranean* (4–7). Illus. by Robert Ingpen. Series: Mysterious Places. 1994, Chelsea LB $19.95 (0-7910-2751-1). 92pp. Ten sites around the Mediterranean are investigated, including Knossos, Rhodes, Delphi, Mistra, the Topkapi Palace, and Hagia Sophia. (Rev: BL 1/15/94; SLJ 5/94) [930.3]

**11868** Wood, Tim. *Ancient Wonders* (4–8). Series: See Through History. 1997, Viking paper $17.99 (0-670-87468-X). 48pp. Introduces famous structures of the ancient world, and tells of their construction and eventual fate. (Rev: BL 10/15/97; SLJ 1/98) [930]

## Egypt and Mesopotamia

**11869** Aliki. *Mummies Made in Egypt* (3–5). Illus. by author. 1979, HarperCollins LB $14.89 (0-690-03859-3); paper $5.95 (0-06-446011-8). 32pp. The burial practices and beliefs of the ancient Egyptians are explored in text and handsome illustrations.

**11870** Anderson, Scoular. *A Puzzling Day in the Land of the Pharaohs* (3–8). Illus. by author. 1996, Candlewick $14.99 (1-56402-877-1). A picture puzzle book that features different aspects of life in ancient Egypt in double-page spreads. (Rev: SLJ 10/96) [932]

**11871** Bendick, Jeanne. *Egyptian Tombs* (4–6). Illus. 1989, Watts LB $22.00 (0-531-10462-1). 64pp. A description of the fascinating Egyptian funerary practices. (Rev: BCCB 4/89; BL 4/15/89; SLJ 5/89)

**11872** Charley, Catherine. *Tombs and Treasures* (4–8). Illus. Series: See Through History. 1995, Viking paper $15.99 (0-670-85899-4). 48pp. An overview of burial practices and the wealth often interred with the body, as in the case of King Tut and other Egyptian pharaohs. (Rev: BL 1/1–15/96; SLJ 1/96) [393.1]

**11873** Clare, John D., ed. *Pyramids of Ancient Egypt* (4–6). Illus. Series: Living History. 1992, Harcourt $16.95 (0-15-200509-9). 64pp. Besides telling about the building of the Pyramids, this book uses human models to describe the daily life of the ancient Egyptians. (Rev: SLJ 10/92) [932]

**11874** Clarke, Sue. *The Tombs of the Pharaohs: A Three-Dimensional Discovery* (2–5). Illus. 1994, Hyperion $16.95 (1-56282-485-6). 10pp. In this interactive book shaped like a pyramid, pop-ups and flaps are used to introduce topics involving ancient Egypt. (Rev: BL 11/15/94) [932]

**11875** Crosher, Judith. *Ancient Egypt* (4–6). Illus. Series: See Through History. 1993, Viking paper $17.99 (0-670-84755-0). 48pp. A visually interesting introduction to the history and accomplishments of

the ancient Egyptians. (Rev: BL 4/15/93; SLJ 8/93) [932]

**11876** David, Rosalie. *Growing Up in Ancient Egypt* (3–5). Illus. by Angus McBride. Series: Growing Up In. 1993, Troll paper $4.95 (0-8167-2718-X). 32pp. Everyday life in the different social classes of ancient Egypt is covered, with a focus on children and their upbringing. (Rev: BL 1/15/94) [932]

**11877** Deem, James M. *How to Make a Mummy Talk* (4–7). Illus. 1995, Houghton $14.95 (0-395-62427-4). 192pp. All kinds of mummies are introduced, with background history of the times in which they were created. (Rev: BCCB 10/95; BL 9/15/95; SLJ 9/95) [393]

**11878** Delafosse, Claude, and Philippe Biard. *Pyramids* (PS–2). Illus. by authors. Series: First Discovery Books. 1995, Scholastic $11.95 (0-590-42786-5). Describes how the pyramids of Egypt were built, as well as mummification and the 7 wonders of the ancient world. (Rev: SLJ 3/96) [932]

**11879** Eschle, Lou. *The Curse of Tutankhamen* (4–6). Illus. Series: Exploring the Unknown. 1994, Lucent LB $22.45 (1-56006-152-9). 48pp. An account of the supposed curse surrounding the opening of Tutankhamen's tomb that also supplies information about this boy king. (Rev: SLJ 4/94) [932]

**11880** Fisher, Leonard Everett. *The Gods and Goddesses of Ancient Egypt* (3–5). Illus. 1997, Holiday LB $16.95 (0-8234-1286-5). 32pp. With accompanying stories, this book introduces 13 Egyptian deities, including Horus and Osiris. (Rev: BL 12/1/97; SLJ 11/97) [299]

**11881** Giblin, James Cross. *The Riddle of the Rosetta Stone: Key to Ancient Egypt* (5–7). Illus. 1990, HarperCollins LB $15.89 (0-690-04799-1). 96pp. Beginning with the British museum, where the Rosetta Stone is now, this is an explanation of its importance. (Rev: BCCB 11/90; BL 9/15/90*; HB 11–12/90; SLJ 9/90) [493]

**11882** Grant, Neil, ed. *The Egyptians* (4–6). Illus. Series: Spotlights. 1996, Oxford paper $9.95 (0-19-521239-8). 46pp. Double-page spreads are used to introduce such topics about ancient Egypt as its history, culture, social life, religion, and political organization. (Rev: SLJ 9/96) [932]

**11883** Harris, Nathaniel. *Everyday Life in Ancient Egypt* (3–6). Illus. by Keith Maddison. Series: Clues to the Past. 1995, Watts LB $20.00 (0-531-14309-0). 32pp. Double-page spreads cover such topics as food, clothing, housing, religion, and education. (Rev: SLJ 3/95) [962]

**11884** Harris, Nathaniel. *Mummies* (4–7). Illus. Series: A Very Peculiar History. 1995, Watts LB $23.00 (0-531-14354-6). 48pp. This account explores the process of mummification and embalming of bodies from ancient Egypt through the ages. (Rev: BL 6/1–15/95; SLJ 7/95) [393.3]

**11885** Hart, Avery, and Paul Mantell. *Pyramids! 50 Hands-on Activities to Experience Ancient Egypt* (3–5). Illus. Series: Kaleidoscope Kids. 1997, Williamson paper $9.95 (1-885593-10-4). 96pp. Some of the craft projects that explore the culture of ancient Egypt are building model pyramids, writing messages in hieroglyphics, and preparing clothes, food, and games for an Egyptian costume party. (Rev: BL 11/15/97) [932]

**11886** Hart, George, ed. *Ancient Egypt* (4–6). Illus. Series: Nature Company Discoveries. 1995, Time Llife LB $15.00 (0-7835-4763-3). 64pp. A handsomely designed book with a brief text that introduces the history and accomplishments of the people of ancient Egypt. (Rev: BL 1/1–15/96; SLJ 1/96) [932]

**11887** Katan, Norma Jean, and Barbara Mintz. *Hieroglyphics: The Writing of Ancient Egypt* (4–6). Illus. 1981, Macmillan $16.00 (0-689-50176-5). 96pp. A fine introduction that includes material on the Rosetta Stone and how to draw and decipher hieroglyphics.

**11888** Koenig, Viviane. *The Ancient Egyptians: Life in the Nile Valley* (5–8). Trans. by Mary K. LaRose. Illus. by Veronique Ageorges. Series: People of the Past. 1992, Millbrook LB $22.40 (1-56294-161-5). 64pp. The daily life of the ancient Egyptians. (Rev: SLJ 8/92) [938]

**11889** Landau, Elaine. *The Assyrians* (4–6). Series: Cradle of Civilization. 1997, Millbrook LB $21.40 (0-7613-0217-4). 64pp. This overview of the Assyrian civilization stresses its history, rulers, and lasting contributions. (Rev: BL 1/1–15/98; SLJ 3/98) [932]

**11890** Landau, Elaine. *The Babylonians* (4–6). Illus. Series: Cradle of Civilization. 1997, Millbrook LB $21.40 (0-7613-0216-6). 64pp. The history, religion, and contributions of this early civilization that invented the wheel and was the first to establish laws and government. (Rev: BL 1/1–15/98; SLJ 3/98) [935]

**11891** Landau, Elaine. *The Curse of Tutankhamen* (4–6). Illus. Series: Mysteries of Science. 1996, Millbrook LB $20.90 (0-7613-0014-7). 48pp. The story of the discovery of King Tut's tomb and of the curse that supposedly plagued the archaeologists that were involved. (Rev: BL 10/15/96; SLJ 11/96) [931]

**11892** Landau, Elaine. *The Sumerians* (4–6). Illus. Series: Cradle of Civilization. 1997, Millbrook LB $21.40 (0-7613-0215-8). 64pp. An overview of the Sumerians, their rulers and gods, and their contributions to science, government, and the arts. (Rev: BL 1/1–15/98; SLJ 3/98) [935]

**11893** Macaulay, David. *Pyramid* (5–8). Illus. by author. 1975, Houghton $18.00 (0-395-21407-6). 80pp. The engineering and architectural feats of the Egyptians are explored with detailed drawings.

**11894** McNeill, Sarah. *Ancient Egyptian People* (4–8). Illus. Series: People and Places. 1997, Millbrook LB $21.90 (0-7613-0056-2). 48pp. This basic introduction to the people of ancient Egypt and how they lived consists of several attractive double-page spreads and brief text. (Rev: BL 2/15/97) [932]

**11895** McNeill, Sarah. *Ancient Egyptian Places* (4–8). Illus. Series: People and Places. 1997, Millbrook LB $21.90 (0-7613-0057-0). 48pp. Some of the great constructions of ancient Egypt are pictured in a series of elegant double-page spreads with a simple text. (Rev: BL 2/15/97) [932]

**11896** Mann, Elizabeth. *The Great Pyramid* (4–7). Illus. Series: Wonders of the World. 1996, Mikaya $18.95 (0-9650493-1-0). 48pp. The building of this architectural marvel is told graphically, with details on the society of ancient Egypt. (Rev: BL 2/1/97; SLJ 6/97*) [932]

**11897** Marston, Elsa. *The Ancient Egyptians* (5–8). Illus. Series: Cultures of the Past. 1995, Benchmark LB $28.50 (0-7614-0073-7). 80pp. A history of ancient Egypt that tells how the people lived and gives information on the various dynasties and the Egyptian religion. (Rev: SLJ 6/96) [932]

**11898** Martell, Hazel M. *The Great Pyramid* (3–5). Illus. Series: Great Buildings. 1997, Raintree Steck-Vaughn LB $24.97 (0-8172-4918-4). 48pp. This title answers questions concerning why, when, where, and how the Great Pyramid in Egypt was built. (Rev: BL 11/15/97) [932]

**11899** Milton, Joyce. *Mummies* (2–3). Illus. by Susan Swan. 1996, Putnam paper $3.99 (0-448-41325-6). 48pp. The purpose and process of mummification are explained, with special reference to ancient Egypt. (Rev: BL 11/15/96; SLJ 6/97) [932]

**11900** Montavon, Jay. *The Curse of King Tut's Tomb* (3–5). Illus. 1991, Avon paper $3.50 (0-380-76220-X). 96pp. Tells about King Tut and the discovery of his tomb, but focuses on the supposed curse that was associated with its opening. (Rev: BL 9/15/91) [932]

**11901** Morley, Jacqueline. *An Egyptian Pyramid* (4–6). Illus. by Mark Bergin and John James. Series: Inside Story. 1991, Bedrick $18.95 (0-87226-346-0). 32pp. This work explains how pyramids were built and their purposes and parts. (Rev: BL 11/15/91; SLJ 12/91) [932]

**11902** Morley, Jacqueline. *How Would You Survive as an Ancient Egyptian?* (4–7). Illus. Series: How Would You Survive? 1995, Watts LB $23.00 (0-531-14345-7). 48pp. Everyday life in Egypt of 1500 B.C. is covered, with material on the preparation of mummies, crops harvested, and the types of food eaten. (Rev: BL 6/1–15/95; SLJ 8/95) [932]

**11903** Odijk, Pamela. *The Egyptians* (4–7). Illus. Series: Ancient World. 1989, Silver Burdett LB $14.95 (0-382-09886-2). 48pp. An introduction to the history of ancient Egypt. (Rev: BL 1/15/90; SLJ 5/90) [932]

**11904** Odijk, Pamela. *The Sumerians* (4–7). Illus. Series: Ancient World. 1990, Silver Burdett LB $14.95 (0-382-09892-7). 48pp. History and contributions of the Sumerians in the Fertile Crescent. (Rev: BL 11/1/90; SLJ 1/91) [935.01]

**11905** Payne, Elizabeth. *The Pharaohs of Ancient Egypt* (6–8). Illus. 1981, Random paper $5.99 (0-394-84699-0). 42pp. A fascinating study of this important period in Egyptian history.

**11906** Perl, Lila. *Mummies, Tombs, and Treasure: Secrets of Ancient Egypt* (5–7). Illus. 1987, Houghton $15.95 (0-89919-407-9). 128pp. An inviting look at the fascinating preservation techniques of the early Egyptians. (Rev: BCCB 6/87; BL 6/15/87; SLJ 8/87)

**11907** Polk, Milbry. *Egyptian Mummies* (3–6). Illus. by Roger Stewart. 1997, Dutton $16.99 (0-525-45839-5). A pop-up book about ancient Egypt in which coffins and pyramids serve as subjects. (Rev: BL 12/15/97; SLJ 12/97) [932]

**11908** Putnam, James. *Pyramid* (4–6). Illus. Series: Eyewitness Books. 1994, Knopf LB $20.99 (0-679-96170-4). 63pp. Using color photos, the author introduces pyramids in many countries, including Egypt, Mexico, and Nubia. (Rev: SLJ 12/94) [932]

**11909** Rees, Rosemary. *The Ancient Egyptians* (3–4). Illus. Series: Understanding People in the Past. 1997, Heinemann LB $14.95 (0-431-07789-4). 64pp. Photos of museum artifacts plus maps, diagrams, and drawings are used liberally to introduce such topics about the ancient Egyptians as their pharaohs, gods, history, pyramids, and mummies. (Rev: SLJ 9/97) [932]

**11910** Steedman, Scott. *The Egyptian News* (4–6). Illus. 1997, Candlewick $15.99 (1-56402-873-9). 32pp. Using a modern newspaper format, this book describes life in ancient Egypt and covers topics like the pyramids, mummies, and pharaohs. (Rev: BL 7/97; SLJ 9/97) [932]

**11911** Steele, Philip. *The Egyptians and the Valley of the Kings* (4–6). Illus. Series: Hidden Worlds. 1994, Dillon $13.95 (0-87518-539-8). 32pp. Some of the topics covered are mummification, hieroglyphics, the Rosetta Stone, and archaeological findings. (Rev: SLJ 12/94) [932]

**11912** Trumble, Kelly. *Cat Mummies* (3–6). Illus. 1996, Clarion $15.95 (0-395-68707-1). 50pp. An introduction to the place of cats in ancient Egypt and

to the process of mummification. (Rev: BCCB 10/96; BL 9/15/96; SLJ 8/96) [932]

**11913** Wright, Rachel. *Egyptians* (3–6). Illus. Series: Craft Topics. 1993, Watts LB $20.00 (0-531-14209-4). 32pp. Through a number of craft projects, the reader learns about the ancient Egyptians, their buildings, and how they lived. (Rev: BL 4/1/93; SLJ 8/93) [932]

## Greece

**11914** Chelepi, Chris. *Growing Up in Ancient Greece* (3–5). Illus. by Christine Molan. Series: Growing Up In. 1993, Troll LB $13.95 (0-8167-2719-8). 32pp. Everyday life in ancient Greece is described, with special attention to the treatment of children, their education, and pursuits. (Rev: BL 1/15/94) [938]

**11915** Chrisp, Peter. *The Parthenon* (3–5). Illus. Series: Great Buildings. 1997, Raintree Steck-Vaughn LB $24.97 (0-8172-4917-6). 48pp. The original architecture and appearance of the Parthenon is covered, as well as later history, when it became a Christian temple and a Muslim mosque. (Rev: BL 11/15/97) [938]

**11916** Clare, John D., ed. *Ancient Greece* (3–6). Illus. Series: Living History. 1994, Harcourt $16.95 (0-15-200516-1). 64pp. An overview of the history of ancient Greece, with emphasis on its heritage and contributions to world civilization. (Rev: BL 4/15/94; SLJ 4/94) [938]

**11917** Descamps-Lequime, Sophie, and Denise Vernerey. *The Ancient Greeks: In the Land of the Gods* (5–8). Trans. by Mary K. LaRose. Illus. by Annie-Claude Martin. Series: People of the Past. 1992, Millbrook LB $22.40 (1-56294-069-4). 64pp. A glimpse into the lives of the ancient Greeks, including the way people dressed and kept their homes. (Rev: SLJ 8/92) [932]

**11918** Edmondson, Elizabeth. *The Trojan War* (5–8). Illus. by Harry Clow. Series: Great Battles and Sieges. 1992, Macmillan LB $13.95 (0-02-733273-X). 32pp. A fine illustrated account of the causes of the Trojan War, its many battles, and the fall of Troy by Greek trickery. (Rev: BL 11/1/92; SLJ 1/93) [939.21]

**11919** Freeman, Charles, ed. *The Ancient Greeks* (4–6). Illus. Series: Spotlights. 1996, Oxford $9.95 (0-19-521238-X). 46pp. Traces the history of ancient Greece, tells about its religion and the pantheon of gods, and supplies generous quotes from original sources. (Rev: SLJ 9/96) [938]

**11920** Hutton, Warwick. *The Trojan Horse* (1–4). Illus. 1992, Macmillan paper $16.00 (0-689-50542-6). 32pp. The old story of the Trojan horse is told, this time from the viewpoint of ordinary people.

(Rev: BCCB 4/92; BL 3/1/92*; HB 5–6/92*; SLJ 4/92*) [398.2]

**11921** Little, Emily. *The Trojan Horse: How the Greeks Won the War* (2–4). Illus. by Mike Eagle. 1988, Random paper $3.99 (0-394-89674-2). 48pp. A lesson in ancient history in this account of the Trojan horse. (Rev: BCCB 1/89; BL 3/1/89; SLJ 2/89) [398.2]

**11922** Loverance, Rowena, and Tim Wood. *Ancient Greece* (4–6). Illus. Series: See Through History. 1993, Viking paper $14.99 (0-670-84754-2). 48pp. An overview in text and interesting illustrations of the life, history, and culture of the ancient Greeks. (Rev: BL 4/15/93; SLJ 8/93) [938]

**11923** MacDonald, Fiona. *A Greek Temple* (4–6). Illus. Series: Inside Story. 1992, Bedrick $18.95 (0-87226-361-4). 48pp. In pictures and text, this is the story of the jewel of the Acropolis: the Parthenon. (Rev: BL 11/1/92; SLJ 1/93) [938.3]

**11924** MacDonald, Fiona. *I Wonder Why Greeks Built Temples and Other Questions About Ancient Greece* (2–4). Illus. Series: I Wonder Why. 1997, Kingfisher $9.95 (0-7534-5056-9). 32pp. Each double-page spread in this book answers 2 or 3 basic questions about the ancient Greeks, how they lived, and their accomplishments. (Rev: SLJ 9/97) [938]

**11925** Odijk, Pamela. *The Greeks* (4–7). Illus. Series: Ancient World. 1989, Silver Burdett LB $14.95 (0-382-09884-6). 48pp. An oversize book that covers history, art, architecture, clothing, and other aspects of ancient Greece. (Rev: BL 1/15/90; SLJ 5/90) [938]

**11926** Pearson, Anne. *Ancient Greece* (4–8). Illus. 1992, Knopf LB $20.99 (0-679-91682-2). 63pp. An attractive overview consisting of 2-page spreads that cover such topics as history, religion, customs, and culture. (Rev: SLJ 12/92) [938]

**11927** Pearson, Anne. *Everyday Life in Ancient Greece* (3–6). Illus. by Ed Dovey. Series: Clues to the Past. 1995, Watts LB $20.00 (0-531-14310-4). 32pp. After a brief history of ancient Greece, introduces such topics as food, education, religion, housing, clothing, and agriculture. (Rev: SLJ 3/95) [938]

**11928** Rees, Rosemary. *The Ancient Greeks* (3–4). Illus. Series: Understanding People in the Past. 1997, Heinemann LB $14.95 (0-431-07790-8). 64pp. Photos of museum artifacts plus maps, diagrams, and drawings are used liberally to introduce such topics about the ancient Greeks as their history, accomplishments, buildings, Olympic games, theater, family life, and trade. (Rev: SLJ 9/97) [938]

**11929** Simpson, Judith. *Ancient Greece* (4–7). Illus. Series: Nature Company Discoveries. 1997, Time Life $16.00 (0-7835-4801-X). 64pp. Various aspects of the history and culture of Ancient Greece are cov-

ered in this account that begins with the Minoan civilization and ends with the fall of Greece to Rome. (Rev: SLJ 12/97) [938]

**11930** Tyler, Deborah. *The Greeks and Troy* (4–7). Illus. Series: Hidden Worlds. 1993, Dillon $13.95 (0-87518-537-1). 32pp. The story of the Trojan War is retold, along with a tour of the ruins of Troy and a recreation of what it once was. (Rev: BL 12/1/93) [938]

**11931** Woodford, Susan. *The Parthenon* (6–8). Illus. 1981, Cambridge Univ. Pr. paper $11.95 (0-521-22629-5). 48pp. The history and structure of the Parthenon and a description of the religion of ancient Greece.

**11932** Wright, Rachel. *Greeks* (3–6). Illus. Series: Craft Topics. 1993, Watts LB $20.00 (0-531-14246-9). 32pp. Presents the everyday life of the ancient Greeks; their dress and their buildings come alive through an interesting text and several craft projects. (Rev: BL 4/1/93; SLJ 8/93) [938]

## Rome

**11933** Andrews, Ian. *Pompeii* (4–6). Illus. 1978, Cambridge Univ. Pr. paper $11.95 (0-521-20973-0). 48pp. A description of the city of Pompeii and of its destruction.

**11934** Baxter, Nicola. *Romans* (3–6). Illus. 1992, Watts LB $20.00 (0-531-14143-8). 32pp. In this overview of the Roman Empire, such craft projects as creating a mosaic and building a Roman villa are presented. (Rev: BL 11/1/92; SLJ 12/92) [937]

**11935** Burrell, Roy. *The Romans* (5–7). Illus. by Peter Connolly. 1998, Oxford paper $14.95 (0-199-17102-5). 112pp. A brief overview of Rome's history from its legendary beginnings to the Barbarian invasions. (Rev: SLJ 1/92) [937]

**11936** Chrisp, Peter. *The Colosseum* (3–5). Illus. Series: Great Buildings. 1997, Raintree Steck-Vaughn LB $24.97 (0-8172-4916-8). 48pp. The history of the Colosseum, its construction, and its uses through the centuries is detailed in this nicely illustrated title. (Rev: BL 11/15/97) [937]

**11937** Chrisp, Peter. *The Roman Empire* (3–6). Illus. Series: Make It Work. 1996, World Book $13.95 (0-7166-1727-7); paper $7.95 (0-7166-1728-5). 48pp. Activities and projects are used to convey information about the Roman Empire and how people lived during these ancient times. (Rev: BL 11/15/96) [276]

**11938** Clare, John D., ed. *Classical Rome* (3–6). Illus. Series: Living History. 1993, Harcourt $16.95 (0-15-200513-7). 64pp. With informative text and photos showing people in period costume, this is a good introduction to ancient Rome. (Rev: BL 2/15/93) [937.06]

**11939** Corbishley, Mike. *Everyday Life in Roman Times* (3–5). Illus. Series: Clues to the Past. 1994, Watts LB $20.00 (0-531-14288-4). 32pp. Some of the topics covered about life in ancient Rome include food, clothing, homes, dress, markets, and schools. (Rev: BL 3/15/95) [937]

**11940** Corbishley, Mike. *Growing Up in Ancient Rome* (3–5). Illus. by Christine Molan. Series: Growing Up In. 1993, Troll paper $4.95 (0-8167-2722-8). 32pp. The social life and customs of ancient Rome are covered, with a particular focus on the life-style of children. (Rev: BL 1/15/94) [937]

**11941** Ganeri, Anita. *How Would You Survive as an Ancient Roman?* (4–7). Illus. Series: How Would You Survive? 1995, Watts LB $24.00 (0-531-14349-X). 48pp. Typical entertainment, education, and religious beliefs in ancient Rome are covered, with sidebars on the proper way to appear before a court of law or how to become a Vestal Virgin. (Rev: BL 6/1–15/95; SLJ 8/95) [937]

**11942** Harris, Jacqueline L. *Science in Ancient Rome* (5–7). Illus. 1998, Watts $24.00 (0-531-20354-9); paper $8.95 (0-531-15916-7). 96pp. A description of Roman achievements in applied science. (Rev: BL 12/15/88)

**11943** Haywood, John, ed. *The Romans* (4–6). Illus. Series: Spotlights. 1996, Oxford paper $9.95 (0-19-521240-1). 46pp. This attractive introduction to the history and political organization of ancient Rome also includes material on its cultural and social life. (Rev: SLJ 9/96) [937]

**11944** Humphrey, Kathryn L. *Pompeii: Nightmare at Midday* (4–6). Illus. 1995, Houghton $9.28 (0-395-73265-4). 64pp. The destruction caused by the eruption of Mount Vesuvius in A.D. 79. (Rev: BL 4/15/90) [937]

**11945** James, Louise. *The Romans* (3–6). Illus. Series: How We Know About. 1997, Bedrick LB $17.95 (0-87226-534-X). 32pp. Using both contemporary photos and many reconstructions, this book describes how people lived in ancient Rome, along with material on how archaeologists have determined these facts. (Rev: BL 12/15/97; SLJ 10/97) [937.6]

**11946** Langley, Andrew, and Philip De Souza. *The Roman News* (4–7). Illus. 1996, Candlewick $15.99 (0-7636-0055-5). 32pp. Using the format of a tabloid newspaper, this book highlights the history of ancient Rome. (Rev: BL 10/1/96; SLJ 1/97) [937]

**11947** Macaulay, David. *City: A Story of Roman Planning and Construction* (6–8). Illus. by author. 1983, Houghton $18.00 (0-395-19492-X); paper $7.95 (0-395-34922-2). 112pp. The imaginary Roman city of Verbonia is constructed through accurate and finely detailed drawings.

**11948** MacDonald, Fiona. *I Wonder Why Romans Wore Togas and Other Questions About Ancient Rome* (2–4). Illus. Series: I Wonder Why. 1997, Kingfisher $9.95 (0-7534-5057-7). 32pp. Each double-page spread in this book answers 2 or 3 basic questions about the ancient Romans, how they lived, their empire, and their accomplishments. (Rev: SLJ 9/97) [937]

**11949** MacDonald, Fiona. *The Roman Colosseum* (4–6). Illus. Series: Inside Story. 1997, Bedrick LB $18.95 (0-87226-275-8). 48pp. In a series of double-page spreads, the world of ancient Rome is introduced, focusing on the structure and functions of the Colosseum. (Rev: BL 2/15/97) [937]

**11950** Morley, Jacqueline. *A Roman Villa* (4–6). Illus. by John James. Series: Inside Story. 1992, Bedrick LB $18.95 (0-87226-360-6). 48pp. Through many double-page spreads and cutaway drawings, the interiors and exteriors of Roman villas are explored. (Rev: BL 12/15/92; SLJ 1/93) [937]

**11951** Nardo, Don. *The Age of Augustus* (5–8). Series: World History. 1996, Lucent LB $22.45 (1-56006-306-8). 112pp. The rise of Augustus Caesar is chronicled with material on his political and military career and his effects on the Roman Empire. (Rev: SLJ 2/97) [937]

**11952** Ochoa, George. *The Assassination of Julius Caesar* (5–8). Series: Turning Points in World History. 1991, Silver Burdett LB $14.95 (0-382-24130-4). 64pp. The events that led to the assassination of Julius Caesar in Rome. (Rev: BL 3/15/92) [937]

**11953** Odijk, Pamela. *The Romans* (4–7). Illus. Series: Ancient World. 1989, Silver Burdett LB $14.95 (0-382-09885-4). 48pp. An oversize book about the ancient Romans and their way of life. (Rev: BL 1/15/90; SLJ 5/90) [937]

**11954** Ridd, Stephen, ed. *Julius Caesar in Gaul and Britain* (5–8). Illus. Series: History Eyewitness. 1995, Raintree Steck-Vaughn LB $24.26 (0-8114-8283-9). 48pp. An edited version of Caesar's fascinating accounts of the Gallic Wars, with pictures and maps. (Rev: BL 4/15/95; SLJ 5/95) [937]

**11955** Roberts, Paul C., ed. *Ancient Rome* (4–6). Series: Nature Company Discoveries. 1997, Time Life $16.00 (0-7835-4909-1). 64pp. Using a series of double-page spreads, the culture and history of ancient Rome are covered, with outstanding illustrations. (Rev: BL 9/15/97; SLJ 12/97) [937]

**11956** Steele, Philip. *Food and Feasts in Ancient Rome* (4–8). Illus. Series: Food and Feasts. 1994, New Discovery LB $14.95 (0-02-726321-5). 32pp. A description of food and food preparation in ancient Rome and how it differed among the classes, as well as a selection of tasty recipes. (Rev: BCCB 10/94; SLJ 12/94) [937]

**11957** Tanaka, Shelley. *The Buried City of Pompeii* (4–7). Illus. Series: I Was There. 1997, Hyperion $16.95 (0-7868-0285-5). 48pp. The facts concerning the destruction of the city of Pompeii are told through the fictionalized account of one of its victims. (Rev: BL 12/1/97; SLJ 3/98)

**11958** Watkins, Richard. *Gladiator* (4–7). Illus. 1997, Houghton $17.00 (0-395-82656-X). 64pp. This attractive book surveys the gladiators of ancient Rome, their training, their performances, and their fights. (Rev: BL 11/1/97*; SLJ 10/97*) [796.8]

**11959** Whittock, Martyn. *The Roman Empire* (4–6). Illus. Series: Biographical History. 1996, Bedrick $17.95 (0-87226-118-2). 64pp. A history of the Roman Empire, its expansion, and life in the Republic are given, with many short biographies and excerpts from both primary and secondary sources. (Rev: SLJ 9/96) [937]

# Middle Ages

**11960** Aliki. *A Medieval Feast* (2–6). Illus. by author. 1983, HarperCollins LB $14.89 (0-690-04246-9); paper $6.95 (0-06-446050-9). 32pp. A visit from the king provides the occasion for a well-described feast.

**11961** *Castles* (PS–3). Illus. Series: First Discovery Book. 1993, Scholastic $11.95 (0-590-46377-2). 30pp. A highly visual introduction to castles that supplies basic information with an interactive approach. (Rev: BL 10/1/93; SLJ 8/93) [940.1]

**11962** Child, John, et al. *The Crusades* (4–6). Illus. Series: Biographical History. 1996, Bedrick $17.95 (0-87226-119-0). 64pp. Describes the nature and the causes of the various Crusades and covers important events, battles, and people. (Rev: SLJ 9/96) [940.1]

**11963** Clare, John D. *Fourteenth-Century Towns* (3–6). Illus. Series: Living History. 1993, Harcourt $16.95 (0-15-200515-3). 64pp. Life in a medieval town is portrayed with double-page spreads and informative text. (Rev: BL 2/15/923) [307]

**11964** Clare, John D., ed. *Knights in Armor* (3–6). Illus. 1992, Harcourt $17.00 (0-15-200508-0). 64pp. Photos of people in period costume help bring to life this historical era. (Rev: BL 12/1/92; SLJ 11/92) [940]

**11965** Clements, Gillian. *The Truth About Castles* (2–5). Illus. 1990, Carolrhoda LB $14.95 (0-87614-401-6). 40pp. Humorous cartoon-style drawings and text show castles and their structure. (Rev: SLJ 10/90) [725]

**11966** Corbishley, Mike. *The Medieval World* (5–7). Illus. Series: Timelink. 1993, Bedrick LB $18.95 (0-

87226-362-2). 64pp. Using a chronological approach, this book covers the years 450 through 1500 in Europe, Asia, Africa, and the Americas. (Rev: SLJ 8/93) [940.1]

**11967** Corzine, Phyllis. *The Black Death* (5–8). Series: World History. 1996, Lucent LB $22.45 (1-56006-299-1). 112pp. Traces the spread of the bubonic plague from Asia and its effects in Europe, including the breakdown of feudalism. (Rev: SLJ 2/97) [940.1]

**11968** Dawson, Imogen. *Food and Feasts in the Middle Ages* (4–8). Series: Food and Feasts. 1994, New Discovery LB $14.95 (0-02-726324-X). 32pp. This account re-creates the culinary aspects of the Middle Ages, with material on farming, dishes, and town and city fare plus several recipes and many attractive illustrations. (Rev: BCCB 10/94; SLJ 12/94) [940.1]

**11969** Gibbons, Gail. *Knights in Shining Armor* (PS–3). Illus. 1995, Little, Brown $14.95 (0-316-30948-6). 32pp. A picture book about knights, tournaments, chivalry, and armor, with brief introductions to such famous knights as St. George. (Rev: BL 11/1/95; SLJ 10/95) [394]

**11970** Gravett, Christopher. *Castle* (4–8). Illus. Series: Eyewitness Books. 1994, Knopf LB $20.99 (0-679-96000-7). 64pp. The structure of a medieval castle is described, with a discussion of life in the Middle Ages. (Rev: BL 10/15/94; SLJ 9/94) [623.1]

**11971** Gravett, Christopher. *Knight* (4–8). Illus. Series: Eyewitness Books. 1993, Knopf LB $20.99 (0-679-93882-6). 63pp. Spanning a period from the 9th through the 17th centuries, this book traces the history of knighthood. (Rev: SLJ 8/93) [940.1]

**11972** Gravett, Christopher. *The World of the Medieval Knight* (4–6). Illus. 1997, Bedrick LB $19.95 (0-87226-277-4). 64pp. Various aspects of knighthood — from armor and jousting to castle life and the Crusades — are presented. (Rev: BL 1/1–15/97; SLJ 3/97) [940.1]

**11973** Howarth, Sarah. *Medieval People* (4–6). Illus. 1992, Millbrook LB $21.90 (1-56294-153-4). 48pp. Arranged by topic, this material covers the period from the 5th to the 15th century. (Rev: BL 3/1/92; SLJ 3/92) [909.07]

**11974** Howarth, Sarah. *Medieval Places* (4–6). Illus. 1992, Millbrook LB $21.90 (1-56294-152-6). 48pp. A look at the castle, guild hall, and university, among other places, from the 5th to the 15th century. (Rev: BL 3/1/92; SLJ 3/92) [909.07]

**11975** Howarth, Sarah. *The Middle Ages* (4–8). Illus. Series: See Through History. 1993, Viking paper $14.99 (0-670-85098-5). 48pp. In a series of thickly illustrated double-page spreads, various topics related to the Middle Ages are presented, e.g., social structure, food, clothing, and dwellings. (Rev: BL 12/15/93; SLJ 2/94) [940.1]

**11976** Howarth, Sarah. *What Do We Know About the Middle Ages?* (4–7). Illus. Series: What Do We Know About . . .? 1996, Bedrick LB $18.95 (0-87226-384-3). 40pp. The way people lived in the Middle Ages in Western Europe is described in a series of double-page spreads. (Rev: BL 6/1–15/96) [940.1]

**11977** Howe, John. *Knights* (3–6). Illus. 1995, Orchard $18.95 (0-531-09456-1). 16pp. Aspects of the Middle Ages — like castles, armor, and the Crusades — come alive in this pop-up book. (Rev: BL 2/1/96) [940]

**11978** Langley, Andrew. *Medieval Life* (4–8). Illus. Series: Eyewitness Books. 1996, Knopf LB $20.99 (0-679-98077-6). 63pp. This book takes one behind the scenes of life in a castle during the Middle Ages, explaining and illustrating its parts and how people lived within its walls. (Rev: BL 6/1–15/96; SLJ 7/96) [940.1]

**11979** Macaulay, David. *Castle* (5–8). Illus. by author. 1977, Houghton $18.00 (0-395-25784-0); paper $7.95 (0-395-32920-5). 80pp. Another of the author's brilliant, detailed works, this one on the planning and building of a Welsh castle.

**11980** MacDonald, Fiona. *A Medieval Castle* (4–6). Illus. by Mark Bergin. Series: Inside Story. 1990, Bedrick LB $18.95 (0-87226-340-1). 48pp. An oversize volume that surveys the development of castles and highlights life in the Middle Ages. (Rev: BL 3/1/91; SLJ 6/91) [940.1]

**11981** MacDonald, Fiona. *Medieval Cathedral* (3–6). Illus. by John James. Series: Inside Story. 1991, Bedrick $18.95 (0-87226-350-9). 48pp. This book explains in many pictures how cathedrals were built in the Middle Ages, their various parts and the roles they played in medieval civilization. (Rev: BL 12/1/91; SLJ 12/91) [726.6]

**11982** MacDonald, Fiona. *The Middle Ages* (4–6). Illus. 1993, Facts on File $19.95 (0-8160-2788-9). 80pp. Two-page spreads feature topics of the Middle Ages — feudalism, food and family, houses, family life, and so on. (Rev: BL 8/85; SLJ 9/85)

**11983** Maynard, Christopher. *Incredible Castles and Knights* (1–3). Illus. 1994, DK Publg. paper $4.95 (1-56458-730-4). 32pp. An attractive pictorial introduction to the parts of a castle and their knightly inhabitants. (Rev: BL 1/15/95) [929.72]

**11984** Morgan, Gwyneth. *Life in a Medieval Village* (5–7). Illus. by author. 1991, HarperCollins paper $13.50 (0-06-092046-7). A story of activities in a medieval village and of the effects of the church on life in the Middle Ages.

**11985** Nicolle, David. *Medieval Knights* (4–8). Series: See Through History. 1997, Viking paper $17.99 (0-670-87463-9). 48pp. An introduction to knights, their functions, weapons, quests, and accomplishments. (Rev: BL 10/15/97; SLJ 1/98) [940]

**11986** Nikola-Lisa, W. *Till Year's Good End: A Calendar of Medieval Labors* (1–4). Illus. by Christopher Manson. 1997, Simon & Schuster $16.00 (0-689-80020-7). 32pp. This book provides a fresh look at the Middle Ages by observing the chores performed in a year by the peasant class. (Rev: BL 10/15/97; SLJ 12/97) [942.02]

**11987** Osband, Gillian. *Castles* (4–6). Illus. by Robert Andrew. 1991, Orchard $18.95 (0-531-05949-9). 16pp. Impressive and informative pop-ups add to the appeal of this book. (Rev: BL 9/15/91) [728.8]

**11988** Pernoud, Regine. *A Day with a Noble-woman* (4–6). Trans. by Dominique Clift. Illus. Series: A Day With. 1997, Runestone LB $22.60 (0-8225-1916-X). 48pp. Using as a focus the life of Blanche of Champagne, a French noblewoman of the Middle Ages, this book traces a typical day in her life. (Rev: BL 1/1–15/98; SLJ 2/98) [944]

**11989** Pernoud, Regine. *A Day with a Stonecutter* (3–6). Illus. 1997, Runestone LB $22.60 (0-8225-1913-5). 48pp. Includes both an introduction to medieval society and a case study of a stonecutter who is working on a project for an abbey. (Rev: BL 11/1/97; SLJ 1/98) [731.4]

**11990** Pipe, Jim. *Medieval Castle* (4–6). Illus. Series: Mystery History. 1996, Millbrook LB $23.90 (0-7613-0495-9). 31pp. Games, brainteasers, and jokes are combined with good factual material to make an entertaining introduction to the parts of a castle and its surrounding land. (Rev: SLJ 7/97) [940.1]

**11991** Platt, Richard. *Castles* (4–7). Illus. by Stephen Biesty. Series: Cross-Sections. 1994, DK Publg. $16.95 (1-56458-467-4). 32pp. Detailed drawings depict the parts of a 14th-century castle and supply details on the everyday life of its inhabitants, from knights to the lowliest worker. (Rev: BL 11/1/94; SLJ 10/94) [940.1]

**11992** Ross, Stewart. *Knights* (5–7). Illus. Series: Fact or Fiction. 1996, Millbrook LB $24.90 (0-7613-0453-3). 48pp. In double-page spreads with many illustrations, facts are separated from fiction about knights from King Arthur's time to soldiers of the U.S. Cavalry. (Rev: BL 3/15/96; SLJ 6/96) [940.1]

**11993** Sabbagh, Antoine. *Europe in the Middle Ages* (5–8). Trans. by Anthea Ridett. Illus. 1988, Silver Burdett $17.98 (0-382-09484-0). 77pp. Details the harshness of medieval society. (Rev: BL 2/15/89; SLJ 2/89)

**11994**  Sabuda, Robert. *The Knight's Castle* (PS–K). Illus. 1994, Golden Bks. $8.95 (0-307-17626-6). 12pp. This pop-up book for preschoolers takes the reader inside a castle. Also use *The Mummy's Tomb* (1994). (Rev: BL 11/15/94) [728.8]

**11995**  Scarry, Huck. *Looking into the Middle Ages* (3–6). Illus. 1985, HarperCollins $12.50 (0-06-025224-3). 12pp. This 12-page pop-up book literally allows readers to look into the Middle Ages — into castles, cathedrals, jousting tournaments. (Rev: BCCB 6/85; BL 9/15/85)

**11996**  Smith, Beth. *Castles* (5–7). Illus. 1988, Watts LB $10.40 (0-531-10511-3). 72pp. Castle history and construction are explained as well as details on how they changed throughout history. (Rev: BCCB 6/88; BL 5/1/88; SLJ 11/88)

**11997**  Steele, Philip. *Castles* (5–7). Illus. 1995, Kingfisher $15.95 (1-85697-547-9). 64pp. In this oversized, well-designed book, castles, jousting, armor, and feast days are described. (Rev: BL 8/95; SLJ 4/95) [940.1]

**11998**  Steffens, Bradley. *The Children's Crusade* (4–7). Series: World Disasters. 1991, Lucent LB $19.95 (1-56006-019-0). 64pp. This slim volume traces the causes and tragic consequences of the Children's Crusade. (Rev: SLJ 5/92) [940]

**11999**  Williams, Brian. *Forts and Castles* (4–8). Illus. Series: See Through History. 1995, Viking paper $16.99 (0-670-85898-6). 48pp. A lavishly illustrated account of the structure and parts of such structures as forts and castles. (Rev: BL 10/15/95) [728.81]

**12000**  Wright, Rachel. *Knights* (3–6). Illus. Series: Craft Topics. 1992, Watts LB $20.00 (0-531-14163-2). 32pp. Children can make stained-glass windows and build a castle with easy-to-find materials such as cardboard. (Rev: BL 10/15/92) [745.5]

**12001**  Yue, Charlotte, and David Yue. *Armor* (4–7). Illus. 1994, Houghton $14.95 (0-395-68101-4). 90pp. Describes the origin, use, and types of armor in the Middle Ages in Europe as well as in other cultures. (Rev: BL 11/15/94; SLJ 12/94) [355.8]

## Renaissance

**12002**  Fradon, Dana. *The King's Fool: A Book About Medieval and Renaissance Fools* (4–7). Illus. 1993, Dutton paper $14.99 (0-525-45074-2). 40pp. Using the biographies of real people as examples, this book re-creates the life of Renaissance court jesters. (Rev: BCCB 1/94; BL 11/15/93; SLJ 11/93) [792.7]

**12003**  Halliwell, Sarah, ed. *The Renaissance: Artists and Writers* (5–8). Series: Who and When? 1997, Raintree Steck-Vaughn LB $27.83 (0-8172-4725-4). 96pp. This introduction to 13 artists and 3 writers of the Renaissance relies heavily of Giorgi Vasari and his eyewitness book about Renaissance art. (Rev: SLJ 1/98) [940.2]

**12004**  Morley, Jacqueline. *A Renaissance Town* (4–6). Illus. Series: Inside Story. 1997, Bedrick LB $18.95 (0-87226-276-6). 48pp. This richly illustrated book focuses on Florence during the Renaissance, with material on government, social life, customs, art, and the economy. (Rev: BL 2/15/97) [945]

**12005**  Wood, Tim. *The Renaissance* (4–8). Illus. Series: See Through History. 1993, Viking paper $17.99 (0-670-85149-3). 48pp. Various topics related to the Renaissance — like city states, trade with the East, and the position of women — are covered in a series of double-page spreads. (Rev: BL 12/15/93; SLJ 2/94) [940.2]

## World War I

**12006**  Clare, John D., ed. *First World War* (5–8). Illus. Series: Living History. 1995, Gulliver $16.95 (0-15-200087-9). 64pp. Excellent visuals and a vivid text are used in this history of World War I. (Rev: SLJ 6/95) [940.53]

**12007**  Cooper, Michael L. *Hell Fighters: African American Soldiers in World War I* (5–8). Illus. 1997, Dutton paper $16.99 (0-525-67534-5). 96pp. The story of the heroic African American World War I infantry regiment that became known as "Hell Fighters." (Rev: BCCB 2/97; BL 2/15/97; SLJ 2/97*) [940.4]

**12008**  Dolan, Edward F. *America in World War I* (5–8). Illus. 1996, Millbrook LB $27.40 (1-56294-522-X). 96pp. A large-format book that introduces background material on World War I and specific information on the role the United States played in it. (Rev: BL 6/1–15/96; SLJ 5/96) [940.3]

**12009**  Gay, Kathlyn, and Martin Gay. *World War I* (5–8). Illus. Series: Voices from the Past. 1995, Twenty-First Century LB $18.90 (0-8050-2848-X). 64pp. The causes, major battles, and effects of World War I are covered, with many excerpts from personal accounts. (Rev: BL 12/15/95; SLJ 2/96) [940.3]

**12010**  McGowen, Tom. *World War I* (5–7). Illus. 1993, Watts LB $21.00 (0-531-20149-X). 64pp. A fact-filled introduction to World War I with many photographs and maps. (Rev: BL 6/1–15/93) [940.3]

# World War II

**12011** Abells, Chana Byers. *The Children We Remember* (2–5). Illus. 1986, Greenwillow LB $15.93 (0-688-06372-1). 48pp. A compelling photographic remembrance of the horror of the Holocaust, intended for a young audience. (Rev: BCCB 10/86; BL 10/1/86; HB 11–12/86)

**12012** Adler, David A. *Child of the Warsaw Ghetto* (3–6). Illus. by Karen Ritz. 1995, Holiday LB $15.95 (0-8234-1160-5). 32pp. The story of the Warsaw Ghetto during World War II as seen through the eyes of a survivor. (Rev: BCCB 5/95; BL 4/1/95; SLJ 7/95) [943.8]

**12013** Adler, David A. *Hiding from the Nazis* (3–5). Illus. by Karen Ritz. 1997, Holiday LB $15.95 (0-8234-1288-1). 32pp. This picture book for older children tells how Lore, a young Jewish girl, is hidden and cared for by a Dutch family during World War II. (Rev: BL 11/1/97; SLJ 2/98) [940.53]

**12014** Adler, David A. *Hilde and Eli: Children of the Holocaust* (3–5). Illus. by Karen Ritz. 1994, Holiday $15.95 (0-8234-1091-9). 32pp. A picture book that tells the true stories of 2 Jewish children who were killed in the Holocaust. (Rev: BCCB 11/94; BL 9/15/94; SLJ 12/94) [940.54]

**12015** Adler, David A. *We Remember the Holocaust* (4–7). 1995, Holt paper $10.95 (0-8050-3715-2). 147pp. Through interview excerpts, the terrible days of the Holocaust are remembered. (Rev: SLJ 12/89) [940.54]

**12016** Auerbacher, Inge. *I Am a Star: Child of the Holocaust* (5–7). Illus. 1993, Puffin paper $5.99 (0-14-036401-3). 80pp. The memoirs of a former child survivor of the Terezin concentration camp in Czechoslovakia. (Rev: BCCB 7–8/87; BL 6/1/87; SLJ 4/87)

**12017** Besson, Jean-Louis. *October 45: Childhood Memories of the War* (4–6). Illus. 1995, Harcourt $22.00 (0-15-200955-8). 96pp. A memoir of a childhood spent in German-occupied France, chiefly Paris, during World War II. (Rev: BCCB 2/96; BL 12/15/95*; SLJ 1/96) [940.54]

**12018** Black, Wallace B., and Jean F. Blashfield. *America Prepares for War* (5–7). Illus. Series: World War II 50th Anniversary. 1991, Macmillan LB $12.95 (0-89686-554-1). 48pp. The U.S. entry into World War II, with numerous photos. (Rev: BL 6/15/91; SLJ 9/91) [940.53]

**12019** Black, Wallace B., and Jean F. Blashfield. *Bataan and Corregidor* (5–7). Illus. Series: World War II 50th Anniversary. 1991, Macmillan LB $12.95 (0-89686-557-6). 48pp. Using documentary photos, this book examines the major events in the

struggle over the Philippines in World War II. (Rev: BL 12/1/91; SLJ 2/92) [940.54]

**12020** Black, Wallace B., and Jean F. Blashfield. *Battle of Britain* (5–7). Illus. Series: World War II 50th Anniversary. 1991, Macmillan LB $12.95 (0-89686-553-3). 48pp. The story of Britain's valiant stand against the German power. Also use: *Blitzkrieg* (1991). (Rev: BL 6/15/91; SLJ 9/91) [940.53]

**12021** Black, Wallace B., and Jean F. Blashfield. *Battle of the Atlantic* (5–7). Illus. Series: World War II 50th Anniversary. 1991, Macmillan LB $12.95 (0-89686-558-4). 48pp. The war in the Atlantic Ocean during World War II, when the Allies tried to keep the seas open for the movement of troops and supplies, is retold in text and pictures. (Rev: BL 12/1/91; SLJ 2/92) [940.54]

**12022** Black, Wallace B., and Jean F. Blashfield. *Battle of the Bulge* (5–7). Illus. Series: World War II 50th Anniversary. 1993, Macmillan LB $12.95 (0-89686-568-1). 48pp. This account describes Hitler's desperate offensive and his gamble to split the Allied army in 2. (Rev: BL 4/15/93) [940.54]

**12023** Black, Wallace B., and Jean F. Blashfield. *Bombing Fortress Europe* (5–7). Illus. Series: World War II 50th Anniversary. 1992, Macmillan LB $12.95 (0-89686-562-2). 48pp. The thrilling, heroic exploits of British and American airmen and their war over the skies of Europe are retold in this illustrated account. (Rev: BL 8/92; SLJ 1/93) [940.54]

**12024** Black, Wallace B., and Jean F. Blashfield. *D-Day* (5–7). Illus. Series: World War II 50th Anniversary. 1992, Macmillan LB $12.95 (0-89686-566-5). 48pp. The fateful day when the Allied forces invaded France during World War II. (Rev: BL 2/1/93; SLJ 4/93) [940.54]

**12025** Black, Wallace B., and Jean F. Blashfield. *Desert Warfare* (5–7). Illus. Series: World War II 50th Anniversary. 1992, Macmillan LB $12.95 (0-89686-561-4). 48pp. This account chronicles the Allied campaigns in North Africa against the desert forces of the Germans and Italians. (Rev: BL 8/92; SLJ 1/93) [940.54]

**12026** Black, Wallace B., and Jean F. Blashfield. *Flattops at War* (5–7). Illus. Series: World War II 50th Anniversary. 1991, Macmillan LB $12.95 (0-89686-559-2). 48pp. The use of aircraft carriers in the Pacific area of combat is described in this account. (Rev: BL 12/1/91) [940.54]

**12027** Black, Wallace B., and Jean F. Blashfield. *Guadalcanal* (5–7). Illus. Series: World War II 50th Anniversary. 1992, Macmillan LB $12.95 (0-89686-560-6). 48pp. The war in the South Pacific, as revealed in the battle of Guadalcanal during 1942-1943, is retold in text and pictures. (Rev: BL 8/92; SLJ 1/93) [940.54]

**12028**  Black, Wallace B., and Jean F. Blashfield. *Hiroshima and the Atomic Bomb* (5–7). Illus. Series: World War II 50th Anniversary. 1993, Macmillan LB $12.95 (0-89686-571-1). 48pp. This is a chronicle of President Truman's decision to drop the atomic bomb on Hiroshima and Nagasaki and the results of that decision. (Rev: BL 4/15/93; SLJ 10/93) [940.54]

**12029**  Black, Wallace B., and Jean F. Blashfield. *Invasion of Italy* (5–7). Illus. Series: World War II 50th Anniversary. 1992, Macmillan LB $12.95 (0-89686-565-7). 48pp. This book describes the campaign by the Allied forces to liberate Italy from the Axis. (Rev: BL 2/1/93; SLJ 4/93) [940.54]

**12030**  Black, Wallace B., and Jean F. Blashfield. *Island Hopping in the Pacific* (5–7). Illus. Series: World War II 50th Anniversary. 1992, Macmillan LB $12.95 (0-89686-567-3). 48pp. The campaign to retake Pacific islands from the Japanese is described in brief text and many photos. (Rev: BL 2/1/93; SLJ 4/93) [940.54]

**12031**  Black, Wallace B., and Jean F. Blashfield. *Iwo Jima and Okinawa* (5–7). Illus. Series: World War II 50th Anniversary. 1993, Macmillan LB $12.95 (0-89686-569-X). 48pp. The story of the savage battles that the Allies faced while taking these 2 islands from the Japanese during World War II. (Rev: BL 4/15/93; SLJ 10/93) [940.54]

**12032**  Black, Wallace B., and Jean F. Blashfield. *Jungle Warfare* (5–7). Illus. Series: World War II 50th Anniversary. 1992, Macmillan LB $12.95 (0-89686-563-0). 48pp. This generously illustrated account recreates the World War II campaigns waged in the jungle of southeastern Asia. (Rev: BL 8/92; SLJ 1/93) [940.54]

**12033**  Black, Wallace B., and Jean F. Blashfield. *Pearl Harbor!* (5–7). Illus. Series: World War II 50th Anniversary. 1991, Macmillan LB $4.95 (0-89686-555-X). 48pp. The Japanese surprise attack that shocked the United States into World War II. (Rev: BL 6/15/91; SLJ 9/91) [940.53]

**12034**  Black, Wallace B., and Jean F. Blashfield. *Russia at War* (5–7). Illus. Series: World War II 50th Anniversary. 1991, Macmillan LB $12.95 (0-89686-556-8). 48pp. Describes the role played by Russia in World War II and how they stopped the Germans in spite of terrible losses, with many documentary photographs. (Rev: BL 12/1/91; SLJ 2/92) [940.54]

**12035**  Black, Wallace B., and Jean F. Blashfield. *Victory in Europe* (5–7). Illus. Series: World War II 50th Anniversary. 1993, Macmillan LB $12.95 (0-89686-570-3). 48pp. This account outlines the events that led to the Allied victory in Europe including the Russian advance and the fall of Berlin. (Rev: BL 4/15/93) [940.54]

**12036**  Black, Wallace B., and Jean F. Blashfield. *War Behind the Lines* (5–7). Illus. Series: World War II 50th Anniversary. 1992, Macmillan LB $12.95 (0-89686-564-9). 48pp. This book tells about the many gallant underground movements that tried to undermine the Fascist powers from within. (Rev: BL 2/1/93; SLJ 4/93) [940.54]

**12037**  Bliven, Bruce. *The Story of D-Day* (5–8). 1963, Random LB $8.99 (0-394-90362-5). The story of June 6, 1944, and its effect on the outcome of World War II.

**12038**  Chaikin, Miriam. *A Nightmare in History: The Holocaust 1933–1945* (4–6). Illus. 1992, Houghton paper $10.00 (0-395-61580-1). 128pp. From the history of Judaism, the author traces the horror of the Holocaust. (Rev: BL 12/15/87)

**12039**  Coerr, Eleanor. *Sadako* (1–5). Illus. by Ed Young. 1993, Putnam $17.95 (0-399-21771-1). 40pp. A picture book version of the story of a young Japanese girl dying of leukemia as a result of the bombing of Hiroshima. (Rev: BCCB 12/93; BL 11/1/93*; SLJ 12/93*) [362.1]

**12040**  Cross, Robin. *Children and War* (4–7). Illus. Series: World War II. 1994, Thomson Learning LB $24.26 (1-56847-180-7). 48pp. True case histories of children in various circumstances during World War II, including in a gulag, the resistance movement, and a death camp. (Rev: BL 12/15/94; SLJ 2/95) [940.53]

**12041**  Daily, Robert. *The Code Talkers: American Indians in World War II* (4–8). Illus. Series: First Books on World War II. 1995, Watts LB $22.00 (0-531-20190-2). 63pp. Describes the roles that Native Americans played in World War II, both as soldiers and as translators. (Rev: SLJ 10/95) [940.54]

**12042**  Davis, Gary. *Submarine Wahoo* (3–5). Illus. Series: Those Daring Machines. 1995, Macmillan paper $5.95 (0-382-24753-1). 48pp. A brief account of the exploits of the World War II submarine that distinguished itself in the Pacific campaign. (Rev: BL 2/15/95) [940.54]

**12043**  Devaney, John. *America Goes to War: 1941* (5–8). Illus. 1991, Walker LB $17.85 (0-8027-6980-2). 192pp. Almost daily notations cover events of the times in 1941. (Rev: BL 10/1/91) [940.53]

**12044**  Dolan, Edward F. *America in World War II: 1943* (5–8). Illus. Series: America in World War II. 1991, Millbrook paper $6.95 (1-878-84181-5). 64pp. The events of 1943 as they related to the United States and World War II are retold in text and many full-color illustrations. (Rev: BL 4/1/92; SLJ 5/92) [940.54]

**12045**  Drogues, Valerie. *Battleship Missouri* (3–5). Illus. Series: Those Daring Machines. 1995, Macmillan LB $13.95 (0-89686-825-7). 48pp. A short, well-illustrated description of the battleship *Missouri* and its amazing record during World War II. (Rev: BL 2/15/95) [359.3]

**12046** Drucker, Olga L. *Kindertransport* (5–8). 1995, Holt $14.95 (0-8050-1711-9); paper $7.95 (0-8050-4251-2). 146pp. A true account of a Jewish girl sent from Germany to live in England until she could join her parents in New York City in 1945. (Rev: BCCB 1/93; SLJ 11/92) [940.54]

**12047** Gay, Kathlyn, and Martin Gay. *World War II* (5–8). Illus. Series: Voices from the Past. 1995, Twenty-First Century LB $18.90 (0-8050-2849-8). 64pp. World War II is covered, from causes to consequences, with quotes from many original sources. (Rev: BL 12/15/95; SLJ 2/96) [940.53]

**12048** Green, Robert. *"Vive La France": The French Resistance During World War II* (5–8). Illus. Series: First Books on World War II. 1995, Watts LB $22.00 (0-531-20192-9). 63pp. The story of the role played by the French underground during World War II. (Rev: SLJ 10/95) [940.54]

**12049** Hopkinson, Deborah. *Pearl Harbor* (4–6). Illus. Series: Places in American History. 1991, Macmillan LB $14.95 (0-87518-475-8). 72pp. A visual and narrative introduction to this well-known site of World War II. (Rev: BL 2/15/92; SLJ 4/92) [940.54]

**12050** Kodama, Tatsuharu. *Shin's Tricycle* (5–8). Trans. by Kazuko Hokumen-Jones. Illus. by Noriyuki Ando. 1995, Walker LB $16.85 (0-8027-8376-7). 32pp. A father recalls the life of his young son, who was killed in the bombing of Hiroshima. (Rev: BCCB 12/95; BL 9/1/95*; SLJ 12/95) [940.54]

**12051** Krull, Kathleen. *V Is for Victory: America Remembers World War II* (5–8). Illus. 1995, Knopf $24.00 (0-679-86198-X). 116pp. Through original documents and illustrations, the atmosphere and events of World War II, both the fighting and on the home front, are recaptured. (Rev: BCCB 7–8/95; BL 7/95; SLJ 10/95) [940.53]

**12052** Lawson, Don, and Wendy Barish. *The French Resistance* (5–7). 1984, Simon & Schuster LB $8.79 (0-671-50832-6). 192pp. A description of a spy network that existed during World War II.

**12053** McGowen, Tom. *"Go for Broke": Japanese-Americans in World War II* (5–8). Illus. Series: First Books on World War II. 1995, Watts LB $22.00 (0-531-20195-3). 63pp. An attractive, accessible presentation that describes the fate of Japanese Americans during World War II. (Rev: SLJ 10/95) [940.54]

**12054** McGowen, Tom. *World War II* (5–7). Illus. 1993, Watts $21.00 (0-531-20150-3). 64pp. An action-filled account that introduces key battles and people connected with World War II. (Rev: BL 6/1–15/93) [940.53]

**12055** Maruki, Toshi. *Hiroshima No Pika* (3–6). Illus. by author. 1982, Lothrop $16.00 (0-688-01297-

3). 48pp. The story of a 7-year-old girl and the bombing of Hiroshima in 1945.

**12056** Marx, Trish. *Echoes of World War II* (5–8). Illus. 1994, Lerner LB $19.93 (0-8225-4898-4). 96pp. The true stories of 6 children from all over the world whose lives were changed dramatically by World War II. (Rev: BCCB 5/94; BL 9/15/94; SLJ 5/94) [940.53]

**12057** Milman, Barbara. *Light in the Shadows* (5–8). Illus. 1997, Jonathan David paper $14.95 (0-8246-0401-6). 82pp. This account tells the stories of 5 Holocaust survivors illustrated with powerful woodcut prints. (Rev: BL 11/15/97) [940.53]

**12058** Mochizuki, Ken. *Passage to Freedom: The Sugihara Story* (3–5). Illus. by Dom Lee. 1997, Lee & Low $15.95 (1-880000-49-0). 32pp. The story of Chiune Sugihara, the Japanese consul in Lithuania, and how he issued visas during the Holocaust that enabled Polish Jews to escape. (Rev: BL 5/15/97; HB 11–12/97; SLJ 7/97) [940.53]

**12059** Pettit, Jayne. *A Time to Fight Back: True Stories of Wartime Resistance* (5–8). 1996, Houghton $14.95 (0-395-76504-8). 176pp. Eight true stories about courageous acts involving young people during World War II. (Rev: BCCB 3/96; BL 4/1/96; SLJ 4/96) [940.53]

**12060** Pfeifer, Kathryn B. *The 761st Tank Battalion* (5–8). Illus. Series: African-American Soldiers. 1994, Twenty-First Century LB $17.90 (0-8050-3057-3). 80pp. An account of the achievements of members of the African American soldiers of the 761st Tank Battalion in World War II. (Rev: BL 9/1/94; SLJ 11/94) [940.54]

**12061** Pringle, Laurence. *One Room School* (1–4). Illus. by Barbara Garrison. 1998, Boyds Mills $15.95 (1-56397-583-1). This is a memoir by the noted author in which he remembers the year 1944, when he was attending a one-room school and collecting scrap metal for the war effort. (Rev: BL 3/1/98; SLJ 4/98) [371]

**12062** Sauvain, Philip. *El Alamein* (4–8). Illus. by Harry Clow. Series: Great Battles and Sieges. 1992, Macmillan $13.95 (0-02-781081-X). 32pp. An account of the decisive World War II battle fought on the sands of North Africa. (Rev: BL 11/1/92; SLJ 1/93) [940.54]

**12063** Siegal, Aranka. *Upon the Head of the Goat: A Childhood in Hungary* (6–8). 1981, Farrar $16.00 (0-374-38059-7); NAL paper $2.25 (0-451-12084-1). 214pp. The destruction of a family at the hands of the Nazis during World War II.

**12064** Simon, Charnan. *Hollywood at War: The Motion Picture Industry and World War II* (4–8). Illus. Series: First Books on World War II. 1995, Watts LB $22.00 (0-531-20193-7). 63pp. Chronicles the role of the movie industry during World War II in supplying propaganda and entertainment. (Rev: SLJ 10/95) [940.54]

**12065** Sinnott, Susan. *Doing Our Part: American Women on the Home Front During World War II* (4–8). Illus. Series: First Books on World War II. 1995, Watts LB $22.00 (0-531-20198-8). 63pp. The role of women at home and in defense industries during World War II is covered in this interesting account. (Rev: SLJ 10/95) [940.54]

**12066** Sinnott, Susan. *Our Burden of Shame: Japanese-American Internment During World War II* (5–8). Illus. Series: First Books on World War II. 1995, Watts LB $22.00 (0-531-20194-5). 63pp. The story of the heartbreaking internment of Japanese Americans during World War II is told in this easily understood, well-illustrated volume. (Rev: SLJ 10/95) [940.54]

**12067** Sloan, Frank. *Bismarck!* (5–8). Illus. Series: First Books. 1991, Watts LB $12.40 (0-531-20002-7). 64pp. One of the great sea battles of World War II occurred when the British sank the German battleship Bismarck. (Rev: BL 5/15/91; SLJ 6/91) [940.54]

**12068** Stein, R. Conrad. *The Story of D-Day* (4–6). Illus. by Tom Dunnington. 1977, Children's LB $13.27 (0-516-04609-8); paper $3.95 (0-516-44609-6). 32pp. Events surrounding the landing in Normandy, June 6, 1944.

**12069** Stein, R. Conrad. *The Story of the Battle for Iwo Jima* (4–6). Illus. by Len W. Meents. 1977, Children's LB $13.27 (0-516-04607-1). 32pp. The heartbreaking story of the battle that cost thousands of American lives.

**12070** Stein, R. Conrad. *World War II in Europe: "America Goes to War."* (5–7). Illus. Series: American War. 1994, Enslow LB $19.95 (0-89490-525-2). 128pp. An unbiased account of the European theater of war during World War II, with emphasis on American participation. (Rev: BL 10/15/94; SLJ 1/95) [940.54]

**12071** Stein, R. Conrad. *World War II in the Pacific: Remember Pearl Harbor* (5–7). Illus. Series: American War. 1994, Enslow LB $19.95 (0-89490-524-4). 128pp. A well-organized, concise account of the Pacific war from the attack on Pearl Harbor to V-J Day that describes key battles and important personnel. (Rev: BL 7/94; SLJ 7/94) [940.54]

**12072** Steins, Richard. *The Allies Against the Axis: World War II (1940–1950)* (5–8). Series: First Person America. 1994, Twenty-First Century LB $18.90 (0-

8050-2586-3). 64pp. The story of World War II and early postwar conditions are covered, with generous use of primary sources. (Rev: SLJ 12/94) [940.54]

**12073** Taylor, Theodore. *Air Raid — Pearl Harbor: The Story of December 7, 1941* (5–8). 1991, Harcourt paper $6.00 (0-15-201655-4). 179pp. A fine account of why the attack occurred and the effects that were felt around the world. A revised edition. (Rev: SLJ 12/91) [940.54]

**12074** Whitman, Sylvia. *Uncle Sam Wants You!* (5–7). Illus. 1993, Lerner LB $19.95 (0-8225-1728-0). 80pp. This work describes the experiences of the many men and women who served in the various armed forces during World War II. (Rev: BL 5/1/93) [940.54]

**12075** Whitman, Sylvia. *V Is for Victory: The American Home Front During World War II* (4–7). Illus. 1993, Lerner LB $21.27 (0-8225-1727-2). 80pp. Such things as Rosie the Riveter, ration stamps, and the relocation of Japanese Americans are included in this look at the United States in another time. (Rev: BL 2/15/93) [973.9]

**12076** Wills, Charles A. *Pearl Harbor* (5–7). Illus. Series: Turning Points in American History. 1991, Silver Burdett LB $14.95 (0-382-24125-8); paper $7.95 (0-382-24119-3). 64pp. Through text and pictures, the "Day of Infamy" that brought America into World War II is re-created. (Rev: BL 1/15/92) [940.54]

**12077** Younkin, Paula. *V-2 Rockets* (3–5). Illus. Series: Those Daring Machines. 1995, Silver Burdett paper $5.95 (0-614-09467-4). 48pp. The history of the development of the V-2 rocket by Germany, its use against the British in World War II, and the career of its developer, Wernher von Braun. (Rev: BL 2/15/95) [940.54]

## Modern History

**12078** Adams, Simon. *Visual Timeline of the 20th Century* (5–8). Illus. 1996, DK Publg. $15.95 (0-7894-0997-6). 48pp. Important events in the 20th century are described in chronological order. (Rev: BL 12/1/96; SLJ 1/97) [909.8]

**12079** Avikian, Monique. *The Mejii Restoration and the Rise of Modern Japan* (5–8). Illus. Series: Turning Points in World History. 1991, Silver Burdett LB $14.95 (0-382-24132-0); paper $7.95 (0-382-24139-8). 64pp. The major factors that led to Japan's economic superiority are discussed. (Rev: BL 3/15/92) [952.03]

**12080** Lye, Keith. *The World Today* (4–6). Illus. 1986, Facts on File $15.95 (0-8160-1072-2). 64pp. This large-size volume gives an overview of communication and transportation links. (Rev: BL 8/86)

**12081** Steins, Richard. *The Postwar Years: The Cold War and the Atomic Age (1950–1959)* (5–8). Series: First Person America. 1994, Twenty-First Century LB $18.90 (0-8050-2587-1). 64pp. Coverage of the 1950s includes first-person material on the Cold War, the Korean conflict, and developments on the home front. (Rev: SLJ 12/94) [940.55]

# Geographical Regions

## Africa

### General

**12082** Ayo, Yvonne. *Africa* (4–8). Illus. Series: Eyewitness Books. 1995, Knopf LB $20.99 (0-674-97334-6). 64pp. This introduces the continent of Africa, with its amazing diversity of people, places, wildlife, and cultures. (Rev: BL 12/15/95) [960]

**12083** Chambers, Catherine. *Africa* (4–7). Illus. Series: Origins. 1997, Watts LB $19.30 (0-531-14416-X). 32pp. The story of emigration from Africa, the slave trade, and the conditions that African Americans have faced through history on their arrival in the United States. (Rev: BL 4/15/97; SLJ 7/97) [960]

**12084** Georges, D. V. *Africa* (2–4). Illus. 1986, Children's LB $19.00 (0-516-01287-8). 48pp. A brief survey of this complex and diverse continent. (Rev: SLJ 5/87)

**12085** Halliburton, Warren J. *African Industries* (4–6). Illus. Series: Africa Today. 1993, Macmillan LB $13.95 (0-89686-672-6). 48pp. Since colonialism, Africans have tried to develop such industries as agriculture, fishing, and mining. (Rev: BL 4/15/93) [338]

**12086** Halliburton, Warren J. *African Landscapes* (4–6). Illus. Series: Africa Today. 1993, Silver Burdett LB $13.95 (0-89686-673-4). 48pp. From tropical forests to freezing mountain tops and arid deserts, this book describes the African landscape and geography. (Rev: BL 4/15/93) [916]

**12087** Halliburton, Warren J. *Africa's Struggle for Independence* (4–6). Illus. Series: Africa Today. 1992, Macmillan LB $13.95 (0-89686-679-3). 48pp. An overview of the people and kingdoms of Africa, slave trade, colonial invasion, and the fight of individual nations for freedom. (Rev: BCCB 2/93; BL 3/1/93; SLJ 2/93) [960]

**12088** Halliburton, Warren J. *Africa's Struggle to Survive* (4–6). Illus. 1993, Macmillan LB $13.95 (0-89686-675-0). 48pp. This book describes the natural disasters and forces of nature dictating the lives of the people of Africa. (Rev: BL 4/15/93) [960]

**12089** Halliburton, Warren J. *Celebrations of African Heritage* (4–6). Illus. Series: Africa Today. 1992, Macmillan LB $13.95 (0-89686-676-9). 48pp. This book describes African holidays and celebrations and tells how some of these have been brought to America. (Rev: BL 2/15/93; SLJ 2/93) [394.2]

**12090** Haskins, Jim, and Kathleen Benson. *African Beginnings* (3–7). Illus. by Floyd Cooper. 1998, Lothrop $18.00 (0-688-10256-5). 48pp. Eleven ancient African cultures, including the Egyptian, are described, beginning with Nubia around 3800 B.C. (Rev: BL 2/15/98) [960]

**12091** Ibazebo, Isimeme. *Exploration into Africa* (4–6). Illus. Series: Exploration Into . . . 1994, New Discovery paper $7.95 (0-382-24732-9). 48pp. An account of the foreign influences in the history of Africa, including the slave trade, and how these have changed its history. (Rev: SLJ 5/95) [960]

**12092** Jones, Schuyler. *Pygmies of Central Africa* (5–8). Illus. 1989, Rourke LB $16.67 (0-86625-268-1). 48pp. A vivid look into the lives of these fascinating people. (Rev: BL 5/15/89)

**12093** Kreikemeier, Gregory Scott. *Come with Me to Africa: A Photographic Journey* (PS–3). Illus. 1993, Golden Bks. $11.95 (0-307-15660-5). 64pp. A 6-month safari to 13 African countries is described, with pictures of the people and wildlife that were encountered. (Rev: BCCB 12/93; BL 1/1/94; SLJ 2/94) [916]

**12094** Musgrove, Margaret. *Ashanti to Zulu: African Traditions* (3–5). Illus. by Leo Dillon and Diane Dillon. 1976, Dial LB $15.89 (0-8037-0358-9); paper $4.95 (0-8037-0308-2). A Caldecott Medal winner (1977) that describes distinctive life-styles of 26 African tribes in text and stunning pictures.

## Central and Eastern Africa

**12095** Arnold, Helen. *Kenya* (1–3). Illus. Series: Postcards From. 1996, Raintree Steck-Vaughn LB $21.40 (0-8172-4024-1). 32pp. An overview of Kenya as portrayed in 13 postcards that describe the capital city, markets, parks, transportation, customs, and important sights. (Rev: SLJ 3/97) [967.62]

**12096** Ayodo, Awuor. *Luo* (4–7). Illus. Series: Heritage Library of African Peoples. 1995, Rosen LB $15.95 (0-8239-1758-4). 64pp. A portrait of the culture, history, and society of the Luo people, who lived on the shores of Lake Victoria in Kenya. (Rev: BL 3/1/96) [967.8]

**12097** Bangura, Abdul Karim. *Kipsigis* (5–8). Illus. Series: Heritage Library of African Peoples. 1994, Rosen LB $15.95 (0-8239-1765-7). 64pp. An attractive title that deals with the history and present status of the Kipsigis people of Kenya. (Rev: SLJ 5/95) [967.62]

**12098** Baroin, Catherine. *Tubu: The Teda and the Daza* (5–7). Illus. Series: Heritage Library of African Peoples. 1997, Rosen LB $16.95 (0-8239-2000-3). 64pp. The history and contemporary life of these African peoples who now live in Central Africa, including Chad, Libya, Niger, and the Sudan. (Rev: BL 4/15/97) [967.43]

**12099** Blauer, Ettagale, and Jason Lauré. *Uganda* (5–8). Illus. Series: Enchantment of the World. 1997, Children's LB $36.00 (0-516-20306-1). 128pp. This introduction to Uganda covers such topics as geography, climate, plants and animals, history, religion, culture, and daily life. (Rev: BL 7/97) [967.61]

**12100** Burnham, Philip. *Gbaya* (5–7). Illus. Series: Heritage Library of African Peoples. 1997, Rosen LB $15.95 (0-8239-1995-1). 64pp. Covers the contemporary culture and the significant history of the Gbaya people, who live in Cameroon, Central African Republic, Congo, and Zaire. (Rev: BL 4/15/97) [967]

**12101** *Ethiopia in Pictures* (5–8). Illus. 1994, Lerner LB $19.93 (0-8225-1836-8). 64pp. Land, history and government, culture, education, religion, education, and health are covered. (Rev: BL 2/1/89)

**12102** Fox, Mary V. *Somalia* (5–8). Illus. Series: Enchantment of the World. 1996, Children's LB $32.00 (0-516-20019-4). 127pp. An introduction to the land and people of this Muslim republic, which occupies the eastern horn of Africa. (Rev: BL 1/1–15/97) [967.73]

**12103** Gish, Steven. *Ethiopia* (4–7). Illus. Series: Cultures of the World. 1996, Marshall Cavendish LB $34.21 (0-7614-0276-4). 128pp. After general background information on Ethiopia, such topics as lifestyles, religion, and language are discussed. (Rev: BL 8/96; SLJ 8/96) [963]

**12104** Greenberg, Keith E. *Rwanda: Fierce Clashes in Central Africa* (1–4). Photos by John Isaac. Series: Children in Crisis. 1996, Blackbirch LB $14.95 (1-56711-185-8). 30pp. A harrowing eyewitness account in text and photos of the effects of the war in Rwanda on the lives of children in the refugee camps. (Rev: SLJ 6/97) [967]

**12105** Holtzman, Jon. *Samburu* (5–8). Illus. Series: Heritage Library of African Peoples. 1995, Rosen LB $15.95 (0-8239-1759-2). 64pp. A detailed account of the culture, history, and life-styles of these Kenyan people. (Rev: SLJ 5/95) [967.62]

**12106** *Kenya in Pictures* (5–8). Illus. 1997, Lerner LB $19.93 (0-8225-1830-9). 64pp. Information on all aspects of life in this African country, including extensive coverage of its history. (Rev: BL 4/15/88; SLJ 11/88)

**12107** Klyce, Katherine P., and Virginia O. McLean. *Kenya, Jambo!* (2–5). Illus. 1989, Redbird $21.95 (0-9606046-4-2). 36pp. In photos and simple text, a 10-year-old girl tells of her family's vacation in Kenya. (Rev: BL 12/1/89) [916]

**12108** Kurtz, Jane. *Ethiopia: The Roof of Africa* (5–8). Illus. Series: Discovering Our Heritage. 1991, Macmillan LB $14.95 (0-87518-483-9). 128pp. Beginning with a map and 2 pages of basic facts, this account gives an introduction to the land, people, and modern problems of Ethiopia. (Rev: BL 2/1/92; SLJ 5/92) [963]

**12109** Lindblad, Lisa. *The Serengeti Migration: Africa's Animals on the Move* (3–7). Photos by Sven-Olof Lindblad. 1994, Hyperion $15.95 (1-56282-668-9). 40pp. A short text and stunning photos describe the annual migration of zebras and wildebeests through Tanzania and Kenya. (Rev: BCCB 5/94; BL 7/94*; SLJ 5/94) [599.73]

**12110** *Malawi in Pictures* (5–8). Illus. 1989, Lerner LB $19.93 (0-8225-1842-2). 64pp. An overview of climate, history, geography, culture, education, and other aspects of life. (Rev: BL 2/1/89)

**12111** Matthews, Jo. *I Remember Somalia* (3–5). Illus. Series: Why We Left. 1995, Raintree Steck-Vaughn LB $22.83 (0-8114-5606-4). 32pp. Basic facts about Somalia are covered in this account describing the feelings of a refugee child who has left his country. (Rev: SLJ 7/95) [967]

**12112** Ng'weno, Fleur. *Kenya* (4–7). Illus. Series: Focus on. 1992, Trafalgar $22.95 (0-237-60194-X). 32pp. Discusses Kenya's history, peoples, and lifestyles. (Rev: SLJ 8/92) [967.6]

**12113** Njoku, Onwuka N. *Mbundu* (5–7). Illus. Series: Heritage Library of African Peoples. 1997, Rosen LB $15.95 (0-8239-2004-6). 64pp. An introduction to the history and contemporary culture of this people of the African republic of Zaire. (Rev: BL 4/15/97) [9678.3]

**12114** Okeke, Chika. *Kongo* (5–7). Illus. 1997, Rosen LB $15.95 (0-8239-2001-1). 64pp. The Kongo people of Angola, Congo, and Zaire in central Africa are featured, with material on their history and contemporary culture. (Rev: BL 4/15/97) [967]

**12115** Parris, Ronald. *Rendille* (5–8). Illus. Series: Heritage Library of African Peoples. 1994, Rosen LB $15.95 (0-8239-1763-0). 64pp. With extensive use of black-and-white and color photos, introduces the history and customs of the Rendille people of Kenya. (Rev: SLJ 5/95) [967.62]

**12116** Pateman, Robert. *Kenya* (4–7). Illus. Series: Cultures of the World. 1993, Marshall Cavendish LB $34.21 (1-85435-572-4). 128pp. The background story of Kenya is revealed through color photos and a text that also covers present concerns. (Rev: BL 8/93) [967.62]

**12117** Sayre, April Pulley. *If You Should Hear a Honey Guide* (K–3). Illus. by S. D. Schindler. 1995, Houghton $14.95 (0-395-71545-8). 32pp. An imaginative guide to the animals and plants that are found in the savanna region of Kenya. (Rev: BL 9/1/95; HB 11–12/95; SLJ 10/95*) [598.7]

**12118** Stein, R. Conrad. *Kenya* (4–6). Illus. Series: Enchantment of the World. 1985, Children's LB $32.00 (0-516-02770-0). 127pp. The country's national park system is highlighted. (Rev: BL 3/1/86; SLJ 5/86)

**12119** Stewart, Judy. *A Family in Sudan* (4–6). Illus. 1988, Lerner LB $18.60 (0-8225-1682-9). 32pp. Customs, work, and play are covered in this look at life in this African land. (Rev: BL 8/88)

**12120** *Sudan in Pictures* (5–8). Illus. 1990, Lerner LB $19.93 (0-8225-1839-2). 64pp. An overview of history, culture, geography, economy, education, and health. (Rev: BL 2/1/89)

**12121** Swinimer, Ciarunji C. *Pokot* (5–8). Illus. Series: Heritage Library of African Peoples. 1994, Rosen LB $15.95 (0-8239-1756-8). 64pp. Using a good balance of text and visuals, this account describes the history, culture, and present status of the Pokot people of Kenya. (Rev: SLJ 5/95) [967.62]

**12122** *Tanzania in Pictures* (5–8). Illus. 1989, Lerner LB $19.93 (0-8225-1838-4). 64pp. Part of the Visual Geography series, contains information on

history, geography, economy, religion, and culture. (Rev: BL 2/1/89)

**12123** Wangari, Esther. *Ameru* (5–8). Illus. Series: Heritage Library of American Peoples. 1995, Rosen LB $15.95 (0-8239-1766-5). 64pp. A history and description of the culture of the Ameru people of Kenya and the humiliation of being conquered by the British. (Rev: SLJ 11/95) [967.62]

**12124** Wilkes, Sybella. *One Day We Had to Run!* (5–8). Illus. 1995, Millbrook LB $20.90 (1-56294-557-2). 61pp. A moving document that was produced from interviews with 3 young African children who were in a refugee camp in Kenya. (Rev: SLJ 12/95) [967.62]

**12125** Willis, Terri. *Serengeti Plain* (4–7). Illus. Series: Wonders of the World. 1995, Raintree Steck-Vaughn LB $25.64 (0-8114-6368-0). 64pp. A look at the national park in Tanzania, its wildlife, and the native Masai and their culture. (Rev: SLJ 6/95) [967.1]

**12126** Zeleza, Tiyambe. *Maasai* (5–8). Illus. Series: Heritage Library of African Peoples. 1994, Rosen LB $15.95 (0-8239-1757-6). 64pp. An introduction to these people of Kenya and Tanzania, their culture, customs, and history. (Rev: SLJ 5/95) [967.62]

**12127** Zeleza, Tiyambe. *Mijikenda* (5–8). Illus. Series: Heritage Library of American Peoples. 1995, Rosen LB $15.95 (0-8239-1767-3). 64pp. The history and present-day life-style of this group that lives in Kenya and is made up of 9 peoples. (Rev: SLJ 11/95) [967.62]

## Northern Africa

**12128** Fox, Mary V. *Tunisia* (5–8). Illus. Series: Enchantment of the World. 1990, Children's LB $32.00 (0-516-02724-7). 128pp. This country in North Africa is introduced. (Rev: BL 1/1/91) [961.1]

**12129** Hermes, Jules. *The Children of Morocco* (3–6). Illus. 1995, Carolrhoda LB $21.27 (0-87614-857-7); paper $7.95 (0-87614-899-2). 48pp. Features children from various Moroccan settings, such as cities like Casablanca and nomadic desert settlements. (Rev: BL 5/1/95; SLJ 7/95) [964]

**12130** Kagda, Falaq. *Algeria* (4–7). Illus. Series: Cultures of the World. 1997, Marshall Cavendish LB $34.21 (0-7614-0680-8). 128pp. This book on Algeria emphasizes the people and how they live. (Rev: BL 8/97) [965]

**12131** *Libya in Pictures* (5–8). Illus. Series: Visual Geography. 1996, Lerner LB $19.93 (0-8225-1907-0). 64pp. Introduces this North African country's geography, history, and people, with many illustrations. (Rev: BL 11/15/96) [961.2]

**12132** Malcolm, Peter. *Libya* (4–7). Illus. 1993, Marshall Cavendish LB $34.21 (1-85435-573-2). 128pp. Well-chosen photos and readable text give good background information as well as material on present problems. (Rev: BL 8/93) [961.2]

**12133** Mann, Kenny. *Egypt, Kush, Aksum: Northeast Africa* (4–6). Illus. Series: African Kingdoms of the Past. 1997, Dillon LB $15.95 (0-87518-655-6); paper $7.95 (0-382-39657-X). 105pp. Describes these famous ancient African civilizations as well as northeast Africa today. Also use *Zenj, Buganda: East Africa*. (Rev: SLJ 9/97) [967]

**12134** Stewart, Judy. *A Family in Morocco* (2–4). Illus. 1986, Lerner LB $18.60 (0-8225-1664-0). 32pp. Basic geography and the facts of daily living, focusing on one child in a family. (Rev: BL 5/15/86; SLJ 10/86)

## Southern Africa

**12135** Biesele, Megan, and Kxao Royal. *San* (5–7). Series: Heritage Library of African Peoples. 1997, Rosen LB $16.95 (0-8239-1997-8). 63pp. The San people of Botswana, Namibia, and South Africa are featured in this account that tells of their rich tradition and their struggle for freedom. (Rev: BL 9/15/97) [968.06]

**12136** Blauer, Ettagale, and Jason Lauré. *Swaziland* (5–8). Illus. Series: Enchantment of the World. 1996, Children's LB $32.00 (0-516-20020-8). 128pp. This landlocked kingdom north of South Africa is introduced, with material on its physical features, history, and economy. (Rev: BL 1/1–15/97) [968.87]

**12137** Bolaane, Maitseo, and Part T. Mgadla. *Batswana* (5–7). Series: Heritage Library of African Peoples. 1997, Rosen LB $15.95 (0-8239-2008-9). 64pp. Discusses the Batswana people, who live in Botswana and South Africa, with material on their history, culture, and present status. (Rev: BL 1/1–15/98) [968]

**12138** Brandenburg, Jim. *Sand and Fog: Adventures in Southern Africa* (5–8). Illus. 1994, Walker LB $17.85 (0-8027-8233-7). 44pp. A stunning photoessay about the wildlife found in Namibia in southwest Africa. (Rev: BCCB 5/94; BL 3/1/94*; HB 5–6/94; SLJ 5/94) [968.1]

**12139** Dawson, Zoe. *South Africa* (K–3). Illus. Series: Postcards From. 1995, Raintree Steck-Vaughn LB $21.40 (0-8172-4015-2). 32pp. In double-page spreads, points of interest in South Africa are described. (Rev: SLJ 3/96) [968]

**12140** Flint, David. *South Africa* (5–8). Illus. Series: Modern Industrial World. 1996, Raintree Steck-Vaughn $24.26 (0-8172-4554-5). 48pp. The present economic status of South Africa is studied through

personal narratives and case studies. (Rev: BL 2/15/97) [968]

**12141** Green, Jen. *A Family from South Africa* (3–5). Illus. Series: Families Around the World. 1997, Raintree Steck-Vaughn LB $17.48 (0-8172-4902-6). 32pp. Everyday life in South Africa is covered through the daily activities of a hard-working family at home and at school. (Rev: BL 2/1/98) [306.85]

**12142** Green, Rebecca L. *Merina* (5–7). Illus. Series: Heritage Library of African Peoples. 1997, Rosen LB $15.95 (0-8239-1991-9). 64pp. This account tells of the life, past and present, of this African tribal group that lives on the island of Madagascar. (Rev: BL 4/15/97) [969.1]

**12143** Heinrichs, Ann. *South Africa* (2–4). Illus. Series: True Book: Countries. 1997, Children's LB $21.00 (0-516-20340-1). 48pp. South Africa is introduced, with material on its history, geography, economy, and peoples. (Rev: BL 9/15/97) [968]

**12144** Inserra, Rose, and Susan Powell. *The Kalahari* (5–8). Illus. Series: Ends of the Earth. 1997, Heinemann LB $14.95 (0-431-06932-8). 48pp. An introduction to the desert region of southern Botswana, eastern Namibia, and western South Africa. (Rev: SLJ 11/97) [968]

**12145** Kaschula, Russel. *Xhosa* (5–7). Series: Heritage Library of African Peoples. 1997, Rosen LB $15.95 (0-8239-2013-5). 64pp. The Xhosa people of South Africa are introduced with stunning photos and coverage of their past as well as present culture and life-styles. (Rev: BL 1/1–15/98) [968]

**12146** Lauré, Jason. *Angola* (5–8). Illus. Series: Enchantment of the World. 1990, Children's LB $32.00 (0-516-02721-2). 128pp. The troubled history of Angola is given, and geography and key people are introduced. (Rev: BL 1/1/91) [967.3]

**12147** Lauré, Jason. *Botswana* (5–8). Illus. Series: Enchantment of the World. 1993, Children's LB $32.00 (0-516-02616-X). 128pp. An introduction to this republic in southern Africa, which gained independence in 1964 and is famous for its gold and wildlife preserves. (Rev: BL 11/1/93; SLJ 4/94) [968.83]

**12148** Lauré, Jason. *Namibia* (5–8). Illus. Series: Enchantment of the World. 1993, Children's LB $32.00 (0-516-02615-1). 128pp. The story of this African nation — formerly South-West Africa — and its history and present problems. (Rev: BL 8/93) [968.81]

**12149** Lauré, Jason. *Zambia* (4–6). Illus. Series: Enchantment of the World. 1989, Children's LB $36.00 (0-516-02716-6). 128pp. The land and people of Zambia are covered with special material in a 10-page section of important facts. (Rev: BL 1/1/90) [941.5]

**12150** Lauré, Jason. *Zimbabwe* (4–7). Illus. 1989, Children's LB $36.00 (0-516-02704-2). 128pp. The history, culture, people, and customs of this African land. (Rev: BL 8/88)

**12151** Leigh, Nila K. *Learning to Swim in Swaziland: A Child's-Eye View of a Southern African Country* (2–4). Illus. 1993, Scholastic $15.95 (0-590-45938-4). 48pp. Nila's first-person account of her year in Swaziland. (Rev: BCCB 3/93; BL 1/15/93; SLJ 5/93) [968.8]

**12152** Lowis, Peter. *South Africa: Free at Last* (4–6). Illus. Series: Topics in the News. 1995, Raintree Steck-Vaughn LB $22.83 (0-8172-4175-2). 32pp. The background, history, and present-day (1995) situation in South Africa are described in a newspaper format using text and pictures. (Rev: BL 3/1/96) [305.8]

**12153** *Madagascar in Pictures* (5–8). Illus. 1988, Lerner LB $19.93 (0-8225-1841-4). 64pp. Covers geography, history, culture, economics, religion, and health. (Rev: BL 2/1/89)

**12154** Ngwane, Zolani. *Zulu* (5–7). Series: Heritage Library of African Peoples. 1997, Rosen LB $15.95 (0-8239-2014-3). 64pp. Introduces the past history and culture of the Zulus of South Africa. Also use *Sukuma* and *Luba* (both 1997). (Rev: BL 9/15/97) [968.06]

**12155** Nwaezeigwe, Nwankwo T. *Ngoni* (5–7). Illus. Series: Heritage Library of African Peoples. 1997, Rosen LB $15.95 (0-8239-2006-2). 64pp. Describes the history, traditions, and struggle for freedom of this African group in Malawi. (Rev: BL 4/15/97) [968.97]

**12156** Oluikpe, Benson O. *Swazi* (5–7). Illus. Series: Heritage Library of African Peoples. 1997, Rosen LB $15.95 (0-8239-2012-7). 64pp. The Swazi people live in Swaziland and South Africa, and this book describes their history, traditions, and struggles for freedom. (Rev: BL 4/15/97; SLJ 12/97) [968]

**12157** Rogers, Barbara R. *Zambia* (3–5). Illus. by Stillman Rogers. Series: Children of the World. 1991, Stevens LB $12.95 (0-8368-0257-8). 64pp. The social and community life of Zambia is introduced through the lives and activities of some typical children. (Rev: BL 12/15/91; SLJ 7/92) [968.94]

**12158** Rosemarin, Ike. *South Africa* (4–7). Illus. Series: Cultures of the World. 1993, Marshall Cavendish LB $34.21 (1-85435-575-9). 128pp. Historical and modern concerns are covered in this look at South Africa. (Rev: BL 8/93) [968]

**12159** Schneider, Elizabeth Ann. *Ndebele* (5–7). Illus. Series: Heritage Library of African Peoples. 1997, Rosen LB $15.95 (0-8239-2009-7). 64pp. Topics covered about the Ndebele people of South Africa include environment, history, religion, social organi-

zation, politics, and customs. (Rev: BL 4/15/97) [968]

**12160** *South Africa in Pictures* (5–8). Illus. 1996, Lerner LB $19.93 (0-8225-1835-X). 64pp. Focusing on climate, geography, wildlife, and the history of this troubled country. (Rev: BL 8/88)

**12161** Stark, Al. *Zimbabwe: A Treasure of Africa* (4–7). Illus. 1986, Macmillan $14.95 (0-87518-308-5). 160pp. The colorful history, culture, wildlife, geography, and diversity of these people are detailed. (Rev: BL 6/15/86; SLJ 5/86)

**12162** Udechukwu, Ada. *Herero* (5–7). Illus. Series: Heritage Library of African Peoples. 1996, Rosen LB $15.95 (0-8239-2003-8). 64pp. The history, customs, and culture of the Herero people are described. (Rev: BL 3/15/96; SLJ 6/96) [968.8]

**12163** Van Wyk, Gary N. *Basotho* (5–7). Illus. Series: Heritage Library of African Peoples. 1996, Rosen LB $15.95 (0-8239-2005-4). 63pp. Describes the Basotho people, who live in Lesotho and South Africa, with material on their history, religion, social organization, and customs. (Rev: BL 11/15/96; SLJ 3/97) [968]

**12164** Van Wyk, Gary N., and Robert Johnson. *Shona* (5–7). Series: Heritage Library of African Peoples. 1997, Rosen LB $15.95 (0-8239-2011-9). 64pp. The Shona people of Zimbabwe are presented in outstanding photos, with a text that covers their past, their culture, and their present living conditions and problems. (Rev: BL 1/1–15/98) [968]

**12165** *Zimbabwe in Pictures* (5–8). Illus. 1997, Lerner LB $19.93 (0-8225-1825-2). 64pp. Many photos highlight this overview of Zimbabwe's history, climate, wildlife, and culture. (Rev: BL 4/15/88)

## Western Africa

**12166** Adeeb, Hassan, and Bonnetta Adeeb. *Nigeria: One Nation, Many Cultures* (4–8). Illus. Series: Exploring Cultures of the World. 1995, Benchmark LB $25.64 (0-7614-0190-3). 64pp. Opening with an account of a legendary figure, this book continues with an introduction to Nigeria that emphasizes its culture and how the people live. (Rev: SLJ 6/96) [966.9]

**12167** Adeleke, Tunde. *Songhay* (5–7). Illus. Series: Heritage Library of African Peoples. 1996, Rosen LB $15.95 (0-8239-1986-2). 63pp. Both historical information and material on contemporary life are given in this account of the African people who live chiefly in Mali, Niger, and Benin. (Rev: BL 11/15/96) [960]

**12168** Anda, Michael O. *Yoruba* (5–7). Illus. Series: Heritage Library of African Peoples. 1996, Rosen LB $15.95 (0-8239-1988-9). 64pp. Looks at the environment, history, religion, social organization, politics, customs, and culture of the Yoruba people. (Rev: BL 3/15/96; SLJ 6/96) [960]

**12169** Azuonye, Chukwuma. *Edo: The Bini People of the Benin Kingdom* (5–7). Illus. Series: Heritage Library of African People. 1996, Rosen LB $15.95 (0-8239-1985-4). 64pp. In this discussion of the Edo people of Nigeria, such topics as history, religion, customs, and culture are covered. (Rev: BL 3/15/96) [966.9]

**12170** Beaton, Margaret. *Senegal* (5–8). Illus. Series: Enchantment of the World. 1997, Children's LB $32.00 (0-516-20304-5). 128pp. An introduction to this West African nation, its people, and its cities, including the capital, Dakar. (Rev: BL 7/97) [916.63]

**12171** Boateng, Faustine Ama. *Asante* (5–7). Illus. Series: Heritage Library of African Peoples. 1996, Rosen LB $15.95 (0-8239-1975-7). 63pp. This African people living in present-day Ghana is described — its history, traditions, and life-style. (Rev: BL 11/15/96; SLJ 3/97) [966.7]

**12172** Brace, Steve. *Ghana* (4–8). Illus. Series: Economically Developing Countries. 1995, Thomson Learning LB $24.26 (1-56847-242-0). 48pp. Rich and poor rural and urban families are introduced in this attractive book on Ghana, its past, and its present. (Rev: SLJ 7/95) [966.7]

**12173** Chicoine, Stephen D. *A Liberian Family* (3–5). Photos by author. Series: Journey Between Two Worlds. 1997, Lerner LB $22.60 (0-8225-3411-8); paper $8.95 (0-8225-0975-6). 64pp. Explains why a family was forced to leave Liberia to escape persecution. Also gives a history of this land and its people. (Rev: SLJ 2/98) [966]

**12174** Chocolate, Deborah M. *Kente Colors* (PS–3). Illus. by John Ward. 1996, Walker LB $16.85 (0-8027-8389-9). 32pp. The history and traditions of kente cloth of Ghana are told, along with a description of its meaning and colors. (Rev: BL 2/15/96; SLJ 6/96) [391]

**12175** *Cote d'Ivoire (Ivory Coast) in Pictures* (5–8). Illus. 1988, Lerner LB $19.93 (0-8225-1828-7). 64pp. Covering all aspects of life in this overview, with pictorial emphasis and coverage on possible future developments. (Rev: BL 4/15/88; SLJ 11/88)

**12176** *Ghana in Pictures* (5–8). Illus. 1988, Lerner LB $19.93 (0-8225-1829-5). 64pp. Photos, maps, and charts enhance this overview. (Rev: BL 8/88)

**12177** Goodsmith, Lauren. *The Children of Mauritania: Days in the Desert and by the River Shore* (3–6). Illus. Series: World's Children. 1994, Carolrhoda LB $15.95 (0-87614-782-1). 56pp. The lives of 2 children growing up in Mauritania in northwest Africa are described, as well as their different environments, one from a desert and the other from a river valley. (Rev: BCCB 4/94; BL 2/1/94) [966.1]

**12178** Hathaway, Jim. *Cameroon in Pictures* (5–8). Illus. Series: Visual Geography. 1992, Lerner LB $19.93 (0-8225-1857-0). 64pp. With numerous charts, maps, and photos, the country of Cameroon is introduced. (Rev: BL 9/15/89) [967]

**12179** Hetfield, Jamie. *The Yoruba of West Africa* (PS–2). Illus. Series: Celebrating the Peoples and Civilizations of Africa. 1996, Rosen/Power Kids Pr. LB $15.93 (0-8239-2332-0). 24pp. A simple introduction to the Yoruba people of West Africa, with material on their culture, food, rituals, and life-style. (Rev: SLJ 11/96) [966.9]

**12180** Koslow, Philip. *Dahomey: The Warrior Kings* (5–8). Illus. Series: The Kingdoms of Africa. 1996, Chelsea LB $17.95 (0-7910-3137-3); paper $8.95 (0-7910-3138-1). 63pp. A history of the West African kingdom that flourished in the 17th and 18th centuries and how the slave trade affected it. (Rev: SLJ 12/96) [960]

**12181** Kummer, Patricia K. *Cote d'Ivoire* (5–8). Illus. Series: Enchantment of the World. 1996, Children's LB $32.00 (0-516-02641-0). 124pp. An introduction to the small French-speaking African republic Ivory Coast, which gained its freedom in 1960 and is now known as Cote d'Ivoire. (Rev: BL 7/96) [966.68]

**12182** Levy, Patricia. *Nigeria* (4–7). Illus. Series: Cultures of the World. 1993, Marshall Cavendish LB $34.21 (1-85435-574-0). 128pp. Information on history, geography, life-styles, people, and culture. (Rev: BL 8/93) [966.9]

**12183** *Liberia in Pictures* (5–8). Illus. 1996, Lerner LB $19.93 (0-8225-1837-6). 64pp. Covers climate, geography, wildlife, vegetation, and natural resources. (Rev: BL 8/88)

**12184** Mack-Williams, Kibibi V. *Mossi* (5–7). Illus. Series: Heritage Library of African People. 1996, Rosen LB $15.95 (0-8239-1984-6). 64pp. The history, social organization, and culture of the Mossi people of West Africa are described. (Rev: BL 3/15/96) [966.25]

**12185** Mann, Kenny. *Ghana, Mali, Songhay: The Western Sudan* (4–8). Illus. Series: African Kingdoms of the Past. 1996, Silver Burdett $15.95 (0-87518-656-4); paper $7.95 (0-382-39176-4). 108pp. After retelling a heroic African folktale, this account describes the once powerful empires of Ghana, Mali, and Songhay. (Rev: SLJ 9/96) [967]

**12186** *Nigeria in Pictures* (5–8). Illus. 1995, Lerner LB $19.93 (0-8225-1826-0). 64pp. A visual focus on this African land. (Rev: BL 8/88)

**12187** Nwanunobi, C. O. *Malinke* (5–7). Illus. Series: Heritage Library of African Peoples. 1996, Rosen LB $15.95 (0-8239-1979-X). 63pp. Features the culture, history, and contemporary lifeways of the

Malinke people, now living along the western coast of Africa. (Rev: BL 11/15/96) [966.23]

**12188** Nwanunobi, C. O. *Soninke* (5–7). Illus. Series: Heritage Library of African Peoples. 1996, Rosen LB $15.95 (0-8239-1978-1). 63pp. This African people — found in such countries as Ghana, Mali, Nigeria, and Senegal — is discussed, with material on its history, customs, and present living conditions. (Rev: BL 11/15/96) [966]

**12189** Ogbaa, Kalu. *Igbo* (5–8). Illus. Series: Heritage Library of American Peoples. 1995, Rosen LB $15.95 (0-8239-1977-3). 64pp. An introduction to the Igbo people, who are one of the 3 most important ethnic groups in Nigeria. (Rev: SLJ 11/95) [966.9]

**12190** Onyefulu, Ifeoma. *Ogbo: Sharing Life in an African Village* (1–5). Illus. 1996, Harcourt $15.00 (0-15-200498-X). 32pp. In a Nigerian village, people in the same age group, called ogbo, work together for the good of the community. (Rev: BCCB 4/96; BL 4/15/96; HB 9–10/96; SLJ 4/96*) [306]

**12191** Parris, Ronald. *Hausa* (5–7). Illus. Series: Heritage Library of African Peoples. 1996, Rosen LB $15.95 (0-8239-1983-8). 63pp. The Hausa people of Niger and Nigeria are discussed, with material on history and contemporary life. (Rev: BL 11/15/96) [966]

**12192** Peffer-Engels, John. *The Benin Kingdom of West Africa* (K–2). Illus. Series: Celebrating the Peoples and Civilizations of Africa. 1996, Rosen/Power Kids Pr. LB $15.93 (0-8239-2334-7). 24pp. This account describes the Benin kingdom home of the Edo people, how many were enslaved and taken to the United States, and of their present culture and life-style. (Rev: SLJ 1/97) [966.9]

**12193** Sallah, Tijan M. *Wolof* (5–7). Illus. Series: Heritage Library of African Peoples. 1996, Rosen LB $15.95 (0-8239-1987-0). 64pp. Using maps, many color illustrations, and text, the Wolof people of Africa are introduced. (Rev: BL 3/15/96; SLJ 7/96) [966.3]

**12194** *Senegal in Pictures* (5–8). Illus. 1989, Lerner LB $19.93 (0-8225-1827-9). 64pp. A look at the geography, history, culture, and economics of Senegal. (Rev: BL 4/15/89; SLJ 11/88)

**12195** Tenquist, Alasdair. *Nigeria* (5–8). Illus. Series: Economically Developing Countries. 1996, Raintree Steck-Vaughn LB $24.26 (0-8172-4527-8). 48pp. This introduction to Nigeria emphasizes present-day government and economic conditions. (Rev: BL 3/1/97; SLJ 9/97) [330]

**12196** Zimmermann, Robert. *The Gambia* (5–8). Illus. Series: Enchantment of the World. 1994, Children's LB $32.00 (0-516-02625-9). 128pp. This tiny West African country is introduced in text and color

photos that cover all major topics related to this new nation. (Rev: BL 12/15/94; SLJ 4/95) [966.51]

# Asia

## General

**12197** Wilkinson, Philip, and Michael Pollard. *The Magical East* (4–7). Illus. by Robert Ingpen. Series: Mysterious Places. 1994, Chelsea LB $19.95 (0-7910-2754-6). 92pp. An oversize volume that highlights several places and cities of importance in the history of the Orient. (Rev: BL 1/15/94; SLJ 4/94) [930.1]

## China

**12198** *China in Pictures* (5–8). Illus. 1994, Lerner LB $19.93 (0-8225-1859-7). 64pp. Covers history and government, cities, minerals, vegetation, and wildlife. (Rev: BL 5/1/89)

**12199** Dawson, Zoe. *China* (K–3). Illus. Series: Postcards From. 1995, Raintree Steck-Vaughn LB $21.40 (0-8172-4007-1). 32pp. Using different postcards as a focus, this account describes salient features of China. (Rev: SLJ 3/96) [951]

**12200** Dramer, Kim. *China* (3–6). Illus. Series: Games People Play. 1997, Children's LB $23.50 (0-516-20308-8). 64pp. After an introduction to China, this book discusses a number of recreational pursuits, including those practiced at festivals and those that are universally popular, like kite flying, chess, and several sports. (Rev: BL 10/15/97) [790]

**12201** Ferroa, Peggy. *China* (4–7). Illus. Series: Cultures of the World. 1991, Marshall Cavendish LB $34.21 (1-85435-399-3). 128pp. Unusual facts highlight this look at China, with emphasis on culture. (Rev: BL 2/15/92; SLJ 3/92) [951]

**12202** Flint, David. *China* (2–4). Series: On the Map. 1994, Raintree Steck-Vaughn LB $15.98 (0-8114-3421-4). 32pp. Alternating a page of color photos with a page of text, such topics as China's geography, education, industry, and family life are covered. (Rev: BL 2/1/94; SLJ 7/94) [951]

**12203** Ganeri, Anita. *I Remember China* (3–6). Illus. Series: Why We Left. 1995, Raintree Steck-Vaughn LB $22.83 (0-8114-5608-0). 32pp. Through personal narratives of refugee children, the turmoil and problems of modern China are discussed, with some background material. (Rev: SLJ 6/95) [951]

**12204** Harkonen, Reijo. *The Children of China* (4–6). Illus. by Matti Pitkanen. Series: The World's Children. 1990, Carolrhoda LB $21.27 (0-87614-

394-X). 40pp. A travelogue narrative with striking color photos. (Rev: BL 6/15/90; SLJ 9/90) [951]

**12205** Haskins, Jim. *Count Your Way Through China* (3–5). Illus. 1987, Carolrhoda LB $19.93 (0-87614-302-8); Lerner paper $5.95 (0-87614-486-5). 24pp. Concepts about China are introduced with the use of numbers 1 through 10. (Rev: BL 10/15/87; SLJ 9/87)

**12206** Heinrichs, Ann. *China* (2–4). Illus. Series: True Book: Countries. 1997, Children's LB $20.00 (0-516-20329-0). 48pp. This introduction to China includes material on the land, people, history, and culture. (Rev: BL 9/15/97; SLJ 11/97) [951]

**12207** Kent, Deborah. *Beijing* (3–6). Illus. Series: Cities of the World. 1996, Children's LB $25.00 (0-516-20023-2). 64pp. A history of Beijing, photos of its famous landmarks, and details on how its residents live are covered in this well-illustrated account. (Rev: BL 1/1–15/97) [951]

**12208** Lazo, Caroline. *The Terra Cotta Army of Emperor Qin* (5–8). Illus. 1993, Macmillan LB $14.95 (0-02-754631-4). 80pp. The story of the 7,500 terra-cotta figures that guard the tomb of China's first emperor. (Rev: BL 7/93; SLJ 8/93) [931]

**12209** McLenighan, Valjean. *China: A History to 1949* (5–8). Illus. 1983, Children's LB $32.00 (0-516-02754-9). 128pp. China from its earliest days to the founding of the People's Republic in 1949.

**12210** McMahon, Patricia. *Six Words, Many Turtles, and Three Days in Hong Kong* (4–6). Illus. 1997, Houghton $16.00 (0-395-68621-0). 64pp. A photoessay about middle-class life in modern Hong Kong. (Rev: BL 7/97; SLJ 12/97) [306.85]

**12211** Mann, Elizabeth. *The Great Wall* (4–6). Illus. Series: Wonders of the World. 1997, Mikaya $18.95 (0-9650493-2-9). 48pp. The story of the building of this great structure, with a special focus on the history of the period of its construction. (Rev: BL 1/1–15/98; SLJ 12/97) [951]

**12212** Martell, Hazel M. *The Ancient Chinese* (4–6). Illus. Series: World of the Past. 1993, Macmillan $14.95 (0-02-730653-4). 64pp. A history of early China with emphasis on culture and accomplishments. (Rev: BL 8/93) [951]

**12213** Mason, Sally. *Take a Trip to China* (1–3). Illus. 1981, Watts LB $10.90 (0-531-04317-7). 32pp. The geography, principal cities, and ways of life are introduced simply.

**12214** Odijk, Pamela. *The Chinese* (4–7). Illus. Series: Ancient World. 1991, Silver Burdett LB $14.95 (0-382-09894-3). 47pp. Brief, informative, and eye-catching treatment of the Chinese, including their influences on medicine and architecture. (Rev: BL 1/15/92) [951]

**12215** Prior, Katherine. *The History of Emigration from China and Southeast Asia* (4–7). Series: Origins. 1997, Watts LB $20.00 (0-531-14442-9). 32pp. Outlines the political, social, and economic conditions in China that led to people leaving during different periods in its history, as well as material on where they went and their reception. (Rev: BL 12/15/97; SLJ 2/98) [951]

**12216** Reynolds, Jan. *Mongolia* (3–5). Photos by author. Series: Vanishing Cultures. 1994, Harcourt $16.95 (0-15-255312-6); paper $8.95 (0-15-255313-4). A handsome photoessay about the land and the nomadic people of Mongolia. (Rev: SLJ 4/94) [951]

**12217** Shemie, Bonnie. *Houses of China* (4–7). Illus. Series: Native Dwellings. 1996, Tundra $13.95 (0-88776-369-3). 24pp. The various cultures of China, past and present, are introduced through an examination of 10 traditional houses. (Rev: SLJ 2/97) [951]

**12218** Simpson, Judith, ed. *Ancient China* (4–6). Illus. Series: Nature Company Discoveries. 1996, Time Life $16.00 (0-8094-9248-2). 64pp. A special feature of this introduction to the history, people, and culture of ancient China is an 8-page foldout featuring an exciting scene from history. (Rev: BL 6/1–15/96; SLJ 7/96) [931]

**12219** Steele, Philip. *Journey Through China* (3–5). Illus. by Martin Camm. Series: Journey Around the World. 1990, Troll LB $13.95 (0-8167-2112-2); paper $4.95 (0-8167-2113-0). 32pp. From its northern desert wastelands to lush southern countryside, the culture, history, and geography of China are explored. (Rev: BL 5/15/91; SLJ 5/91) [951]

**12220** Stepanchuk, Carol. *Red Eggs and Dragon Boats: Celebrating Chinese Festivals* (3–6). Illus. 1994, Pacific View $16.95 (1-881896-08-0). 48pp. Five traditional Chinese festivals, including the Dragon Boat Festival and Moon Festival, are introduced, with details on customs and traditions plus recipes for food. (Rev: BL 3/15/94; SLJ 4/94) [394]

**12221** Tao, Wang. *Exploration into China* (4–7). Illus. Series: Exploration Into. 1996, Dillon LB $15.95 (0-02-718087-5); paper $7.95 (0-382-39185-3). 48pp. The story of Chinese history until the opening up of the country by Europeans is given, with a brief overview of its recent history and contemporary life. (Rev: BL 8/96) [951]

**12222** Teague, Ken. *Growing Up in Ancient China* (3–5). Illus. Series: Growing Up In. 1993, Troll paper $4.95 (0-8167-2716-3). 32pp. An introduction to life in ancient China, with information on history, customs, schooling, food, clothing, and daily activities. (Rev: BL 1/15/94) [931]

**12223** Waterlow, Julia. *China* (4–7). Illus. Series: Country Insights. 1997, Raintree Steck-Vaughn LB $24.96 (0-8172-4787-4). 48pp. Compares the social conditions — home life, employment, schooling, and recreation — in a large city and a rural village in China. (Rev: BL 7/97; SLJ 8/97) [951]

**12224**  Williams, Suzanne. *Made in China: Ideas and Inventions from Ancient China* (4–6). Illus. 1997, Pacific View LB $18.95 (1-881896-14-5). 48pp. Covers such topics as papermaking, medicine, and inventions as they were developed in ancient China. (Rev: BL 2/1/97; SLJ 7/97) [931]

**12225**  Zhang, Song Nan. *The Children of China* (3–6). Illus. 1996, Tundra $17.95 (0-88776-363-4). 32pp. Children of nomadic minorities in China (e.g., Mongolians) are highlighted in this well-illustrated account. (Rev: BL 2/1/96) [759.11]

**12226**  Zhang, Song Nan. *Cowboy on the Steppes* (4–7). Illus. 1997, Tundra $15.95 (0-88776-410-X). 32pp. The true story of an 18-year-old Chinese boy and the first 8 months he spent living in the steppes of Mongolia, where he has been sent during the Cultural Revolution to herd sheep. (Rev: BL 2/15/98; SLJ 2/98) [951.7]

## India

**12227**  Cumming, David. *The Ganges* (4–7). Photos by author. Series: Rivers of the World. 1994, Raintree Steck-Vaughn LB $24.26 (0-8114-3105-3). 48pp. The historical, environmental, and economic importance of the Ganges River on eastern India and Bangladesh are discussed. (Rev: SLJ 2/94) [954]

**12228**  Cumming, David. *The Ganges Delta and Its People* (5–8). Illus. Series: People and Places. 1994, Thomson Learning LB $24.26 (1-56847-168-8). 48pp. An introduction to the Ganges delta, the people who live there, the economy it supports, and the tragedy of its frequent flooding. (Rev: BL 10/15/94) [954]

**12229**  Cumming, David. *India* (4–7). Illus. Series: Our Country. 1998, Raintree Steck-Vaughn $24.96 (0-8172-4797-1). 48pp. Several young inhabitants introduce India and describe life, customs, food, and their homes. (Rev: BL 12/1/89; SLJ 3/92) [954]

**12230**  Das, Prodeepta. *I Is for India* (2–5). Photos by author. 1996, Silver Pr. LB $13.95 (0-382-39278-7). Using an alphabet book format, this account describes India and its geography, culture, religions, and peoples. (Rev: SLJ 11/96) [954]

**12231**  Dhanjal, Beryl. *Amritsar* (3–6). Illus. Series: Holy Cities. 1994, Dillon LB $13.95 (0-87518-571-1). 46pp. A colorful introduction to the holy city of Amritsar in northern India and to the religion of Sikhism. (Rev: SLJ 8/94) [915.404]

**12232**  Ganeri, Anita. *Exploration into India* (4–6). Illus. Series: Exploration Into . . . 1994, New Discovery $15.95 (0-02-718082-4); paper $7.95 (0-382-24733-7). 48pp. A history of India and its people that

focuses on the outside individuals and empires that were influences through exploration and exploitation. (Rev: SLJ 5/95) [954]

**12233**  Ganeri, Anita. *I Remember India* (3–6). Illus. Series: Why We Left. 1995, Raintree Steck-Vaughn LB $22.83 (0-8114-5609-9). 32pp. Basic material about India is introduced, along with descriptions by refugee children of why their parents left to find a better life elsewhere. (Rev: SLJ 6/95) [954]

**12234**  Ganeri, Anita, and Rachel Wright. *India* (4–6). Illus. by John Shackell. Series: Country Topics for Craft Projects. 1994, Watts LB $20.00 (0-531-14314-7). 32pp. Basic information is given about India, with projects and activities, such as how to prepare a curry dish and how to tie-dye a scarf. (Rev: SLJ 3/95) [954]

**12235**  Ghose, Vijaya. *India* (5–8). Illus. Series: Women in Society. 1994, Marshall Cavendish LB $19.95 (1-85435-564-3). 128pp. The position of women in India is explored through milestones in history, daily lives, famous figures, and societal attitudes. (Rev: SLJ 10/94) [954]

**12236**  Haskins, Jim. *Count Your Way Through India* (3–5). Illus. by Liz B. Dodson. Series: Count Your Way. 1990, Carolrhoda LB $19.93 (0-87614-414-8). 24pp. Using a numbers approach, this book introduces the culture, climate, and people of India. (Rev: BL 4/1/91) [954]

**12237**  Hermes, Jules. *The Children of India* (3–6). Illus. Series: World's Children. 1994, Carolrhoda LB $15.95 (0-87614-759-7). 48pp. A brief look at the diversity of children and their cultures in the vast subcontinent of India. (Rev: BCCB 4/94; BL 2/1/94) [305.23]

**12238**  Howard, Dale E. *India* (4–6). Illus. Series: Games People Play! 1996, Children's LB $23.00 (0-516-04437-0). 64pp. This book describes the recreational pursuits of the Indian people, including soccer, cricket, and sports and games that originated in the Indian subcontinent. (Rev: SLJ 11/96) [954]

**12239**  *India in Pictures* (5–8). Illus. 1995, Lerner LB $19.93 (0-8225-1852-X). 64pp. Basic coverage of people, religion, history, government, vegetation, and wildlife. (Rev: BL 5/1/89)

**12240**  Lewin, Ted. *Sacred River* (2–4). Illus. 1995, Clarion $14.95 (0-395-69846-4). 32pp. In a series of beautiful watercolors and brief text, the holy city of Benares (Varanasi) and its dominating force, the River Ganges, are introduced. (Rev: BL 6/1–15/95; SLJ 8/95) [954.1]

**12241**  McNair, Sylvia. *India* (5–8). Illus. Series: Enchantment of the World. 1991, Children's LB $32.00 (0-516-02719-0). 128pp. Such topics as civilization, ethnic groups, and history are treated in this lively introduction to India. (Rev: SLJ 5/91) [954]

**12242** Moorcroft, Christine. *The Taj Mahal* (4–7). Illus. Series: Great Buildings. 1997, Raintree Steck-Vaughn $24.94 (0-8172-4920-6). 48pp. The story of the Moghul emperor who planned this building as a mausoleum for his wife is also a tale filled with treachery and murder. (Rev: BL 2/1/98) [726]

**12243** Prior, Katherine. *Indian Subcontinent* (4–7). Illus. Series: Origins. 1997, Watts LB $19.30 (0-531-14418-6). 32pp. Describes the conditions in India, Pakistan, and Bangladesh that led to emigration, where their people went, and their reception in such countries as the United States and Great Britain. (Rev: BL 4/15/97; SLJ 7/97) [304.8]

**12244** Srinivasan, Rodbika. *India* (5–8). Illus. Series: Cultures of the World. 1990, Marshall Cavendish LB $34.21 (1-85435-298-9). 128pp. Covers the land, peoples, cultural diversity, and current concerns of India. (Rev: BL 3/1/91) [954]

## Japan

**12245** Baines, John. *Japan* (3–5). Illus. Series: Country Fact Files. 1994, Raintree Steck-Vaughn LB $24.26 (0-8114-1847-2). 45pp. Contemporary Japan is introduced under such headings as landscape, climate, trade, and daily life. (Rev: SLJ 10/94) [952]

**12246** Blumberg, Rhoda. *Commodore Perry in the Land of the Shogun* (5–8). Illus. 1985, Lothrop $17.00 (0-688-03723-2). 128pp. Japan was a mysterious country when Perry arrived in 1853 to open its harbors to American ships. (Rev: BL 11/1/85; SLJ 10/85)

**12247** Bornoff, Nick. *Japan* (4–7). Illus. Series: Country Insights. 1997, Raintree Steck-Vaughn LB $24.96 (0-8172-4786-6). 48pp. This description of modern life in the city of Okazaki and in the village of Narai compares home life, employment, schooling, and recreation. (Rev: BL 7/97; SLJ 8/97) [952]

**12248** Cobb, Vicki. *This Place Is Crowded: Japan* (3–5). Illus. by Barbara Lavallee. Series: Imagine Living Here. 1992, Walker LB $15.85 (0-8027-8146-2). 32pp. The focus is on the concept of space in this book that provides basic information about living in a highly populated nation of islands. (Rev: BL 9/1/92; SLJ 8/92) [952.04]

**12249** Dawson, Zoe. *Japan* (K–3). Illus. Series: Postcards From. 1995, Raintree Steck-Vaughn LB $21.40 (0-8172-4011-X). 32pp. Points of interest in Japan are described through a series of postcards. (Rev: SLJ 3/96) [952]

**12250** Galvin, Irene F. *Japan: A Modern Land with Ancient Roots* (4–6). Illus. Series: Exploring Cultures of the World. 1996, Benchmark LB $25.64 (0-7614-0188-1). 64pp. This introduction to Japan includes good background information plus coverage

on the arts, religion, sports, and traditions. (Rev: SLJ 6/96) [952]

**12251** Haskins, Jim. *Count Your Way Through Japan* (3–5). Illus. 1987, Carolrhoda LB $19.93 (0-87614-301-X); paper $5.95 (0-87614-485-7). 24pp. "Two chopsticks" and other numbers help to introduce the culture of Japan. (Rev: BL 10/15/87; SLJ 9/87)

**12252** Heinrichs, Ann. *Japan* (4–6). Series: True Books: Countries. 1997, Children's LB $20.00 (0-516-20336-3). 48pp. This simple, colorful photoessay includes material on Japanese geography, history, culture, and how the people live. (Rev: BL 9/15/97; SLJ 11/97) [952]

**12253** *Japan in Pictures* (5–8). Illus. Series: Visual Geography. 1994, Lerner LB $19.93 (0-8225-1861-9). 64pp. The land and people of Japan are profiled, with many illustrations. (Rev: BL 9/15/89; SLJ 5/90) [952]

**12254** Kent, Deborah. *Tokyo* (3–6). Illus. 1996, Children's LB $25.00 (0-516-00354-2). 64pp. An introduction in text and many pictures to the principal sights of the capital of Japan. (Rev: BL 11/1/96; SLJ 10/96) [952]

**12255** Littlefield, Holly. *Colors of Japan* (3–4). Illus. by Helen Byers. 1997, Carolrhoda $19.93 (0-87614-885-2); paper $5.95 (1-57505-215-6). 24pp. A picture book that uses different colors to explore various aspects of Japanese culture. (Rev: SLJ 1/98) [952]

**12256** MacDonald, Fiona. *A Samurai Castle* (4–6). Illus. Series: Inside Story. 1995, Bedrick LB $18.95 (0-87226-381-9). 48pp. This account supplies details of the Samurai culture of the 17th century, with material on daily life and activities and detailed illustrations of a Samurai castle. (Rev: BL 1/1–15/96; SLJ 3/96) [952]

**12257** MacMillan, Dianne M. *Japanese Children's Day and the Obon Festival* (3–5). Series: Best Holiday. 1997, Enslow LB $18.95 (0-89490-818-9). 48pp. The original of these closely related Japanese holidays are described, with material on how they are celebrated. (Rev: BL 12/15/97; SLJ 8/97) [952]

**12258** Metcalf, Florence E. *A Peek at Japan: A Lighthearted Look at Japan's Language and Culture* (3–6). Illus. by Tomoko. 1992, Metco paper $14.95 (0-9631684-3-6). 136pp. After a section on Japanese language and vocabulary, this book deals with Japan's culture, games, origami, and unusual facts. (Rev: SLJ 7/92) [952]

**12259** Odijk, Pamela. *The Japanese* (4–7). Illus. Series: Ancient World. 1991, Silver Burdett LB $14.95 (0-382-09898-6). 47pp. This brief, informative volume includes sections on famous figures and places. (Rev: BL 1/15/92) [952]

**12260** Schemenaur, Elma. *Japan* (2–3). Illus. Series: Faces and Places. 1997, Child's World LB $22.79 (1-

56766-371-0). 32pp. A simple introduction to Japan, with many color photos and basic information on geography, history, people, and customs. (Rev: BL 2/1/98) [952]

**12261** Tames, Richard. *Exploration into Japan* (5–7). Illus. Series: Exploration. 1996, Dillon LB $15.95 (0-02-751390-4); paper $7.95 (0-382-39186-1). 48pp. A brief history of Japan is given, including the effects of early Western influences. (Rev: BL 8/96) [952]

**12262** Tames, Richard. *Journey Through Japan* (3–5). Illus. by Martin Camm. Series: Journey Around the World. 1990, Troll LB $13.95 (0-8167-2114-9); paper $4.95 (0-8167-2115-7). 32pp. Japan is explored, including its crowded cities, natural beauty, ceremonies, and modern technological advances. (Rev: BL 5/15/91; SLJ 5/91) [952]

**12263** Tames, Richard, and Sheila Tames. *Japan* (4–6). Illus. Series: Country Topics for Crafts. 1994, Watts LB $20.00 (0-531-14315-5). 48pp. The culture of Japan is explored in text, pictures, and a number of appropriate craft projects. (Rev: BL 3/15/95) [952]

**12264** Tyler, Deborah. *Japan* (3–5). Illus. Series: Discovering. 1993, Crestwood LB $13.95 (0-89686-773-0). 32pp. A brief introduction to modern Japan that stresses its distinctive culture and modern accomplishments. (Rev: BL 2/1/94) [952]

**12265** Zurlo, Tony. *Japan: Superpower of the Pacific* (5–8). Illus. Series: Discovering Our Heritage. 1991, Macmillan LB $14.95 (0-87518-480-4). 128pp. Following a section on basic facts, this book concentrates on modern history and the problems of this island kingdom. (Rev: BL 2/1/92; SLJ 4/92) [952]

## Other Asian Lands

**12266** *Afghanistan in Pictures* (5–8). Illus. 1997, Lerner LB $19.93 (0-8225-1849-X). 64pp. Includes sections on vegetation and wildlife, minerals, cities, history, and government. (Rev: BL 5/1/89)

**12267** Ali, Sharifah Enayat. *Afghanistan* (4–7). Illus. Series: Cultures of the World. 1995, Marshall Cavendish LB $34.21 (0-7614-0177-6). 128pp. After general background information, this account focuses on the arts, leisure activities, and festivals of the people of Afghanistan. (Rev: BL 1/1–15/96; SLJ 4/96) [958.1]

**12268** Ashby, Gwynneth. *A Family in South Korea* (3–6). Illus. 1987, Lerner LB $18.60 (0-8225-1675-6). 32pp. Some native words and details of daily life help give a good sense of how South Korean children live. (Rev: BL 2/1/88)

**12269** Bennett, Gay. *A Family in Sri Lanka* (3–6). Illus. 1985, Lerner LB $18.60 (0-8225-1661-6).

32pp. The focus is on one family member in this look at the everyday life of a family in this small nation. (Rev: BL 11/15/85)

**12270** Brace, Steve. *Bangladesh* (4–8). Illus. Series: Economically Developing Countries. 1995, Thomson Learning LB $24.26 (1-56847-243-9). 48pp. An overview of life in Bangladesh told in a simple, large-print text and many color photos. (Rev: SLJ 7/95) [954.9]

**12271** Brill, Marlene T. *Mongolia* (5–8). Illus. Series: Enchantment of the World. 1992, Children's LB $32.00 (0-516-02605-4). 128pp. This little-known and isolated Asian country is introduced with material on its history, people, and geography. (Rev: BL 6/1/92) [951.7]

**12272** Brown, Marion M. *Singapore* (4–6). Illus. Series: Enchantment of the World. 1989, Children's LB $28.70 (0-516-02715-8). 128pp. In this introduction, topics covered include geography, history, key attractions, and important people. (Rev: BL 1/1/90; SLJ 4/90) [959.57]

**12273** Burbank, Jon. *Nepal* (4–7). Illus. Series: Cultures of the World. 1991, Marshall Cavendish LB $34.21 (1-85435-401-9). 128pp. The emphasis is on culture as well as the basics of geography, history, government, and people. (Rev: BL 2/15/92) [954.96]

**12274** *Cambodia in Pictures* (5–8). Illus. Series: Visual Geography. 1996, Lerner LB $19.93 (0-8225-1905-4). 64pp. Cambodia is introduced, with accurate text and many photos, maps, and charts. (Rev: BL 11/15/96) [959.6]

**12275** Cha, Dia. *Dia's Story Cloth* (3–5). Illus. by Chue Cha and Nhia Thao Cha. 1996, Lee & Low $15.95 (1-880000-34-2). 32pp. The story of the author's family, who fled first from Laos and then from Thailand to settle in the United States. (Rev: BCCB 7–8/96; BL 6/1–15/96; SLJ 7/96) [973]

**12276** Clifford, Mary Louise. *The Land and People of Afghanistan* (5–7). Illus. 1989, HarperCollins LB $14.89 (0-397-32339-5). 240pp. An introduction to past life in this central Asian country. A reissue.

**12277** Cromie, Alice. *Taiwan* (5–8). Illus. Series: Enchantment of the World. 1994, Children's LB $32.00 (0-516-02627-5). 128pp. In an attractive format with many color photos, this Asian nation is introduced, with material on such topics as history, government, people, and economy. (Rev: BL 12/15/94) [951.24]

**12278** Day, Noreha Yussof. *Kancil and the Crocodiles: A Tale from Malaysia* (K–3). Illus. by Britta Teckentrup. 1996, Simon & Schuster paper $16.00 (0-689-80954-9). 32pp. Kancil, a trickster mouse, fools the crocodiles so that he can have a delicious meal. (Rev: BCCB 1/97; BL 12/15/96; SLJ 12/96) [398.2]

**12279** Dolphin, Laurie. *Our Journey from Tibet* (3–6). Illus. 1997, Dutton paper $15.99 (0-525-45577-9). 40pp. Told in text and photos, this is the story of young Sonam, who fled Tibet to live in the Tibetan Children's Village in India. (Rev: BL 8/97; SLJ 8/97) [951]

**12280** Foster, Leila M. *Afghanistan* (5–8). Illus. Series: Enchantment of the World. 1996, Children's LB $32.00 (0-516-20017-8). 127pp. This introduction to the troubled land torn by civil war emphasizes its history, geography, and people. (Rev: BL 1/1–15/97) [958.1]

**12281** Garland, Sherry. *Vietnam: Rebuilding a Nation* (4–6). Illus. 1990, Macmillan $14.95 (0-87518-422-7). 127pp. This overview of Vietnam describes landscape, people, history, and culture. (Rev: BL 4/1/90*) [959.7]

**12282** Gogol, Sara. *A Mien Family* (4–7). Illus. Series: Journey Between Two Worlds. 1996, Lerner LB $22.60 (0-8225-3407-X); paper $8.95 (0-8225-9745-4). 64pp. The story of a refugee family from the mountainous area of Laos and of its journey to the United States. (Rev: BL 11/15/96; SLJ 1/97) [306.85]

**12283** Goodman, Jim. *Thailand* (4–6). Illus. Series: Cultures of the World. 1991, Marshall Cavendish LB $34.21 (1-85435-402-7). 128pp. This account stresses both the history and the culture of Thailand as well as the contemporary problems it is facing. (Rev: BL 3/15/92) [959.3]

**12284** Goom, Bridget. *A Family in Singapore* (3–4). Illus. 1986, Lerner LB $18.60 (0-8225-1663-2). 32pp. With the focus on one child in one family, readers discover what life is like in Singapore. (Rev: BL 5/15/86; SLJ 10/86)

**12285** Hansen, Ole Steen. *Vietnam* (5–8). Illus. Series: Economically Developing Countries. 1996, Raintree Steck-Vaughn LB $24.26 (0-8172-4526-X). 48pp. This introduction to Vietnam includes background information and material on its emerging economy. (Rev: BL 3/1/97) [959.7]

**12286** Heinrichs, Ann. *Nepal* (5–8). Illus. Series: Enchantment of the World. 1996, Children's LB $29.70 (0-516-02642-0). 123pp. Using color photos on each page, this attractive book introduces the history, geography, and people of Nepal. (Rev: BL 7/96) [954.96]

**12287** Heinrichs, Ann. *Tibet* (5–8). Illus. Series: Enchantment of the World. 1996, Children's LB $32.00 (0-516-20155-7). 160pp. An introduction to the history, land, and people of this country, now under the occupation of China. (Rev: BL 1/1–15/97) [951]

**12288** Huynh, Quang Nhuong. *Water Buffalo Days* (4–6). Illus. 1997, HarperCollins LB $13.89 (0-06-024958-7). 128pp. This is the story of growing up in rural Vietnam in the late 1940s and of a family's water buffalo, Tank. (Rev: BL 11/15/97; SLJ 2/98*) [636.2]

**12289** Jacobs, Judy. *Indonesia: A Nation of Islands* (4–8). Illus. Series: Discovering Our Heritage. 1990, Macmillan LB $14.95 (0-87518-423-5). 127pp. History and geography of the major Indonesian islands. (Rev: SLJ 9/90) [959.8]

**12290** Jacobsen, Karen. *Korea* (1–4). Illus. Series: New True Books. 1989, Children's LB $21.00 (0-516-01174-X). 48pp. In its exploration of Korea and its culture, this book contains old prints and other historical illustrations as well as modern color photos. (Rev: BL 2/1/90; SLJ 5/90) [951.9]

**12291** Jacobsen, Karen. *Vietnam* (1–4). Illus. Series: New True Books. 1992, Children's LB $20.00 (0-516-01147-2). 48pp. Through pictures and a simple text, Vietnam, now united, is introduced. (Rev: BL 5/15/92) [959.7]

**12292** Jung, Sung-Hoon. *South Korea* (5–8). Illus. Series: Economically Developing Countries. 1997, Raintree Steck-Vaughn LB $24.26 (0-8172-4530-8). 48pp. This overview of current economic conditions in South Korea describes the country's success with electronic exports and provides case studies of family-run companies. (Rev: BL 5/15/97) [951.95]

**12293** Kalman, Bobbie. *Vietnam: The Culture* (3–5). Illus. Series: Lands, Peoples, and Cultures. 1996, Crabtree LB $19.16 (0-86505-225-5); paper $7.95 (0-86505-305-7). 32pp. With many color illustrations, this account discusses such topics as Vietnamese arts, festivals, processions, food, and games. (Rev: BL 8/96; SLJ 11/96) [959.7]

**12294** Kalman, Bobbie. *Vietnam: The Land* (3–5). Illus. Series: Lands, Peoples, and Cultures. 1996, Crabtree LB $19.16 (0-86505-223-9); paper $7.95 (0-86505-303-0). 32pp. The geography of Vietnam is introduced with sections on farming, cities, and famous monuments. (Rev: BL 8/96; SLJ 11/96) [959.7]

**12295** Kalman, Bobbie. *Vietnam: The People* (3–5). Illus. Series: Lands, Peoples, and Cultures. 1996, Crabtree LB $19.16 (0-86505-224-7); paper $7.95 (0-86505-304-9). 32pp. Covers such topics related to Vietnam family life, life in the country and in the city, clothes, and daily life. (Rev: BL 8/96; SLJ 11/96) [959.7]

**12296** Karkonen, Reijo. *The Children of Nepal* (4–6). Illus. by Matti Pitkanen. Series: World's Children. 1990, Carolrhoda LB $21.27 (0-87614-395-8). 40pp. Comments on life in Nepal, with striking color photos. (Rev: BL 6/15/90; SLJ 8/90) [954.96]

**12297** Koh, Frances M. *Korean Holidays and Festivals* (2–5). Illus. by Liz B. Dodson. 1990, EastWest LB $15.95 (0-9606090-5-9). 32pp. Nine holidays and cultural festivals that are celebrated in South Korea are described. (Rev: BL 3/1/91; SLJ 6/91) [394.25]

**12298** *Laos in Pictures* (5–8). Illus. Series: Visual Geography. 1996, Lerner LB $19.93 (0-8225-1906-2). 64pp. The past and present of Laos are introduced using a simple text and many illustrations, including maps and charts. (Rev: BL 11/15/96) [959.4]

**12299** Lauré, Jason. *Bangladesh* (5–8). Illus. Series: Enchantment of the World. 1992, Children's LB $32.00 (0-516-02609-7). 126pp. The history, culture, and economic problems of this crowded Asian land are covered. (Rev: BL 11/15/92; SLJ 1/93) [954.92]

**12300** Layton, Lesley. *Singapore* (5–8). Illus. Series: Cultures of the World. 1990, Marshall Cavendish LB $34.21 (1-85435-295-4). 128pp. As well as history and economy, this introduction to Singapore includes coverage on life-styles and current problems. (Rev: BL 3/1/91; SLJ 6/91) [959.57]

**12301** Levy, Patricia. *Tibet* (4–7). Illus. Series: Cultures of the World. 1996, Marshall Cavendish LB $34.21 (0-7614-0277-2). 128pp. Tibet is introduced with general background information, followed by material on its people and their culture, festivals, and food. (Rev: BL 8/96; SLJ 9/96) [951.1]

**12302** Lorbiecki, Marybeth. *Children of Vietnam* (4–7). Photos by Paul P. Rome. Series: The World's Children. 1997, Carolrhoda LB $21.27 (1-57505-034-X). 45pp. Beginning in the north and working south, this photoessay describes the people of Vietnam and the lives of their children. (Rev: SLJ 2/98) [959.7]

**12303** McNair, Sylvia. *Indonesia* (5–8). Illus. Series: Enchantment of the World. 1993, Children's LB $32.00 (0-516-02618-6). 128pp. Introduces the history, geography, and peoples of this vast country, the world's largest island group. (Rev: BL 11/1/93; SLJ 3/94) [959.8]

**12304** McNair, Sylvia. *Korea* (4–6). Illus. 1986, Children's LB $32.00 (0-516-02771-9). 127pp. Geography, culture, economy, and history are featured, as well as tourist sights. (Rev: BL 8/15/86; SLJ 10/86)

**12305** *Malaysia in Pictures* (5–8). Illus. 1997, Lerner LB $19.93 (0-8225-1854-6). 64pp. Basic coverage from people to the land in this Visual Geography addition. (Rev: BL 5/1/89)

**12306** Matthews, Jo. *I Remember Vietnam* (3–6). Photos by Tim Page. Illus. Series: Why We Left. 1995, Raintree Steck-Vaughn LB $22.83 (0-8114-5605-6). 32pp. The geography, history, culture, and social institutions of Vietnam are introduced through the eyes of refugee children who have left their homeland with their parents. (Rev: SLJ 6/95) [959.7]

**12307** Mirpuri, Gouri. *Indonesia* (5–8). Illus. Series: Cultures of the World. 1990, Marshall Cavendish LB $34.21 (1-85435-294-6). 128pp. Present-day problems and concerns of Indonesia are covered, as well as information on history and geography. (Rev: BL 3/1/91) [959.8]

**12308** Moiz, Azra. *Taiwan* (4–7). Illus. Series: Cultures of the World. 1995, Marshall Cavendish LB $34.21 (0-7614-0180-6). 128pp. The accomplishments, life-style, and religious festivals of the people of Taiwan are covered, along with its history and geography. (Rev: BL 1/1–15/96; SLJ 9/96) [957.24]

**12309** Munan, Heidi. *Malaysia* (5–8). Illus. Series: Cultures of the World. 1990, Marshall Cavendish LB $34.21 (1-85435-296-2). 128pp. Cultural diversity and life-styles of the people are 2 topics covered in this introduction to Malaysia. (Rev: BL 3/1/91) [959.5]

**12310** Oshihara, Yuzuro. *Malaysia* (3–7). Illus. 1987, Stevens LB $25.27 (1-55532-160-7). 64pp. A child's life is portrayed, as are reference facts about this land. (Rev: BL 6/1/87)

**12311** *Pakistan in Pictures* (5–8). Illus. Series: Visual Geography. 1996, Lerner LB $19.93 (0-8225-1850-3). 64pp. Photos, charts, and maps help to introduce the country of Pakistan. (Rev: BL 9/15/89) [954.9]

**12312** Ramulshah, Mano. *Pakistan* (3–8). Illus. 1992, Viking $22.95 (0-237-60193-1). 32pp. Famous landmarks, social and political life, and history are discussed. (Rev: SLJ 8/92) [954]

**12313** Reynolds, Jan. *Himalaya: Vanishing Cultures* (3–5). Illus. Series: Vanishing Cultures. 1991, Harcourt $17.00 (0-15-234465-9). 32pp. A photoessay in the National Geographic style about people whose way of life is disappearing. (Rev: BCCB 11/91; BL 9/1/91; SLJ 10/91) [954.96]

**12314** Rowell, Jonathan. *Malaysia* (5–8). Illus. Series: Economically Developing Countries. 1997, Raintree Steck-Vaughn LB $24.26 (0-8172-4531-6). 48pp. The growth and development of Malaysia are traced, with material on its new technology ventures. Also use in this series *Peru* and *Mexico* (both 1996). (Rev: BL 5/15/97) [959.505]

**12315** Schmidt, Jeremy, and Ted Wood. *Two Lands, One Heart: An American Boy's Journey to His Mother's Vietnam* (3–5). Illus. 1995, Walker LB $16.85 (0-8027-8358-9). 48pp. A young boy is introduced to the culture and life of contemporary Vietnam when he visits his mother's homeland. (Rev: BCCB 6/95; BL 5/1/95; SLJ 4/95) [915.97]

**12316** Schwabach, Karen. *Thailand: Land of Smiles* (5–8). Illus. Series: Discovering Our Heritage. 1991, Macmillan LB $14.95 (0-87518-454-5). 128pp. Explores the land and people of Thailand, with a chapter on the immigrants who have come to the United States. (Rev: BL 4/1/91; SLJ 7/91) [959.3]

**12317** Sheehan, Sean. *Cambodia* (4–7). Illus. Series: Cultures of the World. 1996, Marshall Cavendish LB $34.21 (0-7614-0281-0). 128pp. The troubled land of Cambodia is introduced, with emphasis on its people, their life-styles, and culture. (Rev: BL 8/96; SLJ 9/96) [959]

**12318** Sheehan, Sean. *Pakistan* (5–8). Illus. Series: Cultures of the World. 1993, Marshall Cavendish LB $34.21 (1-85435-583-X). 128pp. This informative account describes the history and culture of Pakistan, with coverage of its economy and how its people live. (Rev: SLJ 2/94) [954.9]

**12319** *South Korea in Pictures* (5–7). Series: Visual Geography. 1997, Lerner LB $19.93 (0-8225-1868-6). 64pp. Introduction to South Korea that focuses on its politics and economy. (Rev: SLJ 5/90) [951.9]

**12320** *Thailand in Pictures* (5–8). Illus. Series: Visual Geography. 1994, Lerner LB $19.93 (0-8225-1866-X). 64pp. Thailand is presented in this well-illustrated account. (Rev: BL 9/15/89; SLJ 5/90) [959.3]

**12321** Thomson, Ruth, and Neil Thomson. *A Family in Thailand* (4–6). Illus. 1988, Lerner LB $18.60 (0-8225-1684-5). 32pp. Thai children point out the characteristics of life in their country. (Rev: BL 8/88)

**12322** *Vietnam in Pictures* (5–8). Illus. Series: Visual Geography. 1994, Lerner LB $19.93 (0-8225-1909-7). 64pp. This well-illustrated account of Vietnam covers its history, geography, people, government, and economy. (Rev: BL 11/1/94) [915.97]

**12323** Wanasundera, Nanda P. *Sri Lanka* (4–7). Illus. Series: Cultures of the World. 1991, Marshall Cavendish LB $195.02 (1-85435-397-7). 128pp. The history, geography, and culture of Sri Lanka are introduced with an emphasis on contemporary problems. (Rev: BL 2/15/92) [954.93]

**12324** Withington, William A. *Southeast Asia* (5–8). Illus. 1988, Gateway $16.95 (0-934291-32-2). 160pp. Sections on life-style, land and climate, history and government, festivals, sports, arts, and crafts. (Rev: BL 12/1/88)

**12325** Wright, David K. *Brunei* (5–8). Illus. Series: Enchantment of the World. 1991, Children's LB $32.00 (0-516-02602-X). 128pp. The country of Brunei is introduced with many photographs covering its geography, history, and culture. (Rev: BL 2/1/92) [959.55]

**12326** Wright, David K. *Burma* (5–8). Illus. Series: Enchantment of the World. 1991, Children's LB $32.00 (0-516-02725-5). 128pp. The land and people of Myanmar (Burma), together with its culture and history, are covered in this colorful introduction. (Rev: BL 8/91; SLJ 9/91) [788.9]

**12327** Wright, David K. *Hong Kong* (3–5). Illus. Series: Children of the World. 1991, Stevens LB $12.95 (0-8368-0382-5). 64pp. Daily life in Hong Kong, including activities at school and at home, is shown through the eyes of one child. (Rev: BL 7/91) [951]

**12328** Wright, David K. *Vietnam* (4–7). Illus. 1989, Children's LB $36.00 (0-516-02712-3). 128pp. Standard information is highlighted by color illustrations and war coverage. (Rev: BL 8/89; SLJ 1/90) [959.7]

**12329** Yu, Ling. *Taiwan in Pictures* (5–8). Illus. Series: Visual Geography. 1997, Lerner LB $19.93 (0-8225-1865-1). 64pp. The history and geography of Taiwan are introduced, with coverage on cities, culture, religion, and economy. (Rev: BL 9/15/89) [915.1]

**12330** Yusufali, Jabeen. *Pakistan: An Islamic Treasure* (4–8). Illus. Series: Discovering Our Heritage. 1990, Macmillan LB $14.95 (0-87518-433-2). 128pp. This book covers the country of Pakistan from its foundation in 1947 to the present, with coverage on economy, geography, and more. (Rev: BL 7/90; SLJ 8/90) [954.91]

**12331** Zimmermann, Robert. *Sri Lanka* (5–8). Illus. Series: Enchantment of the World. 1992, Children's LB $32.00 (0-516-02606-2). 128pp. In addition to background information on the history and geography of Sri Lanka, this book provides material on its current problems. (Rev: BL 6/1/92) [954.93]

## Australia and the Pacific Islands

**12332** Arnold, Caroline. *A Walk on the Great Barrier Reef* (4–7). Illus. 1988, Lerner LB $14.95 (0-87614-285-4). 48pp. Exploring one of the great natural wonders of the world. (Rev: BL 7/88; SLJ 8/88)

**12333** Browne, Rollo. *An Aboriginal Family* (3–6). Illus. 1985, Lerner LB $13.95 (0-8225-1655-1). 32pp. A taste of aboriginal culture is highlighted with color photos. (Rev: BCCB 6/85; BL 6/15/85; SLJ 10/85)

**12334** Cooper, Rod, and Emilie Cooper. *Journey Through Australia* (3–5). Illus. Series: Journey Around the World. 1994, Troll LB $13.95 (0-8167-2757-0). 32pp. This brief tour of Australia introduces its most important regions and cities. (Rev: SLJ 8/94) [919.4]

**12335** Darian-Smith, Kate. *Exploration into Australia* (5–7). Illus. Series: Exploration. 1996, Dillon LB $15.95 (0-02-718088-3); paper $7.95 (0-382-39227-2). 48pp. Descriptions are given of the prehistory of Australia and the changes made after European exploration. (Rev: BL 8/96; SLJ 9/96) [994]

**12336** Darian-Smith, Kate, and David Lowe. *The Australian Outback and Its People* (4–7). Illus. Series: People and Places. 1995, Thomson Learning LB $24.26 (1-56847-337-0). 48pp. A well-organized guide to the Australian outback, its exploration and history, flora and fauna, mining, environmental issues, and people. (Rev: SLJ 7/95) [994]

**12337** Dolce, Laura. *Australia* (5–7). Illus. 1990, Chelsea LB $19.95 (0-7910-1105-4). 127pp. An introduction to Australia concentrating on history, geography, and life-styles. (Rev: SLJ 8/90) [994]

**12338** Fox, Mary V. *New Zealand* (5–8). Illus. Series: Enchantment of the World. 1991, Children's LB $32.00 (0-516-02728-X). 128pp. This island country is introduced in text and pictures that cover geography, history, the people, and key attractions. (Rev: BL 10/1/91) [992]

**12339** Gallagher, Debbie. *The Kimberley* (5–8). Illus. Series: Ends of the Earth. 1997, Heinemann $14.95 (0-431-06933-6). 48pp. The story of this remote part of Western Australia. (Rev: SLJ 11/97) [994]

**12340** Hermes, Jules. *The Children of Micronesia* (4–6). Illus. Series: World's Children. 1994, Carolrhoda LB $21.27 (0-87614-819-4). 48pp. A look at growing up in these South Pacific islands, including the Caroline, Gilbert, and Marshall island groups. (Rev: BCCB 9/94; BL 9/15/94) [996.5]

**12341** Keyworth, Valerie. *New Zealand: Land of the Long White Cloud* (4–7). Illus. Series: Discovering Our Heritage. 1990, Macmillan LB $14.95 (0-87518-414-6). 111pp. New Zealand is introduced with information on people, history, culture, and geography. (Rev: SLJ 1/91) [993.1]

**12342** Kinkade, Sheila. *Children of the Philippines* (3–6). Illus. Series: World's Children. 1996, Carolrhoda LB $21.27 (0-87614-993-X). 48pp. Through the stories of children, the history, geography, and culture of the Philippines are covered. (Rev: BL 12/1/96; SLJ 12/96) [959.9]

**12343** Krasno, Rena. *Kneeling Carabao and Dancing Giants: Celebrating Filipino Festivals* (4–6). Illus. by Ileana C. Lee. 1997, Pacific View $19.95 (1-881896-15-3). 48pp. Contains information on Filipino festivals, customs, folktales, games, and activities. (Rev: BL 12/1/97) [394]

**12344** Lepthien, Emilie U. *The Philippines* (4–7). 1986, Children's LB $32.00 (0-516-02782-4). 128pp. These islands are introduced through a discussion of their history, geography, and culture.

**12345** Lowre, David, and Andrea Shimmen. *Australia* (5–8). Illus. Series: Modern Industrial World. 1996, Raintree Steck-Vaughn LB $24.26 (0-8172-4553-7). 48pp. The present economic status, living

standards, educational system, and industry in Australia are covered. (Rev: BL 2/15/97) [919.4]

**12346** Macdonald, Robert. *Islands of the Pacific Rim and Their People* (5–8). Illus. Series: People and Places. 1994, Thomson Learning LB $24.26 (1-56847-167-X). 48pp. An overview of the islands of the Pacific Ocean and their people, different environments, and economies. (Rev: BL 10/15/94; SLJ 10/94) [990]

**12347** Meisel, Jacqueline D. *Australia: The Land Down Under* (3–5). Illus. Series: Exploring Cultures of the World. 1997, Marshall Cavendish LB $25.64 (0-7614-0139-3). 64pp. A description of various aspects of life in Australia, with material on the range of races and life-styles. (Rev: BL 7/97; SLJ 4/98) [994]

**12348** NgCheong-Lum, Roseline. *Tahiti* (4–7). Illus. Series: Cultures of the World. 1997, Marshall Cavendish LB $34.21 (0-7614-0682-4). 128pp. Background material on history and geography is given, with information on how Tahitians live today. (Rev: BL 8/97) [919.62]

**12349** Nile, Richard. *Australian Aborigines* (4–7). Illus. Series: Threatened Cultures. 1993, Raintree Steck-Vaughn LB $24.26 (0-8114-2303-4). 48pp. The aboriginal culture of Australia is presented. (Rev: BL 8/93; SLJ 8/93) [305]

**12350** Rajendra, Vijeya, and Sundran Rajendra. *Australia* (4–7). Illus. Series: Cultures of the World. 1991, Marshall Cavendish LB $34.21 (1-85435-400-0). 128pp. Beyond the basics, this volumes highlights contemporary problems and concerns in the Land Down Under. (Rev: BL 2/15/92; SLJ 3/92) [994]

**12351** Reynolds, Jan. *Down Under: Vanishing Cultures* (3–6). Illus. Series: Vanishing Cultures. 1992, Harcourt $16.95 (0-15-224182-5). 32pp. A close look at the Tiwi aborigines of Australia, who live as they have for thousands of years. (Rev: BCCB 4/92; BL 3/15/92; SLJ 5/92) [994.8]

**12352** Sullivan, Margaret. *The Philippines: Pacific Crossroads* (4–8). Illus. Series: Discovering Our Heritage. 1993, Macmillan LB $14.95 (0-87518-548-7). 127pp. A history with emphasis on relations with the United States and current developments. (Rev: SLJ 8/93) [959.9]

**12353** Tope, Lily R. *Philippines* (4–7). Illus. Series: Cultures of the World. 1991, Marshall Cavendish LB $34.21 (1-85435-403-5). 128pp. With emphasis on contemporary problems and concerns, the land and culture of the Philippines are introduced in text and well-chosen color photographs. (Rev: BL 2/15/92) [959.9]

**12354** Truby, David. *Take a Trip to Australia* (2–4). Illus. 1981, Watts LB $10.90 (0-531-00988-2). 32pp.

A brief account giving basic material on geography and the way of life in Australia.

**12355** Wilson, Barbara K. *Acacia Terrace* (2–4). Illus. by David Fielding. 1990, Scholastic $13.95 (0-590-42885-3). 40pp. This is the story of a family's fortunes and misfortunes through the years in a small section of Australia. (Rev: BL 2/15/90) [994.4]

# Europe

## General

**12356** Durbin, Chris. *The European Community* (4–6). Illus. Series: Places and Peoples. 1994, Watts LB $20.80 (0-531-14261-2). 32pp. A view of the European Community, its composition, purposes, and economy. (Rev: BL 12/1/94) [914]

## Central and Eastern Europe

**12357** Baralt, Luis A. *Turkey* (5–8). Illus. Series: Enchantment of the World. 1997, Children's LB $32.00 (0-516-20305-3). 128pp. A visually attractive book that covers such topics as Turkey's population, natural resources, historic landmarks, and people. (Rev: BL 8/97) [915.61]

**12358** Burke, Patrick. *Eastern Europe* (3–6). Illus. Series: Country Fact Files. 1997, Raintree Steck-Vaughn LB $24.26 (0-8172-4628-2). 45pp. An overview of current governmental, economic, and social conditions in the Czech Republic, Slovakia, Bulgaria, Romania, Poland, and Hungary. (Rev: BL 7/97; SLJ 8/97) [947]

**12359** Carran, Betty B. *Romania* (4–7). Illus. 1988, Children's LB $32.00 (0-516-02703-4). 124pp. Coverage includes geography, culture, history, and politics. (Rev: BL 8/88)

**12360** *Cyprus in Pictures* (5–8). Illus. Series: Visual Geography. 1992, Lerner LB $19.93 (0-8225-1910-0). 64pp. In addition to describing the history and geography of this rugged island, efforts to reunite its Turkish and Greek zones are described. (Rev: BL 2/1/93) [956.45]

**12361** *Czech Republic in Pictures* (5–8). Illus. Series: Visual Geography. 1995, Lerner LB $19.93 (0-8225-1879-1). 64pp. Text, pictures, charts, and maps provide a basic introduction to the new Czech Republic. (Rev: BL 8/95) [943.7]

**12362** Feinstein, Steve. *Turkey in Pictures* (5–8). Illus. 1989, Lerner LB $19.93 (0-8225-1831-7). 64pp. Lots of visual coverage in this overview. (Rev: BL 8/88)

**12363** Flint, David. *Bosnia: Can There Ever Be Peace?* (4–6). Illus. Series: Topics in the News. 1995,

Raintree Steck-Vaughn LB $22.83 (0-8172-4176-0). 32pp. In a newspaperlike format, this book describes in text and pictures the Bosnian situation as of 1995. (Rev: BL 3/1/96) [949.7]

**12364** Fox, Mary V. *Cyprus* (5–8). Illus. Series: Enchantment of the World. 1993, Children's LB $32.00 (0-516-02617-8). 128pp. An introduction to this Mediterranean island, its troubled history, and its present division between Turkey and Greece. (Rev: BL 11/1/93; SLJ 3/94) [956.93]

**12365** Ganeri, Anita. *I Remember Bosnia* (3–6). Illus. Series: Why We Left. 1995, Raintree Steck-Vaughn LB $22.83 (0-8114-5607-2). 32pp. An introduction to Bosnia that gives good background material and an explanation of the recent political and military problems. (Rev: BCCB 3/95; SLJ 6/95) [949.702]

**12366** Greenberg, Keith E. *Bosnia: Civil War in Europe* (3–5). Photos by John Isaac. Series: Children in Crisis. 1996, Blackbirch LB $14.95 (1-56711-186-6). 31pp. The hardships faced by children in Bosnia because of the civil war are re-created through first-person accounts and many photos. (Rev: SLJ 12/96) [949.6]

**12367** Greene, Carol. *Austria* (4–6). Illus. 1986, Children's LB $32.00 (0-516-02756-5). 126pp. This book features tourist sights, work and lives of the people, and general information. (Rev: BL 8/86; SLJ 10/86)

**12368** Hintz, Martin. *Switzerland* (4–6). Illus. 1986, Children's LB $32.00 (0-516-02790-5). 128pp. Standard, useful information highlighted by color photos. (Rev: BL 4/1/87; SLJ 5/87)

**12369** *Hungary in Pictures* (5–8). Illus. Series: Visual Geography. 1993, Lerner LB $19.93 (0-8225-1883-X). 64pp. With concise text and extensive photographs, the past and present of Hungary are introduced. (Rev: BL 12/1/93; SLJ 12/93) [943.9]

**12370** Kagda, Sakina. *Lithuania* (4–7). Illus. Series: Cultures of the World. 1997, Marshall Cavendish LB $34.21 (0-7614-0681-6). 128pp. The story of this small republic, once part of the Soviet Union, and of its distinctive culture, traditions, and customs. (Rev: BL 8/97; SLJ 10/97) [947.93]

**12371** Levy, Patricia. *Switzerland* (4–6). Illus. Series: Cultures of the World. 1994, Marshall Cavendish LB $34.21 (1-85435-591-0). 128pp. This attractive introduction to Switzerland includes material on lifestyles, economy, geography, arts, and leisure. (Rev: SLJ 7/94) [949.4]

**12372** Pfeiffer, Christine. *Poland: Land of Freedom Fighters* (5–8). Illus. 1991, Macmillan LB $14.95 (0-87518-464-2). 144pp. An introduction to the land and people of Poland and of their migration to the United States.

**12373** Ricchiardi, Sherry. *Bosnia: The Struggle for Peace* (5–8). Illus. 1996, Millbrook LB $23.40 (0-7613-0031-7). 64pp. An account that emphasizes the recent history (through 1995) of Bosnia. (Rev: BL 7/96; SLJ 7/96) [949]

**12374** *Romania in Pictures* (5–8). Illus. Series: Visual Geography. 1993, Lerner LB $19.95 (0-8225-1894-5). 64pp. In addition to background material on history and geography, this account gives a good picture of contemporary life in Romania. (Rev: BL 9/1/93) [949.8]

**12375** Schrepfer, Margaret. *Switzerland: The Summit of Europe* (4–7). Illus. Series: Discovering Our Heritage. 1989, Macmillan LB $14.95 (0-87518-405-7). 142pp. Four ethnic groups plus Switzerland's ancient and modern history are covered in this introduction. (Rev: BL 7/89; SLJ 10/89) [949.4]

**12376** Sheehan, Sean. *Austria* (4–7). Illus. Series: Cultures of the World. 1992, Marshall Cavendish LB $34.21 (1-85435-454-X). 128pp. This introduction to Austria covers its history, life-styles of the people, and contemporary problems. (Rev: BL 10/15/92) [943.6]

**12377** Sheehan, Sean. *Turkey* (4–7). Illus. Series: Cultures of the World. 1993, Marshall Cavendish LB $34.21 (1-85435-576-7). 128pp. This introduction to Turkey covers history, culture, economics, and present-day concerns. (Rev: BL 8/93) [956.1]

**12378** *Slovakia in Pictures* (5–8). Illus. Series: Visual Geography. 1995, Lerner LB $19.93 (0-8225-1912-7). 64pp. Coverage on this newly formed nation is enhanced by many recent photos, maps, charts, and a clear text. (Rev: BL 11/15/95) [942.7305]

**12379** Steins, Richard. *Hungary: Crossroads of Europe* (3–5). Illus. Series: Exploring Cultures of the World. 1997, Marshall Cavendish LB $25.64 (0-7614-0141-5). 64pp. Current conditions in Hungary are covered, along with good background information about its people, culture, and history. (Rev: BL 7/97; SLJ 1/98) [943.9]

**12380** *Switzerland in Pictures* (5–8). Illus. Series: Visual Geography. 1996, Lerner LB $19.95 (0-8225-1895-3). 64pp. With a generous number of color pictures, this account traces the history and geography of Switzerland, with emphasis on the present day and its people. (Rev: BL 9/15/96; SLJ 8/96) [949.4]

**12381** Waterlow, Julia. *A Family from Bosnia* (3–5). Illus. 1997, Raintree Steck-Vaughn LB $24.98 (0-8172-4901-X). 32pp. A moving account of a family in Bosnia and the incredible hardships they endured during the war with Serbia. (Rev: BL 12/15/97) [949.703]

## France

**12382** Arnold, Helen. *France* (1–3). Illus. Series: Postcards From. 1995, Raintree Steck-Vaughn LB $21.40 (0-8172-4004-7). 32pp. France is introduced through a series of postcards written by fictitious children. (Rev: SLJ 2/96) [944]

**12383** Benedict, Kitty C. *The Fall of the Bastille* (5–8). Series: Turning Points in World History. 1991, Silver Burdett LB $14.95 (0-382-24129-0); paper $7.95 (0-382-24135-5). 64pp. The major factors that led to the establishment of a new France are chronicled. (Rev: BL 3/15/92) [944.04]

**12384** Butler, Daphne. *France* (2–4). Illus. Series: On the Map. 1993, Raintree Steck-Vaughn LB $22.83 (0-8114-3675-6). 32pp. An overview of life in France, with coverage of geogrphy, industry, customs, and landmarks. (Rev: BL 9/1/93) [944]

**12385** Dunford, Mick. *France* (5–8). Illus. Series: Modern Industrial World. 1994, Thomson Learning LB $24.26 (1-56847-263-3). 48pp. An introduction to modern France that gives information about government, people, economic conditions, and recent history. (Rev: BL 1/15/95) [944]

**12386** Fisher, Teresa. *France: City and Village Life* (4–7). Illus. Series: Country Insights. 1997, Raintree Steck-Vaughn LB $24.96 (0-8172-4788-2). 48pp. A specific city and village are used to compare and contrast 2 life-styles in contemporary France. (Rev: SLJ 8/97) [944]

**12387** Gamgee, John. *Journey Through France* (K–3). Illus. Series: Journey Around the World. 1994, Troll LB $13.95 (0-8167-2759-7). 32pp. An introduction to contemporary life in France using color photos and a brief text. (Rev: SLJ 9/94) [914.4]

**12388** Gilbert, Adrian. *The French Revolution* (4–6). Series: Revolution! 1995, Thomson Learning LB $24.26 (1-56847-390-7). 48pp. Beginning with the execution of Louis XVI in 1793, this account moves back in time to trace the history of the French Revolution. (Rev: SLJ 2/96) [944]

**12389** Gofen, Ethel C. *France* (4–7). Illus. Series: Cultures of the World. 1992, Marshall Cavendish LB $34.21 (1-85435-449-3). 128pp. This account provides information on the history, culture, and people of France and discusses the current problems and concerns. (Rev: BL 10/15/92) [944]

**12390** Haskins, Jim, and Kathleen Benson. *Count Your Way Through France* (2–4). Illus. by Andrea Shine. Series: Count Your Way. 1996, Carolrhoda LB $19.93 (0-87614-874-7); paper $5.95 (0-87614-972-7). 24pp. Using the numbers 1 through 10, each page contains useful information about the history, traditions, and people of France. (Rev: BL 9/15/96; SLJ 8/96) [944]

**12391** Moss, Peter, and Thelma Palmer. *France* (4–6). Illus. 1986, Children's LB $32.00 (0-516-02761-1). 128pp. Part of the Enchantment of the World series; covers all aspects of French life. (Rev: BL 4/1/87; SLJ 5/87)

**12392** Munro, Roxie. *The Inside-Outside Book of Paris* (K–3). Illus. 1992, Dutton paper $15.00 (0-525-44863-2). 48pp. This visual city guide offers many views for the young armchair traveler. (Rev: BCCB 2/92; BL 1/15/92; HB 3–4/92; SLJ 2/92) [914.4]

**12393** Powell, Jillian. *A History of France Through Art* (5–8). Illus. Series: History Through Art. 1996, Thomson Learning LB $24.26 (1-56847-441-5). 48pp. In 21 double-page spreads, the history of France is re-created through text and art reproductions. (Rev: BL 3/1/96; SLJ 2/96) [944]

**12394** Shuter, Jane, ed. *Helen Williams and the French Revolution* (5–8). Illus. Series: History Eyewitness. 1996, Raintree Steck-Vaughn LB $24.26 (0-8114-8287-1). 48pp. An abridged firsthand account describes the causes and the course of the French Revolution. (Rev: BL 5/15/96; SLJ 6/96) [944.04]

**12395** Stein, R. Conrad. *Paris* (3–6). Illus. Series: Cities of the World. 1996, Children's LB $25.00 (0-516-20026-7). 64pp. The City of Light is introduced, with material on its history, people, culture, and present status. (Rev: BL 1/1–15/97) [944]

**12396** Sturges, Jo. *France* (3–5). Illus. Series: Discovering. 1993, Crestwood LB $13.95 (0-89686-778-1). 32pp. This brief review of French life covers geography, history, holidays, food, entertainment, and landmarks. (Rev: BL 2/1/94; SLJ 12/93) [944]

## Germany

**12397** Ayer, Eleanor. *Germany: In the Heartland of Europe* (4–6). Illus. Series: Exploring Cultures of the World. 1996, Benchmark LB $25.64 (0-7614-0189-X). 64pp. Good background material on Germany is presented, with special emphasis on the arts, sports, leisure, holidays, and festivals. (Rev: SLJ 6/96) [943]

**12398** Ballard, Robert D. *Exploring the Bismarck* (5–8). Illus. 1991, Scholastic $15.95 (0-590-44268-6). 64pp. This is an account of the history and rediscovery of the German battleship Bismarck, which was sunk over 50 years ago. (Rev: BL 1/1/91; SLJ 8/91) [943]

**12399** Flint, David. *Germany* (2–4). Illus. Series: On the Map. 1993, Raintree Steck-Vaughn LB $22.83 (0-8114-3418-4). 32pp. In text and color photos, unified Germany is introduced and such topics as geography, industry, customs, and landmarks are covered. (Rev: BL 2/1/94) [943]

**12400** Fuller, Barbara. *Germany* (4–7). Illus. Series: Cultures of the World. 1992, Marshall Cavendish LB $34.21 (1-85435-530-9). 128pp. In addition to the usual information on the history and geography of Germany, this account stresses how the people live and their traditions. (Rev: BL 1/1/93) [943]

**12401** *Germany in Pictures* (5–8). Illus. Series: Visual Geography. 1994, Lerner LB $19.93 (0-8225-1873-2). 64pp. The new Germany is introduced with a basic text and copious illustrations, including maps, charts, and attractive photos. (Rev: BL 1/15/95) [943]

**12402** Hargrove, Jim. *Germany* (5–8). Illus. Series: Enchantment of the World. 1991, Children's LB $32.00 (0-516-02601-1). 128pp. German geography, people, culture, and history through reunification are covered in text and pictures. (Rev: BL 2/1/92) [943]

**12403** Haskins, Jim. *Count Your Way Through Germany* (2–4). Illus. by Helen Byers. Series: Count Your Way. 1990, Carolrhoda LB $19.93 (0-87614-407-5). The reader is introduced to Germany through numbers. (Rev: SLJ 8/90) [943]

**12404** Lord, Richard. *Germany* (3–5). Illus. Series: Festivals of the World. 1997, Gareth Stevens LB $19.93 (0-8368-1682-X). 32pp. Such German festivals as St. Martin's Day, Karneval, St. Nikolaus Day and Christmas, Oktoberfest, and Walpurgis Night are introduced and described. (Rev: SLJ 1/98) [943]

**12405** Mirable, Lisa. *The Berlin Wall* (5–8). Series: Turning Points in World History. 1991, Silver Burdett LB $14.95 (0-382-24133-9); paper $7.95 (0-382-24140-1). 64pp. How the fall of the Berlin Wall dramatically changed German history. (Rev: BL 3/15/92) [943.1]

**12406** Peters, Sonja. *A Family from Germany* (3–5). Series: Families Around the World. 1997, Raintree Steck-Vaughn LB $15.48 (0-8172-4905-2). 32pp. Introduces the Pfitzner family of Cologne and such everyday activities as a swimming lesson, a carnival parade, and the beginnings of a Lenten observance. (Rev: BL 2/15/98) [943]

**12407** Pollard, Michael. *The Rhine* (5–8). Illus. Series: Great Rivers. 1997, Benchmark LB $21.36 (0-7614-0500-3). 45pp. The history of the Rhine is told, with material on legends, canals, tributaries, tourism, habitats, and current ecological problems. (Rev: SLJ 3/98) [943]

**12408** Shuter, Jane, ed. *Christabel Bielenberg and Nazi Germany* (5–8). Illus. Series: History Eyewitness. 1996, Raintree Steck-Vaughn LB $24.26 (0-8114-8285-5). 48pp. Using a first-person narrative as a framework, this account traces the growth, flowering, and defeat of Nazism in Germany. (Rev: BL 5/15/96; SLJ 6/96) [943]

**12409** Steele, Philip. *Germany* (3–5). Illus. Series: Discovering. 1993, Crestwood LB $13.95 (0-89686-777-3). 32pp. A brief introduction to modern Germany, with good background material on its culture and reunification. (Rev: BL 2/1/94; SLJ 2/94) [943]

**12410** Stein, R. Conrad. *Berlin* (3–6). Series: Cities of the World. 1997, Children's LB $25.00 (0-516-20582-X). 64pp. Describes present-day Berlin, Germany, its landmarks, people, geography, and history, including the division during the Communist period. (Rev: BL 1/1–15/98) [943]

## Great Britain and Ireland

**12411** Arnold, Caroline. *Stone Age Farmers Beside the Sea: Scotland's Prehistoric Village of Skara Brae* (4–7). Illus. by Arthur P. Arnold. 1997, Clarion $15.95 (0-395-77601-5). 48pp. A stunning volume that introduces the ruins of the village of Skara Brae on Scotland's Orkney Islands, which was inhabited between 3100 and 2500 B.C. (Rev: BCCB 4/97; BL 4/15/97; SLJ 7/97) [936.1]

**12412** Baxter, Nicola. *Invaders and Settlers* (5–8). Illus. by Ed Dovey. Series: Craft Topics. 1994, Watts LB $20.00 (0-531-14338-4). 32pp. An overview of the invaders of Great Britain, like the Romans and the Anglo-Saxons, with such craft projects as making a Celtic shield and creating an illuminated manuscript page. (Rev: SLJ 2/95) [941.06]

**12413** Blashfield, Jean F. *England* (4–7). Illus. Series: Enchantment of the World. 1997, Children's $32.00 (0-516-20471-8). 144pp. This fine introduction to England gives material on its history, politics, the royal family, religion, and daily life. (Rev: BL 2/1/98) [942]

**12414** Fisher, Leonard Everett. *The Tower of London* (4–6). Illus. by author. 1987, Macmillan paper $15.95 (0-02-735370-2). 32pp. Thirteen stories tell the bloody history of the Tower of London. (Rev: BCCB 11/87; BL 10/15/87)

**12415** Flint, David. *Great Britain* (5–8). Illus. Series: Modern Industrial World. 1996, Raintree Steck-Vaughn LB $24.26 (0-8172-4555-3). 48pp. Modern Great Britain is the focus of this volume, which concentrates on the economy and industrial development. (Rev: BL 2/15/97) [330.941]

**12416** Flint, David. *The United Kingdom* (3–6). Illus. Series: Country Fact Files. 1994, Raintree Steck-Vaughn LB $24.26 (0-8114-1849-9). 48pp. A fact-filled introduction to the United Kingdom, with coverage of such topics as its economy, daily life, climate, and traditions. (Rev: BL 9/1/94; SLJ 7/94) [941]

**12417** Fradin, Dennis B. *The Republic of Ireland* (4–7). Illus. 1984, Children's LB $32.00 (0-516-02767-0). 128pp. An introduction to this country that touches briefly on many subjects.

**12418** Fuller, Barbara. *Britain* (4–6). Illus. Series: Cultures of the World. 1994, Marshall Cavendish LB $34.21 (1-85435-587-2). 128pp. This fact-filled, heavily illustrated account gives a good overview of life in Great Britain today. (Rev: SLJ 7/94) [941.06]

**12419** Haskins, Jim, and Kathleen Benson. *Count Your Way Through Ireland* (2–4). Illus. by Beth Wright. Series: Count Your Way. 1996, Carolrhoda LB $19.93 (0-87614-872-0); paper $5.95 (0-87614-974-3). 24pp. After a brief introduction, each double-page spread, numbered from 1 to 10, gives interesting facts about Ireland. (Rev: BL 9/15/96; SLJ 8/96) [941.5]

**12420** Hirst, Mike. *The History of Emigration from Scotland* (4–7). Series: Origins. 1997, Watts LB $19.30 (0-531-14441-0). 32pp. Details on the political, social, and economic conditions in Scotland through various periods in its history that led to emigration to the United States and other lands. (Rev: BL 12/15/97; SLJ 2/98) [941.106]

**12421** *Ireland in Pictures* (5–8). Illus. 1997, Lerner LB $19.93 (0-8225-1878-3). 64pp. Contemporary Ireland is highlighted in this illustrated account. (Rev: BL 12/1/90) [941.5]

**12422** Kent, Deborah. *Dublin* (3–6). Illus. Series: Cities of the World. 1997, Children's LB $25.00 (0-516-20302-9). 64pp. This introduction to the Irish capital introduces its history, people, and famous sights. (Rev: BL 8/97) [941.8]

**12423** Killeen, Richard. *The Easter Rising* (4–6). Illus. Series: Revolution! 1995, Thomson Learning LB $24.26 (1-56847-391-5). 48pp. Presents, in a well-paced text, the story of the 1916 Irish Easter Rebellion, during which the Fenians fought for independence from British rule. (Rev: SLJ 2/96) [941.508]

**12424** Levy, Patricia. *Ireland* (4–7). Illus. Series: Cultures of the World. 1993, Marshall Cavendish LB $34.21 (1-85435-580-5). 128pp. An account that traces the role of women in Irish history to the present day. (Rev: SLJ 2/94) [941]

**12425** Levy, Patricia. *Ireland* (4–7). Illus. Series: Women in Society. 1994, Marshall Cavendish LB $19.95 (1-85435-563-5). 128pp. Such topics as history, geography, government, economy, culture, and people are covered in this general introduction to Ireland. (Rev: SLJ 10/94) [941.5]

**12426** Martell, Hazel M. *The Celts* (5–8). Illus. Series: See Through History. 1996, Viking paper $16.99 (0-670-86558-3). 48pp. A visually attractive, fact-filled look at the Celts and how they lived, with interior shots of their homes, fortresses, and burial sites. (Rev: SLJ 3/96) [299]

**12427** *Northern Ireland in Pictures* (3–5). Illus. Series: Visual Geography. 1991, Lerner LB $19.95 (0-8225-1898-8). 64pp. Using photos, maps, charts, and a concise text, the land and history of this troubled country are covered. (Rev: BL 2/15/92) [941.6]

**12428** Prior, Katherine. *Ireland* (4–7). Illus. Series: Origins. 1997, Watts LB $19.30 (0-531-14415-1). 32pp. Tells of the conditions in Ireland that led to emigration, where the Irish went, and their reception in Great Britain, the United States, and elsewhere. (Rev: BL 4/15/97) [941.5]

**12429** Sauvain, Philip. *Hastings* (4–8). Illus. by Claire Rothero. Series: Great Battles and Sieges. 1992, Macmillan $13.95 (0-02-781079-8). 32pp. Describes the 1066 victory of the Duke of Normandy, which brought Norman rule to England. (Rev: BL 10/1/92; SLJ 2/93) [942.02]

**12430** Smith, Nigel. *The Houses of Parliament* (4–7). Illus. Series: Great Buildings. 1997, Raintree Steck-Vaughn LB $24.97 (0-8172-4921-4). 48pp. As well as giving a history of the British Houses of Parliament, this book tells about the British form of government. (Rev: BL 2/1/98) [725]

**12431** Sproule, Anna. *Great Britain: The Land and Its People* (4–6). Illus. 1991, Silver Burdett LB $14.95 (0-382-24243-2). 48pp. An overview of history, people, religion, and industry is highlighted by numerous illustrations. (Rev: BL 11/15/87)

**12432** Stein, R. Conrad. *London* (3–6). Illus. Series: Cities of the World. 1996, Children's LB $26.00 (0-516-00351-8). 64pp. A brief introduction to London, its history, and famous landmarks, together with information about its people and their life-styles. (Rev: BL 11/15/96; SLJ 10/96) [942.1]

**12433** Sutherland, Dorothy B. *Wales* (4–6). Illus. 1987, Children's LB $36.00 (0-516-02794-8). 128pp. Color photos help to explain the history, geography, and culture of Wales. (Rev: BL 10/15/87)

**12434** *Wales in Pictures* (5–8). Illus. 1994, Lerner LB $19.93 (0-8225-1877-5). 64pp. Wales is introduced and material is given on history and current conditions. (Rev: BL 12/1/90) [942.9]

## Greece and Italy

**12435** Allard, Denise. *Greece* (K–2). Illus. Series: Postcards From. 1996, Raintree Steck-Vaughn LB $21.40 (0-8172-4022-5). 32pp. Using a postcard format, this book supplies a brief overview of the geography, culture, and sights of Greece. (Rev: SLJ 2/97) [938]

**12436** Butler, Daphne. *Italy* (2–4). Illus. 1992, Raintree Steck-Vaughn LB $22.83 (0-8114-3677-2). 32pp. A broad overview of Italy, described in terms of topography and life-style. (Rev: BL 3/15/93) [945]

**12437** Clark, Colin. *Journey Through Italy* (K–3). Illus. Series: Journey Around the World. 1994, Troll LB $13.95 (0-8167-2763-5). 32pp. A look at present-day life in Italy in a brief text and many color photographs. (Rev: SLJ 9/94) [914.5]

**12438** Dubois, Jill. *Greece* (4–7). Illus. Series: Cultures of the World. 1992, Marshall Cavendish LB $34.21 (1-85435-450-7). 128pp. This book supplies an introduction to Greece with emphasis on its culture and life-styles. (Rev: BL 10/15/92) [949.5]

**12439** *Greece in Pictures* (5–8). Illus. Series: Visual Geography. 1996, Lerner LB $19.93 (0-8225-1882-1). 64pp. Through photographs, maps, charts, and concise text, the land and people of Greece are introduced. (Rev: BL 10/1/92) [949.5]

**12440** Guittard, Charles. *The Romans: Life in the Empire* (4–6). Trans. by Mary K. LaRose. Illus. by Annie-Claude Martin. Series: Peoples of the Past. 1992, Millbrook LB $22.40 (1-56294-200-X). 64pp. This account presents an overview of how life was lived in the Roman Empire and gives information on such topics as history, culture, and religion. (Rev: BL 10/15/92) [937]

**12441** Haskins, Jim. *Count Your Way Through Italy* (2–4). Illus. by Beth Wright. Series: Count Your Way. 1990, Carolrhoda LB $19.93 (0-87614-406-7). Introduces the geography and culture of Italy through numbers. (Rev: SLJ 8/90) [945]

**12442** Haskins, Jim, and Kathleen Benson. *Count Your Way Through Greece* (2–4). Illus. by Janice L. Porter. Series: Count Your Way. 1996, Carolrhoda LB $19.93 (0-87614-875-5); paper $5.95 (0-87614-973-5). 24pp. Greece is introduced in a counting book that goes from 1 to 10. (Rev: BL 9/15/96; SLJ 8/96) [949.5]

**12443** Pirotta, Saviour. *Rome* (4–6). Illus. Series: Holy Cities. 1993, Dillon LB $13.95 (0-87518-570-3). 46pp. This account focuses on Rome as the center of the pagan religion during the ancient empire and its evolution into the heart of the largest Christian denomination in the world. (Rev: BL 9/15/93; SLJ 8/93) [263]

**12444** Stein, R. Conrad. *Athens* (3–6). Illus. Series: Cities of the World. 1997, Children's LB $25.00 (0-516-20300-2). 64pp. A heavily illustrated account that describes Athens, gives a brief history, tells about its famous landmarks, and introduces its people. (Rev: BL 8/97) [949.5]

**12445** Stein, R. Conrad. *Greece* (4–7). Illus. 1988, Children's LB $32.00 (0-516-02759-X). 128pp. Photos and maps highlight this overview of an ancient land. (Rev: BL 5/15/88)

**12446** Stein, R. Conrad. *Italy* (5–7). Illus. 1985, Children's LB $32.00 (0-516-02768-9). 128pp. Everyday life as well as the history, economy, culture, and geographic features are covered in this overview. (Rev: BL 5/15/85)

**12447** Stein, R. Conrad. *Rome* (3–6). Series: Cities of the World. 1997, Children's LB $25.00 (0-516-20465-3). 64pp. This account gives a basic history of Rome and its current status, with additional material on important sights, the people, and present-day problems. (Rev: BL 1/1–15/98) [945]

**12448** Winter, Jane K. *Italy* (5–8). Illus. Series: Cultures of the World. 1992, Marshall Cavendish LB $34.21 (1-85435-453-1). 128pp. Gives geographic and historical information about Italy and tells about its people and their concerns. (Rev: BL 10/15/92) [945]

**12449** Zinovieff, Sofka. *Greece* (4–7). Illus. Series: Origins. 1997, Watts LB $20.00 (0-531-14417-8). 32pp. Studies the conditions in Greece at various times in history that led to emigration to the United States and Canada, and the experiences of these immigrants. (Rev: BL 4/15/97) [949.5]

## Low Countries

**12450** Fradin, Dennis B. *The Netherlands* (5–7). Illus. 1983, Children's LB $32.00 (0-516-02779-4). 128pp. An introduction to the history, geography, and the people of the Netherlands.

**12451** Kent, Deborah. *Amsterdam* (3–6). Illus. Series: Cities of the World. 1997, Children's LB $25.00 (0-516-20299-5). 64pp. In this introduction to Amsterdam, readers are given a tour of the city, told about its history, and given a picture of its people. (Rev: BL 8/97; SLJ 2/98) [949.2]

**12452** Lepthien, Emilie U. *Luxembourg* (4–6). Illus. Series: Enchantment of the World. 1989, Children's LB $32.00 (0-516-02714-X). 128pp. This tiny European country is introduced with a special section on key facts and important people. (Rev: BL 1/1/90) [949.35]

**12453** Pateman, Robert. *Belgium* (4–7). Illus. Series: Cultures of the World. 1995, Marshall Cavendish LB $34.21 (0-7614-0176-8). 128pp. After a brief introduction to the history and geography of Belgium, this book focuses on the populace, how they live, and their major contributions to the world. (Rev: BL 1/1–15/96; SLJ 9/96) [949.3]

**12454** Sheehan, Patricia. *Luxembourg* (4–7). Illus. Series: Cultures of the World. 1997, Marshall Cavendish LB $34.21 (0-7614-0685-9). 128pp. Includes information on this tiny European country's history, culture, and life-styles. (Rev: BL 8/97) [914.935]

## Russia and the Former Soviet States

**12455** *Armenia* (5–8). Illus. Series: Then and Now. 1993, Lerner LB $23.93 (0-8225-2806-1). 64pp. A source of background information on this ancient western Asian territory, a former USSR state. (Rev: SLJ 3/93) [947]

**12456** Arnold, Helen. *Russia* (1–3). Illus. Series: Postcards From. 1995, Raintree Steck-Vaughn LB $21.40 (0-8172-4006-3). 32pp. In this quick overview of Russia, such topics as food, shopping, transportation, money, and language are covered. (Rev: SLJ 2/96) [947]

**12457** Bassis, Volodymyr. *Ukraine* (4–7). Illus. Series: Cultures of the World. 1997, Marshall Cavendish LB $34.21 (0-7614-0684-0). 128pp. An introduction to this former Soviet state, with emphasis on current history and culture. (Rev: BL 8/97; SLJ 10/97) [947.7]

**12458** *Belarus* (5–8). Illus. 1993, Lerner LB $23.93 (0-8225-2811-8). 56pp. This is a portrait of the former Soviet Republic, sometimes called "White Russia," situated between Poland and the Russian federation. (Rev: BL 5/15/93) [947]

**12459** Bradley, John. *Russia: Building Democracy* (4–6). Illus. Series: Topics in the News. 1995, Raintree Steck-Vaughn LB $22.83 (0-8172-4177-9). 32pp. Using pages designed as a newspaper, this account stresses current developments in Russia's search for democracy and possible future developments. (Rev: BL 2/15/96; SLJ 3/96) [947]

**12460** Brewster, Hugh. *Anastasia's Album* (5–8). Illus. 1996, Hyperion $17.95 (0-7868-0292-8). 64pp. The story of the young daughter of the last of the Romanov czars. (Rev: BCCB 1/97; BL 10/1/96; SLJ 12/96*) [947.08]

**12461** Carrion, Esther. *The Empire of the Czars* (4–7). Illus. Series: World Heritage. 1994, Children's LB $15.00 (0-516-08319-0). 34pp. An overview of Russian history from early times to the breakup of the Soviet Union, with special material on Russia's famous sights, such as Red Square, the Kremlin, and St. Petersburg. (Rev: SLJ 5/95) [947.07]

**12462** Cumming, David. *Russia* (5–8). Illus. Series: Modern Industrial World. 1994, Thomson Learning LB $24.26 (1-56847-240-4). 48pp. An introduction to Russia that stresses current conditions and the economic upheaval that the breakup of the USSR has caused. (Rev: BL 1/15/95; SLJ 3/95) [947]

**12463** Dhilawala, Sakina. *Armenia* (4–7). Illus. Series: Cultures of the World. 1997, Marshall Cavendish LB $34.21 (0-7614-0683-2). 128pp. An introduction to this troubled land that describes how its people live, their life-styles, and culture. (Rev: BL 8/97) [945.56]

**12464** Engholm, Chris. *The Armenian Earthquake* (5–7). Illus. by Maurie Manning. Series: World Disasters. 1990, Lucent LB $19.95 (1-56006-004-2). 64pp. This account explores the European disaster that killed hundreds. (Rev: SLJ 8/90) [947]

**12465** Flint, David. *The Baltic States: Estonia, Latvia, Lithuania* (4–6). Illus. Series: Former Soviet States. 1992, Millbrook LB $21.90 (1-56294-310-3). 32pp. A brief look at the geography, history, and outlook for these former Soviet states. (Rev: BL 1/15/93; SLJ 1/93) [947.4]

**12466** Flint, David. *Russia* (2–4). Illus. Series: On the Map. 1993, Raintree Steck-Vaughn LB $22.83 (0-8114-2941-5). 32pp. A simple introduction to Russia that uses many color photos and simple text to cover geography, landmarks, resources, and how the people live. (Rev: BL 9/1/93) [947]

**12467** Flint, David. *The Russian Federation* (4–6). Illus. Series: Former Soviet States. 1992, Millbrook LB $21.90 (1-56294-305-7). 32pp. Examines this area, which contains more than half of the population of the former USSR, and its current problems. (Rev: BL 1/15/93; SLJ 1/93) [947]

**12468** *Georgia: Then and Now* (5–8). Illus. Series: Then and Now. 1994, Lerner $23.93 (0-8225-2807-X). 56pp. This former Soviet Republic is introduced, and such topics as topography, ethnic makeup, history, economy, and future challenges are discussed. (Rev: BL 2/1/94; SLJ 3/94) [947.95]

**12469** Gosnell, Kelvin. *Belarus, Ukraine, and Moldova* (4–6). Illus. Series: Former Soviet States. 1992, Millbrook LB $21.90 (1-56294-306-5). 32pp. This account highlights the vast Ukraine, the breadbasket of the region, plus 2 smaller lands. (Rev: BL 1/15/93; SLJ 1/93) [947]

**12470** Harvey, Miles. *The Fall of the Soviet Union* (3–6). Illus. Series: Cornerstones of Freedom. 1995, Children's LB $19.50 (0-516-06694-3). 30pp. A highly readable text that begins with the revolution in 1917 and ends with Gorbachev's resignation in December 1991. (Rev: SLJ 8/95) [947]

**12471** Haskins, Jim. *Count Your Way Through Russia* (3–5). Illus. 1987, Carolrhoda LB $19.93 (0-87614-303-6); paper $5.95 (0-87614-488-1). Snowshoes and folk dancers are 2 of the concepts used with numbers to highlight Russian culture. (Rev: BL 10/15/87; SLJ 9/87)

**12472** Jacobsen, Karen. *The Russian Federation* (2–4). Illus. Series: New True Book. 1994, Children's LB $20.00 (0-516-01060-3). 48pp. A simple introduction with large print and many color pictures of the area we now know as Russia. (Rev: BL 7/94) [947]

**12473** *Kazakhstan* (5–8). Illus. Series: Then and Now. 1993, Lerner LB $23.93 (0-8225-2815-0).

56pp. This book introduces the second largest republic of the former U.S.S.R. and supplies details on climate, geography, history, and the life of the people. (Rev: BL 9/1/93; SLJ 9/93) [958.45]

**12474** Kendall, Russ. *Russian Girl: Life in an Old Russian Town* (3–5). Illus. 1994, Scholastic $14.95 (0-590-45789-6). 40pp. This book introduces rural Russian life by telling about the life and activities of 9-year-old Olga Surikova, who lives in a town in western Russia. (Rev: BCCB 1/94; BL 1/15/94; SLJ 3/94*) [947]

**12475** Kent, Deborah. *St. Petersburg* (3–6). Series: Cities of the World. 1997, Children's LB $25.00 (0-516-20467-X). 64pp. This introduction to St. Petersburg, Russia, covers its history from the days of Peter the Great, its landmarks (e.g., the Hermitage), and its current urban problems. (Rev: BL 3/15/98) [947]

**12476** Lychack, William. *Russia* (4–7). Illus. Series: Games People Play. 1996, Children's LB $23.50 (0-516-04441-9). 64pp. Gives some historical information about the country but primarily explores the leisure activities of Russians, including their sports, famous athletes, and Olympic Games contributions. (Rev: SLJ 5/97) [947]

**12477** Lye, Keith. *Passport to Russia* (4–7). Illus. 1996, Watts LB $22.90 (0-531-14384-8). 48pp. An introduction to Russia and its people that covers events through 1994. (Rev: BL 7/96) [947]

**12478** *Moldova* (5–8). Illus. Series: Then and Now. 1993, Lerner LB $23.93 (0-8225-2809-6). 64pp. Background data on this newly formed former USSR country. (Rev: SLJ 3/93) [947]

**12479** Nadel, Laurie. *The Kremlin Coup* (5–8). Illus. Series: Headliners. 1992, Millbrook LB $23.40 (1-56294-170-4). 64pp. The story of the coup by Communist hard-liners that began on August 19, 1991, and almost returned the Communists to power in the former USSR. (Rev: BL 12/1/92) [947]

**12480** Resnick, Abraham. *The Commonwealth of Independent States: Russia and the Other Republics* (5–8). Illus. Series: Enchantment of the World. 1993, Children's LB $32.00 (0-516-02613-5). 144pp. Following a description of the fall of Communism, this title introduces the geography, history, society, and economies of each of the independent republics. (Rev: SLJ 9/93) [947]

**12481** Roberts, Elizabeth. *Georgia, Armenia, and Azerbaijan* (4–6). Illus. Series: Former Soviet States. 1992, Millbrook LB $21.90 (1-56294-309-X). 32pp. This account highlights the politically tumultuous Caucasian states and explores the unrest between Azerbaijan and Armenia. (Rev: BL 1/15/93; SLJ 1/93) [947.9]

**12482** Sallnow, John, and Tatyana Saiko. *Russia* (3–6). Illus. Series: Country Fact Files. 1997, Raintree Steck-Vaughn LB $24.26 (0-8172-4625-8). 45pp. Russia's journey from communism to capitalism is traced, with information on current economic and social conditions. (Rev: BL 7/97; SLJ 8/97) [947]

**12483** Schomp, Virginia. *Russia: New Freedoms, New Challenges* (4–6). Illus. Series: Exploring Cultures of the World. 1996, Benchmark LB $25.64 (0-7614-0186-5). 64pp. As well as providing background information on Russia, this account stresses current conditions, with an emphasis on culture and the arts. (Rev: SLJ 6/96) [947]

**12484** *Tajikistan* (5–8). Illus. Series: Then and Now. 1993, Lerner LB $23.93 (0-8225-2816-9). 56pp. An introduction to the land and people of this remote former Soviet republic located north of Afghanistan. (Rev: BL 10/15/93; SLJ 11/93) [958.6]

**12485** Thomas, Paul. *The Central Asian States* (4–6). Illus. Series: Former Soviet States. 1992, Millbrook LB $21.90 (1-56294-307-3). 32pp. The 4 southern states of the former U.S.S.R. are examined. (Rev: BL 1/15/93; SLJ 1/93) [977.3]

**12486** *Ukraine* (5–8). Illus. Series: Then and Now. 1993, Lerner LB $22.95 (0-8225-2808-8). 64pp. A former USSR state is introduced. (Rev: BCCB 3/93; SLJ 3/93) [947]

**12487** *Uzbekistan* (5–8). Illus. 1993, Lerner LB $23.93 (0-8225-2812-6). 56pp. This area in west-central Asia with Tashkent as its capital is highlighted with information on its possible future as a new republic. (Rev: BL 5/15/93) [958.7]

**12488** Wilkins, Frances. *Uzbekistan* (4–6). Illus. 1988, Chelsea $14.95 (0-7910-0178-4). 96pp. Daily life in this little-known republic. (Rev: BL 4/1/89)

## Scandinavia, Iceland, Greenland, and Finland

**12489** Atkinson, Ian. *The Viking Ships* (5–8). Illus. 1979, Cambridge Univ. Pr. paper $11.95 (0-521-21951-5). 48pp. A book originally published in England that concentrates on Viking activities in Europe.

**12490** Carlsson, Bo Kage. *Sweden* (5–8). Illus. Series: Modern Industrial World. 1995, Thomson Learning LB $24.26 (1-56847-436-9). 48pp. This account focuses on modern Sweden, its industries, economy, resources, and people. (Rev: BL 12/15/95) [949.4]

**12491** Clare, John D., ed. *The Vikings* (3–6). Illus. 1992, Harcourt $16.95 (0-15-200512-9). 64pp. Period costumes and period settings help to dramatize this historical era. (Rev: BL 12/1/92; SLJ 11/92) [948]

**12492** *Denmark in Pictures* (5–8). Illus. Series: Visual Geography. 1997, Lerner LB $19.93 (0-8225-1880-5). 64pp. In photos, maps, charts, and concise text, the land of Denmark and its people are introduced. (Rev: BL 4/1/91; SLJ 7/91) [948]

**12493** *Finland in Pictures* (5–8). Illus. Series: Visual Geography. 1995, Lerner LB $19.93 (0-8225-1881-3). 64pp. This well-illustrated account introduces Finland and describes its people, history, geography, and government. (Rev: BL 12/15/91) [948.97]

**12494** Gan, Delice. *Sweden* (4–7). Illus. Series: Cultures of the World. 1992, Marshall Cavendish LB $34.21 (1-85435-452-3). 128pp. This introduction to Sweden gives special coverage on the people and their life-styles. (Rev: BL 10/15/92) [948.5]

**12495** Hintz, Martin. *Norway* (4–6). Illus. 1982, Children's LB $32.00 (0-516-02780-8). 128pp. The land and the people of Norway are introduced in text and pictures.

**12496** *Iceland in Pictures* (5–8). Illus. Series: Visual Geography. 1996, Lerner LB $19.93 (0-8225-1892-9). 64pp. The history, government, people, and economy of the northern republic of Iceland are covered in words and pictures. (Rev: BL 8/91) [949.12]

**12497** James, Louise. *The Vikings* (3–6). Illus. Series: How We Know About. 1997, Bedrick LB $17.95 (0-87226-535-8). 32pp. Using both contemporary photos and many reconstructions, the everyday life of the Vikings is described, with information on how archaeologists determined these facts. (Rev: BL 12/15/97; SLJ 10/97) [948.022]

**12498** Janeway, Elizabeth. *The Vikings* (4–6). 1964, Random paper $4.99 (0-394-84885-3). 160pp. A basic introduction to the Vikings, their explorations, exploits, and contributions.

**12499** Kagda, Sakina. *Norway* (4–7). Illus. Series: Cultures of the World. 1995, Marshall Cavendish LB $34.21 (0-7614-0181-4). 128pp. After general information on Norway's geography and history, this account concentrates on the Norwegian people, how they live, and their artistic accomplishments. (Rev: BL 1/1–15/96; SLJ 9/96) [948.1]

**12500** Lee, Tan Chung. *Finland* (4–7). Illus. Series: Cultures of the World. 1996, Marshall Cavendish LB $34.21 (0-7614-0280-2). 128pp. The small country of Finland with its thousands of lakes is introduced, with emphasis on the people and how they live. (Rev: BL 8/96; SLJ 7/96) [984.97]

**12501** Lepthien, Emilie U. *Greenland* (5–7). Illus. Series: Enchantment of the World. 1989, Children's LB $32.00 (0-516-02710-7). 128pp. Exploring barren Greenland, the world's largest island. (Rev: BL 8/89; SLJ 2/90) [998.2]

**12502** Lepthien, Emilie U. *Iceland* (4–6). Illus. 1987, Children's LB $32.00 (0-516-02775-1). 128pp. Life in Iceland is portrayed in straight text and color photos and maps. (Rev: BL 10/15/87)

**12503** Martell, Hazel M. *Everyday Life in Viking Times* (3–5). Illus. Series: Ones to the Past. 1994, Watts LB $20.00 (0-531-14287-6). 32pp. The daily life of Vikings, including their pursuits and games, is covered in this handsomely illustrated book. (Rev: BL 3/15/95) [940.1]

**12504** Martell, Hazel M. *The Vikings* (6–8). Illus. 1992, Macmillan $14.95 (0-02-762427-7). 64pp. Handsomely illustrated British account of how the Vikings lived. (Rev: BCCB 7–8/86; BL 5/15/86; SLJ 12/92)

**12505** Martell, Hazel M. *The Vikings and Jorvik* (4–7). Illus. Series: Hidden Worlds. 1993, Dillon LB $13.95 (0-87518-541-X). 32pp. A detailed account of how the Vikings lived, based on sound archaeological research. (Rev: BL 10/15/93; SLJ 8/93) [942.8]

**12506** Mason, Antony. *Viking Times* (4–7). Illus. by Michael Welply. Series: If You Were There. 1997, Simon & Schuster paper $16.95 (0-689-81198-5). 29pp. Using many illustrations, a timeline, and a pictorial map, this account describes the homeland of the Vikings, and their wars, explorations, trade, Christianization. (Rev: SLJ 12/97) [948]

**12507** Morley, Jacqueline. *How Would You Survive as a Viking?* (4–7). Illus. Series: How Would You Survive? 1995, Watts LB $23.00 (0-531-14344-9). 48pp. The way Vikings lived in A.D. 1000 is discussed, with information on such topics as their food, forms of worship, and how they settled disputes. (Rev: BL 6/1–15/95; SLJ 8/95) [948]

**12508** Odijk, Pamela. *The Vikings* (4–7). Illus. Series: Ancient World. 1990, Silver Burdett LB $14.95 (0-382-09893-5). 48pp. The exploits, explorations, and contributions of the Vikings. (Rev: BL 7/90; SLJ 8/90) [936]

**12509** Pitkanen, Matti A. *The Grandchildren of the Vikings* (3–6). Illus. Series: World's Children. 1996, Carolrhoda LB $21.27 (0-87614-889-5). 47pp. A photoessay that explores family life in 5 areas settled by the Vikings, including the Faeroe Islands, Iceland, Gotland, Aland, and Lofoten. (Rev: SLJ 2/97) [949]

**12510** *Sweden in Pictures* (5–8). Illus. 1993, Lerner LB $19.93 (0-8225-1872-4). 64pp. Gives the background geography and history of Sweden, along with contemporary material. (Rev: BL 12/1/90) [948.5]

**12511** Tweddle, Dominic. *Growing Up in Viking Times* (3–5). Illus. by Angus McBride. Series: Growing Up In. 1993, Troll paper $3.95 (0-8167-2726-0). 32pp. The upbringing of Viking children is the focus

of this account that also describes everyday life in a Viking community. (Rev: BL 1/15/94) [948]

**12512** Wilcox, Jonathan. *Iceland* (4–7). Illus. Series: Cultures of the World. 1996, Marshall Cavendish LB $34.21 (0-7614-0279-9). 128pp. This remote island republic is introduced, and such topics as history, geography, the people, and culture are covered with many color photos. (Rev: BL 8/96; SLJ 7/96) [949.12]

**12513** Wright, Rachel. *Vikings* (3–6). Illus. Series: Craft Topics. 1993, Watts LB $20.00 (0-531-14210-8). 32pp. Readers learn how the Vikings lived and dressed and about their ships and weapons through a combination of facts and simple craft projects. (Rev: BL 4/1/93; SLJ 8/93) [948]

## Spain and Portugal

**12514** Butler, Daphne. *Spain* (2–4). Illus. Series: On the Map. 1993, Raintree Steck-Vaughn LB $22.83 (0-8114-3678-0). 32pp. An overview of life in Italy that concentrates on family life, leisure, and how the people make a living. (Rev: BL 9/1/93) [946]

**12515** Champion, Neil. *Portugal* (5–8). Illus. Series: Modern Industrial World. 1995, Thomson Learning LB $24.26 (1-56847-435-0). 48pp. Modern Portugal is highlighted in text and pictures, with coverage of its economy, industries, and resources. (Rev: BL 12/15/95) [946.904]

**12516** Chicoine, Stephen D. *Spain: Bridge Between Continents* (3–5). Illus. Series: Exploring Cultures of the World. 1997, Marshall Cavendish LB $25.64 (0-7614-0143-1). 64pp. This introduction to Spain covers geography, history, the people, family life, the arts, festivals, and recreation. (Rev: BL 7/97; SLJ 1/98) [946]

**12517** Cross, Esther, and Wilbur Cross. *Portugal* (4–6). Illus. 1986, Children's LB $32.00 (0-516-02778-6). 127pp. General information on this country is conveyed in simple language and color photos. (Rev: BL 8/86; SLJ 10/86)

**12518** Heale, Jay. *Portugal* (5–8). Illus. Series: Cultures of the World. 1995, Marshall Cavendish LB $34.21 (0-7614-0169-5). 128pp. Present-day conditions in Portugal are emphasized in this account, which also covers history, geography, and culture. (Rev: SLJ 11/95) [914.9]

**12519** Humble, Richard, and Mark Bergin. *A 16th Century Galleon* (4–6). Illus. Series: Inside Story. 1995, Bedrick LB $18.95 (0-87226-372-X). 48pp. A richly illustrated volume that begins with the construction of the galleon from massive tree trunks and continues through its launching and techniques of ocean navigation. (Rev: BL 8/95) [623.8]

**12520** Kohen, Elizabeth. *Spain* (4–7). Illus. Series: Cultures of the World. 1992, Marshall Cavendish LB $34.21 (1-85435-451-5). 128pp. With text, photos, maps, and fact sheets, the land and people of Spain are introduced. (Rev: BL 10/15/92) [946]

**12521** Leahy, Philippa. *Spain* (3–5). Illus. Series: Discovering. 1993, Crestwood LB $13.95 (0-89686-772-2). 32pp. An introduction to Spain that covers geography, history, landmarks, language, customs, food, and entertainment. (Rev: BL 2/1/94; SLJ 11/93) [946]

**12522** Miller, Arthur. *Spain* (4–6). Illus. 1989, Chelsea LB $16.95 (1-55546-795-4). 112pp. Culture, history, geography, and daily life-styles are covered in this introduction. (Rev: BL 4/1/89; SLJ 5/89)

**12523** *Portugal in Pictures* (5–8). Illus. Series: Visual Geography. 1996, Lerner LB $19.93 (0-8225-1886-4). 64pp. Current conditions and problems in Portugal are introduced as well as the standard material on history, geography, and social conditions. (Rev: BL 12/15/91) [946.9]

**12524** Rutland, Jonathan. *Take a Trip to Spain* (2–4). Illus. 1981, Watts LB $10.90 (0-531-00991-2). 32pp. A simple introduction to principal regions, cities, and customs.

**12525** Selby, Anna. *Spain* (4–7). Illus. Series: Country Fact Files. 1994, Raintree Steck-Vaughn LB $24.26 (0-8114-1848-0). 45pp. A well-illustrated introduction to Spain, with coverage of such subjects as current social conditions, the economy, food and farming, and the environment. (Rev: SLJ 7/94) [946]

**12526** *Spain in Pictures* (5–8). Illus. Series: Visual Geography. 1995, Lerner LB $19.93 (0-8225-1887-2). 64pp. Modern Spain is the focus of this introduction, which relies heavily on photos, charts, and maps. (Rev: BL 11/15/95) [914.6]

# The Middle East

## General

**12527** Gay, Kathlyn, and Martin Gay. *Persian Gulf War* (5–8). Illus. Series: Voices from the Past. 1996, Twenty-First Century LB $18.90 (0-8050-4102-8). 63pp. A clearly written, objective overview of the Gulf War that gives material on the recent history of Iraq and Saddam Hussein's rise to power. (Rev: SLJ 2/97) [956.704]

**12528** King, John. *Bedouin* (4–6). Illus. Series: Threatened Cultures. 1992, Raintree Steck-Vaughn LB $24.26 (0-8114-2304-2). 48pp. This book presents the life and culture of the nomadic Bedouins. (Rev: BCCB 7–8/93; BL 8/93; SLJ 9/93) [961]

**12529** Long, Cathryn J. *The Middle East in Search of Peace.* Rev. ed. (4–7). Illus. Series: Headliners. 1996, Millbrook LB $23.40 (0-7613-0105-4). 64pp. An objective account of the conflict between Arabs and Jews in the Middle East, with good historical information and a description of various peace plans. (Rev: SLJ 1/97) [956]

**12530** MacDonald, Fiona. *A 16th Century Mosque* (4–6). Illus. Series: Inside Story. 1995, Bedrick $18.95 (0-87226-310-X). 48pp. After a discussion of the fundamentals of the Muslim faith, this account graphically covers the construction of the Sulemaniye mosque in Constantinople in 1557. (Rev: BL 4/15/95) [297]

**12531** Tubb, Jonathan N. *Bible Lands* (4–8). Illus. Series: Eyewitness Books. 1991, Knopf LB $20.99 (0-679-91457-9). 64pp. In a series of double-page spreads, the Middle East of biblical times is introduced, with many illustrations. (Rev: BL 12/1/91) [220.9]

**12532** Wilkinson, Philip, and Jacqueline Dineen. *The Lands of the Bible* (4–7). Illus. by Robert Ingpen. Series: Mysterious Places. 1994, Chelsea LB $19.95 (0-7910-2752-X). 92pp. An oversize volume that describes various locales in the Bible and explains their importance. (Rev: BL 1/15/94; SLJ 4/94) [220.9]

**12533** *Yemen in Pictures* (5–8). Illus. Series: Visual Geography. 1993, Lerner LB $19.95 (0-8225-1911-9). 64pp. This Middle Eastern republic on the Gulf of Aden is introduced, with concise text and extensive photographs and maps. (Rev: BL 12/1/93; SLJ 12/93) [953.3]

## Egypt

**12534** Arnold, Helen. *Egypt* (K–2). Illus. Series: Postcards From. 1996, Raintree Steck-Vaughn LB $21.40 (0-8172-4017-9). 32pp. The geography, culture, and sights of Egypt are covered in this book that uses a series of postcards as its focus. (Rev: SLJ 2/97) [962]

**12535** Bennett, Olivia. *A Family in Egypt* (3–6). Illus. 1985, Lerner LB $18.60 (0-8225-1652-7). 32pp. Color photos highlight the life of a family in this Middle East land. (Rev: BL 6/15/85; SLJ 10/85)

**12536** Feinstein, Steve. *Egypt in Pictures* (5–8). Illus. 1992, Lerner LB $19.93 (0-8225-1840-6). 64pp. Covers all areas of life in this Middle East land. (Rev: BL 2/1/89)

**12537** Flint, David. *Egypt* (2–4). Illus. Series: On the Map. 1993, Raintree Steck-Vaughn LB $22.83 (0-8114-3420-6). 32pp. Using many color photos, this account covers briefly such topics related to Egypt as geography, religion, history, and landmarks. (Rev: BL 2/1/94) [954.9]

**12538** Harkonen, Reijo. *The Children of Egypt* (4–6). Illus. by Matti Pitkanen. Series: The World's Children. 1991, Carolrhoda LB $21.27 (0-87614-396-6). 40pp. In this profile, 2 of the children highlighted guide tourists to the pyramids, and another is a brickmaker. (Rev: BL 6/1/91) [962]

**12539** Heinrichs, Ann. *Egypt* (4–7). Illus. Series: Enchantment of the World. 1997, Children's $32.00 (0-516-20470-X). 144pp. This fine introduction to Egypt gives substantial information on ancient and modern history, with coverage on religion, daily life, politics and relations with Israel. (Rev: BL 2/1/98) [962]

**12540** King, David C. *Egypt: Ancient Traditions, Modern Hopes* (3–5). Illus. Series: Exploring Cultures of the World. 1997, Marshall Cavendish LB $25.64 (0-7614-0142-3). 64pp. Describes various aspects of life in modern Egypt, with comparisons and contrasts made to past conditions. (Rev: BL 7/97; SLJ 1/98) [932]

**12541** Loveridge, Emma. *Egypt* (3–6). Illus. Series: Country Fact Files. 1997, Raintree Steck-Vaughn LB $24.26 (0-8172-4626-6). 45pp. An overview of current conditions in Egypt, with details on tourism, the growing educational system, and the life-styles of the people. (Rev: BL 7/97; SLJ 9/97) [962]

**12542** Pateman, Robert. *Egypt* (4–7). Illus. Series: Cultures of the World. 1992, Marshall Cavendish LB $34.21 (1-85435-535-X). 128pp. Egypt past and present is introduced in this account that stresses how the people live. (Rev: BL 1/1/93) [962]

**12543** Stein, R. Conrad. *Cairo* (3–6). Illus. Series: Cities of the World. 1996, Children's LB $25.00 (0-516-20024-0). 64pp. Cairo's history and geography are covered, as well as famous sites, festivals, and the people's life-style. (Rev: BL 1/1–15/97) [962]

**12544** Tenquist, Alasdair. *Egypt* (5–7). Illus. Series: Economically Developing Countries. 1995, Thomson Learning LB $24.26 (1-56847-385-0). 48pp. A look at present-day conditions in Egypt and its concerns and problems. (Rev: SLJ 2/96) [962]

**12545** Weber, Valerie, and John D. Rateliff, eds. *Egypt* (3–5). Illus. by Yoshio Komatsu. Series: Children of the World. 1991, Stevens LB $19.93 (1-55532-209-3). 64pp. This book tells about the everyday life of children in Egypt and of their families and social life. (Rev: BL 12/15/91; SLJ 7/92) [962]

## Israel

**12546** Dubois, Jill. *Israel* (4–7). Illus. Series: Cultures of the World. 1992, Marshall Cavendish LB $34.21 (1-85435-531-7). 128pp. This introduction to

Israel emphasizes its culture and the life-styles of the people. (Rev: BL 1/1/93) [956.94]

**12547** Feinstein, Steve. *Israel in Pictures* (5–8). Illus. 1992, Lerner LB $19.93 (0-8225-1833-3). 64pp. An overview of geography, climate, wildlife, and vegetation with photos, maps, and charts. (Rev: BL 8/88)

**12548** Haskins, Jim. *Count Your Way Through Israel* (2–4). Illus. by Rick Handson. Series: Count Your Way. 1990, Carolrhoda LB $19.93 (0-87614-415-6). Using the format of counting from 1 to 10 in Hebrew, the land and people of Israel are introduced. (Rev: SLJ 2/91) [956.94]

**12549** Kuskin, Karla. *Jerusalem, Shining Still* (3–5). Illus. by David Frampton. 1987, HarperCollins paper $5.50 (0-06-443243-2). 32pp. The history of Jerusalem is briefly told in lyrical prose and touches of verse. (Rev: BL 10/1/87; HB 11–12/87; SLJ 11/87)

**12550** Odijk, Pamela. *The Israelites* (4–7). Illus. Series: Ancient World. 1990, Silver Burdett LB $14.95 (0-382-09888-9). 48pp. Covers the early history of the Jewish people, from their origins in Canaan through the Diaspora. (Rev: BL 7/90; SLJ 8/90) [956.94]

**12551** Paris, Alan. *Jerusalem 3000: Kids Discover the City of Gold!* (4–6). Illus. by Peter Gandolfi. 1995, Pitspopany $16.95 (0-943706-59-9). 47pp. This fine introduction to Jerusalem includes material on its history as determined by archaeological research. (Rev: SLJ 12/95) [956.94]

**12552** Patterson, Jose. *Israel* (3–6). Illus. Series: Country Fact Files. 1997, Raintree Steck-Vaughn LB $24.26 (0-8172-4627-4). 45pp. This account covers modern-day Israel and its political and economic status, resources, and people. (Rev: BL 7/97) [956.94]

**12553** Pirotta, Saviour. *Jerusalem* (4–6). Illus. Series: Holy Cities. 1993, Dillon LB $13.95 (0-87518-569-X). 46pp. An oversize volume that introduces Jerusalem, its buildings, holy sites, and the facts and legends surrounding them. (Rev: BL 9/15/93; SLJ 8/93) [956.94]

**12554** Rutland, Jonathan. *Take a Trip to Israel* (1–3). Illus. 1981, Watts LB $10.90 (0-531-04318-5). 32pp. A short, heavily illustrated introduction to the country.

**12555** Scharfstein, Sol. *Understanding Israel* (5–7). Illus. 1994, KTAV paper $14.95 (0-88125-428-2). 144pp. A heavily illustrated introduction to Israel that covers history, religion, government, culture, and current concerns. (Rev: SLJ 10/94) [956.94]

**12556** Taitz, Emily, and Sondra Henry. *Israel: A Sacred Land* (5–7). Illus. 1988, Macmillan LB $14.95 (0-87518-364-6). 160pp. The focus is on everyday life in this Middle East land. (Rev: BL 2/15/88)

**12557** Waldman, Neil. *The Golden City: Jerusalem's 3,000 Years* (4–6). Illus. 1995, Simon & Schuster $15.00 (0-689-80080-0). 32pp. Beginning with Moses, this account traces the important events in the history of Jerusalem during its 3,000-year existence. (Rev: BL 9/1/95; SLJ 11/95) [965.94]

## Other Middle Eastern Lands

**12558** Ansary, Mir T. *Afghanistan: Fighting for Freedom* (5–8). Illus. Series: Discovering Our Heritage. 1991, Macmillan LB $14.95 (0-87518-482-0). 128pp. In text and pictures, this account gives some background information, but concentrates on modern Afghanistan. (Rev: BL 2/1/92; SLJ 3/92) [958.1]

**12559** Augustin, Byron, and Rebecca A. Augustin. *Qatar* (5–8). Illus. Series: Enchantment of the World. 1997, Children's LB $32.00 (0-516-20303-7). 128pp. An introduction to the small oil-producing country on the Persian Gulf that describes its history under British rule and how the people now live. (Rev: BL 7/97) [953.63]

**12560** Bernards, Neal. *The Palestinian Conflict: Identifying Propaganda Techniques* (4–7). Illus. 1990, Greenhaven LB $16.20 (0-89908-602-0). 32pp. Such skills as distinguishing between fact and fiction and detecting bias are stressed in this book. (Rev: BL 6/15/91) [956.04]

**12561** Bratman, Fred. *War in the Persian Gulf* (4–6). Series: Headliners. 1991, Millbrook LB $14.90 (1-56294-051-1); paper $6.95 (1-878-84161-0). 64pp. This book gives a brief, introductory account of the Persian Gulf War, with historical background material on the region and the rise of Saddam Hussein. (Rev: SLJ 12/91) [956]

**12562** Dutton, Roderic. *An Arab Family* (3–6). Illus. 1985, Lerner LB $18.60 (0-8225-1660-8). 32pp. The author focuses mainly on one family member to give fascinating details of life, noting how the discovery of oil has influenced daily activities. (Rev: BL 11/15/85)

**12563** Foster, Leila M. *Jordan* (5–8). Illus. Series: Enchantment of the World. 1991, Children's LB $32.00 (0-516-02603-8). 128pp. An introduction in text and pictures to the geography, history, culture, and important people of Jordan. (Rev: BL 2/1/92) [956.95]

**12564** Foster, Leila M. *Lebanon* (5–8). Illus. Series: Enchantment of the World. 1992, Children's LB $32.00 (0-516-02612-7). 128pp. In addition to a brief introduction to this troubled land, this book covers recent history and gives biographies of famous Lebanese. (Rev: BL 12/1/92; SLJ 10/92) [956.92]

**12565** Foster, Leila M. *Saudi Arabia* (5–8). Illus. Series: Enchantment of the World. 1993, Children's LB $32.00 (0-516-02611-9). 128pp. This oil-rich country is introduced with material on history, geography, culture, and religion. (Rev: BL 8/93; SLJ 8/93) [953.8]

**12566** Foster, Leila M. *The Story of the Persian Gulf War* (3–5). Illus. Series: America at War. 1991, Children's LB $19.50 (0-516-04762-0). 32pp. With simple text and many photos, the story of the desert war is presented in a straightforward manner. (Rev: BL 3/1/92) [956.704]

**12567** Fox, Mary V. *Bahrain* (3–8). Illus. Series: Enchantment of the World. 1992, Children's LB $32.00 (0-516-02608-9). 126pp. This is an introduction to the tiny island sheikdom in the Persian Gulf. (Rev: BL 11/15/92; SLJ 1/93) [953.63]

**12568** Fox, Mary V. *Iran* (5–8). Illus. Series: Enchantment of the World. 1991, Children's LB $32.00 (0-516-02727-1). 128pp. The history of the country once known as Persia is covered along with present-day conditions and brief biographies of famous people. (Rev: BL 10/1/91) [955]

**12569** Ganeri, Anita. *I Remember Palestine* (3–6). Illus. Series: Why We Left. 1995, Raintree Steck-Vaughn LB $22.83 (0-8114-5610-2). 32pp. Material on the history, geography, and current conditions in Palestine are covered, along with stories of refugee children whose parents have emigrated. (Rev: BCCB 3/95; SLJ 6/95) [956.94]

**12570** Haskins, Jim. *Count Your Way Through the Arab World* (3–5). Illus. 1987, Carolrhoda LB $19.93 (0-87614-304-4); Lerner paper $5.95 (0-87614-487-3). 24pp. "Muslims pray to Mecca 5 times a day" and other numbers help to introduce the culture of the Arab world. (Rev: BL 10/15/87; SLJ 9/87)

**12571** Hassig, Susan M. *Iraq* (4–7). Illus. Series: Cultures of the World. 1992, Marshall Cavendish LB $34.21 (1-85435-533-3). 128pp. This introduction stresses the life-styles of the people, their religion, and culture. (Rev: BL 1/1/93) [956.7]

**12572** *Iran in Pictures* (5–8). Illus. 1992, Lerner LB $19.93 (0-8225-1848-1). 64pp. Basic coverage in the Visual Geography series on this Middle East land much in the news. (Rev: BL 5/1/89)

**12573** Janin, Hunt. *Saudi Arabia* (4–7). Illus. Series: Cultures of the World. 1992, Marshall Cavendish LB $34.21 (1-85435-532-5). 128pp. The history, geography, economy, language, and people are discussed in this book about Saudi Arabia. (Rev: BL 1/1/93) [953.8]

**12574** *Jordan in Pictures* (5–8). Illus. 1992, Lerner LB $19.93 (0-8225-1834-1). 64pp. Young readers learn what life is like in this Middle East land. (Rev: BL 2/1/89; SLJ 2/89)

**12575** King, John. *A Family from Iraq* (3–5). Illus. Series: Families Around the World. 1997, Raintree

Steck-Vaughn $17.48 (0-8172-4904-4). 32pp. Chronicles the daily activities of a single family in Iraq, as well as the differences between the older and younger generations. (Rev: BL 2/1/98; SLJ 2/98) [306.85]

**12576** *Lebanon in Pictures* (5–8). Illus. 1992, Lerner LB $19.93 (0-8225-1832-5). 64pp. A country torn apart by strife is the focus of this Visual Geography edition. (Rev: BL 2/1/89)

**12577** Marston, Elsa. *Lebanon: New Light in an Ancient Land* (5–8). Illus. Series: Discovering Our Heritage. 1994, Dillon LB $14.95 (0-87518-584-3). 124pp. A well-organized, readable introduction to the history, geography, and people of Lebanon, together with material on the impact of Lebanese immigration on the United States. (Rev: SLJ 7/94) [956]

**12578** Moktefi, Mokhtar. *The Arabs in the Golden Age* (4–6). Illus. by Veronique Ageorges. 1992, Millbrook LB $22.40 (1-56294-201-8). 64pp. This book takes the reader back to the 8th to the mid-13th century. (Rev: BL 10/15/92) [909]

**12579** Rajendra, Vijeya, and Gisela Kaplan. *Iran* (4–7). Illus. Series: Cultures of the World. 1992, Marshall Cavendish LB $34.21 (1-85435-534-1). 128pp. As well as standard introductory information about Iran, this book tells about how the people live and what the country's present problems are. (Rev: BL 1/1/93) [955]

**12580** Stein, R. Conrad. *The Iran Hostage Crisis* (3–5). Illus. Series: Cornerstones of Freedom. 1994, Children's LB $19.50 (0-516-06681-1). 32pp. This international incident that brought humiliation to the United States and helped cause the fall of a president are vividly re-created. (Rev: BL 1/15/95; SLJ 4/95) [955.05]

**12581** Steins, Richard. *The Mideast After the Gulf War* (5–8). Illus. 1992, Millbrook LB $23.40 (1-56294-156-9). 64pp. This book details what is being done to solve the problems of refugees, political instability, and environmental damage that were the results of the Gulf War. (Rev: BL 12/1/92) [595.3]

# North and South America (Excluding the United States)

## Canada

**12582** Beattie, Owen, and John Geiger. *Buried in Ice: The Mystery of a Lost Arctic Expedition* (4–7). Illus. by Janet Wilson. Series: Time Quest. 1993, Scholastic paper $6.95 (0-590-43849-2). 64pp. The story of Sir John Franklin's unsuccessful 1845 expedition from England to find the Northwest Passage. (Rev: BCCB 3/92; BL 4/1/92; SLJ 4/92*) [919.804]

**12583** Campbell, Kumari. *Prince Edward Island* (3–6). Illus. Series: Hello Canada. 1996, Lerner LB $19.95 (0-8225-2762-6). 72pp. This volume highlights Canada's island province, its inhabitants, history, famous people, and economy. (Rev: BL 4/15/96) [971.7]

**12584** *Canada in Pictures* (4–6). Series: Visual Geography. 1993, Lerner LB $19.93 (0-8225-1870-8). 64pp. In 4 separate sections that explore the land, the history and government, the people, and the economy, the basic facts about Canada and Canadians are presented. (Rev: SLJ 2/90) [971]

**12585** *Christmas in Canada: Christmas Around the World from World Book* (4–6). Illus. 1994, World Book $18.50 (0-7166-0894-4). 80pp. An overview of how several ethnic groups in Canada spend their Christmas, with asides about special rituals and traditions. (Rev: BL 12/15/94) [394.26]

**12586** Cooper, Michael. *Klondike Fever: The Famous Gold Rush of 1898* (5–8). Illus. 1990, Houghton paper $6.95 (0-395-54784-9). 80pp. The events that turned a remote part of the Yukon into a 3-ring circus of gold-hungry prospectors. (Rev: BCCB 1/90; BL 11/15/89; HB 1–2/90) [971.9]

**12587** Daitch, Richard W. *Northwest Territories* (3–6). Illus. Series: Hello Canada. 1996, Lerner $18.95 (0-8225-2761-8). 72pp. A remote northern part of Canada is featured in this book, with material on its people, history, government, and economy. (Rev: BL 4/15/96) [971.9]

**12588** Ekoomiak, Normee. *Arctic Memories* (3–5). Illus. 1990, Holt $15.95 (0-8050-1254-0); paper $5.95 (0-8050-2347-X). 32pp. Memories of an Inuit artist who was raised in the James Bay area of arctic Quebec. (Rev: BCCB 3/90; BL 3/1/90; HB 5–6/90; SLJ 4/90) [998]

**12589** Gibbons, Gail. *The Great St. Lawrence Seaway* (2–5). Illus. 1992, Morrow $15.00 (0-688-06984-3). 40pp. This book shows the progress of a ship as it carries iron from the Atlantic coast through the great seaway toward the Great Lakes. (Rev: BCCB 3/92; BL 3/15/92; SLJ 4/92) [386]

**12590** Greenwood, Barbara. *A Pioneer Sampler: The Daily Life of a Pioneer Family in 1840* (4–6). Illus. 1995, Ticknor $18.95 (0-395-71540-7). 240pp. Everyday life of a Canadian pioneer family is described, with accompanying projects and activities, such as how to make ink. (Rev: BCCB 5/95; BL 4/1/95; HB 5–6/95; SLJ 4/95) [971.3]

**12591** Hamilton, Janice. *Quebec* (3–6). Illus. Series: Hello Canada. 1996, Lerner LB $19.95 (0-8225-2766-9). 72pp. This Canadian province, currently divided about its political future, is featured, with material on its heritage, geography, and economy. (Rev: BL 4/15/96) [971.4]

691

**12592** Hancock, Lyn. *Nunavut* (3–6). Illus. Series: Hello, Canada. 1995, Lerner LB $14.21 (0-8225-2758-8). 76pp. Basic information is given on this Canadian territory founded in 1993 from the eastern part of the Northwest Territories. (Rev: BL 12/15/95) [971.9]

**12593** Harrison, Ted. *O Canada* (2–5). Illus. 1993, Ticknor $14.95 (0-395-66075-0). 32pp. A brief province-by-province tour of Canada, with paintings by the author. (Rev: BCCB 9/93; BL 10/15/93; SLJ 8/93) [971]

**12594** Jackson, Lawrence. *Newfoundland and Labrador* (3–6). Illus. Series: Hello, Canada. 1995, Lerner LB $19.95 (0-8225-2757-X). 72pp. A slim volume that presents a guided tour of these regions of Canada, with coverage on history, economic development, principal cities, and important residents, past and present. (Rev: BL 12/15/95) [971.8]

**12595** Kalman, Bobbie. *Canada: The Culture* (3–5). Illus. Series: Lands, Peoples, and Cultures. 1993, Crabtree LB $19.16 (0-86505-219-0); paper $7.95 (0-86505-299-9). 32pp. Canadian culture is explored in such areas as television, music, film, art, theater, dance, and sports. (Rev: BL 2/1/94) [971]

**12596** Kalman, Bobbie. *Canada: The Land* (3–5). Illus. Series: Lands, Peoples, and Cultures. 1993, Crabtree LB $19.16 (0-86505-217-4); paper $7.95 (0-86505-297-2). 32pp. Topics include Canada's provinces and territories, natural resources, industry, agriculture, transportation, wildlife, and national parks. (Rev: BL 2/1/94) [971]

**12597** Kalman, Bobbie. *Canada: The People* (3–5). Illus. 1993, Crabtree LB $19.16 (0-86505-218-2); paper $7.95 (0-86505-298-0). 32pp. The multicultural nature of the Canadian people is stressed in this portrait that also covers problems in the English-French relationship. (Rev: BL 2/1/94) [306]

**12598** Kalman, Bobbie. *Canada Celebrates Multiculturalism* (3–5). Illus. Series: Lands, Peoples, and Cultures. 1993, Crabtree LB $19.16 (0-86505-220-4); paper $7.95 (0-86505-300-6). 32pp. Some topics covered are the beginnings of multiculturalism in Canada, religious and heritage days, cross-cultural festivals, and the traditions of various ethnic groups. (Rev: BL 2/1/94) [971]

**12599** Law, Kevin. *Canada* (4–6). Illus. Series: Let's Visit Places and Peoples of the World. 1990, Chelsea LB $19.95 (0-7910-1101-1). 128pp. Following a map section, listings of important facts, and a chronology, the land and people of Canada are introduced. (Rev: BL 2/15/90) [971]

**12600** LeVert, Suzanne. *Canada: Facts and Figures* (4–6). Illus. Series: Let's Discover Canada. 1992, Chelsea LB $17.95 (0-7910-1035-X). 64pp. After an introduction, a map, and a chronology, facts about each Canadian province are given. This series also

has separate volumes on each province. (Rev: BL 11/15/92; SLJ 3/93) [971]

**12601** LeVert, Suzanne. *Dominion of Canada* (4–6). Illus. Series: Let's Discover Canada. 1992, Chelsea LB $17.95 (0-7910-1034-1). 64pp. Chapters on Canadian history, cultural issues, and Quebec's history and separatist movement. (Rev: BL 11/15/92) [971]

**12602** LeVert, Suzanne. *Ontario* (4–6). Illus. Series: Let's Discover Canada. 1990, Chelsea LB $17.95 (0-7910-1022-8). 64pp. One of a series of books introducing the history, geography, sights, and people of Canadian provinces. Also use: *Quebec* (1991). (Rev: SLJ 4/91) [971]

**12603** Lourie, Peter. *Yukon River: An Adventure to the Gold Fields of the Klondike* (3–6). Illus. 1992, Boyds Mills LB $15.95 (1-878093-90-8). 48pp. Following the route of prospectors in the 1890s, this book takes the reader on a trip down the Yukon by canoe. (Rev: BCCB 10/92; BL 10/1/92; SLJ 10/92) [917.98]

**12604** Richardson, Gillian. *Saskatchewan* (3–6). Illus. Series: Hello, Canada. 1995, Lerner LB $14.21 (0-8225-2760-X). 72pp. This introduction to Canada's midwestern province and bread basket includes material on history, geography, resources, and famous people. (Rev: BL 12/15/95) [971.24]

**12605** Shepherd, Jennifer. *Canada* (4–7). Illus. 1988, Children's LB $32.00 (0-516-02757-3). 128pp. Geography, history, climate, and people are discussed in this look at the northern U.S. neighbor. (Rev: BL 5/15/88; SLJ 8/88)

**12606** Steltzer, Ulli. *Building an Igloo* (4–6). Illus. 1995, Holt $14.95 (0-8050-3753-5). 32pp. Black-and-white photographs are used to show how an Inuit father and son build an igloo out of snow. (Rev: BL 9/15/95*; SLJ 12/95) [693]

**12607** Tames, Richard. *Journey Through Canada* (3–5). Illus. by Martin Camm. Series: Journey Around the World. 1990, Troll LB $13.95 (0-8167-2110-6); paper $4.95 (0-8167-2111-4). 32pp. This book explores the majestic scenery, history, and bilingual culture of Canada. (Rev: BL 5/15/91) [971]

**12608** Thompson, Alexa. *Nova Scotia* (3–6). Illus. Series: Hello, Canada. 1995, Lerner LB $14.21 (0-8225-2759-6). 76pp. History, geography, and the economy are covered, with material on the various peoples and cultures represented in Nova Scotia. (Rev: BL 12/15/95; SLJ 3/96) [971.6]

**12609** Yates, Sarah. *Alberta* (3–6). Illus. Series: Hello, Canada. 1995, Lerner LB $19.93 (0-8225-2763-4). 76pp. A colorful, slim volume that crams many facts about this western Canadian province, its culture, history, geography, and resources into a few attractive pages. (Rev: BL 12/15/95; SLJ 3/96) [971.23]

## Mexico

**12610** Ancona, George. *Mayeros: A Yucatec Maya Family* (4–6). Illus. 1997, Lothrop LB $15.93 (0-688-13466-1). 40pp. The present-day life of a Mayan family is contrasted with the way these people lived in ancient times. (Rev: BL 4/15/97; SLJ 6/97) [972]

**12611** Ancona, George. *Pablo Remembers: The Fiesta of the Day of the Dead* (3–6). Illus. 1993, Lothrop $16.00 (0-688-11249-8). 48pp. The customs and traditions surrounding the 3-day Mexican celebration, the Fiesta of the Day of the Dead, are described in this photoessay. A Spanish-language edition is also available. (Rev: BCCB 12/93; BL 2/1/94; SLJ 12/93) [393.9]

**12612** Ancona, George. *The Pinata Maker/El Piñatero* (1–3). Illus. 1994, Harcourt $17.00 (0-15-261875-9); paper $9.00 (0-15-200060-7). 40pp. Many Mexican crafts, like the piñata and puppet making, are highlighted when a group of children visit an aged craftsman in this dual-language book. (Rev: BL 2/15/94; HB 7–8/94; SLJ 4/94) [745]

**12613** Arnold, Helen. *Mexico* (1–3). Illus. Series: Postcards From. 1995, Raintree Steck-Vaughn LB $21.40 (0-8172-4012-8). 32pp. A quick overview of Mexico is given through a series of postcards written by fictitious children. (Rev: SLJ 2/96) [972]

**12614** Baquedano, Elizabeth. *Aztec, Inca and Maya* (4–8). Illus. Series: Eyewitness Books. 1993, Knopf LB $20.99 (0-679-93883-4). 64pp. An overview of the history of these Indian civilizations of the Americas, their cultures, and their fate at the hands of the invading Spaniards. (Rev: BL 10/1/93; SLJ 12/93) [972]

**12615** Berendes, Mary. *Mexico* (K–3). Illus. Series: Faces and Places. 1997, Child's World LB $22.79 (1-56766-372-9). 32pp. Concisely describes the land, plants, animals, history, and culture of Mexico. (Rev: SLJ 2/98) [972]

**12616** Bulmer-Thomas, Barbara. *Journey Through Mexico* (3–5). Illus. by Martin Camm. Series: Journey Around the World. 1990, Troll paper $4.95 (0-8167-2117-3). 32pp. Mexico, a mix of Native American traditions and the culture of the conquistadores, is introduced in colorful photos and text. (Rev: BL 5/15/91) [972]

**12617** Burr, Claudia, et al. *Broken Shields* (4–8). Illus. 1997, Douglas & McIntyre $15.95 (0-88899-303-X); paper $6.95 (0-88899-304-8). 32pp. From firsthand eyewitness accounts, this is the story of the betrayal of Montezuma at the hands of the Spanish

conqueror Cortez. (Rev: BL 12/1/97; HB 11–12/97; SLJ 1/98) [972]

**12618** Conlon, Laura. *People of Mexico* (2–4). Illus. Series: South of the Border. 1994, Rourke LB $14.60 (1-55916-052-7). 24pp. Introduces the various peoples of Mexico and where they live in a simple text with many attractive color photos. Also use in this series *Products of Mexico, Visiting Mexico,* and *Wonders of Mexico* (all 1994). (Rev: SLJ 2/95) [972]

**12619** Flint, David. *Mexico* (2–4). Illus. Series: On the Map. 1993, Raintree Steck-Vaughn LB $22.83 (0-8114-3419-2). 32pp. Such topics as geography, history, customs, life-styles, and landmarks are covered in this well-illustrated introduction to Mexico. (Rev: BL 2/1/94) [972]

**12620** Heinrichs, Ann. *Mexico* (4–6). Series: True Books: Countries. 1997, Children's LB $21.00 (0-516-20337-1). 48pp. Basic materials on Mexico — history, geography, culture, and the people — is covered in this attractive title with many bright photos and a map. (Rev: BL 9/15/97; SLJ 11/97) [972]

**12621** Hicks, Peter. *The Aztecs* (4–6). Illus. 1993, Thomson $22.83 (1-56847-058-4). 32pp. Topics related to the Aztecs, such as family life, religion, music, and Montezuma, are covered with special attention to their art and artifacts. (Rev: BL 6/1–15/93) [972]

**12622** Higginson, Mel. *Wildlife of Mexico* (2–4). Illus. Series: South of the Border. 1994, Rourke LB $14.60 (1-55916-055-1). 24pp. The flora and fauna of Mexico are introduced in a heavily illustrated volume with an easy-to-read text. (Rev: SLJ 2/95) [972]

**12623** Kalman, Bobbie. *Mexico: The Culture* (3–5). Illus. Series: Lands, Peoples, and Cultures. 1993, Crabtree LB $19.16 (0-86505-216-6); paper $7.95 (0-86505-296-4). 32pp. Topics covered include arts, crafts, music, dance, literature, legends, cooking, leisure pursuits, and Spanish influences in the Mayan and Aztec cultures. (Rev: BL 2/1/94) [917.2]

**12624** Kalman, Bobbie. *Mexico: The Land* (3–5). Illus. Series: Land, Peoples, and Cultures. 1993, Crabtree LB $19.16 (0-86505-214-X); paper $7.95 (0-86505-294-8). 32pp. Mexican geography and resources are covered, along with a discussion of Mexico's regions, transportation, industries, wildlife, and conservation. (Rev: BL 2/1/94) [917.2]

**12625** Kalman, Bobbie. *Mexico: The People* (3–5). Illus. 1993, Crabtree LB $19.16 (0-86505-215-8); paper $7.95 (0-86505-295-6). 32pp. The various contrasts among the peoples of Mexico — rich and poor, urban and rural — are covered, along with general material on religion, social conditions, and the position of women. (Rev: BL 2/1/94) [972]

**12626** Kent, Deborah. *Mexico: Rich in Spirit and Tradition* (4–8). Illus. Series: Exploring Cultures of the World. 1995, Benchmark LB $25.64 (0-7614-0187-3). 64pp. In addition to basic information on Mexico, this account gives coverage on religion, holidays, festivals, sports, foods, and education. (Rev: SLJ 6/96) [972]

**12627** Lasky, Kathryn. *Days of the Dead* (3–6). Illus. by Christopher G. Knight. 1994, Hyperion LB $16.49 (0-7868-2018-7). 48pp. Through the story of a single Mexican family, the customs and significance of the Days of the Dead are revealed. (Rev: BCCB 10/94; BL 10/15/94; SLJ 10/94) [394.2]

**12628** Lewis, Thomas P. *Hill of Fire* (1–3). Illus. by Joan Sandin. 1971, HarperCollins LB $15.89 (0-06-023804-6); paper $3.75 (0-06-444040-0). 64pp. The eruption of the volcano Paricutin and its effect on the lives of the people.

**12629** Libura, Krystyna, et al. *What the Aztecs Told Me* (4–8). Illus. 1997, Douglas & McIntyre $15.95 (0-88899-305-6); paper $6.95 (0-88899-306-4). 32pp. Based on an original 12-volume work written in the 16th century, this book describes the Aztec people from observation and eyewitness accounts. (Rev: BL 12/1/97; HB 11–12/97; SLJ 12/97) [973]

**12630** MacDonald, Fiona. *How Would You Survive as an Aztec?* (4–7). Illus. Series: How Would You Survive? 1995, Watts LB $24.00 (0-531-14348-1). 48pp. Food, clothing, and everyday life in an Aztec community are covered in a series of double-page spreads. (Rev: BL 6/1–15/95) [972]

**12631** McKissack, Patricia. *Aztec Indians* (1–3). Illus. 1985, Children's LB $21.00 (0-516-01936-8); paper $5.50 (0-516-41936-6). 48pp. Gives the young reader insight into history and modern activities of these native Americans. (Rev: BL 12/1/85; SLJ 4/86)

**12632** MacMillan, Dianne M. *Mexican Independence Day and Cinco de Mayo* (3–5). Series: Best Holiday. 1997, Enslow LB $18.95 (0-89490-816-2). 48pp. The history of Mexico is interwoven in the description of these related holidays, with material on how they are celebrated. (Rev: BL 12/15/97; SLJ 8/97) [972]

**12633** Mason, Antony. *Aztec Times* (4–7). Illus. by Michael White. Series: If You Were There. 1997, Simon & Schuster paper $16.95 (0-689-81199-3). 29pp. Using many illustrations, a timeline, and a pictorial map, this account describes the origins of this civilization, its daily life, customs, and the arrival the Spaniards. (Rev: SLJ 12/97) [972]

**12634** Mathews, Sally S. *The Sad Night: The Story of an Aztec Victory and a Spanish Loss* (3–5). Illus. 1994, Clarion $16.95 (0-395-63035-5). 39pp. A picture book that introduces the Aztecs, their cities, and the dramatic confrontation between Montezuma and Cortés. (Rev: BL 7/94; SLJ 6/94) [972]

**12635** *Mexico in Pictures* (4–7). Illus. 1994, Lerner LB $19.93 (0-8225-1801-5). 64pp. An introduction to our south-of-the-border neighbor. (Rev: BL 8/87)

**12636** Odijk, Pamela. *The Aztecs* (4–7). Illus. Series: Ancient World. 1990, Silver Burdett LB $14.95 (0-382-09887-0). 48pp. A well-illustrated account of the rise and fall of the ancient Mexican civilization. (Rev: BL 7/90; SLJ 8/90) [972]

**12637** Olawsky, Lynn A. *Colors of Mexico* (2–5). Illus. by Janice L. Porter. Series: Colors of the World. 1997, Carolrhoda LB $19.93 (0-87614-886-0); paper $5.95 (1-57505-216-4). 24pp. Ten different colors are used to introduce facts about Mexico, its history, geography, traditions, and people. (Rev: SLJ 10/97) [972]

**12638** Presilla, Maricel E., and Gloria Soto. *Life Around the Lake* (4–6). Illus. 1996, Holt $16.95 (0-8050-3800-0). 30pp. Life around Lake Patzcuaro in central Mexico is reflected in the embroidery of the native women. (Rev: BCCB 6/96; BL 4/1/96; SLJ 6/96) [972]

**12639** Reilly, Mary J. *Mexico* (5–8). Illus. Series: Cultures of the World. 1991, Marshall Cavendish LB $34.21 (1-85435-385-3). 128pp. This account emphasizes the geography, history, economy, and life-styles of the the Mexican people. (Rev: BL 4/1/91) [972]

**12640** Shepherd, Donna Walsh. *The Aztecs* (4–6). Illus. 1992, Watts paper $6.95 (0-531-15634-6). 64pp. Covers the history, culture, and society of the ancient Aztec civilization of Mexico and its fate under the Spanish conquerers. (Rev: BL 6/15/92; SLJ 8/92) [972]

**12641** Silverthorne, Elizabeth. *Fiesta! Mexico's Great Celebrations* (3–6). Illus. by Jan Davey Ellis. 1992, Millbrook LB $21.40 (1-56294-055-4). 64pp. A description of Mexico's most significant celebrations, plus a look at how Indians and the Spanish contributed to this culture. (Rev: BL 1/15/93; SLJ 11/92) [394.2]

**12642** Sola, Michele. *Angela Weaves a Dream* (4–6). Illus. by Jeffrey J. Foxx. 1997, Hyperion LB $17.49 (0-7868-2060-8). 48pp. Present-day Mayan culture is introduced, as well as their art of weaving clothes and other articles using the same techniques as those of their ancestors. (Rev: BCCB 6/97; BL 4/15/97; SLJ 7/97) [746.1]

**12643** Staub, Frank. *Children of Belize* (3–6). Series: The World's Children. 1997, Carolrhoda $15.95 (1-57505-039-0). 45pp. The reader meets a variety of children from this small Central American country with a unique history and a population of remarkable diversity. (Rev: BL 3/15/98; SLJ 3/98) [972.82]

**12644** Staub, Frank. *The Children of the Sierra Madre* (3–6). Illus. Series: The World's Children. 1996, Carolrhoda LB $14.96 (0-87614-943-4); paper

$7.95 (0-87614-967-0). 48pp. The young people of the Sierra Madre and their social conditions are discussed, with additional historical information. (Rev: BL 10/1/96; SLJ 8/96) [972]

**12645** Staub, Frank. *Children of Yucatan* (3–6). Illus. Series: The World's Children. 1996, Carolrhoda LB $21.27 (0-87614-984-0). 48pp. The daily activities and social conditions of children in this remote part of Mexico are featured, along with good background information. (Rev: BCCB 11/96; BL 10/1/96; SLJ 10/96) [972]

**12646** Steele, Philip. *The Aztec News* (4–6). Illus. 1997, Candlewick $15.99 (0-7636-0115-2). 32pp. Using a newspaper format, this account covers a number of topics related to Aztecs and their history, including farming, recreation, religion, and the practice of human sacrifice. (Rev: BL 7/97; SLJ 9/97) [972.01]

**12647** Stein, R. Conrad. *The Aztec Empire* (5–8). Illus. Series: Cultures of the Past. 1995, Benchmark LB $28.50 (0-7614-0072-9). 80pp. As well as telling the history of the Aztecs, this attractive, well-written account describes their everyday life and religion. (Rev: SLJ 6/96) [972]

**12648** Stein, R. Conrad. *Mexico City* (3–6). Illus. Series: Cities of the World. 1996, Children's LB $25.00 (0-516-00352-6). 64pp. History, religion, and the principal sights are covered in this introduction to Mexico City. (Rev: BL 11/1/96; SLJ 9/96) [972]

**12649** Wolf, Bernard. *Beneath the Stone: A Mexican Zapotec Tale* (4–6). Illus. 1994, Orchard LB $17.99 (0-531-08685-2). 48pp. In photos and text, several months in the life of a Zapotec Indian family in Mexico are followed, with descriptions of their holidays and family business. (Rev: BL 3/15/94; SLJ 8/94) [972]

**12650** Wood, Marion. *Growing Up in Aztec Times* (3–5). Illus. by Richard Hook. Series: Growing Up In. 1993, Troll paper $4.95 (0-8167-2724-4). 32pp. Describes Aztec community life and their beliefs, customs, and rituals, with details on the education of children. (Rev: BL 1/15/94) [972]

**12651** Wood, Tim. *The Aztecs* (4–6). Illus. Series: See Through History. 1992, Viking paper $17.99 (0-670-84492-6). 48pp. Enhanced by overlays, this is a well-designed look at an amazing culture. (Rev: BL 10/15/92; SLJ 1/93) [972.018]

## Other Central American Lands

**12652** Adams, Faith. *El Salvador: Beauty Among the Ashes* (4–6). Illus. 1986, Macmillan $14.95 (0-87518-309-3). 136pp. Basic facts on geography, culture, and history are combined with a sensitive look

at the lives of Salvadorans today. (Rev: BCCB 2/86; BL 3/1/86; SLJ 3/86)

**12653** Adams, Faith. *Nicaragua: Struggling with Change* (5–8). Illus. 1987, Macmillan LB $14.95 (0-87518-340-9). 152pp. A balanced telling of a troubled Central American country's story. (Rev: BL 5/15/87; SLJ 8/87)

**12654** Bachelis, Faren M. *El Salvador* (5–8). Illus. Series: Enchantment of the World. 1990, Children's LB $32.00 (0-516-02718-2). 128pp. Background material is given on this small Central American nation that often figures prominently in the news. (Rev: BL 7/90) [972.84]

**12655** Brill, Marlene T., and Harry R. Targ. *Guatemala* (5–8). Illus. Series: Enchantment of the World. 1993, Children's LB $32.00 (0-516-02614-3). 128pp. This introduction to Guatemala covers history, geography, people, and culture. (Rev: BL 8/93) [972.8]

**12656** *Costa Rica in Pictures* (4–7). Illus. 1997, Lerner LB $19.93 (0-8225-1805-8). 64pp. Separate chapters on land, people, government, history, and economy, plus numerous illustrations and revised text. (Rev: BL 8/87)

**12657** Franklin, Kristine L., and Nancy McGirr, eds. *Out of the Dump: Writings and Photographs by Children from Guatemala* (4–8). Illus. 1996, Lothrop LB $18.93 (0-688-13924-8). 56pp. A photographic essay that focuses on the poor children who exist by scavenging in the garbage dump of Guatemala City. (Rev: BCCB 3/96; BL 3/15/96*; SLJ 4/96*) [861]

**12658** Garcia, Guy. *Spirit of the Maya: A Boy Explores His People's Mysterious Past* (4–6). Illus. 1995, Walker LB $17.85 (0-8027-8380-5). 48pp. A young Mayan boy discovers his heritage when he explores the ruins at Palenque and learns of the boy-king Pacal, who is buried there. (Rev: BCCB 12/95; BL 10/1/95; SLJ 1/96) [972]

**12659** Greene, Jacqueline D. *The Maya* (3–5). Illus. Series: First Books. 1992, Watts LB $21.00 (0-531-20067-1). 64pp. This account explores the daily life of the Central American civilization that survived for thousands of years. (Rev: BL 6/15/92; SLJ 8/92) [972.81]

**12660** *Guatemala in Pictures* (4–7). Illus. 1997, Lerner LB $19.93 (0-8225-1803-1). 64pp. Photos and revised text highlight this review of the land, history, people, and culture. (Rev: BL 8/87)

**12661** Hassig, Susan M. *Panama* (4–7). Illus. Series: Cultures of the World. 1996, Marshall Cavendish LB $34.21 (0-7614-0278-0). 128pp. The troubled history of Panama is covered, with material on geography and the life-style and culture of its people. (Rev: BL 8/96) [972.87]

**12662** Haverstock, Nathan A. *Nicaragua in Pictures* (5–8). Illus. 1993, Lerner LB $19.93 (0-8225-1817-

1). 64pp. A visit to this controversial country is highlighted by color photos and clear text. (Rev: BL 10/15/87)

**12663** Hermes, Jules. *Children of Guatemala* (2–4). Photos by author. Series: World's Children. 1997, Carolrhoda LB $21.27 (0-87614-994-8). 48pp. Children from different classes and districts are introduced in this book describing life in Guatemala. (Rev: SLJ 3/98) [917.28]

**12664** *Honduras in Pictures* (4–7). Illus. 1994, Lerner LB $19.93 (0-8225-1804-X). 64pp. Chapters focus on history, culture, education, people, geography, and life-styles. (Rev: BL 8/87)

**12665** McKissack, Patricia. *The Maya* (1–3). Illus. 1985, Children's LB $21.00 (0-516-01270-3); paper $5.50 (0-516-41270-1). 45pp. A simple introduction to the life-style of the Mayan people for beginning readers. (Rev: BL 3/1/86; SLJ 4/86)

**12666** Malone, Michael. *A Guatemalan Family* (4–7). Illus. Series: Journey Between Two Worlds. 1996, Lerner paper $8.95 (0-8225-9742-X). 64pp. The story of a refugee family from Guatemala and of its resettlement in the United States. (Rev: BL 11/15/96; SLJ 1/97) [975.9]

**12667** Morrison, Marion. *Belize* (5–8). Illus. Series: Enchantment of the World. 1996, Children's LB $32.00 (0-516-02639-9). 124pp. An introduction to the small Central American nation, formerly called British Honduras. (Rev: BL 7/96) [972.82]

**12668** Odijk, Pamela. *The Mayas* (4–7). Illus. Series: Ancient World. 1990, Silver Burdett LB $14.95 (0-382-09890-0). 48pp. The history and accomplishments of the Mayas are covered in this illustrated account. (Rev: BL 11/1/90; SLJ 1/91) [972.81]

**12669** *Panama in Pictures* (4–7). Illus. 1996, Lerner LB $19.93 (0-8225-1818-X). 64pp. The life and culture, history, and geography of the people of Panama. (Rev: BL 8/87)

**12670** Parker, Nancy W. *Locks, Crocs, and Skeeters: The Story of the Panama Canal* (3–5). Illus. 1996, Greenwillow $16.00 (0-688-12241-8). 32pp. A history of the Isthmus of Panama, with details of the dangers and triumphs connected with the building of the canal. (Rev: BCCB 6/96; BL 5/15/96; SLJ 4/96) [972.87]

**12671** Sherrow, Victoria. *The Maya Indians* (3–5). Illus. Series: Junior Library of American Indians. 1993, Chelsea LB $15.95 (0-7910-1666-8). 80pp. An account of the Mayan culture, principally of the Yucatan area of Mexico and Guatemala, its destruction by the Spaniards, and the present status of the descendants. (Rev: BL 2/15/94; SLJ 2/94) [973.81]

**12672** Vazquez, Ana Maria B. *Panama* (5–8). Illus. Series: Enchantment of the World. 1991, Children's LB $32.00 (0-516-02604-6). 128pp. In addition to

historical and geographic information, this book discusses the canal and its troubled present. (Rev: BL 2/1/92) [972.87]

**12673** Waterlow, Julia. *A Family from Guatemala* (3–5). Series: Families Around the World. 1997, Raintree Steck-Vaughn LB $15.48 (0-8172-4903-6). 32pp. The everyday activities of the Calabay family of Guatemala are described, including Vicente's project of weaving a blanket, the sale of which will be the family's sole source of income. (Rev: BL 2/15/98; SLJ 3/98) [972.81]

## Puerto Rico and Other Caribbean Islands

**12674** Anthony, Suzanne. *Haiti* (5–8). Illus. Series: Places and Peoples of the World. 1989, Chelsea LB $19.95 (1-55546-796-2). 110pp. Basic information about Haiti, including history, geography, culture, and economy. (Rev: BL 7/89) [972.94]

**12675** Flint, David. *West Indies* (2–4). Illus. Series: On the Map. 1993, Raintree Steck-Vaughn LB $22.83 (0-8114-2942-3). 32pp. Everyday life in the West Indies is explored in this simple account covering basic facts and figures, climate, geography, landmarks, and tourism. (Rev: BL 9/1/93) [917.29]

**12676** Greenberg, Keith E. *A Haitian Family* (4–7). Illus. Series: Journey Between Two Worlds. 1998, Lerner LB $22.60 (0-8225-3410-X). 56pp. The story of the Beaubrun family, the political oppression they suffered in Haiti, and their eventual journey to freedom in the United States. (Rev: BL 3/1/98) [305.9]

**12677** *Haiti in Pictures* (4–7). Illus. 1995, Lerner LB $19.93 (0-8225-1816-3). 64pp. Life in Haiti is pictured, with chapters on the people, history, government, and flora and fauna. (Rev: BCCB 9/87; BL 8/87)

**12678** Haverstock, Nathan A. *Cuba in Pictures* (5–8). Illus. 1997, Lerner LB $19.93 (0-8225-1811-2). 64pp. A look at America's island neighbor, with color photos. Also use: *Dominican Republic in Pictures* (1997). (Rev: BL 10/15/87)

**12679** *Jamaica in Pictures* (5–8). Illus. 1997, Lerner LB $19.93 (0-8225-1814-7). 64pp. Color photos highlight this visit to a popular and beautiful island. (Rev: BL 10/15/87)

**12680** Kent, Deborah. *Puerto Rico* (4–6). Illus. Series: America the Beautiful. 1991, Children's LB $29.40 (0-516-00498-0). 144pp. In a fine combination of text and graphics, the history, geography, and culture of Puerto Rico are introduced. (Rev: BL 1/15/92) [972.95]

**12681** Lindop, Edmund. *Panama and the United States: Divided by the Canal* (5–8). Illus. 1997, Twenty-First Century LB $21.40 (0-8050-4768-9). 128pp. An account that traces United States–Panama relations, from the building of the canal to the present. (Rev: BL 8/97; SLJ 7/97) [327.73]

**12682** McNeese, Tim. *The Panama Canal* (5–8). Illus. Series: Building History. 1997, Lucent LB $22.45 (1-56006-425-0). 96pp. A description of the building of the Panama Canal that also supplies valuable insights into the economic and social conditions of the times. (Rev: BL 8/97; SLJ 7/97) [386]

**12683** *Puerto Rico in Pictures* (4–7). Illus. 1995, Lerner LB $19.95 (0-8225-1821-X). 64pp. Life and history, culture and geography are introduced. (Rev: BL 8/87)

**12684** Sheehan, Sean. *Jamaica* (5–8). Illus. Series: Cultures of the World. 1993, Marshall Cavendish LB $34.21 (1-85435-581-3). 128pp. This informative account describes many facets of Jamaican life, including history, religion, and reggae music. (Rev: SLJ 2/94) [972.92]

**12685** Staub, Frank. *Children of Cuba* (3–6). Illus. Series: World's Children. 1996, Carolrhoda LB $21.27 (0-87614-989-1). 48pp. Interesting background information on Cuba is introduced through the experiences of several children. (Rev: BL 12/1/96; SLJ 2/97) [972.91]

**12686** Telemaque, Eleanor Wong. *Haiti Through Its Holidays* (4–5). Illus. by Earl Hill. 1980, Blyden Pr. $8.50 (0-685-00779-0). 64pp. An introduction to Haiti through its holidays and customs surrounding them.

**12687** Vazquez, Ana Maria B., and Rosa Casas. *Cuba* (4–7). Illus. 1988, Children's LB $32.00 (0-516-02758-1). 128pp. Facts about our Communist neighbor only 90 miles from the United States. (Rev: BL 5/15/88; SLJ 1/89)

## South America

**12688** *Argentina in Pictures* (5–8). Illus. 1994, Lerner LB $19.93 (0-8225-1807-4). 64pp. Overview of climate, wildlife, cities, vegetation, and mineral resources. (Rev: BL 4/15/88; SLJ 5/88)

**12689** Beirne, Barbara. *Children of the Ecuadorean Highlands* (3–6). Illus. Series: The World's Children. 1996, Carolrhoda LB $21.72 (1-57505-000-5). 48pp. Historical and geographical materials are included in this story about young people in Equador. (Rev: BL 10/1/96; SLJ 11/96) [972]

**12690** Bendick, Jeanne. *Tombs of the Ancient Americas* (3–5). Illus. 1993, Watts LB $21.00 (0-531-20148-1). 64pp. This account surveys the burial practices and places of such civilizations as the Incas, Aztecs, and Mayas. (Rev: BCCB 5/93; BL 8/93; SLJ 8/93) [393.1]

**12691** Blashfield, Jean F. *Galápagos Islands* (4–7). Illus. Series: Wonders of the World. 1995, Raintree Steck-Vaughn LB $25.64 (0-8114-6362-1). 64pp. This book describes the history and unusual wildlife of the Galápagos Islands and Darwin's visit there in 1835. (Rev: SLJ 6/95) [918.5]

**12692** *Bolivia in Pictures* (5–8). Illus. 1993, Lerner LB $19.93 (0-8225-1808-2). 64pp. Color photos add to the appeal of this overview of a South American land. (Rev: BL 10/15/87)

**12693** Brill, Marlene T. *Guyana* (5–8). Illus. Series: Enchantment of the World. 1994, Children's LB $32.00 (0-516-02626-7). 127pp. With color photos on each page, this account introduces Guyana and supplies material on its geography, history, peoples, culture, and resources. (Rev: BL 12/15/94) [988.1]

**12694** Carpenter, Mark L. *Brazil: An Awakening Giant* (5–7). Illus. 1988, Macmillan $14.95 (0-87518-366-2). 128pp. A wide range of information is included, with the focus on everyday life. (Rev: BL 2/15/88)

**12695** *Colombia in Pictures* (5–8). Illus. 1996, Lerner LB $19.93 (0-8225-1810-4). 64pp. Many photos highlight this visit to a South American nation. (Rev: BL 10/15/87)

**12696** Dubois, Jill. *Colombia* (5–8). Illus. Series: Cultures of the World. 1991, Marshall Cavendish LB $34.21 (1-85435-384-5). 128pp. Background information on Colombia is given as well as coverage on contemporary concerns. (Rev: BL 4/1/91) [986.1]

**12697** *Ecuador in Pictures* (4–7). Illus. 1994, Lerner LB $19.93 (0-8225-1813-9). 64pp. Illustrations, many in color, highlight basic facts about this country. (Rev: BL 1/1/88)

**12698** Falconer, Kieran. *Peru* (4–7). Illus. Series: Cultures of the World. 1995, Marshall Cavendish LB $34.21 (0-7614-0179-2). 128pp. The focus of this book is on the people of Peru, their life-styles, artistic endeavors, religion, and leisure activities. (Rev: BL 1/1–15/96; SLJ 4/96) [985]

**12699** Foley, Erin. *Ecuador* (5–8). Illus. Series: Cultures of the World. 1995, Marshall Cavendish LB $34.21 (0-7614-0173-3). 128pp. This book supplies good background material on Ecuador but is strongest in describing contemporary conditions. (Rev: SLJ 11/95) [980]

**12700** Gofen, Ethel C. *Cultures of the World: Argentina* (5–8). Illus. Series: Cultures of the World. 1991, Marshall Cavendish LB $195.02 (1-85435-380-2). 128pp. This book provides standard information on history and geography and tells about the contemporary life-styles of the people. (Rev: BL 4/1/91) [962]

**12701** *Guyana in Pictures* (5–8). Illus. 1997, Lerner LB $19.93 (0-8225-1815-5). 64pp. History, climate, wildlife, and major cities are covered in this overview. (Rev: BL 4/15/88)

**12702** Haskins, Jim, and Kathleen Benson. *Count Your Way Through Brazil* (2–4). Illus. by Liz B. Dodson. Series: Count Your Way. 1996, Carolrhoda LB $19.93 (0-87614-873-9); paper $5.95 (0-87614-971-9). 24pp. Facts about Brazil are introduced in a counting book that goes from 1 to 10. (Rev: BL 9/15/96; SLJ 8/96) [981]

**12703** Haverstock, Nathan A. *Brazil in Pictures* (4–7). Illus. 1997, Lerner LB $19.93 (0-8225-1802-3). 64pp. Current data on the political scene, plus chapters on history, people, and culture in this revised text. Also use: *Chile in Pictures* (1988). (Rev: BL 8/87)

**12704** Haverstock, Nathan A. *Paraguay in Pictures* (5–8). Illus. 1995, Lerner LB $19.95 (0-8225-1819-8). 64pp. This overview of Paraguay includes its history to 1987 and possible future developments. (Rev: BL 4/15/88)

**12705** Heinrichs, Ann. *Brazil* (4–6). Series: True Books: Countries. 1997, Children's LB $20.00 (0-516-20328-2). 48pp. Short chapters on Brazil cover such topics as land, people, history, homes, and culture. (Rev: BL 9/15/97) [981]

**12706** Heinrichs, Ann. *Venezuela* (4–6). Series: True Books: Countries. 1997, Children's LB $21.00 (0-516-20344-4). 48pp. Venezuela is introduced with a simple text, many color photos, and a map. (Rev: BL 9/15/97) [987]

**12707** Hermes, Jules. *The Children of Bolivia* (3–5). Illus. Series: World's Children. 1996, Carolrhoda LB $21.27 (0-87614-935-2). 47pp. By focusing on children in the country and in cities, the 2 distinct native cultures of Bolivia are explored. (Rev: SLJ 5/96) [984]

**12708** Hintz, Martin. *Chile* (4–6). Illus. 1985, Children's LB $32.00 (0-516-02755-7). 128pp. Covers basic aspects of life in this South American land.

**12709** Jacobsen, Karen. *Argentina* (1–3). Illus. Series: New True Books. 1990, Children's LB $20.00 (0-516-01101-4). 48pp. The land and people of Argentina are introduced with minimal text. (Rev: BL 1/1/91) [982]

**12710** Jordan, Tanis. *Angel Falls: A South American Journey* (2–4). Illus. by Martin Jordan. 1995, Kingfisher $15.95 (1-85697-541-X). 40pp. Angel Falls in Venezuela is featured, with excellent coverage on the area's flora and fauna. (Rev: BL 8/95) [508.87]

**12711** Kendall, Sarita. *The Incas* (5–6). Illus. Series: World of the Past. 1992, Macmillan LB $14.95 (0-02-750160-4). 64pp. A history of the Incas before, during, and after the Spanish conquest. (Rev: SLJ 11/92) [940.54]

**12712** Kent, Deborah. *Rio de Janeiro* (3–6). Illus. Series: Cities of the World. 1996, Children's LB $25.00 (0-516-00353-4). 64pp. The great energy of this Brazilian city is captured in this simple introduction that includes material on history, population, famous sights, religion, holidays, and ethnic blending. (Rev: SLJ 9/96) [981]

**12713** Lehtinen, Ritva, and Karl E. Nurmi. *The Grandchildren of the Incas* (4–6). Illus. by Matti Pitkanen. Series: The World's Children. 1991, Carolrhoda LB $21.27 (0-87614-397-4). 40pp. Some children herd sheep while others work in the city in this profile of young Incan descendants. (Rev: BL 6/1/91) [980]

**12714** Lepthien, Emilie U. *Ecuador* (5–7). Illus. 1986, Children's LB $32.00 (0-516-02760-3). 128pp. Full of data on history, topography, people, climate, economy, flora and fauna, education, and work. (Rev: BL 7/86)

**12715** Lepthien, Emilie U. *Peru* (5–8). Illus. Series: Enchantment of the World. 1992, Children's LB $32.00 (0-516-02610-0). 128pp. With many photos and clear text, this volume introduces Peru and gives summary materials in separate minifacts sections. (Rev: BL 2/1/93) [985]

**12716** Lewington, Anna. *What Do We Know About the Amazonian Indians?* (4–6). Illus. by Ian Thompson. Series: What Do We Know About . . .? 1993, Bedrick LB $18.95 (0-87226-367-3); paper $8.95 (0-87226-262-6). 43pp. Double-page spreads are used to introduce the history, lives, and cultures of the Indians of the Amazon River. (Rev: SLJ 3/94) [981.1]

**12717** McKissack, Patricia. *The Inca* (1–3). Illus. 1985, Children's LB $20.00 (0-516-01268-1); paper $5.50 (0-516-41268-X). 45pp. Life-styles of the Inca yesterday and today for the beginning reader. (Rev: BL 3/1/86; SLJ 4/86)

**12718** Markham, Lois. *Colombia: The Gateway to South America* (3–5). Illus. Series: Exploring Cultures of the World. 1997, Marshall Cavendish LB $25.64 (0-7614-0140-7). 64pp. The past and present are contrasted in this account that gives good background information about Colombia plus material on its culture and the arts. (Rev: BL 7/97; SLJ 4/98) [986.1]

**12719** Morrison, Marion. *Brazil* (4–7). Illus. Series: Country Insights. 1997, Raintree Steck-Vaughn LB $24.96 (0-8172-4785-8). 48pp. Compares the home life, employment, schooling, and recreation in a large city and in a small village in Brazil. (Rev: BL 7/97; SLJ 8/97) [918.1]

**12720** Morrison, Marion. *Indians of the Andes* (4–6). Illus. 1987, Rourke LB $16.67 (0-86625-260-6). 48pp. With attractive design and numerous color photos, the Indians of the Andes are introduced to young readers. (Rev: BL 1/15/88)

**12721** Morrison, Marion. *Paraguay* (5–8). Illus. Series: Enchantment of the World. 1993, Children's LB $32.00 (0-516-02619-4). 128pp. The history, geography, and people of Paraguay are covered, along with its economy, traditions, and landmarks. (Rev: BL 11/1/93; SLJ 3/94) [989.2]

**12722** Morrison, Marion. *Uruguay* (5–8). Illus. Series: Enchantment of the World. 1992, Children's LB $36.00 (0-516-02607-0). 128pp. Introduces Uruguay, the small South American republic that was once part of Argentina. (Rev: BL 6/1/92) [989.5]

**12723** Morrison, Marion. *Venezuela* (5–8). Illus. Series: Enchantment of the World. 1989, Children's LB $36.00 (0-516-02711-5). 128pp. Economy, geography, history, and people are some of the topics covered. (Rev: BL 8/89; SLJ 2/90) [987]

**12724** Myers, Lynne B., and Christopher A. Myers. *Galapagos: Islands of Change* (4–7). Illus. 1995, Hyperion LB $17.49 (0-7868-2061-6). 48pp. The formation of these islands and the evolution of life on them are covered in text and amazing photographs. (Rev: BL 12/15/95; SLJ 11/95) [508]

**12725** Newman, Shirlee P. *The Incas* (3–5). Illus. Series: First Books. 1992, Watts LB $21.00 (0-531-20004-3); paper $6.95 (0-531-15637-0). 64pp. The story of the Inca empire in South America from 1200 to 1532, when the Spaniards arrived. (Rev: BL 6/15/92; SLJ 8/92) [980]

**12726** Odijk, Pamela. *The Incas* (4–7). Illus. Series: Ancient World. 1990, Silver Burdett LB $14.95 (0-382-09889-7). 48pp. In addition to a history of the civilization that prospered in Peru, there is a time line, glossary, and list of famous names. (Rev: BL 7/90; SLJ 8/90) [985]

**12727** Pateman, Robert. *Bolivia* (4–7). Illus. Series: Cultures of the World. 1995, Marshall Cavendish LB $34.21 (0-7614-0178-4). 128pp. The people of Bolivia, how they live, and their traditions are some of the topics covered in this general introduction. (Rev: BL 1/1–15/96; SLJ 4/96) [984]

**12728** *Peru in Pictures* (5–8). Illus. 1997, Lerner LB $19.95 (0-8225-1820-1). 64pp. Young readers visit this South American land, highlighted by color photos. (Rev: BL 10/15/87)

**12729** Powell, Susan, and Rose Inserra. *Amazonia* (4–6). Illus. Series: Ends of the Earth. 1997, Heinemann LB $14.95 (0-431-06935-2). 48pp. The environment in and around the Amazon is described in text and many photos, maps, and diagrams, with additional material on native Indians. (Rev: SLJ 10/97) [981]

**12730** Reynolds, Jan. *Amazon Basin* (3–6). Illus. Series: Vanishing Cultures. 1993, Harcourt $16.95 (0-15-202831-5); paper $10.00 (0-15-202832-3). 32pp. Examines the daily life of the Indians who live in the Amazon rain forest and explains why their culture is endangered. (Rev: BCCB 11/93; BL 12/1/93; SLJ 10/93) [306]

**12731** Richard, Christopher. *Brazil* (5–8). Illus. Series: Cultures of the World. 1991, Marshall Cavendish LB $34.21 (1-85435-382-9). 128pp. Brazil is introduced with information on such topics as history, economics, people, and modern problems. (Rev: BL 4/1/91) [981]

**12732** St. John, Jetty. *A Family in Chile* (2–4). Illus. 1986, Lerner LB $18.60 (0-8225-1667-5). 32pp. Focusing on one child in a Chilean family, the reader learns of life in this South American land. (Rev: BL 5/15/86; SLJ 10/86)

**12733** Schimmel, Karen. *Bolivia* (4–7). Illus. Series: Places and Peoples of the World. 1990, Chelsea $19.95 (0-7910-1109-7). 111pp. A clearly written account of Bolivia, where native and Spanish cultures mix. (Rev: SLJ 2/91) [984]

**12734** Schwartz, David M. *Yanomami: People of the Amazon* (4–6). Photos by Victor Englebert. Series: Vanishing People. 1995, Lothrop LB $15.93 (0-688-11158-0). 48pp. A profile of the daily life of the Yanomami, an Indian tribe that lives in the Amazon rain forest. (Rev: BL 3/1/95; SLJ 3/95) [981]

**12735** Siy, Alexandra. *The Waorani: People of the Ecuadoran Rain Forest* (4–7). Illus. Series: Global Villages. 1993, Macmillan LB $14.95 (0-87518-550-9). 80pp. Presents the history, culture, and prospects for the future of these people. (Rev: SLJ 8/93) [980]

**12736** Steele, Philip. *The Incas and Machu Picchu* (4–7). Illus. Series: Hidden Worlds. 1993, Dillon LB $13.95 (0-87518-536-3). 32pp. A history of the Inca people and a tour of their ruined fortress city in Peru are included in this fascinating account. (Rev: BL 12/1/93) [985.37]

**12737** *Venezuela in Pictures* (4–7). Illus. 1993, Lerner LB $19.93 (0-8225-1824-4). 64pp. The land, people, and government of this oil-rich country are explored in maps, text, and photos. (Rev: BL 1/1/88)

**12738** Winter, Jane K. *Chile* (5–8). Illus. Series: Cultures of the World. 1991, Marshall Cavendish LB $34.21 (1-85435-383-7). 128pp. The geography, history, government, and economy of Chile are some of the topics covered in this fine introduction. (Rev: BL 4/1/91) [983]

**12739** Winter, Jane K. *Venezuela* (5–8). Illus. Series: Cultures of the World. 1991, Marshall Cavendish LB $34.21 (1-85435-386-1). 128pp. In detailed text and color photographs, the land and people of Venezuela are introduced and coverage is given on contemporary problems and concerns. (Rev: BL 4/1/91) [987]

# Polar Regions

**12740** Aldis, Rodney. *Polar Lands* (5–8). Illus. Series: Ecology Watch. 1992, Macmillan LB $13.95 (0-87518-494-4). 46pp. After describing the polar regions and the life that exists there, this account emphasizes the need for conservation. (Rev: BL 11/1/92) [574]

**12741** Alexander, Bryan, and Cherry Alexander. *An Eskimo Family* (3–6). Illus. 1985, Lerner LB $18.60 (0-8225-1656-X). 32pp. Young readers get a taste of life in the far north in this look at an Eskimo family. (Rev: BL 6/15/85; SLJ 10/85)

**12742** Alexander, Bryan, and Cherry Alexander. *What Do We Know About the Inuit?* (3–6). Illus. Series: What Do We Know About . . .? 1995, Bedrick LB $18.95 (0-87226-380-0). 45pp. An attractive volume that supplies very basic information about the Inuit people and how they live. (Rev: SLJ 1/96) [979.8]

**12743** Asimov, Isaac. *How Did We Find Out About Antarctica?* (5–7). Illus. by David Wool. 1979, Walker LB $11.85 (0-8027-6371-5). Ideas, people, and occupations that have influenced our knowledge of Antarctica.

**12744** Billings, Henry. *Antarctica* (5–8). Illus. Series: Enchantment of the World. 1994, Children's LB $32.00 (0-516-02624-0). 127pp. With color photos on each page, this account covers the history and geography of the Antarctic region, with material on plant and animal life. (Rev: BL 12/15/94) [998.2]

**12745** Cowcher, Helen. *Antarctica* (K–4). Illus. 1990, Farrar $15.00 (0-374-30368-1). 32pp. Minimal text explains the life of emperor penguins, which, along with other species, are threatened by humans on the continent. (Rev: BCCB 5/90; BL 7/90; HB 7–8/90; SLJ 7/90) [998.9]

**12746** Darling, Kathy. *Arctic Babies* (K–3). Illus. by Tara Darling. 1996, Walker LB $16.85 (0-8027-8414-3). 32pp. Using full-color photos of each animal, the author introduces a variety of babies from a lynx kitten to a baby beluga whale. (Rev: BL 4/15/96; SLJ 4/96) [591.9]

**12747** Dunphy, Madeleine. *Here Is the Arctic Winter* (K–4). Illus. by Alan J. Robinson. 1993, Hyperion $14.95 (1-562-82336-1). A look at the land and the animals that survive the long arctic night of winter. (Rev: SLJ 5/93) [998]

**12748** Fleischner, Jennifer. *The Inuit: People of the Arctic* (4–6). Illus. Series: Native Americans. 1995, Millbrook LB $21.90 (1-56294-587-4). 64pp. The Inuit people of the North are introduced, with material on their food, clothing, homes, history, recreation, and art. (Rev: BL 10/15/95) [979.8]

**12749** Forman, Michael H. *Arctic Tundra* (K–3). Illus. Series: Habitats. 1997, Children's LB $24.00 (0-516-20710-5). 31pp. The Arctic and its animals, birds, plants, and insects are introduced in a fine combination of photos, illustrations, and a clear text. (Rev: SLJ 9/97) [575.5]

**12750** George, Michael. *Antarctica* (3–6). Illus. Series: Images. 1994, Creative Ed. LB $16.95 (0-88682-600-4). 40pp. Breathtaking photos are used to give information about the location, geography, climate, and plant and animal life of Antarctica. (Rev: SLJ 6/95) [919.8]

**12751** George, Michael. *Tundra* (3–6). Illus. Series: Images. 1994, Creative Ed. LB $17.95 (0-88682-601-2). 40pp. The Arctic tundra is presented in text and striking photos illustrating location, life, climate, and physical features. (Rev: SLJ 6/95) [551.4]

**12752** Hoyt-Goldsmith, Diane. *Arctic Hunter* (3–6). 1992, Holiday LB $16.95 (0-8234-0972-4). 32pp. Ten-year-old Reggie and his family travel to their camp north of the Arctic Circle to add to their food supply. (Rev: BL 12/15/92; HB 1–2/93; SLJ 11/92*) [979.8]

**12753** Johnson, Rebecca L. *Braving the Frozen Frontier: Women Working in Antarctica* (3–6). Illus. 1997, Lerner LB $23.93 (0-8225-2855-X). 112pp. A profile of positions open to women in Antarctica including those of doctor, cartographer, biologist, and bulldozer driver. (Rev: BCCB 3/97; BL 2/15/97; SLJ 3/97*) [919.8]

**12754** Kaplan, Elizabeth. *Tundra* (4–6). Illus. Series: Biomes of the World. 1995, Marshall Cavendish LB $25.64 (0-7614-0080-X). 64pp. Material is given on the location of this frigid biome and the life it supports. (Rev: BL 12/15/95; SLJ 3/96) [551.4]

**12755** Kendall, Russ. *Eskimo Boy: Life in an Inupiag Eskimo Village* (2–4). Illus. 1992, Scholastic $15.95 (0-590-43695-3). 40pp. An informal photoessay that focuses on 7-year-old Norman Kokeok, who lives on the remote Alaskan island of Shishmaref. (Rev: BCCB 2/92; BL 1/15/92; SLJ 4/92) [979.8]

**12756** Lambert, David. *Polar Regions* (5–8). Illus. 1988, Silver Burdett LB $12.95 (0-382-09502-2). 48pp. Striking color photos, plus maps and diagrams highlight this description of the world's polar regions. (Rev: BL 4/1/88)

**12757** Lewin, Ted. *The Reindeer People* (3–5). Illus. 1994, Macmillan paper $14.95 (0-02-757390-7). 40pp. The story of the Sami people of Lapland, their environment, and their culture are told in text and splendid paintings. (Rev: BL 10/1/94; SLJ 2/95) [948.97]

**12758** McCurdy, Michael. *Trapped by the Ice: Shackleton's Amazing Antarctic Adventure* (3–5). Illus. 1997, Walker LB $17.85 (0-8027-8439-9).

40pp. The breathtaking account of Shackleton's 6-month ordeal living on the ice after his ship sank in the Arctic. (Rev: BL 9/15/97; SLJ 10/97) [919.9804]

**12759** McDonald, Kellie. *Antarctica* (4–6). Illus. Series: Ends of the Earth. 1997, Heinemann LB $14.95 (0-431-06934-4). 48pp. An introduction to this continent, its geography, and the research stations found there. (Rev: SLJ 10/97) [919.8]

**12760** McMillan, Bruce. *Summer Ice: Life Along the Antarctic Peninsula* (4–6). Illus. 1995, Houghton $15.95 (0-395-66561-2). 48pp. A photoessay that describes the geography and the plants and animals that live on the Antarctic Peninsula. (Rev: BL 11/1/95; SLJ 9/95) [508]

**12761** Markle, Sandra. *Pioneering Frozen Worlds* (3–6). Illus. 1996, Simon & Schuster $17.00 (0-689-31824-3). 48pp. The frozen worlds of the polar regions and current research taking place in these areas are described, with several suggested experiments. (Rev: BCCB 2/96; BL 5/1/96; SLJ 5/96) [919.8]

**12762** Markle, Sandra. *Super Cool Science: South Pole Stations Past, Present, and Future* (3–5). Illus. 1998, Walker LB $17.85 (0-8027-8471-2). 32pp. After describing the first research station at the South Pole built in 1956, the author describes the present facilities and their uses, with coverage on plans for a newer, larger station in the future. (Rev: BL 3/15/98; SLJ 4/98) [507]

**12763** Newman, Shirlee P. *The Inuits* (4–6). Illus. Series: First Books. 1993, Watts $21.00 (0-531-20073-6). 64pp. A vivid account of Inuit, or Eskimo, life that supplies information on their homes, food, clothing, family life, and social structure. (Rev: BL 12/1/93) [973]

**12764** Osinski, Alice. *The Eskimo: The Inuit and Yupik People* (1–3). Illus. 1985, Children's LB $21.00 (0-516-01267-3); paper $5.50 (0-516-41267-1). 45pp. Beginning readers are introduced to the land and peoples of the far north. (Rev: BL 3/1/86; SLJ 4/86)

**12765** Penny, Malcolm. *The Polar Seas* (4–6). Illus. Series: Seas and Oceans. 1997, Raintree Steck-Vaughn LB $24.26 (0-8172-4513-8). 48pp. An overview of the history and importance of the polar seas, as well as the dangers that tourism and the search for natural resources now pose. (Rev: BL 7/97) [551.46]

**12766** Poncet, Sally. *Antarctic Encounter: Destination South Georgia* (5–7). Illus. 1995, Simon & Schuster paper $17.00 (0-02-774905-3). 48pp. A photoessay on the bird population of the islands of the Antarctic plus details on the everyday life of the author and her family in this difficult environment. (Rev: BCCB 9/95; BL 6/1–15/95; SLJ 9/95) [508.95]

**12767** Reynolds, Jan. *Frozen Land* (3–6). Illus. Series: Vanishing Cultures. 1993, Harcourt $16.95 (0-15-238787-0); paper $8.95 (0-15-238788-9). 32pp. An Inuit family of caribou hunters is introduced and their daily life described, with material on why their culture is endangered. (Rev: BCCB 11/93; BL 12/1/93; SLJ 2/94) [306]

**12768** Rootes, David. *The Arctic* (3–6). Illus. Series: Endangered People and Places. 1996, Lerner LB $22.60 (0-8225-2776-6). 48pp. A glimpse of the Arctic region and the people who live in this hostile environment. (Rev: BL 11/15/96; SLJ 1/97) [333.73]

**12769** Sayre, April Pulley. *Tundra* (4–7). Illus. Series: Exploring Earth's Biomes. 1994, Twenty-First Century LB $18.90 (0-8050-2829-3). 64pp. The treeless plains found in the northern arctic are described, along with details of the flora and fauna found there. (Rev: BL 1/15/95; SLJ 2/95) [574]

**12770** Shemie, Bonnie. *Houses of Snow, Skin and Bones* (3–6). Illus. 1989, Tundra $13.95 (0-88776-240-9). 24pp. Covers a variety of dwellings used by people of the extreme north. (Rev: BCCB 12/89; BL 12/15/89; SLJ 4/90) [392.36]

**12771** Shepherd, Donna Walsh. *Tundra* (4–6). Illus. 1996, Watts LB $21.00 (0-531-20249-6). 62pp. The climate, life forms, and people of the Arctic tundra are introduced. (Rev: BL 2/1/97; SLJ 4/97) [574.5]

**12772** Steele, Philip. *Tundra* (3–5). Illus. Series: Geography Detectives. 1997, Carolrhoda LB $14.95 (1-57505-040-4). 32pp. The treeless plains of the Arctic and parts of Antarctica are introduced, with material on the people who live there and how these areas have changed through the centuries. (Rev: BL 8/97; SLJ 1/98) [574.5]

**12773** Steger, Will, and Jon Bowermaster. *Over the Top of the World: Explorer Will Steger's Trek Across the Arctic* (4–7). Illus. 1997, Scholastic $17.95 (0-590-84860-7). 64pp. Describes the grueling, dangerous adventures involved in a present-day journey across the Arctic Ocean. (Rev: BCCB 2/97; BL 4/15/97; SLJ 4/97*) [919.804]

**12774** Stewart, Gail B. *In the Polar Regions* (4–6). Illus. Series: Living Spaces. 1989, Rourke LB $21.27 (0-86592-108-3). 32pp. How people adjust to living in polar regions. (Rev: BL 11/1/89) [919.8]

**12775** Stone, Lynn M. *The Arctic* (1–3). Illus. 1985, Children's LB $19.00 (0-516-01935-X). 48pp. Nonfiction source for the very young reader on the animals and people, physical features, and seasons of the Arctic. (Rev: BL 12/1/85)

**12776** Taylor, Barbara. *Arctic and Antarctic* (4–8). Illus. Series: Eyewitness Books. 1995, Knopf $19.00 (0-679-87257-4). 64pp. A profile of the 2 polar regions that contrasts the environments and introduces their plant and animal life. (Rev: BL 8/95; SLJ 9/95) [508.311]

**12777** Winckler, Suzanne. *Our Endangered Planet: Antarctica* (4–7). Illus. Series: Our Endangered Planet. 1992, Lerner LB $22.60 (0-8225-2506-2). 72pp. Introduces the continent of Antarctica, including current environmental concerns. (Rev: BL 5/15/92) [918.8]

**12778** Yolen, Jane. *Welcome to the Ice House* (PS–3). Illus. by Laura Regan. 1998, Putnam $15.95 (0-399-23011-4). 32pp. Using illustrations that portray the bleak arctic landscapes, the poet introduces various animals that live in this inhospitable climate. (Rev: BL 2/15/98; SLJ 3/98*) [591.7586]

**12779** Yue, Charlotte, and David Yue. *The Igloo* (3–6). Illus. 1988, Houghton $13.95 (0-395-44613-9); paper $6.95 (0-395-62986-1). 128pp. Describes the construction and function of igloos. (Rev: BCCB 1/89; BL 9/1/88; SLJ 12/88)

# United States

## General

**12780** Anno, Mitsumasa. *Anno's U.S.A.* (2–5). Illus. by author. 1998, Putnam paper $6.99 (0-698-11678-X). 48pp. A wordless trek across the United States in imaginative and often humorous drawings.

**12781** Ayer, Eleanor. *Our National Monuments* (4–6). Illus. Series: I Know America. 1992, Millbrook LB $20.90 (1-56294-078-3). 48pp. The most important of our national monuments are highlighted and their history explained in this well-illustrated account. (Rev: BL 9/1/92; SLJ 10/92) [973]

**12782** Brandt, Sue R. *State Trees* (3–5). Illus. Series: Our State Symbols. 1992, Watts LB $23.00 (0-531-20000-0). 64pp. This book pictures and describes each of the states' and Puerto Rico's designated trees. (Rev: BL 2/1/93) [582]

**12783** Butler, Daphne. *U.S.A.* (2–4). Illus. 1992, Raintree Steck-Vaughn LB $22.83 (0-8114-3676-4). 32pp. Color photos aid in a broad overview of the United States, described in terms of topography and life-style. (Rev: BL 3/15/93) [973]

**12784** Henderson, Kathy. *The Great Lakes* (2–4). Illus. Series: New True Books. 1989, Children's LB $21.00 (0-516-01163-4). 48pp. The 5 Great Lakes are identified and described in many photos and brief text. (Rev: BL 1/15/90; SLJ 4/90) [551]

**12785** Hicks, Roger. *The Big Book of America* (3–5). Illus. by Sallie Reason, et al. Series: Courage Books. 1994, Running Pr. $9.98 (1-56138-390-2). 56pp. In a single page for each state, basic information is pre-

sented, including symbols, historical facts, and a map. (Rev: SLJ 7/94) [973]

**12786** Holling, Holling C. *Paddle-to-the-Sea* (3–6). Illus. by author. 1980, Houghton $20.00 (0-395-15082-5); paper $9.95 (0-395-29203-4). From Ontario to the Atlantic in a toy canoe, in this classic juvenile tale.

**12787** Johnson, Linda C. *Our National Symbols* (4–6). Illus. Series: I Know America. 1992, Millbrook LB $20.90 (1-56294-108-9). 48pp. American symbols — historical and current, such as yellow ribbons during the Persian Gulf War — are discussed. (Rev: BL 5/15/92; SLJ 7/93) [929.9]

**12788** Landau, Elaine. *State Birds* (3–6). Illus. Series: Our State Symbols. 1992, Watts LB $23.00 (0-531-20058-2). 64pp. For each of the states and for Puerto Rico, the state bird is pictured and described. (Rev: BL 2/1/93) [582]

**12789** Landau, Elaine. *State Flowers* (3–6). Illus. Series: Our State Symbols. 1992, Watts LB $23.00 (0-531-20059-0). 64pp. State flowers for each state and for Puerto Rico are pictured and described. (Rev: BL 2/1/93) [582]

**12790** Stone, Tanya L. *America's Top 10 National Monuments* (3–6). Illus. Series: America's Top 10. 1997, Blackbirch LB $13.95 (1-56711-194-7). 24pp. Presidential memorials in Washington, D.C., and the Mesa Verde National Park are some of the monuments introduced in a series of 2-page spreads. (Rev: SLJ 1/98) [973]

## General History and Geography

**12791** Baines, John. *The United States* (4–8). Illus. Series: Country Facts Files. 1994, Raintree Steck-Vaughn LB $24.26 (0-8114-1857-X). 45pp. In a series of double-page spreads, basic information about the United States is given, including geography, economy, population, industry, education, government, and environment. (Rev: SLJ 7/94) [973]

**12792** Brownell, Barbara. *Spin's Really Wild U.S.A. Tour* (K–4). Illus. 1996, National Geographic paper $7.95 (0-7922-3422-7). An introduction to the geography of the United States that highlights the flora, fauna, and land formations, conducted by Spin from the National Geographic TV series. (Rev: SLJ 6/96) [910]

**12793** Brownstone, David M., and Irene M. Franck. *Natural Wonders of America* (4–7). Illus. 1997, DIANE Publg. paper $10.00 (0-7881-5090-1). 64pp. Forty-two sites of unusual natural beauty, such as the Grand Canyon, are described. (Rev: BL 7/89; SLJ 9/89) [508.73]

**12794** Colman, Penny. *Strike! The Bitter Struggle of American Workers from Colonial Times to the Pre-*

*sent* (4–6). Illus. 1995, Millbrook LB $23.40 (1-56294-459-2). 80pp. A history of labor relations from the first strike in 1677 to the present. (Rev: BL 11/15/95; SLJ 1/96) [331.89]

**12795** Fisher, Leonard Everett. *The White House* (4–8). Illus. 1989, Holiday LB $16.95 (0-8234-0774-8). 96pp. A tour of the White House that traces American history from the perspective of its inhabitants. (Rev: BL 11/15/89*; SLJ 12/89*) [975.3]

**12796** Foster, Genevieve, and Joanna Foster. *George Washington's World.* Rev. ed. (5–8). Illus. 1997, Beautiful Feet paper $15.95 (0-9643803-4-X). 357pp. A new edition of this 50-year-old book that re-creates what was happening in the world during Washington's life, now with expanded coverage on minorities. (Rev: SLJ 3/98) [909]

**12797** Gold, Susan D. *Land Pacts* (5–8). Illus. 1997, Twenty-First Century LB $21.40 (0-8050-4810-3). 128pp. Covers the many international agreements that resulted in the acquisition of land, as in the Louisiana and Alaska purchases. (Rev: BL 5/15/97; SLJ 6/97) [973.5]

**12798** Harness, Cheryl. *Ghosts of the White House* (2–5). Illus. 1998, Simon & Schuster paper $16.00 (0-689-80872-0). 48pp. Sara takes her own tour of the White House, with the ghosts of dead presidents acting as her guides. (Rev: BL 3/1/98; SLJ 4/98) [973]

**12799** Johnstone, Michael. *The History News: Explorers* (4–7). Illus. Series: History News. 1997, Candlewick $15.99 (0-7636-0314-7). 32pp. Famous explorers and their discoveries are covered using a newspaper format that even includes advertisements and letters to the editor, like one from Columbus telling about reaching an island close to Japan. (Rev: BL 2/1/98; SLJ 1/98) [910.92]

**12800** Jones, Rebecca C. *The President Has Been Shot! True Stories of the Attacks on Ten U.S. Presidents* (4–7). Illus. 1996, Dutton paper $15.99 (0-525-45333-4). 144pp. In chronological order, 10 attacks on U.S. presidents are presented in a very readable account. (Rev: BCCB 9/96; BL 7/96; SLJ 9/96) [364.1]

**12801** Kalman, Bobbie, and Greg Nickles. *Spanish Missions* (4–7). Illus. Series: Historic Communities. 1996, Crabtree LB $19.16 (0-86505-436-3); paper $7.95 (0-86505-466-5). 32pp. In double-page spreads, this book covers the building of the mission in the southern United States and of its functions: teaching Christianity, educating children, and supplying housing and food. (Rev: SLJ 4/97) [973]

**12802** King, David C. *First Facts About U.S. History* (4–7). Illus. 1996, Blackbirch LB $24.95 (1-56711-168-8). 112pp. In well-illustrated, double-page spreads, major events in U.S. history are covered. (Rev: BL 7/96; SLJ 7/96) [973]

**12803** Kroll, Steven. *Ellis Island: Doorway to Freedom* (3–5). Illus. by Karen Ritz. 1995, Holiday LB $15.95 (0-8234-1192-3). 32pp. This history, beginning with colonial times, concentrates on the period when Ellis Island's immigration center processed millions of immigrants. (Rev: BL 11/15/95; SLJ 1/96) [325.73]

**12804** Krull, Kathleen. *Wish You Were Here: Emily's Guide to the 50 States* (3–5). Illus. by Amy Schwartz. 1997, Doubleday $19.95 (0-385-31146-X). 118pp. After a description of a quick trip around the 50 states, this book supplies basic information on each. (Rev: BCCB 5/97; BL 6/1–15/97; SLJ 6/97) [917.3]

**12805** McCall, Edith. *Biography of a River: The Living Mississippi* (4–8). 1990, Walker LB $17.85 (0-8027-6915-2). 150pp. The history of the Mississippi River and the part it played in U.S. history. (Rev: BL 8/90) [977]

**12806** Perl, Lila. *It Happened in America: True Stories from the Fifty States* (4–6). Illus. by Ib Ohlsson. 1992, Holt $22.50 (0-8050-1719-4). 288pp. Fifty true accounts in alphabetical (by state) order showing how exciting history can be. (Rev: BL 1/15/93; SLJ 3/93) [973]

**12807** Sandak, Cass R. *The United States* (5–8). Illus. Series: Modern Industrial World. 1996, Raintree Steck-Vaughn LB $24.26 (0-8172-4556-1). 48pp. Examines the present economic and industrial situation in the United States, with additional information on education, living standards, and related subjects. (Rev: BL 2/15/97) [973]

**12808** Stienecker, David L. *States* (2–5). Illus. Series: Discovering Geography. 1997, Marshall Cavendish LB $21.36 (0-7614-0541-0). 32pp. Using a question-and-answer approach, this book teaches youngsters how to read maps that show topics such as terrain, weather, landmarks, population, capitals and products. (Rev: BL 2/1/98) [917.3]

**12809** Straub, Deborah G., ed. *African American Voices* (5–8). Illus. 1996, Gale $63.00 (0-8103-9497-9). 320pp. This is a collection of excerpts from important speeches delivered by a vast array of African Americans, past and present. (Rev: SLJ 2/97) [973]

**12810** Sullivan, Charles, ed. *Children of Promise: African-American Literature and Art for Young People* (4–8). Illus. 1991, Abrams $24.95 (0-8109-3170-2). 126pp. Through poems, songs, literary excerpts, and illustrations, the history of African Americans is traced. (Rev: SLJ 1/92) [973]

**12811** Tesar, Jenny. *America's Top 10 National Parks* (3–6). Illus. Series: America's Top 10. 1997, Blackbirch LB $13.95 (1-56711-190-4). 24pp. The most frequently visited national parks are described with good historical information. Also use *America's Top 10 Rivers* (1997). (Rev: SLJ 1/98) [917.3]

**12812** *United States in Pictures* (5–8). Illus. Series: Visual Geography. 1995, Lerner LB $19.93 (0-8225-1896-1). 64pp. An attractive, basic introduction to the geography, history, and people of the United States. (Rev: BL 8/95) [973]

**12813** Van Zandt, Eleanor. *A History of the United States Through Art* (5–8). Illus. Series: History Through Art. 1996, Thomson Learning LB $24.26 (1-56847-443-1). 48pp. American history is covered in 21 double-page spreads that feature text and famous artworks. (Rev: BL 3/1/96; SLJ 2/96) [973]

**12814** Warren, Andrea. *Orphan Train Rider: One Boy's True Story* (4–6). Illus. 1996, Houghton $16.00 (0-395-69822-7). 80pp. Although it focuses on one child's experiences on the orphan train in 1926, this account also covers the entire history of the phenomenon from 1850 to 1930. (Rev: BCCB 9/96; BL 7/96; HB 9–10/96; SLJ 8/96*) [362.7]

**12815** Weber, Michael. *Our National Parks* (4–6). Illus. Series: I Know America. 1994, Millbrook LB $21.90 (1-56294-438-X). 48pp. Three parks in each of 4 areas of the country are introduced with material on their histories and attractions. (Rev: SLJ 6/94) [917]

## Historical Periods

### INDIANS OF NORTH AMERICA

**12816** Ancona, George. *Earth Daughter: Alicia of Acoma Pueblo* (3–5). Illus. 1995, Simon & Schuster $16.00 (0-689-80322-2). 40pp. This photoessay introduces the people of a New Mexico pueblo of Keres Indians, as well as their culture, traditions, and current lifestyle. (Rev: BL 10/15/95; SLJ 12/95) [978.9]

**12817** Ancona, George. *Powwow* (3–6). Illus. 1993, Harcourt $17.00 (0-15-263268-9); paper $9.00 (0-15-263269-7). 48pp. Colorful photos and sprightly text capture the flavor of the largest powwow held in the United States at Crow Fair. (Rev: BCCB 5/93; BL 3/15/93; HB 5–6/93*; SLJ 4/93*) [394.2]

**12818** Andryszewski, Tricia. *The Seminoles: People of the Southeast* (3–6). Illus. Series: Native Americans. 1995, Millbrook LB $21.90 (1-56294-530-0). 64pp. As well as giving a history of the Seminoles, this account tells about their culture and traditions and includes a recipe, a legend, and instructions for the Seminole pole-ball game. (Rev: SLJ 1/96) [973]

**12819** Arnold, Caroline. *The Ancient Cliff Dwellers of Mesa Verde* (4–7). Illus. by Richard Hewett. 1992, Houghton $15.95 (0-395-56241-4). 64pp. This is the fascinating story of the Anasazi of southwestern Colorado, who made their homes in the cliffs of steep canyons and later abandoned them. (Rev: BL 5/1/92; SLJ 7/92*) [978.8]

**12820** Ashabranner, Brent. *A Strange and Distant Shore: Indians of the Great Plains in Exile* (5–7). Illus. 1996, Dutton paper $16.99 (0-525-65201-9). 64pp. The story of the Great Plains Indians who were exiled to St. Augustine, Florida in 1875. (Rev: BCCB 7–8/96; BL 7/96; HB 9–10/96; SLJ 9/96) [978]

**12821** Baylor, Byrd. *The Desert Is Theirs* (2–4). Illus. by Peter Parnall. 1987, Macmillan $15.00 (0-684-14266-X); paper $5.95 (0-689-71105-0). 32pp. Through colorful, strong pictures and a lyric text, the life of the Papago Indians and their reverence for the desert are revealed.

**12822** Bealer, Alex W. *Only the Names Remain: The Cherokees and the Trail of Tears* (4–6). Illus. by William Sauts Bock. 1996, Little, Brown $15.95 (0-316-08518-9); paper $4.95 (0-316-08519-7). A history of the Cherokees, with emphasis on their tragic exile west of the Mississippi River in 1839.

**12823** Beyer, Don E. *The Totem Pole Indians of the Northwest* (4–6). Illus. Series: First Books. 1991, Watts paper $6.95 (0-531-15607-9). 64pp. This account covers the history and culture of the major tribes of the northwest Pacific Coast. (Rev: BL 10/1/89; SLJ 3/90) [979.5]

**12824** Bonvillain, Nancy. *The Navajos: People of the Southwest* (3–6). Illus. Series: Native Americans. 1995, Millbrook LB $21.90 (1-56294-495-9). 64pp. Traces the history of the Navajo, their tragic encounters with white men, and their culture and life-style, with a recipe and a legend. (Rev: SLJ 1/96) [973]

**12825** Braine, Susan. *Drumbeat . . . Heartbeat: A Celebration of the Powwow* (4–6). Photos by author. Series: We Are Still Here: Native Americans Today. 1995, Lerner LB $21.27 (0-8225-2656-5); paper $6.95 (0-8225-9711-X). 48pp. An introduction to powwows that explains their history, where they are held, and what they mean to American Indians today. (Rev: SLJ 9/95) [973]

**12826** Bruchac, Joseph. *Children of the Longhouse* (3–6). 1996, Dial paper $14.89 (0-8037-1794-6). 160pp. In a story set in the 1490s, a young Mohawk boy faces a moral dilemma and, in doing right, gains some enemies. (Rev: BCCB 6/96; BL 5/1/96; SLJ 7/96)

**12827** Burby, Liza N. *The Pueblo Indians* (3–5). Illus. Series: Junior Library of American Indians. 1994, Chelsea LB $15.95 (0-7910-1669-2); paper $8.95 (0-7910-2485-7). 80pp. An examination of the Pueblo Indian history and culture and how they preserve their traditions today. (Rev: BL 10/15/94; SLJ 11/94) [973]

**12828** Carter, Alden R. *The Shoshoni* (4–6). Illus. Series: First Books. 1989, Watts LB $21.00 (0-531-10753-1); paper $6.95 (0-531-15605-2). 64pp. The Shoshoni people, a hardy desert tribe, are described, including their history, way of life, customs, and art. (Rev: BL 10/1/89) [979.5]

**12829** Claro, Nicole. *The Cherokee Indians* (3–5). Illus. Series: Indians of North America. 1991, Chelsea LB $15.95 (0-7910-1652-8). 80pp. The concentration is on the history of the Cherokee since their contact with Europeans. (Rev: BL 10/15/91) [973]

**12830** Clores, Suzanne. *Native American Women* (3–5). Illus. Series: Junior Library of American Indians. 1995, Chelsea paper $8.95 (0-7910-2480-6). 72pp. The place of women in Native American cultures and their contributions and accomplishments. (Rev: BL 10/15/95) [305.48]

**12831** Cory, Steven. *Pueblo Indian* (5–8). Illus. by Richard Erickson. Series: American Pastfinder. 1996, Lerner LB $21.27 (0-8225-2976-9). 48pp. Color illustrations and maps accompany this account of the Pueblo Indians and the incredible cities that they built. (Rev: BL 7/96) [973]

**12832** Costabel, Eva D. *The Early People of Florida* (4–6). Illus. 1993, Smithmark $3.98 (0-831-72339-4). 34pp. The life of the indigenous peoples of Florida from prehistoric times to 1845. (Rev: BL 2/15/93; SLJ 3/93) [975.9]

**12833** Crum, Robert. *Eagle Drum: On the Powwow Trail with a Young Grass Dancer* (4–7). Illus. 1994, Four Winds paper $16.95 (0-02-725515-8). 48pp. The preparation and execution of a powwow dance is told through the eyes of a 9-year-old Kalispel Indian in Montana. (Rev: BL 10/1/94; SLJ 12/94) [394.3]

**12834** Dewey, Jennifer O. *Stories on Stone: Rock Art, Images from the Ancient Ones* (1–4). Illus. 1996, Little, Brown $16.95 (0-316-18211-7). 32pp. The story of the prehistoric Indians of the Southwest and how they carved images in the rocks. (Rev: BCCB 4/96; BL 5/1/96; SLJ 4/96) [979]

**12835** Doherty, Craig A., and Katherine M. Doherty. *The Iroquois* (4–6). Illus. Series: First Books. 1989, Watts LB $21.00 (0-531-10747-7). 64pp. Topics covered in this history of the Iroquois nation include history, religion, festivals, and customs. (Rev: BL 10/1/89) [970]

**12836** Doherty, Katherine M., and Craig A. Doherty. *The Zunis* (4–6). Illus. Series: First Books. 1993, Watts LB $21.00 (0-531-20157-0). 64pp. Covers the origins of the Zuñis, their matriarchy, religious beliefs, and encounters with the Spanish explorer Coronado. (Rev: BL 2/15/94; SLJ 2/94) [978.9]

**12837** Duvall, Jill D. *The Cayuga* (1–3). Illus. Series: New True Books. 1991, Children's LB $21.00 (0-516-01123-5). 48pp. This book supplies basic introductory material on the Cayuga Indians in simple text and photos, some in color. (Rev: BL 3/1/92) [973]

**12838** Duvall, Jill D. *The Mohawk* (1–3). Illus. Series: New True Books. 1991, Children's LB $21.00 (0-516-01115-4). 48pp. In short chapters and large print, the history, customs, and social life of the Mohawk Indians are introduced. (Rev: BL 12/15/91; SLJ 1/92) [973]

**12839** Duvall, Jill D. *The Oneida* (1–3). Illus. Series: New True Books. 1991, Children's LB $21.00 (0-516-01125-1). 48pp. In large typeface and many illustrations, the history and culture of the Oneida Indians are well presented. (Rev: BL 3/1/92) [973]

**12840** Duvall, Jill D. *The Onondaga* (1–3). Illus. Series: New True Books. 1991, Children's LB $21.00 (0-516-01126-X). 48pp. This is a good basic introduction to the Onondaga Indians, their culture and place in history. (Rev: BL 3/1/92) [973]

**12841** Duvall, Jill D. *The Penobscot* (2–4). Illus. Series: New True Book. 1993, Children's LB $21.00 (0-516-01194-4). 48pp. Large type and many color pictures highlight this account of these Maine Indians and their history. (Rev: BL 7/94) [973]

**12842** Duvall, Jill D. *The Seneca* (1–3). Illus. Series: New True Books. 1991, Children's LB $21.00 (0-516-01119-7). 48pp. The Seneca Indians are introduced in this simple book that covers history, social life, and present status. (Rev: BL 12/15/91; SLJ 1/92) [973]

**12843** Duvall, Jill D. *The Tuscarora* (1–3). Illus. Series: New True Books. 1991, Children's LB $21.00 (0-516-01128-6). 48pp. In simple text and many photos, the history, crafts, culture, and importance of the Tuscarora Indians are covered. (Rev: BL 3/1/92) [973]

**12844** Fisher, Leonard Everett. *Anasazi* (4–6). Illus. 1997, Simon & Schuster $16.00 (0-689-80737-6). 32pp. The Anasazi Indian tribe of the Southwest is introduced, with information on their homes, agriculture, and artwork. (Rev: BL 11/1/97; SLJ 12/97) [973]

**12845** Fleischner, Jennifer. *The Apaches: People of the Southwest* (5–8). Illus. Series: Native Americans. 1994, Millbrook LB $21.90 (1-56294-464-9). 64pp. As well as presenting the history, life-style, and survival of the Apaches, this book includes a representative folktale. (Rev: SLJ 2/95) [973]

**12846** Fradin, Dennis B. *The Cheyenne* (2–4). Illus. 1988, Children's LB $21.00 (0-516-01211-8); paper $5.50 (0-516-41211-6). 48pp. History of this Native American tribe called "the people." (Rev: BL 8/88; SLJ 11/88)

**12847** Fradin, Dennis B. *The Pawnee* (2–3). Illus. 1989, Children's LB $21.00 (0-516-01155-3); paper $5.50 (0-516-41155-1). 48pp. The story of this Native American tribe of the Great Plains. (Rev: BL 5/15/89)

**12848** Fradin, Dennis B. *The Shoshoni* (2–3). Illus. 1989, Children's LB $21.00 (0-516-01156-1); paper $5.50 (0-516-41156-X). 48pp. The story of this Native American tribe of the Pacific Northwest. (Rev: BL 5/15/89)

**12849** Freedman, Russell. *Buffalo Hunt* (4–6). Illus. 1988, Holiday LB $19.95 (0-8234-0702-0). 52pp. How the Plains Indians worshiped and depended on the buffalo. (Rev: BCCB 10/88; BL 10/1/88; SLJ 10/88)

**12850** Freedman, Russell. *An Indian Winter* (4–8). Illus. by Karl Bodmer. 1992, Holiday $21.95 (0-8234-0930-9). 88pp. A fascinating re-creation of the winter of 1833–34 that the German prince Maximilian and a Swiss artist spent with the Indians in North Dakota. (Rev: HB 7–8/92; SLJ 6/92) [970]

**12851** Fulkerston, Chuck. *The Shawnee* (4–6). Illus. by Katherine Ace. Series: Native American People. 1992, Rourke LB $21.27 (0-86625-392-0). 32pp. This account emphasizes the history of the Shawnee and presents material on their everyday life and religion. (Rev: BL 12/15/92) [973]

**12852** Gold, Susan D. *Indian Treaties* (5–8). Illus. 1997, Twenty-First Century LB $21.40 (0-8050-4813-8). 128pp. Tells of the many settlements and treaties that robbed the American Indians of their lands. (Rev: BL 5/15/97; SLJ 6/97) [973]

**12853** Gorsline, Marie, and Douglas Gorsline. *North American Indians* (5–8). Illus. by Douglas Gorsline. 1978, Random paper $3.25 (0-394-83702-9). Major tribes are identified and briefly described.

**12854** Gravelle, Karen. *Growing Up Where the Partridge Drums Its Wings: A Mohawk Childhood* (4–6). Illus. 1997, Watts $24.00 (0-531-11453-8). 64pp. This account focuses on Chantelle Francis and her cousin David Francis and their youth on a Mohawk reservation that bridges Canada and the United States. (Rev: BL 1/1–15/98; SLJ 3/98) [971.4]

**12855** Hagman, Ruth. *The Crow* (1–3). Illus. Series: New True Books. 1990, Children's LB $21.00 (0-516-01103-0); paper $5.50 (0-516-41103-9). 48pp. This book tells in simple text and many pictures the history and present status of the Crow Indians. (Rev: BL 1/1/91) [978]

**12856** Hahn, Elizabeth. *The Blackfoot* (4–6). Illus. by Katherine Ace. Series: Native American People. 1992, Rourke LB $21.27 (1-57103-395-5). 32pp. Told from the Indians' point of view, this account stresses the history of the Blackfoot tribe. (Rev: BL 12/15/92; SLJ 2/93) [973]

**12857** Hahn, Elizabeth. *The Creek* (4–6). Illus. by Katherine Ace. Series: Native American People. 1992, Rourke LB $21.27 (0-86625-393-9). 32pp. History is emphasized in this book that features the

point of view of the Native Americans. (Rev: BL 12/15/92) [976]

**12858** Hahn, Elizabeth. *The Pawnee* (4–6). Illus. by Katherine Ace. Series: Native American People. 1992, Rourke LB $21.27 (0-86625-391-2). 32pp. Everyday life of the Pawnee, their religion, history, and present-day status are covered in this illustrated account. (Rev: BL 12/15/92) [973]

**12859** Hakim, Joy. *The First Americans* (4–8). Illus. Series: History of US. 1993, Oxford LB $14.95 (0-19-507745-8); paper $10.95 (0-19-507746-6). 160pp. An introduction to the Indians of North America and their history and life-styles before and after the arrival of the white man. (Rev: BL 1/15/94; SLJ 2/94) [973]

**12860** Haluska, Vicki. *The Arapaho Indians* (3–5). Illus. Series: Junior Library of American Indians. 1993, Chelsea LB $15.95 (0-7910-1657-9). 80pp. Coverage is given on both the past and the present of this Indian group, with special material on their arts and crafts. (Rev: BL 5/15/93) [973]

**12861** Hirschi, Ron. *People of Salmon and Cedar* (3–6). Photos by Edward S. Curtis. Illus. by Deborah Cooper. 1996, Cobblehill paper $16.99 (0-525-65183-7). 42pp. With a focus on salmon, forests, and the potlatch, this account gives a brief introduction to the American Indians of the Northwest Coast. (Rev: SLJ 9/96) [973]

**12862** Hoyt-Goldsmith, Diane. *Apache Rodeo* (3–5). Photos by Lawrence Migdale. 1995, Holiday LB $15.95 (0-8234-1164-8). 32pp. The current lifestyles and traditions of the Apache people are revealed through the eyes of young Felicita. (Rev: BCCB 2/95; BL 2/1/95; SLJ 6/95) [973]

**12863** Hoyt-Goldsmith, Diane. *Buffalo Days* (3–7). Illus. by Lawrence Migdale. 1997, Holiday LB $16.95 (0-8234-1327-6). 32pp. By focusing on 10-year-old Clarence Three Irons, Jr., the reader is introduced to the Crow Indians of the present and their heritage, which includes celebrating Buffalo Days. (Rev: BL 11/1/97*; SLJ 12/97*) [973]

**12864** Hoyt-Goldsmith, Diane. *Cherokee Summer* (3–5). Illus. by Lawrence Migdale. 1993, Holiday LB $15.95 (0-8234-0995-3). 32pp. The customs, crafts, and home life of the Cherokee Nation are revealed through the eyes of a 10-year-old girl. (Rev: BCCB 4/93; BL 6/1–15/93; SLJ 7/93) [973]

**12865** Hoyt-Goldsmith, Diane. *Potlatch: A Tsimshian Celebration* (4–6). Illus. 1997, Holiday LB $16.95 (0-8234-1290-3). 32pp. A 13-year-old boy explains the meaning of potlatch for the Tsimshian tribe in Alaska and describes the many rituals and activities it involves. (Rev: BL 5/1/97; SLJ 6/97) [394.2]

**12866** Hoyt-Goldsmith, Diane. *Pueblo Storyteller* (3–5). Illus. by Lawrence Migdale. 1991, Holiday LB $16.95 (0-8234-0864-7). 32pp. A present-day account of how a Pueblo family in New Mexico lives. (Rev: BCCB 4/91; BL 3/5/91; SLJ 5/91) [978.9]

**12867** Hoyt-Goldsmith, Diane. *Totem Pole* (2–5). Illus. by Lawrence Migdale. 1990, Holiday LB $16.95 (0-8234-0809-4). 32pp. A boy of the Eagle Clan describes each step in the making of a totem pole. (Rev: BCCB 4/90; BL 5/15/90*; SLJ 5/90) [730]

**12868** Hucko, Bruce. *A Rainbow at Night: The World in Words and Pictures by Navajo Children* (4–6). Illus. 1997, Chronicle $14.95 (0-8118-1294-4). 44pp. Twenty-three Navajo children, ages 5–13, talk about their daily activities, families, culture, and myths. (Rev: BL 3/15/97; SLJ 3/97*) [973]

**12869** Hunter, Sally M. *Four Seasons of Corn: A Winnebago Tradition* (3–6). Illus. 1997, Lerner LB $21.27 (0-8225-2658-1); paper $6.95 (0-8225-9741-1). 40pp. The daily life of a boy who assimilates his Anglo-American heritage, along with the traditional activities of his Winnebago people. (Rev: BL 2/1/97; SLJ 3/97) [394.1]

**12870** Kalbacken, Joan. *The Menominee* (2–4). Illus. Series: New True Book. 1994, Children's LB $20.00 (0-516-01054-9); paper $5.50 (0-516-41054-7). 48pp. A simple introduction to the American Indian people who lived in Wisconsin and Michigan and formed their own Indian nation in 1961. (Rev: BL 7/94) [973]

**12871** Kalman, Bobbie. *Celebrating the Powwow* (2–4). Illus. Series: Crabapples. 1997, Crabtree LB $18.08 (0-86505-640-4); paper $5.95 (0-86505-740-0). 32pp. Using a number of quality photos, this account describes powwows and their various components. (Rev: SLJ 1/98) [973]

**12872** Keegan, Marcia. *Pueblo Boy: Growing Up in Two Worlds* (3–6). Illus. 1991, Dutton paper $15.99 (0-525-65060-1). 48pp. Timmy is growing up in 2 worlds — his contemporary world of computers and the world of his Pueblo Indian ancestors. (Rev: BCCB 4/91; BL 5/1/91; SLJ 7/91) [978.9]

**12873** King, Sandra. *Shannon: An Ojibway Dancer* (4–7). Illus. by Catherine Whipple. 1993, Lerner $19.95 (0-8225-2752-2); paper $6.95 (0-8225-9643-1). 48pp. Thirteen-year-old Shannon Anderson, an Ojibway girl, prepares for the summer powwow and her part in the shawl dance. (Rev: BCCB 1/94; BL 1/15/94; SLJ 2/94) [394]

**12874** Koslow, Philip. *The Seminole Indians* (3–5). Illus. Series: Junior Library of American Indians. 1994, Chelsea LB $15.95 (0-7910-1672-2); paper $8.95 (0-7910-2486-5). 79pp. A re-creation of the way in which prehistoric Seminoles lived plus their

history to the present day. (Rev: BL 10/15/94; SLJ 8/94) [973]

**12875** Krull, Kathleen. *One Nation, Many Tribes: How Kids Live in Milwaukee's Indian Community* (3–7). Illus. Series: A World of My Own. 1995, Dutton $15.99 (0-526-67440-3). 48pp. The story of the daily life and activities of the North American Indian children who are growing up in a community in Milwaukee, Wisconsin. (Rev: BCCB 2/95; BL 2/15/95; SLJ 3/95) [977.5]

**12876** Landau, Elaine. *The Abenaki* (4–6). Illus. Series: First Books: Indian Tribes. 1996, Watts LB $22.00 (0-531-20227-5). 64pp. The story of this northeastern Indian people is given, with material on culture, traditions, and cuisine. (Rev: BL 8/96; SLJ 1/97) [974]

**12877** Landau, Elaine. *The Cherokees* (3–5). Illus. Series: First Books. 1992, Watts paper $6.95 (0-531-15635-4). 64pp. The daily life of the Cherokee, a tribe that occupied a large part of the eastern United States. (Rev: BL 6/15/92) [970]

**12878** Landau, Elaine. *The Ottawa* (4–6). Illus. Series: First Books: Indian Tribes. 1996, Watts LB $21.00 (0-531-20226-7). 64pp. A description of the history, life, and ways of the Great Lakes Ottawa people. (Rev: BL 8/96; SLJ 1/97) [977]

**12879** Landau, Elaine. *The Sioux* (4–6). Illus. 1989, Watts LB $21.00 (0-531-10754-X); paper $6.95 (0-531-15606-0). 64pp. The social and political organization of the Sioux or Dakota Indians is covered. (Rev: BL 10/1/89; SLJ 3/90) [978]

**12880** La Pierre, Yvette. *Native American Rock Art: Messages from the Past* (4–8). Illus. 1994, Thomasson-Grant $17.95 (1-56566-064-1). 48pp. Different types and techniques of American Indian rock art are discussed, with additional information on the cultures that produced this phenomenon. (Rev: BL 12/1/94; SLJ 11/94) [709]

**12881** Lee, Martin. *The Seminoles* (4–6). Illus. 1989, Watts LB $21.00 (0-531-10752-3); paper $6.95 (0-531-15604-4). 64pp. The formation of the Seminole tribe is covered, including how they were forced into the swamps. (Rev: BL 10/1/89; SLJ 3/90) [975]

**12882** Lepthien, Emilie U. *The Cherokee* (1–3). Illus. 1985, Children's LB $21.00 (0-516-01938-4); paper $5.50 (0-516-41938-2). 48pp. Insights into Native American customs and history for the young reader. (Rev: BL 12/1/85; SLJ 3/86)

**12883** Lepthien, Emilie U. *The Choctaw* (2–4). Illus. 1988, Children's LB $21.00 (0-516-01240-1); paper $5.50 (0-516-41240-X). 48pp. History and culture of these Native Americans. (Rev: BL 5/1/88; SLJ 10/88)

**12884** Lepthien, Emilie U. *The Mandans* (2–4). Illus. Series: New True Books. 1989, Children's LB

$21.00 (0-516-01180-4). 48pp. The Mandan Indians are introduced, with many illustrations. (Rev: BL 1/15/90; SLJ 6/90) [973]

**12885** Lepthien, Emilie U. *The Seminole* (1–3). Illus. 1985, Children's LB $21.00 (0-516-01941-4); paper $5.50 (0-516-41941-2). 45pp. Way of life, customs, and history of these Native Americans. (Rev: BL 12/1/85; SLJ 3/86)

**12886** Liptak, Karen. *North American Indian Ceremonies* (3–6). Illus. 1992, Watts LB $21.00 (0-531-20100-7); paper $6.95 (0-531-15639-7). 64pp. American Indian rituals through history and in the modern world. (Rev: BL 12/1/92; SLJ 7/92) [299.74]

**12887** Liptak, Karen. *North American Indian Medicine People* (4–6). Illus. Series: First Books. 1990, Watts LB $21.00 (0-531-10868-6). 64pp. The philosophies and practices of medicine people of different North American tribes. (Rev: BCCB 12/90; BL 2/1/91) [615.8]

**12888** Liptak, Karen. *North American Indian Sign Language* (4–6). Illus. Series: First Books. 1990, Watts LB $21.00 (0-531-10869-4); paper $6.95 (0-531-15641-9). 64pp. An interesting introduction to sign language in several North American tribes. (Rev: BCCB 12/90; BL 2/1/91) [419]

**12889** Liptak, Karen. *North American Indian Survival Skills* (4–6). Illus. Series: First Books. 1990, Watts LB $21.00 (0-531-10870-8). 64pp. An intriguing introduction to survival skills used by various North American tribes. (Rev: BCCB 12/90; BL 2/1/91) [613.6]

**12890** Liptak, Karen. *North American Indian Tribal Chiefs* (4–6). Illus. 1992, Watts LB $21.00 (0-531-20101-5); paper $6.95 (0-531-15643-5). 64pp. Brief biographies of 4 Indian leaders, plus contemporary and historical leadership positions in native American tribes. (Rev: BL 12/1/92; SLJ 7/92) [970]

**12891** Lucas, Eileen. *The Cherokees: People of the Southeast* (5–8). Illus. Series: Native Americans. 1993, Millbrook LB $21.90 (1-56294-312-X). 64pp. Following a map showing where the Cherokee lived, there are 4 chapters covering their origins, culture, interactions with whites, and the people today. (Rev: SLJ 1/94) [973]

**12892** Lucas, Eileen. *The Ojibwas: People of the Northern Forests* (4–6). Illus. Series: Native American. 1994, Millbrook LB $21.90 (1-56294-313-8). 64pp. This account of the Ojibwa (Chippewa) Indians focuses on their history, daily life, and culture, and also includes a folktale and information on their present-day status. (Rev: BL 4/1/94; SLJ 6/94) [973]

**12893** McDaniel, Melissa. *The Powhatan Indians* (3–5). Illus. Series: Junior Library of American Indians. 1995, Chelsea LB $15.95 (0-7910-2494-6); paper $8.95 (0-7910-2495-4). 80pp. The story of the

powerful Indian confederation that existed in coastal Virginia at the time of the settlement at Jamestown. (Rev: BL 1/1–15/96; SLJ 2/96) [975]

**12894** McDaniel, Melissa. *The Sac and Fox Indians* (3–5). Illus. Series: Junior Library of American Indians. 1995, Chelsea LB $15.95 (0-7910-1670-6); paper $7.95 (0-7910-2034-7). 80pp. This account tells of these Wisconsin-based Indians, their near annihilation by the French, and their part in the Black Hawk War. (Rev: BL 1/1–15/96) [977]

**12895** McGovern, Ann. *If You Lived with the Sioux Indians* (2–4). Illus. by Robert Levering. 1992, Scholastic paper $4.95 (0-590-45162-6). Using a question-and-answer technique, the author gives a great deal of information about the daily life of the Sioux and their relationship with white people.

**12896** McKissack, Patricia. *The Apache* (1–4). Illus. 1984, Children's paper $5.50 (0-516-41925-0). 48pp. Day-to-day life, plus history and customs, of the Apache of the Southwest.

**12897** McLerran, Alice. *The Ghost Dance* (3–6). Illus. by Paul Morin. 1995, Clarion $15.95 (0-395-63168-8). The story of the hardships inflicted on Native Americans by whites and of the Ghost Dance, which was believed would magically rid their land of these intruders. (Rev: BCCB 11/95; SLJ 11/95*) [973]

**12898** Margolin, Malcolm, and Yolanda Montijo, eds. *Native Ways: California Indian Stories and Memories* (5–8). Illus. 1996, Heyday paper $7.95 (0-930588-73-8). 128pp. Reminiscences and stories reflect California Indian culture, both past and present. (Rev: BL 7/96) [979.4]

**12899** Martell, Hazel M. *Native Americans and Mesa Verde* (4–7). Illus. Series: Hidden Worlds. 1993, Dillon LB $13.95 (0-87518-540-1). 32pp. The history of the Pueblo Indians, their amazing cliff dwellings, and the Mesa Verde National Park. (Rev: BL 10/15/93; SLJ 8/93) [948.8]

**12900** May, Robin. *Plains Indians of North America* (4–6). Illus. 1987, Rourke LB $16.67 (0-86625-258-4). 48pp. Life-style and customs of the Plains Indians are described in this well-illustrated introduction to these indigenous people, part of the Original Peoples series. (Rev: BL 1/15/88)

**12901** Mayfield, Thomas Jefferson. *Adopted by Indians: A True Story* (5–8). Ed. by Malcolm Margolin. Illus. 1997, Heyday paper $10.95 (0-930588-93-2). 144pp. This is an adaption of the memoirs of a white man who lived with the Choinumne Indians in California for 10 years, beginning in 1850 when he was 8. (Rev: BL 3/1/98) [979.4]

**12902** Mercredi, Morningstar. *Fort Chipewyan Homecoming: A Journey to Native Canada* (3–6). Photos by Darren McNally. 1997, Lerner LB $21.27 (0-

8225-2659-X); paper $6.95 (0-8225-9731-4). 48pp. Twelve-year-old Matthew visits relatives at Fort Chipewyan in Alberta, Canada, and learns a great deal about his Native American heritage. (Rev: SLJ 9/97) [973]

**12903** Meyers, Madeleine, ed. *Cherokee Nation: Life Before the Tears* (4–8). Series: Perspectives on History. 1994, Discovery Enterprises paper $5.95 (1-878668-26-9). 60pp. A history of the Cherokees that emphasizes the leadership of Sequoyah and the life of the tribe before their forced displacement. (Rev: BL 8/94) [970.3]

**12904** Miller, Jay. *American Indian Families* (3–5). Illus. Series: True Book. 1996, Children's LB $21.00 (0-516-20133-6). 47pp. Discusses family structure and importance in various American Indian tribes. (Rev: SLJ 8/97) [973]

**12905** Miller, Jay. *American Indian Festivals* (2–3). Illus. Series: True Books: American Indians. 1996, Children's LB $21.00 (0-516-20134-4). 47pp. Presents various festivals of American Indians, like rain dances and thanksgiving celebrations. (Rev: BL 3/1/97; SLJ 8/97) [394.2]

**12906** Miller, Jay. *American Indian Foods* (2–3). Illus. Series: True Books: American Indians. 1996, Children's LB $21.00 (0-516-20135-2). 47pp. The foods eaten by different American Indian groups are described by region. (Rev: BL 3/1/97; SLJ 8/97) [641.59]

**12907** Miller, Jay. *American Indian Games* (2–3). Illus. Series: True Books: American Indians. 1996, Children's LB $21.00 (0-516-20136-0). 47pp. With a color photograph on each page and brief text, this title presents the games American Indians played in the past, like canoe racing and lacrosse, and how they compare with today's interests. (Rev: BL 3/15/97) [394]

**12908** Miller, Jay. *Native Americans* (2–4). Illus. Series: New True Book. 1993, Children's LB $21.00 (0-516-01192-8). 48pp. Using large type and many illustrations, this is an attractive, brief introduction to the Indians of North America and their cultures. (Rev: BL 7/94) [973]

**12909** Mooney, Martin. *The Comanche Indians* (4–7). Illus. Series: Junior Library of American Indians. 1993, Chelsea LB $15.95 (0-7910-1653-6). 71pp. A historical account of the Comanches from about 1700 to the present. (Rev: SLJ 4/93) [970]

**12910** Mott, Evelyn Clarke. *Dancing Rainbows: A Pueblo Boy's Story* (PS–3). Illus. 1996, Dutton paper $14.99 (0-525-65216-7). 32pp. The celebration of Feast Day on June 24 by the San Juan Pueblo in New Mexico as seen through the eyes of a young Indian boy. (Rev: BL 4/1/96; SLJ 5/96) [978.9]

**12911** Murdoch, David. *North American Indian* (4–8). Illus. Series: Eyewitness Books. 1995, Knopf $19.00 (0-679-86169-6). 64pp. A basic introduction to the history, culture, and present status of North American Indians. (Rev: BL 8/95; SLJ 9/95) [970]

**12912** Myers, Arthur. *The Cheyenne* (4–6). Illus. Series: First Books. 1992, Watts paper $6.95 (0-531-15636-2). 64pp. In addition to a description of social organization and customs of the Cheyenne, this book tells of their history, including the Battle of Little Bighorn. (Rev: BL 6/15/92) [970.004]

**12913** Myers, Arthur. *The Pawnee* (4–6). Illus. Series: First Book. 1993, Watts LB $21.00 (0-531-20165-1). 64pp. The history of the Pawnee Indians is covered, with material on their life-styles and relations with the white man. (Rev: BL 2/15/94) [978.2]

**12914** Newman, Shirlee P. *The Creek* (4–6). Illus. Series: Indians of the Americas. 1996, Watts LB $22.00 (0-531-20236-4); paper $6.95 (0-531-15809-8). 62pp. The history of the Creek (Muskogee) people, who were moved from southeastern United States to Oklahoma. (Rev: BL 12/15/96) [975]

**12915** O'Neill, Laurie A. *Wounded Knee: The Death of a Dream* (4–6). Illus. Series: Spotlight on American History. 1993, Millbrook LB $21.90 (1-56294-253-0). 64pp. The battle of Wounded Knee, in which a large number of Sioux Indians were massacred, is re-created as a dark chapter in American history. (Rev: BL 6/1–15/93; SLJ 5/93) [973.8]

**12916** Osinski, Alice. *The Chippewa* (2–4). Illus. 1987, Children's LB $21.00 (0-516-01230-4); paper $5.50 (0-516-41230-2). 48pp. History, customs, religious beliefs, and the difficulties faced by today's Native Americans. (Rev: BCCB 11/87; BL 11/1/87)

**12917** Osinski, Alice. *The Navajo* (2–4). Illus. 1987, Children's LB $21.00 (0-516-01236-3); paper $5.50 (0-516-41236-1). 45pp. Navajo customs and traditions, history, and religious beliefs. (Rev: BCCB 11/87; BL 11/1/87)

**12918** Osinski, Alice. *The Nez Perce* (3–5). Illus. 1988, Children's LB $21.00 (0-516-01154-5); paper $5.50 (0-516-41154-3). 48pp. Introducing this tribe of Northwest Indians. (Rev: BL 2/15/89)

**12919** Osinski, Alice. *The Sioux* (1–4). Illus. 1984, Children's LB $21.00 (0-516-01929-5); paper $5.50 (0-516-41929-3). 48pp. Brief history of the Sioux, or Dakota, Indians of the Great Plains and material on their customs and social organization.

**12920** Payne, Elizabeth. *Meet the North American Indians* (1–3). Illus. 1965, Random $6.95 (0-394-80060-5). A narrative that introduces many tribes, their locations and life-styles.

**12921** Pennington, Daniel. *Itse Selu: Cherokee Harvest Festival* (K–3). Illus. by Don Stewart. 1994, Charlesbridge paper $6.95 (0-88106-850-0). 32pp.

Little Wolf and his Cherokee family celebrate the Green Corn Festival with rituals and feasting to acknowledge the ripening of the corn. (Rev: BL 5/15/94; SLJ 7/94) [394.2]

**12922** Peters, Russell. *Clambake: A Wampanoag Tradition* (3–5). Illus. by John Madama. Series: We Are Still Here: Native Americans Today. 1992, Lerner LB $21.27 (0-8225-2651-4); paper $6.95 (0-8225-9621-0). 48pp. Origins and present-day observations of the traditional ceremony that we know as a clambake. (Rev: BCCB 11/92; SLJ 12/92) [973]

**12923** Petersen, David. *The Anasazi* (1–3). Illus. Series: New True Books. 1991, Children's LB $21.00 (0-516-01121-9). 48pp. Simple text and color photos cover this branch of the southwestern Pueblo Indians. (Rev: BL 3/1/92) [979.01]

**12924** Philip, Neil, ed. *In a Sacred Manner I Live: Native American Wisdom* (4–8). Illus. 1997, Clarion $20.00 (0-395-84981-0). 93pp. More than 30 American Indian leaders — e.g., Geronimo and Cochise — are quoted on topics related to the conduct of life. (Rev: BL 7/97; SLJ 12/97) [973]

**12925** Powell, Suzanne. *The Pueblos* (4–7). Illus. Series: First Books. 1993, Watts LB $21.00 (0-531-20068-X); paper $6.95 (0-531-15703-2). 64pp. Covers the history and present status of the Pueblos and their ability to survive the harsh weather and terrain of the American Southwest. (Rev: BL 2/15/94) [978.9]

**12926** Quiri, Patricia R. *The Algonquians* (3–5). Illus. Series: First Books. 1992, Watts LB $22.00 (0-531-20065-5); paper $6.95 (0-531-15633-8). 64pp. In addition to coverage of the Algonquians' daily life, religion, and culture, this book describes their past history and present condition. (Rev: BL 6/15/92; SLJ 3/93) [970.004]

**12927** Regguinti, Gordon. *The Sacred Harvest: Ojibway Wild Rice Gathering* (4–8). Illus. by Dale Kakkak. Series: We Are Still Here: Native Americans Today. 1992, Lerner LB $21.27 (0-8225-2650-6). 48pp. The past and present of the ceremony of the harvest by the Ojibways in Minnesota. (Rev: SLJ 12/92) [973]

**12928** Rendon, Marcie R. *Powwow Summer: A Family Celebrates the Circle of Life* (3–6). Illus. 1996, Lerner LB $16.95 (0-87614-986-7); paper $7.95 (0-57505-011-0). 48pp. The Downwind family, which includes 10 children (five of them in foster care), spend the summer attending many powwows in northern Minnesota. (Rev: BL 7/96; SLJ 10/96) [394]

**12929** Roessel, Monty. *Kinaalda: A Navajo Girl Grows Up* (4–7). Illus. 1993, Lerner LB $21.27 (0-8225-2655-7); paper $6.95 (0-8225-9641-5). 48pp. Celinda McKelvey, a Navajo girl, returns to the reservation to participate in her Kinaalda, the coming-of-

age ceremony. (Rev: BCCB 1/94; BL 1/15/94; SLJ 2/94) [392.1]

**12930** Roessel, Monty. *Songs from the Loom: A Navajo Girl Learns to Weave* (3–6). Illus. 1995, Lerner LB $21.27 (0-8225-2657-3); paper $6.95 (0-8225-9712-8). 48pp. A photoessay about weaving the Navajo way that reveals information about the culture and way of life of these people. (Rev: BL 9/15/95; SLJ 11/95) [746.1]

**12931** Sattler, Helen R. *The Earliest Americans* (5–7). Illus. by Jean Day Zallinger. 1993, Houghton $16.95 (0-395-54996-5). 128pp. This account of early human life in North America also discusses the controversy about the origin of the first hunters to arrive here. (Rev: BCCB 6/93; BL 5/1/93; SLJ 6/93*) [970.1]

**12932** Schwabacher, Martin. *The Huron Indians* (3–5). Illus. Series: The Junior Library of American Indians. 1995, Chelsea $15.95 (0-7910-2489-X); paper $8.95 (0-7910-2033-9). 80pp. An introduction to the history and culture of the Huron peoples, with material on how they preserve their traditions today. (Rev: BL 7/95) [392.2]

**12933** Sewall, Marcia. *People of the Breaking Day* (3–6). Illus. 1990, Macmillan $17.00 (0-689-31407-8). 48pp. An in-depth account of the life-style of the Wampanoag Indians, who were living in Massachusetts when the Pilgrims arrived. (Rev: BL 10/1/90; HB 1–2/91; SLJ 1/91) [305.8]

**12934** Seymour, Tryntje Van Ness. *The Gift of Changing Woman* (5–8). Illus. 1993, Holt $16.95 (0-8050-2577-4). 38pp. In a picture book format, the Apache initiation ceremony for young women to mark their change from girls to women is vividly described. (Rev: BCCB 11/93; BL 11/15/93; SLJ 3/94) [299.74]

**12935** Shemie, Bonnie. *Houses of Adobe: Native Dwellings: The Southwest* (3–5). Illus. Series: Native Dwellings. 1995, Tundra $13.95 (0-88776-330-8); paper $6.95 (0-88776-353-7). 24pp. Various dwellings built by Indians of the Southwest — like pit houses and cliff homes — are described in double-page spreads with detailed drawings. (Rev: BL 9/1/95) [392]

**12936** Shemie, Bonnie. *Houses of Bark: Tipi, Wigwam and Longhouse* (3–6). Illus. 1990, Tundra $13.95 (0-88776-246-8). 24pp. The lives of Native Americans in and around their traditional homes. (Rev: BL 1/1/91) [970]

**12937** Shemie, Bonnie. *Mounds of Earth and Shell* (3–6). Illus. Series: Native Dwellings. 1993, Tundra $13.95 (0-88776-318-9). 24pp. Explores the mound-building Indians of North America, where the mounds are located, and why they were built. (Rev: BL 1/1/94) [393.1]

**12938** Sherrow, Victoria. *The Iroquois Indians* (3–5). Series: Junior Library of American Indians. 1993, Chelsea LB $15.95 (0-7910-1655-2). 82pp. History and culture of Iroquis arts and crafts. Includes an 8-page photoessay. (Rev: BL 11/1/92) [973]

**12939** Siegel, Beatrice. *The Basket Maker and the Spinner* (4–6). Illus. 1987, Walker LB $11.85 (0-8027-6695-1). 64pp. The fictionalized lives of a New England colonist named Mary Allen and a Wampanoag Indian woman named Yawata. (Rev: BCCB 9/87; BL 8/87; SLJ 12/87)

**12940** Siegel, Beatrice. *Indians of the Northeast Woodlands* (4–8). Illus. by William Sauts Bock. 1991, Walker LB $14.85 (0-8027-8157-8). 96pp. In question-and-answer format — following the original 1972 edition — this volume contains much information on Native Americans in New England. (Rev: BL 11/15/92) [973]

**12941** Siegel, Beatrice. *Indians of the Woodland, Before and After the Pilgrims* (4–6). Illus. by Baptiste Shunatona. 1972, Walker LB $5.85 (0-8027-6108-9). 96pp. A look at how the Indians lived before the white settlers came and how the Indians' lives were destroyed soon after.

**12942** Siy, Alexandra. *The Eeyou: People of Eastern James Bay* (4–7). Illus. Series: Global Villages. 1993, Macmillan $14.95 (0-87518-549-5). 80pp. Introduces the Indian culture of the Eeyou, a people with their own writing system. (Rev: BCCB 7–8; SLJ 8/93) [970]

**12943** Smith-Baranzini, Marlene, and Howard Egger-Bovet. *Book of the American Indians* (5–7). Illus. Series: Brown Paper Bag USKids History. 1994, Little, Brown $19.95 (0-316-96921-4). 96pp. Original accounts are used — along with many activities, projects, and games — to explain the folklore, daily life, and problems of American Indians from different geographical areas. (Rev: BL 10/1/94; SLJ 9/94) [973]

**12944** Sneve, Virginia Driving Hawk. *The Apaches* (3–6). Illus. by Ronald Himler. Series: First Americans Book. 1997, Holiday LB $16.95 (0-8234-1287-3). 32pp. An overview of the 6 tribes that make up the Apache nation, accompanied by handsome illustrations. (Rev: BL 4/1/97; SLJ 7/97) [973]

**12945** Sneve, Virginia Driving Hawk. *The Cherokees* (3–6). Illus. by Ronald Himler. Series: First Americans. 1996, Holiday LB $15.95 (0-8234-1214-8). 32pp. The story of this large, important Indian group, its culture, and its present status. (Rev: BCCB 5/96; BL 2/15/96; HB 5–6/96; SLJ 4/96) [973]

**12946** Sneve, Virginia Driving Hawk. *The Cheyennes* (K–4). Illus. Series: First Americans. 1996, Holiday LB $15.95 (0-8234-1250-4). 32pp. The story of the Cheyenne, their history, customs, and how the white

man affected their lives. (Rev: BL 9/15/96; SLJ 2/97) [970]

**12947** Sneve, Virginia Driving Hawk. *The Hopis* (3–5). Illus. by Ronald Himler. Series: First Americans Books. 1995, Holiday LB $15.95 (0-8234-1194-X). 32pp. Details are given of the religion, social structure, history, and life-style of the Hopi, along with a creation myth. (Rev: SLJ 10/95) [973]

**12948** Sneve, Virginia Driving Hawk. *The Iroquois* (K–4). Illus. by Ronald Himler. Series: A First American Book. 1995, Holiday LB $16.95 (0-8234-1163-X). 32pp. Provides a history of the Iroquois, as well as their beliefs, way of life, religion, and current situation. (Rev: BL 6/1–15/95; SLJ 7/95) [973]

**12949** Sneve, Virginia Driving Hawk. *The Navajos* (K–3). Illus. by Ronald Himler. Series: First Americans. 1993, Holiday LB $16.95 (0-8234-1039-0). 32pp. After a creation story, the Navajos are introduced with details given on their daily life, society, relations with other Indian groups, and their fortune after the white man came. (Rev: BCCB 10/93; BL 12/15/93; SLJ 10/93) [973]

**12950** Sneve, Virginia Driving Hawk. *The Nez Perce* (K–3). Illus. by Ronald Himler. Series: First Americans Book. 1994, Holiday LB $15.95 (0-8234-1090-0). 32pp. Beginning with a creation myth, this account continues with an exploration of the daily life and history of the Nez Perce. (Rev: BL 10/1/94) [973]

**12951** Sneve, Virginia Driving Hawk. *The Seminoles: A First Americans Book* (3–5). Illus. by Ronald Himler. 1994, Holiday LB $15.95 (0-8234-1112-5). 32pp. Discusses many aspects of the Seminole history and culture, including the career of Osceola, the Seminole Wars, and their living conditions today. (Rev: BCCB 7–8/94; SLJ 4/94) [973]

**12952** Sneve, Virginia Driving Hawk. *The Sioux* (K–3). Illus. by Ronald Himler. Series: First Americans. 1993, Holiday LB $16.95 (0-8234-1017-X). 32pp. The history of the Sioux Indians is given, with information on their social structure, daily life, ceremonies, and contemporary condition. (Rev: BCCB 10/93; BL 12/15/93; SLJ 10/93) [973]

**12953** Sonneborn, Liz. *The Cheyenne Indians* (3–5). Illus. Series: Junior Library of American Indians. 1991, Chelsea LB $15.95 (0-7910-1654-4). 80pp. The history and culture of the Cheyenne are covered in simple text, historic photos, maps, and an 8-page color section on arts and crafts. (Rev: BL 3/1/92) [973.04973]

**12954** Steedman, Scott. *How Would You Survive as an American Indian?* (4–7). Illus. Series: How Would You Survive? 1996, Watts LB $23.00 (0-531-14383-X). 48pp. The life of the Plains Indians is described, with material on hunting, meals, shelter, and festivals. (Rev: BL 5/15/96) [978]

**12955** Steele, Philip. *Little Bighorn* (5–8). Illus. by Richard Hook. Series: Great Battles and Sieges. 1992, Macmillan $13.95 (0-02-786885-0). 32pp. How General George Custer was defeated by Cheyenne and Sioux Indians in 1876. (Rev: BL 10/1/92; SLJ 2/93) [973.8]

**12956** Stein, R. Conrad. *The Battle of the Little Bighorn* (3–5). Illus. Series: Cornerstones of Freedom. 1997, Children's LB $19.50 (0-516-20296-0). 32pp. The fascinating, well-illustrated account of the battle on June 25, 1876, in which Custer was defeated by the combined forces of the Sioux and Cheyenne warriors. (Rev: BL 6/1–15/97) [973.8]

**12957** Stein, R. Conrad. *The Trail of Tears* (3–5). Illus. Series: Cornerstones of Freedom. 1993, Children's LB $19.50 (0-516-06666-8). 32pp. The tragic story of the removal of the Cherokee Indian tribe from their native lands in 1838. (Rev: BL 8/93) [975]

**12958** Stroud, Virginia A. *The Path of the Quiet Elk: A Native American Alphabet Book* (2–5). Illus. by author. 1996, Dial paper $14.89 (0-8037-1718-0). The spiritual life of American Indians and their relationship with nature are explored in this stunning alphabet book. (Rev: SLJ 4/96) [973]

**12959** Swentzell, Rina. *Children of Clay: A Family of Pueblo Potters* (3–5). Illus. by Bill Steen. 1992, Lerner LB $21.27 (0-8225-2654-9). 40pp. The family of Gia Rose of Santa Clara Pueblo takes the reader through the ancient process of pottery making. (Rev: BCCB 3/93; BL 1/15/93; SLJ 2/92) [978.9]

**12960** Tannenbaum, Beulah, and Harold E. Tannenbaum. *Science of the Early American Indians* (5–7). Illus. 1988, Watts LB $10.40 (0-531-10488-5). 96pp. Early discoveries by Native Americans in such fields as astronomy and agriculture. (Rev: BL 5/1/88)

**12961** Thomas, David Hurst, and Lorann Pendleton, eds. *Native Americans* (4–6). Illus. Series: Nature Company Discoveries Library. 1995, Time Life LB $16.00 (0-7835-4759-5). 64pp. This overview of Native Americans and their history and geography contains an 8-page foldout depicting a buffalo hunt. (Rev: BL 1/1–15/96; SLJ 1/96) [970.004]

**12962** Tomcheck, Ann Heinrichs. *The Hopi* (2–4). Illus. 1987, Children's LB $21.00 (0-516-01234-7); paper $5.50 (0-516-41234-5). 48pp. A look at the Hopi, their customs and history, religious beliefs, and difficulties in today's world. (Rev: BCCB 11/87; BL 11/1/87)

**12963** Warren, Scott S. *Cities in the Sand: The Ancient Civilizations of the Southwest* (5–7). Illus. 1992, Chronicle $10.95 (0-8118-0012-1). 56pp. A look at the ancient cultures of the Southwest, with much absorbing information. (Rev: BL 10/1/92; SLJ 8/92) [979.1]

**12964** Warren, Scott S. *Desert Dwellers: Native People of the American Southwest* (4–6). Illus. 1997, Chronicle $11.95 (0-8118-0534-4). 64pp. Introduces the culture and life-styles of 7 desert tribes of North American Indians, e.g., the Pueblo, Hopi, and Navajo. (Rev: BL 9/1/97; SLJ 10/97) [979]

**12965** White Deer of Autumn. *The Native American Book of Knowledge* (5–8). Illus. by Shonto Begay. 1992, Beyond Words paper $5.95 (0-941831-42-6). 88pp. A description of Native American hero figures before Columbus is part of the information in this native view of history and life-styles. (Rev: BL 10/15/92) [970]

**12966** White Deer of Autumn. *The Native American Book of Life* (5–8). Illus. by Shonto Begay. 1992, Beyond Words paper $5.95 (0-941831-43-4). 88pp. In this look at life-styles from the Native American point of view, the focus is on child rearing. (Rev: BL 10/15/92) [970]

**12967** Wittstock, Laura W. *Ininatig's Gift of Sugar: Traditional Native Sugarmaking* (3–5). Illus. by Dale Kakkak. Series: We Are Still Here. 1993, Lerner LB $21.27 (0-8225-2653-0); paper $6.95 (0-8225-9642-3). 48pp. Describes the traditional way of making maple sugar and syrup by Minnesota Indians. (Rev: BL 9/1/93; HB 11–12/93) [338.1]

**12968** Wolfson, Evelyn. *From Abenaki to Zuni: A Dictionary of Native American Tribes* (4–8). Illus. 1988, Walker LB $18.85 (0-8027-6790-7). 215pp. Sixty-eight Native American tribes in alphabetical order. (Rev: BL 6/1/88; HB 1–2/88; SLJ 6–7/89)

**12969** Wolfson, Evelyn. *Growing Up Indian* (5–7). Illus. 1986, Walker LB $11.85 (0-8027-6644-7). 96pp. What it was like to grow up Indian in traditional American culture before the influence of the white race. (Rev: BL 1/15/87; SLJ 3/87)

**12970** Wood, Leigh. *The Crow Indians* (3–5). Illus. Series: Junior Library of American Indians. 1993, Chelsea LB $15.95 (0-7910-1661-7). 80pp. This account tells about the past, present, and culture of the Crow Indians who now live in southeastern Montana. (Rev: BL 5/15/93) [973]

**12971** Wood, Ted, and Wanbli Numpa Afraid of Hawk. *A Boy Becomes a Man at Wounded Knee* (4–6). Illus. 1992, Walker LB $16.85 (0-8027-8175-6). 42pp. An 8-year-old Lakota boy wants to participate in his ancestor's journey to Wounded Knee. (Rev: BCCB 12/92; BL 9/1/92; SLJ 11/92) [973.8]

### DISCOVERY AND EXPLORATION

**12972** Asikinack, Bill, and Kate Scarborough. *Exploration into North America* (5–7). Illus. Series: Exploration Into. 1996, Dillon LB $15.95 (0-02-718086-7); paper $7.95 (0-382-39228-0). 48pp. This account tells the history of North America from prehistory to

European exploration and settlement. (Rev: BL 8/96; SLJ 9/96) [970]

**12973** Bowen, Andy Russell. *The Back of Beyond: A Story About Lewis and Clark* (3–5). Illus. 1997, Carolrhoda LB $19.93 (1-57505-010-2). 64pp. A gripping account of the journey that took Lewis and Clark to the mouth of the Columbia River in 1805. (Rev: BL 9/1/97; HB 11–12/97; SLJ 3/98) [917.804]

**12974** Brenner, Barbara. *If You Were There in 1492* (3–6). Illus. 1991, Macmillan LB $15.00 (0-02-712321-9). 112pp. A time-travel trip back to the year of the explorer's famous voyage. (Rev: BL 9/1/91; HB 1–2/92; SLJ 11/91)

**12975** Craig, Claire. *Explorers and Traders* (4–6). Illus. Series: Nature Company Discoveries. 1996, Time Life $16.00 (0-8094-9373-X). 64pp. The roles played by explorers and traders in the opening up of our country are traced, with many illustrations and an 8-page foldout. (Rev: BL 9/15/96) [948]

**12976** Dyson, John. *Westward with Columbus* (4–6). Illus. by Peter Christopher. 1991, Scholastic paper $6.95 (0-590-43847-6). 64pp. A fictionalized account of the 1492 voyage, theorizing that Columbus used a secret map. (Rev: BL 11/15/91; SLJ 11/91) [910.4]

**12977** Fradin, Dennis B. *The Nina, the Pinta and the Santa Maria* (4–6). Illus. 1991, Watts LB $21.00 (0-531-20034-5). 64pp. The details of the famous voyage of 1492, emphasizing how the ships were built and life on board. (Rev: BL 10/15/91; SLJ 1/92) [970.01]

**12978** Krensky, Stephen. *Christopher Columbus* (1–2). Illus. by Norman Green. 1991, Random paper $3.99 (0-679-80369-6). 32pp. This is an easy-reading book that tells about Columbus's first voyage to America. (Rev: BL 12/1/91; SLJ 12/91) [970.01]

**12979** Krensky, Stephen. *Who Really Discovered America?* (4–6). Illus. 1991, Hastings $12.95 (0-8038-9306-X); Scholastic paper $2.50 (0-590-40854-2). 64pp. A parade of discoverers who came to North or South America are uncovered in the attempt to answer this intriguing question. (Rev: BL 1/15/88; SLJ 4/88) [970.01]

**12980** Leon, George D. *Explorers of the Americas Before Columbus* (4–8). Illus. 1989, Watts LB $21.00 (0-531-10667-5). 64pp. Exploring proven and supposed contacts with the New World before Columbus. (Rev: BL 7/89; SLJ 9/89) [970]

**12981** McGrath, Patrick. *The Lewis and Clark Expedition* (5–8). Illus. 1986, Silver Burdett LB $14.95 (0-382-06828-9); paper $7.95 (0-382-09899-4). 64pp. A straightforward account illustrated with maps, photographs, paintings, and diary entries. (Rev: BCCB 6/86)

**12982** Maestro, Betsy. *Exploration and Conquest: The Americas After Columbus: 1500–1620* (PS–K).

Illus. by Giulio Maestro. 1994, Lothrop LB $15.93 (0-688-09268-3). 48pp. This book, which covers the years 1492–1625, introduces such explorers as Cortés, Pizarro, Verrazano, Cartier, Champlain, and Hudson. (Rev: BL 11/1/94; SLJ 9/94) [970.01]

**12983** Roop, Peter, and Connie Roop, eds. *Off the Map: The Journals of Lewis and Clark* (4–6). Illus. by Tim Tanner. 1993, Walker LB $15.85 (0-8027-8208-6). 40pp. Excerpts from the journals and diaries of Lewis and Clark are used to present a vivid picture of their amazing explorations. (Rev: BL 9/1/93; SLJ 6/93) [917.8]

**12984** Schanzer, Rosalyn. *How We Crossed the West: The Adventures of Lewis and Clark* (3–5). Illus. 1997, National Geographic $18.00 (0-7922-3738-2). 48pp. A richly illustrated volume that deals with the expedition of Lewis and Clark as taken from their journals. (Rev: BL 9/15/97; SLJ 10/97*) [917.8]

**12985** Stefoff, Rebecca. *Lewis and Clark* (4–7). Illus. 1992, Chelsea LB $15.95 (0-7910-1750-8). 80pp. A simple text and pictures of the Lewis and Clark expedition that helped open up the West. (Rev: BL 7/92) [978.02]

**12986** Stein, R. Conrad. *The Story of Marquette and Jolliet* (3–5). Illus. by Richard Wahl. 1981, Children's LB $13.27 (0-516-04630-6). 32pp. A simple account of the exploration of the Mississippi River.

**12987** West, Delno C., and Jean M. West. *Braving the North Atlantic: The Vikings, the Cabots, and Jacques Cartier Voyage to America* (4–6). Illus. 1996, Simon & Schuster $16.00 (0-689-31822-7). 82pp. From St. Brendan and Erik the Red to Henry Hudson, this is a history of the early explorers of North America. (Rev: BCCB 9/96; BL 12/15/96; SLJ 12/96) [970.01]

## COLONIAL PERIOD

**12988** Appelbaum, Diana. *Giants in the Land* (2–4). Illus. by Michael McCurdy. 1993, Houghton $16.00 (0-395-64720-7). 32pp. An ecological story concerning the forests of giant white pines in New England that were destroyed to build ships for the British in the 18th century. (Rev: BCCB 9/93; BL 10/1/93*; SLJ 11/93*) [634.9]

**12989** Barrett, Tracy. *Growing Up in Colonial America* (4–6). Illus. 1995, Millbrook LB $23.40 (1-56294-578-5). 96pp. Colonial settlements in the North and South are contrasted in their theories and practices of child rearing. (Rev: BL 12/15/95; SLJ 12/95) [973]

**12990** Brown, Gene. *Discovery and Settlement: Europe Meets the New World (1490–1700)* (5–7). Series: First Person America. 1993, Twenty-First Century LB $18.90 (0-8050-2574-X). 64pp. Using excerpts from original documents, this book covers the exploration of the United States, the Puritans, and the role of Native Americans, African Americans, and women in early colonial days. (Rev: SLJ 3/94) [973.2]

**12991** Carlson, Laurie. *Colonial Kids: An Activity Guide to Life in the New World* (4–6). Illus. 1997, Chicago Review paper $12.95 (1-55652-322-X). 160pp. Along with facts about colonial America, this book gives directions for many related projects and activities, like tying sailors' knots, steaming clams, dyeing a shirt, and stitching a sampler. (Rev: BL 2/15/98; SLJ 3/98) [973.2]

**12992** Corwin, Judith Hoffman. *Colonial American Crafts: The Home* (3–5). Illus. Series: Colonial American Crafts. 1989, Watts LB $22.00 (0-531-10713-2). 48pp. This book gives an overview of home life in colonial times with instructions for such projects as a sampler, a friendship pillow, and paper dolls. Another in this series is: *Colonial American Crafts: The School* (1989). (Rev: BL 1/15/90; SLJ 3/90) [745.5]

**12993** Daugherty, James. *The Landing of the Pilgrims* (5–7). Illus. by author. 1981, Random paper $5.99 (0-394-84697-4). 160pp. Based on his own writings, this is the story of the Pilgrims from the standpoint of William Bradford.

**12994** Dunnahoo, Terry. *Boston's Freedom Trail* (4–7). Illus. Series: Places in American History. 1994, Dillon LB $14.95 (0-87518-623-8); paper $7.95 (0-382-24762-0). 72pp. An explanation of the historical events of the Colonial period that are commemorated in the famous Boston walking tour. (Rev: BL 1/1/95; SLJ 3/95) [917.4]

**12995** Egger-Bovet, Howard, and Marlene Smith-Baranzini. *US Kids History: Book of the American Colonies* (5–7). Illus. Series: Brown Paper School. 1996, Little, Brown $21.95 (0-316-96920-6); paper $12.95 (0-316-22201-1). 96pp. In an informal writing style with plenty of drawings and activities, the American colonial period is introduced. (Rev: BL 8/96; SLJ 8/96) [973.2]

**12996** Foley, Sheila, ed. *Faith Unfurled: The Pilgrims' Quest for Freedom* (4–8). Series: Perspectives on History. 1993, Discovery Enterprises paper $5.95 (1-878668-24-2). 64pp. Through the diaries, journals, and letters of many people, the story of the journey to the New World by the Pilgrims and their difficulties forming a new colony is retold. (Rev: BL 11/15/93) [974.4]

**12997** Fradin, Dennis B. *The Connecticut Colony* (5–8). Illus. Series: The Thirteen Colonies. 1990, Children's LB $30.00 (0-516-00393-3). 160pp. In large print, this is an appealing look at the Connecticut colony. (Rev: BL 8/90) [974.6]

**12998** Fradin, Dennis B. *The Georgia Colony* (4–7). Illus. Series: The Thirteen Colonies. 1989, Chil-

dren's LB $30.00 (0-516-00392-5). 160pp. This account traces the history of Georgia from prehistory to ratification of the Constitution. (Rev: BL 1/15/90) [975]

**12999** Fradin, Dennis B. *The Maryland Colony* (5–8). Illus. Series: The Thirteen Colonies. 1990, Children's LB $30.00 (0-516-00394-1). 160pp. The history of the Maryland colony from its first settlers to statehood. (Rev: BL 1/1/91) [975.2]

**13000** Fradin, Dennis B. *The New Hampshire Colony* (4–7). Illus. 1988, Children's LB $30.00 (0-516-00388-7). 190pp. The history of the first of the original 13 colonies to form its own government. (Rev: BL 5/15/88)

**13001** Fradin, Dennis B. *The New Jersey Colony* (5–8). Illus. Series: The Thirteen Colonies. 1991, Children's LB $30.00 (0-516-00395-X). 156pp. Life in colonial New Jersey is discussed in this account that ends with the eventual gaining of statehood. (Rev: BL 8/91; SLJ 10/91) [974]

**13002** Fradin, Dennis B. *The New York Colony* (4–7). Illus. 1988, Children's LB $30.00 (0-516-00389-5). 160pp. Tracing the development of New York, beginning in the 1300s with the Algonquian and Iroquois Indian tribes. (Rev: BL 10/1/88)

**13003** Fradin, Dennis B. *The Pennsylvania Colony* (4–7). Illus. 1988, Children's LB $30.00 (0-516-00390-9). 160pp. A history of the Keystone state from the early 1600s. (Rev: BL 3/15/89; SLJ 4/89)

**13004** Fradin, Dennis B. *The Rhode Island Colony* (4–7). Illus. Series: The Thirteen Colonies. 1989, Children's LB $30.00 (0-516-00391-7). 160pp. This is an introduction to the smallest U.S. state — Rhode Island. (Rev: BL 8/89; SLJ 11/89) [974.5]

**13005** Fradin, Dennis B. *The South Carolina Colony* (5–8). Illus. Series: The Thirteen Colonies. 1992, Children's LB $30.00 (0-516-00397-6). 160pp. This illustrated account tells the story of South Carolina from the first settlements to statehood. (Rev: BL 9/1/92) [975.7]

**13006** Fradin, Dennis B. *The Thirteen Colonies* (2–3). Illus. 1989, Children's LB $21.00 (0-516-01157-X); paper $5.50 (0-516-41157-8). 48pp. How the first 13 colonies were discovered and settled. (Rev: BL 5/15/89)

**13007** Fradin, Dennis B. *The Virginia Colony* (4–6). Illus. 1986, Children's LB $30.00 (0-516-00387-9). 160pp. A thorough introduction to one of the 13 original colonies. (Rev: BL 4/1/87)

**13008** Goor, Ron, and Nancy Goor. *Williamsburg: Cradle of the Revolution* (4–6). Illus. 1994, Atheneum $15.95 (0-689-31795-6). 90pp. Describes the people, buildings, and history of Williamsburg, Virginia, immediately before the American Revolution. (Rev: BL 1/15/95; SLJ 6/95) [975.5]

**13009** Hakim, Joy. *Making Thirteen Colonies* (4–8). Illus. Series: History of US. 1993, Oxford LB $14.95 (0-19-507747-4); paper $10.95 (0-19-507748-2). 160pp. Covers the colonial period in American history, from the founding of Jamestown in 1607 to the opening of the Wilderness Road in 1775. (Rev: BL 10/1/93; SLJ 2/94) [973.2]

**13010** Hale, Anna W. *The Mayflower People: Triumphs and Tragedies* (5–8). Illus. 1995, Harbinger $15.95 (1-57140-002-8); paper $9.95 (1-57140-003-6). 96pp. The story of the Pilgrims from their departure at Southampton, England, in 1620 to the death of Squanto in 1622. (Rev: BL 1/1–15/96) [974.4]

**13011** Howarth, Sarah. *Colonial People* (4–8). Illus. Series: People and Places. 1994, Millbrook LB $21.90 (1-56294-512-2). 48pp. Various trades and professions that were important in American colonial days are described. (Rev: BL 5/15/95; SLJ 3/95) [973]

**13012** Howarth, Sarah. *Colonial Places* (4–8). Illus. Series: People and Places. 1994, Millbrook LB $21.90 (1-56294-513-0). 48pp. Highlights various places of importance in everyday colonial life, like the meeting house and the church. (Rev: BL 5/15/95; SLJ 3/95) [973]

**13013** Hubbard-Brown, Janet. *The Secret of Roanoke Island* (4–7). Illus. 1991, Avon paper $3.50 (0-380-76223-4). 96pp. An intriguing look at this bit of history in colonial times. (Rev: BL 12/15/91) [975.63]

**13014** Jackson, Shirley. *The Witchcraft of Salem Village* (4–7). Illus. 1963, Random LB $9.99 (0-394-90369-2); paper $4.99 (0-394-89176-7). An account of the witch-hunting hysteria that hit Salem Village.

**13015** Kalman, Bobbie. *Colonial Crafts* (3–6). Illus. by Antoinette DeBiasi. Series: Historic Communities. 1992, Crabtree LB $19.16 (0-86505-490-8); paper $7.95 (0-86505-510-6). 32pp. This book introduces crafts from Colonial America through those found in the many reconstructed craft shops in Williamsburg, Virginia. Two others in this series dealing with colonial life are: *A Colonial Town: Williamsburg* and *Tools and Gadgets* (both 1992). (Rev: SLJ 7/92) [973.2]

**13016** Kalman, Bobbie. *Colonial Life* (3–6). Illus. Series: Historic Communities. 1992, Crabtree LB $19.16 (0-86505-491-6); paper $7.95 (0-86505-511-4). 32pp. Using many illustrations and simple text, this book describes how people lived during the Colonial period in U.S. history. (Rev: BL 11/1/92) [973.2]

**13017** Kent, Deborah. *African-Americans in the Thirteen Colonies* (3–5). Illus. Series: Cornerstones of Freedom. 1996, Children's LB $19.50 (0-516-06631-5). 32pp. Using many photographs, this is a simple overview of the part played by African Americans during the formative years of the colonial period. (Rev: BL 4/15/96; SLJ 11/96) [973]

**13018** Kent, Deborah. *Salem, Massachusetts* (4–6). Illus. Series: Places in American History. 1995, Silver Burdett LB $14.95 (0-87518-648-3). 72pp. The place of Salem in the country's history, with special emphasis on the witch trials during the colonial period. (Rev: BL 2/15/96; SLJ 1/96) [133.4]

**13019** Kent, Zachary. *Williamsburg* (3–5). Illus. Series: Cornerstones of Freedom. 1992, Children's LB $18.70 (0-516-04854-6). 32pp. This account includes both the history of the once-capital of Virginia and its present restoration. (Rev: BL 6/1/92; SLJ 9/92) [975.5]

**13020** King, David C. *Colonial Days: Discover the Past with Fun Projects, Games, Activities, and Recipes* (3–6). Illus. 1998, Wiley paper $12.95 (0-471-16168-3). 128pp. Focusing on a year in the lives of a fictional colonial family, this book outlines 40 projects, including making a sundial, dyeing yarn, and dipping candles. (Rev: BL 2/1/98) [973]

**13021** Knight, James E. *Blue Feather's Vision: The Dawn of Colonial America* (4–6). Illus. by George Guzzi. 1982, Troll paper $3.50 (0-89375-723-3). 32pp. The first volume of a 10-volume set on Colonial America. Followed by: *Boston Tea Party: Rebellion in the Colonies; The Farm: Life in Colonial Pennsylvania; Jamestown: New World Adventure; Journey to Monticello: Traveling in Colonial Times; Sailing to America: Colonists at Sea* (all 1982); and 4 other titles.

**13022** Krensky, Stephen. *Witch Hunt: It Happened in Salem Village* (2–4). Illus. by James Watling. 1989, Random LB $7.99 (0-394-91923-8); paper $3.99 (0-394-81923-3). 48pp. An easily read account of the 1692 witch trials that took the lives of 19 women. (Rev: BCCB 7–8/90; SLJ 8/89) [345.744]

**13023** Kurelek, William, and Margaret S. Engelhart. *They Sought a New World* (3–7). Illus. 1985, Tundra $16.95 (0-88776-172-0); paper $9.95 (0-88776-213-1). 48pp. The story of European immigration to North America. (Rev: BCCB 1/86; BL 12/15/85; SLJ 2/86)

**13024** Lizon, Karen H. *Colonial American Holidays and Entertainment* (5–8). Illus. Series: Colonial America. 1993, Watts LB $21.00 (0-531-12546-7). 112pp. This discussion of major and lesser-known holidays celebrated in the American colonies includes material on Native Americans, slaves, and indentured servants. (Rev: BL 1/1/94; SLJ 12/93) [973.2]

**13025** Loeper, John J. *Going to School in 1776* (3–6). Illus. 1973, Macmillan $16.00 (0-689-30089-1). 112pp. An interesting account of education and childhood activities in Colonial America.

**13026** McGovern, Ann. *If You Lived in Colonial Times* (2–4). Illus. 1992, Scholastic paper $4.95 (0-590-45160-X). A re-creation of incidents and situations that could have occurred in the colonial period.

**13027** McGovern, Ann. *If You Sailed on the Mayflower* (3–4). Illus. by Anna Devito. 1991, Scholastic paper $5.99 (0-590-45161-8). 80pp. In a question-and-answer format, information is given on the historic voyage and the settlement in New England.

**13028** Maestro, Betsy. *The New Americans: Colonial Times, 1620–1689* (2–5). Illus. by Giulio Maestro. 1998, Lothrop LB $15.93 (0-688-13449-1). 48pp. Describes the various European immigrants to the United States during the colonial period and tells why they came and where they settled. (Rev: SLJ 3/98) [973.2]

**13029** Marrin, Albert. *Struggle for a Continent: The French and Indian Wars, 1690–1760* (5–8). Illus. 1987, Macmillan LB $15.95 (0-689-31313-6). 232pp. History comes to life in this story of the events leading to the French and Indian wars and their contribution to independence for the colonists. (Rev: BL 1/15/88)

**13030** Ochoa, George. *The Fall of Quebec and the French and Indian War* (5–7). Illus. Series: Turning Points in American History. 1990, Silver Burdett LB $14.95 (0-382-09954-0); paper $7.95 (0-382-09950-8). 64pp. Illustrated account of the French and Indian Wars and the importance of the defeat of Montcalm and the taking of Quebec under Wolfe. (Rev: BL 3/1/91) [973.2]

**13031** O'Neill, Laurie A. *The Boston Tea Party* (4–6). Illus. 1996, Millbrook LB $21.90 (0-7613-0006-6). 64pp. The causes and effects of the Boston Tea Party are presented, as well as the battles of Lexington and Concord. (Rev: BL 1/1–15/97; SLJ 3/97) [973.3]

**13032** Penner, Lucille R. *Eating the Plates: A Pilgrim Book of Food and Manners* (3–5). Illus. 1991, Macmillan LB $16.00 (0-02-770901-9). 128pp. The focus is on food and other aspects of life at the Plymouth colony and aboard the Mayflower. (Rev: BCCB 9/91; BL 9/1/91; SLJ 3/92) [394.1]

**13033** Roach, Marilynne K. *In the Days of the Salem Witchcraft Trials* (4–6). Illus. 1996, Houghton $15.00 (0-395-69704-2). 96pp. After a discussion of the Salem witchcraft trials, this account focuses on the way people lived in this period and what they believed. (Rev: BCCB 6/96; BL 5/15/96; SLJ 7/96) [133.4]

**13034** Roop, Connie, and Peter Roop, eds. *Pilgrim Voices: Our First Year in the New World* (4–7). Illus. 1995, Walker LB $17.85 (0-8027-8315-5). 48pp. Using first-person sources, the experiences of the Pilgrims from their sea journey to the first Thanksgiv-

ing are re-created. (Rev: BL 2/1/96; SLJ 1/96) [974.4]

**13035** Sakurai, Gail. *The Jamestown Colony* (3–5). Illus. 1997, Children's LB $17.00 (0-516-20295-2). 32pp. The story of the first permanent English settlement in America and its almost total destruction during Bacon's Rebellion in 1676. (Rev: BL 6/1–15/97) [975.5]

**13036** San Souci, Robert D. *N. C. Wyeth's Pilgrims* (2–5). Illus. by N. C. Wyeth. 1991, Chronicle $14.95 (0-87701-806-5). 40pp. A clear text and stunning reproductions of Wyeth murals combine in a beautiful volume. (Rev: BL 11/15/91; SLJ 10/91) [974.4]

**13037** Sewall, Marcia. *The Pilgrims of Plimoth* (3–6). Illus. 1986, Macmillan $15.95 (0-689-31250-4). 48pp. A first-person account of the landing of the Pilgrims and the first years at Plymouth. (Rev: BL 9/15/86; HB 11–12/86; SLJ 11/86)

**13038** Sewall, Marcia. *Thunder from the Clear Sky* (3–6). Illus. 1995, Simon & Schuster $17.00 (0-689-31775-1). 56pp. The story of the Pilgrims' relations with Wampanoag Indians in 1675, as told from both points of view. (Rev: BCCB 10/95; BL 11/15/95; SLJ 10/95) [973.2]

**13039** Sherrow, Victoria. *Huskings, Quiltings, and Barn Raisings: Work-Play Parties in Early America* (4–7). Illus. by Laura LoTurco. 1992, Walker LB $14.85 (0-8027-8188-8). 78pp. How people in early America helped each other with difficult tasks, such as clearing land and raising barns. (Rev: BL 1/15/93) [973.2]

**13040** Smith, Carter, ed. *The Arts and Sciences: A Sourcebook on Colonial America* (5–8). Illus. Series: American Albums from the Collections of the Library of Congress. 1991, Millbrook LB $25.90 (1-56294-037-6). 96pp. Through many well-captioned illustrations and brief text, this sourcebook traces cultural and scientific life during the U.S. colonial period. (Rev: BL 1/1/92) [973.2]

**13041** Smith, Carter, ed. *Daily Life: A Sourcebook on Colonial America* (5–8). Series: American Albums from the Collections of the Library of Congress. 1991, Millbrook LB $25.90 (1-56294-038-4). 96pp. The everyday life and social customs of the colonists are covered in this sourcebook, with an emphasis on original prints, engravings, and other illustrations. (Rev: BL 1/1/92) [973.2]

**13042** Smith, Carter. *The Jamestown Colony* (5–7). Illus. Series: Turning Points in American History. 1991, Silver Burdett LB $14.95 (0-382-24121-5); paper $7.95 (0-382-24116-9). 64pp. An introduction in text and excellent illustrations to the ill-fated early colony in Virginia. (Rev: BL 1/15/92) [975.5]

**13043** Steen, Sandra, and Susan Steen. *Colonial Williamsburg* (4–7). Illus. 1993, Macmillan LB

$14.95 (0-87518-546-0). 72pp. The historic town of Williamsburg, the birthplace of the Bill of Rights, has been restored to its colonial state through John D. Rockefeller's generosity. (Rev: BL 5/15/93; SLJ 6/93) [975.5]

**13044** Stein, R. Conrad. *The Boston Tea Party* (3–5). Illus. Series: Cornerstones of Freedom. 1996, Children's LB $19.50 (0-516-20005-4). 32pp. After a brief introduction to life in colonial America, the events surrounding the Boston Tea Party and their historical significance are described. (Rev: BL 12/15/96; SLJ 5/97) [973.3]

**13045** Stevens, Bernardine S. *Colonial American Craftspeople* (5–8). Illus. Series: Colonial America. 1993, Watts LB $21.00 (0-531-12536-X). 112pp. The workings of the apprenticeship system are explored, with a discussion of such crafts as woodworking, paper making, printing, and metalworking. (Rev: BL 1/1/94; SLJ 2/94) [680]

**13046** Terkel, Susan N. *Colonial American Medicine* (5–8). Illus. Series: Colonial America. 1993, Watts LB $22.00 (0-531-12539-4). 112pp. The practice of medicine in colonial America is explored, with material on physicians, barbers, midwives, and astrologers. (Rev: BL 1/1/94; SLJ 11/93) [362.1]

**13047** Tunis, Edwin. *Colonial Living* (5–8). Illus. by author. 1976, HarperCollins $25.00 (0-690-01063-X). 160pp. A beautifully illustrated account of everyday life in Colonial America.

**13048** Warner, John F. *Colonial American Home Life* (5–8). Illus. Series: Colonial America. 1993, Watts LB $22.00 (0-531-12541-6). 112pp. Topics covered in this book about colonial home life include the kinds of houses people lived in and their clothing, food, work, and schools. (Rev: BL 1/1/94; SLJ 2/94) [973.2]

**13049** Waters, Kate. *On the Mayflower: Voyage of the Ship's Apprentice and a Passenger Girl* (3–5). Illus. 1996, Scholastic $16.95 (0-590-67308-4). 40pp. A young ship's apprentice on the *Mayflower* tells the story of the historic crossing, with photographs taken during the voyage of *Mayflower II*. (Rev: BL 10/1/96; SLJ 10/96) [973.2]

**13050** Waters, Kate. *Sara Morton's Day: A Day in the Life of a Pilgrim Girl* (4–6). Illus. by Russ Kendall. 1989, Scholastic paper $14.95 (0-590-42634-6). 32pp. A typical day in the life of a girl in the Plymouth plantation of 1627. (Rev: BCCB 1/90; BL 10/1/89; SLJ 11/89) [974.4]

**13051** Waters, Kate. *Tapenum's Day: A Wampanoag Indian Boy in Pilgrim Times* (3–5). Illus. by Russ Kendall. 1996, Scholastic $16.95 (0-590-20237-5). 40pp. Re-enactment photos of the Plimoth Plantation site in Massachusetts enhance this account of a Wampanoag Indian boy in the 1620s. (Rev: BCCB 3/96; BL 5/1/96; HB 5–6/96; SLJ 5/96) [974.4]

## REVOLUTIONARY PERIOD

**13052** Bliven, Bruce. *The American Revolution* (5–7). Illus. 1963, Random LB $9.99 (0-394-90383-8). The causes, principle events, and results of the war are given in this basic overview.

**13053** Brenner, Barbara. *If You Were There in 1776* (4–8). Illus. 1994, Bradbury paper $17.00 (0-02-712322-7). 112pp. The year 1776 is explored, with particular emphasis on the everyday life of young people in the colonies. (Rev: BCCB 6/94; BL 5/15/94; SLJ 6/94) [973.3]

**13054** Carter, Alden R. *The American Revolution: War for Independence* (3–6). Illus. Series: First Books. 1992, Watts LB $22.00 (0-531-20082-5). 64pp. A summary of the main causes, events, and battles, with color paintings, maps, and etchings. (Rev: BL 3/1/92) [973.3]

**13055** Dolan, Edward F. *The American Revolution: How We Fought the War of Independence* (5–8). Illus. 1995, Millbrook LB $27.40 (1-56294-521-1). 112pp. An outline of the American Revolutions that covers key events and profiles of all of the familiar historical figures. (Rev: BL 12/15/95; SLJ 1/96) [973.3]

**13056** Gay, Kathlyn, and Martin Gay. *Revolutionary War* (5–8). Illus. Series: Voices from the Past. 1995, Twenty-First Century LB $18.90 (0-8050-2844-7). 64pp. Eyewitness accounts are used extensively in this account that covers the causes, key events, and results of the Revolutionary War. (Rev: BL 12/15/95; SLJ 3/96) [973.7]

**13057** Hakim, Joy. *From Colonies to Country* (4–8). Illus. Series: History of US. 1993, Oxford LB $14.95 (0-19-507749-0); paper $10.95 (0-19-507750-4). 192pp. A concise, objective history of the American Revolution that deals with causes, effects, battles, and important figures. (Rev: BL 1/15/94; SLJ 2/94) [973]

**13058** Hughes, Libby. *Valley Forge* (4–6). Illus. Series: Places in American History. 1993, Macmillan LB $14.95 (0-87518-547-9). 72pp. The story of Valley Forge, Pennsylvania, and the terrible winter during the American Revolutionary War when more than 3,000 of General Washington's troops died. (Rev: BL 4/15/93; SLJ 7/93) [973]

**13059** Kent, Deborah. *The American Revolution: "Give Me Liberty, or Give Me Death!"* (5–7). Illus. Series: American War. 1994, Enslow LB $19.95 (0-89490-521-X). 128pp. A succinct history of the Revolution that uses many firsthand quotations and period illustrations and maps. (Rev: BL 7/94; SLJ 7/94) [973.3]

**13060** Kent, Deborah. *Lexington and Concord* (3–5). Series: Cornerstones of Freedom. 1997, Children's $18.72 (0-516-20462-9). 32pp. Traces the events leading up to these opening battles in the Revolutionary War, with details on what actually happened and the lasting consequences. (Rev: BL 12/15/97) [973.3]

**13061** King, David. *Lexington and Concord* (4–8). Illus. Series: Battlefields Across America. 1997, Twenty-First Century $23.40 (0-8050-5225-9). 64pp. A straightforward account that gives good background material before describing the battles and the sites as they are today. (Rev: SLJ 1/98) [973.3]

**13062** Kirby, Philippa. *Glorious Days, Dreadful Days: The Battle of Bunker Hill* (4–6). Illus. by John Edens. Series: Stories of America. 1993, Raintree Steck-Vaughn LB $25.68 (0-8114-7226-4). 88pp. Describes the Battle of Bunker Hill and its significance in the history of our Revolution. (Rev: HB 11–12/97; SLJ 9/93) [973.3]

**13063** Marrin, Albert. *The War for Independence: The Story of the American Revolution* (5–8). 1988, Macmillan $19.00 (0-689-31390-X). 288pp. Historical fact woven into the story of the 8-year war for independence. (Rev: BCCB 4/88; BL 7/88)

**13064** Murphy, Jim. *A Young Patriot: The American Revolution as Experienced by One Boy* (5–8). Illus. 1996, Clarion $16.00 (0-395-60523-7). 101pp. The American Revolution as seen through the eyes of a 15-year-old volunteer. (Rev: BCCB 6/96; BL 6/1–15/96*; HB 9–10/96; SLJ 6/96*) [973.3]

**13065** Nordstrom, Judy. *Concord and Lexington* (4–6). Illus. Series: Places in American History. 1993, Macmillan LB $14.95 (0-87518-567-3). 72pp. The history and monuments of these 2 historic towns are covered, plus their place in the history of the Revolution. (Rev: BL 4/15/93; SLJ 7/93) [973.3]

**13066** Rappaport, Doreen. *The Boston Coffee Party* (1–3). Illus. by Emily Arnold McCully. 1988, HarperCollins paper $3.75 (0-06-444141-5). 64pp. Angry women force a greedy merchant to turn over coffee in this true Revolutionary War incident. (Rev: BL 4/1/88; HB 9–10/88; SLJ 5/88)

**13067** Schleifer, Jay. *Our Declaration of Independence* (4–6). Illus. Series: I Know America. 1992, Millbrook LB $20.90 (1-56294-205-0). 48pp. A well-illustrated history of the writing of the Declaration of Independence and its significance. (Rev: BL 9/1/92; SLJ 10/92) [973.3]

**13068** Silox-Jarrett, Diane. *Heroines of the American Revolution: America's Founding Mothers* (4–6). Illus. 1998, Green Angel $19.95 (0-9658065-2-0). 94pp. Profiles of 25 important women who championed the colonists' cause during the American Revolution. (Rev: BL 2/15/98) [973.3]

**13069** Stein, R. Conrad. *Valley Forge* (3–5). Illus. Series: Cornerstones of Freedom. 1994, Children's LB $19.50 (0-516-06683-8). 32pp. The crucial battle that determined the future of the American Revolu-

tion is retold with many illustrations and maps. (Rev: BL 1/15/95; SLJ 3/95) [973.7]

**13070** Steins, Richard. *A Nation Is Born: Rebellion and Independence in America (1700–1820)* (5–8). Illus. Series: First Person America. 1993, Twenty-First Century LB $18.90 (0-8050-2582-0). 64pp. The events preceding and during the American Revolution are covered with extensive first-person narratives, connecting text, and copious illustrations. (Rev: BL 2/1/94; SLJ 2/94) [973.3]

**13071** Weber, Michael. *Yorktown* (4–7). Illus. Series: Battlefields Across America. 1997, Twenty-First Century $23.40 (0-8050-5226-7). 63pp. Background material on the Revolutionary War is given, along with details of the battle and the present-day condition of its site. (Rev: SLJ 1/98) [973.3]

**13072** Wilbur, C. Keith. *Revolutionary Medicine 1700–1800* (4–8). Illus. 1997, Chelsea $19.95 (0-7910-4532-3). 96pp. In a large-book format, this account gives a great deal of information about medicine in 18th-century America. (Rev: BL 6/1–15/97; SLJ 7/97) [973.3]

**13073** Wilbur, C. Keith. *The Revolutionary Soldier 1775–1783* (4–8). Illus. 1997, Chelsea LB $19.95 (0-7910-4533-1). 96pp. Topics covered in this book about the Continental Army include clothing, weapons, camp life, food, hospitals, and leisure activities. (Rev: BL 6/1–15/97; SLJ 7/97) [973.3]

**13074** Young, Robert. *The Real Patriots of the American Revolution* (4–6). Illus. Series: Both Sides. 1997, Dillon LB $13.95 (0-87518-612-2). 72pp. The points of view of Revolutionists, Loyalists, and the British are represented in this account of the causes and important events of the American Revolution. (Rev: BL 9/15/97) [973.3]

**13075** Zeinert, Karen. *Those Remarkable Women of the American Revolution* (5–8). Illus. 1996, Millbrook LB $27.40 (1-56294-657-9). 96pp. A fascinating account of the various roles women played in the American Revolution, from fighting and spying to fund raising. (Rev: BL 12/1/96; SLJ 3/97) [973.3]

### THE YOUNG NATION, 1789–1861

**13076** Baldwin, Robert F. *New England Whaler* (5–8). Illus. by Richard Erickson. Series: American Pastfinder. 1996, Lerner LB $19.95 (0-8225-2978-5). 48pp. Life on a 19th-century whaling ship is detailed, with many maps and color photos. (Rev: BL 7/96; SLJ 6/96) [638.2]

**13077** Bentley, Judith. *"Dear Friend": Thomas Garrett and William Still, Collaborators on the Underground Railroad* (5–8). Illus. 1997, Dutton paper $15.99 (0-525-65156-X). 119pp. A white Quaker, Thomas Garrett, and a freed slave, William Still, work together in the Underground Railroad to smuggle slaves to freedom. (Rev: BCCB 2/97; BL 2/15/97; SLJ 6/97) [973.7]

**13078**  Bial, Raymond. *The Strength of These Arms: Life in the Slave Quarters* (3–6). Illus. 1997, Houghton $15.00 (0-395-77394-6). 48pp. Using photos extensively, this account re-creates the conditions of life during the days of slavery, both in the mansion house and in the slave quarters. (Rev: BL 9/15/97; SLJ 11/97) [975]

**13079**  Bial, Raymond. *The Underground Railroad* (4–7). Illus. 1995, Houghton $16.00 (0-395-69937-1). 48pp. This photoessay re-creates the places involved in the Underground Railroad and the heroism of the people involved. (Rev: BCCB 3/95; BL 4/1/95; HB 7–8/95; SLJ 4/95) [973.7]

**13080**  Bredeson, Carmen. *The Battle of the Alamo: The Fight for Texas Territory* (5–8). Series: Spotlight on American History. 1996, Millbrook LB $21.90 (0-7613-0019-8). 64pp. A well-organized account that describes important events and people involved in the fall of the Alamo, with quotes from original sources and many art reproductions. (Rev: SLJ 4/97) [976.4]

**13081**  Carter, Alden R. *The Mexican War: Manifest Destiny* (3–6). Illus. Series: First Books. 1992, Watts LB $21.00 (0-531-20081-7). 64pp. This account describes the causes, events, and campaigns of the war by which much of California, Texas, and the Southwest became part of the United States. (Rev: BL 3/1/93; SLJ 2/93) [973.6]

**13082**  Carter, Alden R. *War of 1812: Second Fight for Independence* (3–6). Illus. Series: First Books. 1992, Watts LB $21.00 (0-531-20080-9). 64pp. This book outlines the debate over entry into the war plus a description of the battles and results of the War of 1812. (Rev: BL 3/1/92) [973.8]

**13083**  Chambers, Veronica. *Amistad Rising: A Story of Freedom* (3–6). Illus. by Paul Lee. 1998, Harcourt $16.00 (0-15-201803-4). 40pp. A partly fictionalized account of the *Amistad* mutiny that focuses on Cinque and his restlessness. (Rev: BL 2/15/98; SLJ 4/98) [326]

**13084**  Doherty, Craig A., and Katherine M. Doherty. *The Erie Canal* (4–7). Illus. Series: Building America. 1996, Blackbirch LB $15.95 (1-56711-112-2). 48pp. Photos and maps are used effectively in this introduction to the Erie Canal, an engineering marvel. (Rev: BL 2/15/97; SLJ 2/97) [386]

**13085**  Fleischner, Jennifer. *The Dred Scott Case: Testing the Right to Live Free* (4–6). Illus. 1997, Millbrook LB $21.90 (0-7613-0005-8). 64pp. An account of the life of the slave Dred Scott and the historic court case in 1857 against his owner, John Sanford. (Rev: BL 5/1/97; SLJ 4/97) [342.73]

**13086**  Gay, Kathlyn, and Martin Gay. *War of 1812* (5–8). Illus. Series: Voices from the Past. 1995,

Twenty-First Century LB $18.90 (0-8050-2846-3). 64pp. Accounts taken from letters, memoirs, and official reports highlight this well-illustrated history of the War of 1812 and its consequences. (Rev: BL 12/15/95; SLJ 3/96) [973.5]

**13087**  Guccione, Leslie D. *Come Morning* (4–7). 1995, Carolrhoda LB $21.27 (0-87614-892-5). 120pp. A young boy takes over his father's duties as a conductor on the Underground Railroad. (Rev: BCCB 1/96; HB 11–12/95; SLJ 11/95)

**13088**  Hakim, Joy. *The New Nation* (4–8). Illus. Series: History of US. 1994, Oxford LB $14.95 (0-19-507751-2); paper $10.95 (0-19-507752-0). 176pp. An attractive volume that gives, through text and illustrations, a concise history of the United States from independence to the Civil War. (Rev: BL 4/15/94; SLJ 4/94) [973]

**13089**  Hamilton, Virginia. *Many Thousand Gone: African Americans from Slavery to Freedom* (5–8). Illus. by Leo Dillon and Diane Dillon. 1992, Random LB $16.99 (0-394-92873-3); Knopf paper $12.00 (0-679-87936-6). 160pp. General history and personal narratives and biographies of slaves, including the famous and unknown, combine to tell this dramatic story. (Rev: BL 12/1/92*) [973.7]

**13090**  Hansen, Ellen, ed. *The Underground Railroad: Life on the Road to Freedom* (4–8). Illus. Series: Perspectives on History. 1993, Discovery Enterprises paper $5.95 (1-878668-27-7). 61pp. The story of the great freedom movement in which both whites and African Americans participated in an effort to smuggle slaves out of the pre–Civil War South. (Rev: BL 8/94) [973.7]

**13091**  Harness, Cheryl. *The Amazing Impossible Erie Canal* (3–5). Illus. 1995, Simon & Schuster paper $16.00 (0-02-742641-6). 42pp. This history of the Erie Canal concentrates on the festivities during its opening in 1825. (Rev: BCCB 6/95; BL 5/15/95; SLJ 8/95) [977.1]

**13092**  Jacobs, William J. *War with Mexico* (4–6). Illus. Series: Spotlight on American History. 1993, Millbrook LB $21.90 (1-56294-366-9). 64pp. The events of the 1846–1848 war with Mexico are reported, with an objective account of its causes and results. (Rev: BL 12/15/93; SLJ 1/94) [973.6]

**13093**  Jurmain, Suzanne. *Freedom's Sons: The True Story of the Amistad Mutiny* (5–8). Illus. 1998, Lothrop $15.00 (0-688-11072-X). 128pp. Told with true storytelling skill, this fascinating chapter in American history is re-created brilliantly, with a special focus on the nobility of Cinque and his men. (Rev: BL 2/15/98; SLJ 4/98) [326]

**13094**  Kalman, Bobbie. *The General Store* (3–5). Illus. Series: Historic Communities. 1997, Crabtree LB $19.16 (0-86505-432-0); paper $7.95 (0-86505-462-2). 32pp. Using photos of reconstructions in such places as Old Sturbridge Village, this account describes the importance, contents, and workings of the general store in 18th- and 19th-century America. (Rev: SLJ 7/97) [381]

**13095** Kalman, Bobbie. *Life on a Plantation* (3–6). Illus. Series: Historic Communities. 1997, Crabtree LB $19.16 (0-86505-435-5); paper $7.95 (0-86505-465-7). 32pp. Daily life on the plantation for both the owners and their slaves is covered, with details about working in the fields and the roles and duties of various workers. (Rev: BL 7/97) [975]

**13096** Macaulay, David. *Mill* (5–8). Illus. by author. 1983, Houghton $17.95 (0-395-34830-7); paper $8.95 (0-395-52019-3). 128pp. The construction of an early 19th-century spinning mill in Rhode Island.

**13097** McKissack, Patricia, and Fredrick McKissack. *Christmas in the Big House, Christmas in the Quarters* (4–6). Illus. by John Thompson. 1994, Scholastic $17.95 (0-590-43027-0). 80pp. This book describes life on a Virginia plantation in 1859 and includes social life and master-slave relations plus material on how Christmas was celebrated. (Rev: BCCB 10/94; BL 8/94; SLJ 10/94*) [975]

**13098** McKissack, Patricia, and Fredrick McKissack. *Rebels Against Slavery: American Slave Revolts* (5–8). Illus. 1996, Scholastic $14.95 (0-590-45735-7). 176pp. The careers of such leaders of slave revolts as Nat Turner, Toussaint-Louverture, Cinque, and Harriet Tubman are covered in this informative book illustrated with photos. (Rev: BCCB 6/96; BL 2/15/96; SLJ 3/96) [970.00496]

**13099** McNeese, Tim. *America's Early Canals* (4–6). Illus. Series: America on the Move. 1993, Macmillan LB $11.95 (0-89686-730-7). 48pp. An introduction to canals famous in American history, such as the Potomac Canal and the Erie Canal, with discussion of the builders and how the canals were built. (Rev: BL 11/15/93) [386]

**13100** Miller, Marilyn. *The Transcontinental Railroad* (5–8). Illus. 1987, Silver Burdett paper $7.95 (0-382-09912-5). 64pp. The great event that linked East and West by rail is portrayed with numerous illustrations. (Rev: BL 7/87; SLJ 9/87)

**13101** Myers, Walter Dean. *Amistad: A Long Road to Freedom* (5–8). Illus. 1998, Dutton paper $16.99 (0-525-45970-7). 96pp. The fascinating story of the 1839 mutiny and its consequences told with a skillful narrative that emphasizes the courage, strength, and dignity of the mutineers. (Rev: BL 2/15/98) [326]

**13102** Nirgiotis, Nicholas. *Erie Canal: Gateway to the West* (4–7). Illus. 1993, Watts LB $21.00 (0-531-20146-5). 64pp. The story of the construction of the vast superstructure of canals, supervised by DeWitt Clinton, joining Lake Erie and the Hudson River. (Rev: BL 8/93) [386]

**13103** Pelta, Kathy. *Eastern Trails: From Footpaths to Turnpikes* (4–6). Series: American Trails. 1997, Raintree Steck-Vaughn LB $27.83 (0-8172-4071-3). 96pp. Focusing on trails, footpaths, and emerging roads, this account traces the opening up of the American East to settlers and explorers. Also use *Trails to the West: Beyond the Mississippi* (1997). (Rev: BL 10/15/97) [973.6]

**13104** Santella, Andrew. *The Battle of the Alamo* (3–5). Illus. Series: Cornerstones of Freedom. 1997, Children's LB $19.50 (0-516-20293-6). 32pp. The history of the San Antonio, Texas, chapel and the famous siege there in which Davy Crockett and Jim Bowie were killed. (Rev: BL 6/1–15/97) [976.4]

**13105** Shuter, Jane, ed. *Charles Ball and American Slavery* (5–8). Illus. Series: History Eyewitness. 1995, Raintree Steck-Vaughn LB $24.26 (0-8114-8281-2). 48pp. This autobiographical account in simplified language brings the horrors of slavery to life, with period prints and maps. (Rev: BL 4/15/95; SLJ 5/95) [975]

**13106** Simonds, Christopher. *Samuel Slater's Mill and the Industrial Revolution* (5–7). Illus. Series: Turning Points in American History. 1990, Silver Burdett LB $14.95 (0-382-09951-6); paper $7.95 (0-382-09947-8). 64pp. Describes how the pioneer in the cotton textile industry reproduced English machinery and how the Industrial Revolution began in this country. (Rev: BL 3/1/91) [338]

**13107** Smith, Carter, ed. *The Founding Presidents: A Sourcebook on the U.S. Presidency* (5–8). Illus. Series: American Albums. 1993, Millbrook LB $25.90 (1-56294-357-X). 96pp. A visually oriented review of the personal and political lives of the presidents from Washington through James Monroe. (Rev: BL 12/1/93) [973]

**13108** Smith, Carter, ed. *Presidents of a Young Republic: A Sourcebook on the U.S. Presidency* (5–8). Illus. Series: American Albums. 1993, Millbrook LB $25.90 (1-56294-359-6). 96pp. A well-illustrated account that traces U.S. history from the presidency of John Quincy Adams through James Buchanan. (Rev: BL 12/1/93; SLJ 4/94) [973.5]

**13109** Smith-Baranzini, Marlene, and Howard Egger-Bovet. *Brown Paper School USKids History: Book of the New American Nation* (5–7). Illus. 1995, Little, Brown $21.95 (0-316-96923-0); paper $12.95 (0-316-22206-2). 96pp. From George Washington to the building of the Erie Canal, key issues and people in American history are introduced. (Rev: BL 8/95; SLJ 8/95) [973.5]

**13110** Stein, R. Conrad. *The Underground Railroad* (3–5). Illus. Series: Cornerstones of Freedom. 1997, Children's LB $19.50 (0-516-20298-7). 32pp. A well-organized, illustrated account of the Underground Railroad, its routes, how many lives were saved, and the major names connected with this huge humanitarian effort. (Rev: BL 6/1–15/97) [973.7]

**13111** Stepto, Michele, ed. *Our Song, Our Toil: The Story of American Slavery as Told by Slaves* (5–7). Illus. 1994, Millbrook LB $25.90 (1-56294-401-0). 96pp. The history of American slavery is told in a series of excerpts from journals, narratives, autobiographies, and other original documents. (Rev: BL 5/15/94; SLJ 10/94) [973]

**13112** Toynton, Evelyn. *Growing Up in America: 1830 to 1860* (4–6). Illus. 1995, Millbrook LB $24.90 (1-56294-453-3). 96pp. Describes the life of pre-Civil War children from 5 social groups, including Native Americans, slaves, and farmers. (Rev: BL 4/15/95; SLJ 4/95) [973.5]

### PIONEER LIFE
### AND WESTWARD EXPANSION

**13113** Altman, Linda Jacobs. *The California Gold Rush in American History* (4–8). Illus. Series: In American History. 1997, Enslow LB $19.95 (0-89490-878-2). 128pp. After a brief history of the California Gold Rush, this book covers topics like frontier injustice, racial discrimination, and the place of women. (Rev: SLJ 3/98) [979.4]

**13114** Anderson, Joan. *Spanish Pioneers of the Southwest* (3–6). Illus. 1989, Dutton paper $16.99 (0-525-67546-9). 64pp. A photoessay of life in mid-eighteenth-century New Mexico. (Rev: BCCB 4/89; BL 4/15/89; SLJ 5/89)

**13115** Anderson, Peter. *The Pony Express* (3–5). Illus. Series: Cornerstones of Freedom. 1996, Children's LB $19.50 (0-516-20002-X). 32pp. A brief history of the Pony Express, the men involved in its operation, and its contributions to the opening of the American West. (Rev: BL 11/15/96) [383]

**13116** Bacon, Melvin, and Daniel Blegen. *Bent's Fort: Crossroads of Cultures on the Santa Fe Trail* (4–6). Illus. 1995, Millbrook LB $24.90 (1-56294-526-2). 72pp. A fascinating glimpse of life at Bent's Fort in southeastern Colorado on the Santa Fe Trail during the 1840s. (Rev: BL 1/1–15/96; SLJ 11/95) [978.8]

**13117** Bial, Raymond. *Frontier Home* (3–6). Illus. 1993, Houghton $17.00 (0-395-64046-6). 40pp. A description of the exteriors and contents of frontier homes, with many quotes from original sources. (Rev: BCCB 10/93; BL 11/1/93; SLJ 9/93) [978]

**13118** Carlson, Laurie. *Westward Ho! An Activity Guide to the Wild West* (4–6). 1996, Chicago Review paper $12.95 (1-55652-271-1). 160pp. Clear directions accompany this introduction to 50 activities — like hooking rugs or keeping a trapper's journal — associated with the westward movement. (Rev: BL 10/1/96; SLJ 12/96) [978]

**13119** Christian, Mary Blount. *Hats Are for Watering Horses: Why the Cowboys Dressed That Way* (2–4). Illus. by Lyle Miller. 1993, Hendrick-Long $14.95 (0-937460-89-3). 64pp. Explains how every item of clothing worn by a cowboy has a useful purpose. (Rev: BL 3/15/94; SLJ 6/94) [973.7]

**13120** Cobb, Mary. *The Quilt-Block History of Pioneer Days: With Projects Kids Can Make* (3–6). Illus. 1995, Millbrook LB $23.90 (1-56294-485-1). 64pp. A history of America's Western pioneers as seen through the patterns in their quilts plus a number of related craft projects, such as making bookmarks. (Rev: BL 4/15/95; SLJ 6/95) [746.9]

**13121** De Angelis, Gina. *The Black Cowboys* (4–8). Illus. Series: African-American Achievers. 1997, Chelsea LB $19.95 (0-7910-2589-6); paper $8.95 (0-7910-2590-X). 64pp. As well as telling how African Americans helped open up the West, this book describes the contributions of black cowboys in the latter half of the 1800s and gives profiles of some, like Nat Love and Bill Pickett. (Rev: BL 2/15/98) [978]

**13122** Duncan, Dayton. *People of the West* (5–8). Illus. 1996, Little, Brown $19.95 (0-316-19627-4); paper $10.95 (0-316-19633-9). 128pp. Some people — both famous and obscure — tell in their own words about the opening of the West, based on the PBS series. (Rev: BL 8/96; SLJ 10/96) [978]

**13123** Duncan, Dayton. *The West: An Illustrated History for Children* (5–8). Illus. 1996, Little, Brown $19.95 (0-316-19628-2); paper $10.95 (0-316-19632-0). 144pp. A brief history of the opening up of the West, based on the PBS series. (Rev: BL 8/96; SLJ 10/96) [978]

**13124** Emsden, Katharine. *Voices from the West: Life Along the Trail* (4–8). Series: Perspectives on History. 1993, Discovery Enterprises paper $4.95 (1-878668-18-8). 60pp. Through excerpts from diaries, journals, and letters, the hardships and everyday life of pioneers along the Oregon and Santa Fe trails are re-created. (Rev: BL 11/15/93) [978]

**13125** Fisher, Leonard Everett. *The Oregon Trail* (4–6). Illus. 1990, Holiday LB $16.95 (0-8234-0833-7). 64pp. A clear, readable account of the westward expansion in the 1800s. (Rev: BCCB 1/91; BL 12/15/90; HB 3–4/91; SLJ 1/91) [979.5]

**13126** Fox, Mary V. *The Story of Women Who Shaped the West* (3–5). Illus. Series: Cornerstones of Freedom. 1991, Children's LB $19.50 (0-516-04757-4). 32pp. Outstanding women pioneers are highlighted in this book about the settling of the American West. (Rev: BL 6/1/91; SLJ 9/91) [978.02]

**13127** Fradin, Dennis B. *Pioneers* (2–4). Illus. 1984, Children's LB $21.00 (0-516-01927-9). 48pp. The story of the brave people who opened up the American West. (Rev: BL 3/1/85; SLJ 4/85)

**13128** Freedman, Russell. *Children of the Wild West* (5–8). Illus. 1983, Houghton $15.95 (0-89919-143-6); paper $6.95 (0-395-54785-7). 128pp. The life of children on the frontier told in text and old photos.

**13129** Freedman, Russell. *Cowboys of the Wild West* (5–8). Illus. 1990, Houghton paper $7.95 (0-395-54800-4). 128pp. Text and excellent historical photographs describe these romantic figures. (Rev: BCCB 12/85; HB 3–4/86)

**13130** Gibbons, Gail. *Yippee-Yay! A Book About Cowboys and Cowgirls* (1–4). Illus. by author. 1998, Little, Brown $14.95 (0-316-30944-3). Focusing on a period of 30 years after the Civil War, this account describes the life and gear of a cowboy, with strongest coverage on the roundup. (Rev: SLJ 3/98) [978]

**13131** Gorsline, Marie, and Douglas Gorsline. *Cowboys* (3–4). Illus. by Douglas Gorsline. 1980, Random LB $6.99 (0-394-93935-2); paper $3.25 (0-394-83935-8). 32pp. An amazing amount of information is included in this slim text.

**13132** Gorsline, Marie, and Douglas Gorsline. *The Pioneers* (3–5). Illus. by Douglas Gorsline. 1982, Random paper $2.50 (0-394-83905-6). 32pp. A trip along the Oregon Trail is re-created.

**13133** Granfield, Linda. *Cowboy: An Album* (5–7). Illus. 1994, Ticknor $18.95 (0-395-68430-7). 96pp. The history of the cowboy, legends about him, and his daily life are covered, with material on cowboys from minority groups. (Rev: BCCB 3/94; BL 2/1/94; SLJ 1/94*) [636.2]

**13134** Green, Carl R., and William R. Sanford. *The Dalton Gang* (4–8). Illus. Series: Outlaws and Lawmen. 1995, Enslow LB $15.95 (0-89490-588-0). 48pp. The story of the gang of outlaws that roamed the West during pioneer days. (Rev: BL 11/15/95) [978]

**13135** Harness, Cheryl. *They're Off! The Story of the Pony Express* (3–5). Illus. 1996, Simon & Schuster $16.00 (0-689-80523-3). 28pp. A vivid account of the origin of the Pony Express prior to the Civil War and the typical life of a rider. (Rev: BL 11/15/96; SLJ 12/96) [383]

**13136** Kalman, Bobbie. *The Gristmill* (3–6). Illus. Series: Historic Communities. 1991, Crabtree LB $19.16 (0-86505-486-X); paper $7.95 (0-86505-506-8). 32pp. Text and pictures show the construction and operation of the mill as well as the skills of the millers. (Rev: BL 7/91) [664]

**13137** Kalman, Bobbie. *Home Crafts* (3–6). Illus. Series: Historic Communities. 1991, Crabtree LB $19.16 (0-86505-485-1); paper $7.95 (0-86505-505-X). 32pp. How early settlers produced wool and other cloth and made quilts, soap, leather goods, and other necessities. (Rev: BL 7/91) [745.5]

**13138** Kalman, Bobbie. *In the Barn* (3–6). Illus. Series: Historic Communities. 1997, Crabtree LB $19.16 (0-86505-433-9); paper $7.95 (0-86505-463-0). 32pp. Shows how the barn was the center of activity on a settler's farm and supplies details on its design, barn raising, and all the seasonal activities it housed. (Rev: BL 7/97) [631.2]

**13139** Kalman, Bobbie. *The Kitchen* (3–6). Illus. Series: Historic Communities. 1991, Crabtree LB $19.16 (0-86505-484-3); paper $7.95 (0-86505-504-1). 32pp. The kitchen and its utensils as they existed in pioneer times are pictured and described. (Rev: BL 7/91) [643.3]

**13140** Kalman, Bobbie. *A One-Room School* (3–5). Illus. Series: Historic Communities. 1994, Crabtree LB $19.16 (0-86505-497-5); paper $7.95 (0-86505-517-3). 32pp. Through pictures and text, the physical plan of a one-room school is presented, with material on supplies, routines, expected conduct, and school rules. (Rev: SLJ 9/94) [371.7]

**13141** Kalman, Bobbie. *Settler Sayings* (3–5). Illus. Series: Historic Communities. 1994, Crabtree LB $19.16 (0-86505-498-3); paper $7.95 (0-86505-518-1). 32pp. In a conversational text, sayings popular with settlers are described under such headings as the kitchen and the farm. (Rev: SLJ 7/94) [973.8]

**13142** Kalman, Bobbie. *Visiting a Village* (3–6). Illus. Series: Historic Communities. 1991, Crabtree LB $19.16 (0-86505-487-8); paper $7.95 (0-86505-507-6). 32pp. Life in a frontier village is described in this well-illustrated account. (Rev: BL 7/91) [971]

**13143** Kalman, Bobbie, and Tammy Everts. *Customs and Traditions* (3–5). Illus. Series: Historic Communities. 1994, Crabtree LB $19.16 (0-86505-495-9); paper $7.95 (0-86505-515-7). 32pp. Various customs and traditions from the days of the settlers are described and their origins traced in this heavily illustrated volume. (Rev: SLJ 7/94) [973.8]

**13144** Kalman, Bobbie, and David Schimpky. *Fort Life* (3–5). Illus. Series: Historic Communities. 1994, Crabtree LB $19.16 (0-86505-496-7); paper $7.95 (0-86505-516-5). 32pp. This book describes life in a fort, with details on early American defenses and the daily life of soldiers. (Rev: SLJ 9/94) [978]

**13145** Ketchum, Liza. *The Gold Rush* (5–8). Illus. 1996, Little, Brown $19.95 (0-316-59133-5); paper $10.95 (0-316-49047-4). 128pp. An overview of the gold rush in California and its effects on the development of the West, based on the PBS series. (Rev: BL 8/96; SLJ 10/96) [979.4]

**13146** King, David C. *Pioneer Days: Discover the Past with Fun Projects, Games, Activities, and Recipes* (3–6). Illus. by Bobbie Moore. Series: American Kids in History. 1997, Wiley paper $12.95 (0-471-16169-1). 118pp. In chapters arranged by season, the daily life of pioneers is re-created through an assortment of history, culture, crafts, and stories. (Rev: SLJ 2/98) [973.5]

**13147** Klausmeier, Robert. *Cowboy* (4–7). Illus. Series: American Pastfinder. 1996, Lerner LB $21.27 (0-8225-2975-0). 48pp. This account focuses on the huge cattle drives and the men who led them in the years following the Civil War. (Rev: BL 3/1/96; SLJ 3/96) [636.2]

**13148** Knight, Amelia S. *The Way West: Journal of a Pioneer Woman* (2–5). Illus. by Michael McCurdy. 1993, Simon & Schuster paper $16.00 (0-671-72375-8). 32pp. Using parts of a pioneer woman's story of life on the trail from Iowa to Oregon in 1853, this book presents, with stunning woodcuts, a realistic picture of life on the frontier. (Rev: BL 11/15/93; HB 9–10/93; SLJ 9/93) [917.8]

**13149** Krehbiel, Randy. *Little Bighorn* (4–8). Illus. Series: Battlefields Across America. 1997, Twenty-First Century $23.40 (0-8050-5236-4). 64pp. After good background material, this account describes the battle and tells about the site as it is today. (Rev: SLJ 1/98) [973.8]

**13150** Krensky, Stephen. *Striking It Rich: The Story of the California Gold Rush* (2–3). Illus. by Anna DiVito. 1996, Simon & Schuster $15.00 (0-689-80804-6); paper $3.99 (0-689-80803-8). 48pp. A very simple retelling of the excitement and pain involved in the California gold rush. (Rev: BCCB 11/96; BL 9/15/96; SLJ 2/97) [979.4]

**13151** Kroll, Steven. *Pony Express!* (2–5). Illus. 1996, Scholastic $16.95 (0-590-20239-1). 40pp. A history of the Pony Express, with emphasis on the first trip in 1860. (Rev: BCCB 4/96; BL 3/1/96; HB 9–10/96; SLJ 4/96*) [383]

**13152** Miller, Brandon M. *Buffalo Gals: Women of the Old West* (4–7). Illus. 1995, Lerner LB $21.27 (0-8225-1730-2). 88pp. A realistic portrait of the hardships faced by women pioneers during the 19th century on the Western frontier. (Rev: BCCB 7–8/95; BL 5/1/95; SLJ 6/95*) [978]

**13153** Morley, Jacqueline. *How Would You Survive in the American West?* (4–7). Illus. Series: How Would You Survive? 1996, Watts LB $24.00 (0-531-14382-1). 48pp. Information about supplies and shelter are given in this imaginary journey through the American West, with encounters with Native Americans, buffalo, and various obstacles. (Rev: BL 5/15/96) [978]

**13154** Murdoch, David. *Cowboy* (4–8). Illus. Series: Eyewitness Books. 1993, Knopf LB $20.99 (0-679-94014-6). 64pp. The story of the American cowboy, his place in history, and present functions. (Rev: BL 10/1/93; SLJ 1/94) [978]

**13155** Nelson, Sharlene, and Ted Nelson. *Bull Whackers to Whistle Punks: Logging in the Old West*

(4–6). Illus. 1996, Watts LB $22.00 (0-531-20228-3). 63pp. The early days of logging in the West, with descriptions of each of the jobs and the tools used. (Rev: BL 8/96; SLJ 7/96) [634.6]

**13156** Nirgiotis, Nicholas. *West by Waterway: Rivers and U.S. Expansion* (4–6). Illus. 1995, Watts LB $22.00 (0-531-20188-0). 64pp. A history of the opening-up of the West that emphasizes the roles played by boats and inland waterways. (Rev: BL 9/1/95) [386]

**13157** Patent, Dorothy Hinshaw. *West by Covered Wagon: Retracing the Pioneer Trails* (3–6). Illus. by William Munoz. 1995, Walker LB $16.85 (0-8027-8378-3). 32pp. A modern covered-wagon trip is compared to the original journeys accomplished by pioneers as they opened up the West. (Rev: BCCB 11/95; BL 11/1/95; SLJ 10/95*) [978]

**13158** Paul, Ann W. *The Seasons Sewn: A Year in Patchwork* (4–6). Illus. by Michael McCurdy. 1996, Harcourt $16.00 (0-15-276918-8). 40pp. Various squares on historical patchwork quilts reflect life on the American frontier in the late 19th century. (Rev: BCCB 5/96; BL 4/1/96; SLJ 5/96) [746.46]

**13159** Pelta, Kathy. *Cattle Trails: "Git Along Little Dogies."* (4–6). Illus. Series: American Trails. 1997, Raintree Steck-Vaughn LB $27.83 (0-8172-4073-X). 96pp. A thorough discussion of the cattle drives that were a part of Western history from 1850 to 1890. (Rev: BL 7/97; SLJ 12/97) [978]

**13160** Pelta, Kathy. *The Royal Roads: Spanish Trails in North America* (4–6). Illus. Series: American Trails. 1997, Raintree Steck-Vaughn LB $27.83 (0-8172-4074-8). 96pp. The story of Spanish trails in California, Florida, New Mexico, and Texas, and the people who traveled them looking for material or spiritual gains. (Rev: BL 7/97; SLJ 12/97) [970.01]

**13161** Reef, Catherine. *Buffalo Soldiers* (4–6). Illus. 1993, Twenty-First Century LB $22.90 (0-8050-2372-0). 80pp. The story of the African-American regiments that helped protect settlers during the Westward movement. (Rev: BL 8/93) [978]

**13162** Ritchie, David. *Frontier Life* (5–7). Illus. Series: Life in America 100 Years Ago. 1995, Chelsea $19.95 (0-7910-2842-9). 104pp. A concise overview of life on the American frontier that does not gloss over the harsh and often violent aspects. (Rev: SLJ 1/96) [973.5]

**13163** Roop, Peter, and Connie Roop. *Westward, Ho, Ho, Ho!* (3–5). Illus. 1996, Millbrook LB $21.90 (0-7613-0020-1). 40pp. This book mixes a history of the American West with appropriate riddles and cartoons. (Rev: BL 12/15/96; SLJ 1/97) [978]

**13164** Ross, Stewart. *Cowboys* (5–7). Illus. Series: Fact or Fiction. 1995, Millbrook LB $24.90 (1-56294-618-8). 48pp. The life of cowboys during the late 1800s is covered, with information that tries to separate fact from fable. (Rev: BL 7/95; SLJ 5/95) [978.02]

**13165** Russell, Marion. *Along the Santa Fe Trail: Marion Russell's Own Story* (3–5). Adapted by Ginger Wadsworth. Illus. by James Watling. 1993, Albert Whitman LB $16.95 (0-8075-0295-2). 32pp. In a reworking of a memoir of pioneer life, the experiences of a 7-year-old traveling in a wagon train on the Santa Fe Trail are recalled. (Rev: BL 1/15/94; SLJ 12/93) [917.8]

**13166** Santella, Andrew. *The Chisholm Trail* (3–5). Series: Cornerstones of Freedom. 1997, Children's LB $19.50 (0-516-20393-2). 32pp. The history of the cattle trail from San Antonio, Texas, to Abilene, Kansas, with information on its lasting importance. (Rev: BL 12/15/97) [973.6]

**13167** Savage, Jeff. *Cowboys and Cow Towns of the Wild West* (4–7). Illus. Series: Trailblazers of the Wild West. 1995, Enslow LB $14.95 (0-89490-603-8). 48pp. Through the experiences of a single cowboy, the reader learns about his equipment, dangers, leisure time, cattle drives, and roundups. (Rev: SLJ 2/96) [978]

**13168** Savage, Jeff. *Gunfighters of the Wild West* (3–5). Illus. Series: Trailblazers of the Wild West. 1995, Enslow LB $14.95 (0-89490-600-3). 48pp. This book briefly covers the lives and exploits of such gunslingers as Doc Holliday, the Earps, John Fisher King, Billy the Kid, the Jameses, the Daltons, and the Wild Bunch. (Rev: SLJ 1/96) [973.5]

**13169** Savage, Jeff. *Pioneering Women of the Wild West* (3–5). Illus. Series: Trailblazers of the Wild West. 1995, Enslow LB $14.95 (0-89490-604-6). 48pp. The struggles and hardships of women in the Wild West are covered, with particular mention of such famous characters as Calamity Jane and Carrie Nation. (Rev: SLJ 1/96) [973.5]

**13170** Schlissel, Lillian. *Black Frontiers: A History of African-American Heroes in the Old West* (3–6). Illus. 1995, Simon & Schuster $18.00 (0-689-80285-4). 80pp. Through the experiences of a cross-section of African Americans — homesteaders, cowboys, mountain men, and some that defy classification — the history of the American West comes to life. (Rev: BCCB 1/96; BL 1/1–15/96; SLJ 12/95) [978]

**13171** Shuter, Jane, ed. *Francis Parkman and the Plains Indians* (5–8). Illus. Series: History Eyewitness. 1995, Raintree Steck-Vaughn $24.26 (0-8114-8280-4). 48pp. An edited and abridged version of Parkman's autobiographical writing about the opening up of the West and the Oregon Trail. (Rev: BL 4/15/95) [978]

**13172** Shuter, Jane, ed. *Sarah Royce and the American West* (5–8). Illus. Series: History Eyewitness. 1996, Raintree Steck-Vaughn LB $24.26 (0-8114-

8286-3). 48pp. Pioneer life on the American frontier is described, based on the firsthand account of Sarah Royce. (Rev: BL 5/15/96; SLJ 6/96) [978]

**13173** Steedman, Scott. *A Frontier Fort on the Oregon Trail* (4–6). Illus. Series: Inside Story. 1994, Bedrick $18.95 (0-87226-371-1); paper $9.95 (0-87226-264-2). 48pp. An examination of both the exterior and interior of a frontier fort, with details on its construction and everyday life in it. (Rev: BL 10/15/94; SLJ 9/94) [978]

**13174** Stefoff, Rebecca. *Children of the Westward Trail* (4–7). Illus. 1996, Millbrook LB $23.40 (1-56294-582-3). 96pp. An account of the Westward movement that relies heavily on first-person accounts. (Rev: BL 5/15/96; SLJ 7/96) [917.804]

**13175** Stein, R. Conrad. *The California Gold Rush* (3–6). Illus. Series: Cornerstones of Freedom. 1995, Children's LB $19.50 (0-516-06691-9). 30pp. A brief review of the salient facts in the California Gold Rush, beginning at Sutter's sawmill in 1848. (Rev: SLJ 7/95) [979.5]

**13176** Stein, R. Conrad. *The Story of the Gold at Sutter's Mill* (3–5). Illus. by Lou Aronson. 1981, Children's LB $13.27 (0-516-04617-9). 32pp. The thrilling story of the discovery of gold in California.

**13177** Stein, R. Conrad. *The Story of the Pony Express* (3–5). Illus. by Len W. Meents. 1981, Children's LB $13.27 (0-516-04631-4). 32pp. An introduction to this important early form of postal service.

**13178** Toht, David W. *Sodbuster* (3–6). Illus. by Richard Erickson. Series: American Pastfinder. 1996, Lerner LB $21.27 (0-8225-2977-7). 48pp. In double-page chapters, the life of early pioneers is described, with many quotes from original sources. (Rev: SLJ 3/96) [973.6]

**13179** van der Linde, Laurel. *The Pony Express* (5–8). Illus. 1993, Macmillan LB $14.95 (0-02-759056-9). 72pp. A colorful history of the Pony Express that tells about the riders, routes, equipment, and dangers. (Rev: BL 9/1/93; SLJ 7/93) [383]

**13180** Van Steenwyk, Elizabeth. *The California Gold Rush: West with the Forty-Niners* (3–7). Illus. Series: First Books. 1991, Watts LB $22.00 (0-531-20032-9). 64pp. A vivid retelling of a fascinating chapter in America's past, from Sutter's arrival in California in 1839 to glimpses of such pioneers as Levi Strauss and Mark Hopkins. (Rev: BL 1/1/92; SLJ 12/91) [979.4]

**13181** Winslow, Mimi. *Loggers and Railroad Workers* (5–8). Illus. Series: Settling the West. 1995, Twenty-First Century LB $20.40 (0-8050-2997-4). 96pp. The story of the men and machines who settled in the West, cleared the wilderness, and built the railroads that opened the way for agriculture and industry. (Rev: SLJ 9/95) [973.8]

**13182** Wright, Courtni C. *Wagon Train: A Family Goes West in 1865* (3–5). Illus. by Gershom Griffith. 1995, Holiday LB $15.95 (0-8234-1152-4). 32pp. A freed African American family faces the usual hardships of a wagon train moving West plus the burden of prejudice. (Rev: BCCB 5/95; BL 5/15/95; SLJ 6/95) [978]

### THE CIVIL WAR

**13183** Beller, Susan P. *Cadets at War: The True Story of Teenage Heroism at the Battle of New Market* (4–8). Illus. 1991, Betterway $9.95 (1-55870-196-6). 96pp. The story of the cadets at the Virginia Military Institute in 1864. (Rev: BCCB 7–8/91; BL 8/91) [973.7]

**13184** Black, Wallace B. *Blockade Runners and Ironclads: Naval Action in the Civil War* (3–5). Illus. Series: First Book. 1997, Watts $22.00 (0-531-20272-0). 64pp. Introduces naval operations during the Civil War, with material on battles, strategies, ship building, and prominent military personnel. (Rev: BL 2/1/98) [973.7]

**13185** Blashfield, Jean F. *Mines and Minie Balls* (4–6). Illus. Series: First Book: American Civil War. 1997, Watts LB $21.00 (0-531-20273-9). 64pp. Discusses Union and Confederate weapons at the beginning of the Civil War and shows how they became more deadly and sophisticated as the war went on. (Rev: BL 1/1–15/98) [973.7]

**13186** Blashfield, Jean F. *Women at the Front: Their Changing Roles in the Civil War* (4–6). Illus. Series: First Book: American Civil War. 1997, Watts LB $21.00 (0-531-20275-5). 64pp. An introduction to the roles of female nurses, spies, soldiers, and camp followers during the Civil War, with material on women on the home front. (Rev: BL 1/1–15/98) [973.7]

**13187** Carter, Alden R. *The Civil War: American Tragedy* (3–6). Illus. Series: First Books. 1992, Watts LB $22.00 (0-531-20039-6). 64pp. A summary of the war that redefined the meaning of freedom in America. (Rev: BL 3/1/93) [973.7]

**13188** Damon, Duane. *When This Cruel War Is Over* (5–8). Illus. 1996, Lerner LB $21.27 (0-8225-1731-0). 88pp. Behind-the-scenes of Civil War battlefields and the social conditions on the home front are covered. (Rev: BL 8/96; SLJ 8/96*) [973.7]

**13189** Dolan, Edward F. *The American Civil War: A House Divided* (5–8). Illus. 1997, Millbrook LB $28.90 (0-7613-0255-7). 112pp. A chronologically arranged, well-organized account of the Civil War, beginning with the shots fired at Fort Sumter. (Rev: BL 3/1/98; SLJ 3/98) [973.7]

**13190** Fleischman, Paul. *Bull Run* (5–8). 1993, HarperCollins LB $14.89 (0-06-021447-3). 102pp.

An innovative account of the first great battle of the Civil War. (Rev: BCCB 3/93; BL 5-6/93) [973.7]

**13191** Fritz, Jean. *Just a Few Words, Mr. Lincoln: The Story of the Gettysburg Address* (1–3). Illus. by Charles Robinson. 1993, Putnam paper $3.99 (0-448-40170-3). 48pp. An easy-to-read book that tells the background of the Gettysburg Address and explains its importance. (Rev: BL 10/1/93; SLJ 10/93) [973.7]

**13192** Gay, Kathlyn, and Martin Gay. *Civil War* (5–8). Illus. Series: Voices from the Past. 1995, Twenty-First Century LB $18.90 (0-8050-2845-5). 64pp. An introduction to the causes, events, and consequences of the Civil War that relies on eyewitness accounts. (Rev: BL 12/15/95; SLJ 2/96) [973.7]

**13193** Hakim, Joy. *Liberty for All?* (5–8). Illus. Series: History of U.S. 1994, Oxford LB $14.95 (0-19-507753-9); paper $10.95 (0-19-507754-7). 192pp. This lively history of the Civil War is written in an engaging style, with many illustrations and personal asides. (Rev: SLJ 7/94) [973.7]

**13194** Hakim, Joy. *War, Terrible War* (4–8). Illus. Series: History of US. 1994, Oxford LB $14.95 (0-19-507755-5); paper $10.95 (0-19-507756-3). 160pp. A concise, objective history of the U.S. Civil War, with a well-organized text and excellent illustrations. (Rev: BL 9/15/94; SLJ 7/94) [973.7]

**13195** Haskins, Jim. *Black, Blue, and Gray: African Americans in the Civil War* (5–8). Illus. 1998, Simon & Schuster paper $16.00 (0-689-80655-8). 160pp. A concise and rewarding picture of the role of African Americans before, during, and after the Civil War. (Rev: BL 2/15/98; SLJ 3/98*) [973.7]

**13196** Haskins, Jim. *The Day Fort Sumter Was Fired On: A Photo History of the Civil War* (5–8). Illus. 1995, Scholastic paper $6.95 (0-590-46397-7). 96pp. A short, well-illustrated history of the Civil War, with coverage of the roles of women and blacks. (Rev: BL 7/95) [973.7]

**13197** January, Brendan. *The Emancipation Proclamation* (3–5). Series: Cornerstones of Freedom. 1997, Children's LB $19.50 (0-516-20394-0). 32pp. The story of the events leading up to the Emancipation Proclamation, its contents, and its lasting consequences. (Rev: BL 12/15/97) [973.7]

**13198** January, Brendan. *Fort Sumter* (3–5). Series: Cornerstones of Freedom. 1997, Children's LB $19.50 (0-516-20395-9). 32pp. The events leading up to the firing of the first shot in the Civil War are covered, as well as the immediate and lasting results. (Rev: BL 12/15/97) [973.7]

**13199** Kantor, MacKinlay. *Gettysburg* (5–8). Illus. 1963, Random paper $5.99 (0-394-89181-3). This explains how Gettysburg became the site of the bloodiest Civil War battle; a vivid re-creation of the struggle.

**13200** Kent, Zachary. *The Battle of Chancellorsville* (3–5). Illus. Series: Cornerstones of Freedom. 1994, Children's LB $18.70 (0-516-06679-X). 32pp. This crucial battle of the Civil War and its effects on the remainder of the war are covered, with generous use of maps and illustrations. (Rev: BL 1/15/95) [973.7]

**13201** Kent, Zachary. *The Civil War: "A House Divided."* (5–7). Illus. Series: American War. 1994, Enslow LB $19.95 (0-89490-522-8). 128pp. Using many original quotes, period illustrations, and maps, this account gives a concise history of the Civil War. (Rev: BL 7/94; SLJ 9/94) [973.7]

**13202** Lincoln, Abraham. *The Gettysburg Address* (4–6). Illus. by Michael McCurdy. 1995, Houghton $14.95 (0-395-69824-3). 32pp. An illustrated edition of the address, with pictures that show the audience and the thoughts they might have had. (Rev: BL 10/15/95; HB 11–12/95; SLJ 9/95*) [973.7]

**13203** Ray, Delia. *Behind the Blue and Gray: The Soldier's Life in the Civil War* (4–7). Illus. Series: Young Readers' History of the Civil War. 1991, Dutton paper $17.99 (0-525-67333-4). 112pp. This account re-creates the behind-the-front lives of both Union and Confederate soldiers. (Rev: BL 9/1/91; HB 7–8/91) [973.7]

**13204** Reef, Catherine. *Civil War Soldiers* (4–6). Illus. 1993, Twenty-First Century LB $17.90 (0-8050-2371-2). 80pp. The part that African-American soldiers played in preserving the Union. (Rev: BL 8/93) [973.7]

**13205** Reef, Catherine. *Gettysburg* (4–6). Illus. Series: Places in American History. 1992, Macmillan LB $14.95 (0-87518-503-7). 72pp. After background material on the Battle of Gettysburg, this account introduces the national military park of today. (Rev: BL 9/1/92; SLJ 8/92) [973]

**13206** Smith, Carter, ed. *Behind the Lines: A Sourcebook on the Civil War* (5–8). Illus. Series: American Albums from the Collections of the Library of Congress. 1993, Millbrook LB $25.90 (1-56294-265-4). 96pp. A visual sourcebook describing life on the home front and in the army camps. (Rev: BL 3/1/93) [973.7]

**13207** Smith, Carter, ed. *1863: The Crucial Year: A Sourcebook on the Civil War* (5–8). Illus. Series: American Albums from the Collections of the Library of Congress. 1993, Millbrook LB $25.90 (1-56294-263-8). 96pp. Events of 1863, including the Emancipation Proclamation and the battles of Vicksburg and Gettysburg. (Rev: BL 3/1/93) [973.7]

**13208** Smith, Carter, ed. *The First Battles: A Sourcebook on the Civil War* (5–8). Illus. Series: American Albums from the Collections of the Library of Con-

gress. 1993, Millbrook LB $25.90 (1-56294-262-X). 96pp. From the battle of Fort Sumter to the battle of Fredericksburg at the end of 1862. (Rev: BL 3/1/93) [973.7]

**13209** Smith, Carter, ed. *Presidents of a Divided Nation: A Sourcebook on the U.S. Presidency* (5–8). Illus. Series: American Albums. 1993, Millbrook LB $25.90 (1-56294-360-X). 96pp. A heavily illustrated review of the Civil War and Reconstruction from the viewpoint of presidents Lincoln through Grant. (Rev: BL 12/1/93; SLJ 4/94) [973.7]

**13210** Steins, Richard. *The Nation Divides: The Civil War (1820–1880)* (5–8). Illus. Series: First Person America. 1993, Twenty-First Century LB $18.90 (0-8050-2583-9). 64pp. Excerpts from eyewitness accounts and extensive illustrations are used to re-create the causes, events, and aftermath of the Civil War. (Rev: BL 2/1/94; SLJ 2/94) [973.7]

**13211** Steins, Richard. *Shiloh* (4–7). Illus. Series: Battlefields Across America. 1997, Twenty-First Century $23.40 (0-8050-5229-1). 63pp. Background information on the Civil War is followed by a description of this battle and the site as it is today. (Rev: SLJ 1/98) [973.7]

### RECONSTRUCTION TO THE KOREAN WAR, 1865–1950

**13212** Altman, Linda Jacobs. *The Pullman Strike of 1894: Turning Point for American Labor* (4–6). Illus. Series: Spotlight on American History. 1994, Millbrook LB $21.90 (1-56294-346-4). 64pp. This strike caused by wage cuts and firing of union representatives, considered a landmark in the history of the American labor movement, is well re-created with good illustrations. (Rev: BL 9/15/94; SLJ 4/94) [331.89]

**13213** Bartoletti, Susan Campbell. *Growing Up in Coal Country* (5–8). Illus. 1996, Houghton $16.95 (0-395-77847-6). 127pp. The life of child laborers in the coal mines of Pennsylvania 100 years ago is covered in this photoessay. (Rev: BCCB 2/97; BL 12/1/96*; SLJ 2/97*) [331.3]

**13214** Blake, Arthur. *The Scopes Trial: Defending the Right to Teach* (4–7). Illus. Series: Spotlight on American History. 1994, Millbrook LB $21.90 (1-56294-407-X). 64pp. The story of the Great Monkey Trial of 1925 and its significance for American education. (Rev: BL 10/15/94; SLJ 10/94) [344.73]

**13215** Brown, Gene. *The Struggle to Grow: Expansionism and Industrialization (1880–1913)* (5–8). Illus. Series: First Person America. 1993, Twenty-First Century LB $18.90 (0-8050-2584-7). 64pp. Excerpts from original sources and period illustrations are used to create a history of the period 1880–1913 that touches on frontier life, politics, industry, and immigration. (Rev: BL 2/1/94; SLJ 3/94) [973.8]

**13216** Carter, Alden R. *Last Stand at the Alamo* (4–6). Illus. Series: First Books. 1991, Watts LB $21.00 (0-531-10888-0). 64pp. Important incidents and key participants in an account illustrated with period photos. (Rev: SLJ 3/91) [976.4]

**13217** Carter, Alden R. *The Spanish-American War: Imperial Destiny* (3–6). Illus. Series: First Books. 1992, Watts LB $21.00 (0-531-20078-7). 64pp. Including a discussion of the Spanish colonies, this account describes the war that ended Spain's importance in the New World. (Rev: BL 3/1/93; SLJ 2/93) [973.8]

**13218** Clare, John D., ed. *Industrial Revolution* (4–8). Illus. Series: Living History. 1994, Gulliver $16.95 (0-15-200514-5). 64pp. A clear, concise text telling of the revolution that replaced agriculture with industry as the chief economic activity and its effects on the world, particularly the United States. (Rev: SLJ 4/94) [973.8]

**13219** Cohen, Daniel. *Prohibition: America Makes Alcohol Illegal* (4–6). Illus. Series: Spotlight on American History. 1995, Millbrook LB $21.90 (1-56294-529-7). 64pp. A history of America's attitude toward alcohol, from the rise of the temperance movement through the repeal of Prohibition. (Rev: BL 11/1/95; SLJ 11/95) [363.4]

**13220** Cryan-Hicks, Kathryn, ed. *Pride and Promise: The Harlem Renaissance* (4–8). Illus. Series: Perspectives on History. 1994, Discovery Enterprises paper $5.95 (1-878668-30-7). 52pp. The story of the great 20th-century artistic awakening in New York's Harlem and of its many leaders, like Langston Hughes. (Rev: BL 8/94) [305]

**13221** Duden, Jane. *1940s* (3–7). Illus. 1989, Macmillan LB $11.95 (0-89686-475-8). 48pp. The eventful decade of the 1940s, which included World War II and adjustments to a peacetime economy, is covered in this well-illustrated book. (Rev: SLJ 4/90) [973.9]

**13222** Feinberg, Barbara S. *Black Tuesday: The Stock Market Crash of 1929* (4–7). Illus. Series: Spotlight on American History. 1995, Millbrook LB $21.90 (1-56294-574-2). 64pp. The causes and consequences of the great stock market crash of 1929 are interestingly retold with many photographs and illustrations. (Rev: BL 10/15/95) [338.5]

**13223** Freedman, Russell. *Immigrant Kids* (3–7). Illus. 1995, Puffin paper $5.99 (0-140-37594-5). 64pp. An account of the immigration to the United States from 1880 to 1920.

**13224** Gay, Kathlyn, and Martin Gay. *Spanish-American War* (5–8). Illus. Series: Voices from the Past. 1995, Twenty-First Century LB $18.90 (0-

8050-2847-1). 64pp. This coverage of the Spanish-American War uses excerpts from letters, memoirs, and official reports to cover the causes, battles, and results. (Rev: BL 12/15/95; SLJ 3/96) [973.8]

**13225** Hakim, Joy. *Reconstruction and Reform* (4–8). Illus. Series: History of US. 1994, Oxford LB $14.95 (0-19-507757-1); paper $10.95 (0-19-507758-X). 192pp. The period from after the Civil War to the turn of the century is covered in this well-illustrated account. (Rev: BL 10/15/94; SLJ 1/95) [973.8]

**13226** Kalman, Bobbie. *19th Century Girls and Women* (3–5). Illus. 1997, Crabtree LB $19.36 (0-86505-434-7); paper $7.16 (0-86505-464-9). 32pp. A realistic portrait of the life women led in both the working and wealthy classes, with details on home life, chores, health hazards, and stifling clothing. (Rev: BL 7/97; SLJ 8/97) [305.4]

**13227** Kalman, Bobbie, and Tammy Everts. *A Child's Day* (3–5). Illus. by Antoinette DeBiasi. Series: Historic Communities. 1994, Crabtree LB $19.16 (0-86505-494-0); paper $7.95 (0-86505-514-9). 32pp. A day in the life of settlers' children is shown through such activities as doing chores, playing games, going to school, and visiting a fair. (Rev: SLJ 9/94) [978]

**13228** Koral, April. *An Album of the Great Wave of Immigration* (4–7). Illus. 1992, Watts LB $24.00 (0-531-11123-7). 64pp. A look at southern and eastern European immigrants to the United States from 1890 to 1924. (Rev: BL 1/15/93) [304]

**13229** Levinson, Nancy S. *Turn of the Century: Our Nation One Hundred Years Ago* (4–7). Illus. 1994, Dutton paper $16.99 (0-525-67433-0). 144pp. The beginning of the 20th century is surveyed, with material on minorities, immigration, labor, the rise of cities, and America's growing international influence. (Rev: BCCB 1/95; BL 11/15/94; SLJ 12/94) [973.8]

**13230** Loeper, John J. *Going to School in 1876* (4–8). Illus. 1984, Macmillan $16.00 (0-689-31015-3). 96pp. A book about education in 1876 — curriculum, types of schools, recreation, discipline, etc.

**13231** Mettger, Zak. *Reconstruction: America After the Civil War* (5–8). Illus. Series: Young Readers of the Civil War. 1994, Dutton paper $16.99 (0-525-67490-X). 96pp. Firsthand accounts and original documents enliven this excellent history of Reconstruction. (Rev: BL 10/1/94; SLJ 2/95) [973.8]

**13232** Migneco, Ronald, and Timothy Biel. *The Crash of 1929* (5–7). Illus. by Maurie Manning. Series: World Disasters. 1990, Lucent LB $19.95 (1-56006-007-7). 64pp. The stock market crash that ushered in the Great Depression is re-created. (Rev: SLJ 8/90) [973.9]

**13233** Sherrow, Victoria. *The Triangle Factory Fire* (4–6). Illus. Series: Spotlight on American History. 1995, Millbrook LB $21.90 (1-56294-572-6). 64pp. The story of the terrible fire that exposed the shameful labor exploitation in this country and led to needed reforms. (Rev: BL 12/15/95; SLJ 3/96) [363.37]

**13234** Simonds, Patricia. *The Founding of the AFL and the Rise of Organized Labor* (5–7). Illus. Series: Turning Points in American History. 1991, Silver Burdett LB $14.95 (0-382-24123-1); paper $7.95 (0-382-24118-5). 64pp. The inspiring story of the beginning of the labor movement in the United States and its impact on American history and society. (Rev: BL 1/15/92) [331.88]

**13235** Smith, Carter, ed. *Presidents of a Growing Country: A Sourcebook on the U.S. Presidency* (5–8). Illus. Series: American Albums. 1993, Millbrook LB $25.90 (1-56294-358-8). 96pp. Through extensive use of pictorials, a thorough timeline, and concise text, this attractive book traces the presidency from Hayes through McKinley. (Rev: BL 12/1/93; SLJ 4/94) [973.8]

**13236** Smith, Carter, ed. *Presidents of a World Power: A Sourcebook on the U.S. Presidency* (5–8). Illus. Series: American Albums. 1993, Millbrook LB $25.90 (1-56294-361-8). 96pp. The history of our country from Teddy Roosevelt through Franklin Roosevelt is covered, with many excellent illustrations, an overview chapter, good captions, and an extensive timeline. (Rev: BL 12/1/93; SLJ 4/94) [973.91]

**13237** Spedden, Daisy C. S. *Polar the Titanic Bear* (3–5). Illus. by Laurie McGaw. 1994, Little, Brown $17.95 (0-316-80625-0). 64pp. The true story of a toy bear, his many owners, and his rescue from the Titanic. (Rev: BCCB 12/94; BL 12/1/94*; SLJ 1/95) [910.91]

**13238** Stanley, Jerry. *Children of the Dust Bowl: The True Story of the School at Weedpatch Camp* (4–8). Illus. 1992, Crown LB $15.99 (0-517-58782-3). 50pp. A vivid account, with compelling photos, of youngsters in this troubled time. (Rev: BCCB 10/92; BL 9/1/92*; HB 1–2/93*) [371.96]

**13239** Stein, R. Conrad. *The Great Depression* (3–5). Illus. Series: Cornerstones of Freedom. 1993, Children's LB $19.50 (0-516-06668-4). 32pp. The story of the causes and effects of this great economic tragedy, its toll in human suffering, and the gradual recovery. (Rev: BL 2/1/94; SLJ 3/94) [973.91]

**13240** Stein, R. Conrad. *The Roaring Twenties* (3–6). Illus. Series: Cornerstones of Freedom. 1994, Children's LB $19.50 (0-516-06675-7). 31pp. Period photos and ads bring authenticity to this account of life in the days of flappers, prohibition, and speakeasies. (Rev: SLJ 7/94) [973.9]

**13241** Stewart, Gail B. *1900s* (5–8). Illus. Series: Timelines. 1990, Macmillan LB $11.95 (0-89686-471-5). 48pp. Events and trivia of the decade, with many illustrations. Also use: *1910s; 1920s; 1930s* (all 1989). (Rev: SLJ 6/90) [973.9]

**13242** Wetterer, Margaret K., and Charles M. Wetterer. *The Snow Walker* (2–4). Illus. 1996, Carolrhoda LB $13.95 (0-87614-891-7); paper $5.95 (0-87614-959-X). 48pp. During the terrible blizzard of 1888, Milton Daub unselfishly helped his neighbors in the Bronx by delivering needed supplies. (Rev: BCCB 12/96; BL 2/15/96; SLJ 3/96) [973.9]

### THE 1950S TO THE PRESENT

**13243** Coles, Robert. *The Story of Ruby Bridges* (K–4). Illus. by George Ford. 1995, Scholastic $13.95 (0-590-43967-7). 32pp. A re-creation of the trauma faced by a young African American girl who is the first to integrate an all-white school in New Orleans in 1960. (Rev: BCCB 3/95; BL 1/15/95; SLJ 3/95)

**13244** Devaney, John. *The Vietnam War* (3–6). Illus. Series: First Books. 1992, Watts LB $21.00 (0-531-20046-9). 64pp. This book unveils the horrors and controversy surrounding the Vietnam War. (Rev: BL 3/1/93) [959.704]

**13245** Donnelly, Judy. *A Wall of Names: The Story of the Vietnam Veterans Memorial* (2–4). Illus. 1991, Random LB $9.99 (0-679-90169-8); paper $3.99 (0-679-80169-3). How the memorial was developed and constructed, with excellent photographs. (Rev: BCCB 7–8/91; BL 7/91; SLJ 7/91) [959.704]

**13246** Duden, Jane. *1950s* (3–7). 1989, Macmillan LB $11.95 (0-89686-476-6). 48pp. Events and people associated with this eventful decade come to life in this book that is divided by years. It is continued in *1960s* and *1970s* (both 1989). (Rev: SLJ 4/90) [973.9]

**13247** Gay, Kathlyn, and Martin Gay. *Korean War* (6–8). Illus. Series: Voices from the Past. 1996, Twenty-First Century LB $18.90 (0-8050-4100-1). 64pp. A discussion of the often forgotten Korean War — its causes, the battles, and the people involved. (Rev: BL 11/15/96; SLJ 12/96) [951.904]

**13248** Gay, Kathlyn, and Martin Gay. *Vietnam War* (6–8). Illus. Series: Voices from the Past. 1996, Twenty-First Century LB $18.90 (0-8050-4101-X). 64pp. An objective overview of the Vietnam War, illustrated with many black-and-white photos. (Rev: BL 11/15/96; SLJ 12/96) [959.704]

**13249** Haskins, Jim. *The Day Martin Luther King, Jr., Was Shot: A Photo History of the Civil Rights Movement* (4–8). Illus. 1992, Scholastic paper $5.99 (0-590-43661-9). 96pp. Despite its title, this is a photo history of the civil rights struggle from slavery to the present. (Rev: BL 2/1/92; SLJ 5/92) [323.4]

**13250** Kent, Deborah. *The Vietnam War: "What Are We Fighting For?"* (5–7). Illus. Series: American War. 1994, Enslow LB $19.95 (0-89490-527-9). 128pp. An objective overview of this war, its causes, progression, and results. (Rev: BL 10/15/94; SLJ 11/94) [959.704]

**13251** Kent, Zachary. *The Persian Gulf War: "The Mother of All Battles"* (5–7). Illus. 1994, Enslow LB $19.95 (0-89490-528-7). 128pp. The story of the 1991 Gulf War, its causes and effects, told with striking action photos. (Rev: BL 4/15/95; SLJ 2/95) [956.7]

**13252** McGowen, Tom. *The Korean War* (3–6). Illus. Series: First Books. 1992, Watts LB $21.00 (0-531-20040-X). 64pp. The 3-year-long Korean War is described, including important battles and the leadership of General MacArthur. (Rev: BL 3/1/93) [951]

**13253** Smith, Carter. *The Korean War* (4–7). Illus. Series: Turning Points in American History. 1990, Silver Burdett LB $14.95 (0-382-09953-2); paper $7.95 (0-382-09949-4). 64pp. Covers the causes and events of the Korean War, as well as its significance in American history. (Rev: BL 3/1/91; SLJ 5/91) [951]

**13254** Smith, Carter, ed. *Presidents in a Time of Change: A Sourcebook on the U.S. Presidency* (5–8). Illus. Series: American Albums. 1993, Millbrook LB $25.90 (1-56294-362-6). 96pp. A heavily illustrated, attractive review of the presidency from Truman to Clinton. (Rev: BL 12/1/93; SLJ 4/94) [973.92]

**13255** Stein, R. Conrad. *The Korean War: "The Forgotten War"* (5–7). Illus. 1994, Enslow LB $19.95 (0-89490-526-0). 128pp. This well-organized account of the Korean War presents a balanced picture of the war and includes personal observations. (Rev: BL 4/15/95; SLJ 2/95) [951]

**13256** Super, Neil. *Vietnam War Soldiers* (4–8). Illus. Series: African-American Soldiers. 1993, Twenty-First Century LB $17.90 (0-8050-2307-0). 80pp. The story of the contributions of African American soldiers who fought in the Vietnam War. (Rev: BL 2/15/94; SLJ 4/94) [959.704]

**13257** Wade, Linda R. *Montgomery: Launching the Civil Rights Movement* (4–6). Illus. Series: Doors to America's Past. 1992, Rourke LB $22.60 (0-86592-465-1). 48pp. The city of Montgomery, Alabama, is introduced, together with historical information, its role in the civil rights movement, and its present status. (Rev: BL 5/1/92) [305.890]

**13258** Westerfeld, Scott. *Watergate* (5–7). Illus. Series: Turning Points in American History. 1991, Silver Burdett paper $7.95 (0-382-24120-7). 64pp. An objective account in text and pictures of the Watergate break-in during Nixon's presidency and its consequences. (Rev: BL 1/15/92) [364.1]

---

## Regions

### MIDWEST

**13259** Anderson, Kathy P. *Illinois* (3–6). Illus. Series: Hello U.S.A. 1993, Lerner LB $19.93 (0-8225-2723-5). 72pp. Presents the history and geography of this state, and includes biographies of famous native sons and daughters. (Rev: BL 1/15/93) [977.3]

**13260** Armbruster, Ann. *Lake Huron* (2–4). Illus. Series: A True Book. 1996, Children's LB $21.00 (0-516-20012-7). 48pp. An overview of the formation of this lake and the early Indians who lived around it plus additional history and its current importance. Also use *Lake Michigan* and *Lake Superior* (both 1996). (Rev: SLJ 3/97) [917.709]

**13261** Armbruster, Ann. *Lake Ontario* (2–4). Illus. Series: A True Book: Great Lakes. 1996, Children's LB $21.00 (0-516-20014-3). 48pp. A history of Lake Ontario, the role it has played in Canadian-American history, and its importance today. Also use *St. Lawrence Seaway* (1996). (Rev: SLJ 4/97) [917.704]

**13262** Aylesworth, Thomas G., and Virginia L. Aylesworth. *Eastern Great Lakes: Indiana, Michigan, Ohio* (4–7). Illus. Series: State Reports. 1995, Chelsea $19.95 (0-7910-3409-7). 64pp. Information is given for each of the 3 states covered, including major cities, history, geography, climate, and important cities. (Rev: BL 3/15/92) [977]

**13263** Badt, Karin Luisa. *The Mississippi Flood of 1993* (3–5). Illus. Series: Cornerstones of Freedom. 1994, Children's LB $19.50 (0-516-06680-3). 32pp. The causes and effects of this major modern disaster are traced with eyewitness reports. (Rev: BL 1/15/95) [977.033]

**13264** Brandenburg, Jim. *An American Safari: Adventures on the North American Prairie* (4–6). Illus. 1995, Walker LB $17.85 (0-8027-8320-1). 48pp. This American photographer describes in words and pictures the Western prairies and the animals that live there. (Rev: BCCB 6/95; BL 4/15/95; SLJ 8/95) [508.73]

**13265** Bratvold, Gretchen. *Wisconsin* (3–6). Illus. Series: Hello U.S.A. 1991, Lerner LB $19.95 (0-8225-2700-6). 72pp. An introduction to the dairy state, with full-color photos. (Rev: BL 4/15/91; SLJ 7/91) [977.5]

**13266** Brill, Marlene T. *Illinois* (4–8). Illus. Series: Celebrate the States. 1996, Marshall Cavendish LB $32.79 (0-7614-0113-X). 144pp. Maps, diagrams, and photos enliven this introduction to Illinois that gives good coverage of history, geography, and social conditions. (Rev: BL 2/1/97; SLJ 2/97) [913.73]

**13267** Brill, Marlene T. *Indiana* (4–8). Illus. Series: Celebrate the States. 1997, Marshall Cavendish LB $32.79 (0-7614-0147-4). 144pp. An introduction to this Midwest state that covers such topics as agriculture, industries, and famous natives, as well as its history and geography. (Rev: BL 7/97; SLJ 8/97) [977.2]

**13268** Brown, Dottie. *Ohio* (3–6). Illus. Series: Hello U.S.A. 1992, Lerner LB $19.95 (0-8225-2725-1). 72pp. Ohio, the nation's seventh largest state, is described from the days of the Indians and settlers until today. (Rev: BL 11/15/92) [977.1]

**13269** Carlson, Jeffrey D. *A Historical Album of Minnesota* (5–8). Illus. Series: Historical Albums. 1993, Millbrook LB $23.40 (1-56294-006-6). 64pp. A heavily illustrated volume that traces the history of Minnesota from Native American communities through exploration and settlement to present-day concerns. (Rev: SLJ 10/93) [977.6]

**13270** Doherty, Craig A., and Katherine M. Doherty. *The Gateway Arch* (3–6). Illus. Series: Building America. 1995, Blackbirch LB $15.95 (1-56711-105-X). 48pp. A description of the construction and parts of this St. Louis landmark. (Rev: BL 9/15/95; SLJ 7/95) [725]

**13271** Doherty, Craig A., and Katherine M. Doherty. *Mount Rushmore* (3–6). Illus. Series: Build America. 1995, Blackbirch LB $15.95 (1-56711-108-4). 48pp. The story of the planning through the execution of the 4 gigantic heads on Mount Rushmore and the controversy concerning taking the land from the Sioux. (Rev: BL 9/15/95; SLJ 7/95) [730]

**13272** Doherty, Craig A., and Katherine M. Doherty. *The Sears Tower* (3–6). Illus. Series: Building America. 1995, Blackbirch LB $15.95 (1-56711-109-2). 48pp. The story of the design and construction of the world's tallest building and of some of the wonders found inside. (Rev: BL 9/15/95; SLJ 7/95) [725]

**13273** Farris, John. *The Dust Bowl* (5–7). Illus. by Maurie Manning. Series: World Disasters. 1990, Lucent LB $19.95 (1-56006-005-0). 64pp. This book explores the terrible drought that hit the Midwest in the 1930s. (Rev: SLJ 8/90) [978]

**13274** Ford, Barbara. *Saint Louis* (3–5). Illus. Series: Downtown America. 1989, Macmillan LB $13.95 (0-87518-402-2). 64pp. This introduction includes history, geography, and places to visit. (Rev: BL 8/89; SLJ 11/89) [977.8]

**13275** Fradin, Dennis B. *Illinois* (2–5). Illus. Series: From Sea to Shining Sea. 1991, Children's LB $26.00 (0-516-03813-3). 64pp. Many full-color photos add to the attractive coverage of this midwestern state. (Rev: BL 2/1/92) [977.3]

**13276** Fradin, Dennis B. *Iowa* (3–5). Illus. Series: From Sea to Shining Sea. 1993, Children's LB $26.00 (0-516-03815-X). 64pp. This midwestern state is examined, with material on its history, geography, people, industries, and famous residents. (Rev: BL 11/1/93) [922.7]

**13277** Fradin, Dennis B. *Michigan* (3–5). Illus. Series: From Sea to Shining Sea. 1992, Children's LB $26.00 (0-516-03822-2). 64pp. In addition to material on history and geography, this simple introduction includes a 2-page Fact Sheet summary. (Rev: BL 5/1/92) [977.4]

**13278** Fradin, Dennis B. *Missouri* (3–5). Illus. Series: From Sea to Shining Sea. 1994, Children's LB $26.00 (0-516-03825-7). 64pp. Some of the topics covered are Missouri's geography, history, and industries, plus a gallery of famous residents. (Rev: BL 8/94) [977.8]

**13279** Fradin, Dennis B. *Ohio* (3–5). Illus. Series: From Sea to Shining Sea. 1993, Children's LB $26.00 (0-516-03835-4). 64pp. Ohio is covered through such topics as geography, history, industries, and cities. (Rev: BL 7/93) [977.1]

**13280** Fredeen, Charles. *Kansas* (3–6). Illus. Series: Hello U.S.A. 1992, Lerner LB $19.93 (0-8225-2716-2). 72pp. With excellent color illustrations, this account covers the state of Kansas and includes information on history, geography, and social and economic conditions. (Rev: BL 6/1/92) [978.1]

**13281** Heinrichs, Ann. *Arkansas* (4–6). Illus. Series: America the Beautiful. 1989, Children's LB $28.00 (0-516-00450-6). 144pp. In addition to standard information, this book includes a 30-page reference section. (Rev: BL 7/89) [974.1]

**13282** Jameson, W. C. *Buried Treasures of the Great Plains* (5–8). Series: Buried Treasure. 1997, August House paper $11.95 (0-87483-486-4). 192pp. After a general introduction to the area, provides 3 to 7 stories per state about buried treasure in Kansas, Nebraska, North Dakota, Oklahoma, South Dakota, and Texas. (Rev: SLJ 7/97) [977]

**13283** Kent, Deborah. *Iowa* (4–6). Illus. Series: America the Beautiful. 1991, Children's LB $29.40 (0-516-00461-1). 144pp. In addition to geography, history, and economics, this state profile includes special fact sections and a list of important people. (Rev: BL 7/91; SLJ 9/91) [977.8]

**13284** Kent, Deborah. *Ohio* (4–7). Illus. Series: America the Beautiful. 1989, Children's LB $28.00 (0-516-00481-6). 144pp. The land and people of Ohio are introduced, with a special minifacts section. (Rev: BL 7/89) [974.1]

**13285** Kent, Zachary. *Kansas* (4–6). Illus. Series: America the Beautiful. 1990, Children's LB $28.00 (0-516-00462-X). 144pp. History, geography, statistics, and important dates and people are included. (Rev: BL 1/1/91) [978.1]

**13286**  LaDoux, Rita C. *Iowa* (3–6). Illus. Series: Hello U.S.A. 1992, Lerner LB $19.93 (0-8225-2724-3). 72pp. This introduction to Iowa gives capsule biographies, a time line, fact sheets, and chapters on topics like history and geography. (Rev: BL 9/1/92) [977.7]

**13287**  LaDoux, Rita C. *Missouri* (3–6). Illus. Series: Hello U.S.A. 1991, Lerner LB $19.93 (0-8225-2710-3). 72pp. With time lines, capsule biographies, many fact sheets, and the usual information, the state of Missouri is introduced. (Rev: BL 12/1/91) [977.8]

**13288**  LaDoux, Rita C. *Oklahoma* (3–6). Illus. Series: Hello U.S.A. 1992, Lerner LB $19.95 (0-8225-2717-0). 72pp. Oklahoma is introduced with topics that include famous inhabitants, time lines, and fact sheets. (Rev: BL 6/1/92) [976.6]

**13289**  Lamb, Nancy. *One April Morning: Children Remember the Oklahoma City Bombing* (3–6). Illus. by Floyd Cooper. 1996, Lothrop LB $15.93 (0-688-14724-0). 48pp. Interviews with 50 children who were indirectly involved in the 1955 Oklahoma City bombing of the Federal Building. (Rev: BCCB 6/96; BL 5/15/96; SLJ 7/96) [976.6]

**13290**  Murphy, Jim. *The Great Fire* (5–8). Illus. 1995, Scholastic $16.95 (0-590-47267-4). 144pp. A dramatic re-creation of the catastrophic Chicago fire of 1871 that left 100,000 people homeless. (Rev: BCCB 5/95; BL 6/1–15/95*; HB 5–6/95, 9–10/95; SLJ 7/95*) [977.3]

**13291**  Pfeiffer, Christine. *Chicago* (3–6). Illus. 1989, Macmillan LB $13.95 (0-87518-385-9). 60pp. History and modern life in the great midwestern metropolis. (Rev: BL 3/15/89; SLJ 3/89)

**13292**  Pollard, Michael. *The Mississippi* (5–8). Illus. Series: Great Rivers. 1997, Benchmark LB $21.36 (0-7614-0502-X). 45pp. The history of this great river and its influence on American history are covered, with descriptive photos, maps, and diagrams. (Rev: SLJ 3/98) [917.7]

**13293**  Porter, A. P. *Minnesota* (3–6). Illus. Series: Hello U.S.A. 1992, Lerner LB $19.93 (0-8225-2718-9). 72pp. Fact sheets, time lines, and biographies of famous native sons and daughters are included in this introduction to Minnesota. (Rev: BL 6/1/92) [977.6]

**13294**  Ross, Jim, and Paul Myers, eds. *Dear Oklahoma City, Get Well Soon* (3–6). Illus. 1996, Walker LB $17.85 (0-8027-8437-2). 48pp. A sampling of the letters and drawings sent by children to victims of the 1995 bombing of the Oklahoma City Federal Building. (Rev: BCCB 6/96; BL 5/15/96; SLJ 5/96) [976.6]

**13295**  Sanford, William R., and Carl R. Green. *Missouri* (5–7). Illus. Series: America the Beautiful.

1989, Children's LB $29.40 (0-516-00471-9). 144pp. History, geography, government, economy, and people are some of the topics covered. (Rev: BL 1/1/90) [977.6]

**13296**  Sirvaitis, Karen. *Michigan* (3–5). Illus. Series: Hello USA. 1994, Lerner LB $19.93 (0-8225-2722-7). 72pp. With photos on every page, this account supplies a brief trip around Michigan plus historical information and material on resources, cities, and people. (Rev: BL 4/15/94) [977.4]

**13297**  Stein, R. Conrad. *Chicago* (3–6). Illus. Series: Cities of the World. 1997, Children's LB $24.00 (0-516-20301-0). 64pp. A heavily illustrated account that describes Chicago, gives a brief history, and provides a tour of famous landmarks. (Rev: BL 8/97; SLJ 2/98) [977.3]

**13298**  Stein, R. Conrad. *Minnesota* (4–6). Illus. Series: America the Beautiful. 1990, Children's LB $28.00 (0-516-00469-7). 144pp. Historical and geographical coverage, plus a tour of important sites. (Rev: BL 1/1/91) [977.6]

**13299**  Stein, R. Conrad. *Wisconsin* (4–8). Illus. 1987, Children's LB $28.00 (0-516-00495-6). 144pp. Thorough coverage of this dairy state, with emphasis on history and geography. (Rev: BL 5/15/88)

**13300**  Stewart, Gail B. *Chicago* (3–6). Illus. Series: Great Cities of the U.S.A. 1989, Rourke LB $23.93 (0-86592-538-0). 48pp. Describes the history and development of this important Great Lakes port. (Rev: BL 1/1/90) [917]

**13301**  Sturman, Susan. *Kansas City* (3–5). Illus. Series: Downtown America. 1990, Macmillan LB $13.95 (0-87518-432-4). 60pp. The history of Kansas City, Missouri, is covered, with data on sights and cultural life. (Rev: BL 6/1/90) [977.8]

**13302**  Wade, Linda R. *Hannibal: Mark Twain's Boyhood Home* (4–7). Series: Doors to America's Past. 1991, Rourke LB $22.60 (0-86592-466-X). 48pp. After describing Hannibal as it was in Twain's time, this account describes the city as it is today. (Rev: BL 5/1/92; SLJ 3/92) [977]

**13303**  Wills, Charles A. *A Historical Album of Illinois* (4–8). Illus. Series: Historical Albums. 1994, Millbrook LB $23.40 (1-56294-482-7). 64pp. A brief history of Illinois that touches on the most important events from before the white man to the 1990s. (Rev: SLJ 3/95) [977.3]

**13304**  Wills, Charles A. *A Historical Album of Michigan* (4–7). Illus. Series: Historical Albums. 1996, Millbrook LB $23.40 (0-7613-0036-8); paper $7.95 (0-7613-0126-7). 64pp. Using many archival prints, drawings, photographs, and ample text, the history of Michigan is told. (Rev: BL 10/15/96) [977]

**13305**  Wills, Charles A. *A Historical Album of Ohio* (4–7). Illus. Series: Historical Albums. 1996, Millbrook LB $23.40 (1-56294-593-9); paper $6.95 (0-7613-0086-4). 64pp. The history of Ohio is traced from prehistoric times to the present. (Rev: BL 7/96; SLJ 7/96) [977.1]

**13306** Zimmerman, Chanda K. *Detroit* (3–5). Illus. Series: Downtown America. 1989, Macmillan LB $13.95 (0-87518-409-X). 64pp. Physical features and the history of Detroit are covered. (Rev: BL 8/89; SLJ 11/89) [977.4]

## MOUNTAIN STATES

**13307** Anderson, Peter. *A Grand Canyon Journey: Tracing Time in Stone* (4–6). Illus. Series: First Books: Science. 1997, Watts LB $21.00 (0-531-20259-3). 64pp. This tour down the Grand Canyon tells how ancient history has helped shape this terrain and gives information on the origins and geology of each rock layer. (Rev: BL 5/15/97; SLJ 8/97) [917.91]

**13308** Ayer, Eleanor. *Colorado* (4–8). Illus. Series: Celebrate the States. 1997, Marshall Cavendish LB $32.79 (0-7614-0148-2). 144pp. An introduction to the mountain state, with information on its history, geography, and people. (Rev: BL 7/97; SLJ 8/97) [978.8]

**13309** Ayres, Becky. *Salt Lake City* (3–5). Illus. Series: Downtown America. 1990, Macmillan LB $13.95 (0-87518-436-7). 60pp. Introduces Salt Lake City, its sights, sounds, and history. (Rev: BL 2/1/91) [979.2]

**13310** Bledsoe, Sara. *Colorado* (3–6). Illus. Series: Hello USA. 1993, Lerner LB $19.93 (0-8225-2750-2). 72pp. A small volume that covers Colorado's history, geography, people, industries, and landmarks. (Rev: BL 12/1/93) [978.8]

**13311** Doherty, Craig A., and Katherine M. Doherty. *Hoover Dam* (3–6). Illus. Series: Building America. 1995, Blackbirch LB $15.95 (1-56711-107-6). 48pp. Traces the construction of the Hoover Dam on the Colorado River, from its conception through its completion in 1936 to its present importance. (Rev: BL 9/15/95; SLJ 7/95) [627]

**13312** Filbin, Dan. *Arizona* (3–6). Illus. Series: Hello U.S.A. 1991, Lerner LB $19.93 (0-8225-2705-7). 72pp. This account covers all aspects of this southwestern state and includes many color photos. (Rev: BL 4/15/91; SLJ 6/91) [979.1]

**13313** Foster, Lynne. *Exploring the Grand Canyon: Adventures of Yesterday and Today* (3–6). Illus. by Margaret Sanfilippo. 1990, Grand Canyon Natural History Assn. paper $15.95 (0-938216-33-3). 150pp. This work gives a history of the Grand Canyon, the kinds of people who have been involved with it, and tips for the first-time visitor. (Rev: BL 9/1/90) [917]

**13314** Fradin, Dennis B. *Colorado* (3–5). Illus. Series: From Sea to Shining Sea. 1993, Children's LB $26.00 (0-516-03806-0). 64pp. Maps, diagrams, and color photos on each page enliven this introduction to Colorado, its history, geography, landmarks, and people. (Rev: BL 11/1/93; SLJ 1/94) [978.8]

**13315** Fradin, Dennis B. *Montana* (3–5). Illus. Series: From Sea to Shining Sea. 1992, Children's LB $26.00 (0-516-03826-5). 64pp. With many color photos, this introduction to Montana includes material on people, industries, and principal cities. (Rev: BL 5/1/92) [978.6]

**13316** Fradin, Dennis B. *Utah* (3–5). Illus. Series: From Sea to Shining Sea. 1993, Children's LB $26.00 (0-516-03844-3). 64pp. Coverage includes history, geography, people, and famous places. (Rev: BL 7/93) [979.2]

**13317** Fraser, Mary Ann. *In Search of the Grand Canyon: Down the Colorado with John Wesley Powell* (4–6). Illus. 1995, Holt $14.95 (0-8050-3495-1). 69pp. The story of Powell and his amazing exploration of the Colorado River and the Grand Canyon in spite of many disasters. (Rev: BL 7/95; SLJ 7/95*) [979.1]

**13318** Heinrichs, Ann. *Arizona* (4–6). Illus. Series: America the Beautiful. 1991, Children's LB $28.00 (0-516-00449-2). 144pp. This introduction to Arizona includes a chronology, maps, and biographies of important people. (Rev: BL 7/91) [979.1]

**13319** Heinrichs, Ann. *Montana* (4–6). Illus. Series: America the Beautiful. 1991, Children's LB $28.00 (0-516-00472-7). 144pp. After an introduction to Montana, there is a special reference section that contains key facts. (Rev: BL 7/91) [978.8]

**13320** Heinrichs, Ann. *Wyoming* (4–6). Illus. Series: America the Beautiful. 1991, Children's LB $28.00 (0-516-00496-4). 144pp. A logically organized, fact-filled introduction to Wyoming. (Rev: BL 1/15/92; SLJ 2/92) [972.95]

**13321** Herguth, Margaret. *North Dakota* (4–6). Illus. Series: America the Beautiful. 1990, Children's LB $28.00 (0-516-00480-8). 144pp. Such topics as history, economy, government, and culture are covered. (Rev: BL 7/90; SLJ 11/90) [978]

**13322** Kent, Deborah. *Colorado* (4–7). Illus. 1989, Children's LB $28.00 (0-516-00452-2). 144pp. A handsome look at life in this western state. (Rev: BL 4/15/89)

**13323** LaDoux, Rita C. *Montana* (3–6). Illus. Series: Hello U.S.A. 1992, Lerner LB $19.93 (0-8225-2714-6). 72pp. In addition to standard introductory material, coverage includes time lines about Montana and biographies of famous residents. (Rev: BL 5/15/92; SLJ 7/92) [978.6]

**13324** Lauber, Patricia. *Summer of Fire: Yellowstone 1988* (3–5). Illus. 1991, Orchard $19.95 (0-531-05943-X). 64pp. Striking photos dramatize the fires of 1988 and their aftermath in Yellowstone National Park. (Rev: BCCB 10/91; BL 9/1/91; HB 9–10/91*; SLJ 9/91) [581.5]

**13325** Lepthien, Emilie U. *South Dakota* (4–6). Illus. Series: America the Beautiful. 1991, Children's LB $28.00 (0-516-00487-5). 144pp. In addition to basic information, this account supplies various maps, a tour of the state, and profiles of important people. (Rev: BL 6/1/91) [978.3]

**13326** Lillegard, Dee, and Wayne Stoker. *Nevada* (4–6). Illus. Series: America the Beautiful. 1990, Children's LB $28.00 (0-516-00474-3). 144pp. This introduction includes history, geography, life today, and statistics. (Rev: BL 1/1/91) [979.3]

**13327** McCarthy, Betty. *Utah* (5–7). Illus. Series: America the Beautiful. 1989, Children's LB $28.00 (0-516-00490-5). 144pp. The story of Utah is told in pictures and text covering such topics as economy, history, geography, and recreation. (Rev: BL 1/1/90) [979.2]

**13328** Patent, Dorothy Hinshaw. *Yellowstone Fires: Flames and Rebirth* (2–6). Illus. 1989, Holiday LB $14.95 (0-8234-0807-8). 40pp. Covering the events of 1988 plus the continuing evolution of Yellowstone and other forests. (Rev: BCCB 6/90; BL 3/1/90; HB 5–6/90; SLJ 3/90) [574.5]

**13329** Petersen, David. *Bryce Canyon National Park* (2–3). Illus. Series: True Book. 1996, Children's LB $21.00 (0-516-20048-8). 48pp. A well-illustrated introduction to this national park and its amazing rock formations. Also use *Death Valley National Park* (1996). (Rev: SLJ 5/97) [917.91]

**13330** Petersen, David. *Dinosaur National Monument* (2–4). Illus. Series: New True Books. 1995, Children's LB $21.00 (0-516-01074-3). 48pp. A description in text and pictures of the Dinosaur National Monument in Colorado and Utah and of its historical importance. (Rev: BL 7/95; SLJ 8/95) [978.8]

**13331** Petersen, David. *Grand Canyon National Park* (1–3). Illus. Series: New True Books. 1992, Children's LB $21.00 (0-516-02197-4). 48pp. In stunning color photos and simple text, the Grand Canyon National Park in Arizona is described. (Rev: BL 2/1/93) [917.91]

**13332** Petersen, David. *Mesa Verde National Park* (1–3). Illus. Series: New True Books. 1992, Children's LB $21.00 (0-516-01136-7). 48pp. In addition to an introduction to the Mesa Verde National Park in Colorado, this book gives background information on the Pueblo Indians. (Rev: BL 9/1/92; SLJ 3/93) [917.8]

**13333** Petersen, David. *Rocky Mountain National Park* (2–4). Illus. Series: New True Book. 1993, Children's LB $21.00 (0-516-01196-0). 48pp. This attractive book introduces this Colorado national park with simple text and many photos. (Rev: BL 7/94) [978.8]

**13334** Petersen, David. *Yellowstone National Park* (1–3). Illus. Series: New True Books. 1992, Children's LB $19.00 (0-516-01148-0). 48pp. The story of the oldest national park, famous for its scenery, wildlife, and geysers. (Rev: BL 9/1/92; SLJ 3/93) [917.8]

**13335** Porter, A. P. *Nebraska* (3–6). Illus. Series: Hello U.S.A. 1991, Lerner LB $19.93 (0-8225-2708-1). 72pp. With information on the environment as well as on topics like population, industries, symbols, history, and geography, Nebraska is given good coverage. (Rev: BL 12/1/91) [978.2]

**13336** Simon, Seymour. *Wildfires* (3–5). Illus. 1996, Morrow LB $14.93 (0-688-13936-1). 32pp. Describes forest fires and their place in the ecosystem. (Rev: BL 4/1/96; HB 5–6/96; SLJ 5/96) [574.5]

**13337** Sirvaitis, Karen. *Utah* (3–6). Illus. Series: Hello U.S.A. 1991, Lerner LB $19.95 (0-8225-2707-3). 72pp. This introduction to Utah features color illustrations on each page, facts-at-a-glance sections, and a historical time line. (Rev: BL 8/91; SLJ 2/92) [979.2]

**13338** Spies, Karen B. *Denver* (3–5). Illus. 1988, Macmillan LB $13.95 (0-87518-386-7). 60pp. Living in Denver as described by a resident. (Rev: BL 1/15/89; SLJ 3/89)

**13339** Staub, Frank. *Yellowstone Park* (3–5). Illus. 1990, Troll LB $11.50 (0-8167-1737-0). 32pp. A description of Yellowstone Park, covering current ecological topics. (Rev: SLJ 8/90) [978]

**13340** Staub, Frank. *Yellowstone's Cycle of Fire* (3–6). Illus. Series: Earth Watch. 1994, Carolrhoda LB $14.95 (0-87614-778-3). 48pp. The cycle of forest fires and later renewal in Yellowstone Park is described, with major coverage of the huge fire of 1988. (Rev: BL 2/1/94; SLJ 6/94) [574.5]

**13341** Verba, Joan M. *North Dakota* (2–6). Illus. Series: Hello U.S.A. 1992, Lerner LB $19.95 (0-8225-2746-4). 72pp. This guide to the Flickertail State includes coverage of history, geography, and famous North Dakotans. (Rev: BL 12/15/92) [978.4]

**13342** Vieira, Linda. *Grand Canyon: A Trail Through Time* (3–5). Illus. by Christopher Canyon. 1997, Walker $15.95 (0-8027-8625-1). 32pp. A mule trail is the focus of this description of the Grand Canyon, with material on the formation of this wonder and of the various layers of rock that are visible. (Rev: BL 2/1/98) [917.91]

**13343** Wade, Linda R. *Badlands: Beauty Carved from Nature* (4–6). Illus. Series: Doors to America's Past. 1992, Rourke LB $22.60 (0-86592-471-6). 48pp. The history and present importance of Badlands National Park in South Dakota are told in text and illustrations. (Rev: BL 5/1/92; SLJ 1/92) [508.73]

**13344** Wills, Charles A. *A Historical Album of Colorado* (4–7). Illus. Series: Historical Albums. 1996, Millbrook LB $23.40 (1-56294-592-0); paper $6.95 (1-56294-858-X). 64pp. Using many old engravings and photographs, the history of Colorado is traced, beginning with its Native American population. (Rev: BL 7/96; SLJ 7/96) [978.8]

### NORTHEAST

**13345** Adams, Barbara J. *New York City* (3–5). Illus. 1988, Macmillan LB $13.95 (0-87518-384-0). 60pp. Explaining the unique character of this city in words and pictures. (Rev: BL 1/15/89; SLJ 5/89)

**13346** Avakian, Monique. *A Historical Album of Massachusetts* (4–8). Illus. Series: Historical Albums. 1994, Millbrook LB $23.40 (1-56294-481-9). 64pp. A history of Massachusetts that begins with the Native American culture and ends with the 1900s, including basic material on major events and personalities. (Rev: SLJ 2/95) [974.4]

**13347** Avakian, Monique, and Carter Smith, III. *A Historical Album of New York* (5–8). Illus. Series: Historical Albums. 1993, Millbrook LB $23.40 (1-56294-005-8). 64pp. An overview of New York State history from Native Americans settlements to the present day, using extensive archival illustrations. (Rev: SLJ 10/93) [974.7]

**13348** Aylesworth, Thomas G., and Virginia L. Aylesworth. *Southern New England: Connecticut, Massachusetts, Rhode Island* (4–7). Illus. Series: State Reports. 1988, Chelsea LB $19.95 (0-7910-3398-8); paper $8.95 (0-7910-3416-X). 64pp. Southern New England is described in a well-organized text with many illustrations. (Rev: BL 8/90) [974]

**13349** Aylesworth, Thomas G., and Virginia L. Aylesworth. *Upper Atlantic: New Jersey, New York* (3–8). Illus. 1995, Chelsea LB $19.95 (0-7910-3399-6); paper $8.95 (0-7910-3417-8). 64pp. Encyclopedia-like information in this coverage of New York and New Jersey. (Rev: BL 9/1/87; SLJ 11/87)

**13350** Balcer, Bernadette, and Fran O'Byrne-Pelham. *Philadelphia* (3–6). Illus. 1989, Macmillan LB $13.95 (0-87518-388-3). 60pp. All aspects of the old city's history, as well as modern living, are discussed. (Rev: BL 3/15/89; SLJ 3/89)

**13351** Blackstone, Margaret. *This Is Maine* (K–2). Illus. by John Segal. 1995, Holt $15.95 (0-8050-2800-5). 13pp. A picture book that extolls the beauties and natural wonders of Maine, like the seashore and a blueberry patch. (Rev: BL 6/1–15/95; SLJ 6/95) [974.1]

**13352** Brill, Marlene T. *Building the Capital City* (3–5). Illus. Series: Cornerstones of Freedom. 1996, Children's LB $19.50 (0-516-06633-1). 32pp. The story of the planning, building, and growth of Washington, D.C., through the years. (Rev: BL 7/96; SLJ 8/96) [975.3]

**13353** Brooks, Philip. *The United States Holocaust Memorial Museum* (3–5). Illus. Series: Cornerstones of Freedom. 1996, Children's LB $19.50 (0-516-20007-0). 32pp. The story of this Washington, D.C., landmark, its design, its contents, and the tragic events that it commemorates. (Rev: BL 11/15/96) [940.53]

**13354** Brown, Dottie. *Delaware* (3–6). Illus. Series: Hello USA. 1994, Lerner LB $19.93 (0-8225-2733-2). 72pp. A compact book that introduces Delaware's history, geography, resources, and famous people. (Rev: BL 4/15/94) [975.1]

**13355** Brown, Dottie. *New Hampshire* (3–6). Illus. Series: Hello USA. 1993, Lerner LB $19.95 (0-8225-2730-8). 72pp. A brief, colorful introduction to New Hampshire that takes the reader on a tour of the state, covers its history, tells how the people live, and gives biographies of famous residents. (Rev: BL 12/1/93) [974.2]

**13356** Climo, Shirley. *City! Washington, D.C.* (4–6). 1991, Macmillan LB $16.95 (0-02-719036-6). 64pp. An upbeat look at the nation's capital. (Rev: BL 8/91; SLJ 9/91) [917.5304]

**13357** Cytron, Barry. *Fire! The Library Is Burning* (4–7). Illus. 1988, Lerner LB $15.93 (0-8225-0525-8). 56pp. How workers and volunteers helped to restore the Jewish Theological Seminary in New York City when it was nearly destroyed by fire. (Rev: BL 7/88; SLJ 9/88)

**13358** Dean, Julia. *A Year on Monhegan Island* (3–6). Illus. 1995, Ticknor $14.95 (0-395-66476-4). 48pp. A photoessay that describes the seasons and the activities of the residents of this small island off the coast of Maine. (Rev: BCCB 3/95; BL 4/15/95; SLJ 4/95) [974.1]

**13359** Doherty, Craig A., and Katherine M. Doherty. *The Empire State Building* (4–7). 1997, Blackbirch LB $15.95 (1-56711-116-5). 48pp. The story of the planning and construction of this skyscraper, with material on its functions today. (Rev: BL 10/15/97; SLJ 1/98) [917.47]

**13360** Doherty, Craig A., and Katherine M. Doherty. *The Statue of Liberty* (3–6). Illus. Series: Building America. 1996, Blackbirch LB $15.95 (1-56711-111-4). 48pp. The Statue of Liberty, from the original idea to the finished sculpture. (Rev: BL 11/15/96; SLJ 1/97) [974.7]

**13361** Doherty, Craig A., and Katherine M. Doherty. *The Washington Monument* (3–6). Illus. Series: Building America. 1995, Blackbirch LB $15.95 (1-56711-110-6). 48pp. The story of this Washington, D.C. landmark from the original idea, through its phases of construction, to its present use as a tourist attraction. (Rev: BL 9/15/95; SLJ 7/95) [975.3]

**13362** Elish, Dan. *Vermont* (4–8). Illus. Series: Celebrate the States. 1997, Marshall Cavendish LB $32.79 (0-7614-0146-6). 144pp. An introduction to this New England state that covers such topics as famous sights, history, and how the people live. (Rev: BL 7/97; SLJ 8/97) [974.3]

**13363** Engfer, LeeAnne. *Maine* (3–6). Illus. Series: Hello U.S.A. 1991, Lerner LB $19.93 (0-8225-2701-4). 72pp. With many illustrations, this is a solid introduction to the New England state Maine. (Rev: BL 4/15/91; SLJ 6/91) [974.1]

**13364** Fradin, Dennis B. *Maine* (3–5). Illus. Series: From Sea to Shining Sea. 1994, Children's LB $26.00 (0-516-03819-2). 64pp. In addition to providing standard geographical and historical information, this well-illustrated book contains a checklist of important information about Maine, a timeline, maps, and a glossary. (Rev: BL 8/94) [974.1]

**13365** Fradin, Dennis B. *Massachusetts* (2–5). Illus. Series: From Sea to Shining Sea. 1991, Children's LB $26.00 (0-516-03821-4). 64pp. An attractive, informative package covering this New England state. (Rev: BL 2/1/92; SLJ 3/92) [974.4]

**13366** Fradin, Dennis B. *New Hampshire* (3–5). Illus. Series: From Sea to Shining Sea. 1992, Children's LB $26.00 (0-516-03829-X). 64pp. This introduction to New Hampshire tells about its geography, early history, present status, and state symbols. (Rev: BL 1/15/93) [974.2]

**13367** Fradin, Dennis B. *New Jersey* (3–5). Illus. Series: From Sea to Shining Sea. 1993, Children's LB $26.00 (0-516-03830-3). 64pp. A tour of the Garden State is included in this good introduction. (Rev: BL 7/93) [974.9]

**13368** Fradin, Dennis B. *New York* (3–5). Illus. Series: From Sea to Shining Sea. 1993, Children's LB $26.00 (0-516-03832-X). 64pp. This account takes one on a tour of the state, highlighting landmarks and geography, with material on history, industries, and famous New Yorkers. (Rev: BL 11/1/93; SLJ 2/94) [974.7]

**13369** Fradin, Dennis B. *Pennsylvania* (3–5). Illus. Series: From Sea to Shining Sea. 1994, Children's LB $26.00 (0-516-03838-9). 64pp. An attractive portrait of the past and present of Pennsylvania, with

coverage of the people and how they work and play. (Rev: BL 8/94) [974.8]

**13370** Fradin, Dennis B. *Vermont* (3–5). Illus. Series: From Sea to Shining Sea. 1993, Children's LB $26.00 (0-516-03845-1). 64pp. Many photographs and simple text introduce the New England state of Vermont. (Rev: BL 7/93) [974.3]

**13371** Fradin, Dennis B. *Washington, D.C.* (3–5). Illus. Series: From Sea to Shining Sea. 1992, Children's LB $26.00 (0-516-03851-6). 64pp. This introduction to the nation's capital includes a fact summary and a guide to major monuments. (Rev: BL 5/1/92; SLJ 8/92) [975.3]

**13372** Fredeen, Charles. *New Jersey* (3–6). Illus. Series: Hello U.S.A. 1993, Lerner LB $19.95 (0-8225-2732-4). 72pp. The Garden State is introduced with color illustrations and informative text. (Rev: BL 7/93; SLJ 8/93) [974.9]

**13373** Gibbons, Gail. *From Path to Highway: The Story of the Boston Post Road* (2–4). Illus. 1986, HarperCollins LB $14.89 (0-690-04514-X). 32pp. A picturebook history of the road used by early travelers and today's citizens when traveling between Boston and New York. (Rev: BCCB 6/86; BL 6/15/86; SLJ 9/86)

**13374** Gleman, Amy. *Connecticut* (3–6). Illus. 1991, Lerner LB $19.93 (0-8225-2709-X). 72pp. In text and pictures, this book covers history, economics, and interesting features and includes a time line, maps, and charts. (Rev: BL 10/15/91) [974.6]

**13375** Guzzetti, Paula. *The White House* (4–6). Illus. Series: Places in American History. 1995, Silver Burdett LB $14.95 (0-87518-650-5). 72pp. A tour of the White House and its history, with brief asides on some of its inhabitants and their effects on the building. (Rev: BL 2/15/96; SLJ 1/96) [975.3]

**13376** Harrington, Ty. *Maine* (4–7). Illus. Series: America the Beautiful. 1989, Children's LB $28.00 (0-516-00465-4). 144pp. A fine combination of narrative and graphic materials introduces the state of Maine. (Rev: BL 7/89) [974.1]

**13377** Heinrichs, Ann. *Rhode Island* (4–6). Illus. Series: America the Beautiful. 1990, Children's LB $29.40 (0-516-00485-9). 144pp. This profile of tiny Rhode Island includes a chronology and map section. (Rev: BL 7/90) [974]

**13378** Herda, D. J. *Environmental America: The Northeastern States* (4–7). Illus. Series: American Scene. 1991, Millbrook LB $22.40 (1-878841-06-8). 64pp. This volume discusses the condition of the environment and presents information on such topics as water and land pollution in the northeastern states. (Rev: BL 8/91; SLJ 7/91) [639.9]

**13379** Herda, D. J. *Ethnic America: The Northeastern States* (5–7). Illus. Series: American Scene.

1991, Millbrook LB $22.40 (1-56294-014-7). 64pp. In this heavily illustrated account, the ethnic make-up, including Native Americans, is described and the accomplishments detailed. (Rev: BL 2/1/92; SLJ 2/92) [572.973]

**13380** Holland, Gini. *The Empire State Building* (3–5). Illus. Series: Great Buildings. 1997, Raintree Steck-Vaughn LB $24.97 (0-8172-4919-2). 48pp. This account supplies details of the planning and construction of this landmark building and of its present uses. (Rev: BL 11/15/97) [917.347]

**13381** Jacobs, William J. *Ellis Island* (4–6). Illus. 1990, Macmillan $16.00 (0-684-19171-7). 40pp. A well-written introduction to Ellis Island in the you-are-there style. (Rev: BCCB 5/90; BL 4/15/90; SLJ 6/90) [304.8]

**13382** Jakobsen, Kathy. *My New York* (K–4). Illus. 1993, Little, Brown $16.95 (0-316-45653-5). 34pp. A young New Yorker writes to a friend describing all the wonders of New York City, including some that tourists often miss. (Rev: BL 9/1/93*; HB 11–12/93; SLJ 12/93*) [974.7]

**13383** Johnston, Joyce. *Washington, D.C.* (3–6). Illus. Series: Hello USA. 1994, Lerner LB $19.95 (0-8225-2751-0). 72pp. This brief introduction to Washington, D.C., tells about its history, local government, landmarks, and daily life. (Rev: BL 2/1/94) [975.3]

**13384** Kent, Deborah. *Connecticut* (5–7). Illus. Series: America the Beautiful. 1989, Children's LB $28.00 (0-516-00453-0). 144pp. An introduction that covers history, geography, chronology, and landmarks. (Rev: BL 1/1/90) [974.6]

**13385** Kent, Deborah. *Delaware* (4–6). Illus. Series: America the Beautiful. 1991, Children's LB $28.00 (0-516-00454-9). 144pp. Material on history, geography, and economy, plus a tour of the state. (Rev: BL 6/1/91) [975.1]

**13386** Kent, Deborah. *The Lincoln Memorial* (3–5). Illus. Series: Cornerstones of Freedom. 1996, Children's LB $19.50 (0-516-20006-2). 30pp. An account of the design and building of the Lincoln Memorial in 1922 and of the many controversies that surrounded its construction. (Rev: SLJ 2/97) [917.5]

**13387** Kent, Deborah. *New York City* (3–6). Illus. Series: Cities of the World. 1996, Children's LB $25.00 (0-516-20025-9). 64pp. After a history and geography of New York City, such topics as famous buildings, leisure time activities, and cultural institutions are covered. (Rev: BL 1/1–15/97) [974.7]

**13388** Kent, Deborah. *Washington, D.C.* (4–8). Illus. Series: America the Beautiful. 1991, Children's LB $28.00 (0-516-00497-2). 142pp. About half of this book gives the history of the city and the rest tells

about its many sights and government buildings. (Rev: BL 1/1/92; SLJ 5/91) [975.3]

**13389** Krementz, Jill. *A Visit to Washington, D.C.* (K–3). Illus. by author. 1987, Scholastic paper $5.95 (0-590-40583-7). 48pp. A 6-year-old tells of his home town, the nation's capital city. (Rev: BL 5/15/87; HB 7–8/87; SLJ 5/87)

**13390** Lawlor, Veronica. *I Was Dreaming to Come to America* (3–5). Illus. 1995, Viking paper $15.99 (0-670-86164-2). 40pp. A small picture book that draws on the experiences of some of the 12 million people who passed through Ellis Island. (Rev: BL 6/1–15/95; HB 7–8/95; SLJ 6/95) [304.8]

**13391** Loewen, Nancy. *Philadelphia* (3–6). Illus. Series: Great Cities of the U.S.A. 1989, Rourke LB $23.93 (0-86592-542-9). 48pp. The Pennsylvania "City of Brotherly Love" is profiled. (Rev: BL 1/1/90) [917]

**13392** Loewen, Nancy. *Washington, D.C.* (3–6). Illus. Series: Great Cities of the U.S.A. 1989, Rourke LB $23.93 (0-86592-544-5). 48pp. The nation's capital is introduced, with strong historical material. (Rev: BL 1/1/90) [917]

**13393** Lourie, Peter. *Erie Canal: Canoeing America's Great Waterway* (5–8). Illus. 1997, Boyds Mills $17.95 (1-56397-669-2). 48pp. This colorful book about a journey along the Erie Canal also supplies historical facts about its construction and uses. (Rev: BL 7/97; SLJ 9/97) [974.7]

**13394** McNair, Sylvia. *New Hampshire* (4–6). Illus. Series: America the Beautiful. 1991, Children's LB $28.00 (0-516-00475-1). 144pp. Topics such as history, geography, industry, and famous residents are covered. (Rev: BL 1/15/92) [972.95]

**13395** McNair, Sylvia. *Vermont* (4–6). Illus. Series: America the Beautiful. 1991, Children's LB $28.00 (0-516-00491-3). 144pp. This New England state is profiled with material on geography, history, government, important sights, and interesting residents. (Rev: BL 1/15/92; SLJ 2/92) [974.3]

**13396** Miller, Natalie. *The Statue of Liberty* (3–5). Illus. Series: Cornerstones of Freedom. 1992, Children's LB $19.50 (0-516-06655-2). 32pp. The story of the building of the Statue of Liberty and the place it has taken in American history. (Rev: BL 1/1/93; SLJ 1/93) [974.7]

**13397** Monke, Ingrid. *Boston* (3–6). Illus. 1989, Macmillan $13.95 (0-87518-382-4). 60pp. History and modern living in the famous old city. (Rev: BL 3/15/89; SLJ 3/89)

**13398** Munro, Roxie. *The Inside-Outside Book of Washington, D.C.* (1–3). Illus. 1987, Puffin paper $4.99 (0-14-054940-4). 48pp. Views inside and outside the familiar and sometimes spectacular buildings of Washington, D.C. (Rev: BCCB 4/87; BL 5/15/87; SLJ 5/87)

**13399** Peduzzi, Kelli. *Shaping a President: Sculpting for the Roosevelt Memorial* (3–6). Illus. 1997, Millbrook LB $22.40 (0-7613-0207-7); paper $6.95 (0-7613-0325-1). 48pp. This photoessay tells of the work of the sculptor Neil Estrin, who sculpted figures of Franklin, Eleanor, and their dog Fala, for the Roosevelt Memorial in Washington, D.C. (Rev: BL 12/1/97; SLJ 3/98) [730]

**13400** Quiri, Patricia R. *The White House* (4–6). Illus. 1996, Watts LB $21.00 (0-531-20221-6). 63pp. A history of the White House is given, with a description of the exterior design and rooms inside. (Rev: BL 6/1–15/96; SLJ 8/96) [975.3]

**13401** Reef, Catherine. *The Lincoln Memorial* (3–6). Illus. Series: Places in American History. 1994, Dillon $14.95 (0-87518-624-6). 71pp. This guide to one of Washington's landmark buildings also touches on the importance of Lincoln, as well as supplying details on the planning and construction of the monument. (Rev: SLJ 8/94) [975.3]

**13402** Reef, Catherine. *Washington, D.C.* (3–6). Illus. Series: Downtown America. 1989, Macmillan LB $13.95 (0-87518-411-1). 72pp. This introduction includes a "Fast Facts" section, maps, and a time line. (Rev: BL 1/1/90; SLJ 4/90) [975.3]

**13403** Sakurai, Gail. *The Liberty Bell* (3–5). Illus. Series: Cornerstones of Freedom. 1996, Children's LB $19.50 (0-516-06634-X). 32pp. The story of the Liberty Bell from its casting to its final resting place in Philadelphia. (Rev: BL 7/96; SLJ 8/96) [974.8]

**13404** Schnurnberger, Lynn. *Kids Love New York! The A-to-Z Resource Book* (4–8). Illus. 1990, Congdon & Weed paper $9.95 (0-312-92415-1). 224pp. A group of suggestions for various activities in New York City.

**13405** Schomp, Virginia. *New York* (4–8). Illus. Series: Celebrate the States. 1996, Marshall Cavendish LB $22.95 (1-7614-0108-3). 144pp. The Empire State is introduced, with information on history, geography, people, landmarks, and distinguished New Yorkers. (Rev: BL 2/15/97) [917.47]

**13406** Steen, Sandra, and Susan Steen. *Independence Hall* (3–6). Illus. Series: Places in American History. 1994, Dillon LB $14.95 (0-87518-603-3). 71pp. This introduction to Philadelphia's famous landmark tells about its construction, historical importance, and present status, with material on the State House and the Liberty Bell. (Rev: SLJ 8/94) [974.8]

**13407** Stein, R. Conrad. *Ellis Island* (3–5). Illus. Series: Cornerstones of Freedom. 1992, Children's LB $19.50 (0-516-06653-6). 32pp. The history of the island that served as the best-known immigration sta-

tion, plus material on its present function as a museum. (Rev: BL 6/1/92; SLJ 9/92) [325.1]

**13408** Steins, Richard. *Our National Capital* (4–6). Illus. Series: I Know America. 1994, Millbrook LB $20.90 (1-56294-439-8). 48pp. Important government buildings, historical monuments, and other Washington, D.C. attractions are introduced, with some general background information. (Rev: SLJ 6/94) [917.53]

**13409** Stewart, Gail B. *New York* (3–6). Illus. Series: Great Cities of the U.S.A. 1989, Rourke LB $23.93 (0-86592-541-0). 48pp. Good historical background information is included in this profile of America's largest city. (Rev: BL 1/1/90) [917]

**13410** Sullivan, George. *How the White House Really Works* (5–8). Illus. 1990, Scholastic paper $3.95 (0-590-43403-9). Home, office, museum, and tourist attraction — how the White House operates. (Rev: BCCB 5/89; BL 5/15/89; HB 7–8/89)

**13411** Swain, Gwenyth. *Pennsylvania* (3–5). Illus. Series: Hello USA. 1994, Lerner LB $18.95 (0-8225-2727-8). 72pp. After an introductory trip around Pennsylvania, this concise book covers its history, attractions, environment, and famous people. (Rev: BL 4/15/94; SLJ 8/94) [974.8]

**13412** Thompson, Kathleen. *New York* (4–6). Illus. Series: Portrait of America. 1996, Raintree Steck-Vaughn LB $22.83 (0-8114-7377-5). 48pp. The unique aspects of life in New York State are covered in this account that also deals with its history, economy, culture, and what the future might bring. (Rev: SLJ 8/96) [917.47]

**13413** Thompson, Kathleen. *Pennsylvania* (4–6). Illus. Series: Portrait of America. 1996, Raintree Steck-Vaughn LB $22.83 (0-8114-7383-X). 48pp. The history, economy, culture, and the future are covered in this introduction to Pennsylvania, based on the "Portrait of America" TV series. (Rev: SLJ 8/96) [917.48]

**13414** Topper, Frank, and Charles A. Wills. *A Historical Album of New Jersey* (3–5). Illus. Series: Historical Albums. 1995, Millbrook LB $23.40 (1-56294-505-X). 64pp. Beginning with the Native American culture and ending with the present day, the most important events and people in New Jersey history are touched on in a rapid overview. (Rev: SLJ 7/95) [974.9]

**13415** Warner, J. F. *Rhode Island* (3–6). Illus. Series: Hello U.S.A. 1993, Lerner LB $19.95 (0-8225-2731-6). 72pp. In excellent color illustrations and informative text, Rhode Island and its history, geography, cities, and social and economic life are covered. (Rev: BL 1/15/93) [974]

**13416** Waters, Kate. *The Story of the White House* (K–3). 1991, Scholastic $12.95 (0-590-43335-0).

40pp. This photoessay gives a history of the White House, describes its layout, and gives coverage on individual rooms. (Rev: BL 12/15/91; SLJ 8/91) [975.2]

**13417** Wills, Charles A. *A Historical Album of Pennsylvania* (4–7). Illus. Series: Historical Albums. 1996, Millbrook LB $23.40 (1-56294-595-5); paper $6.95 (1-56294-853-9). 64pp. Beginning with a little geography and coverage of the native population, this account traces the history of Pennsylvania to the present. (Rev: BL 7/96; SLJ 7/96) [974.8]

### PACIFIC STATES

**13418** Abbink, Emily. *Missions of the Monterey Bay Area* (4–7). Series: California Missions. 1996, Lerner LB $23.93 (0-8225-1928-3). 80pp. Covers the history of the missions at San Carlos Borromeo de Carmelo, San Juan Bautista, and Santa Cruz. (Rev: BL 2/15/97) [979.4]

**13419** Altman, Linda Jacobs. *California* (4–8). Illus. Series: Celebrate the States. 1996, Marshall Cavendish LB $32.79 (0-7614-0111-3). 144pp. This introduction to California includes chapters on its history, geography, people, achievements, and landmarks. (Rev: BL 2/1/97; SLJ 2/97) [979.4]

**13420** Aylesworth, Thomas G., and Virginia L. Aylesworth. *The Pacific: California, Hawaii* (3–8). Illus. 1995, Chelsea LB $19.95 (0-7910-3407-0); paper $8.95 (0-7910-3425-9). 64pp. People and places are included in this study of the West. (Rev: BL 11/1/87; SLJ 11/95)

**13421** Behrens, June. *Missions of the Central Coast* (4–7). Series: California Missions. 1996, Lerner LB $23.93 (0-8225-1930-5). 80pp. The missions at Santa Barbara, Santa Ines, and La Purisima Concepción are discussed, with material on their history and importance. (Rev: BL 2/15/97) [979.4]

**13422** Blake, Arthur, and Pamela Dailey. *The Gold Rush of 1849: Staking a Claim in California* (5–8). Illus. Series: Spotlight on American History. 1995, Millbrook LB $21.90 (1-56294-483-5). 63pp. This clear overview of the subject tells of the difficulties that miners faced and of their arduous living conditions. (Rev: SLJ 7/95) [979.9]

**13423** Bratvold, Gretchen. *Oregon* (3–6). Illus. Series: Hello U.S.A. 1991, Lerner LB $19.95 (0-8225-2704-9). 72pp. Topics include geography; history; and social, economic, and environmental concerns, with full-color photos. (Rev: BL 4/15/91; SLJ 6/91) [979.5]

**13424** Brower, Pauline. *Missions of the Inland Valleys* (4–7). Series: California Missions. 1996, Lerner LB $23.93 (0-8225-1929-1). 80pp. Examines 4 missions, including San Luis Obispo and San Miguel Arcangel, with material on their early history and

their impact on the existing cultures. (Rev: BL 2/15/97) [979.4]

**13425** Brown, Tricia. *The City by the Bay: A Magical Journey Around San Francisco* (K–3). Illus. by Elisa Kleven. 1993, Chronicle $14.95 (0-8118-0233-7). 32pp. Using an entertaining series of collages, this simple guidebook introduces the famous sights of San Francisco, including Chinatown, the Golden Gate Bridge, and cable cars. (Rev: BL 9/1/93) [917.94]

**13426** Cohen, Daniel. *The Alaska Purchase* (4–7). Illus. Series: Spotlight on American History. 1996, Millbrook LB $21.90 (1-56294-528-9). 64pp. The story of the purchase of Alaska from Russia and how it has affected the history of the United States. (Rev: BL 3/15/96; SLJ 5/96) [979.8]

**13427** Doherty, Craig A., and Katherine M. Doherty. *The Alaska Pipeline* (4–7). Series: Building America. 1997, Blackbirch LB $15.95 (1-56711-115-7). 48pp. All aspects of the building and maintenance of the Alaska pipeline are covered, with accompanying photos — current pictures and reproductions. (Rev: BL 10/15/97; SLJ 4/98) [917.98]

**13428** Doherty, Craig A., and Katherine M. Doherty. *The Golden Gate Bridge* (3–6). Illus. Series: Building America. 1995, Blackbirch LB $15.95 (1-56711-106-8). 48pp. From concept to completion, this is a thorough, engrossing description of the Golden Gate Bridge in San Francisco. (Rev: BL 9/15/95; SLJ 7/95) [624]

**13429** Feeney, Stephanie. *Hawaii Is a Rainbow* (2–6). Illus. 1985, Univ. of Hawaii Pr. $12.95 (0-8248-1007-4). 64pp. Color photos present the people and land of Hawaii as they present the colors of the rainbow. (Rev: BL 2/1/85; SLJ 1/86)

**13430** Fradin, Dennis B. *Alaska* (3–5). Illus. Series: From Sea to Shining Sea. 1993, Children's LB $26.00 (0-516-03802-8). 64pp. With color photos on each page, this attractive account supplies basic information about Alaska, its past and present, and unusual facts that make it unique. (Rev: BL 3/1/94) [979.8]

**13431** Fradin, Dennis B. *California* (3–5). Illus. Series: From Sea to Shining Sea. 1992, Children's LB $26.00 (0-516-03805-2). 64pp. History, geography, famous names, and a chronology are presented in this introduction to California. (Rev: BL 2/1/93; SLJ 4/93) [976.8]

**13432** Fradin, Dennis B. *Hawaii* (3–5). Illus. Series: From Sea to Shining Sea. 1994, Children's LB $26.00 (0-516-03811-7). 64pp. Among the topics covered in this introduction to Hawaii are its natural wonders, economy, history, and people. (Rev: BL 8/94; SLJ 11/94) [996.9]

**13433**   Fradin, Dennis B., and Judith B. Fradin. *Oregon* (3–5). Illus. Series: From Sea to Shining Sea. 1995, Children's LB $26.00 (0-516-03837-0). 64pp. This guide to the Beaver State presents Oregon's geography, history, climate, wildlife, history, and people. (Rev: SLJ 8/95) [917.95]

**13434**   Grabowski, John, and Patricia Grabowski. *The Northwest: Alaska, Idaho, Oregon, Washington* (3–6). Series: State Reports. 1995, Chelsea LB $19.95 (0-7910-3406-2); paper $8.95 (0-7910-3424-0). 64pp. History, geography, state symbols, capitals, principal cities, and places to visit are some of the topics covered in this introduction to these 4 states. (Rev: SLJ 9/92) [978]

**13435**   Haddock, Patricia. *San Francisco* (3–6). Illus. 1989, Macmillan LB $13.95 (0-87518-383-2). 60pp. A close-up look at life in one of America's favorite cities. (Rev: BL 3/15/89)

**13436**   Heinrichs, Ann. *Alaska* (4–6). Illus. Series: America the Beautiful. 1990, Children's LB $28.00 (0-516-00448-4). 144pp. This introduction to Alaska includes a reference section on important dates and people. (Rev: BL 1/1/91) [979.8]

**13437**   Herda, D. J. *Environmental America: The Northwestern States* (4–7). Illus. Series: American Scene. 1991, Millbrook LB $22.40 (1-878841-10-6). 64pp. This account presents information on such topics as pollution, waste, logging, and the general condition of the environment in Idaho, Montana, Oregon, Washington, and Wyoming. (Rev: BL 8/91; SLJ 7/91) [639.9]

**13438**   Johnston, Joyce. *Alaska* (3–6). Illus. Series: Hello USA. 1994, Lerner LB $19.93 (0-8225-2735-9). 72pp. This introduction to Alaska features a trip around the state, historical information, and material on the life-styles of its people. (Rev: BL 4/15/94; SLJ 8/94) [979.8]

**13439**   Kent, Deborah. *San Francisco* (3–6). Series: Cities of the World. 1997, Children's LB $25.00 (0-516-20466-1). 64pp. An introduction to San Francisco that covers its history, communities, landmarks, maps, and a discussion of the city's problems. (Rev: BL 3/15/98) [917.9]

**13440**   Kent, Zachary. *Idaho* (4–6). Illus. Series: America the Beautiful. 1990, Children's LB $28.00 (0-516-00458-1). 144pp. A standard introduction to Idaho with map section, chronology, and key statistics. (Rev: BL 7/90; SLJ 11/90) [978]

**13441**   Lemke, Nancy. *Missions of the Southern Coast* (4–7). Illus. Series: California Missions. 1996, Lerner LB $23.93 (0-8225-1925-9). 80pp. The 3 missions described here are San Diego de Alcala, San Luis Rey de Francia, and San Juan Capistrano. (Rev: BL 9/15/96; SLJ 8/96) [979.4]

**13442**   Loewen, Nancy. *Seattle* (3–6). Illus. Series: Great Cities of the U.S.A. 1989, Rourke LB $23.93 (0-86592-545-3). 48pp. Information on history, climate, people, and so forth is given on the Washington port of Seattle. (Rev: BL 1/1/90) [917]

**13443**   MacMillan, Dianne. *Destination Los Angeles* (4–6). Illus. Series: Port Cities of North America. 1998, Lerner LB $22.60 (0-8225-2786-3). 80pp. Describes Los Angeles and its history but concentrates on the harbor, trade, and the cargo shipped in and out. (Rev: SLJ 3/98) [917.94]

**13444**   MacMillan, Dianne. *Missions of the Los Angeles Area* (4–7). Illus. Series: California Missions. 1996, Lerner LB $23.93 (0-8225-1927-5). 80pp. This volume gives a description and history of 3 missions: San Gabriel Arcangel, San Fernando Rey de España, and San Buenaventura. (Rev: BL 9/15/96; SLJ 8/96) [979.4]

**13445**   Miller, Debbie S. *Disappearing Lake: Nature's Magic in Denali National Park* (K–3). Illus. by Jon Van Zyle. 1997, Walker $15.95 (0-8027-8474-7). 32pp. The story of an area in Alaska's Denali National Park, which is transformed annually into a lake and then, as the waters recede, into a flowering meadow. (Rev: BCCB 2/97; BL 3/15/97; SLJ 4/97*) [508.798]

**13446**   Murphy, Claire R. *A Child's Alaska* (2–5). Illus. by Charles Mason. 1994, Alaska Northwest $15.95 (0-88240-457-1). 48pp. A year-round look at Alaska that describes its climate and wildlife as well as the different life-styles of its people and their children. (Rev: BL 12/1/94*; SLJ 1/95) [979.8]

**13447**   Oberle, Joseph. *Anchorage* (3–5). Illus. Series: Downtown America. 1990, Macmillan LB $13.95 (0-87518-420-0). 60pp. The sights and sounds of Anchorage are captured, along with the city's colorful history and people. (Rev: BL 6/1/90; SLJ 11/90) [979]

**13448**   O'Connor, Karen. *San Diego* (3–5). Illus. Series: Downtown America. 1990, Macmillan LB $13.95 (0-87518-439-1). 60pp. In color photos and brief text, the city of San Diego, California, is introduced. (Rev: BL 2/1/91) [974.94]

**13449**   Pelta, Kathy. *California* (3–5). Illus. Series: Hello USA. 1994, Lerner LB $19.93 (0-8225-2738-3). 72pp. This small book is crammed with basic information about California, including its history, famous attractions, and important residents. (Rev: BL 4/15/94) [979.4]

**13450**   Penisten, John. *Honolulu* (3–6). Illus. Series: Downtown America. 1989, Macmillan LB $13.95 (0-87518-416-2). 72pp. Included in this introduction are maps, a time line, and lists of places to visit. (Rev: BL 1/1/90; SLJ 5/90) [996.9]

**13451** Powell, E. Sandy. *Washington* (3–6). Illus. Series: Hello U.S.A. 1993, Lerner LB $19.95 (0-8225-2726-X). 72pp. A visually attractive book that includes fact sheets, time lines, and capsule biographies. (Rev: BL 3/15/93; SLJ 8/93) [979.7]

**13452** Pratt, Helen Jay. *The Hawaiians: An Island People* (6–8). Illus. 1991, Tuttle paper $9.95 (0-8048-1709-X). 210pp. An account of early Hawaii and its inhabitants, with emphasis on folk customs.

**13453** Rice, Oliver D. *Lone Woman of Ghalas-Hat* (5–7). Illus. by Charles Zafuto. 1993, California Weekly LB $13.00 (0-936778-52-0); paper $6.00 (0-936778-51-2). 32pp. The true story of the Indian woman who lived alone on a California island for 18 years. This was the basis of Island of the Blue Dolphins. A reissue. [979.7]

**13454** Rice, Oliver D. *Student Atlas of California* (4–7). Illus. by Barbara Mitchell. 1993, California Weekly paper $11.00 (0-936778-63-6). 66pp. This atlas contains over 40 historical and geographical maps on California, with figures through the 1992 census. A reissue. [979.7]

**13455** Seibold, J. Otto, and Vivian Walsh. *Going to the Getty: A Book About the Getty Center in Los Angeles* (4–7). Illus. 1997, J. Paul Getty Museum $16.95 (0-89236-493-9). 32pp. This introduction to the Getty Museum in Los Angeles is a patchwork of impressions, photographs, drawings, and reproductions of artworks. (Rev: BL 2/15/98) [708]

**13456** Snelson, Karin. *Seattle* (3–5). Illus. Series: Downtown America. 1992, Macmillan LB $13.95 (0-87518-509-6). 64pp. This introduction to Seattle includes its history, ethnic life, and places to visit. (Rev: BL 6/1/92) [979.7]

**13457** Stefoff, Rebecca. *Oregon* (4–8). Illus. Series: Celebrate the States. 1997, Marshall Cavendish LB $32.79 (0-7614-0145-8). 140pp. Life in this Pacific state is covered, along with topics like its history, famous sights, cities, and industries. (Rev: BL 7/97; SLJ 7/97) [917.95]

**13458** Stein, R. Conrad. *Oregon* (4–6). Illus. Series: America the Beautiful. 1989, Children's LB $28.00 (0-516-00483-2). 144pp. The Pacific state of Oregon is highlighted, covering history, geography, famous people, and important sites. (Rev: BL 7/89) [979.5]

**13459** Stein, R. Conrad. *Washington* (4–6). Illus. Series: America the Beautiful. 1991, Children's LB $28.00 (0-516-00493-X). 144pp. A fine balance of text and pictures presents the geography, history, government, and famous sites. (Rev: BL 1/15/92) [972.95]

**13460** Stewart, Gail B. *Los Angeles* (3–6). Illus. Series: Great Cities of the U.S.A. 1989, Rourke LB $23.93 (0-86592-540-2). 48pp. The sprawling South-

ern California "City of the Angels" is introduced. (Rev: BL 1/1/90) [917]

**13461** Van Steenwyk, Elizabeth. *The California Missions* (4–6). Illus. Series: First Books of Interest. 1995, Watts LB $22.00 (0-531-20187-2). 63pp. A description of the 21 coastal missions founded in California and their history, functions, and workings. (Rev: SLJ 11/95) [979.4]

**13462** White, Tekla N. *Missions of the San Francisco Bay Area* (4–7). Illus. Series: California Missions. 1996, Lerner LB $23.93 (0-8225-1926-7). 80pp. The history of 5 Spanish missions in the San Francisco Bay Area, including Santa Clara de Asis and San Rafael Arcangel. (Rev: BL 9/15/96; SLJ 8/96) [979.4]

**13463** Wills, Charles A. *A Historical Album of California* (4–8). Illus. Series: Historical Albums. 1994, Millbrook LB $23.40 (1-56294-479-7). 64pp. A slim volume that covers the basic history of California, with material on major events and important personalities. (Rev: SLJ 3/95) [979.4]

**13464** Wills, Charles A. *A Historical Album of Oregon* (4–7). Illus. 1995, Millbrook LB $23.40 (1-56294-594-7). 64pp. A history of Oregon from prehistoric times to the present is outlined with many illustrations, some in color. (Rev: BL 12/15/95; SLJ 1/96) [979.5]

### SOUTH

**13465** Aylesworth, Thomas G., and Virginia L. Aylesworth. *The Southeast: Georgia, Kentucky, Tennessee* (3–8). Illus. 1995, Chelsea LB $18.95 (0-7910-3411-9); paper $8.95 (0-7910-3429-1). 64pp. An inviting look at this region, with color photos and map. (Rev: BL 11/1/87; SLJ 11/87)

**13466** Barrett, Tracy. *Virginia* (4–8). Illus. Series: Celebrate the States. 1996, Marshall Cavendish LB $32.79 (0-7614-0110-5). 144pp. This introduction to Virginia covers such topics as history, culture, famous sites, and important Virginians. (Rev: BL 2/15/97) [975.5]

**13467** Bial, Raymond. *Cajun Home* (4–7). Illus. 1998, Houghton $16.00 (0-395-86095-4). 48pp. This is the story of the people who left France to find freedom in Canada, only to be transported to Louisiana where they settled in the backwood swamp areas. (Rev: BL 3/15/98) [976.3]

**13468** Bial, Raymond. *Mist over the Mountains: Appalachia and Its People* (4–7). Illus. 1997, Houghton $14.95 (0-395-73569-6). 48pp. The people and culture of Appalachia are introduced, including history, agriculture, and folk arts. (Rev: BCCB 6/97; BL 3/1/97; SLJ 5/97) [975]

**13469** Brown, Dottie. *Kentucky* (3–6). Illus. Series: Hello U.S.A. 1992, Lerner LB $19.93 (0-8225-2715-

4). 72pp. The visual beauty of the Bluegrass State is captured in text and pictures in this introductory volume. (Rev: BL 5/15/92; SLJ 7/92) [976.9]

**13470** Cocke, William. *A Historical Album of Virginia* (4–7). Illus. 1995, Millbrook LB $23.40 (1-56294-596-3). 64pp. Beginning with Native Americans and ending with the present, this history of Virginia uses many period paintings and prints as illustrations. (Rev: BL 12/15/95; SLJ 1/96) [975.5]

**13471** DiPiazza, Domenica. *Arkansas* (3–6). Illus. Series: Hello USA. 1994, Lerner LB $19.93 (0-8225-2742-1). 72pp. A brief introduction to Arkansas that covers salient facts, history, industries, people, unique features, and famous residents. (Rev: BL 9/15/94) [976.7]

**13472** Fischer, Marsha. *Miami* (3–5). Illus. Series: Downtown America. 1990, Macmillan LB $13.95 (0-87518-428-6). 60pp. This introduction to Miami includes a map, a historical time line, and places to visit. (Rev: BL 6/1/90) [975.9]

**13473** Fisher, Leonard Everett. *Monticello* (4–7). Illus. by author. 1988, Holiday LB $16.95 (0-8234-0688-1). 64pp. Touring the famous home of our third president. (Rev: BCCB 6/88; BL 6/1/88; SLJ 6–7/88)

**13474** Fradin, Dennis B. *Alabama* (3–5). Illus. Series: From Sea to Shining Sea. 1993, Children's LB $26.00 (0-516-03801-X). 64pp. A good introduction to this southern state. (Rev: BL 7/93) [976.1]

**13475** Fradin, Dennis B. *Florida* (3–5). Illus. Series: From Sea to Shining Sea. 1992, Children's LB $26.00 (0-516-03809-5). 64pp. This simple overview of Florida gives material on its history, geography, and people. (Rev: BL 5/1/92; SLJ 8/92) [917.5904]

**13476** Fradin, Dennis B. *Georgia* (3–5). Illus. Series: From Sea to Shining Sea. 1991, Children's LB $26.00 (0-516-03810-9). 64pp. A simple, attractive look at geography, early history, and current status of this southern state. (Rev: BL 2/1/92) [975.8]

**13477** Fradin, Dennis B. *Kentucky* (3–5). Illus. Series: From Sea to Shining Sea. 1993, Children's LB $26.00 (0-516-03817-6). 64pp. A fine introduction to the Bluegrass State. (Rev: BL 7/93) [976.9]

**13478** Fradin, Dennis B. *North Carolina* (3–5). Illus. Series: From Sea to Shining Sea. 1992, Children's LB $26.00 (0-516-03833-8). 64pp. This introduction to North Carolina includes history, geography, and a trip through the state. (Rev: BL 5/1/92) [917.5604]

**13479** Fradin, Dennis B. *Tennessee* (3–5). Illus. Series: From Sea to Shining Sea. 1992, Children's LB $26.00 (0-516-03842-7). 64pp. Tennessee is introduced with coverage of geography, history, people, and their work. (Rev: BL 2/1/93; SLJ 4/93) [976.8]

**13480** Fradin, Dennis B. *Virginia* (3–5). Illus. Series: From Sea to Shining Sea. 1992, Children's LB $26.00 (0-516-03846-X). 64pp. This introduction to Virginia includes standard information on history and geography and an imaginary trip through the state. (Rev: BL 2/1/93) [975.5]

**13481** Fradin, Dennis B., and Judith B. Fradin. *Arkansas* (3–5). Illus. Series: From Sea to Shining Sea. 1994, Children's LB $26.00 (0-516-03804-4). 64pp. A nicely illustrated introduction to Arkansas past and present, with information on natural resources, its cities, and its people. (Rev: BL 8/94) [976.7]

**13482** Fredeen, Charles. *South Carolina* (3–6). Illus. Series: Hello U.S.A. 1992, Lerner LB $19.95 (0-8225-2712-X). 72pp. Time lines and simple biographies add to the appeal of this introduction to South Carolina. (Rev: BL 5/15/92; SLJ 10/92) [975.2]

**13483** George, Jean Craighead. *Everglades* (2–4). Illus. by Wendell Minor. 1995, HarperCollins LB $15.89 (0-06-021229-2). 32pp. A storyteller explains to 5 children the origins and characteristics of the Everglades and the destruction that humans have caused to this ecosystem. (Rev: BCCB 7–8/95; BL 6/1–15/95; SLJ 6/95*) [975.9]

**13484** Gravelle, Karen. *Growing Up in a Holler in the Mountains: An Appalachian Childhood* (4–6). Illus. Series: Growing Up in America. 1997, Watts $24.00 (0-531-11452-X). 64pp. This account focuses on the unique aspects of growing up in the Appalachian mountains by focusing on the childhood of Joseph Ratliff in Kentucky. (Rev: BL 1/1–15/98; SLJ 3/98) [974]

**13485** Herda, D. J. *Environmental America: The South Central States* (4–7). Illus. Series: American Scene. 1991, Millbrook LB $22.40 (1-878841-09-2). 64pp. This account discusses the general state of the environment and presents information on animal species, pollution, waste, and urban sprawl for 10 states, including Georgia, Kansas, Missouri, and Texas. (Rev: BL 8/91; SLJ 7/91) [639.9]

**13486** Johnston, Joyce. *Maryland* (3–6). Illus. Series: Hello U.S.A. 1992, Lerner LB $19.93 (0-8225-2713-8). 72pp. In this overview on Maryland, there are chapters on history and geography, as well as social and economic conditions. (Rev: BL 5/15/92; SLJ 10/92) [975]

**13487** Kent, Deborah. *Maryland* (4–6). Illus. Series: America the Beautiful. 1990, Children's LB $28.00 (0-516-00466-2). 144pp. Special features of this look at Maryland include an outline chronology of the state's history and brief biographies of important citizens. (Rev: BL 7/90) [975]

**13488** Kent, Deborah. *South Carolina* (5–7). Illus. Series: America the Beautiful. 1989, Children's LB $28.00 (0-516-00486-7). 144pp. The state of South

Carolina is introduced with material on government, history, geography, and life today. (Rev: BL 1/1/90) [975.7]

**13489** Krull, Kathleen. *Bridges to Change: How Kids Live on a South Carolina Sea Island* (3–5). Photos by David Hautzig. Series: A World of My Own. 1995, Dutton paper $15.99 (0-525-67441-1). 46pp. The daily life of 2 African American children, their families, and local history as experienced on St. Helena, a beautiful island off the coast of South Carolina. (Rev: BCCB 2/95; BL 2/15/95; SLJ 3/95) [975.7]

**13490** LaDoux, Rita C. *Georgia* (3–6). Illus. Series: Hello U.S.A. 1991, Lerner LB $19.93 (0-8225-2703-0). 72pp. Geography, economics, history, and the environment are some of the topics covered in this look at a southern state. (Rev: BL 4/15/91; SLJ 6/91) [975.8]

**13491** LaDoux, Rita C. *Louisiana* (3–6). Illus. Series: Hello U.S.A. 1993, Lerner LB $19.93 (0-8225-2740-5). 72pp. An introduction to Louisiana with data on famous native sons and daughters. (Rev: BL 7/93) [976]

**13492** LeVert, Suzanne. *Louisiana* (4–8). Illus. Series: Celebrate the States. 1997, Marshall Cavendish LB $32.79 (0-7614-0112-1). 144pp. The unique aspects of life in this southern state are stressed in this introduction that also covers standard background material. (Rev: BL 7/97; SLJ 7/97) [976.3]

**13493** Loewen, Nancy. *Atlanta* (3–6). Illus. Series: Great Cities of the U.S.A. 1989, Rourke LB $23.93 (0-86592-543-7). 48pp. The history of Georgia's capital is given plus material on sights, climate, and people. (Rev: BL 1/1/90) [917]

**13494** Lourie, Peter. *Everglades: Buffalo Tiger and the River of Grass* (4–7). Illus. 1994, Boyds Mills $17.95 (1-878093-91-6). 47pp. An Indian guide points out the sights in the Everglades and explains what the area means to his people. (Rev: BCCB 10/94; BL 12/1/94*; SLJ 10/94) [574.5]

**13495** Lynch, Amy. *Nashville* (3–5). Illus. Series: Downtown America. 1990, Macmillan LB $13.95 (0-87518-453-7). 60pp. The sights and people of the nation's country music capital are introduced. (Rev: BL 2/1/91) [976.8]

**13496** McNair, Sylvia. *Tennessee* (4–6). Illus. Series: America the Beautiful. 1990, Children's LB $28.00 (0-516-00488-3). 144pp. Topics such as government and industry are covered in this introduction to Tennessee. (Rev: BL 7/90) [975]

**13497** McNair, Sylvia. *Virginia* (4–6). Illus. Series: America the Beautiful. 1989, Children's LB $28.00 (0-516-00492-1). 144pp. Such topics as history, geography, and culture are covered in this introduction to the state. (Rev: BL 7/89) [975.5]

**13498** Morgan, Cheryl Koenig. *The Everglades* (3–5). Illus. 1990, Troll paper $3.95 (0-8167-1734-6). 32pp. A description of the everglades with emphasis on ecology. (Rev: SLJ 8/90) [975.9]

**13499** Nichols, Joan Kane. *New Orleans* (3–5). Illus. Series: Downtown America. 1989, Macmillan LB $13.95 (0-87518-403-0). 64pp. History, neighborhoods, and unique features of New Orleans are covered. (Rev: BL 8/89; SLJ 1/90) [976.3]

**13500** Petersen, David. *Great Smoky Mountains National Park* (1–3). Illus. Series: New True Books. 1993, Children's LB $21.00 (0-516-01332-7). 48pp. This national park in the Great Smokies is introduced, along with special sights. (Rev: BL 8/93) [976.8]

**13501** Ready, Anna. *Mississippi* (3–6). Illus. Series: Hello U.S.A. 1993, Lerner LB $19.93 (0-8225-2743-X). 72pp. Such topics as geography, culture, history, and economics are covered in this introduction. (Rev: BL 7/93) [976.2]

**13502** Reef, Catherine. *Arlington National Cemetery* (4–6). Illus. Series: Places in American History. 1991, Macmillan $14.95 (0-87518-471-5). 72pp. The history and development of this cemetery known as "America's greatest national shrine." (Rev: BL 2/15/92; SLJ 3/92) [975.5]

**13503** Reef, Catherine. *Monticello* (4–6). Illus. Series: Places in American History. 1991, Macmillan LB $14.95 (0-87518-472-3). 72pp. Through pictures and text, the fascinating home of President Thomas Jefferson is introduced. (Rev: BL 2/15/92) [973.4]

**13504** Reef, Catherine. *Mount Vernon* (4–6). Illus. Series: Places in American History. 1992, Macmillan LB $14.95 (0-87518-474-X). 72pp. This account not only introduces the home of this first president, but also tells about the life of George Washington. (Rev: BL 9/1/92) [973]

**13505** Richards, Norman. *Monticello*. Rev. ed. (2–5). Illus. Series: Cornerstones of Freedom. 1995, Children's LB $19.50 (0-516-06695-1). 30pp. The construction and furnishing of Monticello are described, as well as their relation to events in Jefferson's life. (Rev: SLJ 9/95) [917.5]

**13506** Schulz, Andrea. *North Carolina* (3–6). Illus. Series: Hello USA. 1994, Lerner LB $19.95 (0-8225-2744-8). 72pp. A colorful introduction to North Carolina's history, geography, landmarks, and lifestyles. (Rev: BL 2/1/94) [975.6]

**13507** Sirvaitis, Karen. *Florida* (3–5). Illus. Series: Hello USA. 1994, Lerner LB $19.93 (0-8225-2728-6). 72pp. With photos on every page, this compact book contains basic background information about Florida, including its history, famous sights, and important residents. (Rev: BL 4/15/94) [973]

**13508**   Sirvaitis, Karen. *Tennessee* (3–6). Illus. Series: Hello U.S.A. 1991, Lerner LB $19.95 (0-8225-2711-1). 72pp. This book covers the geography, history, and socioeconomic conditions, along with time lines and biographies of famous residents. (Rev: BL 12/1/91) [976.8]

**13509**   Sirvaitis, Karen. *Virginia* (3–6). Illus. Series: Hello U.S.A. 1991, Lerner LB $19.95 (0-8225-2702-2). 72pp. With full-color photos, this is a good, fact-filled introduction to Virginia. (Rev: BL 4/15/91; SLJ 6/91) [975.5]

**13510**   Smith, Adam, and Katherine S. Smith. *A Historical Album of Kentucky* (4–7). Illus. Series: Historical Album. 1995, Millbrook LB $23.40 (1-56294-507-6). 64pp. A clear, lavishly illustrated account of Kentucky's history from prehistory to the present, with accompanying fact sheets and a rundown on state symbols. (Rev: SLJ 6/95) [976.9]

**13511**   Snow, Pegeen. *Atlanta* (3–6). Illus. 1989, Macmillan LB $13.95 (0-87518-389-1). 60pp. History and modern life in this growing southern city. (Rev: BL 3/15/89; SLJ 5/89)

**13512**   Stein, R. Conrad. *West Virginia* (4–6). Illus. Series: America the Beautiful. 1990, Children's LB $28.00 (0-516-00494-8). 144pp. The small state of West Virginia is introduced with coverage on government, history, economy, and geography. (Rev: BL 1/1/91) [975.4]

**13513**   Wade, Linda R. *St. Augustine: America's Oldest City* (3–5). Illus. Series: Doors to America's Past. 1991, Rourke LB $22.60 (0-86592-468-6). 48pp. This book traces the history of St. Augustine, Florida, to the present. (Rev: BL 5/1/92; SLJ 1/92) [975.9]

**13514**   Wills, Charles A. *Alabama* (4–7). Illus. Series: Historical Albums. 1995, Millbrook LB $23.40 (1-56294-591-2). 64pp. Using many period paintings and engravings, this account traces the history of Alabama from prehistoric days to today, with a special section on important facts. (Rev: BL 12/15/95; SLJ 1/96) [976.1]

**13515**   Wills, Charles A. *A Historical Album of Florida* (4–8). Illus. Series: Historical Albums. 1994, Millbrook LB $23.40 (1-56294-480-0). 64pp. This compressed history of Florida deals with major events from prehistory through the 1990s. (Rev: SLJ 2/95) [975.9]

**13516**   Wills, Charles A. *A Historical Album of Georgia* (4–7). Illus. Series: Historical Albums. 1996, Millbrook LB $23.40 (0-7613-0035-X); paper $7.95 (0-7613-0125-9). 64pp. With many period illustrations, some in color, and a simple text, the history and geography of Georgia are presented. (Rev: BL 12/15/96) [975.8]

## SOUTHWEST

**13517**   Anderson, Joan. *Cowboys* (4–6). Illus. by George Ancona. 1996, Scholastic $16.95 (0-590-48424-9). 48pp. All of the Eby family, including their young sons and hired cowboys, work during the spring roundup. (Rev: BL 3/15/96*; HB 5–6/96; SLJ 3/96*) [978]

**13518**   Aylesworth, Thomas G., and Virginia L. Aylesworth. *The Southwest: Colorado, New Mexico, Texas* (3–6). Illus. 1995, Chelsea LB $19.95 (0-7910-3412-7); paper $8.95 (0-7910-3430-5). 64pp. An easy-to-use study of 3 southwestern states. (Rev: BL 8/88; SLJ 11/88)

**13519**   Bredeson, Carmen. *The Spindletop Gusher: The Story of the Texas Oil Boom* (4–7). Illus. Series: Spotlight on American History. 1996, Millbrook LB $21.90 (1-56294-916-0). 64pp. A discussion of the Texas oil boom, its effects on the state and its economy, and the present status of the oil industry. (Rev: BL 3/15/96) [338.4]

**13520**   Bredeson, Carmen. *Texas* (4–8). Illus. Series: Celebrate the States. 1996, Marshall Cavendish LB $32.79 (0-7614-0109-1). 144pp. Basic information about Texas is presented in an attractive format with many color photos, maps, and diagrams. (Rev: BL 2/15/97) [976.4]

**13521**   Doherty, Craig A., and Katherine M. Doherty. *The Houston Astrodome* (4–7). Illus. Series: Building America. 1996, Blackbirch LB $15.95 (1-56711-113-0). 48pp. Both building enthusiasts and sports fans will be interested in this account of the Astrodome, its construction, and its maintenance problems. (Rev: BL 2/15/97; SLJ 2/97) [725]

**13522**   Early, Theresa S. *New Mexico* (3–6). Illus. Series: Hello U.S.A. 1993, Lerner LB $19.95 (0-8225-2748-0). 72pp. An introduction to New Mexico that includes geography, history, and social and economic conditions. (Rev: BL 7/93; SLJ 8/93) [978.9]

**13523**   Fradin, Dennis B. *Arizona* (3–5). Illus. Series: From Sea to Shining Sea. 1993, Children's LB $26.00 (0-516-03803-6). 64pp. This account takes the reader on a trip around Arizona, as well as covering its basic history and geography. (Rev: BL 11/1/93; SLJ 1/94) [979.1]

**13524**   Fradin, Dennis B. *Texas* (3–5). Illus. Series: From Sea to Shining Sea. 1992, Children's LB $26.00 (0-516-03843-5). 64pp. A chronology of Texas history and a state map are included in this account. (Rev: BL 2/1/93; SLJ 4/93) [976.4]

**13525**   Fradin, Dennis B., and Judith B. Fradin. *Wyoming* (3–5). Illus. Series: From Sea to Shining Sea. 1994, Children's LB $26.00 (0-516-03850-8). 64pp. An attractive presentation of the geography, history, and people of Wyoming, with maps, glossary, reference section, and thorough index. (Rev: BL 8/94) [978.7]

**13526** Fradin, Judith B., and Dennis B. Fradin. *New Mexico* (3–5). Illus. Series: From Sea to Shining Sea. 1993, Children's LB $26.00 (0-516-03831-1). 64pp. Includes material on such topics as the land, people, history, important sights, and economy. (Rev: BL 11/1/93) [978.9]

**13527** Frisch, Carlienne. *Wyoming* (3–6). Illus. Series: Hello USA. 1994, Lerner LB $19.95 (0-8225-2736-7). 72pp. The famous sights and attractions of Wyoming are covered, along with its history, development, and people. (Rev: BL 4/15/94; SLJ 7/94) [978.7]

**13528** Herda, D. J. *Environmental America: The Southwestern States* (4–7). Illus. Series: American Scene. 1991, Millbrook LB $22.40 (1-878841-11-4). 64pp. This account, which discusses the state of the environment and how it can be changed for the better, covers Arizona, California, Colorado, Nevada, New Mexico, and Utah. (Rev: BL 8/91; SLJ 7/91) [639.9]

**13529** Herda, D. J. *Ethnic America: The Southwestern States* (5–7). Illus. Series: American Scene. 1991, Millbrook LB $22.40 (1-56294-019-8). 64pp. The waves of immigration, including Hispanic, into the southwestern states, including California and Hawaii, are covered in text and many excellent photos. (Rev: BL 2/1/92; SLJ 3/92) [572.973]

**13530** Lee, Sally. *San Antonio* (4–7). Illus. Series: Downtown America. 1992, Macmillan LB $13.95 (0-87518-510-X). 63pp. This introduction to San Antonio covers history, people, festivals, and interesting landmarks like the Alamo, the river walk, and Spanish missions. (Rev: BL 4/15/92; SLJ 5/92) [976]

**13531** Peifer, Charles. *Houston* (3–5). Illus. 1988, Macmillan $13.95 (0-87518-387-5). 60pp. A look at life in this big Texas city. (Rev: BL 1/15/89; SLJ 5/89)

**13532** Rawlins, Carol. *Grand Canyon* (4–8). Illus.

Series: Wonders of the World. 1995, Raintree Steck-Vaughn LB $25.64 (0-8114-6364-8). 64pp. An overview of the Grand Canyon, with good maps and illustrations, that describes how it was formed, its ecosystem, its national-park status, and conservation efforts. (Rev: SLJ 8/95) [978.8]

**13533** Silverstein, Herma. *The Alamo* (4–6). Illus. Series: Places in American History. 1992, Macmillan LB $14.95 (0-87518-502-9). 72pp. A visual and narrative introduction to the historical site in San Antonio that was besieged by Mexican forces. (Rev: BL 9/1/92; SLJ 8/92) [976]

**13534** Stein, R. Conrad. *Texas* (4–6). Illus. Series: America the Beautiful. 1989, Children's LB $28.00 (0-516-00489-1). 144pp. Covers geography, economy, history, famous residents, and historical sites. (Rev: BL 7/89) [976.4]

**13535** Stewart, Gail B. *Houston* (3–6). Illus. Series: Great Cities of the U.S.A. 1989, Rourke LB $23.93 (0-86592-539-9). 48pp. Named after Sam Houston, this Texas city is introduced through text and pictures. (Rev: BL 1/1/90) [917]

**13536** Turner, Robyn Montana. *Texas Traditions: The Culture of the Lone Star State* (4–8). Illus. 1996, Little, Brown $19.95 (0-316-85675-4); paper $12.95 (0-316-85639-8). 96pp. Cultural and historical traditions unique to Texas are covered, with many illustrations. (Rev: BL 7/96; SLJ 4/97) [976.4]

**13537** Tweit, Susan J. *Meet the Wild Southwest: Land of Hoodoos and Gila Monsters* (4–8). Illus. 1996, Alaska Northwest paper $14.95 (0-88240-468-7). 124pp. An impressive collection of facts and curiosities about the natural history of our Southwest, with many appendixes that supply more-traditional information. (Rev: BL 3/1/96) [508.79]

**13538** Wills, Charles A. *A Historical Album of Texas* (4–7). Illus. Series: Historical Album. 1995, Millbrook LB $23.40 (1-56294-504-1). 64pp. This account of the history of Texas from earliest times to today is also particularly noteworthy for its many illustrations. (Rev: SLJ 6/95) [976.4]

# Social Institutions and Issues

# Business and Economics

## General

**13539** Berger, Melvin, and Gilda Berger. *Round and Round the Money Goes: What Money Is and How We Use It* (1–3). Illus. by Jane McCreary. Series: Discovery Readers. 1993, Ideals LB $12.00 (0-8249-8640-7); paper $4.50 (0-8249-8598-2). 48pp. Many topics about money are briefly introduced in this beginner's account, including the forms money takes, why it is necessary, world monetary units, and how banks work. (Rev: SLJ 12/93) [332]

**13540** Burns, Peggy. *The Mail* (3–5). Illus. Series: Stepping Through History. 1995, Thomson Learning LB $22.83 (1-56847-249-8). 32pp. A broad history of mail service, beginning with the ancient Persians and including material on today's computerized mail sorting and the hobby of stamp collecting. (Rev: BL 4/15/95; SLJ 6/95) [383]

**13541** Burns, Peggy. *Money* (3–5). Illus. Series: Stepping Through History. 1995, Thomson Learning LB $22.83 (1-56847-248-X). 32pp. As well as a history of coins and paper money, this account tells of the development of banks, credit cards, and foreign exchange. (Rev: BL 4/15/95; SLJ 6/95) [332.4]

**13542** Cribb, Joe. *Money* (4–8). Illus. Series: Eyewitness Books. 1990, Knopf LB $20.99 (0-679-90438-7). 64pp. A history of currency is given including today's credit card. (Rev: SLJ 9/90) [332.4]

**13543** Maestro, Betsy. *The Story of Money* (2–4). Illus. by Giulio Maestro. 1993, Houghton $17.00 (0-395-56242-2). 48pp. The story of the ancient Sumerians who invented the idea of making money. (Rev: BCCB 3/93; BL 3/1/93; SLJ 4/93) [332.4]

**13544** Otfinoski, Steven. *Kid's Guide to Money: Earning It, Saving It, Spending It, Growing It, Shar-*

*ing It* (4–7). Illus. 1996, Scholastic $12.95 (0-590-53850-0). 128pp. Practical tips on how to manage money, with special coverage on how to earn it. (Rev: BCCB 4/96; BL 4/1/96; SLJ 6/96) [332.4]

**13545** Parker, Nancy W. *Money, Money, Money* (3–6). Illus. 1995, HarperCollins LB $15.89 (0-06-023412-1). 32pp. An explanation of what is on the front and back of our paper currency from $1 to $100,000, with interesting facts about the presidents pictured. (Rev: BCCB 7–8/95; BL 6/1–15/95*; SLJ 6/95) [769.5]

**13546** *Sold! The Origins of Money and Trade* (5–8). Illus. Series: Buried Worlds. 1994, Runestone LB $23.93 (0-8225-3206-9). 64pp. Explains the world origins of commerce and money, with coverage on how the earliest coins were made in the West and how other cultures developed unique forms of currency. (Rev: BL 9/15/94; SLJ 9/94) [737.4]

**13547** Stine, Jane, and Jovial Bob Stine. *Everything You Need to Survive: Money Problems* (5–8). Illus. by Sal Murdocca. 1983, Random paper $1.95 (0-394-85247-8). 96pp. An amusing and fact-filled guide to managing money.

## Consumerism

**13548** Bendick, Jeanne, and Robert Bendick. *Markets: From Barter to Bar Codes* (3–5). Illus. 1997, Watts LB $21.00 (0-531-20263-1). 64pp. Illustrates the history of trade in the Western world by viewing a number of different markets. (Rev: BL 9/1/97; SLJ 1/98) [380.1]

**13549** Burns, Peggy. *Stores and Markets* (3–5). Illus. Series: Stepping Through History. 1995, Thomson Learning LB $22.83 (1-56847-344-3). 32pp. A history of the distribution of goods from ancient markets and bazaars to today's shopping malls. (Rev: BL 7/95) [381]

**13550** Dunn, John. *Advertising* (5–8). Illus. Series: Overview. 1997, Lucent LB $22.45 (1-56006-182-0). 112pp. As well as a history of advertising, this well-organized book tells about present practices, markets, and media. (Rev: BL 5/15/97; SLJ 7/97) [659.1]

**13551** Miller, Marilyn. *Behind the Scenes at the Shopping Mall* (PS–3). Illus. Series: Behind the Scenes. 1996, Raintree Steck-Vaughn LB $21.40 (0-8172-4088-8). 32pp. Using many leading questions and cartoon–style illustrations, this book provides an inside look at the activities that make a shopping mall work. (Rev: BL 4/15/96; SLJ 12/96) [381]

**13552** Schmitt, Lois. *Smart Spending: A Consumer's Guide* (5–8). 1989, Macmillan $13.95 (0-684-19035-4). 112pp. A no-nonsense text incorporating teen-oriented case studies. (Rev: BL 5/1/89)

**13553** Sullivan, George. *How Do They Package It?* (5–7). Illus. 1976, Westminster $8.00 (0-664-32601-3). 144pp. The history and contemporary use of packaging, which also touches on allied facets of conservation and pollution.

**13554** Yardley, Thompson. *Buy Now, Pay Later: Smart Shopping Counts* (2–3). Illus. by author. Series: Lighter Look. 1992, Millbrook LB $20.90 (1-56294-149-6). 39pp. In an entertaining format, facts about smart shopping and recycling are given. (Rev: SLJ 6/92) [640.73]

## Money-Making Ideas

**13555** Barkin, Carol, and Elizabeth James. *Jobs for Kids: The Guide to Having Fun and Making Money* (5–8). Illus. by Roy Doty. 1990, Lothrop LB $11.93 (0-688-09324-8); Morrow paper $6.95 (0-688-09323-X). 113pp. Describes all sorts of jobs suitable for young people. (Rev: SLJ 10/90) [658.1]

**13556** Barkin, Carol, and Elizabeth James. *The New Complete Babysitter's Handbook* (5–7). Illus. 1995, Clarion $16.95 (0-395-66557-4); paper $7.95 (0-395-66558-2). 164pp. A fine manual that covers such topics as first aid, ways to amuse children, and how to get jobs baby-sitting. (Rev: BL 5/1/95; SLJ 6/95) [649.1]

**13557** Bernstein, Daryl. *Better Than a Lemonade Stand! Small Business Ideas for Kids* (4–8). Illus. by Rob Husberg. 1992, Beyond Words paper $7.95 (0-941831-75-2). 170pp. How to start 51 small businesses is the focus of this book by a 15-year-old entrepreneur. (Rev: BL 10/1/92; SLJ 1/93) [650.1]

**13558** Byers, Patricia, and Julia Preston. *The Kids' Money Book* (2–6). Illus. 1983, Liberty paper $4.95 (0-89709-041-1). A number of ways kids can make money.

**13559** Drew, Bonnie, and Noel Drew. *Fast Cash for Kids* (4–7). Illus. 1995, Career Pr. paper $13.99 (1-564-14154-3). 168pp. Many ideas for ways of making money. (Rev: BL 6/15/87)

**13560** Wilkinson, Elizabeth. *Making Cents: Every Kid's Guide to Money* (3–7). Illus. by Martha Weston. 1989, Little, Brown paper $12.95 (0-316-94102-6). 128pp. Many money-making ideas and basic advice on business practices and managing money. (Rev: BL 1/15/90; SLJ 1/90) [332]

**13561** Zakarin, Debra M. *The Ultimate Baby-Sitter's Handbook: So You Wanna Make Tons of Money?* (4–8). Illus. 1997, Price Stern Sloan paper $4.95 (0-8431-7936-8). 128pp. A practical, easily read guide to baby-sitting and setting up a business. (Rev: BL 9/15/97; SLJ 12/97) [649]

## Retail Stores and Other Workplaces

**13562** Jaspersohn, William. *Cookies* (4–6). Illus. 1993, Macmillan LB $14.95 (0-02-747822-X). 48pp. A photoessay that uses a Famous Amos cookie factory in Georgia. (Rev: BCCB 4/93; BL 3/1/93; SLJ 5/93) [664]

**13563** Vaughan, Jenny. *Bank* (3–5). Illus. Series: World at Work. 1989, Silver Burdett $11.96 (0-382-09717-3). 48pp. The day-to-day activities in a bank are covered as well as the different kinds of accounts and how computers are used to help operations. (Rev: SLJ 11/89) [332.1]

**13564** Waters, Alice, et al. *Fanny at Chez Panisse* (4–6). Illus. by Ann Arnold. 1992, HarperCollins $23.00 (0-06-016896-X). 134pp. Young Fanny tells of life in her mother's popular restaurant. (Rev: BL 2/1/93) [647]

# Ecology and Environment

## General

**13565** Aylesworth, Thomas G. *Government and the Environment: Tracking the Record* (5–8). Illus. Series: Better Earth. 1993, Enslow LB $19.95 (0-89490-398-5). 104pp. This book traces the state of the environment and the involvement of the government in its protection. (Rev: BL 8/93) [363.7]

**13566** Butterfield, Moira. *Richard Orr's Nature Cross-Sections* (4–6). Illus. by Richard Orr. 1995, DK Publg. $17.95 (0-7894-0147-9). 30pp. Includes cross-sections of ecosystems, such as a rainforest, and structures, such as a beehive. (Rev: BL 12/1/95; SLJ 1/96) [574.5]

**13567** Chandler, Gary, and Kevin Graham. *Kids Who Make a Difference* (4–8). Illus. Series: Making a Better World. 1996, Twenty-First Century LB $16.98 (0-8050-4625-9). 64pp. Describes various community projects in which young people have played a significant role. (Rev: BL 12/1/96; SLJ 4/97) [363.7]

**13568** Crenson, Victoria. *Bay Shore Park: The Death and Life of an Amusement Park* (3–5). Illus. 1995, W. H. Freeman $13.60 (0-7167-6580-2). 32pp. This fascinating nature book describes how nature gradually reclaimed the area after an amusement park on upper Chesapeake Bay was closed. (Rev: BL 7/95; SLJ 8/95) [752]

**13569** Flatt, Lizann. *My First Nature Treasury* (K–3). Illus. by Allan Cormack. 1995, Sierra Club $12.95 (0-87156-362-2). 48pp. A large-format introduction to biomes, food chains, the classification of animals and plants, and other basic natural-history information. (Rev: BL 6/1–15/95) [508]

**13570** Greene, Carol. *Caring for Our Land* (1–3). Illus. Series: Caring for Our Earth. 1991, Enslow LB $13.95 (0-89490-354-3). 32pp. The concepts of land use and abuse are simply introduced. (Rev: BL 2/15/92; SLJ 5/92) [333.75]

**13571** Hill, Lee S. *Parks Are to Share* (1–3). Series: Building Blocks Books. 1997, Carolrhoda $14.95 (1-57505-068-4). 32pp. This book explores all kinds of parks and their care and uses, from Yosemite National Park to Central Park in New York City. (Rev: BL 3/15/98) [363.6]

**13572** Holmes, Anita. *I Can Save the Earth: A Kid's Handbook for Keeping Earth Healthy and Green* (4–6). Illus. by David Neuhaus. 1993, Simon & Schuster LB $12.95 (0-671-74544-1); paper $7.95 (0-671-74545-X). 96pp. A practical guide that offers many suggestions on ways for young people to actively help in conservation. (Rev: SLJ 7/93) [320.5]

**13573** Javna, John. *50 Simple Things Kids Can Do to Save the Earth* (3–6). Illus. by Michele Montez. 1990, Andrews & McMeel paper $6.95 (0-8362-2301-2). 156pp. This book shows how small changes can help to save the environment. (Rev: BL 6/15/90; SLJ 9/90) [333.7]

**13574** Kerrod, Robin. *The Environment* (4–6). Illus. by Ted Evans. Series: Let's Investigate Science. 1994, Marshall Cavendish LB $25.64 (1-85435-625-9). 64pp. After a discussion of the natural changes that the earth is constantly undergoing, this book describes how such phenomena as farming, mining, pollution, and deforestation are affecting the environment. (Rev: SLJ 4/94) [574.5]

**13575** Landau, Elaine. *Environmental Groups: The Earth Savers* (5–8). Illus. Series: Better Earth. 1993, Enslow LB $19.95 (0-89490-396-9). 112pp. A fine rundown on various governmental groups involved in the environment. (Rev: BL 8/93) [363.7]

**13576** Levine, Shar, and Allison Grafton. *Projects for a Healthy Planet: Simple Environmental Experi-*

*ments for Kids* (3–7). Illus. by Terry Chui. 1992, Wiley paper $10.95 (0-471-55484-7). 64pp. A worthy addition to the many ecology books on the market. (Rev: BL 8/92; SLJ 8/92) [628]

**13577** Lowery, Linda, and Marybeth Lorbiecki. *Earthwise at Home* (3–5). Illus. by David Mataya. 1993, Carolrhoda LB $19.93 (0-87614-730-9). 48pp. This book gives tips on how to recycle, reuse, and preserve materials at home. Others in this series are: *Earthwise at Play* and *Earthwise at School* (both 1993). (Rev: SLJ 5/93) [320]

**13578** Mattson, Mark. *Scholastic Environmental Atlas of the United States* (3–6). Illus. 1993, Scholastic $14.95 (0-590-49354-X). 80pp. In this atlas, natural resources and ecological threats like water pollution and toxic dumps are pictured globally. (Rev: BL 10/15/93; SLJ 4/94) [333.7]

**13579** Parker, Philip. *Your Living Home* (4–6). Illus. Series: Project Eco-City. 1994, Thomson Learning LB $24.26 (1-56847-246-3). 48pp. A study of the various living things, including bacteria, that live in and around one's home. (Rev: BL 3/15/95) [574.5]

**13580** Parker, Philip. *Your Wild Neighborhood* (4–6). Illus. Series: Project Eco-City. 1994, Thomson Learning LB $24.26 (1-56847-247-1). 48pp. Common birds, other animals, and plants that live in a typical neighborhood are introduced. (Rev: BL 3/15/95) [574.5]

**13581** Pringle, Laurence. *Fire in the Forest: A Cycle of Growth and Renewal* (4–6). Illus. by Bob Marstall. 1995, Simon & Schuster paper $16.00 (0-689-80394-X). 32pp. Discusses the effects of forest fires and the cycle of renewal involving plants and animals that follows. (Rev: BL 12/1/95; SLJ 12/95) [574.5]

**13582** Reed, Catherine. *Environment* (4–6). Illus. Series: Science Fair. 1992, Rourke LB $22.60 (0-86625-431-5). 48pp. This book explains the scope and process of doing science fair projects involving ecology and the environment. (Rev: BL 2/15/93) [574.5]

**13583** Reed-Jones, Carol. *The Tree in the Ancient Forest* (K–3). Illus. by Christopher Canyon. 1995, Dawn $16.95 (1-883220-32-7); paper $7.95 (1-883220-31-9). 32pp. The food cycle of interdependence that involves both plants and animals and a 300-year-old fir tree is the subject of this stunning picture book. (Rev: BL 7/95; SLJ 9/95) [574]

**13584** Scott, Michael. *Ecology* (5–8). Illus. Series: Young Oxford. 1996, Oxford LB $27.00 (0-19-521166-9). 166pp. An attractive introduction to the world of ecology, adaptation, conservation, and species diversity. (Rev: BL 3/1/96; SLJ 3/96) [574.5]

**13585** Seibert, Patricia. *Toad Overload: A True Tale of Nature Knocked Off Balance in Australia* (K–3). Illus. by Jan Davey Ellis. 1996, Millbrook LB $21.90

(1-56294-613-7). 32pp. The balance of nature in Australia is upset when large toads are imported to eat marauding beetles. (Rev: BCCB 2/96; BL 2/15/96; SLJ 4/96) [597.8]

**13586** Simon, Seymour. *Earth Words: A Dictionary of the Environment* (3–5). Illus. 1995, HarperCollins LB $15.89 (0-06-020234-3). 48pp. This handy dictionary supplies definitions for such terms as *biome*, *food web*, *PCBs*, and *biodegradable*. (Rev: BL 4/15/95) [363]

**13587** VanCleave, Janice. *Janice VanCleave's Ecology for Every Kid* (4–7). Illus. 1996, Wiley paper $10.95 (0-471-10086-2). 240pp. Clear instructions and many diagrams introduce a series of experiments that highlight environmental issues. (Rev: BL 3/1/96; SLJ 4/96) [574.5]

**13588** Willis, Terri. *Land Use and Abuse* (5–8). Illus. Series: Saving Planet Earth. 1992, Children's LB $30.50 (0-516-05507-0). 128pp. This attractive volume describes how people have changed the land and sometimes misused it, and provides some suggestions for conservation. (Rev: BL 2/1/93) [383.73]

**13589** Yount, Lisa. *Pesticides* (5–8). Illus. Series: Overview Series. 1995, Lucent LB $22.45 (1-56006-156-1). 128pp. Pros and cons on the use of pesticides are explored, with good background information and present-day policies. (Rev: BL 6/1–15/95; SLJ 5/95) [363]

# Cities

**13590** Parker, Philip. *Global Cities* (4–6). Illus. Series: Project Eco-City. 1995, Thomson Learning LB $24.26 (1-56847-286-2). 48pp. This account concentrates on the ecology and balance of nature found in large cities. (Rev: BL 6/1–15/95) [307.76]

**13591** Parker, Philip. *Town Life* (4–6). Illus. Series: Project Eco-City. 1995, Thomson Learning LB $24.26 (1-56847-287-0). 48pp. Animal and plant life in towns and cities and their future welfare are covered. (Rev: BL 6/1–15/95) [307.76]

**13592** Sammis, Fran. *Cities and Towns* (2–5). Illus. Series: Discovering Geography. 1997, Marshall Cavendish LB $21.36 (0-7614-0540-2). 32pp. Using a question-and-answer approach, this account introduces cities and towns and outlines projects in map making, including finding houses along a newspaper route or stores in a mall. (Rev: BL 2/1/98; SLJ 4/98) [307.76]

# Garbage and Waste Recycling

**13593** Bailey, Donna. *What We Can Do About Litter* (4–6). Illus. Series: What Do We Know About . . .? 1991, Watts LB $18.70 (0-531-11016-8). 32pp. Simple writing and color photographs help to explain the problem of litter and what to do about it. (Rev: BL 2/15/92) [363.72]

**13594** Chandler, Gary, and Kevin Graham. *Recycling* (4–8). Illus. Series: Making a Better World. 1996, Twenty-First Century LB $16.98 (0-8050-4622-4). 64pp. Reports on various recycling endeavors and their beneficial results. (Rev: BL 12/1/96; SLJ 4/97) [363.73]

**13595** Coombs, Karen Mueller. *Flush! Treating Wastewater* (3–6). Illus. 1995, Carolrhoda LB $22.60 (0-87614-879-8). 56pp. A history of sanitation through the centuries is given, plus a description of present-day water purification systems. (Rev: BCCB 1/96; BL 12/1/95; SLJ 12/95) [628.3]

**13596** *50 Simple Things Kids Can Do to Recycle* (4–7). Illus. 1994, EarthWorks paper $6.95 (1-879682-00-1). 144pp. A collection of projects and activities that can help recycling efforts at home, at school, and in the community. (Rev: BL 7/94; SLJ 8/94) [363.7]

**13597** Gibbons, Gail. *Recycle! A Handbook for Kids* (PS–3). Illus. by author. 1992, Little, Brown $15.95 (0-316-30971-0). 32pp. In an appealing format, this essential information makes recycling interesting to young readers. (Rev: BL 5/15/92; HB 7–8/92; SLJ 6/92) [628.4]

**13598** Hall, Eleanor J. *Garbage* (5–8). Illus. Series: Overview. 1997, Lucent LB $22.45 (1-56006-188-X). 96pp. A history of how we have handled waste disposal, and current ecological and environmental approaches, including recycling. (Rev: BL 8/97) [363.73]

**13599** Heilman, Joan R. *Tons of Trash: Why You Should Recycle and What Happens When You Do* (3–5). 1992, Avon paper $3.50 (0-380-76379-6). 80pp. This lively tour of processing plants shows how garbage is recycled. (Rev: BL 4/15/92) [363.72]

**13600** Jacobs, Francine. *Follow That Trash! All About Recycling* (K–3). Illus. by Mavis Smith. Series: All Aboard Reading. 1996, Grosset paper $3.95 (0-448-41314-0). 47pp. Discusses landfills, garbage burning, pollution, composting, and what happens at a recycling plant. (Rev: SLJ 3/97) [628.4]

**13601** Kalbacken, Joan, and Emilie U. Lepthien. *Recycling* (2–4). Illus. Series: New True Books. 1991, Children's LB $20.00 (0-516-01118-9). 48pp. This book tells why recycling is necessary, describes

various types, and tells how effective each type is. (Rev: BL 7/91; SLJ 10/91) [363.72]

**13602** Ring, Elizabeth. *What Rot! Nature's Mighty Recycler* (3–5). Illus. 1996, Millbrook LB $23.40 (1-56294-671-4). 32pp. Numerous photos and a lively text describe how nature provides organisms and processes to decompose materials naturally. (Rev: BL 2/15/96; SLJ 4/96) [574.2]

**13603** Seltzer, Meyer. *Here Comes the Recycling Truck!* (PS–3). Illus. 1992, Whitman LB $14.95 (0-8075-3235-5). 32pp. Follow the garbage truck — not to the dump, but to the recycling center! (Rev: BL 5/1/92; SLJ 5/92) [363.7]

**13604** Snodgrass, Mary Ellen. *Solid Waste* (4–6). Illus. Series: Environmental Awareness. 1991, Bancroft-Sage LB $14.95 (0-944280-28-5). 48pp. The techniques and problems of waste removal and recycling, with many color illustrations. Also use: *Water Pollution* (1991). (Rev: BL 2/15/92) [363.73]

**13605** Stwertka, Eve, and Albert Stwertka. *Cleaning Up: How Trash Becomes Treasure* (3–5). Illus. by Mena Dolobowsky. Series: At Home with Science. 1993, Simon & Schuster paper $5.95 (0-671-69467-7). 40pp. This history of waste recycling includes material on current methods. (Rev: SLJ 8/93) [363.7]

**13606** Tesar, Jenny. *The Waste Crisis* (5–8). Illus. 1991, Facts on File $19.95 (0-8160-2491-X). 112pp. This well-illustrated account describes types of waste, the current crisis in disposal, and possible solutions. (Rev: BL 11/15/91) [363.72]

**13607** Wilcox, Charlotte. *Trash!* (3–5). Illus. 1988, Carolrhoda LB $16.95 (0-87614-311-7); Lerner paper $5.95 (0-87614-511-X). 40pp. What happens to garbage after it's collected. (Rev: BL 12/1/88; HB 1–2/89; SLJ 1/89)

# Pollution

**13608** Anderson, Madelyn K. *Oil Spills* (4–8). Illus. Series: First Books. 1991, Watts LB $21.00 (0-531-10872-4). 63pp. Presents the history, uses, and production of oil, and describes the causes and effects of oil spills. (Rev: SLJ 3/91) [363.7]

**13609** Bailey, Donna. *What We Can Do About Noise and Fumes* (4–6). Illus. Series: What Do We Know About . . .? 1992, Watts LB $18.70 (0-531-11018-4). 30pp. The causes and levels of air and noise pollution are discussed. (Rev: BL 5/15/92) [363.7]

**13610** Baines, John. *Protecting the Oceans* (3–6). Illus. Series: Conserving Our World. 1991, Raintree Steck-Vaughn ₊ LB $24.26 (0-8114-2391-3). 48pp. This account explores ocean pollution in a simple text and many illustrations and maps. (Rev: BL 6/1/91) [333.91]

**13611** Bang, Molly. *Chattanooga Sludge* (2–5). Illus. 1996, Harcourt $16.00 (0-15-216345-X). 48pp. A scientist is determined to clean up the industrial sludge that has polluted Chattanooga Creek. (Rev: BCCB 4/96; BL 5/1/96; SLJ 8/96*) [628.4]

**13612** Berger, Melvin. *Oil Spill!* (K–3). Illus. by Paul Mirocha. 1994, HarperCollins paper $4.95 (0-06-445121-6). 32pp. After a description of the *Exxon Valdez* catastrophe, general material on oil spills is presented, including their causes, effects, and how they can be prevented. (Rev: BL 6/1–15/94) [363.73]

**13613** Blashfield, Jean F., and Wallace B. Black. *Oil Spills* (5–8). Series: Saving Planet Earth. 1991, Children's LB $30.50 (0-516-05508-9). 128pp. Beginning with the Persian Gulf oil spills, this book tells about famous oil spills, how some are inevitable, and the terrible consequences of each. (Rev: SLJ 5/92) [363.73]

**13614** Chandler, Gary, and Kevin Graham. *Protecting Our Air, Land, and Water* (4–8). Illus. Series: Making a Better World. 1996, Twenty-First Century LB $16.98 (0-8050-4624-0). 64pp. Such methods of protecting our natural resources as purifying and conserving water and reducing air pollution are described. (Rev: BL 12/15/96; SLJ 1/97) [363.7]

**13615** Cherry, Lynne. *A River Ran Wild* (1–3). Illus. 1992, Harcourt $16.00 (0-15-200542-0). 40pp. Tracing the environmental history and present status of the Nashua River, which runs through New Hampshire and Massachusetts. (Rev: BL 3/15/92; HB 5–6/92; SLJ 5/92) [974.4]

**13616** Cole, Joanna. *The Magic School Bus: At the Water Works* (2–5). Illus. by Bruce Degen. 1995, Scholastic LB $14.95 (0-614-03341-1); paper $4.95 (0-590-40360-5). 40pp. Scientific fun with Ms. Frizzle, the world's strangest teacher and an unflappable naturalist. (Rev: BL 11/15/86; SLJ 1/87)

**13617** Collinson, Alan. *Pollution* (5–8). Illus. Series: Repairing the Damage. 1992, Macmillan LB $13.95 (0-02-722995-5). 46pp. In this well-organized book, complete with many charts and diagrams, the various kinds of pollution are introduced. (Rev: BL 9/15/92) [363.73]

**13618** Cone, Molly. *Come Back, Salmon! How a Group of Dedicated Kids Adopted Pigeon Creek and Brought It Back to Life* (3–5). Illus. 1992, Sierra Club $16.95 (0-87156-572-2). 48pp. Lively text and color photos explain how Jackson Elementary School students in Everett, Washington, adopted and saved polluted Pigeon Creek. (Rev: BCCB 4/92; BL 5/1/92; HB 7–8/92; SLJ 4/92) [639.3]

**13619** Dudley, William. *The Environment: Distinguishing Between Fact and Opinion* (4–7). Illus. Series: Opposing Viewpoints Juniors. 1991, Greenwillow LB $16.20 (0-89908-603-9). 32pp. Various viewpoints are presented on topics such as whether there is an environmental crisis and how serious acid rain is. (Rev: BL 6/15/91) [363.7]

**13620** Greene, Carol. *Caring for Our Air* (1–3). Illus. Series: Caring for Our Earth. 1991, Enslow LB $13.95 (0-89490-351-9). 32pp. In simple text and black-and-white photos, the concept of air pollution is introduced and practical recommendations are suggested. (Rev: BL 2/15/92; SLJ 5/92) [363.73]

**13621** Gutnik, Martin J. *Experiments That Explore Acid Rain* (5–8). Illus. by Sharon L. Holm. Series: Investigate! 1992, Millbrook LB $21.40 (1-56294-115-1). 72pp. After an introduction to acid rain, experiments are outlined with clear instructions and simple drawings. (Rev: BL 2/1/92) [628.5]

**13622** Hoff, Mary, and Mary M. Rodgers. *Our Endangered Planet: Groundwater* (4–7). Illus. Series: Our Endangered Planet. 1991, Lerner LB $16.95 (0-8225-2500-3). 64pp. A discussion of the supply, access, uses, and pollution of groundwater around the world. (Rev: BL 6/15/91; SLJ 5/91) [333.91]

**13623** Johnson, Rebecca L. *Investigating the Ozone Hole* (5–8). Illus. 1994, Lerner LB $23.93 (0-8225-1574-1). 112pp. Using interviews, documents, and firsthand research, the author charts the development and possible consequences of an ozone hole above the Antarctic. (Rev: BL 3/1/94) [551.5]

**13624** Miles, Betty. *Save the Earth: An Action Handbook for Kids* (4–7). Illus. by Nelle Davis. 1991, Knopf paper $6.95 (0-679-81731-X). 106pp. A revised edition of a readable account that explores ecological themes. (Rev: BL 6/15/91; SLJ 7/91) [523.4]

**13625** O'Neill, Mary. *Air Scare* (4–7). Illus. by John Bindon. Series: SOS Planet Earth. 1991, Troll LB $13.50 (0-8167-2082-7); paper $3.95 (0-8167-2083-5). 32pp. An oversize book that deals with the important environmental issue of air pollution. (Rev: BL 6/15/91) [363]

**13626** Powledge, Fred. *Working River* (5–8). Illus. 1995, Farrar $15.00 (0-374-38527-0). 136pp. The history of Maryland's Patuxent river is covered, with details on its present ecosystem, pollution, and current efforts to protect it. (Rev: BCCB 7–8/95; BL 6/1–15/95; SLJ 11/95) [975]

**13627** Pringle, Laurence. *Oil Spills: Damage, Recovery, and Prevention* (3–8). Illus. 1993, Morrow LB $14.93 (0-688-09861-4). 64pp. In addition to describing the importance of petroleum, the author tells of the thousands of annual oil spills, the incredible damage they cause, and how more preventive measures must be taken. (Rev: BL 9/15/93) [363]

**13628** Pringle, Laurence. *Vanishing Ozone: Protecting Earth from Ultraviolet Radiation* (4–8). Illus. Series: Save-the-Earth Books. 1995, Morrow LB $15.93 (0-688-04158-2). 64pp. The exciting but disturbing story of the thinning ozone layer and the conflicts it is producing among governments, environmentalists, and industry. (Rev: SLJ 9/95*) [363.73]

**13629** Snodgrass, Mary Ellen. *Acid Rain* (4–6). Illus. Series: Environmental Awareness. 1991, Bancroft-Sage LB $14.95 (0-944280-30-7). 48pp. Basic, up-to-date information on acid rain. Also use: *Toxic Waste* (1991). (Rev: BL 2/15/92) [363.73]

**13630** Snodgrass, Mary Ellen. *Air Pollution* (4–6). Illus. Series: Environmental Awareness. 1991, Bancroft-Sage LB $14.95 (0-944280-31-5). 48pp. Using color photos, diagrams, and straightforward information, the problems of air pollution are introduced, along with possible solutions. Also use: *Land Pollution* (1991). (Rev: BL 2/15/92) [363.73]

**13631** Stille, Darlene R. *Air Pollution* (1–3). Illus. Series: New True Books. 1990, Children's LB $21.00 (0-516-01181-2). 48pp. Scientific facts are presented in a straightforward manner. (Rev: BL 10/1/90; SLJ 10/90) [363]

**13632** Stille, Darlene R. *The Ozone Hole* (1–3). Illus. Series: New True Books. 1991, Children's LB $21.00 (0-516-01117-0). 48pp. After a brief explanation of the ozone layer, tells how recent air pollution has changed it and how this trend can be reversed. (Rev: BL 9/1/91; SLJ 11/91) [363.73]

**13633** Stille, Darlene R. *Water Pollution* (1–3). Illus. 1990, Children's LB $21.00 (0-516-01190-1). 48pp. Full-color photos and readable text explain water pollution to the young. (Rev: BL 10/1/90; SLJ 10/90) [363.73]

**13634** Zipko, Stephen J. *Toxic Threat: How Hazardous Substances Poison Our Lives* (5–7). Illus. by Malle N. Whitaker. 1990, Simon & Schuster paper $5.95 (0-671-69331-X). 249pp. Many environmental pollutants, including radon and PCBs, are introduced. (Rev: SLJ 8/90) [363.7]

# Population

**13635** Bernards, Neal. *Population: Detecting Bias* (5–7). Illus. Series: Opposing Viewpoints Juniors. 1992, Greenhaven LB $16.20 (0-89908-622-5). 36pp. Pro and con viewpoints are presented about such topics as family planning and the problems of overpopulation. (Rev: BL 1/15/93) [304.6]

**13636** Greene, Carol. *Caring for Our People* (1–3). Illus. Series: Caring for Our Earth. 1991, Enslow LB $13.95 (0-89490-355-1). 32pp. In simple terms and many pictures, the concept and problems of human ecology are introduced and some practical solutions are given. (Rev: BL 2/15/92; SLJ 1/92) [304.2]

**13637** Winckler, Suzanne, and Mary M. Rodgers. *Our Endangered Planet: Population Growth* (4–7). Illus. Series: Our Endangered Planet. 1991, Lerner LB $22.60 (0-8225-2502-X). 64pp. A discussion of the effects that rapid population growth has had on the environment. (Rev: BL 6/15/91; SLJ 5/91) [304.6]

# Government and Politics

## Courts and the Law

**13638** Beaudry, Jo, and Lynne Ketchum. *Carla Goes to Court* (3–6). Illus. 1983, Human Sciences $16.95 (0-89885-088-6); paper $10.95 (0-89885-354-0). 32pp. The court process is explored through Carla's experience after she witnesses a burglary.

**13639** Deegan, Paul J. *Supreme Court Book* (4–6). Illus. Series: Supreme Court Justices. 1992, ABDO LB $14.98 (1-56239-097-X). 50pp. This account explains the various functions of the court and how they have changed from George Washington's time to the present. (Rev: BL 6/1–15/93) [347]

**13640** Goldish, Meish. *Our Supreme Court* (4–6). Illus. Series: I Know America. 1994, Millbrook LB $20.90 (1-56294-445-2). 48pp. An introduction to the Supreme Court that gives its history, composition, and a few historic decisions. (Rev: BL 11/15/94; SLJ 1/95) [347.73]

**13641** Stein, R. Conrad. *Powers of the Supreme Court.* Rev. ed. (3–5). Illus. Series: Cornerstones of Freedom. 1995, Children's LB $19.50 (0-516-06697-8). 30pp. The composition of the Supreme Court, as well as its powers and history, are covered through a discussion of landmark cases. (Rev: SLJ 8/95) [347]

## United Nations and International Affairs

**13642** Burger, Leslie, and Debra L. Rahm. *Red Cross/Red Crescent: When Help Can't Wait* (5–7). Illus. 1996, Lerner $22.60 (0-8225-2698-0). 80pp. The story of the Red Cross and the role it plays in

helping people today. (Rev: BL 1/1–15/97; SLJ 1/97) [361.7]

**13643** Burger, Leslie, and Debra L. Rahm. *United Nations High Commission for Refugees: Making a Difference in Our World* (5–7). Illus. 1996, Lerner LB $22.60 (0-8225-2699-9). 80pp. Describes the plight of refugees worldwide and the aid that this UN agency gives. (Rev: BL 12/15/96; SLJ 1/97) [362.87]

**13644** Rabinowitz, Richard. *What Is War? What Is Peace? Questions and Answers for Kids* (3–6). Illus. by Paul Meisel. 1991, Avon paper $2.95 (0-380-76704-X). 120pp. A book aimed at answering children's concerns about war and peace. (Rev: BL 12/15/91) [355.2]

**13645** Spies, Karen B. *Isolation vs. Intervention: Is America the World's Police Force?* (4–6). Illus. Series: Issues of Our Time. 1995, Twenty-First Century LB $18.90 (0-8050-3880-9). 64pp. Objectively presents arguments, pro and con, concerning involvement in the political and economic problems of other countries. (Rev: SLJ 2/96) [327.73]

## United States

### Civil Rights

**13646** Brill, Marlene T. *Let Women Vote!* (4–6). Illus. Series: Spotlight on American History. 1995, Millbrook LB $15.90 (0-56294-589-0). 64pp. The history of the struggle to gain the vote for U.S. women and of the key personalities involved. (Rev: BL 12/15/95; SLJ 1/96) [324.6]

**13647** Burns, Marilyn. *I Am Not a Short Adult: Getting Good at Being a Kid* (5–7). Illus. by Martha Weston. 1977, Little, Brown paper $12.95 (0-316-11746-3). Many facets of childhood are discussed, including children's legal status and institutions that affect them.

**13648** Colbert, Jan, and Ann M. Harms, eds. *Dear Dr. King: Letters from Today's Children to Dr. Martin Luther King, Jr.* (4–7). Illus. 1998, Hyperion $14.95 (0-7868-0417-3). 64pp. This is a selection of letters written by white and black Memphis school children to Dr. King telling him about themselves and how conditions have changed since his death. (Rev: BL 2/15/98) [323]

**13649** Duncan, Alice Faye. *The National Civil Rights Museum Celebrates Everyday People* (3–6). Photos by J. Gerard Smith. 1995, Troll paper $16.95 (0-8167-3502-6). 64pp. The history, purpose, and contents of the National Civil Rights Museum built on the spot where Martin Luther King, Jr. was shot. (Rev: BCCB 2/95; BL 2/15/95; SLJ 1/95) [326.1]

**13650** Farrar, Hayward. *Leaders and Movements* (4–6). Illus. Series: African American Life. 1995, Rourke LB $23.93 (1-57103-030-1). 48pp. The roles played by African Americans in the civil rights movement is covered, with profiles of key people. (Rev: SLJ 3/96) [323]

**13651** Fox, Mary V. *About Martin Luther King Day* (3–6). 1989, Enslow LB $16.95 (0-89490-200-8). 64pp. After a brief history of slavery and a look at King's accomplishments, this book tells of the struggle to make Martin Luther King Day an official holiday. (Rev: SLJ 11/89) [323.4]

**13652** Greenberg, Keith E. *Adolescent Rights: Are Young People Equal Under the Law?* (5–8). Illus. Series: Issues of Our Time. 1995, Twenty-First Century LB $18.90 (0-8050-3877-9). 64pp. This unbiased account of the controversial subject encourages readers to form their own conclusions. (Rev: SLJ 9/95) [323]

**13653** Harvey, Miles. *Women's Voting Rights* (3–5). Illus. Series: Cornerstones of Freedom. 1996, Children's LB $19.50 (0-516-20003-8). 32pp. With illustrations on each page (many in color), this account traces the history of women's suffrage and the important people who were active in the movement. (Rev: BL 12/15/96; SLJ 2/97) [324.6]

**13654** Haskins, Jim. *Bayard Rustin: Behind the Scenes of the Civil Rights Movement* (5–8). Illus. 1997, Hyperion LB $15.49 (0-7868-2140-X). 128pp. The life of the great civil rights leader and 50 years in the struggle for equality are presented in this exciting biography. (Rev: BL 2/15/97*; SLJ 4/97) [323]

**13655** Haskins, Jim. *Freedom Rides: Journey for Justice* (5–7). Illus. 1995, Hyperion LB $15.49 (0-7868-2037-3). 128pp. This account focuses on a single dramatic aspect of the civil rights movement: the integration of buses and trains. (Rev: BL 1/1/95; SLJ 4/95) [323.1]

**13656** Hirst, Mike. *Freedom of Belief* (4–8). Illus. Series: What Do We Mean by Human Rights? 1997, Watts LB $22.00 (0-531-14435-6). 48pp. An information-packed overview of religious and political freedom and the people who fought and sometimes died for it. (Rev: BL 1/1–15/98) [323.44]

**13657** Jacobs, William J. *Great Lives: Human Rights* (5–8). Illus. 1990, Macmillan $24.00 (0-684-19036-2). 272pp. Profiles of 30 historical figures "united in a commitment to individual rights." (Rev: BL 7/90) [920]

**13658** Johnston, Norma. *Remember the Ladies: The First Women's Rights Convention* (4–6). Illus. 1995, Scholastic paper $3.50 (0-590-47086-8). 169pp. The story of the 1848 Women's Rights Convention in Seneca Falls, New York, includes biographies of its leaders, like Elizabeth Cady Stanton and Lucretia Mott. (Rev: BL 5/1/95) [323.34]

**13659** Kelso, Richard. *Walking for Freedom: The Montgomery Bus Boycott* (3–5). Illus. by Michael Newton. 1993, Raintree Steck-Vaughn LB $24.26 (0-8114-7218-3). 52pp. The events and personalities associated with the Montgomery bus boycott are noted. (Rev: SLJ 8/93) [323.4]

**13660** Kent, Deborah. *The Disability Rights Movement* (3–5). Illus. Series: Cornerstones of Freedom. 1996, Children's LB $19.50 (0-516-06632-3). 32pp. The story of the growth of the movement that preserves and protects the civil rights of people with disabilities. (Rev: BL 7/96) [323.3]

**13661** King, Casey, and Linda B. Osborne. *Oh, Freedom! Kids Talk About the Civil Rights Movement with the People Who Made It Happen* (5–8). Illus. 1997, Knopf $18.00 (0-679-85856-3). 144pp. In 31 interviews, kids ask their parents and neighbors about the part each played in the civil rights movement. (Rev: BL 4/1/97; SLJ 6/97*) [973]

**13662** King, David C. *Freedom of Assembly* (4–6). Illus. Series: Land of the Free. 1997, Millbrook LB $19.90 (0-7613-0064-3). 48pp. This book covers this basic civil right and its many applications in the courts, including those involving militia movements and hate groups. Also use *The Right to Speak Out* (1997). (Rev: BL 5/15/97; SLJ 10/97) [342.73]

**13663** King, Martin Luther, Jr. *I Have a Dream* (4–8). Illus. 1997, Scholastic $16.95 (0-590-20516-1). 40pp. The full text of Dr. King's speech is reprinted, with illustrations by 15 important African American artists. (Rev: BL 2/15/98*; SLJ 11/97) [305]

**13664** Lucas, Eileen. *Civil Rights: The Long Struggle* (5–8). Illus. Series: Issues in Focus. 1996, Enslow LB $19.95 (0-89490-729-8). 112pp. After a discussion of the first 10 amendments to the U.S. Constitution, this account focuses on the civil rights struggles of African Americans. (Rev: SLJ 12/96) [323]

**13665** Lucas, Eileen. *Cracking the Wall: The Struggles of the Little Rock Nine* (3–5). Illus. 1998, Carolrhoda $18.60 (0-87614-990-5). 48pp. A simple narrative that tells of the desegregation of Central High School in Little Rock, Arkansas, and gives background information on the 1953 Supreme Court decision. (Rev: BL 2/15/98) [379.2]

**13666** McKissack, Patricia, and Fredrick McKissack. *The Civil Rights Movement in America from 1865 to the Present* (5–8). Illus. 1991, Children's LB $45.80 (0-516-00579-0). 352pp. Beginning after the Civil War, this book traces the history of civil rights in the United States. (Rev: BL 6/1/87; SLJ 8/87)

**13667** Meyers, Madeleine, ed. *Forward into Light: The Struggle for Woman's Suffrage* (4–8). Illus. Series: Perspectives on History. 1994, Discovery Enterprises paper $5.95 (1-878668-25-0). 64pp. The story of how women fought to get the vote in this country and of their most influential leaders. (Rev: BL 8/94) [324.6]

**13668** O'Neill, Laurie A. *Little Rock: The Desegregation of Central High* (4–7). Illus. Series: Spotlight on American History. 1994, Millbrook LB $21.90 (1-56294-354-5). 64pp. A moving re-creation of the painful integration of the public school in Little Rock, Arkansas, its background, and the aftermath. (Rev: BCCB 11/94; BL 10/15/94; SLJ 10/94) [373.76]

**13669** Pacoe, Elaine. *The Right to Vote* (4–6). Illus. Series: Land of the Free. 1997, Millbrook LB $19.90 (0-7613-0066-X). 48pp. Explores the principles behind the right to vote and how it was gradually awarded to all citizens. (Rev: BL 5/15/97; SLJ 5/97) [324.6]

**13670** Parks, Rosa, and Gregory J. Reed. *Dear Mrs. Parks: A Dialogue with Today's Youth* (4–6). 1996, Lee & Low $16.95 (1-880000-45-8). 112pp. A collection of letters sent to Rosa Parks and the answers this amazing civil rights leader sent back. (Rev: BL 12/1/96; SLJ 12/96) [323]

**13671** Rochelle, Belinda. *Witnesses to Freedom: Young People Who Fought for Civil Rights* (4–7). Illus. 1993, Dutton paper $15.99 (0-525-67377-6). 97pp. The story of the civil rights movement from school desegregation, through bus boycotts, voting rights struggles, and the March on Washington from the viewpoint of young participants. (Rev: BL 11/1/93; SLJ 5/94) [323.1]

**13672** Sherrow, Victoria. *Freedom of Worship* (4–6). Illus. Series: Land of the Free. 1997, Millbrook LB $19.90 (0-7613-0065-1). 48pp. As well as discussing the right to worship as one pleases, this account covers the religious right, religious intolerance, school prayer, and cults. (Rev: BL 5/15/97; SLJ 5/97) [323.44]

**13673** Shuker-Haines, Frances. *Rights and Responsibilities: Using Your Freedom* (3–6). Illus. Series: Good Citizenship. 1993, Raintree Steck-Vaughn LB $24.26 (0-8114-7355-4). 48pp. Covers such topics as the jury system, freedoms of speech and press, voting, taxes, and the juvenile-justice system. (Rev: SLJ 10/93) [323]

**13674** Sullivan, George. *The Day the Women Got the Vote: A Photo History of the Women's Rights Movement* (5–8). Illus. 1994, Scholastic paper $6.95 (0-590-47560-6). 96pp. The women's rights movement from the early suffragists to the feminist movement that started in the 1960s. (Rev: BL 6/1–15/94; SLJ 7/94) [323.34]

**13675** Tillage, Leon W. *Leon's Story* (4–8). Illus. by Susan L. Roth. 1997, Farrar $14.00 (0-374-34379-9). 112pp. An autobiographical account of growing up black and poor in the segregated South and of participating in the civil rights movement. (Rev: BL 10/1/97*; HB 11–12/97; SLJ 12/97) [975.6]

**13676** Wilson, Reginald. *Think About Our Rights: Civil Liberties and the United States* (5–8). Illus. 1991, Walker LB $15.85 (0-8027-8127-6); paper $9.95 (0-8027-7371-0). 128pp. The focus is on such civil rights questions as integration, affirmative action, and women's rights. (Rev: SLJ 1/92) [323.4]

## Constitution

**13677** Dudley, William. *The U.S. Constitution: Locating the Author's Main Idea* (4–7). Illus. Series: Opposing Viewpoints Juniors. 1991, Greenwillow LB $16.20 (0-89908-601-2). 32pp. Various viewpoints are expressed on such topics as how important the Constitution is and whether it should be revised. (Rev: BL 6/15/91) [347]

**13678** Feinberg, Barbara S. *Constitutional Amendments* (4–6). Illus. Series: Inside Government. 1996, Twenty-First Century LB $15.98 (0-8050-4619-4). 80pp. This account tells how constitutional amendments come to be and the meaning of each that is currently in effect. (Rev: BL 9/15/96; SLJ 12/96) [342.73]

**13679** Fritz, Jean. *Shh! We're Writing the Constitution* (3–5). Illus. by Tomie dePaola. 1987, Putnam paper $8.95 (0-399-21404-6). 64pp. Lots of details make it clear that writing the Constitution was no easy task. (Rev: BCCB 6–7/87; BL 6/1/87; SLJ 8/87)

**13680** Johnson, Linda C. *Our Constitution* (4–6). Illus. Series: I Know America. 1992, Millbrook LB $20.90 (1-56294-090-2). 48pp. This history of our Constitution includes an explanation of its important parts. (Rev: BL 9/1/92; SLJ 10/92) [342.73]

**13681** Levy, Elizabeth. *If You Were There When They Signed the Constitution* (2–4). Illus. 1992, Scholastic paper $5.99 (0-590-45159-6). 80pp. All about the delegates and the U.S. Constitution. (Rev: BL 9/15/87; SLJ 11/87)

**13682** Maestro, Betsy, and Giulio Maestro. *A More Perfect Union: The Story of Our Constitution* (2–4). Illus. 1987, Lothrop LB $15.93 (0-688-06840-5); Morrow paper $7.95 (0-688-10192-5). 48pp. The U.S. Constitution is explained for young readers. (Rev: BCCB 10/87; BL 9/1/87; SLJ 9/87)

**13683** Spier, Peter. *We the People: The Constitution of the United States of America* (PS–4). Illus. by author. 1991, Doubleday paper $7.95 (0-385-41903-1). 48pp. Watercolor paintings create images of "We the People." (Rev: BL 10/15/87; SLJ 10/87)

**13684** Stein, R. Conrad. *The Bill of Rights* (3–5). Illus. Series: Cornerstones of Freedom. 1992, Children's LB $19.50 (0-516-04853-8). 32pp. The story of how the various amendments known as the Bill of Rights became part of the U.S. Constitution. (Rev: BL 6/1/92) [347.73]

## Crime and Criminals

**13685** Ballinger, Erich. *Detective Dictionary: A Handbook for Aspiring Sleuths* (4–8). Illus. 1994, Lerner LB $19.93 (0-8225-0721-8). 144pp. An unusual A-to-Z book that looks at various techniques used in crime detection. (Rev: BL 9/15/94) [363.2]

**13686** Barden, Renardo. *Gangs* (5–8). Series: Facts About. 1990, Rourke LB $17.95 (0-865-93073-2). 47pp. An examination of street gangs, their composition, and their frequent links with drugs. (Rev: SLJ 2/90) [394.3]

**13687** Bowers, Vivien. *Crime Science* (3–6). Illus. 1997, Owl paper $10.95 (1-895688-69-8). 64pp. Using 3 case histories that test the reader's powers of detection, this title is a fine introduction to forensic science. (Rev: BL 12/1/97) [363.2]

**13688** Graham, Ian. *Crime-Fighting* (5–8). Illus. Series: Science Spotlight. 1995, Raintree Steck-Vaughn LB $24.26 (0-8114-3840-6). 46pp. A discussion of scientific methods used in analyzing evidence at crime scenes, such as DNA testing. (Rev: SLJ 7/95) [364]

**13689** Graham, Ian. *Fakes and Forgeries* (5–8). Illus. Series: Science Spotlight. 1995, Raintree Steck-Vaughn LB $24.26 (0-8114-3843-0). 46pp. Examines famous scandals in history involving such fakes as the Loch Ness monster, counterfeit money, and the forged Hitler diaries. (Rev: SLJ 7/95) [364]

**13690** Greenberg, Keith E. *Out of the Gang* (5–8). Illus. 1992, Lerner LB $19.93 (0-8225-2553-4). 40pp. A realistic portrait of what gang life is like, revealed by a man who escaped it and a boy who

stayed out of it. (Rev: BCCB 6/92; BL 6/15/92; SLJ 9/92) [364.1]

**13691** Hjelmeland, Andy. *Prisons: Inside the Big House* (4–8). Illus. Series: Pro/Con. 1996, Lerner LB $21.27 (0-8225-2607-7). 112pp. Different viewpoints on the purposes and functions of prisons in today's society are presented in this objective account. (Rev: BL 8/96; SLJ 9/96) [365]

**13692** Jackson, Donna M. *The Bone Detectives: How Forensic Anthropologists Solve Crimes and Uncover Mysteries of the Dead* (5–7). Illus. 1996, Little, Brown $16.95 (0-316-82935-8). 48pp. Explores the role of forensic anthropologists in solving crimes, including murder. (Rev: BCCB 4/96; BL 4/1/96; HB 5–6/96; SLJ 5/96*) [363.2]

**13693** Jones, Charlotte F. *Fingerprints and Talking Bones: How Real Life Crimes Are Solved* (5–8). Illus. 1997, Delacorte $16.95 (0-385-32299-2). 111pp. A clear, concise account of what forensic science means and how it has been applied in real cases. (Rev: BCCB 6/97; BL 6/1–15/97; SLJ 8/97) [363.2]

**13694** Lane, Brian. *Investigation of Murder* (4–6). Illus. Series: Crimebusters. 1996, Millbrook LB $20.90 (0-7613-0527-0). 32pp. A fictitious murder is used as the framework for this discussion of the work of police and forensic experts. (Rev: BL 1/1–15/97; SLJ 1/97) [363.2]

**13695** Larsen, Anita. *Psychic Sleuths* (5–7). 1994, Macmillan LB $14.95 (0-02-751645-8). 112pp. Pros and cons concerning the use of psychics in solving crimes are discussed, with many case studies. (Rev: BL 10/1/94; SLJ 11/94) [363.2]

**13696** Oliver, Marilyn Tower. *Gangs: Trouble in the Streets* (4–8). Illus. 1995, Enslow LB $19.95 (0-89490-492-2). 128pp. A history of gangs since the 19th century plus coverage of the various types and activities of gangs that exist today. (Rev: BL 8/95) [364.1]

**13697** Oxlade, Chris. *Crime Detection* (3–5). Illus. Series: Science Encounters. 1997, Rigby $13.95 (1-57572-090-6). 32pp. An introduction to detective work that covers forensic science, security, fingerprints, and how evidence is chemically treated. (Rev: SLJ 11/97) [364]

**13698** Platt, Richard. *Spy* (4–7). Illus. 1996, Knopf LB $20.99 (0-679-98123-7). 64pp. All aspects of spying, including equipment and techniques, are described, along with profiles of famous spies. (Rev: BL 12/1/96; SLJ 6/97) [327.12]

**13699** Powell, Jillian. *Drug Trafficking* (4–6). Illus. Series: Crimebusters. 1997, Millbrook LB $20.90 (0-7613-0555-6). 32pp. Using a fabricated crime as a focus, this book describes the many avenues of drug trafficking in the United States and how various agencies are combating it. (Rev: BL 6/1–15/97) [364.1]

**13700** Roden, Katie. *Solving International Crime* (4–6). Illus. Series: Crimebusters. 1996, Millbrook LB $20.90 (0-7613-0528-9). 32pp. Drug trafficking, terrorism, and crime rings are discussed in this book on international crime-fighting efforts. (Rev: BL 1/1–15/97; SLJ 1/97) [363.2]

**13701** Roden, Katie. *Terrorism* (4–6). Illus. Series: Crimebusters. 1997, Millbrook LB $20.90 (0-7613-0556-4). 32pp. Using many text boxes, photos, diagrams, file folder formats, and a fabricated crime to set the stage, this book studies the causes and effects of terrorism. (Rev: BL 6/1–15/97; SLJ 9/97) [363.2]

**13702** Ross, Stewart. *Bandits and Outlaws* (5–7). Illus. Series: Fact or Fiction. 1995, Millbrook LB $24.90 (1-56294-649-8). 48pp. From the book's jacket: "The truth about outlaws, highwaymen, smugglers, and robbers from the bandit gangs of ancient China to the desperadoes of today." (Rev: BL 11/15/95; SLJ 1/96) [364.1]

**13703** Ross, Stewart. *Spies and Traitors* (5–7). Illus. Series: Fact or Fiction. 1995, Millbrook paper $24.90 (1-56294-648-X). 48pp. A history of the people who have placed themselves above their country in the dangerous game of espionage and betrayal. (Rev: BL 11/15/95; SLJ 3/96) [355.3]

**13704** Salak, John. *Violent Crime: Is It Out of Control?* (6–8). Illus. Series: Issues of Our Time. 1995, Twenty-First Century LB $18.90 (0-8050-4239-3). 64pp. An honest presentation of why violent crimes are committed more frequently and how young people are becoming increasingly involved in them. (Rev: BL 2/1/96; SLJ 2/96) [364.1]

**13705** Stewart, Gail B. *Gangs* (5–8). Illus. Series: The Other America. 1996, Lucent LB $22.45 (1-56006-340-8). 96pp. This account describes past and present gangs, discusses causes for their formation, tells about their characteristics, and profiles several members. (Rev: SLJ 3/97) [394.3]

**13706** Szumski, Bonnie, and Neal Bernards. *Prisons: Detecting Bias* (4–7). Illus. Series: Opposing Viewpoints Juniors. 1991, Greenhaven LB $16.20 (0-89908-604-7). 32pp. Can prisons rehabilitate and how do they affect criminals are 2 of several issues explored. (Rev: BL 6/15/91) [365]

**13707** Tipp, Stacey L. *Causes of Crime: Distinguishing Between Fact and Opinion* (5–7). Illus. Series: Opposing Viewpoints Juniors. 1991, Greenhaven LB $16.20 (0-89908-615-2). 32pp. A variety of opinions concerning the causes of crime are presented in an objective way to make the reader evaluate the validity of each. (Rev: BL 5/15/92) [364]

**13708** Trapani, Margi. *Working Together Against Gang Violence* (4–8). Illus. Series: Library of Social

Activism. 1996, Rosen LB $16.95 (0-8239-2260-X). 64pp. Covers gangs, their makeup, purposes, activities, and, most important, how to avoid them and their violence. (Rev: SLJ 2/97) [364.1]

**13709** Wiese, Jim. *Detective Science: 40 Crime-Solving, Case-Breaking, Crook-Catching Activities for Kids* (4–7). 1996, Wiley paper $12.95 (0-471-11980-6). 128pp. Presents 40 experiments and activities that illustrate techniques in forensic science related to observing, collecting, and analyzing evidence. (Rev: BL 4/15/96; SLJ 6/96) [363.2]

**13710** Williams, Stanley, and Barbara Cottman Becnel. *Gangs and Drugs* (3–5). Illus. Series: Tookie Speaks Out Against Gang Violence. 1996, Rosen LB $13.95 (0-8239-2348-7). 24pp. A former gang leader and current prison inmate, Tookie Williams tells about the part drugs play in the gang scene. (Rev: BL 2/15/97) [364.1]

**13711** Winkleman, Katherine K. *Police Patrol* (PS–3). Illus. by John S. Winkleman. 1996, Walker LB $16.85 (0-8027-8454-2). 32pp. Activities in a police station and the duties of police are described in words and photos. (Rev: BCCB 1/97; BL 1/1–15/97; SLJ 12/96) [363.2]

## Elections and Political Parties

**13712** Bernards, Neal. *Elections: Locating the Author's Main Idea* (5–7). Illus. Series: Opposing Viewpoints Juniors. 1992, Greenhaven LB $16.20 (1-56510-022-0). 36pp. Eight pro and con viewpoints examine America's election process. (Rev: BL 1/15/93) [324]

**13713** Brown, Gene. *The 1992 Election* (5–8). Illus. Series: Headliners. 1993, Millbrook LB $23.40 (1-56294-080-5). 64pp. This book presents the issues, the campaigns, and the result of the 1992 presidential election. (Rev: BL 4/1/93; SLJ 7/93) [324]

**13714** Feinberg, Barbara S. *Words in the News: A Student's Dictionary of American Government and Politics* (5–8). Illus. 1993, Watts LB $23.60 (0-531-11164-4). 142pp. Five hundred terms connected with American government and politics — for example *electoral college, liberalism,* and *gerrymandering* — are clearly defined, with their origins often included. (Rev: BL 3/1/94) [320.973]

**13715** Fradin, Dennis B. *Voting and Elections* (1–3). Illus. 1985, Children's LB $21.00 (0-516-01274-6); paper $5.50 (0-516-41274-4). 45pp. Beginning readers learn about the election process. (Rev: BL 3/1/86; SLJ 4/86)

**13716** Henry, Christopher. *Presidential Conventions* (4–6). Illus. Series: First Books: Government. 1996, Watts LB $21.00 (0-531-20219-4). 62pp. Discusses the purpose of political party conventions and their place in the election process. (Rev: BL 9/1/96; SLJ 10/96) [324.6]

**13717** Henry, Christopher. *Presidential Elections* (4–6). Illus. Series: First Books: Government. 1996, Watts LB $21.00 (0-531-20222-4). 62pp. Different kinds of candidates plus the techniques and processes of winning elections are discussed. (Rev: BL 9/1/96; SLJ 10/96) [324.6]

**13718** Lindop, Edmund. *Political Parties* (4–6). Illus. Series: Inside Government. 1996, Twenty-First Century LB $15.98 (0-8050-4618-6). 64pp. The origin of political parties and the role they play in elections and the government. (Rev: BL 9/15/96; SLJ 12/96) [324.273]

**13719** Majure, Janet. *Elections* (5–8). Illus. Series: Overview. 1996, Lucent LB $22.45 (1-56006-174-X). 112pp. After a general history of elections, this account explains present-day procedures and practices. (Rev: BL 7/96) [324.7]

**13720** Scher, Linda. *The Vote: Making Your Voice Heard* (3–6). Illus. 1993, Raintree Steck-Vaughn LB $24.26 (0-8114-7357-0). 48pp. A history of voting rights and a discussion of such topics as registration and voting methods. (Rev: SLJ 2/93) [324]

**13721** Spies, Karen B. *Our Presidency* (4–6). Illus. Series: I Know America. 1994, Millbrook LB $21.90 (1-56294-444-4). 48pp. Provides a basic history of the office of the presidency, an explanation of the president's duties and responsibilities, and a rundown of those who have served. (Rev: BL 11/15/94; SLJ 12/94) [353.03]

**13722** Steins, Richard. *Our Elections* (4–6). Illus. 1994, Millbrook LB $20.90 (1-56294-446-0). 48pp. The process of being elected to office (primarily at the national level) is outlined in text, pictures, and diagrams. (Rev: BL 11/15/94; SLJ 12/94) [324.6]

## Federal Government and Agencies

**13723** Bay, Ann Phillips. *The Kid's Guide to the Smithsonian* (4–6). Illus. by Steven Rotblatt. 1996, Smithsonian Institution $24.95 (1-56098-734-0); paper $14.95 (1-56098-693-X). 160pp. A handy guide to historical information on many of the treasures of the Smithsonian. (Rev: BL 9/1/96) [069]

**13724** Berger, Melvin, and Gilda Berger. *Where Does the Mail Go? A Book About the Postal System* (K–3). Illus. by Geoffrey Brittingham. Series: Discovery Readers. 1994, Ideals LB $12.00 (1-57102-022-5); paper $4.50 (1-57102-006-3). 48pp. Explores the U.S. Postal Service by tracing a letter from posting to delivery. (Rev: SLJ 9/94) [353]

**13725** Bolick, Nancy O. *Mail Call! The History of the U.S. Postal Service* (4–6). Illus. Series: First Book. 1995, Watts LB $21.00 (0-531-20170-8).

64pp. From colonial days to the present, this is a chronological survey of the history of the U.S. Postal Service. (Rev: BL 2/15/95; SLJ 6/95) [383]

**13726** Bratman, Fred. *Becoming a Citizen: Adopting a New Home* (3–6). Illus. Series: Good Citizenship. 1993, Raintree Steck-Vaughn LB $24.26 (0-8114-7354-6). 48pp. As well as looking at immigration, past and present, this account deals with requirements for citizenship, visas, refugees, and illegal aliens. (Rev: SLJ 10/93) [323.6]

**13727** Feinberg, Barbara S. *The Cabinet* (4–6). Illus. Series: Inside Government. 1995, Twenty-First Century LB $18.90 (0-8050-3421-8). 64pp. The history and changing composition of the cabinet are traced, with an explanation of each member's duties. (Rev: BL 9/1/95; SLJ 10/95) [353.04]

**13728** Feinberg, Barbara S. *Electing the President* (4–6). Illus. Series: Inside Government. 1995, Twenty-First Century LB $18.90 (0-8050-3422-6). 64pp. A brief history of presidential elections is given, with an outline of the development of the various parties. (Rev: BL 9/1/95) [324.6]

**13729** Feinberg, Barbara S. *The National Government* (4–8). Illus. Series: First Books. 1993, Watts LB $21.00 (0-531-20155-4). 64pp. After an introduction to the federal government, this book explains the functions of each department and how they work together. (Rev: SLJ 1/94) [336.73]

**13730** Feinberg, Barbara S. *Term Limits for Congress?* (4–6). Illus. Series: Inside Government. 1996, Twenty-First Century LB $18.90 (0-8050-4099-4). 64pp. A clear and concise overview of the arguments for and against congressional term limits. (Rev: BL 5/15/96; SLJ 8/96) [328.73]

**13731** Gibbons, Gail. *The Post Office Book: Mail and How It Moves* (K–3). Illus. by author. 1982, HarperCollins LB $14.89 (0-690-04199-3); paper $5.95 (0-06-446029-0). 32pp. A simple description of how the post office works.

**13732** Gourse, Leslie. *The Congress* (4–6). Illus. Series: First Books. 1995, Watts LB $22.00 (0-531-20178-3). 64pp. The powers of the legislative branch are covered, with a history of both houses. (Rev: BL 3/1/95) [328.73]

**13733** Henry, Christopher. *The Electoral College* (4–6). Illus. Series: First Books: Government. 1996, Watts LB $22.00 (0-531-20218-6). 63pp. Introduces the electoral college, its origins, composition, and functions. (Rev: BL 9/1/96; SLJ 10/96) [324.6]

**13734** Maestro, Betsy. *The Voice of the People: American Democracy in Action* (3–5). Illus. by Giulio Maestro. 1996, Lothrop LB $15.93 (0-688-10679-X). 48pp. The election process and the 3 branches of government are 2 of the topics covered in this overview of our government. (Rev: BCCB 5/96; BL 4/1/96; SLJ 6/96) [324.973]

**13735** Patrick, Diane. *The Executive Branch* (4–6). Illus. Series: First Books. 1995, Watts LB $22.00 (0-531-20179-1). 64pp. An introduction to the executive wing, the cabinet, and the duties of the U.S. president. (Rev: BL 3/1/95) [353]

**13736** Patrick, William. *The Food and Drug Administration* (5–8). Illus. 1989, Chelsea LB $14.95 (0-87754-822-6). 96pp. How this agency protects the U.S. consumer. (Rev: BL 8/88)

**13737** Reef, Catherine. *The Supreme Court* (4–7). Illus. Series: Places in American History. 1994, Dillon paper $7.95 (0-382-24722-1). 72pp. An introduction to the Supreme Court, its powers, composition, and landmark decisions. (Rev: BL 1/1/95) [347.73]

**13738** Ricciuti, Edward R. *Wildlife Special Agent: Protecting Endangered Species* (3–5). Illus. Series: Risky Business. 1996, Blackbirch LB $14.95 (1-56711-160-2). 32pp. A look at the exciting work of the people involved in the Law Enforcement Division of the U.S. Fish and Wildlife Service and how it helps protect endangered species. (Rev: SLJ 2/97) [363.11]

**13739** Sandak, Cass R. *Congressional Committees* (4–6). Illus. Series: Inside Government. 1995, Twenty-First Century LB $18.90 (0-8050-3425-0). 64pp. The purposes, structure, and functions of congressional committees are covered in this illustrated account. (Rev: BL 12/15/95) [328.73]

**13740** Sandak, Cass R. *Lobbying* (4–6). Illus. Series: Inside Government. 1995, Twenty-First Century LB $18.90 (0-8050-3424-2). 64pp. An objective account that discusses the history, purposes, and results of lobbying in the U.S. Congress. (Rev: BL 12/15/95; SLJ 1/96) [324]

**13741** Sandak, Cass R. *The National Debt* (4–6). Illus. Series: Inside Government. 1996, Twenty-First Century LB $18.90 (0-8050-3423-4). 64pp. The origins and causes of the national debt are covered, with options for the future. (Rev: BCCB 3/96; BL 5/15/96; SLJ 8/96) [336.3]

**13742** Stein, R. Conrad. *The Powers of Congress.* Rev. ed. (3–5). Illus. Series: Cornerstones of Freedom. 1995, Children's LB $18.70 (0-516-06696-X); paper $5.95 (0-516-46696-8). 30pp. After a general introduction to Congress, the author describes the shifting balance among the 3 branches of government through several important historical crises. (Rev: SLJ 8/95) [320]

**13743** Sullivan, George. *Presidents at Play* (4–6). Illus. 1995, Walker LB $16.85 (0-8027-8334-1). 176pp. An unusual side of U.S. presidents is

explored: the sports and other recreational activities they engaged in. (Rev: BL 1/1/95; SLJ 2/95) [973]

**13744** Weber, Michael. *Our Congress* (4–6). Illus. Series: I Know America. 1994, Millbrook LB $20.90 (1-56294-443-6). 48pp. Provides a history of Congress, its composition, and its duties. (Rev: BL 11/15/94; SLJ 1/95) [328.73]

**13745** Weizmann, Daniel. *Take a Stand!* (5–8). Illus. by Jack Keely. 1996, Price Stern Sloan $6.95 (0-8431-7997-X). 64pp. Introduces American government and describes many ways that young people can get involved. (Rev: SLJ 12/96) [324]

## State Government and Agencies

**13746** Feinberg, Barbara S. *State Governments* (4–8). Illus. Series: First Books. 1993, Watts LB $21.00 (0-531-20154-6). 64pp. Introduces the various parts of a state government, explains how each works, and stresses the need for cooperation among the components. (Rev: SLJ 1/94) [320]

## Municipal Government and Agencies

**13747** Gibbons, Gail. *Check It Out: The Book About Libraries* (K–3). Illus. 1985, Harcourt $15.00 (0-15-216400-6); paper $6.00 (0-15-216401-4). 32pp. An overview of what the library is and how it functions in picture-book format that is lively enough for older readers. (Rev: BCCB 9/85; BL 10/1/85; HB 11–12/85)

**13748** Sobol, Richard. *Mayor: In the Company of Norman Rice, Mayor of Seattle* (3–6). Photos by author. Series: Government in Action. 1996, Cobblehill paper $15.99 (0-525-65198-5). 30pp. This account of the activities of Seattle's mayor, Norman Rice, includes delivering speeches, meeting people, visiting schools, and conducting meetings. (Rev: SLJ 4/96) [320.8]

## Social Problems and Solutions

**13749** Brimner, Larry Dane. *A Migrant Family* (4–8). Illus. 1992, Lerner LB $19.93 (0-8225-2554-2). 40pp. The daily life of 12-year-old Juan and his Mexican American family is captured in this photoessay. (Rev: BCCB 10/92; BL 9/15/92) [305.5]

**13750** Cann, Kate. *Living in the World* (5–8). Illus. by Derek Matthews. Series: Life Education. 1997, Watts LB $18.20 (0-531-14430-5). 32pp. A book that explores group interactions, including racism, prejudice, and social activism. (Rev: SLJ 1/98) [305.8]

**13751** Dee, Catherine. *The Girls' Guide to Life: How to Take Charge of the Issues That Affect You* (5–8). Illus. 1997, Little, Brown paper $14.95 (0-316-17952-3). 160pp. Such female concerns as self-esteem, political awareness, cultural stereotypes, and sexual harassment are introduced through first-person narratives, poetry, and advice. (Rev: BCCB 7–8/97; BL 7/97; HB 7–8/97, 11–12/97) [305.42]

**13752** de Ruiz, Dana C., and Richard Larios. *La Causa: The Migrant Farmworkers' Story* (4–7). Illus. by Rudy Gutierrez. 1992, Raintree Steck-Vaughn LB $25.68 (0-8114-7231-0). 92pp. The story of the founding of the United Farm Workers highlights the work of Cesar Chavez and Dolores Huerta. (Rev: BL 6/1–15/93) [331]

**13753** Fleming, Robert. *Rescuing a Neighborhood: The Bedford-Stuyvesant Volunteer Ambulance Corps* (4–8). Illus. 1995, Walker LB $16.85 (0-8027-8330-9). 48pp. The story of how 2 determined, dedicated men organized emergency response services in their inner-city neighborhood. (Rev: BL 5/1/95; SLJ 9/95) [362]

**13754** Goodman, Alan. *Nickelodeon's The Big Help Book: 365 Ways You Can Make a Difference by Volunteering!* (4–6). 1994, Pocket paper $3.99 (0-671-51927-1). 134pp. Various kinds of community service projects are described, with hints on how to organize and activate them. (Rev: BL 11/15/94) [302.14]

**13755** Greenberg, Keith E. *Family Abuse: Why Do People Hurt Each Other?* (3–6). Illus. 1994, Twenty-First Century LB $18.90 (0-8050-3183-9). 64pp. An easily read book that explores physical, emotional, and sexual abuse of children as well as neglect and abuse of spouses, the elderly, and the disabled. (Rev: SLJ 9/94) [362.7]

**13756** Hauser, Pierre. *Illegal Aliens* (5–8). Illus. Series: Immigrant Experience. 1996, Chelsea LB $19.95 (0-7910-3363-5). 142pp. A history of the attitudes toward immigration is given, followed by a discussion of illegal aliens, where they come from, and the government's policy toward them. (Rev: SLJ 2/97) [932]

**13757** Hoyt-Goldsmith, Diane. *Migrant Worker: A Boy from the Rio Grande Valley* (4–7). Illus. 1996, Holiday LB $15.95 (0-8234-1225-3). 32pp. A photoessay about the grim living conditions endured by an 11-year-old Mexican American migrant worker. (Rev: BCCB 3/96; BL 3/1/96; SLJ 5/96) [331.5]

**13758** Hubbard, Jim. *Lives Turned Upside Down: Homeless Children in Their Own Words and Photographs* (4–7). Illus. 1996, Simon & Schuster paper $17.00 (0-689-80649-3). 40pp. This work contains first-person accounts of 4 youngsters who come from homeless families. (Rev: BCCB 1/97; BL 11/15/96; SLJ 12/96) [362.7]

**13759** Hull, Mary. *Ethnic Violence* (5–8). Illus. Series: Overview. 1997, Lucent LB $22.45 (1-56006-184-7). 112pp. Gives a history of racial prejudice that has led to violence and tells about decisions and policies that currently guide our behavior and attitudes toward this problem. (Rev: BL 8/97; SLJ 9/97) [305.8]

**13760** Hurwitz, Eugene, and Sue Hurwitz. *Working Together Against Homelessness* (4–6). Illus. Series: Library of Social Activism. 1995, Rosen LB $16.95 (0-8239-1772-X). 64pp. A history of homelessness both nationally and globally, its present frequency, and possible solutions. (Rev: BL 2/15/95; SLJ 12/94) [362.5]

**13761** Hyde, Margaret O. *Know About Abuse* (5–7). Illus. 1992, Walker LB $14.85 (0-8027-8177-2). 93pp. Various kinds of abuse in the home are described and information on how to get help is given. (Rev: SLJ 9/92) [362.7]

**13762** Karnes, Frances A., and Suzanne M. Bean. *Girls and Young Women Leading the Way: 20 True Stories About Leadership* (5–8). Illus. 1993, Free Spirit paper $11.95 (0-915793-52-0). 160pp. Contains case histories of 20 girls who changed their communities by starting projects like collecting food for the homeless or starting a recycling program. (Rev: SLJ 12/93) [307.1]

**13763** Lewis, Barbara A. *The Kid's Guide to Service Projects: Over 500 Service Ideas for Young People Who Want to Make a Difference* (4–7). 1995, paper $10.95 (0-915793-82-2). 175pp. After an introduction on how to organize and conduct service projects, this book gives details on 500 ideas from running errands for seniors to working for voter registration. (Rev: SLJ 7/95) [307]

**13764** McGuire, Leslie. *Victims* (5–7). Series: Women Today. 1991, Rourke LB $17.95 (0-86593-120-8). 64pp. This disturbing book tells the story of several women who have been subjected to physical and emotional violence. (Rev: SLJ 2/92) [305]

**13765** Nichelason, Margery G. *Homeless or Hopeless?* (5–8). Illus. Series: Pro/Con. 1994, Lerner LB $21.27 (0-8225-2606-9). 112pp. The causes of homelessness and the plight of those affected are described in this account, which views all sides of this problem. (Rev: BL 6/1–15/94; SLJ 7/94) [362.5]

**13766** O'Neill, Terry. *The Homeless: Distinguishing Between Fact and Opinion* (4–7). Illus. Series: Opposing Viewpoints Juniors. 1991, Greenwillow LB $16.20 (0-89908-605-5). 32pp. Homelessness is explored, with different points of view on how serious the problem is and who is to blame. (Rev: BL 6/15/91) [362.5]

**13767** Rozakis, Laurie. *Homelessness: Can We Solve the Problem?* (5–8). Illus. Series: Issues of Our Time. 1995, Twenty-First Century LB $18.90 (0-8050-3878-7). 64pp. A history of homelessness is given, with various opinions and possible solutions. (Rev: SLJ 9/95) [362.5]

**13768** Siegel, Danny. *Tell Me a Mitzvah: Little and Big Ways to Repair the World* (3–6). Illus. by Judith Friedman. 1993, Kar-Ben paper $7.95 (0-929371-78-X). 64pp. Profiles of 12 people who have made the world a better place by performing mitzvahs, or good deeds. (Rev: SLJ 3/94) [307.1]

**13769** Spelman, Cornelia. *Your Body Belongs to You* (K–3). Illus. by Teri Weidner. 1997, Albert Whitman LB $13.95 (0-8075-9474-1). 24pp. An introduction to child sexual abuse, with a special section of advice for parents. (Rev: BL 9/1/97; SLJ 9/97) [613.6]

**13770** Steins, Richard. *Censorship: How Does It Conflict with Freedom?* (5–8). Illus. Series: Issues of Our Time. 1995, Twenty-First Century LB $18.90 (0-8050-3879-5). 64pp. A clearly written introduction to censorship, its history, and the various positions possible toward it. (Rev: SLJ 9/95) [363.3]

**13771** Tipp, Stacey L. *Child Abuse: Detecting Bias* (5–7). Series: Opposing Viewpoints Juniors. 1991, Greenhaven LB $16.20 (0-89908-611-X). 32pp. Four different issues involving child abuse (e.g., should abusers be sent to prison) are presented from

various points of view. (Rev: BL 5/15/92; SLJ 3/92) [362.7]

**13772** Walker, Richard. *A Right to Die?* (4–8). Illus. Series: Viewpoints. 1997, Watts LB $20.00 (0-531-14413-5). 32pp. This objective account traces traditional views of death, tells how medicine is prolonging life, and discusses topics like suicide, euthanasia, and life support systems and the controversy surrounding each. (Rev: SLJ 5/97) [306.88]

**13773** Wolf, Bernard. *Homeless* (2–4). Illus. 1995, Orchard LB $17.99 (0-531-08736-0). 46pp. The plight of a homeless family caught up in the New York City welfare system is the subject of this affecting picture book. (Rev: BCCB 3/95; BL 2/15/95; HB 5–6/95; SLJ 4/95) [362.5]

**13774** Worth, Richard. *Poverty* (5–8). Illus. Series: Overview. 1997, Lucent LB $22.45 (1-56006-192-8). 96pp. A carefully researched title that gives a history of poverty in America, changing attitudes toward it, and current policies and practices. (Rev: BL 8/97; SLJ 9/97) [362.5]

# Religion and Holidays

## General and Miscellaneous

**13775** Armstrong, Carole. *Lives and Legends of the Saints: With Paintings from the Great Art Museums of the World* (4–7). Illus. 1995, Simon & Schuster $17.00 (0-689-80277-3). 45pp. An introduction to the lives of 20 of the most important saints, with illustrations from the world's great paintings. (Rev: BL 9/1/95*; HB 11–12/95; SLJ 12/95) [270]

**13776** Bial, Raymond. *Amish Home* (3–6). Illus. by author. 1993, Houghton $17.00 (0-395-59504-5). 40pp. A haunting photoessay of Amish life without the Amish themselves because their religious doctrine forbids portraiture. (Rev: BCCB 5/93; BL 2/15/93; SLJ 5/93) [973.08]

**13777** Bial, Raymond. *Shaker Home* (3–6). Illus. 1994, Houghton $15.95 (0-395-64047-4). 35pp. The Shaker way of life is explored in text and color photos that touch on their beliefs, activities, clothing, crafts, and humanitarian activities. (Rev: BCCB 3/94; BL 2/1/94*; HB 5–6/94; SLJ 3/94) [289.8]

**13778** Birdseye, Debbie H., and Tom Birdseye. *What I Believe: Kids Talk About Faith* (4–7). 1996, Holiday $15.95 (0-8234-1268-7). 32pp. Children from 6 faiths explain what their religion means to them. (Rev: BL 12/15/96; SLJ 2/97) [200]

**13779** Bolick, Nancy O., and Sallie G. Randolph. *Shaker Inventions* (4–6). Illus. by Melissa Francisco. 1990, Walker LB $13.85 (0-8027-6934-9). 96pp. A rundown on many inventions by the Shakers, and a general introduction to their way of life. (Rev: SLJ 9/90) [289]

**13780** Bolick, Nancy O., and Sallie G. Randolph. *Shaker Villages* (4–8). Illus. by Laura LoTurco. 1993, Walker LB $13.85 (0-8027-8210-8). 79pp. A history of the Shaker movement. (Rev: SLJ 6/93) [289]

**13781** Carlstrom, Nancy White. *Does God Know How to Tie Shoes?* (PS–K). Illus. by Lori McElrath-Eslick. 1993, Eerdmans $15.00 (0-8028-5074-X). 32pp. A child questions her parents about the nature of God, and the answers are correlated with passages from the Bible. (Rev: BL 12/1/93; SLJ 3/94)

**13782** Chalfonte, Jessica. *I Am Muslim* (1–4). Illus. Series: Religions of the World. 1996, Rosen/Power Kids Pr. LB $15.93 (0-8239-2375-4). 24pp. An introduction to the Muslim religion and the world of Islam as seen through the eyes of Ahmet, a boy living in Detroit. (Rev: SLJ 2/97) [297]

**13783** Demi. *Buddha* (4–6). Illus. 1996, Holt $18.95 (0-8050-4203-2). 32pp. In this picture book for older children, the story of Buddha's life and teachings are effectively retold. (Rev: BCCB 6/96; BL 4/1/96; HB 9–10/96; SLJ 6/96) [294.3]

**13784** Demi. *Buddha Stories* (3–6). Illus. 1997, Holt $16.95 (0-8050-4886-3). 32pp. Ten of the author's favorite Buddha stories, or jakatas, are elegantly retold with excellent illustrations. (Rev: BCCB 4/97; BL 2/15/97; SLJ 6/97) [294.3]

**13785** Dhanjal, Beryl. *What Do We Know About Sikhism?* (3–6). Illus. Series: What Do We Know About . . .? 1997, Bedrick LB $18.95 (0-87226-387-8). 45pp. The history of Sikhism is covered, along with material on its founder, Guru Nanak; the 10 succeeding Gurus; the Sikh Holy Book; and the Golden Temple at Amritsar. (Rev: SLJ 3/97) [294.6]

**13786** Faber, Doris. *The Amish* (3–5). Illus. by Michael Erkel. 1990, Doubleday $17.95 (0-385-44518-0). An enlightening look at the people, who live plainly, in harmony with nature. (Rev: BL 1/15/91) [973.08]

**13787** Fine, Doreen. *What Do We Know About Judaism?* (3–6). Illus. by Celia Hart. Series: What Do We Know About . . .? 1996, Bedrick LB $18.95 (0-

87226-386-X). 45pp. An introduction to Judaism and the Jewish way of life that includes material on Orthodox, Reform, and Conservative Jews. (Rev: SLJ 2/97) [296]

**13788** Ganeri, Anita. *Out of the Ark: Stories from the World's Religions* (4–7). Illus. by Jackie Morris. 1996, Harcourt $18.00 (0-15-200943-4). 96pp. Traditional tales from 7 of the world's major religions are retold in this thematically arranged book. (Rev: BCCB 4/96; SLJ 4/96) [200]

**13789** Ganeri, Anita. *What Do We Know About Buddhism?* (4–7). Illus. Series: What Do We Know About . . .? 1997, Bedrick LB $18.95 (0-87226-389-4). 45pp. Using double-page spreads, basic facts about Buddha's life and teachings are covered, with information on Buddhist beliefs, sacred texts, festivals, and the art and folk literature connected with this religion. (Rev: SLJ 10/97) [294]

**13790** Ganeri, Anita. *What Do We Know About Hinduism?* (3–6). Illus. by Celia Hart. Series: What Do We Know About . . .? 1996, Bedrick LB $18.95 (0-87226-385-1). 45pp. In this introduction to Hinduism, topics like reincarnation, gods and goddesses, the Sacred Scriptures, types of worship, and yoga are presented. (Rev: SLJ 2/97) [294.5]

**13791** Gellman, Marc, and Thomas Hartman. *How Do You Spell God? Answers to the Big Questions from Around the World* (5–8). Illus. by Joseph A. Smith. 1995, Morrow $16.00 (0-688-13041-0). 224pp. A priest and a rabbi have written this introduction to the world's most important religions: Judaism, Christianity, Islam, Buddhism, and Hinduism. (Rev: BCCB 7–8/95; BL 6/1–15/95; SLJ 5/95) [200]

**13792** Gold, Susan D. *Religions of the Western Hemisphere* (5–8). Illus. Series: Comparing Continents. 1997, Twenty-First Century $21.40 (0-8050-5603-3). 96pp. Explores the history and influence of religions, beliefs, and customs on life in the United States, Canada, and Latin America, with material on the roles of religious leaders in the government, economy, and everyday life. (Rev: BL 2/1/98; SLJ 3/98) [200]

**13793** Hewitt, Catherine. *Buddhism* (5–8). Illus. Series: World Religions. 1995, Thomson Learning LB $24.26 (1-56847-375-3). 48pp. The story of Buddha and the religion he founded are covered in this account, with maps showing its spread and present status. (Rev: BL 9/1/95; SLJ 11/95) [294.3]

**13794** Husain, Sharukh. *What Do We Know About Islam?* (4–7). Illus. Series: What Do We Know About . . .? 1997, Bedrick LB $18.95 (0-87226-388-6). 45pp. Covers the major aspects of Islam, including its history, the life-styles of its believers, holidays like Ramadan, dietary obligations, and the Haj pilgrimage to Mecca. (Rev: SLJ 5/97) [297]

**13795** Jaffe, Nina. *The Mysterious Visitor: Stories of the Prophet Elijah* (4–6). Illus. 1997, Scholastic $19.95 (0-590-48422-2). 112pp. Eight Jewish stories that involve the prophet Elijah are retold. (Rev: BCCB 6/97; BL 5/1/97; SLJ 6/97*) [222]

**13796** Kanitkar, V. P. *Hinduism* (4–6). Illus. 1986, Dufour paper $21.00 (1-871402-09-3). History, major tenets, and an explanation of holidays and festivals. (Rev: BL 12/15/86)

**13797** Kenna, Kathleen. *A People Apart* (PS–3). Illus. by Andrew Stawicki. 1995, Houghton $18.00 (0-395-67344-5). 64pp. A photoessay about the Mennonites that supplies important information on their history, customs, and beliefs. (Rev: BCCB 1/96; BL 11/1/95*; SLJ 12/95*) [289.7]

**13798** Krishnaswami, Uma. *The Broken Tusk: Stories of the Hindu God Ganesha* (4–6). Illus. 1996, Linnet LB $19.95 (0-208-02442-5). 98pp. A collection of folktales about the elephant-headed Hindu god Ganesha, the god of good beginnings. (Rev: BCCB 10/96; BL 10/1/96; SLJ 7/97) [294.5]

**13799** Kroll, Virginia. *I Wanted to Know All About God* (PS–1). Illus. by Debra R. Jenkins. 1994, Eerdmans $15.00 (0-8028-5078-2). 32pp. A book about the nature of God that emphasizes human relationships and the wonders of nature. (Rev: BL 2/15/94; SLJ 8/94) [231.2]

**13800** Krull, Kathleen, ed. *Songs of Praise* (PS–1). Illus. by Kathryn Hewitt. 1989, Harcourt paper $5.95 (0-15-277109-3). 32pp. A collection of 15 hymns. (Rev: BCCB 9/88; BL 11/15/88)

**13801** Langley, Myrtle. *Religion* (4–7). Illus. Series: Eyewitness Books. 1996, Knopf LB $20.99 (0-679-98123-3). 59pp. Each double-page spread introduces a different religion, including those of ancient Egypt and Greece as well as Hinduism, Buddhism, Confucianism, Taoism, Sikhism, Judaism, Christianity, and Islam. (Rev: SLJ 12/96) [291]

**13802** Lucas, Daryl J. *The Baker Bible Dictionary for Kids* (3–6). Illus. 1997, Baker Book House $19.99 (0-8010-4345-X). 503pp. More than 2,000 words found in the Bible are simply and clearly explained. (Rev: SLJ 11/97) [222]

**13803** McFarlane, Marilyn. *Sacred Myths: Stories of World Religions* (4–7). 1996, Sibyl $26.95 (0-9638327-7-8). 110pp. A collection of myths from a number of religions, including Judaism, Christianity, Islam, and Hinduism. (Rev: BL 10/1/96; SLJ 1/97) [291.1]

**13804** Mack-Williams, Kibibi V. *People of Faith* (4–6). Illus. Series: African American Life. 1995, Rourke LB $23.93 (1-57103-031-X). 48pp. African American religious life is discussed, with profiles of important religious people. (Rev: SLJ 3/96) [200]

**13805**  Maestro, Betsy. *The Story of Religion* (4–7). Illus. by Giulio Maestro. 1996, Clarion $15.00 (0-395-62364-2). 46pp. Traces the history of religion from the beliefs of primitive peoples to the development of such modern religions as Islam and Christianity. (Rev: BL 10/1/96; SLJ 9/96*) [291]

**13806**  Nomura, Noriko S. *I Am Shinto* (K–3). Illus. Series: Religions of the World. 1996, Rosen/Power Kids Pr. LB $15.93 (0-8239-2380-0). 24pp. In double-page spreads, various aspects of the Shinto religion are introduced, including Dami spirits, shrines, and purification rituals. (Rev: SLJ 11/96) [299]

**13807**  Osborne, Mary Pope. *One World, Many Religions: The Ways We Worship* (4–7). Illus. 1996, Knopf LB $26.99 (0-679-93930-X). 86pp. Six of the world's major religions are introduced in an account that emphasizes their similarities. (Rev: BCCB 1/97; BL 10/1/96; SLJ 11/96) [291]

**13808**  Pandell, Karen. *Learning from the Dalai Lama: Secrets of the Wheel of Time* (3–6). Illus. 1995, Dutton paper $16.99 (0-525-45063-7). 40pp. As well as introducing Buddhism, this book details the construction and significance of a sand wheel of time known as the Kalachakra. (Rev: BCCB 2/96; BL 1/1–15/96; SLJ 3/96) [294.3]

**13809**  Paterson, Katherine. *Who Am I?* (4–6). 1992, Lerner paper $8.00 (0-8028-5072-3). 96pp. This book asks such questions as "Where do I belong?" and "Where in the world is God?" (Rev: BL 12/15/92) [248.8]

**13810**  Raimondo, Lois. *The Little Lama of Tibet* (K–4). Illus. 1994, Scholastic $15.95 (0-590-46167-2). 40pp. This photoessay deals with the everyday life of Ling Rinpoche, a 6-year-old high lama in the Tibetan Buddhist religion. (Rev: BCCB 1/94; BL 1/1/94; HB 9–10/94; SLJ 3/94) [294.3]

**13811**  Rushton, Lucy. *Birth Customs* (4–6). Illus. Series: Religions. 1993, Thomson $13.95 (1-56847-030-4). 32pp. This book examines the rituals and customs associated with birth as found in many of the world's religions. A companion volume is: *Death Customs* (1993). (Rev: BL 6/1–15/93; SLJ 7/93) [291.2]

**13812**  Sevastiades, Philemon D. *I Am Eastern Orthodox* (1–4). Illus. Series: Religions of the World. 1996, Rosen/Power Kids Pr. LB $15.93 (0-8239-2377-0). 24pp. The unique qualities of this church are covered through the story of Anastasia and her brother, who is the priest of her church in Chicago. (Rev: SLJ 2/97) [291]

**13813**  Sevastiades, Philemon D. *I Am Protestant* (1–4). Illus. Series: Religions of the World. 1996, Rosen/Power Kids Pr. LB $15.93 (0-8239-2378-9). 24pp. Focusing on Yvonne, a Southern African American girl who is an Evangelical Protestant, this

and other branches of Protestantism and their beliefs are covered. (Rev: SLJ 2/97) [280]

**13814**  Sevastiades, Philemon D. *I Am Roman Catholic* (K–3). Illus. Series: Religions of the World. 1996, Rosen/Power Kids Pr. LB $15.93 (0-8239-2376-2). 24pp. Such Roman Catholic institutions, beliefs, and rituals as the Trinity, the Pope, baptism, Mass, confession, communion, and confirmation are discussed. (Rev: SLJ 11/96) [282]

**13815**  Sita, Lisa. *Worlds of Belief: Religion and Spirituality* (5–8). Illus. Series: Our Human Family. 1995, Blackbirch LB $21.95 (1-56711-125-4). 80pp. An overview of world religions and religious practices in a book divided into 5 broad geographic areas. (Rev: SLJ 1/96) [210]

**13816**  Sugarman, Joan G., and Grace R. Freeman. *Inside the Synagogue* (K–3). Illus. 1984, UAHC paper $7.00 (0-8074-0268-0). In text and photos the Jewish house of worship is introduced. (Rev: SLJ 3/85)

**13817**  Thorne-Thomsen, Kathleen. *Shaker Children: True Stories and Crafts: 2 Biographies and 30 Activities* (3–6). Illus. 1996, Chicago Review paper $15.95 (1-55652-250-9). 128pp. Presents the biographies of 2 Shakers, one from the 19th century and the other from the 20th, plus a number of Shaker-related crafts and activities. (Rev: BCCB 7–8/96; BL 5/1/96; SLJ 8/96) [298.8]

**13818**  Vishaka. *Our Most Dear Friend: Bhagavad-gita for Children* (K–3). Illus. 1996, Torchlight $14.95 (1-887089-04-7). 30pp. A reworking of this sacred book of the Hindus in which Lord Krishna explains that every living thing has a soul. (Rev: BL 10/1/96) [294.5]

**13819**  Weiss, Bernard P. *I Am Jewish* (1–4). Illus. Series: Religions of the World. 1996, Rosen/Power Kids Pr. LB $15.93 (0-8239-2349-5). 24pp. This explanation of Judaism shows the links between the religion, Jewish history, and the country of Israel. (Rev: SLJ 2/97) [296]

**13820**  Westridge Young Writers Workshop. *Kids Explore America's Jewish Heritage* (4–7). Illus. Series: Kids Explore. 1996, John Muir paper $9.95 (1-56261-274-3). 147pp. This book explores various aspects of Jewish life, from participation in American historical events to material on special holidays, the arts, folktales, foods, and crafts. (Rev: SLJ 11/96) [305.5]

**13821**  Wilcox, Charlotte. *Mummies and Their Mysteries* (5–7). Illus. 1993, Carolrhoda LB $23.93 (0-87614-767-8). 64pp. An account of how throughout history many civilizations and religions have attempted to preserve bodies. (Rev: BCCB 7–8/93*; BL 6/1–15/93*) [393.3]

**13822** Wood, Angela. *Judaism* (5–8). Illus. Series: World Religions. 1995, Thomson Learning LB $24.26 (1-56847-376-1). 48pp. A history of Judaism is covered, with color photos and a clear, understandable text. (Rev: BL 9/1/95; SLJ 11/95) [296]

## Bible Stories

**13823** Aaseng, Rolfe E. *Augsburg Story Bible* (4–8). Illus. by Annegert Fuchshuber. 1992, Augsburg LB $19.99 (0-8066-2607-0). 270pp. This copiously illustrated version of the Bible is only slightly abridged. (Rev: SLJ 7/92) [222]

**13824** Adams, Georgie. *The Bible Storybook: Ten Tales from the Old and New Testaments* (K–3). Illus. by Peter Utton. 1995, Dial paper $15.99 (0-8037-1760-1). 96pp. A retelling of 10 well-known Bible stories, like Moses in the bulrushes and Jesus' birth. (Rev: BL 2/1/95; SLJ 4/95) [220]

**13825** Beaude, Pierre-Marie. *The Book of Creation* (2–8). Trans. by Andrew Clements. Illus. by Georges Lemoine. 1991, Picture Book paper $16.95 (0-88708-141-X). 48pp. The Creation story as it might have been handed down through oral tradition. (Rev: BCCB 7–8/91; BL 7/91; SLJ 7/91) [222]

**13826** Bible. *And It Was Good* (PS–2). Illus. by Harold H. Nofziger. 1993, Herald Pr. $12.99 (0-8361-3634-9). The Creation story is reproduced with brightly colored collages and a text from the New Revised Standard Version of the Bible. (Rev: SLJ 12/93) [222]

**13827** Bible. *The Ark* (PS–2). Illus. by Arthur Geisert. 1988, Houghton $17.95 (0-395-43078-X). 48pp. A richly detailed account that includes both well-known and unusual animals. (Rev: HB 11–12/89)

**13828** Bible. *The Lord Is My Shepherd* (3–7). Illus. by Tasha Tudor. 1989, Putnam $12.95 (0-399-20756-2). 32pp. An illustrated edition of the Twenty-third Psalm.

**13829** Bogot, Howard I., and Mary K. Bogot, retellers. *Seven Animal Stories for Children* (K–3). Illus. by Harry Araten. 1997, Pitspopany $15.95 (0-943706-40-8); paper $9.95 (0-943706-41-6). 45pp. A collection of Bible stories and Jewish folktales that tell about such people as Noah, Solomon, David, and Jonah. (Rev: SLJ 12/97) [226]

**13830** Brunelli, Roberto. *A Family Treasury of Bible Stories: One for Each Week of the Year* (4–8). Illus. by Mikhail Fiodorov. 1997, Abrams $24.95 (0-8109-1248-7). 124pp. A collection of 52 briefly told stories (one for each week) from the Old and New Testaments. (Rev: BL 10/1/97; SLJ 2/98) [220.9]

**13831** Caswell, Helen. *Parable of the Good* (5–8). Illus. 1992, Abingdon $11.95 (0-687-30023-1). 24pp. A simple picture book that retells the story of the Good Samaritan. (Rev: BL 6/15/92) [226.8]

**13832** Chaikin, Miriam. *Children's Bible Stories: From Genesis to Daniel* (4–7). Illus. by Yvonne Gilbert. 1993, Dial LB $17.89 (0-8037-0990-0). 96pp. A handsome collection of 26 Bible stories. (Rev: BL 2/15/93*; SLJ 1/93) [221.9]

**13833** Chaikin, Miriam, adapt. *Exodus* (3–5). Illus. by Charles Mikolaycak. 1987, Holiday LB $15.95 (0-8234-0607-5). 32pp. The story of the Israelites' flight out of Egypt. (Rev: BCCB 5/87; BL 5/15/87; HB 5–6/87)

**13834** Chaikin, Miriam. *Joshua in the Promised Land* (4–8). Illus. by David Frampton. 1990, Houghton paper $6.95 (0-395-54797-0). The story of Moses' success and the Israelites' journey to the Holy Land.

**13835** Clements, Andrew. *Noah and the Ark and the Animals* (PS–2). Illus. 1992, Scholastic paper $4.95 (0-590-44457-3). 28pp. Subdued watercolors enhance this retelling.

**13836** Cooper, Ilene. *The Dead Sea Scrolls* (5–8). Illus. by John Thompson. 1997, Morrow $15.00 (0-688-14300-8). 64pp. This account tells about the discovery of the Dead Sea Scrolls, their content, and archaeological importance. (Rev: BCCB 5/97; BL 3/1/97; HB 9–10/97; SLJ 6/97) [296.1]

**13837** Cousins, Lucy. *Noah's Ark* (PS). Illus. 1993, Candlewick $15.99 (1-56402-213-7). 40pp. A simple, direct retelling of the Bible story of Noah and the ark. (Rev: BL 10/1/93; HB 11–12/93; SLJ 9/93) [222]

**13838** dePaola, Tomie. *Mary: The Mother of Jesus* (K–3). Illus. 1995, Holiday LB $16.95 (0-8234-1018-8). 32pp. This account combines stories from the Bible with popular legends to create a life of Mary. (Rev: BCCB 11/95; BL 9/1/95; SLJ 12/95) [232.91]

**13839** dePaola, Tomie. *The Miracles of Jesus* (3–6). Illus. by author. 1987, Holiday LB $16.95 (0-8234-0635-0). 32pp. These one-page adaptations from the New Testament include the 12 miracles of Jesus. (Rev: BL 11/1/87; SLJ 10/87)

**13840** dePaola, Tomie. *The Parables of Jesus* (3–6). Illus. by author. 1987, Holiday LB $16.95 (0-8234-0636-9). 32pp. Seven retellings of the parables of Jesus, such as "The Good Samaritan" and "The Mustard Seed." (Rev: BL 11/1/87; SLJ 10/87)

**13841** dePaola, Tomie. *Tomie dePaola's Book of Bible Stories* (K–3). Illus. 1990, Putnam $24.95 (0-399-21690-1). 128pp. A collection of stories from the Old and New Testaments. (Rev: BCCB 11/90; BL 10/15/90; SLJ 12/90*) [220]

**13842** De Regniers, Beatrice S. *David and Goliath* (1–3). Illus. by Scott Cameron. 1996, Orchard LB $16.99 (0-531-08796-4). 32pp. The story of the shepherd boy David and his deadly confrontation with Goliath. (Rev: BL 3/15/96; SLJ 3/96) [222]

**13843** Devon, Paddie. *The Grumpy Shepherd* (PS–2). Illus. 1995, Abingdon paper $6.95 (0-687-00129-3). 32pp. A grumpy shepherd named Joram changes his attitude when he meets Jesus. (Rev: BL 12/1/95)

**13844** Eisenberg, Ann. *Bible Heroes I Can Be* (PS). Illus. by Rosalyn Schanzer. 1990, Kar-Ben $8.95 (0-929371-09-7); paper $4.95 (0-929371-10-0). Eleven important figures from the Old Testament are introduced and their stories told. (Rev: SLJ 11/90) [222]

**13845** Eisler, Colin, ed. *David's Songs: His Psalms and Their Story* (4–6). Illus. by Jerry Pinkney. 1992, Dial paper $16.89 (0-8037-1059-3). 64pp. A noted art historian and well-known children's illustrator interpret the psalms for a young audience. (Rev: BL 11/15/92; SLJ 9/92) [223]

**13846** Elliot, Betsy Rosen. *Did Jesus Wear Blue Jeans? Answers to a Child's First Bible Questions* (1–3). Illus. by Don Page. 1993, Standard paper $9.99 (0-87403-978-9). 20pp. Answers to 39 questions raised by children about the Bible, like what was Jesus' last name? (Rev: BL 10/1/93) [220.61]

**13847** Farnsworth, Bill. *The Illustrated Children's Bible* (4–6). Illus. 1993, Harcourt $19.95 (0-15-232876-9). 320pp. Selected stories from both the Old and New Testaments are retold with background information on history, geography, plants, and animals. (Rev: BL 1/1/94) [220.5]

**13848** Figley, Marty R. *Mary and Martha* (PS–4). Illus. by Cat B. Smith. 1995, Eerdmans $15.00 (0-8028-5079-0). 32pp. Two very different sisters are visited by Jesus in this story from the Bible. (Rev: BL 10/15/95; SLJ 12/95) [226.4]

**13849** Figley, Marty R. *The Story of Zacchaeus* (PS–4). Illus. by Cat B. Smith. 1995, Eerdmans $15.00 (0-8028-5092-8). 32pp. From the fragments of information given in the Bible, this is the story of Zacchaeus, who climbed a tree to see Jesus. (Rev: BL 9/1/95; SLJ 6/95) [226.4]

**13850** Fisher, Leonard Everett. *David and Goliath* (K–3). Illus. 1993, Holiday LB $15.95 (0-8234-0997-X). 32pp. An expertly illustrated retelling of the Bible story of the brave lad who saved the land of the Israelites. (Rev: BL 5/1/93*; SLJ 6/93) [222]

**13851** Fisher, Leonard Everett. *Moses* (PS–4). Illus. 1995, Holiday LB $15.95 (0-8234-1149-4). 32pp. The life of Moses and the salvation of the Jewish people are portrayed in double-page spreads. (Rev: BCCB 5/95; BL 5/15/95; SLJ 5/95) [222]

**13852** Gauch, Patricia L. *Noah* (K–3). Illus. by Jonathan Green. 1994, Putnam $14.95 (0-399-

22548-X). 32pp. This is a straightforward retelling of the Noah story showing his courage and leadership. (Rev: BCCB 6/94; BL 3/1/94; HB 7–8/94; SLJ 4/94) [222]

**13853** Geisert, Arthur. *After the Flood* (PS–3). Illus. 1994, Houghton $16.95 (0-395-66611-2). 32pp. Shows what happens after the flood when the ship is overturned to serve as a shelter and the business of repopulating the earth begins. (Rev: BCCB 2/94; BL 3/1/94; HB 7–8/94; SLJ 4/94) [222]

**13854** Gellman, Marc. *Does God Have a Big Toe? Stories About Stories in the Bible* (4–6). Illus. by Oscar de Mejo. 1989, HarperCollins $16.00 (0-060-22432-0); paper $7.95 (0-064-40453-6). 96pp. A look at familiar tales in the Bible through new eyes. (Rev: BL 10/15/89; HB 3–4/90; SLJ 12/89) [221]

**13855** Gellman, Marc. *God's Mailbox: More Stories About Stories in the Bible* (4–7). Illus. by Debbie Tilley. 1996, Morrow $15.00 (0-688-13169-7). 92pp. Some stories retold from the Bible, including the Creation, Garden of Eden, Jacob's ladder, the Exodus, and Moses receiving the Ten Commandments. (Rev: BCCB 5/96; SLJ 3/96) [222]

**13856** Gerstein, Mordicai. *Jonah and the Two Great Fish* (PS–3). Illus. 1997, Simon & Schuster $16.00 (0-689-81373-2). 32pp. The story of Jonah, who is swallowed by a fish, is expanded through the use of Jewish legends. (Rev: BL 10/1/97; SLJ 8/97*) [224]

**13857** Goodhart, Pippa. *Noah Makes a Boat* (PS–2). Illus. by Bernard Lodge. 1997, Houghton $15.00 (0-395-86957-9). 32pp. A picture book that humanizes the story of Noah building the ark and of the flood that covered the earth. (Rev: BL 10/1/97; HB 9–10/97; SLJ 9/97) [222]

**13858** Greenfield, Karen R. *Sister Yessa's Story* (2–5). Illus. by Claire Ewart. 1992, HarperCollins $15.00 (0-06-020278-5). As she walks through the woods, Yessa gathers animals for her brother's ark. (Rev: SLJ 8/92)

**13859** Hastings, Selina. *The Children's Illustrated Bible* (4–7). Illus. 1994, DK Publg. $22.95 (1-56458-472-0). 320pp. Several stories from both testaments of the Bible are retold, with some background material on history and geographical settings. (Rev: BL 6/1–15/94) [220.9]

**13860** Hayward, Linda. *Baby Moses* (K–1). Illus. by Barb Henry. 1989, Random LB $11.99 (0-394-99410-8); paper $13.99 (0-394-89410-3). 32pp. For beginning readers, the story of how Moses was saved in a basket of bulrushes. (Rev: BL 6/1/89; SLJ 12/89) [222]

**13861** Hewitt, Kathryn. *Two by Two: The Untold Story* (4–6). Illus. 1984, Harcourt $12.95 (0-15-291801-9). 32pp. A hilarious retelling of the Ark story.

**13862** Hickman, Martha W. *And God Created Squash: How the World Began* (PS–3). Illus. by Giuliano Ferri. 1993, Whitman LB $15.95 (0-8075-0340-1). 32pp. This is a fanciful retelling of the Creation story. (Rev: BL 3/15/93; SLJ 5/93)

**13863** Hutton, Warwick, adapt. *Moses in the Bulrushes* (PS–1). Illus. by Warwick Hutton. 1992, Simon & Schuster paper $4.95 (0-689-71553-6). 32pp. The story of the infant Moses, doomed to death by the pharaoh and saved by the pharaoh's daughter. (Rev: BL 7/86; HB 5–6/86; SLJ 5/86)

**13864** Janisch, Heinz. *Noah's Ark* (PS–3). Trans. by Rosemary Lanning. Illus. by Lisbeth Zwerger. 1997, North-South LB $16.95 (1-55858-785-3). 28pp. The story of Noah and the ark is embellished with such details as animals carrying umbrellas and the unicorn being left out in the rain. (Rev: BL 10/1/97; SLJ 11/97)

**13865** *Jesus of Nazareth: A Life of Christ Through Pictures* (5–7). Illus. 1994, Simon & Schuster $16.00 (0-671-88651-7). 37pp. The life of Jesus Christ, with words from the King James Bible and illustrations from Washington's National Gallery. (Rev: BL 1/1/95; SLJ 3/95) [232]

**13866** Johnson, James W. *The Creation* (K–4). Illus. by James E. Ransome. 1994, Holiday LB $15.95 (0-8234-1069-2). 32pp. The story of the first 7 days of life is told in the paintings and a poem by a famous African American writer. (Rev: BL 4/15/94; HB 9–10/94; SLJ 5/94*) [811]

**13867** Jonas, Ann. *Aardvarks, Disembark!* (PS). Illus. 1990, Greenwillow LB $15.93 (0-688-07207-0). 40pp. Happy rhymes and songs with appealing design. (Rev: BCCB 11/90; BL 11/15/90; HB 11–12/90*; SLJ 10/90*) [222]

**13868** Kassirer, Sue. *Joseph and His Coat of Many Colors* (1–2). Illus. by Danuta Jarecka. 1997, Simon & Schuster paper $15.00 (0-689-81227-2). 32pp. An easily read version of the Bible story of Joseph and his brothers. (Rev: BL 8/97; SLJ 10/97) [222]

**13869** Kessler, Brad. *Moses in Egypt* (1–3). Illus. by Phil Huling. 1997, Simon & Schuster paper $22.00 (0-689-80226-9). This picture book traces Moses from his birth and upbringing as an Egyptian prince to the flight from Egypt with his people. (Rev: SLJ 12/97) [222]

**13870** Langstaff, John, ed. *Climbing Jacob's Ladder: Heroes of the Bible in African-American Spirituals* (K–6). Illus. by Ashley Bryan. 1991, Macmillan $14.95 (0-689-50494-2). Nine heroes from the Bible, including Noah, are introduced through spirituals. (Rev: BL 1/15/92; HB 1–2/92; SLJ 1/92) [222]

**13871** Le Tord, Bijou. *The Deep Blue Sea* (PS–3). Illus. 1996, Dell paper $4.99 (0-440-41063-0). 32pp. The story of the Creation told through simple language and subdued watercolors. (Rev: BL 3/15/90*; SLJ 5/90) [231.7]

**13872** Le Tord, Bijou. *The Little Shepherd: 23rd Psalm* (PS–2). Illus. 1995, Bantam paper $4.99 (0-440-40961-6). 32pp. Pastel miniatures illustrate the retelling of Psalm 23. (Rev: BL 12/15/91; SLJ 1/92) [223]

**13873** Le Tord, Bijou, ed. *Sing a New Song: A Book of Psalms* (PS–3). Illus. 1997, Eerdmans $15.00 (0-8028-5139-8). 32pp. Verses taken from the biblical psalms, with matching illustrations, reveal the wonders of nature. (Rev: BL 12/15/96; SLJ 3/97) [223]

**13874** McCaughrean, Geraldine. *God's People: Stories from the Old Testament* (4–7). Illus. 1997, Simon & Schuster $19.95 (0-689-81366-X). 128pp. A brilliant retelling of the major stories found in the Old Testament. (Rev: BL 3/1/98*; SLJ 3/98) [221.9]

**13875** Mark, Jan. *The Tale of Tobias* (K–3). Illus. by Rachel Merriman. 1996, Candlewick $15.99 (1-56402-692-2). A story from the Apocrypha about Tobias and how he sets out on a journey with his dog to get help for his blind father. (Rev: BCCB 12/96; SLJ 10/96) [222]

**13876** Metaxas, Eric, reteller. *David and Goliath* (2–5). Illus. by Douglas Fraser. 1996, Simon & Schuster paper $10.95 (0-689-80604-3). A dramatic retelling of the exciting Bible story that begins with Saul being made king of the Israelites. (Rev: SLJ 1/97) [222]

**13877** *Noah's Ark* (PS). Illus. by Jane Ray. 1990, Dutton paper $14.95 (0-525-44653-2). 32pp. An appealing interpretation of the Bible story. (Rev: BCCB 11/92; BL 11/15/90; HB 3–4/91; SLJ 10/90*) [222]

**13878** Oppenheim, Shulamith Levey. *And the Earth Trembled: The Creation of Adam and Eve* (PS–3). Illus. by Neil Waldman. 1996, Harcourt $16.00 (0-15-200025-9). 32pp. The Muslim version of the Adam and Eve story and the creation story involving the clay of the earth. (Rev: BCCB 2/97; BL 10/1/96; SLJ 9/96) [297]

**13879** Orgel, Doris, and Ellen Schecter. *The Flower of Sheba* (2–3). Illus. by Laura Kelly. 1994, Bantam paper $3.50 (0-553-37235-1). 32pp. In this easy-to-read story based on a Jewish folktale, the Queen of Sheba tests Solomon's legendary wisdom. (Rev: BL 2/1/94; SLJ 5/94) [222]

**13880** Paterson, Katherine. *The Angel and the Donkey* (1–4). Illus. by Alexander Koshkin. 1996, Clarion $15.95 (0-395-68969-4). 34pp. Based on passages in the Hebrew Bible, this is the story of Pethor, a soothsayer, and his encounter with Moses. (Rev: BCCB 4/96; BL 3/1/96; SLJ 3/96) [222]

**13881** Pilling, Ann. *Before I Go to Sleep: Bible Stories, Poems, and Prayers for Children* (PS–3). Illus.

by Kady MacDonald. 1991, Crown LB $15.99 (0-517-58019-5). 93pp. Along with 22 stories from the Old and New Testaments, there are religious poems and prayers. (Rev: SLJ 3/91) [222]

**13882** *Psalm Twenty-Three* (PS–3). Illus. by Tim Ladwig. 1997, Eerdmans $16.00 (0-8028-5160-6); paper $8.00 (0-8028-5163-0). 32pp. This version of the famous psalm pictures 2 African American children growing up in a bleak, urban neighborhood. (Rev: BL 10/1/97) [123.2]

**13883** Sasso, Sandy Eisenberg. *But God Remembered: Stories of Women from Creation to the Promised Land* (3–6). Illus. by Bethanne Andersen. 1995, Jewish Lights $16.95 (1-879045-43-5). 32pp. In this picture book, the stories of several almost-forgotten women in the Old Testament are retold. (Rev: BL 9/1/95*; SLJ 12/95) [221.9]

**13884** Schmidt, Gary D. *The Blessing of the Lord: Stories from the Old and New Testaments* (3–7). Illus. 1997, Eerdmans $25.00 (0-8028-3789-1). 160pp. Realistic details add authenticity to this enjoyable retelling of stories from both the Old and New Testaments. (Rev: BL 11/1/97; SLJ 10/97) [220.9]

**13885** Spier, Peter, reteller. *Noah's Ark* (PS–K). Illus. by Peter Spier. 1977, Dell paper $6.99 (0-440-40693-5). 44pp. Vital, humorous, detailed pictures present a panorama of the animals and their voyage in the ark. Caldecott Medal winner, 1978.

**13886** Stoddard, Sandol. *A Child's First Bible* (PS–3). Illus. by Tony Chen. 1991, Dial paper $17.99 (0-8037-0941-2). 96pp. A simple introduction to 40 stories from the Old and New Testament. (Rev: BL 3/1/91; SLJ 5/91) [220]

**13887** *Stories from the Old Testament: With Masterwork Paintings Inspired by the Stories* (4–6). Illus. 1996, Simon & Schuster $18.00 (0-689-80955-7). 45pp. Seventeen Old Testament stories with texts from the St. James Bible are illustrated with paintings by such old masters as Rubens and Rembrandt. (Rev: BL 10/1/96; SLJ 10/96) [221.5]

**13888** *The Story of the Creation: Words from Genesis* (PS–5). Illus. by Jane Ray. 1993, Dutton paper $16.00 (0-525-44946-9). The language of the first book in the Bible is used to tell the story of Creation. (Rev: BCCB 3/93; BL 12/15/92*; SLJ 1/93) [222]

**13889** Topek, Susan Remick. *Ten Good Rules* (PS–K). Illus. by Rosalyn Schanzer. 1992, Kar-Ben paper $5.95 (0-929371-28-3). In modern language, the Ten Commandments and their meanings are presented in an attractive concept book. (Rev: SLJ 7/92) [222]

**13890** Waldman, Neil. *The Two Brothers: A Legend of Jerusalem* (PS–2). Illus. 1997, Simon & Schuster $17.00 (0-689-31936-3). 40pp. King Solomon is so impressed with the unselfishness of 2 brothers that he

builds his temple in their honor. (Rev: BL 10/1/97; SLJ 9/97) [398.2]

**13891** Wildsmith, Brian. *Joseph* (K–4). Illus. 1997, Eerdmans $20.00 (0-8028-5161-4). 40pp. A handsome, well-told version of the biblical story of Joseph. (Rev: BL 2/1/98) [222]

**13892** Wolkstein, Diane. *Esther's Story* (4–6). Illus. by Juan Wijngaard. 1996, Morrow LB $14.93 (0-688-12128-4). 32pp. This picture book for older children tells how Esther saved the Jews from a wicked Persian leader. (Rev: BCCB 2/96; BL 3/15/96; HB 5–6/96; SLJ 3/96) [222]

# Holidays and Holy Days

## General and Miscellaneous

**13893** Ancona, George. *Fiesta U.S.A.* (3–6). Illus. 1995, Dutton paper $15.99 (0-525-67498-5). 48pp. Various Latin American festivals — like Three Kings' Day and the Day of the Dead — are pictured as they are celebrated in various parts of the United States. (Rev: BL 10/1/95; HB 11–12/95; SLJ 9/95) [394.2]

**13894** Barkin, Carol, and Elizabeth James. *The Holiday Handbook* (5–8). Illus. 1994, Clarion $17.00 (0-395-65011-9); paper $8.95 (0-395-67888-9). 240pp. Both religious and secular holidays are described, including Lefthanders Day and National Grouch Day. (Rev: BL 6/1–15/94; SLJ 5/94) [394.2]

**13895** Barth, Edna. *Shamrocks, Harps and Shillelaghs: The Story of St. Patrick's Day Symbols* (3–5). Illus. by Ursula Arndt. 1982, Houghton paper $5.95 (0-89919-038-3). 96pp. Customs and symbols associated with St. Patrick's Day, with the origin of each explained.

**13896** Behrens, June. *Gung Hay Fat Choy: Happy New Year* (2–4). Illus. 1982, Children's LB $18.00 (0-516-08842-4); paper $4.95 (0-516-48842-2). A description of the Chinese New Year and how it is celebrated.

**13897** Bernhard, Emery. *Happy New Year!* (3–5). Illus. by Durga Bernhard. 1996, Dutton paper $15.99 (0-525-67532-9). 32pp. From ancient to modern times, celebrations and rituals connected with the New Year are presented. (Rev: BCCB 10/96; BL 9/1/96; SLJ 9/96) [394.2]

**13898** Brady, April A. *Kwanzaa Karamu: Cooking and Crafts for a Kwanzaa Feast* (4–6). Illus. 1995, Carolrhoda LB $21.27 (0-87614-842-9); paper $6.95 (0-87614-633-7). 64pp. Following a general introduction to Kwanzaa, this book introduces crafts and gives 18 recipes for appropriate food. (Rev: BL 4/15/95) [641.59]

**13899** Brown, Tricia. *Chinese New Year* (3–5). Illus. 1997, Holt paper $6.95 (0-8050-5544-4). 48pp. A description of this centuries-old spring holiday that families celebrate in different ways. (Rev: BL 12/1/87; SLJ 12/87)

**13900** Campbell, Louisa. *A World of Holidays! Family Festivities All Over the World!* (3–5). Illus. by Michael Bryant. Series: Family Ties. 1993, Silver Moon LB $13.95 (1-881889-08-4). 60pp. Using a fictitious framework, 5 holidays from such places as Pakistan, Japan, and Namibia are introduced. (Rev: SLJ 2/94) [394.2]

**13901** Chambers, Catherine. *Chinese New Year* (3–5). Illus. Series: World of Holidays. 1997, Raintree Steck-Vaughn LB $21.40 (0-8172-4605-3). 31pp. With many color photos and several craft ideas, this book supplies background information on this spring celebration of good fortune and success and the rituals that surround it. (Rev: BL 6/1–15/97) [394.261]

**13902** Chocolate, Deborah M. *Kwanzaa* (2–4). Illus. by Melodye Rosales. 1990, Children's LB $18.00 (0-516-03991-1); paper $4.95 (0-516-43991-X). 32pp. How one American family celebrates the 7-day December holiday of Kwanzaa. (Rev: BL 2/1/91; SLJ 4/91) [394.2]

**13903** Erlbach, Arlene. *Happy Birthday, Everywhere!* (3–5). Illus. 1997, Millbrook LB $23.90 (0-7613-0007-4). 48pp. With accompanying food and craft projects, this book describes birthday celebrations around the world. (Rev: BL 12/1/97; SLJ 2/98) [394.2]

**13904** Fradin, Dennis B. *Columbus Day* (2–4). Illus. Series: Best Holiday Books. 1990, Enslow LB $18.95 (0-89490-233-4). 48pp. Highlights of the explorer's life and his 4 voyages. (Rev: BL 5/1/90) [970.01]

**13905** Freeman, Dorothy R. *St. Patrick's Day* (3–5). Illus. Series: Best Holiday Books. 1992, Enslow LB $18.95 (0-89490-383-7). 48pp. This easily read account describes the origins of St. Patrick's Day and how it is celebrated. (Rev: BL 10/1/92) [394.2]

**13906** Freeman, Dorothy R., and Dianne M. MacMillan. *Kwanzaa* (3–5). Illus. Series: Best Holiday Books. 1992, Enslow LB $18.95 (0-89490-381-0). 48pp. A full treatment of this African American holiday. (Rev: BL 10/1/92) [394.2]

**13907** Gardner, Robert. *Celebrating Earth Day: A Sourcebook of Activities and Experiments* (5–8). Illus. 1992, Millbrook LB $22.40 (1-56294-070-8). 96pp. A discussion, with experiments, of such global problems as conservation and overpopulation. (Rev: BL 12/1/92) [333.7]

**13908** Gibbons, Gail. *St. Patrick's Day* (2–4). Illus. 1994, Holiday LB $15.95 (0-8234-1119-2). 32pp. As

well as telling the story of St. Patrick's life, this simple account describes how we celebrate his day and the symbols connected with it. (Rev: BCCB 2/94; BL 2/1/94; SLJ 4/94) [394.2]

**13909** Giblin, James Cross. *Fireworks, Picnics, and Flags: The Story of Fourth of July Symbols* (3–6). Illus. by Ursula Arndt. 1983, Houghton paper $7.95 (0-89919-174-6). 96pp. A history of the Fourth of July holiday and how it was and is celebrated.

**13910** Graham-Barber, Lynda. *Doodle Dandy! The Complete Book of Independence Day Words* (4–7). Illus. by Betsy Lewin. 1992, Macmillan LB $13.95 (0-02-736675-8). 128pp. Thirty-four words and phrases that reflect our history and government and explain how they came to be. (Rev: BCCB 7–8/92; BL 7/92; SLJ 3/92) [394]

**13911** Grier, Ella. *Seven Days of Kwanzaa: A Holiday Step Book* (PS–2). Illus. by John Ward. 1997, Viking $10.99 (0-670-87327-6). Double-page spreads are used for each of the 7 days of Kwanzaa in this book about the rituals and symbols connected with this harvest festival. (Rev: SLJ 10/97) [394.26]

**13912** Hoyt-Goldsmith, Diane. *Celebrating Kwanzaa* (4–6). Illus. by Lawrence Migdale. 1993, Holiday LB $16.95 (0-8234-1048-X). 32pp. A photoessay about a Chicago family's celebration of Kwanzaa that explains the origins and meanings of the Seven Principles. (Rev: BCCB 11/93; BL 10/1/93*) [394.2]

**13913** Hoyt-Goldsmith, Diane. *Mardi Gras: A Cajun Country Celebration* (4–6). Illus. 1995, Holiday LB $15.95 (0-8234-1184-2). 32pp. A story of the rituals of Mardi Gras plus a history of the Cajun people and even a recipe for gumbo. (Rev: BL 10/1/95; SLJ 11/95) [394.2]

**13914** Johnson, Dolores. *The Children's Book of Kwanzaa: A Guide to Celebrating the Holiday* (4–7). Illus. 1996, Simon & Schuster $16.00 (0-689-80864-X). 159pp. This account discusses African American history and the origins of Kwanzaa, its meaning, and its rituals. (Rev: BCCB 11/96; BL 9/1/96) [394.2]

**13915** Kadodwala, Dilip. *Holi* (3–5). Illus. Series: World of Holidays. 1997, Raintree Steck-Vaughn LB $21.40 (0-8172-4610-X). 31pp. A description of this joyous Hindu spring festival and how it is observed. (Rev: BL 6/1–15/97) [294.5]

**13916** Kerven, Rosalind. *Id-ul-Fitr* (3–5). Illus. Series: World of Holidays. 1997, Raintree Steck-Vaughn LB $21.40 (0-8172-4609-6). 31pp. After giving a brief introduction to Islam, describes the celebration that marks the end of the sacred month of Ramadan. (Rev: BL 6/1–15/97) [297]

**13917** Kindersley, Barnabas, and Anabel Kindersley. *Celebrations!* (2–6). Illus. Series: Children Just Like Me. 1997, DK Publg. $17.95 (0-7894-2027-9). 63pp. Using double-page spreads, a number of holidays from around the world are featured, such as Christmas in Germany and Diwali in India. (Rev: SLJ 1/98) [394.2]

**13918** Liestman, Vicki. *Columbus Day* (2–3). Illus. by Rick Hanson. Series: On My Own Books. 1991, Carolrhoda LB $18.60 (0-87614-444-X). 56pp. The history of this holiday, plus the life of the explorer, illustrated with colorful paintings. (Rev: BCCB 10/91; BL 9/1/91; SLJ 9/91) [970.01]

**13919** Livingston, Myra Cohn. *Festivals* (K–3). Illus. by Leonard Everett Fisher. 1996, Holiday LB $16.95 (0-8234-1217-2). 32pp. Fourteen of the world's festivals, both common and obscure, are introduced in poetry and paintings. (Rev: BCCB 5/96; BL 5/1/96; SLJ 7/96) [811]

**13920** MacMillan, Dianne M. *Diwali: Hindu Festival of Lights* (3–5). Illus. Series: Best Holiday. 1997, Enslow LB $18.95 (0-89490-817-0). 48pp. Introduces the Hindu festival Diwali and explains how it is celebrated. (Rev: BL 7/97; SLJ 8/97) [294.5]

**13921** MacMillan, Dianne M. *Mardi Gras* (3–5). Series: Best Holiday. 1997, Enslow LB $18.95 (0-89490-819-7). 48pp. Gives a description and history of this holiday with religious roots, with details on how it is celebrated around the world, particularly in New Orleans. (Rev: BL 12/15/97; SLJ 8/97) [394.2]

**13922** MacMillan, Dianne M. *Martin Luther King, Jr.* (3–5). Illus. Series: Best Holiday Books. 1992, Enslow LB $18.95 (0-89490-382-9). 48pp. This easy-to-read book describes how Martin Luther King, Jr. Day originated and how it is celebrated in schools and towns. (Rev: BL 10/1/92; SLJ 1/93) [323]

**13923** MacMillan, Dianne M. *Presidents Day* (3–5). Illus. Series: Best Holiday. 1997, Enslow LB $18.95 (0-89490-820-0). 48pp. An introduction to the day on which Americans pay tribute to their presidents and a discussion of the ways in which it is celebrated. (Rev: BL 7/97) [973.4]

**13924** Martinet, Jeanne, comp. *The Year You Were Born, 1986* (2–6). Illus. by Judy Lanfredi. Series: Day-By-Day Record Of. 1993, Tambourine paper $7.95 (0-688-11968-9). This book, like the others in the series, gives facts and assorted trivia for each day of the featured year. (Rev: SLJ 2/94) [793.21]

**13925** Most, Bernard. *Happy Holidaysaurus!* (K–3). Illus. 1992, Harcourt $13.95 (0-15-233386-X). 32pp. Contains a parade of dinosaurs that illustrate a year of holidays. (Rev: BL 3/15/92; SLJ 6/92) [394.2]

**13926** Penner, Lucille R. *Celebration: The Story of American Holidays* (3–5). Illus. by Ib Ohlsson. 1993, Macmillan LB $15.95 (0-02-770903-5). 79pp. A discussion of the origins of and celebrations associated with 13 important American holidays, e.g., Columbus Day, Veterans Day, Martin Luther King Day,

Halloween, and New Year's Day. (Rev: SLJ 11/93) [394.2]

**13927** Perl, Lila. *Pinatas and Paper Flowers: Holidays of the Americas in English and Spanish* (4–8). Illus. by Victoria de Larrea. 1985, Houghton paper $6.95 (0-89919-155-X). 91pp. Eight Hispanic holidays are highlighted in this bilingual volume.

**13928** Porter, A. P. *Kwanzaa* (2–4). Illus. by Janice L. Porter. 1991, Carolrhoda LB $18.60 (0-87614-668-X). 56pp. African Americans celebrate their rich history and culture by observing Kwanzaa. (Rev: BCCB 12/91; BL 12/1/91) [394.2]

**13929** Scott, Geoffrey. *Labor Day* (1–4). Illus. by Cherie R. Wyman. 1982, Carolrhoda LB $18.60 (0-87614-178-5). 48pp. A simple book about the first Labor Day.

**13930** Thompson, Jan. *Christian Festivals* (3–6). Illus. Series: Celebrate. 1997, Heinemann $13.95 (0-431-06961-1). 48pp. Familiar Christian holidays like Christmas, Lent, Ascension Day, and Easter are explained through the experiences of 3 children. (Rev: BL 8/97; SLJ 12/97) [263]

**13931** Viesti, Joe, and Diane Hall. *Celebrate! In South Asia* (2–5). Illus. 1996, Lothrop LB $15.93 (0-688-13775-X). 32pp. Nine holidays as celebrated on the Indian subcontinent are introduced. (Rev: BCCB 10/96; BL 9/1/96; SLJ 9/96) [394.2]

**13932** Viesti, Joe, and Diane Hall. *Celebrate! In Southeast Asia* (2–5). Illus. 1996, Lothrop LB $15.93 (0-688-13489-0). 32pp. Such countries as Vietnam, Thailand, Malaysia, and the Philippines are represented in this explanation of 9 celebrations. (Rev: BCCB 10/96; BL 9/1/96; SLJ 9/96) [394.2]

**13933** Viesti, Joe, and Diane Hall. *Celebrate! In Central America* (3–5). Illus. Series: Celebrate! 1997, Lothrop LB $15.93 (0-688-15162-0). 32pp. Describes holidays that are celebrated in various Central American countries, from Guatemala to Panama. (Rev: BL 9/15/97; SLJ 8/97) [394]

**13934** Wilcox, Jane. *Why Do We Celebrate That?* (4–6). Illus. Series: Why Do We . . .? 1996, Watts LB $18.00 (0-531-14393-7). 31pp. This book looks at various cultures, their holidays and festivals, and how they observe birthdays, weddings, and funeral rites. (Rev: SLJ 8/97) [394.2]

## Christmas

**13935** Barth, Edna. *Holly, Reindeer and Colored Lights: The Story of the Christmas Symbols* (3–6). Illus. by Ursula Arndt. 1985, Houghton paper $6.95 (0-89919-037-5). 96pp. Christmas and its symbols from around the world.

**13936** Bible. *The Nativity* (PS–3). Illus. by Julie Vivas. 1988, Harcourt $13.95 (0-15-200535-8). 34pp. A retelling using Bible verses and earthy, sometimes humorous illustrations. A reissue. (Rev: HB 11–12/88)

**13937** Bible. *Visions of Christmas: A Renaissance Nativity* (2–5). 1997, Simon & Schuster paper $18.00 (0-689-81359-7). This elegant Christmas book combines verses from the King James version of the Bible and Renaissance nativity paintings. (Rev: SLJ 10/97) [922]

**13938** Bodker, Cecil. *Mary of Nazareth* (3–5). Trans. by Eric Bibb. Illus. by Bengt A. Runnerstrom. 1989, Farrar $14.95 (91-29-59178-3). 60pp. The story of Mary, mother of Jesus, incorporates what is known from the New Testament sources. (Rev: BL 12/1/89) [232]

**13939** Brent, Isabelle. *The Christmas Story* (PS–4). Illus. 1989, Dial paper $13.95 (0-8037-0730-4). 32pp. A rich portrayal of the Nativity scene. (Rev: BL 10/15/89; HB 11–12/89) [745.6]

**13940** Chambers, Catherine. *Christmas* (3–5). Illus. Series: World of Holidays. 1997, Raintree Steck-Vaughn LB $21.40 (0-8172-4608-8). 31pp. This book explains the origins of Christmas and how it is observed around the world, along with decorating ideas and some craft projects. (Rev: BL 6/1–15/97) [394.2]

**13941** *Christmas in Colonial and Early America* (4–7). Illus. 1996, World Book $15.95 (0-7166-0875-8). 80pp. The evolution of Christmas celebrations is traced through more than 100 years of American history to the end of the 19th century. (Rev: BL 11/1/96) [394.26]

**13942** *Christmas in Switzerland* (4–6). Illus. 1995, World Book $18.50 (0-7166-0895-2). 80pp. This book introduces Swiss customs and traditional activities surrounding Christmas. (Rev: BL 9/15/95) [394.26]

**13943** Conaway, Judith. *Easy-to-Make Christmas Crafts* (2–4). Illus. 1986, Troll LB $12.50 (0-8167-0674-3). 48pp. Simple projects using easily obtained materials for such Christmas items as leaf chains, an elf's house, and a pop-up house for Santa. (Rev: BL 12/1/86)

**13944** *The First Christmas* (3–7). Illus. 1992, Simon & Schuster paper $17.00 (0-671-79364-0). 30pp. This Christmas story, in the words of Isaiah, St. Matthew, and St. Luke, is illustrated with the work of such artists as Botticelli and Fra Filippo Lippi. (Rev: BL 11/1/92) [226]

**13945** Gibbons, Gail. *Christmas Time* (PS). Illus. by author. 1982, Holiday LB $15.95 (0-8234-0453-6). 32pp. A simple explanation of the origins and traditions associated with Christmas.

**13946** Graham, Ruth B. *One Wintry Night* (4–6). Illus. by Richard J. Watson. 1995, Baker $25.00 (0-8010-3848-0). 72pp. A woman tells an injured mountain boy the story of the importance of Christmas after she rescues him from a snowstorm. (Rev: BL 9/1/95)

**13947** Graham-Barber, Lynda. *Ho Ho Ho! The Complete Book of Christmas Words* (4–6). Illus. by Betsy Lewin. 1993, Bradbury $16.00 (0-02-736933-1). 128pp. A collection of words associated with Christmas, with their definitions and derivations. (Rev: BL 10/1/93) [394.2]

**13948** Kelley, Emily. *Christmas Around the World* (2–4). Illus. 1986, Carolrhoda LB $18.60 (0-87614-249-8); Lerner paper $5.95 (0-87614-453-9). 48pp. Traditions and celebrations around the world in simple language. (Rev: BCCB 9/86; BL 7/86)

**13949** Kennedy, Pamela. *A Christmas Celebration: Traditions and Customs from Around the World* (3–6). Illus. 1992, Ideals LB $12.00 (0-8249-8587-7). 32pp. The author presents international customs and those that are particular to certain cultures and emphasizes the whole season of Christmas rather than one day. (Rev: BL 11/1/92) [394.2]

**13950** Kurelek, William. *A Northern Nativity: Christmas Dreams of a Prairie Boy* (1–3). Illus. by author. 1976, Tundra $16.95 (0-88776-071-6); paper $9.95 (0-88776-099-6). Twenty paintings of the Holy Family transferred to various locales, accompanied by a lyrical text.

**13951** Lankford, Mary D. *Christmas Around the World* (2–5). Illus. 1995, Morrow LB $15.93 (0-688-12167-5). 48pp. An examination of Christmas traditions in 12 countries. (Rev: BL 9/15/95) [394.2]

**13952** Leedy, Loreen. *A Dragon Christmas: Things to Make and Do at Christmas* (1–3). Illus. 1988, Holiday LB $13.95 (0-8234-0716-0). 32pp. Ten blue dragons getting ready for Christmas introduce various activities for children. (Rev: BL 11/1/88)

**13953** Rollins, Charlemae H., ed. *Christmas Gif':* *An Anthology of Christmas Poems, Songs, and Stories* (5–8). Illus. by Ashley Bryan. 1993, Morrow $14.00 (0-688-11667-1). 128pp. An anthology first published 30 years ago that contains songs and stories about Christmas and about African Americans from slavery days. (Rev: BL 7/93) [810.8]

**13954** Roop, Peter, and Connie Roop. *Let's Celebrate Christmas* (3–5). Illus. 1997, Millbrook LB $19.90 (0-7613-0115-1); paper $5.95 (0-7613-0283-2). 32pp. As well as a history of the customs surrounding Christmas, this book contains crafts, puzzles, and riddles. (Rev: BL 9/1/97; SLJ 10/97) [394]

## Easter

**13955** Barth, Edna. *Lilies, Rabbits and Painted Eggs: The Story of the Easter Symbols* (3–6). Illus. by Ursula Arndt. 1981, Houghton paper $5.95 (0-395-30550-0). The pagan and Christian origins of many of the celebrations associated with Easter.

**13956** Kennedy, Pamela. *An Easter Celebration: Traditions and Customs from Around the World* (4–6). Illus. 1991, Ideals $10.95 (0-8249-8506-0). 32pp. Color photos and historical drawings add to this handy volume on Easter celebrations. (Rev: BL 3/15/91) [394.2]

**13957** Winthrop, Elizabeth, adapt. *He Is Risen: The Easter Story* (4–7). Illus. by Charles Mikolaycak. 1985, Holiday LB $15.95 (0-8234-0547-8). 32pp. The Easter story taken from parts of the King James version of the Bible and dramatically illustrated. (Rev: BCCB 4/85; HB 7–8/85; SLJ 4/85)

## Halloween

**13958** Barth, Edna. *Witches, Pumpkins and Grinning Ghosts: The Story of the Halloween Symbols* (3–6). Illus. by Ursula Arndt. 1981, Houghton paper $6.95 (0-89919-040-5). 96pp. The origins of Halloween and how it is celebrated in many countries.

**13959** Chambers, Catherine. *All Saints, All Souls, and Halloween* (3–5). Illus. Series: World of Holidays. 1997, Raintree Steck-Vaughn LB $21.40 (0-8172-4606-1). 31pp. An explanation of the origins of this holiday as an observance for the spirits of the dead, customs associated with it, and a number of craft activities. (Rev: BL 6/1–15/97) [394.2]

**13960** Gibbons, Gail. *Halloween* (PS–1). Illus. by author. 1984, Holiday LB $15.95 (0-8234-0524-9); paper $5.95 (0-8234-0577-X). 32pp. Halloween history and traditions are explained in this simple picture book.

**13961** Limburg, Peter R. *Weird! The Complete Book of Halloween Words* (4–7). Illus. by Betsy Lewin. 1989, Macmillan LB $13.95 (0-02-759050-X). 128pp. This book defines 41 words and expressions, such as trick or treat, associated with Halloween. (Rev: BL 9/1/89; SLJ 9/89) [394]

**13962** Roop, Peter, and Connie Roop. *Let's Celebrate Halloween* (3–5). Illus. 1997, Millbrook LB $19.90 (0-7613-0113-5); paper $5.95 (0-7613-0284-0). 32pp. Includes a number of crafts, like making a haunted house and different masks, as well as a history of Halloween and its significance. (Rev: BL 9/1/97; SLJ 8/97) [745.5]

**13963** Wolff, Ferida, and Dolores Kozielski. *Halloween Fun for Everyone* (1–6). Illus. by Judy Lanfredi. 1997, Morrow paper $7.95 (0-688-15257-0).

79pp. After a history of Halloween, this book gives directions on how to make costumes, games, decorations, and holiday food. (Rev: SLJ 1/98) [745.5]

## Jewish Holy Days and Celebrations

**13964** Adler, David A. *The Kids' Catalog of Jewish Holidays* (4–7). Illus. 1996, Jewish Publication Soc. paper $15.95 (0-8276-0581-1). 244pp. Thirteen major and several minor Jewish holidays are introduced, along with activities, songs, and recipes. (Rev: BL 12/15/96; SLJ 3/97) [296.4]

**13965** Adler, David A. *A Picture Book of Jewish Holidays* (PS). Illus. by Linda Heller. 1981, Holiday LB $15.95 (0-8234-0396-3). 32pp. A very simple explanation of the major Jewish holy days.

**13966** Adler, David A. *A Picture Book of Passover* (PS–3). Illus. by Linda Heller. 1982, Holiday $14.95 (0-8234-0439-0). 32pp. A book that tells the history of Passover and ways in which it is celebrated.

**13967** Brinn, Ruth Esrig. *Jewish Holiday Crafts for Little Hands* (PS–4). Illus. by Katherine J. Kahn. 1993, Kar-Ben paper $10.95 (9-929371-47-X). 127pp. Using 11 different Jewish holidays as a focus, this unique craft book gives an average of a dozen simple projects for each. (Rev: SLJ 10/93) [296.4]

**13968** Burns, Marilyn. *The Hanukkah Book* (4–7). Illus. by Martha Weston. 1991, Avon paper $3.99 (0-380-71520-1). 128pp. Not only the history and traditions of this day but also attitudes Jewish children have about Christmas are discussed.

**13969** Burstein, Chaya M. *The Jewish Kids Catalog* (3–7). Illus. by author. 1983, Jewish Publication Soc. paper $14.95 (0-8276-0215-4). 224pp. An introduction to Jewish holidays, traditions, and crafts.

**13970** Chaikin, Miriam. *Menorahs, Mezuzas, and Other Jewish Symbols* (5–8). Illus. by Erika Weihs. 1990, Houghton $15.95 (0-89919-856-2). 102pp. Exploring some of the symbols of the Jewish faith. (Rev: BL 1/1/91; HB 5–6/91; SLJ 1/91) [296.4]

**13971** Cohn, Janice. *The Christmas Menorahs: How a Town Fought Hate* (3–5). Illus. 1995, Albert Whitman LB $16.95 (0-8075-1152-8). 40pp. The true story about the people of Billings, Montana, who put menorahs in their windows to fight bigotry. (Rev: BL 9/15/95) [305]

**13972** Corwin, Judith Hoffman. *Jewish Holiday Fun* (4–6). Illus. by author. 1987, Silver Burdett paper $5.95 (0-671-60127-X). 64pp. All sorts of ways to celebrate plus an explanation of the meaning of each holiday in this reissued book.

**13973** Drucker, Malka. *The Family Treasury of Jewish Holidays* (4–6). Illus. 1994, Little, Brown $22.95 (0-316-19343-7). 180pp. Organized around the Jewish calendar, this collection of fact and fiction introduces the holidays, including the weekly Shabbat. (Rev: BL 11/15/94; SLJ 11/94) [296.4]

**13974** Fishman, Cathy G. *On Rosh Hashanah and Yom Kippur* (4–7). Illus. by Melanie Hall. 1997, Simon & Schuster $16.00 (0-689-80526-8). 40pp. Explores and explains the traditions associated with Jewish High Holidays, with particular emphasis of Rosh Hashanah. (Rev: BL 10/1/97; SLJ 10/97) [296.4]

**13975** Goldin, Barbara D. *Bat Mitzvah: A Jewish Girl's Coming of Age* (5–7). Illus. 1995, Viking $14.99 (0-670-86034-4); paper $5.99 (0-14-037516-3). 160pp. A history of the Bat Mitzvah and its significance from the first one celebrated in the United States in 1922 to the present. (Rev: BL 9/1/95; SLJ 11/95) [296.4]

**13976** Goldin, Barbara D. *The Passover Journey: A Seder Companion* (4–8). Illus. by Neil Waldman. 1994, Viking paper $15.99 (0-670-82421-6). 64pp. Rabbinical stories and excerpts from Exodus are used to re-create the traditions of the Jewish holiday Passover in this attractively illustrated book. (Rev: BCCB 4/94; BL 3/1/94*; HB 5–6/94; SLJ 2/94) [269.4]

**13977** Groner, Judye, and Madeline Wikler. *All About Hanukkah* (K–4). Illus. by Rosalyn Schanzer. 1988, Kar-Ben paper $4.95 (0-930494-82-2). The origins and customs of the ancient celebration. (Rev: BL 12/15/88)

**13978** Hoyt-Goldsmith, Diane. *Celebrating Hanukkah* (3–6). Illus. by Lawrence Migdale. 1996, Holiday $16.95 (0-8234-1252-0). 32pp. A photoessay about Hanukkah and how it is celebrated in the United States. (Rev: BCCB 11/96; BL 9/1/96) [296.4]

**13979** Jaffe, Nina. *The Uninvited Guest and Other Jewish Holiday Tales* (4–6). Illus. by Elivia Savadier. 1993, Scholastic $16.95 (0-590-44653-3). 80pp. Seven Jewish holidays, including Rosh Hashanah, Yom Kippur, and Passover, are highlighted in these delightful folktales. (Rev: BL 11/15/93; SLJ 2/94) [296.4]

**13980** Kimmel, Eric A. *Bar Mitzvah: A Jewish Boy's Coming of Age* (5–7). Illus. 1995, Viking $15.00 (0-670-85540-5). 112pp. Stories, sayings, and factual material intermingle in this account of the ritual involving a Jewish boy's coming of age. (Rev: BL 2/15/95; HB 9–10/95; SLJ 3/95*) [296.4]

**13981** Kolatch, Alfred J. *The Jewish Child's First Book of Why* (PS–4). Illus. by Harry Araten. 1992, Jonathan David $14.95 (0-8246-0354-0). 32pp. Fifteen questions and answers dealing mainly with Jewish holidays. (Rev: BL 4/15/92) [296.4]

**13982** Manushkin, Fran. *Miriam's Cup: A Passover Story* (2–4). Illus. by Bob Dacey. 1998, Scholastic $15.95 (0-590-67720-9). 32pp. An account of the origins of Passover in ancient Egypt and of the role played by Miriam, Moses' sister. (Rev: BL 2/1/98; SLJ 2/98) [222]

**13983** Musleah, Rahel, and Michael Klayman. *Sharing Blessings: Children's Stories for Exploring the Spirit of the Jewish Holidays* (3–5). Illus. 1997, Jewish Lights $18.95 (1-879045-71-0). 64pp. Through the observances of a single family, all the major Jewish holidays are introduced and explained. (Rev: BL 10/1/97; SLJ 9/97) [296.4]

**13984** Rose, David, and Gill Rose. *Passover* (3–5). Illus. Series: World of Holidays. 1997, Raintree Steck-Vaughn LB $21.40 (0-8172-4607-X). 31pp. This book explains the origins of Passover and the Seder that accompanies it, along with many activities and craft projects. (Rev: BL 6/1–15/97) [296.4]

**13985** Ross, Kathy. *Crafts for Hanukkah* (2–4). Illus. 1996, Millbrook LB $21.90 (1-56294-919-5); paper $6.95 (0-7613-0078-3). 48pp. Outlines crafts associated with Hanukkah, like making dreidels and menorahs. (Rev: BL 9/1/96) [745.594]

**13986** Techner, David, and Judith Hirt-Manheimer. *A Candle for Grandpa* (K–3). Illus. by Joel Iskowitz. 1993, UAHC $10.95 (0-8074-0507-8). Using the first anniversary of the death of a boy's grandfather as a focus, this book presents Jewish funeral practices. (Rev: SLJ 10/93) [296.4]

**13987** Wood, Angela. *Jewish Festivals* (4–6). Illus. Series: Celebrate. 1997, Heinemann $13.95 (0-431-06962-X). 48pp. A boy in Jerusalem and a girl in Chicago explain how their families celebrate a number of Jewish holidays and holy days. (Rev: SLJ 12/97) [221.6]

**13988** Yolen, Jane. *Milk and Honey: A Year of Jewish Holidays* (4–6). Illus. by Louise August. 1996, Putnam $21.95 (0-399-22652-4). 80pp. Eight of the most important holidays in the Jewish calendar are discussed, with accompanying folktales, poems, or other forms of literature. (Rev: BCCB 11/96; BL 10/1/96; SLJ 12/96) [296.4]

## Thanksgiving

**13989** Barth, Edna. *Turkeys, Pilgrims and Indian Corn: The Story of the Thanksgiving Symbols* (3–6). Illus. by Ursula Arndt. 1981, Houghton paper $6.95 (0-89919-039-1). 96pp. Historical details about the origin of this festival and how we celebrate it today.

**13990** Conaway, Judith. *Happy Thanksgiving! Things to Make and Do* (2–4). Illus. 1986, Troll LB $12.50 (0-8167-0668-9); paper $3.95 (0-8167-0669-7). 48pp. A Pilgrim belt buckle, a miniature Mayflower, and a mobile are some of the easy-to-do projects in this book. (Rev: BL 12/1/86)

**13991** Corwin, Judith Hoffman. *Harvest Festivals Around the World* (4–6). Illus. 1995, Messner LB $6.95 (0-671-87240-0). 48pp. Fifteen projects, like mask and doll making, that celebrate harvests and thanksgiving globally. (Rev: BL 2/1/96; SLJ 5/96) [394.2]

**13992** Corwin, Judith Hoffman. *Thanksgiving Fun* (2–4). Illus. 1984, Silver Burdett paper $5.95 (0-671-50849-0). 64pp. A number of Thanksgiving projects are outlined, including a big dinner.

**13993** George, Jean Craighead. *The First Thanksgiving* (3–5). Illus. by Thomas Locker. 1993, Putnam $15.95 (0-399-21991-9). 32pp. Text and dramatic pictures complement this sturdy retelling of the first Thanksgiving. (Rev: BL 7/93; SLJ 7/93) [394.2]

**13994** Gibbons, Gail. *Thanksgiving Day* (PS–2). Illus. by author. 1983, Holiday LB $15.95 (0-8234-0489-7); paper $6.95 (0-8234-0576-1). 32pp. A very simple introduction to Thanksgiving Day.

**13995** Graham-Barber, Lynda. *Gobble! The Complete Book of Thanksgiving Words* (4–6). Illus. by Betsy Lewin. 1993, Avon paper $3.99 (0-380-71963-0). 128pp. In readable fashion, all the words associated with this holiday are featured. (Rev: BL 1/1/91; SLJ 11/91) [394.2]

**13996** Hayward, Linda. *The First Thanksgiving* (1–3). Illus. by James Watling. Series: Step into Reading. 1990, Random LB $11.99 (0-679-90218-X); paper $3.99 (0-679-80218-5). 48pp. This easy-to-read book tells about the journey of the Pilgrims and of their first colony. (Rev: BCCB 11/90; BL 12/1/90) [394.2]

**13997** MacMillan, Dianne M. *Thanksgiving Day* (3–5). Illus. Series: Best Holiday. 1997, Enslow LB $18.95 (0-89490-822-7). 48pp. The origins of this holiday are traced, with discussion of the ways in which it is celebrated. (Rev: BL 7/97; SLJ 8/97) [394.2]

### Valentine's Day

**13998** Barth, Edna. *Hearts, Cupids and Red Roses: The Story of the Valentine Symbols* (4–6). Illus. by Ursula Arndt. 1982, Houghton paper $7.95 (0-89919-036-7). 64pp. A fascinating compilation of facts and lore about St. Valentine's Day.

**13999** Brownrigg, Sheri. *Hearts and Crafts* (4–7). Illus. 1995, Tricycle Pr. paper $9.95 (1-883672-28-7). 96pp. Clear instructions on how to complete a variety of Valentine's Day projects, including making necklaces and candles. (Rev: BL 3/1/96; SLJ 3/96) [745.5]

**14000** Fradin, Dennis B. *Valentine's Day* (3–5). Illus. 1990, Enslow LB $18.95 (0-89490-237-7).

48pp. A look at how we have celebrated this holiday over the years. (Rev: BL 8/90; SLJ 2/91) [394.2]

**14001** Gibbons, Gail. *Valentine's Day* (PS–1). Illus. by author. 1986, Holiday LB $15.95 (0-8234-0572-9); paper $6.95 (0-8234-0764-0). 32pp. History, meaning, and customs of Valentine's Day with simple drawings in bright colors. (Rev: BCCB 2/86; BL 12/15/85)

**14002** Graham-Barber, Lynda. *Mushy! The Complete Book of Valentine Words* (4–8). Illus. by Betsy Lewin. 1993, Avon paper $3.50 (0-380-71650-X). 122pp. An explanation of the words, symbols, and customs concerning Valentine's Day. (Rev: BCCB 3/91; BL 2/15/91; SLJ 5/91) [394.2]

**14003** Kessel, Joyce K. *Valentine's Day* (2–4). Illus. by Karen Ritz. 1981, Carolrhoda LB $13.13 (0-87614-166-1); Lerner paper $5.95 (0-87614-502-0). 48pp. An easily read account of the origins of this holiday and the traditions surrounding it.

**14004** Sabuda, Robert. *Saint Valentine* (K–4). Illus. 1992, Macmillan $16.00 (0-689-31762-X). 32pp. Mosaiclike illustrations accompany the story of the gentle Christian physician and priest who lived in Rome during the Christian persecutions. (Rev: BL 11/15/92; SLJ 11/92) [270.1]

## Prayers

**14005** Batchelor, Mary, ed. *Children's Prayers: From Around the World* (4–7). Illus. 1995, Augsburg $13.99 (0-8066-2830-8). 93pp. Two hundred prayers for children from many sources worldwide, with some for special holidays and holy days. (Rev: BL 9/1/95) [242]

**14006** Baynes, Pauline, ed. *Thanks Be to God: Prayers from Around the World* (PS–3). Illus. by Pauline Baynes. 1990, Macmillan paper $13.95 (0-02-708541-4). 32pp. This is a collection of prayers and thanksgiving. (Rev: BCCB 4/90; BL 3/15/90*; SLJ 5/90) [291.4]

**14007** Beckett, Wendy. *A Child's Book of Prayer in Art* (3–6). Illus. 1995, DK Publg. $12.95 (1-56458-875-0). 32pp. Using the work of 15 artists, from Michelangelo to Millet, the editor shows how the act of praying has been represented in art. (Rev: BL 9/1/95*; SLJ 8/95) [242]

**14008** Bernos de Gasztold, Carmen. *Prayers from the Ark* (4–7). Trans. by Rumer Godden. Illus. by Barry Moser. 1995, Puffin paper $5.99 (0-140-54585-9). 32pp. A poem written during World War II by a woman who is now a nun. (Rev: BCCB 12/92; BL 9/1/92; HB 11–12/92) [841]

**14009**   Bible. *Give Us This Day: The Lord's Prayer* (PS–4). Illus. by Tasha Tudor. 1989, Putnam $12.95 (0-399-21442-9). Children in turn-of-the-century New England highlight the lovely paintings that illustrate the words of this Christian prayer. (Rev: BL 2/1/88)

**14010**   *A Child's Book of Prayers* (PS–2). Illus. by Michael Hague. 1985, Holt $14.95 (0-8050-0211-1). 32pp. Twenty familiar prayers and devotions lovingly illustrated. (Rev: BL 3/1/86; SLJ 3/86)

**14011**   *A Family Treasury of Prayers* (5–7). Illus. 1996, Simon & Schuster $16.00 (0-689-80956-5). 93pp. Classic art works illustrate this lovely collection of prayers from famous sources. (Rev: BL 10/1/96; SLJ 10/96) [242]

**14012**   Field, Rachel. *Prayer for a Child* (1–3). Illus. by Elizabeth Orton Jones. 1968, Macmillan LB $14.00 (0-02-735190-4); paper $4.99 (0-02-043070-1). 32pp. A prayer bespeaking the faith, hope, and love of little children. Caldecott Medal winner, 1945.

**14013**   Groner, Judye, and Madeline Wikler. *Thank You, God! A Jewish Child's Book of Prayers* (PS–2). Illus. by Shelly O. Haas. 1994, Kar-Ben $16.95 (0-929371-65-8). 32pp. A series of blessings and prayers involving Jewish traditions, written in Hebrew letters with an English translation. (Rev: BL 3/15/94; SLJ 4/94) [296.7]

**14014**   Hopkins, Lee Bennett, sel. *All God's Chil-* *dren: A Book of Prayers* (K–2). Illus. by Amanda Schaffer. 1998, Harcourt $15.00 (0-15-201499-3). 48pp. A collection of 22 short prayers that are both moving and easy to understand. (Rev: SLJ 3/98) [242]

**14015**   Strickland, Tessa, ed. *One Earth, One Spirit: A Child's Book of Prayers from Many Faiths and Cultures* (K–5). Illus. 1997, Sierra Club $14.95 (0-87156-978-7). 40pp. This handsome book contains 17 prayers from the world's major religions plus several from North American Indians. (Rev: BL 11/1/97; SLJ 11/97) [291.4]

**14016**   Titherington, Jeanne. *A Child's Prayer* (PS–2). Illus. 1989, Greenwillow LB $15.93 (0-688-08318-8). 24pp. With simple prayers and Bible verses, this book shows a boy at prayer with his toys. (Rev: BL 9/1/89*; HB 1–2/90; SLJ 11/89) [242]

**14017**   Willard, Nancy. *The Good-Night Blessing Book* (K–3). Illus. 1996, Scholastic $15.95 (0-590-62393-1). 32pp. This is a good-night prayer illustrated with the author's photographs. (Rev: BL 10/1/96; SLJ 10/96) [811]

**14018**   Yeatman, Linda. *A Child's Book of Prayers* (PS–3). Illus. by Tracey Williamson. 1992, Workman $19.95 (1-55670-251-5). 94pp. Drawn from African-American spirituals and European and American poems and prayers, this is a collection of short poems divided into general categories. (Rev: BL 6/15/92; SLJ 7/92) [242]

# Social Groups

## Ethnic Groups

**14019** Aliotta, Jerome J. *The Puerto Ricans* (5–8). Illus. Series: Land of Immigrants. 1995, Chelsea LB $19.95 (0-7910-3360-0). 110pp. A history of Puerto Rico and its people plus coverage on their traditions and contributions. (Rev: BL 10/15/95) [305]

**14020** Anderson, Kelly C. *Immigration* (4–8). Illus. 1993, Lucent LB $22.45 (1-56006-140-5). 112pp. After supplying some historical background, this account concentrates on the present status and problems concerning immigration. (Rev: SLJ 8/93) [325.73]

**14021** Archibald, Erika F. *A Sudanese Family* (4–7). Illus. Series: Journey Between Two Worlds. 1997, Lerner paper $8.95 (0-8225-9753-5). 56pp. Introduces Dei Jock Dei and his family, who left Sudan to escape religious persecution and, through the help of a church, settled in Atlanta, Georgia. (Rev: BL 6/1–15/97; SLJ 7/97) [975.8]

**14022** Ashabranner, Brent. *To Seek a Better World: The Haitian Minority in America* (5–8). Photos by Paul Conklin. Illus. 1997, Cobblehill paper $16.99 (0-525-65219-1). 88pp. A good portrait of the Haitian American community, the different times when they left their country, where they settled, and their positive contributions to American life. (Rev: SLJ 5/97) [813]

**14023** Bandon, Alexandra. *Asian Indian Americans* (5–8). Illus. Series: Footsteps to America. 1995, New Discovery LB $13.95 (0-02-768144-0). 111pp. An account of the conditions that caused emigration from India and a description of life in the United States for the immigrants. (Rev: SLJ 8/95) [973]

**14024** Bandon, Alexandra. *Dominican Americans* (5–8). Illus. Series: Footsteps to America. 1995, New Discovery $14.95 (0-02-768152-1). 111pp. A readable account of why many residents of the Dominican Republic left their country to come to the United States and the conditions they found when they settled here. (Rev: SLJ 8/95) [973]

**14025** Bandon, Alexandra. *West Indian Americans* (5–8). Illus. Series: Footsteps to America. 1994, New Discovery LB $13.95 (0-02-768148-3). 111pp. Describes why some West Indians left their islands to come to the United States, their reception here, and their present life-styles and contributions to the nation. (Rev: SLJ 12/94) [304.8]

**14026** Berg, Lois Anne. *An Eritrean Family* (4–7). Illus. Series: Journey Between Two Worlds. 1997, Lerner LB $22.60 (0-8225-3405-3); paper $8.95 (0-8225-9755-1). 64pp. The story of the Kiklu family, which fled Eritrea in eastern Africa in 1978, spent 10 years in a refugee camp, and resettled in Minnesota. (Rev: BL 6/1–15/97; SLJ 8/97) [304.895]

**14027** Berger, Melvin, and Gilda Berger. *Where Did Your Family Come From? A Book About Immigrants* (2–3). Illus. by Robert Quackenbush. Series: Discovery Readers. 1993, Ideals LB $12.00 (0-8249-8647-4); paper $4.50 (0-8249-8610-5). 48pp. A simple text about the waves of immigration to the United States. (Rev: BCCB 4/93; BL 7/93; SLJ 6/93) [325.73]

**14028** Birdseye, Debbie H., and Tom Birdseye. *Under Our Skin: Kids Talk About Race* (3–7). Illus. 1997, Holiday LB $15.95 (0-8234-1325-X). 32pp. Six American middle-schoolers from various racial backgrounds talk about their pride in their culture and their feelings of belonging to the human race. (Rev: BL 12/15/97; SLJ 4/98) [305.8]

**14029** Brown, Tricia. *Konnichiwa! I Am a Japanese-American Girl* (2–4). Illus. by Kazuyoshi Arai. 1995, Holt $15.95 (0-8050-2353-4). 48pp. Told through the eyes of Lauren Seiko Kamiya growing up in San

Francisco's Japantown, this book introduces Japanese Americans. (Rev: BL 4/15/95; SLJ 5/95) [973]

**14030** Catalano, Julie. *The Mexican Americans* (5–8). Illus. Series: Immigrant Experience. 1995, Chelsea LB $19.95 (0-7910-3359-7); paper $9.95 (0-7910-3381-3). 100pp. This book traces the reasons for leaving Mexico, the immigrants' reception in the United States, and their contributions and achievements. (Rev: BL 11/15/95; SLJ 1/96) [973]

**14031** Cavan, Seamus. *The Irish-American Experience* (5–7). Illus. Series: Coming to America. 1993, Millbrook LB $22.40 (1-56294-218-2). 64pp. Beginning with the terrible potato famine that forced millions of Irish to come to America, this is the story of the rise of Irish Americans to positions of prominence. (Rev: BCCB 4/93; BL 6/1–15/93) [973]

**14032** Cole, Melanie, et al. *Famous People of Hispanic Heritage* (4–7). Series: Contemporary American Success Stories. 1997, Mitchell Lane LB $21.95 (1-883845-44-0); paper $10.95 (1-883845-43-2). 96pp. This useful series, now in 9 volumes, profiles famous Hispanics, past and present, from around the world. (Rev: BL 3/15/98) [920]

**14033** Cooper, Martha, and Ginger Gordon. *Anthony Reynoso: Born to Rope* (2–4). Illus. 1996, Clarion $14.95 (0-395-71690-X). 32pp. A young Mexican American displays many skills from his native culture, like roping and riding. (Rev: BL 3/15/96; HB 7–8/96; SLJ 6/96) [791.8]

**14034** Daley, William. *The Chinese Americans* (5–8). Illus. 1995, Chelsea LB $19.95 (0-7910-3357-0); paper $9.95 (0-7910-3379-1). 112pp. The background and culture of this group are explained, as well as its adjustment to life in America. (Rev: BL 1/1/88)

**14035** Di Franco, J. Philip. *The Italian Americans* (5–8). Illus. 1995, Chelsea LB $19.95 (0-791-03353-8); paper $9.95 (0-7910-3375-9). 112pp. A heavily illustrated discussion of the culture that Italian immigrants left behind and their contributions to American life. (Rev: BL 1/1/88)

**14036** Emsden, Katharine, ed. *Coming to America: A New Life in a New Land* (4–8). Series: Perspectives on History. 1993, Discovery Enterprises paper $5.95 (1-878668-23-4). 64pp. People from many countries tell of their experiences as immigrants through quotes from their diaries, journals, and letters. (Rev: BL 11/15/93) [325.73]

**14037** Feelings, Tom. *Tommy Traveler in the World of Black History* (3–8). Illus. 1991, Writers & Readers $13.95 (0-86316-202-9). 48pp. This classic comic strip is about a young African American boy who witnesses highlights in the history of his race. (Rev: BL 9/15/91) [741]

**14038** Ferry, Steven. *Russian Americans* (4–6). Illus. Series: Cultures of America. 1996, Marshall Cavendish LB $28.50 (0-7614-0164-4). 80pp. After some background material on Russia, details the traditions, customs, and contributions of Russian Americans. (Rev: BL 5/15/96; SLJ 6/96) [973]

**14039** Gabor, A. *Polish Americans* (4–6). Illus. Series: Cultures of America. 1995, Marshall Cavendish $19.95 (1-7614-0154-7). 80pp. After a description of life in Poland, this account describes the history of Polish Americans and various aspects of their culture. (Rev: BL 7/95) [305.89]

**14040** Galicich, Anne. *The German Americans* (5–8). Illus. Series: Immigrant Experience. 1995, Chelsea LB $19.95 (0-7910-3362-7); paper $9.95 (0-7910-3384-8). 120pp. From the reasons for their leaving Germany and their initial reception in the United States to the present, this account traces the history of German Americans. (Rev: BL 4/1/89) [973]

**14041** Galvan, Raul. *Cuban Americans* (5–8). Illus. Series: Cultures of America. 1995, Marshall Cavendish LB $28.50 (1-85435-786-7). 80pp. Focuses on contemporary conditions in Cuba, tells why people left to come to the United States, and describes their reception here. (Rev: SLJ 8/95) [973]

**14042** Gernand, Renee. *The Cuban Americans* (5–8). Illus. 1995, Chelsea LB $19.95 (0-791-03354-6); paper $9.95 (0-791-03376-7). 112pp. The contributions of Cuban Americans and reasons why they came to America. (Rev: BL 2/1/89)

**14043** Goldish, Meish. *Immigration: How Should It Be Controlled?* (4–6). Illus. Series: Issues of Our Time. 1994, Twenty-First Century LB $18.90 (0-8050-3182-0). 64pp. Contains historical information about immigration plus material on citizenship laws, illegal aliens, and the pros and cons of allowing more immigrants into this country. (Rev: SLJ 7/94) [304.8]

**14044** Graff, Nancy P. *Where the River Runs: A Portrait of a Refugee Family* (5–7). Illus. by Richard Howard. 1993, Little, Brown $17.95 (0-316-32287-3). 71pp. This is the story of a 3-generation family of Cambodian refugees and how they have adjusted to life in Boston. (Rev: BCCB 7–8/93; BL 6/1–15/93; SLJ 8/93) [973]

**14045** Greenfield, Eloise, and Lessie Jones Little. *Childtimes: A Three-Generation Memoir* (5–8). Illus. by Jerry Pinkney. 1979, HarperCollins LB $15.89 (0-690-03875-5); paper $5.95 (0-06-446134-3). 160pp. The childhood of 3 generations of black women.

**14046** Hamanaka, Sheila. *The Journey: Japanese Americans, Racism and Renewal* (4–7). Illus. by author. 1990, Orchard LB $20.99 (0-531-08449-3). 39pp. With brief text, this book is a series of paintings from a large mural that describes the Japanese American experience, including the internment during World War II. (Rev: HB 5–6/90; SLJ 5/90) [940.54]

**14047** Hoobler, Dorothy, and Thomas Hoobler. *The Italian American Family Album* (5–8). Illus. 1994, Oxford $19.95 (0-19-509124-8). 127pp. Using many primary sources, covers such topics as life in Italy, coming to the United States, working, forming a new life, and becoming Italian Americans. (Rev: SLJ 7/94) [973]

**14048** Hoyt-Goldsmith, Diane. *Hoang Anh: A Vietnamese-American Boy* (3–5). Illus. by Lawrence Migdale. Series: Cornerstones of Freedom. 1992, Holiday LB $16.95 (0-8234-0948-1). 32pp. Color photos and a first-person narrative describe the life of a Vietnamese boy living in California. (Rev: BCCB 4/92; BL 4/15/92; HB 5–6/92; SLJ 4/92) [378.1]

**14049** Israel, Fred L. *The Amish* (5–8). Illus. Series: Immigrant Experience. 1996, Chelsea LB $19.95 (0-7910-3368-6). 100pp. The story of this conservative division of the Mennonites, why they settled in the United States and their contributions to the nation. (Rev: BL 7/96; SLJ 10/96) [305.6]

**14050** Kitano, Harry. *The Japanese Americans.* 2nd ed. (5–8). Photos by Richard Hewett. Series: Land of Immigrants. 1995, Chelsea LB $19.95 (0-7910-3358-9); paper $9.95 (0-7910-3380-5). 92pp. The story of Japanese Americans and their history, traditions, and contributions to American life and culture. (Rev: BL 10/15/95) [305]

**14051** Knight, Margy B. *Who Belongs Here? An American Story* (4–7). Illus. by Anne S. O'Brien. 1993, Tilbury $16.95 (0-88448-110-7). 40pp. The story of 10-year-old Nari, who survived the killing fields of Cambodia and found a new life in the United States. (Rev: BL 3/1/94; SLJ 10/93) [305.895]

**14052** Kuropas, Myron B. *Ukrainians in America* (5–7). Illus. Series: In America. 1996, Lerner LB $19.93 (0-8225-1043-X). 80pp. The story of the Ukrainian immigrants to the United States, their cultural traditions, and their contributions to American life. (Rev: BL 3/15/96; SLJ 3/96) [973]

**14053** Leder, Jane M. *A Russian Jewish Family* (4–7). Illus. Series: Journey Between Two Worlds. 1996, Lerner LB $22.60 (0-8225-3401-0); paper $8.95 (0-8225-9744-6). 56pp. Describes the living conditions experienced by a Jewish family in Russia and in their new American home. (Rev: BL 11/1/96; SLJ 11/96) [977.3]

**14054** Lee, Kathleen. *Illegal Immigration* (5–8). Illus. Series: Overview. 1996, Lucent LB $22.45 (1-56006-171-5). 128pp. Explores this current social problem, gives historical background, and explains present-day policies on illegal immigration. (Rev: BL 2/15/96; SLJ 3/96) [325]

**14055** Lee, Kathleen. *Tracing Our Italian Roots* (4–7). Illus. Series: American Origins. 1993, John Muir $12.95 (1-56261-149-6). 48pp. This account describes living conditions in Italy that led to emigration to this country as well as the reception here and the gradual integration of Italian Americans. (Rev: BL 2/15/94; SLJ 12/93) [973]

**14056** Lee, Lauren. *Japanese Americans* (4–6). Illus. Series: Cultures of America. 1996, Marshall Cavendish LB $28.50 (0-7614-0162-8). 80pp. Supplies material on the family life, religion, customs, food, and contributions of Japanese Americans. (Rev: BL 5/15/96) [973]

**14057** Lee, Lauren. *Korean Americans* (4–6). Illus. Series: Cultures of America. 1995, Marshall Cavendish LB $28.50 (0-7614-0151-2). 80pp. An extensive study with well-chosen color photos of the culture of Korean Americans, with coverage of topics like religion and customs. (Rev: BL 7/95) [305.895]

**14058** Lester, Julius. *To Be a Slave* (5–8). Illus. by Tom Feelings. 1968, Dial $16.99 (0-8037-8955-6); Scholastic paper $3.99 (0-590-42460-2). Through the words of the victims themselves, the reader is helped to realize what it was like to be a slave in America.

**14059** Levine, Ellen. *If Your Name Was Changed at Ellis Island* (3–5). Illus. by Wayne Parmenter. 1993, Scholastic $15.95 (0-590-46134-6). 80pp. Informative and lively case histories highlight the stories of the millions who passed through Ellis Island for a new life in America. (Rev: BCCB 4/93; BL 3/1/93; SLJ 3/93) [325.1]

**14060** Lomas Garza, Carmen. *Family Pictures/ Cuadros de Familia* (3–7). Illus. 1990, Children's Book Pr. $15.50 (0-89239-050-6); paper $6.95 (0-89239-108-1). 32pp. A Mexican-American artist shares memories of her childhood in Texas. (Rev: BCCB 10/90; BL 6/1/90; SLJ 11/90*) [306]

**14061** McGill, Allyson. *The Swedish Americans* (5–8). Series: Immigrant Experience. 1997, Chelsea $19.95 (0-7910-4551-X); paper $9.95 (0-7910-4552-8). 107pp. Explains why Swedes have emigrated from their homeland, their reception in the United States, and their contribution to the nation. (Rev: BL 10/15/97) [322.4]

**14062** Maestro, Betsy. *Coming to America: The Story of Immigration* (K–3). Illus. by Susannah Ryan. 1996, Scholastic $15.95 (0-590-44151-5). 40pp. A picture book introduction to what the many waves of immigrants have meant to this country. (Rev: BCCB 2/96; BL 2/1/96; SLJ 5/96) [304]

**14063** Magocsi, Paul R. *The Russian Americans* (5–8). Illus. Series: Immigrant Experience. 1995, Chelsea LB $19.95 (0-7910-3367-8). 110pp. Coverage includes the reasons for leaving Russia, their customs and traditions, their contributions, and famous

Russian Americans. (Rev: BL 11/15/95; SLJ 1/96) [973]

**14064** Martinez, Elizabeth Coonrod. *The Mexican-American Experience* (5–7). Illus. Series: Coming to America. 1995, Millbrook LB $22.40 (1-56294-515-7). 64pp. Conditions in Mexico that produce a flow of immigrants are discussed, with information on the contributions of Mexican Americans and brief biographies of famous Mexican Americans. (Rev: BL 6/1–15/95) [973]

**14065** Meier, Gisela. *Minorities* (5–7). Series: Women Today. 1991, Rourke LB $17.95 (0-86593-124-0). 64pp. An account that explores the financial status of women in minority groups. (Rev: SLJ 2/92) [305.42]

**14066** Mendez, Adriana. *Cubans in America* (5–7). Illus. Series: In America. 1994, Lerner LB $19.93 (0-8225-1953-4). 80pp. An account that describes why Cubans left their homeland, where they live in the United States, their lifestyles, and their contributions to society. (Rev: BL 8/94; SLJ 8/94) [973]

**14067** Moscinski, Sharon. *Tracing Our Irish Roots* (4–7). Illus. Series: American Origins. 1993, John Muir $12.95 (1-56261-148-8). 48pp. Conditions in Ireland that led to a mass exodus are covered, plus material on the reception given Irish immigrants in the United States and the contributions this group has made to this country. (Rev: BL 2/15/94; SLJ 12/93) [973]

**14068** Moy, Tina. *Chinese Americans* (5–8). Illus. Series: Cultures of America. 1995, Marshall Cavendish LB $28.50 (1-85435-785-9). 80pp. An introduction to the living conditions in China that produces the desire to emigrate and the reception immigrants receive when they arrive in the United States. (Rev: SLJ 8/95) [973]

**14069** Muggamin, Howard. *The Jewish Americans* (5–8). Illus. Series: Immigrant Experience. 1995, Chelsea LB $19.95 (0-7910-3365-1); paper $9.95 (0-7910-3387-2). 126pp. This account describes the lands from which many Jewish Americans came and their religion, customs, family life, food, and contributions. (Rev: BL 11/15/95) [973]

**14070** Murphy, Nora. *A Hmong Family* (4–7). Illus. Series: Journey Between Two Worlds. 1997, Lerner LB $22.60 (0-8225-3406-1); paper $8.95 (0-8225-9756-X). 64pp. After fleeing Laos in 1975 to escape the Communists, this family spent time in a refugee camp in Thailand before settling in Minneapolis, Minnesota. (Rev: BL 6/1–15/97; SLJ 8/97) [305.895]

**14071** O'Connor, Karen. *Dan Thuy's New Life in America* (4–8). Illus. 1992, Lerner LB $19.93 (0-8225-2555-0). 40pp. A photoessay of a 13-year-old Vietnamese girl and her family, newly arrived in San Diego. (Rev: BL 9/15/92; SLJ 9/92) [325]

**14072** O'Connor, Karen. *A Kurdish Family* (4–7). Illus. Series: Journey Between Two Worlds. 1996, Lerner LB $22.60 (0-8225-3402-9); paper $8.95 (0-8225-9743-8). 56pp. Describes the living conditions endured by a Kurdish family in their homeland and their new life in the United States. (Rev: BCCB 12/96; BL 11/1/96; SLJ 11/96) [305.891]

**14073** Phillips, David, and Steven Ferry. *Greek Americans* (4–6). Illus. Series: Cultures of America. 1996, Marshall Cavendish LB $28.50 (0-7614-0161-X). 80pp. In addition to coverage of the traditions of Greek Americans and their contributions to American life, there is introductory material on Greece and its customs. (Rev: BL 5/15/96; SLJ 6/96) [973]

**14074** Press, David P., and Elizabeth Kaplan. *Jewish Americans* (4–6). Illus. Series: Cultures of America. 1995, Marshall Cavendish LB $28.50 (0-7614-0153-9). 80pp. After a history of Jewish immigration to the United States, this account covers such topics as holy days, food, customs, and contributions to American life. (Rev: BL 7/95) [305.892]

**14075** Press, Petra. *Mexican Americans* (4–6). Illus. 1995, Marshall Cavendish LB $28.50 (0-7614-0152-0). 80pp. After describing life in Mexico, this book tells about the immigration process, family life, religion, customs, and contributions to the United States of Mexican Americans. (Rev: BL 7/95) [973]

**14076** Press, Petra. *Puerto Ricans* (4–6). Illus. Series: Cultures of America. 1996, Marshall Cavendish LB $19.95 (0-7614-0160-0). 80pp. A nicely illustrated description of the island of Puerto Rico details the customs, traditions, and contributions of its people. (Rev: BL 5/15/96) [973]

**14077** Reimers, David M. *A Land of Immigrants* (5–8). Illus. Series: Immigrant Experience. 1995, Chelsea $19.95 (0-7910-3361-9). 120pp. An overview of how the waves of immigration developed and determined the nature of the United States and its culture. (Rev: BL 10/15/95; SLJ 12/95) [304.8]

**14078** Riehecky, Janet. *Irish Americans* (5–8). Illus. Series: Cultures of America. 1995, Marshall Cavendish LB $28.50 (1-85435-783-2). 80pp. Historical information is given about Ireland, with a description of how, when, and why there were cycles of emigration and the reception the immigrants received here. (Rev: SLJ 8/95) [973]

**14079** Sagan, Miriam. *Tracing Our Jewish Roots* (4–7). Illus. Series: American Origins. 1993, John Muir $12.95 (1-56261-151-8). 48pp. The story of ghetto life in Europe is followed by coverage of the immigration process and assimilation in the United States in this account of Jewish Americans. (Rev: BL 2/15/94; SLJ 2/94) [973]

**14080** Sawyers, June S. *Famous Firsts of Scottish-Americans* (4–8). Illus. 1997, Pelican $13.95 (1-56554-122-7). 160pp. Biographies of 30 Americans of Scottish descent, including Neil Armstrong, Alexander Calder, Herman Melville, and Patrick Henry. (Rev: BL 6/1–15/97) [973]

**14081** Schouweiler, Thomas. *Germans in America* (5–7). Illus. Series: In America. 1994, Lerner LB $14.95 (0-8225-0245-3). 72pp. The causes and results of German immigration to this country are outlined, with good coverage on their contributions and important constituents. (Rev: BL 1/15/95; SLJ 12/94) [973]

**14082** Shalant, Phyllis. *Look What We've Brought You from Vietnam: Crafts, Games, Recipes, Stories, and Other Cultural Activities from New Americans* (3–6). Illus. 1988, Simon & Schuster paper $6.95 (0-671-65978-2). 48pp. Activities to foster an appreciation of Vietnamese culture. (Rev: BL 9/1/88)

**14083** Silverman, Robin L. *A Bosnian Family* (4–7). Illus. Series: Journey Between Two Worlds. 1997, Lerner LB $22.60 (0-8225-3404-5); paper $8.95 (0-8225-9754-3). 64pp. The story of Velma Dusper, her homeland of Bosnia, and her journey with her family to freedom and a new home in North Dakota. (Rev: BL 6/1–15/97; SLJ 7/97) [304.8]

**14084** Stanek, Muriel. *We Came from Vietnam* (4–6). Illus. 1985, Whitman LB $11.95 (0-8075-8699-4). 48pp. Photos and text focus on the Nguyen family from Vietnam, now settled in Chicago. (Rev: BCCB 11/85; BL 11/1/85)

**14085** Stone, Amy. *French Americans* (4–6). Illus. Series: Cultures of America. 1995, Marshall Cavendish LB $28.50 (0-7614-0155-5). 80pp. French Americans are introduced with discussions of their many contributions, lifestyle, influences, and geographical areas of concentration. (Rev: BL 7/95) [973]

**14086** Strom, Yale. *Quilted Landscape: Conversations with Young Immigrants* (5–8). Illus. 1996, Simon & Schuster paper $18.00 (0-689-80074-6). 80pp. Young immigrants from 15 countries tell about their homelands and the lives they now lead in the United States. (Rev: BCCB 2/97; BL 10/15/96; SLJ 12/96) [305.8]

**14087** Washburne, Carolyn K. *Italian Americans* (5–8). Illus. Series: Cultures of America. 1995, Marshall Cavendish LB $28.50 (1-85435-784-0). 80pp. After discussing why, how, and when many Italians left their homeland to come to the United States, this book tells of their life style, customs, and contributions. (Rev: SLJ 6/95) [973]

**14088** Watts, J. F. *The Irish Americans* (5–8). Illus. Series: Immigrant Experience. 1995, Chelsea LB $19.95 (0-7910-3366-X); paper $9.95 (0-7910-3388-0). 110pp. A history of the Irish Americans, how and why they came to this country, their history here, and their contributions. (Rev: BL 10/15/95) [973]

**14089** *We Are All Related: A Celebration of Our Cultural Heritage* (3–6). Illus. 1997, Orca paper $15.95 (0-9680479-0-4). 64pp. Reproduces the collages created by students at a Vancouver, B.C., elementary school during a yearlong arts program that focused on intercultural and intergenerational studies. (Rev: BL 8/97) [704]

**14090** Whitehead, Sandra. *Lebanese Americans* (4–6). Illus. Series: Cultures of America. 1996, Marshall Cavendish LB $28.50 (0-7614-0163-6). 80pp. Outlines the cultural traditions, food, family life, and customs of Lebanese Americans. (Rev: BL 5/15/96; SLJ 6/96) [973]

**14091** Wu, Dana Ying-Hul, and Jeffrey Dao-Sheng Tung. *The Chinese-American Experience* (5–7). Illus. Series: Coming to America. 1993, Millbrook LB $22.40 (1-56294-271-9). 64pp. The story of Chinese immigration to the United States, from exploitation, prejudice, and discrimination to gradual acceptance. (Rev: BL 6/1–15/93) [973]

# Youth Groups

**14092** Boy Scouts of America. *Fieldbook* (5–8). Illus. 1990, Boy Scouts of America paper $16.25 (0-8395-3200-8). 640pp. Intended as a scouting guide, this is also of use to the outdoor enthusiast interested in hiking, camping, and so on. (Rev: BL 8/85)

# Personal Development

# Behavior

## General

**14093** Bell, Neill. *Only Human* (4–6). Illus. by Sandy Clifford. 1983, Little, Brown paper $9.95 (0-316-08818-8). 128pp. A simple explanation of human behavior and psychology.

**14094** Berger, Terry. *I Have Feelings* (1–5). Illus. 1971, Human Sciences $18.95 (0-87705-021-X); paper $10.95 (0-89885-342-7). 32pp. Text and photos show children that their feelings and emotions — good and bad — are natural.

**14095** Gardner, Richard A. *The Girls and Boys Book About Good and Bad Behavior* (3–6). Illus. by Al Lowenheim. 1990, Creative Therapeutics $17.00 (0-933812-21-3). 221pp. This book talks about ethics and values. (Rev: SLJ 12/90) [155.5]

**14096** Harlan, Judith. *Girl Talk: Staying Strong, Feeling Good, Sticking Together* (4–6). Illus. by Debbie Palen. 1997, Walker $15.95 (0-8027-8640-5); paper $8.95 (0-8027-7524-1). 128pp. This collection of facts, advice, and profiles is intended to help girls as they become young women. (Rev: BL 12/1/97) [305.23]

**14097** Inwald, Robin. *Cap It Off with a Smile: A Guide for Making Friends* (K–3). Illus. by author. 1994, Hilson Pr. paper $9.95 (1-885738-00-5). This book offers practical tips to young people on how they can make friends. (Rev: SLJ 12/94) [158]

**14098** James, Elizabeth, and Carol Barkin. *How to Be School Smart: Secrets of Successful Schoolwork* (4–6). Illus. 1988, Morrow $15.00 (0-688-16130-8); Lothrop paper $4.95 (0-688-16139-1). Getting better grades made easier in this easily read practical guide. (Rev: BL 3/15/88; SLJ 5/88)

**14099** Johnston, Marianne. *Dealing with Anger* (2–4). Illus. Series: The Conflict Resolution Library. 1996, Rosen LB $15.93 (0-8239-2325-8). 24pp. This simple introduction to anger defines it, explains its different kinds, and tells how to handle it. (Rev: SLJ 9/96) [152.4]

**14100** Kalb, Jonah, and David Viscott. *What Every Kid Should Know* (4–6). Illus. 1976, Houghton paper $6.95 (0-395-62983-7). 128pp. An introduction to the study of how people behave toward each other.

**14101** Kaufman, Gershen, and Lev Raphael. *Stick Up for Yourself! Every Kid's Guide to Personal Power and Positive Self-Esteem* (4–7). Illus. by Jackie Urbanovic. 1990, Free Spirit paper $9.95 (0-915793-17-2). 81pp. A how-to guide to developing a healthy ego. (Rev: SLJ 10/90) [362.2]

**14102** Kincher, Jonni. *Psychology for Kids II: 40 Fun Experiments That Help You Learn About Others* (4–6). Illus. 1995, Free Spirit paper $16.95 (0-915793-83-0). 157pp. This second volume supplies more activities and projects to help explore the world of human behavior. (Rev: BL 7/95) [155.2]

**14103** Lankford, Mary D. *Quinceañera: A Latina's Journey to Womanhood* (4–7). Photos by Jesse Herrera. 1994, Millbrook LB $20.90 (1-56294-363-4). 47pp. Using the story of a 15-year-old Mexican American girl as a focus, this account describes the rite of passage to womanhood in the Latina culture. (Rev: SLJ 4/94) [305.23]

**14104** Nathan, Amy. *Surviving Homework: Tips from Teens* (4–6). Illus. 1997, Millbrook LB $23.90 (1-56294-185-2). 80pp. Using answers on questionnaires given to middle and high school kids as a focus, this book supplies many useful study tips and suggestions on how to organize one's time. (Rev: BL 6/1–15/97; SLJ 7/97) [372.12]

**14105** Payne, Lauren M. *We Can Get Along: A Child's Book of Choices* (PS–2). Illus. by Claudia Rohling. 1997, Free Spirit paper $15.95 (1-57542-013-9). 36pp. A simple guide on getting along with others and how to be aware of other people's feelings. (Rev: BL 8/97; SLJ 4/97) [302]

**14106** Pendleton, Scott. *The Ultimate Guide to Student Contests, Grades K–6* (4–6). 1998, Walker paper $14.95 (0-8027-7513-6). 208pp. A directory of organizations that sponsor student competitions or reward outstanding student work, arranged by subject. (Rev: BL 3/15/98) [370]

**14107** Pickering, Marianne. *Lessons for Life: Education and Learning* (5–8). Illus. Series: Our Human Family. 1995, Blackbirch LB $21.95 (1-56711-127-0). 80pp. The content and organization of public education are examined around the world in this book divided into 5 broad geographical areas. (Rev: SLJ 1/96) [370]

**14108** Robson, Pam. *Body Language* (2–5). Illus. Series: Hello Out There. 1997, Watts $18.00 (0-531-14468-2). 32pp. As well as giving good advice on reading the body signals of others, this book includes examples from the animal kingdom and a number of suggested activities. (Rev: BL 1/1–15/98; SLJ 3/98) [153.6]

**14109** Romain, Trevor. *How to Do Homework Without Throwing Up* (3–6). Illus. by author. 1997, Free Spirit paper $13.95 (1-57542-011-2). 67pp. Using a humorous text and drawings, this work supplies a positive approach to homework, with many tips on how to do it efficiently. (Rev: SLJ 5/97) [371.3]

**14110** Rosenberg, Ellen. *Growing Up Feeling Good* (4–8). Illus. 1989, Puffin paper $11.99 (0-14-034264-8). 512pp. This book, aimed at older children and young teenagers, describes the process of growing up. (Rev: BL 2/1/90) [612.6]

**14111** Schneider, Meg. *Help! My Teacher Hates Me* (5–8). Illus. 1994, Workman paper $7.95 (1-56305-492-2). 160pp. A book of practical advice on how to weather the problems of getting along in school. (Rev: BL 3/15/95) [371.8]

## Etiquette

**14112** Best, Alyse. *Miss Best's Etiquette for Young People: Manners for Real People in Today's World* (3–7). Illus. 1991, PEP paper $9.95 (0-945033-02-8). 137pp. Advice is given to young people on proper behavior for both formal and informal social events. (Rev: BL 9/15/91) [395]

**14113** Buehner, Caralyn. *It's a Spoon, Not a Shovel* (PS–3). Illus. by Mark Buehner. 1995, Dial paper $14.89 (0-8037-1495-5). 32pp. Using a question-and-answer format, this book proves that teaching manners can be fun. (Rev: BL 6/1–15/95; HB 7–8/95; SLJ 8/95) [395]

**14114** Holyoke, Nancy. *Oops! The Manners Guide for Girls* (3–7). Illus. by Debbie Tilley. Series: American Girl Library. 1997, Pleasant paper $7.95 (1-56247-530-4). 116pp. An amusing book of manners aimed at girls that covers almost any situation. (Rev: SLJ 3/98) [393]

**14115** James, Elizabeth, and Carol Barkin. *Social Smarts: Manners for Today's Kids* (4–7). Illus. 1996, Clarion $15.00 (0-395-66585-X); paper $6.95 (0-395-81312-3). 103pp. Table manners and responsible, appropriate public behavior are 2 topics covered. (Rev: BL 9/1/96; SLJ 9/96) [395]

**14116** Kirtland, Mark. *Why Do We Do That?* (4–6). Illus. Series: Why Do We . . .? 1996, Watts LB $18.00 (0-531-14394-5). 31pp. Using cross-cultural and historical approaches, this book explores etiquette and protocol around the world. (Rev: SLJ 8/97) [395]

**14117** Stewart, Marjabelle Young, and Ann Buchwald. *What to Do When and Why* (4–7). 1988, Luce $14.95 (0-88331-105-4). An easily read introduction to the basics of good manners and behavior.

## Family Relationships

**14118** Aldape, Virginia Totorica. *David, Donny, and Darren: A Book About Identical Triplets* (2–4). Illus. Series: Meeting the Challenge. 1997, Lerner LB $21.27 (0-8225-2584-4). 40pp. Using a first-person narrative, this is the story of one of identical triplets and how his life is different from those of average kids. (Rev: BL 3/15/98) [306.875]

**14119** Banish, Roslyn, and Jennifer Jordan-Wong. *A Forever Family* (K–3). Illus. 1992, HarperCollins paper $5.95 (0-06-446116-5). 44pp. This photoessay takes 8-year-old Jennifer from foster home to adoption into her "forever family." (Rev: BCCB 5/92; BL 3/15/92; HB 5–6/92; SLJ 4/92) [362.7]

**14120** Berman, Claire. *"What Am I Doing in a Step-Family?"* (3–6). Illus. by Dick Wilson. 1982, Carol Publg. $12.00 (0-8184-0325-X). A somewhat superficial view of stepfamilies and the adjustments necessary in these situations.

**14121** Brown, Laurie Krasny, and Marc Brown. *Dinosaurs Divorce: A Guide for Changing Families* (PS–3). Illus. by Marc Brown. 1988, Little, Brown $15.95 (0-316-11248-8); paper $6.95 (0-316-10996-7). 32pp. These dinosaurs are green and somewhat crocodilian and they demonstrate all the feelings and problems children encounter with divorce in the family. (Rev: SLJ 10/86)

**14122** Cole, Joanna. *The New Baby at Your House.* Rev. ed. (PS–1). Illus. by Margaret Miller. 1998, Morrow LB $15.93 (0-688-13898-5). 48pp. A revision of the standard account on adjustments that are made in a family when a new baby arrives. (Rev: BL 3/1/98; SLJ 4/98) [306.875]

**14123** Cooper, Kay. *Where Did You Get Those Eyes? A Guide to Discovering Your Family History* (5–7). Illus. by Anthony Accardo. 1988, Walker LB $14.85 (0-8027-6803-2). A helpful guide for researching the family tree. (Rev: BCCB 11/88; BL 1/15/89; SLJ 2/89)

**14124** Currie, Stephen. *Adoption* (5–8). Illus. Series: Overview. 1997, Lucent LB $22.45 (1-56006-183-9). 96pp. A well-illustrated account of the history of adoption and present-day practices, procedures, and problems. (Rev: BL 5/15/97; SLJ 4/97) [362.7]

**14125** Drescher, Joan. *Your Family, My Family* (K–3). Illus. by author. 1980, Walker LB $13.85 (0-8027-6383-9). 32pp. All kinds of family arrangements, for example, single parents and working mothers, are described.

**14126** Erlbach, Arlene. *The Families Book: True Stories About Real Kids and the People They Live with and Love* (3–6). Photos by Stephen J. Carrera. Illus. by Lisa Wagner. 1996, Free Spirit paper $12.95 (1-57542-002-3). 111pp. The diversity of families is explored in a series of case histories that show wide differences in structure, religion, and problems. (Rev: SLJ 8/96) [306.85]

**14127** Gardner, Richard A. *Boys and Girls Book About Divorce* (5–8). Illus. 1992, Aronson $25.00 (0-87668-664-1); Bantam paper $5.50 (0-553-27619-0). 160pp. A self-help book written for adolescents trying to cope with parental marriage problems.

**14128** Gellman, Marc. *"Always Wear Clean Underwear!" and Other Ways Parents Say "I Love You."* (4–7). 1997, Morrow $15.00 (0-688-14492-6). 128pp. Some kids think that the expressions pictured in this book are a form of parental nagging, but they are really only showing they care. (Rev: BL 10/1/97; SLJ 11/97) [306.874]

**14129** Girard, Linda Walvoord. *We Adopted You, Benjamin Koo* (3–5). Illus. by Linda Shute. 1989, Whitman LB $14.95 (0-8075-8694-3); paper $5.95 (0-8075-8695-1). 32pp. Nine-year-old Benjamin tells how he was adopted from a Korean orphanage. (Rev: BCCB 5/89; BL 5/1/89; SLJ 6/89)

**14130** Greenberg, Keith E. *Zack's Story: Growing Up with Same-Sex Parents* (5–7). Illus. Series: Meeting the Challenge. 1996, Lerner $21.27 (0-8225-2581-X). 32pp. A true account of 11-year-old Zack, who is growing up with his lesbian mother and her

lover, whom he has grown to regard as a second mother. (Rev: BL 10/15/96; SLJ 3/97) [306]

**14131** Ives, Sally B., et al. *The Divorce Workbook: A Guide for Kids and Families* (3–6). Series: Family Pack. 1993, Waterfront $16.95 (0-914525-04-2). 160pp. This book uses drawings by children concerning divorce to explore feelings and to learn how to deal with them. Two others in this series are: *Changing Families* (1988) and *My Kind of Family* (1990), which explore single-parent homes. All 3 are reissues. [306.8]

**14132** Kandel, Bethany. *Trevor's Story: Growing Up Biracial* (2–4). Illus. Series: Meeting the Challenge. 1997, Lerner LB $21.27 (0-8225-2583-6). 40pp. A first-person narrative in which a boy talks about the racism he has had to face growing up with a white mother and an African American father. (Rev: BL 3/15/98) [362.1]

**14133** Koh, Frances M. *Adopted from Asia: How It Feels to Grow Up in America* (5–8). 1993, East-West $16.95 (0-9606090-6-7). 95pp. Using interviews, the author has gathered stories, impressions, and opinions from 11 young people who were born in Korea and adopted by Caucasian Americans. (Rev: BL 2/15/94) [306.874]

**14134** Krementz, Jill. *How It Feels to Be Adopted* (5–8). Illus. 1988, Knopf paper $15.00 (0-394-75853-6). Interviews with 19 young people, ages 8 to 16, on how it feels to be adopted.

**14135** Krementz, Jill. *How It Feels When Parents Divorce* (4–8). Illus. 1988, Knopf paper $15.00 (0-394-75855-2). Boys and girls, ages 8-16, share their experiences with divorced parents.

**14136** Landau, Elaine. *Sibling Rivalry: Brothers and Sisters at Odds* (3–6). Illus. 1994, Millbrook LB $19.90 (1-56294-328-6). 64pp. Factors that influence sibling rivalry, such as family size, gender, and divorce, are discussed, with tips on how to understand and lessen the problem. (Rev: BL 5/1/94; SLJ 4/94) [306]

**14137** LeShan, Eda. *When Grownups Drive You Crazy* (4–7). 1988, Macmillan paper $14.00 (0-02-756340-5). 128pp. A book that tries to bridge the gap of misunderstanding between children and their parents. (Rev: BL 4/15/88; HB 7–8/88; SLJ 6–7/88)

**14138** Mayle, Peter. *Why Are We Getting a Divorce?* (3–6). Illus. 1988, Harmony $16.00 (0-517-56527-7). 32pp. Calm, straightforward text on an emotional issue. (Rev: BL 8/88; SLJ 9/88)

**14139** Perl, Lila. *The Great Ancestor Hunt: The Fun of Finding Out Who You Are* (5–8). Illus. 1989, Houghton $16.00 (0-89919-745-0). 104pp. A how-to book for amateur genealogists. (Rev: BCCB 12/89; BL 11/1/89; SLJ 12/89) [929.1]

**14140** Rofes, Eric E., and Fayerweather Street School. *The Kids' Book of Divorce: By, for and About Kids* (6–8). Illus. 1982, Random paper $10.00 (0-394-71018-5). Youngsters of various ages tell how their parents' divorce affected them.

**14141** Rogers, Fred. *Let's Talk About It: Adoption* (PS–K). Photos by Jim Judkis. Series: Let's Talk About It. 1995, Putnam $15.95 (0-399-22432-7). All of the emotions and adjustments that come with the adoption process are revealed in this account of 3 adoptive families. (Rev: SLJ 6/95) [362.7]

**14142** Rogers, Fred. *Let's Talk About It: Divorce* (PS–2). Illus. by Jim Judkis. 1996, Putnam $15.95 (0-399-22449-1). 32pp. A photoessay that explores the effects of divorce on 3 families. (Rev: BL 5/15/96; SLJ 4/96) [306.89]

**14143** Rogers, Fred. *Let's Talk About It: Stepfamilies* (K–3). Illus. by Jim Judkis. Series: Let's Talk About It. 1997, Putnam $15.95 (0-399-23144-7); paper $7.95 (0-399-23145-5). 32pp. A simple narrative illustrated with photos that explores the practical and emotional situations involved in stepfamily living. (Rev: BL 10/15/97; SLJ 10/97) [646.7]

**14144** Rosenberg, Maxine B. *Being Adopted* (3–5). Illus. 1984, Lothrop LB $15.93 (0-688-02673-7). 48pp. The subject of interracial adoption is explored through 3 stories of adoption.

**14145** Rosenberg, Maxine B. *Living with a Single Parent* (4–7). 1992, Macmillan $14.95 (0-02-777915-7). 160pp. In interview format, this "hot" topic is presented through the opinions of youngsters from 8 to 13. (Rev: BCCB 2/93; BL 11/15/92; SLJ 12/92) [306.85]

**14146** Rotner, Shelley, and Sheila M. Kelly. *Lots of Dads* (PS–1). Illus. 1997, Dial paper $12.89 (0-8037-2089-0). 24pp. A photoessay about all kinds of fathers and how each has a different way of expressing himself. (Rev: BL 8/97; SLJ 12/97) [306]

**14147** Sanders, Pete, and Steve Myers. *Divorce and Separation* (4–8). Illus. by Mike Lacey. Series: What Do You Know About. 1997, Millbrook LB $20.90 (0-7613-0574-2). 32pp. An introduction to separation and divorce, with an emphasis on tips to help youngsters adjust and cope. (Rev: SLJ 10/97) [346]

**14148** Schwartz, Perry. *Carolyn's Story: A Book About an Adopted Girl* (5–7). Illus. Series: Meeting the Challenge. 1996, Lerner $21.27 (0-8225-2580-1). 40pp. Using fictional case histories, various aspects of adoption are explored. (Rev: BL 10/15/96; SLJ 4/97) [362.7]

**14149** Simon, Norma. *All Kinds of Families* (4–6). Illus. by Joe Lasker. 1976, Whitman LB $14.95 (0-8075-0282-0). 40pp. Explores various kinds of families and their problems.

**14150** Stein, Sara Bonnett. *On Divorce* (2–4). Illus. 1979, Walker $10.95 (0-8027-6344-8); paper $4.95 (0-8027-7226-9). Photographs and text cover this subject in an elementary fashion.

**14151** Stein, Sara Bonnett. *That New Baby* (1–3). Illus. Series: Open Family. 1979, Walker $12.95 (0-8027-6175-5); paper $8.95 (0-8027-7227-7). 48pp. A very helpful book in getting youngsters to accept a new member in the family.

**14152** Wasson, Valentina P. *The Chosen Baby* (PS–K). Illus. by Glo Coalson. 1977, HarperCollins $15.00 (0-397-31738-7). 48pp. A later edition of an excellent book on adoption.

**14153** Weitzman, Elizabeth. *Let's Talk About Foster Homes* (K–2). Illus. Series: Let's Talk About Library. 1996, Rosen/Power Kids Pr. LB $13.95 (0-8239-2310-X). 24pp. After defining what a foster home is, this title explains why some children are placed in one and the adjustments that they must make. Other family problems are explored in *Let's Talk About Staying in a Shelter, Let's Talk About When a Parent Dies,* and *Let's Talk About Your Parents' Divorce* (all 1996). (Rev: SLJ 12/96) [362.7]

**14154** Westheimer, Ruth, and Pierre A. Lehu. *Dr. Ruth Talks About Grandparents: Advice for Kids on Making the Most of a Special Relationship* (4–6). Illus. 1997, Farrar $15.00 (0-374-31873-5). 112pp. Sound advice is given on how to get along with grandparents and how to make these relationships pleasant and communicative. (Rev: BL 8/97; SLJ 9/97) [306.874]

**14155** Wolfman, Ira. *Do People Grow on Family Trees? Genealogy for Kids and Other Beginners* (5–8). Illus. by Michael Klein. 1991, Workman paper $9.95 (0-89480-348-4). 179pp. The purposes of genealogy are discussed and information is given on how to trace family history. (Rev: SLJ 1/92) [929]

## Personal Problems

**14156** Brown, Laurie Krasny. *When Dinosaurs Die: A Guide to Understanding Death* (K–3). Illus. by Marc Brown. 1996, Little, Brown $14.95 (0-316-10917-7). 32pp. A beginner's book about death and its meaning. (Rev: BCCB 3/96; BL 4/1/96; HB 9–10/96; SLJ 4/96) [155.9]

**14157** Cohen-Posey, Kate. *How to Handle Bullies, Teasers and Other Meanies: A Book That Takes the Nuisance out of Name Calling and Other Nonsense* (4–7). 1995, Rainbow paper $8.95 (1-56825-029-0). 91pp. A practical book that offers useful suggestions on how to handle bullies. (Rev: BCCB 12/95; BL 11/15/95) [646.7]

**14158** Croft, Priscilla. *Dealing with Jealousy* (2–4). Illus. Series: Conflict Resolution Library. 1996, Rosen LB $13.95 (0-8239-2326-6). 24pp. Using a variety of real-life situations, various types of jealousy are explored. (Rev: BL 12/1/96; SLJ 11/96) [152.4]

**14159** Girard, Linda Walvoord. *Who Is a Stranger and What Should I Do?* (2–5). Illus. by Helen Cogancherry. 1985, Whitman LB $12.95 (0-8075-9014-2); paper $4.95 (0-8075-9016-9). 32pp. Dealing with strangers in different situations, emphasizing that sometimes the best thing to do is to run away. (Rev: BCCB 3/85; BL 4/1/85; SLJ 9/85)

**14160** Heegaard, Mary E. *Coping with Death and Grief* (4–6). 1990, Lerner LB $19.93 (0-8225-0043-4). 64pp. This account helps children understand how the grieving process promotes emotional growth. (Rev: BL 11/1/90; SLJ 11/90) [155.6]

**14161** Johnston, Marianne. *Dealing with Bullying* (K–3). Illus. Series: Conflict Resolution Library. 1996, Rosen/Power Kids Pr. LB $15.93 (0-8239-2374-6). 24pp. A helpful book that helps young people understand bullies while giving them techniques for self-protection. (Rev: SLJ 1/97) [155.5]

**14162** Johnston, Marianne. *Let's Talk About Being Shy* (4–8). Illus. Series: Let's Talk Library. 1996, Rosen LB $15.93 (0-8239-2304-5). 24pp. The causes and possible cures of shyness are covered in this straightforward discussion. Also use *Let's Talk About Being Afraid* (1996). (Rev: BL 3/15/97) [155.4]

**14163** Krementz, Jill. *How It Feels When a Parent Dies* (4–7). Illus. 1988, Knopf paper $15.00 (0-394-75854-4). 128pp. Eighteen experiences of parental death are recounted.

**14164** LeShan, Eda. *Learning to Say Good-bye: When a Parent Dies* (5–7). Illus. by Paul Giovanopoulos. 1976, Avon paper $8.00 (0-380-40105-3). 96pp. A sympathetic explanation of the many reactions children have to death.

**14165** Reef, Catherine. *Think Positive: Cope with Stress* (4–8). Illus. Series: Good Health Guidlines. 1993, Twenty-First Century $15.95 (0-8050-2443-3). 64pp. An informal discussion of the causes and effects of stress with coverage on other topics such as self-esteem and peer pressure. (Rev: SLJ 1/94) [155]

**14166** Roehm, Michelle, comp. *Girls Know Best: Advice for Girls from Girls on Just About Everything!* (5–8). Illus. 1997, Beyond Words paper $8.95 (1-885223-63-3). 160pp. Clear, direct advice is given on such problems as embarrassing situations, staying healthy, participation in activities, and such family issues as divorce and illness. (Rev: SLJ 12/97) [362]

**14167** Rofes, Eric E., ed. *The Kids' Book About Death and Dying by and for Kids* (5–8). 1985, Little, Brown $16.95 (0-316-75390-4). 119pp. Based on a year-long discussion group, 10- to 14-year-old children discuss aspects of death and grief. (Rev: BCCB 7/85; BL 6/1/85)

**14168** Romain, Trevor. *Bullies Are a Pain in the Brain* (3–7). Illus. by author. 1997, Free Spirit paper $9.95 (1-57542-023-6). 105pp. Explains why bullies act the way they do, types of bullying, and ways to cope with it. (Rev: SLJ 2/98) [371.5]

**14169** Sanders, Pete. *Bullying* (4–7). Illus. Series: What Do You Know About. 1996, Millbrook LB $20.90 (0-7613-0537-8). 32pp. The causes of people being bullies are explored, with tips on how to handle them. (Rev: SLJ 3/97) [155.5]

**14170** Simon, Norma. *The Saddest Time* (K–3). Illus. by Jacqueline Rogers. 1986, Whitman LB $12.95 (0-8075-7203-9); paper $4.95 (0-8075-7204-7). 40pp. Three stories talk to children about death — of an uncle, a child accident victim, and a grandparent. (Rev: BCCB 4/86; BL 4/15/86; SLJ 8/86)

**14171** Wachter, Oralee. *No More Secrets for Me* (3–5). Illus. by Jane Aaron. 1984, Little, Brown paper $8.95 (0-316-91491-6). Four stories about sexual abuse of young people.

# Careers

## General and Miscellaneous

**14172**   Bourne, Miriam Anne. *A Day in the Life of a Chef* (3–5). Illus. 1988, Troll LB $12.50 (0-8167-1115-1). 32pp. A close-up look at the daily activities of this important career. (Rev: BL 2/15/88)

**14173**   Bryant, Jennifer. *Carol Thomas-Weaver: Music Teacher* (3–5). Illus. Series: Working Moms. 1991, Twenty-First Century LB $15.95 (0-941477-56-8). 40pp. The day-to-day life of a music teacher, who is also a mother, is profiled. (Rev: BL 6/15/91; SLJ 7/91) [372.8]

**14174**   Cody, Tod. *The Cowboy's Handbook: How to Become a Hero of the Wild West* (4–6). Illus. 1996, Cobblehill paper $12.99 (0-525-65210-8). 29pp. The life of the modern cowboy is introduced, including gear, life on the trail, the chuck wagon, and some craft projects. (Rev: BCCB 3/96; SLJ 6/96) [979.1]

**14175**   Davis, Alvin G. *Day in the Life of a Cowboy* (3–5). Illus. by Bob Moorhouse. Series: A Day in the Life Library. 1990, Troll LB $12.50 (0-8167-2208-0). 32pp. Through a description of a spring roundup on a large ranch, the daily life of a cowboy is introduced. (Rev: BL 4/15/91) [978]

**14176**   Duvall, Jill D. *Chef Ki Is Serving Dinner!* (1–2). Illus. Series: Our Neighborhood. 1997, Children's LB $19.50 (0-516-20313-4). 32pp. Using a photojournalistic style, readers are introduced to a chef who cooks Oriental food. Also use *Mr. Duvall Reports the News* and *Ms. Moja Makes Beautiful Clothes* (both 1997). (Rev: BL 8/97) [641.59519]

**14177**   Fannon, Cecilia. *Leaders* (5–7). Series: Women Today. 1991, Rourke LB $17.95 (0-86593-118-6). 64pp. This book focuses on the lives of 24 women who have succeeded in business, education, science, and medicine. (Rev: SLJ 2/92) [650.1]

**14178**   Flanagan, Alice K. *A Day in Court with Mrs. Trinh* (1–2). Series: Our Neighborhood. 1997, Children's LB $19.50 (0-516-20008-9). 32pp. This career book describes the legal profession through the day-to-day activities of a real-life lawyer named Mrs. Trinh. (Rev: BL 12/15/97; SLJ 1/98) [340]

**14179**   Flanagan, Alice K. *Exploring Parks with Ranger Dockett* (1–2). Series: Our Neighborhood. 1997, Children's LB $19.50 (0-516-20496-3). 32pp. The work of National Park Service personnel is highlighted in this account that features a real member of the force, Ranger Dockett. (Rev: BL 12/15/97) [363.6]

**14180**   Florian, Douglas. *A Fisher* (PS–2). Illus. Series: How We Work. 1994, Greenwillow LB $14.93 (0-688-13130-1). 32pp. A lone fisherman and his daily activities are used to tell about this occupation and the skills and equipment it requires. (Rev: BL 8/94; SLJ 9/94) [331.7]

**14181**   Gaskin, Carol. *A Day in the Life of a Racing Car Mechanic* (2–4). Illus. 1985, Troll LB $12.50 (0-8167-0091-5). 32pp. Brian Dunkel spends the day getting a car ready for a big race in this look at a special career. (Rev: BL 8/85)

**14182**   Greenberg, Keith E. *Window Washer: At Work Above the Clouds* (2–5). Illus. Series: Risky Business. 1995, Blackbirch LB $14.95 (1-56711-154-8). 32pp. The dangers involved and the safety measures required are stressed in this career book about 2 men who wash windows at the World Trade Center in New York City. (Rev: SLJ 8/95) [646.2]

**14183**   Johnson, Neil. *All in a Day's Work: Twelve Americans Talk About Their Jobs* (5–7). Illus. 1989, Little, Brown $14.95 (0-316-46957-2). 89pp. People in various occupations — such as farmer, musician, and judge — show that work can be fun too. (Rev: BCCB 2/90; BL 1/15/90; HB 3–4/90) [331.7]

**14184** Koral, April. *In the Newsroom* (3–6). Illus. 1989, Watts LB $21.00 (0-531-10463-X). 64pp. Spotlight on reporter Anna Bond at a New York television station. (Rev: BL 4/1/89; SLJ 6/89)

**14185** Kurelek, William. *Lumberjack* (5–8). Illus. by author. 1974, Tundra $17.95 (0-88776-052-X). 48pp. Using his own experience as a basis, a Canadian painter describes, through text and pictures, life and work in a lumber camp.

**14186** Lee, Barbara. *Working in Sports and Recreation* (4–8). Illus. Series: Exploring Careers. 1996, Lerner LB $23.93 (0-8225-1762-0). 112pp. Twelve people involved in careers related to sports and recreation talk candidly about their professions. (Rev: BL 2/15/97) [796]

**14187** Maynard, Christopher. *Jobs People Do* (PS–1). Illus. 1997, DK Publg. $12.95 (0-7894-1492-9). 32pp. This large-size book focuses on the world of work and includes children dressed as a firefighter, dancer, surgeon, lawyer, mail carrier, pilot, etc. (Rev: BL 6/1–15/97) [331.7]

**14188** Monteleone, John. *A Day in the Life of a Major League Baseball Player* (3–5). Series: Day in the Life of Library. 1990, Troll LB $12.50 (0-8167-2216-1). 32pp. This career book takes the reader behind the scenes of a major league stadium and preparations for a big-league game. (Rev: BL 4/15/91) [796.357]

**14189** Paige, David. *A Day in the Life of a Librarian* (2–4). Illus. 1985, Troll LB $12.50 (0-8167-0101-6). It's not all books and quiet in the day of a chief librarian. (Rev: BL 8/85; SLJ 9/85)

**14190** Paige, David. *A Day in the Life of a School Basketball Coach* (4–6). Illus. 1981, Troll LB $12.50 (0-89375-452-8). 32pp. After a day of physical education teaching, Coach Stamply coaches the team.

**14191** Schomp, Virginia. *If You Were a Construction Worker* (3–4). Illus. Series: If You Were. 1997, Marshall Cavendish LB $21.36 (0-7614-0617-4). 32pp. This title describes the different jobs involved in a construction project, the various kinds of buildings these people work on, and some of the world's great structures, like the Empire State Building and the pyramids. (Rev: BL 2/15/98) [624]

**14192** Schomp, Virginia. *If You Were an Astronaut* (3–4). Series: If You Were. 1997, Marshall Cavendish LB $21.36 (0-7614-0618-2). 32pp. Covers the education, training and duties of astronauts. (Rev: BL 2/15/98; SLJ 2/98) [629]

**14193** Stockdale, Linda. *ABC Career Book for Girls/El Libro de Carreras para Niñas* (K–3). Illus. by John Schafer. 1996, Columbia Univ. Pr. paper $9.95 (1-884830-00-5). 31pp. Using the letters of the alphabet, this book describes a wide range of occu-

pations in English and Spanish. (Rev: SLJ 2/97) [331.7]

**14194** Trainer, David. *A Day in the Life of a TV News Reporter* (4–6). Illus. 1980, Troll LB $12.50 (0-89375-228-2). 32pp. An exciting career explained through a "typical day" technique.

**14195** Tropea, Judith. *A Day in the Life of a Museum Curator* (3–5). Illus. by John Halpern. Series: A Day in the Life Library. 1990, Troll LB $12.50 (0-8167-2212-9). 32pp. Describes how fossils are collected and identified and how exhibits are prepared. (Rev: BL 4/15/91) [562]

**14196** Wickenden, Martha. *A Day in the Life of a Newspaper Reporter* (3–5). Series: Day in the Life of Library. 1990, Troll LB $12.50 (0-8167-2214-5). 32pp. The activities of a reporter for a daily paper — such as interviewing, checking facts, and writing articles — are presented. (Rev: BL 4/15/91) [070.4]

# Arts and Entertainment

**14197** Duvall, Jill D. *Meet Rory Hohenstein, a Professional Dancer* (1–2). Illus. Series: Our Neighborhood. 1997, Children's LB $19.50 (0-516-20312-6). 32pp. This is a photoessay with simple text on the life, training, and problems faced by a young male professional dancer. (Rev: BL 5/15/97; SLJ 7/97) [792.8]

**14198** Greenberg, Keith E. *Photojournalist: In the Middle of Disaster* (2–4). Illus. Series: Risky Business. 1995, Blackbirch LB $14.95 (1-56711-157-2). 32pp. In this career book, the work of photojournalist John Isaac — a native of India and an official photographer for the United Nations — is highlighted. (Rev: SLJ 2/96) [770]

**14199** Lee, Barbara. *Working in Music* (4–8). Illus. Series: Exploring Careers. 1996, Lerner $23.93 (0-8225-1761-2). 112pp. Such careers as composing, performing, and violin making are covered in this book profiling 12 people who work in the music field. (Rev: BL 2/15/97; SLJ 2/97) [780]

**14200** Lyon, George E. *A Sign* (K–4). Illus. by Chris K. Soentpiet. 1998, Orchard $15.95 (0-531-30073-0). 32pp. As a child, the author wanted to pursue many different careers, but finally she decided on the best one and became a writer. (Rev: BL 2/15/98; SLJ 3/98) [813]

**14201** Martin, John Harding. *A Day in the Life of a Ballet Dancer* (2–4). Illus. 1985, Troll LB $12.50 (0-8167-0089-3). 32pp. Heather's day includes rehearsal and a performance at the New York City Ballet. (Rev: BL 8/85; SLJ 9/85)

**14202** Maze, Stephanie. *I Want to Be a Dancer* (4–6). Illus. Series: I Want to Be. 1997, Harcourt $16.00 (0-15-201299-0). 48pp. Careers in dance are examined, with information on education, training, the history of dance, famous people, and special terms. (Rev: BL 2/1/98; SLJ 12/97) [792.8]

**14203** Schomp, Virginia. *If You Were a Ballet Dancer* (3–4). Illus. Series: If You Were. 1997, Marshall Cavendish LB $21.36 (0-7614-0616-6). 32pp. This introduction to a career in ballet tells about practicing, performing, styles of dance, costumes, and terminology. (Rev: BL 2/15/98; SLJ 2/98) [792.8]

**14204** Shulman, Jeffrey. *Karen Strange: Children's Theater Producer* (3–5). Series: Working Moms. 1991, Twenty-First Century LB $15.95 (0-941477-57-6). 40pp. A day-to-day look at a young woman who combines job and motherhood. (Rev: BL 6/15/91; SLJ 7/91) [792]

**14205** Smith, Betsy. *A Day in the Life of an Actress* (2–4). Illus. 1985, Troll LB $12.50 (0-8167-0105-9). 32pp. One day's activities include acting class and a variety of television and stage shows. (Rev: BL 8/85; SLJ 9/85)

**14206** Vitkus-Weeks, Jessica. *Television* (4–8). Illus. Series: Now Hiring. 1994, Crestwood LB $14.95 (0-89686-783-8). 48pp. Using real people as case histories, this book describes such TV careers as grip, camera operator, production assistant, costume designer, and actor. (Rev: SLJ 8/94) [621.388]

**14207** Wolf, Stephen. *A Day in the Life of a Stunt Person* (3–5). Illus. by Al Edwards. Series: A Day in the Life Library. 1990, Troll LB $12.50 (0-8167-2222-6). 32pp. This account emphasizes the planning, hard training, and special equipment necessary before a stunt person can attempt dangerous stunts for the movies. (Rev: BL 4/15/91) [792]

## Engineering, Technology, and Trades

**14208** Bryant, Jennifer. *Anne Abrams: Engineering Drafter* (3–6). Illus. Series: Working Moms. 1991, Twenty-First Century LB $15.95 (0-941477-51-7). 40pp. The job of a female engineering drafter, who is also a young mother, is described in a day on the job. (Rev: BL 6/15/91; SLJ 7/91) [604.2]

**14209** Martin, John Harding. *A Day in the Life of a High-Iron Worker* (2–4). Illus. 1985, Troll LB $12.50 (0-8167-0107-5). 32pp. The tasks and responsibilities are shown in a day's work high above the city streets. (Rev: BL 8/85; SLJ 9/85)

**14210** Maze, Stephanie. *I Want to Be an Engineer* (4–6). Illus. Series: I Want to Be. 1997, Harcourt $16.00 (0-15-201298-2). 48pp. Engineering and its various branches are introduced, along with the education and training necessary, terms used, and famous engineers. (Rev: BL 2/1/98; SLJ 12/97) [620]

**14211** Maze, Stephanie, and Catherine O. Grace. *I Want to Be an Astronaut* (3–5). Illus. Series: I Want to Be. 1997, Harcourt $16.00 (0-15-201300-8). 48pp. A career book that describes the duties of an astronaut, the educational requirements, and how to get involved in the field. (Rev: BCCB 5/97; BL 4/15/97; HB 5–6/97; SLJ 4/97) [629.45]

## Health and Medicine

**14212** Carter, Adam. *A Day in the Life of a Medical Detective* (2–4). Illus. 1985, Troll LB $12.50 (0-8167-0097-4). 32pp. Clear text and photos highlight the activities and responsibilities during one day in the life of this worker. (Rev: BCCB 10/85; BL 8/85)

**14213** Flanagan, Alice K. *Ask Nurse Pfaff, She'll Help You!* (1–2). Series: Our Neighborhood. 1997, Children's LB $19.50 (0-516-20495-5). 32pp. The life story of a nurse is given in this simple book that tells about nurses and their contributions to a community. (Rev: BL 12/15/97) [610]

**14214** Flanagan, Alice K. *Dr. Kanner, Dentist with a Smile* (1–2). Series: Our Neighborhood. 1997, Children's LB $19.50 (0-516-20493-9). 32pp. What dentists do and their contributions to a community are covered in this book highlighting the work of an actual dentist, Dr. Kanner. (Rev: BL 12/15/97; SLJ 1/98) [617]

**14215** Lee, Barbara. *Working in Health Care and Wellness* (4–8). Illus. Series: Exploring Careers. 1996, Lerner LB $23.93 (0-8225-1760-4). 112pp. Profiles 12 people who are in health care professions, including the pros and cons of each career. (Rev: BL 2/15/97) [610.69]

**14216** Moses, Amy. *Doctors Help People* (PS–2). Illus. Series: Career Books. 1996, Child's World LB $21.36 (1-56766-304-4). 32pp. A career book that describes what doctors do, particularly when they care for children. (Rev: SLJ 3/97) [610]

**14217** Osborn, Kevin. *A Day in the Life of a Seeing Eye Dog Trainer* (3–5). Illus. by John Halpern. Series: A Day in the Life of. 1990, Troll LB $12.50 (0-8167-2218-8). 32pp. This accounts tells how Seeing Eye dogs are trained to lead their owners through busy streets and to avoid obstacles. (Rev: BL 4/15/91) [362.4]

**14218** Paige, David. *A Day in the Life of a Sports Therapist* (2–4). Illus. 1985, Troll LB $12.50 (0-8167-0099-0). 32pp. Fred Caito helps keep football players in shape for the game; all in a day's work. (Rev: BL 8/85; SLJ 9/85)

**14219** Staub, Frank. *A Day in the Life of a Ski Patroller* (3–5). Illus. Series: A Day in the Life of. 1990, Troll LB $12.50 (0-8167-2220-X). 32pp. A description of a day in the lives of ski patrollers, who locate and save victims of avalanches and other mountain disasters. (Rev: BL 4/15/91) [796]

**14220** Witty, Margot. *A Day in the Life of an Emergency Room Nurse* (3–4). Illus. 1980, Troll LB $12.50 (0-89375-226-6). 32pp. A realistic account of a day's experience in this exciting profession.

## Police and Fire Fighters

**14221** Broekel, Ray. *Fire Fighters* (2–3). Illus. 1981, Children's LB $20.00 (0-516-01620-2). 48pp. An easy reader with many color photographs.

**14222** Flanagan, Alice K. *Ms. Murphy Fights Fires* (1–2). Series: Our Neighborhood. 1997, Children's LB $19.50 (0-516-20494-7). 32pp. A modern firefighter is the focus of this book, which describes what these people do and their contributions to a neighborhood. (Rev: BL 12/15/97; SLJ 1/98) [363.77]

**14223** Greenberg, Keith E. *Bomb Squad Officer: Expert with Explosives* (2–4). Illus. Series: Risky Business. 1995, Blackbirch LB $14.95 (1-56711-155-6). 32pp. A career book, set in New Jersey, that explains the work of the men who remove and dismantle or detonate suspicious objects. (Rev: SLJ 2/96) [363]

**14224** Greenberg, Keith E. *Smokejumper: Firefighter from the Sky* (2–5). Illus. Series: Risky Business. 1995, Blackbirch LB $14.95 (1-56711-153-X). 32pp. This career book gives details on the training and skills needed to become a smoke jumper — one who parachutes into forests to fight fires. (Rev: SLJ 8/95) [634.9]

**14225** Greene, Carol. *Firefighters Fight Fires* (2–4). Illus. Series: Career Books. 1996, Child's World LB $21.36 (1-56766-301-X). 32pp. In this career book, readers accompany firefighters to a blazing house where they also rescue a cat. (Rev: SLJ 4/97) [363]

**14226** Greene, Carol. *Police Officers Protect People* (PS–2). Illus. Series: Career Books. 1996, Child's World LB $21.36 (1-56766-311-7). 32pp. This career book shows many of the jobs that police officers do like coping with an accident and helping to find a missing child. (Rev: SLJ 3/97) [363]

**14227** Hines, Gary. *Flying Firefighters* (K–3). Illus. by Anna Grossnickle Hines. 1993, Clarion $14.95 (0-395-61197-0). 32pp. In double-page spreads using watercolors and text, the activities of a fire-fighting crew are depicted. (Rev: BL 10/15/93; SLJ 1/94) [634.9]

**14228** Maass, Robert. *Fire Fighters* (2–3). Illus. 1989, Scholastic paper $4.99 (0-590-41460-7). 32pp. Photos of fire fighters in training, relaxing, and working a fire. (Rev: BCCB 2/89; BL 4/1/89)

**14229** Martin, John Harding. *A Day in the Life of a Police Cadet* (2–4). Illus. 1985, Troll LB $12.50 (0-8167-0103-2). 32pp. Study and training are part of the day's activities for Rafael Mangual as he works toward his future. (Rev: BL 8/85; SLJ 9/85)

**14230** Masoff, Joy. *Fire!* (3–7). Illus. 1998, Scholastic $16.95 (0-590-97872-1). 48pp. The facts about and excitement of firefighting are covered in this fast-paced book filled with pictures, sidebars, screens, and extensive captions. (Rev: BL 2/1/98; SLJ 3/98) [363.37]

**14231** Paige, David. *A Day in the Life of a Police Detective* (4–6). Illus. 1981, Troll LB $12.50 (0-89375-442-0). 32pp. A typical police detective's day, richly illustrated.

**14232** Schomp, Virginia. *If You Were a Firefighter* (3–4). Series: If You Were. 1997, Marshall Cavendish LB $21.36 (0-7614-0615-8). 32pp. In this simple career book, the training and responsibilities of firefighters are introduced. (Rev: BL 2/15/98) [363]

**14233** Schomp, Virginia. *If You Were a Police Officer* (3–4). Series: If You Were. 1997, Marshall Cavendish LB $21.36 (0-7614-0614-X). 32pp. The everyday activities of a police officer are described in this simple career book. (Rev: BL 2/15/98) [363]

**14234** Smith, Betsy. *A Day in the Life of a Firefighter* (4–6). Illus. 1981, Troll LB $12.50 (0-89375-444-7). 32pp. A typical day of a fire fighter told in text and pictures.

**14235** Smith, Carter. *A Day in the Life of an FBI Agent-in-Training* (3–5). Illus. by Franz A. Jantzen. Series: A Day in the Life Library. 1990, Troll LB $12.50 (0-8167-2210-2). 32pp. Through visiting a class at the FBI Academy, the activities of this law enforcement agency are detailed. (Rev: BL 4/15/91) [363]

**14236** Winkleman, Katherine K. *Firehouse* (2–4). Illus. by John S. Winkleman. 1994, Walker $15.85 (0-8027-8317-1). 32pp. Facts about firehouses, past and present, and how they operate are presented in this fascinating behind-the-scenes look. (Rev: BCCB 10/94; BL 10/1/94; SLJ 1/95) [363.37]

# Science

**14237** Duvall, Jill D. *Who Keeps the Water Clean? Ms. Schindler!* (1–2). Illus. Series: Our Neighborhood. 1997, Children's LB $19.00 (0-516-20315-0). 32pp. This unusual book looks at the life and career of a worker in a water treatment plant. (Rev: BL 5/15/97; SLJ 7/97) [628.1]

**14238** Ghez, Andrea Mia, and Judith Cohen. *You Can Be a Woman Astronomer* (3–5). Illus. by David Katz. 1995, Cascade Pass paper $6.00 (1-880599-17-1). 38pp. A career book in which the author tells how she became a scientist and of the excitement and wonder of using telescopes and other tools of the astronomer. (Rev: SLJ 1/96) [520]

**14239** Greenberg, Keith E. *Marine Biologist: Swimming with the Sharks* (2–4). Illus. Series: Risky Business. 1995, Blackbirch LB $14.95 (1-56711-156-4). 32pp. A career book that focuses on the work of marine biologist Dr. Sonny Gruber, who has studied sharks for the past 30 years. (Rev: SLJ 2/96) [574.92]

**14240** Higginson, Mel. *Scientists Who Study Ancient Temples and Tombs* (1–2). Illus. Series: Scientists. 1994, Rourke LB $10.95 (0-86593-376-6). 24pp. A simple introduction to archaeologists, what they do, the education necessary, and some of their important discoveries. (Rev: SLJ 2/95) [930]

**14241** Higginson, Mel. *Scientists Who Study Fossils* (1–2). Illus. Series: Scientists. 1994, Rourke LB $10.95 (0-86593-375-8). 24pp. This basic book describes what paleontologists do, what sort of education and training they require, and some of their important accomplishments. (Rev: SLJ 2/95) [560]

**14242** Higginson, Mel. *Scientists Who Study Ocean Life* (1–2). Illus. Series: Scientists. 1994, Rourke LB $10.95 (0-86593-371-5). 24pp. Describes the science of oceanography, as well as the training required and discoveries of these scientists who study the oceans. (Rev: SLJ 2/95) [551.46]

**14243** Higginson, Mel. *Scientists Who Study the Earth* (1–2). Illus. Series: Scientists. 1994, Rourke LB $10.95 (0-86593-372-3). 24pp. A basic introduction to the work that geologists do and how they prepare for it. (Rev: SLJ 2/95) [557]

**14244** Higginson, Mel. *Scientists Who Study Wild Animals* (1–2). Illus. Series: Scientists. 1994, Rourke LB $10.95 (0-86593-374-X). 24pp. Careers in animal biology are introduced briefly, with a description of the education and training necessary. (Rev: SLJ 2/95) [591]

**14245** Jaspersohn, William. *A Day in the Life of a Marine Biologist* (5–8). Illus. 1982, Little, Brown $15.95 (0-316-45814-7). 96pp. A career portrait of the director of a marine biology program at Woods Hole, Massachusetts.

**14246** Michels, Penny, and Judith Tropea. *A Day in the Life of a Beekeeper* (3–5). Illus. by John Halpern. Series: A Day in the Life Library. 1990, Troll LB $12.50 (0-8167-2206-4). 32pp. In this account, a school student spends a day with a beekeeper and discovers fascinating facts about bees. (Rev: BL 4/15/91) [638.1]

**14247** Paige, David. *A Day in the Life of a Marine Biologist* (4–6). Illus. 1981, Troll LB $12.50 (0-89375-446-3); paper $3.95 (0-89375-447-1). 32pp. Colorful pictures and brief text are used to describe the daily tasks of a marine biologist.

# Transportation

**14248** Bourne, Miriam Anne. *A Day in the Life of a Cross-Country Trucker* (3–5). Illus. 1988, Troll LB $12.50 (0-8167-1117-8). 32pp. Photos highlight this glimpse into the workday of a trucker. (Rev: BL 2/15/88)

**14249** Jaspersohn, William. *A Week in the Life of an Airline Pilot* (4–8). Illus. 1991, Little, Brown $14.95 (0-316-45822-8). 96pp. A close-up look at the duties and lives of members of an airline crew. (Rev: BL 3/15/91; HB 5–6/91; SLJ 5/91) [629.132]

**14250** McKeever, Michael, and Georgeanne Irvine. *A Day in the Life of a Test Pilot* (3–5). Illus. by Ron Garrison. Series: A Day in the Life Library. 1990, Troll LB $12.50 (0-8167-2224-2). 32pp. Some of the activities of a test pilot, such as trying out a jet and training students. (Rev: BL 4/15/91) [629.134]

**14251** Robinson, Fay. *Pilots Fly Planes* (2–4). Illus. Series: Career Books. 1996, Child's World LB $21.36 (1-56766-308-7). 32pp. A career book that shows both male and female pilots going through a typical day of flight preparation and execution. (Rev: SLJ 4/97) [629.13]

**14252** Schleier, Curt. *The Team Behind Your Airline Flight* (4–6). Illus. 1981, Westminster $10.00 (0-664-32678-1). 94pp. An explanation of the people who are behind a safe flight.

**14253** Wilkinson, Sylvia. *I Can Be a Race Car Driver* (1–3). Illus. 1986, Children's LB $14.60 (0-516-01898-1). 32pp. Stressing safety in this account of an exciting but dangerous career. (Rev: BL 1/15/87)

# Veterinarians

**14254** Bryant, Jennifer. *Jane Sayler: Veterinarian* (3–5). Illus. Series: Working Moms. 1991, Children's $21.27 (0-516-07378-8). 40pp. Combining the jobs of animal doctor and mother is the focus of this career book. (Rev: BL 6/15/91; SLJ 6/91) [636]

**14255** Greene, Carol. *Veterinarians Help Animals* (2–4). Illus. Series: Career Books. 1996, Child's World LB $21.36 (1-56766-310-9). 32pp. In this career book, veterinarians care for a number of animals, mainly cats and dogs. (Rev: SLJ 4/97) [636]

**14256** Horenstein, Henry. *My Mom's a Vet* (4–6). Illus. 1994, Candlewick $17.95 (1-56402-234-X); paper $7.99 (1-56402-922-0). 64pp. In this photoessay, young Darcie describes a week in which she helps her mother, a veterinarian. (Rev: BCCB 3/94; BL 5/1/94; HB 5–6/94; SLJ 6/94) [636.089]

**14257** Hurwitz, Jane. *Choosing a Career in Animal Care* (4–8). Illus. Series: World of Work. 1996, Rosen LB $15.95 (0-8239-2268-5). 64pp. Various careers in working with animals are described, along with the education required, desirable personality traits, and ways to break into the field. (Rev: SLJ 8/97) [371.7]

**14258** Lee, Barbara. *Working with Animals* (4–8). Illus. Series: Exploring Careers. 1996, Lerner LB $23.93 (0-8225-1759-0). 112pp. Profiles of 12 careers involving animals, such as veterinarian, animal shelter worker, or pet sitter. (Rev: BL 2/15/97) [591]

**14259** Maze, Stephanie, and Catherine O. Grace. *I Want to Be a Veterinarian* (3–5). Illus. Series: I Want to Be. 1997, Harcourt $16.00 (0-15-201296-6). 48pp. Describes the responsibilities of a veterinarian, educational requirements for the profession, and how to make a start toward getting into the field. (Rev: BCCB 5/97; BL 4/15/97; HB 5–6/97; SLJ 4/97) [636]

**14260** Paige, David. *A Day in the Life of a Zoo Veterinarian* (2–4). Illus. 1985, Troll LB $12.50 (0-8167-0095-8). 32pp. Chicago's Lincoln Park Zoo is the working scene for Dr. Barbara Thomas, who makes "cage calls." (Rev: BL 8/85)

**14261** Schomp, Virginia. *If You Were a Veterinarian* (3–4). Series: If You Were. 1997, Marshall Cavendish LB $21.36 (0-7614-0613-1). 32pp. In this simple career book, the everyday activities of a veterinarian are described, with some information on the educational background necessary. (Rev: BL 2/15/98; SLJ 2/98) [636]

**14262** Stamper, Judith B. *What's It Like to Be a Veterinarian?* (K–3). Illus. by Marcy Ramsey. Series: Young Careers. 1990, Troll LB $12.95 (0-8167-1817-2). 32pp. A young boy learns about the duties and responsibilities of being a veterinarian. (Rev: SLJ 9/90) [371.7]

# Health and the Human Body

## Aging and Death

**14263** Hyde, Margaret O., and Lawrence E. Hyde. *Meeting Death* (5–8). 1989, Walker LB $15.85 (0-8027-6874-1). 144pp. Demystifying death for children while acknowledging that it is the central mystery of our lives. (Rev: BL 1/1/90) [306.9]

## Alcohol, Drugs, and Smoking

**14264** Cohen, Philip. *Tobacco* (5–8). Illus. Series: Drugs — The Complete Story. 1992, Raintree Steck-Vaughn LB $25.68 (0-8114-3202-5). 64pp. This account tells of the social and physiological effects of tobacco. (Rev: SLJ 8/92) [362.2]

**14265** Condon, Judith. *The Pressure to Take Drugs* (5–8). Illus. 1990, Watts LB $20.80 (0-531-10934-8). 64pp. A book that confronts youths who may feel pressured to take drugs. (Rev: BL 8/90) [362.29]

**14266** DeStefano, Susan. *Focus on Opiates* (3–6). Illus. by David Neuhaus. Series: Drug-Alert. 1990, Children's $19.93 (0-516-07359-1). 68pp. This book focuses on the uses and misuses of various opium forms. (Rev: BL 1/1/91) [362.29]

**14267** Grosshandler-Smith, Janet. *Working Together Against Drinking and Driving* (4–8). Illus. Series: Library of Social Activism. 1996, Rosen LB $16.95 (0-8239-2259-6). 64pp. A book that gives advice on how to avoid alcohol and how one can be involved in the crusade against drinking and driving. (Rev: SLJ 2/97) [616.86]

**14268** Harris, Jacqueline L. *Drugs and Disease* (5–8). Illus. Series: Bodies in Crisis. 1993, Twenty-First Century LB $18.90 (0-8050-2602-9). 64pp.

Introduces various drugs and their role in fighting diseases in a simple, well-illustrated format. (Rev: BL 1/15/94; SLJ 1/94) [616.86]

**14269** Haughton, Emma. *A Right to Smoke?* (3–6). Illus. Series: Viewpoints. 1997, Watts LB $20.00 (0-531-14412-7). 32pp. The controversy concerning cigarette advertising and special taxes is covered, along with facts on the effects of smoking. (Rev: BL 6/1–15/97; SLJ 5/97) [362.29]

**14270** Holmes, Pamela. *Alcohol* (5–8). Illus. Series: Drugs — The Complete Story. 1992, Raintree Steck-Vaughn LB $25.68 (0-8114-3203-3). 64pp. Topics covered include how alcohol is produced, the industry, and the effects of alcohol. (Rev: SLJ 8/92) [613.8]

**14271** Hyde, Margaret O. *Know About Drugs*. 4th ed (5–8). 1995, Walker LB $15.85 (0-8027-8395-3). 93pp. An introduction to drugs and their effects, such as marijuana, alcohol, PCP, inhalants, crack/cocaine, heroin, and nicotine. (Rev: BL 7/90; SLJ 3/96) [362.2]

**14272** Hyde, Margaret O. *Know About Smoking*. Rev. ed. (5–8). Illus. 1995, Walker LB $14.85 (0-8027-8400-3). 100pp. After a history of tobacco and nicotine, this book describes their effects on the body, addiction prevention, and the role of advertising in smoking. (Rev: BL 7/90; SLJ 9/95) [362.2]

**14273** Kreiner, Anna. *Let's Talk About Drug Abuse* (1–4). Illus. Series: Let's Talk Library. 1996, Rosen LB $13.95 (0-8239-2302-9). 24pp. Various kinds of drugs and their effects on the human body are introduced. (Rev: BL 3/1/97; SLJ 12/96) [362.29]

**14274** Landau, Elaine. *Hooked: Talking About Addiction* (5–7). Illus. 1995, Millbrook LB $21.90 (1-56294-469-X). 64pp. This account defines addiction broadly — from use of alcohol and drugs to various forms of compulsive behavior — and gives suggestions for recovery. (Rev: BL 1/1–15/96; SLJ 1/96) [362.29]

**14275** Langsen, Richard C. *When Someone in the Family Drinks Too Much* (K–3). Illus. by Nicole Rubel. 1996, Dial paper $14.89 (0-8037-1687-7). This simple picture book explains what alcoholism is, describes the 10 warning signs, and talks about the typical behavior of those suffering from the disorder. (Rev: BCCB 3/96; SLJ 7/96) [616.86]

**14276** Marr, John S. *Breath of Air and a Breath of Smoke* (4–6). Illus. 1971, Evans $4.95 (0-87131-038-4). 48pp. After a description of the respiratory system, there is a description of the effects of smoking on the body.

**14277** Pietrusza, David. *Smoking* (4–7). Illus. Series: Overview. 1997, Lucent LB $22.45 (1-56006-186-3). 112pp. This well-organized account gives a history of smoking, tells about its effects on the human body, and contains information on smokers' rights and lawsuits against tobacco companies. (Rev: BL 8/97; SLJ 7/97) [362.29]

**14278** Pringle, Laurence. *Smoking: A Risky Business* (3–7). Illus. 1996, Morrow $16.00 (0-688-13039-9). 128pp. A history of smoking and its effects and tips on how to quit when you're hooked. (Rev: BL 12/1/96; SLJ 1/97) [362.29]

**14279** Salak, John. *Drugs in Society: Are They Our Suicide Pill?* (5–8). Illus. Series: Issues of Our Time. 1993, Twenty-First Century LB $18.90 (0-8050-2572-3). 64pp. A slim, easily read account that describes the history of drug abuse, its unfortunate byproducts, and important cases involving such people as Manuel Noriega. (Rev: SLJ 2/94) [616]

**14280** Sanders, Pete. *Smoking* (4–7). Illus. Series: What Do You Know About . . . 1996, Millbrook LB $20.90 (0-7613-0536-X). 32pp. Covers the effects of smoking and ways in which youngsters can avoid getting hooked. (Rev: SLJ 3/97) [362.2]

**14281** Sanders, Pete, and Steve Myers. *Drinking Alcohol* (4–8). Illus. by Mike Lacey. Series: What Do You Know About . . . 1997, Millbrook LB $20.90 (0-7613-0573-4). 32pp. An introduction to alcohol use, with material on its dangerous effects on the body and behavior. (Rev: SLJ 10/97) [362.29]

**14282** Shulman, Jeffrey. *Focus on Cocaine and Crack* (3–6). Illus. by David Neuhaus. Series: Drug Alert. 1990, Twenty-First Century LB $14.95 (0-941477-98-3). 56pp. A good account of the dangers of these drugs. (Rev: BL 3/15/90; SLJ 4/90) [362.2]

**14283** Shulman, Jeffrey. *Focus on Hallucinogens* (3–6). Illus. by David Neuhaus. Series: Drug Alert. 1991, Twenty-First Century LB $14.95 (0-941477-92-4). 68pp. The origins and misuses of mind-altering, or hallucinogenic, drugs. (Rev: BL 1/1/91) [362.29]

**14284** Steffens, Bradley. *Addiction: Distinguishing Between Fact and Opinion* (5–7). Illus. Series: Opposing Viewpoints Juniors. 1994, Greenhaven LB $16.20 (1-56510-094-8). 36pp. Critical thinking is encouraged by having the reader study a variety of attitudes and opinions about addiction. (Rev: BL 1/1/94) [362.29]

**14285** Steins, Richard. *Alcohol Abuse: Is This Danger on the Rise?* (5–8). Illus. Series: Issues of Our Time. 1995, Twenty-First Century LB $18.90 (0-8050-3882-5). 64pp. After defining what an alcoholic is, this account describes the physical effects of alcohol and the emotional problems alcoholism causes within families. (Rev: SLJ 2/96) [613.8]

**14286** Super, Gretchen. *Drugs and Our World* (K–3). Illus. by Blanche Sims. 1991, Twenty-First Century LB $14.95 (0-8050-2888-9); Troll paper $3.95 (0-8167-2365-6). 48pp. For young children, this and the 2 other titles in the series, *What Are Drugs?* and *You Can Say "NO" to Drugs* (both 1995), explain what harmful drugs are and how to avoid them. (Rev: SLJ 11/90) [616]

**14287** Talmadge, Katherine S. *Focus on Steroids* (3–6). Illus. by David Neuhaus. Series: Drug-Alert. 1991, Twenty-First Century LB $14.95 (0-8050-2216-3). 64pp. The use and misuse of steroids, with particular attention to sports. (Rev: BL 1/15/91) [362.29]

**14288** Taylor, Clark. *The House That Crack Built* (3–8). Illus. by Jan T. Dicks. 1992, Chronicle $12.95 (0-8118-0133-0); paper $6.95 (0-8118-0123-3). 36pp. An old children's rhyme is turned into a dark verse, with a relentless rap beat, about drugs. (Rev: BL 4/15/92; SLJ 6/92) [362.29]

**14289** Washburne, Carolyn K. *Drug Abuse* (5–8). Illus. Series: Overview. 1996, Lucent LB $22.45 (1-56006-169-3). 112pp. A carefully researched account that gives important background information on drug abuse and present-day practices and problems. (Rev: BL 1/1–15/96) [362.29]

**14290** Wax, Wendy. *Say No and Know Why: Kids Learn About Drugs* (4–7). Illus. by Toby McAfee. 1992, Walker LB $13.85 (0-8027-8141-1). 80pp. A serious look at drug problems as a sixth-grade class in the Bronx, New York, gets a visit from a local nurse and an assistant district attorney. (Rev: BL 1/15/93; SLJ 10/92) [362.29]

**14291** Weitzman, Elizabeth. *Let's Talk About Smoking* (4–8). Illus. Series: Let's Talk Library. 1996, Rosen LB $15.93 (0-8239-2307-X). 24pp. This book tells why people smoke, its effects, and ways to avoid starting, with tips on how to give up. (Rev: BL 3/15/97; SLJ 1/97) [362.29]

**14292** Zeller, Paula K. *Focus on Marijuana* (3–6). Illus. by David Neuhaus. 1990, Twenty-First Century LB $14.95 (0-941477-97-5). 56pp. New findings are discussed about the dangers of this drug. (Rev: BL 3/15/90; SLJ 4/90) [362.29]

# Bionics and Transplants

**14293** Presnall, Judith J. *Artificial Organs* (5–8). Illus. Series: Overview. 1996, Lucent LB $22.45 (1-56006-257-6). 112pp. A history of the use of artificial organs, along with present-day practices and problems. (Rev: BL 1/1–15/96) [617.9]

# Disabilities, Physical and Mental

**14294** Abeel, Samantha. *What Once Was White* (5–8). Illus. by Charles R. Murphy. 1993, Village Press $19.95 (0-941653-13-7). The author is a 13-year-old learning-disabled student who can't tell time but writes sensitive interpretations of a group of watercolor paintings. (Rev: SLJ 9/93*) [618.62]

**14295** Aseltine, Lorraine, et al. *I'm Deaf and It's Okay* (3–5). Illus. by Helen Cogancherry. 1986, Whitman LB $12.95 (0-8075-3472-2). 40pp. A boy copes with the frustrations of deafness. (Rev: BL 5/15/86; SLJ 8/86)

**14296** Bernstein, Joanne E., and Bryna J. Fireside. *Special Parents, Special Children* (4–7). Illus. by Michael J. Bernstein. 1991, Whitman $12.95 (0-8075-7559-3). 64pp. Young people tell what it's like to grow up with one parent who is physically challenged. (Rev: BCCB 1/92*; BL 8/91; SLJ 2/92) [306.874]

**14297** Brown, Fern G. *Special Olympics* (4–7). Illus. 1992, Watts LB $21.00 (0-531-20062-0). 64pp. A recounting of the history of the Special Olympics, which began in 1963. (Rev: BCCB 5/92; BL 6/1/92; SLJ 7/92) [796]

**14298** Dinner, Sherry H. *Nothing to Be Ashamed Of: Growing Up with a Mental Illness in Your Family* (5–8). 1989, Lothrop LB $12.93 (0-688-08482-6); paper $7.95 (0-688-08493-1). 160pp. A psychologist offers straightforward advice on living with a mentally ill family member. (Rev: BL 6/1/89; SLJ 4/89)

**14299** Dunn, Kathryn B., and Allison Boesel. *Trouble with School: A Family Story About Learning Disabilities* (2–4). Illus. by Rick Stromoski. 1993, Woodbine $9.95 (0-933149-57-3). This book tells how a family dealt with their child's learning disability. (Rev: SLJ 8/93) [616]

**14300** Dwight, Laura. *We Can Do It!* (PS–3). Illus. 1992, Checkerboard $7.95 (1-56288-301-1). 36pp.

Children with various disabilities are shown at home, at play, at school. (Rev: BL 1/15/93) [305]

**14301** Dwyer, Kathleen M. *What Do You Mean I Have a Learning Disability?* (3–6). 1991, Walker LB $15.85 (0-8027-8103-9). 48pp. Feelings of inferiority are related in this story of a 10-year-old boy who fails in school. (Rev: BCCB 9/91; BL 9/1/91; SLJ 11/91) [371.9]

**14302** Dwyer, Kathleen M. *What Do You Mean I Have Attention Deficit Disorder?* (4–6). Illus. 1996, Walker LB $15.85 (0-8027-8393-7). 128pp. Patrick doesn't know why he can't pay attention in school until he is diagnosed as having ADD. (Rev: BCCB 9/96; BL 8/96; SLJ 8/96) [618.92]

**14303** Emmert, Michelle. *I'm the Big Sister Now* (3–5). Illus. by Gail Owens. 1989, Whitman LB $14.95 (0-8075-3458-7). 32pp. The younger sister of a child severely handicapped with cerebral palsy explains what life is like for them and their special love. (Rev: BL 1/1/90; SLJ 12/89) [618.92]

**14304** Fisher, Gary L., and Rhoda Cummings. *The Survival Guide for Kids with LD (Learning Differences)* (5–8). 1990, Free Spirit paper $9.95 (0-915793-18-0). 98pp. A supportive book aimed directly at kids with learning problems. (Rev: BL 7/90; SLJ 6/90) [371.9]

**14305** Hall, David E. *Living with Learning Disabilities: A Guide for Students* (5–8). 1993, Lerner LB $19.93 (0-8225-0036-1). 64pp. This book explains what learning disabilities are, what causes them, how they can be detected, and today's techniques for treatment. (Rev: BL 1/1/94; SLJ 4/94) [371.9]

**14306** Kent, Deborah, and Kathryn A. Quinlan. *Extraordinary People with Disabilities* (5–8). Illus. 1996, Children's LB $37.00 (0-516-20021-6). 288pp. A variety of historical and contemporary people with disabilities introduce various disabilities and the adjustments they have made to live with them. (Rev: BL 3/1/97; SLJ 3/97) [363.4]

**14307** *Kids Explore the Gifts of Children with Special Needs* (3–7). Illus. 1994, John Muir paper $9.95 (1-56261-156-9). 118pp. Each of the 10 chapters deals with a case history of a child with a different handicap, including hemophilia, Down's syndrome, dyslexia, and attention deficit disorder. (Rev: BL 5/15/94; SLJ 6/94) [371.91]

**14308** Landau, Elaine. *Blindness* (4–7). Illus. Series: Understanding Illness. 1994, Twenty-First Century LB $15.95 (0-8050-2992-3). 64pp. Both the emotional and scientific aspects of blindness are covered, with an excellent chapter on prevention. (Rev: BL 12/15/94; SLJ 2/95) [617.7]

**14309** Landau, Elaine. *Deafness* (4–7). Illus. Series: Understanding Illness. 1994, Twenty-First Century LB $18.90 (0-8050-2993-1). 64pp. Beginning with the story of a deaf child, this book explores the causes of deafness, the scientific and emotional factors involved, treatments, and problems in adjusting. (Rev: BL 12/15/94; SLJ 2/95) [617.8]

**14310** Lauren, Jill. *Succeeding with LD: 20 True Stories About Real People with LD* (5–8). Illus. 1997, Free Spirit paper $23.95 (1-57542-012-0). 160pp. Case histories of 20 people, ages 10 to 61, who have overcome various learning difficulties. (Rev: BL 6/1–15/97; SLJ 7/97) [371.92]

**14311** McCarthy-Tucker, Sherri. *Coping with Special-Needs Classmates* (5–8). 1993, Rosen LB $16.95 (0-8239-1598-0). 115pp. First-person accounts describe physical, mental, and emotional problems faced by some young people. (Rev: SLJ 8/93) [616]

**14312** MacKinnon, Christy. *Silent Observer* (K–4). Illus. 1993, Gallaudet Univ. $15.95 (1-56368-022-X). 48pp. The journal of a young deaf girl growing up in Nova Scotia at the end of the 19th century and her experiences at a boarding school. (Rev: BL 1/15/94; SLJ 3/94) [362.4]

**14313** McNey, Martha. *Leslie's Story: A Book About a Girl with Mental Retardation* (3–5). Illus. 1996, Lerner LB $21.27 (0-8225-2576-3). 32pp. The lifestyle and limitations of a mentally retarded girl are explained. (Rev: BL 7/96; SLJ 9/96) [362.3]

**14314** Meyer, Donald, ed. *Views from Our Shoes: Growing Up with a Brother or Sister with Special Needs* (4–6). Illus. 1997, Woodbine paper $14.95 (0-933149-98-0). 106pp. Using the words of 45 youngsters ages 4 to 18 as a focus, this book tells what it is like living with a sibling who has a physical or mental disability. (Rev: BL 1/1–15/98; SLJ 4/98) [362.1]

**14315** Moragne, Wendy. *Dyslexia* (5–8). Illus. Series: Medical Library. 1997, Millbrook LB $23.90 (0-7613-0206-9). 96pp. Using interviews with a number of dyslexic teenagers, this book describes the symptoms, treatments, and emotional problems involved with dyslexia. (Rev: SLJ 3/97) [617.7]

**14316** Parker, Steve. *Living with Heart Disease* (5–8). Illus. Series: Living With. 1989, Watts LB $20.40 (0-531-10845-7). 32pp. The causes and effects of heart disease and how people cope with it. (Rev: BL 2/1/90; SLJ 2/90) [616.1]

**14317** Powers, Mary Ellen. *Our Teacher's in a Wheelchair* (PS–1). Illus. by author. 1986, Whitman LB $12.95 (0-8075-6240-8). 32pp. Photoessay showing how a young teacher manages a classroom in a day care center even though he is in a wheelchair. (Rev: BL 11/15/86; SLJ 12/86)

**14318** Roby, Cynthia. *When Learning Is Tough: Kids Talk About Their Learning Disabilities* (4–6). Illus. by Elena Dorfman. 1994, Albert Whitman LB $13.95 (0-8075-8892-X). 32pp. Eight youngsters talk about their learning problems and their accom-

plishments and dreams for the future. (Rev: BL 6/1–15/94; SLJ 9/94) [371.9]

**14319** Stein, Sara Bonnett. *About Handicaps* (2–3). Illus. 1974, Walker $14.95 (0-8027-6174-7); paper $8.95 (0-8027-7225-0). 48pp. A book about learning to accept people who have physical handicaps.

**14320** Taylor, Barbara. *Living with Deafness* (5–8). Illus. Series: Living With. 1989, Watts LB $20.40 (0-531-10842-2). 32pp. Discusses causes of deafness and the ways people cope with this disability. (Rev: BL 2/1/90; SLJ 2/90) [617.8]

**14321** Ward, Brian. *Overcoming Disability* (5–7). Illus. 1989, Watts LB $12.40 (0-531-10645-4). Discussing the most common disabilities of childhood — from poor eyesight to leukemia. (Rev: BCCB 5/89)

**14322** Watson, Esther. *Talking to Angels* (K–3). Illus. 1996, Harcourt $16.00 (0-15-201077-7). 32pp. The subject of autism is introduced through the experiences of the author, who has an autistic sister. (Rev: BCCB 6/96; BL 4/1/96; SLJ 7/96) [618.92]

## Disease and Illness

**14323** Aldape, Virginia Totorica. *Nicole's Story: A Book About a Girl with Juvenile Rheumatoid Arthritis* (3–5). Illus. 1996, Lerner LB $19.95 (0-8225-2578-X). 40pp. The case history of a young girl who has rheumatoid arthritis. (Rev: BL 7/96; SLJ 9/96) [362.1]

**14324** Berger, Melvin. *Germs Make Me Sick!* Rev. ed (K–3). Illus. by Marylin Hafner. Series: Lets-Read-and-Find-Out. 1995, HarperCollins LB $14.89 (0-06-024250-7); paper $4.95 (0-06445-154-2). 32pp. In this easily read book, germs and viruses and their effects on the human body are introduced. (Rev: BL 10/1/95; SLJ 3/96) [616.9]

**14325** Bergman, Thomas. *Determined to Win: Children Living with Allergies and Asthma* (3–5). Illus. Series: Don't Turn Away. 1994, Gareth Stevens LB $19.93 (0-8368-1075-9). 48pp. This photoessay explores 2 medical conditions found increasingly in children, allergies and asthma, with material on each condition and how to cope with it. (Rev: BL 5/1/94) [362.1]

**14326** Bode, Janet. *Food Fight: A Guide to Eating Disorders for Pre-teens and Their Parents* (5–7). 1997, Simon & Schuster paper $16.00 (0-689-80272-2). 144pp. A clearly written account of the physical, psychological, and social aspects of anorexia and bulimia, plus practical suggestions for help. (Rev: BL 6/1–15/97; HB 1–2/97; SLJ 8/97*) [618.92]

**14327** Bryan, Jenny. *What's Wrong with Me? What Happens When You're Sick, and Ways to Stay Healthy* (2–4). Illus. 1995, Thomson Learning LB $21.40 (1-56847-199-8). 32pp. In this book about illnesses, double-page spreads reveal possible causes and treatments for various symptoms. (Rev: BL 3/15/95) [616]

**14328** Carter, Alden R., and Siri M. Carter. *I'm Tougher Than Asthma!* (PS–2). Illus. 1996, Albert Whitman LB $14.95 (0-8075-3474-9). 32pp. In photos and text, the author explores the world of Siri, who suffers from asthma. (Rev: BL 3/1/96; SLJ 8/96) [616.2]

**14329** Connelly, John P., and Leonard Berlow. *You're Too Sweet: A Guide for the Young Diabetic* (4–6). Illus. 1968, Astor-Honor $9.95 (0-8392-1173-2). The cause and treatment of diabetes from the standpoint of a 9-year-old boy.

**14330** Demuth, Patricia. *Achoo! All About Colds* (1–2). Illus. by Maggie Smith. 1997, Putnam $13.99 (0-448-41348-5); paper $3.95 (0-448-41347-7). 48pp. An easy reader that tells about colds, how they happen, and the treatments for them, using a fictional case history as a framework. (Rev: BL 8/97; SLJ 12/97) [616.2]

**14331** Facklam, Howard, and Margery Facklam. *Viruses* (4–7). Illus. Series: Invaders. 1994, Twenty-First Century LB $18.90 (0-8050-2856-0). 64pp. The composition of viruses and their various types, including AIDS, are introduced. (Rev: BL 1/1/95; SLJ 3/95) [576.62]

**14332** Fassler, David, and Kelly McQueen. *What's a Virus, Anyway? The Kids' Book About AIDS* (K–4). 1993, Waterfront $10.95 (0-914525-14-X). 67pp. This book describes what AIDS is through an explanation of what a virus is and how some viruses attack our immune system. A reissue. (Rev: BL 6/1/90) [616]

**14333** Forbes, Anna. *Kids with AIDS* (2–5). Illus. Series: AIDS Awareness Library. 1996, Rosen/Power Kids Pr. LB $15.93 (0-8239-2372-X). 24pp. Essential facts about AIDS are presented simply, with a focus on living with the disease and that being with AIDS- or HIV-infected individuals does not necessarily involve a health risk. (Rev: SLJ 1/97) [616.97]

**14334** Forbes, Anna. *When Someone You Know Has AIDS* (3–5). Illus. Series: The AIDS Awareness Library. 1996, Rosen/Power Kids Pr. LB $15.93 (0-8239-2369-X). 24pp. A simple introduction to AIDS that covers its causes, effects, and treatments. Also use *Where Did AIDS Come From?* (1996). (Rev: SLJ 12/96) [616.97]

**14335** Gold, Susan D. *Alzheimer's Disease* (4–7). Illus. Series: Health Watch. 1995, Silver Burdett LB $15.95 (0-89686-857-5). 48pp. Using a case study as the focus, this account introduces Alzheimer's dis-

ease, its treatment, and current research. (Rev: BL 5/15/96; SLJ 1/96) [362.19]

**14336** Greenberg, Keith E. *Disease Detective: Solving Deadly Mysteries* (4–7). Series: Risky Business. 1997, Blackbirch LB $14.95 (1-56711-162-9). 32pp. Profiles the many services performed by scientists in their quest to find cures for diseases. (Rev: BL 10/15/97; SLJ 1/98) [616]

**14337** Gutman, Bill. *Harmful to Your Health* (5–8). Illus. Series: Focus on Safety. 1996, Twenty-First Century LB $16.98 (0-8050-4144-3). 80pp. Health hazards of AIDS, steroids, drugs, and sexual abuse are covered in a straightforward manner. (Rev: BL 2/1/97; SLJ 2/97) [616.86]

**14338** Harris, Jacqueline L. *Communicable Diseases* (5–8). 1993, Twenty-First Century LB $18.90 (0-8050-2599-5). 64pp. Various contagious diseases are covered, with material on how they are spread and treated. (Rev: BL 1/15/94; SLJ 1/94) [616.9]

**14339** Harris, Jacqueline L. *Hereditary Diseases* (5–8). Illus. Series: Bodies in Crisis. 1993, Twenty-First Century LB $18.90 (0-8050-2603-7). 64pp. Diagnosis, effects, treatments, and possible cures are discussed in relation to hereditary diseases. (Rev: BL 1/15/94; SLJ 1/94) [616]

**14340** Hyde, Margaret O., and Elizabeth Forsyth. *The Disease Book: A Kid's Guide* (5–8). Illus. 1997, Walker LB $17.85 (0-8027-8498-4). 160pp. An overview of the causes, symptoms, and treatments of more than 100 physical and mental diseases. (Rev: BL 9/15/97; SLJ 11/97) [616]

**14341** Hyde, Margaret O., and Elizabeth Forsyth. *Know About AIDS* (4–8). Illus. Series: Know About. 1994, Walker LB $14.95 (0-8027-8346-5). 100pp. Advances in research and current status are covered in this revised edition. (Rev: BL 7/90; SLJ 7/90) [616.97]

**14342** Hyde, Margaret O., and Elizabeth Forsyth. *Know About Mental Illness* (5–8). Illus. 1996, Walker LB $15.85 (0-8027-8429-1). 144pp. In an anecdotal manner, several mental illnesses and their treatments are discussed. (Rev: BL 9/1/96; SLJ 7/96) [616.89]

**14343** Hyde, Margaret O., and Elizabeth Forsyth. *Living with Asthma* (4–6). Illus. 1995, Walker LB $15.85 (0-8027-8287-6). 96pp. The physical and emotional aspects of asthma are introduced, with several case histories of people who cope with this condition. (Rev: BL 6/1–15/95; SLJ 7/95) [362]

**14344** Katz, Bobbi. *Germs! Germs! Germs!* (1–2). Illus. by Steve Bjorkman. Series: Beginning Reader: Science. 1996, Scholastic $3.99 (0-590-67295-9). 40pp. The contributions and havoc caused by germs are revealed from their point of view. (Rev: BL 2/1/97) [616]

**14345** Kehret, Peg. *Small Steps: The Year I Got Polio* (3–5). 1996, Albert Whitman LB $14.95 (0-8075-7457-0). 179pp. The author describes 7 months in her life when, at age 12, she was stricken with polio. (Rev: BCCB 11/96; BL 11/1/96; SLJ 11/96*) [362.1]

**14346** Lampton, Christopher. *Epidemic* (4–6). Illus. Series: Disaster! 1992, Millbrook LB $19.90 (1-56294-126-7). 64pp. The causes and effects of epidemics are covered, plus the possibility of predicting them. (Rev: BL 4/1/92; SLJ 8/92) [614.4]

**14347** Landau, Elaine. *Allergies* (4–7). Illus. Series: Understanding Illness. 1994, Twenty-First Century LB $18.90 (0-8050-2989-3). 64pp. After a case history that explores allergies in personal terms, an objective presentation is given of their causes, effects, and treatment. (Rev: BL 12/15/94; SLJ 2/95) [616.97]

**14348** Landau, Elaine. *Cancer* (4–7). Illus. Series: Understanding Illness. 1994, Twenty-First Century LB $18.90 (0-8050-2990-7). 64pp. This book explains the many types of cancer, their causes, present-day treatments, and possible developments in the future. (Rev: BL 12/15/95; SLJ 2/95) [616.99]

**14349** Landau, Elaine. *Diabetes* (4–7). Illus. Series: Understanding Illness. 1994, Twenty-First Century LB $18.90 (0-8050-2988-5). 64pp. Causes of diabetes, prevention, and treatment are covered, with case studies to describe how people adjust. (Rev: BL 12/15/94; SLJ 2/95) [616.4]

**14350** Landau, Elaine. *Epilepsy* (4–7). Illus. Series: Understanding Illness. 1994, Twenty-First Century LB $18.90 (0-8050-2991-5). 64pp. Following the story of a youngster who has epilepsy, this account describes the disorder, its emotional and medical aspects, and treatments. (Rev: BL 12/15/94; SLJ 2/95) [616.8]

**14351** Manning, Karen. *AIDS: Can This Epidemic Be Stopped?* (6–8). Illus. Series: Issues of Our Time. 1995, Twenty-First Century LB $18.90 (0-8050-4240-7). 64pp. A frank, objective account of how AIDS is transmitted and present treatment strategies. (Rev: BL 2/1/96; SLJ 2/96) [616.97]

**14352** Marx, Trish, and Dorita Beh-Eger. *I Heal: The Children of Chernobyl in Cuba* (3–6). Illus. 1996, Lerner LB $21.27 (0-8225-4897-6). 48pp. This book contains the story of 2 young victims of the Chernobyl nuclear disaster and of their medical treatment in Cuba. (Rev: BCCB 12/96; BL 12/1/96; SLJ 10/96) [618.92]

**14353** Ostrow, William, and Vivian Ostrow. *All About Asthma* (3–5). Illus. by Blanche Sims. 1988, Whitman LB $12.95 (0-8075-0276-6). 40pp. The author, a young boy, and his mother wrote this book about how he has learned to live with his asthma. (Rev: BCCB 12/89; BL 12/15/89; SLJ 3/90) [616.2]

**14354** Pirner, Connie W. *Even Little Kids Get Diabetes* (PS–2). Illus. by Nadine Bernard Westcott. 1991, Whitman LB $12.95 (0-8075-2158-2). 24pp. A young girl tells of her life with diabetes. (Rev: BL 3/1/91; SLJ 4/91) [616.4]

**14355** Seixas, Judith S. *Allergies: What They Are, What They Do* (2–4). Illus. by Tom Huffman. Series: Read Alone. 1991, Greenwillow LB $12.88 (0-688-08877-5). 56pp. In this book for beginning readers, basic information is given on the nature of allergies. (Rev: BCCB 6/91; BL 4/1/91; SLJ 7/91) [616.7]

**14356** Silverstein, Alvin, et al. *Sickle Cell Anemia* (4–8). Illus. Series: Diseases and People. 1997, Enslow LB $19.95 (0-89490-711-5). 112pp. The symptoms, treatment, and screening of this hereditary disorder are explained in a clear, well-organized text. (Rev: SLJ 2/97) [616]

**14357** Simpson, Carolyn. *Coping with Asthma* (4–7). 1995, Rosen LB $16.95 (0-8239-2069-0). 140pp. After discussing the respiratory system and the causes of asthma, this book deals with how to treat it. (Rev: BL 9/15/95) [616.2]

**14358** Terkel, Susan N., and Marlene Lupiloff-Brazz. *Understanding Cancer* (3–7). Illus. 1993, Watts LB $20.40 (0-531-11085-0). 64pp. This account explains the causes and types of cancer, treatments, and advice and support for those affected by this disease. (Rev: BL 10/15/93; SLJ 7/93) [616.994]

**14359** Weiss, Jonathan H. *Breathe Easy: Young People's Guide to Asthma* (4–7). Illus. 1994, Magination paper $9.95 (0-945354-62-2). 64pp. An account that describes the causes of asthma, what happens during an attack, and how to manage this condition. (Rev: BL 2/15/95) [618.92]

**14360** Weitzman, Elizabeth. *Let's Talk About When Someone You Love Has Alzheimer's Disease* (1–4). Illus. Series: Let's Talk Library. 1996, Rosen LB $13.95 (0-8239-2306-1). 24pp. A discussion of the nature of Alzheimer's disease, the changes it causes, and how to adjust to it. (Rev: BL 3/1/97; SLJ 8/96) [618.97]

**14361** Wiener, Lori S., et al. *Be a Friend: Children Who Live with HIV Speak* (1–4). Illus. 1994, Albert Whitman LB $14.95 (0-8075-0590-0). 40pp. The nature of AIDS is made dramatically clear through the voices of several youthful sufferers and their families. (Rev: BCCB 4/94; BL 3/15/94; SLJ 4/94) [362.1]

**14362** Wolf, Bernard. *HIV Positive* (4–6). Illus. 1997, Dutton paper $16.99 (0-525-45459-4). 48pp. A touching photoessay that focuses on 29-year-old Sara, who has AIDS, and her 2 young children. (Rev: BCCB 5/97; BL 3/15/97*; SLJ 6/97) [362.1]

**14363** Zonderman, Jon, and Laurel Shader. *Environmental Diseases* (5–8). Illus. 1993, Twenty-First Century LB $18.90 (0-8050-2600-2). 64pp. This well-illustrated account deals with the causes of and treatment for such diseases as poison ivy, Lyme disease, and hypothermia. Also use *Nutritional Diseases* (1994). (Rev: BL 7/94; SLJ 4/94) [616.9]

## Doctors and Medicine

**14364** Gates, Phil. *The History News: Medicine* (4–7). Illus. Series: History News. 1997, Candlewick $15.99 (0-7636-0316-3). 32pp. The history of doctors and medicine is covered using a newspaper format that even includes advertisements (one announces leeches for sale) and letters. (Rev: BL 2/1/98; SLJ 1/98) [610.9]

**14365** Miller, Brandon M. *Just What the Doctor Ordered: The History of American Medicine* (5–8). Illus. Series: People's History. 1997, Lerner LB $21.27 (0-8225-1737-X). 88pp. A history of American medicine from the extensive use of plants and herbs to the development of laser surgery. (Rev: SLJ 5/97*) [610.9]

**14366** Parker, Steve. *Medicine* (4–6). Illus. Series: Eyewitness Science. 1995, DK Publg. $15.95 (1-56458-882-3). 64pp. In this history of medicine from ancient times to the future, such topics as modern drugs, diagnostic techniques, medical instruments, and fads are introduced. (Rev: SLJ 10/95) [610]

**14367** Van Steenwyk, Elizabeth. *Frontier Fever: The Silly, Superstitious — and Sometimes Sensible — Medicine of the Pioneers* (5–8). Illus. 1995, Walker LB $16.85 (0-8027-8403-8). 160pp. A history of medicine in the United States from colonial times through the 19th century, including information on the training of caregivers. (Rev: BL 7/95; SLJ 12/95) [610]

**14368** Winkler, Kathy. *Radiology* (3–6). Illus. Series: Inventors and Inventions. 1996, Marshall Cavendish LB $25.64 (0-7614-0075-3). 63pp. Provides short profiles of the leaders, past and present, in the field of radiology, with details on how this scientific breakthrough is changing our lives. (Rev: BL 7/96; SLJ 9/96) [616.07]

**14369** Wolfson, Evelyn. *From the Earth to Beyond the Sky: Native American Medicine* (4–8). Illus. 1993, Houghton $14.95 (0-395-55009-2). 86pp. This book explains herbal medicine, the plants used, and how Native Americans' relationship with nature played a role in the development of their medical treatments. (Rev: BCCB 1/94; BL 12/15/93; SLJ 12/93) [615.8]

## Genetics

**14370** Aronson, Billy. *They Came from DNA* (3–6). Illus. by Danny O'Leary. 1993, W. H. Freeman $16.00 (0-7167-9006-8); paper $11.20 (0-7167-6526-8). 80pp. A creature from outer space studies human evolution and the structure of DNA, and imparts his findings to the reader. (Rev: BL 3/1/94; SLJ 7/94) [574.1]

**14371** Bornstein, Sandy. *What Makes You What You Are: A First Look at Genetics* (5–8). Illus. by Frank Cecala. 1989, Silver Burdett paper $6.95 (0-671-68650-X). 115pp. This book affords a fine introduction to cell structure, dominant and recessive traits, and heredity. (Rev: SLJ 1/90) [573.2]

**14372** Swisher, Clarice. *Genetic Engineering* (5–8). Illus. Series: Overview. 1996, Lucent LB $22.45 (1-56006-179-0). 128pp. An introductory account that discusses DNA, how the genetic code can be altered, and some of the people behind these discoveries. (Rev: BL 7/96; SLJ 1/97) [575.1]

**14373** Wells, Donna. *Biotechnology* (3–6). Illus. Series: Inventors and Inventions. 1996, Marshall Cavendish LB $25.64 (0-7614-0046-X). 63pp. Cell structure, DNA, and ways of altering genetic make-up are discussed, with short profiles of past and current leaders in the field. (Rev: BL 7/96; SLJ 9/96) [660]

## Hospitals

**14374** Brink, Benjamin. *David's Story: A Book About Surgery* (3–5). Illus. 1996, Lerner LB $21.27 (0-8225-2577-1). 32pp. A step-by-step account of a boy undergoing surgery. (Rev: BL 12/1/96; SLJ 10/96) [617.5]

**14375** Dooley, Virginia. *Tubes In My Ears: My Trip to the Hospital* (PS–1). Illus. by Miriam Katin. 1996, Mondo paper $4.95 (1-57255-118-6). 32pp. The experiences of a young boy when he goes to a hospital for the first time to treat an ear infection. (Rev: BL 5/1/96; SLJ 6/96) [362.1]

**14376** Howe, James. *The Hospital Book*. Rev. ed. (2–6). Illus. by Mal Warshaw. 1994, Morrow $16.00 (0-688-12731-2). 96pp. This book filled with photos explains hospital procedures to young patients and tries to lessen any fears they might have about hospitals. (Rev: BL 4/1/94; HB 7–8/94) [362.1]

**14377** Miller, Marilyn. *Behind the Scenes at the Hospital* (PS–3). Illus. 1996, Raintree Steck-Vaughn LB $21.40 (0-8172-4087-X). 32pp. The workers and activities that make hospitals function are introduced in a simple question-and-answer format. (Rev: BL 4/15/96; SLJ 12/96) [362.1]

**14378** Rosenberg, Maxine B. *Mommy's in the Hospital Having a Baby* (PS–1). Illus. by Robert Maass. 1997, Clarion $15.00 (0-395-71813-9). 29pp. Questions are answered about what happens in a hospital when mommy is having a baby, including "How do I behave on visits?" (Rev: BL 4/1/97; SLJ 5/97) [618.4]

**14379** Stein, Sara Bonnett. *A Hospital Story* (1–3). Illus. 1984, Walker paper $8.95 (0-8027-7222-6). A fine introduction to hospitals and what a hospital stay involves.

**14380** Vaughan, Jenny. *Hospital* (3–5). Illus. Series: World at Work. 1989, Silver Burdett $11.96 (0-382-09718-1). 48pp. This book contains a glimpse of life in a hospital and how special patients are cared for. (Rev: SLJ 11/89) [332.1]

# The Human Body

## General

**14381** Aliki. *My Feet* (PS–1). Illus. Series: Let's Read-and-Find-Out Science Books. 1990, HarperCollins LB $15.89 (0-690-04815-7). 32pp. Children are asked to consider the uniqueness of their feet. (Rev: BL 10/1/90; HB 11–12/90; SLJ 11/90) [612]

**14382** Allison, Linda. *Blood and Guts: A Working Guide to Your Own Little Insides* (5–8). 1976, Little, Brown paper $11.95 (0-316-03443-6). An off-putting title but a fine explanation of the functions of the human body.

**14383** Balkwill, Fran. *Cells Are Us* (4–5). Illus. by Mic Rolph. 1993, Carolrhoda LB $19.93 (0-87614-762-7). 32pp. This book introduces the many types of cells found in the human body. Other related books by the same author are: *Cell Wars* and *DNA Is Here to Stay* (both 1993). (Rev: SLJ 4/93) [611]

**14384** Berger, Melvin. *Why I Cough, Sneeze, Shiver, Hiccup, and Yawn* (PS–3). Illus. by Holly Keller. 1983, HarperCollins LB $14.89 (0-690-04254-X). 40pp. A clear, interesting introduction and explanation of some basic body functions.

**14385** Bruun, Ruth Dowling, and Bertel Bruun. *The Human Body* (4–7). Illus. by Patricia J. Wynne. 1982, Random LB $15.99 (0-394-94424-0); paper $14.00 (0-394-84424-6). 96pp. A simple account that concentrates on parts of the body and its systems.

**14386** Cole, Joanna. *The Magic School Bus: Inside the Human Body* (2–5). Illus. by Bruce Degen. 1989, Scholastic $14.95 (0-590-41426-7); paper $4.95 (0-590-41427-5). Ms. Frizzle's class goes on a guided

tour of the human body. (Rev: BCCB 4/89; BL 4/15/89; HB 5–6/89)

**14387** Cole, Joanna. *Your Insides* (PS–1). Illus. by Paul Meisel. 1998, Putnam paper $9.99 (0-698-11675-5). Clear overlays help to explain the workings of the human body for the young reader. (Rev: BL 12/1/92) [612]

**14388** Crelinstein, Jeffrey. *To the Limit* (5–8). Illus. Series: Wide World. 1992, Harcourt $17.95 (0-15-200616-8). 64pp. The effects of exercise on the human body are explored in this book containing amazing photographs. (Rev: SLJ 10/92) [932]

**14389** Day, Trevor. *The Random House Book of 1001 Questions and Answers About the Human Body* (5–8). Illus. Series: 1001 Questions and Answers. 1994, Random paper $15.00 (0-679-85432-0). 128pp. A profusely illustrated question-and-answer book that combines up-to-date information on a wide range of fascinating subjects with an attractive format. (Rev: BL 12/1/94; SLJ 7/94) [612]

**14390** *First Questions and Answers About the Human Body: What Is a Bellybutton?* (PS–1). Illus. Series: Library of First Questions and Answers. 1993, Time Life $14.95 (0-7835-0854-9). 47pp. Using a question-and-answer format, this book supplies basic information about bodily functions. (Rev: SLJ 3/94) [612]

**14391** Ganeri, Anita. *Birth and Growth* (2–3). Illus. Series: First Starts. 1994, Raintree Steck-Vaughn LB $21.40 (0-8114-5519-X). 32pp. In double-page spreads, human life is traced from birth to old age and death. (Rev: SLJ 2/95) [612]

**14392** Ganeri, Anita. *Inside the Body* (4–7). Illus. by Giuliano Fornari. 1996, DK Publg. $16.95 (0-7894-0999-2). 12pp. When tabs are lifted, various parts of the human body are revealed. (Rev: BL 12/15/96; SLJ 8/96) [612]

**14393** Gardner, Robert. *Science Projects About the Human Body* (5–7). 1992, Enslow LB $19.95 (0-89490-443-4). 104pp. Simple experiments and activities are used to illustrate various areas of the human body, like the senses, bones, teeth, and hair. (Rev: SLJ 11/93) [612]

**14394** Hanson, Jeanne K. *Your Amazing Body: From Headaches to Sweaty Feet and Everything in Between* (5–7). Illus. 1994, W. H. Freeman paper $7.20 (0-7167-6552-7). 96pp. Such bodily functions and malfunctions as bad breath, gas, headaches, dandruff, and goose bumps are covered, with suggestions on how to treat each. (Rev: BL 12/1/94) [612]

**14395** Hawcock, David. *The Amazing Pop-Up Pull-Out Body in a Book* (2–4). Illus. 1997, DK Publg. $19.95 (0-7894-2052-X). 9pp. Unfolding pages in this book brings out a full-length 3-D skeleton, accompanied by facts about the human body. (Rev: BL 12/15/97) [612]

**14396** *The Human Body* (PS–2). Illus. Series: First Discovery. 1996, Scholastic $11.95 (0-590-73876-3). 24pp. Using an interactive approach, basic questions about the systems of the human body are explained. (Rev: BL 10/15/96) [612]

**14397** Janulewicz, Mike. *Yikes! Your Body, Up Close* (3–5). Illus. 1997, Simon & Schuster paper $15.00 (0-689-81520-4). 32pp. Close-ups of such parts of the body as skin and red blood cells. (Rev: BL 9/1/97; SLJ 12/97) [611]

**14398** Kroll, Virginia. *Hands!* (PS–1). Illus. by Cathryn Falwell. 1997, Boyds Mills $7.95 (1-56397-051-1). 32pp. In this unusual picture book, hands are seen fulfilling a variety of tasks. (Rev: BL 9/15/97; SLJ 12/97) [612]

**14399** Landau, Elaine. *Joined at Birth: The Lives of Conjoined Twins* (4–7). Illus. Series: First Books: Different From Birth. 1997, Watts LB $21.00 (0-531-20331-X). 64pp. This book explains the phenomenon of conjoining and gives several famous examples of these twins. (Rev: BL 9/15/97; SLJ 8/97) [616.043]

**14400** Landau, Elaine. *Short Stature: From Folklore to Fact* (4–7). Illus. Series: First Books: Different from Birth. 1997, Watts LB $21.00 (0-531-20265-8). 64pp. After giving good historical information, this account explains dwarfism and gives several case histories. (Rev: BL 9/15/97; SLJ 8/97) [573.8]

**14401** Landau, Elaine. *Standing Tall: Unusually Tall People* (4–7). Series: First Books: Different from Birth. 1997, Watts LB $21.00 (0-531-20257-7). 64pp. This introduction to tall people gives a history of society's attitudes toward them and coverage on the challenges that they must face even today. (Rev: BL 9/15/97; SLJ 7/97) [612]

**14402** Miller, Jonathan, and David Pelham. *The Human Body* (5–8). Illus. by Harry Willcox. 1983, Viking paper $22.50 (0-670-38605-7). A pop-up book that explains the systems of the human body.

**14403** Ontario Science Centre Staff. *Sportsworks* (4–8). Illus. by Pat Cupples. 1989, Addison-Wesley paper $9.95 (0-201-15296-7). 96pp. Discusses the human body in relation to sports, with a number of experiments and activities. (Rev: BL 6/15/89; SLJ 7/89) [611]

**14404** Parker, Steve. *The Body Atlas: A Pictorial Guide to the Human Body* (3–6). Illus. by Giuliano Fornari. 1993, DK Publg. $19.95 (1-56458-224-8). 64pp. This atlas of the human body pictures bones, organs, and muscles from head to toe. (Rev: BL 6/1–15/93; SLJ 7/93) [611]

**14405** Parker, Steve. *Human Body* (4–8). Illus. Series: Eyewitness Science. 1993, DK Publg. $15.95 (1-56458-325-2). 64pp. Through full-color graphics,

3-D models, and detailed captions, the human body and its systems are covered. (Rev: BL 11/15/93; SLJ 12/93) [612]

**14406** Parker, Steve. *The Human Body* (3–6). Illus. Series: What If. 1995, Millbrook LB $19.90 (1-56294-914-4); paper $5.95 (1-56294-949-7). 32pp. A series of hypothetical questions like "What if we had no skin?" are used to explore the human body and its parts. (Rev: SLJ 1/96) [612]

**14407** Perols, Sylvaine. *The Human Body* (PS–1). Trans. from French by Jennifer Riggs. Illus. by author. Series: First Discovery Book. 1996, Scholastic paper $11.95 (0-590-73876-3). With the uses of transparencies, the skeleton and different systems and organs of the human body are introduced. (Rev: SLJ 2/97) [612]

**14408** Phifer, Kate Gilbert. *Tall and Small: A Book About Height* (4–6). Illus. 1987, Walker LB $12.85 (0-8027-6685-4). 96pp. Lots of data about growth patterns, plus how to chart growth. (Rev: BCCB 4/87; BL 7/87; SLJ 8/87)

**14409** Pringle, Laurence. *Everybody Has a Bellybutton* (PS–3). Illus. by Clare Wood. 1997, Boyds Mills $14.95 (1-56397-009-0). 32pp. A simple account of the growth of a fetus from a single cell to the birth of a baby. (Rev: BL 9/15/97; SLJ 10/97) [612]

**14410** Rice, Chris, and Melanie Rice. *My First Body Book* (2–4). Illus. 1995, DK Publg. $16.95 (1-56458-893-9). 32pp. Excellent illustrations highlight this beginner's book on the human body, with separate sections on each of the senses. (Rev: BL 11/1/95; SLJ 3/96) [612]

**14411** Rowan, Pete. *Some Body!* (4–7). Illus. 1995, Knopf $20.00 (0-679-87043-1). 44pp. Using the Guinness record book as a model, this large-format book on the human body describes each of the systems and identifies record holders involving the largest, smallest, etc. (Rev: SLJ 10/95) [612]

**14412** Royston, Angela. *My Body* (PS–2). Illus. by Richard Manning. 1991, DK Publg. $8.95 (1-879431-07-6). 17pp. A fine basic introduction to anatomy, using photos and drawings. (Rev: SLJ 2/92) [611]

**14413** Sanders, Pete, and Steve Myers. *Bodyworks* (5–7). Illus. by Derek Matthews and Paul Banville. Series: Life Education. 1997, Watts $19.00 (0-531-14427-5). 32pp. Using sidebars, quizzes, and trivia, this informative book surveys the wonders of the human body and gives advice on keeping it healthy. (Rev: SLJ 3/98) [612]

**14414** Saunderson, Jane. *Heart and Lungs* (3–6). Illus. by Andrew Farmer and Robina Green. Series: You and Your Body. 1992, Troll LB $13.95 (0-8167-2096-7); paper $4.95 (0-8167-2097-5). 32pp. Explores both the respiratory and the circulatory systems and explains how they work. (Rev: BL 5/15/92; SLJ 10/92) [612.1]

**14415** Suzuki, David, and Barbara Hehner. *Looking at the Body* (3–6). Illus. Series: Looking At. 1991, Stoddart $24.95 (0-471-54752-2); paper $9.95 (0-471-54052-8). 96pp. A brief introduction to the human body, with a few accompanying activities to explain its parts and their functions. (Rev: SLJ 5/92) [611]

**14416** VanCleave, Janice. *The Human Body for Every Kid: Easy Activities That Make Learning Science Fun* (5–7). Illus. Series: Science for Every Kid. 1995, Wiley $27.95 (0-471-02413-9); paper $11.95 (0-471-02408-2). 240pp. The various systems in the human body are introduced and decribed, with many projects and experiments. (Rev: BL 4/15/95; SLJ 5/95) [612]

**14417** *Why Do We Laugh? Questions Children Ask About the Human Body* (PS–3). Illus. Series: Why. 1996, DK Publg. $9.95 (0-7894-1121-0). 32pp. In a question-and-answer format, important basic facts about the human body are presented. (Rev: BL 12/1/96; SLJ 1/97) [152.3]

## Circulatory System

**14418** Ballard, Carol. *The Heart and Circulatory System* (5–8). Illus. Series: Human Body. 1997, Raintree Steck-Vaughn LB $25.68 (0-8172-4800-5). 48pp. Topics discussed in this nicely illustrated volume include how blood is made, how it is pumped through the body, and how the heart and circulation system work together. (Rev: BL 6/1–15/97; SLJ 8/97) [612.1]

**14419** Bryan, Jenny. *The Pulse of Life: The Circulatory System* (4–6). Illus. Series: Body Talk. 1993, Dillon LB $13.95 (0-87518-566-5). 48pp. A clear, concise introduction to the circulatory system and an explanation of current concerns and research. (Rev: SLJ 10/93) [612]

**14420** Parker, Steve. *Blood* (4–6). Series: Look at Your Body. 1997, Millbrook LB $20.90 (0-7613-0611-0). 32pp. The composition of blood, its uses, and the circulatory system are introduced in this visually appealing, clearly written book. (Rev: BL 1/1–15/98; SLJ 4/98) [612]

**14421** Parker, Steve. *The Heart and Blood* (4–7). Illus. Series: The Human Body. 1989, Watts LB $19.00 (0-531-10711-6). 40pp. Structure, operation, disease, and advances in surgery are covered. (Rev: BL 1/15/90) [612.1]

**14422** Parramon, Merce. *How Our Blood Circulates* (5–7). Illus. by Marcel Socias. Series: Invisible World. 1994, Chelsea LB $15.95 (0-7910-2127-0). 31pp. Double-page spreads introduce the circulatory

system and discuss such topics as blood cells, clotting, the heart and its functions, and the lymphatic system. (Rev: SLJ 8/94) [612]

**14423** Sandeman, Anna. *Blood* (1–3). Illus. Series: Body Books. 1996, Millbrook LB $18.90 (0-7613-0477-0). 32pp. An introduction to the composition and function of blood and the circulatory system, with clearly labeled artwork. (Rev: BL 4/15/96; SLJ 4/96) [612.1]

**14424** Silverstein, Alvin, et al. *The Circulatory System* (5–8). Illus. Series: Human Body Systems. 1994, Twenty-First Century LB $20.40 (0-8050-2833-1). 96pp. After a general introduction to circulation systems in plants and animals, the human system is introduced. (Rev: BL 3/15/95; SLJ 4/95) [612.1]

**14425** Simon, Seymour. *The Brain: Our Nervous System* (3–6). Illus. 1997, Morrow LB $15.93 (0-688-14641-4). 32pp. The anatomy and functions of the nervous system and brain are carefully explained and illustrated with photos and diagrams. (Rev: BL 8/97; HB 9–10/97; SLJ 8/97) [612.8]

**14426** Simon, Seymour. *The Heart: Our Circulatory System* (3–6). Illus. 1996, Morrow LB $15.93 (0-688-11408-3). 32pp. An excellent introduction to the circulatory system, with illustrations on each page. (Rev: BCCB 10/96; BL 7/96*; HB 9–10/96; SLJ 8/96) [612.1]

**14427** Stille, Darlene R. *The Circulatory System* (2–4). Illus. Series: True Book. 1997, Children's LB $20.00 (0-516-20438-6). 48pp. This account tells how the heart works, what blood does, the flow of blood through the body, and how to keep the heart healthy. (Rev: BL 12/1/97; SLJ 2/98) [612.1]

## Digestive and Excretory Systems

**14428** Ballard, Carol. *The Stomach and Digestive System* (5–8). Illus. Series: Human Body. 1997, Raintree Steck-Vaughn LB $25.68 (0-8172-4801-3). 48pp. Topics discussed in this nicely illustrated volume include the digestive organs, how they work together, how food is tasted, and where nutrients are stored. (Rev: BL 6/1–15/97; SLJ 8/97) [612.3]

**14429** Bryan, Jenny. *Digestion: The Digestive System* (4–6). Illus. Series: Body Talk. 1993, Dillon LB $13.95 (0-87518-564-0). 48pp. A clear, informative text and large captioned illustrations tell about the digestive system and related topics. (Rev: SLJ 10/93) [612]

**14430** Burgess, Jan. *Food and Digestion* (5–8). Illus. 1988, Silver Burdett LB $12.95 (0-382-09704-1). 48pp. Advice for staying healthy in this addition to the How Our Bodies Work series. (Rev: BL 4/15/89)

**14431** Cho, Shinta. *The Gas We Pass: The Story of Farts* (PS–2). Trans. by Amanda Mayer Stinchecum.

Illus. 1994, Kane/Miller $11.95 (0-916291-52-9). 28pp. This book tells about the causes, production, and effects of farts in a variety of animals, mainly humans. (Rev: BL 10/1/94; SLJ 11/94) [612.3]

**14432** Ganeri, Anita. *Eating* (2–3). Illus. Series: First Starts. 1994, Raintree Steck-Vaughn LB $21.40 (0-8114-5522-X). 32pp. This simple introduction to the digestive system gives basic information with many color photos and diagrams. (Rev: SLJ 2/95) [612.3]

**14433** Lambourne, Mike. *Down the Hatch: Find Out About Your Food* (2–3). Illus. by Thompson Yardley. Series: Lighter Look Book. 1992, Millbrook LB $20.90 (1-56294-150-X). 39pp. In simple text and cartoonlike illustrations, the story of food and nutrition is presented. (Rev: SLJ 6/92) [641]

**14434** Parker, Steve. *Digestion* (4–6). Series: Look at Your Body. 1997, Millbrook LB $20.90 (0-7613-0603-X). 32pp. An introductory account of the process of digestion with details about each of the organs involved. (Rev: BL 11/15/97) [612]

**14435** Parker, Steve. *Food and Digestion* (5–8). Illus. 1990, Watts LB $19.00 (0-531-14027-X). 48pp. Each organ involved in the digestive system is introduced. (Rev: BL 5/15/90; SLJ 9/90) [612.3]

**14436** Sandeman, Anna. *Eating* (1–2). Illus. Series: Body Books. 1995, Millbrook LB $18.90 (1-56294-945-4). 32pp. Different organs of the body involved in eating and digestion are introduced in this simple book that also touches on nutrition and energy from food. (Rev: BL 12/15/95; SLJ 2/96) [612.3]

**14437** Showers, Paul. *What Happens to a Hamburger?* (1–3). Illus. by Anne Rockwell. 1985, HarperCollins LB $14.89 (0-690-04427-5); paper $4.95 (0-06-445013-9). 32pp. This revision of the 1970 text that introduced the digestive system reflects current views on nutrition. (Rev: BL 6/1/85; SLJ 8/85)

**14438** Silverstein, Alvin, et al. *The Digestive System* (5–8). Illus. Series: Human Body Systems. 1994, Twenty-First Century LB $20.40 (0-8050-2832-3). 96pp. Beginning with food assimilation in plants and animals, this account focuses on the human digestive system. (Rev: BL 3/15/95; SLJ 3/95) [612.3]

**14439** Silverstein, Alvin, et al. *The Excretory System* (5–8). Illus. Series: Human Body Systems. 1994, Twenty-First Century LB $21.90 (0-8050-2834-X). 96pp. Waste elimination in nature is discussed, with emphasis on this function in the human body. (Rev: BL 3/15/95; SLJ 3/95) [612.6]

**14440** Stille, Darlene R. *The Digestive System* (2–4). Illus. Series: True Books: Health. 1997, Children's LB $21.00 (0-516-20439-4). 47pp. Explains the process of digestion and the organs involved, with special coverage on topics like ulcers, diet, and the importance of cleanliness. (Rev: SLJ 2/98) [612]

## Nervous System

**14441** Barmeier, Jim. *The Brain* (5–8). Illus. Series: Overview. 1996, Lucent LB $22.45 (1-56006-107-3). 128pp. Many kinds of graphics, including cartoons and photos, illustrate this description of the brain, its functions, and how we have learned about it. (Rev: BL 3/15/96; SLJ 7/96) [612.8]

**14442** Bryan, Jenny. *Your Amazing Brain* (4–7). Illus. 1996, Reader's Digest $12.99 (0-88705-930-9). 16pp. The functions of the brain are introduced in text and cutaway plastic windows. (Rev: BL 12/15/96) [612]

**14443** Cole, Joanna. *You Can't Smell a Flower with Your Ear! All About Your 5 Senses* (1–3). Illus. by Mavis Smith. 1994, Putnam paper $3.95 (0-448-40469-9). 48pp. Using everyday experiences as examples, the 5 senses are introduced in this easy-to-read book. (Rev: BL 1/1/95) [612.8]

**14444** Lambert, Mark. *The Brain and Nervous System* (5–7). Illus. 1988, Silver Burdett LB $12.95 (0-382-09703-3). 48pp. Diagrams and photos highlight this description. (Rev: BL 4/1/89)

**14445** Mathers, Douglas. *Brain* (3–6). Illus. by Andrew Farmer and Robina Green. Series: You and Your Body. 1992, Troll LB $13.95 (0-8167-2090-8). 32pp. Topics include how the brain passes messages, how people think, and what happens when we sleep. (Rev: BL 5/15/92; SLJ 10/92) [712.8]

**14446** Parker, Steve. *The Brain and Nervous System* (5–8). Illus. Series: Human Body. 1997, Raintree Steck-Vaughn LB $25.68 (0-8172-4802-1). 48pp. Double-page spreads introduce such topics about the nervous system as parts of the brain and their function, what brain waves are, and the nature of sleep and dreams. (Rev: BL 6/1–15/97; SLJ 8/97) [612.8]

**14447** Parker, Steve. *Brain Surgery for Beginners: And Other Major Operations for Minors* (4–7). Illus. 1995, Millbrook LB $21.90 (1-56294-604-8); paper $7.95 (1-56294-895-4). 64pp. After a brief introduction to the human body, this account focuses on the brain, its composition, and its functions. (Rev: BL 5/1/95; SLJ 7/95) [612]

**14448** Sandeman, Anna. *Brain* (1–2). Illus. Series: Body Books. 1996, Millbrook LB $18.90 (0-7613-0490-8). 32pp. With a simple text and full-color photos and diagrams, the brain is explored and explanations are given on how it works. (Rev: BL 10/15/96; SLJ 1/97) [612]

**14449** Showers, Paul. *Sleep Is for Everyone* (PS–1). Illus. by Wendy Watson. Series: Let's-Read-and-Find-Out Science. 1997, HarperCollins LB $14.89 (0-06-025393-2). 32pp. This simple science book explains what sleep is, why it is necessary, and what happens if we do without it. (Rev: BL 8/97; SLJ 8/97) [612.8]

**14450** Silverstein, Alvin, et al. *The Nervous System* (5–8). Illus. Series: Human Body Systems. 1994, Twenty-First Century LB $20.40 (0-8050-2835-8). 96pp. The human nervous system and how it functions and can malfunction are described, with information on the systems of other animals. (Rev: BL 3/15/95; SLJ 5/95) [612.8]

**14451** Smith, Kathie Billingslea, and Victoria Crenson. *Thinking* (1–3). Illus. 1988, Troll LB $11.89 (0-8167-1016-3). 24pp. How the brain works is the focus of this simple introduction. (Rev: BL 3/15/88)

**14452** Stille, Darlene R. *The Nervous System* (3–5). Illus. 1997, Children's LB $21.00 (0-516-20445-9). 48pp. In this introduction to the nervous system, the brain, nerve cells, and muscles are featured, with information on how they interact. (Rev: BL 2/15/98) [612.8]

**14453** Yount, Lisa. *Memory* (5–8). Illus. Series: Overview. 1996, Lucent LB $22.45 (1-56006-172-3). 112pp. A carefully researched account of what we know about memory and what current research is revealing. (Rev: BL 51596; SLJ 8/96) [153.1]

## Respiratory System

**14454** Bryan, Jenny. *Breathing: The Respiratory System* (4–6). Illus. Series: Body Talk. 1993, Dillon LB $13.95 (0-87518-563-0). 48pp. Large captioned photos are used to explain what happens when we breathe plus giving information on health problems associated with the respiratory system. (Rev: SLJ 10/93) [612]

**14455** Ganeri, Anita. *Breathing* (2–3). Illus. Series: First Starts. 1994, Raintree Steck-Vaughn LB $21.40 (0-8114-5520-3). 32pp. A simple overview of the respiratory system in double-page spreads. (Rev: SLJ 2/95) [612]

**14456** Lambert, Mark. *The Lungs and Breathing* (5–7). Illus. 1988, Silver Burdett LB $12.95 (0-382-09701-7). Profusely illustrated addition to the How Our Bodies Work series. (Rev: BL 4/15/89)

**14457** Parker, Steve. *Lungs* (4–6). Illus. Series: Look at Your Body. 1996, Millbrook LB $20.90 (0-7613-0530-0). 32pp. A well-organized, clearly illustrated description of lungs and their functions. (Rev: BL 11/1/96) [612.2]

**14458** Parker, Steve. *The Lungs and Breathing* (4–7). Illus. Series: The Human Body. 1989, Watts LB $19.00 (0-531-10710-8). 40pp. The mechanisms of respiration, how oxygen is transferred, and air pollution are some of the areas covered. (Rev: BL 1/15/90) [612.2]

**14459** Parker, Steve. *The Lungs and Respiratory System* (5–7). Illus. Series: Human Body. 1997, Raintree Steck-Vaughn LB $25.68 (0-8172-4803-X). 48pp. This nicely illustrated volume examines the organs used in breathing, tells how the respiratory system works, and explains what happens when it fails. (Rev: BL 6/1–15/97; SLJ 8/97) [612.6]

**14460** Silverstein, Alvin, et al. *The Respiratory System* (5–8). Illus. Series: Human Body Systems. 1994, Twenty-First Century LB $20.40 (0-8050-2831-5). 96pp. The purpose and process of breathing are discussed generally, with text and pictures focusing on the human respiratory system. (Rev: BL 3/15/95; SLJ 4/95) [612.2]

**14461** Stille, Darlene R. *The Respiratory System* (2–4). Illus. Series: True Books: Health. 1997, Children's LB $21.00 (0-516-20448-3). 47pp. Explains the process of respiration and the role of the lungs, with additional material on topics like asthma, tuberculosis, lung cancer, and emphysema. (Rev: SLJ 2/98) [612]

## Senses

**14462** Aliki. *My Five Senses* (PS–1). Illus. by author. 1989, HarperCollins paper $4.95 (0-06-445083-X). 32pp. A young boy finds that he is learning about the world through the marvels of his 5 senses. (Rev: SLJ 1/90) [152.1]

**14463** Ardley, Neil. *The Science Book of the Senses* (3–6). Illus. Series: Science Books. 1992, Harcourt $9.95 (0-15-200614-1). 28pp. Simple experiments for each of the 5 senses, with clear directions and attractive illustrations. (Rev: BL 3/15/92; HB 9–10/92) [612]

**14464** Bryan, Jenny. *Smell, Taste and Touch: The Sensory Systems* (4–6). Illus. Series: Body Talk. 1994, Dillon LB $13.95 (0-87518-590-8). 48pp. An illustrated introduction to 3 of the senses and how they function. Also use *Sound and Vision* (1994). (Rev: SLJ 8/94) [612.8]

**14465** Byles, Monica. *Experiment with Senses* (2–5). Illus. Series: Science Experiments. 1994, Lerner LB $19.93 (0-8225-2455-4). 32pp. Fifteen experiments explain the senses, how they operate, and how they send messages to the brain. (Rev: BL 3/1/94; SLJ 4/94) [612.8]

**14466** Fowler, Allan. *Seeing Things* (PS–K). Illus. Series: Rookie Read-About Science. 1991, Children's LB $18.50 (0-516-04910-0). 32pp. Among the many illustrations in this easily read book about sight is one that explains how each part of the human eye works. Also use: *Smelling Things* and *Tasting Things* (both 1991). (Rev: SLJ 12/91) [612.8]

**14467** Isadora, Rachel. *I Hear* (PS). Illus. by author. 1985, Greenwillow LB $15.93 (0-688-04062-4). 32pp. Activities in a toddler's day depict familiar scenes. (Rev: BCCB 4/85; BL 3/15/85; SLJ 4/85)

**14468** Isadora, Rachel. *I See* (PS). Illus. by author. 1985, Greenwillow LB $14.93 (0-688-04060-8). 32pp. A little girl sees objects — her ball, her teddy bear. (Rev: BCCB 6/85; BL 3/15/85; SLJ 4/85)

**14469** Isadora, Rachel. *I Touch* (PS). Illus. by author. 1991, Greenwillow paper $6.95 (0-688-10524-6). 32pp. "I touch my bear, he's soft" says this book that calls attention to tactile sensations. (Rev: BL 11/15/85; SLJ 2/86)

**14470** Jedrosa, Aleksander. *Eyes* (3–6). Illus. by Andrew Farmer and Robina Green. Series: You and Your Body. 1992, Troll LB $13.95 (0-8167-2094-0); paper $3.95 (0-8167-2095-9). 32pp. Basic information about the eye is introduced in an appealing format. (Rev: BL 5/15/92) [612.8]

**14471** Litchfield, Ada B. *A Button in Her Ear* (1–3). Illus. by Eleanor Mill. 1976, Whitman LB $14.95 (0-8075-0987-6). 32pp. A simple introduction to hearing problems and correctional devices such as the hearing aid.

**14472** Martin, Paul D. *Messengers to the Brain: Our Fantastic Five Senses* (4–6). Illus. 1984, National Geographic LB $12.50 (0-87044-504-9). 104pp. A well-illustrated explanation of how the organs of the human body send messages to the brain, which acts as a message center.

**14473** Mathers, Douglas. *Ears* (3–6). Illus. by Andrew Farmer and Robina Green. Series: You and Your Body. 1992, Troll LB $13.95 (0-8167-2092-4); paper $3.95 (0-8167-2093-2). 32pp. Explores the structures and functions of the outer, middle, and inner ear. (Rev: BL 5/15/92) [612.8]

**14474** Murphy, Mary. *You Smell: And Taste and Feel and See and Hear* (PS–1). Illus. 1997, DK Publg. $9.95 (0-7894-2471-1). 32pp. Using a curious young dog in drawings, this book introduces the 5 senses to a young audience. (Rev: BL 12/1/97; SLJ 1/98) [612]

**14475** Parker, Steve. *The Eye and Seeing* (4–7). Illus. Series: The Human Body. 1989, Watts LB $19.00 (0-531-10654-3). 40pp. Topics such as structure, function, and modern eye surgery are covered. (Rev: BL 1/15/90; SLJ 4/90) [612.84]

**14476** Parker, Steve. *Senses* (4–6). Series: Look at Your Body. 1997, Millbrook LB $20.90 (0-7613-0602-1). 32pp. In this visually appealing, clearly written book, the 5 senses are introduced and explored, with interesting accompanying activities. (Rev: BL 1/1–15/98) [612]

**14477** Parker, Steve. *Touch, Taste and Smell* (4–7). Illus. Series: The Human Body. 1989, Watts LB $19.00 (0-531-10655-1). 40pp. The sense organs are introduced with data on how they operate. (Rev: BL 1/15/90; SLJ 4/90) [612.8]

**14478** Parramon, J. M., and J. J. Puig. *Hearing* (PS–1). Illus. by Maria Rius. 1985, Barron's paper $6.95 (0-8120-3563-1). 32pp. An easy introduction to the sense of hearing. (Rev: BL 9/1/85)

**14479** Parramon, J. M., and J. J. Puig. *Sight* (PS–1). Illus. by Maria Rius. 1985, Barron's paper $6.95 (0-8120-3564-X). 32pp. The sense of sight is explained to young readers. (Rev: BL 9/1/85; SLJ 11/85)

**14480** Parramon, J. M., and J. J. Puig. *Smell* (PS–1). Illus. by Maria Rius. 1985, Barron's paper $6.95 (0-8120-3565-8). 32pp. An easy explanation of the sense of smell. (Rev: BL 9/1/85)

**14481** Parramon, J. M., and J. J. Puig. *Taste* (PS–1). Illus. by Maria Rius. 1985, Barron's paper $6.95 (0-8120-3566-6). 32pp. Easy reading about the sense of taste. (Rev: BL 9/1/85)

**14482** Parramon, J. M., and J. J. Puig. *Touch* (PS–1). Illus. by Maria Rius. 1985, Barron's paper $6.95 (0-8120-3567-4). 32pp. An easy-to-read explanation of the sense of touch. (Rev: BL 9/1/85)

**14483** Sandeman, Anna. *Senses* (1–2). Illus. Series: Body Books. 1995, Millbrook LB $18.90 (1-56294-944-6). 32pp. Body organs that are involved with the senses, like eyes, are discussed in this simple introduction that also mentions such topics as color blindness and the ears' role in balance. (Rev: BL 12/15/95; SLJ 2/96) [612.8]

**14484** Showers, Paul. *Look at Your Eyes* (PS–2). Illus. by True Kelley. Series: Let's-Read-and-Find-Out Science Books. 1992, HarperCollins LB $15.89 (0-06-020189-4). 32pp. A little boy looks in the bathroom mirror and begins to think about his eyes. (Rev: BL 1/1/93) [612.8]

**14485** Suhr, Mandy. *Taste* (PS–1). Illus. by Mike Gordon. Series: I'm Alive. 1994, Carolrhoda LB $14.95 (0-87614-836-4). 32pp. Why and how we taste is covered in a nontechnical way, with simple activities and projects to amplify the text. From the same series, also use *Touch* (1994). (Rev: SLJ 12/94) [152.1]

**14486** Suzuki, David, and Barbara Hehner. *Looking at Senses* (3–6). Illus. Series: Looking At. 1991, Stoddart $24.95 (0-471-54751-4); paper $9.95 (0-471-54048-X). 96pp. Each of the senses is highlighted, with a series of projects to explain each. (Rev: SLJ 5/92) [612]

**14487** Walpole, Brenda. *Hearing* (K–3). Illus. Series: See for Yourself. 1996, Raintree Steck-Vaughn LB $21.40 (0-8172-4217-1). 30pp. Using a text that answers questions and provides experiments, this is a simple introduction to hearing. Also use *Seeing, Smell and Taste*, and *Touch* (all 1996). (Rev: SLJ 3/97) [612.8]

**14488** Wright, Lillian. *Hearing* (K–2). Illus. Series: First Starts. 1994, Raintree Steck-Vaughn LB $21.40 (0-8114-5516-5). 32pp. An interesting, copiously illustrated book on the sense of hearing that also discusses echoes and noise pollution. Others in this series are *Seeing, Smelling and Tasting,* and *Touching* (all 1994). (Rev: SLJ 3/95) [152.1]

## Skeletal-Muscular System

**14489** Aliki. *My Hands* (1–3). Illus. by author. 1990, HarperCollins LB $14.89 (0-690-04880-7); paper $4.95 (0-06-445096-1). 32pp. The structure and uses of our hands are presented.

**14490** Balestrino, Philip. *The Skeleton Inside You* (2–4). Illus. by True Kelley. 1989, HarperCollins paper $4.95 (0-06-445087-2). 32pp. Color illustrations help to explain the body's structure. (Rev: BL 6/15/89)

**14491** Ballard, Carol. *The Skeleton and Muscular System* (5–8). Illus. Series: Human Body. 1997, Raintree Steck-Vaughn $24.26 (0-8172-4805-6). 48pp. This well-organized book introduces in text and pictures such topics as muscles and how they work, joint diseases, bones, and skeletal diseases. (Rev: SLJ 2/98) [612]

**14492** Barner, Bob. *Dem Bones* (K–3). Illus. 1996, Chronicle $13.95 (0-8118-0827-0). 32pp. The human skeleton is introduced by using the words of the old song "Dem Dry Bones." (Rev: BL 12/1/96; SLJ 11/96) [611]

**14493** Bryan, Jenny. *Movement: The Muscular and Skeletal System* (4–6). Illus. Series: Body Talk. 1993, Dillon LB $13.95 (0-87518-565-7). 48pp. This clear introduction to muscles and bones also discusses such topics as running, weightlessness, joint replacement, genetic engineering, and artificial limbs. (Rev: SLJ 10/93) [612]

**14494** Dineen, Jacqueline. *The Skeleton and Movement* (5–7). Illus. 1988, Silver Burdett $12.95 (0-382-09702-5). An explanation of human body movement. (Rev: BL 4/15/89)

**14495** Ganeri, Anita. *Moving* (2–3). Illus. Series: First Starts. 1994, Raintree Steck-Vaughn LB $21.40 (0-8114-5521-1). 32pp. A simple introduction to the human skeleton, joints, vertebrae, and muscles using a brief text and many illustrations. (Rev: SLJ 2/95) [612.7]

**14496** Grant, Lesley. *Discover Bones: Explore the Science of Skeletons* (3–6). Illus. by Tina Holdcroft. Series: Nature Detective. 1992, Addison-Wesley paper $8.95 (0-201-63237-3). 96pp. "How tall will I be" and "you look like your bones" are only 2 of the chapter titles in this excursion through the world of bones book. (Rev: BL 1/15/93) [596]

**14497** Parker, Steve. *Skeleton* (4–6). Illus. Series: Look at Your Body. 1996, Millbrook LB $20.90 (0-7613-0529-7). 32pp. The human skeleton, its composition, and its uses are covered, with extensive, unusual illustrations like X-rays and CAT scans. (Rev: BL 11/1/96) [611]

**14498** Parker, Steve. *The Skeleton and Movement* (4–7). Illus. Series: The Human Body. 1989, Watts LB $19.00 (0-531-10709-4). 40pp. This book covers such topics as the structure of bones and muscles, how they work, and how they heal. (Rev: BL 1/15/90; SLJ 2/90) [612]

**14499** Saunderson, Jane. *Muscles and Bones* (3–6). Illus. by Robina Green. Series: Your and Your Body. 1992, Troll LB $13.95 (0-8167-2088-6); paper $3.95 (0-8167-2089-4). 32pp. The structure and function of human muscles in a well-designed book. (Rev: BL 5/15/92) [612.7]

**14500** Silverstein, Alvin, et al. *The Muscular System* (5–8). Illus. Series: Human Body Systems. 1994, Twenty-First Century LB $16.95 (0-8050-2836-6). 96pp. Full-color diagrams, drawings, and photographs highlight this survey of the human muscular system. (Rev: BL 3/15/95; SLJ 5/95) [612.7]

**14501** Silverstein, Alvin, et al. *The Skeletal System* (5–8). Illus. Series: Human Body Systems. 1994, Twenty-First Century LB $16.95 (0-8050-2837-4). 96pp. The purpose and nature of the human skeleton, its maintenance and repair, and the composition of bones are 3 topics discussed. (Rev: BL 3/15/95) [612.7]

**14502** Wilkes, Angela. *Incredible Skeleton Secrets* (1–3). Illus. 1994, DK Publg. paper $4.95 (1-56458-727-4). 32pp. Both human and animal bones and their uses are described in this account that relies heavily on pictures. (Rev: BL 1/15/95) [591.4]

## Skin and Hair

**14503** Badt, Karin Luisa. *Hair There and Everywhere* (3–7). Illus. Series: A World of Difference. 1994, Children's LB $21.00 (0-516-08187-X). 32pp. A cross-cultural look at hair, its variant types and different styles. (Rev: BL 1/1/95; SLJ 1/95) [391.5]

**14504** Sandeman, Anna. *Skin, Teeth, and Hair* (1–2). Illus. Series: Body Books. 1996, Millbrook LB $18.90 (0-7613-0489-4). 32pp. For beginning readers, this colorful account explains the composition and use in the human body of skin, teeth, and hair. (Rev: BL 10/15/96; SLJ 1/97) [612]

**14505** Showers, Paul. *Your Skin and Mine* (PS–3). Illus. by Kathleen Kuchera. Series: Let's-Read-and-Find-Out Science Books. 1991, HarperCollins paper $4.95 (0-06-445102-X). 32pp. A look at skin, with simple experiments to show skin reactions. (Rev: BL 10/15/91; SLJ 8/91) [612.7]

### Teeth

**14506** Rockwell, Harlow. *My Dentist* (1–2). Illus. 1975, Morrow paper $4.95 (0-688-07040-X). 32pp. A matter-of-fact, informative book about dentists and the instruments they use.

**14507** Showers, Paul. *How Many Teeth?* (PS–2). Illus. by True Kelley. Series: Let's-Read-and-Find-Out Science Books. 1991, HarperCollins paper $4.95 (0-06-445098-8). 32pp. A full-color, funny, informative book showing a multiracial classroom. (Rev: BL 6/15/91; SLJ 10/91) [612.3]

# Hygiene and Physical Fitness

**14508** Colman, Penny. *Toilets, Bathtubs, Sinks, and Sewers: A History of the Bathroom* (5–8). Illus. 1994, Atheneum $16.00 (0-689-31894-4). 96pp. A fascinating look at sanitation systems and personal hygiene from ancient times to the present. (Rev: BCCB 2/95; BL 1/1/95; SLJ 3/95) [643]

**14509** Hammerslough, Jane. *Everything You Need to Know About Skin Care* (4–8). Illus. Series: Everything You Need to Know About. 1994, Rosen LB $16.95 (0-8239-1686-3). 64pp. This book tells about skin structure, skin types, blemishes, acne, sunburn, warts, freckles, athlete's foot and other skin disorders, with information on skin care products. (Rev: SLJ 9/94) [616.5]

**14510** Kerr, Daisy. *Keeping Clean: A Very Peculiar History* (4–7). Illus. 1995, Watts LB $23.00 (0-531-14353-8). 48pp. A history of sanitation from the ancient world to the present plus a discussion of how sanitation procedures differ in various cultures. (Rev: BCCB 6/95; BL 6/1–15/95) [613]

**14511** Lukes, Bonnie L. *How to Be a Reasonably Thin Teenage Girl: Without Starving, Losing Your Friends or Running Away from Home* (5–8). Illus. 1986, Macmillan $15.00 (0-689-31269-5). 96pp. Sensible advice from an "ex-fatty" directed toward the young teenager. (Rev: BCCB 10/86; BL 1/1/87)

**14512** Parker, Steve. *Professor Protein's Fitness, Health, Hygiene and Relaxation Tonic* (4–6). Illus. by Rob Shone. 1996, Millbrook LB $23.90 (0-7613-0494-0). 48pp. A witty presentation of material about fitness, health, and hygiene, with accompanying humorous cartoons. (Rev: SLJ 1/97) [613]

**14513** Parsons, Alexandra. *Fit for Life* (3–6). Illus. by John Shackell and Stuart Harrison. Series: Life Education. 1996, Watts LB $19.00 (0-531-14372-4).

32pp. A beginner's guide to nutrition, hygiene, and exercise, with coverage of the effects of drugs, smoking, and alcohol. (Rev: SLJ 10/96) [613.2]

**14514** Powell, Jillian. *Exercise and Your Health* (2–5). Illus. Series: Health Matters. 1997, Raintree Steck-Vaughn LB $22.11 (0-8172-4927-3). 32pp. Explains how exercise affects good health and gives tips on types of exercises, warming-up and cooling activities, proper dress, and ways to design a personalized program. (Rev: SLJ 2/98) [613.7]

**14515** Powell, Jillian. *Food and Your Health* (2–5). Illus. Series: Health Matters. 1997, Raintree Steck-Vaughn LB $22.11 (0-8172-4925-7). 32pp. Explains how food is digested, what constitutes good nutrition, problem foods, and data on proper body weight. (Rev: SLJ 2/98) [613.2]

**14516** Reef, Catherine. *Stay Fit: Build a Strong Body* (4–6). Illus. Series: Good Health Guildline. 1993, Twenty-First Century $15.95 (0-8050-2441-7). 64pp. This fitness manual explains how to develop a personalized physical-activity program, presents different exercises, and gives advice on how to live a healthy life. (Rev: SLJ 3/94) [613.7]

**14517** Savage, Jeff. *Aerobics* (4–6). Illus. Series: Working Out. 1995, Silver Burdett LB $15.95 (0-89686-853-2); paper $7.95 (0-382-24945-3). 48pp. This book describes the nature and benefits of aerobic exercise, how to get started, and how to develop a routine. (Rev: SLJ 10/95) [613.7]

**14518** Swinden, Liz. *Look Good, Feel Good* (5–7). Illus. by Kevin Faerber. Series: Life Education. 1997, Watts LB $18.20 (0-531-14428-3). 32pp. A breezy title that explains how diet, physical fitness, hygiene, attitudes, and medicine contribute to well-being. (Rev: SLJ 3/98) [613]

# Safety and Accidents

**14519** Boelts, Maribeth, and Darwin Boelts. *Kids to the Rescue! First Aid Techniques for Kids* (3–6). Illus. by Marina Megale. 1992, Parenting Pr. LB $17.95 (0-943990-83-1). 72pp. This book helps children react properly to 14 different medical emergencies and includes directions for appropriate actions in each case. (Rev: SLJ 9/92) [616.04]

**14520** Cole, Joanna. *Cuts, Breaks, Bruises, and Burns: How Your Body Heals* (2–4). Illus. by True Kelley. 1985, HarperCollins LB $14.89 (0-690-04438-0). 48pp. The work of different body cells, how platelets stop bleeding, how clotting forms a scab, and much more in this explanation of how the body heals. (Rev: BL 3/15/86; HB 11–12/85)

**14521** Gutman, Bill. *Be Aware of Danger* (5–8). Illus. Series: Focus on Safety. 1996, Twenty-First Century LB $16.98 (0-8050-4142-7). 80pp. Situations that could be dangerous to young people are highlighted, with preventive measures outlined. (Rev: BL 2/1/97; SLJ 2/97) [613.6]

**14522** Gutman, Bill. *Hazards at Home* (4–8). Illus. Series: Focus on Safety. 1996, Twenty-First Century LB $20.40 (0-8050-4141-9). 80pp. This account stresses safety at home and how to avoid accidents, with information on first-aid procedures. (Rev: SLJ 9/96) [363.1]

**14523** Gutman, Bill. *Recreation Can Be Risky* (4–8). Illus. Series: Focus on Safety. 1996, Holt LB $20.40 (0-8050-4143-5). 80pp. Using a number of sports as examples, the author gives tips on how to play safely and avoid accidents. (Rev: BL 7/96; SLJ 9/96) [790]

**14524** Loewen, Nancy. *Emergencies* (1–4). Illus. by Penny Dann. 1996, Child's World LB $18.50 (1-56766-259-5). 24pp. Anthropomorphic animals are used to illustrate safety measures and emergency first aid. Also use *School Safety* (1996). (Rev: SLJ 3/97) [617.1]

**14525** *Now I Know Better: Kids Tell About Safety* (4–6). Illus. 1996, Millbrook LB $21.90 (0-7613-0109-7); paper $7.95 (0-7613-0149-6). 96pp. This book on safety features true accounts from children whose lives have been changed by accidents. (Rev: BL 10/15/96; SLJ 2/97) [613.6]

## Sleep and Dreams

**14526** Green, Carl R. *Seeing the Unseen* (4–6). Illus. by Keith Robinson. Series: Exploring the Unknown. 1993, Enslow LB $15.95 (0-89490-454-X). 48pp. The phenomenon of dreams is explored, with material on the nature of sleep, what dreams mean, and how to remember dreams. (Rev: SLJ 12/93) [612.8]

**14527** Silverstein, Alvin, and Virginia Silverstein. *The Mystery of Sleep* (4–6). Illus. by Nelle Davis. 1987, Little, Brown $12.95 (0-316-79117-2). 48pp. A look at why we sleep and dream, how scientists study sleep, and how to deal with sleep problems. (Rev: BL 12/15/87)

# Sex Education and Reproduction

## Babies

**14528** Knight, Margy B. *Welcoming Babies* (K–2). Illus. by Anne S. O'Brien. 1994, Tilbury House $14.95 (0-88448-123-9). A book that gives details on ceremonies in a variety of cultures and religions are used to greet babies. (Rev: BCCB 1/95; SLJ 12/94) [305.23]

**14529** Nanao, Jun. *Contemplating Your Bellybutton* (PS–K). Trans. by Amanda Mayer Stinchecum. Illus. by Tomoko Hasegawa. 1995, Kane/Miller $11.95 (0-916291-60-X). 32pp. Young Tettchan is told how he got his belly button and the purpose it serves. (Rev: BL 1/1–15/96; SLJ 12/95) [611.95]

**14530** Stein, Sara Bonnett. *Oh, Baby!* (PS–1). Illus. by Holly Anne Shelowitz. 1993, Walker LB $15.85 (0-8027-8262-0). 32pp. Using a series of baby pictures, physical and mental developments during the first year of a child's life are outlined. (Rev: BL 3/1/94*; SLJ 12/93*) [305]

**14531** Wilkes, Angela. *See How I Grow* (PS–1). Illus. 1994, DK Publg. $13.95 (1-56458-464-X). 32pp. This is the story of a baby's first 18 months of life, told in photoessay format. (Rev: BL 5/1/94; SLJ 8/94) [612.6]

## Reproduction

**14532** Audry, Andrew C., and Steven Schepp. *How Babies Are Made* (K–3). Illus. 1984, Little, Brown paper $12.95 (0-316-04227-7). 80pp. Explaining intercourse, pregnancy, and birth — using flowers, animals, and humans.

**14533** Cole, Babette. *Mommy Laid an Egg!* (K–3). Illus. 1993, Chronicle $13.95 (0-8118-0350-3). 30pp. After parents try to explain where babies come from, the children tell them the truth. (Rev: BL 7/93) [649]

**14534** Cole, Joanna. *How You Were Born* (PS–3). Illus. by Margaret Miller. 1993, Morrow LB $15.93 (0-688-12060-1); paper $4.95 (0-688-12061-X). 48pp. Fetal development is tracked in text and color pictures, plus tips are given on how to use this book with children. (Rev: BL 6/1–15/93; SLJ 4/93*) [612]

**14535** Girard, Linda Walvoord. *You Were Born on Your Very First Birthday* (PS). Illus. by Christa Kieffer. 1983, Whitman paper $5.95 (0-8075-9456-3). 32pp. A simple introduction to pregnancy and birth.

**14536** Parker, Steve. *The Reproductive System* (5–8). Illus. Series: Human Body. 1997, Raintree Steck-Vaughn $24.26 (0-8172-4806-4). 48pp. A well-organized, straightforward account that covers male and female anatomy, genes, fertility problems, contraception, STDs, and human development from conception to adolescence. (Rev: SLJ 2/98) [613.9]

**14537** Royston, Angela. *Where Do Babies Come From? A Delightful First Look at How Life Begins* (PS–1). Illus. 1996, DK Publg. $9.95 (0-7894-0579-2). 37pp. This simple introduction to reproduction uses the sunflower, ducks, cats, and humans as examples and uses schematic drawings superimposed on photos to show fetuses. (Rev: SLJ 8/96) [613.9]

**14538** Sandeman, Anna. *Babies* (2–4). Illus. Series: Body Books. 1996, Millbrook LB $18.90 (0-7613-0478-9). 31pp. Clear information is given on conception, pregnancy, childbirth, and the growth of babies. (Rev: SLJ 6/96) [613.9]

**14539** Schnitter, Jane T. *Let Me Explain: A Story About Donor Insemination* (2–4). Illus. by Joanne

Bowring. 1995, Perspectives $14.00 (0-944934-12-9). 32pp. A young girl tells how much she adores her father and also explains that she was the product of artificial insemination. (Rev: SLJ 7/95) [618]

**14540** Silverstein, Alvin, et al. *The Reproductive System* (5–8). Illus. Series: Human Body Systems. 1994, Twenty-First Century LB $20.40 (0-8050-2838-2). 96pp. Reproduction in the plant and animal world is introduced, with the focus on the human system and body parts. (Rev: BL 3/15/95; SLJ 5/95) [612.6]

**14541** Taylor, Nicole. *Baby* (3–5). Illus. Series: Images. 1994, Creative Ed. $16.95 (0-88682-595-4). The process of conception is described in text and photos, along with a month-by-month depiction of fetal development and pictures of a birth. (Rev: SLJ 12/94) [306]

# Sex Education

**14542** Bourgeois, Paulette, and Martin Wolfish. *Changes in You and Me: A Book About Puberty, Mostly for Boys* (4–7). Illus. 1994, Andrews & McMeel $14.95 (0-8362-2814-6). 64pp. A straightforward account about the changes, problems, and challenges associated with puberty. A companion volume is *Changes . . . for Girls* (1994). (Rev: BL 2/1/95; SLJ 3/95) [612]

**14543** Brown, Laurie Krasny. *What's the Big Secret? Talking About Sex with Girls and Boys* (2–4). Illus. by Marc Brown. 1997, Little, Brown $15.95 (0-316-10915-0). 32pp. This picture book on sex education discusses sexuality, gender roles, reproduction, and the issue of privacy. (Rev: BL 10/1/97; SLJ 3/98) [613]

**14544** Cole, Joanna. *Asking About Sex and Growing Up: A Question-and-Answer Book for Boys and Girls* (4–6). Illus. by Alan Tiegreen. 1988, Morrow $16.00 (0-688-06927-4); paper $4.95 (0-688-06928-2). 96pp. Answers questions about sex and physical changes that occur as one grows up. (Rev: BCCB 6/88; BL 6/15/88; SLJ 8/88)

**14545** Elgin, Kathleen, and John F. Osterritter. *Twenty-Eight Days* (5–7). Illus. 1973, McKay paper $5.95 (0-679-51382-5). 64pp. A book about the menstrual cycle that includes information on the reproductive organs.

**14546** Girard, Linda Walvoord. *My Body Is Private* (PS–3). Illus. by Rodney Pate. 1984, Whitman LB $12.95 (0-8075-5320-4); paper $4.95 (0-8075-5319-0). 32pp. A girl of 7 or 8 talks about unwarranted touching of one's body by another in this lesson on prevention of sexual abuse.

**14547** Gordon, Sol, and Judith Cohen. *Did the Sun Shine Before You Were Born? A Sex Education Primer* (PS–3). Illus. 1974, Okpaku $12.00 (0-89388-179-1); Prometheus paper $9.95 (0-879-75723-X). A self-styled sex education manual for the very young.

**14548** Gordon, Sol, and Judith Gordon. *A Better Safe Than Sorry Book: A Family Guide for Sexual Assault Prevention* (PS–1). Illus. 1992, Prometheus paper $9.95 (0-87975-768-X). A book that approaches the subjects of sexual abuse and threats from strangers in a nonscary manner. (Rev: BL 11/15/85)

**14549** Gravelle, Karen, and Jennifer Gravelle. *The Period Book: Everything You Don't Want to Ask (but Need to Know)* (4–6). Illus. 1996, Walker $15.95 (0-8027-8420-8); paper $8.95 (0-8027-7478-4). 128pp. A chatty guide to menstruation that also describes reproductive anatomy and the many changes that occur during puberty. (Rev: BCCB 7–8/96; BL 3/15/96; SLJ 3/96) [612.6]

**14550** Harris, Robie H. *It's Perfectly Normal: A Book About Changing Bodies, Growing Up, Sex, and Sexual Health* (4–7). Illus. by Michael Emberley. 1994, Candlewick $19.95 (1-56402-199-8). 96pp. A frank discussion with candid illustrations are contained in this discussion of the changes, problems, and choices that puberty brings. (Rev: BCCB 10/94; BL 9/15/94*; SLJ 12/94*) [613]

**14551** Johnson, Eric W. *People, Love, Sex, and Families: Answers to Questions That Preteens Ask* (5–8). Illus. 1985, Walker LB $14.85 (0-8027-6605-6). 144pp. Information taken from the results of a survey of 1,000 preteens; covers a broad range of topics, from sexual abuse to venereal disease, to divorce and incest. (Rev: BL 3/15/86)

**14552** Marsh, Carole. *AIDS to Zits: A "Sextionary" for Kids* (3–7). 1987, Gallopade $29.95 (1-55609-263-6); paper $19.95 (1-55609-210-5). 28pp. This dictionary contains definitions of about 100 words related to sexuality. (Rev: BL 12/1/89) [613.951]

**14553** Marzollo, Jean. *Getting Your Period: A Book About Menstruation* (5–8). Illus. by Kent Williams. 1989, Dial $6.95 (0-8037-0356-2). 112pp. Explaining the physical and emotional transitions that girls go through during menstruation. (Rev: BL 7/89)

**14554** Nardo, Don. *Teen Sexuality* (5–8). Illus. Series: Overview. 1997, Lucent LB $22.45 (1-56006-189-8). Traces the changing attitudes toward sex and what are considered acceptable practices according to present standards. In this series are also *Suicide, Drugs and Sports*, and *Homeless Children* (all 1997). (Rev: BL 3/15/97) [362.29]

**14555** Rozakis, Laurie. *Teen Pregnancy: Why Are Kids Having Babies?* (5–8). Illus. Series: Issues of Our Time. 1993, Twenty-First Century LB $18.90 (0-

8050-2569-3). 64pp. A slim, easily read account that explains birth control and deplores the fact that teens do not have access to information about it. (Rev: SLJ 2/94) [612.6]

**14556** Thomson, Ruth. *Have You Started Yet?* (4–7). Illus. 1997, Price Stern Sloan $4.95 (0-8431-7950-3). 122pp. This book for girls explains the changes that occur during puberty and supplies information on menstruation and reproductive anatomy. (Rev: BL 11/1/97; SLJ 1/98) [612.6]

**14557** Westheimer, Ruth. *Dr. Ruth Talks to Kids: Where You Came From, How Your Body Changes, and What Sex Is All About* (5–8). Illus. by Diane De Groat. 1993, Macmillan LB $14.00 (0-02-792532-3). 96pp. A chatty, frank discussion of growing up. (Rev: BCCB 7–8/93; SLJ 6/93) [306.7]

# Physical and Applied Sciences

# General Science

## Miscellaneous

**14558** Aaseng, Nathan. *Yearbooks in Science: 1940–1949* (5–8). Illus. Series: Yearbooks in Science. 1995, Twenty-First Century LB $20.40 (0-8050-3434-X). 80pp. An important decade in scientific discovery is chronicled, with emphasis on the impact of these advances on society. (Rev: BL 1/1–15/96; SLJ 5/96) [609]

**14559** Aaseng, Nathan. *Yearbooks in Science: 1930–1939* (5–8). Illus. Series: Yearbooks in Science. 1995, Twenty-First Century LB $20.40 (0-8050-3433-1). 80pp. An overview of the accomplishments in science in the 1930s arranged by such divisions as physics and chemistry. (Rev: BL 12/1/95; SLJ 1/96) [609]

**14560** Allison, Linda, and David Katz. *Gee Wiz! How to Mix Art and Science or the Art of Thinking Scientifically* (5–7). Illus. by Linda Allison. 1983, Little, Brown paper $12.95 (0-316-03445-2). 128pp. A group of science projects and experiments arranged by subject.

**14561** Ash, Russell. *Incredible Comparisons* (4–8). Illus. 1996, DK Publg. $19.95 (0-7894-1009-5). 64pp. Such concepts in nature as speed and weight are discussed in this fascinating book of comparisons. (Rev: BL 12/1/96*; SLJ 3/97) [031.02]

**14562** Cobb, Vicki. *Why Can't I Live Forever? And Other Not Such Dumb Questions About Life* (3–5). Illus. by Mena Dolobowsky. 1997, Lodestar paper $13.99 (0-525-67505-1). 48pp. Answers simple but important questions like "Why are plants green?" and "Why is blood red?" (Rev: SLJ 5/97) [500]

**14563** Ganeri, Anita, and Chris Oxlade. *The Kingfisher First Science Encyclopedia* (2–4). Illus. 1997, Kingfisher $14.95 (0-7534-5089-5). 112pp. This alphabetically arranged book covers about 75 topics in science, such as color, calculators, television, and physics. (Rev: SLJ 11/97) [500]

**14564** Gates, Phil. *Nature Got There First* (5–8). Illus. 1995, Kingfisher $17.95 (1-85697-587-8). 80pp. Using lessons from nature, modern technology has developed such innovations as cameras, safety helmets, and armored cars. (Rev: BL 10/1/95; SLJ 2/96) [508]

**14565** Gutfreund, Geraldine M. *Yearbooks in Science: 1970–1979* (5–8). Illus. Series: Yearbooks in Science. 1995, Twenty-First Century LB $20.40 (0-8050-3437-4). 80pp. A decade of new scientific concepts and inventions is discussed, with profiles of scientists behind them. (Rev: BL 1/1–15/96; SLJ 5/96) [609]

**14566** Kramer, Stephen. *How to Think Like a Scientist: Answering Questions by the Scientific Method* (3–5). Illus. 1987, HarperCollins LB $14.89 (0-690-04565-4). 48pp. An intriguing account of the ways in which questions are asked, and how scientists try to make sure they are answered correctly. (Rev: BCCB 1/87; BL 5/15/87; SLJ 5/87)

**14567** McGowen, Tom. *Yearbooks in Science: 1900–1919* (5–8). Illus. Series: Yearbooks in Science. 1995, Twenty-First Century LB $20.40 (0-8050-3431-5). 80pp. Science landmarks for 1900–1919 are chronicled in a series of articles dealing with different fields. (Rev: BL 12/1/95; SLJ 1/96) [609]

**14568** McGowen, Tom. *Yearbooks in Science: 1960–1969* (5–8). Illus. Series: Yearbooks in Science. 1996, Twenty-First Century LB $20.40 (0-8050-3436-6). 80pp. Developments in the history of science and technology during the 1960s are covered in an exciting step-by-step approach. (Rev: BL 1/1–15/96; SLJ 5/96) [609]

**14569** Martin, Paul D. *Science: It's Changing Your World* (5–8). Illus. 1985, National Geographic LB $12.50 (0-87044-521-9). 104pp. An overview of the science field today, crediting computers and lasers with the vast growth of scientific information. (Rev: BL 9/15/85; SLJ 10/85)

**14570** Newton, David E. *Yearbooks in Science: 1920–1929* (5–8). Illus. Series: Yearbooks in Science. 1995, Twenty-First Century LB $20.40 (0-8050-3432-3). 80pp. The 1920s in science is surveyed, with chapters devoted to each breakthrough. (Rev: BL 12/1/95; SLJ 1/96) [609]

**14571** Rice, David. *Lifetimes* (3–6). Illus. 1997, Dawn $16.95 (1-883220-58-0); paper $7.95 (1-883220-59-9). 32pp. Various activities are interspersed with facts about a number of animals, plants, and astronomical bodies. (Rev: BL 6/1–15/97; SLJ 2/98) [574.3]

**14572** *Science and Technology: The World of Modern Science* (3–6). Illus. Series: Children's Reference. 1993, Oxford $40.00 (0-19-910143-4). 160pp. Using an encyclopedic arrangement, this work covers many topics in the physical sciences under headings like science and materials, space, energy, transport, and information technologies. (Rev: SLJ 1/94) [500]

**14573** Silverstein, Herma. *Yearbooks in Science: 1990 and Beyond* (5–8). Illus. Series: Yearbooks in Science. 1995, Twenty-First Century LB $20.40 (0-8050-3439-0). 80pp. The final volume in this series not only traces recent developments in science and technology but also presents the challenges of the future. (Rev: BL 1/1–15/96) [609]

**14574** Simon, Seymour. *The Dinosaur Is the Biggest Animal That Ever Lived: And Other Wrong Ideas You Thought Were True* (3–5). Illus. by Giulio Maestro. 1984, HarperCollins paper $5.95 (0-06-446053-3). 64pp. Twenty-nine popularly believed science myths are exposed.

**14575** Stein, Sara Bonnett. *The Science Book* (4–8). Illus. by author. 1980, Workman paper $9.95 (0-89480-120-1). 288pp. A whole-earth approach to strange and fascinating science facts.

**14576** Taylor, Charles, and Stephen Pople. *The Oxford Children's Book of Science* (5–8). Illus. 1996, Oxford LB $27.00 (0-19-521164-2). 192pp. A wide variety of science topics — from gravity and cells to the human body and DNA — are presented in a large format. (Rev: BL 10/1/96; SLJ 8/96) [503]

**14577** Wollard, Kathy. *How Come?* (5–8). Illus. 1993, Workman paper $11.95 (1-56305-324-1). 300pp. Includes questions and answers to a number of common scientific questions, like "Do parrots understand what they say?" (Rev: BL 5/1/94) [500]

## Experiments and Projects

**14578** Allison, Linda, and Martha Weston. *Pint-Size Science: Finding-Out Fun for You and Your Young Child* (PS–2). Illus. Series: Brown Paper Preschool. 1994, Little, Brown paper $9.95 (0-316-03467-3). 48pp. With attractive cartoons and an excellent text, this book helps adults guide young children through a series of science activities that explore topics like insects, plants, light, energy, and the 3 states of matter. (Rev: BL 9/15/94) [372.3]

**14579** *The Ben Franklin Book of Easy and Incredible Experiments* (4–6). Illus. 1995, Wiley $29.95 (0-471-07639-2); paper $12.95 (0-471-07638-4). 144pp. From the Franklin Institute Museum in Philadelphia comes a book of experiments involving weather, music, paper, electricity, light, and sound. (Rev: BL 9/15/95; SLJ 4/96) [507.8]

**14580** *The Big Book of Nature Projects* (4–6). Illus. 1997, Thames & Hudson paper $16.95 (0-500-01773-5). 128pp. An attractive large-format paperback that introduces a wide variety of nature projects for both indoors and outdoors with easy instructions. (Rev: BL 7/97; SLJ 1/98) [507.8]

**14581** Bleifeld, Maurice. *Experimenting with a Microscope* (5–8). Illus. 1988, Watts LB $22.50 (0-531-10580-6). 128pp. Step-by-step explanation of how to use a compound microscope. (Rev: BL 1/15/89; SLJ 2/89)

**14582** Bonnet, Bob, and Dan Keen. *Science Fair Projects: The Environment* (3–6). Illus. 1995, Sterling $16.95 (0-8069-0542-5). 96pp. Outlines 60 experiments and projects related to the environment that involve chemistry, biology, behavior, and consumerism. (Rev: BL 12/1/95; SLJ 1/96) [507.8]

**14583** Broekel, Ray. *Experiments with Straws and Paper* (1–3). Illus. Series: New True Books. 1990, Children's LB $20.00 (0-516-01104-9); paper $5.50 (0-516-41104-7). 48pp. With easily found materials and clear instructions, this is a beginning book of science experiments. (Rev: BL 1/1/91; SLJ 5/91) [962]

**14584** Carrow, Robert. *Put a Fan in Your Hat! Inventions, Contraptions, and Gadgets Kids Can Build* (5–8). Illus. by Rick Brown. 1997, McGraw-Hill paper $14.95 (0-07-011658-X). 139pp. A book of useful science project, including making a natural battery, building a motor, and creating a hat with a cooling fan. (Rev: SLJ 5/97) [507]

**14585** Chapman, Gillian, and Pam Robson. *Exploring Time* (3–5). Illus. 1995, Millbrook LB $19.90 (1-56294-559-9). 32pp. Fourteen projects of varying difficulty related to time, such as creating a time line and a sundial. (Rev: BL 11/1/95; SLJ 3/96) [529]

**14586** Cobb, Vicki. *Lots of Rot* (K–3). Illus. by Brian Schatell. 1981, HarperCollins LB $15.89 (0-397-31939-8). 40pp. Decay is explored in a series of interesting experiments.

**14587** Cobb, Vicki. *Science Experiments You Can Eat* (5–7). Illus. by Peter Lippman. 1994, HarperCollins $14.89 (0-060-23551-9). 128pp. Experiments illustrating principles of chemistry and physics utilize edible ingredients. Also use: *More Science Experiments You Can Eat* (1979).

**14588** Cobb, Vicki, and Kathy Darling. *Bet You Can't! Science Impossibilities to Fool You* (5–8). Illus. by Martha Weston. 1983, Avon paper $4.50 (0-380-54502-0). 128pp. Sixty different tricks and experiments involving such scientific subjects as fluids and energy. Also use: *Bet You Can! Science Possibilities to Fool You* (1983).

**14589** Cobb, Vicki, and Kathy Darling. *Wanna Bet? Science Challenges to Fool You* (3–6). Illus. by Meredith Johnson. 1993, Lothrop $15.00 (0-688-11213-7). 128pp. This book of experiments and projects for young people covers such areas as physics, chemistry, mathematics, physiology, and electricity. (Rev: BL 5/1/93; SLJ 8/93) [793]

**14590** Coulter, George, and Shirley Coulter. *Science in Art* (3–4). Illus. Series: Science Projects. 1995, Rourke LB $18.60 (0-86625-519-2). 32pp. Six science activities are included in this volume, each of which explores some aspect of art, color, or artists' materials. Companion volumes are *Science in Food* and *Science in History* (both 1995). (Rev: SLJ 1/96) [507]

**14591** Falk, John H., et al. *Bubble Monster: And Other Science Fun* (PS–3). Illus. by Charles C. Somerville. 1996, Chicago Review paper $17.95 (1-55652-301-7). 168pp. Five scientific areas — patterns, matter, communication, the human body, and technology — are covered in a series of activities that require some adult help. (Rev: SLJ 4/97) [507]

**14592** Gardner, Robert. *Kitchen Chemistry: Science Experiments to Do at Home* (4–8). Illus. 1989, Silver Burdett paper $4.95 (0-671-67576-1). 136pp. Simple experiments that can be performed in the kitchen with everyday equipment and supplies.

**14593** Gardner, Robert. *Projects in Space Science* (4–8). Illus. 1988, Silver Burdett paper $5.95 (0-671-65993-6). 136pp. Science projects involving space travel and astronomy. (Rev: BL 1/15/89; SLJ 2/89)

**14594** Gardner, Robert. *Robert Gardner's Favorite Science Experiments* (5–8). Illus. 1992, Watts LB $22.00 (0-531-11038-9); paper $6.95 (0-531-15255-3). 128pp. This manual contains 30 easy-to-perform experiments that demonstrate a variety of scientific principles. (Rev: BL 5/15/93) [507.8]

**14595** Gardner, Robert. *Science Around the House* (4–6). Illus. 1989, Silver Burdett paper $4.95 (0-671-68139-7). 136pp. Simple experiments using everyday objects are detailed in this reissued project book.

**14596** Gibson, Gary. *Making Shapes* (3–5). Photos by Roger Vlitos. Illus. by Tony Kenyon. Series: Science for Fun. 1995, Millbrook LB $20.90 (1-56294-631-5). 32pp. In double-page spreads, experiments in shape making and shifting are described, as well as how they illustrate various principles of science. (Rev: SLJ 3/96) [507]

**14597** Gibson, Gary. *Making Things Change* (3–5). Illus. Series: Science for Fun. 1995, Millbrook LB $20.90 (1-56294-645-5). 32pp. Double-page spreads are used to introduce a series of experiments and projects that illustrate how objects and materials can change their forms and structures. (Rev: BL 12/15/95) [507.8]

**14598** Gordon, Maria. *Fun with Materials* (2–4). Illus. by Mike Gordon. Series: Simple Science. 1996, Raintree Steck-Vaughn LB $19.97 (0-8172-4505-7). 32pp. Liquids, solids, and gases are discussed, as well as recycling and various kinds of natural and manmade substances, in this account that contains many science activities, some requiring adult help. (Rev: SLJ 4/97) [507]

**14599** Grier, Katherine. *Discover: Mysteries of the Past and Present* (4–6). Illus. by Pat Cupples. 1990, Addison-Wesley paper $8.95 (0-201-52322-1). 96pp. An introduction to the inner workings of a museum. (Rev: SLJ 8/90) [507]

**14600** Hann, Judith. *How Science Works: 100 Ways Parents and Kids Can Share the Secrets of Science* (4–8). Illus. 1991, Reader's Digest $24.00 (0-89577-382-1). 192pp. A large-format book that describes projects and experiments demonstrating basic principles of science. (Rev: SLJ 7/91) [507.8]

**14601** Harlow, Rosie, and Gareth Morgan. *175 Amazing Nature Experiments* (3–6). Illus. by Kuo Kang Chen. 1992, Random paper $14.00 (0-679-82043-4). 172pp. A fresh collection of experiments, games, and crafts involving nature. (Rev: SLJ 6/92) [507]

**14602** Herbert, Don. *Mr. Wizard's Experiments for Young Scientists* (5–8). Illus. by Don Noonan. 1991, Doubleday paper $12.95 (0-385-26585-9). 187pp. Directions for 13 science experiments that can be done easily with equipment found in the home.

**14603** Herbert, Don. *Mr. Wizard's Supermarket Science* (4–7). Illus. by Roy McKie. 1980, Random paper $9.00 (0-394-83800-9). 96pp. More than 100 projects using supermarket items.

**14604** Hirschfeld, Robert, and Nancy White. *The Kids' Science Book: Creative Experiences for Hands-on Fun* (2–5). Illus. by Loretta Braren. Series: Kids

Can! Books. 1995, Williamson paper $12.95 (0-913589-88-8). 157pp. An interesting collection of games, experiments, and activities that illustrate various principles of science and are fun to perform. (Rev: SLJ 12/95) [507]

**14605** Johnson, Kipchak. *Worm's Eye View: Make Your Own Wildlife Refuge* (3–8). Illus. Series: Lighter Look. 1991, Millbrook LB $20.90 (1-878841-30-0). 40pp. After exploring the wildlife found in a patch of vacant ground, the author suggests various projects for cultivating it. (Rev: SLJ 8/91) [507]

**14606** Kerrod, Robin. *How Things Work* (4–8). Illus. Series: Secrets of Science. 1990, Marshall Cavendish LB $10.95 (1-85435-154-0). 32pp. Simple science projects and experiments such as making a compass. Also use: *Is It Magic?* (1990). (Rev: SLJ 10/90) [507]

**14607** Kramer, Alan. *How to Make a Chemical Volcano and Other Mysterious Experiments* (4–7). Illus. by Paul Harvey. 1991, Watts paper $6.95 (0-531-15610-9). 111pp. Thirty experiments for "detectives of chemistry" by a 13-year-old student. (Rev: BCCB 2/90; BL 12/15/89; SLJ 3/90) [532]

**14608** Lambier, Doug, and Robert Stevenson. *Genesis for Kids: Science Experiments That Show God's Power in Creation!* (3–6). Illus. 1997, Thomas Nelson paper $14.99 (0-8499-4034-6). 160pp. Using the 7 days of creation as a focus, this book of science experiments is intended to be a way of discovering the wonders of God and his creations. (Rev: BL 10/1/97) [507.8]

**14609** Levine, Shar, and Leslie Johnstone. *Everyday Science: Fun and Easy Projects for Making Practical Things* (4–6). Illus. by Ed Shems. 1995, Wiley paper $9.95 (0-471-11014-0). 97pp. The science behind everyday objects is explored in this book of 25 simple projects under such headings as Light and Optics, Heat, Earth Science, Electricity, and Chemistry. (Rev: SLJ 8/95) [507]

**14610** Levine, Shar, and Leslie Johnstone. *Science Around the World: Travel Through Time and Space with Fun Experiments and Projects* (3–6). Illus. by Laurel Aiello. 1996, Wiley paper $10.95 (0-471-11916-4). 84pp. This project book presents activities from 10 countries around the world, like making paper and creating a sand timer using Chinese science. (Rev: SLJ 7/96) [507]

**14611** Levine, Shar, and Leslie Johnstone. *Silly Science: Strange and Startling Projects to Amaze Your Family and Friends* (4–6). Illus. by Ed Shems. 1995, Wiley paper $9.95 (0-471-11013-2). 91pp. Twenty-eight seemingly foolish experiments using common materials illustrate important scientific principles and processes. (Rev: SLJ 8/95) [507]

**14612** Markle, Sandra. *Creepy, Spooky Science* (3–7). Illus. by Cecile Schoberle. 1996, Hyperion LB $15.49 (0-7868-2178-7); paper $4.95 (0-7868-1088-2). 72pp. Easy-to-perform experiments and projects are presented using scary titles like "Whip Up Some Blood" and "Bewitch an Egg." (Rev: SLJ 10/96) [507]

**14613** Markle, Sandra. *Exploring Autumn: A Season of Science Activities, Puzzlers, and Games* (4–7). Illus. Series: Exploring Seasons. 1991, Avon paper $3.50 (0-380-71910-X). 160pp. Science, history, myth, quizzes, and more combined in this book on seasonal activities in the classroom and home. (Rev: BL 1/1/91; SLJ 1/92) [574.5]

**14614** Markle, Sandra. *Icky, Squishy Science* (3–7). Illus. by Cecile Schoberle. 1996, Hyperion LB $15.49 (0-7868-2177-9); paper $3.95 (0-7868-1087-4). 70pp. This breezy book of science activities is geared to a youngster's interests and fascination with things unusual and humorous. (Rev: SLJ 8/96) [507]

**14615** Markle, Sandra. *Science to the Rescue* (4–7). Illus. 1994, Atheneum $15.95 (0-689-31783-2). 48pp. Explains the scientific method and shows how science has found solutions to many problems. (Rev: BL 3/15/94; SLJ 4/94) [507.8]

**14616** Markle, Sandra. *Super Science Secrets: Exploring Nature Through Games, Puzzles and Activities* (1–3). Illus. 1997, Longstreet $14.95 (1-56352-396-5). 36pp. Scientific topics like evaporation, static electricity, and animal defenses are examined, with follow-up questions and simple experiments. (Rev: SLJ 9/97) [507]

**14617** Markle, Sandra. *The Young Scientist's Guide to Successful Science* (4–8). Illus. 1990, Lothrop LB $12.93 (0-688-07217-8). 128pp. Step-by-step explanations of what an experiment is and how it works. (Rev: BCCB 9/90; BL 7/90) [507.8]

**14618** Murphy, Pat, et al. *The Science Explorer Out and About: Fantastic Science Experiments Your Family Can Do Anywhere!* (3–8). Illus. by Jason Gorski. Series: Exploratorium Science-at-Home-Book. 1997, Holt paper $12.95 (0-8050-4537-6). 127pp. A wide variety of science experiments are outlined, many that can be performed alone and others that require adult help. (Rev: SLJ 2/98) [507]

**14619** Murray, Peter. *Silly Science Tricks (with Professor Solomon Snickerdoodle)* (2–4). Illus. by Anastasia Mitchell. 1993, Child's World LB $21.36 (0-89565-976-X). 32pp. Seven science tricks in one eye-catching book. (Rev: BL 3/15/93) [507.8]

**14620** Nye, Bill. *Bill Nye the Science Guy's Big Blast of Science* (5–8). Illus. 1993, Addison-Wesley paper $14.00 (0-201-60864-2). 172pp. Several topics, including matter, heat, light, electricity, magnetism, weather, and space, are introduced in this quick tour of the world of science. (Rev: BL 2/15/94) [507.8]

**14621** Nye, Bill, and Ian Saunders. *Bill Nye the Science Guy's Consider the Following: A Way Cool Set of Science Questions, Answers, and Ideas to Ponder* (4–7). Illus. 1995, Disney $14.89 (0-7868-5035-3); paper $9.95 (0-7868-4054-4). 96pp. A series of questions related to one of the branches of science are answered in 4-page spreads, with easily performed experiments. (Rev: BL 12/1/95) [507.8]

**14622** Ontario Science Centre Staff. *Scienceworks: 65 Experiments That Introduce the Fun and Wonder of Science* (4–6). Illus. 1986, Addison-Wesley paper $11.95 (0-201-16780-8). Emphasizing that science can be fun, this book includes numerous experiments, many of them easily mastered puzzles or tricks.

**14623** Richards, Roy. *101 Science Surprises: Exciting Experiments with Everyday Materials* (3–5). Illus. 1993, Sterling $17.95 (0-8069-8822-3). 104pp. The activities and experiments presented in this book represent various branches of science and vary in difficulty. (Rev: BL 9/1/93; SLJ 6/93) [507.8]

**14624** Richards, Roy. *101 Science Tricks: Fun Experiments with Everyday Materials* (4–8). Illus. by Alex Pang. 1992, Sterling $16.95 (0-8069-8388-4). 104pp. Interesting, easy-to-do science and math activities, with emphasis on understanding the principles behind the tricks. (Rev: BL 2/1/92; SLJ 1/92) [507.8]

**14625** Ross, Michael E. *Sandbox Scientist: Real Science Activities for Little Kids* (PS–2). Illus. by Mary Anne Lloyd. 1995, Chicago Review paper $12.95 (1-55652-248-7). 206pp. Simple experiments and activities introduce young children to the principles involving such components as light and water. (Rev: BL 2/1/96) [372.3]

**14626** Simon, Seymour. *How to Be an Ocean Scientist in Your Own Home* (4–7). Illus. by David A. Carter. 1988, Macmillan LB $14.89 (0-397-32292-5). 144pp. Twenty-four experiments and projects mostly using salt and water. (Rev: BCCB 11/88)

**14627** Sobey, Ed. *Wrapper Rockets and Trombone Straws: Science at Every Meal* (4–7). Illus. 1996, McGraw-Hill paper $14.95 (0-07-021745-9). 137pp. Using tableware like glasses, straws, and napkins, a number of simple tricks and experiments are introduced. (Rev: BL 3/1/97; SLJ 6/97) [500]

**14628** Supraner, Robyn. *Science Secrets* (1–3). Illus. by Renzo Barto. 1981, Troll LB $12.50 (0-89375-426-9). 48pp. Science principles like magnetism and gravity are simply explained.

**14629** UNESCO. *700 Science Experiments for Everyone* (5–8). Illus. 1964, Doubleday $17.95 (0-385-05275-8). 252pp. An excellent collection of experi-

ments, noted for its number of entries and breadth of coverage.

**14630** VanCleave, Janice. *Janice VanCleave's Animals* (4–6). Illus. Series: Spectacular Science Projects. 1992, Wiley paper $10.95 (0-471-55052-3). 84pp. This book contains many easy-to-follow projects involving animals. (Rev: BL 1/1/93; SLJ 2/93) [591]

**14631** VanCleave, Janice. *Janice VanCleave's Biology for Every Kid: 101 Easy Experiments That Really Work* (4–7). Illus. 1989, Wiley paper $11.95 (0-471-50381-9). 224pp. Using readily available equipment and supplies, this book outlines simple experiments. (Rev: BL 2/15/90) [574]

**14632** VanCleave, Janice. *Janice VanCleave's Earth Science for Every Kid: 101 Easy Experiments That Really Work* (3–6). Illus. 1991, Wiley $27.95 (0-471-54389-6); paper $11.95 (0-471-53010-7). 231pp. In this book of interesting experiments, such topics as erosion, rocks, weather, and the oceans are introduced. [551]

**14633** VanCleave, Janice. *Janice VanCleave's Guide to the Best Science Fair Projects* (3–6). Illus. 1997, Wiley paper $14.95 (0-471-14802-4). 144pp. An excellent experiment book that covers 50 science projects in the life and physical sciences, astronomy, mathematics, and engineering. (Rev: BL 3/15/97; SLJ 4/97) [507.8]

**14634** VanCleave, Janice. *Janice VanCleave's Play and Find Out About Nature: Easy Experiments for Young Children* (3–5). Illus. 1997, Wiley $27.95 (0-471-12939-9); paper $12.95 (0-471-12940-2). 128pp. Fifty models and activities using common household materials are outlined to help parents and others introduce the natural world to children. (Rev: BL 6/1–15/97; SLJ 7/97) [574]

**14635** VanCleave, Janice. *Janice VanCleave's Play and Find Out About Science: Easy Experiments for Young Children* (2–4). Illus. 1996, Wiley paper $12.95 (0-471-12941-0). 128pp. Topics like sound, magnets, and electricity are explored through more than 50 easy experiments and activities. (Rev: BL 10/15/96; SLJ 10/96) [530]

**14636** VanCleave, Janice. *Janice VanCleave's 202 Oozing, Bubbling, Dripping and Bouncing Experiments* (4–6). Illus. 1996, Wiley paper $12.95 (0-471-14025-2). 120pp. Fun and learning are combined in these experiments that investigate astronomy, biology, chemistry, earth science, and physics. (Rev: SLJ 2/97) [507]

**14637** Walpole, Brenda. *175 Science Experiments to Amuse and Amaze Your Friends* (2–6). Illus. 1988, Random paper $13.99 (0-394-89991-1). 176pp. Science fair ideas — tricks, experiments, and things to make. (Rev: BL 12/1/88; SLJ 1/89)

**14638** Webster, Vera. *Plant Experiments* (1–4). Illus. 1982, Children's LB $21.00 (0-516-01638-5). 48pp. A manual of simple experiments with plants. Also use: *Science Experiments* (1982).

**14639** White, Laurence B., and Ray Broekel. *Shazam! Simple Science Magic* (3–6). 1991, Whitman LB $12.95 (0-8075-7332-9). 48pp. Young magicians are shown how to perform 20 mystifying tricks. (Rev: BL 5/15/91; SLJ 7/91) [793.8]

**14640** Wiese, Jim. *Rocket Science: 50 Flying, Floating, Flipping, Spinning Gadgets Kids Create Themselves* (3–6). Illus. 1995, Wiley paper $12.95 (0-471-11357-3). 128pp. Principles related to physics, electricity, optics, acoustics, and other branches of science are explored in a number of interesting projects and experiments. (Rev: BL 12/1/95; SLJ 3/96) [507.8]

**14641** Wilkes, Angela. *My First Science Book* (K–4). Illus. 1990, Knopf LB $13.99 (0-679-90583-9). 48pp. A large-format, beginning science book with attractive bright objects. (Rev: BL 1/1/91; SLJ 12/90) [507.8]

**14642** Willow, Diane, and Emily Curran. *Science Sensations* (3–5). Illus. by Lady McCrady. Series: Boston Children's Museum Activity Books. 1990, Addison-Wesley paper $11.00 (0-201-07189-4). 95pp. A simple child-tested experiment book using everyday objects. (Rev: SLJ 6/90) [507]

**14643** Wyatt, Valerie. *The Science Book for Girls and Other Intelligent Beings* (3–5). Illus. by Pat Cupples. 1997, Kids Can paper $8.95 (1-55074-113-6).

80pp. Introduces various science experiments from different branches of science, as well as several female scientists, like Mary Leakey and Sally Ride. (Rev: SLJ 10/97) [509]

**14644** Wyler, Rose. *Science Fun with Peanuts and Popcorn* (2–4). Illus. 1986, Simon & Schuster paper $4.95 (0-671-62452-0). 48pp. Simple experiments that explain scientific principles. Also use: *Science Fun with Mud and Dirt* (1986). (Rev: BL 7/86; SLJ 11/86)

**14645** Wyler, Rose. *Science Fun with Toy Boats and Planes* (2–4). Illus. 1986, Simon & Schuster paper $4.95 (0-671-62453-9). 48pp. Experiments that explain the forces that move these vehicles. Also use: *Science Fun with Toy Cars and Trucks* (1988). (Rev: BL 7/86; SLJ 10/86)

**14646** Zubrowski, Bernie. *Messing Around with Baking Chemistry* (4–6). Illus. by Signe Hanson. 1981, Little, Brown paper $7.95 (0-316-98879-0). 64pp. Cake ingredients and their function are examined.

**14647** Zubrowski, Bernie. *Messing Around with Drinking Straw Construction* (4–6). Illus. by Stephanie Fleischer. 1981, Little, Brown paper $9.95 (0-316-98875-8). 64pp. Projects illustrate the principles of construction.

**14648** Zubrowski, Bernie. *Messing Around with Water Pumps and Siphons* (4–6). Illus. by Steven Lindblom. 1982, Little, Brown paper $7.95 (0-316-98877-4). 64pp. Simple experiments show how water can be moved.

# Astronomy

## General

**14649** Asimov, Isaac. *Cosmic Debris: The Asteroids* (3–5). Illus. Series: Isaac Asimov's New Library of the Universe. 1994, Gareth Stevens LB $19.93 (0-8368-1130-5). 32pp. This account explains what asteroids are, theories of their formation, how some have become planetary moons, and their possible uses as the mines of the future. (Rev: BL 2/15/95) [523.4]

**14650** Asimov, Isaac. *Mysteries of Deep Space: Black Holes, Pulsars, and Quasars* (3–5). Illus. Series: Isaac Asimov's New Library of the Universe. 1994, Gareth Stevens LB $19.93 (0-8368-1133-X). 32pp. Outer space is explored in this account of celestial energy, collapsing stars, types of black holes, pulsars, and quasars. (Rev: BL 2/15/95; SLJ 2/95) [523.8]

**14651** Asimov, Isaac, and Francis Reddy. *Astronomy in Ancient Times* (3–4). Illus. Series: Isaac Asimov's New Library of the Universe. 1995, Gareth Stevens LB $19.93 (0-8368-1191-7). 32pp. A breezy, easy-to-read introduction to the history of astronomy from the ancient Greeks to Galileo. (Rev: SLJ 4/95) [523]

**14652** Asimov, Isaac, and Greg Walz-Chojnacki. *The Birth of Our Universe* (3–4). Illus. Series: Isaac Asimov's New Library of the Universe. 1995, Gareth Stevens LB $19.93 (0-8368-1192-5). 32pp. This brief account describes space outside our solar system, with material on nearby stars, quasars, galactic bubbles, and strings. (Rev: SLJ 4/95) [523]

**14653** Bendick, Jeanne. *The Universe: Think Big!* (2–4). Illus. by Lynne Willey and Mike Roffe. Series: Early Bird Astronomy. 1991, Millbrook LB $19.90 (1-878841-01-7). 32pp. Theories and facts about galaxies and the universe are presented in an easy-to-

read fashion with many illustrations. (Rev: BL 9/1/91; SLJ 8/91) [523.1]

**14654** Bonnet, Bob, and Dan Keen. *Science Fair Projects: Flight, Space and Astronomy* (4–6). Illus. by Frances Zweifel. 1997, Sterling $16.95 (0-8069-9450-9). 95pp. A collection of 53 clever astronomy-related experiments that vary considerably in difficulty and in the nature of the equipment involved. (Rev: SLJ 2/98) [520]

**14655** Bortz, Fred. *Martian Fossils on Earth? The Story of Meteorite ALH 84001* (4–6). Illus. 1997, Millbrook LB $21.40 (0-7613-0270-0). 64pp. The story of the meteorite discovered in Antarctica that hints at the fact that life might have once existed on Mars and the massive scientific investigation that it has caused. (Rev: BL 1/1–15/98; SLJ 3/98) [523.5]

**14656** Ciupik, Larry A. *The Universe* (2–4). Illus. 1987, Raintree Steck-Vaughn paper $4.95 (0-8114-8221-9). 48pp. Difficult-to-understand concepts are well handled in this simple account.

**14657** Couper, Heather, and Nigel Henbest. *Big Bang* (5–8). Illus. 1997, DK Publg. $16.95 (0-7894-1484-8). 45pp. Explains, in double-page spreads, the big-bang theory and its implications for the future. (Rev: BL 6/1–15/97; SLJ 8/97) [523.1]

**14658** Couper, Heather, and Nigel Henbest. *The Space Atlas* (5–8). Illus. by Luciano Corbella. 1992, Harcourt $19.00 (0-15-200598-6). 64pp. An oversize book that gives a guided tour of the solar system and outer space through maps, paintings, photos, and charts. (Rev: SLJ 5/92) [523]

**14659** Fradin, Dennis B. *Astronomy* (1–4). Illus. 1983, Children's LB $21.00 (0-516-01673-3). 48pp. The science is introduced in a simple text, many photographs, and a glossary of terms.

**14660** Fradin, Dennis B. *Searching for Alien Life: Is Anyone Out There?* (5–7). Illus. 1997, Twenty-First

Century $20.40 (0-8050-4573-2). 80pp. A history of space travel is followed by an account of attempts to contact life in space and of recent discoveries. (Rev: SLJ 1/98) [523]

**14661** *Galaxies* (3–6). Illus. Series: Windows on the Universe. 1994, Barron's $12.95 (0-8120-6367-8). 32pp. In a series of double-page spreads and full-color illustrations, galaxies are introduced, with special coverage of the Milky Way. (Rev: BL 4/15/94; SLJ 5/94) [523.1]

**14662** Hirst, Robin, and Sally Hirst. *My Place in Space* (3–4). Illus. by Roland Harvey. 1992, Orchard paper $6.95 (0-531-07030-1). 40pp. A sky show from earth to solar system to the outer reaches of the universe. (Rev: BCCB 3/90; BL 4/1/90; HB 5–6/91; SLJ 4/90) [520]

**14663** Kallen, Stuart A. *Exploring the Origins of the Universe* (4–8). Series: Secrets of Space. 1997, Twenty-First Century LB $20.40 (0-8050-4478-7). 64pp. This account tells in simple terms the various major theories about how the universe was created, including creation stories and the big bang theory. (Rev: BL 9/15/97; SLJ 6/97) [523]

**14664** Lewellen, John. *Moon, Sun and Stars* (2–3). Illus. 1981, Children's paper $5.50 (0-516-41637-5). 48pp. Large type and color photographs are featured in this simple account.

**14665** Maynard, Christopher. *The Young Scientist Book of Stars and Planets* (4–7). Illus. 1978, EDC LB $14.95 (0-88110-313-6); paper $6.95 (0-86020-094-9). 32pp. Attractive illustrations and plentiful experiments and projects add to this book's appeal.

**14666** Miotto, Enrico. *The Universe: Origins and Evolution* (4–5). Illus. Series: Beginnings. 1995, Raintree Steck-Vaughn LB $24.26 (0-8114-3334-X). 48pp. From the Big Bang to the possible Big Crunch, the evolution of the universe is explained, along with a basic history of astronomy. (Rev: BL 4/15/95) [523]

**14667** Mitton, Simon, and Jacqueline Mitton. *The Young Oxford Book of Astronomy* (5–8). Illus. Series: Young Oxford Books. 1998, Oxford paper $16.95 (0-19-521445-5). 160pp. A well-written, lavishly illustrated introduction to astronomy with large fact boxes used for special insights into this topic. (Rev: BL 3/15/96; SLJ 6/96) [520]

**14668** Moche, Dinah L. *Astronomy Today: Planets, Stars, Space Exploration* (5–8). Illus. by Harry McNaught. 1982, Random paper $12.99 (0-394-84423-8). 96pp. A survey of astronomy and space exploration.

**14669** Moeschl, Richard. *Exploring the Sky: 100 Projects for Beginning Astronomers* (5–8). Illus. 1992, Chicago Review paper $16.95 (1-55652-160-X). 320pp. Many ideas for experiments and observa-

tions in an information-packed book. (Rev: BL 5/1/89)

**14670** Muirden, James. *Stars and Planets* (4–6). Illus. Series: Visual Factfinder. 1993, Kingfisher paper $10.95 (1-85697-851-6). 93pp. Includes a general introduction to stars and planets and sections on astronomy and space exploration. (Rev: SLJ 2/94) [523]

**14671** Newton, David E. *Black Holes and Supernovae* (4–8). Illus. Series: Secrets of Space. 1997, Twenty-First Century LB $20.40 (0-8050-4477-9). 64pp. A richly illustrated volume that explores theories about black holes and tells the facts concerning them as well as supernovas. (Rev: BL 7/97; SLJ 6/97) [523.8]

**14672** Pearce, Q. L. *The Stargazer's Guide to the Galaxy* (4–8). Illus. by Mary Ann Fraser. 1991, Tor paper $4.99 (0-812-59423-1). 60pp. In this introduction to star gazing in the Northern Hemisphere, material covered includes a look at the night sky in each of the 4 seasons. (Rev: SLJ 12/91) [523]

**14673** Petty, Kate. *The Sun Is a Star: And Other Amazing Facts About the Universe* (1–3). Illus. by Francis Phillips and Ian Thompson. Series: I Didn't Know That. 1997, Millbrook LB $19.90 (0-7613-0567-X). 32pp. As well as introducing the sun, this book describes other parts of the solar system, black holes, the Milky Way, and other parts of the universe. (Rev: SLJ 9/97) [523]

**14674** Schultz, Ron. *Looking Inside Telescopes and the Night Sky* (4–6). Illus. by Nick Gadbois and Peter Aschwanden. Series: X-ray Vision. 1993, John Muir paper $6.95 (1-56261-072-4). 43pp. A rundown of the main optical and radio telescopes as they are today and those proposed for the future. (Rev: SLJ 8/93) [523]

**14675** Shepherd, Donna Walsh. *Auroras: Light Shows in the Night Sky* (4–6). Illus. Series: First Books of Interest. 1995, Watts LB $22.00 (0-531-20181-3); paper $6.95 (0-531-15766-0). 63pp. Provides a definition of auroras plus coverage of where they are found and how they occur. (Rev: SLJ 11/95) [998]

**14676** Simon, Seymour. *The Long View into Space* (3–5). Illus. 1987, Crown $13.95 (0-517-53659-5). A well-organized introduction to the universe, nicely illustrated with photographs.

**14677** Sipiera, Diane M., and Paul P. Sipiera. *The Hubble Space Telescope* (2–4). Illus. Series: True Book: Space. 1997, Children's LB $21.00 (0-516-20442-4). 48pp. As well as describing the Hubble Space Telescope and its uses, this account tells about space explorations that are unsafe for both humans and telescopes. (Rev: BL 12/1/97) [522]

**14678** Steele, Philip. *Astronomy* (4–8). Illus. Series: Pocket Facts. 1991, Macmillan LB $11.95 (0-89686-586-X). 32pp. A concise introduction to astronomy, complemented by color photos and drawings. (Rev: BL 3/15/92) [520]

**14679** Stott, Carole. *Night Sky* (4–6). Illus. Series: Eyewitness Explorers. 1993, DK Publg. $9.95 (1-56458-393-7). 64pp. Outstanding illustrations, good textual material, and numerous activities highlight this introduction to astronomy. (Rev: BL 11/1/93) [520.2]

**14680** Verdet, Jean-Pierre. *The Universe* (PS–2). Illus. Series: First Discovery. 1997, Scholastic $11.95 (0-590-96212-4). 24pp. From the endless cosmos to exploding stars and a view of our blazing sun, this brilliantly illustrated book introduces the universe. (Rev: BL 2/1/98) [520]

**14681** *The Visual Dictionary of the Universe* (4–8). Illus. Series: Eyewitness. 1993, DK Publg. $16.95 (1-56458-335-X). 64pp. Pictures astral bodies from massive galaxies to comets and meteorites plus various telescopes, space exploration equipment, and lunar vehicles. (Rev: BL 12/15/93; SLJ 2/94) [520]

**14682** Vogt, Gregory L. *The Search for the Killer Asteroid* (4–6). Illus. 1994, Millbrook LB $23.90 (1-56294-448-7). 72pp. With some fictional trappings, this account presents the theory that dinosaurs died because of an asteroid's collision with Earth. (Rev: BL 12/1/94; SLJ 1/95) [523.4]

**14683** Wiese, Jim. *Cosmic Science: Over 40 Gravity-Defying, Earth-Orbiting, Space-Cruising Activities for Kids* (4–6). Illus. 1997, Wiley paper $12.95 (0-471-15852-6). 128pp. Principles of astronomy and space technology are explored through a series of engaging projects with common materials that involve topics like gravity, orbits, planets, and space travel. (Rev: BL 7/97; SLJ 7/97) [929.4]

**14684** Wyler, Rose. *The Starry Sky* (K–4). Illus. by Steven J. Petruccio. Series: Outdoor Science. 1989, Simon & Schuster paper $4.95 (0-671-66349-6). 48pp. This book introduces such topics as the earth's rotation, planets, stars, and the phases of the moon. (Rev: SLJ 9/89) [523]

# Earth

**14685** Baker, Wendy, and Andrew Haslam. *Earth* (3–6). Illus. Series: Make It Work! 1993, Macmillan $12.95 (0-689-71662-1). 48pp. Basic concepts about the earth are explained and activities and experiments are provided. (Rev: SLJ 4/93) [551]

**14686** Branley, Franklyn M. *What Makes Day and Night?* (1–3). Illus. by Arthur Dorros. 1986, Harper-Collins paper $4.95 (0-06-445050-3). 32pp. A clear, simple explanation of the rotation of the earth. (Rev: BL 3/15/86; SLJ 9/86)

**14687** Daily, Robert. *Earth* (4–6). Illus. Series: First Books: Solar System. 1994, Watts LB $22.00 (0-531-20158-9). 64pp. Earth's environment, atmosphere, geographical features, and ancient beliefs regarding it are described. (Rev: BL 10/15/94) [525]

**14688** Lauber, Patricia. *How We Learned the Earth Is Round* (K–4). Illus. by Megan Lloyd. 1990, HarperCollins LB $14.89 (0-690-04862-9). 32pp. Showing how perceptions of the earth's shape changed through the years and how it was finally determined. (Rev: BCCB 12/90; BL 10/15/90; HB 11–12/90; SLJ 10/90) [525.1]

**14689** Lauber, Patricia. *Seeing Earth from Space* (3–8). Illus. 1990, Orchard LB $22.99 (0-531-08502-3). 80pp. In a series of photographs taken from the moon and beyond, secrets of our earth are revealed. (Rev: BCCB 9/90; BL 8/90; HB 3–4/91; SLJ 8/90) [525]

**14690** Nicolson, Cynthia P. *The Earth* (2–5). Illus. Series: Starting with Space. 1997, Kids Can $12.95 (1-55074-314-7). 40pp. Appropriate folktales and projects are included, along with information about the Earth and night and day. (Rev: BL 9/1/97; SLJ 9/97) [525]

**14691** *Our Planet: Earth* (3–6). Illus. Series: Windows on the Universe. 1994, Barron's $12.95 (0-8120-6368-6). 32pp. Traces the origins of Earth, its present composition, and the ways in which it is still changing. (Rev: BL 4/15/94; SLJ 5/94) [525]

**14692** Ride, Sally, and Tam O'Shaughnessy. *The Third Planet: Exploring the Earth from Space* (4–7). Illus. 1994, Crown LB $19.99 (0-517-59362-9). 48pp. This book allows viewers to see the planets, including Earth, from a vantage point in space. (Rev: BCCB 6/94; BL 7/94*; HB 7–8/94; SLJ 7/94) [525]

**14693** Vogt, Gregory L. *Earth* (2–4). Illus. Series: Gateway Solar System. 1996, Millbrook LB $19.90 (1-56294-602-1). 32pp. A beginning introduction to Earth, its composition, and its place in the solar system. (Rev: BL 4/15/96; SLJ 5/96) [550]

# Moon

**14694** Asimov, Isaac. *The Moon* (3–5). Illus. Series: Isaac Asimov's New Library of the Universe. 1994, Gareth Stevens LB $19.93 (0-8368-1131-3). 32pp. Explores theories of the origin of the moon, its phases and composition, moon landings, and possible colonies. (Rev: BL 2/15/95) [523.3]

**14695** Asimov, Isaac. *Why Does the Moon Change Shape?* (1–3). Illus. Series: Ask Isaac Asimov. 1991, Stevens LB $19.93 (0-8368-0438-4). 24pp. This book gives a simple description of the moon's phases and explains why they take place. (Rev: SLJ 3/92) [523.3]

**14696** Bourgeois, Paulette. *The Moon* (3–4). Illus. by Bill Slavin. Series: Starting with Space. 1997, Kids Can $12.95 (1-55074-157-8). 40pp. This introduction to the moon includes material on its features, phases, and tides, important lunar landings, and legends about the moon from around the world. (Rev: SLJ 9/97) [523.3]

**14697** Branley, Franklyn M. *The Moon Seems to Change* (2–4). Illus. by Barbara Emberley and Ed Emberley. 1987, HarperCollins paper $4.95 (0-06-445065-1). 32pp. A clear text that discusses our ever-changing knowledge about the moon. (Rev: BL 11/1/87; SLJ 9/87)

**14698** Branley, Franklyn M. *What the Moon Is Like* (1–3). Illus. by True Kelley. 1986, HarperCollins paper $4.95 (0-06-445052-X). 32pp. A description of the moon's composition information gathered from Apollo space missions. (Rev: BL 3/15/86; SLJ 9/86)

**14699** Fowler, Allan. *So That's How the Moon Changes Shape!* (1–2). Illus. Series: Rookie Read-About Science. 1991, Children's LB $18.50 (0-516-04917-8). 32pp. The phases of the moon are introduced in minimal text and many color photographs. (Rev: BL 4/1/92) [523.3]

**14700** Gardner, Robert. *Science Project Ideas About the Moon* (4–7). Illus. Series: Science Project Ideas. 1997, Enslow LB $18.95 (0-89490-844-8). 96pp. After giving basic information about the moon, this book outlines projects involving ways of observing the moon and how to make models to show its movements. (Rev: BL 12/1/97) [523.3]

**14701** Gibbons, Gail. *The Moon Book* (2–4). Illus. 1997, Holiday LB $15.95 (0-8234-1297-0). 32pp. An introductory description of the moon, its orbit and phases, its place in eclipses, and its effects of the Earth's oceans. (Rev: BCCB 7–8/97; BL 5/1/97; SLJ 4/97) [523.3]

**14702** Krupp, E. C. *The Moon and You* (3–6). Illus. by Robin R. Krupp. 1993, Macmillan LB $13.95 (0-02-751142-1). 48pp. In picture book format, this account covers all the basic facts about the moon, including its formation, phases, and exploration. (Rev: BL 11/1/93; SLJ 2/94) [523.3]

**14703** *Our Satellite: The Moon* (3–6). Illus. Series: Window on the Universe. 1994, Barron's $12.95 (0-8120-6369-4). 32pp. In double-page spreads, features of the moon are explained, such as lunar eclipses and the appearance of the moon's far side. (Rev: BL 4/15/94; SLJ 5/94) [523.3]

**14704** Rosen, Sidney. *Where Does the Moon Go?* (2–4). Illus. 1992, Carolrhoda LB $14.95 (0-87614-685-X). 40pp. In excellent photos, clever illustrations, and simple text, the moon and its phases are introduced. (Rev: SLJ 11/92) [523.3]

**14705** Simon, Seymour. *The Moon* (3–6). Illus. 1984, Macmillan LB $16.00 (0-02-782840-9). 32pp. A simple description of the moon and its effect on earth.

# Planets

**14706** Asimov, Isaac. *A Distant Puzzle: The Planet Uranus* (3–5). Illus. Series: Isaac Asimov's New Library of the Universe. 1994, Gareth Stevens LB $19.93 (0-8368-1136-4). 32pp. This updated edition of an introduction to Uranus includes a report on the findings of *Voyager 2*. (Rev: BL 2/15/95) [523.4]

**14707** Asimov, Isaac. *The Red Planet: Mars* (3–5). Illus. Series: Isaac Asimov's New Library of the Universe. 1994, Gareth Stevens LB $19.93 (0-8368-1132-1). 32pp. This richly illustrated account concentrates on the findings of the Mars probes from 1962 through 1992 and speculates on possible futuristic colonies. (Rev: BL 2/15/95) [523.4]

**14708** Bendick, Jeanne. *The Planets: Neighbors in Space* (2–4). Illus. by Mike Roffe. Series: Early Bird Astronomy. 1991, Millbrook LB $19.90 (1-878841-03-3). 32pp. The planets are introduced in a simple, basic text and full-color artwork. (Rev: BL 9/1/91; SLJ 8/91) [523.4]

**14709** Berger, Melvin. *Discovering Jupiter: The Amazing Collision in Space* (3–6). Illus. by Tom Leonard. 1995, Scholastic paper $4.95 (0-590-48824-4). 55pp. After covering the general facts we know about Jupiter, this account tells of the Comet Shoemaker-Levy 9 and its crash into the planet. (Rev: SLJ 3/96) [523.4]

**14710** Fowler, Allan. *The Sun's Family of Planets* (1–2). Illus. Series: Rookie Read-About Science. 1992, Children's LB $18.50 (0-516-06004-X); paper $4.95 (0-516-46004-8). 32pp. The planets are introduced in full-color photos and minimal text. This simple book is also available in an oversized "Big Book" edition. (Rev: BL 12/15/92) [523.4]

**14711** Fradin, Dennis B. *The Planet Hunters: The Search for Other Worlds* (5–8). Illus. 1997, Simon & Schuster paper $19.95 (0-689-81323-6). 160pp. This well-researched book traces how we discovered each of the planets and how we were made aware that the Earth is also a planet. (Rev: BL 12/1/97*; SLJ 1/98) [523.4]

**14712** Getz, David. *Life on Mars* (3–5). Illus. Series: Redfeather. 1997, Holt $14.95 (0-8050-3708-X). 70pp. A simple description of a trip to Mars and what the reader would find there. (Rev: BL 5/15/97; SLJ 6/97) [574]

**14713** Gibbons, Gail. *The Planets* (K–3). Illus. 1993, Holiday LB $15.95 (0-8234-1040-4). 32pp. In a well-illustrated format, this is a good introduction to the planets of our solar system. (Rev: BL 12/15/93; SLJ 10/93) [523.4]

**14714** Kelch, Joseph W. *Millions of Miles to Mars: A Journey to the Red Planet* (4–6). Illus. by Connell P. Byrne. 1995, Messner $16.95 (0-671-88249-X); paper $9.95 (0-671-88250-3). 121pp. A make-believe journey to the Red Planet reveals what we know and do not know about Mars. (Rev: SLJ 9/95) [523.4]

**14715** Landau, Elaine. *Jupiter* (4–6). Illus. Series: First Books. 1991, Watts LB $21.00 (0-531-20015-9). 64pp. A basic introduction to the largest planet and the Galileo mission launched in 1989. (Rev: BL 6/15/91; SLJ 8/91) [523.4]

**14716** Landau, Elaine. *Mars* (4–6). Illus. Series: First Books. 1991, Watts LB $21.00 (0-531-20012-4). 64pp. Current knowledge plus speculation about the red planet. (Rev: BL 6/15/91; SLJ 8/91) [523.4]

**14717** Landau, Elaine. *Neptune* (4–6). Illus. Series: First Books. 1991, Watts LB $21.00 (0-531-20014-0). 64pp. Using information from the 1989 Voyager 2 mission, this account introduces this distant planet and its surrounding moons. (Rev: BL 6/15/91; SLJ 8/91) [523.4]

**14718** Landau, Elaine. *Saturn* (4–6). Illus. Series: First Books. 1991, Watts LB $21.00 (0-531-20013-2). 64pp. The second largest planet is introduced with material on its atmosphere, rings, moons, and the discoveries from the Pioneer II, Voyager I, and Voyager II spacecraft missions. (Rev: BL 6/15/91; SLJ 7/91) [523.4]

**14719** Lauber, Patricia. *Journey to the Planets* (5–8). Illus. 1993, Crown LB $16.99 (0-517-58125-6). 90pp. Information on and insights into the solar system. (Rev: BL 1/1/91) [523.4]

**14720** Moore, Patrick. *The Planets* (K–3). Illus. Series: Starry Sky. 1995, Millbrook LB $18.90 (1-56294-624-2). 24pp. The size and makeup of the planets are discussed in this beginning astronomy book that also looks at the possibility of interplanetary travel. (Rev: SLJ 7/95) [523.4]

**14721** Schloss, Muriel. *Venus* (4–6). Illus. Series: First Books. 1991, Watts LB $21.00 (0-531-20019-1). 64pp. A lively discussion of what we know about Venus and what we think we know. (Rev: BL 6/15/91; SLJ 7/91) [523.4]

**14722** Schraff, Anne. *Are We Moving to Mars?* (3–4). Illus. by Michael Carroll. 1996, John Muir paper $6.95 (1-56261-310-3). 32pp. This account answers the question "What would living on Mars be like?" (Rev: SLJ 2/97) [523.4]

**14723** Shepherd, Donna Walsh. *Uranus* (4–6). Illus. Series: First Books: Solar System. 1994, Watts LB $21.00 (0-531-20167-8). 64pp. From its discovery in 1787 to present-day findings, this book looks at the seventh planet in our solar system. (Rev: BL 10/15/94) [523.4]

**14724** Simon, Seymour. *Jupiter* (2–4). Illus. 1988, Morrow $16.00 (0-688-05796-9); paper $5.95 (0-688-08403-6). 32pp. A detailed look at Jupiter, enhanced by photographs taken mostly from un-manned spacecraft. (Rev: BCCB 12/85; BL 9/15/85; SLJ 10/85)

**14725** Simon, Seymour. *Mars* (2–5). Illus. 1987, Morrow LB $17.93 (0-688-06585-6); paper $5.95 (0-688-09928-9). 32pp. Lucid text and spectacular photos highlight this detailed study of the red planet. (Rev: BL 10/15/87; HB 11–12/87; SLJ 12/87)

**14726** Simon, Seymour. *Mercury* (3–5). Illus. 1992, Morrow LB $16.93 (0-688-10545-9). 24pp. Eye-catching design and illustrations help focus on the planet Mercury. (Rev: BCCB 5/92; BL 3/15/92; HB 5–6/92; SLJ 4/92) [523.4]

**14727** Simon, Seymour. *Neptune* (4–8). Illus. 1991, Morrow LB $17.93 (0-688-09632-8). 32pp. The voyage of Voyager II as it swept past the planet Neptune provided scientists with more information on this planet than they had ever had. (Rev: BCCB 4/91; BL 2/15/91; HB 5–6/91; SLJ 4/91) [523.4]

**14728** Simon, Seymour. *Saturn* (2–4). Illus. 1985, Morrow LB $15.93 (0-688-05799-3); paper $5.95 (0-688-08404-4). 32pp. Lots of information about Saturn and its rings, enhanced with color photographs. (Rev: BL 9/15/85; HB 1–2/86; SLJ 10/85)

**14729** Simon, Seymour. *Uranus* (2–5). Illus. 1987, Morrow paper $6.95 (0-688-09929-7). 32pp. Descriptions and photos of its 5 moons highlight this look at Uranus, which was not recognized as a planet until 1781. (Rev: BL 10/15/87; HB 11–12/87; SLJ 12/87)

**14730** Simon, Seymour. *Venus* (3–5). Illus. 1992, Morrow LB $14.93 (0-688-10543-2). 32pp. Basic information, with excellent photos, about Venus and how we learned about it. (Rev: BCCB 5/92; BL 3/15/92; HB 5–6/92; SLJ 4/92) [523.4]

**14731** Vogt, Gregory L. *Mars* (3–6). Illus. Series: Gateway Solar System. 1994, Millbrook LB $19.90 (1-56294-392-8). 31pp. Color and black-and-white photos and drawings highlight this introduction to Mars and its geography. Also use *Pluto* (1994). (Rev: BL 7/94; SLJ 5/94) [523.4]

**14732** Vogt, Gregory L. *Mercury* (3–6). Illus. Series: Gateway Solar System. 1994, Millbrook LB $19.90 (1-56294-390-1). 32pp. A useful introduction to the planet Mercury that includes material on Project Mariner and its findings. (Rev: BL 7/94; SLJ 5/94) [523.4]

**14733** Vogt, Gregory L. *Neptune* (3–5). Illus. Series: Gateway Solar System. 1993, Millbrook LB $19.90 (1-56294-331-6). 32pp. An overview of the composition, atmosphere, and satellites of the planet next-to-last from our sun. (Rev: SLJ 11/93) [523.2]

**14734** Vogt, Gregory L. *Pluto* (2–4). Illus. Series: Gateway Solar System. 1994, Millbrook LB $19.90 (1-56294-393-6). 32pp. This introduction to Pluto describes its origins plus a history of what we know about it and things we should find out in the future. Also use *Venus* (1994). (Rev: BL 7/94; SLJ 5/94) [523.1]

**14735** Vogt, Gregory L. *Saturn* (3–5). Illus. Series: Gateway Solar System. 1993, Millbrook LB $19.90 (1-56294-332-4). 32pp. This introduction to Saturn includes material on its cloud layers, magnetic field, and thousands of rings. (Rev: SLJ 11/93) [523.2]

**14736** Vogt, Gregory L. *Uranus* (3–5). Illus. Series: Gateway Solar System. 1993, Millbrook LB $19.90 (1-56294-330-8). 32pp. Sharp, full-color illustrations and a brief text introduce the salient features of Uranus, including its moons, rings, and atmosphere. (Rev: SLJ 11/93) [523.2]

## Solar System

**14737** Alessandrello, Anna. *The Earth: Origins and Evolution* (4–8). Illus. Series: Beginnings. 1995, Raintree Steck-Vaughn LB $24.26 (0-8114-3331-5). 48pp. An oversized book that discusses with lavish illustrations the theories concerning the formation of the earth, its structure and composition, and ways in which it is changing. (Rev: BL 4/15/95; SLJ 6/95) [550]

**14738** Aronson, Billy. *Eclipses: Nature's Blackouts* (4–7). Illus. Series: First Books: Science. 1996, Watts LB $22.00 (0-531-20238-0). 63pp. An introduction to both solar and lunar eclipses, with interesting historical information. (Rev: SLJ 3/97) [523.3]

**14739** Aronson, Billy. *Meteors: The Truth Behind Shooting Stars* (4–6). Illus. 1996, Watts LB $21.00 (0-531-20242-9). 63pp. A useful manual that explains the differences between meteors, meteorites, and meteoroids, with general information on their composition and when they can be seen. (Rev: BL 2/15/97; SLJ 3/97) [523.5]

**14740** Asimov, Isaac. *How Did We Find Out About Comets?* (5–7). Illus. 1975, Walker LB $10.85 (0-8027-6204-2). 64pp. The history of comets, their nature, and their effects on people are covered in this overview.

**14741** Asimov, Isaac. *Our Planetary System* (3–5). Illus. Series: Isaac Asimov's New Library of the Universe. 1994, Gareth Stevens LB $19.93 (0-8368-1134-8). 32pp. A clear, well-illustrated account of the formation of the sun and our solar system, the composition of the planets, and a glimpse at the distant future. (Rev: BL 2/15/95; SLJ 2/95) [523.7]

**14742** Asimov, Isaac. *The Sun and Its Secrets* (3–5). Illus. Series: Isaac Asimov's New Library of the Universe. 1994, Gareth Stevens LB $19.93 (0-8368-1135-6). 32pp. This account includes information on the history of sun worship, how we have probed the sun's secrets, and how its resources can be harnessed. (Rev: BL 2/15/95) [523.7]

**14743** Asimov, Isaac. *What Is a Shooting Star?* (1–3). Illus. Series: Ask Isaac Asimov. 1991, Stevens LB $19.93 (0-8368-0436-8). 24pp. This book explains in simple terms what meteors and meteorites are. Also use: *Why Do Stars Twinkle?* (1991). (Rev: SLJ 3/92) [523]

**14744** Bendick, Jeanne. *Comets and Meteors: Visitors from Space* (2–4). Illus. by Mike Roffe. Series: Early Bird Astronomy. 1991, Millbrook LB $19.90 (1-56294-001-5). 32pp. This introduction to comets and meteors is enlivened with many full-color illustrations. (Rev: BL 11/15/91) [523.6]

**14745** Bendick, Jeanne. *Moons and Rings* (2–4). Illus. by Mike Roffe. Series: Early Bird Astronomy. 1991, Millbrook LB $19.90 (1-56294-000-7). 32pp. The concept of satellite moon is explained and examples are shown within our solar system. (Rev: BL 11/15/91) [523.3]

**14746** Branley, Franklyn M. *Comets* (K–3). Illus. by Giulio Maestro. 1984, HarperCollins LB $14.89 (0-690-04415-1). 32pp. A discussion of comets, including Halley's, the most famous of all.

**14747** Branley, Franklyn M. *The Sun and the Solar System* (4–6). Illus. Series: Secrets of Space. 1996, Twenty-First Century LB $20.40 (0-8050-4475-2). 80pp. Traces the origin of the solar system and the place of Earth and Moon within it. (Rev: BL 12/15/96; SLJ 1/97) [523.2]

**14748** Dickinson, Terence. *Other Worlds: A Beginner's Guide to Planets and Moons* (4–8). Illus. 1995, Firefly LB $19.95 (1-895565-71-5); paper $9.95 (1-895565-70-7). 64pp. An entertaining introduction to the solar system, the planets, and the most important moons. (Rev: BL 11/15/95; SLJ 1/96) [523.4]

**14749** Freeman, Mae, and Ira Freeman. *The Sun, the Moon and the Stars* (2–4). Illus. 1979, Random $8.95

(0-394-80110-5). The easy first look at astronomy in a revised edition.

**14750** Gustafson, John. *Planets, Moons and Meteors: The Young Stargazer's Guide to the Galaxy* (4–8). Illus. 1992, Simon & Schuster LB $12.95 (0-671-72534-3); paper $6.95 (0-671-72535-1). 64pp. Studying the solar system by observing the moon, planets, and meteors, plus basic information on the planets. (Rev: BL 11/1/92) [523]

**14751** Hansen, Rosanna, and Robert A. Bell. *My First Book About Space* (3–6). Illus. 1985, Simon & Schuster paper $13.00 (0-671-60262-4). The solar system is explained, including each planet, discussed in terms of appearance, atmosphere, orbit, and revolutions. (Rev: BCCB 7–8/86; BL 12/1/85; SLJ 2/86)

**14752** Harris, Alan, and Paul Weissman. *The Great Voyager Adventure: A Guided Tour Through the Solar System* (4–8). Illus. 1990, Simon & Schuster LB $16.95 (0-671-72538-6). 80pp. An introduction to the missions and discoveries of the Voyager spacecraft. (Rev: BL 2/1/91; SLJ 2/91) [523.4]

**14753** Kelch, Joseph W. *Small Worlds: Exploring the 60 Moons of Our Solar System* (4–8). Illus. 1990, Simon & Schuster LB $16.95 (0-671-70013-8). 160pp. General information about moons, asteroids, and comets, plus a guided tour of the 60 known moons. (Rev: BL 8/90) [523.9]

**14754** Kraske, Robert. *Asteroids: Invaders from Space* (5–7). Illus. 1995, Simon & Schuster $15.00 (0-689-31860-X). 90pp. A history of these cosmic wanderers, their formation, and the results, positive and negative, when they collide with earth. (Rev: BCCB 11/95; BL 7/95; SLJ 9/95) [523.4]

**14755** Leedy, Loreen. *Postcards from Pluto: A Tour of the Solar System* (1–3). Illus. 1993, Holiday LB $15.95 (0-8234-1000-5). 32pp. A group of children are introduced to the solar system via a spaceship tour conducted by a robot, Dr. Quasar. (Rev: BL 10/15/93; SLJ 10/93) [523.2]

**14756** Marsh, Carole. *Asteroids, Comets, and Meteors* (4–6). Illus. Series: Secrets of Space. 1996, Twenty-First Century LB $20.40 (0-8050-4473-6). 64pp. The history of our knowledge of these bodies from outer space is traced, with descriptions of the nature of each. (Rev: BL 12/15/96; SLJ 1/97) [523.4]

**14757** Moore, Patrick. *Comets and Shooting Stars* (K–3). Illus. Series: Starry Sky. 1995, Millbrook LB $18.90 (1-56294-625-0). 24pp. An attractive beginning astronomy book that describes the composition and orbits of comets and shooting stars. (Rev: SLJ 7/95) [523.5]

**14758** Moore, Patrick. *The Sun and Moon* (K–3). Illus. Series: Starry Sky. 1995, Millbrook LB $18.90 (1-56294-622-6). 24pp. A description of the sun and moon is given, with an explanation of their movements and eclipses. (Rev: SLJ 7/95) [523]

**14759** Poynter, Margaret. *Killer Asteroids* (3–6). Illus. Series: Weird and Wacky Science. 1996, Enslow LB $18.95 (0-89490-616-X). 48pp. Violent clashes involving asteroids and the earth are described, along with coverage of the recent encounter of a comet with Jupiter. (Rev: SLJ 5/96) [551.3]

**14760** Rosen, Sidney. *Can You Catch a Falling Star?* (2–4). Illus. by Dean Lindberg. Series: A Question of Science. 1996, Carolrhoda LB $19.93 (0-87614-882-8). 40pp. A simple question-and-answer book that examines meteors, what happens when they fall to earth, and where and when to look for meteorite showers. (Rev: SLJ 4/96) [523.5]

**14761** Rosen, Sidney. *Can You Hitch a Ride on a Comet?* (1–3). Illus. by Dean Lindberg. Series: A Question of Science. 1993, Carolrhoda LB $19.93 (0-87614-773-2). 40pp. Using a question-and-answer format, all sorts of information is given about comets, including their formation, discovery, and tracking. (Rev: BL 10/15/93) [525.6]

**14762** Simon, Seymour. *Comets, Meteors, and Asteroids* (3–5). Illus. 1994, Morrow LB $14.93 (0-688-12710-X). 32pp. These 3 space bodies are described, with material on their composition and differences. (Rev: BL 9/15/94; SLJ 8/94) [523.6]

**14763** Simon, Seymour. *Our Solar System* (2–6). Illus. 1992, Morrow LB $19.93 (0-688-09993-9). 72pp. A quick tour of the solar system, with many of NASA's striking photos. (Rev: BL 10/15/92; HB 11–12/92; SLJ 10/92) [523.2]

**14764** Sipiera, Paul P. *Comets and Meteor Showers* (2–4). Illus. Series: True Books: Space. 1997, Children's LB $21.00 (0-516-20330-4). 48pp. Large print and clear diagrams highlight this description of comets and the way they have been regarded through history. (Rev: BL 9/15/97) [523.6]

**14765** Sipiera, Paul P. *The Solar System* (2–4). Illus. Series: True Books: Space. 1997, Children's $21.00 (0-516-20339-8). 48pp. A brief informative introduction to the solar system, with excellent graphics and a large-print text. (Rev: BL 9/15/97) [523.2]

**14766** Spangenburg, Ray, and Diane Moser. *Exploring the Reaches of the Solar System* (5–8). Illus. 1990, Facts on File $22.95 (0-8160-1850-2). 109pp. An overview of the solar system. (Rev: SLJ 12/90) [523.4]

**14767** Vogt, Gregory L. *Asteroids, Comets, and Meteors* (2–4). Illus. Series: Gateway Solar System. 1996, Millbrook LB $19.90 (1-56294-601-3). 32pp. A beginning introduction to these unusual celestial bodies and their characteristics. (Rev: BL 4/15/96; SLJ 5/96) [523.6]

**14768** Vogt, Gregory L. *The Solar System: Facts and Exploration* (5–8). Illus. Series: Scientific American Sourcebook. 1995, Twenty-First Century LB $22.40 (0-8050-3249-5). 96pp. As well as describing the planets, moons, and small astral bodies, this account gives a history of the space program. (Rev: BL 12/1/95; SLJ 11/95) [523.2]

## Stars

**14769** Apfel, Necia H. *Orion, the Hunter* (3–6). Illus. 1995, Clarion $16.95 (0-395-68962-7). 48pp. The constellation Orion and its separate nebulae are introduced, described, and pictured. (Rev: BL 12/1/95; SLJ 11/95) [523.8]

**14770** Bendick, Jeanne. *The Stars: Lights in the Night Sky* (2–4). Illus. by Chris Forsey. Series: Early Bird Astronomy. 1991, Millbrook LB $19.90 (1-878841-00-9). 32pp. Ideas and theories about stars and their formation are presented in a clear and simple text and with many diagrams. (Rev: BL 9/1/91; SLJ 8/91) [523.8]

**14771** Berger, Melvin, and Gilda Berger. *Where Are the Stars During the Day? A Book About Stars* (3–5). Illus. by Blanche Sims. Series: Discovery Readers. 1993, Ideals LB $12.00 (0-8249-8644-X); paper $4.50 (0-8249-8607-5). 48pp. An easy-to-read book that introduces the stars, sun, and constellations. (Rev: BCCB 4/93; SLJ 5/93) [523]

**14772** Branley, Franklyn M. *The Big Dipper* (K–2). Illus. by Ed Emberley. 1991, HarperCollins paper $4.95 (0-06-445100-3). 32pp. An introduction to the composition, mythology, and location of the Big and Little Dippers.

**14773** Branley, Franklyn M. *The Sky Is Full of Stars* (2–4). Illus. by Felicia Bond. 1981, HarperCollins paper $4.95 (0-06-445002-3). 40pp. A simple introduction to constellations and star watching.

**14774** Branley, Franklyn M. *Star Guide* (4–6). Illus. by Ellen Eagle. 1997, Macmillan paper $9.10 (0-028-62019-4). 64pp. An exploration of what stars are made of, how they change, and how they are formed. (Rev: BL 8/87; SLJ 9/87)

**14775** Clay, Rebecca. *Stars and Galaxies* (4–8). Series: Secrets of Space. 1997, Twenty-First Century LB $20.40 (0-8050-4476-0). 64pp. This account describes the birth and death of stars and gives a description of galaxies and their composition. (Rev: BL 9/15/97; SLJ 6/97) [523.8]

**14776** Dussling, Jennifer. *Stars* (PS–2). Illus. by Mavis Smith. Series: All Aboard Reading. 1996, Grosset LB $13.99 (0-448-41149-0); paper $3.99 (0-448-41148-2). 32pp. A beginning reader that intro-

duces stars and constellations. (Rev: SLJ 8/96) [523.8]

**14777** Gibbons, Gail. *Stargazers* (1–3). Illus. 1992, Holiday LB $15.95 (0-8234-0983-X). 32pp. With full-color artwork, the author explains what stars are and how we look at them. (Rev: BCCB 1/93; BL 10/15/92; SLJ 10/92) [520]

**14778** Gustafson, John. *Stars, Clusters and Galaxies* (5–8). Illus. Series: Young Stargazer's Guide to the Galaxy. 1993, Simon & Schuster LB $12.98 (0-671-72536-X); paper $6.95 (0-671-72537-8). 64pp. Information about stars, clusters, nebulae, and galaxies, plus tips on effective stargazing. (Rev: BL 7/93; SLJ 6/93) [523.8]

**14779** Jobb, Jamie. *The Night Sky Book* (5–8). Illus. by Linda Bennett. 1977, Little, Brown paper $12.95 (0-316-46552-6). A primer for novice stargazers.

**14780** Krupp, E. C. *The Big Dipper and You* (K–3). Illus. by Robin R. Krupp. 1989, Morrow LB $15.93 (0-688-07192-9). 48pp. An introduction to this constellation, its individual stars, and its use in locating the North Star. (Rev: SLJ 10/89) [523]

**14781** Levy, David H., ed. *Stars and Planets* (4–6). Illus. Series: Nature Company Discoveries. 1996, Time Life $16.00 (0-8094-9246-6). 64pp. Stars and planets are introduced with handsome illustrations and a brief text plus an unusual final 8-page foldout. (Rev: BL 6/1–15/96) [523.2]

**14782** Moore, Patrick. *The Stars* (K–3). Illus. Series: Starry Sky. 1995, Millbrook LB $18.90 (1-56294-623-4). 24pp. A beginning astronomy book that describes the birth and death of stars and the composition of the Milky Way and other galaxies. (Rev: SLJ 7/95) [523.8]

**14783** Rey, H. A. *Find the Constellations* (5–7). Illus. 1976, Houghton $20.00 (0-395-24509-5); paper $9.95 (0-395-24418-8). 80pp. Through clear text and illustrations, the reader is helped to recognize stars and constellations in the northern United States. Also use: *The Stars: A New Way to See Them* (1973).

**14784** Rosen, Sidney. *Where's the Big Dipper?* (2–4). Illus. by Dean Lindberg. Series: A Question of Science. 1996, Carolrhoda $14.95 (0-87614-883-6). 40pp. In a question-and-answer format, this book supplies a simple introduction to deep space, with a focus on the Big Dipper. (Rev: SLJ 4/96) [523]

**14785** Santrey, Laurence. *Discovering the Stars* (1–3). Illus. by James Watling. 1982, Troll LB $12.95 (0-89375-568-0); paper $3.50 (0-89375-569-9). 32pp. A simple book that tells about galaxies, constellations, and other astral bodies.

**14786** Simon, Seymour. *Galaxies* (2–5). Illus. 1988, Morrow LB $15.93 (0-688-08004-9); paper $6.95 (0-688-10992-6). 32pp. Engrossing photographs highlight this look at galaxies. (Rev: BCCB 4/88; BL 3/1/88; SLJ 5/88)

**14787** Simon, Seymour. *The Stars* (3–5). Illus. 1986, Morrow LB $16.93 (0-688-05856-6); paper $5.95 (0-688-09237-3). 32pp. Large photos and diagrams highlight the story of the life cycles of stars, giving a sense of their great numbers and relationship to earth. (Rev: BCCB 10/86; BL 9/1/86; SLJ 12/86)

**14788** Sipiera, Diane M., and Paul P. Sipiera. *Constellations* (2–4). Series: True Books: Space. 1997, Children's LB $21.00 (0-516-20331-2). 48pp. A simple, basic introduction to constellations in a highly accessible format. Also use *Black Holes, Galaxies, and Stars* (all 1997). (Rev: BL 9/15/97) [523]

**14789** Zim, Herbert S., and Robert H. Baker. *Stars* (5–8). Illus. by James G. Irving. 1985, Western paper $5.50 (0-307-24493-8). A guide to the constellations, sun, moon, planets and other features of the heavens.

## Sun and the Seasons

**14790** Allison, Linda. *The Reasons for Seasons* (5–7). Illus. by author. 1975, Little, Brown paper $11.95 (0-316-03440-1). 128pp. A project-experiment book that also contains fascinating information about the 4 seasons.

**14791** Bendick, Jeanne. *The Sun: Our Very Own Star* (2–4). Illus. by Mike Roffe. Series: Early Bird Astronomy. 1991, Millbrook LB $19.90 (1-878841-02-5). Astronomy is presented in simple terms and with colorful illustrations. (Rev: BL 9/1/91; SLJ 8/91) [523.4]

**14792** Bourgeois, Paulette. *The Sun* (2–5). Illus. Series: Starting with Space. 1997, Kids Can $12.95 (1-55074-158-6). 40pp. As well as providing information about the sun, stars, and the seasons, this work contains folktales and projects. (Rev: BL 9/1/97; SLJ 9/97) [523.7]

**14793** Branley, Franklyn M. *The Sun: Our Nearest Star* (1–3). Illus. by Don Madden. 1988, Harper-Collins LB $14.89 (0-690-04678-2). 32pp. An easily read book about the sun and its importance in our lives. Update of 1962 edition.

**14794** Branley, Franklyn M. *Sunshine Makes the Seasons* (3–4). Illus. by Giulio Maestro. 1988, HarperCollins paper $4.95 (0-06-445019-8). 32pp. A very simple account that explains the seasons by exploring the relationship of the sun to the earth and its orbit. Update of 1974 edition.

**14795** Fowler, Allan. *How Do You Know It's Fall?* (1–2). Illus. Series: Rookie Read-About Science. 1992, Children's LB $18.50 (0-516-04922-4). 32pp. For beginning readers, the season of autumn is intro-

duced in many color photos and brief text. (Rev: BL 6/15/92) [508]

**14796** Fowler, Allan. *How Do You Know It's Summer?* (1–2). Illus. Series: Rookie Read-About Science. 1992, Children's LB $18.50 (0-516-04923-2). 32pp. Summer and its characteristics are introduced in many color illustrations and minimal text. (Rev: BL 6/15/92) [508]

**14797** Fowler, Allan. *The Sun Is Always Shining Somewhere* (1–2). Illus. Series: Rookie Read-About Science. 1991, Children's LB $18.50 (0-516-04906-2). 32pp. This simple introduction to astronomy tells about the sun and the earth's rotation around it. (Rev: BL 8/91) [523.7]

**14798** George, Michael. *The Sun* (3–8). Illus. 1997, Child's World LB $17.95 (1-567-66385-0). 40pp. This account covers the structure and activity of the sun as well as its effects on the earth. (Rev: BL 12/15/91; SLJ 7/92) [523.7]

**14799** Gibbons, Gail. *Sun Up, Sun Down* (1–3). Illus. by author. 1983, Harcourt $16.00 (0-15-282781-1); paper $6.00 (0-15-282782-X). 32pp. An introductory account of the sun and its effects on earth.

**14800** Jackson, Ellen. *The Winter Solstice* (2–4). Illus. 1994, Millbrook LB $23.40 (1-56294-400-2). 32pp. The customs and beliefs surrounding the winter solstice are explored in many cultures, e.g., the ancient Britons, Romans, and Peruvians. (Rev: BL 2/15/94; SLJ 4/94) [394.2]

**14801** Markle, Sandra. *Exploring Winter* (3–6). Illus. by author. 1984, Avon paper $2.99 (0-380-71321-7). 160pp. Science and recreation are mixed in this book about winter and activities that are associated with it.

**14802** Simon, Seymour. *Spring Across America* (3–5). Illus. 1996, Hyperion LB $16.49 (0-7868-2056-X). 32pp. A book about spring as it develops in various sections of our country. A sequel to *Autumn Across America* (1993) and *Winter Across America* (1994). (Rev: BL 3/1/96; SLJ 4/96) [508.73]

**14803** Simon, Seymour. *The Sun* (3–5). Illus. 1986, Morrow LB $17.93 (0-688-05858-2); paper $5.95 (0-688-09236-5). 32pp. A look at the structure and atmosphere of this "middle-size" star. (Rev: BCCB 10/86; BL 9/1/86; SLJ 12/86)

**14804** Vogt, Gregory L. *The Sun* (2–4). Illus. Series: Gateway Solar System. 1996, Millbrook LB $19.90 (1-56294-600-5). 32pp. An introduction to the star of our solar system and its life-sustaining force. (Rev: BL 4/15/96; SLJ 7/96) [523.7]

**14805** *Why Do Seasons Change?* (PS–3). Illus. Series: Why. 1997, DK Publg. $9.95 (0-7894-1529-1). 24pp. Using a question-and-answer format, the rotation of the Earth is explained and each season is described. (Rev: BL 8/97) [529]

# Biological Sciences

## General

**14806** Biesiot, Elizabeth. *Natural Treasures Field Guide for Kids* (3–6). Illus. 1996, Roberts Rinehart paper $12.95 (1-57098-082-9). 64pp. A paperback that explains the lives of wild animals by examining such evidence as paw prints, nests, and night sounds. (Rev: BL 9/1/96; SLJ 7/96) [591]

**14807** Björk, Christina. *Linnea's Almanac* (3–5). Trans. by Joan Sandin. Illus. by Lena Anderson. 1989, R&S $13.00 (91-29-59176-7). 60pp. Twelve months of nature lore and activities. (Rev: BL 2/15/90; SLJ 4/90) [508]

**14808** Brimner, Larry Dane. *Unusual Friendships: Symbiosis in the Animal World* (4–6). Illus. 1993, Watts LB $21.00 (0-531-20106-6). 64pp. This book presents the various plant and animal relationships in nature in which the host, the guest, or both benefit. (Rev: BL 8/93) [591]

**14809** Burnie, David. *How Nature Works* (3–8). Illus. 1991, Reader's Digest $24.00 (0-89577-391-0). 190pp. Well-organized science topics give young readers solid explanations at their fingertips. (Rev: BL 11/15/91*; SLJ 12/91*) [508]

**14810** Busch, Phyllis S. *Backyard Safaris: 52 Year-Round Science Adventures* (4–6). Illus. 1995, Simon & Schuster $16.00 (0-689-80302-8); paper $8.95 (0-689-80617-5). 142pp. Fifty-two activities that span the 4 seasons and involve simple nature study projects. (Rev: BL 8/95) [508]

**14811** Doris, Ellen. *Woods, Ponds, and Fields* (4–7). Illus. Series: Real Kids Real Science. 1994, Thames & Hudson $16.95 (0-500-19006-2). 64pp. A book that gives background essays as well as step-by-step directions for nature study projects in all seasons. (Rev: BL 9/1/94) [508]

**14812** Graham-Barber, Lynda. *Toad or Frog, Swamp or Bog? A Big Book of Nature's Confusables* (K–5). Illus. by Alec Gillman. 1994, Four Winds paper $16.00 (0-02-736931-5). 48pp. Twenty sets of common science misunderstandings (e.g., the difference between an alligator and a crocodile) are explained. (Rev: BL 8/94; SLJ 7/94) [508]

**14813** Huber, Carey. *Nature Explorer: A Step-by-Step Guide* (3–6). Illus. 1990, Troll LB $11.89 (0-8167-1953-5); paper $2.95 (0-8167-1954-3). 64pp. Through walks and hikes, this book explains how one can become a student of nature. (Rev: SLJ 4/91) [574]

**14814** Kuhn, Dwight. *My First Book of Nature: How Living Things Grow* (PS–3). Illus. 1993, Scholastic $11.95 (0-590-45502-8). 64pp. Close-ups of 5 plants and 25 animals, from earthworms to humans. (Rev: BL 3/1/93; SLJ 3/93) [574.3]

**14815** Lang, Susan. *Nature in Your Backyard: Simple Activities for Children* (2–4). Illus. 1995, Millbrook LB $22.90 (1-56294-451-7). 48pp. Easy activities and experiments that illustrate the principles of science and nature using the backyard as a laboratory. (Rev: BL 5/1/95; SLJ 7/95) [508]

**14816** Lauber, Patricia. *Who Eats What? Food Chains and Food Webs* (K–3). Illus. by Holly Keller. Series: Let's-Read-and-Find-Out Science. 1995, HarperCollins LB $14.89 (0-06-022982-9); paper $4.95 (0-06-445130-5). 32pp. Food webs and chains as they exist both on land and in the water are explained, with such activities as how to create a food chain for everyday foods like milk. (Rev: BCCB 5/95; BL 5/1/95) [574.5]

**14817** Leslie, Clare W. *Nature All Year Long* (2–5). Illus. 1991, Greenwillow $18.00 (0-688-09183-0). 56pp. Describing the plant and animal life in one habitat during the year. (Rev: BCCB 9/91; BL 12/15/91; SLJ 12/91) [508]

**14818** Martin, Linda. *Watch Them Grow* (PS–1). Illus. 1994, DK Publg. $14.95 (1-56458-458-5). 45pp. This book chronicles the early development of plants, animals that hatch from eggs, and animals that are born alive. (Rev: BL 6/1–15/94; SLJ 8/94) [574]

**14819** Quinlan, Susan. *The Case of the Mummified Pigs and Other Mysteries in Nature* (4–6). Illus. 1995, Boyds Mills $15.95 (1-878093-82-7). 128pp. Fourteen mysteries of science are explored, e.g., why the monarch butterfly is so brightly colored. (Rev: BCCB 3/95; BL 1/1/95; HB 5–6/95; SLJ 3/95) [508]

**14820** Reader's Digest, ed. *ABC's of Nature* (4–8). Illus. 1984, Reader's Digest $25.95 (0-89577-169-1). A question-and-answer format is used on topics about flora and fauna.

**14821** Sandak, Cass R. *Living Fossils* (5–7). 1992, Watts LB $21.00 (0-531-20048-5). 64pp. Gives examples of plants and animals that have lived unchanged through the ages. (Rev: SLJ 7/92) [574]

**14822** Schmid, Eleonore. *The Living Earth* (1–3). Illus. 1994, North-South LB $14.88 (1-55858-299-1). 26pp. An introduction to the varied flora and fauna found on the earth and below its surface. (Rev: BL 2/15/95; SLJ 12/94) [574.5]

**14823** Silver, Donald M. *Backyard: One Small Square* (3–6). Illus. by Patricia J. Wynne. 1993, W. H. Freeman $12.00 (0-7167-6510-1). 48pp. Using a single square of backyard ground, the wide range of plant and animal life found there is explored, with plenty of activities for the amateur naturalist. (Rev: BL 9/15/93) [574.5]

**14824** Smith, Miranda. *Living Earth* (3–8). Illus. Series: Eyewitness Books. 1996, DK Publg. $29.95 (0-7894-0644-6). 192pp. All kinds of plants and animals are introduced, with material on how they adapt to various climatic and geographical conditions. (Rev: SLJ 10/96) [574]

**14825** Sussman, Susan. *Big Friend, Little Friend: A Book About Symbiosis* (2–5). Illus. by Robert James. 1989, Houghton $15.95 (0-395-49701-9). 32pp. Examples from the plant and animal worlds show how 2 organisms can help each other to live. (Rev: BCCB 12/89; BL 12/1/89; SLJ 1/90) [574]

**14826** Tesar, Jenny. *Patterns in Nature: An Overview of the Living World* (5–7). Illus. Series: Our Living World. 1994, Blackbirch LB $18.95 (1-56711-058-4). 64pp. Explains basic principles of biology, observation, and biological classification. (Rev: BL 12/1/94) [574]

**14827** Wilkes, Angela. *My First Nature Book* (1–5). Illus. 1990, Knopf LB $13.99 (0-394-96610-4). 48pp. This beginning nature study book introduces such wonders as seeds, tree buds, and common insects. (Rev: BL 5/1/90) [508]

# Animal Life

## General

**14828** Aaseng, Nathan. *Poisonous Creatures* (4–7). Illus. Series: Scientific American Sourcebooks. 1997, Twenty-First Century $22.40 (0-8050-4690-9). 96pp. This book looks at a number of poisonous creatures, including mollusks, spiders, snakes, and insects, with many divisions into subspecies. (Rev: BL 2/1/98) [591.6]

**14829** Aaseng, Nathan. *Vertebrates* (5–8). Illus. 1993, Watts LB $22.50 (0-531-12551-3). 112pp. An introduction to the world of animals with backbones — fish, amphibians, reptiles, birds, and mammals. (Rev: BL 3/15/94; SLJ 3/94) [596]

**14830** Arnold, Tim. *Natural History from A to Z: A Terrestrial Sampler* (4–6). Illus. 1991, Macmillan LB $15.95 (0-689-50467-5). 61pp. Discusses one scientific topic for each letter of the alphabet. (Rev: BL 10/1/91) [591]

**14831** *Atlas of Animals* (PS–2). Illus. Series: First Discovery. 1996, Scholastic $11.95 (0-590-58280-1). 24pp. Using a highly visual approach, this short book discusses the animals found in the basic regions of the world. (Rev: BL 10/15/96) [591]

**14832** Baillie, Marilyn. *Side by Side: Animals Who Help Each Other* (K–4). Illus. by Romi Caron. Series: Amazing Things Animals Do. 1997, Owl $17.95 (1-895688-56-6); paper $6.95 (1-895688-57-4). 32pp. A simple exploration of symbiotic relationships in nature, like the petrel bird that lives with the tuatara lizard to their mutual benefit. (Rev: BL 5/15/97; SLJ 7/97) [591.52]

**14833** Bischhoff-Miersch, Andrea, and Michael Bischhoff-Miersch. *Do You Know the Difference?* (2–4). Illus. by Christine Faltermayr. 1995, North-South LB $14.88 (1-55858-372-6). 24pp. Twelve similar animals (e.g., the camel and the dromedary) are pictured and their differences explained. (Rev: BCCB 5/95; BL 5/1/95; SLJ 6/95)

**14834** Bix, Cynthia O., and Diana Landau. *Animal Athletes: Olympians of the Wild World* (5–8). Illus. 1996, Andrews & McMeel $15.95 (0-8362-2522-8). 96pp. This account describes 15 of the animal kingdom's record holders for being the strongest, fastest, etc. (Rev: BL 12/1/96; SLJ 2/97) [591]

**14835** Bloyd, Sunni. *Animal Rights* (5–7). 1991, Lucent LB $22.45 (1-56006-114-6). 128pp. This book discusses animal rights as it involves such areas as laboratory animals, farm creatures, hunting targets, and fur-bearing animals. (Rev: SLJ 8/91) [346]

**14836** Burnie, David. *Mammals* (4–6). Illus. Series: Eyewitness Explorers. 1993, DK Publg. $9.95 (1-56458-228-0). 64pp. This book gives examples of various mammals and includes brief information on characteristics and habitats. (Rev: BL 3/1/93) [973.7]

**14837** Chermayeff, Ivan. *Furry Facts* (PS–1). Illus. by author. 1994, Gulliver $10.95 (0-15-230425-8). A heavily illustrated introduction to a number of mammals, each of which is given a double-page spread. Also use *Fishy Facts* (1994). (Rev: SLJ 6/94) [591]

**14838** Cohen, Daniel. *Phantom Animals* (4–5). 1993, Pocket paper $2.99 (0-671-75930-2). 111pp. A collection of true material about ghostly animals. (Rev: SLJ 7/91) [133]

**14839** Creagh, Carson. *Things with Wings* (2–4). Illus. Series: Nature Company Young Discoveries. 1996, Time Life $11.95 (0-7835-4838-9). 32pp. A variety of creatures with wings are pictured in a series of double-page spreads. (Rev: BL 12/15/96; SLJ 12/96) [591]

**14840** Davis, Lee. *The Lifesize Animal Opposites Book* (PS–K). Illus. 1994, DK Publg. $12.95 (1-56458-720-7). 32pp. Using large photos of animals, this nature book explores the concept of simple opposites, like big and little. (Rev: BL 12/1/94; SLJ 4/95) [591]

**14841** De Bourgoing, Pascale. *Under the Ground* (PS–2). Illus. by Danièle Bour. Series: First Discovery Books. 1995, Scholastic $11.95 (0-590-20302-9). Various underground animals like moles and ants are pictured in this spiral-bound book with transparencies. (Rev: SLJ 9/95) [591]

**14842** *Do Bears Give Bear Hugs? First Questions and Answers About Animals* (PS–1). Series: Library of First Questions and Answers. 1994, Time Life $14.95 (0-7835-0870-0). 47pp. A fun book that explores some common questions about animals. (Rev: SLJ 8/94) [591]

**14843** Donnelly, Jane. *Fearsome Hunters of the Wild* (K–4). Illus. 1996, DK Publg. $9.95 (0-7894-1111-3). Double-page spreads introduce such predators as the alligator, shark, eagle, cheetah, tiger, and gray wolf. (Rev: SLJ 1/97) [591]

**14844** Elliott, Leslee. *Mind-Blowing Mammals* (3–6). Illus. Series: Amazing Animals. 1995, Sterling $14.95 (0-8069-1270-7); paper $9.95 (0-8069-1271-5). 64pp. Introduces some amazing mammals with full-color photos on each page. (Rev: SLJ 4/95) [591]

**14845** Emory, Jerry. *Nightprowlers: Everyday Creatures Under Every Night Sky* (4–6). Illus. 1994, Harcourt paper $14.95 (0-15-200694-X). 48pp. After an explanation of the day/night cycle, there are sections on the phases of the moon, the senses of nighttime animals, and an introduction to such creatures as owls and bats. (Rev: BL 11/15/94) [591.5]

**14846** Facklam, Howard, and Margery Facklam. *Parasites* (4–7). Illus. Series: Invaders. 1994, Twenty-First Century LB $18.90 (0-8050-2858-7). 64pp.

Various kinds of parasites, like leeches and tapeworms, are highlighted. (Rev: BL 1/1/95; SLJ 3/95) [574.5]

**14847** Fleisher, Paul. *Life Cycles of a Dozen Diverse Creatures* (4–8). Illus. 1996, Millbrook LB $24.90 (0-7613-0000-7). 80pp. The life cycles of 12 animals — including the oyster, honeybee, penguin, butterfly, and sea horse — are covered, with many color illustrations. (Rev: BL 12/1/96*; SLJ 1/97) [591.3]

**14848** Fowler, Allan. *Animals Under the Ground* (1–3). Series: Rookie Read-About Science. 1997, Children's $18.50 (0-516-20427-0). 32pp. An easy-to-read science book that introduces basic material about such animals as moles. (Rev: BL 12/15/97) [591]

**14849** Fowler, Allan. *It Could Still Be a Mammal* (1–2). Illus. Series: Rookie Read-About Science. 1990, Children's LB $18.50 (0-516-04903-8). 32pp. The nature of mammals and some examples are covered in this easily read science book. (Rev: BL 2/1/91) [599]

**14850** Ganeri, Anita. *The Hunt for Food* (1–5). Illus. Series: Life Cycle. 1997, Millbrook LB $21.40 (0-7613-0304-9). 32pp. This book deals with animals in a meadow and their feeding habits throughout the 4 seasons. (Rev: BL 12/1/97; SLJ 1/98) [577.4]

**14851** George, Jean Craighead. *Animals Who Have Won Our Hearts* (3–6). Illus. 1994, HarperCollins LB $14.89 (0-06-021544-5). 64pp. In 10 short chapters, covers the careers and accomplishments of such famous animals as Koko the gorilla, who learned sign language. (Rev: BL 9/1/94; SLJ 10/94) [599]

**14852** George, Lindsay Barrett. *In the Woods: Who's Been Here?* (PS–2). Illus. 1995, Greenwillow LB $14.93 (0-688-12319-8). 40pp. Two youngsters are able to detect the presence of all sorts of wildlife by examining traces of animal activities during a walk in the woods. (Rev: BCCB 5/95; BL 4/15/95; SLJ 4/95) [591]

**14853** Greenway, Shirley. *Dragons, Dolphins, and Dinosaurs: Wacky Facts About Animals* (3–5). Illus. by Michael Evans. 1993, Whispering Coyote $13.95 (1-879085-83-6). 32pp. A collection of curious facts about animals illustrated with humorous cartoons. (Rev: BL 2/1/94; SLJ 2/94) [591]

**14854** Gunzl, Christiane. *Cave Life* (3–6). Illus. by Frank Greenaway. Series: Look Closer. 1993, DK Publg. $9.95 (1-56458-212-4). 32pp. Animal and plant life in caves are introduced with stunning double-page spreads. (Rev: BL 8/93; SLJ 8/93) [574]

**14855** Halliburton, Warren J. *African Wildlife* (4–6). Illus. Series: Africa Today. 1992, Macmillan LB $13.95 (0-89686-674-2). 48pp. Color photos complement this look at 4 areas — savanna, forest, wetlands, and desert — of wildlife habitat in Africa. (Rev: BL 3/1/93) [591]

**14856** Hanly, Sheila. *The Big Book of Animals* (PS–2). Illus. 1997, DK Publg. $14.95 (0-7894-1485-6). 48pp. In a book arranged by habitat, more than 300 familiar or little-known animals are introduced and pictured. (Rev: BL 7/97) [590]

**14857** Hanna, Jack, and Rick A. Prebeg. *Jungle Jack Hanna's Safari Adventure* (3–5). Illus. 1996, Scholastic $12.95 (0-590-67322-X). 44pp. The animals of Kenya and Uganda are introduced in this handsomely illustrated account. (Rev: BL 10/15/96; SLJ 11/96) [591.96]

**14858** Howell, Judd, ed. *Wildlife California* (4–6). Illus. Series: Chronicle Junior Nature. 1991, Chronicle $9.95 (0-87701-886-3). 56pp. Lots of facts about animal life in 3 types of California parks — coastal, mountain, and desert. (Rev: BL 5/15/91) [596]

**14859** Jenkins, Martin. *Wings, Stings and Wriggly Things* (3–5). Illus. Series: SuperSmarts. 1996, Candlewick $11.99 (0-7636-0036-9). 24pp. Double-page spreads are used to introduce such creatures as butterflies, worms, bees, and snails. (Rev: BL 12/1/96; SLJ 2/97) [595.7]

**14860** Jenkins, Steve. *Biggest, Strongest, Fastest* (PS–3). Illus. 1995, Ticknor $14.95 (0-395-69701-8). 32pp. Double-page collages illustrate some of the animal kingdom's record holders. (Rev: BCCB 6/95; BL 2/1/95*; HB 7–8/95; SLJ 5/95*) [591]

**14861** Kerrod, Robin. *Animal Life* (4–6). Illus. by Ted Evans. Series: Let's Investigate Science. 1994, Marshall Cavendish LB $25.64 (1-85435-623-2). 64pp. Beginning with cells and their functions, the author discusses animal groups, habitats, senses, and reproduction. (Rev: SLJ 4/94) [591.3]

**14862** Kitchen, Bert. *When Hunger Calls* (2–4). Illus. 1994, Candlewick $15.95 (1-56402-316-8). 32pp. The eating habits of 12 creatures, including a vulture and a gazelle-eating python. (Rev: BL 9/1/94; SLJ 12/94) [591.5]

**14863** Kite, L. Patricia. *Blood-Feeding Bugs and Beasts* (4–6). Illus. 1996, Millbrook LB $21.90 (1-56294-599-8). 48pp. Fifteen bloodsuckers are described, including mosquitoes, bed bugs, lice, ticks, assassin bugs, vampire moths, tsetse flies, and bats. (Rev: SLJ 6/96) [591]

**14864** Knapp, Ron. *Bloodsuckers* (3–6). Illus. Series: Weird and Wacky Science. 1996, Enslow LB $18.95 (0-89490-614-3). 48pp. An interesting look at such creatures as vampire bats, leeches, fleas, lice, mosquitoes, and lampreys. (Rev: SLJ 6/96) [591]

**14865** Kneidel, Sally. *Slugs, Bugs, and Salamanders: Discovering Animals in Your Garden* (5–7). Illus. by Anna-Maria L. Crum. 1997, Fulcrum paper $15.95 (1-55591-313-X). 120pp. As well as intro-

ducing backyard insects and other small creatures, this account gives a number of tips on growing healthy flowers and vegetables. (Rev: SLJ 10/97) [595.7]

**14866** Krupinski, Loretta. *Into the Woods: A Woodland Scrapbook* (PS–2). Illus. by author. 1997, HarperCollins LB $15.89 (0-06-026444-6). 31pp. Using a scrapbook approach, this charming picture book introduces the flora and fauna of a forest, retells 3 American Indian legends, and has a section on weather. (Rev: SLJ 5/97) [591]

**14867** LaBonte, Gail. *Leeches, Lampreys, and Other Cold-Blooded Bloodsuckers* (3–6). Illus. Series: First Books. 1991, Watts LB $21.00 (0-531-20027-2). 45pp. The world of slimy, sticky, and pesky parasites that get their proteins from the blood of other animals. (Rev: BL 1/15/92; SLJ 4/92) [591.53]

**14868** Lauber, Patricia. *Fur, Feathers, and Flippers: How Animals Live Where They Do* (4–8). Illus. 1994, Scholastic paper $4.95 (0-590-45072-7). 48pp. Using various habitats such as the grasslands of East Africa as examples, this photoessay describes how animals have adapted to their different environments. (Rev: BL 12/1/94*; SLJ 12/94) [591.5]

**14869** Legg, Gerald. *The X-Ray Picture Book of Amazing Animals* (2–6). Illus. 1994, Watts LB $24.00 (0-531-14285-X). 48pp. Graphic pictures of the inner anatomy of a number of animals, including birds, rats, snakes, tigers, elephants, and whales. (Rev: BL 6/1–15/94; SLJ 11/94) [591]

**14870** Lesinski, Jeanne M. *Exotic Invaders: Killer Bees, Fire Ants, and Other Alien Species Are Infesting America!* (4–6). Illus. 1996, Walker LB $17.85 (0-8027-8391-0). 49pp. In separate chapters, 5 pests — sea lampreys, fire ants, zebra mussels, starlings, and African honeybees — are featured, with a description of the harm they do. (Rev: SLJ 5/96) [591]

**14871** Machotka, Hana. *Breathtaking Noses* (2–4). Illus. 1992, Morrow LB $14.93 (0-688-09527-5). 32pp. Using full-color illustrations, the author shows a variety of animal noses and their different uses. (Rev: BCCB 7–8/92; BL 3/15/92; HB 5–6/92; SLJ 4/92) [596]

**14872** Martin, James. *Living Fossils* (4–7). Illus. 1997, Crown LB $17.99 (0-517-59867-1). 48pp. A description of various animals, like the Komodo dragon and the cockroach, that have survived throughout the ages without changing. (Rev: BL 6/1–15/97; SLJ 6/97) [591]

**14873** Maynard, Thane. *Giant Animals* (3–5). Illus. Series: Cincinnati Zoo Books. 1995, Watts LB $23.60 (0-531-11208-X). 64pp. Very large animals — including mammals, birds, reptiles, fish, and insects — are described, along with their habitats, abilities, and the challenges produced by their size. (Rev: SLJ 9/95) [591]

**14874** Moser, Madeline. *Ever Heard of an Aardwolf? A Miscellany of Uncommon Animals* (K–3). Illus. by Barry Moser. 1996, Harcourt $16.00 (0-15-200474-2). 40pp. Unusual animals are introduced in a picture book format. (Rev: BL 9/15/96; SLJ 10/96) [599]

**14875** Most, Bernard. *Catbirds and Dogfish* (1–3). Illus. 1995, Harcourt $13.00 (0-15-292844-8); paper $5.00 (0-15-200779-2). 32pp. Animals named after other animals, such as the dogfish, are the subject of this nature book. (Rev: BL 4/1/95; SLJ 7/95) [591]

**14876** Palazzo, Tony. *The Biggest and the Littlest Animals* (4–7). Illus. by author. 1973, Lion LB $13.95 (0-87460-225-4). 40pp. Many ways of comparing animals, including size and mobility, are explored.

**14877** Patent, Dorothy Hinshaw. *Why Mammals Have Fur* (3–5). Illus. by William Munoz. 1995, Dutton paper $14.99 (0-525-65141-1). 32pp. Using a broad definition of fur to include quills and horns, this book describes its use for warmth, protection, and camouflage in the animal kingdom. (Rev: BL 5/1/95; SLJ 6/95) [599]

**14878** Paul, Tessa. *In Fields and Meadows* (2–5). Illus. Series: Animal Trackers. 1997, Crabtree LB $19.16 (0-86505-585-8); paper $7.95 (0-86505-593-9). 32pp. Using evidence like footprints, teeth marks, holes, nests, and hair or fur, about a dozen creatures that live in fields and meadows are described. (Rev: SLJ 10/97) [591]

**14879** Pearce, Q. L. *Piranhas and Other Wonders of the Jungle* (3–6). Illus. by Mary Ann Fraser. Series: Amazing Science. 1990, Simon & Schuster paper $5.95 (0-671-70690-X). 64pp. Sketches of animals found in the jungle, such as driver ants and vampire bats. (Rev: SLJ 2/91) [591]

**14880** Perham, Molly, and Julian Rowe. *Wildlife* (4–6). Illus. Series: Mapworlds. 1997, Watts LB $19.30 (0-531-14388-0). 32pp. Using an atlaslike format, this work shows where a variety of animals, birds, and insects, are found in the world, with details on their habits and habitats. (Rev: BL 4/15/97) [591.9]

**14881** Pope, Joyce. *Living Fossils: Animals Unchanged by Time* (3–6). Illus. by Stella Stilwell and Helen Ward. Series: Curious Creatures. 1992, Raintree Steck-Vaughn LB $24.26 (0-8114-3151-7). 46pp. Many examples of animals that exist in prehistoric form, from dragonflies to horseshoe crabs, are explored in this volume. A companion volume is *Two Lives: Metamorphosis in the Natural World* (1992). (Rev: SLJ 5/92) [591]

**14882** Presnall, Judith J. *Animals That Glow* (5–7). Illus. Series: First Books. 1993, Watts LB $22.00 (0-531-20071-X). 64pp. From fireflies to tiny sea creatures, this book covers the amazing phenomenon of bioluminescence. (Rev: BL 5/15/93; SLJ 6/93) [591]

**14883** Pringle, Laurence. *Animal Monsters: The Truth About Scary Creatures* (4–6). Illus. 1997, Marshall Cavendish LB $15.95 (0-7614-5003-3). 64pp. The truth about such feared animals as alligators, killer bees, and tarantulas — and why they are not as dangerous as reported. (Rev: BL 9/1/97; SLJ 10/97) [591]

**14884** Purcell, John Wallace. *African Animals* (1–4). Illus. 1982, Children's LB $21.00 (0-516-01665-2); paper $5.50 (0-516-41665-0). 48pp. A brief introduction to the most common animals associated with Africa.

**14885** Ring, Elizabeth. *Tiger Lilies and Other Beastly Plants* (3–5). Illus. by Barbara Bash. 1984, Walker $9.95 (0-8027-6540-8). 32pp. Plants with animal names and their animal counterparts are illustrated.

**14886** Rochford, Dierdre. *Rights for Animals?* (4–8). Illus. Series: Viewpoints. 1997, Watts LB $20.00 (0-531-14414-3). 32pp. After a discussion of the many uses of animals today, this account focuses on their use in cosmetic and pharmaceutical testing, blood sports, and hunting, with additional material on endangered animals and zoos. (Rev: SLJ 5/97) [179.3]

**14887** Roop, Connie, and Peter Roop. *Walk on the Wild Side!* (4–8). Illus. by Anne Canevari Green. 1997, Millbrook LB $21.40 (0-7613-0021-X). 40pp. Short introductions to 14 different animals and their habitats, complete with jokes, riddles, and humorous illustrations. (Rev: SLJ 6/97) [591]

**14888** Ross, Michael E. *Rolypolyology* (4–6). Illus. Series: Backyard Creatures. 1996, Carolrhoda LB $14.95 (0-87614-862-3). 48pp. Several common backyard creatures and their habits are described with interesting accompanying activities. (Rev: BL 3/15/96; SLJ 7/96) [595.3]

**14889** Royston, Angela. *Small Animals* (PS–1). Illus. by Richard Manning. Series: What's Inside? 1991, DK Publg. $8.95 (1-879431-09-2). 17pp. Scorpions and spiders are 2 of the small animals pictured in diagrams that show exterior and interior structures. (Rev: BL 2/15/92; SLJ 3/92) [591]

**14890** Ruiz, Andres L. *Metamorphosis* (3–5). Illus. by Francisco Arredondo. Series: Cycles of Life. 1997, Sterling $12.95 (0-8069-9325-1). 32pp. In double-page spreads, explains how some amphibians and insects transform themselves into another life form, like tadpoles becoming frogs. (Rev: SLJ 6/97) [591]

**14891** Sateren, Shelley Swanson. *The Humane Societies: A Voice for the Animals* (4–6). Illus. 1996, Silver Burdett LB $14.95 (0-87518-622-X); paper $7.95 (0-382-39309-0). 80pp. Introduces animal rights groups and humane societies and the work they do, including prevention of cruelty to animals and ways of controlling pet populations. (Rev: SLJ 11/96) [179.3]

**14892** Sayre, April Pulley. *Put On Some Antlers and Walk Like a Moose* (4–6). Illus. 1997, Twenty-First Century $20.40 (0-8050-5182-1). 80pp. Outlines the many techniques of observation used by scientists to study animals. (Rev: BL 12/1/97; SLJ 2/98*) [590]

**14893** Schubert, Ingrid, and Dieter Schubert. *Amazing Animals* (1–3). Trans. from Dutch by Leigh Sauerwein. 1995, Front Street $15.95 (1-886910-05-7). Using catchy rhymes and pleasant illustrations, this book shows how common animals live, reproduce, and deal with danger. (Rev: SLJ 1/96) [591]

**14894** Shedd, Warner. *The Kids' Wildlife Book: Exploring Animal Worlds Through Indoor/Outdoor Experiences* (2–6). Illus. by Loretta Braren. Series: Kids Can! Books. 1994, Williamson paper $12.95 (0-913589-77-2). 156pp. This book of projects and experiments features common mammals, amphibians, and birds of Canada and the United States. (Rev: SLJ 8/94) [591]

**14895** Silver, Donald M. *Extinction Is Forever* (2–3). Illus. by Patricia J. Wynne. 1995, Simon & Schuster $14.95 (0-671-86769-5); paper $7.95 (0-671-86770-9). 48pp. Beginning with the end of dinosaurs during the Ice Ages and ending with the present, this account traces the reasons why various species have become extinct. (Rev: SLJ 2/96) [575.7]

**14896** Simon, Seymour. *Ride the Wind: Airborne Journeys of Animals and Plants* (3–5). Illus. by Elsa Warnick. 1997, Harcourt $15.00 (0-15-292887-1). 40pp. Highlights nature's air travelers, including the Arctic tern, albatross, snow goose, monarch butterfly, and various seeds. (Rev: BL 4/1/97; SLJ 5/97) [591.52]

**14897** Singer, Marilyn. *A Wasp Is Not a Bee* (2–4). Illus. by Patrick O'Brien. 1995, Holt $15.95 (0-8050-2820-X). 32pp. This book distinguishes between 14 seemingly similar pairs of animals, like a bat and a bird, and a crocodile and an alligator. (Rev: BL 10/15/95; SLJ 1/96) [595]

**14898** Skramstad, Jill. *Wildlife Southwest* (1–4). Illus. by Mike Dunning. Series: Chronicle Junior Nature. 1992, Chronicle $10.95 (0-8118-0126-8). 56pp. In pictures and text, an introduction to the wild animals of the southwestern states. (Rev: BL 8/92; SLJ 8/92) [599]

**14899** Squire, Ann. *101 Questions and Answers About Backyard Wildlife* (3–6). Illus. 1996, Walker LB $16.85 (0-8027-8458-5). 128pp. Birds, bats, and

snails are 3 common creatures explored in a question-and-answer format. (Rev: BL 12/1/96; SLJ 1/97) [591]

**14900** Staple, Michele, and Linda Gamlin. *The Random House Book of 1001 Questions and Answers About Animals* (4–6). 1990, Random LB $12.99 (0-679-90731-9). 160pp. All sorts of questions and answers about all sorts of animals. (Rev: BL 12/15/90; SLJ 2/91) [591]

**14901** Steele, Philip. *Vampire Bats and Other Creatures of the Night* (3–5). Illus. Series: Young Observer. 1995, Kingfisher paper $6.95 (1-85697-575-4). 40pp. An overview of nocturnal animal life that also explains why these creatures live by a reversed time schedule. (Rev: SLJ 1/96) [591]

**14902** Young, Ruth. *Who Says Moo?* (PS–K). Illus. by Lisa Campbell Ernst. 1994, Viking paper $13.99 (0-670-85162-0). 32pp. A simple picture book in which children are asked to identify salient characteristics of a number of animals. (Rev: BL 10/15/94; SLJ 9/94) [591]

**14903** Zim, Herbert S., and Donald F. Hoffmeister. *Mammals* (4–6). Illus. 1987, Western paper $5.50 (0-307-24058-4). 160pp. This is a reliable guide to the most familiar species of mammals.

## Amphibians and Reptiles

### GENERAL AND MISCELLANEOUS

**14904** Ballard, Lois. *Reptiles* (1–4). Illus. 1982, Children's LB $21.00 (0-516-01644-X); paper $5.50 (0-516-41644-8). 48pp. A straightforward, logically arranged introduction.

**14905** Bernhard, Emery. *Salamanders* (2–4). Illus. by Durga Bernhard. 1995, Holiday LB $15.95 (0-8234-1148-6). 32pp. The structure, habitats, and behavior of salamanders are covered, with an introduction to several key species. (Rev: BL 2/1/95; HB 5–6/95; SLJ 3/95) [597.6]

**14906** *Bizarre and Beautiful Tongues* (3–6). Illus. Series: Bizarre and Beautiful. 1993, John Muir $14.95 (1-56261-123-2). 48pp. How and what animals taste is explored, with examples including earthworms, octopuses, and humans. (Rev: BL 4/15/94; SLJ 2/94) [591.1]

**14907** Brenner, Barbara, and Bernice Chardiet. *Where's That Reptile?* (2–4). Illus. Series: Hide and Seek. 1993, Scholastic $10.95 (0-590-45212-6). 32pp. An interactive book that introduces a variety of reptiles to primary-age children. (Rev: BL 10/15/93; SLJ 1/94) [597.9]

**14908** Burns, Diane L. *Frogs, Toads and Turtles* (3–6). Illus. 1997, NorthWord paper $6.95 (1-55971-593-6). 48pp. A paperback field guide that introduces the world of 30 amphibians, with coverage of their habitats, food, and appearance. (Rev: BL 8/97) [597.8]

**14909** Chermayeff, Ivan. *Scaly Facts* (PS–1). Illus. 1995, Harcourt $11.00 (0-15-200109-3). 32pp. Reptiles are introduced through brief, simple text and dynamic illustrations. (Rev: BL 4/1/95; SLJ 7/95) [597.9]

**14910** Creagh, Carson, ed. *Reptiles* (4–6). Illus. Series: Nature Company Discoveries. 1996, Time Life $16.00 (0-8094-9247-4). 64pp. The world of reptiles is introduced with many colorful illustrations, brief text, and a special foldout section. (Rev: BL 6/1–15/96) [597.96]

**14911** Gove, Doris. *Red-Spotted Newt* (3–6). Illus. by Beverly Duncan. 1994, Atheneum $14.95 (0-689-31697-6). 28pp. Using effective watercolor illustrations, this book portrays the life cycle of a red-spotted newt from egg to embryo, larva, eft, and finally to an adult ready to lay her own eggs. (Rev: BL 12/1/94; SLJ 12/94) [597.5]

**14912** Hornblow, Leonora, and Arthur Hornblow. *Reptiles Do the Strangest Things* (2–4). Illus. by Michael K. Frith. 1970, Random $6.95 (0-394-80074-5). 64pp. A description of the major reptiles and their living habits.

**14913** Lamprell, Klay. *Scaly Things* (2–4). Illus. Series: Nature Company Young Discoveries. 1996, Time Life $10.00 (0-7835-4842-7). 32pp. A pictorially beautiful introduction to creatures whose exteriors are scaly. (Rev: BL 12/15/96) [597.9]

**14914** McCarthy, Colin. *Reptile* (4–8). Illus. Series: Eyewitness Books. 1991, Knopf LB $20.99 (0-679-90783-1). 64pp. In a series of 2-page spreads that include careful anatomical drawings, the world of the reptile is explored. (Rev: BL 6/1/91; SLJ 7/91) [557.9]

**14915** Maruska, Edward J. *Salamanders* (3–5). Illus. Series: Naturebooks. 1996, Child's World LB $22.79 (1-56766-273-0). 32pp. Salamanders are introduced in a series of full-page color photos that face each page of text. (Rev: BL 12/15/96) [597.6]

**14916** Murray, Peter. *Chameleons* (3–6). Illus. Series: Naturebooks. 1993, Child's World LB $22.79 (1-56766-016-9). 32pp. Photos show the color transformations of this reptile and its adaptation to various environments. (Rev: BL 3/1/94) [597.95]

**14917** Parker, Nancy W. *Frogs, Toads, Lizards, and Salamanders* (1–4). Illus. by Joan R. Wright. 1990, Greenwillow LB $15.93 (0-688-08681-0). 48pp. An interesting assortment of reptiles and amphibians in picture-book format. (Rev: BCCB 5/90; BL 2/1/90; HB 5–6/90; SLJ 5/90) [597.6]

**14918** Richardson, Joy. *Reptiles* (1–2). Illus. by Angela Owen. Series: Picture Science. 1993, Watts LB $20.00 (0-531-14254-X). 32pp. For the begin-

ning reader, this basic introduction to reptiles contains attractive color illustrations and diagrams. (Rev: BL 3/15/94) [597.9]

**14919** Silverstein, Alvin, et al. *Vertebrates* (3–6). Illus. Series: Kingdom of Life. 1996, Twenty-First Century LB $21.40 (0-8050-3517-6). 64pp. Vertebrates — animals with enclosed spinal cords — are introduced, with many color photos. (Rev: BL 6/1–15/96) [596]

**14920** Snedden, Robert. *What Is a Reptile?* (3–6). Illus. by Adrian Lascom. 1995, Sierra Club $14.95 (0-87156-493-9). 32pp. In double-page spreads, such characteristics of reptiles as body heat, skin, movement, senses, and defenses are covered. (Rev: SLJ 7/95) [597]

**14921** Snedden, Robert. *What Is an Amphibian?* (3–6). Illus. Series: Sierra Club Books for Children. 1994, Sierra Club $14.95 (0-87156-469-6). 32pp. The 3 main families of amphibians are introduced, with information on life cycles, respiration, locomotion, and feeding. (Rev: BL 12/15/94) [597.6]

**14922** Souza, D. M. *Shy Salamanders* (3–5). Illus. Series: Creatures All Around Us. 1995, Carolrhoda LB $14.95 (0-87614-826-7). 40pp. The life cycle of the salamander and its structure, food, and habitats are topics covered with beautiful illustrations. (Rev: BL 4/15/95; SLJ 9/95) [597.6]

**14923** Winner, Cherie. *Salamanders* (3–6). Illus. Series: Nature Watch Books. 1993, Carolrhoda LB $14.95 (0-87614-757-0). 48pp. Various kinds of salamanders are introduced, with material given on life cycle, habits, and endangered status. (Rev: BL 8/93) [597.6]

### ALLIGATORS AND CROCODILES

**14924** Bare, Colleen S. *Never Kiss an Alligator!* (2–4). Illus. 1994, Puffin paper $4.99 (0-140-55257-X). 32pp. Sharp color photos highlight this close-up look at the alligator. (Rev: BCCB 9/89; BL 9/1/89; SLJ 8/89) [597.98]

**14925** Deeble, Mark, and Victoria Stone. *The Crocodile Family Book* (2–5). Illus. Series: Animal Families. 1994, North-South LB $16.88 (1-55858-264-9). 50pp. Crocodiles from the Serengeti National Park are featured in this superbly illustrated book that describes their life, anatomy, and hunting. (Rev: BL 11/15/94; SLJ 11/94) [597.98]

**14926** Dow, Lesley. *Alligators and Crocodiles* (5–8). Illus. 1990, Facts on File $17.95 (0-8160-2273-9). 68pp. This oversize book illustrates various species of alligators and crocodiles. (Rev: BL 11/15/90; SLJ 5/91) [598.98]

**14927** Lauber, Patricia. *Alligators: A Success Story* (3–5). Illus. by Lou Silva. Series: Redfeather. 1994, Holt $14.95 (0-8050-1909-X). 64pp. This small book discusses the history of alligators, their characteristics, and the effort to protect them. (Rev: BL 3/15/94; SLJ 6/94) [597.98]

**14928** Patent, Dorothy Hinshaw. *The American Alligator* (4–6). Photos by William Munoz. 1994, Clarion $15.95 (0-395-63392-3). 77pp. Generous use of color photos enhances this book on the life cycle of the alligator. (Rev: BL 12/15/94) [597.98]

**14929** Perry, Phyllis J. *The Crocodilians: Reminders of the Age of Dinosaurs* (4–6). Illus. Series: First Books: Animals. 1997, Watts LB $22.00 (0-531-20254-2). 64pp. Although the dinosaurs are gone, their descendants — the alligator, gavial, caiman, and crocodile — are still here, and this book describes them and how they live. (Rev: BL 8/97; SLJ 8/97) [597.98]

**14930** Robinson, Claire. *Crocodiles* (2–3). Illus. Series: In the Wild. 1997, Heinemann LB $18.50 (1-57572-133-3). 24pp. A simple introduction to crocodiles that tells how they live, communicate, find food, and raise their young. (Rev: BL 2/1/98; SLJ 4/98) [597.98]

**14931** Souza, D. M. *Roaring Reptiles: A Book About Crocodilians* (3–5). Illus. Series: Creatures All Around Us. 1992, Carolrhoda LB $14.95 (0-87614-710-4). 40pp. Close-up photographs and lively text introduce the types of crocodilians found in North America. (Rev: BL 10/1/92; SLJ 12/92) [597.98]

**14932** Staub, Frank. *Alligators* (2–4). Photos by author. Illus. Series: Early Bird Nature Books. 1995, Lerner LB $19.93 (0-8225-3007-4). 48pp. Discusses the appearance and habits of alligators, as well as the role they play in their environment. (Rev: SLJ 8/95) [597.6]

**14933** Stone, Lynn M. *Alligators and Crocodiles* (2–4). Illus. Series: New True Books. 1989, Children's LB $21.00 (0-516-01170-7). 48pp. An introduction to alligators and crocodiles, their differences and habitats. (Rev: BL 1/15/90) [597]

**14934** Stoops, Erik D., and Debbie L. Stone. *Alligators and Crocodiles* (4–7). Illus. 1995, Sterling $16.95 (0-8069-0422-4). 80pp. Using a question-and-answer format, this book introduces the structure and habits of many alligators and crocodiles. (Rev: BL 1/1/95; SLJ 3/95) [597.98]

## FROGS AND TOADS

**14935** Back, Christine. *Tadpole and Frog* (1–3). Illus. 1986, Silver Burdett LB $9.95 (0-382-09285-6); paper $?.95 (0-382-24021-9). 24pp. A basic science book in full color explaining the reproductive cycle of the frog. (Rev: BL 1/1/87)

**14936** Brown, Ruth. *Toad* (PS–1). Illus. 1997, Dutton paper $15.99 (0-525-45757-7). 32pp. Pond life and a single toad's activities are introduced in this

picture book with amazing watercolors. (Rev: BCCB 3/97; BL 1/1–15/97*; SLJ 3/97) [597.8]

**14937** Chinery, Michael. *Frog* (3–5). Illus. by Martin Camm. Series: Life Story. 1990, Troll LB $12.95 (0-8167-2102-5); paper $4.95 (0-8167-2103-3). 32pp. The life cycle of the frog is revealed through detailed text, color photographs, and other illustrations. (Rev: BL 4/1/91) [597.8]

**14938** Cole, Joanna. *A Frog's Body* (3–5). Illus. 1980, Morrow LB $15.93 (0-688-32228-X). 48pp. An excellent introduction to the anatomy of a young bullfrog.

**14939** Delafosse, Claude. *Frogs* (PS–2). Illus. Series: First Discovery. 1997, Scholastic $11.95 (0-590-93782-0). 24pp. With a highly visual approach, this book introduces frogs using excellent drawings and a brief text. (Rev: BL 2/15/97) [597.8]

**14940** Dewey, Jennifer O. *Poison Dart Frogs* (K–3). Illus. 1998, Boyds Mills $15.95 (1-56397-655-2). This introduction to the many kinds of poison dart frogs of Latin American rain forests explains how they release a poison through their skin that is used by hunters on blowpipe darts. (Rev: BL 3/1/98; SLJ 4/98) [597.8]

**14941** Fowler, Allan. *Frogs and Toads and Tadpoles Too!* (1–2). Illus. Series: Rookie Read-About Science. 1992, Children's LB $18.50 (0-516-04925-9). 32pp. In minimal text and many color photos, the life cycle of frogs and toads is introduced. (Rev: BL 6/15/92) [597.8]

**14942** Gibbons, Gail. *Frogs* (K–3). Illus. 1993, Holiday LB $15.95 (0-8234-1052-8). 32pp. Colorful water scenes and a simple text depict frogs in all stages of development from spawn to maturity. (Rev: BL 10/15/93; SLJ 12/93) [597.8]

**14943** Johnson, Sylvia A. *Tree Frogs* (4–6). Illus. 1986, Lerner LB $22.60 (0-8225-1467-2). 48pp. A look at the characteristics, environment, breeding, and life cycles of the tree frog. (Rev: BL 10/1/86; SLJ 11/86)

**14944** Mara, William P. *The Fragile Frog* (3–6). Illus. 1996, Albert Whitman LB $16.95 (0-8075-2580-4). 48pp. A description is given of the life cycle of this tiny frog, whose existence is now threatened. (Rev: BL 11/1/96; SLJ 11/96) [597.8]

**14945** Martin, James. *Frogs* (4–6). Photos by Art Wolfe. 1997, Crown LB $18.99 (0-517-70906-6). 32pp. This thorough introduction to frogs covers topics like locomotion, physical characteristics, metamorphosis, mating, defense mechanisms, hibernation, and unusual species. (Rev: SLJ 3/98) [597.8]

**14946** Parker, Steve. *Frogs and Toads* (3–6). Illus. Series: Look into Nature. 1994, Sierra Club $16.95 (0-87156-466-1). 57pp. Frogs and toads are introduced, with material on their anatomy, speed, habits, mating, and food, plus a chapter on essential facts about them. (Rev: BL 10/15/94) [597.8]

**14947** Pascoe, Elaine. *Tadpoles* (3–6). Photos by Dwight Kuhn. Series: Nature Close-Up. 1996, Blackbirch LB $16.95 (1-56711-179-3). 48pp. A frog book that concentrates on the growth and development of tadpoles, using excellent color photos. (Rev: SLJ 10/96) [597.8]

**14948** Patent, Dorothy Hinshaw. *Flashy Fantastic Rain Forest Frogs* (K–3). Illus. by Kendahl J. Jubb. 1997, Walker $15.95 (0-8027-8615-4). 32pp. Rain forest frogs, their characteristics, habits, and habitats are introduced in this attractive picture book. (Rev: BCCB 3/97; BL 2/1/97; SLJ 3/97) [597.8]

**14949** Pfeffer, Wendy. *From Tadpole to Frog* (PS–1). Illus. by Holly Keller. Series: Let's-Read-and-Find-Out Stage 1. 1994, HarperCollins LB $14.89 (0-06-023117-3); paper $4.95 (0-06-445123-2). 32pp. This simple science book shows one year in the life cycle of a frog, beginning with the end of its hibernation in the spring. (Rev: BL 8/94; HB 7–8/94; SLJ 11/94) [597.8]

**14950** Souza, D. M. *Frogs, Frogs Everywhere* (3–5). Illus. Series: Creatures All Around Us. 1995, Carolrhoda LB $19.93 (0-87614-825-9). 40pp. Physical and behavioral characteristics of frogs are attractively presented, along with various species and habitats. (Rev: BL 4/15/95; SLJ 9/95) [597.8]

**14951** Starosta, Paul. *The Frog: Natural Acrobat* (3–6). Photos by author. Series: Animal Close-Ups. 1996, Charlesbridge paper $6.95 (0-88106-437-8). 27pp. A simple account with plenty of photos that tells about the various species, habitats, life cycles, and behavior of frogs. (Rev: SLJ 1/97) [597.8]

**14952** White, William. *All About the Frog* (4–8). Illus. 1992, Sterling $14.95 (0-8069-8274-8). 72pp. History, anatomy, reproduction, food, and other aspects of this amphibian are covered, with many illustrations. (Rev: BL 7/92) [597.8]

## LIZARDS

**14953** Darling, Kathy. *Chameleons: On Location* (3–6). Illus. by Tara Darling. 1997, Lothrop LB $15.93 (0-688-12538-7). 40pp. An introduction to chameleons in their natural habitat in Madagascar that tells about their lives, habits, diets, and mating. (Rev: BCCB 5/97; BL 4/1/97; SLJ 4/97) [597.95]

**14954** Darling, Kathy. *Komodo Dragon: On Location* (4–6). Illus. by Tara Darling. Series: On Location. 1997, Lothrop LB $15.93 (0-688-13777-6). 40pp. Color photographs enliven the description of this reptile, its habits, and its habitat on Komodo Island. (Rev: BCCB 5/97; BL 2/15/97; SLJ 4/97) [597.95]

**14955** Maynard, Thane. *Komodo Dragons* (3–5). Illus. Series: Naturebooks. 1996, Child's World LB $22.79 (1-56766-266-8). 32pp. These fierce-looking reptiles are featured in color illustrations with simple text. (Rev: BL 12/15/96; SLJ 3/97) [597.95]

**14956** Patton, Don. *Iguanas* (2–4). Illus. Series: Naturebooks: Animals. 1995, Child's World LB $22.79 (1-56766-190-4). 32pp. The world of the iguana is covered in full-color photos that face each page of large-print text. (Rev: BL 11/15/95) [597.95]

**14957** Schafer, Susan. *The Komodo Dragon* (3–5). Illus. Series: Remarkable Animals. 1992, Macmillan LB $13.95 (0-87518-504-5). 60pp. Evolution, adaptation, habitat and behavior are covered, as well as why this animal is in danger of extinction. (Rev: BL 11/1/92; SLJ 10/92) [597.95]

**14958** Schnieper, Claudia. *Chameleons* (3–6). Illus. by Max Meier. Series: Nature Watch. 1989, Carolrhoda LB $19.93 (0-87614-341-9). 48pp. The life cycle, physical characteristics, and habits of chameleons are introduced. (Rev: BL 9/15/89; HB 11–12/89; SLJ 10/89) [597.95]

**14959** Schnieper, Claudia. *Lizards* (3–6). Illus. by Max Meier. Series: Nature Watch. 1990, Carolrhoda LB $19.95 (0-87614-405-9). 48pp. Characteristics and reproductive patterns are covered, with color photos. (Rev: BCCB 10/90; BL 6/15/90; SLJ 9/90) [597.95]

**14960** Sherrow, Victoria. *The Gecko* (4–6). Illus. 1990, Macmillan LB $13.95 (0-87518-441-3). 60pp. Color photos highlight this introduction to the gecko. (Rev: BL 1/1/90; SLJ 2/91) [597.95]

**14961** Souza, D. M. *Catch Me If You Can: A Book About Lizards* (3–5). Illus. Series: Creatures All Around Us. 1992, Carolrhoda LB $19.93 (0-87614-713-9). 40pp. From race runners to gila monsters, this book describes lizards found in the United States. (Rev: BL 10/1/92; SLJ 12/92) [597.95]

**14962** Stefoff, Rebecca. *Chameleon* (2–4). Illus. Series: From the Living Things. 1996, Marshall Cavendish LB $21.36 (0-7614-0118-0). 32pp. The African chameleon, its life history, and its habits are presented in brief text and colorful photos. (Rev: BL 2/1/97; SLJ 3/97) [597.95]

**14963** Twinem, Neecy. *Changing Colors* (PS–3). Illus. by author. Series: Animal Clues Board Books. 1996, Charlesbridge $4.95 (0-88106-941-8). A picture puzzle book that gives clues through close-up pictures of parts of the chameleon and finally reveals its identity. (Rev: SLJ 12/96) [597.6]

## SNAKES

**14964** Arnosky, Jim. *All About Rattlesnakes* (3–5). Illus. 1997, Scholastic $15.95 (0-590-46794-8). 32pp. This account is filled with information about snakes, from their physical structure to how they behave, with special material on rattlesnakes. (Rev: BL 12/1/97; HB 9–10/97; SLJ 10/97) [597.96]

**14965** Broekel, Ray. *Snakes* (1–4). Illus. 1982, Children's LB $21.00 (0-516-01649-0); paper $5.50 (0-516-41649-9). 48pp. An introduction to snakes for the primary grades.

**14966** Chinery, Michael. *Snake* (3–5). Illus. by Denys Ovenden. Series: Life Story. 1990, Troll LB $12.95 (0-8167-2106-8); paper $3.95 (0-8167-2107-6). 32pp. The life of the corn snake is featured in this colorfully illustrated account. (Rev: BL 4/1/91) [597.96]

**14967** Demuth, Patricia. *Snakes* (1–3). Illus. by Judith Moffatt. 1993, Putnam paper $3.95 (0-448-40513-X). 48pp. An introduction to snakes, their habits, size, and food. (Rev: BL 7/93; SLJ 7/93) [597.66]

**14968** Dewey, Jennifer O. *Rattlesnake Dance: True Tales, Mysteries, and Rattlesnake Ceremonies* (3–6). Illus. 1997, Boyds Mills $17.95 (1-56397-247-6). 48pp. An oversize book that tells about the author's many encounters with rattlesnakes and pit vipers. (Rev: BCCB 3/97; BL 3/15/97; HB 3–4/97; SLJ 4/97) [597.96]

**14969** Fowler, Allan. *It's Best to Leave a Snake Alone* (1–2). Illus. Series: Rookie Read-About Science. 1992, Children's LB $18.50 (0-516-04926-7). 32pp. Interesting facts about snakes are introduced in a brief text and many pictures. This title is also available in an oversized "Big Book" edition. (Rev: BL 7/92) [597.96]

**14970** Gove, Doris. *A Water Snake's Year* (3–5). Illus. by Beverly Duncan. 1991, Macmillan $13.95 (0-689-31597-X). 40pp. This book describes a year in the life of a female snake in the Great Smoky Mountains. (Rev: BL 10/15/91; SLJ 10/91) [597.96]

**14971** Johnson, Sylvia A. *Snakes* (4–6). Illus. 1986, Lerner paper $5.95 (0-8225-9503-6). 48pp. Diagrams help explain the way snakes move; also includes behavior, breeding, life cycles, and environment. (Rev: BL 10/1/86; SLJ 11/86)

**14972** Lauber, Patricia. *Snakes Are Hunters* (PS–2). Illus. by Holly Keller. 1988, HarperCollins LB $14.89 (0-690-04630-8); paper $4.95 (0-06-445091-0). 32pp. Focusing on how snakes hunt and devour their food, this is a well-organized introduction to these often misunderstood creatures. (Rev: BL 2/1/88; HB 7–8/88; SLJ 9/88)

**14973** Lavies, Bianca. *A Gathering of Garter Snakes* (3–6). Illus. 1993, Dutton paper $15.99 (0-525-45099-8). 32pp. The annual life cycle of garter snakes is described, from awakening after hibernation, through migration, hunting, mating, and shed-

ding skins, and back to hibernation. (Rev: BCCB 2/94; BL 12/1/93; SLJ 2/94*) [597.96]

**14974** Ling, Mary, and Mary Atkinson. *The Snake Book* (4–6). Illus. 1997, DK Publg. $12.95 (0-7894-1526-7). 32pp. A fascinating book that introduces 12 varieties of snakes, with a 4-panel foldout of a python. (Rev: BCCB 5/97; BL 7/97; SLJ 9/97) [597.96]

**14975** Llewellyn, Claire. *Some Snakes Spit Poison and Other Amazing Facts About Snakes* (2–4). Illus. Series: I Didn't Know That. 1997, Millbrook LB $19.90 (0-7613-0561-0). 32pp. Strange facts about unusual snakes and their behavior are given along with basic facts about the life span, food, and reproduction of snakes. (Rev: SLJ 10/97) [597.96]

**14976** McClung, Robert M. *Snakes: Their Place in the Sun* (3–5). Illus. by David M. Dennis. Series: Redfeather Book. 1991, Holt LB $14.95 (0-8050-1718-6). 64pp. The focus is on common snakes that might be found on a Pennsylvania farm, with coverage of other types. (Rev: BL 3/1/92; SLJ 7/92) [597.96]

**14977** McDonald, Mary Ann. *Boas* (3–5). Illus. Series: Naturebooks. 1996, Child's World LB $22.79 (1-56766-212-9). 32pp. This account features in text and photos the large snake that crushes its prey. (Rev: BL 12/15/96) [597.96]

**14978** McDonald, Mary Ann. *Cobras* (3–5). Illus. Series: Naturebooks. 1996, Child's World LB $22.79 (1-56766-265-X). 32pp. The exotic world of the cobra is explored through full-page illustrations and large-print text. (Rev: BL 12/15/96) [597.96]

**14979** Maestro, Betsy. *Take a Look at Snakes* (K–3). Illus. by Giulio Maestro. 1992, Scholastic $14.95 (0-590-44935-4). 40pp. Facts about characteristics, habitats, behaviors, and varieties of snakes. (Rev: BL 11/1/92; HB 11–12/92; SLJ 9/92) [597.96]

**14980** Markle, Sandra. *Outside and Inside Snakes* (3–6). Illus. Series: Outside and Inside. 1995, Simon & Schuster paper $5.99 (0-689-81998-6). 40pp. The text clearly presents material on the anatomy and behavior of snakes, with amazing color photographs. (Rev: BCCB 5/95; BL 7/95; HB 7–8/95; SLJ 6/95*) [597.96]

**14981** Parsons, Alexandra. *Amazing Snakes* (1–4). Illus. Series: Eyewitness Juniors. 1990, Knopf LB $11.99 (0-679-90225-2). 32pp. A general introduction to snakes, plus pictures and text on individual species and locomotion. (Rev: BL 8/90) [597.96]

**14982** Patton, Don. *Pythons* (2–4). Illus. Series: Naturebooks: Animals. 1995, Child's World LB $22.79 (1-56766-180-7). 32pp. Amazing full-page photos highlight this introduction to pythons, their structure, and how they live. (Rev: BL 11/15/95; SLJ 4/96) [597.96]

**14983** Penner, Lucille R. *S-S-Snakes!* (1–2). Illus. by Peter Barrett. Series: Step into Reading. 1994, Random LB $11.99 (0-679-94777-9); paper $3.99 (0-679-84777-4). 32pp. An easy-to-read book about snakes, their structure, and their habits. (Rev: BL 1/1/95; SLJ 2/95) [597.96]

**14984** Robinson, Fay. *Great Snakes!* (2–3). Illus. by Jean Day Zallinger. 1996, Scholastic paper $3.50 (0-590-26243-2). 32pp. In an easily read format, this counting book introduces various snakes. (Rev: BL 11/15/96) [597.96]

**14985** Schnieper, Claudia. *Snakes: Silent Hunters* (3–5). Illus. Series: Nature Watch. 1995, Carolrhoda LB $14.95 (0-87614-881-X); paper $5.95 (0-87614-952-2). 48pp. An introduction to snakes organized under such headings as physical characteristics, reproduction, hunting, and self-defense. (Rev: BL 10/1/95; SLJ 12/95) [597.96]

**14986** Simon, Seymour. *Snakes* (3–5). Illus. 1992, HarperCollins LB $15.89 (0-06-022530-0). 32pp. An informative, visually stunning look at an animal feared by many. (Rev: BL 4/15/92*; HB 5–6/92; SLJ 6/92) [597.96]

### TURTLES AND TORTOISES

**14987** Baskin-Salzberg, Anita, and Allen Salzberg. *Turtles* (3–7). Illus. 1996, Watts LB $21.00 (0-531-20220-8). 64pp. From tiny bog turtles to giant sea turtles, many species are presented, along with their habitats and life-styles. (Rev: BL 9/1/96) [597.92]

**14988** Berger, Melvin. *Look Out for Turtles!* (1–4). Illus. by Megan Lloyd. 1992, HarperCollins LB $14.89 (0-06-022540-8). 32pp. Information on all kinds and sizes of turtles and how their shells are so useful for their survival. (Rev: BL 1/1/93; SLJ 3/93) [597.92]

**14989** Fowler, Allan. *Turtles Take Their Time* (1–2). Illus. Series: Rookie Read-About Science. 1992, Children's LB $18.50 (0-516-06005-8). 32pp. For young children, turtles are introduced with a large color photo on each page and very brief text. (Rev: BL 12/15/92) [597.92]

**14990** Gibbons, Gail. *Sea Turtles* (2–4). Illus. 1995, Holiday LB $15.95 (0-8234-1191-5). 32pp. This account covers the anatomy, life cycle, diet, and habitat of the sea turtle and how it differs from other members of its reptile family. (Rev: BL 10/1/95; SLJ 10/95) [597.92]

**14991** Guiberson, Brenda Z. *Into the Sea* (2–4). Illus. by Alix Berenzy. 1996, Holt $15.95 (0-8050-2263-5). 28pp. The life of a sea turtle from being hatched to becoming an egg-laying adult. (Rev: BCCB 9/96; BL 9/15/96; HB 11–12/96; SLJ 9/96*) [597.92]

**14992** Hirschi, Ron. *Turtle's Day* (1–3). Illus. by Dwight Kuhn. 1994, Dutton paper $12.99 (0-525-65172-1). 32pp. In striking photos, a day in the life of an Eastern box turtle is covered, including successful avoidance of danger. (Rev: BL 4/1/94; SLJ 7/94) [597.92]

**14993** Holling, Holling C. *Minn of the Mississippi* (4–6). Illus. by author. 1951, Houghton $20.00 (0-395-17578-X); paper $11.95 (0-395-27399-4). A snapping turtle's trip down the Mississippi.

**14994** Lepthien, Emilie U. *Sea Turtles* (3–4). Illus. Series: True Book: Animals. 1996, Children's LB $21.00 (0-516-20161-1). 48pp. An introduction to sea turtles that cover their environment, physiology, feeding, mating, nesting, and current endangered status. (Rev: SLJ 6/97) [597.92]

**14995** Patton, Don. *Sea Turtles* (3–5). Illus. Series: Naturebooks: Animals. 1995, Child's World LB $22.79 (1-56766-188-2). 32pp. Both land and sea turtles are introduced, with information on their life cycles, habits, and food. (Rev: BCCB 11/95; BL 11/15/95; SLJ 4/96) [597.92]

**14996** Schafer, Susan. *The Galapagos Tortoise* (3–5). Illus. Series: Remarkable Animals. 1992, Macmillan LB $13.95 (0-87518-544-4). 64pp. With text, pictures, and maps, the story of the endangered Galapagos tortoise is told with information on habitat and behavior. (Rev: BL 12/1/92; SLJ 3/93) [597.92]

**14997** Souza, D. M. *What's Under That Shell? A Book About Turtles* (3–5). Illus. Series: Creatures All Around Us. 1992, Carolrhoda LB $14.95 (0-87614-712-0). 40pp. Various varieties of turtles and tortoises are introduced in color photographs and a lively text. (Rev: BL 10/1/92; SLJ 12/92) [597.92]

**14998** Ziter, Cary B. *When Turtles Come to Town* (3–6). 1989, Watts LB $21.00 (0-531-10691-8). 64pp. This book focuses on protecting the eggs of this endangered species along the Florida coast. (Rev: BL 4/1/89)

## Animal Behavior and Anatomy

### GENERAL

**14999** Arnosky, Jim. *Crinkleroot's Book of Animal Tracking* (2–5). Illus. 1989, Macmillan $14.95 (0-02-705851-4). 48pp. In this remake of the 1979 edition, the folksy hero leads a trek through the woods. (Rev: BL 4/15/89)

**15000** Arnosky, Jim. *Secrets of a Wildlife Watcher* (3–6). Illus. by author. 1991, Morrow paper $7.95 (0-688-10531-9). 64pp. Tips on how to examine animal behavior in the wild.

**15001** Bancroft, Henrietta, and Richard G. Van Gelder. *Animals in Winter* (PS–1). Illus. by Helen K.

Davie. Series: Let's-Read-and-Find-Out Science. 1997, HarperCollins LB $14.89 (0-06-027158-2). 32pp. An easily read title that describes how some animals prepare for winter and how others don't. (Rev: BL 12/1/96; SLJ 3/97) [591.54]

**15002** *Bizarre and Beautiful Feelers* (3–6). Illus. Series: Bizarre and Beautiful. 1993, John Muir $14.95 (1-56261-125-9). 48pp. The sense of touch is surveyed in a number of animals, from insects to humans. (Rev: BL 4/15/94; SLJ 2/94) [591.1]

**15003** Brooks, Bruce. *Predator!* (5–8). Illus. 1991, Farrar $13.95 (0-374-36111-8). 74pp. A well-researched and informative look at food chains and how and why animals hunt and protect themselves. (Rev: BL 1/1/92; HB 1–2/92) [591.53]

**15004** Challoner, Jack. *Wet and Dry* (K–4). Illus. Series: Start-Up Science. 1996, Raintree Steck-Vaughn LB $21.40 (0-8172-4322-4). 32pp. Using both text and experiments, discusses the different habitats of water and land and the creatures that exist in/on them. (Rev: SLJ 2/97) [530]

**15005** Crump, Donald J., ed. *How Animals Behave: A New Look at Wildlife* (5–7). Illus. 1984, National Geographic LB $12.50 (0-87044-505-7). 104pp. How animals obtain food, court, raise their young, and protect themselves.

**15006** Crump, Donald J., ed. *Secrets of Animal Survival* (4–8). Illus. 1983, National Geographic LB $12.50 (0-87044-431-X). 104pp. The survival tactics of animals in 5 geographical environments are discussed.

**15007** Duffy, Dee Dee. *Forest Tracks* (PS–1). Illus. by Janet Marshall. 1996, Boyds Mills $8.95 (1-56397-434-7). Tracks and sounds are used as clues to identify such familiar creatures as a woodpecker, rabbit, deer, raccoon, bear, and skunk. (Rev: SLJ 7/96) [591]

**15008** Facklam, Margery. *What Does the Crow Know? The Mysteries of Animal Intelligence* (4–6). Illus. by Pamela Johnson. 1994, Sierra Club $15.95 (0-87156-544-7). 48pp. In a series of questions and answers, various aspects of animal intelligence are explored, such as whether elephants really never forget. (Rev: BL 3/1/94; HB 9–10/94; SLJ 4/94*) [156.3]

**15009** Flegg, Jim, et al. *Animal Hunters* (4–7). Illus. Series: Wild World. 1991, Millbrook LB $17.90 (1-878137-04-2). 32pp. This account describes the hunting techniques of sharks, piranhas, the parasitic wasp, and others. (Rev: BL 7/91; SLJ 7/91) [591.51]

**15010** Flegg, Jim. *Animal Movement* (4–7). Illus. by David Hosking. Series: Wild World. 1991, Millbrook LB $11.90 (1-878137-21-2). 32pp. Various ways animals move and at what speeds are discussed in this

well-illustrated book. (Rev: BL 1/1/91; SLJ 2/92) [591.18]

**15011** Funston, Sylvia. *Animal Smarts* (4–6). Illus. 1997, Firefly $19.95 (1-895688-66-3); paper $9.95 (1-895688-67-1). 48pp. Explores the levels of intelligence in various mammals, birds, and insects, with material on how they think, solve problems, and understand human language. (Rev: BL 2/1/98; SLJ 4/98) [591.5]

**15012** Gardner, Robert, and David Webster. *Science Project Ideas About Animal Behavior* (4–7). Series: Science Project Ideas. 1997, Enslow LB $18.95 (0-89490-842-1). 96pp. A fascinating project book that outlines techniques and easily followed activities that study animal behavior. (Rev: BL 12/15/97; SLJ 2/98) [591]

**15013** Goodman, Susan E. *Unseen Rainbows, Silent Songs: The World Beyond Human Senses* (2–4). Illus. by Beverly Duncan. 1995, Simon & Schuster $16.00 (0-689-31892-8). 40pp. The senses of various animals are explored and compared to the senses found in humans. (Rev: BL 9/15/95; SLJ 9/95) [591.1]

**15014** Greenaway, Theresa. *Paws and Claws* (3–5). Illus. by Ann Savage, et al. Series: Head to Tail. 1995, Raintree Steck-Vaughn LB $24.26 (0-8114-8266-9). 39pp. An appealing introduction to various kinds of animal feet and their uses for movement, digging, climbing, etc. (Rev: SLJ 5/95) [591]

**15015** Hirschi, Ron. *Dance with Me* (2–4). Illus. by Thomas D. Mangelsen. 1995, Dutton paper $14.99 (0-525-65204-3). 32pp. Explains the motions that animals make, like leaping and flapping, and the reasons why they are made. (Rev: BL 9/1/95; SLJ 10/95) [591.51]

**15016** Hirschi, Ron. *A Time for Playing* (K–2). Illus. by Thomas D. Mangelsen. Series: How Animals Live. 1994, Dutton paper $13.99 (0-525-65159-4). 32pp. A stunning picture book that explores the play activities of such animals as squirrels, polar bears, and sea otters. (Rev: BL 10/15/94; SLJ 10/94) [591.51]

**15017** Hirschi, Ron. *A Time for Sleeping* (K–2). Illus. by Thomas D. Mangelsen. 1993, Dutton paper $13.99 (0-525-65128-4). 32pp. A variety of animals are shown sleeping or at rest. (Rev: BL 12/15/93; SLJ 8/93) [591.51]

**15018** Hornblow, Leonora, and Arthur Hornblow. *Animals Do the Strangest Things* (1–3). Illus. by Michael K. Frith. 1990, Random paper $4.95 (0-394-84308-8). 64pp. Interesting facts and habits of such animals as the camel, lion, and polar bear.

**15019** Kerrod, Robin, et al. *Pets and Farm Animals* (2–8). Illus. Series: Encyclopedia of the Animal World. 1990, Facts on File $19.95 (0-8160-1969-X). 96pp. This book describes the body structure of such animals as cats, dogs, donkeys, and horses. (Rev: BL 7/90) [636]

**15020** Kudlinski, Kathleen V. *Animal Tracks and Traces* (3–5). Illus. by Mary Morgan. 1991, Watts LB $21.00 (0-531-10742-6). 48pp. Tracking becomes fun in this introduction to animal signs. (Rev: BL 4/15/91; SLJ 6/91) [591]

**15021** MacDonald, Suse. *Peck Slither and Slide* (PS–1). Illus. 1997, Harcourt $15.00 (0-15-200079-8). 48pp. The ways that animals move and travel are illustrated, and the words that describe their motions — for example, *wade* and *slither* — are explained. (Rev: BL 4/1/97; SLJ 4/97) [591]

**15022** McGrath, Susan. *The Amazing Things Animals Do* (4–7). Illus. 1989, National Geographic $8.95 (0-87044-709-2). 96pp. Unusual animal behavior is shown in such areas as communication, motion, raising young, and survival. (Rev: SLJ 2/90) [591.5]

**15023** Madgwick, Wendy. *Animaze! A Collection of Amazing Nature Mazes* (3–5). Illus. by Lorna Hussey. 1992, Knopf $13.00 (0-679-82665-3). 40pp. Double-page spreads show a maze for each of 12 animals' habitats in different parts of the world. (Rev: BL 8/92; SLJ 9/92) [591]

**15024** Morgan, Sally. *Animals and Their World* (1–4). Illus. Series: Young Discoverers. 1996, Kingfisher LB $13.90 (0-7534-5035-6); paper $6.95 (0-7534-5034-8). 32pp. Various animals and their environments are briefly introduced, with many illustrations. (Rev: BL 12/1/96) [591.1]

**15025** Nail, Jim. *Whose Tracks Are These? A Clue Book of Familiar Forest Animals* (PS–3). Illus. by Hyla Skudder. 1994, Roberts Rinehart $13.95 (1-879373-89-0). Presents 6 guessing games in which readers are challenged to identify various common forest creatures through their tracks and a description of their habits. (Rev: SLJ 9/94) [591]

**15026** Patent, Dorothy Hinshaw. *What Good Is a Tail?* (3–5). Photos by William Munoz. 1994, Dutton paper $14.99 (0-525-65148-9). 32pp. Tells what a tail is, what it is used for, and what it looks like in various species. (Rev: BCCB 2/94; BL 5/1/94; SLJ 2/94) [596]

**15027** Riley, Linda C. *Elephants Swim* (PS–1). Illus. by Steve Jenkins. 1995, Houghton $14.95 (0-395-73654-4). 40pp. This picture book shows how a variety of animals react to water. (Rev: BL 9/1/95*; HB 9–10/95; SLJ 9/95) [591.1]

**15028** Rosenthal, Mark. *Predators* (1–4). Illus. 1983, Children's LB $15.27 (0-516-01707-1). 48pp. Animals that prey on others are briefly introduced in text and fine photos.

**15029** Royston, Angela. *Night-time Animals* (PS). Illus. by Dave King. Series: Eye Openers. 1992, Macmillan paper $7.95 (0-689-71646-X). 22pp.

Each double-page spread contains a large photo of a nocturnal animal plus other illustrations and some text. (Rev: BL 10/15/92; SLJ 2/93) [595.7]

**15030** Savage, Stephen. *Skin* (2–4). Illus. Series: Adaptation for Survival. 1995, Thomson Learning LB $21.40 (1-56847-353-2). 32pp. Describes the skin covering on a variety of animals, including humans and other mammals, reptiles, birds, fish, and shellfish. (Rev: SLJ 3/96) [591]

**15031** Singer, Marilyn. *Bottoms Up!* (3–6). Illus. by Patrick O'Brien. 1998, Holt $14.95 (0-8050-4246-6). 32pp. A book about the behinds of animals and humans, their various uses, and variations in color, size and structure. (Rev: BL 3/15/98) [591.5]

**15032** Sussman, Susan, and Robert James. *Lies (People Believe) About Animals* (3–6). Illus. 1987, Whitman LB $12.95 (0-8075-4530-9). 48pp. A snake's skin is not wet and slimy; this is just one of the fascinating science facts included here. (Rev: BCCB 7–8/87; BL 8/87; SLJ 11/87)

**15033** Wells, Robert E. *What's Faster Than a Speeding Cheetah?* (K–4). Illus. 1997, Albert Whitman LB $14.95 (0-8075-2280-5); paper $6.95 (0-8075-2281-3). 32pp. The author explores the concept of speed in the animal kingdom by focusing on the cheetah, the fastest animal. (Rev: BL 10/1/97; SLJ 1/98) [531]

**15034** Wilkes, Angela. *Incredible Great Hunters* (1–3). Illus. 1994, DK Publg. paper $4.95 (1-56458-729-0). 32pp. An account of nature's great hunters like bears in a book with a pictorial emphasis. (Rev: BL 1/15/95) [591.5]

## BABIES

**15035** *Baby* (PS–1). Illus. Series: What's Inside? 1992, DK Publg. $8.95 (1-56458-004-0). 24pp. With diagrams that peel back, the internal parts of animal babies are revealed. (Rev: BL 4/15/92) [591.3]

**15036** Baillie, Marilyn. *Little Wonders: Animal Babies and Their Families* (K–3). Illus. by Romi Caron. 1995, Owl $14.95 (1-895688-37-X); paper $5.95 (1-895688-31-0). 32pp. The child-rearing habits of 12 animal species around the world are covered in this attractive picture book. (Rev: SLJ 12/95) [591]

**15037** Bauer, Marion Dane. *If You Were Born a Kitten* (PS–3). Illus. by JoEllen M. Stammen. 1997, Simon & Schuster paper $16.00 (0-689-80111-4). 32pp. Each double-page spread shows a different animal — like a cat, sea horse, or porcupine — along with a picture of its newborn. (Rev: BL 10/15/97; SLJ 11/97*) [591.3]

**15038** Collard, Sneed B. *Animal Dads* (PS–2). Illus. by Steve Jenkins. 1997, Houghton $15.95 (0-395-83621-2). 32pp. The role of fathers in the animal kingdom is presented in large type and beautiful collages. (Rev: BCCB 5/97; BL 5/15/97; SLJ 6/97*) [591.56]

**15039** Craig, Claire. *Animal Babies* (2–4). Illus. Series: Nature Company Young Discoveries. 1996, Time Life $10.00 (0-7835-4839-7). 32pp. Double-page spreads and a brief text are used to introduce the young of various species. (Rev: BL 12/15/96) [591.3]

**15040** Darling, Kathy. *Desert Babies* (3–5). Illus. by Tara Darling. 1997, Walker LB $16.85 (0-8027-8480-1). 32pp. An introduction to deserts, with a focus on the young animals found there, their size, food, enemies, and world location. (Rev: BCCB 3/97; BL 4/1/97; SLJ 3/97) [591.909]

**15041** Dekkers, Midas. *Birth Day: A Celebration of Baby Animals* (2–4). Illus. 1995, W. H. Freeman $14.40 (0-7167-6581-0). 88pp. The story of several different baby animals, from conception to birth and post-natal care. (Rev: BL 7/95; SLJ 9/95) [599]

**15042** Dewey, Jennifer O. *Faces Only a Mother Could Love* (K–3). Illus. 1996, Boyds Mills $14.95 (1-56397-046-5). 32pp. Baby pictures of such unusual creatures as hognose snakes, sloths, and giant anteaters are highlighted in this unique picture book. (Rev: BCCB 2/96; BL 1/1–15/96; SLJ 2/96) [591.3]

**15043** Flegg, Jim. *Animal Families* (4–7). Illus. by David Hosking. Series: Wild World. 1991, Millbrook LB $11.90 (1-878137-20-4). 32pp. In pictures and text, this book shows the various ways animals take care of their young. (Rev: BL 1/1/91) [591.51]

**15044** Hirschi, Ron. *A Time for Babies* (K–2). Illus. by Thomas D. Mangelsen. Series: How Animals Live. 1993, Dutton paper $13.99 (0-525-65095-4). 32pp. Color photographs show how animals and their babies live in their natural habitat. (Rev: BL 12/15/93; SLJ 8/93*) [591.3]

**15045** Maynard, Christopher. *Amazing Animal Babies* (1–4). Illus. Series: Eyewitness Juniors. 1993, Knopf paper $9.99 (0-679-83924-0). 32pp. The infancy of a number of animals is pictured and described in a simple text. (Rev: BL 9/15/93) [591.3]

**15046** Priddy, Roger. *Baby's Book of Animals* (PS). 1993, DK Publg. $9.95 (1-56458-278-7). 21pp. An album of photos that contains pictures of 70 animals and their babies. (Rev: SLJ 4/94) [591]

**15047** Ryan, Pam M. *A Pinky Is a Baby Mouse* (K–3). Illus. by Diane De Groat. 1997, Hyperion LB $15.49 (0-7868-2190-6). 32pp. Using rhyming verse, this book introduces the young of several animals and names them, e.g., a baby swan is a cygnet. (Rev: BL 6/1–15/97; SLJ 7/97) [591]

## CAMOUFLAGE

**15048** Arnosky, Jim. *I See Animals Hiding* (K–3). Illus. 1995, Scholastic $12.95 (0-590-48143-6). 32pp. All kinds of camouflage in animals, including seasonal changes, are explored in paintings and large-print text. (Rev: BCCB 2/95; BL 1/15/95; HB 3–4/95; SLJ 4/95) [591.57]

**15049** Fowler, Allan. *Hard-to-See Animals* (1–2). Series: Rookie Read-About-Science. 1997, Children's LB $18.50 (0-516-20548-X). 32pp. This book introduces animal camouflage, with striking photos and minimal text, suitable for beginning readers. (Rev: BL 11/15/97; SLJ 10/97) [591]

**15050** Llewellyn, Claire. *Disguises and Surprises* (3–5). Illus. Series: SuperSmarts. 1996, Candlewick $11.99 (0-7636-0037-7). 24pp. A wide range of creatures are used to explore the topic of camouflage in nature. (Rev: BL 12/1/96; SLJ 2/97) [591.59]

**15051** McDonnell, Janet. *Animal Camouflage* (K–2). Illus. Series: Animal Behavior. 1997, Child's World LB $22.79 (1-56766-400-8). 32pp. The ways that animals can conceal their identities through protective coloration, body shapes, or unusual behavior are covered in text and pictures. (Rev: SLJ 2/98) [591]

**15052** Otto, Carolyn. *What Color Is Camouflage?* (K–4). Illus. by Megan Lloyd. 1996, HarperCollins LB $14.89 (0-06-027099-3). 32pp. How animal coloration is used to provide safety is explored in a series of pictures containing hidden animal life. (Rev: BL 11/1/96; SLJ 12/96) [591.57]

**15053** Perry, Phyllis J. *Hide and Seek: Creatures in Camouflage* (3–5). Illus. Series: First Book. 1997, Watts $22.00 (0-531-20306-9). 63pp. Describes animal camouflage in various groups of animals, including mammals, birds, insects, reptiles, and ocean life. (Rev: SLJ 2/98) [591]

## COMMUNICATION

**15054** Brooks, Bruce. *Making Sense: Animal Perception and Communication* (5–8). Illus. Series: Knowing Nature. 1993, Farrar $17.00 (0-374-34742-5). 74pp. Organized by the 5 senses, this book tells about the perception of several animals and how they communicate. (Rev: BCCB 1/94; BL 12/1/93; SLJ 1/94*) [591.1]

**15055** Facklam, Margery. *Bees Dance and Whales Sing: The Mysteries of Animal Communication* (4–6). Illus. by Pamela Johnson. 1992, Little, Brown $14.95 (0-87156-573-0). 48pp. Fascinating technical information is given on the ways various animals communicate. (Rev: BL 6/15/92; SLJ 8/92) [591.59]

**15056** Flegg, Jim, et al. *Animal Communication* (4–7). Illus. by David Hosking. Series: Wild World. 1991, Millbrook LB $11.90 (1-878137-23-9). 32pp. This account shows how animals communicate with one another through sounds and actions. (Rev: BL 1/1/91) [591.59]

**15057** Kalman, Bobbie. *How Animals Communicate* (2–4). Illus. Series: Crabapples. 1996, Crabtree LB $18.08 (0-86505-635-8); paper $5.95 (0-86505-735-4). 32pp. Discusses sound, scent, touch, color, and movement in such animals as elephants, giraffes, and honeybees. (Rev: SLJ 6/97) [591]

**15058** McDonnell, Janet. *Animal Communication* (K–2). Illus. Series: Animal Behavior. 1997, Child's World LB $22.79 (1-56766-401-6). 32pp. The ways that animals communicate through sounds and movements are explored in this simple science book. (Rev: SLJ 2/98) [591.59]

## DEFENSES

**15059** Bennett, Paul. *Escaping from Enemies* (1–4). Illus. Series: Nature's Secrets. 1995, Thomson Learning LB $21.40 (1-56847-358-3). 32pp. Describes how animals defend themselves by fighting, running, or resorting to trickery. (Rev: SLJ 8/95) [591]

**15060** Jenkins, Steve. *What Do You Do When Something Wants to Eat You?* (PS–3). Illus. 1997, Houghton $16.00 (0-395-82514-8). 32pp. In this thrilling science book illustrated with paper collages, 14 different animals employ unusual tricks of nature to escape their predators. (Rev: BL 12/1/97; SLJ 11/97) [591.47]

**15061** Mirocha, Paul, and Rhod Lauffer. *Back Off! Animal Defensive Behavior* (2–4). Illus. 1994, W. H. Freeman $8.80 (0-7167-6534-9). Pop-ups are used to illustrate how animals defend themselves. Also use *Look Again!* (1994), about animal disguises. (Rev: BL 11/15/94) [591.566]

**15062** Perry, Phyllis J. *Armor to Venom: Animal Defenses* (3–5). Illus. Series: First Books: Animals. 1997, Watts $22.00 (0-531-20299-2). 63pp. This book explores animal defenses and survival mechanisms, from camouflage to venom production. (Rev: SLJ 12/97) [591]

**15063** Sowler, Sandie. *Amazing Armored Animals* (1–4). Illus. Series: Eyewitness Juniors. 1992, Knopf LB $9.99 (0-679-92767-0); paper $6.95 (0-679-82767-6). 32pp. After a general section on armored animals, such individual species as armadillos are pictured in double-page spreads. (Rev: BL 8/92; SLJ 8/92) [591.57]

## HIBERNATION

**15064** Berger, Melvin, and Gilda Berger. *What Do Animals Do in Winter? How Animals Survive the Cold* (2–4). Illus. Series: Discovery Readers. 1995, Ideals LB $12.00 (1-57102-055-1); paper $4.50 (1-57102-041-1). 48pp. Such winter survival tactics as

hibernation and migration are presented with many examples. (Rev: BL 12/1/95; SLJ 2/96) [591.54]

**15065** Facklam, Margery. *Do Not Disturb: The Mysteries of Animal Hibernation and Sleep* (3–5). Illus. by Pamela Johnson. 1989, Little, Brown $15.95 (0-316-27379-1). 48pp. Explaining the mysterious biological processes of hibernation and long winter sleep. (Rev: BL 3/1/89; SLJ 3/89)

## HOMES

**15066** Arnosky, Jim. *Crinkleroot's Guide to Knowing Animal Habitats* (PS–4). Illus. 1997, Simon & Schuster $13.00 (0-689-80583-7). 32pp. In double-page spreads and a chatty text, several habitats — such as wetlands, grasslands, and cornfields — and the animals that live there are introduced. (Rev: BL 6/1–15/97; SLJ 6/97) [591.5]

**15067** Brooks, Bruce. *Nature by Design* (5–8). Illus. 1991, Farrar $13.95 (0-374-30334-7). 80pp. Animal homes and intelligence are discussed in this excellent account that is both entertaining and informative. (Rev: BCCB 1/92; BL 1/1/92; HB 1–2/92) [591.56]

**15068** Crump, Donald J., ed. *Animal Architects* (3–8). Illus. 1987, National Geographic LB $12.50 (0-87044-617-7). 104pp. Chapters on animal builders are divided according to techniques — mound builders, weavers, excavators, and so on. (Rev: BL 12/15/87)

**15069** Dewey, Jennifer O. *Animal Architecture* (PS–1). Illus. 1991, Orchard $16.95 (0-531-05930-8). 72pp. A fascinating volume on how animals build their dwellings. (Rev: BCCB 5/91; BL 2/15/91*; SLJ 4/91) [591.56]

**15070** Flegg, Jim, et al. *Animal Builders* (4–7). Illus. Series: Wild World. 1991, Millbrook LB $17.90 (1-878137-05-0). 32pp. This book shows the different types of housing that all sorts of animals build and live in. (Rev: BL 7/91; SLJ 7/91) [591.564]

**15071** Forsyth, Adrian. *The Architecture of Animals: The Equinox Guide to Wildlife Structures* (5–8). 1989, Camden House $15.95 (0-920656-16-1); paper $9.95 (0-920656-08-0). 72pp. The relationship between the homes animals build and how animal behavior influences home design and location is explored in this fascinating book. (Rev: SLJ 5/90) [591.5]

**15072** Hester, Nigel. *The Living House* (3–5). Illus. Series: Watching Nature. 1991, Watts LB $20.00 (0-531-14120-9). 32pp. With many color photographs, this book explores the different kinds of habitats animals call home. (Rev: SLJ 5/92) [591]

**15073** Kitchen, Bert. *And So They Build* (3–5). Illus. 1993, Candlewick $15.95 (1-56402-217-X). 32pp. Twelve different animals, like swallows and harvest mice, and the amazing structures they build are described in text and detailed paintings. (Rev: BL 1/1/94) [591.56]

**15074** Miranda, Anne. *Does a Mouse Have a House?* (PS). Illus. by author. 1994, Bradbury paper $14.95 (0-02-767251-4). The homes of 17 different insects and other animals are introduced in rhyming couplets and striking collages. (Rev: SLJ 12/94) [591.5]

**15075** Ryan, Pam M. *Armadillos Sleep in Dugouts: And Other Places Animals Live* (K–2). Illus. by Diane De Groat. 1997, Hyperion LB $15.49 (0-7868-2222-8). About 30 animal homes, from a beaver lodge to woody thicket for deer, are described in text and pictures in this simple science book. (Rev: SLJ 12/97) [591]

**15076** Taylor, Barbara. *Animal Homes* (4–6). Illus. Series: Inside Guides. 1996, DK Publg. $15.95 (0-7894-1012-5). 44pp. A heavily illustrated book that introduces various animal dwellings, including nests, burrows, cocoons, and compost heaps. (Rev: SLJ 11/96) [591.56]

**15077** Zoehfeld, Kathleen W. *What Lives in a Shell?* (PS–1). Illus. by Helen K. Davie. Series: Let's-Read-and-Find-Out Stage 1. 1994, HarperCollins LB $14.89 (0-06-022999-3); paper $4.95 (0-06-445124-0). 32pp. A simple science book that introduces such creatures as snails, turtles, crabs, and oysters, that use their shells as homes. (Rev: BL 8/94; HB 11–12/94; SLJ 9/94) [591.4]

### REPRODUCTION

**15078** Burton, Robert. *Egg* (K–3). Illus. by Jane Burton and Kim Taylor. 1994, DK Publg. $13.95 (1-56458-460-7). 45pp. After tracing the development of a chicken embryo, this book describes 27 animals, mostly birds, that hatch from eggs. (Rev: BL 4/1/94; SLJ 6/94) [591.3]

**15079** Seddon, Tony. *Animal Parenting* (5–8). Illus. Series: Nature Watch. 1989, Facts on File $15.95 (0-8160-1654-2). 61pp. Mating, birth, and parenting are covered, from the primitive to the most complex forms of life. (Rev: SLJ 2/90) [591.56]

## Animal Species

### GENERAL AND MISCELLANEOUS

**15080** Ancona, George. *The Golden Lion Tamarin Comes Home* (3–5). Illus. 1994, Macmillan paper $15.95 (0-02-700905-X). 40pp. This account describes how the National Zoo in Washington, D.C. prepares small Brazilian monkeys to return to their natural habitat. (Rev: BL 12/1/94; SLJ 2/95) [639.9]

**15081** Arnold, Caroline. *African Animals* (3–5). Illus. 1997, Morrow LB $15.93 (0-688-14116-1). 48pp. Using color photos, 20 African animals are introduced, arranged by habitat. (Rev: BL 3/15/97; SLJ 3/97) [591.96]

**15082** Arnold, Caroline. *Llama* (4–6). Illus. 1988, Morrow LB $12.88 (0-688-07541-X). 48pp. An engaging introduction to this South American native. (Rev: BCCB 9/88; BL 9/15/88; SLJ 9/88)

**15083** Arnold, Caroline. *Rhino* (3–6). Photos by Richard Hewett. 1995, Morrow LB $15.93 (0-688-12695-2). 48pp. Material on the rhino's habitats, behavior, and family life is given, with a full description of its physical appearance. (Rev: BL 9/15/95; SLJ 12/95) [599.72]

**15084** Arnold, Caroline. *Zebra* (3–7). Illus. 1993, Morrow paper $5.95 (0-688-12273-6). 48pp. Characteristics and behavior of zebras just like Punda, who lives in an animal park in New Jersey. (Rev: BL 9/1/87; SLJ 9/87)

**15085** Arnosky, Jim. *Raccoons and Ripe Corn* (PS–1). Illus. by author. 1991, Morrow paper $4.95 (0-688-10489-4). 32pp. An autumn night with mother and baby raccoon eating corn in the field. (Rev: BL 9/1/87; SLJ 9/87)

**15086** Arthur, Alex. *Shell* (4–8). Illus. Series: Eyewitness Books. 1989, Knopf LB $18.99 (0-394-92256-5). 64pp. All kinds of shelled creatures are highlighted, including mollusks, crustaceans, turtles, and tortoises. (Rev: BL 9/15/89; SLJ 8/89) [594]

**15087** Brimner, Larry Dane. *Polar Mammals* (3–4). Illus. Series: A True Book: Animals. 1996, Children's LB $21.00 (0-516-20042-9). 48pp. An introduction to the Arctic biome, followed by general information on the many different mammals that live there. (Rev: SLJ 4/97) [590]

**15088** Browne, Philippa-Alys. *A Gaggle of Geese: The Collective Names of the Animal Kingdom* (PS–2). Illus. by author. 1996, Simon & Schuster $15.00 (0-689-80761-9). In this imaginative picture book, the collective names of 26 animals are given. (Rev: HB 5–6/96; SLJ 3/96) [591]

**15089** Butterfield, Moira. *Fast, Strong, and Striped: What Am I?* (PS–3). Illus. by Wayne Ford. Series: What Am I? 1997, Raintree Steck-Vaughn LB $19.97 (0-8172-4583-9); paper $5.95 (0-8172-7229-1). 32pp. Using double-page spreads, clues are given about an animal by introducing its physical characteristics, habitat, and diet and then identifying it. Also use *Brown, Fierce, and Furry: What Am I?* (1997). (Rev: SLJ 7/97) [591]

**15090** Cooper, Ann. *In the Forest* (1–3). Illus. by Dorothy Emerling. Series: Wild Wonders. 1996, Roberts Rinehart paper $7.95 (0-916278-71-9). An intriguing look at woodland animals that contains life-size paw prints, a treasure map of the forest floor, and a look at animal life on each forest level. (Rev: SLJ 8/96) [591]

**15091** Craig, Claire. *Incredible Creatures* (2–4). Illus. Series: Nature Company Young Discoveries. 1997, Time Life $10.00 (0-7835-4840-0). 32pp. Some of nature's oddities are introduced in double-page spreads with a simple text. (Rev: BL 2/15/97) [591]

**15092** Creagh, Carson. *Mammals* (4–6). Illus. Series: Nature Company Discoveries. 1996, Time Life $16.00 (0-8094-9372-1). 64pp. A wide range of mammals are introduced in text and illustrations, with an 8-page foldout. (Rev: BL 9/15/96) [599]

**15093** Crump, Donald J., ed. *Amazing Animals of Australia* (5–8). Illus. 1985, National Geographic LB $12.50 (0-87044-520-0). 104pp. Creatures of the rain forest, ocean, outback, and Tasmania are highlighted with color photos. (Rev: BL 6/1/85)

**15094** Everts, Tammy, and Bobbie Kalman. *Really Weird Animals* (2–5). Illus. Series: Crabapples. 1995, Crabtree LB $18.08 (0-86505-627-7); paper $5.95 (0-86505-727-3). 32pp. A brief introduction to 13 strange animals, including the armadillo, tarsier, hagfish, and the smelliest animal in the world, the zorilla. (Rev: SLJ 6/96) [591]

**15095** Fichter, George S. *Poisonous Animals* (3–5). Illus. 1991, Watts LB $21.00 (0-531-20050-7). 64pp. A look at such animals as the black widow spider and the tarantula. (Rev: BL 12/15/91; SLJ 2/92) [591.9]

**15096** Fowler, Allan. *The Biggest Animal on Land* (PS–3). Illus. Series: Rookie Read-About Science. 1996, Children's LB $18.50 (0-516-06050-3). 31pp. This easy-to-read science book describes some of the world's largest animals, like the elephant, and includes full-color pictures of each. (Rev: SLJ 8/96) [591]

**15097** Fowler, Allan. *Smart, Clean Pigs* (1–2). Illus. Series: Rookie Read-About Science Big Books. 1993, Children's LB $18.00 (0-516-49644-1). 32pp. The world of the pig is covered briefly in this easily read book that explains a pig's anatomy, habits, and reputation. Rocky Mountain sheep are the subject of *Woolly Sheep and Hungry Goats* (1993). (Rev: BL 9/1/93; SLJ 9/93) [636.4]

**15098** Ganeri, Anita. *Small Mammals* (3–6). Illus. by John Parsons. Series: Nature Detective. 1993, Watts LB $19.30 (0-531-14249-3). 32pp. A richly illustrated book that describes such animals as squirrels, rabbits, bats, and mice, with descriptions of where they live and the footprints they leave. (Rev: BL 12/15/93) [599]

**15099** Greenaway, Theresa. *Powerful Beasts of the Wild* (2–3). Illus. Series: Mighty Animals. 1997, DK Publg. $9.95 (0-7894-1509-7). 21pp. A slim volume that gives information on the characteristics, size, and habits of a variety of beasts known for their strength. (Rev: BL 6/1–15/97; SLJ 7/97) [590]

**15100** Greenaway, Theresa. *Weird Creatures of the Wild* (2–3). Illus. Series: Mighty Animals. 1997, DK Publg. $9.95 (0-7894-1510-0). 21pp. This slim volume gives material about the structure, habits, and habitats of such unusual creatures as the babirusa, echidna, and cassowary. (Rev: BL 6/1–15/97; SLJ 7/97) [590]

**15101** Harman, Amanda. *Rhinoceroses* (3–5). Illus. Series: Endangered! 1996, Benchmark LB $21.36 (0-7614-0290-X). 32pp. The ferocious rhinoceros is described, with material on its habits, habitats, and why it is on the endangered list. (Rev: SLJ 2/97) [599.72]

**15102** Hirschi, Ron. *Faces in the Forest* (1–3). Illus. Series: Wildlife Watcher's First Guide. 1997, Dutton paper $15.99 (0-525-65224-8). 40pp. Various forest animals, like the woodpecker and the black bear, are introduced in this informal account. (Rev: BL 9/15/97; SLJ 3/98) [591.52]

**15103** Hirschi, Ron. *Faces in the Mountains* (1–3). Illus. Series: Wildlife Watcher's First Guide. 1997, Dutton paper $15.99 (0-525-65225-6). 40pp. The snow-shoe hare, moose, coyote, and other animals that live in the mountains are introduced. (Rev: BL 9/15/97; SLJ 3/98) [599]

**15104** Hoban, Tana. *A Children's Zoo* (PS). Illus. 1985, Greenwillow LB $16.93 (0-688-05204-5). 24pp. Appealing portraits of 11 common zoo animals. (Rev: BCCB 10/85; BL 9/1/85; SLJ 10/85)

**15105** Johnson, Sylvia A. *Ferrets* (3–6). Illus. 1997, Carolrhoda LB $19.93 (1-57505-014-5). 48pp. Several types of wild and domestic ferrets and their cousins, including otters and skunks, are introduced, with a concentration on efforts to save the black-footed ferret. (Rev: BL 7/97; SLJ 8/97) [636]

**15106** Kalbacken, Joan. *Badgers* (3–4). Illus. Series: A True Book. 1996, Children's LB $21.00 (0-516-20157-3). 48pp. In text and photos, the badger is introduced, with material on its physical characteristics, life-style, breeding, and survival. (Rev: SLJ 4/97) [599.74]

**15107** Knight, Linsay. *The Sierra Club Book of Great Mammals* (3–6). Illus. 1992, Sierra Club $16.95 (0-87156-507-2). 68pp. A photoessay with dramatic photos and intriguing text, asking and answering such questions as why whales get stranded on beaches. (Rev: BL 12/1/92) [599.2]

**15108** Knight, Linsay. *The Sierra Club Book of Small Mammals* (5–7). Illus. 1993, Sierra Club $16.95 (0-87156-525-0). 68pp. An oversized, well-illustrated introduction to small mammals in North America and around the world. (Rev: BL 3/15/93; SLJ 6/93) [599]

**15109** LaBonte, Gail. *The Llama* (4–6). Illus. 1989, Macmillan $13.95 (0-87518-393-X). 60pp. Introducing this gentle-natured member of the camel family. (Rev: BL 3/1/89)

**15110** Lepthien, Emilie U. *Buffalo* (1–3). Illus. Series: New True Books. 1989, Children's LB $21.00 (0-516-01161-8). 48pp. The bison or buffalo are introduced in many colorful pictures and a simple text that gives historic background. (Rev: BL 9/1/89) [599.73]

**15111** Lepthien, Emilie U. *Llamas* (3–4). Illus. Series: True Book: Animals. 1996, Children's LB $21.00 (0-516-20160-3). 48pp. An introduction to llamas and their relatives that tells about body structure, wool, and habits. (Rev: SLJ 6/97) [599.7]

**15112** Lepthien, Emilie U. *Skunks* (2–4). Illus. Series: New True Book. 1993, Children's LB $21.00 (0-516-01197-9). 48pp. Using a simple text, large type, and many attractive illustrations, skunks and their world are introduced. (Rev: BL 7/94) [599.74]

**15113** Leslie-Melville, Betty. *Walter Warthog* (3–5). 1989, Doubleday $12.95 (0-385-26378-3). 46pp. The story of how an American family in Nairobi adopted a warthog. (Rev: BL 10/15/89; SLJ 1/90) [599]

**15114** Maynard, Thane. *A Rhino Comes to America* (4–6). Illus. Series: Cincinnati Zoo Book. 1993, Watts LB $23.60 (0-531-11173-3). 40pp. This account of how a rhino is captured in Sumatra and taken to the Cincinnati Zoo also contains material about the problems of endangered species. (Rev: BL 9/15/93; SLJ 9/93) [636]

**15115** Midge, Tiffany. *Buffalo* (PS–3). Illus. by Diana Magnuson. Series: Animal Lore and Legend. 1995, Scholastic $4.95 (0-590-22489-1). 32pp. The food, habitats, and behavior of buffalo are described, along with 3 Indian folktales about them. (Rev: SLJ 3/96) [591.52]

**15116** Nicholson, Darrel. *Wild Boars* (2–4). Illus. 1987, Carolrhoda LB $14.95 (0-87614-308-7). 48pp. Full-color photos highlight the habits and characteristics of the boar, introduced in the United States at the turn of the century. (Rev: BCCB 9/87; BL 7/87; SLJ 9/87)

**15117** Parker, Steve. *Mammal* (4–8). Illus. 1989, Knopf LB $20.99 (0-394-92258-1). 64pp. Various kinds of mammals are introduced with material on life cycle, development, habits, and habitation. (Rev: BL 9/15/89; SLJ 8/89) [599]

**15118** Parsons, Alexandra. *Amazing Mammals* (1–4). Illus. by Jerry Young. Series: Eyewitness Juniors. 1990, Knopf LB $11.99 (0-679-90224-4); paper $9.99 (0-679-80224-X). 32pp. Good introductions to mammals and how they care for their young. (Rev: BL 8/90) [599]

**15119** Patton, Don. *Armadillos* (2–4). Illus. Series: Naturebooks: Animals. 1995, Child's World LB $22.79 (1-56766-182-3). 32pp. Color photos on each page and a simple text highlight this introduction to armadillos, their structure, and habitats. (Rev: BL 11/15/95; SLJ 4/96) [599.3]

**15120** Pearce, Q. L. *Armadillos and Other Unusual Animals* (4–6). Illus. by Mary Ann Fraser. Series: Amazing Science Books. 1989, Simon & Schuster paper $5.95 (0-671-68645-3). 64pp. Unusual animals and their habits are introduced in this well-organized volume. (Rev: SLJ 4/90) [599]

**15121** Pembleton, Seliesa. *The Armadillo* (2–5). Illus. Series: Amazing Animals. 1992, Macmillan $13.95 (0-87518-507-X). 60pp. The story of the armed mammal, the armadillo, telling where and how it lives and why it is presently endangered. (Rev: BL 11/1/92; SLJ 10/92) [599.3]

**15122** Peters, David. *Giants of Land, Sea and Air, Past and Present* (3–6). Illus. 1986, Knopf LB $15.99 (0-394-97805-6). 64pp. Oversize book offering basic information on 72 oversize animals. (Rev: BCCB 2/87; BL 12/15/86; SLJ 2/87)

**15123** *Polar Animals* (PS–2). Illus. by Paul Hess. 1996, De Agostini $6.95 (1-899883-36-3). Humorous rhymes accompany paintings that describe 8 animals from the polar regions. (Rev: SLJ 12/96) [591]

**15124** Rothaus, Don P. *Hyenas* (2–4). Illus. Series: Naturebooks: Animals. 1995, Child's World LB $22.79 (1-56766-183-1). 32pp. The nocturnal life of the hyena, the African scavenger, is presented in full-page illustrations and simple text. (Rev: BL 11/15/95) [599.74]

**15125** Rothaus, Don P. *Warthogs* (2–4). Illus. Series: Naturebooks: Animals. 1995, Child's World LB $22.79 (1-56766-185-8). 32pp. Important facts about warthogs are presented in a clear, large-print text and full-page color photos. (Rev: BL 11/15/95) [599.73]

**15126** Ryder, Nora L. *In the Wild* (PS–1). Illus. 1995, Holt $11.95 (0-8050-1775-5). 20pp. Flaps are used to depict parts of animals' bodies in this guessing game to determine each creatures' identity. (Rev: BL 12/15/97; SLJ 5/97) [591]

**15127** Schlaepfer, Gloria G., and Mary Lou Samuelson. *The African Rhinos* (3–5). Illus. Series: Remarkable Animals. 1992, Macmillan LB $13.95 (0-87518-505-3). 60pp. Full-color photos help tell the story of this great animal and why it is in danger of extinction. (Rev: BL 11/1/92; SLJ 10/92) [599]

**15128** Seidensticker, John, and Susan Lumpkin, eds. *Dangerous Animals* (4–6). Illus. Series: Nature Company Discoveries. 1995, Time Life LB $16.00 (0-7835-4762-5). 64pp. A number of ferocious animals are introduced in stunning pictures and brief text, with an eye-catching 8-page foldout. (Rev: BL 1/1–15/96; SLJ 1/96) [591]

**15129** Selsam, Millicent E., and Joyce Hunt. *A First Look at Animals That Eat Other Animals* (1–3). Illus. by Harriett Springer. Series: A First Look At. 1990, Walker LB $12.85 (0-8027-6896-2). A simple nature book that introduces the world of carnivores. (Rev: SLJ 4/90) [599]

**15130** Selsam, Millicent E., and Joyce Hunt. *A First Look at Animals with Horns* (2–3). Illus. by Harriett Springer. 1989, Walker LB $11.85 (0-8027-6872-5). 48pp. A straightforward look at animals with horn-like appendages. (Rev: BL 4/15/89; SLJ 6/89)

**15131** Sherrow, Victoria. *The Porcupine* (4–6). Illus. Series: Remarkable Animals. 1991, Macmillan LB $13.95 (0-87518-442-1). 60pp. The life cycle and habits of the porcupine are explored in colorful photographs and informative text. (Rev: BL 8/91; SLJ 1/92) [599.32]

**15132** Short, Joan, et al. *Platypus* (3–4). Illus. by Andrew Wichlinski. 1997, Mondo paper $4.95 (1-57255-195-X). 22pp. There is coverage on the anatomy, habits, and habitat of this unusual animal, with a cross-section drawing of its underground burrow. (Rev: SLJ 8/97) [599]

**15133** Sill, Cathryn. *About Mammals: A Guide for Children* (1–2). Illus. by John Sill. 1997, Peachtree $14.95 (1-56145-141-X). 32pp. In this very simple volume with full-color paintings, several mammals and their habits are introduced to young children. (Rev: BL 6/1–15/97; SLJ 6/97) [500]

**15134** Silverstein, Alvin, et al. *The Black-Footed Ferret* (4–7). Illus. Series: Endangered in America. 1995, Millbrook LB $22.40 (1-56294-552-1). 64pp. An introduction to this endangered species and efforts being made to ensure its survival. (Rev: BL 10/15/95; SLJ 1/96) [333.95]

**15135** Snedden, Robert. *What Is a Mammal?* (3–6). Illus. Series: Sierra Club Books for Children. 1994, Sierra Club $14.95 (0-87156-468-8). 32pp. The characteristics of mammals are described, including such topics as locomotion, life cycles, and temperature control. (Rev: BL 12/15/94) [599]

**15136** Stone, Lynn M. *Back from the Edge: The American Bison* (4–6). Series: Animal Odysseys. 1991, Rourke LB $16.95 (0-86593-101-1). 48pp. The history of the American buffalo and the conservation efforts to prevent its extinction. Also use from this series: *The Wildebeest's Great Migration* (1991). (Rev: SLJ 3/92) [591.52]

**15137** Stuart, Dee. *The Astonishing Armadillo* (3–6). Illus. Series: Nature Watch Books. 1993, Carolrhoda LB $19.93 (0-87614-769-4). 48pp. The amazing armadillo is featured in text and sharp color photos. (Rev: BL 8/93) [599.3]

**15138** Swanson, Diane. *Buffalo Sunrise: The Story of a North American Giant* (4–7). Illus. 1996, Sierra Club $16.95 (0-87156-861-6). 58pp. A glimpse at the fascinating history, appearance, and habits of the buffalo (bison) and current efforts to save the species. (Rev: BCCB 6/96; BL 5/1/96; SLJ 6/96) [599.73]

**15139** Tee-Van, Helen D. *Small Mammals Are Where You Find Them* (5–7). Illus. by author. 1966, Knopf LB $5.99 (0-394-91643-3). Seven small species of mammals from the United States are introduced with maps and identifying data.

**15140** Tesar, Jenny. *What on Earth Is an Echidna?* (3–5). Illus. Series: What On Earth? 1995, Blackbirch LB $14.95 (1-56711-098-3). 32pp. This spiny, egg-laying mammal is introduced with material on where and how it lives. (Rev: SLJ 11/95) [597]

**15141** Thornhill, Jan. *Before and After: A Book of Nature Timescapes* (PS–3). Illus. 1997, National Geographic $16.00 (0-7922-7093-2). 32pp. Using different habitats, this book pictures a variety of animals and plants using a single dramatic incident, like the charge of a lioness, to show before-and-after situations. (Rev: BL 10/1/97; SLJ 9/97) [577]

**15142** Toda, Kyoko. *Animal Faces* (PS). Trans. from Japanese by Amanda Mayer Stinchecum. Photos by Akira Satoh. 1996, Kane/Miller $16.95 (0-916291-62-6). 53pp. This book shows how animal faces differ, even within a particular species. (Rev: SLJ 11/96) [591]

**15143** Walker, Sally M. *Rhinos* (4–6). Illus. 1996, Carolrhoda LB $14.96 (1-57505-008-0). 48pp. An introduction to rhinos that stresses their present near extinction and conservation efforts. (Rev: BL 12/1/96; SLJ 12/96*) [599.72]

**15144** Whayne, Susanne S. *Night Creatures* (3–6). Illus. by Steven Schindler. 1993, Simon & Schuster paper $15.00 (0-671-73395-8). 45pp. Five nocturnal animals are introduced and described. (Rev: BL 7/93; SLJ 7/93) [591]

### APE FAMILY

**15145** Ashby, Ruth. *The Orangutan* (4–6). Illus. Series: Remarkable Animals. 1994, Dillon LB $13.95 (0-87518-600-9). 60pp. As well as a description of the orangutan and its environment, this account discusses conservation efforts being undertaken to save this endangered species. (Rev: SLJ 8/94) [599.88]

**15146** Darling, Tara, and Kathy Darling. *How to Babysit an Orangutan* (2–4). Illus. 1996, Walker LB $16.85 (0-8027-8467-4). 32pp. The description of the activities and functions of Camp Leakey on Borneo, where orphaned orangutans are cared for. (Rev: BL 12/15/96; HB 11–12/96; SLJ 10/96) [599.88]

**15147** DaVolls, Linda. *Tano and Binti: Two Chimpanzees Return to the Wild* (K–3). Illus. by Andy DaVolls. 1994, Clarion $14.95 (0-395-68701-2).

32pp. A true story of how 2 young chimps born in captivity react when they are let loose in the wilds of central Africa. (Rev: BCCB 6/94; BL 3/15/94; SLJ 5/94) [599.88]

**15148** Gelman, Rita G. *Monkeys and Apes of the World* (2–5). Illus. 1990, Watts LB $19.00 (0-531-10749-3). 64pp. Apes and monkeys are compared and contrasted in this well-illustrated study. (Rev: BL 7/90; SLJ 8/90) [599.8]

**15149** Goodall, Jane. *The Chimpanzee Family Book* (4–6). Illus. 1997, North-South paper $8.95 (1-558-58803-5). 72pp. Illustrated with photographs, this is an affectionate portrayal of a family of chimps. (Rev: BL 7/89; HB 7–8/89; SLJ 6/89) [599.88]

**15150** Grace, Eric S. *Apes* (4–6). Illus. 1995, Sierra Club $15.95 (0-87156-365-7). 64pp. The evolution of primates is covered, with details on the behavior, anatomy, and life cycles of species like chimpanzees, gorillas, and orangutans. (Rev: BL 12/1/95) [599.98]

**15151** Hansard, Peter. *I Like Monkeys Because . . .* (PS–1). Illus. by Patricia Casey. Series: Read and Wonder. 1993, Candlewick $14.95 (1-56402-196-3). 32pp. A simple introduction to apes and monkeys around the world. (Rev: BL 10/15/93; SLJ 10/93) [599.8]

**15152** Harman, Amanda. *South American Monkeys* (4–6). Illus. Series: Endangered! 1996, Benchmark LB $21.36 (0-7614-0218-7). 32pp. The monkeys of South America are introduced, with material on how they differ from their African counterparts and why they are endangered. (Rev: SLJ 8/96) [599.88]

**15153** Horton, Casey. *Apes* (3–6). Illus. Series: Endandered! 1996, Benchmark LB $21.36 (0-7614-0212-8). 32pp. Several species of great and lesser apes are introduced, with material on habitats, physical traits, behavior, and endangered status. (Rev: SLJ 3/96) [599.88]

**15154** Lumley, Kathryn Wentzel. *Monkeys and Apes* (1–4). Illus. 1982, Children's LB $21.00 (0-516-01633-4); paper $5.50 (0-516-41633-2). An introduction in simple language with many color illustrations.

**15155** Maynard, Thane. *Primates: Apes, Monkeys, Prosimians* (4–6). Illus. 1995, Watts LB $23.60 (0-531-11169-5). 64pp. Three species of primates and their subgroups are described, with details on habits, geographical locations, and behavior. (Rev: BL 8/95; SLJ 5/95) [599.8]

**15156** Milton, Joyce. *Gorillas: Gentle Giants of the Forest* (1–3). Illus. by Bryn Barnard. Series: Step into Reading. 1997, Random paper $3.99 (0-679-87284-1). 48pp. This easy-to-read account introduces gorillas, where they live, what they eat, and how they move. (Rev: BL 5/1/97; SLJ 8/97) [598.98]

**15157** Patton, Don. *New World Monkeys* (2–4). Illus. Series: Naturebooks: Animals. 1995, Child's World LB $22.79 (1-56766-189-0). 32pp. This species of monkey is introduced, with each page of text faced by a full-color photograph. (Rev: BL 11/15/95) [599.8]

**15158** Redmond, Ian. *Gorilla* (4–8). Illus. Series: Eyewitness Books. 1995, Knopf LB $20.99 (0-679-97332-X). 64pp. Illustrations highlight this introduction to the life, personality, and environment of the gorilla. (Rev: BL 12/15/95; SLJ 1/96) [599.8]

**15159** Robinson, Claire. *Chimpanzees* (2–3). Illus. Series: In the Wild. 1997, Heinemann $12.95 (1-57572-136-8). 24pp. A simple introduction to chimpanzees with close-up views of family life, information on how apes use tools, and material about their endangered status. (Rev: BL 2/1/98) [599.885]

**15160** Stone, Lynn M. *Baboons* (1–3). Illus. Series: Monkey Discovery Library. 1991, Rourke LB $10.95 (0-86593-067-8). 24pp. A brief introduction to baboons: physical traits, behavior, and habitats. Also use: *Chimpanzees; Gorillas;* and *Snow Monkeys* (all 1990). (Rev: SLJ 6/91) [599.8]

### BATS

**15161** Ackerman, Diane. *Bats: Shadows in the Night* (4–6). Illus. 1997, Crown $18.00 (0-517-70919-8). 32pp. The author reports on her bat-watching experiences in the Big Bend National Park in Texas and of the amazing observations she made concerning these unusual creatures. (Rev: BL 10/1/97; SLJ 10/97*) [599.4]

**15162** Arnold, Caroline. *Bat* (3–6). Illus. by Richard Hewett. 1996, Morrow LB $15.93 (0-688-13727-X). 48pp. The structure, behavior, habitats, and mythology of bats are covered. (Rev: BCCB 10/96; BL 8/96; SLJ 9/96) [599.4]

**15163** Bash, Barbara. *Shadows of Night: The Hidden World of the Little Brown Bat* (4–6). Illus. 1993, Sierra Club $16.95 (0-87156-562-5). 32pp. The first year in the life of a little brown bat is created in text and stunning watercolor illustrations. (Rev: BL 4/15/93; HB 7–8/93; SLJ 6/93*) [599.4]

**15164** Earle, Ann. *Zipping, Zapping, Zooming Bats* (2–3). Illus. by Henry Cole. 1995, HarperCollins LB $14.89 (0-06-023480-6). 32pp. Coverage is given on various types of bats and their body structure, senses, eating habits, and homes. (Rev: BCCB 2/96; BL 8/95; SLJ 8/95) [599.4]

**15165** Glaser, Linda. *Beautiful Bats* (PS–K). Illus. by Sharon L. Holm. 1997, Millbrook LB $21.40 (0-7613-0254-9). Basic information about bats is given in the body of this simple science book, with 6 pages of additional details at the back of the book. (Rev: SLJ 12/97) [599.4]

**15166** Greenaway, Frank. *Amazing Bats* (1–4). Illus. by Jerry Young. Series: Eyewitness Juniors. 1991, Knopf LB $11.99 (0-679-91518-4); paper $9.99 (0-679-81518-X). 32pp. In amazing photos spread over 2 pages, the world of bats and their habits is introduced. (Rev: BL 10/1/91) [599.4]

**15167** Maestro, Betsy. *Bats: Night Fliers* (K–3). Illus. by Giulio Maestro. 1994, Scholastic $15.95 (0-590-46150-8). 32pp. An attractive picture book that exposes the myths concerning this night flier and replaces them with the truth. (Rev: SLJ 12/94) [599.4]

**15168** Markle, Sandra. *Outside and Inside Bats* (4–6). Illus. 1997, Simon & Schuster $16.00 (0-689-81165-9). 40pp. A straightforward examination of bats that covers topics like their anatomy, physiology, senses, and habits. (Rev: BL 10/1/97; SLJ 11/97) [599.8]

**15169** Milton, Joyce. *Bats: Creatures of the Night* (1–3). Illus. by Judith Moffatt. 1993, Putnam paper $3.95 (0-448-40193-2). 48pp. Simple vocabulary and short sentences are used to convey basic information about bats and their habits. (Rev: BL 12/1/93; SLJ 2/94) [599.4]

**15170** Penny, Malcolm. *How Bats "See" in the Dark* (3–5). Illus. Series: Nature's Mysteries. 1996, Benchmark LB $21.36 (0-7614-0455-4). 32pp. The facts about bats are interestingly presented with details on how we uncovered their secrets and what questions remain unanswered. (Rev: SLJ 2/97) [599.4]

**15171** Stuart, Dee. *Bats: Mysterious Flyers of the Night* (3–6). Illus. Series: Nature Watch. 1994, Carolrhoda LB $19.93 (0-87614-814-3). 48pp. With outstanding photographs, this is a fine introduction to bats and their habits, food, and habitats. (Rev: BL 9/15/94; SLJ 10/94) [599.4]

### BEARS

**15172** Clark, Margaret G. *The Threatened Florida Black Bear* (4–6). Illus. 1995, Dutton paper $15.99 (0-525-65196-9). 64pp. This account describes the life and habits of the Florida black bear and the methods used to ensure its survival. (Rev: BL 1/1–15/96; SLJ 12/95) [599.72]

**15173** Crewe, Sabrina. *The Bear* (K–3). Illus. by Robert Morton. Series: Life Cycles. 1996, Raintree Steck-Vaughn LB $21.40 (0-8172-4367-4). 32pp. Double-page spreads are used to present material on the black bear, its anatomy, behavior, and habitats. (Rev: SLJ 4/97) [599.74]

**15174** Down, Mike. *Bear* (3–5). Illus. Series: Life Story. 1993, Troll $12.95 (0-8167-2765-1); paper $3.95 (0-8167-2766-X). 32pp. Bears and their life

cycle are introduced in this short, well-illustrated book. (Rev: BL 2/1/94) [599.74]

**15175** DuTemple, Lesley A. *Polar Bears* (2–3). Series: Early Bird Nature Books. 1998, Lerner LB $19.95 (0-8225-3025-2). 48pp. An easily read, extremely attractive introduction to polar bears that covers their life cycle and habitats. (Rev: BL 3/15/98) [599.74]

**15176** Fair, Jeff. *Black Bears: Black Bear Magic for Kids* (2–4). 1991, Stevens LB $21.27 (0-8368-0760-X). 48pp. This introduction to black bears and their behavior includes special material on hibernation. (Rev: BL 6/1/92; SLJ 7/92) [599.74]

**15177** Gilks, Helen. *Bears* (2–5). Illus. by Andrew Bale. 1993, Ticknor $15.95 (0-395-66899-9). 32pp. Besides giving basic information about bears and where they live, this account introduces 8 different types. (Rev: BL 7/93; SLJ 8/93) [599.72]

**15178** Greene, Carol. *Reading About the Grizzly Bear* (K–3). Illus. Series: Friends in Danger. 1993, Enslow LB $17.95 (0-89490-423-X). 32pp. Grizzlies are introduced along with material on how they live and raise their young, and on their endangered status. (Rev: BL 9/1/93; SLJ 8/93) [599.74]

**15179** Hodge, Deborah. *Bears: Polar Bears, Black Bears and Grizzly Bears* (K–3). Illus. by Pat Stephens. Series: Wildlife. 1997, Kids Can $10.95 (1-55074-269-8). 32pp. Discusses bears' food, habitats, hibernation, and life cycle. (Rev: BL 9/15/97; SLJ 9/97) [599.78]

**15180** Horton, Casey. *Bears* (3–5). Illus. Series: Endangered! 1996, Benchmark LB $21.36 (0-7614-0211-X). 32pp. Different species of bears are introduced, with their habitats, physical traits, behavior, and endangered status. (Rev: SLJ 3/96) [599.74]

**15181** Kuchalla, Susan. *Bears* (K–3). Illus. by Kathie Kelleher. 1982, Troll LB $12.95 (0-89375-674-1); paper $3.50 (0-89375-675-X). 32pp. Colorful illustrations and easy vocabulary are present in this brief introduction.

**15182** Lepthien, Emilie U. *Grizzlies* (3–4). Illus. Series: A True Book. 1996, Children's LB $21.00 (0-516-20159-X). 48pp. Many photos and a large typeface are used in this book introducing grizzly bears, their characteristics and habitats. (Rev: SLJ 4/97) [599.74]

**15183** Lepthien, Emilie U. *Polar Bears* (1–3). Illus. Series: New True Books. 1991, Children's LB $21.00 (0-516-01127-8); paper $5.50 (0-516-41127-6). 48pp. Through brief, readable text and many color photos, the characteristics and habitats of the polar bear are explored. (Rev: BL 2/1/92; SLJ 2/92) [599.74]

**15184** McDonald, Mary Ann. *Grizzlies* (3–5). Illus. Series: Naturebooks. 1996, Child's World LB $22.79

(1-56766-213-7). 32pp. This fierce North American bear is highlighted in full-page pictures and large-print text. (Rev: BL 12/15/96) [599.74]

**15185** Miller, Debbie S. *A Polar Bear Journey* (K–4). Illus. by Jon Van Zyle. 1997, Little, Brown $15.95 (0-316-57244-6). 32pp. Dramatic paintings add to the impact of this picture book about the life cycle of polar bears, as seen through the experiences of a single bear and her cubs. (Rev: BL 12/15/97; SLJ 10/97) [599.74]

**15186** Patent, Dorothy Hinshaw. *Looking at Bears* (2–5). Photos by William Munoz. 1994, Holiday LB $15.95 (0-8234-1139-7). 40pp. An attractive book on bears that covers such subjects as classification, behavior, food, reproduction, hibernation, and evolution. (Rev: BL 12/1/94; SLJ 1/95) [599.74]

**15187** Patent, Dorothy Hinshaw. *The Way of the Grizzly* (4–7). Illus. 1991, Houghton paper $5.95 (0-395-58112-5). 64pp. An examination of the life and habits of this feared animal. (Rev: BL 6/1/87; HB 9–10/87; SLJ 8/87)

**15188** Pfeffer, Wendy. *Polar Bears* (K–3). Illus. 1996, Dillon LB $14.95 (0-382-39327-9); paper $5.95 (0-382-39326-0). 32pp. An account of the first 2 years of a polar bear's life, with material on its habitat. (Rev: BCCB 10/96; BL 8/96; SLJ 9/96) [599]

**15189** Robinson, Claire. *Bears* (2–3). Series: In the Wild. 1997, Heinemann $12.95 (1-57572-134-1). 24pp. In this simple introduction to bears, such topics as food, care of cubs, and communication are covered. (Rev: BL 2/15/98) [599.74]

**15190** Rosenthal, Mark. *Bears* (1–4). Illus. 1983, Children's paper $5.50 (0-516-41675-8). 48pp. Various bears and their habits are introduced, mainly through color photographs.

**15191** Schwartz, Alvin. *Fat Man in a Fur Coat: And Other Bear Stories* (5–8). Illus. 1984, Farrar $14.00 (0-374-32291-0); paper $3.50 (0-374-42273-7). 167pp. A collection of factual and fictional material on bears.

**15192** Stirling, Ian. *Bears* (4–6). Illus. Series: Sierra Club Wildlife Library. 1992, Sierra Club $14.95 (0-87156-574-9). 64pp. This slim volume supplies an attractive introduction to various species of bears. (Rev: BL 5/1/92; SLJ 7/92) [599.74]

**15193** Stone, Lynn M. *Grizzlies* (3–6). Illus. Series: Nature Watch. 1993, Carolrhoda LB $19.95 (0-87614-800-3). 48pp. Outstanding color photos and clear text are used to introduce grizzlies, their habitats, food, and family life. (Rev: BL 1/15/94; SLJ 2/94) [599.74]

**15194** Wallace, Karen. *Bears in the Forest* (1–3). Illus. by Barbara Firth. Series: Read and Wonder. 1994, Candlewick $15.99 (1-56402-336-2). 32pp.

Many facts are covered in this novel about 2 bear cubs that are cared for by their mother from birth through their second summer. (Rev: BL 11/1/94) [599.74]

## BIG CATS

**15195** Arnold, Caroline. *Bobcats* (2–3). Series: Early Bird Nature Books. 1998, Lerner LB $19.93 (0-8225-3021-X). 48pp. An extremely attractive introduction to the world of the bobcat and its life cycle. (Rev: BL 3/15/98; SLJ 3/98) [599.74]

**15196** Arnold, Caroline. *Lion* (3–6). Photos by Richard Hewett. 1995, Morrow LB $15.93 (0-688-12693-6). 48pp. The physical features of lions are discussed, with material on their habitats, behavior, and family life. (Rev: BL 9/15/95; SLJ 12/95) [599.74]

**15197** Ball, Jacqueline A., and Kit Carlson. *The Leopard Son: A True Story* (3–5). Illus. 1996, McGraw-Hill $14.95 (0-07-016061-9). 32pp. The animals and vegetation of the Serengeti are seen through the eyes of a young leopard. (Rev: BL 11/1/96; SLJ 1/97) [599.74]

**15198** Bonners, Susan. *Hunter in the Snow: The Lynx* (2–4). Illus. 1994, Little, Brown $15.95 (0-316-10201-6). 32pp. A picture book that explores a year in the life of a female lynx. (Rev: BL 12/15/94; SLJ 10/94*) [599.74]

**15199** Dupont, Philippe, and Valerie Tracqui. *The Cheetah: Animal Close-Ups* (2–4). Illus. 1992, Charlesbridge paper $6.95 (0-88106-425-4). 28pp. A large-format paperback with excellent color photos that focus on the animal's family life. (Rev: BL 2/1/93) [599]

**15200** DuTemple, Lesley A. *Tigers* (2–4). Photos by Lynn M. Stone. Series: Early Bird Nature Books. 1996, Lerner LB $19.95 (0-8225-3010-4). 48pp. Beginning readers will find this an interesting introduction to tigers, their characteristics, and their endangered status. (Rev: SLJ 9/96) [599.74]

**15201** Esbensen, Barbara J. *Swift as the Wind: The Cheetah* (2–5). Illus. by Jean Cassels. 1996, Orchard LB $16.99 (0-531-08797-2). 32pp. The appearance and habits of the cheetah, the fastest animal alive, are covered in text and pictures. (Rev: BL 3/15/96; HB 7–8/96; SLJ 5/96) [599.74]

**15202** Harman, Amanda. *Leopards* (3–5). Illus. Series: Endangered! 1996, Benchmark LB $14.95 (0-7614-0223-3). 32pp. Introduces the 3 species of leopards and their characteristics and describes the circumstances that have caused them to be placed on the endangered list. (Rev: SLJ 8/96) [599.74]

**15203** Harman, Amanda. *Tigers* (4–6). Illus. Series: Endangered! 1996, Benchmark LB $21.36 (0-7614-0215-2). 32pp. The world of the tiger is introduced, with material on hunting skills, habitats, parenting habits, and its endangered status. (Rev: SLJ 4/96) [599.74]

**15204** Hodge, Deborah. *Wild Cats: Cougars, Bobcats and Lynx* (K–3). Illus. by Nancy Gray Ogle. Series: Wildlife. 1997, Kids Can $10.95 (1-55074-267-1). 32pp. Double-page spreads cover such topics about these big cats as their homes, food, habits, and relations with humans. (Rev: BL 9/15/97; SLJ 9/97) [599.75]

**15205** Hofer, Angelika. *The Lion Family Book* (3–5). Trans. by Patricia Crampton. Illus. 1988, Picture Book paper $15.95 (0-88708-070-7). 52pp. An overview of the lives of a family of lions. (Rev: BL 1/15/89; HB 1–2/89; SLJ 11/88)

**15206** Hopcraft, Xan, and Carol C. Hopcraft. *How It Was with Dooms: A True Story from Africa* (2–4). Illus. 1997, Simon & Schuster $19.95 (0-689-81091-1). 64pp. A scrapbook of pictures about Xan — the beloved pet cheetah of the Hopcraft family — who died in Africa at age 12. (Rev: BCCB 6/97; BL 5/15/97; SLJ 4/97) [599.74]

**15207** Lumpkin, Susan. *Small Cats* (5–8). Illus. 1993, Facts on File $17.95 (0-8160-2848-6). 68pp. A handsome oversized volume about the smaller wild cats, with many photos and charts. (Rev: BL 2/15/93) [599.74]

**15208** McDonald, Mary Ann. *Leopards* (1–3). Illus. 1996, Child's World LB $22.79 (1-56766-211-0). 30pp. Large print and color photos give basic information about leopards. (Rev: SLJ 4/96) [599.74]

**15209** MacMillan, Dianne M. *Cheetahs* (3–5). Illus. Series: Nature Watch. 1998, Carolrhoda $19.93 (1-57505-044-7). 48pp. An attractive title that introduces the cheetah and tells about its anatomy, habitats, behavior, and its endangered status. (Rev: BL 2/15/98) [599.74]

**15210** Milton, Joyce. *Big Cats* (1–3). Illus. by Silvia Duran. Series: All Aboard Reading. 1994, Putnam paper $3.95 (0-448-40564-4). 48pp. An easy-to-read book that introduces such big cats as leopards, tigers, lions, jaguars, cougars, and cheetahs. (Rev: BCCB 4/95; BL 1/1/95; HB 3–4/94; SLJ 2/95) [599.74]

**15211** Perry, Phyllis J. *The Snow Cats* (4–6). Illus. Series: First Books: Animals. 1997, Watts LB $21.00 (0-531-20267-4). 64pp. Describes the anatomy and characteristics of such winter cats as the Siberian tiger, lynx, bobcat, cougar, and snow leopard. (Rev: BL 8/97; SLJ 8/97) [599.74]

**15212** Robinson, Claire. *Lions* (2–3). Series: In the Wild. 1997, Heinemann LB $18.59 (1-57572-132-5). 24pp. A heavily illustrated introduction to lions that uses double-page spreads to cover such topics as behavior, food, habitats, and care of young. (Rev: BL 2/15/98) [599.74]

**15213** Ryden, Hope. *Your Cat's Wild Cousins* (3–5). Illus. 1992, Dutton paper $16.00 (0-525-67354-7). 48pp. A look at 18 feline species, explaining similarities and differences between domestic and wild cats. (Rev: BL 1/1/92) [599.74]

**15214** Schneider, Jost. *Lynx* (4–7). Illus. 1994, Carolrhoda LB $19.95 (0-87614-844-5). 48pp. The life cycle, habits, and behavior of the lynx, a member of the cat family, are described. (Rev: BL 1/15/95; SLJ 3/95) [599.74]

**15215** Silverstein, Alvin, et al. *The Florida Panther* (4–7). Illus. Series: Endangered in America. 1997, Millbrook LB $22.40 (0-7613-0049-X). 64pp. Explains why the Florida panther has become endangered, with material on its life cycle and behavior and the efforts being made to save it. (Rev: BL 3/15/97; SLJ 6/97) [599.74]

**15216** Simon, Seymour. *Big Cats* (K–3). 1991, HarperCollins LB $16.89 (0-06-021647-6). 40pp. The life and characteristics of big cats all over the world, with large color photos. (Rev: BCCB 6/91; BL 5/1/91; SLJ 5/91) [599.74]

**15217** Smith, Roland. *Cats in the Zoo* (4–6). Photos by William Munoz. Series: New Zoo. 1994, Millbrook LB $21.90 (1-56294-319-7). 64pp. Describes what happens to big cats after their capture and tells of their lives in a modern zoo. (Rev: BL 10/1/94; SLJ 10/94) [599.74]

**15218** Stone, Lynn M. *Cougars* (2–3). Series: Early Bird Nature Books. 1997, Lerner LB $19.93 (0-8225-3013-9). 48pp. These large cats, noted for their speed and ferocity, are introduced with stunning photos and a simple text. (Rev: BL 9/15/97; SLJ 10/97) [599.74]

### COYOTES, FOXES, AND WOLVES

**15219** Arnold, Caroline. *Fox* (3–6). Illus. by Richard Hewett. 1996, Morrow LB $15.93 (0-688-13729-6). 48pp. By focusing on a single fox, the habits, anatomy, and homes of the species are introduced. (Rev: BCCB 10/96; BL 8/96; SLJ 9/96) [599.74]

**15220** Brandenburg, Jim. *To the Top of the World: Adventures with Arctic Wolves* (5–7). Illus. 1993, Walker LB $17.85 (0-8027-8220-5). 44pp. Amazing color photographs highlight this account of a photographer's experiences living near a pack of Arctic wolves. (Rev: BCCB 11/93; BL 1/1/94*; SLJ 12/93*) [599.74]

**15221** Gibbons, Gail. *Wolves* (2–4). Illus. 1994, Holiday LB $15.95 (0-8234-1127-3). 32pp. The habitat, life cycle, and habits of the gray (timber) wolf are explored in large color drawings and a detailed text. (Rev: BL 9/15/94; SLJ 9/94) [599.74]

**15222** Havard, Christian. *The Fox: Playful Prowler* (PS–3). Illus. Series: Animal Close-Ups. 1995,

Charlesbridge paper $6.95 (0-88106-434-3). 28pp. Using clear, colorful photos and a simple text, this is an attractive introduction to foxes and their lifestyle. (Rev: BL 4/15/95) [599.74]

**15223** Heinz, Brian J. *The Wolves* (K–3). Illus. by Bernie Fuchs. 1996, Dial LB $15.89 (0-8037-1636-9). 32pp. The life of wolves and the activities of the pack are chronicled in this entertaining picture book. (Rev: BL 9/15/96*; SLJ 10/96) [599.74]

**15224** Hodge, Deborah. *Wild Dogs: Wolves, Coyotes and Foxes* (K–3). Series: Wildlife. 1997, Kids Can $10.95 (1-55074-360-0). 32pp. Effective illustrations highlight these double-page spreads introducing these "wild dogs" and their lives, food, habits, and sleep. (Rev: BL 9/15/97; SLJ 11/97) [599.74]

**15225** Horton, Casey. *Wolves* (3–5). Illus. Series: Endangered! 1996, Benchmark LB $21.36 (0-7614-0213-6). 32pp. Different species of wolves are discussed, with material on habitats, physical traits, behavior, and endangered status. (Rev: SLJ 3/96) [599.74]

**15226** Howker, Janni. *Walk with a Wolf* (PS–3). Illus. by Sarah Fox-Davies. 1998, Candlewick $15.99 (0-7636-0319-8). 32pp. An eloquent picture book that introduces the life of a wolf in the Far North, with scenes that deal with hunting, family life, training the pups, and resting. (Rev: BL 3/15/98; SLJ 4/98) [599.74]

**15227** Johnson, Sylvia A., and Alice Aamodt. *Wolf Pack: Tracking Wolves in the Wild* (5–8). Illus. 1985, Lerner paper $6.95 (0-8225-9526-5). 96pp. Fascinating details of the lives of these animals that travel in packs and share hunting, raising the young, and protection. (Rev: BCCB 12/85; BL 2/1/86; SLJ 1/86)

**15228** Laukel, Hans Gerold. *The Desert Fox Family Book* (4–6). Trans. by Rosemary Lanning. Illus. 1996, North-South LB $17.88 (1-55858-580-X). 32pp. Desert foxes of the Sahara are featured in this account, using excellent color photos. (Rev: BL 5/15/96; SLJ 5/96) [599.74]

**15229** Lawrence, R. D. *Wolves* (4–6). Illus. 1990, Sierra Club $18.95 (0-316-51676-7). 64pp. An oversize, well-organized volume with maps and diagrams and outstanding color photos. (Rev: BCCB 2/91; BL 1/1/91; HB 1–2/91) [599.74]

**15230** Lepthien, Emilie U. *Coyotes* (1–3). Illus. Series: New True Books. 1993, Children's LB $21.00 (0-516-01331-9). 48pp. This distant cousin of the dog is introduced in simple text and attractive photos. (Rev: BL 8/93) [333.9]

**15231** Lepthien, Emilie U. *Wolves* (1–3). Illus. Series: New True Books. 1991, Children's LB $21.00 (0-516-01129-4). 48pp. The habits and habitats of wolves are discussed in this easily read, well-illustrated volume. (Rev: BL 2/1/92) [962]

**15232** Lepthien, Emilie U., and Joan Kalbacken. *Foxes* (2–4). Illus. Series: New True Book. 1993, Children's LB $21.00 (0-516-01191-X). 48pp. For primary graders, this is a simple introduction to foxes and their habits and homes. (Rev: BL 7/94) [599.74]

**15233** Ling, Mary. *Amazing Wolves, Dogs, and Foxes* (1–4). Illus. by Jerry Young. 1991, Knopf LB $11.99 (0-679-91521-4); paper $9.99 (0-679-81521-X). 32pp. The wolf family and relatives are pictured in double-page spreads. (Rev: BL 10/1/91) [598.29]

**15234** Ling, Mary. *Fox* (PS–1). Illus. by Jane Burton. Series: See How They Grow. 1992, DK Publg. $7.95 (1-56458-114-4). 24pp. A glimpse of natural history with the aid of color photos. (Rev: BL 11/1/92; HB 1–2/93; SLJ 2/93) [599]

**15235** Mason, Cherie. *Wild Fox* (3–5). Illus. by JoEllen M. Stammen. 1993, Down East $15.95 (0-89272-319-X). 32pp. This picture book tells about the author's encounter with a lame red fox. (Rev: BL 6/1–15/93; SLJ 8/93*) [599.7]

**15236** Matthews, Downs. *Arctic Foxes* (2–4). Photos by Dan Guravich and Nikita Ovsyanikov. 1995, Simon & Schuster $16.00 (0-689-80284-6). 32pp. A description of the Arctic fox that supplies details about its food, housing, mating habits, and adjustments to its cruel environment. (Rev: BL 10/1/95; HB 9–10/95; SLJ 12/95) [599.73]

**15237** Patent, Dorothy Hinshaw. *Gray Wolf, Red Wolf* (4–7). Illus. by William Munoz. 1990, Houghton $15.95 (0-89919-863-5). 64pp. Two native species of North American wolf are covered. (Rev: BL 12/1/90; HB 1–2/91) [777.74]

**15238** Ryden, Hope. *Your Dog's Wild Cousins* (3–5). Photos by author. 1994, Lodestar paper $16.99 (0-525-67482-9). 36pp. Wolves, foxes, and coyotes are just 3 of the many members of the canine family described in a series of double-page spreads. (Rev: SLJ 9/94) [599.74]

**15239** Samuelson, Mary Lou, and Gloria G. Schlaepfer. *The Coyote* (3–5). Illus. Series: Remarkable Animals. 1993, Dillon LB $13.95 (0-87518-560-6). 60pp. An introduction to this renegade of the dog family, its habits, anatomy, and family life. (Rev: BL 11/1/93) [599.74]

**15240** Silverstein, Alvin, et al. *The Red Wolf* (4–8). Illus. Series: Endangered Species. 1994, Millbrook LB $22.40 (1-56294-416-9). 48pp. The story of the red wolf, once thought to have become extinct in the United States, and the recent efforts to reintroduce it in North Carolina. (Rev: BL 4/15/95) [333.95]

**15241** Simon, Seymour. *Wolves* (2–4). Illus. 1993, HarperCollins LB $16.89 (0-06-022534-3). 32pp. Dramatic full-page photos of wolves are accompanied by a text that describes their appearance and how they live. (Rev: BCCB 11/93; BL 10/1/93; HB 11–12/93; SLJ 11/93) [599.74]

**15242** Smith, Roland. *Journey of the Red Wolf* (4–8). Illus. 1996, Dutton paper $16.99 (0-525-65162-4). 60pp. What caused the near extinction of the red wolf and efforts to preserve the species are covered in this fascinating account. (Rev: BCCB 2/96; BL 5/1/96; SLJ 5/96) [599.7]

**15243** Stoops, Erik D., and Dagmar Fertl. *Wolves and Their Relatives* (3–6). Illus. 1997, Sterling $16.95 (0-8069-0926-9). 80pp. Different wolves from around the world are featured in this account, with material on their eating habits, self-defense, and reproduction. (Rev: BL 11/1/97; SLJ 12/97) [599.74]

**15244** Wallace, Karen. *Red Fox* (PS–1). Illus. by Peter Melnyczuk. Series: Read and Wonder. 1994, Candlewick $14.95 (1-56402-422-9). 32pp. A story that introduces a red fox and his hunting habits. (Rev: BL 12/1/94) [599.74]

**15245** Weide, Bruce, and Patricia Tucker. *There's a Wolf in the Classroom!* (3–5). Illus. 1995, Carolrhoda LB $16.95 (0-87614-939-5). 56pp. After a general introduction to gray wolves, this book gives details on raising Koani, from cub to an adult wolf that can be taken into classrooms. (Rev: BCCB 12/95; BL 9/1/95; SLJ 10/95) [599.74]

**15246** Winner, Cherie. *Coyotes* (3–6). Illus. Series: Nature Watch. 1995, Carolrhoda LB $19.93 (0-87614-938-7). 48pp. With color photos on each page and an interesting text, the world of the coyote is introduced, with material on its habitats, family life, and place in America's folklore. (Rev: BL 10/15/95) [599.74]

**15247** Wolpert, Tom. *Wolf Magic for Kids* (2–4). Illus. Series: Animal Magic for Kids. 1991, Stevens LB $21.27 (0-8368-0662-X). 48pp. The world of the wolf and its habits and habitats are introduced in this colorful book. (Rev: BL 4/15/91) [599.74]

## DEER FAMILY

**15248** Arnold, Caroline. *Tule Elk* (3–6). Illus. by Richard Hewett. Series: Nature Watch. 1989, Carolrhoda LB $14.95 (0-87614-343-5). 48pp. This account is highlighted with data on structure, habits, and preservation techniques on this nearly extinct species of elk. (Rev: BL 9/15/89; HB 11–12/89; SLJ 9/89) [599.73]

**15249** Arnosky, Jim. *All About Deer* (K–3). Illus. 1996, Scholastic $15.95 (0-590-46792-1). 32pp. The species, life cycles, and habits of deer are introduced. (Rev: BL 9/15/96; SLJ 9/96) [599.73]

**15250** Bare, Colleen S. *Never Grab a Deer by the Ear* (2–4). Illus. by author. 1993, Dutton paper $13.00 (0-525-65112-8). 32pp. Interesting facts

about deer in a smooth narrative. (Rev: BL 2/15/93) [599]

**15251** Berman, Ruth. *American Bison* (3–6). Illus. by Cheryl Walsh Bellville. Series: Nature Watch. 1992, Carolrhoda LB $19.93 (0-87614-697-3). 48pp. The life-style, habitat, and current status of the American bison is covered in text and pictures. (Rev: BL 8/92; SLJ 10/82) [599.73]

**15252** Bernhard, Emery. *Reindeer* (2–4). Illus. by Durga Bernhard. 1994, Holiday LB $15.95 (0-8234-1097-8). 32pp. The life cycle of reindeer is presented in watercolors and large type. (Rev: BL 9/15/94; SLJ 9/94) [599.73]

**15253** Clark, Margaret G. *Save the Florida Key Deer* (3–5). Illus. 1998, Dutton paper $16.99 (0-525-65232-9). 48pp. The story of the fight to save these tiny deer, no bigger than a large dog, from extinction. (Rev: BL 3/1/98; SLJ 2/98) [333.95]

**15254** Goodman, Susan E. *The Great Antler Auction* (4–7). Illus. 1996, Simon & Schuster $16.00 (0-689-80131-9). 32pp. Describes the annual auction in Jackson, Wyoming, of antlers gathered by Boy Scouts. (Rev: BCCB 10/96; BL 9/1/96; SLJ 9/96) [599.73]

**15255** Guiberson, Brenda Z. *Teddy Roosevelt's Elk* (2–4). Illus. by Patrick O'Brien. 1997, Holt paper $15.95 (0-8050-4296-2). 32pp. A book that combines information about Teddy Roosevelt, the elk named after him, and national parks. (Rev: BL 9/15/97; SLJ 10/97) [599.65]

**15256** Kalbacken, Joan. *White-Tailed Deer* (1–3). Illus. Series: New True Books. 1992, Children's LB $20.50 (0-516-01138-3). 48pp. In short chapters with many illustrations, the white-tailed deer and its habits and habitats are introduced. (Rev: BL 5/1/92) [599.73]

**15257** Lepthien, Emilie U. *Reindeer* (2–4). Illus. Series: New True Book. 1994, Children's $12.45 (0-516-01059-X). 48pp. These creatures of the northlands, their characteristics, and the lore surrounding them are covered in this simple book. (Rev: BL 7/94; SLJ 9/94) [599.73]

**15258** Miller, Debbie S. *A Caribou Journey* (2–4). Illus. by Jon Van Zyle. 1994, Little, Brown $15.95 (0-316-57380-9). 32pp. This picture book explores the characteristics and habits of caribou in this story of a caribou and her calf. (Rev: BL 9/15/94; SLJ 10/94*) [599.73]

**15259** Patent, Dorothy Hinshaw. *Deer and Elk* (4–6). Photos by William Munoz. 1994, Clarion $15.95 (0-395-52003-7). 78pp. The deer family and its branches are described, with coverage of mating, caring for young, overpopulation, hunting, and harvesting. (Rev: BL 5/1/94; HB 7–8/94; SLJ 6/94) [599.73]

**15260** Wolpert, Tom. *Whitetail Magic for Kids* (2–4). Illus. Series: Animal Magic for Kids. 1991, Stevens LB $21.27 (0-8368-0661-1). 48pp. The whitetail deer and its habits and habitats are introduced in text and illustrations. (Rev: BL 4/15/91) [599.73]

## ELEPHANTS

**15261** Blakeman, Sarah. *Elephant* (3–5). Illus. Series: Life Story. 1993, Troll LB $12.95 (0-8167-2769-4). 32pp. A nicely illustrated brief account that traces the life cycle of an elephant. (Rev: BL 2/1/94) [599.6]

**15262** Blumberg, Rhoda. *Jumbo* (2–4). Illus. by Jonathan Hunt. n.d., Smithmark $4.98 (0-765-10075-4). The story of the famous African elephant whose name has become our word for "huge." (Rev: BCCB 1/93; BL 11/1/92; SLJ 10/92) [791]

**15263** Caras, Roger A. *A Most Dangerous Journey: The Life of an African Elephant* (5–8). Illus. 1995, Dial paper $15.99 (0-8037-1880-2). 208pp. A story of an African bush elephant from birth to adulthood that also tells about its habitat and endangered status. (Rev: BL 10/15/95; SLJ 10/95) [599.4]

**15264** Dorros, Arthur. *Elephant Families* (2–3). Illus. Series: Let's-Read-and-Find-Out. 1994, Harper-Collins paper $4.95 (0-06-445122-4). 32pp. The African elephant and its family structure are introduced. (Rev: BL 9/15/94; SLJ 7/94) [599.6]

**15265** Douglas-Hamilton, Oria. *The Elephant Family Book* (3–5). Illus. 1996, North-South paper $8.95 (1-558-58549-4). 60pp. A beautifully illustrated book about this endangered species. (Rev: BL 1/1/91; HB 9–10/90; SLJ 4/91) [599.6]

**15266** George, Dick. *Ruby: The Painting Pachyderm of the Phoenix Zoo* (3–5). Illus. 1995, Delacorte $14.95 (0-385-32100-7). 48pp. The story of Ruby, an Asian elephant who learned to paint at the Phoenix Zoo. (Rev: BL 9/15/95; SLJ 6/95) [636]

**15267** Grace, Eric S. *Elephants* (3–6). Illus. Series: Sierra Club Wildlife Library. 1993, Sierra Club $15.95 (0-87156-538-2). 62pp. Various aspects of elephants — from their habitats to life cycles, food, and anatomy — are described in a simple text with drawings and photographs. (Rev: BL 11/1/93; SLJ 12/93) [599.6]

**15268** Harman, Amanda. *Elephants* (3–5). Illus. Series: Endangered! 1996, Benchmark LB $21.36 (0-7614-0221-7). 32pp. After an introduction to the 2 species of elephants and their characteristics, this book describes why they are considered endangered. (Rev: SLJ 8/96) [599.6]

**15269** MacMillan, Dianne M. *Elephants: Our Last Land Giants* (3–6). Illus. Series: Nature Watch. 1993, Lerner $19.93 (0-87614-770-8). 48pp. A well-organized look at the animal's physical, social, and

behavioral characteristics, with excellent full-color photos. (Rev: BL 1/15/94; SLJ 2/94) [599.6]

**15270** Moss, Cynthia. *Little Big Ears: The Story of Ely* (K–3). Illus. by Martyn Colbeck. 1996, Simon & Schuster paper $17.00 (0-689-80031-2). 32pp. The true story of Ely, the elephant that triumphed over a birth defect. (Rev: BCCB 2/97; BL 1/1–15/97; SLJ 3/97) [599.6]

**15271** Overbeck, Cynthia. *Elephants* (4–7). Illus. 1981, Lerner LB $22.60 (0-8225-1452-4). 48pp. Elephants and their life cycle and habitats are discussed in this well-illustrated volume.

**15272** Patent, Dorothy Hinshaw. *African Elephants: Giants of the Land* (3–5). Illus. by Oria Douglas-Hamilton. 1991, Holiday LB $14.95 (0-8234-0911-2). 40pp. Absorbing text and colorful photos document the lives of these awesome beasts of the jungle. (Rev: BL 1/1/92; SLJ 1/92) [599.6]

**15273** Robinson, Claire. *Elephants* (2–3). Series: In the Wild. 1997, Heinemann $12.95 (1-57572-135-X). 24pp. A heavily illustrated introduction to elephants that covers topics like how they move, find food, and raise their young. (Rev: BL 2/15/98) [599.6]

**15274** Schmidt, Jeremy. *In the Village of the Elephants* (3–6). Illus. by Ted Wood. 1994, Walker LB $16.85 (0-8027-8227-2). 32pp. This book focuses on an elephant keeper who works with other mahouts and their elephants in a wildlife sanctuary in India. (Rev: BCCB 3/94; BL 4/15/94; SLJ 5/94) [636]

**15275** Smith, Roland. *African Elephants* (2–4). Photos by Gerry Ellis. Illus. Series: Early Bird Nature Books. 1995, Lerner LB $19.93 (0-8225-3006-6). 48pp. Beginning with a map of Africa, this account describes the African elephant, its habits and habitats, and why it is scarce and valuable. (Rev: SLJ 8/95) [599.6]

## GIRAFFES

**15276** Arnold, Caroline. *Giraffe* (3–7). Illus. 1987, Morrow LB $12.88 (0-688-07070-1). 48pp. The life of Easter the giraffe, who lives in a park in New Jersey. (Rev: BL 9/1/87; SLJ 9/87)

**15277** *Giraffe* (PS–1). Photos by Peter Anderson. Illus. Series: See How They Grow. 1993, DK Publg. $7.95 (1-56458-311-2). 24pp. In very simple text and outstanding color photos, this brief account traces the life of a giraffe from birth to adulthood. (Rev: BL 11/1/93) [599.73]

**15278** Lepthien, Emilie U. *Giraffes* (3–4). Illus. Series: True Book: Animals. 1996, Children's LB $21.00 (0-516-20158-1). 48pp. This introduction to giraffes includes coverage on its physiology, habitat, food, and life-style. (Rev: SLJ 6/97) [599.7]

## MARSUPIALS

**15279** Arnold, Caroline. *Koala* (3–6). Illus. 1992, Morrow paper $5.95 (0-688-11503-9). 48pp. Karen, a newborn, is on her way from her home in Australia to a new life in the San Francisco Zoo. (Rev: BL 6/1/87; HB 5–6/87; SLJ 5/87)

**15280** Darling, Kathy. *Tasmanian Devil: On Location* (3–5). Illus. by Tara Darling. Series: On Location. 1992, Lothrop LB $15.93 (0-688-09727-8). 40pp. An introduction to one of the world's least likable marsupials, the well-named Tasmanian devil. (Rev: BL 12/1/92; SLJ 10/92) [599.2]

**15281** Lepthien, Emilie U. *Koalas* (1–3). Illus. Series: New True Books. 1990, Children's LB $21.00 (0-516-01108-1). 48pp. In large type and many photographs, the Koala bear and its habits and habitats are described. (Rev: BL 3/1/91) [599.2]

**15282** Sotzek, Hannelore, and Bobbie Kalman. *A Koala Is Not a Bear!* (1–3). Illus. by Barbara Bedell. Series: Crabapples. 1997, Crabtree LB $18.08 (0-86505-639-0); paper $5.95 (0-86505-739-7). 32pp. After distinguishing between this marsupial and bears, this book introduces their subspecies and traits and habits. (Rev: SLJ 9/97) [599.1]

**15283** Tesar, Jenny. *What on Earth Is a Quokka?* (3–4). Illus. Series: What on Earth? 1996, Blackbirch LB $14.95 (1-56711-104-1). 32pp. Describes the characteristics and habitat of this cat-sized marsupial that lives in Australia. (Rev: SLJ 3/97) [599.1]

**15284** Twinem, Neecy. *High in the Trees* (PS–3). Illus. by author. Series: Animal Clues Board Books. 1996, Charlesbridge $4.95 (0-88106-940-X). Close-up pictures of parts of an animal are revealed to be those of a koala bear in this picture puzzle book. (Rev: SLJ 12/96) [599.74]

## PANDAS

**15285** Dudley, Karen. *Giant Pandas* (3–6). Illus. Series: Untamed World. 1997, Raintree Steck-Vaughn LB $26.40 (0-8172-4566-9). 64pp. This presentation includes material on the panda's classification, life span, behavior, and endangered status, plus the myths and legends that surround this animal. (Rev: SLJ 8/97) [599.74]

**15286** Fowler, Allan. *Giant Pandas: Gifts from China* (1–2). Illus. Series: Rookie Read-About Science. 1995, Children's LB $18.50 (0-516-06031-7). 32pp. The life of the giant panda is explored, with information about its habitats, food, and endangered-species status. (Rev: BL 7/95) [599.74]

**15287** Jiguang, Xin, and Markus Kappeler. *The Giant Panda* (5–7). Trans. by Noel Simon. Illus. 1984, China Books paper $9.95 (0-8351-1388-4). 118pp. China's giant panda introduced in its natural habitat. (Rev: BL 12/15/86; HB 1–2/87; SLJ 12/86)

**15288** Lee, Sandra. *Giant Pandas* (K–3). Illus. Series: Naturebooks. 1994, Child's World LB $22.79 (1-56766-009-6). 30pp. With stunning photos, the giant panda is introduced, with coverage on anatomy, habitat, food, and its endangered-species status. (Rev: SLJ 6/94) [599.74]

**15289** Wong, Ovid K. *Giant Pandas* (2–4). Illus. 1988, Children's LB $21.00 (0-516-01241-X). 48pp. A look at the animals called China's "national treasure." (Rev: BL 5/1/88)

## RODENTS

**15290** Barkhausen, Annette, and Franz Geiser. *Rabbits and Hares* (5–7). Illus. Series: Animal Families. 1994, Gareth Stevens LB $21.27 (0-8368-1004-X). 48pp. With color pictures on each page, this is an attractive account of the habits, structure, reproduction, and family raising of rabbits and hares. (Rev: BL 7/94) [599.32]

**15291** Bernhard, Emery. *Prairie Dogs* (1–4). Illus. by Durga Bernhard. 1997, Harcourt $15.00 (0-15-201286-9). 40pp. With text and double-page watercolors, this handsome book introduces the prairie dog, its home and habits, and the symbiotic relationship it has with large grazing animals. (Rev: BL 12/1/97; HB 11–12/97; SLJ 12/97) [599.32]

**15292** Crewe, Sabrina. *The Prairie Dog* (K–2). Illus. by Graham Allen. Series: Life Cycles. 1996, Raintree Steck-Vaughn LB $21.40 (0-8172-4365-8). 32pp. Discusses the life cycle of the prairie dog, including a cross-section of a burrow and information on similar rodents. (Rev: SLJ 3/97) [599.32]

**15293** Hirschi, Ron. *Where Are My Prairie Dogs and Black-Footed Ferrets?* (1–3). Illus. by Erwin Bauer and Peggy Bauer. Series: One Earth. 1992, Bantam paper $8.00 (0-553-35471-X). 48pp. This account introduces prairie dogs and ferrets and makes the reader aware of wildlife conservation. (Rev: BL 10/15/92; SLJ 1/93) [333.95]

**15294** Jarrow, Gail, and Paul Sherman. *Naked Mole-Rats* (4–7). Illus. Series: Nature Watch. 1996, Carolrhoda LB $19.95 (0-87614-995-6). 48pp. An informative introduction to the naked mole-rat, a most unusual animal that seems to copy habits from a variety of other species. (Rev: SLJ 10/96) [599.32]

**15295** Johnson, Sylvia A. *Bats* (4–7). Illus. 1985, Lerner LB $16.95 (0-8225-1461-3); paper $5.95 (0-8225-9500-1). 48pp. Characteristics and behavior patterns of this flying mammal. (Rev: BCCB 3/86; BL 4/15/86; SLJ 2/86)

**15296** Lepthien, Emilie U. *Woodchucks* (1–3). Illus. Series: New True Books. 1992, Children's LB $21.00 (0-516-01140-5). 48pp. Brief text and many photos highlight the life cycle and habits of the woodchuck. (Rev: BL 5/1/92) [599.32]

**15297** Murray, Peter. *Porcupines* (K–3). Illus. Series: Naturebooks. 1994, Child's World LB $22.79 (1-56766-019-3). 30pp. The anatomy, life cycle, and habits of this unusual rodent are presented in a simple text and color photographs. (Rev: SLJ 5/94) [599.32]

**15298** Patent, Dorothy Hinshaw. *Prairie Dogs* (3–6). Illus. by William Munoz. 1993, Clarion $15.95 (0-395-56572-3). 63pp. The varieties, habits, features, and habitats of prairie dogs are described, with coverage of their plight today because of land development. (Rev: BCCB 9/93; BL 10/1/93; SLJ 9/93) [599.32]

**15299** Powell, Sandy. *Rats* (2–4). Illus. 1994, Lerner LB $19.95 (0-8225-3003-1). 48pp. The characteristics, habits, and life cycle of various species of rats are described. (Rev: BL 1/1/95) [599.32]

**15300** Ricciuti, Edward R. *What on Earth Is a Capybara?* (3–5). Illus. Series: What On Earth? 1995, Blackbirch LB $14.95 (1-56711-097-5). 32pp. The habitat, characteristics, and behavior of this unusual rodent are described in pictures and text. (Rev: SLJ 11/95) [636.3]

**15301** Ring, Elizabeth. *Lucky Mouse* (2–4). Illus. by Dwight Kuhn. 1995, Millbrook LB $21.40 (1-56294-344-8). 32pp. The life cycle, structure, habits, and enemies of a wild deer mouse are presented with full-color illustrations. (Rev: BL 12/1/95; SLJ 1/96) [599.32]

**15302** Rogers, Bettye. *Prairie Dog Town* (1–3). Illus. by Deborah Howland. Series: Smithsonian Wild Heritage Collection: Great Plains. 1993, Soundprints $11.95 (1-56899-005-7); paper $4.95 (1-56899-201-7). 31pp. The life and habits of prairie dogs are introduced through the activities of a one-year-old male and his family. (Rev: SLJ 5/94) [599.32]

### SHEEP AND GOATS

**15303** Damerow, Gail. *Your Goats: A Kid's Guide to Raising and Showing* (4–7). Illus. 1993, Storey paper $16.95 (0-88266-825-0). 176pp. This is a complete guide to raising, breeding, and showing goats, with many useful tips and helpful illustrations. (Rev: BL 5/15/94; SLJ 1/94) [636.3]

**15304** Fowler, Allan. *Woolly Sheep and Hungry Goats* (1–2). Illus. Series: Rookie Read-About Science. 1993, Children's Book Pr. LB $18.50 (0-516-06014-7). 32pp. Sheep and goats and their habits are introduced with a simple text, color pictures on each page, and a small format. (Rev: BL 9/1/93; SLJ 9/93) [636.3]

**15305** Staub, Frank. *Mountain Goats* (2–5). Photos by author. Series: Early Bird Nature Books. 1994, Lerner LB $19.93 (0-8225-3000-7). 48pp. A simple text and excellent photos are used to introduce mountain goats of the American Northwest. (Rev: SLJ 8/94) [599]

## Birds

### GENERAL AND MISCELLANEOUS

**15306** Alderton, David. *Birds* (5–7). Illus. by Louis R. Galante. Series: Ladybird Explorers. 1997, Ladybird paper $4.99 (0-7214-5772-X). 38pp. This introduction to birds arranges different species by type of diet, such as seed eaters, fish eaters, and fruit eaters. (Rev: SLJ 2/98) [598]

**15307** Arnold, Caroline. *House Sparrows Everywhere* (3–6). Illus. Series: Nature Watch. 1992, Carolrhoda LB $19.95 (0-87614-696-5). 48pp. Gives details on the house sparrow's life cycle, how it was introduced into the United States, and how its population has grown. (Rev: BL 7/92) [598.8]

**15308** Arnold, Caroline. *Ostriches and Other Flightless Birds* (3–6). Illus. by Richard Hewett. Series: Nature Watch. 1990, Carolrhoda LB $19.95 (0-87614-377-X). 48pp. Smooth text and sharp photos tell of the amazing ostrich and other flightless birds. (Rev: BL 3/1/90; SLJ 7/90) [598.5]

**15309** Arnosky, Jim. *Crinkleroot's 25 Birds Every Child Should Know* (PS–3). Illus. 1993, Bradbury LB $14.00 (0-02-705859-X). 32pp. In this junior field guide, 25 common birds are identified and depicted in engaging watercolor drawings. (Rev: BL 9/1/93; SLJ 9/93) [598]

**15310** Back, Christine, and Jens Olesen. *Chicken and Egg* (1–3). Illus. 1986, Silver Burdett LB $9.95 (0-382-09284-8); paper $3.95 (0-382-09959-1). Basic science explaining how the reproductive cycle operates. (Rev: BL 1/1/87)

**15311** Bailey, Jill, and David Burnie. *Birds* (4–6). Illus. Series: Eyewitness Explorers. 1997, DK Publg. paper $5.95 (0-7894-2212-3). 64pp. This book includes general information on avian biology and behavior. (Rev: BL 2/1/93; SLJ 8/92) [598]

**15312** Barrett, Norman. *Flightless Birds* (3–5). Illus. Series: Picture Library. 1991, Children's paper $4.95 (0-516-95611-6). 32pp. Various examples of flightless birds are introduced in pictures and text. (Rev: BL 7/91) [598.2]

**15313** Berman, Ruth. *Peacocks* (2–5). Photos by Richard Hewett. Series: Early Bird Nature Books. 1996, Lerner LB $19.95 (0-8225-3009-0). 47pp. A clear, succinct text and full-color photographs are used to introduce the members of the peafowl family. (Rev: SLJ 5/96) [598]

**15314** *Birds* (PS–3). Illus. by Rene Mettler. Series: First Discovery. 1993, Scholastic $11.95 (0-590-46367-5). 29pp. Includes basic information about birds — including their beaks, claws, nests, feathers, and food — in a series of transparencies in a spiral-bound book. (Rev: BL 10/1/93; SLJ 8/93) [598.2]

**15315** Bishop, Nic. *The Secrets of Animal Flight* (3–6). Illus. 1997, Houghton $14.95 (0-395-77848-4). 32pp. An explanation of why birds fly is followed by a discussion of how they do it, different types of wings, and various modes of flight. (Rev: BCCB 6/97; BL 3/15/97; HB 5–6/97; SLJ 4/97*) [591.9]

**15316** Brown, Mary B. *Wings Along the Waterway* (PS–1). Illus. 1992, Orchard $18.95 (0-531-05981-2). 80pp. With striking illustrations and readable text, this volume highlights 21 water birds and includes basic information. (Rev: BCCB 5/92; BL 3/1/92; HB 9–10/92; SLJ 4/92) [598.29]

**15317** Burnie, David. *Bird* (4–7). Illus. 1988, Knopf LB $16.99 (0-394-99619-4). 64pp. A photoessay giving an armchair tour of fine museums and introducing various kinds of birds. (Rev: BL 8/88; SLJ 8/88)

**15318** Chermayeff, Ivan. *Feathery Facts* (PS–1). Illus. 1995, Harcourt $11.00 (0-15-200110-7). 32pp. Short, simple text and attractive illustrations are used to introduce the world of birds. (Rev: BL 4/1/95; SLJ 7/95) [598]

**15319** Damerow, Gail. *Your Chickens: A Kid's Guide to Raising and Showing* (4–7). Illus. 1993, Storey paper $14.95 (0-88266-823-4). 160pp. A straightforward, practical guide on raising prize-winning chickens that is both thorough and filled with information. (Rev: BL 5/15/94; SLJ 1/94) [636.5]

**15320** Demuth, Patricia. *Cradles in the Trees: The Story of Bird Nests* (1–3). Illus. by Suzanne Barnes. 1994, Macmillan LB $14.95 (0-02-728466-2). 32pp. Describes and pictures a number of different bird nests and the way in which each meets the special needs of a species. (Rev: BL 9/15/94; SLJ 11/94) [598.2]

**15321** Doris, Ellen. *Ornithology* (4–7). Illus. Series: Real Kids Real Science. 1994, Thames & Hudson $16.95 (0-500-19008-9). 64pp. An excellent manual on how to study birds in their natural habitats, with accompanying activities for all seasons. (Rev: BL 9/1/94) [598]

**15322** Flanagan, Alice K. *Desert Birds* (2–4). Illus. Series: New True Books. 1996, Children's LB $21.00 (0-516-01087-5). 48pp. Using rich illustrations and an easy-to-read text, deserts are introduced, with special focus on the various bird species found in them. (Rev: BL 6/1–15/96; SLJ 8/96) [598.29]

**15323** Flanagan, Alice K. *Night Birds* (2–4). Illus. Series: New True Books. 1996, Children's LB $21.00 (0-516-01089-1). 48pp. Various species of nocturnal birds are introduced, with special empha-

sis on how they live and hunt. (Rev: BL 6/1–15/96; SLJ 8/96) [598.251]

**15324** Flanagan, Alice K. *Songbirds* (2–4). Illus. Series: New True Books. 1996, Children's LB $21.00 (0-516-01095-6). 48pp. A number of birds noted for their songs are described and pictured in this easily read science book. (Rev: BL 6/1–15/96; SLJ 12/96) [598.8]

**15325** Flanagan, Alice K. *Talking Birds* (2–4). Illus. Series: New True Books. 1996, Children's LB $21.00 (0-516-01096-4). 48pp. Parrots and crows are 2 of the bird species highlighted in text and pictures in this book about birds that can be taught to speak. (Rev: BL 6/1–15/96; SLJ 12/96) [636.6]

**15326** Fowler, Allan. *The Chicken or the Egg?* (1–2). Illus. Series: Rookie Read-About Science. 1993, Children's LB $18.50 (0-516-06008-2). 31pp. This small-format book with large print and color photos on each page traces the development of an egg and the hatching of a chick. (Rev: BL 9/1/93; SLJ 9/93) [636.5]

**15327** Fowler, Allan. *Turkeys That Fly and Turkeys That Don't* (1–2). Illus. Series: Rookie Read-About Science. 1994, Children's LB $18.00 (0-516-06029-5). 32pp. The world of the turkey, its different species, and its structure and habits are all covered in this simple science book. (Rev: BL 7/95) [598.6]

**15328** Friedman, Judi. *Operation Siberian Crane: The Story Behind the International Effort to Save an Amazing Bird* (4–7). 1992, Macmillan LB $13.95 (0-87518-515-0). 96pp. Ron Sauey and George Archibald founded the International Crane Foundation and concentrated on the most endangered species. (Rev: BL 1/15/93; SLJ 1/93*) [639.9]

**15329** Gans, Roma. *How Do Birds Find Their Way?* (PS–3). Illus. by Paul Mirocha. Series: Let's-Read-and-Find-Out. 1996, HarperCollins LB $14.89 (0-06-020225-4); paper $4.95 (0-06-445150-X). 32pp. Various kinds of birds that migrate are introduced, and the mysteries connected with their semiannual flights are explored. (Rev: BL 2/1/96; SLJ 4/96) [598.2]

**15330** Garelick, May. *What Makes a Bird a Bird?* (K–3). Illus. 1995, Mondo paper $4.95 (1-57255-008-2). 32pp. In a series of questions and answers, the distinctive characteristics of birds are enumerated. (Rev: BL 8/95) [598.2]

**15331** Gibbons, Gail. *The Puffins Are Back* (3–4). Illus. 1991, HarperCollins LB $14.89 (0-06-021604-2). 32pp. An intriguing look at these "clowns of the sea." (Rev: BL 4/1/91; HB 7–8/91; SLJ 5/91) [598.3]

**15332** Harrison, George H. *Backyard Bird Watching for Kids* (2–5). Illus. 1997, Willow Creek $13.95 (1-57223-089-4). 64pp. Describes the joys of bird watching and introduces 20 popular backyard birds, with material on their calls, food, and habitats. (Rev: BL 12/1/97) [598]

**15333** Hickman, Pamela M. *Birdwise* (4–8). Illus. by Judie Shore. 1989, Addison-Wesley paper $9.95 (0-201-51757-4). 96pp. This introduction to birds discusses anatomy, habits, habitats, and family life. (Rev: BL 10/15/89; SLJ 3/90) [598]

**15334** Hirschi, Ron. *What Is a Bird?* (PS–3). Illus. 1987, Walker LB $11.85 (0-8027-6721-4). 31pp. Birds in flight, leaping, dancing, and sleeping are depicted and identified. Also use: *Where Do Birds Live?* (1987). (Rev: BL 2/1/88)

**15335** Horton, Casey. *Parrots* (3–6). Illus. Series: Endangered! 1996, Benchmark LB $21.36 (0-7614-0222-5). 32pp. This account focuses on 8 species of parrots from around the world and why they are endangered. (Rev: SLJ 9/96) [598.71]

**15336** Jenkins, Priscilla B. *A Nest Full of Eggs* (1–3). Illus. by Lizzy Rockwell. 1995, HarperCollins LB $14.89 (0-06-023442-3). 32pp. By observing a pair of robins build a nest and raise a family, 2 youngsters learn about birds and their habits. (Rev: BCCB 7–8/95; BL 6/1–15/95; SLJ 8/95) [598.8]

**15337** Johnson, Jinny. *Simon & Schuster Children's Guide to Birds* (4–7). Illus. 1996, Simon & Schuster paper $19.95 (0-689-80199-8). 96pp. After each of the major types of birds is described, one bird from each group is highlighted. (Rev: BL 5/15/96) [676.2]

**15338** Johnson, Sylvia A. *Albatrosses of Midway Island* (3–6). Illus. by Frans Lanting. 1990, Carolrhoda LB $19.93 (0-87614-391-5). 48pp. Amazing facts and statistics about the wondrous albatross. (Rev: BL 3/1/90; SLJ 7/90) [598.4]

**15339** Klein, Tom. *Loon Magic for Kids* (2–4). Illus. 1990, NorthWord paper $6.95 (1-55971-121-3). 48pp. This colorful account includes information on the behavior and life cycle of the loon. (Rev: BL 6/1/90; SLJ 3/91) [598.4]

**15340** Kuchalla, Susan. *Birds* (K–3). Illus. by Gary Britt. 1982, Troll paper $3.50 (0-89375-657-1). 32pp. A simple introduction with a few short sentences and many illustrations.

**15341** Legg, Gerald. *Amazing Tropical Birds* (1–4). Illus. by Jerry Young. 1991, Knopf LB $9.99 (0-679-91520-6). 32pp. In double-page photo spreads, the world of tropical birds is introduced. (Rev: BL 10/1/91) [598.29]

**15342** Lepthien, Emilie U. *Ostriches* (2–4). Illus. Series: New True Book. 1993, Children's LB $21.00 (0-516-01193-6). 48pp. Ostriches and their habits and habitats are introduced in this simple account using large type and many illustrations. (Rev: BL 7/94) [598.5]

**15343** Lerner, Carol. *Backyard Birds of Summer* (4–6). Illus. 1996, Morrow LB $15.93 (0-688-13601-X). 48pp. Common summer birds are pictured and described in this handsome volume, with additional information on how young people can make these birds welcome in the backyard. (Rev: BL 2/15/96; HB 5–6/96; SLJ 4/96) [598.297]

**15344** Lerner, Carol. *Backyard Birds of Winter* (3–5). Illus. 1994, Morrow LB $15.93 (0-688-12820-3). 48pp. An attractive introduction to more than 20 common winter birds, with material on their anatomies, diets, and habits, plus tips on backyard feeders. (Rev: BL 11/15/94; SLJ 10/94*) [598]

**15345** Llamas, Andreu. *Birds Conquer the Sky* (4–8). Illus. by Miriam Ferrón and Miguel Ferrón. Series: Development of the Earth. 1996, Chelsea LB $15.95 (0-7910-3455-0). 32pp. A science book that explains the evolution of birds from prehistoric land birds onward and defines their characteristics. (Rev: SLJ 7/96) [598]

**15346** Lynne, Cherry. *Flute's Journey: The Life of a Wood Thrush* (K–3). Illus. 1997, Harcourt $15.00 (0-15-292853-7). 40pp. The story of a single wood thrush's journey from Maryland to a Central American rain forest and back. (Rev: BCCB 5/97; BL 4/1/97; SLJ 7/97) [599.8]

**15347** McDonald, Mary Ann. *Woodpeckers* (3–5). Illus. Series: Naturebooks. 1996, Child's World LB $22.79 (1-56766-218-8). 32pp. These birds with chisel-like bills that drill into wood are pictured in full-page illustrations with simple text. (Rev: BL 12/15/96) [598.7]

**15348** McMillan, Bruce. *A Beach for the Birds* (4–6). Illus. 1993, Houghton $15.95 (0-395-64050-4). 32pp. This book introduces the sea swallow and discusses its life cycle, behavior, and habitats. Information is also given on its endangered status. (Rev: BCCB 6/93; BL 4/1/93; SLJ 4/93) [598.3]

**15349** McMillan, Bruce. *Wild Flamingos* (3–5). Illus. 1997, Houghton $15.00 (0-395-84545-9). 32pp. Introduces the flamingos of Bonaire in the Caribbean using clear text and spectacular photos. (Rev: BL 7/97; HB 9–10/97; SLJ 8/97*) [598.3]

**15350** McNulty, Faith. *Peeping in the Shell: A Whooping Crane Is Hatched* (2–4). Illus. by Irene Brady. 1986, HarperCollins $11.95 (0-06-024134-9). 64pp. The process of hatching a whooping crane egg, with a personal narrative. (Rev: BCCB 10/86; BL 1/1/87; SLJ 12/86)

**15351** Markle, Sandra. *Outside and Inside Birds* (2–4). Illus. 1994, Bradbury paper $17.00 (0-02-762312-2). 40pp. The anatomy of different birds is described and pictured in color photos on every page. (Rev: BCCB 11/94; BL 11/1/94; SLJ 11/94) [598]

**15352** Marshall, Jody. *In the Air and Everywhere: The Scientific American Pop-up Book of Birds* (3–6). Illus. by Elizabeth McClelland. 1994, W. H. Freeman $12.80 (0-7167-6547-0). Birds in various habitats emerge realistically from their environments in this pop-up book. (Rev: BL 11/15/94) [598]

**15353** Maynard, Thane. *Ostriches* (3–5). Illus. Series: Naturebooks. 1996, Child's World LB $22.79 (1-56766-274-9). 32pp. This swift-footed, flightless bird is featured in a series of color illustrations and simple text. (Rev: BL 12/15/96; SLJ 5/97) [598.5]

**15354** Mazzola, Frank, Jr. *Counting Is for the Birds* (K–3). Illus. 1997, Charlesbridge $15.95 (0-88106-951-5); paper $6.95 (0-88106-950-7). 32pp. Different birds and their characteristics are introduced in this counting book that progresses in pairs to 20. (Rev: BL 4/15/97; SLJ 5/97) [598]

**15355** Murray, Peter. *Parrots* (3–4). Illus. Series: Naturebooks. 1993, Child's World LB $22.79 (1-56766-015-0). 30pp. Basic information about parrots is given, including material on their physical characteristics, behavior, and adaptations. (Rev: SLJ 4/94) [598.71]

**15356** Parsons, Alexandra. *Amazing Birds* (1–4). Illus. by Jerry Young. Series: Eyewitness Juniors. 1990, Knopf LB $11.99 (0-679-90223-6); paper $9.99 (0-679-80223-1). 32pp. After a general introduction to birds, this book has large double-page spreads of a single species plus smaller photos and charts. (Rev: BL 8/90) [598]

**15357** Patent, Dorothy Hinshaw. *Feathers* (4–7). Illus. by William Munoz. 1992, Dutton paper $15.99 (0-525-65081-4). 64pp. A fact-filled, attractive volume discussing birds, which make up over 40 percent of vertebrates. (Rev: BL 5/15/92; HB 5–6/92; SLJ 7/92*) [598.2]

**15358** Patent, Dorothy Hinshaw. *Pelicans* (4–7). Illus. by William Munoz. 1992, Houghton $14.95 (0-395-57224-X). 64pp. Lots of facts and excellent color photos tell the story of the pelican, which is "flight transformed." (Rev: BL 11/15/92; SLJ 12/92) [598.2]

**15359** Patent, Dorothy Hinshaw. *Pigeons* (3–6). Illus. 1997, Clarion $16.00 (0-395-69848-0). 78pp. An introduction to pigeons that covers their history, homes, uses, and intelligence. (Rev: BL 9/1/97; SLJ 10/97) [598.6]

**15360** Patton, Don. *Flamingos* (2–4). Illus. Series: Naturebooks: Animals. 1995, Child's World LB $22.79 (1-56766-184-X). 32pp. A striking introduction to flamingos, with each page of text facing a large color illustration. (Rev: BL 11/15/95) [598.3]

**15361** Pembleton, Seliesa. *The Pileated Woodpecker* (3–5). Illus. 1989, Macmillan LB $13.95 (0-87518-392-1). 60pp. A report on the physical characteristics

and life cyle of this large woodpecker. (Rev: BL 2/1/89; SLJ 4/89)

**15362** Pfeffer, Wendy. *Mute Swans* (PS–3). Illus. Series: Creatures in White. 1996, Silver Pr. LB $18.95 (0-382-39325-2). Using 2-page spreads, the reader follows 2 swans through nest building, protecting the eggs, raising their young, and migrating south. (Rev: SLJ 2/97) [598.4]

**15363** Powell, Jillian. *Eggs* (3–5). Illus. Series: Everyone Eats. 1997, Raintree Steck-Vaughn LB $22.83 (0-8172-4759-9). 32pp. This book introduces eggs — their sizes, from caviar to ostrich; the construction, production, and nutritional value of chickens' eggs; rituals connected with eggs; and 2 recipes. (Rev: SLJ 8/97) [598.6]

**15364** Rauzon, Mark. *Hummingbirds* (4–6). Illus. Series: First Books: Animals. 1997, Watts LB $22.00 (0-531-20260-7). 63pp. Describes the anatomy and characteristics of the smallest and most active bird and introduces various species, such as the rufous, sword-billed, and ruby-throated hummingbird. (Rev: BL 8/97; SLJ 8/97) [598.8]

**15365** Rauzon, Mark. *Parrots* (4–6). Illus. 1996, Watts LB $21.00 (0-531-20244-5). 62pp. Types of parrots, their mating and nesting habits, and their life cycles are discussed. (Rev: BL 1/1–15/97; SLJ 4/97) [598.7]

**15366** Rauzon, Mark. *Seabirds* (4–6). Illus. 1996, Watts LB $21.00 (0-531-20246-1). 64pp. Various seabirds and how each lives, raises nestlings, and gathers food are covered, with material on endangered species. (Rev: BL 1/1–15/97; SLJ 4/97) [598.29]

**15367** Rauzon, Mark. *Vultures* (4–6). Illus. Series: First Books: Animals. 1997, Watts LB $21.00 (0-531-20271-2). 63pp. Discusses the important role these scavengers play in the ecology and describes various species, such as the condor, lammergeier, and Egyptian vulture. (Rev: BL 8/97) [598.9]

**15368** Ricciuti, Edward R. *Birds* (4–6). Illus. Series: Our Living World. 1993, Blackbirch LB $18.95 (1-56711-038-X). 64pp. This introduction covers general topics related to birds. (Rev: SLJ 8/93) [598]

**15369** Roop, Peter, and Connie Roop. *Seasons of the Crane* (2–6). Illus. 1989, Walker LB $15.85 (0-8027-6860-1). 48pp. With outstanding photos and lucid text, the migratory habits of this endangerd bird are described. (Rev: BL 8/89; SLJ 9/89) [598.31]

**15370** Royston, Angela. *Birds* (PS). Illus. by Dave King. Series: Eye Openers. 1992, Macmillan $7.95 (0-689-71644-3). 22pp. In 8 double-page spreads, each containing a large photo and small illustrations, various birds are introduced. (Rev: BL 10/15/92; SLJ 2/93) [598]

**15371** Sill, Cathryn. *About Birds: A Guide for Children* (3–6). Illus. by John Sill. 1991, Peachtree $14.95 (1-56145-028-6). 40pp. This very simple introduction to birds describes common species and their characteristics. (Rev: BL 12/15/91; SLJ 2/92*) [598]

**15372** Smith, Roland. *Vultures* (2–3). Series: Early Bird Nature Books. 1998, Lerner LB $19.93 (0-8225-3011-2). 48pp. A sympathetic, easily read introduction to the world of the vulture, including the ways they find and eat their food, their life cycle, and habitats. (Rev: BL 3/15/98; SLJ 3/98) [598]

**15373** Snedden, Robert. *What Is a Bird?* (3–5). Illus. by Adrian Lascom. 1993, Sierra Club $13.95 (0-87156-539-0). 32pp. Each of the distinct characteristics of birds is highlighted in this basic introduction with fine color photographs. (Rev: BL 5/15/93; SLJ 8/93) [598.2]

**15374** Spaulding, Dean T. *Feeding Our Feathered Friends* (4–6). Series: Birder's Bookshelf. 1997, Lerner LB $19.93 (0-8225-3175-5). 56pp. This book covers many aspects of backyard bird feeding, like how to build bird feeders, where and when to hang them, their contents, and how to keep squirrels away. (Rev: BL 3/15/98; SLJ 4/98) [598]

**15375** Spaulding, Dean T. *Housing Our Feathered Friends* (4–6). Illus. Series: Birder's Bookshelf. 1997, Lerner LB $19.93 (0-8225-3176-3). 56pp. As well as supplying information on nests and other conveniences birds use as homes, this book gives directions on how to make a number of birdhouses. Also use: *Protecting Our Feathered Friends* (1997). (Rev: BL 10/15/97; SLJ 9/97) [690]

**15376** Spaulding, Dean T. *Watching Our Feathered Friends* (4–6). Series: Birder's Bookshelf. 1997, Lerner LB $19.93 (0-8225-3177-1). 56pp. This book introduces the hobby of bird watching, with material on its history, how to use a field guide, the best times and places for birding, and the necessary equipment. (Rev: BL 3/15/98) [598]

**15377** Stone, Lynn M. *Sandhill Cranes* (2–3). Series: Early Bird Nature Books. 1998, Lerner LB $19.95 (0-8225-3027-9). 48pp. This easily read, beautifully illustrated account introduces the sand hill crane and its life cycle, with material on its habitat, food, and enemies. (Rev: BL 3/15/98) [597]

**15378** Taylor, Barbara. *The Bird Atlas: A Pictorial Atlas of the World's Birds* (4–6). Illus. by Richard Orr. 1993, DK Publg. $19.95 (1-56458-327-9). 64pp. An oversize, brilliantly colored volume that introduces birds by their habitats. (Rev: SLJ 11/93) [598.2]

**15379** Tesar, Jenny. *What on Earth Is a Bustard?* (3–5). Illus. Series: What on Earth? 1996, Blackbirch LB $14.95 (1-56711-102-5). 32pp. Examines the world of the bustard, a ground-dwelling bird found in grasslands on several continents. (Rev: SLJ 2/97) [598]

**15380** Voeller, Edward. *The Red-Crowned Crane* (3–6). Illus. 1989, Macmillan LB $13.95 (0-87518-417-0). 60pp. A book about the amazing Japanese red-crowned crane and a retelling of the folktale it inspired, The Grateful Crane. (Rev: BL 12/15/89; SLJ 3/90) [598.31]

**15381** Wallace, Karen. *My Hen Is Dancing* (PS–1). Illus. by Anita Jeram. 1994, Candlewick $14.95 (1-56402-303-6). 32pp. The anatomy and habits of a chicken are explained simply with color drawings and large type. (Rev: BL 5/1/94; SLJ 7/94) [636.5]

**15382** Wildsmith, Brian. *Birds by Brian Wildsmith* (K–4). Illus. by author. 1967, Oxford paper $9.95 (0-19-272117-8). Excellent illustrations of common birds.

**15383** Williams, Nick. *How Birds Fly* (3–5). Illus. Series: Nature's Mysteries. 1996, Benchmark LB $21.36 (0-7614-0454-6). 32pp. The flight of birds is explained through an investigation of the internal and external design of their bodies in this book that gives many different examples and descriptions to amplify the text. (Rev: SLJ 2/97) [598]

**15384** Willis, Nancy C. *The Robins in Your Backyard* (K–3). Illus. 1996, Cucumber Island Storytellers $15.95 (1-887813-21-7). 32pp. The life of robins is covered, with material on mating habits and nest building. (Rev: BCCB 6/97; BL 1/1–15/97; SLJ 7/97) [598.8]

**15385** Zim, Herbert S., and Ira N. Gabrielson. *Birds* (5–8). Illus. 1991, Western paper $21.27 (0-307-64053-1). A guide to the most commonly seen birds, with accompanying illustrations and basic materials.

### BEHAVIOR

**15386** Bash, Barbara. *Urban Roosts: Where Birds Nest in the City* (3–5). Illus. 1992, Little, Brown paper $6.95 (0-316-08312-7). 32pp. This unusual nature study shows that wildlife can thrive in an urban setting. (Rev: BCCB 3/91; BL 1/1/91*; HB 1–2/91; SLJ 11/90*) [598]

**15387** Johnson, Sylvia A. *Inside an Egg* (5–8). Illus. 1982, Lerner LB $22.60 (0-8225-1472-9); paper $5.95 (0-8225-9522-2). 48pp. The chicken egg, from fertilization to hatching.

**15388** Peters, Lisa Westberg. *This Way Home* (K–3). Illus. by Normand Chartier. 1994, Holt $14.95 (0-8050-1368-7). 32pp. Using a brief text and attractive watercolors, this book tells of a migratory flight of sparrows from Minnesota to the Gulf Coast. (Rev: BCCB 10/94; BL 12/1/94; SLJ 1/95) [592]

**15389** Selsam, Millicent E. *Egg to Chick* (K–3). Illus. by Barbara Wolff. 1970, HarperCollins paper

$3.75 (0-06-444113-X). 64pp. A concise guide to how an egg develops.

## DUCKS, GEESE, AND SWANS

**15390** Beaty, Dave. *Waterfowl* (3–6). Illus. Series: Naturebooks. 1993, Child's World LB $22.79 (1-56766-006-1). 32pp. Various kinds of waterfowl, such as ducks and geese, are introduced in large color photos facing each page of text. (Rev: BCCB 6/96; BL 3/1/94) [598.4]

**15391** Horton, Tom. *Swanfall: Journey of the Tundra Swans* (4–6). Illus. by David Harp. 1991, Walker LB $16.85 (0-8027-8107-1). 48pp. All about migration and the life of a swan family for one year. (Rev: BCCB 2/92; BL 12/15/91) [598.4]

**15392** Kalas, Sybille. *The Goose Family Book* (2–4). Illus. by author. 1986, Picture Book paper $15.95 (0-88708-019-7). 53pp. A family of goslings from hatching to adulthood is detailed. (Rev: BL 6/15/86; HB 7–8/86; SLJ 11/86)

**15393** Loomis, Jennifer A. *A Duck in a Tree* (K–3). Illus. 1996, Stemmer $18.95 (0-88045-136-X). 40pp. A year in the lives of 2 wood ducks includes raising a family and migrating to Florida. (Rev: BL 2/1/97) [598.4]

**15394** Savage, Stephen. *Duck* (K–2). Illus. by Stephen Lings. Series: Observing Nature. 1995, Thomson Learning LB $21.40 (1-56847-328-1). 32pp. Using double-page spreads, very basic information is given on the life cycle of the mallard duck. (Rev: SLJ 10/95) [598.4]

**15395** Selsam, Millicent E., and Joyce Hunt. *A First Look at Ducks, Geese, and Swans* (1–3). Illus. by Harriett Springer. Series: A First Look At. 1990, Walker LB $12.85 (0-8027-6976-4). 32pp. Features and species are covered in this introduction. Also use: *A First Look at Bats* (1991). (Rev: BL 12/1/90; SLJ 2/92) [598.2]

**15396** Stone, Lynn M. *Swans* (2–3). Series: Early Bird Nature Books. 1997, Lerner LB $19.95 (0-8225-3019-8). 48pp. A well-written introduction for beginners to these handsome birds, with a simple text and many color photos. (Rev: BL 9/15/97; SLJ 10/97) [598.4]

## EAGLES, HAWKS, AND OTHER BIRDS OF PREY

**15397** Arnold, Caroline. *Hawk Highway in the Sky* (4–6). Illus. 1997, Harcourt $18.00 (0-15-200868-3); paper $8.00 (0-15-200040-2). 48pp. Describes Hawk Watch in the Goshute Mountains of Nevada, where scientists and volunteers catch, measure, and trace flight patterns of hawks, eagles, and falcons. (Rev: BL 6/1–15/97; SLJ 6/97) [598.9]

**15398** Arnold, Caroline. *On the Brink of Extinction: The California Condor* (4–6). Photos by Michael Wallace. 1993, Harcourt $17.95 (0-15-257990-7); paper $8.95 (0-15-257991-5). 48pp. The California condor is introduced and material is given on its history and current efforts to help it escape extinction. (Rev: BL 4/15/93*; HB 5–6/93; SLJ 6/93*) [598.9]

**15399** Arnold, Caroline. *Saving the Peregrine Falcon* (4–6). Illus. 1985, Lerner paper $7.95 (0-87614-523-3). 48pp. Once threatened because its eggs were weakened by DDT, the peregrine falcon can now be seen in the city of Los Angeles. The story of their comeback. (Rev: BCCB 3/85; BL 4/1/85; SLJ 3/85)

**15400** Bernhard, Emery. *Eagles: Lions of the Sky* (PS–3). Illus. by Durga Bernhard. 1994, Holiday LB $15.95 (0-8234-1105-2). 32pp. Many aspects of the life of eagles, including mating, eating, flying, hunting, and parenting, are discussed in this richly illustrated book. (Rev: BL 2/1/94; HB 5–6/94; SLJ 5/94) [598.9]

**15401** Craighead, Charles. *The Eagle and the River* (2–4). Photos by Tom Mangelsen. 1994, Macmillan paper $16.00 (0-02-762265-7). 32pp. Stunning photographs provide an eagle-eye view of the Snake River in Wyoming as the bird goes out hunting. (Rev: BL 9/15/94; SLJ 12/94*) [591.5]

**15402** Gieck, Charlene. *Bald Eagles: Bald Eagle Magic for Kids* (2–4). 1991, Stevens LB $21.27 (0-8368-0761-8). 48pp. This book tells about the historical significance of this bird and discusses its life cycle and habits. (Rev: BL 6/1/92; SLJ 7/92) [598]

**15403** Horton, Casey. *Eagles* (4–6). Illus. Series: Endangered! 1996, Benchmark LB $21.36 (0-7614-0214-4). 32pp. The endangered eagle is presented with individual chapters on 8 species. (Rev: SLJ 4/96) [598.9]

**15404** Jenkins, Priscilla B. *Falcons Nest on Skyscrapers* (K–3). Illus. by Megan Lloyd. Series: Let's-Read-and-Find-Out Science. 1996, HarperCollins paper $4.95 (0-06-445149-6). 32pp. The story of Scarlett, the first peregrine falcon raised in captivity, is used to introduce the species that recently faced extinction. (Rev: BL 8/96; SLJ 7/96) [598.9]

**15405** Johnson, Sylvia A. *Raptor Rescue! An Eagle Flies Free* (3–5). Illus. 1995, Dutton paper $15.99 (0-525-45301-6). 32pp. The work of the Gabbert Raptor Center in Minnesota to help eagles, hawks, vultures, and other birds of prey. (Rev: BL 9/15/95; SLJ 10/95) [639.9]

**15406** Lang, Aubrey. *Eagles* (4–6). Illus. by Wayne Lynch. 1995, Little, Brown paper $7.95 (0-316-51383-0). 64pp. An attractive, well-organized look at these fascinating birds. (Rev: BCCB 2/91; BL 1/1/91; HB 3–4/91) [598.9]

**15407** Olsen, Glenda P. *Birds of Prey* (3–6). Illus. Series: Naturebooks. 1993, Child's World LB $22.79 (1-56766-059-2). 32pp. In this introductory account, each double-page spread contains a color picture and descriptive text on such birds as eagles, hawks, and falcons. (Rev: BL 3/1/94) [598.9]

**15408** Parry-Jones, Jemima. *Amazing Birds of Prey* (1–4). Illus. by Mike Dunning. Series: Eyewitness Juniors. 1992, Knopf LB $11.99 (0-679-92771-9); paper $9.99 (0-679-82771-4). 32pp. Following a brief explanation of a bird of prey, several double-page spreads show various species. (Rev: BL 11/1/92; SLJ 5/93) [598.9]

**15409** Patent, Dorothy Hinshaw. *Eagles of America* (4–6). Photos by William Munoz. 1995, Holiday $15.95 (0-8234-1198-2). 40pp. Bald and golden eagles are described, with information on their habits and endangered status. (Rev: BL 3/1/96; SLJ 2/96) [598.9]

**15410** Patent, Dorothy Hinshaw. *Where the Bald Eagles Gather* (4–7). Illus. by William Munoz. 1990, Houghton paper $5.95 (0-395-52598-5). 64pp. A description of our national bird, its habits, and behavior.

**15411** Silverstein, Alvin, et al. *The Peregrine Falcon* (4–7). Illus. Series: Endangered in America. 1995, Millbrook LB $22.40 (1-56294-417-7). 64pp. The story of how the peregrine falcon became an endangered species, its life cycle, and efforts to restore the population. (Rev: BL 6/1–15/95) [598.9]

**15412** Stone, Lynn M. *Eagles* (2–4). Illus. Series: Bird Discovery Library. 1989, Rourke LB $14.60 (0-86592-321-3). 24pp. A brief overview of the life cycle and habitats of the eagle. Also use: *Pelicans* (1989). (Rev: BL 4/1/89; SLJ 11/89) [598]

**15413** Stone, Lynn M. *Vultures* (3–6). Illus. Series: Nature Watch Books. 1993, Carolrhoda LB $14.95 (0-87614-768-6). 48pp. The life cycle of the vulture is covered, and material is given on its habitat and food. (Rev: BL 8/93; SLJ 8/93*) [598.9]

### GULLS AND OTHER SEA BIRDS

**15414** Arnosky, Jim. *Watching Water Birds* (1–4). Illus. 1997, National Geographic $16.00 (0-7922-7073-8). 32pp. An informal introduction to such diving birds as loons, grebes, mallards, wood ducks, Canada geese, gulls, and herons. (Rev: BL 10/1/97; SLJ 10/97*) [598.179]

**15415** Flanagan, Alice K. *Seabirds* (2–4). Illus. Series: New True Books. 1996, Children's LB $21.00 (0-516-01088-3). 48pp. Using color photos and a simple text, this account introduces various marine birds, their special habitats, and how they live. (Rev: BL 6/1–15/96; SLJ 8/96) [589.29]

**15416** Gibbons, Gail. *Gulls . . . Gulls . . . Gulls* (3–5). Illus. 1997, Holiday LB $15.95 (0-8234-1323-3). 32pp. Brief text and watercolor pictures are used to explore the world of the gull, its structure, diet, habits, mating behavior, and migration. (Rev: BL 9/1/97; SLJ 9/97) [598.3]

**15417** Holling, Holling C. *Seabird* (4–6). 1978, Houghton $18.00 (0-395-18230-1); paper $8.95 (0-395-26681-5). A gull accompanies a whaling expedition.

**15418** Kress, Stephen W., and Pete Salmansohn. *Project Puffin: How We Brought Puffins Back to Egg Rock* (3–6). Illus. 1997, Tilbury $16.95 (0-88448-170-0). 40pp. A first-person narrative about the project starting in 1973 that had as a goal bringing puffins back to Eastern Egg Rock, off the Maine coast. (Rev: BCCB 7–8/97; BL 8/97) [636.9]

**15419** McMillan, Bruce. *Nights of the Pufflings* (2–4). Illus. 1995, Houghton $15.00 (0-395-70810-9). 32pp. On an island off the coast of Iceland, children help young puffins succeed in their first flight. (Rev: BCCB 3/95; BL 3/15/95; SLJ 3/95*) [598.3]

**15420** O'Connor, Karen. *The Herring Gull* (3–5). Illus. Series: Amazing Animals. 1992, Macmillan $13.95 (0-87518-506-1). 60pp. This introduction to the herring gull discusses its evolution, habitat, behavior, and the reasons why it is endangered. (Rev: BL 11/1/92) [598]

**15421** Patent, Dorothy Hinshaw. *Ospreys* (4–7). Illus. by William Munoz. 1993, Houghton $14.95 (0-395-63391-5). 64pp. Covers topics that are related to the osprey, such as feeding habits, body structure, nesting patterns, and life cycle. (Rev: BL 6/1–15/93) [598]

**15422** Staub, Frank. *Herons* (2–5). Illus. Series: Early Bird. 1997, Lerner LB $19.93 (0-8225-3017-1). 48pp. Text and wonderful photos introduce a variety of heron species and their behavior and habitats. (Rev: BL 7/97; SLJ 8/97) [598.3]

### OWLS

**15423** Arnosky, Jim. *All About Owls* (K–3). Illus. Series: All About . . . 1995, Scholastic $15.95 (0-590-46790-5). 32pp. The physical features of owls and their habits are discussed, with an introduction to some common species. (Rev: BL 9/1/95; SLJ 10/95*) [598.9]

**15424** Brown, Fern G. *Owls* (3–6). Illus. Series: First Books. 1991, Watts LB $21.00 (0-531-20008-6). 64pp. The appearance and habits of owls are followed by descriptions of different types. (Rev: BL 6/15/91) [598.9]

**15425** Browne, Vee. *Owl* (PS–3). Illus. by Diana Magnuson. Series: Animal Lore and Legend. 1995, Scholastic paper $4.95 (0-590-22488-3). 32pp. Factual information is given about owls on their characteristics, habitats, species, and food, as well as 3 folktales. (Rev: SLJ 3/96) [598.9]

**15426** Epple, Wolfgang. *Barn Owls* (3–6). Illus. by Manfred Rogl. Series: Nature Watch. 1992, Carolrhoda LB $19.93 (0-87614-742-2). 48pp. This informative book looks at the life cycle, habitat, and feeding habits of the mighty hunter, the barn owl. (Rev: BCCB 1/93*; BL 10/1/92; SLJ 1/93) [598.97]

**15427** Esbensen, Barbara J. *Tiger with Wings: The Great Horned Owl* (3–5). Illus. by Mary B. Brown. 1991, Orchard $16.95 (0-531-05940-5); paper $5.95 (0-531-07071-9). 32pp. This deadly hunter, with stripes and a catlike face, is known as a tiger with wings. (Rev: BL 9/1/91; HB 9–10/91; SLJ 8/91*) [598.97]

**15428** Guiberson, Brenda Z. *Spotted Owl: Bird of the Ancient Forest* (3–6). Illus. 1994, Holt $14.95 (0-8050-3171-5). 38pp. The life and habits of the spotted owl are introduced, with material on conservation efforts and the controversies surrounding them. (Rev: BL 1/1/95; SLJ 1/95) [696.83]

**15429** Jarvis, Kila, and Denver W. Holt. *Owls: Whoo Are They?* (3–5). Illus. 1996, Mountain paper $12.00 (0-87842-336-2). 64pp. This introduction to owls includes descriptions of the 19 species found in North America. (Rev: BL 8/96; SLJ 12/96) [598.9]

**15430** Ling, Mary. *Owl* (PS–1). Illus. by Kim Taylor. Series: See How They Grow. 1992, DK Publg. $7.95 (1-56458-115-2). 24pp. In a brief text written from the owl's viewpoint and many photographs, the first months of an owl's life are shown. (Rev: BL 11/1/92; HB 1–2/93; SLJ 3/93) [598]

**15431** Sattler, Helen R. *The Book of North American Owls* (3–6). Illus. 1995, Clarion $15.95 (0-395-60524-5). 64pp. After a general introduction to owls, their habits, and habitats, there is a rundown on 21 species. (Rev: BCCB 5/95; BL 4/15/95; HB 5–6/95; SLJ 5/95) [598]

**15432** Silverstein, Alvin, et al. *The Spotted Owl* (4–8). Illus. Series: Endangered Species. 1994, Millbrook LB $22.40 (1-56294-415-0). 48pp. The story of the spotted owl, its endangered status, efforts to protect it, and the conflicts with the timber industry. (Rev: BL 4/15/95) [333.95]

**15433** Stefoff, Rebecca. *Owl* (K–3). Series: Living Things. 1997, Marshall Cavendish LB $21.36 (0-7614-0443-0). 32pp. This simple introduction to the owl contains short bits of basic information and many colorful photos. (Rev: BL 2/15/98) [598.9]

## PENGUINS

**15434** Barkhausen, Annette, and Franz Geiser. *Penguins* (5–7). Illus. Series: Animal Families. 1994, Gareth Stevens LB $21.27 (0-8368-1002-3). 48pp.

Different kinds of penguins are described and pictured, with information on habitats, behavior, and reproduction. (Rev: BL 7/94) [598.4]

**15435** Bonners, Susan. *A Penguin Year* (K–4). Illus. by author. 1981, Delacorte $9.43 (0-440-00170-6). 48pp. An introduction to the life-style of penguins of the South Pole.

**15436** Cousteau Society. *Penguins* (PS–3). Illus. 1992, Simon & Schuster $3.95 (0-671-77058-6). 20pp. The Gentoo penguin is introduced in simple text and color photos. (Rev: BL 5/1/92; SLJ 7/92) [598.4]

**15437** Fontanel, Beatrice. *The Penguin: A Funny Bird* (2–4). Illus. by Andre Fatras. 1992, Charlesbridge paper $6.95 (0-88106-426-2). 28pp. The growth, development, and behavior of this "funny bird" are presented in color photos and large format. (Rev: BL 2/1/93) [598]

**15438** Johnson, Sylvia A. *Penguins* (4–7). Illus. 1981, Lerner LB $22.60 (0-8225-1453-2). 48pp. Handsome photographs enliven the text of this introduction to penguins and their habitats.

**15439** Kalman, Bobbie. *Penguins* (2–4). Illus. Series: Crabapple. 1995, Crabtree LB $18.08 (0-86505-624-2); paper $5.95 (0-86505-724-9). 32pp. Color photos and text are used to give basic facts about the habits, anatomy, food, and enemies of penguins. (Rev: SLJ 5/96) [598.4]

**15440** Lepthien, Emilie U. *Penguins* (1–4). Illus. 1983, Children's LB $21.00 (0-516-01683-0); paper $5.50 (0-516-41683-9). 48pp. This account is distinguished by a simple text and fine color photographs.

**15441** Ling, Mary. *Penguin* (3–5). Photos by Nell Fletcher. Illus. Series: See How They Grow. 1993, DK Publg. $7.95 (1-56458-312-0). 24pp. This first-person account uses a simple text and stunning color photos to trace the life of a penguin from birth to having a chick of its own. (Rev: BL 11/1/93) [598]

**15442** McMillan, Bruce. *Penguins at Home: Gentoos of Antarctica* (3–6). Illus. 1993, Houghton $15.95 (0-395-66560-4). 32pp. A photoessay on the Gentoo penguins of Antarctica that describes their anatomy, behavior, and mating cycle. (Rev: BCCB 9/93; BL 11/15/93; SLJ 12/93) [598]

**15443** McMillan, Bruce. *Puffins Climb, Penguins Rhyme* (PS–1). Illus. 1995, Harcourt $14.00 (0-15-200362-2). 32pp. A rhyming text is used to describe various activities of penguins and puffins. (Rev: BL 4/1/95; SLJ 5/95) [598.3]

**15444** Patent, Dorothy Hinshaw. *Looking at Penguins* (3–5). Illus. by Graham Robertson. 1993, Holiday LB $16.95 (0-8234-1037-4). 40pp. Various kinds of penguins are introduced, with material on their world habitats and on the endangered emperor penguin. (Rev: BL 1/1/94; SLJ 1/94*) [598]

**15445** *Penguins* (PS–2). Illus. Series: First Discovery. 1996, Scholastic $11.95 (0-590-73877-1). 24pp. Using interactive techniques and interesting visuals, answers basic questions about penguins, such as where they live. (Rev: BL 10/15/96) [598.441]

**15446** Robinson, Claire. *Penguin* (3–5). Illus. Series: Life Story. 1993, Troll paper $3.95 (0-8167-2772-4). 32pp. The habits and habitats of penguins are covered in this brief, illustrated volume. (Rev: BL 2/1/94) [594.4]

**15447** Robinson, Claire. *Penguins* (2–3). Series: In the Wild. 1997, Heinemann LB $18.50 (1-57572-137-6). 24pp. A heavily illustrated introduction to penguins that uses double-page spreads to cover such topics as behavior, food, habitats, and care of young. (Rev: BL 2/15/98; SLJ 4/98) [598.4]

**15448** Schlein, Miriam. *What's a Penguin Doing in a Place Like This?* (3–5). Illus. 1997, Millbrook LB $23.90 (0-7613-0003-1). 48pp. A guide to 17 species of penguins, arranged by habitat. (Rev: BL 6/1–15/97; SLJ 7/97) [598.4]

**15449** Stefoff, Rebecca. *Penguin* (K–3). Series: Living Things. 1997, Marshall Cavendish LB $21.36 (0-7614-0446-5). 32pp. Using double-page spreads and many color photos, the habits, homes, and behavior of penguins are introduced very simply. (Rev: BL 2/15/98) [598.4]

**15450** Stone, Lynn M. *Penguins* (2–4). Series: Bird Discovery Library. 1989, Rourke LB $14.60 (0-86592-325-6). 24pp. Introduces penguins, with brief text, color photos, and a glossary on the effects of pollution on penguins. Also use: *Vultures* (1989). (Rev: SLJ 11/89) [598.4]

## Conservation and Endangered Species

**15451** Bailey, Donna. *What We Can Do About Protecting Nature* (4–6). Illus. Series: What Do We Know About . . .? 1992, Watts LB $18.70 (0-531-11080-X). 30pp. This volume explains why protecting wildlife is important and what can be done about it. (Rev: BL 5/15/92) [363.7]

**15452** Chandler, Gary, and Kevin Graham. *Guardians of Wildlife* (4–8). Illus. Series: Making a Better World. 1996, Twenty-First Century LB $16.98 (0-8050-4626-7). 64pp. Solutions to overhunting, poaching, and overfishing are explored, as well as new wildlife management techniques. (Rev: BL 12/15/96; SLJ 4/97) [639.9]

**15453** Cohen, Daniel. *The Modern Ark* (4–8). Illus. 1995, Putnam $15.95 (0-399-22442-4). 128pp. An account of modern efforts to save such species as the red wolf, California condor, panda, and cheetah. (Rev: BL 12/1/95; SLJ 2/96) [333.95]

**15454** Curtis, Patricia. *Animals You Never Even Heard Of* (3–5). Illus. 1997, Sierra Club $16.95 (0-87156-594-3). 32pp. Information on 12 of the world's lesser-known animals on the brink of extinction, like the axolotl and the pudu. (Rev: BL 9/1/97; SLJ 9/97) [591]

**15455** Dobson, David. *Can We Save Them? Endangered Species of North America* (4–5). Illus. by James M. Needham. 1997, Charlesbridge $15.95 (0-88106-823-3); paper $6.95 (0-88106-822-5). 32pp. Features 12 North American species of endangered wildlife, including Florida panthers, tree snails, gray bats, peregrine falcons, and wildflowers. (Rev: BL 4/1/97; SLJ 7/97) [591.52]

**15456** Facklam, Margery. *And Then There Was One: The Mysteries of Extinction* (3–5). Illus. by Pamela Johnson. 1990, Little, Brown $15.95 (0-316-25984-5). 56pp. Covers extinction and the human interaction that causes the decline or demise of native species. (Rev: BCCB 9/90; BL 7/90; SLJ 9/90*) [591.52]

**15457** Few, Roger. *Macmillan Children's Guide to Endangered Animals* (5–8). Illus. 1993, Macmillan LB $17.95 (0-02-734545-9). 96pp. Using a geographical approach, this account profiles the world's endangered animals in pictures and descriptive text. (Rev: BL 10/1/93; SLJ 12/93) [592.52]

**15458** Galan, Mark. *There's Still Time: The Success of the Endangered Species Act* (2–5). Illus. 1997, National Geographic $15.00 (0-7922-7092-4). 40pp. A heartening account of the animals that have been saved from extinction as a result of the Endangered Species Act. (Rev: BL 12/15/97; SLJ 10/97) [333.95]

**15459** Gates, Richard. *Conservation* (1–4). Illus. 1982, Children's LB $21.00 (0-516-01618-0). 48pp. A simple but informative introduction intended for the primary grades.

**15460** Greene, Carol. *Caring for Our Animals* (1–4). Illus. Series: Caring for Our Earth. 1991, Enslow LB $13.95 (0-89490-352-7). 32pp. A simple text and photos help to introduce wildlife conservation. (Rev: BL 2/15/92) [333.95]

**15461** Gutfreund, Geraldine M. *Vanishing Animal Neighbors* (4–6). Illus. 1993, Watts LB $21.00 (0-531-20060-4). 64pp. Five different endangered species are introduced with a discussion of why they are decreasing and what their loss can mean. (Rev: BL 7/93; SLJ 6/93) [591]

**15462** Hoff, Mary, and Mary M. Rodgers. *Life on Land* (4–7). Illus. Series: Our Endangered Planet. 1992, Lerner LB $22.60 (0-8225-2507-0). 72pp. This account covers such topics as the interdependence of all living things, pollution, and necessary food sources. (Rev: BL 1/15/93; SLJ 2/93) [333]

**15463** Irvine, Georgeanne. *Protecting Endangered Species at the San Diego Zoo* (3–5). Illus. 1990, Simon & Schuster paper $14.95 (0-671-68776-X). 48pp. The efforts made to preserve endangered animals at the zoo. (Rev: BL 11/15/90; HB 11–12/90; SLJ 12/90) [636.08]

**15464** Kessler, Cristina. *All the King's Animals* (3–6). Illus. 1995, Boyds Mills $17.95 (1-56397-364-2). 64pp. The story of the conservationist Ted Reilly and the wildlife preserve he started in Swaziland to help endangered species. (Rev: BL 10/15/95; SLJ 12/95) [591]

**15465** Long, Matthew, and Thomas Long. *Any Bear Can Wear Glasses: The Spectacled Bear and Other Curious Creatures* (4–6). Illus. 1995, Chronicle $14.95 (0-8118-0809-2). 32pp. This entertaining book focuses on a number of endangered species, with informative essays on what the animal looks like, where it lives, how it behaves, and why it is threatened. (Rev: BL 12/1/95; SLJ 12/95) [591]

**15466** Lovett, Sarah. *Extremely Weird Endangered Species* (3–6). Illus. by Mary Sundstrom and Sally Blakemore. Series: Extremely Weird. 1997, Davidson LB $21.27 (1-884756-26-3); John Muir paper $5.95 (0-56261-280-8). 48pp. This colorful book introduces such unusual endangered species as manatees, bats, guan, rhinos, and condors. (Rev: SLJ 7/92) [574]

**15467** McClung, Robert M. *Lost Wild America: The Story of Our Extinct and Vanishing Wildlife. Rev. ed* (5–8). Illus. by Bob Hines. 1993, Shoe String LB $27.50 (0-208-02359-3). 272pp. Describes America's past and present wildlife management and gives a rundown on extinct and endangered animals. (Rev: BL 1/1/94; SLJ 2/94*) [591.5]

**15468** Maynard, Thane. *Endangered Animal Babies: Saving One Species at a Time* (4–8). Illus. 1993, Watts LB $23.60 (0-531-11077-X). 56pp. A number of endangered species are presented with forecasts for their future. (Rev: BL 8/93; SLJ 8/93) [639.9]

**15469** Maynard, Thane. *Saving Endangered Birds: Ensuring a Future in the Wild* (4–6). Illus. 1993, Watts LB $23.60 (0-531-11094-X). 56pp. This guide to 25 endangered birds includes pictures of each, tells about their characteristics and habitats, and gives information about various efforts to save them. (Rev: BL 5/15/94) [333.95]

**15470** Nirgiotis, Nicholas, and Theodore Nigiortis. *No More Dodos: How Zoos Help Endangered Wildlife* (5–8). Illus. 1996, Lerner $23.95 (0-8225-2856-8). 112pp. An introduction to the many organizations that are trying to protect and preserve endangered wildlife worldwide. (Rev: BCCB 2/97; BL 2/15/97*; SLJ 2/97) [639.9]

**15471** O'Neill, Mary. *Nature in Danger* (4–7). Illus. by John Bindon. Series: SOS Planet Earth. 1991,

Troll LB $13.50 (0-8167-2285-4); paper $5.95 (0-8167-2286-2). 32pp. Background information and history lead into the problem of animals in danger. (Rev: BL 6/15/91) [333.7]

**15472** Patent, Dorothy Hinshaw. *Places of Refuge: Our National Wildlife Refuge System* (4–6). Illus. 1992, Houghton $15.95 (0-89919-846-5). 80pp. The nationwide system of wildlife refuges is described, with many photos. (Rev: BCCB 7–8/92; BL 8/92; SLJ 8/92) [333.95]

**15473** Sayre, April Pulley. *Endangered Birds of North America* (4–6). Illus. Series: Scientific American Sourcebooks. 1997, Twenty-First Century $22.40 (0-8050-4549-X). 96pp. After giving some general facts about birds, the author devotes one chapter to each of 5 endangered species. (Rev: BL 12/1/97; SLJ 1/98) [333.95]

**15474** Sherrow, Victoria. *Endangered Mammals of North America* (5–8). Illus. Series: Scientific American Sourcebook. 1995, Twenty-First Century LB $22.40 (0-8050-3253-3). 96pp. A general introduction to the causes of endangered species, like pollution, followed by specific mammals affected, like the bowhead whale and the red wolf. (Rev: BL 12/1/95; SLJ 1/96) [599]

**15475** Stone, Lynn M. *Endangered Animals* (1–3). Illus. 1984, Children's LB $21.00 (0-516-01724-1); paper $5.50 (0-516-41724-X). 48pp. Explores why some species become endangered and what can be done about it.

**15476** Stuart, Gene S. *Wildlife Alert: The Struggle to Survive* (3–6). Illus. 1980, National Geographic LB $12.50 (0-87044-323-2). 104pp. This book outlines the steps being taken to help endangered animals around the world.

**15477** Taylor, Dave. *Endangered Forest Animals* (3–5). Illus. Series: Endangered Animals. 1992, Crabtree LB $19.16 (0-86505-529-7); paper $7.95 (0-86505-539-4). 32pp. In this heavily illustrated book, several endangered animals and forest ecology are highlighted. (Rev: BL 11/15/92) [591]

**15478** Taylor, Dave. *Endangered Grassland Animals* (3–5). Series: Endangered Animals. 1992, Crabtree LB $19.16 (0-86505-528-9); paper $7.95 (0-86505-538-6). 32pp. Animals of the African, Australian, and North American grasslands are introduced, with many full-color photos. (Rev: BL 12/15/92) [591]

**15479** Taylor, Dave. *Endangered Wetland Animals* (3–5). Illus. Series: Endangered Animals. 1992, Crabtree LB $19.16 (0-86505-530-0); paper $7.95 (0-86505-540-8). 32pp. Wetlands are described, and several wetlands animals currently considered endangered are pictured. Also use *Endangered Mountain Animals* (1992). (Rev: BL 11/15/92; SLJ 11/92) [591]

**15480** Turbak, Gary. *Mountain Animals in Danger* (1–4). Illus. by Lawrence Ormsby. 1994, Northland LB $14.95 (0-87358-573-9). 32pp. Introduces 10 endangered species, like the graywolf, bald eagle, and spotted owl. (Rev: BL 2/1/95; SLJ 2/95) [599]

**15481** Turbak, Gary. *Ocean Animals in Danger* (1–4). Illus. by Lawrence Ormsby. 1994, Northland LB $14.95 (0-87358-574-7). 32pp. Ten endangered marine animals are introduced, including sea otters, fur seals, sockeye salmon, brown pelicans, and manatees. (Rev: BL 11/15/94; SLJ 2/95) [574.92]

**15482** Whitman, Sylvia. *This Land Is Your Land: The American Conservation Movement* (5–7). Illus. 1994, Lerner LB $21.27 (0-8225-1729-9). 88pp. A history of the conservation movement from its beginnings in 1870 when there were efforts to save Yellowstone and ending with today's major problems, like oils spills and the need to recycle. (Rev: BL 12/15/94; HB 3–4/94; SLJ 12/94) [363.7]

## Insects and Arachnids

### GENERAL AND MISCELLANEOUS

**15483** Anderson, Margaret J. *Bizarre Insects* (3–6). Illus. Series: Weird and Wacky Science. 1996, Enslow LB $18.95 (0-89490-613-5). 48pp. Fascinating facts and lots of pictures highlight this account of unusual insects and their habits. (Rev: SLJ 6/96) [595.7]

**15484** Baker, Wendy, et al. *Insects* (4–7). Illus. Series: Make It Work! 1994, Thomson Learning $15.95 (1-56847-257-9). 48pp. Through a series of projects, the world of insects is introduced, with material on how they eat, hear, see, and survive. (Rev: BL 10/15/94) [595]

**15485** Bentley, Dawn. *If You Were a Bug: A Pop-up Book About Bugs and You* (PS–4). Illus. 1996, Random $6.99 (0-679-87823-8). A pop-up book that introduces a spider, ant, grasshopper, bee, and dragonfly. (Rev: BL 12/15/96) [581]

**15486** Berger, Melvin. *Killer Bugs* (4–8). Illus. 1990, Avon paper $3.50 (0-380-76036-3). 88pp. This account explores the world of killer bees, fire ants, and other such bugs. (Rev: BL 12/15/90) [595.7]

**15487** Bernhard, Emery. *Dragonfly* (1–3). Illus. by Durga Bernhard. 1993, Holiday LB $15.95 (0-8234-1033-1). 32pp. Detailed drawings are used to introduce facts about the dragonfly, including its life cycle, food, and behavior. (Rev: BL 9/15/93; SLJ 1/94) [595.7]

**15488** Booth, Jerry. *Big Bugs: Getting to Know Little Creatures Up Close* (4–6). Illus. 1994, Harcourt paper $14.95 (0-15-200693-1). 48pp. In addition to introducing a number of common insects, this book

contains many activities and recipes using insects as ingredients. (Rev: BL 11/15/94) [595.7]

**15489** Brenner, Barbara, and Bernice Chardiet. *Where's That Insect?* (2–4). Illus. by Carol Schwartz. 1995, Scholastic paper $4.95 (0-590-45211-8). 32pp. Simple facts are presented about 14 kinds of insects. (Rev: BL 8/93; SLJ 3/93) [595.7]

**15490** Dallinger, Jane. *Grasshoppers* (4–7). Illus. 1981, Lerner paper $5.95 (0-8225-9568-0). 48pp. The life cycle of grasshoppers, well illustrated.

**15491** Dewey, Jennifer O. *Bedbugs in Our House: True Tales of Insect, Bug, and Spider Discovery* (4–6). Illus. 1997, Marshall Cavendish LB $14.95 (0-7614-5006-8). 64pp. Using personal encounters with insects as a focus, the author presents details about all sorts of creatures, including fireflies, locusts, and spiders. (Rev: BL 1/1–15/98) [595.7]

**15492** Doris, Ellen. *Entomology* (4–6). Illus. by Len Rubenstein. 1993, Thames & Hudson $16.95 (0-500-19004-6). 64pp. In this project book, the classification of insects is covered, along with their habitats and metamorphosis and ideas for field trips and collecting specimens. (Rev: BL 10/1/93; SLJ 9/93) [595.7]

**15493** Else, George, et al., eds. *Insects and Spiders* (4–6). Series: Nature Company Discoveries. 1997, Time Life $16.00 (0-7835-4881-8). 64pp. Using a series of double-page spreads, several different insects and spiders are introduced, with material on their structure and habits given through a brief text and outstanding illustrations. (Rev: BL 9/15/97) [595]

**15494** Facklam, Howard, and Margery Facklam. *Insects* (4–7). Illus. Series: Invaders. 1994, Twenty-First Century LB $18.90 (0-8050-2859-5). 64pp. The characteristics and types of insects are introduced, with material on some of the more exotic ones. (Rev: BL 1/1/95; SLJ 3/95) [595]

**15495** Facklam, Margery. *The Big Bug Book* (1–3). Illus. by Paul Facklam. 1994, Little, Brown $15.95 (0-316-27389-9). 32pp. Thirteen large insects, such as a walking stick and Goliath beetle, are introduced in pictures and text. (Rev: BL 4/1/94*; SLJ 6/94*) [595.7]

**15496** Fischer-Nagel, Heiderose, and Andreas Fischer-Nagel. *The Housefly* (3–6). Illus. Series: Nature Watch. 1990, Carolrhoda LB $19.95 (0-87614-374-5). 48pp. A well-organized text with many details about the housefly. (Rev: BL 6/15/90; SLJ 9/90) [595.7]

**15497** Fowler, Allan. *It's a Good Thing There Are Insects* (1–2). Illus. Series: Rookie Read-About Science. 1990, Children's LB $18.50 (0-516-04905-4). 32pp. Insects and their characteristics are introduced in this beginner's science book. (Rev: BL 2/1/91) [595.7]

**15498** Gaffney, Michael. *Secret Forests* (1–4). Illus. 1994, Western Artists & Writers $14.95 (0-307-17505-7). 32pp. Double-page spreads introduce several small animals, chiefly insects, as well as the life found on the floor of various kinds of forests. (Rev: BL 11/15/94; SLJ 1/95) [595]

**15499** Ganeri, Anita. *Insects* (3–6). Illus. by Danny Flynn. Series: Nature Detective. 1993, Watts LB $19.30 (0-531-14225-6). 32pp. Shows how to identify a number of insects and gives details on their life cycles, where they live, and how they interact with their environment. (Rev: BL 12/15/93) [595.7]

**15500** Goldsen, Louise. *The Ladybug and Other Insects* (PS–2). Illus. by Sylvaine Perols. Series: First Discovery. 1991, Scholastic $11.95 (0-590-45235-5). Through painted overlays, the transformation of a larva to a ladybug is depicted, and information is given on the habits and habitats of this and other insects. (Rev: SLJ 6/92) [595.7]

**15501** Greenbacker, Liz. *Bugs: Stingers, Suckers, Sweeties, Swingers* (4–6). Illus. 1993, Watts LB $22.00 (0-531-20072-8). 64pp. Covers insects and spiders that are commonly found, plus data on other animals in their habitats. (Rev: BL 8/93) [595.7]

**15502** Gribbin, Mary. *Big Bugs* (PS–3). Illus. by Andrew Tewson. Series: Ladybird First Explorers. 1996, Ladybird paper $5.99 (0-7214-5691-X). 25pp. Devoting 2 pages per creature, this book describes in text and pictures several of the largest insects, with additional drawings that show each one's activities. (Rev: SLJ 1/97) [595.7]

**15503** Hawes, Judy. *Fireflies in the Night* (PS–3). Illus. by Ellen Alexander. Series: Let's Read and Find Out. 1991, HarperCollins $13.95 (0-06-022484-3); paper $4.95 (0-06-445101-1). 32pp. Full-color illustrations help to explain the world of fireflies. A remake of the original 1963 edition. (Rev: BL 11/15/91; SLJ 3/92) [595.76]

**15504** Hornblow, Leonora, and Arthur Hornblow. *Insects Do the Strangest Things* (3–8). Illus. by Michael K. Frith. 1990, Random paper $4.99 (0-394-84306-1). 64pp. A glimpse at the fascinating world of insects.

**15505** *Insects* (PS–1). Illus. Series: What's Inside? 1992, DK Publg. $8.95 (1-56458-003-2). 24pp. The inside parts of insects are shown in illustrations that peel back to show the interiors. (Rev: BL 4/15/92; SLJ 9/92) [581]

**15506** Johnson, Jinny. *Children's Guide to Insects and Spiders* (3–5). Illus. 1997, Simon & Schuster $19.95 (0-689-81163-2). 64pp. Using a large format, the author identifies and describes families of insects and spiders and furnishes drawings and photos of

body parts and stages of life cycles. (Rev: BL 5/1/97; SLJ 11/97) [595.7]

**15507** Johnson, Sylvia A. *Fireflies* (4–6). 1986, Lerner LB $22.60 (0-8225-1485-0). 48pp. Life cycle, breeding, environment, and characteristics of the firefly. (Rev: BL 10/1/86; SLJ 11/86)

**15508** Johnson, Sylvia A. *Ladybugs* (5–8). Illus. by Yuko Sato. 1983, Lerner LB $22.60 (0-8225-1481-8). 48pp. A description of the ladybug, its habits, behavior, and uses.

**15509** Johnson, Sylvia A. *Water Insects* (3–6). Illus. by Modoki Masuda. 1989, Lerner LB $22.60 (0-8225-1489-3). 48pp. Various kinds of aquatic insects are pictured and described. (Rev: BL 2/15/90; SLJ 4/90) [595]

**15510** Kneidel, Sally. *Pet Bugs: A Kid's Guide to Catching and Keeping Touchable Insects* (4–6). Illus. 1994, Wiley paper $10.95 (0-471-31188-X). 117pp. Describes 25 insects; how they live, eat, and reproduce; and how they can be kept as specimens. (Rev: BL 7/94; SLJ 9/94) [638]

**15511** Lavies, Bianca. *Backyard Hunter: The Praying Mantis* (K–3). Illus. 1995, Puffin paper $4.99 (0-14-055494-7). 32pp. The stages in this insect's life are described with striking photos. (Rev: BL 3/15/90*; SLJ 6/90) [595.7]

**15512** Lavies, Bianca. *Compost Critters* (3–5). Illus. 1993, Dutton paper $14.99 (0-525-44763-6). 32pp. Amazing photos and simple text introduce such organisms as mites, various bugs, and snails in compost piles. (Rev: BCCB 6/93; BL 7/93*; SLJ 7/93*) [591]

**15513** Llewellyn, Claire. *Some Bugs Glow in the Dark: And Other Amazing Facts About Insects* (1–3). Illus. by Mike Taylor, et al. Series: I Didn't Know That. 1997, Millbrook LB $19.90 (0-7613-0562-9). 32pp. As well as explaining what insects are, this book covers truly amazing facts about their speed, size, weight, metamorphosis, and unusual behavior. (Rev: SLJ 9/97) [595.7]

**15514** McLaughlin, Molly. *Dragonflies* (2–6). Illus. 1988, Walker LB $15.85 (0-8027-6847-4). 48pp. The life cycle of dragonflies plus information on different varieties are provided with outstanding photographs. (Rev: BCCB 10/89; BL 8/89*; SLJ 9/89) [595.7]

**15515** Markle, Sandra. *Creepy, Crawly Baby Bugs* (3–5). Illus. 1996, Walker LB $16.85 (0-8027-8444-5). 32pp. The growth cycle of insects is explored, with emphasis on each infant stage. (Rev: BL 11/15/96; SLJ 4/97*) [595.7]

**15516** Merrick, Patrick. *Ticks* (2–4). Illus. Series: Creepy Crawlers. 1997, Child's World LB $22.79 (1-56766-384-2). 32pp. Different kinds of ticks are presented, with material on their life cycle, method of locomotion, habitat, food, and defense mechanisms.

Also use *Walkingsticks* (1997). (Rev: SLJ 3/98) [595.4]

**15517** Mound, Laurence. *Amazing Insects* (1–4). Illus. Series: Eyewitness Juniors. 1993, Knopf paper $9.99 (0-679-83925-9). 32pp. The world of insects is introduced through a series of unusual color photos and a simple text. (Rev: BL 9/15/93; SLJ 10/93) [595.7]

**15518** Mound, Laurence. *Insects* (4–8). Illus. Series: Eyewitness Books. 1990, Knopf LB $20.99 (0-679-90441-7). 64pp. Common insects are introduced and coverage is given on habitats, behavior, and anatomy. (Rev: SLJ 9/90) [595.7]

**15519** Parker, Nancy W., and Joan Richards Wright. *Bugs* (K–3). Illus. by Nancy Winslow Parker. 1987, Greenwillow LB $15.93 (0-688-06624-0); Morrow paper $4.95 (0-688-08296-3). A picture-book format provides solid facts on bugs — including 16 common insects. (Rev: BL 11/1/87; SLJ 10/87)

**15520** Parker, Steve. *Insects* (4–6). Illus. Series: Eyewitness Explorers. 1992, DK Publg. $10.99 (1-56458-026-1). 64pp. Exploring insect characteristics, types, specific habitats, and more. (Rev: BL 2/1/93; SLJ 8/92) [595.7]

**15521** Penner, Lucille R. *Monster Bugs* (1–3). Illus. by Pamela Johnson. Series: Step into Reading Books. 1996, Random LB $11.99 (0-679-96974-8); paper $3.99 (0-679-86974-3). 44pp. An easy-to-read introduction to large insects in a series of double-page spreads. (Rev: BCCB 5/96; SLJ 9/96) [595.7]

**15522** Podendorf, Illa. *Insects* (2–3). Illus. 1981, Children's LB $20.00 (0-516-01627-X); paper $5.50 (0-516-41627-8). 48pp. An easy reader that introduces common insects.

**15523** Ross, Michael E. *Cricketology* (4–6). Illus. Series: Backyard Buddies. 1996, Carolrhoda LB $19.93 (0-87614-985-9). 48pp. The classification, life cycle, and habits of crickets are discussed in this science activity book. (Rev: BL 7/96; SLJ 8/96) [595.7]

**15524** Ross, Michael E. *Ladybugology* (3–5). Photos by Brian Grogan. Illus. by Darren Erickson. Series: Backyard Buddies. 1998, Carolrhoda $14.95 (1-57505-051-X). 48pp. This introduction to ladybugs describes their structure and habits and outlines a number of activities that involve capturing and observing them. (Rev: SLJ 3/98) [595.7]

**15525** Royston, Angela. *Insects and Crawly Creatures* (PS). Illus. by Jerry Young. Series: Eye Openers. 1992, Macmillan $8.99 (0-689-71645-1). 22pp. Various insects and crawling animals are introduced to preschoolers through brief text and large photos. (Rev: BL 10/15/92; SLJ 3/93) [595.7]

**15526** Selsam, Millicent E., and Ron Goor. *Backyard Insects* (K–3). Illus. 1988, Scholastic paper $4.99 (0-590-42256-1). 40pp. How backyard insects camouflage themselves for protection.

**15527** Snedden, Robert. *What Is an Insect?* (2–5). Illus. by Adrian Lascom. 1993, Sierra Club $13.95 (0-87156-540-4). 32pp. Fine color photographs and a lucid text explain the characteristics and types of insects and give details of their life cycles. (Rev: BL 5/1/93; SLJ 8/93) [595.7]

**15528** Souza, D. M. *Insects Around the House* (3–5). Illus. Series: Creatures All Around Us. 1991, Carolrhoda LB $19.95 (0-87614-438-5). 40pp. Describes household insects, from termites under the front steps to caterpillars in the carpet. Also use: *Insects in the Garden* (1991). (Rev: BL 4/15/91; SLJ 7/91) [595.7]

**15529** Souza, D. M. *What Bit Me?* (3–5). Illus. Series: Creatures All Around Us. 1991, Carolrhoda LB $14.95 (0-87614-440-7). 40pp. In pictures and text, this book introduces creatures that can bite and sting, such as water bugs, ticks, and mosquitoes. (Rev: BL 4/15/91; SLJ 7/91) [595.7]

**15530** Van Dyck, Sara. *Insect Wars* (4–6). Illus. Series: First Books: Animals. 1997, Watts LB $21.00 (0-531-20261-5). 64pp. Shows how farmers, restaurant owners, and theme park operators are using beneficial insects to destroy harmful ones, rather than relying on pesticides. (Rev: BL 5/15/97; SLJ 8/97) [632]

**15531** Wangberg, James K. *Do Bees Sneeze? and Other Questions Kids Ask About Insects* (4–6). Illus. 1997, Fulcrum paper $17.95 (1-55591-963-4). 194pp. A noted entomologist answers 200 questions about insects that were actually asked him by children, like "Do bugs have emotions?" (Rev: BL 1/1–15/98; SLJ 4/98) [595.7]

**15532** Watts, Barrie. *Dragonfly* (K–3). Illus. 1989, Silver Burdett LB $9.95 (0-382-09799-8). 25pp. From egg through the nymph stage to adult, this is the life story of the dragonfly. (Rev: SLJ 1/90) [595.7]

**15533** Whayne, Susanne S. *The World of Insects* (PS–3). Illus. by Ebet Dudley. 1990, Simon & Schuster paper $9.95 (0-671-69018-3). 48pp. A large-format book for browsing, with color paintings on every page. (Rev: BL 1/1/91) [595.7]

**15534** *The World in Your Backyard: And Other Stories of Insects and Spiders* (3–5). Illus. 1990, Zaner-Bloser $10.95 (0-88309-132-1). 63pp. Eighteen articles and stories from *Highlights for Children* magazine. (Rev: SLJ 6/90) [595.7]

**15535** Zakowski, Connie. *The Insect Book: A Basic Guide to the Collection and Care of Common Insects for Young Children* (3–5). Illus. 1996, Rainbow paper $8.95 (1-56825-037-1). 64pp. A practical beginner's guide to collecting, caring for, and studying insects. (Rev: BL 12/1/96; SLJ 5/97) [595.7]

**15536** Zim, Herbert S., and Clarence Cottam. *Insects* (4–7). Illus. 1991, Western paper $21.27 (0-307-64055-8). A guide to familiar American insects.

## ANTS

**15537** Berman, Ruth. *Ants* (2–3). Illus. Series: Early Bird Nature Book. 1996, Lerner LB $19.93 (0-8225-3012-0). 48pp. The formica ant and its community are described in this introduction to the ant world. (Rev: BL 8/96; SLJ 7/96) [595.78]

**15538** Brenner, Barbara. *Thinking About Ants* (2–3). Illus. by Carol Schwartz. 1997, Mondo $14.95 (1-57255-210-7). 32pp. In a readable style, 11 types of ants are introduced, with material on their bodies, colors, diet, colonies, and enemies. (Rev: BL 6/1–15/97; SLJ 10/97) [595.79]

**15539** Chinery, Michael. *Ant* (3–5). Illus. by Nichola Armstrong. Series: Life Story. 1997, Troll paper $4.95 (0-8167-2099-1). 32pp. Life in an anthill is introduced in this informative text with color photographs. (Rev: BL 4/1/91) [595.79]

**15540** Demuth, Patricia. *Those Amazing Ants* (PS–2). Illus. by S. D. Schindler. 1994, Macmillan paper $14.95 (0-02-728467-0). 32pp. Fascinating facts are given concerning the food, homes, society, and breeding of ants. (Rev: BL 10/1/94; SLJ 10/94) [595.79]

**15541** Dorros, Arthur. *Ant Cities* (K–2). Illus. by author. 1987, HarperCollins LB $15.89 (0-690-04570-0); paper $4.95 (0-06-445079-1). 32pp. A simplified explanation of the ant world: jobs of worker ants, operation of the ant hill, social divisions of the ant colony. (Rev: BCCB 3/87; BL 2/15/87; SLJ 8/87)

**15542** Overbeck, Cynthia. *Ants* (3–5). Illus. 1982, Lerner LB $22.60 (0-8225-1468-0); paper $5.95 (0-8225-9525-7). 48pp. A description of the parts of an ant's body, plus an introduction to their complex society.

**15543** Ross, Edward S. *Ants* (3–6). Illus. Series: Naturebooks. 1993, Child's World LB $22.79 (1-56766-056-8). 32pp. Excellent photos and text explain how ants live and work, and supply details on their homes and food. (Rev: BL 3/1/94; SLJ 5/94) [595.79]

**15544** Sabin, Francene. *Amazing World of Ants* (1–3). Illus. by Eulala Conner. 1982, Troll paper $3.50 (0-89375-559-1). 32pp. An examination of an ant colony, its inhabitants, and construction.

**15545** Stefoff, Rebecca. *Ant* (K–3). Series: Living Things. 1997, Marshall Cavendish LB $21.36 (0-7614-0447-3). 32pp. A colorful introduction to the

world of ants that describes colonies, homes and food. (Rev: BL 2/15/98; SLJ 3/98) [595.79]

## BEES AND WASPS

**15546** Chinery, Michael. *How Bees Make Honey* (3–5). Illus. Series: Nature's Mysteries. 1996, Benchmark LB $21.36 (0-7614-0453-8). 32pp. In this introduction to bees, such topics as a bee's anatomy, life cycle, enemies, nectar gathering, and honey production are covered. (Rev: SLJ 2/97) [595.79]

**15547** Cole, Joanna. *The Magic School Bus Inside a Beehive* (3–5). Illus. by Bruce Degen. 1996, Scholastic $15.95 (0-590-44684-3). 48pp. Mrs. Frizzle's school bus becomes a beehive in this exploration of the anatomy, activities, and social structure of bees. (Rev: BCCB 10/96; BL 9/1/96; HB 11–12/96; SLJ 10/96) [585.79]

**15548** Crewe, Sabrina. *The Bee* (K–3). Illus. by Stuart Lafford. Series: Life Cycles. 1996, Raintree Steck-Vaughn LB $21.40 (0-8172-4362-3). 32pp. Honey bees are introduced in a number of double-page spreads that cover such topics as anatomy, characteristics, and social life. (Rev: SLJ 4/97) [595.79]

**15549** Davis, Kathleen, and Dave Mayes. *Killer Bees* (3–5). Illus. Series: Remarkable Animals. 1993, Dillon LB $13.95 (0-87518-582-7). 60pp. This well-illustrated account explains where these Africanized honeybees come from, their habits, and the damage they can cause. (Rev: BL 11/1/93) [599.79]

**15550** Delafosse, Claude. *Bees* (PS–2). Illus. Series: First Discovery. 1997, Scholastic $11.95 (0-590-93780-4). 24pp. Basic information about bees and their colonies is given concisely in this interactive book with overlays. (Rev: BL 2/15/97) [595.79]

**15551** Fischer-Nagel, Heiderose, and Andreas Fischer-Nagel. *Life of the Honeybee* (2–5). Illus. 1986, Carolrhoda paper $6.95 (0-87614-470-9). 48pp. A simply written science book showing the work of 3 kinds of bees. (Rev: BCCB 4/86; BL 4/15/86; SLJ 2/86)

**15552** Gibbons, Gail. *The Honey Makers* (1–4). Illus. 1997, Morrow LB $15.93 (0-688-11387-7). 32pp. An informative picture book that introduces honeybees and their society. (Rev: BCCB 4/97; BL 3/15/97; SLJ 5/97) [595.79]

**15553** Johnson, Sylvia A. *Wasps* (4–6). Illus. 1984, Lerner LB $22.60 (0-8225-1460-5). 48pp. A year in the life of a wasp is presented in a clear text and fascinating illustrations.

**15554** Lavies, Bianca. *Killer Bees* (4–6). Illus. 1994, Dutton paper $15.99 (0-525-45243-5). 32pp. An account of African honeybees, which cause horror and hardship whenever they swarm. (Rev: BL 2/1/95; SLJ 3/95*) [595]

**15555** Micucci, Charles. *The Life and Times of the Honeybee* (3–5). Illus. 1995, Ticknor $15.00 (0-395-65968-X). 32pp. Detailed drawings on double-page spreads introduce the anatomy, habits, and behavior of honeybees. (Rev: BCCB 7–8/95; BL 2/1/95*; SLJ 4/95*) [595.79]

**15556** Ross, Edward S. *Yellowjackets* (3–6). Illus. Series: Naturebooks. 1993, Child's World LB $22.79 (1-56766-017-7). 32pp. This species of wasp, its life cycle, and its habits are featured in this attractive picture book with stunning full-page color illustrations. (Rev: BL 3/1/94; SLJ 5/94) [596.79]

**15557** Watts, Barrie. *Honeybee* (PS–3). Illus. Series: Stopwatch. 1990, Silver Burdett LB $9.95 (0-382-24011-1). 25pp. The life of the honeybee, beginning with newly laid eggs, is revealed in clear photos and text. (Rev: BL 6/15/90) [595]

### BEETLES

**15558** Fischer-Nagel, Heiderose, and Andreas Fischer-Nagel. *Life of the Ladybug* (2–5). Illus. 1986, Carolrhoda LB $19.95 (0-87614-240-4). 48pp. The life cycle of the ladybug with full-color, informative photographs. (Rev: BCCB 3/86; BL 5/15/86; SLJ 4/86)

**15559** Johnson, Sylvia A. *Beetles* (4–7). Illus. 1982, Lerner LB $22.60 (0-8225-1476-1). 48pp. Color photography highlights this account that concentrates on the scarab beetle.

**15560** Murray, Peter. *Beetles* (3–6). Illus. Series: Naturebooks. 1993, Child's World LB $22.79 (1-56766-000-2). 32pp. Each double-page spread introduces a different beetle in this attractive book with simple, large-type text and color photos. (Rev: BL 3/1/94) [595.76]

### CATERPILLARS, BUTTERFLIES, AND MOTHS

**15561** Beaty, Dave. *Moths and Butterflies* (3–6). Illus. Series: Naturebooks. 1993, Child's World LB $22.79 (1-56766-001-0). 32pp. Large color photos face each page of text in this attractive introduction to butterflies and moths. (Rev: BL 3/1/94) [595.78]

**15562** Cassie, Brian, and Jerry Pallotta. *The Butterfly Alphabet Book* (PS–2). Illus. by Mark Astrella. 1995, Charlesbridge paper $6.95 (0-88106-894-2). From an Apollo butterfly to a Zephyr Metalmark, this alphabet book features amazing butterflies with descriptions of their characteristics. (Rev: SLJ 12/95) [595.78]

**15563** Chinery, Michael. *Butterfly* (3–5). Illus. by Helen Senior. Series: Life Story. 1990, Troll LB $12.95 (0-8167-2100-9); paper $4.95 (0-8167-2101-7). 32pp. A butterfly's life and its transformations are revealed in this book with color photographs. (Rev: BL 4/1/91) [595.789]

**15564** Delafosse, Claude. *Butterflies* (PS–2). Illus. Series: First Discovery. 1997, Scholastic $11.95 (0-590-93781-2). 24pp. The life cycle of butterflies and their movements are pictured in this beginning book with impressive pictures. (Rev: BL 2/15/97) [595.78]

**15565** Facklam, Margery. *Creepy, Crawly Caterpillars* (3–5). Illus. by Paul Facklam. 1996, Little, Brown $15.95 (0-316-27391-0). 32pp. Explains the structure, life cycle, and important varieties of caterpillars. (Rev: BCCB 7–8/96; BL 5/15/96*; HB 7–8/96; SLJ 5/96) [595.78]

**15566** Feltwell, John. *Butterflies and Moths* (4–6). Illus. Series: Eyewitness Explorers. 1993, DK Publg. $9.95 (1-56458-227-2). 64pp. Different kinds of butterflies and moths are pictured in colorful double-page spreads and brief text. (Rev: BL 3/1/93) [595.79]

**15567** Fischer-Nagel, Heiderose, and Andreas Fischer-Nagel. *Life of the Butterfly* (4–6). Illus. 1987, Lerner paper $7.95 (0-87614-484-9). 48pp. Clear, readable text and color photos detail the life of a peacock butterfly. (Rev: BL 4/1/87; SLJ 5/87)

**15568** French, Vivian. *Caterpillar Caterpillar* (PS–3). Illus. by Charlotte Voake. 1993, Candlewick $14.95 (1-56402-206-4). 32pp. From her observations and answers supplied by her grandmother, a young girl learns about the caterpillars she sees in the garden. (Rev: BL 10/15/93; SLJ 12/93) [595.78]

**15569** Gibbons, Gail. *Monarch Butterfly* (1–3). Illus. 1989, Holiday LB $15.95 (0-8234-0773-X). 32pp. The basic life cycle of the monarch butterfly from egg to adult. (Rev: BCCB 12/89; BL 11/1/89; HB 11–12/89; SLJ 12/89) [595.78]

**15570** Hamilton, Kersten. *The Butterfly Book: A Kid's Guide to Attracting, Raising, and Keeping Butterflies* (3–6). Illus. 1997, John Muir paper $7.95 (1-56261-309-X). 40pp. Introduces 20 species of butterflies and how to attract and keep them, as well as describing their life cycle, anatomy, and habits. (Rev: BL 7/97) [595.78]

**15571** Hariton, Anca. *Butterfly Story* (2–4). Illus. 1995, Dutton paper $14.99 (0-525-45212-5). 32pp. The 5-week process of turning a caterpillar into a butterfly is described in words and pictures. (Rev: BL 1/15/95; SLJ 4/95) [595.78]

**15572** Heiligman, Deborah. *From Caterpillar to Butterfly* (PS–1). Illus. by Bari Weissman. Series: Let's-Read-and-Find-Out Science. 1996, HarperCollins LB $14.89 (0-06-024268-X); paper $4.95 (0-06-445129-1). 31pp. Using a classroom setting, this book shows children watching the miracle of the metamorphosis from caterpillar to butterfly. (Rev: SLJ 8/96) [595.78]

**15573** Hogan, Paula Z. *The Butterfly* (1–3). Illus. by Geri K. Strigenz. 1979, Raintree Steck-Vaughn LB

$21.40 (0-8114-8176-X). 32pp. Large, bright illustrations highlight this introductory account.

**15574** Lasky, Kathryn. *Monarchs* (4–6). Illus. by Christopher G. Knight. 1993, Harcourt $16.95 (0-15-255296-0); paper $10.00 (0-15-255297-9). 64pp. The life cycle of the monarch butterfly is presented with details of its mammoth migration. Also tells how communities have helped preserve this species. (Rev: BCCB 11/93; BL 11/15/93; HB 11–12/93; SLJ 9/93*) [595.78]

**15575** Lavies, Bianca. *Monarch Butterflies: Mysterious Travelers* (4–7). Illus. 1992, Dutton paper $15.99 (0-525-44905-1). 32pp. A secluded forest in Mexico's Sierra Madres is the winter home of these beautiful butterflies that summer in the eastern United States and Canada. (Rev: BL 1/15/93; SLJ 4/93*) [595.78]

**15576** Lepthien, Emilie U. *Monarch Butterflies* (1–3). Illus. Series: New True Books. 1989, Children's LB $21.00 (0-516-01165-0). 48pp. This species is presented in simple, concise text with many color photos. (Rev: BL 9/1/89) [595.78]

**15577** Ling, Mary. *Butterfly* (PS–1). Illus. by Kim Taylor. Series: See How They Grow. 1992, DK Publg. $7.95 (1-56458-112-8). 24pp. Excellent color photos help to give children a glimpse of natural history. (Rev: BL 11/1/92; HB 1–2/93; SLJ 12/92) [595.789]

**15578** Merrick, Patrick. *Caterpillars* (2–4). Illus. Series: Creepy Crawlers. 1997, Child's World LB $22.79 (1-56766-380-X). 32pp. Describes various kinds of caterpillars, how they move, their habitats, diets, and enemies, with material on their complete life cycle. (Rev: SLJ 3/98) [595.78]

**15579** Pascoe, Elaine. *Butterflies and Moths* (3–6). Photos by Dwight Kuhn. Illus. Series: Nature Close-Up. 1996, Blackbirch LB $16.95 (1-56711-180-7). 48pp. After a general introduction to butterflies and moths, this book shows how they can be caught, housed, fed, and observed. (Rev: SLJ 4/97) [595.78]

**15580** Pringle, Laurence. *An Extraordinary Life: The Story of a Monarch Butterfly* (3–6). Illus. by Bob Marstall. 1997, Orchard LB $19.99 (0-531-33002-8). 32pp. The life cycle of a single monarch butterfly and its migration from Massachusetts to Mexico. (Rev: BCCB 5/97; BL 3/15/97*; HB 5–6/97; SLJ 5/97) [595.78]

**15581** Ring, Elizabeth. *Night Flier* (1–3). Photos by Dwight Kuhn. 1994, Millbrook LB $21.90 (1-56294-467-3). 32pp. The life cycle of the cecropia moth is chronicled from its hatching from the cocoon. (Rev: BL 10/1/94; SLJ 12/94) [595.78]

**15582** Ross, Michael E. *Caterpillarology* (3–5). Photos by Brian Grogan. Illus. by Darren Erickson. Series: Backyard Buddies. 1998, Carolrhoda LB

$19.93 (1-57505-055-2). 48pp. A great deal of scientific information is presented about caterpillars in an entertaining way, with experiments and instructions on how to capture and release them. (Rev: SLJ 3/98) [595.78]

**15583** Rowan, James P. *Butterflies and Moths* (1–4). Illus. 1983, Children's paper $5.50 (0-516-41692-8). 48pp. A nicely organized and well-illustrated introduction for young readers.

**15584** Sabin, Louis. *Amazing World of Butterflies and Moths* (1–3). Illus. by Jean Helmer. 1982, Troll paper $3.50 (0-89375-561-3). 32pp. A simple account for young readers with brief text and many illustrations.

**15585** Whalley, Paul. *Butterfly and Moth* (4–8). Illus. 1988, Knopf LB $20.99 (0-394-99618-6). 64pp. Camouflage, life cycles, and migration of these insects are explored. (Rev: BL 12/1/88; SLJ 12/88)

## SPIDERS

**15586** Back, Christine. *Spider's Web* (1–3). Illus. 1986, Silver Burdett paper $3.95 (0-382-24020-0). 25pp. How the garden spider spins its web and uses it as a food trap. (Rev: BL 1/1/87)

**15587** Bailey, Jill. *How Spiders Make Their Webs* (3–5). Illus. Series: Nature's Mysteries. 1996, Benchmark LB $21.36 (0-7614-0456-2). 32pp. Using a large number of illustrations, this account describes a variety of spider constructions and how they are made. (Rev: SLJ 2/97) [595.4]

**15588** Chinery, Michael. *Spider* (3–5). Illus. by Alan Male. Series: Life Story. 1990, Troll paper $3.95 (0-8167-2109-2). 32pp. The life of the common spider is introduced in detailed text and unusual photos. (Rev: BL 4/1/91) [595.4]

**15589** Clyne, Densey. *Spotlight on Spiders* (4–6). Illus. Series: Small Worlds. 1996, Allen & Unwin paper $6.95 (1-86373-862-2). 32pp. Australian spiders, their habits and structure, are described in this colorful import. (Rev: SLJ 7/96) [595.4]

**15590** Dallinger, Jane. *Spiders* (4–7). Illus. 1981, Lerner LB $22.60 (0-8225-1456-7); paper $5.95 (0-8225-9534-6). 48pp. Excellent color photographs complement the text.

**15591** Fowler, Allan. *Spiders Are Not Insects* (PS–3). Illus. Series: Rookie Read-About Science. 1996, Children's LB $18.50 (0-516-06054-6). 31pp. A beginning reader that introduces spiders and features such species as the tarantula, bird spider, and the black widow. (Rev: SLJ 8/96) [595.4]

**15592** Gibbons, Gail. *Spiders* (1–2). Illus. 1993, Holiday LB $15.95 (0-8234-1006-4). 32pp. An introductory account with stunning drawings of spiders, plus their structure, behavior, and important species. (Rev: BL 4/15/93; SLJ 7/93) [595.4]

**15593** Kalman, Bobbie. *Web Weavers and Other Spiders* (2–5). Illus. Series: Crabapple. 1997, Crabtree LB $18.08 (0-86505-632-3); paper $5.95 (0-86505-732-X). 32pp. A description of how spiders live is given, with material on physical characteristics, web building, defenses, and mating behavior. (Rev: BL 7/97; SLJ 7/97) [595.4]

**15594** Llewellyn, Claire. *Spiders Have Fangs: And Other Amazing Facts About Arachnids* (1–3). Illus. by Mike Taylor and Jo Moore. Series: I Didn't Know That. 1997, Millbrook LB $19.90 (0-7613-0610-2). 32pp. A fascination book that reveals little-known facts about spiders and other arachnids. (Rev: SLJ 3/98) [595.4]

**15595** Markle, Sandra. *Outside and Inside Spiders* (4–6). Illus. 1994, Bradbury paper $17.00 (0-02-762314-9). 40pp. The spider's anatomy is described, along with material on mating, habitats, and behavior. (Rev: BL 4/1/94; HB 5–6/94; SLJ 6/94) [595.4]

**15596** Murray, Peter. *Scorpions* (3–5). Illus. Series: Naturebooks. 1996, Child's World LB $22.79 (1-56766-217-X). 32pp. This book features in color photos and simple text the spiderlike creature with a dreaded sting in its tail. (Rev: BL 12/15/96) [595.4]

**15597** Murray, Peter. *Tarantulas* (3–6). Illus. Series: Naturebooks. 1993, Child's World LB $22.79 (1-56766-060-6). 32pp. Amazing full-page photos highlight this simple introduction to tarantulas, how they live, and how they gather food. (Rev: BL 3/1/94) [595.4]

**15598** Parsons, Alexandra. *Amazing Spiders* (1–4). Illus. Series: Eyewitness Juniors. 1990, Knopf LB $11.99 (0-679-90226-0). 32pp. After the nature of spiders is discussed, various kinds are introduced. (Rev: BL 8/90) [595.4]

**15599** Podendorf, Illa. *Spiders* (1–4). Illus. 1982, Children's LB $21.00 (0-516-01653-9); paper $5.50 (0-516-41653-7). 48pp. Color photographs and a well-organized text are highlights of this simple introduction.

**15600** Pringle, Laurence. *Scorpion Man: Exploring the World of Scorpions* (4–7). Illus. 1994, Scribners paper $15.95 (0-684-19560-7). 48pp. A profile of the world of scorpions, with material on the life of the man who studied them, Gary Polis. (Rev: BL 1/15/95; SLJ 3/95) [595.4]

**15601** Schnieper, Claudia. *Amazing Spiders* (3–6). Illus. by Max Meier. 1989, Carolrhoda LB $19.93 (0-87614-342-7). 48pp. In often startling photos and a clear text, spiders are introduced. (Rev: BL 9/15/89; HB 11–12/89; SLJ 8/89) [595.4]

**15602** Souza, D. M. *Eight Legs* (3–5). Illus. Series: Creatures All Around Us. 1991, Carolrhoda LB

$19.93 (0-87614-441-5). 40pp. Close-up photographs and clear explanations introduce spiders, scorpions, and other crawling creatures with 8 legs. (Rev: BL 4/15/91; SLJ 7/91) [595.4]

**15603** Storad, Conrad J. *Tarantulas* (2–3). Series: Early Bird Nature Books. 1998, Lerner LB $19.93 (0-8225-3024-4). 48pp. This easily read, beautifully illustrated account introduces the tarantula, its life cycle, and its feeding habits. (Rev: BL 3/15/98) [595.4]

**15604** Tesar, Jenny. *Spiders* (5–8). Illus. by Robert C. Kray. Series: Our Living World. 1993, Blackbirch LB $18.95 (1-56711-043-6). 64pp. A fine introduction to spiders that includes material on their anatomy, behavior, diet, senses, and reproduction. (Rev: SLJ 2/94) [595.4]

## Land Invertebrates

**15605** Aaseng, Nathan. *Invertebrates* (5–8). Illus. 1993, Watts LB $22.50 (0-531-12550-5). 112pp. Describes the varieties of life without backbones, including insects, and how they have diversified through the ages. (Rev: BL 3/15/94; SLJ 3/94) [592]

**15606** Buholzer, Theres. *Life of the Snail* (2–5). Illus. 1987, Carolrhoda LB $19.95 (0-87614-246-3). 48pp. Close-up photos highlight the story of this small, fascinating animal. (Rev: BL 3/15/87; SLJ 6–7/87)

**15607** Doris, Ellen. *Meet the Arthropods* (4–7). 1996, Thames & Hudson $16.95 (0-500-19010-0). 64pp. Such arthropods as the horseshoe crab, potato beetle, and praying mantis are introduced with photographs and activities. (Rev: BL 10/15/96) [595.2]

**15608** Glaser, Linda. *Wonderful Worms* (PS–2). Illus. by Loretta Krupinski. 1992, Millbrook LB $21.90 (1-56294-062-7). 32pp. A close peek at the wriggly world of earthworms. (Rev: BL 1/15/93; SLJ 3/93) [595]

**15609** Johnson, Sylvia A. *Silkworms* (4–7). Illus. 1982, Lerner paper $5.95 (0-8225-9557-5). 48pp. The life cycle of the silkworm, told in text and striking color pictures.

**15610** Johnson, Sylvia A. *Snails* (4–6). Illus. 1982, Lerner LB $12.95 (0-8225-1475-3). 48pp. The structure, habits, and life cycle of a snail.

**15611** McLaughlin, Molly. *Earthworms, Dirt, and Rotten Leaves: An Exploration in Ecology* (4–6). Illus. 1986, Avon paper $3.50 (0-380-71074-9). 96pp. Activities that lead to an understanding of the behavior and appearance of earthworms. (Rev: BCCB 2/87; BL 2/1/87; SLJ 3/87)

**15612** Murray, Peter. *Snails* (2–4). Illus. Series: Creepy Crawlers. 1997, Child's World LB $22.79 (1-

56766-382-6). 32pp. The physical and behavioral characteristics of snails are presented, with additional material on diet, habitats, movements, and enemies. (Rev: SLJ 3/98) [594.3]

**15613** Pascoe, Elaine. *Earthworms* (4–7). Illus. Series: Nature Close-up. 1996, Blackbirch LB $16.95 (1-56711-177-7). 48pp. An account of the anatomy of earthworms and how they live, as well as how to collect and care for them. (Rev: BL 12/1/96) [595.1]

**15614** Ross, Michael E. *Snailology* (4–6). Illus. Series: Backyard Buddies. 1996, Carolrhoda LB $14.95 (0-87614-894-1). 48pp. Various types of snails are introduced, with material on their classification, physical structure, and habits. (Rev: BL 7/96; SLJ 8/96) [594]

**15615** Ross, Michael E. *Wormology* (4–6). Illus. 1996, Carolrhoda LB $14.95 (0-87614-937-9). 48pp. Worms and their classification, structure, and habits are introduced, with several activities and experiments. (Rev: BL 3/15/96; SLJ 7/96) [595.1]

**15616** Silverstein, Alvin, et al. *Invertebrates* (3–6). Illus. Series: Kingdom of Life. 1996, Twenty-First Century LB $20.40 (0-8050-3518-4). 64pp. Animals without backbones are discussed in a brief text with many color photographs. (Rev: BL 6/1–15/96) [592]

## Marine and Freshwater Life

### GENERAL AND MISCELLANEOUS

**15617** Armstrong, Pam. *Young Explorer's Guide to Undersea Life* (3–5). Illus. 1996, Monterey Bay $16.95 (1-878244-10-8). 64pp. Some plants and about 20 animals that live in or around the sea are described. (Rev: BL 9/15/96; SLJ 9/96) [574.92]

**15618** Bendick, Jeanne. *Exploring an Ocean Tide Pool* (3–5). Illus. by Todd Telander. 1994, Holt paper $6.95 (0-8050-3273-8). 56pp. Includes basic information about a tide pool's plants and animals, with full-color photos and black-and-white diagrams and drawings. (Rev: BL 8/92; SLJ 11/92) [574]

**15619** Cooney, Helen. *Underwater Animals* (2–4). Illus. Series: Nature Company Young Discoveries. 1997, Time Life $10.00 (0-7835-4841-9). 32pp. In a series of double-page spreads and impressive illustrations, a number of marine animals are introduced in a simple text. (Rev: BL 2/15/97) [591.92]

**15620** Darling, Kathy. *Seashore Babies* (3–5). Illus. by Tara Darling. 1997, Walker LB $16.85 (0-8027-8477-1). 32pp. Seashores are introduced, with details of the young of the creatures found there and their lives and enemies. (Rev: BL 4/1/97; SLJ 3/97) [591.3]

**15621** Day, Nancy. *The Horseshoe Crab* (3–5). Illus. Series: Remarkable Animals. 1992, Macmillan

$13.95 (0-87518-545-2). 60pp. The evolution of the horseshoe crab is given plus material on its structure, habitats, and behavior. (Rev: BL 12/1/92; SLJ 3/93) [595.3]

**15622** Demuth, Patricia. *Way Down Deep: Strange Ocean Creatures* (1–3). Illus. by Jim Deal. Series: All Aboard Reading. 1995, Putnam paper $3.99 (0-448-40851-1). 48pp. This easy-to-read science book introduces youngsters to the amazing creatures found at the bottom of the ocean. (Rev: BL 1/1–15/96; SLJ 6/96) [551.46]

**15623** Doubilet, Anne. *Under the Sea from A to Z* (3–7). Illus. by David Doubilet. 1991, Crown $16.00 (0-517-57836-0). Astonishing facts about astonishing creatures, such as the blue-ringed octopus and the Japanese cherry blossom jellyfish. (Rev: BL 6/1/91; SLJ 4/91) [591.92]

**15624** Esbensen, Barbara J. *Sponges Are Skeletons* (1–4). Illus. by Holly Keller. Series: Let's-Read-and-Find-Out. 1993, HarperCollins LB $15.89 (0-06-021037-0). 32pp. This account tells about the original bath sponges and how they originated on the ocean floor. (Rev: BL 12/1/93; SLJ 2/94) [593.4]

**15625** Feeney, Stephanie, and Ann Fielding. *Sand to Sea: Marine Life of Hawaii* (2–4). Illus. by Ed Robinson. 1989, Univ. of Hawaii Pr. $13.95 (0-8248-1180-1). 64pp. A look at the fascinating sea life in Hawaii. (Rev: BL 11/1/89) [574]

**15626** Fleisher, Paul. *Tide Pool* (3–5). Illus. Series: Webs of Life. 1997, Marshall Cavendish LB $21.36 (0-7614-0431-7). 40pp. This wet-and-dry environment is introduced, along with the animals and plants that thrive under conditions where flooding occurs twice a day. (Rev: BL 2/15/98; SLJ 4/98) [574.5]

**15627** Greenaway, Theresa. *Swamp Life* (3–6). Illus. by Jane Burton and Kim Taylor. Series: Look Closer. 1993, DK Publg. $9.95 (1-56458-211-6). 32pp. With double-page spreads and many captions, the flora and fauna of swamps are highlighted. (Rev: BL 8/93; SLJ 8/93) [574]

**15628** Gribbin, Mary. *Big Ocean Creatures* (PS–3). Illus. by Peter Bull. Series: Ladybird First Explorers. 1996, Ladybird paper $5.99 (0-7214-5689-8). 25pp. Various large ocean animals, like seals and whales, are introduced in 2-page spreads that give a large picture of the animals and several smaller ones to show habits and activities. (Rev: SLJ 1/97) [591.92]

**15629** Holling, Holling C. *Pagoo* (4–6). Illus. 1957, Houghton $19.95 (0-395-06826-6); paper $8.95 (0-395-53964-1). 96pp. Life cycle of the hermit crab.

**15630** Kalman, Bobbie. *AB Sea* (K–3). Illus. Series: Crabapples. 1995, Crabtree LB $18.08 (0-86505-625-0); paper $5.95 (0-86505-725-7). 32pp. An alphabet book that uses full-color pictures of marine life to illustrate the ABCs. (Rev: SLJ 4/96) [574.92]

**15631** Kite, Patricia. *Down in the Sea: The Sea Slug* (2–4). Illus. 1994, Albert Whitman LB $14.95 (0-8075-1717-8). 32pp. In photos and easily read text, the life, appearance, and habits of the sea slug are explored. (Rev: BL 5/15/94; SLJ 5/94) [594]

**15632** Kovacs, Deborah, and Kate Madin. *Beneath Blue Waters: Meetings with Remarkable Deep-Sea Creatures* (5–8). Illus. 1996, Viking paper $16.99 (0-670-85653-3). 64pp. Text and color photos are used to explore marine life one mile below the ocean's surface. (Rev: BL 12/1/96I; SLJ 1/97) [591.92]

**15633** Matthews, Rupert. *Record Breakers of the Sea* (2–6). Illus. Series: Record Breakers. 1990, Troll LB $9.95 (0-8167-1925-X). 32pp. Contains facts, records, and trivia about amazing sea creatures. Also use: *Record Breakers of the Air; Record Breakers of the Land* (both 1990). (Rev: SLJ 2/91) [591.92]

**15634** Pallotta, Jerry. *The Freshwater Alphabet Book* (1–4). Illus. by David Biedrzycki. 1996, Charlesbridge $15.95 (0-88106-901-9). Freshwater fish and crustaceans are used, along with a mythical monster or 2 in this nicely illustrated alphabet book. (Rev: SLJ 4/96) [597]

**15635** Parker, Steve. *Whales and Dolphins* (3–6). Illus. Series: Look into Nature. 1994, Sierra Club $16.95 (0-87156-465-3). 57pp. Covers topics related to whales and dolphins, including size and shape, speed, food, and mating. (Rev: BL 10/15/94) [599.5]

**15636** Parsons, Alexandra. *Sea Creatures* (K–3). Illus. Series: What's Inside? 1993, DK Publg. $8.95 (1-56458-221-3). 17pp. Exteriors and interiors of the shark, starfish, and other sea creatures are pictured and described in simple text. (Rev: SLJ 7/93) [591.92]

**15637** Paul, Tessa. *By the Seashore* (2–5). Illus. Series: Animal Trackers. 1997, Crabtree LB $19.16 (0-86505-587-4); paper $7.95 (0-86505-595-5). 32pp. Ten creatures found at the seashore are introduced and identified by the evidence they leave behind, like prints, holes, nests, and hair or fur. (Rev: SLJ 10/97) [591]

**15638** Podendorf, Illa. *Animals of Sea and Shore* (1–4). Illus. 1982, Children's LB $21.00 (0-516-01615-6); paper $5.50 (0-516-41615-4). 48pp. A fine introduction to marine life for primary grades.

**15639** Rothaus, Don P. *Moray Eels* (3–5). Illus. Series: Naturebooks: Animals. 1995, Child's World LB $22.79 (1-56766-187-4). 32pp. The mysterious moray eel is discussed, with information on habitats, structure, habits, and diet. (Rev: BL 11/15/95; SLJ 4/96) [597]

**15640** Savage, Stephen. *Animals of the Oceans* (2–6). Illus. Series: Animals by Habitat. 1997, Raintree Steck-Vaughn LB $22.83 (0-8172-4753-X). 32pp. Readers are taken on a tour of vast underwater

habitats and encounter such animals as the moray eel, green turtle, and sea anemone. (Rev: BL 5/15/97; SLJ 8/97) [591.9]

**15641** Shahan, Sherry. *Barnacles Eat with Their Feet: Delicious Facts About the Tide Pool Food Chain* (3–5). Illus. 1996, Millbrook LB $21.40 (1-56294-922-5). 32pp. The plants and animals in a tidal pool and what they eat. (Rev: BL 2/1/96; SLJ 4/96) [574.5]

**15642** Sibbald, Jean H. *Strange Eating Habits of Sea Creatures* (4–8). Illus. 1987, Macmillan LB $13.95 (0-87518-349-2). 112pp. Eating habits of numerous creatures of the sea are divided into techniques — grazers, gulpers, poisoners, and so on. (Rev: BL 12/1/86; SLJ 2/87)

**15643** Silverstein, Alvin, et al. *The Sea Otter* (4–7). Illus. Series: Endangered in America. 1995, Millbrook LB $22.40 (1-56294-418-5). 64pp. The sea otter's habits and life cycle are covered, with details on how the fur trade, oil spills, and other environmental disasters have made it an endangered species. (Rev: BL 6/1–15/95; SLJ 7/95) [599.74]

**15644** Silverstein, Alvin, and Virginia Silverstein. *Life in a Tidal Pool* (4–6). Illus. by Pamela Carroll and Walter Carroll. 1990, Little, Brown $14.95 (0-316-79120-2). 60pp. The tidal pool habitat is explored. (Rev: SLJ 10/90) [574]

**15645** Stefoff, Rebecca. *Sea Horse* (2–4). Illus. Series: From the Living Things. 1996, Marshall Cavendish LB $21.36 (0-7614-0116-4). 32pp. Various kinds of sea horses are described, along with their habits and life cycles. (Rev: BL 2/1/97; SLJ 3/97) [597]

**15646** Taylor, Barbara. *The Really Sinister Savage Shark: And Other Creatures of the Deep* (PS–4). Illus. Series: The Really Horrible Guides. 1997, DK Publg. $9.95 (0-7894-2050-3). This account explores the various ways — like poisonous stings, electric shocks, and pointed tusks — that sea creatures defend themselves. (Rev: SLJ 12/97) [574]

**15647** Taylor, Leighton. *Creeps from the Deep* (4–8). Illus. 1997, Chronicle $13.95 (0-8118-1297-9). 48pp. In startling color photos and a fascinating text, this title examines the strange creatures that live in the deepest regions of the ocean. (Rev: BL 12/15/97; SLJ 4/98) [578.77]

**15648** Tesar, Jenny. *What on Earth Is a Nudibranch?* (3–5). Illus. Series: What On Earth? 1995, Blackbirch LB $14.95 (1-56711-099-1). 32pp. A fascinating look at the sea slug, its habitats, physical features, and behavior. (Rev: SLJ 11/95) [592]

**15649** Treat, Rose. *The Seaweed Book: How to Find and Have Fun with Seaweed* (4–7). Illus. 1995, Star Bright paper $5.95 (1-887724-00-7). 32pp. The identification, collection, and preservation of various kinds of seaweed. (Rev: BL 2/1/96) [589.45]

**15650** Waterlow, Julia. *The Red Sea and the Arabian Gulf* (4–6). Illus. Series: Seas and Oceans. 1997, Raintree Steck-Vaughn LB $24.26 (0-8172-4515-4). 48pp. An overview of the history and importance of these bodies of water, with information on the coral reefs and animals of the Red Sea and oil reserves of the Arabian Gulf. (Rev: BL 7/97) [551.46]

## CORALS AND JELLYFISH

**15651** Cerullo, Mary. *Coral Reef: A City That Never Sleeps* (5–8). Illus. 1996, Dutton paper $17.99 (0-525-65193-4). 58pp. Exceptional photographs highlight the account of coral reefs and the life they support. (Rev: BL 3/1/96; SLJ 1/96*) [574.9]

**15652** Fleisher, Paul. *Coral Reef* (3–5). Series: Webs of Life. 1997, Marshall Cavendish LB $21.36 (0-7614-0432-5). 40pp. This look at life in a coral reef explains how they are formed and the kinds of life found within them. (Rev: BL 2/15/98; SLJ 4/98) [574.9]

**15653** Hulme, Joy N. *Sea Sums* (K–3). Illus. by Carol Schwartz. 1996, Hyperion LB $14.49 (0-7868-2142-6). 32pp. Addition and subtraction are taught through various creatures found in a coral reef. (Rev: BCCB 12/96; BL 12/1/96; SLJ 12/96) [513.2]

**15654** Johnson, Rebecca L. *The Great Barrier Reef: A Living Laboratory* (5–8). Illus. 1991, Lerner LB $23.93 (0-8225-1596-2). 96pp. This account describes the formation and inhabitants of the Great Barrier Reef from an investigative scientist's point of view. (Rev: BL 5/15/92; SLJ 7/92) [574.92]

**15655** Johnson, Sylvia A. *Coral Reefs* (4–7). Illus. by Shohei Shirai. 1984, Lerner LB $22.60 (0-8225-1451-6); paper $5.95 (0-8225-9545-1). 48pp. The creation and composition of coral reefs and the life they support.

**15656** Kalman, Bobbie. *Life in the Coral Reef* (2–5). Illus. Series: Crabapple. 1997, Crabtree LB $16.95 (0-86505-629-3); paper $5.95 (0-86505-729-X). 32pp. A description of how coral reefs are formed, their interdependence with other animals and plants, and methods used to save them. (Rev: BL 7/97) [574.5]

**15657** Kite, Patricia. *Down in the Sea: The Jellyfish* (1–3). Illus. Series: Down by the Sea. 1993, Whitman LB $14.95 (0-8075-1712-7). 32pp. Color photos highlight this introduction to the fascinating jellyfish. (Rev: BL 3/15/93; SLJ 3/93) [593.7]

**15658** Pringle, Laurence. *Coral Reefs: Earth's Undersea Treasures* (4–6). Illus. 1995, Simon & Schuster $16.00 (0-689-80286-2). 45pp. A pictorial account that displays the diversity of life on a coral reef, its uses to humankind, and the dangers of destruction.

(Rev: BL 10/15/95; HB 11–12/95; SLJ 10/95) [574.5]

**15659** Sayre, April Pulley. *Coral Reef* (4–7). Illus. Series: Exploring Earth's Biomes. 1996, Twenty-First Century LB $20.40 (0-8050-4087-0). 80pp. An accurate, interesting explanation of the composition of coral reefs and description of the life forms they support. (Rev: BL 10/15/96; HB 3–4/96; SLJ 1/97) [574.9]

**15660** Siy, Alexandra. *The Great Astrolabe Reef* (5–8). Illus. Series: Circle of Life. 1992, Macmillan $14.95 (0-87518-499-5). 80pp. Color photos help to tell the story of this delicate coral ecosystem. (Rev: BL 9/1/92; SLJ 11/92) [574.5]

**15661** Taylor, Barbara. *Coral Reef* (3–6). Illus. Series: Look Closer. 1992, DK Publg. $9.95 (1-879431-92-0). 32pp. In a series of double-page spreads with brief captions, the origins and composition of coral reefs are explained. (Rev: BL 6/1/92; HB 7–8/92; SLJ 6/92) [591.9]

**15662** Wood, Jenny. *Coral Reefs: Hidden Colonies of the Sea* (3–5). Illus. Series: Wonderworks of Nature. 1991, Stevens LB $21.27 (0-8368-0630-1). 32pp. Three types of reefs are explored — coral, fringe, and barrier — with material on where they can be found and how coral live on them. (Rev: SLJ 9/92) [574.84]

**15663** Wu, Norbert. *A City Under the Sea: Life in a Coral Reef* (3–6). Illus. 1996, Simon & Schuster $16.00 (0-689-31896-0). 32pp. A fascinating glimpse of the life surrounding a coral reef. (Rev: BL 6/1–15/96; SLJ 3/96) [574]

## CRUSTACEANS

**15664** Cerullo, Mary. *Lobsters: Gangsters of the Sea* (4–6). Photos by Jeffrey L. Rotman. 1994, Dutton paper $16.99 (0-525-65153-5). 64pp. A photoessay about the life cycle of lobsters and what happens when they are caught by lobster trappers. (Rev: BL 3/1/94; HB 1–2/94; SLJ 3/94) [595.3]

**15665** Johnson, Sylvia A. *Crabs* (4–6). Illus. 1982, Lerner LB $22.60 (0-8225-1471-0). 48pp. A look at the structure and life cycle of various crabs.

**15666** Johnson, Sylvia A. *Hermit Crabs* (3–5). Illus. by Kazunari Kawashima. Series: Natural Science Books. 1989, Lerner LB $22.60 (0-8225-1488-5). 48pp. An introduction to hermit crabs, with striking photos. (Rev: BL 1/1/90; SLJ 2/90) [595.3]

**15667** Kite, Patricia. *Down in the Sea: The Crab* (2–4). Illus. 1994, Albert Whitman LB $14.95 (0-8075-1709-7). 32pp. Photographs and simple text introduce the crab, with interesting material on how they communicate. (Rev: BL 6/1–15/94; SLJ 5/94) [595.3]

**15668** Ricciuti, Edward R. *Crustaceans* (5–7). Illus. Series: Our Living World. 1994, Blackbirch LB $18.95 (1-56711-046-0). 64pp. Introduces crabs, lobsters, and other crustaceans, and tells about their unique characteristics, senses, metabolisms, and life cycles. (Rev: BL 12/1/94) [595.3]

**15669** Stefoff, Rebecca. *Crab* (K–3). Series: Living Things. 1997, Marshall Cavendish LB $21.36 (0-7614-0444-9). 32pp. Using double-page spreads, the crab is introduced, with material on its structure, habits, and food. (Rev: BL 2/15/98) [595.3]

### DOLPHINS AND PORPOISES

**15670** Fowler, Allan. *Friendly Dolphins* (1–2). Series: Rookie Read-About-Science. 1997, Children's LB $13.87 (0-516-20428-9). 32pp. Introduces dolphins, with striking photos and minimal text, suitable for beginning readers. (Rev: BL 11/15/97; SLJ 10/97) [599.5]

**15671** Grover, Wayne. *Dolphin Adventure: A True Story* (3–5). Illus. by Jim Fowler. 1990, Greenwillow $16.00 (0-688-09442-2). 48pp. An encounter with wild dolphins off the Florida coast. (Rev: BL 9/15/90; SLJ 12/90) [599.5]

**15672** Hatherly, Janelle, and Delia Nicholls. *Dolphins and Porpoises* (5–8). Illus. 1990, Facts on File $17.95 (0-8160-2272-0). 68pp. The habitats, eating habits, and reproduction of these favorite animals are covered along with other topics. (Rev: BL 11/15/90; SLJ 5/91) [599.5]

**15673** Horton, Casey. *Dolphins* (3–5). Illus. Series: Endangered! 1996, Benchmark LB $21.36 (0-7614-0216-0). 32pp. A basic introduction to dolphins, their characteristics, habitats, and structure is given through text and full-color photos. (Rev: SLJ 3/96) [599.5]

**15674** Morris, Robert A. *Dolphin* (K–3). Illus. by Mamoru Funai. 1975, HarperCollins $6.93 (0-06-024337-6). 64pp. A simple account of the first 5 months of this lovable sea mammal.

**15675** Schomp, Virginia. *The Bottlenose Dolphin* (3–5). Illus. 1994, Silver Burdett LB $13.95 (0-87518-605-X). 60pp. Fact and mythology mingle in this account of the dolphin, its life cycle, and its habitats. (Rev: BL 3/1/95) [599.5]

**15676** Smith, Roland. *Whales, Dolphins, and Porpoises in the Zoo* (4–6). Photos by William Munoz. Series: New Zoo. 1994, Millbrook LB $21.90 (1-56294-318-9). 64pp. This account describes what happens to whales, dolphins, and porpoises after their capture and tells of their lives in modern aquariums and zoos. (Rev: BL 10/1/94; SLJ 10/94) [636]

**15677** Stoops, Erik D., et al. *Dolphins* (3–5). Illus. 1997, Sterling $16.95 (0-8069-0568-9). 80pp. An attractive volume that introduces dolphins, their

unique characteristics, eating habits, reproduction, and self-defense. (Rev: BL 5/1/97; SLJ 7/97) [599.5]

### FISH

**15678** Arnosky, Jim. *Crinkleroot's 25 Fish Every Child Should Know* (PS–3). Illus. 1993, Bradbury LB $12.95 (0-02-705844-1). 32pp. A picture book field guide that introduces with paintings and brief text 25 common species of fish. (Rev: BL 9/1/93; SLJ 9/93) [597]

**15679** Bailey, Jill. *How Fish Swim* (3–5). Illus. by Colin Newman. Series: Nature's Mysteries. 1996, Benchmark LB $21.36 (0-7614-0451-1). 32pp. This work covers how fish and other aquatic animals move and the different anatomical specializations that make locomotion possible. (Rev: SLJ 2/97) [597]

**15680** Broekel, Ray. *Dangerous Fish* (1–4). Illus. 1982, Children's LB $21.00 (0-516-01635-0); paper $5.50 (0-516-41635-9). An introduction to some of the less friendly members of the fish family.

**15681** Cole, Joanna. *A Fish Hatches* (3–5). Illus. 1978, Morrow LB $14.93 (0-688-32153-4). 40pp. The story of a trout, from egg to fully grown fish, in text and photographs.

**15682** Crewe, Sabrina. *The Salmon* (K–2). Illus. by Colin Newman. Series: Life Cycles. 1996, Raintree Steck-Vaughn LB $21.40 (0-8172-4371-2). 32pp. The story of the salmon from the hatching of the egg to adulthood, with coverage on the migrations to and from the ocean. (Rev: SLJ 3/97) [597.55]

**15683** Eastman, David. *What Is a Fish?* (K–3). Illus. by Lynn Sweat. 1982, Troll LB $12.95 (0-89375-660-1); paper $3.50 (0-89375-661-X). 32pp. A simple account that shows various kinds of fish.

**15684** Grossman, Susan. *Piranhas* (4–6). Illus. Series: Remarkable Animals. 1994, Dillon LB $13.95 (0-87518-593-2). 60pp. An introduction to piranhas that points out their value to fisherman and that the harm they do to humans is exaggerated. (Rev: SLJ 8/94) [597]

**15685** Parker, Steve. *Fish* (4–8). Illus. Series: Eyewitness Books. 1990, Random LB $20.99 (0-679-90439-5). 64pp. Anatomy, behavior, and habitats of fish are explored. (Rev: SLJ 9/90) [597]

**15686** Perry, Phyllis J. *Sea Stars and Dragons* (3–5). Illus. Series: First Books. 1996, Watts LB $21.00 (0-531-20223-2). 63pp. A concise text introduces the life and habits of the sea star and sea horse. (Rev: SLJ 8/96) [591.92]

**15687** Ricciuti, Edward R. *What on Earth Is a Pout?* (3–5). Illus. Series: What on Earth? 1996, Blackbirch LB $14.95 (1-56711-103-3). 32pp. An introduction to the pout, a bottom-dwelling fish in the Atlantic, that covers its appearance, life-style, and habits. (Rev: SLJ 2/97) [597]

**15688** Snedden, Robert. *What Is a Fish?* (2–5). Illus. 1993, Sierra Club $13.95 (0-87156-545-5). 32pp. Double-page spreads present basic information about fish including anatomy, reproduction, breathing, and food. (Rev: BL 10/1/93; SLJ 1/94) [597]

**15689** Zim, Herbert S., and Hurst H. Shoemaker. *Fishes* (5–8). Illus. by James G. Irving. 1991, Western paper $21.27 (0-307-64059-0). 160pp. This is a basic guide to both fresh and saltwater species.

## OCTOPUS

**15690** Cerullo, Mary. *The Octopus: Phantom of the Sea* (4–8). Illus. 1997, Dutton paper $16.99 (0-525-65199-3). 64pp. The life cycle of this mysterious sea creature is described, with illustrations of its anatomy and of its relatives, like the squid. (Rev: BCCB 2/97; BL 2/1/97; SLJ 12/97*) [594]

**15691** Kite, Patricia. *Down in the Sea: The Octopus* (1–3). Illus. Series: Down by the Sea. 1993, Whitman LB $14.95 (0-8075-1715-1). 32pp. Color photos highlight this introduction to the feared and fascinating octopus. (Rev: BL 3/15/93; SLJ 3/93) [594.56]

**15692** Stefoff, Rebecca. *Octopus* (K–3). Illus. Series: Living Things. 1996, Marshall Cavendish LB $21.36 (0-7614-0119-9). 32pp. This colorful introduction to the formidable sea creature uses short bits of information and many illustrations on double-page spreads. Also use in this series *Starfish, Giant Turtle,* and *Praying Mantis.* (Rev: BL 3/15/97; SLJ 3/97) [597.92]

## SEA MAMMALS

**15693** Boyle, Doe. *Otter on His Own: The Story of a Sea Otter* (K–3). Illus. by Lisa Bonforte. Series: Smithsonian Oceanic Collection. 1995, Soundprints $15.95 (1-56899-129-0). 30pp. Describes the childhood of a sea otter and how, for several months, the mother shares her meals with him until he can dive for his own food. (Rev: SLJ 6/95) [599.74]

**15694** Cossi, Olga. *Harp Seals* (3–6). Illus. 1991, Carolrhoda LB $19.95 (0-87614-437-7). 48pp. The life cycle, migratory patterns, and behavior of the Arctic harp seal are described. (Rev: BCCB 4/91; BL 5/5/91; SLJ 6/91) [599.74]

**15695** Cousteau Society. *Seals* (PS–3). Illus. 1992, Simon & Schuster $4.95 (0-671-77061-6). 24pp. Introducing the harp seal to a young audience with minimal text and color photographs. (Rev: BL 5/1/92; SLJ 7/92) [599.74]

**15696** Darling, Kathy. *Walrus: On Location* (1–4). Illus. by Tara Darling. Series: On Location. 1991, Lothrop $14.95 (0-688-09032-Y). 40pp. Watching the walrus who come to shore every year on Round

Island off the coast of Alaska. (Rev: BL 8/91; SLJ 12/91) [599.74]

**15697** Grace, Eric S. *Seals* (4–6). Illus. by Fred Bruemmer. Series: Sierra Club Wildlife Library. 1994, Little, Brown paper $7.95 (0-316-32291-1). 62pp. This slim, oversized volume supplies an attractive, well-organized introduction to seals and their cousins, sea lions and walruses. (Rev: BL 1/15/92; SLJ 2/92*) [599.74]

**15698** Greene, Carol. *Reading About the River Otter* (K–3). Illus. Series: Friends in Danger. 1993, Enslow LB $17.95 (0-89490-425-6). 32pp. This account discusses the river otter, its life and habitats, and why it is now considered endangered. (Rev: BL 9/1/93; SLJ 7/93) [599.74]

**15699** Harman, Amanda. *Manatees and Dugongs* (3–5). Illus. Series: Endangered! 1996, Benchmark LB $21.36 (0-7614-0294-2). 32pp. These endangered sea creatures are described in text and pictures, with material on their habitats, life-styles, and how they can be helped. (Rev: SLJ 2/97) [599.5]

**15700** Hurd, Edith Thacher. *The Song of the Sea Otter* (4–6). Illus. by Jennifer Dewey. 1989, Sierra Club paper $5.95 (0-316-38323-6). 40pp. In a harbor on the Pacific coast, a baby sea otter explores his world. A reissue.

**15701** Jenkins, Priscilla B. *A Safe Home for Manatees* (PS–3). Illus. by Martin Classen. Series: Let's-Read-and-Find-Out Science. 1997, HarperCollins LB $14.89 (0-06-027150-7); paper $4.95 (0-06-445164-X). 32pp. An introduction to Florida's sea cows, or manatees, their habits, why they are facing extinction, and the efforts being made to save them. (Rev: BL 12/1/97; SLJ 10/97) [599.5]

**15702** Johnson, Sylvia A. *Elephant Seals* (3–6). Illus. 1989, Lerner LB $22.60 (0-8225-1487-7). 48pp. The story of these animals, hunted almost to extinction, along the California and Mexico coasts. (Rev: BL 3/1/89)

**15703** Lepthien, Emilie U. *Manatees* (1–3). Illus. Series: New True Books. 1991, Children's LB $21.00 (0-516-01114-6). 48pp. This elusive, now endangered aquatic mammal is introduced in simple text and many color photographs. (Rev: BL 8/91) [599.52]

**15704** Lepthien, Emilie U. *Otters* (2–4). Illus. Series: New True Book. 1994, Children's LB $21.00 (0-516-01056-5). 48pp. The habits and life cycles of both sea and river otters are covered, with material on the sea otter's endangered status. (Rev: BL 7/94) [599.74]

**15705** Lepthien, Emilie U. *Walruses* (3–4). Illus. Series: True Book: Animals. 1996, Children's LB $21.00 (0-516-20162-X). 48pp. Introduces the walrus and its life at sea, anatomy, food, child rearing, and habits. (Rev: SLJ 6/97) [599.7]

**15706** Matthews, Downs. *Harp Seal Pups* (3–5). Illus. by Dan Guravich. 1997, Simon & Schuster paper $17.00 (0-689-80014-2). 32pp. The life of a harp seal pup and her fight for survival against her enemies are covered in text and appealing photos. (Rev: BL 1/1–15/97; SLJ 2/97) [599.74]

**15707** Rinard, Judith E. *Amazing Animals of the Sea* (5–8). Illus. 1981, National Geographic LB $12.50 (0-87044-387-9). 104pp. Whales, dolphins, sea otters, sea lions, seals, manatees, and other marine mammals are described.

**15708** Sherrow, Victoria. *Seals, Sea Lions and Walruses* (4–7). Illus. Series: First Books. 1991, Watts LB $12.40 (0-531-20028-0). 64pp. An appealing book with much information and good photos. (Rev: BL 12/15/91; SLJ 12/91) [599]

**15709** Sibbald, Jean H. *The Manatee* (4–7). Illus. 1990, Macmillan LB $13.95 (0-87518-429-4). 60pp. The life of this gentle sea mammal is examined, along with material on how its survival is threatened by humans. (Rev: BL 6/15/90; SLJ 8/90) [599.5]

**15710** Silverstein, Alvin, et al. *The Manatee* (4–7). Illus. Series: Endangered in America. 1995, Millbrook LB $23.90 (1-56294-551-3). 64pp. A profile of this sea creature, its lifestyle and habits, and how it became an endangered species. (Rev: BL 10/15/95; SLJ 1/96) [599.5]

**15711** White, Sandra V., and Michael Filisky. *Sterling: The Rescue of a Baby Harbor Seal* (3–6). Illus. 1989, Crown $14.95 (0-517-57112-9). 32pp. The true story of the rescue of an orphaned harbor seal. (Rev: BL 7/89) [639.9]

### SHARKS

**15712** Batten, Mary. *Shark Attack Almanac* (4–7). Illus. by Carol Lyon. Series: KidBacks. 1997, Random paper $5.99 (0-679-87769-X). 64pp. Using a shark attack as a focus, this book introduces sharks, their structure, habits, and unique qualities. (Rev: SLJ 8/97) [597.31]

**15713** Berger, Gilda. *Sharks* (2–5). Illus. 1987, Doubleday $10.95 (0-385-23418-X). 48pp. Much detail about the behavior and characteristics of 20 shark species. (Rev: BL 8/87; SLJ 8/87)

**15714** Cole, Joanna. *Hungry, Hungry Sharks* (1–3). Illus. by Patricia J. Wynne. 1986, Random LB $11.99 (0-394-97471-9); paper $3.99 (0-394-87471-4). 48pp. Different kinds of sharks are explained in simple terms. (Rev: BL 8/86)

**15715** Coupe, Sheena. *Sharks* (5–7). Illus. Series: Great Creatures of the World. 1990, Facts on File $17.95 (0-8160-2270-4). 72pp. Many kinds of sharks

are identified and pictured with information on their structures, habits, and methods of attack. (Rev: BL 4/1/90; SLJ 7/90) [597]

**15716** Del Prado, Dana. *Terror Below! True Shark Stories* (2–3). Illus. by Stephen Marchesi. Series: All Aboard Reading, Level 3. 1997, Grosset paper $3.95 (0-448-41124-5). 47pp. Three true stories about encounters with sharks in which the victims lived to tell their stories. (Rev: SLJ 10/97) [597.31]

**15717** Fowler, Allan. *The Best Way to See a Shark* (1–2). Illus. Series: Rookie Read-About Science. 1995, Children's LB $18.50 (0-516-06032-5). 32pp. In a small format, this colorful book introduces sharks and their bodies, types, and habits. (Rev: BL 7/95) [596.31]

**15718** Gibbons, Gail. *Sharks* (2–4). Illus. 1992, Holiday LB $15.95 (0-8234-0960-0). For the primary level, this account presents basic general facts as well as specific data on 12 common sharks. (Rev: BL 5/1/92; SLJ 7/92) [597.31]

**15719** Gourley, Catherine. *Sharks! True Stories and Legends* (4–7). Illus. 1996, Millbrook LB $27.40 (0-7613-0001-5). 96pp. Both fact and fiction involving sharks are presented in this informal, readable account. (Rev: BCCB 1/97; BL 10/15/96; SLJ 12/96) [597]

**15720** Harman, Amanda. *Sharks* (4–6). Illus. Series: Endangered! 1996, Benchmark LB $21.36 (0-7614-0220-9). 32pp. This account concentrates on 3 kinds of sharks — the great white, the whale, and the basking — and tells about the differences in their anatomies and why they are endangered. (Rev: SLJ 8/96) [597]

**15721** Maestro, Betsy. *A Sea Full of Sharks* (3–6). Illus. by Giulio Maestro. 1997, Scholastic paper $4.99 (0-590-43101-3). 32pp. An informative look at this feared but fascinating creature. (Rev: BL 1/1/91; SLJ 10/90) [597.31]

**15722** Markle, Sandra. *Outside and Inside Sharks* (3–5). Illus. Series: Outside and Inside. 1996, Simon & Schuster $16.00 (0-689-80348-6). 40pp. The exterior structure and inside anatomy of sharks are described. (Rev: BCCB 7–8/96; BL 6/1–15/96; HB 5–6/96; SLJ 3/96) [597]

**15723** Maynard, Christopher. *Informania: Sharks* (4–7). Illus. 1997, Candlewick $14.99 (0-7636-0328-7). 92pp. A spiral-bound book that attractively presents basic material about sharks in a series of different formats, including a foldout model. (Rev: SLJ 1/98) [597.31]

**15724** Parker, Steve. *Sharks* (3–5). Illus. Series: What If. 1996, Millbrook LB $19.90 (0-7613-0456-8); paper $6.95 (0-7613-0471-1). 32pp. Using questions and answers, various characteristics of sharks are highlighted. (Rev: SLJ 6/96) [597.13]

**15725** Simon, Seymour. *Sharks* (2–4). Illus. 1995, HarperCollins LB $15.89 (0-06-023032-0). 32pp. Basic information about sharks, including life cycles, anatomy, and habits, is given with full-color illustrations. (Rev: BL 10/15/95; HB 11–12/95; SLJ 9/95) [597]

**15726** Zoehfeld, Kathleen W. *Great White Shark: Ruler of the Sea* (PS–3). Illus. by Steven J. Petruccio. Series: Smithsonian Oceanic Collection. 1995, Soundprints $15.95 (1-56899-122-3). 31pp. The life cycle of a great white shark, the Ruler of the Sea, which grows to 20 feet in length in adulthood. (Rev: SLJ 6/95) [597]

### SHELLS

**15727** Abbott, R. Tucker. *Seashells of the World* (3–6). Illus. 1991, Western paper $5.50 (0-307-24410-5). 100pp. A basic guide, well illustrated; revised edition. Also use: *Seashells of North America* (1969).

**15728** Lember, Barbara Hirsch. *The Shell Book* (K–3). Photos by author. 1997, Houghton $14.95 (0-395-72030-3). 32pp. Two-page layouts are used to introduce and describe several seashells that are found along the North American coastline. (Rev: SLJ 4/97) [594]

**15729** Patchett, Lynne. *My Shell* (PS–1). Illus. by Fiona Pragoff. Series: First Step Science. 1995, Gareth Stevens LB $19.93 (0-8368-1188-7). 32pp. Different kinds of seashells are introduced in simple text and interesting activities, with added information on other kinds of shells and basic scientific concepts. (Rev: BL 7/95) [574.4]

**15730** Royston, Angela. *Shells* (PS–1). Illus. by Richard Manning. Series: What's Inside? 1991, DK Publg. $8.95 (1-879431-10-6). 17pp. Using double-page spreads, the exteriors and interiors of a variety of shells are pictured and simply described. (Rev: BL 2/15/92; SLJ 3/92) [591]

### WHALES

**15731** Arnold, Caroline. *Killer Whale* (3–5). Illus. by Richard Hewett. 1994, Morrow LB $14.93 (0-688-12030-X). 48pp. Using the facilities of Sea World in California, the anatomy and behavior of killer whales are examined in the wild and in captivity. (Rev: BL 9/15/94; HB 11–12/94; SLJ 10/94) [599.5]

**15732** Carrick, Carol. *Whaling Days* (3–6). Illus. by David Frampton. 1993, Houghton $15.95 (0-395-50948-3). 40pp. With an emphasis on conservation, this is a history of whaling, from ancient times to the present. (Rev: BCCB 7–8/93; BL 5/1/93*; HB 5–6/93; SLJ 5/93*) [639.2]

**15733** Chrisp, Peter. *The Whalers* (4–6). Illus. 1995, Thomson Learning LB $24.26 (1-56847-421-0). 48pp. A history of whaling from ancient to modern times, with information on present-day efforts to protect whales. (Rev: BL 2/15/96; SLJ 3/96) [639.2]

**15734** Davies, Nicola. *Big Blue Whale* (PS–1). Illus. by Nick Maland. 1997, Candlewick $15.99 (1-56402-895-X). 28pp. Using a picture book format, the characteristics, habits, and behavior of the blue whale are explored. (Rev: BL 9/1/97; HB 5–6/97; SLJ 7/97) [599.5]

**15735** Delafosse, Claude, and Ute Fuhr. *Whales* (PS–3). Illus. Series: First Discovery Book. 1993, Scholastic $11.95 (0-590-47130-9). 24pp. This interactive, highly visual beginner's book introduces whales, how and where they live, and what they eat. (Rev: BL 11/15/93; HB 3–4/93; SLJ 4/94) [599.5]

**15736** Dow, Lesley. *Whales* (5–7). Illus. Series: Great Creatures of the World. 1990, Facts on File $17.95 (0-8160-2271-2). 68pp. Different types of whales are identified and material is given on habits and structure. (Rev: BL 4/1/90; SLJ 7/90) [599.5]

**15737** DuTemple, Lesley A. *Whales* (2–3). Illus. Series: Early Bird Nature Book. 1996, Lerner LB $19.95 (0-8225-3008-2). 48pp. Several kinds of whales are introduced, with descriptions of their appearance and behavior. (Rev: BL 8/96; SLJ 7/96) [599.5]

**15738** Esbensen, Barbara J. *Baby Whales Drink Milk* (PS–1). Illus. by Lambert Davis. Series: Lets-Read-and-Find-Out Science Stage I. 1994, HarperCollins LB $14.89 (0-06-021552-6); paper $4.95 (0-06-445119-4). 32pp. This book explains why whales are not fish and in so doing covers the characteristics of mammals. (Rev: BL 2/15/94; SLJ 3/94) [599.5]

**15739** Fowler, Allan. *The Biggest Animal Ever* (1–2). Illus. Series: Rookie Read-About Science. 1992, Children's paper $4.95 (0-516-46001-3). 32pp. With many color photos and sparse text, whales are introduced to very young readers. (Rev: BL 12/15/92; SLJ 2/93) [599.5]

**15740** Gibbons, Gail. *Whales* (PS–1). Illus. 1991, Holiday LB $15.95 (0-8234-0900-7). 32pp. The world of the fascinating whale, with good photos. (Rev: BL 10/15/91; HB 11–12/91; SLJ 12/91) [599.5]

**15741** Gourley, Catherine. *Hunting Neptune's Giants: True Stories of American Whaling* (5–8). Illus. 1995, Millbrook LB $27.40 (1-56294-534-3). 96pp. A fascinating history of whaling in this country, with generous excerpts from original sources. (Rev: BCCB 1/96; BL 11/1/95*; SLJ 12/95) [639.3]

**15742** Harman, Amanda. *Whales* (4–6). Illus. Series: Endangered! 1996, Benchmark LB $21.36 (0-7614-0219-5). 32pp. Different species of whales are introduced, with coverage on why they have been hunted to near extinction and the efforts being made to save them. (Rev: SLJ 8/96) [599.5]

**15743** Hodge, Deborah. *Whales: Killer Whales, Blue Whales and More* (K–3). Series: Wildlife. 1997, Kids Can $10.95 (1-55074-356-2). 32pp. In a series of double-page spreads, various whales are introduced, with material on food, habitats, and mobility. (Rev: BL 9/15/97; SLJ 11/97) [599.5]

**15744** Kraus, Scott, and Kenneth Mallory. *The Search for the Right Whale* (3–6). Illus. 1993, Crown LB $14.99 (0-517-57845-X). 36pp. Efforts of scientists from the New England Aquarium in Boston to track down the remaining right whales, a species hunted to near extinction. (Rev: BL 7/93; SLJ 8/93*) [599.2]

**15745** Lauber, Patricia. *Great Whales: The Gentle Giants* (3–5). Illus. by Pieter Folkens. Series: Redfeather Book. 1991, Holt LB $14.95 (0-8050-1717-8); paper $4.95 (0-8050-2894-3). 64pp. Characteristics and habits of great whales are explored as well as a look at whale hunting and conservation efforts. (Rev: BL 3/1/92; SLJ 4/92) [599.5]

**15746** McMillan, Bruce. *Going on a Whale Watch* (PS–3). Illus. 1993, Scholastic $19.95 (0-590-72826-1). 40pp. Readers go on a whale watch and watch 2 children watching the whales. (Rev: BL 10/15/92; SLJ 4/93) [599.5]

**15747** Matero, Robert. *The Birth of a Humpback Whale* (5–8). Illus. 1996, Simon & Schuster $16.00 (0-689-31931-2). 53pp. A narrative with pencil drawings that covers the birth of a humpbacked whale and its journey from Hawaii to Alaska. (Rev: BL 4/1/96; SLJ 6/96) [599.5]

**15748** Papastavrou, Vassili. *Whale* (4–8). Illus. Series: Eyewitness Books. 1993, Knopf LB $20.99 (0-679-93884-2). 64pp. A well-illustrated introduction to whales, the various types, their food, travels, and life cycle. (Rev: BL 10/1/93; SLJ 12/93) [599.5]

**15749** Patent, Dorothy Hinshaw. *Killer Whales* (2–4). Illus. by John K. Ford. 1993, Holiday LB $15.95 (0-8234-0999-6). 30pp. Physical structure, social habits, and habitats are described for the killer whale. (Rev: BL 8/93; SLJ 8/93) [599.5]

**15750** Posell, Elsa. *Whales and Other Sea Mammals* (1–4). Illus. 1982, Children's LB $21.00 (0-516-01663-6); paper $5.50 (0-516-41663-4). A description of these sea animals in large type and many color illustrations.

**15751** Selsam, Millicent E., and Joyce Hunt. *A First Look at Whales* (2–3). Illus. by Harriett Springer. 1980, Walker LB $12.85 (0-8027-6388-X). Descriptions of whales are included that show the various species and how they differ from fish.

**15752** Short, Joan, and Bettina Bird. *Whales* (3–5). Illus. by Deborah Savin. 1997, Mondo paper $4.95 (1-57255-190-9). 31pp. Colorful illustrations are used to cover such particulars about whales as anatomy, swimming, breathing, feeding, and communication. (Rev: SLJ 9/97) [599.5]

**15753** Smyth, Karen C. *Crystal: The Story of a Real Baby Whale* (3–6). Illus. 1986, Down East paper $9.95 (0-89272-327-0). 96pp. The first year in the life of a humpback whale. (Rev: BL 8/86; SLJ 4/87)

**15754** Stoops, Erik D., et al. *Whales* (3–6). Illus. 1995, Sterling $16.95 (0-8069-0566-2). 80pp. Using a question-and-answer format, provides basic facts about the whale, such as why they don't drown. (Rev: BL 12/1/95; SLJ 1/96) [599.5]

**15755** Whitfield, Philip. *Can the Whales Be Saved?* (5–6). Illus. 1989, Viking LB $16.95 (0-670-82753-3). 96pp. The worldwide crisis concerning the depletion of the whale population and the efforts that are being taken to help save them. (Rev: SLJ 1/90) [599.5]

**15756** Wolpert, Tom. *Whale Magic for Kids* (2–4). Illus. Series: Animal Magic for Kids. 1991, Stevens LB $21.27 (0-8368-0660-3). 48pp. Through text and full-color photographs, whales, with their varieties and habits, are introduced. (Rev: BL 4/15/91) [599.5]

## Microscopes and Microbiology

**15757** Facklam, Howard, and Margery Facklam. *Bacteria* (4–7). Illus. Series: Invaders. 1994, Twenty-First Century LB $18.90 (0-8050-2857-9). 64pp. A concise explanation of bacteria and their composition and functions. (Rev: BL 1/1/95; SLJ 3/95) [589.9]

**15758** Levine, Shar, and Leslie Johnstone. *The Microscope Book* (5–8). Illus. by David Sovka. 1997, Sterling $19.95 (0-8069-4898-1); paper $9.95 (0-8069-4899-X). 80pp. An excellent introduction to microscopes, with material on parts of the microscope, lenses, how to focus and produce slides, and tips on keeping a journal. (Rev: SLJ 7/97) [502]

**15759** Loewer, Peter. *Pond Water Zoo: An Introduction to Microscopic Life* (5–8). Illus. 1996, Simon & Schuster $16.00 (0-689-31736-0). 86pp. Various life forms found in a drop of pond water are revealed by the microscope. (Rev: BCCB 12/96; BL 9/15/96; SLJ 2/97) [576]

**15760** Ricciuti, Edward R. *Microorganisms: The Unseen World* (5–7). Illus. Series: Our Living World. 1994, Blackbirch LB $18.95 (1-56711-040-1). 64pp. Introduces microorganisms and explains their unique characteristics, how they function, and their purpose in the web of life. (Rev: BL 12/1/94) [576]

**15761** Selsam, Millicent E. *Greg's Microscope* (K–3). Illus. by Arnold Lobel. 1963, HarperCollins paper $3.75 (0-06-444144-X). 64pp. Greg and his parents observe small household items through a microscope.

**15762** Silverstein, Alvin, et al. *Monerans and Protists* (3–6). Illus. Series: Kingdoms of Life. 1996, Twenty-First Century LB $21.40 (0-8050-3521-4). 64pp. The authors explain scientific classification and include information on viruses, bacteria, protozoa, and algae. (Rev: BL 6/1–15/96; SLJ 7/96) [576]

**15763** Snedden, Robert. *Yuck! A Big Book of Little Horrors* (2–5). Illus. 1996, Simon & Schuster $15.00 (0-689-80676-0). 32pp. Everyday materials like hair and food particles are magnified to look like horrifying objects. (Rev: BCCB 6/96; BL 6/1–15/96; SLJ 5/96) [778.31]

**15764** Stwertka, Eve, and Albert Stwertka. *Microscope: How to Use It and Enjoy It* (5–7). Illus. 1989, Simon & Schuster LB $9.95 (0-671-63705-3); paper $4.95 (0-671-67060-3). An instructive introduction to the use of the microscope. (Rev: BL 3/1/89; SLJ 4/89)

## Oceanography

### GENERAL

**15765** Carter, Katharine. *Oceans* (1–4). Illus. 1982, Children's LB $21.00 (0-516-01639-3); paper $5.50 (0-516-41639-1). 48pp. A well-organized, simple account for the primary grades.

**15766** Cole, Joanna. *The Magic School Bus on the Ocean Floor* (3–5). Illus. by Bruce Degen. 1992, Scholastic $15.95 (0-590-41430-5). 48pp. Miss Frizzle's class takes a class trip down to the ocean to study the animals and plants that live there. (Rev: BCCB 12/92; BL 6/15/92; SLJ 8/92*) [591.92]

**15767** Dipper, Frances. *The Ocean Deep* (4–6). Illus. Series: Mysteries Of. 1996, Millbrook LB $22.90 (0-7613-0454-1); paper $6.95 (0-7613-0469-X). 40pp. Describes the composition and formation of the oceans, with details on exploration of the ocean floor and sunken treasure. (Rev: SLJ 6/96) [591.92]

**15768** Fodor, R. V. *The Strange World of Deep-Sea Vents* (5–8). Illus. Series: Earth Processes. 1991, Enslow LB $16.95 (0-89490-249-0). 64pp. This book describes the discovery of hydrothermal vents in the ocean and the life forms found around these deep-sea vents. (Rev: BL 1/15/91) [551.46]

**15769** Ganeri, Anita. *I Wonder Why the Sea Is Salty: And Other Questions About the Oceans* (PS–2). Illus. by Tony Kenyon, et al. Series: I Wonder Why. 1995, Kingfisher $9.95 (1-85697-549-5); paper $6.95 (0-85697-664-5). 32pp. Amazing and commonplace facts about marine life are presented in a question-and-answer format with entertaining drawings. (Rev: SLJ 7/95) [551.46]

**15770** Haslam, Andrew, and Barbara Taylor. *Oceans* (3–6). Series: Make it Work! 1997, World Book $11.95 (0-7166-5110-6). 48pp. In a series of double-page spreads, basic material about oceans is presented, with a strong emphasis on activities like making models. (Rev: BL 12/15/97) [551.46]

**15771** Heinrichs, Susan. *The Atlantic Ocean* (2–4). Illus. 1986, Children's LB $21.00 (0-516-01289-4). 48pp. An introduction to the Atlantic — shorelines, currents, flora and fauna. (Rev: BL 5/1/87)

**15772** Heinrichs, Susan. *The Pacific Ocean* (2–4). Illus. 1986, Children's LB $15.27 (0-516-01295-9). 48pp. The world's largest ocean is described. (Rev: BL 5/1/87)

**15773** Hoff, Mary, and Mary M. Rodgers. *Our Endangered Planet: Oceans* (4–6). Illus. Series: Our Endangered Planet. 1992, Lerner LB $16.95 (0-8225-2505-4); paper $8.95 (0-8225-9628-8). 72pp. This volume gives a good overview of oceans and the major environmental concerns they present. (Rev: BL 5/15/92; SLJ 7/92) [551.46]

**15774** Kraske, Robert. *The Voyager's Stone* (4–6). Illus. 1995, Orchard LB $16.99 (0-531-08740-9). 96pp. The framework of a message in a bottle cast into the sea is used to introduce oceanography, currents, and sea life. (Rev: BCCB 3/95; BL 3/1/95; SLJ 3/95) [551.46]

**15775** Lambert, David. *The Kingfisher Young People's Book of Oceans* (4–6). Illus. 1997, Kingfisher $19.95 (0-7534-5098-4). 95pp. A colorful look at oceans and marine biology is given in a series of double-page spreads. (Rev: SLJ 3/98) [551.46]

**15776** Lambert, David. *The Mediterranean Sea* (4–6). Illus. Series: Seas and Oceans. 1997, Raintree Steck-Vaughn LB $24.26 (0-8172-4512-X). 48pp. Describes the role of the Mediterranean throughout history, its features and formations, and the plant and animal life it supports. (Rev: BL 7/97) [551.46]

**15777** Lambert, David. *The Pacific Ocean* (4–6). Illus. Series: Seas and Oceans. 1996, Raintree Steck-Vaughn LB $24.26 (0-8172-4507-3). 48pp. Ocean life, currents, the formation of islands, and pollution are a few of the topics discussed in this introduction to the Pacific Ocean. (Rev: BL 1/1–15/97) [551.46]

**15778** Lambert, David. *Seas and Oceans* (5–8). Illus. 1988, Silver Burdett LB $12.95 (0-382-09503-0). 48pp. Covers waves, tides, currents, underwater exploration, and ocean life. (Rev: BL 4/1/88)

**15779** MacQuitty, Miranda. *Ocean* (4–8). Illus. Series: Eyewitness Books. 1995, Knopf LB $20.99 (0-679-97331-1). 64pp. Illustrations highlight the world's oceans. (Rev: BL 12/15/95) [551.46]

**15780** Morgan, Nina. *The Caribbean and the Gulf of Mexico* (4–6). Illus. Series: Seas and Oceans. 1996, Raintree Steck-Vaughn LB $24.26 (0-8172-4508-1). 48pp. For these 2 bodies of water, material is presented on such topics as ocean life, shipping, tourism, currents, and people. (Rev: BL 1/1–15/97) [917.29]

**15781** Morgan, Nina. *The North Sea and the Baltic Sea* (4–6). Illus. Series: Seas and Oceans. 1996, Raintree Steck-Vaughn LB $24.26 (0-8172-4510-3). 48pp. These 2 European bodies of water are introduced, with coverage on their importance, history, shipping routes, and plant and animal life. (Rev: BL 1/1–15/97) [551.46]

**15782** Mudd-Ruth, Maria. *The Ultimate Ocean Book* (2–5). Illus. by Virge Kask and Beverly E. Benner. 1995, Golden Bks. paper $19.95 (0-307-17628-2). Creatures like lobsters, fish, and the octopus pop up on pages that explore ocean life. (Rev: BL 2/1/96; SLJ 1/96) [551.46]

**15783** Penny, Malcolm. *The Indian Ocean* (4–6). Illus. Series: Seas and Oceans. 1997, Raintree Steck-Vaughn LB $24.26 (0-8172-4514-6). 48pp. The history of the world's third-largest ocean, the migration and exploration paths that people took from Europe to Asia, and the marine life it supports. (Rev: BL 7/97) [551.46]

**15784** Ricciuti, Edward R. *Ocean* (4–6). Illus. Series: Biomes of the World. 1995, Marshall Cavendish LB $25.64 (0-7614-0079-6). 64pp. With clear explanations and full-color photos, the world's ocean environment and its animal and plant life are introduced. (Rev: BL 12/15/95) [551.46]

**15785** Robinson, W. Wright. *Incredible Facts About the Ocean: The Land Below, the Life Within, vol. 2* (4–8). Illus. 1987, Macmillan LB $13.95 (0-87518-358-1). 120pp. Maps, diagrams, color photos, and glossary add to this detailed explanation. (Rev: BL 11/1/87; SLJ 10/87)

**15786** Sabin, Louis. *Wonders of the Sea* (1–3). Illus. by Bert Dodson. 1982, Troll LB $12.95 (0-89375-578-8); paper $3.50 (0-89375-579-6). 32pp. An easy-to-read account for primary grades that covers basic topics.

**15787** Sauvain, Philip. *Oceans* (3–5). Illus. Series: Geography Detectives. 1997, Carolrhoda LB $19.95 (1-57505-043-9). 32pp. This account identifies and describes the world's oceans, explains the saltwater ecosystem, and explores coastlines, the ocean floor, tides, and marine plant and animal life. (Rev: BL 8/97; SLJ 1/98) [551.46]

**15788** Sayre, April Pulley. *Ocean* (4–7). Illus. Series: Exploring Earth's Biomes. 1996, Twenty-First Century LB $20.40 (0-8050-4084-6). 80pp. An introduction to the nature and composition of oceans and the animal and plant life that they support. (Rev: BL 10/15/96; SLJ 1/97) [551.46]

**15789** Simon, Seymour. *Oceans* (2–5). Illus. 1990, Morrow LB $15.93 (0-688-09454-6). 32pp. Covers the geography of the ocean floor, major currents, and more. (Rev: BL 10/15/90; HB 1–2/91; SLJ 12/90) [551.46]

**15790** Talbot, Frank H., ed. *Under the Sea* (4–6). Illus. Series: Nature Company Discoveries. 1995, Time Life LB $16.00 (0-7835-4760-9). 64pp. Marine life, both plant and animal, is introduced in this handsome book with lavish illustrations and an 8-page foldout section. (Rev: BL 1/1–15/96; SLJ 1/96) [551.46]

**15791** Tesar, Jenny. *Threatened Oceans* (5–8). Illus. 1991, Facts on File LB $19.95 (0-8160-2494-4). 112pp. Explains the decline of the world's large bodies of water. (Rev: SLJ 1/92) [551.46]

**15792** Twist, Clint. *Seas and Oceans* (5–8). Illus. Series: Ecology Watch. 1991, Macmillan LB $13.95 (0-87518-491-X). 45pp. Ethical issues are discussed in this attractive, oversize volume dealing with problems of the earth's seas and oceans. (Rev: BL 3/1/92) [333.95]

**15793** VanCleave, Janice. *Janice VanCleave's Oceans for Every Kid: Easy Activities That Make Learning Science Fun* (5–7). Illus. Series: Science for Every Kid. 1996, Wiley paper $12.95 (0-471-12453-2). 256pp. This book gives good background information about oceans plus a number of entertaining and instructive projects and activities. (Rev: BL 4/15/96; SLJ 5/96) [551.46]

**15794** Waterlow, Julia. *The Atlantic Ocean* (4–6). Illus. Series: Seas and Oceans. 1996, Raintree Steck-Vaughn LB $24.26 (0-8172-4509-X). 48pp. Such topics as geography, currents, history, and economic and recreational importance are covered in relation to the Atlantic Ocean. (Rev: BL 1/1–15/97) [551.46]

**15795** Waters, John F. *Deep-Sea Vents* (4–6). Illus. 1994, Dutton paper $14.99 (0-525-65145-4). 48pp. Discusses exploration of the deepest parts of the ocean, the new technology used, and types of marine life found there. (Rev: BCCB 3/94; BL 1/15/94; SLJ 3/94) [551.46]

**15796** *Why Are There Waves?* (PS–3). Illus. Series: Why. 1997, DK Publg. $9.95 (0-7894-1531-3). 24pp. Using a question-and-answer format, the text covers basic science material related to oceans and lakes. (Rev: BL 8/97; SLJ 8/97) [553.7]

**15797** Wu, Norbert. *Beneath the Waves: Exploring the Hidden World of the Kelp Forest* (3–7). Illus. 1992, Chronicle $12.95 (0-87701-835-9). 40pp. The undersea kelp forests are the food source for many sea creatures, such as jellyfish, snails, sea otters, and others. (Rev: BL 7/92; SLJ 7/92*) [574.5]

## CURRENTS, TIDES, AND WAVES

**15798** Lampton, Christopher. *Tidal Wave* (4–6). Illus. Series: Disaster! 1992, Houghton paper $5.70 (0-395-62464-9). 40pp. This explanation of the causes and effects of tidal waves includes many color photos and detailed descriptions of important tidal-wave disasters of the past. (Rev: BL 3/15/92) [363.3]

## SEASHORES

**15799** Cohat, Elisabeth. *The Seashore* (PS–2). Illus. by Pierre de Hugo. Series: First Discovery Books. 1995, Scholastic $11.95 (0-590-20303-7). A spiral-bound book with transparencies that show the many organisms found in tidal pools. (Rev: SLJ 9/95) [591]

**15800** Cooper, Ann. *Along the Seashore* (3–5). Illus. Series: Wild Wonders. 1997, Roberts Rinehart paper $9.95 (1-57098-121-2). 46pp. A little book that introduces animals associated with seas and seashores: the seal, cormorant, hermit crab, raccoon, osprey, sea star, dolphin, gull, and sea trout. (Rev: BL 7/97; SLJ 8/97) [577.7]

**15801** Malnig, Anita. *Where the Waves Break: Life at the Edge of the Sea* (3–5). Illus. 1985, Carolrhoda LB $14.95 (0-87614-226-9); Lerner paper $6.95 (0-87614-477-6). 48pp. An introduction to life at the sea's edge, including descriptions of starfish, brittle stars, snails, and seaweed. (Rev: BL 6/1/85; HB 9–10/85; SLJ 5/85)

**15802** Parker, Steve. *Seashore* (4–6). Illus. by Dave King. 1989, Knopf LB $18.99 (0-394-92254-9). 64pp. Life on a seashore is introduced with handsome, well-captioned illustrations. (Rev: BL 10/15/89; SLJ 1/90) [591]

**15803** Sayre, April Pulley. *Seashore* (4–7). Illus. Series: Exploring Earth's Biomes. 1996, Twenty-First Century $20.40 (0-8050-4085-4). 80pp. The composition of seashores and the life that they support are covered in this nicely illustrated account. (Rev: BL 10/15/96; SLJ 1/97) [574.5]

**15804** Stolz, Mary. *Night of Ghosts and Hermits: Nocturnal Life on the Seashore* (3–5). Illus. 1985, Harcourt $12.95 (0-15-257333-X). 48pp. After 3 brothers play on the beach during the day, high drama takes place at night with the emergence of marine life. (Rev: BL 10/1/85; SLJ 1/86)

**15805** Taylor, Barbara. *Shoreline* (3–6). Illus. by Frank Greenaway. Series: Look Closer. 1993, DK Publg. $9.95 (1-56458-213-2). 32pp. The plants and animals found along the seashores are introduced. (Rev: BL 8/93; SLJ 8/93) [674]

**15806** Zim, Herbert S., and Lester Ingle. *Seashores* (5–8). Illus. 1991, Western paper $21.27 (0-307-64496-0). 160pp. This is a guide to animals and plants found along the beaches.

## UNDERWATER EXPLORATION

**15807** Ballard, Robert D. *Exploring the Titanic* (4–8). Illus. by Ken Marschall. 1988, Scholastic $14.95 (0-590-41953-6). A compelling description of the undersea search for the missing ocean liner, for young readers. (Rev: BCCB 10/88; HB 5–6/89; SLJ 11/88)

**15808** Gennings, Sara. *The Atocha Treasure* (4–7). Illus. 1988, Rourke LB $22.60 (0-86592-874-6). 32pp. The 20-year search for 2 Spanish treasure ships lost off the Florida Keys in 1622. (Rev: BL 12/1/88; SLJ 12/88)

**15809** Gibbons, Gail. *Sunken Treasure* (2–5). Illus. 1988, HarperCollins LB $14.89 (0-690-04736-3); paper $5.95 (0-06-446097-5). 32pp. Searching for the cargo of the Atocha, a Spanish galleon sunk off Florida in 1622. (Rev: BCCB 10/88; BL 10/15/88; HB 9–10/88)

**15810** Rawlinson, Jonathan. *Discovering the Titanic* (4–7). Illus. 1988, Rourke LB $22.60 (0-86592-873-8). 32pp. The successful search for the ship sunk 70 years before on its maiden voyage. (Rev: BL 12/1/88; SLJ 12/88)

# Pets

## GENERAL AND MISCELLANEOUS

**15811** Chrystie, Frances N. *Pets: A Comprehensive Handbook for Kids*. 4th ed. (4–6). Illus. 1995, Little, Brown paper $8.95 (0-316-14281-6). 261pp. A new edition of this basic work on a variety of pets and how to care for them. (Rev: BL 5/15/95; SLJ 7/95) [636]

**15812** Curran, Wanda L. *Your Guinea Pig: A Kid's Guide to Raising and Showing* (4–6). Illus. 1995, Storey paper $14.95 (0-88266-889-7). 160pp. Topics in this book on how to keep guinea pigs as pets include selecting, feeding, mating, and showing. (Rev: BL 9/1/95) [636]

**15813** Engfer, LeeAnne. *My Pet Hamster and Gerbils* (2–4). Photos by Andy King. Series: All About Pets. 1998, Lerner LB $22.60 (0-8225-2261-6); paper $7.95 (0-8225-9794-2). 64pp. Real-life situations are used to give details of the selection, care, and feeding of hamsters and gerbils. (Rev: SLJ 3/98) [636]

**15814** Evans, Mark. *Guinea Pigs* (3–6). Illus. Series: ASPCA Pet Care Guides for Kids. 1992, DK Publg. $9.95 (1-56458-125-X). 48pp. The physical characteristics of guinea pigs are described, plus tips are given on how to choose one and care for it as a pet. (Rev: BL 4/1/93; SLJ 2/93) [636]

**15815** Evans, Mark. *Hamster* (3–6). Illus. Series: ASPCA Pet Care Guides for Kids. 1993, DK Publg. $9.95 (1-56458-223-X). 45pp. Discusses the care and feeding of hamsters and how to keep them as happy pets. (Rev: BL 8/93) [636]

**15816** Evans, Mark. *Rabbit* (3–5). Illus. Series: ASPCA Pet Care Guides for Kids. 1992, DK Publg. $9.95 (1-56458-128-4). 46pp. This book offers a wide variety of data for the brand-new pet owner. (Rev: BL 12/15/92) [636]

**15817** Greenlaw, M. Jean. *Welcome to the Stock Show* (3–5). Illus. 1997, Dutton paper $15.99 (0-525-67525-6). 48pp. Three animal breeders describe the route from birth to the showing of a rabbit, a goat, and a dairy cow. (Rev: BL 9/15/97; SLJ 9/97) [636.08]

**15818** Gutman, Bill. *Becoming Best Friends with Your Hamster, Guinea Pig, or Rabbit* (3–6). Illus. 1997, Millbrook LB $21.90 (0-7613-0201-8). 64pp. Practical advice on the care of these pets, with tips on how to make their lives comfortable. (Rev: BCCB 6/97; BL 8/97; SLJ 7/97) [636]

**15819** Gutman, Bill. *Becoming Your Bird's Best Friend* (3–6). Illus. 1996, Millbrook LB $21.90 (1-56294-662-5). 64pp. Various species of birds are described, as well as information on how to care for them as pets. (Rev: BL 12/1/96; SLJ 11/96) [636.9]

**15820** Hansen, Elvig. *Guinea Pig* (3–6). Illus. 1992, Carolrhoda LB $19.95 (0-87614-681-7). 48pp. Charming, informative photos explore the life and care of guinea pigs. (Rev: BL 6/15/92; SLJ 8/92) [636]

**15821** King-Smith, Dick. *Dick King-Smith's Animal Friends: Thirty-One True Life Stories* (3–5). Illus. by Anita Jeram. 1996, Candlewick $19.99 (1-56402-960-3). 96pp. The famous English writer of children's books recalls some of the interesting pets he has had. (Rev: BL 12/1/96; SLJ 12/96) [591]

**15822** King-Smith, Dick. *I Love Guinea Pigs* (PS–3). Illus. by Anita Jeram. 1995, Candlewick $15.99 (1-56402-389-3). 32pp. Three of the topics explored about guinea pigs are their habits, physical features, and history. (Rev: BCCB 4/95; BL 3/15/95; SLJ 5/95) [636]

**15823** McPherson, Mark. *Choosing Your Pet* (3–5). Illus. 1996, Troll paper $2.95 (0-8167-0112-1). 48pp. A simply written guide to owning a first pet. (Rev: BL 7/1/85; SLJ 10/85)

**15824** Petty, Kate. *Rabbits* (1–3). Illus. Series: First Pets. 1993, Barron's paper $4.95 (0-8120-1473-1). 24pp. This manual explains the characteristics, habits, and care of rabbits. (Rev: BL 10/1/89; SLJ 4/90) [636.932]

**15825** Simon, Seymour. *Pets in a Jar: Collecting and Caring for Small Wild Animals* (4–6). Illus. by Betty Fraser. 1979, Puffin paper $5.99 (0-14-049186-4). How to catch and care for such small wild creatures as snails, toads, and ants.

**15826** Squire, Ann. *101 Questions and Answers About Pets and People* (4–6). Illus. 1988, Macmillan $13.95 (0-02-786580-0). 96pp. Common questions on a range of topics, such as relationships, behavior, physiology. (Rev: BL 11/1/88; SLJ 2/89)

**15827** Watts, Barrie. *Hamster* (1–3). Illus. 1986, Silver Burdett LB $9.95 (0-382-09281-3); paper $3.95 (0-382-09957-5). 28pp. Well-organized, basic scientific information, with full-color photos. (Rev: BL 1/1/87)

**15828** Wexler, Jerome. *Pet Gerbils* (2–5). Illus. 1990, Whitman LB $15.95 (0-8075-6523-7). 48pp. Raising these rodents, with intriguing photos. (Rev: BCCB 11/90; BL 9/15/90; SLJ 11/90) [636]

**15829** Wexler, Jerome. *Pet Hamsters* (3–6). Illus. 1992, Whitman LB $15.95 (0-8075-6525-3). 48pp. Personal advice from a hamster raiser on the care and handling of these pets. (Rev: BCCB 2/93; BL 2/15/93; SLJ 2/93) [636]

## CATS

**15830** Arnold, Caroline. *Cats: In from the Wild* (4–7). Photos by Richard Hewett. 1993, Carolrhoda LB $19.95 (0-87614-692-2). 48pp. Domestic and wild cats are highlighted with comparisons and contrasts. (Rev: BL 8/93) [636.8]

**15831** Bare, Colleen S. *Toby the Tabby Kitten* (PS–3). Illus. 1995, Dutton paper $13.99 (0-525-65211-6). 32pp. Basic facts about cats are revealed in this photoessay about Toby, a tailless tabby cat. (Rev: BL 11/15/95; SLJ 2/96) [636.8]

**15832** Clutton-Brock, Juliet. *Cat* (4–8). Illus. Series: Eyewitness Books. 1991, Knopf LB $20.99 (0-679-91458-7). 64pp. With careful anatomical drawings and several charts, the basic facts about cats are given. (Rev: BL 12/1/91) [599.74]

**15833** Engfer, LeeAnne. *My Pet Cats* (2–4). Photos by Andy King. Series: All About Pets. 1998, Lerner LB $22.60 (0-8225-2258-6); paper $7.95 (0-8225-9793-4). 64pp. Tips on cat selection and care are found in this book that focuses on a girl who adopts 2 cats from a shelter and raises them to adulthood. (Rev: SLJ 3/98) [636.8]

**15834** Evans, Mark. *Kitten* (3–6). Illus. Series: Pet Care Guides for Kids. 1992, DK Publg. $9.95 (1-56458-126-8). 48pp. The structure and behavior patterns of cats are described, plus tips are given on how to choose a kitten and care for it. (Rev: BL 4/1/93; SLJ 2/93) [636.8]

**15835** Fowler, Allan. *It Could Still Be a Cat* (1–2). Illus. Series: Rookie Readers. 1993, Children's LB $18.50 (0-516-06015-5). 32pp. The cat family is introduced in this easy-to-read book for beginners. (Rev: BL 3/1/94) [636.8]

**15836** Gibbons, Gail. *Cats* (PS–2). Illus. by author. 1996, Holiday LB $15.95 (0-8234-1253-9). Watercolor illustrations are used to introduce a number of breeds of cats, their characteristics, and behavior. (Rev: SLJ 12/96) [636.8]

**15837** Gutman, Bill. *Becoming Your Cat's Best Friend* (3–6). Illus. Series: Pet Friends. 1997, Millbrook LB $21.90 (0-7613-0200-X). 64pp. This book expresses the cat's point of view and gives advice on how to make the pet and its owner happy with the relationship. (Rev: BCCB 6/97; BL 8/97; SLJ 7/97) [636.8]

**15838** Ivory, Lesley A. *Meet My Cats* (4–6). Illus. by author. 1994, Puffin paper $5.99 (0-14-054920-X). 32pp. Twelve cats introduced in an appealing picture-book format. (Rev: BL 12/15/89; SLJ 2/90) [636.8]

**15839** Jessel, Camilla. *The Kitten Book* (1–4). Illus. 1994, Candlewick paper $4.99 (1-56402-278-1). 32pp. The record, in marvelous photographs, of the birth process for a Burmese cat. (Rev: BL 2/1/92; SLJ 4/92) [636.8]

**15840** Lauber, Patricia. *The True-or-False Book of Cats* (2–4). Illus. 1998, National Geographic $15.95 (0-7922-3440-5). 32pp. Cat behavior is explored through the answers to 15 true-or-false statements like, "Cats have nine lives." (Rev: BL 2/15/98) [636.8]

**15841** Overbeck, Cynthia. *Cats* (4–6). Illus. by Shin Yoshino. 1983, Lerner LB $22.60 (0-8225-1480-X). 48pp. This work concentrates on domestic cats and their habits and appearance.

**15842** Petersen-Fleming, Judy, and Bill Fleming. *Kitten Training and Critters, Too!* (PS–2). Illus. by Darryl Bush. 1996, Morrow LB $15.93 (0-688-13387-8). 39pp. This account gives basic tips on how to care for and train kittens, with plenty of fascinating additional information about the training of wild animals at Marine World Africa USA in Vallejo, California. (Rev: SLJ 5/96) [636.7]

**15843** Rosen, Michael J., ed. *Purr . . . Children's Book Illustrators Brag About Their Cats* (2–5). Illus. 1996, Harcourt $18.00 (0-15-200837-3). 48pp. Paintings and text illustrate the moods and activities of a variety of cats. (Rev: BL 4/1/96; SLJ 5/96) [636.8]

**15844** Scott, Carey. *Kittens* (K–5). Illus. 1997, DK Publg. $12.95 (0-7894-2132-1). 37pp. Beautiful photos are featured in this book about kittens and how to choose and care for one as a pet. (Rev: SLJ 2/98) [636.8]

**15845** Selsam, Millicent E. *How Kittens Grow* (1–2). Illus. by Esther Bubley. 1992, Scholastic paper $2.99 (0-590-44784-X). Photographs and simply written text describe the stages in a kitten's growth.

**15846** Selsam, Millicent E., and Joyce Hunt. *A First Look at Cats* (1–4). Illus. by Harriett Springer. 1981, Walker LB $9.85 (0-8027-6399-5). 32pp. A primer for identifying both wild and domestic cats.

## DOGS

**15847** Arnold, Caroline. *A Guide Dog Puppy Grows Up* (3–5). Photos by Richard Hewett. 1991, Harcourt $16.95 (0-15-232657-X); paper $7.00 (0-15-201557-4). 48pp. The life and training of a golden retriever named Honey. (Rev: BCCB 3/91; BL 4/15/91; HB 5–6/91; SLJ 5/91) [362.4]

**15848** Bare, Colleen S. *Sammy, Dog Detective* (K–3). Illus. 1998, Dutton $15.99 (0-525-65253-1). 32pp. A photoessay about the life and work of a police dog, Sammy, who is part of the K-9 team in Modesto, California. (Rev: BL 1/1–15/98; SLJ 1/98) [363.2]

**15849** Calmenson, Stephanie. *Rosie: A Visiting Dog's Story* (PS–3). Illus. by Justin Sutcliffe. 1994, Houghton $16.00 (0-395-65477-7). 48pp. The true story of the dog Rosie, who is being trained to be a visiting dog to help those who are sad or lonely. (Rev: BL 4/15/94; HB 7–8/94; SLJ 4/94) [636.7]

**15850** Clutton-Brock, Juliet. *Dog* (4–8). Illus. Series: Eyewitness Books. 1991, Knopf LB $20.99 (0-679-91459-5). 64pp. The anatomical features of dogs and their different types and outstanding characteristics are covered in this heavily illustrated book. (Rev: BL 12/1/91) [599.74]

**15851** *The Complete Dog Book for Kids* (3–6). Illus. 1996, Macmillan $34.95 (0-87605-458-0); paper $22.95 (0-87605-460-2). 274pp. This publication of the American Kennel Club is an excellent handbook on the various breeds of dogs and how to choose, care for, and train a dog. (Rev: BL 1/1–15/97) [636.7]

**15852** Cooper, Michael. *Racing Sled Dogs: An Original North American Sport* (4–8). Illus. 1988, Houghton $13.95 (0-89919-499-0). 96pp. An account of the Iditarod Trail International Sled Dog Race in Alaska. (Rev: BL 2/1/89; SLJ 3/89)

**15853** Darling, Kathy. *ABC Dogs* (PS–3). Illus. by Tara Darling. 1997, Walker LB $16.85 (0-8027-8635-9). 32pp. This ABC book introduces various breeds of dogs and shows them in photographs, both as puppies and as adults. (Rev: BL 10/15/97; SLJ 10/97) [636.7]

**15854** Evans, Mark. *Puppy* (3–5). Illus. Series: ASPCA Pet Care Guides for Kids. 1992, DK Publg. $9.95 (1-56458-127-6). Intended for the child who is a brand-new pet owner, this book offers much information and full-color photos. (Rev: BL 12/15/91) [636.7]

**15855** Gibbons, Gail. *Dogs* (K–2). Illus. by author. 1996, Holiday LB $15.95 (0-8234-1226-1). An easy-to-read overview of dogs and their history, breeds, and anatomy. (Rev: BCCB 5/96; HB 5–6/96; SLJ 9/96) [636.7]

**15856** Gutman, Bill. *Becoming Your Dog's Best Friend* (3–6). Illus. 1996, Millbrook LB $21.90 (1-56294-661-7). 64pp. In addition to providing information about caring for and training dogs, several breeds are introduced. (Rev: BL 12/1/96; SLJ 11/96) [636.7]

**15857** Jessel, Camilla. *The Puppy Book* (1–4). Illus. 1994, Candlewick paper $4.99 (1-56402-279-X). 32pp. Saffy, a Labrador retriever, is about to give birth, captured in marvelous photographs. (Rev: BL 2/1/92; SLJ 7/92) [636.7]

**15858** Jones, Robert F. *Jake: A Labrador Puppy at Work and Play* (3–5). Illus. 1992, Farrar $15.00 (0-374-33655-5). 32pp. At the age of 8 weeks, Jake goes to a family to begin his training as a hunting dog. (Rev: BCCB 1/92; BL 11/1/92; SLJ 12/92) [636.7]

**15859** King-Smith, Dick. *Puppy Love* (PS–1). Illus. by Anita Jeram. 1997, Candlewick $15.99 (0-7636-0116-0). 32pp. Charmingly illustrated with watercolor-and-ink drawings, this book tells about the many wonderful dogs that Dick King-Smith has as pets. (Rev: BL 12/15/97; SLJ 11/97) [636.7]

**15860** McMains, Joel M. *Dog Training Projects for Young People* (5–8). Illus. 1996, Macmillan paper $14.95 (0-87605-506-4). 288pp. A manual that supplies practical information on dog training. (Rev: BL 5/15/96) [636.7]

**15861** Moore, Eva. *Buddy: The First Seeing Eye Dog* (2–3). Illus. by Don Bolognese. 1996, Scholastic paper $3.99 (0-590-26585-7). 48pp. In simple prose, traces the beginning of the Seeing Eye movement in the 1930s. (Rev: BL 11/15/96) [392.4]

**15862** Patent, Dorothy Hinshaw. *Dogs: The Wolf Within* (3–6). Illus. by William Munoz. 1993, Carolrhoda LB $19.93 (0-87614-691-4); paper $7.95 (0-87614-604-3). 48pp. This book describes the relationship between the habits of the domesticated dog and its distant ancestor, the wolf. (Rev: BCCB 7–8/93; BL 6/1–15/93) [599]

**15863** Patent, Dorothy Hinshaw. *Hugger to the Rescue* (2–5). Illus. by William Munoz. 1994, Dutton paper $13.99 (0-525-65161-6). 32pp. An account of the training and use of a team of Newfoundland dogs in search-and-rescue operations around Bigfork, Montana. (Rev: BCCB 6/94; BL 7/94; SLJ 7/94) [636.7]

**15864** Petersen-Fleming, Judy, and Bill Fleming. *Puppy Care and Critters, Too!* (1–3). Illus. by Debra Reingold-Reiss. 1994, Morrow $15.00 (0-688-12563-8). 40pp. This manual focuses on raising, feeding, and caring for a puppy, with material on other kinds of pets. (Rev: BL 4/1/94; SLJ 6/94) [636.7]

**15865** Pinkwater, Jill, and Daniel Pinkwater. *Superpuppy* (4–6). Illus. 1977, Houghton paper $9.95 (0-89919-084-7). 208pp. All one needs to know about choosing and rearing the "best possible" dog.

**15866** *Puppies* (3–6). Illus. 1997, DK Publg. $12.95 (0-7894-2133-X). 37pp. Using double-page spreads, several breeds of dogs are introduced, with good tips for their proper care. (Rev: BL 10/15/97; SLJ 2/98) [636.7]

**15867** Ring, Elizabeth. *Performing Dogs* (3–5). Illus. Series: Good Dogs. 1994, Millbrook LB $19.90 (1-56294-296-4). 32pp. A history of dogs in various areas of show business, with life stories of some of the most famous. (Rev: BL 8/94; SLJ 12/94) [791.2]

**15868** Ring, Elizabeth. *Search and Rescue Dogs* (3–5). Illus. Series: Good Dogs. 1994, Millbrook LB $19.90 (1-56294-294-8). 32pp. This account tells of the amazing accomplishments of these dogs in saving human lives and of their special training. Also use *Ranch and Farm Dogs* (1994). (Rev: BL 8/94; SLJ 12/94) [636.7]

**15869** Rossiter, Nan P. *Rugby and Rosie* (1–3). Illus. by author. 1997, Dutton paper $14.99 (0-525-45484-5). Background information about guide dogs is given in this story about a young boy who keeps a puppy for a year before it leaves to be trained as a guide dog. (Rev: BCCB 3/97; SLJ 2/97) [636.7]

**15870** Selsam, Millicent E. *How Puppies Grow* (1–2). Illus. 1990, Scholastic paper $2.99 (0-590-42736-9). 32pp. The stages in a puppy's life — from birth through walking, seeing, eating, and playing — described in excellent photographs and simple text.

**15871** Selsam, Millicent E., and Joyce Hunt. *A First Look at Dogs* (1–3). Illus. by Harriett Springer. 1981, Walker LB $9.85 (0-8027-6421-5). 32pp. A history of dogs and an introduction to present breeds.

**15872** Siegel, Mary-Ellen, and Hermine M. Koplin. *More Than a Friend: Dogs with a Purpose* (5–8). Illus. 1984, Walker LB $11.85 (0-8027-6566-1). 128pp. Purebred and mongrel dogs are shown in their work as valuable helpers to human companions.

**15873** Silverstein, Alvin, and Virginia Silverstein. *Dogs: All About Them* (5–8). Illus. 1986, Lothrop $16.00 (0-688-04805-6). 256pp. Coverage on history, anatomy, and breeds. (Rev: BCCB 11/86; SLJ 9/86)

**15874** Squire, Ann. *Understanding Man's Best Friend: Why Dogs Look and Act the Way They Do* (5–7). 1991, Macmillan LB $14.95 (0-02-786590-8). 128pp. A history and analysis of dog breeds and behavior. (Rev: BCCB 7–8/91; BL 6/15/91; SLJ 9/91) [636.7]

**15875** Storer, Pat. *Your Puppy, Your Dog: A Kid's Guide to Raising a Happy, Healthy Dog* (4–6). Illus. 1997, Storey paper $14.95 (0-88266-959-1). 172pp. Chapters in this complete dog care manual cover such subjects as feeding, walking, playing, grooming, and toilet needs. (Rev: BL 12/15/97) [636.7]

**15876** Tildes, Phyllis L. *Calico Picks a Puppy* (2–4). Illus. 1996, Charlesbridge $15.95 (0-88106-892-6). 32pp. Various breeds of dogs are pictured as Calico the cat tries to choose a perfect pet. (Rev: BL 11/1/96) [636.7]

**15877** White, Nancy. *Why Do Dogs Do That?* (2–4). Illus. by Gioia Fiammenghi. 1995, Scholastic paper $4.99 (0-590-26597-0). 32pp. Through answers to 24 simple questions, such common canine behavior as tail wagging is explained. (Rev: BL 2/15/96) [599]

### FISH

**15878** Evans, Mark. *Fish* (3–6). Illus. Series: Pet Care Guides for Kids. 1993, DK Publg. $9.95 (1-56458-222-1). 45pp. The setting up of an aquarium is discussed as well as various kinds of fish and their care. (Rev: BL 8/93) [636.6]

**15879** Halstead, Bruce, and Bonnie L. Landa. *Tropical Fish* (4–8). Illus. 1975, Golden Bks. paper $5.50 (0-307-24361-3). 160pp. A handbook on types and characteristics of specific species, plus tips on their care.

**15880** Pfeffer, Wendy. *What's It Like to Be a Fish?* (1–3). Illus. by Holly Keller. 1996, HarperCollins LB $14.89 (0-06-024429-1); paper $4.95 (0-06-445151-8). 32pp. In this easily read science book, the structure and habits of goldfish are described, with hints on caring for them as pets. (Rev: BL 3/15/96; HB 7–8/96; SLJ 4/96) [597]

### HORSES AND PONIES

**15881** Ancona, George. *Man and Mustang* (3–6). Illus. 1992, Macmillan LB $15.95 (0-02-700802-9). 48pp. Black-and-white photos help to tell the story of how the Bureau of Land Management manages the growing population of wild mustangs. (Rev: BCCB 4/92; BL 3/15/92; HB 7–8/92; SLJ 4/92) [636.1]

**15882** Budd, Jackie. *Horses* (3–8). Illus. 1995, Kingfisher $15.95 (1-85697-566-5). 64pp. Drawings and text cover such subjects related to horses as anatomy, breeds, care, and grooming. (Rev: BL 10/1/95; SLJ 12/95) [636.1]

**15883** Clutton-Brock, Juliet. *Horse* (4–8). Illus. Series: Eyewitness Books. 1992, Knopf LB $20.99 (0-679-91681-4). 64pp. In attractive 2-page spreads, the horse is introduced in detailed anatomical draw-

ings and other diagrams. (Rev: BL 6/1/92; SLJ 2/93) [636.1]

**15884** Cole, Joanna. *A Horse's Body* (3–6). Illus. 1981, Morrow $16.00 (0-688-00362-1). 48pp. The evolution of the horse and its present structure.

**15885** Cole, Joanna. *Riding Silver Star* (K–3). Illus. by Margaret Miller. 1996, Morrow LB $14.93 (0-688-13896-9). 48pp. A nonfiction account of how young Abby cares for her horse, Silver Star, and of the activities they share. (Rev: BCCB 3/96; BL 4/1/96; HB 5–6/96; SLJ 5/96) [798.2]

**15886** Farley, Walter. *Man O' War* (4–6). Illus. 1983, Random paper $4.99 (0-394-86015-2). 352pp. The story of the famous racehorse.

**15887** Fowler, Allan. *Horses, Horses, Horses* (1–2). Illus. Series: Rookie Read-About Science. 1992, Children's LB $18.50 (0-516-04921-6). 32pp. With a minimum of text and lots of pictures, this account introduces various kinds of horses and tells how they help people. (Rev: BL 7/92) [636.1]

**15888** Henry, Marguerite. *Album of Horses* (5–8). Illus. by Wesley Dennis. 1951, Macmillan paper $11.99 (0-689-71709-1). 112pp. A beautifully illustrated guide to 20 breeds of horses.

**15889** Isenbart, Hans-Heinrich. *Birth of a Foal* (2–5). Illus. 1986, Carolrhoda LB $19.93 (0-87614-239-0). 48pp. Complemented by color photos, the phases of fetal development and the birth process are detailed. (Rev: BL 4/1/86; HB 5–6/86; SLJ 3/86)

**15890** Jauck, Andrea. *Assateague: Island of the Wild Ponies* (2–4). Illus. 1997, Sierra Club paper $7.95 (0-939365-59-6). 32pp. A color photoessay to interest horse fans. (Rev: BCCB 5/93; BL 3/15/93; SLJ 6/93) [599.72]

**15891** Kalas, Sybille. *The Wild Horse Family Book* (2–4). Trans. by Patricia Crampton. Illus. 1990, Picture Book paper $15.95 (0-88708-110-X). 52pp. In photos and text, the life and habits of the wild horses of Iceland are explored. (Rev: BL 3/1/90; SLJ 5/90) [636.1]

**15892** LaBonte, Gail. *The Miniature Horse* (3–5). Illus. 1990, Macmillan LB $13.95 (0-87518-424-3). 60pp. The origin of these tiny horses, some no more than 25 inches tall. (Rev: BCCB 4/90; BL 4/1/90; SLJ 7/90) [636.1]

**15893** Ling, Mary. *Foal* (PS–1). Illus. by Gordon Clayton. Series: See How They Grow. 1992, DK Publg. $7.95 (1-56458-113-6). 24pp. This simple picture book shows the development of a horse from birth through the first months. (Rev: BL 11/1/92; HB 1–2/93) [559.72]

**15894** McMillan, Bruce. *My Horse of the North* (K–3). Illus. 1997, Scholastic $15.95 (0-590-97205-7). 32pp. Three Icelandic youngsters tell about the horses that were originally brought there by the Vikings. (Rev: BL 9/1/97; HB 9–10/97; SLJ 9/97) [636.3]

**15895** Meltzer, Milton. *Hold Your Horses! A Feedbag Full of Fact and Fable* (4–8). Illus. 1995, HarperCollins LB $14.89 (0-06-024478-X). 160pp. The place of horses in history is explored in this account that tells about horses in art, war, sports, and work. (Rev: BCCB 12/95; BL 11/15/95; SLJ 12/95*) [636.1]

**15896** Parker, Jane. *The Fantastic Book of Horses* (4–6). Illus. Series: Fantastic Book of . . . 1997, Millbrook LB $22.40 (0-7613-0566-1). 40pp. The care, uses, and breeds of horses are introduced in this copiously illustrated book with foldout sections. (Rev: SLJ 8/97) [636.1]

**15897** Patent, Dorothy Hinshaw. *Horses* (3–5). Illus. by William Munoz. 1994, Carolrhoda LB $19.95 (0-87614-766-X). 48pp. This excellent introduction to the world of horses includes material on their history, types, behavior, and current uses. (Rev: BCCB 3/94; BL 4/1/94; SLJ 3/94) [636.1]

**15898** Patent, Dorothy Hinshaw. *Where the Wild Horses Roam* (PS–2). Illus. by William Munoz. 1989, Houghton $15.95 (0-89919-507-5). 72pp. The history of wild horses that roam the West and the problems they cause. (Rev: BL 7/89; HB 9–10/89; SLJ 8/89) [639.9]

**15899** Peterson, Cris. *Horsepower: The Wonder of Draft Horses* (K–4). Photos by Alvis Upitis. 1997, Boyds Mills paper $15.95 (1-56397-626-9). A photoessay that introduces the history, physical characteristics, and functions of the draft horse, with special coverage on Belgians, Percherons, and Clydesdales. (Rev: BCCB 4/97; SLJ 4/97) [636.1]

**15900** Posell, Elsa. *Horses* (2–3). Illus. 1981, Children's LB $21.00 (0-516-01623-7); paper $5.50 (0-516-41623-5). 48pp. Color photographs and simple text are used in this introductory volume.

**15901** Silverstein, Alvin, et al. *The Mustang* (4–7). Illus. Series: Endangered in America. 1997, Millbrook LB $22.40 (0-7613-0048-1). 64pp. Examines the life cycle and behavior of the mustang, the reasons it has become endangered, and the techniques employed to ensure survival. (Rev: BL 3/15/97; SLJ 6/97) [599.72]

**15902** van der Linde, Laurel. *From Mustangs to Movie Stars: Five True Horse Legends of Our Time* (4–7). Illus. 1995, Millbrook LB $23.40 (1-56294-456-8). 71pp. Biographies of 5 famous horses are recounted, from the racer Native Dancer to Cass Olé, who was the star of the film *The Black Stallion*. (Rev: BCCB 12/95; SLJ 12/95) [636.1]

**15903** *The Visual Dictionary of the Horse* (5–8). Illus. Series: Eyewitness Visual Dictionaries. 1994,

DK Publg. $16.95 (1-56458-504-2). 64pp. This pictorial study includes information on anatomy, breeds, grooming, racing, jumping, and equipment. (Rev: BCCB 7–8/94; SLJ 7/94) [636]

## Zoos and Marine Aquariums

**15904** Aliki. *My Visit to the Aquarium* (K–3). Illus. 1993, HarperCollins LB $14.89 (0-06-021459-7). 40pp. Facts about fish are given as a boy tours an aquarium and examines various species. (Rev: BL 10/15/93; SLJ 1/94*) [597]

**15905** Aliki. *My Visit to the Zoo* (PS–2). Illus. 1997, HarperCollins LB $14.89 (0-06-024943-9). 40pp. A young girl acts as guide in a zoo and introduces the purposes of zoos as well as many of the animals that are kept there. (Rev: BL 7/97; HB 9–10/97; SLJ 10/97) [590]

**15906** Altman, Joyce. *Dear Bronx Zoo* (3–6). Illus. by Sue Goldberg. 1992, Avon paper $3.50 (0-380-71649-6). 102pp. The answers to questions most frequently asked by Bronx Zoo visitors. (Rev: BL 1/1/91; SLJ 3/91) [590.74]

**15907** Epstein, Sam, and Beryl Epstein. *You Call That a Farm? Raising Otters, Leeches, Weeds, and Other Unusual Things* (3–6). Illus. 1991, Farrar $13.95 (0-374-38705-2). 64pp. A description of 8 unusual farms that produce rare plants, shrimp, alligators, and other "nonfarm" animals. (Rev: BL 10/15/91; SLJ 1/92) [636]

**15908** Gerstenfeld, Sheldon L. *The Aquarium Take-Along Book* (4–6). Illus. by Paul Harvey. 1994, Viking paper $14.99 (0-670-84386-5). 128pp. All kinds of sea life that one might encounter in an aquarium are introduced, from clams and different fish to corals and kelp. (Rev: SLJ 6/94) [639.3]

**15909** Gerstenfeld, Sheldon L. *Zoo Clues: Making the Most of Your Visit to the Zoo* (4–6). Illus. by Eldon C. Doty. 1993, Puffin paper $4.99 (0-140-32813-0). 113pp. This is a survey of 28 different groups of animals that are found in zoos. (Rev: SLJ 7/91) [590.74]

**15910** McMillan, Bruce. *The Baby Zoo* (1–6). 1995, Scholastic LB $13.95 (0-590-44634-7); paper $4.95 (0-590-44635-5). 40pp. A survey of 16 baby animals in 2 American zoos. (Rev: HB 3–4/92; SLJ 5/92) [599]

**15911** Patent, Dorothy Hinshaw. *Back to the Wild* (4–6). Photos by William Munoz. 1997, Harcourt $18.00 (0-15-200280-4). 69pp. This account shows how present-day zoos are helping save endangered animals and gives 4 case studies where tamarins, red wolves, lemurs, and the black-footed ferret have been rescued. (Rev: SLJ 4/97) [590]

**15912** Pfeffer, Wendy. *Popcorn Park Zoo: A Haven with a Heart* (3–6). Illus. by J. Gerard Smith. 1992, Simon & Schuster LB $16.95 (0-671-74589-1). 64pp. A unique zoo in New Jersey that cares for animals that are sick, old, hurt, abused, or unwanted. (Rev: BL 6/1/92; SLJ 7/92) [590]

**15913** Riley, Linda C. *Aquarium: Bringing the Seas Inside* (4–6). Illus. by Michael Baytoff. 1993, W. H. Freeman $14.40 (0-7167-6509-8). 80pp. A behind-the-scenes look at a modern aquarium, with information on how its inhabitants are caught, housed, and cared for, and additional material on specific species, like sharks. (Rev: BL 1/1/94; SLJ 2/94) [639.3]

**15914** Rinard, Judith E. *Zoos Without Cages* (5–8). Illus. 1981, National Geographic LB $12.50 (0-87044-340-2). 104pp. An examination of zoos where the enclosures are like natural habitats.

**15915** Yancey, Diane. *Zoos* (5–8). Illus. Series: Overview Series. 1995, Lucent LB $22.45 (1-56006-163-4). 128pp. A history of zoos explaining present-day practices and the controversy that surrounds them. (Rev: BL 6/1–15/95; SLJ 3/95) [590]

# Botany

## Flowers

**15916** Bryant-Mole, Karen. *Flowers* (K–3). Photos by Barrie Watts. Series: See for Yourself. 1995, Raintree Steck-Vaughn LB $21.40 (0-8172-4211-2). 30pp. After basic facts about flowers are presented, questions are posed and various appropriate activities are outlined. (Rev: SLJ 4/96) [583.13]

**15917** Burnie, David. *Flowers* (4–6). Illus. Series: Eyewitness Explorers. 1992, DK Publg. $10.99 (1-56458-024-5). 64pp. In double-page spreads, flowers and their parts are introduced. (Rev: BL 2/1/93; SLJ 2/93) [582.13]

**15918** *Flowers* (PS–3). Illus. Series: First Discovery Book. 1993, Scholastic $11.95 (0-590-46383-7). 30pp. In this interactive book, various kinds of flowers and their parts are introduced. (Rev: BL 10/1/93; SLJ 8/93) [582.13]

**15919** Fowler, Allan. *What's Your Favorite Flower?* (1–2). Illus. Series: Rookie Read-About Science. 1993, Children's paper $4.95 (0-516-46007-2). 32pp. A variety of flowers and their parts are introduced to the very young. (Rev: BL 12/15/92) [635.9]

**15920** Johnson, Sylvia A. *Morning Glories* (4–7). Illus. 1985, Lerner LB $22.60 (0-8225-1462-1). 48pp. Color photographs display the stages of this plant's development. (Rev: BCCB 3/86; BL 4/15/86; SLJ 4/86)

**15921** Johnson, Sylvia A. *Roses Red, Violets Blue: Why Flowers Have Colors* (5–8). Illus. by Yuko Sato. 1991, Lerner LB $23.95 (0-8225-1594-6). 64pp. An explanation of the role color plays in the lives of plants. (Rev: BCCB 12/91; BL 12/1/91) [582.13]

**15922** Landau, Elaine. *Wildflowers Around the World* (4–6). Illus. Series: First Books. 1991, Watts LB $21.00 (0-531-20005-1); paper $6.95 (0-531-15649-4). 64pp. With many illustrations and attractive format, the beautiful world of wildflowers is explored. (Rev: BL 5/15/91; SLJ 7/91) [582.13]

**15923** Murray, Peter. *Roses* (3–5). Illus. Series: Nature Books. 1995, Child's World LB $22.79 (1-56766-192-0). 32pp. The beauty and variety of roses are highlighted in stunning full-page photographs and large-type text. (Rev: BL 12/15/95) [583]

**15924** Velghe, Anne. *Wildflowers: A Garden Primer* (1–4). Illus. 1994, Farrar $15.00 (0-374-38430-4). 28pp. A beautifully illustrated guide to common wildflowers and to garden animals found among them. (Rev: BL 6/1–15/94; SLJ 10/94) [582.13]

**15925** Winner, Cherie. *The Sunflower Family* (4–7). Illus. 1996, Carolrhoda LB $14.95 (1-57505-007-2); paper $7.95 (1-57505-029-3). 48pp. Growth patterns, structures, and reproduction are topics covered in this account of the sunflower family, including thistles, daisies, and asters. (Rev: BL 10/1/96; SLJ 10/96) [583]

**15926** Zim, Herbert S., and Alexander C. Martin. *Flowers* (5–8). Illus. 1991, Western paper $21.27 (0-307-64054-X). 160pp. An identification guide that describes many species in words and pictures.

## Foods and Farming

### GENERAL

**15927** Lampton, Christopher. *Famine* (4–6). Illus. Series: Disaster Book. 1994, Millbrook LB $19.90 (1-56294-317-0). 48pp. The causes and effects of famines are covered, with information on some of the historic disasters to strike the world. (Rev: BL 6/1–15/94; SLJ 4/94) [363.8]

**15928** Morgan, Sally. *Flowers, Trees, and Fruits* (1–4). Illus. Series: Young Discoverers. 1996, Kingfisher LB $13.90 (0-7534-5033-X); paper $6.95 (0-7534-5032-1). 32pp. In addition to general information about plants, this account suggests many simple activities. (Rev: BL 12/1/96) [581]

### FARMS AND RANCHES

**15929** Anderson, Joan. *The American Family Farm* (4–6). Illus. by George Ancona. 1989, Harcourt $18.95 (0-15-203025-5). 96pp. A photo tour of a dairy farm. (Rev: BCCB 11/89; BL 11/15/89; SLJ 10/89*) [630.973]

**15930** Bial, Raymond. *Portrait of a Farm Family* (4–7). Illus. 1995, Houghton $15.95 (0-395-69936-3). 48pp. A behind-the-scenes look at a dairy farm in Illinois that gives details on day-to-day operations and problems. (Rev: BCCB 10/95; BL 9/1/95*; HB 11–12/95; SLJ 12/95) [338.1]

**15931** Fowler, Allan. *If It Weren't for Farmers* (1–2). Illus. Series: Rookie Readers. 1993, Children's LB $18.50 (0-516-06009-0). 32pp. For beginning readers, this is an introduction to what farmers do and how various foods are grown. (Rev: BL 3/1/94) [630]

**15932** Fowler, Allan. *Thanks to Cows* (1–2). Illus. Series: Rookie Read-About Science. 1992, Children's LB $18.00 (0-516-04924-0). 32pp. With large color photos and simple text, this book introduces cattle and their importance. (Rev: BL 6/15/92) [636.2]

**15933** Geisert, Bonnie, and Arthur Geisert. *Haystack* (K–3). Illus. 1995, Houghton $15.95 (0-395-69722-0). 32pp. The story of how haystacks are made and of their uses on farms. (Rev: BCCB 10/95; BL 9/15/95; HB 11–12/95; SLJ 9/95) [633.2]

**15934** Gibbons, Gail. *Farming* (PS–2). Illus. by author. 1988, Holiday LB $15.95 (0-8234-0682-2); paper $6.95 (0-8234-0797-7). 32pp. Farm landscapes through the seasons. (Rev: BL 6/1/88; SLJ 8/88)

**15935** Graff, Nancy P. *The Strength of the Hills: A Portrait of a Family Farm* (4–6). Illus. by Richard Howard. 1989, Little, Brown $14.95 (0-316-32277-6). 80pp. This account highlights life on a family dairy farm in Vermont. (Rev: BL 11/15/89; SLJ 4/90*) [338.1]

**15936** Guiberson, Brenda Z. *Winter Wheat* (1–3). Illus. by Megan Lloyd. 1995, Holt $15.95 (0-8050-1582-5). 32pp. The cycle of planting, growing, and harvesting winter wheat as seen through the eyes of Albert and his animal friends. (Rev: BL 11/15/95; SLJ 11/95) [633.1]

**15937** Halley, Ned. *Farm* (4–8). Illus. Series: Eyewitness Books. 1996, Knopf LB $20.99 (0-679-98078-4). 63pp. This book takes one behind the scenes at a farm, explaining with many illustrations its inner workings and the problems and rewards involved in managing one. (Rev: BL 6/1–15/96; SLJ 7/96) [630]

**15938** Hill, Lee S. *Farms Feed the World* (1–3). Series: Building Blocks Books. 1997, Carolrhoda LB $19.93 (1-57505-075-7). 32pp. This book takes the reader on a visit to many kinds of farms around the world, from a wheat field in Montana to a rice paddy in Indonesia. (Rev: BL 3/15/98) [630]

**15939** Jacobsen, Karen. *Farm Animals* (4–6). Illus. by author. 1981, Children's LB $21.00 (0-516-01619-9). 48pp. Large typeface is used in this simple introduction with many color photographs.

**15940** Lambert, Mark. *Farming and the Environment* (3–6). Illus. Series: Conserving Our World. 1991, Raintree Steck-Vaughn LB $24.26 (0-8114-2392-1). 48pp. This book explores the methods used by modern farmers and how these are changing the environment. (Rev: BL 6/1/91) [978.02]

**15941** Olney, Ross R. *The Farm Combine* (4–8). Illus. 1984, Walker LB $10.85 (0-8027-6568-8). 64pp. The development of the reaper and thrasher is discussed plus information on today's combine.

**15942** Peterson, Cris. *Extra Cheese, Please! Mozzarella's Journey from Cow to Pizza* (PS–2). Illus. by Alvis Upitis. 1994, Boyds Mills $15.95 (1-56397-177-1). 30pp. Dairy farms and the treatment of dairy cattle are described in this explanation of how cheese is made. (Rev: BL 3/15/94; SLJ 4/94) [637.219]

**15943** Smith, E. Boyd. *The Farm Book* (2–5). Illus. by author. 1982, Houghton paper $8.95 (0-395-54951-5). 64pp. A picture book that details many activities associated with farm life.

**15944** Willard, Nancy. *Cracked Corn and Snow Ice Cream* (4–6). Illus. 1997, Harcourt $18.00 (0-15-227250-X). 64pp. Farm life and the families of the author and illustrator are highlighted in this book that ushers in each season and month with photos, poems, and a list of important dates and festivals. (Rev: BL 11/1/97; SLJ 10/97) [031.02]

### FOODS

**15945** Aliki. *Milk: From Cow to Carton* (K–3). Illus. Series: Let's Read-and-Find-Out Science Books. 1992, HarperCollins LB $14.89 (0-06-020435-4). 32pp. This revision of the 1974 edition features full-color artwork in this explanation of how milk is processed. (Rev: BL 11/1/92) [637]

**15946** Back, Christine. *Bean and Plant* (1–3). Illus. 1986, Silver Burdett LB $9.95 (0-382-09286-4); paper $3.95 (0-382-24014-6). 25pp. A basic science book in full color telling how beans grow. (Rev: BL 1/1/87)

**15947** Badt, Karin Luisa. *Pass the Bread!* (3–7). Illus. Series: A World of Difference. 1995, Children's LB $20.30 (0-516-08191-8). 32pp. Different kinds of bread found around the world are highlighted, as well as their methods of production and how they are related to their various cultures. (Rev: BL 7/95; SLJ 12/95) [394.1]

**15948** Bryant-Mole, Karen. *Food* (PS–3). Illus. Series: Picture This! 1997, Rigby LB $12.95 (1-57572-150-3). 24pp. Various kinds of food are introduced, cooking methods are discussed, and the principles of good nutrition are mentioned. (Rev: BL 10/15/97; SLJ 12/97) [641.3]

**15949** Burns, Diane L. *Cranberries: Fruit of the Bogs* (3–5). Illus. by Cheryl Walsh Bellville. 1994, Carolrhoda LB $22.60 (0-87614-822-4). 48pp. A book about cranberry growing in various parts of the country and activities during and after harvesting. (Rev: BL 12/1/94; SLJ 3/95) [633.76]

**15950** Burns, Diane L. *Sugaring Season: Making Maple Syrup* (1–5). Illus. 1990, Carolrhoda $16.95 (0-87614-420-2); paper $5.95 (0-87614-554-3). 32pp. Crisp photos and good diagrams help to explain the maple syrup process. (Rev: BL 11/1/90; SLJ 12/90) [664]

**15951** Chandler, Gary, and Kevin Graham. *Natural Foods and Products* (4–8). Illus. Series: Making a Better World. 1996, Twenty-First Century LB $16.98 (0-8050-4623-2). 64pp. This work discusses genetically engineered foods, safe eco-friendly methods of growing crops, and companies that engage in safe practices. (Rev: BL 12/15/96; SLJ 1/97) [333.76]

**15952** Charles, Oz. *How Does Soda Get into the Bottle?* (2–4). Illus. 1996, Silver Burdett paper $4.95 (0-382-24375-7). 32pp. A brief photoessay on this manufacturing process that takes the reader into a bottling plant. (Rev: BL 4/15/88)

**15953** D'Amico, Joan, and Karen Eich Drummond. *The Science Chef: 100 Fun Food Experiments and Recipes for Kids* (4–6). Illus. 1994, Wiley paper $12.95 (0-471-31045-X). 192pp. Simple experiments introduce various properties of foods and give youngsters a chance to be good cooks. (Rev: BL 11/1/94; SLJ 12/94) [641.3]

**15954** dePaola, Tomie. *The Popcorn Book* (1–3). Illus. 1978, Holiday LB $15.95 (0-8234-0314-9); paper $6.95 (0-8234-0533-8). 32pp. While Tony makes a plate of popcorn, Tiny tells interesting facts about this delicious food.

**15955** Egan, Robert. *From Wheat to Pasta* (PS–2). Series: Changes. 1997, Children's LB $23.00 (0-516-20709-1). 32pp. Beginning with a wheat farm and the production of flour, this account tells about the origins of pasta and explains its different shapes. (Rev: BL 10/15/97; SLJ 9/97) [664.755]

**15956** Erlbach, Arlene. *Soda Pop* (3–6). Illus. 1994, Lerner LB $19.95 (0-8225-2386-8). 48pp. Tells about the origins, history, and manufacture of soda pop, with recipes for making various kinds at home. Also use *Peanut Butter* (1994). (Rev: BL 5/1/94) [663]

**15957** Gibbons, Gail. *The Milk Makers* (1–4). Illus. 1985, Macmillan LB $14.95 (0-02-736640-5); paper $5.99 (0-689-71116-6). 32pp. Young readers learn all about cows and how milk is produced and distributed. (Rev: BCCB 5/85; BL 4/15/85; SLJ 4/85)

**15958** Griffin, Margaret, and Deborah Seed. *The Amazing Egg Book* (2–5). Illus. by Linda Hendry.

1990, Addison-Wesley paper $6.95 (0-201-52334-5). 64pp. This book from Canada focuses on the commonplace but still amazing egg. (Rev: BL 4/15/90) [745]

**15959** Harbison, Elizabeth M. *Loaves of Fun: A History of Bread with Activities and Recipes from Around the World* (3–6). Illus. 1997, Chicago Review paper $12.95 (1-55652-311-4). 91pp. A history of bread from ancient times to the present day, with several activities and 24 recipes. (Rev: BL 5/1/97; SLJ 9/97) [641.8]

**15960** Hausherr, Rosmarie. *What Food Is This?* (1–3). Illus. 1994, Scholastic $14.95 (0-590-46583-X). 40pp. Questions about common foods we eat are answered in simple text and luscious photos. (Rev: BCCB 5/94; BL 4/15/94; SLJ 5/94) [641.3]

**15961** Jaspersohn, William. *Ice Cream* (3–5). Illus. 1988, Macmillan LB $14.95 (0-02-747821-1). 48pp. How ice cream is made, using Ben and Jerry's ice cream plant in Vermont. (Rev: BL 11/1/88; SLJ 12/88)

**15962** Keller, Stella. *Ice Cream* (PS). Illus. by John Holm. Series: Real Readers. 1989, Raintree Steck-Vaughn LB $21.40 (0-8172-3523-X). 32pp. This easily read account describes the history of ice cream. (Rev: BL 2/1/90) [637.4]

**15963** King, Elizabeth. *Chile Fever: A Celebration of Peppers* (3–5). Illus. 1995, Dutton paper $14.99 (0-525-45255-9). 32pp. Using the annual chile festival in Hatch, New Mexico, as a beginning, this book explores the history, varieties, and uses of chile peppers. (Rev: BL 4/15/95; HB 5–6/95; SLJ 5/95) [641.3]

**15964** Knight, Bertram T. *From Cow to Ice Cream* (PS–2). Illus. Series: Changes. 1997, Children's LB $24.00 (0-516-20706-7). 32pp. This book explains how ice cream is made, including the cow's role, pasteurization, the ice cream factory, the sugar refinery, and flavorings. (Rev: BL 10/15/97; SLJ 9/97) [637]

**15965** Lasky, Kathryn. *Sugaring Time* (4–7). Illus. 1998, Center for Applied Research paper $4.95 (0-87628-350-4). 64pp. Through photos and text, the process of maple sugar production in New England is described.

**15966** Mandell, Muriel. *Simple Kitchen Experiments: Learning Science with Everyday Foods* (4–6). Illus. 1994, Sterling paper $4.95 (0-8069-8415-5). 128pp. The kitchen becomes a chemistry lab in this book of simple experiments and projects like degassing beans. (Rev: BL 5/1/94; SLJ 8/93) [641.3]

**15967** Martino, Teresa. *Pizza!* (PS). Illus. by Brigid Faranda. Series: Real Readers. 1989, Raintree Steck-Vaughn LB $21.40 (0-8172-3533-7). 32pp. This easy-to-read account describes the development of pizza from its beginnings 1,000 years ago. (Rev: BL 2/1/90) [641.8]

**15968** Micucci, Charles. *The Life and Times of the Peanut* (1–4). Illus. 1997, Houghton $15.95 (0-395-72289-6). 32pp. A lively combination of words and pictures that describe the peanut, where it is grown, and its many uses. (Rev: BCCB 5/97; BL 5/1/97*; SLJ 5/97) [641.3]

**15969** Nottridge, Rhoda. *Sugars* (3–6). Illus. Series: Food Facts. 1993, Carolrhoda LB $14.95 (0-87614-796-1). 32pp. Covers such topics as the various forms of sugars, the ways they are made, and their uses, with some simple recipes and activities. (Rev: SLJ 10/93) [613.2]

**15970** Paulsen, Gary. *The Tortilla Factory* (1–4). Illus. by Ruth W. Paulsen. 1995, Harcourt $15.00 (0-15-292876-6). 32pp. Simple text and painting show how kernels of corn become flour and eventually tortillas. (Rev: BL 6/1–15/95; HB 7–8/95; SLJ 7/95) [641.8]

**15971** Peterson, Cris. *Harvest Year* (1–3). Illus. by Alvis Upitis. 1996, Boyds Mills $15.95 (1-56397-571-8). 28pp. Using a month-by-month arrangement, various crops grown in the United States are highlighted. (Rev: BL 9/15/96; SLJ 11/96) [641]

**15972** Powell, Jillian. *Food* (5–7). Illus. Series: Traditions Around the World. 1995, Thomson Learning LB $24.26 (1-56847-346-X). 48pp. Each one of the continents is represented in this survey of the many different kinds of food found in various cultures. (Rev: BL 9/15/95) [394.1]

**15973** Powell, Jillian. *Milk* (3–5). Illus. Series: Everyone Eats. 1997, Raintree Steck-Vaughn LB $22.83 (0-8172-4766-1). 32pp. This book introduces milk from different animals, but it focuses on the production, uses, and nutritional value of cow's milk. (Rev: SLJ 8/97) [636.2]

**15974** Powell, Jillian. *Pasta* (1–4). Illus. Series: Everyone Eats. 1997, Raintree Steck-Vaughn LB $22.83 (0-8172-4760-2). 32pp. A tour of a pasta-producing facility and a guide to the various shapes of pasta highlight this account, which includes a few tasty recipes. (Rev: SLJ 7/97) [664]

**15975** Ripley, Catherine. *Why Does Popcorn Pop? and Other Kitchen Questions* (PS–3). Illus. by Scot Ritchie. Series: Question and Answer Storybook. 1997, Owl $17.95 (1-895688-70-1); paper $6.95 (1-895688-71-X). 32pp. Everyday questions about food are posed, with answers on the same page, in this delightfully illustrated book. (Rev: BL 12/1/97; SLJ 2/98) [500]

**15976** Seelig, Tina L. *Incredible Edible Science* (4–8). Illus. 1994, W. H. Freeman paper $11.20 (0-7167-6507-1). 80pp. Includes recipes and a number of interesting related science facts, like what causes

the difference between white and dark meat. (Rev: BL 7/94; SLJ 8/94) [641.5]

**15977** Tames, Richard. *Food: Feasts, Cooks and Kitchens* (3–6). Illus. Series: Timelines. 1994, Watts LB $22.00 (0-531-14312-0). 48pp. This book presents a history of hunting, growing, preparing, and eating food around the world, with amazing cutaways, reconstructions, and diagrams. (Rev: BL 7/94) [641.3]

**15978** Thomson, Peggy. *Siggy's Spaghetti Works* (1–3). Illus. by Gloria Kamen. 1993, Morrow LB $13.93 (0-688-11374-5). 32pp. During a tour of a spaghetti factory, 7 kids learn how pasta is made. (Rev: BL 10/1/93; SLJ 1/94) [664]

**15979** Thomson, Ruth. *Rice* (3–5). Illus. by Prodeepta Das. Series: Threads. 1990, Garrett LB $15.93 (0-944483-71-2). 26pp. The story of rice, from its growth in paddies to its uses in many cultures. (Rev: BL 2/1/91; SLJ 5/91) [633.1]

**15980** Ventura, Piero. *Food: Its Evolution Through the Ages* (4–8). Illus. by author. 1994, Houghton $16.95 (0-395-66790-9). 64pp. A history of food, food preparation, and methods of preservation are presented in a well-organized, visually attractive way. (Rev: SLJ 11/94) [664]

**15981** Wardlaw, Lee. *Bubblemania* (4–8). 1997, Simon & Schuster paper $4.99 (0-689-81719-3). 176pp. Provides a thorough history of chewing gum and describes how gum is made, marketed, and distributed. (Rev: BL 10/1/97; SLJ 1/98) [641.3]

**15982** Watts, Barrie. *Tomato* (PS–3). Illus. 1990, Silver Burdett LB $9.95 (0-382-24008-1). 25pp. The growth of a tomato plant is shown above and below ground. (Rev: BL 6/15/90; SLJ 9/90) [635]

**15983** *What Makes Popcorn Pop? First Questions and Answers About Food* (K–2). Series: Library of First Questions and Answers. 1994, Time Life $14.95 (0-7835-0862-X). 47pp. Cartoonlike illustrations help answer such questions about food as how potato chips are made and why Swiss cheese has holes. (Rev: SLJ 8/94) [641]

**15984** Young, Robert. *The Chewing Gum Book* (3–5). Illus. 1989, Macmillan LB $12.95 (0-87518-401-4). 72pp. Some related topics include history, production, ingredients, and effects on health. (Rev: BL 9/1/89; SLJ 11/89) [664]

**15985** Zubrowski, Bernie. *Soda Science: Designing and Testing Soft Drinks* (5–8). Illus. 1997, Morrow LB $14.93 (0-688-13917-5). 96pp. More than 50 experiments explore the properties of soft drinks and give directions for producing and bottling one's own product. (Rev: BL 8/97; SLJ 10/97) [641.8]

## FRUITS

**15986** Bourgeois, Paulette. *The Amazing Apple Book* (3–5). Illus. by Linda Hendry. Series: Children's Activities. 1990, Addison-Wesley paper $8.95 (0-201-52333-7). 64pp. The commonplace but amazing apple is the focus of this book from Canada. (Rev: BL 4/15/90) [641.3]

**15987** Coldrey, Jennifer. *Strawberry* (K–3). Illus. 1989, Silver Burdett LB $9.95 (0-382-09801-3). 25pp. This simple account traces the development of the strawberry and describes how the use of runners creates new plants. (Rev: SLJ 1/90) [582]

**15988** Davies, Kay, and Wendy Oldfield. *My Apple* (PS–1). Illus. by Fiona Pragoff. Series: First Step Science. 1994, Gareth Stevens LB $19.93 (0-8368-1114-3). 32pp. Introduces the characteristics of an apple, its parts, and its uses. Also use *My Drum* (1994). (Rev: BL 2/15/95) [634]

**15989** Goldsen, Louise. *Fruit* (PS–2). Illus. by P. M. Valet. Series: First Discovery. 1991, Scholastic paper $11.95 (0-590-45233-9). Through the use of overlays, several kinds of fruit are depicted in various stages, such as the ripening of an apple. (Rev: SLJ 6/92) [641]

**15990** Johnson, Sylvia A. *Apple Trees* (5–8). Illus. by Hiro Koike. 1983, Lerner LB $22.60 (0-8225-1479-6). 48pp. The story of the apple tree and seed and fruit formation.

**15991** Lember, Barbara Hirsch. *A Book of Fruit* (PS–K). Illus. 1994, Ticknor $14.95 (0-395-66989-8). 32pp. Expressive photographs are used to introduce 14 fruits and where they grow. (Rev: BCCB 2/95; BL 7/94; SLJ 9/94) [634]

**15992** McMillan, Bruce. *Apples, How They Grow* (3–7). Illus. 1979, Houghton $18.00 (0-395-27806-6). 48pp. A well-presented work on the life cycle and uses of the apple, as revealed in a series of captioned photographs.

**15993** Maestro, Betsy. *How Do Apples Grow?* (5–8). Illus. by Giulio Maestro. Series: Let's-Read-and-Find-Out. 1992, HarperCollins LB $15.89 (0-06-020056-1). 32pp. The development of the apple from bud to fruit. (Rev: BL 12/15/91; HB 1–2/92; SLJ 2/92) [582]

**15994** Powell, Jillian. *Fruit* (1–4). Illus. Series: Everyone Eats. 1997, Raintree Steck-Vaughn LB $22.83 (0-8172-4765-3). 32pp. Describes how fruit are grown, and some of the varieties, legends, and traditional customs surrounding them, with a few tasty recipes. (Rev: SLJ 7/97) [634]

**15995** Robinson, Fay. *We Love Fruit!* (1–2). Illus. Series: Rookie Read-about Science. 1992, Children's LB $18.50 (0-516-06006-6). 32pp. Various kinds of fruit are pictured in color photos and identified in a simple text. An oversized edition of this title is available. (Rev: BL 12/15/92; SLJ 2/93) [641.3]

**15996** Watts, Barrie. *Apple Tree* (PS–2). Illus. 1987, Silver Burdett LB $9.95 (0-382-09436-0). 24pp. Photos help to show the annual cycle of an apple tree. (Rev: BL 11/15/87)

**15997** *Why Are Pineapples Prickly?* (PS–3). Illus. Series: Why. 1997, DK Publg. $9.95 (0-7894-1530-5). 24pp. Using a question-and-answer format, this account discusses various plants and their characteristics. (Rev: BL 8/97; SLJ 8/97) [641.3]

## NUTRITION

**15998** Burns, Marilyn. *Good for Me! All About Food in 32 Bites* (5–8). Illus. by Sandy Clifford. 1978, Little, Brown paper $11.95 (0-316-11747-1). Nutrition and digestion are the major topics discussed in this book.

**15999** Inglis, Jane. *Fiber* (4–6). Illus. Series: Food Facts. 1993, Carolrhoda LB $19.93 (0-87614-793-7). 32pp. This nutrition book focuses on the natural fiber the body needs and how to obtain it. (Rev: BL 11/15/93; SLJ 10/93) [613.2]

**16000** Inglis, Jane. *Proteins* (3–6). Illus. Series: Food Facts. 1993, Carolrhoda LB $14.95 (0-87614-780-5). 32pp. After introducing proteins' structure and uses, this book outlines simple experiments and recipes. (Rev: SLJ 10/93) [574.19]

**16001** Leedy, Loreen. *The Edible Pyramid: Good Eating Every Day* (K–2). Illus. 1994, Holiday LB $15.95 (0-8234-1126-5). 30pp. A waiter in a restaurant introduces the nutritional pyramid that the U.S. Department of Agriculture has developed. (Rev: BCCB 2/95; BL 11/15/94; SLJ 4/95) [613.2]

**16002** Nottridge, Rhoda. *Additives* (4–6). Illus. Series: Food Facts. 1993, Carolrhoda LB $19.93 (0-87614-794-5). 32pp. The value of such food additives as preservatives and flavorings is discussed, with an analysis of their possible harmful effects. (Rev: BL 11/15/93; SLJ 10/93) [664]

**16003** Nottridge, Rhoda. *Fats* (4–6). Illus. Series: Food Facts. 1993, Lerner $19.93 (0-87614-779-1). 32pp. Introduces both saturated and unsaturated fats and tells how much should be consumed in the daily diet. (Rev: BL 11/15/93; SLJ 10/93) [613.2]

**16004** Nottridge, Rhoda. *Vitamins* (3–6). Illus. Series: Food Facts. 1993, Carolrhoda LB $14.95 (0-87614-795-3). 32pp. This book introduces the classification of vitamins, where they are found, their properties and uses, and some experiments and recipes connected with vitamins. (Rev: SLJ 10/93) [613.2]

**16005** Patent, Dorothy Hinshaw. *Nutrition: What's in the Food We Eat* (3–6). Illus. by William Munoz.

1992, Holiday $15.95 (0-8234-0968-6). 40pp. The purpose of food is explained, along with the major food categories and the concept of vitamins and minerals. (Rev: BCCB 2/93; BL 1/15/93; SLJ 2/93) [612.3]

**16006** Reef, Catherine. *Eat the Right Stuff: Food Facts* (4–8). Illus. Series: Good Health Guidelines. 1993, Twenty-First Century LB $15.95 (0-8050-2442-5). 64pp. This basic guide to nutrition and digestion also explores the food pyramid, explains weight control, and discusses the use of vitamins. (Rev: SLJ 1/94) [664]

**16007** Silverstein, Alvin, et al. *Fats* (4–7). Illus. by Anne Canevari Green. Series: Food Power. 1992, Millbrook LB $20.90 (1-56294-208-5). 48pp. With full-color drawings and much boxed information, the various kinds of fats and their roles in one's diet are explored. (Rev: BL 11/15/92; SLJ 1/93) [612.3]

**16008** Silverstein, Alvin, et al. *Proteins* (4–7). Illus. by Anne Canevari Green. Series: Food Power. 1992, Millbrook LB $20.90 (1-56294-209-3). 48pp. Explains the functions of proteins and amino acids in nutrition, as well as the nitrogen cycle. (Rev: BL 11/15/92; SLJ 1/93) [612.3]

**16009** Thompson, Paul. *Nutrition* (5–8). Illus. 1981, Watts LB $10.40 (0-531-04328-2). 72pp. An explanation of food groups, the digestive system, and the importance of good nutrition.

### VEGETABLES

**16010** Aliki. *Corn Is Maize: The Gift of the Indians* (2–4). Illus. by author. 1976, HarperCollins LB $14.89 (0-690-00975-5); paper $4.95 (0-06-445026-0). 40pp. A simply written, comprehensive treatment of corn, its origins, how it is husbanded and harvested, and its many uses.

**16011** Bial, Raymond. *Corn Belt Harvest* (4–6). Illus. 1991, Houghton $17.00 (0-395-56234-1). 48pp. A photoessay about how corn is grown and harvested. (Rev: BCCB 1/92; BL 12/15/91; SLJ 2/92) [633.1]

**16012** Brown, Laurie Krasny. *The Vegetable Show* (PS–3). Illus. 1995, Little, Brown $14.95 (0-316-11363-8). 32pp. The characteristics and importance of vegetables are explored in this imaginative picture book that is framed as a vaudeville show. (Rev: BL 6/1–15/95; SLJ 6/95) [641.6]

**16013** De Bourgoing, Pascale, and Gallimard Jeunesse. *Vegetables in the Garden* (PS–3). Illus. by Gilbert Houbre. Series: First Discovery Book. 1994, Scholastic $11.95 (0-590-48326-7). 24pp. In this well-illustrated interactive book, small children learn about gardens and different kinds of vegetables and how they grow. (Rev: BL 11/15/94) [635]

**16014** Fowler, Allan. *Corn — on and off the Cob* (1–2). Illus. Series: Rookie Read About Science. 1994, Children's LB $18.50 (0-516-06027-9). 32pp. An easily read science book about different kinds of corn and their uses. (Rev: BL 4/15/95) [633.1]

**16015** King, Elizabeth. *The Pumpkin Patch* (PS–3). Illus. 1990, Dutton paper $14.99 (0-525-44640-0). 40pp. A visually satisfying photoessay of the pumpkin. (Rev: BCCB 12/90; BL 9/1/90; HB 11–12/90; SLJ 9/90) [625]

**16016** Robinson, Fay. *Vegetables, Vegetables!* (1–2). Illus. Series: Rookie Read About Science. 1994, Children's LB $18.50 (0-516-06030-9). 32pp. An easily read book that introduces various vegetables and shows ways in which they are prepared for food. (Rev: BL 4/15/95) [635]

**16017** Watts, Barrie. *Potato* (1–3). Illus. 1988, Silver Burdett LB $9.95 (0-382-09527-8); paper $3.95 (0-382-24018-9). How a potato grows and is harvested. (Rev: BL 10/1/88; SLJ 10/88)

## Fungi

**16018** Arnold, Katya, and Sam Swope. *Katya's Book of Mushrooms* (3–6). Illus. 1997, Holt $16.95 (0-8050-4136-2). 45pp. A field book of edible and poisonous mushrooms, how to find and identify them, and folklore surrounding them. (Rev: BCCB 4/97; BL 4/1/97; HB 5–6/97; SLJ 4/97) [589.2]

**16019** Frazer, Simon. *The Mushroom Hunt* (1–4). Illus. by Penny Dale. Series: Read and Wonder. 1995, Candlewick $15.99 (1-56402-500-4). 32pp. Facts and lore about the much-misunderstood mushroom are entertainingly presented. (Rev: BL 7/95; SLJ 7/95) [589.2]

**16020** Murray, Peter. *Mushrooms* (3–5). Illus. Series: Naturebooks: Plants. 1995, Child's World LB $22.79 (1-56766-193-9). 32pp. Edible and poisonous mushrooms are discussed, with information on how and where mushrooms grow and reproduce. (Rev: BL 12/1/95) [589.2]

**16021** Silverstein, Alvin, et al. *Fungi* (3–6). Illus. Series: Kingdom of Life. 1996, Twenty-First Century LB $21.40 (0-8050-3520-6). 64pp. All kinds of fungi and molds are pictured, with brief text. (Rev: BL 6/1–15/96) [589.2]

**16022** Tesar, Jenny. *Fungi* (5–7). Illus. Series: Our Living World. 1994, Blackbirch LB $18.95 (1-56711-044-4). 64pp. A volume that explains what a fungus is, how the various types reproduce and grow, their unique characteristics, and how they fit into food webs and chains. (Rev: BL 12/1/94) [589.2]

## Leaves and Trees

**16023** Arnosky, Jim. *Crinkleroot's Guide to Knowing the Trees* (2–4). Illus. 1992, Macmillan $15.00 (0-02-705855-7). 40pp. Crinkleroot the woodsman guides young readers through the wilderness, teaching nature along the way. (Rev: BL 2/1/92; SLJ 3/92) [582.1]

**16024** Bash, Barbara. *Ancient Ones: The World of the Old-Growth Douglas Fir* (3–6). Illus. 1994, Sierra Club $16.95 (0-87156-561-7). 32pp. The cycle of natural growth and renewal as witnessed by a Douglas fir in the Pacific Northwest. (Rev: BL 9/15/94; SLJ 10/94*) [585]

**16025** Bash, Barbara. *In the Heart of the Village: The World of the Indian Banyan Tree* (3–6). Illus. 1996, Sierra Club $16.95 (0-87156-575-7). 32pp. A discussion of activities and animal life associated with a banyan tree in an Indian village. (Rev: BL 9/15/96; SLJ 11/96*) [583]

**16026** Brandt, Keith. *Discovering Trees* (1–3). Illus. by Christine Willis Nigoghossian. 1982, Troll LB $12.95 (0-89375-566-4); paper $3.50 (0-89375-567-2). 32pp. How a tree is born and how it grows.

**16027** Brockman, Frank C. *Trees of North America* (5–8). Illus. by Rebecca Merrilees. 1968, Golden Bks. paper $11.95 (0-307-13658-2). 280pp. More than 700 species in 76 families are introduced.

**16028** Burnie, David. *Tree* (4–8). Illus. 1988, Knopf LB $20.99 (0-394-99617-8). 64pp. This photoessay covers different leaves, needles, and scales. (Rev: BL 12/1/88; SLJ 12/88)

**16029** Dorros, Arthur. *A Tree Is Growing* (2–4). Illus. by S. D. Schindler. 1997, Scholastic $15.95 (0-590-45300-9). 32pp. In double-page spreads, various types of trees and leaves are introduced, with material on how trees grow. (Rev: BCCB 6/97; BL 2/1/97; SLJ 3/97) [582.16]

**16030** Fischer-Nagel, Heiderose, and Andreas Fischer-Nagel. *Fir Trees* (3–6). Illus. Series: Nature Watch. 1989, Carolrhoda LB $19.93 (0-87614-340-0). 48pp. The development and growth of the conifers. (Rev: BL 10/15/89; SLJ 1/90) [585.2]

**16031** Fleisher, Paul. *Oak Tree* (3–5). Illus. Series: Webs of Life. 1997, Marshall Cavendish LB $21.36 (0-7614-0434-1). 40pp. Describes an Eastern deciduous forest and the plant and animal life that surrounds an oak tree. (Rev: BL 2/15/98) [583]

**16032** Fowler, Allan. *It Could Still Be a Tree* (1–2). Illus. Series: Rookie Read-About Science. 1990, Children's LB $18.50 (0-516-04904-6). 32pp. With simple text and many photos, the characteristics of trees are introduced. (Rev: BL 2/1/91) [582.12]

**16033** Gardner, Robert. *Science Project Ideas About Trees* (4–7). Illus. Series: Science Project Ideas. 1997, Enslow LB $18.95 (0-89490-846-4). 96pp. The parts of trees and their functions are described, with activities involving leaves, seeds, flowers, roots, and twigs. (Rev: BL 12/1/97; SLJ 2/98) [582.16]

**16034** Henderson, Douglas. *Dinosaur Tree* (2–4). Illus. 1994, Bradbury paper $16.00 (0-02-743547-4). 32pp. The story of a 500-year-old tree that is now in the Petrified Forest National Park. (Rev: BL 1/1/95; SLJ 2/95*) [560]

**16035** Jennings, Terry. *Wood* (3–5). Illus. by Ed Barber. Series: Threads. 1991, Garrett LB $15.93 (1-56074-002-7). 28pp. Various types of wood products are pictured with facts on how they are produced and used. (Rev: BL 11/15/91) [674]

**16036** Johnson, Sylvia A. *How Leaves Change* (3–5). Illus. 1986, Lerner LB $22.60 (0-8225-1483-4); paper $5.95 (0-8225-9513-3). 48pp. Leaves change color in the fall; this book explains how and why. (Rev: BCCB 4/87; BL 1/15/87; SLJ 3/87)

**16037** Jorgensen, Lisa. *Grand Trees of America: Our State and Champion Trees* (4–7). Illus. 1992, Roberts paper $8.95 (1-879373-15-7). 120pp. This book describes the official tree of each state and introduces the National Register of Big Trees. (Rev: BL 2/15/93) [582.16]

**16038** Kittinger, Jo S. *Dead Log Alive!* (4–7). Illus. Series: A First Book: Biology. 1996, Watts LB $21.00 (0-531-20237-2). 63pp. A description of the animals, insects, birds, and fungi that live in or on dead trees. (Rev: SLJ 5/97) [586.16]

**16039** Lauber, Patricia. *Be a Friend to Trees* (2–4). Illus. by Holly Keller. Series: Lets-Read-and-Find-Out Science. 1994, HarperCollins LB $14.89 (0-06-021529-1). 32pp. The many uses of trees — such as providing homes for birds and supplying wood for construction — are outlined, with material on trees' structure, parts, and how their leaves make food. (Rev: BCCB 1/94; BL 6/1–15/94; SLJ 3/94) [582.16]

**16040** Maestro, Betsy. *Why Do Leaves Change Color?* (K–4). Illus. by Loretta Krupinski. Series: Lets-Read-and-Find-Out Science. 1994, HarperCollins LB $14.89 (0-06-022874-1). 32pp. This book explains the process that causes leaf color change in the autumn and why leaves fall from the trees. (Rev: BCCB 11/94; BL 11/15/94; SLJ 7/95) [582.16]

**16041** Miller, Cameron, and Dominique Falla. *Woodlore* (3–5). Illus. 1995, Ticknor $14.95 (0-395-72034-6). 32pp. Various kinds of wood and their uses are explored in text and full-color illustrations. (Rev: BCCB 3/95; BL 3/1/95; SLJ 3/95) [674.8]

**16042** Murray, Peter. *Redwoods* (3–5). Illus. Series: Naturebooks: Plants. 1996, Child's World LB $22.79 (1-56766-216-1). 32pp. The majestic redwoods, how they grow, and the characteristics of a single tree are highlighted in this colorful book. (Rev: BL 1/1–15/97) [585]

**16043**  Oppenheim, Joanne. *Have You Seen Trees?* (K–3). Illus. by Jean Tseng and Mou-Sien Tseng. 1995, Scholastic $14.95 (0-590-46691-7). 40pp. Various trees, their uses, and how they change during the seasons are featured in this picture book. (Rev: BL 1/15/95; SLJ 4/95*) [582.16]

**16044**  Patent, Dorothy Hinshaw. *Apple Trees* (2–3). Series: Early Bird Nature Books. 1998, Lerner LB $19.93 (0-8225-3020-1). 48pp. An easily read introduction to the apple tree and its life cycle, told in a simple text with attractive color photographs. (Rev: BL 3/15/98; SLJ 4/98) [582.16]

**16045**  Pfeffer, Wendy. *A Log's Life* (K–3). Illus. by Robin Brickman. 1997, Simon & Schuster paper $16.00 (0-689-80636-1). 32pp. The life cycle of an oak tree and its many uses in the forest ecology. (Rev: BL 9/15/97; SLJ 9/97) [574.5]

**16046**  Russo, Monica. *The Tree Almanac: A Year-Round Activity Guide* (4–7). Photos by Kevin Byron. 1993, Sterling $16.95 (0-8069-1252-9). 128pp. Introduces various species of trees, their changes during the 4 seasons, and their many enemies, including diseases and insects. (Rev: BL 12/15/93; SLJ 1/94) [582.16]

**16047**  Tesar, Jenny. *Shrinking Forests* (5–8). Illus. Series: Our Fragile Earth. 1991, Facts on File $19.95 (0-8160-2492-8). 112pp. A worldwide survey of the decline of forests. (Rev: SLJ 1/92) [582.16]

**16048**  Thornhill, Jan. *A Tree in a Forest* (2–4). Illus. by author. 1992, Simon & Schuster paper $15.00 (0-671-75901-9). In picture-book format, the life story of a maple tree from seedling to destruction. (Rev: SLJ 7/92) [582.12]

**16049**  Vieira, Linda. *The Ever-Living Tree: The Life and Times of a Coast Redwood* (2–5). Illus. by Christopher Canyon. 1994, Walker LB $15.85 (0-8027-8278-7). 32pp. The life of a 2,000-year-old redwood, with details of some important events that occurred during its life. (Rev: BL 3/1/94; SLJ 5/94) [584]

**16050**  Wadsworth, Ginger. *Giant Sequoia Trees* (2–4). Photos by Frank Staub. Series: Early Bird Nature Books. 1995, Lerner LB $19.93 (0-8225-3001-5). 48pp. A photoessay about the world's largest tree, the sequoia, with details on its parts, environment, and life cycle. (Rev: SLJ 10/95) [582]

**16051**  Zim, Herbert S., and Alexander C. Martin. *Trees* (5–8). Illus. 1991, Western paper $21.27 (0-307-64056-6). 160pp. A small, handy volume packed with information and color illustrations that help identify our most important trees.

## Plants

**16052**  Aaseng, Nathan. *Meat-Eating Plants* (3–6). Illus. Series: Weird and Wacky Science. 1996, Enslow LB $18.95 (0-89490-617-8). 48pp. Such plants as bladderworts, sundews, pitcher plants, and Venus flytraps are described, along with their methods of obtaining food. (Rev: SLJ 5/96) [581.5]

**16053**  Alderton, David. *Plants* (5–7). Illus. by Sudio Boni/Galante and Ivan Stalio. Series: Ladybird Explorers. 1997, Ladybird paper $4.99 (0-7214-5771-1). 38pp. This introduction to various plants arranges them by habitat and adaptation. (Rev: SLJ 2/98) [581.5]

**16054**  Ardley, Neil. *The Science Book of Things That Grow* (3–6). Illus. Series: Science Books. 1991, Harcourt $9.95 (0-15-200586-2). 29pp. With everyday equipment and step-by-step procedures, the process of plant growth is explained. (Rev: BL 10/15/91) [581]

**16055**  *Atlas of Plants* (1–3). Illus. by Sylvaine Perols. Series: First Discovery Atlases. 1996, Scholastic $11.95 (0-590-58113-9). Using extensive captions and maps, this atlas tells where plants come from. (Rev: SLJ 9/96) [581.5]

**16056**  Baker, Wendy, and Andrew Haslam. *Plants* (3–6). Illus. Series: Make It Work! 1993, Macmillan $12.95 (0-689-71664-8). 48pp. Such concepts as photosynthesis are introduced and activities and experiments are provided. (Rev: SLJ 4/93) [581]

**16057**  Bash, Barbara. *Desert Giant: The World of the Saguaro Cactus* (3–6). Illus. 1989, Little, Brown $16.95 (0-316-08301-1); paper $5.95 (0-685-33583-6). 32pp. The Tohono O'odham Indians — the Desert People — gather the fruit of the saguaro in a centuries-old harvest ritual. (Rev: BL 3/15/89; HB 3–4/89)

**16058**  Burnie, David. *Plant* (4–8). Illus. Series: Eyewitness Books. 1989, Knopf LB $20.99 (0-394-92252-2). 64pp. The nature of plants — structure, parts, and types — is covered. (Rev: BL 11/15/89; SLJ 1/90) [581]

**16059**  Byles, Monica. *Experiment with Plants* (2–5). Illus. Series: Experiment With. 1994, Lerner LB $19.93 (0-8225-2456-2). 32pp. Various types of plants, parts of plants, their uses, and how they grow are covered in this book filled with simple experiments. (Rev: BL 3/1/94; SLJ 5/94) [537]

**16060**  Carolin, Roger, ed. *Incredible Plants* (4–6). Illus. Series: Nature Company Discoveries. 1997, Time Life $16.00 (0-7835-4799-4). 64pp. A fine introduction to plants, their various forms and uses, and different growing areas. (Rev: BL 6/1–15/97; SLJ 7/97) [581]

**16061** Coil, Suzanne M. *Poisonous Plants* (3–6). Illus. Series: First Books. 1992, Watts paper $6.95 (0-531-15647-8). 64pp. An attractive format with lots of information about these plants and with many illustrations. (Rev: BL 5/15/91; SLJ 7/91) [582]

**16062** Dowden, Anne O. *The Clover and the Bee: A Book of Pollination* (5–8). Illus. 1990, HarperCollins LB $17.89 (0-690-04679-0). 90pp. A beautifully illustrated book with much information on plant pollination. (Rev: BCCB 6/90; SLJ 7/90*) [647]

**16063** Dowden, Anne O. *Poisons in Our Path: Plants That Harm and Heal* (4–7). Illus. 1994, HarperCollins LB $17.89 (0-06-020862-7). 64pp. An examination of the properties, appearance, and habitats of many plants that have been important in the past or present in medicine or magic. (Rev: BCCB 4/94; BL 7/94; HB 7–8/94; SLJ 6/94) [581.6]

**16064** Fleisher, Paul. *Saguaro Cactus* (3–5). Series: Webs of Life. 1997, Marshall Cavendish LB $21.36 (0-7614-0433-3). 40pp. An introduction to this gigantic cactus found in the Southwest, with material on how it survives in a hostile environment. (Rev: BL 2/15/98) [635.9]

**16065** Ganeri, Anita. *Plants* (3–6). 1992, Watts LB $19.30 (0-531-14194-2). 32pp. In this British nature detective book, each section addresses one aspect, such as why do plants have leaves. (Rev: BL 1/15/93; SLJ 12/92) [581]

**16066** Garassino, Alessandro. *Plants: Origins and Evolution* (4–8). Illus. Series: Beginnings. 1995, Raintree Steck-Vaughn LB $24.26 (0-8114-3332-3). 48pp. Important concepts of plant evolution are well presented, with coverage of modern botany and its functions. (Rev: BL 4/15/95) [581.3]

**16067** Gjersvik, Marianne Haug. *Green Fun: Plants as Play* (3–6). Illus. 1997, Firefly $19.95 (1-55209-105-8); paper $7.95 (1-55209-096-5). 48pp. A book that not only presents many projects and crafts using common flowers but also describes the plants, flowers, and care of gardens. (Rev: BL 8/97) [745.5]

**16068** Halpern, Robert R. *Green Planet Rescue: Saving the Earth's Endangered Plants* (5–8). Illus. Series: Cincinnati Zoo Book. 1993, Watts LB $23.60 (0-531-11095-8). 64pp. After citing the terrible destruction of plant life in such areas as the Amazon River basin and Madagascar, this account describes some successful ventures in rescuing endangered plants. (Rev: BL 3/15/94; SLJ 4/94) [581.5]

**16069** Jenkins, Martin. *Fly Traps! Plants That Bite Back* (PS–3). Illus. by David Parkins. Series: Read and Wonder. 1996, Candlewick $15.99 (1-56402-896-8). 32pp. In a picture book format with simple text, this book entertainingly introduces such flesh-eating flora as the Venus flytrap and bladderworts. (Rev: BCCB 1/97; BL 11/15/96; SLJ 12/96) [583]

**16070** Johnson, Sylvia A. *Wheat* (4–6). Illus. by Masaharu Susuki. 1990, Lerner LB $22.60 (0-8225-1490-7). 48pp. The life cycle of the wheat plant is described, with material on harvesting and processing. (Rev: BL 4/15/90; SLJ 8/90) [633.1]

**16071** Kalman, Bobbie. *How a Plant Grows* (3–5). Illus. by Barbara Bedell. Series: Crabapples. 1996, Crabtree LB $18.08 (0-86505-628-5); paper $5.95 (0-86505-728-1). 32pp. An introduction to plants that covers topics like structure, photosynthesis, pollination, carnivorous plants, and the importance of plants in the food chain. (Rev: SLJ 7/97) [581.5]

**16072** Kerrod, Robin. *Plant Life* (4–7). Illus. by Ted Evans. Series: Let's Investigate Science. 1994, Marshall Cavendish LB $17.95 (1-85435-627-5). 64pp. A well-organized introduction to the plant kingdom, with material on classification, photosynthesis, movement, and reproduction. (Rev: SLJ 12/94) [581.5]

**16073** Kite, L. Patricia. *Dandelion Adventures* (PS–2). Illus. by Anca Hariton. 1998, Millbrook $20.90 (0-7613-0037-6); paper $6.95 (0-7613-0377-4). 32pp. This appealing picture book describing the life cycle of a dandelion begins with the landing of seed parachutes and ending with new plants producing their own flowers and seeds. (Rev: BL 3/15/98) [583]

**16074** Kite, L. Patricia. *Insect-Eating Plants* (3–5). Illus. 1995, Millbrook LB $21.90 (1-56294-562-9). 64pp. Several types of carnivorous plants are introduced, with tips on how to grow them. (Rev: BL 9/1/95) [583]

**16075** Landau, Elaine. *Endangered Plants* (4–6). Illus. Series: First Books. 1992, Watts paper $6.95 (0-531-15645-1). 64pp. Color photos enhance this look at plants in danger of extinction. (Rev: BL 6/1/92; SLJ 7/92) [581.5]

**16076** Lerner, Carol. *Cactus* (4–7). Illus. 1992, Morrow LB $14.93 (0-688-09637-9). 32pp. After explaining the parts of the cactus and how it can exist in near-waterless environments, this account describes different species. (Rev: BCCB 10/92; HB 1–2/93; SLJ 12/92) [635.7]

**16077** Lewin, Betsy. *Walk a Green Path* (1–4). Illus. 1995, Lothrop $15.00 (0-688-13425-4). 32pp. Different kinds of plants are introduced in a series of memorable paintings and short poems. (Rev: BL 6/1–15/95; SLJ 4/95) [581]

**16078** Llamas, Andreu. *Plants Under the Sea* (4–6). Illus. by Luis Rizo. Series: Incredible World of Plants. 1996, Chelsea LB $15.95 (0-7910-3468-2). 32pp. Familiar and less common ocean plants are described and pictured, along with their relation to aquatic animal life. Also use *The Vegetation of Rivers, Lakes, and Swamps* (1996). (Rev: SLJ 7/96) [581]

**16079** Lucht, Irmgard. *The Red Poppy* (K–3). Trans. by Frank Jacoby-Nelson. Illus. 1995, Hyperion LB $14.49 (0-7868-2043-8). 32pp. A year in the life of a poppy plant is explored in this large-format picture book. (Rev: BCCB 6/95; BL 4/1/95; SLJ 6/95*) [583]

**16080** McDonald, Mary Ann. *Sunflowers* (3–5). Illus. Series: Naturebooks: Plants. 1996, Child's World LB $22.79 (1-56766-272-2). 32pp. The growth cycle of sunflowers and their characteristics are covered in this colorful introduction to the popular, useful plant. (Rev: BL 1/1–15/97) [583]

**16081** Murray, Peter. *Cactus* (3–5). Illus. Series: Nature Books. 1995, Child's World LB $22.79 (1-56766-191-2). 32pp. Full-page photographs facing large-type pages of text introduce various cacti and their habitats and life. (Rev: BL 12/15/95; SLJ 3/96) [581]

**16082** Murray, Peter. *Orchids* (3–5). Illus. Series: Naturebooks: Plants. 1995, Child's World LB $22.79 (1-56766-194-7). 32pp. The structure, habitats, and growth patterns of orchids are introduced with colorful photographs. (Rev: BL 12/1/95) [584]

**16083** Nielsen, Nancy J. *Carnivorous Plants* (4–8). Illus. 1992, Watts paper $6.95 (0-531-15644-3). 64pp. A look, with the help of color photos, at flesh-eating plants, such as the Venus flytrap. (Rev: BL 6/1/92; SLJ 7/92) [581.5]

**16084** Overbeck, Cynthia. *Cactus* (3–6). Illus. by Shabo Hans. 1982, Lerner paper $5.95 (0-8225-9556-7). 48pp. A description of the cactus and how it lives.

**16085** Overbeck, Cynthia. *Carnivorous Plants* (4–8). Illus. by Kiyashi Shimizu. 1982, Lerner LB $22.60 (0-8225-1470-2). 48pp. How these plants exist is discussed, plus a mention of several types.

**16086** Penny, Malcolm. *How Plants Grow* (3–5). Illus. by Stuart Lafford. Series: Nature's Mysteries. 1996, Benchmark LB $21.36 (0-7614-0452-X). 32pp. Topics like flowering, pollination, seed production, and growth are covered in this elementary book about plants. (Rev: SLJ 2/97) [581.5]

**16087** *Plants* (PS–1). Illus. Series: What's Inside? 1992, DK Publg. $8.95 (1-56458-005-9). 24pp. The internal parts of plants are shown in simple text and diagrams that peel back to reveal the insides. (Rev: BL 4/15/92; SLJ 9/92) [581]

**16088** Pope, Joyce. *Practical Plants* (4–8). Illus. Series: Plant Life. 1991, Facts on File $15.95 (0-8160-2424-3). 62pp. How people use plants for food, medicine, paper and cloth fiber, housing material, and pleasure. (Rev: BL 6/15/91) [581.6]

**16089** Reading, Susan. *Desert Plants* (4–8). Illus. Series: Plant Life. 1991, Facts on File $15.95 (0-8160-2421-9). 63pp. Varieties of cacti and other desert plants are described with many full-color photos. (Rev: BL 6/15/91) [581]

**16090** Reading, Susan. *Plants of the Tropics* (4–8). Illus. Series: Plant Life. 1991, Facts on File $15.95 (0-8160-2423-5). 62pp. Touring the rain forest to see the variety of plants, how they survive, and their relationship with animals. (Rev: BL 6/15/91) [581]

**16091** Silverstein, Alvin, et al. *Plants* (3–6). Illus. Series: Kingdoms of Life. 1996, Twenty-First Century LB $21.40 (0-8050-3519-2). 64pp. Scientific classification of life on earth is explained, focusing on the world of plants and its diversity. (Rev: BL 6/1–15/96; SLJ 7/96) [581]

**16092** Storad, Conrad J. *Saguaro Cactus* (3–5). Photos by Paula Jansen. Series: Early Bird Nature Books. 1994, Lerner LB $19.95 (0-8225-3002-3). 48pp. After a general introduction to cacti, this account focuses on the physical appearance and life cycle of the saguaro. (Rev: SLJ 8/94) [583]

**16093** VanCleave, Janice. *Janice VanCleave's Plants: Mind-Boggling Experiments You Can Turn into Science Fair Projects* (3–7). Illus. 1997, Wiley paper $10.95 (0-471-14687-0). 96pp. Twenty projects and experiments involving plants, their parts, and their growth cycles are presented with clear, easy-to-follow instructions. (Rev: BL 2/15/97; SLJ 3/97) [581]

**16094** Watts, Barrie. *Dandelion* (PS–3). Illus. 1987, Silver Burdett LB $9.95 (0-382-09438-7); paper $3.95 (0-382-24016-2). 24pp. The simple dandelion in close-up photography. (Rev: BL 12/1/87)

**16095** Wexler, Jerome. *Queen Anne's Lace* (3–6). Illus. 1994, Albert Whitman LB $13.95 (0-8075-6710-8). 32pp. An examination of this common weed that explores its structure, roots, seeds, and flowers. (Rev: BCCB 6/94; BL 4/15/94; SLJ 6/94) [583]

**16096** Wexler, Jerome. *Sundew Stranglers: Plants That Eat Insects* (4–6). Illus. 1995, Dutton paper $15.99 (0-525-45208-7). 48pp. Various insect-eating plants are introduced, with special focus on the structure and characteristics of the sundew plants. (Rev: BCCB 7–8/95; BL 6/1–15/95; HB 7–8/95; SLJ 7/95) [583]

## Seeds

**16097** Burns, Diane L. *Berries, Nuts and Seeds* (4–7). Illus. by John F. McGee. 1996, NorthWord paper $6.95 (1-55971-573-1). 42pp. Each page in this guide is devoted to a description of a single berry, nut, or seed, like the raspberry, pecan, cattail, and thistle blossom. (Rev: BL 2/15/97) [582.13]

**16098** Gibbons, Gail. *From Seed to Plant* (PS–3). Illus. 1991, Holiday LB $15.95 (0-8234-0872-8). 32pp. How seeds grow into plants and how flowering plants produce seeds. (Rev: BL 3/1/91; HB 7–8/91; SLJ 7/91) [581.3]

**16099** Jordan, Helene J. *How a Seed Grows* (3–6). Illus. by Loretta Krupinski. Series: Let's-Read-and-Find-Out Science Books. 1992, HarperCollins LB $15.89 (0-06-020185-1); paper $4.95 (0-06-445107-0). 32pp. A boy and a girl plant seeds and watch them grow. (Rev: BL 8/92; SLJ 7/92) [582]

**16100** Kuchalla, Susan. *All About Seeds* (K–3). Illus. by Jane McBee. 1982, Troll LB $12.95 (0-89375-658-X); paper $3.50 (0-89375-659-8). 32pp. A sim-

ple account that explains how and where seeds grow.

**16101** Overbeck, Cynthia. *How Seeds Travel* (4–6). Illus. 1982, Lerner LB $22.60 (0-8225-1474-5); paper $5.95 (0-8225-9569-9). 48pp. An explanation of the various ways seeds are dispersed.

**16102** Pascoe, Elaine. *Seeds and Seedlings* (4–7). Illus. Series: Nature Close-up. 1996, Blackbirch LB $16.95 (1-56711-178-5). 48pp. The growth cycle of seeds is explained, with many projects on how to plant and raise seedlings. (Rev: BL 12/1/96; SLJ 3/97) [582]

# Chemistry

**16103** Fitzgerald, Karen. *The Story of Nitrogen* (4–6). Illus. Series: First Books: Chemical Elements. 1997, Watts LB $21.00 (0-531-20248-8). 64pp. Nitrogen is introduced, with material on its atomic structure, properties, uses, and production. (Rev: BL 9/1/97; SLJ 10/97) [546]

**16104** Mebane, Robert C., and Thomas R. Rybolt. *Salts and Solids* (4–6). Illus. Series: Everyday Material Science Experiments. 1995, Twenty-First Century LB $18.90 (0-8050-2841-2). 64pp. Each of the experiments that explore the properties of salts and solids is accompanied by an explanation of what should happen and why. (Rev: BL 9/15/95; SLJ 8/95) [530]

**16105** Newmark, Ann. *Chemistry* (3–6). Illus. Series: Eyewitness Science. 1993, DK Publg. $15.95 (1-56458-231-0). 64pp. A very attractive book covering the structure of matter, various types of chemical reactions, and the role of chemistry in world history. (Rev: SLJ 9/93) [540]

**16106** VanCleave, Janice. *Janice VanCleave's Molecules* (4–6). Illus. 1992, Wiley paper $10.95 (0-471-55054-X). 86pp. The principles of cohesion, adhesion, density, diffusion, and emulsion are explored, with clear line drawings. (Rev: BL 1/15/93; SLJ 2/93) [540]

**16107** Watson, Philip. *Liquid Magic* (4–6). Illus. by Elizabeth Wood and Ronald Fenton. 1983, Morrow paper $7.95 (0-688-00974-3). 48pp. Through clear, simple experiments, the properties of liquids are introduced.

# Geology and Geography

## Earth and Geology

**16108**  Anderson, Alan, et al. *Geology Crafts for Kids: 50 Nifty Projects to Explore the Marvels of Planet Earth* (4–7). Illus. 1996, Sterling $21.95 (0-8069-8156-3). 144pp. This is a combined craft book and geology text with directions for such projects as building a seismograph and growing crystals. (Rev: SLJ 2/97) [551]

**16109**  Ardley, Neil. *The Science Book of Gravity* (3–6). Illus. Series: Science Books. 1992, Harcourt $9.95 (0-15-200621-4). 28pp. Each 2-page spread contains information about the properties of gravity and includes projects to demonstrate it. (Rev: BL 10/15/92; SLJ 1/93) [531]

**16110**  Arnold, Caroline. *Coping with Natural Disasters* (5–7). Illus. 1988, Walker LB $14.85 (0-8027-6717-6). 128pp. How a community returns to life after a natural disaster. (Rev: BCCB 6/88; BL 6/15/88)

**16111**  Bannan, Jan G. *Letting off Steam* (3–7). Illus. 1989, Carolrhoda LB $19.95 (0-87614-300-1). 48pp. This book explains and illustrates how underground heat can cause hot springs, geysers, and other phenomena. (Rev: BCCB 12/89; BL 9/15/89; HB 9–10/89; SLJ 9/89) [551.3]

**16112**  Barnes-Svarney, Patricia L. *Born of Heat and Pressure: Mountains and Metamorphic Rock* (5–8). Illus. Series: Earth Processes. 1991, Enslow LB $16.95 (0-89490-276-8). 64pp. This book tells how the earth's internal heat and pressure cause mountains and metamorphic rock to form. (Rev: BL 1/15/91) [552.4]

**16113**  Burton, Virginia Lee. *Life Story* (3–5). Illus. by author. 1989, Houghton $20.00 (0-395-16030-8); paper $9.95 (0-395-52017-7). A work about the changes that have taken place on the earth and in its flora and fauna, from the beginning of time until the present.

**16114**  Campbell, Ann-Jeanette, and Ronald Rood. *The New York Public Library Incredible Earth: A Book of Answers for Kids* (4–7). Illus. 1996, Wiley paper $12.95 (0-471-14497-5). 192pp. Questions and answers involving science, collected from the reference department of the New York Public Library. (Rev: BL 9/15/96; SLJ 1/97) [550]

**16115**  Clifford, Nick. *Incredible Earth* (4–7). Illus. Series: Inside Guides. 1996, DK Publg. $15.95 (0-7894-1013-3). 44pp. Earth's composition and other geological topics are described in double-page spreads. (Rev: BL 12/1/96; SLJ 2/97) [551]

**16116**  Cole, Joanna. *The Magic School Bus: Inside the Earth* (2–5). Illus. by Bruce Degen. 1987, Scholastic $15.95 (0-590-40759-7); paper $4.95 (0-590-40760-0). 48pp. In picture-book format, geology is introduced as a school bus journeys to the center of the earth. (Rev: BL 1/1/88)

**16117**  Cox, Shirley. *Earth Science* (4–6). Illus. 1992, Rourke LB $22.60 (0-86625-429-3). 48pp. An introduction to the process of doing a science fair project. (Rev: BL 2/15/93) [550]

**16118**  Crump, Donald J., ed. *Exploring Your World: The Adventure of Geography* (4–7). Illus. 1990, National Geographic $40.00 (0-87044-726-2). 608pp. Excellent photos and a dictionary-style format. (Rev: BL 5/5/90) [910.3]

**16119**  Gallant, Roy A. *Geysers: When Earth Roars* (3–6). Illus. 1997, Watts LB $22.00 (0-531-20288-7). 64pp. As well as explaining what geysers are and why they erupt, this account takes the reader on a tour of famous geysers in Russia, Iceland, New Zealand, and the United States. (Rev: BL 12/1/97; SLJ 12/97) [551.2]

**16120** Gibbons, Gail. *Planet Earth/Inside Out* (2–4). Illus. 1995, Morrow LB $16.00 (0-688-09681-6). 32pp. Theories about the earth's formation are discussed, and information about the earth's interior is given. (Rev: BCCB 9/95; BL 8/95; SLJ 10/95) [550]

**16121** Goodman, Billy. *Natural Wonders and Disasters* (4–7). Illus. Series: Planet Earth. 1991, Little, Brown $17.95 (0-316-32016-1). 96pp. Full-color photos help to explain the earth's natural wonders as well as such disasters as floods and typhoons. (Rev: BL 12/1/91; SLJ 1/92) [550]

**16122** Goodwin, Peter. *Landslides, Slumps, and Creep* (4–6). Illus. Series: First Books. 1997, Watts LB $21.00 (0-531-20332-8). 64pp. Different types of landslides and avalanches are introduced, with material on their causes and effects and an account of some of the major ones. (Rev: BL 11/1/97; SLJ 1/98) [551.3]

**16123** Hoffman, Mary. *Earth, Fire, Water, Air* (3–7). Illus. by Jane Ray. 1995, Dutton paper $19.99 (0-525-45420-9). 80pp. The author combines religion, mythology, and history with today's ecological concerns in an attractive description of Earth's basic components: earth, fire, water, and air. (Rev: BCCB 1/95; BL 1/1–15/96*; SLJ 2/96) [304.2]

**16124** Hooper, Meredith. *The Pebble in My Pocket: A History of Our Earth* (3–5). Illus. by Chris Coady. 1996, Viking paper $14.99 (0-670-86259-2). 40pp. From molten rock to the formation of mountains, this is a concise history of the earth. (Rev: BL 7/96; SLJ 4/96) [552]

**16125** Lauber, Patricia. *You're Aboard Spaceship Earth* (K–3). Illus. by Holly Keller. Series: Let's-Read-and-Find-Out Science. 1996, HarperCollins LB $14.89 (0-06-024408-9); paper $4.95 (0-06-445159-3). 32pp. The author describes Earth and its contents as though it were a gigantic spaceship. (Rev: BL 8/96; HB 9–10/96; SLJ 8/96) [550]

**16126** McNulty, Faith. *How to Dig a Hole to the Other Side of the World* (2–4). Illus. by Marc Simont. 1979, HarperCollins paper $4.95 (0-06-443218-1). 32pp. A journey to the center of the earth.

**16127** O'Neill, Catherine. *Natural Wonders of North America* (4–6). Illus. 1984, National Geographic LB $12.50 (0-87044-519-7). 104pp. Many of the wonders of North America, such as a Mexican volcano and life far north in Alaska, are shown in color photographs.

**16128** Parker, Steve. *The Earth* (3–6). Illus. Series: What If. 1995, Millbrook LB $19.90 (1-56294-913-6); paper $5.95 (1-56294-948-9). 32pp. A series of hypothetical questions like "What if the earth were twice as big?" are used to explore the various properties and attributes of the earth. (Rev: SLJ 1/96) [550]

**16129** Perham, Molly, and Julian Rowe. *Resources* (4–6). Illus. Series: Mapworlds. 1997, Watts LB $19.30 (0-531-14387-2). 32pp. Using an atlaslike format, this work shows where such natural resources as minerals, oil, and coal are found in the world. (Rev: BL 4/15/97) [333.7]

**16130** *Planet Earth: World Geography* (4–8). Illus. 1994, Oxford $40.00 (0-19-910144-2). 160pp. This well-illustrated volume introduces both world geography and earth science. (Rev: SLJ 5/94) [910]

**16131** Robbins, Ken. *Earth: The Elements* (3–6). Illus. 1995, Holt $16.95 (0-8050-2294-5). 46pp. A poetic introduction in photographs and text to the earth's formation and its many different landscapes. (Rev: BL 4/15/95; SLJ 5/95) [550]

**16132** Rothaus, Don P. *Canyons* (2–4). Illus. Series: Biomes of Nature. 1996, Child's World LB $22.79 (1-56766-322-2). 32pp. This book describes what canyons are and how they were formed, along with material on the world's most famous canyons. (Rev: SLJ 3/97) [551.4]

**16133** Sattler, Helen R. *Our Patchwork Planet: The Story of Plate Tectonics* (4–8). Illus. by Giulio Maestro. 1995, Lothrop LB $15.93 (0-688-09313-2). 48pp. The story of the earth's constant motion caused by plate tectonics and how this can cause earthquakes and volcanoes. (Rev: BCCB 4/95; BL 2/15/95; SLJ 4/95) [551.1]

**16134** Savan, Beth. *Earthwatch: Earthcycles and Ecosystems* (3–7). Illus. by Pat Cupples. 1992, Addison-Wesley paper $9.95 (0-201-58148-5). 96pp. Earth cycles — such as those of water, earth, and air — are explained; contemporary ecology problems are introduced; and simple activities are outlined. (Rev: SLJ 7/92) [550]

**16135** Silver, Donald M. *Earth: The Ever-Changing Planet* (4–6). Illus. by Patricia J. Wynne. 1989, Random LB $12.99 (0-394-99195-8). 96pp. From the outer crust to the inner core, the earth's composition is described. (Rev: SLJ 5/90) [550]

**16136** Stacey, Tom. *Earth, Sea, and Sky* (2–6). Illus. by Chris Forsey. Series: Tell Me About Books. 1991, Random paper $4.99 (0-679-80861-2). 40pp. With questions and answers, this book explores mountains, waterfalls, night and day, and weather. (Rev: SLJ 7/91) [551]

**16137** Steele, Philip. *Rocking and Rolling* (1–3). Illus. Series: SuperSmarts. 1997, Candlewick $11.99 (0-7636-0303-1). 24pp. A general introduction to the Earth that presents basic information on volcanoes, earthquakes, and other geological phenomena. (Rev: SLJ 3/98) [551]

**16138** VanCleave, Janice. *Janice VanCleave's Gravity* (4–6). Illus. 1992, Wiley paper $10.95 (0-471-55050-7). 86pp. Problems that explain how gravity affects the environment, with clear line drawings. (Rev: BL 1/15/93; SLJ 2/93) [531]

**16139** Van der Meer, Ron, and Ron Fisher. *The Earth Pack* (4–7). Illus. 1995, National Geographic $40.00 (0-7922-2957-6). 15pp. Interactive devices, a booklet of terms, and an audiotape explain such phenomena as hurricanes, volcanoes, and earthquakes. (Rev: BL 2/1/96) [551]

**16140** Van Rose, Susanna. *The Earth Atlas* (4–8). Illus. 1994, DK Publg. $19.95 (1-56458-626-X). 64pp. An oversize atlas that describes the geography of the earth, supplies cutaways of the interior structure, and introduces various kinds of rocks. (Rev: BL 12/1/94) [912]

**16141** Verdet, Jean-Pierre. *Atlas of the Earth* (PS–2). Illus. Series: First Discovery. 1997, Scholastic $11.95 (0-590-96211-6). 24pp. This atlas introduces the different surfaces and regions of the earth, from the ocean floor to the dry stretches of the Sahara desert. (Rev: BL 2/1/98) [550]

**16142** Watson, Nancy. *Our Violent Earth* (4–8). Illus. 1982, National Geographic LB $12.50 (0-87044-388-7). 104pp. Includes earthquakes, volcanoes, drought, fire and water, and stormy weather.

**16143** White, Larry. *Gravity* (3–6). Illus. by Laurie Hamilton. Series: Simple Experiments for Young Scientists. 1995, Millbrook LB $20.90 (1-56294-470-3). 48pp. Questions and answers concerning the mysteries of gravity are explored in a series of easily performed projects using simple materials. (Rev: SLJ 9/95) [531]

**16144** Zike, Dinah. *The Earth Science Book: Activities for Kids* (3–6). Illus. by Jessie J. Flores. 1993, Wiley paper $12.95 (0-471-57166-0). 119pp. Earth science concepts and environmental issues are presented. (Rev: SLJ 7/93) [551]

**16145** Zoehfeld, Kathleen W. *How Mountains Are Made* (K–4). Illus. by James G. Hale. 1995, HarperCollins LB $14.89 (0-06-024510-7). 32pp. In a simple text, such topics as various kinds of mountains, the earth's interior, and plate tectonics are introduced. (Rev: BCCB 9/95; BL 8/95; SLJ 9/95*) [551.8]

## Earthquakes and Volcanoes

**16146** Archer, Jules. *Earthquake!* (5–7). Illus. Series: Nature's Disasters. 1991, Macmillan LB $12.95 (0-89686-593-2). 48pp. This colorful account discusses the causes and effects of earthquakes and includes a list of famous quakes of the past. (Rev: BCCB 7–8/91; BL 8/91) [551.2]

**16147** Asimov, Isaac. *How Did We Find Out About Volcanoes?* (5–7). Illus. by David Wool. 1981, Avon paper $1.95 (0-380-59626-1). 64pp. An overview of volcanoes, from Pompeii to Mount St. Helens.

**16148** Barrett, Norman. *Volcanoes* (3–5). Illus. Series: Picture Library. 1990, Watts LB $20.00 (0-531-10841-4). 32pp. Full-color photos highlight this basic coverage of volcanoes. (Rev: BL 5/1/90) [551.2]

**16149** Booth, Basil. *Earthquakes and Volcanoes* (5–8). Illus. Series: Repairing the Damage. 1992, Macmillan LB $13.95 (0-02-711735-9). 46pp. A well-organized photoessay that explains the interrelationship between earthquakes and volcanoes. (Rev: BL 9/15/92) [551.2]

**16150** Branley, Franklyn M. *Volcanoes* (1–3). Illus. by Marc Simont. 1986, HarperCollins paper $4.95 (0-06-445059-7). 32pp. A simple look at the whys and hows of volcanoes. (Rev: BL 6/15/89; HB 5–6/85; SLJ 9/85)

**16151** Challand, Helen J. *Earthquakes* (1–4). Illus. 1982, Children's LB $20.00 (0-516-01636-9). The causes and effects of earthquakes, simply told.

**16152** Elting, Mary, et al. *Volcanoes and Earthquakes* (4–7). Illus. by Courtney. 1990, Simon & Schuster paper $9.95 (0-671-67217-7). 40pp. Disasters are covered with a you-are-there approach. (Rev: BL 2/1/91) [551.2]

**16153** Lampton, Christopher. *Volcano* (4–6). Illus. Series: Disaster! 1991, Millbrook LB $19.90 (1-56294-028-7). 64pp. Maps, charts, and diagrams enhance this up-to-date text. (Rev: BL 1/1/92; SLJ 12/91) [551.2]

**16154** Lauber, Patricia. *Volcano: The Eruption and Healing of Mount St. Helens* (2–5). Illus. 1986, Macmillan $16.95 (0-02-754500-8); paper $8.99 (0-689-71679-6). 64pp. Color photos augment the dramatic story of the eruption, aftermath, and gradual return to life of the volcano. (Rev: BCCB 9/86; BL 8/86; HB 9–10/86)

**16155** Levy, Matthys, and Mario Salvadori. *Earthquake Games* (5–8). Illus. 1997, Simon & Schuster $16.00 (0-689-81367-8). 128pp. Games, experiments, and a lucid text answer such questions as what causes earthquakes and volcanoes and what their effects are. (Rev: BL 9/1/97; SLJ 12/97) [551.22]

**16156** Moores, Eldridge M., ed. *Volcanoes and Earthquakes* (4–6). Illus. Series: Nature Company Discoveries Library. 1995, Time Life LB $16.00 (0-7835-4764-1). 64pp. This handsome overview of volcanoes and earthquakes contains many attractive illustrations, including an 8-page foldout. (Rev: BL 1/1–15/96; SLJ 1/96) [551.2]

**16157** Murray, Peter. *Earthquakes* (3–5). Illus. Series: Naturebooks: Natural Disasters. 1995, Child's

World LB $22.79 (1-56766-198-X). 32pp. Using examples from around the world, this account describes the causes and effects of earthquakes. (Rev: BL 12/1/95; HB 7–8/95) [581.2]

**16158**  Murray, Peter. *Volcanoes* (3–5). Illus. Series: Naturebooks: Natural Disasters. 1995, Child's World LB $22.79 (1-56766-197-1). 32pp. The structure and causes of volcanoes are covered, with examples from around the world. (Rev: BL 12/1/95; HB 5–6/95; SLJ 3/96) [551.2]

**16159**  Newton, David E. *Earthquakes* (3–6). Illus. Series: First Books. 1993, Watts LB $21.00 (0-531-20054-X); paper $6.95 (0-531-15664-8). 64pp. Causes and effects of earthquakes and how they are measured. (Rev: BL 7/93) [551.2]

**16160**  Ruiz, Andres L. *Volcanoes and Earthquakes* (4–7). Series: Sequences of Earth and Space. 1997, Sterling $12.95 (0-8069-9744-3). 32pp. This book covers such topics as tectonic plates, quakes, and tsunamis plus the formation, structure, and eruption of volcanoes. (Rev: BL 12/1/97) [551.21]

**16161**  Simon, Seymour. *Earthquakes* (3–5). Illus. 1991, Morrow LB $14.88 (0-688-09634-4). 32pp. Direct text and color photos add to the fascination of this fact-filled book. (Rev: BCCB 7–8/91; BL 8/91*; HB 9–10/91; SLJ 9/91) [551.2]

**16162**  Simon, Seymour. *Volcanoes* (1–3). Illus. 1988, Morrow LB $15.88 (0-688-07412-X). 32pp. How volcanoes are formed and erupt, with well-known examples. (Rev: BCCB 10/88; HB 9–10/88; SLJ 12/88)

**16163**  Thomas, Margaret. *Volcano!* (5–7). Illus. Series: Nature's Disasters. 1991, Macmillan LB $12.95 (0-89686-595-9). 48pp. This book gives solid information about the causes of volcanic eruptions and their effects and includes famous volcanic disasters of the past. (Rev: BL 8/91) [551.2]

**16164**  VanCleave, Janice. *Earthquakes: Mind-Boggling Experiments You Can Turn into Science Fair Projects* (4–6). Illus. Series: Spectacular Science Projects. 1993, Wiley paper $10.95 (0-471-57107-5). 88pp. This is a collection of projects involving the movements of the earth, along with good scientific explanations and simple directions. (Rev: BL 5/1/93; SLJ 7/93) [551.2]

**16165**  VanCleave, Janice. *Janice VanCleave's Volcanoes: Mind-Boggling Experiments You Can Turn into Science Fair Projects* (4–7). Illus. 1994, Wiley paper $10.95 (0-471-30811-0). 89pp. Twenty experiments that explore the properties of erupting volcanoes using simple materials that can often be found around the house. (Rev: BL 7/94; SLJ 8/94) [551.2]

**16166**  Van Rose, Susanna. *Volcano and Earthquake* (4–7). Illus. Series: Eyewitness Books. 1992, Knopf LB $20.99 (0-679-91685-7). 61pp. With emphasis on

the visual, this book explains how volcanoes and earthquakes occur and the efforts to predict them. (Rev: SLJ 12/92) [551.2]

**16167**  Vogel, Carole G. *Shock Waves Through Los Angeles: The Northridge Earthquake* (3–6). Illus. 1996, Little, Brown $15.95 (0-316-90240-3). 32pp. The 1994 earthquake close to Los Angeles is covered, including causes, rescues, and the incredible destruction. (Rev: BL 10/1/96; SLJ 10/96) [363.3]

**16168**  Vogt, Gregory L. *Volcanoes* (3–6). Illus. Series: First Books. 1993, Watts LB $21.00 (0-531-20151-1). 63pp. This book highlights some of the world's most important volcanoes, the causes for their formation, and eruptions. (Rev: BL 7/93) [551.2]

**16169**  Walker, Sally M. *Earthquakes* (3–6). Illus. Series: Earth Watch. 1996, Carolrhoda LB $19.93 (0-87614-888-7). 48pp. A clearly written text and powerful color photos highlight this award-winning book. (Rev: BL 4/15/96; SLJ 6/96) [551.2]

**16170**  Walker, Sally M. *Volcanoes: Earth's Inner Fire* (3–6). Illus. Series: Earth Watch. 1994, Carolrhoda LB $14.95 (0-87614-812-7). 56pp. Many color photographs and clear text are used to explain the causes, locations, and effects of volcanoes. (Rev: BL 1/15/95) [551.2]

**16171**  *Why Do Volcanoes Erupt?* (PS–3). Illus. Series: Why. 1997, DK Publg. $9.95 (0-7894-1532-1). 24pp. Using a question-and-answer format, volcanoes are introduced, with material on the causes and effects of volcano eruptions. (Rev: BL 8/97) [550]

# Icebergs and Glaciers

**16172**  Fowler, Allan. *Icebergs, Ice Caps, and Glaciers* (1–3). Series: Rookie Read-About Science. 1997, Children's LB $13.87 (0-516-20429-7). 32pp. Large type and color illustrations are used to introduce these ice formations, with material on how glaciers move and how pieces of ice caps become icebergs. (Rev: BL 11/15/97) [551.31]

**16173**  George, Michael. *Glaciers* (3–8). Illus. 1991, Creative Ed. LB $16.95 (0-88682-401-X). 40pp. Formations and types of glaciers, as well as their future effects, are explained. (Rev: BL 12/15/91; SLJ 3/92) [551.3]

**16174**  Walker, Sally M. *Glaciers: Ice on the Move* (4–7). Illus. 1990, Carolrhoda LB $19.93 (0-87614-373-7). 48pp. This book explains how glaciers are formed, where they are found, and how they move. (Rev: BCCB 9/90; BL 6/15/90; SLJ 8/90) [551.3]

# Physical Geography

## General and Miscellaneous

**16175** Armbruster, Ann. *Wildfires* (4–6). Illus. Series: First Books: Science. 1996, Watts LB $21.00 (0-531-20250-X). 63pp. Introduces types of wildfires, their causes, effects, and possible prevention. (Rev: BL 1/1–15/97) [363.37]

**16176** Benedick, Jeanne. *Caves!* (4–7). Illus. 1995, Holt $15.95 (0-8050-2764-5). 74pp. A handbook on caves that explains their formation, their uses, and how ancients created art works on their walls. (Rev: BL 2/1/96) [551.4]

**16177** Collard, Sneed B. *Our Natural Homes* (3–6). Illus. by James M. Needham. Series: Our Perfect Planet. 1996, Charlesbridge LB $15.88 (0-88106-930-2); paper $6.95 (0-88106-928-0). An introduction to the plant and animal life found in such North and South American biomes as tundra, boreal forest, mountains, grasslands, deserts, rain forests, and chaparral. (Rev: SLJ 10/96) [910]

**16178** Cone, Molly. *Squishy, Misty, Damp and Muddy: The In-Between World of Wetlands* (1–3). Illus. 1996, Sierra Club $15.95 (0-87156-480-7). 31pp. A pictorial description of the wetlands, with an introduction to their flora and fauna. (Rev: BL 6/1–15/96; SLJ 8/96) [574.5]

**16179** Cone, Patrick. *Wildfire* (3–7). Illus. 1996, Carolrhoda $14.95 (0-87614-936-0); paper $7.95 (1-57505-027-7). 48pp. After a general description of wildfires, discusses their causes, effects, and possible preventive measures that can be taken. (Rev: BL 2/15/97; SLJ 1/97) [574.5]

**16180** Dunphy, Madeleine. *Here Is the Wetland* (K–3). Illus. by Wayne McLoughlin. 1996, Hyperion LB $15.49 (0-7868-2136-1). An attractive introduction to wetlands and the animals and plants found there, with colorful full-page paintings. (Rev: SLJ 12/96) [331.91]

**16181** George, Jean Craighead. *One Day in the Alpine Tundra* (4–7). Illus. by Walter Gaffney-Kessell. 1984, HarperCollins LB $15.89 (0-690-04326-0). 48pp. An introduction to the geology and ecology of the Alpine Tundra and an exciting story are woven together.

**16182** Gibbons, Gail. *Caves and Caverns* (2–4). Illus. by author. 1993, Harcourt $16.00 (0-15-226820-0). An interesting introduction to caves, where they are found, their various types, and how they were formed. (Rev: SLJ 1/94) [551.4]

**16183** Gibbons, Gail. *Marshes and Swamps* (2–3). Illus. 1998, Holiday LB $15.95 (0-8234-1347-0). 32pp. Fresh and saltwater wetlands are introduced, as

well as the amazing variety of animals and plants that are found in them. (Rev: BL 3/15/98) [551.41]

**16184** Kramer, Stephen. *Caves* (3–6). Photos by Kenrick L. Day. Series: Caves. 1995, Carolrhoda LB $19.93 (0-87614-447-4); paper $7.95 (0-87614-896-8). 48pp. Using color photos, diagrams, and maps plus an interesting text, this book supplies a fascinating introduction to caves and their exploration. (Rev: BCCB 7–8/95; BL 4/15/95; SLJ 7/95) [557.4]

**16185** Lavies, Bianca. *Mangrove Wilderness: Nature's Nursery* (4–6). Illus. 1994, Dutton paper $15.99 (0-525-45186-2). 32pp. The ecology of a mangrove swamp on the southwest coast of Florida is described with striking photographs. (Rev: BL 6/1–15/94; SLJ 6/94*) [583]

**16186** Lepthien, Emilie U. *Wetlands* (1–3). Illus. Series: New True Books. 1993, Children's LB $21.00 (0-516-01334-3). 48pp. The ecology of wetlands is covered with material on plant and animal life found there. (Rev: BL 8/93) [333.9]

**16187** Liptak, Karen. *Saving Our Wetlands and Their Wildlife* (4–7). Illus. Series: First Books. 1991, Watts LB $21.00 (0-531-20092-2); paper $6.95 (0-531-15648-6). 64pp. A description of the unique ecosystems in swamps, bogs, and other areas that support plant and animal life flourishing nowhere else. (Rev: BL 1/1/92; SLJ 1/92) [333.91]

**16188** Luenn, Nancy. *Squish! A Wetland Walk* (PS–2). Illus. by Ronald Himler. 1994, Atheneum $16.00 (0-689-31842-1). 32pp. A boy's walk in a wetland is used to introduce the plants and animals found there. (Rev: BL 11/1/94; SLJ 11/94) [574.5]

**16189** Lye, Keith. *Coasts* (4–7). Illus. 1989, Silver Burdett LB $12.95 (0-382-09790-4). 48pp. The effects and explanation of receding and advancing coastlines. (Rev: BL 5/1/89)

**16190** McCormick, Anita Louise. *Vanishing Wetlands* (5–8). Illus. Series: Overview Series. 1995, Lucent LB $22.45 (1-56006-162-6). 112pp. A general history of wetlands and their ecology is given, plus coverage on present-day policies and controversies. (Rev: BL 6/1–15/95) [574.5]

**16191** Maynard, Caitlin, and Thane Maynard. *Rain Forests and Reefs: A Kid's-Eye View of the Tropics* (4–8). Illus. 1996, Watts LB $23.60 (0-531-11281-0). 64pp. The flora and fauna of rain forests and coral reefs in Belize are described in text and stunning photos. (Rev: BL 2/15/97; SLJ 3/97*) [574.5]

**16192** Perenyi, Constance. *Wild Wild West: Wildlife Habitats of Western North America* (K–3). Illus. 1993, Sasquatch $14.95 (0-912365-82-X); paper $8.95 (0-912365-90-0). 32pp. Ten geographical areas, including the Arctic tundra, Rocky Mountains, Sonoran Desert, and a coral reef, are described and pictured in colorful collages. (Rev: BL 12/15/93; SLJ 12/93) [508.78]

**16193** Podendorf, Illa. *Jungles* (1–4). Illus. 1982, Children's LB $21.00 (0-516-01631-8). The flora and fauna in jungles described simply in this introductory volume.

**16194** Ricciuti, Edward R. *Chaparral* (5–7). Illus. Series: Biomes of the World. 1996, Benchmark LB $25.64 (0-7614-0137-7). 64pp. The climate, vegetation, and life cycles are described in the chaparral, the biome situated between desert and grassland or forest and grassland, as in western North America from Oregon to Baja California. (Rev: SLJ 7/96) [574.5]

**16195** Robbins, Ken. *Fire: The Elements* (2–5). Illus. 1996, Holt $16.95 (0-8050-2293-7). 48pp. Various forms of fire, including electricity, are covered, with photographs. (Rev: BL 5/1/96; SLJ 6/96) [541.3]

**16196** Sauvain, Philip. *Rivers and Valleys* (4–7). Illus. Series: Geography Detective. 1996, Carolrhoda $14.95 (0-87614-996-4). 32pp. In 2-page spreads, rivers and valleys are introduced, with material on geology, flood control, wildlife, and tourism. (Rev: SLJ 3/97) [551.48]

**16197** Sayre, April Pulley. *Wetland* (4–7). Illus. Series: Exploring Earth's Biomes. 1996, Twenty-First Century LB $20.40 (0-8050-4086-2). 80pp. The nature of wetlands and the life they support are covered in text and many illustrations. (Rev: BL 6/1–15/96; SLJ 6/96) [574.5]

**16198** Schultz, Ron. *Looking Inside Caves and Caverns* (4–8). Illus. by Nick Gadbois and Peter Aschwanden. Series: X-Ray Vision. 1993, John Muir paper $6.95 (1-56261-126-7). 46pp. This introduction to caves describes their formation, characteristics, the life found inside them, their preservation, and the sport of spelunking. (Rev: SLJ 2/94) [551.4]

**16199** Silver, Donald M. *One Small Square: Cave* (3–5). Illus. 1994, W. H. Freeman $12.00 (0-7167-6514-4). 48pp. This science book explains caves and cave life with a number of activities and experiments. (Rev: BL 8/94) [796.5]

**16200** Staub, Frank. *America's Wetlands* (4–6). Illus. 1995, Carolrhoda LB $19.93 (0-87614-827-5). 48pp. The ecology of wetlands is described, with emphasis on their importance for the survival of wildlife. (Rev: BL 4/1/95; SLJ 5/95) [574.5]

**16201** Steele, Philip. *Islands* (3–5). Illus. Series: Geography Detective. 1996, Carolrhoda LB $19.93 (0-87614-997-2). 32pp. Double-page spreads introduce islands, their composition, and how they have been changed by humankind. (Rev: BL 9/1/96; SLJ 9/96) [551.4]

**16202** Wood, Jenny. *Waterfalls: Nature's Thundering Splendor* (3–5). Illus. Series: Wonderworks of Nature. 1991, Stevens LB $21.27 (0-8368-0633-6). 32pp. Such waterfalls as Niagara, Sutherland, and Victoria are described with information also on rapids, cascades, and hydroelectric power. (Rev: SLJ 9/92) [551.48]

**16203** Young, Allen M. *Lives Intertwined: Relationships Between Plants and Animals* (4–6). Illus. Series: A First Book: Biology. 1996, Watts LB $21.00 (0-531-20251-8). 63pp. Using the Central American rain forest as a lab, this account explores the complex relationships and interdependence of its plant and animal life. (Rev: SLJ 4/97) [574.5]

## Deserts

**16204** Arnold, Caroline. *Watching Desert Wildlife* (3–6). Photos by Arthur Arnold. 1994, Carolrhoda LB $14.95 (0-87614-841-0). 48pp. The desert environment is first explained, and then its wildlife is introduced in text and excellent photographs. (Rev: BL 12/1/94; SLJ 1/95) [574.5]

**16205** George, Jean Craighead. *One Day in the Desert* (3–6). Illus. by Fred Brenner. 1983, HarperCollins LB $14.89 (0-690-04341-4). 48pp. A day in the desert with both record heat and torrential rain.

**16206** Hirschi, Ron. *Desert* (K–3). Illus. by Barbara Bash. 1992, Bantam $13.00 (0-553-08012-1); paper $4.99 (0-553-35497-3). 32pp. This is an introduction to animals that live in the desert, with clues so that young readers can guess the animal's identity. (Rev: BL 12/15/92) [591]

**16207** Jenkins, Martin. *Deserts* (3–6). Illus. Series: Endangered People and Places. 1996, Lerner LB $22.60 (0-8225-2775-8). 48pp. In this account that combines geography and sociology, deserts and the survival of their inhabitants are described. (Rev: BL 11/15/96; SLJ 11/96) [333.73]

**16208** Jernigan, Gisela. *Sonoran Seasons: A Year in the Desert* (3–6). Illus. by E. Wesley Jernigan. 1994, Harbinger paper $10.95 (0-943173-91-4). For every month of the year, a different plant from the Sonoran Desert is introduced, most of them edible. (Rev: SLJ 6/94) [581.5]

**16209** Landau, Elaine. *Desert Mammals* (1–3). Illus. Series: A True Book. 1996, Children's LB $21.00 (0-516-20038-0). 48pp. After brief coverage on what and where deserts are, this account describes some indigenous mammals, like camels, kangaroo rats, antelope jack rabbits, and addaxes. (Rev: SLJ 3/97) [591]

**16210** Lesser, Carolyn. *Storm on the Desert* (K–3). Illus. by Ted Rand. 1997, Harcourt $15.00 (0-15-272198-3). 40pp. Pictures and text depict what happens in a desert before, during, and after a violent storm. (Rev: BL 5/1/97; SLJ 5/97) [574.5]

**16211** Low, Robert. *Peoples of the Desert* (2–5). Illus. Series: People and Their Environments. 1996, Rosen LB $13.95 (0-8239-2296-0). 24pp. Two nomadic tribes, one from the Sahara and the other from the Kalahari, are featured in this discussion of human life in a desert environment. (Rev: BL 10/15/96; SLJ 1/97) [966]

**16212** Lye, Keith. *Deserts* (4–6). Illus. 1987, Silver Burdett LB $12.95 (0-382-09501-4). 48pp. A well-illustrated survey that describes the locations, climate, evolution of, and plant and animal life in the world's deserts. (Rev: BL 2/1/88)

**16213** McLeish, Ewan. *The Spread of Deserts* (3–6). Illus. Series: Conserving Our World. 1990, Raintree Steck-Vaughn LB $24.26 (0-8114-2390-5). 48pp. This slightly oversized book explains how deserts are formed, where the principal ones are found, and how to prevent their spread. (Rev: BL 3/1/91) [910.02]

**16214** MacQuitty, Miranda. *Desert* (4–8). Series: Eyewitness Books. 1994, Knopf LB $20.99 (0-679-96003-1). 63pp. Describes the environment and wildlife found in several deserts, mainly in North Africa and the Middle East. (Rev: BL 10/15/94; SLJ 8/94) [574.5]

**16215** Posell, Elsa. *Deserts* (1–4). Illus. 1982, Children's LB $21.00 (0-516-01613-X); paper $5.50 (0-516-41613-8). 48pp. Straightforward, simple text and fine color photographs are highlights of this book.

**16216** Ricciuti, Edward R. *Desert* (4–6). Illus. Series: Biomes of the World. 1996, Benchmark LB $25.64 (0-7614-0134-2). 64pp. Deserts of the world are identified and described, with coverage on their plant and animal life. (Rev: SLJ 7/96) [574.9]

**16217** Sabin, Louis. *Wonders of the Desert* (1–3). Illus. by Pamela Baldwin Ford. 1982, Troll LB $12.95 (0-89375-574-5); paper $3.50 (0-89375-575-3). 32pp. A fine array of desert flora and fauna is simply introduced.

**16218** Savage, Stephen. *Animals of the Desert* (3–6). Illus. Series: Animals by Habitat. 1997, Raintree Steck-Vaughn LB $22.83 (0-8172-4750-5). 32pp. After a discussion of the world's deserts and how they differ, this book introduces 5 basic animals groups found in deserts, like mammals, birds, and reptiles. (Rev: BL 5/15/97; SLJ 8/97) [591.5]

**16219** Sayre, April Pulley. *Desert* (4–7). Illus. Series: Exploring Earth's Biomes. 1994, Twenty-First Century LB $18.90 (0-8050-2825-0). 64pp. After a general introduction to deserts, a specific one is explored in brief chapters with excellent illustrations. (Rev: BL 1/1/95*; SLJ 1/95) [574.5]

**16220** Silver, Donald M. *Cactus Desert* (3–5). Illus. Series: One Small Square. 1995, Scientific American $12.00 (0-7167-6573-X). 48pp. Using a 24-inch square for observation, the life found in a desert is explored in this heavily illustrated account. (Rev: BL 9/15/95) [574.5]

**16221** Simon, Seymour. *Deserts* (2–5). Illus. 1990, Morrow LB $15.93 (0-688-07416-2). 32pp. The focus is mainly on North American deserts. (Rev: BL 10/15/90; HB 1–2/91; SLJ 12/90) [551.4]

**16222** Spencer, Guy J. *A Living Desert* (3–5). Illus. 1988, Troll LB $11.50 (0-8167-1169-0); paper $3.95 (0-8167-1170-4). 32pp. An adventure in Arizona's Sonoran Desert. (Rev: BL 8/88)

**16223** Steele, Philip. *Deserts* (4–6). Illus. Series: Geography Detective. 1996, Carolrhoda LB $19.93 (0-87614-998-0). 32pp. This introduction to deserts and the life found in them discusses such topics as the differences between hot and cold deserts, their landscape features, and how they are still being created. (Rev: SLJ 9/96) [574.5]

**16224** Stewart, Gail B. *In the Desert* (4–6). Illus. Series: Living Spaces. 1989, Rourke LB $21.27 (0-86592-106-7). 32pp. The hardships faced by people who live in a desert environment. Two other landscapes explored are: *In the Mountains* (1980) and *On the Water* (1989). (Rev: BL 11/1/89) [304.2]

**16225** Taylor, Barbara. *Desert Life* (3–6). Illus. by Frank Greenaway. Series: Look Closer. 1992, DK Publg. $9.95 (1-879431-93-9). 32pp. Clear photos highlight the inhabitants of the desert. (Rev: BL 6/1/92; HB 7–8/92; SLJ 6/92) [574.909]

**16226** Twist, Clint. *Deserts* (5–8). Illus. Series: Ecology Watch. 1991, Macmillan LB $13.95 (0-87518-490-1). 45pp. An informative, attractive survey of the specific problems related to the world's deserts, their plants, and animals. (Rev: BL 3/1/92; SLJ 4/92) [574.5]

**16227** Wallace, Marianne D. *America's Deserts: Guide to Plants and Animals* (3–5). Illus. 1996, Fulcrum paper $15.95 (1-55591-268-0). 48pp. After a general discussion of the flora and fauna of deserts, this account focuses on specific deserts, like Mojave and Death Valley. (Rev: BL 4/1/96; SLJ 7/96) [574.973]

**16228** Wright-Frierson, Virginia. *A Desert Scrapbook: Dawn to Dusk in the Sonoran Desert* (3–5). Illus. 1996, Simon & Schuster $16.00 (0-689-80678-7). 32pp. A day in the life of the Sonoran Desert is described in words and watercolors painted by the author. (Rev: BL 8/96; SLJ 6/96*) [574]

**16229** Yolen, Jane. *Welcome to the Sea of Sand* (K–3). Illus. by Laura Regan. 1996, Putnam $15.95 (0-399-22765-2). 32pp. A depiction in text and paintings of the amazing creatures found in a seemingly lifeless desert. (Rev: BL 4/15/96; SLJ 5/96*) [508]

## Forests and Rain Forests

**16230** Aldis, Rodney. *Rainforests* (5–8). Illus. Series: Ecology Watch. 1991, Macmillan LB $13.95 (0-87518-495-2). 45pp. In an attractive, oversized format, this book discusses how the rain forest evolved, why it is threatened, and the plants and animals specific to it. (Rev: BL 3/1/92; SLJ 4/92) [574.5]

**16231** Anderson, Robert. *Forests: Identifying Propaganda Techniques* (5–7). Illus. Series: Opposing Viewpoints Juniors. 1992, Greenhaven LB $16.20 (0-89908-099-5). 36pp. This book examines such issues as acid rain and saving the rain forests from various viewpoints. (Rev: BL 1/15/93) [574.5]

**16232** Bellamy, David. *The Forest* (2–4). Illus. 1988, Crown $12.00 (0-517-56800-4). 24pp. The forest environment rendered in watercolors. (Rev: BCCB 7–8/88; BL 8/88; SLJ 10/88)

**16233** Challand, Helen J. *Vanishing Forests* (5–8). Illus. 1991, Children's LB $30.50 (0-516-05505-4). 128pp. This account shows the value of forests and what will happen if we continue to destroy them. (Rev: SLJ 3/92) [574.5]

**16234** Crump, Donald J., ed. *Explore a Tropical Forest* (K–3). Illus. by Barbara Gibson. Series: National Geographic Action Books. 1989, National Geographic $16.00 (0-87044-757-2). Pop-ups and flaps are used to give a 3-dimensional look at a tropical rain forest and its flora and fauna. (Rev: SLJ 3/90) [574.5]

**16235** Darling, Kathy. *Rain Forest Babies* (K–3). Illus. by Tara Darling. 1996, Walker LB $16.85 (0-8027-8412-7). 32pp. All kinds of baby animals found in the rain forest are introduced in text and full-page color photographs. (Rev: BL 4/15/96; SLJ 4/96) [591]

**16236** Dorros, Arthur. *Rain Forest Secrets* (3–5). Illus. 1990, Scholastic $15.95 (0-590-43369-5). 32pp. A picture-book introduction to rain forests. (Rev: BCCB 9/90; BL 9/1/90; SLJ 2/91) [574.5]

**16237** Forsyth, Adrian. *How Monkeys Make Chocolate: Foods and Medicines from the Rainforests* (5–8). Illus. 1995, Firefly $16.95 (1-895688-45-0); paper $9.95 (1-895688-32-9). 48pp. An account of the interdependence of plants, animals, and humans in the world's rain forests. (Rev: BL 12/1/95; SLJ 1/96) [581.6]

**16238** Forsyth, Adrian. *Journey Through a Tropical Jungle* (4–8). Illus. 1996, Firefly paper $2.99 (0-920-77526-8). 80pp. A trek through the rain forest in Costa Rica. (Rev: BCCB 4/89; BL 6/1/89; SLJ 5/89)

**16239** George, Jean Craighead. *One Day in the Tropical Rain Forest* (3–6). Illus. by Gary Allen. 1990, HarperCollins $14.95 (0-690-04767-3). 64pp. The tropical rain forest is introduced in a narrative that proceeds through the course of a day. (Rev: BCCB 3/90; BL 4/15/90; HB 5–6/90; SLJ 8/90) [508]

**16240** George, Jean Craighead. *One Day in the Woods* (3–5). Illus. by Gary Allen. 1988, HarperCollins LB $14.89 (0-690-04724-X). 48pp. Following Rebecca's search in the forest for an oven-bird. (Rev: BL 12/15/88; SLJ 2/89)

**16241** Gibbons, Gail. *Nature's Green Umbrella: Tropical Rain Forests* (3–5). Illus. 1994, Morrow LB $15.93 (0-688-12354-6). 32pp. The ecosystem of the rain forest is explained, with material on how these resources should be protected and preserved. (Rev: BL 6/1–15/94; SLJ 7/94) [574.5]

**16242** Gilliland, Judith Heide. *River* (K–3). Illus. by Joyce Powzyk. 1993, Clarion $14.95 (0-395-55963-4). 32pp. Beautiful paintings are used to help introduce the Amazon River and its amazing rain forest. (Rev: BL 11/1/93; SLJ 12/93) [508.81]

**16243** Goodman, Billy. *The Rain Forests* (4–7). Illus. Series: Planet Earth. 1992, Little, Brown $17.95 (0-316-32019-6). 96pp. The rain forests of the world are described in photos and slight text. (Rev: BL 2/15/92; SLJ 5/92) [574.5]

**16244** Goodman, Susan E. *Bats, Bugs, and Biodiversity: Adventures in the Amazonian Rain Forest* (4–6). Illus. by Michael J. Doolittle. 1995, Simon & Schuster $16.00 (0-689-31943-6). 46pp. Some junior high students learn first-hand about the Amazon rain forest and its endangered ecology. (Rev: BCCB 10/95; BL 8/95; SLJ 7/95*) [508]

**16245** Greene, Carol. *Caring for Our Forests* (1–3). Illus. Series: Caring for Our Earth. 1991, Enslow LB $13.95 (0-89490-353-5). 32pp. This book explains what happens when forests are destroyed and suggests ways young people can help preserve them. (Rev: BL 2/15/92; SLJ 5/92) [574.5]

**16246** Grupper, Jonathan. *Destination: Rain Forest* (4–6). Illus. 1997, National Geographic $16.00 (0-7922-7018-5). 32pp. Using brilliant photos, this book introduces the rain forest as a habitat, as well as the animals found there. (Rev: BL 11/1/97; SLJ 10/97) [578.734]

**16247** Jenike, David, and Mark Jenike. *A Walk Through a Rain Forest: Life in the Ituri Forest of Zaire* (4–7). Illus. 1995, Watts LB $23.60 (0-531-11168-7); paper $9.95 (0-531-15721-0). 64pp. Well-captioned photos highlight the plant and animal life found in this African rain forest. (Rev: BL 4/15/95; SLJ 6/95) [574.5]

**16248** Kaplan, Elizabeth. *Taiga* (5–7). Illus. Series: Biomes of the World. 1996, Benchmark LB $25.64

(0-7614-0135-0). 64pp. This account discusses the climate, animal and plant life, soil, and seasonal changes in the taiga, the extensive forest in the Northern Hemisphere. (Rev: SLJ 7/96) [574.5]

**16249** Kaplan, Elizabeth. *Temperate Forest* (4–6). Illus. Series: Biomes of the World. 1995, Marshall Cavendish LB $25.64 (0-7614-0082-6). 64pp. Four types of temperate forests are introduced, with material on locations, animals, plants, and possible future problems. (Rev: BL 12/15/95; SLJ 3/96) [574.5]

**16250** Klum, Mattias, and Hans Odoo. *Exploring the Rain Forest* (2–5). Illus. 1998, Sterling $14.95 (0-8069-9873-3). 64pp. A chatty, informal guide to the rain forest, with excellent photos and captions. (Rev: BL 3/1/98; SLJ 2/98) [578.734]

**16251** Knapp, Brian. *What Do We Know About Rainforests?* (4–6). Illus. Series: Caring for Environments. 1992, Bedrick LB $15.95 (0-87226-358-4). 40pp. A colorful book that surveys the location, terrain, ecology, and importance of rain forests. (Rev: BL 2/15/93; SLJ 1/93) [574]

**16252** Lampton, Christopher. *Forest Fire* (4–6). Illus. Series: Disaster! 1974, Millbrook paper $5.95 (1-56294-779-6). 64pp. High interest and low reading level mark this colorful description, especially valuable for scientific insights on causes and results of forests fires. (Rev: BL 1/1/92; SLJ 12/91) [634.9]

**16253** Landau, Elaine. *Temperate Forest Mammals* (3–4). Illus. Series: A True Book: Animals. 1996, Children's LB $21.00 (0-516-20043-7). 48pp. General information on forests found in temperate climates is followed by material of specific mammals. (Rev: SLJ 4/97) [591]

**16254** Lasky, Kathryn. *The Most Beautiful Roof in the World: Exploring the Rainforest Canopy* (3–5). Illus. 1997, Harcourt $18.00 (0-15-100893-4). The canopy of plants and animals found in the rain forest of Belize is explored by the author, a biologist, and her assistant. (Rev: BL 4/1/97*; HB 5–6/97) [574.5]

**16255** Lepthien, Emilie U. *Tropical Rain Forests* (2–4). Illus. Series: New True Book. 1993, Children's LB $21.00 (0-516-01198-7). 48pp. The nature of tropical rain forests is covered, with material on the animals, plants, and people that live there. (Rev: BL 7/94) [574.5]

**16256** Lewington, Anna. *Antonio's Rain Forest* (3–5). Illus. by Edward Parker. 1993, Carolrhoda LB $22.60 (0-87614-749-X). 48pp. A first-person narrative by an 8-year-old boy of the rain forest. (Rev: BL 3/1/93; SLJ 3/93) [338]

**16257** Low, Robert. *Peoples of the Rain Forest* (2–5). Illus. Series: People and Their Environments. 1996, Rosen LB $13.95 (0-8239-2297-9). 24pp. Human life-styles in a rain forest environment are introduced, with examples from peoples in Africa, South America, and Borneo. (Rev: BL 10/15/96; SLJ 11/96) [304.2]

**16258** Mania, Robert, and Cathy Mania. *A Forest's Life: From Meadow to Mature Woodland* (4–6). Illus. Series: First Book. 1997, Watts LB $22.00 (0-531-20319-0). 64pp. Traces the gradual transformation of a meadow into a forest and of the plants and animals involved. (Rev: BL 12/15/97; SLJ 10/97) [577.3]

**16259** Mutel, Cornelia F., and Mary M. Rodgers. *Our Endangered Planet: Tropical Rain Forests* (4–7). Illus. Series: Our Endangered Planet. 1991, Lerner LB $16.95 (0-8225-2503-8); paper $8.95 (0-8225-9629-6). 64pp. Describes tropical rain forests and the environmental dangers they face. (Rev: BL 6/15/91; SLJ 5/91) [333]

**16260** Oldfield, Sara. *Rain Forests* (3–6). Illus. Series: Endangered People and Places. 1996, Lerner LB $22.60 (0-8225-2778-2). 48pp. The location, geography, and natural life of rain forests are described, plus material on the threats to these regions and how conservation efforts are proceeding. (Rev: BL 11/15/96; SLJ 1/97) [333.75]

**16261** Ricciuti, Edward R. *Rainforest* (4–6). Illus. Series: Biomes of the World. 1995, Marshall Cavendish LB $25.64 (0-7614-0081-8). 64pp. The world's rainforest biome is described, with material on this ecological system, its animals, plants, and current threats of destruction. (Rev: BL 12/15/95) [574.5]

**16262** Ross, Suzanne. *What's in the Rainforest?* (3–5). Illus. by author. 1991, Enchanted Rainforest Pr. paper $5.95 (0-9629895-0-9). 48pp. Using an alphabetical approach, this is a well-organized introduction to the plants and animals found in a rain forest. (Rev: SLJ 3/92) [574.5]

**16263** Rowland-Entwistle, Theodore. *Jungles and Rainforests* (4–6). Illus. 1987, Silver Burdett LB $16.98 (0-382-09500-6). 48pp. Kinds and locations of jungles and rain forests are discussed along with the bad effects of increased farming and timber cutting. (Rev: BL 2/1/88)

**16264** Sabin, Francene. *Wonders of the Forest* (1–3). Illus. by Michael Willard. 1982, Troll LB $12.95 (0-89375-572-9); paper $2.95 (0-89375-573-7). 32pp. An introduction to the trees of the forest in text and pictures. Also use: *Wonders of the Pond* (1982).

**16265** Sauvain, Philip. *Rain Forests* (3–5). Illus. Series: Geography Detectives. 1997, Carolrhoda LB $14.95 (1-57505-041-2). 32pp. Identifies and describes the world's rain forests and the lush plants and diverse peoples and animals that live in them, with information on the many industrial threats to rain forests' survival. (Rev: BL 8/97) [574.5]

**16266** Savage, Stephen. *Animals of the Rain Forest* (3–6). Illus. Series: Animals by Habitat. 1997, Raintree Steck-Vaughn LB $22.83 (0-8172-4751-3).

32pp. The rain forest habitat is introduced, with focus on the 5 categories of animal life found there, such as mammals, birds, and amphibians. (Rev: BL 5/15/97) [591.9]

**16267** Sayre, April Pulley. *Taiga* (4–7). Illus. Series: Exploring Earth's Biomes. 1994, Twenty-First Century LB $18.90 (0-8050-2830-7). 64pp. This book clearly describes the swampy, carnivorous forest and the wildlife found, for example, in northern Canada, where the tundra ends. (Rev: BL 1/15/95; SLJ 2/95) [574.5]

**16268** Sayre, April Pulley. *Temperate Deciduous Forest* (4–7). Illus. Series: Exploring Earth's Biomes. 1994, Twenty-First Century LB $18.90 (0-8050-2828-5). 64pp. Deciduous forests are introduced with material on their composition, uses, and the animal and other plant life found within their community. (Rev: BL 1/1/95*; SLJ 1/95) [574.5]

**16269** Sayre, April Pulley. *Tropical Rain Forest* (4–7). Illus. Series: Exploring Earth's Biomes. 1994, Twenty-First Century LB $15.95 (0-8050-2826-9). 64pp. The structure and contents of rain forests are explored with information on the plants, animals, and people that exist in this habitat. (Rev: BL 1/1/95; SLJ 1/95) [574.5]

**16270** Silver, Donald M. *Why Save the Rain Forest?* (3–5). Illus. by Patricia J. Wynne. 1993, Messner LB $12.98 (0-671-86609-5); paper $6.95 (0-671-86610-9). 48pp. A handsome volume that shows the amazing diversity of life in a rain forest and the consequences of destroying this environment. (Rev: SLJ 3/94) [574.5]

**16271** Spencer, Guy J. *An Ancient Forest* (3–5). Illus. 1988, Troll LB $11.50 (0-8167-1167-4). 32pp. Venturing into the Redwood Forest. (Rev: BL 8/88; SLJ 11/88)

**16272** Taylor, Barbara. *Forest Life* (3–6). Illus. by Kim Taylor and Jane Burton. Series: Look Closer. 1993, DK Publg. $9.95 (1-56458-210-8). 32pp. Plants and animals that live in the forest are covered. (Rev: BL 8/93; SLJ 8/93) [574]

**16273** Taylor, Barbara. *Rain Forest* (3–6). Illus. Series: Look Closer. 1992, DK Publg. $9.95 (1-879431-91-2). 32pp. The flora and fauna of rain forests are covered in a series of double-page spreads with informative captions. (Rev: BL 6/1/92; HB 7–8/92; SLJ 6/92) [591.909]

**16274** Thomson, Ruth. *The Rainforest Indians* (K–2). Illus. Series: Footsteps in Time. 1996, Children's LB $17.00 (0-516-08074-1). 24pp. Humorous rhymes accompany paintings that describe 8 animals from the rain forest. (Rev: SLJ 11/96) [591]

## Mountains

**16275** Cobb, Vicki. *This Place Is High* (3–5). Illus. by Barbara Lavallee. Series: Imagine Living Here. 1989, Walker LB $13.85 (0-8027-6883-0). Set in the high Andes, this is a book on an unusual climate zone in South America. A companion volume is *This Place Is Wet* (1989), about the rain forest of the Amazon River. (Rev: SLJ 10/89) [551.4]

**16276** Collinson, Alan. *Mountains* (5–8). Illus. Series: Ecology Watch. 1992, Macmillan LB $13.95 (0-87518-493-6). 46pp. The flora and fauna of mountainous regions are discussed as well as the need for ecological preservation. (Rev: BL 11/1/92) [574]

**16277** Cumming, David. *Mountains* (5–8). Illus. Series: Habitats. 1995, Thomson Learning LB $24.26 (1-56847-388-5). 48pp. Material covered includes the geology of mountains, their formation, and the life they support. (Rev: BL 2/1/96) [551.4]

**16278** Hirschi, Ron. *Mountain* (K–3). Illus. by Barbara Bash. 1992, Bantam $13.00 (0-553-07998-0). 32pp. An introduction to animals that live in mountain regions. (Rev: BL 12/15/92) [599]

**16279** Landau, Elaine. *Mountain Mammals* (3–4). Illus. Series: A True Book: Animals. 1996, Children's LB $21.00 (0-516-20040-2). 48pp. General information on mountain environments is presented, and several typical mammals found in this biome are introduced. (Rev: SLJ 4/97) [591]

**16280** Low, Robert. *Peoples of the Mountains* (2–4). Illus. Series: Peoples and Their Environments. 1996, Rosen/Power Kids Pr. LB $15.93 (0-8239-2298-7). 24pp. After a definition of a mountain environment, this book tells about people who live in the Himalayas, Andes, and the mountains of China. (Rev: SLJ 1/97) [551.4]

**16281** Lye, Keith. *Mountains* (4–6). Illus. 1987, Silver Burdett LB $12.95 (0-382-09498-0). 48pp. Full-color photos, maps, and diagrams highlight this survey of the world's mountains. (Rev: BL 2/1/88)

**16282** Rotter, Charles. *Mountains* (5–8). Illus. Series: Images. 1994, Creative Ed. LB $16.95 (0-88682-596-2). 40pp. How mountains are formed is discussed, with material on how they change and the life they support. (Rev: SLJ 12/94) [551.4]

**16283** Simon, Seymour. *Mountains* (2–4). Illus. 1994, Morrow LB $14.93 (0-688-11041-X). 40pp. The various kinds of mountains are introduced, with material on how they were formed and beautiful photos. (Rev: BCCB 4/94; BL 3/1/94; SLJ 6/94) [551.4]

**16284** Steele, Philip. *Mountains* (4–8). Illus. Series: Pocket Facts. 1991, Macmillan LB $11.95 (0-89686-587-8). 32pp. A basic introduction to mountains, aided by color photos and drawings. (Rev: BL 3/15/92) [910]

**16285** Stone, Lynn M. *Mountains* (1–4). Illus. 1983, Children's LB $21.00 (0-516-01698-9). 48pp. Mountain ecology is introduced in basic terms with excellent photographs.

**16286** Stronach, Neil. *Mountains* (3–6). Illus. Series: Endangered People and Places. 1996, Lerner LB $22.60 (0-8225-2777-4). 48pp. Geological aspects of mountains are covered, as well as the adjustments people make to live in mountainous regions. (Rev: BL 11/15/96; SLJ 11/96) [333.73]

## Ponds, Rivers, and Lakes

**16287** Amos, William Hopkins. *Life in Ponds and Streams* (PS–3). Illus. 1981, National Geographic LB $16.95 (0-87044-404-2). 32pp. Simple descriptions of pond life, plus outstanding photographs.

**16288** Bains, Rae. *Wonders of Rivers* (1–3). Illus. by Yoshi Miyake. 1982, Troll LB $12.95 (0-89375-570-2); paper $2.95 (0-89375-571-0). 32pp. An explanation of what rivers are and their role in our world.

**16289** Bellamy, David. *The Rock Pool* (2–5). Illus. by Jill Dow. 1988, Crown $9.95 (0-517-56977-9). 32pp. A close look at crabs, starfish, and other creatures at the rock pond. (Rev: BL 1/1/89; SLJ 12/88)

**16290** Cumming, David. *Rivers and Lakes* (5–8). Illus. Series: Habitats. 1995, Thomson Learning LB $24.26 (1-56847-389-3). 48pp. The plant and animal life that is supported in lakes and rivers is introduced, with information on geology and pollution. (Rev: BL 2/1/96) [551.48]

**16291** Ganeri, Anita. *Ponds and Pond Life* (3–6). Illus. by Jamie Medlin. Series: Nature Detective. 1993, Watts LB $19.30 (0-531-14226-4). 32pp. Describes the different types of ponds and their environments plus information on the flora and fauna found in and around them. (Rev: BL 12/15/93) [574]

**16292** Ganeri, Anita. *Rivers, Ponds and Lakes* (5–8). Illus. Series: Ecology Watch. 1992, Macmillan LB $13.95 (0-87518-497-9). 46pp. The nature of pollution and the need for environmental protection are stressed in this introduction to water resources. (Rev: BL 11/1/92) [574]

**16293** Guiberson, Brenda Z. *Spoonbill Swamp* (1–3). Illus. by Megan Lloyd. 1995, Holt $14.95 (0-8050-1583-3); paper $4.95 (0-8050-3385-8). 32pp. This story depicts a day in the lives of a mother spoonbill and a mother alligator in a southern swamp. (Rev: BL 3/15/92; SLJ 3/92) [591.5]

**16294** Haslam, Andrew. *Rivers* (3–6). Illus. Series: Make It Work! 1996, World Book $11.95 (0-7166-1751-X); paper $6.95 (0-7166-1752-8). 48pp. Vari-

ous aspects of the study of rivers are covered, with such related activities as making a model dam and a waterwheel. (Rev: BL 11/15/96) [551]

**16295** Hiscock, Bruce. *The Big Rivers: The Missouri, the Mississippi, and the Ohio* (3–5). Illus. 1997, Simon & Schuster $16.00 (0-689-80871-2). 32pp. As well as examining these 3 rivers, this book gives details on the causes and effects of flooding, with special material on the 1993 floods. (Rev: BL 6/1–15/97; SLJ 7/97) [551.48]

**16296** Hoff, Mary, and Mary M. Rodgers. *Our Endangered Planet: Rivers and Lakes* (4–7). Illus. Series: Our Endangered Planet. 1991, Lerner LB $16.95 (0-8225-2501-1). 64pp. The causes and possible cures of water pollution are examined. (Rev: BL 6/15/91; SLJ 5/91) [363.73]

**16297** Kirkpatrick, Rena K. *Look at Pond Life* (K–2). Illus. 1978, Raintree Steck-Vaughn paper $4.95 (0-8114-6901-8). 32pp. An introduction to the subject through brief text and many illustrations.

**16298** Parker, Steve. *Pond and River* (4–8). Illus. 1988, Knopf LB $20.99 (0-394-99615-1). 64pp. Freshwater fish, mammals, and waterfowl, plus habitats of plants and animals. (Rev: BL 12/1/88)

**16299** *The River* (PS–3). Illus. Series: First Discovery Book. 1993, Scholastic $11.95 (0-590-47128-7). 24pp. Using drawings, overlays, and a concise text, this book for small children describes a river and the life it supports. (Rev: BL 1/1/94) [574.5]

**16300** Rowland-Entwistle, Theodore. *Rivers and Lakes* (4–6). Illus. 1987, Silver Burdett LB $12.95 (0-382-09499-9). 48pp. A fact-filled book that emphasizes the need for conservation and care of these important physical features. (Rev: BL 2/1/88)

**16301** Sayre, April Pulley. *Lake and Pond* (4–7). Illus. Series: Exploring Earth's Biomes. 1996, Twenty-First Century LB $20.40 (0-8050-4089-7). 80pp. Colorful introduction to lake and pond habitats and the life forms found within them. (Rev: BL 6/1–15/96; SLJ 6/96) [574.05]

**16302** Sayre, April Pulley. *River and Stream* (4–7). Illus. Series: Exploring Earth's Biomes. 1996, Twenty-First Century LB $20.40 (0-8050-4088-9). 80pp. In a clearly written, informative style, this book presents material on rivers and streams, their ecology, and the various creatures and plants living in and around them. (Rev: BL 6/1–15/96; SLJ 6/96) [574.5]

**16303** Schwartz, David M. *The Hidden Life of the Pond* (3–5). Illus. 1988, Crown LB $15.00 (0-517-57060-2). 40pp. Animals and plants change and grow in the pond. (Rev: BL 12/15/88; HB 1–2/89; SLJ 2/89)

**16304** Silver, Donald M. *Pond: One Small Square* (3–5). Illus. Series: From the One Small Square. 1995, W. H. Freeman $12.00 (0-7167-6518-7). 48pp.

Using a 24-inch square for observation, the reader is introduced to the plants and animals found in and around a pond. (Rev: BL 3/1/95) [574.5]

**16305** Stone, Lynn M. *Marshes and Swamps* (1–4). Illus. 1983, Children's LB $20.00 (0-516-01681-4). 48pp. The characteristics of these wetlands and their flora and fauna are introduced to the young reader.

**16306** Taylor, Barbara. *Pond Life* (3–6). Illus. Series: Look Closer. 1992, DK Publg. $9.95 (1-879431-94-7). 32pp. Clear photos and basic information highlight life in the pond. (Rev: BL 6/1/92; HB 7–8/92; SLJ 6/92) [591.92]

**16307** Yates, Irene. *From Birth to Death* (1–5). Illus. Series: Life Cycle. 1997, Millbrook LB $21.40 (0-7613-0303-0). 32pp. In double-page spreads, this book gives details on a year of seasonal changes around a pond, with coverage on the interrelationships between plants and animals. (Rev: BL 12/1/97; SLJ 1/98) [571.8]

## Prairies and Grasslands

**16308** Bannatyne-Cugnet, Jo. *A Prairie Year* (3–5). Illus. by Yvette Moore. 1994, Tundra $16.95 (0-88776-334-0). 32pp. A month-by-month account of the experiences and activities involved in prairie life. (Rev: BL 1/15/95; SLJ 2/95) [630]

**16309** Collinson, Alan. *Grasslands* (5–8). Illus. Series: Ecology Watch. 1992, Macmillan $13.95 (0-87518-492-8). 46pp. The flora and fauna of a grassland environment are introduced and the ecological balance needed for them to survive. (Rev: BL 11/15/92) [574.5]

**16310** George, Jean Craighead. *One Day in the Prairie* (3–5). Illus. 1986, HarperCollins LB $14.89 (0-690-04566-2). 48pp. A day spent in the Prairie Wildlife Refuge in southwestern Oklahoma. (Rev: BCCB 12/86; BL 1/1/87; SLJ 12/86)

**16311** Knapp, Brian. *What Do We Know About Grasslands?* (4–6). Illus. 1992, Bedrick LB $15.95 (0-87226-359-2). 40pp. Among the topics covered are the importance of grasslands and their locations, ecology, and outlook. (Rev: BL 2/15/93; SLJ 1/93) [574]

**16312** Landau, Elaine. *Grassland Mammals* (1–3). Illus. Series: A True Book. 1996, Children's LB $21.00 (0-516-20039-9). 48pp. After grasslands are defined and located in the world, this book introduces such indigenous mammals as African elephants, prairie dogs, giraffes, and kangaroos. (Rev: SLJ 3/97) [591]

**16313** Low, Robert. *Peoples of the Savanna* (2–5). Illus. Series: People and Their Environments. 1996, Rosen LB $13.95 (0-8239-2299-5). 24pp. Describes life in a grassland habitat and how this environment

has shaped the life-styles of the people who live there. (Rev: BL 11/15/96; SLJ 1/97) [304.2]

**16314** Patent, Dorothy Hinshaw. *Prairies* (3–6). Illus. by William Munoz. 1996, Holiday LB $15.95 (0-8234-1277-6). 40pp. The ecology of prairie environments is covered, with striking photos and clear text. (Rev: BCCB 2/97; BL 11/1/96; SLJ 2/97) [574.5]

**16315** Ricciuti, Edward R. *Grassland* (4–6). Illus. Series: Biomes of the World. 1996, Benchmark LB $25.64 (0-7614-0136-9). 64pp. The world's grasslands are identified and described, with material on their vegetation and animal life and the environmental threats they face. (Rev: SLJ 7/96) [574.5]

**16316** Rotter, Charles. *The Prairie* (5–8). Illus. Series: Images. 1994, Creative Ed. LB $16.95 (0-88682-598-9). 40pp. The nature of prairie grasslands is introduced, with material on the animals and plants found there. (Rev: SLJ 12/94) [574.5]

**16317** Rowan, James P. *Prairies and Grasslands* (1–4). Illus. 1983, Children's LB $21.00 (0-516-01706-3). 48pp. The flora and fauna in this geographical area are discussed simply.

**16318** Savage, Stephen. *Animals of the Grasslands* (2–6). Illus. Series: Animals by Habitat. 1997, Raintree Steck-Vaughn LB $22.83 (0-8172-4752-1). 32pp. Worldwide locations and characteristics of grasslands are highlighted, with material on such animals as coyotes, zebras, prairie dogs, emus, and termites. (Rev: BL 5/15/97) [591.9]

**16319** Sayre, April Pulley. *Grassland* (4–7). Illus. Series: Exploring Earth's Biomes. 1994, Twenty-First Century LB $18.90 (0-8050-2827-7). 64pp. A well-organized, clearly written account that explains what grasslands are and where they exist and the interaction of the creatures who live in this biome. (Rev: BL 1/15/95; SLJ 2/95) [574.5]

**16320** Schwartz, David M. *The Hidden Life of the Meadow* (3–5). Illus. 1988, Crown LB $12.95 (0-517-57059-9). 40pp. How a meadow stays alive in an ever-changing environment. (Rev: BCCB 12/88; BL 12/15/88; SLJ 2/89)

**16321** Staub, Frank. *America's Prairies* (3–6). Illus. Series: Earth Watch. 1994, Carolrhoda LB $19.93 (0-87614-781-3). 48pp. The 3 kinds of prairies found in the United States are introduced, with coverage of the animals and plants found in each and the environmental hazards. (Rev: BL 2/1/94) [574.5]

**16322** Steele, Philip. *Grasslands* (3–5). Illus. Series: Geography Detectives. 1997, Carolrhoda LB $19.95 (1-57505-042-0). 32pp. Discusses the grassland ecosystem in both temperate and tropical areas, with coverage on how they have been changed by agriculture and urbanization. (Rev: BL 8/97) [574.5]

## Rocks, Minerals, and Soil

**16323** Bourgeois, Paulette. *The Amazing Dirt Book* (3–5). Illus. by Craig Terlson. Series: Children's Activities. 1990, Addison-Wesley paper $8.95 (0-201-55096-2). 80pp. Facts on such appealing matters as dust mites and worms. (Rev: BL 12/1/90; SLJ 3/91) [631.4]

**16324** Bryant-Mole, Karen. *Soil* (K–3). Photos by Barrie Watts. Series: See for Yourself. 1995, Raintree Steck-Vaughn LB $21.40 (0-8172-4213-9). 30pp. After basic facts about the composition and uses of soil are presented, questions are posed and various activities are outlined. (Rev: SLJ 4/96) [631.5]

**16325** Gallant, Roy A. *Sand on the Move: The Story of Dunes* (4–6). Illus. Series: First Book: Earth and Sky Science. 1997, Watts LB $21.00 (0-531-20334-4). 64pp. Explains where sand comes from, how and why dunes are formed, and what animals and plants live on them. (Rev: BL 12/1/97; SLJ 1/98) [551.3]

**16326** Gans, Roma. *Let's Go Rock Collecting* (2–4). Illus. by Holly Keller. 1997, HarperCollins LB $14.89 (0-06-027283-X); paper $4.95 (0-06-445170-4). 32pp. An introduction to rocks, how they were formed, their composition, their uses, and how to collect them. (Rev: BL 5/15/97; SLJ 8/97) [552]

**16327** Gordon, Maria. *Rocks and Soil* (2–4). Illus. by Mike Gordon. Series: Simple Science. 1996, Raintree Steck-Vaughn LB $19.97 (0-8172-4504-9). 32pp. Questions and answers are used to introduce the size, color, and feel of rocks and the composition of soil. Experiments, many requiring adult help, are found at the back of this book. (Rev: SLJ 4/97) [552]

**16328** Hiscock, Bruce. *The Big Rock* (1–4). Illus. 1988, Macmillan $16.00 (0-689-31402-7). 32pp. Tracing the history of an ancient piece of stone. (Rev: BCCB 10/88; BL 11/1/88)

**16329** Kittinger, Jo S. *A Look at Rocks: From Coal to Kimberlite* (4–7). Illus. Series: First Book: Earth and Sky Science. 1997, Watts LB $21.00 (0-531-20310-7). 64pp. This book describes rocks, rock formations, and famous rocks like Mount Rushmore, with added material on how and why rocks change. (Rev: BL 12/1/97; SLJ 1/98) [552]

**16330** Parker, Steve. *Rocks and Minerals* (4–6). Illus. Series: Eyewitness Explorers. 1993, DK Publg. $9.95 (1-56458-394-5). 64pp. The properties of rocks and minerals and their classification are covered with outstanding illustrations and interesting activities. (Rev: BL 11/1/93) [552.2]

**16331** Podendorf, Illa. *Rocks and Minerals* (1–4). Illus. 1982, Children's paper $5.50 (0-516-41648-0). 48pp. A straightforward, well-organized account for the young reader.

**16332** Stangl, Jean. *Crystals and Crystal Gardens You Can Grow* (4–6). Illus. Series: First Books. 1990, Watts LB $21.00 (0-531-10889-9). 64pp. Introduces the nature and structure of crystals and supplies instruction for experiments on their formation. (Rev: BCCB 5/90; BL 5/15/90; SLJ 8/90) [548.5]

**16333** Stille, Darlene R. *Soil Erosion and Pollution* (1–3). Illus. Series: New True Books. 1990, Children's LB $21.00 (0-516-01188-X). 48pp. Explaining soil erosion and pollution to the primary grades. (Rev: BL 10/1/90; SLJ 10/90) [363]

**16334** Symes, R. F., and Robert Harding. *Crystal and Gem* (4–8). Illus. Series: Eyewitness Books. 1991, Knopf LB $20.99 (0-679-90781-5). 64pp. In 2-page spreads, the origins, nature, and value of crystals and gems are explored. (Rev: BL 6/1/91; SLJ 7/91) [548]

**16335** VanCleave, Janice. *Rocks and Minerals* (4–6). Illus. Series: Spectacular Science Projects. 1996, Wiley paper $10.95 (0-471-10269-5). 96pp. In easy-to-follow steps, a series of experiments and other activities illustrate the properties and uses of rocks and minerals. (Rev: BL 3/15/96; SLJ 3/96) [552]

**16336** Winckler, Suzanne, and Mary M. Rodgers. *Our Endangered Planet: Soil* (4–7). Illus. Series: Our Endangered Planet. 1994, Lerner $22.60 (0-8225-2508-9). 72pp. The depletion of our soil resources is the focus of this book, with emphasis on causes and possible solutions. (Rev: BL 5/15/94) [631.4]

# Mathematics

**16337** Adler, David A. *Fraction Fun* (2–4). Illus. by Nancy Tobin. 1996, Holiday LB $15.95 (0-8234-1259-8). A clear, concise introduction to fractions using plenty of real-life situations as examples and for fun. (Rev: BCCB 12/96; SLJ 11/96) [513.2]

**16338** Challoner, Jack. *The Science Book of Numbers* (3–5). Illus. Series: Science Books. 1992, Harcourt $9.95 (0-15-200623-0). 28pp. Through projects described with easy step-by-step procedures, the nature of numbers and counting is explored. (Rev: BL 10/15/92; SLJ 1/93) [513.2]

**16339** Hewitt, Sally. *Measuring* (4–8). Illus. Series: Take Off With. 1996, Raintree Steck-Vaughn LB $14.98 (0-8172-4113-2). 32pp. This brightly illustrated book introduces the mathematical concept of measuring by using puzzles to extend each idea. (Rev: BL 5/15/96) [530.8]

**16340** Leedy, Loreen. *Mission Addition* (PS–3). Illus. 1997, Holiday LB $16.95 (0-8234-1307-1). 32pp. Through many practical applications, the animal creatures of Miss Prime's class explore the mysteries of addition. (Rev: BL 10/15/97; SLJ 8/97) [513.2]

**16341** Losi, Carol A. *The 512 Ants on Sullivan Street* (1–2). Illus. by Patrick Merrell. Series: Hello Math Reader. 1997, Scholastic $3.99 (0-590-30876-9). 32pp. A girl watches ants in a mathematical doubling series (e.g., 1, 2, 4, 8, etc.) as they walk off with picnic food in this easily read math book. (Rev: BL 2/1/98; SLJ 1/98)

**16342** Maganzini, Christy. *Cool Math* (4–7). Illus. 1997, Price Stern Sloan paper $6.95 (0-8431-7857-4). 96pp. This book gives a brief history of math, an outline of its basic concepts, and a number of tricks to play on ones' friends. (Rev: BL 11/1/97) [510]

**16343** Markle, Sandra. *Discovering Graph Secrets: Experiments, Puzzles, and Games Exploring Graphs* (4–6). Illus. 1997, Simon & Schuster $17.00 (0-689-31942-8). 40pp. An entertaining and informative book that introduces 4 different graphs and explains their uses. (Rev: BL 2/15/98; SLJ 3/98) [001.4]

**16344** Murphy, Stuart J. *Betcha!* (1–3). Illus. by S. D. Schindler. Series: MathStart. 1997, HarperCollins LB $14.89 (0-06-026769-0). 40pp. The mathematical skill of estimating is introduced in this concept book about guessing the number of jelly beans in a jar. Other skills are explored in *Elevator Magic* and *Just Enough Carrots* (both 1997). (Rev: BL 10/1/97; SLJ 1/98) [519.5]

**16345** Murphy, Stuart J. *Too Many Kangaroo Things to Do!* (1–3). Illus. by Kevin O'Malley. Series: MathStart. 1996, HarperCollins LB $14.89 (0-06-025884-5). 40pp. Addition and multiplication are introduced through the antics of several animals. (Rev: BL 10/15/96; SLJ 12/96) [513.2]

**16346** Stienecker, David L. *Addition* (3–5). Illus. by Richard Maccabe. Series: Discovering Math. 1995, Benchmark LB $14.95 (0-7614-0593-3). 32pp. An introductory math book that explains the principles of addition and gives puzzles and exercises on applying these concepts. Also use *Division, Fractions*, and *Multiplication* (all 1995). (Rev: SLJ 4/96) [510]

**16347** VanCleave, Janice. *Janice VanCleave's Math for Every Kid: Easy Activities That Make Learning Math Fun* (3–8). Illus. by Barbara Clark. 1991, Wiley $27.95 (0-471-54693-3); paper $11.95 (0-471-54265-2). 215pp. An entertaining look at math concepts with activities and problems given to illustrate each of them. (Rev: SLJ 12/91) [510]

**16348** VanCleave, Janice. *Janice VanCleave's Play and Find Out About Math: Easy Experiments for Young Children* (PS–1). Illus. 1997, Wiley $27.95 (0-471-12937-2); paper $12.95 (0-471-12938-0). 128pp. Simple activities, like measuring one's head and then making a crown, are used to introduce basic math principles. (Rev: BL 12/1/97; SLJ 1/98) [372.7]

**16349** Vorderman, Carol. *How Math Works* (5–8). Illus. 1996, Reader's Digest $24.00 (0-89577-850-5). 192pp. Describes mathematics concepts and history, with many related activities. (Rev: BL 11/1/96) [510]

**16350** Ziefert, Harriet. *Rabbit and Hare Divide an Apple* (1–2). Illus. by Emily Bolam. Series: Viking Math Easy-to-Read. 1998, Viking paper $3.99 (0-14-038820-6). 32pp. In this easy reader, the math concept of fractions is taught through a story about Rabbit, Hare, and wily Mr. Raccoon. (Rev: BL 2/1/98; SLJ 2/98)

# Geometry

**16351** Hansen-Smith, Bradford. *The Hands-On Marvelous Ball Book* (4–7). Illus. 1995, W. H. Freeman $13.60 (0-7167-6628-0). 48pp. Directions are given for making a variety of geometric forms using such everyday materials as paper plates and bobby pins. (Rev: BL 10/15/95) [516]

**16352** Riggs, Sandy. *Circles* (2–4). Illus. by Richard Maccabe. Series: Discovering Shapes. 1996, Benchmark LB $21.36 (0-7614-0458-9). 32pp. Circles are introduced through a series of games, puzzles, and crafts. Also use *Triangles* (1996). (Rev: SLJ 2/97) [516]

**16353** Ross, Catherine. *Circles: Fun Ideas for Getting A-Round in Math* (4–7). Illus. by Bill Slavin. 1993, Addison-Wesley paper $9.95 (0-201-62268-8). 80pp. This book explains the importance of circles in mathematics, physics, and everyday life and includes many related activities and projects. (Rev: BL 6/1–15/93) [516]

**16354** Sharman, Lydia. *The Amazing Book of Shapes* (2–5). Illus. 1994, DK Publg. $14.95 (1-56458-514-X). 37pp. This large-format book uses pictures of objects and people to explore various shapes. (Rev: BL 9/1/94; SLJ 10/94) [516]

**16355** Stienecker, David L. *Rectangles* (2–4). Series: Discovering Shapes. 1996, Benchmark LB $21.36 (0-7614-0460-0). 32pp. A slim volume in which rectangles are explored through games, art ideas, and problems to solve. Also use *Patterns, Polygons,* and *Three-Dimensional Shapes* (all 1996). (Rev: SLJ 2/97) [516]

**16356** VanCleave, Janice. *Geometry for Every Kid: Easy Activities That Make Learning Geometry Fun* (4–6). Illus. Series: Science for Every Kid. 1994, Wiley $27.95 (0-471-31142-1); paper $11.95 (0-471-31141-3). 221pp. Through interesting activities, this book explains geometry from simple shapes and angles to coordinate graphing. (Rev: BL 10/15/94; SLJ 12/94) [516]

# Mathematical Puzzles

**16357** Adler, David A. *Calculator Riddles* (3–5). Illus. by Cynthia Fisher. 1995, Holiday $14.95 (0-8234-1186-9). 42pp. A series of clever riddles and problems in arithmetic that can be answered using a calculator. (Rev: BL 11/1/95; SLJ 11/95) [513.2]

**16358** Adler, David A. *Easy Math Puzzles* (2–5). Illus. by Cynthia Fisher. 1997, Holiday LB $14.95 (0-8234-1283-0). 32pp. A book of challenging, often very tricky math puzzles that sometimes involve the quirks of language and logic. (Rev: BCCB 5/97; BL 3/1/97; SLJ 6/97) [818]

**16359** Anno, Mitsumasa. *Anno's Math Games* (PS–2). Illus. by author. 1997, Putnam paper $12.95 (0-698-11671-2). 112pp. Such puzzling mathematical concepts as number squares, classifications of objects, and graphs are imaginatively introduced. (Rev: BCCB 12/87; BL 1/1/88; SLJ 12/87) [793.7]

**16360** Anno, Mitsumasa. *Anno's Math Games II* (K–3). Illus. 1997, Putnam paper $12.92 (0-698-11672-0). 104pp. Basic math principles are presented in playful games. (Rev: BCCB 11/89; BL 9/15/89*; HB 3–4/90) [793.7]

**16361** Anno, Mitsumasa. *Anno's Math Games III* (K–3). Illus. 1997, Putnam paper $12.95 (0-698-11673-9). 104pp. A treasury of games that help children to understand math principles. (Rev: BL 2/15/91*; HB 5–6/91; SLJ 4/91) [793.7]

**16362** Blum, Raymond. *Math Tricks, Puzzles and Games* (4–7). Illus. 1994, Sterling $14.95 (0-8069-0582-4). 96pp. Kids who like math will particularly enjoy these tricks, mathematical games and puzzles, and calculator riddles. (Rev: BL 11/1/94) [793.7]

**16363** Blum, Raymond. *Mathamusements* (4–6). Illus. by Jeff Sinclair. 1997, Sterling $14.95 (0-8069-9783-4). 95pp. An entertaining collection of math puzzles and activities, many for people with little background in mathematics. (Rev: SLJ 11/97) [513.2]

**16364** Burns, Marilyn. *The I Hate Mathematics! Book* (5–8). Illus. by Martha Hairston. 1975, Little, Brown paper $12.95 (0-316-11741-2). 128pp. A lively collection of puzzles and other mind stretchers that illustrate mathematical concepts. Also use: *Math for Smarty Pants: Or Who Says Mathematicians Have Little Pig Eyes* (1982).

**16365** Gardner, Martin. *Perplexing Puzzles and Tantalizing Teasers* (4–7). Illus. by Laszlo Kubinyi. 1988, Dover paper $5.95 (0-486-25637-5). 256pp. An assortment of math problems, visual teasers, and tricky questions to challenge young, alert minds; perky drawings.

**16366** Markle, Sandra. *Measuring Up! Experiments, Puzzles, and Games Exploring Measurement* (4–7). Illus. 1995, Atheneum $17.00 (0-689-31904-5). 44pp. This book explains through a series of activities how we measure a number of things like temperature, height of trees and flagpoles, weight, and distance. (Rev: SLJ 1/96*) [512]

**16367** *The Mystery of the Sunken Treasure: Sea Math* (3–5). Illus. 1994, Time Life $16.95 (0-8094-9994-0). 63pp. A heavily illustrated book of math games and puzzles that can develop problem-solving skills. (Rev: SLJ 8/94) [510]

**16368** Phillips, Louis. *263 Brain Busters: Just How Smart Are You, Anyway?* (4–6). Illus. by James Stevenson. 1985, Puffin paper $3.99 (0-14-031875-5). 87pp. A knowledge of elementary algebra will be helpful in solving some of these brain busters, not all of which are brain twisters. (Rev: BL 2/15/86; SLJ 2/86)

**16369** Sharp, Richard M., and Seymour Metzner. *The Sneaky Square and 113 Other Math Activities for Kids* (4–8). Illus. 1990, TAB $15.95 (0-8306-8474-3); paper $8.95 (0-8306-3474-6). 134pp. Readers are challenged to solve classic as well as new math and logic problems. (Rev: BL 1/1/91) [793.7]

**16370** Wells, Alison. *Subtraction* (3–5). Illus. by Richard Maccabe. Series: Discovering Math. 1995, Benchmark LB $14.95 (0-7614-0594-1). 32pp. Principles of subtraction are introduced, with many puzzles and games that apply these concepts in problem-solving situations. (Rev: SLJ 4/96) [510]

**16371** Wyler, Rose, and Mary Elting. *Math Fun: Test Your Luck* (4–6). Illus. by Patrick Girouard. Series: Math Fun. 1992, Simon & Schuster LB $10.95 (0-671-74311-2). This book of tricks covers number theory, magic squares, and probabilities. A companion book is: *Math Fun with a Pocket Calculator* (1992). (Rev: SLJ 12/92) [513]

**16372** Wyler, Rose, and Mary Elting. *Math Fun with Money Puzzlers* (3–6). Illus. by Patrick Girouard. Series: Math Fun. 1992, Simon & Schuster paper $5.95 (0-671-74314-7). 64pp. Math activities and concepts are presented in a playful way, with cartoonlike artwork. Also use: *Math Fun with Tricky Lines and Shapes* (1992). (Rev: BL 1/15/93) [513]

# Numbers and Number Systems

**16373** Adler, David A. *Roman Numerals* (2–4). Illus. by Byron Barton. 1977, HarperCollins LB $14.89 (0-690-01302-7). 40pp. The principles involved in Roman numerals and how to write them are detailed.

**16374** Anno, Mitsumasa. *Anno's Mysterious Multiplying Jar* (4–6). Illus. by author. 1983, Putnam $19.95 (0-399-20951-4). 48pp. Everyday objects are used to explain factorials.

**16375** Fisher, Leonard Everett. *Number Art: Thirteen 123's from Around the World* (5–7). Illus. by author. 1982, Macmillan paper $16.95 (0-02-735240-4). 64pp. The development of numbers in various cultures.

**16376** Ganeri, Anita. *The Story of Numbers and Counting* (3–6). Illus. Series: Signs of the Times. 1997, Oxford LB $14.95 (0-19-521258-4). 30pp. A history of the methods of calculating from earliest times to the pocket calculator and computers. (Rev: BL 2/1/97; SLJ 2/97) [513.2]

**16377** Geisert, Arthur. *Roman Numerals I to MM: Numberabillia Romana Uno ad Duo Mila* (2–4). Illus. 1996, Houghton $16.00 (0-395-74519-5). 32pp. Using groups of pigs as examples, Roman numerals are introduced, and later other objects test the reader's knowledge. (Rev: BCCB 3/96; BL 5/1/96; HB 9–10/96; SLJ 9/96) [513.5]

**16378** Hewitt, Sally. *Numbers* (4–8). Illus. Series: Take Off With. 1996, Raintree Steck-Vaughn LB $21.40 (0-8172-4116-7). 32pp. Using colorful photos of everyday objects and interesting puzzles, the concepts of numbers and numbering systems are presented. (Rev: BL 5/15/96; SLJ 6/96) [513.2]

**16379** Massin. *Fun with Numbers* (2–4). Illus. by Les Chats Pelés. 1995, Harcourt $17.00 (0-15-200962-0). A boy and his dog travel through time from ancient Egypt, Mesopotamia, and Rome, to India and Europe to trace the origins and development of numbers and our counting system. (Rev: SLJ 2/96) [512]

**16380** Schwartz, David M. *How Much Is a Million?* (K–3). Illus. by Steven Kellogg. 1985, Lothrop LB $16.93 (0-688-04050-0); Morrow paper $4.95 (0-688-09933-5). 40pp. Using images that children can enjoy — such as "1 million kids standing on each other's shoulders would be taller than . . ." — the concepts of million, billion, and trillion are explained. (Rev: BCCB 7/85; BL 6/15/85; HB 7–8/85)

**16381** Schwartz, David M. *If You Made a Million* (2–5). Illus. by Steven Kellogg. 1989, Lothrop LB $16.93 (0-688-07018-3). 40pp. Exploring mathematical concepts in a delightful way. (Rev: BL 6/15/89)

**16382** Stienecker, David L. *Numbers* (3–5). Illus. by Richard Maccabe. Series: Discovering Math. 1995, Benchmark LB $14.95 (0-7614-0597-6). 32pp. This introductory math book introduces the world of numbers and supplies many problems, with answers at the back of the book. (Rev: SLJ 4/96) [512]

## Statistics

**16383** Cushman, Jean. *Do You Wanna Bet? Your Chance to Find Out About Probability* (3–6). Illus. by Martha Weston. 1991, Houghton $14.95 (0-395-56516-2). 102pp. A slight plot line aids in the explanation of probability and moves on to guessing games, coin tossing, and breaking codes. (Rev: BCCB 2/92; BL 1/1/92; SLJ 12/91) [519.2]

## Time and Clocks

**16384** Branley, Franklyn M. *Keeping Time: From the Beginning and into the 21st Century* (4–6). Illus. by Jill Weber. 1993, Houghton $13.95 (0-395-47777-8). 106pp. Examines the concept of time and how it has been measured from the sundial to digital watches. (Rev: BL 11/1/93; SLJ 8/93) [529]

**16385** Burns, Marilyn. *This Book Is About Time* (5–7). Illus. 1978, Little, Brown paper $12.95 (0-316-11750-1). This work explores many facets of the concept of time, including a history of the calendar.

**16386** Ganeri, Anita. *The Story of Time and Clocks* (3–6). Series: Signs of the Times. 1997, Oxford LB $14.95 (0-19-521326-2). 30pp. With the use of double-page spreads and copious illustrations, this account describes how time has been measured in various cultures and tells how clocks and watches developed. (Rev: BL 9/15/97; SLJ 11/97) [529]

**16387** Murphy, Stuart J. *Get Up and Go!* (1–3). Illus. by Diane Greenseid. Series: MathStart. 1996, HarperCollins LB $14.89 (0-06-025882-9). 40pp. The concept of time as measured by minutes is explored in this imaginative picture book. (Rev: BL 10/15/96; SLJ 12/96) [513.2]

**16388** Verdet, Andre. *All About Time* (PS–2). Illus. by Celine Bour-Chollet, et al. Series: First Discovery Books. 1995, Scholastic $11.95 (0-590-42795-4). This book about time includes material on clocks and watches, time zones, seasons, phases of the moon, months of the year, and how a person can budget time. (Rev: SLJ 3/96) [529]

## Weights and Measures

**16389** Ganeri, Anita. *The Story of Weights and Measures* (3–6). Series: Signs of the Times. 1997, Oxford LB $14.95 (0-19-521328-9). 30pp. With the use of double-page spreads, copious illustrations and sidebars describe a history of measurement and weighing systems. (Rev: BL 9/15/97; SLJ 11/97) [530.8]

# Meteorology

## General

**16390** Tannenbaum, Beulah, and Harold E. Tannenbaum. *Making and Using Your Own Weather Station* (5–8). Illus. by Anne Canevari Green. 1989, Watts LB $12.90 (0-531-10675-6). 128pp. Diagrams and photos help to explain this undertaking. (Rev: BCCB 5/89; BL 5/15/89)

## Air

**16391** Ardley, Neil. *The Science Book of Air* (3–6). Illus. Series: Science Books. 1991, Harcourt $9.95 (0-15-200578-1). 28pp. Step-by-step illustrations for projects involving air. (Rev: BL 3/1/91; SLJ 5/91) [553.6]

**16392** Baines, John. *Conserving the Atmosphere* (5–8). Illus. 1990, Raintree Steck-Vaughn LB $24.26 (0-8114-2388-3). 48pp. How the atmosphere is harmed by pollution and what might be done to save it. (Rev: BL 6/1/90) [363.73]

**16393** Branley, Franklyn M. *Air Is All Around You* (PS–2). Illus. by Holly Keller. 1986, HarperCollins paper $4.95 (0-06-445048-1). 32pp. Cheery children and an orange cat demonstrate the properties of air. (Rev: BL 4/15/86; SLJ 12/86)

**16394** Fitzgerald, Karen. *The Story of Oxygen* (4–6). Illus. 1996, Watts LB $21.00 (0-531-20225-9). 63pp. After a discussion of the discovery of oxygen, its roles in nature and chemistry are covered. (Rev: BL 10/15/96; SLJ 9/96) [546]

**16395** Gardner, Robert. *Science Project Ideas About Air* (4–7). Series: Science Project Ideas. 1997, Enslow LB $18.95 (0-89490-838-3). 96pp. The properties of air are explored in a series of experiments and projects with easy-to-follow directions. (Rev: BL 12/15/97; SLJ 4/98) [678.5]

**16396** Gardner, Robert, and David Webster. *Experiments with Balloons* (4–7). Illus. Series: Getting Started in Science. 1995, Enslow LB $19.95 (0-89490-669-0). 104pp. Over a dozen experiments that explore balloons and the properties of air are presented. (Rev: BL 12/1/95; SLJ 3/96) [507.8]

**16397** Hoff, Mary, and Mary M. Rodgers. *Atmosphere* (4–7). Illus. Series: Our Endangered Planet. 1995, Lerner LB $22.60 (0-8225-2509-7). 72pp. This account describes the atmosphere and current threats that are endangering it — for example, the ozone layer problem. (Rev: BL 8/95; SLJ 12/95) [363.73]

**16398** Mebane, Robert C., and Thomas R. Rybolt. *Air and Other Gases* (4–6). Illus. Series: Everyday Material Science Experiments. 1995, Twenty-First Century LB $18.90 (0-8050-2839-0). 64pp. Basic concepts involving air and other gases are explored in a series of experiments using everyday materials and simple instructions. (Rev: BL 9/15/95; SLJ 8/95) [530.4]

**16399** Murphy, Bryan. *Experiment with Air* (2–4). Illus. Series: Science Experiments. 1992, Lerner LB $19.93 (0-8225-2452-X). 32pp. Introduces, in simple terms, concepts involving air pressure, how things fly, and how sound waves travel. (Rev: BL 6/15/92; SLJ 10/92) [533.6]

**16400** Robbins, Ken. *Air: The Elements* (3–6). Illus. 1995, Holt $16.95 (0-8050-2292-9). 88pp. The composition, properties, and uses of air are described in this handsome photoessay. (Rev: BL 10/1/95; SLJ 1/96) [551.5]

**16401** Santrey, Laurence. *What Makes the Wind?* (1–3). Illus. by Bert Dodson. 1982, Troll LB $12.95

(0-89375-584-2); paper $3.50 (0-89375-585-0). 32pp. A simple, straightforward account on aspects of weather and the atmosphere.

**16402** White, Larry. *Air* (3–6). Illus. by Laurie Hamilton. Series: Simple Experiments for Young Scientists. 1995, Millbrook LB $19.90 (1-56294-471-1). 48pp. Good background information is given, along with a series of simple projects that explore the properties of air. (Rev: SLJ 9/95) [533.6]

**16403** Yount, Lisa, and Mary M. Rodgers. *Our Endangered Planet: Air* (4–7). Illus. Series: Our Endangered Planet. 1995, Lerner LB $22.60 (0-8225-2510-0). 72pp. The emphasis in this book is on how air pollution has become a major environmental issue and how everyone can take action to improve air quality. (Rev: BL 10/15/95) [363.73]

# Storms

**16404** Archer, Jules. *Hurricane!* (5–7). Illus. Series: Nature's Disasters. 1991, Macmillan LB $12.95 (0-89686-597-5). 48pp. In addition to many real-life examples, this book covers the causes of hurricanes and how we can protect ourselves against them. (Rev: BL 8/91) [551.51]

**16405** Archer, Jules. *Tornado!* (5–7). Illus. Series: Nature's Disasters. 1991, Macmillan LB $12.95 (0-89686-594-0). 48pp. Full-color photos add to the drama of this weather phenomenon. (Rev: BL 8/91) [551.55]

**16406** Armbruster, Ann. *Floods* (4–6). Illus. Series: First Books: Science. 1996, Watts LB $21.00 (0-531-20239-9). 63pp. Describes various kinds of floods and preventive measures against them. (Rev: BL 1/1–15/97) [551.48]

**16407** Armbruster, Ann, and Elizabeth Taylor. *Tornadoes* (3–5). Illus. Series: First Books. 1993, Watts paper $6.95 (0-531-15666-4). 64pp. A solid introduction to these fearsome storms, including tracking and safety measures. (Rev: BL 12/1/89; SLJ 12/89) [551.55]

**16408** Branley, Franklyn M. *Flash, Crash, Rumble and Roll* (1–3). Illus. by Ed Emberley and Barbara Emberley. 1985, HarperCollins LB $14.89 (0-690-04425-9); paper $4.95 (0-06-445012-0). 32pp. A simple explanation of the causes and effects of thunderstorms. Update of 1965 edition. Also use: *Rain and Hail* (1983).

**16409** Branley, Franklyn M. *Tornado Alert* (K–4). Illus. by Giulio Maestro. 1988, HarperCollins LB $15.89 (0-690-04688-X); paper $4.95 (0-06-445094-5). 32pp. An explanation of these powerful storms

that hold great fear and fascination for children. (Rev: BCCB 9/88; BL 9/1/88; SLJ 11/88)

**16410** Cole, Joanna. *The Magic School Bus Inside a Hurricane* (2–4). Illus. by Bruce Degen. 1995, Scholastic $14.95 (0-590-44686-X). 48pp. Ms. Frizzle takes her busload of youngsters into the clouds to show where hurricanes come from. (Rev: BCCB 10/95; BL 6/1–15/95; HB 11–12/95; SLJ 9/95) [551.55]

**16411** Erlbach, Arlene. *Hurricanes* (1–3). Illus. Series: New True Books. 1993, Children's LB $20.00 (0-516-01333-5); paper $5.50 (0-516-41333-3). 48pp. With large type and short chapters, this is an introductory account about hurricanes. (Rev: BL 8/93) [551.55]

**16412** Fowler, Allan. *When a Storm Comes Up* (1–2). Illus. Series: Rookie Read-About Science. 1995, Children's LB $18.50 (0-516-06035-X). 32pp. With large type, color photos, and a small format, this effectively introduces storms to young people. (Rev: BL 7/95) [551.55]

**16413** Greenberg, Keith E. *Storm Chaser: Into the Eye of a Hurricane* (4–7). Series: Risky Business. 1997, Blackbirch LB $14.95 (1-56711-161-0). 48pp. Tells about the people who track the paths of hurricanes and of the dangers they often face. (Rev: BL 10/15/97; SLJ 12/97) [551.55]

**16414** Harper, Suzanne. *Lightning: Sheets, Streaks, Beads, and Balls* (4–6). Illus. Series: First Books: Science. 1997, Watts LB $21.00 (0-531-20290-9). 64pp. Describes how thunderclouds form, the causes of lightning, and its various forms. (Rev: BL 5/15/97) [551.5]

**16415** Herman, Gail. *Storm Chasers: Tracking Twisters* (2–3). Illus. by Larry Schwinger. Series: All Aboard Reading. 1997, Grosset $13.99 (0-448-41638-7); paper $3.95 (0-448-41624-7). 47pp. Using a fictitious incident as a focus, this account gives good information about tornadoes, their causes and effects, and what to do during a tornado alert. (Rev: SLJ 11/97) [551.5]

**16416** Hiscock, Bruce. *The Big Storm* (2–5). Illus. 1993, Atheneum $16.00 (0-689-31770-0). 32pp. This picture book traces a violent storm in 1982 from its beginnings on the West Coast, to the deep snows it brought to the Midwest and East Coast. (Rev: BL 11/1/93; SLJ 9/93) [551]

**16417** Kahl, Jonathan D. *Storm Warning: Tornadoes and Hurricanes* (3–6). Illus. Series: How's the Weather? 1993, Lerner LB $21.27 (0-8225-2527-5). 64pp. An introduction to tornadoes and hurricanes with information on their causes, characteristics, and effects. (Rev: BL 5/15/93) [551]

**16418** Kahl, Jonathan D. *Thunderbolt: Learning About Lightning* (4–6). Illus. Series: How's the

Weather? 1994, Lerner LB $21.27 (0-8225-2528-3). 56pp. Causes and effects of lightning and thunder are described, with information on their place in history and in myth. (Rev: BL 6/94; SLJ 5/94) [551.5]

**16419** Kramer, Stephen. *Eye of the Storm* (4–6). Illus. 1997, Putnam $18.95 (0-399-23029-7). 48pp. A photographer who specializes in severe weather describes some dreadful storms and supplies spectacular full-color illustrations. (Rev: BCCB 4/97; BL 3/15/97; HB 3–4/97; SLJ 3/97*) [778.9]

**16420** Kramer, Stephen. *Lightning* (3–6). Illus. by Warren Faidley. Series: Nature in Action. 1992, Carolrhoda LB $19.95 (0-87614-659-0). 48pp. A clear text and many full-color photos explain the hows and whys of lightning. (Rev: BCCB 9/92; BL 6/15/92; SLJ 7/92*) [551.5]

**16421** Kramer, Stephen. *Tornado* (3–6). Illus. Series: Nature in Action. 1992, Carolrhoda LB $14.96 (0-87614-660-4). 48pp. This book shows how and where tornadoes usually form and the damage they can cause. (Rev: BL 11/1/92; SLJ 11/92) [551.53]

**16422** Lampton, Christopher. *Blizzard* (4–6). Illus. Series: Disaster! 1991, Millbrook paper $5.95 (1-56294-775-3). 64pp. This attractive volume gives a detailed description of the causes of blizzards, some famous examples, and methods of protection during these storms. (Rev: BL 1/1/92; SLJ 1/92) [551.5]

**16423** Lampton, Christopher. *Hurricane* (4–6). Illus. Series: Disaster! 1991, Millbrook LB $19.90 (1-56294-030-9). 64pp. A detailed description of the causes of hurricanes, plus some famous historical examples, appears in this brightly illustrated book. (Rev: BL 1/1/92) [551.5]

**16424** Lampton, Christopher. *Tornado* (4–6). Illus. Series: Disaster! 1991, Millbrook paper $5.95 (1-56294-785-0). 64pp. An appealing layout and sharp color photos add to the detailed, informative text with historical data and examples. (Rev: BL 1/1/92) [551.5]

**16425** Lauber, Patricia. *Flood: Wrestling with the Mississippi* (5–8). Illus. 1996, National Geographic $18.95 (0-7922-4141-X). 64pp. An introduction to floods that focuses on the great Mississippi River flood of 1993. (Rev: BL 10/15/96; SLJ 11/96*) [363.3]

**16426** Lauber, Patricia. *Hurricanes: Earth's Mightiest Storms* (4–8). Illus. 1996, Scholastic $16.95 (0-590-47406-5). 64pp. Beginning with an actual hurricane that ravaged Long Island in 1938, this account discusses the causes and effects of these mighty storms. (Rev: BCCB 10/96; BL 10/1/96; HB 9–10/96; SLJ 9/96*) [363.3]

**16427** Lee, Sally. *Hurricanes* (3–6). Illus. 1993, Watts LB $21.00 (0-531-20152-X). 64pp. This book tells how hurricanes are formed, tracked, and pre-

dicted and the devastation they can cause. (Rev: BL 7/93) [551.55]

**16428** Murray, Peter. *Floods* (3–5). Illus. Series: Naturebooks: Natural Disasters. 1996, Child's World LB $22.79 (1-56766-214-5). 32pp. Basic information about floods is given, with full-page color photographs facing each page of text. (Rev: BL 1/1–15/97) [363.3]

**16429** Murray, Peter. *Hurricanes* (3–5). Illus. Series: Naturebooks: Natural Disasters. 1995, Child's World LB $22.79 (1-56766-196-3). 32pp. Basic information is given about hurricanes in striking photographs and informative large-type text. (Rev: BL 12/15/95; SLJ 3/96) [551.55]

**16430** Murray, Peter. *Lightning* (3–5). Illus. Series: Naturebooks: Natural Disasters. 1996, Child's World LB $22.79 (1-56766-215-3). 32pp. The causes and effects of lightning are covered, with many full-page illustrations. (Rev: BL 1/1–15/97) [551.5]

**16431** Murray, Peter. *Tornadoes* (3–5). Illus. Series: Naturebooks: Natural Disasters. 1995, Child's World LB $22.79 (1-56766-195-5). 32pp. Using color photographs and examples from around the world, the wonder and terror of tornadoes are effectively introduced. (Rev: BL 12/15/95; SLJ 3/96) [551.55]

**16432** Otfinoski, Steven. *Blizzards* (4–6). Illus. Series: When Disaster Strikes. 1994, Twenty-First Century LB $18.90 (0-8050-3093-X). 64pp. This book explains why blizzards occur, provides safety tips, and tells about famous storms of the past. (Rev: BL 10/15/94; SLJ 9/94) [363.3]

**16433** Penner, Lucille R. *Twisters!* (2–3). Illus. by Kazushige Nitta. 1996, Random LB $11.99 (0-679-98271-X); paper $3.99 (0-679-88271-5). An easy-to-read introduction to the causes and effects of tornadoes and hurricanes. (Rev: BL 11/15/96) [551.5]

**16434** Rotter, Charles. *Hurricanes* (5–8). Illus. Series: Images. 1994, Creative Ed. LB $16.95 (0-88682-597-0). 40pp. A basic introduction to the causes and effects of hurricanes, with dramatic color photographs. (Rev: SLJ 12/94) [551.55]

**16435** Rozens, Aleksandrs. *Floods* (4–6). Illus. Series: When Disaster Strikes. 1994, Twenty-First Century LB $22.90 (0-8050-3097-2). 64pp. A history of famous floods is given, plus an account of their causes and effects and survival tips. (Rev: BL 10/15/94; SLJ 9/94) [363.3]

**16436** Simon, Seymour. *Lightning* (3–6). Illus. 1997, Morrow LB $15.93 (0-688-14639-2). 32pp. A dramatic, fact-packed description of the causes of lightning, different types, and its effects. (Rev: BL 3/15/97*; SLJ 5/97) [551.319]

**16437** Simon, Seymour. *Storms* (3–5). Illus. 1989, Morrow LB $15.93 (0-688-07414-6); paper $4.95 (0-

688-11708-2). 32pp. Explaining how storms occur. (Rev: BCCB 3/89; BL 3/1/89; SLJ 4/89)

**16438** Souza, D. M. *Hurricanes* (3–6). Illus. Series: Nature in Action. 1996, Carolrhoda LB $19.95 (0-87614-861-5); paper $7.95 (0-87614-955-7). 48pp. The causes and effects of hurricanes are covered, as well as forecasting devices. (Rev: BL 8/96; SLJ 11/96) [551.55]

**16439** Twist, Clint. *Hurricanes and Storms* (5–8). Illus. Series: Repairing the Damage. 1992, Macmillan LB $13.95 (0-02-789685-4). 46pp. This oversized book is a logically organized explanation of the causes and effects of violent storms and hurricanes, with information on famous disasters. (Rev: BL 9/15/92; SLJ 10/92) [551.55]

**16440** Walters, John. *Flood!* (5–7). Illus. Series: Nature's Disasters. 1991, Macmillan LB $12.95 (0-89686-596-7). 48pp. The dramatic story of floods is enhanced by full-color photos. (Rev: BL 8/91) [551.48]

# Water

**16441** Ardley, Neil. *The Science Book of Water* (3–6). Illus. Series: Science Books. 1991, Harcourt $9.95 (0-15-200575-7). 28pp. Sinking, floating, and displacement are some of the science projects presented in this full-color book. (Rev: BL 3/1/91; SLJ 5/90) [532]

**16442** Asch, Frank. *Water* (PS–1). Illus. 1995, Harcourt $14.00 (0-15-200189-1). 32pp. A simple explanation of the nature of water and its uses, from tears to floodwaters. (Rev: BCCB 4/95; BL 4/15/95; HB 3–4/95; SLJ 5/95) [553.7]

**16443** Berger, Melvin, and Gilda Berger. *Water, Water Everywhere: A Book About the Water Cycle* (2–4). Illus. Series: Discovery Readers. 1995, Ideals LB $12.00 (1-57102-056-X); paper $4.50 (1-57102-042-X). 48pp. In addition to the water cycle, this book discusses a city's water system, sewage, and how to conserve water. (Rev: BL 12/1/95; SLJ 2/96) [551.48]

**16444** Brandt, Keith. *What Makes It Rain?* (1–3). Illus. by Yoshi Miyake. 1982, Troll LB $12.95 (0-89375-582-6); paper $3.50 (0-89375-583-4). 32pp. A simple book about the water cycle.

**16445** Branley, Franklyn M. *Down Comes the Rain* (5–8). Illus. by James G. Hale. Series: Let's–Read-and-Find-Out. 1997, HarperCollins LB $14.89 (0-06-025338-X). 32pp. An introduction to rain and hail as well as the water cycle. (Rev: BL 9/1/97; SLJ 10/97) [551.57]

**16446** Fiarotta, Noel, and Phyllis Fiarotta. *Great Experiments with H₂O* (4–6). Illus. 1997, Sterling paper $9.95 (0-8069-4259-5). 80pp. These simple hands-on experiments demonstrate such properties of water as why it freezes, rises as steam, condenses, or evaporates. (Rev: BL 12/1/97) [553.7]

**16447** Fowler, Allan. *It Could Still Be Water* (1–2). Illus. Series: Rookie Read-About Science. 1992, Children's LB $18.50 (0-516-06003-1). 32pp. This is a simple introduction to water and its many uses. It is also available in an oversized "Big Book" edition. (Rev: BL 12/15/92) [553.7]

**16448** Hathorn, Libby. *The Wonder Thing* (K–4). Illus. by Peter Gouldthorpe. 1996, Houghton $14.95 (0-395-71541-5). On the last page, the reader is told that the Wonder Thing described in the book is water. (Rev: SLJ 3/96) [532]

**16449** Locker, Thomas. *Water Dance* (3–5). Illus. 1997, Harcourt $16.00 (0-15-201284-2). 32pp. Using a fictionalized format, this account poetically traces the phases of the water cycle. (Rev: BCCB 5/97; BL 3/1/97; SLJ 4/97) [551]

**16450** Lucas, Eileen. *Water: A Resource in Crisis* (5–8). Illus. Series: Saving Planet Earth. 1992, Children's LB $30.50 (0-516-05509-7). 128pp. A well-organized look at the state — dangerous — of the world's water supply and what some people and countries are doing about it. (Rev: BL 5/15/92) [363.73]

**16451** Marzollo, Jean. *I Am Water* (1–2). Illus. by Judith Moffatt. 1996, Scholastic paper $3.50 (0-590-26587-3). 32pp. In a beginning reader, the various forms of water are introduced. (Rev: BL 9/15/96*) [553.7]

**16452** Mebane, Robert C., and Thomas R. Rybolt. *Water and Other Liquids* (4–6). Illus. Series: Everyday Material Science Experiments. 1995, Twenty-First Century LB $18.90 (0-8050-2840-4). 64pp. The properties of water and other liquids are identified and explored in a series of experiments using everyday materials. (Rev: BL 9/15/95; SLJ 8/95) [530.4]

**16453** Morgan, Sally, and Adrian Morgan. *Water* (4–7). Illus. Series: Designs in Science. 1994, Facts on File $16.95 (0-8160-2982-2). 48pp. The importance and uses of water are described, with information on water storage, filtering, and conservation, plus activities and experiments. (Rev: BL 7/94) [533.7]

**16454** Murphy, Bryan. *Experiment with Water* (2–4). Illus. 1992, Lerner LB $19.93 (0-8225-2453-8). 32pp. Color photos help demonstrate the properties of water through simple activities. (Rev: BL 6/15/92; SLJ 10/92) [532]

**16455** O'Neill, Mary. *Water Squeeze* (4–7). Illus. by John Bindon. Series: SOS Planet Earth. 1991, Troll

LB $13.50 (0-8167-2080-0); paper $5.95 (0-8167-2081-9). 32pp. Recent problems, such as a massive die-off of seals, are discussed in this look at the threats to our water supply. (Rev: BL 6/15/91) [363.73]

**16456** Rauzon, Mark, and Cynthia O. Bix. *Water, Water Everywhere* (K–4). Illus. 1994, Sierra Club $18.95 (0-87156-598-6). 32pp. An attractive book that conveys the importance of water to life and ways we can protect our water resources. (Rev: BL 5/15/94; SLJ 5/94) [551.48]

**16457** Robbins, Ken. *Water* (3–4). Photos by author. Illus. Series: Elements. 1994, Holt $16.95 (0-8050-2257-0). Water is introduced in its 3 states, with material on its uses, pollution, and the natural beauty of water. (Rev: BCCB 11/94; SLJ 12/94) [508.316]

**16458** Robinson, Fay. *Where Do Puddles Go?* (1–2). Illus. Series: Rookie Read-About Science. 1995, Children's LB $18.50 (0-516-06036-8). 32pp. In very simple language and many color photographs, the water cycle is introduced to young children. (Rev: BL 7/95) [551.57]

**16459** Sauvain, Philip. *Water* (4–6). Illus. 1992, Macmillan LB $13.95 (0-02-781078-X). 48pp. A collection of information about water, including uses, sewage, and purification. (Rev: SLJ 8/92) [333.91]

**16460** Schmid, Eleonore. *The Water's Journey* (1–3). Illus. 1990, North-South $14.95 (1-55858-013-1). 32pp. This book explains the water cycle in text and pictures. (Rev: BCCB 6/90; BL 6/1/90; SLJ 11/90) [551.48]

**16461** Souza, D. M. *Powerful Waves* (3–6). Illus. 1992, Carolrhoda LB $19.95 (0-87614-661-2). 48pp. Deals with tsunamis — misnamed tidal waves — how they develop, and the disasters they cause. (Rev: BL 11/1/92; SLJ 11/92) [551]

**16462** Walker, Sally M. *Water Up, Water Down: The Hydrologic Cycle* (3–6). Illus. Series: Earth Watch. 1992, Carolrhoda LB $14.95 (0-87614-695-7). 48pp. This includes a description of the water cycle and material on erosion, flooding, caves, and other interesting aspects. (Rev: BL 1/15/93; SLJ 12/92) [551]

**16463** Walpole, Brenda. *Water* (3–5). Illus. by Ed Barber. Series: Threads. 1990, Garrett LB $15.93 (0-944483-72-0). 26pp. The nature of water is explored in a number of simple projects. (Rev: BL 2/1/91; SLJ 5/91) [546.1]

**16464** White, Larry. *Water* (3–6). Illus. by Laurie Hamilton. Series: Simple Experiments for Young Scientists. 1995, Millbrook LB $20.90 (1-56294-472-X). 48pp. The properties of water and its 3 states are explored in a series of questions and answers, accompanied by simple projects and experiments. (Rev: HB 3–4/95; SLJ 9/95) [553]

**16465** Wick, Walter. *A Drop of Water* (3–6). Illus. 1997, Scholastic $16.95 (0-590-22197-3). 40pp. The properties of water are explored in amazing photographs and activities. (Rev: BCCB 2/97; BL 2/1/97*; HB 3–4/97, 9–10/97; SLJ 3/97) [546]

**16466** Williams, John. *Water Projects* (3–5). Illus. Series: Design and Create. 1997, Raintree Steck-Vaughn LB $22.11 (0-8172-4890-0). 32pp. Among the 12 nicely presented projects in this book are directions on making a drink machine, a waterwheel, a dredger, and many types of boats. (Rev: BL 2/1/98; SLJ 4/98) [532]

**16467** Wyler, Rose. *Raindrops and Rainbows* (K–4). Illus. by Steven J. Petruccio. Series: Outdoor Science. 1989, Simon & Schuster paper $4.95 (0-671-66350-X). 48pp. Many aspects of water and refraction are covered in this simple science book. (Rev: SLJ 9/89) [551.4]

**16468** Zubrowski, Bernie. *Making Waves: Finding Out About Rhythmic Motion* (4–8). Illus. Series: Boston Children's Museum Activity Book. 1994, Morrow LB $14.93 (0-688-11787-2). 96pp. Step-by-step instructions are given for creating a wave machine, plus activities to observe waves in various media. (Rev: BL 7/94; SLJ 8/94) [532]

# Weather

**16469** Ardley, Neil. *The Science Book of Weather* (3–6). Illus. Series: Science Books. 1992, Harcourt $9.95 (0-15-200624-9). 28pp. The different kinds of weather and their causes are described and illustrated. (Rev: BL 10/15/92; SLJ 1/93) [551.5]

**16470** Berger, Melvin, and Gilda Berger. *How's the Weather? A Look at Weather and How It Changes* (K–2). Illus. by John E. Cymerman. Series: Discovery Readers. 1993, Ideals LB $12.00 (0-8249-8641-5); paper $4.50 (0-8249-8599-0). 48pp. A basic introduction to weather that touches on such topics as air pressure, water vapor, weather maps, lightning, hurricanes, and tornadoes. (Rev: SLJ 3/94) [551.5]

**16471** Branley, Franklyn M. *It's Raining Cats and Dogs: All Kinds of Weather and Why We Have It* (3–6). Illus. 1987, Houghton $16.00 (0-395-33070-X). 128pp. Strange happenings, such as pink and green snowstorms, are mixed in with scientific accounts of the weather. (Rev: BL 7/87; HB 9–10/87)

**16472** Branley, Franklyn M. *Snow Is Falling* (PS–2). Illus. by Holly Keller. 1986, HarperCollins paper $4.95 (0-06-445058-9). 32pp. Includes snow's role in ecology and some simple experiments for preschool and primary grades. (Rev: BL 9/15/86; SLJ 12/86)

**16473** Casey, Denise. *Weather Everywhere* (K–3). Photos by Jackie Gilmore. 1995, Simon & Schuster paper $15.00 (0-02-717777-7). 36pp. A simplified introduction to weather that gives explanations of seasons, wind, precipitation, and clouds. (Rev: SLJ 8/95) [551.5]

**16474** Cosgrove, Brian. *Weather* (4–8). Illus. Series: Eyewitness Books. 1991, Knopf LB $20.99 (0-679-90784-X). 64pp. Colorful drawings, charts, and diagrams illustrate each of the 2-page spreads that explore the world of weather. (Rev: BL 6/1/91; SLJ 7/91) [551.5]

**16475** DeWitt, Lynda. *What Will the Weather Be?* (K–3). Illus. by Carolyn Croll. Series: Let's Read and Find Out. 1993, HarperCollins paper $4.95 (0-06-445113-5). 32pp. An illustrated introduction to weather forecasting. (Rev: BCCB 6/91; BL 5/1/91; SLJ 7/91) [551.6]

**16476** Dickinson, Terence. *Exploring the Sky by Day: The Equinox Guide to Weather and Atmosphere* (3–7). Illus. 1989, Firefly $17.95 (0-920656-73-0); paper $9.95 (0-920656-71-4). 72pp. Spectacular photos add to the fascination of this weather explanation. (Rev: BL 3/1/89)

**16477** Elsom, Derek. *Weather Explained: A Beginner's Guide to the Elements* (4–8). Illus. Series: Your World Explained. 1997, Holt $18.95 (0-8050-4875-8). 68pp. Basic material on clouds and winds are introduced, followed by a discussion of the world's changing climate, the causes and effects of El Niño, and the problem of global warming. (Rev: BL 3/1/98; SLJ 2/98) [551.5]

**16478** Facklam, Howard, and Margery Facklam. *Avalanche!* (5–7). Illus. Series: Nature's Disasters. 1991, Macmillan $12.95 (0-89686-598-3). 48pp. Real-life examples and full-color photos add to the drama of this weather phenomenon. (Rev: BL 8/91) [551.3]

**16479** Fowler, Allan. *What Do You See in a Cloud?* (PS–3). Illus. Series: Rookie Read-About Science. 1996, Children's LB $18.50 (0-516-06056-2). 31pp. Various kinds of clouds and what each signifies are covered in this easy-to-read science book. (Rev: SLJ 8/96) [551.6]

**16480** Ganeri, Anita. *Weather* (3–6). Illus. by Mike Atkinson and Mark Machin. Series: Nature Detective. 1993, Watts $19.30 (0-531-14250-7). 32pp. A richly illustrated book that includes such topics as types of clouds, how weather is predicted, and sayings about the weather, with an array of easy projects. (Rev: BL 12/15/93) [551.5]

**16481** Gardner, Robert. *Science Project Ideas About Rain* (4–7). Series: Science Project Ideas. 1997, Enslow LB $18.95 (0-89490-843-X). 96pp. Clear explanations and functional drawings and diagrams for a number of activities that study rain, its causes,

and its effects. (Rev: BL 12/15/97; SLJ 1/98) [551.55]

**16482** Gibbons, Gail. *Weather Forecasting* (K–3). Illus. by author. 1987, Macmillan $14.00 (0-02-737250-2); paper $5.99 (0-689-71683-4). 32pp. Touring a weather station during the 4 seasons. (Rev: BCCB 4/87; BL 4/15/87; SLJ 4/87)

**16483** Gibbons, Gail. *Weather Words and What They Mean* (1–3). Illus. by author. 1990, Holiday LB $15.95 (0-8234-0805-1). Various broad terms — such as temperature, air pressure, moisture, and wind — are defined, with breakdowns into more-specific terms. (Rev: BCCB 4/90; SLJ 5/90) [551.6]

**16484** Harper, Suzanne. *Clouds: From Mare's Tails to Thunderheads* (4–6). Illus. Series: First Books: Science. 1997, Watts LB $22.00 (0-531-20291-7). 64pp. As well as discussing the types of clouds and how they affect climate, this book tells how to predict weather by studying cloud patterns. (Rev: BL 5/15/97) [551.57]

**16485** Haslam, Andrew, and Barbara Taylor. *Weather* (3–6). Series: Make it Work! 1997, World Book $11.95 (0-7166-5112-2). 48pp. In a series of double-page spreads, basic material about the weather is presented, with a strong emphasis on activities like making models and conducting experiments. (Rev: BL 12/15/97) [551.5]

**16486** Inkpen, Mick. *Kipper's Book of Weather* (PS–K). Illus. by author. 1995, Harcourt paper $6.00 (0-15-200644-3). Different kinds of weather are introduced through the experiences of Kipper, a lovable dog. (Rev: SLJ 8/95) [551.6]

**16487** Kahl, Jonathan D. *Hazy Skies: Weather and the Environment* (4–6). Illus. 1998, Lerner LB $21.27 (0-8225-2530-5). 64pp. After providing a history of air pollution, this book links it to such weather-related topics as the ozone layer and global warming. (Rev: BL 3/15/98) [363.73]

**16488** Kahl, Jonathan D. *Weather Watch: Forecasting the Weather* (4–6). Illus. Series: How's the Weather. 1996, Lerner LB $21.27 (0-8225-2529-1). 72pp. Covers the various methods of predicting weather, the history of weather forecasting, and possible future developments. (Rev: BL 6/1–15/96; SLJ 6/96) [551.6]

**16489** Kahl, Jonathan D. *Weatherwise: Learning About the Weather* (4–6). Illus. 1992, Lerner LB $21.27 (0-8225-2525-9). 64pp. Topics covered include atmosphere, winds, storms, and forecasting. (Rev: SLJ 8/92) [551.6]

**16490** Kahl, Jonathan D. *Wet Weather: Rain Showers and Snowfall* (4–6). Illus. Series: How's the Weather. 1992, Lerner LB $21.27 (0-8225-2526-7). 64pp. A book that concentrates on rain and snow, weather fronts, and such extremes as floods and blizzards. (Rev: BL 1/15/93; SLJ 9/92) [551.577]

**16491** Kramer, Stephen. *Avalanche* (3–6). Illus. by Patrick Cone. Series: Nature in Action. 1992, Carolrhoda LB $14.95 (0-87614-422-9). 48pp. Examining different types of snowslides, and how and when they occur. (Rev: BCCB 9/92; BL 6/15/92; SLJ 9/92) [551.57]

**16492** Lambert, David. *Weather* (3–5). Illus. 1990, Troll LB $12.95 (0-8167-1979-9); paper $4.95 (0-8167-1980-2). 32pp. An explanation of various kinds of weather and their causes.

**16493** Llewellyn, Claire. *Wild, Wet and Windy* (3–5). Series: SuperSmarts. 1997, Candlewick $11.99 (0-7636-0304-X). 24pp. This nicely illustrated book describes various kinds of weather and their causes. (Rev: BL 11/15/97) [551.5]

**16494** McMillan, Bruce. *The Weather Sky* (4–6). Illus. 1991, Farrar $16.95 (0-374-38261-1). 40pp. A challenging weather book that young children are able to follow. (Rev: BCCB 4/91; BL 4/15/91; HB 7–8/91; SLJ 5/91) [551.6]

**16495** Mandell, Muriel. *Simple Weather Experiments with Everyday Materials* (4–7). Illus. by Frances Zweifel. 1991, Sterling paper $4.95 (0-8069-7295-5). 128pp. Includes dozens of carefully described experiments, covering various weather types, instruments, and forecasting. (Rev: BL 7/89; SLJ 4/91) [551.6]

**16496** Markle, Sandra. *A Rainy Day* (K–3). Illus. by Cathy Johnson. 1993, Orchard LB $16.99 (0-531-08576-7). 32pp. A simple explanation of how clouds form and why rain falls. (Rev: BCCB 3/93; BL 3/1/93; SLJ 7/93) [551]

**16497** Morgan, Sally. *Weather* (4–6). Illus. Series: Nature Company Discoveries. 1996, Time Life $16.00 (0-8094-9370-5). 64pp. Types of weather, their causes, and prediction possibilities are 3 topics covered, with many colorful illustrations. (Rev: BL 9/15/96) [551.5]

**16498** Simon, Seymour. *Weather* (4–6). Illus. 1993, Morrow LB $14.93 (0-688-10547-5). 40pp. Simple explanations are given for such phenomena as snow and hail, cold and warm fronts, and the atmosphere in this concise introduction to weather. (Rev: BCCB 10/93; BL 9/1/93; HB 11–12/93; SLJ 11/93) [551.5]

**16499** Souza, D. M. *Northern Lights* (5–7). Illus. 1994, Carolrhoda LB $19.95 (0-87614-799-6); paper $7.95 (0-87614-629-9). 48pp. A description of northern lights and an explanation of what causes them. (Rev: BL 1/15/94) [538]

**16500** Steele, Philip. *Frost: Causes and Effects* (3–6). Illus. Series: Weather Watch. 1991, Watts LB $20.00 (0-531-11025-7). 32pp. A brief overview with full-color photos of how frost forms and what it does. (Rev: BL 4/1/92) [551.5]

**16501** Steele, Philip. *Heatwave: Causes and Effects* (3–6). Illus. Series: Weather Watch. 1991, Watts LB $20.00 (0-531-11023-0). 32pp. Brief discussion of a heat wave, with color photos. (Rev: BL 4/1/92) [551.5]

**16502** Stille, Darlene R. *The Greenhouse Effect* (1–3). Illus. Series: New True Books. 1990, Children's LB $21.00 (0-516-01106-5). 48pp. The causes and results of the greenhouse effect are explained. (Rev: BL 1/1/91) [363.73]

**16503** Stonehouse, Bernard. *Snow, Ice and Cold* (5–7). 1993, Macmillan LB $13.95 (0-02-788530-5). 45pp. This work tells about how cultures and individuals have adjusted to severe cold climates. (Rev: SLJ 7/93) [551.6]

**16504** Suzuki, David, and Barbara Hehner. *Looking at Weather* (3–6). Illus. Series: Looking At. 1991, Stoddart $24.95 (0-471-54753-0); paper $9.95 (0-471-54047-1). 96pp. A brief introduction to various kinds of weather and what causes them, with suggestions for activities and projects. (Rev: SLJ 5/92) [551.6]

**16505** VanCleave, Janice. *Janice VanCleave's Weather: Mind-Boggling Experiments You Can Turn into Science Fair Projects* (3–6). Illus. Series: Janice VanCleave's Spectacular Science Projects. 1995, Wiley paper $10.95 (0-471-03231-X). 89pp. Intriguing questions about the weather are answered in 20 easily performed experiments and projects. (Rev: SLJ 8/95) [551.6]

**16506** Webster, Vera. *Weather Experiments* (1–4). Illus. 1982, Children's LB $21.00 (0-516-01662-8); paper $5.50 (0-516-41662-6). 48pp. A simple explanation of how weather evolves is presented through some activities.

**16507** Williams, Terry Tempest, and Ted Major. *The Secret Language of Snow* (4–8). Illus. by Jennifer Dewey. 1984, Pantheon $10.95 (0-394-96574-X). 144pp. Different words for snow in the Eskimo language are used to explore this phenomenon.

**16508** *Wind and Weather* (4–6). Illus. Series: Voyages of Discovery. 1995, Scholastic $19.95 (0-590-47646-7). 45pp. Using die-cut pages, transparencies, foldouts, and stickers, this attractively illustrated book explains the atmosphere, weather, storms, climates, and precipitation. (Rev: SLJ 5/96) [551.5]

# Physics

## General

**16509** Cash, Terry. *101 Physics Tricks: Fun Experiments with Everyday Materials* (4–7). Illus. 1993, Sterling $17.95 (0-8069-8786-3). 104pp. Presents exercises that demonstrate the laws of force, air, and sound. (Rev: BL 3/1/93) [530]

**16510** Challoner, Jack. *Big and Small* (K–4). Illus. Series: Start-Up Science. 1996, Raintree Steck-Vaughn LB $21.40 (0-8172-4319-4). 32pp. Information and experiments are combined in this attractive beginner's science book about size. (Rev: SLJ 2/97) [153.7]

**16511** Challoner, Jack. *Floating and Sinking* (K–4). Illus. Series: Start-Up Science. 1996, Raintree Steck-Vaughn LB $21.40 (0-8172-4317-8). 32pp. The concepts of floating and sinking are explored in a simple, conversational text with many attractive pictures. (Rev: SLJ 2/97) [530]

**16512** Cooper, Christopher. *Matter* (4–8). Illus. Series: Eyewitness Science. 1992, DK Publg. $15.95 (1-879431-88-2). 64pp. Lavish illustrations and clear text help to make difficult scientific principles understandable. (Rev: BL 1/15/93; SLJ 12/92) [535]

**16513** Darling, David J. *From Glasses to Gases: The Science of Matter* (4–8). Illus. Series: Experiment! 1992, Macmillan LB $13.95 (0-87518-500-2). 60pp. The properties of matter are described, and through a series of experiments the underlying principles are demonstrated. (Rev: BL 10/1/92; SLJ 11/92) [530.3]

**16514** Davies, Kay, and Wendy Oldfield. *My Boat* (3–6). Illus. Series: First Step Science. 1994, Gareth Stevens LB $19.93 (0-8368-1115-1). 32pp. This simple presentation explains why boats float or sink, stay upright, and can be propelled, with a series of simple activities. (Rev: BL 2/15/95) [623.8]

**16515** de Pinna, Simon. *Forces and Motion* (3–5). Series: Science Projects. 1998, Raintree Steck-Vaughn $24.97 (0-8172-4962-1). 48pp. A brief explanation of force and motion is followed by a series of activities, with each double-page spread dealing with a different aspect of the subject. (Rev: BL 3/15/98) [531.6]

**16516** Durant, Penny R. *Bubblemania! Learn the Secrets to Creating Millions of Spectacular Bubbles!* (4–8). 1994, Avon paper $3.99 (0-380-77373-2). 86pp. Through a series of easy experiments, surface tension, bubble formation, and the uses of bubbles are explained. (Rev: SLJ 7/94) [530]

**16517** Friedhoffer, Robert. *Physics Lab in a Hardware Store* (5–8). Illus. Series: Physical Science Labs. 1996, Watts LB $20.80 (0-531-11292-6). 112pp. Using objects like nails, axes, and ladders, a number of principles in physics are introduced. (Rev: BL 12/1/96; SLJ 5/97) [621.9]

**16518** Friedhoffer, Robert. *Physics Lab in a Housewares Store* (5–8). Illus. Series: Physical Science Labs. 1996, Watts LB $20.80 (0-531-11293-4). 96pp. Various concepts in physics are demonstrated using such household items as a garlic press and a can opener. (Rev: BL 12/1/96; SLJ 1/97) [621.9]

**16519** Gardner, Robert. *Experiments with Bubbles* (4–7). Illus. Series: Getting Started in Science. 1995, Enslow LB $18.95 (0-89490-666-6). 104pp. The properties of bubbles are explored in a series of experiments, each a little more complex than the last. (Rev: BL 12/1/95; SLJ 3/96) [530.4]

**16520** Gardner, Robert. *Experiments with Motion* (4–7). Illus. 1995, Enslow LB $18.95 (0-89490-667-4). 112pp. Projects using simple equipment illustrate the laws of motion and the ways motion differs in various situations. (Rev: BL 2/1/96; SLJ 2/96) [531]

**16521** Gibson, Gary. *Making Things Float and Sink* (3–5). Illus. Series: Science for Fun. 1995, Millbrook LB $20.90 (1-56294-617-X). 32pp. About a dozen projects are outlined on double-page spreads, each exploring the principles of buoyancy. (Rev: BL 7/95) [532]

**16522** Gibson, Gary. *Pushing and Pulling* (3–5). Photos by Roger Vlitos. Illus. by Tony Kenyon. Series: Science for Fun. 1995, Millbrook LB $20.90 (1-56294-630-7). 32pp. In double-page spreads, experiments are described that demonstrate principles of gravity, weight, friction, hydraulic forces, fluid drag, and pulleys. (Rev: SLJ 3/96) [530]

**16523** Lafferty, Peter. *Light and Sound* (4–8). Illus. by Terry Hadler. Series: Let's Investigate Science. 1996, Benchmark LB $25.64 (0-7614-0030-3). 64pp. Through experiments and a clever, well-illustrated text, the properties of light and sound are covered, the nature of their waves explained, and the uses of such applications as mirrors and lenses discussed. (Rev: SLJ 7/96) [535]

**16524** Morgan, Sally, and Adrian Morgan. *Materials* (4–7). Illus. Series: Designs in Science. 1994, Facts on File $16.95 (0-8160-2985-7). 48pp. Basic properties of matter and materials are explored in a series of experiments using everyday materials. (Rev: BL 7/94) [620.1]

**16525** Skurzynski, Gloria. *Zero Gravity* (2–4). Illus. 1994, Bradbury paper $15.00 (0-02-782925-1). 32pp. Weightlessness in space shuttles is explained, with a discussion of orbiting and zero gravity. (Rev: BCCB 10/94; BL 10/15/94; SLJ 10/94) [531]

# Energy and Motion

## General

**16526** Ardley, Neil. *The Science Book of Energy* (3–6). Illus. Series: Science Books. 1992, Harcourt $9.95 (0-15-200611-7). 28pp. This book of experiments introduces the concepts of force and energy through a series of 2-page projects. (Rev: BL 3/15/92; HB 9–10/92) [531.6]

**16527** Ardley, Neil. *The Science Book of Motion* (3–6). Illus. Series: Science Books. 1992, Harcourt $9.95 (0-15-200622-2). 28pp. This attractive book of experiments discusses the types and characteristics of motion and includes 12 projects to illustrate each. (Rev: BL 10/15/92; SLJ 1/93) [531]

**16528** Bonnet, Bob, and Dan Keen. *Science Fair Projects: Energy* (4–6). Illus. 1998, Sterling $16.95 (0-8069-9793-1). 96pp. Such sources of energy as sunlight, batteries, microwave ovens, and lightbulbs are used in this collection of 55 simple activities

about energy and the various forms it takes. (Rev: BL 3/1/98) [531]

**16529** Challoner, Jack. *Energy* (3–6). Illus. Series: Eyewitness Science. 1993, DK Publg. $15.95 (1-56458-232-9). 64pp. A very attractive book that explores the role of energy in our lives and describes its sources and uses. (Rev: SLJ 9/93) [621]

**16530** Chandler, Gary, and Kevin Graham. *Alternative Energy Sources* (4–8). Illus. Series: Making a Better World. 1996, Twenty-First Century LB $16.98 (0-8050-4621-6). 64pp. This account explores many varieties of alternative energy and the use of natural resources in environmentally safe ways. (Rev: BL 12/15/96; SLJ 1/97) [333.79]

**16531** Cobb, Vicki. *Why Doesn't the Earth Fall Up? And Other Not Such Dumb Questions About Motion* (2–4). Illus. by Ted Enik. 1989, Dutton paper $14.99 (0-525-67253-2). 40pp. The principles of physics explained for the young. (Rev: BCCB 2/89; BL 11/15/88; SLJ 2/89)

**16532** Doherty, Paul, and Don Rathjen. *The Cool Hot Rod and Other Electrifying Experiments on Energy and Matter* (4–8). Illus. Series: Exploratorium Science Snackbook. 1996, Wiley paper $10.95 (0-471-11518-5). 128pp. Based on exhibits at the Exploratorium in San Francisco, this book supplies activities that demonstrate the properties of energy and matter. (Rev: BL 4/15/96; SLJ 7/96) [531]

**16533** Doherty, Paul, and Don Rathjen. *The Spinning Blackboard and Other Dynamic Experiments on Force and Motion* (4–8). Illus. Series: Exploratorium Science Snackbook. 1996, Wiley paper $10.95 (0-471-11514-2). 128pp. The many activities in this well-organized, attractive book reveal important characteristics of force and motion. (Rev: BL 4/15/96; SLJ 6/96) [531]

**16534** Gutnik, Martin J., and Natalie B. Gutnik. *Projects That Explore Energy* (5–8). Illus. Series: Investigate. 1994, Millbrook LB $21.40 (1-56294-334-0). 72pp. A lucid, well-organized series of projects and experiments that explore power, force, and energy sources and resources. (Rev: BL 8/94; SLJ 6/94) [333.79]

**16535** Hawkes, Nigel. *Energy* (4–6). Illus. Series: New Technology. 1994, Twenty-First Century LB $16.90 (0-8050-3419-6). 32pp. Energy sources like water, wind, sunlight, and nuclear fission are described in a series of double-page spreads. (Rev: BL 7/94; SLJ 8/94) [621.044]

**16536** Kerrod, Robin. *Force and Motion* (4–6). Illus. by Ted Evans. Series: Let's Investigate Science. 1994, Marshall Cavendish LB $25.64 (1-85435-622-4). 64pp. Topics covered include the nature of force and motion, the laws of motion, and atomic, electric, and magnetic forces. (Rev: SLJ 5/94) [530]

**16537** Lafferty, Peter. *Force and Motion* (4–8). Illus. Series: Eyewitness Science. 1992, DK Publg. $15.95 (1-879431-85-8). 64pp. This account emphasizes the history of scientific discoveries and theories concerning force and motion. (Rev: BL 1/15/93; SLJ 12/92) [531]

**16538** Rybolt, Thomas R., and Robert C. Mebane. *Environmental Experiments About Renewable Energy* (3–5). Illus. Series: Science Experiments for Young People. 1994, Enslow LB $18.95 (0-89490-579-1). 96pp. This book contains 16 easy experiments to answer questions about renewable energy. (Rev: SLJ 2/95) [531]

**16539** Schultz, Ron. *Looking Inside Sports Aerodynamics* (5–8). Illus. by Peter Aschwanden. Series: X-Ray Vision. 1992, John Muir paper $6.95 (1-56261-065-1). 48pp. Using the effects of gravity, turbulence, drag, and lift, this book explains what happens when we throw or hit a ball or other object. (Rev: BL 1/15/93) [796]

**16540** Taylor, Kim. *Action* (3–5). Illus. 1992, Wiley $12.95 (0-471-57193-8). 32pp. Explains the principles of movement, including gliding and jumping. (Rev: SLJ 11/92) [530]

**16541** White, Larry. *Energy* (3–6). Illus. by Laurie Hamilton. Series: Simple Experiments for Young Scientists. 1995, Millbrook LB $19.90 (1-56294-473-8). 48pp. Simple projects using easily found materials supply answers to a number of questions about energy. (Rev: SLJ 9/95) [531]

**16542** Woelfle, Gretchen. *The Wind at Work: An Activity Guide to Windmills* (4–6). Illus. 1997, Chicago Review paper $14.95 (1-55652-308-4). 144pp. The history and uses of windmills are covered, with many fascinating activities. (Rev: BL 9/1/97; SLJ 10/97*) [621.4]

**16543** Woodruff, John. *Energy* (3–5). Series: Science Projects. 1998, Raintree Steck-Vaughn $24.97 (0-8172-4961-3). 48pp. The properties, uses, and kinds of energy are covered in a series of double-page spreads that give brief explanations followed by simple activities. (Rev: BL 3/15/98) [333]

## Coal, Gas, and Oil

**16544** Mitgutsch, Ali. *From Swamp to Coal* (2–3). Illus. 1985, Carolrhoda LB $18.60 (0-87614-233-1). 24pp. Much information is simply explained in this account of how coal is formed.

**16545** Stephen, R. J. *Oil Rigs* (2–4). Illus. 1987, Watts LB $11.90 (0-531-10185-1). 32pp. Photos and diagrams help to explain the workings of the compli-

cated and monstrous oil rigs. (Rev: BCCB 4/87; BL 5/15/87; SLJ 4/87)

## Nuclear Energy

**16546** Hawkes, Nigel. *Nuclear Power* (4–6). Illus. 1990, Rourke LB $13.95 (0-685-36380-5). 48pp. Safety and waste disposal, radioisotopes, and an explanation of fission are included in this heavily illustrated book.

**16547** Holland, Gini. *Nuclear Energy* (3–6). Illus. Series: Inventors and Inventions. 1996, Marshall Cavendish LB $25.64 (0-7614-0047-8). 63pp. The story of the discoverers of nuclear energy, its uses, and current problems and possibilities are covered, with many color photos. (Rev: BL 7/96; SLJ 9/96) [333.692]

**16548** O'Neill, Mary. *Power Failure* (4–7). Illus. by John Bindon. Series: SOS Planet Earth. 1991, Troll LB $13.50 (0-8167-2288-9); paper $4.95 (0-8167-2289-7). 32pp. The Chernobyl nuclear disaster is just one of the problems discussed in this look at an important environmental danger. (Rev: BL 6/15/91) [333.79]

**16549** Wilcox, Charlotte. *Powerhouse: Inside a Nuclear Power Plant* (4–8). Illus. 1996, Carolrhoda LB $16.95 (0-87614-945-X); paper $7.95 (0-87614-979-4). 48pp. A history of nuclear energy is followed by a description of how a power plant operates and the dangers that are present. (Rev: BL 10/1/96; SLJ 9/96) [621.48]

## Solar Energy

**16550** Asimov, Isaac. *How Did We Find Out About Solar Power?* (5–7). Illus. by David Wool. 1981, Walker LB $12.85 (0-8027-6423-1). 64pp. An account that explains what solar power is and how we use it.

**16551** Fowler, Allan. *Energy from the Sun* (1–3). Series: Rookie Read-About Science. 1997, Children's LB $18.00 (0-516-20432-7). 32pp. An easy-to-read science book that introduces solar energy and how it is captured and used. (Rev: BL 12/15/97) [697.78]

**16552** Gardner, Robert. *Science Project Ideas About the Sun* (4–7). Series: Science Project Ideas. 1997, Enslow LB $18.95 (0-89490-845-6). 96pp. The sun and solar energy are the subjects of this book that illustrates important concepts through a number of interesting projects and experiments. (Rev: BL 12/15/97; SLJ 1/98) [697.78]

# Heat

**16553** Darling, David J. *Between Fire and Ice: The Science of Heat* (4–8). Illus. Series: Experiment! 1992, Macmillan LB $13.95 (0-87518-501-0). 60pp. After a discussion of the scientific method, characteristics of heat are described and simple experiments are given to demonstrate these properties. (Rev: BL 10/1/92; SLJ 11/92) [536]

**16554** Gardner, Robert, and Eric Kemer. *Science Projects About Temperature and Heat* (4–8). Series: Science Projects. 1994, Enslow LB $19.95 (0-89490-534-1). 128pp. Using household materials, this book clearly outlines procedures and results involving projects that explore heat and temperature. (Rev: SLJ 1/95) [536]

**16555** Lafferty, Peter. *Heat and Cold* (4–8). Illus. by Terry Hadler. Series: Let's Investigate Science. 1996, Benchmark LB $25.64 (0-7614-0033-8). 64pp. The properties of heat and cold, their effects on living things, and how we use them are explained in this attractive science book that also contains many experiments. (Rev: SLJ 7/96) [536]

# Light and Color

**16556** Ardley, Neil. *Light* (4–6). Illus. 1992, Macmillan $13.95 (0-02-705667-8). 48pp. How various objects — including the eye, cameras, telescopes, and eyeglasses — use light. (Rev: SLJ 8/92) [535]

**16557** Ardley, Neil. *The Science Book of Color* (3–6). Illus. Series: Science Books. 1991, Harcourt $9.95 (0-15-200576-5). 28pp. Clear color photos enhance the step-by-step directions for science experiments involving color. (Rev: BL 3/1/91; SLJ 5/91) [535.6]

**16558** Ardley, Neil. *The Science Book of Light* (3–6). Illus. Series: Science Books. 1991, Harcourt $9.95 (0-15-200577-3). 28pp. Large-type instructions and full-color photographs are included in this book on science experiments involving light. (Rev: BL 3/1/91; SLJ 5/91) [535]

**16559** Asimov, Isaac. *How Did We Find Out About Lasers?* (5–7). Illus. by Erika Kors. 1990, Walker LB $13.85 (0-8027-6936-5). 64pp. A readable introduction to laser science by the veteran writer. (Rev: BL 8/90; SLJ 11/90) [621.36]

**16560** Branley, Franklyn M. *Day Light, Night Light: Where Light Comes From* (K–3). Illus. by Stacey

Schuett. Series: Let's-Read-and-Find-Out Science. 1998, HarperCollins LB $14.89 (0-06-027295-3). 32pp. In this book about light, topics like darkness, heat, light sources, reflection, vision, and the speed of light are discussed. (Rev: BL 12/1/97; SLJ 2/98) [535]

**16561** Burnie, David. *Light* (4–8). Illus. Series: Eyewitness Science. 1992, DK Publg. $15.95 (1-879431-79-3). 64pp. Clear explanations and a handsome format make these scientific principles readable. (Rev: BL 1/15/93) [535]

**16562** Darling, David J. *Making Light Work: The Science of Optics* (3–6). Illus. Series: Experiment! 1991, Macmillan LB $13.95 (0-87518-476-6). 64pp. An introduction, with experiments, to the principles of light. (Rev: BL 6/1/92) [535]

**16563** Day, Trevor. *Light* (3–5). Illus. Series: Science Projects. 1998, Raintree Steck-Vaughn $24.97 (0-8172-4943-5). 48pp. With explanatory text and simple activities, this account covers such topics as the nature of light, vision, shadows, photography, reflections, refraction, and color. (Rev: BL 3/15/98) [538]

**16564** Doherty, Paul, et al. *The Magic Wand and Other Bright Experiments on Light and Color* (4–8). Illus. 1995, Wiley paper $10.95 (0-471-11515-0). 128pp. A clearly written, well-organized text with fascinating activities that explore the properties of light and color. (Rev: BL 1/1–15/96; SLJ 1/96) [535]

**16565** Fox, Mary V. *Lasers* (3–6). Illus. Series: Inventors and Inventions. 1996, Benchmark LB $25.64 (0-7614-0067-2). 63pp. The history of laser technology, with profiles of several scientists involved in this branch of science and its effects in such areas as medicine. (Rev: BL 3/15/96; SLJ 6/96) [621.36]

**16566** Gardner, Robert. *Experiments with Light and Mirrors* (4–7). Illus. 1995, Enslow LB $18.95 (0-89490-668-2). 112pp. Using equipment like mirrors and cardboard, the properties of light are explained and demonstrated. (Rev: BL 2/1/96; SLJ 3/96) [535.2]

**16567** Gardner, Robert. *Science Projects About Light* (4–8). Series: Science Projects. 1994, Enslow LB $19.95 (0-89490-529-5). 128pp. This project book contains a wealth of demonstrations that explain the basic principles of light. (Rev: SLJ 1/95) [535]

**16568** Gibson, Gary. *Light and Color* (3–5). Illus. Series: Science for Fun. 1995, Millbrook LB $20.90 (1-56294-616-1). 32pp. Underlying scientific principles involving color and light are covered in a series of double-page spreads, each with a different project. (Rev: BL 7/95) [535]

**16569** Hecht, Jeff. *Optics: Light for a New Age* (5–8). Illus. 1988, Macmillan $15.95 (0-684-18879-1). 44pp. An overview of optics, including properties of light, optical instruments and laser technology. (Rev: BL 4/1/88)

**16570** Morgan, Nina. *Lasers* (3–6). Illus. Series: 20th Century Inventions. 1997, Raintree Steck-Vaughn LB $24.26 (0-8172-4812-9). 48pp. This oversize book describes types of lasers and their applications in such fields as CDs and medicine. (Rev: BL 6/1–15/97) [621.36]

**16571** Tomecek, Steve. *Bouncing and Bending Light* (4–8). Illus. by Arnie Ten. Series: Phantastic Physical Phenomena. 1995, Freeman $12.00 (0-7167-6541-1); paper $8.00 (0-7167-6591-8). 48pp. Facts are deduced from a series of experiments using common materials about the nature of light waves. (Rev: SLJ 10/95) [535.078]

**16572** *Why Are Zebras Black and White? Questions Children Ask About Color* (PS–3). Illus. 1996, DK Publg. $9.95 (0-7894-1122-9). 32pp. Common questions about colors (e.g., Why is the sea blue?) are answered in simple prose. (Rev: BL 12/1/96; SLJ 1/97) [574.5]

**16573** Whyman, Kathryn. *Light and Lasers* (4–6). Illus. 1986, Watts LB $12.40 (0-531-17033-0). 32pp. Large-print text and clear explanations of scientific principles for young children. (Rev: BL 12/1/86)

**16574** Zubrowski, Bernie. *Mirrors: Finding Out About the Properties of Light* (4–7). Illus. by Roy Doty. 1992, Morrow LB $13.93 (0-688-10592-0). 112pp. In this hands-on approach to science, games and activities entice the reader. (Rev: BL 7/92; SLJ 8/92) [535]

**16575** Zubrowski, Bernie. *Shadow Play: Making Pictures with Light and Lenses* (4–6). Illus. by Roy Doty. Series: Boston Children's Museum Activity Book. 1995, Morrow LB $15.93 (0-688-13210-3); paper $7.95 (0-688-13211-1). 112pp. Carefully outlines all sorts of projects involving shadows, from using mirrors to creating a shadow box and a box camera. (Rev: BL 9/1/95; SLJ 10/95) [771]

## Magnetism and Electricity

**16576** Ardley, Neil. *Electricity* (4–6). Illus. 1992, Macmillan $13.95 (0-02-705665-1). 48pp. This book tells about the types of electricity and how they are produced. (Rev: SLJ 8/92) [537]

**16577** Ardley, Neil. *The Science Book of Electricity* (3–6). Illus. Series: Science Books. 1991, Harcourt

$9.95 (0-15-200583-8). 29pp. Full-page spreads show step-by-step procedures for projects involving electricity. (Rev: BL 10/15/91) [535]

**16578** Ardley, Neil. *The Science Book of Magnets* (3–6). Illus. Series: Science Books. 1991, Harcourt $9.95 (0-15-200581-1). 29pp. Basic properties of magnets and magnetism are explored through a series of projects with clear directions and attractive illustrations. (Rev: BL 10/15/91) [528.4]

**16579** Bains, Rae. *Discovering Electricity* (1–3). Illus. by Joel Snyder. 1982, Troll LB $12.95 (0-89375-564-8); paper $2.95 (0-89375-565-6). 32pp. A simple explanation of what makes electricity work.

**16580** Berger, Melvin. *Switch On, Switch Off* (K–3). Illus. by Carolyn Croll. 1989, HarperCollins LB $15.89 (0-690-04786-X); paper $4.95 (0-06-445097-X). 32pp. Explaining the mysteries of electricity. (Rev: BL 4/15/89; HB 5–6/89)

**16581** Bonnet, Bob, and Dan Keen. *Science Fair Projects with Electricity and Electronics* (4–8). Illus. 1996, Sterling $16.95 (0-8069-1300-2). 96pp. Details of 46 projects and experiments involving such topics as electric motors and resistance. (Rev: BL 12/1/96; SLJ 12/96) [507.8]

**16582** Branley, Franklyn M. *What Makes a Magnet?* (K–3). Illus. by True Kelley. 1996, HarperCollins LB $14.89 (0-06-026442-X). 32pp. Elementary information and a few simple experiments are given on magnets and how they work. (Rev: BL 11/1/96; HB 11–12/96; SLJ 12/96) [538.4]

**16583** Cole, Joanna. *The Magic School Bus and the Electric Field Trip* (2–4). Illus. by Bruce Degen. Series: Magic School Bus. 1997, Scholastic $15.95 (0-590-44682-7). 56pp. Mrs. Frizzle's class visits a power plant to find out how electricity is made in this entertaining science book filled with facts, jokes, and puns. (Rev: BL 10/15/97; SLJ 11/97) [621.3]

**16584** Cosner, Sharon. *The Light Bulb* (4–6). Illus. 1984, Walker LB $10.85 (0-8027-6527-0). 64pp. A history of various forms of lighting, the light bulb, and the electrical industry.

**16585** de Pinna, Simon. *Electricity* (3–5). Series: Science Projects. 1998, Raintree Steck-Vaughn $24.97 (0-8172-4945-1). 48pp. The properties of electricity are covered in a series of double-page spreads, each of which covers a different aspect of the subject and outlines 3 or 4 simple acitivties. (Rev: BL 3/15/98) [621.3]

**16586** Fowler, Allan. *What Magnets Can Do* (1–2). Illus. Series: Rookie Read-About Science. 1995, Children's LB $18.50 (0-516-06034-1). 32pp. A basic introduction to magnets and magnetism, with photos, large type, and coverage of interesting topics. (Rev: BL 7/95) [538]

**16587** Gardner, Robert. *Science Projects About Electricity and Magnets* (4–8). Series: Science Projects. 1994, Enslow LB $19.95 (0-89490-530-9). 128pp. A wealth of projects that cover the basic principles of electricity and magnetism. (Rev: SLJ 1/95) [537]

**16588** Gibson, Gary. *Playing with Magnets* (3–5). Illus. 1995, Millbrook LB $20.90 (1-56294-615-3). 32pp. Each double-page spread is devoted to a different project illustrating various aspects of magnetism. (Rev: BL 5/15/95; SLJ 12/95) [538]

**16589** Gibson, Gary. *Understanding Electricity* (3–5). Photos by Roger Vlitos. Illus. by Tony Kenyon. Series: Science for Fun. 1995, Millbrook LB $20.90 (1-56294-629-3). 32pp. Using a 6-volt battery and a six-volt lightbulb along with other simple household products, electricity is explored in a series of experiments. (Rev: SLJ 3/96) [621.3]

**16590** Glover, David. *Batteries, Bulbs, and Wires: Science Facts and Experiments* (3–6). Illus. Series: Young Discoverers. 1993, Kingfisher paper $6.95 (1-85697-933-4). 31pp. Concepts related to magnetism and electricity are revealed in double-page spreads with many activities and connecting text. (Rev: SLJ 12/93) [507]

**16591** Levine, Shar, and Leslie Johnstone. *The Magnet Book* (4–6). Illus. 1997, Sterling $19.95 (0-8069-9943-8). 80pp. Clear drawings, photos, and instructions enhance this book containing more than 30 experiments dealing with magnetism and electricity. (Rev: BL 2/1/98) [538]

**16592** Parker, Steve. *Electricity* (4–8). Illus. Series: Eyewitness Science. 1992, DK Publg. $15.95 (1-879431-82-3). 64pp. In double-page spreads with many diagrams and photos, this book covers a history of our knowledge of electricity. (Rev: BL 1/15/93) [537]

**16593** Skurzynski, Gloria. *Waves: The Electromagnetic Universe* (4–7). Illus. 1996, National Geographic $16.95 (0-7922-3520-7). 48pp. Wave theory is explained, with many examples from nature and an explanation of the theory's importance. (Rev: BL 12/1/96; SLJ 11/96*) [539.2]

**16594** Tomecek, Steve. *Simple Attractions: Phantastic Physical Phenomena* (4–7). Illus. by Arnie Ten. 1995, W. H. Freeman $12.00 (0-7167-6601-9); paper $9.95 (0-7167-6632-9). 48pp. A collection of experiments related to magnetic attraction and static cling. (Rev: SLJ 3/96) [538]

**16595** VanCleave, Janice. *Janice VanCleave's Electricity: Mind-Boggling Experiments You Can Turn into Science Fair Projects* (5–7). Illus. 1994, Wiley paper $10.95 (0-471-31010-7). 96pp. As well as providing a discussion on the nature of electricity, this book offers 20 informative experiments that move from the very simple to the more complex. (Rev: BL 12/1/94; SLJ 11/94) [537]

**16596** VanCleave, Janice. *Janice VanCleave's Magnets: Mind-Boggling Experiments You Can Turn into Science Fair Projects* (4–6). Illus. Series: Spectacular Science Projects. 1993, Wiley paper $10.95 (0-471-57106-7). 88pp. Using magnets and the principles of magnetism, this book offers clear directions in developing many interesting science projects. Also use: *Animals; Gravity;* and *Molecules* (all 1993). (Rev: BL 5/1/93; SLJ 7/93) [538]

**16597** Whalley, Margaret. *Experiment with Magnets and Electricity* (2–5). Illus. Series: Experiment With. 1994, Lerner LB $19.93 (0-8225-2457-0). 32pp. Principles of magnetism and electricity are covered through a series of simple, fun-to-do experiments using everyday materials. (Rev: BL 3/1/94; SLJ 5/94) [537]

**16598** Wong, Ovid K. *Experimenting with Electricity and Magnetism* (5–8). Illus. Series: Venture Books. 1993, Watts LB $22.00 (0-531-12547-5). 128pp. This book includes 42 fairly easy experiments that explore properties of electricity and magnetism; also gives good background information. (Rev: SLJ 7/93) [537]

# Optical Illusions

**16599** Banyai, Istvan. *Re-Zoom* (K–5). Illus. by author. 1995, Viking paper $13.99 (0-670-86392-0). A remarkable visual journey in which viewers see something that turns out to be part of something larger. (Rev: BCCB 1/96; SLJ 9/95) [152]

**16600** Baum, Arline, and Joseph Baum. *Opt: An Illusionary Tale* (1–4). Illus. by authors. 1989, Puffin paper $4.99 (0-14-050573-3). A young prince has a birthday party in the land of Opt, where objects appear and disappear. (Rev: BL 5/15/87; HB 9–10/87; SLJ 6–7/87)

**16601** Churchill, E. Richard. *Optical Illusion Tricks and Toys* (4–7). Illus. by James Michaels. 1989, Sterling $12.95 (0-8069-6868-0). 128pp. Sixty-plus opportunities to demonstrate that things look different from what they really are. (Rev: BL 7/89) [152.1]

**16602** Cobb, Vicki, and Josh Cobb. *Light Action: Amazing Experiments with Optics* (5–8). Illus. 1993, HarperCollins LB $15.89 (0-06-021437-6). 208pp. Activities involving optics such as shadows, focus, reflection, and color. (Rev: BL 1/15/94) [535]

**16603** Doherty, Paul, et al. *The Cheshire Cat and Other Eye-Popping Experiments on How We See the World* (4–8). Illus. 1995, Wiley paper $10.95 (0-471-11516-9). 128pp. Based on exhibits at the Exploratorium in San Francisco, this attractive volume outlines activities and experiments that explore optics and vision. (Rev: BL 1/1–15/96; SLJ 1/96) [152.14]

**16604** Hawetson, Sarah. *Eye Magic: Fantastic Optical Illusions — An Interactive Pop-up Book* (4–7). Illus. by Phil Jacobs. 1994, Golden Bks. $19.95 (0-307-17625-8). 11pp. All kinds of optical illusions, like kaleidoscopes and fun-house mirrors, are featured in this pop-up book. (Rev: BL 11/15/94) [152.1]

**16605** Jennings, Terry. *101 Amazing Optical Illusions: Fantastic Visual Tricks* (4–7). Illus. 1997, Sterling $17.95 (0-8069-9462-2). 96pp. In a large-format book, easily followed instructions are given for optical illusions, divided into 3 groups: sight, perception, and movement. (Rev: BL 9/15/97; SLJ 8/97) [152.14]

**16606** Simon, Seymour. *The Optical Illusion Book* (4–6). Illus. by Constance Flera. 1976, Morrow LB $12.93 (0-688-03255-9); paper $6.95 (0-688-03254-0). 80pp. In addition to illustrations that show several optical illusions, there are explanations for each illusion and a chapter on illusion in art.

**16607** Westray, Kathleen. *Picture Puzzler* (3–7). Illus. 1994, Ticknor $13.95 (0-395-70130-9). 32pp. An oversize book that depicts a number of optical illusions and shows how proper focusing can produce different visual patterns. (Rev: BCCB 10/94; BL 7/94; HB 11–12/94; SLJ 8/94*) [152.14]

**16608** Wood, Robert W. *Physics for Kids: 49 Easy Experiments with Optics* (4–7). Illus. 1990, TAB $16.95 (0-8306-8402-6); paper $9.95 (0-8306-3402-9). 176pp. Good experiments are suggested for students using reasonable caution. (Rev: BL 2/15/91) [535]

## Simple Machines

**16609** Asimov, Isaac, and Elizabeth Kaplan. *What Happens When I Flush the Toilet?* (K–3). Illus. 1993, Stevens LB $19.93 (0-8368-0801-0). 24pp. In simple diagrams and clear text, this book explains how the flush toilet works. (Rev: BL 6/1–15/93) [628.3]

**16610** Lampton, Christopher. *Bathtubs, Slides and Roller Coaster Rails: Simple Machines That Are Really Inclined Planes* (3–5). Illus. by Carol Nicklaus. Series: Gateway Simple Machines. 1991, Millbrook paper $4.80 (1-878841-44-0). 32pp. A slim volume that introduces children to the inclined plane. Also use: *Seesaws, Nutcrackers, Brooms: Simple Machines That Are Really Levers* (1991). (Rev: BL 6/15/91) [621]

**16611** Whittle, Fran, and Sarah Lawrence. *Simple Machines* (3–5). Illus. Series: Design and Create. 1997, Raintree Steck-Vaughn $22.12 (0-8172-4889-

7). 32pp. How to make a cookie crusher and a bubble machine are among the 12 projects nicely presented in double-page spreads to outline each activity and give background information. (Rev: BL 2/1/98) [621.8]

## Sound

**16612** Ardley, Neil. *The Science Book of Sounds* (3–6). Illus. Series: Science Books. 1991, Harcourt $9.95 (0-15-200579-X). 29pp. The properties of sound are explored through a series of projects, with each explained in a 2-page spread. (Rev: BL 10/15/91) [534]

**16613** Baker, Wendy, and Andrew Haslam. *Sound* (3–6). Illus. Series: Make It Work! 1993, Macmillan $12.95 (0-689-71665-6). 48pp. The principles of sound are introduced and explained through a series of activities and experiments. (Rev: SLJ 4/93) [530]

**16614** Broekel, Ray. *Sound Experiments* (1–4). Illus. 1983, Children's LB $21.00 (0-516-01686-5). 48pp. Simple experiments that introduce the principles of sound to primary school children.

**16615** Darling, David J. *Sounds Interesting: The Science of Acoustics* (3–6). Illus. 1992, Macmillan LB $13.95 (0-87518-477-4). 64pp. A straightforward text provides an in-depth exploration of the science of sound. (Rev: BL 5/1/92) [523]

**16616** de Pinna, Simon. *Sound* (3–5). Series: Science Projects. 1998, Raintree Steck-Vaughn $24.97 (0-8172-4944-3). 48pp. The properties of sound are explored in a series of double-page spreads that give simple explanations followed by 3 or 4 simple activities. (Rev: BL 3/15/98) [534]

**16617** Gibson, Gary. *Hearing Sounds* (3–5). Illus. Series: Science for Fun. 1995, Millbrook LB $20.90 (1-56294-614-5). 32pp. Basic concepts involving sound are introduced through a series of simple activities and projects, with simple instructions and clear, often amusing illustrations. (Rev: BL 7/95) [534]

**16618** Kaner, Etta. *Sound Science* (3–5). Illus. by Louise Phillips. 1992, Addison-Wesley paper $9.95 (0-201-56758-X). 96pp. The 40-plus experiments and projects in this book, which can be done with easily obtained materials, explore various aspects of sound. (Rev: SLJ 6/92) [530]

**16619** Morgan, Sally, and Adrian Morgan. *Using Sound* (4–7). Illus. Series: Designs in Science. 1994, Facts on File $16.95 (0-8160-2981-4). 48pp. The properties of sound and their relation to everyday life are covered in the text and a number of experiments using readily available materials. (Rev: BL 7/94) [534]

# Space Exploration

**16620**  Alston, Edith. *Let's Visit a Space Camp* (2–4). Illus. Series: Let's Visit. 1990, Troll LB $11.50 (0-8167-1743-5); paper $3.50 (0-8167-1744-3). 32pp. Captivating photos of the U.S. Space Camp in Huntsville, Alabama. (Rev: BL 5/1/90; SLJ 7/90) [629.45]

**16621**  Baird, Anne. *Space Camp: The Great Adventure for NASA Hopefuls* (3–7). Illus. by Robert Koropp. 1992, Morrow LB $13.93 (0-688-10228-X). 48pp. A group of children enjoy 6 days at the U.S. Space Camp in Huntsville, Alabama, which was built to look like a proposed space station. (Rev: BCCB 6/92; BL 3/1/92; SLJ 5/92) [629.45]

**16622**  Baird, Anne. *The U.S. Space Camp Book of Rockets* (4–6). Illus. by David Graham. 1994, Morrow $15.00 (0-688-12228-0). 48pp. The past and future history of space exploration is traced through a visit by Space Camp trainees to the Rocket and Space Museum in Huntsville, Alabama. (Rev: BL 4/1/94; SLJ 5/94) [629.45]

**16623**  Baker, David. *Danger on Apollo 13* (4–7). Illus. 1988, Rourke LB $22.60 (0-86592-871-1). 32pp. The account of the 1970 explosion on a space flight that threatened the lives of 3 U.S. astronauts. (Rev: BL 12/1/88; SLJ 12/88)

**16624**  Baker, David. *Factories in Space* (4–8). Illus. 1987, Rourke LB $23.93 (0-86592-409-0). 48pp. The focus is on NASA's plans for a space-orbiting lab. (Rev: BL 2/15/88)

**16625**  Baker, David. *Peace in Space* (4–8). Illus. 1987, Rourke LB $23.93 (0-86592-408-2). 48pp. A look at the Strategic Defense Initiative, whose purpose is to stop enemy missiles before they reach the earth. (Rev: BL 2/15/88)

**16626**  Becklake, Sue. *Space, Stars, Planets and Spacecraft* (4–7). Illus. by Brian Delf and Luciano Corbella. Series: See and Explore. 1991, DK Publg. $12.95 (1-879-43114-9). 64pp. An explanation of how complex machines work in space and their contribution to life on earth. (Rev: BL 3/1/92; SLJ 5/92) [629.4]

**16627**  Berliner, Don. *Living in Space* (4–6). Illus. 1993, Lerner LB $22.60 (0-8225-1599-7). 72pp. The living conditions of travelers in space are covered. (Rev: BL 7/93) [629.47]

**16628**  Branley, Franklyn M. *Floating in Space* (K–3). Illus. by True Kelley. Series: Lets-Read-and-Find-Out Science. 1998, HarperCollins LB $15.89 (0-06-025433-5). 32pp. Life in space is covered in this book describing weightlessness, space suits, the food astronauts eat, and the activities aboard a space shuttle. (Rev: BL 12/1/97; SLJ 2/98) [629.47]

**16629**  Branley, Franklyn M. *Is There Life in Outer Space?* (1–3). Illus. by Don Madden. 1986, HarperCollins paper $4.95 (0-06-445049-X). 32pp. In cartoon format, the intriguing question of life in outer space is explored for the young.

**16630**  Branley, Franklyn M. *Venus: Magellan Explores Our Twin Planet* (4–6). Illus. 1994, HarperCollins LB $15.89 (0-06-020384-6). 64pp. This is an account of the *Magellan* space probe and what it has learned about the structure, motion, and features of the planet Venus. (Rev: BL 8/94; SLJ 6/94) [523.4]

**16631**  Brenner, Barbara. *Planetarium: The Museum That Explores the Many Wonders of Our Solar System* (1–4). Illus. by Ron Miller. Series: Bank Street Museum Book. 1993, Bantam LB $9.50 (0-533-35428-0). 48pp. On a trip to a planetarium, the reader visits outer space and learns about the solar system. (Rev: BL 9/1/93; SLJ 8/93) [520]

**16632**  Briggs, Carole S. *Women in Space: Reaching the Last Frontier* (4–6). Illus. 1988, Lerner LB $22.60 (0-8225-1581-4); paper $5.95 (0-8225-9547-8). 80pp. Profiles of women astronauts, American and Russian. (Rev: BL 9/1/88; SLJ 10/88)

**16633**  Burns, Khephra, and William Miles. *Black Stars in Orbit: NASA's African American Astronauts* (4–6). Illus. 1994, Harcourt $19.00 (0-15-200432-7); paper $8.95 (0-15-200276-6). 64pp. A history of the contributions of African Americans to NASA and a record of the discrimination they had to overcome. (Rev: BCCB 2/95; BL 2/15/95; SLJ 2/95*) [629.45]

**16634**  Burrows, William E. *Mission to Deep Space: Voyagers' Journey of Discovery* (4–6). Illus. 1993, W. H. Freeman $14.40 (0-7167-6500-4). 80pp. An account of the *Voyager* missions to explore the planets of the solar system and what they found. (Rev: BL 11/15/93; SLJ 12/93) [523.4]

**16635**  Butterfield, Moira. *Space* (3–8). Illus. Series: Look Inside Cross-Sections. 1994, DK Publg. paper $5.95 (1-56458-682-0). 32pp. Double-page spreads introduce such space explorers as *Apollo, Mercury, Viking, Voyager,* and the *Hubble Telescope*. (Rev: BL 2/1/95; SLJ 2/95) [629.47]

**16636**  Campbell, Ann-Jeanette. *The New York Public Library Amazing Space: A Book of Answers for Kids* (5–8). Illus. by Jessica Wolk-Stanley. 1997, Wiley paper $12.95 (0-471-14498-3). 186pp. This question-and-answer book introduces space exploration, the solar system, individual planets, galaxies, and related phenomena. (Rev: SLJ 7/97) [523]

**16637**  Campbell, Peter A. *Launch Day* (2–4). Illus. 1995, Millbrook LB $21.40 (1-56294-611-0). 32pp. An account of the shuttle *Atlantis*, including preparations, launching, and the flight and return. (Rev: BL 12/1/95; SLJ 3/96) [629.454]

**16638**  Charleston, Gordon. *Armstrong Lands on the Moon* (3–6). Illus. Series: Great 20th Century Expeditions. 1994, Dillon LB $13.95 (0-87518-530-4). 32pp. This handy account covers a history of space exploration from the first rockets to the moon landing. (Rev: SLJ 11/94) [523]

**16639**  Clay, Rebecca. *Space Travel and Exploration* (4–8). Illus. Series: Secrets of Space. 1997, Twenty-First Century LB $20.40 (0-8050-4474-4). 64pp. A history of modern space exploration, covering manned flights, space stations, space probes, and telescopes. (Rev: BL 7/97; SLJ 1/98) [629.5]

**16640**  Cole, Michael D. *Challenger: America's Space Tragedy* (4–6). Illus. Series: Countdown to Space. 1995, Enslow LB $18.95 (0-89490-544-9). 48pp. This tragic milestone in the history of our space program is movingly described. Two other titles in this series are *Friendship 7: First American in Orbit* and *Vostok 1: First Human in Space* (both 1995). (Rev: SLJ 2/96) [523]

**16641**  Engelbert, Phillis. *Astronomy and Space: From the Big Bang to the Big Crunch* (4–8). Illus. 1997, Gale $84.00 (0-7876-0942-0). 600pp. Three hundred alphabetically arranged entries about space exploration, including material on the laws and features of the universe, the history of astronomy,

important astronauts, famous observatories, and the greenhouse effect. (Rev: SLJ 5/97) [523]

**16642**  English, June A., and Thomas D. Jones. *Mission: Earth: Voyage to the Home Planet* (4–7). Illus. 1996, Scholastic $16.95 (0-590-48571-7). 48pp. The space program is introduced, with special coverage on the flights of the shuttle *Endeavor* in 1994 and its environmental studies. (Rev: BL 10/15/96; SLJ 10/96) [550]

**16643**  Fallen, Anne-Catherine. *USA from Space* (4–7). Illus. 1997, Firefly $19.95 (1-55209-159-7); paper $7.95 (1-55209-157-0). 48pp. Excellent satellite pictures of parts of the Earth are contained in this book, which also explains the value of satellite imagery in tracking pollution, population, and natural disasters. (Rev: BL 3/1/98; SLJ 12/97) [917.3]

**16644**  Fox, Mary V. *Rockets* (3–6). Illus. Series: Inventors and Inventions. 1996, Benchmark LB $25.64 (0-7614-0063-X). 63pp. Rocket pioneers are profiled, along with their discoveries and the changes these have caused in the modern world. (Rev: BL 3/15/96; SLJ 3/96) [621.43]

**16645**  Fox, Mary V. *Satellites* (3–6). Illus. Series: Inventors and Inventions. 1996, Marshall Cavendish LB $25.64 (0-7614-0049-4). 63pp. Details in an informal text and many interesting photos the story of satellites, their uses, and their creators. (Rev: BL 7/96; SLJ 8/96) [629.43]

**16646**  Kennedy, Gregory. *The First Men in Space* (5–7). Illus. Series: World Explorers. 1991, Chelsea LB $19.95 (0-7910-1324-3). 111pp. This book covers the early years and accomplishments of both Soviet and American space programs. (Rev: SLJ 8/91) [629.44]

**16647**  Kettelkamp, Larry. *ETs and UFOs: Are They Real?* (5–8). Illus. 1996, Morrow $16.00 (0-688-12868-8). 86pp. This account tries to sort out the truth from the massive amount of material on extraterrestrials and unidentified flying objects. (Rev: BL 12/15/96; SLJ 1/97) [001.9]

**16648**  Kettelkamp, Larry. *Living in Space* (5–7). Illus. 1993, Morrow $14.00 (0-688-10018-X). 128pp. Tells how astronauts live in space and discusses plans for space exploration in the future. (Rev: BL 10/1/93; SLJ 9/93) [629.4]

**16649**  Markle, Sandra. *Pioneering Space* (5–8). Illus. 1992, Macmillan LB $14.95 (0-689-31748-4). 40pp. Presents basic information on space travel and how people will live in space. (Rev: BL 9/1/92; SLJ 2/93) [629.4]

**16650**  Marsh, Carole. *Unidentified Flying Objects and Extraterrestrial Life* (4–6). Illus. 1996, Twenty-First Century LB $20.40 (0-8050-4472-8). 64pp. Covers a wide variety of topics associated with UFOs, including the history of famous sightings. (Rev: BL 12/1/96; SLJ 12/96) [001.9]

**16651** Maurer, Richard. *Junk in Space* (4–8). Illus. 1989, Simon & Schuster paper $5.95 (0-671-67767-5). 48pp. Discussing the various kinds of space garbage orbiting earth. (Rev: BL 11/15/89) [363]

**16652** Moche, Dinah L. *The Astronauts* (1–3). Illus. 1979, Random paper $3.25 (0-394-83901-3). A description of various spacecraft and how astronauts are trained to use them.

**16653** Petty, Kate. *You Can Jump Higher on the Moon and Other Amazing Facts About Space Exploration* (2–4). Illus. Series: I Didn't Know That. 1997, Millbrook LB $19.90 (0-7613-0564-5). 32pp. Each double-page spread in this book is used to introduce fascinating facts about space travel and present some related experiments and activities. (Rev: SLJ 10/97) [523]

**16654** Ride, Sally, and Susan Okie. *To Space and Back* (3–7). Illus. 1986, Lothrop $19.00 (0-688-06159-1); Morrow paper $12.95 (0-688-09112-1). 96pp. The first American woman in space describes her experiences aboard the shuttle. (Rev: BCCB 10/86; BL 11/1/86; SLJ 11/86)

**16655** Ride, Sally, and Tam O'Shaughnessy. *Voyager: An Adventure to the Edge of the Solar System* (3–5). Illus. 1992, Crown $17.00 (0-517-58157-4). 36pp. With photos from NASA, the focus is mainly on discoveries by Ride, the first U.S. woman in space, about 4 planets. (Rev: BL 8/92; SLJ 6/92) [523.4]

**16656** Robinson, Fay. *Space Probes to the Planets* (2–4). Illus. 1993, Whitman LB $14.95 (0-8075-7548-8). 32pp. Stunning color photos and clear text tell the story of the space probe. (Rev: BL 2/15/93; SLJ 3/93) [523.4]

**16657** Rockwell, Anne, and David Brion. *Space Vehicles* (PS–1). Illus. by authors. 1994, Dutton paper $13.99 (0-525-45270-2). A simple introduction to such devices as rockets, space probes, satellites, and spaceships. (Rev: SLJ 12/94) [523]

**16658** Scott, Elaine. *Adventure in Space: The Flight to Fix the Hubble* (4–7). Illus. 1995, Hyperion LB $16.89 (0-7868-2031-4). 64pp. A behind-the-scenes look at NASA and the mission to repair the Hubble telescope in 1993. (Rev: BL 7/95*; SLJ 4/95*) [522]

**16659** Sipiera, Diane M., and Paul P. Sipiera. *Project Apollo* (2–4). Illus. Series: True Book: Space. 1997, Children's $21.00 (0-516-20435-1). 48pp. Using large type and many photos, this book chronicles one of the landmark space projects. (Rev: BL 12/1/97) [629.45]

**16660** Sipiera, Diane M., and Paul P. Sipiera. *Project Mercury* (2–4). Illus. Series: True Book: Space. 1997, Children's $21.00 (0-516-20443-2). 48pp. An account of this space venture told in large type with many clear photos. (Rev: BL 12/1/97; SLJ 1/98) [629.45]

**16661** Sipiera, Diane M., and Paul P. Sipiera. *Space Stations* (2–4). Illus. 1997, Children's $20.00 (0-516-20450-5). 48pp. This simple account explains what space stations are, their history, the Mir station, and plans for the future. (Rev: BL 2/1/98) [629.44]

**16662** Smith, Howard E. *Daring the Unknown: A History of NASA* (5–8). Illus. 1987, Harcourt $16.95 (0-15-200435-1). 128pp. Many photos add interest to this story of NASA — the National Aeronautics and Space Administration — its accomplishments, successes, and failures. (Rev: BL 1/15/88)

**16663** Solomon, Maury. *An Album of Voyager* (4–7). Illus. 1990, Watts LB $13.90 (0-531-10876-7). 64pp. An outstanding collection of captioned photos of the journeys of the 2 Voyagers to various planets. (Rev: BL 12/1/90; SLJ 2/91) [523.2]

**16664** Souza, D. M. *Space Sailing* (4–6). Illus. 1994, Lerner LB $21.50 (0-8225-2850-9). 64pp. The history and development of these solar-powered spacecraft are covered plus future developments. (Rev: BL 1/1/95) [629]

**16665** Steele, Philip. *Space Travel* (4–8). Illus. Series: Pocket Facts. 1991, Macmillan LB $11.95 (0-89686-585-1). 32pp. An introduction to space exploration, featuring basic facts and color illustrations. (Rev: BL 3/15/92) [629.4]

**16666** Stein, R. Conrad. *Apollo 11* (3–5). Illus. Series: Cornerstones of Freedom. 1992, Children's LB $19.50 (0-516-06651-X). 32pp. In simple text and many pictures, the story of the Apollo 11 flight to the moon. (Rev: BL 6/1/92) [629.45]

**16667** Stewart, Gail B. *In Space* (4–6). Illus. Series: Living Spaces. 1989, Rourke LB $21.27 (0-86592-116-4). 32pp. A richly illustrated account of life in a space colony. (Rev: BL 11/1/89) [919.9]

**16668** Stott, Carole. *Space Exploration* (4–8). Series: Eyewitness Books. 1997, Knopf LB $20.99 (0-679-98563-8). 60pp. An overview of the history of space exploration, with material on the various missions and their findings. (Rev: BL 12/15/97; SLJ 1/98) [523]

**16669** Suen, Anastasia. *Man on the Moon* (PS–2). Illus. by Benrei Huang. 1997, Viking paper $15.99 (0-670-87393-4). 32pp. A retelling in picture book format of the history-making flight of the Apollo 11 space mission, which put men on the moon. (Rev: BL 11/1/97; SLJ 11/97) [629.45]

**16670** Sullivan, George. *The Day We Walked on the Moon: A Photo History of Space Exploration* (5–8). Illus. 1990, Scholastic paper $4.95 (0-685-58532-8). 80pp. The history of U.S. space exploration, showing the accomplishments of both the United States and the Soviet Union. (Rev: BL 9/1/90; SLJ 2/91) [629.4]

# Technology, Engineering, and Industry

## General and Miscellaneous Industries and Inventions

**16671** Alphin, Elaine M. *Vacuum Cleaners* (3–5). Illus. Series: Household History. 1997, Carolrhoda LB $16.95 (1-57505-018-8). 48pp. A fascinating history of the vacuum cleaner with an explanation of how it works. (Rev: BL 1/1–15/98) [683]

**16672** Bender, Lionel. *Invention* (4–8). Illus. Series: Eyewitness Books. 1991, Knopf LB $18.99 (0-679-90782-3). 64pp. With careful drawings and charts, the world of inventions and inventors is explored. (Rev: BL 6/1/91; SLJ 7/91) [609]

**16673** Bryant-Mole, Karen. *Toys* (PS–3). Series: Picture This. 1997, Rigby LB $12.95 (1-57572-057-4). 24pp. Many toys are shown in this heavily illustrated, interactive book. Also use *Games* (1997). (Rev: BL 10/15/97; SLJ 12/97) [745.592]

**16674** Cash, Terry. *Plastics* (3–5). Illus. by Ed Barber. Series: Threads. 1990, Garrett LB $15.93 (0-944483-70-4). 26pp. An introduction to plastics that shows everyday things made of plastic and how they are made and recycled. (Rev: BL 2/1/91) [668.4]

**16675** Chandler, Jane. *Glass* (3–5). Illus. by Ed Barber. Series: Threads. 1991, Garrett LB $15.93 (1-56074-004-3). 28pp. A history of glass plus coverage of present-day production and uses. (Rev: BL 11/15/91) [666.1]

**16676** Corey, Melinda. *Let's Visit a Spaghetti Factory* (2–4). Illus. Series: Let's Visit. 1990, Troll LB $11.50 (0-8167-1741-9). 32pp. This is the story of how durum wheat is used for the pasta dough that is formed into different shapes. (Rev: BL 5/1/90; SLJ 7/90) [670]

**16677** Crump, Donald J., ed. *How Things Work* (5–7). Illus. 1984, National Geographic LB $12.50 (0-87044-430-1). 104pp. A handsome volume that explains how a variety of objects, from toasters to space shuttles, work.

**16678** Davis, Gary. *From Rock to Fireworks* (3–6). Series: Changes. 1997, Children's LB $23.00 (0-516-20739-3). 32pp. A photoessay that shows each of the steps in the process of manufacturing fireworks, with some activities for the reader. (Rev: BL 2/15/98) [662.1]

**16679** Dixon, Annabelle. *Paper* (2–5). Illus. by Ed Barber. Series: Threads. 1991, Garrett LB $15.93 (1-56074-003-5). 28pp. The origins of paper are described, and information is given on current production. (Rev: BL 11/15/91) [676]

**16680** Erlbach, Arlene. *The Kids' Invention Book* (4–6). Illus. 1997, Lerner LB $22.60 (0-8225-2414-7). 64pp. Beginning with 15-year-old Chester Greenwood, who invented earmuffs in 1873, this book introduces over a dozen young people and their inventions. (Rev: BL 2/1/98) [608]

**16681** Erlbach, Arlene. *Teddy Bears* (3–5). Illus. 1997, Carolrhoda LB $16.95 (1-57505-019-6); paper $7.95 (1-57505-222-9). 48pp. Provides the history of the teddy bear, discusses the problem of identifying the first maker, and describes the industry today. (Rev: BL 1/1–15/98) [745.594]

**16682** Forman, Michael H. *From Wax to Crayon* (2–3). 1997, Children's LB $24.00 (0-516-20708-3). 32pp. Traces the various processes and materials that go into producing the common wax crayon. (Rev: BL 10/15/97) [609]

**16683** Graham, Ian, ed. *How Things Work* (4–6). Illus. Series: Nature Company Discoveries. 1996, Time Life $16.00 (0-8094-9249-0). 64pp. This handsome, well-illustrated volume explains the inner workings of everyday machines and appliances with a special foldout section. (Rev: BL 6/1–15/96) [600]

**16684** Hellman, Hal. *Beyond Your Senses: The New World of Sensors* (4–6). Illus. 1997, Lodestar paper $16.99 (0-525-67533-7). 87pp. Sensors that respond to light, heat, and motion — as in toasters and burglar alarms — are described, with material on robots and their future uses. (Rev: BCCB 7–8/97; SLJ 9/97) [609]

**16685** Jones, Charlotte F. *Accidents May Happen: Fifty Inventions Discovered by Mistake* (4–6). Illus. 1996, Delacorte $16.95 (0-385-32162-7). 96pp. Fifty products, like dynamite and yo-yos, that came into being by accident. A sequel to *Mistakes That Worked* (1991). (Rev: BCCB 9/96; BL 6/1–15/96; SLJ 6/96) [124]

**16686** Jones, Charlotte F. *Mistakes That Worked* (4–6). Illus. by John O'Brien. 1994, Doubleday paper $10.95 (0-385-32043-4). 82pp. An entertaining look at successful mistakes, such as the ice cream vendor who ran out of dishes and invented the cone. (Rev: BCCB 10/91; BL 10/15/91*; SLJ 10/91) [609]

**16687** Jones, George. *My First Book of How Things Are Made: Crayons, Jeans, Peanut Butter, Guitars and More* (3–5). Illus. 1995, Scholastic $12.95 (0-590-48004-9). 64pp. The manufacturing process of 8 objects common in children's lives — including grape jelly, footballs, orange juice, blue jeans, and books — are enumerated. (Rev: SLJ 2/96) [658.5]

**16688** Karnes, Frances A., and Suzanne M. Bean. *Girls and Young Women Inventing: Twenty True Stories About Inventors Plus How You Can Be One Yourself* (4–8). Illus. 1995, Free Spirit paper $12.95 (0-915793-89-X). 168pp. The story of Jennifer Donabar and her electric clock invention plus material on other inventions by young women. (Rev: SLJ 12/95) [658.5]

**16689** Kerrod, Robin. *Communications* (4–6). Illus. by Ted Evans. Series: Let's Investigate Science. 1994, Marshall Cavendish LB $25.64 (1-85435-624-0). 64pp. From signs and signals to complex electronic devices like radar and space satellites, this book explores various facets of communication. (Rev: SLJ 5/94) [501.4]

**16690** Kuklin, Susan. *From Head to Toe: How a Doll Is Made* (1–3). Illus. 1994, Hyperion $15.95 (1-56282-666-2). 32pp. The step-by-step creation of a doll is shown using imaginative photos and a text that introduces each worker. (Rev: BCCB 5/94; BL 5/1/94*; HB 5–6/94; SLJ 5/94) [688.7]

**16691** Lampton, Christopher. *Chemical Accident* (4–6). Illus. Series: Disaster Book. 1994, Millbrook LB $19.90 (1-56294-316-2). 48pp. Introduces the chemical industry and explains what happens when chemical accidents occur, their effects, and how to

prevent them. (Rev: BL 6/1–15/94; SLJ 4/94) [363.17]

**16692** *Machines and Inventions* (5–8). Illus. Series: Understanding Science and Nature. 1993, Time Life $17.95 (0-8094-9704-2). 152pp. Double-page spreads are used to explain such inventions as the box camera, printing press, and dynamite. (Rev: BL 1/15/94; SLJ 6/94) [621.8]

**16693** Markle, Sandra. *Science Surprises* (4–5). Illus. by June Otani. 1996, Scholastic paper $2.99 (0-590-48401-X). 63pp. Six science surprises — like the invention of photography and the discoveries of penicillin and Velcro™ — are described, along with 11 fascinating experiments to expand on scientific principles. (Rev: SLJ 7/97) [507]

**16694** Mebane, Robert C., and Thomas R. Rybolt. *Plastics and Polymers* (4–6). Illus. Series: Everyday Material Science Experiments. 1995, Twenty-First Century LB $18.90 (0-8050-2843-9). 64pp. The composition, uses, and structure of plastics and polymers are covered in a series of projects with easy procedures and easily procured materials. (Rev: BL 9/15/95; SLJ 10/95) [547.7]

**16695** Mitgutsch, Ali. *From Rubber Tree to Tire* (K–2). Illus. by author. 1986, Carolrhoda LB $18.60 (0-87614-297-8). 24pp. The production of rubber explained in easy text. (Rev: BL 12/15/86)

**16696** Mitgutsch, Ali. *From Sea to Salt* (2–3). Illus. by author. 1985, Carolrhoda LB $18.60 (0-87614-232-3). 24pp. Beginning with the salt trapped in the earth, simple text and pictures explain the steps that put it on the table. (Rev: BL 7/85; SLJ 9/85)

**16697** Mitgutsch, Ali. *From Wood to Paper* (K–2). Illus. by author. 1986, Carolrhoda LB $18.60 (0-87614-296-X). 24pp. Full-color illustrations and easy text explain how paper is made. (Rev: BL 12/15/86)

**16698** Parker, Steve. *Fifty-Three and a Half Things That Changed the World and Some That Didn't!* (3–6). Illus. by David West. 1995, Millbrook LB $21.90 (1-56294-603-X). 62pp. A lighthearted look at how various inventions — like clocks, toilets, and the printing press — have changed human history. (Rev: SLJ 8/95) [608]

**16699** Paterson, Alan J. *How Glass Is Made* (5–8). Illus. 1985, Facts on File $14.95 (0-8160-0038-7). 32pp. Glossary, diagrams, and color photos highlight this informative look at the business of making glass. (Rev: BL 6/15/85; SLJ 2/86)

**16700** Platt, Richard. *Inventions Explained: A Beginner's Guide to Technological Breakthroughs* (4–8). Illus. Series: Your World Explained. 1997, Holt $18.95 (0-8050-4876-6). 69pp. An in-depth look at the changing world of technological innovations, with coverage on systems of transportation, energy, medicine, machinery, and computing. (Rev: BL 3/1/98; SLJ 2/98) [609]

**16701** Platt, Richard. *The Smithsonian Visual Timeline of Inventions* (3–6). Illus. 1994, DK Publg. $16.95 (1-56458-675-8). 64pp. Using a timeline of world events as a framework, a history of inventions is detailed in 4 main areas of endeavor: communications, health, industry, and travel. (Rev: BL 12/15/94; SLJ 2/95) [609]

**16702** Reid, Struan. *Inventions and Trade* (5–8). Illus. Series: Silk and Spice Routes. 1994, Silver Burdett LB $15.95 (0-02-726316-9). 48pp. A history of the trade between China and Europe along the Spice Route and of the technological advances that occurred because of this cultural exchange. (Rev: BL 12/15/94; SLJ 12/94) [382.09]

**16703** Royston, Angela. *Toys* (PS–2). Illus. by Richard Manning. Series: What's Inside? 1991, DK Publg. $8.95 (1-879431-08-4). 17pp. A look inside such toys as a teddy bear, a doll house, a robot, and a jack-in-the-box. (Rev: SLJ 2/92) [745]

**16704** Skurzynski, Gloria. *Almost the Real Things: Simulation in Your High Tech World* (5–8). 1991, Macmillan $16.95 (0-02-778072-4). 64pp. Tells how engineers and scientists simulate events from weightlessness to complex animation. (Rev: BCCB 10/91; BL 10/15/91; HB 11–12/91; SLJ 10/91) [620]

**16705** Smith, Elizabeth Simpson. *Paper* (4–8). Illus. 1984, Walker LB $10.85 (0-8027-6569-6). 64pp. The manufacture of paper is described plus its many uses.

**16706** Soucie, Gary. *What's the Difference Between . . . Lenses and Prisms and Other Scientific Things?* (3–6). Illus. by Jeff Domm. 1995, Wiley paper $9.95 (0-471-08626-6). 85pp. This book describes the differences in technology between 2 similar commodities, e.g., soap and detergent; iron and steel. (Rev: SLJ 2/96) [609]

**16707** Tucker, Tom. *Brainstorm! The Stories of Twenty American Kid Inventors* (4–7). 1995, Farrar $15.00 (0-374-30944-2). 148pp. A history of young American inventors who produced such innovations as waterskiing, Popsicles, and ear muffs. (Rev: BCCB 10/95; BL 8/95; SLJ 10/95) [609]

**16708** Turvey, Peter. *Everyday Things and How They Work* (3–8). Illus. by Nicholas Hewetson. Series: X-Ray Picture Books. 1995, Watts LB $24.00 (0-531-14347-3). 48pp. With detailed illustrations and good descriptions, the inner workings of such devices as clocks, cars, engines, cameras, computers, calculators, and lasers are revealed. (Rev: SLJ 12/95) [600]

**16709** Turvey, Peter. *Inventions: Inventors and Ingenious Ideas* (3–6). Illus. Series: Timelines. 1992, Watts $13.95 (0-531-15243-X). 48pp. This book gives the history of important inventions from the

Stone Age to today's high technology. (Rev: BL 9/15/92; SLJ 3/93) [609]

**16710** Wilcox, Jane. *Why Do We Use That?* (4–6). Illus. Series: Why Do We . . .? 1996, Watts LB $18.00 (0-531-14395-3). 31pp. Explains the origin of such common household items as toothbrushes, pencils, garden tools, games, and toys. (Rev: SLJ 3/97) [608]

**16711** Wood, Richard, ed. *Great Inventions* (4–6). Illus. Series: Nature Company Discoveries. 1995, Time Life $16.00 (0-7835-4766-8). 64pp. Some of the world's greatest inventions and inventors are briefly discussed in this well-illustrated book, with a final 8-page foldout section. (Rev: BL 1/1–15/96) [609]

**16712** Wulffson, Don L. *The Kid Who Invented the Popsicle and Other Surprising Stories About Inventions* (3–6). 1997, Dutton paper $13.99 (0-525-65221-3). 128pp. An alphabetically arranged presentation of the stories behind such inventions as animal crackers and zippers. (Rev: BL 2/15/97; SLJ 3/97) [609]

## Aeronautics and Airplanes

**16713** Asimov, Isaac, and Elizabeth Kaplan. *How Do Airplanes Fly?* (K–3). Illus. Series: Ask Isaac Asimov. 1992, Stevens LB $19.93 (0-8368-0800-2). 24pp. In this easily read book, there is an explanation of how birds and planes overcome the forces of gravity and air resistance. (Rev: BL 6/1–15/93) [629.13]

**16714** Baker, Sanna Anderson. *Grandpa Is a Flyer* (2–4). Illus. by Bill Farnsworth. 1995, Albert Whitman LB $15.95 (0-8075-3033-6). 32pp. The life story of a man who was fascinated by flying even as a child in the 1920s. (Rev: BL 4/1/95; SLJ 7/95) [629.1]

**16715** Barton, Byron. *Airplanes* (PS). Illus. by author. 1986, HarperCollins LB $14.89 (0-690-04532-8). 32pp. Simple words and brightly colored artwork portray the roles of airplanes. (Rev: BL 8/86; SLJ 9/86)

**16716** Bellville, Cheryl Walsh. *The Airplane Book* (2–5). Illus. 1991, Carolrhoda LB $22.60 (0-87614-686-8); paper $5.95 (0-87614-618-3). 48pp. A simple history of flight, from Icarus to the Voyager mission. (Rev: SLJ 2/92) [629.1]

**16717** Berliner, Don. *Aviation: Reaching for the Sky* (5–8). Illus. Series: Innovators. 1997, Oliver LB $16.95 (1-881508-33-1). 144pp. A thorough history of aviation, beginning with early hot-air balloons and dirigibles and continuing through the Wright Brothers and Sikorsky's helicopter to supersonic jets. (Rev: SLJ 7/97) [629.133]

**16718** Berliner, Don. *Before the Wright Brothers* (4–7). Illus. 1990, Lerner LB $22.60 (0-8225-1588-1). 72pp. The story of the struggle to fly that went on before the Wright brothers. (Rev: BL 6/15/90; SLJ 9/90) [629.133]

**16719** Crisfield, Deborah. *An Air Show Adventure* (3–5). Illus. by Donald Emmerich. Series: Let's Take a Trip. 1990, Troll LB $11.50 (0-8167-1735-4). 32pp. An account of the air show held each year at Oshkosh, Wisconsin. (Rev: SLJ 8/90) [629]

**16720** Curlee, Lynn. *Ships of the Air* (3–6). Illus. 1996, Houghton $14.95 (0-395-69338-1). 32pp. An attractively presented history of dirigibles and hot-air ballooning. (Rev: BCCB 10/96; BL 9/1/96; HB 11–12/96; SLJ 9/96) [629.133]

**16721** Darling, David J. *Up and Away: The Science of Flight* (3–6). Illus. 1992, Macmillan LB $13.95 (0-87518-479-0). 64pp. Color photos, clear text, and in-depth experiments explain the science of flight. (Rev: BL 5/1/92; SLJ 3/92) [629.19]

**16722** Davis, Meredith. *Up and Away! Taking a Flight* (2–4). Illus. by Ken Dubrowski. 1997, Mondo paper $4.95 (1-57255-214-X). 23pp. An international flight is covered from entering the airport to reaching the final destination. (Rev: SLJ 1/98) [629.133]

**16723** Goold, Ian. *The Rutan Voyager* (4–7). Illus. 1988, Rourke LB $22.60 (0-86592-869-X). 32pp. The around-the-world, nonstop flight of Richard Rutan and Jeana Yeager in 1986. (Rev: BL 12/1/88; SLJ 12/88) [910.4]

**16724** Haskins, Jim. *Black Eagles: African Americans in Aviation* (5–8). Illus. 1995, Scholastic $14.95 (0-590-45912-0). 176pp. This account traces the contributions made to aviation history by African Americans from before World War I to the astronaut Mae Jemison. (Rev: BL 2/15/95; SLJ 4/95) [629]

**16725** Hewish, Mark. *The Young Scientist Book of Jets* (4–7). Illus. 1978, EDC paper $6.95 (0-86020-051-5). An attractive, semicomic book format is used to cover basic material.

**16726** Holland, Gini. *Airplanes* (3–6). Illus. Series: Inventors and Inventions. 1996, Benchmark LB $25.64 (0-7614-0068-0). 63pp. A history of airplanes from their beginnings to the present, with brief profiles of some of the great inventors and pilots. (Rev: BL 3/15/96; SLJ 3/96) [629.133]

**16727** Horton, Madelyn. *The Lockerbie Airline Crash* (5–8). Illus. Series: World Disasters. 1992, Lucent LB $19.45 (1-56006-017-4). 64pp. This book gives background information on the Pan Am flight that crashed in December 1988, its consequences, and how the investigation has been carried out. (Rev: SLJ 7/92) [629]

**16728** Jefferis, David. *Flight: Fliers and Flying Machines* (3–6). Illus. 1991, Watts $13.95 (0-531-

15233-2). 48pp. Beginning with the legend of Icarus, this book chronicles flight to modern times. (Rev: BL 12/15/91; SLJ 3/92) [629.13]

**16729** Jennings, Terry. *Planes, Gliders, Helicopters and Other Flying Machines* (3–5). Illus. Series: How Things Work. 1993, Kingfisher LB $10.95 (1-85697-684-X); paper $6.95 (1-85697-869-9). 40pp. In very simple terms with many illustrations, the principles of flight are introduced with many examples of flying machines pictured and identified. (Rev: BL 6/1–15/93) [629]

**16730** Johnstone, Michael. *Planes* (3–6). Illus. Series: Look Inside Cross-Sections. 1994, DK Publg. paper $5.95 (1-56458-520-4). 32pp. Cross-sections of such planes as the Fokker triplane, the Concorde, the Boeing 314, and the U.S. B-17 bomber are presented. (Rev: BL 10/15/94; SLJ 9/94) [629.133]

**16731** Kerrod, Robin. *Amazing Flying Machines* (1–4). Illus. Series: Eyewitness Juniors. 1992, Knopf LB $9.99 (0-679-92765-4); paper $6.95 (0-679-82765-X). 32pp. In attractive double-page spreads, each featuring a large color illustration, the history of flight and airplanes is covered. (Rev: BL 8/92; SLJ 9/92) [629.13]

**16732** Lindblom, Steven. *Fly the Hot Ones* (4–8). Illus. 1991, Houghton $17.95 (0-395-51075-9). 102pp. Drawings, diagrams, and photos help the reader to experience piloting 8 "hot" aircraft. (Rev: BL 7/91) [629]

**16733** Lopez, Donald, ed. *Flight* (4–6). Illus. Series: Nature Company Discoveries. 1995, Time Life $16.00 (0-7835-4761-7). 64pp. A brief, well-illustrated history of human attempts to conquer the skies, with a final 8-page foldout section. (Rev: BL 1/1–15/96) [629.1]

**16734** Magee, Doug, and Robert Newman. *Let's Fly from A to Z* (PS–3). Illus. 1992, Dutton paper $15.99 (0-525-65105-5). 32pp. Lots of information about airplanes and crisp photography make this an attractive book for the aviation enthusiast. (Rev: BL 10/15/92; SLJ 11/92) [629.133]

**16735** Maynard, Christopher. *Airplane* (PS–4). Illus. Series: Mighty Machines. 1995, DK Publg. paper $9.95 (0-7894-0211-4). 21pp. Many airplanes are pictured and described, with information on other airport machines and the helicopter. (Rev: BL 12/1/95) [629.136]

**16736** Miller, Marilyn. *Behind the Scenes at the Airport* (PS–3). Illus. 1996, Raintree Steck-Vaughn LB $21.40 (0-8172-4086-1). 32pp. Using a question-and-answer approach, the activities that make an airport work are pictured. (Rev: BL 4/15/96; SLJ 12/96) [387.7]

**16737** Millspaugh, Ben. *Aviation and Space Science Projects* (5–8). Illus. 1992, TAB paper $9.95 (0-

8306-2156-3). 133pp. The principles of flight are explored in 19 projects that vary in difficulty and complexity. (Rev: SLJ 6/92) [629.1]

**16738** Nahum, Andrew. *Flying Machine* (4–8). Illus. Series: Eyewitness Books. 1990, Knopf LB $20.99 (0-679-90744-0). 64pp. With charts and diagrams, this account presents the story of airplanes and other flying machines. (Rev: BL 11/15/90; SLJ 1/91) [629.1]

**16739** Otfinoski, Steven. *Taking Off: Planes Then and Now* (2–4). Illus. Series: Here We Go! 1996, Benchmark LB $21.36 (0-7614-0407-4). 32pp. A history of airplanes that is notable for its informative large-print text and spectacular photos. (Rev: SLJ 2/97) [629.133]

**16740** Pallotta, Jerry, and Fred Pallotta. *The Airplane Alphabet Book* (2–4). Illus. by Rob Bolster. 1997, Charlesbridge $15.95 (0-88106-907-8). 32pp. Presents 26 airplanes plus information about the history of flight. (Rev: BL 2/1/97; SLJ 7/97) [629]

**16741** Parker, Steve. *High in the Sky* (3–5). Illus. Series: Supersmarts. 1997, Candlewick $11.99 (0-7636-0128-4). 24pp. This introduction to airplanes and flight uses a magazine-style format, with bright illustrations, many sidebars, quizzes, and double-page spreads. (Rev: BL 8/97; SLJ 1/98) [629.13]

**16742** Parker, Steve. *What's Inside Airplanes?* (4–8). Illus. Series: What's Inside? 1995, Bedrick LB $17.95 (0-87226-394-0). 45pp. Elaborate illustrations are used to show various types of airplanes and describe their parts, including pistons, propellers, fuel tanks, and landing gear. (Rev: SLJ 12/95) [629.133]

**16743** Provensen, Alice, and Martin Provensen. *The Glorious Flight Across the Channel with Louis Bleriot* (1–5). Illus. by authors. 1983, Puffin paper $4.95 (0-317-63651-0). 40pp. The story of a historic flight by a French aviation pioneer. Caldecott Medal winner, 1984.

**16744** Ross, Wilma S. *X-15 Rocket Plane* (3–5). Illus. Series: Those Daring Machines. 1995, Macmillan LB $13.95 (0-89686-831-1). 48pp. A brief history of rocket aircraft is given, with details on the *X-15* and its career. (Rev: BL 2/15/95) [629.133]

**16745** Royston, Angela. *Planes* (PS). Illus. by Tim Ridley. Series: Eye Openers. 1992, Macmillan paper $8.99 (0-689-71564-1). 32pp. The concept of airplanes is introduced for preschoolers in this sturdy book with many photographs. (Rev: BL 8/92; SLJ 10/92) [629]

**16746** Saunders, Rupert. *Balloon Voyage* (4–7). Illus. 1988, Rourke LB $22.60 (0-86592-870-3). 32pp. The 1987 attempt to cross the Atlantic in a hot-air balloon. (Rev: BL 12/1/88; SLJ 12/88)

**16747** Stein, R. Conrad. *The Spirit of St. Louis* (3–5). Illus. Series: Cornerstones of Freedom. 1994, Children's LB $19.50 (0-516-06682-X). 32pp. The record-breaking, trans-Atlantic flight of Lindbergh is re-created with details on the airplane that he flew. (Rev: BL 1/15/95) [629.13]

**16748** Stein, R. Conrad. *The Story of the Flight at Kitty Hawk* (3–5). Illus. by Len W. Meents. 1981, Children's LB $13.27 (0-516-04614-4). 32pp. The landmark flight of the Wright brothers.

**16749** Stille, Darlene R. *Airplanes* (2–4). Illus. Series: True Books: Transportation. 1997, Children's LB $21.00 (0-516-20325-8). 48pp. After a short history of flight, this book describes many airplanes and explains how they work. (Rev: BL 9/15/97) [629.133]

**16750** Stille, Darlene R. *Helicopters* (2–4). Series: True Books: Transportation. 1997, Children's LB $21.00 (0-516-20335-5). 48pp. A number of types of helicopters are introduced in a simple format with an explanation of how they work. (Rev: BL 9/15/97) [629]

**16751** *The Story of Flight* (4–6). Illus. Series: Voyages of Discovery. 1995, Scholastic $19.95 (0-590-47643-2). 45pp. Using die-cut pages, transparencies, foldouts, and stickers, this attractive book traces the history of flight and airplanes from ancient times to the present. (Rev: SLJ 5/96) [629]

**16752** Sullivan, George. *How an Airport Really Works* (4–6). Illus. 1993, Dutton paper $15.99 (0-525-67378-4). 128pp. The history of airports and how their functions have changed through the years are recounted in this book that also contains many black-and-white photographs. (Rev: BCCB 5/93; BL 4/15/93; SLJ 3/93) [387.7]

**16753** Taylor, Richard L. *The First Unrefueled Flight Around the World: The Story of Dick Rutan and Jeana Yeager* (4–6). Illus. 1994, Watts LB $22.00 (0-531-20176-7). 64pp. The story of this remarkable flight around the world during 1986 in a specially designed plane. (Rev: BL 3/15/95; SLJ 3/95) [629.13]

**16754** Tessendorf, K. C. *Barnstormers and Daredevils* (5–8). Illus. 1988, Macmillan LB $14.95 (0-689-31346-2). 96pp. True tales for the aviation buff. (Rev: BCCB 4/88; BL 9/15/88; SLJ 10/88)

**16755** Tessendorf, K. C. *Wings Around the World: The American World Flight of 1924* (4–8). Illus. 1991, Macmillan LB $14.95 (0-689-31550-3). 104pp. The thrilling story of the 4 teams that were involved in the first around-the-world flight in 1924. (Rev: SLJ 11/91) [629.132]

**16756** Weiss, Harvey. *Strange and Wonderful Aircraft* (4–7). Illus. 1995, Houghton $15.95 (0-395-68716-0). 64pp. Humankind's various attempts to conquer the skies are highlighted, from ancient myths to the success of the Wright brothers. (Rev: BL 2/1/96; SLJ 12/95) [629.13]

**16757** Younkin, Paula. *Spirit of St. Louis* (3–5). Illus. Series: Those Daring Machines. 1995, Macmillan LB $13.95 (0-89686-832-X). 48pp. A description of Lindbergh's airplane and the trans-Atlantic flight that made history. (Rev: BL 2/15/95) [629.13]

# Building and Construction

## General

**16758** Adam, Robert. *Buildings: How They Work* (4–6). Illus. 1996, Sterling $14.95 (0-8069-0958-7). 48pp. This well-illustrated volume discusses dwellings, from primitive caves to skyscrapers, and their design, materials, and uses. (Rev: BL 2/15/96) [721]

**16759** *Architecture and Construction* (4–6). Illus. Series: Voyages of Discovery. 1995, Scholastic $19.95 (0-590-47644-0). 45pp. An introduction to architecture that spans the subject from simple shelters to such constructions as a Japanese paper house, skyscrapers, castles, and Frank Lloyd Wright's Fallingwater, with brief text and many illustrations, transparencies, foldouts, stickers, and a spiral binding. (Rev: SLJ 5/96) [720]

**16760** Boring, Mel. *Incredible Constructions: And the People Who Built Them* (4–7). Illus. 1985, Walker LB $13.85 (0-8027-6560-2). Hoover Dam, the Statue of Liberty, and other structures are featured in this history of engineering marvels. (Rev: BL 6/1/85; SLJ 8/86)

**16761** Bortz, Fred. *Catastrophe! Great Engineering Failure — and Success* (4–6). Illus. 1995, W. H. Freeman $16.00 (0-7167-6538-1); paper $11.20 (0-7167-6539-X). 80pp. Highlights catastrophic events involving such structures as the Tacoma Narrows Bridge, DC-10 airplanes, and nuclear power plants. (Rev: BL 6/1–15/95; SLJ 8/95) [620]

**16762** Cash, Terry. *Bricks* (3–5). Illus. by Ed Barber. Series: Threads. 1990, Garrett LB $15.93 (0-944483-68-2). 26pp. The history of bricks, how they are made, and their many uses are explored. (Rev: BL 2/1/91; SLJ 5/91) [666]

**16763** Corbishley, Mike. *The World of Architectural Wonders* (5–8). Illus. 1997, Bedrick LB $19.95 (0-87226-279-0). 48pp. The story of 14 worldwide architectural wonders, including Stonehenge, the pyramids of Egypt, Chartres Cathedral, the Taj Mahal, and Hoover Dam. (Rev: BL 6/1–15/97; SLJ 7/97) [720]

**16764** Darling, David J. *Spiderwebs to Skyscrapers: The Science of Structures* (3–6). Illus. Series: Experiment! 1991, Macmillan LB $13.95 (0-87518-478-

2). 57pp. From natural phenomena like birds' nests and spiderwebs to bridges, skyscrapers, and dams, structural engineering is explained with some projects included. (Rev: SLJ 3/92) [690]

**16765** Delafosse, Claude. *Construction* (PS–2). Illus. Series: First Discovery. 1997, Scholastic $11.95 (0-590-93783-9). 24pp. Various forms of building and their processes are introduced simply with interesting visuals that encourage interaction. (Rev: BL 2/15/97) [338.476]

**16766** *Do Buildings Have Bones? First Questions and Answers About Buildings* (PS–3). Illus. Series: Time-Life Library of First Questions and Answers. 1995, Time Life $14.95 (0-7835-0900-6). 48pp. A series of questions and answers supplies basic information about buildings and construction. (Rev: BL 8/95) [720]

**16767** Dunn, Andrew. *Skyscrapers: Structures* (4–7). Illus. Series: Structures. 1993, Thomson $13.95 (1-56847-027-4). 32pp. After a discussion of the whys of tall buildings, this account explains how they are made. (Rev: BL 6/1–15/93) [720.4]

**16768** Ford, Barbara. *The Elevator* (4–7). Illus. 1982, Walker LB $8.85 (0-8027-6451-7). 64pp. The innovation of the elevator and its effects on construction are discussed.

**16769** Gibbons, Gail. *Up Goes the Skyscraper!* (PS–1). Illus. by author. 1986, Simon & Schuster $14.95 (0-02-736780-0). 32pp. Equipment, construction phases, and workers are depicted in the simple tale of the rise of a skyscraper. (Rev: BL 4/15/86; SLJ 5/86)

**16770** Hawkes, Nigel. *Structures and Buildings* (4–6). Illus. Series: New Technology. 1994, Twenty-First Century $16.90 (0-8050-3418-8). 32pp. The structures described are modern and include the English Channel tunnel and Biosphere 2 and such proposed projects as a U.S. space station and a huge Japanese skyscraper. (Rev: BL 7/94; SLJ 8/94) [624.1]

**16771** Hill, Lee S. *Bridges Connect* (1–3). Illus. Series: Building Blocks. 1997, Carolrhoda $19.93 (1-57505-021-8). 32pp. Using color photos and a simple text, the structure of bridges is introduced. Also use *Canals Are Water Roads* and *Dams Give Us Power* (both 1997). (Rev: BL 9/15/97; SLJ 7/97) [624]

**16772** Hill, Lee S. *Roads Take Us Home* (1–3). Illus. Series: Building Blocks. 1997, Carolrhoda LB $14.95 (1-57505-022-6). 32pp. Types of roads and their construction are introduced in color photos and a simple text. Also use *Towers Reach High* (1997). (Rev: BL 9/15/97; SLJ 7/97) [388.1]

**16773** Hunter, Ryan Ann. *Cross a Bridge* (PS–2). Illus. by Edward Miller. 1998, Holiday LB $15.95

(0-8234-1340-3). A simple picture book that describes various kinds of bridges. (Rev: SLJ 3/98) [625]

**16774** Lynch, Anne. *Great Buildings* (4–6). Illus. Series: Nature Company Discoveries. 1996, Time Life $24.95 (0-8094-9371-3). 64pp. Some of the world's most impressive structures are introduced, with illustrations and an 8-page foldout. (Rev: BL 9/15/96; SLJ 3/97) [720.9]

**16775** Macaulay, David. *Unbuilding* (5–8). Illus. by author. 1980, Houghton $18.00 (0-395-29457-6); paper $6.95 (0-395-45360-7). 128pp. A book that explores the concept of tearing down the Empire State Building.

**16776** Macaulay, David. *Underground* (5–8). Illus. by author. 1983, Houghton $16.95 (0-395-24739-X); paper $8.95 (0-395-34065-9). An exploration in text and detailed drawings of the intricate network of systems under city streets.

**16777** Mann, Elizabeth. *The Brooklyn Bridge* (4–7). Illus. Series: Wonders of the World. 1996, Mikaya $18.95 (0-9650493-0-2). 48pp. The story of the building of the Brooklyn Bridge is told through the eyes of a family. (Rev: BL 2/1/97; SLJ 6/97*) [624]

**16778** Millard, Anne. *Pyramids* (4–6). Illus. 1996, Kingfisher $15.95 (1-85697-674-2). 64pp. The design, construction, and use of pyramids are explained, primarily those found in Egypt. (Rev: BL 5/1/96; SLJ 6/96) [932]

**16779** Platt, Richard. *Stephen Biesty's Incredible Explosions: Exploded Views of Astonishing Things* (4–7). Illus. by Stephen Biesty. 1996, DK Publg. $19.95 (0-7894-1024-9). 32pp. Various aspects of buildings, construction, and technology are shown in this book of cutaway illustrations that includes material on such diverse subjects as London's Tower Bridge, the city of Venice, and a futuristic space station. (Rev: SLJ 10/96) [690]

**16780** Ricciuti, Edward R. *America's Top 10 Bridges* (3–7). Illus. Series: America's Top 10. 1997, Blackbirch LB $13.95 (1-56711-197-1). 24pp. Using double-page spreads, this book describes such famous American bridges as the Golden Gate. (Rev: BL 1/1–15/98; SLJ 2/98) [388]

**16781** Robbins, Ken. *Bridges* (PS–2). Illus. 1991, Dial LB $13.89 (0-8037-0930-7). 32pp. Sixteen different bridges are presented in this photo catalog. (Rev: BCCB 6/91; BL 4/15/91; HB 9–10/91; SLJ 6/91) [624.2]

**16782** Sauvain, Philip. *Skyscrapers* (4–6). Illus. Series: How We Build. 1991, Garrett LB $17.26 (0-944483-78-X). 48pp. Explains the processes and problems of building skyscrapers, with many examples pictured and a number of simple projects. (Rev: BL 6/15/91) [690]

**16783** Tarsky, Sue. *The Busy Building Book* (PS–2). Illus. by Alex Ayliffe. 1998, Putnam $15.95 (0-399-23137-4). 32pp. An appealing book that uses collages to describe the building of a skyscraper. (Rev: BL 1/1–15/98; SLJ 3/98) [690]

**16784** Wilkinson, Philip. *Amazing Buildings* (4–7). Illus. by Paolo Donati. 1993, DK Publg. $16.95 (1-56458-234-5). 48pp. Twenty famous buildings from around the world are pictured in 2-page spreads that include exterior and interior pictures and floor plans. (Rev: BL 9/1/93; SLJ 8/93) [720]

**16785** Wilkinson, Philip. *Building* (4–8). Illus. Series: Eyewitness Books. 1995, Knopf $19.00 (0-679-87256-6). 64pp. This introduction to structures discusses engineering, building materials, and types of construction. (Rev: BL 8/95; SLJ 8/95) [690]

**16786** Wilkinson, Philip. *Super Structures* (4–6). Illus. Series: Inside Guides. 1996, DK Publg. $15.95 (0-7894-1011-7). 44pp. In double-page spreads, the interiors of such structures as oil rigs, skyscrapers, and undersea tunnels are pictured and explained. (Rev: BL 12/15/96; SLJ 2/97) [624.1]

## Houses

**16787** Bown, Deni. *Open House* (K–4). Illus. by Steve Noon. 1996, DK Publg. $16.95 (0-7894-1049-4). 10pp. By pulling tabs, the interiors of houses around the world are revealed. (Rev: BL 12/15/96) [690]

**16788** Knight, Bertram T. *From Mud to House* (3–6). Illus. Series: Changes. 1997, Children's LB $24.00 (0-516-20737-7). 32pp. This book traces the materials and processes used in manufacturing bricks and of their many uses, including the construction of houses. (Rev: BL 2/15/98) [666]

**16789** McGraw, Sheila. *This Old New House* (3–5). Illus. by author. 1989, Annick paper $4.95 (1-55037-034-0). From arranging for permits to the final product, this is the story of the renovation of a house. (Rev: SLJ 9/89) [728]

**16790** Oxlade, Chris. *Houses and Homes: Activities, Things to Make, Facts* (3–6). Photos by Martyn Chillmaid. Illus. by Raymond Turvey. Series: Technology Craft Topics. 1994, Watts LB $20.00 (0-531-14330-9). 32pp. In addition to a history of houses through the ages, this book gives instructions on how to make 5 models plus a solar heater. (Rev: SLJ 1/95) [690]

**16791** Ventura, Piero. *Houses: Structures, Methods, and Ways of Living* (4–8). Illus. by author. 1993, Houghton $16.95 (0-395-66792-5). 64pp. Beginning with caves and ending with modern apartments, this account traces the various kinds of homes people have had throughout history. (Rev: SLJ 12/93) [690]

**16792** White, Sylvia. *Welcome Home!* (3–7). Illus. Series: A World of Difference. 1995, Children's LB $21.00 (0-516-08193-4). 32pp. Family dwellings around the world are explored in text and pictures, with material on how they have evolved for different climates and environments. (Rev: BL 7/95; SLJ 12/95) [391.36]

**16793** Wood, Tim. *Houses and Homes* (4–8). Series: See Through History. 1997, Viking paper $17.99 (0-670-86777-2). 48pp. A well-illustrated examination of different kinds of houses and homes, their variations through history, and their structure and parts. (Rev: BL 11/15/97; SLJ 4/98) [690]

**16794** Yardley, Thompson. *Down the Drain: Explore Your Plumbing* (3–8). Illus. Series: Lighter Look. 1991, Millbrook LB $20.90 (1-878841-28-9). 40pp. This book discusses household plumbing and how it works — and sometimes malfunctions — and gives tips on water conservation. (Rev: SLJ 8/91) [728]

## Clothing, Textiles, and Jewelry

**16795** Badt, Karin Luisa. *On Your Feet!* (3–7). Illus. Series: A World of Difference. 1994, Children's LB $21.00 (0-516-08189-6). 32pp. Using many drawings, this account describes shoes, their styles, and their purposes in various societies and times. (Rev: BL 1/1/95; SLJ 1/95) [391]

**16796** Bryant-Mole, Karen. *Clothes* (K–3). Illus. Series: Picture This! 1997, Rigby LB $12.95 (1-57572-149-X). 24pp. This book shows what clothes are made of and which should be worn on different occassions. (Rev: BL 10/15/97) [646]

**16797** Carlson, Laurie. *Boss of the Plains: The Hat That Won the West* (K–4). Illus. by Holly Meade. 1998, DK Publg. $16.95 (0-7894-2479-7). 32pp. The story of John Batterson Stetson and the broad-brimmed hat he produced to protect himself from the sun and the rain in California. (Rev: BL 3/1/98; SLJ 4/98) [338.7]

**16798** Cole, Trish. *Why Do We Wear That?* (4–6). Illus. Series: Why Do We . . .? 1996, Watts LB $18.00 (0-531-14396-1). 31pp. An overview of fashion in clothes from World War II to the present. (Rev: SLJ 3/97) [646]

**16799** *Dazzling! Jewelry of the Ancient World* (5–8). Illus. Series: Buried Worlds. 1995, Lerner LB $23.93 (0-8225-3203-4). 64pp. Using archaeological methods, this account reveals the wonders and beauty of jewelry from various ancient civilizations. (Rev: BL 7/95; SLJ 4/95) [739.27]

**16800** Dixon, Annabelle. *Wool* (3–5). Illus. by Ed Barber. Series: Threads. 1990, Garrett LB $15.93 (0-944483-73-9). 26pp. The nature of wool, its origins, and its uses are explored in text and pictures. (Rev: BL 2/1/91) [677.31]

**16801** Greenberg, Keith E. *Bill Bowerman and Phil Knight: Building the Nike Empire* (3–4). Illus. by Dick Smolinski. Series: Partners. 1994, Blackbirch LB $13.95 (1-56711-085-1). 47pp. The story of the pair who created the Nike empire and the production of the first "waffle sole" using a waffle iron. (Rev: SLJ 1/95) [391]

**16802** Kalman, Bobbie. *18th Century Clothing* (3–6). Illus. Series: Historic Communities. 1993, Crabtree LB $19.16 (0-86505-492-4); paper $7.95 (0-86505-512-2). 32pp. Many illustrations and simple text show how people of all levels of society dressed in the 18th century. A companion volume is: *19th Century Clothing* (1993). (Rev: BL 8/93; SLJ 9/93) [391]

**16803** Keeler, Patricia A., and Francis X. McCall, Jr. *Unraveling Fibers* (3–5). Illus. 1995, Simon & Schuster $16.00 (0-689-31777-8). 36pp. An introduction to plant, animal, and synthetic fibers and how they are used to produce various kinds of cloth. (Rev: BCCB 6/95; BL 8/95; HB 5–6/95; SLJ 6/95) [677]

**16804** Lawlor, Laurie. *Where Will This Shoe Take You? A Walk Through the History of Footwear* (5–8). Illus. 1996, Walker LB $18.85 (0-8027-8435-6). 144pp. This is a history of footwear, from sandals worn by the ancients to the sneakers popular today. (Rev: BCCB 1/97; BL 11/15/96; SLJ 5/97) [391]

**16805** L'Hommedieu, Arthur J. *From Plant to Blue Jeans* (3–6). Illus. Series: Changes. 1997, Children's LB $24.00 (0-516-20738-5). 32pp. This book begins with the planting of cotton seeds and ends with children wearing blue jeans. (Rev: BL 2/15/98) [687]

**16806** Morris, Ann. *Shoes, Shoes, Shoes* (PS–2). Illus. 1995, Lothrop LB $14.93 (0-688-13667-2). 32pp. Thirty-one shoes from a variety of cultures are identified and pictured. (Rev: BCCB 10/95; BL 10/1/95; SLJ 1/96) [391]

**16807** Nichelason, Margery G. *Shoes* (3–5). Illus. 1997, Carolrhoda $16.95 (1-57505-047-1). 48pp. From the first shoes worn by the Egyptians to today's latest trends, this is the surprising history of footwear through the years. (Rev: BL 1/1–15/98) [391.4]

**16808** Power, Vicki. *Vanity* (4–7). Illus. Series: A Very Peculiar History. 1995, Watts LB $20.00 (0-531-14356-2). 48pp. A history of fashion, jewelry, makeup, and other beautifying trends. (Rev: BL 6/1–15/95) [391.6]

**16809** Pressling, Robert. *My Sweater* (PS–1). Illus. by Fiona Pragoff. Series: First Step Science. 1995, Gareth Stevens LB $19.93 (0-8368-1187-9). 32pp. Covers how a sweater is produced, along with an explanation of its parts and care, in this beginning science book. (Rev: BL 7/95) [646.4]

**16810** Rowland-Warne, L. *Costume* (4–8). Illus. Series: Eyewitness. 1992, Knopf $19.00 (0-679-81680-1). 64pp. With numerous illustrations and brief text, this book supplies a history of fashion and design. (Rev: BL 8/92; SLJ 2/93) [391]

**16811** Smith, Elizabeth Simpson. *Cloth* (5–8). Illus. 1985, Walker LB $10.85 (0-8027-6577-7). 60pp. The discovery of fiber and how cloth is made. (Rev: BL 8/85; SLJ 11/85)

**16812** Straus, Lucy. *The Story of Shoes* (PS). Illus. by Mas Miyamoto. Series: Real Readers. 1989, Raintree Steck-Vaughn LB $21.40 (0-8172-3534-5). 32pp. This easily read account describes how shoes evolved from ancient times. (Rev: BL 2/1/90) [391]

**16813** Tythacott, Louise. *Jewelry* (4–8). Illus. Series: Traditions Around the World. 1995, Thomson Learning LB $24.26 (1-56847-229-3). 48pp. A history of jewelry, why it is worn, and the variety of materials and designs used. (Rev: SLJ 7/95) [739.27]

**16814** Young, Robert. *Sneakers: The Shoes We Choose* (3–5). Illus. 1991, Macmillan LB $14.95 (0-87518-460-X). 64pp. A discussion of the history, development, manufacture, and promotion of the shoes that everybody wears. (Rev: BL 6/1/91; SLJ 7/91) [685.31]

**16815** Yue, Charlotte, and David Yue. *Shoes: Their History In Words and Pictures* (5–8). Illus. 1997, Houghton $14.95 (0-395-72667-0). 96pp. A history of footwear arranged around topics like protection, status, and fashion. (Rev: BCCB 6/97; BL 4/1/97; HB 5–6/97; SLJ 4/97) [391]

# Computers and Automation

**16816** Ahmad, Nyla. *CyberSurfer: The OWL Internet Guide for Kids* (4–7). Illus. 1996, Firefly $19.95 (1-895688-50-7). 72pp. Using cartoons, a fast-paced text, and a demonstration disc, the author introduces the Internet, its functions, and important addresses. (Rev: BL 4/1/96; SLJ 9/96) [004.6]

**16817** Baker, Christopher W. *Let There Be Life! Animating with the Computer* (4–6). Illus. 1997, Walker LB $17.85 (0-8027-8473-9). 48pp. An overview of the basics of computer animation, illustrated with stills from feature films, shorts, and commercials. (Rev: BL 1/1–15/98) [778.2]

**16818** Brimner, Larry Dane. *E-Mail* (2–5). Illus. Series: True Books: Computers. 1997, Children's LB $21.00 (0-516-20332-0). 47pp. A basic introduction to electronic mail that covers topics like what it is,

how it works, advantages and disadvantages, symbols, and acronyms. (Rev: SLJ 11/97) [004]

**16819** Fowler, Allan. *It Could Still Be a Robot* (1–3). Illus. Series: Rookie Read-About Science. 1997, Children's LB $18.50 (0-516-20431-9). 32pp. In this easy-to-read book, robots are introduced, along with the tasks they can and cannot do. (Rev: BL 12/1/97) [629.8]

**16820** Gascoigne, Marc. *You Can Surf the Net!* (4–7). Illus. 1996, Penguin paper $3.99 (0-14-038265-9). 153pp. After introductory material on how to connect into the Internet, there is an annotated directory of Web sites. (Rev: BL 12/15/96) [004.6]

**16821** Gralla, Preston. *Online Kids: A Young Surfer's Guide to Cyberspace* (4–7). Illus. 1996, Wiley paper $14.95 (0-471-13545-3). 288pp. An informal guide to online services that includes important addresses. (Rev: BL 7/96; SLJ 9/96) [025.04]

**16822** Greenberg, Keith E. *Steven Jobs and Stephen Wozniak: Creating the Apple Computer* (3–4). Illus. by James Spence. Series: Partners. 1994, Blackbirch LB $13.95 (1-56711-086-X). 47pp. This book focuses on the pair that worked together to create the Apple Computer empire. (Rev: SLJ 1/95) [004]

**16823** Jortberg, Charles A. *The Internet* (4–6). Illus. Series: Kids and Computers. 1997, ABDO LB $15.95 (1-56239-727-3). 38pp. A history of the Internet, how to use it, and a listing of important sites for kids. (Rev: BL 6/1–15/97) [004.6]

**16824** Jortberg, Charles A. *Virtual Reality and Beyond* (4–6). Illus. Series: Kids and Computers. 1997, ABDO LB $15.95 (1-56239-728-1). 38pp. An explanation of virtual reality, its uses at present and in the future, and career possibilities. (Rev: BL 6/1–15/97) [006]

**16825** Kazunas, Charnan, and Tom Kazunas. *The Internet for Kids* (2–5). Illus. Series: True Book: Computers. 1997, Children's LB $20.00 (0-516-20334-7). 47pp. An easy and attractive introduction that covers such topics as search-and-retrieval tools, networks, addresses, and parts of the Internet, like e-mail and newsgroups. (Rev: SLJ 10/97) [004]

**16826** Kazunas, Charnan, and Tom Kazunas. *Personal Computers* (2–4). Illus. Series: True Books: Computers. 1997, Children's LB $21.00 (0-516-20338-X). 47pp. Such computer topics as hardware, software, and peripherals are covered, as well as a history of computers from the room-sized ENIAC to modern laptops. (Rev: SLJ 1/98) [004]

**16827** Kazunas, Charnan, and Tom Kazunas. *The World Wide Web* (2–4). Illus. Series: True Books: Computers. 1997, Children's LB $21.00 (0-516-20345-2). 47pp. Terms like *bookmarks, search engines, hyperlinks,* and *Internet service providers* are explained in this excellent introduction to the World Wide Web. (Rev: SLJ 1/98) [004]

**16828** Koehler, Lora. *Internet* (3–5). Illus. Series: New True. 1995, Children's LB $20.00 (0-516-01079-4). 48pp. Introduces the Information Highway, ways in which it can be used, and basic concepts and terms. (Rev: BL 9/1/95; SLJ 10/95) [004.6]

**16829** Lampton, Christopher. *Home Page: An Introduction to Web Page Design* (4–8). Illus. 1997, Watts LB $22.00 (0-531-20255-0). 64pp. The author explains to youngsters clearly and simply how they can design their own Web home pages using offline time. (Rev: BL 7/97; SLJ 2/98) [005.7]

**16830** Lampton, Christopher. *The World Wide Web* (4–8). Illus. 1997, Watts LB $21.00 (0-531-20262-3). 64pp. Aspects of the World Wide Web that would be of value and interest to children are covered, with practical suggestions for effective searching. (Rev: BL 7/97; SLJ 2/98) [025.04]

**16831** Lauber, Patricia. *Get Ready for Robots!* (K–3). Illus. by True Kelley. 1987, HarperCollins $12.95 (0-690-04576-X). 32pp. An introduction to robots that work in space, under water, and in factories. (Rev: BCCB 3/87; BL 2/15/87; SLJ 6–7/87)

**16832** Sabbeth, Carol. *Kids' Computer Creations: Using Your Computer for Art and Craft Fun* (3–6). Illus. by Loretta Braren. Series: Kids Can Books. 1995, Williamson paper $12.95 (0-913589-92-6). 158pp. An interesting collection of computer activities grouped by subjects like "Around the House," "Fun and Games," and "Wearable Art." (Rev: SLJ 6/96) [005.1]

**16833** Skurzynski, Gloria. *Robots: Your High-Tech World* (4–7). Illus. 1990, Macmillan LB $16.95 (0-02-782917-0). 64pp. An overview of robotics and history and an explanation of how robots work. (Rev: BL 11/15/90; HB 1–2/91; SLJ 9/90) [629.8]

**16834** Steinhauser, Peggy L. *Mousetracks: A Kid's Computer Idea Book* (K–5). Illus. 1997, Tricycle Pr. paper $12.95 (1-883672-48-1). 94pp. The 70 projects in this book are designed to help youngsters develop their computer skills. (Rev: SLJ 8/97) [004]

**16835** Wright, David. *Computers* (3–6). Illus. Series: Inventors and Inventions. 1996, Benchmark LB $25.64 (0-7614-0064-8). 63pp. The development of the computer is traced, with brief profiles of important people who brought it into being and an account of the effects of computers on today's world. (Rev: BL 3/15/96; SLJ 6/96) [004]

**16836** Zomberg, Paul G. *Computers* (2–4). Illus. 1985, Raintree Steck-Vaughn $15.99 (0-8172-1409-7). 48pp. Programming is explained in this look at how the computer works, highlighted with large color photos. (Rev: BL 8/85)

**16837** Zomberg, Paul G. *A Look Inside Computers* (4–7). Illus. 1984, Raintree Steck-Vaughn LB $15.99 (0-8172-1409-7). 48pp. A clear, concise introduction with illustrations, which includes historical information and explanations of program languages.

## Electronics

**16838** Baker, Wendy, and Andrew Haslam. *Electricity* (3–6). Illus. Series: Make It Work! 1993, Macmillan $12.95 (0-689-71663-X). 48pp. The principles of electricity and how they are applied are explained and activities are provided. (Rev: SLJ 4/93) [537]

**16839** Bridgman, Roger. *Electronics* (4–8). Illus. Series: Eyewitness Science. 1993, DK Publg. LB $15.95 (1-56458-325-4). 64pp. The field of electronics is introduced through full-color graphics, 3-D models, and detailed captions that explain important experiments, equipment, and concepts. (Rev: BL 11/15/93; SLJ 12/93) [621.38]

**16840** Oxlade, Chris. *Electronic Communication* (2–5). Illus. Series: Hello Out There. 1997, Watts $18.00 (0-531-14474-7). 32pp. This is a fine introduction to the various ways people communicate electronically, with coverage on such new innovations as the portable digital assistant. (Rev: BL 1/1–15/98; SLJ 2/98) [621.382]

## Machinery

**16841** Baker, Wendy, et al. *Machines* (4–7). Illus. Series: Make It Work! 1994, Thomson Learning $15.95 (1-56847-256-0). 48pp. The science of gravity, force, and friction are introduced through a series of projects involving building simple machines and examining the uses of each part. (Rev: BL 10/15/94; SLJ 11/94) [621.8]

**16842** Barton, Byron. *Machines at Work* (PS). Illus. 1987, HarperCollins LB $14.89 (0-690-04573-5). 32pp. All sorts of workers — men and women — with picks and drills and cranes and steamrollers parade across the pages. (Rev: BL 10/1/87)

**16843** Berger, Melvin, and Gilda Berger. *Telephones, Televisions and Toilets: How They Work and What Can Go Wrong* (2–3). Illus. by Don Madden. Series: Discovery Readers. 1993, Ideals LB $12.00 (0-8249-8645-8); paper $4.50 (0-8249-8608-3). 48pp. Cartoons and simple text explain the inner workings of these 3 machines. (Rev: BL 7/93) [632.6]

**16844** Biesty, Stephen. *Stephen Biesty's Incredible Pop-up Cross-Sections* (3–6). Illus. 1995, DK Publg.

$16.95 (0-7894-0199-1). Pop-ups are used to show cross-sections of a fire engine, helicopter, and space shuttle. (Rev: BL 2/1/96) [690]

**16845** Bridgman, Roger. *Technology* (4–6). Illus. Series: Eyewitness Science. 1995, DK Publg. $15.95 (1-56458-883-1). 64pp. Describes how the development of machines and materials has affected the areas of communication, farming, medicine, and more. (Rev: SLJ 10/95) [600]

**16846** Gibbons, Gail. *Trucks* (PS–2). Illus. by author. 1985, HarperCollins paper $4.95 (0-06-443069-3). 32pp. A very simple introduction to trucks and what they do.

**16847** Hoban, Tana. *Dig, Drill, Dump, Fill* (K–2). Illus. by author. 1975, Greenwillow LB $15.93 (0-688-84016-7); Morrow paper $3.95 (0-688-11703-1). 32pp. Catching heavy-duty machinery in action.

**16848** Jennings, Terry. *Cranes, Dump Trucks, Bulldozers and Other Building Machines* (3–5). Illus. Series: How Things Work. 1993, Kingfisher paper $6.95 (1-85697-865-6). 40pp. All sorts of large equipment used in construction are pictured with simple explanations of their functions and how they operate. (Rev: BL 6/1–15/93; SLJ 6/93) [690]

**16849** Kirkwood, Jon. *The Fantastic Cutaway Book of Giant Machines* (4–6). Illus. 1996, Millbrook LB $23.90 (0-7613-0491-6). 40pp. Such giant machines as monster trucks, tunnel borers, and nuclear submarines are introduced in double-page spreads. (Rev: BL 2/15/97) [629.04]

**16850** Macaulay, David. *The Way Things Work* (5–8). Illus. by author. 1988, Houghton $29.95 (0-395-42857-2). 400pp. An imaginative look at machine technology. (Rev: BCCB 1/89; BL 1/15/89; HB 3–4/89)

**16851** Parker, Steve. *The Random House Book of How Things Work* (4–8). Illus. 1991, Random LB $19.99 (0-679-90908-7). 157pp. More than 300 everyday machines and processes are examined in this book for the curious. (Rev: BL 5/15/91; SLJ 7/91) [600]

**16852** Royston, Angela. *Big Machines* (PS–3). Illus. by Terry Pastor. 1994, Little, Brown $12.95 (0-316-76070-6). 32pp. In double-page spreads, 9 machines — like the backhoe, harvester, and concrete mixer — are pictured and described. (Rev: BL 3/15/94; SLJ 5/94) [629.2]

**16853** Siegel, Beatrice. *The Sewing Machine* (3–6). Illus. 1984, Walker LB $10.85 (0-8027-6532-7). 64pp. The story of the sewing machine, its inventors Howe and Singer, and its effects on the world.

**16854** Siegel, Beatrice. *The Steam Engine* (4–6). Illus. 1986, Walker LB $10.85 (0-8027-6656-0). 64pp. The development of the steam engine through the ages. (Rev: BL 11/1/86; SLJ 3/87)

**16855** VanCleave, Janice. *Janice VanCleave's Machines: Mind-Boggling Experiments You Can Turn into Science Fair Projects* (4–6). Illus. Series: Spectacular Science Projects. 1993, Wiley paper $10.95 (0-471-57108-3). 88pp. Simple machines that can be made and operated are featured in this collection of fascinating science projects. (Rev: BL 5/1/93; SLJ 7/93) [521.8]

## Metals

**16856** Fitzgerald, Karen. *The Story of Iron* (4–6). Illus. Series: First Books: Chemical Elements. 1997, Watts LB $21.00 (0-531-20270-4). 64pp. Iron's properties, characteristics, uses, and methods of procurement are discussed. (Rev: BL 9/1/97; SLJ 10/97) [669]

**16857** Mebane, Robert C., and Thomas R. Rybolt. *Metals* (4–6). Illus. Series: Everyday Material Science Experiments. 1995, Twenty-First Century LB $18.90 (0-8050-2842-0). 64pp. At various levels of difficulty, this is a collection of experiments using common objects that identify and explore the properties of metals. (Rev: BL 9/15/95; SLJ 10/95) [669]

## Telegraph, Telephone, and Telecommunications

**16858** Ganeri, Anita. *The Story of Communications* (3–6). Series: Signs of the Times. 1998, Oxford LB $14.95 (0-19-521411-0). 32pp. A history of communication from prehistoric times to the modern use of telecommunications is given in this well-illustrated account. (Rev: BL 3/15/98) [302]

**16859** Holland, Gini, and Amy Stone. *Telephones* (3–6). Illus. 1995, Marshall Cavendish LB $25.64 (0-7614-0065-6). 63pp. This well-organized account tells of the beginnings of the telephone and the inventors involved. (Rev: BL 3/15/96; SLJ 3/96) [621.385]

**16860** Oxlade, Chris. *Telecommunications* (3–6). Illus. Series: 20th Century Inventions. 1997, Raintree Steck-Vaughn LB $24.26 (0-8172-4813-7). 48pp. After a brief introduction to telecommunications, this account focuses on such topics as the telephone, telegraph, radio, television, and computers. (Rev: BL 6/1–15/97) [384]

**16861** Skurzynski, Gloria. *Get the Message: Telecommunications in Your High-Tech World* (4–6). Illus. 1993, Macmillan LB $17.00 (0-02-778071-6). 64pp. This simple account explains the workings of such machines as the telephone and the fax and the new uses of fiber optics. (Rev: BCCB 5/93; BL 8/93*; HB 7–8/93; SLJ 6/93) [384]

## Television, Motion Pictures, Radio, and Recording

**16862** Anderson, Carol D., and Robert Sheely. *Techno Lab: How Science Is Changing Entertainment* (4–6). Illus. 1995, Silver Moon $13.95 (1-881889-63-7). 64pp. This fascinating book traces the influence of science and technology on movies, recorded music, television, video games, and virtual reality. (Rev: BL 1/1–15/96; SLJ 12/95) [791.4]

**16863** Bendick, Jeanne, and Robert Bendick. *Eureka! It's Television!* (2–4). Illus. by Sal Murdocca. Series: Inventing. 1993, Millbrook paper $6.95 (1-56294-718-4). 48pp. The exciting story of how television was invented. (Rev: BL 3/1/93; SLJ 6/93) [621]

**16864** Bentley, Nancy, and Donna Guthrie. *The Young Producer's Video Book: How to Write, Shoot and Direct Your Own Videos* (4–7). Illus. 1995, Millbrook LB $21.90 (1-56294-566-1); paper $7.95 (1-56294-688-9). 64pp. A complete step-by-step manual that begins with choosing equipment and script writing and ends with the finished video. (Rev: BL 2/1/96; SLJ 1/96) [791.45]

**16865** Biel, Jackie. *Video* (3–6). Illus. Series: Inventors and Inventions. 1996, Marshall Cavendish LB $25.64 (0-7614-0048-6). 63pp. The story of this important modern invention and the people who brought it into being. (Rev: BL 7/96; SLJ 8/96) [621.388]

**16866** Dahl, Lucy. *James and the Giant Peach: The Book and Movie Scrapbook* (3–6). Illus. 1996, Disney $15.95 (0-7868-3106-5); paper $7.95 (0-7868-4085-4). 64pp. Roald Dahl's daughter tells about the making of the movie of her father's book *James and the Giant Peach.* (Rev: BCCB 6/96; BL 4/1/96) [791.43]

**16867** Hahn, Don. *Disney's Animation Magic: A Behind-the-Scenes Look at How an Animated Film Is Made* (4–6). Illus. 1996, Disney $16.89 (0-7868-5041-8). 96pp. Using a team from the Disney studio as case studies, this book traces the various steps and processes involved in creating an animated film. (Rev: BL 9/1/96; SLJ 10/96) [791.43]

**16868** Merbreier, W. Carter. *Television: What's Behind What You See* (4–6). Illus. 1996, Farrar $16.00 (0-374-37388-4). 32pp. A grab bag of information about television technology and behind-the-scenes operations of a TV station. (Rev: BCCB 2/96; BL 4/15/96; SLJ 3/96) [384.55]

**16869** Oxlade, Chris. *Movies* (3–5). Illus. Series: Science Encounters. 1997, Rigby $13.95 (1-57572-088-4). 32pp. An introduction to movie making that gives a basic history of motion pictures, tells how the film camera works, and covers stunts, different types of film, animation, and computer enhancement. (Rev: SLJ 11/97) [791]

**16870** Platt, Richard. *Film* (4–8). Illus. Series: Eyewitness Books. 1992, Knopf $19.00 (0-679-81679-8). 64pp. Through many 2-page spreads, the mechanics of motion pictures are explored. (Rev: BL 6/1/92; SLJ 2/93) [791.43]

**16871** Riehecky, Janet. *Television* (3–6). Illus. Series: Inventors and Inventions. 1996, Marshall Cavendish LB $25.64 (0-7614-0045-1). 63pp. The history of television and the people behind its development are chronicled, with many photographs and an informal text. (Rev: BL 7/96; SLJ 8/96) [384.55]

**16872** Scott, Elaine. *Movie Magic: Behind the Scenes with Special Effects* (4–7). Illus. 1995, Morrow $16.00 (0-688-12477-1). 96pp. The techniques used to produce special effects in movies are explained, with special material on the use of computers. (Rev: BL 2/15/96) [791.43]

**16873** Stwertka, Eve, and Albert Stwertka. *Tuning In: The Sounds of the Radio* (3–5). Illus. by Mena Dolobowsky. Series: At Home with Science. 1993, Simon & Schuster paper $5.95 (0-671-69466-9). 40pp. A history of radio technology. (Rev: SLJ 8/93) [621]

**16874** Thomas, Bob. *Disney's Art of Animation: From Mickey Mouse to Beauty and the Beast* (1–8). Illus. 1991, Hyperion $39.95 (1-56282-997-1). 208pp. The achievements of Disney and his company are traced from the techniques used at the beginning to the special effects found in Beauty and the Beast. (Rev: SLJ 3/92) [791.43]

**16875** Wallace, Shelagh. *The TV Book: The Kid's Guide to Talking Back* (5–8). Illus. 1996, Annick paper $12.95 (1-55037-480-X). 96pp. This book teaches young people to look at television with critical eyes. (Rev: BL 2/1/97) [302.23]

## Transportation

### General

**16876** Badt, Karin Luisa. *Let's Go!* (3–7). Illus. Series: A World of Difference. 1995, Children's LB $21.00 (0-516-08195-0). 32pp. A look at various methods of transportation around the world and how they reflect the cultures in which they are found. (Rev: BL 7/95) [629.04]

**16877** Burns, Peggy, and Peter Chrisp. *Travel* (3–5). Illus. Series: Stepping Through History. 1995, Thomson Learning LB $21.40 (1-56847-343-5). 32pp. A history of travel and transportation from ancient days to the superjets of today. (Rev: BL 7/95) [629]

**16878** Davies, Eryl. *Transport: On Land, Road and Rail* (3–6). Illus. Series: Timelines. 1992, Watts $22.00 (0-531-14376-7). 48pp. This survey gives facts, illustrations, and ancedotes about various ways people have traveled on land. (Rev: BL 9/15/92) [629.04]

**16879** Gibbons, Gail. *Tunnels* (1–4). Illus. by author. 1987, Holiday paper $5.95 (0-8234-0670-9). 32pp. Different kinds of tunnels are pictured and described.

**16880** Graham, Ian. *Cars, Bikes, Trains, and Other Land Machines* (3–5). Illus. Series: How Things Work. 1993, Kingfisher paper $6.95 (1-85697-871-0). 40pp. This book gives a very simple explanation in words, diagrams, and line drawings of how various vehicles operate. (Rev: BL 6/1–15/93; SLJ 5/93) [629.04]

**16881** Hawkes, Nigel. *Transportation on Land and Sea* (4–6). Illus. Series: New Technology. 1994, Twenty-First Century LB $16.90 (0-8050-3415-3). 32pp. A report on the present status of transportation and a rundown on possible future developments. (Rev: BL 7/94; SLJ 8/94) [629.04]

**16882** Oxlade, Chris. *Canals and Waterways* (4–6). Illus. Series: Technology Craft Topics. 1994, Watts $20.00 (0-531-14331-7). 32pp. Numerous construction projects involving canals and other waterways are outlined in double-page spreads, with interesting asides on building problems and history. (Rev: BL 12/15/94) [627]

**16883** Oxlade, Chris. *Fantastic Transport Machines* (3–8). Illus. by David Salariya. Series: X-Ray Picture Books. 1995, Watts LB $24.00 (0-531-14351-1). 48pp. Introduces in double-page spreads such transport machines as motorcycles, cars, trains, ships, submarines, airplanes, and space vehicles. (Rev: SLJ 12/95) [629]

**16884** Parker, Steve. *Making Tracks* (3–5). Illus. Series: Supersmarts. 1997, Candlewick $11.99 (0-7636-0129-2). 24pp. This introduction to various forms of transportation uses bold illustrations, many sidebars, quiz questions, page foldouts, and double-page spreads. (Rev: BL 8/97; SLJ 1/98) [629.04]

**16885** Sauvain, Philip. *Roads* (4–6). Illus. Series: How We Build. 1991, Garrett LB $17.26 (0-944483-77-1). 48pp. Using many color pictures and some simple projects using everyday materials, this book explains various ways of building roads. (Rev: BL 6/15/91) [625.7]

**16886** Stille, Darlene R. *Blimps* (2–4). Series: True Books: Transportation. 1997, Children's LB $21.00 (0-516-20327-4). 48pp. A simple introduction to dirigibles and how they work. (Rev: BL 9/15/97) [629]

**16887** Wilson, Anthony. *The Dorling Kindersley Visual Timeline of Transportation* (4–8). Illus. 1995, DK Publg. $16.95 (1-56458-880-7). 48pp. A history of transportation from prehistory to possible future developments. (Rev: BL 12/15/95; SLJ 1/96) [629.04]

## Automobiles and Trucks

**16888** Barton, Byron. *Trucks* (PS). Illus. by author. 1986, HarperCollins LB $14.89 (0-690-04530-1). 32pp. Bright colors and simple text describe the role of trucks. (Rev: BL 8/86; SLJ 9/86)

**16889** Bendick, Jeanne. *Eureka! It's an Automobile!* (2–4). Illus. by Sal Murdocca. Series: Inventing. 1992, Millbrook LB $22.40 (1-56294-057-0). 48pp. Beginning with early inventions, this book, which speaks to young children in the form of direct address, challenges them to design cars. (Rev: BCCB 11/92; BL 1/15/93; SLJ 1/93) [629.2]

**16890** Bingham, Caroline. *Big Rig: And Other Massive Machines* (K–3). Illus. Series: Mighty Machines. 1996, DK Publg. $9.95 (0-7894-0575-X). 21pp. Eight examples of large machinery and vehicles are used in a series of double-page spreads. Also use *Race Car: And Other Speed Machines* (1996). (Rev: BL 6/1–15/96; SLJ 7/96) [629.224]

**16891** Bingham, Caroline. *Fire Truck* (PS–4). Illus. Series: Mighty Machines. 1995, DK Publg. paper $9.95 (0-7894-0212-2). 21pp. A large-size picture book that supplies fascinating facts and pictures about all kinds of fire trucks. (Rev: BL 12/1/95; SLJ 3/96) [628.9]

**16892** Bingham, Caroline. *Race Car* (PS–3). Illus. Series: Mighty Machines. 1996, DK Publg. $9.95 (0-7894-0574-1). 21pp. In a large-size format with lots of visual details, this account introduces special vehicles, how they work, and how powerful they are. (Rev: BL 6/1–15/96) [629.222]

**16893** Boucher, Jerry. *Fire Truck Nuts and Bolts* (K–3). Illus. 1993, Carolrhoda LB $22.60 (0-87614-783-X); paper $5.95 (0-87614-619-1). 40pp. An examination of the construction of a fire truck and its many parts. (Rev: BL 11/1/93; SLJ 12/93) [629.255]

**16894** Butterfield, Moira. *Bulldozers* (3–8). Illus. Series: Look Inside Cross-Sections. 1995, DK Publg. $5.95 (0-7894-0012-X). 32pp. In several richly illustrated double-page spreads, the inner and outer sections of the bulldozer and its parts are introduced along with technical data. (Rev: BL 8/95) [629.225]

**16895** Cole, Joanna. *Cars and How They Go* (2–4). Illus. by Gail Gibbons. 1983, HarperCollins LB $14.89 (0-690-04262-0). 32pp. In picture-book format, here is a simple description of cars and how they operate.

**16896** Davies, Kay, and Wendy Oldfield. *My Car* (PS–1). Illus. by Fiona Pragoff. Series: First Step Science. 1995, Gareth Stevens LB $19.93 (0-8368-1185-2). 32pp. Using large print and photographs, children learn about the automobile and perform basic activities. (Rev: BL 7/95) [530]

**16897** Guttmacher, Peter. *Jeep* (4–6). Illus. Series: Those Daring Machines. 1995, Macmillan LB $13.95 (0-89686-830-3). 48pp. A history of this vehicle and its evolution into today's popular sports automobile. (Rev: BL 2/15/95) [629]

**16898** Italia, Bob. *Great Auto Makers and Their Cars* (4–6). Illus. 1993, Oliver LB $16.95 (1-881508-08-0). 160pp. The founders of 10 automobile companies — like Henry Ford, Horace Dodge, Karl Benz, Soichiro Honda, and Ferruccio Lamborghini — are profiled with details on the obstacles they overcame. (Rev: SLJ 11/93) [629.2]

**16899** Johnstone, Michael. *Cars* (3–8). Illus. 1994, DK Publg. paper $5.95 (1-56458-681-2). 32pp. Inner and outer details of a wide selection of European and American cars are pictured, ranging from the Model T to the Jeep and Ferrari. (Rev: BL 2/1/95; SLJ 2/95) [629]

**16900** Kanetzke, Howard. *The Story of Cars* (2–4). Illus. 1987, Raintree Steck-Vaughn paper $4.49 (0-8114-8217-0). 48pp. A brief history of cars, plus material on their parts and construction. Reissue of 1978 edition.

**16901** Marston, Hope I. *Big Rigs* (2–4). Illus. 1993, Dutton paper $14.99 (0-525-65123-3). 48pp. This book explores the outside and inside of the mammoth trucks seen on major highways. (Rev: BL 1/7/93) [629]

**16902** Marston, Hope I. *Fire Trucks* (2–5). Illus. 1996, Dutton paper $14.99 (0-525-65231-0). 48pp. All sorts of fire-fighting equipment are introduced in text and color photographs. (Rev: BL 10/15/96; SLJ 9/96) [628.9]

**16903** Meijer, Marie. *The Car Book* (PS–2). Illus. by Goran Uggla. 1993, Chronicle $18.95 (0-8118-0514-X). 50pp. Using a spiral-book format, this wordless picture book features 5 different vehicles and their interiors. (Rev: BL 3/15/94) [629.2]

**16904** Otfinoski, Steven. *Behind the Wheel: Cars Then and Now* (2–4). Illus. Series: Here We Go! 1996, Benchmark LB $21.36 (0-7614-0403-1). 32pp. A simple text and spectacular photos are used to give a brief history of cars — past, present, and future. (Rev: SLJ 2/97) [629.27]

**16905** Otfinoski, Steven. *To the Rescue: Fire Trucks Then and Now* (1–3). Illus. Series: Here We Go! 1996, Benchmark LB $21.36 (0-7614-0406-6). 32pp. A well-illustrated history of fire trucks, from the horse-drawn ones of yesteryear to the fast, efficient trucks of today. (Rev: SLJ 6/97) [628.9]

**16906** Savage, Jeff. *Demolition Derby* (3–6). Illus. Series: Action Events. 1996, Crestwood LB $14.95 (0-89686-891-5); paper $4.95 (0-382-39294-9). 48pp. Large action photos are used to convey the thrills of this event, which also highlights car designs and builders and members of the driver's team. Also use *Monster Trucks* and *Trucks and Tractor Pullers* (both 1996). (Rev: SLJ 2/97) [629.23]

**16907** Schaefer, Margaret A. *Let's Build a Car* (3–5). Illus. by Patrick T. McRae. 1992, Ideals paper $4.95 (0-8249-8536-2). 32pp. Every page shows just one step in car production. (Rev: BL 12/1/90) [629.23]

**16908** Simonds, Christopher. *The Model T Ford* (5–7). Illus. Series: Turning Points in American History. 1991, Silver Burdett LB $14.95 (0-382-24122-3); paper $7.95 (0-382-24117-7). 64pp. The invention and development of the Model T and its impact on America. (Rev: BL 1/15/92) [629.222]

**16909** Somerville, Louisa. *Rescue Vehicles* (3–8). Illus. Series: Look Inside Cross-Sections. 1995, DK Publg. $5.95 (1-56458-879-3). 32pp. In a series of double-page spreads, different kinds of emergency vehicles are pictured, with detailed diagrams of their interiors and how they work. (Rev: BL 8/95) [629.04]

**16910** Steele, Philip. *Cars and Trucks* (3–4). Illus. Series: Pocket Facts. 1991, Macmillan $11.95 (0-89686-521-5). 32pp. An illustrated compendium of basic facts about cars and trucks. (Rev: SLJ 9/91) [629.28]

**16911** Stille, Darlene R. *Trucks* (2–4). Series: True Books: Transportation. 1997, Children's LB $19.00 (0-516-20343-6). 48pp. A simple but informative guide to various kinds of trucks and their uses with a list of places, including Web sites, to get further information. (Rev: BL 9/15/97) [629.24]

**16912** Sutton, Richard. *Car* (4–8). Illus. Series: Eyewitness Books. 1990, Knopf LB $20.99 (0-679-90743-2). 64pp. The past, present, and future of the automobile are presented. (Rev: BL 11/15/90; SLJ 1/91) [598.98]

**16913** Walker, Sloan, and Andrew Vasey. *The Only Other Crazy Car Book* (3–6). Illus. 1984, Walker LB $11.85 (0-8027-6517-3). 48pp. There is usually one "oddball" auto to a page, including origins and special features, such as the "Roach Coach," which looks like a giant insect.

**16914** Whitman, Sylvia. *Get Up and Go! The History of American Road Travel* (5–8). Illus. 1996, Lerner LB $21.27 (0-8225-1735-3). 88pp. From primitive pathways to modern superhighways, this is a history of American roads and the vehicles that traveled them. (Rev: BL 10/15/96; SLJ 10/96) [388.1]

**16915** Wilkinson, Sylvia. *Automobiles* (1–4). Illus. 1982, Children's $15.27 (0-516-01608-3). 48pp. A history of the automobile, plus a brief description of how it operates.

## Railroads

**16916** Anderson, Peter. *The Transcontinental Railroad* (3–5). Illus. Series: Cornerstones of Freedom. 1996, Children's LB $19.50 (0-516-06635-8). 30pp. The story of building the transcontinental railroad, its many tragedies, and final triumph, with numerous illustrations. (Rev: BL 8/96) [385]

**16917** Barton, Byron. *Trains* (PS). Illus. by author. 1986, HarperCollins LB $14.89 (0-690-04534-4). 32pp. Explaining the role of trains for the youngest readers. (Rev: BL 8/86; SLJ 9/86)

**16918** Crews, Donald. *Freight Train* (PS–K). Illus. by author. 1978, Greenwillow LB $15.93 (0-688-84165-1); Morrow paper $3.95 (0-688-11701-5). 32pp. A description in text and pictures of the various cars included in a freight train, from engine to caboose.

**16919** Fraser, Mary Ann. *Ten Mile Day and the Building of the Transcontinental Railroad* (3–6). Illus. 1993, Holt $15.95 (0-8050-1902-2). 36pp. This account re-creates the building of the transcontinental railroad, the problems, the prejudice and, at last, the hammering of the Golden Spike. (Rev: BCCB 7–8/93; BL 4/15/93; SLJ 5/93) [385]

**16920** Gibbons, Gail. *Trains* (PS–1). Illus. by author. 1987, Holiday LB $15.95 (0-8234-0640-7); paper $6.95 (0-8234-0699-7). 32pp. Describing the essentials of train transportation. (Rev: BL 5/1/87; SLJ 5/87)

**16921** Johnstone, Michael. *Look Inside Cross-Sections: Trains* (3–8). Illus. Series: Look Inside Cross-Sections. 1995, DK Publg. paper $5.95 (0-7894-0319-6). 32pp. Cross-sectional drawings with descriptive text are given for 10 past and present locomotives. (Rev: BL 9/15/95) [625.1]

**16922** Kanetzke, Howard. *Trains and Railroads* (2–4). Illus. 1978, Raintree Steck-Vaughn paper $4.49 (0-8114-8222-7). 48pp. A good overview of the subject, with simple explanations.

**16923** Levinson, Nancy S. *She's Been Working on the Railroad* (5–8). Illus. 1997, Dutton paper $16.99 (0-525-67545-0). 96pp. A history of women's roles as railway workers, including the famous Harvey Girls of the late 1800s. (Rev: BL 9/15/97; SLJ 12/97) [331.4]

**16924** McNeese, Tim. *America's First Railroads* (4–8). Illus. by Chris Duke. Series: Americans on the Move. 1993, Macmillan $11.95 (0-89686-729-3). 48pp. A history of early railroads and their impact on U.S. history. (Rev: SLJ 8/93) [385]

**16925** Murphy, Jim. *Across America on an Emigrant Train* (5–8). Illus. 1993, Clarion $17.00 (0-395-63390-7). 150pp. The cross-country train trip by Robert Louis Stevenson in 1879 is used to present material about the history of railroads. (Rev: BCCB 1/94; BL 12/1/93; SLJ 12/93*) [828]

**16926** Otfinoski, Steven. *Riding the Rails: Trains Then and Now* (1–3). Illus. Series: Here We Go! 1996, Benchmark LB $21.36 (0-7614-0404-X). 32pp. A copiously illustrated history of trains, with material on how they have evolved through the years. (Rev: SLJ 6/97) [625.4]

**16927** Petty, Kate. *Some Trains Run on Water: And Other Amazing Facts About Rail Transportation* (1–3). Illus. by Ross Walton and Jo Moore. Series: I Didn't Know That. 1997, Millbrook LB $19.90 (0-7613-0609-9). 32pp. Strange-but-true facts involving trains, past and present, presented with several projects that don't require adult supervision. (Rev: SLJ 3/98) [625.2]

**16928** Smith, E. Boyd. *The Railroad Book* (2–4). Illus. by author. 1984, Houghton $18.95 (0-395-34832-3). 56pp. An introduction to railroads via a book originally published in 1913.

**16929** Steele, Philip. *Trains* (3–4). Illus. Series: Pocket Facts. 1991, Macmillan LB $11.95 (0-89686-523-1). 32pp. The history of trains plus material on parts, bridges, subways, and the English Channel tunnel. (Rev: SLJ 9/91) [625.2]

**16930** Stein, R. Conrad. *The Story of the Golden Spike* (3–6). Illus. 1978, Children's LB $13.27 (0-516-04621-7). 32pp. The building and completion in 1869 of the transcontinental railroad.

**16931** Stille, Darlene R. *Trains* (2–4). Illus. Series: True Books: Transportation. 1997, Children's LB $21.00 (0-516-20342-8). 48pp. A history of railroading is followed by a description of various trains, how they operate, and the men who work on them. (Rev: BL 9/15/97) [625.1]

**16932** Yancey, Diane. *Camels for Uncle Sam* (4–7). Illus. 1995, Hendrick-Long $14.95 (0-937460-91-5). 92pp. The story of the experiment to import camels to the Southwest in the 1850s to help in railroad construction. (Rev: BL 9/15/95) [357]

**16933** Young, Robert. *The Transcontinental Railroad: America at Its Best?* (4–6). Illus. Series: Both Sides. 1997, Dillon LB $13.95 (0-87518-611-4). 72pp. Various point of view — including those of the workers, business people, and American Indians — are included in this history of the transcontinental railroad. (Rev: BL 9/15/97) [385]

## Ships, Boats, and Lighthouses

**16934** Asimov, Isaac, and Elizabeth Kaplan. *How Do Big Ships Float?* (K–3). Illus. Series: Ask Isaac Asimov. 1992, Stevens LB $19.93 (0-8368-0802-9). 24pp. This book explains simply how gravity and buoyancy keep ships afloat. (Rev: BL 6/1–15/93) [623.4]

**16935** Barton, Byron. *Boats* (PS). Illus. by author. 1986, HarperCollins LB $14.89 (0-690-04536-0). 32pp. Recreational and functional roles of boats are explained in simple text and bright colors. (Rev: BL 8/86; SLJ 9/86)

**16936** *Boats* (PS–1). Illus. Series: What's Inside? 1992, DK Publg. $8.95 (1-56458-006-7). 24pp. Through peeled-back illustrations and simple captions, the internal parts of boats are shown. (Rev: BL 4/15/92) [523.8]

**16937** *Boats* (PS–3). Illus. Series: First Discovery Book. 1993, Scholastic $11.95 (0-590-47131-7). 24pp. A book for small children that introduces boats from around the world and explains their differences. (Rev: BL 1/1/94) [623.8]

**16938** *Boats and Ships* (4–6). Illus. 1996, Scholastic $19.95 (0-590-47647-5). 48pp. Transparencies, flaps, and windows are used to introduce various ships and boats. (Rev: BL 12/15/96) [623]

**16939** Butterfield, Moira. *Look Inside Cross-Sections: Record Breakers* (3–8). Illus. Series: Look Inside Cross-Sections. 1995, DK Publg. paper $5.95 (0-7894-0320-X). 32pp. The inner workings of a number of record-breaking speed machines are pictured in a series of cross-sectional diagrams that supply amazing details. (Rev: BL 9/15/95) [629.05]

**16940** Butterfield, Moira. *Ships* (3–6). Illus. Series: Look Inside Cross-Sections. 1994, DK Publg. paper $5.95 (1-56458-521-2). 32pp. Cross-sections of a variety of ships are shown, including the sunken *Mary Rose* (1545), an old Chinese junk, a fishing trawler, and a World War II aircraft carrier. (Rev: BL 10/15/94; SLJ 9/94) [623.8]

**16941** Gibbons, Gail. *Beacons of Light: Lighthouses* (1–3). Illus. 1990, Morrow $16.00 (0-688-07379-4). 32pp. The development of the lighthouse from a hilltop bonfire to the electronic wonders of today. (Rev: BCCB 3/90; BL 2/15/90; HB 3–4/90; SLJ 4/90) [387.1]

**16942** Graham, Ian. *Boats, Ships, Submarines and Other Floating Machinery* (4–7). Illus. Series: How Things Work. 1993, Kingfisher LB $13.90 (1-85697-682-3); paper $6.95 (1-85697-867-2). 40pp. This

book explains such scientific principles as wind power and buoyancy and how they apply to a wide range of water crafts that include such unusual crafts as hydrofoils and Hovercrafts. (Rev: BL 6/1–15/93; SLJ 5/93) [623.8]

**16943** Guiberson, Brenda Z. *Lighthouses: Watchers at Sea* (3–6). Illus. 1995, Holt $15.95 (0-8050-3170-7). 70pp. A history of lighthouses, including their construction, uses, and some exciting stories connected with them. (Rev: BCCB 12/95; BL 11/1/95; SLJ 1/96) [387.1]

**16944** Hubble, Richard. *Ships: Sailors and the Sea* (3–6). Illus. Series: Timelines. 1991, Watts $13.95 (0-531-15234-0). 48pp. Includes cutaway views of such ships as the Titanic and a modern destroyer. (Rev: BL 12/15/91; SLJ 3/92) [387.2]

**16945** Humble, Richard. *Submarines and Ships* (4–8). Series: See Through History. 1997, Viking paper $17.99 (0-670-86778-0). 48pp. A well-illustrated account that examines several historical ships and submarines and identifies different structures and uses. (Rev: BL 11/15/97) [387.2]

**16946** Kent, Deborah. *The Titanic* (3–5). Illus. Series: Cornerstones of Freedom. 1993, Children's LB $19.50 (0-516-06672-2). 32pp. A slim volume with illustrations on each page that describes the building and tragic first voyage of the ocean liner. (Rev: BL 2/1/94; SLJ 3/94) [910.9]

**16947** Kentley, Eric. *Boat* (4–8). Illus. Series: Eyewitness Books. 1992, Knopf LB $20.99 (0-679-91678-4). 64pp. Two-page spreads show both the exteriors and the interiors of many historical ships and boats. (Rev: BL 6/1/92) [623.8]

**16948** Lewis, Thomas P. *Clipper Ship* (1–3). Illus. by Joan Sandin. 1992, HarperCollins paper $3.75 (0-06-444160-1). 64pp. An easily read account of our sailing ships.

**16949** Lincoln, Margarette. *Amazing Boats* (1–4). Illus. by Mike Dunning. Series: Eyewitness Juniors. 1992, Knopf paper $7.99 (0-679-82770-6). 32pp. What a boat is and what it can do, followed by large photos that show various kinds of boats and ships, plus a text with good general information. (Rev: BL 11/1/92) [623.8]

**16950** Maass, Robert. *Tugboats* (1–3). Photos by author. 1997, Holt $15.95 (0-8050-3116-2). This introduction to tugboats explains their types and functions. (Rev: SLJ 5/97) [387.2]

**16951** Macaulay, David. *Ship* (4–8). Illus. 1993, Houghton $19.95 (0-395-52439-3). 96pp. Using a fictional caravel as subject matter, details the parts of the ship, built in 1504, and the work undertaken to explore its sunken remains. (Rev: BCCB 11/93; BL 10/15/93; SLJ 11/93) [387.2]

**16952** McNeese, Tim. *Clippers and Whaling Ships* (4–8). Illus. by Chris Duke. Series: Americans on the Move. 1993, Macmillan $11.95 (0-89686-735-8). 48pp. Early American shipping and commerce are discussed. Also use: *West by Steamboat* (1993). (Rev: SLJ 8/93) [623.8]

**16953** Maestro, Betsy, and Giulio Maestro. *Ferry-boat* (PS–1). Illus. by Giulio Maestro. 1986, Harper-Collins LB $14.89 (0-690-04520-4). 32pp. The story of ferryboats, centered around one river crossing. (Rev: BCCB 7–8/86; BL 6/15/86; HB 5–6/86)

**16954** Otfinoski, Steven. *Into the Wind: Sailboats Then and Now* (2–4). Illus. Series: Here We Go! 1996, Benchmark LB $21.36 (0-7614-0405-8). 32pp. This simple, well-illustrated account gives a history of sailboats and shows many types and sizes from all over the world, with details on their important features. (Rev: HB 9–10/96; SLJ 2/97) [623.8]

**16955** Platt, Richard. *Shipwreck* (4–8). Series: Eyewitness Books. 1997, Knopf LB $20.99 (0-679-98569-X). 60pp. An overview of the causes and consequences of the world's most famous maritime disasters. (Rev: BL 12/15/97) [363]

**16956** Platt, Richard. *Stephen Biesty's Cross-Sections Man-of-War* (4–7). Illus. by Stephen Biesty. Series: Incredible Cross-Sections. 1993, DK Publg. $16.95 (1-56458-321-X). 32pp. From stem to stern, this is a tour, both inside and outside, of an 18th-century British man-of-war. (Rev: BCCB 1/94; BL 10/1/93; SLJ 1/94*) [359.1]

**16957** Purcell, Cindy. *From Glass to Boat* (3–6). Series: Changes. 1997, Children's LB $24.00 (0-516-20736-9). 32pp. This photoessay shows the process of producing a fiberglass boat with many activities that allow the reader to participate. (Rev: BL 2/15/98) [387.2]

**16958** Stacey, Tom. *The Titanic* (5–7). Illus. by Maurie Manning. Series: World Disasters. 1990, Lucent LB $19.95 (1-56006-006-9). 64pp. Describes the sinking of the "unsinkable" ocean liner. (Rev: SLJ 8/90) [387.2]

# Weapons, Submarines, and the Armed Forces

**16959** Baker, David. *Future Fighters* (4–8). Illus. Series: Military Aircraft. 1989, Rourke LB $18.60 (0-86592-535-6). 48pp. Possible future fighter planes are featured in illustrations and brief text. Also use: *Navy Strike Planes* (1989). (Rev: SLJ 1/90) [358.4]

**16960** Day, Malcolm. *The World of Castles and Forts* (4–6). Illus. 1997, Bedrick LB $19.95 (0-87226-278-2). 46pp. This account covers a world history of fortifications, from ancient walled cities to the modern Maginot Line and nuclear bastions. (Rev: BL 3/1/97; SLJ 2/97) [355.7]

**16961** Ferrell, Nancy Warren. *The U.S. Air Force* (4–8). Illus. 1990, Lerner LB $23.93 (0-8225-1433-8). 72pp. This book includes coverage on how to enlist, the ranking system in the Air Force, and today's use of modern technology. (Rev: BL 5/15/91) [358.4]

**16962** Ferrell, Nancy Warren. *The U.S. Coast Guard* (4–8). Illus. 1989, Lerner LB $23.93 (0-8225-1431-1). 72pp. History, duties, and opportunities in this story of an arm of the U.S. military. (Rev: BL 5/1/89)

**16963** Gonen, Rivka. *Charge! Weapons and Warfare in Ancient Times* (5–8). Illus. 1993, Lerner LB $23.93 (0-8225-3201-8). 72pp. Traces the development of weapons from the sticks and stones of cave dwellers to those used in later warfare, like battering rams. (Rev: BCCB 12/93; BL 2/1/94; SLJ 2/94) [355.8]

**16964** Holmes, Richard. *Battle* (4–8). Illus. Series: Eyewitness Books. 1995, Knopf LB $20.99 (0-679-97333-8). 64pp. Dramatic illustrations are used in this introduction to warfare and its consequences. (Rev: BL 12/15/95) [355]

**16965** Hughes, Libby. *West Point* (4–6). Illus. Series: Places in American History. 1993, Macmillan LB $14.95 (0-87518-529-0). 72pp. The story of the military academy founded in 1802 and of the life of cadets trained there. (Rev: BL 4/15/93; SLJ 7/93) [355]

**16966** Humble, Richard. *A World War Two Submarine* (3–6). Illus. by Mark Bergin. Series: Inside Story. 1991, Bedrick LB $18.95 (0-87226-351-7). 48pp. This account explores the design, construction, and parts of a World War II submarine. (Rev: BL 12/1/91; SLJ 1/92) [359.9]

**16967** Keeler, Barbara, and Don Keeler. *Sailing Ship Eagle* (3–5). Illus. Series: Those Daring Machines. 1995, Macmillan paper $5.95 (0-382-24751-5). 48pp. A brief look at the construction and exploits of the U.S. Coast Guard ship. (Rev: BL 2/15/95) [359.9]

**16968** Meltzer, Milton. *Weapons and Warfare: From the Stone Age to the Space Age* (5–8). Illus. 1996, HarperCollins LB $16.89 (0-06-024876-9). 96pp. Describes the evolution of weapons from clubs to the H-bomb, including how these weapons have been used and misused through the ages. (Rev: BCCB 2/97; BL 12/1/96; SLJ 1/97) [355.02]

**16969** Moran, Tom. *The U.S. Army* (4–8). Illus. 1990, Lerner LB $23.93 (0-8225-1434-6). 88pp. A solid overview of the development of the U.S. Army. (Rev: BL 1/1/91) [335]

**16970** Pelta, Kathy. *The U.S. Navy* (5–7). Illus. 1990, Lerner LB $22.95 (0-8225-1435-4). 88pp. History and present status and activities of the U.S. Navy. (Rev: BL 12/1/90) [359]

**16971** Reef, Catherine. *Black Fighting Men: A Proud History* (4–8). Illus. Series: African-American Soldiers. 1994, Twenty-First Century LB $17.90 (0-8050-3106-5). 80pp. A general overview of the contributions that African Americans have made in the armed services. (Rev: BL 9/15/94; SLJ 11/94) [355]

**16972** Robertshaw, Andrew. *A Soldier's Life: A Visual History of Soldiers Through the Ages* (4–7). Illus. 1997, Dutton paper $16.99 (0-525-67550-7). 48pp. Describes a soldier's uniform, equipment, and weapons through the ages, beginning with a Roman soldier in A.D. 50. (Rev: BCCB 6/97; BL 6/1–15/97; SLJ 6/97) [355.02]

**16973** Rowan, N. R. *Women in the Marines: The Boot Camp Challenge* (4–8). Illus. Series: Armed Services. 1994, Lerner LB $23.93 (0-8225-1430-3). 72pp. Covers the harrowing basic training that women face in the Marines. (Rev: BCCB 4/94; BL 2/15/94; SLJ 4/94) [359.9]

**16974** Schulson, Rachel. *Guns: What You Should Know* (1–3). Illus. by Mary Jones. 1997, Albert Whitman LB $13.95 (0-8075-3093-X). 24pp. An unbiased, appealing book that describes the parts of a gun, introduces different types, explains the destructive power of a bullet, and tells children what to do if they find a gun. (Rev: BL 10/15/97; SLJ 12/97) [363.3]

**16975** Stein, R. Conrad. *The Manhattan Project* (3–5). Illus. Series: Cornerstones of Freedom. 1993, Children's LB $19.50 (0-516-06670-6). 32pp. The history of the development of the atomic bomb in this country, culminating in its use in World War II. (Rev: BL 11/1/93) [355.8]

**16976** Stephen, R. J. *The Picture World of Submarines* (3–7). Illus. Series: Picture World. 1990, Watts LB $12.40 (0-531-14011-3). 32pp. Includes information on both diesel and nuclear submarines. (Rev: BL 7/90) [359.95]

**16977** Warner, J. F. *The U.S. Marine Corps* (4–8). Illus. Series: Armed Services. 1991, Lerner LB $22.95 (0-8225-1432-X). 88pp. From how to enlist to a discussion of the new technology, this is a well-organized introduction to the U.S. Marine Corps. (Rev: BL 2/1/92; SLJ 2/92) [359.6]

**16978** Weiss, Harvey. *Submarines and Other Underwater Craft* (3–7). Illus. 1990, HarperCollins LB $13.89 (0-690-04761-4). 64pp. A good history of submarines that explains many peacetime uses. (Rev: BCCB 6/90; BL 7/90; HB 7–8/90; SLJ 5/90) [359.3]

# Recreation

# Crafts

## General and Miscellaneous

**16979**  Bingham, Caroline, and Karen Foster, eds. *Crafts for Play* (4–7). Illus. Series: Millbrook Arts Library. 1993, Millbrook LB $22.90 (1-56294-096-1). 48pp. Toys, games, puzzles, and puppets from many cultures are introduced, with directions for simple craft projects. (Rev: BL 7/93; SLJ 10/93) [745]

**16980**  Birdseye, Tom. *A Kids' Guide to Building Forts* (5–8). Illus. by Bill Klein. 1993, Harbinger paper $10.95 (0-943173-69-8). 62pp. A guide to the building of 19 kinds of forts, from the very simple to the more complex, some of which can be turned into clubhouses. (Rev: SLJ 9/93) [745.5]

**16981**  Borlenghi, Patricia, and Rachel Wright. *Italy* (2–4). Illus. by Teri Gower. Series: Country Topics for Craft Projects. 1994, Watts LB $20.00 (0-531-14264-7). 32pp. Introduces interesting craft projects and recipes associated with Italy, like preparing a pizza and making mosaics from eggshells. (Rev: SLJ 6/94) [745]

**16982**  Caney, Steven. *Steven Caney's Playbook* (3–5). Illus. 1975, Workman paper $9.95 (0-911104-38-0). 240pp. All sorts of activities involving discarded or inexpensive materials, thoroughly and clearly presented.

**16983**  Carlson, Laurie. *EcoArt! Earth-Friendly Art and Craft Experiences for 3- to 9-Year-Olds* (K–4). Illus. by Loretta Braren. 1993, Williamson paper $12.95 (0-913589-68-3). 160pp. Over 100 arts and crafts activities using natural, recyclable, or reusable materials. (Rev: BL 2/15/93; SLJ 4/93) [745.5]

**16984**  Castaldo, Nancy Fusco. *Rainy Day Play! Explore, Create, Discover, Pretend* (PS–1). Illus. by Loretta Braren. Series: A Little Hands Book. 1996, Williamson paper $12.95 (1-885593-00-7). 142pp. A collection of 64 ideas for activities, crafts, and games that are attractively presented and will afford hours of enjoyment. (Rev: SLJ 2/97) [745.5]

**16985**  Chapman, Gillian, and Pam Robson. *Art from Fabric: With Projects Using Rags, Old Clothing and Remnants* (3–5). Illus. Series: Salvaged! 1995, Thomson Learning LB $21.40 (1-56847-381-8). 32pp. This book contains several creative projects and crafts using old fabrics or fibers, on double-page spreads. (Rev: SLJ 1/96) [745.5]

**16986**  Cole, Joanna, and Stephanie Calmenson. *The Rain or Shine Activity Book* (3–5). Illus. by Alan Tiegreen. 1997, Morrow $20.00 (0-688-12131-4). 192pp. This rich compendium includes many craft projects, word games, magic tricks, jokes, riddles, and tongue twisters. (Rev: BL 8/97; SLJ 9/97) [793]

**16987**  Conaway, Judith. *Fun-to-Make Nature Crafts* (1–3). Illus. by Renzo Barto. 1981, Troll LB $12.50 (0-89375-440-4). 48pp. Simple, easy-to-make projects from toys to terrariums.

**16988**  Conaway, Judith. *Great Gifts to Make* (2–4). Illus. 1986, Troll LB $12.50 (0-8167-0676-X). 48pp. Homemade gifts for all occasions made with easily obtainable materials. (Rev: BL 12/1/86)

**16989**  Conaway, Judith. *Springtime Surprises! Things to Make and Do* (2–4). Illus. 1986, Troll LB $12.50 (0-8167-0670-0). 48pp. Included are easy projects with Easter, nature, and gardening themes. (Rev: BL 12/1/86)

**16990**  Connor, Nikki. *Cardboard Boxes* (1–4). Illus. by Sarah-Jane Neaves. Series: Creative Crafts From. 1996, Millbrook LB $19.90 (0-7613-0538-6). A craft book that transforms cardboard boxes into trains, cars, and ships using a few paints, paper, scissors, and a pencil. Also use *Cardboard Tubes, Plastic Bot-*

*tles*, and *Plastic Cups* (all 1997). (Rev: SLJ 8/97) [745.5]

**16991** Corwin, Judith Hoffman. *Christmas Fun* (3–6). Illus. by author. 1982, Silver Burdett paper $5.95 (0-671-49583-6). 64pp. A collection of simple projects that are useful for this holiday, including designs for gifts and decorations.

**16992** Corwin, Judith Hoffman. *Easter Crafts* (K–3). Illus. by author. Series: Holiday Craft Book. 1994, Watts LB $21.00 (0-531-11145-8). 48pp. A collection of Easter crafts in which bunnies star. (Rev: SLJ 8/94) [745]

**16993** Corwin, Judith Hoffman. *Easter Fun* (2–4). Illus. by author. 1984, Silver Burdett paper $5.95 (0-671-53108-5). 64pp. Foods and crafts associated with this holiday are highlighted.

**16994** Corwin, Judith Hoffman. *Halloween Crafts: A Holiday Craft Book* (3–5). Illus. Series: Holiday Crafts. 1995, Watts LB $21.00 (0-531-11148-2). 48pp. Following a brief history of Halloween, the author outlines related crafts, including decorations, foods, and costumes. (Rev: BL 9/15/95) [745.594]

**16995** Corwin, Judith Hoffman. *Halloween Fun* (3–6). Illus. 1983, Silver Burdett paper $5.95 (0-671-49756-1). 64pp. A wide variety of holiday activities, including party hints and projects.

**16996** Corwin, Judith Hoffman. *Latin American and Caribbean Crafts* (4–6). Illus. 1992, Watts LB $20.00 (0-531-11014-1). 48pp. A basic introduction to the region plus clear instructions on creating arts and crafts. (Rev: BL 10/1/92; SLJ 8/92) [745.5]

**16997** Corwin, Judith Hoffman. *Valentine Crafts* (K–3). Illus. by author. Series: Holiday Craft Book. 1994, Watts LB $20.60 (0-531-11146-6). 48pp. Simple Valentine projects are included, as well as rebuses, games, and directions for writing secret codes. (Rev: SLJ 8/94) [745]

**16998** Corwin, Judith Hoffman. *Valentine Fun* (3–6). Illus. by author. 1983, Silver Burdett paper $5.95 (0-671-49755-3). 64pp. Recipes and craft projects highlight this book of activities.

**16999** Craig, Diana. *Making Models: 3-D Creations from Paper and Clay* (4–6). Illus. Series: First Guide. 1993, Millbrook paper $9.95 (1-56294-710-9). 93pp. A craft book that is short on specific directions but filled with interesting projects that will require adult supervision. (Rev: SLJ 10/93) [745]

**17000** Curti, Anna. *My Very First Nature Craft Book* (PS–2). Illus. 1997, Simon & Schuster $9.99 (0-689-81276-0). 37pp. This large-format book details a number of craft projects using simple materials but often requiring adult supervision. (Rev: BL 2/1/97; SLJ 3/97) [745.5]

**17001** Deshpande, Chris. *Festival Crafts* (4–7). Illus. Series: World Wide Crafts. 1994, Gareth Stevens LB $21.27 (0-8368-1153-4). 32pp. Thirteen craft projects that relate to such multicultural festivals as Mardi Gras and Mexico's All Soul's Day. (Rev: BL 3/1/95; SLJ 1/95) [745.5]

**17002** Deshpande, Chris. *Food Crafts* (4–7). Illus. Series: World Wide Crafts. 1994, Gareth Stevens LB $21.27 (0-8368-1154-2). 32pp. Foods become craft materials in this well-illustrated book containing 13 projects. (Rev: BL 3/1/95) [745.5]

**17003** Diehn, Gwen, and Terry Krautwurst. *Kid Style Nature Crafts: 50 Terrific Things to Make with Nature's Materials* (4–7). Illus. 1995, Sterling $21.95 (0-8069-0996-X). 144pp. Fifty unusual projects that follow the seasons and use objects from nature as materials. (Rev: BL 11/15/95; SLJ 10/95) [745.5]

**17004** Diehn, Gwen, and Terry Krautwurst. *Nature Crafts for Kids* (4–8). Illus. 1992, Sterling $21.95 (0-8069-8372-8). 144pp. Crisp color photos and challenging projects make this an entertaining and unusual craft book. (Rev: BL 7/92) [745.5]

**17005** Drake, Jane, and Ann Love. *The Kids' Summer Handbook* (4–7). Illus. by Heather Collins. 1994, Ticknor $15.95 (0-395-68711-X). 208pp. A handbook of all sorts of outdoor crafts and activities, with several involving whittling, weaving, and knotting. (Rev: BL 4/1/94; SLJ 6/94) [790.1]

**17006** Ehlert, Lois. *Snowballs* (PS–3). Illus. 1995, Harcourt $16.00 (0-15-200074-7). 32pp. All kinds of materials are used to create and decorate a snow family in this book of craft ideas. (Rev: BCCB 11/95; BL 12/1/95; SLJ 11/95)

**17007** Fiarotta, Noel, and Phyllis Fiarotta. *Music Crafts for Kids: The How-to Book of Music Discovery* (3–6). Illus. by authors. 1994, Sterling $19.95 (0-8069-0406-2). 160pp. As well as supplying background information on musical topics like the notes of the scale, music theory, and history, this book supplies directions for a number of music-related crafts. (Rev: SLJ 4/94) [745]

**17008** Ganeri, Anita, and Rachel Wright. *France* (2–4). Illus. by John Shackell. Series: Country Topics for Craft Projects. 1994, Watts LB $20.00 (0-531-14256-6). 32pp. Introduces interesting craft projects and recipes associated with France, like preparing a croque-monsieur sandwich and making jewelry from flowers. (Rev: SLJ 6/94) [745]

**17009** Gayle, Katie. *Snappy Jazzy Jewelry* (4–7). Illus. 1996, Sterling $14.95 (0-8069-3854-4). 48pp. Making necklaces and earrings are 2 of the craft projects described, with many helpful photographs. (Rev: BL 5/15/96; SLJ 6/96) [745.594]

**17010** Gillis, Jennifer S. *In a Pumpkin Shell: Over 20 Pumpkin Projects for Kids* (3–6). Illus. by Patti Delmonte. 1992, Storey paper $9.95 (0-88266-771-8). 64pp. This book tells how to grow pumpkins and how to have fun with them through a number of craft projects. (Rev: SLJ 10/92) [745.5]

**17011** Hebert, Holly. *60 Super Simple Crafts* (3–6). Illus. by Leo Abbett. 1996, Lowell House paper $6.95 (1-56565-385-8). 80pp. Simple instructions are given for 60 crafts projects, most of which involve material found in the home or at local craft shops. (Rev: SLJ 2/97) [745.5]

**17012** Hogrogian, Nonny. *Handmade Secret Hiding Places* (3–5). Illus. by author. 1990, Overlook $9.95 (0-87951-033-1). 48pp. The construction of 6 hiding places from a mud hut to a hideaway made from blankets over chairs is described in words and pictures.

**17013** Kerina, Jane. *African Crafts* (5–8). Illus. by Tom Feelings and Marylyn Katzman. 1970, Lion LB $13.95 (0-87460-084-7). Many projects arranged geographically by the region in Africa where they originated.

**17014** King, Penny, and Clare Roundhill. *Out of This World: Lots of Space Pictures to Make* (2–6). Illus. Series: Making Pictures. 1997, Rigby $14.95 (1-57572-193-7). 29pp. This craft book introduces 12 space-related activities, like making a rocket from a cardboard tube. Others in the series are *Secrets of the Sea: Lots of Underwater Pictures to Make* and *Spooky Things: Lots of Spooky Pictures to Make* (both 1997). (Rev: SLJ 12/97) [745.5]

**17015** Lehne, Judith Logan. *The Never-Be-Bored Book: Quick Things to Make When There's Nothing to Do* (4–6). Illus. by Morissa Lipstein. 1993, Sterling $17.95 (0-8069-1254-5). 128pp. Over 40 projects are included in this useful craft book, plus recipes for many ingredients including clay, dough, and natural dyes. (Rev: BL 5/15/93) [745.5]

**17016** McGraw, Sheila. *Gifts Kids Can Make* (4–8). Photos by Sheila McGraw and Joy von Tiedemann. 1994, Firefly LB $19.95 (1-895565-36-7); paper $9.95 (1-895565-35-9). 96pp. A craft book that gives directions for making 14 simple gifts, like a cotton sock doll and a hobby horse, by using easily obtainable materials. (Rev: SLJ 12/94) [745]

**17017** Marchon-Arnaud, Catherine. *A Gallery of Games* (5–7). Illus. by Marc Schwartz. Series: Young Artisan. 1994, Ticknor $12.95 (0-395-68379-3). 60pp. Historical information, clear directions, and rules of each game are supplied, but young novices might find some of these projects difficult. (Rev: BL 4/1/94; SLJ 3/94) [745]

**17018** Milhous, Katherine. *The Egg Tree* (PS–3). Illus. by author. 1971, Macmillan $15.00 (0-684-12716-4); paper $5.95 (0-689-71568-4). 32pp. This picture book tells how to make a delightful Easter egg tree. Caldecott Medal winner, 1951.

**17019** Milord, Susan. *Hands Around the World: 365 Creative Ways to Build Cultural Awareness and Global Respect* (3–6). Illus. 1992, Williamson paper $12.95 (0-913589-65-9). 160pp. One craft, recipe, or project is offered for each day of the year. (Rev: BL 1/1/93; SLJ 1/93) [306]

**17020** Murray, Anna, and Lynda Watts. *My Christmas Craft Book for Kids* (3–6). Illus. 1993, Western $9.99 (0-307-16750-X). 64pp. Felt tree ornaments and Santa puppets are 2 of the attractive Christmas craft projects clearly outlined in this book. (Rev: BL 12/15/93) [745.5]

**17021** Owen, Cheryl. *My Nature Craft Book* (2–6). Illus. 1993, Little, Brown $15.95 (0-316-67715-9). 96pp. An oversized craft book with such projects as lavender bags and painted stones. (Rev: BL 3/15/93; SLJ 8/93) [745.5]

**17022** Pfiffner, George. *Earth-Friendly Holidays: How to Make Fabulous Gifts and Decorations from Reusable Objects* (3–6). Illus. 1995, Wiley paper $12.95 (0-471-12005-7). 128pp. A total of 29 easily executed craft projects for all sorts of holidays, including Valentine's Day, Christmas, and Kwanzaa. (Rev: SLJ 11/95) [745.5]

**17023** Pfiffner, George. *Earth-Friendly Outdoor Fun: How to Make Fabulous Games, Gardens, and Other Projects from Reusable Objects* (3–6). Illus. by author. 1996, Wiley paper $12.95 (0-471-14113-5). 128pp. Reusable materials like plastic shopping bags, cardboard, and soda bottles are used to produce a number of items like kites, bowling pins, and a scarecrow. (Rev: SLJ 4/96) [745.5]

**17024** Press, Judy. *The Little Hands Big Fun Craft Book: Creative Fun for 2- to 6-Year-Olds* (PS–1). Illus. by Loretta Braren. Series: Little Hands Books. 1996, Williamson paper $12.95 (0-913589-96-9). 142pp. A collection of 75 simple craft projects grouped under such headings as "Animals and Trees," "Friendship," and "Family Fun." (Rev: SLJ 7/96) [745.5]

**17025** Press, Judy. *Vroom! Vroom! Making 'Dozers, 'Copters, Trucks, and More* (2–6). Illus. by Michael Kline. Series: Little Hands Books. 1997, Williamson paper $12.95 (1-885593-04-X). 160pp. Both craft and transportation enthusiasts can uses this simple guide to making several vehicles with ordinary materials and good step-by-step directions. (Rev: SLJ 8/97) [745.5]

**17026** Randall, Ronne. *Thanksgiving Fun: Great Things to Make and Do* (4–6). Illus. by Annabel Spenceley. 1994, Kingfisher paper $4.95 (1-85697-500-2). 29pp. A wonderful book of autumn crafts and projects that also contains material on harvest time traditions around the world. (Rev: SLJ 10/94) [745]

**17027** Rhodes, Vicki. *Pumpkin Decorating* (4–8). Illus. 1997, Sterling $10.95 (0-8069-9574-2). 96pp. Clear direction and full-color photos show how to decorate more than 80 pumpkins. (Rev: SLJ 12/97) [745.5]

**17028** Rice, Melanie. *The Complete Book of Children's Activities* (PS–K). Illus. by Chris Barker. 1993, Kingfisher paper $9.95 (1-85697-907-5). 120pp. For the very young, this is a collection of learning activities, games, and construction projects. (Rev: BL 5/1/93) [372]

**17029** Robins, Deri. *Christmas Fun* (3–6). Illus. by Maggie Downer. 1995, Kingfisher paper $4.95 (1-85697-567-3). 32pp. Crafts, games, and foods are highlighted in this book featuring all sorts of Christmas activities. (Rev: BL 10/1/95) [745]

**17030** Robins, Deri, et al. *The Kids Can Do It Book: Fun Things to Make and Do* (PS–3). Illus. by Charlotte Stowell. 1993, Kingfisher paper $9.95 (1-85697-860-5). 80pp. Simple activities like making potato prints, planting a garden, preparing a picnic, and sewing a bath mat are outlined in this delightful book. (Rev: SLJ 1/94) [745]

**17031** Roche, Denis. *Loo-Loo, Boo, and Art You Can Do* (1–4). Illus. 1996, Houghton $14.95 (0-395-75921-8). 32pp. Eleven art projects are introduced by Loo-Loo and her dog, Boo. (Rev: BCCB 9/96; BL 9/15/96; SLJ 8/96) [704]

**17032** Ross, Kathy. *Crafts for Easter* (K–3). Illus. by Sharon L. Holm. 1996, Millbrook LB $21.90 (1-56294-918-7). 48pp. With simple, clear instructions, Easter-related crafts using everyday objects, like making baskets, are described. (Rev: BL 3/1/96) [745.594]

**17033** Ross, Kathy. *Crafts for Halloween* (1–3). Illus. by Sharon L. Holm. 1994, Millbrook LB $21.90 (1-56294-411-8). 48pp. Colorful illustrations help explain a number of Halloween craft projects for primary-school youngsters. (Rev: BL 10/15/94; SLJ 1/95) [745]

**17034** Ross, Kathy. *Crafts for Kids Who Are Wild About Dinosaurs* (3–5). Illus. Series: Crafts for Kids Who Are Wild About. 1997, Millbrook LB $22.40 (0-7613-0053-8); paper $7.95 (0-7613-0177-1). 48pp. Twenty projects involving dinosaurs and using everyday objects are described. (Rev: BL 2/1/97; SLJ 6/97) [745.5]

**17035** Ross, Kathy. *Crafts for Kids Who Are Wild About Outer Space* (3–5). Illus. Series: Crafts for Kids Who Are Wild About. 1997, Millbrook LB $22.40 (0-7613-0054-6); paper $7.95 (0-7613-0176-3). 48pp. Various aspects of outer space are presented in 20 craft projects that use commonplace items. (Rev: BL 2/1/97; SLJ 6/97) [745.5]

**17036** Ross, Kathy. *Crafts for Valentine's Day* (2–5). Illus. by Sharon L. Holm. Series: Holiday Crafts for Kids. 1995, Millbrook LB $21.90 (1-56294-489-4). 47pp. Twenty simple holiday projects using readily available materials are described on double-page spreads, with color illustrations and step-by-step instructions. (Rev: SLJ 4/95) [745.5]

**17037** Ross, Kathy. *Crafts from Your Favorite Fairy Tales* (1–5). Illus. by Vicky Enright. 1997, Millbrook LB $22.40 (0-7613-0259-X). 47pp. An unusual craft book that uses such tales as *Cinderella* and *Jack and the Beanstalk* as the inspiration for 20 activities. (Rev: SLJ 12/97) [745.5]

**17038** Ross, Kathy. *Every Day Is Earth Day* (2–4). Illus. by Sharon L. Holm. Series: Holiday Crafts for Kids. 1995, Millbrook LB $21.90 (1-56294-490-8). 47pp. After a general discussion of Earth Day, presents 20 crafts that reflect an interest in conserving natural resources and recycling materials. (Rev: SLJ 5/95) [745.5]

**17039** Ross, Kathy. *Gifts to Make for Your Favorite Grownup* (3–6). Illus. by Anne Canevari Green. 1996, Millbrook LB $24.90 (1-56294-274-3). 95pp. Simple directions and easily found materials are included in this volume that describes how to make 43 different gifts for adults. (Rev: BCCB 12/96; SLJ 10/96) [745.5]

**17040** Sattler, Helen R. *Recipes for Art and Craft Materials* (3–6). Illus. by Marti Shohet. 1987, Lothrop $16.00 (0-688-07374-3). 128pp. Formulas for making craft materials like paints and pastes. A reissue of the 1973 edition.

**17041** Simons, Robin. *Recyclopedia: Games, Science Equipment and Crafts from Recycled Materials* (5–8). Illus. by author. 1976, Houghton paper $13.95 (0-395-59641-6). Clear directions complemented by good illustrations characterize this book of interesting projects using waste materials.

**17042** Sohi, Morteza E. *Look What I Did With a Leaf!* (3–6). Illus. Series: Nature Craft. 1993, Walker LB $15.85 (0-8027-8216-7). Combines nature crafts with field guide material and explains how to make collage animals out of leaves. (Rev: SLJ 12/93) [745]

**17043** Solga, Kim, and Priscilla Hershberger. *Craft Fun!* (2–6). Photos by Pamela Monfort. Series: Art and Activities for Kids. 1997, North Light paper $19.99 (0-89134-834-4). 216pp. This activity book introduces crafts projects on a variety of topics, including card making, costumes, and clothes. (Rev: SLJ 1/98) [745.5]

**17044** Supraner, Robyn. *Happy Halloween! Things to Make and Do* (1–3). Illus. by Renzo Barto. 1981, Troll LB $12.50 (0-89375-420-X); paper $3.50 (0-89375-421-8). 48pp. Games, decorations, disguises, and more.

**17045** Supraner, Robyn. *Rainy Day Surprises You Can Make* (1–3). Illus. by Renzo Barto. 1981, Troll LB $12.50 (0-89375-428-5). 48pp. Simple handicrafts made with accessible materials.

**17046** Temko, Florence. *Traditional Crafts from Africa* (2–5). Illus. 1996, Lerner LB $16.95 (0-8225-2936-X). 64pp. Clear instructions and excellent illustrations are used in the presentation of several African craft projects. (Rev: BL 9/1/96; SLJ 10/96) [745]

**17047** Temko, Florence. *Traditional Crafts from Mexico and Central America* (3–6). Photos by Robert L. Wolfe and Diane Wolfe. Illus. by Randall Gooch. Series: Culture Crafts. 1996, Lerner LB $22.60 (0-8225-2935-1). 64pp. After a brief introduction to the area, this book describes 8 traditional crafts with clear instructions and a number of helpful illustrations. (Rev: BCCB 2/97; SLJ 12/96) [745.5]

**17048** Thomas, John E., and Danita Pagel. *The Ultimate Book of Kid Concoctions* (PS–4). Illus. by Robb Durr and Zachariah Durr. 1998, Kid Concoctions paper $14.95 (0-9661088-0-9). 80pp. Features about 65 recipes and activities using common kitchen supplies to make items like sidewalk chalk, finger paints, and scratch-and-sniff stickers. (Rev: SLJ 3/98) [745.5]

**17049** Treinan, Sarah Jane, ed. *Better Homes and Gardens Incredibly Awesome Crafts for Kids* (4–8). Illus. 1992, Meredith paper $14.95 (0-696-01984-1). 168pp. More than 75 projects — many requiring supervision — for interesting patterns and crafts. (Rev: BL 4/15/92) [745.5]

**17050** Umnik, Sharon D., ed. *175 Easy-to-Do Halloween Crafts* (3–5). Illus. 1995, Boyds Mills $6.95 (1-56397-372-3). 63pp. Masks, costumes, and decorations are some of the objects made from common materials in this holiday craft book. (Rev: BL 9/15/95; SLJ 12/95) [745.5]

**17051** Wallace, Mary. *I Can Make Toys: So Easy to Make!* (1–3). Photos by author. Series: Greey de Pencier Books. 1994, Firefly $17.95 (1-895688-23-X); paper $9.95 (1-895688-16-7). 31pp. This book contains 11 easy-to-make projects, including a glider, car, bunny, train, and furniture. (Rev: SLJ 11/94) [745]

**17052** West, Robin. *My Very Own Birthday: A Book of Cooking and Crafts* (2–4). Photos by Robert L. Wolfe and Diane Wolfe. Illus. by Jackie Urbanovic. Series: My Very Own Holiday. 1996, Carolrhoda LB $19.95 (0-87614-980-8). 64pp. Five birthday parties using different themes are described, along with recipes and craft projects. (Rev: SLJ 5/96) [745.5]

**17053** West, Robin. *My Very Own Christmas: A Book of Cooking and Crafts* (PS–1). Illus. by Susan S. Burke. 1993, Carolrhoda LB $19.95 (0-87614-722-8). 64pp. This book contains a variety of Christ-mas crafts and a number of recipes. (Rev: BL 8/93) [394.2]

**17054** Wilkes, Angela. *My First Christmas Activity Book* (4–6). Illus. 1994, DK Publg. $12.95 (1-56458-674-X). 48pp. This Christmas craft book concentrates on cards, decorations, and gift-wrapping paper. (Rev: BL 8/94) [745]

**17055** Wiseman, Ann S. *Making Things: The Handbook of Creative Discovery*. Rev. ed. (4–8). Illus. by author. 1997, Little, Brown $12.95 (0-316-94756-3). 161pp. Children are able to create an amazing array of objects by using this attractive craft book, which also includes many inspirational quotes and sayings. (Rev: SLJ 8/97) [745.5]

**17056** *A World of Things to Do* (2–5). Illus. 1987, National Geographic LB $12.50 (0-87044-615-0). 104pp. All sorts of activities for even the most hard to please, from kitchen science experiments to holiday ideas. (Rev: BL 5/15/87)

**17057** Zweifel, Frances. *The Make-Something Club Is Back!* (PS–3). Illus. by Ann Schweninger. 1997, Viking paper $14.99 (0-670-86727-6). 32pp. With a single project for each month, youngsters are shown, for example, how to build an ant hill and how to grow plants. (Rev: BL 2/1/97; SLJ 3/97) [745.5]

## American Historical Crafts

**17058** *Addy's Craft Book: A Look at Crafts from the Past with Projects You Can Make Today* (3–5). Illus. Series: American Girls Pastimes. 1994, Pleasant paper $5.95 (1-56247-124-4). 44pp. A book of handicrafts that re-creates projects popular in 19th-century America during the days of slavery. (Rev: BL 12/15/94) [745.5]

**17059** Beard, D. C. *The American Boys' Handy Book: What to Do and How to Do It* (5–7). Illus. 1983, Godine paper $12.95 (0-87923-449-0). 392pp. A facsimile edition of a manual first published in 1882.

**17060** Caney, Steven. *Steven Caney's Kids' America* (4–7). Illus. 1978, Workman paper $13.95 (0-911104-80-1). 416pp. Activities that focus on getting children to rediscover parts of America's past.

**17061** D'Amato, Janet, and Alex D'Amato. *Indian Crafts* (1–4). Illus. by authors. 1968, Lion LB $13.95 (0-87460-088-X). An excellent introduction to Indian crafts through projects and activities.

**17062** *Felicity's Craft Book: A Look at Crafts from the Past with Projects You Can Make Today* (3–5). Illus. Series: American Girls Pastimes. 1994, Pleasant paper $5.95 (1-56247-121-X). 44pp. This craft book outlines projects that were current during the

American colonial period. (Rev: BL 12/15/94) [745.5]

**17063** Greenwood, Barbara. *Pioneer Crafts* (2–5). 1997, Kids Can paper $4.95 (1-55074-359-7). 40pp. Directions for 17 projects involving such crafts as candle making, soap carving, and basket weaving. (Rev: BL 9/15/97; SLJ 9/97) [745.5]

**17064** Kalman, Bobbie. *Pioneer Projects* (3–6). Illus. by Marc Crabtree. Series: Historic Communities. 1997, Crabtree LB $19.16 (0-86505-437-1); paper $7.95 (0-86505-467-3). 32pp. Authentic crafts and activities engaged in by early American settlers are outlined, including step-by-step directions for building a model of a pioneer town. (Rev: BL 7/97; SLJ 8/97) [745.5]

**17065** *Kirsten's Craft Book: A Look at Crafts from the Past with Projects You Can Make Today* (3–5). Illus. Series: American Girls Pastimes. 1994, Pleasant paper $5.95 (1-56247-112-0). 45pp. Outlines a number of craft projects that pioneer children enjoyed, like making a calendar stick and a yarn doll. (Rev: BL 12/15/94; SLJ 12/94) [680]

**17066** Merrill, Yvonne Y. *Hands-On Rocky Mountains: Art Activities About Anasazi, American Indians, Settlers, Trappers, and Cowboys* (3–6). Illus. 1996, Kits paper $16.95 (0-9643177-2-9). 83pp. People associated with the West are introduced, and, for each, a series of activities and projects are outlined. (Rev: BL 1/1–15/97; SLJ 4/97) [745.5]

**17067** *Molly's Craft Book: A Look at Crafts from the Past with Projects You Can Make Today* (3–5). Illus. Series: American Girls Pastimes. 1994, Pleasant paper $5.95 (1-56247-118-X). 44pp. Through a series of craft projects, life between the world wars is re-created. (Rev: BL 12/15/94) [745.5]

**17068** Penner, Lucille R. *The Little Women Book: Games, Recipes, Crafts, and Other Homemade Pleasures* (3–6). Illus. by Diane De Groat. 1995, Random $12.00 (0-679-87405-4). 45pp. Various indoor activities are introduced, with information about the social life and recreational pursuits of children in the days of *Little Women*. (Rev: SLJ 1/96) [745.5]

**17069** *Samantha's Craft Book: A Look at Crafts from the Past with Projects You Can Make Today* (3–5). Illus. Series: American Girls Pastimes. 1994, Pleasant paper $5.95 (1-56247-115-5). 44pp. Twentieth-century American history is reflected in a series of interesting craft projects. (Rev: BL 12/15/94) [745.5]

**17070** Temko, Florence. *Traditional Crafts from Native North America* (2–4). Illus. Series: Culture Crafts. 1997, Lerner LB $22.60 (0-8225-2934-3). 64pp. Introduces the major cultural areas of North American Indians and gives directions for making such objects as baskets, cornhusk dolls, and dream catchers. (Rev: BL 10/1/97; SLJ 7/97) [745.5]

**17071** Yamane, Linda. *Weaving a California Tradition: A Native American Basketmaker* (3–6). Illus. Series: We Are Still Here. 1996, Lerner $21.27 (0-8225-2660-3); paper $6.95 (0-8225-9730-6). 48pp. The story of California basket weaving, its present status, and the people who engage in it. (Rev: BL 1/1–15/97; SLJ 2/97) [746.41]

## Clay and Other Modeling Crafts

**17072** Dixon, Annabelle. *Clay* (3–5). Illus. by Ed Barber. Series: Threads. 1990, Garrett LB $15.93 (0-944483-69-0). 26pp. The nature of clay, where it is found, and its uses in pottery and model crafts are discussed. (Rev: BL 2/1/91; SLJ 4/91) [553.6]

**17073** MacLeod-Brudenell, Iain. *Animal Crafts* (4–7). Illus. Series: World Wide Crafts. 1994, Gareth Stevens LB $21.27 (0-8368-1151-8). 32pp. The creation of various models of animals related to different cultures is the focus of this craft book containing more than a dozen projects. (Rev: BL 3/1/95; SLJ 1/95) [745.5]

**17074** Rowe, Christine. *The Children's Book of Pottery* (4–7). Illus. 1989, Trafalgar $19.95 (0-7134-5995-6). 64pp. A good British import about pottery making. (Rev: BL 12/1/89) [738.1]

**17075** Solga, Kim. *Make Sculptures!* (2–5). Illus. Series: Art and Activities for Kids. 1992, North Light $11.99 (0-89134-420-9). 48pp. This book supplies easy-to-follow instructions on constructing simple sculptures. (Rev: BL 9/1/92; SLJ 11/92) [745.5]

## Costume and Jewelry Making

**17076** Casey, Moe. *The Most Excellent Book of Dress Up* (3–5). Illus. Series: Most Excellent Book Of. 1997, Millbrook LB $19.90 (0-7613-0550-5); paper $6.95 (0-7613-0575-0). 32pp. Using many photos and drawings, this colorful book gives easy, step-by-step instructions for making various costumes. (Rev: BL 6/1–15/97; SLJ 8/97) [646.4]

**17077** Chernoff, Goldie Taub. *Easy Costumes You Don't Have to Sew* (3–6). Illus. by Margaret A. Hartelius. 1984, Macmillan LB $13.95 (0-02-718230-4). 48pp. Paper bags, cartons, and old cloth are 3 of the materials used in making these simple costumes.

**17078** Conaway, Judith. *Happy Haunting! Halloween Costumes You Can Make* (2–4). Illus. 1986, Troll LB $12.50 (0-8167-0666-2); paper $3.50 (0-8167-0667-0). 48pp. Simple costumes made with easily obtainable materials. (Rev: BL 12/1/86)

**17079** Doney, Meryl. *Jewelry* (5–8). Illus. Series: World Crafts. 1996, Watts LB $20.00 (0-531-14406-2). 32pp. A number of excellent jewelry-making projects from around the world are outlined with easy-to-follow directions and good background cultural information. (Rev: SLJ 1/97) [739.27]

**17080** Grisewood, Sara. *Making Jewelry* (3–6). Illus. Series: Step-by-Step. 1995, Kingfisher LB $13.90 (1-85697-589-4); paper $6.95 (1-85697-588-6). 40pp. A brightly illustrated craft book that tells how to make many kinds of jewelry out of salt dough, modeling clay, felt, and papier mâché. (Rev: SLJ 1/96) [745.5]

**17081** Gryski, Camilla. *Friendship Bracelets* (3–6). Illus. 1993, Morrow paper $6.95 (0-688-12437-2). 48pp. Instructions are given on how to make friendship bracelets from different materials, plus material on creating other forms of jewelry. (Rev: BL 10/1/93; SLJ 9/93) [746]

**17082** Gryski, Camilla. *Lanyard: Having Fun with Plastic Lace* (3–6). Illus. by Linda Hendry. 1994, Morrow $15.00 (0-688-13324-X). 32pp. Directions for making a number of bracelets, key chains, and earrings out of lanyards — strips of plastic or other materials. (Rev: BL 3/15/94; SLJ 7/94) [745.57]

**17083** Hershberger, Priscilla. *Make Costumes! For Creative Play* (2–5). Illus. Series: Art and Activities for Kids. 1992, North Light $11.99 (0-89134-450-0). 48pp. This oversized book describes how to make simple costumes with easy to follow directions. (Rev: BL 9/15/92; SLJ 12/92) [616.4]

**17084** Lincoln, Margaret. *The Most Excellent Book of Face Painting* (3–5). Illus. Series: Most Excellent Book Of. 1997, Millbrook LB $19.90 (0-7613-0551-3); paper $6.95 (0-7613-0576-9). 32pp. Simple step-by-step instructions are given on how to create a wide variety of brilliant faces. (Rev: BL 6/1–15/97; SLJ 8/97) [745.5]

**17085** MacLeod-Brudenell, Iain. *Costume Crafts* (4–7). Illus. Series: World Wide Crafts. 1994, Gareth Stevens LB $21.27 (0-8368-1152-6). 32pp. Multicultural projects involving dress and body decoration are featured in this easily followed craft book. (Rev: BL 3/1/95; SLJ 1/95) [745.5]

**17086** Reid, Margarette S. *A String of Beads* (2–4). Illus. by Ashley Wolff. 1997, Dutton paper $14.99 (0-525-45721-6). 32pp. A unique history of beads and beadwork, combined with a craft book that gives ideas for youngsters creating their own strings of beads. (Rev: BL 8/97*; SLJ 11/97*) [745.5]

**17087** Sadler, Judy Ann. *Beads* (1–4). Illus. Series: Easy Crafts. 1997, Kids Can paper $4.95 (1-55074-182-9). 32pp. Simple to more difficult projects involved with creating beadwork and bead jewelry are presented in this appealing book. (Rev: BL 12/1/97) [746.5]

**17088** Sadler, Judy Ann. *Easy Braids, Barrettes and Bows* (3–7). Illus. 1997, Kids Can paper $4.95 (1-55074-325-2). 40pp. Discusses various hairstyles, like cornrows and ponytails, and gives instructions on making pieces of hair jewelry. (Rev: BL 10/15/97; SLJ 11/97) [646.7]

**17089** Sensier, Danielle. *Costumes* (5–7). Illus. Series: Traditions Around the World. 1994, Thomson Learning LB $24.26 (1-56847-227-7). 48pp. The rituals and uses involved in costumes are introduced, as well as a general discussion of clothing in various regions and cultures. (Rev: BL 2/1/95; SLJ 3/95) [391]

**17090** Solga, Kim. *Make Clothes Fun* (2–5). Illus. Series: Art and Activities for Kids. 1992, North Light $11.95 (0-89134-421-7). 48pp. This oversize book gives easy-to-follow instructions on how to make clothes. Also use: *Make Gifts!* (1991). (Rev: BL 9/1/92; SLJ 11/92) [746.9]

**17091** Wallace, Mary. *I Can Make Jewelry* (2–4). Illus. 1997, Firefly $17.95 (1-895688-62-0); paper $6.95 (1-895688-63-9). 32pp. Rings, beads, hair decorations, and necklaces are some of the jewelry for which there are directions to make and wear. (Rev: BL 8/97) [745.5]

**17092** Wilkes, Angela. *Dazzling Disguises and Clever Costumes* (4–6). Illus. 1996, DK Publg. $14.95 (0-7894-1001-X). 48pp. Step-by-step instructions on how to make a variety of costumes, the materials needed, and information on clever disguises. (Rev: BCCB 11/96; BL 10/1/96; SLJ 12/96) [646.8]

# Drawing and Painting

**17093** Ames, Lee J. *Draw Fifty Airplanes, Aircraft and Spacecraft* (3–7). Illus. by author. 1987, Doubleday paper $8.95 (0-385-23629-8). 64pp. Simple directions for drawing various airborne articles, from the Wright brothers' plane to the Saturn V rocket. Also use: *Draw Fifty Boats, Ships, Trucks and Trains* (1976); *Draw Fifty Vehicles* (1997); *Draw Fifty Buildings and Other Structures* (1980).

**17094** Ames, Lee J. *Draw Fifty Beasties and Yugglies and Turnover Uglies and Things That Go Bump in the Night* (3–6). Illus. 1988, Doubleday $12.95 (0-385-24625-0). 64pp. Step-by-step drawing instructions introduce a zany cast of characters. (Rev: BCCB 1/89; BL 2/1/89; SLJ 2/89)

**17095** Ames, Lee J. *Draw Fifty Cars, Trucks, and Motorcycles* (4–6). Illus. 1986, Doubleday $10.95 (0-385-19059-X). 64pp. Step-by-step directions to method drawing. Also use: *Draw Fifty Athletes* (1989). (Rev: BL 7/86; SLJ 10/86)

**17096** Ames, Lee J. *Draw Fifty Cats* (4–7). Illus. 1986, Doubleday paper $8.95 (0-385-24640-4). 64pp. Step-by-step method of drawing different breeds and poses of cats. Also use: *Draw Fifty Holiday Decorations* (1987). (Rev: BL 11/15/86)

**17097** Ames, Lee J. *Draw Fifty Dogs* (4–6). Illus. by author. 1981, Doubleday $10.95 (0-385-15686-3); paper $8.95 (0-385-23431-7). 64pp. Six steps are used to draw several species. Also use: *Draw Fifty Animals* (1985); *Draw Fifty Dinosaurs and Other Prehistoric Animals* (1977); *Draw Fifty Horses* (1984).

**17098** Ames, Lee J. *Draw Fifty Famous Cartoons* (4–6). Illus. by author. 1985, Doubleday paper $8.95 (0-385-19521-4). 64pp. How to draw such characters as Dick Tracy and the Flintstones.

**17099** Ames, Lee J. *Draw Fifty Monsters, Creeps, Superheroes, Demons, Dragons, Nerds, Dirts, Ghouls, Giants, Vampires, Zombies and Other Curiosa* (4–6). Illus. by author. 1986, Doubleday paper $8.95 (0-385-17639-2). 64pp. How to draw a variety of curiosities.

**17100** Ames, Lee J., and Ray Burns. *Draw Fifty Creepy Crawlies* (3–6). Illus. by authors. 1991, Doubleday $13.00 (0-385-41190-1). With step-by-step directions, readers are shown how to draw a variety of insects, spiders, and mollusks. (Rev: SLJ 2/92) [741]

**17101** Arnosky, Jim. *Drawing from Nature* (4–8). Illus. 1987, Morrow paper $8.95 (0-688-07075-2). 64pp. A reissue of this acclaimed book to accompany the television series *Drawing from Nature*. (Rev: BL 10/15/87)

**17102** Arnosky, Jim. *Drawing Life in Motion* (4–8). Illus. 1984, Lothrop $16.00 (0-688-03803-4). 48pp. Full-color photos highlight this reissue of a widely acclaimed book. (Rev: BL 10/15/87)

**17103** Arnosky, Jim. *Sketching Outdoors in Autumn* (4–7). Illus. 1988, Lothrop $12.95 (0-688-06288-1). 48pp. Sketching animal tracks and signs as the artist follows the "animals' autumn." Also use: *Sketching Outdoors in Winter* (1988). (Rev: BL 10/1/88; HB 1–2/89; SLJ 12/88)

**17104** Arnosky, Jim. *Sketching Outdoors in Summer* (4–7). Illus. 1988, Lothrop $12.95 (0-688-06286-5). 48pp. The artist's appreciation of nature can inspire young enthusiasts. Also use: *Sketching Outdoors in Spring* (1987). (Rev: BL 6/15/88; HB 7–8/88; SLJ 6–7/88)

**17105** Baron, Nancy. *Getting Started in Calligraphy* (4–7). Illus. by author. 1979, Sterling paper $12.95 (0-8069-8840-1). A well-organized text from an experienced teacher of lettering.

**17106** Baxter, Leon. *The Drawing Book* (3–5). Illus. 1990, Ideals $13.95 (0-8249-8475-7). 64pp. An appealing guide to sketching people, animals, and objects. (Rev: BL 12/1/90) [741.2]

**17107** Butterfield, Moira. *Fun with Paint* (4–8). Illus. Series: Creative Crafts. 1994, Random paper $6.99 (0-679-83942-3). 47pp. This simple introduction to painting covers various media and a number of creative projects, including making your own paints. (Rev: SLJ 3/94) [745]

**17108** Corbett, Grahame. *You Can Draw Fantastic Animals: A Step-by-Step Guide for Young Artists* (3–6). Illus. Series: You Can Draw. 1997, DK Publg. $9.95 (0-7894-1501-1). 21pp. Photos and clever illustrations are used to enliven this book that explains in simple steps how to draw a number of weird animals. (Rev: SLJ 2/98) [741.2]

**17109** DuBosque, Doug. *Draw Desert Animals* (3–6). Illus. 1996, Peel paper $8.95 (0-939217-26-0). 64pp. Beginning with simple shapes like circles and squares, teaches the reader to draw a variety of desert animals. (Rev: BL 12/15/96; SLJ 3/97) [743]

**17110** DuBosque, Doug. *Draw Dinosaurs*. Rev. ed. (3–6). Illus. 1997, Peel paper $8.95 (0-939217-22-8). 64pp. A fine art book that presents easily followed directions for drawing a wide variety of dinosaurs, with interesting facts about each. (Rev: BL 12/15/97) [743.6]

**17111** DuBosque, Doug. *Draw! Grassland Animals: A Step-by-Step Guide* (4–7). Illus. by author. 1996, Peel paper $8.95 (0-939217-25-2). 63pp. A step-by-step description of how to draw 31 animals from grasslands around the world. (Rev: SLJ 9/96) [741]

**17112** DuBosque, Doug. *Learn to Draw Now!* (5–8). Illus. by author. Series: Learn to Draw. 1991, Peel paper $7.95 (0-939217-16-3). 64pp. A simple, easily followed manual on how to draw that contains many interesting practice exercises. (Rev: SLJ 8/91) [743]

**17113** DuBosque, Doug. *Learn to Draw 3-D* (4–8). Illus. Series: Learn to Draw. 1992, Peel paper $8.95 (0-939217-17-1). 80pp. A step-by-step guide with exercises that show how to add depth to a drawing. (Rev: BL 1/1/93) [742]

**17114** Emberley, Ed. *Ed Emberley's Big Green Drawing Book* (2–4). Illus. by author. 1979, Little, Brown $15.95 (0-316-23595-4). A do-it-yourself drawing book using basic shapes, explained by a master. Also use: *Ed Emberley's Big Purple Drawing Book* (1981).

**17115** Emberley, Ed. *Ed Emberley's Big Orange Drawing Book* (2–5). Illus. 1980, Little, Brown paper $9.95 (0-316-23419-2). 96pp. Emberley teaches you to draw many orange things, mostly associated with Halloween.

**17116** Emberley, Ed. *Ed Emberley's Drawing Book: Make a World* (2–4). Illus. by author. 1972, Little, Brown $15.95 (0-316-23598-9); paper $6.95 (0-316-

23644-6). Illustrations and examples on how to draw objects from flags to faces.

**17117** Emberley, Ed. *Ed Emberley's Drawing Book of Faces* (2–5). Illus. 1992, Little, Brown paper $5.95 (0-316-23655-1). 32pp. Step-by-step instructions on how to produce an amusing character from a simple shape.

**17118** Emberley, Ed. *Ed Emberley's Great Thumbprint Drawing Book* (1–4). Illus. by author. 1992, Little, Brown $16.95 (0-316-23648-9). How to make faces and other objects by adding lines to thumbprints.

**17119** Gamble, Kim. *You Can Draw Amazing Faces: A Step-by-Step Guide for Young Artists* (3–6). Illus. Series: You Can Draw. 1997, DK Publg. $9.95 (0-7894-1502-X). 21pp. Photos and clever illustrations highlight this easy-to-follow drawing book that concentrates on how to create all sorts of faces. (Rev: SLJ 2/98) [741.2]

**17120** Goyallon, Jerome. *Drawing Prehistoric Animals* (3–6). Trans. from French by Keith Schiffman. Illus. by author. 1996, Sterling paper $5.95 (0-8069-0979-X). 80pp. Using a system of grids and simple directions, youngsters can draw 30 primitive and prehistoric mammals and Neanderthal man. (Rev: SLJ 5/97) [741.2]

**17121** Haldane, Suzanne. *Painting Faces* (2–5). Illus. by author. 1995, Puffin paper $4.99 (0-14-055611-7). 32pp. Face painting is linked to cultural traditions around the world. (Rev: BCCB 9/88; BL 10/15/88; SLJ 12/88)

**17122** Kallen, Stuart A. *Eco-Arts and Crafts* (3–4). Illus. Series: Target Earth. 1993, ABDO LB $15.98 (1-56239-208-5). 46pp. In these recycling projects, youngsters are taught how to create their own art supplies, including paper. (Rev: SLJ 3/94) [745]

**17123** Lewis, Amanda. *Lettering: Make Your Own Cards, Signs, Gifts and More* (3–7). Illus. 1997, Kids Can paper $4.95 (1-55074-232-9). 48pp. Demonstrates lettering techniques, shows how to make letterhead stationery on the computer, and gives material on calligraphy, type, and displays. (Rev: BL 10/15/97; SLJ 1/98) [745.6]

**17124** Lightfoot, Marge. *Cartooning for Kids* (3–5). Illus. by author. Series: Greey de Pencier Books. 1993, Firefly $16.95 (1-895688-03-5); paper $8.95 (0-920775-84-5). 64pp. This useful introduction to cartooning shows how to break down figures to basic shapes, how to show movement and gesture, and how to place people into settings. (Rev: SLJ 2/94) [741.5]

**17125** Lynn, Sara, and Diane James. *Play with Paint* (PS–3). Illus. 1993, Carolrhoda LB $19.95 (0-87614-755-4). 24pp. This beginning craft book contains simple projects with brief explanations using every-day materials. A companion volume is: *Play with Paper* (1993). (Rev: BL 5/1/93) [750]

**17126** Martin, Judy, ed. *Painting and Drawing* (3–6). Illus. 1994, Millbrook LB $23.90 (1-56294-203-4). 96pp. A thorough, step-by-step guide to drawing and painting, from choosing materials and explanations of basic elements of art to suggestions for executing different kinds of paintings. (Rev: BL 3/1/94; SLJ 4/94) [741.2]

**17127** Pellowski, Michael M. *The Art of Making Comic Books* (4–8). Illus. 1995, Lerner LB $21.27 (0-8225-2304-3). 80pp. A history of comic books, with coverage of techniques and details on how to become a comic book artist. (Rev: BCCB 2/96; BL 1/1–15/96; SLJ 1/96) [741.5]

**17128** Reinagle, Damon J. *Draw! Medieval Fantasies* (4–8). Illus. 1995, Peel paper $8.95 (0-939217-30-9). 64pp. A how-to drawing book that gives simple instructions on creating such medieval subjects as dragons and castles. (Rev: BL 1/1–15/96; SLJ 3/96) [743]

**17129** Reinagle, Damon J. *Draw Alien Fantasies* (3–6). Illus. 1996, Peel paper $8.95 (0-939217-31-7). 64pp. Easy-to-follow directions are given for drawing a number of creatures from outer space. (Rev: BL 12/15/96; SLJ 3/97) [741.2]

**17130** Sirett, Dawn. *My First Paint Book* (3–5). Illus. Series: My First. 1994, DK Publg. $12.95 (1-56458-466-6). 48pp. An oversize book that presents many projects, like painting T-shirts and making papier-mâché pins, in double-page spreads. (Rev: BL 5/15/94; SLJ 7/94) [745.5]

**17131** Solga, Kim, et al. *Art Fun!* (1–6). Photos by Pamela Monfort. Illus. Series: Art and Activities for Kids. 1997, North Light paper $19.99 (0-89134-833-6). 216pp. This activity book introduces projects involving painting, drawing, printmaking, and sculpting. (Rev: SLJ 1/98) [741.2]

**17132** Solga, Kim. *Draw!* (2–5). Illus. 1991, North Light $11.99 (0-89134-385-7). 48pp. Ten drawing projects that use color pencils, crayons, charcoal, watercolors, and felt-tip pens. Also use: *Paint!* (1991). (Rev: BL 1/15/92; SLJ 2/92) [741.2]

**17133** Thomson, Ruth. *Drawing* (K–3). Illus. Series: Get Set . . . Go! 1994, Children's LB $16.00 (0-516-07989-1). 24pp. Various drawing techniques utilizing pencils and crayons are introduced in a simple large-print text and colorful illustrations. (Rev: BL 3/15/95) [741.2]

**17134** Wallace, Mary. *I Can Make Art* (4–8). Photos by author. Series: I Can Make. 1997, Firefly $17.95 (1-895688-64-7); paper $6.95 (1-895688-65-5). 31pp. Art and craft combine in these 12 projects involving such techniques as watercolor, still life, chalk drawing, print-making, and collage. (Rev: SLJ 12/97) [741.2]

**17135** Welton, Jude. *Drawing: A Young Artist's Guide* (4–8). Illus. 1994, DK Publg. $14.95 (1-56458-676-6). 45pp. Many aspects of drawing — like using the proper tools and creating texture — are explained in this book produced with the cooperation of the Tate Gallery in London, England. (Rev: BL 1/15/95; SLJ 3/95) [741.2]

## Masks and Mask Making

**17136** Beaton, Clare. *Masks* (2–4). Illus. Series: Make and Play. 1995, Fitzgerald LB $15.95 (1-887238-02-6). 24pp. Step-by-step directions for making 7 different masks. (Rev: BL 1/1/91; SLJ 2/91) [731.785]

**17137** Doney, Meryl. *Masks* (4–6). Illus. Series: World Crafts. 1996, Watts LB $20.00 (0-531-14397-X). 32pp. Masks from various cultures are introduced, with simple step-by-step instructions to make duplicates. (Rev: SLJ 7/96) [745.5]

**17138** Earl, Amanda, and Danielle Sensier. *Masks* (5–7). Illus. Series: Traditions Around the World. 1994, Thomson Learning $24.26 (1-56847-226-9). 48pp. This multicultural introduction to masks discusses their origins and uses in religion, festivals, and the theater. (Rev: BL 2/1/95; SLJ 3/95) [391.43]

**17139** Flanagan, Alice K. *Masks!* (3–7). Illus. Series: A World of Difference. 1996, Children's LB $21.00 (0-516-08213-2). 32pp. Describes and illustrates masks from many places and time periods, reflecting different cultures. (Rev: BL 9/15/96; SLJ 11/96) [391]

**17140** *Masks* (4–7). Illus. 1997, DK Publg. $19.95 (0-7894-2454-1). 12pp. Through the use of pop-ups, masks from around the world — including Nigeria, Europe, and Colombia — are presented. (Rev: BL 12/15/97) [646.4]

**17141** Russon, Jacqueline. *Face Painting* (3–7). Illus. Series: First Arts and Crafts. 1994, Thomson Learning LB $21.40 (1-56847-197-1). 32pp. An amazing number of ideas for creative face painting, with clear instructions and many illustrations. (Rev: BL 1/1/95; SLJ 12/94) [745.5]

**17142** Supraner, Robyn. *Great Masks to Make* (5–7). Illus. by Renzo Barto. 1981, Troll LB $12.50 (0-89375-436-6). 48pp. Bright, full-color illustrations highlight this simple craft book.

## Paper Crafts

**17143** Araki, Chiyo. *Origami in the Classroom* (4–7). Illus. 1965, Tuttle vol. 1 $14.95 (0-8048-0452-4); vol. 2 $14.95 (0-8048-0453-2). In 2 volumes; each deals with paper crafts for 2 of the seasons.

**17144** Borja, Robert, and Corinne Borja. *Making Chinese Papercuts* (4–7). Illus. by authors. 1980, Whitman LB $14.95 (0-8075-4948-7). A clear explanation of an ancient art with many examples and photographs.

**17145** Churchill, E. Richard. *Fabulous Paper Airplanes* (4–8). Illus. by James Michaels. 1991, Sterling $14.95 (0-8069-8342-6). 128pp. Detailed instructions for creating 29 paper airplanes, some requiring staples, clips, straws, or tape in addition to paper. (Rev: BL 1/15/92; SLJ 4/92) [745.592]

**17146** Churchill, E. Richard. *Fantastic Flying Paper Toys* (5–7). Illus. by James Michaels. 1990, Sterling paper $5.95 (0-8069-7460-5). 96pp. Designs for 30 different toys made from ordinary household objects. (Rev: BL 3/1/91) [745.592]

**17147** Churchill, E. Richard. *Fast and Funny Paper Toys You Can Make* (3–7). Illus. by James Michaels. 1989, Sterling $14.95 (0-8069-5770-0). 128pp. This book takes the reader into a world of toys that move. (Rev: BL 2/1/90; SLJ 4/90) [745.592]

**17148** Churchill, E. Richard. *Holiday Paper Projects* (3–6). Illus. by James Michaels. 1993, Sterling $14.95 (0-8069-8512-7). 128pp. Various paper crafts related to holidays are outlined with simple instructions that usually only involve cutting, folding, and pasting. (Rev: SLJ 12/93) [745]

**17149** Corwin, Judith Hoffman. *Papercrafts: Origami, Papier-Mâché, and Collage* (1–5). Illus. 1988, Watts LB $20.00 (0-531-10465-6). 72pp. Twenty-four things to do with origami and other paper crafts. (Rev: BL 4/1/87; SLJ 10/88)

**17150** Doney, Meryl. *Papercraft* (4–8). Illus. Series: World Crafts. 1997, Watts LB $20.00 (0-531-14446-1). 32pp. A look at paper-crafting around the world is followed by a number of projects, including making paper flowers, a pinwheel, origami, and bookbinding. (Rev: SLJ 12/97) [745.5]

**17151** Fiarotta, Phyllis, and Noel Fiarotta. *Papercrafts Around the World* (4–6). Illus. 1996, Sterling $19.95 (0-8069-3990-7). 96pp. Paper crafts and projects from 31 countries are included with easy-to-follow instructions. (Rev: BL 7/96; SLJ 8/96) [745.54]

**17152** Fleischman, Paul. *Copier Creations* (3–8). Illus. by David Cain. 1993, HarperCollins $15.00 (0-

060-21052-4). 128pp. This craft book shows how to make such items as stationery and decals by using copying machines and common materials. (Rev: BL 7/93) [760]

**17153** Grummer, Arnold E. *Paper by Kids* (5–7). Illus. 1990, Macmillan $12.95 (0-87518-191-0). 116pp. A clear, well-organized guide to papermaking.

**17154** Haas, Rudi, et al. *Egg-Carton Zoo II* (3–7). Illus. 1989, Oxford paper $11.95 (0-19-540718-0). 64pp. How to make animal figures such as a rhino, shark, and pelican with simple tools and egg cartons. (Rev: BL 1/1/90) [745]

**17155** Henry, Sandi. *Cut-Paper Play! Dazzling Creations from Construction Paper* (K–5). Illus. by Norma Jean Jourdenais. Series: Kids Can! Book. 1997, Williamson paper $12.95 (1-885593-05-8). 160pp. In this book, which indicates the relative difficulty of each activity, there are projects that include making a desktop robot, a frog, and a mosaic snowman. (Rev: SLJ 9/97) [745.5]

**17156** Irvine, Joan. *How to Make Holiday Pop-Ups* (3–6). Illus. 1996, Morrow LB $15.93 (0-688-13609-5). 64pp. Directions for making pop-ups for holidays observed in a number of religions. (Rev: BCCB 9/96; BL 9/15/96; SLJ 9/96) [745.594]

**17157** Irvine, Joan. *How to Make Pop-Ups* (3–7). Illus. by Barbara Reid. 1988, Morrow paper $6.95 (0-688-07902-4). 96pp. Instructions on how to create 3-dimensional wonders. (Rev: BL 4/15/88; SLJ 3/88)

**17158** Irvine, Joan. *How to Make Super Pop-Ups* (4–7). Illus. 1992, Morrow $14.00 (0-688-10690-0); paper $6.95 (0-688-11521-7). 96pp. Lots of ideas and directions for making 3-dimensional paper constructions with moving parts. (Rev: BL 1/15/93) [745]

**17159** Kelly, Emery J. *Paper Airplanes: Models to Build and Fly* (4–8). Illus. 1997, Lerner LB $23.93 (0-8225-2401-5). 64pp. This is a practical manual on making and flying paper airplanes, with good coverage of the principles of aerodynamics. (Rev: BL 12/1/97; SLJ 2/98) [745.592]

**17160** McGraw, Sheila. *Papier-Mâché for Kids* (3–6). Illus. 1991, Firefly $17.95 (0-920668-92-5); paper $9.95 (0-920668-93-3). 72pp. A well-designed craft book with instructions for 8 projects. (Rev: BL 1/15/92; SLJ 3/92) [745.54]

**17161** Robins, Deri. *Papier Mâché* (3–6). Illus. by Jim Robins. Series: Step-by-Step. 1993, Kingfisher paper $6.95 (1-85697-926-1). 40pp. This craft book shows how to create such objects as masks, bowls,

puppets, and mobiles with papier-mâché. (Rev: SLJ 3/94) [745.54]

**17162** Sarasas, Claude. *The ABC's of Origami* (4–6). Illus. 1964, Tuttle $14.95 (0-8048-0000-6). Directions on how to create 26 figures from an albatross to a zebra are given.

**17163** Schmidt, Norman. *Paper Birds That Fly* (5–8). Illus. 1997, Sterling $19.95 (1-895569-01-X); paper $12.95 (1-895569-11-7). 96pp. Using the simplest of materials — like paper, patterns, pencils, ruler, scissors, and glue — it is possible to make birds that fly. (Rev: SLJ 7/97) [745.5]

**17164** Solga, Kim. *Make Cards!* (2–5). Illus. Series: Art and Activities for Kids. 1992, North Light $11.99 (0-89134-481-0). 48pp. With easy-to-follow instructions, this oversize craft book tells how to make greeting cards for a number of occasions. (Rev: BL 9/15/92; SLJ 12/92) [745.594]

**17165** Stowell, Charlotte. *Making Cards* (3–6). Illus. Series: Step-by-Step. 1995, Kingfisher LB $13.90 (1-85697-591-6); paper $6.95 (1-85697-590-8). 40pp. Directions for making all sorts of greeting cards, including popups, mobiles, and cards for different holidays. (Rev: SLJ 1/96) [745.5]

**17166** Supraner, Robyn. *Fun with Paper* (1–3). Illus. by Renzo Barto. 1981, Troll LB $12.50 (0-89375-430-7). 48pp. Simple projects with easy directions.

**17167** Temko, Florence. *Paper Gifts and Jewelry* (2–6). Illus. by John Walls. Series: Paper Magic. 1997, Millbrook LB $20.90 (0-7613-0209-3). 45pp. Simple paper projects outlined in this useful craft book include making pleated earrings, unusual gift wraps, and special storage boxes. Also use *Paper Tags and Cards* (1997). (Rev: SLJ 9/97) [745.5]

**17168** Temko, Florence. *Planes and Other Flying Things* (3–6). Illus. 1996, Millbrook LB $20.90 (0-7613-0041-4); paper $7.95 (0-7613-0082-1). 48pp. This guide to making 19 different paper airplanes begins with the basic glider and moves on to more-complicated spaceships and helicopters. (Rev: BCCB 1/97; BL 1/1–15/97) [745]

**17169** Thomson, Ruth. *Collage* (K–3). Illus. Series: Get Set . . . Go! 1994, Children's LB $16.00 (0-516-07988-3). 24pp. With simple instructions, youngsters are introduced to making collages with readily available materials. (Rev: BL 3/15/95) [702]

**17170** Valenta, Barbara. *Pop-o-Mania: How to Create Your Own Pop-Ups* (4–6). Illus. 1997, Dial paper $16.99 (0-8037-1947-7). 16pp. Pop-ups and instructions are included in this craft book that will require help from an adult. (Rev: BL 12/15/97; HB 5–6/97; SLJ 6/97) [745.5]

**17171** Walter, F. Virginia. *Super Toys and Games from Paper* (4–6). Illus. 1993, Sterling $19.95 (1-895569-06-0). 104pp. Directions are given for almost 90 paper toys and games, such as newspaper golf clubs and cardboard-tube hammers. (Rev: BL 1/1/94; SLJ 12/93) [745.592]

**17172** West, Robin. *Dinosaur Discoveries: How to Create Your Own Prehistoric World* (3–6). Illus. 1989, Carolrhoda LB $14.95 (0-87614-351-6). 72pp. Directions for creating models of dinosaurs using scissors, glue, and construction paper. (Rev: BL 11/15/89; SLJ 12/89) [745.54]

## Printmaking

**17173** Sadler, Judy Ann. *Prints* (3–7). Illus. 1997, Kids Can paper $4.95 (1-55074-083-0). 32pp. Step-by-step, labeled drawings introduce such printmaking techniques as potato and sponge printing. (Rev: BL 10/15/97; SLJ 1/98) [760]

## Sewing and Needle Crafts

**17174** Bial, Raymond. *With Needle and Thread: A Book About Quilts* (4–7). Illus. 1996, Houghton $14.95 (0-395-73568-8). 48pp. An attractive introduction to quilts, their history, how they are made, and the people who sew them. (Rev: BCCB 2/96; BL 3/1/96; SLJ 6/96) [746.46]

**17175** O'Reilly, Susie. *Knitting and Crochet* (3–5). Illus. Series: Arts and Crafts. 1994, Thomson Learning LB $21.40 (1-56847-221-8). 32pp. A good handicraft book that explains the basic stitches, gives directions for many projects, and encourages young knitters to create their own patterns. (Rev: SLJ 1/95) [745.5]

**17176** Sadler, Judy Ann. *Sewing* (1–4). Illus. Series: Easy Crafts. 1997, Kids Can paper $4.95 (1-55074-101-2). 32pp. Step-by-step illustrations and directions are given for projects like making placemats and decorating clothing. (Rev: BL 12/1/97) [646.2]

## Toys and Dolls

**17177** Björk, Christina. *Big Bear's Book by Himself* (2–4). Illus. 1994, Farrar $17.95 (91-29-62912-8). 76pp. A history of the teddy bear plus some bedtime tales, a list of toy museums, and a bear bibliography, as told by Big Bear. (Rev: BL 2/15/95) [394.3]

**17178** Churchill, E. Richard. *Paper Science Toys* (4–8). Illus. by James Michaels. 1990, Sterling $14.95 (0-8069-5834-0). 128pp. Forty-eight different toys made from easily obtainable materials. (Rev: BL 2/15/91) [745]

**17179** Corbett, Sara. *What a Doll!* (3–7). Illus. Series: A World of Difference. 1996, Children's LB $21.00 (0-516-08211-6). 32pp. Dolls from various world cultures show the similarities and differences in societies. (Rev: BL 9/15/96; SLJ 11/96) [745]

**17180** Kay, Helen. *The First Teddy Bear* (K–3). Illus. by Susan Detweiler. 1985, Stemmer $14.95 (0-88045-042-8). 40pp. A simple tale of the history of this well-loved stuffed animal. (Rev: BCCB 2/86; BL 11/15/85; SLJ 1/86)

**17181** McGraw, Sheila. *Dolls Kids Can Make* (4–6). Illus. 1995, Firefly LB $19.95 (1-895565-75-8); paper $9.95 (1-895565-74-X). 72pp. Gives directions for making dolls out of washrags, gloves, and old fabrics, with clear instructions on the stitches and techniques involved. (Rev: BL 11/15/95; SLJ 3/96) [745]

**17182** Morris, Ann. *How Teddy Bears Are Made: A Visit to the Vermont Teddy Bear Factory* (PS–3). Photos by Ken Heyman. 1994, Scholastic $10.95 (0-590-47152-X). This photoessay covers the manufacture of teddy bears, from their design to filling orders in a Vermont factory. (Rev: SLJ 10/94) [688.7]

**17183** Pfiffner, George. *Earth-Friendly Toys* (3–6). Illus. 1994, Wiley paper $12.95 (0-471-00822-2). 128pp. The author gives clear directions for making a number of dolls using everyday objects like toilet paper tubes and egg cartons. (Rev: BL 7/94) [745]

## Woodworking

**17184** Gibbons, Gail. *Tool Book* (K–3). Illus. by author. 1982, Holiday LB $15.95 (0-8234-0444-7); paper $6.95 (0-8234-0694-6). 32pp. An introduction to various simple tools and their uses.

**17185** Jensen, Vickie. *Carving a Totem Pole* (3–6). Illus. 1996, Holt $14.95 (0-8050-3754-3). 30pp. A photoessay on the 3-month period it takes master carver Norman Tait and his family to carve a totem pole. (Rev: BCCB 6/96; BL 4/15/96; SLJ 6/96) [730]

**17186** Walker, Lester. *Housebuilding for Children* (4–7). Illus. 1977, Overlook paper $13.95 (0-87951-332-2). 176pp. The construction of 6 different kinds of houses, including a tree house, is clearly described in text and pictures.

# Hobbies

## General and Miscellaneous

**17187** Adkins, Jan. *The Art and Industry of Sand-castles* (4–6). Illus. 1982, Walker paper $9.95 (0-8027-7205-6). This is an illustrated guide to basic construction of sandcastles plus amazing background information.

**17188** Adkins, Jan. *String: Tying It Up, Tying It Down* (5–8). Illus. 1992, Macmillan LB $13.95 (0-684-18875-9). 48pp. With a text that reads like a novel, this book instructs and entertains readers in the art of knot tying. (Rev: BL 4/15/92; SLJ 6/92) [677]

**17189** Dobkin, Bonnie. *Collecting* (1–2). Illus. by Rick Hackney. Series: Rookie Readers. 1993, Children's LB $17.00 (0-516-02015-3). 32pp. For beginning readers, this rhyming story tells about the joys and problems of being a collector. (Rev: BL 3/1/94) [737]

**17190** Goodman, Michael. *Model Railroading* (5–8). Illus. Series: Hobby Guides. 1993, Crestwood LB $12.95 (0-89686-620-3). 48pp. As well as describing the basics of model railroading as a hobby, this account discusses clubs, displays, and organizations. (Rev: SLJ 2/94) [625.1]

**17191** Goodman, Michael. *Radio Control Models* (5–8). Illus. Series: Hobby Guides. 1993, Crestwood LB $12.95 (0-89686-622-X). 48pp. Gives practical advice on getting started in this fascinating hobby, with good background information on radio control models plus coverage on equipment, competitions, and organizations. (Rev: SLJ 2/94) [621]

**17192** Hayes, Ann. *Onstage and Backstage at the Night Owl Theater* (K–3). Illus. by Karmen Thompson. 1997, Harcourt $15.00 (0-15-200782-2). 32pp. Readers follow all the stages of putting on a stage production, from tryouts and first readings to set design, lighting, and performance. (Rev: BL 11/1/97; SLJ 11/97) [792]

**17193** Kiralfy, Bob. *The Most Excellent Book of How to Be a Cheerleader* (3–5). Series: Most Excellent Book Of. 1997, Millbrook LB $19.90 (0-7613-0617-X); paper $5.95 (0-7613-0631-5). 32pp. A step-by-step guide to cheerleading, with examples of moves and chants and tips on how to look the part. (Rev: BL 11/15/97; SLJ 3/98) [761.6]

**17194** Mitchelson, Mitch. *The Most Excellent Book of How to Be a Juggler* (3–5). Series: Most Excellent Book Of. 1997, Millbrook LB $19.90 (0-7613-0618-8); paper $6.95 (0-7613-0632-3). 32pp. A step-by-step guide to juggling, with examples of techniques, routines, and tips for giving an effective performance. (Rev: BL 11/15/97) [790]

**17195** Owens, Thomas S. *Collecting Baseball Cards* (4–6). Illus. 1993, Millbrook LB $22.40 (1-56294-254-9). 80pp. A basic introduction to this hobby, with a history of baseball cards and how they can be priced. (Rev: BL 8/93; SLJ 6/93) [796]

**17196** Owens, Thomas S. *Collecting Baseball Memorabilia* (4–6). Illus. 1996, Millbrook LB $23.40 (1-56294-579-3). 96pp. Ticket stubs, team schedules, autographs, and other related items are described, with hints for collectors on how to get them and how to organize and preserve a collection. (Rev: SLJ 6/96) [796.357]

**17197** Owens, Thomas S. *Collecting Comic Books: A Young Person's Guide* (5–8). Illus. 1995, Millbrook LB $25.90 (1-56294-580-7). 80pp. A beginner's guide to comic book collecting, with sections on kinds of collections, sources, and organizations. (Rev: BL 2/1/96; SLJ 1/96) [741.5]

**17198** Perkins, Catherine. *The Most Excellent Book of How to Be a Clown* (3–5). Illus. 1996, Millbrook

LB $19.90 (0-7613-0486-X); paper $6.95 (0-7613-0499-1). 32pp. Hints on makeup and presentations plus suggestions for routines are given for aspiring clowns. (Rev: BL 6/1–15/96; SLJ 6/96) [791.3]

**17199** Walker, Lester. *Block Building for Children: Making Buildings of the World with the Ultimate Construction Toy* (2–6). Illus. 1995, Overlook $22.95 (0-87951-609-7). 167pp. The 18 block-building projects in this book include a city of the future and the Emerald City of Oz. (Rev: SLJ 1/96) [621]

**17200** Young, Robert. *Miniature Vehicles* (4–6). Illus. Series: Collectibles. 1993, Dillon LB $13.95 (0-87518-518-5). 71pp. A guide for young collectors of miniature vehicles that tells about current sources, how models are manufactured, and where famous collections can be found. (Rev: BL 10/1/93) [629.22]

# Cooking

**17201** *Addy's Cook Book: A Peek at Dining in the Past with Meals You Can Cook Today* (3–5). Illus. Series: American Girls Pastimes. 1994, Pleasant paper $5.95 (1-56247-123-6). 44pp. This cookbook deals with foods prepared and served during the days of slavery in 19th-century America. (Rev: BCCB 2/95; BL 12/15/94; SLJ 4/95) [641.5]

**17202** Bisignano, Alphonse. *Cooking the Italian Way* (5–8). Illus. 1982, Lerner LB $19.93 (0-8225-0906-7). 48pp. Fifteen recipes plus a description of the country, markets, and dinner tables.

**17203** Björk, Christina. *Elliot's Extraordinary Cookbook* (3–5). Trans. by Joan Sandin. Illus. by Lena Anderson. 1991, R&S $11.95 (91-29-59658-0). 64pp. A friendly book that takes the reader step by step through food preparation. (Rev: BCCB 5/91; SLJ 5/91) [641]

**17204** Blain, Diane. *The Box Car Children Cookbook* (3–5). Illus. by L. Kate Deal and Eileen M. Neill. 1991, Whitman LB $14.95 (0-8075-0859-4); paper $9.95 (0-8075-0856-X). 96pp. Each of the simple recipes in this book is related to the Boxcar Children series. (Rev: BL 1/15/92; SLJ 11/91) [641]

**17205** Brown, Karen. *Kids Are Cookin': All-Time-Favorite Recipes That Kids Love to Cook* (3–6). Illus. 1997, Meadowbrook Pr. LB $8.00 (0-671-57552-X). 200pp. This attractive book of kids' favorite recipes includes franks and beans, grilled cheese, and milkshakes plus a number of breakfast dishes, snacks, and desserts. (Rev: BL 6/1–15/97; SLJ 7/97) [641.5]

**17206** Buck-Murray, Marian. *The Mash and Smash Cookbook: Fun and Yummy Recipes Every Kid Can Make!* (3–6). Illus. 1997, Wiley paper $12.95 (0-471-17969-8). 128pp. A collection of recipes that are

named to appeal to kids, with interesting sidebars containing background information about the ingredients. (Rev: BL 1/1–15/98; SLJ 2/98) [641.5]

**17207** Chung, Okwha, and Judy Monroe. *Cooking the Korean Way* (5–7). Illus. 1988, Lerner LB $19.93 (0-8225-0921-0). 48pp. Tempting recipes and a brief look at where they come from. (Rev: BL 8/88; SLJ 9/88)

**17208** Colen, Kimberly. *Peas and Honey: Recipes for Kids (with a Pinch of Poetry)* (3–6). Illus. 1995, Boyds Mills $15.95 (1-56397-062-7). 64pp. A collection of recipes for each daily meal plus appropriate poetry and food facts. (Rev: BL 1/1/95; SLJ 3/95) [641.5]

**17209** Cook, Deanna F. *The Kids' Multicultural Cookbook: Food and Fun Around the World* (3–6). Illus. 1995, Williamson paper $12.95 (0-913589-91-8). 160pp. This collection of activities, recipes, and games includes material on various regions of the world. (Rev: BL 3/15/96; SLJ 2/96) [641.59]

**17210** Coronado, Rosa. *Cooking the Mexican Way* (5–8). Illus. 1982, Lerner LB $19.93 (0-8225-0907-5); paper $5.95 (0-8225-9614-8). 48pp. Easy-to-follow instructions are given for typical Mexican foods.

**17211** Corwin, Judith Hoffman. *Cookie Fun* (4–6). Illus. by author. 1988, Simon & Schuster paper $5.95 (0-671-55019-5). 64pp. Simple recipes for delicious cookies in this reissued cookbook.

**17212** Coyle, Rena. *My First Baking Book* (4–6). Illus. by Tedd Arnold. 1988, Workman paper $9.95 (0-89480-579-7). 144pp. Bialosky Bear offers several fun treats to make, with the emphasis on cooking safety. (Rev: BL 1/1/89; SLJ 1/89)

**17213** Coyle, Rena. *My First Cookbook* (4–7). Illus. 1985, Workman paper $10.95 (0-89480-846-X). 128pp. Fifty recipes, including pancakes, salads, and tacos, and an emphasis on safety. (Rev: BL 4/15/86; SLJ 4/86)

**17214** D'Amico, Joan, and Karen Eich Drummond. *The Science Chef Travels Around the World* (4–7). Illus. 1996, Wiley paper $12.95 (0-471-11779-X). 192pp. Recipes from around the world also include the scientific principles of various cooking and baking processes. (Rev: BL 2/1/96; SLJ 3/96) [641.5]

**17215** Denny, Roz. *A Taste of Britain* (4–6). Illus. Series: A Taste Of. 1994, Thomson Learning LB $22.83 (1-56847-184-X). 48pp. As well as covering basic facts about Britain's culture and geography, recipes are given for such dishes as Welsh rarebit, shepherd's pie, and apple crumble. (Rev: BL 7/94; SLJ 8/94) [641]

**17216** Denny, Roz. *A Taste of China* (4–6). Illus. Series: A Taste Of. 1994, Thomson Learning LB $22.83 (1-56847-183-1). 48pp. Spicy spare ribs and stir fry vegetables are 2 recipes in this book, which also covers the land, climate, crops, and farming methods of the Chinese. (Rev: BL 7/94; SLJ 8/94) [641.595]

**17217** *Desserts Around the World* (4–6). Illus. by Robert L. Wolfe and Diane Wolfe. Series: Easy Menu Ethnic Cookbooks. 1992, Lerner LB $19.93 (0-8225-0926-1). 56pp. This book gives recipes and background material on simple desserts as prepared in different countries and cultures. (Rev: BL 6/15/92) [641.8]

**17218** Dooley, Norah. *Everybody Cooks Rice* (K–3). Illus. 1991, Carolrhoda LB $19.93 (0-87614-412-1); paper $6.95 (0-87614-591-8). 32pp. A story that shows the different ways Americans cook and eat rice. (Rev: BCCB 5/91; BL 4/15/91; SLJ 6/91) [641.6]

**17219** *Felicity's Cook Book: A Peek at Dining in the Past with Meals You Can Cook Today* (3–5). Illus. Series: American Girls Pastimes. 1994, Pleasant paper $5.95 (1-56247-120-1). 44pp. This book, a mixture of history and recipes, re-creates meals that were current during the colonial period in American history. (Rev: BL 12/15/94) [641.5]

**17220** Fison, Jolsie, and Felicity Dahl. *Roald Dahl's Revolting Recipes* (4–6). Illus. by Quentin Blake. 1994, Viking paper $15.99 (0-670-85836-6). 32pp. Recipes are given for all the dishes mentioned in Roald Dahl's books. (Rev: BCCB 3/95; BL 1/15/95; SLJ 3/95) [641.5]

**17221** Germaine, Elizabeth, and Ann L. Burckhardt. *Cooking the Australian Way* (3–7). Illus. by Robert L. Wolfe and Diane Wolfe. Series: Easy Menu Ethnic Cookbooks. 1990, Lerner LB $19.93 (0-8225-0923-7). 48pp. Recipes from Australia and an introduction to their food and eating habits. (Rev: SLJ 2/91) [641]

**17222** Goodwin, Bob, and Candi Perez. *A Taste of Spain* (4–6). Illus. Series: Food Around the World. 1995, Thomson Learning LB $22.83 (1-56847-188-2). 48pp. Basic information is given about the history and culture of Spain, followed by material on Spanish food and a group of representative recipes. (Rev: SLJ 3/95) [641]

**17223** Gore, Sheila. *My Cake* (PS–1). Illus. by Fiona Pragoff. Series: First Step Science. 1995, Gareth Stevens LB $19.93 (0-8368-1186-0). 32pp. The process of making a chocolate birthday cake is explained step by step, with added activities and background scientific information. (Rev: BL 7/95) [641.8]

**17224** Hargittai, Magdolna. *Cooking the Hungarian Way* (5–7). Illus. 1986, Lerner LB $19.93 (0-8225-0916-4). 48pp. An Easy Menu Ethnic Cookbook, with information about Hungarian history and food. (Rev: BL 10/15/86)

**17225** Harrison, Supenn, and Judy Monroe. *Cooking the Thai Way* (5–7). Illus. 1986, Lerner LB $19.93 (0-8225-0917-2). 48pp. Such recipes as Thai salads are included in this Easy Menu Ethnic Cookbook, along with history and information about Thai food. (Rev: BL 10/15/86)

**17226** Hill, Barbara W. *Cooking the English Way* (5–8). Illus. 1982, Lerner LB $19.93 (0-8225-0903-2). 48pp. Menus from breakfast through dinner are outlined plus national customs.

**17227** *Holiday Cooking Around the World* (4–6). Illus. 1988, Lerner LB $19.93 (0-8225-0922-9); paper $5.95 (0-8225-9573-7). 52pp. Recipes for holiday treats from around the world. (Rev: BL 1/15/89; SLJ 1/89)

**17228** Hughes, Helga. *Cooking the Swiss Way* (5–8). Photos by Robert L. Wolfe and Diane Wolfe. Illus. Series: Easy Menu Ethnic Cookbooks. 1995, Lerner LB $19.93 (0-8225-0930-X). 47pp. After a general introduction to Switzerland, this book colorfully discusses its food and produce and gives a number of tempting recipes. (Rev: SLJ 7/95) [641]

**17229** Jacobson, Michael, and Laura Hill. *Kitchen Fun for Kids: Healthy Recipes and Nutrition Facts for 7- to 12-Year-Old Cooks* (3–6). Illus. by Loel Barr. 1991, Holt $14.95 (0-8050-1609-0). 128pp. A cookbook and nutritional guide that asks young readers to think tuna, yogurt, vegetables, and whole-grain loaves! (Rev: BL 8/91; SLJ 10/91) [641.5]

**17230** Katzen, Mollie, and Ann Henderson. *Pretend Soup and Other Real Recipes: A Cookbook for Preschoolers and Up* (PS–3). Illus. by Mollie Katzen. 1994, Tricycle Pr. $16.95 (1-883672-06-6). 95pp. Using pictures as well as text, 17 simple recipes are presented that are easy enough for youngsters to prepare with little supervision. (Rev: HB 7–8/94; SLJ 6/94*) [641]

**17231** Kaufman, Cheryl Davidson. *Cooking the Caribbean Way* (5–7). Illus. 1988, Lerner LB $19.93 (0-8225-0920-2). 48pp. A variety of dishes featuring the spices and fresh fruits that come from these islands. (Rev: BL 8/88; SLJ 9/88)

**17232** *Kirsten's Cook Book: A Peek at Dining in the Past with Meals You Can Cook Today* (3–5). Illus. Series: American Girls Pastimes. 1994, Pleasant paper $5.95 (1-56247-111-2). 44pp. Describes the food that pioneer Swedish families ate in the United States and gives 17 simple recipes. (Rev: BCCB 2/95; BL 12/15/94; SLJ 10/94) [641.5]

**17233** MacDonald, Kate. *The Anne of Green Gables Cookbook* (4–7). Illus. by Barbara Dilella. 1987, Oxford $14.95 (0-19-540496-3). 48pp. The granddaughter of the Anne series, MacDonald combines heritage and expertise in 25 enticing recipes. (Rev: BL 1/1/87)

**17234**  Mack-Williams, Kibibi V. *Food and Our History* (4–6). Illus. Series: African American Life. 1995, Rourke LB $23.93 (1-57103-033-6). 48pp. The contributions of African Americans to world cuisine are outlined, with a number of excellent recipes for traditional dishes. (Rev: SLJ 3/96) [641]

**17235**  McKenley, Yvonne. *A Taste of the Caribbean* (4–6). Illus. Series: Food Around the World. 1995, Thomson Learning LB $22.83 (1-56847-187-4). 48pp. Describes the food of the Caribbean islands, gives several recipes, and supplies basic background information on Caribbean history and culture. (Rev: SLJ 3/95) [641]

**17236**  Madavan, Vijay. *Cooking the Indian Way* (5–8). Illus. 1985, Lerner LB $19.93 (0-8225-0911-3). 52pp. Cultural information is detailed plus both vegetarian and nonvegetarian recipes. (Rev: SLJ 9/85)

**17237**  Medearis, Angela Shelf, and Michael R. Medearis. *Cooking* (5–8). Illus. 1997, Twenty-First Century $20.40 (0-8050-4484-1). 80pp. This account traces the contributions of African Americans to cooking and food. (Rev: BL 2/15/98; SLJ 11/97) [641.59]

**17238**  *Molly's Cook Book: A Peek at Dining in the Past with Meals You Can Cook Today* (3–5). Illus. Series: American Girls Pastimes. 1994, Pleasant paper $5.95 (1-56247-117-1). 44pp. A look at life between the world wars is given in this cookbook with recipes that reflect those times. (Rev: BL 12/15/94) [641.5]

**17239**  Monroe, Lucy. *Creepy Cuisine: Revolting Recipes that Look Disgusting but Taste Divine* (4–7). Illus. by Dianne O. Burke. 1993, Random paper $5.99 (0-679-84402-3). 79pp. Recipes that bear such revolting names as Pus Pockets and Worms au Gratin actually contain directions for preparing delicious food, plus all sorts of cooking techniques and tips. (Rev: BCCB 10/93; SLJ 12/93) [641]

**17240**  Moore, Carolyn E., et al. *Young Chef's Nutrition Guide and Cookbook* (4–6). Illus. 1990, Barron's $13.95 (0-8120-5789-9). 281pp. This cookbook supplies tasty recipes and includes material on nutrition and good eating habits. (Rev: SLJ 8/90) [641.5]

**17241**  Morris, Ting, and Neil Morris. *No-Cook Cooking* (4–6). Illus. Series: Sticky Fingers. 1994, Watts LB $20.00 (0-531-14283-3). 32pp. Tasty recipes that involve no cooking are given, including a Halloween cake, a Caribbean salad, and historic notes on the ingredients. (Rev: BL 3/15/95; SLJ 1/95) [641.5]

**17242**  Nabwire, Constance. *Cooking the African Way* (5–8). Illus. 1988, Lerner LB $19.93 (0-8225-0919-9); paper $5.95 (0-8225-9564-8). 48pp. Clear instructions highlight these African recipes. (Rev: BCCB 5/89; BL 3/15/89)

**17243**  Nathan, Joan. *The Children's Jewish Holiday Kitchen: 70 Ways to Have Fun with Your Kids and Make Your Family's Celebrations Special* (4–6). Illus. 1995, Schocken $18.00 (0-8052-4130-2). 176pp. Seventy recipes arranged by holiday and by the degree of difficulty and need for supervision. (Rev: BL 10/15/95) [641.5]

**17244**  Nguyen, Chi, and Judy Monroe. *Cooking the Vietnamese Way* (5–8). Illus. 1985, Lerner LB $19.93 (0-8225-0914-8). 48pp. Information about the country is given plus recipes for native dishes and even how to eat with chopsticks. (Rev: SLJ 9/85)

**17245**  Numeroff, Laura. *Mouse Cookies: 10 Easy-to-Make Cookie Recipes* (2–4). Illus. by Felicia Bond. Series: Laura Geringer Books. 1995, Harper-Festival $13.95 (0-694-00633-5). 25pp. A spiral-bound book that contains amusing illustrations and 10 recipes that are spinoffs from the author's *If You Give a Mouse a Cookie* (1985). (Rev: SLJ 11/95) [641]

**17246**  Osseo-Asare, Fran. *A Good Soup Attracts Chairs: A First African Cookbook for American Kids* (4–8). Illus. 1993, Pelican $18.95 (0-88289-816-7). 160pp. The more than 35 recipes from Ghana found in this book include peanut butter stew and palm nut soup. (Rev: BL 10/15/93; SLJ 8/93) [641.5]

**17247**  Parnell, Helga. *Cooking the German Way* (5–7). Illus. 1988, Lerner LB $19.93 (0-8225-0918-0). 48pp. Includes such treats as Black Forest Torte and Apple Cake. (Rev: BL 8/88)

**17248**  Parnell, Helga. *Cooking the South American Way* (4–6). Illus. by Robert L. Wolfe and Diane Wolfe. 1992, Lerner LB $19.93 (0-8225-0925-3). 48pp. Great recipes and basic data about where the foods come from. (Rev: BL 6/15/92) [641]

**17249**  Perl, Lila. *Hunter's Stew and Hangtown Fry: What Pioneer America Ate and Why* (5–8). Illus. by Richard Cuffari. 1979, Houghton $16.95 (0-395-28922-X). 176pp. Eating habits and preferences, cooking techniques, and 20 recipes are included in this volume.

**17250**  *The Please Touch Cookbook* (K–3). Illus. 1990, Silver Burdett LB $7.95 (0-671-70558-X). 64pp. A good beginning cookbook with some 70 recipes. (Rev: SLJ 10/90) [641.5]

**17251**  Plotkin, Gregory, and Rita Plotkin. *Cooking the Russian Way* (5–7). Illus. 1986, Lerner LB $19.93 (0-8225-0915-6). 48pp. Included along with history and information are such recipes as Russian honey spice cake, in this Easy Menu Ethnic Cookbook. (Rev: BL 10/15/86)

**17252**  Porter, Cheryl. *Gross Grub: Wretched Recipes That Look Yucky but Taste Yummy* (3–8). Illus. by

Will Suckow. Series: KidBacks. 1995, Random paper $5.99 (0-679-86693-0). 80pp. Recipes are given for disgusting-sounding and -looking foods like Cat Litter Casserole and Diaper Dumps Porridge. (Rev: SLJ 6/95) [641]

**17253** Pulleyn, Micah, and Sarah Bracken. *Kids in the Kitchen: 100 Delicious, Fun and Healthy Recipes to Cook and Bake* (3–5). Illus. 1994, Sterling $24.95 (0-8069-0447-X). 112pp. Gives background information on food preparation for boys and girls plus lots of recipes, many of which require no cooking. (Rev: BL 7/94; SLJ 8/94) [641.5]

**17254** Ralph, Judy, and Ray Gompf. *The Peanut Butter Cookbook for Kids* (5–7). Illus. 1995, Hyperion LB $15.49 (0-7868-2110-8); paper $10.95 (0-7868-1028-9). 96pp. An amazing collection of recipes involving peanut butter, including soups, snacks, and main dishes. (Rev: BL 10/1/95; SLJ 9/95) [641.6]

**17255** Rotner, Shelley, and Julia P. Hellums. *Hold the Anchovies!* (K–2). Illus. 1996, Orchard LB $16.99 (0-531-08857-X). 32pp. The pizza, its ingredients, and methods of preparation are presented with a recipe for basic pizza dough. (Rev: BL 9/15/96; SLJ 10/96) [641.8]

**17256** *Samantha's Cook Book: A Peek at Dining in the Past with Meals You Can Cook Today* (3–5). Illus. Series: American Girls Pastimes. 1994, Pleasant paper $5.95 (1-56247-114-7). 44pp. Twentieth-century American history is reflected in a series of recipes for easily prepared meals. (Rev: BL 12/15/94; SLJ 10/94) [641]

**17257** Scherie, Strom. *Stuffin' Muffin: Muffin Pan Cooking for Kids* (4–6). Illus. by Dave Ferry. 1982, Young People's Pr. paper $18.95 (0-9606964-9-0). 100pp. A variety of foods without sugar or salt that can be made in muffin tins.

**17258** Skrepcinski, Denice, et al. *Cody Coyote Cooks! A Southwest Cookbook for Kids* (4–6). Illus. 1996, Tricycle Pr. paper $14.95 (1-883672-37-6). 96pp. Recipes along with legends, history, and geographical facts highlight this book about cooking and eating in Texas, Arizona, and New Mexico. (Rev: BL 10/15/96; SLJ 10/96) [641]

**17259** Supraner, Robyn. *Quick and Easy Cookbook* (1–3). Illus. by Renzo Barto. 1981, Troll LB $12.50 (0-89375-438-2). 48pp. A good introductory cookbook with 22 recipes.

**17260** Van der Linde, Polly, and Tasha Van der Linde. *Around the World in Eighty Dishes* (3–7). Illus. by Horst Lemke. 1971, Scroll $10.95 (0-87592-007-1). 88pp. The compilers and testers of these recipes from many continents are 2 little girls, 8 and 10 years old.

**17261** *Vegetarian Cooking Around the World* (5–7). Illus. Series: Easy Menu Ethnic Cookbooks. 1992, Lerner LB $19.95 (0-8225-0927-X). 48pp. Vegetarian meal recipes from the Americas, Africa, Asia, Europe, and Australia. (Rev: BL 2/15/93) [641.5]

**17262** Villios, Lynne W. *Cooking the Greek Way* (5–8). Illus. 1984, Lerner LB $19.93 (0-8225-0910-5). 52pp. The young cook is introduced to the cuisine of Greece, with a chapter covering utensils and ingredient needs and a glossary of basic cooking terms. Recipes are varied and easy to prepare.

**17263** Waldee, Lynne Marie. *Cooking the French Way* (5–8). Illus. 1982, Lerner LB $19.93 (0-8225-0904-0). 48pp. A nicely illustrated introduction to French recipes including breads and sauces.

**17264** Walker, Barbara M. *The Little House Cookbook* (5–7). Illus. by Garth Williams. 1979, HarperCollins paper $7.95 (0-06-446090-8). 256pp. Frontier food, such as green pumpkin pie from the Little House books, served up in tasty, easily used recipes.

**17265** Ward, Brenda C., and Jane C. Jarrell. *Good 'n Healthy!* (2–5). Illus. Series: Teachable Moments Cookbooks for Kids. 1995, Word $9.99 (0-8499-3671-3). 80pp. Values such as patience and kindness are dealt with, in addition to recipes that stress good nutrition. (Rev: BL 2/15/96) [641.5]

**17266** Ward, Brenda C., and Jane C. Jarrell. *Snack Attack!* (2–5). Illus. Series: Teachable Moments Cookbooks for Kids. 1995, Word $9.99 (0-8499-3670-5). 80pp. This book contains a number of tasty snack recipes grouped around a discussion of important values in life. (Rev: BL 2/15/96) [641.5]

**17267** Warner, Margaret Brink, and Ruth Ann Hayward. *What's Cooking? Favorite Recipes from Around the World* (5–8). Illus. 1981, Little, Brown $16.95 (0-316-35252-7). Eighty-nine recipes from teenagers around the world are given in simple terms.

**17268** Webb, Lois S. *Holidays of the World Cookbook for Students* (5–8). 1995, Oryx paper $26.95 (0-89774-884-0). 264pp. This excellent cookbook contains 388 recipes that represent holidays in 136 countries, including many from various regions of the United States. (Rev: SLJ 1/96) [641]

**17269** Weston, Reiko. *Cooking the Japanese Way* (5–8). Illus. 1983, Lerner LB $19.93 (0-8225-0905-9). 48pp. Directions for preparing traditional foods are given along with lists of terms, ingredients, and utensils.

**17270** White, Linda. *Cooking on a Stick: Campfire Recipes for Kids* (3–6). Illus. 1996, Gibbs Smith paper $8.95 (0-87905-727-0). 48pp. In addition to covering campfire cooking, this book discusses equipment and fire making. (Rev: BL 4/1/96) [641.5]

**17271** Wilder, Laura Ingalls. *The Laura Ingalls Wilder Country Cookbook* (5–8). Photos by Leslie A. Kelly. 1995, HarperCollins $24.95 (0-06-024917-X).

160pp. A collection of 73 recipes that were used during the author's life. (Rev: SLJ 11/95) [641]

**17272** Wilkes, Angela. *The Children's Quick and Easy Cookbook* (4–6). Illus. 1997, DK Publg. $16.95 (0-7894-2026-0). 96pp. Not nearly as "quick and easy" as the title would suggest, this book nevertheless contains some good recipes in an attractive format. (Rev: BL 12/15/97; SLJ 1/98) [641.5]

**17273** Wilkes, Angela. *My First Cookbook* (4–7). Illus. 1989, Knopf $15.00 (0-394-80427-9). 48pp. Step-by-step photos and clear directions, but some adult assistance will be needed. (Rev: BL 11/1/89; SLJ 12/89) [641]

**17274** Williamson, Sarah A., and Zachary Williamson. *Kids Cook! Fabulous Food for the Whole Family* (4–6). Illus. by Loretta Trezzo-Baren. 1992, Williamson paper $12.95 (0-913589-61-6). 157pp. Using recipes at 3 levels of difficulty, this book contains 153 recipes of foods that are fun to prepare. (Rev: SLJ 7/92) [641.5]

**17275** Winston, Mary, ed. *American Heart Association Kids' Cookbook* (3–7). Illus. by Joan Holub. 1993, Times Bks. $15.00 (0-8129-1930-0). 128pp. An exceptional cookbook with outstanding healthful recipes and many nutritional tips. (Rev: BL 10/1/93*) [641.5]

**17276** Wishik, Cindy S. *Kids Dish It Up . . . Sugar-Free: A Versatile Teaching Tool for Beginning Cooks* (3–5). Illus. 1982, Peninsula paper $11.95 (0-918146-22-4). 160pp. From soup to nuts with sugar-free recipes.

**17277** Yu, Ling. *Cooking the Chinese Way* (5–8). Illus. 1982, Lerner LB $19.93 (0-8225-0902-4). 48pp. From appetizers to desserts, with attractive illustrations.

**17278** Zalben, Jane Breskin. *Beni's Family Cookbook: For the Jewish Holidays* (4–8). Illus. 1996, Holt $19.95 (0-8050-3735-7). 91pp. This entertaining collection of recipes is arranged around the Jewish calendar. (Rev: BL 9/15/96; SLJ 2/97) [641.5]

**17279** Zamojska-Hutchins, Danuta. *Cooking the Polish Way* (5–8). Illus. 1984, Lerner LB $19.93 (0-8225-0909-1). 52pp. Simple Polish recipes include traditional dishes such as pierogi. Glossary of terms, plus listing of utensils and ingredients used.

**17280** Zanzarella, Marianne. *The Good Housekeeping Illustrated Children's Cookbook* (5–8). Illus. 1997, Morrow $17.95 (0-688-13375-4). 176pp. A visually appealing cookbook containing a number of recipes that require adult supervision. (Rev: BL 12/15/97; SLJ 1/98) [641.5]

# Gardening

**17281** Björk, Christina. *Linnea's Windowsill Garden* (1–5). Trans. by Joan Sandin. Illus. by Lena Anderson. 1988, Farrar $13.00 (91-29-59064-7). 60pp. Linnea takes readers on a tour of her indoor garden. (Rev: BCCB 12/88; BL 1/15/89; SLJ 11/88) [635]

**17282** Creasy, Rosalind. *Blue Potatoes, Orange Tomatoes* (1–4). Illus. by Ruth Heller. 1994, Sierra Club $15.95 (0-87156-576-5). 48pp. This beginner's gardening book starts with soil preparation and covers various kinds of seeds and plants and how to care for them. (Rev: BL 4/1/94; SLJ 7/94) [635]

**17283** Dietl, Ulla. *The Plant-and-Grow Project Book* (PS–3). Illus. 1994, Sterling $14.95 (0-8069-0456-9). 48pp. Contains a series of projects involving indoor gardening and growing such plants as cotton, corn, eggplant, and wheat. (Rev: BL 1/15/94) [635.9]

**17284** Herck, Alice. *The Enchanted Gardening Book: Ideas for Using Plants to Beautify Your World, Both Indoors and Out* (3–6). Illus. 1997, Random $14.99 (0-679-88096-8). 39pp. Basic gardening tips and techniques are covered, with material on creating specialized gardens like a rock or doll garden. (Rev: BL 7/97; SLJ 5/97) [635.9]

**17285** Kite, L. Patricia. *Gardening Wizardry for Kids* (3–6). 1995, Barron's paper $14.95 (0-8120-1317-4). 220pp. A guide to windowsill and kitchen gardens, with informative explanations, projects and experiments. (Rev: BL 8/95) [635]

**17286** Lerner, Carol. *My Backyard Garden* (4–6). Illus. 1998, Morrow $16.00 (0-688-14755-0). 48pp. Advice and inspiration are supplied in this book about planting and caring for a backyard vegetable garden. (Rev: BL 3/15/98; SLJ 4/98) [635]

**17287** Morris, Ting, and Neil Morris. *Growing Things* (4–6). Illus. Series: Sticky Fingers. 1994, Watts LB $20.00 (0-531-14284-1). 32pp. A variety of interesting gardening activities are outlined for different seasons of the year. (Rev: BL 3/15/95) [635.9]

**17288** Rhoades, Diane. *Garden Crafts for Kids: 50 Great Reasons to Get Your Hands Dirty* (3–6). Illus. 1995, Sterling $21.95 (0-8069-0998-6). 144pp. A complete guide for the beginning gardener, from choosing the right spot, to selecting seeds and plants, preparing the soil, and growing healthy plants. (Rev: SLJ 8/95*) [635]

**17289** Talmage, Ellen. *Container Gardening for Kids* (4–6). Illus. 1996, Sterling $16.95 (0-8069-1378-9). 80pp. Simple gardening projects for both indoors and outdoors are carefully described. (Rev: BL 8/96; SLJ 10/96) [635]

**17290** Van Hage, Mary An. *Little Green Thumbs* (3–6). Photos by Lucy Tizard. Illus. by Bettina Paterson. 1996, Millbrook LB $21.40 (1-56294-270-0). 32pp. An activity book that offers 12 indoor and outdoor projects for each of the seasons, like building a dinosaur-theme terrarium or planting an orange tree. (Rev: SLJ 7/96) [635]

**17291** Walker, Lois. *Get Growing! Exciting Indoor Plant Projects for Kids* (2–6). Illus. 1991, Wiley paper $12.95 (0-471-54488-4). 101pp. This project book shows how to grow 11 common food plants, such as beans and pineapples, indoors. (Rev: SLJ 11/91) [635]

# Magic

**17292** Baker, James W. *Illusions Illustrated: A Professional Magic Show for Young Performers* (5–8). Illus. by Jeanette Swofford. 1994, Lerner paper $6.95 (0-8225-9512-5). 120pp. Directions on how to put on a magic show with 10 different tricks.

**17293** Bird, Malcolm, and Alan Dart. *The Magic Handbook* (5–8). Illus. 1992, Chronicle $12.95 (0-8118-0284-1). 92pp. Appealing cartoon drawings demonstrate magic tricks. (Rev: BL 11/1/92; SLJ 1/93) [793.8]

**17294** Broekel, Ray, and Laurence B. White. *Abra-Ca-Dazzle: Easy Magic Tricks* (3–5). Illus. by Mary Thelen. 1982, Whitman LB $12.95 (0-8075-0121-2). 48pp. Twenty-five simple but impressive tricks for the beginner.

**17295** Broekel, Ray, and Laurence B. White. *Hocus Pocus: Magic You Can Do* (4–6). Illus. by Mary Thelen. 1984, Whitman LB $12.95 (0-8075-3350-5). 48pp. Twenty simple tricks for beginners.

**17296** Brown, Dave, and Paul Reeve. *Amazing Magic Tricks* (3–6). Illus. 1995, DK Publg. $12.95 (1-56458-877-7). 48pp. Extensive explanations and bright photographs highlight this book describing classic tricks and how to perform them like a professional. (Rev: BL 8/95; SLJ 10/95) [793.8]

**17297** Charles, Kirk. *Amazing Coin Tricks* (3–5). Illus. 1995, Child's World LB $21.36 (1-56766-084-3). 24pp. Ten simple coin tricks, including how to pull one from the air, are presented in this beginner's magic book. Also use *Amazing String Tricks* (1995). (Rev: BL 11/15/95) [793.8]

**17298** Cobb, Vicki. *Magic . . . Naturally! Science Entertainments and Amusements* (4–6). Illus. 1993, HarperCollins LB $14.89 (0-06-022475-4). 150pp. A group of experiments that demonstrate the magic found in many scientific phenomena. (Rev: BL 10/15/93; SLJ 10/93) [793.8]

**17299** Conaway, Judith. *Detective Tricks You Can Do* (2–4). Illus. 1986, Troll paper $3.50 (0-8167-0673-5). 48pp. How to make and compare fingerprints and make up a special detective kit. (Rev: BL 12/1/86)

**17300** Day, Jon. *Let's Make Magic: Over 40 Tricks You Can Do* (4–7). Illus. by Chris Fisher. 1992, Kingfisher paper $9.95 (1-85697-806-0). 96pp. Using items generally found at home, the author shows readers how they can make magic. (Rev: BL 10/15/92; SLJ 11/92 & 7/93) [793.2]

**17301** Eldin, Peter. *The Most Excellent Book of How to Be a Magician* (3–5). Illus. 1996, Millbrook LB $19.90 (0-7613-0458-4); paper $6.95 (0-7613-0473-8). 32pp. Practical advice for would-be magicians, with simple tricks explained and tips on presentation. (Rev: BL 6/1–15/96; SLJ 6/96) [793.8]

**17302** Friedhoffer, Robert. *Magic and Perception: The Art and Science of Fooling the Senses* (5–7). Illus. 1996, Watts LB $20.80 (0-531-11254-3). 109pp. Simple directions for magic tricks that involve altering perceptions. (Rev: BL 7/96; SLJ 9/96) [793.8]

**17303** Friedhoffer, Robert. *Magic Tricks, Science Facts* (5–8). Illus. by Richard Kaufman. 1990, Watts LB $22.00 (0-531-10902-X). 160pp. In this easy-to-follow book, the "madman of magic" gets reluctant scientists interested in magic tricks that also demonstrate science. (Rev: BL 7/90; SLJ 2/91) [793.8]

**17304** Gordon, Henry. *It's Magic* (4–6). Illus. 1989, Prometheus paper $10.95 (0-87975-545-8). 92pp. A treasury of simple magic tricks. (Rev: BL 12/1/89) [793.8]

**17305** Lewis, Shari, and Dick Zimmerman. *Shari Lewis Presents 101 Magic Tricks for Kids to Do* (2–6). Illus. by Jon Buller. 1990, Random LB $9.99 (0-394-92059-7). 90pp. The star of children's television presents a variety of tricks. (Rev: SLJ 8/90) [793.8]

**17306** Leyton, Lawrence. *My First Magic Book: A Life-Size Guide to Making and Performing Magic Tricks* (3–5). Illus. 1993, DK Publg. $12.95 (1-56458-319-8). 48pp. A large-format book that explains how to perform some puzzling tricks and make the props to accompany them. (Rev: BL 12/15/93; SLJ 4/94) [793.8]

**17307** McMaster, Shawn. *60 Super Simple Magic Tricks* (3–6). Illus. by Leo Abbett. 1996, Lowell House paper $6.95 (1-56565-384-X). 80pp. Simple instructions are used to describe clearly 60 magic tricks, with additional information on effective presentations and examples of magician's patter. (Rev: SLJ 2/97) [783.9]

**17308** Rigney, Francis. *A Beginner's Book of Magic* (4–6). Illus. 1963, Devin $9.95 (0-8159-5103-5). This is a do-it-yourself book of tricks, magic, and stunts.

**17309** Russell, Tom. *Magic Step-by-Step* (3–6). Illus. 1997, Sterling $17.95 (0-8069-9533-5). 80pp. Step-by-step instructions for such areas of magic as disappearing acts and tricks involving cards and coins. (Rev: SLJ 8/97) [793.8]

**17310** White, Laurence B., and Ray Broekel. *Razzle Dazzle! Magic Tricks for You* (3–6). Illus. 1987, Whitman LB $13.95 (0-8075-6857-0). 48pp. A clever collection of mystifying tricks explained clearly in text, diagrams, and witty cartoonlike illustrations. (Rev: BL 1/1/88)

**17311** Wyler, Rose, and Gerald Ames. *Spooky Tricks* (1–3). Illus. 1994, HarperCollins LB $14.89 (0-06-023026-6); paper $3.75 (0-06-444172-5). 64pp. Magic tricks with spooky trappings are explained clearly, with helpful illustrations. (Rev: BL 9/15/94; SLJ 7/95) [793.8]

## Model Making

**17312** Harris, Jack C. *Plastic Model Kits* (5–8). Illus. Series: Hobby Guides. 1993, Crestwood LB $12.95 (0-89686-623-8). 48pp. The hobby of making plastic models from kits is introduced, with good background information for both the novice and the expert. (Rev: SLJ 2/94) [745]

**17313** Simon, Seymour. *The Paper Airplane Book* (3–6). Illus. by Byron Barton. 1971, Puffin paper $4.99 (0-14-030925-X). Using how-to-make paper airplanes as the takeoff point, the author explains why planes fly and how changes in their construction can cause variations in flight.

## Photography and Filmmaking

**17314** Arnosky, Jim. *Bring 'Em Back Alive! Capturing Wildlife on Home Video* (4–7). Illus. 1997, Little, Brown paper $9.95 (0-316-05105-5). 48pp. A useful manual that describes how to photograph with a video camera wildlife and backyard animals. (Rev: BL 5/1/97; SLJ 6/97) [778.59]

**17315** Evans, Art. *First Photos: How Kids Can Take Great Pictures* (4–6). Illus. 1993, paper $9.95 (0-9626508-7-0). 64pp. Focuses on disposable cameras and gives good tips on topics like composition, light,

point of view, and camera handling. (Rev: BL 12/15/92; SLJ 9/93) [770]

**17316** Gibbons, Gail. *Click! A Book About Cameras and Taking Pictures* (K–3). Illus. 1997, Little, Brown $14.95 (0-316-30976-1). 32pp. As well as describing the workings of a camera, this simple guide tells how to take good pictures indoors and out. (Rev: BL 4/1/97; SLJ 5/97) [771]

**17317** Hilton, Jonathan, and Barrie Watts. *Photography* (4–6). Illus. Series: First Guide. 1994, Millbrook LB $23.90 (1-56294-398-7). 96pp. Basic photographic equipment is introduced, with techniques and tips on taking a variety of photos, from still lifes to portraits. (Rev: BL 12/15/94) [770]

**17318** Holland, Gini. *Photography* (3–6). Illus. Series: Inventors and Inventions. 1995, Marshall Cavendish LB $25.64 (0-7614-0066-4). 63pp. The invention of photography and the people responsible for its development are covered in this well-written text. (Rev: BL 3/15/96; SLJ 3/96) [770]

**17319** King, Dave. *My First Photography Book* (4–7). Illus. Series: My First. 1994, DK Publg. $12.95 (1-56458-673-1). 48pp. A manual on how to use your camera creatively, with many interesting projects outlined. (Rev: BL 1/15/95; SLJ 12/94) [771]

**17320** Lasky, Kathryn. *Think Like an Eagle: At Work with a Wildlife Photographer* (3–7). Illus. by Christopher G. Knight and Jack Swedberg. 1992, Little, Brown $15.95 (0-316-51519-1). 48pp. Following a wildlife photographer through the seasons and across the country. (Rev: BCCB 3/92; BL 6/1/92; SLJ 4/92) [778.9]

**17321** Morgan, Terri, and Shmuel Thaler. *Photography: Take Your Best Shot* (5–8). Illus. 1991, Lerner LB $21.27 (0-8225-2302-7). 72pp. A comprehensive and well-put-together guide to photography. (Rev: BL 10/1/91) [771]

**17322** Price, Susanna, and Tim Stephens. *Click! Fun with Photography* (4–8). Illus. 1997, Sterling $14.95 (0-8069-9541-6). 48pp. A fine introduction to photography that covers both beginning and advanced topics including the operation of various cameras, exposure, lighting, different types of photography, and filters. (Rev: SLJ 8/97) [770]

## Stamp and Coin Collecting

**17323** Granger, Neill. *Stamp Collecting* (4–6). Illus. Series: First Guide. 1994, Millbrook LB $23.90 (1-56294-399-5). 96pp. A good beginner's book on the history of postage stamps and how to start, develop, and display a collection. (Rev: BL 12/15/94) [769.56]

# Jokes, Puzzles, Riddles, Word Games

## Jokes and Riddles

**17324** Adler, David A. *The Carsick Zebra and Other Animal Riddles* (K–3). Illus. by Tomie dePaola. 1983, Holiday LB $14.95 (0-8234-0479-X). 64pp. A wonderful collection of animal riddles, humorously illustrated.

**17325** Adler, David A. *The Dinosaur Princess and Other Prehistoric Riddles* (2–6). Illus. 1988, Holiday LB $14.95 (0-8234-0686-5). 64pp. An assortment of jokes and riddles and laughs with dinosaurs as the focus. (Rev: BL 5/1/88; SLJ 9/88)

**17326** Adler, David A. *A Teacher on Roller Skates and Other School Riddles* (2–5). Illus. by John Wallner. 1989, Holiday LB $14.95 (0-8234-0775-6). 64pp. Theme riddles all about school. (Rev: BL 10/15/89; SLJ 3/90) [818.5]

**17327** Adler, David A. *Wild Pill Hickok and Other Old West Riddles* (2–6). Illus. by Glen Rounds. 1988, Holiday LB $14.95 (0-8234-0718-7). 64pp. Giggle inducers concerning the Old West. (Rev: BL 2/15/89; HB 1–2/89; SLJ 1/89)

**17328** Beisner, Monika. *Monika Beisner's Book of Riddles* (2–4). Illus. by author. 1987, Farrar paper $3.95 (0-374-45317-9). 32pp. The answers to these 101 riddles are found in the illustrations.

**17329** Bernstein, Joanne E., and Paul Cohen. *Dizzy Doctor Riddles* (3–5). Illus. by Carl Whiting. 1989, Whitman LB $8.95 (0-8075-1648-1). 32pp. More than 100 riddles about everything medical. (Rev: BL 1/15/90; SLJ 3/90) [818]

**17330** Bernstein, Joanne E., and Paul Cohen. *Sporty Riddles* (2–5). Illus. by Paul Harvey. 1989, Whitman LB $8.95 (0-8075-7590-9). 32pp. Theme riddles all about sports. (Rev: BL 10/15/89; SLJ 11/90) [818.5]

**17331** Bierhorst, John. *Lightning Inside You and Other Native American Riddles* (2–6). Illus. by Louise Brierley. 1992, Morrow $14.00 (0-688-09582-8). 104pp. Many subjects and difficulty levels are presented in this collection of 140 riddles from North, South, and Central America. (Rev: BCCB 7–8/92; BL 6/15/92; HB 9–10/92; SLJ 7/92) [398.6]

**17332** Brown, Marc. *Spooky Riddles* (1–4). Illus. by author. 1983, Random $7.99 (0-394-86093-4). 48pp. Simply read riddles involving ghosts, vampires, and so on.

**17333** Burns, Diane L., and Andy Burns. *Home on the Range: Ranch-Style Riddles* (2–5). Illus. by Susan S. Burke. Series: You Must Be Joking. 1994, Lerner LB $14.60 (0-8225-2341-8). A collection of zany riddles about life on the range. (Rev: SLJ 8/94) [818]

**17334** Calmenson, Stephanie. *What Am I? Very First Riddles* (3–6). Illus. by Karen Gundersheimer. 1989, HarperCollins LB $12.89 (0-06-020998-4). 32pp. Snappy one-liners for the young set. (Rev: BCCB 5/89; BL 5/1/89; HB 5–6/89)

**17335** Charlip, Remy. *Arm in Arm: A Collection of Connections, Endless Tales, Reiterations, and Other Echolalia* (K–3). Illus. 1997, Tricycle Pr. $15.95 (1-883672-50-3). 48pp. Verbal and visual plays on words are revealed through a series of riddles, jokes, and puzzles. (Rev: BL 9/1/97) [808]

**17336** Christopher, Matt. *Baseball Jokes and Riddles* (2–4). Illus. 1996, Little, Brown paper $3.95 (0-316-14081-3). 48pp. Trivia and lots of jokes and riddles about baseball highlight this amusing collection. (Rev: BL 4/1/96; SLJ 6/96) [796.357]

**17337** Christopher, Matt. *Football Jokes and Riddles* (4–7). Illus. 1997, Little, Brown paper $3.95 (0-316-14197-6). 48pp. A treasury of riddles and jokes about football that are bound to produce both giggles and groans. (Rev: BL 10/15/97)

**17338** Cole, Joanna, and Stephanie Calmenson. *The Laugh Book: A New Treasury of Humor for Children* (4–6). Illus. by Marylin Hafner. 1986, Doubleday $14.95 (0-385-18559-6). 320pp. Hundreds of laughs, with something for everyone, from novel excerpts to tricks and games, to Mother Goose. (Rev: BL 12/15/86)

**17339** Cole, Joanna, and Stephanie Calmenson, eds. *Ready . . . Set . . . Read — and Laugh! A Funny Treasury for Beginning Readers* (1–3). Illus. 1995, Doubleday $17.95 (0-385-32119-8). 144pp. This easy-to-read book contains a small collection of stories, jokes, and riddles. (Rev: BL 10/1/95; SLJ 10/95)

**17340** Cole, Joanna, and Stephanie Calmenson. *Why Did the Chicken Cross the Road? And Other Riddles Old and New* (2–4). Illus. by Alan Tiegreen. 1994, Morrow LB $14.93 (0-688-12203-5). 64pp. A lively collection of clever riddles arranged by broad subject or type. (Rev: BL 10/15/94; SLJ 9/94)

**17341** Eckstein, Joan, and Joyce Gleit. *The Best Joke Book for Kids Number 4* (3–6). Illus. by Joe Kohl. 1991, Avon paper $3.50 (0-380-76263-3). 64pp. There are riddles, knock-knocks, jokes, and tongue twisters in this book arranged by subjects. (Rev: BL 9/15/91) [793.73]

**17342** Haley, Gail E., reteller. *Mountain Jack Tales* (2–6). Illus. by Gail E. Haley. 1992, Dutton paper $16.99 (0-525-44974-4). 144pp. Poppyseed, a mountain woman, tells 9 Jack tales in a North Carolina dialect. (Rev: BCCB 1/93; HB 1–2/93; SLJ 12/92) [398.2]

**17343** Hall, Kathy, and Lisa Eisenberg. *Mummy Riddles* (1–3). Illus. by Nicole Rubel. Series: Dial Easy-to-Read. 1997, Dial paper $12.89 (0-8037-1847-0). 48pp. A zany easy-to-read book of riddles about mummies. (Rev: BL 8/97; SLJ 11/97)

**17344** Hall, Katy, and Lisa Eisenberg. *Batty Riddles* (2–4). Illus. by Nicole Rubel. 1993, Dial LB $11.89 (0-8037-1218-9). 48pp. A collection of riddles about bats, with goofy illustrations. (Rev: BL 12/1/93; SLJ 9/93) [818]

**17345** Hall, Katy, and Lisa Eisenberg. *Buggy Riddles* (1–3). Illus. by Simms Taback. 1986, Dial LB $9.89 (0-8037-0140-3); paper $4.95 (0-8037-0554-9). 48pp. Forty-two jokes and riddles to attract beginning readers. (Rev: BCCB 5/86; BL 4/15/86; SLJ 5/86)

**17346** Hall, Katy, and Lisa Eisenberg. *Fishy Riddles* (1–4). Illus. by Simms Taback. 1983, Dial paper $4.99 (0-8037-2419-5). 48pp. An easy-to-read book of riddles on ocean life.

**17347** Hall, Katy, and Lisa Eisenberg. *Grizzly Riddles* (1–3). Illus. by Nicole Rubel. 1989, Dial LB $9.89 (0-8037-0377-5). 48pp. An easily read book of riddles, with grizzly bears as the topic. (Rev: BL 12/1/89; HB 11–12/89; SLJ 1/90) [818]

**17348** Hall, Katy, and Lisa Eisenberg. *Puppy Riddles* (1–2). Illus. by Thor Wickstrom. 1998, Dial paper $13.89 (0-8037-2129-3). 48pp. A beginning reader that contains 42 riddles about dogs and hilarious full-color cartoons. (Rev: BL 2/1/98)

**17349** Hall, Katy, and Lisa Eisenberg. *Sheepish Riddles* (1–3). Illus. 1996, Dial paper $12.89 (0-8037-1536-6). 48pp. Funny riddles about sheep. (Rev: BL 4/1/96; SLJ 4/96) [818]

**17350** Hall, Katy, and Lisa Eisenberg. *Spacey Riddles* (1–3). Illus. by Simms Taback. 1992, Dial paper $10.89 (0-8037-0815-7). 48pp. A collection of 42 easily read riddles about outer space. (Rev: BL 2/1/92; SLJ 6/92) [818]

**17351** Hartman, Victoria. *The Silliest Joke Book Ever* (2–4). Illus. by R. W. Alley. 1993, Lothrop LB $13.93 (0-688-10110-0). 32pp. A lively riddle book with cheerful drawings. (Rev: BCCB 4/93; BL 5/1/93) [818]

**17352** Jansen, John. *Class Act: Riddles for School* (3–5). Illus. by Susan S. Burke. Series: You Must Be Joking. 1995, Lerner LB $14.60 (0-8225-2345-0); paper $3.95 (0-8225-9673-3). Riddles that take schools, students, and teachers as their subjects. Also use *Playing Possum: Riddles About Kangaroos, Koalas, and Other Marsupials* (1995). (Rev: SLJ 9/95)

**17353** Keller, Charles. *Astronuts: Space Jokes and Riddles* (1–4). Illus. 1991, Simon & Schuster paper $2.95 (0-671-73984-0). Mostly original, clever jokes on a popular subject. (Rev: BCCB 6/85; BL 6/15/85; SLJ 9/85)

**17354** Keller, Charles. *Ballpoint Bananas and Other Jokes for Kids* (3–6). Illus. by David Barrios. 1976, Simon & Schuster paper $5.95 (0-671-66965-6). Zany American riddles, rhymes, and contemporary jokes.

**17355** Keller, Charles. *Driving Me Crazy: Fun on Wheels Jokes* (2–6). Illus. by Lee Lorenz. 1989, Pippin $13.95 (0-945912-05-6). A collection of jokes and riddles that deal with driving and vehicles. (Rev: BL 7/89) [398]

**17356** Keller, Charles. *It's Raining Cats and Dogs: Cat and Dog Jokes* (2–6). Illus. by Robert Quackenbush. 1988, Pippin $13.95 (0-945912-01-3). 40pp. Pleasing nonsense for young readers. Also use: *Colossal Fossils: Dinosaur Riddles* (1991, Simon & Schuster paper). (Rev: BCCB 11/88; BL 2/15/89; SLJ 2/89)

**17357** Keller, Charles. *King Henry the Ape: Animal Jokes* (2–6). Illus. by Edward Frascino. 1990, Pippin LB $13.95 (0-945912-08-0). 40pp. Animal guffaws sure to delight young readers. (Rev: BL 3/15/90; SLJ 4/90) [818]

**17358** Keller, Charles. *The Planet of the Grapes: Show Biz Jokes and Riddles* (2–5). Illus. by Mischa Richter. 1992, Pippin $13.95 (0-945912-17-X). All the performing arts are included in this collection of zany jokes. (Rev: SLJ 12/92) [808.7]

**17359** Keller, Charles, ed. *Take Me to Your Liter: Science and Math Jokes* (3–6). Illus. by Gregory Filling. 1991, Pippin LB $13.95 (0-945912-13-7). 40pp. Jokes and silly riddles about a serious subject. (Rev: BL 5/15/91; SLJ 7/91) [398.2]

**17360** Keller, Charles, and Richard Baker. *The Star-Spangled Banana and Other Revolutionary Riddles* (3–6). Illus. by Tomie dePaola. 1974, Prentice Hall $3.95 (0-13-842971-5). 62pp. Outrageous puns and jokes that celebrate the Spirit of '76.

**17361** Kohl, Marguerite, and Frederica Young. *Jokes for Children* (4–8). Illus. by Bob Patterson. 1963, Farrar paper $4.95 (0-374-43832-3). 128pp. Over 650 rhymes, riddles, puns, and jokes.

**17362** Levine, Caroline. *Riddles to Tell Your Cat* (PS–3). Illus. by Meyer Seltzer. 1992, Whitman LB $8.95 (0-8075-7006-0). 32pp. Feline riddles to make your cat purr, such as "Why did the teacher fail the cat? Because he was a cheetah." (Rev: BL 11/15/92; SLJ 7/93) [818]

**17363** Lewis, J. Patrick. *Riddle-icious* (4–8). Illus. by Debbie Tilley. 1996, Knopf $15.00 (0-679-84011-7). 32pp. Twenty-eight challenging riddles presented in verse form. (Rev: BCCB 6/96; BL 6/1–15/96; HB 7–8/96; SLJ 6/96) [818]

**17364** Maestro, Giulio. *Halloween Howls: Riddles That Are a Scream* (2–5). Illus. by author. 1983, Puffin paper $4.99 (0-14-036115-4). 64pp. There are almost 60 riddles related to Halloween in this collection.

**17365** Maestro, Giulio. *Macho Nacho and Other Rhyming Riddles* (1–3). Illus. 1994, Dutton paper $12.99 (0-525-45261-3). 48pp. A series of riddles whose answers are 2 words that rhyme, as in the book's title. (Rev: BL 1/15/95; SLJ 10/94) [818]

**17366** Maestro, Giulio. *Riddle Roundup* (3–5). Illus. 1989, Houghton paper $6.95 (0-89919-537-7). 64pp. Puns, homonyms, and homographs for wordplay lovers. (Rev: BL 12/15/89; SLJ 2/90) [818]

**17367** Maestro, Giulio. *What's Mite Might? Homophone Riddles to Boost Your Word Power!* (4–6). Illus. 1986, Houghton paper $5.95 (0-89919-435-4). 64pp. Sixty-one homophone riddles concerning words that have different meanings and spellings but sound the same. (Rev: BL 1/1/87; SLJ 3/87)

**17368** Maestro, Marco, and Giulio Maestro. *Riddle City, USA: A Book of Geography Riddles* (2–4). Illus.

1994, HarperCollins LB $14.89 (0-06-023369-9). 64pp. These playful riddles that use place names in the United States as answers will cause many laughs and some groans. (Rev: BL 6/1–15/94; SLJ 7/94)

**17369** Maestro, Marco, and Giulio Maestro. *What Do You Hear When Cows Sing? And Other Silly Riddles* (1–3). Illus. 1996, HarperCollins LB $14.89 (0-06-024949-8). 48pp. Silly riddles and even sillier answers are found in this delightful joke book. (Rev: BL 1/1–15/96; SLJ 3/96) [398.8]

**17370** Marzollo, Jean. *I Spy Spooky Night* (2–5). Illus. by Walter Wick. 1996, Scholastic $12.95 (0-590-48137-1). 40pp. Riddles give clues to objects hidden in accompanying pictures. (Rev: BL 9/15/96; SLJ 9/96*) [793.73]

**17371** Mathews, Judith, and Fay Robinson. *Oh, How Waffle! Riddles You Can Eat* (2–4). Illus. by Carl Whiting. 1993, Whitman LB $8.95 (0-8075-5907-5). 32pp. Delicious and messy food riddles with a contemporary emphasis. (Rev: BL 1/15/93; SLJ 4/93) [818]

**17372** Most, Bernard. *Pets in Trumpets and Other Word-Play Riddles* (1–3). Illus. 1991, Harcourt $12.95 (0-15-261210-6). 32pp. Finding words within other words is the basis of this wordplay book. (Rev: BL 10/15/91; SLJ 3/92) [818]

**17373** Most, Bernard. *Zoodles* (PS–2). Illus. 1992, Harcourt $13.95 (0-15-299969-8). 32pp. An iguana who hogs all the food is a "piguana" in this riddle book that combines animal names. (Rev: BL 10/15/92; SLJ 1/93) [818]

**17374** Peterson, Scott. *Plugged In: Electric Riddles* (3–5). Illus. by Susan S. Burke. Series: You Must Be Joking. 1995, Lerner LB $14.60 (0-8225-2344-2); paper $1.98 (0-8225-9700-4). Very funny jokes and riddles that involve appliances found around the house. (Rev: SLJ 9/95)

**17375** Phillips, Louis. *Keep 'em Laughing: Jokes to Amuse and Annoy Your Friends* (3–5). Illus. by Michael Chesworth. 1996, Viking paper $12.99 (0-670-86009-3). 64pp. This lively joke book also contains short pieces that can be performed in front of an audience. (Rev: BL 1/1–15/96; SLJ 6/96) [818]

**17376** Rosen, Michael, sel. *Walking the Bridge of Your Nose* (1–5). Illus. by Chloe Cheese. 1995, Kingfisher $14.95 (1-85697-596-7). 61pp. A collection of riddles, puns, tongue twisters, sayings, and chants that have fun with the English language. (Rev: SLJ 1/96) [818]

**17377** Rosenbloom, Joseph. *Biggest Riddle Book in the World* (3–6). Illus. by Joyce Behr. 1979, Sterling paper $6.95 (0-8069-8884-3). About 2,000 old and new riddles arranged under various subjects and amusingly illustrated.

**17378** Rosenbloom, Joseph. *Spooky Riddles and Jokes* (2–4). Illus. by Sanford Hoffman. 1987, Sterling paper $4.95 (0-8069-6736-6). 128pp. Riddles based on ghosts, werewolves, and other creatures. Also use: *Giggles, Gags and Groaners* (1987). (Rev: BL 11/1/87)

**17379** Rosenbloom, Joseph. *Sports Riddles* (2–5). Illus. by Sam Q. Weissman. 1982, Harcourt $8.95 (0-15-277994-9). 64pp. A collection of riddles divided by various sports.

**17380** Rosenbloom, Joseph. *The World's Best Sports Riddles and Jokes* (2–6). Illus. by Sanford Hoffman. 1988, Sterling paper $3.95 (0-8069-6846-6). 128pp. Young sports fans will enjoy these gaffaws. (Rev: BL 5/1/88)

**17381** Rosenbloom, Joseph. *The Zaniest Riddle Book in the World* (3–6). Illus. by Sanford Hoffman. 1984, Sterling paper $4.95 (0-8069-6252-6). 128pp. A riddle book arranged by topics.

**17382** Rothaus, Jim. *Animal Jokes* (1–3). Illus. by Viki Woodworth. 1993, Child's World LB $19.93 (0-89565-861-5). 31pp. A delightful collection of jokes and riddles. (Rev: BL 6/1–15/93) [818]

**17383** Schwartz, Alvin. *Witcracks: Jokes and Jests from American Folklore* (3–6). Illus. by Glen Rounds. 1973, HarperCollins LB $14.89 (0-397-31475-2). 128pp. All sorts of humor associated with America's past, from old riddles to knock-knock jokes.

**17384** Seltzer, Meyer. *Petcetera: The Pet Riddle Book* (2–5). Illus. 1988, Whitman LB $8.95 (0-8075-6515-6). 32pp. Jokes and riddles about animals. (Rev: BL 10/15/88; SLJ 12/88)

**17385** Sloat, Teri, and Robert Sloat. *Rib-Ticklers: A Book of Punny Animals* (2–4). Illus. 1995, Lothrop $15.00 (0-688-12519-0). 32pp. Using different animals as focal points, this book contains a choice collection of jokes, puns, and riddles. (Rev: BL 6/1–15/95; SLJ 7/95) [818]

**17386** Spires, Elizabeth. *With One White Wing* (1–4). Illus. by Erik Blegvad. 1995, Simon & Schuster paper $14.00 (0-689-50622-8). 32pp. A collection of literate riddles culled from sources like Mother Goose and Tolkien. (Rev: BCCB 2/96; BL 10/1/95; SLJ 9/95*) [811]

**17387** Steig, William. *C D B!* (3–6). Illus. by author. 1987, Simon & Schuster paper $3.95 (0-671-66689-4). 48pp. When each set of letters and/or numbers is repeated aloud and riddle buffs apply a bit of imagination, the amusing caption accompanying each cartoon becomes apparent. Also use: *C D C!* (1986, Farrar).

**17388** Swanson, June. *Out to Dry: Riddles About Deserts* (2–5). Illus. by Susan S. Burke. Series: You Must Be Joking. 1994, Lerner LB $14.60 (0-8225-

2343-4). A cornucopia of groaners dealing with deserts. More riddles can be found in *Summit Up: Riddles About Mountains* (1994). (Rev: SLJ 8/94) [818.5]

**17389** Terban, Marvin. *Funny You Should Ask: How to Make Up Jokes and Riddles with Wordplay* (4–6). Illus. by John O'Brien. 1992, Houghton paper $5.95 (0-395-58113-3). 64pp. How word manipulation works and how kids can become schoolyard hams. (Rev: BCCB 2/93; BL 10/1/92; SLJ 12/92) [808.7]

**17390** Thaler, Mike. *Frankenstein's Pantyhose* (2–4). Illus. 1990, Avon paper $2.50 (0-380-75613-7). 92pp. This collection of jokes and riddles contains a special section of cigar jokes. (Rev: BL 3/15/90)

**17391** Young, Frederica. *Super-Duper Jokes* (3–6). Illus. by Chris Murphy. 1993, Farrar $13.00 (0-374-37301-9); paper $4.95 (0-374-47353-6). 97pp. An enjoyable collection of various kinds of jokes, including silly definitions. (Rev: BL 7/93; SLJ 7/93) [818]

**17392** Ziefert, Harriet. *Math Riddles* (1–3). Illus. by Andrea Baruffi. 1997, Penguin paper $3.50 (0-14-038541-X). 32pp. Comic riddles using numbers are amusingly presented in this easy reader. (Rev: BL 8/97; SLJ 12/97)

# Puzzles

**17393** Adshead, Paul. *Puzzle Island* (2–5). Illus. 1991, Child's Play $13.99 (0-85953-402-2); paper $7.99 (0-85953-403-0). 24pp. This puzzle book contains visual clues to decode a secret message and learn the identity of an extinct species. (Rev: BL 6/1/91) [793.73]

**17394** Baxter, Nicola. *Parallel Universe* (4–6). Illus. by Mike Taylor. 1997, Watts LB $23.00 (0-531-14465-8). 41pp. Picture puzzles in which the reader must find 20 anachronisms in each of 13 scenes from different historical periods. (Rev: SLJ 2/98)

**17395** Brown, Osa. *The Metropolitan Museum of Art Activity Book* (3–6). Illus. 1990, Abrams paper $12.95 (0-8109-2437-4). An activity book of puzzles, games, and activities involving the collection of the Metropolitan Museum of Art.

**17396** Burns, Marilyn. *The Book of Think (or How to Solve a Problem Twice Your Size)* (5–7). Illus. by Martha Weston. 1976, Little, Brown paper $12.95 (0-316-11743-9). A stimulating collection of puzzles to make children think; informally and entertainingly presented.

**17397** Chalk, Gary. *Hide and Seek in History* (K–3). Illus. by author. 1997, DK Publg. $14.95 (0-7894-1500-3). Using double-page spreads, this picture book introduces 8 periods in history from ancient Egypt and Rome to the French Revolution and the U.S. Wild West. (Rev: SLJ 12/97) [793.73]

**17398** Gardner, Martin. *Classic Brainteasers* (4–6). Illus. 1995, Sterling $14.95 (0-8069-1260-X). 96pp. An entertaining book of classic puzzles that involve math, science, and logic. (Rev: BL 5/1/95) [793.73]

**17399** Handford, Martin. *Where's Waldo? In Hollywood* (3–6). Illus. 1993, Candlewick $14.95 (1-56402-044-4). 32pp. Waldo can be found in a series of movie sets from silent movies and lavish musicals to the present-day blockbuster. (Rev: BL 12/15/93; SLJ 2/94)

**17400** McMillan, Bruce. *Sense Suspense: A Guessing Game for the Five Senses* (PS–1). Illus. 1994, Scholastic $15.95 (0-590-47904-0). 32pp. A puzzle book that introduces the 5 senses and challenges youngsters to determine objects from close-up details. (Rev: BCCB 12/94; BL 12/1/94; SLJ 12/94*) [793.73]

**17401** Madgwick, Wendy. *Citymaze!* (3–5). Illus. 1995, Millbrook LB $17.90 (1-56294-561-0). 40pp. Each of the maze puzzles in this book introduces a famous city, e.g., Moscow, Delhi, Paris, and London. (Rev: BCCB 4/95; BL 3/1/95; SLJ 6/95) [793.73]

**17402** Marzollo, Jean. *I Spy: A Book of Picture Riddles* (K–4). Illus. 1992, Scholastic $12.95 (0-590-45087-5). 48pp. Readers are asked to search out certain items from collages or montages. (Rev: BCCB 2/92; BL 5/15/92; SLJ 4/92) [793.73]

**17403** Marzollo, Jean. *I Spy Fantasy: A Book of Picture Riddles* (1–3). Illus. by Walter Wick. 1994, Scholastic $12.95 (0-590-46295-4). 40pp. In a series of photographic collages, children are challenged to find hidden objects. (Rev: BL 12/1/94; SLJ 10/94) [793.3]

**17404** Marzollo, Jean. *I Spy Super Challenger! A Book of Picture Riddles* (PS–2). Illus. by Walter Wick. Series: I Spy. 1997, Scholastic $12.95 (0-590-34128-6). 32pp. This detailed picture puzzle book defies the reader to find a needle in the haystack, as well as other eye-dazzling problems. (Rev: BL 10/1/97; SLJ 9/97) [793.735]

**17405** Messenger, Norman. *Famous Faces* (3–6). Illus. by author. 1995, DK Publg. $14.95 (1-56458-686-3). By mixing and matching the split images of the faces of 12 celebrities — like Groucho Marx and Ronald Reagan — more than 2,500 new faces can be created. (Rev: SLJ 7/95)

# Word Games

**17406** Agee, Jon. *Go Hang a Salami! I'm a Lasagna Hog! And Other Palindromes* (3–6). Illus. 1992, Farrar $12.21 (0-374-33473-0). 74pp. A humorous look at groups of letters or numbers that read the same backward and forward. (Rev: BCCB 10/92*; BL 2/1/93) [793]

**17407** Christensen, Bonnie. *Rebus Riot* (2–4). Illus. 1997, Dial paper $14.89 (0-8037-2000-9). 32pp. A clever book that tells humorous rhymes through the use of rebus poetry. (Rev: BL 5/15/97; HB 5–6/97; SLJ 3/97) [811]

**17408** Cole, Joanna, and Stephanie Calmenson, eds. *Six Sick Sheep: 101 Tongue Twisters* (3–6). Illus. by Alan Tiegreen. 1993, Morrow LB $14.93 (0-688-11140-8). 64pp. Some well-known tongue twisters as well as games, contests, and stories. (Rev: BL 3/15/93; SLJ 4/93) [818]

**17409** Davis, Lee. *P. B. Bear's Treasure Hunt* (K–2). Photos by Dave King. 1995, DK Publg. $12.95 (0-7894-0214-9). Toys and other objects are used to represent 88 words in this intriguing rebus book. (Rev: SLJ 4/96)

**17410** McMillan, Bruce, and Brett McMillan. *Puniddles* (2–4). Illus. 1982, Houghton paper $6.95 (0-395-32076-3). Objects in photographs are used to illustrate word combinations.

**17411** Most, Bernard. *Hippopotamus Hunt* (1–3). Illus. 1994, Harcourt $14.95 (0-15-234520-5). 32pp. Explores the pastime of finding words within words and, using *hippopotamus* as an example, comes up with 53 new words. (Rev: BL 9/1/94; SLJ 11/94)

**17412** Rosenbloom, Joseph. *World's Toughest Tongue Twisters* (3–5). Illus. 1987, Sterling paper $4.95 (0-8069-6596-7). 128pp. More than 500 tongue twisters, alphabetically from A to Z.

**17413** Schnur, Steven. *Autumn: An Alphabet Acrostic* (K–3). Illus. by Leslie Evans. 1997, Clarion $15.00 (0-395-77043-2). 32pp. An alphabet book that uses autumn and acrostic poems as a framework. (Rev: BL 9/1/97; SLJ 9/97) [793.73]

**17414** Van Dyke, Janice. *Captivating Cryptograms* (5–8). 1996, Sterling paper $5.95 (0-8069-4890-6). 128pp. A collection of 400 cryptograms based on famous quotes, with the names of the authors also included. (Rev: SLJ 8/96) [793.73]

# Mysteries, Monsters, Curiosities, and Trivia

**17415** Allen, Eugenie. *The Best Ever Kids' Book of Lists* (4–8). Illus. 1991, Avon paper $2.95 (0-380-76357-5). 128pp. Trivia buffs will enjoy these data bits under such headings as Nature's Most Lethal Weapons and Revolting Eating Habits. (Rev: BL 12/15/91) [031.02]

**17416** Asimov, Isaac, and Greg Walz-Chojnacki. *UFOs: True Mysteries or Hoaxes?* (3–4). Illus. Series: Isaac Asimov's New Library of the Universe. 1995, Gareth Stevens LB $19.93 (0-8368-1198-4). 32pp. This brief account examines the supposed sightings of alien craft from a skeptical viewpoint. (Rev: SLJ 4/95) [001.9]

**17417** Ballinger, Erich. *Monster Manual: A Complete Guide to Your Favorite Creatures* (5–8). Illus. 1994, Lerner LB $19.93 (0-8225-0722-6). 144pp. This A-to-Z introduction to monsters includes Dracula, King Kong, and Rambo plus activities and material on people behind some of these creations, like Boris Karloff. (Rev: BL 12/1/94; SLJ 3/95) [001.9]

**17418** Bernards, Neal. *UFO Abductions* (4–6). Illus. 1995, Lucent LB $22.45 (1-56006-161-8). 48pp. Reports of people who claim to have seen UFOs highlight this account that mixes fact and speculation. (Rev: BL 2/15/95) [001.9]

**17419** Bursell, Susan. *Haunted Houses* (4–6). Illus. Series: Exploring the Unknown. 1994, Lucent LB $22.45 (1-56006-153-7). 48pp. A series of case studies in which ghosts have appeared in a variety of settings, including a castle and a yacht. (Rev: SLJ 4/94) [001.9]

**17420** Choron, Sandy, and Harry Choron. *The Book of Lists for Kids* (4–6). Illus. 1995, Houghton paper $9.95 (0-395-70815-X). 396pp. Amazing trivia on such subjects as toys, books, education, online services, and family and friends is included in this volume that is fun for browsing. (Rev: BL 2/15/96) [031.02]

**17421** Cohen, Daniel. *Ghost in the House* (4–6). Illus. by John Paul Caponigro. 1993, Dutton paper $13.99 (0-525-65131-4). 64pp. This book presents 9 accounts of haunted houses, including one in Washington, D.C., which is supposedly haunted by Dolley Madison. (Rev: BL 7/93) [133.1]

**17422** Cohen, Daniel. *Ghosts of the Deep* (5–7). 1993, Putnam $14.95 (0-399-22435-1). 103pp. A collection of ghost stories involving sailors and pirates who met untimely ends. (Rev: BL 11/15/93; SLJ 3/94) [133.1]

**17423** Cohen, Daniel. *The Ghosts of War* (4–6). 1990, Putnam $13.95 (0-399-22200-6). 82pp. Tales about spirits who died in war. (Rev: BCCB 9/90; BL 6/1/90) [133.1]

**17424** Cohen, Daniel. *Phone Call from a Ghost: Strange Tales from Modern America* (4–6). Illus. 1990, Pocket paper $3.50 (0-671-68242-3). 112pp. Stories about weird happenings to famous and average people. (Rev: BCCB 11/88; BL 6/1/88; SLJ 8/88)

**17425** Cohen, Daniel. *Raising the Dead* (5–7). 1997, Dutton paper $14.99 (0-525-65255-8). 160pp. A collection of trivia about such gruesome topics as zombies, grave robbers, Eva Peron's corpse, and Frankenstein's mother. (Rev: BL 10/1/97; SLJ 11/97) [001.9]

**17426** Cohen, Daniel. *The World's Most Famous Ghosts* (6–8). 1989, Pocket paper $2.99 (0-671-69145-7). 112pp. A report in 10 short chapters of better-known incidents accredited to ghosts.

**17427** Cohen, Daniel. *Young Ghosts*. Rev. ed. (4–8). Illus. 1994, Dutton paper $13.99 (0-525-65154-3). 112pp. Includes supposedly true stories about ghost children and ghosts that have appeared to children. (Rev: BL 9/1/94; SLJ 10/94) [133.1]

**17428** Corbett, Sara. *Hold Everything!* (3–7). Illus. Series: A World of Difference. 1996, Children's LB $21.00 (0-516-08212-4). 32pp. Containers like pots and pourers from various cultures of the world are used to illustrate human diversity. (Rev: BL 9/15/96) [688.8]

**17429** Deem, James M. *How to Find a Ghost* (5–8). Illus. 1990, Avon paper $3.25 (0-380-70829-9). 144pp. Explaining what one can do to have a supernatural experience. (Rev: BCCB 11/88; BL 11/1/88; SLJ 11/88)

**17430** Deem, James M. *How to Hunt Buried Treasure* (4–7). Illus. by True Kelley. 1992, Houghton $16.95 (0-395-58799-9). 192pp. Tales of lost mines and pirate ships are part of the lure of this attractive guidebook. (Rev: BL 9/15/92; SLJ 10/92) [622.19]

**17431** Deem, James M. *How to Read Your Mother's Mind* (5–7). Illus. by True Kelley. 1994, Houghton $17.00 (0-395-62426-6). 192pp. Various aspects of ESP are introduced, including the pros and cons about its existence and a test to determine one's own ESP powers. (Rev: BCCB 3/94; BL 3/1/94; SLJ 7/94) [133.8]

**17432** Elfman, Eric. *The Very Scary Almanac* (4–6). Illus. by Will Suckow. 1993, Random paper $4.99 (0-679-84401-5). 80pp. Superstitions, witchcraft, aliens, dangerous animals, and cannibalism are just a few of the topics covered in this treat for the occult-minded. (Rev: SLJ 1/94) [001.9]

**17433** Emert, Phyllis R. *The 25 Scariest Places in the World* (5–7). Illus. by Lauren Jarrett. 1995, Lowell House paper $5.95 (1-56565-277-0). 64pp. Highlights places around the world where ghosts, deadly beasts, or strange monsters live, like the Tower of London or the jungles of West Bengal. (Rev: SLJ 3/96) [001.9]

**17434** Farndon, John. *Eyewitness Question and Answer Book* (2–4). Illus. Series: Eyewitness Juniors. 1993, DK Publg. $16.95 (1-56458-347-3). 64pp. A browsing book that answers all sorts of questions in 3 categories: nature, history, and inventions. (Rev: BL 1/1/94) [031]

**17435** Herbst, Judith. *The Mystery of UFOs* (3–5). Illus. by Greg Clarke. 1997, Simon & Schuster $16.00 (0-689-31652-6). 40pp. An open-minded history of reported encounters with UFOs and aliens from space. (Rev: BL 12/1/97; HB 11–12/97; SLJ 11/97) [001.9]

**17436** Hubbard-Brown, Janet. *The Curse of the Hope Diamond* (4–7). Illus. 1991, Avon paper $2.99 (0-380-76222-6). 96pp. A mystery style introduces historical information. (Rev: BL 12/15/91) [736.23]

**17437** Jackson, Ellen. *The Book of Slime* (2–4). Illus. by Jan Davey Ellis. 1997, Millbrook LB $21.40 (0-7613-0042-2). 32pp. Describes various forms of slime in nature, including human mucus and saliva, along with their uses, slime jokes, and some recipes. (Rev: BL 3/15/97; SLJ 6/97) [001.9]

**17438** Jenkins, Steve. *Duck's Breath and Mouse Pie: A Collection of Animal Superstitions* (2–4). Illus. 1994, Ticknor $14.95 (0-395-69688-7). 48pp. With breathtaking collages, 17 superstitions about animals and their origins are explored. (Rev: BL 10/1/94; SLJ 9/94) [398.24]

**17439** Keats, Robin. *Slime Lives! And Other Weird Facts That Will Amaze You* (3–5). 1995, Avon paper $3.50 (0-380-77304-X). 80pp. A book of weird curiosities involving such subjects as vampires and ancient rituals. (Rev: BL 1/15/95) [031]

**17440** Knight, David C. *Best True Ghost Stories of the 20th Century* (5–8). Illus. 1984, Simon & Schuster paper $5.95 (0-671-66557-X). 64pp. Twenty tales of apparitions and poltergeists.

**17441** Landau, Elaine. *ESP* (4–6). Illus. Series: Mysteries of Science. 1996, Millbrook LB $20.90 (0-7613-0012-0). 48pp. The amazing phenomenon known as extrasensory perception is explored in an account that separates fact from fiction. (Rev: BL 10/15/96; SLJ 11/96) [133.8]

**17442** Landau, Elaine. *Fortune Telling* (4–6). Illus. Series: Mysteries of Science. 1996, Millbrook LB $20.90 (0-7613-0013-9). 48pp. Various methods of future telling are covered, with material that debunks the claims of supposed clairvoyants. (Rev: BL 10/15/96; SLJ 11/96) [133.3]

**17443** Landau, Elaine. *Ghosts* (4–6). Illus. Series: Mysteries of Science. 1995, Millbrook LB $20.90 (1-56294-544-0). 48pp. A slim volume that presents information pro and con on the controversy concerning the existence of ghosts. (Rev: BL 12/15/95; SLJ 4/96) [133.1]

**17444** Landau, Elaine. *The Loch Ness Monster* (4–6). Illus. Series: Mysteries of Science. 1993, Millbrook LB $20.90 (1-56294-347-2). 48pp. Evidence for and against the existence of the Loch Ness Monster is presented in a compact format with drawings and color photos. (Rev: BL 1/1/94; SLJ 2/94) [001.9]

**17445** Landau, Elaine. *Near-Death Experiences* (4–6). Illus. Series: Mysteries of Science. 1995, Millbrook LB $20.90 (1-56294-543-2). 48pp. An objective account that surveys the evidence concerning the possible truth behind reported near-death experiences. (Rev: BL 12/15/95; SLJ 4/96) [133.9]

**17446** Landau, Elaine. *Sasquatch: Wild Man of North America* (4–6). Illus. Series: Mysteries of Science. 1993, Millbrook LB $20.90 (1-56294-348-0). 48pp. Sightings and arguments concerning the supposed existence of this monster from the American

Northwest are presented in a concise text and attractive format. (Rev: BL 1/1/94) [001.9]

**17447** Landau, Elaine. *UFOs* (4–6). Illus. Series: Mysteries of Science. 1995, Millbrook LB $20.90 (1-56294-542-4). 48pp. The controversy concerning UFO sightings is reported in an objective way, with many intriguing photographs. (Rev: BL 12/15/95; SLJ 4/96) [001.9]

**17448** Landau, Elaine. *Yeti: Abominable Snowman of the Himalayas* (4–6). Illus. Series: Mysteries of Science. 1993, Millbrook LB $20.90 (1-56294-349-9). 48pp. The controversy surrounding the possible existence of this Himalayan creature is explored objectively with fascinating details. (Rev: BL 1/1/94; SLJ 2/94) [001.9]

**17449** Levine, Michael. *The Kid's Address Book: Over 2,000 Addresses of Celebrities, Athletes, Entertainers, and More . . . Just for Kids* (3–8). Illus. 1994, Putnam paper $9.95 (0-399-51875-4). 219pp. This directory lists the names and addresses of over 2,000 celebrities, sports figures, and politicians. (Rev: BL 1/1/95) [920]

**17450** Morgan, Rowland. *In the Next Three Seconds* (3–6). Illus. by Rod Josey and Kira Josey. 1997, Lodestar paper $13.99 (0-525-67551-5). 32pp. This book of curiosities outlines events that could occur in 3 seconds, minutes, hours, days, weeks, and so on, to 3 million years. (Rev: SLJ 9/97) [001.9]

**17451** Nickell, Joe. *The Magic Detectives: Join Them in Solving Strange Mysteries* (3–7). Illus. 1989, Prometheus paper $9.95 (0-87975-547-4). 115pp. Each of the 30 brief chapters explores a mysterious phenomenon, such as Bigfoot. (Rev: BCCB 12/89; BL 12/1/89) [133]

**17452** *1001 Questions and Answers* (3–7). Illus. 1995, DK Publg. $16.95 (1-7894-0205-X). 64pp. More than 1,000 fascinating questions and amazing answers covering science and invention, history, the natural world, and recreation are detailed, with matching photographs. (Rev: BL 1/1–15/96) [031.02]

**17453** O'Neill, Catherine. *Amazing Mysteries of the World* (3–8). Illus. 1983, National Geographic LB $12.50 (0-87044-502-2). 104pp. Stonehenge, Easter Island, and Bigfoot are 3 of the many mysteries explored.

**17454** Parker, Steve. *Frankenstein* (4–6). Illus. Series: In the Footsteps Of. 1995, Millbrook LB $21.90 (1-56294-647-1). 40pp. This introduction to the Mary Shelley novel supplies background information, the basic story, and a description of the screen adaptations. (Rev: SLJ 1/96) [398.24]

**17455** Pipe, Jim. *Dracula* (4–6). Illus. Series: In the Footsteps Of. 1995, Millbrook LB $21.90 (1-56294-646-3). 40pp. The origins and content of Bram Stoker's novel are examined, with information on other

vampire stories and a rundown on bloodsucking insects and animals. (Rev: SLJ 1/96) [001.9]

**17456** Powell, Jillian. *Body Decoration* (4–8). Illus. Series: Traditions Around the World. 1995, Thomson Learning LB $24.26 (1-56847-276-5). 48pp. An interesting book that explains the uses of body decoration in history and discusses tattooing, face painting, and body piercing. (Rev: SLJ 7/95) [617]

**17457** Powell, Jillian. *The Supernatural* (4–6). Illus. Series: Mysteries Of. 1996, Millbrook LB $22.90 (0-7613-0455-X). 40pp. Topics like ghosts, UFOs, alien abductions, witchcraft, and out-of-body experiences are discussed. (Rev: SLJ 6/96) [001.9]

**17458** Ross, Stewart. *Secret Societies* (5–7). Illus. Series: Fact or Fiction. 1996, Millbrook $6.95 (0-7613-0510-6). 48pp. This colorful work explores cults, gangs, and secret clans throughout history, from ancient Japan to today. (Rev: BL 10/15/96; SLJ 4/97) [366]

**17459** Schwartz, Alvin. *Gold and Silver, Silver and Gold: Tales of Hidden Treasure* (4–8). Illus. 1993, Farrar paper $8.95 (0-374-42583-3). All sorts of treasure tales, from Captain Kidd to buried coins in a vacant lot. (Rev: BCCB 1/89; HB 3–4/89; SLJ 2/89)

**17460** Simon, Seymour. *Strange Mysteries from Around the World*. Rev. ed. (4–6). Illus. 1997, Morrow $16.00 (0-688-14636-8). 64pp. An updating of the 1980 title that describes 9 unusual events, such as strange lights that periodically appear in the sky. (Rev: BL 2/15/97; SLJ 4/97) [001.9]

**17461** Steffens, Bradley. *The Loch Ness Monster* (4–6). Illus. 1995, Lucent LB $22.45 (1-56006-159-6). 48pp. A history of Loch Ness's Nessie and the controversy surrounding the reality of this marine monster. (Rev: BL 2/15/95; SLJ 2/95) [001.9]

**17462** Tesar, Jenny. *America's Top 10 Curiosities* (3–7). Illus. Series: America's Top 10. 1997, Blackbirch LB $13.95 (1-56711-199-8). 24pp. Using double-page spreads, this book describes such phenomena as the Marfa Mystery Lights in Texas, the Flaming Fountain in South Dakota, and the Seattle Space Needle. (Rev: BL 1/1–15/98) [508.73]

**17463** Walker, Paul R. *Bigfoot and Other Legendary Creatures* (4–6). Illus. by William Noonan. 1992, Harcourt $18.00 (0-15-207147-4). 56pp. Facts, legends, and 7 original stories are included in this collection of material about several legendary creatures. (Rev: BL 2/15/92; SLJ 3/92) [001.9]

**17464** Watts, Claire, and Robert Nicholson. *Super Heroes* (3–6). Illus. Series: Info Adventure. 1995, Thomson Learning $9.95 (1-56847-409-1); paper $4.95 (1-56847-316-8). 31pp. An introduction to many mythical and legendary heroes plus coverage on such modern marvels as Batman, James Bond,

Tarzan, the Terminator, and Indiana Jones. (Rev: SLJ 12/95) [001.9]

**17465** Wilkinson, Philip. *A Celebration of Customs and Rituals of the World* (5–8). Illus. 1996, Facts on File $35.00 (0-8160-3479-6). 224pp. Discusses customs and rituals connected with birth, death, marriage, and coming-of-age. (Rev: BL 4/1/96) [394.2]

**17466** Wilson, Colin. *Mysteries of the Universe* (5–8). Illus. Series: Unexplained. 1997, DK Publg. $14.95 (0-7894-2165-8). 37pp. Such world mysteries as the Shroud of Turin, showers of fish, and life on Mars are explored. Also use *UFOs and Aliens* (1997). (Rev: BL 2/1/98; SLJ 2/98) [001.9]

**17467** Wood, Ted. *Ghosts of the Southwest: The Phantom Gunslinger and Other Real-Life Hauntings* (4–6). Illus. 1997, Walker LB $17.85 (0-8027-8483-6). 48pp. A trip through Arizona, New Mexico, Texas, and Oklahoma, with stops in locales where ghosts reside. (Rev: BL 3/1/97; SLJ 4/97) [133.1]

**17468** Yolen, Jane, and Heidi E. Y. Stemple. *Meet the Monsters* (K–2). Illus. by Patricia Ludlow. 1996, Walker LB $16.85 (0-8027-8442-9). A number of strange creatures — like zombies, vampires, mummies, and Medusa — are introduced in double-page spreads. (Rev: SLJ 11/96) [001.9]

# Sports and Games

## General and Miscellaneous

**17469**  Aaseng, Nathan. *True Champions: Great Athletes and Their Off-the-Field Heroics* (5–8). Illus. 1993, Walker LB $15.85 (0-8027-8247-7). 130pp. These stories illustrate brave true-life sports incidents. (Rev: SLJ 6/93) [793]

**17470**  Allison, Linda. *The Sierra Club Summer Book* (3–6). Illus. by author. 1989, Little, Brown paper $7.95 (0-316-03433-9). 160pp. All sorts of activities on how to spend a summer day in this updated activity book.

**17471**  Alter, Judith. *Rodeos: The Greatest Show on Dirt* (4–7). Illus. Series: First Books: Performances and Entertainment. 1996, Watts LB $21.00 (0-531-20245-3). 64pp. Includes a history of rodeos, standard events, rules, legendary performers, and women in rodeos. (Rev: SLJ 3/97) [791.8]

**17472**  Barrett, Norman. *Hang Gliding* (3–5). Illus. 1988, Watts LB $20.00 (0-531-10350-1). 32pp. Basic techniques of this thrill-seeking sport. (Rev: BL 5/15/88; SLJ 11/88)

**17473**  Bellville, Cheryl Walsh. *Flying in a Hot Air Balloon* (3–5). Illus. 1993, Carolrhoda LB $22.60 (0-87614-750-3). 48pp. An introduction to hot-air ballooning past and present that uses a rally in Minnesota as a framework. (Rev: BCCB 3/94; BL 1/1/94; SLJ 2/94) [797.5]

**17474**  Bellville, Cheryl Walsh. *Rodeo* (1–3). Illus. by author. 1985, Lerner paper $5.95 (0-87614-492-X). 32pp. A brief introduction to rodeos, highlighted with color photos. (Rev: BL 4/1/85; HB 7–8/85; SLJ 4/85)

**17475**  Boardman, Bob. *Red Hot Peppers: The Skookum Book of Jump Rope Games, Rhymes, and Fancy Footwork* (3–6). Illus. by Diane Boardman. 1993, Sasquatch paper $8.95 (0-912365-74-9). 64pp. A collection of directions for jump rope and other games, from simple to highly complex. (Rev: BL 7/93) [796.2]

**17476**  Brimner, Larry Dane. *Bobsledding and the Luge* (2–4). Series: True Books: Sports. 1997, Children's LB $21.00 (0-516-20436-X). 48pp. An introduction to the history, rules techniques, and people involved in these 2 hazardous winter sports. (Rev: BL 1/1–15/98; SLJ 2/98) [796]

**17477**  Brimner, Larry Dane. *Rock Climbing* (4–6). Illus. 1997, Watts LB $21.00 (0-531-20269-0). 64pp. Equipment, techniques, and safety tips are covered in this basic introduction to rock climbing. (Rev: BL 6/1–15/97) [796.5]

**17478**  Brimner, Larry Dane. *Rolling . . . In-Line!* (3–5). Illus. 1994, Watts LB $21.00 (0-531-20171-6). 63pp. In-line skating and its present incarnation, rollerblading, are described, with a section of how to select suitable skates. (Rev: BL 2/15/95) [796.2]

**17479**  Brooks, Philip. *United States* (4–6). Illus. Series: Games People Play! 1996, Children's LB $23.50 (0-516-04442-7). 64pp. Amateur and professional sports in the United States are covered, along with games we play and other forms of recreation. (Rev: SLJ 11/96) [796]

**17480**  Brown, Marc. *Finger Rhymes* (1–3). Illus. by author. 1980, Dutton paper $15.99 (0-525-29732-4). 32pp. This book contains instructions for 14 finger plays and accompanying rhymes.

**17481**  Bryant-Mole, Karen. *Games* (PS–3). Series: Picture This! 1997, Rigby LB $12.95 (1-57572-151-1). 24pp. Various games are introduced, with material on where they are played and the importance of healthy recreation. (Rev: BL 10/15/97) [790]

**17482** Chalmers, Aldie. *In-Line Skating* (3–6). Illus. Series: Fantastic Book Of. 1997, Millbrook LB $22.40 (0-7613-0623-4). 40pp. This introduction to in-line skating covers equipment, safety gear, stretching exercises, drills, techniques, and tips for beginners. (Rev: SLJ 3/98) [796.9]

**17483** Cole, Joanna. *Anna Banana: 101 Jump-Rope Rhymes* (2–4). Illus. by Alan Tiegreen. 1989, Morrow $16.00 (0-688-07788-9); paper $6.95 (0-688-08809-0). 64pp. Rhymes grouped according to jumping style. (Rev: BL 5/1/89)

**17484** Cole, Joanna, and Stephanie Calmenson. *The Eentsy, Weentsy Spider* (PS–1). Illus. by Alan Tiegreen. 1991, Morrow LB $13.93 (0-688-09439-2); paper $6.95 (0-688-10805-9). 64pp. Thirty-eight rhymes that demonstrate the fun children have performing the actions. (Rev: BL 10/15/91; SLJ 10/91) [793.4]

**17485** Cole, Joanna, and Stephanie Calmenson. *Pin the Tail on the Donkey and Other Party Games* (K–3). Illus. by Alan Tiegreen. 1993, Morrow LB $14.93 (0-688-11892-5). 48pp. A picture book with 20 simple party games. (Rev: BL 8/93) [793]

**17486** Cooper, Kay. *Too Many Rabbits and Other Fingerplays About Animals, Nature, Weather, and the Universe* (PS–1). Illus. 1995, Scholastic $12.95 (0-590-45564-8). 48pp. Various scientific principles are introduced in a series of entertaining fingerplays using animal characters and other subjects like stars, snow, and seeds. (Rev: BL 9/1/95; SLJ 3/96) [500]

**17487** Corbett, Pie, sel. *The Playtime Treasury* (PS–4). Illus. by Moira Maclean and Colin Maclean. 1989, Doubleday $9.95 (0-385-26448-8). 125pp. All kinds of games — singing, jumping, counting, and guessing — are included in this attractive collection. (Rev: SLJ 8/90) [796]

**17488** Crisfield, Deborah. *Winning Volleyball for Girls* (5–7). Illus. 1995, Facts on File $24.95 (0-8160-3033-2). 160pp. An excellent introduction to volleyball that gives girls information on rules, strategies, and techniques. (Rev: BCCB 3/96; BL 9/1/95) [796.32]

**17489** Crisman, Ruth. *Racing the Iditarod Trail* (4–6). Illus. 1993, Macmillan LB $14.95 (0-87518-523-1). 72pp. The origins and history of the great Alaskan dog sledding race, the Iditarod. (Rev: SLJ 6/93) [979.8]

**17490** Crum, Robert. *Let's Rodeo! Young Buckaroos and the World's Wildest Sport* (3–5). Illus. 1996, Simon & Schuster paper $17.00 (0-689-80075-4). 48pp. Various events in a typical rodeo are covered in this interesting photoessay. (Rev: BCCB 12/96; BL 11/1/96; SLJ 9/96) [791.8]

**17491** Davidson, Bob. *Hillary and Tenzing Climb Everest* (4–6). Illus. Series: Great 20th Century Expeditions. 1993, Dillon LB $13.95 (0-87518-534-7). 32pp. A description in text and photographs of many early attempts to conquer Everest, with emphasis on the successful 1953 expedition. (Rev: BL 9/15/93; SLJ 9/93) [796.5]

**17492** Dolan, Ellen M. *Susan Butcher and the Iditarod Trail* (5–7). Illus. 1993, Walker LB $15.85 (0-8027-8212-4). 112pp. This book tells about the history of the Iditarod sled dog race and of Susan Butcher who entered the race in 1978. (Rev: BL 4/1/93; SLJ 4/93) [798.8]

**17493** Doney, Meryl. *Games* (5–8). Illus. Series: World Crafts. 1996, Watts LB $21.00 (0-531-14405-4). 32pp. Directions for building a number of games from around the world, with cultural information and a helpful "How to Play" section. (Rev: SLJ 1/97) [790.1]

**17494** Edwards, Chris. *The Young Inline Skater* (4–6). Illus. 1996, DK Publg. $15.95 (0-7894-1124-5). 35pp. From skate maintenance to important techniques, this book describes inline skating, with an emphasis on safety. (Rev: BL 11/15/96; SLJ 11/96) [792.2]

**17495** Erlbach, Arlene. *Sidewalk Games Around the World* (3–5). Illus. 1997, Millbrook LB $23.90 (0-7613-0008-2). 64pp. Informal sidewalk games from 26 countries are introduced, with material on the country and the games and their rules. (Rev: BL 5/1/97; SLJ 5/97) [796.1]

**17496** Fine, John C. *Free Spirits in the Sky* (3–5). Illus. 1994, Atheneum $14.95 (0-689-31705-0). 32pp. With color photos on each page, this book gives a history of ballooning, tells how balloons fly, and explains the different types. (Rev: BL 1/15/94; SLJ 3/94) [797.5]

**17497** Flowers, Sarah. *Sports in America* (5–8). Illus. 1996, Lucent LB $22.45 (1-56006-178-2). 112pp. Problems in the modern sports world like commercialism, racism, and drugs are discussed in a straightforward way. (Rev: BL 9/1/96) [306.4]

**17498** Gay, Kathlyn. *They Don't Wash Their Socks! Sports Superstitions* (3–5). Illus. by John Kerschbaum. 1990, Walker LB $14.85 (0-8027-6917-9). 114pp. Superstitions from many sports are highlighted. (Rev: SLJ 6/90) [796]

**17499** Gilbert, Nancy. *The Special Olympics* (4–6). Illus. Series: Great Moments in Sports. 1991, Creative Ed. LB $14.95 (0-88682-311-0). 32pp. An overview of a subject rarely covered, with color photographs. (Rev: BL 1/1/92) [796]

**17500** Grayson, Marion F. *Let's Do Fingerplays* (PS–2). Illus. by Nancy Weyl. 1962, Luce $14.95 (0-88331-003-1). Comprehensive collection of finger plays under such headings as "Things That Go," "Animal Antics," and "Holidays."

**17501** Greenberg, Keith E. *Rodeo Clown: Laughs and Danger in the Ring* (2–5). Illus. Series: Risky Business. 1995, Blackbirch LB $14.95 (1-56711-152-1). 32pp. This career book goes behind the scenes at a rodeo and shows that there is a great deal of danger involved in being a rodeo clown. (Rev: BCCB 9/95; SLJ 8/95) [791.8]

**17502** Gryski, Camilla. *Cat's Cradle, Owl's Eyes: A Book of String Games* (4–7). Illus. by Tom Sankey. 1984, Morrow LB $15.93 (0-688-03940-5); paper $6.95 (0-688-03941-3). 80pp. Explanations of 21 string figures, plus variations.

**17503** Gryski, Camilla. *Many Stars and More String Games* (4–8). Illus. by Tom Sankey. 1985, Morrow paper $7.95 (0-688-05792-6). 80pp. Figures taken from a range of cultures to be mastered by agile fingers. (Rev: BL 12/15/85; SLJ 1/86)

**17504** Gryski, Camilla. *Super String Games* (4–6). Illus. by Tom Sankey. 1988, Morrow paper $6.95 (0-688-07684-X). 80pp. Advanced string games with harder-to-learn patterns. (Rev: BL 3/1/88; SLJ 8/88)

**17505** Hall, Godfrey. *Games* (5–7). Illus. Series: Traditions Around the World. 1995, Thomson Learning LB $24.26 (1-56847-345-1). 48pp. An oversize book that covers, in text and large color pictures, various games played in geographical regions around the world. (Rev: BL 6/1–15/95; SLJ 9/95) [790.1]

**17506** Hammond, Tim. *Sports* (4–8). Illus. 1988, Knopf LB $20.99 (0-394-99616-X). 64pp. Two dozen varieties of sports, including equipment, history, and rules. (Rev: BCCB 11/88; BL 12/1/88; SLJ 12/88)

**17507** Harris, Jack C. *Adventure Gaming* (5–8). Illus. Series: Hobby Guides. 1993, Crestwood $13.95 (0-89686-621-1). 48pp. Clear, easy-to-read information is given, with coverage of all kinds of adventure games, including war and role-playing games and those that deal with magic and sorcery. (Rev: SLJ 2/94) [793.92]

**17508** Kramer, S. A. *To the Top! Climbing the World's Highest Mountain* (2–4). Illus. by Thomas La Padula. 1993, Random paper $3.99 (0-679-83885-6). 47pp. An account of how Edmund Hillary and Tenzing Norgay conquered Mount Everest in 1953. (Rev: BCCB 6/93; SLJ 8/93) [796.5]

**17509** Krause, Peter. *Fundamental Golf* (5–8). Photos by Andy King. Series: Fundamental Sports. 1995, Lerner LB $21.27 (0-8225-3454-1). 64pp. A clear introduction to golf that covers history, equipment, swings, rules, and courses. (Rev: SLJ 9/95) [796.352]

**17510** Lankford, Mary D. *Hopscotch Around the World* (2–4). Illus. by Karen Milone. 1992, Morrow LB $15.93 (0-688-08420-6). 48pp. A description of 19 hopscotch variations played in 16 countries

around the world. (Rev: BCCB 6/92; BL 3/15/92; SLJ 4/92) [796.2]

**17511** Lankford, Mary D. *Jacks Around the World* (3–5). Illus. by Karen M. Dugan. 1996, Morrow LB $15.93 (0-688-13708-3). 40pp. How the game of jacks is played in various countries around the world. (Rev: BCCB 12/96; BL 7/96; HB 9–10/96; SLJ 9/96) [796.2]

**17512** Mayo, Terry. *The Illustrated Rules of In-line Hockey* (3–5). Illus. by Ned Butterfield. Series: Illustrated Sports. 1996, Ideals paper $6.95 (1-57102-064-0). 32pp. An introduction to in-line hockey, with a history of the sport, an explanation of the rules, a look at different positions and signals, and discussion of sportsmanship. (Rev: SLJ 8/96) [796.2]

**17513** Miller, Thomas. *Taking Time Out: Recreation and Play* (5–8). Illus. Series: Our Human Family. 1995, Blackbirch LB $21.95 (1-56711-128-9). 80pp. Divided into 5 broad geographic areas, this account describes how people enjoy themselves at play in various cultures. (Rev: SLJ 1/96) [794]

**17514** Nash, Bruce, and Allan Zullo. *The Greatest Sports Stories Never Told* (4–6). Illus. by John Gampert. 1993, Simon & Schuster paper $8.95 (0-671-75938-8). 96pp. From a variety of sports, this is a collection of 27 unusual but true stories. (Rev: BL 5/15/93; SLJ 6/93) [796]

**17515** Orozco, Jose-Luis. *Diez Deditos and Other Play Rhymes and Action Songs from Latin America* (PS–1). Illus. by Elisa Kleven. 1997, Dutton paper $18.99 (0-525-45736-4). 48pp. Thirty-four finger rhymes and songs in English and the original Spanish are included in this attractive collection. (Rev: BL 1/1–15/98) [782.42]

**17516** Paros, Lawrence, and Ben Joshua Paros. *Smash Caps: The Official Milkcap Fun Book* (3–6). Illus. by Kuo W. Yang. 1995, Avon paper $7.99 (0-380-78459-9). 55pp. An introduction to POGS, a game originally from Hawaii, which is played with caps from different bottles. (Rev: SLJ 1/96) [796]

**17517** Patent, Dorothy Hinshaw. *A Family Goes Hunting* (4–8). Illus. by William Munoz. 1991, Houghton $14.95 (0-395-52004-5). 64pp. One family is followed through hunting season in this photoessay. (Rev: BCCB 11/91; BL 12/15/91; SLJ 11/91) [799]

**17518** Perry, Phyllis J. *Ballooning* (4–6). Illus. 1996, Watts LB $22.00 (0-531-20234-8). 63pp. Following a history of ballooning, this account describes the parts of balloons and provides race statistics. (Rev: BL 2/1/97; SLJ 2/97) [629.133]

**17519** Perry, Phyllis J. *Soaring* (4–7). Illus. Series: First Books: Sports and Recreation. 1997, Watts LB $21.00 (0-531-20258-5). 64pp. Covers the history of gliders, scientific principles — like lift, thrust, and drag — and the sport of soaring and the equipment needed for it. (Rev: BL 7/97) [797.5]

**17520** *Racing on the Tour de France: And Other Stories of Sports* (4–6). Illus. 1989, Zaner-Bloser $10.95 (0-88309-546-7). 63pp. A collection of sports articles reprinted from the past 20 years of the magazine Highlights for Children. (Rev: SLJ 3/90) [796]

**17521** Robbins, Ken. *Rodeo* (2–5). Photos by author. 1996, Holt $14.95 (0-8050-3388-2). Such rodeo events as bronco riding, bull riding, steer wrestling, calf roping, and barrel racing are described, along with the role of the rodeo clown. (Rev: BCCB 12/96; SLJ 10/96) [791.8]

**17522** Rowe, Julian. *Recreation* (4–7). Illus. Series: Science Encounters. 1997, Rigby $13.95 (1-57572-092-2). 32pp. Shows how science is used in theme park rides, backpacking and camping equipment, computer games, television, scuba diving, and hang gliding. (Rev: SLJ 10/97) [796]

**17523** Rowe, Julian. *Sports* (4–7). Illus. Series: Science Encounters. 1997, Rigby $13.95 (1-57572-089-2). 32pp. Shows how science is used in such sports-related topics as the design of equipment, protective clothing, and sports medicine. (Rev: SLJ 10/97) [796]

**17524** Shahan, Sherry. *Dashing Through the Snow: The Story of the Jr. Iditarod* (4–7). Illus. 1997, Millbrook LB $22.40 (0-7613-0208-5); paper $9.95 (0-7613-0143-7). 48pp. All aspects of the 150-mile Junior Iditarod are touched upon in this account, including how these young mushers communicate with their dogs. (Rev: BL 3/1/97; SLJ 4/97) [798]

**17525** Sheely, Robert, and Louis Bourgeois. *Sports Lab: How Science Has Changed Sports* (4–7). Illus. Series: Science Lab. 1994, Silver Moon $13.95 (1-881889-49-1). 60pp. Traces the effect on sports of applying findings from such branches of science as aerodynamics, psychology, and medicine. (Rev: SLJ 9/94) [617.1]

**17526** Sobol, Donald J. *Encyclopedia Brown's Book of Wacky Sports* (3–6). Illus. by Ted Enik. 1984, Morrow $16.00 (0-688-03884-0). 112pp. A spin-off from the popular series, this is actually a book about wacky "happenings" in sports, covering a wide range of high school, college, and pro sports.

**17527** Steiner, Andy. *A Sporting Chance: Sports and Gender* (5–7). Illus. 1995, Lerner LB $22.60 (0-8225-3300-6). 96pp. The lack of equality between men and women in sports is covered in this account, ranging from Little League to professional levels. (Rev: BL 1/1–15/96; SLJ 1/96) [796]

**17528** Sullivan, George. *Any Number Can Play* (3–7). Illus. by John Caldwell. 1990, HarperCollins LB $13.89 (0-690-04814-9). 128pp. This anecdotal book tells about the myths and facts surrounding

numbers on various sports uniforms. (Rev: BL 6/15/90; SLJ 7/90) [796]

**17529** Sullivan, George. *In-Line Skating: A Complete Guide for Beginners* (4–8). Illus. 1993, Dutton paper $14.99 (0-525-65124-1). 48pp. This is a fine introduction to rollerblading that begins with choosing equipment and ends with entering tournaments. (Rev: BL 4/1/93; SLJ 7/93*) [796.2]

**17530** Warner, Penny. *Splish, Splash: Water Fun for Kids* (3–5). Illus. 1996, Chicago Review paper $12.95 (1-55652-262-2). 155pp. More than 120 water-related activities, including games and crafts, are outlined for various settings, e.g., pools and beaches. (Rev: BL 6/1–15/96) [797.2]

**17531** Wood, Ted. *Iditarod Dream: Dusty and His Sled Dogs Compete in Alaska's Jr. Iditarod* (2–5). Illus. 1996, Walker LB $17.85 (0-8027-8407-0). 48pp. Dusty, a 15-year-old Alaskan boy, prepares for and later enters the 158-mile Junior Iditarod. (Rev: BCCB 4/96; BL 3/15/96; SLJ 5/96) [798]

**17532** Young, Robert. *Sports Cards* (3–6). Illus. Series: Collectibles. 1993, Macmillan LB $13.95 (0-87518-519-3). 71pp. This book presents a history of trading cards and gives material both on their production and on how to collect them. (Rev: SLJ 8/93) [796]

# Automobile Racing

**17533** Andretti, Michael, et al. *Michael Andretti at Indianapolis* (3–7). Illus. by Douglas Carver. 1993, Simon & Schuster paper $5.95 (0-671-79674-7). 64pp. Readers experience the Indianapolis 500 from the driver's viewpoint. (Rev: BL 7/92; SLJ 6/92) [796.7]

**17534** Benson, Michael. *Crashes and Collisions* (5–8). Illus. Series: Race Car Legends. 1997, Chelsea $15.95 (0-7910-4435-1). 64pp. This exciting book chronicles several multicar pileups and gives short profiles of some who have survived them. (Rev: SLJ 2/98) [629.228]

**17535** *Formula 1 Motor Racing Book* (5–8). Illus. 1996, DK Publg. $16.95 (0-7894-0440-0). 64pp. A fascinating introduction to the world of Grand Prix racing with material on car care and maintenance. (Rev: BL 12/15/96) [796.72]

**17536** Kirkwood, Jon. *The Fantastic Book of Car Racing* (4–6). Illus. Series: Fantastic Book of . . . 1997, Millbrook LB $22.40 (0-7613-0565-3). 39pp. A heavily illustrated book with foldout sections on the subject of car racing, its excitement, and its allure. (Rev: SLJ 8/97) [796.7]

**17537** Savage, Jeff. *Drag Racing* (4–8). Illus. Series: Action Events. 1996, Crestwood LB $14.95 (0-89686-890-7); paper $4.95 (0-382-39293-0). 48pp. The thrill of drag racing is conveyed through action photos and a simple text. Also use *Mud Racing* and *Super Cross Motorcycle Racing* (both 1996). (Rev: SLJ 2/97) [796.7]

**17538** Weber, Bruce. *The Indianapolis 500* (4–6). Illus. Series: Great Moments in Sports. 1991, Creative Ed. LB $14.95 (0-88682-321-8). 32pp. A history of the Indianapolis Speedway race and mention of important winners. (Rev: BL 1/1/92) [796.7]

**17539** Wood, Tim. *Motor Racing* (K–3). Illus. Series: My Sport. 1989, Watts LB $11.40 (0-531-10828-7). 32pp. Basic facts about car racing are told through the experiences of a real race car driver. (Rev: SLJ 5/90) [796.7]

# Baseball

**17540** Anderson, Joan. *Batboy: An Inside Look at Spring Training* (3–6). Illus. 1996, Dutton paper $15.99 (0-525-67511-6). 48pp. A photoessay that highlights the work and pleasures of being a bat boy. (Rev: BCCB 3/96; BL 4/1/96; HB 5–6/96; SLJ 3/96) [796.357]

**17541** Aylesworth, Thomas G. *The Kids' World Almanac of Baseball* (4–8). Illus. 1996, World Almanac paper $8.95 (0-88687-787-3). 288pp. An entertaining compendium of baseball facts. (Rev: BL 6/1/90) [796.357]

**17542** Broekel, Ray. *Baseball* (1–4). Illus. 1982, Children's $12.90 (0-516-01616-4). 48pp. A clear, nicely organized introduction to this sport.

**17543** Christopher, Matt. *Great Moments in Baseball History* (3–5). 1996, Little, Brown paper $4.95 (0-316-14130-5). 104pp. Describes 9 important baseball events, involving such luminaries as Babe Ruth and Reggie Jackson. (Rev: SLJ 5/96) [796.357]

**17544** Dunnahoo, Terry, et al. *Baseball Hall of Fame* (4–6). Illus. Series: Halls of Fame. 1994, Macmillan LB $13.95 (0-89686-849-4). 48pp. In addition to providing a description of the Cooperstown, N.Y., museum, this book discusses the origins of the game, rules, and great players. (Rev: BL 9/1/94) [796.357]

**17545** Egan, Terry, et al. *The Good Guys of Baseball: Sixteen True Sports Stories* (3–6). Illus. 1997, Simon & Schuster paper $18.00 (0-689-80212-9). 111pp. Sixteen true stories, many featuring well-known players, that celebrate the hard work and dedication that baseball demands of a serious player. (Rev: SLJ 5/97) [796.357]

**17546** Egan, Terry, et al. *The Macmillan Book of Baseball Stories* (4–6). Illus. 1992, Macmillan LB $16.00 (0-02-733280-2). 112pp. These sentimental, true baseball stories demonstrate strong values, tradition, and the fun of the game. (Rev: BL 1/15/93) [796]

**17547** Frommer, Harvey. *A Hundred and Fiftieth Anniversary Album of Baseball* (4–8). Illus. 1988, Watts LB $24.00 (0-531-10588-1). 96pp. The evolution of the modern game from 1839. (Rev: BL 2/1/89; SLJ 1/89)

**17548** Gardner, Robert, and Dennis Shortelle. *The Forgotten Players: The Story of Black Baseball in America* (5–8). Illus. 1993, Walker LB $13.85 (0-8027-8249-3). 120pp. The trials of black baseball in America are revealed along with little-known aspects of U.S. baseball. (Rev: BL 2/15/93; SLJ 4/93) [769.357]

**17549** Gay, Douglas, and Kathlyn Gay. *The Not-So-Minor Leagues* (5–8). Illus. 1996, Millbrook LB $22.40 (1-56294-921-7). 96pp. The history, importance, and present status of the minor leagues in baseball. (Rev: BL 5/15/96; SLJ 6/96) [796.357]

**17550** Gergen, Joe. *World Series Heroes and Goats* (5–8). Illus. 1982, Random paper $1.95 (0-394-85018-1). 160pp. The best and the worst from America's October classic.

**17551** Hanmer, Trudy J. *The All-American Girls Professional Baseball League* (5–8). Illus. Series: American Events. 1994, New Discovery LB $14.95 (0-02-742595-9). 96pp. As well as discussing the AAGPBL, this account describes women in baseball prior to the league and recent attempts to play at all levels from Little League to the majors. (Rev: SLJ 3/95) [796.357]

**17552** Healy, Dennis. *The Illustrated Rules of Baseball* (3–5). Illus. Series: Illustrated Sports. 1995, Ideals paper $6.95 (1-57102-017-9). 32pp. The baseball diamond, playing positions, equipment, and rules are covered in this introduction to baseball. (Rev: BL 7/95; SLJ 5/95) [798.357]

**17553** Horenstein, Henry. *Baseball in the Barrios* (2–4). Illus. 1997, Harcourt $16.00 (0-15-200499-8). 36pp. A fifth-grader introduces baseball as it is played in the barrios of Caracas, Venezuela. (Rev: BL 4/15/97; HB 7–8/97; SLJ 6/97) [796.357]

**17554** Hughes, Dean, and Tom Hughes. *Baseball Tips* (2–5). Illus. by Dennis Lyall. 1993, Random LB $9.99 (0-679-93642-4). 96pp. In an easy-to-read format, here is a collection of useful pointers for the Little League set. (Rev: BL 5/15/93; SLJ 8/93) [796.357]

**17555** Jensen, Julie. *Beginning Baseball* (3–5). Photos by Andy King. Series: Beginning Sports. 1995, Lerner LB $14.96 (0-8225-3505-X). 80pp. The fundamentals of baseball — like throwing, hitting, fielding, and baserunning — are presented, along with a history of the game. (Rev: SLJ 2/96) [796.357]

**17556** Kreutzer, Peter, and Ted Kerley. *Little League's Official How-to-Play Baseball Handbook* (4–8). Illus. 1990, Doubleday $19.95 (0-385-41227-4); paper $10.95 (0-385-24700-1). 210pp. This guidebook covers all the basics of baseball and supplies strategies for playing various positions. (Rev: BL 5/15/90) [796.357]

**17557** Layden, Joe. *The Great American Baseball Strike* (5–8). Illus. Series: Headliners. 1995, Millbrook LB $23.40 (1-56294-930-6). 64pp. A story of the baseball strike that did great damage to the sport and alienated the fans. (Rev: BL 11/15/95; SLJ 1/96) [331.89]

**17558** Macy, Sue. *A Whole New Ball Game: The Story of the All-American Girls Professional Baseball League* (5–8). Illus. 1993, Holt $14.95 (0-8050-1942-1). 140pp. A fascinating look at the All-American Girls Professional Baseball League that functioned from 1945 to 1954. (Rev: SLJ 5/93*) [796.357]

**17559** Nash, Bruce, and Allan Zullo. *The Baseball Hall of Shame: Young Fans' Edition* (5–8). Illus. 1990, Pocket paper $2.99 (0-671-69354-9). 133pp. Baseball blunders by players, managers, umpires, and even groundskeepers are reported on. (Rev: SLJ 7/90) [796.357]

**17560** Newman, Gerald. *Happy Birthday, Little League* (3–6). Illus. 1989, Watts LB $22.00 (0-531-10687-X). 64pp. A half-century tribute to Little League baseball, filled with impressive statistics. (Rev: BCCB 4/89; BL 4/1/89; SLJ 5/89)

**17561** Ritter, Lawrence S. *Leagues Apart: The Men and Times of the Negro Baseball Leagues* (1–4). Illus. by Richard Merkin. 1995, Morrow LB $14.93 (0-688-13317-7). 40pp. This story of the Negro Baseball Leagues highlights the careers of 21 famous players, including Jackie Robinson. (Rev: BCCB 3/95; BL 2/15/95; HB 9–10/95; SLJ 3/95) [796.357]

**17562** Ritter, Lawrence S. *The Story of Baseball* (4–8). Illus. 1990, Morrow $17.95 (0-688-09056-7); paper $9.95 (0-688-09057-5). 192pp. In this revision of a standard introduction, the author includes coverage through the 1980s with updated statistics. (Rev: BL 7/90; HB 7–8/90; SLJ 9/90) [796.357]

**17563** Solomon, Chuck. *Major-League Batboy* (3–4). Illus. 1991, Crown LB $12.99 (0-517-58245-7). 32pp. A photoessay of many youngsters' dream: being a major league batboy. (Rev: BCCB 3/91; BL 2/15/91; HB 5–6/91; SLJ 9/91) [796.357]

**17564** Sublett, Anne. *The Illustrated Rules of Softball* (3–5). Illus. by Patrick Kelley. Series: Illustrated Sports. 1996, Ideals paper $6.95 (1-57102-063-2). 32pp. After a brief history of baseball, this account presents an explanation of rules and a look at various

positions and signals, plus a glossary and discussion of sportsmanship. (Rev: SLJ 8/96) [796.357]

**17565** Sullivan, George. *All About Baseball* (4–6). Illus. 1989, Putnam paper $9.95 (0-399-21734-7). 128pp. The basics of the game in an appealing format. (Rev: BL 5/1/89)

**17566** Sullivan, George. *Glovemen: Twenty-Seven of Baseball's Greatest* (4–7). Illus. 1996, Simon & Schuster $18.00 (0-689-31991-6). 72pp. A history of the role of defensemen in baseball and profiles of 27 of the greatest. (Rev: BL 5/15/96; SLJ 8/96) [796.357]

**17567** Sullivan, George. *Pitcher* (3–6). Illus. by Don Madden. 1986, HarperCollins LB $11.89 (0-690-04539-5). 64pp. Tips on mastering the art of pitching, aimed at Little Leaguers. (Rev: BCCB 6/86; BL 4/1/86; SLJ 5/86)

# Basketball

**17568** Anderson, Dave. *The Story of Basketball* (4–8). Illus. 1997, Morrow $16.00 (0-688-14316-4). 208pp. An updated introduction to the history, rules, players, and teams involved in basketball. (Rev: BL 1/1–15/98; SLJ 10/97) [796.32]

**17569** Bennett, Frank. *The Illustrated Rules of Basketball* (3–5). Illus. 1994, Ideals paper $6.95 (1-57102-021-7). 32pp. Following the history of basketball, provides a detailed discussion of each rule. (Rev: BL 9/15/94; SLJ 11/94) [796.323]

**17570** Dunnahoo, Terry, et al. *Basketball Hall of Fame* (4–6). Illus. Series: Halls of Fame. 1994, Macmillan LB $13.95 (0-89686-850-8). 48pp. As well as describing the functions of the Basketball Hall of Fame, this book explains how the sport evolved and tells about some of the great players. (Rev: BL 9/1/94; SLJ 8/94) [796.323]

**17571** Kasoff, Jerry. *Baseball Just for Kids: Skills, Strategies and Stories to Make You a Better Ballplayer* (3–7). Illus. 1996, paper $12.95 (0-9645826-7-8). 159pp. Baseball rules, techniques, tips, jokes, and trivia are included in this book that shows that the author loves the game. (Rev: SLJ 4/97) [796.357]

**17572** Kramer, S. A. *Hoop Stars* (2–3). Illus. by Mitchell Heinze. 1995, Putnam paper $3.95 (0-448-40943-7). 48pp. Hakeem Olajuwon, Charles Barkley, Shaquille O'Neal, and David Robinson are the NBA stars briefly profiled in this beginning reader. (Rev: BL 1/1–15/96; SLJ 3/96) [796.323]

**17573** Lace, William W. *The Houston Rockets Basketball Team* (5–8). Series: Great Sports Teams. 1997, Enslow LB $18.95 (0-89490-792-1). 48pp. A profile of the Houston Rockets, with sketches of their key players. (Rev: BL 10/15/97) [796.323]

**17574** McGuire, William. *The Final Four* (4–6). Illus. Series: Great Moments in Sports. 1991, Creative Ed. LB $14.95 (0-88682-310-2). 32pp. A well-illustrated history and highlights of the National Collegiate Athletic Association (NCAA) basketball tournament. (Rev: BL 1/1/92) [796.3]

**17575** Morris, Greggory. *Basketball Basics* (4–6). Illus. by Tim Engelland. 1979, Prentice Hall $6.95 (0-13-072256-1). A player and coach explain 4 specific skills to young players.

**17576** Mullin, Chris, and Brian Coleman. *The Young Basketball Player* (4–7). Illus. 1995, DK Publg. $15.95 (0-7894-0220-3). 45pp. Such basketball techniques as dribbling, passing, and scoring are described, along with brief material on the history of the sport and on equipment. (Rev: BL 11/1/95; SLJ 1/96) [796.323]

**17577** Owens, Thomas S. *The Chicago Bulls Basketball Team* (5–8). Illus. Series: Great Sports Team. 1997, Enslow LB $18.95 (0-89490-793-X). 48pp. A history of the Chicago Bulls, with emphasis on the various stars who have made the team famous. (Rev: BL 10/15/97) [796.323]

**17578** Pietrusza, David. *The Phoenix Suns Basketball Team* (5–8). Series: Great Sports Teams. 1997, Enslow LB $18.95 (0-89490-795-6). 48pp. Introduces the history of the Phoenix Suns and their key players. (Rev: BL 10/15/97) [796.323]

**17579** Preller, James. *NBA Game Day: An Inside Look at the NBA* (3–8). Illus. 1997, Scholastic paper $10.95 (0-590-76742-9). 48pp. A photoessay on a day in the life of the NBA, from the morning workout to the custodian sweeping the court after the evening game. (Rev: BL 1/1–15/98) [796.323]

**17580** Rogers, Glenn. *The San Antonio Spurs Basketball Team* (5–8). Series: Great Sports Teams. 1997, Enslow LB $18.95 (0-89490-797-2). 48pp. Profiles of important players and stories behind important games are included in this profile of the San Antonio Spurs. (Rev: BL 10/15/97) [796.323]

**17581** Rosenthal, Bert. *Basketball* (2–4). Illus. 1983, Children's paper $5.50 (0-516-41674-X). 48pp. For the very young reader, an introduction utilizing many color photographs and a glossary.

**17582** Stevenson, Amy. *The NBA Finals* (4–6). Illus. Series: Great Moments in Sports. 1991, Creative Ed. LB $14.95 (0-88682-314-5). 32pp. The history of the world series of basketball, with mention of a few famous players, in this well-illustrated album. (Rev: BL 1/1/92) [796.323]

**17583** Sullivan, George. *All About Basketball* (5–8). Illus. 1991, Putnam paper $9.95 (0-399-21793-2). 160pp. An ideal explanation for those who know lit-

tle or nothing about the game. (Rev: BL 1/1/92) [296.323]

**17584** Vancil, Mark. *NBA Basketball Offense Basics* (4–8). Illus. 1996, Sterling $16.95 (0-8069-4892-2). 96pp. Action photos and lively text demonstrate such techniques as dribbling, passing, and shooting. (Rev: BL 9/1/96) [796.332]

# Bicycles

**17585** Brimner, Larry Dane. *Mountain Biking* (5–7). Illus. 1997, Watts LB $21.00 (0-531-20243-7). 64pp. An attractive book that includes information on the history of mountain bikes, their construction, and how to choose, use, and maintain one. (Rev: BL 9/1/97; SLJ 8/97) [796.6]

**17586** Erlbach, Arlene. *Bicycles* (3–5). Illus. Series: How It's Made. 1994, Lerner LB $19.93 (0-8225-2388-4); paper $6.95 (0-8225-9740-3). 48pp. The story of the bicycle is told, from its early design to the sleek machines of today. (Rev: BL 3/15/95) [629]

**17587** Francis, John. *Bicycling* (3–6). Illus. Series: How to Play the All-Star Way. 1996, Raintree Steck-Vaughn LB $24.26 (0-8114-6598-5). 48pp. This introduction to bicycling describes its history, types of bicycles, safety rules and racing possibilities. (Rev: SLJ 6/96) [629.2]

**17588** Gibbons, Gail. *Bicycle Book* (K–4). Illus. 1995, Holiday LB $15.95 (0-8234-1199-0). 32pp. A short book that covers such topics as the history of the bicycle, its types, care tips, and safety rules. (Rev: BL 12/1/95; SLJ 1/96) [629.227]

**17589** Hautzig, David. *1,000 Miles in 12 Days: Pro Cyclists on Tour* (3–6). Illus. 1995, Orchard LB $16.99 (0-531-08746-8). 32pp. Using as a framework the Tour Du Pont bicycle race in the southeastern United States, many facts are given about bicycle racing and the behind-the-scenes support team. (Rev: BL 2/1/95; SLJ 3/95) [796.2]

**17590** Hautzig, David. *Pedal Power: How a Mountain Bike Is Made* (4–6). Illus. 1996, Dutton paper $15.99 (0-525-67508-6). 32pp. A fascinating account of the processes, materials, and machinery involved in making mountain bikes, with material on how to choose and maintain one. (Rev: BL 4/15/96; SLJ 4/96) [629.227]

**17591** Jensen, Julie. *Beginning Mountain Biking* (4–6). Photos by Andy King. Series: Beginning Sports. 1996, Lerner LB $21.27 (0-8225-3509-2). 63pp. A very simple, short account that introduces mountain biking to a young audience. (Rev: SLJ 2/97) [796.6]

**17592** Loewen, Nancy. *Bicycle Safety* (K–2). Illus. by Penny Dann. 1996, Child's World LB $18.50 (1-56766-260-9). 24pp. Safety rules for bicycle riding are outlined and then illustrated by cartoons that show right and wrong behavior. Also use *Traffic Safety* (1996). (Rev: SLJ 1/97) [629.227]

**17593** Lord, Trevor. *Amazing Bikes* (1–4). Illus. by Peter Downs. Series: Eyewitness Juniors. 1992, Knopf paper $7.99 (0-679-82772-2). 32pp. An explanation of bicycles plus many illustrations showing various types. (Rev: BL 11/1/92) [629.227]

**17594** McManners, Hugh. *Biking: An Outdoor Adventure Handbook* (4–7). Illus. 1996, DK Publg. paper $10.95 (0-7894-1105-9). 48pp. Clothing, equipment, and basic skills are discussed in this introductory guide to biking. (Rev: BL 12/1/96) [796.6]

**17595** Maestro, Betsy, and Giulio Maestro. *Bike Trip* (2–4). Illus. 1992, HarperCollins LB $16.00 (0-06-022731-1). 32pp. Young Joshua tells a simple story of a bike trip he takes with his family from their rural home into town. (Rev: BL 1/1/92; SLJ 3/92) [796.6]

**17596** Otfinoski, Steven. *Pedaling Along: Bikes Then and Now* (1–3). Illus. Series: Here We Go! 1996, Benchmark LB $21.36 (0-7614-0402-3). 32pp. A copiously illustrated history of bicycles, from their invention to modern bikes. (Rev: SLJ 6/97) [629]

## Camping and Backpacking

**17597** Drake, Jane, and Ann Love. *The Kids Campfire Book* (4–6). Illus. 1998, Kids Can paper $9.95 (1-55074-539-5). 128pp. A thorough guide to good camping that includes such topics as how to choose wood for the fire, recipes for cooking over the fire, games and songs, tips on wildlife exploration, and stories to tell around the campfire. (Rev: BL 3/15/98; SLJ 4/98) [796.54]

**17598** Kuller, Alison M. *An Outward Bound School* (3–6). Illus. Series: Let's Take a Trip. 1990, Troll LB $11.50 (0-8167-1731-1). 32pp. An account of the Hurricane Island Outward Bound School in Rockland, Maine. (Rev: BCCB 5/90; BL 5/1/90) [796.54]

**17599** McManners, Hugh. *The Outdoor Adventure Handbook* (3–6). Illus. 1996, DK Publg. $16.95 (0-7894-1035-4); paper $12.95 (0-7894-0468-0). 64pp. In this useful manual, information is given on such outdoor activities as camping and hiking, with additional material on cooking, first aid, fire making, and putting up a tent. (Rev: SLJ 6/96) [796.54]

**17600** McManus, Patrick F. *Kid Camping from Aaaaiii! to Zip* (5–7). Illus. by Roy Doty. 1979, Avon paper $3.99 (0-380-71311-X). 128pp. A practical camping guide presented in an amusing way.

## Chess

**17601** Kidder, Harvey. *The Kids' Book of Chess* (4–8). Illus. by Kimberly Bulcken. 1990, Workman paper $14.95 (0-89480-767-6). 96pp. Using their origins in the Middle Ages as a focus, this book explains each chess piece and the basics of the game. (Rev: SLJ 2/91) [794.1]

**17602** Nottingham, Ted, et al. *Chess for Children* (4–6). Illus. 1994, Sterling $16.95 (0-8069-0452-6). 128pp. Three experts explain chess, the meaning and use of each piece, strategies, famous games, and the accomplishments of famous players. (Rev: BL 5/1/94) [794.1]

## Fishing

**17603** Arnosky, Jim. *Fish in a Flash: A Personal Guide to Spin-Fishing* (4–6). Illus. by author. 1991, Macmillan LB $14.95 (0-02-705854-9). 63pp. This book combines basic fishing instructions concerning equipment, tackle, and techniques with the author's personal experiences. (Rev: SLJ 10/91) [799.1]

**17604** Morey, Shaun. *Incredible Fishing Stories for Kids* (3–6). Illus. 1993, Incredible Fishing Stories paper $11.95 (0-9633691-1-3). 96pp. These true stories tell how young anglers have made record catches. (Rev: BL 9/1/93)

**17605** Schmidt, Gerald D. *Let's Go Fishing: A Book for Beginners* (4–7). Illus. by Brian W. Payne. 1990, Roberts Rinehart paper $11.95 (0-911797-84-X). 96pp. This practical guide to freshwater fishing includes material on tackle and kinds of fish. (Rev: BL 3/1/91; SLJ 5/91) [799.1]

## Football

**17606** Anderson, Dave. *The Story of Football* (4–8). Illus. 1997, Morrow $16.00 (0-688-14314-8). 208pp. A revision of the 1985 edition — a fine introduction to football, major teams and players, and the rules of the game. (Rev: BL 1/1–15/98; SLJ 10/97) [796.48]

**17607** Broekel, Ray. *Football* (1–4). Illus. 1982, Children's $13.05 (0-516-01629-6). 48pp. A colorfully illustrated introduction for primary grades.

**17608** DiLorenzo, J. J. *The Miami Dolphins Football Team* (5–8). Series: Great Sports Teams. 1997, Enslow LB $18.95 (0-89490-796-4). 48pp. A history of the Miami Dolphins that focuses on their brightest stars and best moments on the field. (Rev: BL 10/15/97) [796.332]

**17609** Dunnahoo, Terry, et al. *Pro Football Hall of Fame* (4–6). Illus. Series: Halls of Fame. 1994, Macmillan LB $13.95 (0-89686-851-6). 48pp. The story of the Football Hall of Fame, its contents and history, plus many asides about the origins of American football and its star players. (Rev: BL 7/94; SLJ 8/94) [796.332]

**17610** Kessler, Leonard. *Kick, Pass, and Run* (1–2). Illus. 1996, HarperCollins LB $14.89 (0-06-027105-1); paper $3.75 (0-06-444210-1). 64pp. An easily read reissue of a book that introduces football and its rules. (Rev: BL 11/15/96) [796.332]

**17611** Lace, William W. *The Dallas Cowboys Football Team* (5–8). Illus. Series: Great Sports Team. 1997, Enslow LB $18.95 (0-89490-791-3). 48pp. After discussing the Dallas championship in 1973, this book traces the history of the team and supplies plenty of sports action. (Rev: BL 10/15/97) [796.332]

**17612** Patey, R. L. *The Illustrated Rules of Football* (3–5). Illus. by Eleanor Hoyt. Series: Illustrated Sports. 1995, Ideals paper $6.95 (1-57102-049-7). 32pp. Introduces football's basic plays and techniques, equipment, and the rules. (Rev: BL 10/15/95; SLJ 1/96) [796.332]

**17613** Sullivan, George. *All About Football* (3–5). Illus. 1990, Putnam paper $9.95 (0-399-21907-2). 128pp. Numerous photos aid in the telling of the game's development, history, complexities, and notable personalities through the years. (Rev: BCCB 12/87; BL 2/1/88)

# Gymnastics

**17614** Barrett, Norman. *Gymnastics* (3–5). Illus. 1991, Children's paper $4.95 (0-516-94614-5). 32pp. A fast-paced introduction to the sport. (Rev: BL 4/15/89)

**17615** Bragg, Linda Wallenberg. *Fundamental Gymnastics* (3–6). Photos by Andy King. Illus. Series: Fundamental Sports. 1995, Lerner LB $19.93 (0-8225-3453-3). 80pp. A brief history of gymnastics is given, including 6 events for boys and 4 for girls and basic moves and workouts. (Rev: SLJ 3/96) [796.44]

**17616** Gutman, Dan. *Gymnastics* (5–8). Illus. 1996, Viking paper $14.99 (0-670-86949-X). 212pp. In addition to a history of gymnastics from the ancient Greeks to the 1996 Olympics, this account explains the different competitive events and how they are judged. (Rev: BL 5/1/96; SLJ 8/96) [796.44]

**17617** Jackman, Joan. *The Young Gymnast* (4–7). Illus. 1995, DK Publg. $15.95 (1-56458-677-4).

45pp. After a history of the sport, the required equipment and clothing are outlined, followed by extensive material on each of the specific skills involved. (Rev: BL 9/1/95; SLJ 7/95) [796.44]

**17618** Kuklin, Susan. *Going to My Gymnastics Class* (4–6). Illus. 1991, Macmillan LB $13.95 (0-02-751236-3). 40pp. The experiences of preschoolers at gymnastics class. (Rev: BCCB 10/91; BL 8/91; SLJ 12/91) [796.44]

**17619** Readhead, Lloyd. *Gymnastics* (3–6). Illus. Series: Fantastic Book Of. 1997, Millbrook LB $22.40 (0-7613-0622-6). 32pp. Covers gymnastics techniques, training, warm-up exercises, and equipment, with an 8-page foldout section on competitions. (Rev: BL 3/15/98) [796.44]

**17620** Schmidt, Diane. *I Am a Jesse White Tumbler* (3–8). Illus. 1990, Whitman LB $14.95 (0-8075-3444-7). 40pp. The story of the Jesse White Tumblers, young Chicago inner-city gymnasts, as seen by a member. (Rev: BCCB 2/90; BL 2/1/90; HB 7–8/90; SLJ 5/90) [796.4]

**17621** Wood, Tim. *Gymnastics* (K–3). Illus. Series: My Sport. 1989, Watts LB $11.40 (0-531-10826-0). 32pp. This is an introduction to gymnastics as it involves a young female gymnast and her activities. (Rev: SLJ 5/90) [796.4]

# Horsemanship

**17622** Damrell, Liz. *With the Wind* (PS–1). Illus. by Stephen Marchesi. 1991, Smithmark $4.98 (0-831-76779-0). 32pp. The feelings of a boy as he goes horseback riding through the country. (Rev: BL 3/1/91; SLJ 6/91) [799.1]

**17623** Green, Lucinda. *The Young Rider* (4–6). Illus. 1993, DK Publg. $15.95 (1-56458-320-1). 64pp. A wide range of topics are covered in this introduction to riding and horse care. (Rev: BL 10/15/93; SLJ 12/93) [798.2]

**17624** Haas, Jessie. *Safe Horse, Safe Rider: A Young Rider's Guide to Responsible Horsekeeping* (4–7). Illus. 1994, Storey paper $14.95 (0-88266-700-9). 160pp. This guide to horsemanship stresses safety and covers such topics as understanding horse behavior. (Rev: BL 1/1/95) [636.1]

**17625** Harris, Jack C. *The Kentucky Derby* (4–6). Illus. Series: Great Moments in Sports. 1991, Creative Ed. LB $21.36 (0-88682-312-9). 32pp. This well-illustrated account gives a brief history of the famous horse race and mentions the famous participants. (Rev: BL 1/1/92) [798.4]

**17626** Kirksmith, Tommie. *Ride Western Style: A Guide for Young Riders* (4–8). Illus. 1991, Howell

Book House $16.95 (0-87605-895-0). 212pp. A guide on Western-style riding for use in conjunction with a supervised riding program. (Rev: BL 4/1/92) [798.2]

**17627** Winter, Ginny L. *The Riding Book* (K–3). Illus. by author. 1963, Astor-Honor $8.95 (0-8392-3031-1). An introductory account for the very young rider.

## Ice Hockey

**17628** Ayers, Tom. *The Illustrated Rules of Ice Hockey* (3–5). Illus. by Eleanor Hoyt. Series: Illustrated Sports. 1995, Ideals paper $6.95 (1-57102-048-9). 32pp. This book introduces the dimensions and parts of a hockey rink, the player's equipment, and basic rules of ice hockey. (Rev: BL 10/15/95; SLJ 1/96) [796.962]

**17629** Barrett, Norman. *Ice Sports* (3–5). Illus. 1989, Watts LB $20.00 (0-531-10627-6). 32pp. Numerous photos highlight the basic details of fun sports on the ice. (Rev: BL 5/15/88)

**17630** Foley, Mike. *Fundamental Hockey* (4–8). Photos by Andy King. Series: Fundamental Sports. 1996, Lerner LB $21.27 (0-8225-3456-8). 80pp. The basics of ice hockey are introduced, plus a brief history of the sport and an explanation of what the various players do. (Rev: SLJ 3/96) [796.962]

**17631** Jensen, Julie, adapt. *Beginning Hockey* (4–8). Photos by Andy King. Series: Beginning Sports. 1996, Lerner LB $21.27 (0-8225-3506-8). 80pp. An introduction to hockey, its history, and the techniques and skills used by the players. (Rev: SLJ 3/96) [796.964]

**17632** McGuire, William. *The Stanley Cup* (4–6). Illus. Series: Great Moments in Sports. 1991, Creative Ed. LB $14.95 (0-88682-316-1). 32pp. A brief history of the "world series" of professional hockey, with important teams and famous players. (Rev: BL 1/1/92) [796.962]

**17633** Solomon, Chuck. *Playing Hockey* (2–4). Illus. 1990, Crown LB $10.99 (0-517-57415-2). 40pp. With photos, this book shows how hockey is played on a country pond and on a city rink. (Rev: BCCB 9/90; BL 6/15/90) [796.96]

## Ice Skating

**17634** Brimner, Larry Dane. *Speed Skating* (2–4). Illus. Series: True Books: Sports. 1997, Children's $21.00 (0-516-20451-3). 48pp. The story of speed skating: its history, equipment, techniques, and place in the Olympic Games. (Rev: BL 1/1–15/98; SLJ 2/98) [796.91]

**17635** Gutman, Dan. *Ice Skating: From Axels to Zambonis* (5–8). Illus. 1995, Viking paper $14.99 (0-670-86013-1). 196pp. A complete guide to ice skating that includes a history, information on techniques, biographies, a chronology, and a list of champions. (Rev: BL 10/1/95; SLJ 12/95) [796.91]

**17636** Winter, Ginny L. *The Skating Book* (K–3). Illus. by author. 1963, Astor-Honor $8.95 (0-8392-3035-4). A beginning account for the young skater.

## Indoor Games

**17637** Cole, Joanna, and Stephanie Calmenson. *Crazy Eights and Other Card Games* (2–5). Illus. by Alan Tiegreen. 1994, Morrow $16.00 (0-688-12199-3). 80pp. Twenty tried-and-true card games, like spit and go fish, are explained with easy instructions. (Rev: BL 4/15/94; SLJ 6/94) [795.4]

**17638** Collis, Len. *Card Games for Children* (K–6). Illus. by Terry Carter and Bob George. 1989, Barron's paper $5.95 (0-8120-4290-5). 95pp. A collection of 41 card games with easily followed directions involving different numbers of players. (Rev: SLJ 3/90) [795.4]

**17639** Eldin, Peter. *The Most Excellent Book of How to Do Card Tricks* (3–5). Illus. Series: Most Excellent Book Of. 1996, Millbrook LB $19.90 (0-7613-0525-4); paper $5.95 (0-7613-0504-1). 32pp. This how-to book also contains "easy step-by-step instructions for a brilliant performance." (Rev: BL 10/15/96; SLJ 2/97) [795.4]

**17640** Erlbach, Arlene. *Video Games* (4–6). Illus. 1995, Lerner LB $19.95 (0-8225-2389-2). 48pp. An explanation of how video games came to be, how they are constructed, and how they work. (Rev: BL 8/95; SLJ 6/95) [794.8]

**17641** Hetzer, Linda. *Rainy Days and Saturdays* (3–6). Illus. 1996, Workman paper $9.95 (1-56305-513-9). 227pp. About 150 activities are outlined on topics like sports, science, and cooking for youngsters confined indoors. (Rev: BL 6/1–15/96; SLJ 7/96) [793]

**17642** Lankford, Mary D. *Dominoes Around the World* (3–5). Illus. 1998, Morrow $16.00 (0-688-14051-3). 40pp. After providing the history of dominoes, the author presents 8 versions of the game as played in such places as Malta, Vietnam, and the United States. (Rev: BL 3/15/98; SLJ 4/98) [795.3]

**17643** McCoy, Elin. *Cards for Kids: Games, Tricks and Amazing Facts* (3–6). Illus. by Tom Huffman.

1991, Macmillan $13.95 (0-02-765461-3). 150pp. Tells the history of playing cards and introduces 42 games suitable for youngsters. (Rev: SLJ 3/92) [795.4]

**17644** Sheinwold, Alfred. *101 Best Family Card Games* (4–8). Illus. by Myron Miller. 1993, Sterling paper $4.95 (0-8069-8635-2). 128pp. A book filled with games enjoyed by many age groups. (Rev: BL 2/15/93) [795.4]

**17645** Silbaugh, Elizabeth. *Let's Play Cards! A First Book of Card Games* (2–3). Illus. by Jef Kaminsky. 1996, Simon & Schuster $14.00 (0-689-80802-X); paper $3.99 (0-689-80801-1). 47pp. Five card games, including one type of solitaire, are introduced, along with a history of playing cards and a description of the deck. (Rev: BCCB 9/96; SLJ 10/96) [795.4]

**17646** Skurzynski, Gloria. *Know the Score: Video Games in Your High-Tech World* (4–6). Illus. 1994, Bradbury $16.95 (0-02-782922-7). 64pp. The history and design of video games are discussed, with material on necessary hardware and current technology in the field. (Rev: BCCB 7–8/94; BL 3/1/94; SLJ 4/94) [794.8]

## Olympic Games

**17647** Anderson, Dave. *The Story of the Olympics* (4–6). Illus. 1996, Morrow $16.00 (0-688-12954-4). 192pp. Beginning with the ancient Greeks, this survey covers the highlights of the Olympic Games. (Rev: BL 7/96; SLJ 4/96*) [796.49]

**17648** Brimner, Larry Dane. *The Winter Olympics* (2–4). Illus. Series: True Books: Sports. 1997, Children's $21.00 (0-516-20456-4). 48pp. Describes the various sports in the Winter Olympics and gives a general history of the games and their goals and symbols. (Rev: BL 1/1–15/98; SLJ 2/98) [796.98]

**17649** Crowther, Robert. *Robert Crowther's Pop-up Olympics* (3–5). Illus. 1996, Candlewick $19.99 (1-56402-801-1). 12pp. A history of the Olympics is given, and many of the events are illustrated with pop-ups. (Rev: BL 2/1/96) [796.4]

**17650** Dinn, Sheila. *Hearts of Gold: A Celebration of Special Olympics and Its Heroes* (4–7). Illus. 1996, Blackbirch LB $21.95 (1-56711-163-7). 96pp. After a short history of the Olympics, the author focuses on the Special Olympics, each sport involved, and important athletes and events. (Rev: BL 3/1/96; SLJ 7/96) [796]

**17651** Glubok, Shirley, and Alfred Tamarin. *Olympic Games in Ancient Greece* (5–8). Illus. 1976, Harper-Collins LB $16.89 (0-06-022048-1). 128pp. Using a

fictitious Olympiad set in the 5th century B.C., the authors offer a great deal of background information in an imaginative, satisfying way.

**17652** Harris, Jack C. *The Winter Olympics* (4–6). Illus. Series: Great Moments in Sports. 1991, Creative Ed. LB $14.95 (0-88682-317-X). 32pp. Each event of the Winter Olympics is described, with mention of the famous players. (Rev: BL 1/1/92) [796.98]

**17653** Haycock, Kate. *Skiing* (4–8). Illus. Series: Olympic Sports. 1992, Macmillan LB $13.95 (0-89686-669-6). 32pp. The Winter Olympic events in skiing are discussed. (Rev: SLJ 4/92) [796.93]

**17654** Hennessy, B. G. *Olympics* (PS–3). Illus. by Michael Chesworth. 1996, Viking paper $14.99 (0-670-86522-2). 32pp. A profile of what happens at the Olympics, including preparations and the actual competitions. (Rev: BL 4/1/96; SLJ 5/96) [796.48]

**17655** Kristy, Davida. *Coubertin's Olympics: How the Games Began* (5–8). Illus. 1995, Lerner LB $23.93 (0-8225-3327-8); paper $10.95 (0-8225-9713-6). 128pp. The story of Baron Pierre de Coubertin, who established the modern Olympic Games. (Rev: BL 8/95; SLJ 11/95) [338.4]

**17656** McGuire, William. *The Summer Olympics* (4–6). Illus. Series: Great Moments in Sports. 1991, Creative Ed. LB $14.95 (0-88682-318-8). 32pp. A history of the events of the Summer Olympics, with highlights and important athletes. (Rev: BL 1/1/92) [796.48]

**17657** Sandelson, Robert. *Ice Sports* (4–8). Illus. Series: Olympic Sports. 1992, Macmillan LB $13.95 (0-89686-667-X). 32pp. Discusses Winter Olympic events, such as bobsledding and ice hockey. (Rev: SLJ 4/92) [796.91]

## Running and Jogging

**17658** Savage, Jeff. *Running* (4–6). Illus. Series: Working Out. 1995, Silver Burdett LB $15.95 (0-89686-855-9); paper $7.95 (0-382-24948-8). 48pp. An introduction to running and its benefits, with information on how to begin, safety considerations, and a training schedule. (Rev: SLJ 10/95) [796.4]

## Sailing and Boating

**17659** Barrett, Norman. *Sailing* (3–5). Illus. 1988, Watts LB $20.00 (0-531-10351-X). 32pp. Basic tips and techniques, with numerous photos. (Rev: BL 5/15/88)

**17660** Hackler, Lew. *Boating with Cap'n Bob and Matey: An Encyclopedia for Kids of All Ages* (K–3). Illus. by Bobby Basnight. 1989, Seascape $12.95 (0-931595-03-7). 32pp. A guide for the very young on boating, which includes basic terms and useful tips. (Rev: SLJ 10/89) [796.125]

**17661** Kalman, Bobbie. *A Canoe Trip* (2–4). Illus. 1995, Crabtree LB $18.08 (0-86505-619-6); paper $5.95 (0-86505-719-2). 32pp. Covers the parts of a canoe, safety considerations, and basic strokes. Also use *Summer Camp* (1994). (Rev: SLJ 7/95) [797.1]

**17662** Wilson, Rich. *Racing a Ghost Ship: The Incredible Journey of Great American II* (3–6). Illus. 1996, Walker LB $17.85 (0-8027-8417-8). 48pp. Photos, maps, and diagrams enliven this account of a voyage from San Francisco around the Cape Horn to Boston in 1993. (Rev: BL 10/1/96; SLJ 11/96) [910.4]

## Self-Defense

**17663** Blot, Pierre. *Karate for Beginners* (5–8). Illus. 1996, Sterling $19.95 (0-8069-3874-9). 144pp. After interesting background information, important karate techniques are covered. (Rev: BL 8/96; SLJ 7/96) [796.8]

**17664** Casey, Kevin K. *Judo* (4–6). Illus. by Jean Dixon. Series: Illustrated History of Martial Arts. 1994, Rourke LB $14.95 (0-86593-369-3). 32pp. How-to information on judo is given, plus a fascinating history of this martial art. Also use, from the same series, *Kung Fu* and *Tae Kwon Do* (both 1997). (Rev: SLJ 1/95) [796.8]

**17665** Leder, Jane M. *Karate* (3–5). Illus. 1992, Bancroft-Sage LB $14.95 (0-944280-34-X); paper $5.95 (0-944280-39-0). 47pp. Some topics covered are the history of karate, basic stances, kicks and punches, and different kinds of competitions. (Rev: SLJ 10/92) [796.8]

**17666** Mitchell, David. *The Young Martial Arts Enthusiast* (5–8). Photos by Andy Crawford. 1997, DK Publg. $15.95 (0-7894-1508-9). 64pp. Double-page spreads and plenty of full-color photos are used in this history of the martial arts, which explains how to perform various stances and self-defense techniques. (Rev: SLJ 7/97) [796.8]

**17667** Morris, Ann. *Karate Boy* (K–3). Illus. 1996, Dutton paper $15.99 (0-525-45337-7). 32pp. A visit to David's karate class is used as an opportunity to explain the basics of this sport. (Rev: BCCB 9/96; BL 8/96; SLJ 8/96) [796.815]

**17668** Rafkin, Louise. *The Tiger's Eye, the Bird's Fist: A Beginner's Guide to the Martial Arts* (4–7).

Illus. 1997, Little, Brown paper $12.95 (0-316-73464-0). 144pp. Short articles cover such topics as the history of the martial arts, lore and legends associated with them, techniques, and several biographical profiles of important people in the field. (Rev: BL 6/1–15/97; SLJ 7/97) [796.8]

## Snowboarding

**17669** Brimner, Larry Dane. *Snowboarding* (4–6). Illus. Series: First Books. 1997, Watts LB $21.00 (0-531-20313-1). 64pp. Introduces the sport of snowboarding, its equipment, clothing, rules, techniques, and competitions. (Rev: BL 11/1/97; SLJ 2/98) [796.9]

**17670** Iguchi, Bryan. *The Young Snowboarder* (5–8). Illus. 1997, DK Publg. $15.95 (0-7894-2062-7). 37pp. Using middle-schoolers as models in the photos, this account describes basic skills, equipment, and techniques plus material on freestyle riding and slalom racing. (Rev: BL 11/15/97; SLJ 2/98) [796.1]

**17671** Jensen, Julie, adapt. *Beginning Snowboarding* (4–8). Photos by Jimmy Clarke. Illus. Series: Beginning Sports. 1996, Lerner LB $21.27 (0-8225-3507-6). 64pp. Snowboarding is introduced, with material on equipment, basic maneuvers, types of competitions, and advanced stunts. (Rev: SLJ 3/96) [796.9]

**17672** Lurie, John. *Fundamental Snowboarding* (4–8). Photos by Jimmy Clarke. Illus. Series: Fudamental Sports. 1996, Lerner LB $21.27 (0-8225-3457-6). 64pp. With eye-catching photos, the equipment and principles of snowboarding are covered, with material on basic and advanced maneuvers, skills, and stunts. (Rev: SLJ 3/96) [796.9]

**17673** Sullivan, George. *Snowboarding: A Complete Guide for Beginners* (4–6). Illus. 1997, Penguin paper $5.99 (0-14-056181-1). 48pp. A complete manual to snowboarding, a new sport that gained Olympic status in 1998. (Rev: BL 1/1–15/97; SLJ 3/97) [796.9]

## Soccer

**17674** Fischer, George. *The Illustrated Laws of Soccer* (3–5). Illus. 1994, Ideals paper $6.95 (1-57102-020-9). 32pp. The history, equipment, field, and rules of soccer are given. (Rev: BL 9/15/94; SLJ 11/94) [796.334]

**17675** Goodman, Michael. *The World Cup* (4–6). Illus. Series: Great Moments in Sports. 1991, Creative Ed. $12.95 (0-88682-320-X). 32pp. This heavily illustrated brief account describes the history and present status of this important international soccer event. (Rev: BL 1/1/92) [796.334]

**17676** Howard, Dale E. *Soccer Around the World* (3–6). Illus. 1994, Children's LB $22.00 (0-516-08046-6). 48pp. This introduction to soccer describes its history and how it is played around the world, including in the United States. (Rev: BL 9/1/94) [796.334]

**17677** Howard, Dale E. *Soccer Stars* (3–6). Illus. 1994, Children's LB $22.00 (0-516-08047-4). 48pp. As well as introducing key U.S. players, this account includes a glossary of soccer terms. (Rev: BL 9/1/94) [796.334]

**17678** Lineker, Gary. *The Young Soccer Player* (2–5). Illus. 1994, DK Publg. $9.95 (1-56458-592-1). 32pp. A seasoned soccer player gives a good introduction to the sport, many useful tips for beginners, and techniques for improving one's game. (Rev: BL 7/94; SLJ 7/94) [796.334]

## Swimming and Diving

**17679** Barrett, Norman. *Scuba Diving* (3–5). Illus. 1989, Watts LB $20.00 (0-531-10631-4). 32pp. Many illustrations highlight this introduction. (Rev: BL 4/15/89)

**17680** Rouse, Jeff. *The Young Swimmer* (3–6). Illus. 1997, DK Publg. $15.95 (0-7894-1533-X). 37pp. An illustrated introduction to swimming that provides history, techniques, and a rundown on various strokes. (Rev: BL 8/97; SLJ 2/98) [797.2]

## Tennis

**17681** Gilbert, Nancy. *Wimbledon* (4–6). Illus. Series: Great Moments in Sports. 1991, Creative Ed. LB $14.95 (0-88682-319-6). 32pp. This brief history of the famous tennis tournament in England highlights some of the major players. (Rev: BL 1/1/92) [796.342]

**17682** Tym, Wanda. *The Illustrated Rules of Tennis* (3–5). Illus. Series: Illustrated Sports. 1995, Ideals paper $6.95 (1-57102-016-0). 32pp. Such topics as equipment, the tennis court, scoring, and the rules are covered in this introduction to tennis. (Rev: BL 7/95; SLJ 6/95) [796.342]

**17683** Vicario, Arantxa S. *The Young Tennis Player* (4–6). Illus. 1996, DK Publg. $15.95 (0-7894-0473-7). 45pp. Different types of play, tennis techniques, and warm-up exercises are covered in text and striking illustrations. (Rev: BL 5/1/96; SLJ 6/96) [796.342]

## Track and Field

**17684** Jackson, Colin. *The Young Track and Field Athlete* (4–7). Illus. 1996, DK Publg. $15.95 (0-7894-0855-4); paper $9.95 (0-7894-0474-5). 32pp. Each track and field event is explained thoroughly in text and pictures, with tips on techniques and conditioning exercises. (Rev: BL 4/15/96; SLJ 8/96) [796.42]

# Author Index

Authors are arranged alphabetically by last name. Authors' and joint authors' names are followed by book titles — which are also arranged alphabetically — and the text entry number. Book titles may refer to those that appear as a main entry or as an internal entry in the text. All fiction titles are indicated by (F), following the entry number.

*West Indian Americans*, 14025

Bang, Molly. *Chattanooga Sludge*, 13611
  *Common Ground*, 3536(F)
  *Dawn*, 8822
  *Delphine*, 759(F)
  *Goose*, 1394(F)
  *The Grey Lady and the Strawberry Snatcher*, 687(F)
  *One Fall Day*, 760(F)
  *The Paper Crane*, 761(F)
  *Ten, Nine, Eight*, 294(F)
  *Wiley and the Hairy Man*, 9315
  *Yellow Ball*, 2395(F)
Bangura, Abdul Karim. *Kipsigis*, 12097
Banim, Lisa. *American Dreams*, 3745(F)
  *Drums at Saratoga*, 7589(F)
  *The Hessian's Secret Diary*, 7590(F)
  *A Spy in the King's Colony*, 7591(F)
Banish, Roslyn. *A Forever Family*, 14119
Banks, Jacqueline T. *Egg-Drop Blues*, 7347(F)
  *The New One*, 7347(F)
  *Project Wheels*, 7347(F)
Banks, Kate. *Alphabet Soup*, 762(F)
  *And If the Moon Could Talk*, 463(F)
  *Baboon*, 4207(F)
  *Spider Spider*, 763(F)
Banks, Lynne Reid. *Angela and Diabola*, 6241(F)
  *The Fairy Rebel*, 8506(F)
  *Harry the Poisonous Centipede*, 6242(F)
  *The Indian in the Cupboard*, 6243(F)
  *The Mystery of the Cupboard*, 6244(F)
  *The Return of the Indian*, 6245(F)
  *The Secret of the Indian*, 6246(F)
Banks, Merry. *Animals of the Night*, 4208
Banks, Sara H. *A Net to Catch Time*, 3746(F)
  *Under the Shadow of Wings*, 7855(F)
Bannan, Jan G. *Letting off Steam*, 16111
Bannatyne-Cugnet, Jo. *A Prairie Year*, 16308
Bannerman, Helen. *Little Black Sambo*, 764(F)
  *The Story of Little Babaji*, 764(F)
Bantle, Lee F. *Diving for the Moon*, 7348(F)
Bany-Winters, Lisa. *On Stage*, 11663
Banyai, Istvan. *Re-Zoom*, 16599
  *REM*, 765(F)
  *Zoom*, 688(F)
Baquedano, Elizabeth. *Aztec, Inca and Maya*, 12614
Baralt, Luis A. *Turkey*, 12357
Barasch, Lynne. *Rodney's Inside Story*, 1395(F)
Barber, Antonia. *Catkin*, 8507
  *The Enchanter's Daughter*, 766(F)
  *The Ghosts*, 6247(F)
  *The Mousehole Cat*, 1396(F)
  *Shoes of Satin, Ribbons of Silk*, 11626
Barber, Barbara E. *Allie's Basketball Dream*, 2396(F)
  *Saturday at The New You*, 2397(F)
Barber, Nicola. *The Search for Gold*, 11839
  *The Search for Lost Cities*, 11819
  *The Search for Sunken Treasure*, 11820
Barber, Phyllis. *Legs*, 5829(F)

Barbosa, Rogerio Andrade. *African Animal Tales*, 8684
Barbot, Daniel. *A Bicycle for Rosaura*, 1397(F)
Barbour, Karen. *Little Nino's Pizzeria*, 2797(F)
  *Mr. Bow Tie*, 4003(F)
Barden, Renardo. *Gangs*, 13686
Bare, Colleen S. *Never Grab a Deer by the Ear*, 15250
  *Never Kiss an Alligator!* 14924
  *Sammy, Dog Detective*, 15848
  *Toby the Tabby Kitten*, 15831
Barish, Wendy (jt. author). *The French Resistance*, 12052
Barker, Margot. *What Is Martin Luther King, Jr. Day?* 4600
Barker, Marjorie. *Magical Hands*, 4644(F)
Barkhausen, Annette. *Penguins*, 15434
  *Rabbits and Hares*, 15290
Barkin, Carol. *The Holiday Handbook*, 13894
  *Jobs for Kids*, 13555
  *The New Complete Babysitter's Handbook*, 13556
Barkin, Carol (jt. author). *How to Be School Smart*, 14098
  *How to Write a Great School Report*, 11468
  *How to Write Your Best Book Report*, 11469
  *Sincerely Yours*, 11470
  *Social Smarts*, 14115
Barklem, Jill. *Autumn Story*, 3537(F)
Barmeier, Jim. *The Brain*, 14441
Barner, Bob. *Dem Bones*, 14492
Barnes, Joyce Annette. *The Baby Grand, the Moon in July, and Me*, 6052(F)
  *Promise Me the Moon*, 7097(F)
Barnes-Murphy, Frances. *The Fables of Aesop*, 9061
Barnes-Svarney, Patricia L. *Born of Heat and Pressure*, 16112
Baroin, Catherine. *Tubu*, 12098
Baron, Alan. *Red Fox and the Baby Bunnies*, 1398(F)
  *The Red Fox Monster*, 1399(F)
Baron, Nancy. *Getting Started in Calligraphy*, 17105
Barracca, Debra. *The Adventures of Taxi Dog*, 1400(F)
  *Maxi, the Hero*, 1401(F)
  *Maxi, the Star*, 1402(F)
  *A Taxi Dog Christmas*, 4694(F)
Barracca, Sal (jt. author). *The Adventures of Taxi Dog*, 1400(F)
  *Maxi, the Hero*, 1401(F)
  *Maxi, the Star*, 1402(F)
  *A Taxi Dog Christmas*, 4694(F)
Barraclough, John. *Mohandas Gandhi*, 11227
  *Mother Teresa*, 11270
Barrett, John M. *Daniel Discovers Daniel*, 2798(F)
Barrett, Judith. *Animals Should Definitely Not Act Like People*, 3276(F)
  *Animals Should Definitely Not Wear Clothing*, 3276(F)
  *Benjamin's 365 Birthdays*, 4645(F)
  *Cloudy with a Chance of Meatballs*, 767(F)
  *Pickles to Pittsburgh*, 768(F)

*When Clay Sings*, 11344

Baynes, Pauline, ed. *Thanks Be to God*, 14006

Baynton, Martin. *Why Do You Love Me?* 2801(F)

Bazilian, Barbara. *The Red Shoes*, 8508(F)

Beach, Milo Cleveland. *The Adventures of Rama*, 8804

Bealer, Alex W. *Only the Names Remain*, 12822

Beales, Valerie. *Emma and Freckles*, 5832(F)

Bean, Suzanne M. (jt. author). *Girls and Young Women Inventing*, 16688

*Girls and Young Women Leading the Way*, 13762

Beard, D. C. *The American Boys' Handy Book*, 17059

Beard, Darleen Bailey. *The Flimflam Man*, 7976(F)

*The Pumpkin Man from Piney Creek*, 4880(F)

Beaton, Clare. *Masks*, 17136

Beaton, Margaret. *Senegal*, 12170

Beattie, Owen. *Buried in Ice*, 12582

Beatty, Patricia. *Sarah and Me and the Lady from the Sea*, 7776(F)

*Who Comes with Cannons?* 7752(F)

Beatty, Terry (jt. author). *ElfQuest*, 6523(F)

Beaty, Dave. *Moths and Butterflies*, 15561

*Waterfowl*, 15390

Beaude, Pierre-Marie. *The Book of Creation*, 13825

Beaudry, Jo. *Carla Goes to Court*, 13638

Bechard, Margaret. *My Mom Married the Principal*, 6055(F)

*My Sister, My Science Report*, 8199(F)

*Really No Big Deal*, 7099(F)

*Star Hatchling*, 8318(F)

Beck, Ian. *Emily and the Golden Acorn*, 773(F)

*Peter and the Wolf*, 9081

Becker, Bonny. *The Quiet Way Home*, 3541(F)

Beckett, Wendy. *A Child's Book of Prayer in Art*, 14007

*The Duke and the Peasant*, 11347

Becklake, Sue. *Space, Stars, Planets and Spacecraft*, 16626

Becnel, Barbara Cottman (jt. author). *Gangs and Drugs*, 13710

Bedard, Michael. *The Divide*, 10232

*Emily*, 6808(F)

*Glass Town*, 11452

Beh-Eger, Dorita (jt. author). *I Heal*, 14352

Behan, Brendan. *The King of Ireland's Son*, 8960

Behn, Harry. *Trees*, 3542

Behrens, June. *Fiesta!* 2802(F)

*Gung Hay Fat Choy*, 13896

*Missions of the Central Coast*, 13421

Behrman, Carol H. *Fiddler to the World*, 10196

Beil, Karen M. *Grandma According to Me*, 2803(F)

Beirne, Barbara. *Children of the Ecuadorean Highlands*, 12689

Beisner, Monika. *Monika Beisner's Book of Riddles*, 17328

Bell, Anthea. *Jack in Luck*, 8899

*Swan Lake*, 11627

Bell, Lili. *The Sea Maidens of Japan*, 3750(F)

Bell, Neill. *The Book of Where*, 11669

*Only Human*, 14093

Bell, Robert A. (jt. author). *My First Book About Space*, 14751

Bellairs, John. *The Curse of the Blue Figurine*, 6259(F)

*The Doom of the Haunted Opera*, 6264(F)

*The Drum, the Doll, and the Zombie*, 5484(F)

*The Figure in the Shadows*, 6260(F)

*The Ghost in the Mirror*, 6261(F)

*The House with a Clock in Its Walls*, 6260(F)

*The Letter, the Witch and the Ring*, 6260(F)

*The Mansion in the Mist*, 6262(F)

*The Mummy, the Will, and the Crypt*, 6259(F)

*The Secret of the Underground Room*, 5483(F)

*The Spell of the Sorcerer's Skull*, 6259(F)

*The Vengeance of the Witch-Finder*, 6263(F)

Bellamy, David. *The Forest*, 16232

*The Rock Pool*, 16289

Beller, Susan P. *Cadets at War*, 13183

Belloc, Hilaire. *Jim, Who Ran Away from His Nurse, and Was Eaten by a Lion*, 7977(F)

Bellows, Cathy. *The Grizzly Sisters*, 1405(F)

Bellville, Cheryl Walsh. *The Airplane Book*, 16716

*Flying in a Hot Air Balloon*, 17473

*Rodeo*, 17474

Belpré, Pura. *Firefly Summer*, 7523(F)

Belton, Sandra. *Ernestine and Amanda*, 6809(F)

*Ernestine and Amanda: Summer Camp, Ready or Not!* 6810(F)

*May'naise Sandwiches and Sunshine Tea*, 3169(F)

*Members of the C.L.U.B*, 6811(F)

Bemelmans, Ludwig. *Madeline*, 3751(F)

*Madeline and the Bad Hat*, 3752(F)

*Madeline and the Gypsies*, 3752(F)

*Madeline in London*, 3752(F)

*Madeline's Christmas*, 4695(F)

*Madeline's Rescue*, 3752(F)

Ben-Ezer, Ehud. *Hosni the Dreamer*, 9170

Benagh, Jim. *Sports Great Herschel Walker*, 11105

Benchley, Nathaniel. *George the Drummer Boy*, 3753(F)

*A Ghost Named Fred*, 5062(F)

*Oscar Otter*, 5063(F)

*Red Fox and His Canoe*, 5064(F)

*Sam the Minuteman*, 3754(F)

*The Strange Disappearance of Arthur Cluck*, 5064(F)

Bender, Lionel. *Invention*, 16672

Bender, Robert. *The A to Z Beastly Jamboree*, 296(F)

*A Most Unusual Lunch*, 1406(F)

*Toads and Diamonds*, 8509

Bendick, Jeanne. *Comets and Meteors*, 14744

*Egyptian Tombs*, 11871

*Eureka! It's an Automobile!* 16889

*Eureka! It's Television!* 16863

*Exploring an Ocean Tide Pool*, 15618

*Markets*, 13548

*Moons and Rings*, 14745

*The Planets*, 14708

*The Stars*, 14770

*The Sun*, 14791

Breese, Gillian. *The Amazing Adventures of Teddy Tum Tum*, 1432(F)

Breitenbucher, Cathy. *Bonnie Blair*, 11143

Brennan, Herbie. *The Mystery Machine*, 8319(F)

Brennan, Linda Crotta. *Flannel Kisses*, 2418(F)

Brenner, Anita. *The Boy Who Could Do Anything and Other Mexican Folk Tales*, 9400

Brenner, Barbara. *Annie's Pet*, 5079(F)

  *Beavers Beware!* 5078(F)

  *Chibi*, 4217

  *The Color Wizard*, 5079(F)

  *Group Soup*, 1433(F)

  *If You Were There in 1492*, 12974

  *If You Were There in 1776*, 13053

  *Moon Boy*, 5080(F)

  *Planetarium*, 16631

  *Thinking About Ants*, 15538

  *Two Orphan Cubs*, 4216(F)

  *Wagon Wheels*, 5081(F)

  *Where's That Insect?* 15489

  *Where's That Reptile?* 14907

Brenner, Barbara, ed. *The Earth Is Painted Green*, 9857

Brenner, Martha. *Abe Lincoln's Hat*, 10672

Brent, Isabelle. *The Christmas Story*, 13939

Breslow, Susan. *I Really Want a Dog*, 4218(F)

Bresnick-Perry, Roslyn. *Leaving for America*, 3763

Brett, Jan. *Annie and the Wild Animals*, 1434(F)

  *Armadillo Rodeo*, 1435(F)

  *Berlioz Bear*, 1436(F)

  *Christmas Trolls*, 4699(F)

  *Comet's Nine Lives*, 1437(F)

  *Fritz and the Beautiful Horses*, 1438(F)

  *The Hat*, 1439(F)

  *The Mitten*, 8867

  *Town Mouse, Country Mouse*, 1440(F)

  *Trouble with Trolls*, 787(F)

  *The Wild Christmas Reindeer*, 4700(F)

Brett, Jan, reteller. *Beauty and the Beast*, 8881

Brewster, Hugh. *Anastasia's Album*, 12460

Brewster, Patience. *Rabbit Inn*, 1441(F)

Brewton, Sara, ed. *Of Quarks, Quasars and Other Quirks*, 9788

Bridgman, Roger. *Electronics*, 16839

  *Technology*, 16845

Bridwell, Norman. *Clifford at the Circus*, 1442(F)

  *Clifford Goes to Hollywood*, 1442(F)

  *Clifford Takes a Trip*, 1442(F)

  *Clifford the Big Red Dog*, 1442(F)

  *Clifford the Small Red Puppy*, 1442(F)

  *Clifford's Good Deeds*, 1442(F)

  *Clifford's Halloween*, 4881(F)

  *Clifford's Tricks*, 1442(F)

Briggs, Carole S. *Women in Space*, 16632

Briggs, Katharine. *An Encyclopedia of Fairies, Hobgoblins, Brownies, Bogies, and Other Supernatural Creatures*, 8961

Briggs, Raymond. *The Bear*, 788(F)

  *Father Christmas*, 4701(F)

  *Jim and the Beanstalk*, 789(F)

  *The Man*, 6814(F)

  *The Snowman*, 691(F)

Briggs-Bunting, Jane. *Laddie of the Light*, 5835(F)

Bright, Robert. *Georgie*, 790(F)

  *Georgie and the Robbers*, 790(F)

Brill, Marlene T. *Allen Jay and the Underground Railroad*, 5082(F)

  *Building the Capital City*, 13352

  *Diary of a Drummer Boy*, 7753(F)

  *Guatemala*, 12655

  *Guyana*, 12693

  *Illinois*, 13266

  *Indiana*, 13267

  *James Buchanan*, 10620

  *John Adams*, 10615

  *Journey for Peace*, 11253

  *Let Women Vote!* 13646

  *Mongolia*, 12271

Brillhart, Julie. *The Dino Expert*, 3286(F)

  *When Daddy Came to School*, 2819(F)

  *When Daddy Took Us Camping*, 2297(F)

Brimner, Larry Dane. *Bobsledding and the Luge*, 17476

  *E-Mail*, 16818

  *If Dogs Had Wings*, 1443(F)

  *Merry Christmas, Old Armadillo*, 4702(F)

  *A Migrant Family*, 13749

  *Mountain Biking*, 17585

  *Polar Mammals*, 15087

  *Rock Climbing*, 17477

  *Rolling . . . In-Line!* 17478

  *Snowboarding*, 17669

  *Speed Skating*, 17634

  *Unusual Friendships*, 14808

  *The Winter Olympics*, 17648

Brinckloe, Julie. *Fireflies!* 3547(F)

Brink, Benjamin. *David's Story*, 14374

Brink, Carol Ryrie. *Caddie Woodlawn*, 6059(F)

Brinn, Ruth Esrig. *Jewish Holiday Crafts for Little Hands*, 13967

Brion, David (jt. author). *Space Vehicles*, 16657

Brisson, Pat. *Hot Fudge Hero*, 5083(F)

  *Kate Heads West*, 2419(F)

  *Kate on the Coast*, 2419(F)

  *The Summer My Father Was Ten*, 2420(F)

  *Wanda's Roses*, 2421(F)

Britt, Grant. *Charlie Sifford*, 11167

Brittain, Bill. *All the Money in the World*, 6279(F)

  *Devil's Donkey*, 6280(F)

  *Dr. Dredd's Wagon of Wonders*, 5490(F)

  *The Ghost from Beneath the Sea*, 6281(F)

  *The Mystery of the Several Sevens*, 6282(F)

  *Shape-Changer*, 8320(F)

  *Who Knew There'd Be Ghosts?* 5491(F)

  *Wings*, 6283(F)

  *The Wish Giver*, 6280(F)

Brock, Betty. *No Flying in the House*, 1444(F)

Brockman, Frank C. *Trees of North America*, 16027

Brodie, James Michael (jt. author). *Sweet Words So Brave*, 11458

*Someone Is Hiding on Alcatraz Island*, 5496(F)
*Summer Wheels*, 6815(F)
*Sunflower House*, 3553(F)
*Sunshine Home*, 2826(F)
*Train to Somewhere*, 7670(F)
*Trouble on the T-Ball Team*, 2299(F)
*A Turkey for Thanksgiving*, 5004(F)
*Twinnies*, 4020(F)
*The Valentine Bears*, 5022(F)
*The Wall*, 2827(F)
*The Wednesday Surprise*, 2828(F)
*Your Move*, 7111(F)
Bunting, Jane. *My First ABC*, 18(F)
Burandt, Harriet. *Tales from the Homeplace*, 7780(F)
Burbank, Jon. *Nepal*, 12273
Burby, Liza N. *The Pueblo Indians*, 12827
Burch, Joann J. *Chico Mendes*, 10884
  *A Fairy-Tale Life*, 10216
  *Fine Print*, 10861
  *Marian Wright Edelman*, 10746
Burch, Robert. *Christmas with Ida Early*, 7908(F)
  *Ida Early Comes over the Mountain*, 6060(F)
  *Queenie Peavy*, 7112(F)
Burckhardt, Ann L. (jt. author). *Cooking the Australian Way*, 17221
Burden-Patmon, Denise. *Imani's Gift at Kwanzaa*, 7909(F)
Burford, Betty. *Chocolate by Hershey*, 10532
Burger, Leslie. *Red Cross/Red Crescent*, 13642
  *Sister Cities in a World of Difference*, 11671
  *United Nations High Commission for Refugees*, 13643
Burgess, Gelett. *The Little Father*, 9789
Burgess, Jan. *Food and Digestion*, 14430
Burgess, Melvin. *The Cry of the Wolf*, 5840(F)
  *The Earth Giant*, 6288(F)
Burgess, Thornton W. *Old Mother West Wind*, 1477(F)
Burgie, Irving. *Caribbean Carnival*, 11501
Burke, Patrick. *Eastern Europe*, 12358
Burke, Timothy R. *Tugboats in Action*, 3767(F)
Burke-Weiner, Kimberly. *The Maybe Garden*, 2430(F)
Burleigh, Robert. *Black Whiteness*, 9971
  *Flight*, 10008
  *Hoops*, 9905
  *A Man Named Thoreau*, 10291
  *Who Said That?* 10315
Burnard, Damon. *Pork and Beef's Great Adventure*, 6289(F)
Burnett, Frances Hodgson. *A Little Princess*, 6061(F)
  *The Secret Garden*, 6816(F)
Burnford, Sheila. *The Incredible Journey*, 5841(F)
Burnham, Philip. *Gbaya*, 12100
Burnie, David. *Bird*, 15317
  *Flowers*, 15917
  *How Nature Works*, 14809
  *Light*, 16561
  *Mammals*, 14836
  *Plant*, 16058

*Tree*, 16028
Burnie, David (jt. author). *Birds*, 15311
Burningham, John. *Cloudland*, 802(F)
  *Come Away from the Water, Shirley*, 803(F)
  *Granpa*, 2829(F)
  *Hey!* 4232(F)
  *John Patrick Norman McHennessy — The Boy Who Was Always Late*, 804(F)
  *Mr. Gumpy's Motor Car*, 2300(F)
  *Mr. Gumpy's Outing*, 2300(F)
Burns, Andy (jt. author). *Home on the Range*, 17333
Burns, Bree. *Harriet Tubman*, 10453
Burns, Diane L. *Berries, Nuts and Seeds*, 16097
  *Cranberries*, 15949
  *Frogs, Toads and Turtles*, 14908
  *Home on the Range*, 17333
  *Sugaring Season*, 15950
Burns, Kate. *Hide and Seek*, 3554(F)
Burns, Khephra. *Black Stars in Orbit*, 16633
Burns, Marilyn. *The Book of Think (or How to Solve a Problem Twice Your Size)*, 17396
  *Good for Me!* 15998
  *The Greedy Triangle*, 805(F)
  *The Hanukkah Book*, 13968
  *How Many Feet? How Many Tails?* 308(F)
  *I Am Not a Short Adult*, 13647
  *The I Hate Mathematics! Book*, 16364
  *Math for Smarty Pants*, 16364
  *This Book Is About Time*, 16385
Burns, Peggy. *The Mail*, 13540
  *Money*, 13541
  *News*, 11455
  *Stores and Markets*, 13549
  *Travel*, 16877
  *Writing*, 11456
Burns, Ray (jt. author). *Draw Fifty Creepy Crawlies*, 17100
Burr, Claudia. *Broken Shields*, 12617
Burrell, Roy. *Oxford First Ancient History*, 11861
  *The Romans*, 11935
Burrows, William E. *Mission to Deep Space*, 16634
Bursell, Susan. *Haunted Houses*, 17419
Bursik, Rose. *Amelia's Fantastic Flight*, 806(F)
Burstein, Chaya M. *The Jewish Kids Catalog*, 13969
  *The Jewish Kids' Hebrew-English Wordbook*, 11416
Burton, Katherine. *One Gray Mouse*, 309
Burton, Marilee Robin. *My Best Shoes*, 2431(F)
Burton, Robert. *Egg*, 15078
Burton, Tim. *The Nightmare Before Christmas*, 7910(F)
Burton, Virginia Lee. *Katy and the Big Snow*, 4555(F)
  *Life Story*, 16113
  *The Little House*, 2432(F)
  *Mike Mulligan and His Steam Shovel*, 4555(F)
Buscaglia, Leo. *A Memory for Tino*, 6817(F)
Busch, Phyllis S. *Backyard Safaris*, 14810
Bush, John. *The Fish Who Could Wish*, 1478(F)
Bush, Lawrence. *Emma Ansky-Levine and Her Mitzvah Machine*, 6290(F)

*Ms. Moja Makes Beautiful Clothes,* 14176
*The Oneida,* 12839
*The Onondaga,* 12840
*The Penobscot,* 12841
*The Seneca,* 12842
*The Tuscarora,* 12843
*Who Keeps the Water Clean? Ms. Schindler!* 14237
Duvoisin, Roger. *Petunia,* 1588(F)
Dwight, Laura. *We Can Do It!* 14300
Dwyer, Kathleen M. *What Do You Mean I Have a Learning Disability?* 14301
*What Do You Mean I Have Attention Deficit Disorder?* 14302
Dwyer, Mindy. *Aurora,* 886(F)
Dwyer, Mindy, reteller. *Coyote in Love,* 9213
Dyer, Jane. *Animal Crackers,* 487(F)
Dygard, Thomas J. *Quarterback Walk-On,* 8441(F)
Dyson, John. *Westward with Columbus,* 12976


Eager, Edward. *Half Magic,* 6365(F)
*Knight's Castle,* 6363(F)
*Magic by the Lake,* 6364(F)
*Magic or Not?* 6365(F)
*Seven-Day Magic,* 6365(F)
*The Time Garden,* 6366(F)
*The Well Wishers,* 6366(F)
Eagle Walking Turtle. *Full Moon Stories,* 9214
Earl, Amanda. *Masks,* 17138
Earle, Ann. *Zipping, Zapping, Zooming Bats,* 15164
Early, Margaret. *Robin Hood,* 8978
*Sleeping Beauty,* 8884
*William Tell,* 8868
Early, Theresa S. *New Mexico,* 13522
Easley, Maryann. *I Am the Ice Worm,* 5537(F)
Eastman, David. *Story of Dinosaurs,* 11723
*What Is a Fish?* 15683
Eastman, P. D. *Are You My Mother?* 5140(F)
*The Cat in the Hat Beginner Book Dictionary,* 11420
Eastman, Patricia. *Sometimes Things Change,* 5141(F)
Easton, Patricia H. *A Week at the Fair,* 5538(F)
Easwaran, Eknath. *The Monkey and the Mango,* 3577(F)
Eaton, Deborah. *No One Told the Aardvark,* 887(F)
Eccleshare, Julia, ed. *First Poems,* 9538
Eckert, Allan W. *Incident at Hawk's Hill,* 5857(F)
Eckhouse, Morris. *Bob Feller,* 10977
Eckstein, Joan. *The Best Joke Book for Kids Number 4,* 17341
Edens, Cooper. *An ABC of Fashionable Animals,* 27(F)
*Favorite Fairy Tales,* 8518
*How Many Bears?* 327(F)
*Nicholi,* 4736(F)
*Santa Cows,* 4737(F)
Edens, Cooper (jt. author). *The Christmas We Moved to the Barn,* 4727(F)
Edmonds, I. G. *Ooka the Wise,* 8823

Edmonds, Walter. *The Matchlock Gun,* 7569(F)
Edmondson, Elizabeth. *The Trojan War,* 11918
Eduar, Gilles. *Jooka Saves the Day,* 1589(F)
Edwards, Chris. *The Young Inline Skater,* 17494
Edwards, Michelle. *A Baker's Portrait,* 4050(F)
*Eve and Smithy,* 3188(F)
Edwards, Pamela Duncan. *Barefoot,* 3788(F)
*Dinorella,* 1590(F)
*Four Famished Foxes and Fosdyke,* 1591(F)
*Livingstone Mouse,* 1592(F)
*Some Smug Slug,* 1593(F)
Edwards, Richard. *Fly with the Birds,* 2477(F)
*Moles Can Dance,* 1594(F)
*Moon Frog,* 9715
*Ten Tall Oaktrees,* 3578(F)
*You're Safe Now, Waterdog,* 2478(F)
Edwards, Roberta. *Five Silly Fishermen,* 5142(F)
Edwards, Roland. *Tigers,* 1595(F)
Egan, Robert. *From Wheat to Pasta,* 15955
Egan, Terry. *The Good Guys of Baseball,* 17545
*The Macmillan Book of Baseball Stories,* 17546
Egan, Tim. *Burnt Toast on Davenport Street,* 1596(F)
*Chestnut Cove,* 3325(F)
*Distant Feathers,* 888(F)
*Friday Night at Hodges' Cafe,* 1597(F)
*Metropolitan Cow,* 1598(F)
Egger-Bovet, Howard. *US Kids History,* 12995
Egger-Bovet, Howard (jt. author). *Book of the American Indians,* 12943
*Brown Paper School USKids History,* 13109
Egielski, Richard. *Buz,* 889(F)
*The Gingerbread Boy,* 8979
Ehlert, Lois. *Circus,* 2479
*Color Farm,* 217(F)
*Color Zoo,* 218(F)
*Cuckoo/Cucu,* 9405
*Eating the Alphabet,* 28(F)
*Feathers for Lunch,* 3579(F)
*Fish Eyes,* 328(F)
*Growing Vegetable Soup,* 2480(F)
*Hands,* 2481(F)
*Mole's Hill,* 1599(F)
*Moon Rope,* 9442
*Nuts to You!* 1600(F)
*Planting a Rainbow,* 2480(F)
*Red Leaf, Yellow Leaf,* 3580(F)
*Snowballs,* 17006(F)
*Under My Nose,* 10240
Ehrlich, Amy. *Leo, Zack, and Emmie,* 5143(F)
*Leo, Zack, and Emmie Together Again,* 5144(F)
*Lucy's Winter Tale,* 4051(F)
*Parents in the Pigpen, Pigs in the Tub,* 1601(F)
*The Story of Hanukkah,* 4954
Ehrlich, Amy, ed. *When I Was Your Age,* 10027
Ehrlich, Fred. *A Class Play with Ms. Vanilla,* 5145(F)
Eichenberg, Fritz. *Ape in a Cape,* 29(F)
Eisen, Armand, reteller. *Goldilocks and the Three Bears,* 8980
Eisenberg, Ann. *Bible Heroes I Can Be,* 13844

Gan, Delice. *Sweden*, 12494

Ganeri, Anita. *Birth and Growth*, 14391
  *Breathing*, 14455
  *Eating*, 14432
  *Exploration into India*, 12232
  *France*, 17008
  *How Would You Survive as an Ancient Roman?*
    11941
  *The Hunt for Food*, 14850
  *I Remember Bosnia*, 12365
  *I Remember China*, 12203
  *I Remember India*, 12233
  *I Remember Palestine*, 12569
  *I Wonder Why the Sea Is Salty*, 15769
  *India*, 12234
  *Insects*, 15499
  *Inside the Body*, 14392
  *The Kingfisher First Science Encyclopedia*, 14563
  *Moving*, 14495
  *Out of the Ark*, 13788
  *Plants*, 16065
  *Ponds and Pond Life*, 16291
  *Rivers, Ponds and Lakes*, 16292
  *The Search for Tombs*, 11825
  *Small Mammals*, 15098
  *The Story of Communications*, 16858
  *The Story of Maps and Navigation*, 11687
  *The Story of Numbers and Counting*, 16376
  *The Story of Time and Clocks*, 16386
  *The Story of Weights and Measures*, 16389
  *The Story of Writing and Printing*, 11391
  *Weather*, 16480
  *What Do We Know About Buddhism?* 13789
  *What Do We Know About Hinduism?* 13790
  *The Young Person's Guide to the Orchestra*, 11569

Ganeri, Anita (jt. author). *The Search for Sunken
    Treasure*, 11820

Gannett, Ruth. *The Dragons of Blueland*, 8046(F)
  *Elmer and the Dragon*, 8046(F)
  *My Father's Dragon*, 8046(F)

Gans, Roma. *How Do Birds Find Their Way?* 15329
  *Let's Go Rock Collecting*, 16326

Gantos, Jack. *Happy Birthday, Rotten Ralph*, 4659(F)
  *Heads or Tails*, 5555(F)
  *Heads or Tales*, 7526(F)
  *Jack's New Power*, 7526(F)
  *Not So Rotten Ralph*, 1639(F)
  *Rotten Ralph*, 1640(F)
  *Rotten Ralph's Rotten Christmas*, 4747(F)
  *Rotten Ralph's Rotten Romance*, 5026(F)
  *Rotten Ralph's Show and Tell*, 1641(F)
  *Rotten Ralph's Trick or Treat*, 4892(F)
  *Worse Than Rotten, Ralph*, 1640(F)

Gantschev, Ivan. *The Christmas Teddy Bear*, 4748(F)
  *Where Is Mr. Mole?* 1642(F)

Gao, R. L. *Adventures of Monkey King*, 8769(F)

Garassino, Alessandro. *Life*, 11805
  *Plants*, 16066

Garaway, Margaret K. *Ashkii and His Grandfather*,
    3802(F)

Garay, Luis. *The Long Road*, 3803(F)
  *Pedrito's Day*, 3804(F)

Garcia, Guy. *Spirit of the Maya*, 12658

Gardella, Tricia. *Casey's New Hat*, 2498(F)
  *Just Like My Dad*, 2499(F)

Garden, Nancy. *Fours Crossing*, 6385(F)
  *Mystery of the Secret Marks*, 6386(F)
  *Watersmeet*, 6385(F)

Gardiner, John Reynolds. *General Butterfingers*,
    5556(F)
  *Stone Fox*, 6001(F)
  *Top Secret*, 8047(F)

Gardner, Jane M. *Henry Moore*, 10099

Gardner, Martin. *Classic Brainteasers*, 17398
  *Perplexing Puzzles and Tantalizing Teasers*, 16365

Gardner, Richard A. *Boys and Girls Book About
    Divorce*, 14127
  *The Girls and Boys Book About Good and Bad
    Behavior*, 14095

Gardner, Robert. *Celebrating Earth Day*, 13907
  *Experiments with Balloons*, 16396
  *Experiments with Bubbles*, 16519
  *Experiments with Light and Mirrors*, 16566
  *Experiments with Motion*, 16520
  *The Forgotten Players*, 17548
  *Kitchen Chemistry*, 14592
  *Projects in Space Science*, 14593
  *Robert Gardner's Favorite Science Experiments*,
    14594
  *Science Around the House*, 14595
  *Science Project Ideas About Air*, 16395
  *Science Project Ideas About Animal Behavior*,
    15012
  *Science Project Ideas About Rain*, 16481
  *Science Project Ideas About the Moon*, 14700
  *Science Project Ideas About the Sun*, 16552
  *Science Project Ideas About Trees*, 16033
  *Science Projects About Electricity and Magnets*,
    16587
  *Science Projects About Light*, 16567
  *Science Projects About Temperature and Heat*,
    16554
  *Science Projects About the Human Body*, 14393

Garelick, May. *Look at the Moon*, 497(F)
  *What Makes a Bird a Bird?* 15330

Garelick, May (jt. author). *Two Orphan Cubs*,
    4216(F)

Garfield, James B. *Follow My Leader*, 7360(F)

Garland, Michael. *The Mouse Before Christmas*,
    4749(F)

Garland, Sarah. *Tex the Cowboy*, 8048(F)

Garland, Sherry. *Cabin 102*, 6387(F)
  *The Lotus Seed*, 6002(F)
  *The Silent Storm*, 5557(F)
  *The Summer Sands*, 2500(F)
  *Vietnam*, 12281

Garne, S. T. *One White Sail*, 338(F)

Garner, Alan. *Once upon a Time*, 8612

Garner, Alan, reteller. *The Little Red Hen*, 8989

Garrigue, Sheila. *The Eternal Spring of Mr. Ito*, 7864(F)

Garrison, Christian. *The Dream Eater*, 8824

Garrison, Susan. *How Emily Blair Got Her Fabulous Hair*, 3339(F)

Garwood, Val. *The World of the Pirate*, 11841

Garza, Hedda. *Frida Kahlo*, 10077

Gascoigne, Marc. *You Can Surf the Net!* 16820

Gaskin, Carol. *A Day in the Life of a Racing Car Mechanic*, 14181

Gates, Doris. *Blue Willow*, 6104(F)
  *A Fair Wind for Troy*, 9466
  *Lord of the Sky*, 9467
  *Mightiest of Mortals*, 9468
  *The Warrior Goddess*, 9469

Gates, Phil. *The History News*, 14364
  *Nature Got There First*, 14564

Gates, Richard. *Conservation*, 15459

Gatti, Anne, reteller. *The Magic Flute*, 11489

Gauch, Patricia L. *Aaron and the Green Mountain Boys*, 7599(F)
  *Bravo, Tanya*, 4057(F)
  *Christina Katerina and Fats and the Great Neighborhood War*, 3193(F)
  *Christina Katerina and the Great Bear Train*, 2892(F)
  *Christina Katerina and the Time She Quit the Family*, 2893(F)
  *Noah*, 13852
  *Tanya and Emily in a Dance for Two*, 3194(F)
  *Tanya and the Magic Wardrobe*, 2501(F)
  *Tanya Steps Out*, 2502(F)
  *This Time, Tempe Wick?* 7600(F)

Gauthier, Gail. *My Life Among the Aliens*, 8335(F)

Gay, Douglas. *The Not-So-Minor Leagues*, 17549

Gay, Kathlyn. *Civil War*, 13192
  *Emma Goldman*, 10751
  *Korean War*, 13247
  *Persian Gulf War*, 12527
  *Revolutionary War*, 13056
  *Spanish-American War*, 13224
  *They Don't Wash Their Socks!* 17498
  *Vietnam War*, 13248
  *War of 1812*, 13086
  *World War I*, 12009
  *World War II*, 12047

Gay, Kathlyn (jt. author). *The Not-So-Minor Leagues*, 17549

Gay, Marie-Louise. *Fat Charlie's Circus*, 3340(F)

Gay, Marie-Louise, adapt. *Rumpelstiltskin*, 8902

Gay, Martin (jt. author). *Civil War*, 13192
  *Emma Goldman*, 10751
  *Korean War*, 13247
  *Persian Gulf War*, 12527
  *Revolutionary War*, 13056
  *Spanish-American War*, 13224
  *Vietnam War*, 13248
  *War of 1812*, 13086
  *World War I*, 12009
  *World War II*, 12047

Gayle, Katie. *Snappy Jazzy Jewelry*, 17009

Geeslin, Campbell. *In Rosa's Mexico*, 919(F)

Gehret, Jeanne. *The Don't-Give-Up-Kid and Learning Differences*, 4058(F)

Geiger, John (jt. author). *Buried in Ice*, 12582

Geis, Jacqueline. *Where the Buffalo Roam*, 9869

Geiser, Franz (jt. author). *Penguins*, 15434
  *Rabbits and Hares*, 15290

Geisert, Arthur. *After the Flood*, 13853
  *The Etcher's Studio*, 920(F)
  *Oink*, 1643(F)
  *Oink Oink*, 698(F)
  *Pigs from A to Z*, 34(F)
  *Pigs from 1 to 10*, 339(F)
  *Roman Numerals I to MM*, 16377

Geisert, Arthur (jt. author). *Haystack*, 15933

Geisert, Bonnie. *Haystack*, 15933

Gelber, Carol. *Masks Tell Stories*, 11842

Gellman, Marc. *"Always Wear Clean Underwear!" and Other Ways Parents Say "I Love You,"* 14128
  *Does God Have a Big Toe?* 13854
  *God's Mailbox*, 13855
  *How Do You Spell God?* 13791

Gelman, Rita G. *Monkeys and Apes of the World*, 15148
  *Queen Esther Saves Her People*, 4956

Gennings, Sara. *The Atocha Treasure*, 15808

Gentieu, Penny. *Wow! Babies!* 2894(F)

Geoghegan, Adrienne. *Dogs Don't Wear Glasses*, 3341(F)

George, Dick. *Ruby*, 15266

George, Jean Craighead. *Animals Who Have Won Our Hearts*, 14851
  *Arctic Son*, 3805(F)
  *The Case of the Missing Cutthroats*, 5558(F)
  *The Cry of the Crow*, 5865(F)
  *Everglades*, 13483
  *The First Thanksgiving*, 13993
  *Julie*, 5559(F)
  *Julie of the Wolves*, 5560(F)
  *Julie's Wolf Pack*, 5561(F)
  *Look to the North*, 4294(F)
  *The Missing 'Gator of Gumbo Limbo*, 5562(F)
  *My Side of the Mountain*, 5563(F)
  *On the Far Side of the Mountain*, 5564(F)
  *One Day in the Alpine Tundra*, 16181
  *One Day in the Desert*, 16205
  *One Day in the Prairie*, 16310
  *One Day in the Tropical Rain Forest*, 16239
  *One Day in the Woods*, 16240(F)
  *The Summer of the Falcon*, 7167(F)
  *The Talking Earth*, 5565(F)
  *The Tarantula in My Purse*, 10246
  *There's an Owl in the Shower*, 5866(F)

George, Kristine O'Connell. *The Great Frog Race and Other Poems*, 9870

George, Lindsay Barrett. *Around the Pond*, 3595(F)
  *In the Snow*, 3596(F)
  *In the Woods*, 14852

George, Michael. *Antarctica*, 12750

Greenberg, Martin H., ed. *Great Writers and Kids Write Spooky Stories*, 6405(F)
  *A Newbery Christmas*, 7926(F)
  *A Newbery Halloween*, 5574(F)
  *A Newbery Zoo*, 8444(F)
Greenberg, Melanie H. *Aunt Lilly's Laundromat*, 3822(F)
  *Blessings*, 4960
Greenblatt, Miriam. *Franklin D. Roosevelt*, 10698
Greenburg, Dan. *Dr. Jekyll, Orthodontist*, 6406(F)
  *A Ghost Named Wanda*, 6407(F)
  *Great-Grandpa's in the Litter Box*, 6408(F)
  *I'm Out of My Body . . . Please Leave a Message*, 6406(F)
  *My Son, the Time Traveler*, 8340(F)
  *Through the Medicine Cabinet*, 6408(F)
  *Zap! I'm a Mind Reader*, 6407(F)
Greene, Bette. *Philip Hall Likes Me, I Reckon Maybe*, 6847(F)
Greene, Carol. *Austria*, 12367
  *Benjamin Franklin*, 10518
  *Caring for Our Air*, 13620
  *Caring for Our Animals*, 15460
  *Caring for Our Forests*, 16245
  *Caring for Our Land*, 13570
  *Caring for Our People*, 13636
  *Firefighters Fight Fires*, 14225
  *The Golden Locket*, 3348(F)
  *Hi, Clouds*, 5160(F)
  *Ice Is . . . Whee!* 5160(F)
  *The Jenny Summer*, 6848(F)
  *John Chapman*, 10493
  *John Muir*, 10887
  *John Philip Sousa*, 10147
  *Margaret Wise Brown*, 10227
  *Margarete Steiff*, 10123
  *Martin Luther King, Jr.*, 10400
  *Police Officers Protect People*, 14226
  *Rachel Carson*, 10813
  *Reading About the Grizzly Bear*, 15178
  *Reading About the River Otter*, 15698
  *Robert Louis Stevenson*, 10286
  *Roberto Clemente*, 10970
  *Shine, Sun!* 5160(F)
  *Thomas Jefferson*, 10656
  *Thurgood Marshall*, 10422
  *Veterinarians Help Animals*, 14255
  *Wolfgang Amadeus Mozart*, 10143
Greene, Constance C. *Beat the Turtle Drum*, 7183(F)
  *A Girl Called Al*, 6849(F)
  *Isabelle the Itch*, 8056(F)
Greene, Ellin. *Billy Beg and His Bull*, 8994
  *Ling-Li and the Phoenix Fairy*, 8770
Greene, Jacqueline D. *The Maya*, 12659
  *One Foot Ashore*, 7474(F)
Greene, Rhonda Gowler. *Barnyard Song*, 1661(F)
  *When a Line Bends . . . A Shape Begins*, 264(F)
Greene, Stephanie. *Owen Foote, Second Grade Strongman*, 8235(F)
  *Owen Foote, Soccer Star*, 8445(F)

Greenfield, Eloise. *Africa Dream*, 3823(F)
  *Big Friend, Little Friend*, 2517(F)
  *Childtimes*, 14045
  *Daddy and I*, 2517(F)
  *Daydreamers*, 940(F)
  *First Pink Light*, 2903(F)
  *For the Love of the Game*, 9906
  *Grandmama's Joy*, 2904(F)
  *Grandpa's Face*, 2905(F)
  *Honey, I Love*, 3196(F)
  *Honey, I Love, and Other Love Poems*, 9692
  *I Make Music*, 2517(F)
  *Koya DeLaney and the Good Girl Blues*, 6003(F)
  *Mary McLeod Bethune*, 10360
  *My Doll, Keshia*, 2517(F)
  *Nathaniel Talking*, 9693
  *Night on Neighborhood Street*, 2518(F)
  *On My Horse*, 3196(F)
  *Rosa Parks*, 10432
  *She Come Bringing Me That Little Baby Girl*, 2906(F)
  *Sister*, 6106(F)
  *Under the Sunday Tree*, 9551
  *William and the Good Old Days*, 2907(F)
Greenfield, Karen R. *Sister Yessa's Story*, 13858(F)
Greenfield, Monica. *Waiting for Christmas*, 4752(F)
Greenlaw, M. Jean. *Welcome to the Stock Show*, 15817
Greenstein, Elaine. *Mattie's Hats Won't Wear That!* 941(F)
  *Mrs. Rose's Garden*, 942(F)
Greenwald, Sheila. *Mariah Delany's Author-of-the-Month Club*, 8057(F)
  *My Fabulous New Life*, 7184(F)
  *Rosy Cole: She Grows and Graduates*, 8058(F)
  *Rosy Cole: She Walks in Beauty*, 8059(F)
Greenway, Shirley. *Dragons, Dolphins, and Dinosaurs*, 14853
Greenwood, Barbara. *Pioneer Crafts*, 17063
  *A Pioneer Sampler*, 12590
Greer, Gery. *Billy the Ghost and Me*, 5161(F)
  *Max and Me and the Time Machine*, 6409(F)
  *Max and Me and the Wild West*, 8341(F)
  *This Island Isn't Big Enough for the Four of Us!* 8060(F)
Greger, C. Shana. *Cry of the Benu Bird*, 8703
Greger, C. Shana, reteller. *The Fifth and Final Sun*, 9408
Gregg, Andy. *Great Rabbit and the Long-Tailed Wildcat*, 9237
Gregoire, Caroline. *Uglypuss*, 4302(F)
Gregory, Kristiana. *Across the Wide and Lonesome Prairie*, 7683(F)
  *Orphan Runaways*, 7791(F)
  *The Stowaway*, 7627(F)
  *The Winter of Red Snow*, 7601(F)
Gregory, Philippa. *Florizella and the Wolves*, 8524(F)
Gregory, Tony. *The Dark Ages*, 11862
Gregory, Valiska. *Kate's Giants*, 3824(F)
  *Looking for Angels*, 2519(F)

Hofer, Angelika. *The Lion Family Book*, 15205

Hoff, Carol. *Johnny Texas*, 7688(F)

Hoff, Mary. *Atmosphere*, 16397
 *Gloria Steinem*, 10789
 *Life on Land*, 15462
 *Our Endangered Planet: Groundwater*, 13622
 *Our Endangered Planet: Oceans*, 15773
 *Our Endangered Planet: Rivers and Lakes*, 16296

Hoff, Syd. *Albert the Albatross*, 5200(F)
 *Arturo's Baton*, 3360(F)
 *Barkley*, 5201(F)
 *Barney's Horse*, 5202(F)
 *Danny and the Dinosaur*, 5203(F)
 *Danny and the Dinosaur Go to Camp*, 5204(F)
 *Duncan the Dancing Duck*, 1715(F)
 *Grizzwold*, 5205(F)
 *Happy Birthday, Danny and the Dinosaur!* 5206(F)
 *The Lighthouse Children*, 5207(F)
 *Mrs. Brice's Mice*, 5208(F)
 *Sammy the Seal*, 5203(F)
 *Stanley*, 5209(F)
 *Where's Prancer?* 4765(F)

Hoffman, E. T. A. *The Nutcracker*, 8936
 *The Strange Child*, 8937

Hoffman, Mary. *Amazing Grace*, 6006(F)
 *An Angel Just Like Me*, 4766(F)
 *Boundless Grace*, 3839(F)
 *Earth, Fire, Water, Air*, 16123
 *The Four-Legged Ghosts*, 6439(F)
 *Henry's Baby*, 4074(F)

Hoffmeister, Donald F. (jt. author). *Mammals*, 14903

Hofsepian, Sylvia A. *Why Not?* 2550(F)

Hofsinde, Robert. *Indian Sign Language*, 11406

Hogan, Paula Z. *The Butterfly*, 15573

Hogrogian, Nonny. *The Cat Who Loved to Sing*, 1716(F)
 *The Contest*, 9092
 *The First Christmas*, 4767
 *Handmade Secret Hiding Places*, 17012
 *One Fine Day*, 8871

Holabird, Katharine. *Alexander and the Magic Boat*, 974(F)
 *Angelina and Alice*, 1717(F)
 *Angelina and the Princess*, 1718(F)
 *Angelina at the Fair*, 1717(F)
 *Angelina Ballerina*, 1719(F)
 *Angelina on Stage*, 1717(F)
 *Angelina's Baby Sister*, 1720(F)
 *Angelina's Christmas*, 4768(F)

Holcomb, Nan. *Andy Finds a Turtle*, 4075(F)
 *Danny and the Merry-Go-Round*, 4075(F)
 *How about a Hug*, 4075(F)

Holden, Dwight. *Grand-Gran's Best Trick*, 7196(F)

Holden, Robert. *The Pied Piper of Hamelin*, 8938

Holder, Heidi. *Carmine the Crow*, 1721(F)
 *Crows*, 359(F)

Holeman, Linda. *Promise Song*, 7397(F)

Holl, Kristi D. *First Things First*, 7197(F)
 *Hidden in the Fog*, 6998(F)
 *Just Like a Real Family*, 6117(F)

*No Strings Attached*, 6118(F)

Holland, Gini. *Airplanes*, 16726
 *The Empire State Building*, 13380
 *Nelson Mandela*, 11249
 *Nuclear Energy*, 16547
 *Photography*, 17318
 *Rosa Parks*, 10433
 *Telephones*, 16859

Holland, Isabelle. *The Journey Home*, 7689(F)
 *The Promised Land*, 7630(F)

Holland, Marion. *A Big Ball of String*, 5210(F)

Holler, Anne. *Pocahontas*, 10594

Holling, Holling C. *Minn of the Mississippi*, 14993
 *Paddle-to-the-Sea*, 12786
 *Pagoo*, 15629
 *Seabird*, 15417
 *Tree in the Trail*, 7690(F)

Hollyer, Belinda. *Stories from the Classical Ballet*, 11635

Holm, Anne. *North to Freedom*, 7870(F)

Holman, Felice. *Slake's Limbo*, 5607(F)

Holmes, Anita. *I Can Save the Earth*, 13572

Holmes, Barbara W. *Charlotte Shakespeare and Annie the Great*, 8240(F)
 *My Sister the Sausage Roll*, 6119(F)

Holmes, Burnham. *Paul Robeson*, 10203

Holmes, Pamela. *Alcohol*, 14270

Holmes, Richard. *Battle*, 16964

Holsonback, Anita. *Monkey See, Monkey Do*, 4324(F)

Holt, Denver W. (jt. author). *Owls*, 15429

Holtzman, Jon. *Samburu*, 12105

Holub, Joan. *Boo Who?* 4901(F)

Holyoke, Nancy. *Oops!* 14114

Honeycutt, Natalie. *The All New Jonah Twist*, 8241(F)
 *The Best-Laid Plans of Jonah Twist*, 8241(F)
 *Invisible Lissa*, 8242(F)
 *Josie's Beau*, 6862(F)
 *Twilight in Grace Falls*, 6999(F)

Hong, Lily T. *The Empress and the Silkworm*, 3840(F)
 *How the Ox Star Fell from Heaven*, 8773
 *Two of Everything*, 8774

Hoobler, Dorothy. *Florence Robinson*, 7797(F)
 *The Italian American Family Album*, 14047
 *Lost Civilizations*, 11827
 *Priscilla Foster*, 7573(F)
 *South American Portraits*, 11178

Hoobler, Dorothy (jt. author). *Sally Bradford*, 7758(F)

Hoobler, Thomas. *Sally Bradford*, 7758(F)

Hoobler, Thomas (jt. author). *Florence Robinson*, 7797(F)
 *The Italian American Family Album*, 14047
 *Priscilla Foster*, 7573(F)
 *South American Portraits*, 11178

Hooker, Ruth. *Matthew the Cowboy*, 975(F)

Hooks, William H. *The Ballad of Belle Dorcas*, 7631(F)
 *Circle of Fire*, 6007(F)

*The Growing Story*, 3636(F)
*A Hole Is to Dig*, 174(F)
*A Very Special House*, 4091(F)
Krautwurst, Terry (jt. author). *Kid Style Nature Crafts*, 17003
*Nature Crafts for Kids*, 17004
Krehbiel, Randy. *Little Bighorn*, 13149
Kreikemeier, Gregory Scott. *Come with Me to Africa*, 12093
Kreiner, Anna. *Let's Talk About Drug Abuse*, 14273
Kreisler, Ken (jt. author). *Citybook*, 2711(F)
*Faces*, 2712
*Nature Spy*, 3687
*Ocean Day*, 3688(F)
Krementz, Jill. *How It Feels to Be Adopted*, 14134
*How It Feels When a Parent Dies*, 14163
*How It Feels When Parents Divorce*, 14135
*A Visit to Washington, D.C.*, 13389
Krensky, Stephen. *Breaking into Print*, 11396
*Christopher Columbus*, 12978
*Four Against the Odds*, 10798
*Lionel and His Friends*, 5238(F)
*Lionel and Louise*, 5239(F)
*Lionel at Large*, 5240(F)
*Lionel in the Fall*, 5240(F)
*Lionel in the Spring*, 5241(F)
*My Teacher's Secret Life*, 4524(F)
*Striking It Rich*, 13150
*Who Really Discovered America?* 12979
*Witch Hunt*, 13022
Krensky, Stephen (jt. author). *Dinosaurs, Beware! A Safety Guide*, 2424(F)
*Perfect Pigs*, 1463(F)
Kress, Camille. *Tot Shabbat*, 4969(F)
Kress, Stephen W. *Project Puffin*, 15418
Kreutzer, Peter. *Little League's Official How-to-Play Baseball Handbook*, 17556
Krisher, Trudy. *Kathy's Hats*, 4092(F)
Krishnaswami, Uma. *The Broken Tusk*, 13798
*Stories of the Flood*, 8620
Kristy, Davida. *Coubertin's Olympics*, 17655
*George Balanchine*, 10157
Kroeber, Theodora. *A Green Christmas*, 4783(F)
*Ishi, Last of the Tribe*, 10583
Kroeger, Mary Kay. *Paperboy*, 3860(F)
Krohn, Katherine E. *Elvis Presley*, 10199
*Lucille Ball*, 10158
Kroll, Steven. *Andrew Wants a Dog*, 4347(F)
*The Big Bunny and the Magic Show*, 4869(F)
*The Biggest Pumpkin Ever*, 4912(F)
*By the Dawn's Early Light*, 11518
*The Candy Witch*, 1028(F)
*Ellis Island*, 12803
*Gone Fishing*, 2593(F)
*Happy Father's Day*, 4616(F)
*It's April Fools' Day!* 1825(F)
*It's Groundhog Day!* 4617(F)
*Lewis and Clark*, 10006
*Loose Tooth*, 1826(F)

*Mary McLean and the St. Patrick's Day Parade*, 4618(F)
*New Kid in Town*, 8456(F)
*Oh, What a Thanksgiving!* 5012(F)
*Patrick's Tree House*, 6879(F)
*The Pigrates Clean Up*, 1827(F)
*Pony Express!* 13151
*Queen of the May*, 8536(F)
*Santa's Crash-Bang Christmas*, 4784(F)
*The Tyrannosaurus Game*, 1029(F)
Kroll, Virginia. *Africa Brothers and Sisters*, 3861(F)
*Beginnings*, 2981(F)
*Butterfly Boy*, 2982(F)
*Can You Dance, Dalila?* 4093(F)
*A Carp for Kimiko*, 3862(F)
*Faraway Drums*, 1030(F)
*Fireflies, Peach Pies and Lullabies*, 4094(F)
*Hands!* 14398
*I Wanted to Know All About God*, 13799
*Masai and I*, 7422(F)
*Pink Paper Swans*, 3224(F)
*The Seasons and Someone*, 3637(F)
*Sweet Magnolia*, 3863(F)
*Wood-Hoopoe Willie*, 1031(F)
Kroninger, Stephen. *If I Crossed the Road*, 1032(F)
Krudop, Walter L. *Something Is Growing*, 1033(F)
Krueger, Richard. *The Dinosaurs*, 11738
Krull, Kathleen. *Bridges to Change*, 13489
*Lives of the Artists*, 10033
*Lives of the Athletes*, 10937
*Lives of the Musicians*, 10034
*Lives of the Writers*, 10035
*Maria Molina and the Days of the Dead*, 3864(F)
*One Nation, Many Tribes*, 12875
*V Is for Victory*, 12051
*Wilma Unlimited*, 11132
*Wish You Were Here*, 12804
Krull, Kathleen, ed. *Gonna Sing My Head Off!* 11519
*Songs of Praise*, 13800
Krumgold, Joseph. *. . . And Now Miguel*, 7225(F)
*Onion John*, 7225(F)
Krupinski, Loretta. *Into the Woods*, 14866
*Lost in the Fog*, 5633(F)
Krupp, E. C. *The Big Dipper and You*, 14780
*The Moon and You*, 14702
Kruusval, Catarina. *No Clothes Today!* 2594(F)
*Where's the Ball?* 2594(F)
Kuchalla, Susan. *All About Seeds*, 16100
*Bears*, 15181
*Birds*, 15340
Kudler, David. *The Seven Gods of Luck*, 8831
Kudlinski, Kathleen V. *Animal Tracks and Traces*, 15020
*Facing West*, 7699(F)
*Night Bird*, 7554(F)
*Pearl Harbor Is Burning!* 7874(F)
*Rachel Carson*, 10816
*Shannon*, 7809(F)
*Shannon, Lost and Found*, 7810(F)
Kudrna, C. Imbior. *To Bathe a Boa*, 1828(F)

Lehrman, Robert. *The Store That Mama Built*, 7814(F)

Lehtinen, Ritva. *The Grandchildren of the Incas*, 12713

Lehu, Pierre A. (jt. author). *Dr. Ruth Talks About Grandparents*, 14154

Leigh, Nila K. *Learning to Swim in Swaziland*, 12151

Leigh, Tom. *The Sesame Street Word Book*, 11431

Leighton, Audrey O. *A Window of Time*, 2990(F)

Leighton, Maxinne R. *An Ellis Island Christmas*, 4787(F)

Leitch, Patricia. *Cross-Country Gallop*, 5922(F)
*Pony Club Rider*, 5923(F)

Leland, Dorothy K. *Sallie Fox*, 7706(F)

Lelooska, Chief. *Echoes of the Elders*, 9249

Lember, Barbara Hirsch. *A Book of Fruit*, 15991
*The Shell Book*, 15728

LeMieux, A. C. *Dare to Be, M.E.!* 7227(F)
*Fruit Flies, Fish and Fortune Cookies*, 7228(F)

Lemieux, Margo. *The Fiddle Ribbon*, 2991(F)

Lemieux, Michele. *Peter and the Wolf*, 9099

Lemke, Nancy. *Missions of the Southern Coast*, 13441

L'Engle, Madeleine. *Meet the Austins*, 6140(F)
*A Ring of Endless Light*, 8354(F)
*A Swiftly Tilting Planet*, 8354(F)
*The Twenty-Four Days Before Christmas*, 7941(F)
*Wind in the Door*, 8354(F)
*A Wrinkle in Time*, 8354(F)

Lenski, Lois. *Strawberry Girl*, 7815(F)

Lent, Blair. *Bayberry Bluff*, 2600(F)
*Molasses Flood*, 1049(F)

Leon, George D. *Explorers of the Americas Before Columbus*, 12980

Leon, Sharon (jt. author). *Sir Isaac Newton*, 10894
*Thurgood Marshall*, 10423

Leon, Vicki. *Outrageous Women of Ancient Times*, 11179

Lepthien, Emilie U. *Buffalo*, 15110
*The Cherokee*, 12882
*The Choctaw*, 12883
*Coyotes*, 15230
*Ecuador*, 12714
*Foxes*, 15232
*Giraffes*, 15278
*Greenland*, 12501
*Grizzlies*, 15182
*Iceland*, 12502
*Koalas*, 15281
*Llamas*, 15111
*Luxembourg*, 12452
*Manatees*, 15703
*The Mandans*, 12884
*Monarch Butterflies*, 15576
*Ostriches*, 15342
*Otters*, 15704
*Penguins*, 15440
*Peru*, 12715
*The Philippines*, 12344
*Polar Bears*, 15183

*Reindeer*, 15257
*Sea Turtles*, 14994
*The Seminole*, 12885
*Skunks*, 15112
*South Dakota*, 13325
*Tropical Rain Forests*, 16255
*Walruses*, 15705
*Wetlands*, 16186
*Wolves*, 15231
*Woodchucks*, 15296

Lepthien, Emilie U. (jt. author). *Recycling*, 13601

Lerman, Rory S. *Charlie's Checklist*, 1843(F)

Lerner, Carol. *Backyard Birds of Summer*, 15343
*Backyard Birds of Winter*, 15344
*Cactus*, 16076
*My Backyard Garden*, 17286

Leroe, E. W. *Hairy Horror*, 6526(F)
*Monster Vision*, 6526(F)
*Nasty the Snowman*, 6526(F)
*Pizza Zombies*, 6526(F)

Leroe, Ellen. *Ghost Dog*, 6527(F)
*H.O.W.L. High*, 6528(F)
*Racetrack Robbery*, 5641(F)

Leroux, Gaston. *The Phantom of the Opera*, 5642(F)

LeShan, Eda. *Learning to Say Good-bye*, 14164
*When Grownups Drive You Crazy*, 14137

Le Sieg, Theo. *Eye Book*, 5246(F)
*I Wish That I Had Duck Feet*, 5246(F)
*Ten Apples Up on Top*, 5246(F)
*Wacky Wednesday*, 374(F)

Lesinski, Jeanne M. *Exotic Invaders*, 14870

Leslie, Clare W. *Nature All Year Long*, 14817

Leslie-Melville, Betty. *Walter Warthog*, 15113

Lessem, Don. *Bigger Than T. Rex*, 11744
*Dinosaur Worlds*, 11745
*The Iceman*, 11832
*Jack Horner*, 10868
*Ornithomimids*, 11746
*Raptors!* 11747
*Seismosaurus*, 11748
*Supergiants!* 11749
*Troodon*, 11750

Lessem, Don (jt. author). *Digging Up Tyrannosaurus Rex*, 11737

Lesser, Carolyn. *Dig Hole, Soft Mole*, 4350(F)
*The Goodnight Circle*, 528(F)
*Great Crystal Bear*, 4351(F)
*Storm on the Desert*, 16210
*What a Wonderful Day to Be a Cow*, 3642(F)

Lester, Alison. *Alice and Aldo*, 59(F)
*Clive Eats Alligators*, 2601(F)
*Isabella's Bed*, 1050(F)
*The Journey Home*, 1051(F)
*My Farm*, 3869
*Tessa Snaps Snakes*, 3227(F)
*When Frank Was Four*, 2602(F)
*Yikes!* 2335(F)

Lester, Helen. *Author*, 10261
*It Wasn't My Fault*, 3380(F)
*Listen, Buddy*, 1844(F)

*Dakota Spring*, 7708(F)
*My Lone Star Summer*, 7237(F)
Loveday, John. *Goodbye, Buffalo Sky*, 7709(F)
Lovelace, Maud H. *Betsy and Tacy Go Downtown*, 8267(F)
*Betsy and Tacy Go over the Big Hill*, 8267(F)
*Betsy in Spite of Herself*, 8267(F)
*Betsy-Tacy*, 8267(F)
*Betsy-Tacy and Tib*, 8267(F)
*Heaven to Betsy*, 8267(F)
*The Trees Kneel at Christmas*, 7943(F)
Loverance, Rowena. *Ancient Greece*, 11922
Loveridge, Emma. *Egypt*, 12541
Lovett, Sarah. *Extremely Weird Endangered Species*, 15466
Low, Alice. *The Macmillan Book of Greek Gods and Heroes*, 9478
*Stories to Tell a Five-Year-Old*, 1063(F)
Low, Alice, ed. *The Family Read-Aloud Christmas Treasury*, 4794
*Stories to Tell a Six-Year-Old*, 8268(F)
Low, Joseph. *Mice Twice*, 1887(F)
Low, Robert. *Peoples of the Desert*, 16211
*Peoples of the Mountains*, 16280
*Peoples of the Rain Forest*, 16257
*Peoples of the Savanna*, 16313
Low, William. *Chinatown*, 4620(F)
Lowe, David (jt. author). *The Australian Outback and Its People*, 12336
Lowell, Melissa. *Breaking the Ice*, 8457(F)
Lowell, Susan. *The Bootmaker and the Elves*, 1064(F)
*I Am Lavina Cumming*, 7817(F)
*Little Red Cowboy Hat*, 3388(F)
*The Three Little Javelinas*, 1888(F)
*The Tortoise and the Jackrabbit*, 9072(F)
Lowery, Linda. *Earth Day*, 4621
*Earthwise at Home*, 13577
*Earthwise at Play*, 13577
*Earthwise at School*, 13577
*Georgia O'Keeffe*, 10104
*Laurie Tells*, 7017(F)
*Martin Luther King Day*, 10405
*Somebody Somewhere Knows My Name*, 7238(F)
*Twist with a Burger, Jitter with a Bug*, 2615(F)
*Wilma Mankiller*, 10587
Lowis, Peter. *South Africa*, 12152
Lowre, David. *Australia*, 12345
Lowry, Lois. *All about Sam*, 8110(F)
*Anastasia, Absolutely*, 8106(F)
*Anastasia Again!* 8108(F)
*Anastasia, Ask Your Analyst*, 8108(F)
*Anastasia at This Address*, 8107(F)
*Anastasia at Your Service*, 8108(F)
*Anastasia Has the Answers*, 8109(F)
*Anastasia Krupnik*, 8108(F)
*Anastasia on Her Own*, 8109(F)
*Anastasia's Chosen Career*, 8110(F)
*Attaboy, Sam!* 8111(F)
*Number the Stars*, 7877(F)

*The One Hundredth Thing About Caroline*, 8112(F)
*See You Around, Sam!* 8113(F)
*Stay! Keeper's Story*, 6548(F)
*Switcharound*, 8114(F)
*Us and Uncle Fraud*, 6148(F)
Lucas, Daryl J. *The Baker Bible Dictionary for Kids*, 13802
Lucas, Eileen. *The Cherokees*, 12891
*Civil Rights*, 13664
*Cracking the Wall*, 13665
*The Ojibwas*, 12892
*Vincent van Gogh*, 10071
*Water*, 16450
Lucht, Irmgard. *The Red Poppy*, 16079
Luenn, Nancy. *The Miser on the Mountain*, 9253
*Mother Earth*, 3650(F)
*Nessa's Fish*, 3885(F)
*Nessa's Story*, 3886(F)
*Otter Play*, 4366(F)
*Songs for the Ancient Forest*, 1065(F)
*Squish!* 16188
*Unicorn Crossing*, 1066(F)
Luger, Harriett. *Bye, Bye, Bali Kai*, 7018(F)
Lukes, Bonnie L. *How to Be a Reasonably Thin Teenage Girl*, 14511
Lumley, Kathryn Wentzel. *Monkeys and Apes*, 15154
Lumpkin, Susan. *Small Cats*, 15207
Lumpkin, Susan (jt. author). *Dangerous Animals*, 15128
Lunn, Carolyn. *A Whisper Is Quiet*, 5265(F)
Lunn, Janet. *Come to the Fair*, 2616(F)
*The Root Cellar*, 6549(F)
Lupiloff-Brazz, Marlene (jt. author). *Understanding Cancer*, 14358
Lurie, John. *Fundamental Snowboarding*, 17672
Lurie, Jon. *Allison's Story*, 8269
Lussert, Anneliese. *The Christmas Visitor*, 4795(F)
Luttrell, Ida. *The Bear Next Door*, 5266(F)
Luttrell, Wanda. *Home on Stoney Creek*, 7577(F)
Lychack, William. *Russia*, 12476
Lydon, Kerry Raines. *A Birthday for Blue*, 3887(F)
Lye, Keith. *Coasts*, 16189
*Deserts*, 16212
*Mountains*, 16281
*Passport to Russia*, 12477
*The World Today*, 12080
Lynch, Amy. *Nashville*, 13495
Lynch, Anne. *Great Buildings*, 16774
Lynch, Chris. *Babes in the Woods*, 8115(F)
*Johnny Chesthair*, 8115(F)
*Scratch and the Sniffs*, 8116(F)
Lyne, Alice. *A My Name Is . . .*, 67(F)
Lyne, Sandford, comp. *Ten-Second Rainshowers*, 9602
Lynn, Sara. *Clothes*, 177(F)
*Play with Paint*, 17125
*Play with Paper*, 17125
Lynne, Cherry. *Flute's Journey*, 15346
Lyon, David. *The Biggest Truck*, 4577(F)
*The Runaway Duck*, 1889(F)

Lyon, George E. *Ada's Pal*, 4367(F)
  *Cecil's Story*, 3888(F)
  *Come a Tide*, 2617(F)
  *Counting on the Woods*, 377
  *Dreamplace*, 3889(F)
  *Five Live Bongos*, 3003(F)
  *Mama Is a Miner*, 3004(F)
  *The Outside Inn*, 1067(F)
  *A Regular Rolling Noah*, 3389(F)
  *A Sign*, 14200
  *Together*, 3229
  *Who Came down That Road?* 2618(F)
  *A Wordful Child*, 10263
Lyons, Mary E. *Catching the Fire*, 10122
  *Master of Mahogany*, 10059
  *Painting Dreams*, 10067
  *Starting Home*, 10111
  *Stitching Stars*, 10112
Lyons, Mary E., ed. *Raw Head, Bloody Bones*, 9359

Maass, Robert. *Fire Fighters*, 14228
  *Tugboats*, 16950
  *UN Ambassador*, 10490
  *When Autumn Comes*, 3651
  *When Spring Comes*, 3652
  *When Summer Comes*, 3653
McAllister, Angela. *The Enchanted Flute*, 1068(F)
Macaulay, David. *BAAA*, 6550(F)
  *Castle*, 11979
  *Cathedral*, 11348
  *City*, 11947
  *Mill*, 13096
  *Pyramid*, 11893
  *Rome Antics*, 7489(F)
  *Ship*, 16951
  *Shortcut*, 2619(F)
  *Unbuilding*, 16775
  *Underground*, 16776
  *The Way Things Work*, 16850
  *Why the Chicken Crossed the Road*, 1890(F)
McBratney, Sam. *The Caterpillow Fight*, 1891(F)
  *The Dark at the Top of the Stairs*, 1892(F)
  *Guess How Much I Love You*, 538(F)
  *Just One!* 1893(F)
MacBride, Roger L. *In the Land of the Big Red Apple*, 7710(F)
  *Little Farm in the Ozarks*, 7711(F)
  *Little House on Rocky Edge*, 7712(F)
  *New Dawn on Rocky Ridge*, 7713(F)
  *On the Other Side of the Hill*, 7714(F)
McCall, Edith. *Biography of a River*, 12805
McCall, Francis X., Jr. (jt. author). *Unraveling Fibers*, 16803
Maccarone, Grace. *Cars! Cars! Cars!* 4578(F)
  *The Gym Day Winner*, 5267(F)
  *The Lunch Box Surprise*, 5268(F)
  *Monster Math School Time*, 178(F)
  *My Tooth Is About to Fall Out*, 5269(F)
  *Recess Mess*, 5270(F)

  *Sharing Time Troubles*, 5271(F)
Maccarone, Grace (jt. author). *The Best Teacher in the World*, 4498(F)
McCarthy, Betty. *Utah*, 13327
McCarthy, Colin. *Reptile*, 14914
McCarthy, Ralph F. *The Inch-High Samurai*, 8835
  *The Moon Princess*, 8836
McCarthy, Victoria (jt. author). *A Child's Anthology of Poetry*, 9662
McCarthy-Tucker, Sherri. *Coping with Special-Needs Classmates*, 14311
McCaughrean, Geraldine. *God's People*, 13874
  *The Golden Hoard*, 9451
  *Greek Myths*, 9479
  *A Pack of Lies*, 6551(F)
  *The Random House Book of Stories from the Ballet*, 11638
  *The Silver Treasure*, 8624
  *Unicorns! Unicorns!* 1894(F)
McCaughrean, Geraldine, adapt. *Moby Dick*, 7642(F)
Maccaulay, David. *Black and White*, 8392(F)
McClain, Margaret S. *Bellboy*, 5656(F)
McClintock, Barbara. *Animal Fables from Aesop*, 9073
  *The Fantastic Drawings of Danielle*, 3890(F)
McClintock, Mike. *Stop That Ball!* 5272(F)
McCloskey, Kevin. *Mrs. Fitz's Flamingos*, 1069(F)
McCloskey, Robert. *Blueberries for Sal*, 3005(F)
  *Burt Dow, Deep-Water Man*, 3390(F)
  *Centerburg Tales*, 8117(F)
  *Homer Price*, 8117(F)
  *Lentil*, 3391(F)
  *Make Way for Ducklings*, 4368(F)
  *One Morning in Maine*, 3005(F)
  *Time of Wonder*, 3654(F)
McClung, Robert M. *America's First Elephant*, 4369(F)
  *Lost Wild America*, 15467
  *Snakes*, 14976
McColley, Kevin. *The Walls of Pedro Garcia*, 7529(F)
McCord, David. *All Day Long*, 9603
  *One at a Time*, 9604
McCormick, Anita Louise. *Vanishing Wetlands*, 16190
McCormick, Dell J. *Paul Bunyan Swings His Axe*, 9360
McCourt, Lisa. *I Love You, Stinky Face*, 539(F)
  *The Rain Forest Counts!* 378(F)
McCoy, Elin. *Cards for Kids*, 17643
McCullough, L. E. *Plays of America from American Folklore for Children Grades K–6*, 9928
  *Plays of the Wild West*, 9929
  *Plays of the Wild West: Grades K–3*, 9929
  *Stories of the Songs of Christmas*, 11557
McCully, Emily Arnold. *The Ballot Box Battle*, 10787
  *Beautiful Warrior*, 3891(F)
  *The Bobbin Girl*, 7643(F)
  *First Snow*, 1895(F)
  *The Grandma Mix-Up*, 5273(F)

McGeorge, Constance W. *Boomer Goes to School*, 4372(F)

*Boomer's Big Day*, 4373(F)

*Snow Riders*, 1074(F)

McGibbon, Robin. *New Kids on the Block*, 10190

McGill, Allyson. *The Swedish Americans*, 14061

MacGill-Callahan, Sheila. *And Still the Turtle Watched*, 3656(F)

*The Children of Lir*, 9016

*To Capture the Wind*, 5657(F)

McGilvray, Richard. *Don't Climb Out of the Window Tonight*, 542(F)

McGirr, Nancy (jt. author). *Out of the Dump*, 12657

McGough, Roger. *Until I Met Dudley*, 4580(F)

McGovern, Ann. *If You Lived in Colonial Times*, 13026

*If You Lived with the Sioux Indians*, 12895

*If You Sailed on the Mayflower*, 13027

*The Lady in the Box*, 4798(F)

*The Secret Soldier*, 10784

*Too Much Noise*, 9017

McGovern, Ann, adapt. *Stone Soup*, 8888

McGowan, Christopher. *Discover Dinosaurs*, 11755

McGowen, Tom. *"Go for Broke,"* 12053

*The Korean War*, 13252

*World War I*, 12010

*World War II*, 12054

*Yearbooks in Science: 1900–1919*, 14567

*Yearbooks in Science: 1960–1969*, 14568

McGrath, Bob. *Uh Oh! Gotta Go!* 2623

McGrath, Patrick. *The Lewis and Clark Expedition*, 12981

McGrath, Susan. *The Amazing Things Animals Do*, 15022

McGraw, Eloise. *The Moorchild*, 6555(F)

*Tangled Webb*, 5658(F)

McGraw, Sheila. *Dolls Kids Can Make*, 17181

*Gifts Kids Can Make*, 17016

*Papier-Mâché for Kids*, 17160

*This Old New House*, 16789

McGregor, Merideth. *Cowgirl*, 2624

MacGrory, Yvonne. *The Secret of the Ruby Ring*, 8358(F)

McGugan, Jim. *Josepha*, 7715(F)

McGuigan, Mary Ann. *Where You Belong*, 6886(F)

McGuire, Leslie. *Brush Your Teeth, Please*, 1905(F)

*This Farm Is a Mess*, 5278(F)

*Victims*, 13764

McGuire, Richard. *Night Becomes Day*, 2625(F)

*What Goes Around Comes Around*, 3396(F)

*What's Wrong with This Book?* 179(F)

McGuire, William. *The Final Four*, 17574

*The Stanley Cup*, 17632

*The Summer Olympics*, 17656

McGuire-Turcotte, Casey A. *How Honu the Turtle Got His Shell*, 1906(F)

Machado, Ana María. *Niña Bonita*, 1075(F)

McHargue, Georgess. *Beastie*, 6556(F)

Machotka, Hana. *Breathtaking Noses*, 14871

*Pasta Factory*, 2626

Macht, Norman L. *Babe Ruth*, 11014

*Christy Mathewson*, 10994

*Cy Young*, 11026

*Frank Robinson*, 11003

*Jimmie Foxx*, 10978

*Lou Gehrig*, 10980

*Sandra Day O'Connor*, 10768

*Satchel Paige*, 10997

*Sojourner Truth*, 10450

*Ty Cobb*, 10973

McInerney, Claire. *Find It!* 11397

Mack, Stan. *Ten Bears in My Bed*, 381(F)

Mack-Williams, Kibibi V. *Food and Our History*, 17234

*Mossi*, 12184

*People of Faith*, 13804

Mackay, Claire, sel. *Laughs*, 8119(F)

Mackay, Claire (jt. author). *Bats About Baseball*, 3384(F)

McKay, Hilary. *The Amber Cat*, 6557(F)

*Dog Friday*, 5932(F)

*The Exiles*, 6150(F)

*The Exiles at Home*, 6151(F)

McKay, Lawrence, Jr. *Caravan*, 3894(F)

McKean, Thomas. *The Secret of the Seven Willows*, 6558(F)

McKee, David. *Elmer Again*, 1907(F)

*Elmer and Wilbur*, 1908(F)

*Elmer in the Snow*, 1909(F)

*I Can Too!* 1910(F)

*The School Bus Comes at Eight O'Clock*, 3010(F)

*Zebra's Hiccups*, 1911(F)

McKeever, Michael. *A Day in the Life of a Test Pilot*, 14250

Mackel, Kathy. *A Season of Comebacks*, 8458(F)

McKellar, Shona, ed. *A Child's Book of Lullabies*, 543(F)

McKelvey, Douglas Kaine. *The Angel Knew Papa and the Dog*, 6559(F)

Macken, Walter. *Island of the Great Yellow Ox*, 5659(F)

McKenley, Yvonne. *A Taste of the Caribbean*, 17235

McKenna, Colleen O'Shaughnessy. *Camp Murphy*, 6887(F)

*Fifth Grade*, 7240(F)

*Live from the Fifth Grade*, 8271(F)

*Mother Murphy*, 8120(F)

McKenna, Virginia. *Back to the Blue*, 4374(F)

McKenzie, Ellen Kindt. *A Bowl of Mischief*, 6560(F)

*The King, the Princess, and the Tinker*, 6561(F)

*The Perfectly Orderly House*, 70(F)

*Stargone John*, 7241(F)

*Under the Bridge*, 7020(F)

McKibbon, Hugh William. *The Token Gift*, 7450(F)

McKinley, Robin. *The Door in the Hedge*, 8552(F)

*My Father Is in the Navy*, 3011(F)

MacKinnon, Christy. *Silent Observer*, 14312

MacKinnon, Debbie. *Billy's Boots*, 2627(F)

*Cathy's Cake*, 2627(F)

*Daniel's Duck*, 2628(F)

*Sugar Isn't Everything*, 7380(F)
*What Are We Going to Do About David?* 7048(F)
*What Could Go Wrong?* 5735(F)
Robertshaw, Andrew. *A Soldier's Life*, 16972
Robertson, Keith. *Henry Reed, Inc.*, 8157(F)
  *Henry Reed's Baby-Sitting Service*, 8157(F)
  *Henry Reed's Big Show*, 8157(F)
  *Henry Reed's Journey*, 8157(F)
Robertus, Polly M. *The Dog Who Had Kittens*, 4415(F)
Robinet, Harriette G. *Children of the Fire*, 7834(F)
  *If You Please, President Lincoln*, 7532(F)
  *The Twins, the Pirates, and the Battle of New Orleans*, 7650(F)
  *Washington City Is Burning*, 7651(F)
Robins, Deri. *Christmas Fun*, 17029
  *The Kids Can Do It Book*, 17030
  *Papier Mâché*, 17161
Robins, Joan. *Addie Meets Max*, 5357(F)
  *Addie Runs Away*, 5357(F)
Robinson, Aminah B. *A Street Called Home*, 2702(F)
Robinson, Barbara. *The Best Christmas Pageant Ever*, 7953(F)
  *The Best School Year Ever*, 8158(F)
  *My Brother Louis Measures Worms and Other Louis Stories*, 8159(F)
Robinson, Claire. *Bears*, 15189
  *Chimpanzees*, 15159
  *Crocodiles*, 14930
  *Elephants*, 15273
  *Lions*, 15212
  *Penguin*, 15446
  *Penguins*, 15447
Robinson, Fay. *Great Snakes!* 14984
  *Pilots Fly Planes*, 14251
  *Space Probes to the Planets*, 16656
  *Vegetables, Vegetables!* 16016
  *We Love Fruit!* 15995
  *Where Did All the Dragons Go?* 1179(F)
  *Where Do Puddles Go?* 16458
Robinson, Fay, ed. *A Frog Inside My Hat*, 9630
Robinson, Fay (jt. author). *Nathaniel Willy, Scared Silly*, 9362
  *Oh, How Waffle!* 17371
Robinson, Marc. *Cock-A-Doodle-Doo! What Does It Sound Like to You?* 4416
Robinson, Mary. *The Amazing Valvano and the Mystery of the Hooded Rat*, 5736(F)
Robinson, Nancy K. *Angela and the Broken Heart*, 6170(F)
  *Countess Veronica*, 7286(F)
Robinson, W. Wright. *Incredible Facts About the Ocean*, 15785
Robson, Pam. *Body Language*, 14108
Robson, Pam (jt. author). *Art from Fabric*, 16985
  *Exploring Time*, 14585
  *Making Shaped Books*, 11386
Roby, Cynthia. *When Learning Is Tough*, 14318
Roche, Denis. *Brave Georgie Goat*, 2063(F)
  *Loo-Loo, Boo, and Art You Can Do*, 17031

*Ollie All Over*, 2703(F)
*Only One Ollie*, 420(F)
Rochelle, Belinda. *Jewels*, 3938(F)
  *When Jo Louis Won the Title*, 3075(F)
  *Witnesses to Freedom*, 13671
Rochford, Dierdre. *Rights for Animals?* 14886
Rock, Gail. *The House Without a Christmas Tree*, 7954(F)
Rocklin, Joanne. *For Your Eyes Only*, 8288(F)
  *One Hungry Cat*, 421(F)
  *Sonia Begonia*, 5737(F)
Rockwell, Anne. *Ducklings and Pollywogs*, 3682(F)
  *Fire Engines*, 4588(F)
  *The First Snowfall*, 3684(F)
  *Halloween Day*, 4931(F)
  *Hugo at the Park*, 2064(F)
  *I Fly*, 2346(F)
  *Mr. Panda's Painting*, 236(F)
  *No! No! No!* 4137(F)
  *Once upon a Time This Morning*, 2704(F)
  *The One-Eyed Giant and Other Monsters from the Greek Myths*, 9489
  *Our Yard Is Full of Birds*, 4417
  *Pots and Pans*, 2705(F)
  *The Robber Baby*, 9490
  *Show and Tell Day*, 4534(F)
  *Space Vehicles*, 16657
  *The Storm*, 3683(F)
  *The Story Snail*, 5358(F)
  *Sweet Potato Pie*, 5359(F)
  *What We Like*, 2706
Rockwell, Anne, reteller. *Romulus and Remus*, 9491
Rockwell, Harlow. *My Dentist*, 14506
Rockwell, Harlow (jt. author). *The First Snowfall*, 3684(F)
Rockwell, Norman. *Willie Was Different*, 2065(F)
Rockwell, Thomas. *How to Eat Fried Worms*, 8160(F)
Rodanas, Kristina. *The Eagle's Song*, 9280
Rodanas, Kristina, adapt. *The Dragonfly's Tale*, 9279
Rodda, Emily. *Finders Keepers*, 8370(F)
  *The Pigs Are Flying*, 6646(F)
  *Power and Glory*, 3452(F)
  *Yay!* 3453(F)
Roddie, Shen. *Toes Are to Tickle*, 2707(F)
  *Too Close Friends*, 2066(F)
Rodell, Susanna. *Dear Fred*, 4138(F)
Roden, Katie. *The Mummy*, 6647(F)
  *Solving International Crime*, 13700
  *Terrorism*, 13701
Rodgers, Frank. *Who's Afraid of the Ghost Train?* 4139(F)
Rodgers, Mary. *A Billion for Boris*, 8161(F)
  *Freaky Friday*, 8161(F)
  *Summer Switch*, 8161(F)
Rodgers, Mary M. (jt. author). *Atmosphere*, 16397
  *Life on Land*, 15462
  *Our Endangered Planet: Air*, 16403
  *Our Endangered Planet: Groundwater*, 13622
  *Our Endangered Planet: Oceans*, 15773

Samuelson, Mary Lou (jt. author). *The African Rhinos*, 15127

Sanchez, Enrique O. (jt. author). *Maria Molina and the Days of the Dead*, 3864(F)

Sand, George. *The Castle of Pictures and Other Stories*, 8572(F)

Sandak, Cass R. *Congressional Committees*, 13739
*Living Fossils*, 14821
*Lobbying*, 13740
*The National Debt*, 13741
*The United States*, 12807

Sandburg, Carl. *Abe Lincoln Grows Up*, 10683
*Grassroots*, 9636
*Rootabaga Stories*, 8168(F)
*Rootabaga Stories: Part Two*, 8169(F)
*The Sandburg Treasury*, 9637(F)
*The Wedding Procession of the Rag Doll and the Broom Handle and Who Was in It*, 1201(F)

Sandelson, Robert. *Ice Sports*, 17657

Sandeman, Anna. *Babies*, 14538
*Blood*, 14423
*Brain*, 14448
*Eating*, 14436
*Senses*, 14483
*Skin, Teeth, and Hair*, 14504

Sanders, Eve. *What's Your Name?* 109(F)

Sanders, Pete. *Bodyworks*, 14413
*Bullying*, 14169
*Divorce and Separation*, 14147
*Drinking Alcohol*, 14281
*Smoking*, 14280

Sanders, Scott R. *Aurora Means Dawn*, 3946(F)
*The Floating House*, 3947(F)
*Here Comes the Mystery Man*, 3948(F)
*Meeting Trees*, 3696(F)
*A Place Called Freedom*, 3949(F)
*Warm as Wool*, 3950(F)

Sanderson, Ruth. *Papa Gatto*, 8573
*Rose Red and Snow White*, 8574(F)
*The Twelve Dancing Princesses*, 8949

Sandin, Joan. *The Long Way to a New Land*, 3951(F)
*The Long Way Westward*, 7839(F)
*Pioneer Bear*, 5377(F)

Sandoval, Dolores. *Be Patient, Abdul*, 3952(F)

Sandved, Kjell B. *The Butterfly Alphabet*, 110(F)

Sanfield, Steve. *Bit by Bit*, 3461(F)
*The Girl Who Wanted a Song*, 1202(F)
*Just Rewards, or Who Is That Man in the Moon and What's He Doing Up There Anyway?* 8784
*A Natural Man*, 9371
*Strudel, Strudel, Strudel*, 9156

Sanford, William R. *Babe Didrikson Zaharias*, 11173
*Babe Ruth*, 11016
*Bill Pickett*, 10198
*Billie Jean King*, 11117
*Brigham Young*, 10576
*Buffalo Bill Cody*, 10506
*Calamity Jane*, 10503
*Chief Joseph*, 10584
*Daniel Boone*, 9969

*Davy Crockett*, 9987
*Dorothy Hamill*, 11151
*Geronimo*, 10579
*Jackie Robinson*, 11012
*Jesse Owens*, 11131
*Jim Thorpe*, 11139
*Joe DiMaggio*, 10976
*Joe Namath*, 11093
*John C. Fremont*, 9999
*Kareem Abdul-Jabbar*, 11028
*Kit Carson*, 9972
*Missouri*, 13295
*Muhammad Ali*, 11078
*Osceola*, 10588
*Quanah Parker*, 10589
*Red Cloud*, 10597
*Richard King*, 10546
*Sacagawea*, 10601
*Sandy Koufax*, 10991
*Sitting Bull*, 10607
*Zebulon Pike*, 10017

Sanford, William R. (jt. author). *Allan Pinkerton*, 10565
*Billy the Kid*, 10498
*Butch Cassidy*, 10505
*The Dalton Gang*, 13134
*Doc Holliday*, 10535
*Jesse James*, 10541
*Judge Roy Bean*, 10497
*Wild Bill Hickok*, 10533
*Wyatt Earp*, 10509

San Jose, Christine. *The Little Match Girl*, 8576
*Sleeping Beauty*, 8577

San Jose, Christine, reteller. *Cinderella*, 8575(F)

San Souci, Robert D. *The Boy and the Ghost*, 1203(F)
*Cut from the Same Cloth*, 9372
*The Enchanted Tapestry*, 8785
*Even More Short and Shivery*, 8645
*The Faithful Friend*, 9431
*The Hired Hand*, 9373
*The House in the Sky*, 9432
*Kate Shelley*, 10785
*The Little Seven-Colored Horse*, 9374
*N. C. Wyeth's Pilgrims*, 13036
*Nicholas Pipe*, 8578(F)
*Pedro and the Monkey*, 1204
*The Red Heels*, 6659(F)
*Sootface*, 9287
*The Talking Eggs*, 9376
*Two Bear Cubs*, 9288
*Young Arthur*, 9031
*Young Guinevere*, 9032
*Young Lancelot*, 9033

San Souci, Robert D., reteller. *The Firebird*, 11643
*Sukey and the Mermaid*, 9375
*A Weave of Words*, 8876
*The White Cat*, 8579(F)

Sant, Thomas. *The Amazing Adventures of Albert and His Flying Machine*, 3462(F)

Slobodkina, Esphyr. *Caps for Sale*, 3476(F)

Slotboom, Wendy. *King Snake*, 2119(F)

Slote, Alfred. *Finding Buck McHenry*, 8470(F)

 *Hang Tough, Paul Mather*, 7382(F)

 *My Robot Buddy*, 8374(F)

 *My Trip to Alpha I*, 8374(F)

 *Omega Station*, 8374(F)

 *The Trading Game*, 8471(F)

 *The Trouble on Janus*, 8375(F)

Slote, Elizabeth. *Nelly's Garden*, 2120(F)

Slovenz-Low, Madeline (jt. author). *Lion Dancer*, 4640

Slyder, Ingrid. *The Fabulous Flying Fandinis*, 3477(F)

Small, David. *Fenwick's Suit*, 6689(F)

 *George Washington's Cows*, 6690(F)

 *Imogene's Antlers*, 1236(F)

 *Paper John*, 1237(F)

Smalls, Irene. *Because You're Lucky*, 4156(F)

 *Dawn and the Round To-It*, 3107(F)

 *Irene Jennie and the Christmas Masquerade*, 3960(F)

 *Jenny Reen and the Jack Muh Lantern*, 4937(F)

Smalls-Hector, Irene. *Jonathan and His Mommy*, 2738(F)

Smath, Jerry. *Pretzel and Pop's Closetful of Stories*, 5415(F)

Smax, Willy. *Jack Tractor*, 1238(F)

Smee, Nicola. *The Tusk Fairy*, 1239(F)

Smith, A. G. *Where Am I? The Story of Maps and Navigation*, 11690

Smith, Adam. *A Historical Album of Kentucky*, 13510

Smith, Beth. *Castles*, 11996

Smith, Betsy. *A Day in the Life of a Firefighter*, 14234

 *A Day in the Life of an Actress*, 14205

 *Jimmy Carter, President*, 10628

Smith, Cara Lockhart. *Twenty-Six Rabbits Run Riot*, 2121(F)

Smith, Carter. *A Day in the Life of an FBI Agent-in-Training*, 14235

 *The Jamestown Colony*, 13042

 *The Korean War*, 13253

Smith, Carter, ed. *The Arts and Sciences*, 13040

 *Behind the Lines*, 13206

 *Daily Life*, 13041

 *1863*, 13207

 *The First Battles*, 13208

 *The Founding Presidents*, 13107

 *Presidents in a Time of Change*, 13254

 *Presidents of a Divided Nation*, 13209

 *Presidents of a Growing Country*, 13235

 *Presidents of a World Power*, 13236

 *Presidents of a Young Republic*, 13108

Smith, Carter, III (jt. author). *A Historical Album of New York*, 13347

Smith, Dodie. *The Hundred and One Dalmatians*, 6691(F)

Smith, Doris Buchanan. *Best Girl*, 7057(F)

 *A Taste of Blackberries*, 7308(F)

Smith, E. Boyd. *The Farm Book*, 15943

 *The Railroad Book*, 16928

Smith, E. S. *Bear Bryant*, 11084

Smith, Elizabeth Simpson. *Cloth*, 16811

 *Coming Out Right*, 9974

 *Paper*, 16705

Smith, Elva (jt. author). *The Year Around*, 9872

Smith, Howard E. *Daring the Unknown*, 16662

Smith, Janice Lee. *The Kid Next Door and Other Headaches*, 6181(F)

 *The Monster in the Third Dresser Drawer and Other Stories About Adam Joshua*, 6181(F)

 *Serious Science*, 8298(F)

 *Wizard and Wart at Sea*, 5416(F)

Smith, Katherine S. (jt. author). *A Historical Album of Kentucky*, 13510

Smith, Kathie Billingslea. *Thinking*, 14451

Smith, L. J. *Heart of Valor*, 6692(F)

Smith, Lane. *The Big Pets*, 1240(F)

 *Glasses*, 8172(F)

 *The Happy Hocky Family*, 1241(F)

Smith, Linda W. *Louis Pasteur*, 10900

Smith, Maggie. *Counting Our Way to Maine*, 434(F)

Smith, Marisa, ed. *Afternoon of the Elves*, 9934

 *Anne of Green Gables*, 9934

 *The Seattle Children's Theatre*, 9934

Smith, Mark. *Pay Attention, Slosh!* 7383(F)

Smith, Miranda. *Living Earth*, 14824

Smith, Nigel. *The Houses of Parliament*, 12430

Smith, Patricia C. (jt. author). *As Long As the Rivers Flow*, 10311

Smith, Pohla. *Superstars of Women's Figure Skating*, 10950

Smith, Robert K. *Chocolate Fever*, 8173(F)

 *Jelly Belly*, 7309(F)

 *The War with Grandpa*, 6182(F)

Smith, Roland. *African Elephants*, 15275

 *Cats in the Zoo*, 15217

 *Jaguar*, 5759(F)

 *Journey of the Red Wolf*, 15242

 *Thunder Cave*, 5760(F)

 *Vultures*, 15372

 *Whales, Dolphins, and Porpoises in the Zoo*, 15676

Smith, Rosie (jt. author). *Detective Donut and the Wild Goose Chase*, 6760(F)

 *Whatley's Quest*, 5808

Smith, Sherwood. *Court Duel*, 6693(F)

 *Crown Duel*, 6694(F)

 *Wren to the Rescue*, 6695(F)

 *Wren's War*, 6696(F)

Smith, Susan M. *The Booford Summer*, 5977(F)

Smith, William J. *Laughing Time*, 9840

Smith, William J., comp. *The Sun Is Up*, 9895

Smith-Baranzini, Marlene. *Book of the American Indians*, 12943

 *Brown Paper School USKids History*, 13109

Smith-Baranzini, Marlene (jt. author). *US Kids History*, 12995

Smothers, Ethel Footman. *Down in the Piney Woods*, 6028(F)

*The Moon Lady*, 7461(F)

Tan, Sheri. *Seiji Ozawa*, 10194

Tanaka, Shelley. *The Buried City of Pompeii*, 11957(F)

*Discovering the Iceman*, 11815

*On Board the Titanic*, 5783(F)

Tang, Fay (jt. author). *Sing for Your Father, Su Phan*, 7455(F)

Tannenbaum, Beulah. *Making and Using Your Own Weather Station*, 16390

*Science of the Early American Indians*, 12960

Tannenbaum, Harold E. (jt. author). *Making and Using Your Own Weather Station*, 16390

*Science of the Early American Indians*, 12960

Tao, Wang. *Exploration into China*, 12221

Tapahonso, Luci. *Navajo ABC*, 120(F)

Targ, Harry R. (jt. author). *Guatemala*, 12655

Tarpley, Natasha A. *I Love My Hair!* 2747(F)

Tarsky, Sue. *The Busy Building Book*, 16783

Tashjian, Janet. *Tru Confessions*, 6190(F)

Tashjian, Virginia A., sel. *Juba This and Juba That*, 11610(F)

Tate, Eleanora E. *A Blessing in Disguise*, 7064(F)

*Don't Split the Pole*, 6719(F)

*The Secret of Gumbo Grove*, 5784(F)

Tate, Lindsey. *Claire and the Friendly Snakes*, 1257(F)

Taylor, Barbara. *Animal Homes*, 15076

*Arctic and Antarctic*, 12776

*The Bird Atlas*, 15378

*Coral Reef*, 15661

*Desert Life*, 16225

*Forest Life*, 16272

*Living with Deafness*, 14320

*Pond Life*, 16306

*Rain Forest*, 16273

*The Really Deadly and Dangerous Dinosaur*, 11783

*The Really Sinister Savage Shark*, 15646

*Shoreline*, 15805

Taylor, Barbara (jt. author). *Oceans*, 15770

*Weather*, 16485

Taylor, C. J. *The Ghost and Lone Warrior*, 9298

*How We Saw the World*, 9299

*The Secret of the White Buffalo*, 9300

Taylor, Charles. *The Oxford Children's Book of Science*, 14576

Taylor, Clark. *The House That Crack Built*, 14288

Taylor, Dave. *Endangered Forest Animals*, 15477

*Endangered Grassland Animals*, 15478

*Endangered Mountain Animals*, 15479

*Endangered Wetland Animals*, 15479

Taylor, Elizabeth (jt. author). *Tornadoes*, 16407

Taylor, George. *Imagination in Art*, 11335

Taylor, Harriet P. *Brother Wolf*, 9301

*Coyote and the Laughing Butterflies*, 9302

*Coyote Places the Stars*, 9303

*When Bear Stole the Chinook*, 9304

Taylor, Kim. *Action*, 16540

Taylor, Leighton. *Creeps from the Deep*, 15647

Taylor, Livingston. *Can I Be Good?* 4458(F)

Taylor, Lolita (jt. author). *Old Meshikee and the Little Crabs*, 9292

Taylor, M. W. *Harriet Tubman*, 10459

Taylor, Mark. *Henry the Explorer*, 2362(F)

Taylor, Mildred D. *The Friendship*, 6035(F)

*The Gold Cadillac*, 6036(F)

*Let the Circle Be Unbroken*, 6191(F)

*Mississippi Bridge*, 6037(F)

*Roll of Thunder, Hear My Cry*, 6191(F)

*Song of the Trees*, 6191(F)

*The Well*, 7845(F)

Taylor, Nicole. *Baby*, 14541

Taylor, Paul D. *Fossil*, 11784

Taylor, Penny (jt. author). *The Kwanzaa Contest*, 7945(F)

Taylor, Richard L. *The First Flight*, 10920

*The First Flight Across the United States*, 10023

*The First Human-Powered Flight*, 10010

*The First Solo Flight Around the World*, 10021

*The First Unrefueled Flight Around the World*, 16753

Taylor, Sydney. *All-of-a-Kind Family*, 6192(F)

*Ella of All-of-a-Kind Family*, 6192(F)

Taylor, Theodore. *Air Raid — Pearl Harbor*, 12073

*The Cay*, 6927(F)

*The Hostage*, 5981(F)

*Maria Taylor*, 7961(F)

*The Odyssey of Ben O'Neal*, 5785(F)

*Teetoncey*, 5785(F)

*Teetoncey and Ben O'Neal*, 5785(F)

*Timothy of the Cay*, 5786(F)

*The Trouble with Tuck*, 5982(F)

*Tuck Triumphant*, 5983(F)

Taylor, William. *Agnes the Sheep*, 5984(F)

*Knitwits*, 5787(F)

*Numbskulls*, 5787(F)

Tazewell, Charles. *The Littlest Angel*, 1258(F)

Tchana, Katrin H. *Oh, No, Toto!* 3969(F)

Teague, Allison L. *Prince of the Fairway*, 11170

Teague, Ken. *Growing Up in Ancient China*, 12222

Teague, Mark. *Baby Tamer*, 3489(F)

*The Field Beyond the Outfield*, 1259(F)

*How I Spent My Summer Vacation*, 2363(F)

*Pigsty*, 2169(F)

*The Secret Shortcut*, 1260(F)

Teague, Mark (jt. author). *The Flying Dragon Room*, 1335(F)

Techner, David. *A Candle for Grandpa*, 13986

Teckentrup, Britta. *Rumble in the Jungle*, 2170(F)

Tee-Van, Helen D. *Small Mammals Are Where You Find Them*, 15139

Teeters, Peggy. *Jules Verne*, 10296

Telemaque, Eleanor Wong. *Haiti Through Its Holidays*, 12686

Temko, Florence. *Paper Gifts and Jewelry*, 17167

*Paper Tags and Cards*, 17167

*Planes and Other Flying Things*, 17168

*Traditional Crafts from Africa*, 17046

*Traditional Crafts from Mexico and Central America*, 17047

Weiss, Ellen. *The Adventures of Ratman*, 8192(F)
  *Color Me Criminal*, 5806(F)
Weiss, Ellen (jt. author). *Born to Be Wild*, 6702(F)
Weiss, George D. *What a Wonderful World*, 11612(F)
Weiss, Harvey. *Strange and Wonderful Aircraft*,
  16756
  *Submarines and Other Underwater Craft*, 16978
Weiss, Jacqueline Shachter. *Young Brer Rabbit*, 9449
Weiss, Jonathan H. *Breathe Easy*, 14359
Weiss, Leatie. *My Teacher Sleeps in School*, 2234(F)
Weiss, Mitch (jt. author). *Stories in My Pocket*, 11466
Weiss, Nicki. *If You're Happy and You Know It*,
  11541
  *Stone Men*, 3985(F)
  *Where Does the Brown Bear Go?* 592(F)
Weissman, Paul (jt. author). *The Great Voyager
  Adventure*, 14752
Weitzman, David. *Great Lives*, 10803
  *My Backyard History Book*, 11858
  *Old Ironsides*, 7658(F)
Weitzman, Elizabeth. *Let's Talk About Foster Homes*,
  14153
  *Let's Talk About Smoking*, 14291
  *Let's Talk About Staying in a Shelter*, 14153
  *Let's Talk About When a Parent Dies*, 14153
  *Let's Talk About When Someone You Love Has
  Alzheimer's Disease*, 14360
  *Let's Talk About Your Parents' Divorce*, 14153
Weizmann, Daniel. *Take a Stand!* 13745
Welch, Catherine A. *Clouds of Terror*, 7743(F)
  *Danger at the Breaker*, 5435(F)
  *Margaret Bourke-White*, 10050
Welch, R. C. *Scary Stories for Stormy Nights*,
  6756(F)
Welch, Sheila K. *Don't Call Me Marda*, 7388(F)
Welch, Willy. *Playing Right Field*, 2763(F)
Well, Ann (jt. author). *Raul Julia*, 10484
Weller, Frances W. *Madaket Millie*, 2370(F)
  *Riptide*, 4470(F)
Wellington, Monica. *Baby at Home*, 2764(F)
  *Baby Goes Shopping*, 2764(F)
  *Baby in a Buggy*, 2765(F)
  *Baby in a Car*, 2766(F)
  *Night House, Bright House*, 1302(F)
  *Night Rabbits*, 4471(F)
Wells, Alison. *Subtraction*, 16370
Wells, Donna. *Biotechnology*, 14373
Wells, H. G. *The Time Machine*, 8379(F)
Wells, Robert E. *Is a Blue Whale the Biggest Thing
  There Is?* 285(F)
  *What's Faster Than a Speeding Cheetah?* 15033
  *What's Smaller Than a Pygmy Shrew?* 286(F)
Wells, Rosemary. *Bunny Cakes*, 2235(F)
  *Bunny Money*, 2236(F)
  *Edward in Deep Water*, 2237(F)
  *Edward Unready for School*, 2237(F)
  *Edward's Overwhelming Overnight*, 2237(F)
  *First Tomato*, 2238(F)
  *Forest of Dreams*, 3721(F)
  *Fritz and the Mess Fairy*, 2239(F)

*Hazel's Amazing Mother*, 2240(F)
*The Island Light*, 2238(F)
*The Language of Doves*, 3986(F)
*Lassie Come-Home*, 5990(F)
*Lucy Comes to Stay*, 4472(F)
*McDuff and the Baby*, 4473(F)
*McDuff Comes Home*, 4474(F)
*McDuff Moves In*, 4475(F)
*Max and Ruby's First Greek Myth*, 2241(F)
*Max's Chocolate Chicken*, 4875(F)
*Max's Christmas*, 4856(F)
*Moss Pillows*, 2238(F)
*Night Sounds, Morning Colors*, 3136(F)
*Noisy Nora*, 2242(F)
*Read to Your Bunny*, 2243(F)
*Shy Charles*, 2244(F)
*Stanley and Rhoda*, 2245(F)
*Timothy Goes to School*, 4545(F)
*Waiting for the Evening Star*, 3137(F)
Wells, Rosemary, reteller. *Jack and the Beanstalk*,
  9042
Wells, Ruth. *A to Zen*, 128(F)
  *The Farmer and the Poor God*, 8849
Welton, Jude. *Drawing*, 17135
Weninger, Brigitte. *Lumina*, 1303(F)
  *Ragged Bear*, 2767(F)
  *What Have You Done, Davy?* 2246(F)
  *What's the Matter, Davy?* 2247(F)
  *Where Have You Gone, Davy?* 2248(F)
  *Will You Mind the Baby, Davy?* 2249(F)
Wenzel, David. *Fairy Tales of the Brothers Grimm*,
  8593
Werlin, Nancy. *Are You Alone on Purpose?* 7389(F)
Wesley, Mary. *Haphazard House*, 6757(F)
Wesley, Valerie W. *Freedom's Gifts*, 6202(F)
West, Alan. *José Martí*, 10267
  *Roberto Clemente*, 10972
West, Colin. *"Buzz, Buzz, Buzz," Went the
  Bumblebee*, 2250(F)
  *One Day in the Jungle*, 258(F)
West, Delno C. *Braving the North Atlantic*, 12987
West, Jean M. (jt. author). *Braving the North
  Atlantic*, 12987
West, Robin. *Dinosaur Discoveries*, 17172
  *My Very Own Birthday*, 17052
  *My Very Own Christmas*, 17053
West, Tracey. *Fire in the Valley*, 7849(F)
  *Mr. Peale's Bones*, 7659(F)
  *Voyage of the Half Moon*, 6758(F)
Westall, Robert. *Christmas Spirit*, 7965(F)
  *Ghost Abbey*, 6759(F)
  *Stormsearch*, 5807(F)
Westcott, Nadine Bernard. *The Giant Vegetable
  Garden*, 1304(F)
  *I Know an Old Lady Who Swallowed a Fly*, 11542
  *I've Been Working on the Railroad*, 11543
  *The Lady with the Alligator Purse*, 9845(F)
  *Peanut Butter and Jelly*, 3504(F)

Wynne-Jones, Tim. *Some of the Kinder Planets*, 6790(F)

Wyss, Johann D. *Swiss Family Robinson*, 5818(F)


Xiong, Blia. *Nine-in-One, Grr! Grr!* 8857


Yaccarino, Dan. *Good Night, Mr. Night*, 597(F)
*If I Had a Robot*, 1338(F)
*An Octopus Followed Me Home*, 3516(F)
*Zoom! Zoom! Zoom! I'm Off to the Moon*, 1339(F)

Yamaka, Sara. *The Gift of Driscoll Lipscomb*, 243(F)

Yamane, Linda. *Weaving a California Tradition*, 17071

Yancey, Diane. *Camels for Uncle Sam*, 16932
*Zoos*, 15915

Yao-wen, Li (jt. author). *Sweet and Sour*, 8776

Yarbrough, Camille. *Tamika and the Wisdom Rings*, 7086(F)

Yardley, Joanna. *The Red Ball*, 1340(F)

Yardley, Thompson. *Buy Now, Pay Later*, 13554
*Down the Drain*, 16794

Yashima, Taro. *Crow Boy*, 4547(F)
*Umbrella*, 2778(F)

Yates, Elizabeth. *Amos Fortune, Free Man*, 10383

Yates, Irene. *From Birth to Death*, 16307

Yates, Sarah. *Alberta*, 12609

Ye, Ting-xing. *Three Monks, No Water*, 8793

Yeatman, Linda. *A Child's Book of Prayers*, 14018

Yee, Patrick. *Rosie Rabbit's Colors*, 244(F)
*Rosie Rabbit's Numbers*, 244(F)
*Rosie Rabbit's Opposites*, 244(F)
*Rosie Rabbit's Shapes*, 244(F)
*Winter Rabbit*, 2277(F)

Yee, Paul. *Ghost Train*, 6791(F)

Yee, Wong H. *Big Black Bear*, 2278(F)
*Eek! There's a Mouse in the House*, 3517(F)
*Fireman Small*, 2779(F)
*Mrs. Brown Went to Town*, 2279(F)
*The Officer's Ball*, 2280(F)

Yektai, Niki. *Bears at the Beach*, 451(F)

Yen, Clara. *Why Rat Comes First*, 1341(F)

Yeoman, John. *Arabian Nights*, 9182
*The Seven Voyages of Sinbad the Sailor*, 9182

Yep, Laurence. *The Butterfly Boy*, 1342(F)
*The Case of the Goblin Pearls*, 5819(F)
*The City of Dragons*, 1343(F)
*The Cook's Family*, 8195(F)
*The Curse of the Squirrel*, 1344(F)
*Dragon of the Lost Sea*, 6792(F)
*The Dragon Prince*, 8794
*The Ghost Fox*, 8598(F)
*Hiroshima*, 7897(F)
*The Imp That Ate My Homework*, 6793(F)
*The Junior Thunder Lord*, 8795
*The Khan's Daughter*, 8757
*Later, Gator*, 5994(F)
*The Man Who Tricked a Ghost*, 8796
*Ribbons*, 7087(F)

*The Shell Woman and the King*, 8797
*Thief of Hearts*, 6041(F)
*Tiger Woman*, 8798
*Tree of Dreams*, 8657

Yerxa, Leo. *Last Leaf First Snowflake to Fall*, 3728(F)

Yezerski, Thomas F. *Together in Pinecone Patch*, 3258(F)

Yolen, Jane. *Animal Fare*, 9847
*Baby Bear's Bedtime Book*, 598(F)
*The Ballad of the Pirate Queens*, 5820(F)
*Child of Faerie, Child of Earth*, 4947(F)
*The Devil's Arithmetic*, 7898(F)
*The Emperor and the Kite*, 8799
*Encounter*, 7535(F)
*The Girl in the Golden Bower*, 1345(F)
*Grandad Bill's Song*, 4185(F)
*Here There Be Angels*, 6794(F)
*Here There Be Dragons*, 6795(F)
*How Beastly!* 9848
*Jane Yolen's Mother Goose Songbook*, 679
*Jane Yolen's Old MacDonald Songbook*, 11546
*A Letter from Phoenix Farm*, 10310
*Letting Swift River Go*, 3729(F)
*Meet the Monsters*, 17468
*Merlin*, 6796(F)
*Merlin and the Dragons*, 6797(F)
*Milk and Honey*, 13988
*Miz Berlin Walks*, 3259(F)
*The Musicians of Bremen*, 8955
*Nocturne*, 3730(F)
*O Jerusalem*, 9679
*Once upon a Bedtime Story*, 8658
*The Originals*, 9753
*Owl Moon*, 4485(F)
*Passager*, 6798(F)
*Picnic with Piggins*, 2281(F)
*Piggins*, 2281(F)
*Piggins and the Royal Wedding*, 2281(F)
*Ring of Earth*, 9901
*Sacred Places*, 9680
*Sea Watch*, 9754
*Sky Dogs*, 9313
*Tam Lin*, 9046
*The Three Bears Holiday Rhyme Book*, 4642
*Water Music*, 9902
*Welcome to the Green House*, 3731
*Welcome to the Ice House*, 12778
*Welcome to the Sea of Sand*, 16229
*Wizard's Hall*, 6799(F)

Yolen, Jane, ed. *Alphabestiary*, 9752
*Camelot*, 9045
*Jane Yolen's Songs of Summer*, 11545
*The Lap-Time Song and Play Book*, 678
*Mother Earth, Father Sky*, 9899
*Once upon Ice*, 9900
*Sky Scrape/City Scape*, 9681
*Sleep Rhymes Around the World*, 599
*Street Rhymes Around the World*, 9682
*Weather Report*, 9903

# Illustrator Index

Illustrators are arranged alphabetically by last name, followed by book titles — which are also arranged alphabetically — and text entry number. All fiction titles are indicated by (F), following the entry number.

*Buffalo Bill and the Pony Express*, 5112(F)
*First Flight*, 5407(F)
*George the Drummer Boy*, 3753(F)
*Pocahontas*, 10596
*Sacajawea*, 10598
*Wagon Wheels*, 5081(F)
*The Warrior Goddess*, 9469
Bolster, Rob. *The Airplane Alphabet Book*, 16740
*Going Lobstering*, 2679(F)
Bomzer, Barry. *Dirt Bike Racer*, 8416(F)
Bond, Denny. *Sleepy Little Owl*, 1652(F)
Bond, Felicia. *The Big Green Pocketbook*, 2694(F)
*Big Red Barn*, 4223(F)
*If You Give a Moose a Muffin*, 1987(F)
*If You Give a Mouse a Cookie*, 1988(F)
*Mouse Cookies*, 17245
*Poinsettia and Her Family*, 1424(F)
*The Sky Is Full of Stars*, 14773
Bond, Higgins. *Susie King Taylor*, 10445
*When I Was Little*, 2950(F)
Bonforte, Lisa. *Otter on His Own*, 15693
Boni/Galante, Sudio. *Plants*, 16053
Bonner, Rog. *Moo Moo, Brown Cow*, 450(F)
Bonners, Susan. *A Penguin Year*, 15435
Bonsall, Crosby. *The Case of the Scaredy Cats*, 5070(F)
*Mine's the Best*, 5071(F)
*Piggle*, 5072(F)
*What Spot?*, 5074(F)
*Who's a Pest?*, 5075(F)
*Who's Afraid of the Dark?*, 5076(F)
Booth, George. *The Ballymara Flood*, 3487(F)
*Possum Come a-Knockin'*, 2187(F)
*Wacky Wednesday*, 374(F)
Booth, Graham. *Henry the Explorer*, 2362(F)
Bootman, Colin. *Oh, No, Toto!*, 3969(F)
*Young Frederick Douglass*, 10371
Borja, Corinne. *Making Chinese Papercuts*, 17144
Borja, Robert. *Making Chinese Papercuts*, 17144
Bornstein, Ruth. *Little Gorilla*, 1426(F)
*Mama One, Mama Two*, 3012(F)
Borovsky, Paul. *The Blabbermouths*, 3400(F)
Bosson, Victor. *The Magic Ear*, 8833
Bostock, Mike. *Imagine You Are a Crocodile*, 4468(F)
*Pond Year*, 3639(F)
Boucher, Joelle. *The Seventh Walnut*, 3677
Bouma, Paddy. *Valentine*, 2835(F)
Bour, Danièle. *Little Brown Bear Does Not Want to Eat*, 1837(F)
*Under the Ground*, 14841
Bour-Chollet, Celine. *All About Time*, 16388
Bowen, Betsy. *Shingebiss*, 9307
Bowen, Keith. *Snowy*, 4509(F)
Bowler, Ray. *The Beast in the Bathtub*, 2139(F)
Bowman, Leslie. *Balloons and Other Poems*, 9524
*The Canada Geese Quilt*, 7217(F)
*The Copper Lady*, 5362(F)
*The Cuckoo Child*, 5904(F)
*El Guero*, 7525(F)

*The Fiddler of the Northern Lights*, 1015(F)
*The Fourth-Grade Four*, 7230(F)
*Hannah*, 7390(F)
*Hello, Crow*, 4380(F)
*The Night the Bells Rang*, 7806(F)
*Orcas Around Me*, 2678
*Rich Lizard and Other Poems*, 9709
*Shadows*, 7191(F)
Bowring, Joanne. *Let Me Explain*, 14539
Brace, Eric. *The Krazees*, 1253(F)
*My Brother Is from Outer Space*, 3048(F)
Brady, Irene. *Peeping in the Shell*, 15350
Braginetz, Donna. *Seismosaurus*, 11748
Brammer, Erin M. *The Sea Maidens of Japan*, 3750(F)
Brandenberg, Alexa. *I Am Me!*, 2415(F)
Brandi, Lillian. *Encyclopedia Brown, Boy Detective*, 5767(F)
*Encyclopedia Brown Saves the Day*, 5768(F)
Braren, Loretta. *EcoArt!*, 16983
*Kids' Computer Creations*, 16832
*The Kids' Science Book*, 14604
*The Kids' Wildlife Book*, 14894
*The Little Hands Big Fun Craft Book*, 17024
*Rainy Day Play!*, 16984
*Shapes, Sizes and More Surprises!*, 202(F)
Brazell, Derek. *Cleversticks*, 4489(F)
Breebaart, Piet. *When I Die, Will I Get Better?*, 1431(F)
Brenner, Fred. *The Drinking Gourd*, 7646(F)
*One Day in the Desert*, 16205
Brent, Isabelle. *The Fairy Tales of Oscar Wilde*, 8565(F)
*Fairy Tales of the Brothers Grimm*, 8566(F)
*Just So Stories*, 1019(F)
Brett, Jan. *Annie and the Wild Animals*, 1434(F)
*Fritz and the Beautiful Horses*, 1438(F)
*The Mother's Day Mice*, 4602(F)
*Noelle of the Nutcracker*, 6473(F)
*The Owl and the Pussycat*, 9811
*St. Patrick's Day in the Morning*, 4604(F)
*Scary, Scary Halloween*, 4884(F)
*The Valentine Bears*, 5022(F)
Brewster, Patience. *Bear and Mrs. Duck*, 2266(F)
*Bear and Roly-Poly*, 2267(F)
*Bear's Christmas Surprise*, 4858(F)
*Queen of the May*, 8536(F)
*There's More . . . Much More*, 1360(F)
*Yoo Hoo, Moon!*, 5067(F)
Brickman, Robin. *A Log's Life*, 16045
*Swallows in the Birdhouse*, 4455
Bridwell, Norman. *Clifford's Good Deeds*, 1442(F)
*Clifford's Halloween*, 4881(F)
Brier, Peggy. *Southern Fried Rat and Other Gruesome Tales*, 9321
Brierley, Louise. *Beauty and the Beast and Other Stories*, 8521
*Lightning Inside You and Other Native American Riddles*, 17331
*Peacock Pie*, 9531

*Junie B. Jones Loves Handsome Warren*, 5339(F)
*The Karate Class Mystery*, 5252(F)
*Samantha the Snob*, 4041(F)
Brusca, Maria C. *Three Friends*, 307(F)
*When Jaguars Ate the Moon*, 8601
Bryan, Ashley. *All Night, All Day*, 11499
*Beat the Story-Drum, Pum-Pum*, 8687
*The Cat's Purr*, 1474(F)
*Christmas Gif'*, 13953
*Climbing Jacob's Ladder*, 13870
*The Story of the Three Kingdoms*, 1119(F)
*The Sun Is So Quiet*, 9691
*What a Morning!*, 11556
*What a Wonderful World*, 11612(F)
Bryan, Diana. *The Fisherman and His Wife*, 8910
*The Monkey People*, 9448
Bryant, Michael. *Bein' with You This Way*, 9701
*Booker T. Washington*, 10464
*Come Sunday*, 2522(F)
*Family Celebrations*, 4628
*Good-bye Hello*, 2532(F)
*Lost in the Tunnel of Time*, 5536(F)
*Madam C. J. Walker*, 10462
*Treemonisha*, 7820(F)
*A World of Holidays!*, 13900
*Zora Neale Hurston*, 10256
Bryer, Diana. *Cleo and the Coyote*, 4352(F)
*The Girl Who Loved Coyotes*, 9312
Bubley, Esther. *How Kittens Grow*, 15845
Buchanan, Yvonne. *Follow the Drinking Gourd*,
7619(F)
*Juneteenth Jamboree*, 7964(F)
Buchs, Thomas. *One Giant Leap*, 5724(F)
Buehner, Mark. *The Adventures of Taxi Dog*, 1400(F)
*Fanny's Dream*, 2823(F)
*Harvey Potter's Balloon Farm*, 1126(F)
*It's a Spoon, Not a Shovel*, 14113
*A Job for Wittilda*, 796(F)
*Maxi, the Hero*, 1401(F)
*My Life with the Wave*, 843(F)
Buetter, Barbara M. *Simple Puppets from Everyday
Materials*, 11649
Buetter, George. *Simple Puppets from Everyday
Materials*, 11649
Bulcken, Kimberly. *The Kids' Book of Chess*, 17601
Bull, Peter. *Big Ocean Creatures*, 15628
Buller, Jon. *Shari Lewis Presents 101 Magic Tricks
for Kids to Do*, 17305
Bullock, Kathleen. *It Chanced to Rain*, 1476(F)
Burchard, Peter. *Squanto, Friend of the Pilgrims*,
10610
Burdick, Jeri. *Sailor Cats*, 2252(F)
Burford, Kay. *Kimako's Story*, 2585(F)
Burger, Carl. *The Incredible Journey*, 5841(F)
*Old Yeller*, 5869(F)
Burgess, Mark. *Harriet and the Crocodiles*, 2214(F)
Burke, Dianne O. *Creepy Cuisine*, 17239
Burke, Susan S. *Class Act*, 17352(F)
*Home on the Range*, 17333
*My Very Own Christmas*, 17053

*Out to Dry*, 17388
*Plugged In*, 17374(F)
Burkert, Nancy E. *A Child's Calendar*, 3716
Burningham, John. *Chitty Chitty Bang Bang*, 6376(F)
*Come Away from the Water, Shirley*, 803(F)
*Granpa*, 2829(F)
*Mr. Gumpy's Motor Car*, 2300(F)
*The Wind in the Willows*, 6402(F)
Burns, Howard M. *The Boy Who Saved the Town*,
3957(F)
Burns, Ray. *Draw Fifty Creepy Crawlies*, 17100
Burroughes, Jo. *Mud, Moon and Me*, 9897
Burrowes, Adjoa J. *My Steps*, 2464(F)
Burstein, Chaya M. *The Jewish Kids Catalog*, 13969
*The Jewish Kids' Hebrew-English Wordbook*, 11416
Burton, Jane. *Egg*, 15078
*Forest Life*, 16272
*Fox*, 15234
*Swamp Life*, 15627
Burton, Virginia Lee. *Life Story*, 16113
*The Little House*, 2432(F)
*Mike Mulligan and His Steam Shovel*, 4555(F)
Bush, Darryl. *Kitten Training and Critters, Too!*,
15842
Bushe, Claire. *Angels, Prophets, Rabbis and Kings*,
9149
Butcher, Jim. *Jackie Robinson and the Story of All-
Black Baseball*, 11010
Butler, Jerry. *Sweet Words So Brave*, 11458
Butler, John. *Baby Animals*, 4309(F)
*Bashi, Elephant Baby*, 4408(F)
Butterfield, Ned. *The Illustrated Rules of In-line
Hockey*, 17512
Butterworth, Nick. *My Dad Is Awesome*, 2830(F)
*The Rescue Party*, 807(F)
Buttner, Thom. *Smoking Stinks!!*, 7181(F)
Byard, Carole. *Africa Dream*, 3823(F)
*The Black Snowman*, 4808(F)
*Grandmama's Joy*, 2904(F)
*Have a Happy . . .*, 7963(F)
*Working Cotton*, 2769(F)
Byers, Helen. *Colors of Japan*, 12255
*Count Your Way Through Germany*, 12403
Bynum, Jane K. *Bubbe and Gram*, 2917(F)
Byrd, Robert. *The Emperor's New Clothes*, 8542(F)
Byrd, Samuel. *Abraham Lincoln*, 10681
*Dancing with the Indians*, 2647(F)
*Keep on Singing*, 10152
*A Picture Book of Frederick Douglass*, 10369
*A Picture Book of Harriet Tubman*, 10452
Byrne, Connell P. *Millions of Miles to Mars*, 14714


Cable, Annette. *I Fly*, 2346(F)
*Me on the Map*, 11692
Cain, David. *Copier Creations*, 17152
Calder, Nancy E. *On Christmas Eve*, 4704(F)
Caldwell, John. *Any Number Can Play*, 17528
Cameron, Rod. *Breaking the Chains of the Ancient
Warrior*, 8478(F)

*Parade*, 2454(F)
*Rain*, 3627(F)
*School Bus*, 4561(F)
*Ten Black Dots*, 322(F)
*Tomorrow's Alphabet*, 113(F)
*Truck*, 694(F)
*When This Box Is Full*, 175(F)
Crews, Nina. *I'll Catch the Moon*, 847(F)
Cristini, Ermanno. *In My Garden*, 695(F)
Crocker, Debbie. *Learn the Value of Trust*, 152
Crockett-Blassingame, Linda. *See the Ocean*, 3561(F)
Croll, Carolyn. *The Big Balloon Race*, 5111(F)
*Clara and the Bookwagon*, 5249(F)
*Switch On, Switch Off*, 16580
*What Will the Weather Be?*, 16475
Crompton, Jack. *Mountains to Climb*, 4181(F)
Crossland, Caroline. *Ten Tall Oaktrees*, 3578(F)
Crowe, Elizabeth. *Jirohattan*, 7881(F)
Crowther, Robert. *My Pop-up Surprise ABC*, 23(F)
*My Pop-up Surprise 123*, 323(F)
Crum, Anna-Maria L. *Slugs, Bugs, and Salamanders*, 14865
Cruz, Ray. *Alexander and the Terrible, Horrible, No Good, Very Bad Day*, 3129(F)
*Alexander, Who Used to Be Rich Last Sunday*, 5434(F)
*Baseball Fever*, 8453(F)
*The Gorilla Did It*, 3355(F)
Cuffari, Richard. *The Cartoonist*, 7114(F)
*Hunter's Stew and Hangtown Fry*, 17249
*Mightiest of Mortals*, 9468
*Nothing Is Impossible*, 10272
*The Odyssey of Ben O'Neal*, 5785(F)
*Thank You, Jackie Robinson*, 8436(F)
*The TV Kid*, 7355(F)
*The Winged Colt of Casa Mia*, 6292(F)
Cummings, Pat. *C Is for City*, 35(F)
*Go Fish*, 6188(F)
*I Need a Lunch Box*, 2434(F)
*Just Us Women*, 2301(F)
*My Mama Needs Me*, 3135(F)
*Storm in the Night*, 4164(F)
Cummins, Jim. *The Valentine Mystery*, 5032(F)
Cunningham, David. *The Memory Box*, 2795(F)
Cupples, Pat. *Discover*, 14599
*Earthwatch*, 16134
*Hands On, Thumbs Up*, 11405
*The Science Book for Girls and Other Intelligent Beings*, 14643
*Sportsworks*, 14403
Curless, Allan. *Outcast of Redwall*, 6465(F)
Curry, Tom. *The Bootmaker and the Elves*, 1064(F)
Cushman, Doug. *Aunt Eater Loves a Mystery*, 5126(F)
*Halloween Mice!*, 4930(F)
*How Do You Make a Bubble?*, 5211(F)
*Porcupine's Pajama Party*, 5174(F)
*Valentine Mice!*, 5033(F)

Cvijanovic, Adam. *The Ledgerbook of Thomas Blue Eagle*, 7547(F)
Cymerman, John E. *How's the Weather?*, 16470
Czernecki, Stefan. *Pancho's Pinata*, 4726
*The Sleeping Bread*, 9402
*Zorah's Magic Carpet*, 849(F)

Da Rif, Andrea. *Where Did You Put Your Sleep?*, 556(F)
Dabcovich, Lydia. *Feathers*, 9143
*Hurry Home, Grandma!*, 4818(F)
*The Polar Bear Son*, 9185
*Sleepy Bear*, 4256(F)
Dacey, Bob. *Miriam's Cup*, 13982
Dale, Penny. *The Mushroom Hunt*, 16019
*Once There Were Giants*, 2759(F)
*Wake Up, Mr. B.!*, 851(F)
*When the Teddy Bears Came*, 3133(F)
Dallinger, Rebecca. *Allison's Story*, 8269
Daly, Carla. *Damien the Dragon*, 6649(F)
Daly, Jude. *Gift of the Sun*, 3486(F)
Daly, Niki. *The Dinosaurs Are Back and It's All Your Fault Edward!*, 3354(F)
*Not So Fast, Songololo*, 3783(F)
*One Round Moon and a Star for Me*, 3024(F)
*Red Light, Green Light, Mama and Me*, 2406(F)
D'Amato, Alex. *Indian Crafts*, 17061
D'Amato, Janet. *Indian Crafts*, 17061
Daniel, Alan. *Big David, Little David*, 4518(F)
*Bunnicula*, 8077(F)
*Bunnicula Escapes!*, 5611(F)
*The Orchestra*, 11575
*Return to Howliday Inn*, 8080(F)
*Sody Salleratus*, 9324
Daniel, Lea. *Bunnicula Escapes!*, 5611(F)
*Sody Salleratus*, 9324
Dann, Penny. *Bicycle Safety*, 17592
*Bon Appetit, Bertie!*, 3374(F)
*Emergencies*, 14524
Darley, Felix O. *Rip Van Winkle and the Legend of Sleepy Hollow*, 6457(F)
Darling, Louis. *Ellen Tebbits*, 7998(F)
*The Enormous Egg*, 7990(F)
*Henry Huggins*, 8000(F)
*Mr. Bass's Planetoid*, 8322(F)
*Otis Spofford*, 8001(F)
*Ramona the Pest*, 6074(F)
*Runaway Ralph*, 8002(F)
Darling, Tara. *ABC Dogs*, 15853
*Amazon ABC*, 24(F)
*Arctic Babies*, 12746
*Chameleons*, 14953
*Desert Babies*, 15040
*Komodo Dragon*, 14954
*Rain Forest Babies*, 16235
*Seashore Babies*, 15620
*Tasmanian Devil*, 15280
*Walrus*, 15696

*My Favorite Ghost*, 5738(F)
*Soccer Circus*, 5569(F)
*Soccer Mania!*, 8475(F)
DeSaix, Deborah Durland. *The Girl Who Danced with Dolphins*, 4262(F)
*Hilary and the Lions*, 1576(F)
*Meg and Dad Discover Treasure in the Air*, 3673(F)
*Returning Nicholas*, 866(F)
DeSantis, Laura. *Come Home with Me*, 2574(F)
de Seve, Peter. *Finn McCoul*, 8991
Desimini, Lisa. *Adelaide and the Night Train*, 567(F)
*Anansi Does the Impossible!*, 8662
*The Great Peace March*, 11602
*How the Stars Fell into the Sky*, 9273
*Love Letters*, 9508
*The Magic Weaver of Rugs*, 9274
*Northwoods Cradle Song*, 596(F)
*Tulip Sees America*, 2349(F)
Detweiler, Susan. *The First Teddy Bear*, 17180
DeVelasco, Joe. *The Twenty-Four Days Before Christmas*, 7941(F)
Devito, Anna. *If You Sailed on the Mayflower*, 13027
Devlin, Harry. *Cranberry Easter*, 4864(F)
*Old Black Witch!*, 868(F)
Dewar, Bob. *Ivan*, 9085
Dewdney, Anna. *Shadow over Second*, 8425(F)
*What You Do Is Easy, What I Do Is Hard*, 2268(F)
Dewey, Ariane. *Alligator Arrived with Apples*, 25(F)
*Alligators and Others All Year Long*, 1581(F)
*April Showers*, 2104(F)
*Birthday Rhymes, Special Times*, 4661
*The Chick and the Duckling*, 1649(F)
*Come Out and Play, Little Mouse*, 1820(F)
*Five Little Ducks*, 419(F)
*Gregory, the Terrible Eater*, 2109(F)
*Herman the Helper*, 1821(F)
*Mushroom in the Rain*, 2156(F)
*One Duck, Another Duck*, 417(F)
*Rockabye Crocodile*, 1368(F)
*They Thought They Saw Him*, 4453(F)
*We Hide, You Seek*, 246(F)
*Where Does the Sun Go at Night?*, 931(F)
Dewey, Jennifer. *New Questions and Answers About Dinosaurs*, 11780
*The Secret Language of Snow*, 16507
*The Song of the Sea Otter*, 15700
*Young Kangaroo*, 4226(F)
de Wolf, Alex. *Melinda and Nock and the Magic Spell*, 5431(F)
Diamond, Donna. *Beat the Turtle Drum*, 7183(F)
*Bridge to Terabithia*, 6903(F)
*Mustard*, 5871(F)
*Riches*, 6005(F)
Dianov, Alisher. *The Enchanted Storks*, 9181
*Melanie*, 814(F)
Diaz, David. *December*, 4707(F)
*Going Home*, 3765(F)
*Just One Flick of a Finger*, 7236(F)
*Neighborhood Odes*, 9651
*Smoky Night*, 2429(F)

*Wilma Unlimited*, 11132
Dick, Judy. *Sefer Ha-Aggadah*, 9154
Dicks, Jan T. *The House That Crack Built*, 14288
*The Little Seven-Colored Horse*, 9374
Dickson, Mora. *Tales of an Ashanti Father*, 8680
Didier, Les. *Carlos Finlay*, 10846
Dieterichs, Shelley. *Uh Oh! Gotta Go!*, 2623
DiFiori, Larry. *I Can Do It!*, 5045(F)
Di Grazia, Thomas. *Holiday Tales of Sholem Aleichem*, 7900(F)
Dilella, Barbara. *The Anne of Green Gables Cookbook*, 17233
Dillon, Diane. *Aida*, 11492
*Ashanti to Zulu*, 12094
*Brother to the Wind*, 1295(F)
*The Color Wizard*, 5079(F)
*The Girl Who Dreamed Only Geese and Other Stories of the Far North*, 9189
*Her Stories*, 9332
*Honey, I Love, and Other Love Poems*, 9692
*The Hundred Penny Box*, 6156(F)
*Many Thousand Gone*, 13089
*The People Could Fly*, 9333
*Pish, Posh, Said Hieronymus Bosch*, 1314
*Songs and Stories from Uganda*, 8736
*The Sorcerer's Apprentice*, 1315(F)
*The Tale of the Mandarin Ducks*, 8840
*What Am I?*, 147(F)
*Who's in Rabbit's House?*, 8676
*Why Mosquitoes Buzz in People's Ears*, 8677
Dillon, Leo. *Aida*, 11492
*Ashanti to Zulu*, 12094
*Brother to the Wind*, 1295(F)
*The Color Wizard*, 5079(F)
*The Girl Who Dreamed Only Geese and Other Stories of the Far North*, 9189
*Her Stories*, 9332
*Honey, I Love, and Other Love Poems*, 9692
*The Hundred Penny Box*, 6156(F)
*Many Thousand Gone*, 13089
*The People Could Fly*, 9333
*Pish, Posh, Said Hieronymus Bosch*, 1314
*Songs and Stories from Uganda*, 8736
*The Sorcerer's Apprentice*, 1315(F)
*The Tale of the Mandarin Ducks*, 8840
*What Am I?*, 147(F)
*Who's in Rabbit's House?*, 8676
*Why Mosquitoes Buzz in People's Ears*, 8677
DiSalvo-Ryan, DyAnne. *Adiós, Anna*, 4059(F)
*The American Wei*, 2690(F)
*The Bravest Cat!*, 5136(F)
*The Christmas Knight*, 8972
*George Washington's Mother*, 10791
*Kate Skates*, 5318(F)
*The Mommy Exchange*, 2929(F)
*Nina, Nina Ballerina*, 5321(F)
*Nina, Nina, Star Ballerina*, 5322(F)
*Now We Can Have a Wedding!*, 2450(F)
*The Real Hole*, 2305(F)
*Say Hola, Sarah*, 5158(F)

*True Blue*, 5146(F)
*What Did Mommy Do Before You?*, 2992(F)
DiVito, Anna. *I Want Answers and a Parachute*, 7043(F)
*Striking It Rich*, 13150
Dixon, Jean. *Judo*, 17664
Dixon, Tennessee. *Berchick*, 4213(F)
*The Heroine of the Titanic*, 3757(F)
*Jessica and the Wolf*, 4103(F)
*The Princess and the Peacocks*, 7401(F)
Dobson, Steven. *Rachel Carson*, 10813
*Robert Louis Stevenson*, 10286
Dodd, Lynley. *Hairy Maclary from Donaldson's Dairy*, 1580(F)
Dodge, Katharine. *Sweet Dreams of the Wild*, 485
Dodson, Bert. *Buffalo Thunder*, 3996(F)
*Chicken Soup for Little Souls*, 4022(F)
*Daniel Boone*, 9967
*Grandpa Was a Cowboy*, 2360(F)
*Hannah's Fancy Notions*, 7837(F)
*Supergrandpa*, 2351(F)
*What Makes the Wind?*, 16401
*Wonders of the Sea*, 15786
*Young Frederick Douglass*, 10376
Dodson, Liz B. *Count Your Way Through Brazil*, 12702
*Count Your Way Through India*, 12236
*Korean Holidays and Festivals*, 12297
Dolobowsky, Mena. *Cleaning Up*, 13605
*Tuning In*, 16873
*Why Can't I Live Forever?*, 14562
Domanska, Janina. *If All the Seas Were One Sea*, 635
*The Trumpeter of Krakow*, 7481(F)
Domm, Jeff. *Gray Wolf Pup*, 4214(F)
*What's the Difference Between . . . Lenses and Prisms and Other Scientific Things?*, 16706
Donahue, Dorothy. *Maybe Yes, Maybe No, Maybe Maybe*, 7271(F)
Donati, Paolo. *Amazing Buildings*, 16784
Doner, Kim. *Green Snake Ceremony*, 3981(F)
Doney, Todd L. W. *January Rides the Wind*, 3669(F)
*Old Salt, Young Salt*, 3001(F)
*Red Bird*, 4623(F)
*Sleeping Beauty*, 11636
Doniger, Nancy. *Morning, Noon, and Night*, 9663
Donnelly, Liza. *Dinosaur Beach*, 873(F)
Donohue, Dorothy. *Believing Sophie*, 4079(F)
*Dear Daddy*, 3093(F)
*Turkey Pox*, 5000(F)
Donze, Lisa. *Squanto and the First Thanksgiving*, 10611
Dooling, Michael. *A Long Way to Go*, 7825(F)
*Mary McLean and the St. Patrick's Day Parade*, 4618(F)
*Straw Sense*, 7428(F)
*Thomas Jefferson*, 10655
Doolittle, Michael J. *Bats, Bugs, and Biodiversity*, 16244
Dore, Gustave. *Perrault's Fairy Tales*, 8893
Dorfman, Elena. *When Learning Is Tough*, 14318

Dorros, Arthur. *Ant Cities*, 15541
*Feel the Wind*, 3573(F)
*This Is My House*, 3787
*What Makes Day and Night?*, 14686
Dorsey, Bob. *The Pet-Sitters*, 5970(F)
Doty, Eldon C. *Zoo Clues*, 15909
Doty, Roy. *How to Write Your Best Book Report*, 11469
*Jobs for Kids*, 13555
*Kid Camping from Aaaaiii! to Zip*, 17600
*Mirrors*, 16574
*Shadow Play*, 16575
*Tales of a Fourth Grade Nothing*, 7985(F)
Doubilet, David. *Under the Sea from A to Z*, 15623
Douglas-Hamilton, Oria. *African Elephants*, 15272
Dovey, Ed. *Everyday Life in Ancient Greece*, 11927
*Invaders and Settlers*, 12412
Dow, Jill. *The Rock Pool*, 16289
Downer, Maggie. *Christmas Fun*, 17029
Downing, Chris. *Seven Sillies*, 1585(F)
Downing, Julie. *Cabbage Rose*, 8528(F)
*Daniel's Gift*, 4759(F)
*The Magpies' Nest*, 8982
*Mr. Griggs' Work*, 2719(F)
*A Ride on the Red Mare's Back*, 1047(F)
*Sonia Begonia*, 5737(F)
*Water Voices*, 8395(F)
*White Snow, Blue Feather*, 3574(F)
Downs, Peter. *Amazing Bikes*, 17593
Doyle, Richard. *King of the Golden River or the Black Brother*, 6652(F)
Drake, Gary. *The Morgans Dream*, 9649
Draper, Rochelle. *The World at His Fingertips*, 11195
Drescher, Henrik. *Klutz*, 3322(F)
*Runaway Opposites*, 9671
*Simon's Book*, 882(F)
Drescher, Joan. *Eaton Stanley and the Mind Control Experiment*, 7969(F)
*My Mother's Getting Married*, 2872(F)
*Your Family, My Family*, 14125
Drucker, Mort. *Whitefish Will Rides Again!*, 3519(F)
Dubanevich, Arlene. *Pig William*, 1582(F)
Dubois, Claude K. *I Love You So Much*, 1978(F)
du Bois, William Pene. *A Certain Small Shepherd*, 7912(F)
*Magic Finger*, 6346(F)
*Twenty and Ten*, 7856(F)
*Twenty-One Balloons*, 8029(F)
*William's Doll*, 3165(F)
DuBosque, Doug. *Draw! Grassland Animals*, 17111
*Learn to Draw Now!*, 17112
Dubowski, Mark. *Pirate School*, 5137(F)
Dubrowski, Ken. *Up and Away!*, 16722
Dudley, Ebet. *The World of Insects*, 15533
Duffy, Daniel. *The Great Pony Hassle*, 6185(F)
*On the Right Track*, 5503(F)
*Out of Place*, 5504(F)
*Theodoric's Rainbow*, 7483(F)
Dufort, Antony. *Ballet Steps*, 11631
Dugan, Karen M. *Bicycle Riding*, 9588

Garrison, Ron. *A Day in the Life of a Test Pilot*, 14250

Gates, Donald. *The Summer of Stanley*, 2331(F)

Gay, Marie-Louise. *Fat Charlie's Circus*, 3340(F)
 *Rumpelstiltskin*, 8902

Gazsi, Edward S. *The Seven Ravens*, 8903

Geehan, Wayne. *Twenty Thousand Leagues Under the Sea*, 5795(F)

Geer, Charles. *Plain Girl*, 7312(F)

Gehm, Charles C. *The House Without a Christmas Tree*, 7954(F)
 *Soup*, 6906(F)

Geisert, Arthur. *Aesop and Company*, 9060
 *The Ark*, 13827
 *Oink*, 1643(F)
 *Pigs from A to Z*, 34(F)
 *Pigs from 1 to 10*, 339(F)

Geldart, William. *The Fairy Rebel*, 8506(F)

George, Bob. *Card Games for Children*, 17638

George, Jean Craighead. *My Side of the Mountain*, 5563(F)

George, Lindsay B. *Box Turtle at Long Pond*, 3597(F)
 *Secret Places*, 9572

Gerard, Elena. *Even a Little Is Something*, 7444(F)

Gergely, Tibor. *Wheel on the Chimney*, 4225(F)

Gerig, Sibyl G. *The Worry Stone*, 9208

Gerrard, Roy. *The Favershams*, 10241
 *Matilda Jane*, 3806(F)
 *A Pocket Full of Posies*, 665
 *Sir Cedric*, 3809(F)
 *Sir Francis Drake*, 9990

Gershom, Griffith. *Journey to Freedom*, 7662(F)

Gerstein, Mordicai. *Behind the Couch*, 925(F)
 *Frankenstein Moved in on the Fourth Floor*, 5645(F)
 *The Mountains of Tibet*, 3812(F)
 *Something Queer at the Library*, 5648(F)
 *Something Queer in Outer Space*, 5649(F)
 *Something Queer in the Wild West*, 5651(F)

Geter, Tyrone. *Dawn and the Round To-It*, 3107(F)
 *White Socks Only*, 3775(F)
 *Willie Jerome*, 2873(F)

Giannini, Enzo. *Caterina, the Clever Farm Girl*, 9075

Gibbons, Gail. *Boat Book*, 4566(F)
 *Cars and How They Go*, 16895
 *Cats*, 15836
 *Caves and Caverns*, 16182
 *Christmas Time*, 13945
 *Dogs*, 15855
 *Easter*, 4866
 *Farming*, 15934
 *Fire! Fire!*, 2504(F)
 *Halloween*, 13960
 *New Road!*, 4568(F)
 *Paper, Paper Everywhere*, 2506(F)
 *Playgrounds*, 151(F)
 *The Post Office Book*, 13731
 *Recycle!*, 13597
 *The Seasons of Arnold's Apple Tree*, 3599(F)

*Sun Up, Sun Down*, 14799
 *Thanksgiving Day*, 13994
 *Tool Book*, 17184
 *Trains*, 16920(F)
 *Trucks*, 16846(F)
 *Tunnels*, 16879
 *Up Goes the Skyscraper!*, 16769
 *Valentine's Day*, 14001
 *Weather Forecasting*, 16482
 *Weather Words and What They Mean*, 16483
 *Yippee-Yay!*, 13130

Gibson, Barbara. *Explore a Tropical Forest*, 16234
 *Star Wars*, 8380(F)

Giffard, Hannah. *Is There Room on the Bus?*, 413(F)

Gilbert, Anne Y. *A Christmas Star Called Hannah*, 4744(F)

Gilbert, Lyn. *While You Sleep*, 552(F)

Gilbert, Yvonne. *Children's Bible Stories*, 13832
 *Per and the Dala Horse*, 968(F)

Gilchrist, Jan S. *Big Friend, Little Friend*, 2517(F)
 *Everett Anderson's Christmas Coming*, 4718(F)
 *First Pink Light*, 2903(F)
 *For the Love of the Game*, 9906
 *Honey, I Love*, 3196(F)
 *Lemonade Sun and Other Summer Poems*, 9536
 *Lift Ev'ry Voice and Sing*, 11515
 *Nathaniel Talking*, 9693
 *Night on Neighborhood Street*, 2518(F)
 *Singing Down the Rain*, 845(F)
 *Waiting for Christmas*, 4752(F)
 *William and the Good Old Days*, 2907(F)

Gilfoy, Bruce. *Whisper Whisper Jesse, Whisper Whisper Josh*, 4128(F)

Gill, Madelaine. *Where Is the Bear at School?*, 4530(F)
 *Where Is the Bear in the City?*, 3425(F)

Gill, Margery. *Dawn of Fear*, 6828(F)

Gilleece, David. *In the Land of the Big Red Apple*, 7710(F)
 *Little House on Rocky Edge*, 7712(F)

Gillespie, Jessie. *The Birds' Christmas Carol*, 7966(F)

Gillman, Alec. *Fast Eddie*, 6312(F)
 *Green Truck Garden Giveaway*, 2643(F)
 *Radio Boy*, 3786(F)
 *Toad or Frog, Swamp or Bog?*, 14812

Gilman, Phoebe. *Once upon a Golden Apple*, 8544(F)

Ginsburg, Max. *The Friendship*, 6035(F)
 *Kate Shelley*, 10785
 *Mississippi Bridge*, 6037(F)

Giovanopoulos, Paul. *How Many Miles to Babylon?*, 5553(F)
 *Learning to Say Good-bye*, 14164

Girouard, Patrick. *Math Fun*, 16371
 *Math Fun with Money Puzzlers*, 16372
 *More or Less a Mess*, 5232(F)

Glanzman, Louis. *The Bears' House*, 8290(F)
 *The Noonday Friends*, 6926(F)
 *Pippi Longstocking*, 8105(F)

Glass, Andrew. *Ananse's Feast*, 8727

Lechon, Daniel. *The Desert Is My Mother/El Desierto Es Mi Madre*, 9887
Leder, Dora. *I Was So Mad!*, 4154(F)
  *I'm Busy, Too*, 4543(F)
  *Julian's Glorious Summer*, 5100(F)
  *Just a Little Ham*, 5846(F)
  *Mama Cat's Year*, 4443(F)
  *Oh, That Cat!*, 4444(F)
  *One More Thing, Dad*, 440(F)
  *The Plum Tree War*, 6913(F)
Lee, Alan. *Black Ships Before Troy*, 9493
  *The Wanderings of Odysseus*, 9494
Lee, Brian. *The Ghost Pirate*, 5485(F)
Lee, Dom. *Baseball Saved Us*, 4117(F)
  *Heroes*, 6018(F)
  *Passage to Freedom*, 12058
Lee, Ileana C. *Kneeling Carabao and Dancing Giants*, 12343
Lee, Jeanne M. *The Butterfly Boy*, 1342(F)
  *The Ch'i-lin Purse*, 8768
  *Toad Is the Uncle of Heaven*, 8853
Lee, Jody. *Anne of Green Gables*, 7253(F)
Lee, Katie. *Who Comes?*, 9710
Lee, Paul. *Amistad Rising*, 13083
Lee, Robert J. *The Magic Pumpkin*, 4920(F)
  *The Summer Sands*, 2500(F)
Lee, Victor. *Where Did All the Dragons Go?*, 1179(F)
Leedy, Loreen. *The Dragon Halloween Party*, 4914(F)
  *Pingo the Plaid Panda*, 1841(F)
  *The Potato Party and Other Troll Tales*, 1046(F)
  *Waiting for Baby*, 2806(F)
Leer, Rebecca. *A Spoon for Every Bite*, 2530(F)
Leghorn, Lindsay. *Proud of Our Feelings*, 2599(F)
Lehman, Barbara. *Moonfall*, 1307(F)
  *Something for Everyone*, 1308(F)
Leigh, Tom. *Bone Poems*, 9612
  *Kermit and Robin's Scary Story*, 1970(F)
  *Miss Piggy's Night Out*, 1730(F)
Leiner, Alan. *Poems That Sing to You*, 9659
Leister, Bryan. *Gutenberg's Gift*, 10863
Lelooska, Chief. *Echoes of the Elders*, 9249
Lemelman, Martin. *The Wise Shoemaker of Studena*, 3876(F)
Lemieux, Michele. *Amahl and the Night Visitors*, 4809(F)
  *There Was an Old Man*, 9815
Lemke, Horst. *Around the World in Eighty Dishes*, 17260
Lemoine, Georges. *The Book of Creation*, 13825
  *The Wicked Prince*, 8503(F)
Lennox, Elsie. *Little Obie and the Kidnap*, 7741(F)
Lenoir, Jane. *Barney the Bear Killer*, 5969(F)
Lenski, Lois. *Betsy-Tacy*, 8267(F)
  *Strawberry Girl*, 7815(F)
Lent, Blair. *Bayberry Bluff*, 2600(F)
  *The Funny Little Woman*, 8839
  *The Little Match Girl*, 8489(F)
  *Tikki Tikki Tembo*, 8782
Leonard, Richard. *The Story of Sacajawea*, 10599

Leonard, Tom. *Discovering Jupiter*, 14709
  *Under the Sun and the Moon and Other Poems*, 9858
Les Chats Pelés. *Fun with Numbers*, 16379
Lessac, Frane. *The Bird Who Was an Elephant*, 7447(F)
  *Caribbean Carnival*, 11501
  *The Chalk Doll*, 3062(F)
  *The Distant Talking Drum*, 9890
  *O Christmas Tree*, 4825(F)
  *Queen Esther Saves Her People*, 4956
  *The Wonderful Towers of Watts*, 11360
Lester, Alison. *Clive Eats Alligators*, 2601(F)
  *Tessa Snaps Snakes*, 3227(F)
  *Yikes!*, 2335(F)
Levering, Robert. *If You Lived with the Sioux Indians*, 12895
Levert, Mireille. *Tiny Toes*, 2572(F)
Levin, Ted. *Cactus Poems*, 9854
  *Sawgrass Poems*, 9855
Levine, David. *Fables of Aesop*, 9054
Levine, Melinda. *Eight Days of Hanukkah*, 4999(F)
Levitt, Sidney. *You Don't Get a Carrot Unless You're a Bunny*, 4917(F)
Lewin, Betsy. *Araminta's Paint Box*, 3733(F)
  *The Boy Who Counted Stars*, 9556
  *Doodle Dandy!*, 13910
  *Gobble!*, 13995
  *Ho Ho Ho!*, 13947
  *The Lunch Box Surprise*, 5268(F)
  *Mushy!*, 14002
  *My Tooth Is About to Fall Out*, 5269(F)
  *No Such Thing*, 524(F)
  *Rapunzel*, 8952
  *Recess Mess*, 5270(F)
  *Sharing Time Troubles*, 5271(F)
  *Somebody Catch My Homework*, 9801
  *A Thousand Cousins*, 9557
  *Weird!*, 13961
  *What If the Shark Wears Tennis Shoes?*, 553(F)
Lewin, Ted. *Ali, Child of the Desert*, 3883(F)
  *The Always Prayer Shawl*, 3923(F)
  *American Too*, 2399(F)
  *Brother Francis and the Friendly Beasts*, 3838
  *Cowboy Country*, 2352(F)
  *The Day of Ahmed's Secret*, 3832(F)
  *The Great Pumpkin Switch*, 3007(F)
  *Herds of Thunder, Manes of Gold*, 5850(F)
  *The Horse in the Attic*, 5518(F)
  *Just in Time for Christmas*, 4698(F)
  *Lost Moose*, 4447(F)
  *Matthew's Meadow*, 6273(F)
  *National Velvet*, 5828(F)
  *The Originals*, 9753
  *Paperboy*, 3860(F)
  *Peppe the Lamplighter*, 3748(F)
  *The Potato Man*, 2621(F)
  *Sami and the Time of the Troubles*, 3833(F)
  *Sea Watch*, 9754
  *The Search for Grissi*, 7305(F)

Macey, Barry. *Paddington on Screen*, 7987(F)
McGaw, Laurie. *Polar the Titanic Bear*, 13237
  *Something to Remember Me By*, 2817(F)
McGee, John F. *Berries, Nuts and Seeds*, 16097
McGinley-Nally, Sharon. *Django*, 9318
  *First Snow, Magic Snow*, 9082
  *Hazel's Circle*, 4260(F)
  *My Grandmother's Journey*, 3770(F)
  *Pigs Go to Market*, 7903(F)
  *Pigs in the Pantry*, 1385(F)
  *Pigs on a Blanket*, 1386(F)
  *Pigs Will Be Pigs*, 1387(F)
McGraw, DeLoss. *Hippity Hop, Frog on Top*, 447(F)
McGraw, Sheila. *This Old New House*, 16789
McGregor, Barbara. *Purple Delicious Blackberry
  Jam*, 3433(F)
McGuire, Leslie. *This Farm Is a Mess*, 5278(F)
Machin, Mark. *Weather*, 16480
Macht, Merle. *Doodle Soup*, 9793
McIntosh, Jon. *Witch Way to the Beach*, 1095(F)
Mack, Stan. *Ten Bears in My Bed*, 381(F)
Mackain, Bonnie. *One Hundred Hungry Ants*, 415(F)
  *A Remainder of One*, 416(F)
MacKay, Donald. *The Stone-Faced Boy*, 7161(F)
McKay, Robert A. *Grandfather's Day*, 6194(F)
McKeating, Eileen. *Laura Ingalls Wilder*, 10307
  *Ozzie on His Own*, 6866(F)
  *Roz and Ozzie*, 6126(F)
McKee, David. *Elmer in the Snow*, 1909(F)
  *I Can Too!*, 1910(F)
Mackie, Clare. *Twin Pickle*, 2871(F)
McKie, Roy. *Mr. Wizard's Supermarket Science*,
  14603
McKinley, John. *The Great Gerbil Roundup*, 8125(F)
McLean, Andrew. *Switch Cat*, 4265(F)
Maclean, Colin. *Nursery Rhyme Songbook with Easy
  Music to Play for Piano and Guitar*, 619(F)
  *The Nursery Treasury*, 620
  *The Playtime Treasury*, 17487
McLean, Meg. *Laughing All the Way*, 2106(F)
Maclean, Moira. *Nursery Rhyme Songbook with Easy
  Music to Play for Piano and Guitar*, 619(F)
  *The Nursery Treasury*, 620
  *The Playtime Treasury*, 17487
McLoughlin, Wayne. *Here Is the Wetland*, 16180
  *Voices of the Wild*, 5931(F)
McMillan, Bruce. *Ghost Doll*, 1077(F)
  *Mary Had a Little Lamb*, 624
  *The Remarkable Riderless Runaway Tricycle*,
  1078(F)
  *Step by Step*, 3015(F)
McMullan, Jim. *Hey, Pipsqueak!*, 1079(F)
McMullen, Nigel. *The Monster Party*, 1042(F)
McNaught, Harry. *Astronomy Today*, 14668
McNaughton, Colin. *Boo!*, 1916(F)
McNeill, Shannon. *Albert Goes to Town*, 999(F)
  *The Trouble with Mister*, 1004(F)
McPhail, David. *Andrew's Bath*, 3397(F)
  *Angel Pig and the Hidden Christmas*, 4852(F)
  *The Bear's Bicycle*, 1915(F)

*The Bear's Toothache*, 1920(F)
*A Big Fat Enormous Lie*, 4152(F)
*The Dream Child*, 545(F)
*Emma's Vacation*, 1921(F)
*Farm Morning*, 2634(F)
*First Flight*, 1922(F)
*Fix-It*, 1923(F)
*The Ice Cream Store*, 9817
*If You Were My Bunny*, 544(F)
*In Flight with David McPhail*, 10265
*Moony B. Finch, the Fastest Draw in the West*,
  1083(F)
*The Mother Goose Songbook*, 11592
*Night Sounds, Morning Colors*, 3136(F)
*The Nightgown of the Sullen Moon*, 1313(F)
*On a Starry Night*, 1016(F)
*Pig Pig Grows Up*, 1927(F)
*Sisters*, 3016(F)
*Snow Lion*, 5281(F)
*Ten Cats Have Hats*, 385(F)
*Uncle Terrible*, 6767(F)
*Who Gets the Sun out of Bed?*, 812(F)
*Why a Disguise?*, 3429(F)
McRae, Patrick T. *Let's Build a Car*, 16907
McTaggart, David. *John's Picture*, 1072(F)
Madama, John. *Clambake*, 12922
Madden, Don. *Is There Life in Outer Space?*, 16629
  *Pitcher*, 17567
  *The Sun*, 14793
  *Telephones, Televisions and Toilets*, 16843
  *The Wartville Wizard*, 1087(F)
Maddison, Keith. *Everyday Life in Ancient Egypt*,
  11883
Maddox, Tony. *Ducks Disappearing*, 399(F)
Maeno, Itoko. *Minou*, 1411(F)
  *Shadow and the Ready Time*, 4439(F)
Maestro, Giulio. *Bats*, 15167
  *Big City Port*, 4581(F)
  *Comets*, 14746
  *The Dinosaur Is the Biggest Animal That Ever
  Lived*, 14574
  *Eight Ate*, 11438
  *Exploration and Conquest*, 12982
  *Ferryboat*, 16953
  *Guppies in Tuxedos*, 11439
  *Halloween Howls*, 17364
  *How Do Apples Grow?*, 15993
  *In a Pickle and Other Funny Idioms*, 11440
  *It Figures!*, 11482
  *The New Americans*, 13028
  *Our Patchwork Planet*, 16133
  *A Sea Full of Sharks*, 15721
  *Snow Day*, 3658
  *The Story of Money*, 13543
  *The Story of Religion*, 13805
  *Sunshine Makes the Seasons*, 14794
  *Take a Look at Snakes*, 14979
  *Taxi*, 2635(F)
  *Too Hot to Hoot*, 11443
  *Tornado Alert*, 16409

*The House on Maple Street*, 3930(F)
*How Many Days to America? A Thanksgiving Story*, 5003(F)
*Matthew and Tilly*, 3215(F)
*The Thanksgiving Visitor*, 7120(F)
Peck, Marshall H. *Amazing Rescues*, 5406
Pedersen, Janet. *A Weed Is a Seed*, 2774(F)
Pedersen, Judy. *Gather Up, Gather In*, 3611(F)
*On the Road of Stars*, 9194
*Seedfolks*, 6000(F)
Peek, Merle. *Roll Over! A Counting Song*, 412(F)
Peet, Bill. *Big Bad Bruce*, 1144(F)
*The Caboose Who Got Loose*, 1145(F)
*Cowardly Clyde*, 2006(F)
*Eli*, 2007(F)
*Encore for Eleanor*, 2008(F)
*The Gnats of Knotty Pine*, 2009(F)
*Jennifer and Josephine*, 1146(F)
*Whingdingdilly*, 2010(F)
*The Wump World*, 3671(F)
Peguero, Adrian. *Lionel and Amelia*, 2012(F)
Peguero, Gerard. *Lionel and Amelia*, 2012(F)
Pelizzoli, Francesca. *Lao Lao of Dragon Mountain*, 771(F)
Pelletier, Gilles. *Come to the Fair*, 2616(F)
*A Happy New Year's Day*, 4605(F)
*The Sugaring-Off Party*, 4106(F)
Pels, Winslow. *Stone Soup*, 8888
Penney, Ian. *A Noteworthy Tale*, 1118(F)
Percy, Graham. *The Cock, the Mouse, and the Little Red Hen*, 8963
*A Cup of Starshine*, 9515
*Pigasus*, 1973(F)
*24 Strange Little Animals*, 2013(F)
Perkins, Lynne Rae. *Clouds for Dinner*, 3054(F)
Perlman, Janet. *The Emperor Penguin's New Clothes*, 8563(F)
Perols, Sylvaine. *Atlas of Plants*, 16055
*Colors*, 220
*The Human Body*, 14407
*The Ladybug and Other Insects*, 15500
Perrin, Gerry. *Hau Kola Hello Friend*, 10247
Perrone, Donna. *The Rajah's Rice*, 3747(F)
Perry, Rebecca. *Lots of Limericks*, 9820
Pertzoff, Alexander. *Three Names*, 3896(F)
Peters, David. *Supergiants!*, 11749
Peters, Patricia. *Nursery Rhymes from Mother Goose Told in Signed English*, 607
Petersham, Maud. *The Rooster Crows*, 664
Petersham, Miska. *The Rooster Crows*, 664
Peterson, Betty. *The Bunny Who Found Easter*, 4876(F)
Peterson, Dawn. *Ellie Bear and the Fly-Away Fly*, 2074(F)
Peterson, Donna. *Gran's Bees*, 3120(F)
Petricic, Dusan. *Bone Button Borscht*, 9137
Petruccio, Steven J. *Great White Shark*, 15726
*Raindrops and Rainbows*, 16467
*The Starry Sky*, 14684
Pfiffner, George. *Earth-Friendly Outdoor Fun*, 17023

Pfister, Marcus. *Penguin Pete, Ahoy!*, 2018(F)
Pfleger, Andrea F. *Surprising Myself*, 10243
Phillips, Francis. *The Sun Is a Star*, 14673
Phillips, Louise. *Sound Science*, 16618
Phillips-Duke, Barbara J. *Digby*, 5181(F)
Pidgeon, Jean. *Brush Your Teeth, Please*, 1905(F)
*The Snowball*, 743(F)
Pienkowski, Jan. *Boats*, 4585(F)
*Colors*, 235(F)
*Sally Go Round the Moon*, 11521
Pierard, John. *My Babysitter Is a Vampire*, 8072(F)
*My Teacher Fried My Brains*, 8327(F)
Pilkey, Dav. *The Dumb Bunnies*, 1566(F)
*The Dumb Bunnies' Easter*, 1567(F)
*The Dumb Bunnies Go to the Zoo*, 1568(F)
*Make Way for Dumb Bunnies*, 1569(F)
*The Silly Gooses*, 2024(F)
Pincus, Harriet. *Tell Me a Mitzi*, 3096(F)
*The Wedding Procession of the Rag Doll and the Broom Handle and Who Was in It*, 1201(F)
Pinkney, Brian. *The Ballad of Belle Dorcas*, 7631(F)
*Bill Pickett*, 10197
*The Boy and the Ghost*, 1203(F)
*Cut from the Same Cloth*, 9372
*The Dark-Thirty*, 9361
*Dear Benjamin Banneker*, 10807
*The Elephant's Wrestling Match*, 2113(F)
*The Faithful Friend*, 9431
*Happy Birthday, Martin Luther King*, 10407
*Seven Candles for Kwanzaa*, 4629
*Sukey and the Mermaid*, 9375
*A Wave in Her Pocket*, 9425
*When I Left My Village*, 7429(F)
*Wiley and the Hairy Man*, 9290
Pinkney, Jerry. *The Adventures of Spider*, 8682
*Back Home*, 2686(F)
*Childtimes*, 14045
*David's Songs*, 13845
*Drylongso*, 7187(F)
*Further Tales of Uncle Remus*, 9353
*The Green Lion of Zion Street*, 6837(F)
*Half a Moon and One Whole Star*, 486(F)
*The Hired Hand*, 9373
*Home Place*, 2473(F)
*I Want to Be*, 2663(F)
*In for Winter, Out for Spring*, 9853
*John Henry*, 9354
*The Jungle Book*, 5912(F)
*The Last Tales of Uncle Remus*, 9356
*The Man Who Kept His Heart in a Bucket*, 8543(F)
*Mary McLeod Bethune*, 10360
*Minty*, 10458
*Mirandy and Brother Wind*, 1076(F)
*More Tales of Uncle Remus*, 9357
*New Shoes for Silvia*, 2561(F)
*The Patchwork Quilt*, 2884(F)
*Rabbit Makes a Monkey of Lion*, 8671
*Rikki-Tikki-Tavi*, 6509(F)
*Roll of Thunder, Hear My Cry*, 6191(F)
*Sam and the Tigers*, 1055(F)

*The Goose Girl*, 8941
*I Know Not What, I Know Not Where*, 9096
*Operation*, 8143(F)
*Sirko and the Wolf*, 8872
*The Storm*, 3683(F)
*The Story of the Tooth Fairy*, 1142(F)
*The Swan Maiden*, 8568(F)
Saunders, Dave. *Brave Jack*, 2085(F)
  *Dibble and Dabble*, 2086(F)
  *Down by the Pond*, 3306(F)
  *Snowtime*, 2087(F)
Sauvant, Henriette. *The Seven Ravens*, 8923
Sauve, Gordon. *Dinosaurs*, 11756
Savadier, Elivia. *A Bedtime Story*, 494(F)
  *Billy and the Bad Teacher*, 4499(F)
  *Treasure Map*, 2916(F)
  *The Uninvited Guest and Other Jewish Holiday Tales*, 13979
Savage, Ann. *Paws and Claws*, 15014
Savin, Deborah. *Whales*, 15752
Savitt, Sam. *Lad*, 5985(F)
Sawaya, Linda D. *How to Get Famous in Brooklyn*, 2546(F)
  *The Little Ant/La Hormiga Chiquita*, 2043(F)
Sawyer, Lori. *Grandmother Five Baskets*, 9245(F)
Say, Allen. *The Bicycle Man*, 3953(F)
  *The Boy of the Three-Year Nap*, 8843
  *Grandfather's Journey*, 3090(F)
  *How My Parents Learned to Eat*, 2887(F)
  *River Dream*, 1205(F)
Sayles, Elizabeth. *Albie the Lifeguard*, 2411(F)
  *The Little Black Truck*, 4570(F)
  *The Marvelous Toy*, 3052(F)
  *The Night Crossing*, 7853(F)
  *Not in the House, Newton!*, 929(F)
  *The Thunderherd*, 4198(F)
Scarry, Richard. *Pie Rats Ahoy!*, 2089(F)
  *Richard Scarry's Best Word Book Ever*, 11434
  *Richard Scarry's Lowly Worm Word Book*, 197(F)
Schachner, Judith Byron. *I Know an Old Lady Who Swallowed a Pie*, 5011(F)
  *The Prince of the Pond*, 6591(F)
  *What Shall I Dream?*, 1036(F)
Schaer, Miriam. *Katie-Bo*, 2883(F)
Schafer, John. *ABC Career Book for Girls/El Libro de Carreras para Niñas*, 14193(F)
Schaffer, Amanda. *All God's Children*, 14014
  *How Now, Brown Cow?*, 9839
Schaffer, Vern. *North American Indian Arts*, 11346
Schaffhausen, Suzanne. *Morgan's Baby Sister*, 4082(F)
Schanzer, Rosalyn. *All About Hanukkah*, 13977
  *Bible Heroes I Can Be*, 13844
  *Ten Good Rules*, 13889
Scharl, Josef. *The Complete Grimm's Fairy Tales*, 8906
Schatell, Brian. *Lots of Rot*, 14586
  *The McGoonys Have a Party*, 3464(F)
Scheffler, Axel. *Juice the Pig*, 1991(F)
Schick, Eleanor. *Navajo ABC*, 120(F)

Schick, Joel. *My Robot Buddy*, 8374(F)
  *Wayside School Is Falling Down*, 8289(F)
Schields, Gretchen. *The Chinese Siamese Cat*, 4457(F)
  *The Moon Lady*, 7461(F)
Schille, Marjett. *How Many Bears?*, 327(F)
Schindelman, Joseph. *Charlie and the Chocolate Factory*, 6342(F)
Schindler, S. D. *The Bat in the Dining Room*, 3321(F)
  *Betcha!*, 16344
  *Big Pumpkin*, 1231(F)
  *Catwings*, 6524(F)
  *Children of Christmas*, 7956(F)
  *Don't Fidget a Feather!*, 2115(F)
  *The Earth Is Painted Green*, 9857
  *Every Living Thing*, 5965(F)
  *The Ghost of Nicholas Greebe*, 6486(F)
  *How Many Fish?*, 5115(F)
  *I Love My Buzzard*, 3469(F)
  *If You Should Hear a Honey Guide*, 12117
  *Is This a House for Hermit Crab?*, 1903(F)
  *Little Vampire and the Midnight Bear*, 5244(F)
  *Madame La Grande and Her So High, to the Sky, Uproarious Pompadour*, 3332(F)
  *Not the Piano, Mrs. Medley!*, 3643(F)
  *Oh, What a Thanksgiving!*, 5012(F)
  *The Pied Piper of Hamelin*, 958(F)
  *The Smash-up Crash-up Derby*, 2731(F)
  *Those Amazing Ants*, 15540
  *The Three Little Pigs and the Fox*, 9344
  *A Tree Is Growing*, 16029
  *Tundra Mouse*, 4797(F)
  *Whoo-oo Is It?*, 4371(F)
  *Whuppity Stoorie*, 9043
Schindler, Steven. *Night Creatures*, 15144
Schmid, Eleonore. *The Squirrel and the Moon*, 2091(F)
  *The Three Feathers*, 8929
Schmidt, Diane. *Where's Chimpy?*, 3066(F)
Schmidt, Karen L. *Going to the Zoo*, 11604
  *Hannah the Hippo's No Mud Day*, 1707(F)
  *My Sister the Sausage Roll*, 6119(F)
  *Stop that Garbage Truck!*, 2509(F)
Schneider, Christine M. *Jeremy's Muffler*, 3424(F)
Schneider, Howie. *Blumpoe the Grumpoe Meets Arnold the Cat*, 4394(F)
Schoberle, Cecile. *Creepy, Spooky Science*, 14612
  *Icky, Squishy Science*, 14614
Schodorf, Timothy. *Baseball Card Crazy*, 6133(F)
Schoenherr, Ian. *Jonkonnu*, 3881(F)
  *Marie in Fourth Position*, 7487(F)
  *Newf*, 4342(F)
Schoenherr, John. *Gentle Ben*, 5937(F)
  *Incident at Hawk's Hill*, 5857(F)
  *Julie of the Wolves*, 5560(F)
  *Owl Moon*, 4485(F)
  *Pigs in the Mud in the Middle of the Rud*, 3436(F)
  *Rascal*, 5952(F)
Scholder, Fritz. *Anpao*, 9241

Wheeler, Cindy. *Bookstore Cat*, 4476(F)

Wheeler, Jody. *An Old Fashioned Thanksgiving*, 7899(F)

Whipple, Catherine. *Shannon*, 12873

Whipple, Rick. *Maria Tallchief*, 10210

Whitaker, Malle N. *Toxic Threat*, 13634

White, Keinyo. *Jenny Reen and the Jack Muh Lantern*, 4937(F)
*Uh-oh! It's Mama's Birthday!*, 3119(F)

White, Michael. *Aztec Times*, 12633

White, Michael P. *The Library Dragon*, 857(F)
*The Secret of Old Zeb*, 5531(F)

White, Mike. *Nelson Mandela*, 11249

White, Rosalyn. *Heart of Gold*, 8809

Whiting, Carl. *Dizzy Doctor Riddles*, 17329
*Oh, How Waffle!*, 17371

Whitman, Candace. *Zoo-Looking*, 4289(F)

Whitney, Jean. *I'm Frustrated*, 4039(F)

Whyte, Mary. *Boomer Goes to School*, 4372(F)
*Boomer's Big Day*, 4373(F)
*I Love You the Purplest*, 2964(F)
*Snow Riders*, 1074(F)

Wiberg, Harald. *Christmas in the Stable*, 4791(F)
*The Tomten*, 3879(F)

Wichlinski, Andrew. *Platypus*, 15132

Wick, Walter. *I Spy Christmas*, 4805
*I Spy Fantasy*, 17403
*I Spy School Days*, 184(F)
*I Spy Spooky Night*, 17370
*I Spy Super Challenger! A Book of Picture Riddles*, 17404

Wickstrom, Sylvie. *Five Silly Fishermen*, 5142(F)
*Hey! I'm Reading!*, 5301(F)
*Mothers Can't Get Sick*, 3140(F)
*This Old House*, 2374(F)
*Wheels on the Bus*, 11608

Wickstrom, Thor. *The Brothers' Promise*, 9144
*Chickie Riddles*, 5168
*I'm Not Moving, Mama!*, 1507(F)
*Noah's Square Dance*, 1296(F)
*Puppy Riddles*, 17348(F)

Widener, Terry. *Lou Gehrig*, 10979

Widom, Dianne. *Go Home, River*, 3659(F)

Wiese, Kurt. *Five Chinese Brothers*, 3281(F)
*The Story About Ping*, 3796(F)

Wiesner, David. *Free Fall*, 722(F)
*Man from the Sky*, 5468(F)
*Night of the Gargoyles*, 801(F)

Wijngaard, Juan. *Emma Bean*, 2754(F)
*Esther's Story*, 13892
*Going to Sleep on the Farm*, 530(F)
*A Piece of Home*, 3874(F)
*Sir Gawain and the Green Knight*, 8996
*Sir Gawain and the Loathly Lady*, 8997
*Thunderstorm!*, 5790(F)

Wik, Lars. *Baby's First Words*, 135

Wikland, Ilon. *I Don't Want to Go to Bed*, 531(F)
*I Want to Go to School, Too!*, 4526(F)
*Lotta's Christmas Surprise*, 4792(F)
*Lotta's Easter Surprise*, 4870(F)

Wikler, Linda. *Alfonse, Where Are You?*, 2255(F)

Wilbur, Richard. *Opposites*, 206

Wilburn, Kathy. *The Gingerbread Boy*, 8990

Wilcox, Cathy. *Andrew Jessup*, 3204(F)

Wildsmith, Brian. *Birds by Brian Wildsmith*, 15382
*Brian Wildsmith's Amazing World of Words*, 11446
*The Circus*, 11625
*Daisy*, 2257(F)
*The Hunter and His Dog*, 2258(F)
*Jack and the Meanstalk*, 1312(F)
*Mother Goose*, 649
*The Myths of the Norsemen*, 9502
*Professor Noah's Spaceship*, 1311(F)
*Seasons*, 3723(F)
*What the Moon Saw*, 207(F)
*Wild Animals*, 3724(F)

Wildsmith, Rebecca. *Jack and the Meanstalk*, 1312(F)

Wilgus, David. *Here There Be Dragons*, 6795(F)

Wilhelm, Hans. *I'll Always Love You*, 4480(F)
*More Bunny Trouble*, 2259(F)
*Tyrone the Horrible*, 2261(F)

Wilkes, Larry. *The Companions*, 6274(F)

Wilkin, Eloise. *Poems to Read to the Very Young*, 9543

Wilkon, Jozef. *Atuk*, 4258(F)
*Katie and the Big, Brave Bear*, 1111(F)

Willard, Michael. *Wonders of the Forest*, 16264

Willcox, Harry. *The Human Body*, 14402

Willebeck le Mair, Henriette. *Granny's Little Rhyme Book*, 676

Willey, Bee. *The Golden Hoard*, 9451
*Michael Rosen's ABC*, 105(F)
*Nonsense Songs*, 9810
*The Silver Treasure*, 8624

Willey, Lynne. *The Universe*, 14653

Williams, Berkeley. *Grandfather Tales*, 9319

Williams, Dan. *The Magpie Song*, 2793(F)

Williams, Garth. *Bedtime for Frances*, 5198(F)
*Beneath a Blue Umbrella*, 666
*Charlotte's Web*, 6761(F)
*Chester Cricket's Pigeon Ride*, 2101(F)
*The Cricket in Times Square*, 6676(F)
*Emmett's Pig*, 5426(F)
*The Family Under the Bridge*, 6821(F)
*The Gingerbread Rabbit*, 1752(F)
*Harry Kitten and Tucker Mouse*, 1211(F)
*J.B.'s Harmonica*, 2095(F)
*The Little House Cookbook*, 17264
*Little House in the Big Woods*, 6204(F)
*The Little Silver House*, 6146(F)
*Ride a Purple Pelican*, 9835
*Wait Till the Moon Is Full*, 3549(F)

Williams, Jared T. *Return of the Wolf*, 5955(F)

Williams, Kent. *Getting Your Period*, 14553

Williams, Marcia. *Greek Myths for Young Children*, 9498
*The Iliad and the Odyssey*, 9499

Williams, Richard. *Herbie Jones and the Dark Attic*, 6875(F)

Wormell, Christopher. *A Number of Animals*, 343(F)
Wormell, Mary. *The Spotty Pig*, 1796(F)
Wright, Beth. *Count Your Way Through Ireland*, 12419
*Count Your Way Through Italy*, 12441
Wright, Blanche Fisher. *Real Mother Goose*, 652
*The Real Mother Goose Clock Book*, 653
Wright, Jane C. *The Sun Is Up*, 9895
Wright, Joan R. *Frogs, Toads, Lizards, and Salamanders*, 14917
Wright-Frierson, Virginia. *First Grade Can Wait*, 4488(F)
*We're Growing Together*, 3069(F)
Wyatt, David. *True Ghost Stories*, 6350(F)
Wyeth, Jamie. *Cabbages and Kings*, 1209(F)
Wyeth, N. C. *N. C. Wyeth's Pilgrims*, 13036
*Rip Van Winkle*, 6455(F)
*Robin Hood*, 8969
*The Yearling*, 5959(F)
Wyman, Cherie R. *Labor Day*, 13929
Wynne, Patricia J. *Backyard*, 14823
*Earth*, 16135
*Extinction Is Forever*, 14895
*The Human Body*, 14385
*Hungry, Hungry Sharks*, 15714
*Why Save the Rain Forest?*, 16270


Yaccarino, Dan. *Bam Bam Bam*, 2650(F)
*Carnival*, 11621
*One Hole in the Road*, 400(F)
Yalowitz, Paul. *Catty-Cornered*, 7076(F)
*Moonstruck*, 3296(F)
*Nell Nugget and the Cow Caper*, 2309(F)
*Somebody Loves You, Mr. Hatch*, 4158(F)
*The Spooky Eerie Night Noise*, 4411(F)
Yamazaki, Sanae. *Ooka the Wise*, 8823
Yang, Kuo W. *Smash Caps*, 17516
Yardley, Joanna. *The Bracelet*, 7891(F)
*The Hand-Me-Down Horse*, 3929(F)
*The Red Ball*, 1340(F)
Yardley, Thompson. *Buy Now, Pay Later*, 13554
*Down the Hatch*, 14433
Yashima, Taro. *Crow Boy*, 4547(F)
*Umbrella*, 2778(F)
Ybanez, Terry. *The Christmas Tree/El Arbol de Navidad*, 4689(F)
Yee, Patrick. *Winter Rabbit*, 2277(F)
Yee, Wong H. *Eek! There's a Mouse in the House*, 3517(F)
Yezerski, Thomas F. *Spy in the Sky*, 7761(F)
Yoder, Dot. *Andy Finds a Turtle*, 4075(F)
Yoshi. *A to Zen*, 128(F)
*The Farmer and the Poor God*, 8849
*The First Story Ever Told*, 9446
*Magical Hands*, 4644(F)
Yoshida, Hideo C. *Why Rat Comes First*, 1341(F)
Yoshino, Shin. *Cats*, 15841
Young, Dan. *Big Brother Dustin*, 2836(F)
Young, Ed. *All of You Was Singing*, 9410

*Bicycle Rider*, 10444
*Bitter Bananas*, 3924(F)
*Dreamcatcher*, 561(F)
*The Emperor and the Kite*, 8799
*The First Song Ever Sung*, 1104(F)
*Foolish Rabbit's Big Mistake*, 8814
*Happy Prince*, 8594(F)
*I Wish I Were a Butterfly*, 1727(F)
*Iblis*, 9179
*October Smiled Back*, 3674(F)
*Pinocchio*, 6315(F)
*Sadako*, 12039
*The Turkey Girl*, 9276
*White Wave*, 8792
*Yeh-Shen*, 8780
*Young Fu of the Upper Yangtze*, 7449(F)
Young, Jerry. *Amazing Bats*, 15166
*Amazing Birds*, 15356
*Amazing Mammals*, 15118
*Amazing Tropical Birds*, 15341
*Amazing Wolves, Dogs, and Foxes*, 15233
*Insects and Crawly Creatures*, 15525
Young, Kathy O. *Once upon a Princess and a Pea*, 8512(F)
Young, Mary O. *Sea, Salt, and Air*, 4004(F)
Young, Noela. *Finders Keepers*, 8370(F)
*The Pigs Are Flying*, 6646(F)
Young, Ruth. *One Crow*, 292(F)
Young, Selina. *First Poems*, 9538
Younker, Linda Q. *What Is a Cat?*, 4320
*What Is a Horse?*, 4321
*Where Do Cats Live?*, 4322
Yuditskaya, Tatyana. *The Four Gallant Sisters*, 8940
*A Spy in the King's Colony*, 7591(F)


Zabar, Abbie. *55 Friends*, 452(F)
Zafuto, Charles. *Lone Woman of Ghalas-Hat*, 13453
Zak, Drahos. *The Pied Piper of Hamelin*, 8938
Zalben, Jane Breskin. *Beni's First Chanukah*, 4995(F)
*Inner Chimes*, 9548
*The Walrus and the Carpenter*, 9791
Zallinger, Jean Day. *The Earliest Americans*, 12931
*Great Snakes!*, 14984
Zallinger, Peter. *Prehistoric Animals*, 11793
Zarins, Joyce A. *The Go-Around Dollar*, 2375
*How to Survive Third Grade*, 4525(F)
*The Story of Things*, 11848
Zawadzki, Marek. *Okino and the Whales*, 893(F)
Zeldich, Arieh. *I Wish I Had My Father*, 4155(F)
Zeldis, Malcah. *A Fine Fat Pig*, 9728
*Honest Abe*, 10680
*Martin Luther King*, 10397
*Spring*, 9758
Zelinsky, Paul O. *Dear Mr. Henshaw*, 7127(F)
*The Enchanted Castle*, 6597(F)
*The Lion and the Stoat*, 2286(F)
*The Random House Book of Humor for Children*, 8150(F)

# Title Index

This index contains both main entry titles and internal titles cited in the entries. References are to entry numbers, not page numbers. All fiction titles are indicated by (F), following the entry number.

A Is for Africa, 90(F)
A Is for Aloha, 3795(F)
A Is for Angry: An Animal and Adjective Alphabet, 13(F)
A Is for Animals: An Animal ABC, 96(F)
A Is for Apple, W Is for Witch, 6354(F)
A Is for Artist, 11285
A Is for Asia, 21(F)
A, My Name Is Alice, 8(F)
A. Nonny Mouse Writes Again! 3443
A. Philip Randolph, 10442
A. Philip Randolph and the Labor Movement, 10441
The A to Z Beastly Jamboree, 296(F)
A to Zen: A Book of Japanese Culture, 128(F)
A Was Once an Apple Pie, 9807
A You're Adorable, 53(F)
Aani and the Tree Huggers, 7432(F)
Aardvarks, Disembark! 13867
Aaron and the Green Mountain Boys, 7599(F)
Aaron's Awful Allergies, 4066(F)
Aaron's Shirt, 2514(F)
AB Sea, 15630
The Abacus Contest: Stories from Taiwan and China, 7464(F)
Abandoned on the Wild Frontier, 7694(F)
Abby (Illus. by Steven Kellogg), 2832(F)
  (Illus. by Alan Marks), 5881(F)
ABC: The Alef-Bet Book, 79(F)
ABC: The Museum of Modern Art, New York, 80(F)

An ABC Bestiary, 10(F)
The ABC Bunny, 33(F)
ABC Career Book for Girls/El Libro de Carreras para Niñas, 14193(F)
ABC Dogs, 15853
The ABC Exhibit, 32(F)
ABC I Like Me! 19(F)
ABC of Crawlers and Flyers, 108(F)
An ABC of Fashionable Animals, 27(F)
ABC Yummy, 48(F)
ABCDrive! A Car Trip Alphabet, 44(F)
ABC's of Nature, 14820
The ABC's of Origami, 17162
Abe Lincoln Goes to Washington, 1837–1865, 10677
Abe Lincoln Grows Up, 10683
Abe Lincoln's Hat, 10672
Abel's Island, 6707(F)
The Abenaki, 12876
Abigail's Drum, 7645(F)
Abiyoyo: Based on a South African Lullaby and Folk Story, 8735
An Aboriginal Family, 12333
About Birds: A Guide for Children, 15371
About Dying, 4162(F)
About Handicaps, 14319
About Mammals: A Guide for Children, 15133
About Martin Luther King Day, 13651
About Phobias, 4162(F)
About the B'nai Bagels, 8096(F)
Abra-Ca-Dazzle: Easy Magic Tricks, 17294

Abracadabra, 1207(F)
Abraham Lincoln, 10679
  (Illus. by Ingri D'Aulaire), 10673
Abraham Lincoln: A Man for All the People, 10681
Abraham Lincoln: 16th President of the United States, 10684
Abraham Lincoln: Sixteenth President of the United States, 10676
Absolutely Normal Chaos, 7143(F)
The Absolutely True Story: My Trip to Yellowstone Park with the Terrible Rupes (No Names Have Been Changed to Protect the Guilty) by Lewis Q. Dodge, 5728(F)
Abuela, 875(F)
Abuela's Weave, 3769(F)
Abuelita's Heart, 3563(F)
Abuelita's Paradise, 3042(F)
Acacia Terrace, 12355
The Accident, 4025(F)
Accidents May Happen: Fifty Inventions Discovered by Mistake, 16685
Ace: The Very Important Pig, 6499(F)
Achoo! All About Colds, 14330
Acid Rain, 13629
Across America on an Emigrant Train, 16925
Across Five Aprils, 7760(F)
Across the Blue Mountains, 3299(F)
Across the Lines, 7766(F)
Across the Stream, 1648(F)

Rat Teeth, 6980(F)
The Rat War, 7239(F)
Rats, 15299
Rats! 8016(F)
The Rats' Daughter, 8607
Rats on the Range and Other
  Stories, 5292(F)
Rats on the Roof: And Other
  Stories, 1940(F)
A Rat's Tale, 6674(F)
The Rattlebang Picnic, 3018(F)
Rattlebone Rock, 4878(F)
Rattlesnake Dance: True Tales,
  Mysteries, and Rattlesnake
  Ceremonies, 14968
Raul Julia, 10484
Raven: A Trickster Tale from the
  Pacific Northwest, 9256
Raven and River, 1508(F)
Raw Head, Bloody Bones:
  African-American Tales of the
  Supernatural, 9359
Ray Charles: Soul Man, 10164
Razzle Dazzle! Magic Tricks for
  You, 17310
Re-Elect Nutty! 8244(F)
Re-Zoom, 16599
Reach Higher, 11064
Read-Aloud Rhymes for the Very
  Young, 9627
Read for Me, Mama, 3067(F)
Read Me a Fairy Tale: A Child's
  Book of Classic Fairy Tales,
  8530(F)
Read to Your Bunny, 2243(F)
Reading About the Grizzly Bear,
  15178
Reading About the River Otter,
  15698
Ready, Set, Go! 5420(F)
Ready . . . Set . . . Read! The
  Beginning Reader's Treasury,
  5120(F)
Ready . . . Set . . . Read — and
  Laugh! A Funny Treasury for
  Beginning Readers, 17339(F)
Ready . . . Set . . . Robot!
  5197(F)
A Real Christmas This Year,
  7967(F)
Real Heroes, 7213(F)
The Real Hole, 2305(F)
The Real Johnny Appleseed,
  10496
Real Kids, Real Adventures,
  Book 4, 9954
Real Mother Goose, 652
The Real Mother Goose Clock
  Book, 653

The Real Patriots of the
  American Revolution, 13074
The Real Plato Jones, 6942(F)
The Real-Skin Rubber Monster
  Mask, 4888(F)
The Real Thief, 6709(F)
The Real Tooth Fairy, 2971(F)
The Really Deadly and
  Dangerous Dinosaur: And
  Other Monsters of the
  Prehistoric World, 11783
Really No Big Deal, 7099(F)
The Really Sinister Savage
  Shark: And Other Creatures of
  the Deep, 15646
Really Weird Animals, 15094
The Reason for Janey, 7083(F)
The Reasons for Seasons, 3598
  (Illus. by Linda Allison), 14790
Rebecca of Sunnybrook Farm,
  6203(F)
Rebel, 4434(F)
The Rebellion of Humans: An
  African Spiritual Journey,
  3528(F)
Rebels Against Slavery:
  American Slave Revolts, 13098
The Rebus Bears, 5356(F)
Rebus Riot, 17407
Recess Mess, 5270(F)
Rechenka's Eggs, 1161(F)
Recipes for Art and Craft
  Materials, 17040
Reconstruction: America After
  the Civil War, 13231
Reconstruction and Reform,
  13225
Record Breakers of the Air,
  15633
Record Breakers of the Land,
  15633
Record Breakers of the Sea,
  15633
Recreation, 17522
Recreation Can Be Risky, 14523
Rectangles, 16355
Recycle! A Handbook for Kids,
  13597
Recycling, 13594, 13601
Recyclopedia: Games, Science
  Equipment and Crafts from
  Recycled Materials, 17041
The Red Ball, 1340(F)
The Red Balloon, 3866(F)
Red Bird, 4623(F)
Red, Blue, Yellow Shoe, 225(F)
Red Cloud: Sioux Warrior, 10597
The Red Comb, 7531(F)
Red Cross/Red Crescent: When
  Help Can't Wait, 13642

The Red-Crowned Crane, 15380
Red Dancing Shoes, 3051(F)
Red-Dirt Jessie, 5946(F)
Red Dog, 7742(F)
The Red-Eared Ghosts, 6217(F)
Red Eggs and Dragon Boats:
  Celebrating Chinese Festivals,
  12220
Red Fairy Book, 8537(F)
Red Fox, 15244
Red Fox and His Canoe, 5064(F)
Red Fox and the Baby Bunnies,
  1398(F)
The Red Fox Monster, 1399(F)
Red Fox Running, 4231(F)
The Red Heels, 6659(F)
Red Hen and Sly Fox, 1636(F)
Red-Hot Hightops, 8423(F)
Red Hot Peppers: The Skookum
  Book of Jump Rope Games,
  Rhymes, and Fancy Footwork,
  17475
Red Leaf, Yellow Leaf, 3580(F)
Red Light, Green Light, 2425(F)
Red Light, Green Light, Mama
  and Me, 2406(F)
Red Light Stop, Green Light Go,
  3375(F)
The Red Planet: Mars, 14707
The Red Poppy, 16079
Red Racer, 3515(F)
Red Riding Hood, 8514
  (Illus. by James Marshall),
  8945
The Red Sea and the Arabian
  Gulf, 15650
The Red Shoes, 8508(F)
Red Sky at Morning, 7852(F)
Red-Spotted Newt, 14911
A Red Wagon Year, 739(F)
Red Wizard, 6703(F)
The Red Wolf, 15240
Red Wolf Country, 4364(F)
The Red Woolen Blanket,
  2515(F)
Redbird at Rockefeller Center,
  4802(F)
Redheaded Orphan, 7736(F)
Redwall, 6467(F)
Redwoods, 16042
Reflections, 2583(F)
Reflections on a Gift of
  Watermelon Pickle and Other
  Modern Verse, 9537
Regards to the Man in the Moon,
  1003(F)
Regina's Big Mistake, 4528(F)
A Regular Flood of Mishap,
  7980(F)
A Regular Rolling Noah, 3389(F)

# Subject/Grade Level Index

All entries are listed within specific subjects and then according to grade level suitability (see the key at the foot of pages for grade level designations). Subjects are arranged alphabetically and subject heads may be subdivided into nonfiction (e.g., "Trucks") and fiction (e.g., "Trucks — Fiction"). References to entries are by entry numbers, not pages.

## A

**Aardema, Verna**
PI: 10214

**Aardvarks — Fiction**
P: 1448, 1452–53, 1456, 1458, 1461

**Aaron, Hank**
I: 10957–58

**Abbott, Jim**
PI: 10960
I: 10959

**Abdul, Paula**
I: 10150

**Abdul-Jabbar, Kareem**
I: 11028
IJ: 11027

**Abenaki Indians**
I: 12876

**Abenaki Indians — Folklore**
P: 9201
I: 9197

**Abernathy, David**
IJ: 10358

**Aborigines (Australia)**
I: 12333, 12349, 12351

**Aborigines (Australia) — Fiction**
P: 3735
IJ: 5805

**Aborigines (Australia) — Folklore**
I: 8864

**Accidents**
P: 14524
I: 14519
IJ: 14522

**Accidents — Fiction**
P: 4034, 5445
I: 6806, 7136, 7183
IJ: 6985

**Acid rain**
I: 13619, 13629
IJ: 13621

**Acting**
I: 11663

**Acting — Fiction**
PI: 8068

**Actors — Biography**
PI: 10193
I: 10191, 10205–6, 10211
IJ: 10036, 10192, 10202, 10484

**Actors — Fiction**
PI: 8068
I: 7156, 8081

**Actresses — Biography**
I: 10175, 10177
IJ: 10176

**Actresses — Careers**
PI: 14205

**Actresses — Fiction**
PI: 8010
I: 8240

**Adams, Ansel**
I: 10047

**Adams, John**
I: 10615

**Adams, John Quincy**
PI: 10616
I: 10617

**Adams, Samuel**
PI: 10489
IJ: 10488

**Addams, Jane**
IJ: 10724–25

**Addictions**
IJ: 14274

**Addition**
P: 16340, 16345
PI: 16346

**Adolescence**
I: 14103

**Adoption**
P: 3006, 14119, 14141, 14152
PI: 14144
IJ: 14124, 14133–34, 14148

**Adoption — Fiction**
P: 1400, 1657, 2253, 2811, 2832, 2846, 2864, 2883, 2897, 2970, 2978, 2981, 3000, 3034, 3053, 3126, 4114, 4146, 5217
PI: 1445, 7304
I: 7012, 7388, 8418, 14129
IJ: 5983, 6021, 6084, 6974, 8464

P = Primary; PI = Primary–Intermediate; I = Intermediate; IJ = Intermediate–Junior High

P = Primary; PI = Primary–Intermediate; I = Intermediate; IJ = Intermediate–Junior High

## Africa — Peoples — Fiction
P: 3024

## Africa — Plants
P: 3781

## African Americans
*See also* Africa; Civil rights;
Civil War (U.S.); Kwanzaa;
Slavery; and names of indi-
viduals, e.g., Robinson,
Jackie
P: 2983, 10457, 11499, 17561
PI: 3847, 10397, 13110, 13182,
13659, 13665, 14132
I: 7735, 12089, 13083, 13085, 13095,
13170, 13257, 13648, 13650–51,
13668, 13670–71
IJ: 7655, 12007, 12060, 13090,
13093, 13101, 13121, 13195,
13661, 13663–64, 13675

## African Americans — Armed forces
IJ: 10382, 13256, 16971

## African Americans — Arts
I: 11351

## African Americans — Biography
P: 2913, 3028, 4600, 10152, 10369,
10381, 10396, 10407, 10410–11,
10807, 10928, 11005, 11128,
17572
PI: 10030, 10153–55, 10204, 10217,
10254, 10256, 10322, 10325,
10343, 10345, 10352, 10360–62,
10367, 10370–71, 10373–74,
10376, 10378, 10380, 10384,
10393, 10399–400, 10405–6,
10413, 10416, 10420–22,
10424–25, 10428–30, 10432–35,
10440–41, 10444–46, 10448,
10451–52, 10456, 10458, 10462,
10464–67, 10469–71, 10823–24,
10827, 10837, 10908, 10916,
10930, 10988, 10998–99, 11004,
11010, 11056, 11070, 11114,
11125, 11129, 11132
I: 9965, 9975–76, 10001–2,
10038–40, 10122, 10140, 10151,
10165, 10177, 10181, 10187–89,
10198, 10201, 10211–13, 10253,
10269–70, 10300–1, 10318–19,
10327–28, 10331, 10350–51,
10357, 10363–66, 10372, 10377,
10379, 10385–87, 10391,
10394–95, 10401–2, 10404, 10417,
10419, 10427, 10431, 10437,
10447, 10449, 10454–55,
10460–61, 10806, 10812,
10825–26, 10870, 10941, 10943,

10946, 10957–58, 10966, 10983,
10995, 10997, 11003, 11007–9,
11012–13, 11020–23, 11028,
11030, 11033–34, 11037, 11040,
11042, 11044, 11047–49, 11054,
11060–61, 11068–69, 11074,
11078, 11088, 11095–97, 11099,
11102, 11104, 11116, 11122–24,
11130–31, 11133, 11167
IJ: 10011–12, 10031, 10044, 10067,
10111–12, 10126, 10128, 10164,
10166, 10168, 10185, 10203,
10218, 10222, 10248, 10255,
10312, 10326, 10330, 10348,
10358–59, 10368, 10382–83,
10388–90, 10392, 10398, 10403,
10408–9, 10412, 10418, 10423,
10426, 10436, 10438–39,
10442–43, 10450, 10453, 10459,
10463, 10835, 10927, 10944,
10963, 10982, 10987, 11006,
11011, 11024, 11027, 11029,
11032, 11035, 11038–39, 11041,
11043, 11046, 11050, 11057,
11059, 11062–65, 11067, 11071,
11073, 11075–76, 11083, 11089,
11094, 11098, 11103, 11126–27,
11162, 13098, 16724
All: 10156

## African Americans — Cookbooks
PI: 17201

## African Americans — Crafts
P: 4633
PI: 17058

## African Americans — Dance
IJ: 11639

## African Americans — Diseases
IJ: 14356

## African Americans — Fiction
P: 275, 294, 332, 410, 1030–31, 1109,
1176–78, 1203, 1354, 1912, 2301,
2397, 2429, 2445, 2457, 2517,
2554, 2579, 2647, 2662, 2685,
2747–48, 2769, 2771, 2832,
2843–44, 2853, 2873, 2884, 2901,
2903, 2941–42, 2950, 2956–58,
2960, 3031, 3045, 3056–57, 3067,
3075, 3089, 3107, 3111, 3119,
3135, 3157, 3169, 3182, 3196–97,
3207, 3211, 3215, 3245, 3247,
3560, 3628, 3648, 3660, 3699,
3775, 3823, 3831, 3839, 3846,
3861, 3895, 3912, 3938, 3949,
3994, 3997, 4024, 4029, 4063,
4076, 4081, 4093, 4164, 4171,
4327, 4718, 4752, 4766, 4830,
4872, 4937, 4939, 5081, 5100,

5163, 5221, 5315, 6006, 6067,
7085
PI: 2544, 2686, 2702, 2943, 3234–35,
3259, 3848, 3880–81, 3911, 3960,
4648, 4808, 5675, 6026, 6057,
6145, 7086, 7094, 7187, 7417,
7422, 7531, 7617, 7631–33, 7646,
7654, 7662, 7764, 7820, 7823,
7829, 7945, 7963–64, 8206, 8463,
8473, 9853, 13243
I: 2455, 2815, 5510, 5678, 5997,
6003, 6029, 6035–36, 6098, 6129,
6202, 6809, 6832, 6837, 6854,
6877, 7075, 7108, 7188, 7244,
7337, 7592, 7619, 7622, 7624,
7637, 7644, 7650, 7652, 7719,
7765, 7797, 7826, 7834, 8128,
8305, 8470, 13087
IJ: 5469, 5784, 5999, 6007, 6011,
6021–22, 6028, 6037, 6048, 6100,
6106, 6110, 6157, 6191, 6208,
6446, 6802, 6811, 6886, 6927,
6991, 7073, 7139, 7206, 7352,
7580, 7611, 7623, 7625, 7628,
7648, 7653, 7657, 7661, 7716,
7757, 7794, 7830, 7841, 7845,
8301

## African Americans — Folklore
P: 9290, 9339–40, 9355, 9363, 9375,
9385, 9390
PI: 9329, 9354, 9358, 9373
I: 8615, 9337, 9357
IJ: 9332–33, 9338, 9353, 9356, 9359,
9361

## African Americans — Food
I: 17234
IJ: 17237

## African Americans — History
P: 3849
PI: 10289, 13017
I: 13078, 13097, 13161, 13204
IJ: 10502, 11836, 12809–10, 13089,
13111, 13220, 13249, 14037,
14045, 14058

## African Americans — Holidays
P: 4607, 4634
PI: 4629, 13902, 13906, 13928
IJ: 13953

## African Americans — Literature
IJ: 11458

## African Americans — Music
PI: 10029
I: 11496
IJ: 11490–91

P = Primary; PI = Primary–Intermediate; I = Intermediate; IJ = Intermediate–Junior High

P = Primary; PI = Primary–Intermediate; I = Intermediate; IJ = Intermediate–Junior High

P: 14275
IJ: 14285

**Alcoholism — Fiction**
P: 4042, 4172
PI: 7069
I: 7154, 8452
IJ: 6989, 7049

**Alcott, Louisa May — Fiction**
P: 4853

**Alexander, Grover Cleveland**
I: 10961

**Alexander the Great**
I: 11186
IJ: 11187

**Algeria**
I: 12130

**Algonquin Indians**
I: 12926
IJ: 12940

**Algonquin Indians — Folklore**
P: 9260

**Ali, Muhammad**
I: 11078
IJ: 11076–77

**Aliens**
*See* Extraterrestrial life; Illegal aliens; Immigration (U.S.); Science fiction

**All-American Girls Professional Baseball League**
IJ: 17551, 17558

**All Souls' Day — Mexico**
I: 12611, 12627

**All Souls' Day — Mexico — Fiction**
P: 3864

**Allen, Richard**
IJ: 10359

**Allergies**
PI: 14325, 14355
I: 14347

**Allergies — Fiction**
P: 4066
PI: 8015
I: 7308

**Alligators and crocodiles**
P: 16293

PI: 14924–25, 14927, 14930, 14932–33
I: 14928–29, 14931, 14934
IJ: 14926

**Alligators and crocodiles — Fiction**
P: 198, 549, 1368, 1544, 1570, 1710, 1733, 1809, 2075, 2079, 2149, 2194–95, 2204–5, 3457, 4468, 5310
PI: 2214
I: 5994
IJ: 5562

**Alligators and crocodiles — Folklore**
P: 8705, 8808

**Alphabet — History**
IJ: 11483–84

**Alphabet books**
P: 1–11, 13–14, 16–20, 22–38, 40–48, 50–60, 62–76, 81, 83–96, 98–99, 101–2, 104–7, 109–27, 129–31, 198, 205, 296, 369, 1221, 4611, 9562, 11285, 11417, 14193, 15562, 15630, 15634, 15853, 17413
PI: 12, 15, 21, 39, 49, 61, 77–78, 80, 82, 100, 108, 128, 9686, 11403, 11409, 11722, 12230, 12958, 16740
I: 11333, 11378, 15623
IJ: 97, 5808, 10056, 11299, 11445

**Alphabet books — Hebrew**
PI: 79

**Alvarez, Luis W.**
PI: 10805

**Alzheimer's disease**
P: 14360
I: 14335

**Alzheimer's disease — Fiction**
P: 2795, 2910, 4044, 4085, 4089, 4143
PI: 7077
I: 7055

**Amazon River**
P: 16242
I: 12716, 12729–30

**Amazon River — Fiction**
P: 52
I: 5782
IJ: 5903

**Ambulances**
IJ: 13753

**America — Discovery and exploration**
*See also* United States — Discovery and exploration
P: 9979, 12978, 12982
PI: 9978, 9982
I: 9981, 12974, 12976–77, 12979
IJ: 9980, 9983–84, 12980

**America — Discovery and exploration — Fiction**
PI: 7393, 7535
IJ: 7545

**American Revolution**
*See* Revolutionary War (U.S.)

**Ameru**
IJ: 12123

**Amish**
PI: 13786
I: 13776
IJ: 14049

**Amish — Fiction**
P: 2899, 3029, 4692
I: 6049, 6997, 7312
IJ: 7029, 7233–34

***Amistad* mutiny**
I: 13083
IJ: 13093, 13101

**Amphibians**
*See also* specific animal names, e.g., Frogs and toads
P: 93, 14917
I: 14908, 14921

**Amritsar, India**
I: 12231

**Amsterdam, Netherlands**
I: 12451

**Amundsen, Roald**
IJ: 9951

**Amusement parks**
P: 3408
I: 11617

**Amusement parks — Fiction**
P: 2672, 3453
I: 5553, 5734, 6336

**Anabaptists — Fiction**
I: 7479

**Anasazi Indians**
I: 12844

**Anastasia (Romanov)**
IJ: 12460

P = Primary; PI = Primary–Intermediate; I = Intermediate; IJ = Intermediate–Junior High

P = Primary; PI = Primary–Intermediate; I = Intermediate; IJ = Intermediate–Junior High

14840–42, 14848, 14852, 14856,
14860, 14866, 14874, 14884,
14889, 14893, 14898, 14902,
15001, 15089–90, 15096,
15099–100, 15102–4, 15118,
15126, 15129, 15133, 15141–42,
15525, 15905, 16206, 16209,
16278, 16312
PI: 377, 14812, 14825, 14832–33,
14839, 14843, 14850, 14853,
14859, 14869, 14873, 14878,
14885, 14890, 14894, 14897,
15004, 15091, 15094–95, 16253,
16279, 16318
I: 11550, 14806, 14830, 14836,
14844, 14851, 14861, 14872,
14876, 14879–81, 14883, 14888,
14899–900, 14903, 15098, 15120,
15122, 15128, 15135, 15907,
15909, 15939
IJ: 14821, 14834, 14887, 15108,
15139

**Animals — Habitats**
PI: 15066
IJ: 14868

**Animals — Harmful**
I: 14828

**Animals — Hibernation**
PI: 14896

**Animals — Homes**
P: 4197, 15069, 15074–75, 15077
PI: 15072–73
I: 15076
IJ: 14868, 15067–68, 15070–71

**Animals — Homes — Fiction**
P: 5205

**Animals — Intelligence**
I: 15008, 15011
IJ: 15067

**Animals — Jokes and riddles**
P: 17324, 17373, 17382
PI: 17357, 17384–85

**Animals — Life cycles**
P: 14818
IJ: 14847

**Animals — Locomotion**
P: 15021
PI: 15033

**Animals — Marine and
  freshwater,** 15617–15756

**Animals — Mythology**
PI: 9670

**Animals — Names**
P: 14875, 15088

**Animals — Nocturnal**
I: 15144

**Animals — Nursery rhymes**
P: 633

**Animals — Pets,** 15811–15903

**Animals — Picture books,**
  1356–2290, 4188–4485

**Animals — Play behavior**
P: 15016

**Animals — Poetry**
P: 55, 485, 9634, 9705, 9710–11,
9715, 9718, 9721, 9725, 9729,
9735–36, 9738, 9740, 9746–49,
9751, 9811–12
PI: 9585, 9708, 9712–13, 9728, 9731,
9744, 9752, 9760, 9765, 9842
I: 9706, 9709, 9714, 9716–17, 9732,
9745, 9753, 9893
IJ: 9733, 9739

**Animals — Puzzles**
PI: 17393

**Animals — Senses**
I: 14906, 15002

**Animals — Sleep**
P: 15017

**Animals — Songs**
P: 11546

**Animals — Sounds**
P: 4283, 4438, 4484, 15007

**Animals — Tails**
PI: 15026

**Animals — Tracks**
P: 15007, 15025
PI: 14999, 15020
I: 17103

**Animals — Winter**
PI: 15064

**Animation — Computers**
I: 16817

**Animation (motion pictures)**
I: 16867
All: 16874

**Animation (motion pictures) —
  Biography**
I: 10062
IJ: 10182

**Anning, Mary — Fiction**
IJ: 7504

**Antarctic**
*See also* Arctic; Polar regions
P: 15436, 15440
PI: 12745, 12758, 12762, 15435,
15450
I: 12750–51, 12753, 12759–60
IJ: 12743–44, 12766, 12777, 15438

**Anteaters — Fiction**
P: 2201, 4703, 5126

**Antelopes**
P: 8695

**Anthony, Susan B.**
P: 10728
PI: 10726–27

**Anthropology**
P: 11794
PI: 11798, 11813
I: 10874, 11795, 11800, 11806, 11810
IJ: 10882, 11796–97, 11803, 11807,
11814

**Anthropology — Biography**
I: 10803
IJ: 10873

**Antonnetty, Evelina Lopez**
PI: 10472

**Antonyms**
P: 14840

**Antonyms — Fiction**
P: 2144

**Ants**
P: 15537–38, 15540–41, 15544–45
PI: 15539, 15542
I: 15543

**Ants — Fiction**
P: 415, 2040, 2156, 2186
PI: 3221
I: 8124

**Apache Indians**
P: 12896
PI: 12862
I: 12944
IJ: 12845, 12934

**Apache Indians — Biography**
PI: 10578
I: 10577

**Apache Indians — Fiction**
IJ: 5573

P = Primary; PI = Primary–Intermediate; I = Intermediate; IJ = Intermediate–Junior High

P = Primary; PI = Primary–Intermediate; I = Intermediate; IJ = Intermediate–Junior High

P = Primary; PI = Primary–Intermediate; I = Intermediate; IJ = Intermediate–Junior High

P = Primary; PI = Primary–Intermediate; I = Intermediate; IJ = Intermediate–Junior High

P = Primary; PI = Primary–Intermediate; I = Intermediate; IJ = Intermediate–Junior High

P = Primary; PI = Primary–Intermediate; I = Intermediate; IJ = Intermediate–Junior High

**Basketball — Poetry**
P: 9912
PI: 9906
I: 9911
IJ: 9905

**Basketball Hall of Fame**
I: 17570

**Basset hounds — Fiction**
P: 4415

**Bassoons — Fiction**
P: 1005

**Bastille**
IJ: 12383

**Bat boys**
I: 17540

**Bat mitzvah**
IJ: 13975

**Bathrooms**
P: 2700
IJ: 14508

**Baths and bathing**
P: 3698

**Baths and bathing — Fiction**
P: 682, 1828, 2139, 2538, 2830, 3397,
3513, 5442

**Bats (animal)**
P: 15164–67, 15169
PI: 15170
I: 15161–63, 15168, 15171, 15295

**Bats (animal) — Fiction**
P: 1487, 1826, 2113, 3555
PI: 8229
I: 6474

**Bats (animal) — Jokes and
riddles**
PI: 17344

**Battered women — Fiction**
I: 6956

**Battles**
*See* under names of specific
battles, e.g., Bull Run, Battle
of

**Battleships**
PI: 12045

**Bauer, Marion Dane**
IJ: 10223

**Baum, L. Frank**
I: 10041

**Beaches**
*See also* Seashores
P: 2744, 3621

**Beaches — Fiction**
P: 873, 990, 1944, 2343, 2500, 2537,
2586, 2597, 3643, 3675, 3683,
3686, 3720
PI: 4004, 4010
I: 6056

**Beaches — Poetry**
P: 2630

**Beads — Crafts**
P: 17087

**Beagles — Fiction**
IJ: 5950

**Bean, Judge Roy**
I: 10497

**Beans — Fiction**
P: 15946

**Bears**
*See also* specific kinds, e.g.,
Polar bears
P: 11599, 15173, 15175, 15178–79,
15181, 15183, 15189–90, 15194,
15284
PI: 15174, 15176–77, 15180, 15182,
15184–86
I: 15172, 15187, 15192–93
IJ: 15191

**Bears — Fiction**
P: 11, 36, 140–41, 210, 232, 302, 381,
542, 545, 547, 589–90, 598, 719,
723, 1017, 1229, 1357–58,
1369–72, 1374–75, 1379, 1405,
1408, 1432, 1436, 1504, 1506,
1515, 1563, 1623, 1630–32, 1659,
1664, 1680, 1708–9, 1724, 1776,
1810, 1838, 1915, 1920–23, 1925,
1959, 1971, 1979, 2001, 2025,
2092, 2095, 2106–7, 2200, 2215,
2266, 2271, 2347, 2369, 2637,
2780, 3145, 3425, 4180, 4216,
4243, 4246, 4256–57, 4295, 4336,
4351, 4362, 4402, 4645, 4654,
4728, 4746, 4785, 4815, 4858,
4995, 4997, 5022, 5065, 5067,
5072, 5164, 5189, 5194, 5205,
5246, 5266, 5309, 5356, 5377,
5438–39, 6578, 6580
PI: 1552, 1744, 6579, 7987–88
I: 6360, 7511, 7537, 7986
IJ: 5618, 5937

**Bears — Folklore**
P: 8927, 8959, 8980, 8987, 9018,
9028, 9095

PI: 9124
I: 9119

**Bears — Jokes and riddles**
P: 17347

**Bears — Nursery rhymes**
P: 629, 673

**Bears — Plays**
PI: 9916

**Beatles (musical group)**
PI: 10160
IJ: 10161

**Beauty, Personal**
I: 16808

**Beauty pageants**
IJ: 11618

**Beavers — Fiction**
P: 1503, 1689, 1898, 5078

**Bedouins**
I: 12528

**Beds — Fiction**
P: 412, 475, 513, 746, 5164

**Bedtime books**
P: 83, 205, 381, 453–58, 460–510,
512–60, 562, 564–75, 577–85,
587–98, 601, 718, 879, 1971, 5198,
5260
PI: 599–600, 9194

**Bedtime books — Poetry**
P: 476, 511, 563, 576, 586

**Bedtime books — Prayers**
P: 14017

**Bees**
P: 15548, 15550, 15552, 15557
PI: 14246, 15546–47, 15549, 15551,
15555
I: 15554

**Bees — Fiction**
P: 3120, 8525
I: 6369, 7308

**Beethoven, Ludwig van**
PI: 10133
IJ: 10132

**Beethoven, Ludwig van —
Fiction**
I: 7491

**Beetles**
I: 15559–60

P = Primary; PI = Primary–Intermediate; I = Intermediate; IJ = Intermediate–Junior High

P = Primary; PI = Primary–Intermediate; I = Intermediate; IJ = Intermediate–Junior High

P = Primary; PI = Primary–Intermediate; I = Intermediate; IJ = Intermediate–Junior High

P = Primary; PI = Primary–Intermediate; I = Intermediate; IJ = Intermediate–Junior High

P = Primary; PI = Primary–Intermediate; I = Intermediate; IJ = Intermediate–Junior High

# C

P = Primary; PI = Primary–Intermediate; I = Intermediate; IJ = Intermediate–Junior High

**Cambodia**
I: 12317
IJ: 12274

**Cambodia — Fiction**
P: 3868
IJ: 5478

**Cambodia — Folklore**
P: 8852, 8855

**Cambodian Americans**
I: 14051
IJ: 14044

**Camels — Fiction**
PI: 1018, 3883
IJ: 6138

**Cameras**
P: 17316

**Cameroon**
IJ: 12178

**Campanella, Roy**
I: 10966

**Camps and camping**
P: 2357
I: 17270, 17597–99
IJ: 17600

**Camps and camping — Fiction**
P: 2094, 2295, 2297, 2303, 2319,
    2427, 2462, 3154, 3358, 3402,
    3539, 4112, 5124, 5153, 5193,
    5220, 6842, 6899
PI: 3091, 3295, 5332, 6120, 6839
I: 2188, 5741, 5749, 6810, 6826,
    6871, 6901, 6912, 7309, 7325,
    8060, 8075, 8079, 8420
IJ: 5618, 6141, 6836, 6887, 6902,
    7132, 7197, 7800

**Canada**
P: 3900
PI: 10081, 12588, 12593, 12595–98,
    12607, 14312
I: 12583–85, 12587, 12591–92,
    12594, 12599–601, 12604–5,
    12608–9, 12742
IJ: 12582

**Canada — Cookbooks**
I: 17233

**Canada — Fiction**
P: 3389, 3738, 3857, 4106, 5793
PI: 3759, 4247, 5587, 7102
I: 5486, 6129, 6834, 7373, 7399–400,
    7864, 8261
IJ: 5841, 5981, 6262, 6549, 7253,
    7397

**Canada — Folklore**
PI: 7406

**Canada — History**
IJ: 13029–30

**Canada — History — Fiction**
IJ: 7394

**Canada — Poetry**
P: 9817
PI: 9519
IJ: 9739

**Canals**
I: 13084, 13099
IJ: 12681–82, 13393

**Canals — Crafts**
I: 16882

**Cancer**
I: 14348, 14358

**Cancer — Fiction**
P: 4092, 4177
I: 6189
IJ: 6995

**Candy — Fiction**
P: 4870, 4885

**Canine family**
PI: 15238

**Canoes and canoeing**
PI: 17661

**Canoes and canoeing — Fiction**
P: 2372, 5064
I: 7671

**Canseco, José**
IJ: 10967

**Canyons**
PI: 16132

**Capri — Fiction**
I: 6639

**Capybaras**
PI: 15300

**Caras, Roger**
PI: 10811

**Card games**
P: 17645
PI: 17637–39
I: 17643
IJ: 17644

**Card tricks**
PI: 17639

**Careers,** 14172–14262
*See also* Occupations and work;
    and specific professionals,
    e.g., Teachers
P: 14187, 14193

**Careers — Fiction**
P: 2415, 2683

**Caribbean Islands**
PI: 12675
I: 12676
IJ: 12684, 14022, 14025

**Caribbean Islands —
    Cookbooks**
I: 17235
IJ: 17231

**Caribbean Islands — Crafts**
I: 16996

**Caribbean Islands — Fiction**
P: 314, 338, 1999, 3630, 3756,
    3810–11, 3828, 3989
PI: 797, 5003, 7531, 7937
I: 5957
IJ: 5786, 6927, 7523, 7526

**Caribbean Islands — Folklore**
P: 9417–20, 9422, 9427–28, 9430,
    9432, 9434–36
PI: 9425
I: 8615, 9424, 9433

**Caribbean Islands — Music**
All: 11501

**Caribbean Islands — Poetry**
P: 9578
PI: 9551
I: 9553

**Caribbean Sea**
I: 15780

**Caribou**
P: 4290
PI: 15252, 15257–58

**Caribou — Fiction**
P: 91, 685

**Carle, Eric**
IJ: 10052

**Carmichael, Stokely**
I: 10365

**Carnivals**
P: 11621

**Carnivals — Fiction**
P: 2291, 3784, 4139

P = Primary; PI = Primary–Intermediate; I = Intermediate; IJ = Intermediate–Junior High

P = Primary; PI = Primary–Intermediate; I = Intermediate; IJ = Intermediate–Junior High

P = Primary; PI = Primary–Intermediate; I = Intermediate; IJ = Intermediate–Junior High

**Chicago, Illinois**
I: 13291, 13297, 13300

**Chicago, Illinois — Fiction**
PI: 5677

**Chicago, Illinois — Poetry**
PI: 9685

**Chicago Bulls (basketball team)**
IJ: 17577

**Chicago Fire (1871)**
IJ: 13290

**Chicago Fire (1871) — Fiction**
I: 7834

**Chickasaw Indians — Folklore**
P: 9191

**Chicken pox — Fiction**
P: 4087, 5000

**Chickens**
P: 15310, 15326, 15381, 15389
I: 15319
IJ: 15387

**Chickens — Fiction**
P: 311, 749, 1054, 1384, 1612, 1626,
1648–49, 1685, 1687–88, 1738,
1778, 1786, 1890, 1941, 1990,
2005, 2154, 3324, 3440, 4260,
4300, 4413, 4868, 5191
PI: 8590
I: 5853, 7990, 8148

**Chickens — Folklore**
P: 8958, 8963, 8985–86, 9090, 9436

**Chickens — Poetry**
P: 9526

**Child abuse**
P: 13769
I: 13755
IJ: 13761, 13771

**Child abuse — Fiction**
P: 4160, 4168
I: 7017, 7041, 7284

**Child care — Biography**
IJ: 10911

**Child labor**
PI: 10544
IJ: 13213

**Child labor — Biography**
IJ: 10534

**Child labor — History**
I: 10756

**Childhood — Poetry**
I: 9563

**Children**
I: 11674

**Children — Art**
P: 2525, 9615
I: 11327

**Children — Legal rights**
I: 10746–47

**Children — Poetry**
P: 9615

**Children (U.S.) — History**
I: 13112

**Children's Crusade**
IJ: 11998

**Chile**
PI: 12732
I: 12708
IJ: 12738

**Chimpanzees**
P: 15147, 15159
PI: 10857
I: 15149

**Chimpanzees — Fiction**
P: 1469–70, 5193–95

**China**
P: 12199, 12213
PI: 12202, 12206, 12219, 15289
I: 12200, 12203–5, 12207, 12210–11,
12223, 12225–26
IJ: 12198, 12201, 14068, 15287

**China — Calendars — Fiction**
P: 1341

**China — Cookbooks**
I: 17216
IJ: 17277

**China — Emigration**
I: 12215

**China — Festivals**
I: 12220

**China — Fiction**
P: 855, 970, 2864, 3281, 3796, 3840,
3867, 4457, 8540
PI: 859, 883, 3891, 7456, 7458, 7955
I: 5971, 6013, 7457, 7461
IJ: 7404, 7449, 7857, 7860, 7892

**China — Folklore**
P: 8761, 8763, 8765, 8767, 8773–74,
8777–78, 8781–89, 8791–93,
8795–97, 8799, 8801–3
PI: 8758, 8762, 8768, 8780, 8790,
8798, 8800
I: 8759, 8766, 8770–72, 8775, 8794
IJ: 8760, 8764, 8776, 8779

**China — History**
PI: 12222
I: 10019, 12212, 12214, 12218,
12221, 12224
IJ: 10242, 11201, 12208–9

**China — Houses**
I: 12217

**China — Poetry**
PI: 9605

**China — Short stories**
I: 7438

**Chinese Americans**
P: 2983, 4606, 4640
I: 10355, 12203
IJ: 14034, 14068, 14091

**Chinese Americans —
Biography**
I: 11147
IJ: 10057, 10089

**Chinese Americans — Fiction**
P: 2441, 2671, 2690, 4169, 4489,
4620, 5113
PI: 6791
I: 6013, 7032, 7461, 8195
IJ: 5819, 6041, 7087, 7668

**Chinese language**
PI: 11379
IJ: 11383

**Chinese language — Writing**
P: 11382
PI: 11464

**Chinese New Year**
P: 4606, 4608, 4640
PI: 13896
I: 13899

**Chinese New Year — Crafts**
PI: 13901

**Chinese New Year — Fiction**
P: 4620, 4638
PI: 6027

**Chinn, May**
I: 10828

P = Primary; PI = Primary–Intermediate; I = Intermediate; IJ = Intermediate–Junior High

**Chinook Indians — Folklore**
I: 9259

**Chipmunks — Fiction**
P: 4305, 5075

**Chippewa Indians**
PI: 12916
I: 12873, 12892
IJ: 12927

**Chippewa Indians — Fiction**
P: 561, 3719

**Chippewa Indians — Folklore**
P: 9215, 9246, 9292
PI: 9271, 9287, 9307
I: 9216

**Chisholm, Shirley**
PI: 10367

**Chisholm Trail**
PI: 13166

**Chocolate — Biography**
I: 10532

**Chocolate — Fiction**
PI: 6301
I: 6342, 8124, 8173

**Choctaw Indians — Folklore**
P: 9239

**Choctaw Indians — History**
PI: 12883

**Choinumne Indians**
IJ: 12901

**Chores — Fiction**
I: 6926, 7116, 7732, 8249

**Christiana Riot — Fiction**
IJ: 7653

**Christianity**
I: 13809

**Christianity — Fiction**
IJ: 7405

**Christianity — Holy days**
I: 13930

**Christmas**
P: 4625, 4709, 4726, 4750, 4767,
   13936, 13945, 13950
PI: 13937, 13939, 13948, 13951,
   13954
I: 12585, 13935, 13941–42, 13944,
   13947, 13949

**Christmas — Anthologies**
PI: 4794

**Christmas — Carols**
*See* Christmas — Songs and
carols

**Christmas — Crafts**
P: 13952, 17053
PI: 13940, 13943, 13954
I: 16991, 17020, 17029, 17054

**Christmas — Fairy tales**
I: 8564

**Christmas — Fiction**
P: 130, 961, 1291, 1550, 2645, 2758,
   2922, 2939, 3526, 4172, 4689–707,
   4711–18, 4720–22, 4724–25,
   4727–41, 4743–49, 4752–54,
   4756–63, 4765–66, 4768–69, 4772,
   4774–88, 4790–93, 4795–804,
   4806–7, 4809–11, 4813–20,
   4822–32, 4835, 4837–47, 4849–58,
   4860, 5306
PI: 4723, 4742, 4751, 4808, 4848,
   4859, 6085, 7586, 7902, 7910,
   7915, 7929, 7931, 7935–38, 7942,
   7962, 7966
I: 7901, 7911–13, 7917, 7921, 7927,
   7933–34, 7940–41, 7943–44, 7946,
   7950, 7953, 13946
IJ: 7035, 7908, 7920, 7922–23, 7932,
   7947, 7949, 7961, 7965, 7967–68

**Christmas — Folklore**
P: 4833, 8939
PI: 9403

**Christmas — History**
I: 13097

**Christmas — Jokes and riddles**
P: 4805

**Christmas — Plays**
All: 9924

**Christmas — Poetry**
P: 4789, 4812, 4836, 7958, 9761,
   9763, 9767, 9773–77
PI: 9760, 9765, 9778
IJ: 9783

**Christmas — Short stories**
I: 7926, 7956
IJ: 7948

**Christmas — Songs and carols**
P: 4764, 11555, 11558, 11560,
   11562–64
PI: 11548, 11551, 11553–54, 11557,
   11559, 11561
I: 11549–50, 11552, 11556
IJ: 13953

**Christmas trees — Fiction**
P: 4708, 4710, 4719, 4755, 4770–71,
   4821, 4834, 4861
I: 7954

**Christopher, Saint**
P: 11202

**Chumash Indians — Folklore**
P: 9309

**Churchill, Winston**
IJ: 11203–4

**Cid, El**
IJ: 11205

**Cincinnati Zoo**
I: 15114

**Circles**
PI: 16352
I: 16353

**Circulation system**
P: 14423
PI: 14427
I: 14414, 14419–21, 14426
IJ: 14316, 14418, 14422, 14424

**Circuses**
P: 318, 2479, 11622, 11625
I: 11624
IJ: 11620

**Circuses — Biography**
IJ: 10159

**Circuses — Fiction**
P: 256, 1170, 1608, 1631, 2008, 2200,
   2367, 3370, 3406, 3892, 4234,
   4263, 4293, 5188
PI: 4051
I: 5701, 5978
IJ: 8076

**Cisneros, Evelyn**
PI: 10478

**Cisneros, Henry**
I: 10480
IJ: 10479

**Cities**
PI: 13592
IJ: 11671

**Cities and city life**
*See also* names of specific
cities, e.g., Boston,
Massachusetts
P: 2469, 2739
PI: 7252, 17401
I: 2494, 11963, 13590–91
IJ: 16776

P = Primary; PI = Primary–Intermediate; I = Intermediate; IJ = Intermediate–Junior High

P = Primary; PI = Primary–Intermediate; I = Intermediate; IJ = Intermediate–Junior High

P = Primary; PI = Primary–Intermediate; I = Intermediate; IJ = Intermediate–Junior High

P = Primary; PI = Primary–Intermediate; I = Intermediate; IJ = Intermediate–Junior High

**Containers**
I: 17428

**Contests**
I: 14106

**Contests — Fiction**
I: 8093

**Cookbooks**
P: 17053, 17218, 17230, 17250,
  17259
PI: 17048, 17203–4, 17245, 17253,
  17265–66, 17276
I: 15953, 17205–6, 17208–9,
  17211–13, 17220, 17229,
  17239–41, 17257–58, 17270,
  17272, 17274–75
IJ: 15976, 17237, 17249, 17252,
  17254, 17261, 17264, 17268,
  17271, 17273, 17280

**Cookbooks — Ethnic**
P: 2392
PI: 17232
I: 17215–17, 17221–22, 17227,
  17233, 17235, 17243, 17248,
  17260
IJ: 17202, 17207, 17210, 17224–26,
  17228, 17231, 17236, 17242,
  17244, 17246–47, 17251,
  17262–63, 17267, 17269,
  17277–79

**Cookbooks — Historical**
PI: 17201, 17219, 17238, 17256

**Cookies**
PI: 17245
I: 13562, 17211

**Cooking**
*See* Cookbooks; Cooks and
  cooking

**Cooks and cooking**
P: 2493, 17223
I: 17214

**Cooks and cooking — Careers**
P: 14176
I: 14172

**Cooks and cooking — Fiction**
P: 2551, 3331
PI: 8011, 8294
I: 8093

**Cooks and cooking — Poetry**
P: 2475

**Coolidge, Calvin**
I: 10636

**Cooperation**
P: 9518

**Cooperation — Fiction**
P: 1612

**Coquelle Indians — Folklore**
P: 9213

**Coral reefs**
P: 15653
PI: 15652, 15656, 15662
I: 15658–59, 15661, 15663
IJ: 15651, 15654–55, 15660, 16191

**Corn**
P: 16014
PI: 16010
I: 16011

**Cortés, Hernando**
IJ: 9985

**Cosby, Bill**
I: 10165, 10167
IJ: 10166, 10168

**Costa Rica**
I: 12656

**Costa Rica — Fiction**
P: 3591
PI: 7522
IJ: 5595

**Costumes and costume making**
PI: 17076, 17078, 17083
I: 17077, 17085, 17092
IJ: 17089

**Costumes and costume making
— History**
I: 16802
IJ: 16810

**Cougars**
P: 15204, 15218
I: 15211

**Counting books**
P: 43, 133, 158, 204–5, 288–326,
  328–34, 336–68, 370–72, 374–76,
  378, 381–97, 399–406, 408–14,
  416–52, 664, 680, 703, 4558, 4936,
  4946, 4948, 14984, 15354, 15653
PI: 335, 377, 379–80, 398, 407,
  12403, 12441–42, 12548, 12702
I: 12205, 12236, 12471, 12570

**Countries**
PI: 11857

**County fairs**
P: 11623

**Courage — Biography**
IJ: 9952

**Courts**
I: 13638–39

**Cowardice — Fiction**
P: 3808

**Cowboys**
P: 10415, 13130
PI: 13119, 13131
I: 13167, 13517, 14174
IJ: 13121, 13129, 13133, 13154,
  13164

**Cowboys — Biography**
P: 10197
I: 10206

**Cowboys — Careers**
PI: 14175

**Cowboys — Fiction**
P: 975, 2352, 2360, 2534, 2713, 3330,
  3490, 3855
PI: 2330, 6534

**Cowboys — Folklore**
P: 9349

**Cowboys — Poetry**
I: 9574

**Cowgirls — Fiction**
P: 3855

**Cows**
P: 15932, 15957

**Cows — Fiction**
P: 306, 993, 1611, 1797, 1967, 2257,
  3270, 4125, 4273, 4316, 4405,
  4427, 4437, 4557, 4737

**Cows — Folklore**
P: 8713
PI: 8967

**Cows — Poetry**
PI: 9839

**Coyotes**
P: 15224, 15230
PI: 15238–39
I: 15246

**Coyotes — Fiction**
P: 1888

**Coyotes — Folklore**
P: 9192, 9273
I: 9294, 9296

**Crabs**
P: 15669

P = Primary; PI = Primary–Intermediate; I = Intermediate; IJ = Intermediate–Junior High

P = Primary; PI = Primary–Intermediate; I = Intermediate; IJ = Intermediate–Junior High

P = Primary; PI = Primary–Intermediate; I = Intermediate; IJ = Intermediate–Junior High

**Death**
P: 3028, 13986, 14156, 14170
I: 13811, 14160, 17445
IJ: 13772, 14163–64, 14167, 14263

**Death — Fiction**
P: 735, 1431, 1515, 1883, 2191, 2256,
2817, 2885, 2926, 3083, 3122,
3127, 3132, 3158, 3176, 3921,
4013, 4019, 4025–26, 4029,
4034–35, 4038, 4045, 4077, 4082,
4094, 4097, 4124, 4141, 4157,
4162, 4176, 4179, 4182, 4185,
4187, 4367, 4480, 5114
PI: 3118, 4123, 4128, 4420, 5896,
5988, 5992, 6047, 6194, 7005,
7123, 7192, 7196, 7211, 7246,
7332, 7335
I: 5557, 5936, 5986, 6721, 6828,
6861, 6960, 6970, 7015, 7040,
7047, 7119, 7138, 7150, 7183,
7302, 7308, 7329, 7337, 7881,
7950, 8217
IJ: 5482, 5489, 5827, 6164, 6212,
6357, 6680, 6903, 6995, 7022,
7038, 7053, 7089, 7118, 7144,
7186, 7203, 7210, 7215, 7219,
7250, 7290, 7297, 7313, 7327,
7342, 7352, 7376, 7465, 7835,
7858, 7968

**Death — Folklore**
P: 9326

**Declaration of Independence
(U.S.)**
PI: 10530
I: 13067
IJ: 13053

**de Coubertin, Pierre**
IJ: 17655

**Deer**
P: 15249, 15256
PI: 15250, 15253, 15260
I: 15259

**Deer — Fiction**
P: 4199
IJ: 5827, 5959, 5968, 8587

**Deer mice**
PI: 15301

**Defecation**
P: 2511

**Degas, Edgar**
IJ: 10060, 11315

**Degas, Edgar — Fiction**
P: 7487

**de la Renta, Oscar**
IJ: 10481

**Delaware**
I: 13354, 13385

**Denali National Park (Alaska)**
P: 13445

**Denmark**
IJ: 12492

**Denmark — Fiction**
I: 5539, 7472
IJ: 5540, 7863, 7877

**Dentists**
P: 14506

**Dentists — Careers**
P: 14214

**Dentists — Fiction**
P: 2131

**Denver, Colorado**
I: 13338

**dePaola, Tomie — Fiction**
P: 2869

**Department stores — Fiction**
P: 2410

**De Passe, Suzanne**
IJ: 10744

**Depression, Great**
PI: 13239
IJ: 13232, 13238

**Depression, Great — Fiction**
P: 3877, 3968, 4009, 4761, 5430
PI: 3759, 7002, 7832
I: 6195, 7006, 7058, 7442, 7788,
7833, 7838, 7851
IJ: 5946, 6191, 7202, 7277, 7780,
7782–83, 7808, 7845, 8073

**Depression (mental state) —
Fiction**
IJ: 6998

**Des Moines, Iowa — Fiction**
IJ: 8114

**Desegregation**
PI: 13665

**Deserts**
P: 3664, 16206, 16210, 16215, 16217,
16229
PI: 12821, 15322, 16211, 16220–21,
16227–28

I: 12828, 16057, 16084, 16204–5,
16207–8, 16212–13, 16216, 16219,
16222–25
IJ: 12144, 16089, 16214, 16226

**Deserts — Animals**
P: 16209
PI: 15040
I: 16218, 17109

**Deserts — Fiction**
P: 2629, 3550, 4191
PI: 3883
I: 5831, 8382

**Deserts — Poetry**
P: 9887
PI: 49, 9859
I: 9706, 9854, 9893

**DesJarlait, Patrick**
IJ: 10061

**Desktop publishing**
IJ: 11398

**Desserts**
I: 17217

**Detectives**
PI: 17299
I: 13709
IJ: 13685

**Detectives — Biography**
IJ: 10565–66

**Detroit, Michigan**
PI: 13306

**Devers, Gail**
I: 11121

**Devil — Fiction**
I: 6234–35
IJ: 5727

**Devil — Folklore**
P: 8874
PI: 8908

**Dewey Decimal System**
PI: 11389

**Diabetes**
P: 14354
I: 14329, 14349

**Diabetes — Fiction**
I: 7380

**Diana, Princess of Wales**
I: 11214
IJ: 11213

P = Primary; PI = Primary–Intermediate; I = Intermediate; IJ = Intermediate–Junior High

**Diaries**
IJ: 11449, 11479

**Diaries — Fiction**
PI: 7393, 7433
I: 7131, 7971
IJ: 6106, 6244, 7614, 7787, 7794, 8157

**Dickens, Charles**
IJ: 10237–38

**Dickens, Charles — Fiction**
I: 7620

**Dickinson, Emily — Fiction**
PI: 6808

**Dictators — Fiction**
P: 3829

**Dictionaries**
*See also* Word books
P: 11420, 11434
IJ: 12968

**Diets**
IJ: 14430, 14511

**Digestion**
P: 14432–33, 14437
PI: 14440
I: 14429, 14434
IJ: 14430, 14435, 14438

**Digestive system**
P: 14436
IJ: 14428

**DiMaggio, Joe**
I: 10975–76

**Diners — Fiction**
P: 1524, 3858

**Dingoes — Fiction**
P: 2193

**Dinosaur National Monument**
PI: 13330
IJ: 11698

**Dinosaurs**
*See also* Paleontology;
  Prehistoric animals; and
  names of specific dinosaurs,
  e.g., Tyrannosaurus rex
P: 3548, 4391, 4398, 11694, 11696,
  11702, 11707–8, 11711, 11713,
  11717–18, 11723, 11728–29,
  11734–35, 11762–66, 11769,
  11772, 11775, 11791, 11793,
  14121, 14895
PI: 9785, 11693, 11695, 11701,
  11712, 11722, 11730, 11732,

11738–39, 11748, 11756–57,
  11777, 11780–82
I: 11704–5, 11715–16, 11719–21,
  11733, 11737, 11740–44,
  11746–47, 11749–53, 11755,
  11760–61, 11767, 11770, 11776,
  11778, 11786–88, 11790, 11792,
  11812, 14682, 17110, 17172
IJ: 11703, 11706, 11710, 11724,
  11726–27, 11745, 11754, 11758,
  11768, 11779

**Dinosaurs — Crafts**
PI: 17034

**Dinosaurs — Defenses**
PI: 11783

**Dinosaurs — Directories**
IJ: 11736

**Dinosaurs — Fiction**
P: 873–74, 1029, 1131, 1414, 1510,
  1513, 1574, 1790, 1968, 2094,
  2152, 2261, 2321, 2424, 3286,
  3294, 3415, 4027, 4209, 4281,
  4734, 5203–4, 5214, 5328
PI: 5155
I: 5503–4, 6414, 6482, 7990
IJ: 5747, 7504

**Dinosaurs — Jokes and riddles**
PI: 17325

**Dinosaurs — Models**
I: 11699

**Dinosaurs — Poetry**
PI: 9612, 9744

**Dirigibles**
PI: 16886
I: 16720

**Dirigibles — Fiction**
PI: 7831

**Disabilities,** 14294–14322
PI: 13660

**Diseases**
*See also* Doctors; Illness;
  Medicine; and specific dis-
  eases, e.g., AIDS
PI: 14327
I: 14336
IJ: 14321, 14338–40, 14356, 14363

**Disney, Walt**
I: 10062, 10064–65
IJ: 10063

**Disney World — Fiction**
I: 8093

**Divorce**
*See also* Family problems
P: 14121, 14142
PI: 14150
I: 14131, 14138
IJ: 14127, 14135, 14140, 14147

**Divorce — Fiction**
P: 2893, 4032, 4138, 4173, 7085,
  7177
PI: 4155, 6965, 6968, 7056, 8020,
  8025
I: 5835, 6537, 6543, 6939, 6943,
  6945, 6980, 7037, 7039, 7042,
  7071, 7078, 7081, 7281, 8467
IJ: 5812, 6870, 6892, 6946, 6967,
  6969, 6972–73, 7001, 7010, 7035,
  7048, 7083, 7099, 8114

**Diwali (Hindu holiday)**
PI: 13920

**Diwali (Hindu holiday) —
  Fiction**
I: 7445

**Dix, Dorothea**
I: 10745

**DNA**
I: 14370, 14373
IJ: 14372

**Doctors**
P: 2417
I: 14366, 14368

**Doctors — Biography**
PI: 10846, 10897
I: 10809, 10812, 10828, 10881,
  10903, 10909
IJ: 10796, 10835, 10865, 10917

**Doctors — Careers**
P: 14216
PI: 14212, 14218

**Doctors — Fiction**
P: 2564
IJ: 6140

**Dogs**
*See also* Guide dogs; Sled
  dogs; and individual species,
  e.g., Dachshunds
P: 3900, 5422, 15233, 15848–49,
  15853, 15855, 15857, 15859,
  15861, 15864, 15869–71
PI: 14217, 15847, 15854, 15863,
  15867–68, 15876–77
I: 15851, 15856, 15862, 15865–66,
  15875, 17097
IJ: 15850, 15852, 15860, 15872–74

P = Primary; PI = Primary–Intermediate; I = Intermediate; IJ = Intermediate–Junior High

P = Primary; PI = Primary–Intermediate; I = Intermediate; IJ = Intermediate–Junior High

I: 6535, 7439
IJ: 809

**Dreams and dreaming**
I: 14526–27

**Dreams and dreaming —
Fiction**
P: 517, 557, 793, 1154, 1159, 2165,
4103, 4281, 5210
PI: 1277, 3889

**Dreams and dreaming —
Folklore**
P: 8824

**Dred Scott case**
I: 13085

**Drew, Charles**
IJ: 10835

**Droughts**
IJ: 13273

**Droughts — Fiction**
PI: 7187
I: 5490

**Drugs and drug problems**
*See also* Alcoholism
P: 14273, 14286
PI: 13710
I: 13699, 14266, 14282–83, 14287,
14292
IJ: 10982, 13736, 14265, 14268,
14271, 14279, 14284, 14288–90

**Drugs and drug problems —
Fiction**
P: 4174
IJ: 5796

**Dublin, Ireland**
I: 12422

**Du Bois, W. E. B.**
PI: 10378
I: 10379

**Ducks and geese**
P: 4217, 15393–95
PI: 15392
I: 15390

**Ducks and geese — Fiction**
P: 417, 419, 1161, 1588, 1649,
1662–63, 1709, 1767, 1858, 1886,
1889, 2032, 2040, 2086–87, 2106,
2161, 2166, 2197, 2212, 2227,
2258, 2266, 2867, 3796, 4368,
4413, 4423, 4434, 4505, 4728,
5088, 5179, 5243, 8502

PI: 2041, 5633, 6630, 8546
I: 1167, 5833, 6709

**Ducks and geese — Folklore**
P: 9228
PI: 8840

**Dugongs**
PI: 15699

**Dugongs — Fiction**
P: 5424

**Duncan, Isadora**
IJ: 10169

**Dust Bowl**
IJ: 13273

**Dust Bowl — Fiction**
P: 3801
I: 7838
IJ: 7277

**Dwarfism**
I: 14400

**Dwarves — Fiction**
P: 8545
IJ: 6718, 6726

**Dwarves — Folklore**
P: 8928

**Dyslexia**
IJ: 14315

**Dyslexia — Fiction**
P: 4058
I: 6854, 7347, 7349–50, 7366, 8019

# E

**Eagles**
*See also* Birds of prey
P: 15400
PI: 15401–2, 15405, 15412
I: 15397, 15403, 15406, 15409
IJ: 15410

**Eagles — Folklore**
P: 9293

**Earhart, Amelia**
PI: 9996
I: 9991–93
IJ: 9994–95, 9997

**Earp, Wyatt**
IJ: 10509

**Earrings — Fiction**
P: 3496

**Ears**
I: 14473

**Earth**
*See also* Geology
P: 11676, 14686, 14797, 14799,
16125
PI: 3691, 11681, 14688, 14690,
14693, 16113, 16116, 16120,
16126, 16136, 16145
I: 14687, 14691–92, 16114, 16123,
16128–29, 16131, 16135
IJ: 14689, 14737, 14798

**Earth — Atlases**
IJ: 16140

**Earth — Experiments and
projects**
I: 14685

**Earth — Fiction**
P: 3532

**Earth — Folklore**
I: 9263

**Earth — Geology,** 16108–16145

**Earth Day**
P: 4621
IJ: 13907

**Earth Day — Crafts**
PI: 17038

**Earth Day — Fiction**
P: 5341

**Earth sciences**
I: 16144

**Earth sciences — Experiments
and projects**
I: 14632, 16117

**Earthquakes**
P: 16151
PI: 16157
I: 16139, 16156, 16159–61, 16167,
16169
IJ: 12464, 16142, 16146, 16149,
16152, 16166

**Earthquakes — Experiments
and projects**
I: 16164
IJ: 16155

**Earthquakes — Fiction**
P: 3791, 4243
IJ: 5524, 6692

P = Primary; PI = Primary–Intermediate; I = Intermediate; IJ = Intermediate–Junior High

**Earthworms**
I: 15613

**Easter**
P: 4866, 4874
I: 13955–57

**Easter — Crafts**
P: 16992, 17018, 17032
PI: 16993

**Easter — Fiction**
P: 4862–65, 4867–70, 4872–73,
4875–76

**Easter — Poetry**
P: 4871, 9766
PI: 9768, 9782

**Eastern Europe — Fiction**
P: 4965

**Eastern Europe — Folklore,**
8866–8880

**Eastern Orthodox religion**
P: 13812

**Eastman, Charles**
I: 10836

**Eastwood, Alice**
PI: 10837

**Eating — Poetry**
P: 9846

**Eating disorders**
IJ: 14326

**Eating disorders — Fiction**
IJ: 7227

**Echidna**
PI: 15140

**Eclipses**
I: 14738

**Ecology and environment**
*See also* Conservation;
Pollution
P: 13569–70, 13583, 13585, 14816,
14822, 16186, 16192
PI: 10702, 13568, 13577, 16236,
16241
I: 13378, 13437, 13485, 13528,
13566, 13572–74, 13578–81,
13590–91, 13625, 14823, 15471,
15940, 16123, 16134, 16177,
16251, 16321
IJ: 12740, 12777, 13565, 13567,
13575, 13584, 13588, 13624,
13907, 15792, 16187, 16230,
16276, 16309

**Ecology and environment —
Dictionaries**
PI: 13586

**Ecology and environment —
Experiments and projects**
I: 13576, 13582, 13587

**Ecology and environment —
Fiction**
P: 1279, 3536, 3559, 3656, 3882,
4232
PI: 3528, 3729, 5390, 7178
I: 7057, 7555
IJ: 5464, 5533

**Ecuador**
I: 12689, 12697
IJ: 12699, 12714

**Ecuador — Fiction**
PI: 4181

**Edelman, Marian Wright**
I: 10746–47

**Edison, Thomas Alva**
PI: 10841
I: 10839–40
IJ: 10838

**Edison, Thomas Alva — Fiction**
P: 3915

**Edmonds, Emma**
IJ: 10748–49

**Edo**
P: 12192
IJ: 12169

**Education**
IJ: 14107

**Educators — Biography**
PI: 10360–62, 10446, 10464
I: 10363–64, 11254
IJ: 10556, 11255

**Eels**
PI: 15639

**Eeyou Indians**
I: 12942

**Eggs**
P: 15078, 15310, 15326, 15389
PI: 15363, 15958
IJ: 15387

**Eggs — Fiction**
P: 1161, 1688, 3283, 3380–81, 3612,
4862, 4873
PI: 2035
I: 6329, 7990, 8272

**Egypt**
P: 12534
PI: 12537, 12540, 12545
I: 12535, 12538–39, 12541–43
IJ: 12536, 12544

**Egypt — Fiction**
P: 3832, 7430
I: 7416, 7427
IJ: 6132, 6921

**Egypt — Folklore**
P: 8692, 8712
I: 8708
IJ: 8702

**Egypt — History**
P: 5134, 11878, 11899
PI: 11278, 11869, 11874, 11876,
11880, 11885, 11898, 11900,
11909
I: 10822, 11206–7, 11277, 11871,
11873, 11875, 11877, 11879,
11882–84, 11886–87, 11891,
11896, 11901–3, 11907–8,
11910–13, 16778
IJ: 11263–64, 11831, 11870, 11872,
11881, 11888, 11893–95, 11897,
11905–6, 13821

**Egypt — History — Fiction**
P: 3807
I: 7423
IJ: 6277

**Egypt — Mythology**
I: 8703
IJ: 9450

**Ehlert, Lois**
PI: 10240

**Einstein, Albert**
I: 10842–43

**Eisenhower, Dwight D.**
I: 10334, 10637, 10640
IJ: 10638–39, 10641

**Eisner, Michael**
IJ: 10510

**El Alamein, Battle of**
IJ: 12062

**El Chino**
I: 11147

**El Greco**
PI: 10066

**El Salvador**
I: 12652
IJ: 12654

P = Primary; PI = Primary–Intermediate; I = Intermediate; IJ = Intermediate–Junior High

P = Primary; PI = Primary–Intermediate; I = Intermediate; IJ = Intermediate–Junior High

P = Primary; PI = Primary–Intermediate; I = Intermediate; IJ = Intermediate–Junior High

P = Primary; PI = Primary–Intermediate; I = Intermediate; IJ = Intermediate–Junior High

**Fairies**
P: 1001, 1054, 2430, 2971, 4711
PI: 6367
I: 6413, 6598, 8772

**Fairies — Folklore**
P: 8981
IJ: 8656

**Fairies — Poetry**
P: 9725

**Fairs**
P: 11623

**Fairs — Fiction**
P: 127, 936, 2428, 2447, 2453, 2616, 2731
PI: 5538

**Fairy tales**
P: 4963, 5177, 8483–85, 8491, 8494, 8497–502, 8504, 8507–10, 8512–14, 8516–18, 8520, 8523, 8525–26, 8528–29, 8531–34, 8536, 8540, 8542–45, 8551, 8554, 8556–60, 8562–63, 8567–68, 8571, 8574, 8576–77, 8580, 8582–83, 8591–92, 8595, 8597, 8599, 8743, 8774, 8797, 8827, 8884, 8900, 9064, 9131
PI: 1140, 3466, 4723, 8482, 8487–88, 8493, 8495–96, 8511, 8522, 8527, 8539, 8546–47, 8549, 8553, 8570, 8575, 8578–79, 8584, 8586, 8588, 8598, 8932
I: 6313–14, 8481, 8486, 8489–90, 8492, 8503, 8505–6, 8515, 8521, 8524, 8530, 8535, 8537–38, 8548, 8550, 8555, 8564–66, 8569, 8572–73, 8581, 8585, 8589, 8593–94, 8596, 8634, 8693, 8816
IJ: 8519, 8541, 8552, 8561, 8587

**Fairy tales — Crafts**
PI: 17037

**Falcons**
P: 15404
I: 15397, 15399, 15411

**Falcons — Fiction**
P: 4219
IJ: 7167

**Families**
P: 14146

**Family life**
P: 2988, 3036, 3038
I: 14126
IJ: 14128, 14155

**Family life — Fiction**
P: 1957
PI: 3121
IJ: 7068

**Family life — Poetry**
P: 2785, 9597, 9648
PI: 9557
I: 9563
IJ: 9614

**Family problems**
P: 14125, 14151–53
PI: 14132, 14144, 14150
I: 14120, 14131, 14136, 14138, 14145, 14149
IJ: 14127, 14134–35, 14137, 14140

**Family problems — Fiction**
P: 2476, 2872, 2897, 2910, 3069, 3392, 4007, 4044, 4062, 4064, 4082, 4100, 4156, 4168, 4622, 5440, 7919
PI: 6170, 6959, 7014, 7056, 7060, 7079, 7086, 7301, 8022
I: 2815, 5775, 5880, 6088, 6179, 6183, 6786, 6938–39, 6943, 6945, 6953–54, 6956–57, 6960, 6962, 6970–71, 6975, 6978, 6980, 6983, 6986, 6992–93, 7006–7, 7012–13, 7024, 7026, 7037, 7039–42, 7047, 7051–52, 7057–58, 7062–63, 7067, 7070, 7072, 7074, 7076, 7080, 7286, 7813, 7851
IJ: 5495, 5527, 5812, 5864, 6687, 6940–41, 6946, 6949–50, 6955, 6958, 6961, 6963–64, 6966–67, 6969, 6973–74, 6976–77, 6979, 6982, 6984–85, 6987–91, 6994–96, 6998–7001, 7003–4, 7008–9, 7011, 7019–23, 7025, 7027–28, 7030–31, 7034–36, 7045–46, 7048–50, 7053, 7059, 7061, 7064–66, 7073, 7084, 7087–88, 7161, 7791, 7799, 7818, 7852

**Family relationships,**
14118–14155

**Family stories**
P: 2860, 2915, 3031, 3090, 3092, 3099, 3119–20, 5096, 6067
PI: 3113, 6057
I: 6056, 6176, 7518, 8113
IJ: 6053, 6101, 6137, 6716

**Family stories — Fiction**
P: 1424, 1776, 2319, 2732, 2759, 2782–84, 2786, 2788–89, 2794, 2796–802, 2805–9, 2811, 2813–14, 2820, 2828–32, 2834–38, 2840, 2842, 2849, 2851–52, 2854–56, 2859, 2861, 2865, 2867–68, 2870, 2874, 2876–80, 2883–84, 2886, 2888–89, 2891–93, 2896–901, 2903, 2905–6, 2908, 2910–11, 2913, 2916, 2918–20, 2922–23, 2925, 2927, 2929, 2932, 2934–37, 2941–42, 2944–49, 2952, 2954–57, 2959–60, 2964, 2967–68, 2970–71, 2974–75, 2977–85, 2987, 2992–96, 2998–99, 3002–5, 3008, 3010–13, 3015–16, 3018, 3020, 3022–24, 3027, 3030, 3037, 3040, 3046–50, 3052–58, 3062–63, 3065–66, 3068, 3070, 3072, 3074, 3076–78, 3080, 3085–88, 3094, 3096–97, 3100, 3102–3, 3106–7, 3109, 3111, 3114, 3116, 3123–26, 3128–31, 3134–36, 3139–42, 3145, 3147, 3149–50, 3152–57, 3159, 3161–65, 3186, 3369, 3376, 3535, 3672, 3833, 3845, 3904, 3956, 4031, 4114, 4252, 4485, 4527, 4603, 4656, 4678, 4708, 5058, 5092, 5151, 5222, 5317, 6086, 6149, 7980
PI: 2593, 2850, 2887, 2904, 2943, 3039, 3118, 4628, 4648, 5967, 5969, 6047, 6051, 6062, 6070–71, 6073–74, 6080, 6085, 6089, 6111, 6113, 6115, 6119–20, 6122, 6124–28, 6131, 6143–45, 6147, 6154, 6159, 6167–68, 6173, 6181, 7122, 7146, 7793, 7929, 8014–15, 8111
I: 2882, 5576, 5877, 6003, 6044, 6050, 6052, 6054, 6059–60, 6065–66, 6068–69, 6076–79, 6081–82, 6087–88, 6091–95, 6097, 6099, 6102, 6104, 6112, 6114, 6117, 6121, 6134, 6139, 6142, 6146, 6148, 6151, 6153, 6155–56, 6160–61, 6165–66, 6172, 6175, 6178, 6182, 6185, 6187, 6192–93, 6195–96, 6202–3, 6206, 6209, 6838, 6947, 7043, 7075, 7150, 7418, 7692, 7704, 7740, 7785, 7846, 7983, 8074
IJ: 5582, 6028, 6042–43, 6045–46, 6048, 6055, 6063–64, 6072, 6075, 6084, 6100, 6106, 6109–10, 6118, 6123, 6130, 6132, 6136, 6138, 6140–41, 6150, 6152, 6157–58, 6162–64, 6169, 6171, 6180, 6190–91, 6198, 6200, 6204–5, 6208, 6507, 7038, 7054, 7186, 7297, 7345, 7437, 7808, 7817, 8144, 8183

**Famines**
I: 15927

**Famines — Fiction**
I: 7506
IJ: 7720

P = Primary; PI = Primary–Intermediate; I = Intermediate; IJ = Intermediate–Junior High

**Famines — Folklore**

P: 9279

**Fantasy**

*See also* Fables; Folklore; Imaginary animals; Mythology; Science fiction; Supernatural; Tall tales; Time travel — Fiction

P: 473, 687, 714, 724–30, 732–41, 743–47, 750–64, 766–67, 769, 771–76, 778–95, 798–808, 811–22, 824–31, 833–37, 839–45, 847–53, 857–58, 860–82, 884–90, 892–900, 902–3, 905–26, 928–33, 935–36, 938–56, 958–94, 996–1017, 1019–22, 1024, 1027–37, 1039, 1041–42, 1044–63, 1065–67, 1069, 1071–81, 1083–118, 1120–22, 1124–39, 1141–44, 1147, 1149–56, 1159–61, 1163–65, 1168–70, 1172–75, 1177–80, 1182–95, 1197–203, 1205–7, 1209–10, 1212–26, 1228–40, 1242–44, 1246–69, 1271–76, 1278, 1280–85, 1287–98, 1300–5, 1307–13, 1315–21, 1323–27, 1329–43, 1345–55, 1420, 1432, 1913, 1934, 2274, 2569, 2867, 3296, 3448, 3700, 3739, 3866, 3879, 4002, 4673, 4780, 5060, 5080, 5090, 5183, 5204, 5227, 5229, 5282, 5358, 5383, 5431, 5437, 6282, 6311, 6392, 6578, 6580, 6611, 6613, 6626, 6664

PI: 742, 748, 765, 797, 846, 856, 859, 891, 901, 904, 927, 937, 1018, 1038, 1064, 1068, 1070, 1123, 1148, 1162, 1171, 1181, 1241, 1245, 1270, 1277, 1306, 1322, 1328, 1344, 3771, 5248, 5641, 5699, 5910, 5913, 6215, 6231, 6239, 6242–43, 6255–56, 6267, 6274, 6284, 6286, 6289, 6293, 6301, 6305, 6309, 6312, 6315, 6328, 6332, 6345, 6349, 6353–54, 6371, 6382, 6388, 6398–99, 6401, 6404, 6406, 6408, 6415, 6423–24, 6430, 6435, 6439, 6443, 6447–48, 6451, 6456, 6481, 6483, 6486, 6502–6, 6508–12, 6515–16, 6518, 6520, 6524–25, 6529–30, 6532, 6552, 6559, 6561, 6566, 6568–69, 6571–73, 6575, 6579, 6581–83, 6585, 6587, 6607, 6625, 6627, 6630, 6633–34, 6637–38, 6643, 6645, 6649–51, 6672, 6678, 6683–84, 6690–91, 6701–2, 6704, 6711–13, 6723, 6736, 6738–39, 6746, 6748–49, 6760–61, 6764, 6766, 6768–69, 6773, 6782, 6787, 6791, 7910, 8192, 8553, 8598

I: 1167, 1211, 2188, 5674, 5914, 5976, 6061, 6078, 6210, 6220, 6222–23, 6225, 6227, 6229–30, 6232–38, 6240, 6246–50, 6254, 6258, 6270–71, 6273, 6275–76, 6279–81, 6287–88, 6290–92, 6302, 6316, 6320–21, 6324–25, 6327, 6329–30, 6335, 6341–44, 6346, 6348, 6356, 6360–66, 6368–70, 6372–73, 6376, 6379, 6393, 6396–97, 6403, 6410–12, 6414, 6416, 6418, 6422, 6426, 6428, 6434, 6437–38, 6440–41, 6449, 6454, 6459, 6463, 6470–75, 6482, 6487–90, 6493–94, 6497–501, 6521–23, 6531, 6535, 6540, 6542–43, 6546–47, 6553–55, 6557, 6562–63, 6565, 6574, 6577, 6584, 6586, 6588, 6591, 6594–99, 6604–6, 6609–10, 6612, 6615–16, 6624, 6629, 6636, 6639, 6641, 6646, 6654, 6656–57, 6660–62, 6665–66, 6673–77, 6681–82, 6685, 6697, 6699–700, 6707–9, 6714, 6717, 6719–21, 6724, 6727, 6729–31, 6734, 6737, 6744–45, 6751–54, 6762, 6765, 6767, 6770, 6774–76, 6778, 6784–85, 6793, 6798–99, 6801, 6816, 7377, 8290

IJ: 1119, 3462, 5715, 5791, 5794, 6211, 6213–14, 6216–19, 6221, 6224, 6226, 6241, 6244–45, 6253, 6257, 6259–60, 6262, 6266, 6269, 6277–78, 6283, 6294–96, 6298, 6300, 6303, 6317, 6322–23, 6326, 6331, 6337, 6357–59, 6377–78, 6381, 6383, 6385, 6387, 6391, 6395, 6402, 6421, 6425, 6431–32, 6436, 6444–45, 6455, 6457–58, 6460–62, 6464–68, 6484, 6491–92, 6495–96, 6513–14, 6517, 6528, 6533, 6538–39, 6544, 6548, 6550–51, 6560, 6570, 6589, 6593, 6600–1, 6603, 6608, 6614, 6619, 6621, 6623, 6631–32, 6642, 6648, 6652–53, 6655, 6658–59, 6663, 6680, 6686, 6688–89, 6692–96, 6703, 6705, 6710, 6715–16, 6718, 6722, 6726, 6732, 6750, 6759, 6763, 6771–72, 6777, 6789–90, 6792, 6796–97, 6800, 7212

**Fantasy — Poetry**

P: 823, 1026, 1299

**Fantasy — Short stories**

PI: 6567

I: 6390, 6400

IJ: 6380, 6476, 6479

**Farm animals — Fiction**

P: 508, 716, 3576, 4448, 4479, 5278, 5316, 5428

**Farm life**

P: 4280, 11505, 11526–27, 15931, 15934, 15936, 15938, 15945, 15957

PI: 3869, 10824, 15943

I: 10825, 13138, 15907, 15929–30, 15935, 15939, 15944, 16336

IJ: 13039, 15019, 15937, 15941

**Farm life — Fiction**

P: 87, 119, 292, 297, 450, 906, 1057, 1143, 2212, 2336, 2382, 2611, 2633–34, 2661, 2722, 2762, 2858, 3098, 3191, 3288, 3381, 3389, 3426, 3594, 3624, 3655, 3714, 3799, 3888, 4054, 4110, 4125, 4221, 4223, 4268–69, 4293, 4306, 4316, 4380, 4389, 4456, 4557, 4790–91, 5278

PI: 721, 1171, 1328, 2686, 3816, 6131, 6882, 7014, 7216, 7778, 8042, 8180

I: 5790, 5842, 6091, 6094, 6343, 7082, 7323, 7495, 7529, 7838, 7851, 7899, 8121

IJ: 6028, 6152, 6201, 6507, 7021, 7625, 7827, 7848, 7852

**Farm life — Folklore**

P: 9279

**Farm life — Poetry**

P: 9577, 9880

**Farm workers — Biography**

PI: 10475

IJ: 10473, 10483

**Farmer, James**

PI: 10380

**Farnsworth, Philo**

I: 10845

**Farragut, David**

IJ: 10511

**Fashion design**

IJ: 10549, 10759

**Fashion design — Biography**

IJ: 10481

**Fashion design — History**

IJ: 16810

**Fathers**

P: 3036, 14146

**Fathers — Fiction**

P: 2819, 2833, 2841, 2963, 3001, 3059, 3070, 3073, 3093, 6103

I: 6058

P = Primary; PI = Primary–Intermediate; I = Intermediate; IJ = Intermediate–Junior High

P = Primary; PI = Primary–Intermediate; I = Intermediate; IJ = Intermediate–Junior High

**Fishing — Folklore**
P: 8663

**Flags**
P: 5427
I: 11365, 11369

**Flags — Fiction**
PI: 8203

**Flags (U.S.)**
P: 10783, 11366–67, 11373
PI: 11372
I: 10782, 11362–63, 11370–71
IJ: 11374

**Flags (U.S.) — States**
PI: 11364
IJ: 11368

**Flamingos**
PI: 15349, 15360

**Flamingos — Fiction**
P: 3630

**Flatulence**
P: 14431

**Fleas — Fiction**
P: 3514

**Fleming, Alexander**
IJ: 10847

**Flies**
I: 15496

**Flies — Fiction**
P: 831, 1404

**Flightless birds**
PI: 15312
I: 15308

**Flipper, Henry O.**
IJ: 10382

**Floods**
PI: 13263, 16428
I: 16406, 16435
IJ: 16425, 16440

**Floods — Fiction**
P: 2617, 7117
PI: 6559, 7792
I: 5568
IJ: 7629

**Florida**
PI: 13475, 13483, 13498, 13507, 15671
I: 13494, 14998
IJ: 10834

**Florida — Fiction**
P: 1503, 4777
I: 6519, 7554, 7815, 7984
IJ: 5562, 5565, 5705, 5959, 7084, 8282

**Florida — Folklore**
P: 9318

**Florida — History**
P: 12885
I: 12832, 12881
IJ: 13515

**Florida — Poetry**
I: 9855

**Florida black bears**
I: 15172

**Florida Keys deer**
PI: 15253

**Florida panthers**
IJ: 15215

**Flour mills**
I: 13136

**Flowers**
P: 15916, 15918–19, 15924
PI: 10837, 16080
I: 12789, 15917, 15920, 15922, 16095
IJ: 15921, 15926

**Flowers — Fiction**
P: 63, 382, 2326, 2563, 3556, 3980

**Flowers — Folklore**
P: 8767, 9209

**Flutes**
IJ: 11579

**Flutes — Fiction**
PI: 1068

**Flying — Fiction**
P: 535, 727, 818, 1295, 1337, 1922
I: 6868
IJ: 6517

**Flying — Folklore**
P: 8791

**Flying — Poetry**
I: 9593, 9883

**Folk art**
P: 446
I: 11336, 11353

**Folk songs**
P: 11502–5, 11508, 11511, 11516, 11520, 11523, 11525–30, 11535–39, 11541, 11544–47

PI: 11500, 11521, 11524, 11531, 11542
I: 9351, 11497, 11507, 11532
IJ: 11498, 11519
All: 11506, 11510, 11514

**Folklore, 8600–9449**
*See also* under specific countries and continents, e.g., Germany — Folklore

**Folklore — Anthologies**
P: 540, 8603, 8608, 8612, 8623, 8637, 8642, 8658, 8905, 9157
PI: 8600, 8602, 8606, 8613–14, 8630, 8639, 8654, 8736, 8741, 8841, 9203, 9248, 9320, 9328
I: 8383, 8609–11, 8618, 8620–22, 8626, 8628–29, 8631–34, 8638, 8640, 8646–49, 8651, 8653, 8657, 8661, 8775, 8810, 8844, 8860, 8880, 8893, 8906, 9006–7, 9117, 9149, 9162, 9165, 9207, 9263, 9337, 9372, 9381, 9391, 9443, 9449
IJ: 8605, 8616, 8624–25, 8645, 8652, 8660, 8700, 8702, 8760, 8764, 8776, 8811, 8848, 8856, 8915, 8961, 8965, 8971, 9078, 9163–64, 9175, 9266, 9321, 9333, 9338, 9353, 9359, 9361, 9365, 9379–80, 9400
All: 8644

**Folklore — General**
P: 5055, 5388, 8518, 8604, 8607, 8650, 8655, 8659
I: 8617

**Folklore — Jokes and riddles**
I: 17383

**Folklore — Plays**
PI: 9926
I: 9928, 9933, 9938

**Folklore — Poetry**
P: 5389

**Fonda, Jane**
I: 10175

**Food**
P: 2460, 2701, 12906, 14433, 14437, 15931, 15948, 15960, 15971, 15975, 15983, 16001
PI: 13032
I: 17206, 17234
IJ: 13736, 14430, 14435, 15951, 15972, 15976, 15998, 16006

**Food — Crafts**
I: 17002

P = Primary; PI = Primary–Intermediate; I = Intermediate; IJ = Intermediate–Junior High

**Food — Experiments and projects**
PI: 14644
I: 15953, 15966

**Food — Fiction**
P: 28, 767, 1531, 2109, 2392, 2510, 2531, 2562, 2601, 2720, 3061, 3315, 3433, 3444, 5233
PI: 8234
I: 6236, 8147, 8160
IJ: 8090

**Food — Folklore**
P: 9402

**Food — History**
I: 15977
IJ: 11956, 15980

**Food — Jokes and riddles**
PI: 17371

**Food — Middle Ages**
PI: 11960

**Food — Poetry**
P: 3504
PI: 9797, 9802, 9827
I: 9507, 9633

**Food additives**
I: 16002

**Food and Drug Administration (U.S.)**
IJ: 13736

**Food chains**
P: 14816

**Food chains — Fiction**
P: 1406

**Football**
P: 17607, 17610
PI: 17612
I: 17613
IJ: 17608, 17611

**Football — Biography**
P: 11085
I: 10938–39, 10947, 10954, 11080, 11082, 11088, 11092–93, 11095–97, 11099, 11101–2, 11104, 11106–8
IJ: 10926, 10987, 11081, 11083–84, 11086–87, 11089–91, 11094, 11098, 11100, 11103, 11105, 11109

**Football — Fiction**
P: 2350, 4486, 5293

I: 8432, 8434, 8474
IJ: 8441, 8468

**Football — History**
I: 17609
IJ: 17606

**Football — Jokes and riddles**
I: 17337

**Force (physics)**
I: 16536
IJ: 16537, 16539

**Force (physics) — Experiments and projects**
PI: 16515

**Ford, Gerald**
I: 10643

**Ford, Henry**
I: 10848

**Foreign languages**
P: 9682

**Foreign languages — Poetry**
P: 9621

**Foreign policy (U.S.)**
I: 13645

**Foreman, Michael**
IJ: 10068

**Forensics**
I: 13687, 13694, 13709
IJ: 13692–93

**Forest fires**
P: 14227
PI: 13328, 13336, 14224
I: 13324, 13340, 13581

**Forest fires — Fiction**
P: 2953

**Forests**
*See also* Rain forests
P: 14866, 15498, 16045, 16245, 16264
PI: 15477, 16232
I: 16249, 16252, 16258, 16268, 16271–72
IJ: 16047, 16230–31, 16233, 16243, 16248

**Forests — Animals**
P: 15102
PI: 16253

**Forests — Fiction**
P: 1065
I: 16240

**Fort Sumter, Battle of**
PI: 13198
IJ: 13208

**Forts**
PI: 13144
I: 16960
IJ: 11999, 16980

**Fortune, Amos**
IJ: 10383

**Fortune telling**
I: 17442

**Fortune telling — Fiction**
P: 2137, 3267
PI: 5548

**Fossils**
*See also* Paleontology
P: 11694, 11718, 11774
PI: 11695
I: 11700, 11740, 11771
IJ: 11724, 11773, 11784

**Fossils — Fiction**
P: 3540
PI: 5511
I: 7659
IJ: 5747

**Foster care**
P: 14119, 14153

**Foster care — Biography**
PI: 10753

**Foster care — Fiction**
P: 3012
PI: 6009
I: 6838, 6993, 7119, 7270
IJ: 6819, 6952, 6994, 7068, 7340

**Foster homes — Fiction**
I: 6784

**Fourth of July**
*See* July Fourth

**Fox Indians**
PI: 12894

**Foxes**
P: 15222, 15224, 15233–34, 15244
PI: 15232, 15235–36, 15238
I: 15219, 15228

**Foxes — Fiction**
P: 583, 1265, 1626, 1648, 1677, 1738, 1752, 1912, 1941, 2176, 2227, 2232, 3481, 3714, 4231, 5035, 5064, 5285, 5288–91, 5409, 8484
PI: 5108, 5885, 8590

P = Primary; PI = Primary–Intermediate; I = Intermediate; IJ = Intermediate–Junior High

I: 5789, 5842, 6343, 6463
IJ: 5917

**Foxes — Folklore**
P: 8963, 9005, 9344
IJ: 9442

**Foxes — Poetry**
P: 9526

**Foxx, Jimmie**
I: 10978

**Fractions**
P: 373
PI: 16337

**Fractions — Fiction**
P: 16350

**France**
P: 11608, 12382, 12387
PI: 12384, 12390, 12396
I: 12386, 12389, 12391, 12395
IJ: 12385

**France — Cookbooks**
IJ: 17263

**France — Crafts**
PI: 17008

**France — Fiction**
P: 2185, 3379, 3890, 3905
PI: 7869
I: 7356, 7856

**France — Folklore**
P: 8881–83, 8885–88, 8890–91,
8894–95, 8897–98
PI: 8889, 8896
I: 8892–93

**France — History**
I: 11236, 12388
IJ: 11200, 11258, 12024, 12036,
12048, 12052, 12383, 12393–94

**Francis of Assisi, Saint**
P: 3838, 11220
I: 11219

**Frank, Anne**
PI: 11221
I: 11222–23, 11226
IJ: 11224–25

**Frankenstein**
I: 17454

**Franklin, Benjamin**
P: 10513, 10518–19
PI: 7595, 10512, 10515, 10517
IJ: 10514, 10516

**Franklin, Benjamin — Fiction**
IJ: 8100

**Franklin, Sir John**
IJ: 12582

**Fredericksburg, Battle of**
IJ: 13208

**Fremont, John C.**
I: 9999

**French Americans**
I: 14085

**French and Indian Wars**
IJ: 13029–30

**French Canada — Fiction**
PI: 4605

**French Revolution**
I: 12388

**Frescoes**
I: 11349

**Friendship**
P: 14097

**Friendship stories**
P: 1045, 1663, 1717, 3166–80,
3182–83, 3185, 3187–89, 3191–94,
3197–220, 3222–23, 3227–28,
3230–32, 3236–44, 3246–57,
3260–62, 3734, 4030, 4134, 4500,
4503, 4546, 5118, 5143–44, 5154,
5199, 5216–17, 5219–20, 5230,
5238, 5245, 5256–57, 5320, 6842,
6891, 6893, 6899–900, 6932, 7428,
14105
PI: 3184, 3195, 3221, 3234–35,
3258–59, 4181, 5237, 6643, 6805,
6808, 6813–15, 6821–23, 6829,
6831, 6840, 6843–44, 6848,
6856–57, 6860, 6866–67, 6869,
6875–76, 6879–81, 6884–85,
6896–98, 6913, 6916, 6928–29,
6934–35, 6937, 7764, 7812, 7850,
7995, 8021, 8177, 8267, 8456
I: 5662, 5754, 5838, 5977, 6166,
6541, 6806–7, 6809–10, 6816–17,
6820, 6824–28, 6832–34, 6837–38,
6841, 6847, 6852–55, 6861,
6863–65, 6868, 6871–73, 6877,
6883, 6888–89, 6901, 6907–8,
6911–12, 6914–15, 6918, 6922–23,
6925–26, 6930–31, 6933, 7148,
7348–49, 7472, 7776, 7810, 7994,
8133, 8237, 8293, 8306
IJ: 3190, 5506, 5508, 5672, 6802–4,
6811, 6818–19, 6830, 6836,
6845–46, 6849–51, 6858–59, 6862,
6870, 6874, 6878, 6886–87, 6890,
6892, 6894–95, 6902–6, 6917,

6919–21, 6924, 6927, 6936, 7120,
7133, 7359, 7391, 7668, 7703,
7877, 8132, 8187, 8451, 8477

**Friendship stories — Poetry**
P: 3229, 9607
PI: 9692
IJ: 9592

**Fright — Fiction**
P: 2967, 3170, 3305, 3356, 3549,
3999, 4002, 4018, 4027, 4139,
4142, 4164, 4938, 5076, 5174,
5284, 5363
PI: 8004
I: 5927, 5989, 6069, 6828, 6868, 8202
IJ: 7140, 7893

**Fritz, Jean**
PI: 10243
IJ: 10242

**Frogs and toads**
P: 14935–36, 14939–42, 14948–49
PI: 14937–38, 14950
I: 14908, 14943–47, 14951
IJ: 14952

**Frogs and toads — Fiction**
P: 709, 745, 1014, 1199, 1287, 1352,
1393, 1539, 1572, 1663, 1668,
1767, 1771, 1788, 1791, 1864,
1868, 1877, 2122, 2134, 2196–97,
2254, 3584, 4403, 5257, 5326,
5381, 8510
PI: 6328
I: 6590–91
IJ: 6402

**Frogs and toads — Folklore**
P: 8825, 8913
IJ: 8853

**Frogs and toads — Nursery rhymes**
P: 612

**Frogs and toads — Poetry**
I: 9870

**Frontier life (Canada)**
I: 12590

**Frontier life (U.S.)**
P: 3761, 5250, 7730
PI: 9966, 10345, 13094, 13115,
13126–27, 13132, 13140–41,
13143–44, 13148, 13163, 13165,
13168–69, 13182, 13227
I: 9988, 10333, 10504, 10652, 13103,
13114, 13116–18, 13120, 13125,
13136–39, 13142, 13146, 13153,
13156–61, 13170, 13173–74,
13178

P = Primary; PI = Primary–Intermediate; I = Intermediate; IJ = Intermediate–Junior High

# G

P = Primary; PI = Primary–Intermediate; I = Intermediate; IJ = Intermediate–Junior High

**Garner, John Nance, IV**
I: 10522

**Garrison, Zina**
I: 11116

**Garter snakes**
I: 14973

**Gates, Bill**
I: 10523

**Gateway Arch (St. Louis)**
I: 13270

**Gays**
*See* Homosexuality; Lesbian mothers

**Gbaya**
IJ: 12100

**Geckos**
I: 14960

**Geese**
*See* Ducks and geese

**Gehrig, Lou**
PI: 10979
I: 10980

**Geisel, Theodor**
I: 10244

**Gems**
IJ: 16334

**Genealogy**
IJ: 14123, 14139, 14155

**Generals — Biography**
I: 10437

**Genetics**
I: 14370, 14373
IJ: 14339, 14371–72

**Genetics — Biography**
I: 10880
IJ: 10883

**Genghis Khan**
PI: 11230

**Genies**
I: 6677

**Geography**
P: 3641, 11676, 16141
PI: 11675, 11681, 11855, 12808, 13592
I: 11667, 11670, 11672, 11677–78, 11680, 11684, 16118
IJ: 11673, 16130

**Geography — Experiments and projects**
I: 11683
IJ: 11669

**Geology**
*See also* Rocks and minerals
P: 11676, 16125, 16137, 16141
PI: 16116, 16120, 16124
I: 13307, 16114–15, 16127, 16131, 16134–35, 16139, 16144, 16329
IJ: 14737, 16112, 16121, 16130, 16142

**Geology — Careers**
P: 14243

**Geology — Crafts**
I: 16108

**Geometry**
PI: 16354
I: 16351, 16356

**Geometry — Fiction**
P: 147

**George, Jean Craighead**
I: 10245–46

**George III, King of England**
I: 11229

**George Washington Bridge — Fiction**
P: 4594

**Georgia**
PI: 13476
I: 13490, 13516, 13562
IJ: 13465

**Georgia — Fiction**
P: 2908, 3746
I: 6029, 7112, 7395
IJ: 6028

**Georgia Colony**
IJ: 12998

**Georgia (republic)**
I: 12481
IJ: 12468

**Geothermal energy**
I: 16111

**Gerbils**
PI: 15813, 15828

**Gerbils — Fiction**
I: 8125

**German Americans**
IJ: 14040, 14081

**German Americans — Fiction**
P: 4731
I: 7688
IJ: 6141, 7639

**Germany**
PI: 12399, 12403, 12406, 12409
I: 12397, 12410
IJ: 12400–2

**Germany — Cookbooks**
IJ: 17247

**Germany — Fiction**
PI: 7879
I: 7373
IJ: 7493, 7499, 7871

**Germany — Folklore**
P: 958, 5425, 8899–903, 8905, 8907, 8909, 8911–14, 8916–22, 8924–28, 8933–34, 8939–40, 8944–48, 8950, 8952, 8955, 8957
PI: 8904, 8908, 8910, 8923, 8931, 8937–38, 8942–43, 8949, 8953–54
I: 8593, 8906, 8930, 8935–36, 8941, 8956
IJ: 8915, 8929, 8951

**Germany — History**
IJ: 11235, 11268, 12398, 12405, 12408

**Germany — Holidays**
PI: 12404

**Geronimo**
PI: 10578
I: 10577, 10579

**Gershwin, George**
PI: 10138
I: 10137
IJ: 10139

**Getty Museum (Los Angeles, Calif.)**
P: 11285
I: 13455

**Gettysburg, Battle of**
I: 13205
IJ: 13199, 13207

**Gettysburg Address**
P: 13191
I: 13202

**Geysers**
I: 16119

**Ghana**
P: 12174
IJ: 12172, 12176

P = Primary; PI = Primary–Intermediate; I = Intermediate; IJ = Intermediate–Junior High

**Ghana — Cookbooks**
IJ: 17246

**Ghana — Folklore**
P: 8685
I: 8718

**Ghosts**
*See also* Haunted houses
P: 733, 790, 832, 950, 1077, 1152,
1156, 1190, 1203, 1231, 1261,
2304, 2338, 4922, 5047, 5049,
5062, 5388, 6747
PI: 6427, 6439, 6782
I: 5491, 5684, 6228, 6247, 6251,
6281, 6325, 6374, 6419, 6452,
6527, 6592, 6778, 8040, 14838,
17419, 17423–24, 17443, 17467
IJ: 3226, 5469, 5592, 5640, 5713–14,
5727, 5738, 5745, 6212, 6224,
6294, 6300, 6303, 6307, 6318,
6326, 6386, 6421, 6442, 6453,
6457, 6480, 6484, 6621, 6648,
6772, 6781, 8039, 9361, 17422,
17426–27, 17429, 17440

**Ghosts — Fiction**
P: 973, 1106, 2296, 4890, 4945
PI: 6407, 6640, 6743, 6758, 6780,
6783
I: 5639, 5748, 6263–64, 6272, 6308,
6333, 6351–52, 6375, 6389, 6622,
6635, 6667, 6728, 6779, 6786
IJ: 6252, 6268, 6306, 6350, 6698,
6725, 7965, 8286, 9367

**Ghosts — Folklore**
P: 8796, 9035, 9331
PI: 9320
IJ: 8616, 9379–80

**Ghosts — Jokes and riddles**
P: 17332
PI: 17378

**Ghosts — Poetry**
IJ: 9668

**Ghosts — Short stories**
I: 6384, 6433, 6469

**Giants — Fiction**
P: 842, 959, 1332, 8516, 8735
I: 6341, 6604
IJ: 6718

**Giants — Folklore**
P: 8975, 9020
PI: 8904
I: 8864

**Gibb, Lois**
IJ: 10798

**Gifted children — Fiction**
PI: 8206
I: 8216
IJ: 6859, 8220

**Gilbert and Sullivan — Songs**
IJ: 11609

**Ginsburg, Ruth Bader**
I: 10525–26
IJ: 10524

**Giraffes**
P: 15277
PI: 15278
I: 15276

**Giraffes — Fiction**
P: 2057, 3776
I: 5829, 6370

**Girl Scouts of America**
*See* Scouts and scouting

**Girlfriends — Fiction**
IJ: 7993, 8201

**Gish, Lillian**
IJ: 10176

**Glacier National Park —
Fiction**
P: 4246

**Glaciers and icebergs**
P: 16172
PI: 5792
IJ: 16173–74

**Glass**
PI: 16675
IJ: 16699

**Glasses — Fiction**
P: 1452, 3141, 4133
PI: 7230, 8172
I: 6397

**Gliders**
PI: 16729
IJ: 17519

**Globe Theatre**
I: 11665

**Globes**
*See* Maps and globes

**Gnats — Fiction**
P: 2009

**Gnomes**
P: 1052

**Gnomes — Folklore**
P: 8921

**Gnus — Fiction**
P: 1678

**Goats**
P: 15304
PI: 15305
I: 15303

**Goats — Fiction**
P: 1091, 1415, 2109, 2269, 2331,
4433
I: 7322

**Goats — Folklore**
P: 9115, 9122

**Gobi Desert**
IJ: 11725

**Goble, Paul**
PI: 10247

**Goblins**
P: 1214, 4965, 5047
IJ: 6726

**Goblins — Folklore**
P: 8829

**Goddard, Robert**
IJ: 10856

**Goddesses**
I: 9454

**Gogh, Vincent van**
P: 10069
PI: 10071
IJ: 10070, 11316

**Gogh, Vincent van — Fiction**
P: 3740

**Gold — History**
I: 11839

**Gold Rush (Alaska) — Fiction**
I: 7786

**Gold Rush (California)**
P: 13150
PI: 13176
I: 13175, 13180
IJ: 13113, 13145, 13422

**Gold Rush (California) —
Fiction**
P: 3872
I: 8037
IJ: 7440

**Gold Rush (Yukon)**
IJ: 12586

**Goldberg, Whoopi**
I: 10177

P = Primary; PI = Primary–Intermediate; I = Intermediate; IJ = Intermediate–Junior High

**Golden Fleece (mythology)**
PI: 9483
IJ: 9457

**Golden Gate Bridge**
I: 13428

**Golden retrievers — Fiction**
PI: 8162
I: 7378

**Goldfish**
P: 15880

**Goldfish — Fiction**
PI: 6684

**Goldman, Emma**
IJ: 10751

**Golem**
I: 9153, 9166

**Golf**
IJ: 17509

**Golf — Biography**
I: 11167, 11173
IJ: 11169–70

**Golf — Fiction**
PI: 8165

**Gonzalez, Juan**
I: 10981

**Good Samaritan (Bible)**
IJ: 13831

**Goodall, Jane**
PI: 10857
I: 10858, 10860
IJ: 10859

**Gooden, Dwight**
IJ: 10982

**Gophers — Fiction**
P: 5266

**Gorbachev, Mikhail**
IJ: 11231

**Gore, Albert**
PI: 10528
I: 10527

**Gore, Tipper**
I: 10752

**Gorillas**
P: 15156
IJ: 15158

**Gorillas — Fiction**
P: 391, 1426, 1467, 1469, 1725, 3355

PI: 4111
I: 5900

**Gorman, R. C.**
IJ: 10072

**Goslar, Hannah**
IJ: 11225

**Gospel music**
I: 11513

**Government**
See United States —
  Government and politics

**Goya, Francisco**
PI: 10073
IJ: 10074

**Graham, Martha**
IJ: 10178–79

**Grammar**
IJ: 11481

**Grand Canyon National Park**
P: 13329, 13331
PI: 13342
I: 13307, 13313, 13317
IJ: 10022, 13532

**Grandfathers — Fiction**
P: 579, 871, 902, 1031, 1265, 2351,
  2358, 2360, 2382, 2547, 2621,
  2783, 2787, 2790–91, 2795, 2812,
  2816, 2822, 2829, 2839, 2844,
  2865, 2869, 2875, 2881, 2885,
  2905, 2908, 2922, 2927, 2930,
  2950–51, 2953, 2958, 2960, 2962,
  2982, 2989–90, 2997, 3009, 3013,
  3075, 3081, 3083, 3112, 3123,
  3132, 3158, 3186, 3233, 3541,
  3545, 3645, 3719, 3802, 3823,
  3884, 3896, 3921, 3926, 3935,
  4038, 4046, 4118, 4145, 4162,
  4164, 4185, 4380, 4663, 4706,
  4748, 4938, 5305
PI: 2961, 3014, 5551, 5753, 5874,
  6047, 6105, 6107, 6174, 6188,
  6194, 6207, 6875, 7191, 7196,
  7902
I: 6092, 6182, 6339, 6983, 7115,
  7330, 7555, 8471
IJ: 5566, 5803, 6184, 6201, 6444,
  7084, 7352

**Grandfathers — Folklore**
IJ: 8760

**Grandmothers**
P: 11600

**Grandmothers — Fiction**
P: 875, 1050, 1226, 1503, 1602, 2590,
  2617, 2782, 2784, 2793, 2803,
  2810, 2817–18, 2826, 2828, 2838,
  2845, 2870, 2879, 2884, 2890,
  2907, 2909, 2916–17, 2924, 2928,
  2937, 2939, 2976–77, 2986, 2994,
  3017, 3021, 3025, 3033, 3042–43,
  3051, 3061, 3071, 3078, 3084,
  3098, 3117, 3122, 3134, 3138,
  3142–45, 3149, 3165, 3384, 3433,
  3470, 3507, 3695, 3769–70, 3830,
  3885, 3902, 3928, 4044–45, 4085,
  4089, 4094, 4143, 4698, 4785,
  4818, 4953, 5274–75
PI: 2904, 3118, 4664, 7077, 7126,
  7192, 7246, 7708, 7825, 8178
I: 5528, 6050, 6066, 6077, 6091,
  6135, 6189, 6344, 6347, 6776,
  6939, 6960, 7055, 7217, 7485,
  7772, 7821, 8217
IJ: 6053, 6116, 6130, 6150, 6200,
  6224, 6539, 6988, 7273, 7313

**Grandmothers — Folklore**
PI: 8800

**Grandparents**
P: 2744, 2857
I: 14154

**Grandparents — Fiction**
P: 521, 2858, 2926, 2931, 2946, 2991,
  3007, 3088–89, 3095, 3511, 3717,
  5273
PI: 3725, 4004, 5007, 6096, 6131,
  7211, 7332, 8438
I: 2863, 6097, 6117, 7267, 7363,
  7740, 7775, 8103, 8461
IJ: 7021, 7048

**Grant, Amy**
I: 10180

**Grant, Ulysses S.**
I: 10645–46

**Graphs**
I: 16343

**Grasshoppers**
IJ: 15490

**Grasshoppers — Fiction**
P: 5258

**Grasslands**
P: 16317
PI: 15478, 16313, 16322
I: 16311, 16315, 16319
IJ: 16309, 16316

P = Primary; PI = Primary–Intermediate; I = Intermediate; IJ = Intermediate–Junior High

P = Primary; PI = Primary–Intermediate; I = Intermediate; IJ = Intermediate–Junior High

P = Primary; PI = Primary–Intermediate; I = Intermediate; IJ = Intermediate–Junior High

**Hanukkah — Short stories**
I: 7957

**Harbors — Fiction**
P: 4560, 4581

**Hardaway, Anfernee**
I: 11034
IJ: 11035

**Harding, Warren G.**
IJ: 10647

**Hares**
*See also* Rabbits

**Hares — Fiction**
P: 4215
IJ: 6468

**Harlem Renaissance**
IJ: 13220

**Harmonicas — Fiction**
P: 2095, 3391

**Harris, La Donna**
I: 10580

**Harrison, Benjamin**
I: 10648

**Harrison, William H.**
IJ: 10649

**Harvey, William**
IJ: 10865

**Haskins, Francine**
P: 2913

**Hastings, Battle of**
IJ: 12429

**Hats**
PI: 16797

**Hats — Fiction**
P: 780, 823, 1220, 1393, 1647, 2498,
2658, 2941, 3342, 3371, 3383,
3476, 3819, 4092, 5316
PI: 7811

**Haunted houses**
P: 1152, 1361, 4883, 5363
PI: 5449
I: 5519, 6546, 6616, 17421
IJ: 5594

**Hausa — Folklore**
I: 8718

**Hawaii**
PI: 13429, 13432
IJ: 13420, 13452, 13529

**Hawaii — Biography**
PI: 10555

**Hawaii — Fiction**
P: 2326, 2909, 3795, 4630
I: 7403, 7874
IJ: 6180

**Hawaii — Folklore**
P: 8865
PI: 9366
IJ: 9317

**Hawaii — History**
I: 11241

**Hawaii — Marine animals**
PI: 15625

**Hawking, Stephen**
IJ: 10866

**Hawks**
*See also* Birds of prey
PI: 15405
I: 15397

**Hawks — Fiction**
P: 4235
I: 5831, 6273

**Hayes, Rutherford B.**
I: 10650

**Haystacks**
P: 15933

**Health and medicine,**
14263–14527
*See also* Diseases; Hygiene;
Illness; Medicine
I: 14512
IJ: 14337, 14518

**Health and medicine —
Biography**
PI: 10730

**Health and medicine —
Careers**
PI: 14212, 14218, 14220
IJ: 14215

**Hearing**
*See also* Deaf
P: 14467, 14471, 14478, 14487–88
I: 14473

**Hearing — Fiction**
P: 247

**Heart**
IJ: 14418

**Heart disease**
IJ: 14316

**Heart disease — Fiction**
IJ: 7162, 7352

**Heat**
IJ: 16555

**Heat — Experiments and
projects**
IJ: 16553–54

**Hebrew — Fiction**
I: 8197

**Hebrew language**
P: 11416

**Hedgehogs — Fiction**
P: 1956, 2213, 5276

**Heisman Trophy**
IJ: 10926

**Helicopters**
PI: 16729, 16750

**Helicopters — Fiction**
P: 961, 1349

**Helium — Fiction**
P: 1121

**Heller, Ruth**
PI: 10249

**Helpfulness — Fiction**
P: 1442, 1821

**Henio, Katie**
I: 10581

**Henry, John (folklore)**
PI: 9354

**Henry, Patrick**
P: 10531

**Henson, Jim**
IJ: 10182

**Henson, Matthew**
PI: 9956
I: 10001–2

**Hercules (mythology)**
PI: 9477, 9482
I: 9468, 9488

**Heredity**
IJ: 14123, 14371

**Herero (African people)**
IJ: 12162

**Herod of Judea**
I: 11233

P = Primary; PI = Primary–Intermediate; I = Intermediate; IJ = Intermediate–Junior High

P = Primary; PI = Primary–Intermediate; I = Intermediate; IJ = Intermediate–Junior High

P = Primary; PI = Primary–Intermediate; I = Intermediate; IJ = Intermediate–Junior High

**Horses — Poetry**
IJ: 9739

**Horses, Miniature**
PI: 15892

**Hospitals**
P: 14375, 14377–79
PI: 14374, 14376, 14380
I: 10881

**Hospitals — Fiction**
P: 2476, 2892
I: 7382
IJ: 5506, 7142, 7199

**Hot-air balloons**
*See* Ballooning

**Hotels — Fiction**
I: 6592
IJ: 8054

**Houdini, Harry**
IJ: 10183

**House of Representatives (U.S.)**
*See* Congress (U.S.); United
States — Government and
politics

**Houses**
*See also* Building and construc-
tion
P: 2505, 2664, 3787
PI: 16787, 16789
I: 11950, 12936, 16788
IJ: 16791, 16793–94, 17186

**Houses — Crafts**
I: 16790

**Houses — Fiction**
P: 169, 1861, 2374, 2398, 2432, 2465,
2473, 2659, 2733, 2777, 2898,
3027, 3077, 3550, 3707, 4048
I: 5472, 5518, 6146, 7610

**Houses — History**
PI: 11309
I: 16792

**Houses — Poetry**
P: 5086

**Houses of Parliament (London,
England)**
I: 12430

**Housework — Fiction**
P: 5331

**Housework — Folklore**
P: 9116

**Houston, Sam**
PI: 10537
IJ: 10536

**Houston, Sam — Fiction**
I: 7636

**Houston, Texas**
I: 13531, 13535

**Houston Astrodome**
I: 13521

**Houston Rockets (basketball
team)**
IJ: 17573

**Howe, James**
P: 10252

**Hubble, Edwin**
IJ: 10869

**Hubble space telescope**
PI: 14677
I: 16658

**Huerta, Dolores**
IJ: 10483

**Hughes, Langston**
PI: 10254
I: 10253

**Hull, Brett**
I: 11152

**Human body**
*See also* specific parts and systems of the human body, e.g.,
Circulation system
P: 3623, 3698, 14381, 14384, 14387,
14390–91, 14396, 14407, 14412,
14417
PI: 14386, 14395, 14397, 14410
I: 11800, 14383, 14404, 14406,
14408, 14411, 14415
IJ: 14382, 14385, 14388–89, 14392,
14394, 14402–3, 14405, 14413,
14501

**Human body — Experiments
and projects**
IJ: 14393, 14416

**Human body — Fiction**
P: 2377, 2592, 2691

**Humanitarians — Biography**
PI: 11271–72
I: 11181, 11275
IJ: 11273, 11283

**Hummingbirds**
I: 15364

**Hummingbirds — Fiction**
P: 3690

**Humorous poetry**
*See* Poetry — Humorous

**Humorous stories**
P: 478, 745, 768, 928, 938, 1081,
1319, 1516, 2089, 2142, 2272,
2344, 2707, 2823, 2932, 3003,
3048, 3175, 3181, 3263–94,
3296–97, 3299–303, 3305–28,
3330–43, 3345–56, 3358–62,
3364–66, 3368–71, 3373–75,
3377–81, 3383–98, 3400–5, 3407,
3409–11, 3414–37, 3439–42,
3444–57, 3459–61, 3463–65,
3467–72, 3474–84, 3486–518,
3520–24, 3594, 3631, 3643, 3752,
3792, 3809, 3963, 4522, 4533,
4539, 4846, 5044, 5094, 5189,
5246, 5261, 5270, 5289, 5309,
5329–31, 5336, 5370–71, 5374,
5378, 5391–97, 7980, 8030, 8139,
8141, 8235, 8256
PI: 1601, 2330, 3295, 3298, 3344,
3363, 3367, 3372, 3413, 3438,
3466, 3485, 3519, 4069, 5147,
5332, 5663, 5851, 6096, 6119,
6713, 6897, 7522, 7970, 7973,
7976, 7981–82, 7987–88, 7995,
7997–98, 8000, 8002, 8004,
8006–11, 8014–18, 8020, 8022,
8025, 8031–33, 8042–43, 8048–52,
8055, 8058–59, 8063, 8066,
8068–69, 8083–85, 8087, 8089,
8098–99, 8104, 8111, 8130–31,
8137, 8140, 8146, 8151–53, 8158,
8162, 8165–66, 8172, 8174,
8176–78, 8180, 8192–94, 8265,
8280–81, 8298, 8328, 8401
I: 5746, 5855, 5904, 6234, 6339,
6565, 6907–10, 7344, 7953, 7969,
7971–72, 7975, 7977–79, 7983–84,
7986, 7989–91, 7994, 7996, 7999,
8001, 8012, 8019, 8023–24,
8026–27, 8029, 8035–37, 8040–41,
8045–47, 8053, 8056–57, 8060–62,
8064, 8067, 8070–72, 8074–75,
8077, 8079–82, 8086, 8092–93,
8096–97, 8101, 8103, 8105–6,
8108, 8113, 8117–18, 8121,
8123–26, 8128–29, 8134–36,
8142–43, 8147–48, 8154–56, 8160,
8163–64, 8170–71, 8173, 8182,
8189–91, 8195–97, 8244–45, 8259,
8272, 8289, 9381
IJ: 3462, 5954, 5984, 6906, 7034,
7132, 7262, 7326, 7854, 7974,
7993, 8003, 8005, 8034, 8038–39,
8044, 8054, 8065, 8073, 8076,
8078, 8088, 8090–91, 8094–95,
8100, 8102, 8107, 8109–10, 8112,

P = Primary; PI = Primary–Intermediate; I = Intermediate; IJ = Intermediate–Junior High

8114–16, 8119–20, 8122, 8127, 8132, 8138, 8144–45, 8149, 8157, 8161, 8167, 8175, 8179, 8181, 8184–87, 8199, 8236, 8260, 8364

**Humorous stories — Anthologies**
I: 8013
IJ: 6297

**Humorous stories — Short stories**
I: 8150, 8159, 8168–69

**Hungary**
PI: 12379
IJ: 11283, 12369

**Hungary — Cookbooks**
IJ: 17224

**Hungary — Fiction**
P: 3836, 4225

**Hungary — Folklore**
P: 8866, 8873
IJ: 8877

**Hungary — History — Fiction**
I: 7495

**Hunters and hunting**
IJ: 12931, 17517

**Hunters and hunting — Fiction**
P: 2007, 2328, 2347
I: 5486, 5789
IJ: 5917

**Hunters and hunting — Folklore**
PI: 9298
I: 9187

**Huron, Lake**
PI: 13260

**Huron Indians**
PI: 12932

**Hurricanes**
P: 16411, 16433
PI: 16410, 16429
I: 16413, 16417, 16423, 16427, 16438
IJ: 16404, 16426, 16434, 16439

**Hurricanes — Fiction**
P: 734, 2371, 3654
I: 5557

**Hurston, Zora Neale**
P: 3028
PI: 10256
IJ: 10255

**Hussein, Saddam**
I: 12561

**Hutchinson, Anne**
IJ: 10755

**Hybernation — Fiction**
P: 2001

**Hyenas**
PI: 15124

**Hygiene**
*See also* Health and medicine
P: 2700
I: 14512–13

**Hymns**
P: 13800
PI: 11493
I: 11513
IJ: 10560, 11512

**Hyperactivity — Fiction**
I: 8056

# I

**Iacocca, Lee**
IJ: 10538

**Ice ages**
P: 11866

**Ice cream**
P: 15962, 15964
I: 15961

**Ice formations — Poetry**
I: 9900

**Ice hockey**
PI: 8421, 17628, 17633
I: 17629, 17632
IJ: 17630–31, 17657

**Ice hockey — Biography**
I: 10933, 11148–49, 11152, 11158, 11163
IJ: 11150, 11160

**Ice hockey — Fiction**
P: 2359, 2426
I: 8409–12, 8420, 8439
IJ: 8440

**Ice skating**
P: 17636
I: 11168, 17629
IJ: 17635, 17657

**Ice skating — Biography**
PI: 11142, 11144
I: 10950, 11141, 11151, 11153, 11161, 11171–72
IJ: 11143, 11145, 11157

**Ice skating — Fiction**
P: 5318
PI: 8442, 8447, 8460
I: 8457

**Icebergs**
*See* Glaciers and icebergs
P: 16172

**Iceland**
P: 15894
PI: 15419
I: 12502, 12512
IJ: 12496

**Iceland — Folklore**
I: 9127

**Iceman (Switzerland)**
I: 11815

**Id-w-Fitr (Islamic holiday)**
PI: 13916

**Idaho**
I: 13437, 13440

**Idioms**
I: 11442

**Iditarod**
PI: 2353, 17531
I: 11146, 17489
IJ: 17492

**Iditarod — Fiction**
P: 4211
PI: 5991
IJ: 5697

**Iditarod (Junior)**
PI: 17531
I: 17524

**Igbo**
IJ: 12189

**Iglesias, Julio**
IJ: 10184

**Igloos**
I: 12606, 12779

**Iguanas**
PI: 14956

**Iguanas — Fiction**
P: 4244

P = Primary; PI = Primary–Intermediate; I = Intermediate; IJ = Intermediate–Junior High

**Illegal aliens**
IJ: 13756

**Illegal aliens — Fiction**
PI: 7318
IJ: 5998

**Illinois**
PI: 13275
I: 13259
IJ: 13266

**Illinois — Fiction**
I: 7305
IJ: 7760

**Illinois — History**
IJ: 13303

**Illness,** 14323–14363
*See also* Diseases; and specific
illnesses, e.g., Diabetes
PI: 14327

**Illness — Fiction**
P: 1520, 1664, 3062, 3081, 3101,
3140, 3240, 3885, 3935, 4046,
4695, 5240
I: 7217
IJ: 7068

**Illustrators — Biography**
PI: 10106
I: 10272, 11354

**Imaginary animals — Fiction**
*See also* Aesop fables; Animals;
Mother Goose; and specific
real or imaginary animals,
e.g., Bears; Dragons
P: 5–6, 11, 27, 34, 104, 140–41, 183,
197, 210, 215, 258, 302, 306, 321,
339, 345, 348, 363, 381, 419, 449,
455, 462, 483, 542, 544–45, 547,
549–50, 571, 573, 583, 589–90,
598, 629, 634, 670, 674, 682–84,
696, 698–700, 704–5, 715, 719,
723, 731, 749, 770, 777, 854, 1004,
1012, 1043, 1067, 1158, 1284,
1310, 1336, 1356–58, 1360–416,
1418–19, 1421–27, 1429–43,
1446–65, 1467–83, 1485–509,
1511–44, 1546, 1548, 1550–51,
1553–79, 1581–600, 1602,
1604–13, 1615–40, 1642–706,
1708–22, 1724–43, 1745–64,
1766–70, 1772, 1775–90, 1792–97,
1799–800, 1802–27, 1829–35,
1837–39, 1841–70, 1872–74,
1876–80, 1882–931, 1933–39,
1941–48, 1950–2009, 2011–32,
2034, 2036–40, 2042–54, 2056–57,
2059–60, 2062–76, 2078–88,
2090–100, 2102–22, 2124–41,

2143–50, 2153–67, 2169–78,
2180–87, 2189–213, 2215–30,
2232–72, 2275–81, 2284–90, 2975,
3145, 3355, 3373, 3398, 3450,
3476, 3481, 3537, 3671, 3892,
4105, 4118, 4180, 4222, 4588,
4602, 4617, 4645, 4650. 4654–55,
4659, 4666, 4680–81, 4690, 4703,
4728, 4737, 4745–47, 4785, 4836,
4842, 4845, 4855, 4858, 4862–63,
4865, 4867–69, 4875, 4891, 4912,
4917, 4942, 4995, 4997, 5004,
5021–22, 5034–35, 5049, 5063,
5065, 5067, 5072, 5074–75, 5119,
5126, 5131, 5148, 5164, 5174,
5176, 5179, 5182, 5187–96,
5198–200, 5231, 5235, 5257,
5259–61, 5263–64, 5266, 5276,
5279, 5283, 5285, 5288–92,
5309–11, 5325–26, 5345, 5356,
5372, 5375, 5379, 5381, 5391,
5395–97, 5404, 5409–10, 5414–15,
5418, 5420, 5424, 5433, 5438–39,
5441–42, 9191, 11428, 11502,
11585, 11599, 13952

PI: 623, 721, 1417, 1428, 1444–45,
1484, 1547, 1549, 1552, 1601,
1641, 1744, 1774, 1798, 1801,
1836, 1875, 1881, 1940, 1949,
2010, 2033, 2035, 2041, 2058,
2101, 2123, 2151, 2179, 2214,
2231, 2273, 2282, 4111, 5108,
5398, 5502, 5511, 5677, 5700,
5905, 6571, 7987–88, 8002, 8417,
9336, 9378

I: 1603, 1707, 1932, 2077, 5473,
5850, 7986, 7990, 8077, 8101,
8125, 8148

IJ: 5632, 6462, 8100, 8102, 8334

**Imaginary animals — Poetry**
P: 1580, 1765, 5405
PI: 1773, 9885
I: 9743

**Immigration (U.S.)**
P: 3763, 14027, 14062
PI: 12803, 13028, 13390, 13396,
13407, 14059
I: 12215, 12282, 12420, 12676,
13023, 13223, 13228, 13381,
14021, 14026, 14038, 14043,
14053, 14055–56, 14067, 14070,
14072, 14079, 14083, 14090
IJ: 12083, 12243, 12316, 12372,
12428, 12449, 13379, 13529,
13756, 14020, 14022–25, 14036,
14040–41, 14047, 14049, 14054,
14061, 14068, 14077–78, 14081,
14086

**Immigration (U.S.) — Fiction**
P: 2966, 3080, 3186, 3940, 3951,
3980, 4787
PI: 3982, 5003, 6004, 7715
I: 6172, 7819
IJ: 7777, 7795, 7842

**In-line hockey**
PI: 17512

**In-line skating**
PI: 17478
I: 17482, 17494

**Incas**
P: 12717
I: 12711, 12713, 12725–26, 12736
IJ: 12614, 12617

**Incas — Fiction**
IJ: 7524

**Incas — Folklore**
PI: 9447

**Independence Hall
(Philadelphia, Pa.)**
I: 13406

**India**
PI: 12230, 13915
I: 12227, 12229, 12231, 12233–34,
12236–37, 12242, 15274
IJ: 11228, 12228, 12235, 12239,
12241, 12243–44, 14023

**India — Biography**
P: 11227, 11270

**India — Cookbooks**
IJ: 17236

**India — Fiction**
P: 1020, 3577, 3747, 5915
PI: 5910, 5913, 7432–33, 7435, 7447,
7450
I: 7445
IJ: 5945, 7460

**India — Folklore**
P: 5055, 8808, 8812–15, 8817,
8819–21
PI: 8809
I: 8804–7, 8810, 8816, 8818
IJ: 8811

**India — History**
I: 12232

**India — Holidays**
PI: 13920, 13931

**India — Poetry**
P: 9664
IJ: 9582

P = Primary; PI = Primary–Intermediate; I = Intermediate; IJ = Intermediate–Junior High

P = Primary; PI = Primary–Intermediate; I = Intermediate; IJ = Intermediate–Junior High

**Indians of North America —
Medicine**
IJ: 14369

**Indians of North America —
Poetry**
P: 9599
PI: 9849, 11601
I: 9704, 9852
IJ: 9850–51

**Indians of North America —
Prayers**
P: 9297
PI: 14015

**Indians of North America —
Songs**
P: 596
IJ: 9851

**Indians of North America —
Sports**
P: 12907

**Indians of North American —
Women**
PI: 12830

**Indians of South America**
PI: 12690
I: 12716, 12720, 12730, 12735

**Indians of South America —
Folklore**
PI: 8601, 9439
IJ: 9441

**Indians of South America —
Jokes and riddles**
PI: 17331

**Indians of the West Indies —
Fiction**
PI: 7535
IJ: 7545

**Indonesia**
IJ: 12289, 12303, 12307

**Indonesia — Fiction**
P: 4445

**Industrial health and safety**
I: 10864

**Industrial Revolution (U.S.)**
IJ: 13106, 13218

**Influenza epidemic, 1918 —
Fiction**
IJ: 7796

**Injuries**
PI: 14520

**Insects**
*See also* names of specific
    insects, e.g., Butterflies
P: 15495, 15497–98, 15500, 15502–3,
    15505, 15511, 15513, 15517,
    15519, 15521–22, 15525–26,
    15532–33, 15541, 15544, 15557,
    15569, 15573, 15576–77,
    15583–84
PI: 15485, 15489, 15506, 15512,
    15514, 15527–29, 15534–35,
    15539, 15542, 15551, 15558,
    15563, 15565
I: 14870, 15483–84, 15488,
    15491–94, 15496, 15499, 15501,
    15507, 15509–10, 15515, 15520,
    15530–31, 15553, 15559,
    15566–67, 15575, 17100
IJ: 14865, 15486, 15490, 15504,
    15508, 15518, 15536, 15585,
    15605

**Insects — Fiction**
P: 367, 601, 723, 1493, 2069, 4370,
    4454, 5280
PI: 108
I: 6275
IJ: 5632

**Insects — Homes**
P: 15074

**Insects — Poetry**
P: 9727
PI: 9723
I: 9720

**Insects — Songs**
P: 11603

**Internet (computers)**
PI: 16825, 16828
I: 16816, 16820, 16823
IJ: 16829–30

**Internet (computers) — Fiction**
I: 8368

**Interracial marriages —
Fiction**
P: 2866
I: 6040

**Inuit**
*See* Eskimos

**Inventions**
*See* Inventors and inventions;
    and specific inventions, e.g.,
    Telephones

**Inventors and inventions**
*See also* Scientists; and specific
    inventions, e.g., Telephones

P: 5226
PI: 11848
I: 2591, 13779, 16570, 16680,
    16685–86, 16693, 16698, 16701,
    16707, 16709–12, 16860
IJ: 16672, 16688, 16692, 16700,
    16702

**Inventors and inventions —
Biography**
P: 10513, 10518–19, 10920
PI: 10083, 10512, 10515, 10517,
    10841
I: 10085, 10427, 10794, 10808,
    10839–40, 10844–45, 10849–50,
    10870
IJ: 10084, 10354, 10514, 10838,
    10919

**Inventors and inventions —
Fiction**
PI: 8031, 8049
I: 8053, 8062, 8196

**Invertebrates**
*See also* Animals; Insects; etc.
I: 15616
IJ: 15605

**Iowa**
PI: 13276
I: 13283, 13286

**Iowa — Fiction**
I: 8075

**Iran**
PI: 12580
I: 12579
IJ: 12568, 12572

**Iran — Folklore**
P: 9171

**Iran hostage crisis**
PI: 12580

**Iraq**
*See also* Persian Gulf War
    (1991)
PI: 12575
I: 12571
IJ: 12527

**Iraq — Folklore**
P: 9181

**Ireland**
PI: 12419
I: 12424–25
IJ: 12417, 12421, 12428, 14078

**Ireland — Fiction**
P: 3766, 3820, 3910

P = Primary; PI = Primary–Intermediate; I = Intermediate; IJ = Intermediate–Junior High

I: 7171, 7506, 7513
IJ: 5659, 5933, 6614, 7505, 7720

**Ireland — Folklore**
P: 8975–76, 8991, 8994, 9014, 9016
PI: 8960
I: 8977, 9006
IJ: 8965, 9012

**Ireland — History**
P: 11260
I: 12423

**Ireland — Poetry**
IJ: 9672

**Ireland, Northern**
PI: 12427

**Irish Americans**
I: 14067
IJ: 14031, 14078, 14088

**Irish Americans — Fiction**
P: 4618
IJ: 7808

**Irish setters — Fiction**
IJ: 5916

**Iron and steel**
I: 16856

**Iroquois Indians**
PI: 12948
I: 12835

**Iroquois Indians — Biography**
IJ: 10582

**Iroquois Indians — Crafts**
I: 12938

**Iroquois Indians — Folklore**
PI: 9195
IJ: 9193

**Ishi**
IJ: 10583

**Islam**
P: 13782
PI: 4612, 13916
I: 12570, 13794

**Islam — Fiction**
I: 6015
IJ: 7441

**Islam — Folklore**
P: 9179

**Islam — History**
I: 12578

**Islamic Americans — Fiction**
I: 6015

**Islands**
*See also* Caribbean Islands; and
specific islands, e.g., Cuba
P: 3970, 5361
PI: 12755, 15890, 16201
IJ: 13453

**Islands — Fiction**
P: 2600, 2986, 3009, 4776, 5178
PI: 2282, 2850, 4344, 5704, 5753
I: 2077, 5684, 6092, 6639, 6707,
6914, 7468, 7513, 7616, 7874,
8060
IJ: 5616, 5659, 5698, 5738, 5802,
6262, 6688, 7385, 7545, 7563,
8122

**Islands — Poetry**
P: 9865

**Israel**
P: 12554, 13819
PI: 79, 12548
I: 12546, 12551–53
IJ: 12547, 12555–56

**Israel — Biography**
PI: 11262
IJ: 11243

**Israel — Fiction**
P: 3768, 3977
I: 7884
IJ: 7275, 7405

**Israel — History**
IJ: 11212

**Israeli-Arab relations**
IJ: 12560

**Italian Americans**
I: 14055
IJ: 14035, 14047, 14087

**Italian Americans — Fiction**
P: 2399, 2797, 2870, 3186
PI: 3748
I: 6209

**Italy**
P: 12437
PI: 12436, 12441
I: 12447
IJ: 12446, 12448

**Italy — Cookbooks**
IJ: 17202

**Italy — Crafts**
PI: 16981

**Italy — Fiction**
P: 4776
PI: 7470
IJ: 6984, 7486, 7882

**Italy — Folklore**
P: 4733, 8925, 9065–68, 9070, 9075
PI: 9069
I: 8573, 9077
IJ: 9062

**Italy — History**
I: 11806
IJ: 12029

**Ivory Coast**
IJ: 12175, 12181

**Iwo Jima, Battle of**
I: 12069
IJ: 12031

---

# J

**Jacks (game)**
PI: 17511

**Jackson, Andrew**
I: 10335, 10652

**Jackson, Bo**
I: 11088
IJ: 10987, 11089

**Jackson, Jesse**
I: 10386

**Jackson, Michael**
IJ: 10185

**Jackson, Reggie**
PI: 10988

**Jackson, Stonewall**
I: 10539
IJ: 10540

**Jacobs, Harriet**
I: 10387

**Jaguars — Fiction**
P: 4253
PI: 4428

**Jaguars — Poetry**
I: 9704

**Jamaica**
IJ: 12679, 12684

**Jamaica — Fiction**
P: 3062, 3828, 4065

---

P = Primary; PI = Primary–Intermediate; I = Intermediate; IJ = Intermediate–Junior High

P = Primary; PI = Primary–Intermediate; I = Intermediate; IJ = Intermediate–Junior High

PI: 13985
I: 13984

**Jewish holy days — Fiction**
P: 690, 1301, 4949, 4952–53,
4957–59, 4961–66, 4969, 4971,
4976–80, 4983–84, 4987–88,
4991–92, 4995, 4997–99
PI: 4950, 7951, 7960
I: 7900, 7925, 7939
IJ: 7959

**Jewish holy days — Poetry**
P: 4974–75
PI: 9770

**Jewish holy days — Short
stories**
I: 7957

**Jewish Theological Seminary**
I: 13357

**Jews**
I: 13820, 14053

**Jews — Biography**
I: 11223
IJ: 10281

**Jews — Fiction**
P: 2838, 3041, 3080, 3225, 3768,
3876, 3918, 3923, 3929, 3932,
3985, 4822, 4830, 4996
PI: 3234, 3920, 6004, 6070, 6080,
7429, 7476, 7836, 7853, 7914,
7938
I: 6172, 6175, 6192, 6290, 7103,
7204, 7484, 7814, 7872, 7889,
7913
IJ: 6005, 7029, 7098, 7389, 7405,
7494, 7777, 7795, 7842, 7861–62,
7876, 7882–83, 7885, 7893

**Jews — History**
*See also* Holocaust;
Immigration (U.S.); Israeli-
Arab relations; World War II
PI: 12011
I: 12038, 12550, 13833
IJ: 11224, 12015–16, 12046, 12063,
13834

**Joan of Arc, Saint**
I: 11236

**Jobs, Steven**
PI: 16822

**Jockeys — Biography**
I: 11154–55

**Jockeys — Women —
Biography**
PI: 11156

**Jogging**
*See* Running and jogging

**John Paul II, Pope**
I: 11237–38

**Johnson, Andrew**
I: 10660
IJ: 10661

**Johnson, Isaac**
IJ: 10389

**Johnson, John H.**
IJ: 10390

**Johnson, Lyndon B.**
I: 10334
IJ: 10662–63

**Johnson, Magic**
I: 11040, 11042
IJ: 11039, 11041

**Johnson, Walter**
IJ: 10989

**Johnstown Flood (1899) —
Fiction**
PI: 7792

**Jokes and riddles**
P: 184, 4805, 5167–68, 5341, 5438,
8543, 8675, 17324, 17332, 17335,
17339, 17343, 17345–50, 17353,
17362, 17365, 17369, 17372–73,
17382, 17386, 17392
PI: 4925, 5169, 11614, 13163, 16986,
17325–31, 17333, 17336, 17340,
17342, 17344, 17351–52,
17355–58, 17364, 17366, 17368,
17370–71, 17374–76, 17378–80,
17384–85, 17388, 17390
I: 8646, 11443–44, 17334, 17337–38,
17341, 17354, 17359–60, 17367,
17377, 17381, 17383, 17387,
17389, 17391
IJ: 17361, 17363

**Jokes and riddles — Folklore**
I: 8880

**Jokes and riddles — Poetry**
IJ: 9661

**Jolliet, Louis**
PI: 12986

**Jones, Frederick McKinley**
I: 10870

**Jones, John Paul**
PI: 10543

**Jones, Mother**
I: 10756
IJ: 10757–58

**Joplin, Scott**
I: 10140

**Jordan**
IJ: 12563, 12574

**Jordan, Barbara**
I: 10391

**Jordan, Michael**
I: 11044–45, 11047
IJ: 11043, 11046

**Jordan, Michael — Poetry**
PI: 9906

**Joseph (Bible)**
P: 13868
PI: 13891

**Joseph (Nez Perce chief)**
I: 10584

**Journalists — Biography**
PI: 10467, 10733, 10735
I: 10276, 10318, 10734, 10789

**Journalists and journalism**
P: 11463
PI: 11455
IJ: 11449

**Journalists and journalism —
Careers**
PI: 14196

**Joyce, William**
I: 11356

**Joyner, Florence Griffith**
I: 11122–23

**Joyner-Kersee, Jackie**
PI: 11125
I: 11124
IJ: 11126

**Juana de la Guz, Sister**
I: 10257

**Juarez, Benito**
PI: 11240
I: 11239

**Judaism**
*See also* Jews; Jews — History;
Religion; Sabbath (Jewish)
P: 13816, 13819

P = Primary; PI = Primary–Intermediate; I = Intermediate; IJ = Intermediate–Junior High

I: 13787, 13820
IJ: 13822

**Judo**
I: 17664

**Jugglers and juggling**
PI: 17194

**Jugglers and juggling — Fiction**
P: 4729
PI: 4051

**Julia, Raul**
IJ: 10484

**July Fourth**
I: 13909
IJ: 13910

**July Fourth — Fiction**
P: 4622, 4636–37, 4641

**Jumbo (elephant)**
PI: 15262

**Jungles**
P: 4425, 16193
PI: 12710
I: 14879, 16263
IJ: 12032, 16238

**Jungles — Fiction**
P: 874, 997, 1278, 1392, 2323, 5281
IJ: 5478

**Junior Iditarod**
*See* Iditarod (Junior)

**Jupiter (planet)**
PI: 14724
I: 14709, 14715

# K

**Kahlo, Frida**
I: 10078
IJ: 10076–77

**Kaiulani, Princess of Hawaii**
I: 11241

**Kalahari Desert**
IJ: 12144

**Kalispel Indians — Dances**
I: 12833

**Kangaroos — Fiction**
P: 1792, 4226, 5119

**Kansas**
I: 13280, 13285

**Kansas — Fiction**
P: 5081
PI: 2772
I: 6139, 7689
IJ: 5844

**Kansas City, Missouri**
PI: 13301

**Karan, Donna**
IJ: 10759

**Karate**
*See also* Martial arts
P: 17667
PI: 17665
IJ: 17663

**Karate — Fiction**
PI: 4127
I: 8403
IJ: 8478

**Karuk Indians — Folklore**
P: 9252

**Kato Indians — Folklore**
PI: 9282

**Kazakhstan**
IJ: 12473

**Keats, Ezra Jack**
I: 10079

**Keller, Helen**
PI: 10760–61
I: 10762
IJ: 10354

**Kelley, Florence**
PI: 10544

**Kelly, Jim**
IJ: 11090

**Kemp, Shawn**
I: 11048

**Kennedy, John F.**
PI: 10664, 10666–67
I: 10334, 10665, 10669
IJ: 10668

**Kennedy, Robert**
IJ: 10545

**Kenny, Elizabeth**
I: 10871

**Kente cloth**
P: 12174

**Kentucky**
PI: 13477
I: 13469, 13484
IJ: 13465

**Kentucky — Fiction**
I: 7319
IJ: 6985

**Kentucky — History**
I: 13510

**Kentucky Derby**
I: 17625

**Kenya**
P: 12095
PI: 12107, 15113
I: 12096, 12112, 12116, 12118
IJ: 12106, 12123, 12127

**Kenya — Animals**
P: 12117

**Kenya — Fiction**
P: 3978, 4195
PI: 4525
I: 5829

**Keres Indians**
PI: 12816

**Kerrigan, Nancy**
I: 11153

**Key, Francis Scott**
P: 3899
PI: 11518
I: 10258

**Kherdian, Jeron**
IJ: 11242

**Kidd, Captain — Fiction**
I: 8101

**Kidnapping**
P: 8692

**Kidnapping — Fiction**
P: 959, 1734, 2329, 5212, 5243, 5374
PI: 5466
I: 5572, 6806, 8346, 8420
IJ: 5495, 5527, 5583, 5591, 5673, 5705, 5729, 7493, 7552, 7558, 7623

**Killer bees**
PI: 15549
I: 15554

**Killer whales**
PI: 15731

P = Primary; PI = Primary–Intermediate; I = Intermediate; IJ = Intermediate–Junior High

**Kindergarten**
P: 4519, 4540

**Kindergarten — Fiction**
P: 4031, 4500, 4503, 4538, 4541
PI: 6074

**King, Billie Jean**
I: 11117

**King, Coretta Scott**
PI: 10393
I: 10394
IJ: 10392

**King, Martin Luther, Jr.**
P: 4600, 10396, 10407, 10410–11
PI: 10397, 10399–400, 10405–6,
10413–14, 13922
I: 10395, 10401–2, 10404, 13648
IJ: 10398, 10403, 10408–9, 10412,
13663

**King, Richard**
I: 10546

**King Philip's War**
I: 10591

**Kings — Biography**
PI: 11230

**Kings — Fiction**
P: 1220, 1933, 3513, 5347
PI: 1140, 6561
I: 8596

**Kings — Folklore**
P: 8604, 8695, 8729, 8738, 8767,
8773
I: 8805

**Kipling, Rudyard**
I: 10259

**Kipsigis**
IJ: 12097

**Kisses — Fiction**
P: 784

**Kitchens — Fiction**
P: 2414, 2705

**Kitchens — History**
I: 13139

**Kites — Fiction**
P: 237, 1237, 1261, 1855, 2059, 2755,
3199, 3935, 4169, 5364
PI: 379

**Klee, Paul**
PI: 10080

**Knight, Philip**
IJ: 10547

**Knights**
P: 11969, 11983
I: 11964, 11972, 11977
IJ: 11971, 11985, 11992

**Knights — Crafts**
I: 12000

**Knights — Fiction**
P: 1088, 1573, 3356, 3809
PI: 7502, 8130
I: 5746, 6363, 7477, 9021
IJ: 7519, 9024

**Knights — Folklore**
PI: 8995, 9001
I: 8935, 8996, 9000
IJ: 8993, 8997, 9002, 9026–27

**Knitting**
PI: 17175

**Knitting — Fiction**
P: 1414, 3256, 3383, 3407

**Knot tying**
IJ: 17188

**Koalas**
P: 15281–82, 15284
I: 15279

**Koalas — Fiction**
P: 1627, 1667

**Kollek, Teddy**
IJ: 11243

**Komodo dragons**
PI: 14955
I: 14954, 14957

**Komodo dragons — Fiction**
P: 3420, 4445

**Kongo**
IJ: 12114

**Korea**
*See also* Korea, North; Korea,
South
IJ: 12292

**Korea — Fiction**
P: 2883, 3772
PI: 7434
I: 7451
IJ: 7437

**Korea — Folklore**
P: 8742–43, 8745, 8747–54

PI: 8756
IJ: 8755

**Korea, North**
P: 12290

**Korea, South**
P: 12290
I: 12268, 12304
IJ: 12319

**Korea, South — Cookbooks**
IJ: 17207

**Korea, South — Holidays**
PI: 12297

**Korean Americans**
I: 14057
IJ: 14133

**Korean Americans — Fiction**
P: 2429, 2845, 2925, 3053, 3772,
4522–23, 8255
PI: 6144
I: 6044, 14129
IJ: 5983, 5996, 6010

**Korean language**
I: 12268

**Korean War**
I: 13252
IJ: 13247, 13253, 13255

**Korean War — Fiction**
IJ: 7437

**Korematsu, Fred**
I: 10548

**Kossman, Nina**
IJ: 11244

**Koufax, Sandy**
I: 10990–91

**Krone, Julie**
PI: 11156
I: 11154–55

**Ku Klux Klan — Fiction**
IJ: 6007

**Kung fu — Fiction**
PI: 3891

**Kurd**
I: 14072

**Kurelek, William**
PI: 10081

**Kuskin, Karla**
PI: 10260

P = Primary; PI = Primary–Intermediate; I = Intermediate; IJ = Intermediate–Junior High

**Kwan, Michelle**
IJ: 11157

**Kwanzaa**
P: 4607, 4611, 4632, 4634, 4639, 13911
PI: 4629, 13902, 13906, 13928
I: 13898, 13912, 13914

**Kwanzaa — Crafts**
P: 4633

**Kwanzaa — Fiction**
PI: 7909, 7945, 7963

**Kyrgyzstan**
I: 12485

# L

**Labor Day**
P: 13929

**Labor movements**
I: 12794, 13212
IJ: 10757, 13234

**Labor movements — Biography**
PI: 10441, 10544
IJ: 10758

**Labor movements — Fiction**
IJ: 7803

**Labrador**
I: 12594

**Labrador retrievers**
PI: 15858

**Labrador retrievers — Fiction**
IJ: 5841, 5982

**La Brea Tar Pits (Calif.)**
IJ: 11785

**Ladybugs**
P: 15500
PI: 15524, 15558
IJ: 15508

**Ladybugs — Fiction**
P: 1493

**Lakes**
P: 15796
PI: 13260–1
I: 16300–1
IJ: 16290

**Lakota Indians**
*See also* Dakota Indians

**Lakota Indians — Folklore**
P: 9233
PI: 9285
IJ: 9229

**Lambs — Fiction**
P: 4318

**Lancelot (knight)**
PI: 9033

**Landscape architecture**
I: 10561

**Landslides**
I: 16122

**Lange, Dorothea**
I: 10082

**Language and languages**
*See also* Dictionaries; Spanish language — Fiction; Word books
P: 4416, 11377, 11380, 11438
PI: 11427, 11430
I: 11381, 11437, 11439–41
IJ: 11299, 11375

**Language and languages — Fiction**
P: 6086, 17411
PI: 7561

**Laos**
PI: 12275
I: 12282
IJ: 12298

**Laos — Folklore**
I: 8857

**Laotian Americans**
I: 14070

**Lapland**
PI: 12757

**Lasers**
I: 16565, 16570, 16573
IJ: 14569

**Latchkey children — Fiction**
P: 4159
I: 6954
IJ: 7065

**Latin America**
*See also* Caribbean Islands; Central America; South America; national and ethnic groups, e.g., Hispanic

Americans; and specific countries, e.g., Mexico

**Latin America — Folklore,**
9393–9449
P: 9444
PI: 9438
I: 9440
IJ: 9437

**Latkes — Fiction**
P: 4953, 4961, 4964

**Latvia**
I: 12465

**Laughter — Fiction**
P: 2413, 3945

**Lauren, Ralph**
IJ: 10549

**Lavoisier, Antoine**
I: 10872

**Law, Ruth**
P: 10005

**Lawrence, Jacob**
I: 11355

**Lawyers — Biography**
PI: 10485
I: 10385

**Lawyers — Careers**
P: 14178

**Lazarus, Charles P.**
IJ: 10550

**Laziness — Fiction**
PI: 7110

**Leakey, Louis and Mary**
IJ: 10873

**Leakey, Mary**
I: 10874

**Learning disabilities**
*See also* Mental handicaps
PI: 14299
I: 14301, 14318
IJ: 14294, 14304–5, 14310

**Learning disabilities — Fiction**
PI: 7383
I: 7357, 7367, 8213
IJ: 7054, 7275

**Leaves**
*See also* Trees
PI: 16040
I: 16036

P = Primary; PI = Primary–Intermediate; I = Intermediate; IJ = Intermediate–Junior High

P = Primary; PI = Primary–Intermediate; I = Intermediate; IJ = Intermediate–Junior High

P = Primary; PI = Primary–Intermediate; I = Intermediate; IJ = Intermediate–Junior High

**Low, Juliette Gordon**
I: 10763

**Lowry, Lois**
IJ: 10262

**Lucas, John**
I: 11049

**Ludington, Sybil**
I: 10764

**Luge**
PI: 17476

**Lullabies**
*See also* Bedtime books; Songs
P: 459, 479, 516, 536–37, 543, 558, 572

**Lumberjacks — Careers**
IJ: 14185

**Lungs**
I: 14457
IJ: 14459

**Luo (African people)**
I: 12096

**Luxembourg**
I: 12452, 12454

**Lying**
P: 8677

**Lying — Fiction**
P: 4121, 4152, 4501, 5100
PI: 5883, 7224
I: 6054, 8434
IJ: 5715, 8003

**Lynx**
P: 15195, 15204
PI: 15198
I: 15211, 15214

**Lyon, George Ella**
PI: 10263

**Lyon, Mary**
IJ: 10556

# M

**MacArthur, Douglas**
I: 10557
IJ: 10558

**McAuliffe, Christa**
PI: 10009

*Macbeth* **(play)**
IJ: 9942, 9945

**McClintock, Barbara**
I: 10880

**MacCready, Paul B.**
IJ: 10010

**Machinery**
P: 4573, 4584, 16847, 16852, 16890
PI: 16848
I: 16683, 16786, 16844–45, 16853
IJ: 15941, 16692, 16850–51

**Machinery — Experiments and projects**
PI: 16611
I: 16841

**Machinery — Fiction**
P: 4555, 4586

**Machinery — Poetry**
P: 4554
I: 9565

**Machines**
P: 4571
I: 16849

**Machines — Fiction**
PI: 4580

**Machines — Picture books — Fiction,** 4548–4599

**Machu Picchu (Peru)**
I: 12736

**Mackenzie, Alexander**
P: 3900

**McKinley, William**
IJ: 10685

**MacKinnon, Christy**
PI: 14312

**McKissack, Patricia**
PI: 10264

**McNair, Ronald**
IJ: 10011–12

**McPhail, David**
PI: 10265

**Madagascar**
IJ: 12142, 12153

**Madagascar — Folklore**
PI: 8733

**Maddux, Greg**
I: 10992
IJ: 10993

**Madison, Dolley**
I: 10689

**Madison, James**
I: 10686, 10688–89
IJ: 10687

**Madison, James — Fiction**
IJ: 7651

**Magarec, Joe**
IJ: 9382

**Magellan, Ferdinand**
I: 9950, 9959

*Magellan* **(spacecraft)**
I: 16630

**Magicians and magic**
P: 8709, 17311
PI: 17297, 17299, 17301, 17305–6
I: 14589, 14639, 17294–96, 17298, 17300, 17304, 17307–10
IJ: 10183, 17292–93, 17302–3

**Magicians and magic — Fiction**
P: 429, 531, 755, 906, 917, 1054, 1282, 1628, 2134, 2366, 3498, 4695, 4869, 5048, 8528
PI: 1270, 1344, 4644, 6309, 6328, 6423, 6735, 8043, 8069
I: 5736, 6094, 6220, 6346, 6364–66, 6597, 6774, 6799, 6877, 8012, 8103, 8293, 8323
IJ: 6260, 6631

**Magicians and magic — Folklore**
P: 8797
PI: 8937

**Magnetism**
P: 16582, 16586

**Magnetism — Experiments and projects**
PI: 16588, 16597
I: 16578, 16590–91, 16594, 16596
IJ: 16587, 16598

**Mahy, Margaret**
PI: 10266

**Mailcarriers — Fiction**
P: 2539

**Maine**
P: 13351
PI: 13364
I: 13358, 13363, 13376, 15418, 17598

**Maine — Fiction**
P: 3005, 3390, 3654
PI: 2850, 6633, 6879

P = Primary; PI = Primary–Intermediate; I = Intermediate; IJ = Intermediate–Junior High

I: 6203, 6971
IJ: 5616, 5643–44, 5652, 7570, 7582

**Maine — History**
P: 3970

**Malamutes — Fiction**
IJ: 6198

**Malawi**
IJ: 12110

**Malawi — Fiction**
P: 3988

**Malaysia**
I: 12310
IJ: 12305, 12309, 12314

**Malaysia — Folklore**
P: 12278

**Malcolm X**
PI: 10416
I: 10417, 10419
IJ: 10418

**Mali — Folklore**
PI: 8739

**Mammals**
P: 14849, 15118, 15133, 15738
PI: 15087
I: 14836, 14844, 14903, 15092, 15098, 15107, 15135
IJ: 15108, 15117, 15139

**Mammoths**
P: 11697

**Mammoths — Fiction**
P: 1979, 3808

**Man O' War (racehorse)**
I: 15886

**Manatees**
P: 15701, 15703
PI: 15699
I: 15710
IJ: 15709

**Manatees — Fiction**
P: 4325

**Mandan Indians**
PI: 12884

**Mandan Indians — Fiction**
IJ: 7709

**Mandela, Nelson**
PI: 11246–47, 11249–50, 11252
IJ: 11248, 11251

**Mangrove swamps**
I: 16185

**Manhattan Project**
PI: 16975

**Mankiller, Wilma P.**
PI: 10587
I: 10586
IJ: 10585

**Manners**
P: 2381, 14105, 14113
I: 14112, 14114–16
IJ: 14117

**Manners — Fiction**
P: 1463, 1710, 2061, 3304, 4083
PI: 3438

**Manufacturing**
P: 2626
PI: 16687

**Manx cats — Folklore**
P: 9037

**Maori — Folklore**
P: 8858, 8861

**Maple sugar and syrup**
PI: 12967, 15950
I: 15965

**Maple sugar and syrup — Fiction**
P: 3606

**Maps and globes**
P: 11668, 11686, 11692
PI: 11682, 11689, 11691
I: 11685, 11687–88, 14880, 16129
IJ: 11690, 13454, 16140

**Maps and globes — Experiments and projects**
PI: 13592

**Maps and globes — Fiction**
P: 157, 957

**Mardi Gras**
PI: 13921
I: 13913

**Mardi Gras — Fiction**
P: 4624

**Marijuana**
I: 14292

**Marijuana — Fiction**
I: 8432

**Marin, Don Luis Monez**
IJ: 10559

**Marine animals**
*See also* Fish; Reptiles; and specific animals, e.g., Sharks
P: 4426, 15481, 15622, 15628, 15630, 15634, 15636, 15638, 15769, 15904
PI: 15618–19, 15633, 15637, 15640, 15766, 15800
I: 15623, 15627, 15644, 15650, 15776, 15783, 15797
IJ: 11759, 15632, 15642, 15647, 15707, 15792

**Marine animals — Defenses**
PI: 15646

**Marine animals — Fiction**
P: 815, 3688

**Marine animals — Hawaii**
PI: 15625

**Marine animals — Poetry**
PI: 9754

**Marine biology**
PI: 15617

**Marine biology — Careers**
PI: 14239
I: 14247
IJ: 14245

**Marine life**
PI: 15787
I: 15790, 16078

**Marine life — Fiction**
P: 4262

**Marine plants**
PI: 15618
I: 15627, 15797

**Marionettes**
*See* Puppets and marionettes

**Markets**
PI: 13548
I: 13549

**Markets — Fiction**
P: 2581, 2603, 2655, 3825, 3907, 3971

**Marquette, Jacques**
PI: 12986

**Mars (planet)**
PI: 14707, 14712, 14722, 14725
I: 14714, 14716, 14731

**Marsalis, Wynton**
I: 10187–88

P = Primary; PI = Primary–Intermediate; I = Intermediate; IJ = Intermediate–Junior High

**Marshall, Thurgood**
PI: 10420–22, 10424–25
IJ: 10423, 10426

**Marshes**
P: 16183, 16305

**Marsupials**
PI: 15280
IJ: 15093

**Martha's Vineyard, Massachusetts — Fiction**
I: 7375

**Martí, José J.**
IJ: 10267

**Martial arts**
*See also* Karate
I: 17668
IJ: 17666

**Martin, Rafe**
I: 10268

**Martin Luther King Day**
PI: 13922
I: 13651

**Martinez, Maria**
PI: 10091
IJ: 10092

**Martinez, Vilma**
PI: 10485

**Martinique — Folklore**
PI: 9431

**Mary, Mother of Jesus**
P: 13838
PI: 13938

**Maryland**
PI: 13568
I: 13486–87

**Maryland — Fiction**
IJ: 5594, 6163, 6200, 6989

**Maryland Colony**
IJ: 12999

**Masai**
I: 12125
IJ: 12126

**Masai — Fiction**
PI: 7422

**Masai — Folklore**
P: 8676, 8730

**Masks**
PI: 17136

I: 17137, 17139–40
IJ: 11842, 17138, 17142

**Mass media**
I: 16862

**Massachusetts**
PI: 13365

**Massachusetts — Fiction**
P: 3655, 4470
PI: 3729, 4344, 7571, 7643
I: 7616, 7837, 8142
IJ: 5797, 7580, 7587, 7649

**Massachusetts — History**
IJ: 13346

**Materials**
I: 16524

**Mathematical puzzles**
P: 327, 16359–61
PI: 16346, 16357–58, 16367, 16370
I: 16338, 16356, 16362–63, 16366, 16368, 16371–72
IJ: 16364–65, 16369

**Mathematical puzzles — Fiction**
P: 4539

**Mathematicians — Biography**
I: 10806, 10842
IJ: 10879

**Mathematics**
*See also* Mathematical puzzles; Numbers; Puzzles; Statistics
P: 181, 360, 16344
PI: 16337, 16346, 16370, 16379, 16382
I: 16342, 16376
IJ: 16347, 16349

**Mathematics — Experiments and projects**
P: 16348

**Mathematics — Fiction**
P: 415, 424, 16341, 16350
PI: 7165
I: 8216
IJ: 8167

**Mathematics — Jokes and riddles**
I: 17359

**Mathematics — Poetry**
PI: 9568

**Mathewson, Christy**
I: 10994

**Matisse, Henri**
PI: 10093
I: 11333

**Matter (physics)**
I: 16524
IJ: 16512

**Matter (physics) — Experiments and projects**
IJ: 16513

**Matzeliger, Jan**
I: 10427

**Mauritania**
I: 12177

**Maximilian, Prince**
IJ: 12850

**Mayan Indians**
P: 12665
PI: 12659, 12671
I: 12610, 12642, 12658, 12668
IJ: 12614

**Mayan Indians — Fiction**
P: 3995

**Mayan Indians — Folklore**
P: 9396, 9405–6
I: 9399, 9416

**Mayan Indians — Poetry**
I: 9704

*Mayflower* (ship)
P: 5001
PI: 13049

*Mayflower* (ship) — Fiction
P: 5008
I: 7575

**Mayo, William and Charles**
I: 10881

**Mays, Willie**
I: 10995

**Mbundu**
IJ: 12113

**Mead, Margaret**
IJ: 10882

**Meadows**
I: 16320

**Mealtime — Fiction**
P: 1067, 1959, 2164
PI: 2887

P = Primary; PI = Primary–Intermediate; I = Intermediate; IJ = Intermediate–Junior High

P = Primary; PI = Primary–Intermediate; I = Intermediate; IJ = Intermediate–Junior High

P = Primary; PI = Primary–Intermediate; I = Intermediate; IJ = Intermediate–Junior High

P = Primary; PI = Primary–Intermediate; I = Intermediate; IJ = Intermediate–Junior High

I: 13559–60
IJ: 13555, 13557

**Money-making ideas — Fiction**
P: 1926, 3522
PI: 6856
I: 6873, 7249, 7264, 8024, 8040, 8126
IJ: 6921, 7197, 7336, 8157

**Money management**
I: 13544

**Mongolia**
PI: 12216
I: 12226
IJ: 12271

**Mongolia — Folklore**
P: 8757

**Mongols — Biography**
PI: 11230

**Mongooses — Fiction**
P: 1020

**Monhegan Island (Maine)**
I: 13358

**Monk, Thelonious**
I: 10189

**Monkeys**
P: 15151, 15154
PI: 15080, 15148, 15157
I: 15152, 15155

**Monkeys — Fiction**
P: 104, 216, 316–17, 1282, 2057, 2059, 2676–77, 3066, 3476, 3924, 5279
PI: 2058, 5450
I: 5960, 6682, 8105

**Monkeys — Folklore**
P: 8670, 8808, 8859

**Monologues — Anthologies**
IJ: 9920

**Monsters**
P: 17468
I: 17099, 17457, 17463
IJ: 17417, 17425

**Monsters — Fiction**
*See also* Fantasy; Folklore; Mythology; Supernatural; Tall tales
P: 117, 406, 428, 488, 502, 513, 515, 548, 562, 595, 793, 850, 882, 895, 914, 916, 980–82, 1005, 1100, 1187, 1196, 1216, 1259, 1319, 2028, 2079, 2139, 3305, 3493,

3497, 3521, 4152, 4529, 4939, 5335
PI: 1840, 6567
I: 6330
IJ: 5714, 6556

**Monsters — Mythology**
PI: 9461, 9475–76
I: 9463, 9479

**Monsters — Poetry**
P: 900, 1614
PI: 9670

**Montana**
PI: 12970, 13315
I: 13319, 13323, 13437

**Montana — History**
I: 12912
IJ: 12955

**Montana — History — Fiction**
I: 11742

**Montana, Joe**
I: 11092
IJ: 11091

**Montessori, Maria**
I: 11254
IJ: 11255

**Montgomery, Alabama**
PI: 10432
I: 10431

**Montgomery bus boycott**
I: 13257

**Months**
*See also* Calendars; Seasons

**Months — Fiction**
P: 3468, 3608, 3642, 3674

**Months — Poetry**
P: 3716, 9879

**Monticello (Va.)**
PI: 13505
I: 13473, 13503

**Moon**
P: 576, 14695, 14698–99, 14758
PI: 14694, 14696–97, 14701, 14704, 16666
I: 14702–3, 14705, 14738, 16638
IJ: 16670

**Moon — Experiments and projects**
I: 14700

**Moon — Fiction**
P: 424, 466, 551, 811–12, 970, 1003, 1271, 1307, 1313, 1371, 1374, 2183, 3543, 3695, 3702, 3826, 5067, 5080
PI: 5724, 6585, 8586
I: 6636

**Moon — Folklore**
P: 9118, 9192
PI: 8614, 8744

**Moons**
PI: 14745
IJ: 14753

**Moore, Henry**
PI: 10099

**Moose — Fiction**
P: 1359, 1363, 1834, 1886, 1987, 4304, 4338, 4447, 5439

**Moral education**
P: 2403

**Moray eels**
PI: 15639

**Mormons — Biography**
I: 10576

**Morocco**
PI: 12134
I: 12129

**Morris, Samuel**
I: 11256

**Morrison, Toni**
I: 10269

**Mosaics**
IJ: 11339

**Moses, Grandma**
IJ: 10100

**Moses (Bible)**
P: 13860, 13863, 13869
PI: 13851
IJ: 13834

**Mosques**
I: 12530

**Mosquitoes — Fiction**
P: 3475

**Mosquitoes — Folklore**
P: 8677

**Moss, Cynthia**
I: 10886

**Mother Goose**
*See also* Nursery rhymes
P: 2, 603–4, 607, 609, 613, 617, 622,
634, 642–43, 645–59, 663, 665–66,
669, 671, 675, 679–80, 1528,
11535, 11592
PI: 660

**Mothers**
P: 2969, 3038

**Mothers — Fiction**
P: 3082, 3108

**Mother's Day — Fiction**
P: 4602
PI: 6113

**Moths**
P: 15581, 15583–84
I: 15561, 15566, 15579
IJ: 15585

**Motion (physics)**
PI: 16531, 16540
I: 16520, 16527, 16536
IJ: 16537

**Motion (physics) —**
**Experiments and projects**
PI: 16515
IJ: 16533

**Motion pictures**
*See also* Animation (motion
pictures)
PI: 16869
I: 10065, 10175, 10866–67, 16872
IJ: 10063, 10510, 11655, 16870
All: 16874

**Motion pictures — Biography**
PI: 10343
I: 10208

**Motion pictures — Careers**
PI: 14207

**Motion pictures — Directors —**
**Biography**
IJ: 10209

**Motion pictures — Fiction**
IJ: 6442

**Motion pictures — History**
I: 11656, 11658
IJ: 11659, 12064

**Motorcycles — Fiction**
PI: 8002
I: 8416

**Mount, William Sidney**
I: 10101

**Mount Everest**
PI: 17508
I: 10003, 17491
IJ: 10004

**Mount Rushmore (S.D.)**
I: 13271

**Mount St. Helens (Wash.)**
PI: 16154

**Mount Vernon (Va.)**
I: 13504

**Mountain and rock climbing**
PI: 17508
I: 17491

**Mountain animals**
P: 16278

**Mountain biking**
I: 17591
IJ: 17585

**Mountain goats**
PI: 15305

**Mountain States (U.S.)**
*See* specific states, e.g.,
Colorado

**Mountaineering — Biography**
I: 10003
IJ: 10004

**Mountains**
P: 16278, 16285
PI: 15479, 16145, 16275, 16280,
16283
I: 16281, 16286
IJ: 16112, 16276–77, 16282, 16284

**Mountains — Animals**
P: 15103
PI: 16279

**Mountains — Fiction**
P: 3385, 3675, 3706
I: 5623, 6185

**Mourning, Alonzo**
I: 11052
IJ: 11051

**Moving — Fiction**
P: 1507, 2207, 2394, 2409, 2577,
2875, 3168, 3471, 4021, 4031,
4043, 4107, 5159, 5255, 5357
PI: 6071, 6880, 7271, 8021, 8083
I: 5518, 5849, 6104, 6971, 7047,
7245, 7846, 8070, 8142

IJ: 5570, 5943, 6118, 6171, 6199,
6201, 7106, 7182

**Mozambique — Fiction**
I: 7418

**Mozart, Wolfgang Amadeus**
P: 10144
PI: 10142–43
IJ: 10145

**Mud — Fiction**
P: 3680

**Mugabe, Robert**
IJ: 11257

**Muir, John**
PI: 10887, 10889–90
I: 10891
IJ: 10798, 10888

**Mules — Fiction**
P: 1354

**Mullin, Chris**
IJ: 11053

**Multiplication**
P: 16345

**Mummies**
P: 11899
PI: 11869, 11900
I: 11815, 11830, 11871, 11877,
11884, 11907
IJ: 11831, 11906, 13821

**Mummies — Fiction**
I: 6647
IJ: 6564

**Municipal government (U.S.)**
I: 13748

**Murals**
IJ: 11293

**Muscles**
P: 14495
I: 14493, 14498–99
IJ: 14491, 14494, 14500

**Muscular dystrophy — Fiction**
I: 7378

**Museums**
I: 11325, 13723, 14599
IJ: 15317

**Museums — Careers**
PI: 14195

**Museums — Fiction**
P: 1634, 1790, 2306, 2423, 4496,
5203

P = Primary; PI = Primary–Intermediate; I = Intermediate; IJ = Intermediate–Junior High

P = Primary; PI = Primary–Intermediate; I = Intermediate; IJ = Intermediate–Junior High

**National Basketball Association**
IJ: 17579

**National Civil Rights Museum**
I: 13649

**National debt**
I: 13741

**National Gallery (Washington, D.C.)**
IJ: 11359

**National Gallery (Washington, D.C.) — Fiction**
P: 1350

**National monuments (U.S.)**
I: 12790

**National Museum of American Art**
I: 11353

**National Park Service — Careers**
P: 14179

**National parks (U.S.)**
*See also* specific national parks, e.g., Yellowstone National Park
P: 13329, 13445, 13571
I: 5758, 12793, 12811, 12815, 13307, 15472
IJ: 13532

**Native Americans**
*See* Eskimos; Indians of North America; and specific Indian tribes, e.g., Arapaho Indians

**Natural disasters**
IJ: 16110, 16121

**Nature**
P: 3600
I: 17103–4
IJ: 13537, 14820, 17101

**Nature — Crafts**
P: 16987
PI: 17021
IJ: 17004

**Nature — Fiction**
P: 230, 504, 3534–35, 3646–47, 3663, 3670, 3685, 3709, 3719, 3722, 4284, 5141
PI: 3725
IJ: 5952

**Nature — Folklore**
P: 9129

**Nature — Photography**
I: 17320

**Nature — Poetry**
P: 3662, 9755, 9858, 9860, 9869, 9888, 9894
PI: 9730, 9857, 9864, 9867, 9877–78, 9885, 9890
I: 9861, 9863, 9870, 9884, 9886, 9896
IJ: 9862, 9871, 9899

**Nature study**
P: 194, 3531, 3538, 3586, 3732, 13569, 14814
PI: 10275, 14807, 14812, 14815, 14817, 14827
I: 13566, 14806, 14810–11, 14813, 14823, 14888

**Nature study — Biography**
I: 10836, 10860
IJ: 10299

**Nature study — Crafts**
I: 17005

**Nature study — Experiments and projects**
I: 14580, 14601, 17003
IJ: 14605, 14809

**Nature study — Fiction**
P: 2459, 2997, 3527, 3541, 3563, 3583, 3592, 3596, 3660, 3708, 3717
PI: 4299

**Navajo Indians**
P: 12949
PI: 12917
I: 10581, 12824, 12868, 12929–30

**Navajo Indians — Fiction**
P: 120, 1415, 2313, 3239, 3423, 3802, 3937
PI: 7246, 7551
I: 7536
IJ: 6023, 7763

**Navajo Indians — Folklore**
P: 9243
PI: 9274

**Navel**
P: 14529

**Navy, Caryn**
PI: 10892

**Nazis**
*See* Germany — History; Holocaust; World War II

**Ndebele**
IJ: 12159

**Ndebele — Art**
P: 11286

**Nebraska**
I: 13335

**Nebraska — Fiction**
I: 5740
IJ: 7784

**Needlecrafts — Fiction**
P: 2483

**Negro League baseball**
IJ: 17548

**Negro League baseball — Fiction**
PI: 8473

**Neighborhoods — Fiction**
P: 1026, 4015

**Nelson, Gaylord**
IJ: 13907

**Nepal**
I: 12296
IJ: 12273, 12286

**Neptune (planet)**
PI: 14733
I: 14717
IJ: 14727

**Nervous system**
P: 14451
PI: 14452
I: 14425, 14445
IJ: 14444, 14446, 14450

**Netherlands**
IJ: 12450

**Netherlands — Fiction**
P: 3740, 3821, 3841
I: 7468, 7474, 7888
IJ: 7885, 7894

**Netherlands — Folklore**
P: 8869

**Nevada**
I: 13326

**Nevada — Fiction**
P: 3706

**New England**
*See also* specific states, e.g., Massachusetts
IJ: 13348

P = Primary; PI = Primary–Intermediate; I = Intermediate; IJ = Intermediate–Junior High

**New England — Fiction**
P: 3827, 4731, 4754
PI: 8042
I: 5490
IJ: 6084

**New Hampshire**
PI: 13366
I: 13355, 13394

**New Hampshire — Fiction**
I: 6108, 7899
IJ: 7614

**New Hampshire Colony**
I: 13000

**New Jersey**
PI: 13367
I: 13372
IJ: 13349

**New Jersey — Fiction**
PI: 7600
I: 6155, 6824, 7984, 8148
IJ: 8157

**New Jersey — History**
PI: 13414

**New Jersey Colony**
IJ: 13001

**New Kids on the Block (rock group)**
IJ: 10190

**New Market, Battle of**
IJ: 13183

**New Mexico**
PI: 12866, 13526
I: 13518, 13522

**New Mexico — Fiction**
IJ: 6090

**New Mexico — History**
I: 13114

**New Orleans, Louisiana**
PI: 13499

**New Orleans, Louisiana — Fiction**
P: 3907

**New Year's Day**
PI: 13897

**New Year's Day — Fiction**
PI: 4605

**New Year's Eve — Fiction**
P: 4630

**New York City**
P: 2739, 3941
PI: 80, 13242, 13382, 13396, 13407
I: 13345, 13357, 13381, 13387, 13409
IJ: 13359, 13404, 13753, 16775

**New York City — Fiction**
P: 875, 1178, 1217, 1475, 1576, 2205, 2306, 2590, 2750, 2778, 2845, 2994, 3198, 3208, 3220, 3439, 3471, 3943, 4594
PI: 2101, 3748, 3778, 6004, 6349, 7774, 7844, 7962, 8083, 8400
I: 1211, 5553, 5580, 6013, 6142, 6192, 6674, 6676–77, 6854, 7245, 7328, 7592, 7840, 7847, 7868, 7917, 8222
IJ: 3967, 5607, 5631, 5954, 6564, 6617, 6763, 7159, 7182, 7805, 7808

**New York City Ballet — Fiction**
PI: 14201

**New York State**
PI: 13091, 13368
I: 13412
IJ: 9193, 13349, 13393, 13405

**New York State — Fiction**
PI: 7781
I: 6452, 6454, 6868, 7105
IJ: 5563, 6453, 6455, 6457, 6977, 7106, 7569, 7629

**New York State — Folklore**
P: 9330

**New York State — History**
I: 13102
IJ: 13347

**New York State Colony**
I: 13002

**New York Zoological Park**
I: 15906

**New Zealand**
I: 12341
IJ: 12338

**New Zealand — Fiction**
PI: 5660
I: 5662
IJ: 5664

**New Zealand — Folklore**
P: 8861

**Newfoundland, Canada**
I: 12594

**Newfoundlands (dog) — Fiction**
P: 4342

**Newspapers**
P: 11463
PI: 14196
IJ: 11449

**Newspapers — Biography**
PI: 10468

**Newspapers — Fiction**
P: 1838, 2684
I: 8086
IJ: 8207

**Newton, Isaac**
I: 10893
IJ: 10894

**Newton, John**
IJ: 10560, 11512

**Newton, John — Fiction**
I: 7634

**Newts**
I: 14911

**Nez Perce Indians**
P: 12950
PI: 12918

**Ngoni**
IJ: 12155

**Nicaragua**
IJ: 12653, 12662

**Nicaragua — Fiction**
I: 7533

**Nicaragua — Folklore**
I: 9404

**Nice, Margaret Morse**
PI: 10895
I: 10896

**Nigeria**
P: 90
PI: 12190
I: 12182
IJ: 12166, 12186, 12189, 12195

**Nigeria — Fiction**
P: 3924–25
I: 7426

**Nigeria — Folklore**
P: 8699, 8722
PI: 8687, 8728

P = Primary; PI = Primary–Intermediate; I = Intermediate; IJ = Intermediate–Junior High

**Night**
P: 3681
I: 14845

**Night — Fiction**
P: 486, 1538, 2472, 2566, 2576, 3730, 4411

**Night — Poetry**
P: 2698, 9880
PI: 9660

**Nightingale, Florence**
P: 11259

**Nightingales — Fiction**
PI: 8482

**Nile River — Fiction**
P: 1570

**Nimoy, Leonard**
I: 10191

**Nitrogen**
I: 16103

**Nixon, Richard M.**
I: 10337
IJ: 10690, 13258

**Noah (Bible)**
P: 3382, 4635, 13827, 13835, 13837, 13852–53, 13867, 13877, 13885
I: 13861
IJ: 14008

**Noah's Ark**
*See also* Animals — Ark;
Animals — Ark — Fiction;
Noah (Bible)
P: 1894, 13857, 13864

**Noah's Ark — Fiction**
P: 1296, 2182

**Nobel Peace Prizes**
PI: 11271–72
I: 11275
IJ: 10722, 11174, 11273

**Nobel Peace Prizes — Women**
IJ: 11182

**Nobel Prizes**
PI: 10805, 10829
I: 10800, 10843
IJ: 10847

**Noble, Sarah — Fiction**
I: 7567

**Nocturnal animals**
P: 15029

PI: 14901
I: 14845

**Nocturnal animals — Fiction**
P: 4208

**Nomo, Hideo**
I: 10996

**Normandy, Duke of**
IJ: 12429

**North, Sterling — Fiction**
IJ: 5952

**North America**
IJ: 11673, 11844

**North America — Discovery and exploration**
I: 12987

**North America — Folklore,**
9183–9392

**North Carolina**
PI: 13478
I: 13506

**North Carolina — Fiction**
PI: 2686

**North Dakota**
PI: 13341
I: 13321

**North Dakota — History**
IJ: 12850

**North Pole**
*See also* Arctic; Polar regions
I: 10016

**North Pole — Biography**
PI: 9956

**North Sea**
I: 15781

**Northeast (U.S.)**
PI: 13373
IJ: 13379

**Northern Ireland**
*See* Ireland, Northern

**Northern lights**
I: 14675
IJ: 16499

**Northern lights — Fiction**
P: 1015

**Northwest Passage**
IJ: 12582

**Northwest Territories, Canada**
I: 12587

**Norway**
I: 12495, 12499

**Norway — Fiction**
P: 3789
I: 7878

**Norway — Folklore**
P: 9113–16, 9120–23, 9126
PI: 9124, 9500
I: 9117, 9119, 9503

**Norway — Mythology**
I: 9501–2, 9937

**Noses — Fiction**
IJ: 6391

**Nova Scotia**
PI: 14312
I: 12608

**Nuclear energy**
I: 16546–47
IJ: 16549

**Nuclear power plants**
I: 16548

**Nuclear power plants — Accidents**
I: 14352

**Nuclear weapons — Fiction**
P: 1219

**Nudibranch**
PI: 15648

**Numbers**
*See also* Counting books;
Mathematics; Statistics
P: 354, 16380
PI: 16373, 16377, 16379, 16381–82
I: 16338, 16374
IJ: 16375, 16378

**Numbers — Fiction**
P: 349

**Numbers — Poetry**
PI: 9568

**Nunavut**
I: 12592

**Nursery rhymes**
*See also* Mother Goose; Poetry
P: 316–17, 337, 602–22, 624–39, 641–59, 661–67, 669–80, 909, 9634, 11592
PI: 623, 640, 660, 668

P = Primary; PI = Primary–Intermediate; I = Intermediate; IJ = Intermediate–Junior High

**Nursery schools — Fiction**
P: 4504

**Nurses — Biography**
P: 11259
PI: 10731
I: 10871
IJ: 10732

**Nurses — Careers**
P: 14213
PI: 14220

**Nurses — Fiction**
P: 2204

**Nursing homes — Fiction**
P: 4044
PI: 6207, 6935

*Nutcracker* (ballet)
P: 2568, 4706, 5177
PI: 11634

**Nutrition**
P: 2422, 14433, 14437, 16001
PI: 14515
I: 8147, 14513, 15999, 16005, 17229, 17240
IJ: 14511, 15998, 16006–9

# O

**Oak trees**
P: 3870, 16045

**Oakley, Annie**
P: 10769–71

**Oakley, Annie — Fiction**
IJ: 7807

**Obesity**
IJ: 14511

**Obesity — Fiction**
P: 1942
I: 6827, 7104, 7309, 8212

**Occupations and work**
*See also* Careers; and specific occupations, e.g., Automobile mechanics
IJ: 14183

**Occupations and work — Fiction**
P: 2173, 2411, 2533, 2719, 2808, 2874, 3065, 3124, 5290
I: 6079, 6165
IJ: 7621

**Oceanography**
P: 15765, 15769, 15786
PI: 15766, 15771–72
I: 15767, 15773–74, 15781, 15795, 15798
IJ: 15768, 15778, 15791

**Oceanography — Careers**
P: 14242

**Oceans**
*See also* Beaches; Marine animals; Oceanography; Seashores; and specific oceans, e.g., Atlantic Ocean
P: 3621, 15796
PI: 15782, 15787, 15789
I: 13610, 15770, 15775, 15784, 15788, 15790, 15794, 15797
IJ: 13608, 13613, 14626, 15779, 15785, 15792

**Oceans — Experiments and projects**
IJ: 15793

**Oceans — Fiction**
P: 785, 803, 815, 899, 1267, 2206, 3704, 3713, 5200
I: 5795, 6497
IJ: 5770

**Oceans — Folklore**
P: 9121
I: 8860

**Oceans — Nursery rhymes**
P: 635

**Oceans — Plants**
I: 16078

**Oceans — Poetry**
PI: 9898

**O'Connor, Sandra Day**
PI: 10766
I: 10765, 10767
IJ: 10768

**Octopuses**
P: 15691–92
IJ: 15690

**Octopuses — Fiction**
P: 1821, 2128, 2206
I: 6193

*Odyssey* (mythology)
I: 9456

**Oglala Sioux Indians — Biography**
IJ: 10597

**Oglala Sioux Indians — Folklore**
P: 9300

**O'Grady, Scott**
IJ: 10013

**Ogres**
PI: 891

**Ohio**
PI: 13279
I: 13268, 13284

**Ohio — Fiction**
PI: 7172, 7929
I: 7821

**Ohio — History**
I: 13305

**Ohio River**
PI: 16295

**Oil**
I: 13519

**Oil drilling — Fiction**
I: 7846

**Oil rigs**
P: 16890
PI: 16545

**Oil spills**
P: 13612
IJ: 13608, 13613, 13627

**Oil spills — Fiction**
P: 3604, 4409

**Ojibwa Indians**
*See* Chippewa Indians

**O'Keeffe, Georgia**
PI: 10104
I: 10103
IJ: 10102

**Oklahoma**
I: 13288, 16310

**Oklahoma — Fiction**
I: 7554, 7833
IJ: 5946, 6201

**Oklahoma — History**
I: 12822

**Oklahoma City bombing (1995)**
I: 13289, 13294

**Olajuwon, Hakeem**
I: 11058, 11060–61
IJ: 11059

P = Primary; PI = Primary–Intermediate; I = Intermediate; IJ = Intermediate–Junior High

*Old Ironsides* (ship) — **Fiction**
I: 7658

**Older readers — Fiction,**
5446–8480

**Olmos, Edward James**
PI: 10193
IJ: 10192

**Olmsted, Frederick Law**
I: 10561

**Olympic Games**
P: 11128, 17654
PI: 11129, 17648–49
I: 11122–24, 11130–31, 11168, 11173, 17647, 17650, 17652, 17656
IJ: 11127, 17651, 17653, 17655, 17657

**O'Malley, Grania**
P: 10014

**Onassis, Jacqueline Kennedy**
I: 10772

**O'Neal, Shaquille**
PI: 11056
I: 11054–55
IJ: 11057

**Oneida Indians**
P: 12839

**Online services**
I: 16821

**Onondaga Indians**
P: 12840

**Ontario, Canada**
I: 12602

**Ontario, Lake**
PI: 13261

**Opera**
I: 10201
IJ: 11488, 11492

**Opera — Fiction**
P: 1734, 4809
PI: 7820

**Opera — Plots**
IJ: 11489

**Opera houses — Fiction**
I: 5642

**Opossums — Fiction**
P: 1628, 1667, 2187
I: 6078

**Opposites**
*See* Concept books — Opposites

**Optical illusions**
P: 16600
PI: 16599
I: 16601, 16604–7

**Optics**
IJ: 16559, 16569

**Optics — Experiments and projects**
IJ: 16602–3, 16608

**Orangutans**
PI: 15146
I: 10851, 15145

**Orangutans — Fiction**
P: 1962

**Orchestras**
PI: 11575
I: 11569
IJ: 11571

**Orchestras — Fiction**
P: 1733, 2596, 2951

**Orchids**
PI: 16082

**Oregon**
PI: 13433
I: 13423, 13458
IJ: 13457

**Oregon — Fiction**
P: 2349
I: 7999
IJ: 5940

**Oregon — History**
I: 13464

**Oregon — Poetry**
I: 9587

**Oregon Territory — Fiction**
I: 7734

**Oregon Trail**
PI: 13132, 13148
I: 13173
IJ: 13124

**Oregon Trail — Fiction**
PI: 7691
I: 7683–84, 7739, 7751

**Organ transplants**
IJ: 14293

**Origami**
PI: 17149
I: 12258, 17143, 17162

**Orion (constellation)**
I: 14769

**Orkney Islands**
I: 12411

**Ornithology — Biography**
PI: 10895

**Orphan train**
I: 12814

**Orphans — Fiction**
P: 3518, 4845, 8540
PI: 4751, 6512
I: 6060–61, 6223, 6374, 7093, 7109, 7553, 7689, 7772, 8037
IJ: 6140, 6544, 7253, 7397, 7647, 7673, 7784

**Orphans — Folklore**
P: 8730
PI: 9230

**Orpheus (mythology)**
PI: 8822

**Osceola (Seminole chief)**
PI: 12951
I: 10588

**Ospreys**
IJ: 15421

**Ostriches**
PI: 15342, 15353
I: 15308

**Ostriches — Fiction**
P: 2011, 3380
I: 5904

**Ostriches — Folklore**
I: 8688

**Ottawa Indians**
I: 12878

**Otters**
P: 3635, 4202, 15693, 15698
PI: 15704
I: 15643

**Otters — Fiction**
P: 472, 4366, 5063, 5174
PI: 5108

**Outer space — Fiction**
P: 1003, 1198, 1311

P = Primary; PI = Primary–Intermediate; I = Intermediate; IJ = Intermediate–Junior High

**Outer space — Jokes and riddles**
P: 17350, 17353

**Outward Bound schools**
I: 17598

**Overprotection — Fiction**
I: 6806

**Owens, Jesse**
P: 11128
PI: 11129
I: 11130–31

**Owls**
P: 15423, 15425, 15430, 15433
PI: 15427, 15429
I: 15424, 15426, 15428, 15431
IJ: 15432

**Owls — Fiction**
P: 800, 1056, 1061, 1525, 1538, 1722, 1736, 2181, 2217, 4371, 4485, 5174, 5261
PI: 5866

**Owls — Poetry**
P: 9811–12
IJ: 9733

**Oxen — Folklore**
P: 8773
PI: 9348
I: 9360, 9369

**Oxygen**
I: 14458, 16394
IJ: 14456

**Ozarks — Fiction**
P: 2474, 3161

**Ozawa, Seiji**
IJ: 10194

**Ozone layer**
P: 13632
IJ: 13623, 13628

# P

**Pachciarz, Judith**
PI: 10897

**Pacific Northwest**
*See* Pacific states (U.S.)

**Pacific Ocean**
PI: 15772
I: 15777

**Pacific Ocean — Islands**
IJ: 12346

**Pacific Ocean — Islands — Fiction**
P: 3854

**Pacific Ocean — World War II**
I: 12069
IJ: 12026–27, 12030–31

**Pacific states (U.S.)**
*See also* specific states, e.g., Oregon
P: 355
I: 12823, 13434, 13437

**Pacific states (U.S.) — Animals**
P: 41

**Pacific states (U.S.) — Fiction**
P: 1065

**Pacifists and pacifism**
IJ: 8625, 11174

**Pacifists and pacifism — Biography**
I: 11175

**Pacifists and pacifism — Fiction**
I: 8386
IJ: 7752, 7866

**Packaging**
IJ: 13553

**Paige, Satchel**
PI: 10998
I: 10997

**Painters — Biography**
PI: 10073, 10080–81, 10087, 10098, 10110, 10114
I: 10078, 10085
IJ: 10048, 10054, 10060, 10074, 10076, 10100, 10102, 10113, 10130

**Painting**
*See* Drawing and painting

**Paiute Indians — Biography**
PI: 10614

**Pakistan**
IJ: 12243, 12311–12, 12318, 12330

**Paleontology,** 11693–11793
*See also* Dinosaurs; Fossils; Prehistoric animals
P: 3673, 11774
PI: 11738, 11757

I: 11716, 11719, 11721, 11733, 11746–47, 11750, 11752, 11760, 11767, 11770–71, 11787, 11812
IJ: 11724–25, 11745, 11773, 11779, 11784–85

**Paleontology — Biography**
I: 10868

**Paleontology — Careers**
P: 14241
PI: 14195

**Paleontology — Fiction**
P: 4209
I: 5503–4, 7659
IJ: 7504

**Palestine**
I: 12569

**Palestine — Fiction**
I: 7884

**Palestinian Americans**
I: 12569

**Palestinians**
IJ: 12560

**Palestinians — Fiction**
P: 3922

**Palindromes**
I: 11413, 11443, 17406

**Panama**
PI: 12670
I: 12661, 12669
IJ: 12672, 12681

**Panama — Fiction**
P: 3903, 3927

**Panama Canal**
IJ: 12681–82

**Panama Canal — Fiction**
I: 7527

**Pandas**
P: 15286, 15288
PI: 15289
I: 15285
IJ: 15287

**Pandas — Fiction**
P: 242, 1841
I: 5971

**Pandora's box (mythology)**
P: 2241

**Panthers**
IJ: 15215

P = Primary; PI = Primary–Intermediate; I = Intermediate; IJ = Intermediate–Junior High

**Pantomime — Fiction**
P: 862

**Papago Indians**
PI: 12821

**Paper**
P: 16697
PI: 16679
IJ: 16705

**Paper — Fiction**
P: 2506

**Paper crafts**
P: 17166
PI: 17149, 17155, 17164, 17167
I: 10215, 11462, 17143–44,
17147–48, 17151, 17154,
17156–58, 17160–62, 17168,
17170–72
IJ: 17146, 17150, 17152–53, 17159,
17163, 17178

**Papermaking — Fiction**
P: 3942

**Papier-mâché**
PI: 17149
I: 17160–61

**Parades — Fiction**
P: 2454, 4433
PI: 5669
IJ: 7961

**Paraguay**
IJ: 12704, 12721

**Parakeets — Fiction**
P: 5376

**Parasites**
I: 14846, 14867

**Paris, France**
P: 12392
I: 12395

**Paris, France — Fiction**
P: 1411, 1560, 1571, 1797, 3374,
3752, 3818–19, 3866, 3892
PI: 1774, 6821

**Parker, Charlie**
P: 2695

**Parker, Quanah (Comanche
chief)**
I: 10589

**Parkman, Francis**
IJ: 13171

**Parks**
P: 4016, 13571

**Parks — Fiction**
P: 1704, 2064, 3467
I: 6837

**Parks, Rosa**
PI: 10429–30, 10432–34
I: 10431, 13670

**Parrish, Maxfield**
I: 11354

**Parrots**
PI: 15355
I: 15335, 15365

**Parrots — Fiction**
P: 4335
I: 5576, 5627

**Parthenon (Greece)**
PI: 11915
I: 11923
IJ: 11931

**Parties**
See also Birthdays

**Parties — Fiction**
P: 1703, 1739, 3451, 3464, 5353
PI: 6860, 7198
I: 7240, 7498

**Passover**
P: 4955, 13966
PI: 13982
IJ: 13976

**Passover — Crafts**
I: 13984

**Passover — Fiction**
P: 4972, 4978–79, 4983, 4986
PI: 6080
I: 7904
IJ: 7862

**Passover — Poetry**
P: 4975

**Pasta**
P: 2626, 15955, 15974, 15978
PI: 16676

**Pasteur, Louis**
PI: 10899
IJ: 10898, 10900–1

**Paterson, Katherine**
IJ: 10271

**Patrick, Saint**
P: 11260

**Patton, George**
I: 10562

**Patuxent River (Md.)**
IJ: 13626

**Pauling, Linus**
IJ: 10902

**Pavlova, Anna**
IJ: 10195

**Pawnee Indians**
I: 12858, 12913

**Pawnee Indians — Folklore**
P: 9206

**Pawnee Indians — History**
P: 12847

**Peace**
See also Pacifists and pacifism
I: 13644

**Peace — Fiction**
I: 8386

**Peace — Folklore**
IJ: 8625

**Peace — Poetry**
I: 9629

**Peace — Songs**
I: 11602

**Peaches — Fiction**
PI: 6345

**Peaches — Folklore**
P: 8828, 8886

**Peacocks**
PI: 15313

**Peale, Charles Willson**
IJ: 10105

**Peanut butter**
IJ: 17254

**Peanuts**
P: 15968

**Pearl Harbor — Fiction**
I: 7874

**Pearl Harbor — History**
I: 12049
IJ: 12033, 12073, 12076

**Peary, Robert E.**
PI: 9956
I: 10016
IJ: 9951, 10015

**Peet, Bill**
PI: 10106

P = Primary; PI = Primary–Intermediate; I = Intermediate; IJ = Intermediate–Junior High

P = Primary; PI = Primary–Intermediate; I = Intermediate; IJ = Intermediate–Junior High

P = Primary; PI = Primary–Intermediate; I = Intermediate; IJ = Intermediate–Junior High

I: 11841, 11847, 11850
IJ: 11852, 11854

**Pirates — Biography**
P: 10014
PI: 9961
IJ: 9998

**Pirates — Fiction**
P: 1080, 1082, 1827, 2312, 2365, 3241, 5137, 5212
PI: 5753, 5820
I: 5661, 7627
IJ: 5467, 5590, 6484, 8039

**Pizarro, Gonzalo**
I: 10018

**Pizza**
P: 15967, 17255

**Plagues**
IJ: 11967

**Plagues — Fiction**
IJ: 7507

**Plains Indians**
I: 12900

**Plains Indians — Fiction**
P: 934

**Plains Indians — Folklore**
P: 9220, 9224, 9226, 9228, 9275
I: 9219
IJ: 9231

**Plains Indians — History**
P: 12847
I: 12849

**Plains (U.S.)**
*See also* specific states, e.g., Nebraska

**Plains (U.S.) — History — Fiction**
I: 7838

**Planetariums**
P: 16631

**Planets**
*See also* specific planets, e.g., Mars (planet)
P: 14710, 14713, 14720, 14755
PI: 14708, 14733–36, 16656
I: 14670, 14692, 14715, 14721, 14731–32, 14781, 16630
IJ: 14711, 14719, 14748

**Planets — Fiction**
P: 825

**Plantation life**
I: 13078, 13095, 13097

**Plants**
*See also* specific plants, e.g., Cactus
P: 3744, 15928, 15997, 16055, 16077, 16087, 16098
PI: 10827, 16071, 16086
I: 16060–61, 16065, 16072, 16075, 16091
IJ: 14821, 16053, 16058, 16062, 16066, 16068, 16083, 16085, 16088–90

**Plants — Crafts**
I: 16067

**Plants — Experiments and projects**
P: 14638
PI: 16059
I: 16054, 16056, 16093

**Plants — Fiction**
P: 789, 1479, 3711, 8516, 15946

**Plants — Folklore**
P: 9003, 9008
I: 8983
IJ: 9204

**Plants — Life cycles**
P: 14818

**Plants — Medicine**
I: 16063

**Plants — Oceans**
I: 16078

**Plants, Poisonous**
I: 16063

**Plastics**
PI: 16674

**Plastics — Experiments and projects**
I: 16694

**Plate tectonics**
IJ: 16133

**Platypuses**
PI: 15132

**Play — Fiction**
P: 2660

**Playgrounds — Fiction**
P: 2688

**Plays**
*See also* Theater
P: 5145, 6006

PI: 5756, 5817, 9916–18, 9927
I: 7173, 7912, 7941, 7953, 8240, 9919, 9928–29, 9937
IJ: 7908, 9921, 9925, 9934, 9936, 11666

**Plays — Anthologies**
PI: 9914, 9926
I: 9913, 9915, 9930–33, 9938
IJ: 9920, 9923
All: 9924

**Plays — Multiculturalism**
P: 9922

**Plays — Production**
P: 17192
I: 11453
IJ: 11664

**Plays — Shakespeare**
I: 9944
IJ: 9939–43

**Pledge of Allegiance**
P: 5427

**Plotkin, Mark**
IJ: 10904

**Plumbing**
I: 14510
IJ: 16794

**Pluto (planet)**
PI: 14734

**Plymouth Colony — Fiction**
P: 5012

**Poarch Creek Indians — Fiction**
PI: 9245

**Pocahontas**
P: 10596
PI: 10592
I: 10593, 10595
IJ: 10594

**Poetry**
*See also* Nursery rhymes; as a subdivision of other subjects, e.g., Animals — Poetry; and as subdivision of countries or ethnic groups, e.g., England — Poetry
P: 29, 134, 226, 291, 340, 404, 406, 491, 815, 1026, 1217, 1299, 1314, 1614, 2631, 3229, 3716, 5242, 9515, 9518, 9526, 9536, 9539, 9556, 9569, 9573, 9588, 9599, 9608–9, 9617, 9620, 9622, 9634,

P = Primary; PI = Primary–Intermediate; I = Intermediate; IJ = Intermediate–Junior High

9638, 9652, 9655, 9658, 9664, 9674, 9677, 9683, 9691, 9725
PI: 1040, 3691, 9511, 9513, 9524, 9533, 9544, 9548, 9551, 9586, 9590, 9600, 9613, 9618, 9631, 9643, 9649, 9654, 9656–57, 9666, 9673, 9692, 9707
I: 6474, 9506–7, 9531, 9534–35, 9559, 9587, 9593–95, 9625, 9636, 9640, 9644–45, 9650–51, 9671, 9676, 9678, 9680, 9743
IJ: 9514, 9517, 9545–46, 9554, 9598, 9616, 9624, 9637, 9639, 9641, 9661, 9667, 9672, 9757, 14008
All: 9522

**Poetry — Animals**
P: 9722
I: 9741

**Poetry — Anthologies**
P: 9538, 9543, 9552, 9561–62, 9564, 9566, 9572, 9581, 9627, 9630, 9632, 9663, 9696, 9751, 9755, 9766–67, 9843
PI: 9519, 9527, 9532, 9547, 9571, 9585, 9626, 9768, 9770–71, 9797, 9832, 9903
I: 9512, 9530, 9540, 9555, 9558, 9560, 9565, 9580, 9583, 9591, 9628, 9659, 9662, 9669, 9684, 9732, 9762, 9764, 9772, 9872, 9907, 9910, 11467
IJ: 9537, 9567, 9575, 9592, 9602–4, 9668, 9733, 9788, 9820, 9851, 9862, 9871

**Poetry — Humorous**
P: 900, 3329, 3349, 3443, 9521, 9721, 9735, 9748, 9786, 9789–90, 9792, 9804, 9807, 9809–14, 9816–17, 9823–26, 9828, 9830–31, 9833, 9835–36, 9841, 9843, 9845–46, 9848, 9912
PI: 9712, 9731, 9785, 9794, 9796–97, 9799, 9801–3, 9806, 9815, 9818–19, 9821, 9829, 9832, 9837, 9839–40, 9842, 9847
I: 9769, 9784, 9787, 9791, 9793, 9795, 9798, 9800, 9805, 9808, 9822, 9834, 9838, 9844
IJ: 9788, 9820

**Poetry — Spanish**
PI: 9523

**Poetry — Women**
PI: 9547

**POGS**
I: 17516

**Poison dart frogs**
P: 14940

**Poisonous animals and plants**
P: 14940
PI: 15095
I: 16061
IJ: 15486

**Pokot**
IJ: 12121

**Poland**
I: 11282
IJ: 12372

**Poland — Cookbooks**
IJ: 17279

**Poland — Fiction**
P: 4787
I: 7498
IJ: 7481, 7883, 7887, 7898

**Polar bears**
P: 15175, 15183, 15188
PI: 15185

**Polar bears — Fiction**
P: 1555, 4286–87, 4351

**Polar regions**
P: 12746, 12775
PI: 15087
I: 12741, 12761, 12765, 12774
IJ: 9971, 12740, 12743, 12756, 12776, 16503

**Polar regions — Animals**
P: 12778, 15123, 15175, 15183, 15188

**Polar regions — Animals — Fiction**
P: 1555, 4286–87, 4351

**Police — Careers**
P: 13711, 14226
PI: 14229, 14233
I: 14231

**Police — Fiction**
P: 2595

**Police dogs**
P: 15848

**Police dogs — Fiction**
P: 4410

**Polio**
PI: 14345
I: 10871

**Polish Americans**
I: 14039

**Polish Americans — Fiction**
PI: 8219
I: 7819

**Political parties**
I: 13716, 13718

**Politicians — Biography**
I: 10563, 10773

**Polk, James K.**
I: 10336
IJ: 10693

**Pollination**
IJ: 15921, 16062

**Pollution**
P: 16333
I: 13578, 13619, 13629, 15462
IJ: 13553, 13614, 13617, 13624, 13626, 13634, 15474, 15791, 16292, 16450

**Pollution — Fiction**
P: 1311, 2122, 3552, 3656, 3671, 3700
PI: 4385
I: 5750, 6519
IJ: 8343

**Pollution, Air**
P: 13620, 13631–32
I: 13609, 13625, 13630, 16397, 16403, 16487
IJ: 16392

**Pollution, Marine**
P: 13612
I: 13610
IJ: 13608, 13613, 13627

**Pollution, Marine — Fiction**
P: 770

**Pollution, Noise**
I: 13609

**Pollution, Water**
P: 13615, 13633
PI: 13611, 13618
I: 16296, 16455
IJ: 16292

**Polo, Marco**
I: 10019

**Polynesia — Fiction**
I: 7403
IJ: 5770

**Polyphemus (mythology)**
PI: 9461

P = Primary; PI = Primary–Intermediate; I = Intermediate; IJ = Intermediate–Junior High

**Pompeii, Italy**
I: 11933, 11944

**Pompeii, Italy — Fiction**
I: 11957

**Ponce de Leon, Juan**
IJ: 10020

**Ponds**
P: 16287, 16297
PI: 16289, 16304, 16307
I: 16291, 16301, 16303, 16306
IJ: 15759, 16298

**Ponds — Fiction**
P: 3584, 3595, 3639, 3682, 4440

**Ponies**
PI: 15890

**Ponies — Fiction**
P: 5186, 5351

**Pony Express**
PI: 13115, 13135, 13151, 13177
IJ: 13179

**Poodles — Fiction**
PI: 4298

**Pool — Fiction**
I: 8404

**Pop-up books**
P: 11616
I: 10085, 11987, 11995, 17156
IJ: 14402

**Pop-up books — Fiction**
P: 466, 1579, 2304, 3751

**Popcorn**
P: 15954

**Popcorn Park Zoo**
I: 15912

**Popes — Biography**
I: 11237–38

**Popes — Folklore**
I: 8930

**Poppies**
P: 16079

**Population**
P: 13636
IJ: 13635, 13637

**Porcupines**
P: 15297
I: 15131

**Porcupines — Fiction**
P: 1846, 5174

**Porpoises**
I: 15676
IJ: 15672

**Portugal**
I: 12517
IJ: 12515, 12518, 12523

**Post, Wiley**
I: 10021

**Postal Service (U.S.)**
P: 5250, 10381, 13724, 13731
I: 13725

**Postal Service (U.S.) — Fiction**
P: 2719, 5410
PI: 2734

**Postal Service (U.S.) — History**
PI: 13540

**Postal Service (U.S.) — Poetry**
P: 9606

**Potatoes**
P: 16017

**Potatoes — Folklore**
P: 8976

**Potlatch**
I: 12865

**Potter, Beatrix**
P: 10274
I: 10272–73

**Potters and pottery**
PI: 12959, 17072
I: 17074
IJ: 11340

**Potters and pottery — Biography**
IJ: 10092

**Pout (fish)**
PI: 15687

**Poverty**
P: 2715
I: 13760
IJ: 12657, 13765, 13774

**Poverty — Fiction**
P: 3088, 3801, 4005, 4017
PI: 6145, 7002, 7185, 7238, 7251
I: 6061, 6142, 7080, 7155, 7247, 7364, 7506, 7529, 7788, 7911
IJ: 6158, 7016, 7018, 7141

**Poverty — Women**
IJ: 14065

**Powell, Colin**
PI: 10435, 10440
I: 10437
IJ: 10436, 10438–39

**Powell, John Wesley**
I: 13317
IJ: 10022

**Powers, Harriet**
IJ: 10112

**Powhatan Indians**
PI: 12893

**Powhatan Indians — Biography**
PI: 10592
I: 10593
IJ: 10594

**Powwows**
PI: 12871
I: 12817, 12825, 12833, 12873, 12928

**Powwows — Fiction**
P: 4623

**Prague — Fiction**
P: 3906

**Prairie dogs**
P: 15291–93, 15302
I: 15298

**Prairies**
PI: 16308
I: 16314

**Prairies (U.S.)**
P: 16317
I: 13264, 16310, 16321

**Prairies (U.S.) — Fiction**
P: 2345, 3897, 3972, 3975
PI: 7717
I: 7692
IJ: 7134

**Prayers**
P: 13881, 14006, 14010, 14012, 14014, 14016–18
PI: 14009, 14015
I: 14005, 14007
IJ: 14008, 14011

**Prayers — Jewish**
P: 14013

**Praying mantises**
P: 15511

**Predatory animals**
P: 15028, 15129, 15408

P = Primary; PI = Primary–Intermediate; I = Intermediate; IJ = Intermediate–Junior High

PI: 148620
IJ: 15003, 15009

**Pregnancy**
IJ: 14555

**Pregnancy — Fiction**
PI: 7122
IJ: 6989

**Pregnant teenagers**
IJ: 14555

**Prehistoric animals**
*See also* Dinosaurs; Mammoths
P: 11731, 11762, 11793
PI: 11789
I: 11704, 11709, 11790, 17120
IJ: 11759, 11816

**Prehistoric animals — Defenses**
PI: 11783

**Prehistoric animals — Fiction**
P: 708, 5043

**Prehistoric life**
IJ: 11807

**Prehistoric peoples**
PI: 11798, 11811, 11817
I: 11795, 11801, 11808, 11832, 11862
IJ: 11802, 11809, 11814, 11816, 11827

**Prehistoric peoples — Fiction**
P: 1348, 3749, 3808, 5209
PI: 7408, 7414
I: 7410, 7415
IJ: 7409, 7411–12

**Prejudice**
PI: 13971
IJ: 13759

**Prejudice — Fiction**
P: 4171
PI: 4181
I: 5510, 6020, 6040
IJ: 5786, 6845

**Prepositions**
PI: 11422

**Preschool**
P: 2388

**Preschool — Fiction**
P: 4493

**Presidents Day (U.S.)**
PI: 13923

**Presidents (Mexico) — Biography**
PI: 11240
I: 11239

**Presidents (U.S.)**
PI: 12798
I: 11465, 13721, 13743
IJ: 12795, 13107–8, 13209, 13235–36, 13254

**Presidents (U.S.) — Biography**
*See also* individual presidents, e.g., Clinton, Bill
P: 10623, 10653, 10670, 10672, 10677–78, 10680–81, 10695, 10714–15
PI: 10616, 10631–32, 10654, 10656, 10664, 10666–67, 10673, 10675, 10682, 10702, 10704, 10719
I: 10313, 10334–38, 10615, 10617–18, 10620–22, 10624–25, 10629, 10633, 10635–37, 10640, 10643, 10645–46, 10648, 10650, 10652, 10655, 10657, 10659–60, 10665, 10669, 10671, 10676, 10686, 10688–89, 10692, 10694, 10701, 10706–7, 10710, 10717, 10738, 12800
IJ: 10344, 10347, 10353, 10619, 10626–28, 10630, 10634, 10638–39, 10641–42, 10644, 10647, 10649, 10651, 10658, 10661–63, 10668, 10674, 10679, 10683–85, 10687, 10690–91, 10693, 10696–700, 10703, 10705, 10708–9, 10711–13, 10716, 10718, 10720–23

**Presidents (U.S.) — Children**
I: 10314

**Presidents (U.S.) — Elections**
I: 13728
IJ: 13713

**Presidents (U.S.) — Fiction**
P: 1448
I: 8047, 8061

**Presidents (U.S.) — Wives — Biography**
P: 10774–75
PI: 10632, 10739, 10742
I: 10323, 10621, 10689, 10737, 10741, 10743, 10772, 10778, 10781, 10792
IJ: 10626, 10740, 10754, 10776–77, 10779–80

**Presley, Elvis**
IJ: 10199–200

**Price, Leontyne**
I: 10201

**Prime ministers (Great Britain) — Biography**
IJ: 11203, 11276

**Prime ministers (Zimbabwe) — Biography**
IJ: 11257

**Prince Edward Island, Canada**
I: 12583

**Prince Edward Island, Canada — Fiction**
PI: 4247

**Princes — Fiction**
P: 559, 1668, 8510, 8529, 8545, 8560
PI: 4848, 8549, 8579
I: 6591, 6604, 6657, 8548, 8550, 8594
IJ: 5550

**Princes — Folklore**
P: 8897, 8913, 8927–28, 9110
PI: 8739, 9088

**Princesses — Biography**
I: 11199, 11214, 11241

**Princesses — Fiction**
P: 1088, 1222, 1244, 1287, 8504, 8512, 8523
PI: 8549
I: 6061, 6554, 6807, 8524, 8548, 8550
IJ: 6277, 6564, 6695

**Princesses — Folklore**
P: 8670, 8753, 8786, 8799, 8886, 8919, 9004
PI: 8606, 8908, 8931, 8949

**Pringle, Laurence**
P: 12061
PI: 10275

**Printers — Biography**
PI: 10862
I: 10861, 10863

**Printing**
*See* Books and printing

**Printmaking**
I: 11306, 17173

**Prisons**
IJ: 13691, 13706

**Prisons — Fiction**
P: 2831
PI: 4073, 7320
I: 7147

---

P = Primary; PI = Primary–Intermediate; I = Intermediate; IJ = Intermediate–Junior High

**Private schools — Fiction**
I: 8261
IJ: 8122

**Pro Football Hall of Fame**
I: 17609

**Probability**
I: 16383

**Prohibition (U.S.)**
I: 13219

**Pronouns**
PI: 11426

**Proteins**
I: 16000
IJ: 16008

**Protestantism**
P: 13813

**Proverbs**
P: 8619

**Proverbs — Fiction**
I: 6719

**Proverbs — Spanish**
PI: 11421

**Psalms (Bible)**
P: 13872–73, 13882
I: 13828, 13845

**Psychic powers — Fiction**
I: 6081
IJ: 7345

**Psychology**
I: 14093, 14102
IJ: 14110

**Pterosaurs**
IJ: 11703

**Puberty**
I: 14103, 14542, 14550, 14556

**Public speaking**
IJ: 11459, 11475

**Publishers and publishing**
P: 11384, 11463
I: 11391
IJ: 11398

**Publishers and publishing —
Biography**
IJ: 10225, 10390

**Puckett, Kirby**
PI: 10999

**Pueblo Indians**
P: 12910, 13332

PI: 12827, 12959
I: 12872, 12899, 12925
IJ: 12831

**Pueblo Indians — Biography**
PI: 10091

**Pueblo Indians — Fiction**
PI: 3889
I: 7537

**Pueblo Indians — Folklore**
P: 9281
PI: 9254

**Pueblo Indians — History**
P: 12923
IJ: 12819, 12963

**Puerto Rican Americans**
I: 14076
IJ: 14019

**Puerto Rican Americans —
Biography**
PI: 10472, 10970
I: 10968, 10971
IJ: 10969

**Puerto Rican Americans —
Fiction**
PI: 5995
I: 7063

**Puerto Rico**
I: 12680, 12683
IJ: 10559

**Puerto Rico — Fiction**
P: 984, 1112, 3042, 3784
PI: 7531
IJ: 7523

**Puerto Rico — Folklore**
P: 9422, 9426, 9428–29

**Puffins**
P: 15443
PI: 15331, 15419
I: 15418

**Puffins — Fiction**
P: 5074

**Pulaski, Casimir**
IJ: 11261

**Pumpkins**
P: 16015
I: 17010

**Pumpkins — Crafts**
IJ: 17027

**Pumpkins — Fiction**
P: 3505, 4906, 4909, 4912, 4920,
4923
PI: 1171

**Puppets and marionettes**
P: 11649, 11653
PI: 11651, 11654
I: 11650, 11652

**Puppets and marionettes —
Biography**
IJ: 10182

**Puppets and marionettes —
Fiction**
P: 1389, 4086
PI: 6315, 8052
I: 6313–14, 7452

**Purim**
P: 4956

**Purim — Fiction**
P: 4976, 4987, 4992

**Puritans — Fiction**
PI: 7576

**Puzzles**
*See also* Games; Mathematical
puzzles; Picture puzzles;
Word games and puzzles
P: 634, 16360–61, 17403
PI: 12, 15023, 17393, 17401
I: 8647, 17395, 17398–99
IJ: 14613, 17396

**Puzzles — Fiction**
P: 248, 339, 2168, 2321, 2513, 4530
PI: 380
IJ: 8167

**Puzzles — Poetry**
I: 5481
IJ: 9661

**Pygmies**
IJ: 12092

**Pyle, Ernie**
I: 10276

**Pyramids**
P: 11878
PI: 11898
I: 11873, 11875, 11896, 11901,
11908, 12538, 16778
IJ: 11893

**Pythons**
PI: 14982

P = Primary; PI = Primary–Intermediate; I = Intermediate; IJ = Intermediate–Junior High

# Q

**Qatar**
IJ: 12559

**Qin, Emperor of China —
Tomb**
IJ: 12208

**Quakers — Fiction**
P: 5082
I: 7635
IJ: 7752

**Quebec, Canada**
I: 12591

**Queen Anne's lace**
I: 16095

**Queens — Biography**
I: 11207, 11216

**Queens — Fiction**
P: 1091, 8491, 8525
PI: 4104

**Quicksand — Fiction**
P: 3571

**Quilts**
P: 95
I: 13120, 13158, 17174
IJ: 10112

**Quilts — Fiction**
P: 996, 2582, 2884, 2909, 3058, 3122,
3792, 3961, 4687, 5114
PI: 241

**Quinn, Anthony**
IJ: 10202

**Quintanilla, Guadalupe**
IJ: 10486

**Quokka**
PI: 15283

# R

**Rabbits**
P: 15824
PI: 15816
I: 15818
IJ: 15290

**Rabbits — Fiction**
P: 33, 320, 345, 571, 573, 682–84,
812, 1299, 1379, 1395, 1403, 1433,
1441, 1462, 1464, 1502, 1647,
1663, 1709, 1752, 1814–15, 1902,
1960, 2030–31, 2034, 2049, 2072,
2085, 2121, 2124, 2135, 2161,
2165, 2177, 2238, 2241, 2259,
2290, 2754, 3328, 3575, 4118,
4363, 4381, 4404, 4471, 4654,
4690, 4862–63, 4865, 4867, 4869,
4875, 4917, 5019, 5034, 5075,
5375, 5415
PI: 2033, 6768–69
I: 1167, 5948, 6522, 8077, 8080
IJ: 6211

**Rabbits — Folklore**
P: 8671, 8676, 8722, 8814, 9055,
9339–40
I: 9337, 9357, 9449
IJ: 9338

**Rabin, Itzhak**
PI: 11262

**Raccoons**
P: 15085

**Raccoons — Fiction**
P: 3549, 4477, 4617, 5235
PI: 6312
IJ: 5844, 5934, 5952

**Racism**
IJ: 13750

**Radio — Fiction**
P: 3786
IJ: 7854, 7930

**Radio — History**
I: 16873

**Radio control models**
IJ: 17191

**Radiology**
I: 14368

**Radium**
PI: 10829
I: 10830–31

**Railroads and trains**
P: 4552, 4583, 16917–18, 16927
PI: 16880, 16922, 16931
IJ: 16921

**Railroads and trains — Fiction**
P: 72, 506, 567, 1061, 1086, 1145,
2451, 2553, 2748, 2939, 3815,
4382, 4564, 4586, 4592, 4851,
5202, 5436, 16920

PI: 5516, 7666
I: 2455

**Railroads and trains — History**
P: 16926
PI: 10785, 16916, 16928–29
I: 16919, 16930, 16932–33
IJ: 13100, 13181, 16923–25

**Railroads and trains (model)**
IJ: 17190

**Rain**
*See also* Acid rain
P: 16444, 16496
I: 16481, 16490

**Rain — Fiction**
P: 1476, 2156, 2548, 2578, 2641,
3581, 3627, 3638, 3699, 3704,
3713, 3722

**Rain — Folklore**
P: 8665

**Rain forests**
*See also* Forests
P: 3731, 3991, 16234–35, 16242
PI: 100, 9890, 16236, 16241, 16250,
16254–57, 16262, 16265, 16270
I: 12729–30, 12734–35, 16203,
16239, 16244, 16246–47, 16251,
16260–61, 16263, 16269, 16273
IJ: 10904, 16090, 16191, 16230,
16237–38, 16259

**Rain forests — Animals**
P: 16274
I: 16266

**Rain forests — Fiction**
P: 52, 3559, 3564, 3591, 3629
PI: 6239
I: 6577

**Rainbows**
PI: 16467

**Rainbows — Fiction**
P: 907

**Ramadan**
PI: 4612

**Ramayana — Folklore**
I: 8804

**Ramsay, Kathleen**
I: 10905

**Ranches and ranch life**
P: 2624
I: 10546

P = Primary; PI = Primary–Intermediate; I = Intermediate; IJ = Intermediate–Junior High

**Ranches and ranch life —
Fiction**
P: 427, 2499
PI: 3898, 5972
I: 6292, 7789
IJ: 6090, 7046

**Randolph, A. Philip**
PI: 10441
IJ: 10442

**Rap music — Fiction**
PI: 6835

**Rap musicians — Biography**
I: 10181

**Rats**
PI: 15299

**Rats — Fiction**
P: 117, 1526, 1734, 1777, 5292
I: 5736, 6316, 6674
IJ: 6317, 6402, 6467, 6608, 7239

**Rats — Folklore**
P: 8607

**Rattlesnakes**
PI: 14964
I: 14968

**Rattlesnakes — Fiction**
P: 9191

**Reading — Fiction**
P: 2438, 2677, 2828, 3233, 5116,
5225, 5249, 5396
PI: 6840
I: 6034, 7175, 7278, 8213, 8251
IJ: 8282

**Reading — Poetry**
P: 9566

**Reading Rainbow (TV
program)**
PI: 11660

**Reagan, Ronald**
P: 10695
I: 10337, 10694
IJ: 10696

**Realistic stories — Picture
books,** 2291–4599

**Rebuses**
P: 647

**Rebuses — Fiction**
P: 5356

**Recipes**
*See* Cookbooks

**Reconstruction (U.S.)**
IJ: 13225, 13231

**Recreation,** 16979–17684
IJ: 17513

**Rectangles**
PI: 16355

**Recycling, Waste**
*See* Waste recycling

**Red Cloud (Oglala Sioux chief)**
IJ: 10597

**Red Cross**
IJ: 13642

**Red Sea**
I: 15650

**Redwoods**
PI: 16042
I: 16271

**Refugees**
PI: 12275
IJ: 12124, 12581, 13643, 14044

**Refugees — Fiction**
P: 4119
I: 7856

**Reilly, Ted**
I: 15464

**Reincarnation — Fiction**
P: 3812
IJ: 6132

**Reindeer**
PI: 15252, 15257–58
I: 13935

**Reindeer — Fiction**
P: 961, 4700, 4824

**Religion**
*See also* Bible stories; Prayers;
and specific religions, e.g.,
Christianity
P: 4610, 13799, 13818
PI: 4612, 4628
I: 13778, 13788, 13803–5, 13807,
13809, 13811
IJ: 11984, 13791–92, 13815, 13821

**Religion — Fiction**
P: 3812, 4609, 13781
IJ: 7009

**Religion — History**
I: 13801
IJ: 10359, 10755, 11931

**Religion — Poetry**
I: 9680

**Rembrandt van Rijn**
PI: 10114
IJ: 10113

**Rembrandt van Rijn — Fiction**
I: 7474

**Renaissance**
I: 12002, 12004
IJ: 12005

**Renaissance — Art**
IJ: 12003

**Renaissance — Fiction**
I: 7482, 7490
IJ: 7480, 7486

**Rendille**
IJ: 12115

**Reno, Janet**
PI: 10569
I: 10567–68

**Renoir, Auguste**
PI: 10116
IJ: 10115

**Reproduction**
P: 14533–35, 14537
PI: 14538, 14541
IJ: 14540

**Reptiles**
*See also* specific reptiles, e.g.,
Alligators and crocodiles
P: 14904, 14909, 14917–18
PI: 14907, 14912–13
I: 14910, 14920
IJ: 14914

**Rescue dogs**
PI: 15863, 15868

**Respiration**
P: 14455
PI: 14461
I: 14276, 14414, 14454, 14457–58
IJ: 14456, 14459–60

**Restaurants**
P: 2493
I: 13564

**Restaurants — Fiction**
P: 2613, 2662, 2797

**Retirement — Fiction**
I: 6117

P = Primary; PI = Primary–Intermediate; I = Intermediate; IJ = Intermediate–Junior High

**Revere, Paul**
P: 10570
PI: 10571

**Revere, Paul — Fiction**
IJ: 8102

**Revere, Paul — Poetry**
P: 9601
PI: 9600

**Revolutionary War (U.S.)**
P: 10570, 10714–15, 13066
PI: 10489, 10521, 10571, 13060, 13069
I: 10319, 10717, 10764, 13054, 13058, 13062, 13065, 13071, 13074
IJ: 10572, 10716, 13052–53, 13055–57, 13059, 13061, 13063–64, 13070, 13072–73

**Revolutionary War (U.S.) — Biography**
P: 10531
PI: 10616
I: 10784
IJ: 10488, 10516, 11261

**Revolutionary War (U.S.) — Fiction**
P: 3753, 3899, 3939, 7608
PI: 3754, 3973, 7589–91, 7595, 7598, 7600, 7603, 7609
I: 7592–93, 7597, 7599, 7605, 7607
IJ: 6480, 7588, 7594, 7596, 7601, 7604, 7606

**Revolutionary War (U.S.) — Jokes and riddles**
I: 17360

**Revolutionary War (U.S.) — Poetry**
P: 9601
PI: 9600

**Revolutionary War (U.S.) — Songs**
P: 11504

**Revolutionary War (U.S.) — Women**
IJ: 13075

**Rhine River**
IJ: 12407

**Rhinoceroses**
P: 11762
PI: 15101
I: 15083, 15114, 15127, 15143

**Rhinoceroses — Fiction**
P: 246, 1846, 2116

**Rhode Island**
P: 3657
I: 13377, 13415

**Rhode Island — Fiction**
IJ: 5469

**Rhode Island — History**
IJ: 13096

**Rhode Island Colony**
IJ: 13004

**Rice**
P: 17218
PI: 15979

**Rice, Jerry**
I: 11095
IJ: 11094

**Rice, Norman**
I: 13748

**Richards, Ann**
I: 10773

**Richards, Ellen**
I: 10906

**Riddles**
*See* Jokes and riddles

**Ride, Sally**
I: 16654

**Rio de Janeiro, Brazil**
I: 12712

**Ripken, Cal, Jr.**
I: 11001
IJ: 11000

**Rivera, Diego**
IJ: 10117

**Rivers**
*See also* Streams
P: 3837, 13615, 16288, 16299
PI: 15401, 16295
I: 12227, 12603, 12730, 12786, 14993, 16196, 16294, 16300, 16302
IJ: 5903, 12228, 16290, 16298

**Rivers — Fiction**
P: 3645, 3704, 3713

**Roads**
P: 16772
I: 16885

**Roads — Fiction**
P: 2618, 4568
IJ: 7113

**Roanoke Island — History**
I: 13013

**Robbers and robbery — Fiction**
P: 790, 1237, 1401, 1524, 1726, 1789, 2292, 3998, 5131, 5333
PI: 5449, 5453, 5521, 5614, 5667
I: 5468, 5542, 5553–54, 5567, 5754, 6527, 7147, 7452, 7729, 8040
IJ: 7493

**Robbers and robbery — Folklore**
PI: 9092, 9177
I: 8992
IJ: 8969, 9025

**Robeson, Paul**
IJ: 10203

**Robin Hood**
P: 8964
PI: 8973–74, 8978, 8999, 9044
I: 9022

**Robins**
P: 15336, 15384

**Robinson, Brooks**
I: 11002

**Robinson, David**
PI: 11070
I: 11068–69
IJ: 11065–67

**Robinson, Frank**
I: 11003

**Robinson, Jackie**
P: 11005
PI: 11004, 11010
I: 11007–9, 11012–13
IJ: 11006, 11011

**Robots**
P: 16819, 16831
I: 16684
IJ: 16833

**Robots — Fiction**
P: 1338, 5197
PI: 8314, 8375
I: 8312, 8317, 8359, 8374
IJ: 8313, 8315–16

**Rock art**
I: 11343
IJ: 12880

P = Primary; PI = Primary–Intermediate; I = Intermediate; IJ = Intermediate–Junior High

P = Primary; PI = Primary–Intermediate; I = Intermediate; IJ = Intermediate–Junior High

**Royce, Sarah**
IJ: 13172

**Rubber**
P: 16695

**Rudolph, Wilma**
PI: 11132
I: 11133

**Runaways**
*See* Running away

**Running and jogging**
I: 17658

**Running and jogging — Fiction**
PI: 1744

**Running away — Fiction**
P: 1215, 1464, 4062, 4148
PI: 6821
I: 6336, 6413, 6993, 7093, 7704,
  7977, 8037
IJ: 6946, 6994, 7095, 7201, 7805,
  7858

**Running away — Folklore**
PI: 9347

**Russell, Charles**
PI: 10121

**Russia**
P: 12456
PI: 82, 12466, 12472, 12474
I: 12459, 12467, 12471, 12477,
  12482–83, 12488, 14053
IJ: 11244, 12462, 12479–80

**Russia — Biography**
IJ: 11284

**Russia — Cookbooks**
IJ: 17251

**Russia — Fiction**
P: 1305, 3763, 3770, 3800, 3874,
  3923, 4308, 4971, 9099
I: 7484–85
IJ: 6391

**Russia — Folklore**
P: 2076, 3928, 9079–84, 9087,
  9089–90, 9093–95, 9098, 9100,
  9102–4, 9106, 9110, 9112, 11643
PI: 9085–86, 9088, 9091–92, 9101,
  9105, 9107–8, 9352
I: 9096, 9109, 9111
IJ: 9078

**Russia — History**
I: 12461, 12470
IJ: 11231, 12034, 12460

**Russia — Sports**
IJ: 12476

**Russian Americans**
I: 14038
IJ: 14063

**Russian Americans — Fiction**
P: 2977, 3770, 4823
PI: 3064
I: 7814
IJ: 7795, 7842

**Rustin, Bayard**
IJ: 13654

**Rustling — Fiction**
P: 2316

**Ruth, Babe**
I: 11014, 11016
IJ: 11015

**Ruth, Babe — Fiction**
I: 8446

**Rwanda**
P: 12104

**Rwanda — Folklore**
I: 8672

**Ryan, Nolan**
I: 11018
IJ: 11017

**Rylant, Cynthia**
I: 10277

# S

**Sabbath (Jewish)**
P: 4973

**Sabbath (Jewish) — Fiction**
P: 4991

**Sabbath (Jewish) — Folklore**
PI: 9159

**Sabin, Florence**
I: 10909

**Sac Indians**
PI: 12894

**Sacagawea**
P: 10598
I: 10599–602

**Sacagewea — Fiction**
IJ: 7725

**Sadat, Anwar**
IJ: 11263–64

**Safety**
P: 14524
I: 14525
IJ: 14521–22

**Safety — Fiction**
P: 1504, 1915, 2424
PI: 7128

**Safety — Sports**
IJ: 14523

**Saguaro cactus**
PI: 16064

**Sailing and boating**
P: 17660
I: 17659, 17662

**Sailing and boating — Fiction**
P: 2308
I: 8399

**Sailing and boating — History**
PI: 16954

**Sailing ships**
P: 16948

**Saint Augustine, Florida**
PI: 13513

**Saint Bernards**
PI: 5171

**St. James, Lyn**
I: 10956

**Saint Lawrence Seaway**
PI: 12589

**Saint Louis, Missouri**
PI: 13274

**Saint Louis, Missouri — Fiction**
PI: 6026
I: 7723

**Saint Patrick's Day**
PI: 13895, 13905, 13908

**Saint Patrick's Day — Fiction**
P: 4604, 4618, 4627

**St. Petersburg, Russia**
I: 12475

**Saints**
I: 13775

**Saints — Biography**
P: 11202, 11260
I: 11219, 11236

P = Primary; PI = Primary–Intermediate; I = Intermediate; IJ = Intermediate–Junior High

**Salamanders**
PI: 14905, 14915, 14922
I: 14911, 14923

**Salamanders — Fiction**
P: 4388

**Salem, Massachusetts — Fiction**
I: 7573, 7581

**Salem, Massachusetts — History**
PI: 13022
I: 13018, 13033
IJ: 13014

**Salmon**
P: 3837, 15682
PI: 13618

**Salmon — Fiction**
P: 2230

**Salmon — Folklore**
P: 9289
I: 9270

**Salt**
P: 16696

**Salt — Experiments and projects**
I: 16104

**Salt Lake City, Utah**
PI: 13309

**Samburu**
IJ: 12105

**Sami (Lapland)**
PI: 12757

**Sampras, Pete**
PI: 11118
IJ: 11119

**Sampson, Deborah**
I: 10784

**Samurai — Fiction**
I: 7453
IJ: 7454

**San Antonio, Texas**
I: 13530

**San Antonio Spurs (basketball team)**
IJ: 17580

**San Diego, California**
PI: 13448

**San Francisco, California**
P: 4606, 13425
I: 13435, 13439

**San Francisco, California — Fiction**
P: 3791
PI: 7875
I: 5799, 7809–10
IJ: 6205, 6294, 7817

**San Francisco, California — History**
I: 13462

**San Juan Capistrano, California — Fiction**
P: 4401

**San Martín, José de**
I: 11265

**Sand castles**
I: 17187

**Sand dunes**
I: 16325

**Sandburg, Carl**
I: 10278

**Sanders, Barry**
I: 11096–97
IJ: 11098

**Sanders, Deion**
I: 11099

**Sandhill cranes**
P: 15377

**Sanitation**
PI: 16443
I: 13595, 14510
IJ: 14508

**Santa Claus — Fiction**
P: 961, 3928, 4700–1, 4721, 4725, 4773, 4783–84, 4799, 4857, 4865
I: 6908, 7917

**Santa Claus — Poetry**
P: 4812, 9773–74, 9777

**Santa Fe Trail**
I: 13116
IJ: 13124

**Santa Fe Trail — Fiction**
I: 7690

**Sasaki, Sadako**
PI: 11266

**Saskatchewan, Canada**
I: 12604

**Sasquatch**
I: 17446

**Saturn (planet)**
PI: 14728, 14735
I: 14718

**Saudi Arabia**
*See also* Arabia
I: 12562, 12573
IJ: 12565

**Sautuola, Maria de**
PI: 11267

**Scandinavia**
*See* Denmark; Finland; Norway; Sweden; Vikings

**Scandinavia — Fiction**
P: 3879

**Scarecrows — Fiction**
P: 872, 3191
PI: 6882

**Schindler, Oskar**
IJ: 11268

**School integration**
I: 13668

**School stories**
P: 116, 123, 151, 254, 705, 804, 838, 1321, 1456, 1534, 1725, 1833, 2234, 2554, 2973, 3230, 3244, 3268, 3283, 3285, 3366, 3405, 3434, 3446, 3524, 3751, 3952–53, 4098, 4134, 4486–90, 4492, 4494–99, 4501–2, 4505–19, 4521–24, 4526–37, 4539–42, 4544–47, 4782, 4888, 5002, 5051, 5066, 5106, 5116, 5139, 5144–45, 5149, 5157–59, 5192, 5247, 5268, 5270–71, 5339–41, 5419, 6282, 8227–28, 8233, 8235, 8253–56, 8302
PI: 77, 1322, 3221, 4491, 4520, 4525, 5152, 5343, 5756, 5995, 7124, 7176, 7198, 7241, 7280, 7299, 7304, 8140, 8158, 8165, 8194, 8203, 8206, 8215, 8218–19, 8223, 8226, 8229, 8232, 8234, 8238–39, 8247–48, 8252, 8257–58, 8262–67, 8270, 8273, 8278–81, 8283, 8285, 8287, 8291–92, 8294–99, 8303–4, 8333, 8448
I: 5626, 6020, 6177, 6396, 6825, 6834, 6847, 6872, 6944, 6962, 6980, 7078, 7092, 7127, 7156, 7169, 7190, 7232, 7303, 7361, 7379, 7969, 8001, 8086, 8097, 8156, 8188, 8190, 8198, 8200, 8202, 8204–5, 8209, 8212–14, 8216–17, 8222, 8225, 8230–31,

8237, 8240–43, 8245, 8249–51,
8259, 8261, 8271–72, 8275, 8277,
8284, 8288–90, 8293, 8300,
8305–7, 8403, 8437

IJ: 6022, 6055, 6340, 6692, 6710,
6812, 6846, 6917, 6950, 6969,
7034, 7099, 7298, 7343, 8199,
8201, 8207, 8210–11, 8220–21,
8224, 8236, 8260, 8274, 8276,
8282, 8286, 8301, 8402, 8441,
8468, 8472

**Schools**
PI: 13140
IJ: 13230, 14111

**Schools — Colonial Period (U.S.)**
I: 13025

**Schools — Jokes and riddles**
PI: 17326

**Schools — Poetry**
P: 9529, 9569, 9642, 9647, 9675,
9830
PI: 9579, 9584, 9799, 9801
I: 9528, 9805

**Schumann, Clara**
I: 10146

**Science,** 14558–16978

**Science — Experiments and projects**
*See also* under specific branch-es of science, e.g., Electricity — Experiments and projects
P: 14578, 14583, 14586, 14591,
14616, 14625, 14628, 14638,
16472, 16506, 16614
PI: 14590, 14596–98, 14604, 14619,
14623, 14634–35, 14637,
14642–45, 16399, 16454, 16463,
16540, 16618
I: 11755, 13576, 13582, 14463,
14579–80, 14582, 14589, 14595,
14599, 14601, 14603, 14607–12,
14614–15, 14621–22, 14627,
14630, 14632–33, 14636,
14639–40, 14646–48, 14685,
15966, 16054, 16056, 16106–7,
16109, 16117, 16138, 16164,
16391, 16441, 16469, 16509,
16526–27, 16557–58, 16562,
16577–78, 16596, 16612–13,
16693, 16721, 16764, 16838,
16855, 17298
IJ: 13621, 14581, 14584, 14587–88,
14592–94, 14600, 14602, 14605–6,
14617–18, 14620, 14624, 14626,
14629, 14631, 14665, 14669,

14790, 16390, 16495, 16513,
16553, 16598, 16608, 16737

**Science — General**
P: 3566
PI: 13616, 14562–63, 14641
I: 13566, 14572, 14574, 14621, 14819
IJ: 14561, 14564, 14569, 14575–77,
16850, 17303

**Science — History**
IJ: 11942, 12960, 13040, 14558–59,
14565, 14567–68, 14570, 14573

**Science — Jokes and riddles**
I: 17359

**Science — Methodology**
I: 14566
IJ: 14560

**Science — Projects**
*See* Science — Experiments and projects

**Science fiction**
*See also* Fantasy; Supernatural
P: 736, 825, 1025, 1197, 5197, 5380
PI: 5147, 8308, 8310, 8314, 8319,
8328, 8340, 8345, 8351, 8365–67,
8375, 8377, 8379–80
I: 6450, 6669, 8208, 8309, 8312,
8317–18, 8321–23, 8326–27, 8329,
8332, 8335, 8337–39, 8341,
8346–49, 8353, 8357, 8359–63,
8368, 8370–74, 8378
IJ: 8311, 8313, 8315–16, 8320,
8324–25, 8330–31, 8334, 8336,
8342–44, 8350, 8352, 8354–56,
8364, 8369, 8376, 8381

**Scientists**
PI: 10824, 10827
I: 10825

**Scientists — Biography**
PI: 10804, 10823, 10829, 10892,
10899, 10908, 10912, 10914
I: 10800, 10826, 10830, 10843,
10851–53, 10872, 10875, 10885,
10893, 10906
IJ: 10799, 10802, 10847, 10854,
10878, 10882–83, 10894, 10898,
10900–2

**Scientists — Women**
IJ: 10802

**Scilly Islands — Fiction**
I: 7518

**Scoliosis — Fiction**
IJ: 7351

**Scopes trial (1925)**
I: 13214

**Scorpions**
PI: 15596, 15602
I: 15600

**Scotch terriers — Fiction**
P: 4282

**Scotland**
*See also* Great Britain
IJ: 16727

**Scotland — Emigration**
I: 12420

**Scotland — Fiction**
PI: 5990
I: 2077, 6091–92, 6320, 6833, 7517
IJ: 6444–45, 6556, 7385

**Scotland — Folklore**
P: 9005, 9043
I: 8977

**Scotland — History**
I: 12411

**Scottish Americans — Biography**
IJ: 14080

**Scouts and scouting**
IJ: 14092

**Scouts and scouting — Biography**
PI: 11188
I: 10763

**Scouts and scouting — Fiction**
P: 3313, 5429, 6899–900

**Scouts and scouting — Songs**
I: 11583
IJ: 11590

**Scuba diving**
I: 17679

**Sculley, John**
IJ: 10910

**Sculptors and sculpture**
PI: 17075

**Sculptors and sculpture — Biography**
PI: 10099
IJ: 10051

**Sculptors and sculpture — Fiction**
I: 7490
IJ: 8065

P = Primary; PI = Primary–Intermediate; I = Intermediate; IJ = Intermediate–Junior High

P = Primary; PI = Primary–Intermediate; I = Intermediate; IJ = Intermediate–Junior High

I: 14470, 14472–73, 14475–77, 14486
IJ: 15054

**Senses — Animal**
PI: 15013

**Senses — Experiments and projects**
PI: 14465
I: 14463

**Sensors**
I: 16684

**Sequoia (tree)**
PI: 16050

**Sequoyah (Cherokee chief)**
I: 10603–4

**Serengeti National Park (Tanzania)**
I: 12109, 12125

**Serengeti National Park (Tanzania) — Animals**
PI: 14925

**Sewing**
P: 17176

**Sewing machines**
I: 16853

**Sex education**
P: 14532–33, 14537, 14546–48
PI: 14538, 14541, 14543
I: 14542, 14544, 14550, 14552
IJ: 14536, 14545, 14551, 14553–54, 14557

**Sex roles — Fiction**
P: 3862

**Sexual abuse**
P: 13769, 14546, 14548
PI: 14159, 14171
IJ: 14551

**Shabbat**
P: 4968, 4970

**Shackleton, Ernest**
PI: 12758

**Shadows — Fiction**
P: 146, 153, 166, 464, 897, 1285, 2177, 3025
PI: 6427
I: 2682, 6426

**Shaka (Zulu chief)**
PI: 11269

**Shakers (religion)**
PI: 11493

I: 13777, 13779, 13817
IJ: 13780

**Shakers (religion) — Fiction**
P: 3934
IJ: 7681

**Shakespeare, William**
I: 9944, 11665
IJ: 9939–43, 9945, 10279

**Shapes — Experiments and projects**
PI: 14596

**Sharing — Fiction**
P: 965, 2019, 4140, 4183

**Sharks**
P: 15714, 15716–17, 15726
PI: 15713, 15718, 15722, 15724–25
I: 15712, 15719–21
IJ: 15715, 15723

**Sharks — Fiction**
P: 3692
IJ: 5615

**Shawnee Indians**
I: 12851

**Shawnee Indians — Biography**
PI: 10612
IJ: 10613

**Sheba, Queen of (Bible)**
P: 13879

**Sheep**
P: 15304

**Sheep — Fiction**
P: 367, 453, 1655, 1897, 1983, 2088, 2155, 3802, 3950, 4354–55, 4681, 4891, 5404
IJ: 5984, 6550

**Sheep — Nursery rhymes**
P: 624

**Sheepdogs — Fiction**
P: 2315, 4296
PI: 5511, 5824, 5884, 5892
I: 6500

**Shelley, Kate**
PI: 10785

**Shells**
P: 15077, 15728–30

**Shells — Fiction**
P: 990

**Shenandoah National Park — Fiction**
P: 4132

**Shepherds — Fiction**
P: 1983, 2605, 3569, 4759, 4776

**Sherburne, Andrew**
IJ: 10572

**Sherman, William T.**
IJ: 10573

**Shiloh, Battle of**
I: 13211

**Shintoism**
P: 13806

**Ships and boats**
*See also* Sailing and boating; and specific ships, e.g., *Titanic* (ship)
P: 16934–37, 16948–50, 16953
PI: 5133, 16967
I: 12977, 16514, 16938, 16940, 16942, 16944, 16956–57
IJ: 9970, 12026, 16945, 16947

**Ships and boats — Experiments and projects**
PI: 14645

**Ships and boats — Fiction**
P: 734, 773, 899, 905, 946, 974, 1364, 1659, 1759, 1787, 2070, 2679, 3379, 3777, 4560, 4566, 4569, 4579
PI: 2850, 5633, 7393, 7656
I: 6488, 7403, 7613
IJ: 5471, 5783, 5788, 5807, 6322, 7563

**Ships and boats — Folklore**
P: 9098, 9106

**Ships and boats — History**
IJ: 16951–52

**Ships and boats — Poetry**
P: 9674

**Shipwrecks**
PI: 16946
IJ: 11837, 16955

**Shipwrecks — Fiction**
P: 2306, 5178
PI: 6738
IJ: 5818

**Shoemakers — Fiction**
P: 3044

P = Primary; PI = Primary–Intermediate; I = Intermediate; IJ = Intermediate–Junior High

P = Primary; PI = Primary–Intermediate; I = Intermediate; IJ = Intermediate–Junior High

PI: 12895, 12956
I: 12879, 12971

**Sioux Indians — Biography**
PI: 10609
I: 10607–8
IJ: 10597, 10605–6

**Sioux Indians — Fiction**
IJ: 7709

**Sioux Indians — Folklore**
P: 9300
PI: 9211, 9225

**Sisters — Fiction**
P: 2847, 2871, 2933, 3022
PI: 6197, 6839

**Sitting Bull (Sioux chief)**
PI: 10609
I: 10607–8
IJ: 10605–6

**Sitting Bull (Sioux chief) —
  Fiction**
IJ: 7538

**Size — Fiction**
P: 2446

**Sizes and shapes**
*See* Concept books — Sizes
  and shapes

**Skateboarding — Fiction**
I: 8427

**Skeletons**
P: 14492, 14495, 14502
PI: 14490
I: 14493, 14496–99
IJ: 14491, 14494, 14501

**Skeletons — Fiction**
P: 4905, 5043–44

**Ski patrollers — Careers**
PI: 14219

**Skin**
P: 14505
PI: 15030

**Skin care**
IJ: 14509

**Skis and skiing**
PI: 14219
IJ: 17653

**Skis and skiing — Fiction**
P: 1481
PI: 7256

**Skunks**
PI: 15112

**Skunks — Fiction**
P: 2239, 3482, 4411
I: 8371–72

**Sky — Poetry**
I: 9882

**Skyscrapers**
P: 16769, 16783
I: 16767, 16782

**Slater, Samuel**
IJ: 13106

**Slavery**
*See also* African Americans;
  Civil War (U.S.);
  Underground Railroad
P: 3849, 10369, 10457
PI: 10288, 10373, 10376, 10451,
  13110, 17201
I: 7622, 10387, 10449, 10500, 10790,
  13078–79, 13083, 13085, 13095,
  13097
IJ: 7655, 10383, 10389, 10450,
  10501, 11218, 11512, 11836,
  12180, 13077, 13089–90, 13093,
  13098, 13101, 13105, 13111,
  14058

**Slavery — Biography**
PI: 10289, 10370–71, 10375, 10445,
  10458
I: 10377
IJ: 10443, 10502

**Slavery — Fiction**
P: 3831, 3852, 3949, 3994, 3997,
  4937
PI: 3788, 3848, 3960, 7531, 7617,
  7631–33, 7654, 7662, 7964
I: 7424, 7532, 7592, 7619, 7634,
  7637–38, 7644, 7650, 7652, 7765,
  13087
IJ: 6011, 6446, 7530, 7580, 7611,
  7623, 7625, 7628, 7648, 7653,
  7657, 7661, 7757, 7794

**Slavery — Folklore**
P: 9076, 9161
PI: 9358

**Slavery — Poetry**
P: 9698

**Sleator, William**
I: 10282

**Sled dog races**
*See also* Iditarod
PI: 2353

I: 17489, 17524
IJ: 15852, 17492

**Sled dogs — Fiction**
P: 4258, 4397
PI: 5991
I: 6001
IJ: 5697, 6198

**Sleep**
P: 14449
I: 14526–27

**Sleep — Fiction**
P: 500–1, 504, 530, 2923, 3514
I: 6472, 8657

*Sleeping Beauty* **(ballet)**
I: 11645

**Slime**
PI: 17437

**Slovakia**
IJ: 12378

**Slumber parties — Fiction**
P: 3177

**Smalls, Robert**
IJ: 10443

**Smell (sense)**
P: 14480

**Smith, Emmitt**
I: 11102
IJ: 11103

**Smithsonian Institution**
I: 13723

**Smoking**
I: 14269, 14276, 14278, 14280
IJ: 14264, 14272, 14277, 14291

**Smoking — Fiction**
PI: 7181

**Smuggling — Fiction**
I: 7878
IJ: 5796, 8184

**Snails**
PI: 15606, 15612
I: 15610, 15614

**Snails — Fiction**
P: 342, 1192, 1861, 2130, 4255, 5190

**Snake River (U.S.)**
PI: 15401

**Snakes**
*See also* individual species,
  e.g., Pythons

P = Primary; PI = Primary–Intermediate; I = Intermediate; IJ = Intermediate–Junior High

P: 14965, 14967, 14969, 14972, 14979, 14981, 14983–84
PI: 14964, 14966, 14970, 14975–76, 14985
I: 14968, 14971, 14973–74, 14980, 14986

**Snakes — Fiction**
P: 444, 1020, 1257, 1762, 1828, 2185, 2210, 3275, 3426, 4332
PI: 4377, 5847, 8004

**Snakes — Folklore**
P: 9191

**Sneakers**
PI: 16801, 16814

**Snider, Duke**
I: 11019

**Snow**
P: 5250, 16472
I: 16490
IJ: 16507

**Snow — Crafts**
P: 17006

**Snow — Fiction**
P: 819, 1218, 1264, 1288, 1783, 1815, 1895, 2222, 2336, 2356, 2418, 2439, 2457, 2497, 2549, 2667, 2752, 2776, 3626, 3628, 3640, 3684, 3835, 4532, 5300
PI: 748
I: 2437

**Snow — Folklore**
P: 9082

**Snow — Poetry**
P: 3678

**Snow leopards**
I: 15211

**Snowboarding**
I: 17669, 17673
IJ: 17670–72

**Snowboarding — Fiction**
I: 8428

**Snowmen — Fiction**
P: 691
PI: 4808

**Soaring**
IJ: 17519

**Soccer**
PI: 17678
I: 17674–77

**Soccer — Biography**
IJ: 11166

**Soccer — Fiction**
P: 706, 5235, 5297, 8445
PI: 5296, 5647, 5824, 8401, 8475
I: 5569, 7013, 7302, 8415, 8429–30, 8454
IJ: 8402, 8477

**Social groups**
*See* Scouts and scouting; and ethnic groups, e.g., Hispanic Americans

**Social problems**
IJ: 13750, 13762

**Social problems — Women**
IJ: 13751

**Social service**
I: 13754

**Social workers — Biography**
IJ: 10724–25

**Sod houses**
P: 7730

**Soft drinks**
PI: 15952
I: 15956

**Soft drinks — Experiments and projects**
IJ: 15985

**Softball**
PI: 17564

**Soil**
P: 16324

**Soil ecology**
PI: 15512, 16323
I: 16336

**Soil erosion**
P: 16333

**Solar energy**
P: 16551
IJ: 16550

**Solar energy — Experiments and projects**
I: 16552

**Solar system**
*See also* Astronomy; Comets; Extraterrestrial life; Meteors; Moon; Planets; Space exploration; Stars; Sun
P: 14755

PI: 14734, 14741, 14745, 14749, 14763, 14765
I: 14731–32, 14747, 14751
IJ: 14711, 14719, 14748, 14766, 14768

**Soldiers — Fiction**
P: 8499–500

**Soldiers — History**
I: 16972
IJ: 13073

**Solomon, King (Bible)**
P: 13879

**Somalia**
PI: 12111
IJ: 12102

**Songs**
*See also* Folk songs; and under specific countries, cultural groups, and regions, e.g., African Americans — Songs
P: 53, 412, 419, 537, 545, 551, 619–20, 671, 678–79, 1104, 1213, 1795, 2503, 4764, 11503, 11508–9, 11511, 11517, 11528–29, 11534, 11537, 11540, 11543–44, 11546–47, 11562–63, 11584–89, 11591–93, 11595–96, 11599–600, 11603–8, 11611–13, 11616
PI: 1040, 11551, 11557, 11581, 11610, 11614–15
I: 11522, 11532, 11552, 11583, 11602
IJ: 11590, 11594, 11609
All: 11598

**Songs — Fiction**
P: 4847

**Sonoran Desert**
PI: 16228

**Sound**
*See also* Concept books — Sounds
PI: 16617
I: 16615
IJ: 16523

**Sound — Experiments and projects**
P: 16614
PI: 16616, 16618
I: 16612–13, 16619

**Sound — Fiction**
P: 569, 1537, 1736, 3102

**Sousa, John Philip**
PI: 10147

P = Primary; PI = Primary–Intermediate; I = Intermediate; IJ = Intermediate–Junior High

**South Africa**
P: 12139
PI: 11247, 11250, 12141, 12143
I: 12152, 12158
IJ: 11248, 11251, 12140, 12160

**South Africa — Biography**
PI: 11246, 11249, 11252

**South Africa — Fiction**
P: 3783, 3845, 3875, 3909, 4327, 7428
PI: 3959
I: 5941, 6019
IJ: 3958, 5777, 7420, 7425

**South Africa — Folklore**
P: 8731
I: 8734, 8740

**South America**
PI: 16275
IJ: 11673, 11844

**South America — Biography**
IJ: 11178

**South America — Cookbooks**
I: 17248

**South America — Crafts**
I: 16996

**South America — Fiction**
P: 3971
IJ: 7563

**South America — Folklore**
I: 9443, 9449

**South America — History**
I: 11189–90, 11265

**South America — Songs**
PI: 11548

**South Carolina**
PI: 13489
I: 13482
IJ: 13488

**South Carolina — Fiction**
IJ: 5784

**South Carolina Colony**
IJ: 13005

**South Dakota**
I: 13325, 13343

**South Dakota — Fiction**
I: 7712

**South Pacific — Fiction**
PI: 5598

**South Pacific — Folklore**
I: 8860

**South (U.S.)**
*See also* specific states, e.g.,
Florida
I: 13485

**South (U.S.) — Fiction**
P: 3775
I: 6820

**South (U.S.) — Folklore**
P: 9376
I: 9319, 9334, 9387

**Southeast Asia**
IJ: 12324

**Southeast Asia — Emigration**
I: 12215

**Southeast Asia — History**
IJ: 12032

**Southeast Asia — Holidays**
PI: 13932

**Southwest (U.S.)**
*See also* specific states, e.g.,
Arizona
P: 14898
PI: 11344
I: 13528
IJ: 13529, 13537

**Southwest (U.S.) — Folklore**
P: 9341

**Southwest (U.S.) — History**
IJ: 12963

**Southwest (U.S.) — Poetry**
P: 9869, 9888

**Soviet Union — History**
I: 12470

**Soweto — Fiction**
PI: 3959

**Space colonies**
I: 16667

**Space debris**
IJ: 16651

**Space exploration**
*See also* Astronauts;
Extraterrestrial life; National
Aeronautics and Space
Administration (U.S.);
Planets; Space colonies, etc.
P: 16628–29, 16631, 16657
PI: 14724–25, 16620, 16637, 16653,
16655–56, 16659–60

I: 14670, 14692, 16622, 16627,
16630, 16634, 16638, 16640,
16643, 16658, 16664
IJ: 9958, 14593, 14660, 14668,
14719, 14727, 14752, 14766,
16635–36, 16639, 16641, 16646,
16648–49, 16662–63, 16665,
16668, 16670

**Space exploration — Crafts**
PI: 17035

**Space exploration — Fiction**
PI: 5480, 6310
I: 6657

**Space exploration — Poetry**
P: 9564, 9653
IJ: 9646

**Space satellites**
I: 16645

**Space shuttles**
I: 16654

**Space stations**
PI: 16661
I: 16627
IJ: 16624, 16639

**Spacecraft**
*See also* specific spacecraft,
e.g., *Voyager II* (spacecraft)
PI: 16716
I: 16642, 17093
IJ: 16623, 16626

**Spacecraft — Fiction**
P: 758, 1198, 1510
I: 8323, 8371
IJ: 8352

**Spain**
PI: 12514, 12516, 12521, 12524
I: 12520, 12522, 12525
IJ: 12526

**Spain — Biography**
IJ: 10109

**Spain — Cookbooks**
I: 17222

**Spain — Fiction**
I: 7475, 7477
IJ: 5582, 7339, 7469

**Spain — Folklore**
P: 9128–29, 9131, 9133
PI: 9130, 9132
I: 8585

P = Primary; PI = Primary–Intermediate; I = Intermediate; IJ = Intermediate–Junior High

**Spain — History**
I: 12519
IJ: 11205

**Spanish American War**
I: 13217
IJ: 13224

**Spanish American War — Fiction**
P: 3842

**Spanish language**
P: 3482, 3664, 3785
PI: 9523, 11376

**Spanish language — Alphabet books**
P: 14193

**Spanish language — Counting books**
P: 307, 390

**Spanish language — Fiction**
P: 103, 894, 2610, 2805, 3076, 3237, 3790, 4689
PI: 6831, 7522
I: 6229, 7533

**Spanish language — Finger plays**
P: 17515

**Spanish language — Folklore**
P: 9129, 9394, 9420
I: 9404
IJ: 9442

**Spanish language — Holidays**
IJ: 13927

**Spanish language — Nonfiction**
PI: 10485, 10805, 10846
IJ: 5899

**Spanish language — Numbers**
P: 349

**Spanish language — Poetry**
P: 9505, 9510, 9576, 9610

**Spanish language — Songs**
P: 11586

**Sparrows**
P: 15388
I: 15307

**Speaking**
I: 11467

**Special Olympics**
I: 14297, 17499, 17650

**Speech disorders — Fiction**
PI: 7272

**Speed skating**
PI: 17634

**Sphinx — Fiction**
P: 7430

**Spiders**
P: 8721, 15586, 15591–92, 15594, 15598–99, 15603
PI: 15095, 15506, 15534, 15587–88, 15593, 15602
I: 15491, 15493, 15589, 15595, 15597, 15601, 17100
IJ: 15590, 15604

**Spiders — Fiction**
P: 1496, 1658, 3021, 4376, 4719, 4911
PI: 5700, 6761

**Spiders — Folklore**
P: 8706
I: 9404, 9433
IJ: 8682

**Spiders — Poetry**
PI: 9723

**Spielberg, Steven**
I: 10208
IJ: 10209

**Spies**
I: 13698
IJ: 12036, 12052, 13703

**Spies — Biography**
I: 11183
IJ: 10748

**Spies — Fiction**
IJ: 5566, 7762

**Spies — Women — Biography**
I: 11183

**Spirituals**
P: 11499
PI: 13870
I: 11556

**Spock, Benjamin**
IJ: 10911

**Sponges**
P: 15624

**Spoonbills**
P: 16293

**Sports**
See also Games; and specific sports, e.g., Baseball

P: 12907
I: 12238, 17479, 17514, 17520, 17525–26, 17528
IJ: 12476, 16539, 17469, 17497, 17506, 17522–23

**Sports — African Americans**
PI: 10930

**Sports — Biography,** 17469–17684
See also under specific sports, e.g., Baseball — Biography
P: 10936
PI: 10940
IJ: 10944, 10951

**Sports — Careers**
IJ: 14186

**Sports — Experiments and projects**
IJ: 14403

**Sports — Fiction**
P: 2798, 2888, 5267
I: 8406

**Sports — Jokes and riddles**
PI: 17330, 17379–80

**Sports — Poetry**
I: 9904, 9908–9

**Sports — Safety**
IJ: 14523

**Sports — Superstitions**
PI: 17498

**Sports and games,** 10921–11173

**Sports cards**
I: 17195, 17532

**Sports medicine**
I: 17525

**Spotted owls**
I: 15428
IJ: 15432

**Spotted owls — Fiction**
PI: 5866

**Spring**
P: 3617, 3652
PI: 14802, 16989

**Spring — Fiction**
P: 830, 987, 3634, 3644, 3689, 5241
PI: 3602, 5792

**Spring — Poetry**
P: 9758
I: 9866

P = Primary; PI = Primary–Intermediate; I = Intermediate; IJ = Intermediate–Junior High

**Springs (water) — Fiction**
I: 6237

**Squanto (Pawtuxet Indian)**
P: 10611
I: 10610

**Squirrels — Fiction**
P: 1360, 1600, 4330, 4450
PI: 1344

**Sri Lanka**
I: 12269
IJ: 12323, 12331

**Stamp collecting**
I: 17323

**Stanley, Henry M.**
IJ: 9960

**Stanley Cup (hockey)**
I: 17632

**Stanton, Elizabeth Cady**
PI: 10787
I: 10786, 10788

***Star-Spangled Banner***
P: 3899
PI: 11518
I: 11582

***Star Trek* (TV show)**
I: 8353

**Stargell, Willie**
I: 11020

**Stars**
P: 14772, 14776–77, 14780, 14782,
   14785
PI: 14650, 14652–53, 14770–71,
   14773, 14784, 14786–87
I: 14670, 14769, 14774, 14781
IJ: 14672, 14750, 14775, 14778–79,
   14783, 14789

**Stars — Fiction**
P: 484, 514

**Stars — Folklore**
P: 8778, 9223, 9273
PI: 8758, 9230
I: 9216
IJ: 9266, 9268

**Stars — Mythology**
I: 9496

**State birds (U.S.)**
P: 3727
I: 12788

**State flowers (U.S.)**
P: 3727
I: 12789

**State government (U.S.)**
IJ: 13746

**State trees (U.S.)**
PI: 12782

**States (U.S.) — Signs and
symbols**
PI: 12785

**Statistics**
I: 16383

**Statue of Liberty**
PI: 13396
I: 13360, 16760

**Statue of Liberty — Fiction**
P: 3524, 5362

**Stealing — Fiction**
P: 4079
PI: 5466, 7600, 8017
I: 5608, 5613, 5635, 5637, 6864,
   6954, 7147, 8212
IJ: 5541, 5573, 6259

**Stealing — Folklore**
I: 9294

**Steam engines**
I: 16854

**Steamboats**
I: 10849

**Steamboats — Fiction**
IJ: 6998

**Stearner, Phyllis**
PI: 10912

**Steel**
*See* Iron and steel

**Steiff, Margarete**
PI: 10123

**Steinbeck, John**
IJ: 10283

**Steinem, Gloria**
I: 10789

**Stepchildren — Fiction**
P: 3409
I: 7007
IJ: 6421, 6940

**Stepchildren — Folklore**
P: 8890–91, 9016

**Stepfathers — Fiction**
P: 2938

**Stepparents**
P: 14143
I: 14120

**Stepparents — Fiction**
P: 2849, 2967, 4008, 4100, 8560
PI: 4072, 6948, 7717
I: 6087, 6099, 6992
IJ: 5658, 6940, 7000, 7066, 7084

**Stepparents — Folklore**
P: 8743, 9080, 9084, 9094
PI: 8780, 9101

**Steroids**
I: 14287

**Stevenson, James**
P: 3966

**Stevenson, Robert Louis**
P: 9674, 10286
IJ: 10284–85

**Stine, R. L.**
I: 10287

**Stock market crash (1929)**
*See also* Depression, Great
I: 13222
IJ: 13232

**Stockton, John**
IJ: 11072

**Stomach**
IJ: 14428

**Stone, Lucy**
I: 10790

**Stone cutters**
I: 11989

**Stonehenge**
IJ: 11827, 17453

**Stores**
P: 2528
PI: 13094
I: 13549

**Stores — Fiction**
P: 2486, 2526, 4921
PI: 6328, 6739, 7962
I: 8082
IJ: 6551

**Stories without words**
P: 22, 222, 271, 359, 681–85, 687–92,
   694–702, 704–19, 722–23, 1550,
   3817, 16903

P = Primary; PI = Primary–Intermediate; I = Intermediate; IJ = Intermediate–Junior High

P = Primary; PI = Primary–Intermediate; I = Intermediate; IJ = Intermediate–Junior High

**Supernatural**
*See also* Fantasy; Folklore;
Mystery stories; Tall tales;
and specific supernatural
creatures, e.g., Ghosts
P: 801, 3312
I: 6285, 6394, 6450, 6545, 6602,
6620, 6628, 6647, 6706, 6741,
17432, 17457
IJ: 6350, 6478, 6526, 6686, 6740,
17429

**Supernatural — Fiction**
PI: 6486, 6575
I: 6265, 6299, 6351, 6788
IJ: 5761, 6405, 6477, 6618, 6756

**Supernatural — Folklore**
IJ: 9359

**Supernatural — Poetry**
PI: 9516
I: 9525, 9623, 9798
IJ: 9624

**Superstitions**
PI: 17438

**Superstitions — Fiction**
P: 3312

**Supreme Court (U.S.)**
PI: 13641
I: 13639–40, 13737

**Supreme Court (U.S.) —
Biography**
PI: 10420–22, 10424–25, 10766
I: 10447, 10525–26, 10765, 10767
IJ: 10423, 10426, 10524, 10768

**Surfing — Fiction**
P: 1995

**Surgery — Fiction**
IJ: 7162, 7199

**Survival stories**
I: 9954

**Survival stories — Fiction**
I: 5488, 5604–5
IJ: 5690, 5786, 7068, 7142

**Swahili — Fiction**
P: 31, 333

**Swahili — Folklore**
P: 8671, 8713

**Swallows — Fiction**
P: 4401
I: 8594

**Swamps**
P: 16183, 16305
I: 15627, 16185

**Swamps — Fiction**
P: 4927
IJ: 5592

*Swan Lake* **(ballet)**
PI: 11627
I: 11633

**Swans**
P: 15362, 15395–96
I: 15390–91

**Swans — Fiction**
P: 1721, 8504
I: 6762

**Swanson, Anne Barrett**
PI: 10914

**Swazi**
IJ: 12156

**Swaziland**
PI: 12151
I: 15464
IJ: 12136

**Sweaters**
P: 16809

**Sweden**
IJ: 12490, 12494, 12510

**Sweden — Fiction**
P: 2351, 3755, 4790
PI: 8539
I: 7267, 8105
IJ: 7471

**Swedish Americans**
PI: 17232
IJ: 14061

**Swedish Americans — Fiction**
P: 3951
PI: 7839
I: 7733

**Swimming**
I: 17680

**Swimming — Fiction**
P: 793, 1533, 2411, 2495, 3073, 4090
PI: 6504
I: 7075, 8479
IJ: 8435

**Switzerland**
PI: 5171

I: 12368, 12371
IJ: 12375, 12380

**Switzerland — Christmas**
I: 13942

**Switzerland — Cookbooks**
IJ: 17228

**Switzerland — Folklore**
P: 8870
PI: 8868

**Symbiosis**
PI: 14825
I: 14808

**Synagogues**
P: 13816

**Synagogues — Fiction**
P: 4965

# T

**T-ball — Fiction**
P: 2299

**Tadpoles**
I: 14947

**Tadpoles — Fiction**
P: 4403

**Taft, William H.**
I: 10707

**Tahiti**
I: 12348

**Taiga**
I: 16267
IJ: 16248

**Taino Indians — Fiction**
IJ: 6387

**Taino Indians — Folklore**
P: 9423

**Taiwan**
I: 12308
IJ: 12277, 12329

**Taiwan — Fiction**
P: 3935
IJ: 7464

**Taj Mahal**
I: 12242

P = Primary; PI = Primary–Intermediate; I = Intermediate; IJ = Intermediate–Junior High

P = Primary; PI = Primary–Intermediate; I = Intermediate; IJ = Intermediate–Junior High

P = Primary; PI = Primary–Intermediate; I = Intermediate; IJ = Intermediate–Junior High

P = Primary; PI = Primary–Intermediate; I = Intermediate; IJ = Intermediate–Junior High

P = Primary; PI = Primary–Intermediate; I = Intermediate; IJ = Intermediate–Junior High

**Tuskegee Institute**
PI: 10464

**Tutankhamen, King**
PI: 11278, 11900
I: 11277, 11879, 11891

**Twain, Mark**
PI: 10294
IJ: 10295, 13302

**Twins**
I: 14399

**Twins — Fiction**
P: 455, 2788, 2973, 3357, 4020, 4903, 5312
PI: 5666–67, 5669–70, 6096, 6128, 6735–36
I: 6179, 6185, 6206, 6440, 6519, 6824, 6915, 7166, 7292, 7620, 7913, 8204, 8359, 8596
IJ: 3226, 6109, 6241, 8440

**Tyler, John**
IJ: 10711

**Tyrannosaurus rex**
I: 11753, 11776

# U

**U.S. Postal Service**
*See* Postal Service (U.S.)

**UFOs**
PI: 17416, 17435
I: 16650, 17418, 17447
IJ: 16647

**UFOs — Fiction**
P: 1023
IJ: 6063

**Uganda**
IJ: 12099

**Uganda — Folklore**
PI: 8736

**Uganda — Songs**
PI: 8736

**Ukeleles — Folklore**
P: 8735

**Ukraine**
I: 12457, 12469
IJ: 12486

**Ukraine — Fiction**
IJ: 7494

**Ukraine — Folklore**
P: 8867, 8872, 8878, 9097

**Ukrainian Americans**
IJ: 14052

**Umbrellas — Fiction**
P: 818, 2778

**Underground Railroad**
*See also* Slavery
P: 10457
PI: 10452, 13110
I: 10454–55, 13079
IJ: 10453, 10459, 13077, 13090

**Underground Railroad — Biography**
PI: 10456

**Underground Railroad — Fiction**
P: 1176, 3994, 5082
PI: 3788, 7646, 7662
I: 5536, 7619, 7624, 7637–38, 7765, 13087
IJ: 5584–85, 7615, 7657

**Underwater archaeology**
I: 11820
IJ: 11828, 11836–37, 16951

**Underwater exploration**
PI: 15809
I: 11835
IJ: 15807–8, 15810

**Underwater exploration — Fiction**
PI: 5577

**Unemployment — Fiction**
IJ: 6999

**Unicorns**
P: 939, 1066
PI: 78, 1949

**Unidentified flying objects**
*See* UFOs

**United Farm Workers**
I: 13752

**United Kingdom**
*See* England; Great Britain; Ireland, Northern; Scotland; Wales

**United Nations**
IJ: 13643

**United Nations — Fiction**
PI: 8393

**United States**
*See also* specific regions, states, and cities, e.g., Midwest (U.S.); California; Chicago, Illinois
IJ: 12807

**United States — Aerial views**
I: 16643

**United States — Biography**
I: 10349

**United States — Civil War**
*See* Civil War (U.S.)

**United States — Colonial Period**
*See* Colonial Period (U.S.)

**United States — Congress**
*See* Congress (U.S.)

**United States — Constitution**
*See* Constitution (U.S.)

**United States — Crafts**
I: 17060

**United States — Discovery and exploration**
PI: 12986
I: 12975, 12983
IJ: 12972, 12981, 12985

**United States — Folklore**
P: 4838, 9034, 9318, 9322–26, 9330–31, 9340–43, 9345–46, 9350, 9355, 9362–64, 9370, 9375, 9377, 9383–84, 9386, 9388–89, 9392
PI: 9315, 9320, 9328, 9335, 9347, 9352, 9378
I: 8615, 9327, 9334, 9337, 9357, 9371–72, 9381, 9387, 9391
IJ: 9321, 9333, 9338, 9353, 9359, 9361, 9365, 9367, 9379–80
All: 11506

**United States — Frontier life**
*See* Frontier life (U.S.)

**United States — Geography**
P: 2670
PI: 12780, 12783, 12792, 12804, 12808
I: 12786, 12793
IJ: 12791, 12812

**United States — Government and politics**
PI: 10322, 13734, 13742
I: 13727, 13735
IJ: 13729, 13745

P = Primary; PI = Primary–Intermediate; I = Intermediate; IJ = Intermediate–Junior High

**United States — Government
and politics — Biography**
I: 10508, 10529
IJ: 10545

**United States — Government
and politics — Dictionaries**
IJ: 13714

**United States — Government
and politics — Women**
PI: 10490
IJ: 10342

**United States — History**
*See also* specific periods and
events, e.g., Colonial Period
(U.S.); Civil War (U.S.)
P: 3870
PI: 12783
I: 12802, 12806
IJ: 12797, 12812–13

**United States — History —
Songs**
I: 11522

**United States — Immigration**
*See* Immigration (U.S.)

**United States — National
monuments**
I: 12781, 12790

**United States — Revolutionary
War**
*See* Revolutionary War (U.S.)

**United States — Sports**
I: 17479

**United States (1789–1861) —
Fiction**
PI: 7646, 7654, 7656
I: 7616, 7624, 7663, 7723, 7732, 7742
IJ: 7611, 7614, 7621, 7623, 7649

**United States (1789–1861) —
History**
I: 13112, 13226
IJ: 13088, 13096, 13100, 13107–9

**United States (1865–1950) —
Fiction**
P: 3743, 3951
PI: 7802, 7844
I: 5798, 7772, 7785, 7815, 7821,
7828, 7837, 7840, 7847
IJ: 7773, 7827, 7835, 7841, 7848

**United States (1865–1950) —
History**
I: 13221, 13223, 13228–29, 13240

IJ: 13215, 13225, 13230–32,
13235–36, 13241

**United States (1951– ) —
History**
PI: 13245
I: 10366, 12080, 13244, 13246,
13252, 13257
IJ: 13253–54, 13258

**United States Air Force**
IJ: 16959, 16961

**United States Army**
IJ: 16969

**United States Army —
Biography**
I: 10557, 10562
IJ: 10388, 10438–39, 10558

**United States Coast Guard**
PI: 16967
IJ: 16962

**United States Fish and Wildlife
Service**
PI: 13738

**United States Marine Corps**
IJ: 16977

**United States Military
Academy — History**
I: 16965

**United States Navy**
IJ: 16970

**United States Navy —
Biography**
PI: 10543
IJ: 10572

**United States Postal Service**
*See* Postal Service (U.S.)

**United States Space Camp**
I: 16621

**Universe**
P: 14680
IJ: 14657

**Uranus (planet)**
PI: 14706, 14729, 14736
I: 14723

**Uruguay**
IJ: 12722

**Utah**
PI: 13316
I: 13337
IJ: 11698, 13327

**Uzbekistan**
I: 12485, 12488
IJ: 12487

# V

**Vacations — Fiction**
P: 1453, 1921
I: 5543, 5863, 6335, 6364

**Vacuum cleaners**
PI: 16671

**Valentine, Saint**
PI: 14004

**Valentine's Day**
P: 14001
PI: 14000, 14003
I: 13998–99
IJ: 14002

**Valentine's Day — Crafts**
P: 16997
PI: 17036
I: 16998

**Valentine's Day — Fiction**
P: 1732, 4158, 5019–36
PI: 5670

**Valentine's Day — Poetry**
P: 9766, 9781
I: 9772

**Valley Forge, Battle of**
PI: 13069
I: 13058

**Valleys**
I: 16196

**Values**
P: 2403
PI: 17265–66

**Vampires — Fiction**
P: 1157, 1231
I: 5719, 6699, 8072, 8077, 8080

**Van Buren, Martin**
IJ: 10712–13

**Van Meter, Vicki**
I: 10024

**Vatican City**
I: 12443

P = Primary; PI = Primary–Intermediate; I = Intermediate; IJ = Intermediate–Junior High

P = Primary; PI = Primary–Intermediate; I = Intermediate; IJ = Intermediate–Junior High

P = Primary; PI = Primary–Intermediate; I = Intermediate; IJ = Intermediate–Junior High

P = Primary; PI = Primary–Intermediate; I = Intermediate; IJ = Intermediate–Junior High

P = Primary; PI = Primary–Intermediate; I = Intermediate; IJ = Intermediate–Junior High

**Wilson, Woodrow**
IJ: 10722–23

**Wimbledon (tennis tournament)**
I: 17681

**Wind — Fiction**
P: 1349, 3556, 3573, 3793, 5316
PI: 3632, 7641

**Windmills**
I: 16542

**Window washers — Careers**
PI: 14182

**Winfrey, Oprah**
I: 10212–13

**Winnemucca, Sarah**
PI: 10614

**Winter**
P: 3618, 15001
PI: 15064
I: 14801

**Winter — Fiction**
P: 819, 979, 1865, 2222, 2232, 3108, 3554, 3574, 3607, 3620, 3649, 3728, 4360
PI: 4247
I: 2437

**Winter — Poetry**
P: 3678
I: 9891

**Winter solstice**
PI: 14800

**Winter sports**
*See* Ice hockey; Ice skating; Skis and skiing

**Wisconsin**
PI: 16719
I: 13265
IJ: 13299

**Wisconsin — Fiction**
I: 6059, 6094, 7047, 7813
IJ: 6204, 7210, 8480

**Wishes and wishing — Fiction**
P: 816, 1290, 1478, 1988, 2136, 3180, 8499–500
PI: 6399, 6448
I: 6078, 6279, 6365, 6397, 8506
IJ: 6513

**Wishes and wishing — Folklore**
P: 8957, 9121

**Witchcraft trials**
PI: 13022
IJ: 13014

**Witchcraft trials — Salem**
I: 13018, 13033

**Witchcraft trials — Salem — Fiction**
I: 7573
IJ: 7580

**Witches — Fiction**
P: 756, 794, 796, 808, 828, 838, 863, 868, 908, 933, 944, 995, 1001, 1028, 1042, 1095, 1135, 1144, 1231, 1243, 1274, 1281, 3334, 4779, 4877, 4895, 4903, 4905, 5016, 5047, 5319, 8499–500, 8529
PI: 1038, 1322, 2010, 6354, 6516, 6567
I: 5822, 6265, 6280, 6347, 6369, 6588, 6595, 6604–5, 6785
IJ: 5727, 6261, 6528, 7384, 7583

**Witches — Folklore**
P: 8914, 8944, 8948, 9066, 9080, 9084, 9094, 9118

**Witches — Poetry**
I: 9669

**Witt, Katarina**
I: 11168

**Wizards — Fiction**
P: 1331
PI: 6255–56, 6735–36
I: 6210, 6223, 6429, 6562, 6599, 6799
IJ: 6257, 6357–59, 6703

**Wolof (African people)**
IJ: 12193

**Wolves**
P: 5308, 8514, 15223–24, 15226, 15231, 15233
PI: 15221, 15225, 15238, 15241, 15247
I: 15229, 15237, 15243, 15245, 15862
IJ: 15220, 15227, 15240, 15242

**Wolves — Fiction**
P: 934, 1363, 1528, 1778, 2028, 4214, 4234, 4258, 4364, 4439, 4481, 4863, 5915, 8567
PI: 1417, 4294, 5834, 5930, 7414
I: 5559, 5758, 5953, 5955, 8524
IJ: 5560–61, 5840, 5933, 6642

**Wolves — Folklore**
P: 8918, 8945, 9029, 9034, 9099
PI: 8800

**Wombats — Fiction**
P: 2193

**Women**
*See also* Battered women; Businesswomen; Feminism; and as a subdivision of other subjects, e.g., Frontier life (U.S.) — Women
I: 16632, 16654

**Women — Armed forces**
IJ: 16973

**Women — Bible**
I: 13883

**Women — Careers**
PI: 14254
I: 12753, 14204, 14208
IJ: 14177

**Women — Collective biography**
I: 11179
IJ: 10317

**Women — Folklore**
I: 8621, 8634, 9372

**Women — History**
I: 13226
IJ: 16923

**Women — Sports**
IJ: 17527

**Women's rights**
PI: 3758, 13653
I: 10786, 10788–90, 13646, 13658
IJ: 10751, 13667, 13674

**Women's rights — Biography**
P: 10728
PI: 10726–27, 10787

**Women's rights — Fiction**
PI: 7825
IJ: 7790

**Wood**
PI: 16041

**Wood, Grant**
IJ: 10127

**Wood, Michele**
IJ: 10128

**Wood thrushes**
P: 15346

**Woodpeckers**
PI: 15347
I: 15361

P = Primary; PI = Primary–Intermediate; I = Intermediate; IJ = Intermediate–Junior High

**Woods**
PI: 16035

**Woods, Tiger**
IJ: 11169–70

**Woodson, Carter G.**
PI: 10470

**Woodworking**
IJ: 17186

**Woodworking — Biography**
IJ: 10059

**Woodworking — Fiction**
P: 1806, 5088

**Wool**
PI: 16800

**Wool — Fiction**
P: 3910

**Wooly mammoths**
*See* Mammoths

**Word books**
*See also* Dictionaries
P: 13, 144, 2699, 5103, 11415–16,
11419, 11424, 11428–29,
11431–33, 11436, 11438, 11448
PI: 11418, 11423, 11425, 11427,
11446
I: 11437, 11439–41, 11443–44,
11447, 13961, 13995, 14552
IJ: 206, 11414, 13910

**Word games and puzzles**
P: 2666, 17372, 17409, 17411, 17413
PI: 17407, 17410
I: 17367, 17406, 17408, 17412

**Words**
I: 11413

**Words — Fiction**
P: 738

**Work — Fiction**
P: 2683

**Working mothers**
PI: 14173, 14254
I: 14204, 14208

**World Cup (soccer)**
I: 17675

**World history,** 11838–12081
I: 11849, 11851
IJ: 11859–60, 12078

**World Series (baseball)**
IJ: 17550

**World War I**
IJ: 12006–10

**World War I — Fiction**
P: 3931
PI: 7825
I: 7806
IJ: 5945, 6920

**World War I — Poetry**
I: 9550

**World War II**
P: 3966, 12061
PI: 12011, 12013, 12042, 12045,
12058, 12077, 16975
I: 10548, 10557, 10562, 10637,
10640, 11223, 12012, 12017,
12038, 12040, 12049, 12055,
12068–69, 12075, 13221, 16966
IJ: 10558, 10638–39, 10641, 10698,
10700, 11224–25, 12015–16,
12018–33, 12035–37, 12041,
12043–44, 12046–48, 12051–54,
12056–57, 12059–60, 12062–67,
12070–74, 12076

**World War II — Biography**
I: 10276

**World War II — Fiction**
P: 3745, 3770, 3794, 3901, 3918,
3929, 3986
PI: 3920, 4117, 7500, 7869, 7875,
7891
I: 6038, 6828, 7373, 7439, 7856,
7864, 7868, 7872–74, 7878, 7881,
7884, 7886, 7888, 7890, 7896
IJ: 6039, 6942, 7273, 7497, 7854–55,
7857–60, 7863, 7865–67, 7870–71,
7876–77, 7880, 7882–83, 7885,
7887, 7892, 7894–95, 7898

**World Wide Web (computers)**
PI: 16827
IJ: 16829–30

**Worms**
P: 15608
PI: 16323
I: 15611, 15613, 15615
IJ: 15609

**Worms — Fiction**
P: 197, 1867
PI: 7149
I: 8160
IJ: 8334

**Wounded Knee, Battle of**
I: 12915

**Wozniak, Steve**
PI: 10918, 16822

**Wrestlers — Folklore**
P: 8827

**Wrestling — Fiction**
P: 2113
I: 8433
IJ: 8472

**Wright, Frank Lloyd**
I: 10129

**Wright, Richard — Fiction**
PI: 3911

**Wright, Wilbur and Orville**
P: 10920
IJ: 10919

**Wright, Wilbur and Orville — Fiction**
P: 5407

**Writers — African American**
PI: 10219
I: 10297

**Writers — Biography**
P: 2743, 2857, 10220, 10226–27,
10241, 10252, 10274, 10286,
10309
PI: 10106, 10214, 10216–17, 10219,
10229, 10232, 10235, 10240,
10243, 10247, 10249, 10251,
10254, 10256, 10260–61,
10263–65, 10275, 10288–89,
10294, 10298, 10306
I: 10035, 10039, 10041, 10215,
10228, 10231, 10239, 10244–46,
10253, 10258–59, 10268–70,
10273, 10276–78, 10282, 10287,
10291–93, 10300–2, 10304–5,
10307–8, 10310
IJ: 10026–27, 10031, 10218,
10221–24, 10230, 10233–34,
10236–38, 10242, 10248, 10255,
10262, 10267, 10271, 10279–81,
10283–85, 10290, 10295–96,
10299, 10303

**Writing**
PI: 11392, 11451–52, 11456–57,
11464, 11480
I: 11391, 11467, 11473, 11482,
11485, 17105
IJ: 11449–50, 11478–79, 11481

**Writing — Careers**
PI: 14200
I: 11474

**Writing — Fairy tales**
I: 11462

P = Primary; PI = Primary–Intermediate; I = Intermediate; IJ = Intermediate–Junior High

**Writing — Fiction**
P: 5106
PI: 6062
I: 7127
IJ: 7139

**Writing — History**
IJ: 11477, 11484

**Writing — Letters**
PI: 11472
I: 11470

**Writing — Poetry**
I: 9580
IJ: 11471

**Writing — Reports**
I: 11468–69

**Wyoming**
PI: 13525
I: 13320, 13527

**Wyoming Territory — Fiction**
I: 7742

## X

**X-rays**
PI: 10907

**Xhosa**
IJ: 12145

## Y

**Yahi Indians — Biography**
IJ: 10583

**Yamaguchi, Kristi**
I: 11171–72

**Yangtze River — Fiction**
P: 3796

**Yanomami — Fiction**
I: 5782

**Yeager, Chuck**
PI: 10025

**Yellow fever**
PI: 10846

**Yellowjackets**
I: 15556

**Yellowstone National Park**
P: 13334
PI: 13328, 13336, 13339
I: 13324, 13340

**Yellowstone National Park — Fiction**
I: 5758

**Yeltsin, Boris**
IJ: 11284

**Yemen**
IJ: 12533

**Yeti**
I: 17448

**Yiddish — Fiction**
P: 2838

**Yolen, Jane**
I: 10310

**Yom Kippur**
IJ: 13974

**Yom Kippur — Fiction**
P: 4994

**Yom Kippur — Folklore**
I: 9147

**Yorktown, Battle of**
I: 13071

**Yoruba (African people)**
P: 12179
IJ: 12168

**Young, Andrew**
PI: 10471

**Young, Brigham**
I: 10576

**Young, Cy**
I: 11026

**Young, Steve**
I: 11106–8
IJ: 11109

**Younger Brothers**
I: 10324

**Younger readers, Books for,**
1–5445

**Yugoslavia**
I: 12365

**Yukon**
IJ: 12586

**Yukon — Fiction**
PI: 5587

**Yukon River**
I: 12603

## Z

**Zacchaeus (Bible)**
PI: 13849

**Zaharias, Babe Didrikson**
I: 11173

**Zaire**
I: 16247

**Zaire — Folklore**
P: 8674

**Zambia**
PI: 12157
I: 12149

**Zapotec Indians**
I: 12649

**Zebras**
I: 12109, 15084

**Zebras — Fiction**
P: 1911, 1962, 2011, 4466

**Zeus (mythology)**
I: 9467

**Zhang, Song Nan**
IJ: 10131

**Zimbabwe**
I: 12150, 12161
IJ: 12165

**Zimbabwe — Fiction**
P: 4451

**Zimbabwe — History**
IJ: 11257

**Zodiac**
I: 9496

**Zodiac — Chinese**
P: 2283

**Zoology — Biography**
PI: 10916

**Zoos**
P: 3329, 3668, 15104, 15905
PI: 15463, 15910
I: 15906, 15909, 15911–12
IJ: 15470, 15914–15

**Zoos — Careers**
PI: 14260

P = Primary; PI = Primary–Intermediate; I = Intermediate; IJ = Intermediate–Junior High

P = Primary; PI = Primary–Intermediate; I = Intermediate; IJ = Intermediate–Junior High